WISDEN

ANTHOLOGY
1978-2006

WISDEN

ANTHOLOGY
1978-2006

CRICKET'S AGE
OF REVOLUTION

EDITED BY

Stephen Moss

FOREWORD BY

Richie Benaud

JOHN WISDEN & CO LTD
13 Old Aylesfield, Golden Pot, Alton, Hampshire GU34 4BY

Reader feedback: **almanack@wisdengroup.com**
Websites
www.cricinfo.com
www.wisden.com

Typeset in Minion by Palimpsest Book Production Ltd, Grangemouth, Stirlingshire
Printed in Great Britain by William Clowes Ltd, Beccles, Suffolk

ISBN-10 1-905625-00-6
ISBN-13 978-1-905625-00-0
Leatherbound edition: ISBN-10 1-905625-06-5
Leatherbound edition: ISBN-13 978-1-905625-06-2

Distributed by Macmillan Distribution Ltd
Distributed in Australia by Hardie Grant Books, Melbourne

Ah, nostalgia!

MATTHEW ENGEL, *Notes by the Editor*, 1995

After the rained-out one-day international between England and New Zealand in May, a woman from Chelmsford wrote to the *Daily Express* to congratulate the BBC for showing an old match from 1979 instead. "It was a joy to watch cricket of yester-year when the crowds were happy, and there was no abuse or rowdiness."

Ah, yes: 1979, the Golden Age of the game – the Packer schism, sledging, Lillee's aluminium bat, bouncer wars. . . No abuse or rowdiness, indeed! We live in the age of Lara and Warne. A love of cricket goes together with an appreciation of the past. But, for heaven's sake, don't overdo it.

Contents

Contents

SECTION ONE: The Revolution

SECTION TWO: The Test-Playing Countries

SECTION THREE: The Players

SECTION FOUR: The World Cup

SECTION FIVE: The Counties

SECTION SIX: The Bigger Picture

SECTION SEVEN: Farewells

LIST OF ILLUSTRATIONS

Continued overleaf

PHOTOGRAPHIC ACKNOWLEDGMENTS

The publishers wish to thank the suppliers of the following images:

Patrick Eagar – pages 8, 22, 71, 89, 115, 196, 214, 230, 274, 296, 335, 438, 515, 547, 594, 669, 675, 697, 736, 757, 770, 780, 803, 829, 911, 1027, 1105, 1158, 1170, 1209, 1218, 1246.

Getty Images – pages 43, 145, 149, 177, 325, 355, 380, 420, 447, 452, 476, 612, 645, 789, 862, 971.

Graham Morris – pages 156, 1035.

Philip Brown – page 718.

Colorsport – page 727.

ACKNOWLEDGMENTS

When I first undertook the task of turning the past 30 years of *Wisden* in to one more or less coherent volume, I fear I forgot to do the maths – 40,000 pages, 15 million words, goodness knows how many matches. At times, the task seemed completely impossible and I was contemplating buying a one-way ticket to South America. That I did not in the end do so – and that the book kept to something resembling the original schedule – is entirely down to the excellent team *Wisden* assembled to produce a large and complicated book. Christopher Lane, *Wisden*'s managing director, marshalled the side expertly, offering constant encouragement and forgiving the occasional dropped catch; Nicky Thompson made the birth far less painful than it might otherwise have been; Peter Ward produced an elegant and attractive design; Simon Webber was the ever-thorough proofreader; Hugh Chevallier, Steven Lynch and Philip Bailey all made invaluable contributions, and Hilary Bird compiled the indexes. Thanks are also due to the many *Wisden* contributors whose work is reprinted here for the warmth with which they embraced the idea (and for not demanding repeat fees), to Richie Benaud for providing an illuminating foreword, and to the typesetting team at Palimpsest who skilfully put together this most complicated jigsaw.

STEPHEN MOSS

Foreword

Wisden tells us everything about the game of cricket, always has from the time of the first issue. From the moment I read my first copy during the Australian tour of 1953, I've always thought that a story lies in every one of the hundreds of pages. One of the very biggest, part of cricket's evolution, came in the 1978 edition. This covered the 1977 formation of World Series Cricket, and the ensuing meetings of the International Cricket Conference and the High Court hearing. After 31 days, Mr Justice Slade found on all counts for World Series Cricket and for the three players, Tony Greig, John Snow and Mike Procter. He ruled that the ICC resolutions had been in "unreasonable restraint of trade". In a delicious touch of irony, the 1978 *Wisden* story began opposite an item on page 122 recalling that coloured shirts, which had been commonly worn, had disappeared from cricket in the period 1880–1895.

World Series Cricket began in 1977, but the seeds that would produce cricket's age of revolution had been sown earlier. In 1976, Channel Nine had offered the Australian Board of Control $1,500,000 for three years' television coverage of Australian cricket; the Board, though, accepted a $200,000 offer for three years from the Australian Broadcasting Commission – quite a difference by way of income for grass-roots cricket. No one, other than the people concerned on the Board and those from Channel Nine, had any inkling this had happened.

By chance, however, this coincided with meetings of aggrieved and extremely disgruntled Australian cricketers who had been trying for four years, without the slightest success, to improve their payments from the Board. One of the players' meetings had been with Bob Hawke, a cricket-lover and astute politician who had advised the players that under no circumstances in their discussions with the Board should they indicate they were thinking along the lines of forming a union. It should only be noted as a Players' Association.

One of the more significant happenings had occurred in 1975 when Ian Chappell was captain of the Australian team that travelled to England via Canada, for the inaugural World Cup. Chappell, who was both international cricketer and professional journalist, had advised the Australian Cricket Board he would be writing articles for newspapers whilst on tour. He received a letter informing him that this was not possible and he was not, under any circumstances, to have cricket articles published during the tour. Both Chappell and I were members of the Australian Journalists' Association which in May 1975 wrote to Sir Donald Bradman expressing concern that Chappell and Ashley Mallett, also a professional journalist, appeared to be bound by restrictive Cricket Board legislation that affected their livelihoods.

Sir Donald was sufficiently concerned to make enquiries in several areas. As a result, he was left in no doubt; if the Australian cricket authorities challenged either the Journalists' Association or the players, Chappell and Mallett, the Board would certainly lose the case because they were *restraining the trade* of the two cricketers: a significant phrase, given what was to happen in the High Court in 1977.

The biggest change in Australian cricket came with the staging of matches under lights. The second summer of World Series Cricket, in 1978–79, coincided with a traditional Ashes series, when Australia and England played six Tests, England winning the series 5–1. On November 28, 1978, just before the First Test, WSC Australia played a limited-overs match against WSC West Indies at the Sydney Cricket Ground, the first night-time cricket in this great arena. There were traffic jams approaching Moore Park and, by the dinner-break, more than 25,000 people were already in the ground. Kerry Packer then ordered the gates be thrown open. It was estimated by the ground authorities that more than 52,000 people watched the match, played in one of the more extraordinary and exciting atmospheres I have ever known.

New players were being signed by World Series Cricket for year three, and there was no doubt about the success of the organisation in the second season, after a slow start 12 months earlier. The new players meant that, in 1979–80, WSC's competition would have teams from Australia, West Indies, Pakistan and a World XI made up of Indian, English and South African cricketers.

Two things stand out. Packer started WSC on 6 April 1977 in his office in Sydney and he ended it on 13 February 1979, when he flew to Adelaide and had morning tea in Sir Donald Bradman's Holden Street home. During an hour-long meeting, he set out an impressive list of WSC's plans for the future. He outlined the new players signed, the new tours to take place and confirmed burgeoning figures for day/night games and television ratings. His suggestion was that it was time for a settlement.

At the next Australian Board of Control meeting, Don is reported to have looked at all those present and said that before the meeting was concluded an agreement between the two parties would be on the table. And it all happened because of the tea and scones at Holden Street. It concluded the greatest revolution the game of cricket has known and completely changed for the better the manner in which television covered all sports, not just cricket, for billions of people around the world. It also ensured that cricketers would in future receive proper financial reward for their skills.

Kerry Packer passed away on Boxing Day 2005, and one of the many obituaries on his life appears in this Anthology. He was a remarkable man who changed for ever the manner in which cricket would be programmed, and at what time of the day, or night, it would take place.

RICHIE BENAUD

Preface

When the publishers of *Wisden* asked me to anthologise the almanacks since the Centenary Test of 1977 – terrain barely covered by previous anthologies – the prospect appealed on several scores. First, it is never a chore to read *Wisden* – how quickly one is drawn into the great games of the past. Second, by the early 1970s cricket was for me already an obsession. I remember as a fourth-former being chastised in a geography lesson for listening to a Test in the great Ashes series of 1972 on the radio. These are my heroes, my history. As I made my choices I remembered where I was during each of those games, though I will for the most part spare you the personal details, even for the semi-final of the 1979 World Cup between West Indies and Pakistan at The Oval – the greatest assembly of cricketers I have ever seen in the flesh, and a match for which I got a ticket from a tout *at less than face value*. Truly, a joyous, unforgettable, buoyantly multicultural experience. The third reason was the publisher's brief: to make this not just a compendium of facts and figures, a jumble of memories, but a coherent picture of a sport that has been transformed in the past 30 years. Like the game itself, the book must be fun – but fun with a purpose.

My first suggestion was that the book begin with the Kerry Packer "circus", as its many critics at the time called it. World Series Cricket, to use its official title, was the alternative circuit with which Packer, the late Australian television mogul, successfully challenged the established order. He turned the cricket world upside down, and much of what followed in the decades after its inception in 1977 flowed from Packer. The quaint days of chaps with three initials running the game were numbered. Money, commerce, helmets, coloured clothing, TV calling the shots, the dominance of international over domestic cricket – a new world was dawning, and *Wisden* often hated what it was seeing.

As I began to make selections, my initial belief that modern cricket more or less began with Packer in 1977 appeared naive. Indeed, as I discuss in my introduction to the section on what I have termed "The Packer Experiment", there is a good argument to be made that it was the revolution already under way in cricket that had enticed the big man and his even bigger bucks. The safest conclusion to draw is that Packer crystallised and accelerated many of the changes: they happened in three years, rather than the ten or 20 they might have taken without his intervention.

Thirty years on, for better and sometimes for worse, the game has changed radically: the top players now form a highly paid elite who rarely venture into first-class cricket beyond the international arena; television calls the tune; the political balance of power is shifting towards Asia; Test cricket in the subcontinent faces a perpetual threat from the thirst, among spectators and TV executives alike, for one-day cricket; scoring-rates universally have increased; batting records are set with almost unseemly frequency; bowlers have rarely been so abused.

I hope the structure chosen for grouping my selections is logical. Section One attempts a historical overview, dealing with the great themes of the period – Packer, politics, the crisis in behaviour in the 1980s, the growing power of television and commercialism, the poison of corruption that threatened the game in the 1990s, the growing centrality of international cricket and the attendant decline in domestic competitions.

Section Two looks at how each of the ten principal cricketing countries (one cannot quite say "Test-Playing" as Zimbabwe is now in limbo) have fared over the period. Section Three offers portraits of the great players. Section Four details each of the seven World Cups played in the past 30 years (the great 1975 final, though strictly speaking outside the period, is included in a prefatory chapter almost invented for the purpose – how could one ignore it?) These World Cups have been eccentric, often unsatisfactory affairs, yet as I relived them I warmed to the notion of this batty global festival of cricket and looked forward to the future of the event with greater confidence. Section Five charts the performance of the 18 first-class counties – as a Glamorgan devotee, I like to believe they still have a place, even in this absurd age of international cricketers arriving to play the odd fortnight for them. What sort of *team* can that create?

Section Six samples *Wisden*'s less easily categorisable offerings, with contributions on village cricket, the world beyond the Test-playing countries (cricket in Antarctica?), umpires, pundits and women's cricket. Section Seven includes as many of Wisden's marvellous obituaries as I have been able to squeeze in. Section Eight contains a chronology of the period, statistical highlights and a list of Cricketers of the Year.

It struck me as I constructed this anthology that all conclusions are provisional. Cricket's history is a river, forever flowing; the scores on Ceefax or Cricinfo constantly changing, the balance of power shifting. The 1978 and 2006 Almanacks, which bookend this Anthology, both recount England regaining the Ashes. The widely celebrated triumph of 2005 makes it possible to see England's journey – a long and painful decline that ultimately ends in glorious resurrection – as a major theme. Hurrah! But neither cricket, nor history, work quite like that. Yes, the Ashes was a magical moment – and the culmination of six or seven years during which England have finally pulled themselves from the depths that Wisden was bemoaning at the turn of the millennium. But nothing stands still. England went to Pakistan and were well beaten by a vibrant Pakistan side. Perhaps Pakistan, underachievers for much of this period, are now themselves about to surge.

The Pakistan series is included – in the chapter on Pakistan – because it may be a significant moment in that country's cricket, but the Darrell Hair controversy which engulfed the game and led to Pakistan forfeiting the Oval Test in August 2006 is not. Some said the Hair debacle was akin to Bodyline in its seismic impact on cricket. I see it less apocalyptically than that: similar to the fortnight of frenzy occasioned by the Atherton "dirt in pocket" affair in 1994. The fiasco at The Oval posed numerous important questions for the game, but it was not quite the catastrophe that some, anxious to see a racial faultline running through the sport, were keen to paint. For Pakistan, the question was the time-honoured one: was a potentially powerful team, sadly undermined on the 2006 tour of England by injuries to its strike bowlers, going once more to be dogged by administrative uncertainty and political bickering?

Three remarkable games happened too late for inclusion in the 2006 *Wisden* and so too late for inclusion in this Anthology. The first is the extraordinary game between South Africa and Australia at Johannesburg in March 2006 when both sides broke the record for team totals in one-day internationals (beaten once more since then); the second is the Sri Lanka v South Africa Test in July in which Jayawardene and Sangakkara established a new record partnership for first-class cricket of 624; and the third is the incredible Test in Fatullah in April in which the world champs Australia squeezed home by three wickets against world chumps Bangladesh. Who knows what the last of those three epic matches presages: Australian atrophy, Bangladeshi boom? The first chapter of the next Anthology is already being written.

Cricket today must be almost unrecognisable to the gnarled old pros of the 1950s, when run-rates of two and a bit an over were the norm, international "stars" used to arrive at Tests the day before the match having been playing a county game at the other end of the country, gentlemen were still segregated from players, MCC controlled the game, and *Wisden* seemed to have an article on Gubby Allen most years. Actually, even by the late 1970s, the annual "Gubby feature" was still a fixture, but everything else was changing.

Some may still bemoan what has been lost – the rootedness of players within their county set-ups, the relative modesty of the game, its refusal to shout. But I believe the game today to be in rude health. Yes, money and television cast long shadows; much of the coverage of the game is crass; many made-for-TV one-day matches are routine, forgettable, devoid of meaning; there is too much Test cricket; tours have been abbreviated to a ridiculous degree; back-to-back Tests are bad for players, fans and cricket generally; the fact that the game is now administered from Dubai rather than Lord's speaks volumes. And yet, despite all that, what an extraordinary amount of fantastic cricket has been played in the past decade.

The game has weathered its triple crisis – Packer, player behaviour, corruption and come up trumps. The return of South Africa, the brilliance of the Australians and the fanatical devotion of India have added a new depth and richness to the global game. As long as India's billions (money, not people) do not seduce that country's power-brokers into their own form of Packerism – there have been one or two signs that they might want to edge away from ICC control – the game looks to have an exciting future. Or perhaps one should say exciting and terri-fying – for no sport seems as malleable as cricket. Tests, one-dayers, Twenty20; greentops and dust bowls; all out for 12 or all out for 1,107; a ten-day match (drawn, unfinished) or a ten-over slog. There are no boundaries in cricket. Therein lie both its fascination and its danger. It is capable of great beauty – and of being turned into a bastardised form of baseball. Happily, *Wisden* is there to watch, warn and sometimes wonder.

Finally, a note about Matthew Engel, whose first *Wisden* as editor was 1993. There is a great deal of Engel's spirited, witty but uncompromising writing in this volume. One piece that sadly I did not have space for was his paean in 2005 to Sydney Pardon, who Engel calls *Wisden*'s "greatest editor". No doubt the accolade is richly deserved – Pardon clocked up more than three decades as editor at the turn of the 20th century, was instrumental in eliminating the scourge of throwing, and in large part created the Almanack. But I would contend that Engel, too, is a great editor – hugely improving the quality of the writing in *Wisden*, reshaping the Almanack for the internet age, welcoming a "global" game without swallowing whole the ICC's propaganda that there will eventually be dozens of countries capable of playing Tests, above all striking a balance between reverence for cricket and the realisation that it is just a game. Engel understands what cricket means, tells the truth unvarnished, and does it with the style of a Hammond or a Gower. What more can one ask? A great, if mildly eccentric, editor of a great and perhaps more than mildly eccentric book.

STEPHEN MOSS

Dates at the right of all headings – often following the name of the writer – refer to the edition of Wisden *in which the extract first appeared. For example, the 2005 Ashes series was published in (*Wisden*) 2006.*

SECTION ONE

The Revolution

The World Before Packer

I t may seem perverse to begin an anthology of *Wisden* 1978–2006 with extracts from the *Wisdens* of 1976 and 1977, but to understand how cricket changed in this phase we need some sense of where it started. When I set out to anthologise this period in cricket's history – and, in anthologising it, to attempt to come to terms with the nature and extent of cricket's "revolution" – I had a simple conviction: modern cricket began with Kerry Packer and World Series Cricket. From that sprang all the virtues and vices of the modern age – commercialism, coloured clothing, the dominance of television, the cult of one-day cricket, the separation of elite cricket from the rest. The world began in 1977 – this was year zero. What followed was the triumph of hype over experience. That was my starting point.

I had always intended to include some material from one or two previous *Wisdens* to demonstrate my case, using extracts from the mid-1970s to paint a picture of slow run-scoring, attritional Test matches, and a game dominated by tweedy men with three initials. The death of Neville Cardus in 1975, marked in the 1976 *Wisden*, might, I thought, provide another benchmark. The Age of Cardus – elegiac, rooted, literate – replaced by the Age of Packer – energetic, rootless, numerate. But it never pays to be too schematic. At university, I was taught medieval history by an extremely clever young tutor who was just winning his academic spurs, a natural iconoclast adept at dismantling simple solutions. We like to see the Battle of Hastings as a seminal moment in English, perhaps even British, history – 1066 and all that. He argued that the Norman Conquest changed very little – how could a small gang of Normans possibly remake the Anglo-Saxon world overnight? It was an attractive thesis and I seem to remember recycling it to good effect in my final exams. Now, it might serve as a warning to we ardent schematisers. Was Packer the instigator of change or the result of changes already under way?

Many of the obituaries of Packer, who died in December 2005, opted for my original contention. "The man who took a bulldozer to the sacred temple of sport" was the headline on an article by *The Times*'s chief sports writer, Simon Barnes. "Before Packer, sport in general and cricket in particular were bowed under the weight of the pseudo-sacred," said Barnes. "Packer changed all that. . . Packer was cricket's Luther. Athletes, especially cricketers, had been held in check by the notion that 'no player is bigger than the game', the war cry of the blazers. Packer, a blazer-free zone, told the world that the players *are* the game."

Cricket's Luther – the progenitor of the great reformation. It's an attractive notion; it chimes with my original conception; it has a pleasing simplicity; and clearly there is some truth in it. Not for nothing did *The Times*'s cricket correspondent, Christopher

Martin-Jenkins, in his obsequy, rank Packer alongside W. G. Grace as the defining figures of the game. But my old tutor would say it's too neat, too simple: cause and effect don't work that way; did Luther make the world, or did the world make Luther?

Norman Preston's Editor's Notes in the 1976 Almanack quickly made it evident to me that this was not a monochrome world to which Packer suddenly added a splash of colour – the colour of money. After all, 1975 saw the brilliantly successful inaugural World Cup, the "volatile" Tony Greig captaining England, the vandalisation of the pitch at Headingley on behalf of George Davis (whatever happened to him?) and a streaker at Lord's. Clearly, even before Packer there was a trend in the affairs of man. Packer would turn it into a flood.

Wisden, under Preston, was perhaps but dimly aware that the tectonic plates were shifting. His preface to the 1977 *Wisden* nicely sums up his view of a well-ordered world, with God in His heaven, the Queen in her palace and the Australians at Lord's. "In this The Queen's Silver Jubilee year when there will be celebrations over a period of six months throughout the country, it is with much pleasure that I present the 114th consecutive edition of *Wisden*. Most appropriately we have as our guests the Australians on their 28th official tour of Britain. This time the first Test will be at Lord's and it will be called the Jubilee Test."

Preston was making an assumption of continuity even when much of the evidence – the success of that first World Cup, the attraction of one-day cricket, the growth of sponsorship – pointed in the direction of change. Some of these straws in the wind are represented below – the TCCB's search for a sponsor for the County Championship, the storming by women players of the citadel of Lord's (long before they could become MCC members), the complaints about noise levels at the 1976 Tests (no affectionate embrace for the Barmy Army then). But there are also some delightful examples of the *ancien régime* hanging on. MCC's dismissal of India's charges that the England side (which then still officially represented MCC and played under that name) had deliberately applied Vaseline to the ball to make it swing is splendidly imperious, indeed imperial. "Whilst this may have caused an inadvertent technical breach of the Law," it concluded, "the Council totally reject inferences that the individuals concerned, or the England team, were indulging in any form of sharp practice." No Englishman could cheat, was the subtext.

Even more redolent of a disappearing world was Ian Peebles' eulogy to Gubby Allen, part of which appears below. One phrase in Peebles' piece struck me as the key to much of what has changed in the past 30 years: "With the MCC at the centre of all cricket matters, a position it has retained in a changing world. . ." This could still be said in 1977 – cricket was lagging about 20 years behind the rest of the world and was only just waking up to decolonisation. Chaps in the City – men like Allen – still ran the game, made the rules, called the shots. *Wisden* devoted 60 pages to public-school cricket. The universities (or two of them, anyway) absorbed another 30 pages, with full lists of "Blues". The Eton v Harrow match got a couple of pages, with a useful list of results since 1950. Truly, another world – and another *Wisden*.

Gubby Allen now feels like a figure from the distant, patrician past, yet this encomium was published only a generation ago. That sums up how quickly this revolution in cricket has been effected. The chaps are on the retreat in all areas of British life; MCC has been emasculated; the law-maker in the game is now the International Cricket Council, and the fact that it bases itself in Dubai reflects cricket's commercial imperatives and global ambitions. Here then is a world on the brink of change: a few seeds have been planted, some previously unseen vegetation is sprouting, but the keepers of cricket can still see only English lawns and striped marquees. No doubt it was a similar story in Versailles in 1788.   S. M.

SIR NEVILLE CARDUS – A TRIBUTE   Alan Gibson, 1976

Born April 2, 1889; Died February 27, 1975. CBE 1964; Knighted 1967. At a memorial service in St Paul's, Covent Garden, more than 700 people joined in an occasion brimming over with joyous music and amusing talk. The service had great warmth and style, as had Cardus himself. Alan Gibson set the tone on the day with this tribute.

Since we are in a church, I thought it proper that we should have a text. Hear then these words from the prophet Blake (I am not sure whether Blake was one of Sir Neville's favourites, though he has recalled how enthusiastically he would join in "Jerusalem" in his days with the Ancoats Brotherhood). Blake wrote, in *Auguries of Innocence*:

> Joy and woe are woven fine,
> A clothing for the soul divine;
> Under every grief and pine
> Runs a thread of silken twine.

On an occasion such as this, joy and woe are inseparable companions: thanksgiving for such a life, sadness that it has ended. But more than that: it was the mingling of joy and woe that made Sir Neville such a writer – the sensitivity to the human condition, not least his own; the ability to observe it, and to communicate what he saw, with detachment and yet with passion. His books are full of humour: rich comedy, sometimes almost slapstick, and yet he keeps us hovering between tears and laughter. For always he is conscious, and makes us conscious, of the fragility of happiness, of the passing of time. He loved the good moments all the more avidly because he knew they were fleeting.

There is no need to recite his achievement. His autobiographical books, the crown of his life's work, have done that already. His early cricket books gave him a reputation for fancy writing. The words lyrical, rhapsodical, were sometimes applied to him, usually by people who would not know a lyric from a rhapsody. These terms were still jostled about long after they had any possible justification, to Sir Neville's wry amusement. His mature prose was marked by clarity, balance, and indeed by restraint, though he never shrank from emotion or from beauty. Perhaps George Orwell was as good a writer of prose; or you may think of P. G. Wodehouse, or Bernard Darwin – everyone has his own favourites – but in this century it is not easy to think of many more in the same class.

I remember clearly how I was introduced to Cardus's writing. It was in August, 1935. We were on holiday in Cornwall, at St Ives, and my father was buying me a book, because of some small family service I had done. I said I would like a cricket book, and the choice narrowed to two: a book of reminiscences attributed to Hendren, I think it was, and *Good Days*, by Neville Cardus. I doubt if I had heard of Cardus then, because it was difficult to get *The Manchester Guardian* in the south of England. I was inclined to Hendren, but father was inclined to Cardus. Father won. We bought *Good Days*. Father read it before I did, though I have more than made up for that since. Most of us, perhaps half a dozen times in our lives, read books – not always famous books – which change us, change our thinking, books which open doors, revelatory books. That was one of mine. It was the essay on Emmott Robinson that did it – do you remember it? – when Cardus imagined that the Lord one day gathered together a heap of Yorkshire clay, and breathed into it, and said "Emmott Robinson, go on and bowl at the pavilion end for Yorkshire". And then the next bit, about how Emmott's trousers were always on the point of falling down, and he would remember to grab them just in time.

All cricket writers of the last half-century have been influenced by Cardus, whether they admit it or not, whether they have wished to be or not, whether they have tried to copy him or tried to avoid copying him. He was not a model, any more than Macaulay, say, was a model for the aspiring historian. But just as Macaulay changed the course of the writing of history, Cardus changed the course of the writing of cricket. He showed what could be done. He dignified and illuminated the craft. It was, it has occurred to me, fortunate for cricket that Bradman and Cardus existed at the same time: fortunate for them, too, since the best of batsmen was recorded by the best of critics. Each was worthy of the other.

Perhaps the most remarkable episode in the life of Cardus, going by what he said himself, and one to which we should refer here, was his conversion. I think the word is properly used: I mean his conversion to music. It was achieved by one of the minor saints: Edward German. He was watching a production of a light opera, *Tom Jones*, at the Prince's Theatre, Manchester. He had gone there because he was reading Henry Fielding, but, he says, "the music of Edward German got past my ears and entered into my mind behind my back". Only 20 months after that first experience, he was listening to the first performance of Elgar's *Symphony in A Flat*, and wondering, with the other musicians in the audience, how Elgar was going to cope with such a long first subject.

He used to say that he was baffled that it should have been Edward German who had first revealed the light: yet he should not have been. It was all of a piece with the man and his thought. When Beecham and MacLaren, and Bradman and Ranjitsinhji, and Elgar came within the experience of Cardus, he rose to them and did them justice – but he was capable of being moved, such was his sense of humanity, by men who were no more than good county bowlers, Emmott Robinson or Edward German.

DAVID STEELE   Alex Bannister, *Five Cricketers of the Year*, 1976

Few events in the heady summer of 1975 occasioned greater public delight than the part played by David Stanley Steele in rousing England from fast-fading faith to the dignity of a fighting force at least able to match Australia on equal terms. Test cricket has not enjoyed such a romantic story for decades. In the space of three matches, and at the age of 33, after 12 seasons with Northamptonshire on the county circuit, Steele emerged as the much-needed national hero with the skill, nerve and character to stand up and offer fair fight to Lillee, Thomson and Co. His selection in the shake-up following the disaster at Edgbaston was inspired. He applied a refreshingly new outlook, confidence and patriotism to a daunting task, and perfectly complemented the drive of the captain, Tony Greig. At the end of the series Greig said that Steele's inclusion was the best thing that had happened to England – and none challenged the opinion as exaggerated praise.

Steele, born at Stoke-on-Trent on September 29, 1941, did more than accumulate 365 runs and bat almost without fault for 19 hours in six innings. He showed how a sensible technique, concentration and courage could be an effective shield to the brilliant aggression of Lillee, at least on English pitches. Here was a batsman, not in mourning for the recent past or overawed by occasions, but cocking a snook at bowlers who had carried all before them for so long. Defeat was no longer the expected ritual, and at last England had a No. 3 exuding defiance and dependability. His Test initiation was to take part in a stand of 96 with Greig after the first four wickets had gone for 49, all to Lillee. Long stands with either Greig or John Edrich became the expected bonus of every innings. All cricket posed the understandable question: why had this clearly talented cricketer been ignored for so long? It is not easy to answer except that 1975 was statistically Steele's second-best season with 1,756 runs (including a century for Northamptonshire off the Australians), and an average of 48.77. And the selectors were reaching a state of near-desperation.

Overall, Steele, with the extra recommendation of a first-class catcher close to the wicket and a slow left-arm bowler, was a consistent rather than a spectacular performer. He needed seven seasons from his arrival in 1963 to reach an average of 30 – partly because of the variable pitches of the period – and in the last six seasons his average has fluctuated from a modest 25 to 52 in 1972 when, not surprisingly, he thought his last chance of playing for England had disappeared. Perhaps unfairly he was branded as almost exclusively a front-foot batsman. Steele protests that he is neither front nor back, but a close watcher of the ball which is then played strictly on its merits. What better technique can there be? What the selectors did not know until it was put to the test was his incredible temperament and superb response to a challenge. "I regard it as a tremendous privilege to play for my country," he pronounces with simple directness. "It makes you want to try until it hurts."

THE 1975 WORLD CUP
1976

The first World Cup, officially called The Prudential Cup, proved an outstanding success. Blessed by perfect weather, ideal conditions prevailed. Altogether 15 single-innings matches, each confined to 60 overs, were played in England between June 7 and June 21. There were a few one-sided contests among some tremendous and keenly fought struggles. The highlight came in the final at Lord's where Australia and West Indies were in combat from 11 a.m. until 8.45 p.m. when the Duke of Edinburgh presented the Cup to Clive Lloyd, West Indies captain.

Eight countries took part, but unfortunately not South Africa [*Wisden* in this period could never quite understand why South Africa had been excluded from international competition]. The Prudential put £100,000 in the kitty and the overall takings came to more than £200,000, with an aggregate attendance of 158,000. Lord's was packed for the final, with 26,000 present and receipts, a record for one day, of £66,000. The winners received £4,000. Australia, runners-up, £2,000 and the losing semi-finalists, England and New Zealand, £1,000 each.

When the ICC met in London towards the end of June member countries were invited to submit ideas for the next World Cup. India had already said that they were keen to act as hosts, but several members thought it was hard to beat England as the venue. The main view for this reasoning was the longer period of daylight in England in June when 60 overs for each side can be completed the same day.

The World Cup final: Australia v West Indies
At Lord's, June 21, 1975. West Indies won by 17 runs. 1976

Prince Philip presented the Cup amidst hilarious scenes to West Indies' talented captain and Man of the Match, Clive Lloyd, just before nine o'clock on a glorious summer's evening. From 11 a.m. till 8.43 p.m. the cricketers from the Caribbean had been locked in a succession of thrills with the cricketers from the Southern

That winning feeling: Clive Lloyd lifts the inaugural World Cup at Lord's in 1975. He did the same four years later when West Indies won again.

Cross. It might not be termed first-class cricket, but the game has never produced better entertainment in one day.

The deciding factor was the wonderful hundred by Clive Lloyd after Ian Chappell had won the toss and invited West Indies to bat. Until Lloyd arrived at 50 for three, Chappell had set a fairly tight field and his battery of quick seam bowlers had kept West Indies under subjection. Australia gained the initiative when Fredericks hooked a bouncer high over fine leg for six only to lose his balance and tread on his wicket. Greenidge spent 80 minutes crawling to 13 and a rash cut by Kallicharran ended in a flick to the wicket-keeper.

Then came Lloyd and at once he showed himself master of the situation. He hooked Lillee in majestic style, square for six, and then cut Walker off the back foot past cover with disdainful ease. At the other end Lloyd had the dependable Kanhai as a willing anchor man – he did not score for 11 overs – and so the pair put on 149 together in 36 overs. Lloyd hit two sixes and 12 fours and was at the crease only one hour and 48 minutes while making his scintillating hundred off 82 balls. More powerful hitting came from Boyce and Julien so that Australia required 292 to lift the Cup.

Although they challenged to the very end and might have won had they shown some discretion when trying to steal precious runs, they contributed to their own destruction, for as many as five men were run out by the brilliant West Indies fielders. The amazing Kallicharran begun their troubles with a dazzling slip catch which removed McCosker, then Richards threw down the stumps twice from backward square leg and also enabled Lloyd to break the wicket at the bowler's end when Ian Chappell hesitated and then set off for the third impossible run.

Nevertheless, Turner and particularly Ian Chappell played extremely well before their mishaps, but West Indies always had the edge until near the end when Thomson and Lillee threw their bats, adding 41 in their attempt to win a lost cause. It was the longest day of the year; the longest day in cricket history, and one that those who were there and the millions who watched it on television will never forget.

Australia v West Indies, 1975   World Cup Final
At Lord's, June 21, 1975. Result: West Indies won by 17 runs.

WEST INDIES

R. C. Fredericks hit wkt b Lillee 7	B. D. Julien not out 26	
C. G. Greenidge c Marsh b Thomson 13	†D. L. Murray c and b Gilmour 14	
A. I. Kallicharran c Marsh b Gilmour 12	V. A. Holder not out 6	
R. B. Kanhai b Gilmour 55	L-b 6, n-b 11 17	
*C. H. Lloyd c Marsh b Gilmour 102		
I. V. A. Richards b Gilmour 5	1-12 2-27 3-50 4-199 (8 wkts, 60 overs) 291	
K. D. Boyce c G. S. Chappell b Thomson . . 34	5-206 6-209 7-261 8-285	

A. M. E. Roberts did not bat.

Lillee 12–1–55–1; Gilmour 12–2–48–5; Thomson 12–1–44–2; Walker 12–1–71–0;
G. S. Chappell 7–0–33–0; Walters 5–0–23–0.

AUSTRALIA

A. Turner run out	40	M. H. N. Walker run out	7
R. B. McCosker c Kallicharran b Boyce	7	J. R. Thomson run out	21
*I. M. Chappell run out	62	D. K. Lillee not out	16
G. S. Chappell run out	15	B 2, l-b 9, n-b 7	18
K. D. Walters b Lloyd	35		
†R. W. Marsh b Boyce	11	1-25 2-81 3-115 4-162 5-170 (58.4 overs)	274
R. Edwards c Fredericks b Boyce	28	6-195 7-221 8-231 9-233 10-274	
G. J. Gilmour c Kanhai b Boyce	14		

Julien 12–0–58–0; Roberts 11–1–45–0; Boyce 12–0–50–4; Holder 11.4–1–65–0; Lloyd 12–1–38–1.

Toss won by Australia   UMPIRES H. D. Bird and T. W. Spencer
MAN OF THE MATCH C. H. Lloyd

G. O. B. ALLEN – MR CRICKET

Ian Peebles, 1977

In September 1976, George Oswald Browning Allen ("Gubby" to the entire cricket world) retired as treasurer of MCC, an office he had held for 12 years. At that point he could well claim to have achieved a wider experience of the practicalities of the game of cricket than any predecessor for, in the course of a remarkable career, no man can have held so many different cricket appointments. As a player, selector and administrator, he had seen at first hand every aspect of the game with the possible exceptions of umpiring and scoring. His immediate background has always been Lord's for, besides his own prominence in MCC affairs, he has been a great power in his own club, Middlesex; but his sphere of action has extended to the widest boundaries of the cricket-playing countries.

With MCC at the centre of all cricket matters, a position it has retained in a changing world, the club has been well served by a succession of competent and devoted men without material reward and often in the face of sharp and, occasionally, ill-informed criticism. Two names immediately come to mind as men of Lord's who, by their outstanding talents as players and administrators, are pre-eminent in the 20th century. They are Lord Harris and Sir Pelham Warner. Few contemporaries would dispute the addition of Gubby Allen's name to complete an illustrious trio.

Allen was born in Sydney on July 31, 1902 and came to this country when six years old. At Summerfields Preparatory School he captained the XI before going on to Eton, where his cricket career came under the influence of two remarkable men, C. M. ("Father") Wells and George Hirst. Two fruitful years at Cambridge brought sharply contrasting fortunes in the University Match. When Oxford were completely routed in 1922 he took nine wickets for 78 runs. When, in the following year, the pattern of events was diametrically reversed, he played under protest that he was unfit, the truth of which was confirmed at an early stage in the game and he took but little part in it. This setback had its compensations for, almost as a last resort [Allen had had a history of back trouble, potentially career-ending for a fast bowler], he sought the services of a Mr Blake, a famous chiropractor of the day, and, although always rather prone to strains, he was thenceforward free from back trouble.

Allen was picked for the Gentlemen at Lord's in 1925 but it was not until late in the decade that he fulfilled his early promise for, as a hard-working business man, the time he could devote to cricket was strictly limited. Allen's playing career reached its zenith when he visited his native Australia with Douglas Jardine's MCC side of 1932–33. Playing in all five Test matches, he bowled magnificently, batted respectably and proved himself a first-class close fielder. As praiseworthy as his success on the field was his fibre in resisting the strong pressure his captain brought on him to bowl to the packed leg side or bodyline field of which he strongly disap-proved. By the mid-thirties Allen was clearly the best qualified cricketer to lead England and he was duly appointed captain in 1936 for the series against India. He proved himself a most competent leader and additionally did well himself, taking 20 wickets cheaply in the defeat of India by two matches to nil.

Allen became chairman of the selectors in 1955 and held the position for seven years. From 1956 until he became president in 1963, he was chairman of the MCC Cricket Committee, at that time the most influential body in existence where the laws of the game were concerned. As concurrently he was chairman of the selectors and chairman of the Umpires Committee, he was as dominating a figure in domestic and international circles as the popular title of "Mr Cricket" would imply.

ENGLAND V WEST INDIES 1976
Norman Preston, 1977

The tenth West Indies side to visit England after gaining Test status 50 years ago covered themselves in glory under the astute direction of their captain, Clive Lloyd, and the manager Clyde Walcott, of the Three Ws fame. Blessed by ideal condi-tions such as they enjoy in their own islands, for it was the hottest summer within living memory, they kept the *Wisden* Trophy, outclassing England in the last three Tests after drawing the first two.

Only a few months earlier the West Indies men had undergone a disastrous tour in Australia and then met India in four Tests on their own soil where they won two and were beaten once. Before they arrived in England in May it was questioned whether they would be stale from so much continuous cricket. Many of their batting performances in Australia had been reckless, but apart from a repetition of this malady in the first innings of the Lord's Test they generally knuckled down to the business on hand and showed themselves to be a splendid set of players who enjoyed their cricket as well as providing first-class enter-tainment.

Only four of the 17 players were strangers to first-class cricket in England, Michael Holding, Raphick Jumadeen, Collis King and Albert Padmore, but King had played for Nelson in 1974 and 1975. The majority had extensive experience in county cricket and, indeed, several were indebted to their individual counties for their development into top-class Test performers.

By the time they had completed the tour Lloyd and his team claimed easily the best first-class record of any West Indies combination in England, for their results were even better than the glamorous 1950 side when those two spinners, Ramadhin and Valentine, mystified the cream of England's batsmen. In Holding, Roberts, Holder and Daniel, West Indies had four hostile and genuine fast bowlers. Holding, on his first visit to this country, was exceptionally fast, and set up two West Indies records at The Oval where he took eight first-innings wickets for 92 and altogether 14 in the match for 149 runs. Roberts had already made his name in England with his county, Hampshire, and though he had to be content with two victims in the first Test at Trent Bridge, he was at his best at Lord's where he took five wickets in each innings and in the third contest at Old Trafford where, with Holding and Daniel, England were routed for totals of 71 – their lowest against West Indies – and 126.

At times the excessive use of the bouncer by Holding, Roberts and Daniel caused a storm of criticism, notably on the Saturday evening at Old Trafford where Edrich and Close were subjected to a cruel bombardment. Holding was warned by umpire Alley following three successive bouncers at Close. After that condemnation the bowlers concentrated more on attacking the stumps than their opponents' bodies. So the wickets fell sooner and the change of tactics was not only welcome but also proved that intimidation was unnecessary. It was in this match that Roberts had three chances of a hat-trick and his third attempt was only ruined when the usually dependable Greenidge dropped Selvey in the slips.

Turning to the batting, this West Indies side was very rich in talent, with Vivian Richards, Gordon Greenidge and the left-handed Fredericks the main exponents. Richards was exceptionally brilliant and must be ranked among the finest West Indies batsmen of all time, worthy to be coupled with the great George Headley of pre-war fame, even if perhaps he did not have to deal with the same class of bowling. Illness kept Richards out of the Lord's Test, yet in seven innings in the other four Tests he made 829 runs, average 118.42, with two gems, his 232 at Trent Bridge and 291 at The Oval. His aggregate of 829 has been exceeded only three times – Bradman 974 for Australia against England 1930, Hammond 905 for England in Australia 1928–29 and Harvey 834 for Australia in South Africa, 1952–53. Richards and Bradman batted only seven times, Hammond and Harvey nine. During the year of 1976, Richards scored 1,710 runs in Tests and in under 12 months beginning with the first Test in Australia in November 1975 his runs in a year record was 1,811. But mere figures cannot convey his perfect style and strokeplay. His cover driving was superb and with his feet always in the right position the way he flicked the ball on his leg stump to square leg had to be seen to be believed.

For once, Lloyd was seen in a lesser light with the bat, with 84 at The Oval his top Test score in which he contributed to a total of 687 for eight declared, West Indies' highest-ever total against England. The real Lloyd was seen at Swansea in August when he hit a double-century in exactly two hours, equalling the record by Gilbert Jessop for Gloucestershire against Sussex at Hove in 1903. When Lloyd declared he had made 201 not out, out of 287 in partnership with Rowe in 124 minutes with Rowe 78 and extras eight. He hit seven sixes and 28 fours, and 91 of his runs came from the bowling of his namesake Barry Lloyd, whose last two overs cost 41 (6–4–2–4; 4–6–4–6–4–1).

TCCB SUMMER MEETING
Crowd Noise Intimidatory

The Test and County Cricket Board spent much of its summer meeting on August 6 discussing noise at Tests, which was considered not only irritating but sometimes intimidatory to players and umpires. West Indies players were among those who found it disconcerting and Clive Lloyd, their captain, was to be asked to cooperate in appealing for relative quiet at the last Test at The Oval. (Appeals by both captains produced the required results.)

Price Rise

The ground admission price for the Tests against Australia in 1977 was raised to £2 from £1.50 and there was a 50p increase for the three one-day internationals, to £2.50, and the Benson and Hedges final, to £3. The board also suggested to counties that there should be a minimum 75p ground admission to Championship matches.

Sponsorship

The board considered three ways of raising additional money by sponsorship: (a) of the County Championship; (b) of the first-class season as a whole; (c) of the five Tests as a package. The Public Relations sub-committee was to go into the matter and report to the board at its winter meeting.

THE MADRAS INCIDENT

Inferences that John Lever, England's left-arm fast bowler, cheated during the third Test against India in Madras in January were totally rejected by the Cricket Council in London immediately after the match. Lever and Bob Willis, his fellow fast bowler, briefly wore gauze strips, fastened by Vaseline, about the eyebrows in an attempt to stop sweat dripping into their eyes. The scheme did not work. Willis removed his strips at once and, after one over, so did Lever. It was alleged that the grease was being used to keep the shine on the ball, a violation of Law 46 regarding fair and unfair play.

The Indian Board of Control impounded the ball and sent the offending strips for analysis. They stated that they were unable to decide whether "the intentions of the bowler were deliberate or not" and asked MCC to deal with the matter. From Lord's came this statement: "The Cricket Council has been in communication with the manager and captain of the MCC with regard to the highly publicised incident in Madras. The Council fully accept the explanation given that the wearing of gauze strips by both Willis and Lever was solely to prevent sweat getting into their eyes. Whilst this may have caused an inadvertent technical breach of the Law, the Council totally reject inferences that the individuals concerned, or the England team, were indulging in any form of sharp practice."

WOMEN AT LORD'S
Netta Rheinberg, 1977

The most memorable event in a Golden Jubilee season packed with cricket as well as social functions was the falling, to women cricketers, of the last stronghold of cricket, Lord's, and with the blessing of MCC and amidst a considerable flurry from the press, England played Australia on Wednesday, August 4 in a 60-over match and history was made. Fate had also played a certain part as this match, originally scheduled for Sunbury, was moved to Lord's when Middlesex CCC failed to reach the Gillette Cup quarter-final. There was a good crowd which swelled during the day, many spectators coming from a distance to be present at this unique event on a flawless summer day. A centrally pitched wicket was provided and countless press, broadcasting and television personnel took an active interest. England celebrated the day fittingly with an eight-wicket victory.

The Packer Experiment

The Packer experiment was, first and foremost, about elitism. Its premise was that you could separate the top 50 players in the world from the rest and they could play in their own little bubble. *Wisden's* attitude to Packer was oddly non-committal: "The Public Will Decide" was a subhead in editor Norman Preston's first, characteristically brief assessment of Packerism. He clearly disliked the duplicity at work in the signing up of players during the Centenary Test between Australia and England, and he didn't think England players should be allowed to pick and choose when they played for their country, but in general his reaction was very understated. Indeed, he seemed rather taken with the Packer innovations of night-time cricket and the white ball.

Wisden could not, however, bring itself to take the World Series Cricket matches themselves very seriously. No reports of games were offered, and the scorecards of the "Super Tests" were hidden away at the back – on page 1,001 of the 1979 *Wisden*, just after the list of Sheffield Shield winners. This despite the fact that the WSC games were highly competitive and packed with virtually all the greatest players of the period. Take the World XI that beat the Australians by an innings and 73 runs in Perth in late January 1978: Barry Richards, Gordon Greenidge, Viv Richards, Clive Lloyd, Asif Iqbal, Tony Greig, Imran Khan, Alan Knott, Andy Roberts, Wayne Daniel, Derek Underwood. Zaheer Abbas and Joel Garner were available but not selected! Has a greater side than this ever taken the field? Yet *Wisden*, not condemning the enterprise but not quite accepting that it constituted meaningful cricket either, did not provide its usual couple of hundred words summarising the game. It was being treated with polite disdain, so we never did get a description of Barry Richards' double-hundred and the centuries by his namesake Viv and by Greenidge in a commanding total of 625 (scored at five and a half an over).

Wisden's attitude was, I think, an odd one. Preston was almost trying to pretend that it wasn't happening, when the reports from his correspondents covering domestic cricket in Australia and the West Indies were making it painfully clear that the sport was groaning under the strain of the split. The perfunctory Editor's Notes in 1979 are laughable in the way they ignore Packerism, concentrating instead on the game in England, which, with fewer "defectors" and in any case a far larger pool of players, had been much less affected. "England rich in young talent"; "Brearley's indifferent form"; "Sussex thrive under Arnold Long"; "Whither Somerset and Essex?". These were the issues on which Preston chose to concentrate, seemingly unaware that globally cricket was at a crossroads.

Wisden left its main treatment of Packerism to associate editor Gordon Ross, who in three long articles in 1978, 1979 and 1980 dealt authoritatively and, on the whole, objectively with the split in world cricket. Ross's pieces are reprinted, with minor cuts where his desire to reproduce official documents at length perhaps ran away with him, below. Occasionally, when, for example, Ross uses the word "circus" to describe the Packer matches without qualifying quotation marks (this term was always the one thrown at Packer by his enemies), he shows whose side he was on, and once he lashes out, saying that "to seasoned and ardent followers of the game, Packer's offering was almost a masquerade of the game of cricket". But generally he is fair and assiduous in charting the chronology of the extraordinary affair (even when roused, he puts in that qualifying "almost"), and his summaries are still valuable in understanding a subject that cries out for a detailed and impartial history.

Ross quickly pinpointed the key question raised by the Packer experiment: "In this age of extreme partisanship, had non-partisan cricket any future? Does the world not want to see England beat Australia, or Arsenal beat Tottenham, or England beat Wales at Twickenham – or vice versa, according to particular loyalties? Could a collection of players, however great, stimulate public interest, when there was nothing on the end of it, except a considerable amount of money for the participants?" The initial answer was no: despite the galaxy of stars on offer, attendances were poor. In sport, as one always suspected, tribalism matters more than the aesthetics of the game; a cover-drive may be a beautiful thing, but once you've seen one you've seen them all; context is everything. But Packer was more successful at attracting spectators to one-day games, especially those played at night, and started to attract a different sort of audience – young, some said loutish, there for a raucous night out rather than participation in some time-honoured ritual, seeking casual cricket rather than a long-term relationship.

Moreover, there were signs that Packer was winning. The World Series "Super Test" series between "Australia" and "West Indies" in the Caribbean in 1979 was, in effect, a proper five-Test series. Packer had all the best West Indian players and most of the best Australians; it was the only international cricket being played in the islands; the fans would not have been unduly concerned that the matches were not officially sanctioned by the ICC. If it walks like a duck, talks like a duck, and many of the batsmen facing an attack comprising Roberts, Holding, Croft and Garner are getting out for ducks, then it's a duck.

Tony Cozier's report on the 1979 season, which appeared in the 1980 *Wisden*, pulled no punches. "The 1979 first-class season in the West Indies was so dominated by the tour of World Series Cricket through the region that public interest in the Shell Shield competition was acutely diminished," he wrote. "Major matches, such as those between Barbados and Trinidad, Barbados and Guyana, and Trinidad and the Combined Islands, which attracted crowds in excess of 10,000 on the best days in the past, were attended by fewer than 1,000 on several occasions. There was no crowd larger than 5,000, several attendances were in three figures, and only 51 paying spectators watched the final day of the Trinidad v Guyana match at the Queen's Park Oval (capacity 28,000)."

Elite cricket was winning. West Indian crowds didn't care that it was alleged to be a "television circus" or who the ringmaster was. It was good, hard cricket being played between two top-flight sides. Australia, though outgunned, somehow hung on for a 1-1 draw. The all-conquering West Indies team of the 1980s emerged from World Series Cricket almost fully formed and duly beat the official Australians (with their Packer players restored) in the first post-Packer series in Australia in 1979-80 - their first series victory in Australia. As I scanned the matches, I made a note of the West Indies side that won the Melbourne Test by ten wickets: Greenidge, Haynes, Richards, Kallicharran, Rowe, Lloyd, Murray, Roberts, Garner, Holding, Croft. There is endless debate over the relative merits of the great West Indies side of the 1980s and the Australians of the 1990s. Which would win some hypothetical across-the-generations series? *Pace* Shane Warne, my money would be firmly on the West Indians if this XI were in the field, and the game wasn't being played in, say, Hyderabad.

The extracts I have chosen attempt to capture the febrile atmosphere of the Packer years. While Norman Preston was apparently sleeping easily in Bromley and fretting only about "Whither Somerset and Essex?", elsewhere in the volume he edited there was plenty of evidence of deep turmoil. The Australian board did not capitulate to Packer for nothing - it faced financial ruin, and the game in Australia and West Indies was in crisis. Gordon Ross's three reports provide the spine of the analysis of this great moment in world cricket, but the reports on the conventional Test series played during this period and the analyses of the impact of World Series Cricket on the domestic game in Australia, West Indies and South Africa will, one hopes, help us to form some understanding of how deep the rift was.

The death of Kerry Packer in December 2005 provided commentators and obit-uarists with an opportunity to assess his legacy almost 30 years on. He got an extraordinarily good press: the ogre of 1977 - the unscrupulous magnate who had bought up the world's greatest players and debased the soul of the game - had been transfigured into something approaching a saviour. It was a nice irony that the Australians, engaged in a Test against South Africa when Packer died on Boxing Day, accorded him a minute's silence before the start of the game. Ehsan Mani, the president of the International Cricket Council, successor to Packer's bitter adversary the International Cricket Conference, paid an even more remarkable tribute, saying the Australian "took the game by the scruff of the neck and dragged it into the modern era. Day-night cricket, white balls and black sightscreens, coloured clothing and cutting-edge television coverage are all aspects of the game that modern cricket fans take for granted and all of them are down to one man - Kerry Packer."

Packer "provided the catalyst that improved the lot of the player in what had become an exceedingly smug game", said Mike Selvey in *The Guardian*, which also quoted Richie Benaud's encomium: "It's because of what happened then, cricket's so strong now." A few days later, Selvey wrote an article arguing that it was the Centenary Test in March 1977 that triggered Packer's interest in staging his own "Super Tests", but his chronology may be faulty. If much of the signing up of players was done during that unforgettable match, it seems fair to assume that plans were already well laid. The match must simply have confirmed his belief that cricket could supply a vast audience for broadcasters.

Cricket's modern age did not start with Packer - the success of the Gillette Cup and the International Cavaliers in the 1960s, the launch of the John Player League in 1969 and the inaugural World Cup in 1975 all signposted where the game was heading. But Packer compressed what might have taken a generation into three brief, traumatic years. Christopher Martin-Jenkins, cricket correspondent of *The Times*, recognised this in his measured assessment of Packer. "Since the game has always reflected social trends," he wrote, "the changes would probably have come sooner or later anyway. Perhaps, indeed, the effective control of all professional sport now exercised by television, and the consequences of more matches, more tours and much better-rewarded players, was inevitable." Packer is thus more catalyst than creator. The game was changing, albeit slowly, and in the case of those who sought to protect traditional values, the county structure and the honourable traditions of I Zingari, reluctantly. The players were already ousting the gentlemen. Packer speeded the process up – with a vengeance.

The report below on the Australian season immediately following the Australian Cricket Board's capitulation to Packer and its hearty conversion to Packerism demonstrates that all the elements of contemporary cricket were immediately put in place: short tours, one-day series, white balls and night cricket, long-winded mechanisms to eliminate just one team (ironically, in this first, supposedly money-making triangular series, the hosts Australia), "sophisticated" TV presentation, a plethora of marketing gimmicks, hype. The brave new world was born and cricket has been struggling with it ever since.

"With the possible exception of W. G. Grace, there has been no more influential figure in the history of cricket than Kerry Packer," said Martin-Jenkins after the Australian mogul's death. "He changed cricket beyond recall, recognising its commercial potential as no one had, spotting that the leading players were underpaid for the entertainment they gave and pioneering night cricket in coloured clothing, not everyone's cup of tea but arguably his greatest legacy to the game. He was seen then as the enemy of the established game, but the revolution he created hastened the process by which television now both pays the piper and calls the tune. Whether it changed international cricket for the better or for worse is a matter of opinion."

Martin-Jenkins resists giving his opinion, though as the spiritual heir to the Norman Preston and E. W. Swanton school, which wanted cricket to be an ideal as well as a sport, a way of life as well as a game, he no doubt has misgivings. The game, as he suggests, has become "brasher"; money and television rule; the Test and one-day international roundabout never stops, one series blending into another; domestic cricket has been marginalised; the elite in each of the Test-playing countries take most of the cake; the county and state players, once local gods, are left with the crumbs; Packer's elitist experiment has conquered the world. We are still coming to terms with the consequences. But that is for subsequent chapters. Here we concentrate on *Wisden*'s treatment of those dramatic years at the end of the 1970s in which, for better or worse, cricket was remade. S. M.

WISDEN'S INITIAL REACTION TO PACKER Norman Preston, *Notes by the Editor*, 1978

The summer of 1977 will be remembered by most people for the Queen's Silver Jubilee. For lovers of cricket there were two other important topics. First, England won back the Ashes and secondly, there came the announcement in May that Kerry Packer, the Australian newspaper and television magnate, had secretly signed up at fabulous fees thirty-five Test stars from England, Australia, the West Indies, South Africa and Pakistan.

Earlier in the year at Melbourne, Australia and England had celebrated the centenary of the first Test Match in that city in 1877. It was a wonderful occasion with 200 former Test players present and it produced some splendid cricket. Many Australians had by then made up their minds to break with tradition to earn as much as they could from the game whatever the consequences. Mr Packer's eyes may have opened wider to the amount which big cricket itself could attract by the happenings at Melbourne, but this could not be put forward as the reason for his determination to skim the game of its cream. The lack of response from the Australian Cricket Board to his overtures for TV rights for his Channel Nine commercial station was clearly at the root of the trouble, and this was further illustrated both during Mr Packer's visit to Lord's to meet the International Cricket Conference and the protracted High Court case in London in which Mr Justice Slade came down heavily against the cricket authorities. By then the world of cricket outside Australia had been drawn into an intricate and complicated web of other people's making.

No one can be positive for the time being about the success or failure of Mr Packer's venture. It is said that he would be willing to spend as much as nine million Australian dollars to put his World Series Cricket firmly on the map, but in the end it will be the public who will pronounce the verdict, mainly by their attendance at his matches and the time they devote to his TV presentations. The big test will come at the end of the year when England visit Australia for cricket of the traditional kind in another struggle for the Ashes. Moreover, the England selectors will have to bear this tour in mind when picking the teams to face Pakistan and New Zealand in the dual tours this summer. I cannot see how room can be made for the Packer men like Greig, Underwood, Knott, Woolmer and Amiss when they will not be available later to play in Australia, unless before then there is a compromise, which is possible.

As things stand at the time of writing at the New Year no solution would appear to be in sight and the cricket authorities, particularly those in England, who spend thousands of pounds raising young talent to the top level, run the risk of losing players to any rich entrepreneur, for Packer could only be the first in the line. I feel that those who signed for Packer were placed in a dilemma – loyalty to those that nurtured them or the attraction of financial reward for playing another kind of cricket that excludes them from first-class recognition because it is outside the bounds of the International Cricket Conference.

FLOODLIT CRICKET AND WHITE BALL   Norman Preston, *Notes by the Editor*, 1978

With the long hours of daylight which prevail in England, cricket in mid-summer can be played until 9 p.m., as was the case at Lord's in 1975, and the need for flood-lighting is unnecessary. In other parts of the cricket world, the sun goes down much earlier and now Packer has staged the first floodlit cricket in Australia with a white ball against a dark sightscreen. For the first session the traditional red ball was in use, but when the Australians batted against the West Indians, spectators and cricketers alike found the white ball much easier to follow, though it was questionable whether it swung as much. It is possible that night cricket has come to stay in Australia.

PACKER: THE EXPLOSION

Gordon Ross, 1978

First news of what was to become, virtually, "The Packer Explosion", came from South Africa towards the end of April 1977 when South Africa's *Sunday Times* broke the news that four South African cricketers had signed lucrative contracts to play an eight-week series of matches throughout the world. It was said that when the team visited South Africa and played local teams it would have immeasurable benefits for the game there.

In the middle of May, *The Bulletin*, Australia's 97-year-old magazine owned by The Australian Consolidated Press Limited (chairman, Kerry Packer) announced the completion of a huge sporting deal in which 35 top cricketers had been signed for three years to play specially arranged matches, beginning with a series of six five-day Test matches, six one-day games, and six three-day round-robin tournaments in Australia in 1977–78. Prize money would be $100,000. The deal had been put together by JP Sports and Television Corporation Limited, proprietors of Channel Nine in Sydney (chairman, Kerry Packer).

Many of the signings were carried out during the Centenary Test match in Melbourne and the New Zealand-Australia series. Austin Robertson and John Kitto (secretary and attorney of the Television Corporation Group) flew to the West Indies where West Indies were playing Pakistan, and then to Britain to finalise the arrangements with the English and South African players. The Australian team was already in England. The manager, Len Maddocks, was quoted as having said: "I do not envisage the present development having a detrimental effect upon this tour. But if any of them play for a side contrary to the jurisdiction of the Australian Board, they will place their careers in jeopardy."

On May 13 the Cricket Council issued a statement at the end of an emergency meeting to the effect that Tony Greig was not to be considered as England's captain in the forthcoming series against Australia. The statement went on: "His action has inevitably impaired the trust which existed between the cricket authorities and the captain of the England side." F. R. Brown, chairman of the council, added: "The captaincy of the England team involves close liaison with the selectors in the management, selection and development of England players for the future and clearly Greig is unlikely to be able to do this as his stated intention is to be contracted elsewhere during the next three winters."

At the end of May, Packer arrived in England, and at a press conference, said: "It is not a pirate series but a Super-Test series. I have sent telegrams to all the cricketing bodies but they don't reply. I am willing to compromise but time is running out." He referred to cricket as the easiest sport in the world to take over, as nobody had bothered to pay the players what they were worth.

At this point the only cricket subject being discussed from the highest committee room in the land to the saloon bar of the tiniest inn was "Packer", and from all the multifarious points raised, one was likely to be proved the dominant factor in the end. In this age of extreme partisanship, had non-partisan cricket any future? Does the world not want to see England beat Australia, or Arsenal beat Tottenham, or England beat Wales at Twickenham – or vice versa, according to particular loyalties? Could a collection of players, however great, stimulate public interest, when there was nothing on the end of it, except a considerable amount of money for the participants? The fact that tennis players and golfers are a constant attraction was irrelevant; they are individuals playing for no one but themselves. And moreover, the whole crux of this matter was linked to big business – the business of television, and not so much to the furtherance of cricket or cricketers.

Mr Packer, as chairman of Channel Nine of Australia, was bitterly disappointed that an offer he had made to the Australian Board of Control for television rights for conventional Test cricket had not been given the due consideration which Mr Packer felt the offer had merited. Out of this frustration, his scheme was born and nurtured. Meanwhile, unanimous agreement on their attitude to Packer's television circus was reached at the emergency meeting of the International Cricket Conference on June 14. Mr Packer, who left Heathrow that evening for the United States, was to be invited to discuss his plans with representatives of the ICC at the earliest possible moment. This meeting was arranged for June 23, but negotiation was not found possible on one salient point – Mr Packer demanded exclusive television rights from the Australian Board of Control from 1981 when their present contract with the Australian Broadcasting Commission ended. The ICC representatives told him that it would be totally wrong in principle if this were taken as a condition of agreement. The representatives of all the countries present were unanimous that no member country should be asked to submit to such a demand.

Afterwards, Packer said: "I will take no steps at all to help anyone. It isn't 40 players, it's 51." It seemed clear that his purpose in signing up the players was essentially as a bargaining weapon to help him to secure the exclusive television rights he so badly wanted. Names of other players to have joined Packer were being announced from day to day – D. L. Amiss, A. I. Kallicharran, C. L. King, B. D. Julien, C. G. Greenidge. Zaheer Abbas was yet another to defect from cricketing authority, making the known total at that time 41, except that it was announced that Jeff Thomson had withdrawn, as indeed had Kallicharran, according to Mr David Lord, the Australian agent for them both. Packer swiftly answered this possible damage to his cause by setting out for England to talk to them. Lord, who also acted for Vivian Richards, said: "I shall be offering them the same advice that I have given to Jeff. I am going to make it my job to see as many players as I can to try and persuade them to follow this example."

Mr Packer then announced that he would apply for an injunction and damages in the High Court against the International Cricket Conference and Test and County Cricket Board, and a similar action was to be started against Mr David Lord, claiming that Mr Lord had wrongfully induced players to break their contracts with the company. A temporary injunction was granted against Lord, but the TCCB gave an undertaking that no Packer player would be banned until the court hearing.

A TCCB meeting at Lord's on August 10 produced the following conditions:

1. No player who, after October 1, 1977, has played or made himself available to play in a match previously disapproved by the ICC shall thereafter be

The man who changed the face of cricket: Kerry Packer (left), the Australian media mogul, with the deposed England captain Tony Greig outside the High Court in London in 1977, after the establishment of Packer's breakaway World Series Cricket.

eligible to play in any Test match without the express consent of the Conference.

2. No county shall be entitled to play in any competitive county cricket match, any cricketer who is and remains precluded from playing in a Test match on the above grounds before the expiration of a period of two years immediately following the date of the last day of the last match previously disapproved by the ICC in which he has played or made himself available to play.

This, of course, was subject to any High Court ruling which might follow. The name of Bob Woolmer was added to the list of Packer players. On Monday September 26 the High Court hearing began, and it lasted 31 days. The judgment, occupying 221 foolscap pages, took five and a half hours to deliver.

Mr Justice Slade granted three English cricketers who had contracted to play for Mr Kerry Packer's World Series Cricket Pty Ltd declarations that all the changes of the rules of the International Cricket Conference and all their resolutions banning them from Test cricket are *ultra vires* and void as being in unreasonable restraint of trade. So, too, are the Test and County Cricket Board's proposed rules governing qualification and registration of cricketers in Test and competitive and county cricket. His Lordship also granted similar declarations to World Series Cricket. The plaintiffs were Mr Tony Greig, Mr John Snow and Mr Michael Procter.

His Lordship said that as a result of the entry of World Series Cricket into cricket promotion, the International Cricket Conference in July, 1977, changed its rules in a manner which, if implemented, was likely effectively to disqualify any of the individual plaintiffs from playing in official international Test cricket for an indefinite time if he played in any cricket match organised by WSC. The TCCB proposed, subject to the court's decision, to change its rules in a manner which was likely to disqualify any of the plaintiffs from playing in English county cricket for at least several years if he played WSC cricket. Judgment was given for the plaintiffs in both actions with costs.

PACKER: THE IMPACT
Gordon Ross, 1979

It was announced from Lord's on Thursday, February 2, 1978 that an appeal against the High Court ruling by Mr Justice Slade the previous November in favour of Mr Kerry Packer and some of his players would not be in the best interests of international cricket. Mr Jack Bailey, secretary of the International Cricket Conference, said that once the delegates had agreed there should be no appeal – the first item on the agenda – all discussions that followed were in the light of the High Court judgment. No pressure could be brought to bear upon member countries about whom they should select to play; the ICC could not make stipulations concerning this aspect. Mr Bailey told a press conference that, though it was felt that both the ICC and the TCCB had reasonable grounds for appeal, there was no guarantee of success, and to appeal just for the sake of appeal would be churlish. The selectors of individual countries will, as now, be responsible for making their own decisions and there may be different criteria used – consideration of the short-term or long-term requirements of that particular country.

As far as the TCCB were concerned, Peter Lush, the spokesman on their behalf, said that the selection by counties of World Series Cricket players was a matter for individual members; just as, in the case of the ICC, the TCCB was not in a position to make recommendations. At this moment, six England players were under contract to WSC – Greig, Amiss, Snow, Knott, Underwood and Woolmer. The ICC meeting, which lasted two days, agreed that the costs of the High Court hearing would be divided between the ICC and the TCCB. The question of making contractual arrangements with players had been aired, but no collective decision was taken. If individual countries were approached by WSC, any discussion would have to be with the ICC as a whole.

Meanwhile, WSC were continuing to sign up players; or rumour had it that they were. On February 3, *The Sydney Sun* claimed that Sunil Gavaskar and Bishan Bedi were to be offered lucrative contracts for the next season, though Bedi said he knew of no such offer, and was loath to comment further until he did. On February 7 it was revealed that Greig and Sydney promoter David Lord had had lengthy discussions with a view to effecting a compromise between WSC and the ICC, with a new international series, under the auspices of the ICC, to be played in addition to scheduled Test series. In what struck observers as a most curious finale to their discussions, it was stated that Greig had not signed the joint statement because it did not constitute a perfectly true expression of his views. The

Australian board's view has never wavered from its original course; that if WSC wished to reopen talks with the Board, it should do so through the ICC in London. On this they stood firm.

On the same day, in England, a meeting of Kent's full committee decided to have back all their four Packer players should they wish to return. Hampshire announced at the same time that Greenidge, Richards and Roberts would again be playing for them in the summer. Inevitably, all shades of opinion were being expressed. A letter to *The Times* from Surrey's chairman, Raman Subba Row, advocated a genuine discussion between the ICC and the rival system; two days later, Oliver Popplewell, QC, in a letter to the same newspaper, stated that the authorities should stand firm and beware the siren song of compromise until such time as Kerry Packer notified them that players signed by him would be released for the whole of the England tour of Australia in 1978–79.

During these diverse expressions of opinion, the WSC Packer matches were taking place in Australia to attendances considerably smaller than Packer would have hoped for. The exceptions were matches played in floodlight, which obviously had a novelty attraction and were well patronised. Before a crowd of 2,716 WSC Australia prevented a run of three defeats at the hands of the WSC World XI by winning by 41 runs. Comparative failure by Australia, in any sport, is something that appeals less to Australian crowds than to those in most other cricketing countries, and the Australian team's performance clearly could not have aided the Packer cause.

The true financial picture of this first series may not emerge for some time – if ever – but estimates put the loss in excess of £2m; derived from an outlay of some three and a half million, with receipts from advertising revenue about a million, and gate receipts of a shade under half a million. Packer's comment was: "We are still amateurs, but we are more professional than we were, and will become even more professional."

When the dust was allowed to settle on this first adventure, followers of traditional cricket throughout the world had some comfort that this adventurer, Mr Kerry Packer, had clearly not met with the resounding success for which he had hoped. On the other hand, any new enterprise is subject to teething troubles. Moreover, Mr Packer's make-up is such that he was most unlikely to throw in the towel after a disastrous first round, and suffer a loss of pride as well as of money. In the end, of course, he may have to decide how much money he can afford to spend on pride. At a much later date a new managing director, Andrew Caro, emerged, clearly with the brief to make WSC pay, and to fight what, at that stage, appeared to be a battle with authority.

In Australia, one factor in the whole affair had remained constant – the unwavering line pursued by the Australian board. Just as Australia was firm, Pakistan, too, was doing its best to follow the hard line. When the Board of Control for Cricket in Pakistan announced the names of about 30 players to attend the training camp in preparation for the tour of England, Majid, Imran, Mushtaq and Zaheer were omitted. The board stated they were prepared to consider the Packer players, provided they could guarantee their availability to play for Pakistan, not only on the tour of England but for all future commitments. This, they could not give; and there followed a raging controversy, the result of which was a meeting called on March 26 under the chairmanship of the chief martial law administrator and attended by former Pakistan captains, prominent cricket organisers, and representatives from every province. At the end of it, the administrator ruled that Packer players would not be included in the Pakistan team. The poor showing of the Pakistan team, deprived of the Packer players, was later to generate some rethinking.

West Indies, perhaps the most vulnerable of all the ICC members in the matter of cricket finance, was placed in an increasingly difficult position. The distance between the islands – 1,200 miles, for instance, between Jamaica and Barbados – and multifarious other problems have made it an intense struggle for any treasurer of the West Indies board to make ends meet; and a West Indies team that was virtually a second team would impair this rickety financial structure even more. It is not surprising, therefore, that West Indies had taken the most moderate line with Packer players. The board were against the original ICC ban, although subsequently voting for it in the interests of unity, and they decided to continue to play their Packer men, provided they made themselves available. Anyone with first-hand knowledge of West Indies cricket will readily understand their thinking.

In the series beginning in the Caribbean in March, West Indies included the Packer players; Australia did not. As a result, West Indies won the first two Tests with some ease – by an innings and 106 runs, and by nine wickets. But just before the Third Test, at Georgetown, Guyana, a balloon of sizeable dimensions went up. When the West Indies team was announced, three Packer players – Haynes and Austin, recently signed, and Deryck Murray, secretary of the West Indies Players' Association – were dropped and replaced by non-Packer players. Clive Lloyd made an immediate protest and resigned as captain, although the board stated they had not been officially informed by Lloyd of his decision. Lloyd then sought a meeting between the board and the Packer players, but by the time the board's president, Jeffrey Stollmeyer, arrived in Guyana, the Packer set had already written to the board withdrawing from the Test, which was due to start the day after Stollmeyer's arrival.

The result was that West Indies took the field for the Third Test with six players new to Test cricket. [Basil] Williams joined the cricketing elite by scoring a century in his first Test, and Gomes also scored a hundred in a huge second-innings total of 439. This looked to have secured the match, but for the second time in a 1977–78 series Australia scored more than 300 in the fourth innings to win a Test; they had done so to win the second Test against India in Perth.

Australia's dramatic recovery provided the West Indies board with another headache. A match had been narrowly lost; the presence of the Packer players in the West Indies side would almost certainly (as certain as a game of cricket can be) have produced a different result. The board, understandably, had already announced that the Packer players would take no further part in the series, because the players had been unable to give an assurance that they would be available for the tour of India and Sri Lanka.

The board had set March 23 as the date for a decision from the players. Packer himself flew to Georgetown and held a press conference. And in the grand manner, he sent his jet aircraft to pick up former West Indies players who had problems in getting flights to a dinner party he gave at the Sandy Lane Hotel, Barbados, using his visit to put his case on television, and to win over his receptive audience. Events followed events and immeasurably widened the gulf between the board and the Packer players. The West Indies board, so far the only ICC member to play their Packer men, were now realising they were on a collision course. There was precious little evidence that Packer was looking for an amicable compromise.

The international position at this moment was that Australia, England and Pakistan were not playing Packer players, West Indies, though having done so, were now in line with the others; India, New Zealand and South Africa were not specifically concerned, though India and New Zealand could conceivably be in the future. South Africa, not playing Test cricket, would not.

An important factor was to affect the thinking of both the West Indies and Pakistan boards; the opinion of cricket followers in both countries. Clearly, throughout the Caribbean, sympathy was with the Packer players; or more precisely with West Indies always fielding the best available side in Test cricket. The same applied in Pakistan; if anything, feeling was heightened by the palpably poor performance of the Pakistan side in England. Attempts were made by Pakistan's supporters to make martyrs out of the discarded Packer players and ridicule the team, at a time when it needed firm support. Clearly, something had to be done, especially by the West Indies board who faced the stark reality of a huge financial loss on the series with Australia; it was rumoured to be in the region of £100,000.

It was not so much a turn-about, therefore, as facing reality when the West Indies board recommended that dialogue between the International Cricket Conference and World Series Cricket be reopened at the earliest opportunity; and, if necessary, on the initiative of the ICC. The second resolution offered the board's services to initiate such discussions. Meanwhile, WSC, which had named Deryck Murray as its Caribbean representative, was writing to the clubs responsible for the major grounds in West Indies, plus Antigua and St Lucia, to set up a West Indies v Australia WSC series in 1978–79. The West Indies board were to have the enemy on their doorstep – if enemy they were to be – doing irreparable damage to the future of organised cricket in the West Indies. It left the board with virtually no option but to seek a peaceful solution.

World opinion and interest was now focused on the International Cricket Conference meeting that was to begin at Lord's on Tuesday, July 25, and this was not without its dramatic overture. On the eve of proceedings, Mr David Clark, president of MCC and thus chairman of the ICC, resigned from the Kent County Cricket Club committee, on which he had served for 30 years, following Kent's decision to offer new contracts to the three WSC players: Asif, Woolmer and Underwood. Mr Clark's position, in the light of this decision, left him with no option but to resign, otherwise he could have been accused of double-dealing.

Kent's decision to make their policy known when they did was considered by many to have political implications; it was felt they were trying to influence ICC thinking, and perhaps give the impression that all English counties felt the same way. There were also rumours that the players concerned were bringing pressure to bear on Kent during the week before the Benson and Hedges Cup final at Lord's; Kent were finalists and obviously would not want disruptions during the run-up to a final. The county had previously met legal requirements by offering contracts of only one year to Packer employees; Knott, being one of them, withdrew (for the time being at any rate) from first-class cricket. Despite the two sides being poles apart, it was agreed that the dialogue should be continued, and that WSC be asked to reconsider their proposals. A sub-committee was to be set up to monitor all future developments. It had, in any case, been understood by both parties that no alteration to tours already arranged for the coming winter was possible. Andrew Caro, managing director of WSC, gave his version of events as showing the first real chink of light (some chink, and some light, a few would say!) and followed at a press conference by calling the WSC proposals a working document and giving a few nebulous alternative ideas.

Just what sort of a hand was WSC playing? Did they hold all the honours or not? If they were contemptuous of organised cricket, and in no need of it, why bother to submit proposals? The plot deepens. One feasible explanation could be that Packer, like a good union official or shop steward, must put on a good front on behalf of his players and be seen to give them confidence in the future. Clearly, such terms as those outlined above would create the impression of negotiating from strength, while, at the same time, playing for time. Packer would obviously want to know how WSC matches fare in Australia with an official Australia v England series going on. That would give him some guide as to the depth of his roots.

It was said in the early days that Packer resented the use of the word "circus" in relation to his cricket, which was to be serious stuff at the highest level. Hardly the highest level in September when his stars went to New York and, as World All Stars, met an American All Stars XI for a rather undistinguished trophy given by a Brooklyn sporting goods shop – and lost! Mr Greig announced that he would be back in a year's time – and win. Perhaps with players like Greig, Sobers, Hookes, Majid Khan and Fredericks in the Packer contingent, it was better mileage to lose, so creating a big story. Who knows?

In the meantime, Pakistan, smarting from the very poor showing of their side in England, turned back to their Packer players. General K. M. Azhar, responsible for cricket in Pakistan, said: "We do not have the schedule of the Packer series, but if there is no clash of fixtures and nothing in their [the Packer players'] contracts to stand in the way, then we should welcome them." Five Pakistani players were then under contract to Packer – Imran Khan, Majid Khan, Mushtaq Mohammad, Zaheer Abbas and Asif Iqbal.

It had already been rumoured that Richard Hadlee, who had improved his reputation in England in the summer of 1978, was now on the Packer list of potentials. It was said that Hadlee's involvement would be limited to a series of professional matches to be staged in New Zealand between November 2 and November 16; before WSC opened their second Australian season. There was also talk that Geoff Howarth, the other New Zealander to play well against England, was a candidate. With Richard Hadlee's father, Walter Hadlee, chairman of the New Zealand board, it was a ticklish situation for him, and one he would almost inevitably want to leave to the other members of his board, hoping they could reach agreement without needing the chairman's casting vote.

In England, at the end of the summer, attention was focused on two players at the opposite ends of the earth: Dennis Amiss in Warwickshire and Jeff Thomson in Australia. Amiss was told by Warwickshire that, as a Packer player, he would not be retained by the county in 1979. Thomson, despite being under contract to the official Australian Cricket Board, signed a three-year contract with World Series Cricket. It was announced that the board would be seeking legal advice.

To take Warwickshire first. The announcement that Amiss would not be retained caused a furore amongst Warwickshire members. Their view was: why should Warwickshire deplete their ranks when Kent, who had just won the Championship, were retaining their Packer men, as were a few other counties? It seemed that Warwickshire cricket was split right down the middle, and it was no great surprise when a special general meeting was convened for Tuesday, September 26. The surprise was that at the request of Amiss himself, the meeting was called off. Why? There is a ready answer. It appears, almost for the first time since the Packer saga began, that the Cricketers' Association was able to play a substantial part in striving for peace.

They apparently advised Amiss that if, during the winter, talks between WSC and the ICC could establish some sort of peace, Warwickshire would obviously be happy to retain a player who had scored over 2,000 runs for them in the summer; especially as the player himself wanted to stay. If nothing was achieved, then Amiss could rethink the situation. In any event, the Cricketers' Association had one or two crucial resolutions to deal with at their next meeting, and they felt that these would be better kept on ice until the outcome of any talks during the winter.

It seemed that both the Cricketers' Association and some of the Packer players were anxious for WSC and the ICC to get together as soon as possible, to see if the framework of an agreement could be worked out. Warwickshire were alone in standing on principles, but their supporters' view that what is good for the goose is good for the gander is readily understandable. Dennis Amiss, at this point, emerged from the furore with honour, as did the Cricketers' Association.

Thomson's move, however, represented yet another twist in his topsy-turvy relationship with Packer. First he signed; then he withdrew on the advice of his agent, who was taken to court by Packer. Now, on the eve of an Ashes series, he has defected again in breach of another contract. The Australian board are particularly unfortunate, because obviously Thomson was Australia's principal drawing-card in the series against England. Packer knew this well, and countered with a contract and a cheque book; in 1978, the two together seem to be a passport to anywhere.

In the subsequent court action, Mr Justice Kearney decided, after a 12-day hearing, that Thomson, who has said he will never play Test cricket for Australia again, was bound by a contract he signed with the Australian Cricket Board earlier in the year. He could not, therefore, play for Packer until April. Judge Kearney said that some of Thomson's evidence before the court had been quite unreliable. He awarded costs against Thomson and World Series Cricket. Thomson replied by saying that he would probably spend the summer as a professional fisherman off the Queensland coast rather than play grade cricket; in the words of the famous Bing Crosby song – "Gone Fishin'".

PACKER: THE RESOLUTION

Gordon Ross, 1980

The supreme test for Packer's brand of jet-age razzmatazz cricket was to come in the winter of 1978–79 when an official Ashes series would take place in Australia at the same time. To seasoned and ardent followers of the game, Packer's offering was almost a masquerade of the game of cricket; to young Australians, however, especially when it was staged at night with the right sort of refreshment available, WSC was certainly having appeal. To them, whether or not it conformed to the accepted standards of the game of cricket was immaterial, as long as it provided dramatic entertainment. So it seemed likely that as well as two separate series being played, they would be watched by two quite diverse species of Australian life.

Tony Lewis, reporting from Sydney, in January 1979, had this to say of the World Series Cricket game in a feature in the *Sunday Telegraph*: "The most dangerous act in the entertainment business these days is not balancing on the high wire nor even putting a head in the lion's mouth. It is, without doubt, batting in Kerry Packer's Flying Circus. Fast bowling and repeated bouncers are destroying some of the best batsmen we have ever seen. I have never seen so many bouncers bowled in a session as by the World team against the West Indies in a one-day game last week."

Tony Greig, in the *Sun Herald*, gave the true flavour of WSC cricket when he wrote: "The competition in WSC is so intense, teams can no longer afford to allow the opposition tailenders to hang around. Consequently the pace bowlers are dishing out an unprecedented amount of bouncers to the 'rabbits'. So it is pleasing to see that cricketers like Dennis Lillee and Garth le Roux have got the message, swallowed their pride, and are wearing helmets."

Are these cricketers, or mercenaries risking their skin for a sizeable bag of gold? *The Australian* reported the conclusion of one game as follows: "Last night's game ended dramatically when number 11 batsman, Joel Garner, playing with a broken left middle finger from an accident only nine days previously, was struck on the finger by a short ball from World XI all-rounder Clive Rice. Garner was in considerable pain and walked from the field, giving the World XI a win by 35 runs."

While the circus moved from place to place for one-day stands, the Ashes series was taking the course the Australian Cricket Board had reason to fear most. Their team, without the cream of its talent who had defected to Packer, were no match for a competent England side, except for a little splutter in the middle of the series when Australia won the Third Test at Melbourne by 103 runs. England won the series by five Tests to that solitary one. The Australian public (and who can blame them?) have little stomach for the second-best in sport, and this, to a measurable degree, was reflected in attendances. On the other hand, Packer gave the public free parking at Sydney, free transport out to the Waverley ground in Melbourne, and played his matches when spectators have time to watch – at night, and with a white ball which they can see better. In addition, with his television network, he promoted his stars as Hollywood used to theirs in the thirties. They became household names, and faces. It was all a personality cult.

There had been many estimates as to how much the Packer organisation had lost in its first season of WSC cricket. But much of the enormous outlay of capital expenditure would not apply a second time round. At this stage, Packer seemed to have the edge over the Australian Cricket Board on the question of balancing budgets. The official Test series in what was once the greatest of sporting series – the "Fight for the Ashes" – had done financially worse than any series before it; much worse.

As far as Packer's next move was concerned, the spotlight switched to England, where there was considerable conjecture as to what might happen at the next Cricketers' Association meeting. Would the players in English domestic cricket, especially those who constituted the present England team, vote for a ban on Packer players? If they did, Packer had always threatened to bring his circus to England, and no one ever doubted that Packer meant what he said. When Ian Davis, a bank employee, was refused leave to join Packer's tour to the West Indies, Packer sharpened his teeth and promptly withdrew two very substantial accounts.

From the start, there had been a strong feeling in cricket's higher echelon that Packer would never be able to find suitable grounds in Britain. But there was an equally strong body of confident opinion that he would. A great number of cricket grounds are not owned by the county which plays on them. Take, as an example, St Helen's, Swansea, which belongs to the City Corporation. Could they possibly refuse a glittering cash guarantee from Packer if he wanted to play there? Glamorgan could reply by refusing to play there again if the corporation sold out to Packer, but would that matter as much to the corporation as it might to Glamorgan?

Packer had always claimed that his first season of WSC was a disappointment, mainly because, to quote him, "People had been so heavily indoctrinated against the idea." The reprisal this time was to indoctrinate people in favour of the idea in preference to orthodox cricket. Almost every Australian newspaper had a former player who was on the Packer payroll banging the drum, and Packer's own television network remorselessly did the same. Still, not everyone was taken in. In a letter to an Australian newspaper, D. M. Elliston of Tasmania wrote: "Are these posturing gum-chewing yahoos who participate in that rather poor standard television production called or perhaps miscalled World Series Cricket members of actors equity? With sadness I remember back to the days when some of them were cricketers."

Packer admitted that he was fading himself into the background. "I spent a disproportionate amount of time on cricket at first – it's only three or five per cent of the business." He told Alan Lee in an interview in February that, if he had been asked "Would you do it all over again?" he would probably have said "No". He was "still prepared to compromise for the good of cricket, but the longer it goes on the less eager I shall be." Lee, writing of this interview in the *Sunday Telegraph*, concluded: "World Series Cricket has grown beyond being a temporary intrusion on the game, and its threat to England adds completely new pressures to every county player at their crucial April meeting. Packer is awaiting their decision with something more than indifference."

It was reported, however, that a group of England players who toured

Australia were stepping up their campaign against players affiliated to World Series Cricket. They were proposing to the annual meeting of the Cricketers' Association that no county should be allowed to sign a player dismissed by another county because of his links with Kerry Packer. Additionally, they said that no county should recruit any further players on the WSC payroll, or known to be about to sign for the organisation. They would reserve the right to refuse to play against them. Some England players, however, were hoping for an encouraging statement before the association's meeting from the International Cricket Conference about talks held with Packer representatives in Australia. If these gave some hint of compromise, then their proposals could be dropped. But there were still proposals on the table which could seriously affect the coming Prudential World Cup, calling, as they did, for English players to refuse to play with or against any of the Packer men. Certainly, West Indies and Pakistan would select their Packer players, so confrontation and disruption of the World Cup was, at that stage, a serious possibility. Packer, in the meantime, was turning his attention to the West Indies. His organisation's half-year financial report had suggested that a possible profit on the cricket operation depended largely on the financial success of the current WSC Australian tour of the West Indies. There must be considerable sympathy for the West Indies board who, by the nature of events in the Caribbean, operate within the framework of the most slender financial resources at the best of times. Their position had worsened considerably since the arrival of Packer.

For the season 1978–79, with the absence of the Packer men – a team and a half of them – and with West Indies committed to sending a team to India and Sri Lanka, there was not a single first-class match in any of the territories until the end of March. Then within a few weeks, because a large number of their players would be due back in England, the Shell Shield matches – once the backbone of cricket in the West Indies – would have to be rushed through. Meanwhile, the Packer circus was on the road in the Caribbean; and as it contained all the top players of both countries, the attraction was inevitable and immediate.

In the desperate necessity to stay afloat financially, the West Indies board had only one option – to seek some stability, regardless of where it came from. Of course, it came from Packer. E. W. Swanton wrote: "There is, however, one consolation at the moment for West Indies cricket. The various territories are getting from WSC both rentals for grounds and a portion of the gate over an agreed figure; also – let us give the devil his due – the board itself is to receive an ex-gratia payment which will at least do something to compensate for the inevitable diminution of interest in its own Shell Shield and the absence of opportunity of discovering new talent until the tail-end of the season."

Mr Swanton went on: "So, although the International Cricket Conference has done all possible from the start to accommodate any reasonable proposals put forward by the opposition – and I gather, by the way, that the January talks at Sydney between the ICC representatives and Kerry Packer were decorously conducted – the boards of individual countries can only proceed on the basis that, in the foreseeable future, the two systems may co-exist."

With Packer in the West Indies, the cricket world had by now accepted conditionally that his influence on the game was likely to be of a permanent nature. It was not a pie in the sky that would go as it came, simply because of the established business principle that he could now negotiate from strength. When the much-heralded Cricketers' Association meeting took place at Edgbaston on April 5, however, all the anticipated heat was taken out of it by news that something was in the wind. In the words of their president, John Arlott: "We have been asked not to rock the boat. We have been given assurances, but not facts, that close negotiations are going on between the two sides and that a settlement is hoped for in weeks rather than months." The Australian board was due to meet on April 23 and 24 to make what was expected to be their final decision on their television contract, the root of all the turmoil in the first place.

It was agreed at the Edgbaston meeting that, should there be no settlement, another meeting of the association would be held on July 5, when the much tougher proposals laid down a year previously would certainly be debated with a fair chance of being carried. By then, however, the Prudential World Cup would have been completed. The representatives were also assured that traditional cricket would not be the loser from any settlement made. It was felt that this did, at least, open up the way for Warwickshire and Amiss to be reunited, for when Warwickshire made their decision the previous September not to renew Amiss's contract, they did say it could be changed if an agreement between ICC and WSC was reached or thought to be imminent. This proved to be the case, and an agreement between Warwickshire and Amiss followed closely on the heels of this meeting.

Towards the end of April there came the Australian Cricket Board's long-expected granting to Kerry Packer's Channel Nine of exclusive television rights for Test and other matches in Australia. What Packer had tried to achieve in 1976 he had achieved in 1979, at a damaging cost all round. It will remembered that the board had said throughout that they would put this contract out to tender when the time came for its renewal.

Opinion at this latest news was cautious, to say the least. Much more detail was needed, but the agreement apparently was for three years and the board would benefit by an estimated £600,000. As to the future of World Series Cricket, it was reported that this would be disbanded from January 31, 1980. It need never have started had Packer accepted that the Australian Cricket Board was bound by a contract to the Australian Broadcasting Commission until 1979, and that his money was likely to win the prize he so dearly sought when the time came.

This news of Packer winning the television contract was largely expected and was nothing like the bombshell which exploded upon the cricket world a month later when, from the outside, it appeared that from being arch-enemies with no compromise possible in any set of circumstances, the parties had wed and were now hand in hand for, as they said, the future good of cricket. Whether the rest of the world thought so was quite another matter. The feeling in many quarters was that when the Australian board first found Packer at their throats, the rest of the cricket world had supported them to the hilt; even to the extent of highly expensive court cases which cricket could ill afford. Now, when it suited Australia, they had brushed their friends aside to meet their own ends. Let us, first of all, look at the text of the statement made by the chairman of the Australian Cricket Board, Bob Parish.

"I am pleased to announce that the agreement between the Australian Cricket board and PBL Sports Pty Ltd has been signed and will be lodged with the Trade

Practices Commissioner. Under the agreement the board has granted PBL Sports Pty Ltd the exclusive right, for a term of ten years, to promote the programme of cricket organised by the board and to arrange the televising and merchandising in respect of that programme. For the first three years of the agreement the board has agreed that PBL Sports Pty Ltd may arrange a contract for the televising of the programme with the Channel Nine network.

"World Series Cricket Pty Ltd will cease to promote cricket matches in Australia or elsewhere during the term of the agreement. However, under the programme the World Series logo will continue to be worn in international one-day matches by Australian players.

"The Australian Board will have the exclusive responsibility for the selection of Australian teams and has agreed that no player will be excluded from selection by reason only of that player having participated prior to the commencement of the 1979–80 cricket season in any match not authorised by the board. There will be no change in board policy that Australian teams will be selected only from those players who participate in Sheffield Shield cricket.

"It is envisaged that the programme each season will comprise five or six Test matches and an international one-day series, to be known as the Benson and Hedges World Series Cup, of 15 matches plus a final which will be the best of five matches. These international matches will involve two overseas teams and the Australian team. The programme will also include the Sheffield Shield competition and a one-day series of nine matches between the states.

"Playing conditions of all matches will be under the control of the board, and the board has agreed to consider favourably the introduction of the 30-yard circle in limited-overs matches, day/night matches and, on an experimental basis, the use of coloured clothing in Benson and Hedges World Series one-day limited-overs international matches.

"The programme for the 1979–80 season will not be finally determined for some weeks. England and India have accepted invitations to come to Australia in 1979–80. The board has agreed to ask the Indian board to defer their visit until next season, 1980–81, and will invite the West Indian board to send an official team to participate in the 1979–80 programme."

India, of course, had more reason than most to be unhappy, because their scheduled tour of Australia was to be deferred. New Zealand, too, must have wondered what might happen to them as one of the lesser crowd-pulling cricketing countries. Would the new deal mean that the weak would go under because they would have too little television appeal?

Throughout the debate, the sixty-four thousand dollar question was "Why has the Australian board done this?", and the sixty-four thousand dollar answer can be succinctly given in one word – "Money". For the first time in the history of the Ashes, an Australia v England series had lost money. Faced with nothing in the kitty, and a tour by India – and this was bound to lose money – the Australian board could see the spectre of bankruptcy close round the corner. It was left with precious little bargaining power.

Packer had all the cards in his hand. It could be said that, in the circumstances, Australia had come out of it pretty well. Financially, of course, they may have, but time alone will tell whether the Australian board – a very small dog, with Packer as a very large tail – will find that the tail wags the dog on any issue of divided opinion. It easily could.

Knowing the dilemma the Australian board was in after losing an estimated £445,000 in the two-year dispute, it was not too surprising that the International Cricket Conference, at its annual meeting at Lord's, approved the Australian board's agreement with Packer's PBL Pty Ltd. They were satisfied that PBL would be the agent of the board, not its master. The ICC announced that it was likely that England and West Indies would go to Australia in the coming winter, India and New Zealand in 1980–81, and West Indies and Pakistan in 1981–82, so, for all countries, honour was satisfied. India accepted a year's postponement with good grace on the assurance that, in the three-year programme of international cricket currently being worked out, they will have an equitable share of Test series, home and away. The Australian board's agreement with PBL was for ten years, but there is no commitment to have two tours every Australian season, and England's next visit after the coming winter should be for a full season.

Although some say that this will have little effect on established cricket in England, this view might have to be taken with a pinch of salt. It is practically impossible for one of the major components of a small unit – the countries involved in international cricket – to commit itself to such far-reaching proposals as these without some of the implications rubbing off elsewhere. A glut of one-day cricket could be one example, as could the development of a new breed of cricketer who seeks the quick pickings of easy money in preference to the long hard road of becoming thoroughly accomplished. Will the watcher lose all sense of the aesthetic qualities of cricket because, in a one-day game, snicks through an unguarded slip area count for as much as the beauty of the supreme cover-drive?

The Test and County Cricket Board swiftly put some uneasy minds at rest when they announced that, although they reluctantly agreed to compete in the ICC-approved one-day competition involving Australia and West Indies, they have told the Australians they want the next tour in 1982–83 to revert to the traditional format of five or six Tests. The TCCB added: "The Australian board have agreed to a significant reduction in one-day international cricket from their original programme. England are strongly of the opinion that there are still too many of these matches as opposed to Tests than is desirable."

The TCCB also insisted that "no abnormal conditions" be imposed for the limited-overs series. This obviously meant that England would refuse to play in coloured clothing and suffer any of the other intolerable gimmicks of WSC television presentation. Furthermore, they had their way over the position of the Ashes in the three-Test series, and these were not at stake.

One immediate example of the new "all money" attitude by the Australian board was the length of time it took for the TCCB to negotiate terms for the recent winter tour, which, in the first instance, were unacceptable. In fact, whether or not the tour was on was touch and go for some time. Agreement was finally reached for an announcement to be made on October 4, and even then an estimated £30,000 to be divided among the counties seemed paltry reward for a tour which was not really wanted, and was purely a gesture to help Australia – and Packer, too. The illogicality of it all had surely reached its peak.

CRICKET IN AUSTRALIA 1977–78 Brian Osborne, 1979

There were many calls in Australia for compromise between what has loosely been described as "establishment cricket" and WSC, but no effectual moves were made during the season; nor did the emotionally charged situation suggest that this would take place at any early date. In fact, expressions of antagonism and division of opinion have been more pronounced in Australia than elsewhere, no doubt because the move to introduce the WSC form of cricket professionalism was developed by an Australian and its operation was initially commenced during a cricket season in this country.

WSC experienced frustrations and serious disappointments in its initial year, notably in the attendances at early matches, but no one could deny that the organisers' professional approach was intrepid as they methodically pressed on through the stalemate period with a series of image-capturing innovations to cope with venue problems and establish a form of WSC cricket most suited to engage public patronage. The introduction of the excellent glass-house-grown portable pitches, night cricket, the white ball, and recognition that public preference was for the limited-overs WSC game were all enlightening forms of progress achieved within just one season, during which the game of cricket, by any standards, took on new and wider dimensions. The opportunity for wider use of major grounds is to follow. Independent public opinion polls are favourable to WSC cricket and, in another area, there has been keen appreciation of the improved and unparalleled television presentation through greater use of cameras and the intimacy of the personalised coverage. While this was proceeding, "establishment cricket" had to take close note of improvements to its players' payments and conditions and contend with the continuing dwindling attendances.

WSC Australian XI v WSC West Indies XI

At VFL Stadium, Melbourne, December 2, 3, 4, 1977. WSC West Indies XI won by three wickets.

WSC AUSTRALIAN XI	First innings		Second innings
R. B. McCosker c Richards b Roberts	0	– c Fredericks b Daniel	47
I. C. Davis hit wkt b Holding	15	– b Roberts	0
*I. M. Chappell c Daniel b Holding	34	– lbw b Roberts	3
G. S. Chappell c Fredericks b Holding	0	– lbw b Daniel	28
D. W. Hookes b Holding	0	– c Lloyd b Roberts	63
K. D. Walters c Holford b Roberts	16	– lbw b Roberts	5
†R. W. Marsh c Holding b Daniel	23	– lbw b Holding	12
R. J. Bright c Greenidge b Roberts	69	– not out	16
D. K. Lillee c Fredericks b King	37	– c Allen b Holding	5
M. H. N. Walker c Richards b Daniel	30	– b Holding	1
L. S. Pascoe not out	26	– b Daniel	7
B 2, l-b 3, n-b 1	6	L-b 4, n-b 1	5

1-0 2-33 3-39 4-39   256   1-4 2-12 3-58 4-126   192
5-66 6-66 7-119 8-187 9-207 10-256   5-139 6-158 7-158 8-168 9-171 10-192

First innings – Roberts 15–5–52–3; Holding 12–1–60–4; Daniel 11.2–0–51–2; King 8–0–46–1; Holford 10–2–41–0.
Second innings – Roberts 13–1–52–4; Holding 12–1–72–3; Daniel 8.6–0–45–3; King 2–0–12–0; Holford 1–0–6–0.

WSC West Indies XI

	First innings		Second innings	
R. C. Fredericks b Pascoe	24	–	c Hookes b Walker	42
C. G. Greenidge lbw b Lillee	22	–	c Lillee b Pascoe	16
M. A. Holding lbw b Pascoe	1			
I. V. A. Richards c Marsh b Hookes	79	–	(3) c Hookes b Walker	56
J. C. Allen lbw b Walker	8	–	(4) b Lillee	12
*C. H. Lloyd c I. M. Chappell b Walker	19	–	(5) c Davis b Pascoe	44
C. L. King c Davis b Pascoe	5	–	(6) c I. M. Chappell b Walker	4
†D. L. Murray c Hookes b Lillee	29	–	(7) not out	36
D. A. J. Holford c Lillee b Bright	11	–	(8) c Marsh b Lillee	0
A. M. E. Roberts run out	13	–	(9) not out	13
W. W. Daniel not out	0			
W 1, n-b 2	3		L-b 14	14

1-33 2-47 3-47 4-68   **214**   1-30 2-113 3-116   **(7 wkts) 237**
5-150 6-156 7-165 8-185 9-214 10-214   4-130 5-147 6-186 7-190

First innings – Lillee 16–4–77–2; Pascoe 14–3–70–3; Walker 14–4–43–2; Hookes 2–0–6–1; Bright 3–0–15–1.
Second innings – Lillee 20–1–100–2; Pascoe 13–2–56–2; Walker 13–3–43–3; Hookes 2–0–14–0; Bright 2.7–1–10–0.

Umpires J. R. Collins and D. Sang Hue

WSC Australian XI v WSC World XI

At the Showground, Sydney, January 14, 15, 16, 17, 18, 19, 1978. WSC World XI won by four wickets.

WSC Australian XI

	First innings		Second innings	
B. M. Laird b Garner	106	–	lbw b Roberts	5
R. B. McCosker lbw b Procter	5	–	b Procter	3
*I. M. Chappell run out	44	–	c Fredericks b Roberts	19
R. S. Langer c Knott b Garner	39	–	b Roberts	12
G. S. Chappell c I. V. A. Richards b Garner	35	–	b Roberts	0
M. F. Kent c I. V. A. Richards b Underwood	10	–	c Knott b Garner	31
†R. W. Marsh c Lloyd b Procter	8	–	c Knott b Roberts	6
G. J. Gilmour c Knott b Roberts	10	–	b Roberts	26
R. J. Bright c Knott b Procter	9	–	c Knott b Garner	11
M. H. N. Walker b Procter	22	–	c Knott b Garner	0
W. Prior not out	1	–	not out	7
B 6, l-b 2, n-b 7	15		B4, l-b 4	8

1-8 2-113 3-203 4-204   **304**   1-8 2-8 3-25 4-25   **128**
5-252 6-252 7-270 8-270 9-303 10-304   5-44 6-54 7-86 8-113 9-113 10-128

First innings – Roberts 16–3–53–1; Garner 22–2–71–3; Procter 9.7–1–33–4; Underwood 24–4–77–1; Greig 11–1–55–0.
Second innings – Roberts 12–2–69–6; Garner 7.4–1–26–3; Procter 9–1–25–1.

WSC WORLD XI

	First innings		Second innings	
R. C. Fredericks c Marsh b Gilmour	4	– b Gilmour		13
B. A. Richards b Gilmour	57	– c Marsh b Walker		48
C. G. Greenidge c Marsh b Walker	23	– b Gilmour		50
I. V. A. Richards c Gilmour b Walker	119	– c Marsh b Walker		18
C. H. Lloyd c I. M. Chappell b Walker	1	– (8) not out		0
*A. W. Greig c I. M. Chappell b Walker	38	– (5) c Langer b Gilmour		8
†A. P. E. Knott b Gilmour	2	– (6) b Gilmour		0
M. J. Procter c Marsh b Walker	6	– (7) not out		5
A. M. E. Roberts c Marsh b Walker	10			
J. Garner c Laird b Walker	24			
D. L. Underwood not out	3			
N-b 3	3	L-b 3		3

1-7 2-59 3-95 4-124	290	1-15 2-82	(6 wkts) 145
5-218 6-227 7-253 8-253 9-275 10-290		3-124 4-140 5-140 6-141	

First innings – Prior 11–1–66–0; Gilmour 25–2–103–3; Walker 28.3–9–88–7; Bright 4–1–21–0;
G. S. Chappell 6–1–9–0.
Second innings – Prior 13–0–74–0; Gilmour 4–1–26–4; Walker 10.5–1–42–2.

UMPIRES J. R. Collins and D. Sang Hue

WSC Australian XI v WSC World XI

At Gloucester Park, Perth, January 27, 28, 29, 30, 1978. World XI won by an innings and 73 runs.

WSC WORLD XI

B. A. Richards c G. S. Chappell b Bright	207
C. G. Greenidge c Marsh b Bright	140
I. V. A. Richards c Walker b Lillee	177
C. H. Lloyd c G. S. Chappell b Lillee	37
Asif Iqbal c G. S. Chappell b Lillee	1
*A. W. Greig c Edwards b Lillee	14
Imran Khan c Walker b Bright	15
†A. P. E. Knott c Walker b Bright	20
A. M. E. Roberts c G. S. Chappell b Gilmour	1
W. W. Daniel b Bright	1
D. L. Underwood not out	0
B 4, l-b 4, n-b 4	12

1-369 2-461 3-481 4-522 5-571 6-587	625
7-613 8-622 9-624 10-625	

Greenidge retired hurt at 234 and resumed at 481.

Lillee 27-1-149-4; Gilmour 33-3-141-1; Walker 14-1-115-0; Bright 30.3-3-149-5;
I. M. Chappell 3-0-22-0; G. S. Chappell 6-0-37-0.

WSC AUSTRALIAN XI	*First innings*		*Second innings*
B. M. Laird c Knott b Imran	6	– b Imran	20
I. C. Davis c Knott b Roberts	2	– b Daniel	7
*I. M. Chappell c sub b Underwood	62	– (8) not out	13
M. F. Kent c Knott b Imran	0	– (3) c Greig b Imran	0
R. Edwards b Roberts	34	– c Roberts b Underwood	39
G. S. Chappell c Knott b Imran	174	– (4) c I. V. A. Richards b Greig	26
†R. W. Marsh lbw b Roberts	27	– (6) c Roberts b Underwood	23
G. J. Gilmour c Roberts b Underwood	9	– (7) c I. V. A. Richards b Greig	13
R. J. Bright not out	41	– b Greig	0
D. K. Lillee lbw b Greig	1	– b Imran	8
M. H. N. Walker c Asif Iqbal b Greig	10	– b Imran	4
B 10, l-b 3, w 2, n-b 12	27	B3, n-b 3	6

1-3 2-19 3-19 4-73 5-150 6-209 7-251   **393**   1-18 2-23 3-30 4-91 5-102 6-126   **159**
8-367 9-368 10-393   7-136 8-136 9-155 10-159

First innings – Roberts 17-2-65-3; Imran 19-1-79-3; Daniel 10-1-59-0; Underwood 24-5-79-2;
Greig 20.4-1-75-2; Asif Iqbal 2-0-9-0.
Second innings – Roberts 8-2-18-0; Imran 7-1-24-4; Daniel 7-1-30-1; Underwood 15-3-54-2;
Greig 10-2-27-3.

UMPIRES G. Duperouzel and P. R. Enright

WEST INDIES V AUSTRALIA 1978

Tony Cozier, 1979

Australia's fourth tour of the West Indies was depressingly dominated more by events off the field than on them. The inauguration of Kerry Packer's World Series Cricket, which had created such chaos throughout the cricket world, had considerable influence over the series.

The Australian Cricket Board of Control adamantly refused to select any of the Packer players, with the result that they sent a young and inexperienced party under the captaincy of the veteran Bobby Simpson, recalled from retirement to lead his country in the earlier series against India. The West Indies board, on the other hand, decided they would choose players contracted to WSC on the grounds that they had never refused to play for their country and had now made themselves available.

With the two teams thus constituted, West Indies proved far superior in the first two Tests, which they won by large margins inside three days. By the end of the Second Test, however, it was clear that relations between the board and the Packer players were becoming strained. The board was "to say the least, extremely disappointed" when three young players – Austin, Croft and Haynes – signed contracts with WSC despite an earlier, verbal assurance not to do so. The West Indies board felt the Packer representatives were militant in their financial negotiations, seeking substantial increases just before the First Test.

For their part, the players were irritated by the decision to relieve Deryck

Murray, their spokesman, of the vice-captaincy in mysterious circumstances on the opening day of the series. They detected a coldness in the board's attitude towards them and, when they were handed a March 23 deadline to state whether they would be available for the tour of India and Sri Lanka later in the year, saw it as unwarranted pressure because of their Packer associations. The board, however, simply stated that they wanted to be prepared for the India and Sri Lanka trip. When they received no definite response by the date set, the selectors decided to replace three WSC signees – Austin, Haynes and Deryck Murray – with three who had no such ties – Gomes, David Murray and Williams – for the Third Test. Clive Lloyd made an almost immediate protest, announcing his resignation from the captaincy he had held for 29 successive Tests since 1974. It was time the West Indies board made "very clear the principles underlying the selection of the present team," he said.

Within two days, other West Indian players contracted to WSC also withdrew from the team in solidarity with Lloyd. Although a meeting between Lloyd, some of the players involved, and the West Indies board – headed by the president, Mr J. B. Stollmeyer – was held on the eve of the Third Test, nothing was resolved. West Indies then named a new team, appointing Alvin Kallicharran captain for the remaining three Tests and banning the Packer players for the rest of the series.

The impasse caused an emotional explosion throughout the Caribbean, with heated arguments raging everywhere. Groups in Trinidad and Jamaica called for the public to boycott the Fourth and Fifth Tests; the board and the selectors were widely criticised and urged to resign. In response, the board declared that they had bent over backwards to accommodate the Packer players and charged that they were "vacillating" and "were under the domination of WSC".

With the teams more evenly matched as a result of the dispute, the final three Tests produced far keener cricket. Australia won the third narrowly, and West Indies the fourth to regain the Sir Frank Worrell Trophy they had last held in 1965. Australia were on the verge of victory in the fifth when the crowd, reacting violently against an umpiring decision, halted play by throwing stones, bottles and debris on the field. When an attempt was made to restart the match on an unscheduled sixth day to make up lost time, it did not meet the approval of one of the umpires and the match had to be left abandoned as a draw – the final bizarre twist in a series bedevilled throughout by acrimony and confusion.

There were other incidents as well, and even if they were overshadowed by the confrontation between the players and the board, they were nonetheless unsavoury. The Australians, ill-equipped to cope with the formidable West Indian fast bowling early on, suffered several injuries that affected their team balance. Several batsmen were struck and some took to wearing protective headgear. In the end it brought a public protest from the manager, Mr Fred Bennett, against the short-pitched bowling of Croft in the Guyana match, describing it as "a direct contravention of both the law and the tour conditions". At least twice, Simpson was so at odds with the umpire that he called for the tour conditions to be brought on to the field for scrutiny; a most unusual occurrence.

AUSTRALIA V ENGLAND 1978–79 Alex Bannister, 1980

A lone trumpeter on the sparsely filled Hill at Sydney grimly symbolised Australia's embarrassing defeats, domestic confusions and divided loyalties, by sounding the Last Post as England won the Sixth Test inside four days and the series by five to one. For Brearley, a comfortable victor over Greg Chappell in the home summer of 1977, it was a continuation of his trumphant progress since he took over the captaincy from Greig. In the space of 20 months he defeated Australia eight times in 11 Tests, and it is not uncharitable to say that his one defeat at Melbourne might have been avoided if he had not lost an important toss. No England captain, or for that matter any captain, had won five Tests in a series in Australia, although J. W. H. T. Douglas (1911–12), A. P. F. Chapman (1928–29) and D. R. Jardine (1932–33) had comparable records in taking four matches in a five-Test rubber.

Brearley's critics will no doubt argue that Australia, drained by defections to World Series Cricket, have never been weaker in the 102 years of struggle between the two countries. In another era Brearley might not have succeeded as he did, but he had disposed of an Australian team full of Packer players by three-nil in 1977. He was expected to win in Australia, and, to his credit, he did all that was expected of him.

The competition from World Series Cricket put heavy demands on the Australian authorities, and the game at large suffered from an over-heavy programme and too much exposure on television. The well-oiled and professional WSC publicity machine often distracted attention from the Ashes series, and the public grew tired of supporting a losing team. An original error was perhaps made in playing two Tests on the over-worked ground at Sydney, where Packer was strongly established. A brave effort was made to stimulate interest with skydivers arriving with the match ball, or the coin, marching displays and athletic events during the intervals. But the essential factor of a winning Australian team was missing and attendances dropped to alarming levels by the final Test.

CRICKET IN AUSTRALIA 1978–79 Brian Osborne, 1980

Victoria won the Sheffield Shield for the first time since 1973–74, and did so most handsomely. However, in a season in which the changing fortunes of the leading states should have attracted good crowds, the further decline in public interest in the competition was a matter of great concern. At one stage or another, four states were favourably placed to take the Shield, and yet the official attendance figures (only 134,552 for 25 matches) were an alarming 37% below 1977–78 returns.

A number of reasons were advanced for the dramatic fall in public interest, but the general view was that a need existed for the immediate overhaul of cricket's administration to bring it up to date with the far-reaching changes of recent times. Even setting aside the problems caused by World Series Cricket, it was evident that the Sheffield Shield programme suffered from the division of interest within a wide range of Australian Cricket Board of Control matches. Eight Tests and other major matches against the England and Pakistan touring teams drew the best Shield players. There was, as well, increased interest in the equally extensive WSC programme. Moreover, spectators included those from sections of the public not previously attracted to cricket, either by attendance or the media.

CRICKET IN THE WEST INDIES 1979   Tony Cozier, 1980

The 1979 first-class season in the West Indies was so dominated by the tour of World Series Cricket through the region that public interest in the Shell Shield competition was acutely diminished. Major matches, such as those between Barbados and Trinidad, Barbados and Guyana, and Trinidad and the Combined Islands, which attracted crowds in excess of 10,000 on the best days in the past, were attended by fewer than 1,000 on several occasions. There was no crowd larger than 5,000, several attendances were in three figures, and only 51 paying spectators watched the final day of the Trinidad v Guyana match at the Queen's Park Oval (capacity 28,000).

Such depressing statistics were worrying to the West Indies Cricket Board of Control, which had announced a loss of close on £100,000 for the year ending September 30, 1978. The Shield, after all, remains the premier first-class competition in the West Indies and, over the years, has stimulated keen public enthusiasm.

The presence of WSC also had a peculiar effect on the composition of the teams fielded by Barbados, the eventual champions, whose triumph was their third in successive years and their eighth (once shared) in the 13 seasons of the Shield. With seven of their players engaged with WSC, they were forced to call on their reserve strength in the opening two matches against Jamaica and the Combined Islands. They did so well that Barbados had accumulated 18 of a possible 24 points at that stage. For the final two games, the WSC players were available and were chosen.

WSC West Indies v WSC Australia
At Kingston, February 23, 24, 25, 26, 1979. WSC West Indies won by 369 runs.

Toss: WSC West Indies. **WSC West Indies 188** (I. V. A. Richards 31, C. H. Lloyd 56; D. K. Lillee 4-68)
and 481 (R. C. Fredericks 69, I. V. A. Richards 48, C. H. Lloyd 197, A. M. E. Roberts 89, Extras 39;
D. K. Lillee 4-100); **WSC Australia 106** (C. E. H. Croft 3-34, W. W. Daniel 3-24) **and 194**
(I. M. Chappell 41, R. J. Bright 47*, M. F. Kent 30; M. A. Holding 3-37, C. E. H. Croft 3-70)

WSC West Indies v WSC Australia

At Port-of-Spain, March 16, 17, 18, 19, 20, 1979. WSC Australia won by 24 runs.

Toss: WSC Australia. **WSC Australia 246** (B. M. Laird 122, R. W. Marsh 34, D. K. Lillee 30; M. A. Holding 5-48, A. M. E. Roberts 3-39) **and 282** (M. F. Kent 45, G. S. Chappell 150; A. L. Padmore 6-81); **WSC West Indies 230** (I. V. A. Richards 44, C. H. Lloyd 39, A. M. E. Roberts 50*; J. R. Thomson 5-78, L. S. Pascoe 3-35) **and 274** (C. G. Greenidge 37, R. C. Fredericks 72, I. V. A. Richards 46; D. K. Lillee 3-77, I. M. Chappell 3-35).

The other three "Super-Tests" were drawn. The game at Bridgetown in March was abandoned because of crowd disturbances.

INDIA V AUSTRALIA 1979
Dicky Rutnagur, 1981

The Australians' third full tour of India was of historic interest on two counts. It was Australia's final campaign before the compromise between the Australian Cricket Board of Control and World Series Cricket took effect, and it was important from their opponents' viewpoint because India won a series (2–0) against Australia for the first time. The two countries had previously contested seven rubbers over 31 years, during which India had won only five Tests to Australia's 19, with six drawn.

The result of the Test series was not unexpected, for the Australians were relatively inexperienced, ten of the party of 15 never having toured before. Moreover, they were all new to conditions on the Indian subcontinent. The main Australian gain of the tour was the tremendous advance made by two batsmen, Hughes and Border. Between the First Test and the last there was a marked development in Hughes's technique of playing spin bowling, and happily the heavy burden of captaincy had no adverse effect on his batting.

The series marked the end of an era in Indian cricket as, for the first time in 11 years, India took the field without any of their three great contemporary spinners, Chandrasekhar, Bedi and Prasanna. Venkataraghavan also lost his place after the first two Tests. The main wicket-taker, with 28 victims, was pace bowler Kapil Dev, who showed how much he had benefited from the tour of England.

AUSTRALIA V ENGLAND 1979–80
Peter Smith, 1981

Forty-eight hours before England's cricketers flew out of Melbourne for the last time, Alec Bedser was asked by the Australian authorities to present his considered view of the experimental twin-tour programme, the first product of the marriage between the Australian Cricket Board and World Series Cricket which had taken place some nine months earlier. He gave it a definite thumbs-down. It was a strictly personal view, sought not in his capacity as England's tour manager or as chairman of England's selectors but from a man who has had the closest possible association with the game through four decades. He received majority support from those who had the best interests of cricket at heart, particularly Australian cricket below Test level. This had been swamped by the accent on Test and one-day internationals, neatly parcelled to present a cricketing package suitable for maximum exploitation on television.

Privately, at least, the Australian players agreed with Bedser. With a programme of six Test matches – three each against England and West Indies – plus the triangular one-day competition for the Benson and Hedges World Series Cup, the Australian players became very much a touring side inside their own country. So anxious was their captain Greg Chappell to rejoin a family he had hardly seen for two months that

Still time for a beer: Mike Brearley (left) and Greg Chappell, rival captains in the 1979–80 series between England and Australia, share a drink after the Second Test at Sydney.

he was flying home to Brisbane within an hour of bringing the final Test against England in Melbourne to a swift and victorious conclusion.

England's cricketers were just as unhappy with the complicated programme of matches that brought a constant switch from one-day to five-day cricket with few three-day matches in between. It could be claimed that England's verdict was coloured by their 3–0 series defeat in the Tests, but Clive Lloyd, West Indies' captain, was just as critical immediately after his side's two-nil series win – their first in Australia at the sixth attempt – and their victory in the World Series Cup.

It was not only the match programme but the whole atmosphere that the England players found disagreeable. Their captain, Brearley, was the subject of a disgraceful campaign wherever he went, and a large section of the Melbourne crowd was so abusive that the Australian team manager, John Edwards, was moved to issue a statement in which he said they made him ashamed to be an Australian. The childish behaviour of Lillee during the aluminium bat affair during the First Test in Perth and his baiting of Brearley during a one-day international in Sydney proved as distasteful to them as the treatment they received from the crowd in the early night games under the Sydney floodlights when they became the target of an assortment of missiles.

The show-business style presentation of the one-day matches by the marketing company advising the Australian Cricket Board succeeded in appealing to a new public, but the loutish, drunken behaviour of many of the newcomers posed additional headaches for the ground authorities. Both in Melbourne and Sydney costly extra security measures were taken, along with a restriction on the amount of alcohol sold inside the grounds or taken in. This improved the behaviour but not the language.

In losing the actual Test series against this background it could be said that England achieved all that was expected of them when they arrived in Australia. For the first time for three years, the Australians had available their full complement of players, with Lillee and Thomson, destroyers of England in two previous series, on hand to team up with Hogg, who had taken 41 Test wickets against England the previous winter. Greg Chappell was back to provide the leadership and batting expertise missing 12 months earlier, and there were half a dozen others rich in Test experience. The availability of these players promised to provide England with their toughest opposition since Brearley assumed the captaincy in 1977. Against more modest bowling attacks, England's batting had proved brittle in the in-between years. Against Australia it failed to function as a unit, even though Thomson was seldom fit to take part and Hogg disappeared from the series, losing both his confidence and fitness after a severe mauling from West Indies.

There were pockets of resistance in each Test match, such as Boycott's unbeaten 99 in the second innings in the First Test in Perth when trying to save the game, Gower's unbeaten 98 in the second innings of the Second Test in Sydney, Gooch's 99 in the first innings of the final Test in Melbourne and Botham's 119 not out in the second innings to delay Australia's victory. Brearley, too, offered stern resistance in every Test; but Lillee proved that, at 30, he was still a match-winning bowler, even if he had lost that explosive edge. He took 23 wickets in the series, 11 of them in the final Test in Melbourne when he cut his pace and produced a mixture of leg-and off-cutters which drew the highest praise from Brearley.

With problems in all departments, Brearley was not as positive as he might have been in countering them. He is not a captain for laying down the law. The England sides under his command have been happy sides, and he seemed reluctant to risk spoiling that harmony by remonstrating with his batsmen even when they continued to display a lack of discipline and sense of responsibility. In fairness, Brearley was also burdened at the start of the tour with additional tasks that should have been no part of his brief and that led directly to his unpopularity with sections of the Australian crowd. Communication difficulties with the Australian board resulted in England and West Indies arriving with the playing conditions still to be finalised. Renewed pressure was put on Brearley to accept conditions already rejected by the Test and County Cricket Board, namely the wearing of coloured stripes on shirts, flannels and sweaters, using a white ball in day-time matches, and restrictive fielding circles – as used in World Series Cricket – for the one-day internationals. As the spokesman outlining England's objections to conditions which seemed designed principally for television, Brearley was portrayed as a whingeing Pom, which was grossly unfair. It must be hoped that no future captain is ever landed with such a burden.

Australia v England   First Test

At Perth, December 14, 15, 16, 18, 19, 1979. Australia won by 138 runs.

It was unfortunate that Australia's victory at the end of an enthralling match was soured by Lillee's unsavoury behaviour in seeking to use an aluminium bat in the first innings despite objections from Brearley, the umpires and his own captain. He caused play to be held up for ten minutes before being persuaded by Chappell to exchange it for the traditional willow. The incident served only to blacken Lillee's reputation and damage the image of the game as well as, eventually, the reputation of the Australian authorities because of their reluctance to take effective disciplinary action. Lillee's behaviour also partly overshadowed other individual performances more in keeping with the spirit of the game, notably the bowling of Botham and Dymock, the batting of Hughes and Border, and Boycott's gallant attempt to save England on the final day.

Toss: England. **Australia 244** (K. J. Hughes 99, R. W. Marsh 42; I. T. Botham 6-78) **and 337**
(J. M. Wiener 58, B. M. Laird 33, A. R. Border 115, G. S. Chappell 43; I. T. Botham 5-98,
D. L. Underwood 3-82); **England 228** (J. M. Brearley 64, G. R. Dilley 38*; D. K. Lillee 4-73,
G. Dymock 3-52) **and 215** (G. Boycott 99*; G. Dymock 6-34).

Australia v West Indies 1979–80   Tony Cozier, 1981

West Indies achieved an historic and satisfying triumph over Australia in their three-match series that formed part of an unusual and revolutionary season for that country in 1979–80. In five previous tours of Australia, West Indies had always been the losers, defeat often so great as to amount to humiliation. This time they were not to be denied, converting their clear superiority over Australia into massive victories in the last two Tests after the first had been drawn.

The result was especially pleasing as this team included nine of those who had endured the 5–1 drubbing four years earlier, captain Lloyd and vice-captain Deryck Murray among them. However, they were well prepared, all but six of the party having been members of the World Series Cricket West Indies squad which had played in Australia over the two previous seasons.

Not only did West Indies retain the Frank Worrell Trophy by securing the Test series; they also confirmed their standing as the game's most efficient limited-overs combination by defeating England in the finals of the limited-overs Benson and Hedges World Series Cup. The large proportion of the major honours – and the prize money – was theirs. Vivian Richards was voted the outstanding player of both the Test and limited-overs series, and Gordon Greenidge the player of the limited-overs finals. The team's winnings amounted to $A86,000.

West Indies' success was based principally on the magnificent batting of Richards and on their quartet of fast bowlers – Roberts, Holding, Garner and Croft – who maintained persistent pressure on opposing batsmen and were well supported by safe-handed close-catching. In addition, an intensive physical fitness schedule paid dividends in reducing injuries to a minimum.

Few individuals have so dominated a season as Richards did this one. Statistics help tell some of the story. In the Tests, he scored 140 at Brisbane, 96 at Melbourne, and 76 and 74 at Adelaide. In the World Series Cup, his sequence was 9, 153 not out, 62, 85 not out, 88, 23 and 65. Outside the Tests he batted in only two first-class innings, scoring 79 and 127. He gathered his runs with the command and range of strokes of the truly great batsmen, scoring freely against bowling of every type. That he was suffering at the time from groin and back trouble so acute that he was often forced to limp painfully emphasised the extraordinary nature of his performance.

The batting of his team-mates suffered by comparison. None of them could find consistent form although Lloyd, at the end of a season troubled by injury and self-doubt, contributed a vital and typically belligerent century on the first day of the final Test. Greenidge improved steadily from an uncertain beginning and played two sterling innings in the one-day finals, while Kallicharran chose the very last opportunity to register his only significant score of the series, a century in the second innings of the final Test. In the field, Lloyd always had at his disposal an almost irresistible form of attack, he and his co-selectors adhering rigidly to a policy of pace to the exclusion of spin.

Whereas West Indies possessed a stronger, fitter and better prepared team than they had four years earlier, the Australians were nothing like the force they were then. Greg Chappell, reinstated as captain, and Lillee, slower but shrewder, remained their outstanding individuals. Yet too much depended on these two, and the strain told. Chappell, after batting with all his old authority in the first Test, fell three times in his last four innings to the bouncer. His vice-captain, Hughes, played freely in the second innings at Brisbane and Melbourne, but the only batsman who scored with any consistency was the diminutive Western Australian opener, Laird. In his first Test series, Laird showed determination and courage, passing 50 in four of his six innings.

Perhaps Australia's biggest disappointments were in the lack of support for Lillee, the failure of Marsh's batting, and the lack of an adequate all-rounder. There were well-founded local hopes that, with Lillee and Thomson now joined by Hogg, the pace of the West Indians would be matched ball for ball. Instead, Thomson, troubled by injury, was not half the menace he had been, and Hogg was also reduced by injury, a disheartening blow following his exploits of the previous season against England. It was left to the veteran left-armer Dymock to fill the gap, which he tried nobly to do. Australia might have turned more to spin, but in the event the three spinners used, Bright, Higgs and Mallett, each played in only a single Test against West Indies.

Arranged as it was with the emphasis on the Tests and limited-overs internationals, the tour offered little opportunity for the reserve players, whose cricketing education suffered as a result. It was this aspect of the experimental, triangular international arrangement which caused most concern, although there was a body of opinion that the format of this exceptional season would be the prototype of future international cricket.

Australia v West Indies ⠀⠀⠀⠀⠀⠀⠀⠀⠀⠀⠀⠀⠀⠀⠀⠀⠀⠀ Second Test
At Melbourne, December 29, 30, 31, 1979, January 1, 1980. West Indies won by ten wickets.

In winning with a day to spare, West Indies emphatically overcame their jinx at the Melbourne Cricket Ground, where they had lost every one of their previous seven Tests. They took a grip on the match from the start, bowling Australia out for 156 and replying with 103 for one off eighteen overs by the close on the first day.

Toss: Australia. **Australia 156** (J. M. Wiener 40; M. A. Holding 4-40, C. E. H. Croft 3-27, J. Garner 3-33) **and 259** (B. M. Laird 69, K. J. Hughes 70; A. M. E. Roberts 3-64, C. E. H. Croft 3-61); **West Indies 397** (C. G. Greenidge 48, I. V. A. Richards 96, A. I. Kallicharran 39, C. H. Lloyd 40, A. M. E. Roberts 54; D. K. Lillee 3-96, G. Dymock 4-106, J. D. Higgs 3-122) **and 22-0.**

Australia v West Indies ⠀⠀⠀⠀⠀⠀⠀⠀⠀⠀⠀⠀⠀⠀⠀⠀⠀⠀ Third Test
At Adelaide, January 26, 27, 28, 29, 30, 1980. West Indies won by 408 runs.

West Indies needed only a draw to clinch their first series in Australia; instead, they so outplayed their dispirited opponents that their victory was one of the most overwhelming in Tests between the two countries. As usual, their formula for success was consistent batting, irresistible fast bowling and athletically alert fielding.

Toss: Australia. **West Indies 328** (I. V. A. Richards 76, L. G. Rowe 40, C. H. Lloyd 121; D. K. Lillee 5-78) **and 448** (C. G. Greenidge 76, I. V. A. Richards 74, A. I. Kallicharran 106, L. G. Rowe 43, C. H. Lloyd 40, Extras 32; G. Dymock 5-104); **Australia 203** (B. M. Laird 52, K. J. Hughes 34, A. R. Border 54; A. M. E. Roberts 3-43, C. E. H. Croft 4-57) **and 165** (B. M. Laird 36, G. S. Chappell 31; M. A. Holding 4-40).

BENSON AND HEDGES WORLD SERIES CUP 1979–80 ⠀⠀⠀⠀⠀⠀⠀⠀ 1981

For the second time in the space of eight months, West Indies proved them-selves the outstanding limited-overs side in cricket when they won the trian-gular Benson and Hedges World Series Cup in Australia by beating England twice in the best-of-three final. Their victory, in the end, was as emphatic as it had been the previous June at Lord's when the same 11 players defeated England in the final of the World Cup. West Indies stumbled in the first of the final matches, in Melbourne, two run-outs almost certainly costing England their chance of victory. England finished two runs short. That scare behind them West Indies quickly made sure the third scheduled final match would be unnecessary by overwhelming England in the second final at Sydney two days later. Here Greenidge and Richards made light of the task of scoring the 209 runs their side required to capture the first prize of £16,000. The outcome of the triangular tournament, in which each side played the other four times in a qualifying round with the two most successful teams going into the final, was largely a battle between West Indies' heavy artillery and England's professional, limited-overs expertise based on containment and the ability to frustrate batsmen. The West Indian fire-power, usually supplied by Greenidge and Richards, generally won the day. Strangely, however, West Indies encountered difficulties whenever they came across the Australians, who bowled for wickets instead of adopting the run-saving line and length approach of England. Lloyd's team, having lost three of their four qualifying matches against Australia, all at Sydney, had had to rely on beating England to reach the finals.

Winning the limited-overs competition gave Lloyd as much pleasure as taking the Test series against Australia, although for different reasons. He felt their triumph confirmed he was leading the best side to emerge from the Caribbean, not only for their ability but also for their determination to fight back when events had gone against them. This had not often been a feature of West Indies' sides on tour. The failure of the Australians to qualify for the finals was a major disappointment for the home crowd, the Channel Nine television company for which the competition had been specially tailored, and the Australian cricket authorities who were relying on an Australia-West Indies final to attract the crowds and help pay the costs of staging a twin tour.

ENGLAND v WEST INDIES 1980   **Benson and Hedges World Series Final**

Best of three matches – West Indies won 2–0 with third match not required.

England v West Indies   **First Match**

At Melbourne, January 20, 1980. West Indies won by two runs.

Toss: England. **West Indies 215-8** (50 overs) (C. G. Greenidge 80, A. I. Kallicharran 42, C. L. King 31*; I. T. Botham 3-33); **England 213-7** (50 overs) (G. Boycott 35, P. Willey 51, W. Larkins 34; A. M. E. Roberts 3-30).

England v West Indies   **Second Match**

At Sydney, January 22, 1980 (day/night). West Indies won by eight wickets.

Toss: England. **England 208-8** (50 overs) (G. Boycott 63, I. T. Botham 37); **West Indies 209-2** (47.3 overs) (C. G. Greenidge 98*, I. V. A. Richards 65).

CRICKET IN AUSTRALIA 1979–80   Peter McFarline, 1981

The season, the first after the amalgamation of the Australian Cricket Board and World Series Cricket, proved a financial disaster. Despite the return to the fold of most of the country's best players, losses suffered by the various state associations totalled more than £125,000. Leading administrators sought vainly to find a formula that would bring the crowds back. The introduction of the six-ball over in the 1979–80 season did not bring the faster over-rate that was hoped for. In addition, a packed itinerary meant that several of the better-known players were rarely available for their states. Kim Hughes, of Western Australia, did not play in a single Shield match, owing to the late return of the Australian side from the 1979 tour of India and a heavy schedule of international commitments.

The matter of player behaviour also had an adverse effect on attendances. South Australian captain Ian Chappell was twice disciplined by the board following umpires' reports. He received a three-week suspension for abusive language in the game against Tasmania in Devonport early in the season, and later a suspended sentence for alleged misconduct in South Australia's game against the touring Englishmen. Before the 1980–81 season began, the players themselves drew up a code of behaviour which the board agreed should be administered by the players. Thus, for the first time in sporting history, the matter of player conduct was given solely to the participants.

But the overriding cause of poor attendances could be traced directly to the saturation of international cricket in Australia. With joint tours now a fact of life, and 20 limited-overs internationals scheduled for each season, it became apparent that Australian cricket-lovers had decided, rightly or wrongly, that the Sheffield Shield was scarcely worthy of their attention or their money.

Cricket in the West Indies 1980   Tony Cozier, 1981

Barbados won the Shell Shield for the fifth consecutive time and, in doing so, created a record by winning all four matches outright. After two seasons in the doldrums, with public interest being drained by the loss of leading players to World Series Cricket, the Shield was revitalised. The scheduled Indian tour was cancelled so that there was no counter-attraction, and the majority of those engaged in the tour of Australia and New Zealand answered the board's plea to return home for the competition. The result was increased enthusiasm and, generally speaking, large crowds.

The Passing of WSC   John Woodcock, *Notes by the Editor*, 1981

On the surface, the end of traditional cricket's acrimonious dispute with Mr Kerry Packer brought a reasonably harmonious return to normality. But at what cost to the game? Cricketers who were previously paid too little are now, in some cases, being paid more than the game can afford or they themselves are worth. Money has become the talk of the first-class dressing-rooms, with the average county cricketer feeling that Test players are getting a disproportionately large slice of the cake.

In Australia, one worrying aspect of the settlement which led to the running-down of World Series Cricket is the new structure of the first-class game there, this now being devised to accommodate commercial television. When England were in Australia in the winter of 1979–80, a tour they shared with West Indies, such was the confusion of fixtures that attendances and authenticity both suffered. The public seemed not to know what to expect next, or indeed for what trophy any given match was being played. As for the players, they were given little chance to settle down to any one type of cricket, whether one-day, four-day or five-day, all of which call for different tactics and not necessarily the same skills.

The World After Packer

A t one time, I had planned to conclude this long, synoptic chapter with Tim de Lisle's paean – from the 2003 *Wisden*, which he edited as a unique one-off – to Steve Waugh's Australia and the way they had revolutionised Test cricket, dragging the game into "the age of speed". Then, I thought perhaps that all-important final piece should be Matthew Engel's celebration of cricket in 2003, from his Notes in the 2004 *Wisden*, which included a compelling Test series between England and South Africa, record-breaking batting performances all round the world, the extraordinarily successful debut of Twenty20 cricket (what would Norman Preston have made of that?), and a sunny English summer. I also had to keep a weather eye on the 2006 *Wisden*, due to land on my desk as I worked and sure to be full of encomia to England's Ashes heroes.

And yet, and yet, being British, it was not in my nature to end in so celebratory a fashion – to say that cricket has come through its travails and emerged in robust health. It is, I believe, possible to construct such an argument. The Packer experiment was a grave threat to cricket and forced a transformation that may have been unhealthily rapid. Subsequent chapters in this section will deal with some of the negative effects of Packerism – overcommercialism, the ill-discipline that reached crisis proportions in the 1980s, the bribery scandals that the proliferation of largely meaningless one-day matches facilitated. But as cricket administration professionalised itself – the introduction of "neutral" umpires was a crucial step in taking the heat out of incendiary situations and improving player behaviour – many of these difficulties were met and overcome, and by 2000 the game was presenting a bold and confident face to the world.

But still I refuse to be too Panglossian. In part, this is out of self-defence: what if this volume appears shortly after England have been crushed in a Test series and the Ashes triumph of 2005 has been, if not forgotten, put into some sort of perspective? The annual swings of emotion, depending on how well the national side is performing, are remarkable for their ferocity. The glorious Ashes series of 2005 was not a terminus, the full stop that marked the end of a generation of revolutionary change. It was part of the story. We should beware a Whig interpretation of cricketing history: we have lived through some gloriously exciting years, and later sections of this book will celebrate great games and great players, but time never stands still, nothing should be taken for granted, anything could happen. The golden age is a chimera: it exists only in the eye of the the the beholder. All ages are combinations of lead and gold.

England's defeat in Pakistan, a few months after the national party that culminated in Trafalgar Square and saw Andrew Flintoff embark on one of the most monumental benders in recorded history, was a reminder that events will always confute us. When the Berlin Wall fell, Francis Fukuyama declared the end of history and his thesis became very fashionable... until it was replaced by the "Clash of Civilisations" and what looked very much like a new history. So all conclusions are provisional, which is why I eventually chose a characteristically wry piece by Engel from the notes he wrote on his return from the cricket-shy US. Engel, a little out of the loop, was struggling to come to terms with Twenty20, Duckworth/Lewis, squad numbers, and Dominic Cork's Alice band. (Sorry to harp on about this, but what would Norman Preston have made of Dominic Cork's Alice band? *Wisden* decorated Hugh Chevallier's report on the inaugural Twenty20 finals with a large photograph of Jenny Frost of the pop group Atomic Kitten, who performed at Trent Bridge on finals day, and a rather smaller picture of Azhar Mahmood. "From Norman Preston to Atomic Kitten" would, I think, be quite an engaging – and evocative – title for this volume.)

Engel's returning squib contains a veiled warning not to see Twenty20 as necessarily the saviour of county cricket. Look what happened to the John Player League, he says, to which crowds, and BBC TV cameras, once flocked on Sunday afternoons. There was another warning, too. As I started to write the introduction to this section, India were telling the ICC that they did not wish to participate in the Champions Trophy after 2006, preferring to stage their own money-spinning tournaments. Commentators were quick to see the seeds of a rift within the game: India, cricket's global superpower, might choose to go its own way. A game that lives by the rupee might die by the rupee.

In fact, in the end even Engel's delightful return-from-exile piece was supplanted by his shriek of rage in the 2006 *Wisden* at the ICC's growing commercialism, as reflected in the absurd and thankfully disastrous "Super Series'" between Australia and the Rest of the World (Packerism reborn?) and its crass dalliance with super-subs and powerplays. To my mind, Engel's apocalyptic tone is a little overcooked: these initiatives were daft and won't be repeated; there are pros and cons to letting the minnows swim in the 2007 World Cup and at least this time the structure will allow them to be swallowed reasonably swiftly. But if *Wisden* doesn't protect the authenticity of the game, who will?

This tension between enthusiasm for a new, dynamic, barely containable global sport and fear of what the ultimate consequences might be underpins, and I hope energises, the articles I have chosen for this chapter. They are more than mere period pieces because the issues remain central to the evolution of cricket: the relationship of Tests to one-day matches; of the national team to the rest of the domestic programme; of commercialism to what might, a little pompously, be called the eternal verities of the game.

In the 1980s and early '90s, Tests did appear to be an endangered species and writers in *Wisden* were close to despair. It was the cricketing equivalent of television abandoning Kenneth Clark's *Civilisation* for an endless supply of *Big Brother*. The public watched, but their minds were being poisoned by the pap. But Test cricket fought back – *Civilisation* on television has yet to make the same recovery – and now appears to be buoyant in most parts of the world, though as *Wisden* editors never tire of telling us, ignoring the paradox, there are simply too many quickfire Test series.

The greatest change recorded by *Wisden* in this period of almost 30 years, and prefigured in the previous chapter, is that international cricket has been virtually divorced from the domestic game. The implications of this have yet to be digested. As Graeme Wright argued in his final Notes in 2002 (reprinted below), England retains a 19th-century county set-up but with no support base or local funding to justify it. Who are these games being played for: a few diehard fans, the players themselves, the good of the England team? The County Championship – Cardus's "background music to an English summer" – is played this way because it has always been played this way. But need it be, forever? And is it really sustainable? Will the television money, gained by selling rights to England matches, always be there? These are huge questions for English domestic cricket – and, to a lesser extent perhaps, for other countries too. The revolution really isn't over.

Wright's suggestion – then fashionable but now, in the wake of the money-spinning success of Twenty20, largely forgotten – was to base domestic cricket around cities rather than counties. I seem to recall making a similar argument once, but I'm not sure I ever really believed it: would any supporter really feel empathy with a team called London? Of course not. Our sympathies are with smaller entities – or, oddly, somewhat bogus entities such as counties. I was born in Gwent (formerly and now again called Monmouthshire), but fell in love with Glamorgan, the neighbouring county which contrives to represent all Wales. I still follow their scores on the internet, on Ceefax and in the newspapers (though I avert my eyes if, as in 2005, they are excruciatingly bad), but I rarely see them play, living 150 miles away from the county ground. What does my affinity add up to? Would I miss them if they were gone? What could replace them? Not Cardiff, I hope, for which I would feel no affection. So, Wales, or Wales and the West?

The issues are, as always, intractable. Should the weaker counties go to the wall? How many teams should there be? How many overseas players should counties field? As several commentators below point out, we have now reached the ludicrous position where the home-grown talents, centrally contracted, rarely turn out for their counties, but all sorts of here today, gone tomorrow foreign stars, eager to earn a fast buck, do a month here and there, leaving spectators confused and destroying the notion of a county allegiance. Majid Khan, Glamorgan's batting star in my youth (though his hundreds usually evaded my eyes), was an honorary Welshman; Rohan Kanhai and Alvin Kallicharran men of Warwickshire; Barry Richards and Gordon Greenidge synonymous with Hampshire. Those days are gone. Now many counties will plump for a fringe Test player able to plug a gap in August in a bid to fend off relegation. It leaves county cricket looking tawdry and hollow. Simon Heffer, in his devastating critique of the county game in 2002, says turn the clock back – to three-day cricket, uncovered pitches, a more relaxed international schedule. A good Tory response from the biographer of Carlyle, but I don't see the ECB buying it, somehow. Some more radical solution will have to be found.

The diminution of the status of the first-class domestic game is by no means only an English phenomenon. The 1976 *Wisden* devoted 20 pages to full Sheffield Shield scorecards. The 2001 *Wisden* provides five pages of abbreviated scores on the Pura Milk Cup (I suppose the fact they have been condensed has a certain logic). *Wisden* might argue that the full scores are available in its baggy-green Australian sibling, but I see it as part of a trend: these historic clashes between the Australian states just don't matter as much any more: to fans, administrators or pundits. The national team takes up all our attention; tours have really just become sets of Test matches and one-day internationals; the action is now downtown rather than up-country. Cricket, in the public mind at least, has lost its context: all that matters now is the cream – and I'm not referring here to the Pura Cup.

The articles below are arranged roughly chronologically, though I have occasionally grouped them thematically where pieces from different years were making similar points. They offer a fascinating insight into cricket's preoccupations over the past 30 years and show *Wisden* itself having to adapt to a game that was changing with extraordinary speed.

Three final thoughts. First, I see the International Cricket Council's move to Dubai in 2005 as a symbol of the changes that have taken place in the past three decades: the shift in power from west to east, the marginalisation of MCC, and the switch from a patrician hierarchy to a commercially minded secretariat (Dubai was chosen for tax reasons as well as to reflect a globalising game). Somehow Dubai seems perfect for modern cricket – slick, fast-moving, multi-ethnic, at times anonymous. Second, beware blanket condemnations of the one-day game. *Wisden* editors have sometimes been guilty of this, I have sometimes been guilty of this, too – all these pointless and predictable games in which the side batting first will almost invariably make 256. That is how I have always seen it, and yet I was in the gym a few days before I tackled this introduction, watching Sky without commentary, and I found a one-day match between South Africa and Sri Lanka compelling watching. It was part of one of those absurd triangular series in Australia in which it takes about a dozen games to eliminate one team – they have always struck me as the *reductio ad absurdum* of sport – yet the South African fielders were so intense and the Sri Lankans so crestfallen in defeat that I could not bring myself to despise the game for its lack of a legitimate context. It was exciting; the players were fired up; in that moment it had reality, even if two days later it was forgotten.

My final thought is, beware predictions. In an excellent piece on the future of the game from 1986 (also reprinted below), Sir Donald Bradman bemoaned the death of the leg-spinner, killed off by one-day cricket. A few years later, you-know-who arrived on the scene – in fairness, Pakistan's Abdul Qadir had blazed the trail – to recreate the art, propel Australia to greatness and, if this is not too grand a claim, change the whole feel of cricket. It once more has subtlety and artistry; Roberts, Marshall, Garner, Holding were an irresistible force of nature; Warne was a gift from God. Or perhaps, we England supporters would say, the Devil.   S. M.

WHY THE AUSTRALIAN "ESTABLISHMENT" GAVE IN   R. J. Parish, 1984

The Australian season of 1983–84 completed the fifth year of the agreement between the Australian Cricket Board and World Series Cricket. It was in May 1977 that World Series Cricket burst upon the cricketing world and in May 1979 that agreement was reached between the two factions; after two years of trauma, disastrous law suits and internecine disputes.

Much has been written as to the reasons why a private promoter entered the field of the commercial promotion of international cricket. It is not my intention to recapitulate those reasons or to attempt to justify arguments one way or the other. However, it would be wrong of me not to take this opportunity to clarify the Australian board's motive and method in reaching the agreement it did. The board has been, and is still, concerned that its action has not been fully understood.

In June 1977, at a special meeting of the International Cricket Conference, the effect of the private promotion of international cricket was fully discussed and it was unanimously agreed that there should be no unilateral attempts to reach a compromise or solution. ICC set up a sub-committee to pursue negotiations with WSC with a view to achieving an agreement eagerly sought by several of the Test-match-playing countries. By late 1978 it was becoming more and more apparent that, if a solution were to be reached, it would depend on the attitude and initiative of the Australian board.

In January 1979 the chairman of ICC gave written authorisation to the Australian board to hold unilateral talks with WSC. Both the chairman and secretary of ICC were informed in February 1979 that continuing talks raised hopes of achieving a solution. Detailed negotiations continued, and on April 24, 1979, the board announced that it had accepted, in principle, an offer from PBL Sports Pty Ltd. On April 27 a telex was sent to the secretary of ICC setting out the relevant details as they affected other countries. It was made clear that Australia had not committed and would not commit ICC or other countries but could only use their best endeavours to implement what had been agreed.

The non-disclosure of the financial conditions caused some consternation. However, it has always been the Australian board's policy not to make public the financial conditions relating to television fees and sponsorships. ICC was assured that the agreement provided no bonanza for the Australian board, and whether or not the agreement was financially successful would depend on the ability of the promoters to encourage attendance at the programme of matches. The board had acted honourably and entered into the agreement in the best interests, as they saw them, of international cricket.

Now, what has happened over the past five years? It was understandable that, in arriving at a solution, the promoters of WSC should want a combination of what they saw as the best of their own cricket with the best of the traditional game. So, out of the negotiations came a mixture of traditional Test cricket with one-day internationals.

The control of the game reverted to the Australian board while PBL undertook, with their considerable expertise, to promote the programme. This provided for two visiting Test-playing countries to be involved each season. Initially it was agreed that each visiting country would play three Tests against Australia. Interspersed would be a total of 15 one-day internationals with a final the best of five matches. Test cricket would maintain its traditional red ball and white clothing. The one-day competition would use a white ball, coloured clothing and play a number of day/night matches.

By agreement, the first participants in this new era were England and West Indies in 1979–80. India, who had been invited to tour Australia in that season agreed to transfer to 1980–81 and to combine with New Zealand. West Indies and Pakistan agreed to tour together in 1981–82. The 1979–80 joint tour was not easy to arrange. England were not happy about the number of one-day internationals, finally agreeing to play a total of eight preliminary games, four each against West Indies and Australia and a final the best-of-three. Coloured clothing was unacceptable, even though it was considered essential for night games. England were also apprehensive about using the white ball in one-day daylight matches, though one of the reasons for using the white ball in both day and day/night matches was to differentiate between traditional Test cricket and the series of one-day internationals. Finally, after weeks of discussion, the joint tour by England and West Indies was confirmed, though England were not agreeable to their three-match Test series being for the Ashes. Australia also agreed with England that after the first three years of this type of programme the Board would give consideration to reverting to the traditional Ashes programme for England's 1982–83 tour of Australia.

The 1979–80 season was successful. A total of 228,936 attended the three Tests against England and 216,659 the three against West Indies. Australia failed to qualify for the final of the Benson and Hedges World Series Cup, and one preliminary match, England against West Indies, scheduled to be played at Melbourne, was completely abandoned because of rain. Nevertheless, a total of 258,825 attended the eleven preliminary and two final matches. The total attendance for the international season in Australia of 703,420 compared favourably with previous figures.

A survey taken during the season showed that support for Test cricket and the limited-overs games was more or less equally divided. A majority supported the use of coloured clothing in one-day games. It became apparent during the season that the mixing of Test cricket and one-day internationals was somewhat confusing to the public and difficult for the players. Some of the players found it hard to adapt from normal Test cricket to the hustle and bustle of the interspersed limited-overs games. Nevertheless, a similar type of programme as that provided in the original agreement was confirmed for the seasons 1980–81 (India and New Zealand) and 1981–82 (West Indies and Pakistan).

In 1980–81 the world attendance record for a one-day game was broken in Melbourne when 52,990 attended the first final between New Zealand and Australia. In 1981–82, again in Melbourne, a West Indies-Australia preliminary one-day match attracted 78,142 spectators. Financially, the three seasons 1979–80, 1980–81, and 1981–82 were successful, especially when compared with 1977–78 and 1978–79, the seasons of the rift, both of which had shown substantial losses.

With the experience of the three previous seasons and in the light of the assurance given to England in 1979–80 to review the type of programme for their 1982–83 tour, it was decided to revert to the traditional five-Test tour for the Ashes series and to play the Tests first, followed by 15 one-day games and a best-of-three final. The result was a success. At a preliminary match, between England and Australia in Melbourne, a new record attendance for one-day limited-overs matches of 84,360 was established. The overall attendance at international cricket in 1982–83 totalled almost 1,100,000 – a substantial increase over the total for 1979–80.

It has to be remembered that only two-thirds of the Australian population are now of Anglo-Saxon origin. The other third, principally European, has never been exposed to cricket. But it is pleasing to note the increasing interest in cricket from members of ethnic groups.

Cricket is a players' game. Test cricket is the game preferred by the players, the one for which they have been trained. However, they appreciate the financial need to play a combination of traditional and limited-overs cricket. Administrators must judge the success of a players' game by the number of participants. In Australia there are more players than ever before. A public opinion poll conducted in June 1983 showed that the most popular sport in Australia is cricket. Long may that continue.

In the late 1970s, R. J. Parish was chairman of the Australian Cricket Board, and thus the man who sued for peace with Packer. Wisden *presented this as Parish's "first account of the war and peace with Packer". Editor John Woodcock described it, in his preface, as "of definitive interest". Even* Wisden, *it seems, was learning the value of hype.*

THE NIGHT EXPERIMENT

John Woodcock, *Notes by the Editor*, 1981

New to the English scene in 1980 was night cricket, played on football grounds. Though the cricket itself was of no consequence, a germ has been implanted. There are, in cricketing administration today, marketing men whose desire to bring money into the game causes them to trifle with its origins and gamble with its charm. Night cricket in Sydney, being on a genuine cricket ground, indeed a great one, can be a dazzling spectacle, not far removed from the real thing; at Stamford Bridge it smacks of gimmickry. Should it ever catch on, it may have to be given another name, which is not to dismiss it as being of no threat to the present game. I have not included in this edition of *Wisden* the scores of the three night matches played in England last summer because they were meaningless.

EASY PICKINGS

E. M. Wellings, 1980

Is too much money too easily earned today? Do we set our sights too low? Should commentators encourage complacency by using the currently favourite BBC adverb "extremely" so freely? It is not an extremely good stroke when a supposedly Test-class batsman drives a half-volley, for most No. 11s can do that. For that matter, should commentators on TV talk as much as they do while play is actually in progress? Perhaps our low standard exists because the incentive to strive for perfection is insufficient.

Journalist E. M. Wellings's famously (perhaps infamously is a better word) ferocious views on England's hapless batsmen appear on page 227.

TOO MUCH TEST CRICKET John Woodcock, *Notes by the Editor*, 1981

The reason most often given for the decline in interest in the first-class game in Australia is that it has reached the point of saturation. The same applies to association football in England. There is too much of it, just as there is now, to my mind, too much Test cricket. Between the middle of July 1979 and the middle of February 1980, a matter of seven months, India played 17 Test matches. A series between them and West Indies, due to have taken place in March and April 1980, was cancelled simply because both countries were surfeited with Test cricket. Between December 1974 and the first week of September this year, England will have played Australia no fewer than 31 times. This is more than twice the rate at which they met until only a few years ago. In 1981, for the first time in England, Australia are playing six Test matches. We must be careful not to kill the goose that lays the golden egg.

Also for the first time in England there will be Test cricket on Sundays in 1981 – not in every Test but at Trent Bridge, Edgbaston and Old Trafford. The case for this, by those keen to make it, was strengthened by the loss of so much play on the first three days of last year's Centenary Test. Both captains expressed the view then that the Sunday should have been set aside for making up time lost. The decision now taken to implement Sunday play means that in three of this season's Test matches there will be no rest day. Thinking, as I do, that both players and public need one, and being opposed to the advancing tide of Continentalism on Sundays, this is a barrier which I would rather had not been broken down. So, no doubt, would John Player and Sons who, since their Sunday League began in 1969, have had Sunday afternoons more or less to themselves.

MORE TESTS, LESS CRICKET John Woodcock, *Notes by the Editor*, 1982

It is interesting to compare the itinerary of the 1981 Australians with that, for example, of Joe Darling's side in 1905. The old-timers played 113 days' cricket, 15 of them in Tests; last year Kim Hughes's side played 67, including 28 in Tests. As shorter tours, though with more Test matches, become the fashion, much enjoyable cricket, played in some of the pleasantest places, is being foregone by visiting teams.

It is not generally realised, I think, that county cricketers also play less cricket now than they did. Soon after the last war a couple of dozen bowlers would get through several hundred more overs in a season than anyone does today. Even as late as the 1960s, Lord's staged over 100 days of cricket in a season; this was down last year to 58.

A GLIMPSE INTO THE PAST
John Woodcock, *Notes by the Editor*, 1985

Many followers of the game were of the opinion that the most agreeable cricket they watched in 1984 was played on the first two days of the Test match against Sri Lanka at Lord's, when our visitors were batting. Their batsmen stood in the natural position, rather than with bat aloft; they used their feet, and bouncers were few and far between.

It would have been a very different story, I know, had the West Indians, not England, been bowling, or if England themselves had had a fast attack, but it was quite like the old days while it lasted. This was a great occasion for Sri Lanka, on which they won many new admirers. Wettimuny's 190 will have made him something of a legend.

So small, though, were the crowds which the match attracted, even over a holiday weekend, and England played so feebly, that there was no escaping the effects of the present surfeit of international cricket. The more there is of it the more the senior players, as well as the public, tend to take it for granted. Allegations that the England team to New Zealand and Pakistan in the winter of 1983–84 had been taking drugs would have seemed unthinkable, even in an age when it is common practice, but for the amount of touring they now do. England embarked of 15 Test matches in 1984, not to mention numerous one-day internationals.

THE WRONG KIND OF CRICKET
Graeme Wright, *Notes by the Editor*, 1988

The escalation of international cricket in the last ten years has been immense; but if the professional players are to be better paid, they have to perform for their rewards. The spectre of another Packer-style circus and rebel tours to South Africa still haunts the game's administrators. To alleviate what has correctly been described as a treadmill, one answer would be a reduction in the number of one-day internationals – but that is unlikely. Across the world the public prefers them to Test matches; and as economists tell us, the consumer dictates the market. Most children will eat hamburgers and chips in preference to a healthy, well-balanced meal when given a choice.

Early in 1987, the Sri Lankan opening batsman, Sidath Wettimuny, who in his country's first Test in England, at Lord's in 1984, scored 190, announced his retirement from cricket at the age of 30. Not considered for the one-day internationals, he felt that with the number now being played by touring sides he was not getting sufficient match practice for Test cricket. He had, he said, stopped enjoying the game. Towards the end of the year, India dropped one of the Test matches scheduled against West Indies in favour of two extra one-day matches. If, as has been seen in India and Pakistan, attendances at Test matches fall away, will sponsorship be found to keep them going? England, having given birth to the one-day competition, could find itself the last bastion of the Test match. Let us hope that there are still cricketers able to play in them.

THE COUNTIES' STRUGGLE TO SURVIVE Philip Carling, 1983

For most of its history, county cricket has lurched from one financial crisis to another. Only during the two immediate post-war periods did large crowds invade county grounds to provide relative security for clubs and players alike. Yet in spite of seemingly regular predictions that the end for cricket, or rather professional cricket, was nigh, the game has survived for the most part in a form which would have been immediately recognisable to its practitioners in late Victorian England. This thought is at the same time both reassuring and worrying. It is reassuring because the warmth of feeling for the game throughout English society has seen it safely through these crises; it is worrying lest today's administrators rely too heavily on this history of survival.

Cricket has traditionally provided for its professionals no more than a reasonable way of life and the hope, not always realised, of a rewarding benefit which would provide secondary employment when limbs or faculties forced a reluctant retirement. It became abruptly apparent, however, during the 1960s, that the game could not for very much longer support such an existence, even for a quite small number of players. As a result, a period of commercialism began with the advent of the knockout cup, sponsored on its inception by Gillette. Along with the growing awareness of the need to attract spectators back to cricket came the realisation that cricket could not survive without commercial support. It would be industry which would replace the wealthy benefactors of inter-war years. But there would be an important difference. Sponsorship is a reward-seeking, commercial activity and not an exercise in altruism. Cricket would have to adjust to its new partner and to a new image.

The limited-overs knockout competition was to bring its own problems. Above all, attitudes changed, and success on the field, previously the plaything of a small group of the more heavily populated counties, became paramount. Whereas overseas players helped to redress the county population imbalance, they increased the pressure to win. Financial rewards for international cricketers needed to be improved and the best English cricketers did not expect to lag behind the cricketing mercenaries.

The profound shock waves which swept through the cricket establishment worldwide at the formation of World Series Cricket in 1977 are proof that the commercial opportunities which offered themselves, once the Gillette sponsorship was adopted, were declined. Cricket was admittedly saved for the seventies, but other sports were left to capitalise on the interest newly shown by business and commercial organisations. Open tennis saw players' earnings multiply many times over, and golf's great achievement in Britain was to increase substantially the prize-money for the winner of its Open Championship while subjugating the size of the winner's purse to the prestige and traditional value of winning itself – proof that heavy commercialisation need not necessarily detract from tradition and the purity of a game.

Much of it had happened before. The parallels between William Clarke's operation in the mid-19th century and World Series Cricket are obvious. Clarke, in earning for himself considerable sums of money, clashed frequently with the established county game, with Lord's, and eventually with a rival organisation set up by James Dean and John Wisden, two of his own players who believed his profit margins were excessive.

The immediate rewards offered by World Series Cricket in 1977 were too good for a large number of international cricketers to refuse, but such an experiment, parasitic as it was and superimposed on the established game, could not survive as a long-term threat. The commercial success of the Melbourne Centenary Test match in March 1977 underlined both cricket's commercial potential at the highest level and the relatively poor rewards accepted until then by its top players. Thus World Series Cricket provided a logical if unwelcome jolt for the professional game. It provoked a new approach and a greater acceptance of the need for further commercialism. It posed many new problems, but solving them also helped to overcome previously unresolved difficulties. As a result, a hesitant acceptance of the need to improve cricketers' salaries, particularly at the highest level, has been at the heart of the flurry of commercial activity undertaken both by individual counties and centrally by the Test and County Cricket Board since 1977. Professional cricket could survive only if it could provide a rewarding career for its players.

Necessity has indeed proved the mother of invention. The marketing department of the Test and County Cricket Board, now a full-time operation, oversees an income to English cricket approaching £3m. Ironically, as it became apparent that the prices charged for national sponsorships were commercially unrealistic and could be increased, Gillette were the first major casualty. To a large extent, they were the victims of their own success. Gillette's name had become synonymous with cricket's knockout cup during a sponsorship lasting 18 years. The popularity of the competition had increased the value of a sponsorship which started at £6,500 to a startling £250,000, a sum which rather more than compensates for inflation. Gillette declined the increased cost and the National Westminster Bank were pleased to become involved in cricket. Gillette departed from the scene content that their long involvement with the game had been beneficial both to their own company objectives and to cricket.

Of course the John Player League (1969) and the Benson and Hedges Cup (1972) had been in existence well before 1977. The former had been a competition designed for purely commercial reasons and sold simultaneously to the sponsor and to television. Both have proved successful, and the price to their sponsors has been dramatically increased in 1982 and 1983 respectively. In a further heightening of commercialism, the County Championship became the Schweppes Championship in 1977. The major innovation, however, was the sponsorship of Test matches in England by the Cornhill Insurance Group.

This was a sponsorship hurriedly undertaken in the confusion which followed the formation of World Series Cricket, and represented something of a gamble for the Cornhill company. It has proved so successful that the Test and County Cricket Board has been able more than to double its asking price for a continuation of the agreement in 1983 – a price which Cornhill are prepared to pay. The Cornhill sponsorship of Test cricket in England is acknowledged as one of the outstanding successes in the general field of sports sponsorship. Public awareness of the Cornhill name increased from 2% to 17% as a direct result of their sponsorship and put the company into the top five in insurance for instant recognition.

This new, more businesslike approach to the finances of the game, adopted in recent years at national level, has been mirrored, again of necessity, at county level, with considerable local success. The counties have been forced to use their facilities and their grounds to the full. Investment has been made in executive boxes, entertaining suites and, in some counties, in the building of squash courts. Local firms have responded to this encouragement, and the partnerships at county level between business and cricket have increased considerably the game's income. In recent years perimeter advertising and lotteries have also bolstered the game. Both have produced huge sums of money. Cricket has achieved more television time than any other sport, and the advertising industry has been quick to take advantage of the sites on cricket grounds. Counties have managed to swell their coffers in a way previously undreamt of.

The fruits of this dramatic growth of commercialism reached their peak in 1981. An entertaining and heavily attended Ashes series coincided with this peak, and nearly all the first-class counties reported profits for the year. Surpluses in excess of six figures were returned in some cases. To underline this achievement it has to be remembered that global expenditure on cricket and cricketers had almost trebled in a little over three years. But the financial situation changed considerably in 1982, and although there is a strong temptation to place the blame for this on a poorly attended Test series with India, that would be hiding the whole truth. The fear must be that if income has been maximised both nationally and in the counties, and yet, as in 1982, large losses still result, then cricket has still not got the equation right. Although there are still pockets of income to be tapped, we are left with the harrowing thought that another financial crisis is imminent. There are signs that income from perimeter advertising and from lotteries is decreasing, and the recession has led to a rationalisation of business involvement at county level.

A number of solutions have been advanced: more cricket, less cricket, a four-day County Championship with one-day cricket at weekends. Cricketing arguments augment and sometimes override financial considerations. The only certain conclusion is that administrators cannot rely on the game's history of survival. There remains a general short-sightedness in the county game. It was always stressed by the TCCB that receipts from an Australian series would produce considerably more income for each county than the Test matches of 1982, against India and Pakistan. With West Indies coming second in the league table of attendances, it seems financially advisable to make sure that they and Australia do not come to England in successive years.

Yet the sharp fluctuation in financial fortunes between 1981 and 1982 does suggest poor county budgeting, which, in most cases, is an annual exercise. It means, effectively, that a county will spend virtually all its income in any one year to try to achieve success on the field. Pressure from the Cricketers' Association for a minimum earnings level for all cricketers and the move to longer contracts for players have played havoc with one-year budgets. A more sophisticated financial approach is required. The high number of redundant players at the end of 1982 is testimony to this.

Philip Carling was a former chief executive of Nottinghamshire and, at the time of writing, secretary-designate of Glamorgan.

The Four-Day Lobby

John Woodcock, Notes by the Editor, 1985

In 1985 come the first four-day first-class matches to be played in England outside the Test arena, other than the occasional game between England and The Rest. They feature – eight of them – in the programme for the Australian touring team and could be seen as a pilot scheme. There is a school of thought which views a four-day County Championship (16 four-day matches, played in midweek, as opposed to 24 of three days) as the answer to England's ills. It would reduce the heavy load of cricket played and cut down the travelling. Also, so it is claimed, it would provide a better preparation for five-day Test matches.

Against that, it would be unpopular with county members, who constitute an indispensable source of revenue, and might well lead to more slow play. It is said, in addition, that it would mean better pitches, though this I doubt. Most groundsmen already do all they can to meet the requirements of the TCCB.

It is not the current Championship which the players find so wearing, and which breeds careless batting habits and negative bowling, but the abundance of one-day cricket. In purely technical terms the standard of English batsmanship can seldom, if ever, have been so low. Even among the Test side there is an absence of basic, orthodox footwork, while the bat, time and again, comes through across the line of the ball. Why? Because four competitions out of five, from the cradle to the grave, are now played on a limited-overs basis, culminating in a slog. There is even a tendency in certain counties to think of the Championship as being little more than an interlude between one one-day competition and the next. The reverse sweep, an abomination of a stroke and one which I doubt whether any of the great batsmen of the past ever played, is redolent of today's "instant" cricket.

Whither Cricket Now?

Sir Donald Bradman, 1986

At the request of the editor I wrote a short piece for the 1939 *Wisden*. My main theme then was a plea for cricket to adapt itself to the quickening tempo of modern life, for administrators to consider ways of speeding up the game, to provide more modern scoreboards (especially in England), to face up to financial problems, and so on. Little did I appreciate at the time what a revolution would engulf cricket before another 50 years had passed.

The great stadiums of Sydney and Melbourne now display huge electronic scoreboards costing millions of dollars and giving a wealth of information to the spectators. The enormous electric light towers turn night into day at the flick of a switch. That, in turn, demands the use of a white ball, and to satisfy the television and marketing moguls the players turn out in a variety of coloured outfits.

The whole scene stirs up human emotions ranging from those of a largely new and young audience (more liberally sprinkled with females than of yore), who yell and scream their support, to those of the dyed-in-the-wool lovers of Test cricket, who yearn for more peaceful, bygone days. As with so many things, it becomes well-nigh impossible to bring about a reconciliation between the opposing attitudes. But where does the truth lie and what about the future?

Despite my deep feeling for the traditional game, and my conviction that a vast majority of players and the public still regard Test cricket as the supreme contest, we must accept that we live in a new era. If Sir Neville Cardus were alive today, I can well imagine how eloquently he would bemoan the huge attendances at pop concerts compared with the lack of support for opera or a Beethoven evening. But I am sure he would also admit that, irrespective of the quality of the music or the musicians, the public are primarily interested in entertainment. Perhaps he would throw in his well-known reference to an eagle, no matter how beautiful in flight, being no match for the Concorde. I am satisfied that one-day cricket, especially day/night cricket, is here to stay. If there is a threat to the survival of the game of cricket, that threat lies in the first-class arena, and it behoves the administrators to understand the challenge and face up to it.

I confess to a love for both types of game. Nothing can match the continuous cut and thrust of a Test match, where the advantage seesaws and the result is unpredictable to the last ball. I can't imagine any sporting event being more exciting than the tied Test between West Indies and Australia. It wasn't only the finish. Here you had two teams of great players, led by imaginative and intelligent captains determined from the first ball to pursue victory by adhering to the principles upon which the game was founded. The match had spin and speed, superb batting and fielding; every facet of the game was manifested as both sides strove for victory. It starkly revealed the Achilles' heel of the limited-overs match, namely the premium placed on defensive bowling and negative and defensive field-placing. One can get bored to death watching countless singles being taken when even the world's fastest bowler may be operating with no slips and five men on the boundary.

But let me turn to the good thing about one-day cricket. It rids the game of the unutterable bore who thinks occupancy of the crease and his own personal aggrandisement are all that matter. It demands fieldsmen of great speed and agility with good throwing arms. The standard of fielding at all levels of cricket has undoubtedly been lifted. Running between the wickets, too, has taken on a new dimension. Risks must be taken to maintain the essential run-rate. Umpires are put under enormous pressure, having to adjudicate frequently on split-second issues: to their credit, I believe they have responded in a very positive manner and improved their standards.

Inevitably one sees the odd umpiring mistake, graphically portrayed by the modern marvel of the instant replay on television. With this new aid available, I should see no loss of face or pride if umpires were to agree, when in doubt about a decision, to seek arbitration from the box. This could never apply to LBW, but for run-outs, and on odd occasions, for stumpings or a disputed catch, it would seem logical.

My first-class playing career began in 1927, and I remain a trustee of the Adelaide Oval and a member of the main South Australian Cricket Association committee. Having watched first-class cricket in 1921, I have seen as observer, player or administrator, all the great players of the last 65 years. Indeed, I can probably claim to span 75 years because many of the 1920–21 players also played before the Great War. It is still absolutely fascinating to me to watch and compare players of different generations.

How often I was asked in 1985 whether Clive Lloyd's West Indians were the best team of all time. Unhesitatingly I replied that they were the best fielding combination I have seen. But no matter how competent their batting, bowling and fielding, they were so reliant on fast bowlers that they became out of balance on a slow, turning pitch. In addition, their batting became vulnerable, which was proved in Sydney when Australia's two spinners, Bennett and Holland, tore the heart out of the West Indian batting to win a convincing victory for Australia. And without detracting from the skill of Bennett and Holland, it was clear to any knowledgeable observer that they were not of the quality of O'Reilly and Grimmett. To me these facts are indisputable and tend to place matters in their proper perspective. Australia's victory confirmed my view that my 1948 side was the best I ever saw, with Lloyd's 1984–85 team and Armstrong's 1920–21 Australian side not far behind. And my reading of history causes me to think Joe Darling's 1902 Australians were perhaps equal to any. How lovely to be able to speculate without having to prove the answer.

Many cricket enthusiasts claim that the one-day game has brought in its wake a decline in batting technique. This may have some validity, but it is not necessarily true. People get confused between a normal mode of play and the essential improvisation needed to circumvent defensive fields. Vivian Richards and Clive Lloyd are marvellous examples of batsmen capable of coping quite adequately in both types of cricket without sacrificing any basic soundness of technique. The main difference in their one-day attitude has been a willingness to take the risk of lofting the ball over fieldsmen's heads. I doubt if modern players in general cut or pull quite as well as some of their forebears did, but I attribute this largely to the ultra-heavy bats they use. These hinder shots other than those of the perpendicular kind, such as the drive.

Undeniably the limited-over game caters for a plethora of fast and medium-pace bowlers who tend to bowl just short of a length. In general it discourages, in fact it almost tolls the knell of, the slow leg-spinner. But here again one must acclaim the marvellous leg-spin bowling of the young Indian, Sivaramakrishnan, who proved against the best batting in the world in Sydney and Melbourne early in 1985 that he could bowl his ten-overs stint, get wickets, and still be economical. I don't doubt that O'Reilly, Grimmett, Benaud, Verity and others would have done the same. So perhaps, after all, the game is highlighting the fact that top-quality spinners can and will survive any challenge.

An interesting facet of the limited-overs game is the general rule governing bouncers. It unquestionably controls them in a sensible and practical way, and is a rule which I believe should be adopted in all grades of cricket without delay. It clearly reveals the way experimental laws could be used in one-day games to ascertain their effectiveness and/or desirability in first-class matches.

I also believe we have now reached the stage when some limitation in the length of a bowler's run-up is warranted. It would be the first and most logical step towards speeding up the over-rate. In Australia that magnificent player, Malcolm Marshall (excluding Frank Tyson, the fastest bowler I have seen since Larwood), has repeatedly shown us that a short run-up is sufficient to generate maximum speed.

The money now being paid to players has spawned professionalism beyond anything dreamed of 50 years ago. With so much money at stake I doubt if the modern professionals enjoy their cricket as much as did the players who were financially independent of the game and played purely for the love of it. Perhaps, too, monetary reward is responsible for some of the theatrical performances and even bad manners occasionally portrayed in recent years on the field. Happily I feel this unhealthy phase is on the wane, as players understand that good sportsmanship and keen competitiveness are not incompatible.

Most people agree that too much cricket was played during the Australian summer of 1984–85, owing to the Melbourne anniversary tournament being added to the schedule. It highlighted the need to strike a proper balance between one-day games and normal first-class matches. The attendances at Sheffield Shield matches were adversely affected. Indeed, the mounting losses on Shield games, now amounting to hundreds of thousands of dollars annually, constitute the most seemingly intractable problem confronting Australia cricket today. We need the Shield to produce Test cricketers, but can receipts from sponsorship, television rights etc, continue to make up the losses?

A MELBOURNE JAMBOREE   John Woodcock, *Notes by the Editor*, 1986

India's victory in Melbourne in March, in the so-called World Championship of Cricket, a one-day tournament arranged to mark the 150th anniversary of the founding of the state of Victoria, was as much of a surprise as their triumph over West Indies at Lord's in the final of the 1983 World Cup. The tournament itself was no more than a qualified success, the Australian public having by that stage of their season had more than enough one-day cricket. "They are killing a good product," said Border on the over-exposure of the one-day game, a warning all countries would do well to heed. Having flown on to Australia from India, where they did so well, England made disappointingly little contribution to this Melbourne jamboree, though they did share with Australia the privilege of playing in the first match under the new Melbourne floodlights, watched by 84,494 people.

CRICKET IN THE FAST-FOOD AGE   Graeme Wright, *Notes by the Editor*, 1987

"Just heard that India won the Lord's Test," wrote a correspondent from overseas last summer. "I have been an ardent supporter of England for over 50 years, and am both grieved and surprised at this defeat. I am still at a loss to understand: (a) The poor standard of cricket in the two premier Universities – Cambridge and Oxford. In the past they have always produced clever Test captains and cricketers of Test standard. (b) The lack of a firm, resolute captain of the calibre of Douglas Jardine and Len Hutton, both of whom rescued England when in the doldrums. (c) The loss of English grit and determination in their batting. I wonder whether one-day cricket is killing Test cricket in England."

The influence of one-day, or limited-overs, cricket was also very much in the minds of those who prepared the Report of the TCCB Enquiry into the Standards of Play of English Cricket in Test and First-Class County Cricket: the Palmer Report, so named after the enquiry's chairman, C. H. Palmer. Reading that report, full of valid points, I was nevertheless left wondering to what extent it, like the letter above, was out of tune with what England and English cricket have become and are becoming.

We live today in the age of the instant, be it the microwave oven, the fast-food outlet or the cricket match. So it seems inevitable that, if the public wants action and a winner to cheer, a match it can watch from beginning to end, the counties will supply it; not only because there is public interest but also because where there is public interest there will be sponsors. For the Test and County Cricket Board, on one hand trying to improve playing standards for Test matches while on the other planning the economic welfare of the county game, the dichotomy is that what is good for the game is not always good for the business.

In the same year that the Palmer Report considered limited-overs cricket to be the main cause of the decline in standards of batting and bowling in English cricket (and before the Indians and New Zealanders had shown the extent of that decline), the TCCB introduced a second limited-overs competition for the county Second XIs; and this summer the number of games in that competition has been virtually doubled by the playing of home and away ties in the three zonal rounds. Yet the Palmer Report advised: "The young cricketer now entering the first-class county game as presently organised has greater difficulty in acquiring the skills for success in all types of cricket because of insufficient opportunity to serve a good apprenticeship in three-day cricket."

I am reminded of the television programme, *Yes Minister*, in which the civil service's answer to any call for action was to set up an enquiry. By the time it had reached its conclusion, everyone would have forgotten why it had been commissioned. The Palmer Report deserves better than to be shelved and forgotten, and it was appropriate that 1986 provided a timely reminder of its origins: widespread disappointment and genuine concern about the standards of play at Test and county level following the series of failures in Australia in 1982–83, in New Zealand and Pakistan in 1983–84, and against West Indies in England in 1984. Yet how quickly fortunes change.

England had just retained the Ashes in Australia, making Wright fearful that Palmer's report would, indeed, be shelved.

COMINGS AND GOINGS   Graeme Wright, *Notes by the Editor*, 1987

I am intrigued by the number of itinerant spear-bearers who have joined the play in recent years, bringing on or taking off helmets, glasses of water, dry batting gloves, salt tablets. Sometimes they are mentioned by name over the public address system: perhaps it's in the spear-bearers' union agreement. But thinking about it, the spectator has a right to know the extra's name, having paid to see this interruption to his day's cricket.

More serious are other comings and goings. One first-class umpire told me last year of an international fast bowler who, at the end of his spell, took his sweater and kept walking until he was back in the pavilion, without even telling his acting-captain that he was going, let alone requesting the umpire's consent. This consent is not just a courtesy (the day seems long past when courtesy is considered commonplace); it is a requirement of the Laws.

TIME PRESENT AND TIME PAST
Vic Marks, 1987

Comparisons may well be odious but they are also irresistible. Who's the greater: Laver or Borg, Joe Davis or Steve, Bradman or Richards? Such debates are often endless and always fruitless, yet cricket enthusiasts, as well as slightly desperate biographers, can rarely shun picking their All-Time World XI. Usually the selectors plump for the heroes of their own era, and with an ageing population the lament that "Things ain't what they used to be" grows gradually louder. However, I do not intend here to deliver a polemic in defence of the modern cricketer; rather to examine some of the changes of the last few decades, as well as to observe some surprising similarities between cricketers past and present.

In the 1960s, cricket was compelled to react to the force of economic necessity. County clubs' coffers were like colanders, and the authorities' response was the introduction of instant cricket: the Gillette Cup knockout in 1963, the John Player Sunday League in 1969 and the Benson and Hedges competition in 1972. In addition, they permitted the influx of non-qualified overseas players in 1968. In retrospect, the authorities, so easily maligned, should be congratulated for ensuring the survival of all the first-class counties. Now the treasurer of a county cricket club is less susceptible to (stress-induced) ulcers than his counterpart in the Football League.

Cricket has survived, but not without sacrifices. Instant cricket has created a demand for instant success; with four competitions each year there is less excuse if your club does not win one of them. Newcomers are now expected to match the contributions of their more experienced colleagues immediately. In 1964, Dennis Amiss could be assured of a slow and gentle baptism to first-class cricket, a luxury no longer afforded James Whitaker in 1984.

The advent of these new competitions had far-reaching consequences, such as the installation of a computer in the pavilion at Lord's and a complete transformation of the fixture list. The county cricket season has become one prolonged, frenetic dash around the highways and byways of the country. County cricketers no longer check train schedules but instead tune into motoring flashes as they lurch from a JPL game at Canterbury back to a championship match at Northampton. Our car insurance premiums have, unsurprisingly, rocketed.

These domestic changes have been mirrored at international level. In 1975 the first World Cup was a spectacular success and one-day internationals became a financial necessity. As a result, the commercial wizards planning a tour of Australia now insist that the intervals between Test matches are spent, not with missionary visits to the outback but in a series of lucrative one-day games. A modern international cricketer, when asked his impression of Australia, is scarcely able to give anything more than a vivid description of the airport lounges of Sydney, Melbourne and Perth. Many enthusiasts will have been astounded by Graham Gooch's decision not to tour last winter, but a regular tourist with a young family will understand his position much more easily. So, while our predecessors may envy the increased financial rewards available at the highest level, the modern player might yearn for the more leisurely existence of the 1950s – 32 Championship games and nothing else, with the chance to play golf on Sundays.

As the governing bodies, amidst general approval, have become more commercially minded, it is not surprising that some players have reacted in the same way, often to general condemnation. Modern players sometimes employ agents to maximise their earning capacity through endorsements and the newspapers during their short lifespan as a cricketer. This august Almanack has noted this trend: "Too many Australian and England cricketers appeared to be governed by commercial interests and cricket suffered accordingly." That was written by the editor of *Wisden* in 1964. Surely, then, it is a misconception to believe that it is only the cricketers of the last decade who have been rather keen to make some money from their prowess? Indeed, the established county player is unimpressed by the theory occasionally expressed in the columns of the *Daily Telegraph* that cricketers are overpaid. He earns approximately £8,500, a figure he is unlikely to match in the winter months and one which does not compare that favourably with the £10 a week that leading professionals received in 1933. And they didn't have to dive in the field.

Before England's tour to Australia in 1986, the TCCB in their tour contracts imposed restrictions on the players regarding their contributing to national newspapers. Those concerned, notably Phil Edmonds and Ian Botham, acquiesced and signed the contracts, presumably at some financial loss to themselves. However, this was no new problem. No doubt in Adelaide Sir Donald Bradman allowed himself a wry chuckle, recalling that he was in a similar position in 1932 when his newspaper released him from his contract, with full pay, to allow him to play against Jardine's tourists. Who can blame Bradman or Botham or the lesser mortals for trying to exploit their brief stay at the top? Cricket is a precarious profession: you might be dropped next week.

Today's cricketers have an uneasy relationship with the press. They enjoy praise and being offered writing contracts; they usually tolerate criticism of their performances on the field; but they detest the constant intrusions into their private lives. Of late, cricket tours have been covered by a gaggle of 50 or so pressmen, not just cricket reporters but newsmen as well, hunting for some saucy snippets for the tabloids.

"Dullness is feared and avoided. So unfortunately is fact. The news room has invaded sport and on the occasion of Test matches, the cricket correspondent is often reinforced by a columnist or news-hawk, who, with furrowed brow, scours hotels and pavilions on his dark and dubious assignments. The technique of the game now ranks far below the 'story' and you will often hear reporters at the end of a full day's cricket lamenting that 'nothing has happened'. No one has fallen dead while taking guard or been arrested while placing the field."

To my surprise, that analysis of the press was written by R. C. Robertson-Glasgow in 1949, so bang goes the theory that such attention is a new phenomenon. However, the problem still remains, and it is sometimes exacerbated by the TV cameras. Every smile, every grimace, every expression of disappointment is relayed unerringly into our sitting-rooms so that a cricketer's behaviour is under the microscope as never before.

Finally, let me turn to what actually happens on the field. Have standards dropped to the extent that some of our commentators would have us believe? I can begin with confidence by making two assertions. Firstly, the overall level of fielding has improved as a result of one-day cricket; even Fred Trueman would agree with that. Secondly, the standard of wrist-spin has declined dramatically; no quarrels there even from Kim Barnett, one of the few left. Thereafter the picture becomes more blurred.

In an attempt to gain some perspective about the changes in the game, I examined the 1964 season; Simpson's Australians retained the Ashes 1–0; Worcestershire, led by Don Kenyon, won the County Championship; Sussex, under Dexter, retained the Gillette Cup in its second year; and Geoffrey Boycott was one of *Wisden*'s Five Cricketers of the Year. Like any gnarled old pro I turned to the averages. Although I recognise that averages can be very misleading, especially when they refer to my own performances, certain trends were clearly established when placing them alongside those of 1986; namely that batsmen today dominate the game to a far greater extent and that spin bowlers in particular have become less effective over the last two decades. Here are some statistics: in 1964, 13 batsmen averaged over 40: in 1986, 48 batsmen averaged over 40, with Geoff Boycott, inevitably, being the common denominator.

Unsurprisingly, the converse applies when examining the bowling averages. In 1964, 39 bowlers averaged under 22; in 1986, nine bowlers averaged under 22 (common denominator – N. Gifford). Out of the top 30 bowlers in each year, 12 were spinners in 1964, only four in 1986. One obvious explanation for the change is that the full covering of wickets, introduced in 1980, made batting a less precarious occupation and deprived spinners of 20 wickets per annum. However, I think that this trend has been exaggerated by the advent of one-day cricket, which has damaged our bowlers far more than our batsmen.

In the 1950s and '60s, the great English bowlers such as Bedser, Laker, Titmus and Shackleton presumably rediscovered their optimum length and line in a net every April and they persevered with it until the Scarborough Festival. Minor adjustments might be made for individual players, but basically there was just one place to bowl – a good length at off-stump – and they became superb bowling machines programmed solely for Championship and Test cricket. Now, every Sunday evening captains around the country are beseeching their bowlers to bowl anything but a good-length ball at off-stump because such deliveries give the batsman too much room to swing his bat as he searches for that match-winning swat over mid-wicket at the end of the innings. Good-length bowling becomes a liability. Spinners are asked to attack leg-stump as quickly as possible, in complete contrast to the requirements of Saturday and Monday. Even Norman Gifford admits that it's hard to make the adjustment, so what chance has Richard Illingworth?

While one-day cricket has demanded greater aggression from the batsmen, often causing them to discover new, uncharted talents, as in the cases of Glenn Turner and Ravi Shastri, it has nurtured a negative, containing approach in many of our bowlers. Maidens rather than wickets become the goal. It may be no co-incidence that the two leading wicket-takers in Test history, Ian Botham and Dennis Lillee, have seldom been feted for their prowess as limited-overs bowlers. Today's cricketers have had to become more adaptable as they turn their attentions to the differing demands of the various competitions, and unfortunately there is less scope for the out-and-out specialist. I'm afraid they have had to become fitter as well. They also need a comprehensive road atlas, a reliable car, an understanding wife and a thick skin. Whether they are any better or worse than their predecessors, I don't know. All I can say is that Hobbs and Hammond, May and Trueman, Botham and Gower would have triumphed in any era.

Vic Marks, the Somerset off-spinner and batsman, retired two years after this article appeared, and became cricket correspondent of The Observer.

A TRULY SPORTING OCCASION Graeme Wright, *Notes by the Editor*, 1988

English cricket, it seems to me, needs to be lifted beyond the routine performance. That the game is capable still of freeing the spirit was evidenced during the MCC Bicentenary match at Lord's. Moreover, it offered a personal insight into one of the problems which sport faces today. Following any game made competitive by nationalism or commercialism can blind the spectator to those aspects of sport – enjoyment and entertainment – which are as important as winning.

Sport was not meant to be a war substitute, and cricket must not find itself being forced into that role. Winning is not everything. This should be one of sport's primary lessons to society. Satisfaction can come from giving of one's best and even, in those few exquisite moments, from surpassing personal expectations. Participants and spectators both need to be reminded of that from time to time, and at Lord's in August I was grateful for the reminder.

Although the rewards were generous, personal pride was the spur that drew from the players their best. Good manners prevailed, batsmen walked, bouncers were used sparingly and so were effective in surprising both the batsman and the spectator. In terms of technique, the game was a delight; from batsmen and bowlers there was variety. And throughout there was friendliness.

Yet, honesty compels the admission, at first I was not enchanted. Something seemed to be missing. It was the edge, some would call it needle, which after years of watching top-class sport I had come to accept as part of

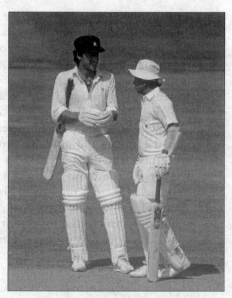

Unlikely partners: Pakistan's Imran Khan (left) and Sunil Gavaskar of India, whose countries were often on the brink of warfare, bat together in the showpiece MCC Bicentenary match at Lord's in 1987.

the occasion. Without it, that first day of the MCC Bicentenary match was like the first day without a cigarette after years of smoking. The next day, having realised why the fault was mine, I rejoiced in the occasion of cricket sportingly and well played.

That morning I had sat on my station, with the sun on my back, reading a favourite book. I walked with the crowds to Lord's, all of us looking forward to a great day's cricket. We had not come to see anyone win or lose. We had come to see fine cricketers give of their best and it was a wonderful feeling.

MCC Bicentenary Match

At Lord's, August 20, 21, 22, 24, 25, 1987. Drawn. Rain washed out the last day's play with the Rest of the World 13 for one overnight, needing another 340 to win.

Toss: MCC. **MCC 455-5 dec.** (C. G. Greenidge 52, G. A. Gooch 117, M. W. Gatting 179, C. E. B. Rice 59*, Extras 30) **and 318-6 dec.** (C. G. Greenidge 122, G. A. Gooch 70, D. I. Gower 40, R. J. Hadlee 36); **Rest of the World XI 421-7 dec.** (S. M. Gavaskar 188, Imran Khan 82; M. D. Marshall 3-53, R. J. Shastri 3-130) **and 13-1.**

A GAME OF TWO HALVES

Matthew Engel, *Notes by the Editor*, 1993

Cricket can appeal to the athlete and the aesthete alike; it can veer between lyric poetry, differential calculus and Thai kick-boxing. No game has such range, such depth. But it is all extremely fragile. Editors of *Wisden* have been worrying about the game in these pages for most of the Almanack's existence. It has always been in crisis of one sort or another.

Last year the crisis moved into an acute phase. It was nothing to do with ball-tampering, dissent, TV umpiring, coloured clothing nor any of the other issues that dominated the cricketing press in 1992. Cricket, at the highest level, has acquired a unique and insoluble problem by turning itself into two separate sports. There is traditional cricket, a game that has stood the test of time as a satisfying pastime and way of life, but which finds it increasingly hard to get an audience. And there is one-day cricket, which is popular among spectators but is regarded with varying degrees of contempt by the professionals forced to play it, administrators forced to stage it, and journalists forced to report it. It distorts cricket's skills and produces a mutant game which, while it might on occasion be tense, is essentially shallow.

The winter of 1992–93 has produced some wonderfully vivid Test cricket in Australia particularly. There have been huge crowds in Melbourne and Calcutta. But with the Indian authorities frightened even to schedule a full Test series, these still look like upward blips on a downward graph. The highest form of the game may have reached the point county cricket was at in the 1950s when the audience found other things to do.

The autumn of 1992 brought the first Tests in South Africa for 23 years and the first ever in Zimbabwe. This should have been a glorious time for cricket. The village-sized attendances in Harare and Bulawayo may have been inevitable; there is no cricket-watching base in Zimbabwe. But what happened in South Africa? The crowds at Durban, for their first-ever Test against India, were actually lower than the low figures put out by the ground authority. The idea that the longest-awaited cricket match in history would attract just 5,000 people on its opening day would have been regarded throughout the years of boycott as insane.

All this is gradually ceasing to be a surprise. Players and administrators appear to have forgotten that Test cricket was ever meant to be a public entertainment. The boring passage of play, the possibility of the draw, the long block – all these have their place in cricket tactics. But when they become the entire strategy, the effects are disastrous.

The series between South Africa and India, which was desperately important to the future of the game, was played throughout at a level that might have been carefully designed to repel the casual spectator. Zimbabwe's inaugural Test in Harare against India was screamingly dull. A little boy sitting behind me (one of a couple of hundred spectators) asked his mother impatiently: "Who's winning?" "Sssh," she said, "nobody". She was right too. Do you think he'll be clamouring for a ticket next time there is a Test match? The Zimbabwe coach John Hampshire defended his team (406 for five after two days) by saying they had to learn – in which case they should do so in private. There are very few books to buy in Harare these days and I had no knitting. But the South Africans and Indians, with no excuses, were even worse. The scoring rate over five days in the Test at Cape Town was 1.83 an over. It was an affront to a beautiful setting.

In the 1960s cricketers were enjoined to play "brighter cricket". At the start of every tour, like politicians promising better times, captains said they would play it. Now they would probably regard such an idea as insulting. Brighter cricket? Entertainment? We do all that in the one-dayers.

Fortunately, cricket is a resilient game. One great match (like West Indies' one-run victory over Australia in Adelaide), one victory (India over England in Calcutta) can galvanise the local public and wipe out the memory of many wretched days. But if Test cricket is to thrive, as well as survive, there have to be many more Adelaides than Harares.

These fears for the future of Test cricket were voiced in Matthew Engel's first set of Editor's Notes. He succeeded Graeme Wright in 1993.

DAWNING OF THE AGE OF WARNE   Matthew Engel, *Notes by the Editor*, 1994

Shortly after lunch on the first day of the Edgbaston Test in 1993, Shane Warne was bowling leg-breaks to Alec Stewart, who had momentarily discarded both his helmet and his faded baseball cap in favour of a real, old-fashioned, three-lions-of-England version. As he pushed forward, he looked the image of his father at the crease. Behind the stumps, there was Ian Healy wearing his baggy cap and air of ageless Australian aggression. And there was Warne, bowling beautifully with a method thought to have been relegated to the museum. For a moment the years seemed to roll away. The detail of the cricket was suspended; the game was overtaken by the timelessness of the scene. It was summer in England and all was well. Then, of course, Stewart got out and everything became secondary to the fact that we were being licked again.

In a number of respects cricket had a very good year in 1993. In England, India and Australia, crowds showed they would respond to the thrill of an exciting Test series, as well as to the gimcrack appeal of one-day cricket. Warne was the most talked-about player of the year and single-handedly did a huge amount to switch cricket back into a game where the batsman's fear is of mental torture rather than physical. South Africa and Zimbabwe began to play more of a part in the comity of Test-playing nations. The women's World Cup was a success, and a success for England at that. And, cautiously, the game began to show signs of expansion round the world. It is best not to get over-excited about the prospects: soccer is not on the brink of being dethroned.

Indeed, in some of cricket's heartlands, in the West Indies and the English cities, the game is under threat from simpler, cheaper pastimes: basketball on the one hand, computer games on the other. But when Malaysia talks of achieving Test status by the year 2020, it would be wise not to be too dismissive: things happen in that part of the world when they put their minds to it.

The year also saw the transformation of the International Cricket Council, newly independent of MCC and with its headquarters in a discreet little office on the other side of Lord's in what used to be the staff canteen. This, rather than the pavilion, is now the centre of power in world cricket. But it is the new secretary of MCC, Roger Knight, who gets the room with the view. From his office, the ICC chief executive, David Richards, can see about a square yard of the outfield. In other respects, the new world order has brought changes, starting with the arrival of what they would prefer us not to call "neutral" umpires (all umpires are neutral, these are "third-country"), one in each Test for at least the next three years. This seems to me as essential a rite of passage for cricket as the change in ICC itself.

However, 1993 was also the year when the system of umpiring by video spread to engulf the Test-playing world. I may be in a minority; I remain utterly convinced that this is a disaster. Umpires can now call for help from a third official watching the TV replay on run-outs, stumpings and, sometimes, boundary decisions; indeed, they can hardly not do so. It is true that last year one or two players in Test matches may have been given in or out more accurately than would otherwise have been the case. What we also saw was very good umpires virtually giving up on their duties at square leg, knowing there was no point in even contemplating making a judgment: it could only get them into trouble; why take the risk?

Remember that it was a couple of outrageously wrong decisions that led to the demand for this system, not a lot of marginal ones. We saw players starting to pressurise umpires if they did not call for a replay. And we saw increasing demands (sometimes on the field) for the system to be extended to close catches as well. The heart of the game, the finality of the umpire's verdict, is being eaten away.

CRICKET V CASH

Matthew Engel, *Notes by the Editor*, 1994

The 1994 first-class season in England was the first given over to four-day cricket. By the end of it even the most conservative of cricket's constituencies, the county members, appeared to have accepted the principle of the change. Undoubtedly four-day cricket is better than three-day cricket had become on the dead wickets of modern England. There is no evidence yet that it is any better than three-day cricket once was.

The orthodoxy of the moment is that players have to be allowed to build innings of Test-match length. One is now terrified to shout "Get on with it" to a boring blocker, in case this in some way inhibits the development of the poor darling. I believe that if the counties played less one-day cricket their players would be better able to develop classical technique and still entertain the public.

The other changes wrought by the Murray Report, which the counties were forced to accept *en bloc*, were, predictably, less successful. The 50-over Sunday League was a hopeless compromise between irreconcilable objectives – proper cricket and junk marketing – and was dumped after a season. At least a 40-over Sunday game does not go on too long. The idea of an all-knockout Benson and Hedges Cup was not wholly bad but it was imbecilic to schedule the opening round in April, leaving the knocked-out teams dismayed before they have had the chance to peel off the first layer of sweaters. That reform will be repealed before 1995. One-day cricket is purely a revenue-raising exercise and it ought to be staged as late in the season as possible, when the players can cope with it. The main reason for staging it in April and May is to enable the selectors to assess one-day form before the one-day internationals in late May, as if that mattered a jot compared to getting the Test team right.

In 1994 there are once again two Texaco Trophies, one against New Zealand and one against South Africa. How can a trophy have any credibility if it is won twice in a season? In this particular case, I am astonished that the TCCB has never taken the chance to stage a couple of extra one-day games and make the Texaco a minia-ture World Series Cup. New Zealand v South Africa at Worcester or Canterbury or somewhere, during the period when the teams overlap, would be a nice little earner.

These twin-tour summers are always unsatisfactory. The South Africans – understandably after such a frantic reintroduction to world cricket – did not want a full series in 1994. But great Test cricket needs a full series to boil up, to get the public aware of the characters, for the drama, and all the subplots, to develop. The 1993 Ashes series was a glorious illustration. One hopes that, even with nine [Bangladesh had yet to be admitted] Test-playing countries, administrators are not going to lose sight of that.

NEW WORLD (DIS)ORDER

Jack Bailey, 1994

On February 2 1993, what was almost certainly the most acrimonious and sham-bolic meeting in the history of the ICC broke up amid signs of lasting anguish. The central debating point had been the venue for the next World Cup. So strongly had feelings run on all sides that a one-day meeting had gone on well into the night. The issue of the World Cup was finally resolved on the morning of the second day. It would be played in India, Pakistan and Sri Lanka – this in spite of a decision in favour of England at a previous ICC meeting.

The announcement of the World Cup decision was followed *sotto voce* – as an afterthought, almost – by a statement to the effect that David Richards, chief executive of the Australian Cricket Board, had been appointed chief executive of the International Cricket Council. He would take up his duties, at Lord's, five months later.

The meeting focused on the World Cup marked an alarming departure from the way business had been conducted within the ICC from its foundation as the Imperial Cricket Conference in 1909. Since then, the name had changed to the International Cricket Conference and then to the International Cricket Council, and the ICC had seen some contentious times. But that 1993 meeting was something different. It was the outward and visible sign, if one were needed, that the playing of cricket as a game, so long the chief preoccupation of those gathered round the tables of the MCC committee room at Lord's, and pursued invariably with an attitude of quiet and civilised deference, had been overtaken.

The meeting had been prolonged, almost beyond endurance, by a series of legal quibbles concerning an interpretation of ICC rules. There were frequent adjournments so that India's two chief representatives (of the nine apparently present at various times) could seek the support of India's Lord Chief Justice for their contention that a simple majority of those voting was all that was necessary to determine the destination of the next World Cup.

This had been the case with the allocation of previous World Cups. By rule, the 19 associate members had one vote; the Test-playing countries, with two votes each, mustered 18 between them. But because this put the associate members in a position of strength, unwarranted in the eyes of full members, the voting had been changed. A binding resolution now required a simple majority of those present. But that would apply only if support were given by two-thirds of the full members, of whom at least one had to be a foundation member (England or Australia).

Complicated perhaps; but, since this rule change had been made with the backing of India and the other full members, not, one would have thought, questionable. The new voting system applied to all decisions categorised as binding. From all accounts, the position of India and her supporters was to question that the World Cup vote should fall into the category of a binding decision. Here the mind boggles. If a decision as to where the World Cup would be staged, at a meeting called specifically to decide the issue, was not considered binding, then what was?

Madhavrao Scindia, the President of the Indian board and one-time Minister of Civil Aviation and Tourism, was supported by representatives of Pakistan and Sri Lanka in a determined and prolonged attempt to win the day. The intrusion of legalistic arguments into the game had already become familiar to Sir Colin Cowdrey, chairman of the meeting. The Pakistan tour of England, with its ball-tampering row and the swift interventions by lawyers employed by Pakistan, had surely prepared him and the MCC secretariat, or should have done. The obduracy of India and others in the face of the ICC's own lawyers must have come as a shock, however, and the meeting degenerated. All that cricket used to stand for was thrown out of the committee-room window.

Politicking and favour-seeking among member countries by those from the subcontinent had apparently begun well before the meeting. Those representing the associate members were aware that substantial funds would be made available. India had supported Zimbabwe's elevation to full membership; talk was rife of favours being called in.

After the ICC meeting, an unprecedented press conference was called by the chief executive of the British Test and County Cricket Board, A. C. Smith. Never one to volunteer information ("no comment but don't quote me" has often been put forward as one of his more adventurous remarks), Smith went to town. "We endured a fractious and unpleasant meeting beset by procedural wrangling," he said. "There was no talk of anything like cricket. It was, by a long way, the worst meeting I have ever attended." He confirmed that although his board felt that a previous minute nominating England as the next host country for the World Cup was still valid, they had finally succumbed in the best and wider interests of the world game. Smith also confirmed that a price for his board's compliance had been that they would definitely host the World Cup after next. As part of the deal, they also ensured that the profits of the tournament supposed to be held in 1995 (which is actually now scheduled for early 1996) would fund the new ICC secretariat.

For the Marylebone Cricket Club, the agreement to appoint Richards was an outward manifestation of a notably unwelcome passage in their history. They would no longer help to administer the international scene, even peripherally. Their last remaining influence on the world stage of cricket was officially at an end. It was a turn of events presaged by the appointment in 1988 of a chairman, Cowdrey, who, though nominated by the President of MCC, was ostensibly, for the first time, an appointment of the ICC itself. What had happened since then had been a far cry from the original idea when Francis Lacey, the secretary of MCC, came together in conference with Australia and South Africa on June 15, 1909.

A memorandum was published in *The Times* a week later. There were two parts to the memorandum. The first set out the regulations for Test matches between the three member countries: England, Australia and South Africa. Most of these regulations were still in existence in the 1980s. The other set out a programme of matches between the three countries, including a triangular contest in England in 1912. In general it was agreed that every team should pay and receive a visit from each other country in every cycle of four years.

As Test cricket spread, so the founder members protected themselves with a power of veto, almost never used but there just in case. India, New Zealand and West Indies became members in 1926. The newly created Pakistan took its place in 1953. South Africa left the Commonwealth and the ICC in 1961. In 1965 the rules were changed, the title International Cricket Conference was adopted and the first associate members, with strictly limited voting powers, were allowed inside, including, now that Imperial had been dropped, the United States.

Gradually, as governments throughout the world became more interested in sport, recognising the prestige it could bring, more and more countries applied for associate membership. The first World Cup brought an avalanche of them. MCC paid for all the administration and there were few barriers in the way of any country that could show that cricket was firmly established and organised. A loose-knit family was gradually formed: representation regarding the Laws could be made; full members were given the task of encouraging cricket in countries nearby. Other areas of common concern were tackled, but until the 1970s two issues above all others were kept strictly out of the ICC's province: finance and politics. Without these two erratic and sometimes unpleasant strands of human existence to consider, the ICC remained for a long time a benevolent but only mildly persuasive body. Goodwill prevailed.

Thus the ICC was a source of guidance rather than a central bureaucracy. There were times when guidance had to be firm, but this applied in the main strictly to cricketing matters. The isolation of South Africa became the subject of a ruling only in the 1970s. For almost a decade after they left the Conference in 1961, their fellow founder members continued to visit them. These unofficial Test matches remained outside the province of the Conference, and England and Australia saw that they remained so. Yet the ICC, in conjunction with MCC, acted swiftly enough after the Bodyline controversy in the 1930s, came to an agreement about the spate of throwing that developed early in the 1960s, and formed a united (if not successful) front against Kerry Packer and his rebel players in the 1970s. Throughout, undefined but pervading all contentious issues, was the same spirit of fair play that prevailed on the cricket field.

Often, the ICC was the merest shadow of a co-ordinating, let alone a ruling, body. At times Australia, for instance, wanted little part of a world governing organisation and would often make the point during the post-war years, sometimes by sending local representatives with limited powers to the annual meeting. The Anglo-Australian axis with its special position remained firmly against any thought of centralised power in the cricket world, although comparative newcomers such as Pakistan beavered away at achieving it.

For them, and for other emergent countries, a way to advancement lay through a homogenisation of world cricket. The dominance of England and Australia was all very well – but. The persistence of the Pakistani board president Air Marshal Nur Khan led to the appointment of observers, forerunners of the Test match referees. They were powerless, but their appointment, even if only to view Test matches in Pakistan, was a small step in what Pakistan considered to be the right direction. Gradually, the days when Billy Griffith, secretary of the ICC and MCC between 1962 and 1974, would issue brief communiqués to the press agencies at the end of a two-day meeting receded. Often in later years cricket writers were disappointed at the apparent lack of progress on the world front. But there was no short cut to decision-taking if even one of the Test-playing countries did not want there to be. Consequently, as secretary of the ICC I found that the items of hard news to give to the press concerned only South Africa, the World Cup or Kerry Packer. So many other issues which were the subject of fierce, sometimes brilliant, debate could be frustrated by one or two dissidents who could not, by code of practice, be publicly named. Yet, by and large, cricket prospered.

It was inevitable, perhaps, that in the end there had to be a centralised administration employed by the ICC itself. The appointment of Test match referees was a visible sign of an attempt to stamp the views of a central authority on cricket throughout the Test-playing world. Commercialism is snowballing.

From 1994, at least one neutral umpire will stand in each Test match, a development abhorrent to the purists. Central control, with a chief executive answering to ICC sub-committees, and to the full panoply of countries probably more than a once a year, was the almost certain outcome. Financial and political considerations will come high on the agenda. The welding together of many disparate points of view and aspirations will be a tough job.

It is hard to imagine a combination better suited to deal with issues which confront them than the newly elected chairman, Clyde Walcott, and chief executive, David Richards. Clyde's name as a cricketer puts him in a position of high regard, even from those for whom commercial and political gain is more important than the game itself. He is a modest man, a man of wit, with a strong sense of fair play and a shrewdness which underlies his genial exterior, and since he represents West Indies – strong in playing ability, less fortunate in terms of home-produced funds – he will see the point of view of the less well-off.

David Richards has not played first-class cricket, although he was a more than useful grade cricketer. He is a professional cricket administrator, tough, likeable and efficient. As secretary of the Victorian Cricket Association he played a pivotal role in the staging of the 1977 Centenary Test match in Melbourne and we hardened cricket administrators marvelled at the industry and ability he displayed in getting together former cricketers from all over the world. Since then, he has served with distinction as chief executive of the Australian board, having to come to terms early with the commercialisation of the game and the apparent lack of authority vested in the board itself after the deal had been struck with World Series Cricket. A fixture list dominated by one-day cricket was one outcome, the brash commercialism generated by the board marketeers who had previously acted on behalf of the Packer organisation was another. Whether or not PBL, the organisation responsible for marketing World Series Cricket for Kerry Packer, or the Australian board were calling the shots became a matter for conjecture, but Richards rode it all with equanimity and emerged not only unscathed but with a reputation sufficiently enhanced to hand him the number one job in cricket.

Still in his forties, Richards has the additional advantage of having come through a particularly hard school in which not too many words are minced before delivery. He also has positive views on the future and is backed by a cricket committee which includes Bob Cowper, a fellow Australian and formidable Test batsman, who, as a banker in Monte Carlo, knows his way around the financial world. Stationed at Lord's, but beholden to nothing and nobody other than his international role, Richards and his operation will be financed by a levy on World Cup income and membership fees from all members of the ICC. "Victoria and Australia no longer claim my loyalties in a cricketing sense," he says. "It is a global sport and it will be a large part of my job to look at the year 2003 and make sure the game holds its place in global sports then." One move has been to form an off-shore company to deal with the ICC's commercial activities. Richards sees a role for the ICC in cricket at all levels and he is unashamedly in favour of all the recent innovations at Test-match level: TV aids, referees, sponsorship of umpires, more stringent regulations. Aware of traditional values, he will not be bound by them.

Already many of the ties which bound his predecessors (in their joint roles) no longer apply to him. His empire seems bound to grow well beyond the two assistants now at his elbow. He will be a target for the media. He will need patience in dealing with strident politicians. He will need to be most things to all men, but never all things to anybody. One can only wish him, and cricket, well.

Jack Bailey was secretary of MCC, and therefore of the ICC, from 1974 to 1987. He previously played for Oxford University and Essex.

TIME FOR A WORLD CHAMPIONSHIP   Matthew Engel, *Notes by the Editor*, 1995

The most immediate problem facing the game is little discussed: England remains the home of cricketing self-analysis, and the greatest triumph of English cricket (amidst its manifest failures) has been to maintain and enhance the status of Test cricket as the game's apogee. Full-length, i.e. five-match, Test series are extinct where neither England nor Australia are involved. And even West Indies v Australia this year is down to four matches.

One-day internationals, in a bewildering variety of competitions with no legitimacy beyond the profit motive, continue to attract vast crowds from Ahmedabad to Wellington. In Test cricket the picture is very patchy indeed: suddenly encouraging in South Africa after a slow start on their return; in India, often better in the smaller and less blasé cities; variable in the West Indies, except when boosted by English mass tourism; excellent in Australia at the moment but, one suspects, heavily dependent on the team's success; dismal in Pakistan, New Zealand, Sri Lanka and Zimbabwe.

It is hard to explain why a Test match between two mighty sides, Pakistan and Australia, should attract crowds barely touching four figures in Lahore, not a city famous for its range of competing leisure attractions. Tickets are often too expensive; it is cheaper and easier to watch one day rather than five; live TV coverage may be a hindrance. But Test cricket, crucially, depends on context. It needs a five-Test series (six is too long) for the personalities to emerge and the battle to capture the public imagination. These half-hearted one-off Tests rarely work.

There is a possible solution which would cost next to nothing, could bring in major sponsorship, and would give shape to the present mish-mash of world cricket, raise the game's profile and give it something it badly needs: a true world champion team to go alongside the one-day world champions, who are after all the winners of just one tournament. All the Test countries need do is undertake to play at least one Test home and away against all the others in a four-year cycle, which they are edging towards anyway. (In this context, it is worth saying that England's decision to play six Tests against West Indies in 1995 instead of inviting Zimbabwe is a rather churlish and unworthy exception.)

In an Ashes series, the World Championship would merely be a subplot and the whole series could count in the final table: two points, say, for the winner; one each if it were drawn. For countries which just played a single Test against each other, then the one game would count for everything. It would thus add particular pith to the matches that now seem least important. There is no reason why this Championship could not be instituted almost at once. It can do no harm and could be very good for the game.

THE WISDEN WORLD CHAMPIONSHIP

Matthew Engel, 1997

The idea of a World Championship of Test cricket is hardly brand-new. In 1912 the three major playing nations of the time – England, Australia and South Africa – gathered in England for the Triangular Tournament, and played a nine-Test round-robin. The combination of a very wet summer, a boycott by the leading Australians, and a weak South African team proved disastrous. The 1913 *Wisden* warned the experiment might not be repeated in this generation. This was optimistic. The number of Test cricketing nations grew, but South Africa's apartheid policies (and such lesser difficulties as the trans-Tasman snobbery that stopped Australia playing New Zealand) meant that only England had a playing relationship with all the teams. And even that ceased with South Africa's exile from the game after 1970.

Thus the idea went to sleep. Cricket had other problems and priorities. The one-day World Cup began in 1975, but for some years the West Indians were so dominant in Test cricket that the question of who might be champions rarely caused much discussion. In the 1990s the situation changed. The emergence of the new South Africa and the promotion of Zimbabwe brought the number of Test countries to nine. At the same time, West Indies ceased to be cricket's undisputed superpower. When Australia took the Frank Worrell Trophy in May 1995 for the first time in almost two decades, they were widely described as the new world champions. But this judgment was complicated by the steady form of the South Africans, the spasmodic brilliance of Pakistan, and India's near-invincibility at home.

Sometimes a Test World Cup was suggested, but the logistics were horrendous: everyone would have to gather in one place for months. It took a while to work round that. But in my Editor's Notes in the 1995 *Wisden*, I suggested an ongoing Championship, using normal Test fixtures. The thought was well-received, but brought forth no official response. Then, in the November 1996 edition of *Wisden Cricket Monthly*, I argued the case in greater detail, calling for minor changes to the international fixture list so that such a Championship could be formally started. *Wisden* also set up a prototype, unofficial, table using the present incomplete schedule.

On this occasion the timing was right. The United Cricket Board of South Africa formally endorsed the *Wisden* plan and said it would recommend its adoption at the ICC in 1997. Administrators from other countries reacted more guardedly but, in almost every case, sympathetically. There was by now a growing recognition of the need to ensure the safety of traditional cricket in countries where the popularity of the one-day game was in danger of overwhelming it. And respected figures across the cricketing world were coming up with similar thoughts. Clive Lloyd called for a Championship. Sir Richard Hadlee and Ian Chappell independently proposed not dissimilar schemes for what Hadlee called "Supertests", leading to a grand final every four years. The former Australian batsman Ross Edwards suggested a points system involving the top six nations. These ideas have the drawback of requiring substantial reconstruction of the fixture list and, in some cases, are rather complex.

The *Wisden* Championship has the advantages of simplicity, practicality – and a working model. The proposal is that each country should agree to play the other eight in at least one Test – home and away – every four years, the existing cycle for the traditional confrontations such as England v Australia. A handful of extra Tests would be needed on top of current schedules. Each series of whatever length – counting a one-off game as a series – would be worth the same: two points for winning the series, one for drawing and none for losing. The competition would be continuous, like the world ranking systems in golf and tennis, but every time a series was contested it would replace the corresponding one in the table.

The system used in the prototype *Wisden* Championship is identical. But since not every country has played everyone else (e.g. Australia and West Indies have yet to play Tests against Zimbabwe), the difference between points gained and series played determines the standings. Series not renewed since 1990 are also excluded; this date will be subject to periodic review.

In January 1997 Australia's success in their home series against West Indies made them undisputed leaders of the *Wisden* table. This fact was prominently reported not merely in many papers across the cricketing world but at the top of the sports page in the *International Herald Tribune*, which is aimed primarily at expatriate Americans.

This helps back up *Wisden*'s contention that a World Championship offers the chance to ignite interest in Test matches even among non-cricketers. I believe it could secure the future of the traditional game, and offer the authorities and players commercial opportunities beyond the easy pickings of one-day internationals. I hope the ICC will take the small steps necessary to make the competition official. It has been a while since 1912. In the meantime, *Wisden* will continue to publish its own Championship table.

THE *WISDEN* CHAMPIONSHIP TABLE

(as at March 14, 1997)

		Series played	Points	Difference
1.	Australia	14	21	+7
2.	South Africa	12	17	+5
3.	India	13	17	+4
4.	West Indies	11	14	+3
5.	Pakistan	12	14	+2
6.	Sri Lanka	14	12	-2
7.	England	14	11	-3
8.	Zimbabwe	10	4	-6
9.	New Zealand	16	6	-10

In 1999, Wisden adjusted its table so that ranking was determined by average points per series. The system was formally adopted by the ICC in 2001, but with one-off Tests excluded for ranking purposes.

THE WRONG CHAMPIONS

Tim de Lisle, 2003

In January, the ICC Test Championship mace passed from Australia, one of the best teams ever, to South Africa, who were not even the best South African team ever. By no stretch of the imagination were they the best team in the world. They went top partly on the strength of fine victories in India and the West Indies, but largely because they had had the political will to play the minnows.

This didn't make the Test Championship a bad idea, but it did show up severe flaws in its execution. Something had to be done. The ICC agreed on a new format, to begin in June 2003, at their meeting the day before the World Cup final, but did not say what it was. The only clue was that it would take account of every match. In other words, it would get more complicated. The best thing about the original idea, floated in these pages by Matthew Engel in 1995 and known as the *Wisden* World Championship until 2001, was its simplicity. You could explain it on the back of a bus ticket. Two points for a series win, one for a draw, none for a defeat; count only the latest meeting between each pair of teams, home and away; take an average until such time as all play all. Engel's championship began with South Africa top, but that was then – Hansie Cronje wasn't yet a crook, and Australia, under Mark Taylor, were only three-quarters of the way to becoming the victory machine of today.

Once Australia went top, only a dud system could dislodge them. The ICC made an elementary error in counting South Africa's two one-off Tests against Zimbabwe in 1999–2000, home and away, as a two-Test home series for South Africa: it wasn't. They made a more general blunder in not allowing one-off Tests to count. A single Test is enough for a series between the strong and the weak; Bangladesh would surely have learned more and suffered less if they didn't have to keep playing two-Test series. Better still, Bangladesh's results could be discounted for their opponents as well as for them. We can only hope the ICC get it right second time.

THE ICC TEST CHAMPIONSHIP
(as at March 31, 2003)

		Series played	Won	Lost	Drawn	Points	Average
1.	South Africa (2)	17	13	3	1	27	**1.59**
2.	Australia (1)	13	9	2	2	20	**1.54**
3.	New Zealand (5)	17	8	5	4	20	**1.18**
4.	Sri Lanka (3)	16	8	6	2	18	**1.13**
5.	England (4)	16	6	6	4	16	**1.00**
6.	India (8)	15	5	6	4	14	**0.93**
7.	West Indies (6)	17	7	9	1	15	**0.88**
8.	Pakistan (7)	16	4	8	4	12	**0.75**
9.	Zimbabwe (9)	16	3	11	2	88	**0.50**
–	Bangladesh (–)	7	0	7	0	0	**0.00**

Previous year's positions in brackets.

BE CAREFUL WHAT YOU WISH FOR   Matthew Engel, *Notes by the Editor*, 2004

Modern *Wisden* editors generally welcome the cancellation of cricket tours, because there is too much international cricket to cram into this book already. This one is saddened as well as irritated by the surfeit. Writing these notes between 1993 and 2000, when I took a break, I fought hard for the World Test Championship. Be careful what you wish for, as they say.

The Championship was intended to be like a *salwar kameez*, a loose-fitting outfit within which the air could flow. The ICC instead imposed a straitjacket. The promotion of Bangladesh (now universally recognised as a mistake, certainly in the way it was done), the outlawing of one-off Tests, the imposition of too many one-dayers and the proliferation of back-to-back Tests have all made the schedule too onerous for the players and ill-designed to promote the game. The refusal to persevere with the original simple Championship concept (which went wrong only through ICC neglect) means that we have a system probably understood only by its deviser, my friend David Kendix, who is a clever mathematician. It is not a championship; it is a ratings system and it means damn-all to the man on the Clapham or Colombo omnibus, thus defeating the object.

It is right that everyone should play everyone else, if possible. But this schedule elevates one-sided cricket at the expense of the best cricket. As the 2003 England-South Africa series proved, there is nothing – absolutely nothing – in this game to touch a five-Test series between well-matched teams, in which the battle can ebb and flow. Now there are no five-Test series that do not involve England. But who on earth, outside the ICC, ever says "OK, best of two then"? So much time is taken up with bad cricket, there is not enough time for the really good stuff. To compensate, cricket has to think up gimmicks like the Top Team v Rest of the World artifice, proposed for 2005.

NO PLACE FOR SPONTANEOUS ENTHUSIASM   Matthew Engel, *Notes by the Editor*, 1996

During the Benson and Hedges Cup final, someone was spotted in the Lord's pavilion wearing an AIDS ribbon. It was a reminder, besides anything else, that MCC is no longer, if it ever was, an exclusive club for irascible colonels. All kinds and conditions of men belong, though not many young ones, as is inevitable in a club where the main qualification for membership is the patience to endure 20 years on the waiting list.

Many people have noticed that attitudes at the club have lately become a little less narrow too. This has been a gradual process, but it has accelerated since Roger Knight became secretary. There are imaginative rebuilding plans. And the atmosphere for non-members seems less intimidating; a little more in keeping with a place of entertainment at the end of the 20th century and less with the glasshouse at Catterick circa 1942. Perhaps eventually this mood will reach the membership as a whole and they will realise the extent to which their attitude towards the half of the human race excluded by birth from MCC makes not just them but the whole game look stupid.

But the most urgent problem, at Lord's as at other major grounds, is not getting into the pavilion but into the ground itself. In perhaps the bravest piece of cricket reporting last summer, Andrew Longmore of *The Times* discovered that it was indeed possible, just about, to buy a ticket on the day. He queued four hours for returns at the back of the Mound Stand. So did dozens of others. By the time Longmore was saved by a friendly passer-by with a spare, the grand total of two people had gained admission. After all that, he was rather angry to discover that the person in the seat in front of him, an MCC member, spent the afternoon reading *The Spectator* instead of being one.

It was noticeable in 1995 that West Indian supporters were virtually absent from the Tests. Spontaneous enthusiasm now is out; buy a ticket months in advance or stay at home is the message. There is a danger that soon the disadvantaged, the unconnected and – worst of all – the young will all be missing. This needs coherent thought and care from the game's authorities. Why not a couple of thousand tickets for the Saturday and Sunday of a Test match kept back and sold at affordable prices? The small loss of short-term revenue would be more than cancelled out by long-term gains. How many of today's cricket fans got hooked because they were able to get a glimpse of some big game when they were young? And how many of tomorrow's?

HANDLE WITH CARE
Matthew Engel, *Notes by the Editor*, 1997

One evening last July I was sitting at Worcester watching Durham, who were bottom of the County Championship, play Worcestershire, who were then 15th. It was precisely the sort of cricket match people who never watch the game keep saying is entirely worthless.

After tea on the first day, the Durham spearhead Simon Brown reduced Worcestershire to 11 for four. Only Graeme Hick stood between Durham and probable victory. Both men were playing for a place in the Test team against Pakistan the following week. Hick had also made himself unpopular with some Worcestershire members by missing the previous home match, pleading exhaustion. This was the very stuff of cricket: wheels within wheels, confrontations within the confrontation, games within the game. I thought it was utterly enthralling. In the event, Hick stood in Brown's way through the evening and much of the next day as well; the supporters decided they loved him again; and so did the England selectors, who chose both him and Brown for the next Test – then dropped them.

At the end of August, I was at Bristol for an even deader match: Gloucestershire playing Northamptonshire, two counties going nowhere. There was a young off-spinner, Jeremy Snape, bowling to an old slogger, Courtney Walsh, with three men on the leg-side boundary while Walsh tried to give them jumping practice; there too was an even younger batsman, Alec Swann – apparently impassive behind his grille but heart pounding – facing the master bowler Walsh, as he played his very first innings in county cricket.

At Taunton a few days later, I saw Derbyshire, thirsting for their first Championship in 60 years, bounding on to the field in bright sunshine with their hyperactive wicket-keeper Karl Krikken shouting "keep working" even before a ball had been bowled – and his captain, Dean Jones, then providing a running commentary which became noticeably more intermittent as the Somerset score moved towards 194 for one.

The 1996 cricket season in England was in some respects the most depressing in memory, almost entirely due to the continual disasters that afflicted the national team. A calendar year which began with the dreadful conclusion to the tour of South Africa, and a wretched performance in the World Cup, ended with England's glum failures in Zimbabwe. An indifferent summer was sandwiched in between; and a pall of gloom descended on the game. But every time I went to a county match I enjoyed myself hugely, no matter how few people might have been around to share that enjoyment.

The debate in English cricket is sometimes said to be between conservatives and radicals. Yet it seems to me that every true cricket lover is, in a sense, a conservative, or at any rate that the game represents the conservative side of our nature: our love of summer days and our youth. More often, the debate – such as it is – goes on between sleepwalkers on one side and hysterics on the other. Fleet Street cricket correspondents no longer report the game as such. Nearly all the time they just cover the soap opera of the England team: *EastEnders* without the varying storylines. Before contemplating the future of cricket – and, most daunting of all, English cricket – it makes sense to pause, and to give thanks for a wonderful game. It needs to change; but it has to be changed with care and love.

TOMORROW THE WORLD?   Matthew Engel, *Notes by the Editor*, 1997

Taking a global perspective, the game of cricket is thriving. Sri Lanka's success in the World Cup has sent a whole country cricket-crazy. Between harvests, when the rice paddies are dry, they are said to be filled with youngsters playing with any implements that approximate to bats and balls; indeed, doctors there are concerned about the injuries being done by flying stones. In rural South Africa, you see black people – women as well as men – playing impromptu versions of a game that was once effectively denied them. In Australia, the national team's success has helped restore cricket's role as the country's most potent unifying factor. In India, a remarkable proportion of the national income is now being channelled into the game, and the players' pockets.

In the subcontinent the success of the one-day game has wreaked havoc in other directions; the 1996–97 Duleep Trophy final in Mohali, a first-class match of some significance, was said to have begun with an attendance of one. But South Africa has shown that people can be won back to traditional cricket. When India visited there for the first post-isolation Tests in 1992–93, crowds varied between the patchy and the pitiful; four years on, when India returned, the support was tremendous.

The buzzword among optimists now is "globalisation", the belief that cricket can and must colonise new lands where the game is little known. It happened once before (through imperialism rather than television), which is why cricket is an international sport and not a quaint Olde English pastime. The evidence that it can happen again is not overwhelming. Thus far only two new countries, Kenya and Bangladesh, remotely look as if they might be able to stage Test cricket in the foreseeable future. The fear is that what globalisation might actually mean is more and more piddling one-day tournaments staged in more and more *recherché* places for the benefit of Asian satellite TV. This is exacerbated by the perception that Indian cricket is keener on short-term financial gains than the long-term welfare of the game.

These considerations have informed a year of intense debate among the members of the International Cricket Council, following the failure of the controversial secretary of the Indian board, Jagmohan Dalmiya, to be elected ICC chairman at the 1996 meeting. The past few months have been taken up with intense negotiations over a plan devised by Sir John Anderson, the chairman of New Zealand Cricket, to put a new executive committee in place, with devolved powers to sub-committees covering cricket, finance and marketing, and development. In the long run, that is likely to mean a beefed-up secretariat, with less power for the non-Test-playing countries, and perhaps less importance attached to the post of chairman.

Within the ICC, there are faint glimmerings of a consensus, particularly over the need to get a balance between one-day internationals and Tests. Two years ago, I made the case for an ongoing World Championship of Test cricket. *Wisden*'s own version of this now exists and has gathered a gratifying amount of interest throughout the cricketing world. The principle of a World Championship now seems to command overwhelming support.

If there were a Test Championship, it would be reasonable to consider a similar framework for international one-day cricket. South Africa has floated the idea of staging the World Cup every two years instead of four; others are interested in an ongoing one-day Championship culminating in a mini-World Cup between, say, the top four teams. The World Cup provides cricket with a showcase for the most popular form of the game, and it would certainly be preferable to clone that rather than continue with the present absurd situation in which meaningless trilateral and quadrilateral tournaments fill the international calendar and TV time to no sporting purpose whatever.

Whichever way this goes, part of the pattern is clear: a more seamless year, with cricket in many countries even during the English summer; and shorter, more intense, competitions that may render the concept of touring obsolete. Indeed, while the English were earnestly debating whether or not overseas players should be allowed to play county cricket, hardly anyone seemed to notice that the decision was being taken for them because the players were rapidly becoming unavailable. More than ever, one suspects, leading international cricketers will be just that and nothing else – they will be representing their country, or preparing to do so, or recovering and resting.

A WIND BLOWS FROM THE EAST
Mihir Bose, 1997

Napoleon's warning that the world should beware when China awakes has, in the last year, been translated into a wholly unexpected warning for the cricket world from another part of Asia – the Indian subcontinent. It has happened, not on the cricket field, but off it. On the field, the subcontinent has been a major power since 1971, when India won back-to-back series away from home in the West Indies and England. Sri Lanka's recent rise has merely confirmed this trend: three of the last four World Cups have been won by the subcontinent.

However, it is the money that the subcontinent can now generate through cricket that is posing a challenge to the established power centres. It is transforming the traditional image of the subcontinent as the land of magical spinners, wristy batsmen and (in Pakistan) devilish fast bowlers, into a place whose rich cricket administrators can dictate the future of the game.

This sounds like a contradiction. With a combined population of well over a billion, South Asia remains one of the poorest regions of the world. But, while much of this population lives just above the poverty line, there is also a well-off nation within the poor one. Six hundred million Indians may not get more than a square meal a day; but India also has 250 million people – almost the population of the United States – with a standard of living not far behind that of the West. Inside the subcontinent's thin man, there is a fat man trying to get out – and desperate to advertise his wealth.

A hint of this had come in 1993 when India, Pakistan and Sri Lanka, after the most fractious meeting ever of the International Cricket Council, won the right to stage the 1996 World Cup. The key to victory was the way the three countries got the ICC's associate members – hitherto treated much as the Soviet Union used to treat its eastern European satellites – on their side by promising them £100,000 each. England, who believed they had a gentleman's agreement guaranteeing them the 1996 tournament, had offered £60,000 each, and throughout the meeting seemed to assume this was yet another cosy old boys' gathering. The Asians wheeled in politicians and lawyers and treated the event as if it were an American presidential convention. They outflanked England, and won a rich prize. How rich only became evident when the 1996 World Cup began.

Unlike the Olympic Games, or soccer's World Cup and European Championships, the cricket World Cup is not an event owned by the international authority that runs the game. The country staging it, in effect, owns the competition. In five previous World Cups this had made little difference: the host country had made money, but not so much as to raise eyebrows. The 1996 World Cup changed everything.

As soon as they had won the competition the hosts set about selling it. Their biggest success was auctioning the television rights for a staggering $US14m, using a hitherto unknown agent of Indian extraction based in the United States, Mark Mascarenhas. The UK rights alone fetched $7.5m, compared to $1m in 1992. In addition the tournament was marketed on a scale never before seen in cricket. There was an official sponsor for every conceivable product, including the official World Cup chewing gum.

Cricket goes commercial: not much doubt about the identity of the
official drinks supplier of the 1996 World Cup.

A few years earlier, the world's most famous soft-drink manufacturers had
not even been allowed to sell their products in India. Now Coca-Cola and Pepsi-
Cola battled it out to be the official drink supplier. Coke won – but they had to
pay $3.8m, more than Benson and Hedges paid the Australians to be the main
sponsor of the 1992 World Cup. That role went to Wills, the Indian tobacco
offshoot of BAT, who paid $12m.

The organisers loved the rivalry. They were aware that they could keep all the
profits, once they had met their expenses, which included a fee of £250,000 to
each of the competing Test countries. This amount did not even cover the expenses
of some of the teams, but the hosts pocketed a profit of almost $50m. Contrast
this with the 1996 European Soccer Championship in England: where UEFA, as
owners of the championships, made a profit of £69m, England, the hosts, made
a loss of £1.7m.

It could be argued that the cricket administrators of the rest of the world were
naive to agree to such an arrangement. But in five previous World Cups nobody
had sought, let alone achieved, such commercial success. Not everyone on the
subcontinent foresaw it. The Sri Lankans, co-hosts of the tournament along with
India and Pakistan, clearly had doubts: they did not agree to underwrite the costs,
so did not participate in any of the profits.

The man who drove the commercial juggernaut was Jagmohan Dalmiya,
secretary of the Indian board. He hails from the Marwari community of India
whose business skills are both feared and respected. The joke in India is that a
Marwari can do business with a Scotsman and a Jew and still make money. The

other joke, less flattering, is that if you should see a Marwari and a tiger together in the jungle, you should shoot the Marwari first. Even within the Indian board, there are some who are less than enamoured of Dalmiya. He was responsible for the opening ceremony in Calcutta, which was widely regarded as a disaster. But few have ever had doubts about his financial acumen.

Had the subcontinent been content with its World Cup killing, this would have been an interesting marketing story. What has made it an explosive cricketing one is the use the triumphant administrators made of their new-found financial power. They launched a two-pronged attack. The short-term aim was to make Dalmiya chairman of the ICC. The long-term aim was to make sure that the subcontinent was at the centre of the cricket world.

The first battle came to a head during the annual ICC meeting at Lord's in July. With Sir Clyde Walcott coming to the end of his term, Dalmiya stood for the chairmanship, along with Malcolm Gray from Australia and Krish Mackerdhuj of South Africa. On the basis of a simple majority, Dalmiya, bolstered by the associate countries, had the votes. But he did not command the majority of the Test-playing countries. The rules were less than clear, but the Indians, having taken the advice of a QC, contended that the election should be decided by a simple majority. Walcott argued that any successful chairman must have the backing of a two-thirds majority of the Test-playing countries: six out of nine. Underlying this was concern about what a Dalmiya chairmanship might do. Before the meeting, his thoughts on the future development of the game had been extensively quoted in the media. These included a suggestion that Tests should become more like one-day matches, with every innings limited to certain numbers of overs.

The meeting ended in stalemate. Various suggestions to resolve it, including a second term for Walcott or for future chairmen to rotate country-by-country, were left hanging. But as 1996 turned into 1997, intense negotiations suggested a possible compromise framework: a rotating short-term chairmanship (probably starting with Dalmiya); a new, authoritative executive committee; less power for the associates. In the meantime Walcott carried on. The wider issue remains: how can the ICC accommodate the new power? The Asians want to be at the top table. As one administrator put it: "We do not want to come to Lord's for ICC and just nod our heads like little schoolboys as we used to. Now we come with fully prepared plans and want to be heard as equals."

It is interesting to note that on this issue the old racial solidarity displayed when the ICC tackled apartheid in South Africa no longer holds. In subcontinental eyes the West Indies are part of the old power structure, marshalled by England and Australia. Cricket has evolved no mechanism to cope with a changing situation. In 1974 the world football body FIFA elected the Brazilian, Joao Havelange, as president. He defeated Sir Stanley Rous, the symbol of the old European control, by shrewdly aligning the footballing centres of Latin America with the emerging countries. The Europeans have never been totally reconciled to him, but co-existence has been possible because Europe is still the economic powerhouse of the game. New centres such as Africa have come through and football has flourished.

Cricket has never had to cope with a Havelange. The ICC may no longer be a creature of MCC, but its offices are still at Lord's. [It moved to Dubai in 2005.] And the two men who have presided over it since the MCC President stopped being automatically head of the ICC, Sir Colin Cowdrey and Sir Clyde Walcott, have been old-world figures. In such a setting, Dalmiya is seen as a parvenu out to wreck the game. As one (non-Asian) administrator put it: "Dalmiya, personally, may not have been acceptable, and his tactics of trying to storm the citadel were probably wrong. But we have to realise that the subcontinent is a major power in world cricket. The television market there alone makes it very important."

The fear is that if Asia is not kept sweet, it could use its money to seduce Test-playing countries into something like a rival cricket circuit. Here cricket's very structure could be a help. The game is still organised in the 19th-century way. Apart from the World Cup every four years, and England's regular series with Australia, there are no fixed dates on the calendar. This means entrepreneurs can, almost at will, construct lucrative cricket tournaments. In 1996 the cricket boards of India and Pakistan, together with Mark McCormack's company TWI, staged five one-day matches in Toronto, the first time official internationals had been played in North America. The enterprise was underpinned by the ability to sell television rights, at $1m a match, to a satellite company keen to broadcast to the subcontinent.

In May 1997 the Indians are planning to hold a tournament to celebrate 50 years of their independence. Traditionally, the idea of playing in India in May was considered preposterous. But in order to avoid the worst of the intense heat, the Indians intend to start matches at about 3.30 in the afternoon and play until midnight. The Indians can contemplate this because the profits of the World Cup have helped them install lights on most of their grounds. And they know the TV rights will fetch large sums of money. Already, cricket in Sri Lanka from August has cut into the latter half of the northern summer, which used to be the exclusive cricket preserve of England. A tournament in May will be another dent.

The end result could be a far more powerful ICC – more like FIFA or the International Olympic Committee than the present small-scale set-up consisting of David Richards, the chief executive, a couple of assistants and a few phones. The subcontinent may not even want such an outcome: its bid for power should be seen as more akin to the barons at Runnymede extracting concessions from King John. But just as Magna Carta led to consequences undreamt of by the barons, so this could make the ICC the real powerhouse of cricket.

But is this what cricket wants, or needs? At present the game has no centralised bureaucracy, no Havelange at its helm. Does it really want to exchange the cosy club – admittedly biased in favour of the older cricketing countries – for an elective dictatorship at the mercy of the richest? In such a situation the subcontinent may even find that it has created an animal it cannot always control.

Mihir Bose is sports correspondent of the Daily Telegraph. *Among his books is* A History of Indian Cricket.

MR DALMIYA GOES TO LORD'S   Matthew Engel, *Notes by the Editor*, 1998

In 1996, the possibility that the Indian businessman Jagmohan Dalmiya might take control of the International Cricket Council had caused such consternation that it was almost split asunder. In 1997 he assumed office as President of the ICC for a three-year term without a murmur of dissent. And the first public utterance of a man previously painted as a sort of money-mad barbarian was to congratulate Colin Cowdrey on his elevation to the House of Lords. ("The most radical revolutionary will become a conservative on the day after the revolution" – Hannah Arendt.)

Dalmiya's job had never existed before. His predecessor, Sir Clyde Walcott, had been called chairman. Dalmiya's title sounded grander, but the reality was less imposing. The work done by Sir John Anderson, head of New Zealand Cricket, in reconstructing the ICC's decision-making processes had ensured a presidency with influence rather than power. There is now an 18-member executive board, with subsidiary committees covering cricket, finance and development. At long last, there are the glimmerings of a proper decision-making structure.

None the less, the game over which Dalmiya presided was one he had played a major part in creating, as Indian cricket's chief power-broker. There were 110 one-day internationals played in 1997 (plus two washouts). Most blurred into each other. The most significant may well have been the least noticed: those in Nairobi during October between Zimbabwe, Kenya and Bangladesh in front of tiny crowds and no TV cameras. After the ICC Trophy earlier in the year, when Bangladesh beat Kenya in the final, both countries had been promoted to a new, intermediate status, above the other associate countries but behind the Test-playing nations. This enabled them to play one-day internationals, as a possible preliminary move to full Test status – very soon, officials hoped.

In Nairobi, the two aspirants proved themselves hopelessly inferior to the newest of the nine Test-playing teams. Zimbabwe's professionalism and athleticism totally outclassed their rivals, and it rapidly became clear that neither would be ready for Test status in the near future. [Bangladesh were given Test status in 2000.]

It is important not to be dog-in-the-manger about this. There is huge interest in cricket in Bangladesh (which should be harnessed when all the major countries visit for a quickie tournament in October this year), and great playing potential in Kenya. Both countries need an injection of resources to develop stars capable of playing Tests, and the ICC is right to encourage them and others. Toronto and Singapore now stage one-day internationals; the ICC is salivating about the potential of playing in Florida. The more countries that play cricket the better.

But sports politicians can get carried away by their own rhetoric. Dalmiya was quoted as saying this January that the game had to spread to all corners of the world to survive. That is nonsense. If cricket were to mutate into something different simply to try and sell itself to the American market, or anywhere else, it wouldn't be cricket and it wouldn't be worth having.

"The idea that the poor should have leisure," observed Bertrand Russell, "has always been shocking to the rich." He might well have had cricket in mind. Inevitably, much cricket goes on while most people are working. But in England they have lately left bank holidays blank. The guardians of the greensward have not moved rapidly to take the opportunity of staging the game at sociable hours.

Happily, times are at last changing. In the nethermost crannies of the minutes of the International Cricket Council's meeting in July 1997 lurked an item of inestimable significance to the future of Test cricket. In the event of bad light, the ICC said, play could continue under floodlights. And at Perth in November, between Australia and New Zealand, it happened for the first time. At a time when the game's highest form of expression is struggling in several countries to justify its existence as a commercial entity, the advent of Tests with supper intervals cannot be far away.

Of all the advances in the competitive arts since the second world war, nothing, not even the satellite dish, can match the cultural significance of the pylon. Here is sport freed from the tyrannies of the working day. Here, moreover, is sport in Technicolor and Sensurround. The lights do not merely illuminate; they appear to magnify and intensify. To be among the 15,000 present at Edgbaston on a balmy Wednesday night in July 1997, for English cricket's first floodlit flannelled foolery of any consequence, was to wonder why the counties had dallied for so long. Here was cricket without an exclusion zone, a family affair complete with crèche and bouncy castle.

All this happened a mere 119 years after floodlights were first tried on an English cricket ground. The ground, though, was Bramall Lane, Sheffield, and the sport was football: in October 1878, 12,000 paid to see a game featuring two Sheffield representative teams and the novelty of electricity; another 8,000 sneaked in free, because no one thought to light the entrances.

The nearest cricket came to such an experiment was at The Oval in 1889, when the second day of Yorkshire's Championship match with Surrey was extended until 7 p.m. because the game was almost over and neither captain wanted to come back next day. It was late August and daylight saving had not been invented, so it was already dark. The players had to rely on the gas lamps from the streets of Kennington.

Typically, it was America which really blazed the trail. When he went there in the 1930s to turn professional, Fred Perry found himself lobbing and smashing in exhibition halls and skating rinks. In 1935 the Cincinnati Reds hosted baseball's first major league night game. English sport was slower on the uptake. When the Arsenal manager, Herbert Chapman, tried to push the idea to meet the growing challenge of greyhound racing, he was rebuffed by football officials. The first floodlit Football League match did not come until February 1956.

Cricket, inevitably, endured an even lengthier awakening. In 1932, the Western Suburbs grade players in Sydney practised under lights, but the bowlers complained that the dew made the white ball hard to grip. There was the odd experiment in the 1950s: the enterprising Middlesex spinner Jack Young staged a benefit match at Highbury, and there was one midsummer night's frolic in Brisbane, but it took Kerry Packer to transform the ugly gosling into a golden goose.

Spurred by the initial public apathy towards World Series Cricket and the promise of a prime-time television audience, toes were dipped at VFL Park on December 14, 1977. Late arrivals from offices and factories swelled the gate to 6,300, the largest to date for Packer's seemingly vainglorious revolution. The sightscreens were turned around and painted black. The lights were switched on at 6.30, after which a white ball was used, yellow and orange having been deemed unsuitable. Tony Greig, the World XI captain, opted to bat first, reasoning that any voluntary confrontation with Dennis Lillee under such unfamiliar conditions, even though bouncers were to be barred, would be an act of hubris; the Australians still prevailed at a canter. For the defence, a skier held with aplomb by Imran Khan served as Exhibit A. Exhibit B was Ian Chappell's decisive 69, compiled first in bright sunlight, then in the twilight, then lit by high-wattage bulbs.

English reactions ranged from distaste to prescience. John Woodcock observed that Australians, "being always early with their evening meal", were "well-suited by night-time sport". David Frith attributed his nausea to fatigue: "If I'm prejudiced at all perhaps it is in favour of cricket in God's sunshine." Alan Lee's conclusion was unarguable. Packer had "struck gold" and would "arouse the envy of the traditional authorities".

Before long, Dayglo kit was *de rigueur* and WSC was attracting the young and unjaundiced, expanding the audience. State funds provided pylons in Brisbane and Perth. English concessions to all this garish modernity were hesitant and fleeting. There was the Lambert and Butler Cup, held at football grounds in 1981; even though Clive Lloyd, Ian Botham and David Gower were on parade, the semi-finals and final at Stamford Bridge drew a paltry 2,500. By the 1990s, portable pylons were a possibility, so cricket grounds could get temporary lighting. But a Sixes event at The Oval in 1994 was the least propitious attempt yet. It was cancelled halfway through when the principals demanded payment, which the organisers could not provide. The headline in *The Times* alluded to a broader scepticism: "Rotten enterprise worthy of contempt."

The Indian Board of Control used profits from the last World Cup to install floodlights at its principal venues. Dennis Amiss, the Warwickshire chief executive, has estimated the total cost of equipping every first-class county headquarters at £4m, a far from prohibitive sum. But after unveiling his blueprint for the future of the game Lord MacLaurin, chairman of the ECB, admitted that the possibility had not even been discussed. Given the unalloyed success of Edgbaston, an encouraging attempt in poor weather at Hove and a reasonably well-attended Roses friendly at Old Trafford, it was an astonishing oversight. Here, surely, was the sugar to coat the pill of a two-divisional Championship for the reluctant counties.

Technically, the main problem is the ball. Since the white model used in the one-day game is felt to lack durability, the preferred projectile for the Sheffield Shield's inaugural day/night fixture, between Western Australia and Queensland at Perth in November 1994, was a traditional model tanned in yellow. Some batsmen complained about visibility; but the damp atmosphere and seaming pitch apparently had rather more to do with their tribulations. In Britain, dew is also a concern, hence the dispensation granted to Sussex to drag a rope through the outfield, though Tony Pigott, the club's chief executive, maintains that, when he inspected the pitch at 10 p.m. the previous evening, it was "as dry as a bone".

Such objections, Pigott argues, are petty, so typical of the game's aversion to change. It is hard to disagree. Some estimate that batting first in a day/night international is worth a start of 20 to 30 runs, but in a longer game of cricket, there is a stronger likelihood of any imbalances evening out. Besides, the vagaries and uncertainties can only add spice to our favourite dish. Further self-denial is senseless. Unless, that is, the aim is to prove Bertrand Russell right.

CRICKET MAX · 1998

In October 1997, England sent a 12-man squad to New Zealand for the three-match Cricket Max series against the Max Blacks. Cricket Max, the brainchild of former New Zealand Test batsman Martin Crowe, is a form of one-day cricket in which both teams have two innings of ten overs each, with hits into the "max zone" – an area near the boundary and behind the bowler – counting double. England's side, led by Matthew Maynard, included Test players such as Phillip DeFreitas, Chris Lewis and Robin Smith. Although the Max Blacks were unable to call on New Zealand's stars, who were touring Australia, they had more experience of the format.

England won the first match, at Auckland, by four wickets, thanks to an unbeaten 50 from 17 balls from Dominic Ostler, who finished the series as England's top scorer by far with 152 runs. In all, he hit two 12s, seven eights, a four and three twos. The Max Blacks hit back to win the second match, at Hamilton, by 13 runs and the decider, at Wellington, by ten wickets.

MCC AND WOMEN · Matthew Engel, Notes by the Editor, 1999

The replay screens at the Tests in England last year were sponsored by the car firm Citroën. And so, during intervals at the Lord's Test, the screen kept showing Citroën's current advert, which consisted of the model Claudia Schiffer descending a staircase and getting into a car while simultaneously removing every item of her clothing. She did this, in about twice life-size, in full view of the Lord's pavilion. It was a remarkable disjunction.

At the time, a blocking minority of MCC had just ensured the continuation of the club's ban on women members. In normal times, that might have been the end of the subject for another generation. But an unusually determined MCC President, Colin Ingleby-Mackenzie, accompanied by threatening noises from the sports minister, Tony Banks, had a remarkable effect. Essentially, members were told to keep thinking and voting until they came up with the right decision. In September, they did: 69.8% of those who voted were in favour of change, above

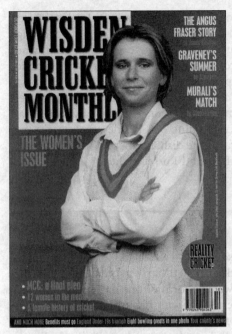

Girl power: *Wisden Cricket Monthly* encouraged MCC to allow lady members in October 1998 by putting woman cricketer Isabelle Duncan, mischievously wearing the club's sweater, on its cover.

the two-thirds majority required, compared with 55.7% in February. And in early 1999 five women were duly invited to become playing members.

What was notable about the continuing debate was that the arguments advanced against the admission of women were generally stupid, mostly peevish and entirely selfish. The minority never explained how a game battling against heavy odds to retain its place in British hearts could do so if its most famous organisation so wantonly alienated half the population. What they talked about were their own privileges.

The change has come, and it is very welcome. But in practice, of course, MCC discriminates against almost all the population. The 57 million Britons who are not members have second-class access to the game's greatest occasions, as the World Cup final in June will show yet again, even though, on that occasion, members will actually have to pay their way. A random elite is still accorded privileges that would be unthinkable if the game were to start from scratch. What MCC needs to ask itself is what its function is to be in the 21st century. If it did not happen to own England's biggest and most historic cricket ground (an increasingly well-appointed one), MCC's entrance requirements would be of no more interest than those of Free Foresters or I Zingari. But it does matter, because Lord's matters. Does MCC exist primarily for the benefit of cricket as a whole? Or is it just a rich organisation whose first obligation is to its own members? Admitting women is a start. But only a start.

BEFORE I NOD OFF. . .   Matthew Engel, *Notes by the Editor*, 2000

In his autobiography, *Tiger by the Tail*, Lord MacLaurin, the chairman of the ECB, has the following passage: "It is no longer possible to capture the somnolence of John Arlott's poem 'Cricket at Worcester, 1938', when 'Drowsing in deck-chair's gentle curve, through half closed eyes, I watched the cricket.' Those times are long gone." I am not entirely sure what Lord MacLaurin is on about. He is right in the sense that there are no deck-chairs at Worcester these days, rather those plastic tip-up thingies, which are less conducive to drowsing. I still don't find it impossible. I half-dozed very happily on a sunny September afternoon last year; there was even someone called Hutton batting. Does he think county cricket isn't somnolent any more? Has he *been* to Worcester lately?

Heaven knows, I am not against reforming cricket where it is desirable and essential. I have been banging on about it in this space for the past eight years, and Lord MacLaurin can go on tinkering with the game in his way if he insists. But he really ought to leave us snoozers alone. They have done away with the deck-chairs. There are those whose future plans for cricket would include doing away with Worcester. Do away with somnolence, and you will do away with cricket once and for all. And England with it, probably.

ENGLAND CLAIM THEIR CRICKETERS   Graeme Wright, *Notes by the Editor*, 2001

There are new Test sponsors, npower, presumably providing power, if not funding, to the nth degree. But financing the county game continues to tax cricket's administrators, and some counties have good reason to be concerned about their futures. So do their members, and 2000 gave them plenty to talk about, with the introduction of the two-division County Championship, a summer of almost continuous international cricket (the blueprint for summers ahead) and the arrival of central contracts for Test cricketers. Some of them, anyway. The system, which essentially put those with central contracts under England's management rather than their county's, was by no means perfect. Counties losing players who were not under contract complained they did not receive the same level of compensation.

However, lessons were learned, and adjustments have been made. In principle, the system worked. At first sight, it appeared more beneficial for bowlers than batsmen to have time off between Tests, though England's 37-year-old wicket-keeper-all-rounder-cum-one-day-opening-batsman-cum-stand-in-captain will have appreciated not having to drive back to The Oval for a county game, as he would in days gone by. County members see central contracts as one more downgrading of the domestic game; the counties themselves recognise who butters their bread and have gone along with them.

Craig White's emergence as a strong candidate to be England's cricketer of the year was worth celebrating. England look all the better for having a fast-bowling all-rounder on board, and always have; the search for one has gone on too long. If White fits the bill, it will also take some pressure off Andrew Flintoff, of whom too much was expected too soon. He was in danger of becoming the Moby Dick of English cricket, forever pursued by his potential.

Graeme Wright, who last edited Wisden *in 1992, returned to do a further stint as editor when Matthew Engel, perhaps undermined by England's continuing on-field struggles, took a sabbatical. Wright edited the 2001 and 2002 Wisdens, Tim de Lisle did 2003, and Engel returned in 2004.*

TEST CRICKET'S TEN-YEAR PLAN

Graeme Wright, *Notes by the Editor*, 2001

Last year, the ICC agreed an eight-year television deal worth a minimum $US550m (£355m), to include the 2003 World Cup in South Africa, 2007 in the Caribbean, and other tournaments. Such is the attraction of one-day internationals, mostly to viewers in the subcontinent. So that Test cricket also has a focus over and above traditional rivalries and piecemeal series, the ICC has agreed a ten-year programme, in which the Test-playing countries meet each other home and away over two five-year periods, and introduced a Test Championship along the lines of the *Wisden* World Championship. Each series will comprise two or more Tests, accompanied by a one-day series – perhaps as a way of countering the profusion of "offshore" tournaments regarded by some as the feeding-ground of illegal bookmakers and their bribes.

CRYING OUT FOR LESS

Christopher Martin-Jenkins, 2003

"They are as sick that surfeit with too much, as they that starve with nothing."
– The Merchant of Venice

As usual Shakespeare hit the nail bang in the middle, and as usual we do well to listen to his wisdom. There is too much cricket. There has been too much cricket for far too long and if we do not act now to stop the rot, we will all be driven to distraction: players, media, spectators; umpires, groundsmen, administrators; everyone with a stake in the game.

The media have to take it on the chin: we make a lifelong living from the game and there are ways of sharing the load. But for players there is sometimes no way off the treadmill. In January 2003, the nucleus of England's team made a vain attempt to spend three precious nights at home between the end of the VB Series in Australia and the start of their preparations for the World Cup in South Africa. They were away from October to March, an acceptable absence, perhaps, in the days of sea travel, infrequent tours and mothers who expected to change every nappy; hardly so today, if there is to be any balance in their lives.

No wonder Graham Thorpe opted out altogether for a time and others such as Jonty Rhodes have chosen to retire from one form of the game. No wonder India's team made the same plea for a break at home in the midst of a remorseless programme last year when, hard on the heels of the contentious series in South Africa late in 2001, they played host to England and Zimbabwe, toured the West Indies and England, went hot-foot to the Champions Trophy in September, then began a series of three Tests and seven one-day internationals against West Indies – and fitted in a Test series and seven more one-dayers in New Zealand by mid-January.

When Nasser Hussain made a plea for a break towards the end of England's tour of Australia, he was echoing the *cri de coeur* made by a number of Test captains over the years, among them the Australians Kim Hughes and Allan Border. In 1989–90 Border resigned the captaincy of Queensland, publicly asking the Australian Cricket Board what point there was in leading his state team when he was able to play for them only twice a season.

It is a reminder that this is not a new problem, only one that becomes a little more exacerbated with every year that passes, like creeping rheumatism in an ageing body. Each year cricket boards round the world agree to just a little more to feed the insatiable appetites of the television companies. The leading players do not want to play more, and they risk injury by doing so, but they are sucked in, knowing that someone else will take their place should they desist, and feeling that they might as well take the money on offer while they can. The result is shorter careers and shorter tempers; more wearisome travel, more soulless hotels; more tired players playing to preserve their batteries as well as to win; less time with loved ones and less enjoyment.

In 1972, 14 Tests started around the world and only three one-day internationals, all between England and Australia, the pioneers. By 1982, the totals had risen gently to 33 one-dayers and 28 Tests. In 1992, it was 89 one-dayers and only 26 Tests, but that had something to do with it being a World Cup year; in 1993, there were 36 Tests. By 2002, the total was 145 one-day internationals and 54 Tests. Last year, the ICC permitted, no, encouraged, a bigger Champions Trophy. And this year they let the World Cup expand again, to 14 countries playing what was intended to be 54 matches in 43 days.

For 20 years after the Packer Revolution – the event that started this rapid proliferation – the ICC did nothing to prevent the steady rise in the amount of cricket. Then came their plan for a ten-year programme of Tests, already disrupted by political disputes. It was a laudable attempt to bring some order to the whole programme, but it was designed less to put a sensible limit on the number of matches than to give a framework for a rolling world championship table.

Domestic professional cricket in every country is completely dependent for its viability on income generated by internationals. But it has to be an inter-dependent system. Without first-class cricket, players of the necessary quality to make Tests and one-day internationals attractive would be very hard to find, if not impossible. They would have to learn their advanced skills on the big stage, and there are few players good enough to do that. That is why it is vitally impor-tant for the county game in England, and for domestic cricket elsewhere, to find a sensible balance in the programme.

Cricket was looked forward to more eagerly by all involved in the days when there were clearly defined seasons. Once upon a time, only England staged cricket between May and September: these days West Indies have Tests in June, Sri Lanka and Zimbabwe in July, Pakistan in August. Australia have taken to playing indoors in Melbourne at the height of the British summer and now they are to have outdoor Tests in the tropical north as well. England's response has been to organise even more incoming tours. Since 1997, they have gone from three one-day inter-nationals and six Tests to 13 one-dayers and seven Tests in 2003. Every extra inter-national event makes enthusiasm for the major occasions of county cricket that much less. Every quarter-final of the Cheltenham & Gloucester Trophy that does not fill all the seats and marquees means a greater dependence on the international profits. So the vicious circle turns. It all revolves around money: that is inevitable for any professional sport.

Therefore, what used to be called the $64,000 question (probably about $550m by now) is this: has the surfeit become counter-productive not just for players, media and others closely involved, but also for paying spectators and subscribing television viewers? There is much evidence to suggest that it has. Swathes of empty seats could be seen last year at Tests from Christchurch to Old Trafford. Channel 4's coverage, good as it is, tends to attract smaller audiences than the BBC did. On the phone to me in the later stages of England's tour of Australia, one of the keenest followers of sport I have ever known said: "I'm afraid I stopped reading, watching and listening after we lost in Perth." So he had taken no close interest in Michael Vaughan's hundreds at Melbourne and Sydney, two of the most attractive innings anyone could hope to see.

Surely heed has to be taken of the implications. The aim should be a happy medium – providing enough cricket for the game to remain solvent, but not so much that when the keen follower sees in his morning paper that there is another match to watch today he feels complete indifference or, worse, a heart-sinking revulsion. The answer, as the Test captains have argued, is for the ICC to impose limits on each nation, for the good of all involved. Home and away, 12 Tests and 20 one-day internationals a year seems now to be a reasonable and realistic maximum for any country. Within the bounds it would be possible for each nation to suit its programme to its particular needs. Perhaps India, with its uniquely large market, apparently unquenchable enthusiasm for the one-day game and no need to compete with anything so formidable as the market for football in Britain, might be treated as a special case, adding, if politics will permit, an Asian tournament to its commitments in the ICC's Test and one-day championships.

Long before Shakespeare had his say, Solomon had put it equally succinctly: "To everything there is a season and a time to every purpose under the heaven."

TIME FOR CITIES TO REPLACE COUNTIES   Graeme Wright, *Notes by the Editor*, 2002

Some years have passed since the baby and its bathwater appeared in these Notes. Contrary to the warning of the saw-sayers, the time may have come to throw them both out. It is not only that the water is cold; the baby is old and should have been lifted out long ago.

Which is a long-winded way of saying that the time is approaching to reform the first-class county structure, as opposed to merely meddling with the cricket and the fixture list. Not that a little meddling would go amiss: the passing of the Benson and Hedges Cup this summer provides just the opportunity for fewer games, less travelling and more preparation. But I would like these Notes to open a wider-ranging, longer-term debate, aimed at revivifying professional cricket. And however loath I am to say it, I believe the county system runs counter to a positive future for English cricket at the highest level.

What we have at the moment is a Victorian institution that resisted reform in the 20th century and struggled into the 21st on subsidies rather than public support. It isn't that the counties haven't changed. A number have become like businesses rather than members' clubs, which is not to say they have become more businesslike. To be commercially viable, they have to satisfy their dual market needs. Because professional sport is essentially in the entertainment game, they should be able to attract and entertain an audience; and, such is the framework of English cricket, they must provide the right players for the national teams that generate much of the ECB's income. This is a well-rehearsed argument; it hardly requires repeating any more than the fact that many counties no longer seem capable of fulfilling these conditions. The system survives on a confederacy of mediocrity.

It is easy to understand, to sympathise even, with resistance to radical reform. There are livelihoods and grand traditions at stake. But if 18 counties cannot pay their way without subsidy, and if they fail the needs of the national team, do we need so many? What happens if the subsidy dries up? If nothing else, it might be prudent for county cricket to reform its structure before circumstances force it to change.

Some 60% of the ECB's revenue comes from television. Government and lottery funding are essential for many projects, in particular the much vaunted National Cricket Academy. Cricket, compared with other sports, does well out of the lottery. This suggests that it still has a place in national life, but that place depends on the profile of the national team. Unlike football clubs, the counties have little national reference; rather, for much of the population and the media, county cricket drifts along in a backwater. Without the annual injection of more than a million pounds each, most counties would be further up the creek without a paddle.

Changes have been introduced in attempts to improve standards: among them, four-day matches, two divisions, pitch penalties and smaller-seamed balls. But they have not brought spectators to first-class cricket and they have not provided the core of players able to step up to international level. Some argue that the gap between county and Test cricket is so wide that another tier, regional cricket, is needed. It seems unlikely to happen, but its very presence in the debate is further confirmation that the county structure is failing England. An England squad system, giving players more time to practise and work together as a team, would be more worthwhile than a regional tier. The success England have enjoyed abroad these past few winters is a strong argument in favour of developing the squad system at home.

In fairness to the counties, there are simply not enough good young English players coming into professional cricket to sustain an environment that produces Test cricketers. The Australian board are able to put 25 cricketers under contract; the ECB manage just a dozen. That can't only be a matter of economics; England would be hard pushed to name 25 ready for international cricket. Take out the centrally contracted bowlers – six last year, three from Yorkshire – and the standard of county bowling is deplorably low. Batsmen hit 118 more centuries in 2001 than in the previous year and twice the number of double-hundreds. The other counties can only envy Yorkshire's bowling depth; England are merely covetous.

The counties themselves acknowledge the paucity of home-grown talent by increasing the intake of overseas players with British passports or flying the European Union's flag of convenience. There were ten in 2001; the Professional Cricketers' Association estimate a 150% increase in 2002. Many come from South Africa, where political decrees on team selection and the country's changing economic circumstances hamper the career prospects of young white cricketers. They won't be able to play for England without meeting the ECB's qualification requirements, but they will have their salaries subsidised by income generated by Team England.

In the meantime, seven counties are receiving £50,000 each towards accredited local academies that will identify players aged between 13 and 18, and help them become first-class cricketers. The need for these academies is a sorry commentary on the way sport, especially cricket, has been downgraded in schools by greater emphasis on exams, the selling-off of sports grounds and the paperwork that absorbs teachers' time, energy and desire. The problem is not new but it has taken cricket time to address it.

It was not so long ago that Lord MacLaurin, chairman of the ECB, was calling the counties themselves English cricket's 18 academies. This was back when the media wanted a national academy along Australian lines; last year their demand was met. It had become so apparent that the so-called "academies" were not producing the right calibre of cricketer to mix it with the best that the board bowed to the inevitable and hired an Australian to do the job properly. Admittedly, they didn't have any premises at the time; happily Rod Marsh, the man they appointed, knew just the place and so England's National Cricket Academy began life at the Australian Academy in Adelaide, where Marsh had previously been director. New Labour are trying something similar with the National Health Service, sending patients abroad for treatment.

In the same way that the board chairman called the counties "academies", his chief executive Tim Lamb took to calling them "centres of excellence", which did nothing for the counties but made him sound like one of those well-spun politicians whose peculiar notion of excellence is applied in defence of failing institutions. Last year he took to describing the counties as "businesses". But, as the farming industry is currently debating, what happens to the business if the subsidy diminishes or disappears?

Given that the ECB's television agreement expires in 2005, this is not idle speculation. Channel 4's viewing figures for cricket have dropped each year since they began to televise the game in 1999. They put a brave face on this, comparing reductions in audiences for other sports. But however the numbers are interpreted, they mean fewer people have been watching cricket on television, and falling figures are anathema to any broadcaster dependent on advertising income. Cricket may not be living on borrowed time; some counties clearly are. I suspect there is already a tendency to let the weakest go to the wall. Natural wastage, businessmen call it.

Maybe that's the answer; it is pragmatic, and lately English cricket has been learning to live with pragmatism. But it would add interest to the debate to hear something more radical being discussed; something that would take into account England in the 21st century rather than the 19th. It has become an urban society, built on cities and conurbations. Why not a professional circuit based on these, rather than on shires and counties, however romantically their names resonate? The grounds are already firmly established in cities.

It is a given that cricket does not exist on membership and gate money. Total membership for the 18 counties in 2001 was 128,234, with Yorkshire attracting 15,331 and Derbyshire 1,877 (including 16 dogs), a fair reflection of their Championship positions if ever there was. But one in every 330 adults in England and Wales belonging to a county cricket club is not a fair reflection of the national interest in cricket. It demonstrates mostly the extent to which professional cricket has to market itself. Becoming part of a city's life by name as well as location would assist this process. The cricket club could incorporate civic identity, and benefit from the commercial and sponsorship opportunities such an association would provide. Yorkshire would doubtless claim to be an exception.

Assuming the globalisation of cricket continues apace, it will be only a matter of time before there is a television-driven demand for international inter-city tournaments. Cities are marketable commodities in a way that counties, states and provinces are not. This may seem fanciful now, but looking ahead often does. Cricket may never have the lion's share of the television sports market in England, but it has immense potential elsewhere. English cricket should not simply be aware of this potential but positioned to exploit it when the opportunity arises. Cricket has trundled along traditional lines for a long time, but the pace of change and growth is faster now than it has ever been.

A Game in Flux
Simon Heffer, 2002

It is easy to forget this, but professional cricket in England took off in the 19th century because people were prepared to pay to watch it. In those days, spectators – whether club members, or people charged at the gate – provided the revenues to pay the players. Now, television companies and corporate sponsors perform that function. Therefore, it might be argued, the public deserves no consideration when it comes to the scheduling of matches, or the composition of the teams that participate in them.

That is certainly how a great many county members have come, in recent years, to regard the cricket authorities' attitude to the sides they support, and the first-class competition in which those sides play. True, it would seem eccentric now to attempt to market county cricket as a viable leisure activity. But first-class county cricket has been changed to an extent at which it seems designed actively to drive spectators away. If this was the plan, it is working brilliantly.

The first step was to play county cricket over four days instead of three. With slow over-rates – why bowl 20 an hour when you can get away with bowling 15 or 16? – and four days to fill, the play became attritional. Only the retired have the time, and then not always the inclination, to watch such a contest. It is a contest made all the more soporific and irrelevant in recent seasons by the introduction of central contracts for England players and an extended international programme. This means that the best English players hardly ever appear for their clubs – and then, for good measure, they complain about the "lack of support" given them by their county committees. The two-division County Championship has suspended some ancient rivalries, an important ingredient of any sporting fixture list, added to which games are often either not scheduled for, or have finished by, the weekend, when people might have time to watch.

Indeed, all the major changes in the last 15 years have been made with complete disregard for the paying public. No doubt this reflects how little cash they actually bring into the game, but there is more to it than that. When counties have tried to stand up for their members' interests, they have been castigated for obstructing "progress". It is a chicken-and-egg argument. The public drifted away from cricket because it became progressively more unattractive as a spectacle. First-class county cricket is nigh unwatchable: it almost beggars belief that anybody should find it a recreation preferable to, say, sitting in his or her own garden and watching the flowers grow. The county supporter's emotional tie to his or her side is considered sentimental and uncommercial. It seems to be the view of the ECB that the counties exist solely to breed England players. As soon as they are bred they are whisked off, not to be seen again until they have proved inadequate for the international task, returning to their counties in a useful state of demoralisation. This shows contempt for the counties themselves, for the players and for the paying public. The ECB don't appear to realise that if the last of those is a far smaller constituency than it used to be – and it is – it is largely the board's own fault, and that of their forerunner. Moreover, this decline matters. Those who lose the habit of paying to watch county cricket will in time lose the habit of paying to watch Test cricket, too.

The way the ECB treat the counties is reckless. At the going rate, there will be hardly any paying supporters for first-class cricket, and greatly reduced county memberships, before the end of the decade. After all, why should members pay to see boring cricket, played (by definition) by those who are not especially good cricketers? And just as this is driving away individuals, so it is driving away the corporate clients who were so in evidence in the 1980s and 1990s. The fewer people who go into county grounds, the less money that will be spent there. The begging bowl, which counties already hold out to the ECB, will be thrust more and more aggressively and desperately in the board's face. The choice will be either to pump more money into these loss-making enterprises, or accept blithely that a club or two will go bankrupt.

The counties have behaved stupidly themselves. Large staffs packed with mediocrities are simply not acceptable. Too many cricketers make it quite clear they hate playing cricket, and the game should not tolerate them. Their attitude is like a cancer dragging down the professional game, while reliance on subsidy has prevented some clubs from challenging the forces of decline head on.

It does not, however, need to be like that. The board should realise, first, that their greed in scheduling so much international cricket – and thereby taking county players away for so much of the season – will in time prove counterproductive, as the currency of such contests is devalued. They should also realise that they achieve little by demanding that England-contracted players "rest" from matches in between Tests, thereby missing opportunities to stay in or get back into form, while at the same time entertaining county supporters. They should see, too, that four-day cricket is not working. If those with an interest in cricket were told that first-class matches would be played over three days, on uncovered wickets, featuring the best players in between an old-style international programme, then first-class county cricket might become attractive to them again.

At the moment, it is dying a painful death because of the attitude that counties, in return for providing international players, deserve no consideration other than the regular filling of the begging bowl. Yet it is madness to let what, in many cases, could be viable businesses go into terminal decline. We must not expect the ECB to be vulnerable to sentimental arguments about the place of county clubs in the history of English cricket. We might, though, expect the board to want to maximise the appeal of cricket and to make these clubs strong. After all, they are not just a source of players for England, but also of generating interest in English cricket: without such interest the game dies altogether.

At the time of writing, Simon Heffer was a columnist on the Daily Mail. *He later moved to the* Daily Telegraph.

COUNTY CRICKET LOSES THE PLOT   Matthew Engel, *Notes by the Editor,* 2005

One of the arguments privately advanced for the Sky deal [exclusively to cover England's Test matches] is that otherwise "several counties would have gone to the wall". This is something that has echoed down the ages: Derbyshire were supposedly going out of business in 1910; Northamptonshire almost crashed in 1929, shortly after Wall Street. Yet they have all proved remarkably resilient.

Let them go. This is not said the way the county game's enemies say it, but in the belief that if counties were pushed back on their own resources, they would emerge even stronger, and with a clearer sense of purpose, than the subsidy junkies of today. Either the people of Derbyshire, Northamptonshire and Leicestershire (to choose only the most obvious examples) want county cricket or they don't. If the social-security cheques from Test revenues dried up, the experience might prove not just salutary but liberating. Four-day cricket played by moderate players on dead pitches is never likely to be a major 21st-century entertainment, but the county game is now in danger of sliding from its position on the margins of British life into total oblivion.

Some of this is old news. Some isn't. The very reforms credited with helping the England team have actually had a dire effect lower down: there are no local heroes any more because the best English players almost never play for their counties. And whereas England have learned the value of settled side with its own *esprit de corps*, counties happily spend their subsidies flying in international allsorts who barely even know which side they are representing, never mind who their teammates might be.

A few of the evils may be mitigated by the new system of using handouts to reward counties that develop their own players, and by a belated mini-tightening of the rules on overseas signings from 2006. And help may be at hand from a very unexpected source. The new draft European Constitution (Article III-182) recognises the "specific nature" of sport, implying that the Kolpak ruling, which has allowed counties to sign cricketers from anywhere that has a trade agreement with the EU, will be open to challenge.

But Brussels won't change the fact that the county game is increasingly unwatchable and pointless. Precisely as predicted here six years ago, the introduction of two divisions has forced counties into short-term signings instead of long-term development of players. And the fear of relegation made first-division cricket last summer absolutely wretched.

I did propose an idea to try to pep up county cricket by merging the Championship and the one-day league to create a real champion county, something the public would understand. It was endorsed by an ECB working party but rejected by the county chairmen, as a side-effect of their determination to stop the fixture list being slashed. "The Championship is a great competition," snorted their spokesman, Mike Soper, "and to muddle it up with one-day games seems completely stupid." Great competition? Are we on the same planet?

Anyway, on December 23 (a traditional date for burying bad news – there really was no one home at the ECB) Soper's own working party announced a new one-day cricketing set-up from 2006 rendering what was previously confused entirely incomprehensible. The one competition everyone could understand, the knockout cup, is to be abolished, which is a dreadful decision. Instead, there will be three competitions, indistinguishable to the naked eye except for their length: 20, 40 and 50 overs. If and when the sheen wears off Twenty20, as it probably will once international cricket muscles in, county cricket may then finally wither for good and all.

TWENTY20 VISION
Hugh Chevallier, 2004

At 9.30 p.m. precisely on Saturday July 19, the longest day of cricket anyone could remember ended, almost 11 hours after it began. It was a paradoxical conclusion for a competition whose very *raison d'etre* was to be over quickly. In fact, finals day of the Twenty20 Cup – with the first semi beginning at 10.45 a.m. and the winner not due to be decided till 10 p.m. – was far from the star turn of the venture. Even so, the 15,000 who spent the day in the Nottingham sunshine seemed to go home satisfied. Such was the popularity of what the ECB termed short-form cricket that its rationale could be turned on its head and it would still work.

Attendances were the key. In 1998, the ECB, concerned at dwindling gates for county matches, had mooted a reduced form of cricket. The First-Class Forum – the game's powerbase, comprising the 18 first-class counties and MCC – had not taken to the idea, and it was shelved. By 2001, though, attendances were still falling, concern had become alarm, and the scheme was resurrected. And this time, it was backed by substantial investment in market research.

More than 30 focus groups later, the ECB knew a great deal more about why the public were spurning county cricket: they did not know how, when or even where to watch the game; and they thought the grounds were intimidating, like private members' clubs that met only when most people were at work or school. A programme of 4,000 15-minute face-to-face interviews revealed that about two-thirds of the population either hated or had little interest in county cricket. Prominent among the rejectors were children, people aged 16–34, women, ethnic minorities and lower social strata. But when these rejectors were offered a game that went like the clappers, was wrapped up in well under three hours on a weekday evening and included some intriguing innovations, around half flocked to join the middle-aged, middle-class white males in the tolerators' camp. Faced with these findings, the First-Class Forum voted in April 2002 by 11–7 (with MCC abstaining) in favour of short-form cricket. The great experiment had begun.

Not that there was *carte blanche* to redefine how the game was played. As Stuart Robertson, marketing manager at the ECB during the genesis of the project, put it: "The Twenty20 is not an end in itself, but a means to an end. The hope is that a 20-over game after work or school will be the first rung on a cricket-watching ladder that has a Championship game at its top." And so some of the more creative ideas were discarded. (At one stage, there were *It's A Knockout*-style plans for captains to play a joker – a "golden over" in which all the runs counted double.)

There was no watering down of the format's philosophy of speed, though: limit each side to 20 overs, allow just 15 minutes between innings, give the incoming batsman a maximum of 90 seconds to reach the crease after the fall of a wicket, and come down like a ton of bricks on a slow over rate. Critics had long accused cricket of being far too slow a game, but here was a version that fizzed like a Shoaib Akhtar yorker – very, very fast, but would it be well directed? Would the ECB show a decent return on their research budget of £200,000?

They wisely stacked the odds in their favour by spending another £250,000 on marketing. The contrast with the Twenty20's near-invisible predecessor, sponsored by the tobacco pariah Benson and Hedges (which, towards the end, was legally barred from poking its head above the parapet), could hardly have been greater. Shoppers at Sainsbury's were encouraged to redeem their loyalty vouchers for tickets, and countless newspaper adverts pushed the tournament hard. For all the hype, though, the ECB had failed to find a main sponsor for the competition, and there were plenty who would delight in the brash, profligate new kid on the block coming an embarrassing cropper.

So it was a bold move to launch the tournament on Friday 13th. Brave – or foolhardy – to trust the British weather, too; there were provisions for Duckworth/Lewis to step in, though even a short weather delay could scupper a game already pared to the bone, timewise. But in glorious midsummer sunshine, Twenty20 made a faultless debut. Everything went right, and the wails of the Jeremiahs were soon drowned by the appreciative roars of the hordes, who couldn't seem to get enough.

Initially there was some doubt about what it was that the crowds couldn't get enough of. "The acid test," wrote Mike Selvey in *The Guardian*, "will come when the cricket rather than the peripheral attractions are perceived to be the main event." He had a point. In the ECB's understandable desire to make sure things started with a bang, the cricket was in danger of being forgotten. Jacuzzis, fair-

ground rides, bouncy castles, face-painting, barbecue zones, boy bands, girl bands –
you name it, it was there as a sideshow. Rather more in your face were the banks
of loudspeakers blaring out frequent musical snatches – "I don't like cricket, I love
it" from 10cc (remixed for our times by the United Colours of Sound) greeted
boundaries, while Queen's "Another one bites the dust" taunted dismissed batsmen
as they sprinted for the dug-out.

The dug-out and loudspeakers were symbols of two important tenets of the
Twenty20 concept. To demystify the game and to bring play closer to the paying
public, batsmen rejoined their colleagues beside the boundary rather than retreat
into the confines of a dark pavilion to do who knew what. For the glitzy opening
match, between Hampshire and Sussex at Southampton and televised on Sky, the
dug-out was a sophisticated affair, all smoked curving glass; for the next game at
the Rose Bowl, this had become a couple of garden benches.

The loudspeakers – to the relief of the fuddy-duddier members of the crowd –
also diminished in size when the television cameras weren't there. For that first
game, some were oddly pointing toward the square, and the players struggled to
make themselves heard over the din. Snatches of song were a fundamental part
of the Twenty20 package, which was designed to bring sport and music together,
a move seemingly welcomed by many, especially the younger ticket-holders. But
in a sign that Selvey did not have too much to worry about, Mis-teeq, a high-
profile girl band hired to pep up the opening fixture at the Rose Bowl, saw more
than half their substantial crowd filter out of the ground after the game – and
before their set had begun.

All seemed to agree that, with or without Mis-teeq, they had been well entertained. The pace had indeed been fast and furious, the batting blistering, the
fielding phenomenal, the bowling hittable (but occasionally devastating), the
innovations lapped up by a crowd unusually representative of the population at
large. Here were women, girls, teenagers, boys and, yes, a few regular cricket-
goers, too. Reception from press and public alike was massively positive. Some
children even admitted they found it more exciting than football, and nobody
was in the mood to take issue. Surely something had to go wrong, but just as
the sun seemed to shimmer all summer long, so the Twenty20 went from strength
to strength.

At Edgbaston, advance ticket sales were so encouraging that Warwickshire
rushed to lay on extra car-park space. For the Roses clash at Old Trafford, an astonishing crowd of almost 15,000 turned out. No one could remember an occasion
outside Lord's when so many had paid to see a county match. The comparison
with the old B&H from the previous year was not entirely fair, but irresistible. By
sensibly retaining the zonal groups, the ECB ensured that local derbies lived on,
and in all 45 group games, the gates were up on 2002, often gigantically. Fifteen
matches were sell-outs, and the total attendance mushroomed from under 67,000
for the B&H to around 240,000.

The 16th sell-out of the tournament was the finals day. In another break
with tradition, this was not held at Lord's – ruled out because their application
for a concert licence was turned down by Westminster Council – but at Trent
Bridge. It certainly made sense for an occasion scheduled to last until ten at
night to be located close to a motorway hub. The finals day was arguably the

least pleasing part of the whole jamboree. Playing both semi-finals and the final on the same pitch meant scores became progressively lower, and having four sets of supporters ensured at last half the audience were always neutral. And there were endless hiatuses, despite two more bands – Atomic Kitten and United Colours of Sound – playing to a moderately enthusiastic crowd before the final began.

As luck would have it, the best game of the day – between the two strongest sides, Gloucestershire and Surrey – was the semi. Still, it felt right that Surrey lifted the first Twenty20 after defeating Warwickshire. They had the deepest resources and played the most ruthless cricket, though it was a shame that, in a contest designed to eliminate the drabness of a one-sided limited overs game, that was how the final turned out. There was talk of abandoning the three-game format for 2004, but the ECB decided to stick with it for one more year.

For both the finals and the group games, England's leading lights were elsewhere, either taking part in the NatWest Challenge against Pakistan, or enjoying enforced rest. More's the pity: Lancashire could have done with Andrew Flintoff, for whom this competition could have been made. The stars all shone, though, particularly those from the southern hemisphere. Time and again, the dominant figures, especially with the bat, were Australian. Ian Harvey hit the competition's only hundred, a feat made all the more astounding by the fact that Gloucestershire, habitually batting second after winning the toss, were chasing just 135 against Warwickshire. He took just 50 balls for his century, but would probably have been upstaged by Andrew Symonds had Kent been set a stiffer target by Hampshire. Symonds, who ended unbeaten on 96 from 37 balls, was thwarted by his colleagues scoring too quickly. Symonds didn't quite fire on all cylinders again, but his meteoric strike rate of 226 per 100 balls was comfortably the best. Mike Hussey, from Northamptonshire, and Essex's Andy Flower never appeared to miss out, and Brad Hodge sneaked past 300 runs for the competition during Leicestershire's semi-final defeat by Warwickshire.

England-qualified players produced only one of the five heaviest scorers, Nick Knight, and won only 25 of the 48 match awards. Overseas players did not have things quite so much their own way in the bowling. Medium-pace was the order of the day, and those who took the pace off the ball often proved far more penetrative than their fierier counterparts. Adam Hollioake, the Surrey captain, and Derbyshire's Dominic Hewson, with 16 and ten wickets respectively, were cases in point. Surrey, in fact, had three of the four most successful bowlers in terms of wickets. Azhar Mahmood picked up a dozen (and hit 114 runs), while James Ormond demolished Warwickshire in the final. Jason Brown and Collins Obuya, from Northamptonshire and Warwickshire, showed that spinners could be a potent weapon by taking 21 wickets between them. But arguably as important was economy. Gloucestershire's Mike Smith averaged a fraction more than four an over; respectable enough in 50-over cricket but truly outstanding in Twenty20.

For that, he could in part thank the most agile fielding of all 18 counties. Following the example of Jonty Rhodes, Gloucestershire took standards of catching, stopping, diving and throwing to new heights. In fact, every team fielded with an athleticism and commitment unseen only a few years before – one of the things which made Twenty20 cricket so good to watch. Less obvious but just as remarkable was the trend for wicket-keepers to stand up to the stumps for all but the quickest bowlers.

Once the counties realised quite what a financial success they had on their hands, there was a huge temptation to increase the number of games. Some argued for two groups of nine, raising the preliminary games from 45 to 72, while others warned of killing the goose that laid the golden egg. The ECB sagely decided to leave largely alone, the two substantial changes being the introduction of quarter-finals and the removal of the whole competition into July. All that was needed now was major sponsorship. For contractual reasons, a name sponsor was unlikely. But it was no secret that the ECB were hoping for what the marketing people call an FMCG (fast-moving consumer goods) brand to get involved. They had hoped this before. This time they might even get lucky.

THE AGE OF SPEED
Tim de Lisle, *Notes by the Editor*, 2003

If you had to choose one word to sum up cricket in the early 21st century, what would it be? Some might say Australia, others Tendulkar or Murali. The cynical observer would be tempted to go for match-fixing or chucking; a South African might just say aaaarrrghh. A more persuasive contender might be something else altogether. In 2003, the name of the game is speed. The concentrated verve of Steve Waugh's Australians has galvanised international cricket as a whole.

For most of the past 126 years, Test cricket was conducted at a leisurely pace. The occasional burst of frenzied activity only emphasised that the standard tempo was sedate. Nowadays, the longest form of the game – of any game – rattles along like a good television drama (which it is). It helps that two of the fastest bowlers ever, Brett Lee and Shoaib Akhtar, are in their prime, turning every ball into theatre. But they are only a fraction of a second faster than their predecessors, if that: Shoaib's 100mph delivery to Nick Knight at Cape Town, while pressing useful buttons in the minds of small boys and journalists, had the benefit of a wind roaring in from the Antarctic, and still, like Lee's 100mph ball a week later, gave Knight no trouble. The more meaningful acceleration has come at the other end. The great dramatic art of fast bowling has been joined by that of fast batting.

Two of the fastest-scoring calendar years in Test history have been 2001 and 2002. Four of the five fastest Test double-centuries of all time in terms of balls were made in the year to January 2003. In 2001–02, two marauding Australian left-handers, Matthew Hayden and Justin Langer, reinvented the business of opening the innings, seeing it as their job to blaze a trail rather than lay a foundation. Fast scoring is no longer the province of the occasional showman, a Botham or Jessop, but a stratagem used by whole teams, all day long. Beyond the turnstiles, life in general is moving faster, and for once the game is keeping up. Always a dance to the music of time, Test cricket is no longer a quadrille: it is a quickstep, maybe even a jive.

Far from being undermined or overshadowed by the growth of one-day internationals, Test cricket has sharpened up its act. One-day cricket, often regarded as a little trollop lowering her older sister's standards, has actually enabled her to let her hair down. When you consider the electricity of the fielding and the exuberance of the fans, the immaculate virtuosity of Tendulkar, the flawed genius of Lara and Warne, the mysteries of the new-model off-spinners, the spread of express bowling to New Zealand and India, the classical crafts-manship of McGrath and Dravid, the rampaging audacity of Adam Gilchrist, the wiles of Stephen Fleming and Nasser Hussain, the Greek tragedy of South Africa and the Ealing comedy of Pakistan, Test cricket may be more entertaining now than it has ever been.

A BRILLIANT YEAR FOR CRICKET   Matthew Engel, *Notes by the Editor*, 2004

Let's start by celebrating. In many respects, 2003 was a brilliant year for cricket. It began with a World Cup won by the team that was not merely the best but, quite conceivably, the best there has ever been. It went on to produce a couple of Test series – England v South Africa and Australia v India – that in their different ways might stand comparison with any in history.

Some of cricket's most resonant records were smashed. There was the first offi-cial 100mph ball, bowled by Shoaib Akhtar in Cape Town. Then West Indies, cricket's fallen giants, rose from the canvas to pull off Test cricket's biggest-ever successful run-chase and beat mighty Australia. In Perth, Matthew Hayden took perhaps the game's most magical number – the highest individual Test score – to a new peak of 380. Even the poor, sad, whipping boys from Bangladesh took part in a fantastic Test match, when they came within one wicket of beating Pakistan in remote Multan.

Australia scored their Test runs in 2003 at a phenomenal rate of 4.08 per over. Everywhere, the pace of batting, and the dominance of bat over ball, seemed rather like global warming: terrifying when you contemplate what it means for the fragile ecology of cricket, with bowlers potentially being driven to the edge of extinction, but thoroughly pleasant when contemplated from a deck-chair on a summer's afternoon.

In England, the sun really did blaze down, and the much-derided England and Wales Cricket Board (ECB) produced a new tournament – the Twenty20 Cup – that struck the motherlode of public affection for cricket that runs just below the surface crust of apparent indifference.

Arguably, the game has been better run for the past few years than at any time in history. The ECB has been thinking hard and, I believe, creatively about the prob-lems it faces. At the international level, match-fixing has almost certainly not been eradicated from the game, any more than chucking and dissent have. But at least corruption is handled with a sense of urgency and vigour unthinkable less than a decade ago, when the crisis first emerged and the International Cricket Council (ICC) pretended it was not their problem. And with what was either astonishing acuity or luck, the ICC managed to secure a TV deal for the 2003 and 2007 World Cups at the very top of the TV-rights market, which was a remarkable piece of business.

Cricket's development strategy is showing gains and, in places far more improbable than Multan, the game appears to be taking a grip. Some of the gains might be overhyped, but the reality is impressive enough. Our Round the World section reports how an Afghan warrior laid down his arms to join in a match. In the United States, the shimmering fairytale castle (so impregnable! But, oh, so full of treasure!) which cricket's rulers keep glimpsing through the mist, Asian migrants are giving cricket a currency it has not had there since the mid 19th-century. More enticing yet, the Chinese government are said to be keen on encouraging this mysterious sport, believing it will teach their people useful virtues. Think of that.

For those of us who already love the game, the year's events provided regular infusions of delight, reinforcing our romance with this strangely bewitching, ineffably complex and maddeningly beautiful pastime. Maddening? Oh, yes. Definitely maddening.

A RETURNED EXILE WRITES   Matthew Engel, *Notes by the Editor*, 2004

As some readers may know, I returned to edit *Wisden* having spent two years on the heathen shores of the United States. But cricket changes so fast these days that even after a short absence one comes back entirely disorientated. In a way, the arrival of Twenty20 cricket was the least of it. I am delighted by its success but also remember the initial ecstatic response to 65-over cricket (1963) and 40-over cricket (1969). Actually, Twenty20 went on a bit too long for my own taste. I shall try to hang on for Ten10 or maybe Five5.

Other things were also different. All the county players seemed to have changed, or at least changed counties. Of the few in their familiar place, Matthew Maynard had hair poking out from the back of his cap, and it had either gone completely grey or been dyed blond. Maybe both. Players seem, indeed, an entirely different breed. Last year Alamgir Sheriyar of Kent was injured, having cut his hand while washing up, while Saqlain Mushtaq fell downstairs holding his baby. Such injuries never happened to Lord Harris or D. R. Jardine. Dominic Cork turned out for Derbyshire wearing an Alice band; I am reliably informed that Copson and Pope did not wear Alice bands when they bowled Derbyshire to the Championship in 1936. In hot weather, the umpires now officiate at county games wearing polo shirts. Since, in the nature of things, not all of them are as svelte as they used to be, and the shirt is sometimes worn over a substantial paunch, it makes them look less like figures of authority and more as if they've wandered in from a game of crazy golf with the grandchildren.

The battle to get players' names on their shirts in the Championship has, surprisingly, largely been won. Unfortunately, my eyes have deteriorated too much in the meantime for them to be any use to me. (It remains mysterious that all spectators who come to a Test match are automatically expected to be able to recognise everyone under their helmets and sunhats; the commentators can't always do it – how can the customers?) And occasionally last summer the terrified cry would go up "The PLO is coming!" Only in county cricket does this refer, not to the Palestine Liberation Organisation, but to the Pitch Liaison Officer. Meanwhile, squad numbers, Duckworth/Lewis, "overs remaining", "overs per bowler" and the obsessive recording of extras have combined to render scoreboards more incomprehensible than ever.

One ground, however, is offering a potentially vital service. Signs round Trent Bridge say: "Would spectators experiencing any problems please inform an official or steward." Nottinghamshire have always had a reputation as a helpful club, but this is a breakthrough in customer care: "Excuse me, steward. My wife doesn't understand me." "I've got this pain on my left side and the doctor says it's indigestion, but I don't think it is." "The council haven't fixed the holes in the road." Other counties, please copy.

THE LONG AND THE SHORT OF IT   Matthew Engel, *Notes by the Editor*, 2006

The ICC has shown a gung-ho approach even in abiding by its own regulations, but it took some brass neck for it to jettison the first sentence of the Laws of Cricket: Law 1.1 – "A match is played between two sides, each of 11 players. . ."

This was the attempt to jazz up one-day internationals by introducing the "supersub", who arrived in 2005 along with the "powerplay", a tactical innovation so obscure that captains couldn't be bothered to think about it. The supersub concept destroyed essential strategies and principles of the game without bringing in a single extra spectator (except perhaps the substitute's mother). And as I write, it looks as though the idea will be chucked out of the 11th-floor window, and thank heaven for that.

Both these silly ideas were supposed to pep up something deemed to have become tired. But you can't improve a bad product, and 50-over cricket has always been a dreary formula, which has grown worse with repetition. When the Gillette Cup first began in England, in 1963, it provided 65-over cricket for the first season; then it (and its successor, the NatWest Trophy) was a 60-over tournament for 35 happy summers until 1998, and declined thereafter when it conformed and went down to 50 overs. This seems not to be coincidental.

The early World Cups were all 60 overs, and the one-day matches that linger in the memory (the moonlit Old Trafford Gillette semi-final of 1971; the 1975 and 1983 World Cup finals; the succession of wonderful NatWest games in 1981) nearly all took place in this format. It injected urgency into the ancient framework of a cricket match without discounting the essential skills of attacking bowling and defensive batting.

The 60-over game had to go because, before floodlights became so widespread, there was not enough daylight to schedule them outside England. And they were still not concise enough for broadcasting tastes. But 50-over cricket was always inferior and, with endless usage, one-day internationals turned into trench warfare, with everything done according to a predetermined plan. They have become mathematical exercises in fancy dress: too short to be real cricket, and too long to have any of the zing that has made Twenty20 such a hit.

The beauty of Twenty20 does not derive only from its brevity, though it does fit nicely into normal schedules: you can do a day's work, and still watch the match. Right now, it remains novel for the players as well as the spectators: nobody yet knows what they are doing. Each team is trying new ideas and different techniques, and conventional wisdom is being turned on its head all the time. That at least makes it fresh and vibrant. Let's just hope it stays that way. While it does, a Twenty20 World Cup is something even traditionalists should support. If the format's sensible.

CAN I PHONE A FRIEND?

Matthew Engel, *Notes by the Editor*, 2006

With Ashes fever raging after the Old Trafford Test, the Radio 4 programme *Today* asked me, as a presumed expert, to provide a short cricketing quiz designed to catch out the saloon-bar bluffers who were suddenly proclaiming they knew it all. So I obliged.

Is Shane Warne a leg-spinner or an off-spinner? What's the difference between a draw and a tie? Which is the bogus fielding position: deep extra cover, fourth man, backward short leg or silly mid-on? Good questions, they said. Who are the county champions? The producer sent a polite message: "Please think of something else. That one's too difficult."

One of the perverse consequences of the Ashes is that it led to less interest in county cricket rather than more. The narrative of the Test series was so strong it was able to withstand the expected competition from football (exploding, more by luck than judgment, the arguments of those of us who said the series should have been staged earlier in the summer). But the extra newspaper space devoted to umpteen Ashes reports, sidebars and columns came largely at the expense of county coverage, especially in those papers most committed to the game, like *The Times* and *Daily Telegraph*.

Wisden readers can probably remember who the current champions are. But there are now six sort-of trophies spread among the 18 counties, including the two second-division titles. This suits the county chairmen, who can pretend they are successful, on average, once every three years. But can you name the winners of them all in 2005? Harder still, try assigning the correct division for each team in both the Championship and the whatever-it's-called-this-year League.

On second thoughts, don't bother. The unified championship I have talked about before – merging the main four-day and one-day competitions – would mitigate this problem. But it's a reform that would interfere with the general pretence of success.

Last year I asked a county chief executive if he could describe the purpose of a county cricket club. To win trophies? To provide pleasure for the members? To enhance cricket within the county? To provide players for the England team? To make money? All of these? If so, which takes precedence when they conflict? He said that was an interesting philosophical discussion, in the tone of one who was far too busy ever to have philosophical discussions. But unless he is clear about the answer, I don't see how he can do his job.

THE GREATEST SERIES? QUICK, RUN AWAY! Matthew Engel, *Notes by the Editor*, 2006

Not everyone was around to enjoy the Ashes. In the ten days between the Lord's and Edgbaston Tests, Malcolm Speed, chief executive of the International Cricket Council, turned the key and locked the poky offices behind the Compton Stand at Lord's where the ICC had been based for the previous dozen years. A few days later, it re-emerged 3,500 miles away in Dubai, in more spacious if less evocative premises, on the 11th floor of an anonymous office block. In the new reception area, the pictures were not of Grace or Bradman, but of the local ruling family.

There were sound reasons for the move, but the timing typified the ICC year. For a start, the temperature in Dubai hit 50°C (122°F) as soon as the staff arrived. And it was a wretched time for any cricket-lover to leave Britain, as thousands of holidaymakers who had opted to spend August in Provence or Tuscany could tell you. They spent the month staring at computers, plaintively asking friends the score on their mobiles, or twiddling radios, desperately trying to get a faint crackle of Radio 4.

Destination Dubai: ICC's chief executive Malcolm Speed locks the office door at Lord's for the last time before cricket's ruling body moved to its "Dubaivory tower".

In their Dubaivory tower, the ICC rose above all this. There were other pre-occupations. The game's most intractable crisis – Zimbabwe – burbled on without resolution in 2005: the country got worse, its cricket got worse, and the ICC's hand-wringing hopelessness got worse. It became hard to imagine what outrage the country's politicians or cricket administrators might have to commit to provoke a response at last. Eventually, early in 2006, the Zimbabweans had to pull themselves out of Test cricket because the ICC refused to kick them out, despite the manifest inadequacy of the team, the incompetence (at best) of the officials, and the wickedness of the system in which they operated. This had a clear and direct effect on Speed's authority. When he mildly chastised players for their behaviour – which is his job – Tim May, of the international players' association FICA, quite rightly flung Zimbabwe back in his face.

The one chink of light on this issue came when Jagmohan Dalmiya, the supremo of Indian cricket for almost two decades, fell from power in November, suggesting an end to the strange alliance that had formed between India and Zimbabwe. But the private rejoicing among Dalmiya's former colleagues round the Dubai boardroom table (kept very discreet for fear that he couldn't possibly be gone for good) was more to do with the hope that his fall would end the administrative chaos he fostered inside Indian cricket. The filing system for the most influential national organisation in the game was basically inside Dalmiya's head, which was driving everyone crazy. Dalmiya at least worked through the council, when necessary subverting it to his own ends. In their early weeks, anyway, his successors at the Indian board seemed prepared to challenge its authority directly. Not a bad idea, you might think. It is time someone did, because the ICC's entrepreneurial role is damaging its regulatory one.

There was a crucial symbolic change when its web address switched from .org to .com. It constantly now has to refer to its own financial interests – exacerbated by the fraught TV deal with the Global Cricket Corporation, which expires in 2007 – rather than the good of cricket, which should be its only concern. Every year, it insists, there has to be an ICC tournament of some kind, whether anyone wants it or not. It would be hard to imagine cricket more ill-timed and ill-presented than the 2004 Champions Trophy in England. But the bad ideas keep coming: the Australia v World XI Super Series, held in Australia in October 2005, was OK in theory, but the World XI players didn't want to be there (the Australians, a month after the Ashes, were happy to kick any available arses), and nor did the people of Sydney or Melbourne. It wasn't even the cricket season.

This might have worked as a full-length Test series if there was ever time for such a thing. But there wasn't, and there isn't. Coming up: yet another ugly-looking Champions Trophy, to the delight only of TV channels with more airtime than content. Year after year, the wonderful folks at the ICC assemble the world's best players and get them to play bad cricket. If they staged W. G.'s XI v The Don's XI at the Elysian Oval with S. F. Barnes bowling to Victor Trumper, they would find some way of making the occasion dismal. It's a gift, really: a form of anti-showmanship. Even the 2007 World Cup will be badly flawed. What should be cricket's greatest tournament will last 47 days (the Olympics: 16, football World Cup: 31), the first two weeks of which will mainly comprise no-contests. The ballooning of the World Cup derives from one fact alone: the delusion of expansion. From well-intentioned beginnings, this has now become an outright menace. The error is right up there at the start of the ICC's mission statement. It will lead, it says, "by promoting the game as a global sport". It should change its mission statement.

In modern times cricket has only really spread within existing cricketing cultures: to the Afrikaners and, to a limited extent, the urban black community in South Africa; and from the cities to the countryside in South Asia. None of the four countries elevated to Test status since the Second World War represents a gain of territory: Pakistan and Bangladesh were simply new political entities carved out of India; in cricketing terms, the same is true of Zimbabwe which – as Rhodesia – played in South African domestic cricket; and the rise of Sri Lanka was just a matter of degree.

Our Round the World section passes its century in 2006: in 14 years we have reported on cricket in 103 countries and territories. It's a part of *Wisden* I love. But with minor exceptions (Afghanistan, for instance, where war refugees brought the game back from their camps in Pakistan) it does not report on true expansion – although our far-flung correspondents understandably over-egg the pudding sometimes. Overwhelmingly, the game in non-traditional countries is played by expatriates, mostly South Asian. Journalists were kidded into believing that cricket was about to burst on China, on the basis of some warm comments by civil servants and a couple of coaching courses. I have seen not one shred of evidence to back this up. Are the kids playing with tapeballs on the streets of Shanghai? Are they heck!

But we have to pretend, don't we? Eight teams at a World Cup doesn't sound global enough, other sports would sneer, and what *would* the International Olympic Committee think? So there have to be 16. Indeed, from now on, the leading associate members will get one-day international status whenever they play a senior country. This will add another layer of distortion to cricket's poor old statistics. Far more often than not, it will also create yet more bad cricket, leaving less time for the great contests which the public want to watch. Two terrible events, the Champions Trophy and the Afro-Asian Cup, have already been justified by the need to raise money for expansion. Millions of pounds later and – aside from the thoroughly dubious case of Kenya – what has emerged?

The top two of the five teams who qualified for the World Cup via the ICC Trophy are Scotland and Ireland. Well, whoop-de-doo! In cricketing terms, these are not separate countries. It is just a historical quirk that the England cricket team is not called Britain or the British Isles. Every Scotsman and Irishman who gets good at cricket wants to play for England, and always has done. Of course they do. And we have enough formlines to go on to know how good these teams are: stronger than a Minor County; worse than the weakest first-class county. About where they have always been. The idea that they can provide proper opposition for any genuine Test team is ludicrous. But the World Cup will be substantially ruined to perpetuate this myth. If I ever get the chance to report the first China v England Test at Guangzhou, I would be delighted to celebrate with a plateful of sweet-and-sour hat. But it is time to stop wrecking the game we do have in the vain pursuit of the one we don't.

Mammon

A fair amount of the previous two chapters was about the commercialism of the sport which Kerry Packer's *démarche* accelerated. But here I have brought together some specific reflections on the way money was changing the game. Matthew Engel, in lambasting the Australian Cricket Board's decision to replace the Sheffield Shield – revered name of great antiquity, in Australian terms anyway – with the Pura Milk Cup, approvingly quoted a remark of ECB chief executive Tim Lamb, who said that professional cricket was "a business inside a game" not "a game inside a business". *Wisden* has been preoccupied with getting that balance right, and has fought strenuously to protect the traditions of the game from being sullied by an excess of commercialism. Its contention might be that if the game is only played for money, it isn't worth playing.

Norman Preston always made a point of mentioning injections of money into the game, and complimenting new sponsors, but his approach remained delightfully old-fashioned. As he says in the item printed below, "When one also takes into account the £1,500 awarded each month by Bonusbonds – £1,000 to the County Cricketer of the Month and £250 each to the batsman with most runs and bowler with most wickets, plus all the luncheons and teas provided by various people and firms at most county matches, first-class cricket has much to be thankful for." It is unlikely that the players of the pre-Packer era saw it that way, and Jack Bannister's minute examination of the increase in players' (and umpires'!) salaries in the 1980s demonstrates how Packerism benefited them.

The struggle between god and gold, game and business, is at heart a philosophical one, and *Wisden* editor Graeme Wright adopted suitably apocalyptic tones to discuss it in 1990. "Profit is important, but it is not all, and in its concern with the checks and balance of profit and loss, the TCCB is always in danger of losing sight of the beauty of cricket itself." He even quoted Victorian sage Thomas Carlyle on "the infinite, absolute character of Virtue". Or, rather, the lack of it.

The late 1980s were in many ways depressing days. More recently, Shane Warne and Andrew Flintoff have shown us how to make oodles of money while still playing (and loving) a great game. We should be ever vigilant – Paul Kelso's piece explaining why this is the Age of the Agent shows that the spirit of calculation is strong – but, compared with football, tennis, golf or the corporate beanfeasts that are American sports, cricket retains some degree of innocence. It has not yet sold its soul to the financial devil. Packerism transformed it without destroying it. Carlyle could probably just about live with it, though I'm not so sure about Gubby Allen.

S. M.

CORNHILL'S £1 MILLION

Norman Preston, *Notes by the Editor,* 1979

For a period of five years, beginning in 1978, Cornhill Insurance sponsorship will inject £1,000,000 into Test cricket. In 1977–78 the basic tour fee for each England player was increased from £3,000 to £5,000, and last summer each player collected £1,000 for a single Test appearance. In addition, Test umpires' fees went up from £175 to £750 a match. This meant that Cornhill's outlay in 1978 was something like £175,000. It was reckoned that Schweppes provided £175,000 for the County Championship; Benson and Hedges £130,000 for their cup; John Player roughly the same for the Sunday League; and Gillette at least £100,000. This summer, Prudential are giving £250,000 for the World Cup and they also sponsor the one-day internationals. When one also takes into account the £1,500 awarded each month by Bonusbonds – £1,000 to the County Cricketer of the Month and £250 each to the batsman with most runs and bowler with most wickets, plus all the luncheons and teas provided by various people and firms at most county matches, first-class cricket has much to be thankful for. There is also the generous support of the county club members. Nor must one forget the three "Ws": the Wrigley Cricket Foundation, now in its ninth year of encouraging young cricketers; Whitbread Brewery, who sent young talent to Australia in the winter; and Wilkinson Sword Blades, who sponsored the Under-19 team which went to Australia at the beginning of the year under the guidance of Freddie Brown, chairman of the National Cricket Association.

A FINANCIAL REVOLUTION

Jack Bannister, 1986

Whatever the rights and wrongs of the Packer issue, it accelerated changes in English first-class cricket, some of which were already in the pipeline, so rapidly that within a decade there has taken place the biggest financial revolution in the history of the game. Starting from the top, the Test match payments to players and umpires have increased roughly sevenfold, and even at the bottom end of the scale, the successful introduction of a minimum wage in 1979 has more or less tripled county players' salaries. For players with the affluent clubs it may have done even more, and for very few has it done any less.

At the beginning of the 1977 season, an England player received £74 for a one-day international, £210 for five-day Test match, and around £3,000 for an overseas tour. Add to that a county salary of £3,500, and a top regular England player in a year containing six home Test matches could earn directly from his skills a maximum of £4,500 from Test cricket and £8,000 in all, the equivalent of, say, £20,000 today.

Comparative figures for last year were £500 for a one-day international, £1,500 for a five-day Test, a touring fee of at least £12,000, and a county salary of only marginally less. That adds up to nearly £35,000, and extra awards available from Cornhill, Texaco and the domestic sponsors mean that the top half-dozen England players earned in 1985 around £40,000 from actually playing cricket. Other spin-offs, including individual sponsorship and advertising contracts, as well as the loan of a car, vary according to the individual.

Nor have umpires been left behind, the ratio increase in their big-match fees being similar to that of the players. Ten years ago the fee for standing in a one-day international was £68 and in a full Test match £173. The corresponding figures are now £400 and £1,200 respectively, and a study of the difference in basic salaries available in 1977 and 1986 explains why there is now an umpires' waiting list, compared with a decade ago, when, annually, there was the threat of a shortage. By last year their annual basic salary had moved from £1,740 to £7,300, with a likely increase of around 5% for 1986. For a top Test match umpire, standing in two Test matches and a one-day international, the marked improvement in the game's finances has brought an increase in annual salary from £2,154 to £10,460. Again, obviously, the improvement is less in real terms, after inflation has been evaluated, but it still marks a considerable upgrading, and the salary is for only about 90 days' work. Also, like the players, umpires live for most of the summer off an overnight expense figure, from which they would not make a loss, and they have their meals provided during matches. The seven-month close-season affords other earning opportunities, either through businesses they have established at the end of their playing careers, the majority of umpires being ex-players, or through other employment, including coaching at home or overseas.

As a result of this increased remuneration, there is now a reserve list of three umpires in addition to the full list of 24, and there was no shortage of applicants last winter even for the reserve list. Another point is that the average age of the arbiters has been dramatically reduced in the last few years: only one umpire is now near the retiring age of 65, and with one exception the remainder are under 55.

And what about the average county player? Here, too, there has been a considerable improvement; but before the comparative figures are given for now and 1979, the progress towards the reluctant acceptance of a minimum wage by the clubs should be explained. The year of its introduction was 1979, and the arguments against it were many. No two clubs paid the same salaries, or even by the same method. Widely differing loyalty bonuses and appearance fees were paid, with expenses particularly variable. Another argument was that few clubs could afford the big increase in their overall wage bill: this would be inevitable, particularly for the younger players. There was also the implied threat that reductions in county staffs would have to be made with so much extra money to be found. The argument for the introduction of a minimum scale was that in 1977 one reserve county wicket-keeper received £400.

Another consideration in favour of the minimum scale was that it would lessen the chances of wealthier clubs luring away the more promising youngsters from other clubs. By persuading those clubs to generate more income and pay higher wages, fears of increased movement by players between clubs would accordingly be reduced. The counties finally agreed to dip their toes into the water in 1979, but only on a voluntary basis for the first year. Experience showed that some clubs were already meeting or exceeding the agreed target figure of £4,500 as a minimum wage. Others had shortfalls to meet of varying amounts, in one case £18,000.

Many argue that despite this improvement the gap between the Test star and the bread-and-butter county cricketer is too wide to be explained satisfactorily by the argument that extra skills merit extra rewards. Indeed, because senior England players in the early eighties agreed with this, there have been only nominal increases in Test fees in the last four years.

The result of this wage explosion is that the overall county wage bill in 1978 of £700,000 has risen to at least £2,000,000. Yet the argument that such an increase would bring about a reduction in the size of county staffs has been rebutted by an increase in the number of registered and contracted players from 300 eight years ago to a current 350. It is also irrefutable that the introduction of a regularised minimum scale has made the game financially more attractive to youngsters as a profession. The other fear, held by some clubs, that cricket would follow soccer into bankruptcy is unfounded because, unlike the winter game where players make their wage demands individually and with little concern for football's financial structure, negotiators for the Cricketers' Association, being aware of the TCCB's overall annual income, know what can and cannot be afforded.

But how have the counties found so much extra money? A greater awareness of the need to maximise the use of their facilities all the year round would not alone have sufficed. There has been, as well, a remarkable increase in the income from sponsorship generated at board level. At the beginning of the 1977 season, the TCCB's Marketing Committee had contracts worth £476,000. In 1985 these totalled £2,321,000. Therein lies one of the satisfactory effects of the Packer revolution. Although such a process was already slowly evolving in English cricket, it was undoubtedly accelerated.

Umpires' complaints that, with so much extra money to be won, their job is being made nearly intolerable have to be tempered by the commensurate increase in their own rewards. But on-field behaviour does seem to have declined marginally, accompanied by more attempts to pressurise umpires. With money comes power and responsibility, and the players must make a conscious effort to prevent the first-class game from travelling even the shortest step down the wrong path, as seems to have happened in Australia. There, the extra rewards have driven players and umpires apart. First-class cricket in England provides the only fulltime professional circuit in the world, and in that it is unique. In its standards of on-field behaviour it is also unique, and to see that that continues to be so is the responsibility of everyone, particularly the players. Having got the rewards they asked for, they must show that they deserve them.

LOSING SIGHT OF THE BEAUTIFUL AND GOOD

Graeme Wright, *Notes by the Editor*, 1990

"This is not a religious age," Thomas Carlyle wrote more than 150 years ago. "The infinite, absolute character of Virtue has passed into a finite, conditional one; it is no longer a worship of the Beautiful and Good, but a calculation of the profitable." Profit is important, but it is not all, and in its concern with the checks and balance of profit and loss, the TCCB is always in danger of losing sight of the beauty of cricket itself. This is a legacy of the decision to make county cricket fully professional; to make it a business. The game is no longer an end in itself; it has become in several respects the means to an end.

This being so, are the interests of the national summer game best served by the Cricket Council as it is now constituted? While at first glance it appears that the Cricket Council is the governing body, closer inspection reveals that the true power lies with the Test and County Cricket Board, particularly as the chairman has the casting vote and the chairman, since the Council was reconstituted in 1983, has always been the chairman of the TCCB. Effectively, therefore, English cricket is controlled by the professional game.

The late Sir George Allen, one of the foremost administrators of cricket and one of those responsible for setting up the Cricket Council in 1969, resigned from the Council in 1982 in protest at the strengthening of the TCCB's position, expressing his opposition to a national game being virtually controlled by a body that is mainly concerned with its professional side.

Writing in *Wisden* at the time, John Woodcock drew his readers' attention to what had happened in Australia when the say of the marketing people had taken precedence over that of the cricketers. "Beware the small, executive sub-committee of businessmen," he wrote, "to whom the charm of cricket is little more than a technicality: that was the burden of Mr Allen's message."

SYMBOLISM IN THE OUTFIELD

Graeme Wright, *Notes by the Editor*, 1992

The logo on the outfield is a symbol. It is a symbol of the level to which English cricket has to go to earn a crust. Indeed, it brings to mind that tragic figure of Victorian melodrama: the mother who goes out on the street to support her family in hard times. (Not that the editor of *Wisden* is best placed to cast the first stone.) But it is a symbol, too, of the influence which the marketing committee has within the Test and County Cricket Board, and of the diminishing influence of those whose first concern is for the game of cricket itself. The periphery, one feels, has become more important than the middle.

IMPURE MILK

Matthew Engel, *Notes by the Editor*, 2000

With the 1999–2000 competition already under way, the Sheffield Shield, Australian cricket's inter-state Championship for the last 107 years, suddenly ceased to exist. The competition had acquired a sponsor and, as part of the deal, the trophy itself was immediately retired, as were both parts of the name. Inter-state first-class cricket was henceforth to be contested for – one can hardly bring oneself to write it – the Pura Milk Cup. The very phrases that have been part of the fabric of the Australian language for generations were effectively banned: Shield cricket, Shield records, Shield player.

This is not sponsorship. It is an act of vandalism against both cricket's past and its future: an attempt to blank out future generations from any understanding of the game's history. Tradition is harder to come by in Australia than in England, and therefore more highly valued. *The Age* in Melbourne rightly called the decision abhorrent.

Domestic first-class cricket is hard to sell and the game has to make a living. But this time cricket has sold its dignity as well as its advertising space. Tim Lamb, chief executive of the ECB, once said, in perhaps his happiest piece of phrase-making, that professional cricket was "a business inside a game" not "a game inside a business".

He should have that drawn up as a motto in appliqué work and distributed at the next ICC meeting to be stuck up in every chief executive's office around the globe.

GROUND RULES

Matthew Engel, *Notes by the Editor*, 2000

New Zealand's remarkable Test win over West Indies (who were 276 for nought on the first day) in Hamilton took place, apparently, at Westpac Trust Park. Other recent Tests in Hamilton were held at Trust Bank Park. Before that they were at Seddon Park. Trust is hardly the word here: the unwary might imagine that Hamilton is unusually well-served with cricket grounds, like Colombo.

This is, of course, a single ground changing its name at sponsors' whims. It is a spreading phenomenon: Lancaster Park in Christchurch is now the Jade Stadium. In South Africa, brand-new Springbok Park, Bloemfontein, has become Goodyear Park, and Centurion Park is now, hideously, SuperSport Park. This is particularly sad: the town of Centurion (which originally had the apartheid-tainted name of Verwoerdburg) was, rather charmingly, renamed after the cricket ground.

Such changes pose unique difficulties for *Wisden*. We have an obligation to try and ensure that, long after these contracts end and the names have changed again, future readers can learn where cricket matches were played. And thus we have to be as unhelpful as possible to the deal-makers in this regard. We will stick with cricket grounds' traditional and original names wherever possible.

CALL MY AGENT

Paul Kelso, 2004

The birth of the sports agent can be traced, so the story goes, to England's 1948–49 tour of South Africa, when Denis Compton handed a suitcase to the journalist, Reg Hayter. It contained hundreds of letters that Compo, a man hardly cut out for admin, could not face opening. Hayter began ploughing through them and found scores of what would now be called commercial opportunities. Among the invitations to after-dinner speaking engagements and public appearances was an offer of £2,000 to write a column for the *News of the World*. There was also a further letter, written two months later, withdrawing the offer because the paper had not received a reply.

Hayter passed the suitcase on to Bagenal Harvey, a publisher who quickly abandoned books to devote himself to the promotion of sportsmen. Harvey secured the £1,000-a-year Brylcreem contract that put Compton's face and gleaming hair on posters across the country, and happily trousered a 10% fee for himself. His success with Compton had the leading lights of other sports scurrying to his office, among them Fulham footballers Jimmy Hill and Johnny Haynes. Hill was campaigning for an end to football's £20 maximum wage (that was £20 per week, not per minute) and, when he succeeded in 1961, Harvey was well placed to secure Haynes the first £100-a-week contract.

Ever since then, football has dwarfed cricket, where players of limited profile and modest income have presented few opportunities for agents following in Harvey's footsteps. There have been exceptions for exceptional players. The eccentric entrepreneur "Lord" Tim Hudson sparkled briefly, promising to take Ian Botham, the most marketable English cricketer since Compton, to Hollywood and make him the "new Errol Flynn". (Nothing came of it and Hudson, down on his luck, was reduced to living in a caravan adjoining the Cheshire estate he owned in his pomp.) David Gower, meanwhile, is still represented by Jon Holmes, a friend of his and Gary Lineker's from their Leicester days, whose SFX agency grew huge from its provincial roots.

Botham and Gower stood out because they were marketable well beyond the county grounds. For the average county player, however, sponsorship opportunities in the 1970s and 1980s were limited to a car from the local garage and the occasional tryst with a Benson and Hedges cigarette girl. Players were reluctant to share 10% of either. In the past five years, however, changes to the structure of the domestic game, increased television revenues and more aggressive marketing of the sport have led to an increase in cricket's fortunes. And in sport, where there's brass, there are agents.

There are now more than a dozen agencies representing English cricket's 350-odd middling players. (There are even agents operating outside the first-class structure. For instance, Paul Carrick, a civil servant based in the north-east, offers overseas professionals to league clubs via his website.) For evidence of their growing influence, you have only to turn to the acknowledgments page of Michael Vaughan's hastily ghosted book, *A Year in the Sun*. There, in a list that includes his parents, his brother and sundry Yorkshire coaches, England's captain thanks the team at International Sports Management for guiding his career thus far. James Anderson was at it too when he stepped up to receive his award for the 2003 Young Cricketer of the Year at the Cricket Writers' Club annual dinner. "Thanks to everyone at ISM," stuttered the tyro.

When Vaughan had the captaincy thrust upon him, much was made of his old-fashioned virtues. He wore an England cap to his first press conference, and his former captain David Byas revealed that Vaughan was known as "the Amateur" at Headingley. In fact Vaughan is far more Player than Gentleman and, along with Anderson, Andrew Flintoff and others, is one of a new generation of English international cricketers benefiting from an unprecedented degree of professionalism in the management both of their careers and their bank accounts.

Vaughan's agent is Andrew "Chubby" Chandler, a modestly talented former European Tour golf professional who realised there were better ways to make money out of other golfers than losing to them, and established ISM. His core business is still golf, a game awash with money. However, Chandler has moved into cricket and established a specialist division headed by the former England batsman Neil Fairbrother, a man with excellent contacts in the Lancashire dressing-room and beyond. As well as Vaughan and Flintoff, ISM represent just a handful of the most marketable and high-profile players, including Muttiah Muralitharan and Marcus Trescothick, reasoning that once you move away from the elite, cricketers make little commercial sense. With the average county pro earning around £50,000 and with limited potential to make more, agents have to represent a lot of players before they can make a decent living.

"The idea is to have a small group of players you do a real proper job for," says Chandler. "We are starting to see crossover opportunities between cricket and golf;

we do pro-am days and have clients out for dinner with the players. There's potential there. The difference between cricket and golf is that cricket's a team game, so I can't put a logo on Freddie's helmet. If I could, I'd get him £200,000. But our cricket broke even in the first year and we'll make some money in the years to come."

Chandler may focus on the elite, but it is among the modest ranks of the game that the growth in player representation is most marked, thanks mainly to the easing of restrictions on overseas cricketers, a rise in the number of players moving counties and the advent of the EU-qualified cricketer. Richard Thompson is chairman of cricket at Surrey CCC and managing director of Merlin Elite, a sports management company, so he is both poacher and gamekeeper and has watched the process at first hand.

"More and more counties are looking for dual-passport players because they are cheaper and cost nothing to develop," says Thompson. "You can have as many as six effectively foreign players in a team now, and the agents are selling these players to clubs. I am constantly getting lists of players from agents via fax and e-mail. I'm sure most players could get by with just a good lawyer advising them, but agents are useful sometimes. In cricket we deal with a lot of fathers, and in some ways I'd rather deal with an agent than a parent."

Thompson recently took on Alec Stewart in a non-executive role, but has stuck to representing golfers and footballers rather than cricketers, partly because of the potential conflict of interest, and partly because of money. "The finances of the cricket agent's business are tight," he says. "A senior pro, capped and with six years behind him, will earn on average £50,000, and have a bat and kit deal worth around £10,000. At Surrey we also offer personal player sponsorship deals to companies. For between £10,000 and £15,000 the client gets, say, five personal appearances a year from the player, who will also be around during Oval Test matches and come along and say hello when the sponsor has guests in his box. But even taken together, a cricketer's income is small by the standards of other sports."

Despite the modest returns, there are more agents then ever, and the ECB and the Professional Cricketers' Association have introduced a registration system to ensure that counties deal only with approved agents. Their role remains controversial. In football, agents are blamed for unsettling players and encouraging them to move so the agent can pocket a commission. Cricket remains more stable, largely thanks to the benefit system, but young players are far more restless than they used to be. And when they need a new county, an agent will help them find one. "Youngsters are unlikely to linger in Second XI cricket at their first county for more than a season or two now," says Thompson. "At Surrey, the bulk of the home-grown players – Thorpe, Bicknell, Butcher and Stewart – spent up to four years on the fringes of the first team before nailing down their places. That wouldn't happen now."

Given English cricket's obsession with all things Australian, it comes as no surprise to hear that the man widely considered the best in the business grew up in Adelaide. David Ligertwood, born in Oxford but raised in Australia, played first-class cricket for Surrey and Durham. In 1999, he founded athletes1, a management company with offices in London, Melbourne and Adelaide, and more than 150 cricketers worldwide on its books, including Mark Butcher, Michael Bevan, Stuart MacGill, Chaminda Vaas, Henry Olonga and around 30% of the English game's first-class stock. Ligertwood says cricketers are commercially viable to his firm for two reasons:

volume, and because they offer their clients more than occasional contract advice. "The easy part of representing a player is getting them a county and doing the contract. All you need for that is a few contacts. What we offer the players is the whole deal. We do all their legal work and accounting, financial planning, deal with the taxman, source sponsorship opportunities for them, open their mail when they are on tour. If you sit down with a player and say 'we can save you £10,000 this year and it's going to cost you £1,000', you often find they are interested."

Ligertwood is starting to bring some of the more sophisticated strategies common in other sports into cricket. For example, county salaries are made up of two strands, one for playing and another for promotional work on the county's behalf. One method employed by athletes1 is to separate those streams and siphon the money for the promotional work into a separate company. It is common practice in football where image rights are recognised as one of the key assets a player has, but it is relatively new in cricket.

"These are all pretty straightforward, tax-efficient ways of doing things, but they are just coming into the game in this country," says Ligertwood. Ligertwood is frank about the marketing opportunities presented by England's current first-class stock. "The game here is not nearly as marketable as it is in Australia. There the players are massive, huge stars, as big as any footballer here. But in England there is so much competition and, unless you are really special, you are not going to make a fortune. International players will have their central contract, a bat deal worth up to £60,000 and then a bit of media work, but it's still a long way off golf. Vaughan is marketable because the captain always is. Butcher is fantastic and if he was captain he'd be huge. He's got personality, he's a top bloke and a rounded guy, he plays the guitar, and he's had a bit of sketchy publicity about his personal life. He's easy to market.

"Anderson's all right, but he's done nothing yet apart from dye his hair red. You have to be absolutely outstanding as a bowler to get really big because all the focus is on the batters. Darren Gough, who was the most marketable Englishman since Botham, was only just good enough in a poor side to be worth it, and that was because he had such charisma on top of his ability."

Ligertwood forecasts that for now cricketers' earnings will remain modest compared to golf, tennis and football. "None of the really big agencies, the Octagons and IMGs, have an interest in cricket at the moment, so outside India we've not seen any mega-deals, the sort you get in football where Coke or Pepsi buy up a whole team of players and use them across the board."

He does see richer times ahead, however. In 2002 the ICC approved a change in regulations to allow players to display the name of any sponsor on their bats. Prior to this, only kit manufacturers were permitted to advertise in that space, a rule famously broken by Arjuna Ranatunga who displayed an ad for Sam's Chicken and Ribs at Trent Bridge in 1998. At the moment the space available is restricted to ten square inches on the back of the bat, which is barely visible on a stump cam – and even that is illegal at ICC events such as the World Cup and the Champions' Trophy. Discussions continue, however, and if the players get their way, cricketers' incomes could be transformed. "If you had a large space on the front of the bat you could see players getting up to £200,000 each. If four kit manufacturers can push it up to £60,000, imagine what open competition could do," says Ligertwood. When that day comes, you can be sure no cricketer will ever have to open his own mail again.

The Television Takeover

O h, my Laker and my Peter West long ago. Yes, it was once so simple. When I became addicted to cricket as a teenager in the 1970s, the BBC had a divine right to show games on television, and show them it did – every ball, as far as I recall. No interruptions from dreadful daytime TV; no interruptions from the great Jim Laker either sometimes – on the basis of pounds for words, his fee must have been colossal. The Sunday League dominated the BBC Sunday schedule, too, and, in retrospect, was taken absurdly seriously, with John Arlott presiding as commentator – akin to getting Sir John Gielgud to play Buttons in *Cinderella*. Happy days – even if it did mean my entire adolescence was spent on the sofa watching Asif Iqbal, Clive Lloyd and Colin Dredge (aka the "Demon of Frome").

The long-time domination of the airwaves by the BBC – and the conservatism of its coverage – may account for the paucity of articles about TV coverage of cricket in the 1980s *Wisden*s. Everything else in the game was changing; the BBC was the one constant. There was no upstart commercial station to challenge the mighty Beeb, as had happened in Australia. ITV, apart from showing occasional Roses cricket, wasn't interested – it attracted a niche audience and took up too much valuable television time. Only the BBC, with two channels, could do it. . . Until, of course, Channel 4 started taking an interest, and then Sky decided it wanted not just a piece of the action, but all the action. That's when *Wisden*, fearing both the tawdrification of the game and its exile on a minority satellite channel, took guard. It accepted that the BBC's lacklustre approach was damaging the game; that the time had come for change. But it was quick to see the dangers of a satellite takeover – the scenario that has, indeed, now come to pass. *Wisden* has always warned that giving coverage exclusively to a satellite channel would sacrifice the long-term health of the game for short-term financial benefits. That dire prediction is now being tested.

S. M.

HOW TELEVISION CALLS THE TUNE   Graeme Wright, *Notes by the Editor*, 1992

Last summer's decision by the first-class counties to ignore the advice of the TCCB's cricket committee, with regard to the future of the Sunday League, and instead to take on board the plans of the marketing men, illustrates the struggle for the soul of the game.

For sound cricketing reasons – and perhaps for good commercial ones, too – the cricket committee advocated playing the Sunday League in two divisions of nine teams each, with a knockout stage to determine the season's champions. While cutting the number of 40-overs games – technically more damaging to playing standards than other forms of cricket – this would also have offered variety for spectators by freeing some Sundays for either 55-overs Benson and Hedges Cup matches or for Championship cricket. Instead, the TCCB rejected these proposals, voting in favour of the existing format and also for teams to wear coloured clothing and play with a white ball against black sightscreens.

Somehow the marketing men and the counties – Kent, Leicestershire, Middlesex and Surrey excepted – got it badly wrong. For a start they were flying in the face of members' opinion; not that members' opinions worry committee men much, until the members get their act together and vote them out of office.

Replying to a questionnaire sent out prior to the special meeting of the TCCB in May last year, the majority of county members who replied gave an emphatic thumbs-down to coloured clothing. So did Refuge Assurance, the sponsors of the Sunday League. They chose not to renew their contract. But even worse, no one else wanted to sponsor the board's colourful new package either.

This does raise a question. If members opposed coloured clothing, and sponsors didn't want it, for whom was it intended? Television? Only a small minority of potential viewers watch Sunday League cricket on television, now that the broadcasting rights reside with BSkyB, the satellite network. To realise how few of the game's supporters bother with BSkyB, one had only to hear the thunderous applause which greeted the announcement at Lord's during the NatWest Trophy final that the BBC would again cover the Benson and Hedges Cup, as well as continuing to screen the NatWest and all international matches in England.

Money should not be the only determining factor when it comes to broadcasting rights. Cricket is not such a popular sport that audience figures can afford to be ignored, especially with cricket being played at fewer schools and young people being offered a whole range of alternative leisure activities.

Cricket needs maximum exposure more than ever. Thousands of viewers in Britain will have watched the World Cup [in Australia and New Zealand in February/March 1992], perhaps hundreds of thousands. The fact that it would have been millions had the World Cup been shown on the BBC or ITV should be of concern to the TCCB. One feels it is not.

A Tightrope Walk   Matthew Engel, *Notes by the Editor*, 1998

In its first year the ECB conveyed, much of the time, an air of efficiency and progressiveness. It became, however, increasingly obsessed with its efforts to persuade the Government to remove Test cricket from the list of events that have to be seen on terrestrial TV, so the rights can be sold to the highest bidder. Ideally, the board wants Test cricket to stay on the BBC so it can be seen by the widest audience. But it understandably and rightly wants more money, and argues that 180 hours of Test cricket a year cannot be compared to 12 minutes for the Grand National and the Derby. This is a tightrope walk, though. Rugby's viewing figures have plummeted since it moved to Sky TV. The financial gains are short-term. The damage is not.

GETTING THE PICTURE
Matthew Engel, *Notes by the Editor*, 1999

When the dust from the World Cup settles, cricket followers in England will wake up to a very different world. The BBC has lost its immemorial right to cover home Test matches, and deservedly so. For many years, its presentation of cricket has been (as with other sports) complacent and dreary. Many new techniques for broadcasting the game have been developed in the past two decades – from the blindingly obvious (showing the score continuously) to the technically magical (super slo-mo). So far as I am aware, not a single one has emanated from the BBC, though they cheerfully pinched the ideas from others.

The viewing figures will probably fall when Tests move to Channel 4 (and they will plummet for the one Test a year to be shown live only on Sky TV, which is unavailable in most homes), though I am not sure cricket will lose anyone who has really been watching. The coverage may or may not be an improvement. But it was a reasonable gamble by the ECB, which will enliven future bidding rounds without shunting too much of the game into the ghetto of satellite TV. The BBC lost out not because of its poverty, but because of its poverty of ideas.

So what has Channel 4 got to show first time out, on the bounce from what everyone hopes will be a successful World Cup [a forlorn hope, of course]? A clutch of Tests against New Zealand, the world's least charismatic team. It was an absurdity to give them four Tests this year, having allowed Sri Lanka only one in 1998. But there should be two occasions that would be a little bit special: 1999 marks the centenary of Test cricket at both Headingley and Trent Bridge. However, you'll never guess which two grounds have not been awarded Test matches this year. Oh, you've guessed, haven't you?

FROM RICHIE TO, ER, RICHIE
Marcus Berkmann, 2000

In May 1999, in a louche bar near the Old Bailey, Channel 4 finally launched its long-awaited cricket coverage to a hushed and expectant press. Tim Lamb of the ECB, his blazer buttons gleaming with pride, introduced Mark Sharman, the station's head of sport, who enthusiastically revealed the many exciting innovations he had planned for the summer and beyond.

That is, we assumed he did, as few of us were paying much attention at the time. Behind Sharman a massed bank of TV screens was relaying live pictures of the one-day international between England and Pakistan in Sharjah and, as he began to speak, Ijaz Ahmed thumped Robert Croft for a huge six over long-off, breaking a hole in the roof of the stand. Instead of hearing about Channel 4, the cream of the nation's cricketing journalists were watching Sky Sports.

Sharman, by coincidence, had recently moved from BSkyB, and returned there later in the year. In the interim, though, he presided over a new approach to cricket broadcasting that both impressed the critics and charmed the public (84% of *Wisden Cricket Monthly* readers registered their approval).

Instead of dull old Richie Benaud, Channel 4 employed vibrant young Richie Benaud, who to universal relief greeted his audience each day with the same words ("Morning, everyone") he had used every previous Test match day for 35 years. Mark Nicholas was imported from Sky as anchorman and introduced millionsofnewviewers. To. His. Unusual. Mode. Of. Delivery. Simon Hughes and Dermot Reeve supplied technical analysis with the aid of super slo-mo cameras, although they often struggled to find anything interesting to say. Sybil Ruscoe ran around breathlessly interviewing supporters dressed as nuns or giant vegetables. And the snickometer emerged as cricket's equivalent of the lie-detector test, showing time and again that the batsman really had hit it when all other evidence (and the batsman's furious expression) suggested otherwise.

Reviews were favourable, though Nicholas came in for some stick. ("His absurd swept-back hair and veneer of laminated self-regard have turned him into a premature parody of Roger Moore," wrote Adam Sweeting in *The Guardian*. "The camera loves him," wrote Giles Smith in the *Daily Telegraph*, "and its love does not, shall we say, go unrequited.") Channel 4 had some luck: the weather was fair, and the new theme tune went straight to number one. But its main advantage was that it wasn't the BBC.

AN EYE TO THE FUTURE
Simon Hughes, 2002

Reruns of *Botham's Ashes*, broadcast to coincide with the arrival of Steve Waugh's Australians for the 2001 series, made enjoyable, revealing watching. Enjoyable for the sheer satisfaction of seeing rampant Aussies for once cut down to size; revealing because they brought the great advances of television technology into sharp focus. Those pictures from 20 years ago looked so primitive: single-end coverage, so that every other over was viewed from behind the wicket-keeper; four cameras at most; grainy, jerky replays; and stationary shots of scoreboards to update the match situation.

Compare that with what we take for granted now. More than 30 cameras, some in stumps that can pan with the bowler as he's running in, some capable of zooming in so close you can see the stubble a player missed when he shaved that morning, one on rails that whizzes up and down the boundary like a dog-track hare. Countless (sometimes too many) replays of a wicket, the pictures pin-sharp, stump microphones, snickometers, clever graphics that superimpose red mats on the pitch, statistics galore and the score permanently displayed in the top corner of the screen. The viewer is left in no doubt as to what has occurred, and why, from ten different angles.

Magic marker: technological aids such as Hawk-Eye, which tracks the trajectory of each ball, have helped TV viewers crack cricket's mysteries.

Britain had already established itself as a world leader in sports-television broadcasting before last summer's revolutionary, and controversial, development: the introduction of Hawk-Eye on Channel 4 and Sky Scope. Based on missile guidance systems, Hawk-Eye uses six small cameras positioned round the ground to monitor the flight, trajectory, speed and movement of the ball, both out of the bowler's hand and off the pitch. This information is then fed into a computer that almost instantly produces an exact replay of the ball in virtual reality, adding in the ball's predicted path if it hadn't cannoned into the batsman's pad, or been hit by his bat.

Suddenly television was not only relaying what had happened in explicit detail, but also what would have happened in different circumstances (i.e. if the batsman hadn't been there). It was predicting a probability as well as portraying the past. This was very new and very daring and not everyone liked it, fearing it would irreparably damage the fabric of the game, remove its glorious uncertainty. Umpires cowered in dark corners muttering, "Soon I'll only be there to count to six. . . it'll be the death of us."

They are anticipating the day when there will be cameras in the bats, balls and fielders' helmets, and a speaker in the stumps delivering a computer-generated "That's out" verdict (in a North Country accent if so desired) to send the batsman on his way. In fact, an electronic device, similar to the bleeper in tennis, that signals instantly to the players that a no-ball has just been bowled is already available. Paradoxically, it would probably pose more problems than it solved: "Wasn't that a no-ball then?" "No, it was a car horn in St John's Wood Road." Reassuringly, from an aesthetic point of view, it will be a while before cricket's international body feel they can sanction its use.

But are the umpires' fears justified? Is cricket soon to be presided over only by wired-up men in little boxes? Will bowlers of the future be yelling "Howzat?" to a set of traffic lights rather than an umpire? Well, Hawk-Eye hasn't yet been programmed to see that far ahead. But the short answer to the umpires' understandable worry is that they are likely to be there, doing roughly the same job, 20 years from now. In the same way that closed-circuit TV hasn't made the local bobby redundant, so too television's all-seeing eye does not spell the end of the umpire.

As the technological side of TV coverage develops further, it will just alter the style of his decision-making. Instead of him making instant, hairline judgments, a voice in his headset will give him a bit of guidance. "Pitched outside leg," the voice will say, or "a bit high". These morsels from the third umpire in the TV control unit will take less than five seconds to transmit; the delay will be imperceptible. In fact, the umpire will probably have made up his mind a good deal quicker than Steve Bucknor usually does. But most importantly, the umpire in the middle will still have the final say. It will be up to him to sift all the information he receives, as he does now, and then make his decision. Machines are supplying the information, but, vitally, humans are still interpreting and applying it.

Many supporters of the game will find this scenario disturbing. But you can't turn the clock back. Technological aids generally enhance the viewer's appreciation of the event and will increase in number and sophistication as rival television companies joust for reputation and airtime. For the viewer to have seen exactly what has happened, while the umpire remains more or less in the dark, is unacceptable. Players, too, expect every decision to be as right as it can possibly be. One problem that needs addressing immediately is the way officials are allowed to use technology. At the moment, cameras can be used to arbitrate whether a ball has gone for four or six, but not whether it has hit the batsman's glove or elbow before being caught. In other words, a relatively minor decision in the scheme of things – deciding whether the ball cleared the rope – is made to appear more significant than a potentially vital one, namely a batsman's dismissal. With more appropriate use of technology, Mike Atherton would have been reprieved in both innings at Trent Bridge last summer (he was given out caught off his arm guard to the second ball of the match) and Australia might not have taken an unassailable 3–0 lead.

The ICC's decision to declare a shortlist of elite umpires worldwide and to employ members of that panel whenever possible is absolutely the right approach. Because one thing Hawk-Eye, the snickometer, the red zone and all the other gimmicks reaffirmed was the supreme quality of the best officials. Men like Peter Willey, David Shepherd, Steve Bucknor and Rudi Koertzen get 95% of the hairline decisions right, often under extreme provocation. They should be paid a prince's ransom and then supplied – as subtly and quickly as possible – with all the televisual information necessary to ensure they aren't made to look fools to the viewer at home.

Television has illuminated and enhanced cricket. All the intricate skills and mysterious strategies of the game have been explained and explored, making it easier to understand and appreciate. Players young and old have benefited from the highlighting of their art. Ultimately, umpires will as well. They think they're the fallguys, but television should help them become even better snap-decision makers.

The technology people are on their side. The men in white coats are part of the fabric of cricket, maintaining its human factor. The day umpires are abolished, leaving the running of the game to people watching monitors, is the day cricket ceases to be sport and becomes, instead, more closely associated with the security industry. Law suits would be filed for "wrongful dismissal" and Test matches would be sponsored by legal firms rather than finance houses and power companies.

It will never happen. It is vital for cricket's credibility that the game played by highly paid international stars is still vaguely recognisable as the same recreation that 22 players indulge in come Saturday afternoon on Putney Common or beside the M62 at Milnrow. What would life be without the sight of a batsman staring incredulously at the umpire's raised finger? Or the bowler glaring at the umpire's implacable gaze and grunting, "But it were knocking all three down." A game without emotion is no game at all.

THE POWER OF BABEL

Mihir Bose, 2005

A curious thing happened during the Champions Trophy final between England and West Indies at The Oval last summer. At various times during the match the scoreboard flashed messages in Sanskrit, an Indian language as dead as Latin. The Sanskrit words are part of the logo of Bharat Petroleum, an Indian oil company using the occasion to advertise to the audience back home, in the country that now provides 60% of world cricket's income.

Every second person watching cricket anywhere in the world is an Indian, and major cricket tournaments like the Champions Trophy or the World Cup could not exist without being sold to an Indian TV company. India is the classic case of the fat man inside a thin man trying to get out. Most of its population still lead lives only marginally changed by the passing centuries, but another 300 million of the 1.1 billion now count as middle class. Most are not rich by western standards, but the sheer weight of numbers gives them phenomenal purchasing power. Cricket, particularly one-day cricket, is the great marketing tool for companies to reach them. Hence Sanskrit words flashed on the Oval scoreboard on a September afternoon.

The rise of the Indian television juggernaut is one of the great untold stories of cricket. In 1977, when the last major revolution in cricket took place, led by the Australian magnate Kerry Packer, India had barely entered the television age. There were fewer than 700,000 sets in a country whose population was already over 600 million: barely one per thousand. All that was on offer was the state channel, Doordarshan, showing programmes about as professional and entertaining as those available in the Soviet bloc. Not a single ball of cricket had ever been televised in India.

Today there are still remote villages where people will gather to watch the one communal TV set: a flickering screen powered by an unreliable generator. But the *pan* shops, offering betel nuts and crackly radio commentary, now have competition from smart restaurants, often with large screens. And 80 million homes, containing maybe a third of the population, have their own sets. The 1977 schism came about because the Australian Cricket Board refused to consider Packer's offer of $US3.25m to show five years of cricket in Australia. In the autumn of 2004, Zee TV offered $308m for four years of cricket in India: a hundred times as much. Inflation cannot entirely explain this away.

Various factors came together to produce this explosion. By coincidence, they reached a critical mass together. The turning point was 1991, when changes in cricket were matched by changes in society. That year, under pressure from the World Bank, India was forced to open up its economy and allow foreign investment into what had been one of the most protected markets on the planet. It was the year of the first Gulf War; suddenly Indians learned it was possible to follow world events on television rather than just through newspapers and cinema newsreels. And that was also when cricket at last became one family: South Africa, having shed its apartheid past, was readmitted into the game and finally played a non-white country, launching its rebirth with a one-day series in India. The historic tour made the Indian board realise it had television rights, which it could sell. Before that, Doordarshan had televised big games in India but, far from paying anything, it had often demanded fees from the board to cover the cost of production.

Now two South African channels wanted to show the games. Amrit Mathur, an official who worked for the then Indian board president Madhavrao Scindia, recalls: "We had to find out first who owned the rights and then how much they were worth." Mathur discovered that they belonged to the Indian board, and that they were surprisingly valuable. So as South Africa realised what it is to play against someone outside the white commonwealth, the Indians realised that they were sitting on a goldmine.

They might never have dug for the gold but for the intervention of one man. Mark Mascarenhas, a Bangalore boy who went to live in Connecticut, was convinced cricket could make big money. He bought the rights for the 1996 World Cup held in the subcontinent, and guaranteed $10m to the host countries; he delivered $30m. At the time, seasoned broadcasters thought Mascarenhas was mad. Hardly – he also became Sachin Tendulkar's agent and a big power in the game before his death in a car crash in 2002. And the Indian board's profits, as they ruthlessly commercialised the World Cup, enabled every major cricket ground in the country to be equipped with floodlights.

This was the turning point for TV rights in general, and India in particular. By 1996 India had also gone from two channels to 50, provided by more than 60,000 cable operators. Now there are 200 channels, and this Babel makes it easier to watch cricket, and even English football, than it is in England; I have watched Tottenham play Manchester City, a fixture not shown live at home, on a Saturday night in Darjeeling.

The government could not control this situation on the ground: there was no organised road digging, as in Britain or the USA – the companies just flung the wires over treetops and verandahs. They could not control the situation in the sky either, and two global media giants were now crucial players: Rupert Murdoch and the Disney Corporation. Murdoch owned Star, the Asian equivalent of Sky, and Disney had the sports channel ESPN. At first they competed furiously, then formed a curious and interesting alliance. They started a joint venture company called ESPN Star Sports and decided not to bid against each other, effectively carving up the cricket market. They continued to run their own separate sports channels, broadcast from Singapore, but divided up Indian cricket between them.

They have little else in common. ESPN remains a specialist sports channel, while Star is now the number one TV company in India. Its programme *Who Wants to be a Crorepati?* (Who wants 10 million rupees?), modelled on the UK's *Who Wants to be a Millionaire?* and hosted by the Bollywood star Amitabh Bachchan, is the country's most popular show. Doordarshan is still in the market and showed India's games from 1999 to 2003, paying $55m. To an extent this mirrored the triangular cricket television market in the UK in which the BBC, Channel 4 and Sky have all been regarded as potential bidders.

In Britain it makes a big difference to the audience who gets the rights, as each station has its own style and Sky's coverage is still only received by a minority. In India the audience is largely indifferent to which channel is showing the game. But the TV companies are not, and in 2000 the picture changed dramatically when another outfit, which had previously shown no interest, made the biggest bid cricket has ever seen.

The story of Zee TV is one of those extraordinary and very Indian tales. Its founder, Subhas Chandra, started making cooking oil when he was 19 and then earned money exporting grain to Russia. In 1992, a year after India opened up its markets, he set up Zee, funded by money from the Indian diaspora. For eight years Zee concentrated on films, sitcoms and the like. But in the summer of 2000, when the ICC met in Paris to allocate world rights for the 2003 and 2007 World Cups and other tournaments, Zee tabled the biggest bid in the history of the game: $660m, $110m more than the group backed by Rupert Murdoch.

Cricket decided to play safe. Murdoch seemed a more solid bet than Chandra, and the lower bid was accepted. Three years later, there was another surprising Indian intervention. This was from Sony, which for some years had been running a general entertainment channel with occasional forays into cricket, but now bid nearly $230m for the Indian rights for the 2003 and 2007 World Cups, an amazing amount given that the Murdoch company, the Global Communications Corporation, had struggled to sell coverage elsewhere. Outside India, the 2003 Cup was mainly on Murdoch-owned stations.

Sony showed the 2003 World Cup on its Max channel. With many of the top commentators contracted to ESPN Star, they had to bring in a relatively untried bunch of ex-cricketers, and the doyen, Sunil Gavaskar, had to spend the World Cup broadcasting from a flat in Cape Town. Sony's chief executive, Kunal Dasgupta, was very clear about the logic of his bid: "Cricket is the only product in India which unites the whole country, north, south, east, west. It transcends class, religion, regional and language differences. You do not require words to explain Sachin Tendulkar or Rahul Dravid."

Just as Murdoch had used Premier League football in England to drive the sales of satellite dishes, and attract the free-spending young males who so delight advertisers, so Sony was using cricket. The same thought inspired Zee in the autumn of 2004, when the Indian board began auctioning the rights for the next four years of international cricket. After a complex series of manoeuvres, Zee emerged on top with that bid of $308m, easily trumping ESPN Star, Doordarshan and Sony. But the tender document had said the rights would only go to a broadcaster that broadcasts cricket, which Zee so far has not. The case ended up in the Supreme Court, which in February 2005 ruled 3-2 against Zee, meaning the process had to start again. Sources inside the Indian board admit that it started the negotiations too late, and messed things up both strategically and legally. As a result, the Australian tour last autumn was almost blacked out.

Even more competitors could soon be on the scene: Ten, best known as a company producing cricket broadcasts for other networks, has its own channel. In contrast to Britain, where TV rights may now remain with the same company forever, all things are possible. Except, perhaps, order.

On the one hand, India's cricketers are the country's greatest stars. Individually and as a team, they are on TV adverts the whole time, endorsing all the consumer products of the new India. Yet the game is still run in a chaotic and often inept manner. To that extent, India hasn't changed at all.

HELLO SKY, GOODBYE WORLD
Steven Barnett, 2005

While cricket supporters reputedly jammed the England and Wales Cricket Board switchboard to vent their anger over the decision to move English Test cricket off Channel 4 and on to satellite television, the trade magazine *Broadcast* had a rather different angle. Its response to the news was headlined "C4's cricket loss frees 200 hours". For independent television producers and Channel 4's commissioning editors – not to mention its finance director – this was definitely not a bad-news story.

From the summer of 2006, not a single ball of live Test cricket will be available to viewers on free-to-air terrestrial television, for the first time in 60 years. This loss of mass exposure will without doubt have unfortunate consequences for promoting cricket amongst young and less devoted followers. The ECB decided to trade coverage for cash on the basis that this would not be forever, and that when the next deal starts in 2010, cricket could again be widely available. This misunderstands the nature of the broadcasting world.

When the ECB explained its reasoning – and in particular Channel 4's inability to match the four-year package of £220m primarily generated by BSkyB – a number of commentators condemned Channel 4 for its failure to commit itself to cricket. What they failed to appreciate was the unique difficulty of scheduling cricket in the heart of a mainstream TV channel that makes its living from selling commercials.

Cricket is a scheduler's nightmare. It takes up a huge amount of airtime, during most of which – to the uninitiated – not a great deal happens. It alienates large sections of the potential audience, especially women. Its finish time depends on the over rate and is therefore unpredictable, which collides with the first rule of scheduling: always transmit your key early-evening shows at predictable times. In a competitive broadcasting environment, the early evening is critical to building audiences for the rest of the night. If two million switch on at 6 p.m. to watch *The Simpsons*, only to find an unknown Sri Lankan batsman playing for the close, they are unlikely to hang around. That is disastrous for the channel's revenue.

On top of that, there are the hours to fill when poor weather prevents play: the cricket lover isn't interested in time-fillers and the non-believer thinks the cricket is on. So the channel loses twice over. Channel 4 can't even make do with old movies because it has a strict quota of original programming which would be severely compromised.

All these uncertainties have a cost, which in Channel 4's case is measurable. At its best, when England are doing well and a match is well poised, the channel can break even. At its worst, it loses money. Its original highlights package at 7.30 was drawing an average of 700,000 viewers instead of the usual 1.5 million. None of this diminished the enthusiasm with which Channel 4 embraced the game. To almost universal acclaim, it revolutionised coverage and demonstrated vividly how lazy and unimaginative the BBC's approach had become. From Hawk-Eye to regular and concise explanations of some of the more eccentric laws, it made the game accessible and fun to watch.

It also demonstrated its commitment off the air. Part of the ECB's rationale in 1998, when it dumped the BBC, was that Channel 4 could exploit its trendy image to appeal to a new, younger and multicultural audience. And indeed the station has invested money in inner-city cricket programmes, teaching packs for schools, a community cricket ground in Lambeth, and themed cultural events encouraging ethnic Indian and West Indian communities to participate. It has kept its side of the bargain.

But over the next five years, the commercial environment will become much tougher. C4's new chief executive, Andy Duncan, has projected a funding gap of over £100m by 2012 and is already appealing to government for some kind of public subsidy for the first time in the channel's history. Against that kind of background, Channel 4 could hardly be blamed for not matching BSkyB's offer.

Unfortunately, the ECB doesn't seem to understand how difficult it will be to re-establish contact with terrestrial television. ITV's complete indifference to cricket – compared to rugby union, motor racing or European soccer – is one measure of the sport's lack of commercial viability. Channel 5 may have committed itself to a highlights package at 7.15, but against *Coronation Street, EastEnders* and *Emmerdale* it will be lucky to attract an audience of half a million. Five certainly won't touch ball-by-ball coverage.

That leaves the non-commercial BBC, which for 60 years was televised cricket's natural home but this time did not even put in a bid. As it prepares for the decennial review of the BBC charter and makes its case for continued licence fee funding, many cricket fans have been wondering why cricket should not be an integral part of the public-service rationale. There are several reasons.

First, the new director-general, Mark Thompson, has made it clear he intends to move away from a populist approach. That means making more room for some of the core public-service areas such as current affairs, documentaries, arts, music and children's programming. While cricket lovers may be keen to add their sport to the public-service list, there are too many other programme areas being vacated by the commercial channels, and which the BBC is under growing pressure to prioritise.

Second, the BBC has existing obligations to sports which have stayed loyal or returned to it. Wimbledon tennis, rugby union, the FA Cup and football highlights all have a place in the BBC's sports pantheon. Once a sport takes itself off to a competitor, the BBC can't be expected to wait patiently in the wings for a change of mind; its sports resources and personnel will have been diverted elsewhere.

Third, schedules need to be filled. As *Test Match Special* producer Peter Baxter put it, "the problem with moving a sport off a mainstream channel is that the hole closes over". Commitments are made not just to other sports but to other programming areas, often with long lead times. Something in the current schedule – which will probably have built its own loyal audience – would have to make way, particularly for such a huge chunk of television time as Test cricket consumes.

Meanwhile, BSkyB has a very different agenda. With three dedicated sports channels, there is no shortage of airtime, and subscribers who are willing and able to pay upwards of £400 per year will see full coverage. More importantly, it is live and exclusive sport which drives the BSkyB business. After years of facing very little competition in the multichannel world, it is now finding life more difficult against Freeview, the BBC's digital offering which requires only a set-top box and no monthly subscription – but offers a much smaller range of channels. Sky's monthly rate of signing up new households has been declining and the number of Freeview homes accelerating. Exclusive Test cricket is a valuable carrot to persuade an additional tranche of otherwise reluctant subscribers to join the BSkyB club and boost its subscription base.

This won't detract from the proven quality of Sky's coverage. But for Sky, as with all its exclusive sports, cricket is a commodity which it will want to buy as cheaply as possible next time around. And when the ECB starts looking in 2009 for competing bids from mainstream channels, it will be lucky to find any other potential takers for a sport which makes such enormous and unpredictable demands on airtime. Sky knows when it has a free run, and will be bidding accordingly – and the pot of gold which the ECB discovered this time round could prove to be a very short-lived cash bonanza.

There is one potential game-saving approach, which would depend on the government intervening to do what the ECB hasn't done and recognise the national significance of the game. Until 1998 home Test matches were among ten "listed events", the crown jewels of sport which were judged to be of such cultural value to the nation that live rights could not be sold exclusively to a non-terrestrial broadcaster. After intense lobbying from the ECB – and a much-touted "gentlemen's agreement" between the board chairman Lord MacLaurin and the cabinet minister in charge of sport, culture secretary Chris Smith, that the game would not disappear from mainstream television – home Test matches were removed from the "A" list of protected events.

Unfortunately, the harsh reality of commercial life does not allow for agreements between gentlemen. So it is worth remembering the words of Chris Smith in June 1998 when he acceded to the request: "This is something for which the ECB and county cricket clubs have specifically asked. I expect to see their freedom used responsibly, with continued access for all viewers to a substantial proportion of live Test coverage. If those expectations are not fulfilled then I may, of course, need to review the listed criteria again."

Both Smith and MacLaurin have gone now, but it may be time for the government to act on Smith's threat. The English Rugby Football Union recognised its mistake in selling its Six Nations matches at Twickenham to BSkyB when live TV audiences allegedly plummeted to a tenth of their BBC1 size. The RFU understood the potential damage that was being done to maintaining a healthy grassroots interest in the sport, and reversed their decision. A rugby match is about one twenty-fifth the length of a Test match, so the BBC could easily accommodate them. The same will not be true for cricket in 2009.

Steven Barnett is professor of communications at the University of Westminster. His books include Games and Sets, *an analysis of sport on television.*

REACH FOR THE SKY   Matthew Engel, *Notes by the Editor*, 2005

English cricket followers will get substantial benefits from the deal whereby live cricket in England will cease to be shown on terrestrial television, starting from 2006, and instead move to the satellite network, Sky Sports. The insidious process by which Test match days have had to start earlier and earlier so that they finish in time for the evening schedules will cease. Coverage will no longer have to be interrupted to accommodate horse races or other irrelevances. Cricket will have the benefit of being covered by a network with a proven commitment to the game and a reasonably innovative approach to it (even if the commentary is often banal). The subsidiary deal with Channel 5, which is a terrestrial station, ensures that the highlights package will be shown in the early evening and not, as has increasingly happened on the present Test-match station Channel 4, after midnight and shortly before the mud wrestling.

Readers who are unfamiliar with British TV may not grasp the passion attached to this argument. While the BBC, which showed home Test matches until 1998, and Channel 4 are available to everyone on payment of an annual licence fee (and Channel 5 to most people), Sky Sports has to be purchased by subscription, costing about £400 a year. Only a minority of the population makes this payment, but, as the defenders of the deal have pointed out, it is thought half of households with children do pay, and these are the people cricket is most anxious to get at.

And from what one can gather, the ECB ran short of options. The BBC did not bid at all; Channel 4 entered only half-heartedly; Sky made it clear that, while not demanding all or nothing, it wanted all or would pay a great deal less. ECB sources say the funding gap between the Sky deal and any alternative package would have been about £20m per year, about a quarter of the board's annual budget. What matters here is the politics, not the economics. Had the ECB management board accepted a lesser deal, the counties would almost certainly have rebelled. Those responsible would have been voted out at best, strung up from Father Time at worst. That's today's reality.

Let us now consider tomorrow's reality. The pattern of TV viewing is indeed changing, though not in the way the deal's instigators claim. Giles Clarke, the board's chief negotiator, described terrestrial television as "a dying form". But though all TV is indeed scheduled to be digital by 2012, there will still be mainstream channels, available to all viewers, and specialist ones for paying customers only. On Channel 4, Test matches have a peak audience of just over a million [it was eight times that for the 2005 Ashes series]. No one knows what the figure might be on Sky; the company does not reveal such figures, partly, one suspects, because they are too small to be measurable by any available method; and partly because they would draw derisive laughter. All the anecdotal evidence and one's intuition suggest that Test matches only on Sky get noticed less than others.

Sky's business model does not depend on drawing large audiences. It makes money by accreting minorities who want different aspects of their service. Sky Sports will indeed give a good service to cricket lovers willing to pay the subscription. It will not, however, go beyond them. Cricket's post-war survival in Britain was driven by the BBC. Television and radio attracted not just the obvious audience, but drew in people who knew nothing about the game until they heard or glimpsed it by chance and were captivated. Sky will attract only the already committed.

Some argue that the prime-time highlights package will be a huge bonus, but these programmes really are a dying form, because viewers can now see so much live sport. Others claim football has not suffered from being on Sky, which spectacularly misses the point. A vast amount of football remains on mass audience TV, most especially the two biennial festivals of the game, the World Cup and the European Championship. The 2003 cricket World Cup was only on Sky, and there is little prospect of anything different in 2007.

We are talking here about a situation where the overwhelming majority of the British population will never come across a game of cricket in their daily lives. Never, never, never, never. There will be short-term consequences as sponsors drift away; the longer-term effects will take a generation to unfold. Some believe these could be serious; I think we're looking at a potential catastrophe.

THE COMMONS BLAMES LORD'S
Steven Barnett, 2006

It is a measure of how much controversy the ECB generated when it sold exclusive live TV rights for home Test matches to Sky Sports that its decision was subject to a House of Commons select committee inquiry. As far as MPs were concerned, this was up there with the major issues of the day. The Culture, Media and Sport select committee's report, Broadcasting Rights for Cricket, published in February 2006, did a first-class job in grasping a difficult issue and, in particular, exposing the timidity of most of those involved, but the ECB took the brunt of their criticism.

With the power to call witnesses, including lords of the realm, the committee was able to clarify the 1998 "gentlemen's agreement" between Lord Smith who, as plain Chris Smith, was culture secretary at the time, and Lord MacLaurin, then the ECB's chairman. The government agreed to remove the "listing" that made it compulsory for all home Tests to be sold to terrestrial TV, but what did cricket offer in return? The committee's conclusion was unequivocal. It may not have been legally binding, but there was an agreement: "live Test match cricket played in England was not to be removed completely from free-to-air TV". The claim by the current culture secretary, Tessa Jowell, that the agreement was "somewhat unclear" was rejected. It was scarcely surprising that the committee called in future for "formal binding undertakings".

The broadcasters too were criticised, particularly the BBC. While there was some sympathy for Channel 4 – who lost £16m a year on their cricket coverage – and an appreciation that scheduling a long and unpredictable game was difficult, the committee could not understand why the BBC did not even bid for highlights. But the worst tongue-lashing was reserved for the ECB. While acknowledging the importance of a decent financial settlement for cricket, the committee noted that no other major sport around the world had deliberately removed itself from mass-audience television. It concluded that "the ECB did not do enough to ensure that a non-exclusive deal was brokered". In a very astute passage which suggested the committee had a rather better grasp of rights negotiations than the board, it wrote: "By allowing BSkyB to think they could obtain an exclusive deal, it is self-evident that the broadcaster would reduce any offer for shared rights and ramp up dramatically its bid for exclusive rights."

For the future, it recommends an earlier start to negotiations – although it is hard to see anyone matching the airtime volume and sheer financial muscle of Sky by 2010. In the meantime, the committee said the ECB "must take the blame for any decline in interest in the game".

A STAKE THROUGH CRICKET'S HEART   Matthew Engel, *Notes by the Editor*, 2006

Cricket has become very fond of the fashionable word "stakeholder". I occasionally get communications from official bodies addressed to me that way. One might swank about this, but I suspect my stakeholding is analogous to that of a woman with one share turning up at the Marks & Spencer AGM to moan about the knickers being frumpy. In the case of English cricket, there is now only one stakeholder worth a light: Sky TV, a company which itself is run by one dominant stakeholder. Luckily for cricket, Rupert Murdoch has other things to consider, and Vic Wakeling, the head of Sky Sports, seems a nice, sensible bloke – which is lucky, because if he wakes up one morning and thinks the leg-bye should be abolished, or the tea interval, he only has to pick up the phone.

Let's not go through *all* this again, because it is really too awful. English cricket will be shown live only on Sky Sports until at least 2010. In January 2006, a committee of MPs gave the England and Wales Cricket Board a tap with the ruler for the decision, taking the view, which I share, that this was a bad decision for which the board is primarily, but not wholly, responsible. However, it is the ECB's job to protect English cricket's interests, not the government's, nor parliament's, nor any TV company's. Live cricket has now disappeared from the screens of more than half the homes in the country. The ECB has counted the financial gain from Sky; the damage – just when the game should be poised to reap the full rewards from 2005 – will be incalculable. No amount of money for the counties, even in the unlikely event of them using it wisely, can compensate for what has happened. Had the deal applied last year, and the Ashes been shown only on Sky, the great surge of interest would have been a ripple. No serious broadcasting analyst disputes this. Only the main TV channels have the reach that allows these great national obsessions to develop, whether it is sport, a breaking news story, Darren Gough reinventing himself as a ballroom dancer, or faded stars making prats of themselves on *Celebrity Big Brother*.

It would help if the ECB admitted the disaster, instead of denying it. But the gung-ho gimme-de-money county chairmen who negotiated the wretched deal were in full cry even as the Ashes was proving them wrong. "People are gibbering on about wanting to retain Test cricket on terrestrial TV, but that will not exist in the digital age. . . if the BBC competes in 2010 it will be through a digital channel," said Giles Clarke of Somerset. Mr Clarke is supposed to be a clever man, but he is the gibberer, a condition that seems to have been exacerbated by swallowing some first-year media studies undergraduate's textbook. The word "terrestrial" is irrelevant. But in any conceivable television future, there will still be a vast difference between a free-to-air general channel and a paid-for sports service, which will be watched only by existing fans. It doesn't matter whether the service is being received by aerial, satellite dish or a cable inserted direct into Mr Clarke's brain. Live cricket's presence on a general channel is essential to the game's well-being.

English cricket now thinks wistfully about the Beeb. It was like the game's first wife: it was safe and dull and, by the 1990s, its cricket coverage was bordering on frigid. But she would never have sought a divorce had cricket not walked out for the flashy young bird down the road. Channel 4 was the classic second wife: rekindling the fires with sexiness, imagination and fun. There was always a commitment problem, though. . . so cricket is on to its third wife: a marriage it does not want. No. 3 is rich, and, after two divorces, the game needs the cash – allegedly to help bring up the kids. And it is the next generation who, as ever in these situations, will be the losers.

It's Just Not Cricket –
A Crisis in Behaviour

"It's not cricket" is, of course, a peculiar phrase. As if hurling a rock-hard projectile at somebody while ten other players collaborate to bring about the batsman's downfall was ever a gentlemanly pursuit. And yet somehow cricket did gain the reputation for good manners, sportsmanship, fair play. No doubt something to do with Thomas Arnold and the public-school spirit in the mid-19th century.

It certainly has nothing at all to do with the sport's raffish period in the late 18th century, when gambling-induced bribery and corruption were rife. Derek Pringle, in a useful corrective to the view that cricket was hunky-dory until money infected the game over the past two or three decades, shows how many of the practices that have recently been spotlighted were an accepted part of the game in the past. His piece on the "secret history of cheating", reprinted below, also includes the lovely story of an 18th-century match in which both sides had been bribed to lose. What an inventive encounter that must have been.

And yet, despite this helpful warning not to grow misty-eyed over Corinthian golden ages, I think there is evidence of a crisis in behaviour in the years immediately after the Packer experiment. It is there most vividly in some alarming photographs in the *Wisdens* of the late '70s and '80s – the great and generally placid Michael Holding kicking the stumps over in New Zealand, Dennis Lillee demanding that he be allowed to use his patented aluminium bat, Trevor Chappell bowling the final ball of a one-day match underarm to ensure that a six could not be hit, Chris Broad refusing to leave the field having been given out against Pakistan, the infamous slanging match between England captain Mike Gatting and Pakistani umpire Shakoor Rana.

There does appear, in this period, to have been a breakdown of common courtesies among opponents, and a failure on the part of the administrators to exert a proper authority. One can only guess at the reasons: more money in the game, greater awareness by players of their own power post-Packer, political differences between Test-playing countries as India and Pakistan, in particular, sought to escape the dominance of the so-called "White Commonwealth" countries who for years had set the cricketing rules. All contributed to a crisis that threatened the fabric of the game, demeaned it in the eyes of the public and caused great heartache among the procession of *Wisden* editors, who were all too aware that a great game was being besmirched.

The crisis reached its ugly apogee in 1991, when bowler Rashid Patel brandished a stump at Raman Lamba in the final of the Duleep Trophy. Thereafter, the howls of anguish in *Wisden* become fewer. The Atherton dirt-in-pocket furore could cause some heart-searching, and there were still incendiary incidents such as the Denness affair in South Africa that led to an unofficial Test being played when the ICC withdrew authorisation for a recognised match. But despite such blots on the game, behaviour was improving – in my view, principally because of the introduction of "neutral" umpires. Home-country umpires, no matter how impartial they may have been, were a constant bugbear as sides got it into their heads that they were being done down.

The fiasco of the Oval Test in August 2006, which Pakistan forfeited when they staged a protest over umpire Darrell Hair's decision to penalise them for allegedly tampering with the ball, would appear to fly in the face of these conclusions. Here was a situation that spiralled out of control despite the presence of a third-country umpire and a referee. It was abysmally handled at every level: from Hair's peremptory action, through the Pakistan team's confusion, to the ICC's publication of Hair's confidential emails – a smokescreen to enable adjudication over Pakistan captain Inzamam-ul-Haq to be delayed without jeopardising the one-day series, worth an estimated £15m, between England and Pakistan. In modern cricket, when justice and money collide, there can only be one winner. But, despite the debacle and ICC's cynical stratagem, I continue to believe that standards of both behaviour and administration now are far better than they were 20 years ago, that mutual respect among players is strong – this was evident throughout the England-Pakistan series – and that the system of third-country umpires and referees has been of great benefit.

The Hair affair showed three things: that the laws on ball-tampering are befuddled; that referees must be more visible; and that the latent power struggle between the old "White Commonwealth" members of ICC and their Asian counterparts is the gravest threat to international cricket. The Hair incident echoes the Denness affair in that the cricketers of an Asian country felt they were being unfairly picked on by an official from the old white Commonwealth. Dangerously, arguments over home-country umpires are being supplanted by allegations of bias based on race. An already nightmarish job just got even harder.   S. M.

IT HAS TO STOP   Norman Preston, *Notes by the Editor*, 1980

Alarmed at the growing incidence of bad behaviour by players in all levels of grade cricket – which includes Test players – the New South Wales Cricket Association held a discussion at Cricket House, Sydney, and requested that the following message be printed in a prominent place in each club's annual report. I make no excuse for bringing it forward to wider spheres in the cricket world because the issues raised appertain not solely to Australia, but to most parts of the world where cricket is played. The advent of big prize-money may well be the cause of the spread of excessive bad manners.

"It Has To Stop" is the heading of the NSW message to its members, and here is the context. Bad behaviour by players is bringing the game into disrepute. It is alienating public support and making it almost impossible to recruit and hold umpires. The following examples give rise to concern:

- Fieldsmen making ridiculous appeals in the hope of intimidating umpires into giving a favourable decision.
- Fieldsmen making disparaging remarks about umpires.
- Fieldsmen swearing at a batsman in an attempt to break his concentration.
- Fieldsmen directing a dismissed batsmen to the pavilion with a torrent of abuse.
- Batsmen disputing an umpire's decision by remaining at the crease and making disparaging remarks to the umpire.
- Batsmen making offensive remarks to fieldsmen attempting to field a ball or take a catch.
- Batsmen on the way back to the pavilion banging the bat on the ground, swearing, and throwing the bat on reaching the dressing-room.

UNBRIDLED DISSENT
John Woodcock, *Notes by the Editor*, 1981

There is one aspect of the year under review which is new and of great concern. This is the manner and frequency with which famous players have flouted the authority of the umpires. In all the years that *Wisden* has been published, there can have been no more shocking photograph than that of Michael Holding, the distinguished and richly talented West Indian fast bowler, kicking the stumps out

High dudgeon: Michael Holding, later a respected TV commentator, kicks the stumps in a display of what *Wisden* called "unbridled dissent" after an appeal was turned down at Dunedin during West Indies' fractious tour of New Zealand in 1980. The batsman, John Parker, appears supremely unconcerned.

of the ground in a Test match in New Zealand – for no other reason than that he disagreed with an umpire's decision.

Nor was this an isolated example of such unbridled dissent. In the same Test series Colin Croft, another of the West Indian fast bowlers, having lost his temper, sent an umpire flying as he ran into bowl. In India, at much the same time, the umpires were being denounced by the touring Pakistanis; in Perth, Dennis Lillee, the great Australian, held up play for ten minutes in a Test match between England and Australia while he argued with the umpires and his own captain over the use of an aluminium bat in which he had a proprietorial interest. Technically Lillee had a point, there being nothing in the Laws at that time, though there is now, to say that a bat must be made of wood; morally, as he must have known, he should have done as the umpires asked him.

As disconcerting as these individual cases of defiance was the way in which they were glossed over by those whose responsibility it was to make an example of the players concerned. In New Zealand, the West Indian manager, himself a former Test player, blamed the umpires for what was happening. No wonder that when the West Indians left for home the New Zealand cricketing public, to quote R. T. Brittenden in his summary of the tour, "was glad to see the back of them".

In Australia, the Chairman of the Australian Cricket Board said that he could not understand what all the fuss was about over Lillee's insubordination. Ian Chappell, an outstanding batsman and conspicuously successful captain of Australia, was suspended once, and subsequently given a second suspended sentence, for tilting at the precept that the umpire's decision is final; but in Australia, as elsewhere, the standards of cricketing discipline have in recent years been regularly compromised.

Towards the end of 1980, however, it began to seem as though those who administer the game were themselves seeing the red light. In the West Indies Gerry Gomez, a member of the West Indian Board of Control, advocated a series of fines aimed at calling the players to order. There was a move among members of the International Cricket Conference to appoint independent observers to Test series. From Pakistan came a suggestion that Test umpires should be empowered to send players off the field. Even in Australia the senior players, or most of them, were looking for ways of keeping the hoodlums at bay.

THE CENTENARY FRACAS   John Woodcock, *Notes by the Editor*, 1981

This great jamboree, arranged to celebrate 100 years of Test cricket between England and Australia in England, had been eagerly awaited. Its counterpart, at Melbourne in 1977, had been a wonderful success, but last summer's match was ill-fated from the start.

Some would say that the hours from eleven o'clock until six o'clock on the Saturday were like a nightmare. So incensed were certain members of MCC by the middle of the afternoon that play was not in progress, owing, as they thought, to the obstinacy of the umpires, that a scuffle took place on the steps of the pavilion, in which the umpires, one or two members, and the captains were involved. As a result of it, the umpires were shaken, the reputation of MCC was damaged and the occasion impaired.

Two and a half months later, following what MCC described as a thorough inquiry – which included taking the evidence of the umpires, the captains and a number of members, and studying a BBC film recording of the incident – Peter May, President of MCC, wrote in a letter to all members of the club that "appropriate disciplinary action" had been taken. He made the point, too, that it was no more fitting for members of a club publicly to question the decision of the umpires, let alone abuse them, than for players to do so on the field.

If good is to come from a sorry affair, it will be to see that efforts are redoubled to provide the best possible covering on all first-class grounds, especially those where Test matches are staged. As many have said, it seems laughable to be able to land a man on the moon yet to have discovered no adequate way of protecting the square at Lord's.

Sharp Practice in Melbourne
John Woodcock, *Notes by the Editor*, 1982

Wisden 1981 carried a picture of Michael Holding kicking a stump out of the ground, during a Test match, to show his disapproval of an umpire's decision. This year, in the same disreputable category, is one of Trevor Chappell bowling a sneak in Melbourne, at his brother Greg's behest, to prevent New Zealand from making the six runs they needed to tie a one-day match. Some say it is money that has caused this collapse in the ethics of the game, others that it is the reflection of a graceless age.

In Australia, I am afraid, it is partly the result of weak government. For too long the Australian Cricket Board have been over-tolerant of indiscipline and actions of dubious intent. True cricket-lovers have been as sickened by Lillee's antics as they have been spellbound by his bowling. The latest precept, that Australian players shall penalise each other for misconduct, hardly seems a step in the right direction.

A Disturbing Year
John Woodcock, *Notes by the Editor*, 1983

In 1982, politics cast a shadow across the cricket fields of the world. For this and other reasons it was a disturbing year. Towards the end of 1981 two of the game's outstanding cricketers, Dennis Lillee of Australia and Javed Miandad, who was captaining Pakistan, had been involved in an ugly scuffle in a Test match in Perth; early in 1982, 14 English cricketers were banned for three years from playing Test cricket for touring South Africa together.

To umpire in a Test match, not least in England, was to run the risk of becoming profoundly disaffected. The English season closed with most of the 17 first-class counties in financial difficulties, and no sooner had England's series against Australia, in the winter of 1982–83, begun than shameful scenes, again in Perth, caused concern.

Although the Australian Cricket Board, under urging from Lord's, had given proper priority to the Test matches, over the one-day triangular tournament which is now a regular feature of the Australian season, they had sanctioned from their marketing agents a distasteful film aimed at promoting England's tour. This caricatured, in a gratuitously offensive and quite erroneous way, the English view of Australia's chances. In the event it was a number of Englishmen, bearing Union Jacks and under the influence of drink, who invaded the field during the first Test match in Perth and grappled with the Australian fielders.

In England last summer, during the matches against Pakistan, there were times when Trent Bridge and Edgbaston sounded like football grounds. The same has begun to happen on Sundays at John Player League matches and at Lord's in the one-day finals. For some years now, on high days and holidays, the Hill at Sydney and the southern stand at Melbourne have been places where no one wanting an agreeable day at the cricket would choose to go. The unruliness which has removed so much of the pleasure from watching football is even less compatible with cricket.

If, in Perth, young expatriate Englishmen started the trouble, as they clearly did, the players themselves, particularly Lillee, have much to answer for, owing to their inflammatory gestures on the field of play. In Mr Packer's World Series Cricket these were necessary because of the absence of any authentic atmosphere. Test cricket is competitive enough without them. When, in Perth, a blow was aimed at Alderman, the Australian bowler, by one of England's so-called supporters, and some of the Australian side retaliated by setting on him, it was another sad manifestation of the violence that is the bane of modern sport.

AUSTRALIA V PAKISTAN 1981–82   Brian Osborne, 1983

Javed Miandad led the side and batted well throughout, although his confrontation with Lillee during the Perth Test was a wretched affair and he did not appear to have the full support of his whole team at times. He was also involved in strong but unsuccessful requests by the Pakistan management to have the umpires replaced for the Second Test.

The confrontation between Miandad and Lillee [in the First Test at Perth] was one of the most undignified incidents in Test history. Miandad, batting to Lillee, had turned a ball to the on side and was in the course of completing a comfortable single when he was obstructed by Lillee. In the ensuing fracas Lillee kicked Miandad, who responded by shaping to strike him with his bat. The Australian team imposed a $200 fine (£120 approx.) on Lillee and sought an apology from Miandad for his part in the affair. However, the umpires, who had assisted in quelling the incident, objected to the penalty as too lenient and the matter was dealt with at a Melbourne hearing before Mr R. Merriman, the co-ordinator of the Australian Cricket Board's Cricket sub-committee. His ruling was that Lillee's penalty, set by the players, was not sufficient and he imposed a suspension from Australia's two ensuing one-day internationals – against Pakistan and West Indies. No apology was forthcoming from Miandad, whose participation in the incident was also referred to in the umpires' report.

Confrontation: Javed Miandad reacts angrily to Dennis Lillee's kick at him while he was running, during the Test between Australia and Pakistan at Perth in 1981. The swift intervention of umpire Tony Crafter probably prevented an ugly incident from developing into something far worse.

CROWD CONTROL
John Woodcock, *Notes by the Editor*, 1986

To guard against the hooliganism that has so harmed the image and marred the enjoyment of association football, the cricketing authorities are having to restrict licensing hours on grounds and to make special appeals for orderly behaviour. After the field at Headingley had been prematurely invaded at the end of the first Test match, in anticipation of the winning hit, steps were taken to avoid the same thing happening in the remaining Tests.

It is a pity when many have to be denied their ordinary pleasures in order to restrain the few, but it was for the best. The one-day finals are also having to be more tightly controlled, while even in Derbyshire it was considered necessary to express publicly the county's concern at "the type of people" who were being attracted to Sunday games.

LAW OR ANARCHY
Graeme Wright, *Preface*, 1988

The year past seems to have been one in which both the spirit and the letter of the Laws have been threatened by malevolence and near anarchy. Can this really be what happens when the Laws are omitted from *Wisden*?

In the 1987 Wisden, *Wright had at the last moment been forced to drop the Laws for space reasons.*

149

MALEVOLENCE AND MISCHIEF
Graeme Wright, *Notes by the Editor*, 1988

The first two of the summer's Test matches between England and Pakistan were badly affected by the weather. At Old Trafford there were constant interruptions; at Lord's, there was no play on the second, fourth and fifth days. For players, managers and press, there was time to fill, and as an old saw has it, Satan finds some mischief still for idle hands to do. Certainly some mischief emanated from the enforced intervals of those two matches and the ramifications were to be bitter and widespread.

England and Pakistan had arrived at the Test series still tasting success from their winter series, Pakistan having drawn with West Indies at home and beaten India in India, England having retained the Ashes and won two international one-day tournaments in Australia. In terms of international prestige in the world of cricket, much was at stake in this series.

With Imran Khan unable to bowl at Old Trafford, Pakistan were seriously handicapped, and as England set about building on the advantage secured by Robinson's century, Pakistan began to play for time. The weather was always going to be their ally, and the longer England batted, the better were Pakistan's chances of a draw. At one stage on the second day, they managed to bowl no more than 11 overs in an hour, and this without one bowler boasting a long run-up. Players came and substitutes went, and the rhythm of play was broken. Imran himself was off the field at the time, having required an X-ray of an injured thumb, and it was Javed Miandad who conducted the stalling operation.

That it was deliberate time-wasting cannot be questioned. Unfortunately, all countries do it, and that England have been no exception is something England's newly appointed team manager, M. J. Stewart, should have considered when, at the evening's press conference, he criticised Pakistan's tactics. Commenting on the poor over-rate, and the need for a tightening-up on the use of substitutes, he said, "I feel there has to be a stricter control over what constitutes a genuine injury".

Some of the following morning's newspapers made a great play of Mr Stewart's comments. Later that day, a rain-interrupted Saturday, Imran and the Pakistan manager, Haseeb Ahsan, replied to the criticisms levelled at them. "We get slagged off and called cheats and I object to that," said Imran. "Maybe if I'd been in the field I'd have stepped things up. But both umpires said it was fine." Haseeb said, "The series has started off on the wrong foot. We've been labelled as cheats. I respect Stewart but he shouldn't have said what he did. If there's any problem we can sit down and talk it out. The umpires said there was no problem, and yet talk of dirty tricks and all that nonsense has appeared in the press."

The battle lines had been drawn up: a fuse had been lit and it was to smoulder unchecked for another six months until, at Faisalabad in December, the charge exploded. Could not something have been done to defuse the situation before that? Or were the administrators at the TCCB aware even that there was a situation to defuse? At Lord's, along with the rain, came a leak from the Pakistan management which was as subtle as any from a government department to parliamentary correspondents. Its effect was to make public the TCCB's decision not to accede to Pakistan's request to remove two umpires, D. J. Constant and K. E. Palmer, from the Test match panel. Mr Constant had officiated in the Headingley Test match of the 1982 series between England and Pakistan, after which Imran had been critical of the umpiring, claiming that errors had cost his side the match and so the series.

Pakistan's request in 1987 was not the first time that a visiting side had requested Mr Constant's omission from the Test match list. In 1982 the Indians, who came to England ahead of the Pakistanis, requested that he be replaced. This might have been a retaliatory move following complaints by England about umpiring standards in India during the previous winter: the 1981–82 tour on which the captain, K. W. R. Fletcher, expressed his dissent at an umpire's decision by hitting the stumps with his bat, an act which contributed to his being replaced as England's captain after the tour. It was also thought that the Indians had been unhappy with Mr Constant's umpiring during the final Test of the 1979 series. Whatever the reasons behind the Indians' request in 1982, the TCCB complied with it, although paying the umpire his match fee.

Last year, however, not only was the Pakistan request turned down on the grounds of prejudice, but A. C. Smith, the new chief executive of the TCCB, read a statement from the first-class umpires in support of their colleagues on the Test match panel. It was to be a year of supporting statements. All this time Mr Constant was the umpire officiating in the Test match at Lord's, and later both he and K. E. Palmer stood at The Oval in the final Test. At both venues, the Pakistan manager was publicly critical of Mr Constant and his umpiring, at one time describing him as "a disgraceful person". With or without justification, and I am not aware that there really was any, this was conduct unbecoming of a tour manager; but following some of Haseeb's other statements while in England, it surprised no one. At Trent Bridge, during the touring team's match against Nottinghamshire, he attempted to interfere when the umpires officially warned a Pakistani bowler, Mohsin Kamal, for excessive use of the bouncer.

In view of Haseeb's conduct in England, it required the most optimistic of men to expect that England would not encounter some kind of retaliation when they stayed on in Pakistan after the World Cup. Without wishing to be pessimistic, or unduly cynical, little in the history of man's behaviour towards his fellow man, or nation's towards nation, could lead one to expect anything else, especially as Pakistan is a young, aggressive state fired by a fierce nationalism and a strict fundamentalist religion. Moreover, touring teams have repeatedly been critical of umpiring standards there, to the extent that the Pakistanis themselves had initiated a move towards neutral umpires for Test cricket.

At the end of the series in England, P. M. Lush, the England tour manager, said that he did not fear any reprisals. "If we want to have an umpire changed", he said, "there are procedures and I am sure that if we present the evidence on which our complaints is based, we will be given a fair hearing. It will be done without attracting publicity." His faith and his intentions were to be short-lived. By the end of the First Test in Pakistan, England's players and managers were convinced that both the umpires and the conditions favoured the home side.

PAKISTAN V ENGLAND 1987

Martin Johnson, 1989

England's sixth tour to Pakistan was ill-conceived from the outset, coming immediately after the World Cup, when both public and player interest were never going to be high, and following so closely on the five-Test series in England in the summer of 1987. The Pakistanis' visit to England had not been without acrimony, but not even the most hardened pessimist would have forecast that England's tour several months later would lead to some of the most shameful scenes witnessed in any sport, never mind one traditionally associated with fair play, courtesy and high moral values.

At one point, amidst allegations and counter-allegations of cheating, verbal abuse, crisis telephone calls to and from the Test and County Cricket Board at Lord's and a threat of strike action by the visiting players, it looked as if the tour might be abandoned in mid-series. However, after the England captain, Mike Gatting, had been ordered to write an unconditional apology to umpire Shakoor Rana, to which his team-mates reacted by producing an outspoken, contract-breaching statement, protesting at the board's instruction, the Second Test in Faisalabad was eventually completed. So, too, was the tour, which will go down as one of the more squalid in international cricket's history. Just about the only worthy memory of it was the bowling of the leg-spinner, Abdul Qadir, who in becoming only the fourth player to take 30 or more wickets in a three-Test series condemned England to their eighth defeat in 11 series and their third defeat in their last three series against Pakistan.

The seeds of discontent had been blowing in the wind ever since the first meeting between the two countries in Pakistan, on E. R. Dexter's 1961–62 tour. England won the first Test of that series. But they had not won another there, and a succession of visiting teams had returned home thinking that they had not been allowed to. At best they had come to regard the home umpires as incompetent; at worst, cheats. On Pakistan's 1982 tour to England, however, resentment went the other way. In a tight, three-Test series, the teams were level at one apiece before the deciding game at Headingley. There, umpire David Constant gave a decision which had a significant bearing on England squeezing home by three wickets. Afterwards Imran Khan, the Pakistan captain, was critical of the umpiring and blamed it for Pakistan's defeat.

Pakistan, who had been campaigning for neutral umpires since 1980, were further incensed before the start of their 1987 tour of England when the TCCB overruled their objections to umpires Constant and Ken Palmer. Both men stood in two Tests, and at Lord's and again at The Oval, umpire Constant was involved in incidents which aroused controversy. Pakistan's outwardly genial but outspoken manager, Haseeb Ahsan, described Constant as a "disgraceful person" – and when England embarked on their own tour, it was felt by some that Haseeb would orchestrate swift retribution. It was an unhealthy attitude, but one made understandable by suspicions that the pressure on Pakistan to win the Test series, after a nation-numbing defeat in the World Cup semi-finals, and again in the following one-day international series, almost guaranteed some use of shady tactics. In addition, following the retirement of Imran Khan, the captaincy had passed to Javed

Miandad, a volatile character and one viewed with grave misgivings by the England players.

It was in this disagreeable climate that the First Test began in Lahore, and there the long-smouldering bonfire at last caught alight. England's refusal to entertain Pakistan's objections to umpires Constant and Palmer rebounded on them when their own protest about the appointment of the controversial Shakeel Khan was ignored. The English players claimed afterwards that no fewer than nine incorrect decisions had been given in favour of Pakistan's bowlers, while during the match their disgust and disillusion had boiled over in an extraordinary incident involving Chris Broad. Given out, caught at the wicket, by Shakeel, Broad refused to accept the decision, and almost a minute elapsed before he was at last persuaded by his partner, Graham Gooch, to depart the crease.

Pakistan demanded that Broad be sent home as punishment, but the tour manager, Peter Lush, took the view that a stern reprimand would suffice. This was a mistake. Regardless of the provocation to which Mr Lush undoubtedly considered Broad and all the team had been subjected, a heavy fine should have been imposed for such a flagrant breach of discipline. Nor was this the right time for the manager to criticise openly the umpiring, as he did, and call for neutral umpires in Test matches. His statement more or less gave Gatting *carte blanche* to inflame the row publicly after the match, which Pakistan won easily by an innings. Qadir had figures of nine for 56 in the first innings and four for 45 in the second. Gatting, not to put too fine a point on it, accused the umpires of cheating when he said: "We knew roughly what to expect but never imagined it would be quite so blatant. They were desperate to win a Test match, but if I was them I wouldn't be very happy about the way they did it."

And so, in embittered mood – and with many of the players privately considering that Broad had done cricket a service by highlighting what they saw as years of injustice to visiting teams – the touring party moved on to the Montgomery Biscuit Factory at Sahiwal, where there was a three-day match against the Punjab Chief Minister's XI. Absent, however, were the manager and captain. They, along with Gooch and Neil Foster, remained in Lahore for three days before the team travelled to Faisalabad for the Second Test.

There, despite the England management's complaint that their request to be informed of the umpiring appointments in private and in advance had not been met in Lahore, they again learnt only through the local press of the two officials for the match. And they were less than delighted to discover that Shakoor Rana was one of them. The umpire's reputation for upsetting visiting teams, notably when the New Zealand captain, J. V. Coney, led his team off the field in protest during the Karachi Test in 1984–85, was already known to them.

On the second day of the Faisalabad Test match, there had already been one unsavoury incident, following Shakoor's rejection of a bat-pad appeal from Bill Athey, when, three deliveries from the end of play, an extraordinary sequence of events was set in motion by a furious on-the-field row between Gatting and the umpire. Shakoor accused Gatting of sharp practice in allegedly moving a fielder without informing the batsman (which Gatting denied). Within seconds the two were locked in a toe-to-toe, finger-wagging exchange – scenes that were to arouse mixed reactions from TV viewers in Britain. Shakoor accused the England captain of heaping abuse on him; Gatting claimed that he was sworn at first and also called a cheat.

It was not until the following morning that the full magnitude of the row became clear. Shakoor refused to take the field until he received an apology from Gatting, and Gatting declined to apologise unless the umpire reciprocated. The third day's play was lost while officials of both camps strove for an acceptable solution. At one stage a settlement looked forthcoming, but Shakoor (prompted, it is thought, by the Pakistan captain, Javed Miandad) dug his heels in again after initially agreeing to a joint apology.

Negotiations continued through the night and into the rest day, with Shakoor confined to a hotel room. But Mr Lush's exhaustive attempts to resolve the impasses were frequently frustrated by the elusiveness of Pakistani officials. On the afternoon of the abortive third day, Ijaz Butt, secretary of the BCCP, left Faisalabad for Lahore; when Mr Lush undertook the two-and-a-half-hour drive there himself, in the hope of discussing the situation with the BCCP president, Lt-General Safdar Butt, he was told that the general was out to dinner. He was thus forced to stay overnight in Lahore so that he could meet the two Butts next day, along with Haseeb, who was both a BCCP member and chairman of Pakistan's selectors.

Throughout, the England management were in contact with Lord's. By co-incidence, the TCCB's winter meeting was being held on the day that was the rest day in Faisalabad, and it was there that the private decision was taken to instruct Gatting to apologise if no compromise could be reached. Both the manager and the captain were furious at the order, but they had little option but to comply. Consequently, on the morning of the fourth day Gatting handed the umpire the following, hand-written note. "Dear Shakoor Rana, I apologise for the bad language used during the 2nd day of the Test match at Fisalabad (sic). Mike Gatting, 11th Dec 1987."

In London, the TCCB issued a statement which read: "It was unanimously agreed that the current Test match in Faisalabad should restart today after the rest day. The board manager in Pakistan, Peter Lush, was advised of this decision immediately and asked to take whatever action was necessary to implement it. In reaching their decision the members of the board recognised the extremely diffi-cult circumstances of the tour and the inevitable frustration for the players arising from those circumstances, but they believe it to be in the long-term interests of the game as a whole for the match to be completed. The board will be issuing a statement on the tour when it is finished, but in the meantime the chairman and chief executive will be going to Karachi for the final Test next week."

In Faisalabad, Mr Lush issued a statement which read: "The Test and County Cricket Board has instructed me as manager of the England team to do every-thing possible to ensure that this Test match continues today and that we honour our obligations to complete the tour of Pakistan. We have tried to resolve amicably the difference between Mike Gatting and umpire Shakoor Rana following their heated exchange of words which took place on the second day. We all hoped this could have been achieved in private and with a handshake. Umpire Shakoor Rana has stated he would continue to officiate in this match if he received a written apology from Mike Gatting. The umpire has made it clear he will not apologise for the remarks he made to the England captain. In the wider interests of the game Mike Gatting has been instructed by the board to write an apology to Shakoor Rana, and this he has now done."

The players themselves had already agreed to refuse to play on if their captain received such an instruction, but when it came, they eventually decided to continue under protest. This they made public in the form of a fiercely worded statement voicing their unequivocal support for the captain and their disgust with the board. "The England players deplore the fact that it was not possible to effect a compromise solution between Mike Gatting and umpire Shakoor Rana. We would have expected the governing bodies of both countries to use their influence and authority to resolve the problem.

"What is beyond dispute is that the umpire was the first to use foul and abusive language to the England captain. This was clearly heard by England players close to the incident. Mike Gatting was ready to apologise two days ago for his response, provided the umpire would do the same. We also wish to register a unanimous protest that the TCCB should consider it necessary to issue instructions through our manager, Peter Lush, to order the captain to make an unconditional apology to the umpire. By doing so, the captain, in the wider interests of the game, felt he was forced to act against his own free will.

"An earlier statement from the TCCB said that the problem had been left in the hands of the England management to resolve as they thought fit. The instructions issued to the manager last night left him virtually no room for manoeuvre. The TCCB exerted pressure on Mike Gatting and on the rest of us, and we are unanimous in the view that the same 'wider interests of the game' referred to by our board had been completely ignored by the BCCP, who did not exert similar pressure on the umpire. The incident was sad for cricket but the solution forced upon us is even sadder."

There was suspicion in the England camp that the TCCB had bowed to both political and financial pressures, regardless of their wider interest claims. This the board denied, although it was later conceded that a senior Foreign Office official had voiced government concern, and also that a substantial slice of the tour guarantee money had yet to be paid by Pakistan. Such was the strength of feeling conveyed back to Lord's that when Mr A. C. Smith, the board's chief executive, and its chairman, Mr Raman Subba Row, flew out to Karachi, they were in a conciliatory rather than a punitive mood.

Gatting, who had been contemplating resignation, was placated by Mr Subba Row's announcement of the board's full backing for him, plus the concession that the board was at fault – not only for not appreciating the full extent of the team's problems, but also in not sending representatives to Lahore when the first hint of serious unrest surfaced. Furthermore, Mr Subba Row accepted the players' claim that Shakoor had initiated the swearing episode and also had called the England captain a cheat. This, said the board chairman, had been totally unjustified. However, he was less successful in his attempts to secure a belated apology from the umpire, although after the tour it was learnt that Gatting had received a letter from Shakoor Rana. It was not made public by the England captain at the time (during the Third Test) because it was an expression of regret rather than an apology.

Toe to toe: Shakoor Rana and Mike Gatting during their slanging match at Faisalabad in 1987. A whole day's play was lost, with both parties skulking in their tents, until England's captain was ordered to apologise.

It was odd, none the less, that Gatting declined to mention at the time that he had received a communication, however unsatisfactory he personally felt it to be. Even odder, though, was the decision to try to keep secret the award of £1,000 to each player by way of a hardship bonus. When, as it inevitably did, it came into the open, the board was badly placed to fend off allegations that the money had been awarded either by way of a bribe to save the tour or as conscience money for its poor handling of the affair. Mr Subba Row was later reprimanded for acting unilaterally, and it is highly unlikely that the board would have agreed to the payment. Whatever England's grievances, they had received extra financial reward for having performed poorly, both as cricketers and as ambassadors for their country.

All in all, the disgraceful events at Lahore and Faisalabad tended to deflect from the fact that the team performed poorly. Sadder still was the thought that cricket may never again recapture its reputation as a bastion for old-style values.

AN ACCEPTABLE STANDARD OF BEHAVIOUR Graeme Wright, *Notes by the Editor*, 1988

Britain has good reason to be proud of a tradition of civilised behaviour. But in recent years the tradition and indeed the civilisation have been endangered by the unacceptable increase in violent attitudes. I am not referring to criminal violence such as physical assault; rather the ill-tempered outbursts one encounters from otherwise law-abiding citizens. This behaviour is manifest on our roads, on public transport, in restaurants and at sports grounds. Consideration towards those about us is in decline; tolerance has given way to a short-fused temper.

There are some, among whom are our politicians, for whom such attitudes of verbal aggression are a device, a professional posturing. But politicians have a duty to society. When they are heard on the radio and television bickering, shrilly dissenting and by no means behaving in a civil manner, who can throw up his hands when the average citizen emulates those who are regarded as the country's leaders? It was not without significance that Mike Gatting, when called upon by the TCCB to apologise for his behaviour towards the Pakistani umpire, Shakoor Rana, was reported to have said, "Does Maggie [Mrs Thatcher, the prime minister] back down when she's given no choice?" The implication was that he could see no difference between his own outburst against an umpire he felt was behaving unjustly and that of the prime minister against her opponents.

The refusal of Chris Broad, England's opening batsman, to leave the wicket when given out in the First Test in Pakistan cannot be condoned. He received a reprimand but was subject to no other disciplinary measure. On a rainy day at Nottingham, he would do well to read sections one and two of the Professional Golfers' Association code of ethics, and thank his lucky stars he is a professional cricketer and not a golfer. Cited in mitigation were the frustrations of the England players which had been allowed to build up during the tour as a result of some bad umpiring. Sympathy was the prevailing sentiment. In the next Test match, at Faisalabad, Gatting lost his temper and indulged in an unedifying confrontation with Shakoor Rana. The nation was then held spellbound by the spectacle of two grown men standing on their dignity without a square inch of moral ground to support them. At the time of writing, no action had been taken against Gatting.

Whether or not it should have been, time will provide an answer. A glance at what has happened in two other sports, however, suggests it should have been. Rugby Union and tennis have suffered at lower levels from the example of ill discipline at the highest level. When the British Lions rugby team toured South Africa in 1974, and won a series there for the first time, part and parcel of their game plan was the now infamous "99 call". In the event of provocation or aggression against a Lions forward, his fellow forwards would immediately pitch into the opposition. The purpose was twofold. It showed the opposing side that the Lions could not be intimidated, and it made it impossible for the referee to send off any one player for retaliation. The consequences of this policy are still being felt today in club rugby, especially in Wales where a lack of discipline leads to outbursts of violence throughout the season. In tennis, the boorish behaviour of some leading players has permeated through to junior ranks so that coaches in England now complain that their young charges could win Wimbledon on the strength of their tantrums, but lack the tennis skills to match them.

I doubt if there is a cricketer anywhere who has not been upset by an umpire's decision, especially when – as can happen in club and village matches – that umpire has affiliations with the other side. But without the unchallenged acceptance of the principle that the umpire's word is final, what chance does the game have? Professional sportsmen set the standards of behaviour for those who play the game at all levels, just as those in authority have a responsibility to ensure that they do. A cricket master, reporting on his school's season for *Wisden*, informed us that he had lost three senior players for disciplinary reasons. "All I can say after 19 years with the XI," he wrote, "is that a schoolmaster must uphold behaviour standards, even at the cost of losing his best players."

Like it or not, the England captain has a responsibility to England cricket. On the day that the national team left Heathrow for New Zealand, the Cricket Council announced its marketing strategy to introduce Kwik Cricket into primary schools, club colts sections and community groups. There is a significant sponsorship of £550,000 from the Milk Marketing Board. The launch was planned, in advance of the happenings in Pakistan, so that it would coincide with the England team's departure, partly to obtain maximum publicity, partly to show the Cricket Council's concern that cricket should be available to all. In the event, it was perhaps an unfortunate coincidence.

Never has cricket been more in need of firm leadership. The events in Pakistan showed that the management, in which I include the captain, instead of retaining a position from which they could provide leadership, allowed themselves to be drawn into the coterie of the players to the extent that sympathy for them was allowed to outweigh the most important issues. Leadership is not simply issuing commands. As in business, it is a matter of understanding employees, conditions, resources and competition. History is something to be drawn upon; not put behind and forgotten. One wonders if in the offices of the TCCB there is a desk with a drawer filled with past managers' and captains' reports which have never been read again. This past tour was not the first to Pakistan by a cricket team, and nor will it be the last. Gatting had toured there twice before with England teams. He knew what the conditions were like and, as captain, should have helped his side rise above them. He could not; nor, it appears, could the tour manager or the cricket manager. Even the chairman of the Cricket Council and TCCB, Raman Subba Row, was so moved by the players' pity for themselves that, without the sanction of the board, he gave the players a bonus of £1,000 each. My first thought was to wonder how a soldier serving in Northern Ireland felt about that.

Gatting's outburst, of course, drew public support from those who suppose that Britain should stand up to the indignities perpetrated upon it by other countries, especially those of the third world. They ignore that what gives a nation its civilisation is its ability to accept these provocations without feeling a need to retaliate. It is an ability to judge when an issue is so morally wrong that action must be taken which makes a country great. A spat with an umpire in a cricket match is not one of those occasions.

DISGRACE IN INDIA
R. Mohan and Sudhir Vaidya, 1992

While modern batsmen may need more than a wand of willow to protect themselves on the field of play, a degree in law may become a prerequisite for informed cricket journalism in India. To see the game being dragged to the courts was not a unique experience, but the sight of a bowler uprooting a stump to assault a batsman certainly was. Such an extraordinary incident, in the final of the nation's premier tournament, the Duleep Trophy, was the worst instance of the deterioration in standards of behaviour.

The violent action, senseless yet far from unprovoked, of Rashid Patel of West Zone, who went after Raman Lamba of North Zone, stump in hand, will be remembered as the most shameful moment in the history of Indian cricket. It occurred on the final afternoon of the five-day match in Jamshedpur, after Patel had come down the pitch to aim a head-high full toss at the batsman, Lamba. Nor was it the only controversy of a game in which senior players questioned the umpires' decisions and berated officials. Yet in the end, the Board of Control for Cricket in India seemed to draw a veil over the acrimony which found its final expression in the beamer attack, for none of the players were disciplined except for Patel and Lamba, who were banned for 13 and ten months respectively. The sequel to the violence on the pitch was a riot in the crowd, which resulted in the covers and anything else suitable being set alight, bringing the match to a premature conclusion.

The report of this dramatic incident is a little unsatisfactory. The authors say that Patel's action was "far from unprovoked", but we are not told the nature of the provocation. It would have to have been extreme, indeed, to justify an attack first with a beamer and then with a stump. It appears, reading other reports, that a row had been simmering between the two for some time. But perhaps Lamba's real provocation had been to score 180 out of North Zone's monumental first innings of 729 for nine declared. The tragic footnote to this sorry story is that, seven years later, Lamba died when he was struck by the ball while fielding at forward short leg in a club match in Bangladesh. He was 38.

THE DIRT-IN-POCKET AFFAIR

Matthew Engel, *Notes by the Editor*, 1995

Possibly the most bizarre cricketing moment in 1994 was the conversation that took place between Ossie Wheatley, then the chairman of the TCCB cricket committee, and a former Test bowler whose anonymity we will preserve. Wheatley was giving details of his conversations with an Indian rocket scientist working for NASA who had explained to him the aerodynamic principles behind reverse swing. "Horsefeathers" (or something like that), said the Test player. "There's no such thing as reverse swing. It's a complete con."

This was just a postscript to the affair that for a week convulsed English cricket: when Mike Atherton appeared to perform what was officially called, with splendid coyness, "unfamiliar action on the ball" as Darren Gough was trying to induce reverse swing. Several months on, the TV pictures remain puzzling, Atherton's evasiveness remains discreditable.

What is hard to recreate is the febrile atmosphere of the time in which every saloon bar in the land was unanimous that Atherton was cheating, while those best-placed to know how to fiddle with a cricket ball were least convinced – or did not even believe reverse swing existed.

We shall never know the truth unless and until Atherton publishes his memoirs with a chapter headed "Bang to Rights: Of course I did it." But perhaps even Atherton did not know quite what he was doing and why: the human mind is complex and captaining England is a very stressful job. But, according to old team-mates, Atherton bowled with dust in his pockets in his leg-spinning days when he was definitely not trying to reverse swing it. Traditional British justice and common sense suggest that we should not destroy the career of any sportsman unless the evidence of his malfeasance is absolutely clear-cut – and, before anyone says anything, this is not out of line with what *Wisden* said about the Pakistani bowlers in similar circumstances two years ago.

However, the modern British way is to damn people first and ask questions later; it is an attitude of mind promoted by our newspapers and it is having an insidious effect on national life. The American Ring Lardner wrote a short story called *The Champ*, about a boxer who got away with every kind of evil because he was the champ; had Lardner been British he would have written the story the other way round.

Atherton was the right choice to captain England. Nothing has happened to change that. He has made mistakes but has a sense of what needs to be done, and deserves the chance to bring that to fruition. That should not be tossed away lightly, by him or the rest of us.

CHEATING: THE SECRET HISTORY
Derek Pringle, 1995

Cricketers have always crossed over into unfairness in seeking to gain the advantage. In the late 18th century, when cricket was very largely a gambling game, whole teams were bribed to throw matches. In 1817, William Lambert, the greatest batsman of his era, was forced out of cricket for corruption. Around the same time, there was a farcical match between England and Nottinghamshire in which both sides had sold the match, so batsmen were trying to get out to bowlers who were doing their best to avoid taking wickets.

W. G. Grace, the first cricketing superstar, was regularly guilty of irksome subterfuges within the law. He was also a notorious sledger. In 1921, J. W. H. T. Douglas, the England captain in Australia, supposedly threatened to report Arthur Mailey for illegally using resin to grip the ball – until Mailey pointed out that Douglas's own thumbnail had been worn to the flesh picking the seam for his own bowlers.

Until recently most infractions were either ignored by the umpires, or sorted out with a quiet word in the ear of either the culprit or the captain. One umpire just stared at the ball, as treated by an England fast bowler, and said: "You better take six wickets with that or there'll be trouble." The media and television, in particular, have changed all that. As Graham Gooch put it: "What for years were accepted but mildly frowned-upon practices, like picking the seam, have now been labelled cheating. That's a big word. What people would once have had a bit of a laugh about in the bar is now being flatly denied. Nobody wants to be labelled a cheat. It's all the media's fault for going overboard to get their story." The *Sunday Mirror* recently quoted Geoff Boycott admitting that Yorkshire players in his day sometimes played around with the ball. Three of the first 55 words were bombshell, incredible and sensationally.

So administrators have clamped down on practices like seam-lifting, using lipsalve to maintain the shine and, horror of horrors, batsmen getting their spikes into the pitch to break it up once their team is in the ascendancy. All these actions are premeditated. In a court of law, a premeditated crime is considered far worse than one committed on the spur of the moment. But in cricket these have traditionally been regarded far more lightly than the behaviour of the chancer who on the spur of the moment refuses to walk or claims a catch on the bounce.

Picking the seam has been endemic to the professional game for years. Usually, that is the action of the individual bowler not only to try and get an advantage over the batsmen but to get one over on his fellow bowlers by taking more wickets than them and keeping his place in the team. A professional playing a team game has more than one objective in his mind.

In contrast, keeping the ball shiny by using lipsalve requires a team effort. Very often, at county level, this has been sanctioned not only by the captain but also by the ex-players who are umpires. There was an incident that reputedly took place in the law-abiding surroundings of Tunbridge Wells, of all places, where the visiting slip fielders returned the ball to the fast bowler before they had time to rub in whatever substance was being used that day. The bowler bellowed out: "What's this greasy stuff someone's put all over the ball?"

"In my day, everyone cleaned the seam," recalled the former Northamptonshire and England bowler Frank Tyson. "You had to, playing on uncovered wickets. Inevitably, the seam would get lifted as well. Some sides were notorious for it. Brylcreem and hair oil would also find their way on to the ball. Both were widely used as part of the fashion of the day. Of course, it was no bloody use to me. I had no hair to put it on even then."

This was in clear contravention of the Laws and yet, until recently, this sort of thing was far more acceptable than a batsman not walking, though this was not in breach of any written rule. It may have something to do with the fact that, when the distinction still existed, batsmen were a mixture of amateurs and professionals, whereas bowlers were far more likely to be professional. As Bob Appleyard, the former Yorkshire and England bowler, confirmed, when asked if everyone in his day walked: "Ay, mostly. But those who didn't were more likely to be professional. It was, perhaps, easier for amateurs to live up to gentlemanly notions of fair play than for professionals who had a living to scrape together."

However, gentlemanliness always had its limits. In the 1960s and 1970s some well-known batsmen were believed to have built up unblemished reputations for walking when an edged catch was obvious, but standing their ground when less obvious chances were offered in more critical situations, relying on their good name to be given not out. This was a very English phenomenon. Ray Lindwall says none of his contemporaries ever walked – except Neil Harvey, once, for lbw in a Test match.

"To walk or not to walk?" was still a debate on the England tour of Australia in 1982–83. The rest of the world had stopped walking at Test level at least a decade earlier, but England held a team meeting in which Ian Botham vehemently insisted that, if anyone walked, it would be over his dead body. His argument was that England would be getting no favours from Australian umpires and probably bad decisions too. Several players felt uncomfortable with this line and in the end Bob Willis, as captain, left it up to the individual.

Not walking might break the spirit of the game, but it is harder for batsmen to break the Laws. When "Shock" White walked out in the 18th century with a bat wider than the stumps it was not then illegal; and Dennis Lillee was not breaking any existing law when he used an aluminium bat against England in 1979–80. However, it is not unknown for lead weights to be put in the back of bats to make them bottom-heavy, and bowlers these days get annoyed by batsmen using fibreglass tape, which has an abrasive effect on the ball, rather than Elastoplast to bind their bats. No one screams that anyone should be drummed out of the game for this.

Thus fair play is largely a notion that affects bowlers. And far from being a blessing, it is becoming an encumbrance for players as the game finds itself a vehicle for moral and behavioural issues far beyond its compass. The word "cheat" has been much bandied round in the past three seasons when first the Pakistani fast bowlers and then England captain Mike Atherton were accused of illegally helping the ball reverse swing.

The discovery of reverse swing is a perfect example of man's triumph over an unhelpful environment in order to survive. Playing on grassless pitches of low bounce with hard, bare outfields, where cricket balls rapidly deteriorate, Pakistan's bowlers developed a method of swinging an old ball. It requires a creation of opposites on the ball's surface, a kind of Yin and Yang effect where one side is kept smooth and damp while the other is allowed to roughen but is kept scrupulously dry. It has to be a team effort, for any dampness on the rough side will negate the swing.

This has not always been achieved legally, and Imran Khan has admitted once using a bottle-top to scratch one side of the ball to speed up its deterioration. But not long ago, roughing up a ball by rubbing it in the dirt was accepted practice. One county captain was seen to do the job against the concrete on the pavilion steps. Granted, it was done in those days to improve the grip for the spinners, but where's the difference?

So was Atherton cheating? To my eyes, there was no evidence that he was taking any action to alter the state of the ball and there is no regulation to stop a player having a pocketful of soil. There is a danger now that the authorities will be panicked into rewriting the Laws yet again. The contest between bat and ball will work best with a minimum of fuss and a maximum of self-regulation.

THE END OF CHIVALRY
Andrew Longmore, 1998

Now that Eton v Harrow is no longer the great social occasion of an English summer, cricket between English public schools rarely gets much space in the national press. The 1997 match between Marlborough and Radley was different.

On a rain-hit day, Marlborough, who were put in to bat, spent 68.3 overs scoring 170, leaving Radley a mere 18 overs in reply. The Marlborough innings was marred by verbal abuse of the batsmen and a number of deliberate no-balls, while on the boundary tempers flared among the spectators. The warden of Radley admitted that the match was not played in an attractive atmosphere, and fixtures in major sports between these two historic schools were cancelled for the foreseeable future.

Though the most publicised, this was not the only instance of bad sportsmanship to emerge from schools who once epitomised the Corinthian spirit so absolutely that they would remove their goalkeeper if they conceded a penalty, on the grounds that to defend the consequences of foul play would be improper.

In an Under-17 match in Kent, a boy spat at the wicket-keeper after being bowled and had to be forced into the opposition dressing-room at the end of play to apologise. A match between two crack cricketing schools, Tonbridge of Kent and Grey High School from Port Elizabeth, South Africa, with both sides protecting unbeaten records, quickly degenerated from competitiveness into verbal intimidation, and highlighted a clash of prevailing sporting cultures. Tonbridge won, but only after an unpleasant afternoon. One of the umpires deemed the South Africans 80 per cent responsible. "Most schools will now play two or three overseas sides a season," Paul Taylor, the Tonbridge cricket master, said. "That has an influence on the boys. Grey were competitive to a degree our players had not seen before and one of our boys was drawn into that."

Here, in microcosm, is English cricket's dilemma. "We have to get a bit of nastiness into our game," the England vice-captain Nasser Hussain said the day after Australia had secured the Ashes for the fifth consecutive series. "In Australia, even in grade cricket, they are abusing you, rucking you and making it very clear they want you back in the pavilion pretty quick." There is a danger that, because Australia have been winning and England losing, the courtesies which the English gave to the cricketing world get blamed for the problems.

Umpires at every level of the English game report that teams are more voluble, more excitable, harder to control than once they were. Very few batsmen walk; bowlers pout and teapot when decisions go against them. Encouragement by the fielding side too often crosses the thin line between morale-boosting and naked intimidation – an average of three times in each county match, according to one first-class umpire – and ordinary league clubs are framing their own disciplinary code to enforce standards which, old timers will tell you, were once instinctive.

In a NatWest Trophy match, two Devon batsmen were treated to premeditated verbal – and personal – abuse by the Leicestershire players. And an incident of persistent intimidation of the umpires, in a Bassetlaw and District League match, resulted in a nine-match ban for one captain, a deduction of points and the ostracism by his club of one of the umpires.

Some people say that the game merely reflects modern society, which is louder and more aggressive. Cricket's reputation for good manners has always been a convenient mask for skulduggery, from W. G. onwards. If as the anecdote claims, W. G. was bowled and replaced the bails blaming the wind, these days 15 television cameras would have proved him a cheat. Is it too cynical to suggest that a similar thought passed through the head of Ian Healy, the brilliant Australian wicketkeeper, who disclaimed a dubious catch at Lord's and was applauded for his sportsmanship by umpire David Shepherd on the field and by the entire national press the following morning? Healy is not a cheat, but he may be a pragmatist.

The Australians won, however, without any excesses. The series, given the intense scrutiny, was remarkably free of rancour. That is as it should be. Cricket is a contact sport no less than rugby or football, but it is contact of the mind. Its skills are subtler, its rituals more pronounced. The umpires take the field first, the batsmen leave first, generally applauded by the fielding side. In between, the action is more sedate, calculating and thoughtful. There is time for respect and, as Mark Ilott and Robert Croft would doubtless confirm after their puerile shoving match in the NatWest Trophy semi-final, embarrassment. If protocol is breached, if some fielders slip into the pavilion before the opposing batsmen, the game will not collapse in a heap, it will simply be more anarchic and less attractive.

Test cricket ceased to be a metaphor for fair play long before the systematic assault on a batsman's confidence which has become known as sledging became fashionable. The sadness is that the practice has been lauded, mistaken as a prerequisite for excellence. There is an excuse for Test players, earning a hard living from the game, going over the top. There is none for schoolboys.

"We don't want public-school cricket to go back ten years, we've got to move to playing the game relevantly," says Paul Taylor of Tonbridge. "But you can make opposing batsmen feel uncomfortable by bowling and fielding tightly, not by abusing them. Players must respect their opponents as cricketers and people."

The responsibility lies with the headmasters and cricket masters, who in the current cut-throat educational climate can fall prey to the same fear of losing as many football managers. The move towards employing recently retired first-class cricketers as coaches has also consciously or subconsciously encouraged a misplaced sense of professionalism. They, like cricketers from Lord's to Little Snoring, need to be reminded: England did not lose to Australia because they were too well-mannered; they lost because they were not good enough.

SCUFF AND NONSENSE   R. Mohan and Sudhir Vaidya, 1999

For the first time in the 64 seasons of the Ranji Trophy, two teams were debarred from the competition. Tamil Nadu and Delhi were both disqualified after the pitch was scuffed up during a drinks break in their match at Chennai in February. It had seemed safe to assume that one of Tamil Nadu's players was responsible, as they had both motive and opportunity: they had a big score on the board, and the Delhi batsmen, who were wearing rubber-soled shoes, were with the umpires as they took refreshments. The referee ordered that the pitch should be repaired so that play could resume on the final day, a decision some questioned. But the Delhi captain, Ajay Sharma, simply refused to continue the pursuit of Tamil Nadu's score of 473.

It took several months for the Board of Control for Cricket in India to find out who was to blame. Eventually, the Tamil Nadu wicket-keeper Reuben Paul was named, and initially banned for life from first-class cricket. This was later reduced to a one-year ban, and then nothing. In the meantime, rough and ready justice had been administered: Tamil Nadu were suspended for tampering with the pitch, and Delhi for refusing to resume. The innocent players on both sides were the losers.

AN ATMOSPHERE OF LAWLESSNESS   Graeme Wright, Notes by the Editor, 2002

The word "anarchy" appeared in cricket headlines a few times in 2001; not something anyone should be proud of. An atmosphere of lawlessness hung over the first two Tests between Sri Lanka and England in March; by November, India and South Africa had taken the law into their own hands. In Sri Lanka, the umpires were under siege – psychologically if not physically; in South Africa it was the match referee, Mike Denness.

Denness was officiating at the Second Test between South Africa and India at

Port Elizabeth when he imposed penalties on six Indian players and incurred the wrath of a nation. It would be unfair to say he brought the game to the brink of schism; others did that, among them Jagmohan Dalmiya, former president of the ICC and, since September 2001, president of the Indian board. When India took umbrage at Denness's penalties and insisted he be removed as referee for the final Test – otherwise the team would go home and take their lucrative television purse with them – the South African board buckled under the threat of lost revenue. Denness was denied access to the Third Test, at Centurion, and the ICC withdrew their imprimatur. For the time being anyway: past experience warns that one should never take any ICC ruling for granted. But as things stand, the match at Centurion does not count as an official Test.

Viewed dispassionately, it was difficult to gauge what grieved the Indians more: the fact that prime among the penalised was Tendulkar, accorded god-like status by his millions of adoring fans, or that Denness, white and British, a former England captain, was a representative of the old colonial power. Accusations of racism, because he took no action against the South Africans' appeals and sledging, muddied the waters further.

Tendulkar (we'll come to the other five) was caught up in the catch-all crime of bringing the game into disrepute, fined 75% of his match fee and given a one-match suspended ban. Denness, watching on television, had caught him interfering with the ball "by himself and without the on-field umpire's supervision under Law 42.3 (a)(ii) and Law 42.3 (b)". The umpires appear not to have noticed anything untoward, and the condition of the ball had not changed sufficiently to attract their attention, or the statutory five-run penalty. In fact, Tendulkar was most likely cleaning the seam and guilty on a technicality at worst. By the time the headline writers had put their slant on it, the crime was ball-tampering and the incendiaries were burning effigies of Denness.

In another year, the matter might have ended with the unofficial Test. But Denness, as well as fining captain Sourav Ganguly, Virender Sehwag, Harbhajan Singh, Deep Dasgupta and Shiv Sunder Das for other breaches of the code of conduct, also handed out a one-Test suspension to Sehwag, who had earlier hit a hundred on debut at Bloemfontein. In happier circumstances, that would have been the Centurion match. Now, however, India's next Test, as far as the ICC were concerned, was against England at Mohali in December. India, who had not played Sehwag at Centurion, argued otherwise and a period of brinkmanship followed. The Indian selectors included Sehwag in their squad; the ICC's new chief executive, Malcolm Speed, warned in no uncertain manner that the council would not give the Test official status if he played; the ECB said England would not take part in an unofficial match. For a day or two there was the threat of an international split. One deadline passed but eventually, perhaps inevitably, India accepted Speed's offer to set up a "referees commission" to investigate whether Denness had acted in accordance with the code of conduct, the role of referees generally and whether players should have a right of appeal. Given that the ICC executive board had already agreed to strengthen the disciplinary power of referees from April 2002, the commission looked like being about as sabre-toothed as its name.

SOUTH AFRICA V INDIA 2001

Unofficial Test

At Centurion, November 23, 24, 25, 26, 27, 2001.
South Africa won by an innings and 73 runs.

Dicky Rutnagnur and Amit Varma, 2003

The match was neither one thing nor the other. The South African team were told by their board to treat it as unofficial, while India were under orders to treat it as a proper Test. Yet it was South Africa who rolled on methodically and relentlessly, and the Indians who were lacklustre and bored and threw the match away with feckless batting and wayward bowling.

With the ICC officials departed, the South African board appointed two home umpires and a home referee, Denis Lindsay, who was to supervise India's series with England in December. Despite withdrawing Test status, the ICC promised no reprisals. They did not, however, accept that Virender Sehwag's omission here fulfilled his one-Test suspension. Ganguly took the opportunity to rest after back spasms; Connor Williams stepped up for his first game of the tour, an international debut of sorts for him and for Jacques Rudolph, both of whom were left, like Alan Jones after the England v Rest of the World series in 1970, in the limbo of the nearly capped.

In the circumstances, it was little surprise that the Indians were overwhelmed by the South African batsmen. Gibbs and Kirsten shared a century opening partnership; Kallis scored 110 in 234 balls, with 18 fours; and finally Pollock moved the game up a couple of gears, dashing to 113 in 109 balls, with nine fours and seven sixes, before declaring 334 ahead on the fourth morning. Williams and Das batted bravely to reach 92 without loss, but both fell before rain brought an early close. The South Africans needed only six more wickets on the final day, as Srinath and Prasad were both injured. Srinath had managed to bowl 27 overs with a broken finger on his left hand (struck by Hayward on the first evening), while Prasad had hurt his neck. Their colleagues – including Tendulkar, who played ludicrously, as though imitating the wild abandon of Harbhajan's batting in the nets – were bowled out with most of two sessions remaining.

Toss: South Africa. **India 232** (S. S. Das 46, D. B. Dasgupta 36; M. Hayward 4–74) **and 261** (S. S. Das 48, C. C. Williams 42, S. R. Tendulkar 40, Harbhajan Singh 30); **South Africa 566-8 dec.** (H. H. Gibbs 59, G. Kirsten 90, J. H. Kallis 110, N. D. McKenzie 33, L. Klusener 33, S. M. Pollock 113*, M. Ntini 34*, Extras 34).

Bribery and Corruption
(Alleged)

M atthew Engel, in a warning he issued in 2005 about the ever-present dangers of corruption in cricket, said that the spate of betting scandals in the mid-1990s "came close to destroying international cricket". Several leading players were implicated and their careers ended in disgrace; others escaped with fines and suspensions; the life of the man who came to symbolise the canker at the heart of cricket, Hansie Cronje, ended in a plane crash.

It was an ugly, dangerous story that remains clouded in fog. There is a great deal of detail, accusation and counter-accusation, but little clarity. Even Cronje's role, as Rob Steen shows, is still argued over: the former South African captain's claim that he did not throw matches has never been disproved, though clearly he was helping bookmakers to "fix" aspects of matches. Whether certain matches were indeed fixed – Pakistan's defeat against Bangladesh in the 1999 World Cup remains the most notorious suspect – has also never been proven. In the absence of a true "closure", the suspicions remain. "The known facts about match-fixing are bad enough," wrote Engel at the height of the panic in 1999. "What is suspected is terrible. If even a fraction of the rumours doing the rounds are true, it would be diabolical." We still do not know whether the situation was diabolical or just terrible.

What can be said with certainty is that the cricket authorities were wretchedly slow and pusillanimous in dealing with this threat to the integrity of the game. "ICC's policy of damage limitation leaves most questions in this affair unanswered, and leaves Salim Malik's reputation forever besmirched by assumptions and innuendo," wrote David Hopps in the early stages of what, even in 1996, *Wisden* was already calling the "bribes crisis". If only cricket's administrators had been as quick to see the gravity of the situation.

The problem was the division of responsibility between the ICC and the national boards, too many of whom shied away from meeting the crisis head on. "Cricket-watchers have never had much faith in the game's administrators," said *Wisden* in 1999. "But what they expect is incompetence, not cynicism. In fact, the ICC investigation never materialised as such. The national boards, obsessed by territorial imperative, refused to allow it." And so the poison identified by Engel did its work until the inquiry into Cronje's crazy, almost inexplicable actions shed much-needed light on a decade in which Test cricketers, some of them very famous names indeed, thought little of doing deals with bookmakers for a few thousand pounds, selling their sport very cheaply indeed.

In part, they were willing to make that trade because the sport had undermined itself by allowing the number of pointless, instantly forgotten one-day games to multiply. "The international programme, particularly as played by India and Pakistan, is a guaranteed recipe for jiggery-pokery," wrote Engel in 1998. "The one-day tournaments of which these countries are so fond have no real meaning. No one remembers who wins them, so honour can never overcome profit. And the actual rewards for victory are hardly exciting. England's success in the Sharjah Champions Trophy won them just £25,000 between a squad of 14. Champion golfers tip their waiters better than that, never mind their caddies."

It was a system ripe for exploitation – and it was ruthlessly exploited by Indian bookmakers and South African gamblers. Somehow, the sport survived – and in Cronje found something close to a sacrificial victim. But its survival was due more to luck than judgment, and Cronje's death was no catharsis. The only lesson is that the authorities must be eternally vigilant. And that when international cricket teams meet, the encounter ought to be more than merely televised wallpaper.   S. M.

THE BRIBES CRISIS   David Hopps, 1996

Australia's chief executive, Graham Halbish, called it cricket's greatest crisis for 20 years. If the Salim Malik affair is ultimately survived without excessive disorder, it will be largely due to the game's inclination to suppress a scandal rather than investigate it. When three Australian players allege that the captain of Pakistan offered them bribes to throw matches, and when talk is rife of illegal betting scams throughout Asia, which have burgeoned since the introduction of satellite TV coverage, then crisis is a reasonable word.

The International Cricket Council's failure to take a central role by conducting an immediate inquiry – preferring instead to act as a conduit between the two nations involved – identified it as a body hopelessly unempowered to manage the international game convincingly. In an increasingly litigious world, governing bodies in many sports are reluctant to act, for fear that their authority will be undermined in a civil court. There must be a measure of sympathy for their predicament. But the ICC's policy of damage limitation leaves most questions in this affair unanswered, and leaves Salim Malik's reputation forever besmirched by assumptions and innuendo.

Malik *was* cleared of the allegations by an independent inquiry in Pakistan. Frustrated by the ICC's failure to take control, the Pakistan board placed matters in the hands of Fakhruddin G. Ebrahim, a former Pakistani supreme court judge, and one-time attorney-general and governor of Sindh province. Ebrahim's investigation was hampered by Australia's unwillingness to subject their three players – Shane Warne, Tim May and Mark Waugh – to cross-examination in Pakistan, saying they feared for their welfare, and that they would be prepared to travel to London for any ICC inquiry. That left Ebrahim's investigation strictly limited. After studying a sworn statement from the three Australians, and cross-examining Malik, who was represented by counsel, at length, Judge Ebrahim concluded on October 21, 1995: "The allegations against Saleem (*sic*) Malik are not worthy of any credence and must be rejected as unfounded."

He angered the Australian Cricket Board with his final remark, suggesting that the allegations appear to have been concocted for reasons best known to the accusers. The ACB, a week later, condemned such comments as extraordinary and damaging. The Board also contended that ICC should have conducted an inquiry and was empowered to do so, under Rule 2 of its Code of Conduct. That states: "Players and team officials shall not at any time engage in conduct unbecoming to an international player or team official which could bring them or the game into disrepute."

The allegations arose from Australia's tour of Pakistan in late 1994. Warne's sworn statement contended that, on the fourth evening of the Test at Karachi (where Pakistan had never lost a Test, and where illegal bookmakers appear to wield considerable power), he received a phone call from Malik, in the presence of his room-mate, May. According to Warne, he visited Malik's room, whereupon Malik offered him $US200,000 (about £130,000) to bowl badly on the final day. Warne's affidavit assumed the money was to be shared between them; May interpreted it as $200,000 each. Ebrahim refused to believe that Malik "should offer a large sum of money not for any direct personal gain, but for the sake of the nation's pride." The judge appeared unaware of any suggestion that betting might be involved.

Warne's second charge in his affidavit concerned a conversation between Malik and Mark Waugh at a presidential reception before a one-day international in Rawalpindi. It was alleged that Waugh was offered $200,000 for four or five Australian players not to play well the next day. Incredibly, Pakistan did not hear of Australia's accusations for five months, and then only because the facts were deliberately leaked in finest Deep Throat tradition to Phil Wilkins of the *Sydney Morning Herald*. By that time, rumours of corruption on Pakistan's tours of South Africa and Zimbabwe were rife and two players, Rashid Latif and Basit Ali, went into temporary retirement, reportedly to bring matters to a head. Pakistan's loss to Zimbabwe in the First Test in Harare had been one of the greatest upsets in Test history. Before the match, Zimbabwe had been quoted at 40-1 with some Asian bookmakers, but went on to record their first win since becoming a full Test nation.

Intikhab Alam, Pakistan's team manager, confirmed that his team had been asked to swear on the Koran after the series against Australia that they were not involved with any betting syndicates. "I think that people have gone mad," he claimed. "There is no truth in it. It is terrible. These are very serious charges against the Pakistan team." Nevertheless, more than one Pakistani player intimated that bribery and betting activities were out of control and must be addressed. That Judge Ebrahim made no reference to Asia's illegal betting market was a regrettable omission. Betting syndicates in Bombay and the Gulf were credited with enormous influence. Bets were taken not just on the result of matches, but on the toss, individual scores and even the number of runs scored in an over. Ladbrokes thought that their level of cricket betting in England was minuscule by comparison.

The crisis spread its tentacles far and wide. Mushtaq Mohammad said his question to Australia's captain, Allan Border, about how he would react if someone offered him £500,000 to throw the 1993 Edgbaston Test against England had been purely hypothetical, a joke that had been misunderstood. Sarfraz Nawaz, the former Pakistani pace bowler, who had re-emerged as a sports adviser to the Pakistani prime minister, Benazir Bhutto, claimed an anti-corruption committee had launched an investigation the previous year into six or seven players, including Malik. Imran Khan broke off from his wedding preparations with a vehement denial of reports that he had called for any perpetrators, if found guilty, to be hanged. He said the word he used was "banned".

Salim Malik was replaced as captain, and suspended, pending investigation, only for him to return as a batsman on Pakistan's tour of Australia in November 1995. Warne dismissed him, fourth ball, in the First Test in Brisbane. "It shows there is justice in the game," he said.

MUCK AND BRASS
Matthew Engel, *Notes by the Editor*, 1996

Fifteen years ago, Dennis Lillee and Rodney Marsh handed over a couple of notes to a gopher and instructed him to place them on the 500-1 available against England in the betting tent at Headingley. They were playing for the opposition. The most famous odds in the history of cricket produced the most famous win and, in the case of those two, the most disgraceful pay-out.

If the sport were baseball and the country America, they would have been banned forever. Australia and cricket did nothing. Indeed, the Aussies tended to laugh the matter off, as though a pair of lovable larrikins had been caught playing a slightly illegal game of two-up during the factory lunch-hour. So one cannot resist a slightly malicious chuckle at the mess in which Australian cricket has lately found itself.

Some conclusions are easy to draw. There really is no more serious allegation possible within the game than the one Warne, Mark Waugh and Tim May made against Salim Malik. If Malik tried to bribe Warne to throw a match, he is a cheat; alternatively the other three are liars. Whoever is guilty should not be allowed to continue in the game. But which?

There is no point in having an International Cricket Council if it is not to investigate a situation like this, adjudicate on it and issue penalties as appropriate. Who cares how many overs are bowled in a day's cricket, if the overs and the day are tainted? Most outside observers believe the power exists, inherently. The ICC's chief executive, David Richards, believes it should exist, and hopes to get more authority to deal with emergencies, but he was warned against precipitate action by the lawyers. In the old days, the world's great fears were war, famine and pestilence; these days litigation sometimes seems have superseded the lot.

Instead, the only investigation was the one conducted by the retired Pakistani judge Fakhruddin G. Ebrahim. The three Australians, perhaps arrogantly, declined to travel to Pakistan. But if they had no faith in Pakistani justice, they were vindicated. The judge said their allegations were concocted. Now there are still countries in the world where judges sometimes reach a verdict without listening to the defence; it is pretty unusual to get there without listening to the prosecution. Judicial ignorance ("Who are the Beatles?") is a well-known phenomenon, though it is a little baffling that any judge could produce a nine-page summary while apparently ignorant of the relevance of gambling to this case. Judicial pique is less well-documented but it shines through this judge's attitude to the Australians.

Cricket is a splendidly designed game for betting: its mixture of the individual and the general gives an unparalleled range of opportunities for enthusiasts to back their judgments. But, as the northern saying ought to go, where there's brass, there's muck. In Britain, where betting is legal and bookmakers are inclined to cowardice rather than corruption, the problem appears to be controllable; any unusual betting patterns would be spotted at once, and publicly exposed. In the subterranean world of subcontinental betting, too illegal to be subject to the public gaze, too narrowly based to form a mature market, the same checks do not apply. The ICC Code of Conduct belatedly lays down the law and bans players from betting: the sound of stable doors slamming is heard across the globe.

THE VIEW FROM PAKISTAN
Abid Ali Kazi, 1996

Controversies surrounded Pakistan cricket in 1994–95, this time accompanied by failures on the field – a massive Test defeat by South Africa and an historic one by Zimbabwe. Rumours of revolt in the team were supplemented by charges of betting and bribery. The centre of the attention was the Test captain, Salim Malik. At the fag end of the Zimbabwean tour, Rashid Latif, the vice-captain, and Basit Ali suddenly announced their retirement from international cricket. It was believed they were disgusted with Malik. They returned three months later, but in the meantime there were scores of allegations and counter-allegations levelled at each other by team members and other prominent cricketing personalities.

On their return to Pakistan, Malik and Intikhab Alam were sacked as captain and team manager. Malik was suspended from first-class cricket and given seven days' notice to answer the charges. After a six-and-a-half-hour meeting, the board decided he ought to have a chance to cross-examine his accusers and asked the Australian Cricket Board to send May and Warne to Pakistan. The invitation was declined, the ACB citing fears for their safety. Next time a Pakistan team was selected, for the Asia Cup in April, Malik and several others were not considered; wicket-keeper Moin Khan was named captain, only to catch chicken-pox.

IF YOU'RE BROKE, FIX IT
Matthew Engel, Notes by the Editor, 1998

It might be healthier if cricket officials spent a little less time reaching for the sky and paid more attention to what was going on in the gutter. As 1998 began, the rumours that results in one-day internationals were being twisted to suit the interests of betting syndicates operating illegally, mainly in Mumbai and the Gulf, were moving from a murmur to something nearer a roar. Nobody now doubts that this gambling takes place, for large sums, and that cricketers are involved in the process. This does not necessarily mean that players have deliberately thrown matches. It is possible that the substantial number who have made allegations – Tim May, Shane Warne, Manoj Prabhakar, Aamir Sohail and so on – are making mischief or a mistake. Possible, but increasingly implausible. The ICC needs to set up a credible international investigation designed to discover the truth, not what everyone wants to hear.

Anyone with experience of gambling will feel that the amount of smoke billowing out of this story is a pretty reliable indicator of fire. The international programme, particularly as played by India and Pakistan, is a guaranteed recipe for jiggery-pokery. The one-day tournaments of which these countries are so fond have no real meaning. No one remembers who wins them, so honour can never overcome profit. And the actual rewards for victory are hardly exciting. England's success in the Sharjah Champions Trophy in December won them just £25,000 between a squad of 14. Champion golfers tip their waiters better than that, never mind their caddies.

The present system bears a resemblance to the one that was prevalent in tennis a decade or so ago. The top players would turn up in some hick town for what was billed as a showdown. They would split the profits amiably and put on a show for the locals. It was not that they didn't try, but no one except the poor saps watching cared who won. The difference is that the cricketers are not getting rich – not from cricket. A handful do manage to turn their fame to good commercial advantage, but that is not the same thing. It would be astonishing if some of the others had not been tempted by villainy.

THE CORRUPTION OF CRICKET
Mihir Bose, 1999

It had been obvious for some time that cricket's great bribery saga was far from over. The wholly unexpected twist of December 1998 was that the goodies threatened to change places with the baddies.

The original accusation was that the Australians Shane Warne, Tim May and Mark Waugh had been approached by Salim Malik, who allegedly offered them $200,000 bribes to throw matches in October 1994. This first alerted a dozing cricket world to the heavy illegal betting going on in the subcontinent and Sharjah, and to the possibility that players were being bribed to rig matches.

More than four years later, it finally emerged that Warne and Waugh had their own involvement with subcontinental bookmakers and that the Australian Cricket Board knew about this and had covered it up all that time. Suddenly, the rights and wrongs seemed a great deal muddier.

Until the new Australian revelations, the affair had followed a predictable pattern. The Pakistanis had held three inquiries into the allegations, the Indians had held one, Malik had denied everything, nothing had been proven and in four years the only victim had been a journalist. This was Ramaswamy Mohan, for 18 years the cricket correspondent of *The Hindu*, one of India's leading newspapers. The paper has never officially commented on Mohan's departure, although one source there said: "*The Hindu* had to think of the credibility of the paper."*

But everyone's credibility was at stake. In 1997 the Delhi-based magazine *Outlook* published claims by the former Indian Test cricketer Manoj Prabhakar that he was offered 2.5 million rupees (about £40,000) by a team-mate "to play below my usual standards". Prabhakar said the incident happened just before the India-Pakistan fixture (which was rained off anyway) in the Singer World Series in Sri Lanka in September 1994. "I told him to get out of my room," Prabhakar said.

Until then, the Indian board had been looking on Pakistan's difficulties on this issue with a slightly smug and superior air. Now it asked Mr Justice Chandrachud, a former Chief Justice of India, to examine the Prabhakar story. But Prabhakar refused to name the player concerned, so Chandrachud concluded in December 1997 that there was nothing to report. This limp-wristed conclusion pleased no one. The general feeling by now was that betting and match-throwing were part of the subcontinent's cricket culture, and that nothing could be done about it. People began to accept the resigned comment of a Bombay police investigator: "Every side with the exception of Australia and England can be purchased."

This remained the accepted wisdom for another year. In the meantime, the Pakistanis did begin a far more serious inquiry into the issue. Justice Malik Mohammad Qayyum sat in Lahore while Pakistan's cricketing elite made depositions. Inexorably, a picture of casual corruption built up. The International Cricket Council privately promised that, once Qayyum had finished, it would take action. But it was, the rest of the cricketing world thought, primarily Pakistan's problem.

Then, on December 8, 1998, the former Australian cricketer David Hookes mentioned to a Melbourne radio station that two Australians had given information to an Indian bookmaker. This turned the whole story on its head. The new revelation was that, during the same tournament in Sri Lanka in 1994, Waugh and Warne had been approached by an Indian bookmaker identified only as "John", who had asked them to begin giving him apparently innocent information about the weather and the state of the pitch – less, said the players, than they might routinely give free to journalists. For this, Waugh was paid $A6,000 (about £2,500) and Warne $A5,000.

The players had admitted this after making their original allegations about Malik to the Australian Cricket Board, which then fined them slightly more than John paid them ($A10,000 for Waugh and $A8,000 for Warne). But the ACB had said nothing about this publicly for almost four years. However, it informed the ICC at the time, telling Sir Clyde Walcott, the then chairman, and David Richards, the chief executive, to keep it secret, which they did. The news incensed the Australian public, and Waugh was booed during the Adelaide Test against England. Warne escaped this because he was injured. But letter-writers to Australian papers demanded that both be drummed out of the game. Warne and Waugh admitted being "naive and stupid" but insisted they had not been involved in match-fixing in any way.

---

* Note by Matthew Engel, editor of *Wisden* 1999:
Mohan admits having bet on cricket and having passed on routine information, but denies acting as a linkman between players and bookmakers, or any involvement in match-fixing. In the absence of any evidence that would justify his removal, he remains as *Wisden*'s Indian correspondent.

The news also incensed the Pakistanis. Justice Qayyum's inquiry was just nearing its end. Two months earlier, Waugh and Mark Taylor (representing Warne) had given evidence to him during Australia's tour of Pakistan. The Pakistanis had made special arrangements to accommodate their wishes, assembling a special court in a private house. Waugh and Taylor promised to tell the truth, the whole truth and nothing but the truth. They were not asked about "John" and (though Taylor was in on the secret) neither said anything. They did speak loftily about their cricketing ideals, and Justice Qayyum was much impressed by Waugh's testimony – until the news broke. "If he did not have a legal obligation, he had a moral duty to bring it to our notice, and it casts doubt on his credibility," Qayyum said.

Pakistani officials were also angered by the ICC's connivance in the Australian cover-up. "We felt the way ICC was constituted, we could not inform Pakistan," said Richards. "We were of the view that the onus was on the ACB to disseminate the information." Yet when the first Pakistan inquiry, under Justice Fakhruddin G. Ebrahim, suggested that the Australians had concocted their complaints against Malik, the Australians had demanded that ICC hold its own inquiry under Rule 2 of the Code of Conduct.

Now it was the Pakistanis who were making demands. They wanted Waugh and Warne to return to Pakistan to give further evidence. The compromise was that the Pakistani court travelled instead, at the Australian board's expense. A hearing was arranged in Melbourne; it was in effect a Pakistani court, sitting under Pakistani law. Ali Sibtain Fazli, the Pakistan board's lawyer, closely questioned Warne and Waugh about the match that was now felt to be the key to the whole affair. This was the one-day international in Colombo on September 7, 1994, eight days before the washed-out India-Pakistan match, and immediately preceding the Australian Test tour when Malik allegedly made his approach. Australia had scored just 179 for seven; Pakistan, captained by Malik and going well until Saeed Anwar retired with a hamstring injury, had lost by 28 runs. The Singer World Series involved India, who went on to win it, and Sri Lanka as well. It was rapidly becoming the centre of the many allegations; and it was after this tournament that the Pakistani board banned mobile telephones from the dressing-room. A Pakistani bookmaker had previously told the commission in secret that he had given money to two players to fix this game. Both denied it.

When Warne and Waugh were given a grilling by the Pakistani investigators, no new information emerged. And the sense of anti-climax was heightened two days later when the ICC held its much-heralded executive meeting. This was billed as the occasion when the organisation would finally come of age and take some of the powers of policing invested in similar international sporting organisations. Instead, the ICC announced a three-man commission to supervise the investigation of such allegations but left the initial responsibility with the domestic boards.

The belief that this is a Pakistani issue remains deeply ingrained. Yet in the month before the meeting, one Australian – Ricky Ponting – and two England players – Adam Hollioake and Dougie Brown – said they had received approaches from bookmakers. The approach to Ponting was made at a Sydney dog track, a long way from Pakistan. In 1817, it was easy for MCC to ban the miscreant William Lambert and expel the bookmakers from Lord's. The world is a more complex place in 1999. There seemed little sign of this sorry story ever ending, let alone soon.

THE BIGGEST CRISIS SINCE PACKER   Matthew Engel, *Notes by the Editor*, 1999

On a couple of occasions last November, *The Times*, a newspaper which made its reputation by not exaggerating, said cricket faced its worst crisis in 20 years – the Kerry Packer schism being the benchmark for modern cricketing crises. The paper was right, but not in the way it intended. The supposed worst crisis was the bizarre industrial dispute in which the West Indian players refused to start their tour of South Africa and instead holed up in a London hotel for a week. It was settled soon enough.

At the time, the real crisis was being ignored. Justice Qayyum, a Pakistani judge, was in Lahore conducting his investigation into the tangled skein of allegations about gambling and match-fixing. But elsewhere in the cricket world, no one was listening. A month later, the Australian Cricket Board was finally forced to admit something it had known, and covered up, since February 1995. Mark Waugh and Shane Warne, who had made the original allegations of attempted match-fixing against the former Pakistan captain Salim Malik, had themselves accepted thousands of dollars from an Indian bookmaker for providing apparently innocuous information.

Of itself, what Waugh and Warne did was only borderline-reprehensible. My own hunch is that it was a sting that went wrong: the bookmaker, using old spymasters' techniques, tried to draw them into a web of deceit from which there could be no escape, but was too unsubtle. The Waugh–Warne case is just a small but rocky outcrop of the mountain range of corruption that almost certainly still lies shrouded in the mists elsewhere.

But its emergence at last galvanised public opinion, and – on the face of it – the administrators. Suddenly, the Australian board announced that it would hold an investigation. So did the International Cricket Council. "Unfortunately," said ICC chairman Jagmohan Dalmiya, "the very fabric of the great game is being damaged." Yet both bodies had known about Waugh and Warne for four years, since the ACB had informed ICC officials (but no one else) at the time. The fabric, apparently, was damaged only when the public found out.

Cricket-watchers have never had much faith in the game's administrators. But what they expect is incompetence, not cynicism. In fact, the ICC investigation never materialised as such. The national boards, obsessed by territorial imperative, refused to allow it. Instead, a supervisory body was to be set up, although, outside Australia and Pakistan, there were no investigations to supervise.

This did at least appear to constitute an acceptance that the rotten apples had to be removed from the barrel. But that misses the point. The poison is in the barrel itself, and it is likely to seep out again and again in the years ahead. The known facts about match-fixing are bad enough. What is suspected is terrible. If even a fraction of the rumours doing the rounds are true, it would be diabolical.

It is not easy to understand the new world of cricket if you sit in London or even Melbourne. Go to Dalmiya's own patch, though, to a hotel room or a middle-class home with satellite TV, pretty well anywhere in South Asia. There nearly always seems to be a game being broadcast from somewhere, usually a one-day international (India played 48 in 1997–98), otherwise another one-day game. Yes, these matches do have some spectator appeal. But they have as much lasting resonance as the afternoon greyhound meetings staged in Britain for the benefit of betting shops. And since cricket goes on longer than a dog race, it makes better, more cost-effective, visual wallpaper without losing its power as a gambling medium.

This crisis is not merely the worst in 20 years. It is doing more damage than anything since Bodyline because it is eating away at cricket's most vital asset: its reputation for fair play. And Bodyline was easily solved by amending the Laws. This one is far harder to control.

I like a punt myself: I would be sorry if cricket betting had to end. But it is an ironclad rule that unregulated gambling leads to gangsterism, and, when that gets a grip on a game, then radical action is the only solution. It happened in baseball after the First World War. To clean up, the game required strong moral leadership at the time, and constant vigilance thereafter. Cricket's response so far has been pathetic, almost frivolous. Dalmiya almost split world cricket trying to take charge of the ICC. Having succeeded, he has given the game no leadership whatever. He should resign and be replaced by someone capable of providing that leadership.

THE CRONJE AFFAIR
Graeme Wright, *Notes by the Editor*, 2001

In Harvard Square in 1896, a man was knocked off his bike by a wagon and subsequently died. The wagon owners claimed that the accident "could not have been helped". "There are some things which must not happen," retorted Josiah Royce, professor of philosophy at Harvard. There are some things which can be avoided.

Royce's reply came back time and again as Hansie Cronje's reputation was peeled away, leaf by leaf, at the King Commission hearings last summer. It wasn't so much the facts themselves: the bribes from bookmakers, the attempts to fix matches and inveigle his team-mates into corrupting cricket's, indeed sport's, very ethos. It was the date when Cronje first crossed the line and accepted money from the Indian bookmaker, M. K. Gupta: 1996. We would learn later, through India's Central Bureau of Investigation, that Mohammad Azharuddin's involvement with Gupta began a year earlier. Still significant. It was in February 1995, you see, that Mark Waugh and Shane Warne admitted to the Australian Cricket Board that they had accepted money from another bookmaker. Admissions that the ACB, with the compliance of the International Cricket Council, whose chief executive was a former ACB employee, chose to keep under wraps. What I kept wondering was whether Azharuddin and Cronje would have become involved with Gupta had those two supposedly responsible organisations gone public immediately, and made an example of Waugh and Warne. As it was, the sound of silence rang out loud and clear both to bookmakers and cricketers. The game's administrators were not going to interfere in their activities. It took the Indian police to throw some light on cricket's darker side.

As Cronje's complicity was revealed, it was remarked that it was fortunate Jim Swanton was not here to witness this latest shame. It would have broken his heart, some said. Yet that misread the man. He would certainly not have condoned Cronje's behaviour; nor Azharuddin's. He would have been deeply saddened at the way cricket's reputation had once again been sullied by those who set their own interests above those of the game. But he would have been one of the first to find understanding and forgiveness, as well as advocating the appropriate punishment. And he wouldn't have been alone. Towards the end of his lengthy inquiry into match-fixing in Pakistan, Justice Malik Mohammad Qayyum was similarly inclined. "To those disappointed with their fallen heroes," he wrote in his report, "it be suggested that humans are fallible. Cricketers are only cricketers."

Cronje's worst crime was not against cricket – accepting the bookies' bribes or trying to fix matches – but against morality and decency. It was in the way he ensnared the two most vulnerable members of his team, Herschelle Gibbs and Henry Williams. Cronje's white team-mates could afford to send him on his joking way with a rejection; he was just the captain, one of the boys. For Gibbs and Williams, however, even in the rarefied atmosphere of the new South Africa, Cronje was the white man in charge. It takes

Ex-hero: Hansie Cronje, a charismatic captain of South Africa, takes his oath in court after stunning the cricket world in 2000 when he admitted being involved in match-fixing. Cronje died in a plane crash in 2002.

more than a rainbow for generations of social conditioning and economic deprivation to be washed away.

Of the three government-sponsored inquiries into match-fixing, in India, Pakistan and South Africa, India's Central Bureau of Investigation enjoyed much wider scope than the terms of reference that constricted both Qayyum and Justice Edwin King. As the title of their report implied, the Central Bureau of Investigation had freedom to investigate "related malpractices", allowing them to be wonderfully critical of cricket administrators in a way the other two could not. In spite of much post-Cronje posturing, the Central Bureau of Investigation decided, the office-bearers of the Board of Control for Cricket in India (BCCI) had been negligent by not looking thoroughly into alleged malpractices in the past, even though there had been clear indications of the malaise in the game there. The primary reason behind this was "the lack of accountability of the BCCI to anyone". The BCCI, the report made clear for anyone who didn't know it, "perpetuates a system of self-aggrandisement". It is not only in India, either. The men in clover become so besotted by the opiate of their own importance that they lose the will to confront problems. The trappings of power become more important than the judicious exercise of the power.

This might matter less if cricket were still primarily a domestic game, given a touch of glamour by Tests and one-day tournaments. But it isn't. It is an international sport, a multi-million-pound enterprise, and the question of accountability spotlights the dilemma at the heart of the game. Who does administer it? Well-meaning national representatives with other business and personal interests, or a coterie of power-players pursuing their own political or self-serving agendas? The ICC's few years as a governing body – it can hardly be called independent or autonomous – have not been glorious. It is still perceived as little more than a talking shop, not always the sum of its fractious parts and impotent to act without the agreement of its member countries, with their own vested interests.

The ICC's initial response to Cronje's admission of guilt was to resist calls for a worldwide inquiry into match-fixing, preferring that each country should determine its own methods of inquiry. This after India and Pakistan had already held inconclusive inquiries in recent years. It took a little prodding from the ECB's more proactive chairman, Lord MacLaurin, to get the nine full members around a table. In due course, the ICC established its own anti-corruption unit under the former commissioner of London's Metropolitan Police, Sir Paul Condon. Even so, its powers are limited. Although nominally independent, the unit is none the less financed by the ICC and its role is to support the ICC's Code of Conduct Commission. By its own terms of reference, this Commission "recognises and confirms that each member has sovereign rights over its own players, umpires, team officials and administrators and. . . is responsible for all disciplinary matters". In other words, the countries, not the anti-corruption unit, not the Code of Conduct Commission, not the ICC, decide what's what.

Take throwing. Cricket balls this time, rather than matches. On December 31, 1999, the ICC banned the Pakistan fast bowler, Shoaib Akhtar, because of a suspect bowling action. Pakistan alleged racial bias, a card that is beginning to fray at the edges, and appealed directly to the ICC president Jagmohan Dalmiya and cricket chairman Sir Clyde Walcott. In little more than a week, the Rawalpindi Express was steaming in again, though only in one-day internationals. The thinking behind his reprieve had touches of Alice: Shoaib's bouncer was the delivery that concerned the ICC bowling panel; bouncers are not legitimate deliveries in one-day cricket; ergo, Shoaib won't bowl bouncers and his bowling won't be suspect. Just to be on the safe side, the panel's power to suspend bowlers with suspect actions was revoked, and eventually replaced by a three-stage process that initially puts the issue back in the hands of individual countries.

More recently, there have been discussions about relocating the ICC headquarters to a country with a more favourable tax regime. The United Kingdom, currently at any rate, taxes sporting bodies; the suggested alternatives do not. It explains why the finance men slip away from Lord's to do their deals. In addition to this possible move, the ICC needs a new chief executive to replace David Richards when he has worked through the notice he gave last October. The time must be coming for the member countries to put the ICC on a proper business footing, with full-time executives empowered to take decisive, unilateral action as a centrally functioning administration. Otherwise, it makes no odds whether it's in Singapore or Switzerland, Dublin or Dubai.

A GAME IN SHAME

Mihir Bose, 2001

Cricket corruption, like taxes and poverty, may always be with us. But after cricket's *annus horribilis* of 2000 we can, for the first time, understand how a combination of players' greed, dreadful impotence and infighting by cricket administrators, and a radical shift in cricketing power from England to the Indian subcontinent helped create cricket's darkest chapter.

Two incidents illustrate this, and both occurred in India. The first was in 1984, some months after India's unexpected victory in the 1983 World Cup. One evening a Delhi bank clerk, Mukesh Kumar Gupta, was walking near his home in the grimy by-lanes of old Delhi when he saw some people betting small amounts on a cricket match. This, as he would later tell the Central Bureau of Investigation, India's top police investigators, caught his imagination. Having ascertained that the betters were neither well educated nor well informed about cricket, Gupta began to hone his cricket knowledge by listening to the BBC. And over the next decade he would travel the world, following cricket and meeting many of the world's top cricketers. Meeting and bribing. Meanwhile, as Gupta was transforming himself from a lowly bank clerk to cricket's most notorious match-fixer, and enriching himself in the process, cricket was also being reinvented and enriched. By the mid-1990s, even the Ashes Tests, the bedrock of the international game for more than 100 years, had been – away from the insular focus of England – sidelined in favour of one-day internationals.

By 1996, and the heyday of Gupta the match-fixer, there had been an enormous spread of such matches, the greatest expansion in the history of the game, with series in "non-cricketing" venues such as Sharjah, Singapore and Toronto. Sharjah had started by staging benefit matches for Indian and Pakistani cricketers, who had no recourse to an English-style system. Toronto provided a North American haven for India versus Pakistan, not always possible in the subcontinent for political reasons, while Singapore, and similar tournaments, represented the commercial opportunities that limited-overs cricket provided to businessmen seeking to reach the emerging Indian middle-classes.

Companies such as Singer and Pepsi, American but with extensive interests in south Asia, saw the marketing advantages of being associated with subcontinental cricket, and sponsored many of these mini-series. Television companies, in particular Rupert Murdoch's Star, were also keen to reach this new economic group. It is estimated that every second person watching cricket in the world is an Indian, and their insatiable appetite for the one-day game since 1983 has created a market worth cultivating. As Justice Malik Mohammad Qayyum pointed out in his inquiry into match-fixing, submitted to the Pakistan government in 1999, "with the massive influx of money and sheer increase in the number of matches played, cricket has become a business." It was a business, however, that was run like a private members' club.

Not surprisingly, the game's new economic power stimulated the ambitions of Asia's cricket administrators. Our second incident, in the spring of 1996, provided the spur. It happened in the foyer of Taj Bengal, the luxurious Calcutta hotel just opposite the city's zoo, and gathered there were the subcontinent's leading administrators. The World Cup, which was just about to start in the subcontinent, had been thrown into chaos by the refusal of the Australians, for security reasons, to play their group matches in Sri Lanka. The television and sponsorship deals that the Asians had made for the World Cup, which would eventually bring them a profit in excess of $US75m, were in jeopardy, and the game's governing body, the International Cricket Council, seemed powerless to act. It was against this background that Ana Punchihewa, president of the Sri Lankan board, turned to Jagmohan Dalmiya, the Indian convenor of the World Cup organising committee, and said, "We should have an Asian as the next chairman of the International Cricket Council."

Dalmiya picked up the baton and ran his election campaign as if it was an American presidential race, energetically wooing the ICC Associate Members. But despite winning a simple majority in two ballots, he found the old, established members reluctant to accept him. A bitter power struggle, essentially brown versus white (and black), saw England, Australia, New Zealand and West Indies ranged against the subcontinent. It was so vicious that the scars have never healed. The Asian countries resented the grudging acceptance of them by England and Australia; the old powers felt that the new kids on the block were not following the game's gentlemanly ways.

"There was, is, a power struggle in international cricket," one highly placed ICC source admitted, "and the Asian countries are resentful of England, the old colonial power, but then the subcontinent has not helped matters by being very defensive about match-fixing. We have known for years that match-fixing goes on, helped by the fact that betting is illegal and in the hands of criminals there. But in the past, whenever the matter has been raised, they have said we are cricket administrators, not cops. Then a clean-cut white South African, Hansie Cronje, was caught in the net, the game changed and everyone has had to come clean."

Ironically, it was a Delhi crime-branch detective, Ishwar Singh Redhu, who, on April 7, 2000, forced everyone to come clean. Asked to investigate complaints by Delhi businessmen of extortion with menace, he was listening to telephone taps on two suspects when Cronje's name – and the fixing of one-day games in the current series between India and South Africa – cropped up. Then Cronje himself was heard discussing the fixing of matches with a London-based Indian businessman called Sanjeev (also known as Sanjay) Chawla.

Before that moment, five and a half years after Shane Warne, Mark Waugh and Tim May had made allegations of match-fixing against the Pakistan captain, Salim Malik, there had been inquiries in India, Pakistan and Sri Lanka, as well as media investigations led by the Indian magazine *Outlook*. But apart from the fines on Waugh and Warne for receiving $A6,000 and $A5,000 respectively from an Indian bookmaker in return for information, which the Australian board and the ICC had covered up, nothing had been done. It would subsequently emerge that Justice Qayyum had recommended a life ban on Salim Malik, but his report was still to be published.

The immediate reactions to the Delhi police's charges of match-fixing and betting against Cronje and the team-mates he had mentioned to Chawla – Nicky Boje, Herschelle Gibbs, Pieter Strydom and Henry Williams – were of utter disbelief that a born-again Christian like Cronje could be involved. Cronje denied everything – "Absolute rubbish." Ali Bacher, managing director of South African cricket, backed him – "unquestionable integrity and honesty" – and the South Africans denounced the tactics of the Delhi police. In London, *The Observer* quoted a South African journalist as saying he had heard the tapes and it could not be Cronje as the voice had an Indian accent. It later turned out he had heard Indian actors reading transcripts released by the Delhi police. The tapes themselves had been sealed and placed under the jurisdiction of the Delhi High Court.

Four days after detective Redhu's initial announcement, the cricket world was rocked and shocked. Cronje made the first of many confessions, and the shadowy world of M. K. Gupta and his ilk was about to emerge in the public light. Within two months, all the rumours of match-fixing that had been circulating for years were given substance. The Pakistanis, who had been sitting on Justice Qayyum's report since the previous October, were finally obliged to release it. Qayyum accepted that Waugh, Warne and May had told the truth about Malik seeking to corrupt them. Another cricketer, Ata-ur-Rehman, was found guilty of perjury in relation to evidence about Wasim Akram and a life ban recommended. Fines were also recommended for these two, and for Wasim, Mushtaq Ahmed, Waqar Younis, Inzamam-ul-Haq, Akram Raza and Saeed Anwar. The judge found that the evidence of match-fixing against these others had not come up to the level required, but he concluded none the less that Wasim should never again captain Pakistan. The fines were because, within the terms of the inquiry, these players had either brought the name of the Pakistan team into disrepute or, by "partial amnesia" and withholding evidence, had not co-operated fully.

In June, two weeks after the Qayyum report was published, a South African judicial commission under retired judge Edwin King began to hear devastating evidence from South African players. The entire South African team had considered an offer to throw a one-day match in 1996 and, in yet another confession, Cronje admitted he could have taken as much as $US140,000 from Gupta and other bookmakers between 1996 and 2000. But he asked the world to believe that, while he had lied to the bookies about throwing matches, he was telling the truth in saying he had never tried to fix a match. At the beginning of November, the Indian government released the Central Bureau of Investigation's report on match-fixing. By interviewing illegal bookmakers as well as players, this added a new dimension to the story. The result was that, for the first time, a cricketer, former Indian captain Mohammad Azharuddin, admitted to being involved in the fixing of one-day internationals. And drawing on the information from Gupta and other bookies, the Central Bureau of Investigation revealed how international cricketers had been lured and, in some instances, corrupted. What began as a scandal could be seen at last as a conspiracy. Match-fixing could no longer be shrugged off as an isolated instance; there was now a history and a pattern of corruption.

Gupta's first cricket contact was Ajay Sharma, very much a bit-player in international cricket – one Test and 31 one-day internationals for India – but a useful conduit to other cricketers. They first met at a club tournament in Delhi in 1988 when Gupta, impressed by the way Sharma batted, gave him 2,000 rupees (£100 at the current rate of exchange) as a token of his appreciation. Gupta saw this as an investment for the future, and it was to prove a shrewd one. A fortnight later Sharma contacted him and soon the two men had formed a bond which, as the

CBI report made clear, "was to prove beneficial to both". When Sharma toured New Zealand with India in 1990, Gupta claimed he provided him with information about the pitch, weather and the team which he used to make "a good amount of money". Sharma denies he provided any information, but he did later introduce Gupta to Manoj Prabhakar, who was keen to get a new car – "a Maruti Gypsy with wide tyres". On the 1990 tour of England, said Gupta, Prabhakar gave him information about the team and "underperformed" in one of the drawn Tests. Prabhakar got his Maruti Gypsy – he told the CBI he paid for it himself – and Gupta got to know yet more cricketers.

The picture Gupta painted for the Central Bureau of Investigation, which was often backed in testimony from Sharma, Prabhakar, Azharuddin, Ajay Jadeja and even Cronje, shows how frighteningly casual the whole thing was. Gupta goes to Prabhakar's Delhi home for dinner (Prabhakar denies this); Prabhakar rings Gus Logie, who refuses to help (Prabhakar confirms this). When the Sri Lankans tour India in 1990, Prabhakar introduces Gupta to Aravinda de Silva (Prabhakar denies this). He in turn, and over the phone, introduces Gupta to Martin Crowe, and they get on so well that when Gupta visits New Zealand in 1991 – Sri Lanka toured there from January to March – he lunches with Crowe and his wife, Simone, at their home. At a Hong Kong six-a-side tournament, Prabhakar introduces Gupta to Mark Waugh; Gupta flies to Colombo during some festival matches there and, so he claims, meets Dean Jones, Arjuna Ranatunga and Brian Lara. When the winners of the Indian and Pakistani Wills one-day tournaments play in Delhi, Prabhakar introduces him to Salim Malik, and when England tour India in 1993 he introduces him to Alec Stewart. Gupta and Prabhakar agree on this.

Gupta's success with these cricketers varies. During the 1994 Sri Lankan tour of India, he claims, Ranatunga and de Silva agreed to "underperform" – "[they] could manage it since they were the captain and vice-captain", he told the Central Bureau of Investigation – and he profited when Sri Lanka lost the first Test. For this, he says, he paid de Silva $US15,000. There was talk of fixing other Tests, but the odds were too low. Gupta claims he paid Crowe $US20,000 for information, but he refused to fix matches. Jones was offered $US40,000, he says, but while Jones promised to think about it, he did nothing. In Hong Kong, says Gupta, Mark Waugh was paid $US20,000 to provide information "whenever Australia played", but on another occasion, in Sharjah in 1994, he refused to help, as did Salim Malik. Later that year, however, Gupta recalls making good money on Malik's information that Pakistan would lose to Australia in the Singer World Series in Sri Lanka, a match mentioned in both the Central Bureau of Investigation and Qayyum reports. When the West Indians toured India in 1994–95, Gupta says he paid Brian Lara $US40,000 to underperform in two one-day games.

After the CBI report was released, de Silva and Ranatunga denied Gupta's allegations. Crowe said he thought he was dealing with a journalist and was duped. Waugh denied accepting Gupta's money and talked of taking legal action. So did Lara. The most robust denial came from Stewart. According to Gupta, Stewart was paid £5,000 for information but refused to fix matches for him. Stewart not only denied receiving any money but claimed he did not remember knowingly meeting Gupta.

It is possible that in the fevered atmosphere of subcontinental cricket Stewart may have met Gupta: for a long time he was identified only as M.K. Confusingly, he was also known as John, although he was not the John who in 1994 paid Waugh and Warne for information, knew Salim Malik and approached Cronje in 1995 with offers to fix the finals of the Mandela Trophy between South Africa and Pakistan. Not yet caught in the web, Cronje turned him down. But as he and Malik walked on to the field before the first final, the Pakistan captain asked him whether he had spoken to John. Cronje told the King Commission that he felt embarrassed and ashamed and merely nodded in response: he did not want to talk about it. South Africa won both games; as far as Qayyum was concerned, Pakistan lost them in controversial circumstances.

"There was an open dispute within the team about the decision of the toss. Since the matches were day/night games and the lights in Johannesburg were not conducive to batting second, Rashid Latif the vice-captain had strongly recommended that if Malik won the toss Pakistan should bat first. Both times Malik won the toss and put the opposition in [and lost]. In cricketing terms the toss in a day/night game is crucial as it is easier to bat first in natural daylight than under the shadows of floodlights. Even *Wisden* notes that [in the first final] Malik made 'the puzzling decision to field first'. It was also puzzling why, having [fielded] first and lost in the first final, Malik repeated the mistake two days later in the second match as well."

However, whether he was M. K., John or just plain Gupta, there can be no doubt about his intense and close relationship with Azharuddin and Cronje. After Ajay Sharma had introduced Azharuddin to Gupta at the Taj Palace hotel in Delhi in 1995, the two had a relationship that lasted until 1997. During that period, says Gupta, Azhar's wife Sangeeta Bijlani was also involved. He claims he paid Azhar 90 lakh rupees (£150,000: a lakh equals 100,000 rupees) but, finding some of Azhar's predictions "proved incorrect", asked for his money back and was repaid 30 lakh rupees – in instalments from Azharuddin's locker at the Taj Palace.

It was Azhar's unreliability as a forecaster, Gupta told the Central Bureau of Investigation, that made him seek out Cronje late in 1996. Even so, that Indian season had begun well for him. With Sharma's help, he claims to have had the pitch at Delhi's Feroz Shah Kotla ground doctored for the one-off Test between India and Australia, which India won in three and a half days. He was told that the First Test against South Africa at Ahmedabad would not be a draw – India won and Gupta made money – and that India would lose the second; again he made money. In Kanpur for the Third Test, he asked Azharuddin to introduce him to Cronje. The meeting took place on the evening of the third day, with South Africa facing defeat. Azhar introduced him as a diamond merchant, but Gupta quickly told Cronje that he was a match-fixer who wanted to be sure that South Africa would lose. He asked Cronje to obtain the players' co-operation. Cronje would later tell the King Commission, "I led him to believe I would. This seemed an easy way to make money, but I had no intention of doing anything." He accepted $US30,000 from Gupta, hid it in his kit bag and smuggled it out of India, into and out of South Africa, and finally to a bank account in England, so violating the foreign exchange laws of both India and South Africa.

That established the Cronje–Gupta relationship. Cronje says he lied to Gupta about match-fixing but took his money nevertheless. And during the last match of the Indian tour, the entire South African team debated whether to accept Gupta's bribe, variously said to be $US200,000 and $US250,000, to play badly in the one-day international at Mumbai, intended as a benefit match for Mohinder Amarnath. Pat Symcox told the King Commission, "Some guys, including myself, said it was a lot of money and we should look at it. Some guys were for it, some against." In the end the offer was rejected, but it remains the only known instance of a whole team discussing match-fixing.

Cronje met Gupta at three o'clock on the morning of the match to tell him the fix was not on. Yet when India then went to South Africa for three back-to-back Tests and a one-day tournament, also involving Zimbabwe, the relationship developed. Cronje says he kept lying to Gupta about throwing matches but took his money. Gupta says that when Cronje, like Azharuddin, proved an unreliable forecaster, and he suffered huge losses, Cronje apologised and promised to make amends. Here we have a touch of comic opera. According to Gupta, Cronje had promised that, during the one-day tournament, South Africa would lose some matches against India. When they didn't, he told Gupta that India had played so badly and missed so many chances that he couldn't do anything about the result. Poor Gupta: he had invested in both camps and still couldn't get the result he wanted. Could it be that other players were in hock to other bookies seeking a different fix?

The age of Gupta the match-fixer ended in May 1998, and there is some evidence to suggest that the high tide of cricket match-fixing ended then, although Majid Khan, former chief executive of the Pakistan board, remains convinced that Pakistan's two World Cup losses to India and Bangladesh in 1999 were fixed. However, no player or bookie has come forward to provide any details, and the World Cup did not fall within the compass of Justice Qayyum's inquiry.

In fact, it is possible that the world at large would never have heard of Gupta had Cronje not decided he couldn't do without bookies. He would tell Judge King that his behaviour was like that of an alcoholic, who abstains only to return when he has one drink. The fateful "drink" was offered by a South African gambler, Marlon Aronstam. He contacted Cronje on his mobile phone on the fourth evening of the rain-ruined Fifth Test between England and South Africa at Centurion Park in January 2000; they agreed to meet at 10 o'clock in Cronje's hotel room. Aronstam wanted Cronje to "make a game" of the Test by declaring and persuading England to agree to a double forfeiture, something not only unprecedented in Test history but also not sanctioned by the Laws.

Aronstam planned to back both sides at long odds. If Cronje agreed, Aronstam told the King Commission, he was going to give 200,000 rand to a charity of Cronje's choice. (Cronje remembered the figure as 500,000 rand.) He claimed that Cronje implied that the only way to make money from cricket was by fixing matches, and gave the impression that he would be prepared to throw a one-day international "once South Africa has qualified for a final". He also offered to throw the first one-day international against India in Kochi, when South Africa toured there after the triangular series between South Africa, England and Zimbabwe. Cronje would later try to qualify his offers, but it remains extraordinary that he had such a discussion with a man he had only just met. As a result, he "made a match" of the Centurion Test, and Aronstam gave him 53,000 rand plus a leather jacket for his wife, even though it had been too late to place his bets by the time the final day was set up. The money for charity never materialised.

Cronje denied that the match was fixed. But by his own admission he was hooked again on bookmakers, and a fortnight later, when South Africa were in Durban to play Zimbabwe, he was introduced to Chawla. The intermediary was Hamid "Banjo" Cassim, a South African of Indian origin, who had befriended the South African players by giving them biltong (dried meat). When the Indians toured South Africa in 1996–97, he had provided them with biryani, and one of the sights of the Cape Town Test was "Banjo" hauling biryani up to the Indian dressing-room on a rope.

By the time Cronje left Chawla's room, he was clutching a mobile-phone box filled with perhaps as much as $US15,000. It was to prove a fatal relationship. Cronje felt so invincible he did not seem to care who knew about his match-fixing discussions with Chawla. In India he happily discussed the topic on a mobile phone given to him by Chawla. He asked Pieter Strydom to play badly in the First Test in Mumbai, but Strydom refused. Before the Second Test at Bangalore, he asked Mark Boucher, Jacques Kallis and Lance Klusener – "in passing, jokingly" Klusener remembered – whether they were keen "to throw the game for money". Again, his suggestion was rejected. Then, on the morning of the final one-day match at Nagpur, he lured two non-white players, Herschelle Gibbs and Henry Williams, by offering the former $US15,000 if he scored less than 20 runs and the latter a similar amount if his overs cost more than 50 runs. He had, it transpired, told Chawla he would need $US25,000 each for Gibbs and Williams, and later conceded he might have been "trying to cut something" for himself.

In the event, Gibbs scored 74 and Williams was injured in his second over, but Cronje, who had made the offer with a smile, just laughed it off – part of his strategy, perhaps, to convince his players that it could all be a huge practical joke. What Cronje did not know was that the mobile he had been given by Chawla was being tapped. Two weeks later, when the Delhi police held their press conference, releasing transcripts of taped conversations between Cronje and Chawla, the joke was on Cronje. It would lead to the South African board banning him from cricket for life, just as after the CBI report the Indian board would issue life bans on Azharuddin and Sharma. Two other Indians, Jadeja and Prabhakar, received five-year bans; South Africans Gibbs and Williams got six-month suspensions.

Yet, in the end, the joke has been played on cricket's administrators. This became evident when in May the ICC, prompted by Lord MacLaurin, held an emergency session to discuss match-fixing. It was the first time in its seven years as an independent organisation that such a meeting had been held. In the weeks beforehand, the various boards manoeuvred to put themselves in the best possible light. Everyone put pressure on Pakistan to release the Qayyum Report, while in an interview with *The Australian* newspaper, Ali Bacher sought to turn the spotlight away from South Africa with allegations that two 1999 World Cup matches were "manipulated" and that an umpire had been paid to "ensure a certain result in a Test match in England". Questions were raised in the media about ICC president Dalmiya's own conduct during negotiations for television rights for the 1998 ICC knockout tournament in Dhaka. This had brought the ICC £12m, at the time the biggest deal it had transacted.

Just before Dalmiya opened the session, MacLaurin passed round a statement on ECB notepaper, which he asked all the ICC delegates to sign, declaring that they were honest men. Everyone duly complied, but it revealed the curious state of an organisation whose own senior members had to declare they were clean before they could consider corruption among the players. Friends of Dalmiya hinted darkly that this was some English plot. Yet the most persistent questions about the 1998 television deal – whereby Doordarshan, India's state television, had received the rights – were raised in India. Soon, another CBI inquiry would be set up to examine the deal, and also the links between Dalmiya and Mark Mascarenhas, whose media interests include a television company called World-Tel.

Central Bureau of Investigation officers visited Dalmiya's offices in Calcutta and there was also a raid by income-tax officials on his office. Dalmiya, meanwhile, insisted he had done nothing wrong. The ICC, he said, did not lose out, and if Doordarshan paid over the odds that was their responsibility. As for the raids, he claimed they had nothing to do with cricket and were common to all business houses in India.

In a sense, Dalmiya's remarks sum up the problem and the immense cultural divide that the cricket corruption issue raises. In Pakistan, the cricket board is at the mercy of the government; in India, it is autonomous. But in both countries the game is played and administered against a background in which corruption, and police and tax inquiries into prominent persons, are part of life.

In the various countries around the world, the investigations into match-fixing reflect the fact that each country does its own thing. In India, Pakistan and South Africa, the investigations have been either judicial or led by the police but, in all three instances, reporting to the respective governments. In Australia and New Zealand, they are being handled by the cricket bodies and have no legal powers. A strong central cricket administration could have overcome this.

The ICC has taken tentative steps with the setting up of an investigation unit under former London Metropolitan Police commissioner Sir Paul Condon. But, as Sir Paul himself has admitted, he has no legal powers; if he discovers anything, it will be reported to the ICC. He can do nothing to administer justice, he can only react, and what co-ordination he can achieve is through persuasion. It is noteworthy that the very afternoon he held a press conference in London to publicise the work of his new unit, it was overshadowed by the release of the Central Bureau of Investigation report. Sir Paul had to delay his press conference to deal with that.

Since its initial report, the Central Bureau of Investigation has begun looking into links between cricketers, bookmakers and the Indian underworld, and could discover more secrets. The King Commission wants to go back to the beginning of 1992, when South Africa re-emerged into international cricket. It has high hopes of unlocking more secrets, but others in South Africa would prefer to see a line drawn under the whole sorry business. This would be a mistake. The high tide of match-fixing in cricket may have ebbed, but the full story of what happened throughout the 1990s has not yet been told.

DEATH OF A DISGRACED HERO

Obituary, 2003

Wessel Johannes "Hansie" Cronje, South Africa's cricket captain in a record 53 Tests and 138 one-day internationals between 1994 and 2000, died on June 1, 2002 when the cargo plane in which he was travelling crashed on Cradock Peak in the Outeniqua mountain range on its approach to his home town, George, in the Western Cape. He was just 32. Two years earlier, Cronje's admission that he took bribes from book-makers to provide information and fix matches exposed the extent of a corruption scandal that cricket authorities had signally neglected to confront.

At first he had hotly denied charges levelled by the New Delhi police, who during a phone-tapping operation in March 2000 heard him conspiring with an Indian bookmaker, Sanjeev Chawla, to predetermine performances. And such was his standing as a player, captain and sporting ambassador for post-apartheid South Africa that few in the cricket world doubted him, preferring to heap scorn on the Indian investigation. Ali Bacher, managing director of the United Cricket Board of South Africa, spoke of Cronje's "unquestionable integrity and honesty". Then, four days after the accusation, Cronje confessed in a 3 a.m. phone call to Bacher that he had not been "entirely honest". He was immediately stripped of the captaincy, as his side prepared for a one-day series against Australia, and in subsequent testi-mony to the government-appointed King Commission revealed, sometimes in tears, further details of his involvement with bookmakers in match-fixing. The cricket world listened agog as much as aghast. The game's reputation, it seemed, was at an all-time low. Cronje's life and career were in tatters.

It had been so different a decade earlier when, aged 21, he was given the captaincy of Orange Free State. His upbringing and education had groomed him for leadership. His family were of solid, middle-class Afrikaner stock, deeply reli-gious and sporty: Hansie's father, Ewie, had been an off-spinning all-rounder for Free State in the 1960s. The importance of discipline, dedication and hard work had been inculcated in Hansie at an early age, honed at Grey College in his native Bloemfontein, and was made manifest in 1991–92, his second year in charge, when the young Free State team, coached by Eddie Barlow to a level of physical and mental fitness rare even for South African cricket, finished runners-up in the Castle Bowl (formerly the Currie Cup) and won the limited-overs Nissan Shield. The next two seasons brought Castle Cup and one-day doubles, followed by one-day trophies in subsequent years – a total of seven titles in five seasons. International commitments meant the young captain was not ever-present, but his influence remained inspirational.

He had made his debut at 18 in January 1988, joining his brother, Frans, for the Currie Cup games against Transvaal and Northern Transvaal. Innings of two and 16, then a pair, were an inauspicious start for someone who would notch up a record 15 first-class hundreds for the Free State, as well as six in one-day competi-tions. The following season, his unbeaten 105 against Impalas took Orange Free State into the Benson and Hedges Trophy final, where Frans's old school-friend Allan Donald blew Western Province aside with four for 18. Hansie's maiden first-class hundred followed in January 1990 when, captaining South African Universities, he hit 104 against Mike Gatting's English rebels.

Inside the year, South Africa had been readmitted to full membership of the ICC, and the 22-year-old Cronje was one of four non-playing observers – two white, two non-white – taken to India with the first post-isolation side. Three months later, he was bowling five tidy overs for 17 as South Africa, captained by Kepler Wessels, shocked Australia with a nine-wicket victory at Sydney in the World Cup. He played in eight of their nine games in that tournament, including the infamous semi-final against England in which South Africa's target was adjusted after rain from 22 off 13 balls to 21 off one. Then he went to the Caribbean for South Africa's first Test since readmission, and their first ever against West Indies. Cronje scored only five and two, but in 68 Tests would go on to make 3,714 runs at 36.41, as well as taking 43 wickets at 29.95; in 188 one-day internationals he made 5,565 runs at 38.64, took 114 wickets at 34.78 with an economy rate of 4.44, and held 72 catches. His first-class figures from 184 games were 12,103 runs at 43.69 and 116 wickets at 34.43.

With his aggressive batting, intelligent medium-pace bowling and brilliant fielding, Cronje was a formidable competitor. The Indians discovered as much when they visited South Africa in 1992–93 and he took a career-best five for 32 in the opening one-day international, won it with a six with three balls to spare, and conceded only 3.59 an over in the seven-match series. That tour also proved he had the mettle for Test cricket. Going in in the second over at Port Elizabeth, he stayed eight and three-quarter hours (411 balls) until he was last out for 135, the first and highest of his six Test centuries. When Donald took his match haul to 12 wickets, South Africa had their first Test victory of the new era. Cronje's second hundred, 122, came in Colombo the following September to set up South Africa's biggest Test win – an innings and 208 runs – and Sri Lanka's heaviest defeat.

His good form initially held when, the youngest in the side at 24, he was Wessels's vice-captain in Australia in 1993–94. After Wessels broke a finger in the Sydney Test, Cronje took charge on the tense final morning to such effect that Australia, chasing 117 for victory with six wickets in hand, were dismissed for 111; his direct hit to run out Shane Warne from wide mid-off struck a crucial blow. He also took over during the one-day tournament when further injuries forced Wessels home, and at Adelaide became South Africa's second-youngest Test captain, after Murray Bisset in 1898–99.

But there was no fairytale: Australia won by 191 runs to square the series. Wessels was captain again when the two countries resumed hostilities in South Africa, and Cronje wasted no time extracting revenge for Adelaide. In six games in 14 days, he hammered the Aussie bowling for 721 runs: he began with 112 from 120 balls, the higher of his two one-day international hundreds, hit 251, his maiden double-hundred, for Orange Free State and finished with 122 in the First Test, which South Africa won by 197 runs. The double-hundred – next highest score was Gerry Liebenberg's 39 – remained Cronje's best.

This was a period of transition for Australian fast bowling, though. Cronje was given a harder time in England in 1994 and managed only 90 runs in six Test innings as Devon Malcolm and the young Darren Gough exposed a technical weakness against short-pitched bowling directed at his ribs. Spin gave him no such problems, and his armoury against it included a ferocious slog-sweep over mid-wicket, played on one knee. When he made what was then Test cricket's third-fastest fifty, off 31 balls at Centurion in 1998, he reached it by hitting Muttiah Muralitharan, the world's best off-spinner, for 4,666 off successive balls.

In 1995, he expunged his unhappy introduction to English conditions by making 1,362 first-class runs at 50.44 in a one-off season for Leicestershire, whose cricket manager Jack Birkenshaw and all-rounder Gordon Parsons, Cronje's brother-in-law since 1991, participated in Orange Free State's triumphs. Among his four hundreds was 213 against Somerset at Weston-super-Mare. But it would take him 10 Tests and until 1998 to reach 50 against England, whereupon he did so five times on the trot: 81 in South Africa's win at Lord's, 69 not out at Old Trafford, 126 and 67 at Trent Bridge, and 57 (plus a duck) at Headingley, where England took the series 2–1 with help from some inept umpiring. He was South Africa's top-scorer, with 401 runs at 66.83, but it was generally accepted that his unenterprising captaincy had let the rubber slip away. Instead of penetration he went for strangulation, setting defensive fields for his seam bowlers and encouraging them to bowl wide of off stump: what Bob Woolmer, South Africa's coach, called "aggressive containment".

Yet when Cronje succeeded Wessels in 1994, and began the partnership with Woolmer that masterminded South Africa's tactics until the 1999 World Cup, he was welcomed as an adventurous captain; one prepared to gamble. In his first series, against New Zealand in South Africa, he became the first captain since W. G. Grace to win a three-match rubber after being one down. When the teams met again at Auckland in March 1995, Cronje's pre-lunch declaration, setting New Zealand 275 to win in 63 overs, was the catalyst for South Africa's 93-run victory. Something saturnine in his demeanour, however, spoke of arrogance and calculated self-control; his dour expression suggested few concessions to humour or emotion. Yet there were times when the composure snapped. Shortly after becoming South Africa's captain, he received a one-match ban for dissent on dismissal in a Castle Cup game. When the umpires rightly ruled Mark Waugh not out after inadvertently hitting his wicket at Adelaide in 1997–98, and he went on to save the Test, Cronje hurled a stump through their dressing-room door. At Cape Town in 1996, he was fined for imposing his will on umpire Dave Orchard to refer a run-out to the television umpire after Orchard ruled England's Graham Thorpe not out; the decision was overturned and South Africa went on to take the match and the series.

He could certainly be articulate and persuasive. The England bowler Angus Fraser recalled him holding an audience in thrall for 40 minutes, without notes, and reciting "word for word" from Hamlet. "His pre-match talks were often inspirational," Woolmer said, "and he led from the front." His players revered him. The Western Province seamer Craig Matthews credited Cronje with changing his life: "He actually persuaded me that I was good enough to play international cricket." At Cronje's funeral, Shaun Pollock, his successor as national captain, spoke of his love of practical jokes, often used to make newcomers feel at home. Pollock recounted being told to field next to a certain sponsor's advert, only to discover the sponsor had boards scattered all round the ground. As with most great leaders, Cronje's personality comprised a complex skein of qualities.

His captaincy record brooks few arguments. South Africa won 27 and lost only 11 of his 53 Tests in charge, with series victories over every opponent except Australia; in 138 one-day internationals there were 99 wins, as well as a tie. His record made a nonsense of the South African board's decision to appoint him for only the first two Tests against England in 1999–2000, even allowing for a downturn in his form and his apprehensions about the UCBSA's politically motivated policy of selection on racial quotas. Although he was later confirmed as captain for all the Tests and one-day games, his take on the turn of events was apparent in his brooding presence and the fact that he openly flirted with an offer to succeed Duncan Fletcher as Glamorgan coach.

He was still coming to terms, too, with that cataclysmic tie against Australia that cost South Africa a place in the 1999 World Cup final and dashed his boyhood dreams of leading his country to World Cup glory. With one run needed to win their semi-final, and three balls still in hand, South Africa's last pair, Lance Klusener and Donald, contrived the most fatal of run-outs. Cronje, who had been given out for a duck caught off his boot, was magnanimous in defeat as ever, but nothing could mask his anguish. Australia remained his *bête noire*.

He did outdo his Australian rivals Mark Taylor and Steve Waugh in winning a Test series in India, in 2000. South Africa won 2-0 and ended India's sequence of 14 unbeaten home series since 1987. But in that moment of triumph the seeds of his tragedy were quickly taking root. Ensnared in illicit dealings with subcontinental bookmakers after Mohammad Azharuddin introduced him to the match-fixer M. K. Gupta on South Africa's previous tour of India, in 1996, Cronje was now in cahoots with Sanjeev Chawla.

Granted immunity from prosecution, Cronje told the King Commission he received around $US140,000 from bookmakers, including $US110,000 from Gupta for information on team selection, daily forecasts and when he would declare against India at Cape Town in January 1997. He denied ever fixing the actual result of a match. When Cronje rejected further advances from Gupta in November 1997, that might have ended his perfidy. But, as he told Justice King, he had "an unfortunate love of money. . . I am not addicted to alcohol or nicotine, but I believe this is very similar to an alcohol problem".

Neither Justice King nor many others believed they had heard the full story, but enough was known for Cronje to receive a life ban from all cricketing activities. The Qayyum Report had already recommended a life ban for Pakistan's former captain Salim Malik; India's Azharuddin and Ajay Sharma would receive similar sentences before the year was out. And the ICC would eventually publish their own report into corruption in the game and implement a range of measures designed to keep the bookmakers at bay.

Meanwhile, the most intriguing question – why he did it – remained an enigma. In media interviews between his testimony and his ban in October, reputed to have netted a further £100,000, Cronje talked of "greed, stupidity and the lure of easy money" and claimed: "I was arrogant enough to think I would get away with it". A born-again Christian who wore a bracelet with the initials WWJD – What Would Jesus Do? – he talked of how Satan had entered his world when he took his eyes off Jesus and his "whole world turned dark". There was something pre-Christian in this, an echo of Greek heroes blaming the gods rather than themselves for their misfortunes.

Cronje's appeal against his life ban was rejected by the Pretoria High Court in October 2001, and while there was talk of his having some future role in cricket, maybe coaching or in the media, he began to build a life away from the game. He enrolled on a Masters degree course, and in February 2002 joined the Johannesburg-based firm Bell Equipment, which specialised in earth-moving machinery, as financial manager. At the time of his death he was commuting weekly to and from his home on the exclusive Fancourt Estate in George. That fateful weekend, he had hitched a ride with the two pilots of an Air Quarius Hawker Siddeley turbo-prop after his scheduled flight had been grounded by a hailstorm – a risk-taker to the end.

More than a thousand mourners filled the Grey College Chapel for Cronje's funeral, while a thousand more outside watched the service, which was televised nationally, on large screens. It was reported that members of the South African Cricket Board, critical earlier of their captain's betrayal, had been told they would not be welcome, but Bertha Cronje, Hansie's widow, said he would not have agreed with such a ban. The divisions were forgotten as South Africa, a nation rebuilding on forgiveness and reconciliation, mourned, in Gary Kirsten's words, "a great crick-eter, a great performer and a great on-field leader of his country". It was elsewhere that cricket would still consider Hansie Cronje a tarnished hero.

THE MAKING OF A MARTYR
Rob Steen, 2005

Few things ring alarm bells more loudly than a newspaper story pinned on "a survey". But sometimes these can be very instructive. One such survey was conducted by the South African Broadcasting Corporation to discover the "100 Greatest South Africans".

It was hardly a scientific study since the voting methods – phone, text and e-mail – obviously favoured white South Africans. Aware of the potential for embarrassment, the organisers decided in advance that Nelson Mandela would finish first. They did not plan the rest of the ballot well enough to reflect the new South Africa in quite the way they had hoped: Hendrik Verwoerd, the archi-tect of apartheid, finished 14 places above Walter Sisulu, who helped demolish it. Most astonishing of all, to the casual observer, was the name in 11th place, only just behind President Thabo Mbeki and Bishop Desmond Tutu: Hansie Cronje, former captain of the South African cricket team and admitted match-fixer.

As beneficiaries of the estates of Elvis Presley, James Dean and Marilyn Monroe will attest, death can be less a full stop than a colon. And although Cronje was no global superstar, his story was a three-part drama that surpassed even Elvis or Marilyn: after the rise to fame came the disgrace, and then the tragically early death – in a plane crash in June 2002, two years after he had been forced to admit taking bribes from bookmakers. This has given the Hansie story an extraordinary potency, especially among the Afrikaner community from which he sprang, where he remains revered, not so much as a fallen hero but as a martyr.

His afterlife started with Leon Dorfling's Hawker Siddeley Project. Why not recover the wreckage of the 748 freighter on which Cronje hitched a last-minute ride? Holidaymakers in Mossel Bay were soon paying canny Leon 20 rand (about £1.50) per gawk. Then came the opening ceremony for the 2003 World Cup at

Newlands, where the caterers rebranded one of their most popular items. "The Gatsby", a huge and somewhat grotesque roll stuffed with ham, tomato and chips, metamorphosed into "The Hansie". Any symbolism seems to have been accidental, but the men do have something in common: Scott Fitzgerald invented a character who elevated money above honour.

But the process preceded the crash. The King commission of inquiry into match-fixing had barely completed its hearings when the rehabilitation programme kicked into gear. One TV channel aired a three-part homage/interview with the apologetic Cronje over successive evenings: his fee was reportedly in the region of one million rand. The *Hello!*-style footage consisted largely of Cronje and his wife Bertha in their luxury home, or walking lovingly along a sun-kissed beach. In the final instalment, Cronje and the interviewer, Michael Haysman, both in blue shirts and khaki trousers, stood either side of a roaring fire, glass of wine in hand and chatting amiably.

Barred from direct involvement in cricket, Cronje then undertook a series of speaking engagements around the country, set up by a marketing arm of Castle Lager, co-sponsors of the Test team then and now. The audiences were almost exclusively white, middle class and male: the nucleus of the rainbow nation's audience for cricket and rugby. And the talks sold out.

Cronje was widely seen as a victim, who was punished cruelly for his misdemeanours while others involved, especially Australians, escaped. Many took at face value his assertion that he had never tried to lose a match for his country. Others were adamant he was picked on while black government officials get away with corruption. The foreign currency in Cronje's cupboard – for which he went unpunished – is seen as an irrelevance.

The victim thesis, strong enough while Cronje was alive, grew wings after he died. A year after the crash, there came an *Observer* article headlined "Was Hansie Cronje murdered?" "Many senior police officers believe he may have been – and they are working covertly to prove it," said the author, David Murt. "A lot of people wanted Cronje dead," claimed one investigator. "It suits the police to have a closed case." This theory is pooh-poohed by most sources – after all, Cronje only took the plane at the last minute – and was ignored by the official inquiry. But it all helps the myth. "Pictures of Cronje remain on office desks," wrote Murt, "statues are erected in his honour, team-mates proclaim his virtues, his image is emblazoned across T-shirts, and the making of his martyrdom continues to grow."

But this has strange effects. The *Cape Times* recently ran an article headlined "Hansie killed my mother", in which a woman blamed her parent's death on Cronje's misdemeanours and the way they had shattered her belief system. Yet the belief systems of white South Africans, and the Afrikaner community in particular, have endured many shocks over the past decade or so. They have already been obliged to disavow their former political leaders. Who would ever have expected them to have to disavow a cricket captain too?

"Afrikaners do feel embattled, especially on the sporting front, now that there are noises from parliamentary committees that their days are numbered in sport," explained Professor Bruce Murray, author of *Caught Behind*, a study of race and politics in South African cricket. "There is this sense that whites are being robbed of their cricket history. If you go to the corridor leading to the Long Room at the

Wanderers, all the photographs of the old Springboks have been removed and replaced by bats from the World Cup. The grounds are being sanitised, and there's a denial of the white cricketing past."

"There's a widespread feeling that Cronje owned up and came clean," Murray added, "and that it's always the South Africans who get the rough end of things." While that persists, the Cronje story will retain its power.

BEWARE THE SLEEPING DRAGON   Matthew Engel, *Notes by the Editor*, 2005

The new internet betting exchanges now often take far more money on England Tests than they do on even the most important England football matches. This form of gambling is perfectly legal in Britain and pretty much unstoppable anywhere else the internet reaches. There is nothing intrinsically wrong with it either: betting adds spice to cricket, and exchange betting can be very spicy indeed. I am a participant, not a critic.

The figures can be extraordinary, even for routine matches. The biggest exchange, Betfair, took more than £1m on the Essex-Glamorgan totesport League match last September. There was a reason for this: Glamorgan were already champions and fielded a weakened side; Essex were trying like mad to evade relegation. The shrewdies cleaned up over the internet, and in the betting shops of Cardiff. Nothing wrong with that, either.

But the line between that and the jiggery-pokery that came close to destroying international cricket a decade ago can be a thin one. And I suspect English cricket has not woken up to any of this. The ICC has an agreement with Betfair so that unusual betting patterns can be traced and potential match-fixing stamped on. The ECB has to be just as alert.

Politics

Hindsight is a wonderful thing. With hindsight we can see that the isolation of apartheid South Africa in the 1980s and 1990s did the trick – it helped to bring that wretched regime founded on ignorance, stupidity and selfishness to heel. With that hindsight we can also see that *Wisden* was on the wrong side for much of the period. Implicitly – occasionally explicitly – it sought the separation of politics and sport. It believed that visiting cricketers, repositories of enlightenment (*sic*), could bring illumination to that benighted land. Phooey! *Wisden*'s line – with that blessed hindsight – was misconceived. Apartheid in South Africa couldn't be tempered; it had to be dismantled.

Wisden, in the early 1980s, ran two long appeals for the show to be allowed to go on. First, from New Zealand bigwig Walter Hadlee in 1982: "I would hope that unity between the two cricket administrations can be effected," he apostrophised. "With the goodwill and support of all cricketers, greater influence will be possible, and will demonstrate that cricket knows no barriers and sets the highest example of integrated sport, so providing the platform for closer co-operation in the wider spheres of everyday life embracing social, cultural and economic activities." The following year, Kent batsman Graham Johnson went further, praising the benefits of unofficial "England" tours: "Tours such as that by the English SAB XI, provided they are handled correctly, can do a great deal to further changes within South Africa."

As early as 1976 *Wisden* was running longish items about the "normalisation" of cricket in South Africa. Under Norman Preston and John Woodcock, there was deep suspicion of the politicisation of cricket. "There is no knowing where it will all end," wrote Woodcock in 1982. "In the autumn of 1981, while England's tour [of India] was in doubt, the world of cricket came close to being split into two halves, the dividing line being one of colour. The white and non-white countries are, in fact, so interdependent in a cricketing sense that for this to happen would be a setback from which the game might take generations to recover."

There was a failure to see the cricketing wood from the political trees, or to acknowledge the leverage being exerted by the policy of isolating South Africa. Was cricket in South Africa on the road to integration? That was the only question of interest to *Wisden* in the early 1980s. The rest of society could, and probably did, go hang. "To act as they [the TCCB] ultimately did, without doing anything for the cause of cricket in South Africa, smacked more of expediency than strength," wrote Woodcock in 1983 of the ban on rebel tourists to South Africa. "The cause of cricket in South Africa" was the be-all and end-all of *Wisden*'s world view. But sometimes life must take precedence over the game. Who knows cricket who only cricket knows?

Matthew Engel, writing in 1984 as a contributor, moderated *Wisden*'s stance. "The game was integrated in theory, and sometimes in practice," he wrote of a proposed MCC tour to South Africa. "There was a better case for playing South Africa in the '80s than there ever had been in the totally segregated '60s. But even more had changed in the rest of the world: attitudes had hardened and the sports boycott had become a weapon with a wider purpose."

By the late '80s, the attitude of the cricket authorities – faced with a potentially devastating rift between Test-playing countries – had certainly hardened, and anyone who played in South Africa was facing a long ban. The then *Wisden* editor Graeme Wright, who opposed rebel tours, accepted the pragmatic need for such bans, but bemoaned the loss of freedom inherent in punishing individuals for earning a living. "An important principle has been conceded," he wrote in 1989. "If there remains any euphoria that international cricket has been saved – and with it, arguably, England's fully professional circuit with some 400 employees – the citizens of the United Kingdom have had a freedom curtailed at the insistence of other countries. It can be argued that a freedom which allows trade with an unjust society is not so valuable a freedom. None the less it is a freedom within British law. If it is expedient to accept restrictions on legal freedoms, how simple it will be to restrict freedom legally."

But he also recognised, in a way that previous editors had not, the principle that sometimes sport could not be squared with prevailing social conditions. "If the will of the voting class is not for change, no amount of cricket in the townships will destroy apartheid," he wrote. "And it is the ending of apartheid, not the number of black cricketers, which will influence world opinion." That seems to me to be a clear acknowledgment that it was no longer acceptable to have any cricketing contact with South Africa until it had reformed itself. "No amount of cricket in the townships will destroy apartheid" – that is not a phrase which would have appeared in *Wisden* a decade earlier.

It did ultimately reform itself and in 1992 South Africa was welcomed back into the international fold. Its contribution in the years since has been enormous, and it is now firmly established in the upper tier of Test-playing countries. The bitterness of the 1980s seems very distant, yet as the following extracts from *Wisden* show it came close to tearing the game apart, leading to games and tours being cancelled and international careers curtailed.

A decade later, the sport faced the crisis in Zimbabwe, and under Engel's stewardship *Wisden* took a very different line from the "keep sport separate" stance of the '70s and '80s. "Of course morality has a legitimate role to play in deciding whether or not a cricket tour can take place," he wrote in 2004, arguing that Zimbabwe should be shunned. "Any contrary argument is contemptible, especially in a game that went through the decades of torment caused by apartheid." Don't play games with monsters.   S. M.

THE JACKMAN AFFAIR   Michael Melford, 1982

The [England] team had been in Guyana for two days when, early on February 23, they were joined by Robin Jackman, the replacement for Bob Willis who had returned home after breaking down in Trinidad. No attempt was made to conceal the fact that Jackman, like others in the party, had spent winters playing in South Africa. Bairstow had captained a South African province, Griqualand West, in 1977–78 after the signing of the Gleneagles declaration which, in the next few days, was to become the subject of many interpretations, varying according to political taste.

By February 25, three days before the Second Test was due to start, it was known that a radio commentator in Jamaica had suggested that the Guyana government, by admitting Jackman with his South African connections, was in contravention of the Gleneagles Agreement. It was also learned that the Guyana government was taking the matter seriously. The next day the British government stated clearly through the minister for sport, Hector Monro, that the Gleneagles declaration was irrelevant in this case as it made no reference to actions by one country against the nationals of another.

However, later on February 26, the British high commissioner in Georgetown was informed by the Guyanese minister of foreign affairs that Jackman's visitor's permit had been withdrawn and that he must leave the country. A statement was issued simultaneously by the England manager, Alan Smith, in Georgetown and by the Cricket Council meeting at Lord's, saying that England would not play the Second Test as it was no longer possible for the Test team to be chosen without restrictions being imposed. In fact, it had not been envisaged that Jackman, newly arrived from an English winter, would play at all in Guyana, but injuries to Dilley and Old would probably have forced his inclusion if the match had taken place.

This way out: England's team leaves Guyana early in 1981, after Robin Jackman's visa was revoked because of his South African connections. In the second group are David Gower, Jackman, Mike Gatting and Graham Gooch (who would later find himself *persona non grata* after playing in South Africa), while up front are the tour captain Ian Botham, Geoff Miller and Graham Stevenson. Manager A. C. Smith brings up the rear.

Alan Smith, in collaboration with the high commissioner and with sympathy and support from other Caribbean countries, at once set in motion plans to withdraw the England party which, with press, radio and television representatives, was now over 40 strong. This was done next morning and, after a long wait at Georgetown airport, the team arrived that night in Barbados to a warm welcome. A meeting was then convened in Bridgetown between representatives of the governments of Barbados, Montserrat, Antigua and Jamaica, the other islands where England were due to play. Five days later, at 2 a.m. local time on March 4, it was announced that the tour would go on.

The statement of the four governments said that the Gleneagles declaration did not deal with sanctions against nationals of another country. From Lord's, the Cricket Council reaffirmed its support for the right of cricketers to pursue their careers in South Africa, Australia or anywhere else on an individual basis. The Cricket Council also made the highly significant point that such eventualities had been thoroughly discussed with the West Indies board during the year or more in which the tour was being planned. The team had gone only after assurances had been received that the fact that many English players earn their living in the winter by coaching and playing in South Africa would be no stumbling block.

As the dust settled in later weeks, it became even clearer that the case of Jackman was being used by the Guyana government to make a political point. In particular, it was considered elsewhere in the Caribbean to have been largely a reprisal for Lord Avebury's adverse report on election-rigging in Guyana. The main sufferers were the Guyanese cricket public, starved of cricket and, on all the evidence, bitterly disappointed to be deprived of a Test match. The previous match with Guyana had not been played owing to the waterlogged state of the Bourda Oval after days of heavy storms.

POLITICS TAKES OVER
John Woodcock, *Notes by the Editor*, 1982

Before and after the heady days of July and August [1981], when England were beating Australia, the game took some hard knocks. More than in any previous year the question of the South African connections of first-class cricketers kept cropping up. When two countries wish to meet each other, it is no longer a simple matter of their respective boards of control arranging a tour and knowing that it will go ahead. Given half a chance the politicians will use it as a means of applying pressure on South Africa to renounce the system of apartheid.

In February this led to the evacuation from Guyana of the England team and the cancellation of the Test match that was to have been played there. For the next few days, while discussions were taking place between the governments of Antigua, Barbados, Jamaica and Montserrat (the islands in which England had yet to play) as to whether the tour should be allowed to continue, officials of the West Indian Cricket Board and those in charge of the England team were bystanders, no more.

Later in the year New Zealand had a tour to the West Indies cancelled, for no other reason than that as a country they had played rugby football against South

Africa. For a fortnight, too, England's tour of India hung precariously in the balance because two of their chosen team, Boycott and Cook, were on a United Nations blacklist for having been, regularly and quite recently, to South Africa. That Cook had spent some time there coaching non-white children and that Boycott's visits had been mostly of a private kind cut no ice with the Indian government. In the end Mrs Gandhi, their prime minister, relented, but it was a close-run thing.

There is no knowing where it will all end. In the autumn of 1981, while England's tour was in doubt, the world of cricket came close to being split into two halves, the dividing line being one of colour. The white and non-white countries are, in fact, so interdependent in a cricketing sense that for this to happen would be a setback from which the game might take generations to recover.

When it comes to overturning racial prejudice, cricketers believe that the best contribution they can make is to compete together, whether in the same team or on opposite sides. Those administrators who meet each year at Lord's will always do well to remember that they hold the positions they do, not to act as politicians but as guardians of the game of cricket – in South Africa not least.

THE ESCALATING EFFECTS OF POLITICS ON CRICKET   Walter Hadlee, 1982

As I write, the England cricket team is commencing its tour of India. The speculation surrounding the tour has been ended by the Indian government's decision that it may proceed, because it is satisfied that two players selected for England, whilst having had some association with cricket in South Africa, are opposed to the apartheid system enforced by the government.

The cricket world received this decision with a sense of infinite relief. Had the Indian government not given their approval, the tour would have been cancelled by the UK cricket authorities. What then? New Zealand had indicated that they would host the England team. In the same season, Australia were also touring New Zealand. Would India then feel they could no longer play New Zealand, because that country had accepted players who had some links, however remote, with South Africa? Would India feel likewise about Australia, who had visited New Zealand who had played England, whose selected team was not acceptable in India? Would a chain reaction spread throughout the cricket world, threatening those long-standing ties and friendly associations that have been the product of visits frequently exchanged?

In retrospect, cricket – indeed all sport – should be deeply indebted to Mrs Gandhi and her government: in expressing continued opposition to the discriminatory laws of South Africa, and at the same time taking the view that sportsmen and supporters should not be penalised, India has set an example which, if followed, could solve many of the problems confronting cricket in particular and sport in general.

Cricket has had its share of traumatic experiences in recent years. In 1977, World Series Cricket was launched and the game suffered until peace was made. The after-effects, some good, some bad, continue to pose problems. Today, however, the major area of concern centres around boycotts, blacklists, and who will or will not play one another. In 1981, a Test match was cancelled in the West Indies because Guyana refused entry to Robin Jackman. Worse still, the West Indies Board of Control advised the New Zealand Cricket Council that their team would not be welcome in 1982 – not for cricket reasons, but because a rugby tour by a multi-racial team of South Africans was taking place in New Zealand.

This exposes the heart of the issue – South Africa and its policies. A rugby tour of South Africa by New Zealand in 1976 led to the withdrawal of some African nations from the Montreal Olympics, and the Commonwealth Heads of Government, no doubt in an effort to prevent a repetition at the Edmonton Games in 1978, came up with the controversial Gleneagles declaration in June 1977. This declaration is headed Apartheid in Sport. Different interpretations have given rise to endless controversy, much of it still continuing.

From 1970, maybe earlier, sporting bodies had required that South Africa meet the dual criteria of multi-racial sport from club level upwards, and selection on merit. If those conditions were met, South African teams would be accepted at international level.

If the Gleneagles Agreement, with all its imperfections, was intended to apply to apartheid in sport, one would expect that the agreement would not apply when apartheid – surely meaning racial discrimination – in sport no longer existed. Cricket in South Africa could, by September 1977, claim one governing body democratically born by common consent and representing the black, white, and coloured racial groups. The constitution of the South African Cricket Union can leave no doubt as to the intent to provide multi-racial cricket, selection on merit, and a sharing of facilities on all grounds on a common basis. However, since the formation of the South African Cricket Union (SACU), the politically motivated South African Cricket Board (SACB), aligned to the South African Council on Sport (SACOS), has been created as an alternative body, claiming to be non-racial, but with its primary purpose to isolate South Africa from international cricket.

So again the political motive determines attitudes towards sport. The target of those who see sport as a means to an end is the South African government, whose laws are unacceptable to the world in general. There is a widespread desire to enforce change, and to put pressure on South Africa through the isolation of their sportsmen and women, and sports administrative bodies. Governments and anti-apartheid groups never seem to clarify their demands by setting out the precise requirements to be met by either the South African government or the sporting bodies concerned. Gleneagles mentions the detestable policy of apartheid, but does not define apartheid. Does the word mean separate development, or the laws which discriminate against non-whites?

It seems to me that the matter of separate development is for the determination of those who reside in Southern Africa. There is evidence that some ethnic groups prefer separate development and that others do not. If the word apartheid is used in the context of discriminatory laws, there can be no doubt that these are not acceptable, offensive as they are to human dignity.

I have personally opposed all forms of racial discrimination and will continue to do so. I opposed the New Zealand rugby tour of South Africa in

1960, because Maoris were excluded. This was racial discrimination by New Zealanders against New Zealanders. I was also totally opposed to the decision of the South African government to refuse to accept Basil D'Oliveira as a member of the England team in 1968. In 1973, when chairman of the New Zealand Cricket Council, I had the pleasure of meeting for the first time officers of the South African Cricket Association, the former administrative body for white South African cricketers. I indicated that I could support South African cricket only when they achieved multi-racial cricket with selection on merit. They attained this in 1977, and having done so deserve the recognition and encouragement of not only every fair-minded cricket administrator, but of all who oppose racial prejudice.

Independent reports issued by several fact-finding delegations establish that many other sports bodies within South Africa have had similar success in their efforts to provide equal opportunities and integrated sport for members of all ethnic groups. One may well ask, what more is required of the South African Cricket Union and similar national sporting bodies who have rejected discrimination? The discriminatory laws which have been the root cause of many of cricket's problems have been successfully opposed by the South African Cricket Union, who have been in the forefront of the battle for equality in the area in which they exercise most influence – on the cricket field. They can take much of the credit for the fact that practically all barriers to racially mixed sport in South Africa, above school age, have now been removed.

The sporting world has, I believe, had enough of the sabotage of the Olympic Games by those who disrupt them for political reasons, as at Montreal in 1976 and Moscow in 1980. If this pattern continues, sport will become fragmented, and true international sport will not survive. Even now it is under such threat that none can predict who will take part in the Commonwealth Games in 1982 or the Olympics in 1984. All international sports bodies will have to look seriously at what the future holds for their sport. Disciplinary action may be required against those who, without adequate reason, surrender the opportunity to participate. But in the true spirit of sport, no country wishing to take part should be denied the right.

The International Cricket Conference represents the cricketers of the world. Its future can only be threatened if members allow themselves to be involved in politics rather than cricket. To be a truly effective body, it must encourage the development of the game wherever it is played. It must be aware of the problems of member countries, but always believe that sporting contacts, especially through cricket, can be the catalyst in resolving such problems. To revert to the cricket scene in South Africa, I would hope that unity between the two cricket administrations can be effected. With the goodwill and support of all cricketers, greater influence will be possible, and will demonstrate that cricket knows no barriers and sets the highest example of integrated sport, so providing the platform for closer co-operation in the wider spheres of everyday life embracing social, cultural and economic activities.

I would urge that where there are difficulties, let there be understanding; where there is division, let there be dialogue; where there are differences, let there be reconciliation. Cricket, indeed all sport, has much to offer. May it not be misused, but left alone to play its natural role in providing relaxation and pleasure for those who would play and follow it.

Walter Hadlee captained New Zealand and was later chairman of selectors and chairman of the New Zealand Cricket Council.

THE SOUTH AFRICAN DILEMMA

John Woodcock, *Notes by the Editor*, 1983

It was ironic, some thought absurd, that Allan Lamb should be acceptable for England but not the 15 Englishmen, captained by Graham Gooch, who toured South Africa, Lamb's home country, in the spring of 1982 and were disqualified from Test cricket for three years for having done so.

Having had their submission for re-entry into the Test fold persistently rejected, despite meeting in every detail the original conditions for this to happen, South Africa have run out of patience and decided that only with the aid of a cheque book can they give the game there the stimulus of international competition which it needs. They are, accordingly, offering cricketers the chance to become mercenaries.

By the end of 1982 a team of Sri Lankans (the equivalent, perhaps, of Sri Lanka's second XI) had been slipped into South Africa, there, at the expense of their cricket careers at home, to earn more money in few weeks than they could normally do in a lifetime. There are, inevitably, unattractive aspects to this. For one thing, any such operation is likely to be conspiratorially planned, if only to keep the protesters at bay. Although the Englishmen who went to South Africa (12 of them had won Test caps, all except Amiss within the previous 18 months) were not in breach of the Gleneagles Agreement as it is interpreted by the British government (they would have been, of course, had they been an official team), they must have known that there would be repercussions.

Five of the party had only recently returned from the England tour of India, which Mrs Gandhi had threatened to prohibit because of the connections of two of them (Boycott and Cook) with cricket in South Africa. It was hardly surprising, when Gooch, Boycott, Emburey, Lever and Underwood turned up in Johannesburg in March, that the Indians felt let down.

In the autumn of 1981 the Test and County Cricket Board had warned, by letter, all county cricketers that if they went as members of a team to South Africa (the distinction between going collectively and to coach was clearly drawn) they might have to pay for it. In the event, the reaction to their unheralded arrival in South Africa was little short of hysterical. Although they had widespread public support, the English players became, overnight, pawns in a fiercely political game. Predictably, the cricket boards of both India and Pakistan, guided by their governments, threatened to call off their forthcoming visits to England should they be expected to play against the English rebels. One English county, Northamptonshire, so feared the financial consequences of such a cancellation that they called for a life ban, no less, on the offending players. The prime minister, on the other hand, refused to condemn them. Speaking in Parliament, Mrs

Thatcher said "we do not have the power to prevent any sportsmen or women from visiting South Africa or anywhere else. If we did we would no longer be a free country."

Trapped in the maelstrom, the TCCB, by imposing a three-year ban – to preserve international multi-racial cricket – bowed to political pressures, to the consternation not only of the players concerned but also of the average cricket follower. In politics, which this was, even a week is a long time. Three years is an eternity, as it is in a cricketer's career. In time the players appealed for some remission of their sentence. But again politics took over. When the West Indians were asked how they would view it if the players' suspensions were to be reduced from three years to two, they withheld their approval. This although, less than a month before, the ICC had agreed unanimously that on no account should one country be allowed to influence the team selection of another.

If that was not hypocritical, what is? I am sure that at all times the TCCB proceeded, as they thought, in good faith. They did all they could, once they had got wind of the tour, to dissuade the players from embarking on it. For all that, to act as they ultimately did, without doing anything for the cause of cricket in South Africa, smacked more of expediency than strength.

A one-year suspension, with a future tightening of players' contracts, would have been ample. And knowing the West Indians as I do, and the importance they attach to playing cricket against England, quite apart from the joy they get from beating them, I believe that, come 1984, their politicians, like everyone else, would have accepted some reduction of the ban.

PROGRESS TOWARDS NON-RACIAL CRICKET

Graham Johnson, 1983

My initial contact with South African cricket came in 1973, as a member of a strong Derrick Robins XI. The situation was illuminating: it was the first non-racial cricket tour of South Africa, and sharing a room with John Shepherd, a West Indian, gave me an insight into many questions.

In 1978 I was asked by Barclays National Bank of South Africa to spend an English winter in Johannesburg, developing and expanding their already considerable cricket coaching programme and playing in the top Johannesburg league for a non-racial club. With this becoming an annual visit I have gained an intimate knowledge by personal contact of the aspirations and problems of cricket in Johannesburg, and, by contact with the other provinces and the personalities involved, of the situation in other areas.

Two points are central to the Barclays philosophy in cricket development. It is insisted that the scheme benefits cricketers of *all* races (although in prevailing circumstances the major portion of the budget is directed towards non-white cricketers) and the involvement is viewed as a long-term commitment to the establishment of cricket in areas where it has not previously thrived. Taking the population groups within South Africa, cricket in general is well established in the Asian, Coloured and white areas, but is a relatively new sport in most African areas.

Thus for people to expect that with the coming of non-racial cricket within

South Africa some eight years ago, representative sides would immediately become markedly more non-white was unfounded. Few non-white cricketers were of a calibre to compete for places on merit with white players who had had exposure for the development of their talents. It made one realise what an enigma Basil D'Oliveira was, and that his amazing example should not be held as a yardstick for the average product of non-white cricket. A goal to be achieved yes, but not the norm.

Having established the framework in which equal development and opportunity can take place, there is bound to be a lead-in period before the talent develops sufficiently for the non-white players whom the public expect to see representing South Africa, and playing at provincial level, to do so in any numbers. Initially the non-white representation has to come from the Coloured and Asian groups. Almost certainly it will be some time before an African cricketer wears a Springbok cap. Nevertheless, given time, I can see no reason why the development of African cricket should not be along the lines of South African football, which has become an African-dominated sport. It is important that the public overseas accepts this perspective and appreciates that a lot of good is being done within South African cricket and South African sport in general, even if the whole South African XI does not come from Soweto.

Within the Barclays scheme in Johannesburg, evidence of this development has been seen since 1978 with non-white cricketers gaining selection for the Transvaal Schools Under-14, Under-15, open-age group and the senior Transvaal B team on merit. This trend is happening throughout the country, and in the different population groups the progression is bound to continue. There has been an honest and sincere effort by the South African cricket authorities to overcome deep-seated internal problems and prejudices. They have challenged the laws of the land so that their belief in non-racial sport may be realised. It cannot be said of cricket that it is a cosmetic selection of a few talented non-white players for representative sides. It is a major commitment, and one can understand the disappointment of South African cricket representatives, who have made considerable steps forward in their sport, when international bodies seems so reluctant to acknowledge these improvements.

Within South African cricket there is a split allegiance between the South African Cricket Union, the almost universally recognised governing body, and the more politically motivated South African Cricket Board with its predominantly Asian and Coloured membership. This causes continual internal problems, especially for the non-white cricketer. To say that either camp truly has the support of the non-white cricketer is to over-simplify a complicated issue. There is an ebb and flow between the two sides; and that such a difference of opinion exists in a country of so many population groups, with further divisions within each group, is hardly surprising. Despite their different ways of going about them, their aims are basically the same. When different personalities run the SACB set-up, the current differences may be looked back on in years to come as a passing phase. What would be hypocritical is if either side were to adopt an unyielding stance and so create what in effect would be a reverse apartheid system within the game.

Tours such as that by the English SAB XI, provided they are handled correctly, can do a great deal to further changes within South Africa. There is a valid view expressed – about the future of South Africa – that socio-economic trends and principles decree that attitudes and therefore, eventually, laws will *have* to change, and that commercial companies and their attitudes will have a big part to play in forming the country's future. Why, in that case, can the same attitudes and ideas not be applied to cricket and other sports, which, to those playing them, are businesses? The idea of a cricket world split in two, comprising those with and without contacts with South Africa, is disastrous. World cricket can't afford it and South Africa would rather avoid it. But unless constructive contact is made and South Africa's advances are recognised, without threatening a rupture in the world game, there is a real danger that entrepreneurs within South Africa will successfully develop their activities.

I was once asked what I was trying to do in Johannesburg. I replied that, whether through the coaching programme or by playing club cricket, I hoped to help create a system in which everybody had an equal opportunity to play the game; and in which people could meet on equal terms afterwards, learning, through contact, more about each other. Without such contact messages are misunderstood and false images built up, either within the country itself or externally. The philosophy can be applied, I believe, at international level and can help to ensure the natural development of the game.

Graham Johnson played for Kent from 1965 to 1983.

MCC AND SOUTH AFRICA
Matthew Engel, 1984

The summer of 1983 will mainly be remembered as a time when cricket people could forget their troubles and enjoy the game and the sunshine, if only temporarily. The problem of South Africa was never that far away from anyone's consciousness. But its prime manifestation came in a manner that left little damage, and was even rather quaint.

On July 13, the members of the Marylebone Cricket Club voted to support their committee and reject a proposal to send a touring team of their own to South Africa. In the history of one of sport's most intractable crises, it will probably not be regarded as one of the most momentous decisions; in the history of one of sport's most famous and most powerful clubs, it may well have been.

The idea of trying to use MCC as a locomotive to pull South Africa back into world cricket had been conceived a year earlier at a meeting of the six-man executive of the right-wing pressure group, Freedom in Sport: the Conservative MP John Carlisle, Jeff Butterfield, Tommie Campbell, John Reason, Edward Grayson and Lord Chalfont. All except Mr Campbell also happened to be members of MCC. The club had not been directly involved in the issue since 1968. On that occasion the committee, in spite of the cancellation of the 1968–69 tour over South Africa's refusal to admit Basil D'Oliveira, was still defending, though with growing unease, the principle of continuing cricketing links. It beat off liberal opposition, led by two of the less conventional men to captain the England team, the Reverend David Sheppard and Michael Brearley, by a margin of more than three to one.

In the 15 intervening years very little had changed in South Africa's general political outlook. But a great deal had changed in cricket since the formation of the multi-racial South African Cricket Union in 1977. The game was integrated in theory, and sometimes in practice. There was a better case for playing South Africa in the '80s than there ever had been in the totally segregated '60s. But even more had changed in the rest of the world: attitudes had hardened and the sports boycott had become a weapon with a wider purpose.

Something else had changed: MCC no longer had that much authority to do anything about it. 1968 was also the year when it surrendered its role as the ruling body of English cricket and moved into a nebulous position of influence without anything like the same direct power – the house of Lord's in this sense being like the House of Lords. It was associated with the policies made elsewhere in cricket, without being able to change them. As far as the boycott went, cricket was in any case forced largely to comply with policies made elsewhere.

None the less, MCC seemed ideal for Freedom in Sport's purposes. Its supporters could get nowhere with any of cricket's ruling bodies, national or international. But, under Rule 43, it takes only 50 members to demand a special general meeting. Finding 50 was not a problem for Mr Carlisle and his friends. They set up their own committee including the evocative names of Denis Compton and Bill Edrich. There were brief but hopeless talks with the real committee to see if an accommodation could be reached. In April, Jack Bailey, the secretary of MCC, stood at the Grace Gates and received a petition proposing that the members of MCC committee implement the selection of a touring party to tour South Africa in 1983–84. He has been seen looking happier.

The problem Mr Bailey – and cricket – now faced was a curious one. MCC, in theory, had become merely a private club. Plenty of private clubs had been touring South Africa and dispensing discreet aid and comfort throughout the years of supposed isolation. It quickly became clear, because of the sanctions that would almost certainly be applied to any current first-class players who might make the tour, that, if forced to send a team, the committee would have to despatch players not far above customary club level – the men who habitually raise the flag for Marylebone and cricket in places like Bangladesh or the United States. But the very initials MCC have a special power. Few people with a casual involvement in cricket at home and even fewer overseas have cottoned on to the club's diminished role. The last Test-playing tour party to be called MCC had been in 1976–77. After six years the change had still not permeated the consciousness of much of the world's cricketing public. Thus one of the great dangers of the tour would have been mistaken identity. Indeed the most worried man I met before the vote was one of the likely tourists, who thought South Africa might get it wrong and unleash their fastest bowlers at him.

The case put by the 50 members and sent out on their behalf by MCC was that a tour would recognise the progress made by SACU, halt the slide of international sport towards total political influence and possible disintegration, and allow long-suffering sports people to get on with sport. MCC's rebuttal acknowledged that the resolution would appeal to many members and talked about hypocrisy and double standards among South Africa's opponents. But it then argued that such a tour would achieve nothing in cricketing terms, breach the Gleneagles Agreement, which the British government was pledged to support, and endanger the club's remaining positions in the game; as custodian of the Laws, as owner of Lord's, which the black countries might refuse to visit, and in the ICC, for which MCC still automatically provided the president and secretary. Since a number of overseas officials regarded this as an anachronism anyway, Mr Bailey and the incumbent president, Sir Anthony Tuke, were aware they might be the first casualties.

The meeting was fixed for the night prior to the first Test – well after the World Cup and the annual ICC meeting. The World Cup was conducted amid constant rumours that the South Africans, having bought their own teams of English and West Indian rebels in successive years, were now trying to sign anything that moved. A SACU delegation, led by Joe Pamensky, paid its annual, now ritualised visit to the ICC which in an equally ritualised way refused to see them. Mr Pamensky's visit was very public but he said little about the impending MCC vote, beyond saying that any team it sent would be very welcome.

The postal votes began to pile up at MCC's solicitors in the City. There were rumours about these too, most of them saying that the proponents were not far short of the two-thirds majority they would need to carry the motion and well above the simple majority that would be regarded as a huge moral victory and a humiliation for the club's establishment. Everyone Mr Carlisle met at Lord's, he said later, told him they were voting for him. Since his majority at Luton West had gone up from 200 to 12,000 at the June general election, he may well have been feeling invulnerable. His only moment of discomfort came when the prime minister (ineligible to join MCC owing to her sex) came out against the tour in the Commons.

The evening of July 13 turned out to be one of almost unbearable heat. The committee had hired Central Hall, Westminster, the largest available, in the expectation that around 2,000 of the 18,000 members would wish to come. But it was no night for attending meetings voluntarily. Only 1,000 turned up. The meeting was also a little overshadowed. By coincidence, a few hundred yards across Parliament Square, the newly elected House of Commons was debating whether or not to bring back hanging. Some thought that MCC was debating whether or not to hang itself.

Mr Carlisle proposed the motion. His speech – cogent and well received – made much of the argument that it was unfair to treat sporting and business links differently. He was seconded by John Pashley, a former Yorkshire League cricketer, who emphasised the importance of not being pushed around in a speech that was passionate and effective until, for a hot evening, it went on too long.

The motion was opposed by Hubert Doggart, a former president of MCC, who, as in the committee's written argument, conceded part of the case before putting over the official view of the realities of the situation and implying that Mr Carlisle's motives were political rather than sporting. He was seconded, in similar vein, by Colin Cowdrey who, 15 years earlier, had been prominent in the bridge-building school of thought. Both went down well, assisted by their known love for the game and their gentle demeanour which enabled them to disguise some sharp debating points. The floor speakers included another Conservative MP Andrew Hunter, Denis Compton and Brian Johnston (a popular BBC commentator), all for the motion; the antis included two churchmen – David Sheppard, now Bishop of Liverpool, and John Stacey.

But the debate did not matter. As Mr Bailey knew (though he says he did not tell a soul) the Carlisle forces were already beaten. They had lost the postal vote 6,069 to 3,935; they lost the vote in the hall 535 to 409 – an overall total of 6,604 to 4,344 against the resolution, or 60.3% to 39.7.

The expectations that had built up in the past few days now worked heavily against Mr Carlisle and his supporters. The focus was on the committee victory rather than on the perhaps more remarkable fact that 40% of those who voted and almost a quarter of MCC's traditionally docile membership had repudiated the committee on a matter on which it had fought furiously to enforce its point of view. This suggested that MCC's rulers might have many more uncomfortable nights, over all kinds of issues, in the years to come.

Mr Carlisle felt later, in view of what everyone had told him beforehand, that he must have been defeated by the votes of people who never go to Lord's. He thought too that it had been a mistake to pin down the committee by putting a date to the tour, when the important thing was winning the principle. Mr Bailey thought the exercise had cleared the air and enhanced the reputation of the club. Everyone agreed that, whether or not MCC debated the matter again, cricket was not going to be able to forget South Africa.

ENGLAND'S TOUR TO INDIA CANCELLED   Graeme Wright, *Notes by the Editor*, 1989

Mike Gatting did not play in the second Test against West Indies [in 1988], and after doing little in the Third, he asked the selectors not to consider him for the rest of the summer. He also withdrew from consideration for England's tour to India in the winter. Whether or not he would have been missed there became academic when the tour was cancelled on October 7. The Indian government would not grant visas to eight of the players whose names appeared on a list of sportsmen with links with South Africa, and the TCCB, holding to the International Cricket Conference's principle that no country should be allowed to influence the team selection of another, refused to replace those players.

The team which England selected was as follows: Graham Gooch (captain), John Emburey (vice-captain), Robin Bailey, Kim Barnett, John Childs, Graham Dilley, Neil Foster, David Gower, Eddie Hemmings, Allan Lamb, David Lawrence, Phil Newport, Steve Rhodes, Tim Robinson, Jack Russell and Robin Smith. The players about whom objections were raised were Gooch, Emburey, Bailey, Barnett, Dilley, Lamb, Newport and Robinson. Even before the team was announced, on September 7, there had been speculation that the tour might be in jeopardy following the appointment the previous week of Gooch as captain. Gooch had captained the first of the rebel tours to South Africa, for which he (and Emburey) had been banned from Test cricket for three years. Both he and Emburey had been admitted into India and Pakistan for the World Cup in 1987, an expediency which led to accusations of hypocrisy. These did an injustice to the strength of feeling in India against the apartheid policy of South Africa's elected government.

Gooch and Emburey, with others, had gone virtually straight on to South Africa from a tour of India, which had been in doubt because the Indian government found unacceptable the inclusion of Geoffrey Boycott and Geoff Cook, who had recently played in South Africa. Boycott moreover played a part in setting up the team for South Africa, as well as being a member of it. In the circumstances, it should not have been surprising when, on September 9, India's Foreign Ministry announced that no player having or likely to have sporting contact with South

Africa would be granted a visa. Gooch, it was by now known, had intended spending the winter playing in South Africa for Western Province, rather than touring India with England. When he was persuaded to tour as captain of England, he was released from his South Africa contract. It was a situation made, if not designed, to aggravate the Indian government.

In his interview with *The Cricketer*, Peter May was asked if he and his fellow selectors had considered the political repercussions of appointing Gooch. His view was that the selectors' brief was to select the best possible team from the cricketing point of view. "We don't pick teams for political reasons. In any case Graham Gooch had been perfectly acceptable to India for the World Cup. . ." More apt, perhaps, to say that he had been an exception then rather than acceptable; and is it not naive of the chairman and his selectors, at the end of the 1980s, to think it unnecessary to look beyond the cricketing point of view? If the cricketing point of view were all that mattered, it would be possible to ask why Gatting was stripped of the captaincy [over an alleged sexual dalliance with a barmaid]. Sad though it may be, cricket cannot operate as a business without an awareness of the messy world beyond the boundary.

When the tour of India was cancelled, the TCCB agreed to pay the players selected a substantial portion of their £12,000 tour fee. They also tried to arrange a replacement tour. With most countries already committed, this was not an easy task. Eventually, New Zealand arranged a seven-week tour in February and March incorporating two Test matches against England and a triangular limited-overs tournament involving Pakistan, their scheduled touring team. However, when Pakistan changed their mind and refused to play against England in New Zealand, this tour too had to be abandoned. New Zealand, whose finances had suffered the previous season, felt they could not afford to stage a secondary tour involving England which did not include the three-way one-day competition. Pakistan, like India, objected to the presence in the England team of players who had worked in South Africa; yet Pakistan's cricketers were playing at the time in Australia against at least one player, Terry Alderman, who had toured South Africa with rebel sides.

India's decision to exclude the England eight left the TCCB in little doubt that it would have to make concessions on the subject of links with South Africa if it was not to find itself isolated internationally. Certainly it was the opinion of the board's executive that English cricket could not maintain its current financial health without a regular programme of Test matches at home and away. Some counties, no doubt, would have liked to call the bluff of those countries opposed to links with South Africa, but such thinking did not take into account the political opposition in the other ICC countries to apartheid. The reality of the situation demanded a solution. Only time will tell if the solution agreed on will prevent further interference by governments in the composition of touring teams.

At its meeting at Lord's on January 23 and 24, the ICC resolved that, as from April 1, 1989, any cricketer who visits South Africa as a player or coach or in an administrative capacity will automatically be suspended from Test cricket for the following terms according to the player's age: over 16 and under 19, three years; 19 and over, four years. In addition, players participating in an organised tour will be suspended for five years. A register of ineligible players will be kept by the ICC secretariat, and a second or subsequent visit to South Africa could increase the suspension.

The resolution, which was proposed by West Indies and seconded by Sri Lanka, was unopposed and carried by 32 votes: two votes each by the seven Full Members and one by each of the 18 Associate Members. It was preceded by much negotiating, and no doubt there were some on either side of the divide who saw it as a compromise. It is; and the test will come when England tour the West Indies this coming winter with players who worked in South Africa before April 1. For the moment, England's cricketers can be thankful that the resolution was not retrospective. Nevertheless, an important principle has been conceded. If there remains any euphoria that international cricket has been saved – and with it, arguably, England's fully professional circuit with some 400 employees – the citizens of the United Kingdom have had a freedom curtailed at the insistence of other countries. It can be argued that a freedom which allows trade with an unjust society is not so valuable a freedom. None the less it is a freedom within British law. If it is expedient to accept restrictions on legal freedoms, how simple it will be to restrict freedom legally.

Freedom is a strange word to use in any context involving South Africa. Cricket, however, is not free of South Africa. There remains, as I write these Notes, the threat of legal action against the ICC and perhaps the TCCB, the cost of which will be borne by English cricket, not by those countries which instigated the ban on players who ply their trade in South Africa. There is also the possibility that South Africa will continue to attract cricketers from abroad. It would be ironic if this affected England less than other countries, whose seasons are the same as South Africa's. In a material age, money is a powerful persuader.

What the member countries of the ICC have not said in recent years is what they want of South Africa. Perhaps they hope that, as it is no longer on the agenda, the question of South Africa will cease to exist. I wonder if an opportunity has been lost by ignoring what is being done by the South African Cricket Union in taking cricket into the black townships. South Africa has to change if justice is to prevail and each child, regardless of colour, is to begin life equal with the next. That change can come through bloodshed or through the political will of the South African electorate. The second way will take time and education.

I know nothing of the work of the South African Cricket Union except for what I have read. It may be propaganda. But if black South African children are being taught a game which brings them into regular contact with white South African children, might not the latter come to acknowledge the rights of the former and grow to vote out a government which maintains apartheid? Undue optimism? Probably, but I prefer subversion by the cricket bat to subversion by the Kalashnikov. If, however, the will of the voting class is not for change, no amount of cricket in the townships will destroy apartheid. And it is the ending of apartheid, not the number of black cricketers, which will influence world opinion.

AN ILL-TIMED VENTURE

Graeme Wright, *Notes by the Editor*, 1990

By playing as a team in South Africa, Mike Gatting's side – 16 including the captain and David Graveney, the player-manager – become ineligible to play for England for at least five years under the ICC resolution of January 1989. All but Graveney and

Alan Wells have played for England, and eight – Gatting, Barnett, Broad, Dilley, Embury, Foster, Jarvis and Robinson – represented England against Australia in 1989.

Each claimed he was exercising his right to practise his trade as a professional cricketer. And we were told again of the short lifespan of the professional cricketer. Both are valid points in their own ways, but I am inclined to think the argument devalues the professional in this instance.

I also feel that the South African Cricket Union has made a mistake – politically and tactically – in staging this tour. In recent years it has been improving its credentials, both as an opponent of apartheid and as a non-racial administration, through its cricket development programme in the black townships. Now it is gambling that goodwill on a venture that can be seen only as sanctions-busting by the country's black leaders.

If, as a result of the tour, the community leaders turn against the township programmes, it will be a tragedy: not for South African cricket, but for those under-privileged children to whom cricket had offered a means of expressing themselves beyond their segregated environments. Had SACU waited a year, such is the promise of change in South Africa politically that the ICC decision of January 1989 might have been seen as coming too late to be meaningful. As it is, who knows what harm will be done.

WHEN SPORT MEETS TYRANNY
Tim de Lisle, *Notes by the Editor*, 2003

The cricket administrator's favourite charge down the years, the catch-all phrase deployed to deal with naughty boys, has been "bringing the game into disrepute". More often than not, it is hogwash. But early in 2003, the game really was brought into disrepute – by its own rulers. Months before the World Cup began on February 9, it was clear that Zimbabwe was in a desperate state. Robert Mugabe's government, returned to power in a flagrantly fixed election, was running a vicious, thuggish police state, apparently indifferent at best to the famine afflicting millions of its people. Those in Zimbabwe who raised the alarm risked imprisonment or worse: in 2002, the local human-rights forum reported 1,061 cases of torture. As the banners on marches say, if you weren't outraged, you weren't paying attention. This was no place to stage a major sports event.

The 2003 World Cup had not been awarded to Zimbabwe. It had been awarded to South Africa, which decided to make it more African, and more helpful to their World Cup football bid, by handing six matches to Zimbabwe and a couple to Kenya. Irrespective of whether you approved, it was an unmistakably political decision, taken, as the World Cup organiser Dr Ali Bacher was careful to point out, by the government. Politics ran through this World Cup like the zebra-skin logo that bedecked the stands.

One poll after another suggested that three-quarters of UK sports followers thought visiting teams should be allowed to switch their Zimbabwe games to South African venues (which were already on stand-by in case of security problems). Malcolm Speed reacted to this idea like a new father who hears someone criticising his baby. He took umbrage and insisted, to the open-mouthed disbelief of those who had observed their machinations over the years, that the ICC were non-political. It hadn't stopped them stomaching plenty of political activity from the South Africans. It hadn't stopped them letting matches go ahead in Zimbabwe under a repugnant regime. And it didn't stop them standing by in silence as Mugabe's police arrested dozens of people for making polite protests at Australia's game in Bulawayo.

Before the tournament, Nasser Hussain grasped three crucial points: that England and Zimbabwe had a singularly complex relationship, the legacy of colonialism; that the England players could hardly represent their country if their country didn't want them to go; and that they would be making a political statement whether they went to Zimbabwe or not. Speed couldn't see it. The ICC ended up doing something that ought to have been impossible: washing their hands at the same time as burying their heads in the sand.

When the ICC failed to give a lead over Zimbabwe, the England and Wales Cricket Board had the chance to fill the void. Instead, Tim Lamb said: why us? Cricket, he argued, was part of the international leisure and entertainment industry. About 300 British companies were continuing to do business with Zimbabwe; why should cricket alone be expected to take a stand? The answer hardly needs spelling out. A national team has a symbolic dimension that a firm importing mange-touts does not. A cricket board is not a company: it may be businesslike, but it does not exist to make money. It exists to stage cricket, to promote it and protect its good name. Lamb's stance, like Speed's, brought the game into disrepute. How can they govern cricket, who only cricket know?

Not that the administrators were alone in ducking the issue. Ricky Ponting played a great captain's innings in the final, but he hadn't shown much leadership in Bulawayo, where he went with a shrug of the shoulders. The Australians were reportedly asked to wear black armbands and refused. The only visible flickers of conscience in the Australian camp came from Matthew Hayden and Adam Gilchrist, who was so deeply affected that three weeks later, he walked when given not out. Bulawayo was the one moment where Australia missed Steve Waugh: a man who had founded a ward for the daughters of lepers in Calcutta would have been able to see beyond the boundary.

Hussain and his players did better than most. They at least managed to raise the moral issue, before allowing tactical considerations to tilt the argument towards security grounds: that got the ECB on board, and could have given the ICC a way out. The price to be paid for that pragmatism was the loss of the high ground. It looked as if nobody else would come along to claim it, and cricket would have to file for moral bankruptcy. But then, out of nowhere, came two black armbands.

England had got stuck thinking there were only two options: go or don't go, kowtow or boycott. Henry Olonga and Andy Flower, in a far tighter corner, found a more agile solution. The statement they issued at Zimbabwe's first game was calm, dignified and lethally clear. Their stand was not just brave but shrewd: there were two of them, one black, one white, they were both senior players, and they had not even been friends until this episode made them, in Olonga's words, "blood brothers". Together they were responsible for a shining moment in the game's history, which is already on the way to entering its mythology (armbands and the men I sing. . .). The Zimbabwe Cricket Union dropped Olonga, and would have dumped Flower too had it not been for a players' mutiny, thus neatly proving that it was a politicised organisation. Two strips of black tape, more potent than any logo, breathed life back into the game's battered spirit. And the ICC were so blind to this that they asked for the armbands to be taken off.

NOT THE NINE O'CLOCK NEWS   Matthew Engel, *Notes by the Editor*, 2004

"The new right-wing military government in South Africa, which seized power yesterday, has announced that apartheid is to be reintroduced. The black population will be stripped of all voting rights and segregation will be reimposed as soon as practicable. The situation in the country was said to be calm and there were no reports of violence. The International Cricket Council has therefore announced that forthcoming tours to the country can go ahead as normal. . ."

Unthinkable? Which bit is unthinkable? The ICC has made it plain that safety and security are the only legitimate grounds for countries to call off cricket tours. Apartheid South Africa was a very safe place for white men to play cricket against other white men, as anyone who toured there in the 1950s or '60s will tell you. Issues of morality are irrelevant, according to the nine other countries apparently ranged against England on the issue of whether they should play in Zimbabwe. Do the United Cricket Board of South Africa – of all people – really understand what they are saying?

Of course morality has a legitimate role to play in deciding whether or not a cricket tour can take place. Any contrary argument is contemptible, especially in a game that went through the decades of torment caused by apartheid. The ECB's position on whether or not to go to Zimbabwe has been incoherent and inconsistent. But consistency on this subject is probably for the simple-minded.

It is true that it is all too easy to get on a high horse about this. I could have a decent stab at writing a powerful newspaper column arguing the moral case against playing cricket in any place you dare to name, however innocuous it might seem. (Even New Zealand has dirty little secrets, you know. The UK certainly has.) But somewhere in the dust, by no means easy to find, is a line that no decent human being should cross. And I believe the wretched tyranny that is Robert Mugabe's Zimbabwe is now across that line and that no team should tour there.

On the ICC's own miserable terms, Zimbabwe should fail the test. Visiting teams – in their effective house arrest between airport, hotel and cricket ground – would probably be "secure". I doubt if the same could be said for any accompanying journalist with a moderately inquiring mind, or even a curious spectator. If sanctions are invoked against England for refusing to tour such a country, it will be the majority, not the minority, who will have earned themselves the contempt of thoughtful individuals across the globe.

Gear Change –
Helmets, Bats and Balls

What Norman Harris called the "equipment revolution" may not be quite on a par with the changes wrought by Packer, or the impact of television, or the corruption scandals, or the furore over South Africa, but it has been significant – heavier bats, lighter pads, wicket-keeping gloves that make catching easier, and (whisper it to traditionalists) helmets. All have been introduced in the past 30 years and left their mark.

Harris cleverly shows how heavier bats changed the nature of batting. "In just ten years our image of the Test batsman has changed dramatically," he wrote in 1985. "Perhaps distance lends enchantment, but when we reach for a picture of the past we tend to produce, in our mind's eye, someone like Bradman or Compton or Edrich. We see the twinkling feet, and wristy sweeps, hooks and cuts. Nimble is a word we associate with the players of yesteryear, and one which we rarely use now." The picture we have of today's Test batsman is of someone standing tall and quite still. "He wears a helmet, and almost every part of his body is protected. . . Our man's bat may well be raised in advance of the ball being delivered and when it descends it does so firmly, without flourish."

Harris evidently thought something had been lost in the transition to the well-padded, helmeted leviathan wielding his 3lb bat. Other *Wisden* contributors were of the same opinion, with most of their ire directed at helmets. "Today, as often as not, it is impossible to tell who is batting without first consulting a scorecard, so many players being encrusted in helmets and camouflaged by visors," complained Trevor Bailey in 1981. "This gives them a space-age image, devoid of individuality and as dull as dirty denims."

Norman Preston rounded on "ugly" helmets, while making the interesting observation that Patsy Hendren had worn one made by his wife in the 1930s – perhaps there really is nothing new under the sun. Preston doubted whether close fielders should be allowed to wear helmets, believing that it gave them an unfair advantage. Ditto his successor as editor, John Woodcock, though he did recognise that safety concerns meant their growing use was inevitable. At least umpires haven't started wearing them. Yet.

S. M.

THE UGLY HELMET

Norman Preston, *Notes by the Editor*, 1979

Head strong: Dennis Amiss sports the earliest type of batting helmet. Purists hated the new innovation – but it prolonged the career of Amiss, and saved several others' skulls.

The 1978 season will go into cricket history as the one when the ugly helmet was used by many players to protect themselves from injury, not only when batting but also when fielding in the suicide positions. I remember that Patsy Hendren first used one, made by his wife, in the early 1930s when facing Larwood and Voce and the West Indies contingent, but that was an isolated case. Now, when batsmen have been laid low by the spate of bouncers that captains and umpires have tolerated, how could I, as an observer in a safe and comfortable seat, blame the players for wearing something to protect themselves from serious injury? Dennis Amiss, the only batsman to score 2,000 runs, wore one regularly. It was made of fibre-glass in Birmingham and retailed at £29; more than 100 went to the counties.

Whether a fielder should be allowed to wear a helmet is a different matter. When Philip Russell (Derbyshire) was struck in the face at short leg by a shot from Malcolm Nash (Glamorgan) at Chesterfield, the ball lodged in the visor of his helmet. He suffered a fractured cheekbone, but the injury might have been much more serious. It was no catch because umpire Harold Bird promptly called "dead ball"; and that is now the official ruling from Lord's in the event of similar incidents. Nor is the batsman out if the ball bounces off a helmet and without touching the ground is held by a fielder. The TCCB have ruled that the wearing of a helmet gives the fielder an unfair advantage and if the ball rebounds from the helmet the umpire must call "dead ball". However, a catch may be taken if a batsman snicks the ball on to his own helmet.

THE BAT...

Norman Preston, *Notes by the Editor*, 1980

An aluminium bat has been produced in Australia under the direction of Australian express bowler Dennis Lillee, who thought of the idea when bats at his cricket coaching centre continually splintered. Instead of making the pleasant noise one associates when the willow strikes the ball, there is a much louder noise from the metal one. The manufacturers are trying to solve this problem, and they also have to find a substance, such as foam, cork or polystyrene – to fill the inside. For the purpose of practice at the nets, it is durable and would be much cheaper to produce than the willow type. It could not be used in any kind of match, because the new Laws which have just come into force with the beginning of this English season state that the blade of the bat shall be made of wood.

. . . AND THE BALL   Norman Preston, *Notes by the Editor*, 1980

The rising cost of the cricket ball – in England in 1979 the top-grade varied from £16.50 to over £20 each – is causing much concern. There are 15,000 to 20,000 cricket clubs in the United Kingdom. In Australia, the Kookaburra ball costs £12, and in India and Pakistan their Grade A balls range from £6 to £8 each. There are two main manufacturers in England – the Wisden–Duke–Stuart Surridge firm called Tonbridge Sports Industries at Penshurst, and Alfred Reader, of Teston, near Maidstone. With cash from the Cricket Council and the British Sports and Allied Industries, a British Standards Institution team of scientists has been working out a new specification for cricket balls, taking into account size, construction, stitching and the seam of different grades of ball.

DONNING THE HELMET   John Woodcock, *Notes by the Editor*, 1981

Last year was the first in which helmets, or reinforced caps, became standard wear in first-class cricket. When, as more often than not, they have a visor attached, they reduce the batsman, or short-leg fielder, to wretched anonymity. I find it sartorially and aesthetically an objectionable trend. It has, furthermore, detracted from the artistry of batting. As you would expect, old players deplore the sight of a helmeted batsman. Yet if their use saves cricketers from serious injury, they must be allowed. Had short-pitched bowling, over the years, not got so out of hand, they would not be necessary. But it has, and because of the protection which helmets afford, there may in future be more bumpers than ever. This, certainly, is something which umpires will need to watch. The game's administrators would prefer to prohibit the use of helmets in the field. Here too, though, there is the aspect of safety. The helmet, it seems, has come to stay – an unsightly adjunct to an increasingly dangerous game.

ARE HELMETS JUST A GIMMICK?   Trevor Bailey, 1981

One of cricket's many charms used to be the way it was possible to walk into a ground and instantly recognise the batsman at the crease. Apart from his style, he was unmistakable because of his build, features, headgear or hair. Who could have failed to pick out Cyril Washbrook with his cap at a jaunty angle, or Jack Robertson, who wore his with the precision of a guardsman? Then again, there was the hair-style of Herbert Sutcliffe, black patent-leather glinting in the sun, complete with the straightest of partings, the blonde waves of Joe Hardstaff, Reg Simpson's dark curls, and Denis Compton's, so unlike those Brylcreem advertisements, forever unruly. Today, as often as not, it is impossible to tell who is batting without first consulting a scorecard, so many players being encrusted in helmets and camou-flaged by visors. This gives them a space-age image, devoid of individuality and as dull as dirty denims.

Obviously a helmet makes batting, which personally I never considered as even a vaguely dangerous occupation, less dangerous; just as wearing one in a car, or on a bicycle in traffic, would reduce the risk of injury following a road accident. However, assuming the player obeys the fundamental principle of batsmanship and keeps his eye on the ball, he should not be hit on the head by a fast bowler – provided the pitch is reasonable and the batsman compe-tent. He is, in fact, safer than a fieldsman in any of the more suicidal bat-and-pad positions or a wicket-keeper standing up to fast-medium bowling. It is interesting that keepers, who have the riskiest job in cricket, have so far rejected the helmet, perhaps because increased safety fails to compensate for lack of comfort. No batsman with reasonably quick reflexes should be struck on the head, though there is always the risk of his edging a hook into his face. The latter fate is most likely to occur against very fast bowling, especially when the stroke has been attempted against a ball that is too fully pitched for hooking safely.

Although helmets rob batsmen of much of their personality, and are aesthet-ically unattractive, they have become almost standard equipment in first-class cricket. But are they necessary? In an effort to find the answer, I have spoken to a number of very good players who performed in the helmetless era, to discover how often they were struck on the head by fast bowling. I chose cricketers with different techniques – with intriguing results.

Reg Simpson was a tall and graceful back-foot player who never bothered to hook and probably coped better with real pace than any other Englishman in the post-war period. He was never hit or even looked in the slightest danger as he watched the balls fly harmlessly through to the wicket-keeper. Colin Milburn, a stocky, impulsive hooker, was also never hit. This was true, also, of two contrasting West Indians: Clyde Walcott, a big, strong, powerful hooker, with a high backlift, and Everton Weekes, small, neat and very quick-moving.

Garry Sobers never bothered with a thigh pad, so it is difficult to imagine he would have ever required a helmet. He was hit on one occasion, in England at Lord's by a medium-pacer when the ball lifted off a length. Denis Compton, another who never wore a thigh pad, was also hit only once in a long career. It happened when he changed his stroke at the last moment, against a no-ball from Ray Lindwall, and the ball flew off the edge into his face. Brian Close, despite an initial movement forward, had noticeably less difficulty in coping with the genuine speed of Roberts, Holding and Daniel, when in his mid-forties, than his younger colleagues. He, too, was never hit on the head, though he did twice mis-hook medium-paced bowlers, whom he dismissed as trundlers, into his face on dodgy pitches. My own experience, as an essentially forward player and a non-hooker, was being hit on the back of the head when I ducked to a ball from Keith Miller, which failed to rise as much as expected, and unintentionally nodding down a delivery of no more than medium-pace which rose unexpectedly in a Championship match.

It is fair to say that none of the players I have mentioned required a helmet for protection, for either physical or mental reasons, which is, of course, why they are worn. Which leads to the question, has the pace of the bowlers increased dramatically? I don't personally think so. Apart from anything else, the bowlers are now forced to release the ball farther from the batsman than when the law allowed them an enormous drag. Gordon Rorke, for example, actually broke the popping crease with his back foot. On the other hand, there has been a marked increase in the amount of fast, fast-medium and medium-paced seam bowling.

Are the present-day pitches more uneven in bounce? The wickets overseas do appear to have become more receptive to seam and less helpful for batting; but, remembering the ridge at Lord's in the 1950s, this, I think, does not apply in this country. The best reason for wearing a helmet was put forward by Graham Gooch: "In first-class cricket, the helmets are now popular and I wear one all the time. I've got no qualms about it. I just feel more confident and therefore a better player when I'm wearing one. The day can't be far off when batsmen start wearing them in club cricket. If you're tempted to wear one, do so – and if anyone laughs at you, just point to the runs in the scorebook." Although the cynic might point to the runs made by Sir Donald Bradman, Garry Sobers, or Vivian Richards without one, if a helmet gives a player confidence it must be an asset to him. A helmet might have made a considerable difference to a fine county cricketer of my vintage, who regularly clocked up over 2,000 runs a season, yet was so apprehensive that he scored many fewer than he should have done against a team which contained a really quick bowler.

John Snow, who in his time has hit his share of batsmen with the bouncer, favours the helmet because it makes life easier for the members of the later order. It is also interesting that David Gower, who is a lovely mover and has lots of time to play his strokes, has, in a comparatively short career, twice been hit on the head. Once it was his own fault through his ducking into the ball; on the other occasion he mis-hooked into his face. The latter is liable to happen even to as fine a natural hooker as David; but, rather strangely in these circumstances, he scorns the use of a visor with his helmet and the extra protection it provides. One of the first times I saw protective headgear used was by Mike Brearley and Geoff Boycott in a Test match on a placid pitch against bowling of such gentle pace that they seemed much over-dressed; but presumably it gave them extra and valuable confidence. A fascinating, somewhat ironic outcome of the helmet has been the marked increase in the number of batsmen hit on the head and in the face. This can't be put down solely to the increase in fast and medium-paced bowling. What, then is the reason? My view is that the extra protection has meant that batsmen have become less worried and apprehensive. As a result, they are attempting to play, or hook, deliveries which previously they would have been thankful to have avoided. The outcome is that they are not moving quite so quickly, and are being hit.

Whether the helmet is a sensible adjunct to batting, like pads and gloves, or merely a well-marketed gimmick and a modern trend is a matter of opinion. Although on many occasions a helmet is unnecessary, it can hardly be condemned if it provides batsmen as successful as Gooch and Boycott with extra confidence. Less objectionable than the dirt-track crash-helmet type are those that look like caps. I would rather they were not worn in the field – but that is another issue.

HEAVY BATS
John Woodcock, *Notes by the Editor*, 1985

Helmets, especially those with visors attached, are cumbersome to wear. They can weigh as much as 3½lb and inevitably slow down a batsman's reactions. The weight of the modern bat has also led to a change in batting styles, the cut and the hook being the strokes to have suffered most.

In 1956, when Gunn and Moore supplied the Australian touring team with bats, the order was for 16 between 2lb 2oz and 2lb 4oz and one of 2lb 6oz. This last one was for Mackay, who had a method all his own, involving no detectable pick-up of the bat. Today's average weight is nearer 2lb 10oz, not a few being of 3lb and more. Is it surprising, therefore, that it has become fashionable to stand with the bat already raised above the shoulder?

No less an authority than Bradman sees this as a negative and regressive idea and one which detracts greatly from the style and flow of batsmanship. Bradman's own bats weighed 2lb 2oz. So did Compton's. Using a modern mallet they could never have played with such marvellous dexterity.

THE EQUIPMENT REVOLUTION
Norman Harris, 1985

In just ten years our image of the Test batsman has changed dramatically. Perhaps distance lends enchantment, but when we reach for a picture of the past we tend to produce, in our mind's eye, someone like Bradman or Compton or Edrich. We see the twinkling feet, and wristy sweeps, hooks and cuts. Nimble is a word we associate with the players of yesteryear, and one which we rarely use now.

The picture we have of today's Test batsman is of someone standing tall and quite still. He wears a helmet, and almost every part of his body (at least on the side which faces the bowler) is protected, the latest addition being a forearm guard. Yet this padding is not over-voluminous; and it does not stop him running quickly between the wickets. Our man's bat may well be raised in advance of the ball being delivered and when it descends it does so firmly, without flourish. From this short downward movement of the bat we are used to seeing the ball travel quite quickly into the area between mid-wicket and square leg for – typically – a comfortable two runs.

The model for our modern picture is, if you like, the opening batsman, Chris Broad. Of course, other players will bat differently; but the pattern is changing. Certainly at the highest level there is now a different style of batting, and it is clear that it has been influenced by changes in equipment – in particular, bats.

In the mid-1970s the weight of bats had for long been standard, at something around 2¼ pounds; and the shape of the bat had altered very little since the early century. The parameters of length and width were, after all, laid down in the Laws of Cricket and the only area in which manufacturers sought to gain a little advantage was in the springing of handles. Then, in 1974, the long-established bat-makers, Gray-Nicolls, cautiously introduced a bat which they probably feared would offend many traditionalists. The bat, which could be called by no other name than the Scoop, drew its inspiration from the heel-and-toe-weighted golf putter invented by a South African, Dr Arthur Garner. An Englishman named Barry Wheeler, who had some knowledge of physics and was also the agent for an American golf-ball manufacturer, concluded that the perimeter-weighting principle could be applied equally well to cricket bats. By making the centre of the bat's back concave instead of ridge-like, the weight saved could be pushed towards the edges, thus effectively widening the bat's middle. Ian Chappell was a prominent early exponent of the new bat, the demand for which was startling in the first year it was sold in earnest, 1975. Cricket shops could not get enough of them. In that one year alone Gray-Nicolls had to tear up 8,000 orders which they could not fulfil.

The immediate consequence was that other bat-makers – and there were very soon more of them – began to think anew about the shape of cricket bats. Weight could be spread by other means than grooving out the back (for the Scoop had been patented). The hump could simply be flattened and pushed towards the edges. Weight could be moved from higher up the blade, including a fluting of the edges so that these were thicker at the bottom than near the shoulders.

Bats began to bulge at the business end. Heaviness seemed to become almost a greater virtue than balance, and thicker handles were made to help lift these bats. Some amused onlookers began to talk of railway sleepers and to wonder if bats were going to revert to the club-like shapes of the game's origins. It was recalled that in 1820, when William Ward made 278 at Lord's (a score not bettered on that ground for the next 105 years) he used a bat said to weigh over four pounds.

The heaviest of the new bats of the 1970s went above three pounds, which was nearly a 30% weight increase. One was the 3lb 4oz bat (a true weight according to its maker, Duncan Fearnley, because it did not have a thick handle) which Glenn Turner employed in his innings of 311 not out at Worcester in 1982. Turner, a relatively slight figure, argued that if a heavy bat was picked up straight it was less likely to go off line as it came down than a lighter bat might be. He thought of it as a heavy pendulum. Bigger men who have used heavy bats are Clive Lloyd, Ian Botham and Clive Rice. Some also employ the early backlift in which the bat is up and waiting as the bowler delivers. Accordingly, the ball has on occasion (and especially on Sundays) been hit very hard indeed – harder, in the opinion of some, than ever before.

In the process, a different range of shots has emerged. Fewer cuts, pulls and hooks – the hook, in particular – are made, but more are played in the arc between extra cover and mid-on. Indeed, sixes or one-bounce fours over cover are no longer a great rarity. Another popular sector is the one between square leg and mid-wicket.

There is the shot off the legs which races along the ground and rattles the fence in that area; there is the pick-up over mid-wicket; and there is the drive which is mis-hit, but with sufficient power for the ball to squeeze through midwicket for runs.

These, of course, are shots which are made with a single, uncomplicated movement that is essentially downward. The wrists do not have to do much at all. Compare that with the movement required for what might now be regarded as the old-fashioned square cut, for which the bat comes down on top of the ball. That shot is now much less popular than the other oft-termed cut, which is simply a back-foot hit through the covers or square of the wicket – and which is much the easier of the two shots to play with a heavy bat.

The problem for coaches everywhere is that other players, especially youngsters, have struggled to wield bats that are much too heavy for them. It is a trend deplored by the national coach, Les Lenham, and also at the Gover Cricket School in London. Lenham recalls somewhat wistfully that Denis Compton once said he liked his bat to feel like a wand. At Gover's they notice the contrast when visiting Indian and Pakistani players come to practise, with their lighter bats and twirling strokes. At last, though, there are clear signs that the weight of bats is no longer going upwards. Moreover, bat-makers realise that there is a gap in the market, indeed a demand for a lightweight bat. Several plan to introduce one into their range for 1985. But the quest for new ideas is unlikely to stop. It has already produced a bat with small holes in it, a laminated bat with many segments glued together, and a bat with no shoulders; and it has produced names like Magnum, Master, Maestro, Excalibur, Galaxy, Executive.

Where will the next push come from? Some bat-makers have looked again at the handle, introducing steel or fibre-glass, but most now seem to accept cane and rubber as the tried-and-tested combination. Perhaps the manufacturers will look instead at the advances made in the Protection Business, where there has also been innovation. This started with the Tony Greig glove, a one-piece gauntlet. The argument was that the fingers did not need to separate one from the other; and, even if many batsmen do like to experience this feeling, the introduction of the one-piece glove inspired many changes. There are now gloves in which just the first two, most vulnerable, fingers are kept together under heavy padding; gloves in which all the fingers are housed separately but then joined together either partially or completely; and gloves in which the fingers are pre-bent.

More importantly, the padding which protects the fingers has improved markedly from the days of rubber-spiked gloves (an item which lasted for many decades but was discontinued 15 years ago). Cotton-waste has been the standard filling in the rolled gloves – a material perhaps not entirely commensurate with the high-technology age but one which is in plentiful supply in India and Pakistan, where most gloves are made. Now, British manufacturers have introduced PVC foam, which has higher shock-absorbency qualities coupled with lightness, and the leading name in the field, Frank Bryan, has even found it cost-effective to make such gloves in England.

Leg-guards (pads) may no longer be filled with elk hair, covered in best buckskin and have the straps hand-sewn, but they have become lighter and more resilient. And the better materials do not add greatly to cost, allowing even the cheapest leg-guards to offer extra padding across knee and lower leg. Furthermore, today's schoolboy or club batsman will have a thigh pad in his cricket bag, when once only first-class cricketers owned such specialist equipment. The helmet, also, is slowly gaining ground at this level.

But the bat is the item on which most attention will be focused. The innovators will keep experimenting. Some may even follow the example of protective equipment and try to find alternative materials. If non-wood bats are banned, then perhaps an equally resilient but cheaper wood could be found to challenge the hitherto unique willow. Most cricketers, though, will probably go on paying what they are asked to pay for a new, gleaming, white sword which promises to fulfil all their dreams. The top bat in the shops in 1985 is expected to cost £75.

The White Ball

Norman Harris, 1994

Whatever else may have been said about the revamped Sunday League – and the media's response on the opening day was almost uniformly negative – by the end of the season, the white ball was judged a success. That was certainly true for spectators, and it was a view also held by some players. It therefore raises what traditionalists may regard as an heretical question: why not a white ball for all cricket? Football, rugby, hockey and tennis now prefer a ball of the most visible colour – in most cases white. So does cricket's cousin, baseball.

Evidence from the Sunday League is supported by local teams who use a white ball for evening matches, or whose ground is surrounded by trees and has no sightscreen. Such teams may play in normal cricket gear, yet they have found that the ball does not get lost against white clothing, mainly thanks to its black seam. So worries about sightscreens may be a red (or white) herring. When white balls were first considered for the Sunday League they were used in experimental play at Lord's, during which the sightscreens were removed. To general surprise, this made very little difference to the batsmen – even with a background of white seats.

White balls are more difficult to make, in terms of dyeing and stitching. On Sundays last summer, some turned rather grey after a short while. Others retained their whiteness thanks to the addition of polyurethane, which seals the surface but gives an almost permanent dull sheen. This can make it harder for bowlers to get the favoured contrast between a dull side and a polished side.

Ultimate v Optimum

Norman Harris, 1995

Bat-makers have always striven for the extra edge, as you might say, but they are now struggling to go beyond it. At the same time they have reached the end of the line in word-play. "Ultimate" was the name chosen by Gray-Nicolls for their top bat in 1994, but how can you improve on the ultimate? The makers' answer is to call their top 1995 model the "Optimum". We must leave it to lexicographers to debate which word has the greater value.

PLAYING FOR KEEPS

Matthew Engel, *Notes by the Editor*, 2005

Wisden 2004 contained an article, a slightly sentimental one I suppose, in which Pat Murphy lamented the decline of the wicket-keeper's craft. His point was vividly illustrated within 48 hours of publication: Chris Read was dropped from an England team in favour of Geraint Jones, regarded as an inferior wicket-keeper but a better batsman. This was done without the knowledge of the specialist selector, Rod Marsh, who was furious.

The 2000 version of the Laws contained a new provision restricting the use and nature of the webbing on keepers' gloves. This was included at the urging of Bob Taylor, who had noticed players deliberately catching the ball in the webbing rather than their palms, and sensed that the next step was going to be baseball mitts, enabling pretty much anyone with two hands to do the job.

This change barely slowed a global trend that threatens to become irreversible. In Australia, the arguments are even more bitter than in England: Darren Berry, the retired Victorian keeper rated by Shane Warne as the best he has ever seen, described the standard set by Adam Gilchrist and Parthiv Patel in the Chennai Test last year as "disgraceful".

And England's Jones may only be an interim choice: the future, one suspects, belongs to the batsman-keeper rather than the keeper-batsman. A young professional with any kind of fielding aptitude would be well advised to see if he can keep wicket – it might make his career. The day may be approaching when wicket-keeper becomes no more than a quasi-specialist position, like a glorified first slip. The keeper's contribution is unquantifiable, so it doesn't get counted.

SECTION TWO

The Test-Playing Countries

SECTION TWO

The Test-Playing Countries

England Expects
(Too Much, Mostly)

It has not been easy being an England supporter over the past 30 years. Shortly after the disaster of the 1999 World Cup, when England – the hosts – failed to make it to the "Super Six" games, *Wisden*'s editor Matthew Engel took a sabbatical and fled to the US. When the editor of *Wisden* takes a break from cricket, you know things are in a bad way.

English cricket had become a laughing stock. "The script for English cricket now seems to be more like the Book of Job than anything else," Engel wrote in 2000. "The Sabeans have stolen the oxen; the Chaldeans have stolen the camels; and the fire of God has burned up the sheep. Something like that. Anyway, a tournament officially regarded as the English game's make-or-break opportunity to re-establish itself in the public's affection had produced the worst case imaginable: a fall at the first fence.

"And so it went on to the end of that millennium and beyond. England contrived to lose a Test series to New Zealand in almost equally improbable circumstances. In the winter, they effectively lost the series against South Africa in the first half-hour. The Under-19 team performed pretty hopelessly in their World Cup. And the women's team lost to Australia by margins that could terrify anyone who thought the men's team could now get no worse (a sampler: Australia 299 for two; England 79 all out). With the match-fixing scandal temporarily swept under various carpets, the English crisis is now the greatest crisis in world cricket."

Yes, it really was that bad. Engel wondered if England would ever win the Ashes again. They did, of course, in the great series of 2005, which galvanised the country and demonstrated that the British retained a subliminal love of cricket. The euphoria was overdone, inasmuch as England were on the way to becoming a very good team, rather than the finished article, but for a cricket lover it was a delight to see the start of the premature football season obliterated by the dramas of the summer game.

This section traces the fortunes of the England team over the past three decades and reprints some of the reflections on the game in the UK that the evidence of decline produced. My view is that the true nadir of English fortunes was 1988, when England ran through four captains in a series against West Indies that they were lucky to lose only 4–0. In 1984, they were "blackwashed" by a wonderful West Indies team at the height of their powers – possibly the strongest unit of all time. In 1988 England were just woeful – inconsistent in selection, uninspired on the field. "England's selectors did not seem to know where to turn, either for a new captain or for a settled team," wrote Tony Cozier.

The problem in the 1980s may have been that a very capable set of players – indeed, something of a golden batting generation – was beaten into submission by a magnificent West Indies side. In most eras, Gooch, Broad, Robin Smith, Gower, Gatting, Lamb and Botham would have been an overpowering combination, but the teams of Lloyd and Richards were too strong for them, English fast bowling was in the doldrums, and selection policy was amateurish. Only now, when Duncan Fletcher has demonstrated the importance of consistency – of "class" above the old-fashioned notion of picking "form" players – can we see how hopeless were the previous regimes and what a raw deal players got. Central contracts and the emphasis now given to "Team England" have immeasurably strengthened the national team (at the expense of county cricket), and made them competitive internationally in a way they only sporadically were in the previous three decades. England (and happily Engel) are back, but it's been a painful journey. Relive it slowly and in the happy knowledge that the destination is a delirious Oval in 2005.   S. M.

THE CENTENARY TEST (Australia v England, Melbourne, March 1977)

See page 334

ENGLAND V AUSTRALIA 1977   Harold Abel, 1978

Although the day should never come when an Australian cricket team is described as colourless, the 1977 party to England took on a very light shade of grey. A side no more than marginally above average was allowed to beat them, with some comfort, in three Tests in England for the first time since 1886, so winning back the Ashes at home for only the third time this century. The other two Tests ended in draws. Boycott had a vast influence on the series. He chose his own Headingley ground for his 100th century and went on to 191 before being last out. The balance of power had been shifted by this one player who came from a three-year self-imposed exile to average 147.33 in five innings. Before his return there was little between the sides man-for-man.

England v Australia   **Third Test**

At Nottingham, July 28, 29, 30, August 1, 2, 1977. England won by seven wickets.   Norman Preston, 1978

England won by seven wickets ten minutes after tea on the last day. It was England's first victory against Australia at Trent Bridge since 1930. Blessed with fine weather, the ground was packed on the first four days and made a wonderful sight. Moreover, the Queen was in the Midlands for the Silver Jubilee celebrations and visited the ground on the first day. Play was interrupted briefly at 5.30 p.m. when the players and officials were presented to Her Majesty in front of the pavilion.

Memorable mostly from a cricket point of view was the return of Boycott to the England team after three years of self-imposed absence. Naturally, Boycott hoped for success and he exceeded all expectations by scoring 107 and 80 not out. He had the singular experience of batting on all five days of the match and altogether spent over 12 hours at the crease, his second innings taking five and a quarter hours. Botham distinguished his Test match debut by taking five wickets for 74. He moved the ball each way and at one time took four for 13 in 34 balls.

Toss: Australia. **Australia 243** (R. B. McCosker 51, I. C. Davis 33, K. J. O'Keeffe 48*; I. T. Botham 5-74) **and 309** (R. B. McCosker 107, D. W. Hookes 42, R. D. Robinson 34; R. G. D. Willis 5-88); **England 364** (G. Boycott 107, A. P. E. Knott 135, Extras 35; J. R. Thomson 3-103, L. S. Pascoe 4-80) **and 189-3** (J. M. Brearley 81, G. Boycott 80*; M. H. N. Walker 3-40).

England v Australia — Fourth Test

At Leeds, August 11, 12, 13, 15, 1977. England won by an innings and 85 runs. Geoffrey Wheeler, 1978

An historic game was made more memorable by Boycott who, on the opening day, became the first player to score his hundredth century in a Test match. The Yorkshire crowd seemed to regard the achievements of this landmark as inevitable, and Boycott batted with such ease and assurance that he gave his loyal supporters few qualms and the Australian bowlers scant hope. His was a remarkable feat, for he was only the 18th cricketer to reach this goal. Two of the others, Herbert Sutcliffe and Sir Leonard Hutton, were present for at least part of the match. By the time Boycott was finally out for 191, Australia had lost any hope of saving the series.

Toss: England. **England 436** (G. Boycott 191, R. A. Woolmer 37, A. W. Greig 43, G. R. J. Roope 34, A. P. E. Knott 57, Extras 39; J. R. Thomson 4-113, L. S. Pascoe 4-91); **Australia 103** (M. Hendrick 4-41, I. T. Botham 5-21) **and 248** (G. S. Chappell 36, R. W. Marsh 63, M. H. N. Walker 30; R. G. D. Willis 3-32, M. Hendrick 4-54).

LOWER STANDARDS OF TEST PLAYERS

E. M. Wellings, 1980

Anticipation had been more satisfying than was realisation when, having been abroad, I saw cricket for the first time in six years. What was read and heard promised much, but in reality, the standard was disappointingly lower than in 1973, when England's batting was weak enough to admit such as Lewis, Roope and Wood to Test cricket. In retrospect their merits, measured against those of Brearley and Randall, look more attractive.

When I left England, Boycott was our best batsman. When I returned he was the only one of true class. I heard much about young batsmen challenging the present incumbents. The latter were vulnerable, but the challengers were not all they had been painted. Some, notably Larkins and Parker, failed whenever seen on television, and shaped as if they often would do so against class bowling. I did see Tavaré make runs on occasions, but not impressively, and a batsman whose hands work against each other, the one at the top, the other at the bottom of the handle, is much handicapped.

That young players are damaged by over-limited cricket is an obvious excuse – except that it apparently leaves young foreigners like South Africa's Lamb unscathed. Lamb is far ahead of most young Englishmen, those shufflers crippled by bad footwork. He looks correct at the wicket, still and composed, his bat comfortably grounded. His footwork is economical and sure, so that stroke-play is almost a formality.

Willey, Gooch and Gower, in that order, looked Boycott's best supporters. Gooch would surely benefit from a more relaxed stance. His stiff, awkward position with bat unnaturally aloft must surely prove a severe strain when he plays a long innings in a hot country. Gower most obviously has flair, a gift for stroke-making, a fine sense of timing, and certainly a quick eye. His weakness is footwork, for he seldom plays far from the batting crease off either foot. He has been compared to Frank Woolley, but any resemblance does not extend to footwork. It seemed well-nigh impossible to bowl a length when Woolley was on the rampage, reaching far forward or going right back to attack. That is what footwork is about. If footwork was better, there would be no call for those ridiculous helmets.

England v Australia 1981 — John Woodcock, *Notes by the Editor*, 1982

In two unforgettable months, English cricket emerged in 1981 from a period of much gloom to a well-being that was reflected even in the enthusiasm with which ordinary men and women set about their labours. After several weeks of dreadful weather (not a single ball was bowled in any of Gloucestershire's three Championship matches in May), culminating in the loss by England of the first Test match, the sun got the better of the rain and England gained two of the more dramatic victories in the history of the game. A third, soon afterwards, meant that the Ashes were retained.

The change in England's fortunes coincided with Michael Brearley's return as captain. This not only lifted the spirits of the side, it improved its direction and freed Ian Botham of a burden which was threatening to ruin his cricket. Botham's record speaks for itself. In his 12 matches as England's captain, between June 1980 and July 1981, he scored 276 runs at an average of 13.80 (top score 57) and his 35 wickets cost 32 runs apiece. Yet by the end of last season he had made eight Test hundreds and taken five wickets in an innings 17 times – always when without the cares of captaincy.

The seventh of these hundreds, in the Third Test at Headingley, snatched victory from the jaws of defeat; the eighth won the Fifth Test at Old Trafford. With some wonderful hitting Botham reached three figures in 87 balls at Headingley and in 86 at Old Trafford. At Edgbaston, between giving the Australian bowlers two such unmerciful poundings, he finished off the fourth Test by taking five wickets for one run when Australia needed only a handful of runs to win. Botham's catching, too, was back to its prehensile best. Small wonder that Australia's captain, Kim Hughes, said when the series was over that the difference between the two sides was represented by one man and one man only.

No one, I believe, can ever have played a finer Test innings of its type than Botham's at Old Trafford. I have been told that Australia's attack was by no means one of their strongest, and that by the time Botham came in the best of their bowlers, Lillee and Alderman, were on their last legs. To which I will say only that you would never have known it from the way they were bowling. At Headingley and Old Trafford we witnessed the reincarnation of Gilbert Jessop. Those who saw Willis take eight for 43 at Headingley or watched Brearley's cool handling of each succeeding crisis also have a great story to tell – one to last them a lifetime.

Australia came so near to winning three of the first four Test matches, despite losing two of them, that if they felt frustrated when they left for home they had good reason to. Alderman and Border, two of their younger players, made a considerable impression; another, Wellham, became the first Australian this century to score a hundred in England in his maiden Test; Lillee made up in virtuosity what he had lost in pace. Not even collectively, though, could such benefits compensate for the collapses, at vital times, which their batting suffered.

England v Australia　　　　　　　　　　　　　　　　　　　**Third Test**

At Leeds, July 16, 17, 18, 20, 21, 1981. England won by 18 runs.　　Alan Lee, 1982

A match which had initially produced all the wet and tedious traits of recent Leeds Tests finally ended in a way to stretch the bounds of logic and belief. England's victory, achieved under the gaze of a spellbound nation, was the first this century by a team following on, and only the second such result in the history of Test cricket.

The transformation occurred in less than 24 hours, after England had appeared likely to suffer their second four-day defeat of the series. Wherever one looked, there were personal dramas: Brearley, returning as captain like England's saviour; Botham, who was named Man of the Match, brilliant once more in his first game back in the ranks; Willis, whose career has so often heard the distant drums, producing the most staggering bowling of his life when his place again seemed threatened.

Others, too, had good reason to remember this game. It was the first time in 19 Tests that Willey had been a member of a victorious side, there were wicket-keeping records for both Taylor (all first-class cricket) and Marsh (Tests). Dyson made his maiden century for Australia, and Lillee moved further up the list of bowling immortals. But if the statisticians revelled in such facts, they were, for most of us, submerged in the tension of a climax as near to miraculous as a Test ever can have been.

None of this had seemed remotely likely on the opening day when the familiar slate-grey clouds engulfed the chimneys which stretch away from the Kirkstall Lane End. Australia, one up in the series, were unchanged; England made two changes, Woolmer standing down for Brearley and Old returning on his home

Headingley '81: Rod Marsh and bowler Terry Alderman are the only Aussies in view as Ian Botham continues his spectacular assault, which turned the match and the 1981 Ashes series, and enraptured the whole of the country.

ground at the expense of Emburey. England thus went in with four seamers and only Willey to provide a measure of spin. It was a selectorial policy which caused considerable discussion. Brearley later confessed he lost sleep on the first night for fear that it had been a mistake. As things transpired, however, it was largely irrelevant.

Australia, having chosen to bat, ended the first day in fine health at 203 for three, the extra hour having reduced lost time to only 50 minutes. Dyson batted diligently for his century, playing chiefly off the back foot, and survived one chance, to Botham in the gully, when 57. Chappell, who supported Dyson staunchly in a stand of 94 for the second wicket, was twice reprieved – by Gower and Botham again – so England, not for the first time this summer, suffered for their ineptitude in the field.

It will come as a surprise when, in future years, people look back on a Test of such apparently outrageous drama, to know that the second day was pedestrian in the extreme. Botham, to some degree, salvaged English pride by taking five more wickets, all of them in an after-tea spell costing 35 runs, and finishing with six for 95. Naturally, the assumption was drawn that he is a more effective player without leadership duties. Despite his efforts, Australia extended their score to 401 for nine, thanks to half-centuries from Hughes and Yallop. It was another day of patchy weather and patchy cricket, completed when Gooch and Boycott saw out an over apiece from Lillee and Alderman without mishap.

At this stage, the odds seemed in favour of a draw. An England win was on offer generously, though by no means as extravagantly as 24 hours later when Ladbrokes, from their tent on the ground, posted it at 500-1. The reason for their estimate was a truncated day on which England were dismissed for 174 and, following on 227 behind, lost Gooch without addition. Australia's seamers had shown what could be done by bowling straighter and to a fuller length than their counterparts. Other than Botham, who opted for all-out aggression and profited by a swift 50, England at no stage commanded and were occasionally undone by deliveries performing contortions at speed. Botham fell victim to just such a ball from Lillee and the catch by Marsh was his 264th in Tests, beating Knott's record.

The third day ended with unhappy scenes similar to those seen at Lord's, when spectators hurled cushions and abuse at the umpires. On this occasion, Messrs Meyer and Evans had walked to the middle, wearing blazers, at five to six, after a lengthy stoppage for poor light. They consulted their meters and summoned the covers, abandoning play just before the hour. With cruel irony, the light improved instantly, the sun was soon breaking through and the large crowd was incited to wrathful demands for explanations as to why they were not watching the prescribed extra hour.

This heated diversion seemed likely to achieve nothing more than a stay of sentence for England, a view which appeared amply confirmed by late afternoon on the Monday. England were then 135 for seven, still 92 behind, and the distant objective of avoiding an innings defeat surely their only available prize. Lillee and Alderman had continued where Saturday's disturbances had forced them to leave off, and for all Boycott's skilful resistance, the cause seemed lost. Boycott, who batted three and a half hours, was sixth out to an lbw decision he seemed not to relish, and when Taylor followed quickly, the England players' decision to check out of their hotel seemed a sound move. Three hours later, the registration desks around Leeds were coping with a flood of re-bookings, Botham having destroyed the game's apparently set course with an astonishing, unbeaten 145, ably and forcefully aided by Dilley. Together, they added 117 in 80 minutes for the eighth wicket, only seven short of an England record against Australia. Both struck the ball so cleanly and vigorously that Hughes's men were temporarily in disarray; when Dilley departed after scoring 56 precious runs, Old arrived to add 67 more with Botham, who still had Willis as a partner at the close, with England 124 ahead.

Botham advanced his unforgettable innings to 149 not out before losing Willis the next morning, but Australia, needing 130, still remained clear favourites. Then, at 56 for one, Willis, having changed ends to bowl with the wind, dismissed Chappell with a rearing delivery and the staggering turnabout was under way. Willis bowled as if inspired. It is not uncommon to see him perform for England as if his very life depended on it, but this was something unique. In all, he took eight wickets for 43, the best of his career, as Australia's last nine wickets tumbled for 55 runs despite a stand of 35 in four overs between Bright and Lillee. Old bowled straight and aggressively and England rose to the need to produce an outstanding show in the field. Yet this was Willis's hour, watched or listened to by a vast invisible audience. At the end, the crowd gathered to wave their Union Jacks and chant patriotically, eight days in advance of the Royal Wedding.

England v Australia, 1981 — Third Test

At Leeds, July 16, 17, 18, 20, 21, 1981. Result: England won by 18 runs.

AUSTRALIA	First innings		Second innings	
J. Dyson b Dilley	102	– c Taylor b Willis	34
G. M. Wood lbw b Botham	34	– c Taylor b Botham	10
T. M. Chappell c Taylor b Willey	27	– c Taylor b Willis	8
*K. J. Hughes c and b Botham	89	– c Botham b Willis	0
R. J. Bright b Dilley	7	– (8) b Willis	19
G. N. Yallop c Taylor b Botham	58	– (5) c Gatting b Willis	0
A. R. Border lbw b Botham	8	– (6) b Old	0
†R. W. Marsh b Botham	28	– (7) c Dilley b Willis	4
G. F. Lawson c Taylor b Botham	13	– c Taylor b Willis	1
D. K. Lillee not out	3	– c Gatting b Willis	17
T. M. Alderman not out	0	– not out	0
B 4, l-b 13, w 3, n-b 12	32	L-b 3, w 1, n-b 14	18

1-55 2-149 3-196 4-220 5-332 (9 wkts dec.) 401   1-13 2-56 3-58 4-58 5-65   111
6-354 7-357 8-396 9-401   6-68 7-74 8-75 9-110 10-111

First innings – Willis 30–8–72–0; Old 43–14–91–0; Dilley 27–4–78–2; Botham 39.2–11–95–6;
Willey 13–2–31–1; Boycott 3–2–2–0.
Second innings – Botham 7–3–14–1; Dilley 2–0–11–0; Willis 15.1–3–43–8; Old 9–1–21–1; Willey 3–1–4–0.

ENGLAND	First innings		Second innings	
G. A. Gooch lbw b Alderman	2	– c Alderman b Lillee	0
G. Boycott b Lawson	12	– lbw b Alderman	46
*J. M. Brearley c Marsh b Alderman	10	– c Alderman b Lillee	14
D. I. Gower c Marsh b Lawson	24	– c Border b Alderman	9
M. W. Gatting lbw b Lillee	15	– lbw b Alderman	1
P. Willey b Lawson	8	– c Dyson b Lillee	33
I. T. Botham c Marsh b Lillee	50	– not out	149
†R. W. Taylor c Marsh b Lillee	5	– c Bright b Alderman	1
G. R. Dilley c and b Lillee	13	– b Alderman	56
C. M. Old c Border b Alderman	0	– b Lawson	29
R. G. D. Willis not out	1	– c Border b Alderman	2
B 6, l-b 11, w 6, n-b 11	34	B 5, l-b 3, w 3, n-b 5	16

1-12 2-40 3-42 4-84 5-87 6-112   174   1-0 2-18 3-37 4-41 5-105 6-133   356
7-148 8-166 9-167 10-174   7-135 8-252 9-319 10-356

First innings – Lillee 18.5–7–49–4; Alderman 19–4–59–3; Lawson 13–3–32–3.
Second innings – Lillee 25–6–94–3; Alderman 35.3–6–135–6; Lawson 23–4–96–1; Bright 4–0–15–0.

Toss won by Australia   UMPIRES D. G. L. Evans and B. J. Meyer

England v Australia — Fourth Test

At Birmingham, July 30, 31, August 1, 2, 1981. England won by 29 runs.   Derek Hodgson, 1982

A startling spell of bowling by Botham, from the Pressbox End, which brought
him five wickets for one run in 28 deliveries, ended an extraordinary Test match
at 4.30 p.m. on a glorious Sunday afternoon. And so, for a second successive Test,

England contrived to win after appearing badly beaten. As at Leeds, a large crowd helped give the match an exciting and emotional finish, and once again critics, commentators and writers were left looking foolish, a fact that the players of both teams were quick to point out afterwards.

For a third time in the series, after Trent Bridge and Headingley, the pitch was the centre of controversy, though when Brearley elected to bat on a fine sunny morning on what is traditionally regarded as one of the finest surfaces in England, it looked in superb condition. Hughes was reported to have said that it looked good for 800 runs. The outfield was fast and the temperature acceptable to Melbourne. Certainly no one at Edgbaston could have dreamt that this would be the first Test since 1934, anywhere in the world, in which no batsman made a fifty.

Boycott and Brearley opened, a change in the order that had caused misgivings, and had reached 29 in 45 minutes when Alderman's late swing defeated Boycott and then, two overs later, provoked Gower, a reluctant number three, to try, unsuccessfully, to hit over mid-on. Alderman had figures then of 7–4–4–2, and although Brearley denied himself a run for an hour, surviving a vehement appeal for a slip catch by Wood, he and Gooch saw Alderman and Lillee retire. It was Bright, making the spinner's now-customary appearance just before the interval, who tempted Gooch into a rash pull that cost a third wicket at 60.

The afternoon was an English disaster. Bright, from the Pavilion End, used the rough outside the leg stump while Alderman, with Lillee in the unusual role of deputy, and Hogg were straight and swift from the other. By 5.30 p.m. England had been dismissed for 189, of which Brearley had made 48 in just under four hours, four boundaries off Lillee promoting his innings from one of mere resistance. Alderman had taken five for 42 before Old, from that same Pressbox End, then rattled the teaspoons in the Australian dressing-room by removing Dyson and Border, in five overs, for 19 runs by the close.

The pitch, declared England's players the following day, after they had been roasted overnight by the media, was untrustworthy. It was too dry, the surface was less than firm, the occasional ball kept low, and there was turn for the spinner. Shoulder to shoulder, Australia's batsmen were later to demonstrate their solidarity with their English colleagues.

Friday was cool and grey and England did well to restrict the Australian lead to 69. Brearley was at his best, constantly varying pressure on each batsman by his bowling and fielding changes, never losing the initiative, while his men responded admirably, running out Wood and Hogg and causing enough apprehension to deter Australia from attempting up to a dozen further singles. Hughes, batting well through a stormy spell by Willis, whose five bouncers in two overs caused the umpires to confer, was unlucky to be leg-before to a low bounce. Although Brearley fell to Lillee on a gloomy evening, England had narrowed the margin to 20 runs.

Blue sky and Saturday sunshine attracted 15,000 spectators, whose holiday mood was not jollied along by Boycott, who spent three hours three minutes raising his score to 29 – seven short of Cowdrey's Test aggregate record for an Englishman – before falling to Bright. So, too, did Gower, Gooch and Willey, and when Botham was caught behind off Lillee, England's lead was no more than 46, with four wickets standing. Fortunately for England their tail-end batsmen, urged on by the combative Gatting, batted bravely. Emburey, 37 not out, demonstrated that Bright's line allowed him to be swept profitably, while Old hit straight and hard before taking the ball to dismiss Wood in the evening haze. Yet Australia needed only another 142 to win, with two days to play. Miracles, wrote a distinguished correspondent, like lightning, do not strike twice.

Willis, bowling again as if the devil were at his heels, removed Dyson and Hughes in the first 40 minutes on the fourth morning (Sunday), but Border was his resolute self and at 105 for four, with only 46 more needed, Australia seemed to have the match won. However, Border was then desperately unlucky to be caught off his gloves, a ball from Emburey suddenly lifting prodigiously. Brearley, who had ordered Willey to loosen up with the idea of using spin at both ends, in a last gamble, changed his mind and called on a reluctant Botham.

Somerset's giant bowled quicker than for some time, was straight and pitched the ball up, and one after another five Australian batsmen walked into the point of the lance. The crowd, dotted with green and gold, were beside themselves with agony and ecstasy as, only 12 days after Headingley, history amazingly repeated itself. Botham was again named Man of the Match, though Emburey would have been the choice of many.

England v Australia, 1981 — Fourth Test

At Birmingham, July 30, 31, August 1, 2, 1981. Result: England won by 29 runs.

ENGLAND

	First innings		Second innings	
G. Boycott c Marsh b Alderman		13	– c Marsh b Bright	29
*J. M. Brearley c Border b Lillee		48	– lbw b Lillee	13
D. I. Gower c Hogg b Alderman		0	– c Border b Bright	23
G. A. Gooch c Marsh b Bright		21	– b Bright	21
M. W. Gatting c Alderman b Lillee		21	– b Bright	39
P. Willey b Bright		16	– b Bright	5
I. T. Botham b Alderman		26	– c Marsh b Lillee	3
J. E. Emburey b Hogg		3	– (9) not out	37
†R. W. Taylor b Alderman		0	– (10) lbw b Alderman	8
C. M. Old not out		11	– (8) c Marsh b Alderman	23
R. G. D. Willis c Marsh b Alderman		13	– c Marsh b Alderman	2
B 1, l-b 5, w 1, n-b 10		17	L-b 6, w 1, n-b 9	16
		189		**219**

1-29 2-29 3-60 4-101 5-126 6-145 7-161 8-161 9-165 10-189

1-18 2-52 3-89 4-98 5-110 6-115 7-154 8-167 9-217 10-219

First innings – Lillee 18–4–61–2; Alderman 23.1–8–42–5; Hogg 16–3–49–1; Bright 12–4–20–2.
Second innings – Lillee 26–9–51–2; Alderman 22–5–65–3; Hogg 10–3–19–0; Bright 34–17–68–5.

AUSTRALIA	First innings		Second innings
G. M. Wood run out	38	lbw b Old	2
J. Dyson b Old	1	lbw b Willis	13
A. R. Border c Taylor b Old	2	c Gatting b Emburey	40
R. J. Bright lbw b Botham	27	(8) lbw b Botham	0
*K. J. Hughes lbw b Old	47	(4) c Emburey b Willis	5
G. N. Yallop b Emburey	30	(5) c Botham b Emburey	30
M. F. Kent c Willis b Emburey	46	(6) b Botham	10
†R. W. Marsh b Emburey	2	(7) b Botham	4
D. K. Lillee b Emburey	18	c Taylor b Botham	3
R. M. Hogg run out	0	not out	0
T. M. Alderman not out	3	b Botham	0
B 4, l-b 19, n-b 21	44	B 1, l-b 2, n-b 11	14
1-5 2-14 3-62 4-115 5-166 6-203	258	1-2 2-19 3-29 4-87 5-105 6-114	121
7-220 8-253 9-253 10-258		7-114 8-120 9-121 10-121	

First innings – Willis 19–3–63–0; Old 21–8–44–3; Emburey 26.5–12–43–4; Botham 20–1–64–1.
Second innings – Willis 20–6–37–2; Old 11–4–19–1; Emburey 22–10–40–2; Botham 14–9–11–5.

Toss won by England   UMPIRES H. D. Bird and D. O. Oslear

England v Australia   Fifth Test
At Manchester, August 13, 14, 15, 16, 17, 1981. England won by 103 runs.   John Thicknesse, 1982

England regained the Ashes by going three-one up in the series. Like its two predecessors, the Fifth Test was a game of extraordinary fluctuations and drama, made
wholly unforgettable by yet another *tour de force* by Man-of-the-Match Botham,
who, with the pendulum starting to swing Australia's way in England's second
innings, launched an attack on Lillee and Alderman which, for its ferocious yet
effortless power and dazzling cleanness of stroke, can surely never have been
bettered in a Test match, even by the legendary Jessop.

Striding in to join Tavaré in front of 20,000 spectators on the Saturday afternoon when England, 101 ahead on first innings, had surrendered the initiative so
totally that in 69 overs they had collapsed to 104 for five, Botham plundered 118
in 123 minutes. His innings included six sixes and 13 fours, all but one of which,
an inside edge that narrowly missed the off stump on its way to fine leg, exploded
off as near the middle of the bat as makes no odds. Of the 102 balls he faced (86
to reach the hundred), 53 were used up in reconnaissance in his first 28 runs (70
minutes). Then Alderman and Lillee took the second new ball and Botham erupted,
smashing 66 off eight overs by tea with three sixes off Lillee, all hooked, and one
off Alderman, a huge pull far back in the crowd to the left of the pavilion. He
completed his hundred with his fifth six, a sweep, added the sixth with an immense
and perfectly struck blow over the sightscreen, also off Bright, and was caught at
the wicket a few moments later off 22-year-old Mike Whitney. The brisk left-armer,
after only six first-class games (four for New South Wales, two for Gloucestershire),
had been plucked out of obscurity on the eve of the match when Australia learned
that neither Hogg nor Lawson was fit to play.

Unkindly, it was to the greenhorn Whitney, running back from deep mid-off, that Botham, at 32, offered the first of two chances – nearer quarter than half – a high, swirling mis-hit over Alderman's head. The other came at 91 when Dyson, sprinting off the third-man boundary, then sliding forward on his knees and elbows, made an heroic effort to get his hands underneath a sliced square-cut off Lillee.

Of the 149 Botham and Tavaré added for the sixth wicket – after a morning in which England had lost three for 29 off 28 overs – Tavaré's share was 28. But his seven-hour 78, embodying the third-slowest 50 in Test cricket (304 minutes) was the rock on which Knott and Emburey sustained the recovery as the last four wickets added 151.

With the pitch growing steadily easier throughout the match, the full value of Tavaré's survival was seen on the fourth and fifth days when, thanks to Yallop's artistic 114 and a fighting 123 not out in six and three-quarter hours by Border, batting with a broken finger, Australia more than once seemed to be within reach of scoring 506 to win. Border's hundred, taking 373 minutes, was the slowest by an Australian in any Test, beating by four minutes Hughes's time for his hundred against England in 1978–79.

Had Australia managed to win, it would have been in keeping with a bizarre series; but with Lillee buoyantly supporting Border for the eighth wicket, Brearley threw a smokescreen over proceedings by allowing both batsmen singles – and the Australians, suspecting some sinister motive, lost impetus and purpose. The end came with 85 minutes left for play, when Whitney was caught by Gatting at short leg.

Toss: England. **England 231** (C. J. Tavaré 69, M. W. Gatting 32, P. J. W. Allott 52*; D. K. Lillee 4-55, T. M. Alderman 4-88) **and 404** (G. Boycott 37, C. J. Tavaré 78, I. T. Botham 118, A. P. E. Knott 59, J. E. Emburey 57; T. M. Alderman 5-109); **Australia 130** (M. F. Kent 52; R. G. D. Willis 4-63, I. T. Botham 3-28) **and 402** (K. J. Hughes 43, G. N. Yallop 114, A. R. Border 123*, R. W. Marsh 47; R. G. D. Willis 3-96).

ENGLAND IN NEW ZEALAND AND PAKISTAN 1983–84   John Thicknesse, 1985

England's tour of 1983–84 has claims to rank among the unhappiest they have ever undertaken. Ineptly selected, burdened with a bad itinerary and losing three out of 15 players through injury or illness (including the captain), they became the first English team to be beaten in a Test series by New Zealand and Pakistan – and to fill their cup to overflowing they were publicly accused of taking drugs. Following allegations in *The Mail on Sunday* that certain members of Bob Willis's team had smoked pot in New Zealand, the Test and County Cricket Board held an inquiry, which resulted in the party being cleared of having done anything off the field which might have affected their playing performance.

The team's record in their first-class matches was depressing. Out of six Tests and four three-day games, their only win was against Northern Districts in mid-January. Coming immediately before the three-Test series in New Zealand, the victory sent the team into the First Test in Wellington in confident mood. But, inspired by maiden Test hundreds from Martin Crowe and Jeremy Coney, New

Zealand escaped with a draw, after conceding a first-innings lead of 244, and went on to overwhelm England in the Second Test at Christchurch. The 12 hours New Zealand took to win that match represented England's nadir: they put up an exhibition that would have shamed a side in the lower reaches of the County Championship.

Three weeks later, when the team flew on to Pakistan, nobody with an open mind could possibly have argued that the truncated nature of the itinerary was not a factor in England's defeat in the First Test in Karachi. Arriving some ten hours behind schedule, because of engine failure on the flight from Auckland, England not surprisingly found the combination of jetlag and unaccustomed heat and glare too much to cope with when, within 60 hours of touching down, they were confronted by the leg-breaks and googlies of Abdul Qadir on a turning pitch.

Having asked for a short tour, the team in a sense had no one but themselves to blame. But the greater fault lay with the Test and County Cricket Board for indulging them. It begged the question, which was duly asked, who was running English cricket: a coterie of senior players or the board? Willis, typically, remained adamant, sticking to the view that England had a better chance of a respectable performance within a few hours of getting off the aeroplane than they would have had by playing a three-day match up-country and running the risk of illness.

INDIFFERENCE TO DEFEAT
John Woodcock, *Notes by the Editor*, 1985

The TCCB made short work of rejecting the charges made against Willis's team on tour, deciding there was no conclusive evidence to suggest that anything they might have done off the field had adversely affected their performance on it. However, Willis and then Taylor, England's immaculate wicket-keeper, bemoaned the indifference with which some of the England players were inclined to shrug off defeat; Cook, the Northamptonshire captain and the chairman of the Cricketers' Association, felt moved to warn his members to look to their laurels; and Mr F. M. Turner, the Leicestershire secretary, called for English cricket to put its house in order.

I hope more than I can say that Lord's administrators are being sufficiently vigilant. It is always possible to change the Laws of the game, but to restore crumbling traditions is altogether harder. In December the TCCB, prompted by England's lack of success, set up a nine-man working party, under the chairmanship of Mr C. H. Palmer, to investigate the standard and quality of English cricket, from the Test team downwards.

GOWER'S ACCESSION
John Woodcock, *Notes by the Editor*, 1985

Following England's unsuccessful tour, on which, besides their sundry setbacks off the field, they lost to both New Zealand and Pakistan, a change of captaincy was only to be expected. For 19 of his 87 Test matches Willis had tackled the job staunchly. His distinguished career came, though, to a rather muted end. After being forced, through illness, to fly home early from Pakistan, he was still not himself when he returned to county cricket in late May and to Test cricket in June, and on July 21 he played what turned out to be his last match, the Benson and Hedges Cup final at Lord's. His indomitable service to England is handsomely reflected in his great collection of Test wickets. Although often beset with aches and pains, he never spared himself when bowling for his country.

David Gower, Willis's natural successor as England captain, could not have taken over at a more demanding time. I had felt the selectors should have given him the tour to New Zealand and Pakistan, by way of preparation for the series against West Indies which followed it. But that was not to be, and by the end of last summer no one was much the wiser as to whether Gower would, in fact, prove the man to lead England out of the shadows.

More than once, I fancy, he was unhappy with the side the selectors gave him, and for the third year running the TCCB ban on those who had toured South Africa in 1982 precluded the inclusion in the Test side of some of England's best players. Conspicuous among these were Boycott, Gooch, Lever and Underwood, whose collective experience would have been invaluable to Gower. But even with a free choice England would have been unlikely to hold the West Indians at bay [England were "blackwashed" 5–0 in the 1984 home series].

In India, soon afterwards, Gower and his side ran into more difficulties. Having earned the gratitude of the Indian people by staying on in the country despite the assassination of the Indian prime minister and then of a deputy British high commissioner, they proceeded to provide India with their first victory in 32 Test matches.

This year, when the TCCB's ban expires, England should be in a position to field a full side for the first time since early in 1982. This will renew the interest of those to whom the political implications of the TCCB's action were disingenuous. To some extent, at least, it should restore England's playing fortunes.

ENGLAND'S SEARCH FOR PACE   John Woodcock, *Notes by the Editor*, 1985

In August 1984 a sponsored search was launched to unearth, if possible, some *English* fast bowlers. Given the blessing of the Test and County Cricket Board, and under the direction of two former England captains, Dexter and Willis, the intention was to find willing, well-built athletes and to turn them into Larwoods, Snows and Truemans.

Nothing much came of it. What tends to be forgotten, I think, is that fast bowlers of English stock, and I mean genuinely fast, always have been scarce. Between the wars there were no more than three or four of them. In Dexter's opinion there have been only five (Snow, Statham, Trueman, Tyson and Willis) in the last 30 years. Like it or not, English conditions and the structure of the English first-class game (long before the growth of one-day cricket), as well as an Englishman's natural capacity, are not conducive to bowling with what West Indians call "pace like fire".

It would have been splendid had this quest for fast bowlers been successful (so long as four had not been chosen for every Test match); but a more realistic aim would be to improve the *quality* of English bowling. Diversity and ingenuity are in short supply because the call for containment has become the burden of English cricket. The variety in bowling and virtuosity in batting which came as a consequence of uncovered pitches are missing because pitches are now covered. The game suffers, too, from being played with balls which have seams that stand up, at times, like a dog's hackles.

I should like to see a restriction placed on the polishing of the ball. Apart from anything else, it absorbs time. The Clark Report of 1967, which, although the counties rejected it, proved to be quite far-sighted, recommended that no interference with the natural condition of the ball, other than wiping and cleaning, should be allowed. Such a move would have had support at the time from overseas cricket authorities.

ENGLAND V AUSTRALIA 1985
David Frith, 1986

The 1985 Australian touring team, the 30th to play Test cricket in England, disappointed its supporters. After four matches in the Cornhill Test series, England and Australia had a victory apiece, and one further success by Australia in the remaining two Test matches would have ensured their retention of the Ashes. At this point, while England were felt to be the better side, it was beyond most objective pundits to foresee England's two crushing victories, each by an innings, that unveiled a conclusive superiority.

England v Australia   **Fifth Test**
At Birmingham, August 15, 16, 17, 19, 20, 1985.
England won by an innings and 118 runs.   David Field, 1986

Rain, rivalling Australia as England's greatest adversary, rolled away on the final afternoon to allow just enough time for Gower's side to force a thoroughly warranted victory. There was, however, a dark cloud of controversy waiting to shed its gloom. Australia's captain asserted that the crucial, quite freak dismissal of Phillips should not have been allowed, claiming that enough doubt existed for the umpires to have judged in the batsman's favour. Border insisted that the incident cost Australia the match. Phillips hit a ball from Edmonds hard on to the instep of Lamb, who was taking swift evasive action at silly point. The rebound gently stood up for Gower, a couple of yards away, to catch, and 48 minutes later England won when it had seemed that the weather-induced frustrations which prevailed at Manchester would deny them again.

It was a pity Border blamed defeat on this one incident, especially as England had forged their supremacy with a succession of outstanding individual performances, none more so than Ellison's. The Kent swing bowler fought off the debilitating effects of a heavy cold to capture ten for 79 in the match, be named as Man of the Match, and announce his coming-of-age as a

Test bowler. He and Taylor had replaced Agnew and Allott in the England side. Gower, in addition to savouring the fruits of victory and being appointed ahead of schedule for England's winter tour to the West Indies, exquisitely unveiled his strokemaking talents with a career-best 215 on the ground where he had scored his previous double-hundred for England, against India in 1979. Helped by some badly directed bowling, the England captain remorselessly punished Australia in a sumptuous, high-speed partnership of 331 with Robinson. Then Gatting, almost clinically, added a top-quality hundred – resourceful, chanceless and occupying only 125 balls.

Toss: England. **Australia 335** (A. M. J. Hilditch 39, K. C. Wessels 83, A. R. Border 45, G. F. Lawson 53, C. J. McDermott 35; R. M. Ellison 6-77) **and 142** (W. B. Phillips 59; I. T. Botham 3-52, R. M. Ellison 4-27); **England 595-5 dec.** (R. T. Robinson 148, D. I. Gower 215, M. W. Gatting 100*, A. J. Lamb 46, Extras 49).

England v Australia   Sixth Test
At The Oval, August 29, 30, 31, September 2, 1985.
England won by an innings and 94 runs.   John Thicknesse, 1986

Australia's modest chance of salvaging the Ashes effectively vanished on the opening morning when Gower won an exceptionally good toss and was then blessed by a good deal of luck in the first hour of what blossomed into a match-winning second-wicket stand of 351 with Gooch. The Essex opener, who had been rather overshadowed in the first five Tests by Robinson, his opening partner, made a chanceless 196 (27 fours, 423 minutes); but though Gower, too, went on to play brilliantly in scoring 157 (20 fours, 337 minutes), he had started loosely, lobbing the slips at two while attempting to kill a rising ball from McDermott, and surviving further narrow escapes at 31 and 35 during an over from Lawson. Given extra help by ill-directed bowling, much of it over-pitched and leg-side, England had sped to 100 for one off 25 overs by lunch, from which point Australia played like a losing side.

As in 1926 and 1953, when the Ashes were also regained at The Oval, several thousand spectators massed in front of the pavilion when the match was over, to hail the England captain and his team and to give Allan Border a heartfelt cheer. Gooch was named Man of the Match and Gower Player of the Series.

Toss: England. **England 464** (G. A. Gooch 196, D. I. Gower 157, extras 50; G. F. Lawson 4-101, C. J. McDermott 4-108); **Australia 241** (A. R. Border 38, G. M. Ritchie 64*; I. T. Botham 3-64) **and 129** (A. R. Border 58; I. T. Botham 3-44, R. M. Ellison 5-46).

RETAINING THE ASHES   Graeme Wright, *Notes by the Editor*, 1987

When they departed for Australia in October last year, England had gone 11 Test matches without a win, having lost all five in the West Indies, two to India and one to New Zealand. Before the year was out, however, they had beaten Australia twice: at Brisbane in the First Test by seven wickets, having made Australia follow on, and at Melbourne by an innings and 14 runs in three days. The Second and Third Tests, at Perth and Adelaide respectively, were drawn, and so the Ashes, regained by Gower in 1985, were retained by his successor as England's captain, Gatting.

After a year in the wilderness, these victories were a great morale boost for the England players and their supporters. Viewed from a distance, they appear to be the product of a happy, unified team, and much credit for this must be given to the manager, P. M. Lush, and the assistant manager, M. J. Stewart. Between them, they have restored pride to England's players.

Gatting, on his first tour as England's captain, said that he did not enjoy all aspects of the job, in which case success must have tasted all the sweeter. There were times last year when he appeared to be waiting for something to happen, rather than trying to make it happen, and it is hoped that his success in Australia will have given him confidence. Leadership is a matter of initiative as well as command; it is a quality Gatting has always shown in his batting and should, now that he has some wins under his belt, be seen in his captaincy.

Gower's brief reign, in which series victories over India in India and Australia in England in 1985 were offset by 5–0 defeats by West Indies at home and away, ended when he was relieved of the England captaincy following England's defeat by India at Lord's: the first Test of last summer. The cry for a change was widespread. Had it been less strident, who is to say that he would not have been just as successful as Gatting in Australia, especially given Stewart's influence?

AUSTRALIA v ENGLAND 1986–87 — Fourth Test

At Melbourne, December 26, 27, 28, 1986.
England won by an innings and 14 runs.

John Thicknesse, 1988

A combination of excellent out-swing bowling by Small, playing in his first Test of the series, and an inept appraisal by Australia of their best means of success, effectively decided the match, and the destination of the Ashes, by tea on the first day. Australia, put in on a pitch not fully dry, were bowled out for 141 in 235 minutes, Small maintaining a high degree of accuracy to take five for 48 in 22.4 overs. Against the advice of Border [the captain] and R. B. Simpson, Australia's cricket manager, the selectors had omitted Ritchie, a specialist batsman, in favour of an all-rounder, thought to be Matthews, to give the side an extra option in the field. In practice, with Matthews not called upon to bowl in an England innings lasting 120 overs, the decision served only to weaken the batting.

Toss: England. **Australia 141** (D. M. Jones 59; G. C. Small 5-48, I. T. Botham 5-41) **and 194**
(G. R. Marsh 60, A. R. Border 34, S. R. Waugh 49; P. H. Edmonds 3-45); **England 349**
(B. C. Broad 112, M. W. Gatting 40, A. J. Lamb 43; C. J. McDermott 4-83, B. A. Reid 4-78).

Australia v England   Fifth Test

At Sydney, January 10, 11, 12, 14, 15, 1987. Australia won by 55 runs.   John Thicknesse, 1988

When, with one over left, Sleep bowled Emburey to complete Australia's first Test win in more than a year, it was an unexpected as well as welcome victory. Indeed, at the start of the final 20 overs England appeared to have the better chance. Recovering from the loss of four wickets in eight overs, among them Botham first ball to Taylor in his maiden Test, they had been carried to within 90 runs of their target (320) by the pugnacity of Gatting with determined help from Richards in a stand of 131, a record for England's sixth wicket on the ground. Only once before, in 633 Tests, had England scored more than 300 runs to win – at Melbourne in 1928–29 when Hobbs and Sutcliffe shared one of their most celebrated partnerships, 105 on a rain-affected pitch. However, at 230 for five, with Australia faltering, the odds had swung their way. Even when Gatting was caught and bowled by Waugh, four short of his hundred and with only another three on England's total, it was not until Sleep dismissed Richards and Edmonds with successive balls in the 11th over of the final 20 that Australia scented victory.

Small defended resolutely through seven overs until, with only 14 balls remaining, Border at first slip, one of eight men round the bat, claimed a sharp, low catch off Reid. Then, with 12,684 spectators in a state of high excitement, Sleep penetrated Emburey's defence with a grubber to give Australia their first win in 15 Tests. Of Sleep's five for 72, his best figures in a Test, three were taken in his last five overs as England, through neither carelessness nor lack of fight, lost five for 31 in 70 tense minutes.

If their leg-spinner delivered Australia's *coup de grâce*, however, there was no question that their hero was the 30-year-old Taylor, a sandy-haired off-spinner from Sydney's Northern District club who had played only six first-class matches in his life, and only one that season, restricted to few appearances for New South Wales by their three Test spinners. So little was known about him that when Australia announced a XII containing only one opening batsman, Marsh, there was speculation in some quarters that he owed selection to an error in transmission, confusing him with M. A. Taylor, a dour left-handed opener who had been making runs for New South Wales.

There was no substance to the allegations, and in a saga that developed along the lines of a story in *Boy's Own*, the unassuming Taylor gloriously vindicated the selectors' judgment, not to say courage, with a performance of such merit that he was named player of the match. Figures of six for 78 in England's first innings and two for 76 in the second revealed him as a thoughtful bowler with more than average powers of spin. But well as he did in his specialist department, it was his batting – angular, left-handed and blessed with common sense – that made possible Australia's win. Going in at No. 9, he batted for 244 minutes in both innings while 142 runs were scored, enabling Jones to add 111 with his last three partners in the first innings and sharing a stand of 98 with Waugh in the second when Australia's needs were even greater.

Jones, whose 184 not out (540 minutes, 420 balls, on six, twelve fours) was his first Test hundred on home soil, was Australia's other match-winner in a game that produced more runs on every day than the bowlers should have allowed on a pitch which helped spin as well as seam.

Toss: Australia. **Australia** 343 (D. M. Jones 184*, A. R. Border 34; G. C. Small 5-75, P. H. Edmonds 3-79)
and 251 (D. M. Jones 30, A. R. Border 49, S. R. Waugh 73, P. L. Taylor 42; J. E. Emburey 7-78);
England 275 (D. I. Gower 72, C. J. Richards 46, J. E. Emburey 69; P. L. Taylor 6-78)
and 264 (C. W. J. Athey 31, D. I. Gower 37, M. W. Gatting 96,
C. J. Richards 38; P. R. Sleep 5-72).

ENGLAND V WEST INDIES 1988
Tony Cozier, 1989

The morale and reputation of English cricket has seldom been as severely bruised as it was during the 1988 Test series against West Indies. Another resounding loss, with four consecutive and heavy defeats after a drawn First Test, was not unusual – the margins in the previous series between the countries, in 1984 and 1985–86, had been complete; 5–0 to West Indies each time. England even had the satisfaction, brief and illusory though it might have been, of winning all three one-day internationals for the Texaco Trophy. The euphoria ended there and the season was quickly transformed into a sequence of traumatic events, on and off the field.

It began with the dismissal after the First Test of Mike Gatting, the captain since 1986, on the evidence of obscene allegations in the tabloid press of his nocturnal relationship with a young barmaid during the match. The affair, filled with sordid controversy, shook the foundations of English cricket, undermined the confidence of the team, and opened the selectors, under the continued chairmanship of Peter May, to harsh and widespread criticism. It was certainly not the only reason for yet another humiliating demise, for West Indies again proved powerful and confident opponents. Yet England's problems multiplied rapidly after it; under Vivian Richards's increasingly assured captaincy, and with Malcolm Marshall's irresistible fast swing bowling, the West Indians took fullest advantage.

England's selectors did not seem to know where to turn, either for a new captain or for a settled team. Their confusion was evident even in the dismissal of Gatting. While accepting his assertion that nothing improper had taken place with the young woman, they removed him all the same for improper behaviour. After that, they appointed John Emburey for the Second and Third Tests, even though Emburey's place in the team was increasingly tenuous. When they decided that Emburey was not their man, they chose Christopher Cowdrey on the basis of his influence in Kent's current success in the County Championship. Cowdrey, son of a great batsman and former England captain, as well as May's godson, came with well-founded doubts over his ability as a player of Test quality. It was generally taken almost as a blessing in disguise when, after England had lost heavily under him at Headingley, he injured his foot in a county match and was ruled out of the final Test at The Oval. With most of their major candidates exhausted, the selectors made Graham Gooch their fourth captain of the summer. Gooch, a cricketer of vast experience, had relinquished the captaincy of Essex at the end of the previous season in order to concentrate on his batting.

England did somewhat better under him but lost nevertheless, by eight wickets. He confirmed that he remained one of the finest batsmen in the game and was the only Englishman to play in all five Tests, although Allan Lamb, along with him the only century-maker, and Graham Dilley, the leading wicket-taker, were prevented from doing so only by injury. Even David Gower was dropped after reaching the rare landmark of 7,000 runs in his 100th Test, at Headingley. In all, 23 players were chosen for the five Tests, which was a manifesto for failure, especially against opponents quick to spot and exploit the slightest weakness. At the end, England were without either an obvious captain or a single player who had established himself during the series.

Never pressed in any county match, the West Indians would have won many more if that had been their object. In spite of this, however and of England's depressing plight, the tour proved highly profitable, with Lord's recording takings of over £1m, the first time for a Test in England. Corporate sponsorship provided much of the revenue but led to complaints in the media that the genuine lover of the game was being turned away by increased entrance fees. Certainly, the formerly high level of attendance by the West Indian immigrant population was noticeably diminished.

England v West Indies	Third Test

At Manchester, June 30, July 1, 2, 4, 5, 1988.
West Indies won by an innings and 156 runs.   Graham Otway, 1989

With England unable to cope for any length of time with the West Indian fast bowlers, and in particular with Marshall, a Test match which had been scheduled for a minimum of 455 overs ended after 243.1 had been bowled. The game lasted until the fifth day only because of constant interruptions for bad light and rain.

On the final morning, England's only chance of survival lay with the weather, but Manchester dawned bright and steamy. In a shade over an hour, England lost their last seven wickets while only 33 runs were added – and then it rained. Marshall, maintaining a strike-rate of a wicket every 26 balls in the series, was the chief destroyer, sending back five Englishmen to finish with a career-best seven for 22, while Lamb and Emburey fell to the fast-improving Ambrose. The 6ft 7in, 24-year-old Leeward Islander, although unknown to most English followers, was not without local knowledge, having taken more than 100 wickets the previous year in the Central Lancashire League. He kept the ball well up to the bat and relied on pace and movement. The same could be said of Marshall. England could not blame this defeat on the hostility of fast short-pitched bowling. Their undoing was the intelligent use of the conditions by a far superior force.

Toss: England. **England 135** (A. J. Lamb 33; C. A. Walsh 4-46) **and 93** (D. I. Gower 34;
M. D. Marshall 7-22); **West Indies 384-7 dec.** (C. G. Greenidge 45, I. V. A. Richards 47, A. L. Logie 39,
P. J. L. Dujon 67, R. A. Harper 74, M. D. Marshall 43*; G. R. Dilley 4-99).

WHY ENGLAND LOSE
Graeme Wright, *Notes by the Editor,* 1989

Two years ago, when writing the Notes for the 1987 edition of *Wisden,* I took as a centrepiece the Palmer Report; the Report of the TCCB Enquiry into the Standards of Play of English Cricket in Test and First-class County Cricket. It would be appropriate to do so again, for the background to the enquiry remains as apt now as when it was first commissioned. It was the widespread disappointment and genuine concern about the standards of play at Test and county level following England's performances between 1982–83 and 1984. Given the wisdom contained in that report, there should be even greater concern that, in the two years following its publication, the problems and the causes which it highlights remain.

Little has been done to solve the problems. In some instances, as with county pitches, there has been further deterioration rather than a serious attempt to bring about an improvement. But if it is any consolation, little of this is new. And because of that, it might be possible to look forward with a little optimism, if not necessarily with any great confidence.

Much was made of the fact that in 1988 England fielded as many as 23 players in the series against West Indies. For this, and for choosing four captains for the five Tests, the England selectors were castigated.

In 1966, when West Indies beat England by three Tests to one, and their victories were as overwhelming as any achieved last year, England called on 24 players. (When John Price withdrew from the side for the final Test, which England won, John Snow regained his place.) Moreover, of the three England captains that summer, M. J. K. Smith and Colin Cowdrey were replaced following innings defeats inside the distance. Of England's captains last season, only John Emburey could be said to have lost the captaincy because of his form or because his side lost heavily.

"Before the summer ended, the selectors themselves came in for adverse criticism," said Norman Preston in his Notes to the 1967 *Wisden.* But, he went on to say, "Examining the facts, one must remember that compared with other countries England have many more first-class players on the fringe of Test standard, yet few who can be termed automatic choices."

A similar view was expressed by Peter May, in an interview with the editor of *The Cricketer* magazine, following his retirement on November 25 after seven years as chairman of selectors. "We have more players of a certain standard than any other country," he said. "It's often easier to pick a team if you have fewer players to choose from." What is of interest as much as the similarity of views is that Mr May was also an England selector in 1966.

Critics of England's recent record, in which they went 18 Tests without a win, might consider that from 1963 to 1966 England won only twice in 18 home Tests against Australia, South Africa and West Indies. One of those victories was against West Indies at The Oval in 1966; the other, also against West Indies, was in 1963 at Edgbaston where Trueman had match figures of 12 for 119, his best analysis in Test cricket.

In that series, won 3–1 by West Indies, Trueman at the age of 32 took 34 wickets at 17.47 each from 236.4 overs. This remained the record for an England-West

Indies series until last year, when Malcolm Marshall claimed 35 wickets at 12.65 from 203.1 overs. By way of contrast, England's strike bowler, Graham Dilley, had 15 wickets at 26.86 from 136.1 overs in his four Tests last year, although he did have fewer innings in which to bowl. "The shortage of high-class batsmen and bowlers in English cricket could be a passing phase – or is it bound up with current conditions?" asked the editor of *Wisden* after the 1963 series. The old songs always were the best.

It is because of what happened after 1966 that I ponder the possibility of looking ahead with some optimism. I am not necessarily forecasting success for England. There is no reason why, in a country where it is often impossible to have building work done or a motor car serviced properly, its sporting tradesmen should perform any better. But just as craftsmen can sometimes be found, so it is in sport. England, from defeat by West Indies in 1966, went on to win in the West Indies in 1967–68 and did not lose a series, home or away, until 1971, when India won at The Oval and brought to an end England's record run of 26 Test matches without defeat.

If anything constructive emerged from England's performances against West Indies, it was their attitude under Gooch's leadership at The Oval. There seemed to be a positiveness which, to me, had been absent in recent times. I can understand why the selectors wanted to retain him as captain, however disingenuous it was to expect the Indian government to accept him as a touring captain.

There is an authority about Gooch's batting which earns the respect of his colleagues and his opponents, and I think he has an ability to distance himself sufficiently from his team-mates to gain their respect also as a leader. He will not need to be one of the lads. I do not share the concern that Gooch's batting will suffer from his being captain. Essex consider he is capable of doing the job, and they are a county who plan carefully and have a commitment to success.

When, some 20 years ago, I first watched county cricket, what struck me was the discernible gap between the county game and a Test match. This will sound as if I am stating the obvious. But it had not been obvious to me, from the game's literature or from the little international cricket I had seen, that first-class county cricketers did not play to their full potential day in, day out. I think I expected professional cricket to be like the professional theatre, in which one could expect a first-class performance, even at a matinee.

In time I became accustomed to the inertia of county first-class cricket; the game, after all, has many charms. However, it has become more noticeable that players, when selected for England, are not bridging the gap. Their approach in Test match cricket seems little different from the way they play much of their Championship cricket. It is imperative, therefore, that the captain and the cricket manager are men able to lift the players out of their usual mode and keep them playing to the peak of their ability over five days. Little I have seen convinces me that many players are capable of this transition on their own. Achieving this transition is not made easier in home Test matches by the county fixture list. The players have a day together before the Test match and are away to another county game soon after it finishes. The match becomes little more than an interim in what Peter Roebuck calls the "continuum" of county cricket. Given Test cricket's importance both to the financial welfare of the English game and to the morale of the country generally (remember 1981?), a Test match should be seen as more than just an occasion which brings in revenue. It should also be an occasion for pride; not for cynicism and despair.

There is a developing argument in favour of a 16-match, four-day County Championship. If the standard of English cricket is to be improved, it should be supported. Not all the county secretaries and treasurers will agree. If such a programme were implemented, it would mean eight fewer days of cricket per county. What will need to be resisted is any attempt to fill those eight days with more one-day cricket; indeed, cricket of any kind except net practice.

Men and women in other professional sports take time between fixtures to practise; the cricketers of other countries do not spend all their time playing and travelling. One would like to think that players could sort out their problems in the middle, but the modern game, in its various forms and with its pressures for success, does not allow this luxury. Consequently, English county cricket contains a good number of journeymen who make their way from one season to another contract by means of a satisfactory method, rather than the techniques required for Test cricket.

If standards are to improve, so that English cricket is again an example to the world, it will require dedication and discipline. Players will need to work at their game with coaches who can pinpoint and correct the faults that creep in during the season. Matthew Maynard provides an example of this. When I first saw him in 1986 he stood still at the crease, had time to move back or forward to play the ball, and he timed his strokes. He looked a potential Test cricketer. Last season, he was shuffling about at the crease as the bowler was delivering the ball. While some top-class batsmen do make an initial movement, few get away with fidgeting about like a tennis player receiving service.

It cannot be simply coincidence that a number of overseas players in county cricket have been critical of the commitment of their English colleagues. Career professionalism should be English cricket's strength, and yet it is arguable that it is its weakness. In that it gives cricketers of other countries the opportunity to develop their skills, and do so in English conditions, it might be said to be a double weakness.

Yet I would be reluctant to advocate a total restriction on overseas players. They remain an attraction, which was a reason for having them initially, and county cricket generally is richer for their presence. On the other hand, a limit of one overseas player per county does seem sensible. Unfortunately, while paying lip-service to a restriction, the chairmen and their committees put county before country as success is seen in a local rather than a national light.

It has been the same with pitches. When the ball behaves quite differently in a three-day game and a limited-overs game, yet at only a few strips' remove, something strange is happening. No one, apart from batsmen perhaps, is looking for plumb pitches. But pitches which allow the ball to deviate laterally and bounce unevenly, as we have seen recently, serve only the ego and the averages of the bowlers. Certainly they do not help the selectors in their search for bowlers able to do something with the ball on a truer Test-match pitch.

ASHES TO ASHES   Graeme Wright, *Notes by the Editor*, 1990

Living in a country not one's own, one has a different perspective of it from that of the natives. Last season, as England were handsomely and decisively beaten by a well-prepared Australian team, I could see no reason, other than wounded nationalism, for the hollering and head-hunting that followed each Test defeat. What was new? In the four years I have been writing these Notes as editor of *Wisden*, England's cricketers have lost every home series, beaten by India, New Zealand, Pakistan, West Indies and now Australia. Only victory in a one-off Test against Sri Lanka interrupts the sorry tale of England's failure to win a Test match in England since 1985.

Nothing had changed to indicate it would be any different in 1989. All that happened was that the Australians were better than many had expected. And yet, man for man, were they that much better than England's cricketers at the start of the series? It was in their attitude and their approach that they were superior. They played with a purpose that was missing from England's players. As Allan Border once said of his own team, they had forgotten the reason for playing Test cricket: the feeling of national pride.

Not that David Gower, England's captain, would have said such a thing. It was not his style – and as Ted Dexter said when announcing that Gower would captain England for the series, he was looking to him to set the tone and style for the team. For the man who, at the end of the series, said he was not aware of any errors that he made, this was probably his first mistake.

It later emerged that Gower might not have been the first choice of Dexter, chairman of the newly formed England committee, and Micky Stewart, the England team manager. I will return to that. It is the call for tone and style which interests me, for in the context of England performances in recent seasons, character and not style was the requirement. The two are not synonymous, though it has often seemed to me that in England style is mistaken for character. By character I mean mettle: a combination of ability, mental toughness and judgment. Style is apparent; and it has its place in, among other things, the arts, in the art of batting, in fashion and in good manners. Nevertheless, when inner reserves are required, it is character and not style which sees one through.

Gower has shown this in his batting; his leadership has never been so clear-cut. It has been said of him that the quality of life is important to him, but it has seemed sometimes that it is the quality of his own life which is important: his lifestyle. When defeat began to sour his life, Gower was not able to dig deep into his own character to make his players respond to the crisis. Instead, they were carried along by the air of despondency which enveloped him. It was not the tone and style Dexter had envisaged.

Image, however, has an important part to play in Dexter's life. As a public-relations consultant, it is integral to his professional life, and he knew how to employ the tricks of his trade to advance the argument for a new style of selection and management of the England team. In this, he had the support of the chairman of the Test and County Cricket Board, Raman Subba Row, another whose business is public relations.

Both men appreciate the value of the media when it comes to promoting a client – or an idea. Subba Row's objective, in wanting to do away with the old-style selection committee, was to put the management of England's cricket on a more professional basis, streamlining the organisation with the aim of achieving success on the field. Whether this is the right way to go about it, and whether Dexter is the right man, remains to be seen. His vision is wide-ranging; but so are his interests. In its current state, English cricket needs more than just a dash of enthusiasm.

It was another of Subba Row's initiatives which led to the TCCB giving its Cricket Committee chairman a power of veto within the England Committee when, in March, it superseded the selection committee. He felt that, while those responsible for selection should be allowed to concentrate on cricket matters, one of the committee should be able to take a broader view which took into account the overall interests of the board.

In the event, the power of veto was given to Ossie Wheatley, chairman of the cricket committee, a former captain and chairman of Glamorgan, and a contemporary of Dexter's at Cambridge. Towards the end of last year it came to light, in Dexter's report to the board, that the veto had been used to block Mike Gatting's appointment as captain when his name was put forward by Dexter and Stewart. Wheatley, it transpired, felt that the time was not yet right for the Middlesex captain's reinstatement because of events which happened during his term of office as England captain, principally his public dispute with the Pakistani umpire, Shakoor Rana, in Faisalabad in 1987–88.

Though not informed of this decision at the time, the board backed Wheatley's use of the veto, and at the same time regretted the fact that Dexter's confidential report had been leaked to the press. However, as governments repeatedly discover, usually to their embarrassment, secrets of public interest have a habit of finding their way into the public domain.

As much a surprise as the veto was the discovery that Dexter should have wanted Gatting as captain in the first place. That Stewart would is more understandable. He and Gatting had been in charge when England retained the Ashes in Australia in 1986–87 – the only series won by Stewart in his time as England's cricket manager – and had taken England to the final of the World Cup in 1987. Gatting, however, never struck me as Dexter's man, in the same way that it seemed obvious from the time of Dexter's appointment that Gooch would not be retained as captain. The style was wrong.

In the three weeks before the new committee met to choose the captain, Gower was generally thought to be Dexter's favourite for the job; he was the one the new chairman singled out for mention. However, no decision was made at that meeting, which was said to have contained detailed discussion. Five days elapsed before Gower was accorded a press conference at which Dexter announced that he was the committee's choice to captain England for the series. There was just a hint that he might not have been everyone's choice.

The trouble, when things are kept secret, is that people start to look around for explanations other than the authorised version. I've always been one for conspiracy theories. For example, if Dexter wanted Gower, and knew that his No. 2, Stewart, wanted Gatting, the veto could not have been more in Dexter's favour. It gave him the captain he wanted and prevented an initial disagreement with Stewart.

The existence of the veto was known from the outset to the four men on the committee, and Dexter looks the sort who is at home walking the corridors of power. Of course it is equally possible that, some time in March, Stewart persuaded Dexter that Gatting was the man for the job. As I write these Notes, Gatting, the man they apparently wanted, is leading an unofficial tour of England cricketers to South Africa; Gooch, whom they relieved of the captaincy in April, is taking England to the West Indies; and Gower, the man they appointed, is contemplating his future on a health farm.

WEST INDIES V ENGLAND 1990 Alan Lee, 1991

The essential weakness of any statistical record is that it can reflect neither circumstance nor injustice. A potted summary of England's Test series in the Caribbean, early in 1990, indicates merely that they lost 2–1, with one match drawn and the other abandoned. In years to come, that stark scoreline may be read to mean that England did slightly better than anticipated. The truth of the matter is that at worst they merited a shared series, and at best an unimaginable upset of the world champions of Test cricket.

When the tour began, in late January, England were given no chance. They had been beaten 4–0 by Australia in England in their previous series. The response of the selectors to that had been to dismiss David Gower, as both captain and player, and replace him with Graham Gooch, who had never been thought to be inspirational leadership material.

England's nine-wicket victory in the First Test, at Kingston, unarguably qualified to be one of the most outlandish results in Test-cricket history. West Indies were thoroughly outplayed. Georgetown, venue for the Second Test, was struck by atrocious weather which prevented a ball being bowled, but those who maintained that the Jamaica Test result had been an unrepeatable freak were silenced in Trinidad. England, with the benefit of winning an important toss, set up a second victory, which was cruelly denied them by a persistent downpour on the final afternoon. This, if you like, was a real freak.

The tour was never the same after that. With their strongest side, England might have withstood the travesty and risen again. But for the two remaining Tests they were without Gooch, whose captaincy had become even more crucial than his batting, and Angus Fraser, the most dependable member of a startlingly influential four-man seam attack. It was too much to bear. In Barbados England battled ferociously, losing a dramatic and controversial match with half an hour's daylight remaining on the final evening. In Antigua, for the finale, they had nothing left to offer and were beaten, by an innings, before tea on the fourth day.

When it was over, England's dressing-room was a casualty ward, virtually half the party having suffered injuries in the battle. Two, Robin Smith and Nasser Hussain, batted in Antigua with broken bones. The character of the players was beyond question. As Micky Stewart, the team manager, said: "You have to feel so sorry for them, having nothing to show for it."

West Indies v England

First Test

At Kingston, February 24, 25, 26, 28, March 1, 1990. England won by nine wickets.   Alan Lee

England won by nine wickets, their first victory against West Indies in 16 years and 30 Tests. Before this match began, it would have been hard to find one person in the Caribbean willing to give England a chance of victory. When it ended, just before lunch on the final day, the game's established order had been so dramatically overturned that even those within the England party were scarcely able to absorb the fact. Among those who witnessed it were two members of the only previous England team to win in Kingston, 36 years earlier, Sir Leonard Hutton and T. G. Evans.

West Indies were without Logie and Ambrose, both unfit, but their team none the less had a familiar appearance. England gave first caps to Stewart and Hussain and opted, controversially, to include only four bowlers, not one of them a spinner. It was a policy vindicated by subsequent events, and none of the chosen quartet can ever have bowled better.

There was no hint of the sensations to come as West Indies' opening pair were putting on 62. However, Greenidge's run out, as he tried to take a second when Malcolm fumbled at fine leg, was the first of several needlessly sacrificed wickets as all ten went down for the addition of only 102 runs. Not that the West Indies' lowest total against England for 21 years, since the Leeds Test of 1969, was entirely due to slapdash batting. Operating rigidly to an off-stump line, England's four bowlers could not be faulted, and after Small, Malcolm and Capel had taken important top-order wickets, Fraser collected the last five at a personal cost of six runs. To complete one of their best days' cricket in some years, England navigated to close of play for the loss only of Gooch and Stewart, the latter to a viciously rising ball from Bishop which was a sobering reminder of possible reprisals.

The first two sessions of the second day were decisive, with England losing only one wicket as Larkins, Lamb and Smith applied themselves to five-day disciplines with a will not always evident in recent England displays. Lamb and Smith put on 172 for the fourth wicket, and Lamb went on to his tenth Test century, five of them against West Indies. He had been batting for 364 minutes when he was out, and by the close of play England were on 178 with two wickets remaining.

That lead was stretched to 200 early on the third day, which ended with the game all but decided. Despite approaching their second innings more professionally than their first, the West Indians still found some curious ways of getting out on a pitch on which the increasingly low bounce called for the elimination of certain shots. Malcolm bowled fast, and with unsuspected control, taking the crucial wicket when he dismissed Richards (for the second time in the match) to end a partnership of 80 with Best. That wicket fell with West Indies still eight runs short of avoiding an innings defeat, and when three more fell in consecutive overs while they clawed a lead of 29 before the close, it seemed that only the weather could deny England.

This being Jamaica, such a thing could not happen – yet it so nearly did. It rained intermittently on the rest day and again, heavily, overnight. The fourth day's play was abandoned, after numerous inspections, but English prayers were answered when the final day dawned sunny and clear. The two outstanding West

Indian wickets were taken in 20 balls, their confusion ending, as it had begun, in a run-out. England, needing 41 to win, coasted home for the loss of Gooch, who had waited ten years to beat West Indies and now, as captain, deserved to have been there at the end. This, however, was a match of no logic, and while it paid handsome tribute to the preparation and discipline of the England team, it asked more questions than it answered about West Indies.

Toss: West Indies. **West Indies 164** (C. G. Greenidge 32, D. L. Haynes 36; A. R. C. Fraser 5–28)
and 240 (C. G. Greenidge 36, C. A. Best 64, I. V. A. Richards 37; G. C. Small 4–58,
D. E. Malcolm 4–77); **England 364** (W. Larkins 46, A. J. Lamb 132, R. A. Smith 57,
Extras 48; I. R. Bishop 3-72, C. A. Walsh 5-68) **and 41–1**

ENGLAND V INDIA 1990
See page 437

AUSTRALIA V ENGLAND 1990–91
John Thicknesse, 1992

England were badly beaten in Australia, and against a strong and well-knit team they might well have suffered the same fate even had luck been on their side. In the event, deprived of Graham Gooch, the captain, for a month spanning the First Test, Allan Lamb, another mainstay of the batting, for the Second and Third Tests, and Angus Fraser, the best bowler, for the Third and Fifth, they were never in contention.

Australia v England   **First Test**
At Brisbane, November 23, 24, 25, 1990. Australia won by ten wickets.

A Test which looked evenly balanced after two days ended in an astonishingly easy win for Australia on the evening of the third, following a familiar England collapse in the face of Alderman. Outshone by Reid in the first innings, the 34-year-old Western Australian bowled his outswing with excellent control to take six for 47, his best figures in Test cricket. Yet future generations will surely wonder how Marsh and Taylor scored 157 without being parted, a ground record against England, to complete Australia's win, after the first three innings had yielded 194, 152 and 114. The short answer is that England had no bowler to match Alderman or Reid, and that by the third day the pitch had belatedly turned in favour of the bat.

Toss: Australia. **England 194** (D. I. Gower 61, A. J. Lamb 32; B. A. Reid 4-53, M. G. Hughes 3-39)
and 114 (T. M. Alderman 6-47); **Australia 152** (G. R. J. Matthews 35; A. R. C. Fraser 3-33,
G. C. Small 3-34, C. C. Lewis 3-29) **and 157-0** (M. A. Taylor 67*, G. R. Marsh 72*).

REJOICE, REJOICE
Graeme Wright, *Notes by the Editor,* 1992

Twelve months ago, as the Notes to the 1991 *Wisden* were being written, England failed to regain the Ashes in Australia, and were soon to embark on a series of embarrassing defeats in New Zealand. England's cricket, without a doubt, was in desperate straits. What a difference a year makes. Two Test wins over West Indies, and a drawn series, restored the confidence in English cricket which had been badly shaken by the events in Australia and New Zealand.

Although those victories were very much team efforts, they owed everything to individual performances, in particular to the batting of Graham Gooch, the captain, and Robin Smith. No one, however, delighted more than the left-arm spinner, Philip Tufnell, whose own passage from doldrums to buoyancy encapsulated that of the England team. Tufnell turned the final Test against West Indies with a spell of slow bowling on the Saturday which will find its way into cricketing mythology.

ENGLAND v WEST INDIES 1991 — First Test
At Leeds, June 6, 7, 8, 9, 10, 1991. England won by 115 runs.
John Callaghan, 1992

England gained their first home victory over West Indies since 1969, when Illingworth's team also won at Headingley. In addition to Gooch, the outstanding batsman, and DeFreitas, the most successful bowler, they possessed a greater discipline in testing conditions, and this eventually enabled them to outplay their opponents, in their 100th encounter.

Gooch gloriously confirmed his standing on the international stage. His decisive, unbeaten 154 in the second innings was the product of seven and a half hours of careful application. Unyielding concentration carried him through three interruptions for rain on the fourth day, and mental toughness enabled him to survive a series of disasters at the other end. In 331 deliveries, England's captain collected 18 fours and scored two-thirds of his side's runs from the bat as they built on a lead of 25; and he became the first England opener to carry his bat through a completed innings since G. Boycott finished with 99 not out, in a total of 215, against Australia at Perth in 1979–80. Three other England batsmen had achieved the feat, among them Sir Leonard Hutton, the only one previously to do so in England; coincidentally, West Indies were on the receiving end of his unbeaten double-hundred at The Oval in 1950. Gooch's innings also gave him a full set of Test hundreds on each of England's six international grounds.

Although no praise could be too lavish for Gooch, DeFreitas, too, took a prominent role. His match figures of eight for 93 rewarded admirable control and impressive accuracy. Inevitably, as 40 wickets fell for only 785 runs, the pitch attracted a good deal of comment, not all favourable, and batting was never comfortable. The ball moved off the seam and the bounce became a shade variable towards the end; but the damp weather played a part, and far too many batsmen got out to strokes which reflected anxiety about what the ball might do, rather than what it actually did. There was also, at times, some high-class bowling, notably from Ambrose, and three players were run out during the first two innings. As Gooch eventually demonstrated, it was possible to score runs with a sound technique. But it was not a pitch for the flamboyant strokeplayer, and West Indies lost largely because they failed to appreciate this point. Significantly, it was the tenth successive Test on the ground to produce a positive result.

England v West Indies, 1991 — First Test

At Leeds, June 6, 7, 8, 9, 10, 1991. Result: England won by 115 runs.

ENGLAND

Batsman	First innings		Second innings	
*G. A. Gooch c Dujon b Marshall	34	– not out		154
M. A. Atherton b Patterson	2	– c Dujon b Ambrose		6
G. A. Hick c Dujon b Walsh	6	– b Ambrose		6
A. J. Lamb c Hooper b Marshall	11	– c Hooper b Ambrose		0
M. R. Ramprakash c Hooper b Marshall	27	– c Dujon b Ambrose		27
R. A. Smith run out	54	– lbw b Ambrose		0
†R. C. Russell lbw b Patterson	5	– c Dujon b Ambrose		4
D. R. Pringle c Logie b Patterson	16	– c Dujon b Marshall		27
P. A. J. DeFreitas c Simmons b Ambrose	15	– lbw b Walsh		3
S. L. Watkin b Ambrose	2	– c Hooper b Marshall		0
D. E. Malcolm not out	5	– b Marshall		4
L-b 5, w 2, n-b 14	21	B 4, l-b 9, w 1, n-b 7		21

1-13 2-45 3-45 4-64 5-129 6-149   **198**   1-22 2-38 3-38 4-116 5-116 6-124   **252**
7-154 8-177 9-181 10-198   7-222 8-236 9-238 10-252

First innings – Ambrose 26–8–49–2; Patterson 26.2–8–67–3; Walsh 14–7–31–1; Marshall 13–4–46–3.
Second innings – Ambrose 28–6–52–6; Patterson 15–1–52–0; Walsh 30–5–61–1; Marshall 25–4–58–3; Hooper 4–1–11–0; Richards 4–1–5–0.

WEST INDIES

Batsman	First innings		Second innings	
P. V. Simmons c Ramprakash b DeFreitas	38	– b DeFreitas		0
D. L. Haynes c Russell b Watkin	7	– c Smith b Pringle		19
R. B. Richardson run out	29	– c Lamb b DeFreitas		68
C. L. Hooper run out	0	– c Lamb b Watkin		5
*I. V. A. Richards c Lamb b Pringle	73	– c Gooch b Watkin		3
A. L. Logie c Lamb b DeFreitas	6	– c Gooch b Watkin		3
†P. J. L. Dujon c Ramprakash b Watkin	6	– lbw b DeFreitas		33
M. D. Marshall c Hick b Pringle	0	– lbw b Pringle		1
C. E. L. Ambrose c Hick b DeFreitas	0	– c Pringle b DeFreitas		14
C. A. Walsh c Gooch b DeFreitas	3	– c Atherton b Malcolm		9
B. P. Patterson not out	5	– not out		0
L-b 1, n-b 5	6	L-b 1, n-b 6		7

1-36 2-54 3-58 4-102 5-139 6-156   **173**   1-0 2-61 3-77 4-85 5-88 6-136   **162**
7-160 8-165 9-167 10-173   7-137 8-139 9-162 10-162

First innings – Malcolm 14–0–69–0; DeFreitas 17.1–5–34–4; Watkin 14–2–55–2; Pringle 9–3–14–2.
Second innings – Malcolm 6.4–0–26–1; DeFreitas 21–4–59–4; Watkin 7–0–38–3; Pringle 22–6–38–2.

Toss won by West Indies   UMPIRES H. D. Bird and D. R. Shepherd

England v West Indies

Fifth Test

At The Oval, August 8, 9, 10, 11, 12, 1991. England won by five wickets.

David Field, 1992

As if by calculation, Botham struck his only delivery of England's second innings to Compton's corner to complete the victory which secured a drawn series against West Indies for the first time since 1973–74. Compton's famous sweep for the Ashes triumph of 1953 had finished in the same spot, and in many ways this match was just as memorable in Oval Test history. Certainly it could hardly have had a more popular final scene to gladden English hearts, Botham, with his Comptonesque flair for the big occasion, sealing the win in his first Test appearance for two years. It was, moreover, his first taste of victory in 20 Tests against West Indies.

This was the *coup de grâce*, but notwithstanding Smith's hundred, it was the left-arm spinner, Tufnell, who played the key role in a result many thought beyond England, against opposition nearing their formidable best after wins at Nottingham and Birmingham. His six for 25 on a hot Saturday afternoon obliged West Indies to follow on for the first time against England in 22 years and 48 Tests, and presented his captain, Gooch, with a priceless equation of runs and time.

Richards, in his 121st Test and his 50th as captain, was leading West Indies for the last time. He was forced to forgo the services of Logie, who had a knee injury, and called in the Guyanese left-hander, Lambert, for his Test debut. Gooch, winning the toss, decided to have first use of a pitch containing its usual generous bounce. This was exploited fully by West Indies' fast bowlers on the first afternoon, after Gooch and [Hugh] Morris had fought their way to 82 by lunch.

No Law was broken by Ambrose, Patterson and Walsh, but as the bouncer became a regular weapon, the spirit of the game was sorely tested at times. And the attack had the desired effect; England lost three wickets for eight runs in 21 deliveries, with Morris out one ball after a lifter from Ambrose had broken the chinstrap on his helmet. Atherton faced just four balls, but Ramprakash once more battled against the pace, only to fall, for the seventh time in the series, in the 20s. However, Smith, reaching 50 for the 20th time in Tests, and Stewart saw their team to the close at 231 for four, and next day Smith's valiant sixth Test hundred, his second of the series, enabled England to reach 400 against West Indies for the first time in 15 years. His square cut was again profitable, and he hit 13 fours in almost six hours at the wicket.

There were important contributions, too, from Stewart, Botham and Lewis in the late middle order, with Botham dismissed in a bizarre fashion. Attempting to hook Ambrose, he over-balanced and dislodged a bail with his right thigh as he tried to straddle the stumps. Equally unusual was the pause in play late on the second day while stewards cleared away a mass of torn paper from the outfield, emanating from the tiresome Mexican wave. West Indies closed at a comfortable 90 for one, with Haynes and Richardson relieved to have survived a chance each.

The third day belonged to Tufnell, when Richards might have been expected to take command on his farewell stage. From 158 for three, West Indies declined rapidly to 176 all out as Tufnell spun the ball generously in a devastating spell of six for four in 33 deliveries either side of lunch. It has to be said, though, that a rash of reckless strokes contributed to this collapse, which began when Lambert miscued Tufnell's first ball of the day to cover. Marshall cut to slip, Richards, Ambrose and Walsh gave their wickets away in one over, and in Tufnell's next over,

Botham dived for his third catch to dismiss Patterson. Richards had held himself back because of a headache. Haynes, who carried his bat for the second time in Test cricket, faced 198 balls in four and three-quarter hours, and he batted eight minutes under three hours (114 balls) when West Indies followed on 243 behind. England collected three more wickets by the close.

There were no easy pickings for Tufnell on the fourth day, however. Twice Hooper struck him for six during a magnificent display of strokemaking which illuminated the first hour. Then Richards, given a standing ovation to the wicket, put on 97 for the fifth wicket with Richardson to put his side ahead for the first time in the game. Richards began needing 20 runs to guarantee an average of 50 in Tests, and he had gone well past that when he drove Lawrence to mid-on. He left the Test arena to rapturous applause, stopping on the way to raise his bat and maroon cap to both sides of the ground in gracious acknowledgement. Richardson finally reached his hundred, a dedicated effort, after six and a half hours, and West Indies led by 113, with four wickets in hand, on Sunday evening.

Marshall lost his middle stump to DeFreitas's second ball on Monday, Ambrose was lbw off his fourth, and then Lawrence claimed five wickets in a Test innings for the first time when he removed Walsh and, finally, Richardson. This left England to score 143 to level the series, with time no object. However, the West Indian fast bowlers backed Richards's pledge that England would have to fight for victory, and wickets fell too regularly for England's comfort. At 80 for four the cricket was tense, but Stewart's coolness and sure strokeplay saw England to the finishing line. With the scores level, Ramprakash was lbw to Lambert's third ball in Test cricket, bringing in Botham to conclude the match with a little under two hours remaining.

England v West Indies, 1991   Fifth Test

At The Oval, August 8, 9, 10, 11, 12, 1991. Result: England won by five wickets.

ENGLAND	First innings		Second innings	
*G. A. Gooch lbw b Ambrose	60	– lbw b Marshall	29
H. Morris c Lambert b Ambrose	44	– c Dujon b Patterson	2
M. A. Atherton c Hooper b Walsh	0	– c Hooper b Patterson	13
R. A. Smith lbw b Marshall	109	– c Patterson b Walsh	26
M. R. Ramprakash c Lambert b Hooper	25	– lbw b Lambert	19
†A. J. Stewart c Richardson b Patterson	31	– not out	38
I. T. Botham hit wkt b Ambrose	31	– not out	4
C. C. Lewis not out	47		
P. A. J. DeFreitas c Dujon b Walsh	7		
D. V. Lawrence c Richards b Walsh	9		
P. C. R. Tufnell c Haynes b Patterson	2		
B 8, l-b 10, w 1, n-b 35	54	B 4, w 1, n-b 10	15

1-112 2-114 3-120 4-188 5-263 6-336   419   1-3 2-40 3-80 4-80 5-142   (5 wkts) 146
7-351 8-386 9-411 10-419

First innings – Ambrose 36–8–83–3; Patterson 25.1–3–87–2; Walsh 32–5–91–3; Marshall 24–5–62–1; Hooper 34–1–78–1.
Second innings – Ambrose 8–0–48–0; Patterson 9–0–63–2; Marshall 5–3–9–1; Walsh 9–3–18–1; Lambert 0.4–0–4–1.

WEST INDIES	*First innings*		*Second innings*
P. V. Simmons lbw b Lawrence	15	– c Lewis b Botham	36
D. L. Haynes not out	75	– lbw b Lawrence	43
R. B. Richardson c Stewart b Botham	20	– (4) c Gooch b Lawrence	121
C. L. Hooper c Stewart b DeFreitas	3	– (5) c Gooch b Tufnell	54
C. B. Lambert c Ramprakash b Tufnell	39	– (3) lbw b Botham	14
†P. J. L. Dujon lbw b Lawrence	0	– (7) c Stewart b Lawrence	5
M. D. Marshall c Botham b Tufnell	0	– (8) b DeFreitas	17
*I. V. A. Richards c Stewart b Tufnell	2	– (6) c Morris b Lawrence	60
C. E. L. Ambrose c Botham b Tufnell	0	– lbw b DeFreitas	0
C. A. Walsh c Gooch b Tufnell	0	– lbw b Lawrence	14
B. P. Patterson c Botham b Tufnell	2	– not out	1
L-b 9, n-b 11	20	B 7, l-b 5, w 2, n-b 6	20

1-52 2-95 3-98 4-158 5-160 6-161   176   1-53 2-71 3-125 4-208 5-305 6-311   385
7-172 8-172 9-172 10-176   7-356 8-356 9-378 10-385

First innings – DeFreitas 13–6–38–1; Lawrence 16–1–67–2; Tufnell 14.3–3–25–6; Botham 11–4–27–1; Lewis 3–1–10–0.
Second innings – DeFreitas 20–9–42–2; Lawrence 25.5–4–106–5; Lewis 25–12–35–0; Tufnell 46–6–150–1; Botham 16–4–40–2.

Toss won by England   UMPIRES J. W. Holder and M. J. Kitchen

THE LAST DAYS OF GOOCHIE AND TED   Matthew Engel, *Notes by the Editor*, 1994

The Ashes series of 1993 was extremely one-sided – all of them have been, one way or the other, for many years now – and the season was damp. But it was still entirely riveting. The grounds were full and both nations transfixed – in England by the extent of the horror, if nothing else. Before England's victory at The Oval, they had lost nine Tests out of 10. The summer ranked with the worst years of breast-beating and navel-contemplation: 1989, 1988, 1984, 1976. . .

The 1993 series came immediately after a particularly unsuccessful tour of India and Sri Lanka – one well up with the worst of all time. Someone had to carry the can and both Dexter and Gooch did. The manager, Keith Fletcher, largely escaped criticism, even though the desperate sequence began when he took over from Micky Stewart, while Dexter and Gooch had each been in place since 1989, not without some success. Fletcher had the sense to keep his head some distance below the parapet. Dexter, in contrast, stood there with a very English, if slightly batty, heroism as shot and shell flew about him. The people responsible for the absurdly overstated and doltishly brutal abuse in the tabloid press will have to answer to their consciences.

My suspicion is that history will regard Dexter more kindly than either the newspapers or the Test match crowd who cheered his resignation. It might then be easier to put his four years in context with the amateurish shambles that preceded them. Dexter set out to impose a logical system of international recognition for young players, leading up to the England team. He did bring in a more sensible selection system. This did not necessarily mean more sensible selections. But when you see Alan Knott spend an entire match at Abergavenny by the sightscreen with binoculars, to report on whether Colin Metson might be a better wicket-keeper than Jack Russell – something that would have been unthinkable before Dexter – you realise that not every development has been a negative one.

Though Dexter stoically took the blame for everything, he had made a conscious decision to apply a light touch and let the manager and captain take day-to-day control. His touch was almost certainly too light: when he wanted Gatting rather than Gower as captain in 1989 and was blocked by the chairman of the cricket committee, Ossie Wheatley, he should have screamed the place down, not taken it on the chin. I reckon he would have got his way. He should certainly have been more closely involved in 1993.

For a professional public-relations man, he was also surprisingly inept at that part of the operation. In public, he kept silent when explanations were required, and kept talking (eventually saying something that was either daft or could be twisted to sound daft) when he should have shut up. In private, he failed – crucially – to win the support of the county chairmen. They felt slighted when Dexter's system of an England committee, responsible for the best players in all age groups, was first foisted on them, as they saw it, by the TCCB executive. It was accompanied by a great deal of ill-considered propaganda from various sources about the counties being selfish and parochial and holding back the visionaries who wanted to make English cricket great again. Dexter had a powerful vision but he failed to let enough people see the picture.

Part of his legacy will survive: regular A tours, the age-group squads, the system of identifying the best players at every level and giving them the best coaches and facilities. As far as selection is concerned, we now look like returning to a worse version of the old committee-room mess which could lead to the chairman, the manager, the captain and the other selectors all pulling against each other. In the short run, things can only get better than they were last summer. In the long run, I fear the worst.

ENGLAND V AUSTRALIA 1993
For Series Review and First, Second and Fourth Tests, see page 354

For Series Review and First, Second and Fourth Tests, see page 354

England v Australia	**Sixth Test**
At The Oval, August 19, 20, 21, 22, 23, 1993. England won by 161 runs.	Matthew Engel, 1994

To general astonishment, England [who had lost four of the five Tests in the six-Test series] reversed the form of the summer, outplayed Australia and won the final Test deservedly and decisively. The result came more than six and a half years or – as one paper recorded – 2,430 days, 11 hours and 49 minutes after England's last win over Australia, at Melbourne in December 1986. It brought about a halt, at least temporarily, in the mood of national teeth-gnashing that had accompanied England's previous failures. For Australia, who had enjoyed a triumphal progress round the British Isles with only trivial setbacks, the defeat came hours before they flew home; it was like having the perfect holiday and then being nabbed by customs.

The win was a particular triumph for the England captain Mike Atherton, in his second game in charge; he was immediately named as captain for the winter tour to the West Indies. It was a cause for quieter satisfaction for Ted Dexter, the much-vilified chairman of selectors who had announced his resignation two weeks earlier. This was the last team for which he was responsible.

It was a greatly changed team too, but if England finally found the right combination there was as much accident as design and, at last, a bit of luck. Smith was dropped, for the first time, after 45 Tests, along with Ilott and Emburey. Back into the squad came Hick, Tufnell and Malcolm. But the selectors took what might have been a gamble by naming Fraser, whose brief but brilliant Test career had been halted two and a half years earlier by a serious hip injury, as cover for Martin Bicknell, who had a dodgy knee. The evidence that Fraser was back to his best was based on only a couple of games, but when Bicknell did pull out he had to play. It was a turning point. The combination of Fraser, Malcolm and Watkin (who made it into the final 11 this time, while Tufnell did not) on a pacy wicket transformed England. None had played a game before in the series; they shared the 20 wickets between them.

England had to make a fifth change less than an hour before the start when Thorpe was hit on the hand by a net bowler, broke his thumb and fainted; Ramprakash was summoned from Lord's. The short notice meant it had to be someone playing nearby; had Middlesex been at Swansea or Darlington, someone else might have got the chance. As it was, Ramprakash – in his tenth Test – finally passed 30 and began to add a little achievement to his unquestioned promise.

The next bit of English luck came when Atherton won the toss. England made their familiar good start, racing to 143 for one. Australia were again unchanged, except that they were two weeks further along a hard tour and even someone as great-hearted as Hughes was beginning to show signs of weariness. The batsmen were right on top all day but, in familiar English fashion, they got themselves out, often for no good reason – Hick, in particular, was blazing away and hit a regal six to reach 80 two balls before being caught at third man off a thoroughly ill-judged cut.

In the field, Australia seemed more intent on getting mad than getting even and the verbal battle appeared to reach new heights, or depths: the managers were called in for a quieter word by the referee, Clive Lloyd, after the first day. Next morning, England were all out for 380 and the consensus was that they had scored a hundred too few. But that assumed England's attack would live up to past form. Instead, Malcolm's speed, Watkin's resilience and Fraser's relentlessness completely transformed their prospects. The wicket was hard enough to favour strokeplay and to ensure that class bowlers could always make a batsman uncomfortable. England fielded tightly, with the young men darting everywhere and Gooch loyally putting on the short-leg helmet. Australia crumpled to 196 for eight. But then England could not finish them off and the last two wickets took the score past 300.

Australia could have got back in the game but, once again, the top three England batsmen tore into some jaded bowling and by the middle of Saturday afternoon England, at 157 for one, already looked fireproof. The runs included an off-driven four off Reiffel by Gooch which took his score to 21 and his total of Test runs to 8,235, more than David Gower and every other England player. The applause was unstinting, though the moment had a bittersweet touch: Gower might have scored many more if Gooch, as captain, had let him play.

The innings meandered later and England's prospects were hindered on the fourth day by the loss of two hours' play to the weather – only 41 minutes had been lost throughout the series while Australia had been on top. But the presence of the seventh specialist batsman, Ramprakash, enabled England to take the lead to 390 before they were bowled out to save Atherton having to decide whether to risk a declaration.

The rain effectively ruled out the remote chance of an Australian win. Could England do it? Again the luck was with them. The weather improved and umpire Meyer gave them two successive decisions that might have gone the other way: replays showed that Slater was given out caught off his armguard, and the first-ball lbw decision against Boon was not a certain one. Then Taylor played on and it was 30 for three. There was a stand between Mark Waugh and Border, who was caught behind – another decision that was not universally approved – straight after lunch and left an English cricket field for what was presumed to be the last time without once looking up. Mark Waugh and Healy were both out hooking and, though Steve Waugh dug in with Hughes, Malcolm was getting ready for another burst. His first ball back had Waugh leg before.

At 5.18 England won. The heroes of the hour were English but the heroes of the summer were Australian: it was Border who was presented with a replica of the Ashes. What England had won, at the very last minute, was some self-respect.

England v Australia, 1993 — Sixth Test

At The Oval, August 19, 20, 21, 22, 23, 1993. Result: England won by 161 runs.

ENGLAND	First innings		Second innings	
G. A. Gooch c Border b S. R. Waugh	56	–	c Healy b Warne	79
*M. A. Atherton lbw b S. R. Waugh	50	–	c Warne b Reiffel	42
G. A. Hick c Warne b May	80	–	c Boon b May	36
M. P. Maynard b Warne	20	–	c Reiffel b Hughes	9
N. Hussain c Taylor b Warne	30	–	c M. E. Waugh b Hughes	0
†A. J. Stewart c Healy b Hughes	76	–	c M. E. Waugh b Reiffel	35
M. R. Ramprakash c Healy b Hughes	6	–	c Slater b Hughes	64
A. R. C. Fraser b Reiffel	28	–	c Healy b Reiffel	13
S. L. Watkin c S. R. Waugh b Reiffel	13	–	lbw b Warne	4
P. M. Such c M. E. Waugh b Hughes	4	–	lbw b Warne	10
D. E. Malcolm not out	0	–	not out	0
L-b 7, w 1, n-b 9	17		B 5, l-b 12, w 1, n-b 3	21
	380			**313**

1-88 2-143 3-177 4-231 5-253 6-272
7-339 8-363 9-374 10-380 — 380

1-77 2-157 3-180 4-180 5-186 6-254
7-276 8-283 9-313 10-313 — 313

First innings – Hughes 30–7–121–3; Reiffel 28.5–4–88–2; S. R. Waugh 12–2–45–2; Warne 20–5–70–2; M. E. Waugh 1–0–17–0; May 10–3–32–1.

Second innings – Hughes 31.2–9–110–3; Reiffel 24–8–55–3; Warne 40–15–78–3; May 24–6–53–1.

AUSTRALIA	First innings		Second innings
M. A. Taylor c Hussain b Malcolm	70	– (2) b Watkin	8
M. J. Slater c Gooch b Malcolm	4	– (1) c Stewart b Watkin	12
D. C. Boon c Gooch b Malcolm	13	– lbw b Watkin	0
M. E. Waugh c Stewart b Fraser	10	– c Ramprakash b Malcolm	49
*A. R. Border c Stewart b Fraser	48	– c Stewart b Malcolm	17
S. R. Waugh b Fraser	20	– lbw b Malcolm	26
†I. A. Healy not out	83	– c Maynard b Watkin	5
M. G. Hughes c Ramprakash b Watkin	7	– c Watkin b Fraser	12
P. R. Reiffel c Maynard b Watkin	0	– c and b Fraser	42
S. K. Warne c Stewart b Fraser	16	– lbw b Fraser	37
T. B. A. May c Stewart b Fraser	15	– not out	4
B 5, l-b 6, w 2, n-b 4	17	B 2, l-b 6, w 2, n-b 7	17

1-9 2-30 3-53 4-132 5-164 6-181	**303**	1-23 2-23 3-30 4-92 5-95 6-106	**229**
7-196 8-196 9-248 10-303		7-142 8-143 9-217 10-229	

First innings – Malcolm 26–5–86–3; Watkin 28–4–87–2; Fraser 26.4–4–87–5; Such 14–4–32–0.
Second innings – Malcolm 20–3–84–3; Watkin 25–9–65–4; Fraser 19.1–5–44–3; Such 9–4–17–0;
Hick 8–3–11–0.

Toss won by England | UMPIRES M. J. Kitchen and B. J. Meyer

WEST INDIES V ENGLAND 1994
Alan Lee, 1995

When England headed for the Caribbean in January 1994, many people might have predicted that the series would end in a 3–1 win for West Indies. And that, three months later, was how things turned out. So everything went to plan? Well, hardly. Modern tours seldom seem to run along humdrum straight lines, but this one broke all the rules of logic and expectation. It was a tour of exhausting extremes, on which despair gave way to triumph at impossibly short notice and soaring personal achievement attended every game in the series and, it sometimes seemed, every day. Some of the performances – like Curtly Ambrose's amazing bowling to turn the Port-of-Spain Test [he took six for 24 to dismiss England for 46 in their second innings], the heroic deeds from Alec Stewart and Angus Fraser to give England an improbable, indeed almost unthinkable, win in Bridgetown and, above all, Brian Lara's world Test record 375 in Antigua – will be remembered as long as the game is played.

In the final analysis, it was a disappointment for England because, with only a handful of exceptions, the selected players made no obvious progress and, as a unit, they made no impression on the supremacy that West Indies have paraded for so long.

West Indies v England
See page 400
Third Test

West Indies v England — Fourth Test

At Bridgetown, April 8, 9, 10, 12, 13, 1994. England won by 208 runs.

Cricket's aptitude for producing the inexplicable has seldom been so convincingly demonstrated. England arrived at the supposedly impregnable bastion of West Indian cricket with their form and confidence rock-bottom. Even team manager Keith Fletcher admitted a draw would have been considered a triumph: West Indies had won their last 12 Tests on the ground. To win, and win handsomely, becoming the first visiting Test team to succeed at Bridgetown since R. E. S. Wyatt's England team 59 years earlier, and only the second ever, beggared belief. And yet it was no fluke. England dictated the game and won on merit, eight minutes after the scheduled tea interval on the final day. Each of the five days had attracted capacity crowds, swelled by about 6,000 holidaying England supporters, creating a unique and strangely bipartisan atmosphere for a Caribbean Test.

It seemed the familiar pattern had been restored on the second day, when four wickets from Ambrose, at a personal cost of 24, restricted the [England] total to 355. But the West Indian reply was quickly in trouble, despite Haynes surviving a controversial run-out appeal when he eased up, believing his shot had crossed the boundary. Haynes later retired hurt, struck on the finger by Lewis, initiating a disastrous period for West Indies. In his eighth over with the new ball, Fraser dismissed Richardson and Arthurton and, after Lara had seen a lavish drive superbly caught at cover by the substitute, Hussain, he returned for a crucial evening spell which brought him four for one in 17 balls. It was easily his most effective and impressive bowling since his prolonged pelvic injury and, with Tufnell containing skilfully at the other end, West Indies were 205 for eight when Ambrose became a seventh victim for Fraser on the third morning. Chanderpaul's remarkable temperament was again in evidence as he batted five hours in company with the tail, who eventually carried the side past 300. The last three wickets added 170 but Fraser still achieved figures of eight for 75, the best by an Englishman against West Indies, and the best for England since Bob Willis took eight for 43 against Australia at Headingley in 1981.

The lead of 51 was precarious, however, when Walsh quickly dismissed Atherton and Ramprakash. With Smith failing once more, England were tottering until Hick joined Stewart and, with the aid of generous supply of no-balls, added 92 before the close of the third day – delayed, like the previous two, by a desultory over-rate which was to produce a heavy fine for the West Indians. The first session of the fourth day was a critical one. Having survived it for the loss of one more wicket – Hick – they were well-placed. Stewart, who scored only 13 in the two hours to lunch, then advanced rapidly to his second century of the match, the first England player to achieve the feat against West Indies. If his second innings lacked the fluency of his first, it surpassed it for application; he had been batting almost eight hours when he played on, wearily, for the second time in the game. His stand of 150 with Thorpe was a record for England's fifth wicket against West Indies.

Thorpe's breezy 84, made in 188 minutes, permitted Atherton the unaccustomed luxury of a declaration and West Indies, set an improbable 446, 40 more than had ever been made to win a Test, were 47 for two at the close, the retirement of Richardson with a hamstring strain adding to their woes. If Russell had not missed a stumping with Lara on strike, England might have thought they were nearly home; as it was, they had to wait 75 minutes on the fifth morning before, crucially, he mis-hooked Caddick to mid-on where Tufnell took an impressive catch. With Haynes batting down the order with his damaged finger, the rest was not far short of a procession.

West Indies v England, 1994   Fourth Test
At Bridgetown, April 8, 9, 10, 12, 13, 1994. Result: England won by 208 runs.

ENGLAND	First innings		Second innings
*M. A. Atherton c Lara b K. C. G. Benjamin	85	– c Lara b Walsh	15
A. J. Stewart b W. K. M. Benjamin	118	– b Walsh	143
M. R. Ramprakash c Murray b W. K. M. Benjamin	20	– c Chanderpaul b Walsh	3
R. A. Smith c Murray b W. K. M. Benjamin	10	– lbw b K. C. G. Benjamin	13
G. A. Hick c Murray b Ambrose	34	– c Lara b Walsh	59
G. P. Thorpe c sub (P. V. Simmons) b K. C. G. Benjamin	7	– c Arthurton b Walsh	84
†R. C. Russell c Chanderpaul b Ambrose	38	– not out	17
C. C. Lewis c Murray b Ambrose	0	– c Walsh b Adams	10
A. R. Caddick b Ambrose	8		
A. R. C. Fraser c Chanderpaul b Walsh	3		
P. C. R. Tufnell not out	0		
L-b 8, n-b 24	32	B 8, l-b 6, n-b 36	50

1-171 2-223 3-242 4-265 5-290 6-307   355   1-33 2-43 3-79 4-194   (7 wkts dec.) 394
7-307 8-327 9-351 10-355   5-344 6-382 7-394

First innings – Ambrose 24.2–5–86–4; Walsh 24–3–88–1; W. K. M. Benjamin 22–4–76–3; K. C. G. Benjamin 20–5–74–2; Chanderpaul 10–4–23–0.
Second innings – Ambrose 22–4–75–0; Walsh 28–5–94–5; W. K. M. Benjamin 22–3–58–0; K. C. G. Benjamin 20–1–92–1; Chanderpaul 10–3–30–0; Adams 6.5–0–31–1.

WEST INDIES	First innings		Second innings
D. L. Haynes c Atherton b Fraser	35	– (8) c Thorpe b Tufnell	15
*R. B. Richardson c Atherton b Fraser	20	– (1) c Ramprakash b Caddick	33
B. C. Lara c sub (N. Hussain) b Lewis	26	– c Tufnell b Caddick	64
K. L. T. Arthurton c Russell b Fraser	0	– (5) b Tufnell	52
J. C. Adams c Thorpe b Fraser	26	– (2) c Russell b Caddick	12
S. Chanderpaul c Ramprakash b Tufnell	77	– c sub (N. Hussain) b Hick	5
†J. R. Murray c Thorpe b Fraser	0	– c Thorpe b Caddick	5
W. K. M. Benjamin c Hick b Fraser	8	– (9) c Stewart b Tufnell	3
C. E. L. Ambrose c Hick b Fraser	44	– (10) b Lewis	12
K. C. G. Benjamin not out	43	– (4) c Hick b Caddick	0
C. A. Walsh c Tufnell b Fraser	13	– not out	18
L-b 1, n-b 11	12	B 1, l-b 7, n-b 10	18

1-55 2-55 3-95 4-126 5-126 6-126   304   1-43 2-43 3-128 4-150 5-164 6-179   237
7-134 8-205 9-263 10-304   7-195 8-199 9-216 10-237

First innings – Fraser 28.5–7–75–8; Caddick 24–2–92–0; Lewis 17–2–60–1; Tufnell 32–12–76–1.
Second innings – Fraser 17–7–40–0; Caddick 17–3–63–5; Tufnell 36–12–100–3; Lewis 8.2–1–23–1; Hick 4–2–3–1.

Toss won by West Indies   UMPIRES L. H. Barker and D. B. Hair

West Indies v England   **Fifth Test**
See page 401

ENGLAND V SOUTH AFRICA 1994
For Series Review and First Test, see page 487

England v South Africa   **Third Test**
At The Oval, August 18, 19, 20, 21, 1994. England won by eight wickets.   Ted Corbett, 1995

It will always be Malcolm's Match but there was so much more to this astonishing Test than Devon Malcolm's nine for 57 in South Africa's second innings. When the game ended 19 minutes before lunch on the fourth day, only 255.2 overs had been bowled; if the bowlers had kept to the prescribed 90 overs a day, it could have finished at five o'clock on the third day. Runs came at nearly four an over; a wicket fell every 48 balls; Jonty Rhodes went to hospital after being struck on the helmet by Malcolm; Atherton and de Villiers were fined for dissent and both teams for their slow over-rates; and Malcolm delivered himself of a threat so graphic when he was hit in his turn that it has already become part of cricket folklore. The content, excitement and drama were at the level of a *Superman* film; value for money, even at TCCB ticket prices.

Winning the toss meant batting, but this true, fast pitch offered help to the bowlers too. Like South Africa, England had picked four seamers – introducing Benjamin and bringing back Malcolm in place of Fraser and Tufnell. Soon after Rhodes was escorted off the field, four overs beyond lunch, this attack had effectively reduced South Africa to 136 for six. The half-brothers Gary and Peter Kirsten – opening in a Test at The Oval 114 years after the Grace brothers W. G. and E. M. went out there together for England – Cronje, Wessels and Cullinan, playing in place of the out-of-form Hudson, had all been swept aside. The ball from Malcolm that struck Rhodes was fast and nasty. Rhodes ducked so low that Malcolm considered an lbw appeal. Rhodes's team-mates were worried that his epilepsy might make his condition worse. He was taken to the neuro-surgery unit of Maudsley Hospital for a scan, given the all-clear but kept in overnight with concussion. Having handwritten his own lucid account of events rather than be interviewed, he did not return to bat until seven wickets fell in the second innings. McMillan, who was also hit by Malcolm but survived to make 93 in four and a half hours, and Richardson revived South Africa with a sixth-wicket stand of 124 in 30 overs. But Benjamin, a Surrey favourite in his first Test, and DeFreitas picked up four wickets each. Once it was clear that Rhodes would not be returning yet, South Africa were all out for 332 early on the second day.

England made a traumatic start when Atherton was given lbw to his first ball, looked at his bat and shook his head repeatedly as he left: that evening he was summoned before the match referee, Peter Burge, fined half his match fee – £1,250 – and reprimanded. With Gooch also going cheaply, men of Surrey again held sway, as Thorpe made his third successive 70 and Stewart a dashing 62. But the power of Donald got rid of Hick and Crawley, who looked a year short of maturity. Just when it seemed that England had had the worst of the day, DeFreitas and Gough added 59 exhilarating runs in the final half-hour and England were only 28 behind when the innings finished next morning. That was after Gooch had called the team together in Atherton's absence and urged them to rally behind the captain. It was also after Malcolm was hit on the helmet, straight between the eyes, first ball by de Villiers. He was not hurt, only angry. He stared back at the fielders who gathered round. "You guys are going to pay for this," he was reported to have said. "You guys are history."

Malcolm turned his words into action in 99 balls, the most devastating spell by an England bowler since Jim Laker wiped out the Australians in 1956. It was the sixth-best Test analysis ever and, until Cullinan was caught off Gough, it looked as if Malcolm might join Laker by taking all ten. The Kirstens and Cronje had gone for one run and the last six wickets fell for 38, with only Cullinan, who made 94, standing firm for long. Malcolm produced a series of classic deliveries: five catches to slip and wicket-keeper from lifting balls, a bouncer hooked to long-leg, a desperately determined caught and bowled and two sets of stumps sent clattering by yorkers. He answered every question save one. Why did the selectors make him wait so long to bowl against a team who appeared alarmed by fast bowling?

England were left to make 204 and, for the first time since the Trent Bridge Test against New Zealand, Gooch showed the value of his experience. His fitness had been in doubt and Gatting had been called up as cover, but now his bold strokes inspired Atherton so that 56 came in five overs – when Gooch was bowled – 79 off 10 and 107 in 16 by the close. This incisive batting settled the match and the new, mature Hick sealed England's success.

He strode towards an undefeated run-a-ball 81 in the style he had so often displayed for Worcestershire. De Villiers thought he had him caught behind at 53 and expressing doubts about umpire Palmer's verdict cost him 25% of his match fee. By the time his team had been fined 70% of their fees for bowling 14 overs short of their target on the second day, he was left with £70 for his 31 overs, four wickets and 14 runs. England were fined 30% for being six overs short. De Villiers will find it no consolation that he played in one of the great Tests. South Africa's performance was wretched compared with their win at Lord's, but England saw the victory as a rebirth.

By winning this Test, England drew the series, the first time since twin tours were introduced in England in 1965 that a team had not lost a three-match series after falling one behind. Although Devon Malcolm only played in the final Test, he was named England's Man of the Series as well as Man of the Match.

England v South Africa, 1994   Third Test

At The Oval, August 18, 19, 20, 21, 1994. Result: England won by eight wickets.

SOUTH AFRICA

	First innings		Second innings	
G. Kirsten c Rhodes b DeFreitas	2	– (2) c and b Malcolm		0
P. N. Kirsten b Malcolm	16	– (1) c DeFreitas b Malcolm		1
W. J. Cronje lbw b Benjamin	38	– b Malcolm		0
*K. C. Wessels lbw b Benjamin	45	– c Rhodes b Malcolm		28
D. J. Cullinan c Rhodes b DeFreitas	7	– c Thorpe b Gough		94
J. N. Rhodes retired hurt	8	– (9) c Rhodes b Malcolm		10
B. M. McMillan c Hick b DeFreitas	93	– (6) c Thorpe b Malcolm		25
†D. J. Richardson c Rhodes b Benjamin	58	– (7) lbw b Malcolm		3
C. R. Matthews c Hick b Benjamin	0	– (8) c Rhodes b Malcolm		0
P. S. de Villiers c Stewart b DeFreitas	14	– not out		0
A. A. Donald not out	14	– b Malcolm		0
B 8, l-b 10, w 1, n-b 18	37	L-b 5, n-b 9		14

1-2 2-43 3-73 4-85 5-136 6-260   **332**   1-0 2-1 3-1 4-73 5-137 6-143   **175**
7-266 8-301 9-332   7-143 8-175 9-175 10-175

First innings – DeFreitas 26.2–5–93–4; Malcolm 25–5–81–1; Gough 19–1–85–0; Benjamin 17–2–42–4; Hick 5–1–13–0.
Second innings – DeFreitas 12–3–25–0; Malcolm 16.3–2–57–9; Gough 9–1–39–1; Benjamin 11–1–38–0; Hick 2–0–11–0.

ENGLAND

	First innings		Second innings	
G. A. Gooch c Richardson b Donald	8	– b Matthews		33
*M. A. Atherton lbw b de Villiers	0	– c Richardson b Donald		63
G. A. Hick b Donald	39	– not out		81
G. P. Thorpe b Matthews	79	– not out		15
A. J. Stewart b de Villiers	62			
J. P. Crawley c Richardson b Donald	5			
†S. J. Rhodes lbw b de Villiers	11			
P. A. J. DeFreitas run out	37			
D. Gough not out	42			
J. E. Benjamin lbw b de Villiers	0			
D. E. Malcolm c sub (T. G. Shaw) b Matthews	4			
B 1, w 1, n-b 15	17	L-b 6, n-b 7		13

1-1 2-33 3-93 4-145 5-165 6-219   **304**   1-56 2-180   **(2 wkts) 205**
7-222 8-292 9-293 10-304

First innings – Donald 17–2–76–3; de Villiers 19–3–62–4; Matthews 21–4–82–2; McMillan 12–1–67–0; Cronje 8–3–16–0.
Second innings – Donald 12–1–96–1; de Villiers 12–0–66–0; Matthews 11.3–4–37–1.

Toss won by South Africa   UMPIRES R. S. Dunne and K. E. Palmer

AUSTRALIA V ENGLAND 1994–95   John Thicknesse, 1996

England's tour of Australia resembled its predecessor in that a key player suffered severe damage to a finger within a week of arrival, in each case with far-reaching consequences. In 1990–91, Graham Gooch, the captain, was kept out of the First Test, which England duly lost inside three days. In 1994–95, Alec Stewart's broken index finger mended in time for him to play in Brisbane. But when he broke it again in the Second Test in Melbourne, and sustained a further blow to it as soon as he was passed fit to reappear – against Victoria just before the Fourth Test – Mike Atherton was deprived of his regular opening partner in all the last three Tests.

In a series in which it was clear from the start that England needed luck to smile on them, the handicap of Stewart's absence might alone have ensured that Australia kept the Ashes. In the event, England's misfortune with illness and injuries was so uniformly foul that the vice-captain's was merely the first item on a list so long that six replacements were required. Granted Australia's known superiority, especially in bowling through Shane Warne's devastating leg-spin and Craig McDermott's fire and pace, it was no disgrace in the circumstances that, after being two down with three to play, England held the margin to 3–1. The executive committee of the Test and County Cricket Board took a different view, however. Within a month of the tour ending, Keith Fletcher was told by A. C. Smith, the TCCB's chief executive, that his contract as team manager had been terminated midway through its five-year course. Two days later, Smith announced that Ray Illingworth, the chairman of selectors, was in addition to take on Fletcher's duties.

Australia v England   First Test
At Brisbane, November 25, 26, 27, 28, 29, 1994. Australia won by 184 runs.

Yet another display of exceptional all-round cricket took Australia to victory by the now-familiar crushing margin. Warne, who had held England's batsmen spellbound from the moment he bowled Gatting at Old Trafford in 1993, was again the executioner, taking three for 39 and eight for 71 – his best analysis in first-class cricket. It was not until the final innings, though, that he commandeered the spotlight. During the first three days, it was the combined efforts of Slater, Taylor, Mark Waugh, McDermott and Healy which forced the tourists into a position from which there was little prospect of escape.

Toss: Australia. **Australia 426** (M. J. Slater 176, M. A. Taylor 59, M. E. Waugh 140; D. Gough 4-107)
and 248-8 dec. (M. A. Taylor 58, M. J. Slater 45, I. A. Healy 45*; P. C. R. Tufnell 4-79);
England 167 (M. A. Atherton 54; C. J. McDermott 6-53, S. K. Warne 3-39)
and 323 (A. J. Stewart 33, G. A. Hick 80, G. P. Thorpe 67,
G. A. Gooch 56; S. K. Warne 8-71).

WHY? OH WHY?

Matthew Engel, *Notes by the Editor*, 1995

As England were losing to a team from the Australian Cricket Academy at North Sydney Oval late in 1994, one of the most telling but not necessarily the worst of the many humiliations English cricket has suffered these past few years, a plane appeared (not thought on this occasion to be carrying David Gower) and sky-wrote the word WHY? in the clear blue sky.

The question apparently related to Sydney Airport's new runway, not cricket. But, invisibly, it hung there all tour, even after the victory in Adelaide. England are never boring: each time they plummet to a previously uncharted depth, they stage an improbable leap upwards; they were bowled out under 100 three times in 1994, but invariably came back to score a startling victory a Test or two later. None the less, each depth does seem to be lower than the last. I have never seen a team as dismal and demoralised as the England side that slouched around the field on the fourth day of the Melbourne Test. Each time this happens the Why-ing gets more frenzied and less enlightening.

Much of it emanates from the press box, which is not an environment designed for original thought. But, though no one seems to be able to answer the question, everyone seems to know what to do about it. From 1913, when the bigger counties backed off from a threat to break away from the rest, until the 1990s, the idea of two divisions in the County Championship was one of those ideas that rarely got an airing outside the letters columns of the cricket magazines. In the past 12 months, it has been paraded by many writers as the solution to England's problems with the certainty usually reserved for revealed truth. Just as hurriedly and thoughtlessly, the counties tossed it out at their meeting in December 1994.

Such a scheme could have infinitely more far-reaching effects than its enthu-siasts have contemplated. Yes, it would make some Championship matches more pressurised. But it bears no relation to the present evenly spread division of power (consider the recent gyrations in the county table of Glamorgan, Warwickshire and Worcestershire); it would lead to a full-blown transfer system, probably within hours; and it could destroy what the counties actually do well – spotting the talent that is around, and keeping professional cricket alive and within easy reach of the vast majority of the population.

In practice, it could even damage the national team's prospects, because the pressure on teams to stay in the higher division might create club-country battles for the leading players' attention that would be irreconcilable in a short English summer. It seems to me that those who seek to reform English cricket are some-times a bit too rapid in demanding the chucking out of not only the baby with the bathwater, but the bath itself.

But the counties have got to start doing some hard thinking, especially about the amount of one-day cricket they play. In 1995, having returned to a zonal system in the Benson and Hedges Cup, every county will play between 22 and 30 compet-itive one-day matches; 241 are scheduled in all, an unprecedented figure. In the face of all the evidence of the damage this form of the game is doing to English players' technique, this is grotesque and disgraceful.

Since the counties are most unlikely to get rid of the wretched Sunday League,

I propose a small but, I think, elegant interim reform. In future, the Benson and Hedges Cup should be restricted to the top eight Championship teams of the previous season. This would cut out 50 of the least-watched one-day games, avoid the unjust April knockouts of 1993 and 1994, and add more vigour to some of the late-summer mid-table four-day games.

Overall, it is possible to get far too hung up on the tortured logic which suggests that, because Australia beat England, the way to reverse this must be to copy everything Australia does. Australia has only six state teams: quick! get rid of a dozen counties. Australia has a Cricket Academy: gotta-getta-Cricket-Academy. Actually, there has been an Academy of sorts in England for ages, the Lord's groundstaff. But the MCC Young Cricketers now generally provide a second chance for players who have not been signed by a county.

A new structure would be useful only if it were very carefully designed to fit in with what the counties do well (scooping up talent) and what they do badly (making the most of it). To be truthful, the most important asset Australia has over England is its climate, which could be matched only by towing Great Britain a thousand miles nearer the Equator, a proceeding likely to be ruled out on grounds of practicality and cost.

Amidst all this, it is very easy to ignore what is in front of our noses. In 1994–95 Australia had a better cricket team than England. But the gap between the players' inherent abilities was nowhere near as great as some of the performances suggested. Whereas Australia appeared to approach Test cricket open to the best and most up-to-date methods in everything from technical analysis and fitness training to media relations, much of England's thinking proceeded on the basis that what was good enough for our forefathers was good enough now. England, even more than the counties, continue to fail hopelessly to make the most of their human resources.

In March 1994, the counties, as constituents of the TCCB, did try and do something about this. Faced with two contending former England captains as candidates to succeed Ted Dexter as chairman of selectors, they made the surprisingly imaginative decision of choosing Ray Illingworth instead of the safer figure of M. J. K. Smith. Illingworth at once announced that, though he would be heading a committee of five, he would be taking full control of England's affairs, diminishing the role of both the team manager, Keith Fletcher, and the captain, Mike Atherton.

An extraordinary 12 months followed. Illingworth's approach was very different from the po-faced taciturnity that has long been the norm in English cricket. He spoke from the start as though he possessed the answers. Indeed, he spoke non-stop, making individual judgments and criticisms even while players were in the midst of preparing for or playing Test matches in both the West Indies and Australia. Modern warfare is usually accompanied by the sound of armchair generals chuntering over the airwaves about the correct way to invade Kuwait City or Port Stanley; it is not a role normally played by the serving commander-in-chief.

Illingworth abandoned Dexter's elaborate system of observers, making it clear that he would be relying on his observations and intuition. When he did not get his way in the restyled committee (containing Brian Bolus and Fred Titmus as well as Fletcher and Atherton) he made that clear too. But there was no evidence that his judgments were any less fallible than anyone else's.

His assessments of cricketing character were often awry, hence his preference for Martin McCague ahead of Angus Fraser in the initial selection for the Australian tour; he appeared not even to understand the extent to which Australian wickets have slowed up over the past 20 years. Everyone respects Illingworth's feel for the game; but he sometimes seemed to forget that one of the beauties of this most complex pastime is that no one ever has a monopoly of cricketing wisdom. One began to feel that the right adjective was the one that never attached to him in his playing days: amateurish.

Illingworth then went out to Australia for two Tests on the traditional TCCB-funded trip, which past chairmen of selectors used rather like state visits. He arrived with England already 1–0 down and was greeted by some sections of the travelling press as a saviour, which from their point of view he was, since his comments could fill columns of newsprint. In contrast, the tour manager – the same M. J. K. Smith whose approach had been implicitly rejected by the counties in their vote – who was nominally in control, refused to play a part in the explanations of England's performances. The Duke of Norfolk, as manager in 1962–63, was infinitely less remote.

There were edges to this farce that were very serious indeed: England were beaten so badly in Melbourne that one sensed the Australians starting to regard the whole country, not just its cricketers, as a laughing-stock. No one knew who was in charge. The tensions were obvious, overwhelming and, as I write, unresolved, with the captain and one selector, Titmus, firing messages to each other in print about a policy of concentrating on young players, which Atherton wanted but Titmus did not. The situation increased Fletcher's tendency to fatalistic pessimism at a time when England needed an optimist. The tour was organised in a shambolic way, and it must never happen again.

If power is to lie with the chairman of selectors rather than the team manager, then he has to give the job the dedication and commitment he is entitled to expect from his players. He should be the tour manager, taking full responsibility, backed up by keen young coaches and an administrator to cope with the logistics and day-to-day public relations. It is not necessary to be a former England captain to get baggage off carousels.

THOSE FOOLS AT THE NEW-FANGLED ECB   Matthew Engel, *Notes by the Editor*, 1995

In the next year or so the various administrative bodies that have ruled English cricket for the past 27 years are to be merged into something that will probably be called the English Cricket Board. For most people, the main effect may be that they will learn to stop saying, "Look what those fools at the TCCB have done now," and say instead, "Look what those fools at the ECB have done now."

The danger with these reorganisations is always that more people are hired to push the same amount of paper round and everyone involved gets a handsome pay rise and a better car. However, since the new board will control cricket at all levels, it will be in a position to try to bring about the urgent changes that are needed below first-class level. There is a huge amount to be done; in this volume the tattered state of things is revealed even in a section as gentle as League Cricket in England and Wales, which tells of the way overseas players, especially itinerant Australians, manage to dominate the game in the innermost recesses of the country.

Nominally, cricket already has not one but two Second Divisions – but the Minor Counties Championship, now that Durham have departed, is contested by clubs with minimal ambition for themselves (imagine a football club that did not want to be promoted) and is increasingly dominated by ex-first-class players on the way down; there are hardly any potential first-class players on the way up. It might profitably be merged with the Second XI Championship, with the first-class teams using nearby counties as farm clubs, as happens in American baseball.

There is a need for more elite leagues, as Micky Stewart has been saying, especially round the major population centres, getting away from limited-overs games and the 2.30-start-if-everyone-turns-up-on-time mentality. There is a need to recognise that there are not two universities in England but 80, containing a very large percentage of the country's 18 to 22-year-olds, and in many of these institutions cricket is close to collapse because of the contraction of the summer term and a shortage of funds.

The disaster that has overtaken cricket in the state schools has long been recognised, but hardly addressed. Many thousand boys attend sixth-form colleges; but in these schools, funding exists only for specific vocational qualifications, which makes cricket a very low priority indeed, unless pupils are doing physical education A-Level. The concerned rhetoric of the prime minister is very different from his government's policy.

It would also help if the new organisation were less instinctively secretive than the old one. The board will have a massive constituency of county members and players, which could make it even harder to control democratically than the TCCB. But is there any reason why it should not publish its accounts?

Above all, it is going to need strong leadership. In 1990 the counties replaced Raman Subba Row with Frank Chamberlain as chairman, a clear decision not to have an activist in charge. It is time to change again. The game does not need dictatorship; it does need direction.

ENGLAND V WEST INDIES 1995
Tony Cozier, 1996

England and West Indies contested a fascinating, fluctuating series watched by packed houses in a gloriously hot summer. For a variety of reasons, they were more evenly matched than for some time and, fittingly, they shared it 2–2. If West Indies enjoyed the better of the last two drawn, high-scoring Tests, and had the satisfaction of retaining the Wisden Trophy they have held through 22 years and 12 series, captain Richie Richardson's assessment that they performed below their potential was self-evident. In every department their cricket was inconsistent. England showed great spirit to recover from heavy defeats at Headingley and, especially, Edgbaston (where they were routed for 147 and 89) to draw level twice and then bat through difficult last days to safety at Trent Bridge and The Oval when West Indies held the upper hand. The home team overcame injuries that were mainly responsible for the use of 21 players in the six Tests – the longest series ever scheduled between the two teams – and could take considerable comfort from the authoritative leadership of Mike Atherton.

England v West Indies   Second Test

At Lord's, June 22, 23, 24, 25, 26, 1995. England won by 72 runs.   John Etheridge, 1996

A match of startling fluctuations and compelling cricket was finally settled by an historic bowling performance. Dominic Cork, the 23-year-old Derbyshire bowler, returned an analysis of seven for 43, the best by an England player on Test debut and fifth on the list for any country. England levelled the series with the sort of aggression, determination and plain good sense that were so woefully lacking in the First Test [which they had lost by nine wickets]. For West Indies, it was their third defeat in six Tests – a sequence of failure unknown during their two decades of world dominance – and their first at Lord's since 1957.

Toss: England. **England 283** (A. J. Stewart 34, G. P. Thorpe 52, R. A. Smith 61, D. G. Cork 30; C. A. Walsh 3-50) **and 336** (A. J. Stewart 36, G. A. Hick 67, G. P. Thorpe 42, R. A. Smith 90, Extras 42; C. E. L. Ambrose 4-70, C. A. Walsh 3-91, I. R. Bishop 3-56); **West Indies 324** (C. L. Hooper 40, J. C. Adams 54, R. B. Richardson 49, K. L. T. Arthurton 75; A. R. C. Fraser 5-66) **and 223** (S. L. Campbell 93, B. C. Lara 54; D. Gough 3-79, D. G. Cork 7-43).

England v West Indies   Third Test

At Birmingham, July 6, 7, 8, 1995. West Indies won by an innings and 64 runs.   Robert Mills, 1996

Test pitch controversies are normally the preserve of Headingley. But all the talk before, during and after this one-sided contest was of an Edgbaston strip of unusual appearance – shaved at each end and grassy in the middle – which was ultimately lethal to England. West Indies won by an innings and 64 runs, at 12.18 on the third day of a match which lasted for only 172.2 overs. The aftermath was queues of disgruntled ticket-holders arguing over where to direct their anger (Ray Illingworth, Mike Atherton and groundsman Steve Rouse were the candidates) amid claims and counter-claims about who was to blame for a fast pitch of variable bounce which played into the hands of the West Indian pace bowlers. They used it with ruthless efficiency.

Toss: England. **England 147** (A. J. Stewart 37, G. P. Thorpe 30, R. A. Smith 46; C. A. Walsh 3-54, I. R. Bishop 3-18) **and 89** (R. A. Smith 41; C. A. Walsh 5-45, I. R. Bishop 4-29); **West Indies 300** (C. L. Hooper 40, S. L. Campbell 79, R. B. Richardson 69; D. G. Cork 4-69).

SOUTH AFRICA V ENGLAND 1995–96

Scyld Berry, 1997

It was another long and losing tour by England, their fourth in a row, and third under Mike Atherton's captaincy. But it was the first of those three in which they had gone with a fair chance of winning the Test series, which ultimately made their defeat more disappointing than the preceding reverses in the West Indies and Australia. Following their excellent summer, when they held West Indies to 2–2, England would have moved into the upper half of the unofficial table of Test-playing countries if they had beaten South Africa. As it was, they competed on more or less equal terms for the first four Tests, only to disintegrate and lose the series 1–0 and the subsequent one-day internationals 6–1.

South Africa v England

At Johannesburg, November 30, December 1, 2, 3, 4, 1995. Drawn.

Second Test

Scyld Berry, 1997

"One of the great innings of all time," in the opinion of Ray Illingworth, saved England from going 1–0 down. Others acclaimed Atherton's innings as the finest by any England captain, as he had no particular partner until Russell joined him for the last 277 minutes, whereas Peter May had Colin Cowdrey to help repulse Sonny Ramadhin at Edgbaston in 1957. Possibly only the 262 not out by Dennis Amiss at Kingston in 1973–74 was a greater match-saving innings for England.

Atherton, resolutely single-minded in any event, became even more so when he saw his decision to play four fast bowlers and send South Africa in fail badly. This was his bowlers' fault as much as his. Only Cork fired until Malcolm, who had replaced Richard Illingworth, clicked with the second new ball. Gough never got going at all and while Fraser eventually did it was not until the second innings; in the first, Kirsten had frequently clipped him off his legs, and square cut and square-driven his maiden Test hundred. Kirsten also set an example by taking quick singles with Cronje to set South Africa going, whereas England were rudderless in their first innings once Atherton shouldered arms to a ball which just brushed his off stump. He later described his team's disintegration – to a sequence of soft dismissals in the face of some passionate and often short-pitched bowling – as "fairly unforgivable".

England's bowlers, and Cork especially, kept a fuller length than the South Africans. This enabled Russell to take the world record for dismissals in a Test from Bob Taylor, who was at the ground. Russell took 11 catches out of 13 possible chances, all but one standing back. South Africa, in their second innings, scored so freely against defensive fields – Cullinan's dashing strokeplay was reminiscent of Kim Hughes – that they had a lead of 400 well before the third-day close. England's mood brightened a little when they realised they would not have to bat that evening, with the ball still seaming.

South Africa indeed were so cautious that they came off for light that was not unplayably bad when 428 ahead, and with 7.3 overs remaining. Shortly beforehand, McMillan had hooked consecutive balls from Malcolm for six, four and six. Next morning, they went on for 92 more minutes to add 50 superfluous runs – and it was their bowlers who had to do the batting – just so that McMillan could

Captain marvel: Michael Atherton (left) and Jack Russell meet in mid-pitch during their epic match-saving rearguard at Johannesburg in 1995.

complete his second Test hundred, made with three sixes in all off 168 balls.

England therefore had to survive for four overs and five sessions, not two whole days, or more. They had drawn their three previous Tests, but only after batting first and banking large totals. Atherton and Stewart, in his 50th Test, were aspiring to new heights when they set out to save the game – a target of 479 was theoretical. Only a shower was forecast, and that did not materialise. What did help was that the one lively pitch of the series went to sleep once it had fully dried, and its numerous cracks never became influential: fortunately for England, it had been moved half a pitch width in the week before the Test to avoid the worst of them. A full house of 30,000 on the fourth day waited for England to capitulate, and by the close Atherton had lost four partners. Twice in three balls, McMillan hit the stumps with yorkers – Ramprakash beaten in an uncontrolled drive for the second time – and yet they were not scathed again in the next nine hours.

On the fifth morning Atherton took a while to return to his groove, until his feet began moving again. On 99, he forced off his body into Kirsten's hands at short-leg, and straight out again. He hooked his next ball from Donald to bring up his ninth hundred and 4,000 runs in Tests, and celebrated with rare animation, exchanging hugs with Smith. Soon after, Smith's slash was caught at third man and Russell offered a return catch to Pringle when five, which was missed. A draw was still only the faintest of hopes.

Gradually that hope grew stronger. Back home, England's supporters hung on to television and radio commentaries, if not quite as grimly as Atherton and Russell. The captain's tempo was perfect, as he did not try an uncontrolled shot, and restricted his scoring arc to his favourite areas square of the wicket, yet he put away the bad ball to the boundary 28 times to stop the bowlers getting on top. Russell took more than his share of the strike and kept reminding his captain of England's collapse in the Barbados Test of 1989–90.

Cronje made little effort to disturb the batsmen's rhythm by varying his bowlers and fields. Donald had nothing left when the third new ball was taken – and certainly no time to exploit it, owing to the timing of the delayed declaration. Atherton batted for 643 minutes in all – the fourth-longest innings for England – and 492 balls, Russell for 277 minutes and 235 balls.

South Africa v England, 1995–96   Second Test

At Johannesburg, November 30, December 1, 2, 3, 4, 1995. Result: Drawn.

SOUTH AFRICA	First innings		Second innings	
A. C. Hudson c Stewart b Cork	0	–	c Russell b Fraser	17
G. Kirsten c Russell b Malcolm	110	–	c Russell b Malcolm	1
*W. J. Cronje c Russell b Cork	35	–	c Russell b Cork	48
D. J. Cullinan c Russell b Hick	69	–	c Gough b Cork	61
J. N. Rhodes c Russell b Cork	5	–	c Russell b Fraser	57
B. M. McMillan lbw b Cork	35	–	not out	100
†D. J. Richardson c Russell b Malcolm	0	–	c Ramprakash b Malcolm	23
S. M. Pollock c Smith b Malcolm	33	–	lbw b Cork	5
C. E. Eksteen c Russell b Cork	13	–	c Russell b Cork	2
M. W. Pringle not out	10	–	c Hick b Fraser	2
A. A. Donald b Malcolm	0	–	not out	9
B 1, l-b 14, w 2, n-b 5	22		B 5, l-b 12, w 1, n-b 3	21

1-3 2-74 3-211 4-221 5-260 6-260   332   1-7 2-29 3-116 4-145 5-244   (9 wkts dec.) 346
7-278 8-314 9-331 10-332   6-296 7-304 8-311 9-314

First innings – Cork 32–7–84–5; Malcolm 22–5–62–4; Fraser 20–5–69–0; Gough 15–2–64–0;
Hick 15–1–38–1.
Second innings – Cork 31.3–6–78–4; Malcolm 13–2–65–2; Fraser 29–6–84–3; Gough 12–2–48–0;
Hick 15–3–35–0; Ramprakash 4–0–19–0.

ENGLAND	First innings		Second innings	
*M. A. Atherton b Donald	9	–	not out	185
A. J. Stewart c Kirsten b Pringle	45	–	b McMillan	38
M. R. Ramprakash b Donald	4	–	b McMillan	0
G. P. Thorpe c Kirsten b Eksteen	34	–	lbw b Pringle	17
G. A. Hick c and b Eksteen	6	–	c Richardson b Donald	4
R. A. Smith c and b McMillan	52	–	c Pollock b Donald	44
†R. C. Russell c Rhodes b Eksteen	12	–	not out	29
D. G. Cork c Cullinan b Pollock	8			
D. Gough c and b Pollock	2			
A. R. C. Fraser lbw b Pollock	0			
D. E. Malcolm not out	0			
B 6, l-b 1, n-b 21	28		B 4, l-b 7, n-b 23	34

1-10 2-45 3-109 4-116 5-125 6-147   200   1-75 2-75 3-134 4-145 5-232   (5 wkts) 351
7-178 8-193 9-200 10-200

First innings – Donald 15–3–49–2; Pringle 17–4–46–1; Pollock 15–2–44–3; McMillan 10.3–0–42–1;
Eksteen 11–5–12–3.
Second innings – Donald 35–9–95–2; Pringle 23–5–52–1; Pollock 29–11–65–0; McMillan 21–0–50–2;
Eksteen 52–20–76–0; Cronje 3–1–2–0; Kirsten 2–2–0–0.

Toss won by England   UMPIRES D. B. Hair and K. E. Liebenberg

ENGLAND, ILLY'S ENGLAND

Matthew Engel, *Notes by the Editor*, 1996

The calendar year 1995 was not a bad one for the England team. They played 13 Test matches, all against strong teams, won three, lost three and drew seven. The year was immediately preceded by a decisive defeat in Melbourne and followed by one in Cape Town, after which came a 6–1 defeat in a set of one-day internationals against South Africa. The team was then weary, in the way that only cricket teams who have lost an overseas Test series can be weary. Two youngish quality fast bowlers have emerged: Darren Gough was followed by Dominic Cork. They have hardly yet played together in Test cricket, still less played well together. But the potential is there.

The TCCB's decision last March to sack Keith Fletcher and make Ray Illingworth manager as well as chairman of selectors was the only sensible response to the situation that had developed. In the short run, it has been successful. With fewer internal tensions, England's affairs were mostly conducted with more dignity than had been the case beforehand, especially on the hopelessly run 1994–95 tour of Australia. The South African tour, with Illingworth in charge, was mostly harmonious and the arrival of the diplomatic John Barclay as assistant manager was extremely helpful. The handling of gifted but problematic individuals remained woeful. It was hard to fathom what Illingworth thought he was achieving in his dealings with Mark Ramprakash and Devon Malcolm. Other teams are deeply into sports psychology; Illingworth expresses his contempt for the very idea.

Theoretically, Illingworth had more power than anyone has ever had over the national team. And he would regularly flex his muscles, laying down iron principles for the untrammelled exercise of his power and for selecting the team. Then, suddenly, those principles would prove unexpectedly changeable. Ultimately, it became clear that teams were being chosen much as they had been before, by a coalition in which the captain's voice was extremely important. And Mike Atherton's reputation, as a cricketer and captain, had recovered after his difficult 1994; indeed, it was sky-high – both because of the way he held the batting together (saving the Johannesburg Test was merely the most dramatic example) and because of the sensible manner in which he appeared to deal with his master. There was something rather endearing about Illy's claims to total power, which became a great deal less insistent when things were going wrong. It is clear, though, that if the counties are ever to agree to let the England selectors have a say in the way they handle their players, it will come only when Illingworth gives way to a more emollient figure.

To me, the biggest disappointment of Illingworth's reign so far is not that he has exercised too much power but the reverse: he would insist on citing form as a justification for selection instead of backing his judgment about a player's quality and then sticking with it, and facing the consequences. The style of leadership has changed dramatically; the sense that England selection policy will be blown around by the most fickle of winds has not.

Zimbabwe v England 1996–97
See page 610

The English Disease   Matthew Engel, *Notes by the Editor*, 1997

Early in 1997, Archie Henderson, sports editor of a South African newspaper, the *Cape Argus*, wrote a column enthusing about the role television has played in the cricketing boom there. "Cricket, once seemingly destined for extinction, has learned to sell itself," he wrote. "While rugby and soccer have rested on their laurels, cricket has exploited the medium with imaginative innovations. This has extended the audience from largely white and male... the marketing gurus behind the sport have taken every little nuance of a game that is full of nuances and turned them into sub-plots of the greater drama."

Such a column might also be written in Britain, with the word "not" strategically inserted throughout. And this is only in part because the production values of the BBC TV coverage now seem so stereotyped and dated. Amid the general global mood of cricketing expansionism, England is a spectacular and potentially catastrophic exception.

In 1996–97 the national team reached a point where even the good days were bad. They were one run short of victory in the Bulawayo Test and one wicket short at Auckland. It felt as though the English, who were once presumed to have won first prize in the lottery of life, were now on the receiving end of some cosmic practical joke.

At the 1996 World Cup, the England squad resembled a bad-tempered grandmother attending a teenage rave; British delegations at European summits have sometimes behaved in a similar fashion. Unable to comprehend what was happening – on the field or off it – the players just lingered, looking sullen as well as incompetent. They conveyed as bad an impression in Zimbabwe at the end of the year. And, though they appeared to have learned to display a little grace under pressure by the time they reached New Zealand in January 1997, that merely emphasised their earlier petulance. The captain, Mike Atherton, and coach, David Lloyd, were culpable in failing to understand the importance of their roles as public figures. But it was hardly surprising. Until the end of 1996, they were paid by the Test and County Cricket Board, a body that found public relations so difficult that for its last couple of years it simply gave up on the whole business.

All this was merely the superficial expression of a far deeper mess. In England, football has always been more popular than cricket. Ten years ago, when Ian Botham and David Gower were more instantly recognisable than any footballer, and soccer was struggling against the ravages of hooliganism, the gap was a narrow one. It is now a yawning chasm. Play in the Lord's Test was stopped by the roar of delight among the spectators when they heard that England had beaten Spain in the European Championship quarter-final. The idea that the reverse might ever happen at Wembley is unthinkable.

The consistent failure of the England team is the biggest single cause of the crisis, but it is not the crisis itself. The blunt fact is that cricket in the UK has become un-attractive to the overwhelming majority of the population. The game is widely perceived as elitist, exclusionist and dull. The authorities have been accused of worrying too much about marketing. In fact their idea of marketing has usually consisted of sucking up to corporate sponsors and TV executives. If anyone has devoted serious thought to finding innovative ways of bringing young people into cricket grounds, then it must be one of those secrets of which the old TCCB was so fond.

The fixtures are either unpopular or, in some cases, too popular to be accessible. One of the joys of an Oval Test, wrote Terence Rattigan in 1965, is always the presence in force of the very young. How many young people does anyone suppose will be at the 1997 Oval Test when all the tickets will have been sold six months before the event? Equally, how many will be at the many other games where tickets are available and unwanted? Very little has been done to make grounds welcoming and attractive to the young. The message is merely, "Sit down and shut up."

Of course, the biggest possible fillip English cricket could receive is success. It would be tremendous if, by the time they reach The Oval, England have won, are still contesting or even have not utterly disgraced themselves in the fight for the Ashes. But this will not be enough on its own.

ALAS, POOR RAYMOND
Matthew Engel, *Notes by the Editor*, 1997

Raymond Illingworth's three-year reign as chairman of selectors, and briefer period as all-purpose supremo, will not be remembered kindly. It was sad to watch a man whose career embodied so many of the strengths of English cricket flail around and have his failings exposed so hopelessly in the World Cup. He had no long-term strategy, merely faith in his own instincts. It was not enough. A teacher friend of mine has a motto on his wall from an unknown American educator: "In times of change, learners inherit the earth, while the learned find themselves beautifully equipped to deal with the world which no longer exists." It can serve as Illy's cricketing epitaph.

ENGLISH CRICKET – A MANIFESTO
Lord MacLaurin, 1997

Where is cricket going to be in 20 or 30 years? We are under pressure from a host of activities – passive and active. My belief is that the prime task of the new board is to ensure that, by the time we get to the 2020s, cricket in England and Wales is at least as healthy as it is at the moment. And that it remains the national summer sport.

That may sound unadventurous. Obviously we want to grow, to get more and more people playing and watching the game. But we're in an increasingly competitive marketplace – something I've had to cope with in the retail trade – with new leisure activities coming in all the time. Just to stay where we are will be a very sizeable achievement.

How do we ensure that? The main message that Tim Lamb, the new chief executive, and I have been taking to the counties is that the top priority has to be a successful national side. That's the key to our cricket and to our business. I remember when my own son was nine or ten: it is so much easier to capture kids' attention if they've got heroes they can look up to, and try to emulate.

Yet it's been so rare for England to win Test matches that people can almost remember where they were when it happened. We need more results like last year's soccer – England 4 Holland 1 – which will capture the public imagination. Tetley's announcement of their withdrawal from England team sponsorship was depressing. There were all kinds of reasons involving corporate restructuring that were behind that decision, but it can't have been entirely coincidental that England had been so unsuccessful for so long. There are some amber lights flashing over our game, and we have to respond.

In so many ways we have so much going for us. There are as many people playing cricket as have ever played it. Although there is less school cricket, there are now 4,000 clubs with colts' sections. And our finances have never been in better shape. We are a £65m business, and more than £20m in lottery funds have been distributed to the game in one form or another. But to maintain the support of TV, sponsors and the public, the flagship – the England team – has to be successful. People want to be associated with winners.

This doesn't mean the whole of our game is going to be sacrificed on the altar of national success. County cricket is an important, integral part of the game, and of the fabric of the country. So is village cricket. And we wouldn't dream of changing that. But now the whole of cricket is run under one roof, we can give the game a strategic plan and a framework that will move us forward.

Tim Lamb and I are a new team, and we have a blank sheet of paper. We're prepared to talk to the counties about issues that in the past might have been filed under "too hard": the amount of one-day cricket, uncovered wickets, two divisions, anything. Perhaps we will have a more radical agenda than people expect. But, clearly, we've got to get it right at the top level, so all the other levels can thrive.

At the time of writing, Lord MacLaurin was chairman of the new England and Wales Cricket Board. He retired as chairman of Tesco in the summer of 1997.

CRICKET'S PLACE IN COOL BRITANNIA   Matthew Engel, *Notes by the Editor*, 1998

On May 2, 1997, Tony Blair, the leader of the Labour Party, became Britain's prime minister as a result of the general election, and moved into Downing Street. John Major moved out and immediately went to watch Surrey play the universities. At this moment, and for some weeks thereafter, it appears that Britain had, for the first time ever, a prime minister (born 1953) younger than a current county cricketer (John Emburey, born 1952). It also had one who, in contrast to his mad-keen predecessor, regarded cricket as something he had put away when he was a teenager, after a brief fling in which he memorised all the statistics of England's Tests in the mid-1960s.

Unlike fox-hunting, cricket was not in immediate danger of being made illegal under the new government. But among the many subtexts of the election campaign was the one in which the struggling Tories were depicted as the party of England past, wedded to warm beer and cricket, while Labour was hip and youthful, representing cold lager and the people's game. Blair took care to be seen on football grounds.

It was all pretty bogus. But the perception that cricket was a tired old sport remained strong throughout 1997. This was not true everywhere. Whereas cricket was in crisis in England, West Indies, Zimbabwe, and perhaps New Zealand, it flourished in the countries where people had more cause to cheer their national teams. In Sri Lanka, in particular, the boom kept reverberating: when TV showed an interview with Sanath Jayasuriya, the country's electricity demand broke 1,000 megawatts for the first time. In Australia, the traditional Boxing Day start of the Melbourne Test attracted its largest crowd in 22 years, 73,812, and a CD making fun of Bill Lawry's commentaries sold 100,000 copies in no time. Across the globe and into cyberspace, cricketing internet sites were consistently among the busiest on the entire web.

And what was striking even in Britain was the extent to which the public's residual passion for the game could be mobilised. After Denis Compton died in April, the demand for tickets at his memorial service exceeded anything Westminster Abbey had experienced since the death of the TV presenter Richard Dimbleby, at the height of his celebrity, in 1965. Then there was Dickie Bird's autobiography. Here was a book that contained no revelations, no sex (famously so) and a collection of very well-aired anecdotes. By mid-January 1998, it had sold 287,432 copies in hardback. This is an extraordinary figure.

There was a yearning: a need for heroes. English cricket was still awaiting a new one. When he comes, Tony Blair will rush to embrace him. In his absence, a hero from half a century ago and a lovable umpire provided substitutes.

ENGLAND V AUSTRALIA 1997 Tim de Lisle, 1998

The best skyline in English cricket is the one you see from the top of The Oval pavilion, encompassing the gasometer, Big Ben, the incongruous gaudiness of the MI5 headquarters, and, on a clear day, half of London. In 1997, there was an extra attraction: "The World's First Tethered Balloon Ride", in the Harleyford Road. Every so often, a hot-air balloon would rise behind the sightscreen at the Vauxhall End, dangle for a few minutes, and return to earth.

It could have been put there to represent England's summer. They started so commandingly, in the one-day internationals and the First Test, that the nation became more excited about the team's performance than it had been at any time since Kingston 1989–90, arguably since Headingley 1981. But the Australians, undisputed world champions for the first time in many years, dug deep into their reserves of skill and will-power. After having the better of a rainy stalemate at Lord's, they needed only three Test matches to draw level, pull ahead, and then secure both the Ashes and the series. At The Oval, England finished as they had begun, with a pulsating victory. It was too late. The balloon had been tethered all along.

Of all the possible scorelines, 3–2 was the one most likely to satisfy both sides. For Australia, it was a third major victory in nine months, following the series against West Indies and South Africa, and a fifth consecutive series win over England – a sequence they had never achieved in 115 years of the Ashes.

England v Australia

At Birmingham, June 5, 6, 7, 8, 1997. England won by nine wickets.

First Test

John Etheridge, 1998

The ripples of patriotic optimism which followed England's 3–0 victory in the one-day internationals had become a tidal wave of emotion and euphoria by the end of this extraordinary match. There were reasons to think England might perform well – their growing confidence in New Zealand, the whitewash in the one-day internationals, Taylor's personal purgatory, Australia's injuries and general lack of form – but nothing had prepared a disbelieving public for what actually happened.

The game had everything as far as England were concerned: Australia's collapse to 54 for eight on the opening morning, magnificent innings by Hussain and Thorpe, a heroic century by Taylor and a suitably dramatic finale. England won at 6.52 p.m. on Sunday evening, when Stewart cracked Warne to the extra-cover boundary. They passed their target of 118 in just 21.3 overs and the crowd, close to a fourth successive full house, engulfed the field. "They're coming home, they're coming home, Ashes coming home," they sang, to the tune made famous in the Euro 96 soccer championships. Not even the most hard-bitten realists dared argue: the electric, jingoistic atmosphere was a feature of the grand occasion.

Toss: Australia. **Australia 118** (S. K. Warne 47; D. Gough 3-43, A. R. Caddick 5-50) **and 477** (M. T. G. Elliott 66, M. A. Taylor 129, G. S. Blewett 125, S. R. Waugh 33, I. A. Healy 30, S. K. Warne 32, Extras 37; D. Gough 3-123, R. D. B. Croft 3-125, M. A. Ealham 3-60); **England 478-9 dec.** (N. Hussain 207, G. P. Thorpe 138, M. A. Ealham 53*; M. S. Kasprowicz 4-113) **and 119-1** (M. A. Atherton 57*, A. J. Stewart 40*).

England v Australia

At Manchester, July 3, 4, 5, 6, 7, 1997. Australia won by 268 runs.

Third Test

Ken Casellas, 1998

The slumbering giant, aroused by the unaccustomed situation of trailing in a Test series, awoke, flexed its not inconsiderable muscle and demolished the opposition with brutal efficiency. Australia's emphatic triumph put them back on track after a stuttering start and weeks of depressing grey skies and rain. Suddenly, the weather resembled something vaguely like summer, but England's first defeat in eight Tests dampened the optimism springing from their resounding victories in the one-day series and the First Test. The contest had high achievement and occasional drama, but, from the moment Steve Waugh put his stamp on it, the whip hand was held by Australia. Waugh became the first batsman to score twin Ashes hundreds for 50 years; backed up by Warne, who convincingly returned to his best form, he well and truly wrested the initiative from England.

Toss: Australia. **Australia 235** (M. T. G. Elliott 40, S. R. Waugh 108, P. R. Reiffel 31; D. Gough 3-52, D. W. Headley 4-72) **and 395-8 dec.** (M. E. Waugh 55, S. R. Waugh 116, I. A. Healy 47, S. K. Warne 53, P. R. Reiffel 45*; D. W. Headley 4-104); **England 162** (M. A. Butcher 51, A. J. Stewart 30; G. D. McGrath 3-40, S. K. Warne 6-48) **and 200** (J. P. Crawley 83; G. D. McGrath 4-46, J. N. Gillespie 3-31, S. K. Warne 3-63).

England v Australia

Fourth Test

At Leeds, July 24, 25, 26, 27, 28, 1997. Australia won by an innings and 61 runs. Mark Ray, 1998

In the Third Test, Australia had levelled the series through fine work from some of their senior players. The most notable aspect of Australia's comprehensive win in the Fourth Test, which gave them the lead for the first time, was that the protagonists were young players in their first Ashes series. Elliott, aged 25, and Ponting, aged 22, scored centuries to lead Australia out of trouble and into an unbeatable position, after the 22-year-old Gillespie had destroyed England's first innings with seven for 37, the best figures by an Australian in a Headingley Test. England returned to their old ways, bowling and fielding poorly to concede a huge first-innings score, and batting with minimal application under sustained pressure. But the Australians were back to their best, combining tightly disciplined play with just the right amount of risk-taking.

Once again, there was tension between the fierce Headingley stewards and the sometimes raucous spectators in the Western Terrace, especially those keen on the fashion for attending Tests in fancy dress. Two men dressed in a pantomime-cow costume cavorted round the boundary, and were crash-tackled by officials after play: the man playing the rear end, Branco Risek, needed treatment in hospital. Brian Cheesman, a university lecturer dressed as a carrot, was frogmarched from the ground for drunken and abusive behaviour. He vehemently denied the allegations. Mr Cheesman has been attending Headingley Tests in fancy dress since 1982.

Toss: Australia. **England 172** (M. A. Atherton 41; J. N. Gillespie 7-37) **and 268** (N. Hussain 105, J. P. Crawley 72; P. R. Reiffel 5-49); **Australia 501-9 dec.** (M. T. G. Elliott 199, R. T. Ponting 127, I. A. Healy 31, P. R. Reiffel 54*, Extras 54; D. Gough 5-149).

England v Australia

Sixth Test

At The Oval, August 21, 22, 23, 1997. England won by 19 runs. Matthew Engel, 1998

Too late to rescue the Ashes, but not too late to rescue their self-respect, England won a sensational victory after a contest fit to rank with the great games of Ashes history. The match was over at 5.24 on the third day, but the cricket that did take place was amazing, and the climax utterly riveting. Australia, needing only 124 to win, were bowled out for just 104. The Oval crowd celebrated England's triumph in a manner not seen at least since the Edgbaston win, 11 weeks earlier – but that seemed like an awfully long time ago.

Australia's collapse maintained their reputation for vulnerability in a run-chase, and for flunking the Tests that matter least. It was the third time in 1997 they had lost the last match of a series they had already won. It did not much dent their reputation as one of the great Ashes teams. The result meant far more to England. In advance, they would have settled for losing the series 3–2, a result that suggested tangible progress after all the bleak years. And though the ECB had to refund £400,000 to ticket-holders for Sunday (a 16,500 sell-out, like the first three days), the gain was incalculable. The English public had grown weary of failure.

Like so many great matches, this came about thanks to what is convention-ally known as a bad pitch. It was too dry, and by the second day it was crumbling. This came as a surprise to just about everyone. When England were all out on the first day, it was assumed to be yet another pathetic batting failure, and perhaps a terminal one for Atherton's captaincy. The first assumption was correct, because the pitch was still mild and there was no excuse at all for their collapse from 128 for three to 132 for seven. McGrath finished with seven for 76, including England's top six; he did little more than bowl fast and straight.

Tufnell removed Australia's openers in the evening session, but even so England's position looked dire, and direr still when Australia were 94 for two. But then the game changed. Over the years, Tufnell had displayed more than his share of the slow left-armer's traditional eccentricity; now he displayed the breed's quieter virtues. He kept his line and his patience and, in the afternoon, as the pitch began to wear visibly, he reaped his reward. Bowling unchanged for 35 overs, he worked his way through the Australian batting. He, too, finished with seven and, until Warne began slogging him, he conceded hardly more than a run an over.

And so, after tea, England were in again, their hopes renewed. But the first three batsmen were gone before they had even wiped off their narrow deficit. And Saturday began with two blows. Firstly, Australia's first-innings lead was recalcu-lated from 38 to 40 because a four hit by Blewett was ruled a six after the third umpire, Ken Palmer, had pored over the TV evidence. And in this game every run mattered. Then, to the third ball of the morning, Hussain toe-ended a cut straight to Elliott. England were effectively 12 for four.

But the luck had turned. England supporters had long since assumed that injuries happened only to their side. However, Warne had been struggling on the second night, and now it was obvious he had a nasty groin strain. He was only able to lope in off three paces, and it seemed to curb his variety. That did not stop him turning the ball viciously out of the rough, and could not save the likes of Hussain, bent on doing something daft. But the next pair avoided the daft, and put on 79.

Thorpe, not for the first time, failed to convert a fifty into a century but, since he scored the only fifty of the match, that was wholly forgivable. It was an innings of exceptional quality and tenacity. Ramprakash made 48, which was worth at least double, and began at long last to bat for England with the certainty he showed for Middlesex.

At the time it still did not look enough. The England tail was useless yet again – the last four wickets fell for three – and Kasprowicz followed McGrath and

Tufnell in taking seven in an innings; three bowlers had never done this in the same Test. Australia needed just 124 to win. But there was a sense that the situation was not hopeless. The crowd roared Malcolm in as he took the new ball, and he responded by straightening his fourth delivery to dismiss Elliott.

Tufnell bowled over the wicket to turn the ball from the crumbling pitch rather than the footmarks, and applied enough pressure to help the bowler at the other end. The beneficiary was Caddick, who removed Taylor and Blewett, given out caught behind, though TV replays suggested this was a quaint decision – by no means the first – by umpire Barker. The Waughs soon followed. Australia were 54 for five and suddenly all England was agog, even if it was the first day of the league football season.

Ponting and Healy battled back, with a stand of 34. But Tufnell finally trapped Ponting on the back pad, and Caddick took a return catch from Healy, juggled with it one-handed twice, and then clung on. Warne, batting with a runner, tried to lash out again. This time Martin got underneath his first big hit. Since Martin's fielding is willing rather than athletic, and he had dropped Warne badly 24 hours earlier, he seemed a plausible candidate to be the modern answer to Fred Tate. But he took it easily. England were confident now. The last act was Thorpe catching McGrath at mid-off – Tufnell's 11th victim – and his sunglasses falling off as he did so.

This was the first three-day Test at The Oval since 1957. On the Saturday evening Mark Taylor received a replica Ashes urn from the master of ceremonies David Gower, who had waved around a similar copy 12 years earlier. But this was greeted with only casual applause. It was a moment for England, and not just for the team. For the administrators, desperate to keep the game alive in the hearts of the public in difficult times, it was a priceless victory.

England v Australia, 1997   Sixth Test

At The Oval, August 21, 22, 23, 1997. Result: England won by 19 runs.

ENGLAND	First innings		Second innings	
M. A. Butcher b McGrath	5	–	lbw b M. E. Waugh	13
*M. A. Atherton c Healy b McGrath	8	–	c S. R. Waugh b Kasprowicz	8
†A. J. Stewart lbw b McGrath	36	–	lbw b Kasprowicz	3
N. Hussain c Elliott b McGrath	35	–	c Elliott b Warne	2
G. P. Thorpe b McGrath	27	–	c Taylor b Kasprowicz	62
M. R. Ramprakash c Blewett b McGrath	4	–	st Healy b Warne	48
A. J. Hollioake b Warne	0	–	lbw b Kasprowicz	4
A. R. Caddick not out	26	–	not out	0
P. J. Martin b McGrath	20	–	c and b Kasprowicz	3
P. C. R. Tufnell c Blewett b Warne	1	–	c Healy b Kasprowicz	0
D. E. Malcolm lbw b Kasprowicz	0	–	b Kasprowicz	0
B 2, l-b 6, n-b 10	18		B 6, l-b 10, n-b 4	20

1-18 2-24 3-97 4-128 5-131 6-132   180   1-20 2-24 3-26 4-52 5-131 6-138   163
7-132 8-158 9-175 10-180   7-160 8-163 9-163 10-163

First innings – McGrath 21–4–76–7; Kasprowicz 11.4–2–56–1; Warne 17–8–32–2; Young 7–3–8–0.
Second innings – McGrath 17–5–33–0; Kasprowicz 15.5–5–36–7; Warne 26–9–57–2;
M. E. Waugh 7–3–16–1; Young 1–0–5–0.

AUSTRALIA	First innings		Second innings	
M. T. G. Elliott b Tufnell	12	– (2) lbw b Malcolm		4
*M. A. Taylor c Hollioake b Tufnell	38	– (1) lbw b Caddick		18
G. S. Blewett c Stewart b Tufnell	47	– c Stewart b Caddick		19
M. E. Waugh c Butcher b Tufnell	19	– c Hussain b Tufnell		1
S. R. Waugh lbw b Caddick	22	– c Thorpe b Caddick		6
R. T. Ponting c Hussain b Tufnell	40	– lbw b Tufnell		20
†I. A. Healy c Stewart b Tufnell	2	– c and b Caddick		14
S. Young c Stewart b Tufnell	0	– not out		4
S. K. Warne b Caddick	30	– c Martin b Tufnell		3
M. S. Kasprowicz lbw b Caddick	0	– c Hollioake b Caddick		4
G. D. McGrath not out	1	– c Thorpe b Tufnell		1
L-b 3, w 1, n-b 5	9	B 3, l-b 4, w 1, n-b 2		10

1-49 2-54 3-94 4-140 5-150 6-164   220   1-5 2-36 3-42 4-49 5-54 6-88   104
7-164 8-205 9-205 10-220   7-92 8-95 9-99 10-104

First innings – Malcolm 11–2–37–0; Martin 15–5–38–0; Caddick 19–4–76–3; Tufnell 34.3–16–66–7.
Second innings – Malcolm 3–0–15–1; Martin 4–0–13–0; Tufnell 13.1–6–27–4; Caddick 12–2–42–5.

Toss won by England   UMPIRES L. H. Barker and P. Willey

WEST INDIES V ENGLAND 1998   Scyld Berry, 1999

This was a series which a boxing promoter would have been proud to arrange: a middleweight contest between two well-matched teams, one on the way down, the other gradually on the way up. In one corner, West Indies, sliding rapidly from their position as long-standing unofficial world Test champions. They had recently returned from Pakistan where they had lost all three Tests by wide margins amid rumours of disunity, centred on Brian Lara, who had lost his batting mastery under the captaincy of Courtney Walsh. Indeed, the very future of cricket in the West Indies was perceived to be at crisis-point.

In the other corner, England were making modest progress after winning 2–0 in New Zealand and losing only 3–2 to Australia, instead of disintegrating as usual. But they needed to win a major Test series, which they had not done since beating Australia 11 years earlier, to give their recovery substance. Their captain, Mike Atherton, thought that beating West Indies was a realistic objective, and hinted that he would resign if England did not win.

And resign he did – at the very moment Lara, who displaced Walsh as captain before the series, was parading the Wisden Trophy round the ground in Antigua, the 13th successive occasion the West Indies captain had received it. West Indies won the Test series 3–1 (and the one-day series 4–1), but it was only at the end – after a series of continual drama which lived up to its billing – that their superiority was definitively established. Along the way, the pendulum swung from side to side with each Test. West Indies had the stronger team, if only because they had Curtly Ambrose back to something near his peak form, but the final margin was unjustly wide.

After the two Trinidad Tests had been shared, three crucial pieces of luck all went in the home side's favour. In Guyana, Lara won a toss which allowed West Indies to bat before the Bourda pitch disintegrated; in Barbados, rain washed out most of the last day when an England win or a draw were the only realistic results; then in Antigua, West Indies, having won the toss, were able to bowl when the re-laid pitch was so damp – it had been over-watered for fear that it would crack up prematurely – that three chunks came out of it in the first over. It slowly settled. When all three events went against England, Atherton could sustain his captaincy no longer, and resigned at once even though there were five one-day internationals still to be played; Atherton sat them out forlornly while Adam Hollioake took charge.

West Indies v England   **First Test**
At Kingston, January 29, 1998. Drawn.   Matthew Engel, 1999

After the third ball of the match flew off a length past the England captain's nose, one alleged sage turned to his neighbour in the press box and whispered: "Well, we can rule out a draw, that's for sure." This was proved wrong with astonishing rapidity. After just 56 minutes' cricket, the contest – which enthusiasts had been looking forward to with relish for months – was called off in sensational and, at this level, unprecedented circumstances because the umpires considered the pitch to be dangerous.

Sixty-one balls (and a no-ball) were bowled in that time, and the England physio Wayne Morton came on to the field six times to attend batsmen who had suffered direct hits from Ambrose and Walsh. Neither bowled exceptionally well, by their standards. It was unnecessary; almost anyone could have propelled a hard ball lethally off such a surface.

It rapidly became clear that the batsmen were suffering more than the normal terrors England players expect when confronted with a fired-up West Indies attack. They lost three wickets quickly: Butcher for a golden duck. But observers quickly sensed these might be trivial details. The ball was moving so unpredictably that a serious injury looked a near-certainty. Umpire Venkat was on the walkie-talkie to referee Barry Jarman after three overs but, under Law 3, the fitness of the pitch, remains the umpires' responsibility whether there is a referee or not, and Jarman could only offer moral support.

After Stewart was hit for the third time and Thorpe for the second, the end was in sight. Atherton, the England captain, came on to the field and got agreement from his opposite number, Lara, that the game could not go on. After ten minutes' discussion, the umpires led the players off and the final decision to abandon came nearly an hour later. Stewart was left on what was widely agreed to be the most heroic nine not out in history.

It was rough on the three dismissed batsmen, especially Butcher, who had come in as a late replacement when Russell pulled out with diarrhoea. He had not batted since September, owing to England's poor pre-match planning. It was even rougher on spectators who had saved for years for what they thought would be the holiday of a lifetime rather than an all-time fiasco.

West Indies v England, 1998 — First Test

At Kingston, January 29, 1998. Drawn.

ENGLAND

*M. A. Atherton c Campbell b Walsh	.....	2
†A. J. Stewart not out	....	9
M. A. Butcher s S. C. Williams b Walsh	....	0
N. Hussain c Hooper b Ambrose	....	1
G. P. Thorpe not out	....	0
B 4, n-b 1	....	5

1–4 (1) 2–4 (3) 3–9 (4) (3 wkts) 17

J. P. Crawley, A. J. Hollioake, A. R. Caddick, D. W. Headley, A. R. C. Fraser and P. C. R. Tufnell did not bat.

Walsh 5.1–1–10–2; Ambrose 5–3–3–1.

WEST INDIES

S. L. Campbell, S. C. Williams, *B. C. Lara, C. L. Hooper, S. Chanderpaul, J. C. Adams, †D. Williams, I. R. Bishop, C. E. L. Ambrose, N. A. M. McLean and C. A. Walsh.

UMPIRES S. Venkataraghavan and S. A. Bucknor.

ENGLAND V SOUTH AFRICA 1998 — Third Test

At Manchester, July 2, 3, 4, 5, 6, 1998. Drawn.   Tim de Lisle, 1999

It is a requirement of thriller writing that the hero should be taken almost to the point of no return. At the end of the second act, he (or she) will ideally be clinging to a precipice, in a hurricane, by one finger, while the baddie takes leisurely aim, from a sheltered vantage point, with an automatic weapon. This is precisely the position in which the England cricket team found themselves on July 5–6, 1998.

They had followed one follow-on, at Lord's, with another, graver, one at Old Trafford: in reply to South Africa's 552 for five declared, they had scraped 185 all out – a third of the runs, for twice as many wickets. Sent in again by Hansie Cronje, England were soon 11 for two. In terms of competing, chairman of selectors David Graveney admitted, we're just not there. The players were not the only ones who were not there: Old Trafford was nowhere near full. The football World Cup was still raging and, even with England knocked out, the back pages belonged to men in shorts. It wasn't just the cricket team that appeared to be in mortal danger, but English cricket. An SOS went out: Save our Summer, perhaps even Save our Sport.

That second wicket brought together Alec Stewart and Mike Atherton, the new captain and his predecessor. When playing for pride, no one comes prouder than these two. They pooled all their dissimilar skills and similar experience to add 226, the highest of their nine century partnerships. Atherton stayed six hours, Stewart seven, and, with one fast bowler absent (Shaun Pollock) and another injured (Lance Klusener), England's supporters began to hope. But then Atherton

287

and Stewart were caught on the long-leg boundary – captain hook following ex-captain hook. Two more wickets fell immediately. With four left, and only Mark Ramprakash to shield the tail, England were still half a day from safety.

Cometh the three hours, cometh the man. Robert Croft, wicketless all summer and virtually runless for a year, chose this moment to stand up and be counted, to fend off the straight ones and dig out the yorkers, to punch the wide ones through the covers and waft only at anything that was too good for him to get a touch. When Ramprakash was out, there were still nearly two hours to go, but Darren Gough, Croft's soul mate and fellow under-achiever with the bat, also rose to the occasion. At twenty to six, Gough fell to Allan Donald, and the precipice beckoned again: England were still two runs behind. Donald thudded a yorker into Angus Fraser's lower shin. If umpire Cowie's finger had gone up, England could not have won the series. The finger stayed down. Fraser survived 13 balls, and even laid a bat on one of them. Stewart, who had apparently started the recovery with a dressing-room speech on Sunday morning, reserved his most stirring rhetoric for the media: "I'd rather be one down than two down." To say that England never looked back would be overstating the case, but the corner had been turned. Their in-house psychologist, Steve Bull, noted that the result, on paper a losing draw, felt like a victory.

Toss: South Africa. **South Africa 552-5 dec.** (G. Kirsten 210, J. H. Kallis 132, D. J. Cullinan 75, W. J. Cronje 69*; D. Gough 3-116); **England 183** (M. A. Atherton 41, A. J. Stewart 40, M. R. Ramprakash 30; P. R. Adams 4-63) **and 369-9** (M. A. Atherton 89, A. J. Stewart 164, M. R. Ramprakash 34, R. D. B. Croft 37*; A. A. Donald 6-88).

England v South Africa   Fourth Test
At Nottingham, July 23, 24, 25, 26, 27, 1998. England won by eight wickets.   Tim de Lisle, 1999

The next Test, at Trent Bridge, was just as dramatic. Croft was left out, but Gough took five wickets and Fraser ten, to leave England needing 247 to win. Donald hurled himself at Atherton like a man who had taken 24 wickets in the series and had just worked out that he could still finish on the losing side. An irresistible force met an immovable object, and the consequence was one of the great duels in Test history. Atherton was plainly out, caught behind off his glove, for 27, but was not given. Donald pressed even harder on the accelerator. The two men exchanged world-class stares. Eventually, Atherton escaped to the other end, and Donald induced a snick from Nasser Hussain. Mark Boucher, the young wicket-keeper who had made a habit of fumbling only when it didn't matter, dropped the catch. Donald let out a great wounded roar, of the kind normally heard only by tourists *to* South Africa. Within five minutes, he had composed himself to the extent of trotting up from fine leg in mid-over to give Boucher a forgiving pat on the backside. If ever a visiting cricketer deserved to win a Test series, this man did. Atherton went on to 98 not out, depriving himself of a hundred, happy to let Stewart turn a slow march into a waltz. It was 1–1, but the tide was with England.

Toss: England. **South Africa 374** (J. H. Kallis 47, D. J. Cullinan 30, W. J. Cronje 126, S. M. Pollock 50,
S. Elworthy 48; D. Gough 4-116, A. R. C. Fraser 5-60) **and 208** (D. J. Cullinan 56, W. J. Cronje 67,
M. V. Boucher 35; A. R. C. Fraser 5-62, D. G. Cork 4-60); **England 336** (M. A. Butcher 75,
M. A. Atherton 58, M. R. Ramprakash 67*, Extras 34; A. A. Donald 5-109) **and 247-2**
(M. A. Atherton 98*, N. Hussain 58, A. J. Stewart 45*).

England v South Africa	**Fifth Test**
At Leeds, August 6, 7, 8, 9, 10, 1998. England won by 23 runs.	*Tim de Lisle, 1999*

In the Fifth Test at Headingley, as if to emphasise how well-matched they were, the teams held a sort of collapsing competition, assisted by a trigger-happy umpire from Pakistan named Javed Akhtar. South Africa were left to chase 219 in five sessions; they needed only a good start, but after an hour Gough and Fraser had them reeling at 27 for five.

Jonty Rhodes, not far behind Donald in the Men Who Did Not Deserve To Lose stakes, mounted a counter-attack, putting together a stand with Brian McMillan that lasted two and a half hours. By the close, South Africa required only 34 to win with two wickets left. It was then that Donald, whose work with the ball was done, finally put a foot wrong. With the England bowlers weary, the South Africans could have benefited from the extra half-hour. But they failed to ask for it before the umpires called time.

England came out on Monday morning charged up like a mobile phone. Fraser lured Donald into the edge that Donald had not been able to lure him into five weeks earlier. Finally, just before 11.30, Gough had Makhaya Ntini leg-before. It was the tenth lbw in the match and the eighth to be given against South Africa, but that counted for no more in the heat of the moment than it would in the cold print of the scorebook. England had won a big series for the first time since Australia in 1986–87, when Atherton had yet to play first-class cricket. Joy was unconfined, or confined only to the extent that the market for cricket had shrivelled during the years of drought.

The prize that had eluded Atherton, through the longest captaincy stint in England's history, had gone to Stewart at the first time of asking. This was not necessarily an indictment. To a degree, Stewart was reaping what Atherton (once best-known for having earth in his pocket) had sown: a tougher team, better-drilled, still brittle and inconsistent, but no pushovers. What Stewart added was a spark, a dynamism, an old-fashioned directness.

Toss: England. **England 230** (M. A. Butcher 116; A. A. Donald 3-44, S. M. Pollock 3-51, M. Ntini 4-72) **and 240** (M. A. Butcher 37, N. Hussain 94, A. J. Stewart 35; S. M. Pollock 5-53, A. A. Donald 5-71); **South Africa 252** (J. H. Kallis 40, W. J. Cronje 57, J. N. Rhodes 32, S. M. Pollock 31; D. Gough 3-58, A. R. C. Fraser 5-42) **and 195** (J. N. Rhodes 85, B. M. McMillan 54; D. Gough 6-42, A. R. C. Fraser 3-50).

ENGLAND V SRI LANKA 1998

See page 592

A BATTY SUMMER

Matthew Engel, *Notes by the Editor*, 1999

The hero of the English cricket season of 1998 may well have been someone who is not even a cricketer: one David Batty. Batty was the England footballer who missed the crucial penalty in the shoot-out after the World Cup match against Argentina. England had only reached the last 16, but an atmosphere had built up that was already close to hysterical: every competing leisure activity, from eating out to theatre-going, was bleeding as the country went football-mad. English cricket seemed to be haemorrhaging.

It was a cold, damp spring. The Test team was doing badly. The County Championship was hardly registering. If the football team had got to the final, public reaction would probably have surpassed the Relief of Mafeking and VE Day put together: we live in a trivial age. More to the point, had they reached the quarter-final, the game would have been played on Saturday afternoon, in the midst of the Third Test against South Africa.

As it was, the England cricket team got booed off the field at Old Trafford that day. Had there been direct competition from a football match, there might not have been anyone there to boo. These were bleak hours for English cricket. If the papers noticed the game at all, it was usually to print feature articles announcing that it was finished, and that football was now the national summer sport. The ECB issued statements trying to show that cricket was actually doing jolly well, really, but failed to sound as if it had convinced even itself.

The weather got better. So did the Test team. Football went away for a week or two. But May/June 1999 is now looming as the most crucial period the English game has ever faced. The World Cup – the cricket one, that is – comes to Britain for the first time in 16 years. It will not return for a generation. No one inside the game needs reminding what a crucial opportunity this is.

AUSTRALIA V ENGLAND 1998–99

John Etheridge, 2000

England were once more overwhelmed by Australia, who won their sixth successive Ashes series. More than a century earlier, England won eight on the trot, but only one was a five-Test rubber; and the haphazard tours of the 1880s are hardly comparable to the intensity of modern Test cricket. To be realistic, Australia's success in 1998–99 continued a period of unrivalled dominance in Test cricket's most enduring conflict. Since 1989, they had won 20 Tests to England's five. After pushing closer in 1997 when they lost 3–2, England's margin of defeat this time, 3–1, was the same as on their previous tour four years earlier.

So not much had changed. Indeed, rain probably saved England from defeat in the First Test, and an unexpected collapse, blamed by Australia's captain on complacency, allowed England a dramatic victory in the Fourth. It could have been 5–0. Only Nasser Hussain and Mark Ramprakash enhanced their reputations with the bat. Darren Gough was magnificent, and in the second half of the series collected the wickets his skill and hostility deserved, including a hat-trick at

Sydney. Dean Headley had 14 wickets in his last three innings. These four apart, there were few English successes.

MILLENNIAL ANGST
Matthew Engel, *Notes by the Editor*, 2000

On May 30, 1999, *The Observer* newspaper carried an advert offering readers the chance to win tickets for all England's Super Six games in the World Cup. "It is unclear who England will be playing," said the blurb innocently. "However, we know they have qualified." At the time the words were written, that was, if not a mathematical fact, then a reasonable assumption. It's just that reasonable assumptions have no place in discussion of the prospects for the England cricket team. A few hours later, they were out of the World Cup.

The script for English cricket now seems to be more like the Book of Job than anything else: the Sabeans have stolen the oxen; the Chaldeans have stolen the camels; and the fire of God has burned up the sheep. Something like that. Anyway, a tournament officially regarded as the English game's make-or-break opportunity to re-establish itself in the public's affection had produced the worst case imaginable: a fall at the first fence.

And so it went on to the end of that millennium and beyond. England contrived to lose a Test series to New Zealand in almost equally improbable circumstances. In the winter, they effectively lost the series against South Africa in the first half-hour. The Under-19 team performed pretty hopelessly in their World Cup. And the women's team lost to Australia by margins that could terrify anyone who thought the men's team could now get no worse (a sampler: Australia 299 for two; England 79 all out).

With the match-fixing scandal temporarily swept under various carpets, the English crisis is now the greatest crisis in world cricket. It is currently difficult to imagine any circumstances in which England (male version) could face Australia over at least the next three series and have a cat in hell's chance of the Ashes. That's not even good for Australian cricket. It is particularly bad for the future of traditional Test cricket, which depends greatly on English influence wherever it is played.

ENGLAND v WEST INDIES 2000
Tony Cozier, 2001

The extraordinary scenes on a sunlit, early September afternoon at The Oval aptly and vividly illustrated the contrasting states of English and West Indian cricket at the start of the 21st century. England had convincingly won the final Test to secure the series 3–1 and regain the Wisden Trophy that had been in West Indies' assured possession for 27 years. As captain Nasser Hussain and his triumphant players stood on the balcony, showering themselves with champagne, their achievement was hailed by thousands of joyful fans below, many of whom had not been born when Ray Illingworth was the last England captain to claim the Trophy on July 1, 1969.

Confident that this last day of the international summer would bring to an end the prolonged and painful period of Caribbean dominance, so many spectators streamed into the ground that the gates had to be closed within half an hour of the first ball, leaving an estimated 5,000 latecomers outside. Lord's, where England had drawn level with an unimaginable victory in the Second Test, and Headingley, where they had gone one up with their first two-day win since 1912, had witnessed similar public outpourings. This was the climax.

It was a stark contrast to events a year earlier. That summer had seen England eliminated from the World Cup at the group stage and beaten in the subsequent Test series by the unfancied New Zealanders. Hussain, new to the captaincy, was booed and heckled from the same Oval outfield that now cheered him. In 1999, *The Sun*, parodying the *Sporting Times'* famous notice that in 1882 gave rise to the Ashes, had devoted its entire front page to another mock obituary of English cricket. Now headlines and editorials were gushing in their praise. For a fleeting moment, football, the sporting obsession of the British media, was kicked off the front page. There were a few cautionary voices amid the tumult, but the elation was understandable.

For West Indies, it was the passing of an era in more ways than one. Even as they were folding to inevitable defeat, their 13th in 15 overseas Tests, the Oval crowd – and the England team with their guards of honour – bade a warm and generous farewell to the two survivors from the glory years of the 1980s, the great fast bowlers Curtly Ambrose and Courtney Walsh. Their team had gone under despite their yeoman efforts and, as Ambrose walked off a Test ground for the last time, 405 wickets to his account (and with Walsh, on 483, declaring that he would soon follow), it was clear such an enduring and successful partnership was unlikely to emerge in the foreseeable future.

England v West Indies — Second Test

At Lord's, June 29, 30, July 1, 2000. England won by two wickets. — Derek Pringle, 2001

The 100th Test match played at Lord's also proved to be one of the most exciting, with England winning a low-scoring encounter by two wickets to level the series. Many talk about the Lord's Test of 1963 as being the apogee between these two sides: for sheer drama and sustained excitement, this one may have usurped it.

The uncertainty was contagious and, right up until Cork struck the winning boundary just after 7 p.m. on Saturday, it was a match that defied prediction. Momentum in Test cricket is usually a gradual, shifting force, but here it changed hands quicker than a spare ticket among the touts, who, sensing something special, thronged the pavements surrounding the ground. Whether or not the innovation of live music during the lunch break played a part – on the first day it was Third World and the Jools Holland Big Band – business was brisk. On Friday, when 21 wickets fell in 75 overs, including West Indies' second innings for just 54, value for money was given ten times over. In fact, the day saw at least one ball of all four innings, an instance unique in more than 1,500 Tests.

Chasing 188 did not sound much, but on a bouncy seaming pitch, against two of the world's best new-ball bowlers, England's task was stern. If most realists made West Indies favourites, they hadn't reckoned on Atherton and his heir apparent, Vaughan (playing only because of Hussain's injury). Coming together in the sixth over, after Ramprakash had played on to Walsh, they added 92 painstaking runs, each one cheered to the echo by a full house now reaching the point of emotional saturation – itself a rarity at Lord's. With the job only half done, both fell in the forties to Walsh, who took the first six wickets to fall and improved his best figures against England for the second Test running, completing ten in the match for the first time against them.

At 140 for six the pendulum, having creaked England's way, was back in West Indies' territory. When Knight, nursing a cracked finger, fell to Rose for a two that had spanned a courageous hour, their second victory looked assured. However, Cork, dripping adrenalin and with a decisive glint in his eye, had entered the fray at the fall of the sixth wicket. Unfazed by the tension, he set about getting the runs. A lofted drive for four off the tiring Walsh, a pull for six off Rose and sundry stolen singles were all executed with his usual sense of theatre. As Gough kept him company with an admirably straight bat, Cork chipped away at both the total and the heartstrings of the public. Only when he had forced Walsh through the covers for the winning runs was the tension finally released, amid euphoria and ecstasy.

England v West Indies, 2000 — Second Test

At Lord's, June 29, 30, July 1, 2000. Result: England won by two wickets.

WEST INDIES	First innings		Second innings	
S. L. Campbell c Hoggard b Cork	82	– c Gough b Caddick		4
A. F. G. Griffith run out	27	– c Stewart b Gough		1
W. W. Hinds c Stewart b Cork	59	– c Ramprakash b Caddick		0
B. C. Lara c Stewart b Gough	6	– c Cork b Caddick		5
S. Chanderpaul b Gough	22	– c Ramprakash b Gough		9
*J. C. Adams lbw b Gough	1	– lbw b Cork		3
†R. D. Jacobs c Stewart b Cork	10	– c Atherton b Caddick		12
C. E. L. Ambrose c Ramprakash b Cork	5	– c Ramprakash b Caddick		0
F. A. Rose lbw b Gough	29	– c and b Cork		1
R. D. King not out	12	– lbw b Cork		7
C. A. Walsh lbw b Caddick	1	– not out		3
B 1, l-b 8, w 2, n-b 2	13	L-b 8, n-b 1		9
1-80 2-162 3-175 4-185 5-186 6-207	267	1-6 2-6 3-10 4-24 5-24 6-39		54
7-216 8-253 9-258 10-267		7-39 8-39 9-41 10-54		

First innings – Gough 21–5–72–4; Caddick 20.3–3–58–1; Hoggard 13–3–49–0; Cork 24–8–39–4; White 8–1–30–0; Vaughan 3–1–10–0.

Second innings – Gough 8–3–17–2; Caddick 13–8–16–5; Cork 5.4–2–13–3.

ENGLAND	First innings		Second innings
M. A. Atherton c Lara b Walsh	1	– lbw b Walsh	45
M. R. Ramprakash c Lara b Ambrose	0	– b Walsh	2
M. P. Vaughan b Ambrose	4	– c Jacobs b Walsh	41
G. A. Hick b Ambrose	25	– c Lara b Walsh	15
*†A. J. Stewart c Jacobs b Walsh	28	– lbw b Walsh	18
N. V. Knight c Campbell b King	6	– c Jacobs b Rose	2
C. White run out	27	– c Jacobs b Walsh	0
D. G. Cork c Jacobs b Walsh	4	– not out	33
A. R. Caddick c Campbell b Walsh	6	– lbw b Ambrose	7
D. Gough c Lara b Ambrose	13	– not out	4
M. J. Hoggard not out	12		
L-b 5, n-b 3	8	B 3, l-b 8, w 1, n-b 12	24

1-1 2-1 3-9 4-37 5-50 6-85   **134**   1-3 2-95 3-119 4-120 5-140   **(8 wkts) 191**
7-100 8-100 9-118 10-134   6-140 7-149 8-160

First innings – Ambrose 14.2–6–30–4; Walsh 17–6–43–4; Rose 7–2–32–0; King 10–3–24–1.
Second innings – Ambrose 22–11–22–1; Walsh 23.5–5–74–6; Rose 16–3–67–1; King 8–2–17–0.

Toss won by England   UMPIRES J. H. Hampshire and
MAN OF THE MATCH D. G. Cork   S. Venkataraghavan

England v West Indies   **Fourth Test**

At Leeds, August 17, 18, 2000. England won by an innings and 39 runs.   David Hopps, 2001

The first two-day Test win for 54 years – and England's first since crushing South Africa at Old Trafford in 1912 – ensured the 2000 Headingley Test would claim a prominent place in cricket folklore. Inspirational English pace bowling, a mediocre surface and West Indies' continued fallibility against the seaming or swinging ball combined to bring England victory with astonishing haste. It was their first innings win over West Indies since 1966.

West Indies were routed just as they had been at Lord's, dismissed in their second innings for only 61 in 26.2 overs, in seven minutes over two hours. The Leeds crowd, beside itself with excitement, could even crow that, at almost every stage, Yorkshire players led the way. Rarely has a Test bowler spectacularly rounded things off with five for five in 15 balls – including four wickets in an over – and still imagined himself a support act. That, though, was the fate to befall Caddick, of Somerset. White's England career had attracted more than a few dismissive comments over the previous six years, and not three months had passed since he fell unconscious in a Scarborough side street and feared for his long-term health. At 30, his hair was beginning to thin, but his upper body was stronger and the 90mph delivery, once an occasional shock weapon, was now produced with regularity. His reverse swing, delivered from around the wicket to West Indies' procession of left-handers, also proved devastating. On the opening day, he took five in a Test innings for the first time as the tourists were bundled out for 172 inside 49 overs on a damp and uneven surface. Ambrose stalked England's top order with silent and deadly efficiency, both openers going in his first three overs. Atherton's nibble to slip brought him his 400th Test wicket, a feat greeted by the highest of high-fives and a melon smile. With Walsh already well past the mark, two 400-wicket men bowled in tandem for the first time in history. Walsh claimed three victims of his own by the close, two nip-backers ending the partial recovery engineered by Hussain and Thorpe, who added 70 for the third wicket. Hussain's 22 in almost two hours was his highest Test score of a tormented batting summer.

On the second morning, the match swung England's way. Vaughan, on his home midden and batting in the scholarly, slightly formal manner of a country parson, made a Test-best 76. Hick, at No. 8 thanks to Caddick's night-watchman duties, hit a half-century just as composed, especially while cutting. What followed rivalled even the drama of Headingley 1981, when Ian Botham banished the Australians. The bounce had been awkward for batsmen facing bowling from the Rugby Stand End, but West Indies' collapse was primarily brought about by high-quality swing bowling at speed. Gough, twice overshadowed by Yorkshire colleagues, now delivered for the faithful, dismissing a trio of left-handers with in-duckers in his first three overs. Griffith and Hinds both fell first ball, with Griffith's stumps splayed and Hinds struck on the back leg. Lara barely jammed down on the hat-trick ball, but he fell in Gough's next over, lbw without playing a shot for the second time in the match. Cork, eager to join the fray, then struck Jimmy Adams on the hand and, after treatment, caused him to drag on next ball.

After tea, Caddick was finally allowed to switch to the Rugby Stand End, where he produced the most devastating over of his Test career. Jacobs was lbw to the first ball, then the stumps were shattered three times – dismissing McLean, Ambrose and King – in four legitimate deliveries to leave this impassive cricketer wheeling around the outfield in disbelief. It took him another eight balls to complete the job. Five batsmen had departed for ducks in the lowest Test total recorded at Headingley. England took a 2–1 lead and Saturday's sell-out crowd had to make other arrangements.

England v West Indies, 2000   Fourth Test

At Leeds, August 17, 18, 2000. Result: England won by an innings and 39 runs.

WEST INDIES	First innings		Second innings	
S. L. Campbell c Trescothick b Gough	8	– c Hick b Gough		12
A. F. G. Griffith c Stewart b Gough	22	– b Gough		0
W. W. Hinds c Stewart b White	16	– lbw b Gough		0
B. C. Lara lbw b White	4	– lbw b Gough		2
*J. C. Adams b White	2	– b Cork		19
R. R. Sarwan not out	59	– not out		17
†R. D. Jacobs c Caddick b Cork	35	– lbw b Caddick		1
N. A. M. McLean c Stewart b White	7	– b Caddick		0
C. E. L. Ambrose b Cork	1	– b Caddick		0
R. D. King lbw b Gough	6	– b Caddick		0
C. A. Walsh c Caddick b White	1	– b Caddick		3
L-b 2, n-b 9	11	L-b 3, n-b 4		7

1-11 2-50 3-54 4-56 5-60 6-128   172   1-3 2-3 3-11 4-21 5-49 6-52   61
7-143 8-148 9-168 10-172   7-52 8-52 9-53 10-61

First innings – Gough 17–2–59–3; Caddick 10–3–35–0; White 14.4–4–57–5; Cork 7–0–19–2.
Second innings – Gough 10–3–30–4; Caddick 11.2–5–14–5; Cork 5–0–14–1.

ENGLAND

M. A. Atherton c Lara b Ambrose	6	C. White c Jacobs b McLean	0
M. E. Trescothick c Lara b Ambrose	1	D. G. Cork not out	11
*N. Hussain lbw b Walsh	22	D. Gough c Griffith b Walsh	2
G. P. Thorpe lbw b Walsh	46	B 4, l-b 13, w 3, n-b 18	38
†A. J. Stewart c Campbell b Walsh	5		
M. P. Vaughan c Jacobs b Ambrose	76	1-7 2-10 3-80 4-93 5-96 6-124	272
A. R. Caddick c Jacobs b Ambrose	6	7-222 8-224 9-269 10-272	
G. A. Hick st Jacobs b Adams	59		

Ambrose 18–3–42–4; Walsh 24.5–9–51–4; King 11–2–48–0; McLean 22–5–93–1; Adams 6–1–21–1.

Toss won by West Indies

UMPIRES D. B. Cowie and G. Sharp

MAN OF THE MATCH M. P. Vaughan

England v West Indies   Fifth Test

At The Oval, August 31, September 1, 2, 3, 4, 2000. England won by 158 runs.   Richard Hobson, 2001

Earlier in the season, a critic of the sport had described cricket as "a grey game played by grey people". The misguided journalist should have been at The Oval on the final day to see the conclusion of a momentous contest, itself the culmi-

Long wait over: Nasser Hussain holds the *Wisden* Trophy aloft at The Oval in 2000, after England beat West Indies in a series for the first time for 31 years.

nation of a memorable series. This was sport at its vibrant, colourful best, and it rekindled the public's love affair with cricket. Some 18,500 spectators crammed into the ground; thousands more were turned away, left to wander the Harleyford Road, hearing the roar that urged England on to triumph. In a show of admirable common sense, the Surrey club – who also admitted children at no cost – gave several hundred luckier fans access to the executive boxes.

Consensus suggested it was the first sell-out on a final day in England since Hutton, Compton, et al recovered the Ashes here in 1953. Now, as then, England needed merely to hold their nerve. A victory would complete a summer that had already seen Zimbabwe beaten in a Test series, and both West Indies and Zimbabwe overcome in the one-day NatWest Series.

When Cork trapped Walsh 12 minutes after tea to complete the 3–1 win, the jubilant crowd packed in front of the pavilion and stretched back as far as the square to witness the presentation ceremony. Some of them, a year previously, had booed Hussain, the England captain, after a miserable defeat by New Zealand, but such churlishness was long forgotten as England celebrated a first series win against West Indies in 31 years. There could be no doubting the choice of Man of the Match. Atherton, who hinted during the game at retirement after the 2001 Ashes series, top-scored in both innings, in all batting for more than 12 hours on a pitch that showed enough life to keep the bowlers interested throughout.

England v West Indies, 2000 — Fifth Test

At The Oval, August 31, September 1, 2, 3, 4, 2000. Result: England won by 158 runs.

ENGLAND	First innings		Second innings	
M. A. Atherton b McLean	83	– c Jacobs b Walsh	108
M. E. Trescothick c Campbell b Nagamootoo	78	– c Lara b Ambrose	7
*N. Hussain c Jacobs b Nagamootoo	0	– lbw b McLean	0
G. P. Thorpe lbw b Walsh	40	– c Griffith b Walsh	10
†A. J. Stewart lbw b McLean	0	– c Campbell b Nagamootoo	25
M. P. Vaughan lbw b Ambrose	10	– lbw b Walsh	9
G. A. Hick lbw b Ambrose	17	– c Campbell b Walsh	0
C. White not out	11	– run out	18
D. G. Cork lbw b McLean	0	– lbw b McLean	26
A. R. Caddick c Hinds b Walsh	4	– c Jacobs b McLean	0
D. Gough b Walsh	8	– not out	1
B 4, l-b 15, w 1, n-b 10	30	B 1, l-b 7, n-b 5	13

1-159 2-159 3-184 4-184 5-214 6-254   **281**   1-21 2-29 3-56 4-121 5-139 6-139   **217**
7-254 8-255 9-264 10-281   7-163 8-207 9-207 10-217

First innings – Ambrose 31–8–38–2; Walsh 35.4–16–68–3; McLean 29–6–80–3; Nagamootoo 24–7–63–2; Adams 4–0–13–0.

Second innings – Ambrose 22–8–36–1; Walsh 38–17–73–4; McLean 22–5–60–3; Nagamootoo 19–7–29–1; Adams 7–3–11–0.

WEST INDIES	*First innings*		*Second innings*	
S. L. Campbell b Cork	20	–	c Hick b Gough	28
A. F. G. Griffith c Hick b White	6	–	c Stewart b Caddick	20
W. W. Hinds lbw b Cork	2	–	(4) lbw b Caddick	7
B. C. Lara b White	0	–	(3) lbw b Gough	47
*J. C. Adams c Hick b Cork	5	–	c White b Caddick	15
R. R. Sarwan c Trescothick b White	5	–	run out	27
†R. D. Jacobs not out	26	–	c Hick b Caddick	1
M. V. Nagamootoo c Trescothick b Gough	18	–	lbw b Gough	13
C. E. L. Ambrose lbw b Caddick	0	–	(10) c Atherton b Cork	28
N. A. M. McLean b White	29	–	(9) not out	23
C. A. Walsh b White	5	–	lbw b Cork	0
L-b 3, n-b 6	9		L-b 3, w 1, n-b 2	6

1-32 2-32 3-32 4-34 5-39 6-51   125   1-50 2-50 3-58 4-94 5-140 6-142   215
7-74 8-75 9-119 10-125   7-150 8-167 9-215 10-215

First innings – Gough 13–3–25–1; Caddick 18–7–42–1; White 11.5–1–32–5; Cork 8–3–23–3.
Second innings – Gough 20–3–64–3; Caddick 21–7–54–4; White 11–2–32–0; Cork 15–1–50–2;
Vaughan 3–1–12–0.

Toss won by West Indies   UMPIRES D. J. Harper and D. R. Shepherd
MAN OF THE MATCH M. A. Atherton

PAKISTAN V ENGLAND 2000   John Etheridge, 2002

The sun had dipped beneath the horizon and night was fast approaching when England turned a tour of significant progress into one of historic success. It was 5.52 – around 45 minutes after play would normally have been suspended for bad light – when an inside edge by Graham Thorpe gave England victory by six wickets in the deciding Third Test and a 1–0 triumph in the series. England's first tour of Pakistan for 13 years – since Mike Gatting, Shakoor Rana and all that – was always likely to be notable, but their win, and the manner in which it was achieved, was epoch-making. England had not won a Test match in Pakistan since their first full tour in 1961–62.

Nasser Hussain's presence at the wicket when the winning runs were scampered was entirely appropriate. Hussain's year-long struggle for runs continued, and as a batsman he made scant contribution. Yet the England captain was a towering figure. He was tactically sharp, refused to allow the frustrations and restrictions peculiar to touring Pakistan to affect his squad, motivated them superbly and, not least, displayed commendable restraint at being given out incorrectly at least three times on the tour, twice in the Second Test alone.

The technically enhanced television pictures and photographers' stills gave little indication of the darkness at the moment of victory. When Hussain lifted the trophy for winning the series, just 15 minutes later, it could have been midnight. There was hardly time or opportunity for an evening of celebration. There was some beer and wine, courtesy of the British Embassy, but the players soon headed for the airport, intoxicated by their unexpected triumph.

Pakistan v England   Third Test

At Karachi, December 7, 8, 9, 10, 11, 2000. England won by six wickets.   Samiul Hasan

With failing light always going to be a factor, Pakistan captain Moin Khan adopted desperate delaying tactics, for which he was fiercely criticised, after his side were bundled out for 158 on the final afternoon, leaving England a target of 176 in a minimum of 44 overs. His bowlers took 40 minutes to send down the first seven of these before tea, and almost three and a half hours to bowl a total of 41.3 intense, nail-biting overs. Moin, who was warned for his go-slow strategy by referee Ranjan Madugalle during the tea interval, made three unsuccessful appeals for bad light to umpire Steve Bucknor as Thorpe and Hussain resolutely stood their ground. With victory in sight, but little else, Thorpe edged the winning runs. Some of the Pakistani players thought he had been bowled, until the ball was spotted by a searching fielder.

"The fielders in the deep just couldn't pick the ball. I have never played in such poor conditions," said Moin later, though in truth it was his defensive ploys and limited ideas that allowed England to claw their way back after losing Atherton, Trescothick and Stewart in the space of 27 runs with 111 still required from a minimum of 27 overs. "Another five minutes and it would have been complete darkness," said Hussain, who praised Hick and Thorpe for their decisive fourth-wicket stand of 91. Hick, who had failed dismally in his five previous innings, finally played a Test-winning hand with 40. Thorpe remained undefeated on 64, demonstrating to the end the patience and mental toughness that characterised his series.

Toss: Pakistan. **Pakistan 405** (Inzamam-ul-Haq 142, Yousuf Youhana 117; D. Gough 3-82, A. F. Giles 4-94) **and 158** (Saleem Elahi 37; D. Gough 3-30, A. F. Giles 3-38); **England 388** (M. A. Atherton 125, N. Hussain 51, C. White 35, Extras 45; Waqar Younis 4-88) **and 176-4** (G. P. Thorpe 64*, G. A. Hick 40; Saqlain Mushtaq 3-64).

Sri Lanka v England 2001   Hugh Chevallier, 2002

On their first full tour of Sri Lanka, England confirmed their status as the most improved team in Test cricket. While Australia, undisputed masters of the international game, were stumbling to defeat after leading their three-Test series in India, England were striding to success after going behind. It was a clear demonstration of what leadership, conviction and mettle, plus a fair bit of ability, could achieve. By ensuring English heads never bowed, even after their rout at Galle, coach Duncan Fletcher and captain Nasser Hussain could take credit for a fourth consecutive series win. It was almost 22 years since Mike Brearley had led England to a similar run of success.

Throughout the tour, England spectators matched home supporters in numbers and in volume – and far exceeded them in spending power. There had been significant refurbishment of hotels beforehand, and newspapers frequently mentioned the boost to the Sri Lankan economy from the visitors – estimated at 10,000. Given England's past churlishness in granting Sri Lanka only occasional one-off Tests, it was fitting that the hosts should also benefit from the long-overdue tour.

Sri Lanka v England   **Second Test**

At Kandy, March 7, 8, 9, 10, 11, 2001. England won by three wickets.   Hugh Chevallier, 2002

This was a bruising, bar-room brawl of a Test, the type that, pre-Fletcher, England would not have won. But with a now-habitual steel, win it they did, squaring the series. In several respects, Kandy was a classic. Thanks to an exemplary pitch that encouraged strokeplay, rewarded seam and took spin – yet never broke up as predicted – the initiative was batted back and forth like a ping-pong ball. And the drama unfolded against a backdrop of hazy blue mountains, fringed with palm and flame trees.

Undermining it all, however, was more lamentable umpiring. By some counts there were 15 errors, and tempers inevitably boiled over, coming to a head on the explosive third day – ironically a poya day, or "day of peace" for the predominantly Buddhist population. Referee Hanumant Singh issued severe reprimands to Atherton and Sangakkara, as well as fining Jayasuriya 60% of his match fee for dissent and adding a suspended ban of two Tests and two one-day internationals. Both umpires had dreadful games, and most errors favoured England. Home official B. C. Cooray was especially vilified: "BC Bats for England" ran one local headline.

Toss: Sri Lanka. **Sri Lanka 297** (D. P. M. D. Jayawardene 101, R. P. Arnold 65, T. M. Dilshan 36; D. Gough 4-73, A. R. Caddick 4-55) **and 250** (K. C. Sangakkara 95, H. D. P. K. Dharmasena 54, W. P. U. J. C. Vaas 36; D. Gough 4-50, R. D. B. Croft 3-40); **England 387** (N. Hussain 109, G. P. Thorpe 59, A. J. Stewart 54, C. White 39, R. D. B. Croft 33*, Extras 41; M. Muralitharan 4-127, S. T. Jayasuriya 3-76) **and 161-7** (G. P. Thorpe 46; W. P. U. J. C. Vaas 4-39).

Sri Lanka v England   **Third Test**

At Sinhalese Sports Club, Colombo, March 15, 16, 17, 2001.

England won by four wickets.   Hugh Chevallier, 2002

Hard on the heels of Kandy's five-day classic came a three-day thriller at Colombo. On an astounding third day, 22 wickets fell for 229 runs – including ten Sri Lankans for 81 – to give England the series 2–1. True, they made a meal of hitting the required 74, but after losing the First Test by an innings it was a magnificent recovery. It wasn't just the Sri Lankans they overcame; the sun beat down remorselessly, and Thorpe said he had never played in such draining conditions. To widespread relief, the umpiring was of a high standard, and local official Asoka de Silva drew universal praise. With better umpiring came better behaviour, and the referee was invisible.

Toss: Sri Lanka. **Sri Lanka 241** (S. T. Jayasuriya 45, K. C. Sangakkara 45, P. A. de Silva 38, D. P. M. D. Jayawardene 71; R. D. B. Croft 4-56) **and 81** (D. Gough 3-23, A. F. Giles 4-11); **England 249** (G. P. Thorpe 113*; W. P. U. J. C. Vaas 6-73) **and 74-6** (G. P. Thorpe 32*; S. T. Jayasuriya 4-24).

FLETCHER'S IMPACT
Graeme Wright, *Notes by the Editor*, 2001

More than a decade has passed since England held the Ashes and, a year ago, the prospect of winning them back was the stuff of fantasy and stand-up comedians. But from the evidence of 2000, England are again starting to take a grip on their game. It is not only the victories over Zimbabwe, West Indies and Pakistan, impressive and encouraging as they were. It is the way the players approached their cricket. After years of managers and coaches who have talked a useful game, it has been a pleasure, not to say relief, to watch a coach who keeps his words to a minimum and lets his team's cricket do the talking. (Lord MacLaurin, who apparently finds himself being misquoted rather regularly, might want to employ a similar tactic.) Duncan Fletcher will be under no illusions when it comes to taking on Australia. Nor will Nasser Hussain. But between them, England's coach and captain will instil the discipline and pragmatism that underpin the most successful sides.

Some have said there was an element of good fortune in England's success. Marcus Trescothick, for example, one of the summer's finds, was not a first choice: he came into the side because of injury. It would also be possible to subscribe to the theory, given much currency in England's down time, that success comes in cycles. That depends on how long you're prepared to wait. Good fortune and cycles obscure the planning. Not merely the planning that Hussain and Fletcher put into the team itself, but the planning and strategy that have been set in motion for English cricket's long-term future.

Heaven forbid that these Notes should praise men in suits. But it seems to me that Lord MacLaurin came to the ECB convinced of at least two things. English cricket's future lay with the success of the England team: what MacLaurin, with his businessman's nous, called the shop window. The other was the poor quality of county cricket as a provider of Test cricketers. England Test cricketers, at any rate. That was only four years ago. Not really long enough to drag the game, a way of life for many and something of a sinecure for others, out of the 19th century and into the 21st. But he and the ECB could be getting there.

Last year the game bade farewell to one of its oldest sponsors, when Cornhill Insurance called it a day. It was sad to see them go. They came in at a bleak time, during the Packer schism, and remained supportive through less and less thick and lots of thin. It was good they could bow out with England on the rise again.

ENGLAND V AUSTRALIA 2001

For Series Review and First Test, see page 373

England v Australia	**Fourth Test**
At Leeds, August 16, 17, 18, 19, 20, 2001. England won by six wickets.	Jim Holden, 2002

Few cricketers play a Test innings that will become an Ashes legend. Mark Butcher joined this elite when he struck an exhilarating 173 not out to ensure single-handedly that there would be no "greenwash", and show that, for a day at least, McGrath, Gillespie and Warne could be tamed. Butcher's score matched that of Don Bradman in 1948, when Australia made 404 for three here on the last day to win against the odds. But the immediate comparison was with Ian Botham's 149 not out in 1981, when his hitting transformed not only a match but a whole summer, and a whole sport. Butcher's knock was not as important as that. A fairer parallel would be the fabled 1902 innings of Gilbert Jessop, whose attacking shots and endless verve inspired a remarkable Test victory no one thought possible. As here, it was England's only win of the series.

Butcher's innings, entirely out of character with the rest of a one-sided Ashes contest, was Jessopian in vein: he cut anything short of a length with exquisite power and timing, stepped forward to drive McGrath through the covers, and clipped sweet boundaries off his legs when the bowlers erred in line. The Australians could not contain him and, though it was the only such day of the summer, his innings will never be forgotten.

Australia's stand-in captain, Gilchrist, had not thought anything like it was possible when he closed his team's second innings on the fourth evening, with a lead of 314 runs and 110 overs still to play. Rain had seriously disrupted his game plan, taking maybe two sessions of Australian batting time. But Gilchrist's decision spoke volumes for the tourists' aura of invincibility, and their desire to win the series 5–0. Few in England gave the side hope of victory either; only once, at Melbourne in 1928–29, had England scored so many in the fourth innings to win. Yet, by conventional cricketing logic, the target was attainable – even after bad light and further rain removed 17.3 overs that Sunday evening, revising England's task to 311 from 90 overs.

Still, it needed a miraculous performance, and Butcher, whose technique had been modified the previous winter with help from his father, Alan, produced it. He was particularly severe in the overs just after lunch, when it dawned on the capacity crowd that they were witnessing an epic day of cricket. Butcher reached his hundred to a seemingly endless ovation, and when Hussain went, England's sole loss in a session worth 104, their partnership had added 181.

After tea, the outcome was not in doubt. Ramprakash succumbed within sight of the finishing line, leaving Butcher to complete the task. He carved Gillespie for six behind point in an over that brought 19 runs. Finally, he steered Warne away for three and England were home with 20 overs to spare.

England v Australia, 2001

Fourth Test

At Leeds, August 16, 17, 18, 19, 20, 2001. Result: England won by six wickets.

AUSTRALIA	First innings		Second innings	
M. J. Slater lbw b Caddick		21	– (2) b Gough	16
M. L. Hayden lbw b Caddick		15	– (1) c Stewart b Mullally	35
R. T. Ponting c Stewart b Tudor		144	– lbw b Gough	72
M. E. Waugh c Ramprakash b Caddick		72	– not out	24
D. R. Martyn c Stewart b Gough		118	– lbw b Caddick	6
S. M. Katich b Gough		15	– not out	0
*†A. C. Gilchrist c Trescothick b Gough		19		
S. K. Warne c Stewart b Gough		0		
B. Lee c Ramprakash b Mullally		0		
J. N. Gillespie c Atherton b Gough		5		
G. D. McGrath not out		8		
B 5, l-b 15, w 1, n-b 9		30	B 5, l-b 7, n-b 11	23

1-39 (1) 2-42 (2) 3-263 (3) 4-288 (4)   **447**   1-25 (2) 2-129 (3) 3-141 (1)   (4 wkts dec.)   **176**
5-355 (6) 6-396 (7) 7-412 (8) 8-422 (9)   4-171 (5)
9-438 (10) 10-447 (5)

First innings – Gough 25.1–4–103–5; Caddick 29–4–143–3; Mullally 23–8–65–1; Tudor 18–1–97–1;
Butcher 1–0–7–0; Ramprakash 4–0–12–0.
Second innings – Gough 17–3–68–2; Caddick 11–2–45–1; Tudor 4–1–17–0; Mullally 7.3–2–34–1.

ENGLAND	First innings		Second innings	
M. A. Atherton c Gilchrist b McGrath		22	– c Gilchrist b McGrath	8
M. E. Trescothick c Gilchrist b McGrath		37	– c Hayden b Gillespie	10
M. A. Butcher run out		47	– not out	173
*N. Hussain lbw b McGrath		46	– c Gilchrist b Gillespie	55
M. R. Ramprakash c Gilchrist b Lee		40	– c Waugh b Warne	32
U. Afzaal c Warne b McGrath		14	– not out	4
†A. J. Stewart not out		76		
A. J. Tudor c Gilchrist b McGrath		2		
A. R. Caddick c Gilchrist b Lee		5		
D. Gough c Slater b McGrath		8		
A. D. Mullally c Katich b McGrath		0		
B 2, l-b 3, n-b 7		12	B 14, l-b 16, n-b 3	33

1-50 (1) 2-67 (2) 3-158 (4) 4-158 (3)   **309**   1-8 (1) 2-33 (2) 3-214 (4)   (4 wkts)   **315**
5-174 (6) 6-252 (5) 7-267 (8) 8-289 (9)   4-289 (5)
9-299 (10) 10-309 (11)

First innings – McGrath 30.2–9–76–7; Gillespie 26–6–76–0; Lee 22–3–103–2; Warne 16–2–49–0.
Second innings – McGrath 16–3–61–1; Gillespie 22–4–94–2; Warne 18.2–3–58–1; Lee 16–4–65–0;
Waugh 1–0–7–0.

Toss won by Australia
MAN OF THE MATCH M. A. Butcher

UMPIRES D. R. Shepherd and
S. Venkataraghavan

AUSTRALIA V ENGLAND 2002–03

Scyld Berry, 2004

As in 1989 and the six subsequent Ashes series, so it was in 2002–03. The standard of Australia's cricket was so superior that England never came close, and lost for the eighth time running. When the series was alive, in the first three Tests, Australia won by mountainous margins – once by 384 runs, twice by an innings – and so swift was their despatch of England that only 11 days of play were necessary for the destiny of the Ashes to be decided.

After the First Test in Brisbane, the main debate centred not on the outcome of the series, which was taken for granted, but on whether this was the best Australian team of all time. There was plenty of support for the motion, so long as Glenn McGrath and Shane Warne were fit. By the Second Test in Adelaide, Alec Stewart, who had played in seven of the eight disasters, said the gap between England and Australia was the largest he had known. Perhaps the most objective assessment came from Keith Miller, one of the 1948 Invincibles, the other main contenders for the all-time title; Miller accorded it to Steve Waugh's side.

Hussain was widely criticised, not least by himself, for sending Australia in at Brisbane rather than playing to the relative strength of England's batting. But it was hard to see how his depleted attack could have dismissed the home line-up twice at any time while the series was alive. When Australia fielded their first-string attack, however, there was no such thing as a free run. On the generally true pitches which prevailed – in spite of a drought – until the second half of the Sydney Test, their virtue was unrelenting accuracy. England's batsmen, as usual, tried to dominate, but they did not get on top until the first innings at Sydney, when Mark Butcher and Hussain did so only by means of accumulation.

Vaughan was chosen as Man of the Series for his three large hundreds, following four in the English summer. Sooner than his opening partner, Trescothick, he learned to make a clear distinction between defence and attacking shots, rather than blurring the two with open-faced nudges which might have succeeded in England but not on pitches of Australian bounce. His driving all round the wicket was reminiscent of Peter May; his pulling was equally brilliant. Vaughan's footwork had always been outstanding in a generation of English batsmen who either played on the crease or pushed half-forward. Now he used it to move into position to pull the short ball, as perhaps no tall batsman has done better.

Australia v England   **First Test**

At Brisbane, November 7, 8, 9, 10, 2002. Australia won by 384 runs.   Trevor Marshallsea, 2004

It will go down as one of the costliest decisions in Test history. England captain Nasser Hussain had forecast in his last pre-Ashes newspaper column that "the worst nightmare" would be working out what to do if he won the toss. Despite the fact opening batsmen Vaughan and Trescothick were clearly his side's most potent weapons, Hussain sent Australia in. At stumps on day one, Australia were 364 for two. There went the match and the momentum. Hussain's choice will rank up there with David Gower's invitation to the 1989 Australians to bat at Headingley, a gesture repaid by a first-innings score of 601 for seven declared. Australia went on to win that Ashes series 4–0.

Hussain later admitted his mistake, saying it had been based on a belief there would be enough early life in the green-tinged pitch to help his inexperienced seam attack restrict the Australian batting. The pitch quickly dried out into the proverbial belter, and Hayden and Ponting feasted. They put on 272 for the second wicket in 253 minutes, Hayden continuing his incredible 2002 by marching imperiously to 186 not out at stumps, while Ponting fell in the final hour of the day for 123. By then, the young pace bowler Simon Jones had tumbled out of the attack – and the series – when he horribly ruptured knee ligaments in the field. He bowled only seven overs, and dismissed Langer with his ninth ball.

Toss: England. **Australia 492** (J. L. Langer 32, M. L. Hayden 197, R. T. Ponting 123, D. S. Lehmann 30, S. K. Warne 57; A. R. Caddick 3-108, A. F. Giles 4-101) **and 296-5 dec.** (M. L. Hayden 103, D. R. Martyn 64, A. C. Gilchrist 60*; A. R. Caddick 3-95); **England 325** (M. E. Trescothick 72, M. P. Vaughan 33, M. A. Butcher 54, N. Hussain 51, J. P. Crawley 69*; G. D. McGrath 4-87) **and 79** (M. A. Butcher 40; G. D. McGrath 4-36, S. K. Warne 3-29).

Australia v England   **Fifth Test**
At Sydney, January 2, 3, 4, 5, 6, 2003. England won by 225 runs.   Christian Ryan, 2004

England carried over their Melbourne momentum [an improved performance had seen them lose by a mere five wickets] to inflict Australia's first home defeat in four years. It was tempting to blame it on dead-rubber syndrome, but this was a hard-fought, fair-dinkum English victory. Their two previous Test wins against Australia hinged on a miraculous spell by Dean Headley and an even more miraculous innings by Mark Butcher. This time, they played grinding cricket for five days. They did it under a hot sun and an unflinching leader. And maybe, just maybe, they exposed the first crack in a mighty empire.

Banging the ball in purposefully, Caddick made the most of some uneven bounce and undisciplined batting to collect ten wickets in a Test for the first time. Martyn and Love lingered briefly but the rest went down swinging. Waugh's men have achieved many wondrous feats; they don't, however, do draws. Batting seven hours to save a match proved hopelessly beyond them. Their whitewash ambitions scuppered, it completed an irksome few days for the Australians. The previous day, thanks to a mathematical quirk, they had bequeathed their No. 1 ranking in the ICC Test Championship to South Africa. Hussain, long-sleeved white shirt buttoned to his throat and wrists, was his usual gloomy self at the post-match press conference. But he had glimpsed a new world, a brighter world, a world without McGrath and Warne. It was hard to shake the feeling that, after 14 years of ritual Ashes humiliation, the worst for England might finally be over.

Toss: England. **England 362** (M. A. Butcher 124, N. Hussain 75, J. P. Crawley 35*, A. J. Stewart 71; A. J. Bichel 3-86) **and 452-9 dec.** (M. P. Vaughan 183, M. A. Butcher 34, N. Hussain 72, A. J. Stewart 38*, Extras 41; B. Lee 3-132, S. C. G. MacGill 3-120); **Australia 363** (S. R. Waugh 102, A. C. Gilchrist 133, J. N. Gillespie 31*; M. J. Hoggard 4-92, A. R. Caddick 3-121, S. J. Harmison 3-70) **and 226** (A. J. Bichel 49, A. C. Gilchrist 37, B. Lee 46; A. R. Caddick 7-94).

ENGLAND V SOUTH AFRICA 2003
John Etheridge

Five unpredictable and action-laden Test matches, all squeezed into less than seven weeks, gave South Africa's third series in England since readmission an almost non-stop rush of excitement. The buzz started when South Africa scorched to 398 for one on the opening day of the First Test, and finished with England completing a staggering comeback in the Fifth. There was scarcely time to pause for breath. Although South Africa dominated large chunks of the series they will ultimately judge their tour as one of frustration and lack of fulfilment, if not exactly failure. Undoubtedly they played the more consistent cricket, and the final result – a 2–2 draw – gave little clue as to how the matches actually unfolded. More revealing was the number of runs each team averaged per wicket: 44.30 for South Africa, but just 35.81 for England. Graeme Smith, at the age of 22 and on his first major tour as captain, was left to ponder how his side failed to win the rubber by a convincing margin.

Rain probably deprived them of a win in the First Test, although they achieved a victory of sorts when the opposition captain, Nasser Hussain, decided to resign immediately afterwards. They won the Second overwhelmingly, but England drew level after winning a crucial toss in the Third. In the Fourth, at Headingley, South Africa hauled themselves to an unlikely victory after England surrendered at least three positions of superiority, prompting Hussain's replacement, Michael Vaughan, to criticise his players for a lack of ruthlessness. Going into the last match, South Africa could easily have been leading 4–0 rather than 2–1. Instead, Vaughan and England were somehow able to level the series in an astonishing match at The Oval. At 345 for two shortly before the close on the first day, South Africa's position seemed unassailable. But, perhaps because of their own complacency and certainly because of English skill and resolve, the balance of power in the game swung to such an extent that England eventually won by nine wickets.

England v South Africa   **Fifth Test**
At The Oval, September 4, 5, 6, 7, 8, 2003. England won by nine wickets.   Hugh Chevallier

At the start of the second day, bookies were offering 40-1 against an England win – not quite the 500-1 that tempted Rod Marsh and Dennis Lillee at Headingley in 1981, but an indication of the mountain England climbed to claim this epic. South Africa had lost a wicket to the last ball of the first day but, even at 362 for four, a huge score beckoned, and with it victory in the series. That wicket turned out to be the fulcrum on which the match pivoted. From then on, England produced far the sharper cricket. They were especially ruthless in the morning sessions, plundering five wickets for 70 on the second day, hitting 106 without loss on the third and 102 for two on the fourth before scattering the tail to the four winds on the last. On this sublime pitch, South Africa's 484 simply wasn't enough. Only once before in a Test in England, when Arthur Morris and Don Bradman triumphed at Headingley in 1948, had a first-innings total of 450 or more led to defeat.

It was not just the delicious reversal of fortune that made this a classic: there were myriad subplots to intrigue and absorb a packed house for five days. Alec Stewart, at the age of 40 and in his record 133rd and avowedly final Test appearance for England, wrapped himself in the cross of St George for the last time, at least on a cricket pitch. Thorpe, back from the wilderness only because another of Nasser Hussain's brittle bones was broken, achieved redemption with a beautiful hundred. And Bicknell, strutting his stuff on the big stage, hinted at what he might have done as a regular Test cricketer. Huge roars from the crowd regularly filled the air at the exploits of these three, Surrey stalwarts all.

On a pitch aching to give up its runs, Gibbs was first to make hay in the September sunshine, crafting a big, full-blooded hundred bursting with drives and cuts. When he reached three figures, he had studded his tenth Test century with 20 fours and a six; only Flintoff, 18 months earlier in Christchurch, had hit more in boundaries en route to a Test century. Gibbs had reason to spurn ones and twos: in the morning, he had run out his captain, though Smith later had the grace to say he did not back up far enough. It hardly mattered, as Gibbs and Kirsten revelled in the conditions, adding 227 untroubled runs for the second wicket. True, both fell in the last session as Giles gained reward for perseverance, to be followed by McKenzie to the day's last gasp, but South Africa held the match in an iron grip.

It was loosened on the second morning, when they could – and should – have taken the game beyond England. More of what had gone before would have done the job, but England bowled with heart, fielded with zest, and South Africa floundered. There were two early wickets – which meant three had gone for 23 – but Kallis and Pollock looked as safe as houses. They had taken the score well past 400 when disaster struck. Inside 28 balls England's morning lurched from the good to the miraculous: Giles ran out Kallis with a fluky deflection on to the non-striker's stumps, Hall fell for a single, and Adams was beaten by Butcher's throw from the deep. But with the score 432 for nine, was it all too late? Once the resourceful Pollock eked 52 from the last wicket, the door seemed firmly shut.

Gloom-mongers pointed out that England needed 285 to avoid the follow-on, and had adopted an I-told-you-so air when Thorpe, whose last three Test innings against South Africa were ducks, joined Trescothick at 78 for two. But the next five hours left the pessimists squirming. Neither batsman gave a genuine chance as runs came thick, fast and handsome. Thorpe, who likened the occasion to a second debut after dropping out of international cricket 14 months earlier, did what he had done first time round and hit a hundred. Even Pollock, who became the 19th bowler to 300 Test wickets – and at 20.45 the one with the lowest average – when he whipped out Vaughan, came in for uncharacteristic stick during the partnership of 268.

A deafening cheer greeted Stewart, collar up, as he strode through the South Africans' generous guard of honour. Several bat twiddles and knee squats later, he was slotting the ball between the fielders – though not for as long as the crowd wanted. On 38, he played across a straight ball, and a career totalling 8,463 runs at a shade under 40 was almost over. Cue more rapturous applause. Trescothick, meanwhile, was in consummate touch. Recently upbraided for a susceptibility outside off (and for the bad-light nonsense at Headingley), he silenced his critics with a glorious hundred later converted into a maiden double; his best shot was the leave. He faced 374 balls, batted nine and a half hours, and swatted 32 fours and two sixes before holing out for 219.

Yet despite these riches, there was a danger the innings would peter out as the South Africans' had. Early on the fourth morning, England, eight down, led by a gossamer 18. With the forecast predicting that the tail-end of Hurricane Fabian would drown The Oval – and with the pitch as immaculate as Stewart's whites – the sensible money was on a draw. Flintoff treated that logic with utter disdain. Beefy shots flashed from his bat as if it had been Ian Botham's; he hit cleanly, he hit hard and he hit often; 85 came from his last 72 balls. If there was an occasional slog-sweep, it disappeared for six, and the only thing agricultural about his innings was the assured way he farmed the strike: Harmison's contribution to a stand of 99 was a level-headed three. For South Africa, the psychological damage of watching ball after ball sail over the rope was as telling as the runs themselves; for the first time all series, Graeme Smith looked lost.

Shortly before lunch, Vaughan declared 120 ahead. England had bowled decently on the first day, but without fire. Now the South Africans wilted in the heat. Harmison subtly honed his "They don't like it up 'em" technique and deservedly reaped dividends. Bicknell slanted two away-swingers across Rudolph, then bowled a majestic in-swinger, unwisely ignored. By the close – and still no rain to speak of – South Africa, effectively 65 for six, had nowhere to hide.

The noisy fifth-day crowd craved victory, yet hankered for drama. They had to make do with the win. The South African lower order keeled over feebly against more lionhearted bowling, and England, finding it all very easy, tore to their target at nearly five an over. The massive victory allowed Stewart to end his Test career – which also numbered 54 defeats – as he began it, on the winning side.

England v South Africa, 2003 — Fifth Test

At The Oval, September 4, 5, 6, 7, 8, 2003. Result: England won by nine wickets.

SOUTH AFRICA	First innings		Second innings	
*G. C. Smith	run out	18	lbw b Bicknell	19
H. H. Gibbs	b Giles	183	c Stewart b Anderson	9
G. Kirsten	lbw b Giles	90	c Trescothick b Harmison	29
J. H. Kallis	run out	66	lbw b Harmison	35
N. D. McKenzie	c Stewart b Anderson	9	lbw b Flintoff	38
J. A. Rudolph	lbw b Bicknell	0	b Bicknell	8
†M. V. Boucher	c Stewart b Bicknell	8	c Stewart b Bicknell	25
S. M. Pollock	not out	66	c Thorpe b Harmison	43
A. J. Hall	lbw b Flintoff	1	c Smith b Bicknell	0
P. R. Adams	run out	1	not out	13
M. Ntini	b Anderson	11	c Smith b Harmison	1
	B 12, l-b 10, w 4, n-b 5	31	B 1, l-b 7, n-b 1	9
		484		229

1-63 2-290 3-345 4-362 5-365 6-385 7-419 8-421 9-432 10-484

1-24 2-34 3-92 4-93, 5-118 6-150 7-193 8-193 9-215 10-229

First innings – Bicknell 20–3–71–2; Anderson 25–6–86–2; Harmison 27–8–73–0; Giles 29–3–102–2; Flintoff 19–4–88–1; Vaughan 5–0–24–0; Butcher 3–0–18–0.

Second innings – Bicknell 24–5–84–4; Anderson 10–1–55–1; Harmison 19.2–8–33–4; Giles 10–2–36–0; Flintoff 6–2–13–1.

ENGLAND	First innings		Second innings
M. E. Trescothick c Rudolph b Ntini	 219	– not out	69
*M. P. Vaughan c Gibbs b Pollock	 23	– c Boucher b Kallis	13
M. A. Butcher lbw b Hall	 32	– not out	20
G. P. Thorpe b Kallis	 124		
E. T. Smith lbw b Hall	 16		
†A. J. Stewart lbw b Pollock	 38		
A. Flintoff b Adams	 95		
A. F. Giles c Hall b Kallis	 2		
M. P. Bicknell lbw b Pollock	 0		
S. J. Harmison not out	 6		
J. M. Anderson not out	 0		
B 11, l-b 18, w 9, n-b 11	 49	L-b 4, n-b 4	8

1-28 2-78 3-346 4-379 5-480   (9 wkts dec.) 604   1-47   (1 wkt) 110
6-489 7-502 8-502 9-601

First innings – Pollock 39–10–111–3; Ntini 31–4–129–1; Hall 35–5–111–2; Kallis 34–5–117–2;
Adams 17–2–79–1; Rudolph 6–1–28–0.
Second innings – Pollock 6–0–15–0; Ntini 8–0–46–0; Kallis 5.2–0–25–1; Adams 3–0–20–0.

Toss won by South Africa   UMPIRES S. J. A. Taufel and S. Venkataraghavan
MAN OF THE MATCH M. E. Trescothick

WEST INDIES V ENGLAND 2004   Christopher Martin-Jenkins, 2005

Having laboured hard for no reward in Sri Lanka before Christmas, Michael Vaughan's promising England team arrived in the Caribbean in February 2004 and performed even better than Australia had the previous year. They won the first three Tests, then held on for a draw in the final game on a supine pitch in Antigua, after Brian Lara had regained his Test batting record. In the course of an astonishing display of skill and will power, he became the first batsman to reach 400 in a Test innings.

The feat gained precious time for Lara and his team of *ingenus* but he himself said that, in the context of the series, "it was nothing to rant and rave about". That is a matter of opinion. The fact remains that in all too short a span the dream that his side might bounce back from an embarrassing hammering in South Africa was shattered by a united touring team playing harder, more disciplined and more thoughtful cricket.

The unexpectedly lively pitches produced for the first three Tests – a re-action to the bland surfaces on which Australia had built huge totals the previous year – played into the hands of the best group of England fast bowlers to have toured together for a long time. Impressively led by Steve Harmison, easily the most influential bowler on either side, they were arguably the best pack since the briefly invincible years of the 1950s, and certainly since John Snow, Jeff Jones and David Brown led the attack on England's last triumphant tour here in 1967–68.

West Indies v England — First Test

At Kingston, March 11, 12, 13, 14, 2004. England won by ten wickets. — Rob Smyth, 2005

The denouement came like a bolt from the clear blue Kingston skies. For three days this was a gritty arm-wrestle of a match; then, on the fourth morning, West Indies collapsed for 47, their lowest total ever. Steve Harmison, bowling with cold-eyed purpose, finally came of age, taking the cheapest seven-wicket haul in Test history in a performance described by his captain Vaughan as "one of the greatest spells by an England bowler".

This was an exaggeration: only one batsman, Jacobs, got a real snorter. And Harmison himself felt he was to bowl better in Port-of-Spain five days later. No one played any truly appalling shots either, but the chips fell exactly where England wanted. The exception was the last-wicket partnership that inched West Indies past the symbolic mark of 46 – England's total when they were terrorised by Curtly Ambrose in Trinidad ten years earlier.

Harmison's success, though spectacular, was a reward for getting the fundamentals right rather than sudden inspiration. After getting carried away and underpitching in the first innings, he simply increased his length, cut his pace a fraction, and concentrated on the basics. It worked, probably beyond his wildest dreams. Only two bowlers in Test history have taken more wickets in an innings more cheaply: George Lohmann and Johnny Briggs, with eight for seven and eight for 11, both for England in South Africa in the 19th century.

West Indies v England, 2004 — First Test

At Kingston, March 11, 12, 13, 14, 2004. Result: England won by ten wickets.

WEST INDIES	First innings		Second innings	
C. H. Gayle b Harmison	5	c Thorpe b Harmison	9
D. S. Smith st Read b Giles	108	c and b Hoggard	12
R. R. Sarwan lbw b Hoggard	0	lbw b Harmison	0
*B. C. Lara c Flintoff b Jones	23	(5) c Flintoff b Hoggard	0
S. Chanderpaul b Hoggard	7	(4) b Harmison	0
R. O. Hinds c Butcher b Giles	84	c Read b Jones	3
†R. D. Jacobs c Vaughan b Jones	38	c Hussain b Harmison	15
T. L. Best lbw b Harmison	20	c Read b Harmison	0
A. Sanford c Trescothick b Flintoff	1	c Trescothick b Harmison	1
C. D. Collymore not out	3	not out	2
F. H. Edwards c Flintoff b Hoggard	1	c Trescothick b Harmison	0
L-b 6, w 1, n-b 14	21	L-b 4, n-b 1	5

1-17 (1) 2-22 (3) 3-73 (4) 4-101 (5) 5-223 (2) 6-281 (6) 7-289 (7) 8-300 (9) 9-307 (8) 10-311 (11) — **311**

1-13 (1) 2-13 (3) 3-15 (4) 4-16 (5) 5-21 (2) 6-41 (7) 7-41 (8) 8-43 (6) 9-43 (9) 10-47 (11) — **47**

First innings – Hoggard 18.4–3–68–3; Harmison 21–6–61–2; Flintoff 16–3–45–1; Jones 18–2–62–2; Giles 12–0–67–2; Vaughan 1–0–2–0.

Second innings – Hoggard 9–2–21–2; Harmison 12.3–8–12–7; Jones 4–1–10–1.

ENGLAND	First innings		Second innings
M. E. Trescothick b Edwards	7	– not out	6
*M. P. Vaughan c Lara b Edwards	15	– not out	11
M. A. Butcher c Jacobs b Edwards	58		
N. Hussain c sub (D. E. Bernard) b Best	58		
G. P. Thorpe c Sanford b Best	19		
A. Flintoff c Hinds b Sarwan	46		
†C. M. W. Read c Hinds b Best	20		
A. F. Giles b Sanford	27		
M. J. Hoggard not out	9		
S. P. Jones c Sanford b Hinds	7		
S. J. Harmison run out	13		
B 7, l-b 28, w 7, n-b 18	60	B 1, n-b 2	3
	339	(no wkt)	20

1-28 (1) 2-33 (2) 3-152 (3) 4-194 (5)
5-209 (4) 6-268 (6) 7-278 (7)
8-313 (8) 9-325 (10) 10-339 (11)

First innings – Collymore 26–7–55–0; Edwards 19.3–3–72–3; Best 19–1–57–3; Sanford 22–1–90–1;
Hinds 11.5–2–18–1; Gayle 1–0–6–0; Sarwan 4–1–6–1.
Second innings – Best 1.3–0–8–0; Hinds 1–0–11–0.

Toss won by West Indies
MAN OF THE MATCH S. J. Harmison

UMPIRES B. F. Bowden and D. J. Harper

West Indies v England

Second Test

At Port-of-Spain, March 19, 20, 21, 22, 23, 2004. England won by seven wickets.   John Stern, 2005

Less than a fortnight after the start of the series, England secured their main objective of the tour when they retained the *Wisden* Trophy.

Once again Harmison was the dominant figure in England's success, and was responsible for perhaps the crucial moment of the series. This came after West Indies had made an excellent start, with Gayle leading the charge in hot, sunny conditions on a pitch with far less pace than its Sabina Park predecessor. His century opening stand with Devon Smith, containing 82 in boundaries, came up in the 25th over. But at that point, clouds filled the blue sky and light rain started to fall. Harmison, whose first spell of six overs had gone for 27, had just changed ends and he got immediate results, dismissing Gayle, then Smith – and made it three in eight deliveries with the vital wicket of Lara. He hit him on the right hand with one that rose sharply from short of a length, then bounced him next ball: Lara could only fend towards gully as he took his eyes off it. It was the first time in his career that Lara had made successive Test ducks.

Toss: West Indies. **West Indies 208** (C. H. Gayle 62, D. S. Smith 35, R. D. Jacobs 40; S. J. Harmison 6-61)
and 209 (R. D. Jacobs 70, S. Chanderpaul 42; S. P. Jones 5-57); **England 319** (M. A. Butcher 61,
N. Hussain 58, G. P. Thorpe 90, A. F. Giles 37, Extras 45; P. T. Collins 4-71, T. L. Best 3-71) **and 99-3**
(M. A. Butcher 46*).

West Indies v England   **Fourth Test**

See page 422

See page 422

ENGLAND v NEW ZEALAND 2004

Following what Wisden *called England's "historic triumph in the Caribbean", they were pitted against New Zealand in a home series before taking on the demoralised West Indies again. A close series against the Kiwis was anticipated, but they performed disappointingly and were beaten 3–0. The main point of interest was Nasser Hussain's sudden decision to retire after making a hundred at Lord's in the First Test – a nice note on which to finish and surely far better than those careers that just dribble away.*

England v New Zealand   **First Test**

At Lord's, May 20, 21, 22, 23, 24, 2004. England won by seven wickets.   Mike Walters, 2005

Rarely has Lord's witnessed a surge of affection for one of English cricket's grandees to match the final flourish of Nasser Hussain's career, which concluded an extraordinary sequence of events. The theory that a butterfly flapping its wings in Casablanca can lead to a hurricane in Cuba found powerful supporting evidence in this compelling match. It was a wonderful setting for anyone's farewell.

The first twist of a spellbinding plot came three days before a ball had been bowled in anger. Vaughan, the England captain, attempted an innocuous sweep at a 19-year-old net bowler, left-arm spinner Zac Taylor, collapsed in a heap and was carted from the Nursery practice ground with a twisted right knee. The repercussions were momentous: Trescothick stood in as captain for the first time in Tests and the Middlesex captain, Andrew Strauss, not named in the original 13-man squad, became only the fourth player – after Australian Harry Graham (in 1893), England's John Hampshire (1969) and India's Sourav Ganguly (1996) – to launch his Test career with a century at Headquarters.

Strauss was not the only adhesive left-handed opener to make an impact. For more than six hours on a stodgy first day, New Zealand's Richardson was a model of obduracy. He was robbed of a century by a poor lbw decision which disregarded an inside edge. But that helped the innings perk up. There was Astle, with 11 fours in a 77-ball 64, and Oram, with a similarly breezy 67 from 82 balls, and finally there was a performance of awesome power and violence from Cairns. Four times in the space of ten deliveries, Simon Jones, Harmison and Flintoff (twice) disappeared into the back of beyond. In the process, Cairns surpassed Sir Vivian Richards's record of 84 sixes in Tests.

Without their fastest bowler, Bond, the New Zealanders could hardly raise a gallop, and it was England's openers who made all the running with a fluent stand of 190 in 54 overs. Trescothick was finally beaten down the slope by Oram, 14 short of becoming only the third man to score a hundred in his first Test as England captain. But Strauss, batting on his home ground and serenaded by the crowd warbling the "Blue Danube" in his honour, was not to be denied. On 91, he enjoyed a miraculous sliver of good fortune when his inside edge off Martin brushed off stump firmly enough to make the timber wobble but somehow failed to dislodge the bails. Another trail of scorched earth through the covers soon confirmed England's first centurion on debut since Graham Thorpe in 1993, and their superiority. But the applause was accompanied by a sense of wonder: Vaughan would have to come back, and Strauss could hardly be dropped. So who would make way? No one was considering the implications more clearly than a 36-year-old ex-captain already known to be close to retirement.

England led by 55 on first innings, but with Richardson – a man whose batting fills the bars – in occupation again, the pendulum swung back towards New Zealand on the fourth morning. They clawed their way to a 125-run lead with nine wickets in hand. Inexplicably, Trescothick ignored the second new ball and settled for the attrition of Giles, dutifully bowling over the wicket for 35 overs unchanged in a spell of three for 64 to suppress the scoring rate. He could argue that negativity served its purpose, but it took three wickets in 19 balls from Harmison to end the charade. England eventually needed 282 from 95 overs to win – 64 more than they had ever managed in a fourth innings to win in 105 previous Lord's Tests.

A 35 for two, the chase began to look forlorn until Hussain – who had already decided, unknown to his team-mates, that this would be his final Test innings – marched out to join Strauss for his last hurrah. Strauss was the dominant partner in a 108-run stand and was on course for a century in each innings, a feat achieved on debut only by West Indian Lawrence Rowe and Pakistan's Yasir Hameed. Then he sacrificed himself in a Keystone Kops mix-up with Hussain. While the crestfallen Strauss would soon be mollified by the match award, Hussain was distraught after "doing a Boycott on the local lad" – a reference to Geoff Boycott running out Derek Randall against Australia at Trent Bridge 27 years earlier.

Only leading England to victory would atone for Hussain's part in the catastrophe, and they were still 139 away. But few men are blessed with such willpower. Fortified by a succinct pep-talk from fellow warhorse Thorpe – "Stop whingeing and get on with it" – Hussain scrambled to his fifty in 158 deliveries before he was carried to glorious redemption, and the final curtain, on one last rush of adrenalin. His next fifty took only 45 balls; he reached his 14th Test hundred with a lofted on-drive and signature extra-cover drive off successive deliveries to level the scores, and the ovation had not subsided before he collared Martin through the covers again and swayed triumphantly into the sunset. Less than three days later, he confirmed what everybody had suspected from his nostalgic body language: after 96 Tests spanning 14 years, he was giving up the game in a blaze of glory.

Toss: New Zealand. **New Zealand 386** (M. H. Richardson 93, S. P. Fleming 34, N. J. Astle 64, J. D. P. Oram 67, C. L. Cairns 82; S. J. Harmison 4-126, S. P. Jones 3-82) **and 336** (M. H. Richardson 101, B. B. McCullum 96, N. J. Astle 49, Extras 38; S. J. Harmison 4-76, A. F. Giles 3-87); **England 441** (M. E. Trescothick 86, A. J. Strauss 112, N. Hussain 34, A. Flintoff 63, G. O. Jones 46, Extras 41; C. S. Martin 3-94) **and 282-3** (A. J. Strauss 83, N. Hussain 103*, G. P. Thorpe 51*, Extras 37).

ENGLAND V WEST INDIES 2004
Stephen Fay, 2005

Two decades after the successive "blackwash" series that marked the high tide of Caribbean cricketing dominance, England completed a double rout of their own over West Indies so easily that English cricket lovers who had grown stoical in defeat started to take winning for granted. Having won a four-Test away series 3–0 earlier in the year, England swept the four at home, with Michael Vaughan's leadership of a relatively young team growing in skill and conviction all the time.

West Indies' problem was that Lara had no confidence in this team, while his players, awed or fearful, were distanced from him and lacked confidence in themselves. There were talented young cricketers in the squad but, with one exception [Dwayne Bravo], they did not develop. It was emblematic of West Indies' predicament that, while the team and its managers criss-crossed England in a distinctively decorated bus, Lara usually travelled in a silver Mercedes lent him by an admirer. They were destined not just to lose the series, but to be humiliated in a country where whole generations of cricket-lovers had grown up believing West Indies were invincible. Before the final Test, Lara came up with the notion that his side commonly restored their pride in the last match of a series they had already lost. In fact, they were blown away at The Oval. It was a whitewash.

England v West Indies
Second Test
At Birmingham, July 29, 30, 31, August 1, 2004. England won by 256 runs.   Hugh Chevallier, 2005

Crushing defeat inside four days was further proof of West Indian cricket's descent into a vortex of despondency and failure. An abiding memory of this Test – a vignette that could stand for the series – was Lara, the captain, standing at mid-on and rolling his eyes in weary resignation as another wayward ball vanished to the rope. His face in his hands, mulling on the horror of it all, he steeled himself for the pain of it happening all over again. No consolation for the bowler, no word of advice; just lonely, anguished suffering.

In contrast, England went about their business with a *joie de vivre* that bubbled over into everything they did. Typifying this effervescence was Flintoff. Pounding in with the speedo in the high eighties, sweeping up sharp slip catches and swatting the ball to every corner, he did it all with a cheeky grin. And how Edgbaston loved it. In one act of glorious bravado, he lofted Lawson high into the top tier of the Ryder stand. A powerfully built middle-aged man stood up to take the catch. From a crowd of 20,000, Flintoff had somehow picked out his father, who muffed it: the only false move from a Flintoff in the entire Test. Flintoff's 167 – an innings of pace, strength, variety and ebullience – was unforgettable: it came from 191 balls and included 17 fours and seven sixes.

Toss: West Indies. **West Indies 311** (D. S. Smith 108, R. O. Hinds 84, R. D. Jacobs 38; M. J. Hoggard 3-68) **and 47** (S. J. Harmison 7–12); **England 339** (M. A. Butcher 58, N. Hussain 58, A. Flintoff 46, Extras 60; F. H. Edwards 3–72, T. L. Best 3–57) **and 20–0**.

South Africa v England 2004–05

John Etheridge, 2005

England, under the calm yet increasingly bold captaincy of Michael Vaughan, won an often thrilling Test series 2–1 and secured their first victory in South Africa for 40 years. Admittedly, it was only their third Test tour to the country since M. J. K. Smith's team won in 1964–65, but that should not diminish their achievement. Only Australia, twice, had previously won a series in South Africa since their return from sporting isolation in 1991–92. It is a very tough country in which to win.

England failed to reach the standards they established in their demolitions of West Indies and New Zealand in 2004, yet this was a hugely determined performance in the face of a savage and unprecedented schedule – no touring team in history had previously been confronted by five Test matches in 40 days without a game of any description in between. Even David Morgan, the chairman of the ECB, said England must never again agree to such an itinerary, regardless of the financial benefits. Vaughan himself described the result as his best as captain, which is saying something because he had already presided over England's first win in the Caribbean for 36 years and an unprecedented seven victories out of seven during the English summer. Vaughan's reasoning was that England won the Basil D'Oliveira Trophy without playing at their best, making it a triumph for mental resolve as much as for cricketing skill.

Certainly, much of the excitement was generated because these were two flawed and often fatigued teams. England's weariness was obvious when they had to launch into a one-day series immediately afterwards without their star all-rounder, Andrew Flintoff, and lost it 4–1, though it was a series mainly notable for the stirring form of England's latest recruit from South Africa, Kevin Pietersen, who rode the boos from the fans he deserted to score three outstanding centuries.

South Africa v England

First Test

At Port Elizabeth, December 17, 18, 19, 20, 21, 2004. England won by seven wickets. Andrew Miller, 2005

Two made-to-measure innings from Strauss – the first painstaking, the second emphatic – carried England to an unprecedented eighth consecutive Test victory, as they eclipsed the seven in a row last achieved by Percy Chapman's team in 1928–29. Strauss's eight-Test career had now encompassed the entire record-breaking run and, by scoring 126 and an unbeaten 94 on his maiden appearance overseas, he became the first player to score centuries on debut against three consecutive opponents, after his performances against New Zealand and West Indies in the summer. Fittingly, he hit the winning runs as well, outscoring his partner Thorpe by 43 runs to eight as England surged to victory under rain-bearing skies on the final morning.

Toss: South Africa. **South Africa 337** (J. A. Rudolph 93, H. H. Dippenaar 110, S. M. Pollock 31, Extras 31; M. J. Hoggard 3-56, A. Flintoff 3-72) **and 229** (G. C. Smith 55, J. H. Kallis 61; S. P. Jones 4-39); **England 425** (M. E. Trescothick 47, A. J. Strauss 126, M. A. Butcher 79, A. Flintoff 35, Extras 57; M. Ntini 3-75) **and 145-3** (A. J. Strauss 94*, G. P. Thorpe 31*).

South Africa v England — Fourth Test

At Johannesburg, January 13, 14, 15, 16, 17, 2005. England won by 77 runs.   Matthew Engel, 2005

Most of the time, this Test resembled a well-run sightseeing tour (probably to a safari park, since this was definitely Big Game): it was always so varied and interesting no one objected that it seemed certain to lead them back exactly where they started. Then, just after lunch on the final day, the bus was hijacked by Hoggard, with a classical display of swing bowling. The draw all the shrewdies expected never happened, and England managed what eluded them in Durban [where South Africa narrowly escaped defeat]. Once again, they found the onset of darkness harder to beat than South Africa, but this time they just managed it, and went 2–1 up. [South Africa had won the Third Test; the fifth was to be drawn.]

It was their 12th Test win in ten months, and the most improbable of the lot. Vaughan's final-day declaration was a touch conservative, understandably so since his attack was in tatters: the spearhead Harmison had fallen so far that mid-match speculation suggested he might fly home; Flintoff seemed both wounded and distracted; Anderson had not played a first-class match since August, and it showed; even the spinner Giles was hurt. So Hoggard carried the team on his shoulders like Atlas. He bowled them to victory with seven for 61 and match figures of 12 for 205, England's best in 25 years. It was an amazing and thrilling end to a match that often seemed four-sided. The two teams were contending against the ever-unpredictable Highveld summer weather, and the even more mysterious ICC regulations (copies almost unobtainable) and conditions of play [there were disagreements over bad light and the use of floodlights on the second day].

On the final morning, England's lead was only 189 with half the side out; though the draw was hot favourite, a South African win seemed the most viable alternative. Trescothick put paid to that, charging on to 180, mainly supported by Giles, himself struggling with a right thumb dislocated when he had caught Rudolph two days earlier. Vaughan waited for Trescothick to get out before setting South Africa 325 in what seemed a notional 68 overs, because of the likelihood of bad light.

Hoggard found the perfect length, swing in both directions and growing cracks in both the pitch and the batsmen's composure. Soon it was 18 for three, with Kallis nicking a slip catch first ball. Success re-energised England. Hoggard was dauntless; Flintoff gave staunch support; Harmison found enough inspiration at least to worry the batsmen, if not dismiss any. Gibbs, though, galloped to 98 in three hours through the gaps in the aggressive fields, and Smith shrugged off doctor's orders to march in at No. 8 and hold firm. England were anxiously scanning the clouds, and even sent out their spare players (most of whom had not set foot on a field in weeks) to act as ball boys in the absence of a last-day crowd. Twice the sun went in, and England groaned. Twice it came out again. At seven minutes to six, Hoggard induced a nick from last man Steyn. England had their first Test win at the Wanderers in 48 years, and one to rank among their most remarkable anywhere.

South Africa v England, 2004–05 — **Fourth Test**

At Johannesburg, January 13, 14, 15, 16, 17, 2005. Result: England won by 77 runs.

ENGLAND

Batsman	First innings	Second innings
M. E. Trescothick	c Boucher b Steyn 16	c Boucher b Ntini 180
A. J. Strauss	c Kallis b Pollock 147	c de Villiers b Ntini 0
R. W. T. Key	c Smith b Ntini 83	c Kallis b Ntini 19
*M. P. Vaughan	not out 82	c Boucher b Pollock 54
G. P. Thorpe	c Dippenaar b Ntini 0	c and b Kallis 1
M. J. Hoggard	c de Villiers b Ntini 5	(9) c Boucher b Kallis 0
A. Flintoff	c Smith b Ntini 2	(6) c Boucher b Pollock 7
†G. O. Jones	c Smith b Pollock 2	(7) c de Villiers b Pollock 13
A. F. Giles	c Gibbs b Steyn 26	(8) c Gibbs b Kallis 31
S. J. Harmison	not out 30	not out 3
	L-b 13, n-b 5 18	L-b 7, w 6, n-b 11 24

1-45 (1) 2-227 (3) 3-262 (2) (8 wkts dec.) 411
4-263 (5) 5-273 (6) 6-275 (7)
7-278 (8) 8-329 (9)
J. M. Anderson did not bat.

1-2 (2) 2-51 (3) 3-175 (4) (9 wkts dec.) 332
4-176 (5) 5-186 (6) 6-222 (7)
7-272 (8) 8-274 (9) 9-332 (1)

First innings – Pollock 33–12–81–2; Ntini 34–8–111–4; Steyn 21–7–75–2; Kallis 22–2–79–0; Boje 14–2–52–0.
Second innings – Pollock 19–2–74–3; Ntini 20.1–2–62–3; Kallis 21–5–93–3; Steyn 9–0–47–0; Boje 12–0–49–0.

SOUTH AFRICA

Batsman	First innings	Second innings
*G. C. Smith	lbw b Hoggard 29	(8) not out 67
H. H. Gibbs	c Hoggard b Anderson 161	lbw b Giles 98
J. A. Rudolph	c Giles b Hoggard 4	b Hoggard 2
J. H. Kallis	b Hoggard 33	c Trescothick b Hoggard 0
H. H. Dippenaar	c Trescothick b Flintoff 0	c Giles b Hoggard 14
A. B. de Villiers	c Giles b Hoggard 19	(1) lbw b Hoggard 3
†M. V. Boucher	c Strauss b Anderson 64	(6) c Jones b Hoggard 0
S. M. Pollock	lbw b Hoggard 0	(9) c Jones b Flintoff 4
N. Boje	run out 48	(7) c and b Hoggard 18
M. Ntini	b Giles 26	lbw b Flintoff 13
D. W. Steyn	not out 0	c Jones b Hoggard 8
	B 9, l-b 11, w 6, n-b 9 35	B 2, l-b 5, w 1, n-b 12 20

1-64 (1) 2-75 (3) 3-138 (4) 4-149 (5) 419
5-184 (6) 6-304 (7) 7-306 (8)
8-358 (2) 9-399 (9) 10-419 (10)

1-10 (1) 2-18 (3) 3-18 (4) 4-80 (5) 247
5-86 (6) 6-118 (7) 7-163 (2)
8-172 (9) 9-216 (10) 10-247 (11)

First innings – Hoggard 34–2–144–5; Harmison 12.5–4–25–0; Anderson 28–3–117–2; Flintoff 30.1–8–77–1; Giles 8.1–0–25–1; Trescothick 5–1–11–0.
Second innings – Hoggard 18.3–5–61–7; Harmison 14–1–64–0; Flintoff 16–2–59–2; Anderson 6–1–32–0; Giles 5–0–24–1.

Toss won by England
MAN OF THE MATCH M. J. Hoggard

UMPIRES S. A. Bucknor and Aleem Dar

South Africa v England   **Second One-Day International**

At Bloemfontein. February 2, 2005 (day/night). Tied.   Richard Hobson, 2005

Memories of great South African chokes from the past were rekindled as they failed to score three runs from the last six balls to win, producing the 20th tie in 2,219 one-day internationals, and South Africa's fifth in less than six years. The word "eventful" barely does justice to the last over. It began when Boucher swung a chest-high no-ball from the inexperienced Kabir Ali to the boundary, before pulling another full toss straight to Giles in the deep; continued with Prince being run out by Bell; and ended with Hall stumped first ball on a dazed meander from the crease. England celebrated like winners, which they expected to be when Pietersen struck 108 not out from 96 balls, a maiden hundred for his adopted country. With four sharp chances either going to ground or falling short, he enjoyed enough good fortune to last an entire series, and the kiss he planted on his helmet after reaching three figures may have been the most passionate-looking ever witnessed on a cricket field.

Toss: South Africa. **England 270-5** (50 overs) (M. E. Trescothick 37, M. P. Vaughan 42, K. P. Pietersen 108*, P. D. Collingwood 40); **South Africa 270-8** (50 overs) (J. H. Kallis 63, H. H. Gibbs 78, J. M. Kemp 32; Ali 3-56).

South Africa v England   **Fifth One-Day International**

At East London, February 9, 2005 (day/night).
South Africa won by seven runs.   Richard Hobson, 2005

Comic-book baddie to a partisan crowd but an awesome presence to his team-mates, Pietersen completed the fastest hundred by an England player in a one-day international (69 deliveries) when he hit the last ball for his fourth six. Never before had England scored as many as 304 in a losing chase, and if Pietersen had engineered more of the strike late on he might have completed an extraordinary story. Giles and Ali also hit sixes and there was a moment when South Africa began to look alarmed. But Nel and Ntini exercised just enough control in the final overs to win the game, if not to stop Pietersen's personal triumph.

Toss: South Africa. **South Africa 311-7** (50 overs) (G. C. Smith 115*, J. H. Kallis 49, A. G. Prince 34, J. M. Kemp 80; D. Gough 3-52); **England 304-8** (50 overs) (G. O. Jones 37, M. P. Vaughan 70, K. P. Pietersen 100*).

South Africa v England   **Seventh One-Day International**

At Centurion, February 13, 2005. South Africa won by three wickets.   Richard Hobson, 2005

South Africa completed a 4–1 victory when Prince hit the winning runs from the last ball of the penultimate over. But the highlight came earlier when Pietersen rescued England from 68 for six with his third hundred of the series, during which he cleared the leg-side rope six times. His first fifty was a pedestrian affair, from

80 balls, but the second required only 24. Giles reached a one-day international best in support, and the seventh-wicket stand of 104 ensured that another capacity crowd saw a contest not a capitulation. The result also meant that England went home from a tour – successful in its main purpose – with plenty of food for thought, both about their continuing problems in one-day cricket and Pietersen's potential challenge to the established Test players.

Toss: South Africa. **England 240** (49.5 overs) (K. P. Pietersen 116, A. F. Giles 41; A. J. Hall 3-52); **South Africa 241-7** (49 overs) (G. C. Smith 47, J. H. Kallis 36, A. G. Prince 62*, M. V. Boucher 44).

ENGLAND'S REVIVAL: THE ONLY WAY WAS UP Mike Selvey, 2005

Spooky, isn't it, how, quite out of the blue, a tune can capture the moment? Just like that. So sitting there, as you do, pondering the vagaries of English over the past couple of decades, suddenly, over the airwaves from a golden oldies radio station comes the sound of the Tremeloes from 1967 telling us that "Even The Bad Times Are Good". Then, blow me, if not ten minutes later, there are the Mamas and Papas making the pertinent observation that the darkest hour is in fact just before dawn.

Most English cricket followers have grown used to the notion that the darkest hour so far comes before an even darker one. They have become natural pessimists, with much to be pessimistic about. Clouds do not have silver linings: they build up into whopping great anvil-tops and it rains even harder. We glimpse the light down the tunnel and see only a freight train coming the other way. Glass half-full? Not on your life, someone has drunk the lot. But it is not true. The bad times were good in their own way. Sometimes the failures actually dictated that events took a turn for the better. Serendipity: the discovery of new and pleasant things through chance.

Take, for instance, an incident at Lord's in early July 1981. The First Test against Australia has been lost, and the Second is sliding out of reach when England's champion is bowled, for his second nought in the game, and stomps off through the silent, seething hostility of the Long Room, his captaincy in its death throes. That was indeed a dark hour, but it precipitated one of the most uplifting renaissances in cricket history. If Ian Botham's leadership was lying in the gutter at that stage, then as with Oscar Wilde, his career was looking at the stars.

And has English cricket, in all its years, sunk to the depths it managed in the later 1980s, when in successive seasons England were trounced at home by West Indies and then gave up the Ashes with scarcely a whimper, to live only in hope of regaining them ever since?

Now 1988 was a shocker. First came the infamous Rothley Romps, leading to tabloid revelations of high jinks, bare bums and barmaids at a Leicestershire hotel that resulted in the England captain Mike Gatting being sacked – although that was probably an expedient for Lord's officials who regretted not disciplining him for the previous winter's finger-wagging contest with Shakoor Rana at Faisalabad.

The trouble was, there was nowhere to go. The chairman of selectors Peter May dithered, appointing first of all John Emburey and then his own godson Chris Cowdrey. Finally though, from it all, emerged a man who was to lead by example and begin the process of instilling some backbone into the establishment. Graham Gooch, forgiven for his rebel forays to South Africa, led only briefly before David Gower got the job back, but the future was there.

First, though, came 1989, which was probably an even worse year without being lightened by barmaid stories. The nadir came at Old Trafford when David Boon swept the runs that regained the Ashes for Australia. Immediately prior to that came the news that a significant number of the England side had decided to abandon Test cricket and instead, under the leadership of the disgruntled Gatting, partake in another unofficial money-spinner to South Africa. But the game has an immune system. Earlier that year, Angus Fraser, a future stalwart, had made his debut and became the first England bowler to dismiss Steve Waugh in a Test that summer, after he had scored a mere 393 runs in the series. After the defections, in came Mike Atherton. The end of the Ashes campaign brought with it the termination of Gower's captaincy and the appointment of Gooch once more, to take the side to the Caribbean, a cricketing war zone. The response was a resounding win in the First Test at Jamaica, and the debuts of two more future captains in Nasser Hussain and Alec Stewart. Thus, from the carnage and probably even because of it, in the space of eight months, the careers had begun of four players who were to play 390 Tests, and captain England 114 times.

Gooch's period in charge lasted until a doleful resignation at Headingley in 1993 after the Ashes had once more been conceded to Australia. But if the cricket had brought only occasional shafts of sunlight, then he had brought some stability, and a boot-camp sense of discipline as a counterpoint to the laissez-faire that had preceded him. The ethos was changing.

Not that Atherton found it easy going. The next West Indies tour brought with it another failure, including the infamous 46 all out at Trinidad – although the consolation victory in Bridgetown, West Indies' first defeat there for 59 years, was an important milestone. Two winters later, South Africa ultimately proved too much on their home pitches, although Atherton's personal achievement in saving the game at the Wanderers was arguably Test cricket's greatest rearguard innings. The captain's relationship with Ray Illingworth, England's first supremo, was fractious, Illingworth being unable to translate his captaincy skills to management.

England cricket at the highest level still lacked focus, and after a disastrous World Cup in 1996, Illingworth was replaced with the enthusiastic David Lloyd and, a year later, a more self-effacing chairman of selectors in David Graveney. If another nadir was reached that winter in Zimbabwe (what has become known as the "we flippin' murdered 'em tour" after Lloyd's over-excited match report on a draw) then, in the background, the English game was about to undergo a fundamental overhaul that over the next eight years was to transform the way that the England team was regarded.

The old TCCB, which once ran the game with a staff of a dozen, was replaced in 1997 by a far more elaborate operation, with a chief executive, Tim Lamb, and a high-profile chairman, Lord MacLaurin, the chairman of Tesco. MacLaurin viewed the England side as the shop window of the game, and its principal earner. Energies, he decided, should be diverted into maximising this to the benefit of everyone else. England players were offered status not previously accorded them (beginning with the seemingly insignificant gesture of single rooms on tour). Lloyd and Atherton were given the forerunners of the backroom staff that surround the current national side. Counties were told that the England team – Team England as it came to be known – was to be prioritised.

But it was out of the depths of yet another crisis that the England team finally rose to the surface without sinking yet again. Stewart had been given the captaincy when Atherton resigned following another Caribbean failure, in 1998. But he never looked secure and, after England's miserable home World Cup in 1999, was replaced by the brooding, volcanic Hussain. Immediately, a loss to New Zealand at home relegated England to the status of the world's worst team in the then unofficial *Wisden* World Championship. The boos that were directed at the new captain as he stood on the Oval balcony were merely a reflection of public derision: despite all the changes, the team was still a metaphor for humiliating failure.

Before Duncan Fletcher was appointed Lloyd's successor that summer, Hussain had never met him – which is lucky, because they might never have got on. But together, Hussain's volatility and drive and Fletcher's understated organisation and single-mindedness pulled England from the quagmire. Fletcher's ideas began to get credence and support. He wanted control over his players and it came in the form of central contracts, the argument in favour reinforced by previous failures. Today's England players regard themselves as just that, and it has transformed the way they play.

Last summer's surprises were nearly all happy ones. Given a fair wind and fitness, the year might have finished successfully enough for England, with Hussain retiring at the end, and a hatful of runs for Mark Butcher and Graham Thorpe. Happenstance again interfered. A freak injury to Vaughan before the First Test brought a debut century for Andrew Strauss, and precipitated Hussain's departure in a blaze of glory. A couple of bizarre injuries to Butcher let in Rob Key, who responded with a double-century. Finally, an injury to Thorpe gave Ian Bell his chance to make runs. Maybe in an ideal world, each would have been a triumph of selection rather than chance. But, with England, we take what we can get – and hope that all these signs of brightness really do constitute the dawn.

ENGLAND V AUSTRALIA 2005 Stephen Brenkley, 2006

If there has been a more compelling series, history forgot to record it. If there is a better one in the future, you would beg to be there. England regained the Ashes after a gap of 16 years and 42 days, when bad light brought a formal end to the Fifth Test: a series full of extraordinary climaxes and reversals, in the end, just dwindling away in the more usual cricketing fashion to the point where an Australian victory became impossible, even in this summer.

Australia needed 338 runs to win from the 17.2 overs remaining to draw level at 2–2 and retain the Ashes. So 2–1 to England it was, though but for a run here, a wicket there or a catch almost anywhere it could conceivably have been either 4–1 or 0–4. It is somehow soothing to relate the bare facts and the strangely prosaic conclusion. The contest was gripping from the beginning. As it reached the end, not just regular English cricket-followers, but the whole country and the rest of the cricketing world were in its thrall. It was so intense and played with such purpose that it supplanted football on the back pages and much else on the front pages. Television viewing figures went through the roof.

The First Test was topsy-turvy, but eventually resulted in an easy Australian victory, leading most people – including, crucially, the Australians themselves – to assume their dominance would remain unchallenged. The Second ("The Greatest Test", many thought) produced the first sensational finish and a two-run England win. Australia just held out to save the Third. England clung on to edge the Fourth. And, though the Fifth reached a conclusion more bizarre than thrilling, everyone was so galvanised by the whole affair and, in England, by the impending return of the urn that no one minded.

By the halfway mark, a debate had begun about whether it was the best Ashes series of all; it moved swiftly on to whether it was the best Test series ever, with a substantial body of informed opinion thinking it was. At various times, the matches entered that peculiar realm where you could not look away but found it unbearable to keep watching.

But there was another dimension too. The image of England's monumental all-rounder Andrew Flintoff consoling a distraught Brett Lee immediately after England had won the Second Test flashed round Planet Cricket. It seemed to show a world where forgotten virtues of honour, decency, respect and commiseration for your opponent still held sway. After years when every aspect of English cricket had been savaged or mocked, the game was now being reborn in the country where it had been conceived and nurtured, and looking like something with a great deal to teach rival sports and the rest of an often bad-tempered country.

When the series outcome was finally confirmed, after an audacious maiden Test century by Kevin Pietersen prevented Australia from having a decent tilt at the victory they required, there was an outpouring of relief and jubilation. The scenes at The Oval, splendidly refurbished and packed with 23,000 spectators on five successive days, were astonishing enough. There were countless renditions of "Jerusalem" which, like it or not, had become accepted as the team anthem, as well as "Land of Hope and Glory" and "There'll Always Be An England". The little scene when England's captain, Michael Vaughan, planted a kiss on the replica of the Ashes urn brought the house down, in the way that the hoisting of the FA Cup by the winning captain once did. And it was done with the judgment and delicacy of touch that had been apparent in his leadership throughout.

The following day, anything between 100,000 and a quarter of a million people lined the streets of London as the triumphant squad and support staff, wives and in some cases children paraded on an open-topped double-decker bus. Crowd estimates are invariably as trustworthy as a dodgy builder's, but there were decidedly more than the two men and a dog Matthew Hoggard said he was expecting. The procession ended in Trafalgar Square, where roughly 25,000 paid homage to the victors – before they went to Downing Street to meet the prime minister.

Had the players known how many would turn up, they might have postponed the all-night bender that led many of them (not least the player of the series, Flintoff) to report for this extra day of duty somewhere below the level of fitness that sustained them through the series. This prompted a heated, though cooked-up, media discussion on the duty of professional sportsmen to observe the proprieties. The majority, if not quite unanimous, response was that the players were fine, just fine: after emerging from such a titanic struggle, they deserved their booze. Indeed, it seemed to endear them to the public even more.

England v Australia   **Twenty20 International**

At Southampton, June 13, 2005. England won by 100 runs.   Hugh Chevallier, 2006

England won their first Twenty20 international so easily that the crowd taunted Australia, singing "Are you Bangladesh in disguise?" Even Bangladesh seemed unlikely to botch things so badly. Australia's reply was effectively over by the sixth over, at a jaw-dropping 31 for seven, and was officially done by the 15th. They were rusty, playing their first competitive match since March, but Ponting insisted: "We take every game pretty seriously." The crowd were thrilled; the Australian players thought it didn't matter much – history may record that the crowd were right.

Toss: England. **England 179-8** (20 overs) (M. E. Trescothick 41, K. P. Pietersen 34, P. D. Collingwood 46; G. D. McGrath 3-31); **Australia 79** (14.3 overs) (D. Gough 3-16, J. Lewis 4-24).

England v Australia   **NatWest Series Final**

At Lord's, July 2, 2005. Tied.   Julian Guyer, 2006

A thrilling recovery by England resulted in a breathless tie, only the second between these sides and the 21st in all one-day internationals. When England slumped to 33 for five, chasing 197, every cricket fan in the country could be forgiven for thinking "here we go again". But as Collingwood and wicket-keeper Geraint Jones added 116, England dared to think of victory once more. The pair were separated only when Collingwood was run out, with 48 needed from 39 balls; Jones and his namesake Simon followed in the next two overs. But Giles and Gough brought the target down to ten off the last over, from McGrath, who started with a no-ball. Gough needed three from two balls when he was run out going for a single. Giles survived an lbw appeal off the final ball, and a misfield by Lee at third man allowed him to scramble two leg-byes and tie the scores.

Toss: England. **Australia 196** (48.5 overs) (M. E. K. Hussey 62*; A. Flintoff 3-23, S. J. Harmison 3-27); **England 196-9** (50 overs) (P. D. Collingwood 53, G. O. Jones 71; G. D. McGrath 3-25).

England v Australia   First Test

At Lord's, July 21, 22, 23, 24, 2005. Australia won by 239 runs.   David Frith, 2006

The longest period of ambitious anticipation in living memory as far as England's Ashes hopes were concerned came to a juddering halt in the opening encounter. Australia's bowling champions, McGrath and Warne, proved as effective as ever in exploiting both the conditions and batsmen's nerves. Further swaying the outcome was England's failure to hold catches. Seven were grassed. The upshot was that Australia's 71-year unbeaten sequence in Lord's Tests would be extended to at least three-quarters of a century, 1934 to 2009. And, misleadingly, it was assumed that business as had been usual since 1989 was being maintained.

Ponting expressed gratitude that Lord's had been chosen as the opening venue. It remained easily their favourite ground in the world.

Toss: Australia. **Australia 190** (J. L. Langer 40; S. J. Harmison 5-43) **and 384** (M. L. Hayden 34, R. T. Ponting 42, D. R. Martyn 65, M. J. Clarke 91, S. M. Katich 67; S. J. Harmison 3-54); **England 155** (K. P. Pietersen 57, G. O. Jones 30; G. D. McGrath 5-53, B. Lee 3-47) **and 180** (M. E. Trescothick 44, A. J. Strauss 37, K. P. Pietersen 64*; G. D. McGrath 4-29, S. K. Warne 4-64).

England v Australia   Second Test

At Birmingham, August 4, 5, 6, 7, 2005 England won by two runs.   Steven Lynch, 2006

If Australia had been rolled over in a couple of balls on the fourth morning, which was wholly possible, this would still be remembered as a great Test match: it produced exciting, fluctuating, often brilliant cricket from day one. But the crowd that turned up and filled Edgbaston on the Sunday seemed to sense they would be seeing something more worthwhile than three minutes' cricket and a victory singsong.

They still got the win they desperately wanted and expected, but in a manner that will never be forgotten. When the Old Trafford Test began four days later, "The Greatest Test" DVD was on sale. And no one was arguing with the description.

On that sunlit fourth morning, England strode out on to the field with Australia 175 for eight, chasing 282. The main batsmen were all gone, and so was the swaggering confidence that had characterised Australia's Test performances for almost the whole of the previous 16 years.

But sometimes there is nothing quite as invigorating as a hopeless situation. Warne started brightly, Lee jumped solidly behind the ball, collecting bruises as well as runs, and the target ticked down. Warne trod on his stumps with 62 wanted, but still it wasn't over. The bowlers dug the ball in too short and too straight, aiming for catches off the splice rather than in the well-stocked slip cordon. England's confidence turned to concern to alarm to panic. And the last pair, Lee and Kasprowicz – with plenty of help from Extras – whittled the target down towards single figures.

With 15 required, Kasprowicz flicked Flintoff uppishly to third man, where Simon Jones failed to hold on to a difficult catch as he dived forward. England's

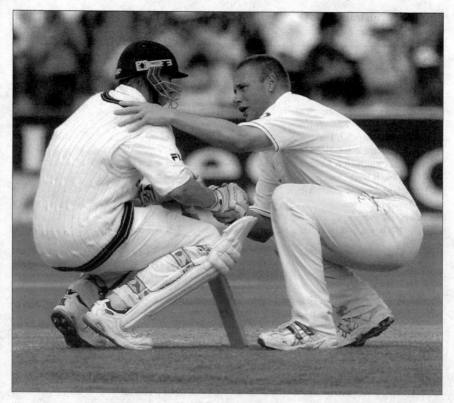

So close: the end of the nail-biting Edgbaston Test of 2005. England's talisman Andrew Flintoff consoles Brett Lee, who shepherded Australia to within three runs of victory. This result set up the greatest of all Test series.

last chance appeared to have gone. But finally, with just three wanted, Harmison banged one into the left glove of Kasprowicz, who hunched down horrified as the ball looped down the leg side and Geraint Jones plunged for the winning catch, the signal for tumultuous celebrations. A mournful Kasprowicz said afterwards, "It just got big quick, and I didn't see too much of it." Nor did umpire Bowden. After umpteen TV replays, it was possible to conclude that Kasprowicz's left hand was off the bat at the moment of impact and, technically, he was not out. Bowden, however, would have needed superhuman vision to see this, and an armed escort involving several regiments to escape the crowd had he actually refused to give it out. It was also the right decision for cricket: 2–0 to Australia would have been the signal for the football season to begin; 1–1 lit the blue touchpaper. The Greatest Test became the Greatest Series, and the pyrotechnics illuminated the summer. The final margin was the closest in England-Australia Tests, edging the three-run thrillers at Old Trafford 1902 and Melbourne 1982 – and neither of those could match this one in its relentless unmissability.

England v Australia, 2005

Second Test

At Birmingham, August 4, 5, 6, 7, 2005. Result: England won by two runs.

ENGLAND	First innings		Second innings	
M. E. Trescothick c Gilchrist b Kasprowicz	90	– c Gilchrist b Lee		21
A. J. Strauss b Warne	48	– b Warne		6
*M. P. Vaughan c Lee b Gillespie	24	– (4) b Lee		1
I. R. Bell c Gilchrist b Kasprowicz	6	– (5) c Gilchrist b Warne		21
K. P. Pietersen c Katich b Lee	71	– (6) c Gilchrist b Warne		20
A. Flintoff c Gilchrist b Gillespie	68	– (7) b Warne		73
†G. O. Jones c Gilchrist b Kasprowicz	1	– (8) c Ponting b Lee		9
A. F. Giles lbw b Warne	23	– (9) c Hayden b Warne		8
M. J. Hoggard lbw b Warne	16	– (3) c Hayden b Lee		1
S. J. Harmison b Warne	17	– c Ponting b Warne		0
S. P. Jones not out	19	– not out		12
L-b 9, w 1, n-b 14	24	L-b 1, n-b 9		10

1-112 (2) 2-164 (1) 3-170 (4) 4-187 (3)   **407**   1-25 (2) 2-27 (1) 3-29 (4) 4-31 (3)   **182**
5-290 (6) 6-293 (7) 7-342 (8)   5-72 (6) 6-75 (5) 7-101 (8)
8-348 (5) 9-375 (10) 10-407 (9)   8-131 (9) 9-131 (10) 10-182 (7)

First innings – Lee 17–1–111–1; Gillespie 22–3–91–2; Kasprowicz 15–3–80–3; Warne 25.2–4–116–4.
Second innings – Lee 18–1–82–4; Gillespie 8–0–24–0; Kasprowicz 3–0–29–0; Warne 23.1–7–46–6.

AUSTRALIA	First innings		Second innings	
J. L. Langer lbw b S. P. Jones	82	– b Flintoff		28
M. L. Hayden c Strauss b Hoggard	0	– c Trescothick b S. P. Jones		31
*R. T. Ponting c Vaughan b Giles	61	– c G. O. Jones b Flintoff		0
D. R. Martyn run out	20	– c Bell b Hoggard		28
M. J. Clarke c G. O. Jones b Giles	40	– b Harmison		30
S. M. Katich c G. O. Jones b Flintoff	4	– c Trescothick b Giles		16
†A. C. Gilchrist not out	49	– c Flintoff b Giles		1
S. K. Warne b Giles	8	– (9) hit wkt b Flintoff		42
B. Lee c Flintoff b S. P. Jones	6	– (10) not out		43
J. N. Gillespie lbw b Flintoff	7	– (8) lbw b Flintoff		0
M. S. Kasprowicz lbw b Flintoff	0	– c G. O. Jones b Harmison		20
B 13, l-b 7, w 1, n-b 10	31	B 13, l-b 8, w 1, n-b 18		40

1-0 (2) 2-88 (3) 3-118 (4) 4-194 (5)   **308**   1-47 (1) 2-48 (3) 3-82 (2)   **279**
5-208 (6) 6-262 (1) 7-273 (8)   4-107 (4) 5-134 (6) 6-136 (7)
8-282 (9) 9-308 (10) 10-308 (11)   7-137 (8) 8-175 (5) 9-220 (9) 10-279 (11)

First innings – Harmison 11–1–48–0; Hoggard 8–0–41–1; S. P. Jones 16–2–69–2; Flintoff 15–1–52–3; Giles 26–2–78–3.
Second innings – Harmison 17.3–3–62–2; Hoggard 5–0–26–1; Giles 15–3–68–2; Flintoff 22–3–79–4; S. P. Jones 5–1–23–1.

Toss won by Australia   UMPIRES B. F. Bowden (NZ) and
MAN OF THE MATCH A. Flintoff   R. E. Koertzen (SA)

England v Australia	Third Test
At Manchester, August 11, 12, 13, 14, 15, 2005. Drawn.	Chloe Saltau, 2006

Cricket had hardly caught its breath after Edgbaston; the superlatives had not even settled. But now 2005 had something else to give. A draw, of all things: the first in 17 Ashes Tests. Yes, five days passed and nobody won. But an estimated 10,000 had to be turned away from Old Trafford on the final morning, and thousands more were turned back before they could get close. Roads were clogged for miles around.

This reflected the mounting enthusiasm for the series, but also the decision to offer last-day tickets for only £10 to adults and £5 for juniors; the black market put their value at around £80. Those who failed to join the 22,000 in the ground had to join the estimated 7.7 million who watched the conclusion on TV. This involved Australia's last pair, Lee and McGrath, keeping out the last 24 balls to save the game, something this Australian team has hardly ever had to contemplate. Two nations held their collective breath yet again. The end was only made possible by an inspirational innings from Ponting. He batted nearly seven hours for 156 after England had set Australia 423 to win. It was the loneliest of hands on a wearing pitch: no one else even got close to 50. When he was ninth out, with four overs still left, he thought he had blown it. Ponting left the field, not with the satisfaction of having played a great innings, but in a fury. He went into the dressing-room and threw a private tantrum...while his tailenders in the middle kept their cool.

Toss: England. **England 444** (M. E. Trescothick 63, M. P. Vaughan 166, I. R. Bell 59, A. Flintoff 46, G. O. Jones 42; B. Lee 4-100, S. K. Warne 4-99) **and 280-6 dec.** (M. E. Trescothick 41, A. J. Strauss 106, I. R. Bell 65; G. D. McGrath 5-115); **Australia 302** (J. L. Langer 31, M. L. Hayden 34, A. C. Gilchrist 30, S. K. Warne 90, Extras 38; S. P. Jones 6-53, A. F. Giles 3-100) **and 371-9** (M. L. Hayden 36, R. T. Ponting 156, M. J. Clarke 39, S. K. Warne 34, Extras 34; A. Flintoff 4-71).

England v Australia	Fourth Test
At Nottingham, August 25, 26, 27, 28, 2005. England won by three wickets.	Lawrence Booth, 2006

The law of averages demanded a dull draw after the showstoppers at Edgbaston and Old Trafford, but this was a series in which the usual laws did not apply. By the time Giles and Hoggard scampered the winning runs on a sun-kissed Sunday, both teams – both nations – had been put through the wringer once more. But now England were ahead, a point not lost on the home supporters. "What's the score, Glenn McGrath, what's the score?" they chanted at the 5–0 predictor on the Australian balcony. He responded with another forecast, holding up two fingers on each hand, but the gesture seemed poignant. Not only was a 2–2 draw the best Australia could still hope for; McGrath himself had now missed two Tests in the series, both lost. [Crucially, he had suffered an ankle injury when he trod on a ball during practice on the morning of the Edgbaston Test; here he was kept out by a problematic elbow.]

The game turned on a partnership between Flintoff and Geraint Jones that was a study in contrasts: the lumbering giant and the nifty urchin; the bully and the pickpocket; the front-foot driver and the back-foot cutter. What they shared was urgency, and they added 177 at high speed. When Flintoff tucked Warne to leg for a single to complete his fifth Test hundred, from only 121 balls, Trent Bridge erupted. Moments later, he aimed across the line against Tait and the fun was over, but the stand had deflated the Australians and ushered England to a third successive first-innings score of 400 for the first time in nearly 19 years of Ashes cricket. Jones fell 15 runs short of three figures, and Australia were left with a session on the second evening in which to chip away at England's 477.

Instead, the breaches came from the bowlers. Hoggard located his away-swinger for the first time in the series in an 11-over burst of three for 32, and Harmison undid Clarke in the last over of the day, as he had at Edgbaston. Both Ponting and Martyn were given out lbw to balls they had edged, but the nicks were imperceptible to the naked eye and could not detract from the truth: Australia were being outplayed again.

The sense that the force was with England was confirmed on the third morning, when Strauss dived full stretch at second slip to hold on to Gilchrist's edge, before Simon Jones, hostile and incisive, cleaned up to take five for 44. Not even Lee's hard-hit 47 could prevent Australia from following on for the first time since Karachi in 1988–89. Still, at 155 for two second time round, they were progressing smoothly. Then Martyn called Ponting for a single, only to see his captain beaten by a direct hit from the covers. Ponting's fury at losing his wicket at a crucial stage was compounded by the identity of the fielder: Gary Pratt, a 23-year-old batsman who had not played a first-class game for Durham all summer, was substituting for Simon Jones, who had limped off with an ankle injury. Pratt's presence on the field was thus legitimate, but the Australians had objected to England's constant use of substitutes, apparently to rest their bowlers, and Ponting vented his feelings towards the England balcony on his way to the pavilion. The outburst would cost him 75% of his match fee. More immediately, his side's momentum was checked. When Martyn feathered Flintoff two overs later, Australia were still 98 behind with six wickets left.

What followed was the most attritional passage of batting in the series yet, as Clarke and Katich added 100 – only Australia's second century stand in four games – in 48 overs to wipe out England's lead. But Hoggard persuaded Clarke to nibble at the second new ball just before lunch on the fourth day, before becoming the first seamer to win an lbw appeal against Gilchrist in his 72 Tests. Harmison mopped up with three wickets, including Katich, who was furious when his 262-minute vigil was ended by a poor lbw decision from Aleem Dar. His all-too-obvious displeasure (he conducted his argument with spectators) earned him a 50% fine, and England were eventually left needing an awkward 129.

At 32 without loss after five overs, they were coasting. But cricket has never had a scene-stealer – not even Ian Botham – who could match Warne. He removed Trescothick and Vaughan with the opening deliveries of his first two overs, then snared Strauss at leg slip in his fifth to make it 57 for three. When Bell hooked

Lee to long leg without addition, the talk was of Australian revenge for Headingley 1981. As on the Sunday morning at Edgbaston and Monday afternoon at Old Trafford, news from Trent Bridge began to savage the peace of a warm August English Sunday.

Pietersen and Flintoff, against type, calmed everyone's nerves by adding 46, but Lee had Pietersen caught behind with the first ball of a new spell and in his next over bowled an incredulous Flintoff with a beauty that proved Australia could produce reverse swing, to tremendous effect. With 13 still needed, Geraint Jones spooned Warne to deep extra cover. England were down to the bowlers. The anxiety was not confined to the spectators. As Hoggard trooped to the crease, Giles provided a cheerless assessment of Lee's bowling: "He's reversing it at 95 miles an hour." Somehow, though, the runs came in dribs and drabs: Giles kept out Warne, Hoggard handled Lee. Catharsis arrived when Hoggard drove a Lee full toss to the cover fence to take England within four runs of their target, and victory was secured in the next over when Giles clipped Warne through mid-wicket.

With more support for Lee and Warne – Kasprowicz and Tait bowled six wicketless overs for 43 between them – Australia might have won. Instead, it was England who celebrated a result which ensured that, for the first time in nine Ashes series, they would not be on the losing side. Could they now take the one last step towards the Ashes?

England v Australia, 2005 — Fourth Test

At Nottingham, August 25, 26, 27, 28, 2005. Result: England won by three wickets.

ENGLAND	First innings		Second innings	
M. E. Trescothick b Tait	65	– c Ponting b Warne	27	
A. J. Strauss c Hayden b Warne	35	– c Clarke b Warne	23	
*M. P. Vaughan c Gilchrist b Ponting	58	– c Hayden b Warne	0	
I. R. Bell c Gilchrist b Tait	3	– c Kasprowicz b Lee	3	
K. P. Pietersen c Gilchrist b Lee	45	– c Gilchrist b Lee	23	
A. Flintoff lbw b Tait	102	– b Lee	26	
†G. O. Jones c and b Kasprowicz	85	– c Kasprowicz b Warne	3	
A. F. Giles lbw b Warne	15	– not out	7	
M. J. Hoggard c Gilchrist b Warne	10	– not out	8	
S. J. Harmison st Gilchrist b Warne	2			
S. P. Jones not out	15			
B 1, l-b 15, w 1, n-b 25	42	L-b 4, n-b 5	9	

1-105 (2) 2-137 (1) 3-146 (4) 4-213 (3) 477   1-32 (1) 2-36 (3) 3-57 (2) (7 wkts) 129
5-241 (5) 6-418 (6) 7-450 (7)   4-57 (4) 5-103 (5) 6-111 (6)
8-450 (8) 9-454 (10) 10-477 (9)   7-116 (7)

First innings – Lee 32–2–131–1; Kasprowicz 32–3–122–1; Tait 24–4–97–3; Warne 29.1–4–102–4; Ponting 6–2–9–1.
Second innings – Lee 12–0–51–3; Kasprowicz 2–0–19–0; Warne 13.5–2–31–4; Tait 4–0–24–0.

AUSTRALIA	First innings		Second innings	
J. L. Langer c Bell b Hoggard		27	– c Bell b Giles	61
M. L. Hayden lbw b Hoggard		7	– c Giles b Flintoff	26
*R. T. Ponting lbw b S. P. Jones		1	– run out	48
D. R. Martyn lbw b Hoggard		1	– c G. O. Jones b Flintoff	13
M. J. Clarke lbw b Harmison		36	– c G. O. Jones b Hoggard	56
S. M. Katich c Strauss b S. P. Jones		45	– lbw b Harmison	59
†A. C. Gilchrist c Strauss b Flintoff		27	– lbw b Hoggard	11
S. K. Warne c Bell b S. P. Jones		0	– st G. O. Jones b Giles	45
B. Lee c Bell b S. P. Jones		47	– not out	26
M. S. Kasprowicz b S. P. Jones		5	– c G. O. Jones b Harmison	19
S. W. Tait not out		3	– b Harmison	4
L-b 2, w 1, n-b 16		19	B 1, l-b 4, n-b 14	19

1-20 (2) 2-21 (3) 3-22 (4) 4-58 (1)   218   1-50 (2) 2-129 (1) 3-155 (3) 4-161 (4)   387
5-99 (5) 6-157 (6) 7-157 (8)   5-261 (5) 6-277 (7) 7-314 (6)
8-163 (7) 9-175 (10) 10-218 (9)   8-342 (8) 9-373 (10) 10-387 (11)

First innings – Harmison 9–1–48–1; Hoggard 15–3–70–3; S. P. Jones 14.1–4–44–5; Flintoff 11–1–54–1.
Second innings – Hoggard 27–7–72–2; S. P. Jones 4–0–15–0; Harmison 30–5–93–3; Flintoff 29–4–83–2; Giles 28–3–107–2; Bell 6–2–12–0.

Toss won by England   UMPIRES Aleem Dar and S. A. Bucknor
MAN OF THE MATCH A. Flintoff

England v Australia   Fifth Test

At The Oval, September 8, 9, 10, 11, 12, 2005. Drawn.   Hugh Chevallier, 2006

The Ashes series ended in the sort of obscure anti-climax which baffled outsiders were inclined to associate with cricket before the summer of 2005. But this time it did not produce bewildered shakes of the head. It delivered one of the most exhilarating moments in the history of English sport, never mind cricket. As England moved towards the draw that clinched the Ashes, the roads went quiet as the nation headed for the TV screens to concentrate on the moment. Next day, the noise was on the streets as England paraded the replica trophy from an open-top bus, and the game's new fans jumped into the Trafalgar Square fountains in delight as they awaited the team's arrival.

Could stuffy old cricket really have caused all this? The answer was yes. The euphoria released when England brought back the Ashes after an absence of 16 years 42 days confirmed that cricket's place in the country's soul had survived eight successive humiliating series against the Australians. But more than that, what was noticeable was how young those in Trafalgar Square were: many were unborn when Mike Gatting's team won in 1986–87. A new genera-tion had been enticed to the game by this amazing summer. Cricket was unmiss-able; cricket was cool.

Perhaps it should have been no surprise. This was the climax of what was already being called the Greatest Series Ever. And despite that impossible billing, it matched expectations in all but its very end. It helped that the stage was perfectly set: with England 2–1 up, only defeat could prevent the triumphant restoration of the Ashes. It meant that tension suffused every move.

Australia trailed by six [on first innings], failing to make 400 in a series of four or more Tests for the first time since 1978–79. Ponting's only option was to blast England out double quick, but the light remained sepulchral. McGrath idiotically bowled a bouncer, and they were off – though not before Warne found extravagant, anxiety-inducing spin to remove Strauss. On their return, in marginally brighter conditions, all the Australian players sported sunglasses. The pantomime caught on: with Warne a constant threat, some spectators theatrically unfurled umbrellas against non-existent rain. Nearby Aussies promptly stripped off their shirts and basked in illusory sunshine. The umbrellas won. To applause that might have been thunder, everyone trooped off. It meant no more cricket; the paying public, for once, didn't care.

The final day dawned, brightly, with every result possible and tension upgraded from danger level to crisis point. England were 34 for one, but they had to get through a notional 98 overs without giving Australia a look-in. With the score on 67, McGrath struck twice with two exquisite deliveries. The hat-trick ball looped into the slips, sparking huge appeals and much queasiness. Somehow, umpire Bowden got it right. Not out: it had hit Pietersen's shoulder. Next over, he was dropped off Warne; had it stuck, England would have been 68 for four. They were nurturing the shoots of a recovery when Lee found Pietersen's edge. The ball flashed at head height to Warne, safest of first slips. He parried it. As his despairing lunge failed to grab the rebound, the stands erupted.

The release of tension was short-lived. Warne snaffled Trescothick and Flintoff to give Australia the edge: at lunch, they were 133 behind, just five wickets to filch and more than 70 overs left. Some found it all too much. David Graveney, the chairman of selectors, headed for the car park to calm himself down, missing an epic shoot-out between Pietersen, oozing conviction, confidence and courage, and Lee, touching 95mph. Supported by Collingwood, whose 72-minute ten justified his selection, and then Giles, Pietersen reeled off shots outrageous in any circumstances, unimaginable in these. By tea, he had pulled, punched, slashed and smashed his way to an extraordinary maiden Test hundred, applauded by Warne (his Hampshire captain), 23,000 in the stands and millions in their living-rooms.

Even then, Australia – 227 behind, three batsmen to dislodge, nearly 50 overs available – had a chance of victory. Not for long. No one could say precisely when the draw and England's Ashes became inescapable: certainly before Pietersen fell for an unforgettable 158, including seven sixes. Giles consolidated his reputation for reliability with 59, his highest Test score, and Warne wheeled away for a lion-hearted six wickets – 12 in the match, a staggering 40 in the series.

Yet the denouement of this Test, unlike the previous three, was pure bathos. Even though there was nothing to be gained from Australia starting their second innings, ICC regulations dragged the players back out. Four meaningless balls later, they came off for the umpteenth and last time, in fading light. The game theoretically remained live for another 16 minutes, and then, to a roar audible in Sydney, the umpires, adding their own piece of theatre, removed the bails: the Ashes were England's.

England v Australia, 2005

Fifth Test

At The Oval, September 8, 9, 10, 11, 12, 2005. Result: Drawn.

ENGLAND	*First innings*		*Second innings*	
M. E. Trescothick c Hayden b Warne	43	– lbw b Warne	33
A. J. Strauss c Katich b Warne	129	– c Katich b Warne	1
*M. P. Vaughan c Clarke b Warne	11	– c Gilchrist b McGrath	45
I. R. Bell lbw b Warne	0	– c Warne b McGrath	0
K. P. Pietersen b Warne	14	– b McGrath	158
A. Flintoff c Warne b McGrath	72	– c and b Warne	8
P. D. Collingwood lbw b Tait	7	– c Ponting b Warne	10
†G. O. Jones b Lee	25	– b Tait	1
A. F. Giles lbw b Warne	32	– b Warne	59
M. J. Hoggard c Martyn b McGrath	2	– not out	4
S. J. Harmison not out	20	– c Hayden b Warne	0
B 4, l-b 6, w 1, n-b 7	18	B 4, w 7, n-b 5	16

1-82 (1) 2-102 (3) 3-104 (4) 4-131 (5)   **373**   1-2 (2) 2-67 (3) 3-67 (4)   **335**
5-274 (6) 6-289 (7) 7-297 (2)   4-109 (1) 5-126 (6) 6-186 (7)
8-325 (8) 9-345 (10) 10-373 (9)   7-199 (8) 8-308 (5) 9-335 (9) 10-335 (11)

First innings – McGrath 27–5–72–2; Lee 23–3–94–1; Tait 15–1–61–1; Warne 37.3–5–122–6; Katich 3–0–14–0.
Second innings – McGrath 26–3–85–3; Lee 20–4–88–0; Warne 38.3–3–124–6; Clarke 2–0–6–0; Tait 5–0–28–1.

AUSTRALIA	*First innings*		*Second innings*	
J. L. Langer b Harmison	105	– not out	0
M. L. Hayden lbw b Flintoff	138	– not out	0
*R. T. Ponting c Strauss b Flintoff	35		
D. R. Martyn c Collingwood b Flintoff	10		
M. J. Clarke lbw b Hoggard	25		
S. M. Katich lbw b Flintoff	1		
†A. C. Gilchrist lbw b Hoggard	23		
S. K. Warne c Vaughan b Flintoff	0		
B. Lee c Giles b Hoggard	6		
G. D. McGrath c Strauss b Hoggard	0		
S. W. Tait not out	1		
B 4, l-b 8, w 2, n-b 9	23	L-b 4	4

1-185 (1) 2-264 (3) 3-281 (4)   **367**   (no wkt)   **4**
4-323 (2) 5-329 (6) 6-356 (7) 7-359 (5)
8-363 (8) 9-363 (10) 10-367 (9)

First innings – Harmison 22–2–87–1; Hoggard 24.1–2–97–4; Flintoff 34–10–78–5; Giles 23–1–76–0; Collingwood 4–0–17–0.
Second innings – Harmison 0.4–0–0–0.

Toss won by England   UMPIRES B. F. Bowden and R. E. Koertzen
MAN OF THE MATCH K. P. Pietersen

Australia and the Rules of Waugh

S uch has been the Australians' dominance over the past 15 years that it is easy to forget what a poor state their cricket was in during the 1980s. There was a grim period between the decline of the Chappell teams of the 1970s and the emergence of Allan Border's Ashes-winning side in 1989 when *Wisden* was bemoaning "the parlous state of Australian cricket" and wondering whether, with West Indies such an overpowering force, the Ashes really was still the best show in town.

Many of Australia's problems in the 1980s were symptoms of that troubled period. Packerism had its most malign influence there – on behaviour, factionalism and interest in domestic cricket. The infamous underarm delivery bowled by Trevor Chappell to ensure that Australia won a one-day match against New Zealand in 1981 stands as a tawdry symbol of this period – winning seemed to be everything and, quite soon, Australia couldn't manage that. They were put to the sword by Gower's England in the Ashes series of 1985 and beaten again by Gatting's side in Australia in 1986–87.

"Writing of the Australian side that toured England in 1985," said Graeme Wright in his 1987 Notes, "my predecessor said he was 'not among those who maintain there is no such thing as a weak Australian side.' Has there ever been one as weak as that beaten by England this past winter?" Wright put the blame squarely on Packerism. "State sides once proud with great names are frequently bare of current Australian players caught up in the commercial whirlpool of international cricket, simply to satisfy the television mogul and his marketing minions."

With Australia – and of course England, too – being routinely beaten by the great West Indies side of the period, were the Ashes losing their lustre? That question was posed by Matthew Engel, then a humble contributor rather than editor, in 1989. "Every four years – immediately after leap year, the American presidential election and the quadrennial shellacking of English cricket by West Indies – the Australians arrive. Is that such a big deal any more?" In fact, he decided that the Ashes *did* retain their aura, despite Australia's fall from grace.

Lucky he did, because that was the year when the wheel turned – Australia, under Allan Border and inspired by the young Steve Waugh, regained the Ashes and hung on to them until 2005. A succession of great sides was built under Mark Taylor, Steve Waugh and Ricky Ponting, and by the end of the 1990s they were well-nigh unbeatable, revolutionising Test cricket with their speed of scoring and refusal to countenance draws – they notched up an extraordinary 16 wins in a row under the remarkable Waugh. The 2005 Ashes victory mattered so much because the Australians were so special, their dominance over England so complete. There was no longer any need to ask whether the Ashes were the brand leader; indeed, the danger now – especially with West Indies having fallen so low – was that it had cornered the market.   S. M.

AUSTRALIA V ENGLAND 1977   **The Centenary Test**
At Melbourne, March 12, 13, 14, 16, 17, 1977. Australia won by 45 runs.   Reg Hayter, 1978

An occasion of warmest reunion and nostalgia, the cricket continuously compelling, a result straining credulity. Hans Ebeling, former Australian Test bowler and the inspiration of it all, should have been christened Hans Andersen Ebeling. From Ebeling, a vice-president of the Melbourne Cricket Club, originated the suggestion to signalise 100 years of Test cricket by a match between England and Australia on the same ground – in 1877 the Richmond Police Paddock – on which David Gregory's team beat James Lillywhite's all-round professional England side.

A masterpiece of organisation resulted in an event which none fortunate enough to be present could forget. Arrangements were made for the England team visiting India to extend their tour to play an official Test in the same month as the 1877 Test, and invitations to attend as guests were sent to the 244 living cricketers who had played for Australia or England in the series. All but 26 of these were able to accept for an event unique in history.

The oldest Australian Test player present was the 87-year-old Jack Ryder. Even though suffering from near-blindness, the 84-year-old Percy Fender made the enervating air journey from Britain as the oldest English representative. He was accompanied by his grandson, Jeremy, who became his cricketing eyes. Poor health alone prevented E. J. (Tiger) Smith and Herbert Sutcliffe from travelling and, for the same reason, Frank Woolley could not leave Canada.

Of those who went to Melbourne, many told unusual stories. Colin McCool was marooned in his Queensland home by floods and had to be hauled up from his front lawn by helicopter for the airport. Jack Rutherford's train broke down and he finished the journey to the airport by taxi. Denis Compton – who else? – left his passport in a Cardiff hotel and, but for the early start to the pre-flight champagne party at London airport which enabled a good friend to test the speed limits on the M4, would have missed the plane.

Some ex-England players – Harold Larwood, Peter Loader, Tony Lock, Barry Knight, Frank Tyson – already lived in Australia and the Australian Neil Hawke flew home from England. The gradual gathering of all at the Hilton Hotel, 200 yards across the Jolimont Park from the Melbourne Oval, brought meetings and greetings of unabated happiness. Fittingly, this was also Melbourne's Mardi Gras, a week called Moomba, the Aboriginal word for "let's get together and have fun".

Greig called correctly to Greg Chappell's spin of the specially minted gold coin and chose for England to field first. Probably he felt apprehension about his batsmen facing Lillee while moisture remained in the pitch. The resolute fast-medium bowling of Willis, Old and Lever, helped by Underwood's customary left-handed accuracy and breathtakingly supported in the field, appeared to justify

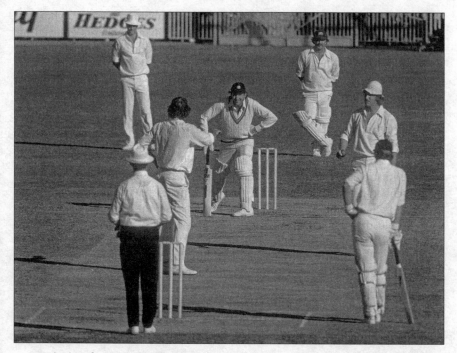

Enjoying the party: Derek Randall taunts Australia's spearhead Dennis Lillee
during the 1977 Centenary Test at Melbourne, the showpiece event staged
to mark 100 years of Test cricket.

Greig's decision in Australia's dismissal for 138 in front of a crowd of over 61,000.
Australia, handicapped by the early departure of McCosker, who fractured his jaw
when a ball from Willis flew off his hand into his face, were always on the defensive. But England's batting buckled even more swiftly against Lillee, at the zenith
of his form and speed, and Walker – Australia's fielding being no whit inferior to
that of England.

That was the last of the bowling mastery. On the second, third and fourth days
Australia increased their first-innings lead of 43 so much that their declaration left
England 463 to win at 40 an hour. Marsh, who had already beaten Grout's record of
187 Test victims, added to his triumph by his first Test century against England, and
Walters joyfully rode his fortune in the manner that has charmed so many cricket
admirers of the cavalier approach to batsmanship. Yet the spotlight centred on the
21-year-old David Hookes, who won his place on the forthcoming tour to England
with an innings straight from the fount of youth. This 6ft 2in powerful left-handed
batsman, who had scored five centuries in 1976–77 Sheffield Shield cricket, strode to
the crease with a confidence even more apparent when he struck Greig for five fours
in an over – off, pull, cover, midwicket, cover. Then it was England's turn. And, in
the presence of the Queen and the Duke of Edinburgh – during an interval they
drove round the ground and were hugely acclaimed – royally did they apply themselves. Well as Amiss, Greig, Knott and Brearley batted, however, the innings to

remember was played by Randall, a jaunty, restless, bubbling character, whose 174 took England to the doorstep of victory. The Australian spectators enjoyed his approach as much as Indian crowds had done on the tour just finished.

Once, when Lillee tested him with a bouncer, he tennis-batted it to the midwicket fence with a speed and power that made many a rheumy eye turn to the master of the stroke, the watching Sir Donald Bradman. Words cannot recapture the joy of that moment. Another time, when Lillee bowled short, Randall ducked, rose, drew himself to his full 5ft 8in, doffed his cap and bowed politely. Then, felled by another bouncer, he gaily performed a reverse roll. This helped to maintain a friendly atmosphere in what, at all times, was a serious and fully competitive match.

The Australians responded. When Randall was 161, umpire Brooks gave him out, caught at the wicket. Immediately Marsh intimated that he had not completed the catch before dropping the ball. After consultation, the umpire called Randall back. Would that this spirit was always so! At the end of the game Randall was awarded the first prize of $1,600 as the Man of the Match. To be chosen ahead of the superb Lillee, whose colleagues chaired him from the field when he finished the match with an analysis of 11 for 165, was a feat indeed.

Some time after it was over, someone discovered that the result of the 226th Test between the two countries – victory by 45 runs – was identical, to the same side and to the very run, with that of the 1877 Test on the same ground. Hans Andersen Ebeling had even scripted the final curtain.

Australia v England, 1977 — The Centenary Test

At Melbourne, March, 12, 13, 14, 16, 17, 1977. Result: Australia won by 45 runs.

AUSTRALIA	*First innings*		*Second innings*	
I. C. Davis lbw b Lever	5	– c Knott b Greig		68
R. B. McCosker b Willis	4	– (10) c Greig b Old		25
G. J. Cosier c Fletcher b Lever	10	– (4) c Knott b Lever		4
*G. S. Chappell b Underwood	40	– (3) b Old		2
D. W. Hookes c Greig b Old	17	– (6) c Fletcher b Underwood		56
K. D. Walters c Greig b Willis	4	– (5) c Knott b Greig		66
†R. W. Marsh c Knott b Old	28	– not out		110
G. J. Gilmour c Greig b Old	4	– b Lever		16
K. J. O'Keeffe c Brearley b Underwood	0	– (2) c Willis b Old		14
D. K. Lillee not out	10	– (9) c Amiss b Old		25
M. H. N. Walker b Underwood	2	– not out		8
B 4, l-b 2, n-b 8	14	L-b 10, n-b 15		25

1-11 2-13 3-23 4-45 5-51   138   1-33 2-40 3-53 4-132 5-187   (9 wkts dec.) 419
6-102 7-114 8-117 9-136 10-138   6-244 7-277 8-353 9-407

First innings – Lever 12–1–36–2; Willis 8–0–33–2; Old 12–4–39–3; Underwood 11.6–2–16–3.
Second innings – Lever 21–1–95–2; Willis 22–0–91–0; Old 27.6–2–104–4; Underwood 12–2–38–1; Greig 14–3–66–2.

ENGLAND	First innings		Second innings
R. A. Woolmer c Chappell b Lillee	9	– lbw b Walker	12
J. M. Brearley c Hookes b Lillee	12	– lbw b Lillee	43
D. L. Underwood c Chappell b Walker	7	– (10) b Lillee	7
D. W. Randall c Marsh b Lillee	4	– (3) c Cosier b O'Keeffe	174
D. L. Amiss c O'Keeffe b Walker	4	– (4) b Chappell	64
K. W. R. Fletcher c Marsh b Walker	4	– (5) c Marsh b Lillee	1
*A. W. Greig b Walker	18	– (6) c Cosier b O'Keeffe	41
†A. P. E. Knott lbw b Lillee	15	– (7) lbw b Lillee	42
C. M. Old c Marsh b Lillee	3	– (8) c Chappell b Lillee	2
J. K. Lever c Marsh b Lillee	11	– (9) lbw b O'Keeffe	4
R. G. D. Willis not out	1	– not out	5
B 2, l-b 2, w 1, n-b 2	7	B 8, l-b 4, w 3, n-b 7	22

1-19 2-30 3-34 4-40 5-40   95   1-28 2-113 3-279 4-290 5-346   417
6-61 7-65 8-78 9-86 10-95   6-369 7-380 8-385 9-410 10-417

First innings – Lillee 13.3–2–26–6; Walker 15–3–54–4; O'Keeffe 1–0–4–0; Gilmour 5–3–4–0.
Second innings – Lillee 34.4–7–139–5; Walker 22–4–83–1; O'Keeffe 33–6–108–3; Gilmour 4–0–29–0; Chappell 16–7–29–1; Walters 3–2–7–0.

Toss won by England   UMPIRES T. F. Brooks and M. G. O'Connell

AUSTRALIA V NEW ZEALAND 1980–81   Henry Blofeld, 1982

To share in the second Australian season of double tours, New Zealand were able to choose a good side, at any rate on paper, even without Glenn Turner, their leading batsman, who could not be persuaded to make the visit. New Zealand arrived in Australia with reasonable hopes of success, especially in the one-day competition for the Benson and Hedges World Series Cup.

They had no complaints about the three-match Test series. In this they were well beaten, losing the first two Tests, in Brisbane and Perth, each in three days, with Australia's seam bowlers uncovering technical flaws in New Zealand's batsmen. New Zealand's main grievance concerned the one-day finals [these were decided on a best-of-five basis] in which they met Australia, India having been eliminated at the preliminary stage. New Zealand won the first of these games, in Sydney, quite comfortably. Two days later, in Melbourne, they lost the second when their batting let them down.

The third, also in Melbourne, produced two lamentable incidents, for which this particular Australian season will be long remembered. The first of them came when Greg Chappell, the outstanding player on either side and Australia's regular match-winner in this competition, was given not out to an appeal for a low, diving catch at mid-wicket by Snedden off Cairns. Australia, batting first, were 131 for one at the time with Chappell in his 50s. With the umpires, somewhat surprisingly, both claiming that they were looking for short runs rather than watching the ball, and therefore unable to give Chappell out, it was left to Chappell to accept Snedden's claim, strongly supported by Howarth, that he had made a clean catch. This he declined to do, though TV pictures showed that there was no question of the ball having been grounded. Chappell went on to make 90 and New Zealand were left with 236 to win.

The second, more far-reaching incident came when, with New Zealand needing six to tie off the last ball of the match, Greg Chappell instructed his brother, Trevor, to bowl an underarm sneak to McKechnie, the New Zealand No. 10, as an insurance against their getting them. Not surprisingly this prompted widespread charges of poor sportsmanship. The Australian Cricket Board, meeting by telephone hook-up, at once agreed that the playing conditions should be changed to prohibit the use of underarm bowling in the remaining matches of the competition. They also decided that, as no existing rule had been infringed, the Melbourne result, however regrettably achieved, must stand.

Mr P. L. Ridings, chairman of the Australian board, said his board "deplored Greg Chappell's action" and had "advised him of their strong feelings on the matter and of his responsibility as Australia's captain to uphold the spirit of the game at all times". Chappell said himself it was something he would not do again. Even the prime ministers of the two countries had things to say, Australia's Mr Malcolm Fraser claiming that Chappell had "made a serious mistake, contrary to the spirit of the game". New Zealand's Mr Robert Muldoon was more outspoken, describing the underarm delivery as "an act of cowardice". It was appropriate, he said, that the Australian team should have been dressed in yellow, a reference to the coloured strip favoured by Australia in these one-day matches.

Australia v New Zealand   **World Series Cup Final: Third Match**
At Melbourne, February 1, 1981. Australia won by six runs.

With New Zealand needing six runs to tie the match off the last ball, Trevor Chappell, instructed to do so by his brother and captain Greg, bowled McKechnie an underarm ball, which caused a furore that could haunt Australian-New Zealand cricket for a long time. Earlier in the day Greg Chappell, when on 52, had refused to walk when Snedden claimed what appeared to be a low but fair catch. Trevor Chappell came on to bowl the last over with 15 still needed and four wickets left. Hadlee straight drove the first ball for four and was lbw to the second. Smith then hit two twos before being bowled, swinging at the fifth ball, leaving New Zealand with six to tie off the now infamous underarm delivery.

Toss: Australia. **Australia 235-4** (50 overs) (G. M. Wood 72, G. S. Chappell 90, M. F. Kent 33);
New Zealand 229-8 (50 overs) (J. G. Wright 42, B. A. Edgar 102*; G. S. Chappell 3-43).

AUSTRALIA V ENGLAND 1982–83   John Woodcock, 1984

England's tour of Australia and, very briefly, New Zealand in the winter of 1982–83 had, for them, two redeeming features: one of the most exciting Test matches ever played, at Melbourne immediately after Christmas, resulted in an English victory, and despite some transparently poor umpiring England played the game in a good spirit. The Ashes, which England had held since 1977, were surrendered, Australia winning the Test series by two victories to one, and, in competition with Australia and New Zealand, England failed, really rather abjectly, to reach the final stages of the Benson and Hedges World Series Cup.

Once again fast bowling proved the decisive factor in the Test series. Although Dennis Lillee and Terry Alderman were injured in the first Test match and unable to play in the last four, Australia were still able to field much the stronger pace attack, Geoff Lawson, Jeff Thomson and Rodney Hogg all being faster and more consistently hostile than anything England could muster. England lost the Second and Third Tests easily enough to go to Melbourne for the Fourth, which they won, in some disarray. Victory there was a great tonic, not only for Bob Willis and his side but for everyone associated with English cricket. Had John Dyson, one of Australia's opening batsmen, been given run out, as he palpably should have been, in the first over of the Fifth Test match, the series might even have been saved and the Ashes retained, though had that happened it would not have reflected Australia's undoubted superiority.

Australia v England	**Second Test**

At Brisbane, November 26, 27, 28, 30, December 1, 1982.
Australia won by seven wickets. John Woodcock, 1984

Batting failures in their first innings, which could not be blamed on the pitch, coupled with some wayward fast bowling, always left England struggling in a match full of incident. Australia, in spite of dropping eight catches in England's second innings, deserved their success, owing much to Wessels, who made a remarkable debut, and to Lawson, who finished with 11 wickets. Other features included a warning to Thomson for intimidatory bowling, and to Willis, Lawson (twice) and Cowans for running through on to the pitch. Crumbling footholds, especially at the Vulture Street End, were partially blamed for this, as they were for the 84 no-balls bowled in the match, this figure including those that were scored off.

Toss: Australia. **England 219** (A. J. Lamb 72, I. T. Botham 40, D. W. Randall 37; G. F. Lawson 6-47) **and 309** (G. Fowler 83, D. I. Gower 34, G. Miller 60, Extras 52; G. F. Lawson 5-87, J. R. Thomson 5-73); **Australia 341** (K. C. Wessels 162, G. S. Chappell 53, B. Yardley 53; R. G. D. Willis 5-66, I. T. Botham 3-105) **and 190-3** (K. C. Wessels 46, K. J. Hughes 39*, D. W. Hookes 66*).

Australia v England	**Third Test**

At Adelaide, December 10, 11, 12, 14, 15, 1982. Australia won by eight wickets. John Woodcock, 1984

For the second time in a fortnight England could find no adequate answer to the Australian fast bowling. With Rackemann not recovered from the groin strain which he suffered in the Second Test, and Lillee and Alderman still unfit, Lawson and Thomson were partnered now by Hogg, playing in his first Test match for nearly 18 months. Hogg's speed and hostility, no less than Lawson's and Thomson's, came as a nasty shock to England's batsmen. Between them these three took 17 wickets in the match, Lawson bringing his tally from the first three Tests to 26.

Toss: England. **Australia 438** (K. C. Wessels 44, J. Dyson 44, G. S. Chappell 115, K. J. Hughes 88, D. W. Hookes 37, B. Yardley 38; I. T. Botham 4-112) **and 83-2** (J. Dyson 37*); **England 216** (D. I. Gower 60, A. J. Lamb 82, I. T. Botham 35; G. F. Lawson 4-56, J. R. Thomson 3-51) **and 304** (G. Fowler 37, D. I. Gower 114, I. T. Botham 58, Extras 31; G. F. Lawson 5-66).

Australia v England   Fourth Test
At Melbourne, December 26, 27, 28, 29, 30, 1982. England won by three runs.   John Woodcock, 1984

A magnificent Test match, to be ranked among the best ever played, produced a finish of such protracted excitement that it had the whole of Australia by the ears. Needing 292 to win, Australia were 218 for nine when Border and Thomson embarked on a last-wicket partnership of epic proportions. At close of play on the fourth day they had taken the score to 255 for nine, leaving another 37 runs to be found on the last morning for Australia, there and then, to regain the Ashes.

Although, on this last day, the match could have been over within moments, 18,000 spectators, admitted free of charge, went to the Melbourne Cricket Ground in the hope of seeing Border and Thomson achieve their improbable goal. All things considered, among them a new ball taken at 259 for nine, Thomson was rarely in trouble; Border never was. By the time Botham began the 18th over of the morning Australia were within four runs of victory. His first ball was short of a length and wide of the off stump. Thomson, sparring at it, edged a none-too-difficult catch to Tavaré, the second of Botham's two slips. Tavaré managed only to parry it, the ball bouncing away behind him but within reach of Miller, fielding at first slip, deeper than Tavaré. With a couple of quick strides Miller reached the catch and completed it, the ball still some 18 inches off the ground.

No one who played in the game or watched it, or who saw it on television, or who listened to it on the radio, many of them from halfway across the world, could have been left unmoved. In terms of runs, the only closer Test match ever played was the Brisbane tie between Australia and West Indies in 1960–61. In 1902, at Old Trafford, the margin between England and Australia was also three runs, on that occasion in Australia's favour.

For the first time in a Test match, Melbourne's huge video scoreboard was in operation, the screen being used to show action replays and advertisements as well as the score and other sundry details. It was, on the whole, well received, although Willis remarked after the match that there had been occasions when, needing to know the score, he found himself looking instead at a picture of a motor car or a meat pie.

Australia v England, 1982–83   Fourth Test
At Melbourne, December 26, 27, 28, 29, 30, 1982. Result: England won by three runs.

ENGLAND	First innings		Second innings	
G. Cook c Chappell b Thomson	10	–	c Yardley b Thomson	26
G. Fowler c Chappell b Hogg	4	–	b Hogg	65
C. J. Tavare c Yardley b Thomson	89	–	b Hogg	0
D. I. Gower c Marsh b Hogg	18	–	c Marsh b Lawson	3
A. J. Lamb c Dyson b Yardley	83	–	c Marsh b Hogg	26
I. T. Botham c Wessels b Yardley	27	–	c Chappell b Thomson	46
G. Miller c Border b Yardley	10	–	lbw b Lawson	14
D. R. Pringle c Wessels b Hogg	9	–	c Marsh b Lawson	42
†R. W. Taylor c Marsh b Yardley	1	–	lbw b Thomson	37
*R. G. D. Willis not out	6	–	not out	8
N. G. Cowans c Lawson b Hogg	3	–	b Lawson	10
B 3, l-b 6, w 3, n-b 12	24		B 2, l-b 9, n-b 6	17
1-11 2-25 3-56 4-217 5-227	**284**		1-40 2-41 3-45 4-128 5-129	**294**
6-259 7-262 8-268 9-278 10-284			6-160 7-201 8-262 9-280 10-294	

First innings – Lawson 17–6–48–0; Hogg 23.3–6–69–4; Yardley 27–9–89–4; Thomson 13–2–49–2; Chappell 1–0–5–0.
Second innings – Lawson 21.4–6–66–4; Hogg 22–5–64–3; Yardley 15–2–67–0; Thomson 21–3–74–3; Chappell 1–0–6–0.

AUSTRALIA	First innings		Second innings	
K. C. Wessels b Willis	47	–	b Cowans	14
J. Dyson lbw b Cowans	21	–	c Tavare b Botham	31
*G. S. Chappell c Lamb b Cowans	0	–	c sub (I. J. Gould) b Cowans	2
K. J. Hughes b Willis	66	–	c Taylor b Miller	48
A. R. Border b Botham	2	–	(6) not out	62
D. W. Hookes c Taylor b Pringle	53	–	(5) c Willis b Cowans	68
†R. W. Marsh b Willis	53	–	lbw b Cowans	13
B. Yardley b Miller	9	–	b Cowans	0
G. F. Lawson c Fowler b Miller	0	–	c Cowans b Pringle	7
R. M. Hogg not out	8	–	lbw b Cowans	4
J. R. Thomson b Miller	1	–	c Miller b Botham	21
L-b 8, n-b 19	27		B 5, l-b 9, w 1, n-b 3	18
1-55 2-55 3-83 4-89 5-180	**287**		1-37 2-39 3-71 4-171 5-173	**288**
6-261 7-276 8-276 9-278 10-287			6-190 7-190 8-202 9-218 10-288	

First innings – Willis 15–2–38–3; Botham 18–3–69–1; Cowans 16–0–69–2; Pringle 15–2–40–1; Miller 15–5–44–3.
Second innings – Willis 17–0–57–0; Botham 25.1–4–80–2; Cowans 26–6–77–6; Pringle 12–4–26–1; Miller 16–6–30–1.

Toss won by Australia   UMPIRES A. R. Crafter and R. V. Whitehead

A draw in the Fifth and final Test at Sydney ensured that Australia won the series 2–1, and thus regained the Ashes which they had lost in England in 1977.

WEST INDIES V AUSTRALIA 1984 — Tony Cozier, 1985

Australia's fifth tour of the West Indies, their first since 1978 when their team was much weakened by the absence of players contracted to World Series Cricket, was a disastrous one. They were comprehensively beaten in the last three Tests, after just managing to hold out for draws in the first two, and lost the one-day internationals 3–1. They also lost friends through a number of unsavoury incidents. An outstanding West Indies team started the series immediately after returning from highly successful visits to India and Australia. Australia, on the other hand, were badly affected by the absence of leading players and injuries at crucial periods.

The retirement from international cricket just prior to the tour of Greg Chappell, Lillee and Marsh had an individual effect on each department of the team as well as the obvious repercussions. What is more, the left-handed Graham Yallop, Australia's leading scorer in the preceding series against Pakistan, was kept at home by a knee injury. Against a team described by their captain, Kim Hughes, at the end of the tour as "the strongest, most professional and most disciplined" he has played against, Australia needed to be at full strength. As it was, they were outplayed in every department of the game, sometimes embarrassingly so. West Indies went through the five Tests without losing a single second-innings wicket, and only the loss of significant amounts of play to the weather denied them victories in the first two Tests. Only once were they dismissed for fewer than 300, they passed 500 once and 450 twice; and five of their batsmen had centuries, two by one of the younger players, Richie Richardson.

Australia, on the other hand, totalled 300 only once while falling for 200 or under four times, including the lowest total over recorded in a Test in Bridgetown, 97, as they collapsed to defeat in the Third Test. Only one of their batsmen, the left-handed Allan Border, found the spirit and technique necessary to score consistently against the strong West Indian bowling, dominated, as usual, by pace. He was top-scorer in half his ten Test innings, scored more than twice as many as anyone else in the team, and averaged nearly three times as many. His 98 and 100 in the Second Test, both undefeated were innings of the utmost courage.

West Indies v Australia — Second Test
At Port-of-Spain. March 16, 17, 18, 20, 21, 1984. Drawn. — Tony Cozier, 1985

Two epic innings by Border stood between Australia and defeat. His undefeated 98 in the first innings lasted five hours 49 minutes, his undefeated century in the second another four and three-quarter hours. He offered not a single chance although batting, each time, under great pressure.

Border received crucial assistance in Australia's cause from other sources. The weather accounted for the equivalent of almost a full day, and finally the tailenders, Hogg and then Alderman, batted with him for the last 160 minutes to frustrate their opponents. In addition, Garner, West Indies' most penetrative bowler, was off the field for half the last day with stomach cramps.

Richards, leading the team in place of the injured Lloyd (pulled hamstring), sent Australia in on a well-grassed pitch; and by the time rain halted play at lunch on the first day, Garner had taken four wickets and Australia were 55 for four. Garner added a fifth early next day, but Jones, in his first Test, helped Border prevent a complete rout with a century stand. Border was denied his century when he was held scoreless on 98 for 12 deliveries, ten from Garner, while the last two wickets fell.

With the early moisture out of the pitch, West Indies took a sizeable first-innings lead through two partnerships of brilliant strokeplay. Richards and Logie added 100, then Dujon, from 187 balls, scored 130 runs by exquisite batting which featured two sixes (hooks off successive balls from Hogg) and 15 fours. Logie, a last-minute replacement for Lloyd, was Dujon's partner while 158 were added, but he fell three short of his century after an unsteady period in the 90s.

Richards's declaration left his bowlers just over an hour of the fourth day and all of the fifth to win the match. Australia entered the last day 55 for three and were all but beaten when their eighth wicket fell 55 minutes before tea, still 17 in arrears. By now, however, Garner was off the field, Richards delayed taking the new ball for 10.2 overs, and Border and his last two partners clung on to deny West Indies a victory which had appeared theirs. Hogg stayed for 55 minutes, and Alderman, whose previous highest Test score was 12, had been batting for 95 minutes when Border reached his century by hitting the last ball of the match to the boundary.

Toss: West Indies. **Australia 255** (A. R. Border 98*, D. M. Jones 48; J. Garner 6-60, W. W. Daniel 3-40) **and 299-9** (K. J. Hughes 33, T. G. Hogan 38, A. R. Border 100*); **West Indies 468-8 dec.** (D. L. Haynes 53, I. V. A. Richards 76, A. L. Logie 97, P. J. L. Dujon 130).

West Indies v Australia   **Third Test**
At Bridgetown, March 30, 31, April 1, 3, 4, 1984. West Indies won by ten wickets.   Tony Cozier, 1985

After scoring their highest total of the series, Australia collapsed limply in their second innings to be all out for the lowest total ever recorded in a Test at Kensington Oval. As late as lunch on the fourth day, neither team had gained a first-innings lead; by lunch on the fifth, the match was over.

Lloyd, returning to the team after injury, followed the recent trend by sending Australia in after winning the toss, but the pitch proved less lively than anticipated, a fact emphasised when he introduced Harper's off-spin before lunch on the opening day. Australia did not make the most of it, nor of a second-wicket stand of 103 between the solid Wood and the adventurous Ritchie. By close of play they were 227 for five, which was extended to 429 as the night-watchman, Hogan, contributed an important 40 and Phillips an uncompromising 120 in 197 balls (four sixes, 14 fours). Phillips was 40 when Hogg joined him, but the West Indians allowed an unusual number of chances to escape them.

Greenidge, dropped early on the third day when 24, and Haynes launched West Indies' reply with a stand of 132 before Greenidge was run out by Smith, whereupon Haynes and Richardson put together a further 145. However, their progress was laboured and West Indies went into the rest day still 128 behind with three wickets down after Haynes and Richards had been bowled with the second new ball in the final hour.

Richardson, who retained his place in the team only after Logie was stricken by 'flu on the eve of the match, was dropped in the gully off Hogg when 37 but proceeded solidly to his first Test century. It was Lloyd, however, who changed the tempo of the match with a brilliant 76 including three sixes and eight fours. Richardson's unbeaten 131 took him seven hours 49 minutes.

Behind by 80 on the first innings, Australia then lost four second-innings wickets for 68 by the end of the fourth day and were undermined on the final morning by magnificent bowling from Marshall (three for 18) and Holding (three for nine from seven overs). The last six wickets fell for 29 in an hour and a quarter, leaving Greenidge and Haynes the formality of scoring 18 to win.

Toss: West Indies. **Australia 429** (G. M. Wood 68, G. M. Ritchie 57, A. R. Border 38, D. W. Hookes 30, T. G. Hogan 40, W. B. Phillips 120, Extras 31; J. Garner 3-110) **and 97** (M. D. Marshall 5-42, M. A. Holding 4-24); **West Indies 509** (C. G. Greenidge 64, D. L. Haynes 145, R. B. Richardson 131*, C. H. Lloyd 76, Extras 36; R. M. Hogg 6-77) **and 21-0.**

West Indies v Australia   Fourth Test
At St John's, Antigua, April 7, 8, 9, 11, 1984.
West Indies won by an innings and 36 runs.   Tony Cozier, 1985

The Australians entered the match only three days after their depressing defeat in Barbados and their problems were compounded by injuries to Wood (broken finger) and Hogg (strained Achilles' tendon) which kept them out of the match. This meant a third pair of openers for the series in Phillips and Ritchie – the latter was unaccustomed to the position – and both fell soon after Hughes had won the toss for the first time in the series.

So it was left to Border again to prop up the first innings with a typically fighting 98. West Indies then accumulated their third successive total in excess of 450, Richards and Richardson making their hometown crowd ecstatic with individual centuries. They put on more in their third-wicket record for West Indies against Australia (308) than Australia totalled in either innings. While Richardson was lucky to survive a straightforward catch to the wicket-keeper off Lawson when 38, Richards offered nothing but a broad bat, striking 30 fours in the highest score yet recorded in a Test at the Recreation Ground. Both were victims of Rackemann, who bowled 27 consecutive overs on the third day and never flagged.

On the fourth day, the Australian batsmen could find neither the spirit nor the technique to cope with their formidable task: the largest contribution to the innings came from 36 extras. Garner and Marshall, who took his 100th and

101st Test wickets by dismissing Woolley and Maguire with successive balls, routed them.

Toss: Australia. **Australia 262** (A. R. Border 98, D. W. Hookes 51; M. A. Holding 3-42,
E. A. E. Baptiste 3-42) **and 200** (Extras 36; M. D. Marshall 3-51, J. Garner 5-63); **West Indies 498**
(R. B. Richardson 154, I. V. A. Richards 178, C. H. Lloyd 38; C. G. Rackemann 5-161,
J. N. Maguire 3-121).

INDIA V AUSTRALIA 1984 Mike Coward, 1986

It took some time for the full relevance of Australia's brief goodwill tour of India, to play a series of one-day internationals, to become apparent. In the end, what started as a public relations exercise to help the Indian authorities celebrate the Golden Jubilee of the Ranji Trophy had a considerable impact on Australian cricket.

From a cricketing standpoint, it was a most successful undertaking. Australia won the five-match series three-nil – the matches at Trivandrum and Jamshedpur were abandoned after rain – which was a considerable achievement after India's success in the World Cup the previous year. However, with the benefit of hindsight, Australia's first success in such a series on the subcontinent can be seen to have been the least significant happening. While he had personal success, Kim Hughes lost support within his team and within a few weeks had resigned the Australian captaincy. The Indian excursion culminated with a gala dinner in Bombay, a priceless moment in the history of Indian cricket, and on their way home several of the Australian players had their first significant contact with representatives of the South African Cricket Union. Clandestine discussions with organisers of rebel teams took place in Singapore, leading in April 1985 to another major crisis for Australia's cricketing authorities.

THE PARLOUS STATE OF
AUSTRALIAN CRICKET Graeme Wright, *Notes by the Editor*, 1987

Writing of the Australian side that toured England in 1985, my predecessor said he was "not among those who maintain there is no such thing as a weak Australian side." Has there ever been one as weak as that beaten by England this past winter?

Yet there are players with the potential to be good. What is missing, it seems, is the tempering of that potential before it is exposed to international cricket. The place for that is not in the succession of airport terminals and one-day internationals through which the leading Australian cricketers pass each season. It is in a healthy domestic first-class competition.

In 1985–86 the Australian selectors called 24 players to the colours. It is worth a glance at the Sheffield Shield matches which appear later in the Almanack. State sides once proud with great names are frequently bare of current Australian players caught up in the commercial whirlpool of international cricket, simply to satisfy the television mogul and his marketing minions. It was understandable that New Zealand, rather than compete for the prize money at the junket in Perth, chose instead to keep their Test men at home, strengthening their domestic competition so that younger players might profit from the experience of playing with and against them.

The loss of experienced players to South Africa did not help Australia's cause either. In improving the earning power of its top players, Mr Packer, the poacher turned gamekeeper, failed to take into account that while many may be called, only 11 are chosen: and that in a land where the dollar and success are the goal-posts, those not chosen would become all too easy prey to the hand with the rand. Yet if the Australians continue to flounder, interest will fall away, not only at the grounds but also in the viewing figures. Even interest in one-day cricket will fall off if Australia are beaten regularly by the likes of New Zealand or India or Sri Lanka. The Australian Cricket Board already is concerned at the standard of the game there, but those who market it might do well to look at their investment if they see cricket as a continuing commodity. There are those, of course, who would like to see the marketing men run even before they cut their losses.

THE SECOND TIED TEST (India v Australia, Madras, September 1986)

See page 432

ENGLAND v AUSTRALIA – THE BRAND LEADER?   Matthew Engel, 1989

The first Australian team to visit England after the war was welcomed in the 1948 *Wisden* by the writer, Vivian Jenkins, who described the Test matches between the two nations as an ever-recurring wonder that stirs the blood of each succeeding generation as they see it come to light anew. Jenkins's generation had just suffered a conflict infinitely more important than any game, and there was indeed a sense of wonder about the renewal of cricket. The Editor's Notes in that volume, refer-ring to the 1947 season, were headed "A Wonderful Season" and the sub-headings included the phrases "Bowlers of Many Types", "Batsmen Excel", "Close Finishes" and "Great Crowds". Despite the present editor's best intentions, the 1989 edition is inevitably a little less upbeat.

This is, in part, the penalty for more than 40 years of peace. Sport has fallen into a routine. Every four years – immediately after leap year, the American pres-idential election and the quadrennial shellacking of English cricket by West Indies – the Australians arrive. Is that such a big deal any more?

Modern cricket, professional and problematical, cannot recapture the delight people felt in the late 1940s simply in being alive and, incidentally, involved in the game again. We have come to take the good things in life for granted. Players and journalists secretly rejoice when a tour is cancelled because it gives them a break from Test matches. Meanwhile, cricket has become a competing brand name in the leisure industry; it has to be sponsored, marketed and packaged for television.

England v Australia is a product. And if it remains the brand leader, it is hard to pretend that is anything to do with superior quality. It is highly improbable that the Test series this summer will be won by the world's best cricket team. If *Which?* magazine was conducting a survey, it would probably rate India against New Zealand a better buy. And yet. Ad-men understand better than anybody the importance of mystique, and in cricket we are absolute suckers for it. Somehow this spring is a little different from last spring, the one before and the one before that. The first grass cuttings smell just a mite sweeter; the tang of anticipation is that tiny bit keener. The Ashes are at stake. In spite of everything, England v Australia is an ever-recurring wonder, even in 1989.

But if it is to stay that way, we perhaps ought to understand the phenomenon a little better. It is probably 28 years since the two teams met as the best cricket teams on earth. Even so, there have been a stack of series and individual games since then that have stirred the blood in a way no other contest could have. Part of this is because, somehow, England and Australia understand each other's cricket. Thinking about this, I wondered whether this might be something to do with the unfashionable concept of kith 'n' kin. But it is not. That rapport is never there with the New Zealanders. Lovely people, of course – but on a tour of New Zealand it soon becomes clear that everyone there would be far more interested if you were playing rugby or, worse, a best-of-50 one-day series. With England and Australia, there is a shared instinct. For more than a century, cricket's founder-nations have managed to rub along together. The relationship has often been terse, even gruff, because both countries prefer it that way. But when problems have arisen – Bodyline, the chuckers and drag artists of the fifties, even the Packer intervention – they have been settled in the end with a mutual regard and sympathy.

It happens that in the 1980s there has been a great deal of personal friendship between the dressing-rooms. This is partly a reaction to the sledging 1970s, and partly due to the personal qualities of the leading players of the era, Allan Border in particular. We have grown used to the sight of Australia's captain playing for Essex, though it would have been inconceivable for his predecessors. On the whole, I am inclined to think that it is a precedent which ought not to be encouraged. This is nothing to do with the desperate theory that England's prospects of winning Test matches are being ruined by the small number of overseas players now allowed to appear in county cricket. It is everything to do with the freshness that Australians still bring to every fourth English summer.

Dean Jones, who was established as one of the world's leading players until he lost form in 1988, is still only a rumour to most English cricket-watchers. Ditto Bruce Reid. One feels that the appeal of the West Indians, for instance, would have been infinitely greater through the 1980s if the sight of Richards and Marshall had been rationed, instead of being on offer seven days a week, summer after summer, to those who bothered to turn up at Taunton and Southampton.

Australian touring teams really do arrive still, unlike Indians and West Indians who sort of coalesce over the course of a few days from exotic winter quarters in places like Oldham. Even with the Aussies, it is not quite the same as in the old days, when the liner would dock at Tilbury, and Woodfull or Bradman would stand on a windswept quayside in a full-length macintosh and make a brief but graceful speech (having had a month on board for preparation, with only formal dinners and deck quoits as distractions) about making friends, playing bright cricket and winning the series.

Nowadays, the players arrive at Heathrow, shortly after finishing their latest set of utterly forgettable one-day internationals against somebody or other. They will be driven to a hotel in central London and troop into a function room, probably with chandeliers. The team will be green-blazered, bleary-eyed, unshaven; if precedent is followed exactly, one or two may be suffering from very severe hangovers indeed. The captain will then make a brief but graceful speech about making friends, playing bright cricket and winning the series.

It is not necessary for anyone to believe this, even the captain. After all, in the past 25 years, Australia have won only one series in Britain – on the hastily arranged tour of 1975. However, he is probably being utterly insincere only if he says he intends to win all the county matches as well. The Australian tour, alone of them all, still retains a sense of occasion outside the Test matches; it remains an event when the team arrives in Northampton or Southampton. It would be an event in Hove or Canterbury, too, but this year Kent and Sussex are likely to get a fixture only by being knocked out of the NatWest Bank Trophy before the semi-finals, which is not something they are going to contrive on purpose. Among spectators, the enthusiasm remains; but it represents the triumph of hope and folk-memory over recent experience. The 1977, 1981 and 1985 Australians played 42 first-class matches between them outside the Tests and drew 31 of them. The last two visiting teams were unbeaten in first-class matches outside the Tests, just as the 1953 team was. It would be nice to see this as a tribute to their strength. Unfortunately, it has more to do with a truncated fixture list, appalling weather and pathetic attitudes on the part of both touring teams and counties.

I hereby propose a minor amendment to either the Laws of the Game or the tour conditions, to apply to (a) any touring captain who says he would have declared but thought that so-and-so needed the batting practice, and (b) any county captain who, on the first morning of the tourists' game, suddenly discovers that all his adult fast bowlers and front-line batsmen happen to have hay fever or groin stains; viz., that they should be taken at once to the traditional beneficiary's barbecue and served up roasted whole with the jacket potatoes.

However, these are the 1980s. If something is to be done, it will probably require a form of sponsorship. An attempt was made a decade ago, with an improbable £100,000 jackpot offered to the touring team if they won every county match. The 1980 West Indians actually got almost halfway – five wins out of 11 – towards scooping the pool before being confounded by that very wet summer. It seems to me that something similar may have to be devised again, this time with an equally juicy bone for the counties to gnaw.

Occasionally, a classic match still happens. For the opening game of first-class cricket on the 1985 tour, the Australians went to Taunton and there were 507 runs on the first day, a marvellous duel between Botham and the visiting attack, and then a burst of fast bowling from Jeff Thomson which implied that he and his team were ready to storm through the summer. It was an illusion, in various ways; but the tour as a whole was unforgettable none the less. One way or another, it always is. Pray heaven it always will be.

ENGLAND V AUSTRALIA 1989 — John Thicknesse, 1990

Allan Border could hardly have dared hope for a more triumphant fourth tour of England, and second as captain, than the one that unfolded in 1989. Arriving with a record which, though markedly better than England's since the 1985 tour – five wins and nine defeats in 30 Tests compared with their hosts' three and 15 in 34 – was still far from satisfactory for one of the co-founders of the Test game, Australia gained such confidence from winning the First Test that when the series ended they had a right to consideration as the next strongest to West Indies in the world.

It was an extraordinary transformation which stemmed from a variety of factors. Among them was the Australians' remarkable freedom from injuries, and the hottest, driest English summer since 1976, which at times not only encouraged the illusion they were playing in Adelaide or Perth but also provided constant match-play. There was no doubt, however, that the biggest factor, by a distance, was the single-minded hunger for success implanted by the leadership.

Border had had neither a successful nor conspicuously happy time as captain since the job was thrust on him by the resignation of Kim Hughes in 1984. He had won only one series out of eight; and even that, against New Zealand in 1987–88, had been in unconvincing circumstances. But his commitment was undiminished, and in the coach, 53-year-old former captain R. B. Simpson, he had a kindred spirit. Like Border, Bob Simpson had been a batsman of enviable natural ability, who by determination and application had become one of the most feared and prolific of his day. Relieving England of the Ashes would have been high on both men's lists of life's priorities; and when the chance was there they grabbed it.

England v Australia — First Test

At Leeds, June 8, 9, 10, 12, 13, 1989. Australia won by 210 runs. — John Callaghan, 1990

England's first match under the new management team headed by E. R. Dexter, and with Gower restored as captain, fell sadly into the sorry pattern of so much that had gone before in that they contributed significantly to their own downfall. It was their fourth successive defeat at Headingley, where the Australians had not won since 1964, and the outcome extended to nine the sequence of positive Test results on the ground.

Australia, very much the outsiders at the start, outplayed England to an embarrassing extent. England's plans were thrown into confusion by injuries to Botham and Gatting. More important were two major errors of judgment by Gower and his advisers. In the first place they left out the spinner, Emburey, so that the attack was desperately short of variety; and, ignoring the groundsman's advice, they then elected to give Australia first use of an excellent pitch. The match was staged on the traditional Test strip, which had been relaid by Keith Boyce, the Headingley groundsman, and although lacking in bounce, so that the occasional delivery kept low, the pitch hardly encouraged the quicker bowlers. The decision to field first was apparently based on the theory that a build-up of cloud might allow movement through the air. In fact it was much too cold and the ball behaved predictably in every way.

All the England seamers persistently bowled short and wide, offering easy runs, and no matter how he juggled his resources, Gower could not change the bowling. This remained undemanding medium-pace so long as any of his specialists were in action. Equally neither Gooch nor Barnett, with his rather rusty leg-spin, challenged the batsmen's authority, and Gower quickly discovered that his reappointment as captain brought with it many familiar problems. Taylor laid the foundations for a massive Australian total with a solid, patient innings. Missed by Gower at slip off DeFreitas when 89, he went on to occupy the crease for 393 minutes while receiving 315 balls and hitting 16 boundaries. Border provided the necessary acceleration before Jones and Waugh shared in the decisive partnership, adding 138 in 31 overs and breaking the back of the English resistance.

Wearing a cap instead of the familiar helmet, Waugh reminded many spectators of a bygone age, despatching the ball stylishly through the gaps and timing his forcing strokes so well that he brought an effortless quality to the proceedings. His unbeaten 177 came in 309 minutes from 242 deliveries and included 24 fours, many of them driven gloriously off the back foot through the off side in the textbook manner. Against this onslaught, only Foster came close to achieving the essential accuracy in terms of length and line.

Lamb held the England innings together with a typical effort in the course of which he savaged anything the least bit short. His 125 involved 205 deliveries in 279 minutes and included 24 fours. However, there was a distinct warning-note in the collapse which followed his departure. England's last six wickets fell for 107 in 31 overs and Australia, left with a lead of 171, now looked to put the match out of England's reach while at the same time giving their bowlers scope to bowl England out a second time. For their part, England needed to bowl tightly and field keenly to put them under pressure. Instead they again fell into error, allowing Australia to maintain a run-rate of four an over without recourse to the unorthodox. Border was able to declare next morning and set England a remote target of 402 for victory.

The more interesting part of the equation, though, related to the minimum 83 overs which were available for the Australian bowlers to dismiss England. In theory, their prospects of success should have been no brighter than the England batsmen's of surviving, but so feeble was England's response to this challenge that Australia had 27 overs to spare in completing their task. Only Gooch, battling through 176 minutes to make 68 from 118 balls, caused Border to worry. Barnett shared in a partnership worth 50 and Gower in one which added 57, both in 12 overs, but England for the most part found the straight ball unplayable.

Gower was caught down the leg side, glancing, as the Australians set a very obvious trap. In many ways that one incident summed up the difference between the two teams. Australia had done their homework and knew exactly what they were trying to do, whereas England lived more in hope than expectation. Alderman finished with match figures of ten for 151 – his best in Test cricket. And as Taylor and Waugh also completed their first centuries at the highest level, Australia collectively and individually claimed all the honours.

England v Australia, 1989 — First Test

At Leeds, June 8, 9, 10, 12, 13, 1989. Result: Australia won by 210 runs.

AUSTRALIA

	First innings		Second innings
G. R. Marsh lbw b DeFreitas	16	– c Russell b Foster	6
M. A. Taylor lbw b Foster	136	– c Broad b Pringle	60
D. C. Boon c Russell b Foster	9	– lbw b DeFreitas	43
*A. R. Border c Foster b DeFreitas	66	– not out	60
D. M. Jones c Russell b Newport	79	– not out	40
S. R. Waugh not out	177		
†I. A. Healy c and b Newport	16		
M. G. Hughes c Russell b Foster	71		
G. F. Lawson not out	10		
L-b 13, w 1, n-b 7	21	B 2, l-b 5, w 9, n-b 5	21

1-44 2-57 3-174 4-273 5-411   (7 wkts dec.) 601   1-14 2-97 3-129   (3 wkts dec.) 230
6-441 7-588

G. D. Campbell and T. M. Alderman did not bat.

First innings – DeFreitas 45.3–8–140–2; Foster 46–14–109–3; Newport 39–5–153–2; Pringle 33–5–123–0; Gooch 9–1–31–0; Barnett 6–0–32–0.
Second innings – Foster 19–4–65–1; DeFreitas 18–2–76–1; Newport 5–2–22–0; Pringle 12.5–1–60–1.

ENGLAND

	First innings		Second innings
G. A. Gooch lbw b Alderman	13	– lbw b Hughes	68
B. C. Broad b Hughes	37	– lbw b Alderman	7
K. J. Barnett lbw b Alderman	80	– c Taylor b Alderman	34
A. J. Lamb c Boon b Alderman	125	– c Boon b Alderman	4
*D. I. Gower c Healy b Lawson	26	– c Healy b Lawson	34
R. A. Smith lbw b Alderman	66	– c Border b Lawson	0
D. R. Pringle lbw b Campbell	6	– c Border b Alderman	0
P. J. Newport c Boon b Lawson	36	– c Marsh b Alderman	8
†R. C. Russell c Marsh b Lawson	15	– c Healy b Hughes	2
P. A. J. DeFreitas lbw b Alderman	1	– b Hughes	21
N. A. Foster not out	2	– not out	1
B 5, l-b 7, w 1, n-b 10	23	B 4, l-b 3, n-b 5	12

1-35 2-81 3-195 4-243 5-323   430   1-17 2-67 3-77 4-134 5-134   191
6-338 7-392 8-421 9-424 10-430   6-153 7-153 8-166 9-170 10-191

First innings – Alderman 37–7–107–5; Lawson 34.5–6–105–3; Campbell 14–0–82–1; Hughes 28–7–92–1; Waugh 6–2–27–0; Border 2–1–5–0.
Second innings – Alderman 20–7–44–5; Lawson 11–2–58–2; Campbell 10–0–42–0; Hughes 9.2–0–36–3; Border 5–3–4–0.

Toss won by England   UMPIRES J. W. Holder and D. R. Shepherd

England v Australia

At Lord's, June 22, 23, 24, 26, 27, 1989. Australia won by six wickets.

Second Test

David Norrie, 1990

Victory not only gave Border's side a 2–0 lead, a position from which England had never come back to win or even draw an Ashes series, but continued the home side's dismal record at the game's headquarters this century against their oldest cricket rivals. England's sole success remained 1934; 21 other contests had brought Australia nine victories, with 12 draws.

The tourists confirmed their Headingley form, while England, again badly hit by injuries, took a different route to defeat. Gower's side struggled badly for three days before staging a spirited fightback which, with a little more help from the rain on Tuesday, would have earned them a reprieve. Gower, cast as the villain for rushing out of Saturday night's press conference to go to the theatre, was hailed as a hero on Monday for scoring his 15th Test century. But character and courage were not enough to repair the earlier damage and, despite the threat of lunchtime rain and then Foster's bowling, Waugh saw Australia through to a conclusive victory just after five o'clock on Tuesday.

Toss: England. **England 286** (G. A. Gooch 60, D. I. Gower 57, R. A. Smith 32, R. C. Russell 64*; T. M. Alderman 3-60, M. G. Hughes 4-71) **and 359** (D. I. Gower 106, R. A. Smith 96, J. E. Emburey 36*; T. M. Alderman 6-128); **Australia 528** (M. A. Taylor 62, D. C. Boon 94, A. R. Border 35, S. R. Waugh 152*, M. G. Hughes 30, G. F. Lawson 74; N. A. Foster 3-129, J. E. Emburey 4-88) **and 119-4** (D. C. Boon 58*; N. A. Foster 3-39).

England v Australia

At Manchester, July 27, 28, 29, 31, August 1, 1989. Australia won by nine wickets.

Fourth Test

Don Mosey, 1990

Australia's win at Old Trafford gave them the series and the Ashes, and Border thus became the first captain since W. M. Woodfull in 1934 to win back the trophy in England. It was a success which was all the more noteworthy because few people in this country gave the tourists much chance of victory when their party was first announced. Paradoxically, England played more positively on the third and fifth days than they had at any stage of the series up to that point, and centuries were scored by Smith, on his return after injury, and Russell who, apart from keeping wicket immaculately and at times spectacularly, registered a maiden first-class hundred, the fourth Englishman to do so in a Test match.

It was a game played not only beneath the familiar Manchester clouds but also others of an even more threatening nature hovering over Gower, the England captain. He had been the object of an increasingly virulent campaign in some newspapers since the first defeat of the series, and even the more sober and responsible journals had expressed disquiet at what seemed to be a lack of positive leadership. Gower's resignation after four Tests appeared to be unavoidable when salvation came from an unexpected quarter. On the final morning of the Test came formal confirmation that a party of 16 players would go to South Africa to play between January and March, thus effectively debarring themselves from playing international cricket for England for the next seven years.

Three of the players named were currently involved in the Fourth Test – Robinson, Emburey and Foster; a fourth, Dilley, had been selected to play but was unfit on the first morning. Five of the others – Gatting, Broad, Jarvis, DeFreitas and Barnett – had already played in the earlier Tests of 1989, and of the remaining seven, six were former internationals. Only Graveney, the Gloucestershire slow left-arm bowler, who was named as player-manager, had not won an England cap.

Toss: England. **England 260** (R. A. Smith 143, D. I. Gower 35, N. A. Foster 39; G. F. Lawson 6-72, T. V. Hohns 3-59) **and 264** (R. C. Russell 128*, J. E. Emburey 64; G. F. Lawson 3-81, T. M. Alderman 5-66); **Australia 447** (M. A. Taylor 85, G. R. Marsh 47, A. R. Border 80, D. M. Jones 69, S. R. Waugh 92; A. R. C. Fraser 3-95) **and 81-1** (M. A. Taylor 37*, G. R. Marsh 31).

England v Australia	**Fifth Test**
At Nottingham, August 10, 11, 12, 14, 1989.	
Australia won by an innings and 180 runs.	Martin Johnson, 1990

On a flat, grassless pitch expected to assist the spinners as the match wore on, England named both Cook and Hemmings in their final XI, and Cook it was who took the first Australian wicket. As it arrived at 12 minutes past 12 on the second day, this was not a matter for great rejoicing. Border, having won an important toss, had then spent the best part of four sessions joining in the applause as Marsh and Taylor went past numerous records in their opening partnership of 329.

The milestones (gravestones?) began just after lunch on the first day with the comparatively modest figure of 89 – Australia's previous highest opening partnership at Trent Bridge – and ended at 323, the highest by two openers in Ashes history, a record that had stood to Hobbs and Rhodes since 1911–12. Moreover, by stumps on Thursday, Marsh and Taylor had become the first pair to bat through a full day's play in a Test match in England, and only the ninth in Test cricket anywhere.

With the notable exception of Smith, there was not much consolation from the England batting. The first wicket went down after four deliveries (740 fewer than England had required to remove the first Australian), and when Atherton made a second-ball nought on his debut, Smith arrived for the start of the second over with the scoreboard reading one for two. His strokeplay, particularly around the off stump, was little short of ferocious. Hughes took a beating, and a pull off Hohns resulted in Boon, at short leg, literally having the helmet torn from his head. It was a miracle that he was helped off in need of nothing more than a couple of aspirin and a lie-down.

Smith's magnificent 150-ball century, bracketed alongside Waugh's unbeaten 177 at Headingley as among the great innings in England v Australia Tests, none the less stood alone amidst another familiarly depressing tale. Following on 347 in arrears on Monday morning, they were bowled out for 167 soon after tea.

Atherton, batting almost three hours for his 47, was the one batsman to make a half-decent fist of it. Only once before, to Bradman's 1948 side, had England lost four home Tests in an Ashes series, and the final ignominy for them in the statistical avalanche was the fact that an innings and 180 runs represented their heaviest defeat in England by Australia.

Toss: Australia. **Australia 602-6 dec.** (G. R. Marsh 138, M. A. Taylor 219, D. C. Boon 73, A. R. Border 65*, Extras 61; N. G. B. Cook 3-91); **England 255** (R. A. Smith 101, E. E. Hemmings 38, Extras 31; T. M. Alderman 5-69) **and 167** (M. A. Atherton 47, E. E. Hemmings 35; M. G. Hughes 3-46).

ENGLAND V AUSTRALIA 1993
John Thicknesse, 1994

Australia's third overwhelming Ashes victory in succession [they had beaten England 3–0 at home in the 1990–91 series] was as well merited as its predecessors in a series that ended Graham Gooch's reign as England captain and Ted Dexter's as chairman of the England committee. The course of the series – Allan Border leading his team to victory at Old Trafford, Lord's, Headingley and Edgbaston before The Oval brought England the consolation of their first win in 19 Tests against Australia – stemmed even more than usual from confidence. In England's case, it was the lack of it, following a tour of India and Sri Lanka on which they lost all four Tests and five one-day internationals out of eight. It was no surprise, then, that when Mike Atherton, taking over the captaincy from Gooch, led England to a big win at The Oval in his second match in charge, the change of fortune aroused relief as much as joy.

Annoying as it was for Australia to stumble at the final hurdle, defeat did no more than tarnish a fine all-round performance, in which 23-year-old leg-spinner Shane Warne played the starring role. Arriving in England after a well-fought series against West Indies in the southern summer, the tourists were into their stride with wins against Worcestershire and Somerset in their first two three-day games, took the Texaco Trophy 3–0, and were in control of the Cornhill series from the moment they won the First Test at Old Trafford by 179 runs. Such was their confidence that when Craig McDermott, their best fast bowler, was forced to fly home for treatment to a twisted bowel with four Tests still to play, it was decided not to send for a replacement. Merv Hughes, who took over McDermott's role as spearhead, shouldered the extra burden with a will that at times came close to heroism, though it was clearly a factor in England's Oval win; Hughes was visibly flagging in the final month. The management's refusal to reinforce the team was an effective means of assuring the remaining players that Border and the coach, Bob Simpson, had full faith in them to do the job.

Although Warne had two startling analyses to his credit in his 11 previous Tests, seven for 52 against West Indies and four for eight against New Zealand, his reputation before the tour was more that of a beach-boy than a budding Test-winner. His shock of dyed blond hair, earring and blobs of white sun-block on the tip of his nose and lower lip lent his appearance a deceptive air of amiability, which an expression of wide-eyed innocence enhanced. However, his incessant niggling of umpires and truculent questioning of unfavourable decisions made it obvious that the sunny exterior hid a graceless streak, which stopped him earning the unqualified respect of his opponents. In his hitherto unexplored method of attack, founded on ferociously spun leg-breaks, as often as not angled a foot or more outside the leg stump from round the wicket, he left no doubt that Australia had uncovered not only a match-winner of singular inventiveness but a cricketer crowds would flock to see.

Thanks to TV, Warne's first ball in Ashes cricket, which bowled Mike Gatting, may become the most famous ever bowled. It was flighted down the line of middle and leg, the fierceness of the spin causing it to swerve almost a foot in its last split-seconds in the air, so that it pitched six inches outside the leg stump. From there, it spun viciously past Gatting's half-formed forward stroke to hit the off stump within two inches of the top. It was unplayable and, by impressing the bowler's capacities on England, it had a profound impact on the series.

England v Australia   First Test
At Manchester, June 3, 4, 5, 6, 7, 1993. Australia won by 179 runs.   Pat Murphy, 1994

An enthralling match of splendid individual achievements was won by Australia with 9.4 overs to spare. A rarity among modern Tests in England, it was shaped by slow bowling and finally decided by leg-spin. Warne, the 23-year-old Victorian, returned match figures of eight for 137. One particular delivery from Warne set the tone for the series. His first ball in an Ashes contest pitched outside leg stump and hit the top of Gatting's off stump. Gatting looked understandably bewildered. Warne also produced a stunning catch at backward square leg to dismiss Caddick in the tense final stages.

Steve Waugh and Healy batted England out of the match with an unbroken stand of 180 in 164 minutes. Healy became the first Australian to make his maiden first-class century in a Test since H. Graham, exactly a hundred years earlier, at Lord's. England were left to score 512 in a day and a half. Gooch and Atherton again batted securely, with the captain notably authoritative. On the final morning he reached his 18th Test hundred and England had the chance of a draw. Yet half an hour after lunch Gooch became the fifth cricketer, and the first

Ball of the century: Mike Gatting is bamboozled by Shane Warne's first delivery in an Ashes Test, at Old Trafford in 1993. Ian Healy, Australia's long-serving wicket-keeper, shows his delight.

Englishman, to be dismissed handled the ball in a Test as he instinctively flicked out with a glove at a ball dropping on to his stumps.

England v Australia, 1993

At Manchester, June 3, 4, 5, 6, 7, 1993. Result: Australia won by 179 runs.

AUSTRALIA	*First innings*		*Second innings*	
M. A. Taylor c and b Such	124	– lbw b Such	9
M. J. Slater c Stewart b DeFreitas	58	– c Caddick b Such	27
D. C. Boon c Lewis b Such	21	– c Gatting b DeFreitas	93
M. E. Waugh c and b Tufnell	6	– b Tufnell	64
*A. R. Border st Stewart b Such	17	– c and b Caddick	31
S. R. Waugh b Such	3	– not out	78
†I. A. Healy c Such b Tufnell	12	– not out	102
B. P. Julian c Gatting b Such	0		
M. G. Hughes c DeFreitas b Such	2		
S. K. Warne not out	15		
C. J. McDermott run out	8		
B 8, l-b 8, n-b 7	23	B 6, l-b 14, w 8	28

1-128 2-183 3-221 4-225 5-232   289   1-23 2-46 3-155 4-234 5-252   (5 wkts dec.) 432
6-260 7-264 8-266 9-267 10-289

First innings – Caddick 15–4–38–0; DeFreitas 23–8–46–1; Lewis 13–2–44–0; Such 33.3–9–67–6; Tufnell 28–5–78–2.
Second innings – Caddick 20–3–79–1; DeFreitas 24–1–80–1; Such 31–6–78–2; Tufnell 37–4–112–1; Hick 9–1–20–0; Lewis 9–0–43–0.

ENGLAND	*First innings*		*Second innings*	
*G. A. Gooch c Julian b Warne	65	– handled the ball	133
M. A. Atherton c Healy b Hughes	19	– c Taylor b Warne	25
M. W. Gatting b Warne	4	– b Hughes	23
R. A. Smith c Taylor b Warne	4	– b Warne	18
G. A. Hick c Border b Hughes	34	– c Healy b Hughes	22
†A. J. Stewart b Julian	27	– c Healy b Warne	11
C. C. Lewis c Boon b Hughes	9	– c Taylor b Warne	43
P. A. J. DeFreitas lbw b Julian	5	– lbw b Julian	7
A. R. Caddick c Healy b Warne	7	– c Warne b Hughes	25
P. M. Such not out	14	– c Border b Hughes	9
P. C. R. Tufnell c Healy b Hughes	1	– not out	0
B 6, l-b 10, n-b 5	21	L-b 11, w 1, n-b 4	16

1-71 2-80 3-84 4-123 5-148   210   1-73 2-133 3-171 4-223 5-230   332
6-168 7-178 8-183 9-203 10-210   6-238 7-260 8-299 9-331 10-332

First innings – McDermott 18–2–50–0; Hughes 20.5–5–59–4; Julian 11–2–30–2; Warne 24–10–51–4; Border 1–0–4–0.
Second innings – McDermott 30–9–76–0; Hughes 27.2–4–92–4; Warne 49–26–86–4; Julian 14–1–67–1.

Toss won by England   UMPIRES H. D. Bird and K. E. Palmer

England v Australia **Second Test**
At Lord's, June 17, 18, 19, 20, 21, 1993. Australia won by an innings and 62 runs. Vic Marks, 1994

England's lamentable record against Australia at Lord's – their last win was in 1934 – continued as the tourists romped to an innings victory. Of more immediate concern, this was England's seventh consecutive Test defeat, prompting a national outcry on a scale more familiar in football. For Australia the match offered reassuring confirmation of the stamina and resourcefulness of a bowling attack deprived of McDermott.

On such a bland surface a draw should have been within England's capabilities, but May and Warne conjured more turn than the English spinners and Hughes, refusing to be daunted by the sluggishness of the pitch or the absence of McDermott – Mark Waugh shared the new ball – was not to be denied. Gooch and Gatting were dismissed in unfamiliar and humiliating ways; Gooch was caught at long leg, hooking, while Gatting, supposedly the master of spin, was bowled through the gate by a perfectly flighted off-break. But the most notable dismissal was that of Smith, who became the first victim in an English Test of trial by television. Smith came down the wicket to May, the ball turned down the leg side and Healy whipped off the bails. Umpire Kitchen signalled to the third umpire, Chris Balderstone, at the top of the pavilion and, after 69 seconds, three TV replays and a brief walkie-talkie conversation, raised his finger.

Only Atherton, who batted 253 minutes for 80, had a clear idea of how to blunt the Australian attack as England were bundled out for 205. Atherton was also the cornerstone of England's second innings, remaining for another 242 minutes until a moment of masochistic madness. After Gooch had succumbed to a perfect Warne leg-break, Atherton and a subdued Gatting had added 104 to offer England hope of scrambling a draw. Atherton had reached 97, batting more fluently than in the first innings, when he clipped a ball to mid-wicket off Border. Both batsmen were swayed by the impending landmark as they debated a third run. Atherton set off, stalled and then slipped as Hughes hurled the ball from the boundary; he was agonisingly stranded as Healy removed the bails. If he had been on seven or 87 a third run would not have been contemplated.

Despite resistance from Hick and Stewart on the fifth day England were unable to recover from this self-inflicted wound. The Australian spinners, who shared 15 wickets in the match, patiently removed the middle order. Warne then took the last two wickets in consecutive balls by bowling Such and Tufnell around their legs, a suitably humiliating end for England. For the Australians there was enough time to spruce themselves up before meeting the Queen who, optimistically, had maintained the tradition of visiting Lord's at tea-time on the Monday, even though, with Sunday play, it was now the final day.

Toss: Australia. **Australia 632-4 dec.** (M. A. Taylor 111, M. J. Slater 152, D. C. Boon 164*, M. E. Waugh 99, A. R. Border 77); **England 205** (M. A. Atherton 80; M. G. Hughes 4-52, S. K. Warne 4-57) **and 365** (M. A. Atherton 99, M. W. Gatting 59, G. A. Hick 64, A. J. Stewart 62; T. B. A. May 4-81, S. K. Warne 4-102).

England v Australia   **Fourth Test**

At Leeds, July 22, 23, 24, 25, 26, 1993.

Australia won by an innings and 148 runs.   Peter Johnson, 1994

England lost the Ashes and, within minutes, their captain too when Graham Gooch honoured his promise to resign. In his final, most unwanted, press conference he explained haltingly: "It is the best way forward... the team might benefit from fresh ideas, a fresh approach, someone else to look up to." His departure was inevitable. This was his 34th Test in charge and, though ten of those ended in victory, this was England's eighth defeat in their last nine. It was by far the most comprehensive and, six weeks earlier, Gooch had said he would go if there was no improvement.

Toss: Australia. **Australia 653-4 dec.** (M. J. Slater 67, D. C. Boon 107, M. E. Waugh 52,
A. R. Border 200*, S. R. Waugh 157*, Extras 43; M. C. Ilott 3-161); **England 200** (M. A. Atherton 55,
G. A. Gooch 59; M. G. Hughes 3-47, P. R. Reiffel 5-65) **and 305** (M. A. Atherton 63, R. A. Smith 35,
A. J. Stewart 78; M. G. Hughes 3-79, P. R. Reiffel 3-87, T. B. A. May 4-65).

England v Australia   **Sixth Test**

See page 258

Why We Beat the Poms   Ian Chappell, 1994

Why do Australia beat England? In general, because Australia play an aggressive brand of cricket and, when the talent is there, they get in position to seek victory more often. Notwithstanding that, Australia couldn't have lost the last three Ashes series even if they had bet heavily on the opposition. England played badly, often. In particular, the bowling was abysmal.

During the summer of 1993 I constantly heard the lament, "What is wrong with English cricket?" In part, the answer is the inability of people directing the English game to recognise the good that there is. For instance, one of the more common moans was "Where are all the England fast bowlers?" Answer: Devon Malcolm was playing for Derbyshire for the first five Tests. Or "What has happened to the old-fashioned English seamer?" Answer: Steve Watkin was playing for Glamorgan for the first five Tests. Or "Why were England 4-0 down after five Tests?" Answer: From the time of the second one-day international when, as captain, Graham Gooch froze like a rabbit caught in the headlights, it was obvious he wasn't the man to lead England to an Ashes victory.

England's ability to over-theorise and complicate the game of cricket is legendary. Ever since I became involved in Ashes battles, I've felt that Australia could rely on some assistance from the England selectors. In 1993 they ran truer to form than many of the players they picked. Their magnanimity gave Australia a four-game start before the penny dropped. They then promoted Mike Atherton to the captaincy and, in no time, England picked a reasonably well-balanced side with an attack that bore some semblance of hostility.

Atherton had one piece of good fortune which every captain needs to be successful. Angus Fraser chose the appropriate moment to return to full form and fitness. But even before that Atherton had displayed considerable cricket wisdom. He said at Edgbaston after only three days in the job: "Our most important task is to identify the talent to win games. Then we must be prepared to stick with them." He was as good as his word in helping to select the touring party for the Caribbean, and in addition he cleverly used his new-found power to make important adjustments to the balance of the side.

Until the advent of Atherton, England's selections had often lacked rhyme or reason. A classic case was the predicament of 21-year-old Mark Lathwell in the one-day international series. At Lord's, Australia had an unbeatable 2–0 lead, so the selectors took the opportunity to play their talented 21-year-old, Damien Martyn. As he made mincemeat of the bowling on his way to a glorious half-century, an MCC member said to me, "How come you Australians always produce good young batsmen?" With Lathwell needlessly sitting in the pavilion watching his third match in a row, the answer wasn't difficult. "We play them," I replied.

Maybe Atherton doesn't need assistants like Keith Fletcher. The England cricket manager seems typical of a mentality that pervades county cricket – if it is difficult, take the easy way out. Fletcher's illogical call during the Ashes series for groundsmen to help England by producing seaming pitches went as it should have done: unheeded. However, Fletcher's behaviour should have caught the attention of officials and received a reprimand.

Not only was the suggestion unfair, his reasoning was astray. This was proved at The Oval where a well-balanced side, capably led and playing good, aggressive cricket, beat Australia on one of the best cricket wickets I've seen in England. There was pace and bounce in Harry Brind's pitch (as usual) and it produced the best match of the series. If the counties followed the examples of Brind and Old Trafford's Peter Marron and, where possible, produced similar pitches, then England's good cricketers would benefit substantially at international level. Unfortunately, the county mentality is often similar to Fletcher's: pitches are prepared either to assist the home side or to blunt a strength in the opposition.

Fletcher incorrectly suggested that England is the only country where helping the home side with pitch preparation is not accepted practice. I haven't played on or seen any green-top fliers in the Caribbean, and my brother Greg has often said: "If you have to bat against four West Indies pace bowlers then the best place to do it is on their own turf."

And in more than 30 years of playing and watching cricket in Australia, I can honestly say that I've never seen a Test pitch that varies greatly from its behaviour during the Sheffield Shield season. In fact, one of the strengths of the Shield competition is that the players perform on pitches which are very close to Test standard. Under this system it's easy to identify the players who stand a chance at Test level, the ones who are capable of playing only first-class cricket and those who will soon return to club cricket.

When Australia hit rock bottom through the 1984–87 period, the standard of

Sheffield Shield cricket was low. The problem was addressed because talented and gutsy young players were encouraged. Now it is a vibrant competition and an excellent breeding ground. England are on the right track with four-day first-class games, but it will take time for the benefits to accrue. I think they should go a step further and reduce the number of teams to make it more competitive, as there are players in the county structure who are not up to first-class standard. Any system that protects incompetence needs changing. If this means having a first and second division then that could be the way to accommodate part-time players who want to combine business and cricket. These changes could be part of a package to convince the counties that they must put England's needs at the top of their list, rather than on a level with deciding which colour to paint the pavilion roof.

Any move to improve the structure should be aimed at increasing pride in playing for the national team. Encouragingly, since Atherton has become involved in the selection process, I detect a move back to the feeling that the England team is for English players. If this is the case it's good news: England was in danger of becoming a haven for career cricketers who were unsure of making it in their own country.

Lack of pride manifests itself in a number of ways and in England's case the most serious has been to capitulate in a Test when trouble loomed. Their players used to be the best in the world at extricating themselves from trouble. This generation needs to rediscover that urge. The inability to save Tests must also have something to do with technique and mental strength. In an age where we have more coaches than ever throughout the cricket world, I query how much good they are doing. I believe in good coaching, but I think players are better to have none (i.e. work it out for themselves), than to have bad coaching.

In Australia, I believe the Cricket Academy could be run more effectively by not removing the young players from their home environment. However, many of the players leaving the Academy are mentally tough and primed for first-class cricket. This is exactly what you would expect with Rod Marsh as head coach and there is no doubt it is having a positive effect on the depth of Australian first-class cricket.

Also, apart from a brief period when Australia, like other teams, were bluffed by West Indies into thinking that pace was the almighty weapon, there has been a broadbrush approach to bowling the opposition out. This includes having leg-spinners once again. In the period when they were forgotten in Australia, Bill "Tiger" O'Reilly was furious. But just as he did in his playing days, O'Reilly saved his most lethal delivery for the old enemy. I can never forgive English cricket, he said, for attempting to kill off leg-spin bowling. O'Reilly thought English captains had no idea how to handle leg-spinners.

This brings me in a roundabout way to uncovered pitches. This is often suggested as a recipe for helping English cricket. I say codswallop. Uncovered pitches at first-class level would encourage the expectancy of easy pickings for the bowlers. Leg-spinners are the antithesis of easy pickings. Another suggestion is that there is too much one-day cricket. This is codswallop too. If young players are taught properly as they progress in the game, the smarter ones learn to adapt their thinking to all sorts of different pitches, bowlers and playing conditions.

Prior to the 1993–94 season, the Australian Cricket Board gave the selectors power to rest a jaded or slightly injured player from one-day internationals, while still receiving full pay. This is recognition that Test cricket is the true measuring stick for a player's skill, but also acknowledges the contribution made by one-day cricket to the game's finances and spreading popularity. It could also be a solution to the vexing problem of the right balance in a touring team's itinerary.

The ACB's edict is an interesting development in the gradual evolution of the professional game, in places other than England. Like so many things, the English invented one-day cricket and other countries have improved on their system, leaving them languishing. There are some signs of modern thinking in the marketing of English cricket but it has taken an inordinate amount of time to occur. In the end, though, the marketing men need a strong England side. So does the whole of cricket.

Ian Chappell captained Australia in 30 Test matches between 1971 and 1975, 16 of them against England.

WEST INDIES V AUSTRALIA 1995 Robert Craddock, 1996

On May 3, 1995, the great wall crashed at last. After 15 years and 29 series, world cricket's longest-lasting dynasty was overthrown by the relentless, underestimated Australians – the most distinguished run of triumphant success gone with the Windies. The last time West Indies lost a series was in March 1980, when Clive Lloyd's tourists lost to Geoff Howarth's New Zealanders. Since then, they had won 20 and drawn nine (including two one-off Tests). Against Australia, the West Indians had won seven and drawn one since their defeat in 1975–76. It was 1972–73 when the last visiting team, Ian Chappell's Australians, had won a series in the Caribbean.

Mark Taylor led Australia to victory by 2–1, despite losing all four tosses. They had other problems: two leading pace bowlers, Craig McDermott and Damien Fleming, missed the series after injuries; only two batsmen – the Waugh twins – averaged over 26; the Australians had been thumped 4–1 in the one-day games; and during the First Test, Australian coach Bob Simpson developed a blood clot in his left leg and was admitted to hospital.

Against all expectations, ball dominated bat in the Tests, despite under-strength or outdated attacks. The Australian bowlers who had been belted to all parts of the Caribbean in the one-day series somehow restricted West Indies to three totals below 200 and a best of 265 in six completed innings. The cricket was like arm-wrestling, with white knuckles tilted back and forth until the strain told, the weaker man snapped and his arm was crunched into the table. It was strike-or-be-struck-down from the opening minutes of the series, when West Indies lost three batsmen for six, to the final wicket on the fourth afternoon of the last match. Two Tests were completed within three days and the winning margins were all landslides – ten wickets, nine wickets and an innings and 53 runs.

How did Australia do it? All discussion must start and finish with Steve Waugh, whose 429 runs at 107.25 represented the most courageous, passionate and decisive batting of his life. With his low-risk, keep-the-ball-along-the-ground game, Waugh scored 189 more than the next Australian – his brother, Mark – and 121 more than West Indies' most prolific batsman, Brian Lara. But his tour was laced with drama from the first day of the First Test, when he claimed a catch off Lara which, seemingly unbeknown to him, had touched the ground as he tumbled. As an unsavoury consequence, he was heckled every time he came to the crease, branded a cheat by local crowds, publicly chastised by Viv Richards and subjected to intimidatory phone calls in the small hours. In Trinidad, he had a verbal clash with Curtly Ambrose, who had to be restrained by captain Richie Richardson.

During the final Test, he woke up to discover a security guard in search of some unsanctioned souvenirs. Weary but undeterred, he went in next morning to conjure one of the best innings by an Australian in decades, batting nearly ten hours for a maiden Test double-century. Every media critic in Australia had, at some stage, branded Steve Waugh gun-shy against short-pitched bowling. Yet at Kingston, he took more than six blows on the hands, arms and body; over the series, he absorbed more than 500 rib-rattlers by ducking or offering a straight defensive bat, sometimes with both feet six inches off the ground. Nineteen Australian wickets fell to the hook, but he refused to play the stroke, arguing it was too risky.

The only other batsman to enjoy much success for Australia was Waugh's brother, Mark, who shared with him in the glorious stand of 231 that decided the series. It sapped West Indian spirits so quickly that they had not put on 100 when Winston Benjamin was spotted in tears. The Waugh twins are opposites in many respects. Steve is the calculating percentage player, the student of cricket history, and Mark the free-spirited gambler, the risk-taker who breezes through life without a harsh thought. But at Sabina Park, where Mark was as tough as his brother, they became a perfect union. They acknowledged their twin centuries without histrionics, declining any show of brotherly emotion for the cameras.

West Indies v Australia	First Test
At Bridgetown, March 31, April 1, 2, 1995. Australia won by ten wickets.	Robert Craddock, 1996

Australia swept to victory with two days to spare – West Indies' first three-day defeat for 30 years. The captain who beat them in 1964–65, Bobby Simpson, now the Australian coach, followed the closing stages from hospital, after succumbing to a thrombosis in his left leg on the second day. It was only West Indies' third defeat at Bridgetown – but their second in successive seasons.

The tone of a pulsating, intense series was set early. The former *Wisden* editor John Woodcock rated the first session one of the best morning's play he had seen in six decades watching cricket. Australia's bare-boned pace attack, deprived of Fleming and McDermott, found a bouncy pitch at last and made the most of it. Julian and Reiffel reduced West Indies to six for three: Williams, Campbell and Richardson managed one run between them. It was the first of many occasions when they missed their bankable opening greats, Greenidge (retired) and Haynes (in dispute with the West Indies board). But joyous Australian backslaps turned to pats of commiseration and concern as a withering counter-attack by Lara and Hooper lifted West Indies to 116 without further loss at lunch. The tide turned so quickly that Warne had a long-on posted in the first hour.

The drama intensified in the afternoon, when Steve Waugh four times juggled a cut shot by Lara as it bobbled beneath his tumbling body. Television replays confirmed the ball had hit the ground but Lara, after loitering a few seconds, trudged off for the most controversial – and perhaps the decisive – moment of the tour. "If I had doubts I would not have claimed it," Waugh said later. "I have called players back before." Setting the pattern for the remaining Tests, Lara's dismissal started a slide that the meek lower order could not arrest. The enigmatic Julian, his form as flukey as a Caribbean breeze, paid his way for the series with four top-order victims – just the injection of self-belief the novice seam attack craved. All ten wickets were caught, nine of them off edges.

Nevertheless, Australia were eyeing a marginal advantage at 194 for five, before Healy scored a stubborn 74 not out in three hours. His stand of 60 with Julian was priceless when runs were trading for gold bars and set up a lead of 151. In reply, West Indies' second innings was another limp effort, with the highest score an unbeaten 39 from Adams. That left a target of only 39, which Taylor and Slater knocked off inside seven overs. McGrath, who had primed himself to be the attacking fist of Australia's bowling in McDermott's absence, took his first five-wicket haul in Tests. But nothing embodied Australia's determination more than Steve Waugh's glorious interception of Murray at mid-wicket – running towards the boundary, glaring skywards and snaring the ball as he dived, never taking his eye off it.

Toss: West Indies. **West Indies 195** (B. C. Lara 65, C. L. Hooper 60; B. P. Julian 4-36, G. D. McGrath 3-46) **and 189** (R. B. Richardson 36, J. C. Adams 39*; S. K. Warne 3-64, G. D. McGrath 5-68); **Australia 346** (M. A. Taylor 55, M. E. Waugh 40, S. R. Waugh 65, I. A. Healy 74*, B. P. Julian 31; W. K. M. Benjamin 3-71) **and 39-0.**

West Indies v Australia   Third Test

At Port-of-Spain, April 21, 22, 23, 1995. West Indies won by nine wickets.   Robert Craddock, 1996

The Australians had a suspicion of trouble when they went looking for the pitch and could barely pick it out from the rest of the gumleaf-green square. It was covered by grass nearly an inch long, suspiciously damp and given only a token shave. Even the winning captain, Richardson, agreed it was unsatisfactory. Fast bowlers looked at it and grinned like fat men about to tackle Christmas dinner. It simply had to be their match, and it was. Ambrose, who had taken three wickets in two Tests, bounced back with nine for 65 on the site where he demolished England a year earlier, while McGrath ripped out six.

Only Steve Waugh reached 50; his unbeaten 63 on this pitch was as admirable as his 200 in the next Test. In Australia's first innings, no one else bettered Boon's 18 and they lost nine wickets to outside edges. West Indies had similar problems. "When the ball seams like that, it does not matter whether you are Brian Lara or Don Bradman; you are not going to get runs consistently," said Australian coach Bob Simpson.

Rain, which cut the first day to 40 overs, hardly helped. Sent in, Australia lost

Taylor and Slater with only two on the board, Mark Waugh, a debonair strokemaker under the most trying conditions, managed only two singles in 25 minutes before he tickled behind. When Boon edged to slip at 37, Australia seemed no certainty to make three figures. But by then Steve Waugh had entered the front line. He stood his ground like John Wayne when Ambrose engaged him in a verbal exchange of fire from two metres; the bowler had to be tugged away by Richardson. "It's Test cricket," the unrepentant Waugh said afterwards. "If you want an easy game, go play netball." Waugh suspected anything approaching 150 would prove competitive and even 128 looked reasonable as McGrath scythed down the West Indians for 136. He did more than let the pitch work for him: he swung the old ball and some of his team-mates rated the out-swinging yorker which Lara edged to slip the ball of the series.

Australia's openers inched ahead on the second evening, but seizing the initiative proved beyond them. In the morning, the upper order struggled to 85 for three, then the last seven departed for 20, four to Ambrose, in a miserable procession that was not entirely the fault of the pitch. West Indies' target of 98 was small enough to clear in one hay-making assault. Richardson and Williams lashed out and Lara delighted his home crowd with the spectacular punchline, a six off Warne in the 21st over, to square the series and restore their confidence for the decider in Kingston. The match took less than 164 overs and, but for rain, might have finished earlier than tea on the third day.

Toss: West Indies. **Australia 128** (S. R. Waugh 63*; C. E. L. Ambrose 5-45, C. A. Walsh 3-50) **and 105** (M. A. Taylor 30; C. E. L. Ambrose 4-20, C. A. Walsh 3-35, K. C. G. Benjamin 3-32); **West Indies 136** (J. C. Adams 42; G. D. McGrath 6-47) **and 98-1** (S. C. Williams 42, R. B. Richardson 38*).

West Indies v Australia   Fourth Test

At Kingston, April 29, 30, May 1, 3, 1995.
Australia won by an innings and 53 runs.   Robert Craddock, 1996

The final Test was settled by a partnership to be cherished in Australian history, the pinnacle of the cricketing lives of Steve and Mark Waugh. In a series featuring only one other century, Steve scored 200 and Mark 126. They added 231 in 57 overs to bankroll the innings victory that regained the Frank Worrell Trophy, surrendered by Simpson's team in 1977–78, and ended West Indies' 15 years without a series defeat.

Batting was meant to be easy on a shiny pitch of rolled mud, as polished as a dance-room floor. When Richardson won his fourth consecutive toss it looked like a decisive advantage: West Indies' first 100 whistled by in 20 overs, with Lara running up a scorching fifty. Quite unexpectedly, he fell for 65, caught behind. It was the first time Warne had dismissed him in eight Tests. Richardson remained, patiently crafting the first hundred of the series before he was eighth out at 251. A moderate total of 265 was West Indies' best in the four Tests and next day Australia were teetering at 73 for three when Steve Waugh joined Mark. From then on, the home side spiralled towards oblivion.

The Waughs hit their stride almost immediately, smacking 67 from 11 overs after lunch. One by one they repelled the pace brigade; the buoyant West Indians were suddenly under siege. Winston Benjamin sat weeping during the drinks break and had to be cajoled to continue; Ambrose bowled only 11 overs in the day, amid whispers of team disunity, and the underachieving Kenny Benjamin was hooted on arrival at the bowling crease. Sabina Park was stunned and some of the Waughs' best boundaries went unapplauded. They applauded each other's centuries (their eighth Test hundreds in both cases) reached by Mark in 146 balls and Steve in 183 – and shook hands, but no more. Mark had left behind his gambler's hat to play a low-risk game. His bravest stroke was a contemptuous laid-back dab off Walsh over the slips for four. He pulled and drove with great rhythm. As usual, Steve hit almost everything along the ground, displaying some attractive back-foot cover drives. He gave just one chance, on 42, when he was grassed by debutant wicketkeeper Courtney Browne (a late replacement for Murray, who was ill).

Mark fell on the second evening, but Steve was 110 at stumps. He retired to his room to get some sleep, after being woken the previous night by a thief. Next day, supported by Blewett and the tail, he advanced to a maiden double-hundred in Tests. He was last out after batting for close on ten hours and 425 balls, more than 150 short-pitched, and had 17 fours, one six, and six aching bruises at the end of his greatest innings.

West Indies faced 14 overs that night; their doom was all but certain when Reiffel dismissed three. Their last chance was the weather, but rain restricted itself to the rest day. Only night-watchman Winston Benjamin and Browne passed 20 and Warne took the last four wickets – his best return of the tour – to complete the West Indians' shattering defeat.

Toss: West Indies. **West Indies 265** (R. B. Richardson 100, B. C. Lara 65; P. R. Reiffel 3-48) **and 213**
(W. K. M. Benjamin 51, C. O. Browne 31*; P. R. Reiffel 4-47, S. K. Warne 4-70); **Australia 531**
(M. E. Waugh 126, S. R. Waugh 200, G. S. Blewett 69, Extras 44; C. A. Walsh 3-103,
K. C. G. Benjamin 3-106).

A NEW WORLD ORDER
Matthew Engel, *Notes by the Editor*, 1996

Before West Indies arrived in England they had lost a series that was seen as a turning-point. Their defeat at home to Australia, their first in any series in 15 years, led to a general declaration that the Australians were now world champions. And it could not have happened to a more deserving team. Mark Taylor's leadership has been forceful but sporting; the batting positive; and Shane Warne's bowling has been among the most welcome developments cricket has had in years. These Notes are being written just before the 1996 World Cup. By the time they are read, it will (fingers crossed) have taken place and people will loosely be declaring someone or other – possibly even England – world champions.

Well, world one-day champions, yes. But even with that proviso, it will be a happy accident if the winners of the World Cup are the planet's best team. The nature of one-day cricket is that any set of capable professionals can beat any other, depending on who performs on the day. And the format chosen for the 1996 World Cup – three weeks of shadow-boxing to reduce 12 teams, including three makeweights, to eight followed by nine days of straight knockouts – was particularly ill-designed for the purpose.

The case for a true Test match World Championship, with minimum disruption to the existing structure, was stated here last year and I will not bang on again – yet. The response from round the world was enthusiastic. The authorities did nothing. It is an idea whose time will come.

England did not win the 1996 World Cup. Sri Lanka did, beating Australia.

AUSTRALIA V WEST INDIES 1996–97 — Greg Baum, 1998

Characterised and hyped as a world-title decider, complete with posters of the opposing captains staring like prize-fighters into each other's eyes, this series became a classic of the genre down to its last detail: the victor emerged almost as battered and bloodied as the vanquished.

As Mark Taylor hoisted the Frank Worrell Trophy again after an overwhelming if inconsequential defeat for Australia in the last Test, the best that could be said of the defending champions was also the least expected of them on their own shores: they won. Many heavy blows had been landed and absorbed by both sides. Taylor himself had such a wretched batting series that his place in the team was in the balance, though his captaincy remained as widely admired as ever. His handling of Michael Bevan, so unorthodox of personality and delivery, when the series was still delicately poised in the Fourth Test probably won it for Australia. He became the first Australian captain to win two series against West Indies, though – given the country's cricketing priorities – some of the shine was lost by the team's failure in the one-day competition.

Only one specialist batsman, Matthew Hayden, made a Test century for Australia, and he still could not win over reputable critics who maintained that his front-foot technique was too limited for Test cricket. Shane Warne, recuperating by painstaking degrees from off-season finger surgery and confronted by up to five left-handers at a time in the West Indian order, never took five wickets in an innings. None the less, he did take 22 in total, and was probably denied several others by the serendipitous emergence of Bevan as a bowler. Injuries, accidents and cumulative stress took a heavy toll, and the expanded and suddenly nervy selection panel exacted another: 16 players appeared for Australia in five different configurations. These did not include Michael Slater, whose shock omission from the First Test was a harbinger of the instability to come.

West Indies, meantime, were wincing from their own wounds, including the knowledge that their decline as the paramount power of world cricket was continuing apace. More than ever, and in stark contrast to Australia, they depended on particular players and pitches. What their Fifth Test victory did above all else was to underline Australia's previous combination of good cricket and good luck in subjugating the two players from whom there was most to fear. West Indies needed Brian Lara and Curtly Ambrose to be at their best, but their big performances were spasmodic and, until the last Test, not contemporaneous.

Australia v West Indies   First Test

At Brisbane, November 22, 23, 24, 25, 26, 1996. Australia won by 123 runs.   Greg Baum, 1998

Campbell, whose previous highest score on the tour was 22, made a last-day century and almost saved this match for West Indies. But Bevan, who had never taken a Test wicket as a spinner, took three – including Campbell's – to win it. Meanwhile, Lara and Warne, the celestials in whose hands the match was thought to rest, were by their usual standards little more than bystanders. Thus was established the series' theme: a predictable enough end achieved by not entirely predictable means or agents.

Toss: West Indies. **Australia 479** (M. A. Taylor 43, R. T. Ponting 88, M. E. Waugh 38, S. R. Waugh 66,
I. A. Healy 161*, Extras 33; C. A. Walsh 4-112, I. R. Bishop 3-105) **and 217-6 dec.** (M. A. Taylor 36,
M. E. Waugh 57, I. A. Healy 45*; I. R. Bishop 3-49); **West Indies 277** (C. L. Hooper 102,
S. Chanderpaul 82; P. R. Reiffel 4-58) **and 296** (S. L. Campbell 113, B. C. Lara 44; G. D. McGrath 4-60,
M. G. Bevan 3-46).

Australia v West Indies   Second Test

At Sydney, November 29, 30, December 1, 2, 3, 1996. Australia won by 124 runs.   Greg Baum, 1998

Trailing by merely 27 on first innings, West Indies threw away a position of near-equality with a fielding display of such incompetence that, even when Mark Waugh and Elliott were lying dazed on the ground after a head-on collision, neither was run out. Left again to negotiate survival rather than campaign for victory, the tourists failed, despite an astonishing rearguard innings from Chanderpaul.

Toss: Australia. **Australia 331** (G. S. Blewett 69, I. A. Healy 44; C. A. Walsh 5-98, I. R. Bishop 3-55)
and 312-4 dec. (M. T. G. Elliott 78*, M. E. Waugh 67, M. G. Bevan 52, G. S. Blewett 47*);
West Indies 304 (S. L. Campbell 77, R. G. Samuels 35, S. Chanderpaul 48, J. C. Adams 30,
I. R. Bishop 48; G. D. McGrath 4-82, S. K. Warne 3-65) **and 215** (C. L. Hooper 57, S. Chanderpaul 71;
G. D. McGrath 3-36, S. K. Warne 4-95).

Australia v West Indies   Fourth Test

At Adelaide, January 25, 26, 27, 28, 1997. Australia won by an innings and 183 runs.   Greg Baum, 1998

In Adelaide four years previously, the sting was in the last ball, when West Indies won by one run. This time, the match and series were as good as decided before the first ball. The late withdrawal of Ambrose dealt a massive psychological blow to West Indies. But Australia's gamble of playing the enigmatic

Bevan as a front-line spinner became a masterstroke. He took ten wickets with his left-arm wrist-spin and scored 85 in an all-round performance of rare efficacy. Early on the fourth morning, West Indies slumped to their second-worst defeat ever at Australia's hands, and Taylor had retained the Frank Worrell Trophy.

Toss: West Indies. **West Indies 130** (J. R. Murray 34; M. G. Bevan 4-31, S. K. Warne 3-42) **and 204** (B. C. Lara 78, C. L. Hooper 45; M. G. Bevan 6-82, S. K. Warne 3-68); **Australia 517** (M. L. Hayden 125, M. E. Waugh 82, G. S. Blewett 99, M. G. Bevan 85*, Extras 41).

SOUTH AFRICA V AUSTRALIA 1997   Jack Bannister, 1998

Mark Taylor became the first visiting captain to win a Test series in South Africa since they returned to official international cricket in 1991. But although it was Australia's sixth successive series win (excluding a one-off defeat by India), Taylor ended the tour with his position in doubt. His form was such that, after averaging 16 over the three Tests and scoring seven and 17 in the first two one-day internationals, he dropped himself for the remaining five games. He had gone 20 innings without a Test fifty, and the fact that he lasted long enough to reach double figures more often than not led his critics to believe that his decline was not a temporary run of bad luck. Taylor was constantly under fire from the travelling media. But he earned respect and admiration from neutral observers for the unflustered and honest way that he dealt with personal questions.

Australia also won the seven-match one-day international series – South Africa's first defeat in a limited-overs series or tournament on home soil since early 1993. It was a surprise result, as Australia had won only five limited-overs games out of 18 following their defeat in the 1996 World Cup final. South Africa had suffered only two defeats in 24 matches in that time, but paid for their tactical error at Centurion Park, where they opted to risk bowling with a wet ball.

The only disappointing feature of a magnificently successful tour for Australia was the poor attendances at the three Tests. Only 135,209 spectators paid to watch what was billed as the unofficial championship of world cricket – compared with 193,739 who watched India earlier in the summer. The lesson for South African administrators was that two short series are not the best option; future tours by West Indies and England have been scheduled for five Tests each.

Australia won the first two Tests in spite of, not because of, the balance of their side. They opted to play an extra batsman and fielded only three specialist bowlers – Glenn McGrath, Jason Gillespie and Shane Warne – backed up by the emerging wrist-spin of Michael Bevan; had Bevan batted at No. 6, they could have included a third pace bowler. Only the inability of South Africa's batsmen to come to terms with Warne and Bevan enabled this gamble to succeed. It could have failed in the marvellous Second Test at St George's Park, and it did fail at Centurion [where South Africa won by eight wickets], when the overworked McGrath finally broke down.

South Africa v Australia

First Test

At Johannesburg, February 28, March 1, 2, 3, 4, 1997.
Australia won by an innings and 196 runs.

Jack Bannister, 1998

Australia recorded their second-biggest victory in 60 Tests against South Africa. The match will be remembered for a record-breaking stand between Steve Waugh and Greg Blewett, which spread across three days. Australia were always in charge, and 12 of the game's 13 sessions were one-way traffic. McGrath brilliantly exploited all-too-familiar South African top-order weaknesses in an opening spell of 10–4–10–3 and South Africa slumped to 195 for 8. Only Cronje's 76 represented any worthwhile resistance – until Richardson enhanced his record as the patron saint of apparently lost causes. He hit an unbeaten 72 from 87 balls, including ten fours and a six, to steer his side to a respectable 302 – still at least 100 under par on a good pitch.

Opening Australia's innings next morning, Taylor was unlucky to play on against Pollock. Otherwise, the much-vaunted South African pace attack made little impression on an unusually slow pitch, although Donald did bounce out Mark Waugh and the left-hander Elliott – whose elegant off-side play was reminiscent of David Gower – in three balls. That brought in Blewett to join Steve Waugh. Shortly afterwards, rain forced an early close, but next day they rewrote the record books.

On the third, wicketless, day, Blewett scored a remorseless 153, and Waugh 123. Waugh's was his 12th hundred in 87 Tests, and Blewett's his third in 14, in which he had also made 99 and four other fifties. Waugh suffered leg cramps after tea but refused to go off, and that final session was worth 101 off 29 overs, following 93 and 94. Blewett's driving and pulling were a revelation, and his eventual 214 beat the previous highest Test score on the ground – Mike Atherton's unbeaten 185, 15 months earlier. Waugh scored 160, in 501 minutes and 366 balls, with 22 fours. When he fell, they had added 385, the second-biggest partnership for the fifth wicket in any Test and the best for any wicket against South Africa, surpassing the 370 by Bill Edrich and Denis Compton at Lord's in 1947.

Taylor's declaration gave his bowlers a minimum of 138 overs to take ten wickets, but they needed only half that. Kallis defended well for almost three hours, but the force was still with Steve Waugh. He ran Hudson out brilliantly and had Cronje caught down the leg side. After that, Warne and Bevan were unstoppable. The last seven wickets fell for 40, with Bevan taking the last four for two runs in 12 balls – two caught at short leg and two bowled. His quickish left-arm wrist-spin was as much a mystery to the batsmen as the wiles of Shane Warne; their combined match figures of 87.4–28–207–12 contrasted vividly with those of Adams, who took one for 163.

Toss: South Africa. **South Africa 302** (W. J. Cronje 76, S. M. Pollock 35, D. J. Richardson 72*; G. D. McGrath 4-77) **and 130** (A. C. Hudson 31, J. H. Kallis 39; S. K. Warne 4-43, M. G. Bevan 4-32); **Australia 628-8 dec.** (M. L. Hayden 40, M. T. G. Elliott 85, S. R. Waugh 160, G. S. Blewett 214, M. G. Bevan 37*, Extras 30).

South Africa v Australia

At Port Elizabeth, March 14, 15, 16, 17, 1997. Australia won by two wickets.

Second Test

Jack Bannister, 1998

Mark Waugh's magnificent fourth-innings 116 clinched a wildly fluctuating Test and, with it, the series. Australia began and finished strongly, but for much of the match South Africa seemed bound to square the series. The key was the pitch, which had such a thick mat of grass that it looked like an Essex ground of the 1950s, Westcliff or Clacton maybe. It was automatic that Taylor would bowl.

Bowling an impeccable line and length at high speed, Gillespie reduced South Africa to 95 for seven. Then the Australians were convinced Richardson was caught behind before scoring, but he remained to add 85 for the eighth wicket with McMillan. A total of 209 was a good one on that pitch. Again, the lack of a third pace bowler hampered Australia, although Warne bowled beautifully in conditions entirely against wrist-spin.

The Australians lost Hayden on the first evening and their reply next day was a peculiar one. They somehow got through the morning with only three wickets down, despite inordinate movement off the greentop. They were helped when Pollock was forced out after tearing a hamstring. The turning point came when Bacher ran out Elliott for 23, the top score of the innings. That started a collapse of seven wickets for 44, and Australia trailed by 101. Donald bowled with fearsome hostility and frequently beat the bat, but Blewett was his only victim in the Test – a statistic almost as extraordinary as the fact that Healy took only one catch. The tourists complained because hessian mats were not used under the tarpaulin covers to reduce overnight sweating, as they were in the First Test.

South Africa's openers extended their advantage to 184 as batting conditions improved, which put them almost out of sight. But on the third day, a red mist cost them all ten wickets for 85. Bacher was responsible for another run-out, but this time the victim was his partner, Kallis, and five more dismissals from rash strokes gave Australia a hope of victory. Only Cronje displayed the necessary obduracy, batting for 21 overs until he failed to read a googly from Bevan, who wrapped up the innings with Warne.

Australia needed 270. Though two and a half days remained, another 40 or 50 might have defeated them. But the chance was there and Mark Waugh took it. He later described it as his best innings in any cricket: it lasted nearly five and a half hours and included a six and 17 fours. Stern defence was twinned with innate elegance after he arrived in a crisis – 30 for two. Taylor failed again, and Hayden was comically run out when he and Elliott lunged for the same crease as Cronje burst between them to knock down the other wicket.

Waugh reached his fifty by the close, when Australia were an encouraging 145 for three, with his brother Steve digging in at the other end. But Kallis had Steve caught in the covers and, when Adams bowled Blewett, at 192 for five, South Africa were back in the match. The crowd, though disappointingly small, was close to delirium. Bevan came in to help Waugh to the brink of victory but, with 12 still wanted, Kallis dismissed Waugh and Cronje had Bevan caught at slip. Warne soon followed. Two wickets were left, five needed. But not for Healy the Hirst-Rhodes tactic of getting them in singles – he swung Cronje high over long leg for six.

Toss: Australia. **South Africa 209** (D. J. Cullinan 34, H. H. Gibbs 31, B. M. McMillan 55, D. J. Richardson 47; J. N. Gillespie 5-54, S. K. Warne 3-62) **and 168** (G. Kirsten 43, A. M. Bacher 49; J. N. Gillespie 3-49, M. G. Bevan 3-18); **Australia 108 and 271-8** (M. T. G. Elliott 44, M. E. Waugh 116; J. H. Kallis 3-29).

PAKISTAN V AUSTRALIA 1998

Mark Ray, 2000

Australia's visit to Pakistan in October 1998 will always be remembered for Mark Taylor's historic 334 not out in the drawn Second Test at Peshawar, yet the most significant event of a tumultuous tour was their victory in the First Test at Rawalpindi. Taylor's effort, equalling Sir Donald Bradman's record for a Test score by an Australian, was a brilliant individual performance, but an excellent team effort in Rawalpindi was the crux of the series victory – Australia's first in Pakistan since Richie Benaud's team won 2–0 in 1959–60.

The First Test win became more and more significant as the other two matches ended in draws. On most of their visits to Pakistan during the 39-year drought, Australia had been beaten in the First Test and then fought back (usually) to draw the other matches. This time, they took the lead and never looked like surrendering it. Their triumph came without leg-spinner Shane Warne, arguably the best bowler in the game before a serious shoulder operation in May 1998.

Pakistan v Australia

First Test

At Rawalpindi, October 1, 2, 3, 4, 5, 1998.
Australia won by an innings and 99 runs.

Mark Ray, 2000

The two first innings of the series indicated the pattern that continued for the rest of the tour: Pakistan played as a loose group of individuals, Australia as a tight unit. The effect was Pakistan's first innings defeat on home soil since they lost to West Indies in 1986–87, and the only result of the series.

Toss: Pakistan. **Pakistan 269** (Saeed Anwar 145, Moin Khan 39; S. C. G. MacGill 5-66) **and 145** (Salim Malik 52*; S. C. G. MacGill 4-47); **Australia 513** (M. J. Slater 108, S. R. Waugh 157, D. S. Lehmann 98, I. A. Healy 82, Extras 30; Wasim Akram 3-111).

Pakistan v Australia

Second Test

At Peshawar, October 15, 16, 17, 18, 19, 1998. Drawn.

Mark Ray, 2000

If ever a sound typified a Test then it was the mellow thwack of the ball meeting the middle of Mark Taylor's bat during his undefeated 334 in this game. On a flat, evenly grassed yellow pitch, which hardly changed appearance over five days,

Taylor played as well as he ever had in his ten-year Test career. After a less than perfect start against some very fast bowling from Shoaib Akhtar, Taylor made barely an error, hitting the ball with the sweet spot of his bat hour after hour. His pulling was brutal, his cutting precise.

After Shoaib's first spectacular spell, which removed Slater with the score at 16, Taylor and Langer settled into a 279-run stand for the second wicket, asserting a dominance of bat over ball which never faltered. Their partnership became the highest for any wicket in Australia-Pakistan Tests, eclipsing 259, also for the second wicket, by another pair of left-handers, Wayne Phillips and Graham Yallop, at Perth in 1983–84. On the second day, Australia added 375 for the loss of three wickets. At stumps, they were 599 for four, with Taylor unbeaten on 334 and level with Bradman's Australian record at Headingley in 1930. He clipped the final ball of the day, from Aamir Sohail, towards square leg, but Ijaz, who had hardly excelled in the field before then, threw down a hand and managed to stop what would have been a record-breaking single.

Taylor had batted for exactly 12 hours and 564 balls, hitting 32 fours and a six. His innings was the seventh-highest score in Test history, the 15th triple-century and the fifth by an Australian. He also became the fourth Australian to pass 7,000 Test runs. Yet more drama followed next morning as the news spread around the ground – and the world – that Taylor had sacrificed the chance of breaking both Bradman's mark and Brian Lara's world record 375 by declaring. Immediately the theorising and myth-making began. The local experts could not believe that Taylor would deny himself a shot at the record. One explanation which quickly gained currency, though it was later denied by Taylor, was that he had refused to pass the record of Bradman. The simplest explanation was the correct one: Taylor thought 599 in two days was more than enough runs, and he wanted to try to win by giving his bowlers a chance at Pakistan's batsmen from the start of the third day. There were a number of team meetings that evening, and several players urged Taylor to bat on and beat Lara. But it was typical of his approach to the game that he should be aware of the record without being obsessed by it.

The declaration did not help. As the Pakistanis came to the crease, it became more and more obvious that this pitch would have been more suitable for a time-less Test than one scheduled for a mere five days. The postscript to the game came weeks later when Taylor visited Bradman at his home in Adelaide, and the Don thanked him – as he had in a letter – for not exceeding his record. The thanks might have been better directed at Ijaz.

Toss: Australia. **Australia 599-4 dec.** (M. A. Taylor 334*, J. L. Langer 116, M. E. Waugh 42, R. T. Ponting 76*) **and 289-5** (M. A. Taylor 92, M. E. Waugh 43, S. R. Waugh 49*, R. T. Ponting 43); **Pakistan 580-9 dec.** (Saeed Anwar 126, Aamer Sohail 31, Ijaz Ahmed 155, Inzamam-ul-Haq 97, Salim Malik 49, Mushtaq Ahmed 48*, G. D. McGrath 3-131)

WEST INDIES V AUSTRALIA 1999

See page 408

ENGLAND V AUSTRALIA 2001

David Frith, 2002

Seldom has such high expectation before an Ashes series ended in such summary demolition. Peter May's 1958–59 England team, which had a truly formidable look about it, was crushed 4–0 by Richie Benaud's eager combination, yet it was 63 days into the series before the Ashes were relinquished. In 2001, with its compressed schedule (five Tests within 54 days), Steve Waugh's Australians made sure of retention in only 31, framing a mere 11 days of combat; Benaud's needed 22.

They arrived in England as outstanding favourites, notwithstanding their reversals at Kolkata and Chennai and the revival in England's performances under Nasser Hussain and coach Duncan Fletcher. At the outset, Steve Waugh knew England were stronger than in recent years, and acknowledged that forecasting was fraught with difficulties. But he did add ominously, "If we can get on top early, we can open up some old scars."

All was triumph for the Australians, whose image had been enhanced by their demeanour. McGrath passed Dennis Lillee's 355 Test wickets, Gilchrist had his 100th dismissal in a record 22 Tests, the Waughs now stood with 47 Test centuries between them, and Australia had won 20 of their last 23 Tests, all of which had had positive conclusions, another record. And still their captain claimed they were a team without stars.

It remained for us to try to assess whether we had been watching the best cricket team of all time. Wasted though the exercise may be, the man in the traffic jam or the halted railway carriage was eager for debate about the relative qualities of the 1902, 1921, 1948 and 1975 Australians, the 1950s England sides, South Africa 1969–70, the West Indies combination of 1984.

England v Australia   **First Test**

At Birmingham, July 5, 6, 7, 8, 2001. Australia won by an innings and 118 runs.   Graeme Wright, 2002

One session was all Australia needed to settle into their defence of the Ashes. When England were 106 for one with an over to lunch, pre-match fears for Hussain's reconstructed team looked overblown. Then Steve Waugh introduced Warne. Butcher pushed a pad at his second ball and gloved a catch to Ponting, diving forward from short cover. It was the beginning of the end. When, in the second innings, Gillespie broke Hussain's little finger with a startling delivery, England's whole campaign was threatened.

Toss: Australia. **England 294** (M. A. Atherton 57, M. A. Butcher 38, A. J. Stewart 65, A. R. Caddick 49*, Extras 34; G. D. McGrath 3-67, S. K. Warne 5-71) **and 164** (M. E. Trescothick 76, M. A. Butcher 41; J. N. Gillespie 3-52, S. K. Warne 3-29); **Australia 576** (M. J. Slater 77, M. L. Hayden 35, M. E. Waugh 49, S. R. Waugh 105, D. R. Martyn 105, A. C. Gilchrist 152, Extras 33; D. Gough 3-152, M. A. Butcher 4-42).

England v Australia   **Fourth Test**
See page 302

AUSTRALIA V SOUTH AFRICA 2001–02
Gideon Haigh, 2003

On the eve of the First Test at Adelaide, South Africa's captain, Shaun Pollock, was asked by a photographer to pose beside the ICC Test Championship mace. He declined, politely, on superstitious grounds: he had posed with the World Cup 30 months earlier, and South Africa's exit from that tournament at Australia's hands was a memory he preferred not to revisit. Pollock's refusal to tempt the fates was wise, but he added to his bad memories anyway. Though the ICC tabulations said South Africa would replace Australia as championship leaders by winning or drawing this three-Test rubber, they never looked like contenders. The tourists were thrice disposed of by big margins, with ample time to spare, and in some disarray.

For Australia, the encounter put further flesh on an already far-from-bony case to be considered the outstanding cricket team of the past decade. The latest weapon in their line-up was the left-handed opening combination of Matthew Hayden and Justin Langer; a *faute de mieux* arrangement in England had flowered on home soil. The hulking Hayden was overpowering, scoring his 429 runs at a strike-rate of around 60 per hundred balls. Always busy, always acquisitive, Langer was less eye-catching but little less effective, having turned his recall at The Oval into a new lease on life. By the end of the series, their average partnership was a hearty 117.90, including four double-century stands in 11 innings.

What the openers left incomplete, Damien Martyn polished off at No. 6, with compact technique and crisp timing. It was hard to believe his centuries at Adelaide and Sydney were his first in home Tests, such was Martyn's composure in the presence of the tail and easeful manipulation of the strike. The Waughs and Gilchrist were less productive than usual, but never really needed.

Despite fielding only four specialist bowlers in each match, Australia's attack contained sufficient variety to cover most contingencies. After their unsuccessful series against New Zealand, Glenn McGrath and Shane Warne were back to their usual steady selves. Brett Lee improved as the Tests progressed, beating Herschelle Gibbs at Sydney with a ball that went through him like an X-ray. The horses-for-courses selections – Andy Bichel in Melbourne and Stuart MacGill in Sydney – paid off nicely, and all were abetted by fielding of the highest quality. Ricky Ponting's 11 catches contained some which justified the invention of the television replay.

Australia v South Africa
First Test

At Adelaide, December 14, 15, 16, 17, 18, 2001. Australia won by 246 runs.
Gideon Haigh, 2003

After an inconclusive series against New Zealand, Australia entered this match with the objective, expressed by Steve Waugh, of proving they were "still a very good cricket side". They accomplished it with ease and a session to spare, although South Africa's final, hasty capitulation made it look a little too easy. Warne returned to something like his best, recovering his menacing drift into the right-hander, and bowling over and round the wicket with all his old facility. His plot to uproot Gibbs was one for the scrapbook: a beguiling leg-break into the footmarks spun round the advancing batsman for Gilchrist to execute the stumping. After bagging five in an innings for the 20th time in Tests, Warne volunteered that a target of 250 in the fourth innings would be demanding: "The pitch is going to get worse, and it will keep lower for the fast bowlers." His prognosis showed why John the Bookie had once valued his opinions.

Toss: Australia. **Australia 439** (J. L. Langer 116, M. L. Hayden 31, R. T. Ponting 54, D. R. Martyn 124*, S. K. Warne 41, B. Lee 32; M. Hayward 3-108, C. W. Henderson 4-116) **and 309-7 dec.** (M. L. Hayden 131, M. E. Waugh 74, Extras 31; C. W. Henderson 3-130, J. H. Kallis 3-45); **South Africa 374** (H. H. Gibbs 78, G. Kirsten 47, C. W. Henderson 30, N. D. McKenzie 87, M. V. Boucher 64; G. D. McGrath 3-94, S. K. Warne 5-113) **and 128** (J. H. Kallis 65*; G. D. McGrath 3-13, S. K. Warne 3-57).

SOUTH AFRICA V AUSTRALIA 2002
Neil Manthorp, 2003

Australians were deeply offended by the fact that a draw in either of their back-to-back series against South Africa would be enough to dislodge them from the top of the ICC Test Championship. Steve Waugh's team had seen off the first half of the challenge at home, giving South Africa such a hammering that the return series might have been a foregone conclusion. But they arrived in February, the tail-end of the African summer, when rain is always a threat, and the possibility that they could be dethroned without a ball being bowled meant there was no shortage of motivation for Australia.

Amazingly, there was no shortage of optimism in South Africa, although it soon turned out to be more a desperate need to stop the pain than a coherent belief that Shaun Pollock's team could actually slay the giant. In the event, Pollock missed all three Tests with a knee injury, fatally weakening the attack, which became even thinner when Allan Donald broke down on the first day of the series and then announced his retirement from Test cricket. His tally of 330 wickets in 72 matches was easily a South African record.

The captaincy passed to Pollock's deputy, the wicket-keeper Mark Boucher, who lost his first Test in charge, at Johannesburg, by an innings and 360 runs. It was the second-heaviest defeat in Test history. "I don't care about the margin of defeat or records," Boucher responded. "Every loss hurts just the same."

Most supporters did care about the scale of the humiliation. The Second Test, at Cape Town, brought four changes to the home side, including three debuts. The Gauteng all-rounder Andrew Hall was picked to provide the team with back-bone, not to mention a verbal riposte or two, after surviving a hijacking, two muggings and a shooting. The swing bowler Dewald Pretorius was rewarded for a fine domestic season, though he was to struggle at Test level. More successful was the powerful left-handed opener Graeme Smith, not unlike a young Graeme Pollock in stance and physique, who was given a chance at No. 3. Paul Adams, Test cricket's least orthodox left-arm spinner, was recalled after nearly a year on the sidelines. With another left-hander, Ashwell Prince, playing his second Test, it was the freshest South African team since readmission in 1991.

The newcomers supplied a welcome antidote to the staggering cynicism shown by one of the country's most senior players on the eve of the match. Daryll Cullinan was called up after several months off with a knee injury, and there was talk of his leading the side when he joined them in Cape Town. But he immediately demanded a national contract for 13 months, until the end of the 2003 World Cup, even though he had previously retired from one-day cricket. When this was refused – the board said they did not offer contracts in mid-season until a player had appeared in two Tests or six one-day internationals, and in any case all current contracts were to expire in April – he refused to play and flew back to Johannesburg. A widespread sense of expectation at the prospect of Cullinan renewing his battle with Shane Warne was frustrated.

Hours later, the new boys appeared at a joint press conference. Led by the 21-year-old Smith, they spoke with passion of the pride they felt. From that point on, South Africa gradually started to compete. They held out for five days in Cape Town before losing a close-fought encounter, and finally registered a victory at Durban a week later.

No amount of praise would flatter Australia, and especially Adam Gilchrist. Even those who had seen 100 or more Tests were astonished by Gilchrist's performance – 473 runs at 157, including what was then the fastest double-hundred in Test cricket. Matthew Hayden brought his prodigious form with him from the first series, narrowly missing five centuries in consecutive Tests. For Steve and Mark Waugh, it was a lean spell that wore on. Steve had been told before departure that he was losing the one-day captaincy to Ricky Ponting, who had a highly successful tour. During the Tests, the twins learned that they were to be dropped altogether from the one-day squad. But their poor Test form simply allowed Gilchrist to spend more time at the crease. Australia scored five Test centuries, South Africa just one – from Herschelle Gibbs.

The scoreboard operators could hardly keep up with Australia's flow of runs, and the flair with which they were scored gave the impression that their batsmen were solely responsible for winning the series. In reality, for the umpteenth time, Warne and Glenn McGrath were instrumental in Australia's triumph. McGrath took 12 wickets at 19, while Warne took 20 and moved into second place in the all-time Test wicket-takers' list. In his 100th Test, at Newlands, he put in a heroic effort, bowling 70 overs in a single innings, and claimed the match award.

The Australians were tactically as well as technically superior in every respect. But the gulf wasn't as wide as the embarrassing scorelines suggested. Above all, it was the imposition of Australia's collective character that the South Africans could not handle – the fact that they were constantly "there", with bat, ball or in the field. After the defeat at Durban, they swiftly hit back to cement their domination: Ponting became the first touring captain to win a one-day series in South Africa since Mark Taylor, one of his predecessors, in 1996–97. Despite the return of Pollock, Australia went five up before conceding one more consolation win. They left the local population with a nasty feeling that they might never beat them over a series again.

South Africa v Australia   First Test

At Johannesburg, February 22, 23, 24, 2002.

Australia won by an innings and 360 runs.   Neil Manthorp, 2003

A single moment summed up the crushing superiority of Australia and the brilliance of their star, Adam Gilchrist. It came when he took a pot shot at an advertising hoarding offering a bar of gold, worth 1.3 million rand (over £80,000), for a direct hit. The sponsor, a local gold mine, hardly seemed in danger: the billboard was 30 feet in the air and well behind the deep mid-wicket boundary, a carry of at least 100 yards.

Gilchrist was 169, and had butchered the entire front-line attack, which badly missed the injured Pollock. With McKenzie bowling gentle medium-pace, he could resist no longer. Like a golfer hitting a wedge approach shot, he scooped a length delivery towards the target – and started to jump up and down as he realised how close it would be. He missed by a couple of feet, but what remained of South Africa's spirit was broken. Gilchrist was playing with them like a cat keeping a half-dead mouse alive for entertainment. And it was only the second day of the series.

The carnage had started the day before with Hayden's fourth century in as many Tests. He was only the eighth player to produce such a purple patch, though the fourth Australian after Don Bradman, who did it three times, Jack Fingleton and Neil Harvey. South Africa had a chance to dam the flow in Ntini's first over when Hayden offered a straightforward catch to second slip. Kallis dropped it, and Hayden blossomed with a muscular display of strokes that brought 18 fours and a pair of sixes. Ntini and Nel tried hard to be hard but were left cowering by his power. A torn hamstring forced Donald off the field, but it could not be blamed for South Africa's inability to compete. Although he trapped Langer with a clever, slow off-cutter, Donald conceded 72 runs in 15.2 overs before his body announced it would no longer play the game for more than a day at a time. He retired from Test cricket after the match.

Even so, Australia's dominance was not quite assured on Hayden's departure at 272 for four. Martyn set out with studious care, taking 130 balls over his first fifty. Like everyone else, he was mesmerised by Gilchrist. But he picked up the tempo as the bowlers sagged drunkenly; his second fifty took only 37 balls, and he went on to a Test-best 133. He was never more than the junior partner, however, in a stand of 317, the second-highest for the sixth wicket in Test history, after Fingleton and Bradman's 346 against England in 1936–37. The afternoon session yielded 190 runs at 7.45 an over: it was dizzying to watch.

Gilchrist reached 200 four balls after tea, with his 19th four from his 212th delivery. For three weeks, it was the quickest Test double in terms of balls, beating Ian Botham's (220 balls) against India at The Oval in 1982. Gilchrist faced one further ball, for a single which raised his highest first-class score, 204 in 293 minutes. He smashed eight sixes, including the one that almost struck gold. Steve Waugh declared at the end of the over on 652 for seven, Australia's highest score against these opponents.

South Africa were so far past relief it was shocking. Not one of them had seen anything like this five-session mauling, and the effect on morale was all too clear. Ashwell Prince marked his debut with a sometimes belligerent 49, defying the pressures of batting at No. 3, but there was little else. They were dismissed in 48 overs for 159 and followed on 493 behind. It was a new low in South African history – but the second innings was even shorter. During the third day, they lost 16 wickets in 54.3 overs, to go down by an innings and 360 runs. The margin was second only to Australia's own beating, by an innings and 579, at The Oval in 1938.

McGrath and Warne bowled beautifully to enforce their stranglehold over the batsmen. Warne's six wickets took him to 438 in Tests, second only to Courtney Walsh, while McGrath wound up the game with four in nine balls.

But if it is possible for a batsman to win a Test in the first innings, Gilchrist did it. Even the parochial, normally hostile crowd were punched into submission by one of the finest, most entertaining and consistently aggressive innings ever played in Test cricket.

Toss: Australia. **Australia 652-7 dec.** (M. L. Hayden 122, R. T. Ponting 39, M. E. Waugh 53, S. R. Waugh 32, D. R. Martyn 133, A. C. Gilchrist 204*); **South Africa 159** (H. H. Gibbs 34, A. G. Prince 49; G. D. McGrath 3-28, B. Lee 3-40) **and 133** (H. H. Gibbs 47; G. D. McGrath 5-21, S. K. Warne 4-44).

South Africa v Australia   Second Test

At Cape Town, March 8, 9, 10, 11, 12, 2002. Australia won by four wickets.   Neil Manthorp, 2003

Shane Warne flew 16 friends and relatives to Cape Town for his 100th Test, and they saw him bowl 98 overs, take eight wickets, score a half-century, win the match award – and propel his team to yet another series triumph, which cemented their place at the head of the Test Championship.

In the end, it was a memorable five-day battle. But that hardly looked likely when South Africa crashed to 92 for six on the opening day in the face of some tremendous fast bowling inspired by McGrath. They clawed their way back to 239, thanks to the street-fighting qualities of Andrew Hall, who scored 70 on debut. Gilchrist was again devastating, but for once South Africa's top five were undaunted, and Australia required 331, the tenth-highest total to win in Test history, though as they were responsible for five of the top nine, history was no barrier.

Langer and Hayden launched the assault in fearless style, sharing their sixth century stand in 14 starts. When Dewald Pretorius, who was mostly outclassed, bowled Langer off an inside edge, Ponting helped take the score to 201 before Hayden edged Kallis to the keeper. He failed by four runs to become the second player to score centuries in five consecutive Tests, after Bradman, who went on to six. Some welcome tension entered the chase when Ntini removed Mark Waugh just before lunch. Then Adams's googlies bowled Steve Waugh and cornered Martyn lbw in successive overs, leaving Australia 268 for five; but Gilchrist effecti`vely finished the job with a carefree, run-a-ball 24. Ponting had the last word in the drama: six short of a meticulous century, but needing only three for victory, he achieved both with a single blow against Adams. The script decreed that Warne should be there at the other end.

Toss: South Africa. **South Africa 239** (A. J. Hall 70, P. R. Adams 35; G. D. McGrath 3-42, J. N. Gillespie 3-52) **and 473** (H. H. Gibbs 39, G. Kirsten 87, G. C. Smith 68, J. H. Kallis 73, N. D. McKenzie 99, M. V. Boucher 37; S. K. Warne 6-161); **Australia 382** (J. L. Langer 37, M. L. Hayden 63, R. T. Ponting 47, A. C. Gilchrist 138*, S. K. Warne 63; M. Ntini 4-93, P. R. Adams 4-102) **and 334-6** (J. L. Langer 58, M. L. Hayden 96, R. T. Ponting 100*).

South Africa v Australia
At Durban, March 15, 16, 17, 18, 2002. South Africa won by five wickets.

Third Test
Neil Manthorp, 2003

Australia found themselves on the back foot for the first time in six Tests when South Africa put them in and reduced them to 182 for five. They still seemed more than capable of retrieving the situation, and claimed a large first-innings lead. But impressive as South Africa's spirit was in pulling off a consolation victory, the truth was that Australia were emotionally and physically spent.

Toss: South Africa. **Australia 315** (R. T. Ponting 89, M. E. Waugh 45, A. C. Gilchrist 91) **and 186**
(R. T. Ponting 34, M. E. Waugh 30, S. R. Waugh 42; M. Ntini 3-65, J. H. Kallis 3-29);
South Africa 167 (H. H. Gibbs 51; B. Lee 4-82, S. K. Warne 4-33) **and 340-5** (H. H. Gibbs 104,
G. Kirsten 64, G. C. Smith 42, J. H. Kallis 61*, A. G. Prince 48).

PAKISTAN V AUSTRALIA 2002
See page 565

AUSTRALIA V ZIMBABWE 2003
Chloe Saltau, 2004

Australia roused themselves from a two-month hiatus to play a Test series at home in October, in a nation preoccupied with the rugby World Cup, and against one of the world's lowliest Test nations. It had all the makings of an unremarkable, predictable series. But Zimbabwe's first Test tour of Australia, one-sided as it was, was better than that. It was better because of Matthew Hayden. He cast a muscular shadow over the series. His Test-record 380 [the record was reclaimed by Brian Lara six months later] at Perth defined and elevated a contest that would otherwise have been lost among the more common pursuits of early Australian spring. The great shame was that only 8,062 people were at the WACA on October 10 – Hayden's day – to witness the 31-year-old Queenslander calmly yet powerfully etch his own number into cricket history, eating up milestones owned by such revered figures as Mark Taylor and Sir Donald Bradman (334), and the West Indian Brian Lara (375), as he went. Not bad for a man repeatedly ignored as a young batsman.

Australia v Zimbabwe
At Perth, October 9, 10, 11, 12, 13, 2003. Australia won by an innings and 175 runs.

First Test

Toss: Zimbabwe. **Australia 735-6 dec.** (M. L. Hayden 380, R. T. Ponting 37, D. R. Martyn 53,
S. R. Waugh 78, D. S. Lehmann 30, A. C. Gilchrist 113*; S. M. Ervine 4-146);
Zimbabwe 239 (T. R. Gripper 53, M. A. Vermeulen 38, C. B. Wishart 46; B. Lee 3-48,
J. N. Gillespie 3-52) **and 321** (M. A. Vermeulen 63, S. V. Carlisle 35, S. M. Ervine 53, H. H. Streak 71*,
R. W. Price 36; A. J. Bichel 4-63, D. S. Lehmann 3-61).

Matt finish: Australia's Matthew Hayden (right) leaves the field at Perth with
Adam Gilchrist after hammering 380 against Zimbabwe in October 2003 to take the
record for the highest Test score from Brian Lara – temporarily, as it turned out,
as Lara reclaimed the mark six months later.

INDIA V AUSTRALIA 2004 Paul Weaver, 2005

A boxing promoter might have been proud of the hyperbolic billing that preceded
this series. The drum roll carried from Mumbai to Melbourne, but the entire
cricket world was aware of a rare frisson of anticipation. Although India were the
world's fourth-ranked side when Australia arrived at the end of September, there
were many who viewed the meeting of these teams as Test cricket's blue-riband
event, based on the epic nature of the preceding two series, in India in 2001 and
in Australia in 2003–04.

But heavyweight match-ups are often a letdown, and this one never went the
distance, as Australia took an unassailable 2–0 lead in the Third Test. Arguably,
the series could have been drawn had it not rained in Chennai with India on top.
But by the end of the series Australia had established themselves as much the
better side, and the 2–1 scoreline rather flattered the Indians. Steve Waugh's "final
frontier" had been breached at last, even if Waugh himself was now back home
in Australia watching the series on TV. The Australians had not won here in 35
years, but the modern team could now claim to have beaten everyone everywhere
(except Bangladesh away, because they had not yet bothered).

India v Australia — First Test

At Bangalore, October 6, 7, 8, 9, 10, 2004. Australia won by 217 runs. Paul Weaver, 2005

Gilchrist, leading Australia in place of Ponting, who was recovering from a broken thumb, called heads. The tottering coin was going to fall tails but then hit one of the larger cracks on the crazy-paving pitch and flipped over the other way. The luck would remain with Australia throughout the match but they also played the better and more purposeful cricket.

Their approach surprised many. Rejecting the nuclear option that had served them so well in recent years, they relied more on conventional warfare: line and length and crease occupation. They played with patient care, sticking to a game plan that had started to evolve since they lost their last series in this country over three years earlier. "I didn't know what it was like to lose a Test match when we lost here last time," said Gilchrist. "I think it's good to have a little fear, to know what it feels like to lose and what it takes to win."

The player of the match, however, was gloriously unscarred by previous battles. Michael Clarke became the 17th Australian to score a century on his Test debut, and the first since Greg Blewett almost a decade earlier. More than that, he played with real audacity, particularly against the spinners, picking the length early and using his feet to get to the pitch of the ball.

If Clarke's innings swung the game Australia's way it was, as so often, Gilchrist who demoralised the opposition. His 11th Test hundred came from just 103 balls and included 13 fours and three sixes.

Toss: Australia. **Australia 474** (J. L. Langer 52, S. M. Katich 81, M. J. Clarke 151, A. C. Gilchrist 104; Harbhajan Singh 5-146, A. Kumble 3-157) **and 228** (M. L. Hayden 30, S. M. Katich 39, D. R. Martyn 45, S. K. Warne 31; Harbhajan Singh 6-78); **India 246** (V. Sehwag 39, S. C. Ganguly 45, V. V. S. Laxman 31, P. A. Patel 46, I. K. Pathan 31; G. D. McGrath 4-55) **and 239** (R. S. Dravid 60, I. K. Pathan 55, Harbhajan Singh 42; J. N. Gillespie 3-33).

India v Australia — Third Test

At Nagpur, October 26, 27, 28, 29, 2004. Australia won by 342 runs. Paul Weaver, 2005

"Looks like home, don't it?" said umpire David Shepherd, in his familiar West Country burr, as he surveyed the strip at the Vidarbha Cricket Association ground on the eve of this match. And, indeed, it looked like an old-fashioned English green seamer. As Australia prepared to cross what had become known as "the final frontier" and win their first series in India for 35 years, even the return of Tendulkar, who had been out of cricket for two months with tennis elbow, was overshadowed by the preparation of the VCA pitch. Ganguly said he had asked the groundsman to remove the grass from the wicket the previous week. "But I don't think he has done much," he said, sounding miffed. "Our strength is our spinners but the pitch is up to him."

India seemed dispirited and when Ganguly withdrew injured on the morning of the match they were thrown into disarray. They were also without Harbhajan Singh, who was suffering from gastroenteritis. The pitch suited tall fast bowlers: Australia had three, India none. McGrath, who became the first Australian fast bowler to win 100 Test caps, bowled with astonishing accuracy, conceding barely a run an over in the first innings. But even he was upstaged by Gillespie, who bowled superbly to take nine wickets.

Toss: Australia. **Australia 398** (J. L. Langer 44, D. R. Martyn 114, D. S. Lehmann 70, M. J. Clarke 91; Z. Khan 4-95, M. Kartik 3-57) **and 329-5 dec.** (J. L. Langer 30, S. M. Katich 99, D. R. Martyn 97, M. J. Clarke 73); **India 185** (M. Kaif 55; G. D. McGrath 3-27, J. N. Gillespie 5-56) **and 200** (V. Sehwag 58, P. A. Patel 32, A. B. Agarkar 44*; J. N. Gillespie 4-24).

India v Australia   Fourth Test
At Mumbai, November 3, 4, 5, 2004. India won by 13 runs.   Paul Weaver, 2005

India won a thrilling match by a wafer-thin margin to release some of the pressure that had been building on them, though the circumstances surrounding their victory detracted from the celebrations. It was achieved on a pitch which turned square from the start and saw 20 wickets fall on the third and final day after 18 had tumbled on the second. "The wicket was no way near to being Test standard," said Ponting, Australia's returning captain. "Forty wickets in two days is almost unheard of. It's been a fantastic series but this has left a sour taste." Even some Indian players agreed.

Ponting returned after missing the first three games through injury. He was anxious to make a belated mark on the series, and also to atone for his wretched experience on his previous tour, when he scored just 17 runs in five innings. It was not to be, and he even lost the toss, breaking Gilchrist's winning sequence. Australia, set 107 to win, were bowled out for 93. As at Headingley in 1981 or Sydney in 1994 – to name only the two most memorable examples – a minuscule fourth-innings target was beyond them.

Toss: India. **India 104** (R. S. Dravid 31*; J. N. Gillespie 4-29, N. M. Hauritz 3-16) **and 205** (V. V. S. Laxman 69, S. R. Tendulkar 55; M. J. Clarke 6-9); **Australia 203** (M. L. Hayden 35, D. R. Martyn 55; A. Kumble 5-90, M. Kartik 4-44) **and 93** (Harbhajan Singh 5-29, M. Kartik 3-32).

West Indies' Fall from Grace

At the beginning of the period covered by this Anthology, the West Indian team was just fomenting into one of the most powerful (perhaps even *the* most powerful) cricket machines of all time. They weren't pretty, but they were mighty effective – and at times frightening. Perm four from Roberts, Garner, Holding, Marshall, Croft, Patterson and Daniel, and you had a strike force of remarkable potency. Add Greenidge, Haynes, Richards, Lloyd, Gomes and Dujon to make a stack of runs; Harper to bowl some spin; and the odd back-up bowler to supplement the ferocity of the spearheads, and one sees what an extraordinary generation of West Indian cricketers this was. Lacking the romance of the teams commanded by Worrell and Sobers, certainly, but far better at winning cricket matches, indeed well-nigh invincible, undisputed heavyweight champions for more than a decade.

Now, no one fears West Indies. Indeed, the batsmen of other countries rub their hands when a West Indian series draws near. Their bowling is inexperienced, raw, unsophisticated – and nothing like as fast or hostile as it used to be. The batting remains capable of compiling a decent score, but it is rarely enough. West Indies' record over the past decade is atrocious, and reflects deep-seated problems in the Caribbean's domestic cricket. It is an issue not just for cricket administrators in the West Indies, but globally, because cricket's eco-system is not so secure that it can afford a greatly weakened West Indies stretching into the future. For the downward spiral could become terminal: the West Indies is said to look towards the US these days; young men who might have played cricket now play basketball.

International cricket bodies must help to secure the future of the sport in the Caribbean. It's not altruism; it's pragmatism. As the rich get stronger and the strong get richer, countries with a weak domestic infrastructure (notably West Indies and Sri Lanka) might get sidelined. West Indian tours to England and Australia are already shorter than they were 20 years ago; how much shorter can they get? A resurgent West Indies would be the best news world cricket could have. After all, variety is the spice of cricketing life.

The series covered in this chapter chart West Indies' precipitous descent. In the early and mid-'90s the greatness of Lara, Ambrose and Walsh masked the true extent of the decline, but as the two fast bowlers aged and Lara periodically fell out with the West Indian board, the truth could no longer be denied. How dismal for Lloyd, Richards and that great '80s generation to see their legacy squandered. Can West Indies recover? That, alongside the question of how India uses its new-found dominance – for good or ill – will be the great question of the next 20 years. We need all those little pals of ours to return to the fold.

S. M.

ENGLAND v WEST INDIES 1980   John Woodcock, *Notes by the Editor*, 1981

Only the weather prevented West Indies from beating England more comfortably than by a single victory. The West Indians, remorseless in certain tactical respects, were a powerful side and less prone than most of their predecessors to self-destruction. They and their manager, Clyde Walcott, were on their guard against such a collapse of morale and discipline as had undermined them in New Zealand earlier in the year.

There can never have been a side more heavily reliant on their fast bowlers than these West Indians, or better served by them. When the Fifth Test match ended in August, West Indies had played ten Tests in 1980 and included a spin bowler in only one of them – that when, against all the odds, they lost to New Zealand in Dunedin. It is a pity, none the less, to see them so committed to speed. A balanced attack adds to the joys of watching cricket; to sit through a day's play in which only 74 overs are bowled, as happened in the Oval Test match, does not.

In England last year Croft, Garner, Holding, Marshall and Roberts, the West Indian fast bowlers, were formidable in attack and effective in defence. Vivian Richards, one of the two Antiguans in the West Indian side, remains the world's most brilliant batsman. Sir Garry Sobers was the last most powerful single influence on the game; before that, Sir Donald Bradman was.

England v West Indies   First Test
At Nottingham, June 5, 6, 7, 9, 10, 1980. West Indies won by two wickets.   Peter Smith, 1981

The bitter split in English cricket caused by the Packer affair was officially healed with Knott and Woolmer being welcomed back into the England side for the first time since they rejected their country in 1977. In all, Kent provided four of the England side. It would have been five but for the omission of Underwood from the England twelve, owing largely to the weather conditions.

Barely 1,000 spectators made the effort to turn up for the final morning with West Indies requiring only 99 runs for victory with eight second innings wickets in hand. But those who saw the ending were rewarded by a gripping and courageous fightback, by England's bowlers in general and Willis in particular, that went close to presenting Botham with a startling victory in his first Test as captain.

Throughout the previous four days the bowlers on both sides had held the upper hand on a wicket that offered extravagant movement off the seam and in conditions conducive to swing bowling. On the final morning even putting bat against ball proved difficult and only Haynes batted with any degree of authority during his three hundred and five minute, match-winning vigil. Willis's heroic bowling was rewarded with nine wickets in the match, and if one of two vital catches on the final day had been taken England might easily have won.

England v West Indies, 1980   First Test

At Nottingham, June 5, 6, 7, 9, 10, 1980. Result: West Indies won by two wickets.

ENGLAND

	First innings		Second innings	
G. A. Gooch c Murray b Roberts		17	– run out	27
G. Boycott c Murray b Garner		36	– b Roberts	75
C. J. Tavare b Garner		13	– c Richards b Garner	4
R. A. Woolmer c Murray b Roberts		46	– c Murray b Roberts	29
D. I. Gower c Greenidge b Roberts		20	– lbw b Garner	1
*I. T. Botham c Richards b Garner		57	– c Richards b Roberts	4
P. Willey b Marshall		13	– b Marshall	38
†A. P. E. Knott lbw b Roberts		6	– lbw b Marshall	7
J. K. Lever c Richards b Holding		15	– c Murray b Garner	4
R. G. D. Willis b Roberts		8	– b Garner	9
M. Hendrick not out		7	– not out	2
B 7, l-b 11, w 3, n-b 4		25	B 19, l-b 13, w 10, n-b 10	52

1-27 2-72 3-74 4-114 5-204 6-208 7-228   263   1-46 2-68 3-174 4-175 5-180 6-183 7-218   252
8-246 9-254 10-263   8-237 9-248 10-252

First innings – Roberts 25–7–72–5; Holding 23.5–7–61–1; Marshall 19–3–52–1; Richards 1–0–9–0; Garner 23–9–44–3.
Second innings – Roberts 24–6–57–3; Holding 26–5–65–0; Marshall 24–8–44–2; Garner 34.1–20–30–4; Greenidge 3–2–4–0.

WEST INDIES

	First innings		Second innings	
C. G. Greenidge c Knott b Hendrick		53	– c Knott b Willis	6
D. L. Haynes c Gower b Willis		12	– run out	62
I. V. A. Richards c Knott b Willis		64	– lbw b Botham	48
S. F. A. F. Bacchus c Botham b Willis		30	– c Knott b Hendrick	19
A. I. Kallicharran b Botham		17	– c Knott b Willis	9
†D. L. Murray b Willis		64	– (7) c Hendrick b Willis	16
*C. H. Lloyd c Knott b Lever		9	– (6) lbw b Willis	3
M. D. Marshall c Tavare b Gooch		20	– b Willis	7
A. M. E. Roberts lbw b Botham		21	– not out	22
J. Garner c Lever b Botham		2		
M. A. Holding not out		0	– (10) not out	0
B 1, l-b 9, w 2, n-b 4		16	L-b 8, n-b 9	17

1-19 2-107 3-151 4-165 5-208 6-227 7-265   308   1-11 2-69 3-109 4-125 5-129 6-165   (8 wkts) 209
8-306 9-308 10-308   7-180 8-205

First innings – Willis 20.1–5–82–4; Lever 20–2–76–1; Hendrick 19–4–69–1; Willey 5–3–4–0; Botham 20–6–50–3; Gooch 7–2–11–1.
Second innings – Willis 26–4–65–5; Lever 8–2–25–0; Hendrick 14–5–40–1; Botham 16.4–6–48–1; Gooch 2–1–2–0; Willey 2–0–12–0.

Toss won by England   UMPIRES D. J. Constant and D. O. Oslear.
MAN OF THE MATCH A. M. E. Roberts

India v West Indies 1983
Dicky Rutnagur, 1985

West Indies went through an arduous itinerary with little challenge to their authority. They won the six-Test series three-nil, which was as big a margin as any previous West Indian side had achieved in India, and made a clean sweep of the five one-day internationals, thus avenging their two shock defeats by India only a few months earlier in the Prudential World Cup in England.

For the second consecutive series, Clive Lloyd was West Indies' main run-getter. Beginning most of his Test innings in something of a crisis, and with the pitches seldom lending themselves to free strokeplay, Lloyd was not the robust, explosive player of old. He batted very circumspectly, but always very soundly, and averaged 82.66 in the Tests. It was a tribute to his character that, despite his 39 years and a nagging back problem, he buckled down to play one long innings after another.

West Indies would not have gained their Test victories so comfortably had their fast bowlers, Malcolm Marshall, Michael Holding and Andy Roberts, not taken turns to play major innings. Marshall finished fourth in the batting averages, while, spearheading the attack, he also claimed 33 wickets to equal West Indies' record for a Test series. He and Holding, who took only three fewer wickets, always looked capable of turning the fortunes of a Test match in one spell. Holding was no less hostile for operating off a short run. Roberts was dogged by injury and played only in the last two Tests. Instead, Wayne Daniel took his opportunity to make a forceful comeback to Test cricket after seven years. With Winston Davis also taking his fair share of wickets, West Indies had no cause to miss the injured Joel Garner.

By the end of the series, India had played 29 consecutive Tests without a victory, their longest barren stretch ever. However, Sunil Gavaskar was back in his accustomed place as the leading India run-getter. A third of the way through the series he told the selectors that he no longer relished going in first and it was when batting at No. 4 that he made 236 not out in the final Test, his 30th century in Test cricket, which took him past Bradman's record.

India v West Indies
Fifth Test

At Calcutta, December 10, 11, 12, 14, 1983.
West Indies won by an innings and 46 runs.
Dicky Rutnagur, 1985

The wide margin that eventually separated the sides belied the close struggle for supremacy over the first two days. The balance was tilted by a long and sound, if dour, innings by Lloyd. Apart from his effort, the match was almost completely dominated by the bowlers. This was surprising, as the pitch was bare and slow – features which prompted West Indies to include a specialist spinner, the hitherto uncapped Harper, for the first time in the series. Roberts also played his first Test of the rubber.

Toss: India. **India 241** (R. M. H. Binny 44, Kapil Dev 69, S. M. H. Kirmani 49; M. D. Marshall 3-65, A. M. E. Roberts 3-56, M. A. Holding 3-59) **and 90** (A. O. Malhotra 30; M. D. Marshall 6-37, M. A. Holding 3-29); **West Indies 377** (C. H. Lloyd 161*, M. D. Marshall 54, A. M. E. Roberts 68; Kapil Dev 4-91, N. S. Yadav 3-80).

WEST INDIES V AUSTRALIA 1984

See page 342

ENGLAND V WEST INDIES 1984 Christopher Martin-Jenkins, 1985

As far as the records are concerned, the 1984 West Indians, under the captaincy of Clive Lloyd, were unique. No country had hitherto achieved a 100% record in a full Test series in England. Apart from one limited-overs international, at Trent Bridge early in their tour, not a game was lost. Only four other rubbers of five games or more in the history of Test cricket have finished with a similar whitewash for one of the competing teams, and Lloyd's West Indians must rank as the equals at least of the others on this very short list: Australia against England in 1920–21 and South Africa in 1931–32, England against India in 1959, and West Indies, under another of their elder statesmen, Frank Worrell, against India in 1961–62.

Blessed by a dry summer, maturely led, strong and adaptable in batting, possessing in Roger Harper the best West Indian off-spinner since Lance Gibbs, and basing their attack on a formidably fit and hostile band of fast bowlers, Lloyd's was a team of almost all the talents. Whatever may have appeared to be the case on paper, they relied on no special individuals. There was a man for every moment.

The most gifted batsman in contemporary world cricket, Vivian Richards, began the tour in the kind of form, and mood, which had enabled him to score 829 runs in seven Test innings in England in 1976. In the two one-day Texaco Trophy matches which West Indies won he totally dominated the England bowling, producing at Old Trafford perhaps the most powerful innings ever seen in one-day cricket at this level. Then, in the First Test at Edgbaston, he made a century almost as a matter of course, playing as if a hundred was the least that he, and everyone else, expected. If this suggests over-confidence, it is no more than the truth. Thereafter he played like a millionaire and in doing so enjoyed no luck, so that it was not Richards but Greenidge and Gomes who took the main batting honours in the Tests. Both hit four first-class centuries on the tour and two against England. Greenidge, in fact, reached a thousand runs in only 16 first-class innings at an average of 82.23. Gomes made 841 from 17 innings at 70.08.

Greenidge batted with the air of a man in control of every situation. Seldom can he have played on such a high plane of inspired brilliance as when seizing the Second Test from England on the last day at Lord's. His second double-hundred of the series, at Old Trafford in the Fourth Test, was less attractive and fluent, yet his defence was seemingly unpierceable and his judgment in attack quite flawless as he set about locking England out of the game.

In the field the West Indians were as impressive as at any time during the Lloyd era. The close-catching and out-fielding were slick and sure. One of the most memorable moments of the tour occurred at Lord's when England's Geoff

Miller, blithely sauntering along on a second run after the ball had been played wide of Eldine Baptiste on the long-leg boundary, was amazed to see a missile fizzing past him to break the stumps at the bowler's end from some 80 yards away. If this stands out ahead of the many brilliant slip catches, taken by a variety of fielders, it is perhaps because the latter were two-a-penny.

But the invincibility of the West Indians was based again upon their relentless fast bowling. Joel Garner, towering above the batsmen, was the most consistently dangerous; Malcolm Marshall, wiry as a whippet, was the fastest. Michael Holding, graceful but intelligently menacing, bowled mainly off a shorter run than of old but was still capable of taking vital wickets with near-unplayable balls; and Baptiste bowled with admirable stamina and accuracy, if not with quite as much ferocity as the others.

It was also at Old Trafford that Harper, built to bowl fast like so many of his team-mates but in fact a slow off-spinner, with a keen cricket brain, sharp spin, accuracy and subtle changes of flight and pace, took six second-innings wickets for 57. He had less opportunity in the other Tests but still took some important wickets, notably those of Ian Botham at Edgbaston and David Gower at Headingley, when each had achieved a rare ascendancy.

There were no passengers in the party. Whenever it was threatened, someone came to the rescue, as when Desmond Haynes, after a lean series, played the match-winning innings in the final victory at The Oval which took West Indies' run of Test successes to eight out of eight, following a one-sided series against Australia in the Caribbean.

Praise must be tempered by two reservations. Before the tour began, the West Indies Cricket Board refused to agree to the Test and County Cricket Board's idea of insisting on a reasonable minimum number of overs in a day, an expedient which had worked well in England in 1982 and 1983. As a result both sides bowled their overs in the Test matches at a rate which was unacceptably low. Over the series, England averaged 13.4 overs an hour, West Indies 13.5. Only at Old Trafford, when Pocock, Cook and Harper bowled long spells, did either side maintain a rate of more than 15 overs an hour.

Equally typical of contemporary cricket, for which West Indies, being the best team in the world, have set the trend, the bouncer was used by their fast bowlers to such an extent that batting against them became as much an exercise in self-defence as in defence of the wicket. Andy Lloyd and Paul Terry both sustained serious injury while playing for England. Several others were hit on the helmet. Uneven pitches and poor batting techniques partially explained this, but so, too, did the West Indian strategy (aped by other teams but most effectively carried out by themselves) of digging the ball in short and watching the hapless batsmen dance to their tune.

England v West Indies   **First Texaco Trophy Match**

At Manchester, May 31, 1984. West Indies won by 104 runs.

A magnificent innings by Richards, which he himself considered to be one of the best he had ever played, dwarfed all else. Almost single-handed he won the match for West Indies after they had been in deep trouble. Having won the toss and chosen to bat, they were 102 for seven in the 26th over, on a pitch which was of little help to the faster bowlers but allowed Miller generous turn with his off-breaks. In a memorable display Richards received 170 balls and hit 21 fours and five sixes, one of these, a straight drive, going out of the ground at the Warwick Road end. In 14 overs for the last wicket Richards and Holding added 106, Richards's share being 93. He batted with daring and immense power, giving only one technical chance, a leg-side stumping off Miller when he was 44.

England v West Indies, 1984   First Texaco Trophy Match

At Manchester, May 31, 1984. West Indies won by 104 runs.

WEST INDIES

C. G. Greenidge c Bairstow b Botham	9	E. A. E. Baptiste c Bairstow b Botham	26
D. L. Haynes run out	1	J. Garner c and b Foster	3
R. B. Richardson c and b Willis	6	M. A. Holding not out	12
I. V. A. Richards not out	189	B 4, 1-b 2, w 1, n-b 3	10
H. A. Gomes b Miller	4		
*C. H. Lloyd c Pringle b Miller	8	1-5 2-11 3-43 4-63 5-89	(9 wkts, 55 overs) 272
†P. J. L. Dujon c Gatting b Miller	0	6-98 7-102 8-161 9-166	
M. D. Marshall run out	4		

Willis 11–2–38–1; Botham 11–0–67–2; Foster 11–0–61–1; Miller 11–1–32–3; Pringle 11–0–64–0.

ENGLAND

G. Fowler c Lloyd b Garner	1	D. R. Pringle c Garner b Holding	6
T. A. Lloyd c Dujon b Holding	15	N. A. Foster b Garner	24
M. W. Gatting lbw b Garner	0	R. G. D. Willis not out	1
*D. I. Gower c Greenidge b Marshall	15	L-b 6, n-b 3	9
A. J. Lamb c Richardson b Gomes	75		
I. T. Botham c Richardson b Baptiste	2	1-7 2-8 3-33 4-48 5-51 6-80	(50 overs) 168
†D. L. Bairstow c Garner b Richards	13	7-100 8-115 9-162 10-168	
G. Miller b Richards	7		

Garner 8–1–18–3; Holding 11–2–23–2; Baptiste 11–0–38–1; Marshall 6–1–20–1; Richards 11–1–45–2; Gomes 3–0–15–1.

Toss won by West Indies   UMPIRES D. J. Constant and D. R. Shepherd.
MAN OF THE MATCH I. V. A. Richards

England v West Indies   First Test

At Birmingham, June 14, 15, 16, 18, 1984.
West Indies won by an innings and 180 runs.   John Thicknesse, 1985

Granted the known disparity between the teams, West Indies were always likely winners on a ground where the previous six Tests had all finished well inside four days. Fresh from three sweeping victories against Australia in the Caribbean, and pitted against an England team which during the previous winter had lost series to New Zealand and Pakistan for the first time, West Indies carried nearly all the guns, especially in bowling. To that extent, the match went according to form, three missed catches being the only blemishes on a powerful all-round performance that exposed to the full the shortcomings of the England team.

Toss: England. **England 191** (I. T. Botham 64, P. R. Downton 33; J. Garner 4-53) **and 235** (P. R. Downton 56, I. T. Botham 38, D. R. Pringle 46*; J. Garner 5-55); **West Indies 606** (H. A. Gomes 143, I. V. A. Richards 117, C. H. Lloyd 71, E. A. E. Baptiste 87*, M. A. Holding 69, Extras 53; D. R. Pringle 5-108).

England v West Indies	Second Test
At Lord's, June 28, 29, 30, July 2, 3, 1984. West Indies won by nine wickets.	Terry Cooper, 1985

England were either level or on top until the last four hours of the match. West Indies then strolled nonchalantly to victory, making the fifth highest score to win a Test. Only Bradman and Hammond have made higher scores in a Lord's Test than Greenidge's 214 not out in West Indies' second innings. Yet despite their overwhelming defeat, England managed several skilful and brave performances. Gower, however, might not have relished the occasion. It was his second defeat as captain at headquarters and he became the first England captain since Yardley in 1948 to declare in the second innings and lose. Lloyd, his opposite number, reached 7,000 Test runs. Greenidge and Botham each passed 4,000.

West Indies had to chase 342 to win in five and a half hours. The swing and movement that had been there all match seemed to have vanished, England's change bowlers looked second-rate, and nobody but Willis bowled the right line or set the right field to the powerful and phlegmatic Greenidge. Although England finally blocked his square cut, the mid-wicket and long-on boundaries saw plenty of Greenidge's 29 fours. It was Greenidge's day, the innings of his life, and his ruthless batting probably made the bowling look worse than it was. He was dropped by an inattentive Botham, the sole slip, off Willis, when he was 110, but by then a West Indies win was certain.

Toss: West Indies. **England 286** (G. Fowler 106, B. C. Broad 55, I. T. Botham 30, Extras 35; M. D. Marshall 6-85) **and 300-9 dec.** (A. J. Lamb 110, I. T. Botham 81; J. Garner 3-91, M. A. Small 3-40); **West Indies 245** (I. V. A. Richards 72, C. H. Lloyd 39, E. A. E. Baptiste 44; I. T. Botham 8-103) **and 344-1** (C. G. Greenidge 214*, H. A. Gomes 92*).

AUSTRALIA v WEST INDIES 1984–85 — Tony Cozier, 1986

Although this was the fourth time that the West Indians had toured Australia in six seasons since the disbanding of World Series Cricket, it was the first full Test series between the teams in Australia since 1975–76 when West Indies, then, as now, under the captaincy of Clive Lloyd, suffered a crushing five-one defeat. It was, therefore, cause for considerable satisfaction for Lloyd and those players who had survived the debacle nine seasons earlier – his vice-captain, Vivian Richards, Gordon Greenidge and Michael Holding – that the roles were reversed this time. Lloyd, in the farewell series of an illustrious career, could enjoy fully the sweeping triumph of his powerful team which won the first three Tests by wide margins, would almost certainly have won the fourth but for a delayed declaration, and had its record tarnished only by defeat in the last. It was Australia who now endured the traumatic effects of a heavy defeat, their captain, Kim Hughes, resigning after two Tests under the pressure of constant criticism, and their selectors using no fewer than 19 players in the series.

The result was not entirely unexpected. West Indies arrived in Australia with an imposing record – comfortable victors over India in India, a similarly emphatic record over much the same Australian team in the Caribbean and a clean sweep over England in England, all accomplished in the preceding year. In Greenidge and Desmond Haynes they possessed the most consistent pair of opening batsmen in the game; in Richards and Lloyd the two most experienced and commanding middle-order batsmen. Even with such credentials, though, the batting was no more formidable than the fast bowling, spearheaded by Holding, Joel Garner and Malcolm Marshall. It is not often the case that a touring team can be said to have had no single individual failure, but it was so with this West Indian team. There may have been disappointments, notably Greenidge and Haynes, but every member could claim to have played some part in the triumph, which extended to the limited-overs World Series Cup tournament, also involving Sri Lanka, that followed the Tests.

Unfortunately, the series was marred by strained relations between the teams, involving verbal altercations on the field and causing an official protest from the West Indians against one Australian player, Lawson. For all that, West Indies, managed again by their former fast bowler, the affable Wesley Hall, retained their popularity with Australian crowds and their captain received fond farewells wherever he went. He was awarded the Order of Australia by the Australian government for his services to the game.

Australia v West Indies — First Test

At Perth, November 9, 10, 11, 12, 1984. West Indies won by an innings and 112 runs. Tony Cozier, 1986

West Indies, with some magnificent fast bowling supported by spectacular catching on a bouncy pitch, ran out overwhelming winners. Yet, midway through the opening day, Australia had established an early advantage after Hughes had decided to bowl first. Two days of rain preceding the match had left the pitch under-prepared and unpredictable and Alderman, on his return to Test cricket on the ground where he had been injured two seasons earlier in a clash with an intruding spectator, took four wickets for five runs from 26 balls to leave West Indies 104 for five.

Gomes and Dujon halted the decline, in spite of blows to the head. Neither was wearing a helmet at the time. Dujon, who was hit by a ball from Alderman before he had scored, called for one but then temporarily retired, complaining of blurred vision. By the end of the first day, at 211 for six, West Indies could not be entirely satisfied. However, Dyson missed a straightforward chance at second slip off Alderman early next day when Gomes was 45, and it was not until an hour after lunch that the partnership was eventually broken, Dujon then being caught behind after hitting 21 fours in four hours' batting. Gomes was last out after a determined innings lasting seven and three-quarter hours.

Australia lost three wickets for 36 in just over the hour available to them on the second afternoon and the result was virtually settled in the first session of the third day when Australia lost eight wickets for 45. All out for their lowest total ever against West Indies, they immediately lost Wessels in the first over when they followed on. West Indies were irresistible, Holding taking six for 21 from 8.2 overs, Garner and Marshall offering no respite at the other end, and the fielders supporting the effort with several brilliant catches. If their cricket became somewhat ragged as Dyson and Wood added 91 in Australia's second innings, with Garner being no-balled six times in an over for overstepping, in the final session Marshall and Walsh claimed two wickets each and only a pugnacious last-wicket partnership of 59 between Lawson and Alderman delayed Australia's inevitable defeat early on the fourth day.

Toss: Australia. **West Indies 416** (C. G. Greenidge 30, D. L. Haynes 56, H. A. Gomes 127, P. J. L. Dujon 139; T. M. Alderman 6-128, R. M. Hogg 4-101); **Australia 76** (M. A. Holding 6-21) **and 228** (J. Dyson 30, G. M. Wood 56, K. J. Hughes 37, G. F. Lawson 38*; J. Garner 3-52, M. D. Marshall 4-68).

WEST INDIES V ENGLAND 1986 John Thicknesse, 1987

It would be less than fair to David Gower and the team he captained in the West Indies to label the tour simply a disaster. Their record, true enough, was all of that – another "blackwash" in the Test series and only two wins, compared to ten defeats, in 14 matches. Much went wrong, too, that with firmer captaincy and management might not have. But there were many mitigating circumstances, of which the brilliance of the opposition, captained by Viv Richards, and the poor quality of too many of the pitches were the most decisive. In cold fact, England never had a hope.

That they could and should have done better, few who saw them would dispute. Their lack of commitment was reflected in their attitude to practice, a department in which West Indies showed them up as amateurs. However, any chance England had of competing in the series – slender at the best of times on the record of West Indies since the middle 1970s – vanished to all practical purposes when the batsmen reached the First Test in Jamaica without having met, in four matches, one pitch on which to find their confidence. On top of that, they had been deprived by injury of Mike Gatting, who had been in better form than anyone. Gatting, the vice-captain, had his nose broken by Malcolm Marshall in the first one-day international, misjudging the ball to hook, and the consequences were long-lasting both in playing terms and psychologically.

Three days after Gatting's injury, England were in the thick of the Test series on a dangerous Kingston pitch, and within two more had been beaten by ten wickets after being demolished twice in 88 overs and two balls. Almost overnight another star fast bowler, Patrick Patterson, had risen in the firmament. Raw at that stage, but very quick, he took seven wickets on his debut and left more mental scars and bruises than Marshall on a fast, uneven pitch. Well grassed for about four yards either side of centre, and bare in the areas forward of the popping creases, the playing surface could not have underlined with greater emphasis the disparity between the two teams' bowling strength if its preparation had been left to West Indies' four-pronged pace attack itself.

West Indies were always certain winners in the conditions that prevailed. It was fitting that Richards should crown their superiority with his devastating 56-ball hundred in the final Test, the fastest ever in Test cricket in terms of balls received. But there are ways and ways of losing. Once England fell love–two behind, they seemed to lose their appetite to fight. There were certain notable exceptions, but for the last month of the tour too many of the team, subconsciously or other-wise, gave the appearance of scoring off the days before they could return to England. At nearly £900 a week per head, they owed the Test selectors, and the British public, a good deal more than that.

West Indies v England	First Test
At Kingston, February 21, 22, 23, 1986. West Indies won by ten wickets.	John Thicknesse, 1987

Only while Gooch and Robinson batted without undue difficulty in the first hour of the match did England promise to give West Indies a harder fight than in 1984. Of the five West Indian victories in that series in England, two were achieved on the fourth day: at Sabina Park, after two England collapses, they had almost an hour to spare on the third when Haynes and Richardson completed the formality of scoring the five runs needed in West Indies' second innings.

Once again the cause of England's defeat was their inability to play excep-tional fast bowling, much of it short-pitched. Their problems were accentuated by a fast, uneven surface and the presence in West Indies ranks of Patterson, a 24-year-old Jamaican who, after failing to make much impact in a handful of games for Lancashire in 1985, forced his way into the West Indies team by his performances in the Shell Shield. Described before the Test as the fastest bowler in the Caribbean after Marshall, Patterson left no doubt in the England batsmen's minds that the order should have been reversed. A heavyweight of 6ft 2in, with a sprinting run and powerful delivery, in England's second innings he bowled at a pace comparable to that of Jeff Thomson of Australia in his prime. Deprived of the new ball by the prior claims of Marshall and Garner, he none the less took seven for 74 in his first Test and won the match award.

Toss: England. **England 159** (G. A. Gooch 51, A. J. Lamb 49; B. P. Patterson 4-30) **and 152**
(P. Willey 71; M. D. Marshall 3-29, J. Garner 3-22, B. P. Patterson 3-44); **West Indies 307**
(C. G. Greenidge 58, D. L. Haynes 32, H. A. Gomes 56, C. A. Best 35, P. J. L. Dujon 54;
R. M. Ellison 5-78) **and 5-0.**

West Indies v England
Fifth Test

At St John's, Antigua, April 11, 12, 13, 15, 16, 1986. West Indies won by 240 runs.   John Thicknesse, 1987

Richards's 110 not out in West Indies' second innings, the fastest Test hundred ever in terms of balls received (56 to reach three figures, 58 in all), made the final Test historic on two counts. The other was West Indies' achievement in emulating Australia, previously the only country to win all five home Tests on more than one occasion. Their previous five-love victory was over India in 1961–62, matching Australia's feats against England (1920–21) and South Africa (1931–32), the series in which Sir Donald Bradman made 806 runs in four completed innings. In addition, West Indies also won all five Tests of the 1984 series in England.

Richards's display would have been staggering at any level of cricket. What made it unforgettable for the 5,000 or so lucky enough to see it was that he scored it without blemish at a time when England's sole aim was to make run-scoring as difficult as possible to delay a declaration. Botham and Emburey never had fewer than six men on the boundary and sometimes nine, yet whatever length or line they bowled, Richards had a stroke for it. His control and touch were as much features of the innings as the tremendous power of his driving. The full innings went: 36126141 (24 off 10) 211 412 1 (36 off 20) 112 2111 (45 off 30) 1 1624441 (68 off 40) 12 664612 (96 off 50) 21 461 (110 off 58). Plundered in 83 minutes out of 146 while he was at the wicket, it had to be, by any yardstick, among the most wonderful innings ever played.

West Indies v England, 1986
Fifth Test

At St John's, Antigua, April 11, 12, 13, 15, 16, 1986. Result: West Indies won by 240 runs.

WEST INDIES	First innings		Second innings
C. G. Greenidge b Botham	14		
D. L. Haynes c Gatting b Ellison	131	– (1) run out	70
R. B. Richardson c Slack b Emburey	24	– (2) c Robinson b Emburey	31
H. A. Gomes b Emburey	24		
*I. V. A. Richards c Gooch b Botham	26	– (3) not out	110
†P. J. L. Dujon b Foster	21		
M. D. Marshall c Gatting b Gooch	76		
R. A. Harper c Lamb b Foster	60	– (4) not out	19
M. A. Holding c Gower b Ellison	73		
J. Garner run out	11		
B. P. Patterson not out	0		
B 2, l-b 11, w 1	14	B 4, l-b 9, w 1, n-b 2	16

1-23 2-63 3-137 4-178 5-232 6-281 7-351   474   1-100 2-161   (2 wkts dec.) 246
8-401 9-450 10-474

First innings – Botham 40–6–147–2; Foster 28–5–86–2; Ellison 24.3–3–114–2; Emburey 37–11–93–2; Gooch 5–2–21–1.
Second innings – Botham 15–0–78–0; Foster 10–0–40–0; Ellison 4–0–32–0; Emburey 14–0–83–1.

ENGLAND	First innings		Second innings
G. A. Gooch lbw b Holding	51	– lbw b Holding	51
W. N. Slack c Greenidge b Patterson	52	– b Garner	8
R. T. Robinson b Marshall	12	– run out	3
*D. I. Gower c Dujon b Marshall	90	– (5) c Dujon b Harper	21
A. J. Lamb c and b Harper	1	– (6) b Marshall	1
M. W. Gatting c Dujon b Garner	15	– (7) b Holding	1
I. T. Botham c Harper b Garner	10	– (8) b Harper	13
†P. R. Downton c Holding b Garner	5	– (9) lbw b Marshall	13
R. M. Ellison c Dujon b Marshall	6	– (4) lbw b Garner	16
J. E. Emburey not out	7	– c Richardson b Harper	0
N. A. Foster c Holding b Garner	10	– not out	0
B 5, l-b 6, n-b 40	51	B 10, l-b 10, w 2, n-b 21	43

1-127 2-132 3-157 4-159	310	1-14 2-29 3-84 4-101	170
5-205 6-213 7-237 8-289		5-112 6-124 7-147	
9-290 10-310		8-166 9-168 10-170	

First innings – Marshall 24–5–64–3; Garner 21.4–2–67–4; Patterson 14–2–49–1; Holding 20–3–71–1; Harper 26–7–45–1; Richards 2–0–3–0.

Second innings – Marshall 16.1–6–25–2; Garner 17–5–38–2; Patterson 15–3–29–0; Holding 16–3–45–2; Harper 12–8–10–3; Richards 3–1–3–0.

Toss won by England   UMPIRES L. H. Barker and C. E. Cumberbatch

---

NEW ZEALAND v WEST INDIES 1987   Tony Cozier, 1988

The unmistakable evidence after the West Indians' tour of New Zealand early in 1987 was that both teams were on the decline and faced a period of rebuilding. Each relied on the same players who had formed the nucleus of its sides for several years; most were over the age of 30 and several had passed their peak. The West Indians, particularly, lacked the all-round brilliance with which they had dominated international cricket for the better part of a decade, their enthusiasm diminished by a glut of cricket. They had come directly from a hectic one-day series in Australia.

The honours were even in the series of three Tests. New Zealand comfortably saved the first after a spirited recovery in their second innings, West Indies won the second, in spite of the loss of more than a day's play to the weather, and New Zealand levelled the rubber in convincing fashion in the last. In the one-day internationals that followed, the West Indians, largely through the batting of their captain, Vivian Richards, in the first and Gordon Greenidge in the last two, were irresistible.

It was the first visit to New Zealand by the West Indians since their ill-tempered tour of 1979–80, and the team manager, the former Test opening batsman and current Board secretary, Stephen Camacho, and captain Richards made a conscious effort to let bygones be bygones. Apart from exchanges during the Second Test between Richards and an umpire, Fred Goodall, which brought a protest from the New Zealand team management, the tour passed smoothly.

New Zealand v West Indies
At Christchurch, March 12, 13, 14, 15, 1987. New Zealand won by five wickets.

Third Test
Tony Cozier, 1988

New Zealand won by five wickets to square the series, inflicting on West Indies their first defeat in three days' play since 1965 when they were beaten by Australia at Port-of-Spain. Unfit conditions on certain parts of the outfield, caused by two days of heavy rain, had led to the abandonment of the first day and had also hindered the proper preparation of the pitch, which was slightly damp when play began promptly on the second morning.

The toss provided New Zealand with an early advantage, and Hadlee and Chatfield capitalised on it against batting lacking application and discipline. The collapse started with the first ball of the third over, when Hadlee went through Haynes's defence to hit the off stump, and only the last-wicket partnership of Gray and Walsh lifted West Indies past 77, their previous lowest total against New Zealand. There were five slip catches as Hadlee, whose first four overs cost 25 runs, returned to maintain the pressure initiated by Chatfield, who bowled his 18 overs unchanged, offering hardly a bad ball.

New Zealand lost both left-handed openers cheaply, Horne, on his debut, and Wright falling to catches at first slip. But the Crowe brothers put them ahead by the end of the day. Both had been dropped by then, Jeff by the wicket-keeper off Marshall when 16, Martin at slip off Richards when 39, and Martin gave a chance to gully off Marshall next day when 75. Their stand was worth 156 when Martin got himself into a tangle over a pull shot against Marshall and was bowled 17 runs short of his third century of the series. Gray then claimed two quick wickets, only for Coney and Bracewell to consolidate New Zealand's advantage by adding 89.

West Indies had a deficit of 232 when Coney declared and Greenidge, who lifted Bracewell for six in the final over, and Haynes had reduced it by 35 at the close. When Haynes was out to the sixth ball and Greenidge to the seventh next morning, all fight seemed to leave the West Indians and they batted with carefree abandon as wickets fell at regular intervals. Richards epitomised his team's approach. Coming in at 80 for three after Hadlee had claimed his 350th Test wicket by having Richardson caught off a miscued hook, he took five fours off the first seven balls he received from Hadlee and was then caught behind, cutting at a ball too close to him, the first of Snedden's five wickets.

Dujon and Marshall delayed the end with a seventh-wicket partnership of 77, but New Zealand were left with the seeming formality of scoring 33. However, Walsh and Gray, bowling with real pace and hostility, made it anything but. Gray supplemented his bowling with two stunning catches, one at slip, the other at gully, but it was little more than a gesture. New Zealand completed their well-deserved victory with 25 minutes remaining of the day. Their fifth wicket in the second innings was that of Coney, their captain, who was given an emotional reception by the crowd in his last Test.

Toss: New Zealand. **West Indies 100** (R. B. Richardson 37; R. J. Hadlee 6-50, E. J. Chatfield 4-30) **and 264** (H. A. Gomes 33, I. V. A. Richards 38, P. J. L. Dujon 39, M. D. Marshall 45; R. J. Hadlee 3-101, M. C. Snedden 5-68); **New Zealand 332-9 dec.** (J. J. Crowe 55, M. D. Crowe 83, J. V. Coney 36, J. G. Bracewell 66, Extras 37; J. Garner 4-79) **and 33-5** (C. A. Walsh 3-16).

ENGLAND V WEST INDIES 1988

See page 243

AUSTRALIA V WEST INDIES 1992–93   Tony Cozier, 1994

A fledgling West Indian team, under a captain in his first full series, showed great resilience in winning the new Frank Worrell Trophy – the original had disappeared – and adding yet another World Series Cup to their collection. It was West Indies' first series against Australia since 1972–73 without the imposing batting talents of Vivian Richards and Gordon Greenidge, the first since 1979–80 without Jeffrey Dujon, their most successful wicket-keeper-batsman, and since 1983–84 without Malcolm Marshall, their leading taker of Test wickets. All had left the international scene since the teams last met in the Caribbean, less than two years earlier, and the failure of the reconstituted team, under new captain Richie Richardson, in the World Cup did not encourage hopes of a quick revival.

When Australia won the Second Test at Melbourne comfortably by 139 runs, having only just been denied victory in the First, and then amassed over 500 in their first innings of the Third at Sydney before removing the openers for 31, West Indies faced a stern test of character. An extraordinary double-century by Brian Lara, assessed by many reputable judges as one of the finest innings of the modern era, revived them. Lara's 277, the fourth-highest Test score by a West Indian, and his third-wicket partnership of 293 with Richardson led to a total of 606, undermined Australia's confidence and proved the turning point in the series. After securing a draw in Sydney, West Indies won every match: the final two Tests to take the series 2–1 and four consecutive World Series Cup games, including the two finals against Australia. A heart-stopping victory by one run, Test cricket's narrowest margin, in an unusually low-scoring match at Adelaide levelled the series. And as they had done in each of their three previous Tests in Perth, they overwhelmed their opponents on a characteristically fast and bouncy pitch.

While Lara's unforgettable performance changed the course of the series, Curtly Ambrose's flawless fast bowling was instrumental in winning it. Hindered by bad luck on unresponsive pitches in the first three Tests, he was irresistible in the more sympathetic conditions of Adelaide and Perth, claiming 19 wickets in the two matches at less than 11 runs each. Using his height to awkward effect, Ambrose was always capable of delivering the unplayable ball at the opportune time. When Australia required only 186 to win at Adelaide, he removed their two most reliable batsmen, David Boon and Allan Border, for a single between them. Then he settled the outcome of the Perth Test after lunch on the first day with a stunning spell of seven for one off 32 balls. He went on to equal the record of 33 wickets in an Australian-West Indian series held by Clarrie Grimmett and Alan Davidson. In the two one-day finals, he took eight wickets for 58.

Australia v West Indies

Third Test

At Sydney, January 2, 3, 4, 5, 6, 1993. Drawn.

Tony Cozier, 1994

An innings of breathtaking quality by Brian Lara towered over everything else in a high-scoring match. In between breaks for rain Lara unleashed a dazzling array of strokes. He needed only 125 balls to reach his maiden Test century in his fifth match. Australia were powerless to stop him until he committed himself to a single to cover off Matthews and could not beat Martyn's return to the wicket-keeper when Hooper sent him back. His 277 was the third-highest individual Test score against Australia (behind L. Hutton and R. E. Foster) and the highest for either side in Tests between Australia and West Indies. He struck 38 fours off 372 balls in seven hours 54 minutes. Lara's pre-eminence on the rain-shortened fourth day was such that he added 156 and struck 23 fours, outscoring his three partners by more than two to one. His solitary chance, low to Steve Waugh at gully off Hughes, was when he was 172.

Toss: Australia. **Australia 503-9 dec.** (D. C. Boon 76, S. R. Waugh 100, M. E. Waugh 57, A. R. Border 74, G. R. J. Matthews 79, I. A. Healy 36*, Extras 30; C. L. Hooper 3-137) **and 117-0** (D. C. Boon 63*, M. A. Taylor 46*); **West Indies 606** (R. B. Richardson 109, B. C. Lara 277, K. L. T. Arthurton 47, J. C. Adams 77*; M. G. Hughes 3-76).

Australia v West Indies

Fourth Test

At Adelaide, January 23, 24, 25, 26, 1993. West Indies won by one run.

Tony Cozier, 1994

Adelaide 1993 took its place as one of the greatest of all Test matches when Craig McDermott failed to get out of the way of a lifter from Courtney Walsh and gloved a catch to give West Indies victory by one run, the narrowest victory anyone has achieved in 116 years of Test cricket. It had been a game of fluctuating fortunes throughout. When Australia, needing 186 to win, lost their eighth second-innings wicket for 102, it appeared to have made its decisive shift. But then the 22-year-old debutant Justin Langer, who came in only when Martyn was injured at pre-match practice, added 42 with the No. 10 Tim May, who was playing his first Test in four years. After that May and the last man McDermott put on another 40 to get Australia within two of their target.

The unfolding drama lifted the TV cricket ratings in Australia to a new record. And, with the Adelaide Oval within walking distance of the city centre, new spectators rushed to the ground. Finally, a short ball from Walsh, pitched on off stump, lifted to brush McDermott's hand on its way through to Murray. Umpire Hair upheld the appeal. The West Indians on the field celebrated emotionally. The crowd who had been singing "Waltzing Matilda" as Australia inched towards their goal were stunned into silence.

The Australian captain Border did not dispute Hair's decision, though he said that, like the result, it was a very close one. "What can you say – one run? I was very confident of getting 186 at the start of the day." His opposite number Richardson said: "I knew Walshy would get a wicket with that very ball. I never lost hope." Both leaders paid tribute to the man who made the result possible: Ambrose consolidated his reputation as the world's leading fast bowler with ten wickets in the match and a burst of three wickets in 19 balls after lunch to dismiss Steve Waugh, Border and Hughes.

Australia v West Indies, 1992–93 — Fourth Test

At Adelaide, January 23, 24, 25, 26, 1993. Result: West Indies won by one run.

WEST INDIES	First innings		Second innings	
D. L. Haynes st Healy b May	45	– c Healy b McDermott		11
P. V. Simmons c Hughes b S. R. Waugh	46	– b McDermott		10
*R. B. Richardson lbw b Hughes	2	– c Healy b Warne		72
B. C. Lara c Healy b McDermott	52	– c S. R. Waugh b Hughes		7
K. L. T. Arthurton c S. R. Waugh b May	0	– c Healy b McDermott		0
C. L. Hooper c Healy b Hughes	2	– c Hughes b May		25
†J. R. Murray not out	49	– c M. E. Waugh b May		0
I. R. Bishop c M. E. Waugh b Hughes	13	– c M. E. Waugh b May		6
C. E. L. Ambrose c Healy b Hughes	0	– st Healy b May		1
K. C. G. Benjamin b M. E. Waugh	15	– c Warne b May		0
C. A. Walsh lbw b Hughes	5	– not out		0
L-b 11, n-b 12	23	L-b 2, n-b 12		14
1-84 2-99 3-129 4-130 5-134 6-189 7-206 8-206 9-247 10-252	252	1-14 2-49 3-65 4-65 5-124 6-137 7-145 8-146 9-146 10-146		146

First innings – McDermott 16–1–85–1; Hughes 21.3–3–64–5; S. R. Waugh 13–4–37–1; May 14–1–41–2; Warne 2–0–11–0; M. E. Waugh 1–0–3–1.

Second innings – McDermott 11–0–66–3; Hughes 13–1–43–1; S. R. Waugh 5–1–8–0; May 6.5–3–9–5; Warne 6–2–18–1.

AUSTRALIA	First innings		Second innings	
M. A. Taylor c Hooper b Bishop	1	– (2) c Murray b Benjamin		7
D. C. Boon not out	39	– (1) lbw b Ambrose		0
J. L. Langer c Murray b Benjamin	20	– c Murray b Bishop		54
M. E. Waugh c Simmons b Ambrose	0	– c Hooper b Walsh		26
S. R. Waugh c Murray b Ambrose	42	– c Arthurton b Ambrose		4
*A. R. Border c Hooper b Ambrose	19	– c Haynes b Ambrose		1
†I. A. Healy c Hooper b Ambrose	0	– b Walsh		0
M. G. Hughes c Murray b Hooper	43	– lbw b Ambrose		1
S. K. Warne lbw b Hooper	0	– lbw b Bishop		9
T. B. A. May c Murray b Ambrose	6	– not out		42
C. J. McDermott b Ambrose	14	– c Murray b Walsh		18
B 7, l-b 3, n-b 19	29	B 1, l-b 8, n-b 13		22
1-1 2-16 3-46 4-108 5-108 6-112 7-181 8-181 9-197 10-213	213	1-5 2-16 3-54 4-64 5-72 6-73 7-74 8-102 9-144 10-184		184

First innings – Ambrose 28.2–6–74–6; Bishop 18–3–48–1; Benjamin 6–0–22–1; Walsh 10–3–34–0; Hooper 13–4–25–2.

Second innings – Ambrose 26–5–46–4; Bishop 17–3–41–2; Benjamin 12–2–32–1; Walsh 19–4–44–3; Hooper 5–1–12–0.

Toss won by West Indies   UMPIRES D. B. Hair and L. J. King.

West Indies v England 1994
For Series Review and Fourth Test, see page 261

West Indies v England   Third Test
At Port-of-Spain, March 25, 26, 27, 29, 30, 1994. West Indies won by 147 runs.   Alan Lee, 1995

The fourth day of this match witnessed an astonishing transformation: when it began England were enviably placed for a victory which would have kept the series alive [they had lost the first two Tests by large margins]; by the end they were threatened by their lowest score in history. Eventually, by a single run, they avoided the ultimate indignity of equalling the 45 all out recorded at Sydney, 107 years earlier, but the England side of 1887 actually won. The 1994 side lost both match and series during a staggering collapse to fast bowling of the highest calibre from Ambrose, who finished with six for 24 in the innings and 11 for 84 in the match. He supplied one of the most devastating spells of even his career, rampaging in as if on springs.

The game lasted only 17 minutes on the final morning, Walsh claiming the last two wickets. As Ambrose was carried shoulder-high from the ground, the great calypsonian Lord Kitchener serenaded his success outside the dressing-room. For England, a match which had promised much for three days had ended in utter humiliation.

West Indies v England, 1994   Third Test
At Port-of-Spain, March 25, 26, 27, 29, 30, 1994. Result: West Indies won by 147 runs.

WEST INDIES	First innings		Second innings
D. L. Haynes b Salisbury	38	– b Lewis	19
*R. B. Richardson lbw b Salisbury	63	– c and b Caddick	3
B. C. Lara lbw b Lewis	43	– c Salisbury b Caddick	12
K. L. T. Arthurton lbw b Lewis	1	– c Stewart b Caddick	42
J. C. Adams c Smith b Lewis	2	– c Russell b Salisbury	43
S. Chanderpaul b Fraser	19	– c Fraser b Caddick	50
†J. R. Murray not out	27	– c Russell b Caddick	14
W. K. M. Benjamin b Fraser	10	– c Fraser b Lewis	35
C. E. L. Ambrose c Thorpe b Fraser	13	– b Caddick	12
K. C. G. Benjamin b Fraser	9	– not out	5
C. A. Walsh lbw b Lewis	0	– lbw b Lewis	1
B 1, l-b 13, w 1, n-b 12	27	B 8, l-b 13, n-b 12	33
1-66 2-158 3-158 4-163 5-164 6-201	252	1-15 2-37 3-51 4-131 5-143 6-167	269
7-212 8-241 9-251 10-252		7-227 8-247 9-267 10-269	

First innings – Fraser 24–9–49–4; Caddick 19–5–43–0; Lewis 25.2–3–61–4; Salisbury 22–4–72–2; Ramprakash 2–1–8–0; Hick 3–1–5–0.
Second innings – Fraser 25–6–71–0; Caddick 26–5–65–6; Lewis 27.5–6–71–3; Salisbury 9–1–41–1.

ENGLAND	First innings		Second innings
*M. A. Atherton c Murray b W. K. M. Benjamin	48	– lbw b Ambrose	0
A. J. Stewart b Ambrose	6	– b Ambrose	18
M. R. Ramprakash c and b W. K. M. Benjamin	23	– run out	1
R. A. Smith lbw b Ambrose	12	– b Ambrose	0
G. A. Hick lbw b Walsh	40	– c Murray b Ambrose	6
G. P. Thorpe c Lara b Ambrose	86	– b Ambrose	3
†R. C. Russell b Ambrose	23	– (8) c sub (P. V. Simmons) b Ambrose	4
C. C. Lewis b Ambrose	9	– (9) c W. K. M. Benjamin b Walsh	6
I. D. K. Salisbury c Lara b Walsh	36	– (7) c Lara b Walsh	0
A. R. Caddick c Lara b W. K. M. Benjamin . .	6	– c Lara b Walsh	1
A. R. C. Fraser not out	8	– not out	0
B 10, l-b 9, w 1, n-b 11	31	L-b 6, n-b 1	7

1-16 2-82 3-87 4-115 5-167 6-249   **328**   1-0 2-1 3-5 4-21 5-26 6-27   **46**
7-273 8-281 9-294 10-328   7-37 8-40 9-45 10-46

First innings – Ambrose 29–6–60–5; Walsh 27.2–3–77–2; K. C. G. Benjamin 20–5–70–0; W. K. M. Benjamin 24–3–66–3; Adams 4–0–18–0; Chanderpaul 5–0–13–0; Arthurton 3–0–5–0.
Second innings – Ambrose 10–1–24–6; Walsh 9.1–1–16–3.

Toss won by West Indies   UMPIRES S. A. Bucknor and S. Venkataraghavan

---

West Indies v England   Fifth Test

At St John's, Antigua, April 16, 17, 18, 20, 21, 1994. Drawn.   Alan Lee, 1995

A contest which scarcely progressed beyond its first innings, tied at 593 runs each, nevertheless earned an eternal place in cricket history by dint of an innings of 375 by Brian Lara, beating by ten runs the record individual score in Test cricket, created 36 years earlier by Sir Garfield Sobers. Lara broke the record from the 530th ball he faced, having batted for the equivalent of more than two days. He had not given a single chance and, until tension and fatigue almost overcame him in the home straight, scarcely made a mistake. Sobers himself came on to the field to shake Lara's hand in the chaotic moments which followed an exultantly pulled four from a short ball by Lewis. It was only Lara's third Test century but the previous two had been 277 and 167, confirming his appetite for the long innings. After the 277 he said he had been thinking of the record. Having achieved it this time, Lara went to Trinidad for a triumphal homecoming before leaving to play county cricket for Warwickshire.

One of the most remarkable aspects of the innings was that it was born out of the adversity of 12 for two, West Indies' makeshift opening pair having lasted barely half an hour on the first morning. Another was that the record, or at least a threat to the old record, looked inevitable by the time Lara had made 50, such was his obvious determination and his absolute mastery of England's bowlers on an utterly inoffensive pitch, only partially offset by a turgidly slow outfield which turned many fours into twos.

All England could aspire to was the not inconsiderable task of batting out time. This they achieved in some comfort, Atherton batting with great authority after being dropped on 46 and Smith profiting from two dismissals off no-balls from Walsh to make an overdue century. The performance of Atherton and Smith also guaranteed only the fourth draw in the last 29 Tests between these teams. Once Russell and Lewis had added half-centuries and the scores had finished level on first innings, only 34 overs remained. Of these, 24 were played out to end a game of total stalemate but glittering memories.

West Indies v England, 1994   Fifth Test

At St John's, Antigua, April 16, 17, 18, 20, 21, 1994. Result: Drawn.

WEST INDIES	First innings		Second innings
P. V. Simmons lbw b Caddick	8	– not out	22
S. C. Williams c Caddick b Fraser	3	– not out	21
B. C. Lara c Russell b Caddick	375		
J. C. Adams c sub (N. Hussain) b Fraser	59		
K. L. T. Arthurton c Russell b Caddick	47		
S. Chanderpaul not out	75		
L-b 3, n-b 23	26		

1-11 2-12 3-191 4-374 5-593   (5 wkts dec.) 593   (no wkt) 43

†J. R. Murray, W. K. M. Benjamin,
C. E. L. Ambrose, K. C. G. Benjamin and
*C. A. Walsh did not bat.

First innings – Fraser 43–4–121–2; Caddick 47.2–8–158–3; Tufnell 39–8–110–0; Lewis 33–1–140–0;
Hick 18–3–61–0.
Second innings – Fraser 2–1–2–0; Caddick 2–1–11–0; Tufnell 6–4–5–0; Hick 8–2–11–0;
Ramprakash 3–1–5–0; Thorpe 2–1–1–0; Stewart 1–0–8–0.

ENGLAND

*M. A. Atherton c Murray b Ambrose	135	A. R. Caddick c W. K. M. Benjamin b Adams 22
A. J. Stewart c Ambrose b K. C. G. Benjamin	24	A. R. C. Fraser b Adams 0
M. R. Ramprakash lbw b K. C. G. Benjamin	19	P. C. R. Tufnell lbw b W. K. M. Benjamin 0
R. A. Smith lbw b K. C. G. Benjamin	175	B 9, l-b 20, n-b 23 52
G. A. Hick b K. C. G. Benjamin	20	
G. P. Thorpe c Adams b Chanderpaul	9	1-40 2-70 3-373 4-393 5-401 6-417 593
†R. C. Russell c Murray b W. K. M. Benjamin	62	7-535 8-585 9-589 10-593
C. C. Lewis not out	75	

Ambrose 40–18–66–1; Walsh 40–9–123–0; W. K. M. Benjamin 41.1–15–93–2;
K. C. G. Benjamin 37–7–110–4; Chanderpaul 24–1–94–1; Adams 22–4–74–2; Arthurton 2–1–4–0.

Toss won by West Indies   UMPIRES S. A. Bucknor and D. B. Hair

ALL CHANGE AT THE TOP   Tony Cozier, 1997

West Indies cricket has never known a more tempestuous period. Dissension and indiscipline within the Test team, which had first surfaced in April 1995 as West

Indies surrendered the Frank Worrell Trophy to Australia for the first time in 17 years, ultimately led to the resignation of their captain, Richie Richardson, and the replacement of their coach, Andy Roberts, both announced midway through the World Cup. At virtually the same time, the president of the West Indies Cricket Board of Control, Peter Short, said he would not seek re-election and the team manager, Wes Hall, announced that he would no longer be available because of business commitments. This meant a complete change of leadership on all fronts in the space of a few weeks.

Richardson, unfairly but not unexpectedly, took most of the blame for the upheavals within the team and for its erratic performances, the nadir being the World Cup loss to Kenya. The upheavals were compounded by the controversies surrounding Brian Lara, West Indies' most celebrated player, who had temporarily walked out of the 1995 tour of England, refused to join the subsequent trip to Australia, twice appeared before the board's disciplinary committee and twice issued public apologies for indiscretions that brought him a fine, a written reprimand and a warning about his future conduct.

Getting wind that the board was about to remove him, Richardson preempted the decision. It was a distressing end to the career of one of the most exciting batsmen and genuine sportsmen of all time. He had led West Indies in 24 of his 86 Tests and played 224 one-day internationals, 87 as captain. His replacement was the 33-year-old fast bowler Courtney Walsh, who had already stood-in when illness forced Richardson to rest a year earlier. This was a short-term choice. But Lara's persistent disciplinary troubles were delaying his elevation to the position for which he has been groomed since he was a teenager.

PAKISTAN V WEST INDIES 1997   Fazeer Mohammed, 1999

West Indies' sixth Test series in Pakistan was an unqualified disaster. The team's gradual decline from their previous high standards accelerated into freefall and they lost all three Tests by embarrassingly wide margins. Not since their first ever series, in England in 1928, had West Indies experienced such a thorough whitewash. Then, they lost all three matches by an innings. Nearly 70 years later, they came within 12 runs of a similar humiliation.

If the manner and extent of Pakistan's victories – the first two by an innings, the third by ten wickets – shocked the cricketing world, they were not altogether surprising to close followers of Courtney Walsh's team. All that was needed was opposition of the right calibre to expose and capitalise upon their inconsistency, indiscipline and complacency. And this time the Pakistanis, often their own worst enemies, displayed a ruthless efficiency under the inspiring leadership of Wasim Akram, restored to the captaincy after the defeat by South Africa.

Wasim himself led the assault, taking 17 wickets, three more than Walsh, who soldiered on manfully with little assistance from his colleagues. By contrast, Wasim had other potent weapons in his arsenal. Leg-spinner Mushtaq Ahmed's 12 wickets included ten in the First Test in Peshawar, while off-spinner Saqlain Mushtaq claimed nine in his only appearance, in the final Test in Karachi. Waqar Younis made an immediate impact on his return to partner Wasim with a spectacular dismissal of Brian Lara in the Second Test in Rawalpindi.

Lara's woes, on and off the field, typified and aggravated West Indies' struggles. Many explanations were sought for his pitiful return of 129 runs at 21.50, most focusing on the dressing-room rather than events in the middle. There were persistent reports of a power struggle between him and Walsh. The West Indies Cricket Board contributed to the furore by not naming an official vice-captain for the tour: Lara had held the position in recent series. Repeated denials by team management, who made him second-in-command anyway, of any rift or general dissension in the ranks failed to quell the almost daily speculation. Manager Clive Lloyd considered it a calculated ploy to unsettle his team. If it was, it worked.

West Indies' batting, so brittle in recent series, plumbed new depths of ineptitude. Only once did they total more than 300 in an innings – and then it was only just. The next best effort was 216, telling a stark tale of players out of their depth, unable – or unwilling – to concentrate for long periods against a challenging attack in testing conditions. Only opener Sherwin Campbell, who scored 248 runs including three half-centuries, suggested any degree of consistency and solidity. Carl Hooper attacked with sublime brilliance for his team's only century of the series, in Karachi, and compiled an equally delightful unbeaten 73 in Rawalpindi. But, typically, his other four scores totalled less than 50. Left-hander Shivnarine Chanderpaul came within five runs of a century in the Second Test yet contributed precious little otherwise. So successful against India in the Caribbean earlier in the year, Chanderpaul found the late swing of Pakistan's pace bowlers an almost insurmountable hurdle.

However, Pakistan's top order weighed in heavily against bowling that was often ordinary and lacking in purpose. An epidemic of dropped catches and generally ragged out-cricket only served to ease Pakistan's passage to totals of 381, 471 and 417 in their three completed innings. Aamir Sohail was the prime beneficiary, compiling identical scores of 160 in each of the final two Tests to earn his team's Man of the Series award. Inzamam-ul-Haq topped the averages with 136.50 thanks to a monumental 177 in Rawalpindi after an unbeaten 92 in Peshawar. Not wanting to miss out on the run-feast, Ijaz Ahmed took over the role of opener from the injured Saeed Anwar in Karachi and hit 151. He shared an opening partnership of 298, a record for Pakistan, with Sohail, who had already put on 323 for the third wicket with Inzamam in the previous Test.

Walsh had little support. Aged 35, he bowled 32 more overs than anyone else, but the burden was too much for even him to carry alone. Curtly Ambrose, a destructive force in three previous series against Pakistan, was a shadow of his old self, taking just one wicket for 139 runs in the first two Tests, before injury forced him out of the Third. A few months later he would take out his frustrations on England. In the meantime, Mervyn Dillon filled the breach effectively. But leg-spinner Rawl Lewis disappointed on debut in Peshawar, another step backwards for West Indian slow bowlers. In these circumstances, Walsh's efforts were nothing short of heroic. The obvious choice as West Indies' Man of the Series, he returned home chastened, and on the brink of losing the captaincy, but having built up his Test aggregate to 353 wickets in 96 Tests.

Pakistan v West Indies   **First Test**

At Peshawar, November 17, 18, 19, 20, 1997.

Pakistan won by an innings and 19 runs.   Fazeer Mohammed, 1999

West Indies crashed to what was – for a fortnight – their heaviest ever defeat at the hands of Pakistan. Coming hard on the heels of their whitewash in the quadrangular limited-overs series, this was another indicator of the decline in Caribbean standards. Mushtaq earned most of the plaudits, with match figures of ten for 106 – even if cynics noted that he bowled in both innings at the end where the local umpire, Said Shah, was presiding.

Toss: West Indies. **West Indies 151** (D. Williams 31, C. E. L. Ambrose 30; Mushtaq Ahmed 5-35) **and 211**
(S. L. Campbell 66, B. C. Lara 37; Wasim Akram 4-65, Mushtaq Ahmed 5-71); **Pakistan 381**
(Saeed Anwar 65, Ijaz Ahmed 65, Inzamam-ul-Haq 92*, Moin Khan 58; C. A. Walsh 5-78,
I. R. Bishop 3-76).

WEST INDIES V ENGLAND 1998

See page 285

See page 285

CHAOS, CONFUSION AND CONTROVERSY   Tony Cozier, 1999

The twin triumphs over England towards the end of the [1998] home season – 3–1 in the Tests, 4–1 in the one-day internationals – came as a timely and immense relief for West Indies cricket. For several months it had been consumed by chaos, confusion and controversy off the field and catastrophe on it. It seemed to be in a self-destruct mode, undermined by a succession of administrative blunders and divisions, and shamed by heavy defeats sustained by its teams at all levels. To have faltered against England, opponents with an unflattering record, would have been a devastating reversal for a sport already beginning to lose its exalted status in the English-speaking Caribbean.

The game plunged back into crisis later in the year when its star players effectively went on strike for a week over pay and conditions, before finally agreeing to start the 1998–99 tour of South Africa. Most of the immediate troubles could be traced to the financial losses incurred by the West Indies Cricket Board in its grandiose schemes of the previous year and to the contentious debate over the captaincy. The decision to extend the 1996–97 season by doubling the number of matches in the first-class tournament, the Red Stripe Cup, playing home and away, and by hosting, for the first time, two separate Test series, proved a serious drain on funds. The retention of 22 players on year-long contracts increased the liability when the relevant governments reneged on pledges of support. Operating profits of over $4m the previous year were transformed into a loss of $267,000. The players' contracts were not renewed and the 1997–98 regional tournament reverted to a one-round format. There was a further setback when it could not find a sponsor; Red Stripe transferred its support to the limited-overs competition, previously the Shell/Sandals Trophy, which became the Red Stripe Bowl.

The debate over the captaincy also proved acrimonious. It was public knowledge that the board had overridden the selectors' recommendation that Brian Lara, a Trinidadian, take over from Courtney Walsh, a Jamaican, for the tours of Pakistan and Sharjah. The rejection was angrily resented by the Trinidad & Tobago board, which issued a statement alleging "a calculated plot to tarnish [Lara's] image and international reputation using past indiscretions as the basis for sowing the seeds of destruction". Lara was heckled by Jamaicans during the Red Stripe Bowl and there were repeated claims of tension within the team – vehemently denied – in Pakistan and Sharjah.

Eventually, Lara was appointed in January for the series against England, his accession eased by Walsh's magnanimity and continuing commitment to the team. It was a significant factor in their success. Yet the problems were not over. West Indies made another entry in the ledger of infamy when the First Test had to be abandoned because of the treacherous and ill-prepared Sabina Park pitch. It was an unwelcome first in Test cricket's history – and, as a substitute Test was hurriedly arranged, a further disruption in the first-class domestic tournament, which halted during international games.

SOUTH AFRICA V WEST INDIES 1998–99 — Geoffrey Dean, 2000

Even though they had been defeated 3–0 in Pakistan a year earlier, the notion that West Indies would suffer a 5–0 series whitewash on their first Test tour of South Africa was inconceivable. On paper, there was little between the two sides. How, then, did the unthinkable come to pass? How did West Indies lose every match in a five-Test series for the first time in their long and distinguished history? It had happened only six times before in Test cricket and, on each of the last three occasions, it was West Indies who had done the humbling.

The pay dispute with the West Indies board, which culminated in crisis talks in London, unsettled the team before the tour even began. Only half the West Indies party arrived in South Africa at the scheduled start of the tour. The rest, including captain Brian Lara and vice-captain Carl Hooper, stayed in London after the Mini World Cup in Bangladesh. The remainder of the squad then flew into Heathrow from South Africa to present a united front to the board, who initially sacked Lara and Hooper, then sought reconciliation.

How united that front really was is open to question: the junior players found themselves dragged into a dispute in which the seniors were largely seeking a pay increase for themselves. Certainly, there was a divided air about the West Indies party for much of the tour. Lara admitted after the Fifth Test that "we are not together as a team". That appeared an understatement, and, for that lack of unity, Lara had to bear some responsibility. His public criticism of two of his bowlers, Nixon McLean and Mervyn Dillon, after the Second Test capitulation, seemed to sap their confidence, and neither bowled consistently all tour. Lara failed to get the best not only from them but also several other unproven Test players.

Lara himself continued to underachieve with the bat, extending his sequence of matches without a Test hundred to 14. There were glimpses of his old genius, but he got himself out all too regularly. The same could be said for Hooper and Shivnarine Chanderpaul, whose dearth of runs critically undermined the West Indian cause. The three middle-order heavyweights generally failed to apply themselves after they were exposed to the new ball in almost every innings. The opening pairings – five combinations were tried – were feeble, showing even less application than the stroke-players. While Jonty Rhodes excelled at No. 6 for South Africa, that position remained highly problematic for the visitors throughout. Jimmy Adams, who would have filled it, was badly missed, having to return home after suffering a mysterious hand injury – reportedly caused by a butterknife – on the flight to Johannesburg.

The most noticeable difference between the sides, however, was the quality of fielding. The run-out count was only 5–4 in South Africa's favour, but the general level of out-cricket did not bear comparison. Rhodes saved a multitude of runs square of the wicket, and his brilliance was matched by Herschelle Gibbs, who held two breathtaking catches to turn the Third Test. Boucher, meanwhile, became the first wicket-keeper to negotiate a five-Test series without conceding a bye.

The one-day series was equally one-sided. Only in the first two games were West Indies competitive and, when injury ruled Lara out for three matches, the batting was hopelessly over-reliant on Chanderpaul and Hooper. An unhappy tour could not end soon enough for a side by now devoid of confidence and spirit.

South Africa v West Indies   First Test

At Johannesburg, November 26, 27, 28, 29, 30, 1998.
South Africa won by four wickets.   Geoffrey Dean, 2000

West Indies came close to winning this First Test and, had they done so, the series might have gone very differently. Just before tea on the fourth day, Jacobs and Hooper, who had joined forces at 80 for five, had inched their side towards a position of strength on a pitch showing increasing signs of unevenness. With their stand worth 68, West Indies were 141 ahead and on course to set a psychologically intimidating target of 200 plus. But both batsmen then fell in successive overs – Jacobs to a dreadful shot – and not long afterwards the final three wickets were frittered away in just four balls. The last gave Pollock his 100th Test victim in the same match, his 26th, in which he had passed 1,000 Test runs. Trevor Goddard was the only South African to achieve this double before.

Set 164, by no means a routine target, South Africa were fortunate that bad light spared them an awkward hour at the end of the fourth day. When play resumed next morning in intense heat, Lara had the problem of marshalling his fast-bowling resources in an extended two-and-a-half hour session. Ambrose and Walsh had superb opening spells, but neither came back as convincingly. With Lara unprepared to risk McLean for more than five overs, Lewis's leg-spin causing few problems and Hooper still hampered by a groin strain, his options were limited. After starting out most uncertainly – creeping to 29 for two from 22 overs – the South Africans at last began to play positively. Once they did so, victory looked increasingly assured. Cullinan and Cronje played aggressive cameos, while Kallis anchored one end. Crucially, the pitch did not deteriorate further.

Toss: West Indies. **West Indies 261** (S. Chanderpaul 74, C. L. Hooper 44, S. C. Williams 35; A. A. Donald 3-91, S. M. Pollock 5-54) **and 170** (C. B. Lambert 33, R. D. Jacobs 42, C. L. Hooper 34; S. M. Pollock 4-49, P. L. Symcox 3-43); **South Africa 268** (G. Kirsten 62, J. H. Kallis 53, W. J. Cronje 41; C. A. Walsh 4-66) **and 164-6** (J. H. Kallis 57*, D. J. Cullinan 35, W. J. Cronje 31; C. A. Walsh 3-45).

WEST INDIES V AUSTRALIA 1999

Mike Coward, 2000

Any series for the Frank Worrell Trophy is something to savour, but in advance it was impossible to foresee quite how fascinating this one would be. In the months preceding the series, West Indies had been humiliated 5–0 in South Africa, while Australia could have defeated England 5–0 but for a tropical storm in Brisbane and arrogant complacency in Melbourne. Rather than a contest for a prize many Australians now treasure as much as the Ashes, this seemed a mismatch with potentially serious consequences for the game. But these series have developed such importance and proud traditions over three decades that both teams played with an intensity which exhausted all who competed and observed.

A squared rubber [two Tests apiece] was a fitting result, although Australia's new captain, Steve Waugh, felt that a tie would have been the most appropriate outcome in Barbados, and that would have given Australia the series. Other, less biased, analysts wondered aloud whether that Test, which West Indies won by one wicket, was the greatest ever played. Certainly, West Indian captain Brian Lara's single-handed orchestration of the match instantly became part of the rich lore of the game. Lara's extraordinary metamorphosis, as a man and leader, breathed new life into the series and, indeed, West Indies cricket. While the seriousness of the problems confronting the game throughout the Caribbean at the end of the 20th century could not be underestimated, Lara showed that, where there is life, there is hope.

West Indies v Australia

First Test

At Port-of-Spain, March 5, 6, 7, 8, 1999. Australia won by 312 runs.   Mike Coward, 2000

Compounding the humiliation of the infamous whitewash in South Africa, West Indies truly reached their nadir when they were dismissed for 51 – their lowest score in 71 years of Test cricket. Their previous worst was 53 in Faisalabad in 1986, and their lowest at home 102 against England in 1935. Only Jacobs reached double figures – the next best was six, by Ambrose. Astonishingly, they lost their last 17 wickets for 69 runs in 31.4 overs, to be ridiculed by critics and crowds alike. The prime target for the vitriol was captain Lara (out second ball). Even doting followers in his native Trinidad showed signs of disaffection, if not anger. When the match ended, after lunch on the fourth day, there were renewed and loud calls for his head.

The capitulation, and the inquisition which inevitably followed, deflected attention from the indefatigable Walsh, who became only the third bowler behind Sir

Richard Hadlee and Kapil Dev to take 400 Test wickets. Going into the Test, his 107th, with 397 wickets, he finished with a match analysis of seven for 131 from 56.2 overs. But it was his counterpart, McGrath, who won the match award, after taking ten wickets in a Test for the first time.

West Indies v Australia, 1999   First Test
At Port-of-Spain, March 5, 6, 7, 8, 1999. Result: Australia won by 312 runs.

AUSTRALIA

	First innings			*Second innings*	
M. J. Slater c Dillon b Collins	23	–	(2) st Jacobs b Adams		106
M. T. G. Elliott lbw b Collins	44	–	(1) c Joseph b Walsh		0
J. L. Langer c Jacobs b Walsh	5	–	c Jacobs b Dillon		24
M. E. Waugh lbw b Walsh	2	–	lbw b Ambrose		33
*S. R. Waugh c Jacobs b Dillon	14	–	c Jacobs b Collins		0
G. S. Blewett lbw b Ambrose	58	–	st Jacobs b Adams		28
†I. A. Healy lbw b Walsh	12	–	lbw b Walsh		0
S. K. Warne c Campbell b Ambrose	21	–	b Walsh		25
J. N. Gillespie not out	28	–	c Lara b Ambrose		22
S. C. G. MacGill b Ambrose	0	–	b Walsh		0
G. D. McGrath c Jacobs b Dillon	39	–	not out		4
L-b 18, n-b 5	23		L-b 7, w 1, n-b 11		19

1-42 2-51 3-53 4-74 5-118 6-153 7-186 8-203   269   1-7 2-45 3-126 4-127 5-193 6-194 7-227   261
9-203 10-269   8-257 9-257 10-261

First innings – Walsh 31–9–60–3; Ambrose 27–15–35–3; Collins 23–8–46–2; Dillon 26.3–4–69–2; Adams 14–2–41–0.
Second innings – Walsh 25.2–2–71–4; Ambrose 18–8–25–2; Collins 21–2–72–1; Dillon 14–1–57–1; Adams 8–1–29–2.

WEST INDIES

	First innings			*Second innings*	
S. L. Campbell lbw b McGrath	9	–	c M. E. Waugh b Gillespie		0
S. Ragoonath run out	9	–	lbw b Gillespie		2
D. R. E. Joseph lbw b McGrath	50	–	c Warne b McGrath		5
*B. C. Lara run out	62	–	c M. E. Waugh b Gillespie		3
J. C. Adams b MacGill	13	–	lbw b McGrath		5
†R. D. Jacobs lbw b MacGill	6	–	lbw b McGrath		19
P. T. Collins lbw b McGrath	1	–	(10) b Gillespie		0
R. I. C. Holder lbw b MacGill	0	–	(7) c M. E. Waugh b McGrath		4
C. E. L. Ambrose c Slater b McGrath	0	–	(8) lbw b McGrath		6
M. Dillon b McGrath	0	–	(9) run out		0
C. A. Walsh not out	0	–	not out		2
B 4, l-b 2, n-b 11	17		B 4, l-b 1		5

1-16 2-28 3-116 4-149 5-156 6-163 7-163 8-163   167   1-3 2-8 3-11 4-16 5-16 6-31 7-47   51
9-167 10-167   8-47 9-49 10-51

First innings – McGrath 14–3–50–5; Gillespie 12–3–34–0; MacGill 16–5–41–3; Warne 14–4–35–0; Blewett 1–0–1–0.
Second innings – McGrath 10–3–28–5; Gillespie 9.1–4–18–4.

Toss won by Australia   UMPIRES E. G. Nicholls and P. Willey
MAN OF THE MATCH G. D. McGrath

West Indies v Australia   Second Test

At Kingston, March 13, 14, 15, 16, 1999. West Indies won by ten wickets.   Mike Coward, 2000

There can have been few more dramatic turnarounds in the history of Test cricket than this. Only Lara could have changed the course of the series after Trinidad, and he did so by defying odds and circumstances that would have crushed most men. On one fantastic, sunny, windy Sunday, Lara seduced the people of a bankrupt nation, resurrected his career as a batsman of rare gifts and reignited cricket throughout the Caribbean. He did it with an unforgettable double-century, which enabled West Indies to reach an imposing 431 and a lead of 175. It was, by universal consent, one of the great Test innings: Tony Cozier, the distinguished Barbadian commentator, thought it was the most significant ever by a West Indian.

Devastated at being put to the sword by Lara, the Australians offered no resistance in the second innings. Off-spinner Nehemiah Perry celebrated his debut in front of his home crowd by taking five for 70, with some assistance from a splendid pitch. The square had been impressively relaid after the highly embarrassing abandonment of the England Test the previous year. West Indies needed only three runs to complete an overwhelming victory, and level the series, early on the fourth morning.

Toss: Australia. **Australia 256** (M. E. Waugh 67, S. R. Waugh 100; C. A. Walsh 4-55, P. T. Collins 3-79)

and 177 (G. S. Blewett 30; C. A. Walsh 3-52, N. O. Perry 5-70); **West Indies 431** (B. C. Lara 213,

J. C. Adams 94, Extras 42; G. D. McGrath 5-93, S. C. G. MacGill 3-84) **and 3-0.**

West Indies v Australia   Third Test

At Bridgetown, March 26, 27, 28, 29, 30, 1999. West Indies won by one wicket.   Mike Coward, 2000

Another transcendent innings by Lara saw West Indies touch the heights of glory just 22 days after they had hit rock bottom in Trinidad. Irrefutably, his undefeated 153 was the hand of a genius. Exhibiting the new awareness and maturity he discovered in Jamaica, he brilliantly orchestrated the conclusion to an unforgettable match. He guided his men to victory as though leading the infirm through a maze.

Two days earlier, West Indies had been 98 for six in response to Australia's imposing 490, and seemed destined to follow on. But they turned the game round so successfully that they found themselves needing 308 to take the lead in the series. It seemed improbable, but it was within Lara's reach. No one else scored more than 38, and the eighth wicket fell with 60 still wanted for victory. But Ambrose obdurately occupied the crease for 82 minutes to be followed by Walsh, who survived five balls, helped by a wide and a no-ball, before Lara crashed Gillespie to the cover boundary to complete a victory even more astonishing than the last one, giving West Indies a 2–1 lead in the series.

It was only the fourth time West Indies had scored more than 300 to win a Test, the last occasion being at Lord's in 1984. Despite the result, Steve Waugh, who survived some extraordinary pace bowling from Ambrose to score a priceless 199, said he had never played in a better match – a telling observation, given that he had appeared in the tied Test against India in 1986. The *Daily Nation* in Barbados headlined this as the Match of the Century, and its writer Haydn Gill said "It will go down in the history books as one of the most spirited-ever revivals, the victory coming from the depths of despair." Even an Australian could not argue with that.

West Indies v Australia, 1999 — Third Test

At Bridgetown, March 26, 27, 28, 29, 30, 1999. Result: West Indies won by one wicket.

AUSTRALIA

	First innings		Second innings	
M. J. Slater c Lara b Ambrose	23	(2) run out	26
M. T. G. Elliott c Jacobs b Walsh	9	(1) c Jacobs b Walsh	0
J. L. Langer b Hooper	51	lbw b Ambrose	1
M. E. Waugh b Ambrose	0	(5) lbw b Walsh	3
*S. R. Waugh lbw b Perry	199	(6) b Collins	11
R. T. Ponting c Hooper b Perry	104	(7) c Griffith b Walsh	22
†I. A. Healy lbw b Walsh	0	(8) c Jacobs b Collins	3
S. K. Warne c Lara b Perry	13	(9) lbw b Walsh	32
J. N. Gillespie not out	23	(4) b Ambrose	14
S. C. G. MacGill run out	17	c Campbell b Walsh	1
G. D. McGrath c Joseph b Hooper	3	not out	8
B 4, l-b 10, n-b 34	48	L-b 5, w 1, n-b 19	25

1-31 2-36 3-36 4-144 5-425 6-427 7-429 8-446 **490**
9-483 10-490

1-0 2-12 3-35 4-46 5-48 6-73 7-81 8-134 **146**
9-137 10-146

First innings – Ambrose 31.3–7–93–2; Walsh 38–8–121–2; Perry 33–5–102–3; Collins 35.3–7–110–0; Hooper 15.4–4–50–2.
Second innings – Walsh 17.1–3–39–5; Ambrose 20–2–60–2; Collins 9–0–31–2; Perry 4–0–11–0.

WEST INDIES

	First innings		Second innings	
S. L. Campbell c S. R. Waugh b Gillespie	105	lbw b McGrath	33
A. F. G. Griffith run out	0	lbw b Gillespie	35
D. R. E. Joseph lbw b McGrath	26	lbw b MacGill	1
P. T. Collins lbw b McGrath	0	lbw b McGrath	0
*B. C. Lara c Healy b Gillespie	8	not out	153
C. L. Hooper c Warne b McGrath	25	c Healy b Gillespie	6
J. C. Adams c M. E. Waugh b McGrath	0	b McGrath	38
†R. D. Jacobs c M. E. Waugh b Ponting	68	lbw b McGrath	5
N. O. Perry lbw b Gillespie	24	lbw b McGrath	0
C. E. L. Ambrose not out	28	c Elliott b Gillespie	12
C. A. Walsh c Slater b Warne	12	not out	0
B 10, l-b 3, n-b 20	33	B 8, l-b 13, w 2, n-b 5	28

1-1 2-50 3-50 4-64 5-98 6-98 7-251 **329**
8-265 9-291 10-329

1-72 2-77 3-78 4-91 5-105 6-238 **(9 wkts) 311**
7-248 8-248 9-302

First innings – McGrath 33–5–128–4; Gillespie 28–14–48–3; Warne 15.5–2–70–1; MacGill 20–5–47–0; Ponting 4–1–12–1; M. E. Waugh 3–0–11–0.
Second innings – McGrath 44–13–92–5; Gillespie 26.1–8–62–3; Warne 24–4–69–0; MacGill 21–6–48–1; S. R. Waugh 5–0–19–0.

Toss won by Australia
MAN OF THE MATCH B. C. Lara

UMPIRES E. G. Nicholls and D. L. Orchard

Australia won the Fourth Test by 176 runs to square the series.

New Zealand v West Indies 1999–2000

Geoffrey Dean, 2001

Less than 12 months after their disastrous tour of South Africa, West Indies' away form showed no signs of improving. Beaten by New Zealand in a Test match for the first time since 1986–87, they went on to suffer only their second series defeat at their hands. Brian Lara's side were then whitewashed 5–0 in the one-day series by a country that had won just four of their previous 25 limited-overs meetings. Lara admitted afterwards: "Everyone is hurt, but there is no one to blame but us. It's a greater hurt than in South Africa because it's a year later and you expect it to make a difference."

A complete management clearout followed the tour, with Lara resigning from the captaincy, Clive Lloyd stepping down as manager and Sir Viv Richards, who was appointed as coach in a caretaker capacity after Malcolm Marshall had fallen ill, being overlooked when the position was advertised on the party's return home. Even Dennis Waight, West Indies' Australian-born physiotherapist, left his job after more than 20 years. Lloyd declared that his frustration in being unable to take part in selection had been a major factor in his decision to resign. "I dislike my contract and my fulfilment of it," he said, having been in the post three years. "These are traumatic times for West Indies cricket. There are a lot of things wrong at the moment."

Personal problems, coupled with a disillusionment with the game, caused Lara not only to give up the leadership of the side but also to take a four-month sabbatical from all cricket. Mentally stale, he made himself unavailable for both home series, against Zimbabwe and Pakistan, that followed the tour. In New Zealand, he appeared weighed down by responsibilities and, while he was not exactly out of form, two fatally irresponsible strokes in the First Test played a large part in what was a catastrophic defeat. Another, West Indies' tenth in succession on foreign soil, followed in the Second Test at the Basin Reserve.

New Zealand v West Indies   **First Test**

At Hamilton, December 16, 17, 18, 19, 20, 1999.
New Zealand won by nine wickets.

Geoffrey Dean, 2001

That West Indies lost this match after being 276 without loss shortly before the close of the first day will long haunt them. From that seemingly impregnable position, they batted so poorly on a docile pitch that they managed only 186 more runs in the match for the loss of 20 wickets. The transformation in New Zealand's bowling, which had been so disappointing on the first day, was equally marked. Their batsmen all made useful contributions against indifferent West Indian bowling, but it was a magnificent all-round effort from Cairns that was primarily responsible for this extraordinary victory. Coming to the wicket at 258 for six, he played some superb attacking shots in a belligerent 72 that gave his side an unexpected first-innings lead of 28. Then he demolished West Indies' second innings, ending with seven for 27, his best figures in Test cricket. In all, he claimed ten for

100, meaning that he and Lance Cairns became the first father and son each to take ten wickets in a Test.

Toss: West Indies. **West Indies 365** (A. F. G. Griffith 114, S. L. Campbell 170; C. L. Cairns 3-73, D. L. Vettori 4-83) **and 97** (R. L. Powell 30; C. L. Cairns 7-27); **New Zealand 393** (M. J. Horne 32, S. P. Fleming 66, N. J. Astle 48, C. D. McMillan 51, C. L. Cairns 72, Extras 32; D. Ramnarine 3-82, R. D. King 4-81) **and 70-1** (C. M. Spearman 30*).

West Indies v Zimbabwe 2000

Craig Cozier, 2001

West Indies began their first home international season of the new millennium, combining Test series against Zimbabwe and Pakistan with the first triangular one-day tournament in the Caribbean, in a state of uncertainty. Smarting from yet another overseas catastrophe – losing both Tests and all five one-day internationals in New Zealand – Brian Lara not only resigned as captain but, reportedly contemplating retirement, took a break from the game, leaving West Indies without their star batsman. Meanwhile, controversy surrounded the appointment of Roger Harper as coach, replacing Sir Viv Richards after just one assignment, the New Zealand tour. When the decision to sack Richards was announced in February, the outcry was most vehement in his native island of Antigua, which is also the headquarters of the West Indies Cricket Board. A large crowd marched through the streets with placards; a window was smashed and a gate vandalised at the board's offices.

A month later, new captain Jimmy Adams joined his players and thousands of fans in a lap around Kingston's Sabina Park to acclaim hard-fought victories in both Tests of the inaugural series with Zimbabwe. The success was made sweeter by the fact that, a day earlier and in front of his Jamaican countrymen, 37-year-old Courtney Walsh had passed India's Kapil Dev as Test cricket's leading wicket-taker. But the ensuing euphoria could not mask the fact that West Indies had been outplayed by Zimbabwe for long periods.

In the First Test at Port-of-Spain, they were let off the hook when Zimbabwe's inexperience and lack of confidence, combined with their own disciplined fast bowling and fielding, saw them home: Zimbabwe collapsed for 63 in pursuit of a mere 99. "We simply did not seem to have that belief in our ability to win," said coach David Houghton. "We led for four days and about one session."

West Indies v Zimbabwe | First Test

At Port-of-Spain, March 16, 17, 18, 19, 20, 2000. West Indies won by 35 runs.   Craig Cozier, 2001

A stirring display of fast bowling on the final day saved West Indies from adding another embarrassing chapter to their recent book of woes. Zimbabwe's bowlers, inspired by Streak, had routed them twice to present their own batsmen with a target of 99 on a worn but still firm pitch. But against Walsh and Ambrose, and with Rose and King rising to the occasion, the Zimbabweans could not grasp the gilt-edged chance, slumping to 63 all out, their first Test total under 100. Ambrose returned figures of 11–6–8–3; there was only one, edged, boundary in 47 overs, and Zimbabwean coach Houghton said that "there was hardly a ball to be hit anywhere off the square". West Indies' escape, one of a number throughout the Walsh-Ambrose era, provided only the second instance of a Test side successfully defending a target below 100 (Australia dismissed England for 77 chasing 85 at The Oval in 1882).

At the start of the final day, when Streak took his match haul to a Test-best nine for 72, Zimbabwe were on the verge of an historic victory. Instead, the traditional West Indian four-pronged pace attack wrote history in their own favour. After Johnson was despatched in Walsh's second over, Grant Flower and Gripper dug deep for an hour until King broke through. Rose flattened the middle order, all to catches by wicket-keeper Jacobs, while at the other end Walsh bowled Grant Flower with one that kept low. In frustration, Flower demolished the stumps to earn a suspended ban and fine; apart from him, no one reached double figures. Ambrose returned before tea to remove the last three in 13 balls and draw alongside Malcolm Marshall on 376 wickets, with only Walsh among West Indians ahead of him. Victory complete, Adams gathered his elated troops in a huddle of prayer on the outfield before setting off on a joyous lap of honour in front of the sparse crowd.

Toss: Zimbabwe. **West Indies 187** (C. H. Gayle 33, W. W. Hinds 46*; H. H. Streak 4-45, B. A. Murphy 3-32) **and 147** (S. Chanderpaul 49; H. H. Streak 5-27); **Zimbabwe 236** (T. R. Gripper 41, A. Flower 113*; C. E. L. Ambrose 4-42, C. H. Gayle 3-25) **and 63** (C. E. L. Ambrose 3-8, F. A. Rose 4-19).

West Indies v Zimbabwe   Second Test

At Kingston, March 24, 25, 26, 27, 28, 2000. West Indies won by ten wickets.   Craig Cozier, 2001

Jamaica's favourite cricketer became Test cricket's leading wicket-taker in front of several thousand ecstatic countrymen. In his 16th international season and 114th Test, Courtney Walsh reached the magical mark of 435 at 5.12 p.m. on the fourth day when Zimbabwe's last man, Olonga, pushed a lifting ball to short leg, where Hinds pouched it left-handed. The catch took Walsh past India's Kapil Dev, who took 434 wickets in 131 Tests.

Walsh started with high fives, then kissed the pitch where he had taken 42 wickets in ten Tests. There were hugs and kisses from his mother, Joan Wollaston, and 13-year-old son Courtney Junior, a lap of honour after the day's play, and special tributes from Kapil (live from Sharjah, where he was coaching India) and Jamaica's prime minister. The next night, Walsh was honoured by the government and presented with a plot of land. Long before that, West Indies had raced to their ten-wicket win, spurred on by Griffith's frenetic 54 in 41 balls with its 11 fours.

Toss: Zimbabwe. **Zimbabwe 308** (M. W. Goodwin 113, A. Flower 66, S. V. Carlisle 44, Extras 34; R. D. King 5-51) **and 102** (C. A. Walsh 3-21); **West Indies 339** (S. L. Campbell 48, J. C. Adams 101*, F. A. Rose 69, Extras 38; H. K. Olonga 3-65, N. C. Johnson 4-77) **and 75-0** (A. F. G. Griffith 54*).

West Indies v Pakistan 2000 — Fazeer Mohammed, 2001

Building on the successes of the previous series against Zimbabwe, and benefiting from generous slices of outrageous good fortune at crucial moments, West Indies narrowly turned back the threat of Pakistan to triumph 1-0 in the three-Test series. The one-wicket victory, earned amid heart-stopping drama and sensational controversy in Antigua on the final day of the tour, was a much-needed fillip for a team going through a period of rehabilitation in the wake of humiliating defeats away from home. Pakistan's expectations had been high when they won the Cable & Wireless triangular one-day tournament that preceded the Tests; instead, they became the latest touring team to leave the Caribbean agonising over lost opportunities.

For the new West Indies captain, Jimmy Adams, and their reconstituted team management, the rediscovery of a sense of determination and team spirit in the continued absence of Brian Lara was as important as the result. More than once, they wriggled out of tight spots as some of their talented young batsmen made vital contributions alongside the dour defiance of their captain.

West Indies v Pakistan — Third Test

At St John's, Antigua, May 25, 26, 27, 28, 29, 2000.
West Indies won by one wicket. — Fazeer Mohammed, 2001

Amid scenes reminiscent of Brian Lara's heroics against Australia in Barbados a year earlier, Adams piloted his team to a nerve-jangling one-wicket victory and West Indies' fourth triumph in five unbeaten home series against Pakistan. Yet a reasoned appraisal of the events of that last afternoon left no doubt that West Indies were extremely fortunate to reach their target of 216. They benefited from two glaring umpiring errors and Saqlain Mushtaq's raw panic when the match was literally in his hands.

Wasim Akram, in an inspired spell of fast bowling as devastating as his first-innings six for 61, had a confident appeal for a catch by Moin Khan off Adams turned down by umpire Doctrove, while an equally vehement claim for a bat-pad dismissal of last man Walsh, off Saqlain, was denied by umpire Cowie. Television replays confirmed that both should have been out. Yet Pakistani fury at the officiating was tempered by Saqlain's bungling of two run-out chances, the second opportunity producing one of the more amazing scenes in the history of Test cricket: both Adams and Walsh seemed hopelessly stranded at the striker's end, only for Saqlain to fail to gather the return cleanly. As the ball ran away from him, Walsh hared through for the leg-bye Adams intended.

After such incredible escapes, it was almost inevitable that the last pair would make the 19 runs they required, and Adams was engulfed by joyous team-mates after scampering the winning run. For Antiguans in particular, it was cause for a double celebration, following the investiture of the former West Indies captain and master batsman, Sir Vivian Richards, at the lunch interval.

West Indies v Pakistan, 2000 — Third Test

At St John's, Antigua, May 25, 26, 27, 28, 29, 2000. Result: West Indies won by one wicket.

PAKISTAN

	First innings			Second innings	
Mohammad Wasim c and b Rose	13	–	b King		21
Imran Nazir c Rose b Ambrose	10	–	c Sarwan b Walsh		0
Younis Khan c Jacobs b Ambrose	4	–	lbw b Ambrose		2
Inzamam–ul–Haq c Griffith b Walsh	55	–	c Jacobs b Rose		68
Yousuf Youhana not out	103	–	lbw b King		42
Abdul Razzaq c Jacobs b Walsh	2	–	(8) run out		0
*†Moin Khan c Jacobs b Rose	24	–	(6) c Hinds b King		10
Wasim Akram c Campbell b King	26	–	(9) c Adams b King		24
Saqlain Mushtaq c Campbell b Walsh	4	–	(7) c Campbell b Ambrose		15
Waqar Younis c Sarwan b Walsh	4	–	c Adams b Ambrose		16
Mushtaq Ahmed c Jacobs b Walsh	0	–	not out		3
L-b 4, n-b 20	24		B 2, l-b 4, n-b 12		18

1-21 2-27 3-33 4-130 5-132 6-173 7-209 8-247   **269**
9-268

1-0 2-3 3-49 4-129 5-150 6-162 7-163 8-186   **219**
9-213

First Innings – Ambrose 14–4–30–2; Walsh 26–2–83–5; Rose 19–4–48–2; King 16–3–48–1; Adams 14–2–40–0; Sarwan 2–0–16–0.

Second Innings – Ambrose 21–5–39–3; Walsh 20–4–39–1; Rose 20–2–69–1; King 23–6–48–4; Adams 6–1–18–0.

WEST INDIES

	First innings			Second innings	
S. L. Campbell c Yousuf Youhana b Mushtaq Ahmed	31	–	c Yousuf Youhana b Wasim Akram		6
A. F. G. Griffith b Mushtaq Ahmed	22	–	c Waqar Younis b Wasim Akram		23
W. W. Hinds run out	26	–	b Wasim Akram		63
S. Chanderpaul b Wasim Akram	89	–	lbw b Abdul Razzaq		31
*J. C. Adams lbw b Waqar Younis	60	–	not out		48
R. R. Sarwan lbw b Wasim Akram	10	–	lbw b Wasim Akram		6
†R. D. Jacobs lbw b Wasim Akram	0	–	run out		5
F. A. Rose c Abdul Razzaq b Wasim Akram	15	–	c Wasim Akram b Mushtaq Ahmed		4
C. E. L. Ambrose c Yousuf Youhana b Wasim Akram	0	–	lbw b Saqlain Mushtaq		8
R. D. King c and b Wasim Akram	3	–	b Wasim Akram		0
C. A. Walsh not out	2	–	not out		4
B 1, l-b 10, n-b 4	15		B 8, l-b 7, n-b 3		18

1-40 2-73 3-84 4-218 5-235 6-243 7-254 8-258   **273**
9-269

1-16 2-31 3-84 4-144 5-161 6-169 7-177 8-194   **216**
9-197

First Innings – Wasim Akram 26.2–7–61–6; Waqar Younis 21–8–41–1; Mushtaq Ahmed 24–3–68–2; Saqlain Mushtaq 23–4–48–0; Abdul Razzaq 12–1–44–0.

Second Innings – Wasim Akram 30–12–49–5; Waqar Younis 11–0–39–0; Mushtaq Ahmed 17–3–61–1; Abdul Razzaq 11–3–14–1; Saqlain Mushtaq 22–7–38–1.

Toss won by West Indies
MAN OF THE MATCH Wasim Akram

UMPIRES B. Doctrove and D. B. Cowie

AUSTRALIA V WEST INDIES 2000–01

Greg Baum, 2002

Before their landmark triumph in the Caribbean in 1995, Australia had beaten West Indies six times in 17 years in Test matches, mostly in dead rubbers. Now they beat them five times in six weeks to register the first clean sweep in series between these countries, though Greg Chappell's Australians won a six-Test series 5–1 in 1975–76, just before the long drought. It was cricket's most graphic example of the boot being on the other foot.

Australia won all 15 internationals – Test and one-day – during the summer, making it 30 out of 31 home internationals over two successive summers. These five Test wins were part of a world record run of 16 successive victories. It did not matter that Australia were without Shane Warne for the entire series. Cricket may famously be described as an individual sport played by teams, but Steve Waugh's Australians had made it a team sport played by individuals, none of whom was either above the team or indispensable to it. This applied even to the leadership: when injury forced out Waugh for a match, Adam Gilchrist, in only his 12th Test, stepped in as captain and the streak continued. Australia were to win all of Gilchrist's first 15 Tests, such was their time of plenty.

The West Indians, in contrast, were at a wretchedly low ebb. By summer's end, they had lost their sixth away series in a row, in which sequence they had won three and lost 21 Tests. They had also lost ten of their last 11 first-class matches, encompassing not only seven Test defeats, but heavy losses against Somerset, Western Australia and a half-strength Victoria. Jimmy Adams, for whom the captaincy was the most poisonous of chalices, remained dignified and gentlemanly throughout, but could provide no inspiration in word or deed. It was scarcely a surprise when he was sacked as leader and player after the tour, and vice-captain Sherwin Campbell went with him. As for the rest, some Caribbean commentators thought that they were on rather better terms with themselves than their achievements warranted.

Australia v West Indies

First Test

At Brisbane, November 23, 24, 25, 2000.
Australia won by an innings and 126 runs.

Greg Baum, 2002

This Test may be summed up in the figures of its central player, McGrath, who bowled 33 overs to take ten for 27 and ensure that Australia would equal the West Indians' record of 11 consecutive Test wins. The pitch – put in place at the end of the Olympic soccer tournament and so providing the first instance of a drop-in pitch in Test cricket – was seamy but slow. On it, West Indies did not so much explode as erode, scoring at 1.9 an over in their innings of 82 (their third total in double figures since June) and 124. Australia also laboured to make 332 at 2.9 an over, but that was more than enough for a resounding innings win. Proceeding at once at a crawl and a rush, the match was over by its scheduled mid-point.

Toss: Australia. **West Indies 82** (G. D. McGrath 6-17) **and 124** (S. Chanderpaul 62*; G. D. McGrath 4-10, B. Lee 3-40); **Australia 332** (M. J. Slater 54, M. L. Hayden 44, S. R. Waugh 41, A. C. Gilchrist 48, B. Lee 62*; M. I. Black 4-83, M. Dillon 3-79).

WEST INDIES v AUSTRALIA 2003 Andrew Ramsey, 2004

As usually happens when Australia tour the Caribbean, the Test series contained cussedness, controversy, a clattering of records and some cracking cricket. All, however, were squeezed into the final Test in Antigua, and the other three were as predictable, flat and lifeless as the shamefully benign pitches on which they were played. The quick, bouncy tracks which once characterised West Indian cricket have gone the way of the phalanx of fearsome fast bowlers who so ruthlessly exploited them. As the Australian captain, Steve Waugh, adroitly noted, ground authorities in the region had to take heed of the connection. Until they produced pitches that encouraged pace bowlers and challenged batsmen, the stagnation of the game in the West Indies would continue.

Stymieing the opposition was effectively confirmed as policy by Brian Lara, reinstated as captain three years after resigning amid much acrimony. Not that his return to the post was much less traumatic. Even allowing for the poisonous political undercurrents that permeate Caribbean cricket, West Indies' lead-up to the Test series was farcical. When Lara was asked to take over from Carl Hooper in the wake of their poor World Cup campaign, Hooper waited until three days before the First Test to declare he was unavailable. Around the same time, the West Indies Cricket Board proudly trumpeted that Bennett King, head of the Australian cricket academy, was their new national coach. Unfortunately, they told the press before contractual negotiations had been completed, and – though King denied his decision had been influenced by a glimpse of the workings of the WICB – he announced he was no longer interested.

On top of these embarrassments, the outstanding young opener, Chris Gayle, was omitted from the First Test team after he preferred a lucrative double-wicket tournament in St Lucia to turning out for Jamaica in the final of the Carib Beer Challenge, the region's first-class competition. In what looked for all the world to be disciplinary action, he missed the first two Tests, though the selection panel, headed by Sir Vivian Richards, muddied the waters by stating that Gayle had been considered, but simply wasn't picked. It all added up to the kind of backstage buffoonery that might have unsettled a team heading into a series against lowly Bangladesh. Against the ultra-professional world champions, it was suicide.

Australia's *modus operandi* in retaining the Frank Worrell Trophy, which they had held since 1995, was as familiar as it was punishing. During the first three Tests, they averaged 550-plus in their first innings at a rate of more than four an over, giving their bowlers enough time and ammunition to knock over a West Indian batting line-up containing more talent than application. A major beneficiary of the Australians' approach was Stuart MacGill, who proved himself the perfect understudy to Warne: the 20 wickets he prised out with his leg-spin were the most by a bowler on either side.

In the end, the epic Fourth Test, which so nearly brought about Australia's first Caribbean whitewash, was decided perhaps as much by the fatigue of the Australian bowlers – enforcing the follow-on at Barbados subjected them to 244 overs off the reel – and by the absence of Ponting as by the courageous and mature batting from Lara's young players.

Boosted by the arrival of fresh reinforcements, Ponting led his World Cup-winning side to four straight victories in the one-day games, taking Australia's record to an astounding 21 consecutive wins. Either a lack of appetite on their part or the brilliance of Wavell Hinds – perhaps both – then let West Indies claw back three consolation victories at the end of a seemingly interminable series.

West Indies v Australia   Fourth Test

At St John's, Antigua, May 9, 10, 11, 12, 13, 2003.
West Indies won by three wickets.   Andrew Ramsey, 2004

Many expected the final Test to bring a disappointing series to an historic conclusion with Australia's first Caribbean clean sweep. Few, though, could have imagined the controversies that the game would bring and still less that West Indies would etch their name in the record books by achieving the largest successful run-chase in 1,645 Tests.

The talking-point on the opening day was in fact more of a whisper. Presented with the most sporting pitch of the tour, [Jermaine] Lawson could scarcely hide his excitement – and exposed hitherto unseen weaknesses in the Australian batting. Fast and furious, he pocketed career-best figures of seven for 78 in Australia's modest 240. But by the end of the day the word was spreading around the Recreation Ground: to many, Lawson's action, which had first drawn the attention of the series referee, Mike Procter, during the First Test in Guyana, looked dubious. The murmurs grew louder when umpires David Shepherd and Venkat called for video evidence. By the fourth day, Procter confirmed that Lawson had been reported to the ICC for a suspect action.

By then, other storm clouds had gathered over St John's. On the second morning, Lara walked out to bat in a bellicose frame of mind, had exchanges with three Australians before he faced his first ball, from Lee, and duly hammered it over point for six. Lara spent the first half-hour of his innings arguing furiously with his tormentors, and at one stage stood toe-to-toe with Waugh, who had moved to short cover to pepper him with more chat, causing umpire Shepherd to intervene briefly. It was an unedifying spectacle, though no further action was taken by umpires or referee.

The game, however, continued to simmer, partly due to the closeness of the contest. West Indies also scored 240, the seventh instance of precise first-innings equality in Test history, and then – with Lawson ostensibly sidelined by a back strain – Dillon finally lived up to his billing as bowling spearhead to keep his team in the match. The importance of his four for 112 cannot be overstated, particularly after Australia raced to 242 from 55 overs on the strength of Langer and Hayden's fifth double-century opening stand, more than any other pair in Test history.

By restricting Australia to 417, about 150 fewer than Waugh had envisaged, West Indies had left themselves a target which, though unlikely, was not impossible now that the pitch had lost its juice if not its bounce. With more than two days available, time at least was on their side. But when West Indies wobbled to 74 for three on the fourth morning, the existing record score to win a Test – the

406 India hit against West Indies in Trinidad 27 years earlier – appeared safe. And hope was all but extinguished when Lara was fourth out at 165, trying to belt MacGill for a fourth huge six down the ground.

But Sarwan and Chanderpaul, who was nursing a broken finger, got on with the task – and under the skin of the Australians, especially McGrath. As Sarwan approached a mature hundred, there were signs that Australia were losing the plot. McGrath, who started the verbal war, became utterly incensed at Sarwan's riposte – he apparently referred to McGrath's wife. After a set-to with the batsman, he wagged his finger at umpire Shepherd, demanding he get involved. Despite this, no official action was taken, though once pictures were beamed round the world both the ACB and the ICC castigated the Australians and called on them immediately to mend their ways.

When Sarwan had taken his score to 105 and his stand with Chanderpaul to 123, he mis-hooked Lee to leave the game perfectly poised: at 288 for five, either 130 runs or five wickets would settle it. The first-ball dismissal of Jacobs, caught behind though he was struck on the elbow, initially tilted things Australia's way. The crowd were furious, and disrupted play by throwing bottles on to the outfield. Through all this – and a rain delay – Chanderpaul kept his concentration to reach a magnificent hundred. By the close, Australia needed four wickets for the clean sweep; West Indies 47 runs to prevent it.

On the final morning, Chanderpaul added only one to his overnight 103 before Lee prised him out, too, leaving West Indies to rely on Banks and Drakes, neither really an all-rounder. But they coolly took care of the 46 needed to reach a stun-

High fives: Omari Banks (right) and Vasbert Drakes celebrate after West Indies reached 418 in the fourth innings – a Test record – to beat Australia in Antigua in May 2003. Stuart MacGill is less impressed.

ning, unparalleled victory. The Australian bowlers, having worked themselves into the ground to set up the series win, now made history as the attack to concede most runs to lose a Test. Lara reckoned the win the zenith of his career.

West Indies v Australia, 2003   Fourth Test

At St John's, May 9, 10, 11, 12, 13, 2003. Result: West Indies won by three wickets.

AUSTRALIA	First innings		Second innings	
J. L. Langer c Banks b Lawson	42	– c Lara b Gayle	111
M. L. Hayden c Drakes b Lawson	14	– run out	177
M. L. Love b Banks	36	– (4) c sub b Banks	2
D. S. Lehmann c Jacobs b Lawson	7	– (5) b Dillon	14
*S. R. Waugh c Jacobs b Dillon	41	– (6) not out	45
†A. C. Gilchrist c Chanderpaul b Dillon	33	– (3) c sub b Banks	6
A. J. Bichel c sub b Lawson	34	– c Smith b Dillon	0
B. Lee c Jacobs b Lawson	9	– c sub b Dillon	18
J. N. Gillespie c Jacobs b Lawson	6	– c Lara b Drakes	5
S. C. G. MacGill c Sarwan b Lawson	2	– c Lara b Dillon	0
G. D. McGrath not out	5	– c Ganga b Drakes	14
B 2, l-b 3, w 2, n-b 4	11	B 4, l-b 9, n-b 12	25

1-27 2-80 3-93 4-128 5-181 6-194 7-224 8-231   240   1-242 2-273 3-285 4-330 5-338 6-343 7-373 8-385   417
9-233   9-388

First Innings – Dillon 18–2–53–2; Lawson 19.1–3–78–7; Drakes 15–2–42–0; Banks 20–2–62–1.
Second Innings – Lawson 6–1–17–0; Dillon 29–3–112–4; Banks 37–5–153–2; Drakes 19–1–92–2;
Gayle 13–1–30–1.

WEST INDIES	First innings		Second innings	
C. H. Gayle b McGrath	0	– c Waugh b Lee	19
D. S. Smith c Gilchrist b Lee	37	– c Gilchrist b Gillespie	23
D. Ganga c Gilchrist b Bichel	6	– lbw b McGrath	8
V. C. Drakes lbw b Lee	21	– (9) not out	27
*B. C. Lara c Langer b Bichel	68	– (4) b MacGill	60
R. R. Sarwan c and b Bichel	24	– (5) c and b Lee	105
S. Chanderpaul b McGrath	1	– (6) c Gilchrist b Lee	104
†R. D. Jacobs run out	26	– (7) c Gilchrist b Lee	0
O. A. C. Banks not out	16	– (8) not out	47
M. Dillon b Lee	9		
J. J. C. Lawson c Love b MacGill	14		
L-b 8, w 3, n-b 7	18	B 9, l-b 9, w 1, n-b 6	25

1-1 2-30 3-73 4-80 5-137 6-140 7-185 8-197 9-224   240   1-48 2-50 3-74 4-165 5-288 6-288 7-372   (7 wkts) 418

First Innings – McGrath 17–6–44–2; Gillespie 17–3–56–0; Bichel 14–4–53–3; Lee 15–2–71–3;
MacGill 2.3–0–8–1.
Second Innings – McGrath 25–10–50–1; Gillespie 25–10–64–1; Lee 23–4–63–4; MacGill 35.5–8–149–1;
Bichel 15–3–49–0; Waugh 5–0–25–0.

Toss won by Australia   UMPIRES D. R. Shepherd and S. Venkataraghavan
MAN OF THE MATCH S. Chanderpaul

CAN IT GET ANY WORSE?

Tony Cozier, 2005

Between November 2003 and August 2004, West Indies cricket passed through the most agonising period in its history, even by recent distressing standards. The optimism created by a record-breaking last-Test win over Australia in May 2003, followed by victory over Sri Lanka, rapidly evaporated during five tightly packed series. In 16 Tests, West Indies suffered ten defeats, one by an innings, three by ten wickets, and two by over 200 runs. They beat Zimbabwe and Bangladesh – the only teams ranked below them in the ICC's Test Championship – in one Test each. Even these two enjoyed the better of West Indies in their other, drawn matches.

South Africa, at home, and England, in the Caribbean, were denied clean sweeps only by two exceptional innings – Dwayne Smith's last-day, run-a-ball hundred in Cape Town, and Brian Lara's unbeaten Test-record 400 in Antigua. There were no such heroics in the return series: England completed the dreaded whitewash at The Oval, where West Indies had formalised their own "blackwash" 20 years earlier. The ICC Champions Trophy final brought a timely triumph only a month later, on the same ground as their Test match humiliation. But this euphoria was soon dissipated in an acrimonious row between the board and the players.

The difficulties had been compounded by Sir Viv Richards's exit after two years as chairman of selectors, before the tour of England. It reflected his frustration at the team's performances and the players' sensitivities. A formal letter of protest to the West Indies Cricket Board from the West Indies Players' Association had alleged that he and other selectors "verbally belittled and threatened" some of its members in public.

Stung by the realisation that, after five years of failure, the situation was getting worse, not better, and the fear that West Indies were losing their global appeal, the board announced drastic changes to the running of the Test team and to the domestic tournaments. "There will be no gain without pain," said Teddy Griffith, the WICB president.

WEST INDIES V ENGLAND 2004

For Series Review and First and Second Tests, see page 309

West Indies v England

Fourth Test

At St John's, Antigua, April 10, 11, 12, 13, 14, 2004. Drawn.

Tony Cozier, 2005

One hundred and eighty-five days after losing his position as scorer of Test cricket's highest innings, Brian Lara reclaimed the record from Matthew Hayden and became the first man to reach 400 in a Test. Twenty-five minutes before lunch on the third day, he danced down the pitch to hoist Batty's invitingly flighted off-break into the stand at long-on for the six that lifted him past his own 375 and level with Hayden at 380. He then swept the next ball, flatter and ill-directed, to fine leg for four, to secure once more the record he had taken from another celebrated West Indian left-hander, Garry Sobers, on the same ground against the same opposition ten years earlier. It was the tenth time the record had changed hands; no one else had ever recovered it.

The reception this time was joyful enough, but less frenetic than first time round. There was no spectator invasion, as in 1994, except for an inappropriate appearance by a government entourage headed by the new prime minister of Antigua and Barbuda, Baldwin Spencer. As in Bridgetown, travelling England supporters formed the majority of the estimated 10,000 in the stands. They politely rejoiced that they were there to see history. Over in the popular, open section adjoining Independence Avenue, where hardly a pale face was to be seen, the celebrations were understandably more bois-terous. The national flags of the independent Caribbean nations that somehow manage to find unity through their cricket team waved ecstatically. For the first time in the series, West Indian voices were no longer drowned out by the deafening, triumphal chants of the Barmy Army and their travelling accomplices.

After handshakes from weary opponents, Lara again stooped to kiss the pitch – prepared under the supervision of Andy Roberts, the formidable fast bowler of an earlier era – that had once more favoured him. Nor was he finished. He stated at the start of the third day that his aim was a total of 750, the highest ever conceded by England in their 820 Tests. Before that, he swept Batty to fine leg again for the single that raised Test cricket's first 400, and the tenth in all first-class cricket. Jacobs hit the next ball for four to take West Indies to 751, and Lara declared at the end of the over.

He had batted two minutes short of 13 hours and faced 582 balls; there were four sixes – in 1994, he had none – and 43 fours. He was so composed, so concen-trated, so invincible that he surely could have carried on to 500, or 600 if he had been so minded. Geraint Jones, who had replaced Read as England wicket-keeper and thus had the closest vantage point, observed how fresh Lara looked throughout, hardly raising a sweat. Although he scored freely in all directions with his full range of strokes, he was, as in 1994, more calculating than extravagant.

Two other men were on the field during both record innings: England's Graham Thorpe, and Australian umpire Darrell Hair. Indeed, Hair had also officiated when Lara scored the first of his 25 Test hundreds – and the first of his seven doubles – 277 in Sydney in 1992–93. Yet, had Hair been persuaded by a convincing appeal for a catch at the wicket, Lara would not have scored a run. His fourth ball, from Harmison, his nemesis in earlier games, produced an indecisive drive. As Jones gath-ered, wicketkeeper, bowler and slips leapt in the certainty that there had been a thin edge. Hair shook his head, and television replays indicated he was correct.

There was nothing more that seriously tested the umpires' judgment. Lara offered one chance, a stinging, low straight drive off Batty that burst through the bowler's hands on its way to the boundary when he was 293. Only Harmison caused him the occasional bother – until his third warning for running on the pitch debarred him from bowling. By then, he had sent down 37 overs and Lara was 359.

The experienced Jacobs entered, with Lara 234, and followed in his slipstream for more than five hours to gather his third Test century. Their stand was worth 282, a sixth-wicket record for West Indies, at the declaration half an hour into the third afternoon. There were some, notably Australia's captain Ricky Ponting, who criticised this delayed closure, claiming it disregarded the goal of winning the match. Lara's response was that his priority was to avoid the ignominy of an unprecedented whitewash.

Had Lara not dropped a juggled catch at slip off Sarwan when Flintoff was 27 late on the third afternoon, West Indies would have been closer to a satisfying triumph. Dropped again at 56 and 67, Flintoff spent nearly five and a half hours over an unbeaten century, skilfully ensuring that the last four wickets yielded 103. England did follow on but, without a genuine spinner, an omission later regretted by Lara, West Indies could make little impression in the second innings on a wearing pitch.

West Indies v England, 2004 — Fourth Test

At St John's, Antigua, April 10, 11, 12, 13, 14, 2004. Result: Drawn.

WEST INDIES

C. H. Gayle c and b Batty	69	†R. D. Jacobs not out	107
D. Ganga lbw b Flintoff	10	B 4, l-b 5, w 2, n-b 5	16
*B. C. Lara not out	400		
R. R. Sarwan c Trescothick b Harmison	90	1-33 (2) 2-98 (1) 3-330 (4)	(5 wkts dec.) 751
R. L. Powell c Hussain b S. P. Jones	23	4-380 (5) 5-469 (6)	
R. O. Hinds c and b Batty	36		

T. L. Best, P. T. Collins, C. D. Collymore and F. H. Edwards did not bat.

Hoggard 18–2–82–0; Harmison 37–6–92–1; Flintoff 35–8–109–1; S. P. Jones 29–0–146–1; Batty 52–4–185–2; Vaughan 13–0–60–0; Trescothick 18–3–68–0.

ENGLAND

	First innings		Second innings	
M. E. Trescothick c Jacobs b Best		16	– c Sarwan b Edwards	88
*M. P. Vaughan c Jacobs b Collins		7	– c Jacobs b Sarwan	140
M. A. Butcher b Collins		52	– c Gayle b Hinds	61
N. Hussain b Best		3	– b Hinds	56
G. P. Thorpe c Collins b Edwards		10	– not out	23
A. Flintoff not out		102	– c Lara b Sarwan	14
†G. O. Jones b Edwards		38	– not out	10
G. J. Batty c Gayle b Collins		8		
M. J. Hoggard c Jacobs b Collins		1		
S. P. Jones lbw b Hinds		11		
S. J. Harmison b Best		5		
B 1, l-b 5, w 4, n-b 22		32	B 4, l-b 7, w 3, n-b 16	30

1-8 (2) 2-45 (1) 3-54 (4) 4-98 (3) 285   1-182 (1) 2-274 (2) 3-366 (3) (5 wkts) 422
5-98 (5) 6-182 (7) 7-205 (8)   4-387 (4) 5-408 (6)
8-229 (9) 9-283 (11) 10-285 (10)

First innings – Collins 26–4–76–4; Edwards 18–3–70–2; Collymore 19–5–45–0; Best 10.3–3–37–3; Hinds 17.3–7–29–1; Sarwan 7–0–18–0; Gayle 1–0–4–0.

Second innings – Best 16–1–57–0; Edwards 20–2–81–1; Collymore 18–3–58–0; Powell 8–0–36–0; Hinds 38–8–83–2; Gayle 17–6–36–0; Sarwan 12–2–26–2; Collins 8–2–34–0.

Toss won by West Indies   UMPIRES Aleem Dar and D. B. Hair
MAN OF THE MATCH B. C. Lara

ENGLAND V WEST INDIES 2004   ICC Champions Trophy Final
At The Oval, September 25, 2004. West Indies won by two wickets.   S. Rajesh, 2005

A tournament full of insipid, forgettable moments ended with one of the most memorable finals in recent years, as West Indies scripted a soul-stirring fightback to put paid to England's hopes of winning their first one-day tournament of any significance. For a region devastated by various opponents on the cricket field, and by Hurricanes Ivan and Jeanne off it, this was a victory to savour. The reactions of the players immediately after Bradshaw struck the winning boundary told the story – the entire West Indian party roared on to the field in semi-darkness, hugging, kissing and screaming, ecstatic yet bewildered by their achievement.

Toss: West Indies. **England 217** (49.4 overs) (M. E. Trescothick 104, A. F. Giles 31; W. W. Hinds 3-24); **West Indies 218-8** (48.5 overs) (S. Chanderpaul 47, C. O. Browne 35*, I. D. R. Bradshaw 34*, Extras 35; A. Flintoff 3-38).

CRICKET'S MIGRANT SOUL   Robert Winder, 2005

The West Indies tour of England in the summer of 2004 [in which the visitors were whitewashed] was marked above all by an absence. There was a missing guest at the feast, and until the astonishing finale at The Oval, when the Champions Trophy ended in a raucous blare of trumpet and conch, it hovered over the summer like a rain cloud, or an elegy. The sad fact, much remarked on by commentators, was that few of Britain's West Indians watched the games from the stands. At a time when Barbados and Antigua have become home matches for scarlet-faced Barmy foot-soldiers, the domestic venues were Caribbean-free. For atmosphere they relied on fancy dress: the grounds were alive with Elvis lookalikes, Heidi replicas, nuns and Vikings. The series felt like an extended rag week – there was none of the clamour that used to carry across the ocean the atmosphere of the tropics.

It could not be called a new phenomenon. After a noisy crescendo in the mid-1980s, the West Indian element in English stadiums has been dissolving for a generation. But now the silence was resounding: the exodus seemed complete. And it felt prompted by something more serious than a mere dip in the team's form. Form, as we are so often told, is temporary, and West Indies may rediscover it any day. But the evaporation of their English support, felt deeper, like a permanent loss.

Some argued that the Caribbean game had been weakened by the Americanisation of the region, with its televised basketball, track-and-field scholarships and trim attention span. Perhaps the increasing disunity of the islands was generating a low-wattage team spirit, compared to the days when cricket was a rallying point for an archipelago of emerging nations. The poor form of the team certainly didn't help – who wanted to support such persistent losers? – but such fluctuations are hardly unusual. Just four years earlier, West Indies themselves had thrashed England in three days at Edgbaston to precipitate similar talk of England as a power in terminal decline.

So perhaps the answer lay not in the Caribbean but in England – in ticket prices that were too high for one of Britain's least affluent ethnic communities, or in the regulations mounted against the percussion for which West Indian fans were famous. Arguments such as these appealed to anyone who liked presuming that the establishment was barring the gate against colonial intruders.

There was probably truth in all of these suggestions. And there were clues outside the game, too, in the social conditions that underpinned West Indian life in Britain. The set text for such matters remains *Beyond a Boundary*, C. L. R. James's teasing assertion of cricket's importance in personal and national life. He saw the game as an English pastime, designed to enact British virtues, but one that had been invaded and internalised by West Indians ("Eton or Harrow had nothing on us"). Excellence at cricket, he thought, could be an ennobling form of dissent, especially for liberated nations seeking fresh fields in which to excel. The thrill of outdoing the masters, on their own immaculate lawns, was extreme.

When West Indies first won in England in 1950, Caribbean men danced in Piccadilly Circus. They didn't stop dancing for 40 years. The Oval became a particular home-from-home. The pioneering migrants who crossed the Atlantic on the *Empire Windrush* in 1948 were sent to an underground shelter in Clapham, and directed to the Brixton Labour Exchange. So Lambeth, with The Oval at its heart, became a Caribbean locale. Would-be travellers could buy the *South London Press* on the harbour front in Kingston, Jamaica, just as they could buy *The Gleaner* on the Railton Road.

Cricket proved a vivid diversion for homesick migrants labouring in unfriendly factories and being cold-shouldered by colour-conscious landlords and employers. Those dreamy days at The Oval, with its exuberant orchestra of cans and bottles, the drumming and cheering, and the whiplash brilliance of the cricketers – if you closed your eyes you could almost have been back in Barbados. It was powerful medicine. In 1976, when Vivian Richards battered nearly three hundred runs across the parched brown outfield, the stands in front of the gasometers shook with West Indian glee.

A generation later, there was hardly a Caribbean fan in sight to witness the capitulation of Brian Lara's 2004 team – just a few mournful elders staring into their drinks. Far from seeing cricket as a stage on which to swagger, today's black Britons saw cricket as a form of collusion or conformity. In media interviews, black spokesmen shrugged and said that cricket was simply not cool. And if you couldn't beat them, the saying seemed to go, then don't join them. Added piquancy was given to the situation by the fact that, the following weekend, London's Afro-Caribbean population swayed through Notting Hill in a well-organised burst of migrant merrymaking. The carnival was going strong, but cricket was neither invited nor included. The old idea that cricket was a West Indian game invented by the English had never seemed more like an anachronism.

The same can be said of some of the arguments surrounding the subject. In the many debates about Britain's West Indians, the fact that they are not "West Indian" is sometimes overlooked. They are British. They may be black, but they are no longer Caribbean. They sink or swim in the football-loving mainstream. There are many times more West Indian-descended sportsmen in football's Premiership than in county cricket. So it may not be a matter of them being too proud to endure the recent failures – on the contrary, they may not be West Indian enough.

History has installed them in a place where cricket has rarely gripped: in England's inner cities, where there are few pitches, fewer coaches, and enough racial animosity to lower anyone's spirits. That all is not well can be seen at a glance. In 2002, only 30% of Caribbean-descended children achieved five GCSE passes at school, against a national average of 51%, with 64% for the Indian community and 73% for the Chinese.

Television hates inert audiences: that is why it sponsors boundary placards and prizes for joke banners, and why its cameras seek out the wildest cheerleaders. So the disappearance of the West Indian fan is a commercial as well as a cultural loss. It is an especially keen setback for England fans. Not long ago, in the heyday of Clive Lloyd's fast-bowling quartets, they could look forward to a home-grown Holding or Marshall of their own. The size and fervour of the migrant population made it seem inevitable. More than a dozen players of Anglo-Caribbean descent have played Test cricket for England since Roland Butcher paved the way 24 years ago, but in the 1990s the flood slowed to a trickle, and now that appears to have dried up.

The English have a soft spot for narratives of decline, but it might be misleading to wonder, in the case of West Indian cricket, how far the mighty have fallen. The real surprise is that the team rose so high, that such a small and poor archipelago should have produced as many superlative sides as they did. In the years after liberation, cricket was the fortunate beneficiary of a brilliant flowering: the invincibles of Sobers, Lloyd and Richards were ruthless, athletic, haughty, joyful, violent and charismatic. It was a rare, perhaps unrepeatable, eruption of cricket energy.

Robert Winder is the author of Bloody Foreigners: The Story of Immigration to Britain.

India – The Tiger Awakes

I ndia, for so long the whipping boys in international cricket – away from their own pitches, at least – are now the dominant force in the game. They have the money, the support base and the talent to shape cricket's future, and how they choose to exercise their new-found power will in large part determine whether the game goes on striking a balance between respecting the old and embracing the new. Too much one-day cricket, too many (alleged) spectator- and TV-friendly rule changes and the sport could be damaged. We must hope India uses its muscle wisely.

At the beginning of the period covered by this book, India's fine, spin-oriented team of the early 1970s had given way to a feebler, more monochrome outfit. The ease with which England (in fact, Botham, more or less single-handedly) beat them in the Jubilee Test at Bombay in 1980 reflected their torpor. Kapil Dev and Vengsarkar managed to keep them competitive in the 1980s – notably achieving a rare series win in England in 1986 – and Azharuddin's brilliance made them attractive in the early '90s, when they remained extremely hard to beat at home. But only in the past six or seven years have they had a team, as opposed to several captivating individuals, who could compete against anyone, anywhere.

"Ever so rarely comes a series that marks a turning point in history," wrote Sambit Bal of India's dramatic tour of Australia in 2003–04. "It may be years or decades before the significance of India's tour can be truly assessed, but in this series they announced themselves as a force in Test cricket, after years of living on promise and vain dazzle. They didn't quite end Australia's reign, but how close they came. . . It ended with a realignment of the world order: the Ashes and the Frank Worrell Trophy could keep their tradition, but the Border-Gavaskar Trophy had emerged as the worthiest in contemporary cricket. And yes, India kept it."

This of course was written at a time when the Ashes appeared to be permanently in Australia's grasp, but his point was a valid one: India had joined the top table and Steve Waugh's Australia saw them as the greatest challenge. Australia's loss of the miraculous Kolkata Test of 2001 is perhaps the moment at which India embraced the new century and thought "this could be ours". For better or worse, it could.   S. M.

INDIA V PAKISTAN 1979-80 Dicky Rutnagur, 1981

Much the same Pakistan side that had totally outplayed India at home a year earlier, and won the series 2–0, went down by the same margin in a tense, controversial rubber of six Tests. The marked turn of fortunes in a year was wrought by several factors, of which India's advantage of playing at home was the least significant. The most prominent reason for India's ascendancy was the development as an opening bowler of Kapil Dev who, with 32 wickets, was the leading wicket-taker of the series for either side. And with an abundant infusion of new players, India were stronger than 12 months earlier, much of the added strength coming from greater mobility in the field and superior catching.

India v Pakistan	Fifth Test
At Madras, January 15, 16, 17, 19, 20, 1980. India won by ten wickets.	Dicky Rutnagur, 1981

Two men shaped this decisive Indian victory – Gavaskar, with an innings of 166, the longest played in a Test match by an Indian (593 minutes), and Kapil Dev, with an outstanding all-round performance. He took 11 wickets in the match, including seven for 56 (the best figures of his Test career) in the second innings, and contributed a boisterous 84 to India's total of 430. His great-hearted bowling minimised India's self-imposed disadvantage of going into the match with only four bowlers, off-spinner Yadav having been left out.

Toss: Pakistan. **Pakistan 272** (Sadiq Mohammad 46, Majid Khan 56, Javed Miandad 45, Asif Iqbal 34, Imran Khan 34; Kapil Dev 4-90, K. D. Ghavri 3-73) **and 233** (Javed Miandad 52, Wasim Raja 57; Kapil Dev 7-56); **India 430** (S. M. Gavaskar 166, Yashpal Sharma 46, Kapil Dev 84, R. M. H. Binny 42*; Imran Khan 5-114, Iqbal Qasim 3-81) **and 78-0** (C. P. S. Chauhan 46*).

INDIA v ENGLAND, 1979–80	Golden Jubilee Test
At Bombay, February 15, 17, 18, 19, 1980. England won by ten wickets.	Dicky Rutnagur, 1981

With the rival sides fatigued, both mentally and physically, at the end of an arduous season, the Test match to celebrate the Golden Jubilee of the Board of Control for Cricket in India produced poor cricket. But it was redeemed by an extraordinary all-round performance by Botham, whose versatility was in full bloom. There was hardly a session on which he did not bring his influence to bear, performing the unprecedented feat of scoring a century and capturing 13 wickets in a Test. Taylor, the England wicket-keeper, also established a new world Test record by taking ten catches in the match. To England, after the Test series in Australia, this success, even if inspired by one man, brought welcome relief. But for India, the defeat ended an unbeaten run of 15 Test matches, four of which they had won.

Toss: India. **India 242** (S. M. Gavaskar 49, D. B. Vengsarkar 34, S. M. Patil 30, S. M. H. Kirmani 40*; I. T. Botham 6-58) **and 149** (Kapil Dev 45*; J. K. Lever 3-65, I. T. Botham 7-48); **England 296** (I. T. Botham 114, R. W. Taylor 43, Extras 31; Kapil Dev 3-64, K. D. Ghavri 5-52) **and 98-0** (G. A. Gooch 49*, G. Boycott 43*).

ENGLAND V INDIA 1986   Graeme Wright, 1987

As the Indians began their tour in cold, rainy weather in the West Country, two questions came to mind. Why were they filling the first half a twin-tour summer when, having toured first in 1982, they could have followed New Zealand in 1986? And could their bowlers, on the evidence presented, bowl England out twice to win a Test match?

The answer to the first question was that it was the choice of India's Board of Control. With two tours of India scheduled for 1986–87, they wanted their international players fresh at the start of the season rather than returning from a tour of England. While sensible, this none the less condemned Kapil Dev's team to the colder, more unsettled half of the English season. And the wisdom of it was called into question when India went into the first one-day international having lost a third of their playing time to the weather. Furthermore, it meant there was no place in the touring team for the leg-spinner, Laxman Sivaramakrishnan, whose art would be nullified by wickets still not hard.

India won the first one-day international; they won the Texaco Trophy; and they beat England in the First Test, so winning their second Test in England and their first at headquarters. In doing so they answered, convincingly, the second question, and they did so again at Headingley, embarrassingly, dismissing England for 102 and 128.

The turning-point came at Northampton, where Kapil Dev, Roger Binny and Chetan Sharma bowled the county side out for 118. This success, and especially that of Kapil who, moving the ball from leg to off or cutting it back, took four wickets in eight balls, brought home to the Indians the vulnerability of English batsmen in English conditions. Subsequently, in the Test series, their seam bowlers adhered to the traditional virtues of line and length, while the selection of two left-arm spinners reinforced the strategy of attacking the England batsmen on and outside off stump. Consequently, players programmed by limited-overs cricket to work the ball to leg were forced to adjust their method. And when the conditions encouraged movement in the air or off the pitch, as they did for the Indian bowlers in all three Tests, the deficiencies in English batting techniques were exposed.

While the technique of England's batsmen was found wanting, that of the Indians was not. Krishnamachari Srikkanth, by the impulsive nature of his game, always gave bowlers a chance, but if Sunil Gavaskar failed to make the same impact as on his four previous Test-match tours, that owed more to his own approach than to any lessening of technique. So often in the past the main course, Gavaskar preferred this time to be a lively *hors d'oeuvre*, whetting the appetite for the batting that followed.

In Dilip Vengsarkar, India had the batsman of the series. At Lord's and at Headingley, his hundreds were the platform from which India pushed for victory. In both innings of both Tests he top-scored for India, was rarely forced to play a false stroke, and made every movement elegant. His 126 not out in the first Test was his third hundred in a Test match at Lord's, unique for an overseas player.

England v India
At Lord's, June 5, 6, 7, 9, 10, 1986. India won by five wickets.

First Test

Graeme Wright, 1987

India's first Test victory at Lord's and only their second in 33 Tests in England was, in addition, England's sixth successive defeat since regaining the Ashes so comprehensively the previous season, and at the end of the match Gower was informed by the chairman of selectors, Mr P. B. H. May, that he had been relieved of the captaincy. Gatting, the vice-captain, was promoted to lead England in the next two Tests.

Toss: India. **England 294** (G. A. Gooch 114, R. T. Robinson 35, D. R. Pringle 63; R. M. H. Binny 3-55,
C. Sharma 5-64) **and 180** (M. W. Gatting 40, A. J. Lamb 39; Kapil Dev 4-52, Maninder Singh 3-9);
India 341 (S. M. Gavaskar 34, M. Amarnath 69, D. B. Vengsarkar 126*, M. Azharuddin 33;
G. R. Dilley 4-146, D. R. Pringle 3-58) **and 136-5** (D. B. Vengsarkar 33).

England v India
At Leeds, June 19, 20, 21, 23, 1986. India won by 279 runs.

Second Test

Graeme Wright, 1987

Hammonds Sauce Works Band, playing in front of the Football Stand, was the indisputable success for England during a match which India won by a resounding margin in under three and a half days. This victory, their first in England outside London, gave them a decisive 2–0 lead in the three-match series. Summing up England's performance, their chairman of selectors said: "We were outplayed in every department." It was an unhappy start to Gatting's term as captain.

Toss: India. **India 272** (S. M. Gavaskar 35, K. Srikkanth 31, R. J. Shastri 32, D. B. Vengsarkar 61,
K. S. More 36*; G. R. Dilley 3-54, D. R. Pringle 3-47) **and 237** (D. B. Vengsarkar 102*, Kapil Dev 31;
J. K. Lever 4-64, D. R. Pringle 4-73); **England 102** (C. W. J. Athey 32; Madan Lal 3-18, R. M. H. Binny 5-40)
and 128 (M. W. Gatting 31*; Maninder Singh 4-26).

INDIA v AUSTRALIA 1986

R. Mohan, 1988

The 11th Test series between Australia and India earned its place in posterity when the first of the three matches, at the Chidambaram Stadium, Chepauk in Madras concluded excitingly in the second tie in Test cricket. It had taken almost 84 years and 498 Tests to produce the first tie, between Australia and West Indies at Brisbane in December 1960; the second came only 26 years later, but there have been so many Test matches of late that this was the 554th Test since that first historic finish at the Gabba.

Apart from the fascination of such a rare result in five-day cricket, there was little of note in the series. The weather did not help by washing out the first three days of the Second Test. In the Third, all Australia sought was an honourable draw and this was achieved. Kapil Dev went without a wicket in a series for the first time, and this certainly dented India's ambition of sustaining the winning vein struck several months earlier in England. Border, on the other hand, had cause to feel satisfied with the way the tour panned out for his young and inexperienced side, even though there was no escaping the conclusion that his side were still heavily reliant on him when they were under pressure.

India v Australia — First Test
At Madras, September 18, 19, 20, 21, 22, 1986. Tied. — R. Mohan, 1988

On a hot and humid Monday, one of the most memorable Test match finishes was witnessed by some 30,000 spectators at Chepauk. For the second time in 1,052 Tests, the result was a tie, and coincidentally Australia had been involved each time. Yet there had been little hint of such a climax on the first four days; indeed, as India were being outplayed on the first three days, the thoughts of some Australians were possibly inclined to an innings victory. Only an inspired century against the odds by the Indian captain, Kapil Dev, precluded the possibility of India having to follow on after Australia had amassed their highest total in India – 574 in 742 minutes.

Border won the toss and Boon set the tone for positive Australian batting with his third Test hundred, all scored against India. On the second day, Jones cemented the solid start, first reaching his maiden Test hundred and then extending it to Australia's first double-hundred in a Test in India. Batting in all for 8 hours 23 minutes, Jones had to battle against the difficult weather conditions and overcome bouts of nausea and leg cramps. Yet he led the way in the partnership of 178 with Border, a record for Australia's fourth wicket against India.

Border declared first thing on the final morning, setting India 348 to win in a minimum of 87 overs. An opening stand of 55 announced what was assumed to be India's intention of a draw, but a century stand between Gavaskar, playing in his 100th consecutive Test match, and Amarnath pointed to different possibilities. When India went in to tea at 190 for two, a last-session chase (158 off 30 overs) against an Australian side reduced to defence was on the cards, and when the final 20 overs began, India were suitably placed with 118 needed and seven wickets in hand. However, at 251 Gavaskar mistimed a cover-drive after 259 minutes' batting, and Kapil Dev, having promoted himself in the order, went two runs later. Azharuddin unsuccessfully tried to charge Bright, but Shastri took control with a clever mixture of outright offence and the safe picking of runs.

With 18 needed off the last 30 balls, the match seemed to be India's, but when Chetan Sharma, caught on the boundary, and More were dismissed in one over by Bright, a third possible result – an Australian victory – was sighted for the first time that day. Yadav, who had struck Matthews for six to take India within seven runs of victory, was next out, bowled off his pads by Bright, leaving India 344 for nine with eight balls remaining. Maninder Singh defended the last two balls from Bright, which gave Shastri the strike for the last over, from Matthews. He blocked the first ball and, scenting victory off the second, hit a shade too eagerly: the ball went in front of deep square leg off a thick inside edge and a misfield enabled two runs to be taken safely. The next ball he placed calmly towards mid-wicket for the single which eliminated the possibility of an Australian win. Maninder defended the fourth ball, with some difficulty, and at 5.18 p.m. was leg-before to Matthews's penultimate delivery. The Australians were jubilant, none more so than a tiring Matthews, who had been bowling since the ninth over and had taken his second five-wicket return, giving him ten in a match for the first time. With Bright also taking five wickets, all ten wickets in India's second innings had fallen to spin.

India v Australia, 1986 — First Test
At Madras, September 18, 19, 20, 21, 22, 1986. Result: Tied.

AUSTRALIA

	First innings		Second innings	
D. C. Boon c Kapil Dev b Sharma	122	lbw b Maninder Singh		49
G. R. Marsh c Kapil Dev b Yadav	22	b Shastri		11
D. M. Jones b Yadav	210	c Azharuddin b Maninder Singh		24
R. J. Bright c Shastri b Yadav	30			
*A. R. Border c Gavaskar b Shastri	106	(4) b Maninder Singh		27
G. M. Ritchie run out	13	(5) c Pandit b Shastri		28
G. R. J. Matthews c Pandit b Yadav	44	(6) not out		27
S. R. Waugh not out	12	(7) not out		2
B 1, l-b 7, w 1, n-b 6	15	L-b 1, n-b 1		2

1-48 2-206 3-282 4-460 (7 wkts dec.) 574   1-31 2-81 3-94 4-125 5-165 (5 wkts dec.) 170
5-481 6-544 7-573
†T. J. Zoehrer, C. J. McDermott and B. A. Reid did not bat.

First innings – Kapil Dev 18–5–52–0; Sharma 16–1–70–1; Maninder Singh 39–8–135–0; Yadav 49.5–9–142–4; Shastri 47–8–161–1; Srikkanth 1–0–6–0.
Second innings – Kapil Dev 1–0–5–0; Sharma 6–0–19–0; Maninder Singh 19–2–60–3; Yadav 9–0–35–0; Shastri 14–2–50–2.

INDIA

	First innings		Second innings	
S. M. Gavaskar c and b Matthews	8	c Jones b Bright		90
K. Srikkanth c Ritchie b Matthews	53	c Waugh b Matthews		39
M. Amarnath run out	1	c Boon b Matthews		51
M. Azharuddin c and b Bright	50	c Ritchie b Bright		42
R. J. Shastri c Zoehrer b Matthews	62	(7) not out		48
C. S. Pandit c Waugh b Matthews	35	(5) b Matthews		39
*Kapil Dev c Border b Matthews	119	(6) c Bright b Matthews		1
†K. S. More c Zoehrer b Waugh	4	(9) lbw b Bright		0
C. Sharma c Zoehrer b Reid	30	(8) c McDermott b Bright		23
N. S. Yadav c Border b Bright	19	b Bright		8
Maninder Singh not out	0	lbw b Matthews		0
B 1, l-b 9, n-b 6	16	B 1, l-b 3, n-b 2		6

1-62 2-65 3-65 4-142 397   1-55 2-158 3-204 4-251 347
5-206 6-220 7-245   5-253 6-291 7-331
8-330 9-387 10-397   8-334 9-344 10-347

First innings – McDermott 14–2–59–0; Reid 18–4–93–1; Matthews 28.2–3–103–5; Bright 23–3–88–2; Waugh 11–2–44–1.
Second innings – McDermott 5–0–27–0; Reid 10–2–48–0; Matthews 39.5–7–146–5; Bright 25–3–94–5; Waugh 4–1–16–0; Border 3–0–12–0.

Toss won by Australia   UMPIRES D. N. Dotiwalla and V. Vikramraju

INDIA V WEST INDIES 1987–88 Dicky Rutnagur, 1989

The interests of cricket were not best served by either the timing of this tour or the cavalier fashion in which the Board of Control for Cricket in India, influenced by financial considerations and driven by internal politics, chopped and changed the itinerary even after the tour had started. The World Cup tournament, which was so vigorously promoted and which had only just ended, left the country with no appetite for any form of international cricket except the overs-limit variety. The Test matches, regrettably, were received as enthusiastically as sandwiches filled with the leftovers of the Christmas turkey. The thrilling First Test, at Delhi, was played before very thin crowds and on no day of the series was any ground completely full.

In such an atmosphere, the first-class games outside the Tests also suffered from lack of support. Member associations of the Indian board were reluctant to host these fixtures, yet all clamoured to stage one-day internationals. To meet this demand, the board went to the extent of cancelling, at the 11th hour, the Second Test match at Nagpur and substituting it with two one-day internationals in addition to the five originally scheduled. West Indies won the one-day series 6–1, and most of their victories were gained decisively. Yet crowds flocked to them. The low attendances at the Test matches, however, left the host associations incurring heavy losses.

The 1–1 result of the four-match Test series was not a true index of the strength of the teams. While West Indies were not the side they once were, they were distinctly superior. A more appropriate result would have been 2–1 in their favour, although even then it would not have been a just one. The Indian victory in the final Test was gained on a Madras pitch that made a mockery of Test cricket.

India v West Indies First Test
At Delhi, November 25, 26, 28, 29, 1987. West Indies won by five wickets. Dicky Rutnagur, 1989

Taken unawares by conditions uncharacteristic of the Feroz Shah Kotla ground – notorious for tall scores and dull draws – both sides were dismissed in the first innings for their lowest totals against each other. Vengsarkar, in his first Test as captain, won the toss and, despite evidence of moisture in the pitch, elected to bat. He foresaw some help in the fourth innings for the spinners, of whom India had three, including a new cap in Arshad Ayub, an off-spinner. On the opening day, however, 17 of the 18 wickets that fell were credited to the fast bowlers. India were bowled out in only 145 minutes for 75, their lowest score in a home Test.

Undermined by a splendid opening spell from Kapil Dev, West Indies at one stage looked unlikely to match India's score, for they were 29 for six after ten overs. However, Haynes, who had not scored then, became the mainstay of the innings, and aided by plucky knocks from Davis, Benjamin and Walsh he put West Indies 52 ahead.

India made another disastrous start in their second innings and, despite a solid 40 by Arun Lal, were only 30 runs ahead when Shastri was fourth out. The early damage this time was done by Patterson, who claimed eight wickets in the match. A flamboyant 44, off only 41 balls, by Kapil Dev turned India's fortunes. His partnership of 73 with Vengsarkar was succeeded by one of 96 for the sixth wicket between Vengsarkar and More, who took care of the second new ball on the third morning. Vengsarkar batted for 405 minutes for his 16th Test century, during which he scored his 6,000th run in Test cricket, and when he and More were out in quick succession, the tail wagged productively.

West Indies were left to score 276 runs on a pitch which had now stopped helping the pace bowlers, but had become dry enough to offer hope to the spinners. Indeed, Ayub, the newcomer, took four wickets, but Maninder Singh bowled poorly. After an opening stand of 62, West Indies declined to 111 for four, but the issue was settled by a brilliant 109 not out off 102 balls from Richards. With Logie and Dujon proving staunch allies, he batted with great responsibility, and yet not without flair. There were 13 fours in his 21st Test hundred, his seventh against India.

Toss: India. **India 75** (B. P. Patterson 5-24, W. W. Davis 3-20) **and 327** (Arun Lal 40, D. B. Vengsarkar 102, Kapil Dev 44, K. S. More 49, Extras 30; B. P. Patterson 3-100, C. A. Walsh 5-54); **West Indies 127** (D. L. Haynes 45; Kapil Dev 3-41, C. Sharma 5-55) **and 276-5** (C. G. Greenidge 33, R. B. Richardson 31, I. V. A. Richards 109*, A. L. Logie 46; Arshad Ayub 4-72).

India v West Indies   **Fourth Test**
At Madras, January 11, 12, 14, 15, 1988. India won by 255 runs.   Dicky Rutnagur, 1989

India's winning margin was the most decisive of their six victories against West Indies. Its main author was a new cap in Hirwani, a bespectacled, 19-year-old leg-spinner, who had the assistance of an underprepared pitch which afforded turn from the opening day. In the circumstances, the scales were tipped heavily in India's favour when Shastri, captaining for the first time in a Test match, won the toss. Hirwani captured eight wickets in each innings to equal the Australian R. A. L. Massie's feat of taking 16 wickets on his debut, against England at Lord's in 1972. If Hirwani was able to give the ball air, as he did, and challenge the batsmen to counter-attack, it was because of India's first-innings total of 382, which was owed principally to a dashing 109 by Kapil Dev, scored off only 119 balls and including 17 fours.

Although the ball turned extravagantly, the seven other spinners in the match, while bowling 154 overs between them, could not take more than seven wickets. The collapse of the West Indians for scores of 184 and 160, the second time in 156 minutes, not only was indicative of their mistrust of the pitch but also underlined the vulnerability of the new generation of their batsmen to leg-spin. Certainly, in conditions which put a premium on experience, they missed Greenidge, who was kept out by an injured thumb. He was replaced by Simmons, hitherto uncapped. Besides Hirwani, India included two newcomers in the all-rounders Raman and Ajay Sharma, and they too played vital roles in shaping India's victory, their first over West Indies since 1979. The pitch, if a nightmare for the batsmen, made equally high demands on the wicket-keepers, and More deserved much credit for stumping six batsmen in the match, five of them in the second innings. Both figures were a record for stumpings in a Test.

India v West Indies, 1987-88

Fourth Test

At Madras, January 11, 12, 14, 15, 1988. Result: India won by 255 runs.

INDIA

	First innings			Second innings	
K. Srikkanth c Davis b Walsh	23	–	lbw b Davis		17
Arun Lal c Logie b Hooper	69	–	lbw b Walsh		1
M. Amarnath c Dujon b Walsh	3	–	(4) c Richardson b Walsh		1
W. V. Raman c Dujon b Davis	9	–	(3) c Dujon b Walsh		83
M. Azharuddin c Haynes b Hooper	47	–	c Davis b Richards		39
A. K. Sharma lbw b Richards	30	–	lbw b Patterson		23
Kapil Dev c Richards b Walsh	109	–	lbw b Patterson		5
*R. J. Shastri b Davis	23	–	not out		20
†K. S. More b Davis	17	–	c Dujon b Walsh		0
Arshad Ayub not out	23	–	not out		3
N. D. Hirwani c Richardson b Davis	1				
B 15, l-b 4, n-b 9	28		B 8, l-b 7, n-b 10		25

1-30 2-38 3-64 4-153 5-156 6-269   **382**   1-3 2-36 3-37 4-124 5-185   (8 wkts dec.) **217**
7-313 8-342 9-369 10-382   6-185 7-190 8-194

First innings – Patterson 15–1–62–0; Walsh 27–3–85–3; Davis 18.1–0–76–4; Butts 24–4–62–0;
Richards 8–1–36–1; Hooper 12–3–42–2.
Second innings – Patterson 9–2–17–2; Walsh 16–5–55–4; Davis 6–0–20–1; Butts 21–1–62–0;
Richards 18–4–28–1; Hooper 6–1–20–0.

WEST INDIES

	First innings			Second innings	
D. L. Haynes c Kapil Dev b Shastri	13	–	lbw b Hirwani		6
P. V. Simmons c and b Kapil Dev	8	–	c Amarnath b Hirwani		14
R. B. Richardson c Azharuddin b Hirwani	36	–	c Amarnath b Arshad Ayub		7
*I. V. A. Richards b Hirwani	68	–	c Kapil Dev b Hirwani		4
A. L. Logie c Azharuddin b Hirwani	12	–	st More b Hirwani		67
C. L. Hooper lbw b Hirwani	2	–	st More b Hirwani		8
†P. J. L. Dujon st More b Hirwani	24	–	st More b Hirwani		2
C. G. Butts c Raman b Hirwani	0	–	c Sharma b Hirwani		38
W. W. Davis lbw b Hirwani	1	–	st More b Hirwani		7
C. A. Walsh c More b Hirwani	8	–	st More b Raman		0
B. P. Patterson not out	0	–	not out		0
B 8, l-b 2, n-b 2	12		B 4, l-b 1, n-b 2		7

1-17 2-47 3-98 4-128 5-132 6-163   **184**   1-22 2-24 3-33 4-41 5-61 6-79   **160**
7-175 8-175 9-183 10-184   7-138 8-153 9-160 10-160

First innings – Kapil Dev 7–0–20–1; Amarnath 3–0–8–0; Shastri 13–6–29–1; Arshad Ayub 28–10–47–0;
Hirwani 18.3–3–61–8; Sharma 4–0–9–0.
Second innings – Kapil Dev 4–3–8–0; Amarnath 2–0–7–0; Shastri 5–0–25–0; Arshad Ayub 14–5–33–1;
Hirwani 15.2–3–75–8; Raman 1–0–7–1.

Toss won by India   UMPIRES R. B. Gupta and P. D. Reporter

ENGLAND V INDIA 1990

R. Mohan, 1991

The theatrical impresarios of London's West End would have been proud to have put on a spectacle like this. The sporting plot was played out on arenas larger than any stage along Shaftesbury Avenue, and it fascinated by its natural twists and turns, supported by bravura performances. Most importantly, the patrons went away delighted by what they had seen. The show was a winner.

The supremacy of cricket as England's summer sport was in question. The preceding Tests against New Zealand had struggled to compete against the circus of soccer's quadrennial showpiece, the World Cup, and neither the knighting of Richard Hadlee nor England's first win in a home series for five years made the impact of the Indian summer which followed. A certain amateur spirit was needed if cricket was to recapture its glory, and the Indian tourists, led by Mohammad Azharuddin, had that spirit. The fear of losing has often been responsible for dull Test cricket, but India, accustomed to winning abroad once in a blue moon, had none of that fear. Moreover, with conditions so dry that hosepipe bans were being imposed in Britain, the Indian batsmen found themselves in their element. They scored heavily from their earliest games, making 15 first-class hundreds, six of them in Tests, and their double victory in the Texaco Trophy one-day internationals suggested how attractively they could perform. The Tests would revolve around their success in using these batting skills to support the notoriously weak bowling.

The fate of the series lay in the toss at Lord's. With so many batsmen among the runs, most captains would have grabbed first strike the moment the coin came down in their favour. This is where captaincy may have let India down. Graham Gooch, soon to make this summer his *annus mirabilis*, may not have believed his ears or his luck when England were asked to bat. For while the mild cloud cover at the time of the toss was contrary to the forecast, any moisture in the pitch could only have been imagined. Not without reason did the sagacious Mike Brearley write that the decision was pusillanimous. Moreover, the divisions in Indian cricket were soon emphasised as the team's cricket manager, Bishan Bedi, was reported to have disassociated himself from the decision to put England in, though he made a belated attempt to assuage the players' feelings by denying the words attributed to him.

Until the last Test, India's batsmen were always left to battle against the odds, chasing one massive England total after another, but their talented line-up, and especially the brilliant Azharuddin, did much to re-establish the virtues of positive batting. The Indian captain's breathtakingly audacious hundred at Lord's signified the difference between the English straight bat, wielded with control rather than subtlety, and oriental wristiness, which lends itself to innovation.

How different the series might have been was suggested by the way India performed when they batted first in the final Test, on a parched Oval pitch as close to their native conditions as they were likely to find. They made the most of it with their highest score against England, who came to appreciate the difference now that it was their turn to bat after the opposition had ground out a huge total. The ball was spinning on the third day, and when England followed on before lunch on Monday, conditions pointed to India's first victory in an overseas Test since Leeds in 1986. But their bowling was exposed yet again. Inflexible tactics and lack of penetration led the Indians to accept the draw long before England could relax to enjoy their first summer without a defeat since 1979.

The Indians nevertheless left England happier for their visit, convinced that the future would be brighter and that a nucleus of players had been found to serve them for some time to come. In the Texaco series they had also rediscovered their talent in the one-day game. Most of all, the series did more for the game than many recent ones, and that in itself was cause for celebration.

England v India	First Test
At Lord's, July 26, 27, 28, 30, 31, 1990. England won by 247 runs.	John Thicknesse, 1991

The Indians, and especially their captain, Azharuddin, had small reason to think so by the end, but the First Test was as brilliant a match as the players could hope to take part in, or spectators to watch. England's winning margin made it look one-sided; and no one would dispute that, from lunch on the first day, when they were 82 for one after being put in, England were in control until the end. Certainly England's win, inspired by Gooch's historic innings of 333 and 123, which broke all kinds of records, was the result of a powerful performance by his team, and following the victory over New Zealand in the last Test of the previous series, it provided the first instance of England winning successive Tests since 1985.

Six appeal: needing 24 to save the follow-on with the No. 11 at the other end at Lord's in 1990, Kapil Dev's response was to blast Eddie Hemmings for four successive sixes: this was the fourth. India still lost the match, in which Graham Gooch scored 333 and 123.

Yet it would not have been the match it was without the vibrant batting of the tourists. Shastri and Azharuddin made splendid hundreds of contrasting styles, and Kapil Dev struck a high-velocity 77 not out, jauntily rounded off with four successive sixes to limit England's lead to 199 and thus save the follow-on. Each was straight-driven off Hemmings's off-spin into the building works that throughout the season masqueraded as the Nursery End.

When India were challenged by Gooch's second declaration to make 472 to win, or bat seven hours on a crusting pitch to draw, it was possible retrospectively to see that they were fighting a losing battle once Fraser and Malcolm had dismissed their openers in eight overs on the fourth evening. Such was the depth of their batting, however, and the dash and artistry with which Vengsarkar and Azharuddin batted on the last morning as they put on 51 at four an over, that it was not until the former was caught at the wicket, trying not to play an off-break, that it became obvious there could be only one result. When Azharuddin followed 20 minutes later, superbly caught at third slip as he tried to turn a straight ball into the leg side, India's spirit cracked, and the score, at one stage 114 for three, was eroded to 181 for eight. A flourish by the last two wickets added 43 and so raised the match aggregate to 1,603, two runs more than the previous record for the ground, established in England's 1930 classic with Australia.

England v India, 1990   First Test

At Lord's, July 26, 27, 28, 30, 31, 1990. Result: England won by 247 runs.

ENGLAND

	First innings			Second innings	
*G. A. Gooch b Prabhakar		333	– c Azharuddin b Sharma		123
M. A. Atherton b Kapil Dev		8	– c Vengsarkar b Sharma		72
D. I. Gower c Manjrekar b Hirwani		40	– not out		32
A. J. Lamb c Manjrekar b Sharma		139	– c Tendulkar b Hirwani		19
R. A. Smith not out		100	– b Prabhakar		15
J. E. Morris not out		4			
B 2, l-b 21, w 2, n-b 4		29	L-b 11		11

1-14 2-141 3-449 4-641   (4 wkts dec.) 653   1-204 2-207 3-250 4-272   (4 wkts dec.) 272

†R. C. Russell, C. C. Lewis, E. E. Hemmings, A. R. C. Fraser and D. E. Malcolm did not bat.

First innings – Kapil Dev 34–5–120–1; Prabhakar 43–6–187–1; Sharma 33–5–122–1; Shastri 22–0–99–0; Hirwani 30–1–102–1.
Second innings – Kapil Dev 10–0–53–0; Prabhakar 11.2–2–45–1; Shastri 7–0–38–0; Sharma 15–0–75–2; Hirwani 11–0–50–1.

INDIA

	First innings			Second innings	
R. J. Shastri c Gooch b Hemmings		100	– c Russell b Malcolm		12
N. S. Sidhu c Morris b Fraser		30	– c Morris b Fraser		1
S. V. Manjrekar c Russell b Gooch		18	– c Russell b Malcolm		33
D. B. Vengsarkar c Russell b Fraser		52	– c Russell b Hemmings		35
*M. Azharuddin b Hemmings		121	– c Atherton b Lewis		37
S. R. Tendulkar b Lewis		10	– c Gooch b Fraser		27
M. Prabhakar c Lewis b Malcolm		25	– lbw b Lewis		8
Kapil Dev not out		77	– c Lewis b Hemmings		7
†K. S. More c Morris b Fraser		8	– lbw b Fraser		16
S. K. Sharma c Russell b Fraser		0	– run out		38
N. D. Hirwani lbw b Fraser		0	– not out		0
L-b 1, w 4, n-b 8		13	B 3, l-b 1, n-b 6		10

1-63 2-102 3-191 4-241   454   1-9 2-23 3-63   224
5-288 6-348 7-393   4-114 5-127 6-140
8-430 9-430 10-454   7-158 8-181 9-206 10-224

First innings – Malcolm 25–1–106–1; Fraser 39.1–9–104–5; Lewis 24–3–108–1; Gooch 6–3–26–1; Hemmings 20–3–109–2.
Second innings – Fraser 22–7–39–3; Malcolm 10–0–65–2; Hemmings 21–2–79–2; Atherton 1–0–11–0; Lewis 8–1–26–2.

Toss won by India   UMPIRES H. D. Bird and N. T. Plews

England v India — Second Test

At Manchester, August 9, 10, 11, 13, 14, 1990. Drawn. — Graham Otway, 1991

Of the six individual centuries scored in this fascinating contest, none was more outstanding than Tendulkar's, which rescued India on the final afternoon. At 17 years and 112 days, he was only 30 days older than Mushtaq Mohammad was when, against India at Delhi in 1960–61, he became the youngest player to score a Test hundred. More significantly, after several of his colleagues had fallen to reckless strokes, Tendulkar held the England attack at bay with a disciplined display of immense maturity.

Tendulkar remained undefeated on 119, having batted for 224 minutes and hit 17 fours. He looked the embodiment of India's famous opener, Gavaskar, and indeed was wearing a pair of his pads. While he displayed a full repertoire of strokes in compiling his maiden Test hundred, most remarkable were his off-side shots from the back foot. Though only 5ft 5in tall, he was still able to control without difficulty short deliveries from the English pacemen.

Toss: England. **England 519** (G. A. Gooch 116, M. A. Atherton 131, D. I. Gower 38, A. J. Lamb 38, R. A. Smith 121*; A. Kumble 3-105, N. D. Hirwani 4-174) **and 320-4 dec.** (M. A. Atherton 74, A. J. Lamb 109, R. A. Smith 61*); **India 432** (S. V. Manjrekar 93, M. Azharuddin 179, S. R. Tendulkar 68; A. R. C. Fraser 5-124) **and 343-6** (S. V. Manjrekar 50, D. B. Vengsarkar 32, S. R. Tendulkar 119*, M. Prabhakar 67*; E. E. Hemmings 3-75).

England v India — Third Test

At The Oval, August 23, 24, 25, 27, 28, 1990. Drawn — David Field, 1991

Gower's sublime strokeplay, unwavering determination and considerable stamina throughout the final day erased India's chances of squaring the series, though their hopes were high when they enforced the follow-on after scoring their third-best score of all time. The six-hour *tour de force* was Gower's 16th hundred in Tests and his fourth on the Kennington ground; with Shastri and Kapil Dev he brought the tally of centuries scored by the two teams to 15, a record for a three-match series.

Toss: India. **India 606-9 dec.** (R. J. Shastri 187, D. B. Vengsarkar 33, M. Azharuddin 78, Kapil Dev 110, K. S. More 61*, Extras 37); **England 340** (G. A. Gooch 85, N. F. Williams 38, R. A. Smith 57, R. C. Russell 35, E. E. Hemmings 51, Extras 30; M. Prabhakar 4-74) **and 477-4 dec.** (G. A. Gooch 88, M. A. Atherton 86, D. I. Gower 157*, J. E. Morris 32, A. J. Lamb 52, Extras 55).

INDIA v SOUTH AFRICA 1996

Colin Bryden, 1998

The Indians had not lost a home series since 1986–87, and had won ten out of 14 Tests at home since 1992–93, the most recent being an emphatic win over Australia in a one-off match at Delhi. South Africa, meanwhile, had not lost any series, or a one-off, since their inaugural Test on rejoining the cricketing world, in April 1992. They had played enough one-day cricket on the subcontinent not to worry unduly about the conditions. But they soon discovered that Tests were different: they lost the series 2–1, sandwiching a win in Calcutta between defeats in Ahmedabad and Kanpur.

The Indians had the bonus of a late flowering from Mohammad Azharuddin. Relieved of the captaincy, he found sublime batting form: his hundred off 74 balls in Calcutta was extraordinary; his unbeaten 163 in Kanpur clinched the series. Javagal Srinath, the First Test match-winner, and Venkatesh Prasad were an effective new-ball pair, while Anil Kumble had an outstanding series in an unexpected role. Showing a straight bat and good sense, he played vital innings in each Test, and there was no diminution either in his powers as a brisk-paced bowler of leg-spin and top-spin. Although his figures were not sensational, the South Africans never mastered him.

India v South Africa — First Test

At Ahmedabad, November 20, 21, 22, 23, 1996. India won by 64 runs. — Colin Bryden, 1998

Devastating pace bowling by Srinath gave India victory on a poor pitch. Though it seemed best suited to the spinners, Srinath's fast, accurate in-swingers and off-cutters brought him career-best figures of six for 21. South Africa crashed for 105 after being set a modest 170 to win.

Toss: India. **India 223** (S. V. Manjrekar 34, S. R. Tendulkar 42, M. Azharuddin 35; A. A. Donald 4-37) **and 190** (R. Dravid 34, V. V. S. Laxman 51, A. Kumble 30*; A. A. Donald 3-32, P. R. Adams 3-30); **South Africa 244** (D. J. Cullinan 43, P. L. Symcox 32, P. S. de Villiers 67*; S. B. Joshi 4-43) **and 105** (W. J. Cronje 48*; J. Srinath 6-21, A. Kumble 3-34).

India v South Africa — Second Test

At Calcutta, November 27, 28, 29, 30, December 1, 1996. South Africa won by 329 runs. — Colin Bryden, 1998

South Africa levelled the series in an invigorating Test watched by an estimated 50,000 people each day. Their batsmen found form on a true pitch and fast outfield and, for the first time, scored four hundreds in one Test. Two came from Kirsten – the third South African to achieve twin centuries. The most sensational century, however, came from Azharuddin. He reached it in 74 deliveries, equalling the fourth-quickest Test hundred recorded in terms of balls. Azharuddin hit debutant Lance Klusener for five successive fours. But Klusener rebounded in remarkable fashion, taking eight for 64 in the second innings, the third-best bowling for South Africa in Tests and the best on debut. He said afterwards he had lacked rhythm in the first innings and, in an unsuccessful team strategy, had peppered Azharuddin with short balls. His triumph came after he shortened his run-up by half a yard and bowled to a fuller length.

Toss: South Africa. **South Africa 428** (A. C. Hudson 146, G. Kirsten 102, H. H. Gibbs 31, D. J. Cullinan 43, D. J. Richardson 36*, Extras 39; B. K. V. Prasad 6-104) **and 367-3 dec.** (G. Kirsten 133, D. J. Cullinan 153*, W. J. Cronje 34); **India 329** (N. R. Mongia 35, R. S. Dravid 31, M. Azharuddin 109, A. Kumble 88; A. A. Donald 3-72) **and 137** (M. Azharuddin 52; L. Klusener 8-64).

India v South Africa

At Kanpur, December 8, 9, 10, 11, 12, 1996. India won by 280 runs.

Third Test

Colin Bryden, 1998

India maintained their unbeaten record in home series for a tenth season with a crushing victory. They managed only 237 in the first innings, but South Africa struggled even more, allowing India, inspired by a breathtaking century from Azharuddin, to take complete control. The South Africans were disconcerted by an under-prepared pitch, which had not been rolled for several days and looked badly cracked. It did not deteriorate as much as expected however, and although batting was never easy on a low, slow surface, it was far from impossible.

Toss: India. **India 237** (N. R. Mongia 41, W. V. Raman 57, S. C. Ganguly 39, S. R. Tendulkar 61; P. R. Adams 6-55) **and 400-7 dec.** (A. Kumble 42, S. C. Ganguly 41, S. R. Tendulkar 36, M. Azharuddin 163*, R. S. Dravid 56); **South Africa 177** (G. Kirsten 43; J. Srinath 3-42, A. Kumble 4-71) **and 180** (A. C. Hudson 31, W. J. Cronje 50, L. Klusener 34*; J. Srinath 3-38, S. B. Joshi 3-66).

INDIA v AUSTRALIA 1998

Dicky Rutnagur, 1999

Australia's sequence of nine victorious Test series, starting with the 1994–95 Ashes, was ended by India, who had not lost a series on home soil for exactly 11 years. There had been one blip in Australia's record before this, also involving India, when they lost a one-off Test in Delhi in October 1996. But India's 2–1 victory – the Australian win came in the dead last game – was only the second time they had had the better of Australia over a Test series. The last was in 1979–80, during the Packer era, when the Australian team was gravely weakened.

Their 1998 successors were not at full strength either. Two frontline fast bowlers, Glenn McGrath and Jason Gillespie, were left at home recovering from injuries. Then Paul Reiffel, one of only two experienced seam bowlers in the party, suffered a recurrence of his shoulder injury; he played no further part after the First Test. Michael Kasprowicz was forced to play the dual role of strike and stock bowler. These misfortunes explain Australia's inability to win, until the very end, but not the two heavy defeats. Their batsmen were the best they could call on, yet they failed time and again against an attack as limited as their own. The two Australia centuries, by Mark Waugh and Mark Taylor, were scored after the series was settled; Michael Slater, too, was slow to make an impact.

The fact that the last series Australia lost was in Pakistan, in 1994, suggested that they are still not at ease touring the subcontinent. But there were no overt signs of unhappiness, except that Shane Warne could not manage the cuisine and had cans of baked beans and spaghetti flown out. A more plausible explanation for the poor performance was tiredness, exacerbated by extreme heat and humidity. In the 17 months since their last visit to India, Australia had played 20 Tests – five against West Indies, six against South Africa, six against England and three against New Zealand. They had also played 33 one-day internationals, culminating with four in New Zealand just before arriving here.

India v Australia   First Test

At Chennai, March 6, 7, 8, 9, 10, 1998. India won by 179 runs.   Dicky Rutnagur, 1999

The head-to-head contest between Sachin Tendulkar and Shane Warne was the key to this opening encounter. Warne's quick conquest of Tendulkar in the first innings gave Australia the initial advantage. But Tendulkar retaliated so devastatingly in the second, scoring 155 not out, that India were able to declare with a lead of 347, and 105 overs to bowl Australia out on a spinners' pitch. They had three men out overnight and won in comfort on the final afternoon.

Toss: India. **India 257** (N. R. Mongia 58, N. S. Sidhu 62, R. Dravid 52, A. Kumble 30; S. K. Warne 4-85, G. R. Robertson 4-72) **and 418-4 dec.** (N. S. Sidhu 64, R. Dravid 56, S. R. Tendulkar 155*, M. Azharuddin 64, S. C. Ganguly 30*, Extras 31); **Australia 328** (M. E. Waugh 66, I. A. Healy 90, G. R. Robertson 57; A. Kumble 4-103, S. L. V. Raju 3-54) **and 168** (I. A. Healy 32*, S. K. Warne 35; A. Kumble 4-46, S. L. V. Raju 3-31).

India v Australia   Second Test

At Calcutta, March 18, 19, 20, 21, 1998.
India won by an innings and 219 runs.   Dicky Rutnagur, 1999

Rather than make amends for their batting failures in the First Test, Australia plumbed new depths. They could not blame the pitch; in between their innings of 233 and 181, India amassed 633 for five, their biggest total ever against Australia and the highest total at Eden Gardens. No Indian was dismissed for less than 65, while only two Australians passed 45. Australia had bad luck with injuries and umpiring errors. But so vast was the chasm that it made little difference as they surrendered the series.

Azharuddin scored his fifth century in six Tests on this ground, and it was one of his masterpieces: 163 not out in 310 minutes with 18 fours and three sixes. But with the pitch so amiable, it was apt that a bowler was named Man of the Match – and it was Srinath, rather than Kumble, whose bag was fuller by two wickets, for Srinath's strikes made the bigger impact. He bowled with pace and accuracy, cutting the ball back and, in the second innings, reverse-swinging it menacingly.

India had picked Laxman at the last minute, from outside their squad of 12, to open the batting with Sidhu. The pairing was a triumph: they put on 191 in only 40 overs. Both openers fell just short of a hundred, Sidhu missing a deflection at Mark Waugh and Laxman edging a square-cut. Tendulkar launched an immediate assault. He bent the bowling to his will, reaching 50 off only 60 balls, but a lapse of concentration cost him his wicket on 79.

Toss: Australia. **Australia 233** (S. R. Waugh 80, R. T. Ponting 60; J. Srinath 3-80, S. C. Ganguly 3-28, A. Kumble 3-44) **and 181** (M. A. Taylor 45, I. A. Healy 38, S. R. Waugh 33; J. Srinath 3-44, A. Kumble 5-62); **India 633-5 dec.** (V. V. S. Laxman 95, N. S. Sidhu 97, R. Dravid 86, S. R. Tendulkar 79, M. Azharuddin 163*, S. C. Ganguly 65, N. R. Mongia 30*).

INDIA V PAKISTAN 1999 Qamar Ahmed, 2000

In January 1999, Pakistan arrived for their first Test series with neighbours India for nine years, and the first on Indian soil since 1987. Though there were only two Tests (a third match at Calcutta, won by Pakistan, was regarded as part of the separate Asian Test Championship), it was probably the most exciting of the 11 series between the rivals. Pakistan won a narrow victory at Chennai, only for India to strike back with a massive win at Delhi. The star players were the spinners, Saqlain Mushtaq of Pakistan and Anil Kumble of India: Kumble provided the sensational conclusion to the series by taking all ten wickets in the final innings.

It was also probably the most important series between the teams from a political standpoint. Three previous attempts to organise a Pakistani tour of India in the 1990s had been aborted because of threats of disruption by right-wing Hindu fundamentalists. In 1998, both countries had tested nuclear weapons, adding a new dimension to their traditional tension. The Shiv Sena party, led by maverick politician Bal Thackeray, were the most prominent opponents of the visit. Early in January, activists dug up the Test pitch in Delhi, forcing the Indian board to move the First Test to Chennai. Shortly afterwards, the board's offices at Mumbai were ransacked and officials manhandled, though this time Shiv Sena denied responsibility. Supporters and opponents of the tour both held processions in the major Indian cities. But prime minister Atal Behari Vajpayee urged the Pakistanis to come, promising maximum security for both teams, and sent a senior minister to negotiate with Thackeray. Shiv Sena sensed that the mood was against them, and they were in danger of being alienated from the coalition government; the day before the tourists arrived, they withdrew the threat of further disruption.

Nevertheless, commandos and plain-clothes officers shadowed the Pakistani team everywhere. The board even engaged snake charmers, after rumours that extremists might release snakes in the crowds or on to the pitch. But the two Tests went off without any trouble: a victory for cricket and diplomacy (when crowd trouble came later, at Calcutta, it was of a less political nature). The tourists' team manager, former diplomat and foreign minister Shaharyar Khan (who subsequently became ambassador to France), and captain Wasim Akram did much to contribute to the success of the series and the goodwill it created. The Chennai Test attracted an estimated 50,000 spectators a day, and the Delhi Test nearly 40,000 a day.

Spin dominated the series, accounting for 55 of the 80 wickets which fell. Both Tests ended in four days as off-spinner Saqlain and leg-spinner Kumble tweaked and turned the ball on slow pitches. Saqlain bowled superbly for 20 wickets at 20.15; he claimed five wickets every innings he bowled, and was named Man of the Series, ahead of Kumble, who collected 21 at 14.85, thanks to his ten in an innings at Delhi. He was only the second man in Test cricket to take a perfect ten; he devastated Pakistan's batting with his lift and bounce, taking his ten wickets for 47. His overall analysis was ten for 74, as against Jim Laker of England, who took ten for 53 against Australia in 1956 – Laker finished with 19 for 90 in the match, to Kumble's 14 for 149.

The pitch was substandard after the vandals' attack, and Kumble was lucky in a couple of decisions from home umpire Jayaprakash who, like Steve Dunne in the First Test, appeared inconsistent. That should not take the credit away from a magnificent performance. "It is a dream. I cannot get over the fact I have got ten wickets," said a delighted Kumble afterwards. "Whenever I am leaving for a match, my mum says 'Get a hat-trick.' Probably next time she will say 'Get ten wickets.'"

India v Pakistan	First Test
At Chennai, January 28, 29, 30, 31, 1999. Pakistan won by 12 runs.	Qamar Ahmed, 2000

A nail-biting finish on the fourth day saw India, chasing 271, slump to 82 for five – two of the wickets controversially given out by umpire Dunne. When Tendulkar and Mongia combined to add 136 for the sixth wicket, however, they seemed to be on their way to victory. Then Mongia was caught for 52. Still Tendulkar kept going, despite a back strain, and India were only 17 from their target when he holed out at mid-off, trying to hit Saqlain Mushtaq out of the ground. He had batted 405 minutes and scored 136, his 18th Test hundred, including 18 fours. But India's last three wickets added only four more runs; Saqlain finished them off with five for 93, giving him ten for 187 in the match. The Pakistanis bowed to the ground in prayer and embarked on a lap of honour, to a standing ovation from the Chennai crowd, whose sporting behaviour won much praise.

India v Pakistan, 1999   First Test
At Chennai, January 28, 29, 30, 31, 1999. Result: Pakistan won by 12 runs.

PAKISTAN	First innings		Second innings	
Saeed Anwar lbw b Srinath	24	– lbw b Prasad	7
Shahid Afridi c Ganguly b Srinath	11	– b Prasad	141
Ijaz Ahmed lbw b Kumble	13	– c and b Kumble	11
Inzamam–ul–Haq c and b Kumble	10	– c Laxman b Tendulkar	51
Yousuf Youhana lbw b Tendulkar	53	– b Tendulkar	26
Salim Malik b Srinath	8	– c Dravid b Joshi	32
†Moin Khan c Ganguly b Kumble	60	– c Mongia b Prasad	3
*Wasim Akram c Laxman b Kumble	38	– c Joshi b Prasad	1
Saqlain Mushtaq lbw b Kumble	2	– lbw b Prasad	0
Nadeem Khan c Dravid b Kumble	8	– not out	1
Waqar Younis not out	0	– c Ramesh b Prasad	5
L-b 5, n-b 6	11	B 1, l-b 4, n-b 3	8

1-32 2-41 3-61 4-66 5-91 6-154   238   1-11 2-42 3-139 4-169 5-275 6-278   286
7-214 8-227 9-237 10-238   7-279 8-279 9-280 10-286

First innings – Srinath 15–3–63–3; Prasad 16–1–54–0; Kumble 24.5–7–70–6; Joshi 21–8–36–0; Tendulkar 3–0–10–1.
Second innings – Srinath 16–1–68–0; Prasad 10.2–5–33–6; Kumble 22–4–93–1; Joshi 14–3–42–1; Tendulkar 7–1–35–2; Laxman 2–0–10–0.

INDIA

	First innings		Second innings	

S. Ramesh lbw b Wasim Akram . . . . 43 – c Inzamam–ul–Haq b Waqar Younis 5
V. V. S. Laxman lbw b Wasim Akram . . . . . . 23 – lbw b Waqar Younis 0
R. Dravid lbw b Saqlain Mushtaq . . . . 53 – b Wasim Akram 10
S. R. Tendulkar
    c Salim Malik b Saqlain Mushtaq . . . . 0 – c Wasim Akram b Saqlain Mushtaq 136
*M. Azharuddin
    c Inzamam–ul–Haq b Saqlain Mushtaq . 11 – lbw b Saqlain Mushtaq 7
S. C. Ganguly
    c Ijaz Ahmed b Shahid Afridi . . . . . . 54 – c Moin Khan b Saqlain Mushtaq 2
†N. R. Mongia
    st Moin Khan b Saqlain Mushtaq . . . . 5 – c Waqar Younis b Wasim Akram 52
A. Kumble
    c Yousuf Youhana b Saqlain Mushtaq . . 4 – (9) lbw b Wasim Akram 1
S. B. Joshi not out . . . . 25 – (8) c and b Saqlain Mushtaq 8
J. Srinath c Ijaz Ahmed b Shahid Afridi . . . 10 – b Saqlain Mushtaq 1
B. K. V. Prasad
    st Moin Khan b Shahid Afridi . . . . . 4 – not out 0
    B 2, l-b 2, n-b 18 22   B 8, l-b 10, n-b 18 36

1-67 2-71 3-72 4-103 5-156 6-166   254   1-5 2-6 3-50 4-73 5-82 6-218   258
7-188 8-229 9-246 10-254   7-254 8-256 9-256 10-258

First innings – Wasim Akram 20–4–60–2; Waqar Younis 12–2–48–0; Saqlain Mushtaq 35–8–94–5; Shahid Afridi 7.1–0–31–3; Nadeem Khan 7–0–17–0.
Second innings – Wasim Akram 22–4–80–3; Waqar Younis 12–6–26–2; Shahid Afridi 16–7–23–0; Saqlain Mushtaq 32.2–8–93–5; Nadeem Khan 13–5–18–0.

Toss won by Pakistan   UMPIRES R. S. Dunne and V. K. Ramaswamy
MAN OF THE MATCH S. R. Tendulkar

India v Pakistan   **Second Test**
At Delhi, February 4, 5, 6, 7, 1999. India won by 212 runs.   Qamar Ahmed, 2000

India won a massive victory, their first over Pakistan since 1980, to draw the series. But the headlines belonged to leg-spinner Anil Kumble. He claimed all ten wickets in Pakistan's second innings, becoming only the second man in history to take ten in a Test innings, following English off-spinner Jim Laker in 1956.

Kumble had bowled six overs without taking a wicket on the fourth morning, mostly from the Football Stand End. Pakistan had little hope of winning after being set a formidable target of 420, but needed only a draw to take the series, and had seemed well placed at 101 without loss. After lunch, Kumble operated from the Pavilion End: he bowled 20.3 overs and claimed ten for 47, aided by some brilliant fielding and a substandard pitch. Pakistan were all out for 207.

Kumble started the slide when Shahid Afridi was given out caught behind dabbing outside off stump. Afridi lingered in protest at the decision by home umpire Jayaprakash, whose performance was much condemned by Pakistani observers. With his next ball, Kumble had Ijaz Ahmed lbw as he stretched forward. Inzamam-ul-Haq averted the hat-trick, but played on off an inside edge minutes later. Yousuf

Youhana, pushing forward, was lbw; Moin Khan was caught low down in the slips; and Saeed Anwar, who had defended for two and a half hours, was caught bat and pad at short leg. Pakistan had slumped to 128 for six, and Kumble had taken six for 15 in 44 balls. "That was the moment when I thought all ten could be mine," he said afterwards.

But he had to wait until after tea for No. 7, as Salim Malik and Wasim Akram held firm in a stand of 58. Then Kumble resumed the demolition. He bowled Malik, trying to pull; Mushtaq Ahmed was caught at gully off an awkward bounce; and the next ball hit Saqlain Mushtaq on the toe and trapped him lbw. That ended Kumble's 26th over, with one wicket remaining. Azharuddin instructed Srinath to bowl a wayward line in his next over. Wasim, who had resisted for an hour and a half, then kept out the hat-trick ball, and the

All ten: Anil Kumble, one of only two bowlers to take ten wickets in a Test innings.

next one, but top-edged Kumble's third ball to Laxman at short leg. Kumble was carried back to the pavilion on his colleagues' shoulders as the crowd rejoiced. "My first reaction is that we have won," he said. "No one dreams of taking ten wickets in an innings, because you can't. The pitch was of variable bounce, and cutting and pulling was not easy. All I had to do was pitch in the right area, mix up my pace and spin, and trap the batsmen. The first wicket was the hardest to get – the openers were cruising." He added that the match award should have gone to a batsman in those conditions.

Back on the opening day, India had claimed first use of the suspect pitch. They scored 252, but would have done even more modestly except for four dropped catches, all off the spinners. Three of those who escaped – Kumble was the other – were the highest scorers of the innings. Pakistan's reply reached only 172, with Kumble first starting to enjoy bowling on this pitch. However, India stretched their lead handsomely. Their second innings was founded on a fine 96 by Ramesh, who batted four and a half hours in only his fourth Test innings before giving Mushtaq Ahmed a return catch. Wasim made history for Pakistan when he trapped Mongia, his 363rd wicket in 85 Tests, passing Imran Khan's record of 362 wickets in 88 Tests. But Ganguly and Srinath put on 100 for the eighth wicket, setting up a lead of 419 before Saqlain finished things off – taking ten in a match for the second Test running.

The rest was history, for Kumble, and for Richard Stokes, a 53-year-old English businessman. As a schoolboy, he had seen Jim Laker take some of his ten wickets at Old Trafford in 1956, and he arrived at Feroz Shah Kotla – on his birthday – just in time to see Kumble repeat the feat.

India v Pakistan   Second Test

At Delhi, February 4, 5, 6, 7, 1999. India won by 212 runs.

INDIA

	First innings		Second innings
S. Ramesh b Saqlain Mushtaq	60	– c and b Mushtaq Ahmed	96
V. V. S. Laxman b Wasim Akram	35	– b Wasim Akram	8
R. Dravid lbw b Saqlain Mushtaq	33	– c Ijaz Ahmed b Saqlain Mushtaq	29
S. R. Tendulkar lbw b Saqlain Mushtaq	6	– c Wasim Akram b Mushtaq Ahmed	29
*M. Azharuddin c Ijaz Ahmed b Mushtaq Ahmed	67	– b Wasim Akram	14
S. C. Ganguly lbw b Mushtaq Ahmed	13	– not out	62
†N. R. Mongia run out	10	– lbw b Wasim Akram	0
A. Kumble c Yousuf Youhana b Saqlain Mushtaq	0	– c Ijaz Ahmed b Saqlain Mushtaq	15
J. Srinath lbw b Saqlain Mushtaq	0	– c Ijaz Ahmed b Saqlain Mushtaq	49
B. K. V. Prasad not out	1	– b Saqlain Mushtaq	6
Harbhajan Singh run out	1	– b Saqlain Mushtaq	0
B 11, l-b 9, n-b 6	26	B 13, l-b 9, n-b 9	31
	252		**339**

1-88 (2) 2-113 (1) 3-122 (4) 4-191 (3)   252
5-231 (6) 6-240 (5) 7-243 (8)
8-247 (9) 9-248 (7) 10-252 (11)

1-15 (2) 2-100 (3) 3-168 (4)   339
4-183 (1) 5-199 (5) 6-199 (7)
7-231 (8) 8-331 (9) 9-339 (10) 10-339 (11)

First Innings – Wasim Akram 13-3-23-1; Waqar Younis 13-5-37-0; Mushtaq Ahmed 26-5-64-2;
Saqlain Mushtaq 35.5-9-94-5; Shahid Afridi 4-1-14-0.
Second Innings – Wasim Akram 21-3-43-3; Waqar Younis 12-2-42-0; Saqlain Mushtaq 46.4-12-122-5;
Mushtaq Ahmed 26-4-86-2; Shahid Afridi 8-1-24-0.

PAKISTAN

	First innings		Second innings
Saeed Anwar c Mongia b Prasad	1	– c Laxman b Kumble	69
Shahid Afridi b Harbhajan Singh	32	– c Mongia b Kumble	41
Ijaz Ahmed, sen. c Dravid b Kumble	17	– lbw b Kumble	0
Inzamam-ul-Haq b Kumble	26	– b Kumble	6
Yousuf Youhana c and b Kumble	3	– lbw b Kumble	0
Salim Malik c Azharuddin b Prasad	31	– (7) b Kumble	15
†Moin Khan lbw b Srinath	14	– (6) c Ganguly b Kumble	3
*Wasim Akram lbw b Harbhajan Singh	15	– c Laxman b Kumble	37
Mushtaq Ahmed c Laxman b Harbhajan Singh	12	– c Dravid b Kumble	1
Saqlain Mushtaq lbw b Kumble	2	– lbw b Kumble	0
Waqar Younis not out	1	– not out	6
B 1, l-b 8, n-b 9	18	B 15, l-b 2, w 2, n-b 10	29
	172		**207**

1-1 (1) 2-54 (2) 3-54 (3) 4-60 (5)   172
5-114 (4) 6-130 (6) 7-139 (7)
8-167 (9) 9-168 (8) 10-172 (10)

1-101 (2) 2-101 (3) 3-115 (4)   207
4-115 (5) 5-127 (6) 6-128 (1)
7-186 (7) 8-198 (9) 9-198 (10) 10-207 (8)

First Innings – Srinath 12-1-38-1; Prasad 11-1-20-2; Harbhajan Singh 17-5-30-3; Kumble 24.3-6-75-4.
Second Innings – Srinath 12-2-50-0; Prasad 4-1-15-0; Kumble 26.3-9-74-10; Harbhajan Singh 18-5-51-0.

Toss won by India   UMPIRES S. A. Bucknor and A. V. Jayaprakash

Australia v India 1999–2000
Dicky Rutnagur, 2001

The Indians failed to live up to having top billing in a season of twin tours. Never before in almost 68 years as a Test nation had an Indian national team been so completely overwhelmed. It wasn't just that they were outclassed in all three Tests. They lost to Queensland on the fourth morning, were soundly beaten by 164 runs in a one-day fixture against the Prime Minister's XI, a team of young aspirants, and lost seven of their eight games in the Carlton & United series. Their only win, other than beating Pakistan once in the one-day series, was against New South Wales, who fielded a depleted side.

Apart from Sachin Tendulkar and Sourav Ganguly, India's batsmen could not come to terms with the pace and bounce of Australia's pitches. Tendulkar, despite being the victim of dubious umpiring decisions in both innings of the First Test, averaged 46.33, scoring a splendid 116 in the Second and two half-centuries. However, V. V. S. Laxman, with some substantial innings early on the tour and a gloriously elegant 167 in the final innings of the rubber, showed that he could have made a bigger impact batting lower down the order. Not yet an established Test player, he was pitchforked by circumstances into opening the innings in the Second and Third Tests. The big disappointment was Rahul Dravid who, to date, had an impressive overseas record. He made a hundred on a lifeless pitch in the drawn game against Tasmania but gathered just 93 runs in six Test innings.

Javagal Srinath was India's best bowler, and his new-ball partner, Ajit Agarkar, toiled hard and bowled at a rapid pace for one who is small of build and whose career had been blighted by frequent injury. Between them they claimed 21 of the 38 Australian wickets in the series, whereas Anil Kumble, who was expected to be a big force on resilient Australian pitches, obtained no more than five. India took early wickets in every innings of the Test matches – Australia's highest opening stand was nine – but never managed to restrict the home side's first innings to under 400, which was a clear reflection of their meagre bowling resources.

So pronounced was the disparity between the two sides that Australia's selectors never contemplated replacing two batsmen who were palpably out of form, Greg Blewett and Mark Waugh. Whenever Australia were hard pressed for runs or momentum, they were unfailingly invigorated by Ricky Ponting, the top run-scorer on either side with 375, and Adam Gilchrist (221), whose wicket-keeping, too, was consistently excellent.

A pace attack headed by Glenn McGrath, at the height of his form, and Damien Fleming was enough of a handful in the opening Test before the Australians further sharpened its edge by introducing 23-year-old Brett Lee, who had hitherto played only 16 first-class matches. The younger brother of Shane Lee, Australia's one-day international all-rounder, he showed remarkable maturity as he combined genuine pace with admirable control, subtlety and an ability to reverse-swing the old ball.

Eight wickets at 41.87 apiece do no justice to Shane Warne's part in a series in which the fast bowlers were the main destroyers. On an easy pitch in Adelaide, however, he took six wickets and in the first innings skimmed off the cream of India's batting: Dravid, Tendulkar and Ganguly. He again bowled superbly in the

Second Test and, although his reward was merely two wickets, struck the mortal blow by dismissing Tendulkar in the second innings.

Australia v India   Third Test
At Sydney, January 2, 3, 4, 2000. Australia won by an innings and 141 runs.   Dicky Rutnagur, 2001

At the instigation of Steve Waugh, the Australians marked their first Test of the new century with a one-off appearance in caps of the style and shade of green worn in 1900. Having made this concession to history, they got down to business as remorselessly as ever, winning in three days to complete their second clean sweep of the summer and extend their run of Test victories to seven. India, their morale in tatters, were ready victims.

Although rain before the start produced conditions choice for pace bowlers, Tendulkar opted to bat first – and duly came to grief. McGrath and Lee went through India in 68 overs, all except Tendulkar looking hopelessly out of their depth. For the fourth time in succession, Agarkar was dismissed first ball – unprecedented in Tests, and another unwelcome record was in store for him. Tendulkar batted with greater abandon than at Adelaide and Melbourne, hitting eight fours in 45 from 53 balls. His dismissal was the climax of a rousing duel with McGrath, who, having been hooked, pulled and driven earlier in the over, sent Tendulkar on his way with an ill-tempered verbal assault. Yet it brought him no more than a mild censure from referee Madugalle.

The pitch rolled out true on the sunny second day, but India had Australia 49 for two, and a further setback looked imminent as Langer struggled. He hung on, though, found his fluency after reaching 50 and prospered to compile the highest score by an Australian against India. His 223 was spread over eight hours 43 minutes, in which he faced 355 balls and hit 30 fours. The Waugh twins – Mark was playing his 100th Test – helped Langer put on 218 and then Ponting, in irresistible form, joined him to add another 190.

Any significant Indian reply was snuffed out when Tendulkar, off the fourth ball he faced, ladled a catch to cover. McGrath methodically unpicked the innings, taking five wickets for the second time in the match. His last was that of poor Agarkar, this time out second ball without scoring to equal the unenviable record of five successive ducks in Test innings. India's honour was saved by a quite remarkable 167 off 198 balls by Laxman, who at the start of his innings had taken a staggering blow on the visor of his helmet. Tall and elegant, he drove with classic grace to all points between cover and mid-wicket and was just as assertive against anything short, cutting and pulling with power.

Toss: India. **India 150** (S. R. Tendulkar 45; G. D. McGrath 5-48, B. Lee 4-39) **and 261**
(V. V. S. Laxman 167; G. D. McGrath 5-55); **Australia 552-5 dec.** (J. L. Langer 223, M. E. Waugh 32,
S. R. Waugh 57, R. T. Ponting 141*, A. C. Gilchrist 45*, Extras 34).

INDIA V AUSTRALIA 2001

Dicky Rutnagur, 2002

Although the Australians began the tour with the awesome achievement of 15 consecutive Test wins, they deemed victory in the series against India as absolutely essential if they were to stand comparison with the greatest teams Australia had fielded. Winning in India was, in their eyes, a conquest of the "final frontier", not least because 31 years and four tours had passed since Australia last left there triumphant.

Steve Waugh's team seemed to be on the point of emulating Bill Lawry's when they won the First Test at Mumbai, by ten wickets in three days, and then made India follow on 274 behind in the Second at Kolkata (formerly Calcutta). However, India not only denied them a winning 2–0 lead there, but rallied strongly enough to achieve one of the most remarkable victories in the history of Test cricket. They went on to win the deciding Test in a gripping finish.

India v Australia

First Test

At Mumbai, February 27, 28, March 1, 2001. Australia won by ten wickets.

Although Australia completed their 16th win in consecutive Tests in three days and by a vast margin, it was not as straightforward as it might appear: in their first innings, they lost five wickets before reaching three figures. Moreover, Steve Waugh's decision to put India in had been a major gamble, given the doubts about the durability of the pitch, even though the Wankhede Stadium invariably offers encouragement for seam bowlers on the first morning. Happily for him, his bowlers met his immediate expectations and later, by dismissing India cheaply a second time, left Australia needing only 47 in the final innings.

McGrath was outstanding, conceding a run an over, and Warne most guileful. But the Indians contributed to their plight through poor technique or misjudgment. True, the pitch was not of the desired quality, with spin accompanying bounce from day one, but they did bat first while it was at its best. Only Dravid and Ganguly were genuinely beaten, and even Tendulkar, meticulous and solid for 139 minutes, eventually succumbed from driving on the up at a widish ball.

Not for the first time in his 16-month Test career, Gilchrist brought about a sudden and dramatic change in Australia's fortunes. His 122 off 112 balls, with 15 fours and four sixes, was almost a replica of his celebrated maiden century against Pakistan at Hobart in November 1999. The spinners could not find the line or length to shackle his sweeping, pulling and pull-driving. He went from 50 to 100 in only 29 balls. Hayden, who had batted stolidly throughout the early collapse, heartily joined in the assault, using much the same methods, and the two left-handers added 197, a record for Australia's sixth wicket against India, in 32 overs.

India's second innings was another shambles, and once Tendulkar, who again batted in masterly fashion, was out to a sensational catch by Ponting, the decline was rapid. Tendulkar, pulling, had struck Langer at short leg on the shoulder, and the impact kept the ball in the air long enough for Ponting to sprint and dive for it. India lost their last eight wickets for 65, including Agarkar's seventh duck in consecutive Test innings against Australia.

Toss: Australia. **India 176** (S. R. Tendulkar 76; G. D. McGrath 3-19, S. K. Warne 4-47) **and 219**

(S. Ramesh 44, R. Dravid 39, S. R. Tendulkar 65; J. N. Gillespie 3-45, M. E. Waugh 3-40);

Australia 349 (M. L. Hayden 119, A. C. Gilchrist 122, S. K. Warne 39; Harbhajan Singh 4-121) **and 47-0.**

India v Australia   **Second Test**

At Kolkata, March 11, 12, 13, 14, 15, 2001. India won by 171 runs.   Dicky Rutnagur, 2002

An astonishing Indian recovery provided several records and culminated in only the third victory in Test history for a side who had followed on. Australia were the victims in the previous instances also, losing to England at Sydney in 1894 and Leeds in 1981. Laxman amassed 281, the highest Test score for India [since exceeded by Sehwag], while his partnership of 376 with Dravid was an Indian fifth-wicket record. Their feats almost overshadowed the outstanding performance of off-spinner Harbhajan Singh, who claimed India's first Test hat-trick while capturing a career-best seven wickets in the first innings, and followed up with a match-winning six in the second.

India lost four wickets before the first-innings deficit of 274 was cleared,

Comeback kids: V. V. S. Laxman (left) and Rahul Dravid during their epic stand of 376 against Australia at Kolkata in March 2001, which helped India win the match after following on – and ended Australia's record run of 16 successive Test victories. Laxman scored 281 and Dravid 180.

but as Dravid's batting recovered its sparkle in Laxman's company, the game was transformed. They batted together for 104 overs, including the whole of the fourth day, when they added 335 in 90 overs. Their stand of 376 overtook India's fifth-wicket record, a mere 214 between Mohammad Azharuddin and Ravi Shastri against England on this ground in 1984–85, and then India's all-wicket record against Australia, an unbroken 298 for the sixth wicket between Dilip Vengsarkar and Shastri at Bombay in 1986. Their efforts not only dispelled India's troubles, but opened up an avenue to a momentous victory. Dravid was eventually run out for a chanceless 180 from 353 balls in seven hours 24 minutes, with 21 fours.

When Ganguly declared with a lead of 383, Australia had to bat out 75 overs for a draw, on a pitch affording turn without being devilish. Their prospects looked good when Hayden, given an early life, and Slater stayed together for 23 overs. But once they were separated, wickets fell at regular intervals. The only pause in the collapse was provided by a fourth-wicket partnership of 50 between Hayden and Steve Waugh. Otherwise, the turning ball proved too disconcerting for the Australians; Harbhajan again did the major damage, and Tendulkar, bowling leg-spin, took three wickets, including the crucial ones of Hayden and Gilchrist – for a king pair. Australia were all out in the 69th over and their record run of Test wins had come to an abrupt and spectacular halt.

India v Australia, 2001 — Second Test

At Kolkata, March 11, 12, 13, 14, 15, 2001. Result: India won by 171 runs.

AUSTRALIA

First innings		Second innings	
M. J. Slater c Mongia b Zaheer Khan	42	(2) c Ganguly b Harbhajan Singh	43
M. L. Hayden c sub (H. K. Badani) b Harbhajan Singh	97	(1) lbw b Tendulkar	67
J. L. Langer c Mongia b Zaheer Khan	58	c Ramesh b Harbhajan Singh	28
M. E. Waugh c Mongia b Harbhajan Singh	22	lbw b Raju	0
*S. R. Waugh lbw b Harbhajan Singh	110	c sub (H. K. Badani) b Harbhajan Singh	24
R. T. Ponting lbw b Harbhajan Singh	6	c Das b Harbhajan Singh	0
†A. C. Gilchrist lbw b Harbhajan Singh	0	lbw b Tendulkar	0
S. K. Warne c Ramesh b Harbhajan Singh	0	(9) lbw b Tendulkar	0
M. S. Kasprowicz lbw b Ganguly	7	(10) not out	13
J. N. Gillespie c Ramesh b Harbhajan Singh	46	(8) c Das b Harbhajan Singh	6
G. D. McGrath not out	21	lbw b Harbhajan Singh	12
B 19, l-b 10, n-b 7	36	B 6, l-b 5, n-b 8	19

1-103 (1) 2-193 (2) 3-214 (3) 4-236 (4)   445
5-252 (6) 6-252 (7) 7-252 (8)
8-269 (9) 9-402 (10) 10-445 (5)

1-74 (2) 2-106 (3) 3-116 (4)   212
4-166 (5) 5-166 (6) 6-167 (7) 7-173 (1)
8-174 (9) 9-191 (8) 10-212 (11)

First innings – Zaheer Khan 28.4–6–89–2; Prasad 30–5–95–0; Ganguly 13.2–3–44–1; Raju 20–2–58–0; Harbhajan Singh 37.5–7–123–7; Tendulkar 2–0–7–0.
Second innings – Zaheer Khan 8–4–30–0; Prasad 3–1–7–0; Harbhajan Singh 30.3–8–73–6; Raju 15–3–58–1; Tendulkar 11–3–31–3; Ganguly 1–0–2–0.

INDIA	First innings		Second innings
S. S. Das c Gilchrist b McGrath	20	– hit wkt b Gillespie	39
S. Ramesh c Ponting b Gillespie	0	– c M. E. Waugh b Warne	30
R. Dravid b Warne	25	– (6) run out	180
S. R. Tendulkar lbw b McGrath	10	– c Gilchrist b Gillespie	10
*S. C. Ganguly c S. R. Waugh b Kasprowicz	23	– c Gilchrist b McGrath	48
V. V. S. Laxman c Hayden b Warne	59	– (3) c Ponting b McGrath	281
†N. R. Mongia c Gilchrist b Kasprowicz	2	– b McGrath	4
Harbhajan Singh c Ponting b Gillespie	4	– (9) not out	8
Zaheer Khan b McGrath	3	– (8) not out	23
S. L. V. Raju lbw b McGrath	4		
B. K. V. Prasad not out	7		
L-b 2, n-b 12	14	B 6, l-b 12, w 2, n-b 14	34
	171	(7 wkts dec.)	657

1-0 (2) 2-34 (1) 3-48 (4) 4-88 (3)
5-88 (5) 6-92 (7) 7-97 (8) 8-113 (9)
9-129 (10) 10-171 (6)

1-52 (2) 2-97 (1) 3-115 (4) (7 wkts dec.)
4-232 (5) 5-608 (3) 6-624 (7) 7-629 (6)

First innings – McGrath 14–8–18–4; Gillespie 11–0–47–2; Kasprowicz 13–2–39–2; Warne 20.1–3–65–2.
Second innings – McGrath 39–12–103–3; Gillespie 31–6–115–2; Warne 34–3–152–1;
M. E. Waugh 18–1–58–0; Kasprowicz 35–6–139–0; Ponting 12–1–41–0; Hayden 6–0–24–0;
Slater 2–1–4–0; Langer 1–0–3–0.

Toss won by Australia
Man of the Match V. V. S. Laxman

Umpires S. K. Bansal and P. Willey

India v Australia — Third Test

At Chennai, March 18, 19, 20, 21, 22, 2001. India won by two wickets.   Dicky Rutnagur, 2002

Appropriately, the deciding Test of an enthralling series, marked by dramatic shifts of fortune, produced a grandstand finish. India, requiring 155 in the final innings, seemed to be heading for a comfortable win, only to encounter a brave, if unavailing, challenge from the Australian bowlers.

The bare pitch prompted both sides to alter the balance of their attacks towards spin. Australia picked Miller as a second spinner for the first time in the series; India included leg-spinner Sairaj Bahutule to back up Harbhajan Singh and the slow left-armer, Kulkarni. While all three shared the workload, the concentrated threat to Australia's batsmen was again posed by Harbhajan, who took 15 wickets. Only leg-spinner Narendra Hirwani, with 16 against West Indies at Madras in 1988, had claimed more wickets in a Test for India.

That Australia took any advantage from their continued luck with the toss was all down to opener Hayden, who was last out for 203 made in 474 minutes off 320 balls. Fifteen fours and six sixes – the most sixes by an Australian in a Test innings – testified to his form and his positive approach regardless of the situation. But support was confined to Langer and the Waugh twins. He added 150 with Mark Waugh, who passed 7,000 Test runs, and 123 with Steve, whose dismissal in circumstances both unfortunate and bizarre triggered his side's collapse.

Australia's captain became only the sixth batsman in Test history to be given out handled the ball. While Waugh's attention was fixed on the umpire after an lbw appeal, following a missed a sweep at Harbhajan, the ball came to ground outside the popping crease and spun back vigorously towards the stumps at bail height. Alerted to the danger by Hayden from the other end, Waugh fatally intercepted the ball with the palm of his hand. Harbhajan now collected the remaining six wickets for 26 in 9.4 overs; Hayden's mastery was emphasised by the fact that he scored all but four runs of the 51 added in that time. Warne made his 23rd duck in Tests, an Australian record.

India's reply, launched by Das and Ramesh with a century partnership, also tapered away after the fall of the fifth wicket. The difference was that their collapse started with the total already at 453, which included four fifties and Tendulkar's superb century. He reached it with his second six off Miller, and also hit 15 fours in his 126. Helped by Tendulkar's 169-run partnership with Dravid, the eventual lead was 110. Hayden and Slater quickly chipped away at this, raising 82 in 18 overs before a diving catch by Zaheer Khan at deep mid-wicket dismissed Hayden. Mark Waugh then added 100 with Langer and Steve Waugh, and the latter, composed and assured, remained unbeaten at the end of the fourth day. Harbhajan had him caught next morning in the eighth over, and this time India's off-spinner took the last six wickets for 15 in 17.1 overs to finish with a career-best eight for 84.

Australia seemed beaten as India reached the hundred mark with only two wickets down. Laxman and Tendulkar were in such firm control that victory looked a formality. However, Gillespie's dismissal of Tendulkar, caught by Mark Waugh at second slip off a ball of lethal speed and aim, was the signal for two more wickets in the next three overs. Laxman was still scoring freely, but after tea, with 20 runs wanted, Mark Waugh removed him with an amazing mid-wicket catch that put the match wide open once more. When the seventh wicket fell at the same score, the balance was tipping Australia's way. Stand-in wicket-keeper Sameer Dighe and Zaheer tilted it back again and, with India nine short, McGrath – suffering from a stomach disorder and having to be sparingly used – was called on to make a final effort. Aided by Mark Waugh's fourth catch of the innings he prised out Zaheer, but it proved to be Australia's last throw. The target was now just four runs. Dighe and Harbhajan picked up a single each and then, fittingly, Harbhajan, voted Man of the Series, nonchalantly pushed a McGrath half-volley square of the wicket for the winning runs.

Toss: Australia. **Australia 391** (M. L. Hayden 203, J. L. Langer 35, M. E. Waugh 70, S. R. Waugh 47; Harbhajan Singh 7-133) **and 264** (M. L. Hayden 35, M. J. Slater 48, M. E. Waugh 57, S. R. Waugh 47; Harbhajan Singh 8-84); **India 501** (S. S. Das 84, S. Ramesh 61, V. V. S. Laxman 65, S. R. Tendulkar 126, R. Dravid 81; G. D. McGrath 3-75, C. R. Miller 3-160) **and 155-8** (V. V. S. Laxman 66; C. R. Miller 3-41).

ENGLAND v INDIA 2002   Rahul Bhattacharya, 2003

A series of more than three Tests is a rare thing these days. Its shifting dynamics embrace such abstractions as momentum, luck, form, intensity – karma, even – as if it were a universe in itself. India's tour of England in 2002 captured the ebb and flow, the up and down, of this strange and enchanting realm. The series was played out by sides that were evenly matched at the start, became absurdly superior to one another at different points, and ended exactly level as if to reconcile themselves to the truth of the original equation. Life, it appeared, had come a complete circle within the space of four Tests.

The scoreline, 1–1, was frustrating but fair. Michael Vaughan, who came of age with three princely hundreds, did not deserve to be on the losing side; nor did Rahul Dravid, who matched him for excellence if not for excitement. The series was India's first of more than three Tests in England since 1979, and in those 23 years Indian ready-meals had sprung up in Marks & Spencer, chicken tikka masala had overtaken fish and chips as the national dish and Britain had become more multicultural, or more comfortable in its multi-culturalism. On hoardings and TV screens, the summer was branded as Indian: there were more Indian movie festivals than anyone could possibly attend, plus the opening season of Andrew Lloyd Webber's musical *Bombay Dreams*. And the lasting flavour of the cricket was Indian.

It was India who made the larger gains, and did so in more valiant fashion. This may seem harsh on England, who at different times were without three, four, even six of their first-choice players. But that must be weighed against India's entire cricket history, which reveals that winning a single Test outside the subcontinent, let alone drawing a series of four matches, is a less frequent occurrence than national elections. India had never drawn a series in England, and although they had won two, in 1971 and 1986, they had lost the other 11 for a combined tally of 41 Tests played, three won and 22 lost.

By the time they finished this, their second long tour in a row following the five-Test series in the Caribbean, India were barking more regularly outside their own border than at any time since 1971. They showed in the one-day triangular series before the Tests, and again in a magnificent fightback from 1–0 down, that they were coming to terms with the mechanisms of digging deep, scrapping and winning against the odds more than ever before. The new, harder India that the captain, Sourav Ganguly, and coach, John Wright, were determined to create was becoming more than just a good idea. Admittedly, circumstances played their part in making India's effort appear more heroic. Their best efforts came from positions of despair, and from the Second Test onwards, a messy and prolonged row over personal sponsorship twisted and turned till its fortunes were followed back home with as much interest as the cricket. India's cricketers were battling not just against the England cricket team, but the ICC and the Board of Control for Cricket in India as well.

The cricket itself, 19 days of it, could be divided into three sets, each shorter than the one before: a first set of almost nine days, a second of about six and a last of four. In the first, Nasser Hussain and Duncan Fletcher flexed their brains, the England batsmen flexed their muscles and India simply did not know what to do. It began with the First Test at Lord's where, in strangely subcontinental conditions, Hussain employed the grand choke upon the free-scoring Indian middle order, and especially Sachin Tendulkar, to carve out a comprehensive win.

The Indians could not be placated even when Ajit Agarkar, a bowling all-rounder who usually did too little with the bat to justify the title, stroked a frilly second-innings century, bringing a high backlift down in lashing arcs like a lesser Brian Lara. They were still ruing the decision to leave out their greatest perpetrator of batting collapses, Harbhajan Singh, on a pitch that would have encouraged him even though it lacked the bounce that he thrives on. Not even an announcement by Graham Thorpe at the end of the match that he was pulling out of all cricket in an effort to resolve his domestic problems could dampen England's joy at winning three consecutive Tests. The first set carried over to the first 11 sessions of the next Test, at Trent Bridge, where England batted like Australia to hammer out a 260-run lead. Four Englishmen had scored centuries by this point, and the runs had flowed at four an over. India were not even in the frame.

The second set began in the second over of India's second innings in the Second Test, when they lost their second wicket with the total barely into double figures. India were in danger of losing the match by an innings, putting a series win beyond their reach. Dravid and Tendulkar came together. A spectacular sun came angling out through the clouds late on the fourth evening. Trent Bridge looked beautiful. Now was the time.

By the next evening, the Test had been saved. Tendulkar made 92 runs of bona-fide brilliance, Ganguly scraped an equally crucial 99, and Dravid's 115 occupied almost as many deliveries as both put together, which was a fair indication of its value. Even little Parthiv Patel, the 17-year-old debutant wicket-keeper with bright wide eyes and chubby cheeks, hung around for an hour and a half at the end, a performance stirring enough for the battle-hardened Alec Stewart, 22 years his elder, to put a fatherly arm around him as the players made their way off the pitch. Like an alcoholic who had hit rock bottom, Team India had risen and reformed themselves.

They took this self-belief to Headingley where, given usual conditions, it was all but written in stone that they must lose. Here they made a series of bold decisions. First, they committed themselves to two spinners knowing full well the history of a ground where even Shane Warne had an average of 90-odd. Second, they resisted the urge to recall the opener Shiv Sunder Das, who had just made 250 in a tour game, preferring the utility man Sanjay Bangar, who could offer back-up as third seamer. Third, in order to give the spinners last use of the pitch, they batted first on winning the toss, well aware that the first day would be no tea party.

Every piece fell into place: defensive batting and then attacking batting, seam bowling and then spin bowling, close catching and outfield catching. Dravid and Bangar guarded their wickets on the opening day as if the hopes of a billion hinged on them, then Tendulkar and Ganguly steamed to a tantalising 249-run partnership at more than four an over. They rattled England, who proceeded to drop four catches in an hour on the third morning. Robert Key, the chunky opener playing his second Test, dropped two more on top of one the previous evening, as his red face kept turning steadily redder.

When it was time to bowl, Anil Kumble produced his greatest performance away from home, and for the first time in a 12-year international career, reaped the rewards. India won by an innings and 46 runs, their largest overseas win. Such was the power of belief. The questions about the mettle of his team that had been asked of Ganguly were now hurled at Hussain. It was one of the great turnarounds.

The third set, which should have been the decider, was the least remarkable.

The teams went to The Oval tied and tired, and left tied and tired. On a surface good for little else than batting for long periods, both sides did exactly that. England finished the first day well placed on 336 for two, and Headingley in reverse was a possibility. But they lost the remaining eight wickets for 179 runs, mostly because of the middle order's unwillingness to seize the initiative as the openers had done. When India passed the follow-on mark, the fate of the series was sealed. The game was a washout even before the last day was rained off.

From Vaughan and Dravid, though, who made 195 and 217 respectively, there were batting masterclasses. This series was meant to revolve around Tendulkar. Speculation at every juncture certainly did. After his three failures at Lord's – in the final of the NatWest series and twice in the First Test – all India was beginning to question his big-occasion temperament. Typically, imperturbably, Tendulkarly, he ended the tour with an average of 66.83 and his reputation restored. But it was Dravid who emerged from the shadows to play the central role. He batted for more than 30 hours and compiled 602 studious and utterly critical runs. If Tendulkar remained India's greatest batsman, Dravid was now established as the one you would want to bat for your life – Steve Waugh with more style. When he lifted the helmet off his sweat-drenched face to kiss the Indian crescent upon reaching his third successive century, you could feel the weight of his efforts, the scrupulous diligence behind every run.

England v India	**NatWest Series Final**
At Lord's, July 13, 2002. India won by two wickets.	Lawrence Booth, 2003

This was one of the most thrillingly topsy-turvy limited-overs internationals ever played. At 146 for five in pursuit of 326 – more than they had ever scored batting second – India were down and out. Their four senior batsmen were all back in the pavilion, and only Yuvraj Singh, aged 20, and Mohammad Kaif, 21, stood between England's bowlers and the tail. But Yuvraj played some punishing strokes off the back foot, Kaif was all wrists through mid-wicket, and the pair added 121 in less than 18 overs. When Yuvraj top-edged a sweep to short fine leg, Harbhajan helped add a quick 47 with Kaif to take India to the brink, but Flintoff tilted the balance once more with two wickets in the 48th over. Even so, India needed just 11 runs off 12 balls. Kaif thick-edged Gough to the third-man boundary to reduce the target to two off six, and Zaheer Khan stole the winning runs with three balls remaining courtesy of an overthrow. As England's players wandered off in a daze, the Indians celebrated in style. In an echo of Flintoff's antics at Mumbai five months earlier, Ganguly whipped off his shirt and whirled it round his head on the players' balcony, before running through the Long Room to kiss the Lord's turf and embrace Kaif. The capacity crowd, many of them Indians, stood and cheered. After nine consecutive defeats in one-day finals, India had made it tenth time lucky.

But for most of the match their losing streak had seemed certain to continue. England's innings of 325 for five, their fourth-highest in this form of the game, had inspired drama of its own. In his 72nd innings, Hussain reached his first one-day international century, a dogged but scratchy innings, full of miscues and failed reverse sweeps. When he reached three figures, from 118 balls, he embarked on an impassioned series of gestures to the press box, where several commentators – "ex-players", Hussain later said – had questioned his position in the batting order. Hussain held up three fingers and gesticulated angrily to the No. 3 on the back of his shirt. It was pure theatre, and almost overshadowed an outstanding display from Trescothick, who added a joyous 185 for the second wicket with Hussain in just 177 balls. Trescothick moved to a 40-ball half-century, his most memorable shot a flick for six over mid-wicket off Zaheer, and motored to his third one-day century in 89 balls with some hammer-on-anvil cover-drives. Flintoff bullied 40 off 32, and England had rewarded Hussain's decision to make first use of a belter.

Needing six and a half an over, India came racing out of the blocks too. Ganguly pummelled his way to fifty in just 35 deliveries, and his opening partnership with the dashing Sehwag had reached 106 in the 15th over when Ganguly aimed an ambitious slog at Tudor and was bowled. It was the first of five wickets to fall for 40 runs in less than ten overs – including Tendulkar, bowled as he made room. The game seemed over. But England had reckoned without the youthful daring and verve of Yuvraj and Kaif.

Toss: England. **England 325-5** (50 overs) (M. E. Trescothick 109, N. Hussain 115, A. Flintoff 40, Extras 31; Zaheer Khan 3-62); **India 326-8** (49.3 overs) (V. Sehwag 45, S. C. Ganguly 60, Yuvraj Singh 69, M. Kaif 87*).

England v India   **First Test**
At Lord's, July 25, 26, 27, 28, 29, 2002. England won by 170 runs.   Tim de Lisle, 2003

England went into the four-Test series against India with a depleted team – no Gough, Caddick or Trescothick, and Thorpe visibly distressed by marital problems – and several scores to settle. They had lost the one-day final here two weeks earlier, they had lost the Test series in India in the winter, and they had lost the only game in which the teams met on India's previous visit, for the 1999 World Cup. In the 12 years since Graham Gooch's 333 at Lord's, England had managed to win only one Test against India, home or away. But you would never have known it from this match. On a pitch that could have been cooked up by Sourav Ganguly's personal chef, England weren't merely greater than the sum of their parts: they were greater than the sum of India's.

It was a personal triumph for Nasser Hussain. He won his third Test in succession, made his highest Test score for five years and spiked India's big guns with rigorous game plans. His team showed a spirit that radiated all the way from the middle to the stands, enthusing the crowd, who in turn inspired the players with the will to take 20 wickets on a blandly unresponsive surface.

Toss: England. **England 487** (N. Hussain 155, J. P. Crawley 64, A. Flintoff 59, C. White 53, S. P. Jones 44, Extras 31; Zaheer Khan 3-90, A. Kumble 3-128) **and 301-6 dec.** (M. P. Vaughan 100, J. P. Crawley 100*, A. J. Stewart 33; A. Kumble 3-84); **India 221** (V. Sehwag 84, R. Dravid 46, V. V. S. Laxman 43*; M. J. Hoggard 3-33) **and 397** (W. Jaffer 53, R. Dravid 63, V. V. S. Laxman 74, A. B. Agarkar 109*; M. J. Hoggard 4-87).

England v India
At Leeds, August 22, 23, 24, 25, 26, 2002. India won by an innings and 46 runs.

Third Test

Tanya Aldred, 2003

England can usually rely on Headingley for home comforts. So it was a nasty shock that this year the old girl turned against them, embracing instead India – out-of-form, contract-disputing India. It was they who were invited to Geoffrey Boycott's pre-match curry buffet and it was they who breathed in the dank Leeds air, looked up at the furious age-old leaden skies, mastered the demons in the pitch, and served up a win by an innings – something they hadn't achieved overseas since routing a Packer-scarred Australia at Sydney in 1978.

It was a magnificent performance, built on a sublime first-day century by Dravid which Hussain graciously described as one of the finest he had seen. With that in the vaults, Tendulkar and Ganguly had the licence to play, and play they did – Tendulkar smoothing his way to his highest Test score against England, and Ganguly producing a knockabout hundred that would have been at home in a seaside cabaret. It was the first time all three had made a century in the same innings, though they had come close only two weeks earlier at Trent Bridge with two nineties and a hundred; Tendulkar passed David Gower to go seventh on the all-time Test runs list. The really unexpected part of the tale was that this excellent batting was matched by wise, wily bowling from an attack much mocked even at home. Anil Kumble, who famously struggles away from his dustbowls, merrily spun his buoyant leg-breaks along to seven wickets and thoroughly deserved his first Test victory outside the subcontinent in 12 years. Agarkar, Bangar and Zaheer Khan did much of the rest – out-Englanding the England bowlers in their mastery of line, length, accuracy and patience.

Before the match Geoffrey Boycott, Fred Trueman, Ray Illingworth and Brian Close gritted their teeth and posed together to open the new East Stand – though such was the financial mess at Yorkshire that no one had much of an idea who was going to pay for it. But the most poignant moment came on Saturday afternoon when the ground stood in complete silence, in memory of Holly Wells and Jessica Chapman, the schoolgirls from Soham whose disappearance had captured the sympathy of the nation.

Toss: India. **India 628-8 dec.** (S. B. Bangar 68, R. Dravid 148, S. R. Tendulkar 193, S. C. Ganguly 128, Extras 50; A. R. Caddick 3-150); **England 273** (R. W. T. Key 30, M. P. Vaughan 61, A. J. Stewart 78*; A. Kumble 3-93, Harbhajan Singh 3-40) **and 309** (R. W. T. Key 34, M. A. Butcher 42, N. Hussain 110, A. J. Stewart 47; A. Kumble 4-66).

AUSTRALIA V INDIA 2003–04

Sambit Bal, 2005

Every once in a while comes a special sporting contest that leaves behind a whiff of glory and magic. Australia and India played one such Test series in 2001; Kolkata was a match for the ages and Chennai not far behind. But ever so rarely comes a series that marks a turning point in history. It may be years or decades before the significance of India's tour of Australia in 2003–04 can be truly assessed, but in this series they announced themselves as a force in Test cricket, after years of living on promise and vain dazzle. They didn't quite end Australia's reign, but how close they came.

To expect anything to match Kolkata was a tough ask. Yet Adelaide, where India came back from the dead to win, was almost a replica. The quality of cricket was admittedly superior in 2001, because bowling was a factor then. This was a series decided by batsmen's rare mistakes; injury kept out leading bowlers from both sides, and the rest were blunted by the flatness of the pitches and a galaxy of batting talent. But throughout, the cricket was captivating, grand and redolent with meaning. It ended with a realignment of the world order: the Ashes and the Frank Worrell Trophy could keep their tradition, but the Border-Gavaskar Trophy had emerged as the worthiest in contemporary cricket. And yes, India kept it.

The 1–1 scoreline did not fully reveal India's gains. These have to be viewed through the prism of their wretched past. The last time they had won a Test series outside the subcontinent was in England in 1986, and not since 1980–81 had they won a Test in Australia (where they had lost seven of their last eight). Their previous tour had left deep scars, for they had come boasting a strong middle order and had sunk without a murmur. Meanwhile, under Steve Waugh, Australia had won 21 out of 25 Tests at home, losing a solitary dead-rubber Test against England the previous season.

For Australia, the series meant a great deal more than the chance to keep their impressive home record intact. A legacy was at stake. Waugh, one of the most innovative of all Test captains, revealed beforehand that he would retire at the end of the series – an announcement whose timing would be questioned repeatedly. Waugh insisted that he had done it to end the speculation; cynics saw a design to maximise the commercial potential of a staged farewell. A spectacle it certainly was, with every city according Waugh its own send-off complete with red rags (provided by the newspapers to whom he was contracted), replicas of his good luck charm. It reached a point where Waugh merely had to touch the ball for an eruption of mass sentiment.

This was not unlike the reception reserved for Tendulkar at every ground in India, and Waugh, a visionary and a doer, deserved every bit of it. Yet when Damien Martyn ran himself out to save Waugh's wicket in the First Test at Brisbane, commentators wondered whether his team-mates were letting emotion affect their good sense. Waugh was uncharacteristically testy at the post-match press conference, saying he had been hurt by the "innuendos and conjecture", and remarking sarcastically that "even the red rags are my fault".

But as the series wore on it became clear that what was affecting Australia more was the absence of the injured Glenn McGrath, who had rarely allowed the Indians a start in 1999–2000, claiming one of the openers in five innings out of six. India's opening partnerships on that tour read 7 and 0, 11 and 5, 10 and 22. Also missing from action in the first two Tests was Brett Lee, who on debut in 1999–2000 had harassed the Indians with pace and movement, claiming 13 wickets in two matches. When he did return, for the Boxing Day Test at the MCG, he cut a sorry figure, unable to land either the ball consistently on a length or his foot behind the bowling crease. In the first innings of the two games he played, he bowled 28 no-balls, and at the SCG he was reduced to delivering from well behind the line. He did unleash a perfect in-swinging yorker that crashed into Ganguly's stumps on the second day, and he celebrated with gusto. But it was too late: India were 570 for five.

If there was less discussion about Australia missing Shane Warne, who was serving a 12-month drugs ban, it was because he had been collared by the Indians before. Warne remained a presence in the Channel Nine commentary box, occasionally straying into the press box to pick a bone with a journalist or two. Stuart MacGill, despite having taken wickets by the dozen against other opponents, turned out to be a poor replacement, and was a perennial source of boundary-balls.

So resplendent was India's top order through the series that it was difficult to guess what effect McGrath might have had. To start with, they had two openers with skill and steel. Virender Sehwag had been pushed up to open in 2002 because no place could be found for him in the middle order and he was too talented a player to sit on the bench. He had expressed reservations about his long-term future in the role, but returned from Australia with his reputation massively enhanced. Once asked, in Sunil Gavaskar's presence, to compare his own technique with the master's, Sehwag insouciantly replied that Gavaskar's technique belonged to that age while he played to the requirement of his. The same insouciance was evident in his batting as he carved the Australian bowlers around the vast MCG, scoring 195 breathless runs in a little over five hours before perishing as he tried to raise his double-hundred with a six. Aakash Chopra, Sehwag's resolute partner, averaged a meagre 23.25, but never failed in any of their first innings.

All the touring batsmen shone, none more dazzlingly than the contrasting pair of Rahul Dravid and V. V. S. Laxman. Yet India's first saviour was an unlikely one. Ganguly, the presumed weak link in the batting, arrived at the crease in Brisbane with the score reading 62 for three, and Dravid and Tendulkar gone in the space of four balls. He departed nearly five hours later, at 329 for six. His 144 was an emphatic assertion of authority, and Ganguly continued to lead by example through the series: he promoted himself during the dying overs of the third evening at Melbourne to protect Tendulkar's wicket at the risk of his own, whereas, in more favourable conditions at Sydney, he gave up his No. 5 spot to Laxman. The weather ensured a draw at the Gabba, but Ganguly's was a decisive innings nevertheless. Here was a team that looked adversity in the eye.

And so they did in the next Test, at Adelaide. They conceded 400 runs on the first day to Australia, and 556 in all in the first innings, and found themselves looking down the barrel at 85 for four on the second afternoon. Yet the matter was routine for Dravid and Laxman, who forged another 300-run partnership, just as at Kolkata, as if batting in a world of their own. They so bedraggled their opponents that the Australian second innings was an exhibition of confusion. India, amazingly, were left with a target of 230 to win, which they achieved with another nerveless innings from Dravid. The defeat prompted John Buchanan to write a letter to his squad, questioning their commitment to the baggy green cap. And, not for the first time, a private missive from Buchanan found its way to the newspapers.

If the collective splendour of the Indian batsmen captured the imagination, the individual exploits of Ricky Ponting, Australia's captain-in-waiting, invited awe. He had spoken about the sobering effects of marriage: at Adelaide and Melbourne, he demonstrated his maturity with back-to-back double-hundreds. The punch and crispness of his strokeplay remained, but the new Ponting was less impetuous, less prone to collaborate in his own dismissals, and keen to consolidate and work the angles when width was denied. At Melbourne, he hardly ever went down the wicket to Anil Kumble until he was in the 190s, ensuring that Australia didn't blow it.

The win at Melbourne set the series up for an extraordinary farewell to Waugh. But Sydney also provided the stage for the redemption of two other giants. From the moment Tendulkar was given out lbw to his third ball at Brisbane, he had had an awful series, with both his driving and self-belief gone astray. He rediscovered himself by limiting his scoring options by one-third: his 241 not out in the first innings featured not a single cover-drive, a stroke that had caused his dismissal a couple of times in the series. After an unbeaten half-century in the second innings, he raised his series average from 16.40 to 76.60. Kumble, a colossus most Indians fail to recognise, harvested 12 wickets, finishing with 24 overall, which made him the most successful bowler on either side. Overshadowing all else was Waugh's farewell.

But the Test, and the series, were drawn. It was ironic that Waugh, whose legacy to Test cricket was the virtual elimination of the draw, ended his career with one. But if India denied Waugh the captain a fitting end, they set the stage for one last scrap from Waugh the warrior batsman. A record fifth-day crowd watched as he made his way in for the final time, with Australia not yet out of danger at 170 for three. He began with a shovel drive that could have got him out and minutes later the crowd gasped as a sweep flew off the edge to fall a few feet short of a fielder running in from deep square leg. But Waugh soon found his nerve, to hit a string of rasping boundaries, and a child held up a banner on Yabba's Hill: WAUGH RULES, OK.

He didn't rule his last series, but he played his part in saving it. The last hour of the match turned into a giant celebration. Willed on by the crowd and needled by young Parthiv Patel for one last blow ("Show some respect," Waugh countered, "you were in nappies when I made my debut."), he made a charge for the hundred and ended his career with a slog-sweep. It did make for a grand entry in the scorebooks: Waugh c Tendulkar b Kumble 80. After an emotional parade around the ground on the shoulders of his team-mates, Waugh walked off, with two of his children in his arms, doting wife beside him, to applause heard around the cricket world.

Australia v India   **Second Test**

At Adelaide, December 12, 13, 14, 15, 16, 2003. India won by four wickets.   Sambit Bal, 2005

After five breathless days it was difficult to decide what was more confounding. Just how had Australia managed to lose after scoring 556 by the second afternoon? Or how had India managed to win after being 85 for four in reply? Only once had a team scored more runs in the first innings of a Test and yet lost, and that 109-year-old record too belonged to Australia: they made 586 at Sydney in the Ashes opener of 1894, enforced the follow-on, and fell 11 short of the 177 needed to win.

So, did India win the match or did Australia lose it? The truth was somewhere in between. It was inevitable that a game yielding more than 1,500 runs would be decided by batting mistakes. Australia's inability to stick to their guns on the fourth day cost them the match. But it was as much a triumph of the Indian spirit, exemplified by none better than Dravid, who was on the field for most of the five days, batting 835 minutes and scoring 305 runs. He was last out in the first innings and there at the end to secure victory. It was a monumental effort, the finest performance by an Indian batsman in an overseas Test, because he made the difference.

The victory was all the more incredible because India had not won a Test in Australia in 23 years, and Australia had not lost a home Test of consequence in five – and because Australia had scored 400 runs on the first day, a record for any day on this ground. Ponting contributed 176 of those, and all the Australians exploited the short square boundaries on a flat pitch against an uninspired attack.

Australia seemed set for at least 600 until Kumble finally had Ponting caught at slip, and followed up with the last two wickets in the same over to restrict the innings to 556. Within a couple of hours it hardly seemed to matter. Bichel, a controversial selection after a poor game in Brisbane, struck three vital blows. He bowled straight to a canny, defensive field set by Waugh (to Sehwag, there were no slips, only a gully) and India slumped from 66 without loss to 85 for four when Ganguly was run out. Laxman joined Dravid. It took Australia 94 overs to separate them. It was not quite Kolkata; there, they had added 376 for the fifth wicket, here it was a mere 303. That made them only the third pair to share two triple-century stands in Tests, after Bradman and Ponsford and, more recently, the South Africans Gibbs and Smith.

This time, it was Dravid's turn to score the double-hundred. He simply played everything on its merits, leaving every ball that carried the threat of an edge alone, while taking advantage of every scoring opportunity. After he played himself in, his cover-driving was sublime, and the only time he was in danger of getting out was when he top-edged a hook off Gillespie. But it sailed over backward square leg and brought up his hundred.

The Test took a decisive turn on the fourth day when a combination of weariness, tight bowling and a fatal urge to dominate the bowlers caused a dramatic Australian collapse. Agarkar bowled his best spell of the series, swinging the ball both ways, to account for Langer and Ponting, and thereafter every top-order batsman fell trying an aggressive stroke on a pitch that had slowed down. India were left to make 230 in 100 overs; Dravid redeemed a pledge to himself by being there to score the winning runs. There was a minor scare when India lost their fourth wicket on 170, but Dravid sealed a historic victory by cutting MacGill to the cover boundary. Waugh chased the ball all the way, retrieved it from the gutter, handed it over to Dravid and said "Well played." Indeed.

Australia v India, 2003–04   Second Test

At Adelaide, December 12, 13, 14, 15, 16, 2003. Result: India won by four wickets.

AUSTRALIA	First innings		Second innings	
J. L. Langer c Sehwag b Kumble	58	– lbw b Agarkar	10
M. L. Hayden c Patel b Pathan	12	– c Sehwag b Nehra	17
R. T. Ponting c Dravid b Kumble	242	– c Chopra b Agarkar	0
D. R. Martyn c Laxman b Nehra	30	– c Dravid b Tendulkar	38
*S. R. Waugh b Nehra	30	– c Dravid b Tendulkar	42
S. M. Katich c Sehwag b Agarkar	75	– c Nehra b Agarkar	31
†A. C. Gilchrist c Sehwag b Agarkar	29	– b Kumble	43
A. J. Bichel c Chopra b Kumble	19	– b Agarkar	1
J. N. Gillespie not out	48	– c Patel b Agarkar	3
B. A. Williams b Kumble	0	– not out	4
S. C. G. MacGill lbw b Kumble	0	– b Agarkar	1
B 1, l-b 7, w 1, n-b 4	13	B 2, l-b 2, w 1, n-b 1	6

1-22 (2) 2-135 (1) 3-200 (4) 4-252 (5)   556   1-10 (1) 2-18 (3) 3-44 (2) 4-109 (4)   196
5-390 (6) 6-426 (7) 7-473 (8)   5-112 (5) 6-183 (7) 7-184 (8)
8-556 (3) 9-556 (10) 10-556 (11)   8-188 (6) 9-192 (9) 10-196 (11)

First innings – Agarkar 26–1–119–2; Pathan 27–3–136–1; Nehra 25–3–115–2; Kumble 43–3–154–5; Sehwag 5–0–21–0; Tendulkar 1–0–3–0.
Second innings – Agarkar 16.2–2–41–6; Pathan 7–0–24–0; Nehra 7–2–21–1; Kumble 17–2–58–1; Tendulkar 6–0–36–2; Sehwag 3–0–12–0.

INDIA	First innings		Second innings	
A. Chopra c and b Bichel	27	– lbw b Gillespie	20
V. Sehwag c Hayden b Bichel	47	– st Gilchrist b MacGill	47
R. Dravid c Bichel b Gillespie	233	– not out	72
S. R. Tendulkar c Gilchrist b Bichel	1	– lbw b MacGill	37
*S. C. Ganguly run out	2	– c Katich b Bichel	12
V. V. S. Laxman c Gilchrist b Bichel	148	– c Bichel b Katich	32
†P. A. Patel c Ponting b Katich	31	– b Katich	3
A. B. Agarkar c MacGill b Katich	11	– not out	0
A. Kumble lbw b MacGill	12		
I. K. Pathan c and b MacGill	1		
A. Nehra not out	0		
B 4, l-b 2, w 2, n-b 2	10	B 3, l-b 6, w 1	10

1-66 (1) 2-81 (2) 3-83 (4) 4-85 (5)   523   1-48 (1) 2-79 (2) 3-149 (4)   (6 wkts) 233
5-388 (6) 6-447 (7) 7-469 (9)   4-170 (5) 5-221 (6) 6-229 (7)
8-510 (8) 9-518 (10) 10-523 (3)

First innings – Gillespie 40.5–13–106–1; Williams 23–7–72–0; Bichel 28–3–118–4; MacGill 44–8–143–2; Katich 16–3–59–2; Waugh 9–2–15–0; Ponting 1–0–4–0.
Second innings – Gillespie 10.2–2–22–1; Williams 14–6–34–0; MacGill 24.4–3–101–2; Bichel 11.4–1–35–1; Katich 8–1–22–2; Waugh 4–0–10–0.

Toss won by Australia   UMPIRES R. E. Koertzen and D. R. Shepherd
MAN OF THE MATCH R. Dravid

Australia v India Third Test

At Melbourne, December 26, 27, 28, 29, 30, 2003. Australia won by nine wickets.   Mike Coward, 2005

Forfeiting a series lead from such an imposing first-day position will long haunt Ganguly and his minions. Opportunities to dictate to world cricket's superpower at the MCG come rarely. But at 329 for four after a rollicking Boxing Day, India were poised to press home the advantage so sensationally established at Adelaide ten days earlier. The abject submission of their batting on the second morning – the last six fell for 16 runs to a mostly unfamiliar attack – was an affront to Sehwag, who had given them a stunning start, and it cleared the way for a spectacular rally by the Australians.

Elite Indian batsmen have often been noted for their quiet demeanour and inscrutability, but Sehwag is representative of a new breed who boast a self-assuredness, even cockiness. A daring opener, he has a simple philosophy and an uncomplicated style, playing by instinct and not by the book. For five hours and 12 minutes he enthralled a first-day crowd of 62,613 – a record for India in Australia – his bold strokeplay bringing 25 fours and five sixes. This was an innings of both brilliance and raw courage. Twice, Sehwag was hit on the helmet by Lee; each time, he barely flinched. In summers past, Indian openers would have wilted against such an attack on the body.

India collapsed next morning, however, and Ponting, riding high after his glorious 242 in Adelaide, and Hayden moved swiftly to avert embarrassment. They pooled their formidable resources and added 234 for the second wicket before Hayden was lbw to the indefatigable Kumble for 136. Ponting completed his 20th Test century two overs later and, although he elicited only modest support from that point, he was in such sublime form that he reached 257, his third double. Before Adelaide, he had made 206 at Port-of-Spain in April; Don Bradman, in England in 1930, is the only other batsman to have scored three Test double-hundreds in a calendar year. With an unforgettable array of cuts, drives and thrilling trademark pulls and clips ahead of square, Ponting batted for ten minutes shy of ten hours. He took the match away from India, much as Dravid and Laxman stole the Second Test from Australia.

Ponting rarely lapsed in concentration, even when the excitement surrounding Waugh's farewell reached fever pitch. On the third morning, the nation that halts for a horse race was stopped in its tracks when Waugh was struck above the left elbow by a short delivery from the enigmatic Agarkar. For one unsettling moment, as Waugh admitted later, he feared his distinguished career was to end in Melbourne and not his beloved Sydney the following week. He left the ground for treatment but, hard as nails, returned after lunch to assist Ponting in advancing the total beyond 500. Characteristically, he made light of the pain and received three standing ovations from a crowd of 33,256 – many there expressly to pay him tribute.

Any lingering doubts as to the quality of India's cricket under duress were dispelled on the fourth day, although it must be said the batting after plucky Patel at No. 7 was lily-livered and inept. The tail's capitulation again undermined the splendid work of Dravid, who batted five and a half hours for 92, and Ganguly, who selflessly promoted himself ahead of Tendulkar in the closing overs of the third day, following the master's first-ball duck in the first innings. Demonstrably leading from the front, Ganguly showed his mettle by returning to the fray after receiving a nasty blow to the head from Williams, and compiling a neat 73. To the unrestrained delight of the entire Indian contingent, Tendulkar played with a quiet effectiveness for 44, suggesting better days might not be far away. But Ponting had the last word; when he swept the winning four to fine leg, he had 1,503 Test runs for the calendar year, a total exceeded only by Viv Richards and Sunil Gavaskar.

Toss: India. **India 366** (A. S. Chopra 48, V. Sehwag 195, R. Dravid 49, S. C. Ganguly 37; S. C. G. MacGill 3-70) **and 286** (R. Dravid 92, S. C. Ganguly 73, S. R. Tendulkar 44; B. A. Williams 4-53); **Australia 558** (M. L. Hayden 136, R. T. Ponting 257, D. R. Martyn 31, Extras 39; A. B. Agarkar 3-115, A. Kumble 6-176) **and 97-1** (M. L. Hayden 53*, R. T. Ponting 31*).

Australia v India

At Sydney, January 2, 3, 4, 5, 6, 2004. Drawn.

Fourth Test

Matthew Engel, 2005

In strict cricketing terms, this should be remembered for the way India batted Australia out of the game, ensuring a drawn series, maintaining their hold on the Border-Gavaskar Trophy and consolidating their presumed new position as No. 1 contenders to Australia's crown. But cricket was a secondary feature of this extraordinary occasion, a mere backdrop. The contest was compelling enough, but it was taken over – hijacked almost – for a farewell the like of which cricket, normally a diffident kind of sport, had never seen.

Steve Waugh's 168th and positively last Test (no one would dare attempt a comeback after this) turned into one long wallow, starting with adulatory wrap-around newspaper souvenir supplements and culminating in Waugh being chaired round the SCG by his team-mates. John Williamson's nostalgic anthem "True Blue" competed with the roars of a record last-day crowd, many waving red rags, Waugh's customary comfort-object. No one had ever left the cricketing stage like this; no one had dared.

The show resulted from a benign (though presumably tacit) conspiracy between Cricket Australia, Waugh's personal management, the broadcasters Channel Nine, and the Murdoch press, to whom Waugh was contracted. Most cricketers, especially captains, go when the selectors choose: Waugh himself was forced out of the one-day captaincy in disagreeable circumstances two years earlier. By announcing his retirement date from Test cricket in advance, he controlled the timing. The other parties were able to leap aboard for the ride, and everyone cashed in. The total crowd of 181,063 had been surpassed at Sydney only by the 1946–47 Ashes Test, which lasted six days.

The Indians? They just dominated the Test match. The most important decision of the game was made by Ganguly, who called correctly and condemned Australia to the field on a belting wicket, in extreme heat, with a weakened attack and less than 72 hours after the previous Test. The crowd had come to watch Waugh, and could indeed watch him throughout the first two days: standing at mid-off, issuing occasional instructions and – provided they didn't blink – bowling a couple of overs.

It was tough for Australia on the first day, which started with a blistering 72 from Sehwag and an outbreak of no-balls from Lee. But there were even more ominous features for Australia. They were set intently, behind the grille of his helmet, and they belonged to Tendulkar. Shrewd observers of the series sensed that he might impose himself in this Test, though no one would have guessed quite how. Tendulkar had thought through his problems to the point of cutting out one of his most distinguished strokes, abandoning the cover-drive and instead just waiting for the chance to hit to leg. He maintained this policy for ten hours 13 minutes and 436 deliveries, scoring an unbeaten 241, his highest first-class score and perhaps the highest ever made by a man still nowhere near his own top form. Twenty-eight of his 33 fours and 188 of his runs came on the leg side. His 32nd Test hundred matched Waugh; only Sunil Gavaskar, on 34, remained ahead. He was also the fourth man to reach 9,000 Test runs, two days ahead of Brian Lara in Cape Town.

Tendulkar put on 353, an Indian fourth-wicket record, with Laxman, whose 178 was of a different order: a lovely innings, full of perfectly timed caresses. The crowd never gave the partnership the credit it deserved, partly because they were obsessed with Waugh, partly because the over-elaborate Sydney scoreboard's failings meant only statisticians noted the 300 stand. When Laxman was out, it was 547 for four, which in a normal series would be deemed unassailable. But Australia had scored 556 in Adelaide and lost, and Ganguly rightly decided to bat on and on, 39 minutes into the third day. This infuriated many Australians, including the TV commentators, who had been anticipating the declaration minute by minute the previous evening. It was yet another sign, however, that India were now playing cricket every bit as ruthlessly as Australia.

When Ganguly finally gave over, at 705 for seven – India's highest Test total, and the second-highest conceded by Australia – the response was predictably savage. The Australian openers put on 147 and the once-introspective Langer played an innings so impertinently confident that he felt able to reach his hundred with a reverse sweep. At 214 for one, Australia might even have been sniffing a first-innings lead.

However, the real difference between the teams lay not in the batting, nor in the modest seam bowling, but in the fact that India had a spinner capable of maintaining control while Australia did not. MacGill had offered a four-ball almost every over; Kumble varied his pace while maintaining his line and was rewarded with eight for 141.

The third-day crowd were mostly interested in Waugh, who scored a cameo 40, after which they streamed out. Waugh himself was still intent on business and refused to doff his helmet, sensing this was not his real farewell innings. Less noticed, Katich became the fourth centurion of the game next day with an innings of lithe grace and huge promise, thus restricting India's lead to 231.

Again, Ganguly was criticised by pundits for not enforcing the follow-on, though again he was right: avoiding any risk of defeat before thinking of victory. Dravid and Tendulkar extended the lead to 442 before Kumble set to work again, sharing the new ball on the fourth evening. Realistically, Australia never had much chance of chasing that. But this match had long since left reality behind.

At 196 for four there was some danger of an Aussie defeat, but that presupposed a failure by Waugh. Not here, not today. He never quite got the century all Australia wanted – though his 15 fours were all cheered as if he had – and certainly never glimpsed victory. But he batted with the ease and grace of a man at the peak of his career, flicking the ball to the off-side boundary whenever the spinners dropped short until he got to 80 and was caught, trying to hit Kumble for six, at deep square leg. "It shows that after 168 Tests you can still lose the plot under pressure," said Waugh.

Katich was staunch again; Kumble finished with 12 for 279. Their achievements were lost amid the hubbub. Then, cricket being cricket, Waugh finally slipped away, not quite to oblivion, merely to New South Wales v Victoria at Newcastle.

Toss: India. **India 705-7 dec.** (A. S. Chopra 45, V. Sehwag 72, R. Dravid 38, S. R. Tendulkar 241*,

V. V. S. Laxman 178, P. A. Patel 62, Extras 38; B. Lee 4-201, J. N. Gillespie 3-135) **and 211-2 dec.**

(V. Sehwag 47, R. Dravid 91*, S. R. Tendulkar 60*); **Australia 474** (J. L. Langer 117, M. L. Hayden 67,

S. R. Waugh 40, S. M. Katich 125, J. N. Gillespie 47, Extras 38; A. Kumble 8-141) **and 357-6**

(J. L. Langer 47, M. L. Hayden 30, R. T. Ponting 47, D. R. Martyn 40,

S. R. Waugh 80, S. M. Katich 77*; A. Kumble 4-138).

PAKISTAN V INDIA 2004

Rahul Bhattacharya, 2005

India's tour of Pakistan, their first full one in 14 years, was extraordinary even before a ball was bowled. Two years earlier, the two countries had appeared on the brink of nuclear war, but the tour gained impetus from what was popularly described as the "wind of brotherhood" blowing at long last between the nations, and also became an agent of change in itself. Sport, far from being an agent of division, turned out to be the centrepiece for something resembling a peace march. For India, there was another dimension. Their rising cricket team shone as never before in Pakistan, winning the Tests 2–1 and the one-day series 3–2. They had never won even a single Test there in 20 previous attempts.

It was a strange Test series, and not as absorbing as it might have been. Within the life of each Test there were few surprises. The last two were mirrors of one another: the side batting first was seamed out on the opening day, before the opposition built a lead too heavy to counter. In the First Test, this form of bullying by runs happened in the very first innings. Sehwag flogged 309 in only 375 balls, India's first triple-century in Tests, while Tendulkar controversially missed a double-hundred when Dravid declared.

The gap between the teams was not merely in batting, which was expected, but also in bowling and fielding. In Anil Kumble, India knew they held the advantage on spin – he was the leading wicket-taker, with 15 – but even their inexperienced seamers, Pathan and Lakshmipathy Balaji, bowled far more incisively than the speedy duo of Shoaib Akhtar and Mohammad Sami. Ganguly later suggested Pakistan had made a mistake by not preparing sparse outfields and dusty pitches to aid reverse swing.

The warmth of the tour radiated beyond cricket. The governments decided to tone down the aggressive posturing at the daily closing-of-the-gates ceremony on the Wagah border. Bollywood film-makers suggested that Indian films should stop pushing anti-Pakistan propaganda. About 15 Pakistani musical bands crossed the border between January and May. And the business sector brimmed with optimism at the potential for trade. Of course, it would be presumptuous for cricket to take credit. What is irrefutable, however, is that the tour provided the highest possible profile for friendship, and the strongest metaphorical way of saying "peace over conflict".

Pakistan v India	First Test

At Multan, March 28, 29, 30, 31, April 1, 2004.

India won by an innings and 52 runs.   Rahul Bhattacharya, 2005

From about 10 a.m. on March 28, a regular thud, rather than the roars associated with cricket in the subcontinent, began to emerge from Multan Cricket Stadium, a modern ground situated on farmland 45 minutes out of town. The stadium was virtually desolate, and the thumps, from Virender Sehwag's bat, were to resound for a day and a half as he constructed India's first triple-century in Test cricket. It laid the foundation of an historic victory, India's first in Pakistan in 21 Tests spread over 49 years. It was also, briefly, their most substantial win in a largely wretched 72 years of Tests away from home.

Sehwag's 309, and his partnership of 336, an Indian third-wicket record, with Tendulkar, who crafted a meticulous century, carried India to their third-highest total, and second-highest away: 675 for five declared. The highest, 705 for seven declared, had come in their previous Test on a similar pitch at Sydney. Sehwag's glitzy epic was not without luck. He was dropped on 68 and 77 during an opening stand of 160 with Chopra – their third century partnership in as many Tests. Later, he offered two chances behind the wicket of Shabbir Ahmed, one ball either side of the four that took him past the Indian record of 281 held by Laxman. None the less, it was an innings of sustained and versatile violence. He thrashed six sixes and 39 fours in 531 minutes and 375 balls; he went from 99 to 105 with a glided six over third man off Shoaib Akhtar, and from 295 to 301 with a roundhouse blast over wide long-on off Saqlain Mushtaq. That was his 364th ball, just two behind Matthew Hayden's 362-ball treble against Zimbabwe five months earlier. Only while nearing his maiden Test double had Sehwag turned circumspect, perhaps stung by the memory of holing out off a full toss on 195 at Melbourne in December.

Toss: India. **India 675-5 dec.** (A. S. Chopra 42, V. Sehwag 309, S. R. Tendulkar 194*, Yuvraj Singh 59, Extras 36); **Pakistan 407** (Imran Farhat 38, Yasir Hameed 91, Inzamam-ul-Haq 77, Yousuf Youhana 35, Abdul Razzaq 47, Extras 40; I. K. Pathan 4-100) **and 216** (Yousuf Youhana 112; A. Kumble 6-72).

Pakistan v India	Third Test

At Rawalpindi, April 13, 14, 15, 16, 2004.

India won by an innings and 131 runs.   Rahul Bhattacharya, 2005

With three and a half days of almost flawless cricket, India not only bettered their thundering victory at Multan for magnitude, but won their first Test series away from home for an entire decade. It was also the first time they had won series in both formats on the same tour, discounting England in 1986, when they won the Tests but were awarded a tied one-day series on run-rate. For Pakistan, the defeat brought to a head the impatience of a nation: two months later, the coach, Javed Miandad, was sacked. Veteran commentator Omar Kureishi described the fourth day, when they finally capitulated, as "the blackest in Pakistan's cricket history", though – match-fixing scandals aside – losing by an innings to Matthew Hayden's bat alone in October 2002 was surely worse.

Like the previous Test, this match was made on day one. Bitten at Lahore [where they chose to bat, struggled in the first session and lost by nine wickets], India chose to field when Ganguly, back from injury, continued Dravid's luck with the toss. There, India had been 107 for four at lunch; here, Pakistan were 96 for four. This included the key wicket of Inzamam-ul-Haq, set up beautifully when Nehra (who replaced Agarkar) had him hunch over an in-swinger before slanting one across for the nick.

Any hopes of recovery were thwarted by Balaji, who extracted three wickets in a nine-over spell after the interval, bending away the middle-aged ball late in its trajectory to leave Pakistan tottering at 137 for eight. The top score was a committed 49 from Mohammad Sami, his highest in Tests; that and a comical 25 from Fazl-e-Akbar managed to lift Pakistan to a modest 224. As Ganguly reflected later, extracting the advantage with the ball on the opening day was perhaps the difference between this and his previous quests for an overseas victory. It led to his 15th win as captain, beating Mohammad Azharuddin's record for India.

It was a colossal 270 from Dravid that put the series beyond Pakistan. In its significance, the innings could stand alongside any ever played by an Indian. Even Dravid agreed, though, that he was not at his most fluent, particularly on the second day, which he ended unbeaten on 134. He was given the benefit of the doubt after an adjacent lbw shout on 21, carelessly dropped at point on 71, and again spared when caught behind off bat-and-boot on 77. In between, he mis-timed more than he had sometimes done through entire tours.

Dravid's strength, however, is in raising his game when most needed. The following day he blossomed. He had already glued together the innings through century stands with Patel and, most delightfully, Laxman; he completed a third with Ganguly, and 98 with Yuvraj. It was a phenomenal physical effort. Between his 73 overs in the field and 175 overs at the crease lay a mere 10-minute break: Sehwag had been out first ball. In all, Dravid batted 12 hours 20 minutes – India's longest Test innings – faced 495 balls, and struck 34 fours and a six. His fifth Test double-hundred was an Indian record, one ahead of Sunil Gavaskar.

Dravid's task was made simpler when, late on the second afternoon, Shoaib Akhtar fell in his follow-through and injured his left thumb and a rib, soon after castling Laxman with a rapid out-swinging full toss. He left the field after six further balls and did not return except to bat. It was the last thing Pakistan needed: their bowling had already been depleted by the absence of Umar Gul, whose replacement, Fazl-e-Akbar, churned out dross to the tune of 162 runs for a single wicket in 41 overs.

Dravid finally fell on the third evening attempting, of all things, to reverse-sweep Imran Farhat's part-time leg-spin. Seven runs later, India were out for an even 600. As in the first innings, the Pakistan openers fell in consecutive overs, leaving the others to battle back from 327 runs behind with two days remaining. They did not even come close, despite the best efforts of India's fielders, who dropped six catches in the first hour next morning, four of them off Balaji. But the potency of his swing, exaggerated by cloud cover, could not be repressed. Before lunch, he added two more wickets, including Inzamam with a peachy away-curler and, between those two, Patel held a superb diving catch down the leg side off Yasir Hameed's glance. For Pakistan, the only pride came via Asim Kamal, defiantly unbeaten on 60 despite a painful elbow.

There was a final twist when Shoaib came out and smote a manic 14-ball 28, all in boundaries, which contrasted greatly with his mulish obduracy in the previous Test. Eyebrows were raised, Inzamam hurled a few barbs moments after the defeat, and Shaharyar Khan and Ramiz Raja, the PCB chairman and chief executive officer, questioned Shoaib's commitment to the team. They ordered a "medical inquiry commission" to see if he had exaggerated his injury or not; it led to further estrangement and nothing more.

Toss: India. **Pakistan 224** (Mohammad Sami 49; L. Balaji 4-63) **and 245** (Yousuf Youhana 48, Asim Kamal 60*; L. Balaji 3-108, A. Kumble 4-47); **India 600** (P. A. Patel 69, R. Dravid 270, V. V. S. Laxman 71, S. C. Ganguly 77, Yuvraj Singh 47; Shoaib Akhtar 3-47).

South Africa – Return of the Exile

The most heartening development in cricket over the past 30 years has been South Africa's return to the international fold, both because they add an extra dimension to the competition between cricket-playing countries, but, more importantly of course, because their return reflected the changed political realities in that country, for so long disfigured by racial politics and a white stranglehold on power.

Wisden's attitude to South Africa in the 1970s and, to a slightly lesser degree the 1980s, was not an edifying one. Politics, it argued had nothing to do with sport, so we should be playing against the South Africans. "From a cricketer's point of view it was a shame that once more South Africa was left in the cold," was the Almanack's blithe verdict on the 1979 World Cup. Editor Norman Preston was evidently unaware that cricket in South Africa had been organised along racial lines, and that, as Donald Woods' fine piece from 1993 (reprinted below) shows, many excellent black cricketers were denied the opportunity to play first-class cricket.

Presumably, those who continued to support sporting ties right up until the end of apartheid would argue that by the late 1970s the South African government was making it possible for black and white cricketers to play alongside each other. By then it was anti-apartheid activists, aware of the potency of the sporting boycott, who put pressure on black players to keep their game separate. But it was too late: any move to readmit South Africa to world cricket would have destroyed the ICC, with West Indies and the Asian countries resisting even if it meant the destruction of the organisation. Cricket had become a means of putting pressure on the apartheid government, and for this writer though not for *Wisden* in the 1970s and '80s, a legitimate one.

The debate is by no means cut and dried, and the policy of not playing sport with abhorrent regimes extremely difficult to apply, but South Africa was about as close to a clear case for a boycott as it is possible to get. *Wisden*, under Matthew Engel, has now adopted a very different position – supporting a boycott of Zimbabwean cricket because of the repressive government of Robert Mugabe. "Don't play cricket with monsters" is now the mantra – a far cry from the moans of the late 1970s that South Africa's noble cricketing chaps weren't being allowed to represent their country. Surely sometimes a country is in so wretched a state that it should be denied such representation, especially when that helps make its sports-mad public aware of the necessity of change.

In 2006 Engel, with South African statistician Andrew Samson, gave all those black players marginalised by apartheid policies and, later, by political pressure from activists a retrospective first-class existence – by accepting as first class 223 matches played by black players under South African Cricket Board (SACB) jurisdiction in the 1970s and '80s. Engel headlined the article "Setting the record straight". The Almanack got it right in the end.

South Africa's return hasn't just been a political story. From the beginning, they also played highly competitive – if, in the early years, somewhat conservative – cricket. By the late 1990s they were vying with Australia (albeit more because of a statistical quirk than any suggestion that they were their equals) to be regarded as the best team in the world. They also seem to bring out the best in England, and the recent series between the two have been humdingers. They have filled the vacuum created by the decline of West Indies. A series against South Africa is now a major event, with hard and often dramatic cricket virtually guaranteed.

South African cricket could have been derailed by the "Cronjegate" nightmare, or by arguments about the use of positive discrimination to get more black players into representative cricket. The corruption exposed by the King Commission and Cronje's death in a plane crash were destabilising, and the question of introducing quotas for black players in South African XIs is still raised from time to time. Yet neither has pushed what remains a resilient and battle-hardened team off course. South Africa was out of world cricket for too long not to give it their utmost now.   S. M.

"NORMAL" CRICKET   Denys Heesom, 1978

A major step forward was taken by the introduction of so-called "normal" cricket involving the merit selection of teams. Indeed, the provinces which did not include coloured players in their teams failed to do so only for lack of the requisite talent, not for the lack of will. Eight such players appeared during the season. All this stemmed from the success of the long and difficult negotiations between the three bodies which have hitherto controlled cricket in South Africa to come together into a single body, the efforts being crowned by success in September 1977. Even so, there remained dissidents – particularly in Western Province and Natal – to emphasise the fact that the welfare of cricket is not always the first consideration in everybody's minds. The upshot is, however, that the South African administrators have now done everything which is required of them to gain re-entry into international competition, but even so it seems highly unlikely that the general political atmosphere will permit this.

THE FORBIDDEN LAND   John Woodcock, Notes by the Editor, 1986

Never a year goes by without South Africa making its presence felt. With no chance of being voted back into membership of the ICC, and aware of the need for international competition to sustain their own game, the South African Cricket Union managed to arrange a full tour, starting in November, by a useful side of Australians, who accepted to go to South Africa in the certain knowledge that they would be banned forthwith from official Australian cricket. The team, led by the former Australian captain, Kim Hughes, was more experienced and arguably stronger than that which had lost the Ashes in England. They went at a time when South Africa was in ferment, and unlike the English side of 1982, the first of the "rebels", their tour coincided with their own domestic season. It thus presented the Australian authorities with a dilemma similar to that in 1977, when they encountered widespread defections to Mr Packer, and they had little alternative but to impose the bans they did. This is not to say that the Australian board's own handling of the matter had been entirely plausible.

Return to the Fold
Frank Heydenrych, 1992

The events of a well-contested South African season were quickly overshadowed by those off the field, which culminated in recognition of South Africa by the International Cricket Council, and the country's long-awaited return to world cricket. The road to acceptance has been a long, often stormy one, and had claimed the Test careers of some of the greatest cricketers South Africa had produced. But that road has now been travelled, and all agree with hindsight that it had to be travelled.

For those in South Africa who had pressed their noses against the shop window of international cricket for two decades, this was the most momentous moment of their sporting lives. English cricket lovers, temporarily deprived of the services of players such as Gooch, Emburey, Gatting and Foster, would have to amplify their frustration a thousand times to get some idea of what South African cricket-lovers had borne for the past 20 years.

India v South Africa 1991
Matthew Engel, 1993

Twenty-one years and eight months after Ali Bacher took a catch at mid-off to dismiss Alan Connolly in a Test at Port Elizabeth, the cricketers of South Africa – isolated ever since because of global opposition to the apartheid policy – rejoined the world by playing three one-day internationals in India. In the intervening years people had often wondered how, when or even whether South Africa's isolation might end: no one could have dared invent an ending quite so ironic and incongruous as this.

The South Africans arrived in Calcutta, four months after rejoining the International Cricket Council, at the insistence of the Board of Control for Cricket in India after Pakistan had called off a scheduled tour because of worsening Hindu-Muslim tensions. The visit was arranged almost as hurriedly as some of the rebel tours in which South Africa had lately specialised. But it was organised with the special blessing of the Marxist government of West Bengal. Thousands of people lined the route from the airport to the hotel to welcome the team, carrying banners with slogans that only a few months before would have been politically unthinkable: "South Africa-India friendship long live". The tourists' plane was said to be the first from South Africa ever to land in India.

Another banner at the hotel welcomed "the Springboks", but this was hurriedly torn down at the insistence of the United Cricket Board of South Africa, which

Happy returns: Clive Rice (centre) leads South Africa into their first official international match for more than 21 years, at Eden Gardens in Calcutta in November 1991.

was anxious not to use a nickname associated with the days of exclusively white sport. The 14-man squad – captained by Clive Rice and managed by Bacher, South Africa's last Test captain before isolation – was all white, but the party included four youngsters, two white and two black, brought along for the experience and to make a political and diplomatic point.

The whole South African team, except Kepler Wessels, who had played for Australia, were making their official international debuts and there were signs of naivete in their tactics both on and off the field. Their self-belief was hit by defeats in the two opening matches and was only partially restored by victory in the third. And the Indians were surprised when, in South Africa's very first game back, Bacher made "an informal protest" about the state of the ball, which had apparently been gouged while the Indians were fielding to help it swing. World-weary observers thought it was a little too soon for South Africa to switch from being cricket's pariah to its preacher. The Indians denied any wrong-doing and the South African board president, Geoff Dakin, was obliged to apologise to his hosts.

However, the team itself was experienced, too experienced in the view of the selectors afterwards. They dropped the two most senior batsmen, 42-year-old Rice and 38-year-old Jimmy Cook, before the World Cup and were intent on doing the same to 36-year-old Peter Kirsten before relenting. South Africa's rheumaticky performance in the field, so alien to the country's cricketing conditions, was one of the most surprising features of the trip.

India v South Africa   First One-Day International

At Calcutta, November 10, 1991. India won by three wickets.   Matthew Engel, 1993

South Africa's first officially blessed representative match in almost 22 years, first one-day international and first-ever game against India attracted a crowd widely claimed as beating the world record for a day's cricket of 90,800. However, Jagmohan Dalmiya, president of the Cricket Association of Bengal, said Eden Gardens now contained 90,452 seats and estimates putting the attendance higher included all the various officials, pressmen, policemen and peanut vendors.

The cricket was a disappointment and India's victory was easier than the margin suggested. South Africa were obliged to bat at 9 a.m. when the ball swung in the Calcutta smog and, understandably, the batting was nervy since 90,000 people, many of them throwing firecrackers, were able to create quite an atmosphere even if they did not break the record. Wessels's 50 was made too slowly. South Africa were given some hope when Donald took three wickets in his first four overs, but Tendulkar and the debutant Praveen Amre took India towards victory. Even in defeat, the South Africans were still overwhelmed by the occasion: "I know how Neil Armstrong felt when he stood on the moon," said their captain Rice.

Toss: India. **South Africa 177-8** (47 overs) (K. C. Wessels 50, A. P. Kuiper 43); **India 178-7** (40.4 overs) (S. R. Tendulkar 62, P. K. Amre 55; A. A. Donald 5-29).

India v South Africa   Second One-Day International

At Gwalior, November 12, 1991. India won by 38 runs.   Matthew Engel, 1993

India ensured victory in the three-match series after another poor performance by South Africa, though the game was overshadowed by the revelation that the touring team had, in effect, accused the Indians of cheating by tampering with the ball during the opening match. Having been put in after fog delayed the start, India's openers, Sidhu and Srikkanth, put on 130 in 28 overs. The later batsmen failed to capitalise on this start and South Africa were going well at 144 for three. But the Indians held some good catches in the deep – Kapil Dev's to dismiss Richardson was superb – and the result was not in doubt for long.

A crowd of 25,000 filled the Roop Singh stadium, chosen because Gwalior was the home town of the Indian Board president, Madhavrao Scindia. There was some rock-throwing but the crowd demonstrated their hospitality by aiming only at the Indians: two fielders, Raju and Sidhu, required treatment.

Toss: South Africa. **India 223-6** (45 overs) (K. Srikkanth 68, N. S. Sidhu 61, S. V. Manjrekar 52*; A. A. Donald 3-36); **South Africa 185-8** (45 overs) (M. Yachad 31, K. C. Wessels 71; S. L. V. Raju 3-43).

India v South Africa   Third One-Day International

At Nehru Stadium, New Delhi, November 14, 1991 (day/night).
South Africa won by eight wickets.   Matthew Engel, 1993

South Africa's first win in a one-day international was professionally executed after India had scored an apparently invulnerable 287 for four. The cricketing validity of the game was somewhat reduced by the use of the city's athletics stadium where the outfield included four separate surfaces: grass, the Tartan of the running track, artificial grass over the long-jump pit and tarpaulins. However, 75,000 watched the run-feast with great enthusiasm even when India started losing. Shastri, having been dropped for the previous game, was brought back as captain and put on 175 for the second wicket with Manjrekar at seven an over. But South Africa made light work of the chase: Wessels's third consecutive half-century was much freer than his previous two and his 90 came off 105 balls; Kuiper's 63 not out took only 41 balls. Firecrackers and thunder-flashes went off all round the stadium continually, regardless of the state of the game.

Toss: India. **India 287-4** (50 overs) (R. J. Shastri 109, K. Srikkanth 53, S. V. Manjrekar 105);
South Africa 288-2 (46.4 overs) (S. J. Cook 35, K. C. Wessels 90, P. N. Kirsten 86*, A. P. Kuiper 63*).

West Indies v South Africa 1992   Geoffrey Dean, 1993

South Africa were beaten in every match on their first-ever tour of the West Indies, but the results were in contrast to the overwhelming political success of the three-week tour. The whole affair would have been cancelled had not South African whites voted in favour of President de Klerk's programme of reform just three weeks earlier. But in the event there were hardly any demonstrations and a South African team with just one non-white player, Omar Henry, was received warmly throughout the Caribbean. In Trinidad, the centre of anti-apartheid demonstrations when England toured six years earlier, the players were given a standing ovation when they came out to jog round the boundary before the game.

There was one significant protest which led to a boycott of the Test match by Barbadian spectators: only a few hundred people watched each day of a momentous Test match. But in an extraordinary twist to history, this was nothing to do with South Africa or the apartheid policy. It was ostensibly caused by the omission of the Barbadian Anderson Cummins from the West Indian team. However, this was the culmination of various grievances against the selectors about the treatment of Barbadian heroes, including the exclusion of Carlisle Best from the previous Bridgetown Test, the passing over of Desmond Haynes for the captaincy and the exclusion of Malcolm Marshall from the World Cup party.

The protesters missed a remarkable game of cricket which appeared certain

478

to end in a triumph for South Africa until the final morning. They had looked far better geared up for the Test than the West Indians, several of whom still seemed to be in one-day mode. The boycott cost the West Indies board an estimated £100,000 in gate receipts but the touring team's expenses were met by the South African arm of the oil company BP, thus ensuring that the West Indies were able to make a profit on a tour for the first time in 15 years. Back in South Africa, the tour was on national TV instead of the satellite channel which showed the World Cup to a predominantly white audience.

The one-day series had been both well-attended and completely uncompetitive. The South Africans went straight into the first game without a practice match 72 hours after their arrival. The nets in both Kingston and Port-of-Spain were unsatisfactory and the team were unable to get used to the perfect batting pitches and, after the white ball of the World Cup, a red ball which hardly swung.

West Indies v South Africa   **Inaugural Test Match**

At Bridgetown, Barbados, April 18, 19, 20, 22, 23, 1992.
West Indies won by 52 runs.   Geoffrey Dean, 1993

An epic inaugural Test between the two countries ended in West Indies' 11th consecutive victory at the Kensington Oval. But South Africa were on top for the first four days, until a dramatic collapse preserved their hosts' 57-year-old unbeaten record in Barbados. Needing only 201 to win, the South Africans were well placed at 122 for two at the start of the fifth day. Quality fast bowling from Ambrose and Walsh removed their last eight wickets while another 26 runs were scored, and they were bowled out for 148, 20 minutes before lunch. Attendances throughout the game were minimal because Barbadians stayed away in protest against West Indian selection policy. The total attendance was only 6,500 and there were fewer than 500 spectators on the ground to witness one of West Indies' finest fightbacks, but scores of them charged ecstatically after their team on its lap of honour. All 11 players linked hands "to show the people of the Caribbean how united we are," said a visibly relieved Richardson. It was his first Test as captain of a West Indian side in transition after the era of Richards, Greenidge, Marshall and Dujon, and missing Logie and Hooper through injury.

Wessels, who played 24 Tests for Australia between 1982–83 and 1985–86, became the 13th player to represent two countries at Test level. He won a good toss, and followed the example set in the previous ten Bridgetown tests by electing to field first. At the end of the third day the tourists appeared to be on the brink of a famous victory. West Indies had had two pieces of extreme good fortune. Haynes played the second ball of the innings, from Donald, on to his off stump without dislodging a bail. Later Lara, who had just reached his maiden Test fifty trod on his off stump going back to Bosch. The incident was clear in television replays, but he was reprieved as neither umpire had seen it. This was the only moment of friction between the teams on the whole tour.

On a pitch that was now uneven, the South Africans quickly lost both openers. But they were manoeuvred into a winning position by Wessels and Kirsten. They had added 95 in 42 overs by the close, but were swept away next morning by Walsh, in an inspired spell of four for eight in 11 overs. Cutting the ball both ways, he found the form that eluded him earlier. Ambrose mopped up the tail.

West Indies v South Africa, 1992

At Bridgetown, April 18, 19, 20, 22, 23, 1992. Result: West Indies won by 52 runs.

WEST INDIES

	First innings		Second innings	
D. L. Haynes c Wessels b Snell		58	– c Richardson b Snell	23
P. V. Simmons c Kirsten b Snell		35	– c Kirsten b Bosch	3
B. C. Lara c Richardson b Bosch		17	– c Richardson b Donald	64
*R. B. Richardson c Richardson b Snell		44	– lbw b Snell	2
K. L. T. Arthurton c Kuiper b Pringle		59	– b Donald	22
J. C. Adams b Donald		11	– not out	79
†D. Williams c Hudson b Donald		1	– lbw b Snell	5
C. E. L. Ambrose not out		6	– c Richardson b Donald	6
K. C. G. Benjamin b Snell		1	– lbw b Donald	7
C. A. Walsh b Pringle		6	– c Richardson b Snell	13
B. P. Patterson run out		0	– b Bosch	11
L-b 7, n-b 17		24	B 17, l-b 11, n-b 20	48
		262		283

1-99 2-106 3-137 4-219 5-240 6-241 7-250 8-255 9-262 10-262

1-10 2-66 3-68 4-120 5-139 6-164 7-174 8-196 9-221 10-283

First innings – Donald 20–1–67–2; Bosch 15–2–43–1; Snell 18–3–83–4; Pringle 18.4–2–62–2.
Second innings – Donald 25–3–77–4; Bosch 24.3–7–61–2; Snell 16–1–74–4; Pringle 16–0–43–0.

SOUTH AFRICA

	First innings		Second innings	
M. W. Rushmere c Lara b Ambrose		3	– b Ambrose	3
A. C. Hudson b Benjamin		163	– c Lara b Ambrose	0
*K. C. Wessels c Adams b Ambrose		59	– c Lara b Walsh	74
P. N. Kirsten c Lara b Benjamin		11	– b Walsh	52
W. J. Cronje c Lara b Adams		5	– c Williams b Ambrose	2
A. P. Kuiper c Williams b Patterson		34	– c Williams b Walsh	0
†D. J. Richardson c Ambrose b Adams		8	– c Williams b Ambrose	2
R. P. Snell run out		6	– c Adams b Walsh	0
M. W. Pringle c Walsh b Adams		15	– b Ambrose	4
A. A. Donald st Williams b Adams		0	– b Ambrose	0
T. Bosch not out		5	– not out	0
B 4, l-b 6, w 1, n-b 25		36	B 4, l-b 3, n-b 4	11
		345		148

1-14 2-139 3-168 4-187 5-279 6-293 7-312 8-316 9-336 10-345

1-0 2-27 3-123 4-130 5-131 6-142 7-142 8-147 9-148 10-148

First innings – Ambrose 36–19–47–2; Patterson 23–4–79–1; Walsh 27–7–71–0; Benjamin 25–3–87–2; Arthurton 3–0–8–0; Adams 21.4–5–43–4.
Second innings – Ambrose 24.4–7–34–6; Patterson 7–1–26–0; Walsh 22–10–31–4; Benjamin 9–2–21–0; Adams 5–0–16–0; Simmons 5–1–13–0.

Toss won by West Indies   UMPIRES D. M. Archer and S. A. Bucknor

SOUTH AFRICA V INDIA 1992–93

Richard Streeton, 1994

A great deal of humdrum cricket failed to detract from the diplomatic and sporting history made when India embarked on a tour of Zimbabwe and South Africa late in 1992. Slow scoring and negative captaincy, coupled with moribund pitches, marred both Zimbabwe's inaugural Test and the first series staged in South Africa for 23 years. The continued failure of the Indians to do themselves justice away from home also militated against the representative games being worthy of these occasions. By the end of the tour India had gone 25 Test matches outside their own country without a win. In the wider context, though, this first tour to South Africa by a recognised non-white side was a success. The visit had the active support of the African National Congress and was almost entirely free from political rancour. More than £650,000 of the profits made by the United Cricket Board of South Africa (UCBSA) went into their development programme for black cricketers. The Indians undertook a heavy schedule of duties off the field, in townships and elsewhere, and proved fine ambassadors.

The tour will be remembered for the introduction of the ICC's scheme for independent umpires and even more for the South African board's experiment using television replays to settle difficult line decisions. It was a successful innovation, welcomed by most players and officials after some initial reservations. Hitherto, for as long as the game has been played, batsmen have received the benefit of an umpire's doubt. When officials on the field felt unable to decide, a third umpire in the pavilion watched video replays to rule on run outs, stumpings, (and hit-wicket decisions, though none arose). A green light signalled that the batsman must go, and the red that he was not out. Invariably the crowd buzzed with excitement as they waited and at some grounds they were able to watch the big-screen replays at the same time. The only major dispute arose when the West Indian umpire Steve Bucknor declined to call for a replay.

South Africa v India   **First One-Day International**

At Cape Town, December 7 (day/night), 1992.
South Africa won by six wickets.

Richard Streeton, 1994

A virtuoso performance by Cronje ensured that South Africa won their first home limited-overs international. His medium pace brought him five for 32 as India failed to build on a good start provided by Jadeja and Raman. Cronje later completed the victory, with three balls to spare, by hitting a six over mid-wicket. South Africa had been pegged back by steady bowling and reached the last two overs still needing 16. Earlier they owed much to Wessels and Kirsten, who both survived chances, though Wessels missed his fifty when he became the first batsman in a one-day international to be ruled out by the video replay.

Toss: India. **India 184** (50 overs) (A. D. Jadeja 48, W. V. Raman 47; W. J. Cronje 5-32);
South Africa 185-4 (49.3 overs) (K. C. Wessels 43, A. C. Hudson 33, P. N. Kirsten 56).

South Africa v India   **Third Test**

At Port Elizabeth, December 26, 27, 28, 29, 1992.

South Africa won by nine wickets.   Richard Streeton, 1994

Hostile fast bowling by Donald, who took 12 wickets, and a solid century by Cronje were the decisive performances as South Africa completed victory with a day to spare. It was their first Test win since they were readmitted to the ICC; their last had been over Australia on the same ground in March 1970. Donald's figures were the fourth-best for South Africa, and Richardson was the first South African wicket-keeper to take nine catches in a Test. A flamboyant hundred by Kapil Dev, coming in when India were 27 for five in their second innings, prolonged the game, but otherwise India were badly let down by their batsmen.

Toss: South Africa. **India 212** (M. Azharuddin 60; A. A. Donald 5-55, B. M. McMillan 3-41) **and 215** (Kapil Dev 129; A. A. Donald 7-84); **South Africa 275** (A. C. Hudson 52, W. J. Cronje 135; A. Kumble 3-81, S. L. V. Raju 3-73 **and 155-1** (K. C. Wessels 95*, A. C. Hudson 33).

African Sunrise   Donald Woods, 1993

In 1992 cricket's prodigal son, South Africa, came back fully to the game's global family through the World Cup competition and the first-ever Test matches against West Indies and India. After decades of isolation from real international competition the South African cricketers had two main points to prove – that South Africa was still among the top cricketing nations and that its team represented a new South Africa, in which apartheid was replaced with positive action to make up for past wrongs.

In theory the new South Africa ought to develop even stronger teams than the powerful combination which crushed Australia in seven of the last nine Tests before the curtain of isolation dropped in 1970, when the batting was so strong that Mike Procter went in as low as eight or nine. The hope is that the new South Africa will in time draw its Test stars from all the cultural groups of the nation instead of only the English-speaking whites, who number no more than 6% of the total population. Until comparatively recently most of the whites, the Afrikaners, were so alienated from cricket that those few making it to Test level were regarded as anglicised and somehow not truly of the Volk. So great was the cultural chasm between the two white groups that when Springbok captain Dudley Nourse introduced his players to the Afrikaner prime minister Dr Daniel Malan on the eve of the 1951 tour to England, Malan told the astonished Nourse that he hoped the team would enjoy their visit to South Africa.

Batsmen such as Andre Bruyns of Stellenbosch, who would probably have been a Springbok captain had there been no isolation, led a new wave of young Afrikaner cricketers to prominence in the mid-1970s. Their deeds in the domestic Currie Cup competition caused such a spread of cricket popularity among Afrikaans schools that by the time of the 1992 World Cup no fewer than four members of the South African team, Cronje, Bosch, Wessels and Donald, came from Afrikaans-speaking homes.

But the main recruitment in the new South Africa will have to come from those previously excluded from all hope of representing their country at cricket: the 84% of South Africans formerly classified under the apartheid lexicon as non-white, the Africans, so-called Coloureds and Indians – until recently subjected to 317 racial laws. If the nation's cricket comes to represent its demography accurately, this black majority of some 30 million will in due course supply about three-quarters of future South African teams. Fortunately for the future of South African cricket there is among this black majority a longer tradition and greater depth of cricket involvement than there was for many years among the Afrikaner whites, so that the integration of black players into the national playing structures should be a somewhat easier process than the integration of Afrikaners. As far back as the turn of the century there was a black fast bowler, Krom Hendricks, good enough to be chosen for South Africa against England, and his omission was the first of many surrenders by white South African cricket administrators to the racial considerations of their political leaders. This system of meddling was described as keeping politics out of sport.

During the years of segregation, young white South Africans idolised their cricketing heroes from Faulkner and Schwarz to the Pollocks and Richards, while young blacks in the country preferred to identify with Nicholls, Salie, Roro, Majola, Malamba, Ntikinca, Barnes, D'Oliveira, Bhamjee, Ntshekisan and Ebrahim – all black players as unknown to their white compatriots as they were to the cricket world at large. They may not have been national figures but they were local and regional heroes, especially in the Cape Province. All the time many whites liked to assume blacks were not interested in cricket. Meanwhile, the only white cricketers cheered on by black cricket fans were those playing *against* South Africa. When Neil Harvey played his epic match-winning innings of 151 not out for Australia against South Africa at Durban in 1950, every scoring stroke he made was cheered from the seating area reserved for blacks, not least by a young lawyer named Nelson Mandela.

How good were the black players of those years? D'Oliveira was the only one given the international opportunity to prove himself, but there is evidence that a number of them were worth Springbok places. Taliep Salie was a googly bowler regarded by Clarrie Grimmett as good enough for any Test team in the world. Among the Africans were Frank Roro, who scored 20 centuries in black inter-provincial cricket, Khaya Majola, Ben Malamba, Edmund Ntikinca and Sam Ntshekisa, all of whom showed skills far above average despite adverse pitches and playing conditions. Tiffie Barnes and Baboo Ebrahim would have been stars in any first-class cricket arena, and as wicket-keepers Chicken Bhamjee and C. J. Nicholls were regarded by some sound judges as being at least as good as their counterparts in the white cricket world. So there was a lot to be sorry for in South Africa's cricketing past; a lot of lost time and opportunity and a lot of wrong to acknowledge and put right as the first-ever South African team chosen consciously on merit-only was assembled for the World Cup in Australia and New Zealand.

On performance grounds alone the South Africans had a good World Cup, reaching the semi-final after beating teams as powerful as West Indies, Australia, India and the eventual winners, Pakistan, and in their first Test matches thereafter they were far from outclassed, despite the long years of isolation. More importantly, however, they showed an intelligent level of acknowledgment of the point of the boycott in a manner which their rugby compatriots failed to emulate. The key to this acknowledgment was the trust developed between Dr Ali Bacher, managing director of the then South African Cricket Union, and Steve Tshwete, chief spokesman on sport for the African National Congress. Their relationship was the tip of an iceberg of more widespread commitment throughout South African cricket. It was also expressed through what had become a genuine commitment to the development of cricket among black children in the townships.

Initially the Township Development Programme had been a limited and exploratory project which, if not entirely window-dressing, was nevertheless paternalistic, lagging well behind the desired return to international cricket in the priorities of most of the white cricket administrators. The catalyst for real change was the last rebel tour, led by Mike Gatting in 1990. The extent of the opposition to it stunned many people in the SACU, who had ignored the warnings of anti-apartheid activists and expected the tour to pass off as peacefully as the previous six. But there were indications even beforehand that some formerly blinkered administrators had begun to realise that the kids in the townships were showing exciting abilities and that the best priority for South African cricket was the mission to black youth. The tour was something of a throwback. Suddenly, almost without realising the transition, Bacher and his colleagues were thinking as real South Africans for the first time in their lives. This was all that Tshwete and his associates had been waiting for, and they responded with generous enthusiasm. From the moment white officials began to view the youth scheme rather than tours as the main priority, the ANC made the tours possible again.

Soon the SACU merged with its old rival, the South African Cricket Board, the new United Board was admitted to the ICC and South African cricket began to be riven instead by the same disputes that characterise the game elsewhere, mostly over the eccentricities of the selectors. This argument reached its peak when Jimmy Cook and Clive Rice were left out of the World Cup squad. But Cook, Rice, Kepler Wessels and Peter Kirsten are all in or approaching their cricketing old age. There is a new generation of stars to find as representatives of the new South Africa.

Donald Woods was editor of the Daily Dispatch *in South Africa until he was arrested for anti-government activities in 1977. At the time he was the only white member of the governing council of the South African Cricket Board. He fled the country in 1978 and was not able to return until August 1990. He died in 2001.*

AUSTRALIA v SOUTH AFRICA 1993–94
Steven Lynch, 1995

The success of South Africa's first tour of Australia for 30 years was assured at Sydney, when a young side – temporarily under the direction of Hansie Cronje, after an injury to the captain Kepler Wessels – pulled off a remarkable victory, dismissing Australia for 111 to win the Second Test by the slender margin of five runs.

That Sydney triumph had looked most unlikely from the first day, when South Africa slid to 169 all out, with Shane Warne taking seven wickets. On an indifferent pitch, Australia's 292 seemed to have insured them against defeat, and when South Africa were 110 for five a premature end was in sight. However, Jonty Rhodes organised the later order to stretch the lead into three figures. Australia's hopes of victory with a day to spare were dashed by the lively Fanie de Villiers, who reduced the home side to 63 for four that night. Next morning Australia soon lost Allan Border, and from then on a crowd of around 12,000 – admitted free – held its collective breath as Australia inched towards the target. All looked lost at 75 for eight, but then Craig McDermott played a forthright innings – until last man Glenn McGrath popped a return catch to de Villiers, who took ten for 123 in the match, to ignite South African celebrations from Sydney to Soweto. Australian batsmen are supposed to be superstitious about 87 rather than Nelson, but 111 had become the unlucky number of Australian cricket, with this collapse joining those against England at Melbourne and Adelaide in 1954–55, Sydney in 1978–79, and Headingley in 1981.

The euphoria of the historic Sydney victory outweighed an anticlimactic end to the tour, defeat in the one-day World Series finals being followed by a comprehensive reverse in the Adelaide Test. Despite this, the Test series was shared, mirroring the performance of South Africa's last two touring teams in Australia, in 1952–53 and 1963–64; the First Test had been ruined by unseasonal weather, which allowed little more than four hours' play over the first three days at Melbourne.

Australia v South Africa, 1993–94   Second Test

At Sydney, January 2, 3, 4, 5, 6, 1994. Result: South Africa won by five runs.

SOUTH AFRICA

	First innings		Second innings	
A. C. Hudson lbw b McGrath	0	–	c Healy b McDermott	1
G. Kirsten st Healy b Warne	67	–	b McDermott	41
W. J. Cronje c Waugh b McDermott	41	–	b McDermott	38
D. J. Cullinan b Warne	9	–	(5) lbw b Warne	2
J. N. Rhodes lbw b Warne	4	–	(6) not out	76
*K. C. Wessels c and b Warne	3	–	(4) b Warne	18
†D. J. Richardson c Taylor b Warne	4	–	lbw b McGrath	24
P. L. Symcox b Warne	7	–	c Healy b McDermott	4
C. R. Matthews c Taylor b Warne	0	–	c Waugh b Warne	4
P. S. de Villiers c Waugh b McDermott	18	–	lbw b Warne	2
A. A. Donald not out	0	–	c Healy b Warne	10
B 1, l-b 4, n-b 11	16		B 13, l-b 1, n-b 5	19

1-1 2-91 3-110 4-133 5-134 6-141   169   1-2 2-75 3-101 4-107 5-110 6-182   239
7-142 8-142 9-152 10-169   7-188 8-197 9-203 10-239

First innings – McDermott 18.1–2–42–2; McGrath 19–5–32–1; Warne 27–8–56–7; May 10–1–34–0.
Second innings – McDermott 28–9–62–4; McGrath 14–3–30–1; May 22–4–53–0; Warne 42–17–72–5; Border 3–1–8–0.

AUSTRALIA	First innings		Second innings	
M. J. Slater b Donald	92	–	(2) b de Villiers	1
M. A. Taylor c Richardson b Donald	7	–	(1) c Richardson b de Villiers	27
D. C. Boon b de Villiers	19	–	c Kirsten b de Villiers	24
M. E. Waugh lbw b Symcox	7	–	(5) lbw b Donald	11
*A. R. Border c Richardson b de Villiers	49	–	(6) b Donald	7
D. R. Martyn c Richardson b de Villiers	59	–	(7) c Hudson b Donald	6
†I. A. Healy c Richardson b Donald	19	–	(8) b de Villiers	1
S. K. Warne c Rhodes b Symcox	11	–	(9) run out	1
C. J. McDermott c Cronje b de Villiers	6	–	(10) not out	29
T. B. A. May not out	8	–	(4) lbw b de Villiers	0
G. D. McGrath b Donald	9	–	c and b de Villiers	1
B 1, l-b 2, n-b 3	6		L-b 3	3

1-10 2-58 3-75 4-179 5-179 6-229   292   1-4 2-51 3-51 4-56 5-63 6-72   111
7-250 8-266 9-281 10-292   7-73 8-75 9-110 10-111

First innings – Donald 31.2–8–83–4; de Villiers 36–12–80–4; Matthews 28–11–44–0; Symcox 46–11–82–2.
Second innings – Donald 17–5–34–3; de Villiers 23.3–8–43–6; Matthews 6–5–9–0; Symcox 10–3–22–0.

Toss won by South Africa	UMPIRES S. G. Randell and W. P. Sheahan

---

AFTER ALL THESE YEARS
Matthew Engel, *Notes by the Editor*, 1994

All being well, there will still be some wonderful moments when the South Africans finally arrive in England, 100 years after their first tour, and 29 after their last. Nothing in cricket has disgraced the game over the years so much as its relationship with South Africa. For two decades after the formal introduction of apartheid, administrators in the white countries did everything possible to avoid consideration of the ethical questions involved, although it was obvious at the time that South African cricket was rooted in a system that was fundamentally evil.

Even after Basil D'Oliveira's exclusion from South Africa they had to be dragged kicking and screaming towards the notion that the relationship must cease; it was the home secretary, James Callaghan, terrified that civil disorder would muck up a general election, who forced the cancellation of the 1970 tour of England. For the next two decades of formal isolation, cricket's attitude was ineffectual and half-hearted. The culture of the game was such that no odium attached to the players who were so well-rewarded for going on the seven rebel tours though, in their own small and moral pygmyish way, they were acting as agents of apartheid.

That war has now been won. The future of South Africa remains clouded with all kinds of terrible possibilities but this summer it will be possible to welcome their cricketers without reservation. Since the collapse of the last rebel tour in 1990, when South African administrators ceased their equivocation about their real intentions and merged into the United Cricket Board, they have done an enormous amount for the good of the game. No country is doing more to spread cricket to its own people; if only Lord's worked as hard in the deprived areas of English cities.

ENGLAND V SOUTH AFRICA 1994

Scyld Berry, 1995

South Africa's first Test series in England since 1965 began in triumph, when they won the First Test at Lord's in four days, vastly superior to England in every facet except spin bowling, in which the tourists chose not to compete at all. However, in the course of the two remaining Test matches, the pendulum swung from one side to the other, as seldom happens in a three-Test series.

England gained the advantage during the Second Test at Headingley and used it to full effect in the Third at The Oval. Indeed, so unsettled were the South Africans on the fast pitch there that they ended in some disarray; and ultimately their complete record on paper, after losing their final one-day game against Holland, was little better than that of the New Zealanders earlier in the summer. After the tour, Mike Procter, one of the most famous names in South African cricket, was replaced as coach by the more technically minded Englishman, Bob Woolmer, and in November Kepler Wessels gave up the captaincy. But because they took England's last two wickets in their Lord's Test, unlike New Zealand, and because they renewed official relationships so diplomatically, the South Africans' tour of 1994 can be judged an overall success.

Amid the harmony which existed between the two teams, and between the South Africans and the public (although the tourists' approach to the county games was often cautious), there was only one controversy, albeit a huge one, and it did not directly concern the tourists at all. The Lord's Test match was played in intense heat, similar to that in the West Indies where England had toured a few months before, and where they had learned a lot about reverse swing. On the Saturday afternoon at Lord's, the England captain, Mike Atherton, was seen on television to be taking dirt from his pocket, which everyone agreed was connected with keeping the ball dry and helping it to reverse swing. Thereafter, public opinion differed sharply during a debate which provoked newspaper editorials and phone-in programmes, and divided even those barely interested in cricket into two factions. One faction thought Atherton was cheating and that this, combined with his economy with the truth in front of the ICC referee Peter Burge, constituted a resignation issue; the other accepted his assertion that he was trying to avoid affecting the ball. It was subsequently inferred that Burge took a very dim view of Atherton's behaviour, since he fined him half his match fee at The Oval for stepping minimally out of line, by shaking his head and looking at the inside edge of his bat after being given leg-before first ball.

If the incident at Lord's was unfortunate for Atherton, coming as it did within the first year of his England captaincy, it was no less so for the South Africans. Public attention was distracted from their magnificent victory – one of only two first-class games that they won – and due credit denied them in the British media. Moreover, Procter remarked after the series that he thought the Atherton affair had had the effect of bringing the England players together, in support of their young captain.

In any event, the tourists never quite recaptured the fervent enthusiasm which they brought to the Lord's match. After 29 years away from England, a sweeping victory at the first attempt proved to be almost a cathartic experience, after which everything else was anticlimax. There may also have been a failure to redefine goals. The two previous South African parties who won Test series in England, in 1935 and 1965, had done so by one game to nil; and on their arrival Wessels and his team had spoken of a similar aim, expecting the win to come at either Headingley or The Oval, the two grounds overtly most suited to their pace bowling. The Test at Lord's was to have been a quiet reintroduction, an acclimatisation. When England capitulated after the opening day of the series, the tourists as much as anyone were taken by surprise and did not readjust their sights upwards.

At Headingley, however, the South Africans still had enough steam to fight back with the tenacity that was their trademark. Apparently doomed at 105 for five in reply to 477, their later order rallied superbly under Peter Kirsten, who drew on five seasons of experience with Derbyshire to make his maiden Test hundred at the age of 39, and the large, burly all-rounder Brian McMillan, whom Atherton considered to be as good a batsman as any on the South African side. What is more, the tourists counter-attacked with aggressive strokeplay, not dogged defence. Once they had saved the follow-on, England made no more than a gesture towards winning.

Still, the cracks which had appeared in South Africa's cricket at Headingley – for instance, the uncertainty of their vice-captain Hansie Cronje against the short-pitched bowling of Darren Gough – England widened in spectacular fashion at The Oval. Pre-tour conjecture had come up with several suggestions as to what South African cricket had missed most during the years of their absence from official cricket because of apartheid, and at The Oval the answer became apparent. In their approach – tenacious spirit, buoyant morale and hard work – the tourists were like the best of Australian teams. But their batsmen shaped more like New Zealanders when confronted with the unfamiliar spectacle of a fast and bouncy pitch. Their top-order batsmen were so startled by it that they were overwhelmed.

By then the senior opening batsman, Andrew Hudson, had been dropped, his self-confidence gone, his shot selection indiscriminate. His one century of the tour was in the final game at Scarborough. But he had made 163 against West Indies in Barbados and perhaps he should have been persuaded to play at The Oval. In his absence, the half-brothers Gary and Peter Kirsten were paired as openers and could not cope with Devon Malcolm at his fastest. Earlier, on slower wickets, the left-handed Gary had demonstrated a fine cover-drive and had set both of South Africa's innings in motion at Lord's; he was also a brave short leg. The tall and front-footed Cronje at No. 3 was ever more at sea as the series went on. For a team which had two of its first three batsmen as non-contributors throughout the series, the tourists did remarkably well.

Procter's overall objective was to make South African cricket more attacking. Thanks largely to the robust methods of McMillan and Richardson in the later order, the Test team scored at more than three runs an over in the series, when in the previous Tests since their return they had scored at only 2.28. Having aimed over the previous two years for respectability, frequently in the shape of draws, the South Africans played a more expansive game in England. It thrillingly paid off at Lord's and in their counter-attack at Headingley. For England, after their deplorable start, a drawn series – only their second at home since 1974 – was a comforting consolation.

England v South Africa **First Test**
At Lord's, July 21, 22, 23, 24, 1994. South Africa won by 356 runs. Matthew Engel, 1995

The first Test between the countries for 29 years began with the word historic being used to the point of monotony but ended with controversy engulfing the England captain, Mike Atherton, and threatening his future. The Atherton affair took over all discussion of the match and the genuinely historic outcome – a devastating South African victory – was all but forgotten amid the fuss.

Normally, England being bowled out for 99 on a sound wicket might have caused a great deal of anguish. However, everyone was preoccupied by the fact that Atherton, fielding on Saturday afternoon, was seen by the TV cameras taking his hand out of his pocket and rubbing it across the ball before passing it back to the bowler. He was called before the referee, Peter Burge, to explain what the official statement called his unfamiliar action and answer suspicions that he had broken Law 42.5 by using an artificial substance to alter the condition of the ball. Burge said he had accepted Atherton's explanation without saying what it was. But the following day, after further TV pictures were shown that looked even more sinister and England's batsmen had crumpled to a humiliating four-day defeat, Atherton admitted publicly that he had not told Burge the truth by saying that he had nothing in his pocket. In fact, he said, he had some dirt there that he picked up to keep his hands dry and prevent moisture getting on the ball while Darren Gough was trying to reverse swing it; the second set of pictures clearly showed some of the dirt falling off it.

Ray Illingworth, the chairman of selectors, immediately fined Atherton £2,000 – half for using the dirt, though that was not a breach of any Law, and half for the lie. He hoped that would close the matter. But over the next 48 hours, there was a tidal wave of public emotion in which almost everyone from the cricket correspondent of the BBC to people who had never seen a match in their lives demanded Atherton's resignation. Illingworth and the TCCB remained staunch in their support, though. The umpires said the condition of the ball had not been changed and the South Africans made no complaint, except to grumble that their triumph had been ignored. Five days after the game ended, Atherton relieved the pressure by emerging from something close to hiding and calling a press conference at which he did not entirely explain away the pictures but stressed repeatedly that he had never cheated at cricket.

If Atherton was a cheat, he was not a very successful one. England's bowlers mostly failed, though not quite as humiliatingly as their batsmen. England had dropped both Such and [Robin] Smith, who had been desperate to play against the country of his birth, and named two uncapped players in their 12: the Hampshire off-spinner Shaun Udal and the Lancashire batsman John Crawley. Udal was then left out of the team in favour of the leg-spinner Salisbury, the 12th man in the last Test against New Zealand. South Africa, concerned that both their spinners were below standard, named an attack entirely comprising right-arm seam bowlers.

The formalities included the officials being presented to Thabo Mbeki, the recently appointed deputy president of South Africa, and reports of the almost as ritualised refusal-of-admission-to-the-pavilion: the victim was the Archbishop of Cape Town, Desmond Tutu, who was out of uniform and not wearing a jacket. On the field, the first day consisted of South Africa winning the toss and their captain, Wessels, playing an innings that epitomised his country's approach to Test cricket: unflashy but utterly determined.

Wessels spent just under five hours scoring 105. His partnerships with his fellow left-hander Gary Kirsten, whose 72 was just as deadpan though it included some high-class cutting, and Rhodes gave the South African first innings its body. At the end of the first day, the game was evenly matched at 244 for six, but it was typical of both sides that South Africa's last four wickets were able to add 116. For no obvious reason, England then collapsed before Donald's pace and de Villiers's swing; no one played a substantial innings, though Hick yet again promised flickeringly before losing his way and then his wicket.

On the third morning, England avoided the follow-on after a brief counter-attack from DeFreitas, but Donald finished off the tail to take five for 74. South Africa began consolidating their lead of 177, a task which – but for the cameras and Atherton – might have been uneventful. Though no South African batsman played a long innings, the bowlers again failed to exercise proper control, except for the occasional off-spinner Hick, who bowled 21 consecutive overs for only 27. Gough looked something close to the spearhead England had been seeking, and apparently did manage to reverse swing the ball on the fourth morning to york Peter Kirsten and Rhodes. But the overall performance of the attack, with DeFreitas out of sorts and Fraser weary, was below par.

South Africa declared at Sunday lunchtime, setting England 456 to win, which would have been improbable in any circumstances. It is difficult to assess the extent to which England were affected by the storm gathering over the captain, who had led his team out in the morning with his hands, insouciantly and provocatively, in his pockets. Atherton and Crawley were both caught in the slips; Hick received an unkind lbw decision from umpire Randell; then Stewart, after an unusually dogged innings, was caught behind and White was out first ball. On five, Gooch had passed Viv Richards to go fourth on the list of all-time Test match run-makers. But from 74 for three, England fell away to 99 all out, England's lowest only since the 46 in the Trinidad Test less than four months earlier.

The new South African flag did flutter in the closing stages, despite MCC's earlier request to the team to obey their regulations banning all flags. The match throughout was played in extreme heat and some humidity, which helped the swing bowlers and, according to Atherton, explained why he needed the dirt to dry his hands. It may also have contributed to the air of frenzy that took over when the cricket finished.

Toss: South Africa. **South Africa 357** (G. Kirsten 72, K. C. Wessels 105, J. N. Rhodes 32, C. R. Matthews 41; D. Gough 4-76, A. R. C. Fraser 3-72) **and 278-8 dec.** (G. Kirsten 44, W. J. Cronje 32, P. N. Kirsten 42, J. N. Rhodes 32, B. M. McMillan 39*, Extras 30; D. Gough 4-46); **England 180** (G. A. Hick 38; A. A. Donald 5-74, P. S. de Villiers 3-28) **and 99** (C. R. Matthews 3-25, B. M. McMillan 3-16).

England v South Africa   **Third Test**
See page 264

SOUTH AFRICA V NEW ZEALAND 1994–95
See page 520

SOUTH AFRICA V PAKISTAN 1995   Inaugural Test Match
At Johannesburg, January 19, 20, 21, 22, 23, 1995. South Africa won by 324 runs.   Qamar Ahmed, 1996

Cronje led South Africa to their biggest ever home victory by runs, while Pakistan surrendered their record of at least one Test victory in their inaugural series against each of their opponents. Waqar Younis and Rashid Latif were declared unfit; rather than replacing Waqar with one of the bowlers to hand, the tour management selected Aamir Nazir, who was still on a 14-hour journey from Pakistan. He landed at Johannesburg an hour before play and entered the field 35 minutes late. Nazir broke down with cramp in his seventh over, but returned after tea, had Rhodes caught at slip to end a 157-run partnership, bowled Richardson next ball, broke down again and returned next day.

South Africa had lost three wickets in the first 75 minutes. But Kirsten and Cronje repaired the damage before Rhodes and McMillan shared South Africa's biggest partnership since their return to international cricket. They put on 157 in 39 overs, Rhodes reaching his first Test fifty since March and McMillan completing a maiden Test hundred from 146 balls. He was then bowled by a no-ball from Wasim: no-balls contributed 36 to the innings. McMillan hit 15 fours and helped South Africa to almost four an over on the first day. After his departure next morning, de Villiers raced to a maiden Test half-century.

De Villiers continued to dominate play, removing Pakistan's top three as they reached 44. The tourists were 177 for six at stumps, with only Salim Malik standing firm. In the morning, he got within one run of a third hundred in successive Tests, but Eksteen held a hard catch at gully to deny him. Pakistan were bowled out for exactly half South Africa's total and faced following on.

Cronje, however, preferred to establish a huge lead rather than bat last on a deteriorating pitch. The openers set off at a run a minute until Steyn received his second doubtful caught-behind decision of the Test. When the batsmen accepted an offer of bad light on the third evening, the advantage was 391, which South Africa extended by 98 before declaring at lunch. The morning saw two first-ball dismissals: Commins, who had a groin strain, forgot he had a runner and ran himself out, while Richardson completed a king pair.

Pakistan needed 490 from five sessions, but the home crowd of 28,000 were already celebrating by the close, with seven down for 149. De Villiers and Donald had grabbed three as the score reached five; Asif Mujtaba survived for nearly three hours, the first 45 minutes on nought, but his dismissal triggered another collapse. Pakistan's only comfort was a battling 95 from Inzamam-ul-Haq. They lost their last three wickets in 6.3 overs on the final morning, when de Villiers became the first South African to take ten wickets and score fifty in a Test. Pakistan manager Intikhab Alam afterwards described their batting as unprofessional, but Salim Malik denied reports of rifts within the team. "All rumours," he insisted.

491

South Africa v Pakistan, 1995   Inaugural Test Match
At Johannesburg, January 19, 20, 21, 22, 23, 1995. Result: South Africa won by 324 runs.

SOUTH AFRICA	First innings		Second innings	
G. Kirsten c Aamir Sohail b Kabir Khan	. . .	62	– b Wasim Akram	42
P. J. R. Steyn c Moin Khan b Wasim Akram	.	1	– c Moin Khan b Aamer Nazir	17
J. B. Commins b Aqib Javed	. . . .	13	– (6) run out	0
D. J. Cullinan c Moin Khan b Aqib Javed	. .	0	– not out	69
*W. J. Cronje c Asif Mujtaba b Kabir Khan	.	41	– (3) c Aamer Sohail b Aqib Javed	48
J. N. Rhodes c Inzamam–ul–Haq				
b Aamir Nazir	. . . .	72	– (5) c Moin Khan b Wasim Akram	16
B. M. McMillan c Moin Khan				
b Aqib Javed	. . . .	113	– c Salim Malik b Kabir Khan	33
†D. J. Richardson b Aamir Nazir	. . . .	0	– lbw b Aqib Javed	0
C. E. Eksteen c Moin Khan b Wasim Akram	.	13	– not out	2
P. S. de Villiers not out	. . . .	66		
A. A. Donald c Inzamam–ul–Haq				
b Aamir Sohail	. . . .	15		
B 4, l-b 18, w 6, n-b 36	. . . .	64	B 6, l-b 5, w 15, n-b 6	32

1-1 2-55 3-59 4-138 5-168 6-325 7-325   460   1-69 2-96 3-155 4-185 5-185   (7 wkts dec.)   259
8-367 9-389 10-460   6-251 7-255

First innings – Wasim Akram 36–11–113–2; Aqib Javed 29.4–6–102–3; Kabir Khan 19.1–4–60–2;
Aamir Nazir 13.1–1–67–2; Aamir Sohail 14.2–2–47–1; Salim Malik 8–0–49–0.
Second innings – Wasim Akram 23–4–53–2; Aqib Javed 26–2–82–2; Aamir Nazir 13–1–55–1;
Kabir Khan 18–0–58–1.

PAKISTAN	First innings		Second innings	
Aamir Sohail c Richardson b de Villiers	. . .	23	– c McMillan b de Villiers	0
Saeed Anwar c Cullinan b de Villiers	. . . .	2	– c de Villiers b Donald	1
Asif Mujtaba c Richardson b de Villiers	. .	0	– c Richardson b McMillan	26
*Salim Malik c Eksteen b Donald	. . . . . .	99	– lbw b de Villiers	1
Ijaz Ahmed b de Villiers	. . . .	19	– (6) c Richardson b McMillan	1
Inzamam–ul–Haq b McMillan	. . . .	19	– (5) c Richardson b de Villiers	95
†Moin Khan c de Villiers b McMillan	. . . .	9	– c Rhodes b Eksteen	0
Wasim Akram b de Villiers	. . . .	41	– c Kirsten b Eksteen	11
Kabir Khan c Richardson b Donald	. . . .	4	– c Eksteen b Donald	10
Aqib Javed not out	. . . .	0	– c Richardson b de Villiers	0
Aamir Nazir b de Villiers	. . . .	0	– not out	1
L-b 5, n-b 9	. . . .	14	B 8, l-b 7, w 1, n-b 3	19

1-20 2-20 3-44 4-106 5-134 6-158 7-193   230   1-3 2-3 3-5 4-98 5-100 6-101 7-124   165
8-207 9-230 10-230   8-164 9-164 10-165

First innings – Donald 17–2–63–2; de Villiers 20.5–4–81–6; McMillan 12–3–46–2; Eksteen 7–1–16–0;
Cronje 9–5–19–0.
Second innings – Donald 15–3–53–2; de Villiers 19.3–11–27–4; McMillan 11–1–33–2;
Eksteen 19–7–34–2; Cronje 5–2–3–0.

Toss won by South Africa   UMPIRES M. J. Kitchen and C. J. Mitchley

AUSTRALIA V SOUTH AFRICA 1997–98 Steven Lynch, 1999

The South Africans arrived with high hopes of recording their first Test series victory over Australia in four attempts since returning to the international fold. In the end, two factors counted against them. A familiar foe, Shane Warne, over-came unseasonal damp weather in the Sydney Test with some wristy magic, which included his 300th Test wicket. And in the Third Test at Adelaide, as the visitors looked set to square the series, uncharacteristically ragged fielding cost them dear. Ten catches went down as Australia just managed to stave off defeat and take the series 1–0.

There was a similar near-miss in the one-day series. South Africa dominated the qualifying stages, winning all four of their matches against Australia and losing only once, to New Zealand. But Australia turned the tables in the best-of-three finals, winning the last two games after another defeat in the first one. The South Africans also failed to win a first-class match on the tour, though they lost only the Test at Sydney.

It seemed almost as if, when pitted against Australia, the South Africans had an inferiority complex – not something they exhibit against other countries nor, indeed, in many other sports. Captaincy came into it too: sometimes, when comparing the thoughtful Mark Taylor with the rather mechanical Hansie Cronje, one was reminded of Dr Who outwitting the Daleks. In the Sydney Test, for example, Cronje delayed posting a short leg during a lightning spell from Allan Donald until after both Waughs had popped up inviting catches there. Later, Taylor posi-tioned Ricky Ponting unusually close at mid-wicket, where he immediately took a sharp low catch to send Adam Bacher back. Good luck – or good judgment?

Their main problem remained the lack of a world-class batsman – a Lara, a Richards (Viv) or, come to that, a Richards (Barry). All their batsmen had work-manlike Test averages in the upper thirties, but none threatened to reach the magic 50 mark. The man most likely to, Daryll Cullinan, ran into trouble against his old nemesis, Warne, and was dropped for the last two Tests. And Cronje let himself down too often with reckless shots after patient starts. Jacques Kallis made an accomplished maiden Test century at Melbourne, and Gary Kirsten, the vice-captain, scored consistently, apart from a double failure in the defeat at Sydney. After the First Test, South African coach Bob Woolmer caused some amusement when he suggested that Bacher had returned to form, moving his feet well in a laboured innings of three in 53 minutes. But the canny Woolmer was proved right when Bacher, who started the tour wretchedly, followed this up with four useful scores.

The tourists had fewer problems in the fast bowling department, although they missed the steadiness of Fanie de Villiers, the match-winner at Sydney four years ago, who was overlooked this time. Donald, who became South Africa's leading Test wicket-taker at Melbourne, was a constant threat. One spell at Sydney, where he bowled after a pain-killing injection in his foot, was as fast as anyone could remember. It was a major blow when he pulled a buttock muscle in the closing stages of the one-day competition and had to miss the final Test. Shaun Pollock responded well in that match, taking seven for 87 on an unhelpful pitch, but Donald's absence probably allowed Australia to stave off defeat. Brian McMillan, who struggled with the bat until the final Test, looked past his best with the ball as well. There were signs of raw promise in Makhaya Ntini, the first black player to play for South Africa. He was given little scope but, in a rare one-day outing, he impressed with his pace with the ball, and, during the Sydney Test, with his fleetness of foot: he took part in an invitation 400-metre race on the outfield. Roared on by his team-mates, he hung on to win.

This series saw the final bow of Dave Richardson, South Africa's polished wicket-keeper. At Melbourne, he broke the national record for Test dismissals, surpassing John Waite. There were occasional signs that his keeping had declined, and he made little impact with the bat, but he managed a rare stumping, his second in Tests and, as it turned out, his last. He also took 150 catches in 42 Tests, having missed only one game between South Africa's return and his retirement. His eventual replacement, Mark Boucher, fretted at the limited scope he was allowed on this tour while his rivals were fully employed at home – but he soon took his chance, quite literally with both hands.

Australia v South Africa — Second Test

At Sydney, January 2, 3, 4, 5, 1998. Australia won by an innings and 21 runs.   Steven Lynch, 1999

Four years earlier, Warne had taken 12 wickets against South Africa at Sydney, but still lost, as Australia were beaten by five runs after collapsing for 111. There was no mistake this time, though: Warne took 11 wickets, including his 300th in Tests, six years to the day after his first: Ravi Shastri on January 5, 1992. This time the landmark victim was Kallis, bemused by a perfect top-spinner which dipped through his forward lunge. "A quality ball for a quality batsman," Taylor called it. Warne was back to his best here: the ball which removed Richardson in the first innings was a near-replica of the famous one which did for Mike Gatting at Old Trafford in 1993. And, with the close fielders backing him up well, another South African escape act proved impossible.

One slight regret for Warne was that few spectators witnessed the final act. Heavy rain on the fourth afternoon sent many home, and it was a surprise when the weather relented enough to allow the players back on. With the floodlights on for the third afternoon running, Australia pushed hard for a four-day victory, claiming the extra half-hour. They were rewarded when, with rain beginning again, Reiffel had Donald caught behind to seal an emphatic innings win.

Toss: South Africa. **South Africa 287** (A. M. Bacher 39, W. J. Cronje 88, H. H. Gibbs 54;
S. K. Warne 5-75) **and 113** (J. H. Kallis 45, P. L. Symcox 38; P. R. Reiffel 3-14, S. K. Warne 6-34);
Australia 421 (M. T. G. Elliott 32, M. E. Waugh 100, S. R. Waugh 85, R. T. Ponting 62, I. A. Healy 46*;
A. A. Donald 3-81, S. M. Pollock 3-71).

South Africa v West Indies 1998–99

See page 406

Colin Bryden and Andrew Samson, 1999

South Africans have long been aware that politics or, more realistically, normal life, cannot be kept separate from cricket. The racial politics of the former South African government had a devastating impact on the country's cricketers, and it was a certainty that the implications of the post-apartheid era would affect the game. The most contentious issue in a season with no shortage of discussion points was the "fast-tracking" of black cricketers, culminating in the selection of Makhaya Ntini for two Test matches against Sri Lanka. He became the first black African to play Test cricket for South Africa.

The race issue resurfaced some four years after South Africa's first fully inclusive general election in April 1994. "The euphoria of the new South Africa two or three years ago has worn off," noted Ali Bacher, managing director of the United Cricket Board. "People are impatient and they want to see results." Unlike rugby, cricket has remained in tune with the government's aspirations, and leading figures, including President Nelson Mandela and Archbishop Desmond Tutu, have been among the most enthusiastic supporters of the national team. Millions of rand have been spent on developing the game and providing facilities in black areas. Yet the continued "white" look of the team attracted criticism from a parliamentary sports committee and some vocal spectators during the Second Test against Pakistan in Durban. There was a small demonstration in Port Elizabeth before the Third Test against Pakistan, leading to a meeting between Bacher and the protest leaders. "In 1998, you cannot have an all-white national team," Bacher said afterwards.

The cynical might read an over-abundance of coincidence into the events which happened quickly thereafter. Bacher made his statement on the first day of the Test match. Fanie de Villiers, 33, announced his retirement the following day, citing family priorities, a lucrative offer to commentate on TV, and a long struggle against injuries. He took Test-best figures of six for 23 on the day after that. It was the worst-kept secret in South Africa that Ntini would play in South Africa's next Test, the first against Sri Lanka, at Newlands less than two weeks later. On the last day of the Newlands game, a delegation from the United Cricket Board had a largely amicable meeting with the parliamentary sports committee.

Bacher outlined the choice for cricket in an article in the *Sunday Times*, South Africa's largest-selling newspaper. "Either we take the majority of South Africans with us or we alienate them," he wrote. He insisted, though, that standards would not be compromised. "We must have excellence," he said in a separate interview. "Although cricket is a team game, you are alone when you have a bat or a ball in your hand. There is no place to hide an inferior player. We want our national team to be truly representative, but there are a lot of pressures, especially on the individuals in contention."

The issue is peculiarly South African and needs to be seen against the background of a country in which whites for decades enjoyed inordinate privileges in employment, education and sporting opportunities. In the new South Africa, there has been an active policy of affirmative action throughout society, with many top jobs being awarded to black people. Affirmative action has been applied either officially or unofficially at various levels of cricket since the formation of the

United Cricket Board in 1991. In the case of players from underprivileged back-grounds, potential is as important as performance. Ntini, from a village near King William's Town in the Eastern Cape, had been noticed while playing soft-ball Mini Cricket, which has introduced many thousands of youngsters to the game. Because of his cricketing ability, Ntini was awarded a scholarship to Dale College, a school with a strong cricket tradition. He quickly proved himself a fine schoolboy fast bowler and won selection to the senior Border provincial team in 1995–96, making his debut against England. His first victim was Alec Stewart. National under-15 and under-19 teams have long reflected the demographics of the "rainbow nation", with Ntini one of many to play at the highest junior level.

Bacher has put the onus on provinces to take the process further. "The selectors cannot be expected to pick black players for the national team when hardly any are playing at provincial level. The problem is not with the national selectors, it is with the provincial A teams. Not enough black players are getting opportunities." The UCB currently has an affirmative action policy up to provincial B level. That, Bacher indicated, may be extended to senior teams. "We are not a normal country. Nobody must delude themselves. Changes must be immediate."

BEWARE POSITIVE DISCRIMINATION
Matthew Engel, *Notes by the Editor*, 1999

In the midst of South Africa's triumphant series against West Indies, the South African selectors were informed that the team was not good enough. Steve Tshwete, the sports minister, said that if an all-white side were sent to the World Cup "it will be difficult for me to support them". The United Cricket Board has been obliged to respond with a policy of positive discrimination, fumbling and unclear at national level, overt and clear-cut below that. The initial objection to the old South Africa was that its teams were not chosen on merit. That is true once again. There is exquisite irony here, but it still makes me feel uneasy. What value is a South African cap to a player who knows he is not there on his own ability?

SOUTH AFRICA V ENGLAND 1999–2000
Colin Bateman, 2001

A unique and totally unexpected victory in the Fifth and final Test against South Africa – albeit subsequently devalued – could not mask another disappointing over-seas trip by England. The South Africans were much too strong and confident, and the revenge they sought for their series defeat in England in 1998, when they believed fate conspired against them, was obtained more comfortably than the 2–1 margin might suggest. England's status as one of the weakest teams in the world did not improve, despite the new stewardship of Nasser Hussain and Duncan Fletcher.

The tour took place against a background of political unrest in South African cricket, which was promoting a policy of "affirmative action". Provincial unions were expected to field teams of mixed colour, making allowances for the degree of ability. It was a thorny issue, and a few consciences were pricked when an all-white Northerns/Gauteng Combined XI was named to play England before the First Test. Displeasure turned to outrage when it was discovered that Geoffrey Toyana, a black batsman from Soweto, had been replaced in the original squad by Sven Koenig, a move prompted by the United Cricket Board president, Ray White. Although injury to David Townsend subsequently allowed the board to bring in Walter Masimula, a black fast bowler who played at the expense of Townsend's original replacement, Rudi Bryson, this eleventh-hour decision smacked of tokenism and the row rumbled on. It ended with White's resignation during the one-day triangular tournament that followed the Test series.

The political brouhaha did not improve the demeanour of South Africa's captain, Hansie Cronje, often a brooding figure, unhappy with his masters and his own form. Already disgruntled at starting the series with a short-term appointment for two Tests only, subsequently extended to cover the remaining Tests and the one-day games against England and Zimbabwe, he reportedly offered to drop himself before the Third at Durban because he strongly opposed the selectors' decision to leave out Jonty Rhodes. Throughout, Cronje was widely criticised for being too cautious tactically, yet at the end he was again a national champion, hailed both for the series victory and for his initiative on the last day at Centurion Park. Within months, however, his career, possibly his life, was in ruins. His captaincy of South Africa had become a source of national shame rather than pride. In April, following allegations of match-fixing by the Indian police – South Africa toured there after England's visit – Cronje confessed to accepting a bookmaker's money in return for "detailed information and forecasting" on the one-day series between India and South Africa. He was immediately stripped of the captaincy, and South Africa set up an inquiry into match-fixing, the King Commission, which heard in June that Cronje's involvement with bookmakers went back to 1995.

Not even the history-making Fifth Test escaped untarnished. After rain for three and a half days, this match at Centurion had appeared destined for a watery grave, the fate it suffered when England played in the inaugural Test there in November 1995. With South Africa still in the first innings of the match on the last morning, Cronje approached Hussain about a contrived finish, suggesting they each forfeit an innings to make a contest of it. Permitted in domestic competitions in similar circumstances, the forfeiting of one innings, let alone two, had never been seen in Test cricket before. At the time the Laws, subject to local playing conditions, allowed the forfeit only of a second innings. After some bartering, a deal was struck and England chased 249 to win in 76 overs, a target they reached with two wickets and five balls to spare.

Defeat ended South Africa's unbeaten sequence of 14 Tests since Headingley 1998, and some traditionalists held up their hands in horror at the "cheapening" of the five-day game. But most agreed, including match referee Barry Jarman and the travelling England supporters who had endured three miserable days without play, that Cronje's enterprise was to be applauded. What subsequently emerged at the King Commission hearing was that Cronje's initiative had been motivated by a Johannesburg bookmaker, Marlon Aronstam, who rewarded the South African captain with 53,000 rand (around £5,000) and a woman's leather jacket. As the odds favoured a draw, a win by either side was the most satisfactory result for bookmakers.

South Africa v England

At Johannesburg, November 25, 26, 27, 28, 1999.
South Africa won by an innings and 21 runs.

First Test

Colin Bateman, 2001

South Africa overpowered a new-look England side who went to the Wanderers full of optimism and left realising the scale of the task ahead. It was South Africa's tenth consecutive home Test win. The match was dominated by South Africa's peerless new-ball pairing of Donald and Pollock, who exploited perfect conditions for fast bowling to claim 19 wickets between them. Poor England. They turned up on the first morning to find a damp, spongy pitch underfoot and heavy, low clouds overhead. Then Cronje won the toss. It took just 17 deliveries to put all England's plans and preparation through a shredder as they lost four wickets for two runs, their worst start to a Test match.

Donald did the principal damage, bowling Atherton second ball with a late in-swinger. Four years earlier, Atherton had batted here for ten hours 43 minutes, scoring an unbeaten 185 to save the Second Test. Donald's devastating first two overs also accounted for Butcher and Stewart, out first ball, so that Chris Adams, coming in at No. 6, found himself batting to prevent a hat-trick within 15 minutes of his debut. With Hussain out third ball to an almost unplayable lifter from Pollock in between, any contest was as good as over. That England achieved 122 owed much to Vaughan, who impressed on his first outing, and some controlled hitting by Flintoff, back in Test cricket after 15 months' absence. But with the ball swinging through the air and seaming off the pitch, batting was a lottery.

Or it appeared that way until England had the ball in their hands. Gough, Caddick and Mullally lacked the potency of South Africa's fast men and, when Hussain turned to his support bowlers, the home team plundered runs at will on the second day as the sun shone and the pitch dried out. Without a specialist spinner to call on, he was unable to assert the necessary control over events. Gibbs and Cullinan were allowed to leave alone far too often against some wasteful bowling as they ensured that South Africa would build a commanding lead – the 15th time in consecutive Tests that England had conceded a first-innings deficit. Gibbs, recalled after missing the two preceding Tests against Zimbabwe through injury, fell 15 short of his first Test century at home, but Cullinan was in no mood to miss out on his fourth Test hundred of 1999. His 108 in four and a quarter hours, including 17 fours, put him alongside Dudley Nourse and Kirsten on a record nine hundreds for South Africa.

Three quick wickets on the third morning gave Gough a flattering five-wicket return. But, after removing Pollock and Donald with successive balls, he was denied the chance of a hat-trick – he had achieved one in his previous Test, back in January at Sydney – by the weather. Before Paul Adams could take guard, the umpires offered the light and the players went off. During the hour-long delay, Cronje declared.

Needing 281 to avoid an innings defeat, England were instantly in trouble. Pollock unleashed a wickedly fast, rising delivery that Atherton could only glove behind to be out first ball, his second pair and 19th duck in Tests. Only Derek Underwood, an *habitué* of the other end of the innings, had made as many for England. Stubborn resistance from Butcher, who spent 220 minutes grafting for 32, and Stewart meant England's innings was not always one-way traffic. Stewart, struck in the ribs by Pollock, put attack before occupation and hit a bold 86, with a six and 14 fours, before becoming Donald's tenth victim of the match. His 11th, Hamilton, was also his 75th against England, equalling in 14 Tests Hugh Tayfield's record from 15 games. More bad light meant the match went into the fourth day, when the lower-order antics of Flintoff and Caddick, who made a Test-best 48, persuaded Cronje to turn to Adams. Spin did the trick, extracting a return catch out of Flintoff, but it also prevented Pollock and Donald from becoming only the seventh pair to claim all 20 wickets in a Test.

Toss: South Africa. **England 122** (M. P. Vaughan 33, A. Flintoff 38; A. A. Donald 6-53, S. M. Pollock 4-16) **and 260** (M. A. Butcher 32, A. J. Stewart 86, A. Flintoff 36, A. R. Caddick 48; A. A. Donald 5-74, S. M. Pollock 4-64); **South Africa 403-9 dec.** (H. H. Gibbs 85, D. J. Cullinan 108, W. J. Cronje 44, L. Klusener 72, Extras 37; D. Gough 5-70, A. D. Mullally 3-80).

South Africa v England   Fifth Test
At Centurion, January 14, 15, 16, 17, 18, 2000. England won by two wickets.   Neil Manthorp, 2001

History was made on the final day when a match apparently reduced to the deadliest of finishes, following three consecutive playless days, was brought back to life by the captains. For the first time in Test cricket, innings were forfeited and this produced a memorable, entertaining climax. When play resumed, with South Africa still in the first innings, the many hundreds of travelling English supporters and a few hundred hardy locals had every reason to expect the worst. What they were treated to was a gripping finale that saw England win with five balls and two wickets remaining.

Five months after the match, however, came the bitterness of deceit when Cronje, South Africa's captain, admitted receiving money and a leather jacket from a bookmaker, who had urged him to initiate a positive result, rather than let the match peter out as a draw. At the King Commission inquiry into match-fixing, which opened in Cape Town in June, he insisted that his motives were "for the good of cricket", but the fact that financial reward formed a part of his motivation tainted the match for ever. History would also record that it was the first Test in which "fixing" was proven.

Hussain, understandably delighted [at the victory], paid special tribute to Cronje at the time. "It was a very special thing that Hansie did and I hope he gets the credit he deserves. It certainly was a great finish to be a part of." But later, when it emerged that corruption had played its regrettable part in the shaping of the final day, he would write in his newspaper column that England's win had been ruined. "We can't get away from that," he said. "It will always be remembered as a Test that was fixed." Yet the cricket was played as hard as both teams were able, and that is some consolation. Cronje's goal was to achieve a positive result and, while a captain without thought of personal gain might have opted for defence and the safety of a draw when the match was slipping away, South Africa did almost pull off a remarkable win.

South Africa v England, 1999–2000   Fifth Test

At Centurion, January 14, 15, 16, 17, 18, 2000. Result: England won by two wickets.

SOUTH AFRICA	First innings		Second innings forfeited
G. Kirsten c Adams b Gough		0	
J. H. Kallis b Caddick		25	
*W. J. Cronje c Maddy b Gough		0	
L. Klusener not out		61	
†M. V. Boucher b Mullally		22	
H. H. Gibbs c Adams b Caddick		3	
D. J. Cullinan c and b Mullally		46	
P. C. Strydom c Stewart b Silverwood		30	
S. M. Pollock run out		30	
P. R. Adams not out		4	
B 2, l-b 11, w 3, n-b 11		27	

1-1 2-15 3-50 4-55 5-102   (8 wkts dec.) 248
6-136 7-196 8-243
M. Hayward did not bat.

Gough 20–2–92–2; Caddick 19–7–47–2; Mullally 24–10–42–2; Silverwood 7–1–45–1;
Vaughan 2–0–9–0.

ENGLAND	First innings forfeited	Second innings
M. A. Butcher	– lbw b Klusener	36
M. A. Atherton	– c Boucher b Pollock	7
*N. Hussain	– c Gibbs b Pollock	25
†A. J. Stewart	– c Boucher b Hayward	73
C. J. Adams	– c Boucher b Hayward	1
M. P. Vaughan	– b Hayward	69
D. L. Maddy	– run out	3
A. R. Caddick	– c Boucher b Pollock	0
D. Gough	– not out	6
C. E. W. Silverwood	– not out	7
	B 4, l-b 9, w 4, n-b 7	24

1-28 2-67 3-90 4-102 5-228   (8 wkts) 251
6-236 7-236 8-240

A. D. Mullally did not bat.

Pollock 20–7–53–3; Hayward 17.1–3–61–3; Klusener 14–4–38–1; Kallis 13–2–44–0; Cronje 5–3–15–0;
Strydom 6–0–27–0.

Toss won by England   UMPIRES R. E. Koertzen and D. B. Hair
MAN OF THE MATCH C. J. Adams

INDIA v SOUTH AFRICA 2000

Dicky Rutnagur, 2001

By beating India 2–0 in a two-match rubber, South Africa ended India's sequence of 14 unbeaten home series since Pakistan won there in March 1987. Consequently, victory also gave them the distinction of becoming the only country in that 13-year period to win series in all three countries of the subcontinent. Sadly, South Africa's achievement would be first undermined by accusations of match-fixing against their captain, Hansie Cronje, and four team-mates, then overshadowed by Cronje's admission to the King Commission in June that he had accepted money from bookmakers since South Africa's tour of India in 1996. Cronje continued to deny all allegations of match-fixing, but the integrity of his captaincy, along with his team's record, had been seriously besmirched.

South Africa, despite the subsequent revelations by and about Cronje, deserve credit for their triumph. Their superiority was testimony to thorough tactical planning, disciplined bowling on and around off stump, and batting that was resolute, if seldom spectacular. Outstanding fast bowlers prevail on all surfaces, and Allan Donald, Shaun Pollock and Nantie Hayward certainly left bold marks on the series. Cronje and Jacques Kallis took important wickets by dint of swing and, with a match haul of seven wickets at Bangalore in only his second Test, left-arm spinner Nicky Boje hoist India with their own petard.

Kallis, the Man of the Series, batted in subdued style but played crucial innings in both Tests. In the low-scoring, closely fought First Test, Kumble and Murali Kartik were bowling venomously on a pitch that had become vicious. Kallis, who had made a tormented, undignified start, held his ground for three hours 11 minutes, if for only 36 not out. In the Second Test, he made 95 and his partnership of 164 with Lance Klusener virtually secured the series for South Africa.

India v South Africa	First Test
At Mumbai, February 24, 25, 26, 2000.	
South Africa won by four wickets.	Dicky Rutnagur, 2001

A pitch made to order could not mask India's shortcomings, but highlighting their weaknesses would not do justice to South Africa's achievement, particularly that of their fast bowlers, in winning with two days to spare. From its appearance – the surface was not just shorn by the mower but also scraped with a wire brush – it was clear that the ball would turn wickedly, and South Africa were persuaded to include both left-arm spinners, Eksteen and Boje, at the expense of the speed of Hayward. Instead it was Donald, Pollock and Kallis, backed up by Cronje, who determined the course of the match with skill and swing more than sheer pace.

Toss: India. **India 225** (S. R. Tendulkar 97, A. B. Agarkar 41*; J. H. Kallis 3-30) **and 113** (R. Dravid 37, S. C. Ganguly 31; S. M. Pollock 4-24, W. J. Cronje 3-23); **South Africa 176** (G. Kirsten 50, H. H. Gibbs 47, L. Klusener 33; J. Srinath 3-45, S. R. Tendulkar 3-10) **and 164-6** (H. H. Gibbs 46, J. H. Kallis 36*; A. Kumble 4-56).

India v South Africa · Second Test

At Bangalore, March 2, 3, 4, 5, 6, 2000.
South Africa won by an innings and 71 runs.   Dicky Rutnagur, 2001

Once again the loss of the toss did not inconvenience the South Africans. Their bowlers turned in another superlative effort to dismiss India on the first day, when the pitch was at its best for batting. Then, as it began to help the spinners, as anticipated, their batsmen played with determination and discipline to put the game and the series out of India's reach.

Toss: India. **India 158** (A. Kumble 36*) **and 250** (M. Azharuddin 102; N. Boje 5-83);
South Africa 479 (G. Kirsten 79, N. Boje 85, J. H. Kallis 95, D. J. Cullinan 53, L. Klusener 97, Extras 31; A. Kumble 6-143, M. Kartik 3-123).

SRI LANKA V SOUTH AFRICA 2000   Neil Manthorp, 2001

Hansie Cronje and South Africa's King Commission into match-fixing did not hang heavily on the minds of the country's cricketers when they departed for Sri Lanka on June 30, even though five of the nine players who testified at the inquiry were on the plane to Colombo. As soon as they arrived, however, many began to realise just how much emotion they had suppressed. Their former captain was everywhere and nowhere, his ghost haunting the senior players and confusing the new faces in the squad.

Shaun Pollock was diplomacy personified, accepting his responsibility as captain to speak honestly and answer questions whenever they were asked. At a packed news conference on the second day, he admitted there were many disillusioned cricket followers in South Africa whose trust and respect had to be regained. He promised that his new-look squad would never contemplate communication, let alone dealings, with bookmakers and that they would give "110 per cent effort" in every game they played.

It took three weeks at least for the players to settle, and to come to terms with the realisation that – for the first time in their careers – Cronje was not on tour. And would not be again. Jonty Rhodes admitted to looking for him at every practice during the first ten days, and while many were still smarting over his betrayal of them as a friend, they none the less missed him as both player and disciplinarian. The team stayed close to their hotel when they were not playing, and they were understandably reserved, waiting to see how they were regarded.

Without their best player of spin, Cronje, to counter the expected troop of spinners led by Muttiah Muralitharan, many expected Pollock's team to struggle in Sri Lanka. The team looked disorientated, and initially could not get to grips with a Sri Lankan side brimming with confidence. Pollock began his reign as Test captain with an innings defeat, Sri Lanka's first victory in six Tests between the two nations. That he and his team fought back to square the series spoke volumes for their character.

Sri Lanka v South Africa

First Test

At Galle, July 20, 21, 22, 23, 2000. Sri Lanka won by an innings and 15 runs.   Neil Manthorp, 2001

Sri Lanka's victory in four days was a triumph of planning and execution, with the match following a course prescribed and predicted from three days before it began. For match-winner Muralitharan, his second-best Test analysis of 13 for 171 provided further evidence that he was the complete off-spinner, the ultimate attacking bowler. For South Africa, it was like being trapped in a nightmare. Everything pointed towards a contest between Muralitharan and the touring batsmen after his domination of them in the preceding Singer Triangular Series. Not one South African had felt comfortable against him; none even pretended to. Consequently, no one was surprised that the match started on a dry, cracked pitch that might have been ready for play two days earlier.

Maintaining complete control over the degree of spin of his stock off-break, revelling in both his "mystery ball", which turned the other way, and a top-spinner that darted towards the knees of the batsman, he reduced batting to a lottery. Cullinan played with immense skill to remain unbeaten with 114 after four and a half hours, yet admitted: "I could have been out three or four times. He's unique." On occasions, Muralitharan almost toyed with the batsmen as he gleefully tossed high, looping deliveries wide and short of off stump, teasing them into stepping back to cut. Rhodes and Boucher were both bowled, and embarrassed, when the ball spun back prodigiously. When South Africa followed on, 284 behind, leg-spinner Chandana had the temerity to take two of the first three wickets to fall. But Murali claimed the last seven to become only the sixth bowler in Tests to dismiss all 11 opposing batsmen. When he achieved his career-best 16 for 220 against England at The Oval in 1998, Alec Stewart's wicket had evaded him.

Toss: Sri Lanka. **Sri Lanka 522** (M. S. Atapattu 54, S. T. Jayasuriya 148, D. P. M. D. Jayawardene 167, W. P. U. J. C. Vaas 54, Extras 34; S. M. Pollock 3-73, P. R. Adams 3-184); **South Africa 238** (D. J. Cullinan 114*; M. Muralitharan 6-87) **and 269** (G. Kirsten 55, J. H. Kallis 40, J. N. Rhodes 63*, N. Boje 35; M. Muralitharan 7-84).

Sri Lanka v South Africa

Second Test

At Kandy, July 30, 31, August 1, 2, 2000. South Africa won by seven runs.   Neil Manthorp, 2001

South Africa avenged their innings defeat at Galle with a narrow victory in a match that was compulsive viewing from first ball to last, attracting larger crowds each day as it neared its climax. They came to see Sri Lanka clinch the series; instead South Africa delivered a knockout blow on the fourth day to square the series.

Winning the toss meant a gamble, for the pitch was a strange hybrid. Prepared as a dry turner, it had then sweated profusely after two days under heavy, tarpaulin covers while it rained incessantly. Jayasuriya unsurprisingly let his bowlers loose on it and South Africa crashed to 34 for five in 19 overs. The recovery was effected by Klusener and Boucher, who opted for a thrilling counter-attack rather than attritional repair work. Hitting the spinners over the top, and thrashing anything vaguely short, they put on 124, a sixth-wicket record for South Africa against Sri Lanka, before Klusener misjudged Muralitharan's agility off his own bowling and Boucher was run out. However, Klusener used his anger at himself constructively, and forged on towards his third Test hundred, squeezing 80 runs from the last two wickets and encouraging rare discipline from Adams and Hayward, who had replaced Ntini. The total slipped past 250 before Klusener was left unbeaten on 118, containing 13 fours and two sixes in 220 balls, an innings he described as his best yet.

In reply, Atapattu produced an exhibition of such impeccable, straight-bat technique that it resembled illustrations from a coaching manual. Together with the pugnacious Ranatunga, in his penultimate Test, he took the score to 286 for four, a lead of 33: Atapattu had a century, Ranatunga a half-century. But a desperate Pollock, bowling with skill and passion, instigated a collapse worth six for 22 in seven overs. Ranatunga had more than one reason to look watery-eyed at umpire Harper when lbw to a rising delivery that struck him on the box.

South Africa lost three wickets working off the arrears, but for almost four hours Kallis survived on a pitch that, by the third day, was offering exotic and quirky bounce. His 87 contained long periods of defence, mainly on the back foot reading the spinners off the pitch, but there were also moments of aggression when he used his feet and charged the bowling. Even so, South Africa's lead was only 137 with two wickets left when they resumed on the fourth morning. Boje, a No. 9 with four first-class hundreds, coaxed another partnership out of Adams, but ultimately Sri Lanka had more than five sessions to make 177.

The start was sensational: Atapattu and Jayasuriya were both lbw first ball, and at lunch Sri Lanka were 41 for four, with Ranatunga already on his way to a 36-ball 50 that made him the second Sri Lankan to pass 5,000 Test runs. No matter what Pollock tried, no matter how defensive his field settings or the bowling, Ranatunga found the middle of the bat and the gaps in the field. Arnold dropped anchor and admired his former captain during a stand of 109 that seemed to be winning the match. Then he lost concentration and was lbw to Boje for 40. Ranatunga's innings, with 15 fours, ended just before tea when Rhodes snapped up a reflex catch at short leg off the full face of the bat. Suddenly South Africa sniffed victory, although Sri Lanka then needed only 16 with three wickets still in hand. Klusener, bowling slow, awkward cutters and "grippers" off just five paces, yorked Chandana first ball after the break, and five overs later Vaas, jittery and nervous, was run out by the injured Zoysa's runner, Jayasuriya, who had gone out himself to avoid exactly this possibility. Muralitharan was then unkindly given out caught behind off his first ball, which summed up an unhappy match for umpires Harper and Gamini Silva, standing in his first Test.

Sri Lanka v South Africa, 2000   Second Test

At Kandy, July 30, 31, August 1, 2, 2000. Result: South Africa won by seven runs.

SOUTH AFRICA

	First innings		Second innings	
G. Kirsten lbw b Vaas		0	– b Dharmasena	13
N. D. McKenzie c Jayawardene b Zoysa		0	– b Zoysa	1
J. H. Kallis lbw b Muralitharan		16	– b Muralitharan	87
D. J. Cullinan b Dharmasena		2	– b Muralitharan	6
J. N. Rhodes b Dharmasena		12	– c Sangakkara b Jayasuriya	33
L. Klusener not out		118	– c Sangakkara b Jayasuriya	4
†M. V. Boucher run out		60	– c Atapattu b Muralitharan	15
*S. M. Pollock c Jayawardene b Chandana		5	– c Sangakkara b Vaas	20
N. Boje lbw b Chandana		0	– c sub b Chandana	27
P. R. Adams c Jayawardene b Dharmasena		6	– not out	14
M. Hayward b Muralitharan		13	– lbw b Chandana	0
B 9, l-b 6, n-b 6		21	B 7, l-b 1, n-b 3	11

1-0 2-4 3-16 4-34 5-34 6-158 7-173 8-173   **253**   1-10 2-37 3-50 4-121 5-128 6-153 7-186   **231**
9-210   8-186 9-231

First Innings – Vaas 8–5–11–1; Zoysa 6–2–16–1; Dharmasena 20–3–58–3; Muralitharan 30.5–3–95–2; Chandana 20–2–58–2.
Second Innings – Vaas 14–6–17–1; Zoysa 5–0–17–1; Dharmasena 16–2–47–1; Muralitharan 36–8–76–3; Chandana 9.5–0–21–2; Jayasuriya 13–1–45–2.

SRI LANKA

	First innings		Second innings	
M. S. Atapattu lbw b Pollock		120	– lbw b Pollock	0
*S. T. Jayasuriya c Kallis b Hayward		28	– lbw b Hayward	0
R. P. Arnold run out		28	– lbw b Boje	40
D. K. P. M. D. Jayawardene c Cullinan b Boje		18	– c Boucher b Hayward	1
†K. C. Sangakkara run out		24	– c Hayward b Kallis	5
A. Ranatunga lbw b Hayward		54	– c Rhodes b Boje	88
H. D. P. K. Dharmasena c Boucher b Pollock		3	– c Rhodes b Klusener	1
W. P. U. J. C. Vaas c Rhodes b Pollock		4	– (9) run out	5
U. D. U. Chandana not out		1	– (8) b Klusener	16
D. N. T. Zoysa b Kallis		3	– not out	2
M. Muralitharan b Kallis		0	– c Boucher b Boje	0
B 6, l-b 12, n-b 7		25	B 1, l-b 6, w 2, n-b 2	11

1-53 2-109 3-142 4-182 5-286 6-296 7-300   **308**   1-0 2-5 3-9 4-21 5-130 6-133   **169**
8-303 9-308   7-161 8-161 9-169

First Innings – Pollock 24–5–83–3; Hayward 22–6–67–2; Kallis 11.4–4–18–2; Boje 15–2–50–1; Klusener 11–2–21–0; Adams 14–1–44–0; Cullinan 2–0–7–0.
Second Innings – Pollock 11–4–38–1; Hayward 5–1–15–2; Kallis 8–1–25–1; Adams 3–1–26–0; Klusener 13–3–34–2; Boje 10.1–4–24–3.

Toss won by Sri Lanka   UMPIRES D. J. Harper and G. Silva
MEN OF THE MATCH L. Klusener and A. Ranatunga

WEST INDIES V SOUTH AFRICA 2001
Tony Cozier, 2002

On their first full tour of the West Indies, nine years after a fleeting visit for their inaugural, unsuccessful post-apartheid Test in April 1992, South Africa became the first team to triumph in twin Test and one-day international series in the Caribbean. They won the Second and Fourth Tests and drew the First and Third before the West Indians gained a consolation victory in the Fifth. Their superiority was even more pronounced in the shorter game, where they won 5–2 after a last-ball setback in the opening match.

Even though West Indies had lost only one Test series at home in 28 years, to the Australians in 1994–95, South Africa's success was not unexpected. Since their 5–0 whitewash of West Indies at home in 1998–99, they had won 12 of their 21 Tests, and lost only two. They had not lost a series since 1998 in England. Their record in limited-overs cricket was similarly impressive. If the embarrassment of Hansie Cronje's dealings with bookmakers lingered, it had no effect, either on or off the field.

The South Africans' strengths were all-round depth, athletic fielding and obvious self-confidence. Their captain, Shaun Pollock, set a fine example. His unbeaten 106 at Bridgetown – his second Test hundred – was one of only five centuries on either side in the Tests, he headed the batting averages with 302 at 75.50, took 20 inexpensive Test wickets, and was the most economical bowler in the one-day internationals. Not only did he collect both Cable & Wireless series trophies, he also won the individual award for the outstanding player of the Tests and limited-overs games.

West Indies v South Africa
Second Test

At Port-of-Spain, March 17, 18, 19, 20, 21, 2001. South Africa won by 69 runs. Tony Cozier, 2002

The promise of a home victory attracted a last-day crowd of 12,000. West Indies started at 32 for one, requiring another 200 to go one up in the series, but lost four for 19 at the start and five for 19 either side of tea to fall well short. In between, Hooper and Sarwan had raised local hopes with a sixth-wicket partnership of 92, but the captain was eventually left stranded and forlorn. For West Indians, and Trinidadians in particular, it was a disappointing finale to what was billed as the Golden Test; Queen's Park Oval was staging its 50th Test, the eighth ground – and first outside England and Australia – to reach its half-century.

The match itself had a golden moment, midway through the third day, when Walsh became the first player to take 500 Test wickets. There were immediate and emotional celebrations. His team-mates formed a guard of honour as they filed off at tea, when the first man to greet him was Donald, his South African counterpart, who also paid tribute after play as the West Indies Cricket Board presented Walsh with a trophy.

West Indies needed 232 to win, the lowest total of the match. But Ntini struck a vital blow on the final morning when he had Lara lbw for his first Test duck on his home ground, leaving them 51 for five. Hooper and Sarwan kept the contest alive with composed batting, until Sarwan was lured into hooking Kallis's third bouncer of the penultimate over before tea straight to square leg. Jacobs was run out by Gibbs's direct hit soon afterwards, and there was nothing Hooper could do to halt the slide as South Africa hurried to victory.

Toss: South Africa. **South Africa 286** (H. H. Gibbs 34, J. H. Kallis 53, D. J. Cullinan 103; N. A. M. McLean 3-60, D. Ramnarine 3-57) **and 287** (H. H. Gibbs 87, D. J. Cullinan 73, M. V. Boucher 38; C. A. Walsh 6-61, M. Dillon 3-58); **West Indies 342** (W. W. Hinds 56, M. N. Samuels 35, R. R. Sarwan 34, C. L. Hooper 53, R. D. Jacobs 93*; A. A. Donald 4-91, S. M. Pollock 3-55) **and 162** (R. R. Sarwan 39, C. L. Hooper 54*; J. H. Kallis 4-40).

TIME FOR A NEW TROPHY
Matthew Engel, *Notes by the Editor*, 2004

England–South Africa matches have been one of the highlights of world cricket ever since South Africa were readmitted. All the Test series have been intensely, sometimes heroically, fought. Yet these encounters, dating back 115 years, still do not have their own trophy to match the Ashes, the *Wisden* Trophy (England–West Indies), the Worrell Trophy (Australia–West Indies) or the Border–Gavaskar (Australia–India). They should have. It would be a nice gesture, and an appropriate one, if the ECB were to suggest that the Nelson Mandela Trophy should be inaugurated during the 2004-05 tour.

D'OLIVEIRA FOR EVER
Matthew Engel, *Notes by the Editor*, 2005

A year ago I proposed in these Notes that Test matches between England and South Africa should have a permanent trophy to match the Ashes, the *Wisden* Trophy, the Border–Gavaskar and so on. I suggested naming it after Nelson Mandela. Instead, South Africa put up the Basil D'Oliveira Trophy, which was an infinitely more elegant and appropriate answer. Dolly is a son of the game, and of both nations. The South African board said it was only for their home Tests, which would be meaningless. The series this winter showed yet again that when these two teams meet, they produce wonderful, well-fought contests (and also, let's say it again, that there is nothing in cricket, and few things in life, to beat a close five-Test series). The D'Oliveira Trophy should be at stake every time they meet.

New Zealand – Hadlee's Heroics

N ew Zealand seem to be eternally the poor relations of Test cricket, tucked away in half-summers here and there, putting up plucky, committed performances in one-day competitions without ever quite setting the world on fire. In some ways this is an unfair perception – because we don't see enough of them, it is difficult to have that identification we have with, say, the Australians. A three-match series once every four years is hardly sufficient to gauge the true quality of New Zealand cricket.

I fear this chapter, too, will give only the most basic sense of New Zealand's performances over the past 30 years – the Hadlee-inspired rise under Jeremy Coney in the mid-1980s, when they were good enough to win series against Australia and England within a period of less than 12 months, the subsequent dip that saw them become international fall guys, and the return to respectability under Stephen Fleming, who fulfilled predictions that his reign would be a long one.

They have produced some very fine players – including Martin Crowe, Fleming himself, Geoff Howarth, John Bracewell, Chris Cairns, Daniel Vettori and Glenn Turner, though the latter's pomp largely preceded the period covered by this Anthology – but they have rarely been able to field an XI that didn't include a few makeweights. In seven-a-side, the New Zealand teams of the past 30 years would have been a match for anyone. Only once, in the period of Richard Hadlee's maturity, did it not matter than New Zealand had the odd weak point. His bowling – with extraordinary analyses such as the one recorded in the 1985 victory over Australia at Brisbane – made up for all deficiencies. In his prime, which came surprisingly late in his career, he counted for three. With him in the side, anything was possible. He combined the genius of Botham with the mind of a computer. Briefly, he turned New Zealand into world-beaters.   S. M.

NEW ZEALAND V ENGLAND 1978   First Test

At Wellington, February 10, 11, 12, 14, 15, 1978. New Zealand won by 72 runs.   Alex Bannister, 1979

After 48 years and in the 48th Test between the two countries, New Zealand beat England for the first time. Though England's form and fortune struck rock bottom in the crucial final innings, it was a great and deserved triumph for New Zealand and for Richard Hadlee.

Success was all the sweeter, and more exciting, because of the remarkable turnaround of the match. At tea on the fourth day the air was loaded with fore-boding for New Zealand; the portents were all for the pattern of history to continue. Willis, supported by superb catching, had caused a collapse of nine for 41 in two hours and England, with time of no concern, had to score a moderate 137 to win.

Only two hours later, New Zealand gloom was transformed into joy as England, with Rose retired with a bruised right arm, tottered on the brink of defeat with eight down for 53. England, in turn, had been routed by Richard Hadlee and Collinge. The next morning, after a frustrating delay of 40 minutes for rain, New Zealand took 49 minutes to complete a famous victory in an understandably emotional atmosphere. The crowd gathered in front of the pavilion and sang "For they are jolly good fellows", followed by three cheers.

Hadlee fittingly took the last two wickets. In the first innings he had four for 74, and in the second six for 26. Apart from one over by Dayle Hadlee, Richard Hadlee and Collinge bowled unchanged as England were dismissed for 64. England's previous lowest total against New Zealand was 181 at Christchurch in 1930 – the first series between the countries. Without detracting in any way from the magnifi-cence of Hadlee and Collinge, who took his 100th Test and 500th first-class wicket during the match – and twice dismissed the key batsman Boycott – it would be kind to draw a discreet veil over England's performance. Both Hadlee and Collinge tore into the attack with hostility, skill, and speed on a pitch of uneven bounce, and England's response, once Boycott was bowled off his pads, was inept in the extreme.

New Zealand v England, 1978 — First Test

At Wellington, February 10, 11, 12, 14, 15, 1978. Result: New Zealand won by 72 runs.

NEW ZEALAND	First innings		Second innings	
J. G. Wright lbw b Botham		55	c Roope b Willis	19
R. W. Anderson c Taylor b Old		28	lbw b Old	26
G. P. Howarth c Botham b Old		13	c Edmonds b Willis	21
*M. G. Burgess b Willis		9	c Boycott b Botham	6
B. E. Congdon c Taylor b Old		44	c Roope b Willis	0
J. M. Parker c Rose b Willis		16	c Edmonds b Willis	4
†W. K. Lees c Taylor b Old		1	lbw b Hendrick	11
R. J. Hadlee not out		27	c Boycott b Willis	2
D. R. Hadlee c Taylor b Old		1	c Roope b Botham	2
R. O. Collinge b Old		1	c Edmonds b Hendrick	6
S. L. Boock b Botham		4	not out	0
B 12, l-b 3, w 1, n-b 13		29	B 2, l-b 9, w 2, n-b 13	26

1-42 2-96 3-114 4-152 5-191 6-193 7-194 8-196   228   1-54 2-82 3-93 4-93 5-98 6-99 7-104   123
9-208 10-228   8-116 9-123 10-123

First innings – Willis 25–7–65–2; Hendrick 17–2–46–0; Old 30–11–54–6; Edmonds 3–1–7–0; Botham 12.6–2–27–2.

Second innings – Willis 15–2–32–5; Hendrick 10–2–16–2; Old 9–2–32–1; Edmonds 1–0–4–0; Botham 9.3–3–13–2.

England	First innings		Second innings
B. C. Rose c Lees b Collinge	21	– not out	5
*G. Boycott c Congdon b Collinge	77	– b Collinge	1
G. Miller b Boock	24	– c Anderson b Collinge	4
†R. W. Taylor c and b Collinge	8	– (7) run out	0
D. W. Randall c Burgess b R. J. Hadlee	4	– (4) lbw b Collinge	9
G. R. J. Roope c Lees b R. J. Hadlee	37	– (5) c Lees b R. J. Hadlee	0
I. T. Botham c Burgess b R. J. Hadlee	7	– (6) c Boock b R. J. Hadlee	19
C. M. Old b R. J. Hadlee	10	– lbw b R. J. Hadlee	9
P. H. Edmonds lbw b Congdon	4	– c Parker b R. J. Hadlee	11
M. Hendrick lbw b Congdon	0	– c Parker b R. J. Hadlee	0
R. G. D. Willis not out	6	– c Howarth b R. J. Hadlee	3
L-b 4, n-b 13	17	N-b 3	3

1-39 2-89 3-108 4-126 5-183 6-188 7-203 8-205   215   1-2 2-8 3-18 4-18 5-38 6-38 7-53 8-53   64
9-206 10-215   9-63 10-64

First innings – R. J. Hadlee 28–5–74–4; Collinge 18–5–42–3; D. R. Hadlee 21–5–47–0;
Boock 10–5–21–1; Congdon 17.4–11–14–2.
Second innings – R. J. Hadlee 13.3–4–26–6; Collinge 13–5–35–3; D. R. Hadlee 1–1–0–0.

Toss won by England   Umpires W. R. C. Gardiner and R. L. Monteith

A Botham-inspired England won the Second Test, and the Third was drawn, so the series was shared.

New Zealand v West Indies 1980   R. T. Brittenden, 1981

New Zealand's first victory in a Test rubber at home should have been a happy occasion, but the New Zealand cricket public, which had looked forward keenly to the West Indians' visit, was glad to see the back of them. New Zealand won the First Test by the narrowest of margins, and drew the remaining two. Yet the West Indians lost more than a Test series. Their reputation for sportsmanship went too. There were several extremely unsavoury incidents on the field in the first two Tests, and the situation was not improved by the extravagant statements made by their harassed manager, Willie Rodriguez.

There could be some sympathy for the West Indians, coming to New Zealand after a particularly demanding tour of Australia and having to do without Richards, because of injury. Their main complaint in New Zealand was about the umpiring, and in retrospect there is little doubt that if both sides suffered from difficult, debatable decisions, more went against West Indies than against New Zealand. Both Mr Rodriguez and the captain, Lloyd, said there should be neutral umpires in Test matches. Such complaints by touring teams are by no means uncommon; they have been made in every cricketing country for years. But Mr Rodriguez, after stating at a press conference in Christchurch that he did not think the umpiring was biased, only incompetent, claimed after his departure that the West Indians had had to get batsmen out nine times before getting a decision. And his allegations went well beyond the bounds of acceptable comment when he claimed the West Indians were "set up; that there was no way we could win a Test"; that New Zealand were celebrating 50 years in Tests and were "determined to do something about it." This thinly veiled suggestion that there had been collaboration between the New Zealand administration and its umpires was highly insulting to men of integrity.

On the field, the West Indian players behaved in an extraordinary fashion. In the First Test Holding, having had an appeal disallowed, kicked the stumps out of the ground at the batsmen's end. When West Indies lost the match, Greenidge showed similar ill-temper as he left the field. At Christchurch in the Second Test, Croft, after being no-balled, flicked off the bails as he walked back, and a little later ran in very close to the umpire, F. R. Goodall – so close that the batsman could not see him – and shouldered Goodall heavily. It was the height of discourtesy when Goodall, wishing on two occasions to speak to Lloyd about Croft's behaviour, had to walk all the way to the West Indian captain, standing deep in the slips. Lloyd took not a step to meet him.

It was in this match that the West Indians refused to take the field after tea on the third day, saying they would not continue unless umpire Goodall was removed. They were finally persuaded to continue 12 minutes late. That evening they emptied their dressing room and there was a distinct prospect that the tour would end there and then. Following protracted negotiations with the New Zealand Board of Control it was agreed to continue the match and the rest of the tour. The board made clear its feeling that Croft, after his attack on Goodall, should not be considered for the Auckland Test, but in the event he did play.

The Auckland Test, the last of the series, produced yet another extraordinary situation. Four senior members of the West Indian team booked flights home which would have required their leaving the ground soon after lunch on the last day of the Test. However, they were dissuaded from this dramatic action after representations from the New Zealand board.

The West Indians, being badly led and managed, were the author of their own misfortunes. For a side described as the best in the world, and the strongest since the 1948 Australians, this was singularly disappointing. It was extraordinary that New Zealand, held in scant regard by the West Indians and everyone else, actually deserved their narrow victory, for they played better cricket and played as a team, whereas the West Indians sulked or stormed in turn.

The West Indian bowlers persistently dropped the ball far too short when there was movement off the seam. They seemed intent on bouncing the New Zealanders out. And when the New Zealand bowlers used a fuller length, the touring batsmen got themselves out trying to cut or hook. In the simplest terms, they failed to adapt to changed conditions. Their outstanding batsman was Haynes, who had the technique and the temperament to counter good, steady bowling when conditions were helpful for seam bowlers – as they were at the start of each Test. The others showed flashes of ability, but lacked discipline. Garner was the best of the bowlers. The fielding was very patchy, a good many catches being dropped.

Howarth and Edgar played some fine innings for New Zealand, and Richard Hadlee, the Man of the Series, bowled most effectively. New Zealand's success was attributable largely, however, to the advance made by the left-arm bowler, Troup, who was sharper of pace, more accurate and more durable than previously. Except for one bad hour at Auckland, New Zealand's fielding was excellent.

A photograph of Michael Holding kicking down the stumps appears on page 145.

New Zealand v West Indies   First Test

At Dunedin, February 8, 9, 10, 12, 13, 1980. New Zealand won by one wicket.   R. T. Brittenden, 1981

Clear evidence of an inability to adjust to New Zealand conditions was given by West Indies' batting on the first day. Lloyd, having won the toss, made a questionable decision in batting first, for the ball often kept rather low and there was sharp movement off the pitch. Only Haynes saw the need to get on to the front foot as much as possible, and against the pace attack he batted several inches outside his crease. He was in for all the three and a half hours of an innings which yielded only 140. Four West Indian batsmen, with their partiality for playing back, were lbw to balls cutting into them. Others lost their wickets trying to hook or cut in conditions which made such shots extremely risky. The first three wickets fell in Hadlee's first 13 balls, for four runs, and after Haynes and Lloyd had fought it out for 112 minutes there was little resistance.

The West Indian bowlers were as much at fault as their batsmen as New Zealand built up a lead of 109. They bowled much too short, unlike the New Zealanders who had made the most of the conditions by keeping the ball up. The New Zealand batsmen took a physical hammering, but they showed considerable determination in grafting for their runs. Edgar was in almost five hours for his 65, Howarth just over two hours for 33, but their stand of 67 was followed by a swift decline against fiercely hostile bowling until the late-order batsmen again came to the rescue. [Lance] Cairns, a powerful hitter, took three sixes in an over from Parry which brought him 20 runs, and Hadlee had nine fours in his 51; their eighth-wicket partnership of 54 took just 35 minutes and swung the game New Zealand's way.

There were only 70 minutes' play on the third day, which left West Indies 18 for one, and the fourth was dominated by Haynes and Hadlee. At 29 for four West Indies were in dire straits, but there were stands of 87 between Haynes and King and 64 between Haynes and Deryck Murray. The West Indian tail failed, however, and New Zealand were left needing only 104 to win. By lunch, under intense pressure, they had fought to 33 for two. About 20 minutes before lunch, Parker was given not out when Holding appealed for a catch by the wicket-keeper, which prompted Holding to demolish the stumps at the batsman's end with a full swing of the right foot. In the afternoon West Indies seemed to have the game won. Howarth was third out at 40, and 15 minutes later New Zealand were 44 for six. Webb went at 54, but once more there was strong resistance from the tailenders. Hadlee and Cairns added 19, with Hadlee playing some fine forcing strokes; Cairns and Troup put on 27, with determination much more of a factor than finesse. At tea it was 95 for eight.

Only one run had been added after tea when Holding beat Cairns, but the ball touched the off stump without dislodging a bail. When Cairns was out at 100, Boock, whose best Test score was eight, saw out the last five balls of Holding's over. Garner bowled the final over. The first ball produced a bye. Boock, the non-striker, tried to make it two runs and turning back was almost run out. Second ball, he survived an appeal for lbw. He kept the next two out and then squeezed two runs backward of point to level the scores. The last ball went from his pads to backward square and the batsmen ran the leg-bye, Parry's return to the non-striker's end going wildly astray. It was the narrowest of victories, but well-earned. Hadlee took 11 wickets for the match and set a Test record of seven leg-before decisions.

New Zealand v West Indies, 1980 — First Test

At Dunedin, February 8, 9, 10, 12, 13, 1980. Result: New Zealand won by one wicket.

WEST INDIES

	First innings		Second innings	
C. G. Greenidge c Cairns b Hadlee	2	lbw b Hadlee	3
D. L. Haynes c and b Cairns	55	c Webb b Troup	105
L. G. Rowe lbw b Hadlee	1	lbw b Hadlee	12
A. I. Kallicharran lbw b Hadlee	0	c Cairns b Troup	0
*C. H. Lloyd lbw b Hadlee	24	c Lees b Hadlee	5
C. L. King c Coney b Troup	14	c Boock b Cairns	41
†D. L. Murray c Edgar b Troup	6	lbw b Hadlee	30
D. R. Parry b Boock	17	c and b Hadlee	1
J. Garner c Howarth b Cairns	0	b Hadlee	2
M. A. Holding lbw b Hadlee	4	c Cairns b Troup	3
C. E. H. Croft not out	0	not out	1
L-b 8, n-b 9	17	L-b 4, n-b 5	9

1-3 2-4 3-4 4-72 5-91 6-105 7-124 8-135 — 140
9-136 10-140

1-4 2-21 3-24 4-29 5-117 6-180 7-186 — 212
8-188 9-209 10-212

First innings – Hadlee 20–9–34–5; Troup 17–6–26–2; Cairns 19.5–4–32–2; Boock 13–4–31–1.
Second innings – Hadlee 36–13–68–6; Troup 36.4–13–57–3; Cairns 25–10–63–1; Boock 11–4–15–0.

NEW ZEALAND

	First innings		Second innings	
J. G. Wright b Holding	21	b Holding	11
B. A. Edgar lbw b Parry	65	c Greenidge b Holding	6
*G. P. Howarth c Murray b Croft	33	c Greenidge b Croft	11
J. M. Parker b Croft	0	c Murray b Garner	5
P. N. Webb lbw b Parry	5	(6) lbw b Garner	5
J. V. Coney b Holding	8	(5) lbw b Croft	2
†W. K. Lees run out	18	lbw b Garner	0
R. J. Hadlee c Lloyd b Garner	51	b Garner	17
B. L. Cairns b Croft	30	c Murray b Holding	19
G. B. Troup c Greenidge b Croft	0	not out	7
S. L. Boock not out	0	not out	2
B 5, l-b 2, n-b 11	18	B 7, l-b 5, n-b 7	19

1-42 2-109 3-110 4-133 5-145 6-159 7-168 8-232 — 249
9-236 10-249

1-15 2-28 3-40 4-44 5-44 6-44 — (9 wkts) 104
7-54 8-73 9-100

First innings – Holding 22–5–50–2; Croft 25–3–64–4; Garner 25.5–8–51–1; King 1–0–3–0; Parry 22–6–63–2.
Second innings – Holding 16–7–24–3; Croft 11–2–25–2; Garner 23–6–36–4.

Toss won by West Indies — UMPIRES F. R. Goodall and J. B. R. Hastie

ENGLAND V NEW ZEALAND 1983   Graeme Wright, 1984

After 52 years, and at the 29th attempt, New Zealand beat England in a Test match in England. For that victory the tenth New Zealand side to England will hold a lasting place in its country's cricket history. Unbeaten outside the Test matches, Geoff Howarth's team may be regarded alongside its most eminent predecessors, although in some respects it failed to fulfil expectations. The other three Tests were lost by convincing margins, two of them in four days, and New Zealand failed to reach the semi-finals of the Prudential Cup, which occupied the team's interest in June before the first-class tour began.

The problems of choosing a team to cope with a programme of limited-overs and first-class cricket have in the past been presented as one reason for the poor performance of touring sides facing dual commitments, but this could not be applied to the 1983 New Zealanders. They represented the core of New Zealand's recent successes in both forms of the game. Howarth, Richard Hadlee and John Wright (as well as Glenn Turner in the Prudential Cup squad) knew English conditions from regular county cricket, while Lance Cairns, Martin Crowe and Evan Gray had recently played league cricket in England. Jeff Crowe had played for South Australia in the Sheffield Shield for five years. No previous New Zealand side to England could boast such experience.

Following the final Test, Willis, the England captain, said there was a need for New Zealand to find some fast bowlers, and certainly, Hadlee apart, the New Zealand attack had held few fears for England's batsmen. Neither Ewen Chatfield nor Martin Snedden, the candidates to share the new ball with Hadlee, was better than a useful fast-medium, with Snedden the quicker of the two and the 33-year-old Chatfield the more accurate. It speaks volumes, perhaps, that Chatfield's five for 95 in sympathetic conditions at Headingley was a personal best in Test cricket. Although surprising batsmen occasionally with unexpected lift and away movement, he lacked that decisive edge to open a Test attack. Snedden failed to do himself justice. Hit for 105 in 12 overs on his first appearance in England (v England in the World Cup at The Oval), he took time to find an English length and had too few weapons on a good wicket. The medium-paced Cairns, whose big hitting frequently provided brief entertainment, also began the tour out of sorts but regained form with eight wickets against Warwickshire on the eve of the Second Test. With ten wickets he played the major role in that historic Headingley victory. In addition to swing he had at his disposal an excellent leg-cutter, a useful slower ball and even a leg-spinner.

Chosen as Man of the Series, Hadlee always lived up to his reputation and his own high standards. His bowling, off a shortened run-up, was a model for an aspiring fast bowler, full of variation, control and hostility. At 33 he remained one of the world's leading fast bowlers, as well as strengthening his claims to a place among the top all-rounders. His left-handed batting had few frills but his approach was undeniably effective. His 21 wickets were a record for a New Zealand bowler against England.

England v New Zealand

Second Test

At Leeds, July 28, 29, 30, August 1, 1983. New Zealand won by five wickets.   John Thicknesse, 1984

New Zealand's first victory in a Test in England, following 17 defeats and 11 draws, arrived shortly after tea on the fourth day when Coney completed their task of scoring 101 with a leg-side four off Botham – the first ball of the only over Willis permitted Botham, so unintelligently had he bowled in New Zealand's first innings. Because England were in almost as hopeless a position after three days as they had been two years earlier in the Test against Australia upon which Botham made such an imperishable impact, only about 3,000 spectators saw the winning hit. But more than 30,000 had watched the game develop and all knew New Zealand's groundwork was well laid. For England, only Willis, who took the nine wickets he needed to become the fourth man to reach 300 in Test cricket, and Gower, with a handsome but unavailing 112 not out in the second innings, had reason to remember it with satisfaction. The toss was admittedly important, enabling Howarth to give his bowlers first use of a pitch that started damp to make it last; but in matters of skill, not excluding team selection, they proved themselves the better side.

It was happy, too, that the man who made the winning hit should have a sense of history: with Willis, charging down the slope at the end from which he took his eight for 43 against Australia in 1981, New Zealand hearts were fluttering when the lanky Coney walked in to bat at 61 for four. Nerves had let them down before in similar positions. A fifth wicket fell, all five to Willis, at 83. But Coney kept a steady head and with Hadlee, watched by father Walter, steered New Zealand home. Later, asked what was in his mind as Willis imperilled what had looked a fairly simple victory, Coney modestly tipped his cap to history by saying: "The main feeling was thinking of all the New Zealand players who have been coming here for 52 years, better players than myself, and making sure that their sweat and effort had not been in vain."

But despite Coney's contribution, and workmanlike efforts by Wright and Edgar in New Zealand's first innings, backed up by a punishing 75 from Hadlee, the match was essentially decided by the performances of the opposing sets of bowlers. In Cairns and Chatfield New Zealand had two whose

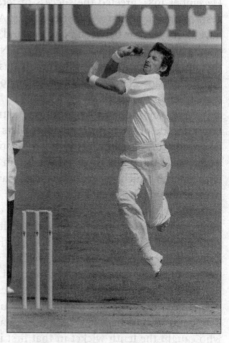

A well-oiled machine: Richard Hadlee, New Zealand's dominant all-rounder and the first bowler to take 400 Test wickets, displays his classical action at Headingley in 1983 as his side wins a Test in England for the first time.

speed was better suited to conditions than their faster England rivals. By bowling a full length they also gave the ball a better chance to swing. The 33-year-old Cairns, who won the Man of the Match award with his first bag of ten wickets in a Test, and Chatfield, who took five for 95 in England's second innings, were New Zealand's obvious heroes. But no miscarriage of justice would have been required for Hadlee to emerge with comparable figures.

Toss: New Zealand. **England 225** (C. J. Tavaré 69, A. J. Lamb 58, I. T. Botham 38; B. L. Cairns 7-74) **and 252** (D. I. Gower 112*; E. J. Chatfield 5-95, B. L. Cairns 3-70); **New Zealand 377** (J. G. Wright 93, B. A. Edgar 84, M. D. Crowe 37, R. J. Hadlee 75; R. G. D. Willis 4-57, N. G. Cowans 3-88) **and 103-5** (R. G. D. Willis 5-35).

AUSTRALIA V NEW ZEALAND 1985–86 — D. J. Cameron, 1987

Perhaps because New Zealand cricket had existed in the shade of Australia for so many decades – one Test was played in 1946, and regular Test exchanges did not start until 1973–74 – Australian cricket loomed over New Zealand. So it was with a sense of wonderment, and delight, that New Zealanders, in November and December 1985, greeted the success of Jeremy Coney's team as they took, by two Tests to one, their first-ever series against Australia. With a little more luck it might have been 3–0, for between New Zealand's innings victory in the first Test at the Gabba and the six-wicket win at Perth, New Zealand narrowly missed victory in the nip-and-tuck struggle at Sydney. It was, in fact, only New Zealand's third series victory outside New Zealand. Pakistan 1969–70 and Sri Lanka 1983–84 provided the earlier instances.

Were New Zealand so good, or Australia so bad? It was a little bit of both. For a decade or so, New Zealand bowlers had toiled on Australian pitches which favoured truly fast bowlers and proficient, shot-making batsmen. New Zealand never had quite enough of either. Yet in late 1985 New Zealand were presented with pitches which, at the vital times, favoured the skilled medium-fast bowler who could hit the seam rather than the man who might hit the helmet. These same pitches, with not enough bounce to delight the cutters and the hookers, were allies to the batsman who played sensibly and straight. In other words New Zealand, and especially Richard Hadlee, the sharpest and finest-tempered of New Zealand's bowling swords, found pitches very much of the New Zealand mould, except for that strip of spinning mischief at Sydney.

From the moment Hadlee laid waste the Australian first innings of the first Test, nine wickets for 52, a display which justified the use of that overworked adjective great, he and the New Zealanders had the Australians in their grip. Hadlee, who caught the tenth wicket in that first innings, took six more in the second. In the second Test, on a drudge of a pitch, he still acquired seven wickets. At Perth, on a bony, slowish pitch, he took another 11, taking his total for the series to 33; few as a result of bouncers, many through the artistry of a medium-fast bowler on pitches which gave him such a vast canvas.

Australia v New Zealand

First Test

At Brisbane, November 8, 9, 10, 11, 12, 1985.

New Zealand won by an innings and 41 runs.

D. J. Cameron, 1987

When Coney sent Australia in to bat on a pitch which seemed to have some moisture in it, and with cloudy, humid weather aiding the faster bowlers, there was no early indication of the drama that this Test would provide. Wessels, 38 not out, led Australia uncertainly to lunch at 72 for two, and he had 69 not out, and Australia 146 for four, when bad light cut short the first day. Hadlee's 15 overs had brought him four wickets for 35, and early on the second, humid morning he dismissed Wessels for 70 (186 balls). He then demolished the Australian innings with one of the outstanding pieces of contemporary Test match bowling, having taken all eight by the time Australia were 175 for eight. He missed the chance of all ten wickets by taking a well-judged catch in the deep from Lawson to give Brown his first wicket in Test cricket, whereupon Brown returned the favour by catching Holland and Australia were all out for 179, with Hadlee returning figures of 23.4–4–52–9. Only J. C. Laker (twice in 1956 at Manchester) and G. A. Lohmann (in 1896 at Johannesburg) had recorded better analyses in Test cricket.

The Australians had no bowler to match Hadlee's control and movement off the pitch, which had lost much of its spite, and staunch batting by Reid (71 not out) and Martin Crowe (58 not out) took New Zealand to 209 for two at stumps. On the third day they tightened New Zealand's grip on the match, reaching their centuries within five minutes of each other. It took a great diving catch by Border to remove Reid when the stand was worth 224. Crowe, however, surged on, accompanied by free hitting from Coney and Jeff Crowe, hitting 26 fours in all before edging a delivery from Matthews into his stumps after 328 balls. Next Hadlee arrived to torment the Australians again and New Zealand were 553 for seven at stumps, their highest score in Tests. Coney declared on the fourth morning with a lead of 374.

In a little more than two hours Hadlee, Chatfield and Snedden had Australia 67 for five, but Border found a stout ally in Matthews, who hit his first Test hundred from 171 balls and then saw Border to his fifteenth from 196 balls. However, when Hadlee took the second new ball 14 minutes from stumps and had Matthews caught for 115, Border, 106 not out, was Australia's last hope as they went into the final day at 266 for six. He stood alone as Hadlee took three of the last four wickets to give him match figures of 52.3–13–123–15, the best match return by a New Zealand bowler. Border's undefeated 152, off 303 balls in just over seven and a half hours, included two sixes and 20 fours.

Toss: New Zealand. **Australia 179** (K. C. Wessels 70, D. C. Boon 31, W. B. Phillips 34; R. J. Hadlee 9-52) **and 333** (A. R. Border 152*, G. R. J. Matthews 115; R. J. Hadlee 6-71, E. J. Chatfield 3-75); **New Zealand 553-7 dec.** (J. G. Wright 46, J. F. Reid 108, M. D. Crowe 188, J. J. Crowe 35, V. R. Brown 36*, R. J. Hadlee 54, Extras 45; G. R. J. Matthews 3-110).

ENGLAND V NEW ZEALAND 1986 Graeme Wright, 1987

To say that Richard Hadlee was the difference between England and New Zealand in the 1986 Test series between the two countries is not an exaggeration. And yet to say so does an injustice to the 15 of his countrymen who comprised the tenth New Zealand side to visit England on a Test-match tour. The record partnership between Bruce Edgar and Martin Crowe at Lord's; Evan Gray's determined half-century and John Bracewell's hundred at Trent Bridge; John Wright's long innings at The Oval: all were essential to the touring party's prime aim. This was to win, for the first time, a series in England, and with victory by eight wickets at Trent Bridge, that aim was realised.

Hadlee's influence, however, cannot be overestimated. At 35 he was a master of the arts of fast-medium seam and swing bowling. Only at The Oval, late in a full season for him, did English batsmen play him with confidence. As New Zealand's only experienced fast bowler, once Ewen Chatfield's broken thumb ruled him out of the first two Tests, Hadlee maintained fitness, form and concentration so that Jeremy Coney, his captain, was able to bowl him in short, demanding spells. Few passed without a wicket falling.

With the consent of the Test and County Cricket Board, Hadlee played in the Test matches only. Otherwise he appeared for his county, Nottinghamshire, who had granted him a benefit in 1986. Regarded by some as a dubious precedent, it was none the less appreciated by the New Zealand Cricket Council, who wanted to use the tour to bring on young seam bowlers. With Chatfield 36 and Lance Cairns retired, replacements for them and Hadlee are New Zealand's greatest need.

In the absence of an established seam attack, New Zealand were fortunate in their contrasting spin bowlers – Bracewell, an off-spinner, and Gray, a slow left-armer. Bracewell, having played a leading part in New Zealand's recent success over Australia, was thought to be the bowler around whom New Zealand's future attack would revolve.

England v New Zealand **Second Test**

At Nottingham, August 7, 8, 9, 11, 12, 1986. New Zealand won by eight wickets. Matthew Engel, 1987

New Zealand's victory was their fourth Test win over England since the 48-year drought broke in 1978. It was a thoroughly deserved and comprehensive one too, dominated by Hadlee, who reacted to the challenge of facing England on his adopted home ground in his customarily combative manner. He took ten wickets in a Test for the seventh time (a feat achieved before only by Barnes, Grimmett and Lillee) and played an important role in New Zealand's first-innings batting recovery, which in the end marked the difference between the teams. When New Zealand were 144 for five, chasing England's 256, the game was nicely balanced. But on the Saturday England's bowlers were outwitted by the capable set of batsmen masquerading as the New Zealand tail, and Bracewell went on to make 110 from 200 deliveries, only the third century of his life.

For New Zealand, this was further confirmation of their new high standing in world cricket; a triumph for Hadlee's exceptional qualities and the whole team's professionalism, resilience and adaptability. For England, it was yet another dismal game, the eighth defeat in ten Tests, and one that was heavily laden with off-the-field murmurings. Gooch was under pressure to announce his availability or other-wise for the tour of Australia (he said no three days after the game); Gower's inclusion had become a matter for debate because his form and spirits had under-standably declined after he had lost the England captaincy; and then, on the rest day, 50 miles away at Wellingborough, Botham broke the Sunday League six-hitting record. It was like a distant thunderclap.

Toss: New Zealand. **England 256** (C. W. J. Athey 55; D. I. Gower 71; R. J. Hadlee 6-80) **and 230** (J. E. Emburey 75; R. J. Hadlee 4-60, J. G. Bracewell 3-29); **New Zealand 413** (J. G. Wright 58, E. J. Gray 50, R. J. Hadlee 68, J. G. Bracewell 110; G. C. Small 3-88) **and 77-2** (M. D. Crowe 48*).

NEW ZEALAND V WEST INDIES 1987
See page 395

SRI LANKA V NEW ZEALAND 1992
Sri Krishnamurthi, 1994

What began as a confidence-boosting exercise to develop some of New Zealand's emerging players turned into a tour through a chamber of horrors. After their expected successes in Zimbabwe – whose promotion to Test status New Zealand had enthusiastically supported – Martin Crowe's youthful side arrived in Colombo prepared for stiffer competition in a three-Test series. But 36 hours later Sri Lanka lost all its idyllic enchantment.

On November 16 several players were taking breakfast on the balconies of their hotel in Colombo when, less than 50 metres away, Sri Lanka's naval commander, Vice-Admiral Clancy Fernando, and three other naval personnel were assassinated by a suicide bomber from the Tamil separatist movement. The tourists saw the horrific results at first hand. Dismembered bodies were strewn over the blood-stained street; even the balconies and walls of the hotel were stained with human debris. Many of the players went into shock.

New Zealand's previous tour of Sri Lanka, led by Crowe's brother Jeff in 1987, was abandoned after a bomb killed over 100 people at the crowded Pettah bus station, which the team had passed at a distance of 150 metres half an hour before. This time, though fewer people died, the incident was much closer. After seeking diplomatic advice, a majority of the tourists voted to leave.

But the chairman of New Zealand Cricket, Peter McDermott, having consulted government officials, flew out to insist that the tour should go on. McDermott was concerned about the cost to his board in tour guarantees and compensation to the Sri Lankan board; the government was concerned about trading relations with Sri Lanka, and particularly about a trade exhibition due to start in Colombo two days later. Despite public promises that there would be no pressure and no recriminations, McDermott was forceful in a three-and-a-half-hour meeting with the players, creating division and acrimony within their ranks.

Mark Greatbatch was particularly angry at attempts to make him stay, and returned home with Rod Latham, Dipak Patel, Gavin Larsen and Willie Watson. Coach Warren Lees also left, and Crowe took over his duties. Ken Rutherford, one of those who changed their minds and stayed, warned other countries against touring Sri Lanka, though he later withdrew his remarks under pressure from the ICC. The departed players were replaced by 38-year-old John Wright, who thought he had played his last Test cricket, Justin Vaughan, Michael Owens and Grant Bradburn. Vaughan, an English-born doctor who played for Gloucestershire in 1992, made himself useful on the flight over by attending a sick woman.

A revised itinerary included two Tests instead of three, reducing the trip by a week. But the players' confidence and will never recovered. After winning all their matches in Zimbabwe apart from the drawn First Test, they lost all in Sri Lanka except the rain-curtailed First Test at Moratuwa and the first of the one-day internationals, washed out when Sri Lanka were in sight of victory. Most humiliating was their first-ever Test defeat by Sri Lanka, whose only previous two Test victories were over India and Pakistan, both in 1985–86.

Sri Lanka v New Zealand   Second Test

At Sinhalese Sports Club, Colombo, December 6, 7, 8, 9, 1992.
Sri Lanka won by nine wickets.   Sri Krishnamurthi, 1994

New Zealand's abysmal performance in their first innings enabled Sri Lanka to record a third victory in their 42nd Test, and their first over New Zealand, with four sessions to spare. The star of the Sri Lankan team was Tillekeratne, who had lost the wicket-keeper's job to Gamini Wickremasinghe, but equalled the record of seven field catches in a Test held by G. S. Chappell and Yajurvindra Singh – after making 93, his highest Test score. Mahanama followed up his maiden Test century at Moratuwa [in the drawn First Test] with a second in successive innings and the Sri Lankan spinners, Warnaweera, Muralitharan – called up to replace seamer Ramanayake – and Anurasiri, shared 15 wickets in the match.

Toss: Sri Lanka. **Sri Lanka 394** (R. S. Mahanama 109, A. Ranatunga 76, H. P. Tillekeratne 93;
M. B. Owens 4-101, G. E. Bradburn 3-134) **and 73-1; New Zealand 102** (J. G. Wright 30;
K. P. J. Warnaweera 4-25, M. Muralitharan 3-22) **and 361** (J. G. Wright 50,
M. D. Crowe 107, K. R. Rutherford 38, A. C. Parore 60; M. Muralitharan 4-134).

SOUTH AFRICA V NEW ZEALAND 1994–95   Jack Bannister, 1996

New Zealand's third tour of South Africa, and first for 33 years, began promisingly, with a well-crafted win in the First Test at Johannesburg, but ended with their squad in disarray. They lost the next two Tests to become the first side since Australia against England in 1888 to lose a three-match series after being ahead. They also failed to win one of their six one-day internationals in the quadrangular Mandela Trophy, and returned to New Zealand to face a barrage of criticism.

The recriminations intensified when Matthew Hart, Dion Nash, Stephen Fleming and Chris Pringle were all suspended – the first three for smoking cannabis, Pringle for unspecified misbehaviour. Manager Michael Sandlant and coach Geoff Howarth resigned in mid-January. Captain Ken Rutherford, who twice fell foul of ICC referee Peter Burge, was sacked after the home season degenerated into a series of traumas. Leading the critics in this series was Sir Richard Hadlee, who was commentating for New Zealand television and attacked the team's lack of discipline. The criticism was difficult to refute: the performances in the Durban and Cape Town Tests bordered on the suicidal. Senior players were not exempt: Martin Crowe and Rutherford set the tone with six dismissals from short deliveries between them, in situations which cried out for applied defence. Adam Parore, Bryan Young, Shane Thomson and the promising Fleming also perished to injudicious hooks and pulls fed by intelligent bowling from the home pace attack, well instructed by new coach Bob Woolmer.

Thomson was the only New Zealander to average over 40 in the series. Fleming was just short but every other batsman, including Crowe and Rutherford, was below 30. Those two aggregated only 290 in their 12 Test innings; one major performance from each would have prevented one, if not both Test defeats. It has to be said that Crowe was carrying a knee injury so inhibiting that he was an embarrassment in the field. As for batting, he could venture only the safest of singles. Apart from his opening innings of 83, he never threatened to score the century he needed to become the first batsman to reach a hundred against the other eight Test-playing countries.

South Africa v New Zealand — Third Test

At Cape Town, January 2, 3, 4, 5, 6, 1995. South Africa won by seven wickets.   Jack Bannister, 1996

Another aggressive South African performance exposed the frailties of their dispirited opponents. On a newly relaid pitch, unusually pacy for Newlands, the fast bowlers overwhelmed New Zealand, but they helped with their own destruction: Crowe, Rutherford, Parore, Young and Fleming all perished to rash hooks and pulls. That they came within 45 minutes of the draw, despite squandering at least six wickets, illustrates their careless approach throughout the later stages of a tour which started so well. Fleming, with two half-centuries at No. 7, seemed to be one of the few still competing.

Toss: New Zealand. **New Zealand 288** (B. A. Young 45, K. R. Rutherford 56, S. P. Fleming 79, C. Pringle 30; S. D. Jack 4-69, B. M. McMillan 4-65) **and 239** (B. A. Young 51, A. C. Parore 34, S. P. Fleming 53; P. S. de Villiers 5-61, B. M. McMillan 3-52); **South Africa 440** (G. Kirsten 64, P. J. R. Steyn 38, W. J. Cronje 112, D. J. Richardson 109; M. N. Hart 3-141, S. A. Thomson 3-65) **and 89-3.**

NEW ZEALAND V SRI LANKA 1997 Peter Bidwell, 1998

The flak surrounding Lee Germon's sacking as New Zealand captain quickly disappeared in the wake of the team's successes against Sri Lanka in March 1997. Under Germon's Canterbury colleague, Stephen Fleming, New Zealand recovered from a disappointing series against England to beat Sri Lanka in both Tests, and squared the one-day internationals 1–1.

Germon had been dismissed a couple of hours after New Zealand beat England in their final one-day international. He had no idea of his fate when he spoke of the forthcoming Sri Lankan series at the closing ceremony, leading to allegations of plots and poor communication. But Germon had come under mounting pressure through the summer and, when he was injured just before the last Test against England, Fleming demonstrated a refreshing attitude and inventiveness as his stand-in. Though he lost, the selectors and coach Steve Rixon took notice and gave him the job full-time against Sri Lanka.

As one of New Zealand's best batsmen, Fleming commanded instant respect within the team and could hardly have dared ask for a better start, with two wins in his first three Tests at the helm – Germon won only one of his 12 Tests, and lost five. Fleming had been looked on as a future Test captain since he scored 92 on debut against India, just before his 21st birthday. When he was officially elevated, aged 23, he had already played 25 Tests and 60 one-day internationals (Germon had taken over in his debut Test, after one limited-overs game) and he talked confidently about a ten-year reign.

New Zealand's Australian coach, Steve Rixon, took time to get to grips with players lacking the ability and bubbling confidence he seemed to expect. By the end of the summer, however, his team looked in better shape. Bryan Young set up New Zealand's first win over Sri Lanka with an unbeaten 267. Too often he had been guilty of failing to build on promising starts, but this time he maintained his dominance for five sessions. Blair Pocock and Matt Horne consolidated their places, while Germon's departure enabled Adam Parore to re-establish himself as a wicket-keeper/batsman. Above all, 18-year-old left-arm spinner Daniel Vettori maintained the extraordinary form he showed against England, and took 11 more wickets at 20.09.

New Zealand v Sri Lanka **First Test**

At Dunedin, March 7, 8, 9, 10, 1997.
New Zealand won by an innings and 36 runs. Peter Bidwell, 1998

New Zealand completed their first home Test win for three years through a remarkable innings from Young backed up by the right-arm swing of Doull. Young scored an unbeaten 267, the seventh double-hundred for New Zealand, and second only to Martin Crowe's 299, also against Sri Lanka, at Wellington in 1991. Likewise, New Zealand's total of 586 for seven had been beaten only by their 671 for four in the same match.

Young's one previous Test century, 120 against Pakistan in 1994, had set up his team's last home victory. He cut and drove with hardly a blemish, and batted right through the innings for 605 minutes, facing 421 balls and striking 37 fours. He shared century partnerships with Horne and Cairns, while his captain, Fleming, hit 51 in 59 balls out of a stand of 76.

Toss: Sri Lanka. **New Zealand 586-7 dec.** (B. A. Young 267*, M. J. Horne 66, S. P. Fleming 51,
C. L. Cairns 70, D. N. Patel 30*, Extras 37; W. P. U. J. C. Vaas 4-144); **Sri Lanka 222**
(H. P. Tillekeratne 55*, R. S. Kaluwitharana 43, G. P. Wickremasinghe 43; S. B. Doull 5-58,
H. T. Davis 3-34) **and 328** (S. T. Jayasuriya 50, R. S. Kaluwitharana 103,
W. P. U. J. C. Vaas 57; S. B. Doull 3-82).

New Zealand v Sri Lanka   Second Test
At Hamilton, March 14, 15, 16, 17, 1997. New Zealand won by 120 runs.   Peter Bidwell, 1998

Teenage left-arm spinner Daniel Vettori took nine for 130 in his fourth Test to give New Zealand their first series win since their visit to Zimbabwe in 1992. It was the first time they had won consecutive Tests since they beat Pakistan twice in 1985. A slow pitch of uneven bounce was below Test standard, and was dug up a few weeks later. Pocock anchored New Zealand's otherwise undistinguished first effort of 222 with 85, an innings whose significance grew clearer as the game developed. It was to be the highest score of the match and further enhanced Pocock's right to the opener's spot. None of his colleagues reached 30 on that first day, and the Sri Lankans struggled even more. Their coach, Bruce Yardley, criticised their lack of patience and shot selection; only Mahanama displayed the necessary commitment, batting 137 minutes for 45. The once-erratic Davis continued his rehabilitation, taking five in an innings for the first time, but Vettori was just behind him with four for 46, his best figures yet, and Sri Lanka conceded a lead of 52.

New Zealand effectively batted them out of the match by extending that to 325, thanks to half-centuries from Young, Fleming and Astle. When off-spinner Muralitharan bowled Fleming, it was his 100th Test wicket – he was the first Sri Lankan to achieve the landmark, in his 27th Test. But, although he picked up six wickets here, he did not seem to bowl with the confidence to put the home batsmen, often suspect against quality spin, under pressure. Vettori, on the other hand, bowled with relish on his own ground. He had come within sight of earning New Zealand victory over England in his second Test; this time he completed the job, improving on the best analysis of his short career yet again by taking another five wickets. Aravinda de Silva, the tourists' star on their visit in 1991, when he scored 493 in five innings, ended a disastrous series with a total of nine runs. For the second time running, New Zealand had won with a day to spare.

Toss: New Zealand. **New Zealand 222** (B. A. Pocock 85, Extras 30; D. N. T. Zoysa 3-47,
M. Muralitharan 3-43) **and 273** (B. A. Young 62, S. P. Fleming 59, N. J. Astle 52, Extras 34;
D. N. T. Zoysa 3-53, M. Muralitharan 3-62); **Sri Lanka 170** (R. S. Mahanama 45; H. T. Davis 5-63,
D. L. Vettori 4-46) **and 205** (R. S. Mahanama 65, A. Ranatunga 33, H. D. P. K. Dharmasena 38*;
S. B. Doull 3-34, D. L. Vettori 5-84).

England v New Zealand 1999

Simon Briggs, 2000

After their humiliating World Cup bellyflop, a four-Test home series against New Zealand was exactly what England might have asked for: a chance to regain lost face, and establish young players, against one of the least-feared sides on the international circuit. England went in as clear favourites. Coming off a not-too-disastrous Ashes tour, and that morale-boosting win over South Africa in 1998, their form was much stronger in Tests than one-day games. And when they turned a 100-run deficit into a cheeky seven-wicket win at Edgbaston, it all looked very predictable. New Zealand, sacrificial victims in three of England's last five winning series, would surely fulfil their customary role once again.

New Zealand's prospects were hardly improved when Simon Doull, the only proven match-winner in their attack, sustained a knee injury that forced him home. English supporters, traditionally pessimistic, found themselves predicting a 4–0 whitewash. But this was not the New Zealand of old. Steeled by their gruff Australian coach, Steve Rixon, these players discovered a defiant streak of self-belief, as well as resilient team spirit that contrasted with the infighting and backbiting of the previous few years. Already this summer, New Zealand had outplayed Australia on their way to a World Cup semi-final. Even their new nickname, the Black Caps, bespoke All-Black aggression rather than vulnerable, flightless prey, and they turned out to be world-class sledgers.

And there was still the Lord's factor to consider. England's haplessness at the home of cricket was a leitmotif of the 1990s: this time, they were 183 for nine by the first-day close, and it took the Dunkirk spirit of Chris Read and Andy Caddick to make New Zealand bat twice. For the fourth year running, England had come away from Edgbaston brimming with confidence, only for it all to drain away down the famous slope. Worse still, Nasser Hussain, who had made an admirably positive start to his term as captain, suffered a broken finger while fielding in the gully. He missed the next match, a rain-ruined draw at Old Trafford, where England's incompetence left New Zealand looking more like a Rest of the World XI.

England v New Zealand   **First Test**

At Birmingham, July 1, 2, 3, 1999. England won by seven wickets.   Jim Holden, 2000

England's new captain, Nasser Hussain, said before the start of play that he expected to encounter ups and downs in the job. By the end of an extraordinary match, he had been through so many that he felt as if he had aged 20 years in the two and a half days it took to claim victory. His emotions were sent spinning every which way, but he never lost control of his thoughts or his strategies. It was an encouraging debut as leader.

Fleming chose to bat first on what everyone feared would be an unpredictable Edgbaston pitch. In fact, it was generous swing which troubled batsmen most, along with their own recklessness and poor shot selection. Twose, the former Warwickshire batsman who emigrated to New Zealand for the chance to play Test cricket, had a miserable return to Birmingham. He was out for a third-ball duck in the first innings and then first ball in the second. His failure set the tone as New Zealand were restricted to 226 on the opening day,

Next morning, England collapsed to 45 for seven before lunch. Hussain ran out Butcher and was then bowled by Doull for 10. Introduced at the deep end, Read and Habib could be forgiven for floundering; they managed one apiece. But Caddick and Tudor struck out positively after lunch and England sneaked to 126. It was still their lowest total at home to New Zealand, and the first-innings deficit was 100.

Hussain gave a stirring speech during the interval, and the bowlers responded with fire. Caddick took five wickets to reduce New Zealand to 52 for eight after tea. Foolish batting was again a contributory factor: Astle's exit, caught behind chasing a wide ball, was inexcusable. England were back in the match, although Stewart dropped another catch at second slip to reprieve Fleming, who nursed the tail to 107. Doull flayed a defiant 46 before he was lured down the pitch by Tufnell, the stumping gratefully accepted by Read. He made six dismissals in the second innings and eight in the match; only Jack Russell and Bob Taylor had done better for England. The youngster [making his debut] looked a natural in his work standing back, but inexperienced standing up to Tufnell. His relish of the occasion was a good sign. Still, the second day was not finished. Stewart contrived to be the 21st victim of Frightening Friday, when the ball swung violently in the sultry atmosphere. He was out third ball again, this time for a duck, ending an unhappy game for him. But it did mean England sent out Tudor as night-watchman.

As dawn broke on the third day, England needed 205 runs with nine wickets in hand. A bright, breezy morning altered conditions, the ball hardly swung, and the target proved easy. Hussain demanded his batsmen be positive, and Tudor, who had not bowled particularly well, batted brilliantly. Anything wide he smacked fiercely through the covers, while he proved equally adept at sweetly timed leg-side boundaries off his feet, cruising past his career-best 56 for Surrey. The moment was spoiled only by Thorpe, who failed to pick up the mood of an ecstatic crowd willing Tudor to a century, and was jeered. With the scores level, Tudor needed five to reach his hundred; a six was asking too much and he could only manage a top-edged four, his 21st, to finish one short.

Nevertheless, his inspirational effort was the pick-me-up English cricket required after their failure in the World Cup a few weeks earlier. It was not a great match, but the excitement and entertainment value were genuine enough. Never mind the quality, feel the pleasure of victory: Hussain had ended the curse of the captain. Since Bob Willis beat India in 1982, his eight successors had all lost their first match in charge. However, few saw it. Crowds were poor and, under the new TV contract, this match was shown live only on Sky, which is in less than a sixth of Britain's homes.

Toss: New Zealand. **New Zealand 226** (A. C. Parore 73; A. R. Caddick 3-57, P. C. R. Tufnell 3-22) **and 107** (S. B. Doull 46; A. R. Caddick 5-32, A. D. Mullally 3-48); **England 126** (A. R. Caddick 33, A. J. Tudor 32*; C. L. Cairns 3-35, D. J. Nash 3-17) **and 211-3** (M. A. Butcher 33, A. J. Tudor 99*, N. Hussain 44).

England v New Zealand   Second Test

At Lord's, July 22, 23, 24, 25, 1999. New Zealand won by nine wickets.   Mike Dickson, 2000

England arrived at Lord's promising to debunk the theory that they are never more vulnerable than at the home of cricket. They departed in something approaching disarray, having done nothing but support the legend that had built up around their performances at Lord's during the 1990s. In just under four days, New Zealand had levelled the series, wiped out the psychological edge England had gained from the First Test and abruptly brought to an end the honeymoon that Hussain had enjoyed since succeeding Stewart.

To make matters worse, Hussain had to spend most of the second part of the match watching from the balcony, after breaking a finger while trying to stop a ball at gully early on Saturday. Thorpe temporarily took over the captaincy in the field. Hussain's humour could not have been helped by the knowledge that his decision to bat first had contributed to the team's downfall, handing his batsmen the worst of the conditions. He himself had battled through for 61 and got a close-up view of an all-too-familiar lack of application from his team-mates. In choosing to bat, Hussain had gambled on the Met Office getting it right when they said that the morning's heavy cloud cover would quickly lift. It did not. For most of the afternoon, at least three scoreboard lights were showing, in murk that a few years earlier would have seen a suspension long before it actually came, shortly after the tea interval. The ball moved considerably and, with some moisture in the pitch, did more off the seam than expected, but there was still huge disappointment among the full house, which saw 102 for two eventually translate itself to 186 all out.

Cairns was a revelation, unveiling a slower ball, learned from former Nottinghamshire colleague Franklyn Stephenson, that dipped viciously to cause panic among the home batsmen. His dismissal of 20-year-old Read was the most spectacular, not to say embarrassing: Read attempted to duck what turned out to be a yorker, and fell away as he was bowled. Ably supported by Nash, who bowled better than his figures suggested, Cairns took six for 77.

The sun shone on the second day, and the conditions finally started to conform to expectations. With the England bowlers finding little to assist them, the hero was the solid if unspectacular Horne. His six-hour century, followed by a delightful 54 from night-watchman Vettori, guided New Zealand to a 172-run lead. Even then, England would have felt that all was not lost, as there was the prospect of the pitch turning as the match progressed.

In fact, their second innings was very much the same as the first, and this time they could not blame the conditions, or inaccurate weather forecasts. Butcher, Stewart and Ramprakash were all guilty, for the second time running, of playing one-day shots in a five-day game, trying to force the pace when it was unnecessary. New Zealand needed just 58 and, shortly after 5 p.m. on the fourth day, Bell hit the winning runs and his team were celebrating their first-ever victory at Lord's. With football dormant, Wimbledon and the British Open gone, this had been England's chance to bask in the public's attention after their premature exit from the World Cup. It appeared they were blinded by the light, and the clamour about the batsmen's failings reached a pitch shriller than ever before.

Toss: England. **England 186** (A. J. Stewart 50, N. Hussain 61; C. L. Cairns 6-77, D. J. Nash 3-50)
and 229 (A. J. Stewart 35, C. M. W. Read 37, A. R. Caddick 45; G. I. Allott 3-36); **New Zealand 358**
(M. J. Horne 100, N. J. Astle 43, R. G. Twose 52, D. L. Vettori 54, C. L. Cairns 31, Extras 40;
A. R. Caddick 3-92, D. W. Headley 3-74) **and 60-1.**

England v New Zealand   Fourth Test

At The Oval, August 19, 20, 21, 22, 1999. New Zealand won by 83 runs.   Hugh Chevallier, 2000

Ten minutes after lunch on the fourth day, Roger Twose, an English emigrant, held a steepling catch at mid-on that gave victory in the match – and the series – to a young and self-confident New Zealand side. The ignominy of a home defeat by the team previously considered the weakest in Test cricket unleashed a hail of criticism on the England players and – after the departure during the summer of the coach and two selectors – what remained of the management. This was no ordinary failure. As almost everyone noticed, the defeat meant that for the first time since the Wisden World Championship was launched in 1996, England were at the bottom of the heap.

In truth, England's performance was not wholly inept. Hussain's captaincy was inventive, the bowling thoughtful and the fielding near-faultless. The batting, though, was execrable. Atherton held the second innings together for a while but, the moment he was out, the familiar, gaping deficiencies were cruelly exposed. The end, as it usually is with England, was swift, painful and rather embarrassing.

Heavy rain meant that the pitch had sweated for two days beneath the covers, prompting Hussain to bowl first. Although the bounce remained constant throughout, the ball swung and spun from the word go; only Cairns, in New Zealand's second innings, overcame the doubt and hesitancy that characterised both teams' shoddy batting. On the first morning, Caddick, bowling a fuller length, was almost unplayable, and at one stage had conceded just four runs from 12 overs. The first wicket took 26 overs to arrive, though, and with New Zealand 45 for one at lunch, it seemed they had weathered the initial storm. But after struggling to make a breakthrough, England took six more wickets with comparative ease.

Having received scant support from the specialist batsmen, Fleming at last found an ally in Nash. Together, they rebuilt the innings from the ruins of 104 for seven but, by the close – and with Nash gone for a battling 18 – New Zealand were a precarious 170 for eight. Next morning, it all went wrong for England. Vettori got runs first from the edge of the bat, then from the middle. He scored 51 in 48 balls, put on 78 for the ninth wicket with Fleming at almost five an over and wrested the initiative.

England made it to lunch at 24 without loss but, just as with New Zealand, concentration wavered after the break. Atherton nibbled at one from Nash, and then Maddy, Atherton's 11th opening partner in Tests, fell to a classic piece of deception from Vettori. He pitched successive balls on the same spot for totally different results and left Maddy playing no shot at a ball which clipped off stump. Later, Hussain blundered into a more obvious trap and hooked Cairns straight to backward square leg. Ramprakash and Caddick put on 47, but early on the third morning England were bowled out for 153, a deficit of 83. Vettori bowled 31 consecutive overs and eventually had cramp in his spinning finger, which had to be uncurled by umpire Venkat.

For the 14th time in a row, England trailed on first innings. But just when the press were yet again preparing to fill their laptops with vitriol, the bowlers produced something special. England's previous six Test wins had come off the back of a first-innings deficit and, with New Zealand hurtling towards disaster at 39 for six – an overall lead of 122 – a seventh was on the cards. Caddick and Giddins had taken three wickets each with intelligent, accurate bowling, and the New Zealand batsmen had rolled over as tamely as their English counterparts. Then Cairns changed everything with an innings of uncompromising, Bothamesque belligerence. Playing off the front foot to minimise the effect of lateral movement, he hit 80 from 94 balls, including four sixes, all off Tufnell, and eight fours. The most audacious of hundreds was denied him when Mullally clung on to a brilliant reflex catch after Cairns had smashed the ball straight back at him. The damage, though, had been done. Despite Tufnell quickly claiming the last two wickets, England were left needing 246, the highest score of the match.

They lost two wickets cheaply but, by the close, sensible batting from Atherton and Thorpe saw them to 91. This switchback of a Test promised an intriguing climax. England needed an overdue hundred from a top-order batsman or, failing that, a century partnership. But, for the first time ever in a home series of more than two Tests, they could produce neither. Once Atherton was fourth out for a positive 64 – the 50th time he had reached 50 in Tests – the batting descended into farce, the remaining six wickets adding 19 runs. Over their two innings, England's last three wickets fell for a total of two runs; New Zealand's 92. Chairman of selectors David Graveney belatedly promised that England would never again pick what amounted to three No. 11s – Mullally, Tufnell and Giddins – in the same Test. The crowd jeered as Hussain collected the loser's cheque.

Toss: England. **New Zealand 236** (S. P. Fleming 66*, D. L. Vettori 51; A. R. Caddick 3-66, P. C. R. Tufnell 3-39) **and 162** (C. L. Cairns 80; A. R. Caddick 3-35, E. S. H. Giddins 3-38); **England 153** (N. Hussain 40, M. R. Ramprakash 30; C. L. Cairns 5-31, D. L. Vettori 3-46) **and 162** (M. A. Atherton 64, G. P. Thorpe 44; D. J. Nash 4-39).

NEW ZEALAND v WEST INDIES 1999–2000

See page 412

AUSTRALIA v NEW ZEALAND 2001–02
Richard Boock, 2003

New Zealand took great satisfaction from their execution of a plan, almost laughable in its simplicity, which nearly added another colourful chapter to Test cricket's book of surprises. In the end, the New Zealanders could not quite pull off victory over the mighty Australians, but they did come through three Tests unbeaten. No tourists had played two or more Tests in Australia without at least one defeat since Kapil Dev's Indian side in 1985–86.

The theory was hatched earlier in 2001, when the New Zealand captain, Stephen Fleming, was in England, watching the Ashes series while playing for Middlesex, and it was fine-tuned and polished until December, at Perth, where Australia were taken to the brink of one of the biggest upsets in living memory. It depended on a quaint, old-fashioned and oft-forgotten virtue – patience.

Though it caused amusement when first mooted, the strategy was later confirmed by the New Zealand coach, Denis Aberhart. Its rationale was that Australia were vulnerable in the last two days of a Test match – provided they had not already annihilated their opposition within the first three. Believing the world champions were so keen for a sprint that they had become unfamiliar with the distance race, New Zealand aimed to weather the initial onslaught and then hang on for dear life. Many Kiwis would claim that they went within a deaf umpire of having the last laugh. The New Zealanders were probably saved by rain at Brisbane – though an over-generous declaration almost let them steal victory – and Hobart. But when they played well enough, in Perth, it all came to fruition. Lou Vincent made a famous debut, scoring one of four centuries in the first innings. True to their promise, New Zealand batted on stubbornly in their second innings, eventually setting Australia the apparently impossible challenge of scoring 440 in a minimum of 107 overs.

This was when Australia were staggering on the ropes. It was surely time for New Zealand to change to Plan B: fix bayonets, jump out of the trenches and finish them off. Another wicket or two on the last morning, and they might have done it. Instead, New Zealand continued to play the waiting game until the batsmen were reasonably settled and, worse, their strike bowler, the slow left-armer Daniel Vettori, was beginning to tire. The longer the innings progressed, the more difficult the bowlers' task became. Sustained by an unbeaten 83 from Adam Gilchrist, Australia ended at 381 for seven, with only Brett Lee and Glenn McGrath left to bat. It remained a spellbinding Test, and, if Ian Robinson had not turned down confident appeals against Steve Waugh and Jason Gillespie, the unfancied Kiwis might still have struck the jackpot.

Australia v New Zealand   **Third Test**

At Perth, November 30, December 1, 2, 3, 4, 2001. Drawn.   Richard Boock, 2003

New Zealand almost snatched an outrageous series victory after challenging their hosts to score the highest fourth-innings total to win a Test. Even more outrageously, Australia came close to doing it, but the series finally ended in its third draw.

Fleming called correctly again and, this time, chose to bat, whereupon Lou Vincent, rushed into the side at the expense of the struggling Bell, made a fairy-tale debut. Asked to open the batting on the world's bounciest pitch against the best pace attack, Vincent set the tone for his country's bold showing with 104 in the first innings and a run-a-ball 54 in the second. He was the sixth New Zealander to score a century on Test debut and, remarkably, only the fourth touring player to achieve the feat in Australia.

Fleming declared on the second evening at 534 for nine, New Zealand's second-biggest total against their neighbours, and seemed likely to make them follow on when they were 192 for six. Australia avoided that thanks mainly to Warne's highest first-class innings: 99 out of 159 added for the remaining four wickets. New Zealand were well served by Chris Martin, who had replaced his fellow-seamer, Tuffey, but the attack was brilliantly led by Vettori, who claimed the prize wickets of the Waughs, sent back the dangerous Gilchrist, outwitted Lee and Gillespie, and deprived Warne of a century. Earlier, Langer's run of hundreds in successive Tests ended when he walked on 75 – only to look up and see the replay screen, which suggested a no-ball.

When Fleming declared on the fourth evening – just after Lee had seen off Bond with abusive language that earned a 75% fine – he set Australia the uphill task of scoring a record 440 in a minimum of 107 overs. It seemed even steeper when they lost Langer and Ponting by the close. In fact, they finished only 59 short with three wickets left, and Gilchrist unbeaten on 83. The Australian batsmen took full advantage of a safety-first approach from Fleming; half-centuries from the Waughs even gave them an outside chance of winning.

It might have been a different story had umpire Robinson agreed that Steve Waugh, then 13, had been caught behind off Vettori midway through the last afternoon. That would have reduced Australia to 203 for five. New Zealand's frustration grew when Robinson refused to accept that Gillespie had gloved a ball from Cairns down the leg side to Parore, which would have been 366 for eight, with seven overs to go. It could have been Australia's first home defeat for three years. Instead, the series ended in stalemate, but the draw had provided five thrilling days of Test cricket.

Toss: New Zealand. **New Zealand 534-9 dec.** (L. Vincent 104, S. P. Fleming 105, N. J. Astle 156*, A. C. Parore 110, Extras 34; J. N. Gillespie 3-112, B. Lee 4-125) **and 256-9 dec.** (M. H. Richardson 30, L. Vincent 54, C. L. Cairns 42, N. J. Astle 40; B. Lee 4-56); **Australia 351** (J. L. Langer 75, R. T. Ponting 31, M. E. Waugh 42, D. R. Martyn 60, S. K. Warne 99; D. L. Vettori 6-87) **and 381-7** (M. L. Hayden 57, M. E. Waugh 86, S. R. Waugh 67, D. R. Martyn 30, A. C. Gilchrist 83*).

NEW ZEALAND v ENGLAND 2002

Lawrence Booth, 2003

England's increasingly polished performances over the winter lost a coat of varnish on the final afternoon of their travels, when they went down to their first Test defeat in New Zealand for 18 years. The result left the series tied at 1–1: not bad against a side that had given Australia a run for their dollars a few months earlier, but an anticlimax after England had bossed the show until the third evening of the Third Test. They had missed a gilt-edged chance to exact revenge – for their defeat at home to New Zealand in 1999 and for the nail-biting 3–2 loss in the one-day series that preceded the Tests.

If the players were physically exhausted after six months' jetting between

England, Zimbabwe, India and New Zealand, they flew home with their emotions in tatters too. News arrived during the Second Test that Ben Hollioake, a popular team-mate throughout the winter programme of 16 one-day internationals, had been killed in a car crash in Perth, after an evening out with his family. It would be wrong to speculate on just how much this tragedy affected England's cricket, but their step lost the spring that had helped them bounce back from bad defeats in the first two one-dayers and then win the First Test. The tour ended in disappointment and in grief.

New Zealand v England   First Test
At Christchurch, March 13, 14, 15, 16, 2002. England won by 98 runs.   Lawrence Booth, 2003

This game will be remembered for perhaps the most glorious failure in the history of Test cricket. When an injured Cairns walked out to join Astle late on the fourth afternoon, New Zealand were 333 for nine, still 217 short of a wildly improbable victory. What happened next had to be seen to be believed. Astle, 134 at the fall of the ninth wicket, proceeded to treat England's attack as if they had been drafted in from the local kindergarten. He smashed his way to by far the fastest double-century in Tests and briefly raised hopes of a jaw-dropping, eye-popping win. In the end, England, thanks to their earlier all-round efforts, prevailed. But this was, and will always be, Astle's match.

A cricket ball had perhaps never been hit so cleanly, so often. Astle's first hundred had come from a brisk 114 deliveries, but he was merely playing himself in. The carnage began in earnest when Hussain took the second new ball: the next four overs, even though they included a wicket maiden from Caddick, yielded 61 runs. Hoggard, unplayable on the second day, was smashed for 41 in two overs – and out of the attack. So Astle turned his attention to Caddick, steaming in with the confidence of a man who had already grabbed six wickets in the innings. But in seven balls spread across two overs, Astle sprayed graffiti all over Caddick's figures by smacking him for 38. One six flew over third man, another landed on the roof of the stand at extra cover, and three more – over cover, mid-wicket, and straight down the ground – came in successive deliveries as the home sections of the crowd began to sing and dance in disbelief. England's supporters, so raucous moments before, were stunned into silence.

Another six off Flintoff, a gentle sweep for a single off Giles, and Astle had raced from 101 to 200 in a scarcely believable 39 balls. He reached his maiden Test double-century in 153, smashing the record – set by Adam Gilchrist at Johannesburg just three weeks earlier – by 59 deliveries. He had taken 217 minutes, three more than Bradman at Leeds in 1930, when the balls were not totted up (but over-rates were generally higher). It was as though Astle had taken two seconds off the 100 metres record.

Two more sixes off Hoggard followed, bringing the deficit down to double figures. England were seriously worried, and Astle later admitted he would have started to look for ones and twos had New Zealand come within 70 runs of victory. So the relief England felt when Astle drove at Hoggard and was caught behind for 222 was palpable. In all, he faced 168 balls in 231 minutes, hitting 28 fours and 11 sixes. He put on 118 with Cairns (in 69 balls), beating his own last-wicket record against England, an unbroken 106 with Danny Morrison at Auckland in 1997, and helped New Zealand to the second-highest total in the fourth innings of a Test, bettered only by England's 654 for five against South Africa at Durban in 1939. And he had done it all in the twinkling of an eye.

Amid the fireworks, it was easy to forget the mistake Astle made at a critical moment in England's second innings. With wickets falling regularly, Thorpe, on four, edged Drum to second slip, but Astle was unable to cling on. Soon after, England had lurched to 106 for five, leading by a precarious 187. But Thorpe survived, and he and Flintoff embarked on a stand that changed the course of the match. Flintoff had managed just eight runs in his previous five Test innings, but within 13 deliveries a burst of searing cuts and drives had taken him to 26. The fifty partnership came in 39 balls, and New Zealand, deprived of Cairns, who had injured his right knee while bowling on the first day, began to wilt. England's lead was a seemingly impregnable 370 by the time Thorpe reached his third century in four Tests in New Zealand, from 121 balls. Flintoff, whose previous Test-best was 42, was even quicker, moving to his hundred from 114 balls with a top-edged hook over the keeper's head. The stand had reached 281, a sixth-wicket record for England, overtaking Peter Parfitt and Barry Knight's 240, also against New Zealand, at Auckland in 1963, when Flintoff picked out deep mid-wicket and departed for 137. Thorpe rattled on to a 231-ball double-hundred, his first in Tests and briefly the third-fastest in Test history, and finished with 28 fours and four sixes in five and a half hours. The ink had barely dried when Astle forced a rewrite.

New Zealand v England, 2002   First Test
At Christchurch, March 13, 14, 15, 16, 2002. Result: England won by 98 runs.

ENGLAND	First innings		Second innings
M. E. Trescothick c Parore b Cairns	0	– c Vettori b Butler	33
M. P. Vaughan c Parore b Cairns	27	– b Butler	0
M. A. Butcher c Butler b Cairns	0	– hit wkt b Butler	34
*N. Hussain lbw b Drum	106	– c Parore b Drum	11
G. P. Thorpe c Fleming b Drum	17	– not out	200
M. R. Ramprakash c Parore b Astle	31	– b Drum	11
A. Flintoff lbw b Astle	0	– c sub (M. N. McKenzie) b Astle	137
†J. S. Foster lbw b Drum	19	– not out	22
A. F. Giles c Drum b Butler	8		
A. R. Caddick lbw b Butler	0		
M. J. Hoggard not out	0		
B 1, l-b 10, n-b 9	20	B 6, l-b 4, n-b 10	20

1-0 (1) 2-0 (3) 3-46 (2) 4-83 (5) 5-139 (6)   228   1-11 (2) 2-50 (1) 3-81 (4) 4-85 (3)   (6 wkts) 468
6-151 (7) 7-196 (8) 8-214 (9) 9-226 (10)   5-106 (6) 6-387 (7)
10-228 (4)

First innings – Cairns 15–4–58–3; Drum 20.2–8–36–3; Butler 16–2–59–2; Astle 18–10–32–2; Vettori 9–1–26–0; McMillan 3–1–6–0.
Second innings – Drum 32–6–130–2; Butler 23–2–137–3; Cairns 4–0–8–0; McMillan 10–0–66–0; Astle 5.4–0–20–1; Vettori 22–3–97–0.

NEW ZEALAND	*First innings*			*Second innings*
M. H. Richardson lbw b Hoggard	2	–	c Foster b Caddick	76
M. J. Horne c Thorpe b Hoggard	14	–	c Foster b Caddick	4
D. L. Vettori c Foster b Hoggard	42	–	(8) c Flintoff b Giles	12
L. Vincent b Hoggard	12	–	(3) c Butcher b Caddick	0
*S. P. Fleming c Giles b Caddick	12	–	(4) c Foster b Flintoff	48
N. J. Astle lbw b Hoggard	10	–	(5) c Foster b Hoggard	222
C. D. McMillan c Vaughan b Hoggard	40	–	(6) c and b Caddick	24
C. L. Cairns c Flintoff b Caddick	0	–	(11) not out	23
†A. C. Parore lbw b Caddick	0	–	(7) b Caddick	1
C. J. Drum not out	2	–	(9) lbw b Flintoff	0
I. G. Butler c Hussain b Hoggard	0	–	(10) c Foster b Caddick	4
L-b 5, n-b 8	13		B 9, l-b 11, w 1, n-b 16	37

1-4 (1) 2-50 (2) 3-65 (3) 4-79 (4) 5-93 (6) **147**
6-117 (5) 7-117 (8) 8-117 (9) 9-146 (7)
10-147 (11)

1-42 (1) 2-53 (3) 3-119 (1) 4-189 (4) 5-242 (6) **451**
6-252 (7) 7-300 (8) 8-301 (9) 9-333 (10) 10-451 (5)

First innings – Caddick 18–8–50–3; Hoggard 21.2–7–63–7; Flintoff 12–2–29–0.
Second innings – Caddick 25–8–122–6; Hoggard 24.3–5–142–1; Giles 28–6–73–1; Flintoff 16–1–94–2.

Toss won by New Zealand
MAN OF THE MATCH G. P. Thorpe

UMPIRES B. F. Bowden and E. A. R. de Silva

New Zealand v England
Third Test

At Auckland, March 30, 31, April 1, 2, 3, 2002. New Zealand won by 78 runs.   Lawrence Booth, 2003

New Zealand dramatically squared the series with their first home Test win over England for 18 years. Time was running out on the fourth afternoon when they were given room to manoeuvre by the Eden Park floodlights, switched on at 5.50. Play continued until shortly before eight o'clock, by which time the moon was shining and New Zealand were beaming, having extended their lead to a decisive 311. It had been a crucial two hours.

Hussain complained that his players were unable to see the ball clearly against the night sky, and the sight of Afzaal fielding as substitute, curled up like an armadillo to protect himself at deep square leg, lent weight to his argument. But the umpires were prepared to offer the light only to the batsmen: England, who nearly 16 months earlier had been more than happy to pursue victory in the gloom at Karachi, had to get on with it. A series that had been theirs for the taking when rain limited play to 54 overs on the first two days was being snatched from under their noses by opponents who had shown more daring – and, ultimately, more desperation.

Fleming declared overnight to set England 312 in 105 overs, and when Butcher and Hussain advanced to 122 for two in the 28th, anything was possible. But the pitch, another drop-in, was becoming a minefield: indentations left by the ball during the damp first three days had hardened, and the occasional delivery exploded disconcertingly from a length. New Zealand had no complaints, and England feared the worst when Astle got one to pop at Butcher, catch the splice and fly to gully. Thorpe followed next over, caught behind off Tuffey to make Parore only the eighth wicket-keeper to complete 200 Test dismissals, and Flintoff was bowled two balls later. Hussain, who passed 4,000 Test runs with some pristine straight drives, and Foster prolonged the inevitable but, at 2.53 p.m. on the final afternoon, Hoggard flashed Adams to slip and New Zealand had levelled the series. It was no less than they deserved.

Toss: New Zealand. **New Zealand 202** (C. Z. Harris 71, C. D. McMillan 41, A. C. Parore 45; A. R. Caddick 4-70, M. J. Hoggard 3-66, A. Flintoff 3-49) **and 269-9 dec.** (A. C. Parore 36, C. Z. Harris 43, N. J. Astle 65, C. D. McMillan 50*; M. J. Hoggard 4-68, A. Flintoff 3-108); **England 160** (G. P. Thorpe 42; D. R. Tuffey 6-54, A. R. Adams 3-44) **and 233** (M. P. Vaughan 36, M. A. Butcher 35, N. Hussain 82; D. R. Tuffey 3-62, C. J. Drum 3-52, A. R. Adams 3-61).

Pakistan and the Art
of the Unpredictable

It is a terrible cliché to apply to Pakistan but no less true for that: they are the most electrifying team when on song and when they are playing for each other, but they can also do bad days like almost no one else. They have raised unpredictability and inconsistency to an art form: you simply never know which Pakistan will turn up. This was taken to an extreme degree in the notorious Test at The Oval in August 2006 when, after tea on the fourth day, they failed to turn up at all, but in fairness to them they had been sorely tested by hamfisted application of an inane law.

The period covered by this Anthology has seen some wonderful Pakistan teams: the starry team of the late 1970s, bursting with batting talent; Imran's great team of the mid-'80s, proud and fiery; the Wasim and Waqar-inspired teams of the early and mid-'90s; and now, perhaps, the ebullient side that put the Ashes-winning England team in their place in Pakistan in 2005.

The great Pakistan sides have been based on attacking bowlers – the pace of Imran, Waqar and Wasim, Shoaib Akhtar; the spin of Abdul Qadir, Mushtaq Ahmed and Saqlain Mushtaq. I was at the final day of the 1996 series against England, at The Oval, and the intensity of Pakistan's out-cricket was remarkable. The bowlers seemed – and eventually proved to be – irresistible. Two contrasting pace bowlers and a brilliant spinner, operating superbly in harness. English resistance ultimately crumbled.

All that has held back Pakistan is internal dissension: the bribery scandals of the late '90s left a legacy of mistrust, exacerbated by personal hostilities and factionalism within the team. Conquer that, create the sort of harmonious team atmosphere that prevailed in 2005, and they are a match – indeed usually more than a match – for anyone.

S. M.

PAKISTAN V INDIA 1978

Dicky Rutnagur, 1980

Pakistan and India, who had confronted each other twice on battlefields since they last played a Test match, resumed cricket contact after almost 18 years when India undertook an eight-week tour of Pakistan which included three Test matches. Pakistan, distinctly the stronger side, won the Second and Third Tests. The First was drawn.

The warmth and enthusiasm with which the Indians were received, plus the cordial relations between the players, made it plain enough that the renewal of cricketing rivalry between the two neighbouring countries was long overdue. Indeed, cricket authorities on both sides of the border are eager to make up for the lost years. Future plans include not only a more frequent exchange of tours at Test level, but also a constant two-way traffic of club and colts sides. In fact, a Pakistan Under-19 side went to India immediately after the Indian Test team returned home. It would be hypocritical to say that the tour and the Test series were totally free of incidents and controversy. But there was no more tension and friction than is usual these days in Test matches between any two countries. However, the tour would have been happier without the notorious Sahiwal incident, on the occasion of the last of three one-day internationals. As the Indians, with plenty of wickets in hand, approached their target, Sarfraz Nawaz indulged in an excess of bumpers which were obviously out of the batsmen's reach. There was no intervention from the umpires, and Bedi, the Indian captain, conceded the match in protest. His action raised controversies both in Pakistan and at home.

The significant feature – and a very happy one – of the Test series was the positive approach of both sides, in bold contrast to the attitudes struck in past series between the two countries. Their two previous rubbers, involving ten Test matches, were all drawn. Pakistani pitches being what they are, the stalemate could well have continued, and had all three Test matches been drawn, the captains and players would have been blameless. Decisive results were obtained only because of the fragility of the Indian batting.

With all their Packer players recalled to the colours, Pakistan were a formidable batting side. Majid Khan, having played little or no competitive cricket since leaving Glamorgan, was not always at his best; but the only failure as such among Pakistan's frontline batsmen was Sadiq Mohammad. The dominant figure was Zaheer Abbas, who amassed 583 runs in five innings, averaging 194.33. The manner in which he scored his runs was even more impressive than their aggregate. Next in Pakistan's honours' list was Javed Miandad, who made two hundreds, besides an exhilarating 62 during the hectic run-chase on the final day of the Third Test. Mushtaq Mohammad and Asif Iqbal both indicated that they could have scored many more runs had the need arisen.

As with most modern captains, Mushtaq relies mainly on his pace bowlers, and despite the heat and the depressing pace of the pitches, Imran Khan and Sarfraz Nawaz responded magnificently, capturing 14 and 17 wickets respectively. Sarfraz was forever probing the batsmen's weaknesses, and although Imran had complained of back trouble before the First Test, he went flat out at every call. Pakistan's catching did not match their agile ground fielding, but, despite advancing years, wicket-keeper Wasim Bari was as brilliant and acrobatic as ever.

Pakistan v India   Second Test

At Gaddafi Stadium, Lahore, October 27, 28, 29, 31, November 1, 1978.
Pakistan won by eight wickets.   Dicky Rutnagur, 1980

Despite a courageous second-innings recovery by India, Pakistan maintained the grip they established on the first day when they bowled out India for a meagre 199. A grassy pitch prompted Mushtaq to put India in first. The wicket was hardly fiery, but it provided enough movement off the seam for Pakistan's pace attack to lay bare the Indian batsmen's flaws in technique. Conditions being what they were, a big innings from Gavaskar was vital to India's well-being. But in the third over, Saleem Altaf, Pakistan's veteran seam bowler, who was given the new ball in preference to Sarfraz Nawaz, produced a beautiful away-going ball to have Gavaskar caught at slip. Soon, India were reduced to 49 for four.

India were fortunate not to be overtaken by further disasters before their total reached three figures, for Vengsarkar made a very shaky start and Mohinder Amarnath survived a chance at backward short leg when he was seven and the total 88. But in the last over before lunch, at 106 for four, Amarnath turned his back on a bumper from Imran – the third of that over – and took a blow on the head. He was forced to retire. (When he resumed his innings, Amarnath trod on his wicket trying to hook yet another short-pitched delivery from Sarfraz.) Kirmani joined Vengsarkar following the injury to Amarnath and the total reached 151 before Pakistan were able to break this fifth wicket partnership. Again, Pakistan missed an important chance by dropping Kirmani when the total was 118. Once he went, however, the innings tapered away rapidly. Vengsarkar was seventh out, having batted four hours 23 minutes for his 76.

Pakistan were unperturbed by the early loss of Mudassar's wicket. A splendid 235 not out by Zaheer Abbas was the centrepiece of Pakistan's innings, but a sizeable total was guaranteed even before he came on the scene, thanks to a breezy night-watchman's innings of 85 by Wasim Bari, who dominated a second-wicket stand of 125 with Majid Khan. Zaheer was in full flight in scoring the third double-century of his Test career. The ease and fluency with which he drove, cut and pulled put Pakistan well ahead of the clock and enabled Mushtaq to declare, midway through the afternoon of the third day, with an awesome lead of 340 runs.

More than half this lead was wiped out by India's opening pair, Gavaskar and Chauhan, with the highest first-wicket partnership to date in India-Pakistan Tests. Little more than eight hours remained when they were parted – and both demonstrated dissatisfaction at the decisions ruling them out, Chauhan at 93 and Gavaskar at 97. Viswanath then took charge of the situation, and though most of his partners looked vulnerable, India continued to prosper. Surinder Amarnath, who made 60, was dropped three times.

A draw looked the most likely result, even 15 minutes before lunch on the last day when Viswanath, drawing back to cut Mudassar, was bowled for 83. India then were 406 for five and their hopes were dimmed further when Mudassar grabbed another important wicket, that of Vengsarkar, a few minutes later. It was due only to a gallant 39 not out by Kirmani that India were now able to extend Pakistan even a little. The final target was 126 runs in a shade over 100 minutes, and with most of their batsmen well versed in the art of chasing runs after long experience in English cricket, Pakistan galloped home with 8.2 overs to spare.

Toss: Pakistan. **India 199** (D. B. Vengsarkar 76; Imran Khan 4-54, Sarfraz Nawaz 4-46) **and 465;**
(S. M. Gavaskar 97, C. P. S. Chauhan 93, Amarnath 60, G. R. Viswanath 83, S. M. H. Kirmani 39*,
Kapil Dev 43; Imran Khan 3-110); **Pakistan 539-6 dec.** (Majid Khan 45, Wasim Bari 85,
Zaheer Abbas 235*, Javed Miandad 35, Mushtaq Mohammad 67) **and 128-2**
(Majid Khan 38, Zaheer Abbas 34*).

Pakistan v Australia 1982

Phil Wilkins, 1984

The premonitions before the Australian team's six-week campaign in Pakistan proved well-founded, and they proved ill-equipped to cope with a Pakistan side beginning to exert its international authority under the leadership of Imran Khan. They failed to win a single one of their nine games. They lost all three Tests comprehensively, the two limited-overs internationals which were completed – the third was abandoned because of spectator disruptions – and drew the three-day first-class matches against invitation XIs.

The triumph of the dominant personality of the Test series, leg-spinner Abdul Qadir, deserved high tribute. Although his selection for the First Test in Karachi was criticised in some quarters, by the end of the series the thick-set wrist-spinner had so frustrated and bewildered the Australians that he had established a new record of 22 wickets for a series against Australia. His remarkable dexterity, variety and accuracy, usually exploited from round the wicket, to find boot marks at the other end, caused the Australians such difficulties that it made his absence from the team which had visited Australia the previous summer all the more inexplicable. His success was achieved, moreover, against batsmen who prided themselves on their ability to cope with the ball tossed into the air and turning from leg. Qadir's ability to turn the ball sharply in both directions eroded the Australians' patience and confidence and frustrated their desires to advance down the pitch to get the better of him.

If, in all aspects of the series, Pakistan were the better side, the tourists' anger was understandable at the interference by spectators during the First Test and third limited-overs international in Karachi and, to a lesser extent, during the games in Hyderabad and Sialkot. Hughes threatened to end the tour and return to Australia if any of his players were hurt by the stone-throwing from the uncovered grandstand – mostly occupied at reduced rates by university students – at the National Stadium in Karachi, which led to two walk-offs during the First Test. He said: "When a player cannot field on the boundary without being hit, then something serious has to be done to make spectators realise it is wrong. People do not deserve to see international cricket when they behave like this." After less than an hour's play in the final limited-overs international in Karachi, by which time Geoff Lawson, Ian Callen and Greg Ritchie had been struck on the body and legs by missiles, Hughes led his players off and returned to the team's hotel. It was a sad end to the tour.

But difficulties and frustrations aside – and all members of the party sooner or later had some illness or other, stemming from the food or water, despite the presence of an accompanying doctor and physiotherapist – there was no denying that for Pakistan it was the country's finest cricketing hour. Their three-nil Test victory was unprecedented in a short series there. Even without Sarfraz Nawaz, whose injury in England and leanings towards retirement prevented him from taking any part in the tour, Pakistan were able to field a versatile and consistent attack, although none of the three specialist pacemen considered to partner Imran Khan – Tahir Naqqash, Jalal-ud-Din and Sikander Bakht – advanced sufficiently to suggest that he would adequately replace Sarfraz in the immediate future. Even so, together with the medium-paced Mudassar Nazar, they all provided moments of perplexity for the Australians, as the scores indicate. It was in spin, though, that Pakistan found themselves with an embarrassment of riches. Qadir and his left-arm orthodox spin partner, Iqbal Qasim, took 30 of the 56 Australian wickets to fall to bowlers in the three Tests. The off-spinner, Tauseef Ahmed, became an indispensable member of the limited-overs side, and was unfortunate not to play in the Tests. The slow left-arm orthodox spinner, Amin Lakhani, appeared of Test potential, and Iqbal Sikander displayed enough leg-spinning talent to remain on the selectors' shortlist for a touring side.

Pakistan also had a much greater depth in batting than Australia, with Mohsin Khan and Mudassar Nazar often providing a substantial start. Mohsin showed remarkable improvement from his brief tour of Australia, when he appeared there as a reinforcement. His century in the Lahore Test caused Hughes to consider him worthy of a position in a World XI. Zaheer Abbas was employed profitably in the middle order. The Australians were convinced of his vulnerability against the new ball, but the superiority of the earlier Pakistan batsmen invariably prevented them from cornering him. Mansoor Akhtar, some ten years younger than Zaheer, occupied the No. 3 position so adequately that he hit his maiden Test century in Faisalabad. Javed Miandad also grew further in stature as an international batsman, his youthful audacity now being supplanted by a technical competence and insatiable appetite for runs.

Pakistan v Australia   **Second Test**

At Faisalabad, September 30, October 1, 2, 4, 5, 1982.

Pakistan won by an innings and three runs.   Phil Wilkins, 1984

So stultifying did the Australians find the pitch that well before stumps on the first day, Pakistan having chosen to bat, Lawson and Thomson were bowling without a slip or gully. Mudassar and Mohsin began with a partnership of 123, Mohsin passing 1,000 Test runs. Mansoor and Zaheer added 155 in 174 minutes for the fourth wicket, with Mansoor poised on 99 for 25 minutes before cover-driving Border to the boundary for his maiden Test century in his ninth Test. Zaheer, dropped when 57 and 119, hit three sixes and 12 fours in his 337-minute innings, including 19 runs from one over by Sleep. Lawson's four for 96 from 33 overs was an effort of sustained pace and fortitude.

Two days in the field had the expected effect on the Australians. With the pitch extremely dry and containing only dead grass, Imran introduced his spinners within an hour of their first innings beginning. Qadir deceived Laird with a top-spinner in his third over and by stumps Australia were up against it. Wood provided genuine resistance, but it was Ritchie who displayed most character in the closing stages of the match. After defying Pakistan's bowlers for almost three hours before being run out in the first innings, when Australia followed on he continued calmly, judiciously and much more aggressively to make his maiden century – an unbeaten 106. Qadir took 11 wickets in the match, and seven in an innings for the first time, receiving clever assistance from his spin-bowling partner, Iqbal Qasim.

Toss: Pakistan. **Pakistan 501-6 dec.** (Mohsin Khan 76, Mudassar Nazar 79, Mansoor Akhtar 111, Zaheer Abbas 126, Haroon Rashid 51; G. F. Lawson 4-97); **Australia 168** (G. M. Wood 49, G. M. Ritchie 34; Abdul Qadir 4-76) **and 330** (B. M. Laird 60, J. Dyson 43, A. R. Border 31, G. M. Ritchie 106*; Abdul Qadir 7-142).

India v Pakistan 1987

R. Mohan, 1988

A run of 11 successive draws between India and Pakistan was dramatically arrested by the quality, or rather lack of quality, of a Test match pitch designed to produce a result. In contrast to the languorous pace at which the first four Tests had been played, the final Test in Bangalore, a centre notorious in the previous decade for flat wickets, was enthralling throughout. After pitches which had blunted the edge of Pakistan's pace attack and provided nothing for spin bowlers against Indian batsmen so accustomed to such bowling, it seemed at times that the batsmen were now treading through a minefield. It was a test of nerve which India, despite having dominated many phases of the first four Tests and having bundled out Pakistan for next to nothing in the first innings, failed. Imran Khan realised Pakistan's and his own ambition to beat India in India; but as much a victory for Pakistan's superior tactical approach to such conditions, it was also a victory born of the despair of the administrators, who sought to break the deadlock brought about by the teams' inability to bowl each other out on any surface other than an underprepared one.

India, unable to develop the advantages won in the Second and Fourth Tests, relied heavily on their batsmen to run up huge totals which would put pressure on Pakistan batsmen lacking experience of slow, turning wickets. But this the Pakistanis, not having agreed to a minimum number of overs in a day's play, could counter tactically. Furthermore, the sharp decline of Kapil Dev as a strike bowler forced India to base their attack on the left-arm spin of Maninder Singh. He had improved enormously in the course of a long season, but he could not clinch the issue for India after opening up a golden avenue with seven for 27 on the first day of the Fifth Test. Considering the odds against which Pakistan's victory came – few sides have gone on to win a Test match after so inauspicious a first innings – theirs was a remarkable triumph.

In the limited-overs series, Pakistan's superiority was beyond dispute. They had a number of utility players in their ranks, any one of whom could fashion a match-winning effort with the bat, and they won the series 5–1. Even that solitary win for India came in somewhat contentious circumstances [the scores ended tied and the umpires failed to notice an infringement of the fielding restrictions by India].

The touring team were subjected to a harrowing time by the crowds in Ahmedabad and Bangalore, where any convenient missile was thrown at the Pakistani players. However, Imran's sporting approach to the niggling problems which occur on a tour of India helped keep matters from getting out of proportion, including those instances when his own colleagues were guilty of over-dramatisation on the field.

India v Pakistan

At Bangalore, March 13, 14, 15, 17, 1987. Pakistan won by 16 runs.

Fifth Test

R. Mohan, 1988

Pakistan recorded their first series win in India, their seventh Test win against India, and only their third victory in any series outside Pakistan. The behaviour of the pitch, so encouraging to spin bowling, provided a match of riveting theatre. Batting first after winning the toss, Pakistan responded to panic induced by the turning ball with extravagant strokeplay that was not so much bold as foolish. Maninder, despite mixing the bad with the good, returned career-best figures of seven of 27, including a spell of four wickets in 13 balls. Pakistan tumbled to their lowest score against India. The home side, in turn, were made to struggle, but Vengsarkar attained the right level of aggression, hitting a six and seven fours, to place India in a splendid position at 119 for four. His first misjudgment in lofting the ball opened the way for Pakistan's counter-attack. On a wicket getting worse by the hour, the Indian batsmen followed the example of their Pakistani counterparts and a lead of 29 was all that eventuated. Iqbal Qasim and Tauseef split the spoils.

The lead was erased by Imran's shrewd move in sending Miandad out to open with Ramiz, but Kapil was not so astute in keeping Maninder on when it became apparent that he was not bowling as effectively as he had in the first innings. Pakistan's middle order was allowed to prosper. Even so, only a ninth-wicket stand of 51 between Yousuf and Tauseef put India in the disadvantageous position of having to score 221 in the fourth innings.

India's cause was not helped when they lost Srikkanth and Amarnath to successive balls and Vengsarkar was bowled on the eve of the rest day. But on the fourth day, on a pitch which allowed even an off-spinner to bowl bouncers, Gavaskar gave a masterly exhibition of technique and judgment. Only when he was out, having batted five hours 23 minutes and faced 266 balls for his 96, caught at slip off a ball that kicked off a good length, could Pakistan assume victory. A late chancey charge by Binny cut the margin to 16, leaving India to consider what might have been had Kapil Dev and Shastri been able to resist the rush of blood that cost them their wickets.

India v Pakistan, 1987 — Fifth Test

At Bangalore, March 13, 14, 15, 17, 1987. Result: Pakistan won by 16 runs.

PAKISTAN

	First innings		Second innings	
Ramiz Raja c Vengsarkar b Kapil Dev	22	–	b Yadav	47
Rizwan–uz–Zaman b Kapil Dev	0	–	(3) b Shastri	1
Salim Malik b Maninder Singh	33	–	(4) b Kapil Dev	33
Javed Miandad c Shastri b Maninder Singh	7	–	(2) c Srikkanth b Shastri	17
Manzoor Elahi c Azharuddin b Maninder Singh	0	–	(7) c More b Maninder Singh	8
*Imran Khan c Amarnath b Maninder Singh	6	–	c Srikkanth b Shastri	39
Wasim Akram b Maninder Singh	0	–	(8) lbw b Maninder Singh	11
†Salim Yousuf c and b Shastri	0	–	(9) not out	41
Iqbal Qasim b Maninder Singh	19	–	(5) c Srikkanth b Yadav	26
Tauseef Ahmed not out	15	–	c Yadav b Shastri	10
Salim Jaffer c Vengsarkar b Maninder Singh	8	–	c Gavaskar b Maninder Singh	0
B 2, l-b 1, n-b 3	6		B 7, l-b 8, n-b 1	16

1-3 2-39 3-60 4-60 5-68   116   1-45 2-57 3-89 4-121 5-142   249
6-68 7-73 8-74 9-98 10-116   6-166 7-184 8-198 9-249 10-249

First innings – Kapil Dev 11–2–23–2; Binny 3–0–25–0; Amarnath 3–1–7–0; Maninder Singh 18.2–8–27–7; Shastri 11–1–19–1; Yadav 3–0–12–0.

Second innings – Kapil Dev 12–2–25–1; Maninder Singh 43.5–8–99–3; Shastri 24–3–69–4; Yadav 15–3–41–2.

INDIA

	First innings			Second innings	
S. M. Gavaskar b Tauseef Ahmed	21	–	c Rizwan–uz–Zaman b Iqbal Qasim		96
K. Srikkanth b Tauseef Ahmed	21	–	lbw b Wasim Akram		6
M. Amarnath b Tauseef Ahmed	13	–	c Salim Yousuf b Wasim Akram		0
D. B. Vengsarkar					
c Manzoor Elahi b Tauseef Ahmed	50	–	b Tauseef Ahmed		19
M. Azharuddin c Manzoor Elahi b Iqbal Qasim	6	–	(6) c and b Iqbal Qasim		26
R. J. Shastri c Salim Malik b Tauseef Ahmed	7	–	(7) c and b Iqbal Qasim		4
*Kapil Dev c Salim Malik b Iqbal Qasim	9	–	(8) b Iqbal Qasim		2
R. M. H. Binny c Tauseef Ahmed b Iqbal Qasim	1	–	(9) c Salim Yousuf b Tauseef Ahmed		15
†K. S. More not out	9	–	(5) lbw b Tauseef Ahmed		3
N. S. Yadav b Iqbal Qasim	0	–	b Tauseef Ahmed		4
Maninder Singh c Salim Yousuf b Iqbal Qasim	0	–	not out		2
B 4, l-b 4	8		B 22, l-b 5		27

1-39 2-56 3-71 4-102 5-126	145	1-15 2-15 3-64 4-80 5-123	204
6-130 7-135 8-137 9-143 10-145		6-155 7-161 8-180 9-185 10-204	

First innings – Imran Khan 5–0–26–0; Wasim Akram 2–0–9–0; Iqbal Qasim 30–15–48–5;
Tauseef Ahmed 27–7–54–5.
Second innings – Wasim Akram 11–3–19–2; Iqbal Qasim 37–11–73–4; Tauseef Ahmed 45.5–12–85–4.

Toss won by Pakistan	Umpires R. B. Gupta and V. K. Ramaswamy

WEST INDIES V PAKISTAN 1988

Qamar Ahmed, 1989

Pakistan's third tour of the West Indies produced an entertaining and absorbing series. Pakistan won the First Test, the Second was drawn, and West Indies won the Third to preserve their unbeaten record at home since 1972–73. It was a result that Pakistan could reflect on with pride, for not since the drawn 1973–74 rubber with England had West Indies failed to win a home series.

Yet there had been a time when Pakistan looked towards the tour with apprehension. Imran Khan, their captain and inspirational all-rounder, was in retirement, Wasim Akram was suffering from groin and hernia injuries which would require surgery before the tour, and Abdul Qadir's recurring knee ailment was again troubling him. However, in mid-January Imran yielded to immense public pressure and a personal request from the President of Pakistan, General Zia-ul-Haq, to come out of retirement and lead the touring team. It was a decision which no one regretted, for the Test series that followed was an epic one.

The early indications were not promising. While Imran, Wasim and Qadir were still regaining match fitness, Pakistan lost the one-day international series 5–0. Worse, Tauseef Ahmed, the economical off-spinner, returned home after only two games because of injury. But once the Test matches began, Pakistan bounced back admirably. West Indies, without Vivian Richards, their captain, and Malcolm Marshall, were beaten in four days at Georgetown, with Imran producing a morale-boosting match return of 11 for 121. The four-day match against against a West Indies Under-23 XI was won by 211 runs, and in the Second Test, at Port-of-Spain,

Pakistan chased a target of 372 with much verve before Qadir played out the final five deliveries to secure a draw in a nail-biting finish. At Barbados, an unbroken ninth-wicket stand of 61 between Jeffrey Dujon and Winston Benjamin squared the series in a match of fluctuating fortunes and high drama.

Unfortunately, the tension at Kensington Oval overflowed into an unsavoury incident on the boundary on the last morning. Qadir, after having appeals against Dujon and Benjamin turned down by umpire Archer, became involved with a 21-year-old spectator, Albert Auguste. Infuriated at an insulting remark, he turned and threw a punch at the heckler, hitting him on the arm. Qadir later received a summons from the police, but with the matter being decided out of court for a settlement of 1,000 US dollars, Auguste did not press charges against the Pakistan leg-spinner.

That Pakistan became the first country to beat West Indies in a home Test since Australia in 1977–78 was due mainly to Imran's spirited performances with the ball and the masterly batting of Javed Miandad. Imran went on to finish the series with 23 wickets, the most by a bowler on either side, while Miandad, who had previously not scored a hundred against West Indies, followed his 114 in the First Test with 102 in the second and was the leading run-getter in the series.

West Indies v Pakistan   **First Test**

At Georgetown, April 2, 3, 4, 8, 1988.
Pakistan won by nine wickets.   Qamar Ahmed, 1989

Contrary to expectations, Pakistan won the First Test convincingly, inflicting on West Indies their first home defeat since April 1978, when Australia beat them, also at Georgetown. Pakistan's success was mainly due to inspired spells of fast bowling by Imran Khan, who finished with match figures of 11 for 121 in his first Test since being coaxed from retirement.

Toss: West Indies. **West Indies 292** (R. B. Richardson 75, A. L. Logie 80, C. L. Hooper 33;
Imran Khan 7-80) **and 172** (C. G. Greenidge 43, C. L. Hooper 30; Imran Khan 4-41,
Abdul Qadir 3-66); **Pakistan 435** (Shoaib Mohammad 46, Javed Miandad 114, Ijaz Ahmed 31,
Salim Yousuf 62, extras 71; B. P. Patterson 3-82, C. A. Walsh 3-80) **and 32-1**.

West Indies v Pakistan   **Second Test**

At Port-of-Spain, April 14, 15, 16, 17, 19, 1988. Drawn.   Qamar Ahmed, 1989

In a nail-biting finish to a dramatic final day which had seen each side achieve a match-winning position, Abdul Qadir, the No. 11 batsman, survived the last five balls from Richards to maintain Pakistan's lead in the series. Requiring 372 to win, Pakistan were 31 runs short of victory after Javed Miandad had drawn them nearer and nearer the target with a flawless 102 compiled over seven hours seven minutes. His 17th Test hundred, it came from 240 balls and contained seven fours and a five. On his dismissal, in the over before the last 20 overs began, 84 were still needed; but when Marshall dismissed the hard-hitting Wasim Akram at 311, the odds favoured West Indies. Salim Yousuf and Ijaz Faqih defended tenaciously until the last over, when Yousuf's dismissal, lbw to the first ball, brought in Qadir to play out the tense last scene.

Toss: Pakistan. **West Indies** 174 (R. B. Richardson 42, I. V. A. Richards 49; Imran Khan 4-38, Abdul Qadir 4-83) and 391 (R. B. Richardson 40, I. V. A. Richards 123, P. J. L. Dujon 106*; Imran Khan 5-115, Abdul Qadir 4-148); **Pakistan** 194 (Salim Malik 66, Salim Yousuf 39; M. D. Marshall 4-55, W. K. M. Benjamin 3-32) and 341-9 (Ramiz Raja 44, Javed Miandad 102, Salim Malik 30, Ijaz Ahmed 43, Salim Yousuf 35, Extras 61; W. K. M. Benjamin 3-73).

West Indies v Pakistan   Third Test

At Bridgetown, April 22, 23, 24, 26, 27, 1988. West Indies won by two wickets.   Qamar Ahmed, 1989

Pakistan's hope of becoming the first team from their country to win a series in the West Indies was dashed at the last by a match-winning stand of 61 between Dujon and Benjamin, who came together at 207 for eight with West Indies needing another 59 to win and defeat in sight. Their unbeaten ninth-wicket stand enabled West Indies to square the series half an hour after lunch on the final day, Benjamin finally hitting the winning boundary off Qadir.

Toss: West Indies. **Pakistan** 309 (Rameez Raja 54, Shoaib Mohammad 54, Aamer Malik 32, Salim Yousuf 32*, Wasim Akram 38; M. D. Marshall 4-79, W. K. M. Benjamin 3-52) and 262 (Mudassar Nazar 41, Shoaib Mohammad 64, Javed Miandad 34, Imran Khan 43*, extras 31; M. D. Marshall 5-65); **West Indies** 306 (D. L. Haynes 48, C. L. Hooper 54, I. V. A. Richards 67, M. D. Marshall 48, W. K. M. Benjamin 31; Imran Khan 3-108, Wasim Akram 3-88) and 268-8 (C. G. Greenidge 35, R. B. Richardson 64, I. V. A. Richards 39, W. K. M. Benjamin 40*; Wasim Akram 4-73).

PAKISTAN v NEW ZEALAND 1990   Qamar Ahmed, 1992

The tour was not without controversy. Even before it began, Imran Khan declined to play in the series, branding the New Zealanders a B team and appealing to the Pakistan Board to cancel the tour altogether. Then, just days before it started, Pakistan withdrew their offer of third-country umpires for the Tests, following reports that Martin Crowe, the New Zealand captain had said that any umpire standing in the series will be better than having two Pakistani umpires, a statement he strongly denied having made. Finally, on the team's return home, the New Zealand manager accused the Pakistan bowlers of doctoring the ball, a claim which they strongly denied. He even admitted that Chris Pringle had experimented with such tactics during the Third Test at Faisalabad, in which he took seven for 52 in the first innings as Pakistan were bowled out for 102, their lowest total against New Zealand.

In the Test matches, Waqar Younis's 29 wickets was a record for a three-match series in Pakistan, and twice he captured ten or more wickets in a match. Shoaib Mohammad scored 506 runs at an average of 169 and had the distinction of scoring five hundreds in five consecutive Tests against the New Zealanders, having begun the sequence in New Zealand in 1989.

ENGLAND V PAKISTAN 1992

Scyld Berry, 1993

The Pakistanis' tour in 1992 was as eventful as any tour of England there has been. Beyond dispute, it was the most lucrative England had staged. For the first time, the formula was five Tests and five one-day internationals and they generated more than the £7m which the Test and County Cricket Board had budgeted. But there were disputes, a rumbling sequence of them, as allegations were made of ball-tampering by Pakistan's fast bowlers and of partiality by England's umpires. In between whiles, especially in the three Tests which ended in four days, there was some magnificent cricket between two sides who were almost opposites in their outlook and method. In winning 2–1, when England felt they had the batting strength to draw the series at least, the Pakistanis confirmed their status as a world power, alongside Australia and West Indies.

It was the first Test series between the two countries since 1987, when Pakistan had won 1–0 both at home and away, and the sores had clearly not healed. Although Mike Gatting was not eligible to represent England, as he was still serving a ban for touring South Africa, his feud with the umpire Shakoor Rana in Faisalabad was never far from the mind. In addition to that incident were the many others – from the David Constant decision at Headingley in 1982 back to Donald Carr's A tour of 1955–56, when the umpire Idris Begh was doused in water – that have so coloured relations between England and Pakistan that slights are perceived where none is intended. And the series came a few weeks after the teams' bizarre encounters in the World Cup: in the first Pakistan were all out for 74 and only stayed in the tournament because it rained; the second was the final, which they won.

Given this background, the atmosphere was heightened from the start. If England's players nursed grievances about the umpiring after their 1987 tour, the World Cup winners arrived with similar suspicions. The Pakistanis' fear of retribution was not allayed when John Holder disappeared from the Test panel: an umpire who had stood in Pakistan as a neutral in their 1989 series against India, Holder was one of the few the tourists were prepared to trust. Again, they saw little of Dickie Bird and David Shepherd, because the TCCB unwisely preferred to use as many as eight umpires in the five Tests. While this may have been a sincere desire on the TCCB's part to spread it around, the effect was an abdication of responsibility, just as there had been in 1987 when Pakistan refused to use their best umpires. There are probably not eight umpires of international standard in the world, let alone in one country.

After a bland and rain-spoiled prelude at Edgbaston, and the tensest of Tests at Lord's the accumulating tensions boiled over at Old Trafford, where Roy Palmer was umpiring in his first Test match. By the fourth evening, the game was a certain draw. But so rife were the tourists' suspicions about the umpiring that tempers overflowed in the most inconsequential of situations, after England had saved the follow-on. It did not help that Palmer's first decision had been to give Ramiz Raja out following an appeal too lukewarm to be called half-hearted; or that he was the younger brother of Ken Palmer, to whom the Pakistanis had objected [on their tour of England] in 1987. Still, there was no excuse for the furore which followed the warning given by Palmer to Aqib Javed for intimidating Devon Malcolm. Aqib reacted with a show of petulance which earned him a fine of half of his match fee by the referee. It was an illustration of Aqib's state of mind that he should then have perceived an insult, when Palmer handed him his sweater, where clearly none was intended. The television replay showed that the sweater caught in the belt of Palmer's coat as he handed it to Aqib and was not thrown at the bowler.

An impartial judge would have to say that for most of the series the tourists' suspicions about the umpiring had no foundation whatsoever. But in the Fourth Test at Headingley there was an impression of bias towards the home team which strengthened the call for third-country umpires. Much was made in Pakistan of a decision by Ken Palmer in Graham Gooch's favour, when replays showed the England captain to have been run out by a yard or two, at a stage in England's second innings when they could still have lost. Blown-up photographs of the run-out were reported to have been displayed on buses in Pakistan. In making much out of split-second judgments such as this, the visiting media in 1992 probably generated as much ill-feeling back home as the English media had done in 1987.

On the England side, meanwhile, there was increasing concern about what was happening to the ball in the hands of Pakistan's two brilliant fast bowlers, Waqar Younis and Wasim Akram. These concerns, however, did not come into the open until after the series, when Allan Lamb, in an article for the *Daily Mirror*, made detailed allegations of ball-tampering. For speaking out and breaking his contract, Lamb was immediately fined an estimated £2,000 and suspended for two matches by Northamptonshire; later, at a TCCB disciplinary hearing, he was fined £5,000, with costs of £1,000, the stiffest penalty of its kind in English cricket to date. This was reduced on appeal, but only to £4,000 (half of it suspended for two years) and £500 costs.

Popular opinion was largely in favour of Lamb, if only for finding an excuse for England staging four spectacular collapses and thereby losing the series: at Lord's they lost their last six wickets for 42 runs in the first innings and 38 in the second; at Headingley their last eight for 28, and at The Oval their last seven for 25. Critical reaction, however, from former players of various countries, was more in support of the Pakistanis. By making the ball swing so effectively, by whatever means, and bowling straight, the tourists returned the focus of the game to the batsman's stumps, not his head and body, which had been the aim of short-pitched bowling in the 1970s and 1980s. While lawsuits and threats of legal action began to fly off the field, Waqar and Wasim made the old ball swing further than most people had over seen. No longer was the ball an especial threat when new but, in defiance of previous theory, when it was 60 or 70 overs old.

The umpires made frequent inspections of the ball, according to their brief, while the ICC match referee was required to examine it at every interval. But only once did anything untoward result, during the fourth one-day international, at Lord's, after it had been carried over into a second day. At the lunch interval, during England's innings, the umpires and the match referee changed the ball for one of similar condition. There was no end to the confusion which followed. The referee, the former West Indian wicket-keeper Deryck Murray, would only say that the ball had been changed, leaving the reason for it open to speculation. One informed source stated that the original ball had been changed under Law 42.5 because it had been tampered with. But Intikhab Alam, the touring team manager, asserted that the ball had been

Dangerous double: Wasim Akram (left) and Waqar Younis gave Pakistan a devastating cutting edge, never more so than in England in 1992, when they were among the first exponents of reverse swing at high pace. And they were in at the end to win that year's Lord's Test with the bat, too.

changed under Law 5.5 – simply because it had gone out of shape. Then, while accusation bred counter-accusation, it emerged that the umpires, according to the regulations for the Texaco Trophy, should have changed the ball for one of inferior, not similar, condition if the original had been deliberately damaged: and in the end, perhaps because of this slip-up in procedure, perhaps because of terror of the lawyers, the ICC finally decided to provide no further elucidation of the matter. In the darkness, further seeds of mistrust and animosity were sown for the future.

One of the most vocal supporters of neutral umpires, Imran Khan, had initially declared himself available for the tour, but withdrew shortly after the World Cup final. He pleaded a shoulder injury, but it was suspected that another factor was his declining popularity within the Pakistan team. Immediately, the prophecy was made that the tourists would go to pieces without Imran as their captain, and that he would be recalled in mid-season. But neither of these expectations was fulfilled. The tourists maintained their unity, except for the two episodes of indiscipline at Old Trafford and Headingley, while Imran was left to play in charity matches which he organised to raise money for a cancer hospital in Lahore.

Had Imran been captain, the tourists would surely still have won the series, but it is doubtful whether they would have achieved such an astonishing record in their first-class county games. In 1987 Imran had shown little interest in them except as practice, but under Javed Miandad the Pakistanis set out to win every one, both as a preparation for the Tests and as an end in itself. They scored rapidly and, led by Wasim and the leg-spinner Mushtaq Ahmed, bowled with a rare aggression. The outcome, nine wins in 12 matches, was the best record against county teams since the 1948 Australians won 15 of their 20 games against first-class counties. There can be no doubt that Tetley Bitter's sponsorship – £2,000 for each victory, and a jackpot of £50,000 for winning a minimum of eight out of 12 – provided a vital incentive which enlivened these matches.

In contrast to his reputation for waywardness, Miandad displayed a high level of leadership. Given three bowlers of a quality beyond anything England could field, he was more flexible in his field-placings than his counterpart, Gooch, and had plenty of experience of English conditions after his seasons with Sussex and Glamorgan. The one lapse into the immaturity which had marked his first attempts at captaincy came at Old Trafford where he failed to work with Roy Palmer in interpreting the law, and was then ostentatiously rude as he made play of Aqib's sweater. Some commentators thought Miandad should have been fined, along with Aqib. Instead, the referee Conrad Hunte simply urged Miandad to uphold standards of behaviour; and this he did in the following Test, when the Pakistanis were upset by a decision against them in England's second innings, and the substitute Rashid Latif threw his cap on the ground and was also fined.

England v Pakistan   **Second Test**

At Lord's, June 18, 19, 20, 21, 1992. Pakistan won by two wickets.   David Norrie, 1993

Wasim Akram drove Salisbury through the covers at 6.40 on Sunday evening to give Pakistan a one-match lead in the series and conclude an astonishing day of Test cricket. Seventeen wickets tumbled and the close-to-capacity crowd could be forgiven for thinking this was a one-day final. Pakistan saw near-certain victory evaporate into near-certain defeat before Wasim and Waqar Younis – as a batting partnership for once – defied England's depleted and tiring attack for the final nerve-racking hour. That last boundary ended England's brave fightback, and provoked some of the most emotional scenes ever seen at Lord's as the Pakistan touring party raced on to the playing surface in celebration.

Wasim's elegant drive also saved the Test and County Cricket Board from facing the wrath of a frustrated crowd for the second successive Test. Had Salisbury bowled a maiden, proceedings for the day would have been concluded. The battle would have resumed on Monday morning with England needing two wickets to tie the Test and Pakistan wanting one run to win. In fact, it would not have been the TCCB's fault: the Pakistanis had rejected the customary provision for an extra half-hour before the tour began. It was not a great Test match, but Sunday was a great Test day, and it would have been dreadful if this ding-dong battle had not been resolved there and then because of a technicality.

The influence of Pakistan's heroes, Wasim and Waqar – with ball and bat – was all the more remarkable because there were serious doubts over both a few weeks earlier. Wasim missed the First Test because of shin trouble, while Waqar used Edgbaston for little more than a trial run after the stress fracture which kept him out of the World Cup. Less than a fortnight later, they put Pakistan in command of this Test with 13 wickets, and then held their nerves for a famous victory.

England v Pakistan, 1992   Second Test

At Lord's, June 18, 19, 20, 21, 1992. Result: Pakistan won by two wickets.

ENGLAND   *First innings*   *Second innings*

*G. A. Gooch b Wasim Akram	69	– lbw b Aqib Javed	13
A. J. Stewart c Javed Miandad b Asif Mujtaba	74	– not out	69
G. A. Hick c Javed Miandad b Waqar Younis	13	– (4) c Moin Khan b Mushtaq Ahmed	11
R. A. Smith c sub (Rashid Latif) b Wasim Akram	9	– (5) b Mushtaq Ahmed	8
A. J. Lamb b Waqar Younis	30	– (6) lbw b Mushtaq Ahmed	12
I. T. Botham b Waqar Younis	2	– (7) lbw b Waqar Younis	6
C. C. Lewis lbw b Waqar Younis	2	– (8) b Waqar Younis	15
†R. C. Russell not out	22	– (9) b Wasim Akram	1
P. A. J. DeFreitas c Inzamam–ul–Haq b Waqar Younis	3	– (10) c Inzamam–ul–Haq b Wasim Akram	0
I. D. K. Salisbury hit wkt b Mushtaq Ahmed	4	– (3) lbw b Wasim Akram	12
D. E. Malcolm lbw b Mushtaq Ahmed	0	– b Wasim Akram	0
B 6, l-b 12, n-b 9	27	B 5, l-b 8, n-b 15	28
	255		**175**

1-123 2-153 3-172 4-197 5-213   1-40 2-73 3-108 4-120 5-137
6-221 7-232 8-242 9-247 10-255   6-148 7-174 8-175 9-175 10-175

First innings – Wasim Akram 19–5–49–2; Aqib Javed 14–3–40–0; Waqar Younis 21–4–91–5; Mushtaq Ahmed 19.1–5–57–2; Asif Mujtaba 3–3–0–1.
Second innings – Wasim Akram 17.4–2–66–4; Aqib Javed 12–3–23–1; Waqar Younis 13–3–40–2; Mushtaq Ahmed 9–1–32–3; Asif Mujtaba 1–0–1–0.

PAKISTAN   *First innings*   *Second innings*

Aamir Sohail c Russell b DeFreitas	73	– b Salisbury	39
Ramiz Raja b Lewis	24	– c Hick b Lewis	0
Asif Mujtaba c Smith b Malcolm	59	– c Russell b Lewis	0
*Javed Miandad c Botham b Salisbury	9	– c Russell b Lewis	0
Salim Malik c Smith b Malcolm	55	– c Lewis b Salisbury	12
Inzamam–ul–Haq c and b Malcolm	0	– run out	8
Wasim Akram b Salisbury	24	– not out	45
†Moin Khan c Botham b DeFreitas	12	– c Smith b Salisbury	3
Mushtaq Ahmed c Russell b DeFreitas	4	– c Hick b Malcolm	5
Waqar Younis b Malcolm	14	– not out	20
Aqib Javed not out	5		
B 4, l-b 3, n-b 7	14	B 2, l-b 5, w 1, n-b 1	9
	293	(8 wkts)	**141**

1-43 2-123 3-143 4-228 5-228   1-6 2-10 3-18 4-41 5-62
6-235 7-263 8-271 9-276 10-293   6-68 7-81 8-95

First innings – DeFreitas 26–8–58–3; Malcolm 15.5–1–70–4; Lewis 29–7–76–1; Salisbury 23–3–73–2; Botham 5–2–9–0.
Second innings – Malcolm 15–2–42–1; Lewis 16–3–43–3; Salisbury 14.1–0–49–3.

Toss won by England   UMPIRES B. Dudleston and J. H. Hampshire

England v Pakistan   **Fifth Test**

At The Oval, August 6, 7, 8, 9, 1992. Pakistan won by ten wickets.   Mark Baldwin, 1993

A game billed as "The Showdown Test" became instead a perfect showcase for the awesome fast bowling talents of Wasim Akram and Waqar Younis. Pakistan won 15 minutes before lunch on the fourth day, a more comprehensive victory than even they could have dared hope for – and the crowning triumph of the summer for their captain Javed Miandad. At last, Miandad was captain in his own right – the unchallenged leader of a young, multi-talented team that no longer needed, or wanted, the paternal and patrician guidance of Imran Khan. Fittingly, too, Imran's record of 21 wickets in a series for Pakistan in England was equalled by Wasim and broken by Waqar, who claimed one more. Their combined total of 43 wickets was the main reason why Pakistan won their fourth successive series against England; at The Oval their haul of 15 left the home nation shattered and outclassed.

Toss: England. **England 207** (A. J. Stewart 31, M. A. Atherton 60, R. A. Smith 33; Wasim Akram 6-67) **and 174** (R. A. Smith 84*; Wasim Akram 3-36, Waqar Younis 5-52); **Pakistan 380** (Aamir Sohail 49, Shoaib Mohammad 55, Javed Miandad 59, Salim Malik 40, Asif Mujtaba 50, Rashid Latif 50, Extras 36; D. E. Malcolm 5-94) **and 5-0.**

PAKISTAN V AUSTRALIA 1994   Mike Coward, 1996

It has long been the view of the vast majority of Australian cricketers that a tour of Pakistan is both exhausting and unrewarding. Yet more often than not they have exaggerated the difficulty of the exercise. This was again the case in 1994, when they squandered precious opportunities to win their first Test match in Pakistan since 1959.

Pakistan v Australia   **First Test**

At National Stadium, Karachi, September 28, 29, 30, October 1, 2, 1994.
Pakistan won by one wicket.
                                                              Mike Coward, 1996

Australia's new era, after the end of Allan Border's decade of captaincy, began with an epic encounter. What looked like their first Test victory in Pakistan for 35 years was turned into a home triumph by the bold batting of Inzamam-ul-Haq and Mushtaq Ahmed on a slow, low pitch. Coming together at 258 for nine with the awesome task of averting Pakistan's first ever defeat at the National Stadium, Inzamam and Mushtaq added 57 on a worn pitch against the redoubtable leg-spin of Warne. To the unrestrained delight of a crowd which steadily grew in number and chanted Allah-O-Akbar (God is great), they accomplished their goal in 8.1 overs, against an attack weakened by the withdrawal of McDermott, who had an infected toe, and then by injuries to McGrath and May. In the end, Warne and Angel, in his second Test, were the only front-line bowlers still standing. Pakistan had never scored as much as 314 in a fourth innings to win; coach Intikhab Alam described the victory as the country's finest. Observers hoped it might revive interest in Test cricket in Pakistan.

Pakistan v Australia, 1994   First Test

At Karachi, September, 28, 29, 30, October 1, 2, 1994. Result: Pakistan won by one wicket.

AUSTRALIA

	First innings		Second innings	
M. J. Slater lbw b Wasim Akram	36	(2) lbw b Mushtaq Ahmed		23
*M. A. Taylor c and b Wasim Akram	0	(1) c Rashid Latif b Waqar Younis		0
D. C. Boon b Mushtaq Ahmed	19	not out		114
M. E. Waugh c Zahid Fazal b Mushtaq Ahmed	20	b Waqar Younis		61
M. G. Bevan c Aamir Sohail b Mushtaq Ahmed	82	b Wasim Akram		0
S. R. Waugh b Waqar Younis	73	lbw b Wasim Akram		0
†I. A. Healy c Rashid Latif b Waqar Younis	57	c Rashid Latif b Wasim Akram		8
S. K. Warne c Rashid Latif b Aamir Sohail	22	lbw b Waqar Younis		0
J. Angel b Wasim Akram	5	c Rashid Latif b Wasim Akram		8
T. B. A. May not out	1	b Wasim Akram		1
G. D. McGrath b Waqar Younis	0	b Waqar Younis		1
B 2, l-b 12, n-b 8	22	B 7, l-b 4, n-b 5		16

1-12 2-41 3-75 4-95 5-216   **337**   1-1 2-49 3-171 4-174 5-174   **232**
6-281 7-325 8-335 9-335 10-337   6-213 7-218 8-227 9-229 10-232

First innings – Wasim Akram 25–4–75–3; Waqar Younis 19.2–2–75–3; Mushtaq Ahmed 24–2–97–3;
Akram Raza 14–1–50–0; Aamir Sohail 5–0–19–1; Salim Malik 1–0–7–0.
Second innings – Wasim Akram 22–3–63–5; Waqar Younis 18–2–69–4; Mushtaq Ahmed 21–3–51–1;
Akram Raza 10–1–19–0; Aamir Sohail 7–0–19–0.

PAKISTAN

	First innings		Second innings	
Saeed Anwar c M. E. Waugh b May	85	c and b Angel		77
Aamir Sohail c Bevan b Warne	36	run out		34
Zahid Fazal c Boon b May	27	c Boon b Warne		3
*Salim Malik lbw b Angel	26	c Taylor b Angel		43
Basit Ali c Bevan b McGrath	0	(6) lbw b Warne		12
Inzamam–ul–Haq c Taylor b Warne	9	(8) not out		58
†Rashid Latif c Taylor b Warne	2	(9) lbw b S. R. Waugh		35
Wasim Akram c Healy b Angel	39	(7) c and b Warne		4
Akram Raza b McGrath	13	(5) lbw b Warne		2
Waqar Younis c Healy b Angel	6	c Healy b Warne		7
Mushtaq Ahmed not out	2	not out		20
L-b 7, n-b 4	11	B 4, l-b 13, n-b 3		20

1-90 2-153 3-154 4-157 5-175   **256**   1-45 2-64 3-148 4-157 5-174   **(9 wkts) 315**
6-181 7-200 8-234 9-253 10-256   6-179 7-184 8-236 9-258

First innings – McGrath 25–6–70–2; Angel 13.1–0–54–3; May 20–5–55–2; Warne 27–10–61–3;
S. R. Waugh 2–0–9–0.
Second innings – McGrath 6–2–18–0; Angel 28–8–92–2; S. R. Waugh 15–3–28–1; Warne 36.1–12–89–5;
May 18–4–67–0; M. E. Waugh 3–1–4–0.

Toss won by Australia   UMPIRES H. D. Bird and Khizar Hayat

Australia v Pakistan 1995

David Hopps, 1997

Pakistan's tour of Australia was widely expected to be one of the most quarrelsome and unsavoury series in Test history. It took place in the aftermath of Australian bribery allegations against the former Pakistani captain, Salim Malik, an affair which had been unsatisfactorily concluded because of the ICC's inability – or unwillingness – to hold its own investigation.

But the three-Test series passed off relatively peacefully, which was testimony to superb leadership on both sides. Mark Taylor had already established himself as a highly principled Australian captain and his authority was emphasised as his players' behaviour remained exemplary, despite their resentment that a Pakistani judge had proclaimed Malik's innocence and effectively called the Australians liars. Taylor said merely: "I think the players feel a little let down." Wasim Akram, reinstated as captain in place of Ramiz Raja, deserved equal commendation for his handling of the Pakistani squad. They had been riven by conflict and mistrust over the allegations of bribery and betting scams but, in trying circumstances, they generally maintained a cordial and dignified air.

Malik himself often cut a peripheral figure, his prevailing mood summed up on the eve of the First Test when he stated: "I hate Australia; it's hell. I just stay in my room all day watching TV." When he required six stitches in a hand wound on the first day of the series, it precipitated the arrival of his brother-in-law Ijaz Ahmed, who not only strengthened the batting, carving a stubborn hundred in the final Test in Sydney, but provided Malik with some much-needed succour.

On the field, Pakistan were far from impressive, going 2–0 down within eight days before gaining a consoling victory in Sydney when Australia eased off with the series already won, just as they had against England the previous summer. Pakistan's fielding was at times inept, one hapless practice session after their defeat in Brisbane being turned into an *It'll Be Alright On The Night* comic sequence by Australian TV. It gave Australia the chance to wipe away their draining experience in Pakistan a year earlier, when they dominated all three Tests, but lost the series 1–0; Taylor had likened that to having his heart torn out.

Australia v Pakistan

First Test

At Brisbane, November 9, 10, 11, 13, 1995.
Australia won by an innings and 126 runs.

David Hopps, 1997

After Warne's match-rigging allegations against Salim Malik, dramatic necessity dictated that the pair should confront each other at the Gabba. Warne dismissed Malik for nought, fourth ball, which was as satisfying in itself for Australia as the entire lop-sided result, achieved with more than five sessions to spare. On the first day Malik had made a splendid diving catch at mid-wicket to dismiss Australia's captain Taylor, and had needed six stitches in split webbing on his left hand. By the time he walked out to bat at No. 8 in Pakistan's second innings, to sporadic abuse, with overwhelming defeat beckoning and his hand heavily strapped, all Australia had cast Warne in the role of avenging angel. Malik offered a hesitant leading edge against a slightly turning top-spinner and McDermott plunged to hold a low catch at mid-off.

The fielders' temperate reaction was testimony to Taylor's positive influence, but Warne, understandably, could not resist commenting after the match. "It showed that there is justice in the game," he said. Warne's match figures of 44–19–77–11 took his record in three Tests at the Gabba, a traditional haven for seam bowling, to 30 wickets at 10.40. Brisbane's extra bounce enabled him to make full use of flight and dip as well as turn. At times, by his own high standards, he did not bowl uncommonly well, but he did not need to, such was his psychological hold over the batsmen.

Toss: Australia. **Australia 463** (M. A. Taylor 69, M. J. Slater 42, D. C. Boon 54, M. E. Waugh 59, S. R. Waugh 112*, G. S. Blewett 57; Waqar Younis 3-101); **Pakistan 97** (Aamir Sohail 32; S. K. Warne 7-23) **and 240** (Aamir Sohail 99, Inzamam-ul-Haq 62; G. D. McGrath 4-76, S. K. Warne 4-54).

WORLD CUP HANGOVER – THE 1995–96 SEASON
Abid Ali Kazi, 1997

The 1995–96 season was overshadowed by the World Cup, the optimistic belief that Pakistan would retain their title and the national trauma when they were knocked out in the quarter-finals. Looking at Pakistan's performances over the previous year, the mess created by the Salim Malik affair, changes in captaincy and management and internal bickering, their chances of remaining champions were always slim. But the media falsely raised the hopes of the nation. After the anti-climax of defeat in the quarter-finals – the first serious hurdle – by arch-rivals India, the mood of both media and people swung sharply from patriotic enthusiasm to wrath against the players. Allegations of bribery were made, resignations were demanded and some disheartened fans even stoned captain Wasim Akram's house in Lahore, forcing him to take refuge with his in-laws in Islamabad.

ENGLAND V PAKISTAN 1996
Peter Johnson, 1997

No tour – save, perhaps, the Australians' first visit after Bodyline – can ever have needed more delicate handling than this one. Yet Pakistan achieved the remarkable feat of spreading goodwill while winning a Test series and administering two hefty defeats on England. When they left England in 1992, feeling falsely accused and deeply insulted, Imran Khan predicted in print that no official Pakistan team would ever set foot in the country again. Though that prophecy always seemed a mite over-emotional, the sentiment was understandable. There was so much mutual mistrust that sporting relations between the two nations could not have survived another series ablaze with accusations of ball-tempering, sweater-throwing and umpire-baiting.

The fact that Pakistan managed to play their usual exhilarating, strong-arm, glamorous cricket, yet still kept the peace, was a diplomatic triumph which must be attributed to tour manager Yawar Saeed and, even more so, to captain Wasim Akram. There was little starch in Yawar's approach to public relations. Unlike the early-season India tourists, Pakistan had no internal troubles to hide. The players were encouraged to mingle, talk and, above all, entertain. They did all three. The world's most fractious team seemed to have found an unprecedented unity since the Pakistan public turned on them after the defeat by India in the World Cup just over three months earlier.

Wasim had been the most cruelly hounded. He was subjected to outrageous insults in local newspapers and effigies of him were burned in the streets. He kept his job and his dignity and, in the process, earned the kind of respect he never enjoyed when his first misguided spell as captain was ended by a players' rebellion. There were, paradoxically, few times during the tour when Wasim looked, with either ball or bat, the great all-rounder he undoubtedly is. Perhaps he expended so much energy damping down emotions that his own game never caught fire. He began the three-match series needing 11 wickets to become only the 11th bowler to take 300 Test wickets. He did not reach that target until a perfect yorker bowled Alan Mullally and ended England's innings in the final Test at The Oval. He finished on his knees, arms upraised in a gesture that was part triumph, part prayer of thanksgiving. Throughout the tour he said he was unworried by his own lack of form. It never got in the way of his job as manipulator of a team so obviously superior that only a freak English pitch or their own suspect temperament threatened to defeat them. He has learned a lot since he first walked into the traditionally down-to-earth, classless, Lancashire dressing-room in 1988 – not only about English conditions but about English attitudes. Nowadays, he is not a man to take offence easily. His leadership is the antithesis of the posturing and confrontational style that made Javed Miandad the detonator for so many of the 1992 explosions. Wasim was always quick to intervene to calm jangling Pakistan nerves, but never theatrical.

Quite a few landmines were laid in his path. Allan Lamb, whose ball-tampering accusations had caused the major crisis on the previous tour, had strategically resigned from Northamptonshire so that Test and County Cricket Board rules could not prevent him raking over the old ashes in a ghosted autobiography; the newspaper serialisation was timed to coincide with the tour. In the event, those embers were cold, grey and unenlightening. The real, hurtful mud was being slung daily in the High Court where, by some mischievous quirk of the legal calendar, the libel case brought against Imran Khan by Ian Botham and Lamb provided a lurid and, at times, unintentionally hilarious curtain-raiser to the First Test at Lord's. England captain Mike Atherton and coach David Lloyd were the most reluctant witnesses, called on the eve of the Test. Lloyd, in particular, protested that it interfered with England's preparations. To his credit, he did not offer that as an excuse for the defeat which settled the course of the series.

There had always been a suspicion that England's 1–0 series win over an underprepared and disorganised India [in the first half of the summer] was something of a false dawn, and that reality would be restored once they were confronted by a team with three world-class bowlers – Wasim, Waqar Younis and Mushtaq Ahmed – and a handful of batsmen of dazzling, if vulnerable, brilliance. So it proved. Though Pakistan may be gloriously unpredictable, England are not. They lost the opening Test through a hopeless batting collapse, drew the second by wasting heaven-sent conditions at Headingley and were overwhelmed by weight of runs and Mushtaq's unrelenting spin at The Oval.

England v Pakistan   **First Test**

At Lord's, July 25, 26, 27, 28, 29, 1996.
Pakistan won by 164 runs.   David Lloyd, 1997

Having beaten India 1–0, England were losers all the way down the line on their second visit of the summer to Lord's. They lost coach David Lloyd and captain Atherton for part of the eve of Test practice session (both being required to give evidence in the Botham and Lamb v Imran libel trial), lost Hussain and Lewis to injuries before the match, lost the toss for choice of ball, lost the principal toss when both teams were anxious to bat first and, finally, lost nine for 75 in little more than two hours on the last afternoon.

Bad luck? England experienced more than their fair share in a match not memorable for outstanding umpiring, but no one could deny Pakistan were worthy winners. Inzamam-ul-Haq's century would have captured many a Man of the Match award. But was overshadowed by some wonderful fast bowling from Waqar Younis, who returned eight for 154.

At Lord's, July 25, 26, 27, 28, 29, 1996. **Pakistan won by 164 runs.** Toss: Pakistan. **Pakistan 340**
(Saeed Anwar 74, Inzamam-ul-Haq 148, Rashid Latif 45; A. D. Mullally 3-44) **and 352-5 dec.**
(Saeed Anwar 88, Shadab Kabir 33, Ijaz Ahmed 76, Inzamam-ul-Haq 70, Wasim Akram 34*;
D. G. Cork 3-86); **England 285** (N. V. Knight 51, A. J. Stewart 39, G. P. Thorpe 77, R. C. Russell 41*;
Waqar Younis 4-69, Ata-ur-Rehman 4-50) **and 243** (M. A. Atherton 64, A. J. Stewart 89,
I. D. K. Salisbury 40; Waqar Younis 4-85, Mushtaq Ahmed 5-57).

England v Pakistan   **Third Test**

At The Oval, August 22, 23, 24, 25, 26, 1996. Pakistan won by nine wickets.   David Norrie, 1997

In a predictable repeat of the Lord's Test, England's batting sank to the leg-spin of Mushtaq Ahmed on the final afternoon after they appeared to be in sight of land at lunchtime. This collapse left Pakistan comfortable winners of their fifth successive series over England. While Mushtaq collected his fifth five-wicket haul in his last six Tests and Pakistan captain Wasim Akram celebrated his 300th Test wicket, retiring chairman of selectors Ray Illingworth suffered his first home series defeat after three years in charge.

For Illingworth, coach David Lloyd and captain Mike Atherton it was a dismal end to a Test summer that had started promisingly at Edgbaston. The long-term worries and discussions centred on England's continuing fast-bowling shortcomings. Yet, badly as they bowled on Friday afternoon, that would not have led to defeat if their batsmen had not played poorly twice on a good pitch. England complained before, during and after the Test that it suited the tourists, but it was difficult to imagine a surface that would have delivered them victory over a side superior in all aspects. Where they must stop handing away the advantage is over the choice of match ball. Once again, Wasim called correctly and chose the Reader ball. For that reason alone, England would have preferred the Dukes. Everywhere else in the world, the home side nominates the type of ball to be used.

Crawley's majestic first-day innings failed to disguise the fact that his teammates had missed their opportunity after Atherton won the toss. Thorpe received a harsh lbw decision and Knight was unlucky to see the ball hit his pad, arm and wicket, but the others also got starts, and got out. Rain kept Crawley waiting until the next afternoon for the six runs he needed for his maiden Test hundred. After that, it was a bad Friday for England. Their total looked woefully inadequate as Saeed Anwar launched into some wayward bowling: the one exception was the new boy, Croft, who showed good skill, temperament, class and a clear pointer to England's spinning future. Pakistan finished the day less than a hundred adrift with only Sohail back in the pavilion. Anwar was already 116, which he took to a Test-best 176 on Saturday, when only 38.3 overs were permitted by rain. England's frustration was evident as Cork pushed Anwar out of the way while fielding the ball. The referee, Peter van der Merwe, spoke to both players, Cork apologised and the matter was closed.

The ingredients of Sunday's principal drama were a puncture on a Mercedes convertible and the late arrival of the most naturally talented and irritating England cricketer of recent times. Lewis's only appearance at The Oval at the correct time was on Illingworth's list for the one-day squad, announced an hour before the start. The man himself appeared 25 minutes later. After a meeting with Atherton, who then discussed the matter with Illingworth and Lloyd, Lewis was replaced in the one-day squad by Kent's Dean Headley. The big crime for the England management was his failure to ring in, even though all the players had been given mobile phones by a sponsor, for just such an eventuality. Lewis's brilliant run-out of Mujtaba later in the day served only to emphasise general bewilderment at his unfulfilled talent and irresponsibility.

On the field, Salim Malik capitalised on Anwar's work with a steady century, his 14th in Tests. Wasim declared 195 ahead; Atherton and Stewart had to survive the 23 overs remaining on the fourth day. They were still together at the close, which came at 7.18, because of rain, after a hostile barrage from the Pakistan fast bowlers. Mushtaq had come on to deliver the tenth over, from the Vauxhall End, and he bowled unchanged until 4.20 on the final afternoon when the innings ended. England had reached 158 for two at lunch – reminiscent of Lord's, where they were 152 for one. This time, they seemed to be in a stronger position, just 37 runs away from making the tourists bat again. But Mushtaq was already bowling round the wicket and Atherton had already gone.

England's last eight wickets went down for 76 in 27 overs. Hussain received no benefit of the doubt from Sri Lankan umpire B. C. Cooray, and Crawley's concentration was disturbed by two streakers, but, generally, it was a sorry display. When Mushtaq bowled Cork to leave England 238 for eight, Wasim had to take the final two wickets to become the 11th member of the 300-club in his 70th Test. This he did in style, dismissing Croft and Mullally with successive balls; he fell to his knees as his team-mates ran to congratulate him. Pakistan completed the formality of scoring 48 to win in less than seven overs.

Groundsman Paul Brind was one of the few Englishmen to come out with any credit. Richie Benaud described his pitch as the perfect Test wicket because, as Pakistan proved, there was something for bowlers with ability who were prepared to bend their backs. England could cope with neither the pitch nor the Pakistanis, which offered Atherton and Lloyd little comfort for the future.

Toss: England. **England 326** (M. A. Atherton 31, A. J. Stewart 44, G. P. Thorpe 54, J. P. Crawley 106; Wasim Akram 3-83, Waqar Younis 4-95) **and 242** (M. A. Atherton 43, A. J. Stewart 54, N. Hussain 51; Wasim Akram 3-67, Mushtaq Ahmed 6-78); **Pakistan 521-8 dec.** (Saeed Anwar 176, Aamir Sohail 46, Ijaz Ahmed 61, Inzamam-ul-Haq 35, Salim Malik 100*, Wasim Akram 40; A. D. Mullally 3-97) **and 48-1.**

SOUTH AFRICA V PAKISTAN 1998

Paul Weaver, 1999

A series between Pakistan, the world's most gifted side, and the heroically resilient South Africans always promised momentous cricket. South Africa had just lost a highly competitive series in Australia 1–0, and Pakistan had recently routed West Indies 3–0 at home. But South Africa had achieved the rare feat of winning a series in Pakistan only four months earlier. Some saw the series as deciding the silver medal position in world cricket.

It was certainly a memorable series, fairly drawn 1–1. But, although there was some outstanding cricket, the mood and shape of the contest was directed by incidents off the field. Not for the first time, a Pakistan tour mixed enthralling cricket with mayhem. Even as the teams gathered for the First Test in Johannesburg, there was a strange atmosphere of peevishness in the air.

South African captain Hansie Cronje, who missed the match with a knee injury, had just been obliged to apologise to the Australian Cricket Board after an incident in Adelaide, when the umpires' door was damaged. Pakistan, meanwhile, had arrived in characteristic disarray. Wasim Akram, the captain and inspiration against West Indies, had been omitted from the party, officially for fitness reasons, and Rashid Latif had become their fourth captain in ten months. With allegations of betting and match-fixing still swirling, the appointment of Latif was seen as an attempt by the Pakistan Cricket Board to loosen the grip of the senior pros and repair the side's tarnished image. He had briefly retired three years earlier after complaining about the behaviour of former captain Salim Malik.

A little more tarnish was just round the corner. The First Test was delayed for 24 hours (Pakistan asked for longer) after fast bowler Mohammad Akram and off-spinner Saqlain Mushtaq claimed they had been mugged outside the team hotel. Later reports said they had been seen at two exotically named nightspots, Club 69 and Blue Orchid, and that the injuries had actually been sustained there. The players could not describe their assailants or agree on the time of the attack.

The seeds of mistrust were sown and poisoned the entire series. The immediate effect was to polarise the two camps. Pakistan developed a siege mentality, which can be a healthy attitude for a touring party, but in this case came close to paranoia. In the face of a sceptical press, some senior players favoured returning home.

Ali Bacher, managing director of the United Cricket Board of South Africa, worked and wheedled frantically to keep the tour on course. "I could have written a best-seller to describe what happened on this tour," he said at the end. Meanwhile the Pakistan manager, Asad Aziz, disappeared to his hotel room when difficult questions were asked and went off to an elephant game park when Wasim controversially returned to the fold for the final Test. Given the history of this most talented but mercurial team, it seemed strange to embark on such a serious tour without a strong manager.

The mugging issue was never resolved. South African officials felt they had been hoodwinked, and the players were in danger of being charged with wasting police time. Even on the day of their departure to Zimbabwe there was trouble: coach Haroon Rashid declared that Shoaib Akhtar and Fazl-e-Akbar were to be sent home for late-night partying, but the decision was reversed.

The First Test ended in a miserable and best-forgotten draw. In Durban, Pakistan briefly fulfilled their vast potential, outclassing South Africa to win more emphatically than a margin of 29 runs suggests, before destroying themselves for the final match. Wasim flew in at the personal request of Khalid Mahmood, chairman of the Pakistan Cricket Board, prompting the immediate resignation of Salim Altaf, the chairman of selectors. The arrival of Wasim, a strong personality, divided the team and they under-performed in the final Test. Wasim himself did not look match-fit.

South Africa v Pakistan — Second Test

At Durban, February 26, 27, 28, March 1, 2, 1998.
Pakistan won by 29 runs.

Paul Weaver, 1999

For once, Pakistan played to their considerable potential to take a 1–0 lead. South Africa were unable to keep pace with their more gifted opponents, though a less determined side would surely have been overwhelmed by a wider margin. Pakistan were put in on a two-paced pitch, and Donald and Pollock reduced them to 89 for five. They were rescued by an outstanding hundred from Azhar Mahmood, his third in six Test innings against South Africa. He consistently drove and cut the fast bowlers backward of point and hit Donald back over his head before hooking him in front of square leg.

Then, on the second day, South Africa were troubled by another youngster. Shoaib, carrying a knee injury, was still quicker than Waqar Younis or Donald the previous day – which arguably made him the fastest bowler in the world at this time. In his third Test, he captured five for 43 and swept away the lower half of the batting after Kallis and Ackerman had put on 83 for the third wicket. Four of his victims were clean bowled and the other lbw. Despite a fluent, undefeated 70 from Pollock, South Africa were all out shortly after tea, trailing by 28.

On the third day, Saeed Anwar and Aamir Sohail built the first century opening stand against South Africa in 45 Tests since their return to international cricket. Anwar batted more than five hours for his fifth Test century, which carried him past 2,000 Test runs. But Pakistan lost their last nine wickets for 67. Set 255 to win, South Africa then faltered against Mushtaq, who used the rough to return figures of six for 78. Once again, they refused to lie down: a ninth-wicket stand of 86 between Boucher and De Villiers gave South Africa sudden, outrageous optimism. But early on the final morning, they suffered their first defeat in six Tests against Pakistan and their first at Kingsmead since England's win in 1964.

Toss: South Africa. **Pakistan 259** (Saeed Anwar 43, Azhar Mahmood 132; A. A. Donald 5-79) **and 226** (Saeed Anwar 118, Aamir Sohail 36; S. M. Pollock 6-50); **South Africa 231** (J. H. Kallis 43, H. D. Ackerman 57, S. M. Pollock 70*; Shoaib Akhtar 5-43, Mushtaq Ahmed 3-71) **and 225** (S. M. Pollock 30, M. V. Boucher 52, P. S. de Villiers 46*; Waqar Younis 3-60, Mushtaq Ahmed 6-78).

South Africa v Pakistan

At Port Elizabeth, March 6, 7, 8, 9, 10, 1998.
South Africa won by 259 runs.

Third Test

Paul Weaver, 1999

Superficially, Pakistan looked even more powerful going into the final Test. Inzamam-ul-Haq, their finest batsman, had recovered from his ankle injury, and their best player, Wasim Akram, who had been left out of the original tour party, flew in. But this move by the Pakistan board, going over the heads of the selectors, appeared to upset the team spirit carefully rebuilt by vice-captain Aamir Sohail in Durban. There was worse. Sohail handed back the captaincy to Rashid Latif, who declared himself fit; but Latif did not appear to possess Sohail's leadership qualities and his authority was not helped when he made a pair and kept wicket erratically. Wasim did not look match-fit, and Inzamam scored six and four. Pakistan imploded and South Africa levelled the series with some ease.

South Africa brought in left-arm wrist-spinner Adams, in place of Klusener, but did not even use him in the first innings. Instead, de Villiers, playing in what he said was his final Test, returned his best figures, six for 23, and had eight for 48 in the match. It was all over 25 minutes into the final day; if rain had not wiped out the second day, Pakistan's humiliation would have been even more obvious.

Toss: Pakistan. **South Africa 293** (G. Kirsten 38, A. C. Hudson 42, W. J. Cronje 85, S. M. Pollock 38, M. V. Boucher 52; Wasim Akram 3-70, Waqar Younis 6-78) **and 206-7 dec.** (G. Kirsten 44, J. H. Kallis 69, H. D. Ackerman 42; Waqar Younis 4-55, Azhar Mahmood 3-49); **Pakistan 106** (Wasim Akram 30*; A. A. Donald 4-47, P. S. de Villiers 6-23) **and 134** (Saeed Anwar 55, Azhar Mahmood 41; A. A. Donald 4-27, P. R. Adams 3-36).

INDIA v PAKISTAN 1999

See page 444

AUSTRALIA V PAKISTAN 1999

Peter Deeley, 2001

Pakistan's cricketers left for Australia following a string of upheavals that seem part and parcel of life in their country. A military coup days before their departure not only overthrew the elected, if almost universally unpopular, government; it also detained the newly appointed chairman of the Pakistan Cricket Board, Mujeeb-ur-Rehman, and replaced the board members with yet another ad hoc committee. The new chairman, Zafar Altaf, had been manager of Pakistan's World Cup team in England. This was shortly preceded by the reinstatement as captain of Wasim Akram, who had been suspended after the World Cup following allegations of match-fixing.

There was a particular piquancy in this meeting between two of the world's leading sides. Four and a half months earlier, Steve Waugh's Australians had trounced Pakistan in the embarrassingly one-sided final of the World Cup at Lord's. And beyond that lay the tension provoked by it being a previous Australian team, under Mark Taylor, which made the match-fixing allegations that led to the judicial inquiry into Pakistan cricket.

Waugh could hardly have dared hope for a clean sweep against a side boasting an all-round attack probably without parallel in the contemporary game. Yet, for a variety of reasons, Pakistan's bowlers failed to live up to their promise. There was never room for both spinners, Mushtaq Ahmed and Saqlain Mushtaq, and Shoaib Akhtar was often too carried away by his reputation as the world's fastest bowler to reproduce his form of earlier in the year. Waqar Younis played in only one Test and appeared to be nearing the end of a wonderful international career. We learned that he felt slighted by the way Wasim had overlooked him. He could respect his captain as a cricketer, he said, but not as a leader.

Despite these problems, Pakistan had their moments. They were in with a chance of victory in a rousing First Test until the fourth afternoon, and they should have won the Second. Indeed, they would have but for an epic partnership between the left-handed Western Australian team-mates, Justin Langer and Adam Gilchrist, and an umpiring decision that swayed the game Australia's way.

Australia v Pakistan   **Second Test**

At Hobart, November 18, 19, 20, 21, 22, 1999. Australia won by four wickets.   Peter Deeley, 2001

Australia achieved an extraordinary victory to secure the series, registering the third-highest fourth-innings total to win a Test match. They had been on the ropes at 126 for five, but Langer and Gilchrist put on 238 in 59 overs, a sixth-wicket record by any country against Pakistan, to take their side to within five runs of their goal. The win was not without controversy. Umpire Parker's refusal to judge Langer caught at the wicket in the first hour of the final morning left Wasim Akram, Pakistan's captain and also the unlucky bowler, almost incandescent with rage. A breakthrough then would have made Pakistan strong favourites. Unfortunately, it was already public knowledge that Parker had apologised to Langer the previous day for giving him out wrongly in the first innings, and in Pakistani minds it all added up to a suspicion that they were not getting a fair rub of the green. Certainly, neither the situation nor the umpire was helped by the fact that, as in Brisbane, the "snickometer" reading was played over and over on the ground television screen and appeared to indicate some contact. Replays of debatable decisions were shown much too frequently. After this latest incident, series referee Reid concluded that they were undermining the umpires and took action to limit their use. Before the final Test the ACB drew the line at one slow-motion replay and one at normal speed.

Toss: Australia. **Pakistan 222** (Mohammad Wasim 91; S. A. Muller 3-68, S. K. Warne 3-45) **and 392**
(Saeed Anwar 78, Ijaz Ahmed 82, Inzamam-ul-Haq 118, Wasim Akram 31; S. K. Warne 5-110);
Australia 246 (M. J. Slater 97, G. S. Blewett 35, J. L. Langer 59; Saqlain Mushtaq 6-46)
and 369-6 (J. L. Langer 127, A. C. Gilchrist 149*).

PAKISTAN v WEST INDIES 2002
Dicky Rutnagur, 2003

In a major departure from practice and tradition, Pakistan played host to West Indies on foreign soil. Two Tests, both of which Pakistan won emphatically, and three one-day internationals were staged at the Sharjah CA Stadium in the space of 18 days. Test matches had been played on neutral territory before, during the Triangular Tournament in England in 1912 and, more recently, when Dhaka staged the final of the Asian Test Championship in 1999. This was different because it was the only alternative to the tour being cancelled, at high cost to the Pakistan Cricket Board. Their finances had already suffered from the abandonment of visits by New Zealand and Sri Lanka in the aftermath of the terrorist attacks on September 11. On top of that, West Indies feared an outbreak of hostilities between Pakistan and India. The ICC therefore approved the transfer to Sharjah, and ruled that the Tests would still count as a home series for Pakistan in the Test Championship.

The original itinerary included three Tests, but was truncated because 18 full days on the same ground was deemed impractical. There were grave doubts about the durability of the pitches at a venue which had been used only for limited-overs cricket (a record 181 internationals since 1983–84). As it happened, they played reasonably well. The spinners were expected to wreak havoc on cracked surfaces, but it was pace and reverse swing that did more damage, claiming 48 wickets to spin's 19.

The Test series was the first played under the surveillance of the ICC's anti-corruption unit, represented by two former police officers from England. The approaches to the dressing-rooms were watched over by closed-circuit television cameras, though these seemed superfluous, because the attendance was so small that every single person at the ground was conspicuous and identifiable. In a stadium seating 20,000, a few hundred turned up for the Tests, until the authorities belatedly decided to admit schoolchildren free. But these figures were immaterial. Hosting the series in Sharjah enabled the Pakistan Board to salvage their much-needed revenue from TV rights.

Pakistan v West Indies

First Test

At Sharjah, January 31, February 1, 2, 3, 4, 2002. Pakistan won by 170 runs.   Dicky Rutnagur, 2003

By the end of the third day, West Indies seemed safe. They had saved the follow-on with only five wickets down, Chanderpaul and the debutant Ryan Hinds were batting fluently, and the first Test at Sharjah, Test cricket's 83rd venue, was heading for a draw. Five sessions later, they had succumbed to another heavy defeat. Waqar Younis was outstanding as he shot out West Indies' lower half for 41 runs on the fourth morning, while Shoaib Akhtar and Abdul Razzaq wrecked them on the final day.

Toss: Pakistan. **Pakistan 493** (Younis Khan 53, Yousuf Youhana 146, Abdul Razzaq 34, Rashid Latif 150; M. Dillon 3-140, C. H. Gayle 3-27) **and 214-6 dec.** (Younis Khan 32, Inzamam-ul-Haq 48, Rashid Latif 47*); **West Indies 366** (C. H. Gayle 68, W. W. Hinds 59, C. L. Hooper 56, S. Chanderpaul 66, R. O. Hinds 62; Waqar Younis 4-93) **and 171** (D. Ganga 34, C. H. Gayle 66; Shoaib Akhtar 5-24, Abdul Razzaq 4-25).

PAKISTAN V NEW ZEALAND 2002

Qamar Ahmed and Samiul Hasan, 2003

New Zealand were originally due to arrive in Pakistan in September 2001, but called the tour off because of security fears after the terrorist attacks in the USA. Seven months later, they honoured their commitment, travelling to Pakistan for three one-day internationals and two Test matches – down from the three Tests originally planned.

Sadly, after all the spadework done by the Pakistan Cricket Board, the tour came to an abrupt and tragic end. A car bomb exploded in front of the Pearl Continental Hotel in Karachi, where both teams were staying, a couple of hours before the start of the Second Test, and killed 14 people, including 11 French engineers who were in Karachi helping the Pakistan Navy to build submarines. None of the players was hurt, though they witnessed some horrific injuries to bystanders, and the New Zealand physiotherapist, Dayle Shackel, was cut by flying glass.

The referee, Mike Procter, swiftly announced the cancellation of the Test, and the tour; the dazed Pakistan officials had no alternative but to agree. But it was depressing news for their board. They had already lost nearly $US20m after India had refused to come to Pakistan for the Asian Test Championship for political reasons, and Sri Lanka and West Indies had also declined to tour after September 11. To fulfil the requirements of the ICC Test Championship, the West Indian series was transferred to Sharjah. Now, the Karachi blast put Test cricket in Pakistan, and the future of the Championship, in jeopardy. The single Test played here did not qualify as a series in the Championship reckoning, and how many times could a tour be rescheduled?

On the field, Pakistan's triumph was total. Their record on home soil had been disappointing in recent years: they had not won a Test series there since beating West Indies in 1997. In the one-day games they achieved their first clean sweep since Zimbabwe's visit in 1996. Shoaib Akhtar unofficially bowled a 100mph delivery, and followed his best figures in one-day internationals, six for 16 at Karachi, with his best in Tests, six for 11 at Lahore. Even he was overshadowed by the hefty figure of Inzamam-ul-Haq, who became the 15th man to score a triple-hundred in Tests. New Zealand crumbled for 73 and went down to the fifth-heaviest defeat in Test history. Once the Second Test was cancelled, however, Pakistan's dominance counted for nothing in the ICC Championship.

Pakistan v New Zealand   First Test

At Lahore, May 1, 2, 3, 2002. Pakistan won by an innings and 324 runs.   2003

In three days, Pakistan recorded the fifth-biggest victory in Test cricket, thanks to two outstanding performances: a triple-century from Inzamam-ul-Haq, and six for 11 from Shoaib Akhtar. Both were hobbling by the end of the second day – Inzamam from cramp, Shoaib after spraining an ankle. But New Zealand were the real casualties. It was all downhill for them after the opening over, when Shahid Afridi gave the new wicket-keeper, Robbie Hart, his first Test dismissal. From then on, both seamers and spinners wilted on the docile pitch as temperatures soared. The first day was dominated by centuries from Imran Nazir, recalled for his first Test in 17 months, and Inzamam. Nazir reached three figures with his third six, just before tea, and they had put on 204 together in just under four hours when he was spectacularly caught by the diving Richardson at mid-on. Inzamam completed his 16th Test hundred in the next over with a crisp four off Vettori. He struck the ball delightfully, driving and cutting at every opportunity, as he added 94 with Yousuf Youhana; his only blemish in a power-packed innings came on 110, when he drove Vettori uppishly but was dropped by Vincent.

Inzamam continued with his usual flamboyance on the second day, advancing to his second double-hundred in Tests shortly before lunch. He had begun to suffer from cramp, and was allowed to use a runner for three overs before the interval; afterwards, the privilege was withdrawn. Struggling to run singles and twos, Inzamam made up for it by hitting more loose deliveries to the fence, or over it. He was 250 when Saqlain was seventh out, after a partnership of 111, but hurried on, pushing a single to cover off Harris after tea to reach Pakistan's second triple-century in Tests, following Hanif Mohammad's 337 against West Indies at Bridgetown in 1958. His first 100 had come in 191 balls, the second in 132, and the third, which contained seven fours and four sixes, at a run a ball. After adding 78 with Shoaib Akhtar – a ninth-wicket record for Pakistan against New Zealand – he hit three sixes in an over from Brooke Walker's leg-breaks and was caught at long-on attempting a fourth. Last out, he had made 329, the tenth-highest score in Test history, in a stay of 579 minutes and 436 balls, from which he smashed 38 fours and nine sixes.

Now it was Shoaib's turn. He did not bowl flat out, as in the one-day series, but controlled his line and length, occasionally slipping in one at a brisker pace. His lethal yorkers claimed four for four in 25 balls – all bowled – to leave New Zealand reeling on 21 for four. Shoaib sprained an ankle, losing his balance in his follow-through, and was absent at the start of the third morning. But he limped back on to finish the innings with two more wickets in eight deliveries, without conceding another run, for a career-best six for 11 from only 8.2 overs. It took his tally for the season to 23 wickets in five Tests at an average of 16.65 and a strike rate of 30. The tourists sank from their overnight 58 for six to 73 all out, the lowest total in Tests at Lahore, and followed on a massive 570 behind.

Shoaib did not return and, despite losing Horne in the first over, New Zealand looked more confident. They were a respectable 186 for three on the third evening, thanks to a captain's innings from Fleming, supported by Vincent and Harris. But the last seven wickets toppled for 60 in 20 overs. Danish Kaneria took his fourth five-for in eight Tests with his bouncy leg-breaks. It was Pakistan's biggest Test victory, surpassing an innings and 264 against Bangladesh in August [2001], and New Zealand's heaviest defeat. Fleming called it "a tough day in the office".

Pakistan v New Zealand, 2002 — First Test

At Lahore, May 1, 2, 3, 2002. Result: Pakistan won by an innings and 324 runs.

PAKISTAN

Imran Nazir c Richardson b McMillan	127	*Waqar Younis c and b McMillan	10
Shahid Afridi c Hart b Tuffey	0	Shoaib Akhtar st Hart b Walker	37
Younis Khan c Fleming b Vettori	27	Danish Kaneria not out	4
Inzamam–ul–Haq c Tuffey b Walker	329	B 1, l-b 8, w 1, n-b 8	18
Yousuf Youhana c Fleming b Martin	29		
Abdul Razzaq lbw b Tuffey	25	1-1 (2) 2-57 (3) 3-261 (1) 4-355 (5) 5-384 (6)	643
†Rashid Latif c and b Harris	7	6-399 (7) 7-510 (8) 8-534 (9) 9-612 (10) 10-643 (4)	
Saqlain Mushtaq b McMillan	30		

Tuffey 25–7–94–2; Martin 31–12–108–1; Vettori 40–4–178–1; Walker 14.5–3–97–2; Harris 29–3–109–1; McMillan 18–1–48–3.

NEW ZEALAND	*First innings*			*Second innings*	
M. H. Richardson b Shoaib Akhtar	8	–	c Rashid Latif b Saqlain Mushtaq		32
M. J. Horne b Shoaib Akhtar	4	–	c Rashid Latif b Waqar Younis		0
L. Vincent c Rashid Latif b Danish Kaneria	21	–	c Rashid Latif b Danish Kaneria		57
*S. P. Fleming b Shoaib Akhtar	2	–	c sub (Mohammad Sami) b Danish Kaneria		66
C. Z. Harris b Shoaib Akhtar	2	–	lbw b Abdul Razzaq		43
C. D. McMillan c Shahid Afridi b Saqlain Mushtaq	15	–	lbw b Danish Kaneria		2
†R. G. Hart lbw b Waqar Younis	4	–	b Danish Kaneria		0
D. L. Vettori c Waqar Younis b Saqlain Mushtaq	7	–	c sub (Shoaib Malik) b Abdul Razzaq		5
B. G. K. Walker lbw b Shoaib Akhtar	0	–	not out		15
D. R. Tuffey not out	6	–	c Younis Khan b Danish Kaneria		12
C. S. Martin b Shoaib Akhtar	0	–	c sub (Shoaib Malik) b Saqlain Mushtaq		0
L-b 1, n-b 3	4		B 4, l-b 6, n-b 4		14

1-12 (2) 2-17 (1) 3-19 (4) 4-21 (5) 5-53 (6)   73   1-3 (2) 2-69 (1) 3-101 (3) 4-186 (5) 5-193 (6)   246
6-57 (3) 7-66 (8) 8-67 (7) 9-73 (9) 10-73 (11)   6-193 (7) 7-204 (8) 8-227 (4) 9-245 (10) 10-246 (11)

First innings – Waqar Younis 10–6–21–1; Shoaib Akhtar 8.2–4–11–6; Danish Kaneria 6–1–19–1; Saqlain Mushtaq 6–1–21–2.
Second innings – Waqar Younis 9–1–38–1; Abdul Razzaq 14–2–47–2; Danish Kaneria 32–2–110–5; Saqlain Mushtaq 17.3–3–38–2; Shahid Afridi 4–1–3–0.

Toss won by Pakistan   UMPIRES S. A. Bucknor and R. E. Koertzen

Pakistan v Australia 2002

Martin Blake, 2004

Pakistan's proximity to trouble-torn Afghanistan, and the aftermath of the Karachi suicide bombing that cut short New Zealand's tour in May, had a lingering impact on Pakistani cricket later in 2002. In August, after months of discontented murmuring from the players, the Australian Cricket Board finally pulled out of their scheduled three-Test tour, citing government advice and security concerns.

Confronted with a choice between finding a neutral venue and cancelling the tour, the Pakistani board discussed grounds in Morocco and Bangladesh. But they finally chose Colombo for the First Test and Sharjah (where they had played West Indies in similar circumstances earlier in the year) for the last two. There were no one-day games. Even then, in the midst of the gathering storm over Iraq, the selection of a Middle Eastern venue caused concern among the Australians. The relocation was a blow to Pakistan; with home advantage seized from their grasp and several key players missing, they were crushed 3-0. Steve Waugh wanted a whitewash and his men delivered. During the Second Test, in the sledgehammer heat of Sharjah, Pakistan unravelled pitifully. Bowled out for 59 and 53, they managed fewer runs in two innings than Matthew Hayden made in one, and slumped to a humiliating innings defeat inside two days. The chairman of the board, Lieutenant General Tauqir Zia, immediately offered his resignation, though it was not accepted. The Australians were equally merciless in the Third Test, in which Pakistan were thrashed by an innings once again. The recriminations would come, but only after the embarrassment was compounded by a poor World Cup.

Pakistan v Australia

First Test

At P. Saravanamuttu Stadium, Colombo, October 3, 4, 5, 6, 7, 2002.
Australia won by 41 runs.

Martin Blake, 2004

A marvellous contest fell Australia's way on the last day after a feisty young Pakistan team almost conjured a miracle. The Australians had dominated until, in their second innings, a breathtaking spell of five wickets in 15 balls by Shoaib Akhtar turned the tide. Set a difficult 316 to win on the final two days, Pakistan were within striking distance at 187 for three. But against unremitting bowling they fell short.

The pivotal moment was Warne's dismissal of Younis Khan for an elegant 51. Five wickets then tumbled for 26 to McGrath and Gillespie with the new ball. Though Gillespie broke down with a calf strain, a few balls later Faisal spooned a catch to Ponting at backward point and it was all over. Once again, Australia's old firm of Warne, who took 11 wickets in total, and McGrath had performed heroically when it mattered most.

Toss: Australia. **Australia 467** (J. L. Langer 72, R. T. Ponting 141, M. E. Waugh 55, S. R. Waugh 31, D. R. Martyn 67, A. C. Gilchrist 66*; Shoaib Akhtar 3-51, Saqlain Mushtaq 4-136) **and 127** (M. L. Hayden 34; Shoaib Akhtar 5-21, Saqlain Mushtaq 4-46); **Pakistan 279** (Younis Khan 58, Faisal Iqbal 83, Rashid Latif 66; S. K. Warne 7-94) **and 274** (Imran Nazir 40, Taufeeq Umar 88, Younis Khan 51, Faisal Iqbal 39; G. D. McGrath 3-38, S. K. Warne 4-94).

Pakistan v Australia
Second Test

At Sharjah, October 11, 12, 2002. Australia won by an innings and 198 runs.   Martin Blake, 2004

Pakistan arrived in Sharjah comfortable with the familiar conditions and buoyed by their competitive performance in Colombo. But their mood would quickly darken as they slumped to a display that, even allowing for their reputation for spasmodic performances, could only be described as a shocker. In 125 years, Test cricket had produced only 16 two-day defeats; here, on a slow, flat pitch and against an Australian side weakened by the absence of the injured Gillespie, Pakistan subsided to the 17th.

After Waqar Younis was granted his wish to bat first on one of world cricket's most benign strips, Pakistan were rolled over for their lowest-ever score, a pathetic 59, three below their previous worst at Perth in 1981. They had lasted less than 32 overs. The openers Imran Nazir and Taufeeq Umar repeated the pair of ducks they managed in the first innings at Colombo, and only Abdul Razzaq, who endured almost two hours for 21, reached double figures. Warne caused the damage again, taking four for 11 and bewitching the batsmen with his new "slider". Pushing forward, they found themselves trapped lbw by deliveries that were doing precisely nothing.

Two balls after tea on the first day, the Australians were already in front. With the temperature pushing 50°C in the middle, Hayden likened it to batting in an oven and wondered whether hell was any hotter. But his sheer hunger for runs came to the fore. While Ponting looked ready to expire by the time he was out for 44, Hayden ground his way relentlessly to 119. Afterwards, Steve Waugh would label Hayden the best batsman in the world. Waugh was celebrating his 150th Test, but a first-ball duck scarcely crowned the event and meant Waugh beat Mike Atherton's record for an established batsman of 20 Test ducks.

Following their mauling in Colombo, the Australians had spent a lot of time devising strategies to counter Shoaib Akhtar's speed and reverse swing. In fact Shoaib could not cope with the heat and proved ineffectual, managing only 14 overs. Waqar Younis bowled just eight, and the batsmen pummelled Danish Kaneria, the young leg-spinner who had come into the team in place of the seamer Mohammad Sami. It meant that Pakistan leaned heavily on Saqlain Mushtaq, who toiled for 34 overs and was rewarded with four for 83, including the Waughs with consecutive balls. However Hayden showed his opponents the determination that the conditions demanded. Dropped twice, he never truly dominated – though he reached three figures with a six off Kaneria – but his seven-hour vigil was exactly what Australia needed.

Australia were aiming for 500; although they managed only 310, it proved more than enough. After Nazir simply turned his back on Taufeeq as he charged through for a run in Pakistan's first over, and Razzaq's wrist was broken by Lee in the sixth, their resolve fractured too. Warne once again imposed his authority, taking four for 13, and the quick bowlers mopped up. Pakistan had lasted less than 25 overs, and were routed for 53. Their record low had lasted only one day.

Pakistan v Australia, 2002 — Second Test

At Sharjah, October 11, 12, 2002. Result: Australia won by an innings and 198 runs.

PAKISTAN

	First innings		Second innings	
Imran Nazir c Warne b McGrath		0	c Gilchrist b Warne	16
Taufeeq Umar b Lee		0	run out	0
Abdul Razzaq c Martyn b Warne		21	retired hurt	4
Younis Khan c Bichel b McGrath		5	lbw b McGrath	0
Misbah–ul–Haq c M. E. Waugh b Bichel		2	c S. R. Waugh b Bichel	12
Faisal Iqbal lbw b Warne		4	c M. E. Waugh b Warne	7
†Rashid Latif not out		4	c M. E. Waugh b Bichel	0
Saqlain Mushtaq lbw b Warne		0	c Warne b Lee	9
Shoaib Akhtar c Gilchrist b Bichel		1	c S. R. Waugh b Warne	2
*Waqar Younis lbw b Warne		0	lbw b Warne	0
Danish Kaneria b Lee		8	not out	1
B 8, l-b 2, n-b 4		14	N-b 2	2

1-0 (1) 2-1 (2) 3-8 (4) 4-23 (5) 5-41 (6)   59
6-46 (3) 7-46 (8) 8-49 (9) 9-50 (10) 10-59 (11)

1-0 (2) 2-13 (4) 3-32 (1) 4-34 (5) 5-36 (7)   53
6-50 (6) 7-52 (8) 8-52 (9) 9-53 (10)

First innings – McGrath 7–4–10–2; Lee 7.5–1–15–2; Bichel 6–2–13–2; Warne 11–4–11–4.
Second innings – McGrath 6–2–5–1; Lee 5–2–16–1; Bichel 7–1–19–2; Warne 6.5–2–13–4.

AUSTRALIA

J. L. Langer run out	37		S. K. Warne c Younis Khan	
M. L. Hayden c Imran Nazir			b Saqlain Mushtaq	19
b Saqlain Mushtaq	119		B. Lee lbw b Abdul Razzaq	12
R. T. Ponting lbw b Danish Kaneria	44		A. J. Bichel not out	2
M. E. Waugh lbw b Saqlain Mushtaq	2		G. D. McGrath lbw b Abdul Razzaq	0
*S. R. Waugh c sub (Imran Farhat)			B 15, l-b 7, n-b 2	24
b Saqlain Mushtaq	0			
D. R. Martyn c Taufeeq Umar b Abdul Razzaq	34		1-55 (1) 2-145 (3) 3-148 (4) 4-148 (5) 5-224 (6)	310
†A. C. Gilchrist c Taufeeq Umar			6-252 (7) 7-285 (8) 8-304 (9) 9-310 (2) 10-310 (11)	
b Shoaib Akhtar	17			

Waqar Younis 8–2–25–0; Shoaib Akhtar 14–3–42–1; Danish Kaneria 26–2–116–1;
Abdul Razzaq 10.1–3–22–3; Saqlain Mushtaq 34–2–83–4.

Toss won by Pakistan   UMPIRES S. A. Bucknor and S. Venkataraghavan
MAN OF THE MATCH M. L. Hayden

PAKISTAN IN SOUTH AFRICA AND ZIMBABWE 2002–03

Neil Manthorp and John Ward, 2004

The most notoriously unpredictable team in international cricket stretched even their own extremes on this tour. In Zimbabwe, they were all-conquering. In South Africa, many of their performances were bad enough to be laughable, yet somehow they produced a single day of brilliance, scoring 335 for six at Port Elizabeth to inflict South Africa's heaviest one-day defeat.

But Pakistan still lost that limited-overs series 4–1, and the two Test matches in South Africa were so one-sided that in a different sport they would have been stopped early. The bowling was routinely tired, and the batting – barring that one rousing day and two gritty but hopeless efforts by Taufeeq Umar in the Second Test – uncommitted. In general, Pakistan were depressingly uninspired. Their form in Zimbabwe on the first part of the trip, when they swept the board against a side wracked by injuries, most importantly to their captain and inspiration, Heath Streak, seemed irrelevant: their humiliation by Australia just beforehand did not.

Even to the naked eye the Pakistani team lacked cohesion and harmony but, in case anyone doubted it, the tour was awash with stories of infighting and argument. Wasim Akram, inevitably, was involved in most of them, and his decision to return home after the one-dayers was greeted with relief among some of his colleagues. The camp was clearly split. Shoaib Akhtar, one of Wasim's acolytes, expressed his contempt for management and team spirit during the First Test in Durban. Having decided he was carrying a knee injury and unable to play, Shoaib revelled in the attention of Durban's big Asian population, boogieing the night away in carefree fashion at a Bollywood extravaganza. Certainly beats bowling 20 overs a day in the heat.

Throughout this disintegrating mess, the captain Waqar Younis remained outwardly calm, but he was clearly resigned to having little influence and even less control. Damage limitation seemed to be the main priority, which led to a highly conservative approach to selection: Pakistan entered the opening Test with just three bowlers plus an all-rounder, with disastrous results, and still fielded only a four-man attack in the Second Test at Cape Town. This time, South Africa piled up 620 for seven, and the bowlers' futile and exhausted efforts were rewarded only by a whopping fine – 100% of the match fee – for a slow over-rate. Had a team ever emerged from a Test so utterly empty-handed?

By way of partial explanation, Pakistan's coach, Richard Pybus, revealed that some members of the squad were "mentally and physically exhausted" and had spent as few as five days at home during the preceding six months. But the end result was a heartless, soulless and headless display that was unworthy of Pakistan's proud reputation and history.

South Africa v Pakistan   Second Test

At Cape Town, January 2, 3, 4, 5, 2003.
South Africa won by an innings and 142 runs.   Neil Manthorp, 2004

Gibbs and Smith destroyed Pakistan's demoralised bowling with an opening stand of 368, at the time South Africa's best for any wicket. Gibbs, in particular, played shots that caused grown men in the stands to miss their mouths with their sandwiches. South Africa reached 445 by the first-day close, more than they had ever before managed in a day.

Having lost a toss he desperately needed to win, Waqar Younis ran in to bowl the first ball looking like a fun-runner completing the last mile of a charity marathon. Like so many that followed, it was wide and harmless. Despite a sad flogging for an understaffed attack in Durban, the selectors had not dipped into their reserves for reinforcement. The injured Abdul Razzaq was replaced by the tall medium-pacer

Mohammad Zahid, playing his first Test in over four years, following major back surgery. He was a very different bowler from the one who took 11 for 130 on debut against New Zealand in November 1996, producing two spells of long-hops and leaking 61 in his first 11 overs. Gibbs skipped down to hit all the bowlers, inside out, over extra cover, while Smith hooked, pulled and hooked again. Length became increasingly inconsequential as they tried to outdo each other, complete with toothy grins.

After tea, Eddie Barlow and Graeme Pollock's 341 for the third wicket at Adelaide in 1964 was erased as South Africa's highest partnership. Soon afterwards, Gibbs reached his double-hundred, from 211 deliveries, the second-fastest ever recorded in terms of balls. He couldn't help dreaming, he later said, of the records that lay within his grasp. But ten overs before the close, he pushed forward with a hint of tiredness to Saqlain Mushtaq, the ball looped off his pad to slip and umpire Venkat raised his finger – to the disbelief of Gibbs and dismay of the crowd. His 228 had lasted six hours 23 minutes and 240 balls, and included 29 fours and six sixes. It was the highest Test score at Newlands.

Next day, Dippenaar and McKenzie helped themselves to very deliberate half-centuries, but it was akin to looting in the aftermath of violent conflict. Pollock's declaration left South Africa two short of their highest total, 622 for nine against Australia at Durban in 1970. "I didn't know," admitted a sheepish Pollock. His uncle Graeme could have reminded him: he scored 274 that day.

By now, most of the Pakistanis seemed to have lost all will to fight, and they would later be fined their entire match fee for a funereal over-rate. The exception was the determined Taufeeq Umar, who led them to 152 for one. On the third morning, though, Pollock trapped Younis Khan lbw, Ntini backed him up and nine wickets fell for 100. Taufeeq, however, had made a serious impression amid the collapse. Short, left-handed and well balanced, with quick feet and even quicker hands, he clearly had more time to play the ball than any of his team-mates and thoroughly deserved his 135, which occupied five and three-quarter hours with a six and 20 fours – most sweetly timed through the covers.

Taufeeq showed more guts during the follow-on, and not just on the field. Having top-scored again, with a classy 67, he watched from the pavilion as Yousuf Youhana launched a frenzied assault. But for a couple of miscues, he would have hit the fastest recorded Test fifty in balls, although 27, with six fours and two sixes was still second quickest. It was also inappropriate to the situation and Taufeeq, in broken English, let it be known how he felt: "I will not speak of that," he seethed through clenched teeth. "I have no comment."

Once Youhana went in the final over of the third day, the rest folded compliantly. And so it was with his second successive massive four-day win – which took South Africa to the top of the ICC Championship – that Shaun Pollock's reign as Test captain ended. Two months later he was sacked. For Gibbs and Smith, memories were not so bitter-sweet.

Toss: South Africa. **South Africa 620-7 dec.** (G. C. Smith 151, H. H. Gibbs 228, J. H. Kallis 31, H. H. Dippenaar 62, N. D. McKenzie 51, S. M. Pollock 36*; Saqlain Mushtaq 3-237); **Pakistan 252** (Taufeeq Umar 135, Younis Khan 46, Inzamam-ul-Haq 32; S. M. Pollock 4-45, M. Ntini 4-62) **and 226** (Taufeeq Umar 67, Inzamam-ul-Haq 60, Yousuf Youhana 50; M. Ntini 4-33).

PAKISTAN V ENGLAND 2005 — John Etheridge, 2006

England's sequence of six successive series victories was brought to an end by a resurgent, united and at times brilliant Pakistan side. Two dramatic final-day collapses, one when in sight of winning the First Test and the other when apparently on the way to securing a comfortable draw in the Third, meant England lost two matches in a series in Pakistan for the first time. Coming so soon after their historic Ashes triumph, the tour was a chastening experience for Michael Vaughan's party. Their batting lacked patience and application, the threat posed by their spin bowlers was minimal and their momentum was disrupted by important players missing matches because of injury or paternity leave. In the end, England were comprehensively outplayed. The champagne of the previous summer was replaced by nothing more intoxicating than a pot of the local green tea. It tasted bitter.

Pakistan, by contrast, improved steadily: their superiority was such by the Third Test that they won by the crushing margin of an innings and 100 runs. Most of the dominant characters were in their ranks. Inzamam-ul-Haq's lowest score in five innings was 53 and he was named Man of the Series. Mohammad Yousuf (formerly Yousuf Youhana, before his conversion from Christianity to Islam) made a double-century in the Third Test, Salman Butt and Kamran Akmal also reached three figures and Danish Kaneria initiated the two series-deciding England collapses with his wrist-spin. But no image captured Pakistan's joy at winning more than the expressive face of Shoaib Akhtar. Eyes wild, hair flowing, sweat spraying, Shoaib re-established himself as one of the true characters of world cricket. He bowled magnificently and with renewed commitment after his unhappy time with Worcestershire earlier in the year and a heavily criticised appearance for the World XI in Australia a few weeks before. Shoaib's bowling was a dazzling cocktail. He mixed 95mph deliveries with superbly disguised 65mph slower balls, not to mention yorkers, bouncers and even the occasional good-length ball. Shoaib took 17 wickets in the three Tests, and could have had more: no England batsman was able to relax against him.

Pakistan v England — First Test
At Multan, November 12, 13, 14, 15, 16, 2005. Pakistan won by 22 runs. — Mike Dickson, 2006

It was a mark of the progress England had made that the team emitted an air of stunned disbelief when they failed to close the deal in yet another riveting Test match. After the Ashes, they appeared to have that basic commodity of modern sport, "mental toughness", by the bucketload. But it was the supposedly more flaky Pakistan side that came through under pressure. Marshalled and inspired by captain Inzamam-ul-Haq, they won by 22 runs early on the final afternoon.

The pivotal passage of play, however, came halfway through the morning session. Chasing 198, England were 64 for one, then lost five wickets in ten overs. That left them on 101 for six with, as it turned out, just too much to do. Some of the dismissals were simply profligate, wasting the hard work put in during the first four days to build a winning position after losing the toss. So often in the previous year, they had squeezed a satisfactory outcome out of the final day; this time, it proved beyond them.

Marcus Trescothick led England for the second time in a Test, again because Michael Vaughan had damaged his right knee. Fears were politely expressed in some quarters that Trescothick would be an inadequate deputy. These were to prove unfounded. He guided his team with tactical astuteness and led by example, with a superb 193 in their first innings dwarfing any other contribution. Not only that, but it later emerged that he was coping with a family crisis. His father-in-law had suffered a severe head injury falling from a ladder and was critically ill in a Bristol hospital; it was serious enough for Trescothick to consider going home, though eventually he decided to stay.

It was the 24th successive Test since Kingston in March 2004 featuring the triumvirate of Hoggard, Harmison and Flintoff; once more taking their lead from Flintoff, they combined superbly to dismiss Pakistan for 274 on a glorious batting surface. The adhesive young opener Salman Butt stood out with 74, before giving Udal his first Test wicket in unusual circumstances: a thick edge flew through Trescothick's hands at slip, pinged off his forehead and was well taken by the alert Jones, diving backwards. But with the last nine wickets falling for 113, there was no doubting which team had the swagger that comes from vanquishing the world champions.

Much of England's batting in the warm-up matches had been flimsy, and this was true again. Bell worked hard for 71, but elsewhere there was an ominous lack of application, with many unable to pick Danish Kaneria's googly. Trescothick was immune. Although he survived a decent lbw shout from Kaneria on 48, he gave only one chance, on 181, when he swept to square leg. He faced 305 balls, hit 20 fours, and twice lofted Kaneria over long-off for six. He had batted for 13 minutes shy of eight hours when, just after lunch on the third day, he nicked the seamer Shabbir Ahmed to leave his team on 388 for seven. The eventual lead was 144. Even so, there was a sense that England could have scored more heavily: they had been 251 for two just before the second-day close.

Pakistan's mainstays were Butt and the stately Inzamam, who despite rising temperatures never took the field without a sleeveless sweater. On the fourth day, the two of them calmly went about the task of trying to bat England out of the game. Butt showed great self-knowledge in his shot selection, working the ball into gaps and minimising risk against the persistent probing of Flintoff and Hoggard. All was to change, however, with the second new ball. Its second delivery trapped Inzamam in front of his wicket, as Hoggard, able to gain conventional swing, got one to hold its line. There was panic in the home dressing-room as Flintoff added two more in quick succession. He had been given the new ball ahead of Harmison, who was bowling slightly less consistently than his peers, though he did chip in with the final two wickets. The last – a lob to square leg – was notable for being Pietersen's first Test catch, after his six spillages against Australia.

Despite losing Trescothick late on the fourth day, England should have overhauled a target of 198 on a benign surface, and looked like doing so at 64 for one. Then three wickets fell in eight balls, starting with Bell, the first of several batsmen looking to be too aggressive against Kaneria's leg-spin. The tourists needed big innings from their big hitters, but Flintoff played a "six or out" swipe that went straight to deep mid-wicket, while Pietersen flailed at a very wide delivery and was caught behind. Jones rallied England, and got them within 32 of victory before he was bowled off bat and pad by Shoaib Akhtar – like Kaneria, much improved from the first innings. It was all over ten balls later. Pakistan's only disappointment was that the umpires later reported the bowling actions of Shabbir and off-spinner Shoaib Malik. As for England, they were reminded that in Test cricket one bad hour is enough to undo four days' good work.

Toss: Pakistan. **Pakistan 274** (Shoaib Malik 39, Salman Butt 74, Younis Khan 39, Inzamam-ul-Haq 53; S. J. Harmison 3-37, A. Flintoff 4-68) **and 341** (Salman Butt 122, Younis Khan 48, Inzamam-ul-Haq 72, Kamran Akmal 33; A. Flintoff 4-88, S. J. Harmison 3-52); **England 418** (M. E. Trescothick 193, I. R. Bell 71, A. Flintoff 45, Extras 42; Shoaib Akhtar 3-99, Shabbir Ahmed 4-54) **and 175** (I. R. Bell 31, G. O. Jones 33; Shoaib Akhtar 3-49, Danish Kaneria 4-62).

Pakistan v England   Third Test
At Lahore, November 29, 30, December 1, 2, 3, 2005.
Pakistan won by an innings and 100 runs.   Matthew Engel, 2006

England were inching towards a draw in this match as though walking a narrow parapet to escape a burning building. They got within touching distance of the fire escape. Then there was a sudden slip, a lurch – and down they plummeted. But there was no gasp of horror from the onlookers. Instead, the crowd did jigs of delight and deafeningly crashed their hands against the plastic seats.

Ian Bell and Paul Collingwood batted the game towards torpor for more than four hours until, just after lunch on the final day, England lost eight for 43 in 70 minutes, ending their supposedly glorious Test year with one of the most startling collapses of recent history. The win was concocted by the enigmatic Shoaib Akhtar, who used both his extreme pace and his near-unreadable slower ball to devastating effect, and the leg-spinner Danish Kaneria. They were briefly awesome.

Overall, on a slow pitch with a fast outfield, batsmen found it easy to stay in once ensconced, but hard to get settled. Thus a turnaround was always plausible: England's batting in the final phase was abject, but not especially incompetent. Their real disaster had come at the start, when they squandered the advantage of winning the toss at last, and let themselves be bowled out for 288. For a while, it was possible to kid oneself that the surface was wicked enough to make this a passable score. But from lunchtime on the third day, as Mohammad Yousuf and Kamran Akmal took utter command, it was clear that England's prime objective – victory to square the series – was unattainable. In the end, the secondary target of a draw proved elusive too. There was no serious argument that Pakistan deserved their 2–0 series victory.

Toss: England. **England 288** (M. E. Trescothick 50, M. P. Vaughan 58, P. D. Collingwood 96, K. P. Pietersen 34; Shoaib Malik 3-58) **and 248** (I. R. Bell 92, P. D. Collingwood 80, Extras 32; Shoaib Akhtar 5-71, Danish Kaneria 4-52); **Pakistan 636-8 dec.** (Mohammad Yousuf 223, Inzamam-ul-Haq 97, Shoaib Akhtar 38, Kamran Akmal 154, Naved-ul-Hasan 42*).

Sri Lanka's Instant Success

S ri Lanka found their feet in Test cricket remarkably quickly. Indeed, in his Notes, *Wisden* editor John Woodcock made a point of applauding their first Test victory, against India in 1985, and pointing out that while it had taken some countries a generation to establish themselves, Sri Lanka had managed it in just three years. Their performance at Lord's in 1984, when Sidath Wettimuny made a memorable 190, established their credentials to a British audience and, as David Hopps points out in an article reprinted here, it was absurd that they had to wait almost 20 years for a full tour to Britain. Even now, we treat them as the *hors d'oeuvre* – laid on in drizzly May before some more enticing series. The old patronising view of Sri Lankan cricket lingers. An odd way to treat a team which has won the World Cup, a trophy which has of course eluded some rather longer-established Test-playing nations. S. M.

The Sri Lankans in England 1981
Henry Blofeld, 1982

Anyone watching the Sri Lankans on their England tour must have been struck by their seemingly old-fashioned approach to the game. Their strength lay with spin – they regularly bowled 20 overs in the hour – while their batsmen went for their strokes as though believing that attack was always the best form of defence. Bandula Warnapura's side, therefore, provided good entertainment wherever they played, even if the inescapable question always remained. How will such methods serve them in Test cricket?

There was no doubting the side's natural talent. The leg-spin of D. S. de Silva and the off-breaks of Lalith Kaluperuma formed a top-class spin pairing. There was also much exotic strokeplay by Sidath Wettimuny, Hemantha Devapriya, Roy Dias, Yohan Gunasekera, Duleep Mendis, Nirmal Hettiaratchy and Anura Ranasinghe, besides the captain himself, which was never better illustrated than when they beat a representative TCCB XI at Trent Bridge. In Sri Lanka, in high heat and humidity, they should always be a difficult side to beat. After Kim Hughes's Australians had played there on their way to England in April, they reckoned that only the West Indians, because of the ferocity of their pace attack, could at the moment be confidently expected to win a Test series there. That, though, is at home. Their seam attack is weak, and in England in 1981 the Sri Lankans won only one of their first-class matches and that on a declaration.

TESTS FOR SRI LANKA

John Woodcock, *Notes by the Editor*, 1982

In 1981 the International Cricket Conference admitted Sri Lanka to full membership, thus increasing to seven, exclusive of South Africa, the number of Test-playing
countries. During a two-months tour of England the Sri Lankan national team
played an engagingly open type of game. They are a welcome addition to the fold.

SRI LANKA V ENGLAND 1982   Inaugural Test Match

At Saravanamuttu Oval, Colombo, February 17, 18, 20, 21, 1982.
England won by seven wickets.

John Thicknesse, 1983

Although they were beaten five minutes from the end of the fourth day, following a
headlong collapse in which seven wickets fell for eight runs, Sri Lanka did enough in
their first Test to show they deserved elevation to full membership of the International
Cricket Conference. Apart from the frustration when, in three-quarters of an hour,
Emburey destroyed their hopes with a spell of five for five, the only disappointment
of a long-awaited moment in the island's history was the smallness of the crowds. The
consequence was a saddening lack of atmosphere, except briefly on the fourth morning
when Sri Lanka, 160 ahead with seven wickets standing on a turning pitch, seemed to
have the makings of a winning score. Ultimately, both the batting and the spin bowling
failed to rise to the occasion, but their overall performance left little doubt that Sri
Lanka have a handful of promising young players.

Sri Lanka v England, 1982   Inaugural Test

At Colombo, February 17, 18, 20, 21, 1982. Result: England won by seven wickets.

SRI LANKA

	First innings		Second innings	
*B. Warnapura c Gower b Willis		2	– c Gooch b Emburey	38
S. Wettimuny c Taylor b Botham		6	– b Willis	9
R. L. Dias c Cook b Willis		0	– c Taylor b Underwood	77
L. R. D. Mendis lbw b Botham		17	– c Willis b Emburey	27
R. S. Madugalle c Gower b Underwood		65	– c Cook b Emburey	3
A. Ranatunga b Underwood		54	– c Fletcher b Emburey	2
D. S. de Silva c Gower b Underwood		3	– c Fletcher b Underwood	1
A. L. F. de Mel c Fletcher b Underwood		19	– c Gower b Emburey	2
L. W. Kaluperuma c Cook b Underwood		1	– c Taylor b Emburey	0
†H. M. Goonatillake not out		22	– not out	2
G. R. A. de Silva c Emburey b Botham		12	– c Willis b Underwood	0
B 2, l-b 4, w 2, n-b 9		17	L-b 6, n-b 8	14

1-9 2-11 3-29 4-34 5-133 6-149   218   1-30 2-113 3-140 4-167 5-169 6-170   175
7-181 8-183 9-190 10-218   7-172 8-173 9-174 10-175

First innings – Willis 19–7–46–2; Botham 12.5–1–28–3; Allott 13–4–44–0; Emburey 19–3–55–0;
Underwood 18–6–28–5.
Second innings – Willis 9–3–24–1; Botham 12–1–37–0; Emburey 25–9–33–6; Underwood 37.5–15–67–3.

ENGLAND	*First innings*		*Second innings*
G. A. Gooch lbw b de Mel	22	– b G. R. A. de Silva	31
G. Cook c Kaluperuma b de Mel	11	– lbw b de Mel	0
C. J. Tavare b de Mel	0	– st Goonatillake b G. R. A. de Silva	85
D. I. Gower c Goonatillake b D. S. de Silva . . .	89	– not out	42
*K. W. R. Fletcher			
c Warnapura b G. R. A. de Silva	45	– not out	0
I. T. Botham b de Mel	13		
†R. W. Taylor not out	31		
J. E. Emburey lbw b G. R. A. de Silva	0		
P. J. W. Allott c Kaluperuma b D. S. de Silva .	3		
D. L. Underwood c Mendis b D. S. de Silva .	0		
R. G. D. Willis run out	0		
L-b 3, n-b 6	9	B 7, l-b 5, n-b 1	13
	223		**(3 wkts) 171**

1-34 2-34 3-40 4-120 5-151 6-200
7-207 8-216 9-216 10-223

1-3 2-84 3-167

First innings – de Mel 17–2–70–4; Warnapura 3–1–9–0; D. S. de Silva 27.5–11–54–3;
Kaluperuma 9–1–29–0; G. R. A. de Silva 30–12–52–2.
Second innings – de Mel 13.1–4–33–1; Warnapura 1–0–1–0; D. S. de Silva 15–5–38–0;
Kaluperuma 12–3–40–0; G. R. A. de Silva 17–6–46–2.

Toss won by Sri Lanka · · · · · · · · · · · · · · · · UMPIRES H. C. Felsinger and K. T. Francis

---

SRI LANKA V NEW ZEALAND 1984 · · · · · · · · · · · · · · Steve McMorran, 1985

Hosting the first full tour by a Test-playing country was the most significant event
in Sri Lanka's cricketing history since their inaugural Test match, against England,
two years earlier. It gave the Sri Lankan board an opportunity to put international
cricket before an eager public for the first extended period in their history.

From that point of view, the tour was a success. All matches were well attended
and Sri Lankans, whose love of the game rivals that of their counterparts anywhere in
the world, gave administrators encouragement for future ventures. The New Zealanders
took first-class cricket to the historic Portuguese settlement of Galle and to Radella,
high in Sri Lanka's tea-planting area, where the game was first played by immigrant
planters more that 150 years ago. They also christened the world's 57th and 58th Test
venues, the Sinhalese Sports Club and Colombo Cricket Club grounds, during a tour
of eight matches, which included three Tests and three one-day internationals.

Sri Lankan officials had hoped that their young team would mark the tour
with their first Test victory. New Zealand commanded the Test series, however,
and carried on to win the one-day series as well. In terms of results this made it
the most successful overseas tour by a New Zealand side. Richard Hadlee was New
Zealand's trump card. His ability to claim vital wickets at crucial moments was a
constant handicap to the Sri Lankans, who were also encumbered by a lack of Test
experience. They lost the First and Third Tests from positions which should have
allowed them to claim a draw, though they did attain a compensatory victory in
the second one-day international.

Sri Lanka v New Zealand   First Test

At Kandy, March 9, 10, 11, 13, 14, 1984. New Zealand won by 165 runs.   Steve McMorran, 1985

Rain, continuing to dog the New Zealanders, washed out the first four sessions of a match which, once it started, was closely contested until Sri Lanka collapsed on the final day. New Zealand were 120 for one by the close of the second day and all out for 276 before tea on the third. Madugalle was the most solid of the Sri Lankans in their first innings, the highlight of which was a last-wicket partnership of 60 between John and a new cap, Amerasinghe, Sri Lanka's best in Test cricket. With Howarth posting a second half-century, New Zealand declared their second innings eight minutes after lunch on the final day. Sri Lanka's collapse, as they chased 263 in 130 minutes plus 20 overs, amazed spectators and led to disturbances which had to be quelled by riot police. Sri Lanka could amass only 97, of which Ranatunga made 51, which prompted a partial recovery from 18 for six to 97 for eight. Hadlee claimed four wickets for eight runs from his first six overs and Boock wrapped up the tail.

Toss: New Zealand. **New Zealand 276** (G. P. Howarth 62, J. G. Wright 45, I. D. S. Smith 30; V. B. John 5-86) **and 201-8 dec.** (G. P. Howarth 60, J. F. Reid 30, I. D. S. Smith 31*; V. B. John 3-73, D. S. de Silva 3-59); **Sri Lanka 215** (R. S. Madugalle 33, A. M. J. G. Amerasinghe 34; R. J. Hadlee 4-35) **and 97** (A. Ranatunga 51; R. J. Hadlee 4-8, S. L. Boock 5-28).

Sri Lanka v New Zealand   Third Test

At Colombo Cricket Club, March 24, 25, 26, 28, 29, 1984.
New Zealand won by an innings and 61 runs.   Steve McMorran, 1985

Hadlee marked his 50th Test appearance with a match-winning haul of ten wickets. He claimed five in each innings, the seventeenth and eighteenth occasions on which he has achieved the feat in his Test career. Sri Lanka's innings was marked by Madugalle's brave 89 in 218 minutes, completed in two parts through his being forced to retire late on the first day when hit behind the left ear by a ball from Hadlee, and for the second time in the series a Sri Lankan record partnership (109 with Ranatunga for the sixth wicket) was brought to an end by injury. New Zealand batted for almost three days in reply for a lead of 203. The left-handed Reid batted for eleven and a half hours for his 180. Playing for a draw, Sri Lanka were 69 for three at the close of the fourth day but, succumbing to Hadlee's venom, were out shortly after lunch on the fifth.

Toss: Sri Lanka. **Sri Lanka 256** (R. S. Madugalle 89*, A. Ranatunga 37; R. J. Hadlee 5-73, E. J. Chatfield 5-63) **and 142** (R. S. Madugalle 38, A. Ranatunga 50; R. J. Hadlee 5-29, S. L. Boock 3-32); **New Zealand 459** (J. F. Reid 180, M. D. Crowe 45, S. L. Boock 35, J. V. Coney 92, I. D. S. Smith 42; V. B. John 3-99, J. R. Ratnayeke 3-128).

England v Sri Lanka 1984

John Woodcock, 1985

For the third time in six years Sri Lanka sent a team to England to play a series of first-class matches, mostly against the counties. In 1979, while they were here, they performed quite creditably in the Prudential World Cup; in 1981 their visit coincided with their election to full membership of the International Cricket Conference. Nothing they had ever done, however, outside their own country, bore any comparison with the remarkable success they enjoyed in the Test match against England at Lord's at the end of August 1984, their first in this country. Having been put in by David Gower, on a morning when the ball was expected to swing, they were still batting two days later, by when Sidath Wettimuny had made 190, the highest score by anyone on his first Test appearance in England, and the Sri Lankan captain, Duleep Mendis, had raced to a hundred in only 112 balls. In the end Sri Lanka gained a first-innings lead of 121 and had the better of a drawn game, Mendis having come, by then, within six runs of making a second century.

Not surprisingly this achievement dwarfed all else on the tour. For the most part the Sri Lankans struggled to hold their own against the counties, of whom they played seven. They failed, in fact, to win a first-class match and lost to Surrey at The Oval. The only two sides they bowled out, even once, were Kent (who scored 420 for five declared in their second innings) and England. This overall record accurately indicated the weakness of their attack. As on their previous tours, they had no one of any real pace, and they were hampered now by injuries.

The batsmen played mostly with a wristy charm and a keen determination not to be subdued. Boosted by their showing at Lord's – they were of the opinion that the pitch there was the best they had ever batted on – they went to Edgbaston where they declared twice against Warwickshire. Amal Silva, a left-hander who made Wettimuny a good opening partner, finished the tour by making 102 not out in the second innings of the Test match – his maiden first class hundred – followed by 161 not out and 70 against Warwickshire. The left-handed Arjuna Ranatunga also played attractively while making 84 at Lord's, and Madugalle looked a well-balanced, quick-footed player. The only disappointment among the batsmen was Roy Dias, though he, too, made his top score in the Test match. A certain portliness among some of the side showed up in the field and reflected the side's carefree, if not pragmatic, approach to the game.

England v Sri Lanka, 1984

At Lord's, August 23, 24, 25, 27, 28, 1984. Drawn.

Test Match

Michael Carey, 1985

Sri Lanka marked their inaugural appearance at Lord's with a splendid performance, especially with the bat, which won them a host of new admirers and in only their twelfth match at this level left few in any doubt about their right to Test status. None of them had played at Lord's before, yet three of their batsmen, Wettimuny, Silva and Mendis, all made centuries. England, by contrast, had many dreadfully inept moments, with both bat and ball, and Gower's leadership was short of imagination. Ironically, the match was expected to give England some respite after their battering by West Indies; instead, it produced more moments of embarrassment, and if Lamb, whose fourth century of the summer made him one of the few successes, had been caught behind when 36, England might even have had to follow on.

Gower's decision to bowl first, made in anticipation of the ball swinging on a hazy morning, proved to be the wrong one, and after two early breakthroughs by Botham and Ellison, Sri Lanka ended the first day at 226 for three, Wettimuny reaching three figures despite being restricted by an attack of cramp. He batted throughout the second day as well, when England took only one wicket and Mendis made an unbeaten 100 from only 112 deliveries with glorious strokes, including three hooks for six off Botham.

England contributed to their problems with inefficiency and mismanagement in the field. Despite the ineffectiveness of their quicker bowlers, Pocock was not seen until mid-afternoon when the score was 366 for four. Three catches went down and Sri Lanka completed England's humiliation by twice refusing offers from the umpires to go off for bad light. Wettimuny and Mendis received standing ovations at the end, and Sri Lanka's progress was checked only on the third morning when Pocock and Allott, the most accurate of the England bowlers, were used in harness and the batsmen deserted their more orthodox methods to try to accelerate.

Wettimuny's tremendous effort ended after ten hours 42 minutes, the longest innings in a Test match at Lord's. His 190 was the highest score by any batsman on his first appearance in a Test in England and had been bettered by a visiting player at Lord's only by Sir Donald Bradman (254), C. G. Greenidge (214 not out), M. P. Donnelly (206), W. A. Brown (206 not out), Mohsin Khan (200) and W. Bardsley (193 not out). The only surprise was that, with three bowlers carrying injuries and an attack which on their tour had bowled out only one county side in 11 innings, Sri Lanka did not go beyond 491 for seven, which was their highest Test total.

But it scarcely mattered, for England continued with the bat as modestly as they had performed in the field. From 27 overs between lunch and tea, the focal point of a Saturday at Lord's, Tavaré and Broad scored only 49 runs. The ground now rang with shouts of derision after the cheers for Sri Lanka, and Gower even apologised to spectators at his Saturday evening press conference, saying: "That kind of cricket is no fun to watch and it is certainly worse to play like it."

England avoided the follow-on with five wickets down on the fourth day, although Lamb's escape and two near things for Ellison, before he had scored, illustrated how hard they found the going against bowling that was no more than workmanlike on a pitch which remained good. D. S. de Silva, a leg-spinner, was able to complete 45 economical overs, despite an ankle injury which had needed an X-ray earlier, and with a lead of 121 Sri Lanka then overcame the loss of two early second-innings wickets to Botham on the last morning and kept England at arm's length afterwards. Mendis narrowly failed to become only the second man, G. A. Headley being the other, to make two centuries in a Lord's Test.

England v Sri Lanka, 1984

Test Match

At Lord's, August 23, 24, 25, 27, 28, 1984. Result: Drawn.

SRI LANKA

	First innings		*Second innings*	
S. Wettimuny c Downton b Allott	190	– c Gower b Botham	13
†S. A. R. Silva lbw b Botham	8	– not out	102
R. S. Madugalle b Ellison	5	– b Botham	3
R. L. Dias c Lamb b Pocock	32	– lbw b Botham	38
A. Ranatunga b Agnew	84	– lbw b Botham	0
*L. R. D. Mendis c Fowler b Pocock	111	– (7) c Fowler b Botham	94
P. A. de Silva c Downton b Agnew	16	– (6) c Downton b Pocock	3
A. L. F. de Mel not out	20	– c Ellison b Botham	14
J. R. Ratnayeke not out	5	– not out	7
B 2, l-b 8, w 2, n-b 8	20	B 5, l-b 4, n-b 11	20

1-17 2-43 3-144 4-292 (7 wkts dec.) 491 1-19 2-29 3-111 4-115 (7 wkts dec.) 294
5-442 6-456 7-464 5-118 6-256 7-276

D. S. de Silva and V. B. John did not bat.

First innings – Agnew 32–3–123–2; Botham 29–6–114–1; Ellison 28–6–70–1; Pocock 41–17–75–2; Allott 36–7–89–1.
Second innings – Agnew 11–3–54–0; Allott 1–0–2–0; Botham 27–6–90–6; Pocock 29–10–78–1; Ellison 7–0–36–0; Lamb 1–0–6–0; Tavare 3–3–0–0; Fowler 1–0–8–0.

ENGLAND

G. Fowler c Madugalle b John	25	P. J. W. Allott b de Mel	0
B. C. Broad c Silva b de Mel	86	P. I. Pocock c Silva b John	2
C. J. Tavare c Ranatunga b D. S. de Silva	14	J. P. Agnew not out	1
*D. I. Gower c Silva b de Mel	55	B 5, l-b 7, w 5, n-b 6	23
A. J. Lamb c Dias b John	107		370
I. T. Botham c sub (D. M. Vonhagt) b John	6	1-49 2-105 3-190 4-210 5-218 6-305	
R. M. Ellison c Ratnayeke b D. S. de Silva	41	7-354 8-354 9-369 10-370	
†P. R. Downton c Dias b de Mel	10		

de Mel 37–10–110–4; John 39.1–12–98–4; Ratnayeke 22–5–50–0; D. S. de Silva 45–16–85–2; Ranatunga 1–1–0–0; Madugalle 3–0–4–0.

Toss won by England

UMPIRES H. D. Bird and D. G. L. Evans

SRI LANKA V INDIA 1985

R. Mohan, 1987

Lacking any kind of match practice for months after the 1984-85 home season had ended, and with a team hastily assembled in August, the Indians were under-prepared for their visit to Sri Lanka. They were also at a further disadvantage in conditions which the Sri Lankan seam attack was accustomed to exploiting. The home team had trained assiduously for months, and for this reason alone the fledgling Test nation deserved the historic and emotive maiden win it scored in the three-match series.

India's bowling was even more limited than usual, but what let the team down was the batting. This never attained the levels it had in the two limited-overs successes earlier in the year – first in Melbourne and then in Sharjah. The political background against which this series was organised, with the Indian government viewing it as a diplomatic initiative, was never likely to inspire confidence in cricketers touring the island in troubled times.

With only two three-day matches and a one-day international before the first Test, the Indians were hardly in a position to find their form before the three Tests were played off the reel. Indeed, with a bit of luck the Sri Lankans might well have won the First Test, rain robbing them of a session of play on the final day. However, the chance that had slipped away was encashed in the Second Test in which the Sri Lankans outbowled and outbatted the Indians. In the final hour, Rumesh Ratnayake dived to take a return catch from a defiant Kapil Dev to end the Indian innings and signal a fine triumph. Sri Lanka had seized the chance which India had given them by losing four first-innings wickets cheaply on the fourth morning, the home batsmen sparkling as they set up a target which the Indians could not be expected to attain. Only some unconvincing umpiring, about which the Indians unfortunately stated their misgivings in very clear terms, detracted from the merits of a splendid victory.

Finding their feet somewhat late on tour, the Indians seized the initiative only in the final Test, but here too the Sri Lankan captain, Duleep Mendis, and his deputy, Roy Dias, were too good for the Indian attack. They increased their rescue stand to 216 on the final day and took their team close to snatching victory from the jaws of defeat. When they were out, both having hit hundreds, the late-order batsmen played out time to force a draw and keep intact the hard-earned lead in the series.

Sri Lanka's victory in the series was a triumph for the seniors in the team such as Mendis, Dias, Ranjan Madugalle and de Mel. They had been fixtures in the Sri Lankan team since the country's Test baptism in February 1982, and they played leading parts in the Test win at the Tamil Union ground in Colombo. Ratnayake, with a slinging action, bowled consistently well throughout the series, the Indian batsmen never learning to judge his change of pace correctly, while Amal Silva, the wicket-keeper, set a new record for a three-Test series with 22 dismissals, including nine in the first Test.

Sri Lanka v India   **Second Test**

At P. Saravanamuttu Stadium, Colombo, September 6, 7, 8, 10, 11, 1985.
Sri Lanka won by 149 runs.   R. Mohan, 1987

Sri Lanka's epochal Test win, in only their 14 Test match, came despite their own slow batting at the start, but their well-directed seam attack, bowling on and outside off stump, put them well in the hunt by establishing a convincing first-innings lead. India's woeful catching on the first day enabled Silva and Madugalle to build a steady foundation of 168 by the close, and Dias's polished 95 increased the advantage on the second day. Although the last six wickets fell for 17, the Sri Lankan bowlers maintained it by capturing three Indian wickets for six runs by the end of the day's play.

Despite half-centuries from Srikkanth, Gavaskar and Amarnath on the third day, India frittered away their margin of safety by losing four quick wickets for 34 runs on the fourth morning. This left Sri Lanka, 141 runs ahead, time to set up a declaration on the fourth afternoon, and Dias and Aravinda de Silva obliged with quick-fire knocks that left their bowlers a whole day to bring about the country's first Test win.

Notwithstanding two dubious decisions on the final morning, India, set a target of 348 in 333 minutes plus 20 overs, could have batted out for a draw. However, Ratnayake swung the match for Sri Lanka by running through the middle order. A defiant 78 by Kapil Dev produced moments of anxiety before Ratnayake dived to take a smart return catch to dismiss the Indian captain and seal the victory which led to a nationwide celebration and a public holiday the following day. Silva's century and nine dismissals in the match were an unprecedented feat by a wicket-keeper in a Test match.

Toss: Sri Lanka. **Sri Lanka 385** (S. A. R. Silva 111, R. S. Madugalle 54, R. L. Dias 95, L. R. D. Mendis 51; C. Sharma 5-118, R. J. Shastri 3-74) **and 206-3 dec.** (S. Wettimuny 32, P. A. de Silva 75, R. L. Dias 60*); **India 244** (K. Srikkanth 64, S. M. Gavaskar 52, M. Amarnath 60; R. J. Ratnayake 4-76, F. S. Ahangama 3-59) **and 198** (Kapil Dev 78; A. L. F. de Mel 3-64, R. J. Ratnayake 5-49).

COVETED VICTORY
John Woodcock, Notes by the Editor, 1986

Sri Lanka's first Test victory, against India in Colombo in September, provided them with a famous landmark. It had taken them three and a half years and 14 Test matches to achieve it. India's first, against England in Madras in 1952, came in their 25th Test and after nearly 20 years of trying, the war intervening; New Zealand's, against West Indies in Auckland in 1956, came only in their 45th Test match.

ENGLAND V SRI LANKA 1991
1992

The third visit to England in four years by a Sri Lankan team did little to alter the impression, given by their predecessors, of talented, natural cricketers lacking experience in competitive first-class cricket. Although in recent years Sri Lanka had allocated first-class status to its top level of club cricket, and had striven to develop a regional competition played over four days, the evidence offered by the tourists again suggested that, in attitude and application, the Sri Lankans in general had still to make the transition from weekend club cricketers to first-class cricketers.

On easy-paced pitches, against bowling offering some latitude outside the off stump, their batsmen delighted by the richness of their strokeplay. In their only win in seven first-class games on the tour, over Somerset, they successfully chased a target of 249 in 49 overs for the loss of only two wickets, with Aravinda de Silva, the captain, and the left-handed Sanath Jayasuriya scoring the last 83 runs in eight overs. But it was another matter entirely when the ball swung, seamed or turned, as it did at Worcester and Bristol, where the tourists suffered heavy defeats. On both occasions, flair and lack of discipline betrayed their generally sound techniques, which could have stood them in good stead.

Jayasuriya, who against Sussex scored the side's only hundred, and de Silva timed the ball exquisitely, as they showed in the Test match, at Lord's. There, de Silva lit up the closing stages of the second day with a startling display of derring-do which, in its virtuosity, matched Hooper's batting for West Indies on the Sunday morning of The Oval Test. However, although it was a stunning catch by Lewis, in the gully, which dismissed de Silva first thing next morning, the situation called for something more temperate from the captain. He was leading a young side, with an average age between 24 and 25, and his players required a standard to emulate. Once or twice on the tour, too, they could have done with a reminder of the tenets of the game with regard to sportsmanship.

The Sri Lankan bowling, always likely to be the weaker of their principal suits, excelled itself at Lord's by bowling out England for 282, which would have been less had Stewart, England's century-maker, not been dropped when he was 24. Rumesh Ratnayake, on his first Test match tour of England, and Sri Lanka's leading wicket-taker in Tests, stood out. With his slinging action he could generate deceptive pace, and in helpful conditions at Bristol he took eight of the 12 Gloucestershire wickets to fall. Champaka Ramanayake maintained a tidy line and length, and was a willing workhorse, but neither he nor Kapila Wijegunawardene possessed the firepower to do more than contain at the highest level. The length of Wijegunawardene's run-up, not to mention his name, was hardly commensurate with his pace.

The left-arm spinner, Don Anurasiri, gained his third tour of England on the strength of his bowling against England A in February and March, and if Ranjith Madurasinghe, the off-spinner, had been able to recapture his form of 1990, when he was the Sri Lankans' leading wicket-taker, the attack would have boasted an experienced and contrasting spin combination to support their faster bowlers. Another off-spinner, Muttiah Muralitharan, failed to take a first-class wicket on tour, finding the pitches generally unsympathetic to his slow turn. However, at 19 he was very much a novice, with time to learn the skills of his trade – if he can get the opportunity in a side which seems more welcome for one-day internationals than for first-class cricket. Of Sri Lanka's 34 Tests, for example, Lord's was only their ninth since April 1987, when New Zealand's tour of the country was abandoned owing to the civil unrest there. In the same period, Sri Lanka had played 49 one-day internationals against the Test-playing countries, all of them, like the Tests, away from home.

England v Sri Lanka   **Test Match**

At Lord's, August 11, 13, 14, 16, 17, 1991. England won by 137 runs.   Norman de Mesquita, 1992

On the final day Sri Lanka needed 344 to win with eight wickets in hand. Tufnell opened the proceedings, and in his seventh over of the morning he bowled Gurusinha round his legs, deceived though the air while trying to sweep. Lawrence had the next success, although de Silva looked surprised to be given caught at the wicket for a stubborn 18. When, just before lunch, Mahanama was taken at slip off Tufnell, half the side had gone for 159. Nevertheless Jayasuriya, who had struck six fours while compiling 30 from only 28 balls before the interval, continued to bat as though he thought Sri Lanka could win. He hurried on to 66 before he was caught behind off the 70th ball he faced, and after that it was simply a matter of time before England won. Tufnell finished with his third five-wicket return in his sixth Test.

Toss: England. **England 282** (G. A. Gooch 38, H. Morris 42, A. J. Stewart 113*, Extras 31;
R. J. Ratnayake 5-69) **and 364-3 dec.** (G. A. Gooch 174, A. J. Stewart 43, R. A. Smith 63*,
Extras 49; S. D. Anurasiri 3-135); **Sri Lanka 224** (U. C. Hathurusinghe 66, P. A. de Silva 42,
R. J. Ratnayake 52; P. A. J. DeFreitas 7-70) **and 285** (A. P. Gurusinha 34, S. T. Jayasuriya 66,
C. P. H. Ramanayake 34*; P. C. R. Tufnell 5-94).

Sri Lanka's Great Game
Christopher Martin-Jenkins, 1994

The really big cricket match in Colombo on March 13, 1993 attracted a crowd of 15,000. There was radio commentary all day long; most of the back-page space in Colombo's two newspapers was devoted to it. The build-up to the great event had been going on all week. President Premadasa (assassinated only a few weeks later) was there on the first day, not so much because he was a cricket enthusiast as because this was the place for a politician to be seen. The match was staged on Sri Lanka's most famous ground, where Test cricket was first played. But this was not a Test match: it was the annual game between two of Colombo's largest schools, Royal College and St Thomas's. The final day of three in the 114th match between the two clashed with the opening day of the Test between Sri Lanka and England and, though cricket followers in other lands may find it hard to believe, it completely put the Test into the shade.

Sri Lanka v England 1993
Test Match

At Sinhalese Sports Club, Colombo, March 13, 14, 15, 17, 18, 1993.
Sri Lanka won by five wickets.
Peter Hayter, 1994

Sri Lanka comprehensively outplayed England and thoroughly deserved their first win against them in five Tests and their fourth in the 43 they had contested since attaining Test status 11 years previously. England joined India, Pakistan and New Zealand on the list of Sri Lankan conquests. Although there were individual performances of some merit from England, collectively this was another bad display. The tourists once again failed to produce the standard of performance required to compete with technically skilled and highly motivated opposition in a hostile environment. In Calcutta, the climatic peculiarity that had caused so much consternation was smog; here it was the steamy heat.

There were also further murmurings regarding the impartiality of Sri Lankan umpiring and the bowling action of Sri Lankan off-spinners Warnaweera and Muralitharan. But, overall, England had nothing and no one to blame but themselves. They had been given a substantial platform by [Robin] Smith, who scored his first century as a Test opener. In partnerships of 112 with Hick and 122 with Stewart he played the anchor role to perfection. His first Test hundred overseas, and his eighth in all, lasted seven and a half hours, a tribute to his stamina as well as his skill. But after he was dismissed at 316 for four the innings soon folded: the last seven wickets fell for 64 runs.

The Sri Lankan batting lived up to its high reputation against some of England's best bowling on the entire tour, particularly from Lewis and Tufnell. De Silva and Ranatunga, their two senior batsmen, displayed the determination to build long innings as well as the exquisite wristy strokeplay so widely admired in world cricket. But the decline of the innings from 330 for three to 376 for eight indicated a brittleness in the lower order to match England's until the fourth morning of the match. England needed almost two hours to take the wickets of two tail-enders who enabled Tillekeratne to finish unbeaten on 93 and build a first-innings lead of 89.

England's batting self-destructed again. Against some penetrative off-spin from Warnaweera, they slumped initially to 96 for five. Atherton completed a miserable tour [England had come to Sri Lanka from India] by adding two to his first-innings 13 to finish with a Test average for the tour of 15.75, while Gatting, Smith and Hick all got out when well set through careless shots. Lewis and Emburey made sure the innings achieved a modicum of respectability at 228 all out on the final morning.

Their efforts might have led to greater things had Sri Lanka, struggling at 61 for four with 79 still required to win, performed as they had done against Australia on the same ground in August 1992. Then they needed 181 to win, reached 127 for two, and lost. This time, however, in front of substantially the biggest crowd of the match – some 10,000 who arrived to witness the historic moment of victory – there was to be no repetition. The England bowlers once more found Tillekeratne impossible to get out. Tufnell and Emburey bowled well in tandem, but Tillekeratne had their measure, cutting hard at anything fractionally short and dancing down the wicket if the opportunity to drive presented itself. At the other end, Ranatunga was batting as though his life depended on it. For him, victory meant too much to be allowed to slip through his grasp. His obvious sadness when he was caught with only four runs needed soon disappeared as Jayasuriya pulled Tufnell's next ball for six.

Toss: England. **England 380** (R. A. Smith 128, G. A. Hick 68, A. J. Stewart 63; K. P. J. Warnaweera 4-90, M. Muralitharan 4-118) **and 228** (R. A. Smith 35, C. C. Lewis 45, J. E. Emburey 59; K. P. J. Warnaweera 4-98); **Sri Lanka 469** (R. S. Mahanama 64, U. C. Hathurusinghe 59, A. P. Gurusinha 43, P. A. de Silva 80, A. Ranatunga 64, H. P. Tillekeratne 93*, Extras 32; P. W. Jarvis 3-76, C. C. Lewis 4-66) **and 142-5** (A. Ranatunga 35, H. P. Tillekeratne 36*).

Sri Lanka's second half of 1993 was mostly notable for bad weather. Their July Test against India in Kandy saw just 50 minutes' play in the five days (12 overs, all on the second day). Then in December, their inaugural Test against the West Indies in Moratuwa had no play on three days.

NEW ZEALAND V SRI LANKA 1995 D. J. Cameron, 1996

For Sri Lanka, triumph. For New Zealand, more agony. By winning the First Test at Napier by 241 runs, Sri Lanka gained their first overseas win in 32 attempts since entering Test cricket in 1982. By working comfortably to a draw in the Second Test at Dunedin, they completed their first series win outside Sri Lanka. As they grew in style and confidence, the tour became a landmark in their history and they left trailing clouds of glory. In total contrast, for New Zealand this was the final act of a season that had degenerated into the script of a horror film. The Sri Lankan tour should have been a pleasant way to round off a celebratory centenary programme. Instead, after months of indiscipline, resignations, defeats and injuries, New Zealand cricket was in crisis even before this. The effect of the injuries was to force the selectors into hasty and ill-considered changes.

The Sri Lankans had been disconcerted to arrive at the Napier ground to find a green pitch prepared, so the gossip had it, for New Zealand's medium-fast bowlers, especially 22-year-old Kerry Walmsley, who had only three first-class games behind him. The New Zealanders rubbed their hands when Sri Lanka had to bat first and were out for 183. But from that point onward they were wringing their hands in despair. The pitch lent itself just as well to the left-arm seam of Chaminda Vaas, who took ten wickets in the match to set up a crushing victory. Even allegations from the New Zealand camp about the action of off-spinner Muttiah Muralitharan, who claimed five in the second innings, could not obscure the brilliance of Vaas's bowling, sharp Sri Lankan catching, and the ability of their batsmen to fight their way out of trouble. Chamara Dunusinghe, Sri Lanka's new wicket-keeper, also emerged as a hero at Napier. His keeping was speculative, but he fought hard as a No. 7 batsman; his second-innings 91 played a major part in securing victory.

On a steadier pitch at Dunedin, Vaas shone again, with a maiden fifty and six more wickets. Despite a 74-run lead, New Zealand's prospects of forcing a win to draw the series disappeared as Asanka Gurusinha and Hashan Tillekeratne scored centuries. The home team were more cheerful when the one-day internationals began, taking the first two high-scoring games, but Sri Lanka finished their tour with a flourish by winning the third at Eden Park.

Although Roshan Mahanama missed the tour, Sri Lanka proved to have a solid batting line-up, despite the lack of any substantial help from the explosive Aravinda de Silva. As for the bowling, the arrival of Vaas, the steadiness of Pramodya Wickremasinghe and the perplexing spin of Muralitharan – plus the versatility of Sanath Jayasuriya and Ruwan Kalpage in the one-day game – gave Sri Lanka an effective all-round attack. Though their opponents were not in good form or humour, the Sri Lankans improved with every passing day; even in form, New Zealand would have had trouble avoiding defeat by what became known as Ranatunga's Raiders.

New Zealand v Sri Lanka

At Napier, March 11, 12, 13, 14, 15, 1995. Sri Lanka won by 141 runs.

First Test

D. J. Cameron, 1996

Needing 427 to win in five sessions, New Zealand were baffled by Muralitharan's bounce and sharp off-spin. Though Murray and Greatbatch counter-attacked to take the score past 100 with only one wicket down, three quick wickets put New Zealand in trouble again. Rutherford and Thomson survived, not at all confidently, until stumps, when John F. Reid, the stand-in New Zealand coach, tastelessly claimed Muralitharan's action was suspect. Next morning, at 141, Rutherford was caught behind off Vaas and Muralitharan ended Thomson's struggle. Vaas ripped out the tail with merciful speed, for match figures of 45.3–13–90–10. No Sri Lankan had taken ten in a Test before.

Toss: New Zealand. **Sri Lanka 183** (D. P. Samaraweera 33, A. Ranatunga 55, W. P. U. J. C. Vaas 33*; D. K. Morrison 3-40, K. P. Walmsley 3-70) **and 352** (P. A. de Silva 62, H. P. Tillekeratne 74, C. I. Dunusinghe 91, W. P. U. J. C. Vaas 36; G. R. Larsen 3-73, D. K. Morrison 4-61); **New Zealand 109** (S. P. Fleming 35, K. R. Rutherford 32; G. P. Wickremasinghe 3-33, W. P. U. J. C. Vaas 5-47) **and 185** (D. J. Murray 36, M. J. Greatbatch 46; W. P. U. J. C. Vaas 5-43, M. Muralitharan 5-64).

PAKISTAN V SRI LANKA 1995

Qamar Ahmed, 1997

Arjuna Ranatunga's Sri Lankans created history by winning a Test series against Pakistan for the first time in six attempts. Their triumph was the more remarkable for the fact that they had lost the First Test by an innings in four days. Over the next fortnight, they came back strongly to level the rubber at Faisalabad and then crush Pakistan at Sialkot. Curiously, they were the third team to come from behind to win a three-Test series in 1995, following South Africa against New Zealand in January, and Pakistan in Zimbabwe a month later; the only previous instance had been England against Australia in 1888. The pattern was repeated in the ensuing one-day series, where Sri Lanka bounced back from a nine-wicket defeat for another 2–1 win. They had never won any series in Pakistan before, Test or limited-overs, but their success followed straight on from their first ever Test win overseas, against New Zealand the previous March. Deservedly, they returned home to a tumultuous welcome, and were driven through the streets of Colombo in a cavalcade.

The tourists' most reliable batsman was Hashan Tillekeratne, who played magnificently in all the Tests and averaged 56.20. He made 115 out of a meagre first-innings 223 to keep Sri Lanka in the game at Faisalabad; Aravinda de Silva scored the century that put them in control in the second innings, but it was one of the few occasions when he came to terms with conditions in Pakistan after his season in English county cricket. Chandika Hathurusinghe was almost as steady as Tillekeratne, and Ranatunga played some fine innings in both series. The most successful bowler was off-spinner Muttiah Muralitharan, with 15 wickets at 27.33, who became Sri Lanka's leading wicket-taker during the tour; left-arm medium-pacer Chaminda Vaas was close behind, with 13 at 19.53. But, after their initial defeat, the Sri Lankans played better cricket all round: they bowled better, fielded better and, in a generally low-scoring series, batted with greater consistency.

Pakistan v Sri Lanka   **Second Test**
At Faisalabad, September 15, 16, 17, 18, 19, 1995. Sri Lanka won by 42 runs.   Qamar Ahmed, 1997

Sri Lanka levelled the series with their first Test win on Pakistani soil, a victory which underlined the rise in their fortunes. They were strengthened by de Silva, who flew in from England after spending a season with Kent and scored what proved a match-winning century. Pakistan, on the other hand, lost another experienced player when Waqar Younis withdrew, saying he needed longer to regain his fitness, and suffered a further heavy blow when a shoulder injury prevented Wasim Akram from bowling in Sri Lanka's second innings.

It was Hathurusinghe and de Silva who turned the game in a stand of 176 in the second innings, a Sri Lankan third-wicket record. Hathurusinghe scored 83, his best in internationals, while de Silva batted more than six and a half hours for 105, his eighth Test hundred, which included 11 fours; he also became the second Sri Lankan to reach 3,000 Test runs, following Ranatunga. Sri Lanka led by 130 when he fell at last but the last four wickets added another 121. Aqib Javed finally saw them off on the fourth evening to complete his first five-wicket haul in Tests.

That left Pakistan to score 252: they were already two down by stumps, with Ramiz out in the final over. On the fifth day, Saeed Anwar advanced to his third fifty in as many innings, but the home batsmen then lost their way against the pace of Vaas and the off-spin of Muralitharan and Dharmasena. Inzamam, allowed to bat at No. 4 despite his absence in the field, still seemed shaky and gave Muralitharan a return catch just before lunch. That wicket, Muralitharan's seventh in the match, made him Sri Lanka's leading Test wicket-taker, overtaking Rumesh Ratnayake with 73. A fighting fifty from Moin Khan, backed up by the injured Wasim, could not deny Sri Lanka their historic victory.

Toss: Pakistan. **Sri Lanka 223** (U. C. Hathurusinghe 47, H. P. Tillekeratne 115; Aqib Javed 3-34, Saqlain Mushtaq 3-74) **and 361** (U. C. Hathurusinghe 83, P. A. de Silva 105, H. D. P. K. Dharmasena 49, W. P. U. J. C. Vaas 40; Aqib Javed 5-84); **Pakistan 333** (Saeed Anwar 54, Saqlain Mushtaq 34, Ramiz Raja 75, Inzamam-ul-Haq 50, Moin Khan 30, Extras 32; M. Muralitharan 5-68) **and 209** (Saeed Anwar 50, Moin Khan 50; W. P. U. J. C. Vaas 4-45, H. D. P. K. Dharmasena 3-43).

Pakistan v Sri Lanka   **Third Test**
At Sialkot, September 21, 23, 24, 25, 26, 1995. Sri Lanka won by 144 runs.   Qamar Ahmed, 1997

Sri Lanka's triumph gave them their first series win over Pakistan. It was Ranatunga's fifth Test win in his 32nd Test in charge, making him easily Sri Lanka's most successful captain. But it was the beginning of the end of Ramiz Raja's brief reign: Pakistan had not lost a home series since the West Indians toured in 1980.

The tide seemed to have turned in Sri Lanka's favour after their victory in Faisalabad; they were able to field an unchanged team and won the toss for the first time, while Pakistan had to make three changes because of injury and dropped the disappointing Ijaz Ahmed junior. Still, the inexperienced home attack, led by Aqib Javed, bowled well in the first innings to keep Sri Lanka down to 232. Gurusinha and Ranatunga began the recovery from 41 for three, but the only batsman to reach fifty was Dharmasena. Coming in at No. 7, he remained unbeaten on 62 after three and a half hours. Pakistan were batting in the first hour of the second morning but ran into trouble after lunch, when they slid from 72 for one to 122 for five. Muralitharan had claimed three men lbw and, backed up by fellow off-spinners Dharmasena and De Silva, finished the innings off for 214 early next morning.

Sri Lanka were to convert a marginal lead of 18 into a strong position in their second innings. Hathurusinghe batted solidly for most of the day, falling just before bad light ended play three overs early, and the forceful Ranatunga continued throughout the fourth morning to score 87. Pakistan took the new ball in the second over of the day but, missing the strike force of Wasim Akram and Waqar Younis, were unable to prevent the tourists from plundering runs. Though a spectacular slip catch by Inzamam-ul-Haq finally removed Ranatunga, a valuable half-century from Tillekeratne gave Sri Lanka the confidence to declare before tea, leaving a target of 357 in four sessions.

Total humiliation for Pakistan was on the cards when Vaas and Wickremasinghe, the sometimes overlooked Sri Lankan seamers, ripped out three wickets with the score on seven and quickly added two more to leave them 15 for five. That brought in Moin Khan to join Basit Ali: they began a desperate struggle to stop the rot by adding 64 for the sixth wicket but, when Basit fell before the close, Moin must have known survival was out of the question. Nevertheless, he batted on into the final afternoon for 117 not out, his second Test hundred, thanks to last man Aamir Nazir, who held out for 75 minutes.

Toss: Sri Lanka. **Sri Lanka 232** (A. P. Gurusinha 45, H. D. P. K. Dharmasena 62*; Aqib Javed 3-47)

and 338-9 dec. (U. C. Hathurusinghe 73, A. Ranatunga 87, H. P. Tillekeratne 50, Extras 41;

Mohammad Akram 3-39); **Pakistan 214** (Aamir Sohail 48; M. Muralitharan 4-72) **and 212**

(Moin Khan 117*, Extras 34; G. P. Wickremasinghe 4-55, W. P. U. J. C. Vaas 4-37).

AUSTRALIA V SRI LANKA 1995–96 Trent Bouts, 1997

Sri Lanka arrived in November to provide the second and, according to most forecasts, the subsidiary act of the Australian summer, following Pakistan and the reincarnated Salim Malik. On their departure ten weeks later, Arjuna Ranatunga's men were so much the main event that the two countries' political leaders were forced to take note.

Sadly, government interest had less to do with the cricket than with the drama it generated. The three Tests barely qualified as contests. Mark Taylor's Australians were both professional and ruthless, winning by an innings and 36 runs in Perth, ten wickets in Melbourne and then by 148 runs in Adelaide. They landed another sweep, although Sri Lanka would argue just how clean it was, in the finals of the one-day World Series, which they won 2–0. But Sri Lanka's very presence in the finals was significant; West Indies, minus Brain Lara, failed to qualify.

Despite the lop-sided scorelines, public interest remained high and ultimately exceeded expectations. In Melbourne, the 55,239 who attended on Boxing Day bettered the equivalent crowd for England 12 months earlier, and a staggering 72,614 watched the first World Series final. The incendiary nature of the summer may have helped: there was certainly no lack of publicity, although it was overwhelmingly at Sri Lanka's expense. They were briefly convicted of doctoring the ball in the First Test, had their leading wicket-taker branded a chucker in the Second and played the Third under a thinly veiled threat to behave if Australia were not to pull out of their upcoming World Cup match in Colombo.

All the while, the Sri Lankans and their supporters, including a significant expatriate population, simmered over umpiring. The players' patience ran out in the one-day decider at Sydney in January, though by then they may have been itching for a dust-up. Several verbal and physical brushes, and probably the disappointment of defeat in a rain-shortened affair, led many Sri Lankans to snub Taylor's outstretched hand at the presentation in full public view. Although competition was stiff, it was probably the least savoury incident of the summer. Earlier that day, Shane Warne had talked about his fears as one of several Australians who had received a death threat. Craig McDermott was told to expect a diet of hand-grenades when he arrived in Colombo. Small wonder the Australian Cricket Board sought advice from the Department of Foreign Affairs and that Sri Lanka mobilised diplomatic resources in an attempt to quell Australian alarm. Though it was a terrorist bomb unconnected with cricket that eventually persuaded the Australians not to go to Colombo, many players were pretty happy to have found an excuse.

The officials got things seriously wrong in the Perth Test. Umpires Khizar Hayat of Pakistan and Peter Parker of Queensland failed to impound the ball when they suspected interference and referee Graham Dowling, the former New Zealand captain, gave the impression that he had made his mind up that the Sri Lankans were guilty even before the post-match hearing began. The ICC overturned his verdict.

When Muttiah Muralitharan was called for throwing by Australian umpire Darrell Hair on the first day of the Melbourne Test, both had a right to ask why the bowler had been able to negotiate 22 Tests, indeed his entire first-class career, in safety until then. Either Hair was wrong or some, if not all, of those who had not called Muralitharan in the past six years were. The ICC divulged that umpires, via match referees, had expressed doubts about his legitimacy for more than two years. But Sri Lanka produced an array of doctors and biomechanists who declared the off-spinner in the clear. None said Muralitharan could not throw, but they argued that the elbow he had been unable to straighten completely since birth could create the visual illusion of a throw, a contention lost on most observers. It was certainly lost on Ross Emerson who, umpiring his first international ten days later, also no-balled Muralitharan repeatedly, even after the distraught bowler resorted to leg-spin. Instead of the intended celebration of the 25th anniversary of one-day internationals, the first such match under lights in Brisbane provided one of the short game's darkest hours. The umpires were booed from the field under police escort and Muralitharan did not play again on tour.

Not surprisingly, the cricket ran a distant second to the trouble all too often. The seeds that would grow into Sri Lanka's historic World Cup triumph within weeks were sown almost without notice. Romesh Kaluwitharana's blazing approach at the top of the one-day order offered some welcome relief but few thought it could last, let alone be embellished by Sanath Jayasuriya, although Jayasuriya's maiden Test century in Adelaide was a glorious thrash. Like the other two Sri Lankan centuries in the series, Jayasuriya's came in the second innings when the match was already all but lost. By contrast, each of Australia's five centuries came in the first innings, as did two 96s in Perth. The Sri Lankans simply could not bowl the Australians out, even before Muralitharan's demise. While the home side declared in every innings, losing 26 wickets in total at an average return of 72.11, Sri Lanka lost all 60 on offer at 28.16.

Australia v Sri Lanka   **Second Test**

At Melbourne, December 26, 27, 28, 29, 30, 1995. Australia won by ten wickets.   Trent Bouts, 1997

Ranatunga gambled by sending Australia in on a fine pitch. But that soon paled against the drama on the first afternoon, when umpire Hair called Muralitharan seven times in three overs for throwing. Unusually, he made his judgment from the bowler's end, and several minutes passed before the crowd realised that Muralitharan's elbow, rather than his foot, was at fault. Many were unimpressed. Ian Meckiff, who retired after being called in Brisbane in 1963, was so affected that he went home. Muralitharan switched ends and bowled until tea on the second day. Then Hair told the Sri Lankans he was ready to call him from square leg. As Muralitharan's career was set adrift, Boon was fighting for his. Since his 20th Test hundred, against England 12 months earlier, he had averaged under 18 in 18 innings. Retained on an unwritten loyalty clause, he ground out 100 in 363 minutes, the slowest of eight centuries in this series by an hour and a half. Steve Waugh was two and a half hours quicker reaching three figures and Ponting again seemed destined for a maiden hundred until he fell to debutant left-arm spinner Jayantha Silva, for 71 from 94 balls. Taylor declared on 500 and had time to take his 100th Test catch before stumps.

Sri Lanka's malaise deepened next day. The dressing-room's attention was divided between Muralitharan's plight and a procession of batsmen, which began when Taylor's punt on the medium-pace of Ponting removed Gurusinha. It was typical of Taylor's refreshing approach, mixing two parts instinct with an ounce of nous: Ponting had troubled him at net practice. Ranatunga stood his ground for 141 minutes and Kaluwitharana cut, hooked and drove a bright fifty off 59 balls. That prompted his promotion to open in one-day games, a move with far-reaching consequences in the World Cup. But De Silva disappointed again and Tillekeratne was struck four times in one over as McGrath exploited his instinctive push forward. McGrath topped and tailed the innings, as well as drilling the middle, to finish with five for 40, and 50 wickets in the calendar year; Warne was to pass 50 for the third year running in the second innings.

Sri Lanka followed on 267 behind and their chances of making Australia bat again seemed distant. But Gurusinha, respected as a good bloke by his opponents, achieved a minor moral victory. He scored 143 – the other ten managed 144 between them – to force a fifth day and ensure that Australia would indeed bat again. It was a brave effort: a painful blow from McGrath meant he could see several balls through watering eyes as he approached his century.

Toss: Sri Lanka. **Australia 500-6 dec.** (M. J. Slater 62, D. C. Boon 110, M. E. Waugh 61, S. R. Waugh 131*, R. T. Ponting 71, I. A. Healy 41) **and 41-0; Sri Lanka 233** (A. Ranatunga 51, R. S. Kaluwitharana 50; G. D. McGrath 5-40) **and 307** (U. C. Hathurusinghe 39, A. P. Gurusinha 143, H. P. Tillekeratne 38; S. K. Warne 4-71).

Sri Lanka v India 1997 Sa'adi Thawfeeq, 1999

Records and bowlers took a beating in the mini-Test series between Sri Lanka and India, but two high-scoring draws led to stalemate. With both sides rich in batting and short of bowling, the only hope would have been a sporting pitch, which neither ground provided. The series proved that Sri Lanka had durable batsmen capable of batting long hours in the middle with unflagging concentration. No one made the point more emphatically than the indomitable left-handed opener Sanath Jayasuriya. His 799 minutes of unwavering concentration on a dead-as-a-dodo pitch at the R. Premadasa Stadium brought him 340 runs, the fourth-highest innings in Tests and the first triple-hundred by a Sri Lankan in first-class cricket.

Jayasuriya had to share some of his glory with Roshan Mahanama, [who scored] a career-best 225. They shared a second-wicket partnership of 576 – the highest for any wicket in Test cricket [it was surpassed in 2006, again by two Sri Lankans, Sangakkara and Jayawardene, who amassed 624 against South Africa]. That mammoth stand enabled Sri Lanka to reach the highest total in Tests – 952 for six, beating England's 59-year-old record of 903 for seven against Australia at The Oval.

Sri Lanka v India First Test

At R. Premadasa Stadium, Colombo, August 2, 3, 4, 5, 6, 1997. Drawn. Sa'adi Thawfeeq, 1999

On the fifth and final morning, crowds gathered to see a Sri Lankan assault the peak of Test cricket. Brian Lara's Test record of 375 [since surpassed by both Matthew Hayden and Lara himself] was under threat from another left-hander, two months his junior: Sanath Jayasuriya. Jayasuriya began the day on 326 and confidently moved to 340 with three fours and two singles. Then an off-break from Chauhan bounced a little more than he expected; he popped a simple catch to silly point to end his hopes of beating Lara. The disappointment was alleviated to some extent by Sri Lanka establishing two other world records: Jayasuriya and Mahanama put on 576, the highest partnership for any Test wicket and only one run short of the all-time first-class record; and Sri Lanka's total of 952 for six was the highest in Test history. "It was a terrible toss to win," said Indian captain Tendulkar. "We should have batted second."

Sri Lanka v India, 1997   First Test

At Colombo, August 2, 3, 4, 5, 6, 1997. Result: Drawn.

INDIA

†N. R. Mongia c Jayawardene b Pushpakumara 7	A. Kumble not out 27
N. S. Sidhu c Kaluwitharana b Vaas 111	R. K. Chauhan c Vaas b Jayasuriya 23
R. Dravid c and b Jayasuriya 69	A. Kuruvilla c Atapattu b Pushpakumara ... 9
*S. R. Tendulkar c Jayawardene b Muralitharan 143	B 10, n-b 12 22
M. Azharuddin c and b Muralitharan 126	1-36 2-183 3-230 4-451 5-451 (8 wkts dec.) 537
S. C. Ganguly c Mahanama b Jayasuriya ... 0	6-479 7-516 8-537

N. M. Kulkarni and B. K. V. Prasad did not bat.

Vaas 23–5–80–1; Pushpakumara 19.3–2–97–2; Jayawardene 2–0–6–0; Muralitharan 65–9–174–2; Silva 39–3–122–0; Jayasuriya 18–3–45–3; Atapattu 1–0–3–0.

SRI LANKA

S. T. Jayasuriya c Ganguly b Chauhan 340	†R. S. Kaluwitharana not out 14
M. S. Atapattu c Mongia b Kulkarni 26	W. P. U. J. C. Vaas not out 11
R. S. Mahanama lbw b Kumble 225	B 28, l-b 9, w 7, n-b 14 58
P. A. de Silva c Prasad b Ganguly 126	
*A. Ranatunga run out 86	1-39 2-615 3-615 4-790 (6 wkts dec.) 952
D. P. M. D. Jayawardene c Kulkarni b Ganguly . 66	5-921 6-924

K. J. Silva, K. R. Pushpakumara and M. Muralitharan did not bat.

Prasad 24–1–88–0; Kuruvilla 14–2–74–0; Chauhan 78–8–276–1; Kumble 72–7–223–1; Kulkarni 70–12–195–1; Ganguly 9–0–53–2; Tendulkar 2–1–2–0; Dravid 2–0–4–0.

Toss won by India   UMPIRES K. T. Francis and S. G. Randell
MAN OF THE MATCH S. T. Jayasuriya

ENGLAND V SRI LANKA 1998   David Hopps, 1999

The Sri Lankans could regard their short tour of England as an unmitigated success. Not only did they win both their sole Test match and the one-day triangular series against England and South Africa, they drew large crowds eager to witness a zestful approach which had become more widely appreciated since their victory in the 1996 World Cup. The English authorities, who had routinely sought to justify the sparse number of matches against Sri Lanka since their elevation to

Test status on economic grounds, confirmed a three-Test tour of the island in 2000–01, with a lengthier Sri Lankan visit to England provisionally scheduled for 2002. The gesture was not before time.

In the wake of a Test series against South Africa of growing and ultimately exhausting intensity, Sri Lanka's exhilarating cricket ensured that the summer finished with a joyous release of tension. The batting, primarily of Sanath Jayasuriya and Aravinda de Silva, and the unique bowling style of Muttiah Muralitharan, whose 16 wickets in the Oval Test confirmed him as the finest off-spinner in the world, made a particular impact. Muralitharan's match figures at The Oval of 16 for 220 represented the fifth-best Test bowling return in history, but it was not achieved without controversy. David Lloyd, the England coach, had reopened the debate about the legality of Muralitharan's bowling action by expressing his reservations to the International Cricket Council after the Emirates tournament. Then, inadvisedly and insensitively, with England on the brink of defeat in the Test, he implied to the media that he still regarded him as a chucker.

It was not surprising that Lloyd, as England coach, should take such a subjective view of matters; an emotional style had proved a vital facet of his success as a dressing-room motivator. His insinuations, nevertheless, were unfortunate, ill-considered and perhaps even a trifle xenophobic.

England v Sri Lanka   **Test Match**
At The Oval, August 27, 28, 29, 30, 31, 1998. Sri Lanka won by ten wickets.   David Hopps, 1999

Only three weeks after a Test series victory against South Africa had encouraged talk that English cricket was embarking upon a more successful era, the unique bowling talents of the Sri Lankan off-spinner, Muralitharan, brought England back down to earth in the final Test of the summer. Muralitharan, the hill-country Tamil and son of a biscuit manufacturer, born with a deformity of the elbow joint and a highly manoeuvrable wrist, produced one of the most phenomenal bowling displays in Test history as Sri Lanka won by ten wickets inside the final hour. Muralitharan's 16 for 220 was the fifth-best match analysis in Test history; his nine for 65 in England's second innings was seventh on the all-time list. On the way, he passed 200 Test wickets in his 42nd Test. Among spinners, only Clarrie Grimmett had reached 200 in fewer Tests; another Australian, Shane Warne, also took 42. Many who observed Muralitharan's prodigious performance wondered whether, given continued fitness, he could become the greatest Test wicket-taker in history.

England had long identified Muralitharan as Sri Lanka's prime bowling threat (indeed, Sri Lanka's captain, Ranatunga, had no compunction in referring to him as his only real asset), and the nature of the Oval surface strengthened that conviction. Slow and largely unresponsive to the seamers, the pitch negated the England trio of Gough, Fraser and Cork that had been central to the defeat of South Africa. Salisbury's leg-spin, seemingly fraught with anxiety, also failed to impress. That left the only battle between Muralitharan, his own exhaustion and the tortuous resistance of the England batsmen. Muralitharan's unorthodox action, angled in from wide of the crease, achieved turn and dip from the outset, and provided an engrossing spectacle, even against batsmen largely committed to survival. As long as the ICC remains satisfied by its legitimacy, it is an unorthodox action that we are privileged to witness. Evidence suggested that only a small minority of spectators at The Oval had much sympathy with England's coach, David Lloyd, when he hinted at his unhappiness with Muralitharan's methods on the fourth evening. Lloyd's remark that "I have my opinions that I have made known to the authorities" brought an official protest to the ECB from the Board of Control for Cricket in Sri Lanka, and led to Lloyd receiving a severe reprimand.

Rarely has a Test innings encouraged more misleading conclusions than England's first. England took not far short of two days to make 445 and were assumed, at the very least, to be safe from defeat: they weren't. Hick's computerised, indeed colourless, century on the first day had been greeted as making his selection for the winter's Ashes series inevitable; thanks to Crawley's subsequent 156, a crisper, more appealing affair, it didn't. And, thirdly, the widespread condemnation of Ranatunga, for putting England in to bat, had to be gradually re-addressed. Ranatunga later crowed that he had wanted Muralitharan to have a rest in between innings, a points-scoring explanation which required us to believe that, had Sri Lanka batted first, they would have automatically made England follow on.

Mystery spinner: Muttiah Muralitharan's perplexing variations won several Tests for Sri Lanka almost single-handed. Here he bowls John Crawley – a first-innings century-maker – in the second innings at The Oval in 1998, on his way to 16 wickets in another victory.

Sri Lanka's Instant Success

England v Sri Lanka, 1998 — Test Match

At The Oval, August 27, 28, 29, 30, 31, 1998. Result: Sri Lanka won by ten wickets.

ENGLAND

	First innings		Second innings	
M. A. Butcher c Jayasuriya b Wickremasinghe	10	– st Kaluwitharana b Muralitharan		15
S. P. James c and b Muralitharan	36	– c Jayawardene b Muralitharan		25
G. A. Hick c Kaluwitharana b Wickremasinghe	107	– lbw b Muralitharan		0
*†A. J. Stewart c Tillekeratne b Perera	2	– run out		32
M. R. Ramprakash c Jayawardene b Muralitharan	53	– c Tillekeratne b Muralitharan		42
J. P. Crawley not out	156	– b Muralitharan		14
B. C. Hollioake c Atapattu b Muralitharan	14	– lbw b Muralitharan		0
D. G. Cork b Muralitharan	6	– c Kaluwitharana b Muralitharan		8
I. D. K. Salisbury b Muralitharan	2	– lbw b Muralitharan		0
D. Gough c Kaluwitharana b Muralitharan	4	– b Muralitharan		15
A. R. C. Fraser b Muralitharan	32	– not out		0
B 1, l-b 11, w 2, n-b 9	23	B 7, l-b 8, w 1, n-b 14		30

1-16 (1) 2-78 (2) 3-81 (3) 4-209 (5) **445**
5-230 (3) 6-277 (7) 7-333 (8) 8-343 (9)
9-356 (10) 10-445 (11)

1-25 (1) 2-25 (3) 3-78 (2) 4-93 (4) **181**
5-116 (6) 6-116 (7) 7-127 (8) 8-127
(9) 9-180 (5) 10-181 (10)

First innings – Wickremasinghe 30–4–81–2; Perera 40–10–104–1; Dharmasena 18–3–55–0; Muralitharan 59.3–14–155–7; Jayasuriya 11–0–38–0.

Second innings – Wickremasinghe 4–0–16–0; Perera 11–2–22–0; Muralitharan 54.2–27–65–9; Dharmasena 19.3–13–12–0; Jayasuriya 28–14–30–0; de Silva 10.3–3–16–0; Jayawardene 2–0–5–0.

SRI LANKA

	First innings		Second innings	
S. T. Jayasuriya c Stewart b Hollioake	213	– not out		24
M. S. Atapattu lbw b Cork	15	– not out		9
D. P. M. D. Jayawardene c Hollioake b Fraser	9			
P. A. de Silva c Stewart b Hollioake	152			
*A. Ranatunga lbw b Gough	51			
H. P. Tillekeratne lbw b Gough	0			
†R. S. Kaluwitharana c Crawley b Cork	25			
H. D. P. K. Dharmasena lbw b Fraser	13			
A. S. A. Perera not out	43			
G. P. Wickremasinghe b Fraser	0			
M. Muralitharan c Stewart b Salisbury	30			
B 15, l-b 20, w 1, n-b 4	40	L-b 4		4

1-53 (2) 2-85 (3) 3-81 (4) 4-450 (5) 5-450 (6) **591**
6-488 (7) 7-504 (4) 8-526 (8) 9-532 (10)
10-591 (11)

(no wkt) **37**

First innings – Gough 30–5–102–2; Fraser 23–3–95–3; Hollioake 26–2–105–2; Cork 36–5–128–2; Salisbury 25.5–7–86–1; Ramprakash 5–0–24–0; Butcher 11–2–16–0.

Second innings – Fraser 2–0–19–0; Cork 2–0–3–0; Hollioake 1–0–11–0.

Toss won by Sri Lanka
MAN OF THE MATCH M. Muralitharan

UMPIRES E. G. Nicholls and D. R. Shepherd

Sri Lanka v Australia 1999

Malcolm Conn, 2001

Not in anyone's wildest dreams could the painful revamping of Sri Lankan cricket have been so emphatically endorsed. The unwieldy and factionalised Board of Control had been tossed out and replaced by an interim committee of respected businessmen, the canny but difficult Arjuna Ranatunga was deposed as captain, and Dav Whatmore returned as coach. Building for the future, after three years basking in past glory, had become essential after a dreadful World Cup. Sanath Jayasuriya was appointed captain, while Ranatunga and Aravinda de Silva were left out of the one-day side.

Bold moves indeed, because the Australians were coming. What would the World Cup champions and Test leaders do against such an unsettled side? Answer: receive the shock of their lives. An upset win over Australia in the final of the Aiwa Cup one-day competition was just the fillip Whatmore and Jayasuriya needed in their drive for youth and fitness. But it was surely an aberration. Australia, after all, had dominated the triangular tournament until then.

Nine days later, Australia tumbled to 60 for seven before lunch on the opening day of the First Test in Kandy. In a flash, the series was decided. Despite some heroics, Australia never recovered; the next two rain-marred games would be drawn. It was their first Test failure against Sri Lanka in 11 matches going back to their inaugural meeting, on the same ground, 16 years earlier.

There were two major factors in Sri Lanka's unexpected success: excellent and exhaustive preparation by Whatmore, assisted by physiotherapist Alex Kountouri, both Australian nationals, and the bowling of Muttiah Muralitharan. Whatever questions remained about his action, particularly the top-spinner, Muralitharan baffled most of the Australian batsmen. His wonderful control and use of flight on slow, turning pitches once again exposed their vulnerabilities on the subcontinent. "He turns it more than any other spinner going around at the moment and I guess we're facing something like the opposition has faced with Shane Warne over the years," said Australian captain Steve Waugh. The left-handed Justin Langer was the one most traumatised by Muralitharan, as the ball constantly turned across him. Australia's misery at Kandy was epitomised by the loss of Jason Gillespie, who broke his right leg and injured his wrist in a dreadful on-field collision with Steve Waugh as they both went for a catch behind square leg. The fast bowler had been Australia's leading wicket-taker in the one-day tournament.

This was a tough time for Waugh as captain. Australia had underperformed in the West Indies, drawing 2–2 against weakened opponents. Had he been able to bat again in the Kandy Test, Australia might have scrambled a victory. Instead, he had a badly broken nose and was being flown by helicopter to a Colombo hospital with Gillespie; he could not even see his men go down fighting. However, Waugh insisted on returning for the Second Test. His presence was not enough to prevent another poor performance, but by the Third his side were playing the better cricket. The weather denied them in Colombo, having rescued them at Galle. As four of Australia's last six Tests on the island had now been ruined by rain, there was a good argument for them visiting Sri Lanka during April in future, rather than the monsoon months of August and September.

Sri Lanka v Australia

At Kandy, September 9, 10, 11, 1999. Sri Lanka won by six wickets.

First Test

Malcolm Conn, 2001

The drama of Test cricket rose to new heights as the sound of a helicopter filled Asgiriya Stadium. Reminiscent of a scene from *Apocalypse Now*, the machine had appeared, dark green and menacing, over the adjoining hill, out of tropical vegetation, and play stopped as it swept low over the back of the ground, touched down briefly, then headed towards Colombo. With it went any possible chance Australia might have had of turning round a Test Sri Lanka always deserved to win.

On board were Steve Waugh, with a badly broken nose, and Gillespie, with a broken leg that would keep him out of the national side throughout the Australian season. They had crashed, horrifically, as Waugh ran back from square leg and Gillespie came in from the boundary, both trying to catch the Sri Lankan vice-captain, Jayawardene. The ball always seemed destined to fall between them.

This freak accident represented Australia's lowest point on a rare lowly tour. When it happened on the second morning, Sri Lanka were already 139 for three in reply to Australia's 188, and threatening to bat them out of the match. Jayawardene and de Silva ran two but abandoned a third when they saw the Australians had forgotten the ball and were huddled around their fallen colleagues. Play was held up for six minutes while they received treatment before Gillespie was carried from the field.

Little had gone right for Steve Waugh since winning the toss had given Australia a record 13 in succession. Minutes before lunch on the opening day, Australia had crumbled to a staggering 60 for seven, first against the left-arm seam attack of Vaas and Zoysa, then the off-spin of Muralitharan. A face-saving century partnership between Ponting and Gillespie was the only high point of a dreadful day's batting. Gillespie stuck for more than two hours, scoring 41, while Ponting remained until the end. On 96, with only McGrath for support, he was in two minds about how best to snatch a hundred and pushed a catch back to Murali.

Sri Lanka were coasting at 177 for three in reply, but fell victim to Warne and inexperience: they were all out for 234, a lead of just 46. Back in the Test side after being dropped in the West Indies, and now acting-captain in Waugh's absence, Warne bowled beautifully for five wickets. Only de Silva, with a patient and polished 78, lasting three hours and containing 13 fours, and Jayawardene, with a more fortunate 46, offered significant contributions. But Australia's batting soon failed again. Without their captain and down to nine men, they mustered only 140, Murali and Vaas grabbing three wickets each. This time Ponting stood alone, with another fifty.

Sri Lanka needed just 95 for an historic first Test victory over Australia, but it was no simple affair. They had stumbled to 39 for three when the new batsman, Jayawardene, spooned the ball towards cover and bowler Miller gathered it left-handed at ground level after a desperate lunge. Australian celebrations were cut short, however. Umpire Manuel, apparently fooled by a puff of dust from Jayawardene's bat, believed it had been a bump ball, despite its slow, looping trajectory, and did not choose to consult either his colleague at square leg or the third umpire. Miller did remove Jayawardene a few overs later, leaving Sri Lanka an uneasy 60 for four, but the old firm of Ranatunga and de Silva ensured glory would not drown in a sea of panic. Riding his luck with the cheeky approach that so annoys the Australians, Ranatunga survived a desperately close lbw appeal and a dropped catch before scoring, then broke the game open with a four and six off successive balls from Warne.

Excitement mounted with every delivery, amid rhythmic clapping and wild cheering. The small and picturesque ground was suddenly so full that the crowd spilled out in front of the sightscreen at one end and could not be moved by police. In the end, Sri Lanka scrambled to a six-wicket victory after three days of drama, tension and controversy.

Toss: Australia. **Australia 188** (R. T. Ponting 96, J. N. Gillespie 41; W. P. U. J. C. Vaas 3-43, D. N. T. Zoysa 3-38, M. Muralitharan 4-63) **and 140** (R. T. Ponting 51; W. P. U. J. C. Vaas 3-15, M. Muralitharan 3-65); **Sri Lanka 234** (P. A. de Silva 78, D. P. M. D. Jayawardene 46; C. R. Miller 4-62, S. K. Warne 5-52) **and 95-4** (P. A. de Silva 31*; C. R. Miller 3-48).

ENGLAND V SRI LANKA 2002   Rob Smyth, 2003

In their 21st year as a Test-playing nation, Sri Lanka's adulthood was finally recognised with the present they most wanted: a first full tour of England. But the party hardly got going at all. They were without Muttiah Muralitharan for the first part of the tour; when he did arrive, they lost the last two Tests comprehensively. England played so well that a 2–0 victory did not flatter them, but Sri Lanka certainly helped gift-wrap it. And the whole thing was conducted in the shadow of a bigger, better jamboree – the football World Cup.

Failure to reach the final of the triangular one-day series compounded an unhappy tour, which was in total contrast to the giddy, all-conquering stopover in 1998. When Sri Lanka's coach, Dav Whatmore, said at the end, "I've seen some positives but we haven't got what it takes to win abroad," only the first bit was debatable.

England v Sri Lanka   **First Test**
At Lord's, May 16, 17, 18, 19, 20, 2001. Drawn.   Stephen Fay, 2003

Sri Lanka had won nine straight Tests when they took the field at Lord's, but English commentators still felt compelled to patronise them. The assumption was that their victories in Asia would be no guide to their form on damp days and seaming wickets in May. The absence of Muttiah Muralitharan, who was being treated for a dislocated shoulder in Melbourne after a bad fall in the field in an inconsequential one-day game in Sharjah, was commonly expected to be decisive. However, on the first day of the series, the buds of May were blossoming and Lord's was like a summer idyll. The sun shone, the less-than-capacity crowd wore their lightest clothes, and the wicket was as flat as Norfolk. After two days of their first fairly full series in England, the only team with a realistic chance of winning was Sri Lanka, and the pundits had turned their attention to the elegance and fluency of their batsmen.

Sri Lanka chose to bat and started as their critics expected them to go on. Sanath Jayasuriya's series began disastrously when he misjudged a third run and was out for 18. Sangakkara edged Hoggard to slip, just as forecast, and Sri Lanka were 55 for two. But they had not studied the script, because nearly four hours later that was 261 for three and England were reeling. Atapattu and Jayawardene batted sumptuously, displaying style and finesse in a stand of 206. Atapattu had already shown his skills before a Lord's audience, whereas Jayawardene was a revelation. He had eight Test centuries to his name, but this was statistical excellence made flesh. At the close Sri Lanka were 314 for three and Duncan Fletcher had unkind words for all his bowlers bar Flintoff.

Sri Lanka added 241 runs less gloriously [on the second day] and Atapattu failed by only 15 to make his sixth Test double-century. England lost Trescothick in the eight remaining overs and 329 runs were still needed just to save the follow-on. But the openers would be back in again the next evening as England collapsed abysmally and failed by 81 runs to make Sri Lanka bat next. The weather had changed overnight and was sufficiently overcast and damp to delay the third-day start by 20 minutes. Butcher soon fell but Vaughan and Hussain took advantage of the benign wicket. Hussain had 11 boundaries in his 57, and there was no rational explanation for what happened after their stand of 106 was broken. Crawley said later that conditions overhead were difficult, but that did not explain Vaughan's undignified heave to fine leg, or the absence of any contribution from Stewart, Flintoff or Cork in what should have been a long batting order.

The result may well have been decided in the first 20 minutes of the bright, fine morning of the fourth day. Jayasuriya, at first slip, dropped Vaughan twice. Both were easy chances. His colleagues consoled their captain after the first, but left him alone after the second, presumably because he was inconsolable. Vaughan, who had apologised to his team-mates for his first-innings indiscretion, added 168 for the first wicket with Trescothick and made a fluent, upright second Test century; theirs were the only wickets to fall that day. England were effectively 41 for two and early wickets on the last morning might have set off a panic, but in the second over Jayasuriya sent four men to the boundary; three more patrolled the covers and there was just one slip. Sri Lanka had accepted the draw.

Toss: Sri Lanka. **Sri Lanka 555-8 dec.** (M. S. Atapattu 185, D. P. M. D. Jayawardene 107, P. A. de Silva 88, R. P. Arnold 50, Extras 40; D. G. Cork 3-93) **and 42-1; England 275** (M. P. Vaughan 64, N. Hussain 57, J. P. Crawley 31, Extras 34; T. C. B. Fernando 3-83, P. D. R. L. Perera 3-48) **and 529-5 dec.** (M. E. Trescothick 76, M. P. Vaughan 115, M. A. Butcher 105, N. Hussain 68, G. P. Thorpe 65, J. P. Crawley 41*, Extras 33).

England v Sri Lanka　　　　Second Test

At Birmingham, May 30, 31, June 1, 2, 2002.
England won by an innings and 111 runs.　　　Hugh Chevallier, 2003

The crucial moment came towards the close of the third day. Not the third day here at Edgbaston, but a fortnight earlier at Lord's, when England had at last roused themselves and remembered how to play cricket. They went on to make a stack of runs and, briefly, bowled with fire in their hearts. Whatever Duncan Fletcher and Nasser Hussain had said as they contemplated the follow-on, it was enough for England to retain an Australian intensity for the duration of the Second Test. For the first time in many a moon, England dictated terms throughout, barely suffering so much as a bad session. Their victory was as clinical as it was crushing.

Toss: England. **Sri Lanka 162** (D. P. M. D. Jayawardene 47; A. R. Caddick 3-47) **and 272**
(M. S. Atapattu 56, D. P. M. D. Jayawardene 59, P. A. de Silva 47, H. P. Tillekeratne 39;
A. R. Caddick 3-67, M. J. Hoggard 5-92); **England 545** (M. E. Trescothick 161, M. P. Vaughan 46,
M. A. Butcher 94, G. P. Thorpe 123, Extras 40; D. N. T. Zoysa 3-93, M. Muralitharan 5-143).

SRI LANKA V ENGLAND 2003 Andrew Miller, 2004

England were under no illusions about the challenge they faced on an intensive 11-week tour of Bangladesh and Sri Lanka. Against Bangladesh, a team that had lost 23 of their 24 Tests, England were such cast-iron favourites that the slightest slip-up invited ridicule. In Sri Lanka, however, they were competing not only against formidable opposition, but also with the legacy of their astonishing series victory in 2001 – arguably England's best performance of the past decade. If that were not enough, another England team 5,000 miles away were adding to the pressure by stealing every available plaudit in winning the rugby World Cup in Australia.

As a consequence the team were dogged by a fear of failure. For ten gruelling weeks they ploughed a lonely and unspectacular furrow, but were nonetheless beginning to tick off their winter's objectives. At the 11th hour, however, their resolve snapped, and in the defining Test in Colombo they tumbled to defeat by an innings and 215 runs. It was England's third-worst beating ever; after that, it was almost impossible to haul any positives out of the wreckage.

The difference between the two sides was simple. For the first time since his 16 wickets at The Oval in 1998, Muttiah Muralitharan was fit and ready to face England on his own terms. The groin and shoulder injuries that had hindered his mobility in 2001 and 2002 were gone, and instead he introduced a wickedly illegible ball known as the "doosra" that spat back into the left-hander and made England's pad-dominated tactics fraught with danger. At the age of 31, and with 459 Test wickets to his name already, Murali had become the most complete bowler in world cricket.

The *doosra* – meaning "second" or "the other one" in Hindi and Urdu – is the off-spinner's leg-break, first introduced by Pakistan's Saqlain Mushtaq in the mid-1990s, but not yet seriously mastered by any non-subcontinental bowler. The new weapon had England in a quandary, and drove a timid squad so deep into their shells that they lost the power to reply. In particular, Murali established a stranglehold over his former nemesis Graham Thorpe, who he dismissed five times out of six to attacking and defensive strokes alike.

One man did attempt to take Murali on – but not with the bat. When Nasser Hussain, who appeared frustrated in his new role of elder statesman, allegedly chose the midpoint of the Kandy Test to cast aspersions on Murali's action, his remarks were tossed to the media and became front-page headlines. The England team muttered darkly that comments made on the field should remain on the field, but Murali won the propaganda battle hands down as well. Even an apparent weakness had been converted into a strength. The Barmy Army made their feelings known with their song to the tune of "Row, Row, Row Your Boat":

> Throw, throw, throw the ball
> Gently down the seam.
> Murali, Murali, Murali, Murali,
> Chucks it like a dream.

Sri Lanka v England | **First Test**
At Galle, December 2, 3, 4, 5, 6, 2003. Drawn. | Lawrence Booth, 2004

Drawn Test matches rarely set the pulse racing. This one nearly induced several coronaries. At tea on the final day, Sri Lanka were three wickets away from completing a sixth successive victory at Galle. Instead, England's tailenders launched one of the most improbable rearguards in Test history. When, after much agonising, the umpires offered the light to the final pair at 5.42, a huge English cheer echoed off the walls of the old Dutch fort that guards the stadium. It was a mixture of relief and disbelief, but not necessarily in that order.

England's week had ended as it began: with a heroic rescue act. Two days before the start of the Test, their off-spinner Gareth Batty was saved from drowning by lifeguards after he was caught in a strong cross-current while body-surfing. Back on *terra firma* six days later, Batty was one of the saviours himself, although by that stage he was used to swimming against the tide.

The Sri Lankans were devastated. As Giles and Hoggard marched briskly to the pavilion, where the English balcony was awash with hugs and high-fives, the fielders lingered in the middle, urging the umpires to double-check their light meters. They had enjoyed the best of the game, but the worst of the umpiring; one home estimate made the error count 10–2 in England's favour. Placatory in public, the Sri Lankans were furious in private.

Toss: Sri Lanka. **Sri Lanka 331** (S. T. Jayasuriya 48, K. C. Sangakkara 71, T. T. Samaraweera 45, M. Muralitharan 38; A. Flintoff 3-42, A. F. Giles 4-69) **and 226** (M. S. Atapattu 35, D. P. M. D. Jayawardene 86*; A. F. Giles 4-63, G. J. Batty 3-55); **England 235** (M. A. Butcher 51, G. P. Thorpe 43; M. Muralitharan 7-46) **and 210-9** (M. A. Butcher 54, P. D. Collingwood 36; M. Muralitharan 4-47).

Sri Lanka v England | **Third Test**
At Sinhalese Sports Club, Colombo, December 18, 19, 20, 21, 2003.
Sri Lanka won by an innings and 215 runs. | Lawrence Booth, 2004

England arrived in Colombo full of optimism. They left dazed and confused, having suffered their third-heaviest defeat in 127 years of Test cricket and their first series loss under Vaughan's captaincy. After the energy-sapping escape acts of the first two Tests, they played with as much edge as a lump of plasticine. For Sri Lanka – and not least for their captain, Tillekeratne, whose conservative brand of leadership had roused the critics – it was a delightful surprise. After failing to beat anyone but Bangladesh since March 2002, they pulled off the most crushing win in their history. To beat England in a proper series for the first time was merely a bonus.

England's 265 was quickly put into perspective. Jayasuriya and Sangakkara waltzed to fifty, and although Sangakkara edged Kirtley to slip soon afterwards, it proved an illusory breakthrough as England's limited attack toiled in the afternoon heat. After two days, Sri Lanka trailed by a single run, and Samaraweera and Jayawardene were doing as they pleased. Even the night-time provided no respite. The hotel management allowed a noisy party to go on till the early hours, infuriating the England players, and on the third morning they duly fielded like insomniacs, Giles dropping Jayawardene at fine leg and Trescothick completing a hat-trick of slip fumbles off Samaraweera.

England needed 363 to avoid an innings defeat – or five and a half sessions to survive. They held out for just over two as Muralitharan became the first bowler to take 100 wickets at a single Test venue. When Kirtley was bowled through the gate to give Murali his 26th wicket of the series, Sri Lanka were home and dry with more than a day to spare. It was no more than they deserved.

Sri Lanka v England, 2003   Third Test

At Colombo (SSC), December 18, 19, 20, 21, 2003. Result: Sri Lanka won by an innings and 215 runs.

ENGLAND	First innings		Second innings	
M. E. Trescothick c Jayawardene b Muralitharan	70	–	c sub (M. G. Vandort) b Vaas	0
*M. P. Vaughan c Jayawardene b Chandana	18	–	c Jayasuriya b Fernando	14
M. A. Butcher c Sangakkara b Fernando	23	–	b Jayasuriya	37
N. Hussain lbw b Vaas	8	–	c Sangakkara b Muralitharan	11
G. P. Thorpe lbw b Muralitharan	13	–	st Sangakkara b Muralitharan	19
A. Flintoff c and b Muralitharan	77	–	(7) c Sangakkara b Fernando	30
G. J. Batty c Atapattu b Chandana	14	–	(6) st Sangakkara b Muralitharan	0
†C. M. W. Read not out	17	–	lbw b Jayasuriya	0
A. F. Giles run out	10	–	b Fernando	13
R. J. Kirtley lbw b Vaas	1	–	b Muralitharan	12
J. M. Anderson lbw b Vaas	1	–	not out	1
B 4, l-b 8, n-b 1	13		B 2, l-b 8, n-b 1	11

1-78 (2) 2-108 (1) 3-114 (3) 4-135 (4) 5-139 (5)   265   1-0 (1) 2-22 (2) 3-44 (4) 4-82 (5) 5-82 (6)   148
6-226 (7) 7-236 (6) 8-258 (9) 9-259 (10)   6-84 (3) 7-84 (8) 8-124 (9) 9-137 (7)
10-265 (11)   10-148 (10)

First innings – Vaas 17–5–64–3; Fernando 12–3–55–1; Samaraweera 4–1–11–0; Chandana 26–7–82–2; Muralitharan 40–21–40–3; Jayasuriya 2–1–1–0.
Second innings – Vaas 7–2–25–1; Fernando 12–4–27–3; Chandana 13–7–18–0; Muralitharan 27–9–63–4; Jayasuriya 9–6–5–2.

Sri Lanka

†K. C. Sangakkara c Trescothick b Kirtley	. . 31	W. P. U. J. C. Vaas run out	 9
S. T. Jayasuriya c Trescothick b Flintoff	 85	M. Muralitharan not out	 21
T. T. Samaraweera run out	142	C. R. D. Fernando not out	 1
D. P. M. D. Jayawardene	. . . .	B 7, l-b 16, w 5, n-b 6	. . . 34
c sub (P. D. Collingwood) b Flintoff	. . 134		
T. M. Dilshan b Giles	 83	1-71 (1) 2-138 (2) 3-400 (4)	(8 wkts dec.) 628
*H. P. Tillekeratne b Giles	 12	4-428 (3) 5-456 (6) 6-582 (5)	
U. D. U. Chandana c Vaughan b Kirtley	. . . 76	7-605 (8) 8-606 (7)	

M. S. Atapattu did not bat.

Kirtley 31–4–131–2; Anderson 24–5–85–0; Flintoff 18–0–47–2; Giles 65–16–190–2; Batty 41–4–137–0; Vaughan 1–0–5–0; Trescothick 2–0–10–0.

Toss won by England UMPIRES Aleem Dar and S. A. Bucknor
MAN OF THE MATCH T. T. Samaraweera

Zimbabwe's Nightmare

T he final Tests before Zimbabwe – of its own volition but fearing ICC sanctions – left the Test arena early in 2006 make grisly reading. *Wisden's* correspondent called the innings defeat against South Africa in Cape Town in March 2005 "the most one-sided of all" Test matches. Zimbabwe were dismissed for 54; South Africa replied with 340 for three in 50 overs and promptly declared. In a way, Graeme Smith's declaration showed pity – many sides would have pressed on to 400 and possibly beyond. But it was also contemptuous: it said that we know there is no way back for you. Cricket, that gloriously unpredictable game, had become utterly predictable.

It was all so different when the Zimbabweans joined the Test club in 1992. They were immediately competitive and fashioned an excellent side based around Dave Houghton, the Flower brothers, Neil Johnson, Murray Goodwin and Paul Strang. They had a powerful batting line-up, gave no quarter in the field, and when Heath Streak came on the scene had a cutting edge, too. But the layer of world-class players was thin, the domestic game undeveloped, and, fatally, Robert Mugabe's despotic regime ready to exploit cricket for political ends. The result is a shambles which has led some to question whether cricket in Zimbabwe will ever recover. Will it play Tests again? Can it be competitive? Can the game put down roots among the black population? It would be a tragedy if Zimbabwe failed to build on the promise of those opening years – part, of course, of a far more affecting human-itarian tragedy. The possibility is a real one, however, and will need drastic remedial action on the part of the ICC and others who want to help the revival of cricket in Zimbabwe. But little can be done without a change of government.   S. M.

CRICKET IN ZIMBABWE 1980–81   1982

In May 1980, Zimbabwe, having severed ties with the South African Cricket Union, organised a programme of three tours to the country. Application was also made for associate membership of the International Cricket Conference, and this was accepted at the ICC meeting held at Lord's in July 1981. In September and October 1980, the English county champions, Middlesex, toured Zimbabwe for three weeks. Of the three first-class matches they played against the Zimbabwe national XI, each side won one and one was drawn. Kenya were the next visi-tors in January 1981, playing two three-day matches against the national XI, both of which Zimbabwe won comfortably. In March 1981, Leicestershire were the visitors. The three first-class matches were all drawn. The outstanding batsman for Zimbabwe was Andrew Pycroft, and the team was well led by the all-rounder Duncan Fletcher.

The Zimbabweans in England 1985 1986

One of the purposes of Zimbabwe's seven-week tour, to give their players experience of English conditions in preparation for the 1986 ICC Trophy, was successfully accomplished, though five days' cricket were lost to rain and all but one of their six first-class matches finished as draws. The tourists won all their one-day games, however. With 895 runs in all matches at an average of 52.65, Graeme Hick looked a world-class player in the making.

Cricket in Zimbabwe 1991–92 Mark Williams, 1993

In their last season as an Associate Member of the ICC before attaining Test status, Zimbabwe had a busy programme, culminating in the World Cup in Australia and New Zealand. If the tour by an Australian XI in September provided the most testing cricket, the highlight of the home season was the one-day international against South Africa at the Harare Sports Club in early February. Although Zimbabwe lost by six wickets the result seemed secondary to the occasion, which marked the restoration of cricketing relations between the two countries and was attended by a packed crowd. The subsequent World Cup campaign was not as successful as the Zimbabweans had hoped – the batting falling short of expectations. But they came within a whisker of beating Sri Lanka, had victory over India in their sights when the rain came and lowered England's colours at Albury. Few would have predicted a better balance sheet.

Zimbabwe v India 1992 Richard Streeton, 1994

A great deal of humdrum cricket failed to detract from the diplomatic and sporting history made when India embarked on a tour of Zimbabwe and South Africa late in 1992. Slow scoring and negative captaincy, coupled with moribund pitches, marred both Zimbabwe's inaugural Test and the first series staged in South Africa for 23 years. The dreary routine that characterised the Tests was started on a lifeless pitch in Harare. Zimbabwe set their sights on avoiding defeat through dour batting and defensive bowling. Perhaps Zimbabwe could be excused a little for their caution, in view of their limited playing resources. Whether they justify their Test status will depend on the success of their schemes to find cricketers among the previously untapped African population.

Zimbabwe v India

At Harare, October 18, 19, 20, 21, 22, 1992. Drawn.

Inaugural Test Match

Richard Streeton, 1994

Against expectation Zimbabwe held the upper hand for long periods in their inaugural Test match, played in very hot weather on a lifeless pitch. Both attacks were rendered innocuous and much of the batting was also excessively cautious, with a run-rate of barely two an over. Zimbabwe, however, had the satisfaction of gaining a first-innings lead of 149 and, as the ninth Test-playing country, went on to become the first to avoid defeat in their initial Test since Australia in 1876-77, when Test cricket began. Their captain, Houghton, became the first player to score a century on his country's debut since Charles Bannerman, on the same occasion. Houghton shared the individual honours with Manjrekar, who scored a hundred for India, and Traicos, the Zimbabwean off-spinner.

At the age of 45, Traicos became the 14th man to represent two countries at Test level, 22 years and 222 days since playing for South Africa in their last Test before exclusion from international cricket – a record gap between Test appearances. He took five for 86 in 50 overs marked by subtle changes of pace and flight. The game will also be remembered as the first Test to have three appointed umpires. A new sponsorship by the British company National Grid meant that Dickie Bird was flown out from England to stand in his 48th Test and equal the world record set by his compatriot, Frank Chester. Bird stood throughout and the two Zimbabwean umpires on alternate days. Attendances throughout the game were tiny.

India, still adjusting to the altitude and short on match preparation, could take only five wickets during the first two days. The Zimbabwean innings was launched by a stand of 100 from Arnott and Grant, the younger of the Flower brothers, who survived a chance to slip off Raju when 21 and had made 82 when he fell just before the close. An early wicket next morning brought in Houghton, for so long the mainstay of his country's batting, to make his Test debut at the age of 35. Curbing his natural attacking instincts, he reached a chanceless hundred in 305 minutes, with 12 fours. He had sound support from Andy Flower, who helped him to add 165 in 68 overs for the sixth wicket, but Zimbabwe quickly lost their last five wickets on the third morning. Houghton was seventh out when he edged a catch behind. He had batted watchfully for 414 minutes, permitting himself just the occasional lofted drive or pull; he hit 15 fours from 322 balls, and played the spinners especially well.

Zimbabwe's eventual total of 456 was easily the highest by a country on Test debut, beating Australia's 245. When they took the field they soon lost Brandes, their only fast bowler, who broke down after two overs and took no further part in the match. Yet they shrugged off this setback, as Traicos subdued the batsmen from the moment he came on; he held a good return catch to dismiss Tendulkar and then had Azharuddin taken at slip. India were thus reduced to 93 for four by the close, still needing 164 to avoid the follow-on.

On the fourth day Traicos claimed the only three wickets to fall. Zimbabwe, though, lost the initiative for the first time when they took the new ball at 113 for five from 75 overs. The switch from Traicos's spin suited Kapil Dev, who made a forceful 60 in 95 balls. Prabhakar and More then stayed with Manjrekar as he dragged the game away from Zimbabwe, pushing and nudging towards his hundred just before the close after 500 minutes, the fourth-slowest Test century. He had faced 397 balls and hit only seven fours. Though he was soon caught at backward point next morning, when India were all out in a further 45 minutes, Zimbabwe could only bat out the match.

Zimbabwe v India, 1992 — Inaugural Test Match

At Harare, October 18, 19, 20, 21, 22, 1992. Result: Drawn.

ZIMBABWE

	First innings		Second innings	
K. J. Arnott c Raman b Kumble	40	– b Prabhakar	32
G. W. Flower c More b Srinath	82	– c More b Kapil Dev	6
A. D. R. Campbell lbw b Kapil Dev	45	– b Kapil Dev	0
A. J. Pycroft c Azharuddin b Prabhakar	39	– lbw b Shastri	46
M. G. Burmester c Azharuddin b Prabhakar	7		
*D. L. Houghton c More b Srinath	121	– (5) not out	41
†A. Flower b Prabhakar	59	– (6) not out	1
G. J. Crocker not out	23		
E. A. Brandes lbw b Srinath	0		
A. J. Traicos b Kumble	5		
M. P. Jarvis c Raman b Kumble	0		
B 1, l-b 19, n-b 15	35	B 11, l-b 4, n-b 5	20

1-100 2-175 3-186 4-199 5-252 6-417 **456**   1-16 2-16 3-93 4-119   **(4 wkts) 146**
7-445 8-445 9-454 10-456

First innings – Kapil Dev 39–13–71–1; Prabhakar 45–15–66–3; Srinath 39–12–89–3; Raju 39–15–79–0; Kumble 35.2–11–79–3; Shastri 17–3–52–0.
Second innings – Prabhakar 14–4–22–1; Kapil Dev 15–4–22–2; Tendulkar 4–3–8–0; Srinath 5–1–15–0; Kumble 9–1–15–0; Raju 7–2–17–0; Shastri 12–4–32–1.

INDIA

	First innings	
R. J. Shastri c Pycroft b Burmester	11
W. V. Raman b Crocker	43
S. V. Manjrekar c sub (S. G. Davies) b Jarvis	104
S. R. Tendulkar c and b Traicos	0
*M. Azharuddin c G. W. Flower b Traicos	9
S. L. V. Raju c Arnott b Traicos	7
Kapil Dev b Traicos	60
M. Prabhakar c Arnott b Traicos	14
†K. S. More c Traicos b Burmester	41
A. Kumble c A. Flower b Burmester	0
J. Srinath not out	6
B 2, l-b 9, n-b 1	12

1-29 2-77 3-78 4-93 5-101 6-197 7-219 8-287 **307**
9-294 10-307

Brandes 2–0–3–0; Burmester 39.4–18–78–3; Jarvis 38–17–73–1; Crocker 35–18–41–1; Traicos 50–16–86–5; G. W. Flower 5–0–15–0.

Toss won by Zimbabwe   UMPIRES H. D. Bird, K. Kanjee and I. D. Robinson

CRICKET IN ZIMBABWE 1992–93 Terry Yates-Round, 1994

The advent of Test cricket gave the Zimbabwean game a new lease of life. Had it not been for the granting of Test status, cricket could easily have dwindled to a third-rate sport. Players who had been thinking of retirement or emigration because of the lack of first-class matches in Zimbabwe turned back to the game with enthusiasm, and the Zimbabwe Cricket Union announced the first domestic first-class tournament, to begin in 1993–94. Meanwhile, it was developing its programme to extend cricket facilities and coaching to schools across the country and to discover fresh talent, especially among the black majority.

ZIMBABWE V PAKISTAN 1995 First Test

At Harare, January 31, February 1, 2, 4, 1995.
Zimbabwe won by an innings and 64 runs. Qamar Ahmed, 1996

Zimbabwe not only created history with their first victory in their 11th Test, but did it with style, by an innings inside four days. The Flowers took control on the first afternoon in a record-breaking fourth-wicket partnership, and Pakistan never got back into the game. Streak forced them to follow on and they folded in 62 overs on their second attempt.

The match had a farcical start when the referee, Jackie Hendriks, demanded a second toss. Salim Malik had called "Bird", the national symbol on one side of the Zimbabwean coin, instead of "Heads"; Andy Flower congratulated him on winning but Hendriks said he had not heard the call. Flower won at the second attempt and chose to bat. Until lunch, Pakistan seemed to shrug off their frustration. Aqib Javed and Wasim Akram dismissed Dekker, Campbell and Houghton as Zimbabwe reached 42. After the interval, Wasim bowled seven maiden overs in succession. But from then on, the Flowers flourished.

Andy, the elder brother, was the dominant partner, reaching his second Test century in three and a half hours. The brothers' stand passed 194, Zimbabwe's all-wicket record set by Campbell and Houghton against Sri Lanka three months earlier, and was 247 at the close, with Andy on 142 and Grant on 88. Next day they took it to 269, overtaking the fraternal Test record of 264 shared by Greg and Ian Chappell for Australia's third wicket against New Zealand in 1974, before Andy was out. But there was no relief for the bowlers. Whittall joined Grant in another double-hundred partnership. Both completed maiden Test centuries; Grant, who had been dropped at 24 and 98, took 343 balls to reach his hundred but then speeded up to convert it to a double in another 177. He had batted for 11 hours and hit only ten fours in a marathon display of discipline and concentration. His brother declared at 544 for four, Zimbabwe's highest Test total, beating their 462 for nine against Sri Lanka in October.

Pakistan lost one wicket on the second evening, to Henry Olonga, the first non-white player to appear for Zimbabwe. His first delivery went for four wides, his second was a bouncer, and Andy Flower caught Saeed Anwar down the leg side off the third.

But Olonga's debut ended in disaster next day. As in the previous tour match, he was no-balled for throwing, by umpire Robinson – the first recognised bowler to be called in a Test since Ian Meckiff for Australia against South Africa in Brisbane in 1963 – and later retired with a side strain. But accurate medium-pace bowling by Streak, with six for 90, brilliant fielding and some careless shots by the batsmen finished off Pakistan 222 in arrears. Aamir Sohail, Salim Malik and Ijaz Ahmed all made a start before getting themselves out; Inzamam-ul-Haq, batting at No. 8 after damaging his shoulder in the slips, showed more authority in making 71.

Inzamam was also the principal source of resistance when Pakistan followed on and collapsed to 35 for five. He and Rashid Latif added 96 but, apart from them and Wasim, no one else reached double figures. There were three wickets each for seamers Streak, who returned the best Test analysis yet for Zimbabwe, Brain and Whittall, as Pakistan were all out for an ignominious 158.

Toss: Zimbabwe. **Zimbabwe 544-4 dec.** (G. W. Flower 201*, A. Flower 156, G. J. Whittall 113*, Extras 48); **Pakistan 322** (Aamir Sohail 61, Salim Malik 32, Ijaz Ahmed 65, Inzamam-ul-Haq 71; H. H. Streak 6-90) **and 158** (Inzamam-ul-Haq 65, Rashid Latif 38; D. H. Brain 3-50, H. H. Streak 3-15, G. J. Whittall 3-58).

Pakistan recovered to win the two subsequent Tests and take the series 2–1.

ZIMBABWE V SOUTH AFRICA 1995

Peter Robinson, 1997

South Africa warmed up for a crowded summer with a quick and highly successful trip north of the Limpopo River. Their inaugural Test with Zimbabwe and two one-day internationals were all played at the picturesque Harare Sports Club before good crowds – an estimated 7,000 turned up on both the Saturday and Sunday of the Test, outstripping anything achieved before in Zimbabwe, outside one-day cricket. However, the visiting team was never seriously challenged.

Zimbabwe's great handicap, as captain Andy Flower was quick to acknowledge, is a shortage of competitive cricket, both at Test and first-class level. Despite Zimbabwe's unexpected win against Pakistan in February, the country's cricketers get most of their practice playing against each other in inter-district competitions. The contrast between the sociable amateurism of the Zimbabweans and the professionalism of the South Africans, driven by their coach, Bob Woolmer, was apparent throughout. It was difficult to see how Zimbabwe could develop their game without extending their existing participation in South Africa's domestic competitions.

Zimbabwe v South Africa   Inaugural Test Match

At Harare, October 13, 14, 15, 16, 1995. South Africa won by seven wickets.   Peter Robinson, 1997

South Africa's first Test against their immediate neighbours was notable mostly for some wonderful fast bowling from Donald as Zimbabwe were beaten inside four days. Coming in off a shortened run but with little noticeable loss of pace,

Donald was simply too quick and too controlled for the Zimbabweans in their second innings. Taking full advantage of a slight ridge, he claimed eight for 71 – the best Test analysis by any South African since their return to international cricket – to leave Zimbabwe at least 100 short of a defensible target.

The Zimbabweans did play with great spirit, none more so than Streak, who bowled and batted with gusto. Their shortage of meaningful competition showed, however, and South Africa had few moments of real anxiety. Most of the Zimbabweans got themselves in the second innings before Donald got them out. Of the recognised batsmen, only Grant Flower failed to reach 20, but only his brother Andy pressed on for a half-century. With most of two days remaining to chase 108 for victory, the South Africans began edgily, losing three for 48. The Zimbabweans, however, seemed torn between sticking with Streak and Lock, who had made the breakthrough, and leg-spinner Paul Strang, their only realistic hope of snatching something from the game. In the event, Strang, was not called up until Cronje had played himself in, and the match ended shortly after lunch. The Zimbabweans were forced to wait before buying their opponents a post-match drink, as South Africa immediately embarked upon a lengthy fielding practice.

Toss: Zimbabwe. **Zimbabwe 170** (H. H. Streak 53; A. A. Donald 3-42, B. N. Schultz 4-54) **and 283**
(D. L. Houghton 30, A. Flower 63, G. J. Whittall 38, P. A. Strang 37; A. A. Donald 8-71);
South Africa 346 (A. C. Hudson 135, B. M. McMillan 98*, A. A. Donald 33; A. C. I. Lock 3-68,
B. C. Strang 5-101) **and 108-3** (W. J. Cronje 56*).

Zimbabwe v England 1996–97
David Lloyd, 1998

The English winter began gloomily in Zimbabwe, where the visitors could do no better than draw both Tests, and lost all three one-day internationals rather humiliatingly [the second half of the tour, in New Zealand, proved more successful]. Worse still, by the time they left Harare for Auckland in early January, few Zimbabweans were sorry to see the back of the England party. They had accomplished the rare double of failing to win a single match of significance while adopting an approach widely regarded as unfriendly, aloof and, thanks to one crass comment from coach David Lloyd, downright rude. It was hard to think how England could have made a bigger mess of their first senior tour to cricket's ninth and newest Test country.

To claim that they underestimated Zimbabwe is to invite argument from the tour management. The facts, however, support the prosecution. England, having already decided 15 players (rather than the usual 16) would be sufficient, declined to replace Dominic Cork, the Derbyshire bowler, when he withdrew from stage one to sort out his troubled personal life. Only four days were set aside to acclimatise to conditions, including the problems created by altitude, before the first match in Zimbabwe. And this was in late November, when most members of the squad had neither bowled nor batted for two months, net practice having been omitted at a training camp in Portugal. Zimbabwe were surprised and somewhat offended by England's apparently cavalier approach. They had gained Test status in 1992 despite English opposition. England had not rushed to play them, so they were more than normally pleased to ambush them.

England were thrashed in two early preparatory games, by the President's XI and Mashonaland, and suddenly began to find that their squad was on the thin side. Atherton, initially handicapped by his chronic back problem, and Graham Thorpe both lost form completely. The management had decided Alec Stewart would be first-choice wicket-keeper, which meant Jack Russell was sent into internal exile; and neither Ronnie Irani nor Andy Caddick was pushing hard for inclusion.

Before long, Craig White was summoned from a holiday in Australia, following his successful A tour, and played a Test within 72 hours of landing in Harare. By that stage, the First Test, in Bulawayo, had been drawn (famously so, with scores level) and coach Lloyd was just about the most unpopular man in Zimbabwe. He told anyone who would listen, and a fair number of locals who did not want to, that "we flippin' murdered them", a claim based on England's almost successful fourth-innings run-chase and Zimbabwe's defensive tactics during the final afternoon, which included far-flung fields and deliberately negative bowling, both sides of the stumps. In an ideal world the umpires would have been stricter in their interpretation of wides. Then again, in an ideal world England's attack would not have squandered the new ball on the opening day. At least Zimbabwe's bowlers were landing the ball roughly where they intended and, if deliveries are not deemed wide in the first hour of a match, then those equally off line during the last should not be penalised, either.

England spent a dreary Christmas minus their families (another poor decision by the tour planners, unlikely to be repeated), but were set to finish the stronger side in the Second Test before rain washed out the final day. Another moral victory? Maybe. But does any Test team dismissed for 156 in its first innings deserve too much sympathy? Nothing but condemnation followed England's performances during the last two one-day internationals: one they lost from a position of power, the other ended in a rout after an inspired spell of swing bowling from Eddo Brandes, who claimed a hat-trick. Zimbabwe celebrated while England were more than happy to say their goodbyes, having underperformed as a unit throughout and failed in their wider obligations as cricketing tourists. "Lord MacLaurin and I were horrified by what we saw in Zimbabwe," ECB chief executive Tim Lamb confirmed later. "We were not happy with the way the England team presented themselves. Their demeanour was fairly negative and not particularly attractive."

Zimbabwe v England   **Inaugural Test Match**

At Queens Sports Club, Bulawayo,
December 18, 19, 20, 21, 22, 1996. Drawn.   David Lloyd, 1998

A gently smouldering match suddenly burst into full flame on the last afternoon when England were left to chase 205 from 37 overs. Often up with the rate but never sufficiently ahead to feel comfortable, they eventually needed three from Streak's final delivery. Knight managed two and this inaugural Test between the two countries earned another place in history: it was the first Test to be drawn with the scores level. Such excitement had seemed unlikely during the first four days, on a slow-turning pitch where both runs and wickets needed chiselling out. Zimbabwe won a useful toss, England swiftly hit back when Gough had Carlisle caught at short leg with his third delivery, and so it continued. First one side then the other put their noses in front, but neither could create a decisive advantage.

The finale, though, was thrilling. Atherton again departed quickly but Knight and, particularly, Stewart, who passed 4,000 Test runs as he scored 73 off 76 balls, gave the run-chase real impetus against increasingly negative bowling and far-flung fields. Stewart's exit, to a miscued pull, when England needed 51 from eight overs, was probably crucial. Three more wickets swiftly followed. Knight, though, brought fresh hope with a glorious square-leg six in Streak's final over and five runs were wanted from three deliveries. The next ball might have been called as a wide by the Zimbabwe umpire Robinson, whose decision-making was questioned several times. There was no signal, however, and Knight could not find the boundary again. Referee Hanumant Singh busied himself during and after the contest, reprimanding England for the manner of their appealing, investigating but taking no action over coach David Lloyd's "we flippin' murdered them" outburst, and fining Streak 15% of his match fee for inferred criticism of the umpires; Streak had said he was lucky not to have been called wide in that last over.

Zimbabwe's finest: Andy Flower drives during his century against England at Bulawayo in December 1996, the first Test to end in a draw with the scores level. Flower, who was eventually hounded out of Zimbabwe, averaged over 50 in Tests.

Zimbabwe v England, 1996-97   First Test

At Bulawayo, December 18, 19, 20, 21, 22, 1996. Result: Drawn.

ZIMBABWE	*First innings*		*Second innings*	
G. W. Flower c Hussain b Silverwood	43	–	lbw b Gough	0
S. V. Carlisle c Crawley b Gough	0	–	c Atherton b Mullally	4
*A. D. R. Campbell c Silverwood b Croft	84	–	b Croft	29
D. L. Houghton c Stewart b Croft	34	–	c Croft b Tufnell	37
†A. Flower c Stewart b Tufnell	112	–	c Crawley b Tufnell	14
A. C. Waller c Crawley b Croft	15	–	c Knight b Gough	50
G. J. Whittall c Atherton b Silverwood	7	–	(8) c Croft b Tufnell	56
P. A. Strang c Tufnell b Silverwood	38	–	(9) c Crawley b Croft	19
H. H. Streak b Mullally	19	–	(10) not out	8
B. C. Strang not out	4	–	(7) c Mullally b Tufnell	3
H. K. Olonga c Knight b Tufnell	0	–	c Stewart b Silverwood	0
L-b 4, w 3, n-b 13	20		B 4, l-b 6, w 2, n-b 2	14

1-3 2-130 3-136 4-206 5-235 6-252 7-331 8-372   **376**   1-6 2-6 3-57 4-82 5-103 6-111 7-178 8-209   **234**
9-376 10-376   9-233 10-234

First innings – Mullally 23–4–69–1; Gough 26–4–87–1; Silverwood 18–5–63–3; Croft 44–15–77–3; Tufnell 26.5–4–76–2.
Second innings – Gough 12–2–44–2; Mullally 18–5–49–1; Croft 33–9–62–2; Silverwood 7–3–8–1; Tufnell 31–12–61–4.

ENGLAND	*First innings*		*Second innings*	
N. V. Knight lbw b Olonga	56	–	run out	96
*M. A. Atherton lbw b P. A. Strang	16	–	b Olonga	4
†A. J. Stewart lbw b P. A. Strang	48	–	c Campbell b P. A. Strang	73
N. Hussain c B. C. Strang b Streak	113	–	c Carlisle b P. A. Strang	0
G. P. Thorpe c Campbell b P. A. Strang	13	–	(6) c Campbell b Streak	2
J. P. Crawley c A. Flower b P. A. Strang	112	–	(5) c Carlisle b Whittall	7
R. D. B. Croft lbw b Olonga	7			
D. Gough c G. W. Flower b Olonga	2	–	(7) not out	3
C. E. W. Silverwood c Houghton b P. A. Strang	0			
A. D. Mullally c Waller b Streak	4			
P. C. R. Tufnell not out	2			
B 4, l-b 4, w 1, n-b 24	33		B 2, l-b 13, w 3, n-b 1	19

1-48 2-92 3-160 4-180 5-328 6-340 7-344 8-353   **406**   1-17 2-154 3-156 4-178 5-182 6-204   (6 wkts) **204**
9-378 10-406

First innings – Streak 36–8–86–2; B. C. Strang 17–5–54–0; P. A. Strang 58.4–14–123–5; Olonga 23–2–90–3; Whittall 10–2–25–0; G. W. Flower 7–3–20–0.
Second innings – Streak 11–0–64–1; Olonga 2–0–16–1; P. A. Strang 14–0–63–2; G. W. Flower 8–0–36–0; Whittall 2–0–10–1.

Toss won by Zimbabwe   UMPIRES I. D. Robinson and R. S. Dunne

David Lloyd, who wrote Wisden's *reports of this tour, is the cricket correspondent of the* Evening Standard, *and not the former Lancashire and England cricketer who was England's coach on this tour.*

Zimbabwe v England   **First One-Day International**

At Queens Sports Club, Bulawayo, December 15, 1996.

Zimbabwe won by two wickets.   David Lloyd, 1998

Zimbabwe overcame their own attack of nerves and the tourists' spirited fight-back to record their eighth one-day international victory in their 64th match – and their third in four against England. While no one made batting look enjoyable on a slow but springy pitch, England's performance was woeful: they failed to survive into their final four overs. Only Hussain, whose 49 included 40 singles, showed sufficient patience as Rennie, a bespectacled medium-pacer, shared the honours with Streak. Chasing only three an over, Zimbabwe should have won more comfortably. But Silverwood, on his international debut, Gough and Mullally gnawed away at home confidence, and, at 106 for seven, with 47 still needed, it was anyone's match. Campbell, batting down the order because of a hand injury, provided the common sense necessary to pass the winning post.

Toss: Zimbabwe. **England 152** (45.5 overs) (N. Hussain 49*; J. A. Rennie 3-37, H. H. Streak 3-30); **Zimbabwe 153-8** (43.5 overs) (A. C. Waller 48, A. D. R. Campbell 32*).

Zimbabwe v England   **Second One-Day International**

At Harare Sports Club, Harare, January 1, 1997.

Zimbabwe won by six runs (D/L method).   David Lloyd, 1998

A 2–0 lead gave Zimbabwe their first limited-overs series win and no one, least of all England's players, could deny that they deserved it. They were struggling at 38 for four and then hanging on grimly when England attacked a revised target, but Zimbabwe simply wanted the win more. Andy Flower, reprieved in the deep when Gough misjudged a catch off Croft's first delivery, masterminded their recovery. Evans and Streak gave excellent support, while gifts – ten wides and three no-balls – were gratefully received. Lunchtime rain allowed the newest recalculation system, the Duckworth/Lewis model, to get in on the act. The target should have been 186 in 42 overs, though it was mistakenly given as 185, an error which proved academic. The challenge looked comfortable enough while Stewart and Crawley were in full cry. Leg-spinner Strang turned the game, however, with three wickets in 17 balls and, when Streak conceded just three from the penultimate over, another piece of cricket history was all but written.

Toss: England. **Zimbabwe 200** (48.5 overs) (A. Flower 63, C. N. Evans 32, H. H. Streak 43*; A. D. Mullally 3-29, D. Gough 4-43); **England 179-7** (42 overs) (A. J. Stewart 41, J. P. Crawley 73; P. A. Strang 3-24).

Zimbabwe v England   Third One-Day International

At Harare Sports Club, Harare, January 3, 1997.
Zimbabwe won by 131 runs.   David Lloyd, 1998

Zimbabwe completed a 3–0 whitewash in an emphatic manner with their biggest win in limited-overs internationals. Captain Campbell set a fine example by scoring a stylish and undefeated 80 but was dramatically upstaged by Brandes. Nearly five years earlier, Brandes had led his country to a shock World Cup win against England in Australia by taking four for 21. Here, during a wonderful exhibition of swing and seam bowling, he captured England's top five wickets, including a hat-trick, as they struggled to 54. Every British newspaper reported that the team had been humiliated by a chicken farmer. England were already facing a stiff target of five an over, and that put them right out of contention. They failed to survive beyond 30 of their 50 overs, and only some late defiance from Croft and Mullally helped them into three figures. England still claimed a points victory in the drawn Test series, but Zimbabwe were one-day winners – by a knockout.

Toss: England. **Zimbabwe 249-7** (50 overs) (G. W. Flower 62, A. D. R. Campbell 80*, A. Flower 35);
England 118 (30 overs) (R. D. B. Croft 30*; E. A. Brandes 5-28).

ZIMBABWE V INDIA 1998   John Ward, 2000

Back in 1992, the Indians obliged Zimbabwe with a hastily arranged tour which included the home country's inaugural Test. Zimbabwe duly surprised the cricketing world by forcing India to fight hard to avoid defeat. The Indians' second tour was again arranged at short notice, when the Mini World Cup in Bangladesh caused the cancellation of what would have been Zimbabwe's first visit from the West Indians. And again Zimbabwe caused widespread surprise – this time by winning a thrilling match, only their second Test victory.

This success was all the more creditable given that they were missing four key players, while India were at full strength. Grant Flower, ending a run of 30 consecutive Tests, Paul Strang and Guy Whittall were injured; Eddo Brandes, despite inspiring victory in the third one-day international, was still not fit enough for five-day cricket. On the other hand, they were strengthened by Neil Johnson, the former South Africa A and Leicestershire all-rounder. He had returned to live in his native Zimbabwe and was cleared to represent them on the eve of the Test. Players and public alike were delighted by the long-awaited success. For several years, Zimbabwe had been a talented if underestimated side which competed well but failed to achieve results, apart from the one-day whitewash of England in 1996–97. As captain Alistair Campbell commented, "you only learn to win by winning".

Zimbabwe v India — Test Match

At Harare, October 7, 8, 9, 10, 1998. Zimbabwe won by 61 runs. — John Ward, 2000

Zimbabwe's second Test victory came after an enthralling match where the balance continually shifted, especially near the end. Their success caught Harare by surprise: until the final moments, on the fourth day, the crowd never numbered more than a few hundred. But those present shared the delight of their team, who played with a passion and rare self-belief. The victory earned a brief mention on the front page of *The Herald*, which has little interest in cricket.

Zimbabwe had begun that final day 160 runs ahead with eight second-innings wickets in hand. There was much speculation as to when Campbell should declare, but his batsmen never gave him the chance. On a pitch offering both turn and bounce, those last eight wickets fell before lunch, with only Andy Flower standing firm. This left India's powerful line-up a target of only 235. Before taking the field, Campbell emphasised to his team that they were not going out merely to compete, but to win. And this they proceeded to do, spearheaded by Streak and Olonga, a pair of Test-class pace bowlers. Four wickets tumbled for 37 before Dravid and Ganguly rallied, as they had done in the first innings. Once they were separated, the end was swift, though Srinath and Harbhajan Singh caused a few anxious flutters during a lusty last-wicket stand. Throughout the game, Campbell used his bowlers effectively in short spells.

Toss: India. **Zimbabwe 221** (G. J. Rennie 47, M. W. Goodwin 42, A. Flower 30; J. Srinath 3-59, A. Kumble 3-42) **and 293** (G. J. Rennie 84, C. B. Wishart 63, M. W. Goodwin 44, A. Flower 41*; A. Kumble 4-87, Harbhajan Singh 3-64); **India 280** (R. Dravid 118, S. R. Tendulkar 34, S. C. Ganguly 47; H. H. Streak 3-62, H. K. Olonga 5-70) **and 173** (R. Dravid 44, S. C. Ganguly 36; N. C. Johnson 3-41).

PAKISTAN V ZIMBABWE 1998 — Waheed Khan, 2000

Zimbabwe made history in November 1998 with their first ever win in an overseas Test – and, thanks to a foggy December which ensured draws in the next two games, converted that into their first series victory. They could not have picked a better time to tour Pakistan. Their hosts were distracted by the judicial inquiry into match-fixing allegations against some of the team's leading cricketers, and had just lost a Test series to Australia for the first time on Pakistan soil since 1959. Moreover, captain Aamir Sohail clearly lacked support and commitment from his team-mates.

Zimbabwe took full advantage of this confusion – but they could not have done so had they not been a much improved and better-equipped side than the one which last toured Pakistan in 1996. Alistair Campbell, captain on both tours, led them well, and clearly he and coach Dave Houghton had done their homework. They gave Pakistan warning by winning the second one-day international, thanks to a hundred by all-rounder Neil Johnson. Pakistan hit back to win the one-day series, but came unstuck in the First Test at Peshawar.

Desperate for a win, they prepared a grassy pitch to help the fast bowlers. They found out too late that Zimbabwe's own pace attack were no longer pushovers. Heath Streak, Henry Olonga and Mpumelelo Mbangwa bowled Pakistan out for just 103 on the third day to set up an unexpected win. But they could not have done it without Johnson, who kept his side in the match with a courageous maiden Test hundred in the first innings.

Pakistan had also given Zimbabwe their first-ever Test win at Harare in 1995, when they won by an innings and 64 runs. The victory at Peshawar was only their third in 32 Tests – but their second in succession, following one against India in October – and their first in 15 Tests away from home.

Pakistan v Zimbabwe   First Test

At Peshawar, November 27, 28, 29, 30, 1998. Zimbabwe won by seven wickets.   Waheed Khan, 2000

Zimbabwe completed their first overseas Test win on the fourth morning, after a run-chase led by Goodwin, who hit an unbeaten 73. Like Johnson, who scored a vital first-innings century, Goodwin had returned to his native Zimbabwe after sharpening his skills overseas; he had played in Australia, Johnson in South Africa and England. But the bowlers who set up the victory by skittling Pakistan in their second innings for just 103 were the black pace men, Olonga and Mbangwa, and their white compatriot Streak, who had all come up through Zimbabwe's ranks.

Toss: Zimbabwe. **Pakistan 296** (Saeed Anwar 36, Ijaz Ahmed 87, Yousuf Youhana 75; H. H. Streak 4-93, M. Mbangwa 3-40) **and 103** (Saeed Anwar 31, Wasim Akram 31; H. K. Olonga 4-42, M. Mbangwa 3-23); **Zimbabwe 238** (N. C. Johnson 107; Wasim Akram 5-52, Waqar Younis 4-78) **and 162-3** (G. W. Flower 31, M. W. Goodwin 73*; Wasim Akram 3-47).

ZIMBABWE V AUSTRALIA 1999   Inaugural Test Match

At Harare, October 14, 15, 16, 17, 1999. Australia won by ten wickets.   Malcolm Conn, 2001

Seven years had passed since Zimbabwe's elevation to Test status but their long overdue first Test against Australia never looked like becoming a David and Goliath story. In the end, Australia required only five runs for a remarkably easy victory, and they managed those within an over, with more than a day to spare.

After their disappointing tour of Sri Lanka, the Australians ruthlessly set about restoring cricket's pecking order, beginning with an unsettling display of fast bowling. Zimbabwe's captain, Campbell, was left to rue his decision to bat first on a pitch that Steve Waugh said he would have bowled on had he won the toss. Zimbabwe had tumbled to 37 for four in the 19th over before Johnson and the dour Andy Flower, who occupied more than two and a half hours scoring 28, added 70 for the fifth wicket. Johnson top scored with a spirited 75.

In circumstances that might have been designed for him, Mark Waugh then took the opportunity to revive his flagging career as Australia took control next day. Arriving in the second over of the morning, with his side an embarrassing seven for two, he ran up his best score in 14 Test innings – 90 in three and a half hours. But it was his brother who ensured that only one team could win. By the time Steve Waugh had finished with Zimbabwe's bowlers on the third day, Australia had amassed a devastatingly unspectacular 422, a first-innings lead of 228, and Waugh, unbeaten on 151, had joined the exclusive 20-Test-century club as the 17th member, three days after the 16th, Sachin Tendulkar. Zimbabwe seemed capable of better things at their second attempt, when they ground their way to 200 for two. But they could not sustain the fight, and lost their last eight in a spectacular collapse for 32 runs in 25 overs. The match would prove to be the last of Healy's 119 Tests for Australia.

Toss: Zimbabwe. **Zimbabwe 194** (N. C. Johnson 75; G. D. McGrath 3-44, S. K. Warne 3-69) **and 232**
(T. R. Gripper 60, G. W. Flower 32, M. W. Goodwin 91; G. D. McGrath 3-46, C. R. Miller 3-66,
S. K. Warne 3-68); **Australia 422** (J. L. Langer 44, M. E. Waugh 90, S. R. Waugh 151*, R. T. Ponting 31,
D. W. Fleming 65; H. H. Streak 5-93) **and 5-0.**

ENGLAND V ZIMBABWE 2000
Stephen Brenkley, 2001

All the elements were in place for Zimbabwe's first full tour of England to end in tears and acrimony. Civil disorder at home was at its zenith, and several players' immediate families, living on isolated farms, were in danger. The long-standing pay dispute between the team and the Zimbabwe Cricket Union festered. When they were humiliated by England in the First Test, it seemed likely that disarray and defeat would accompany the rest of the visit. In the event, Zimbabwe doggedly regrouped and demonstrated again that they are usually greater than the sum of their parts. If the tour did not culminate in resounding triumph, it was testimony to the Zimbabweans' spirit that they gave England a fright in the Second Test of the two-match series and then reached the final of the triangular one-day tournament, having embarrassed both the hosts and West Indies along the way.

Zimbabwe had been waiting a long time for this trip. Eight years had passed since their elevation to Test status, opposed at the time by England, who had subsequently been reluctant to invite them to tour. Thus, Zimbabwe arrived bearing well-concealed grievances, and with points to make. Perhaps it was this, allied to other distractions, which led to their crash at Lord's in mid-May, the earliest Test played in an English summer. Almost to a man, they froze, and the outcome was in little doubt from the first morning when they lost the toss and found themselves at eight for three in the first half-hour of the match. So much for the theory that overseas visitors save their best for Lord's.

Somehow, they put it behind them. The news from Zimbabwe was invariably grim. Farms were being occupied daily as the government insisted that land must be redistributed. The players declared that it was their duty to give those at home something to cheer, although they may have excluded their administrators from such thoughts. They had been frustrated and embittered at the ZCU's refusal to offer more money. The captain, Andy Flower, was one of the more vociferous proponents of a better deal for his team and was unafraid to voice an opinion.

The players did not seek riches, but could not understand why they should be worse off than before they turned professional. Flower's articulate stance was eventually to cost him his job. While giving the captaincy his all, he might not have been too unhappy to shed the responsibility. His other roles as front-line batsman and wicket-keeper already presented him with a full plate. During the Lord's Test his wicket-keeping was constantly poor, presumably because he had too much else to think about.

Flower usually led the side positively, and if Zimbabwe's lack of flair precluded risks, his declaration at Trent Bridge in the Second Test confirmed a sense of adventure. There was a brief period, alarming to English eyes, when they might have sneaked victory. They came to command respect and Murray Goodwin's century revealed him as a batsman of high class.

Goodwin and Neil Johnson, two of the few players in the squad who rose above the rank of journeyman, added to Zimbabwe's travails by announcing their retirement from Test cricket. Both were born in Zimbabwe and had moved elsewhere with their families before returning to establish international careers. Goodwin went back to Australia, Johnson set up home again in South Africa. However, suggestions that Goodwin might have been persuaded to stay, had the right offer been forthcoming, again reflected badly on the ZCU. Life without both would inevitably expose shortcomings in the upper order.

Heath Streak, the vice-captain who was to succeed Andy Flower as skipper, was easily the best bowler. He struggled with fitness, but managed both Tests. His movement and deceptive pace lent them a cutting edge, and without his six wickets in England's only innings at Lord's their plight might have been even sorrier.

If the majority of the squad were workmanlike players and recognised it, there were signs that the further development of cricket amongst the black population would pay future dividends. Tatenda Taibu, a wicket-keeper/batsman aged 16 at the beginning of the tour, was selected solely to gain experience. Yet Andy Flower's poor form at Lord's prompted serious consideration of Taibu keeping wicket in the Second Test. If it was wise to keep him waiting, he demonstrated enough with the gloves and his elegant batting to suggest that more will be heard of him.

It was not lost on Zimbabwe that one of the chief plotters of their downfall was their countryman, Duncan Fletcher, who had once been their captain but was now England's coach. Perhaps it was inevitable that Graeme Hick, also born and bred in Salisbury but long since qualified for England, should score his first Test century at Lord's against them.

England v Zimbabwe

First Test

At Lord's, May 18, 19, 20, 21, 2000. England won by an innings and 209 runs.   Hugh Chevallier, 2001

Another Lord's Test, another humiliating defeat characterised by two abject batting displays. Only this time it was different. England – excepting an ugly passage on the third afternoon – dominated from start to finish. It was Zimbabwe, in their first Test here, who were the whipping boys, giving England their biggest win since they crushed India by an innings and 285, also on this ground, in 1974. England outplayed their opponents in every respect. Even their fielding was faultless: not a catch dropped, not a run given away. No visiting team had won their first Test at Lord's, and circumstances conspired against Zimbabwe. They had just toured the West Indies, and this, the earliest Test staged in England, was played in distinctly un-Caribbean conditions. The damp and chill of an English spring were meat and drink to the English seamers.

Toss: England. **Zimbabwe 83** (A. R. Caddick 3-28, E. S. H. Giddins 5-15) **and 123** (B. C. Strang 37*; D. Gough 4-57, A. R. Caddick 4-38); **England 415** (M. A. Atherton 55, G. A. Hick 101, A. J. Stewart 124*, N. V. Knight 44, Extras 40; H. H. Streak 6-87, G. J. Whittall 3-27).

England v Zimbabwe
Second Test

At Nottingham, June 1, 2, 3, 4, 5, 2000. Drawn.
Simon Briggs, 2001

The Zimbabwean worm turned here. After the obloquy of Lord's – which Andy Flower described as their worst showing since gaining Test status – they produced a sparky performance that finally kick-started their tour. But while Flower's imaginative last-morning declaration may have embarrassed England, rain had already washed away any real chance of a result. Given the loss of four of the first six sessions, Zimbabwe needed to take control much earlier than they did.

England's bowling had none of the sharpness of Lord's, and England had still not shrugged off the inconsistency that dogged their performances throughout the 1990s. Most worryingly, their two young Lancastrians, Flintoff and Schofield, appeared to lack the nous required at the highest level. But Trent Bridge proved to be a Rubicon for Zimbabwe, whose domestic troubles were placing them under increasing strain. On Thursday, the players wore black armbands in honour of Tony Oates, a farmer and friend of several of the team, who had been shot dead on his farm the day before the match.

Toss: Zimbabwe. **England 374** (M. A. Atherton 136, M. R. Ramprakash 56, C. P. Schofield 57, Extras 48; M. L. Nkala 3-82) **and 147** (G. A. Hick 30, M. A. Atherton 34; G. J. Whittall 3-14); **Zimbabwe 285-4 dec.** (M. W. Goodwin 148*, N. C. Johnson 51, A. Flower 42; D. Gough 3-66) **and 25-1.**

INDIA v ZIMBABWE 2000
Anirban Sircar, 2002

A Zimbabwean team in transition landed in India three hours behind schedule, and without their baggage, leg-spinner Brian Murphy or captain Heath Streak. Though all of these eventually caught up, the chaotic start epitomised Zimbabwean cricket's most turbulent phase since they celebrated the granting of Test status in 1992. Against a political backdrop growing ever more volatile with the continuing occupation of white-owned farms, Zimbabwe's shattered economy held no promise for some of its underpaid cricketers. Two of their most valuable players, Murray Goodwin and Neil Johnson, had walked out after an encouraging tour of England, to seek more prosperous lives in Australia and South Africa respectively. Without them, Zimbabwe had lost two home Tests to New Zealand in September. Now on only their second Test tour of India, they confronted an ominous task in the difficult conditions of the subcontinent.

The last time the two sides met, at Harare in 1998, India had committed hara-kiri chasing an achievable target of 235, and folded 62 runs short. They avenged that humiliation with victory at Delhi, which was to give them the Test series 1–0, and then took the one-day series 4–1. But Zimbabwe looked resolute wherever they went on the 40-day tour, and earned their hosts' admiration for their fightback after following on at Nagpur. Wicket-keeper/batsman Andy Flower emerged with great distinction. He stamped his class against spin bowling in particular, amassing 540 runs in the two Tests, where his lowest score was 55 and his highest 232 not out.

Another former captain, Alistair Campbell, finally scored a maiden hundred in his 47th Test. In the one-day series, new guns Trevor Madondo and Mluleki Nkala oozed confidence. Disappointingly, 19-year-old pace bowler Travis Friend, who had troubled the Indians at Sharjah in October and was expected to provide much-needed new-ball support to Streak, missed the Tests through a nagging injury to his left ankle.

India v Zimbabwe	Second Test
At Nagpur, November 25, 26, 27, 28, 29, 2000. Drawn.	Anirban Sircar, 2002

The bandwagon moved southwards to the orange groves of Nagpur, hosting its first Test in three years. The match was poorly attended, with headlines dominated by local political demands for autonomy, the Indian board's hearings into match-fixing, and gossip about captain Ganguly's fling with voluptuous actress Nagma. On the field, however, there was a feast of runs. Six batsmen ran up centuries, culminating in Andy Flower's undefeated 232, the highest Test score by a wicket-keeper, which foiled India's expectations of a series whitewash. Forced to follow on, Flower and his team-mates displayed great grit and poise as they camped at the crease to erase an unnecessarily tall home total of 609, a ground record. For nearly two days, the Indians laboured on a placid track.

The home side were counting down to victory shortly after lunch [on the fourth day], when 21-year-old off-spinner Sarandeep Singh, a newcomer from Punjab, reduced Zimbabwe's second innings to 61 for three, still 166 behind. But the indomitable Andy Flower showed awe-inspiring skill and physical fortitude, remaining unconquered for 544 minutes and 444 balls, to build a career-best 232 not out laced with 30 fours and two sixes. It was his ninth Test century, and first double. The previous best by a Test wicket-keeper was 210 not out by Taslim Arif for Pakistan against Australia at Faisalabad in 1980. Surprisingly, Campbell, who like Flower had played in all of Zimbabwe's 47 Tests, had never previously passed 99, but he put that right now as they added 209 to push their side into the lead. Viljoen, a last-minute fly-in for the injured Paul Strang, then helped Flower put on 113 for the sixth wicket to ensure safety.

Toss: India. **India 609-6 dec.** (S. S. Das 110, S. Ramesh 48, R. Dravid 162, S. R. Tendulkar 201*, S. C. Ganguly 30); **Zimbabwe 382** (G. J. Whittall 84, S. V. Carlisle 51, A. Flower 55, G. W. Flower 106*; J. Srinath 3-81) **and 503-6** (G. J. Rennie 37, A. D. R. Campbell 102, A. Flower 232*, D. P. Viljoen 38, Extras 30; Sarandeep Singh 4-136).

THE CRISIS DEEPENS – THE 2002–03 SEASON
John Ward, 2004

Zimbabwean cricket struggled under the shadow of the nation's political crisis. It should have been a season to rejoice in Zimbabwe's status as junior co-hosts of the 2003 World Cup; it was ruined by controversy over that status and the premature retirements of several senior cricketers, most notably Andy Flower.

The cancellation of Australia's tour in April 2002 was a foretaste. Somewhat belatedly – the political crisis dated back to 2000 – protests flooded in about playing World Cup matches in Zimbabwe. Objections centred on security, but many also brought up moral reasons. A boycott, however, threatened serious damage to Zimbabwean cricket without any impact on the government which was its target. Two ICC delegations declared Zimbabwe safe for visiting teams, and for the Zimbabwe Cricket Union security was never a concern. In the event, only England, after weeks of dithering, forfeited their match, which ultimately meant that Zimbabwe beat them to a place in the Super Six stage without defeating a Test side on the field. As in 1999, Zimbabwe lacked the temperamental fibre to do themselves justice in the Super Six, where the ultimate humiliation was their first defeat by Kenya, whose vibrant enthusiasm showed up the Zimbabweans' strained, careworn demeanour.

Zimbabwe's campaign is more likely to be remembered for the heroism of Andy Flower and Henry Olonga. Before their opening match, they issued a statement speaking out against the political situation, and wore black armbands in mourning for "the death of democracy in our beloved Zimbabwe". Flower had already planned to leave the country; Olonga was prepared to stay and face the consequences. However, rumours of secret police sent to escort him home after Zimbabwe's final game in South Africa forced him into exile.

Flower and Olonga felt they could no longer keep quiet, but this put the ZCU and the other players in a difficult position. They had deliberately not consulted their team-mates, so as not to put pressure on them, and none supported them openly, fearing for their careers and their families' safety. The ZCU faced a serious dilemma. Failure to oppose the protest might be construed as treasonable and invite government interference, which could be disastrous to the game's well-being. Whatever the private views of individual administrators, they felt obliged in public to oppose Flower and Olonga, though they denied that this was why Olonga was promptly dropped – he played only one more game in the tournament. Naturally, the ZCU suffered worldwide condemnation. Next, they had to decide whether to pull out of their tour of England, knowing that the government might force them to do so. But the risk was averted when England promised undisclosed compensation for their World Cup withdrawal and said they would undertake their scheduled tour of Zimbabwe in 2004.

After the World Cup, the struggling Zimbabwe team was further weakened by the loss of some key players. The departure of Andy Flower, 35 in April and still at his peak, was the greatest blow. Besides him and Olonga, Guy Whittall gave up international cricket because of injury, while former captain Alistair Campbell retired after hearing he would not be picked for Sharjah and England; the convener of selectors, Ali Shah, cited a poor attitude to practice. Promising pace bowler Brighton Watambwa had already emigrated to the United States, following Everton

Matambanadzo. Paul Strang retired because of injury, and his brother Bryan had moved to South Africa. They joined a long list of players lost to Zimbabwe over the years, from Graeme Hick to Murray Goodwin, losses that would have debilitated a much stronger team. On the positive side, dynamic all-rounder Andy Blignaut returned after a season's self-imposed absence. But unless problems within the country and in administration can be put to rights, the future of Zimbabwean cricket appears bleak. In the meantime, it needs the support and understanding of the rest of the cricketing world as never before.

ZIMBABWE V SRI LANKA 2004

2005

Sri Lanka's third Test tour of Zimbabwe, through no fault of their own, was a travesty of international cricket from beginning to end. The civil war between Zimbabwe's administrators and cricketers led to the absence of 15 good players in a country desperately short of them. The upshot was a farce in which the Sri Lankans easily won all five one-day internationals and then hammered the team chosen to represent Zimbabwe by record margins in the two Tests.

The International Cricket Council refused to recognise the extent of the crisis until the results of the Test matches meant that they could bury their heads in the sand no longer. They then stepped in to safeguard the Australian tour that followed from similar abuse of international status; the Zimbabwe Cricket Union agreed to postpone those Tests, before they could be stripped of their official standing. But by that time the Sri Lankan series had become a part of cricket history that could not be revoked.

Of the team that did play Sri Lanka, only Tatenda Taibu, who became the youngest Test captain in history eight days before his 21st birthday, Dion Ebrahim and Douglas Hondo had been established members of the team before the boycott. The others consisted mainly of black players from the fringe of the full-strength team, some of whom had already tasted international cricket unsuccessfully, and under-19 players. Two of the latter gave most hope for the future: opening batsman Brendan Taylor, usually the only white left in the team, and pace bowler Tinashe Panyangara.

In the one-day series Zimbabwe averaged 16.75 runs per wicket against Sri Lanka's 36. The disparity would have been greater had the tourists not rested key players after the first couple of games and found difficulty in lifting themselves against opposition so badly below standard. In the two Tests, however, the statistics were ludicrously tilted: Sri Lanka averaged 96.46 runs per wicket against Zimbabwe's 19.

To their credit the young Zimbabweans – Hondo was the grand-daddy at 24 and the average age was just under 20 – never gave up. They were clearly thrilled to be given the chance of playing international cricket, and never really lost heart, although physical and mental exhaustion had its effect. Their batting, though, was horrendously weak, as exemplified by an all-time record low of 35 on the only pitch not prepared with batsmen in mind. Taibu remained unfailingly cheerful and optimistic in his impossible job as captain of a decimated team with no experienced or successful players to support him. He led from the front, with an epic 96 not out on his debut as captain, when both openers had been dismissed without scoring; he even took off his wicket-keeper's pads and bowled to supplement his side's meagre attack.

For Sri Lanka, facing such feeble opposition inevitably meant that they learned little about themselves. Sangakkara scored a massive 270 in Bulawayo, where he shared a record-breaking partnership of 438 with Atapattu. But such records were seriously devalued. Muttiah Muralitharan's seizure of the title of Test cricket's leading wicket-taker was one record likely to have occurred here whatever the quality of the opposition. It was just sad that he could not have overtaken Courtney Walsh's record of 519 wickets in more salubrious circumstances. It was still a memorable occasion, acclaimed rapturously by his team-mates and all of Sri Lanka.

Zimbabwe v Sri Lanka — Third One-Day International
At Harare, April 25, 2004. Sri Lanka won by nine wickets. 2005

On a pitch with a grassier surface than usual, Zimbabwe's youngsters suffered the ultimate humiliation: bowled out for 35, one below the previous worst in a one-day international (set by Canada against Sri Lanka in the 2003 World Cup), and three below their own 38, also against Sri Lanka, at Colombo in 2001. Ironically, an opening stand of five was their best of the series to date. The second wicket fell at 18, when Ebrahim was caught behind for seven, which was to be Zimbabwe's joint top score, along with Extras. The seamers found life and movement in the pitch: Vaas picked up four for 11, which made him the sixth to achieve 300 one-day international wickets, and Maharoof ended the innings with two in three balls, both caught behind. To their credit, Zimbabwe threw everything into their bowling and fielding, and managed to remove Arnold before the inevitable end came 70 minutes before lunch. Jayantha hit a four and six off successive balls to bring this mismatch to an end in 27.2 overs.

Toss: Sri Lanka. **Zimbabwe 35** (18 overs) (W. P. U. J. C. Vaas 4-11, M. F. Maharoof 3-3); **Sri Lanka 40-1** (9.2 overs).

Zimbabwe v Sri Lanka — First Test
At Harare, May 6, 7, 8, 2004. Sri Lanka won by an innings and 240 runs. 2005

The one-day embarrassments turned into a three-day humiliation once the Test series began. The XI that took the field for Zimbabwe had 53 previous Test caps between them, included five debutants. Taibu – the only man apart from Ebrahim whose Test career ran into double figures – became the youngest-ever Test captain at 20 years 358 days. The result was Zimbabwe's heaviest Test defeat, a record that held for nine days.

Atapattu continued his habit of winning the toss and putting Zimbabwe in, despite the benign appearance of the pitch. The openers began with great caution, taking two runs off the first six overs, but to put on 30 against quality bowling was commendable. Only Taibu, however, had the ability and experience to do more than make a start, scoring a determined 40 before walking for a bat-pad catch. The top-scorer, with 45, was Prosper Utseya, who had been chosen for his accurate off-spin but was wicketless throughout this tour. Muralitharan mopped up the last six, and drew level with Courtney Walsh on 519 Test wickets.

Hondo and Tinashe Panyangara, who had shared a spirited last-wicket stand of 50, caused Sri Lanka some concern for two or three overs when they took the new ball; after that it was one-way traffic. The bowlers exhibited enthusiasm and reasonable accuracy, but had little more to offer as Atapattu and Jayasuriya put on 281, a first-wicket record against Zimbabwe. Jayasuriya scored 157 off 147 balls without ever looking to be forcing the pace. The breakthrough finally came on the second afternoon when Taibu took off his pads to bowl his skiddy medium-pacers, only to get his third delivery to bounce unexpectedly from the pitch, off Jayasuriya's gloves and into the gully. Atapattu, leaden-footed, was bowled by the second new ball for 170, during a middle-order slump of five for 45. The later batsmen scored usefully, if gratuitously, on the third morning to give Sri Lanka a first-innings lead of 342.

So unbalanced were the teams that the main question was not even whether Zimbabwe could survive the day, but when Muralitharan would break the record – if he had the chance. Maregwede and Nkala fought back, though, and had just drawn level with Zimbabwe's lowest Test score, 63, when Nkala played forward to Murali and was caught off pad and bat at silly mid-off, giving himself a footnote in history as Muralitharan's 520th Test wicket. The Sri Lankans erupted and embraced their hero. However, of the 200 spectators present to witness the record, few appreciated its true significance.

Toss: Sri Lanka. **Zimbabwe 199** (T. Taibu 40, P. Utseya 45, T. Panyangara 32*; D. N. T. Zoysa 3-53, M. Muralitharan 6-45) **and 102** (D. N. T. Zoysa 5-20); **Sri Lanka 541** (M. S. Atapattu 170, S. T. Jayasuriya 157, D. P. M. D. Jayawardene 37, M. F. Maharoof 40; T. Panyangara 3-101, N. B. Mahwire 3-97).

Zimbabwe v Sri Lanka   Second Test

At Bulawayo, May 14, 15, 16, 17, 2004. Sri Lanka won by an innings and 254 runs.   2005

The First Test showed up the inability of Zimbabwe's reserves to compete at international level; this was even worse. For the second match running, the Zimbabweans suffered the heaviest defeat in their Test history, and this time they managed just three Sri Lankan wickets. Sri Lanka amassed 425 runs for a single wicket [on the second day]. The bowlers did at least carry out their plan against Jayasuriya, keeping him quiet so that his 48 took 95 balls, but they had no answer to Atapattu or Sangakkara, who piled up 438, the sixth-highest stand for any Test wicket. Shortly before the close, Atapattu reached his sixth Test double-century, his third against Zimbabwe and his second in two Tests on this ground. Sangakkara followed him past 200 next day, and both must have had their eyes on 300 or more. Against such weak opposition, it was perhaps a mercy that neither achieved the coveted landmark.

Sri Lanka's lead was 485, and only the pursuit of personal milestones had prevented another three-day victory. A promising 61 by Taylor, studded with handsome off-side strokes, was the fourth day's main feature, Ebrahim again batted well and Panyangara hit merrily at the end. Another total mismatch finally persuaded the ICC that something had to be done to preserve the integrity of Test cricket.

Toss: Sri Lanka. **Zimbabwe 228** (S. Matsikenyeri 45, D. D. Ebrahim 70; W. P. U. J. C. Vaas 3-41) **and 231** (B. R. M. Taylor 61, D. D. Ebrahim 42, T. Panyangara 40*; M. Muralitharan 4-79); **Sri Lanka 713-3 dec.** (M. S. Atapattu 249, S. T. Jayasuriya 48, K. C. Sangakkara 270, D. P. M. D. Jayawardene 100*, T. T. Samaraweera 32*).

Zimbabwe v England 2004

Paul Kelso, 2005

It was entirely in keeping with the ECB's unhappy handling of the Zimbabwe question over the years that the England team should have been stuck yet again in a luxury hotel hundreds of miles away when they should have been preparing to play international cricket. Less than two years earlier, Nasser Hussain's squad had mooched in the Cullinan Hotel, Cape Town, while their employers searched in vain for a solution to the players' objections to visiting Harare for the World Cup. This time the gaudy Italianate Imperial Hotel in Johannesburg's northern suburbs was the venue for a stand-off prompted by the Zimbabwe government's refusal to accredit 13 British journalists, representing nine different media organisations – described as "political" rather than "bona fide" by one official. Those not meeting Zimbabwe's exacting standards included *The Times* and the *Daily Telegraph*.

The media ban, announced 24 hours before the squad were due to land in Harare, prompted an unlikely alliance between press and players. At a team meeting held in the first-class lounge at Jan Smuts airport just an hour before the scheduled departure, Michael Vaughan made it plain to ECB chairman David Morgan, already in Harare, that if the hacks weren't going, nor were the team. As tour manager Phil Neale kindly collected boarding passes from the assembled media so our luggage could be rescued from the aircraft, you could not get a price on the tour going ahead – which only goes to confirm the players' more usual opinion of the press, i.e. we don't know what we're talking about.

Next morning, as the players lounged round the Imperial's vast pool and their new allies discussed the merits of that evening's different flights to Heathrow, came news that Zimbabwe had climbed down. That night Morgan's emissary, John Carr, confirmed the tour was on. David Morgan was delighted at having forced a change of heart in Harare, but in reality the *volte-face* had more to do with internecine feuding within the ruling party ZANU-PF than the ECB chairman's powers of diplomacy. Not that the players would have known it. Wearing the indifferent expressions that international cricketers adopt wherever they are, the squad spent the next ten days insulated from the country's politics and privations by the routine of playing and practising. Transported from ground to hotel to golf course, they saw only sporadic graffiti and one pathetic early-morning protest to illustrate the deeper issues raised by this tour.

The opening mismatch even took place in a festival atmosphere in front of several thousand Harareans who managed to find something to enjoy in it. The next three took place amid general indifference, even among the old Rhodesian diehards in the bars. Black and white alike knew that, whatever it was they were watching, it was not a genuine contest. The players were not fooled either. The administrators present, including the ICC president Ehsan Mani, may have believed this sad tour deserved to be called international cricket. Michael Vaughan certainly didn't.

Zimbabwe v England   First One-Day International

At Harare, November 28, 2004. England won by five wickets.   Paul Kelso, 2005

Shortly before 9.30 a.m., Michael Vaughan finally led an England team on to a Zimbabwean cricket field, three years after their last series in the country and just over 21 months since the acrimonious cancellation of their previous scheduled appearance, in the 2003 World Cup. He had strongly intimated that any attempt to politicise this series would have led to the team's withdrawal. Fortunately, neither Robert Mugabe nor any of his government officials showed up. Instead, around 3,000 spectators, black and white, piled in and by mid-afternoon were contributing to a festival atmosphere. Sadly, the mismatch failed to justify local interest. Chigumbura's 47-ball 52 turned a perilous 90 for five into a respectable 195. England's run-chase was built round a half-century for Bell, and Pietersen eventually hit the winning runs, though not before running out Collingwood and twice almost doing the same to Jones.

Toss: England. **Zimbabwe 195** (49.3 overs) (D. D. Ebrahim 45, E. Chigumbura 52; D. Gough 3-34); **England 197-5** (47.4 overs) (I. R. Bell 75, M. P. Vaughan 56).

CRICKET IN ZIMBABWE, 2003–04   2005

The world has looked on helplessly for several years now as the Zimbabwean government has ruined the country's economy and manipulated elections in its thirst to retain power. In 2004, a similar disaster unfolded in the nation's cricket community, as politically motivated administrators with little love for the game destroyed the competitiveness of the national side – and, potentially, the future of cricket in Zimbabwe – when most of the top players rebelled against their rule. Though the final outcome of the dispute, as with the country's wider political crisis, remains unclear, there is no question that the reputation and health of Zimbabwean cricket has been damaged, perhaps irreparably, by the very people supposed to safeguard it.

Conflict was perhaps inevitable from 2000 when the Zimbabwe Cricket Union, under political pressure, set up an integration task force to draw up a plan for "the rapid evolution of Zimbabwean cricket". Headed by an American management consultant, Dr Richard Zackrison, the group found that "racism was right at the heart of Zimbabwe cricket" and added "Zimbabwe cricket was sitting on a powder keg that was ready to explode". This turned out to be true, but not for the reasons Zackrison thought.

His plan offered a route not merely to fast-track blacks in cricket but effectively to force whites out. Whites dominated cricket at the time, which was hardly a surprise: historically, non-whites in Rhodesia (in contrast to South Africa) barely touched the game, and it takes many years to build a cricket culture. The aim of the task force was to ensure that by 2005 blacks would be in the majority in every area of the game. The intention was that these "goals" – the term "quotas" was never used – should be carried out with "the least possible reduction in individual and team performance". This, unfortunately, was not to be.

Over the next three years, a steady stream of white faces departed the cricketing scene. Most said they were simply disillusioned with ZCU policy and unsatisfactory working conditions, which was perhaps an easy way of getting rid of them. But some were forced out, such as the national team's fitness trainer, Malcolm Jarvis, and the assistant coach, Kevin Curran. The most devastating repercussions, however, were felt in the national team. Murray Goodwin and Neil Johnson quit in 2000. Other white players saw the task force as a direct threat to their careers, and, amid an atmosphere of increasing paranoia, fringe members of the squad – such as Alistair Campbell, Bryan Strang, Gavin Rennie, Douglas Marillier, Brian Murphy and Dirk Viljoen – opted for early retirement rather than fight for a place they feared they would not be able to claim anyway.

It was not only the whites: pace bowlers Everton Matambanadzo and Brighton Watambwa left the game in that period too. Many former academy players, of all colours, were also lost. Yet at the start of 2004, Zimbabwe had a promising young side, with talented players such as Tatenda Taibu, Andy Blignaut, Sean Ervine and Raymond Price. However, Taibu was still the only non-white, with the seamer Douglas Hondo not far behind, who was unquestionably worth his place. It was a situation some black nationalists were unable to stomach. So they brought the house crashing down.

At the age of 29, the captain, Heath Streak, was enjoying the best all-round season of his outstanding career. A fluent Ndebele speaker, he was idolised by the young black cricketers he coached in the township. After a tough start, he had settled into the captaincy and won the respect of the players, although some, such as Andy Flower, thought him too malleable. This may have been true, but also understandable: the Streaks' farm was in danger of being overrun by the "war veterans" unleashed by President Robert Mugabe, and any outspokenness could have had serious consequences for his family.

Even so, Streak and his players were unhappy, and in March 2004 he took a list of the team's grievances to the board. Streak said he threatened retirement if the board failed to act. The ZCU announced he had resigned – although Streak later claimed he had been sacked – and in his place appointed Taibu. Leading Zimbabwe on to the field before his 21st birthday, he became the youngest-ever Test captain. Many viewed his appointment as premature and racially motivated. The players were outraged, and within two weeks most of the regular team, along with several on the fringe, had decided on what was in effect a strike. They demanded not only the reinstatement of their captain, but a reconstruction of both the selection panel and the ZCU board itself, as they believed both were now dominated by those with a political or racial agenda. Their decision to strike rather than pursue the matter through official channels did not help their cause, but years of frustration and aggravation had come to a head. However, all the rebel players were white. They said three "players of colour" had planned to join them, but had been intimidated into withdrawing their support. They were not alone in reporting threats: a Bulawayo reporter, Mehluli Sibanda, wrote an article critical of the ZCU, and claimed to have received menacing phone calls from two board members.

In the past Peter Chingoka, the ZCU chairman, had generally been regarded as a benign figurehead, but as the rift widened he became more hawkish. His claims that Zimbabwe cricket was totally non-racial and, at the AGM in August 2004, that "the future for Zimbabwe cricket has never been brighter" were met with widespread derision. Talks between the rebels and administrators rumbled on, but they were further apart than ever when Sri Lanka arrived in April to play a Zimbabwe team shorn of most of its leading players. Sri Lanka duly won all five one-day internationals, skittling Zimbabwe for a world-record low of 35 in the third match, at Harare, and inflicted on the home side their two heaviest defeats in Test cricket. Zimbabwean cricket would have been a laughing stock, except that tears were more appropriate. Just as it may be decades before the country as a whole recovers from its political misrule, Zimbabwe's fragile cricket culture will take many years to overcome the effects of this disastrous year.

SOUTH AFRICA V ZIMBABWE 2005 — Neil Manthorp, 2006

This was a gruesome tour, embarrassing all who saw it, from the middle, in the stands or on television. The weakened Zimbabwean team was not expected to be any match for South Africa, but the carnage was even worse than forecast. The entire Test series was completed in five days – half its scheduled length – and the one-day matches were just as one-sided.

South Africa v Zimbabwe — First Test

At Cape Town, March 4, 5, 2005. South Africa won by an innings and 21 runs. — Neil Manthorp, 2006

Those who hoped Zimbabwe would rediscover some cohesion, following the return of senior all-rounders Streak and Blignaut, were shocked by the team's performance here. Those expecting the worst were equally shocked: they had no idea how bad the worst could be. Zimbabwe lurched into lunch on the first day at 37 for seven and were dismissed for 54 – their lowest Test total – barely five overs later. The spectacle grew even more horrific when they had to bowl, and the squeamish had to avert their gaze. It took South African openers Smith and de Villiers only 33 overs to reach 200, with Smith helping himself to a run-a-ball century. It ended only when he suffered a guilt attack and slogged 18-year-old leg-spinner Cremer up into the air to give the others a chance. De Villiers followed his example three overs later, two short of an equally gratuitous hundred.

Kallis, freshly ranked as the world's best batsman but never noted for fast scoring, walked out at 234 for two in the 38th over. What would he do? The answer was to beat Ian Botham's 23-year-old record for the fastest fifty in terms of balls. Botham got there in 26 against India at Delhi in December 1981; Kallis was two balls quicker. Smith declared overnight with a lead of 286, true to his pre-series promise to "win quickly rather than hugely". Boucher, who on the first day had become only the third wicket-keeper to make 300 Test dismissals after Australians Ian Healy and Rod Marsh, said: "It's not nice to see young guys being belted all over the ground and being bowled out for 50. Maybe we can have a beer and a chat with them afterwards, help them out a bit."

At 940 deliveries, this was the 11th-shortest completed Test in history but, given that conditions were faultless and there were no illnesses or injuries, surely it was the most one-sided Test of all.

Toss: Zimbabwe. **Zimbabwe 54** (S. M. Pollock 3-9, M. Ntini 3-23, J. H. Kallis 4-13) **and 265**
(D. D. Ebrahim 72, H. Masakadza 46, A. M. Blignaut 61; N. Boje 4-106); **South Africa 340-3 dec.**
(G. C. Smith 121, A. B. de Villiers 98, J. A. Rudolph 49*, J. H. Kallis 54; A. G. Cremer 3-86).

ZIMBABWE V NEW ZEALAND 2005   2006

The most competitive part of this tour came in New Zealand before the players left. A lower-key rerun of the row in Britain about the morality of touring Zimbabwe while the country remained in the grip of Robert Mugabe's regime ended the same way – with the New Zealand government refusing actually to ban the tour, and the ICC refusing to accept any other excuse for the team not turning up.

So Stephen Fleming led his third tour of Zimbabwe – a very different one from his first, in 1997, when Zimbabwe had been the stronger side. Eight years on, this seemed unbelievable, following the premature retirement of numerous top players and the rebellion in 2004 by most of those who remained. Some rebels had been persuaded to return, but by the tour's end there were further rumblings of mutiny.

The team's lack of class, morale and determination made three of Zimbabwe's four matches against New Zealand – Test and limited-overs – virtual walkovers. The two Tests added together lasted five days of a possible 10. The return tour of New Zealand never happened. The government there would not isssue visas to the Zimbabweans.

Zimbabwe v New Zealand   **First Test**
At Harare, August 7, 8, 2005. New Zealand won by an innings and 294 runs.   2006

Zimbabwe's results had been disastrous since the 2004 player rebellion, but with several rebels back onside they hoped for a better showing. Instead, they suffered their heaviest Test defeat – having raised the bar twice against Sri Lanka 15 months earlier – after totalling 158, their lowest aggregate. They lost inside two days for the second time in three Tests, and became only the second team in Test history, after India at Old Trafford in 1952, to be dismissed twice in one day.

Vettori, coming in straight after tea [on the first day], completed New Zealand's fastest Test hundred, off 82 balls, after a freakish escape on 67; he played a ball from Streak on to his wicket, and the leg bail flipped, only to land back on top of the stumps at right angles, miraculously retaining its balance, which, under Law 28.1(b), does not constitute "complete removal".

Toss: Zimbabwe. **New Zealand 452-9 dec.** (S. P. Fleming 73, B. B. McCullum 111, D. L. Vettori 127, S. E. Bond 41*; N. B. Mahwire 3-115); **Zimbabwe 59** (J. E. C. Franklin 3-11, C. S. Martin 3-21) **and 99** (H. Masakadza 42; D. L. Vettori 4-28).

As I write, in summer 2006, Zimbabwe are not playing Tests. They in effect suspended themselves in January, recognising that the matches had become pointlessly one-sided and fearing action on the part of the ICC, which after much prevarication realised that the integrity of the game (and its records) was being imperilled.

Bangladesh – Battered but Hopeful

I t would be tempting to take a pessimistic line on Bangladesh and to suggest, as some of the articles reprinted below do, that they were prematurely pitchforked into Test cricket. But the previous chapter dealt with the real basket case of international cricket, next to whom Bangladesh's statistically dismal introduction to the big league looks almost joyous. They have the numbers, in terms of population; they will benefit from the proximity of India, cricket's commercial powerhouse; and their results are now at last on an upward curve.

Their symbolically important first Test win over a feeble Zimbabwe and, more significantly, their one-day win over Australia in Cardiff in June 2005 may, just may, have been turning points. They again competed admirably with an admittedly jaded Australia in the spring of 2006, though allowing a night-watchman to make a double hundred suggests they have a way to go yet. But let's be positive. Because Sri Lanka and Zimbabwe, before their implosion, established themselves almost immediately, we forget how difficult it can be for new Test-playing nations to join the elite. It took no fewer than 48 years for New Zealand to register their first win over England; the betting man in me says it won't take almost half a century for Bangladesh to do the same.

There is nevertheless a danger that the game – and its records – can be devalued by mismatches, and the ICC has sensibly reduced Bangladesh's Test programme. That way, they get some exposure to top-flight cricket without extended series that serve only to undermine the sport and their own morale. As always, the key will be to create a sound and competitive domestic structure that produces a viable pool of first-rate cricketers. That will take time, but my bet is Bangladesh will make it. A home-grown Murali would aid their cause greatly. Start searching the streets of Dhaka immediately for boys with peculiar bowling actions.   S. M.

SURPRISE FOR SRI LANKA   1994

The first-ever tournament under the auspices of the South Asian Association for Regional Co-operation (SAARC) was organised in Dhaka in December 1992, including strong B teams from India, Pakistan and Sri Lanka, and the Bangladesh national team. The Bangladeshis began the tournament by bowling out the Sri Lankans for 85 and winning by seven wickets. Unfortunately, the match between Bangladesh and the Indians was called off after 35 minutes because crowds had gathered outside the Dhaka Stadium protesting against the demolition of the mosque in the Indian town of Ayodhya, and the organisers eventually abandoned the tournament. Club cricket remains very popular in Bangladesh and crowds of up to 35,000 watched games between leading club sides on four or five occasions in 1992–93.

THE DREAM... Utpal Shuvro, 1998

Cricket in Bangladesh entered a new era when the national team won the 1997 ICC Trophy in Kuala Lumpur, thus achieving their goal of a place in the 1999 World Cup and doing so as champions of the non-Test-playing nations. Not since independence from Pakistan in 1971 had the country celebrated with such togetherness. When the team won their semi-final against Scotland and thus made sure of their World Cup place, processions started all over the country and young people began sprinkling coloured water. Ecstasy was not without its share of undesirable excess: three fatalities were reported. However, good sense prevailed soon. This was evident when Bangladesh beat Kenya in the final: the country seemed to be bathed in a serene spirit of joy. Hundreds of thousands of people thronged the airport to receive the heroes. Each player was given a new car. And Gordon Greenidge, the West Indian batsman whose inspired coaching helped Bangladesh turn a dream into reality, was made a Bangladeshi citizen as a special honour.

The dream had been there for some time. Bangladesh have been competing in the ICC Trophy since it started in 1979. Twice, in 1982 and 1990, they reached the semi-finals. Unfortunately for them, on both occasions they ran into Zimbabwe, then the dominant team among the ICC associate members. It was Zimbabwe's entry into the Test family that helped expand Bangladesh's horizons.

Cricket has a long tradition in Bangladesh. Pakistan played their first home Test match in Dhaka in 1955, and it was a regular Test venue until independence 16 years later. After that, cricket took some time to win its place back – the country was ravaged by war, cricket was labelled elitist in certain quarters, and there was propaganda against it. But the love of the players overcame this.

In 1993 the ICC chief executive, David Richards, was surprised to see a turnout of about 15,000 for a league match at the Dhaka Stadium between two rather unfancied clubs. He was even more astonished when he was told everyone had had to pay. Since Test status is the ultimate target, the longer version of the game is now the priority. Already, the decision has been taken to turn the popular domestic competitions into two-day, 80 overs-a-side affairs, and the national championships will include three-day games.

... AND THE REALITY Utpal Shuvro, 1999

Bangladesh turned into a land of fiesta after their victory in the ICC Trophy in April 1997. Cricket emerged as a new dream, and the cricketers became national heroes. But they failed to fulfil heightened expectations in the season that followed. After the success in Kuala Lumpur, the national squad continued to frustrate their fans. Bangladesh had their busiest-ever season in 1997–98, thanks to the granting of one-day international status, along with the right to play first-class cricket, after their ICC Trophy success. They toured Kenya, India, Pakistan, New Zealand and finally the British Isles, but could not generate much optimism about their likely performance in the 1999 World Cup in England.

Moreover, problems between national coach Gordon Greenidge and the Bangladesh Cricket Control Board became public knowledge when Greenidge told a local newspaper that he was not getting proper co-operation from the board. His outburst came after vice-president Syed Ashrafal Haq called him a "rookie" as a coach. The board took rapid action: Greenidge was not sent with the national side to the Commonwealth Games in Kuala Lumpur, and his position became increasingly difficult, though he was eventually confirmed as coach for the World Cup. Bangladesh did reach one or two memorable landmarks during the season. They had started playing one-day internationals in the 1985–86 season, but could not register a win in any of their first 22 games. The much-cherished victory came at last in the 23rd match, against Kenya in the Coca-Cola Cup in India in May 1998, although it was overshadowed by poor results in the rest of the tournament.

The team made its first-class debut during the New Zealand tour in November. But they lost all four first-class matches, three of them by an innings, and two one-day games. The only notable feat was Bangladesh's maiden first-class century, scored by the talented but enigmatic Al-Shahriar Rokon.

GOODBYE TO GREENIDGE   Utpal Shuvro, 2000

The greatest moment in Bangladesh's cricket history came in 1999, far away in Northampton, when the national team ended their first World Cup campaign with the upset of the tournament: a comprehensive 62-run win over Pakistan. The celebrations in Dhaka revived memories of 1971, the year Bangladesh won independence from Pakistan after a nine-month war. It was nearly midnight at home, but people took to the street, bands played, and children sprinkled coloured waters. There was only one hint of gloom: when the first whispers began about the possibility of the match being rigged. No one in Bangladesh believed it, and they wondered bitterly why their team could not have beaten someone else, to avoid the issue.

There was bitterness, too, for Gordon Greenidge, the former West Indian Test player who had been Bangladesh's director of coaching for three years. Throughout his tenure, Greenidge had had problems with the Bangladesh Cricket board, and there had been signs that he wanted to leave, but he was asked to continue until the World Cup was over. The end came after Greenidge told a press conference that Bangladesh's application for Test status was "ridiculous". He was relieved of his duties the night before the match against Pakistan. Greenidge went to the ground, but only to say goodbye to the players. In July, the board appointed Eddie Barlow, the former South African Test player, director of development.

GRANTED TEST STATUS
Utpal Shuvro, 2001

For the second time in just over a year, Bangladesh turned its gaze towards England, and once again the news coming back to the subcontinent triggered an outpouring of national pride and joy. In 1999, the magical day was May 31, when Bangladesh beat Pakistan against the odds in the World Cup. But June 26, 2000, would become a much more significant date in the nation's cricket heart. It was then that the dream seed, planted as ICC associate membership in 1977, reached full bloom with the unanimous decision of the ICC annual general meeting at Lord's to welcome Bangladesh into the Test family as its tenth member.

BANGLADESH V INDIA 2000
Richard Hobson, 2002

Saber Chowdhury, the president of the Bangladesh Cricket board, described his country's elevation to Test status as the third most historic event in their national life, behind independence and the adoption of a United Nations mother-tongue day commemorating the suppression of the Bengali language under Pakistani rule. A near-capacity crowd of around 40,000 watched the first day's play, which began after a simple but poignant opening ceremony in which parachutists carried flags from each of the ten Test-playing countries into the Bangabandhu Stadium. During the tea interval, Naimur Rahman, the Bangladesh captain, and Yuvraj Singh, a member of the Indian squad, injected four children with a polio vaccine to promote a new immunisation programme. The Bangladesh team delighted supporters as they advanced to 400 over the first two days. Their performance then gradually dropped off; so did attendances, as the later stages coincided with the Muslim festival of Shab-e-Barat, during which Allah is said to write the destiny of all men. Bangladesh's destiny, on this occasion, was defeat.

Bangladesh v India
At Dhaka, November 10, 11, 12, 13, 2000. India won by nine wickets.

Inaugural Test Match
Richard Hobson, 2002

For at least two-thirds of this contest, Bangladesh surpassed all expectations by matching their neighbours, and at times even enjoying the upper hand. Ultimately, they lacked the stamina, experience and, possibly, the self-belief to overcome an Indian side well short of their best. Aminul Islam's 145 was the third century for a country playing their inaugural Test, and the highest since Australian Charles Bannerman retired hurt on 165 in 1877. Only Dave Houghton of Zimbabwe had achieved the feat in between. The discipline Bangladesh showed first time around deserted them [in the second innings], with Mehrab Hossain, driving loosely, and Habibul, hooking compulsively, particularly at fault.

Bangladesh's first-innings 400 had been the second-highest total on Test debut, after Zimbabwe's 456 against India; [their second innings] 91 was the second-lowest, after South Africa's 84 against England in 1888–89.

Bangladesh v India, 2000   Inaugural Test Match

At Dhaka, November 10, 11, 12, 13, 2000. Result: India won by nine wickets.

BANGLADESH	First innings		Second innings	
Shahriar Hossain c Ganguly b Joshi	12	– lbw b Joshi	7
Mehrab Hossain c Karim b Zaheer Khan	4	– c Kartik b Zaheer Khan	2
Habibul Bashar c Ganguly b Zaheer Khan	71	– c Zaheer Khan b Agarkar	30
Aminul Islam c Srinath b Agarkar	145	– lbw b Agarkar	6
Akram Khan c Dravid b Joshi	35	– (6) c Das b Joshi	2
Al Sahariar lbw b Agarkar	12	– (5) c and b Joshi	6
*Naimur Rahman c Das b Joshi	15	– (8) c Ganguly b Srinath	3
†Khaled Mashud c Das b Joshi	32	– (7) not out	21
Mohammad Rafique c Das b Tendulkar	22	– c Ganguly b Srinath	4
Hasibul Hussain not out	28	– lbw b Srinath	0
Bikash Ranjan Das c Ganguly b Joshi	2	– c Das b Kartik	0
B 13, l-b 6, n-b 3	22	B 7, l-b 1, n-b 2	10

1-10 (2) 2-44 (1) 3-110 (3) 4-175 (5) 5-196 (6)   **400**
6-231 (7) 7-324 (8) 8-354 (9) 9-385 (4) 10-400 (11)

1-11 (2) 2-32 (4) 3-43 (1) 4-53 (3) 5-53 (6)   **91**
6-69 (8) 7-76 (1) 8-81 (9) 9-81 (10) 10-91 (11)

In the second innings Shahriar Hossain, when 3, retired hurt at 5 and resumed at 69.

First innings – Srinath 22–9–47–0; Khan 21–6–49–2; Agarkar 31–13–68–2; Joshi 45.3–8–142–5; Kartik 24–9–41–0; Tendulkar 10–2–34–1.
Second innings – Srinath 11–3–19–3; Khan 5–0–20–1; Agarkar 11–4–16–2; Joshi 18–5–27–3; Kartik 1.3–0–1–1.

INDIA	First innings		Second innings	
S. S. Das b Naimur Rahman	29	– not out	22
S. Ramesh b Bikash Ranjan Das	58	– b Hasibul Hussain	1
M. Kartik c sub b Naimur Rahman	43		
R. Dravid c Al Sahariar b Mohammad Rafique	28	– (3) not out	41
S. R. Tendulkar c sub b Naimur Rahman	18		
*S. C. Ganguly c Al Sahariar			
b Naimur Rahman	84		
†S. S. Karim st Shahriar Hossain			
b Naimur Rahman	15		
S. B. Joshi c Al Sahariar			
b Mohammad Rafique	92		
A. B. Agarkar c Bikash Ranjan Das			
b Naimur Rahman	34		
J. Srinath c and b Mohammad Rafique	2		
Zaheer Khan not out	7		
B 13, l-b 4, w 2	19		

1-66 (1) 2-104 (2) 3-155 (4) 4-175 (3) 5-190 (5)   **429**
6-236 (7) 7-357 (6) 8-413 (8) 9-421 (10) 10-429 (9)

1-11 (2)   **(1 wkt) 64**

First innings – Hasibul Hussain 19–2–60–0; Bikash Ranjan Das 19–3–64–1; Naimur Rahman 44.3–9–132–6; Mohammad Rafique 51–12–117–3; Habibul Bashar 8–0–39–0.
Second innings – Hasibul Hussain 6–0–31–1; Bikash Ranjan Das 3–0–8–0; Naimur Rahman 4–0–22–0; Mohammad Rafique 2–0–3–0.

Toss won by Bangladesh   UMPIRES S. A. Bucknor and D. R. Shepherd

Zimbabwe v Bangladesh 2001

John Ward, 2002

Bangladesh, the tenth and youngest Test-playing nation, visited Zimbabwe, the ninth, for their first Test tour in April 2001. They themselves admitted that they did not expect to win but saw the trip as a chance to learn. In that regard they succeeded, improving steadily, without ever posing a real threat to their hosts. Though Zimbabwe were still ranked ninth in the World Test Championship, the difference in experience between the sides was insurmountable. But Bangladesh did show, as in their inaugural Test against India, that they had talented players; with a population of 130 million to draw from, they also had the potential to develop rapidly.

Bangladesh's best bowler was left-arm pace man Manjurul Islam, who took six wickets at Bulawayo, but none at Harare, where the batsmen had worked him out. In the one-day matches, his opening partner Mohammad Sharif, officially just 15 years old, took some good wickets, but the side was surprisingly weak in spin. The Bangladeshis were fine ambassadors for their country, enthusiastic and cheerful, and sporting on the field of play. One wondered how long this would last in the often cynical world of modern Test cricket.

Zimbabwe v Bangladesh

First Test

At Bulawayo, April 19, 20, 21, 22, 2001. Zimbabwe won by an innings and 32 runs.   John Ward, 2002

Bangladesh's inaugural overseas Test, like their first at home, ended in defeat as they were outclassed by the vastly more experienced Zimbabweans. But the home side were often unimpressive and below their best. Indeed, some players felt – as they had in the last home series in September – that their strongest team had not been selected. Gavin Rennie, who scored 93 and 37 when he opened at Wellington in Zimbabwe's previous Test, was dropped in favour of 20-year-old Dion Ebrahim, while Bryan Strang, a pillar of strength in the bowling for several seasons, gave way to newcomers Andy Blignaut and Brighton Watambwa.

On the fourth day, Bangladesh's second innings was virtually a procession from one end while Javed Omar repeated his feat in the second one-day international by carrying his bat. He was only the third batsman, and the first for more than 100 years, to do so on Test debut, following Jack Barrett for Australia at Lord's in 1890 and Pelham Warner for England at Johannesburg in 1899. Omar might well have emulated Warner by reaching a century, too, had the tail given him even moderate support. But his achievement was enough to earn him the match award, a rare honour for a player whose team had lost by an innings. He dedicated it to his brother Asif, who had inspired his cricketing career until his early death in 1995.

Toss: Zimbabwe. **Bangladesh 257** (Javed Omar 62, Aminul Islam 84, Khaled Mashud 30; A. M. Blignaut 5-73) **and 168** (Javed Omar 85*; H. H. Streak 3-42, A. M. Blignaut 3-37); **Zimbabwe 457** (G. J. Whittall 119, A. Flower 73, G. W. Flower 68, H. H. Streak 67, M. L. Nkala 47, B. A. Murphy 30; Manjural Islam 6-81).

AFTER THE HONEYMOON

Utpal Shuvro, 2003

Bangladesh's struggles to compete in Test cricket continued. By the end of their series in Sri Lanka in July 2002, they had lost 12 of their first 13 Tests, mostly inside three days, while rain robbed Zimbabwe in the single draw. And by the ICC Champions Trophy in September, Bangladesh had lost 20 consecutive one-day internationals since their upset against Pakistan in the 1999 World Cup. With their batsmen short of application and their bowlers short of firepower, there was plenty of ammunition for those who had condemned their elevation to Test status.

A DULL THROB

Andrew Miller, 2003

After two years of incessant beatings, the pain of defeat for Bangladesh had given way to a dull throb, and the desire for self-improvement had been swamped by the hopelessness of the task. Long before they bombed out of the World Cup with defeats to Canada and Kenya, their cricketers had been stripped of all dignity. Their players deserved some sympathy for being rushed into Test cricket before they were ready, but the privileged status demanded responsibility. In 14 Tests since August 2001, Bangladesh failed to pass 200 in 20 completed innings, while bowling the opposition out on four meagre occasions. The wider danger was to the reputation of Test cricket itself.

Tests involving Bangladesh were a chore, not a challenge, and by the end of 2002 the record books had been cheapened to the tune of 25 hundreds and 18 five-fors. In the Asian Test Championship in September 2001, two Sri Lankan batsmen were so sated that they retired bored, and 11 months later a virtual Sri Lankan Second XI opted for batting practice instead of helping themselves to an innings victory.

Reputations were as short-lived as public interest. Aminul Islam, a century-maker in Bangladesh's inaugural Test, like two other former captains, Naimur Rahman and Akram Khan, dropped in and out, as a batch of teenagers were drafted into the front line. Partly influenced by Mohammad Ashraful's historic century against Sri Lanka, the chopping and changing also stemmed from a rootless domestic structure – talent had to be plucked before it ripened, or it would wither on the vine. In time, Bangladesh's struggles could transform them into a battle-hardened team. In reality, however, they had reached saturation point. For their sakes and the good of the game, they needed to be sent for a lengthy period of reflection.

AUSTRALIA V BANGLADESH 2003

Steven Lynch, 2004

On the face of it, Bangladesh's first foray into Australia as a fully fledged Test nation was a disaster: both Tests were lost by an innings, and all three one-day internationals by wide margins. Their one-day performances were indeed disappointing, but some encouraging signs of added application did emerge from the Tests and the warm-up games. It was evident that the ministrations of Dav Whatmore, the Australian in his first major outing as Bangladesh's coach after parting company with Sri Lanka (whom he coached to World Cup success in 1996), were having some effect. Nerves took hold on the first day of the First Test, when Bangladesh were shot out for 97; apart from that, the batsmen performed above expectations, especially on the first day of the Second Test on what was expected to be a spiteful pitch.

Australia v Bangladesh   First Test

At Darwin, July 18, 19, 20, 2003. Australia won by an innings and 132 runs.   Steven Lynch, 2004

The first Test to be played at Darwin's Marrara Oval – the 89th Test venue, and the eighth in Australia – was done and dusted in less than half the scheduled playing time. Bangladesh's fate was sealed on the first day when, overwhelmed by the occasion and the reputation of the opposition, they collapsed to 97 all out on a drop-in pitch (prepared in Melbourne and airlifted to Darwin a month before the match), which proved to be low and slow. The Australians also found scoring difficult, at least until Gilchrist joined Waugh and upped the tempo. Play up in the Tropics started at 9.30, so lunch was at 11.30. George Gunn, who insisted on lunching at 1.30 whatever the hours of play, would not have approved.

Toss: Australia. **Bangladesh 97** (G. D. McGrath 3-20, B. Lee 3-23) **and 178** (Hannan Sarkar 35, Habibul Bashar 54, Al Sahariar 36; S. C. G. MacGill 5-65); **Australia 407-7 dec.** (J. L. Langer 71, D. S. Lehmann 110, S. R. Waugh 100*, A. C. Gilchrist 43; Mashrafe Mortaza 3-74).

Australia v Bangladesh   Second Test

At Cairns, July 25, 26, 27, 28, 2003. Australia won by an innings and 98 runs.   Steven Lynch, 2004

Bangladesh put up a spirited performance at Cairns, where the Bundaberg Rum Stadium (formerly Cazaly's Oval) became Test cricket's 90th venue, but they still went down by an innings.

Toss: Australia. **Bangladesh 295** (Hannan Sarkar 76, Habibul Bashar 46, Sanwar Hossain 46, Khaled Mashud 44; J. N. Gillespie 3-57, S. C. G. MacGill 5-77) **and 163** (Hannan Sarkar 55; J. N. Gillespie 4-38, S. C. G. MacGill 5-56); **Australia 556-4 dec.** (M. L. Hayden 50, R. T. Ponting 59, D. S. Lehmann 177, S. R. Waugh 156*, M. L. Love 100*).

PAKISTAN v BANGLADESH 2003   Utpal Shuvro, 2004

Bangladesh embarked on their first full tour of Pakistan with the aim of playing good cricket. And good cricket they played. Their long losing streak continued – Pakistan won all three Tests and five one-dayers – but the scoreline concealed more than it revealed. After enduring three years of humiliation since their elevation in 2000, Bangladesh at last actually looked like a proper international side. In the Second Test, they took a first-innings lead for the first time, and it took a great individual performance from fast bowler Shoaib Akhtar to defeat them. And in the Third, at Multan, they were staring a historic maiden victory full in the face. Before the fourth day, their captain, Khaled Mahmud, put the likelihood of a Bangladesh win at 80%. It did not seem over-optimistic. But they were denied by a monumental innings from Inzamam-ul-Haq. Despite that deep disappointment, Bangladesh ended the series – the first in Pakistan since a bomb blast cut short New Zealand's trip in May 2002 – having taken a big step forward.

It was all very different from the three previous Tests between the sides, where Pakistan's narrowest scrape was a victory by an innings and 169 runs. Two factors played a major part in the turnaround. Firstly, Bangladesh had just returned from Australia, their first tour with Dav Whatmore as coach, having exceeded all expectations, and with their self-belief boosted. By contrast, Pakistan were still rebuilding after an unceremonious exit from the first round of the World Cup.

Pakistan v Bangladesh   **Third Test**

At Multan, September 3, 4, 5, 6, 2003. Pakistan won by one wicket.   Utpal Shuvro, 2004

Inzamam-ul-Haq played one of the innings of his life to save Pakistan from humiliation and break Bangladeshi hearts. On the third afternoon, Bangladesh's first Test win, so desperately longed for during three years of demoralising defeat, was within touching distance. On a pitch helping seamers, Pakistan were 132 for six – still 129 short of victory. But Inzamam stood firm for five hours 17 minutes, and his unbeaten 138 guided Pakistan home. It was only the tenth one-wicket win in Test history, and Inzamam had now been at the crease for two of them. While the 1994 victory over Mark Taylor's Australians came at Karachi, this triumph was in front of his home crowd, who showered him in rose petals as he left the field.

It was cruel for Bangladesh. They dominated from the word go, and despite Inzamam's heroics might still have won, given a bit more luck. But things went against them on the fourth morning. First, Hannan Sarkar at second slip dropped Shabbir Ahmed on nought. It was perhaps the most costly miss in Bangladesh's short Test history: Shabbir and Inzamam went on to add 41 for the eighth wicket. Later, with 49 now needed, eight wickets down and Inzamam farming the strike, the No. 10 Umar Gul survived a run-out despite being beaten by a direct hit. The crestfallen bowler, Mohammad Rafiq, had brushed the stumps and dislodged the bails before the ball struck. In the same over, Rafiq sportingly chose not to run out Gul when he was backing up too far.

By the time Gul was finally run out, after a bad call from Inzamam, they had added 52. Gul's contribution was five. Four runs were now needed, five balls remained in the over and the No. 11 coming to the striker's end was Yasir Ali – a 17-year-old on first-class debut, with only a handful of junior games and a hurried lunchtime batting lesson from Javed Miandad, the Pakistan coach, behind him. But Yasir kept out three balls and then tickled a single into the leg side. Off the last delivery of the over, Inzamam flicked the winning boundary. Ramiz Raja, the former Test batsman, now chief executive of the PCB, called it "one of the best Test innings of modern times". That might have been a little overblown, but Inzamam's concentration had been steely and his hitting authoritative. Supporters rushed on to the field to hug their local hero.

640

Pakistan v Bangladesh, 2003   Third Test

At Multan, September 3, 4, 5, 6, 2003. Result: Pakistan won by one wicket.

BANGLADESH	First innings		Second innings	
Hannan Sarkar c Rashid Latif b Umar Gul		13	– c Rashid Latif b Umar Gul	3
Javed Omar c Younis Khan b Umar Gul		38	– c Inzamam–ul–Haq b Shabbir Ahmed	16
Habibul Bashar c Rashid Latif b Yasir Ali		72	– c Rashid Latif b Umar Gul	3
Mohammad Ashraful lbw b Saqlain Mushtaq		12	– c Salman Butt b Shabbir Ahmed	3
Rajin Saleh run out		49	– c Rashid Latif b Umar Gul	42
Alok Kapali b Umar Gul		11	– c Rashid Latif b Yasir Ali	22
†Khaled Mashud c Rashid Latif b Umar Gul		29	– (8) lbw b Shabbir Ahmed	28
*Khaled Mahmud lbw b Shabbir Ahmed		19	– (7) lbw b Shabbir Ahmed	2
Mohammad Rafique b Shabbir Ahmed		11	– lbw b Umar Gul	4
Tapash Baisya lbw b Shabbir Ahmed		0	– not out	14
Manjural Islam not out		0	– c Younis Khan b Saqlain Mushtaq	5
B 4, l-b 10, n-b 13		27	B 5, l-b 2, w 2, n-b 3	12

1-28 (1) 2-102 (2) 3-136 (4) 4-166 (3) 5-179 (6)   281   1-4 (1) 2-9 (3) 3-23 (4) 4-41 (2) 5-77 (7)   154
6-241 (5) 7-248 (7) 8-278 (9) 9-278 (10) 10-281 (8)   6-91 (6) 7-111 (5) 8-127 (9) 9-137 (8) 10-154 (11)
In the second innings Alok Kapali, when 17, retired hurt at 71 and resumed at 77.

First innings – Shabbir Ahmed 25.2–3–70–3; Umar Gul 32–7–86–4; Yasir Ali 14–4–43–1;
Saqlain Mushtaq 25–5–61–1; Mohammad Hafeez 3–1–7–0.
Second innings – Umar Gul 15–2–58–4; Shabbir Ahmed 23–6–68–4; Yasir Ali 6–1–12–1;
Saqlain Mushtaq 2.3–0–9–1.

PAKISTAN	First innings		Second innings	
Mohammad Hafeez				
lbw b Khaled Mahmud		21	– (2) c sub b Manjural Islam	18
Salman Butt c Khaled Mashud				
b Khaled Mahmud		12	– (1) c sub b Manjural Islam	37
Yasir Hameed b Mohammad Rafique		39	– c sub b Khaled Mahmud	18
Inzamam–ul–Haq c Hannan Sarkar				
b Khaled Mahmud		10	– not out	138
Younis Khan c Khaled Mashud				
b Khaled Mahmud		34	– run out	0
Farhan Adil lbw b Mohammad Rafique		25	– c Habibul Bashar b Mohammad Rafique	8
*†Rashid Latif c Alok Kapali				
b Tapash Baisya		5	– lbw b Khaled Mahmud	5
Saqlain Mushtaq b Mohammad Rafique		9	– c Khaled Mashud b Khaled Mahmud	11
Shabbir Ahmed lbw b Mohammad Rafique		4	– lbw b Mohammad Rafique	13
Umar Gul b Mohammad Rafique		5	– run out	5
Yasir Ali not out		0	– not out	1
B 1, l-b 5, n-b 5		11	L-b 4, w 4	8

1-27 (2) 2-36 (1) 3-50 (4) 4-121 (5) 5-135 (3)   175   1-45 (1) 2-62 (2) 3-78 (3) 4-81 (5)   (9 wkts) 262
6-152 (7) 7-154 (6) 8-166 (9) 9-170 (8) 10-175 (10)   5-99 (6) 6-132 (7) 7-164 (8) 8-205 (9) 9-257 (10)

First innings – Manjural Islam 13–3–42–0; Tapash Baisya 11–2–54–1; Khaled Mahmud 13–1–37–4;
Mohammad Rafique 17.4–7–36–5.
Second innings – Manjural Islam 21–2–64–2; Tapash Baisya 12–0–46–0; Khaled Mahmud 28–9–68–3;
Mohammad Rafique 30–6–80–2.

Toss won by Bangladesh   UMPIRES E. A. R. de. Silva and R. B. Tiffin

BANGLADESH V ENGLAND 2003

Andrew Miller, 2004

England probably expended too much energy in the early weeks of the tour [the main business of which was the three-Test series in Sri Lanka], fretting over the Bangladeshi challenge. But the lessons learned on their horror tour to Zimbabwe seven years earlier – the last time they had travelled as such overwhelming favourites – meant they had no choice but to train like Trojans and perform with the utmost professionalism throughout. Three years earlier, England had turned down the chance to play in Bangladesh's inaugural Test. Now they were pitched against an improving side that had just run Pakistan unspeakably close in a Test in Multan and, under the astute guidance of Dav Whatmore, were looking for all the world like an embarrassment waiting to happen. Until the arrival of Flintoff for the one-day series, caution dogged England's every move. They were outplayed on two of the five days of the Dhaka Test and, though they won comfortably at Chittagong, they were shaken by two dramatic first-innings collapses.

Bangladesh v England   First Test

At Dhaka, October 21, 22, 23, 24, 25, 2003. England won by seven wickets.   Matthew Engel, 2004

The inaugural Test between Bangladesh and England – the last unplayed fixture between any of the ten full members of the ICC – came close to providing an earthquake that would have surpassed anything on the seismograph of England's embarrassments down the years. With a day to go, Bangladesh (previous Test record: P 24, L 23, D 1) had a distinct chance of victory. In the end, England came through comfortably enough and, objectively, Bangladesh's performance was no more than a logical continuation of their improved form since the World Cup and their near miss in Multan six weeks earlier. However, defeat would have caused derision at home and across the cricketing world. As it was, in a contest billed locally as Tigers v Lions, the home-grown cubs at last managed to inflict some scratches on opponents who – certainly on days three and four – looked both mangy and toothless.

Toss: Bangladesh. **Bangladesh 203** (Mushfiqur Rahman 34, Khaled Mashud 51, Mohammad Rafique 32; M. J. Hoggard 3-55, S. J. Harmison 5-35) **and 255** (Hannan Sarkar 59, Habibul Bashar 58, Mushfiqur Rahman 46*; M. J. Hoggard 4-48, S. J. Harmison 4-44); **England 295** (M. E. Trescothick 113, M. P. Vaughan 48, G. P. Thorpe 64; Mashrafe bin Mortaza 3-41, Mohammad Rafique 3-84) **and 164-3** (M. E. Trescothick 32, M. P. Vaughan 81*).

Bangladesh v England   Second Test

At Chittagong, October 29, 30, 31, November 1, 2003. England won by 329 runs.   Andrew Miller, 2004

For six consecutive Tests, coinciding with the arrival of Dav Whatmore as coach, Bangladesh had displayed a slow but steady improvement, and seemed at last to be coming to terms with Test cricket. At Chittagong, however, they were sent scurrying back to the drawing board, as England wrapped up a 2–0 sweep of the series with an emphatic 329-run victory. England's enforcer was Johnson, playing in only his second Test. On debut, against Zimbabwe in June, he had bowled a full, pad-rapping length to pluck out six wickets for 33. Here, he realigned his radar to buzz around the Bangladeshis' midriffs, and gained match figures of nine for 93, becoming the first bowler since Nick Cook in 1983 to pick up five-wicket hauls in his first two Tests.

Johnson had not been an original selection for the tour party. He abandoned his honeymoon in the Maldives when Anderson withdrew with a knee injury, and stepped up to the Test team when Harmison's back gave way after his match-winning efforts at Dhaka. His reward was a fright of a pitch – all green and tufty, like a Martian's chest hair – quite unlike any other that England had encountered on tour. It gave ample assistance to the seamers and no end of problems to Bangladesh's brittle batsmen, who mustered 290 in two innings.

Toss: Bangladesh. **England 326** (M. E. Trescothick 60, M. P. Vaughan 54, N. Hussain 76, R. Clarke 55, C. M. W. Read 37; Mashrafe bin Mortaza 4-60) **and 293-5 dec.** (M. A. Butcher 42, N. Hussain 95, G. P. Thorpe 54, C. M. W. Read 38*; Mohammad Rafique 3-106); **Bangladesh 152** (Rajin Saleh 32; R. L. Johnson 5-49) **and 138** (Khaled Mahmud 33; R. L. Johnson 4-44).

WHAT WENT WRONG?
Utpal Shuvro, 2004

Life got worse for Bangladesh, who had not won a game since entering the Test arena in 2000. Between October 2002 and November 2003, they clocked up 13 more Test defeats, only two reaching the fifth day, and lost 25 one day internationals, interrupted only by two washouts. Though there were chinks of light and two near-misses against Pakistan and England in late 2003, there was a growing feeling within the ICC, which Bangladesh could not ignore, that the country's promotion had been mis-handled. The World Cup was the nadir. In 1999, their first World Cup, Bangladesh had won the most important victory in their cricketing history; beating Pakistan helped them gain Test status. Four years later, in South Africa, Bangladesh owed their only two points to rain, and endured humiliating defeats by Canada and Kenya.

The World Cup disaster evoked a sharp reaction. The Bangladesh Cricket Board set up an inquiry, which interviewed players, coach, manager, board officials past and present, and even journalists. Their explosive report condemned a lack of co-ordination between the captain, Khaled Masud, who was described as autocratic, coach Mohsin Kamal, the former Pakistan bowler, and manager A. S. M. Faruque. By then, all three had gone: Masud had always said he would quit the captaincy after the World Cup, while Mohsin and Faruque were sacked. But the report also pointed to the board's flawed management, criticising president Ali Asghar and cricket committee chairman Mahbubul Anam, and the circumstances of Mohsin's appointment. The most important recommendation was to keep politics out of cricket. The Bangladesh government has deliberately politicised the cricket board, to the detriment of sporting decisions.

BANGLADESH V INDIA 2004 Amit Varma, 2005

India won both [Test and one-day] series, but the headlines were stolen by Bangladesh's stunning one-day victory at Dhaka, when they upset a second-string Indian side to achieve only their third victory over Test-playing opposition in 90 matches.

Bangladesh's place in the order of Test-playing nations was under constant scrutiny, and the fact that they lost the two Test matches convincingly – both by an innings in a little over three days – did nothing to further their cause. Their coach Dav Whatmore pleaded for the cricket world to be patient, but that plea fell on deaf ears – at least until the third day of the Second Test at Chittagong, when Mohammad Ashraful answered the clarion-call of a cricket-mad nation with an innings so pure in its freedom of strokeplay that it invited comparisons to a young Tendulkar. Ashraful's unbeaten 158 suggested that the talent on the streets of Dhaka was not necessarily inferior to that in Colombo, Karachi or Kolkata. That Bangladesh failed to avoid the follow-on, and collapsed to another humiliating defeat, paled in comparison to the self-belief and inspiration they drew from Ashraful's innings.

It proved a catalyst for their one-day victory, when they played out of their skins against a depleted and amateurish Indian side. Ultimately, the tour will be remembered not for Irfan Pathan's five-fors or the centuries from Rahul Dravid, Tendulkar and Gautam Gambhir, but for this single defeat. If critics insist that Bangladesh do not deserve to play international cricket, then the result left India's claims to be the second-best side in the world sounding a touch hollow.

Bangladesh v India **Second One-Day International**

At Dhaka, December 26, 2004 (day/night). Bangladesh won by 15 runs. Amit Varma, 2005

This was the most startling day of India's tour, as a depleted side – missing Tendulkar, Dravid, Harbhajan and Pathan – slid to a sensational 15-run defeat. Bangladesh had never won before at home, but for once 40,000 baying fans at the Bangabandhu had their dreams realised. The upset seemed entirely improbable when Bangladesh slipped to 88 for five, but the tail wagged vigorously, thanks to 67 from the supple-wristed Aftab Ahmed. Even a second-string Indian side should have had no difficulty chasing 230 on an easy pitch against gentle bowling. But they did not factor in the Bangladeshi spirit: their fielders fought for every run, clawed every catch, and struck the stumps every time they had to. The top three failed, and the middle order, led by Sriram, eked out a painful existence. Suddenly, the required rate climbed to a run a ball, and when Kaif ran himself out, the wheels came off, and Dhaka went wild. But even this triumph was badly timed: it was the day of the Asian tsunami, and the result was barely noticed across a traumatised continent.

Toss: Bangladesh. **Bangladesh 229-9** (50 overs) (Aftab Ahmed 67, Mashrafe bin Mortaza 31*);
India 214 (47.5 overs) (S. Sriram 57, M. Kaif 49).

BANGLADESH V ZIMBABWE 2005

First Test

At Chittagong, January 6, 7, 8, 9, 10, 2005. Bangladesh won by 226 runs.   Utpal Shuvro, 2006

At 12.53 p.m. on January 10, the moment all Bangladesh had been waiting for arrived. When Enamul Haque junior had Christopher Mpofu held at silly point, they recorded their maiden victory in their 35th Test. They had been dreaming of this day since gaining Test status in 2000, but first had to endure 31 defeats, three draws and innumerable sleepless nights. Zimbabwe, fielding three debutants, were the weakest opponents they had ever faced, and from beginning to end the Test followed Bangladesh's script. After winning the toss in perfect batting conditions, they amassed their highest Test total, took a sizeable first-innings lead, scored quickly in the second innings to earn ample time to dismiss Zimbabwe again, and completed their historic victory shortly after lunch on the final day.

Captain Habibul Bashar called it the best day of his life. He had led from the front scoring fifties in both innings for the fifth time in Tests. Enamul bowled beautifully, in the first innings without reward; in the second, luck was on his side, and his flight and turn sent wickets tumbling like ripe mangoes. Dismissing last man Mpofu gave him six for 45, the best Test figures for Bangladesh, before cartwheels and a lap of honour kicked off the national celebrations.

Toss: Bangladesh. **Bangladesh 488** (Javed Omar 33, Nafis Iqbal 56, Habibul Bashar 94, Rajin Saleh 89, Khaled Mashud 49, Mohammad Rafique 69, Mashrafe bin Mortaza 48; C. B. Mpofu 4-109) **and 204-9 dec.** (Habibul Bashar 55; D. T. Hondo 3-61, E. Chigumbura 5-54); **Zimbabwe 312** (B. R. M. Taylor 39, T. Taibu 92, E. Chigumbura 71; Mashrafe bin Mortaza 3-59, Mohammad Rafique 5-65) **and 154** (H. Masakadza 56, B. R. M. Taylor 44; Enamul Haque 6-45)

Winning at last: Bangladesh suffered a harsh introduction to Test cricket, losing 31 of their first 34 matches, so the celebrations were joyous when they finally won, against Zimbabwe at Chittagong in January 2005.

BANGLADESHIS IN ENGLAND 2005

Andrew Miller, 2006

Bangladesh's inaugural Test tour of England in 2005 consisted of eight weeks of toil and one glorious day. By defeating the world champions, Australia, at Cardiff, at the start of the one-day NatWest Series, they achieved their greatest ever result, and arguably the biggest upset in the game's history. For the serial whipping-boys of international cricket, one swallow really did make a summer.

Yet the widespread astonishment that greeted their victory merely underlined the inevitable question: how could Bangladesh continue to justify their Test status? In their main business of the summer, a two-Test series that began with a maiden fixture at Lord's, they were on the receiving end of a pair of hidings as numbingly predictable as they were comprehensive: their 32nd and 33rd defeats – the 21st and 22nd by an innings – in 38 Tests. Both Tests were wrapped up on the third morning, and the speed with which Bangladesh were rushed to defeat mirrored the unseemly haste with which they had been elevated to the upper echelons.

England entered the series with eight consecutive home Test wins under their belts, and the defining challenge of their careers, against Australia, fast approaching. With such an intense combination of form and focus, their only struggle was to pretend that Bangladesh posed a credible challenge. By the end, England captain Michael Vaughan had dispensed with the platitudes. The series, he admitted, had simply been too easy.

For once, the statistics told the whole story. England lost just six wickets to Bangladesh's 40, and their three leading scorers, Marcus Trescothick, Ian Bell and Vaughan, outstripped the entire opposition by 736 runs to 622. Trescothick, in particular, was in his element, adding innings of 194 and 151 to the century he had made in the inaugural fixture between these sides, at Dhaka in October 2003. Bell, in his third Test, stroked an effortless maiden hundred at Chester-le-Street which included 105 before lunch on the second day. The declaration left him with a grotesque career average of 297, and a realisation that he would never again have it so good.

England v Bangladesh

First Test

At Lord's, May 26, 27, 28, 2005. England won by an innings and 261 runs.

Pat Gibson, 2006

It had all the trappings of a Lord's Test. The jazz band was in top form under the trees beyond the Grace Gates, the members mingled happily in the splendidly refurbished pavilion, and hordes of schoolchildren brought an exuberant atmosphere to a decent-sized crowd. Even the Bedser twins were there for their customary pre-lunch pint in the Bowlers' Bar. Only the cricket failed to match the occasion. Hoggard and Harmison took a bit longer than John Barnes's Outswingers to hit the right notes, donating nine no-balls in as many overs. But once they, too, were in the swing of things, it became perfectly obvious that Bangladesh's batsmen were completely out of their depth in their first Test in English conditions. "And to think," sighed Sir Alec Bedser, "every one of those wickets is worth the same as Bradman's in the record books."

Bangladesh were bowled out for 108 inside 39 overs. The only question then was how long England wanted to bat against an attack offering little more than glorified practice. The answer turned out to be 112 overs, from which they scored 528 for three. Trescothick, averaging 16 in the County Championship, and Vaughan, averaging 24, both helped themselves to centuries; Vaughan's was his third in successive Test innings at Lord's.

England led by 420, and the prospect of the fifth two-day Test since the Second World War was looming when Bangladesh resumed. But Omar's defence and Aftab's flashing blade got them into a third day, and a spirited ninth-wicket stand of 58 between Khaled Mashud and Anwar Hossain Monir delayed England slightly longer than expected. Not that it mattered. The second-biggest victory in any Lord's Test (behind England's innings and 285-run win over India in 1974) had been so undemanding that, within an hour, England coach Duncan Fletcher had his players back in the middle for fielding practice: naughty-boy nets in reverse.

Toss: England. **Bangladesh 108** (M. J. Hoggard 4-42) **and 159** (Aftab Ahmed 32, Khaled Mashud 44; A. Flintoff 3-44, S. P. Jones 3-29); **England 528-3 dec.** (M. E. Trescothick 194, A. J. Strauss 69, M. P. Vaughan 120, I. R. Bell 65*, G. P. Thorpe 42*, Extras 38).

Australia v Bangladesh
At Cardiff, June 18, 2005. Bangladesh won by five wickets.

NatWest Series ODI
Julian Guyer, 2006

Two days after being humbled by England [who beat them by ten wickets in the first match of the NatWest series], Bangladesh produced the greatest upset in 2,250 one-day internationals to outclass world champions Australia. This match looked like David and Goliath in more ways than one. Mohammad Ashraful's mother had worried about her slightly built son taking on the physically imposing Australians, but he emerged a hero, striking 11 fours in a dazzling, run-a-ball innings. He kissed the pitch after reaching a maiden one-day hundred with a single off McGrath. Bangladesh, chasing 250 to win, now needed just 23 off three overs with six wickets left. Ashraful fell next ball, caught at long-on off Gillespie. But Aftab Ahmed, little taller than Ashraful, and Mohammad Rafique held their nerve, bringing it down to seven off six balls. The murmur of anticipation was now a barely suppressed roar. Aftab struck the first ball of Gillespie's final over for six wide of long-on to level the scores. A scrambled single completed the miracle, only Bangladesh's tenth victory in 108 one-day internationals. Attempts to keep joyful fans off the field were no more successful than Australia's to hold back Bangladesh's batsmen.

Australia's day was awkward from the start. They dropped Symonds after an alcohol-fuelled night in Cardiff, and Lee was injured, but their absence initially seemed trifling – even when Ponting surprisingly batted first, and Mashrafe bin Mortaza's second ball had Gilchrist lbw. Ponting himself managed one run before Tapash Baisya exploited his habit of falling across his stumps early on, leaving Australia nine for two. Martyn and Clarke rallied, and a total of 249 for five seemed more than adequate when Bangladesh were only 81 for three after 25 overs.

But Ashraful was as hot as the weather as he added 130 with Habibul Bashar.

He brought up his fifty flat-batting McGrath over mid-off for four, though he should have been caught two overs later when he hooked Kasprowicz to long leg: Gillespie dropped it. No Welsh try at the nearby Millennium Stadium was ever greeted with a louder roar, and the collapse almost everyone expected never came. "This is probably one of the biggest upsets in the history of cricket, and my worst defeat as captain," said Ponting. Dav Whatmore, the Bangladesh coach and former Australian Test batsman, showed a Kipling-like approach to victory and defeat, but admitted the whole team were "jumping up and down when that six was hit". They were not alone. The reaction of anyone who took the pre-match odds offered by some London bookmakers of 500-1 *on* Australia would have been somewhat different.

Toss: Australia. **Australia 249-5** (50 overs) (M. L. Hayden 37, D. R. Martyn 77, M. J. Clarke 54, M. E. K. Hussey 31*, S. M. Katich 36*; Tapash Baisya 3-69); **Bangladesh 250-5** (49.2 overs) (Mohammad Ashraful 100, Habibul Bashar 47).

SECTION THREE

The Players

SECTION THREE

The Players

The Great and the Good

My original notion, in this section, was to showcase all the "great" players of the past 30 years. But two immediate problems presented themselves. First, what constitutes greatness? Lara, Gooch, Miandad, Gavaskar, Tendulkar, Graeme Pollock and Viv Richards are, clearly, great batsmen – as defined by sheer weight of runs made over a long period, and often by the manner in which those runs were made. They are a cut above, true champions. But what of Gower, Atherton, Hick – all included here. Is there a different sort of greatness?

The choice became horribly subjective – an amalgam of some quality in the player and in the way *Wisden* had memorialised the career. Apologies to the greats who got away, either because of my own or *Wisden*'s poor judgment. The chapter headings in this section are more or less self-explanatory – batsmen, quick bowlers, spinners, all-rounders, keepers, captains and a few characters, men who in a bland age brought something special to the way they played the game, forged a special bond with fans, achieved greatness of a different kind.

Matthew Engel calls picking the Five Cricketers of the Year his annual perk. I have given myself a perk for compiling this book – the chance to pick an XI from the greats who played in the period covered by this volume: Gooch, Greenidge, Viv Richards, Lara, Tendulkar, Botham, Knott, Marshall, Warne, Muralitharan, Waqar Younis. Who should skipper? Several of these were, after all, flawed captains. It may have to be Warne – the great Australian captain who got away. Bird and Shepherd will umpire; Benaud, Arlott and Johnston will commentate; Frindall will score; the game will be played at The Oval. Corporate diners and the singing of "Jerusalem" will be banned. The sun will shine strongly; tickets will not cost £50 or have to be bought nine months in advance; boisterous West Indian fans will be welcome; spectators will not have to squeeze themselves into small plastic seats and sit next to loud young bankers who drink copiously. Now all we need is some decent opposition.　　　　　　　　　　　　　　　　　　　　　　　　　　　S. M.

Batsmen

GEOFFREY BOYCOTT   Terry Brindle, 1978

Geoffrey Boycott's place in cricket folklore was assured long before that warm Headingley evening last summer when he succeeded where only would-be bombers and the infernal weather had succeeded before and stopped an English Test match in its tracks for almost ten minutes.

Boycott's hundredth century – in a Test Match, before his Yorkshire public – was indeed the stuff that dreams are made of. There was hardly a dry contact lens in the house. But the abiding significance of his hundredth century was not simply statistical; Boycott himself conceded that one century on record was much the same as the one before or the one to follow. It was the realisation, vitally important to Boycott himself, that the public were prepared to accept his peace offering after a controversial absence from Test cricket.

Boycott and controversy have shared the longest opening partnership in the game. The owlish, introverted young man who broke into county cricket with Yorkshire in 1962 and who was regarded as a dedicated technician rather than a talented strokemaker developed his skills to prove the unbelievers wrong and neglected his personality to convince his critics they were right. The trauma of Trent Bridge and the Headingley homecoming which followed combined, as never before, Boycott the public man with Boycott the private person. To his unconcealed delight, the public showed themselves ready to accept both.

Cricket tends to traditionalise its heroes, seeking to find in them all the qualities of unselfishness and character which lend an amateur's zeal to a highly professional game. Boycott, complex and warted, refused to fit the pattern and was not easily forgiven. Yet Boycott the technician has rarely been doubted. He is compact, beautifully balanced, professionally expert, arguably the most adroit player of the ball off the wicket in the modern game. The very soundness of his technique tends to detract from the drama of his innings, even of centuries carved with fastidious determination.

Others have created their own legends more extrovertly, more gloriously, more entertainingly. Boycott builds an innings brick by brick, cementing each stroke to the next with that extraordinary power of concentration which frustrates good bowling and intimidates poor. His centuries are an act of will.

That single-mindedness has exposed Boycott to accusations of selfishness which are bound to be levelled from a distance; easier to challenge with an insight into the man and the situation thrust on him as captain of a young and inexperienced

Yorkshire side. Boycott's responsibilities weigh heavily and the proven frailty of Yorkshire's batting has led him to believe he cannot, must not fail. The conviction that his runs are indispensable – and Yorkshire without them would have struggled fearfully in the recent past – feeds an already characteristic strain of stubbornness. Boycott in or out of form cannot contemplate giving his wicket away; the very idea is anathema, an admission of failure. He is, consequently, a player less than ideally suited to limited-overs competition where the ability to improvise is ranked as important as ability itself. He has, consequently, an air of detachment during an innings which shuts out every consideration except the next ball, the requirements of the moment. His intensity is sometimes misdirected, often misinterpreted.

Boycott's character and performance are indivisible; more than any modern player he has been judged in terms of personality. Knowing this, and sometimes wounded by it, he withdrew into the security of the art he knew best and resolved that if he could not be the most popular of players he would be the most effective. A century of centuries insists that he did not fail. His welcome back into Test cricket and the warmth of his reception at Trent Bridge and Headingley tapped a fund of popular sympathy and admiration which Boycott never knew existed. At 5.49 on August 11 Geoffrey Boycott reached one hundred hundreds and realised he could count on the support, understanding and even friendship of one thousand thousand. It would not be easy to decide which he values more.

A photograph of Geoffrey Boycott on the occasion of his hundredth century, in the company of Len Hutton and Herbert Sutcliffe, appears on page 1246.

Derek Hodgson, 1988

Geoffrey Boycott, an egocentric right-hand batsman of great defensive skills and an occasional in-swing bowler, will be remembered as much for his prodigious scoring record as for his impact, over 25 years, perhaps more, on the history of the Yorkshire county club. He has a facility for making enemies much faster than he made his runs, admits to very few friends, yet inspires a loyalty among his admirers that all politicians must envy.

As a cricketer, a batsman converted to opening in his early days with Yorkshire, he had no peers in England during his career. Abroad, only Sunil Gavaskar, the man who overtook Boycott's aggregate of Test match runs, could be compared in application, dedication, attention to detail, tactical acumen, patience and endurance. Even Boycott's critics would agree, too, that his runs were made often in far more difficult circumstances, in English conditions and on English pitches, than Gavaskar's. In batting on seaming or turning pitches, or when the ball cut or swung, Boycott for more than 20 years reigned supreme in the world.

This ability to score runs, albeit slowly, when all around him were grateful merely to survive, indicated that Boycott was far from limited in his strokeplay. All the shots were there, but only rarely was the full armoury uncovered; when he did settle upon an attacking innings, however, the ensuing firework display could be a brilliant memory. Three occasions come to mind, the first a brief burst at Bradford in 1977, when Yorkshire were chasing runs on the third afternoon against

Northamptonshire and Boycott, astonishingly, was charging from his crease to lift the bowling straight. There was a humid Sunday afternoon at Worcester, where Boycott produced a dazzling 60 at a rate not even Milburn would have scorned.

But the outstanding recollection of Boycott in this mood must be of a World Series Cup match against Australia at Sydney during the 1979–80 tour under Mike Brearley. There had been speculation that Boycott might be dropped from the limited-overs side. Brearley, like every other captain, had his difficulties with Boycott, yet their relationship was only occasionally strained; and Brearley was able, as he was with most players, to inspire some remarkable performances. On December 11, Boycott walked out with Derek Randall and, against an attack featuring Lillee, Thomson and Walker, scored 105 off 124 balls, including seven fours. He reduced a rowdy Hill, primed to jeer him, to a respectful silence. Englishmen, by and large, are not disposed to embrace Geoffrey Boycott, but that was one time when he induced considerable emotion among the stiff upper lips.

The more customary Boycott, and the experience of batting with him, was summed up thus by a younger contemporary. "You were always conscious that you were on your own, in that he was one partner unlikely to surrender his wicket to save you and that you were his partner on his terms. That accepted, there was a lot to learn because his mind, computer-like, was always working. He would know who was to bowl and which end they would choose and why. He would anticipate bowling and fielding changes, calculating when and for what reason. He knew most bowlers backwards, most pitches, even the direction of the prevailing wind. You would always know when there was something he didn't like about one particular bowler when you found yourself with more of the strike than normal. Professionally he was a paragon, immaculate in his preparation and turn-out, and for all the jokes it was an education to stand at the other end and watch him play."

GLENN TURNER

Norman Harris, 1983

In retrospect, it almost seems that Glenn Turner was destined to score his 100th hundred on May 29. One would hardly say he had tried *not* to reach the milestone on some other day on some other ground. But, after a run of low scores, a gloriously fine Saturday at Worcester suddenly seemed the obvious setting.

It was also clear that Turner would not want to just score 100 in adding his name to the 18 players who had previously registered the feat. He would surely want to do so in particularly glittering fashion. Securing 100 before lunch was the most obvious way. Almost inevitably, he achieved it.

The occasion seemed even more appropriate, with Billy Ibadulla on hand to come out to the middle with a celebratory gin and tonic. It was Ibadulla, once a coach in Dunedin, New Zealand, who had encouraged Turner to go to England and arrange a trial with Warwickshire. It was Warwickshire who had not been able to offer him a contract, and against whom Turner has always scored particularly heavily. And it was Warwickshire's bowlers who were now suffering again. With Turner 128 at lunch, the afternoon offered a further challenge; as the runs mounted up it became clear that he was after his 300. He reached it at 5.36 and at the declaration, six minutes later, was 311 not out.

DENNIS AMISS

Jack Bannister, 1987

The crisis-ridden career of Dennis Leslie Amiss is an object lesson to those lesser cricketers who, when faced with their first major hurdle in professional cricket, show a deficiency in technique and temperament which precludes further progress. But because Amiss's make-up is generously threaded with toughened steel, in his 44th year – 29 of which have been spent on the Warwickshire staff – he was able to step into the 100 hundreds club, as well as moving past Andrew Sandham into 12th place in the list of the game's most prolific run-scores. He continued to parade a technique and level of concentration which, far from showing the first under-standable signs of decline, were as impressively solid as ever.

Because he has always been a batsman whose approach has been governed by an unflagging self-discipline, it might have been expected that the passing years would dull Amiss's appetite for runs. Instead, it is a measure of the man that he still relishes a batting challenge so voraciously that in 45 innings in 1986, his stumps were hit only four times – and one of those rare dismissals was a fast leg-break from the New Zealand seamer, Watson.

For Amiss, the Holy Grail became the 21st entry card into batting's most exclusive club. It shone brightly enough at the beginning of the summer to draw in, in 17 innings, three of the four hundreds needed for glory, but then there was a tantalising wait as the hundredth century eluded him for 16 more innings, in three of which he topped 50. And although it finally came in slightly anticlimactic fashion – the extra half-hour of a dead game against Lancashire being taken to enable the last 36 runs to be scored – the innings marked the personal high-point of a magnificent career.

A photograph of Dennis Amiss wearing a prototype helmet appears on page 214.

GRAEME POLLOCK

Charles Fortune, 1988

Graeme Pollock, the great South African batsman who too soon was denied occu-pation of cricket's more illustrious creases, retired from the first-class game at the end of the 1986–87 season. In January 1961, aged 16 years and 335 days, he scored his first Currie Cup century in Johannesburg, for Eastern Province against Transvaal B. Twenty-six summers later, with a score of 63 not out and now playing for Transvaal, he was there at the finish of the match which saw his team retain the Castle Currie Cup.

It is for his batting at Trent Bridge in 1965 that, in England, Graeme Pollock is best remembered; and this was the batting of a player only 21 years old. Of his hundred there, *Wisden* said that following the lunch break ". . . he reigned supreme for 70 more minutes while he lashed the bowling for 91 out of 102. . . he offered no chance." The power and the artistry of his strokeplay that day was awesome. Using his height (6ft 2½ in) to full advantage, he drove the English bowling, off back foot and front, through the covers, regardless of length. The ball to which other batsmen would have offered a defensive bat was simply struck to the boundary.

Ted Dexter later wrote of him: ". . . he could hit the good-length ball, given only a modicum of room outside the off stump, actually harder than he could hit the half-volley. Now that takes some doing."

Across the world cricket scene, that was pretty much the end for South Africa. Pollock was to play twice more against Australia in South Africa – Bobby Simpson's side in 1966–67 and Bill Lawry's in 1969–70 – and he was in England in 1970 for the series between England and the Rest of the World, which took the place of the cancelled tour by South Africa. A century in the fifth Test, which incorporated with Garry Sobers a fifth-wicket partnership of 165, was his one big innings. His scores for eight innings averaged 31.25 and were below those of the other Springbok batsmen, Barlow, Procter and Richards.

At home, however, Pollock was consistently a heavy scorer, and in the two series with Australia he was often brilliant. Against Simpson's team came a double-century at Newlands. Four years later, when Lawry brought his team on from India, Pollock at Durban made 274 in the only South African innings and estab-lished a new record score by a South African in Test cricket. Thereafter, his and South Africa's international cricket were to be restricted to home series against breakaway visitors from England, Sri Lanka, the West Indies and Australia. The innings of 144 against an Australian XI with which he bowed out of international cricket in Port Elizabeth in 1987 was both convincing and memorable; it seemed hard to think of him as being 43 in three to four weeks' time.

If it is permissible to attach the word genius to the artistry of a batsman, then Graeme Pollock is such among cricketers. Like others so acknowledged he was ever the master craftsman. Perhaps the all-important factor was that from the start, the bowling he faced was more skilled and demanding than will have come the way of many others. Only Colin Cowdrey among the cricketers I have known has moved so easily up the rungs that take cricket toddlers to a Test match debut. Pollock never underestimated the opposition, nor hesitated to meet a challenge. When 13, he became excited, even entranced, by the skill and application of the Australian, Neil Harvey, like himself a left-handed batsman. It was Harvey's dedi-cation to the task of making runs, and still more runs, that determined Pollock never to yield his wicket while runs were there to be taken.

ZAHEER ABBAS
David Green, 1984

Zaheer Abbas burst upon the world of cricket in 1971 at the age of 23. In the opening match of Pakistan's tour of England that year, at Worcester, he made a rapid 100 and continued in prolific form, scoring 731 runs in May. The first Test match started at Edgbaston on June 3 and by June 4 Zaheer, during the course of a magnificent innings of 274, had completed 1,000 for the season.

Opponents, press and public were struck by the slender, bespectacled newcomer's mastery over an England attack which included Peter Lever, Ray Illingworth and Derek Underwood and had, only the previous winter, proved too strong for the Australians on their own pitches. His elegance, timing and powers of concentration (he batted for over nine hours and hit 38 fours) were acclaimed.

Nevertheless, some reservations were expressed. England, having omitted the out-of-sorts John Snow, had no bowler of high pace to test this young man with the full and curiously looped backlift, and the Edgbaston pitch had been dead. Would the languid-looking Zaheer succeed on quicker wickets or when the ball seamed and swung? One who did not hedge his bets was Ted Dexter, who noted in a broadcast that up to the start of the tour Zaheer had made nine hundreds in only 45 first-class innings. "You must," said Dexter, "be some batsman if you can score a century every five knocks you have."

In the event, Zaheer, or Zed as he has been almost universally known since his association with Gloucestershire began in 1972, has mocked the doubters. He has already made well over 30,000 runs at an average of comfortably more than 50, and on December 12, 1982, his 215 for Pakistan against India at Lahore was his 100th first-class hundred. By September 1983 he had made a century in each innings of a match on eight occasions, and on four of them one of the centuries was a double; both are feats unparalleled in the annals of the game. In Test matches he had scored his 4,000th run and was averaging 46.81.

This bald statistical recital gives the impression that all went smoothly for Zaheer after that remarkable performance in what was only his second Test match – his first had been against New Zealand in 1969 – but this is far from being the case. Zaheer's impressive Test figures mask some inconsistencies. After his triumph at Edgbaston he had to wait three years for his next Test century, which was again a big one and against England – 240 in The Oval Test of 1974. There was another long gap before his third, which was against Australia at Adelaide in 1976. Prosperous series against India and New Zealand in 1978–79 brought him three hundreds, yet in his next 23 Test innings he made only 528 runs. Then came some marvellous batting in Pakistan in 1982–83 against Australia and India, a veritable run-glut which included five Test centuries, the 215 at Lahore among them.

These ups and downs are mentioned less as criticism than as an illustration of the character which Zaheer, a man whose persona is quiet to the point of diffidence, has frequently shown in overcoming adversity. Poor form, for him, is a more serious matter than for most players, for apart from his wife, Najma, their daughters, Rudaba and Roshana, and the immediate circle of his family, cricket and more particularly batting is the breath of life to him. Where such dedication exists, failure is not easily shrugged off, and introspection and worry can compound a player's difficulties.

Technical faults have sometimes been advanced to explain Zaheer's extremes of form, but this seems to me to be nonsense. He has scored a century on every six and a half visits to the crease. Leaving aside the phenomenal Sir Donald Bradman, whose ratio of centuries to innings was one to 2.8, Zaheer's striking-rate, among those who have made 100 hundreds, is excellent. Batsmen who have made a comparable number of runs with a higher career average can be counted on the fingers of one hand. No one with a faulty method could perform at Zaheer's level over 14 seasons, winter and summer, and to attempt to explain his failures in this way is to misunderstand the man and the nature of his art.

Zaheer's love of batting is manifested not through mere sterile occupation of the crease, with runs being scored at a rate dictated by the level of the bowler's competence, but rather through a will to dominate bowlers, almost irrespective of their skill or of the condition of the pitch. This is a characteristic he shares with his great contemporary, Vivian Richards. The shortish ball just outside off stump, which a player more prudent or less talented might studiously ignore, is to him there to be hit, and the same can apply to the straight, good-length ball, from which he scores with an ease and frequency which only Richards and perhaps Greg Chappell have matched in recent years.

Such an ambitious approach carries its own penalties. Inevitably, attacking strokes aimed at good balls leave little margin for error. Zaheer, therefore, more than most, can be affected by slight loss of form; the flowing cover-drive, if edged, carries to slip in a way that the careful defensive prod does not. On balance, however, his attitude is fully justified by his record. The spectator must expect the occasional early dismissal, but in compensation he sees, when Zaheer is going well, strokeplay of a beauty which illuminates a utilitarian age.

SUNIL GAVASKAR
Dicky Rutnagur, *Five Cricketers of the Year*, 1980

Sunil Manohar Gavaskar was born in Bombay on July 10, 1949, with the scent of bat oil in his nostrils, for his father was still a very active club cricketer and his uncle from his mother's side, M. K. Mantri, was Bombay's and India's wicket-keeper. In the circumstances, it was no surprise that a toy cricket bat was among his earliest possessions, and that the infant Gavaskar's afternoon naps were followed by practice against the bowling of a doting mother and the houseboy.

The most prolific Indian batsman ever in Test cricket says that he learnt to read numbers from scoreboards. While children of his age went to bed listening to tales of Red Riding Hood and Goldilocks, Gavaskar had his little ears trained to the radio and the voices of John Arlott and Rex Alston describing the Test matches of 1952, in which uncle Madhav was engaged. For him, the big bad wolf was F. S. Trueman.

When Gavaskar went visiting his uncle, he would ask him to unlock his wardrobe and display his various caps, sweaters and blazers, the colours of Bombay University, Bombay and India. The child that stared at them with awe was to win all those colours himself before he was 20 and to wear them with great distinction.

Last summer's memorable Oval Test, in which Gavaskar scored his epic 221, was his 50th. At that point, with a home season of 13 Test matches to follow, he had played more Test matches than any Indian except Bishan Bedi, Polly Umrigar and Gundappa Viswanath. Gavaskar has made and broken records at all levels of the game. Flip through the statistical section of *Wisden*'s Indian counterpart and his name figures on almost every page. During the recent 1979–80 series against Australia, he became the first Indian to complete 5,000 runs in Test cricket.

Gavaskar's three-figure Test scores include three double-centuries, the first of which was made in only his fourth Test and came on the heels of a century in the first innings of that same game – the fifth Test of India's 1971 series in the West Indies. India went into this Test match, at Trinidad's Queen's Park Oval, leading one-nil, having won the Second Test on the same ground a few weeks earlier. But for Gavaskar's 124 in a total of 360, India would probably have lost that six-day final Test, for West Indies scored 526 in reply. Danger still lurked when Gavaskar scored 220 in the second innings, but eventually India came near to winning it. The remarkable feature of Gavaskar's marathon batting in that match was that both innings were played under the handicap of an agonising toothache which deprived him of adequate sleep. He refused pain-killers lest they made him drowsy or slackened his reflexes.

As is obvious from Gavaskar's Test record, he is capable of intense concentration and discipline. But he summons these virtues only when India are in trouble or when he senses the chance of a win. He is not one for making big scores just for the sake of records. When he sets his sights high, he builds his innings with meticulous craftsmanship, limiting himself to the stroke he plays best – drives through the covers, past the bowler, and between mid-on and mid-wicket. But when he lets his hair down, his range of shots and the power behind them are quite astonishing. He can lay claim to a six at the Melbourne Cricket Ground. As an exhibition of brilliant batsmanship in a Test match, his 205 against West Indies at Bombay two winters ago was outstanding.

A photograph of Sunil Gavaskar batting with Imran Khan appears on page 71.

VIVIAN RICHARDS
Vic Marks, *Five Cricketers of the Century*, 2000

Fast bowlers, usually West Indian, have caused countless sleepless nights and/or some nasty nightmares over the years, but Vivian Richards was the one batsman I've encountered who could intimidate his opponents – even before he had received a ball. His journey to the crease was a declaration of intent. It was usually delayed a fraction to enable the outgoing batsman to disappear from view. Richards did not want any distractions from his entry. He glided slowly to the crease in his own time, checking the light on the way; there was a hint of a swagger, which became more marked as the years rolled by. And there was the cap, the most obvious symbol of his superiority. In a decade when the fast bowler's stock ball whizzed past the batsman's nostrils, Richards was the last hold-out who shunned the helmet. The cap was the reminder that no bowler, however fast, would threaten his domination.

For Richards was never content with mere survival. Bowlers had to be subjugated, to recognise that he was the master. There were occasions when he might sleepily tap back some medium-pacers from a novice who had just graduated from the second team – for Richards was not primarily an avaricious gleaner of runs. But he would always launch a fearsome assault upon anyone with an international reputation. In England, this meant that Derek Underwood and Bob Willis, England's two world-class bowlers of the 1970s, had to be destroyed rather than blunted. Richards's pride demanded nothing less. In fact, it was a compliment to be on the receiving end of an onslaught from him, though the bowlers in question rarely appreciated it at that time.

Richards was capable of technical excellence. His forward defensive stroke, which he sometimes played with exaggerated, ironic care, just to inform the bowler that he could have smashed a boundary but had chosen not to, could be as impenetrable as Boycott's. But he didn't use it that often. More frequently, he ignored the coaching manuals and, relying on the keenest pair of eyes and phenomenal reflexes, just trusted his instincts. He reckoned that, if he played an on-drive in classical style, the ball would simply speed into the hands of mid-on. So instead he continued to turn the wrists and play the ball squarer – through the gaps. His front foot was planted down the wicket and his bat swung across his pad. All wrong, yet Richards made it seem the safest shot in the world. We tried to copy him and were plumb lbw. Despite the lunge of that front foot, his hook shot was the one that astounded his new county colleagues in 1974. No one hooked his fellow Antiguan Andy Roberts, who was terrorising county batsmen for Hampshire, except Richards. We couldn't work out how he did that.

Sir Isaac Vivian Alexander Richards (he was knighted by the Antiguan government in 1999) separated himself from his rivals by his ability to perform at his peak on the grand occasion. He adored Lord's in a way that is peculiar to overseas players, who first pictured the ground while listening to crackling radios in the old colonies. He played in eight Lord's finals, five for Somerset and three for West Indies, and failed – by normal standards – only once. Even that day, the inaugural World Cup final against Australia in 1975, his fielding altered the course of the match. "When I was batting at Lord's," he said, "I wanted to make sure that no one else was going to come in. It was my stage."

When it really mattered, he might proceed a little more cautiously at the start of his innings; he would sweat even more profusely, and then he would set about tinkering with fate as only the great players can. Take two innings at another of his favourite spots, the Recreation Ground at St John's, Antigua. West Indies played their first Test there in 1981 – mostly thanks to the prominence Richards himself had given the island. He willed himself to a hundred, edgy by his standards. Five years later, against England again, his mission was to entertain those who had seen him grow up. One hundred came from 56 balls, the swiftest Test century recorded. Sixes disappeared down the high street. Richards could destroy both clinically and ferociously, provided he had a cause to play for. He usually did.

A photograph of Vivian Richards batting in the 1979 World Cup Final appears on page 803.

David Foot, 1990

There were times when peaks in Viv Richards's career seemed almost predestined. He told David Graveney in bar-room pleasantry one evening that he would be making two hundred against Gloucestershire – and that was what he did next day. In the September of 1979, when Somerset acquired their first title after 104 years of feckless history and eternal optimism, those of us from down in the West Country knew Richards would excel. He gripped his bat tighter than usual, staying from the seventh till the last over to score 117 in the final of the Gillette Cup.

At Sydney, in November 1988 against New South Wales, Richards became the

first West Indian to complete 100 first-class hundreds. In his previous innings –
the first of the tour – he had fashioned his 99th, against South Australia. Clearly
the procrastinations had gone on long enough. That particular landmark was
overdue. In any case, he hated all the talk about records.

His inclusion, as No. 22 on the illustrious list, was always a matter of inevitability.
Judged by his own expansive, often sublime, at times savage standards, the surprise
was that the milestone took him so long. It was still achieved out of only 658 innings.
Yet if the mind, the mood, the fitness and the circumstances had combined rather
more felicitously, his statistics would have carried a greater dramatic eloquence. As
it was, only Bradman (295), Compton (552), Hutton (619) and Boycott (645) had
got there in fewer innings. Of that contrasting quartet, he would be most flattered
to be compared with Compton, because of his impish disregard for reputation and
his innate sense of adventure.

There was a time, early in his career, when Richards was being dubbed "the
black Bradman". It was an absurd analogy: their styles and attitudes were so dissimilar. Almost certainly the great Don kept a furtive eye on the scoreboard a great
deal more than does Richards. I. V. A. could actually look fallible, and that was an
integral part of his charm and his genius.

His departure from Somerset and subsequent loss to county cricket probably
robbed him of another 18 hundreds. Injuries and ill health over recent years have
also restricted him. There are suggestions that the marvellous eyesight and the
almost magical reflexes are at last on the decline, though no doubt he would
contest such notions. Nearly half his hundred hundreds were for Somerset, the
county he loves no more. When he arrived in 1974, they seemed made for each
other. He liked the gentle pace of market-town Taunton, the chummy rustic
boundary banter, the apple-juice buzz of expectancy as overdue success loomed.
It was Richards and Botham growing up together, playing for their countries, doing
wondrous deeds. Somerset had always liked batsmen who got on with it – from
Sammy Woods to Wellard, Guy Earle to the tragic Harold Gimblett. Richards didn't
just do that; he was the best in the world.

His first centuries were at Bristol and Bath, where this writer recalls the
boyish excitement, tempered by disbelief, when word reached him that he was in
the West Indian tour party for India. There was, too, the joy of seeing, at a rough
count, 30 of his hundreds. They varied in quality, never in excitement. He did it
without a helmet. The cap was straight and yet distinctive, in the way that caught
Colin Cowdrey's eye when he first saw Richards, lean and cheerful, swinging a
Caribbean bat that looked almost too heavy for him. In this country, the body
filled out: the muscles flexed and the runs flowed. The aficionados nudged each
other: to admire the sheer stillness of the man as he stood at the crease waiting
for the bowler, then the instinctive way he got into position so quickly to play
his shot. Somehow he was conjuring up half-volleys when they did not exist. He
was hitting beautifully through the covers. And, most beguilingly of all, he was
hitting across the front foot. He was defying generations of coaches as he clipped
the off-stump ball through mid-wicket.

Of his hundred centuries, 44 were scored for West Indies, exactly half of
them in Test matches. No more than eight came from his appearances for
Leeward Islands or Combined Islands. One of those was against Jamaica at

St Kitts. Could there have been a few spectators present that day who had made the journey, a decade earlier, to see him play for Antigua against St Kitts? It was his first zone match and, for him, an infamous one. He refused to walk when given out. There were demonstrations and a two-hour delay. But then Richards has never been completely free of controversy. There have been racial taunts from Yorkshire crowds; angry words with opponents and umpires; the delay over his appointment as captain of West Indies; the acrimonious good-byes at Taunton.

The memory is long, the fuse can be short. The walk to and from the wicket carries a swagger that is seen, perhaps misinterpreted, as arrogance. That unrelenting cricketing diary all round the year has left him at times both weary and cynical. Captaincy has not always gone easily for him. There must be difficulties on occasions in welding a common purpose from talented players of disparate temperaments and varying island homelands. Inter-island rivalries do exist; political implications can be inhibiting. But he has one undeniable bonus. All West Indian cricketers respect his bountiful gifts.

GORDON GREENIDGE AND DESMOND HAYNES
Peter Roebuck, 1992

As Joey "The Lips" Fagan said in *The Commitments*, "Beginnings are everything. Get a start and the rest is inevitable." So it is in cricket. Powerful teams are strong at top and bottom, in their head and their feet. Those early exchanges with bat and ball which so dictate the course of events must be won. Take early wickets, forge an effective opening stand, and the enemy is forever in retreat. And resistance, however heroic, seldom brings victory. As Sir Winston said after the valiant and celebrated withdrawal from Dunkirk, "We cannot afford many victories such as this".

Throughout their 15-year stint as cricket's outstanding team, West Indies have been superb and ruthless in their use of the new ball. At even a hint of grass, or freshness in the pitch, Clive Lloyd or Viv Richards chose to bowl first, confident that his august pace merchants would seize their opportunity. Already their names are legion, and it was these men, Roberts, Holding, Garner, Croft, Marshall, Ambrose and Patterson among them, whom opposing teams feared, for this was West Indies' most potent and irresistible weapon.

And yet this was but half the tale. Throughout their reign as world champions of Test cricket, the West Indians also fielded two of the game's most reliable opening pairs. Greenidge and Fredericks, Greenidge and Haynes. Their names trip off the tongue as smoothly as Laurel and Hardy, Simon and Garfunkel, or Astaire and Rogers; excellent in themselves, brilliant in combination. Time after time they gave their team a secure start, which allowed men such as Viv Richards, Clive Lloyd, Alvin Kallicharran and Richie Richardson to turn strength into domination.

Both pairs feature in the ranks of Test cricket's most productive opening partnerships. Including only those who put on at least 1,000 runs, and averaged 40, Fredericks and Greenidge lie 11th in the list with an average of 57.73, and Haynes and Greenidge 14th with an average of 46.94. Hobbs and Sutcliffe top a list which also includes Hutton and Washbrook (seventh) and Simpson and Lawry (eighth). But in many respects Haynes and Greenidge have been the greatest pair of them all, because they walked out together in 89 games, far, far more than any rival partnership. In terms of longevity, fitness and consistency they are unrivalled.

It helped, of course, that they were so diverse in temperament and technique. Desmond Haynes emerged from his quarters in a back room of his mother's Barbados rum shop as a cheerful, extrovert man, alert to every situation, prepared to hit hard, high and, at first anyhow, to any quarter. To him cricket was a simple and spontaneous game, full of life and love and laughter. He could strike balls over cover, could run like a hare, and hook with a sudden, quick, wristy movement. On his feet he was light, and as he collected his runs he was smiling, charming, crisp and flamboyant.

In time Haynes changed, as men do when they begin to experience the barbs and the bouquets; and though still grinning he began to calculate, and to irritate. If he was just as much a dasher in manner, his performances told a different tale, one of a man now fully versed in the arts of life, a man with a position to protect, and to advance. At the crease he continued to move forward to play off his pads with characteristic Caribbean expertise, or to go back to drive through cover. He was, and is, a creative player, but as his batting gathered discipline, so he personally began to bubble not with the delight of spring, but with the moodiness of autumn.

As his career hardened, as he saw and knew more, Haynes turned from calypso, with its happy chants, to reggae, with its biting edge. Like his captain, Vivian Richards, in maturity he can entertain; and yet, now, a distance is felt, as if the entertainer were no longer as comfortable with himself or his audience. None the less he has continued to improve and stands as arguably the leading opening batsman in world cricket. Moreover his versatility is formidable, for he has scored hundreds on bowlers' pitches, on turning tracks, notably in Sydney, and in one-day matches. If no longer a cavalier, he remains a respected warrior.

Gordon Greenidge had never seemed straightforward: he rarely smiled, rather he lived within himself. His nature was not so much contrary as suspicious, to which trait was added a dangerous colleague, imagination. Born in the West Indies and raised in England, Greenidge had a foot in both camps and a tent in neither. Accordingly he was inclined to set a guard by his door with instructions to challenge all outsiders. "Who are you and what do you want?" Greenidge tried hard, perhaps too hard, to avoid being hurt, and he may have resented his more gregarious and greater contemporary, Vivian Richards. They learned to work together and to play their parts in a formidable team, yet were never as close as thunder and lightning, for all that they were thunder and lightning.

Technically Greenidge was a master, moving further forward and further back than any contemporary, square cutting with withering power or driving straight with bare-knuckle force. He could hook, too, and had a penchant for pick-up shots off his pads, strokes which often despatched the ball into the next parish. And while he could murder spin, it was not with the range of shots used by Haynes, but with the crushing brutality of a tank.

His weakness, apart from a brooding nature, lay in the very muscularity which sometimes destroyed bowling, and in an upbringing on English pitches which left him a less accomplished player on bouncy pitches. He did not score a first-class hundred in Australia until his final visit there, in 1988–89. Perhaps, too, he lacked touch, but no man can have everything. In full flight, Greenidge was a glorious sight, and impossible to contain. So awesome was his power, so complete his authority, that once a bombardment was under way not a ball could be bowled to him. In this mood he was like an orator suddenly aroused with passion, devouring opposition with a tongue lashing which was vivid, inspired and devastating. For hours, weeks, days, he seemed to wander along, holding his own in debate, giving no quarter, until in a moment it would all fit into place and a ferocious harangue would begin. At his best, unleashed, he was intimidating.

And now Greenidge is in retirement and the partnership with Haynes is broken. As a pair they put on fifty 26 times, 100 on twelve occasions and 200 four times. More significantly still, in 48 Tests won by West Indies in their time as praetorian gatemen, their average partnership was 48.83, while in eight games lost they averaged 29.87. Unsurprisingly their average was higher still – 49.57 – in drawn matches, a tribute to some docile pitches. They were, in some measure, unsung heroes, but they will be missed. As a pair they were distinguished, dependable and complementary in all forms of cricket. They performed their awkward task with authority and, sometimes, élan. Repeatedly they defied all manner of peril to cut a path through the foliage along which others might travel at their ease.

DILIP VENGSARKAR   Dicky Rutnagur, *Five Cricketers of the Year*, 1987

The view has always been held overseas that the true test of batsmanship is making runs in England, where conditions can alter with the passing overhead of a cloud and where pitches can vary so much in character. Even in contemporary times of covered pitches, the touring batsman still takes added glory from success in England.

One who has triumphed on every tour of England is Dilip Balvant Vengsarkar, born in Bombay on April 6, 1956, who holds the unique record of scoring a century on every one of his three Test appearances at Lord's. And this tall, elegant batsman reached his zenith in the summer of 1986 when his two hundreds, one at Lord's and another at Headingley, on one of the poorest Test pitches seen in England for some years, went so far towards India's achieving their 2–0 win in the three-match series. He finished it with an average of 90, by some margin the highest of any Indian batsman in England. Any suspicions that these hundreds were scored against a weak England team can be discounted. In each instance, Vengsarkar, having come in at the fall of the second wicket, was still short of his century when joined by the number 11 batsman. They were innings of the highest quality.

India's selectors have seldom been regarded as over-adventurous, but they could scarcely resist picking Vengsarkar in his first season of first-class cricket after seeing him make 110 in less than even time on a turning pitch against Prasanna, Bedi and Minna, a leg-spinner who was then regarded as a Test prospect. This classic innings was played in the annual fixture between the Ranji Trophy champions and the Rest of India, and when Vengsarkar went in, Bombay, the champions, were 100 for three and needing to score 211 to obtain a lead on first innings.

At that time, in 1975, the middle order of the Indian batting was fairly settled and the only vacant place was as Sunil Gavaskar's opening partner. Playing very straight as he did, Vengsarkar seemed to fit the role, but blooded against Sri Lanka, he was not an immediate success. He was out for 0 and 17 and was dropped for the remaining representative games. However, he held the selectors' attention by making a dour century against the touring team for the Indian Universities, and before he was quite 20, he earned himself a place in the tour party to New Zealand and the West Indies in the spring of 1976.

Vengsarkar does not hail from a cricketing family, but his interest in the game was kindled when he was little more than a toddler as his home overlooked a large patch of green which is one of the main nurseries of Bombay cricket. Part of it was the home ground of Dadar Union, a club of high repute and tradition. Young Vengsarkar watched from his bedroom window, and when he was a little older he joined other boys in the neighbourhood in impromptu midweek games. Nor was it just that he lived and grew up in the right environment. He was sent to the right school, King George, which produced many cricketers who played for Bombay and not a few who went on to play for India, including such greats of Indian cricket as Manjrekar and Gupte.

On the first leg of his maiden tour, in New Zealand, Vengsarkar played in all three Tests, opening the innings with Gavaskar each time, but without scoring over 30. There were no major scores either in the two Tests he played in the West Indies, but in the second of them he gave a clear hint of his promise and class. That was the contentious final Test match at Kingston, which was played on a newly laid pitch of very uneven bounce. The West Indies pace bowlers, Holding, Daniel, Holder and Julien, were not averse to pitching short and three Indian batsman took no further part in the match after being injured in the first innings. Indeed, Bedi declared as a protest against West Indies' intimidatory bowling. However, Vengsarkar, using his height to cope with the steep bounce, came out of the struggle with distinction, considering his lack of experience against pace bowling, scoring 39 and then 21 in the second innings, when five Indian batsman were "absent injured".

Nothwithstanding this display of skill, he was not a fixture in the Test side until the tour of Australia in 1977–78, but from then until the series against England last summer he had missed only three Tests. By the time he returned to India for the series against Australia, he had 85 appearances to his name and an aggregate, including 11 centuries, of 4,985; only Gavaskar and Viswanath had scored more runs for India.

Although he frequently passed 50, Vengsarkar had to wait until his 17th Test match before achieving his maiden hundred: an occasion when he shared a record second-wicket stand of 344 with Gavaskar against West Indies, in Calcutta, in 1978–79. He has made runs everywhere, but all his overseas Test hundreds have been scored in England, where his reach and his technique of playing the ball late stand him in such good stead, as he demonstrated so amply last summer.

DAVID GOWER

Michael Carey, *Five Cricketers of the Year*, 1979

The sun scarcely graced the English cricket scene with its presence in 1978, but when it did it seemed to adorn the blond head of David Gower. The young Leicestershire left-hander could do little wrong. He typified a new, precocious breed of stroke-players, imperious and exciting, who added colour and glamour to an otherwise bedraggled English summer. Plucked, to his astonishment, from Grace Road to play for MCC in their early-season showcase for maturing talent, Gower went on to make runs in one-day internationals and Tests almost as of right, becoming the youngest batsman to make a hundred for England since Peter May.

Had all this been combined with helping Kent to cut a controversial swathe through the land as they lifted two trophies, the image would have been complete, for David Ivon Gower was born in that county, in Tunbridge Wells, on April 1, 1957. Leicestershire's secretary-manager Michael Turner has never disguised his astonishment and delight that when he wrote to Kent for permission to offer terms to Gower, it was unhesitatingly granted.

Gower spent his early years in Tanganyika, as it then was, where his father was in the Colonial Service. He came home at the age of six to attend Marlborough House preparatory school at Hawkhurst, Kent. The Leicestershire connection began two years later when his father, after turning down a post in Eastbourne (thus are the fortunes of the counties affected), became registrar of Loughborough Colleges and young Gower was educated for a time in Quorn before moving to King's School, Canterbury, where his cricketing skills began to emerge.

Tours of South Africa with the English Schools and the West Indies with the England Young Cricketers eased his transition from Second XI to Championship cricket. Now, of course, the mantle of cricket's golden boy slips easily over Gower's lithe shoulders. One can imagine many gnarled old professionals who would like to be restarting their careers in this age of sponsorship and handsome pay cheques.

Gower is something of a cerebral cricketer. Away from the game he likes to relax with crossword puzzles or to listen to classical music. He plays squash to maintain his fitness. He may be the envy of hundreds of young players throughout the country, but his rise to fame has not affected his polite, level-headed, and easy-to-approach attitude to life. The world of cricket may, in the next few years, lie at his feet, but those feet are planted firmly on the ground.

Martin Johnson, 1994

In the spring of 1975, as was my custom in those days as cricket correspondent of the *Leicester Mercury*, I turned up to one of Leicestershire's pre-season training sessions to welcome back familiar faces and say hello to one or two unfamiliar ones. Sitting on a bench waiting to take part in a five-a-side football game was a blond, curly-haired young lad I had not seen before. "Hi there, David Gower," he responded to my introduction, and then, in reply to the inevitable follow-up of "what do you do?" he said: "I, um, bat."

In November 1993, when he announced his retirement from cricket at the age of 36, I thought to myself: "I, um, bat?" In retrospect, it was like Michelangelo saying that he dabbled in ceilings, or Mozart that he rattled off the odd tune. Gower's batting was the stuff of poetry, and enriched the lives of those who were privileged to watch him. Following, as it did, the summer retirements of Ian Botham and Viv Richards, his exit represented the completion of one of cricket's nastier hat-tricks, and cricket will be a poorer game for their passing.

However, what made Gower's departure the saddest of all is that, unlike the other two, he was some way short of his sell-by date. Furthermore, it is a matter more for anger than sadness that he was prematurely lost to the game by the fact that the England cricket team had come to regard genius with suspicion, and substituted the ethos that graft was now preferable to craft and perspiration to inspiration. If Beethoven had been employed by the Test and County Cricket Board, he would have been pensioned off with the reference: "It's all very well coming out with a concerto every now and again, but we'd have employed him for a good deal longer if the wretched boy had practised his scales more often."

Gower played in 117 Test matches [then a record], but with more sympathetic handling he might have played many more, and would probably have been adding to his total – not to mention adding to our own enjoyment – at least until his 40th birthday. However, he ultimately became an anachronism in a joyless era of sprints and press-ups. Latterly, this failure to accommodate a class batsman and a true entertainer was a betrayal of cricket's essential romance, and one of the sadder legacies of an era in which the professional game found itself hijacked by marketing men in grey suits.

During the course of a career that spanned 19 summers, Gower collected a good many medals and gongs around the world, but the proudest possession on his mantelpiece at home is a trophy from a national newspaper that does not, on the face of it, mean very much; neither was it accompanied by any financial reward. It is a plaque inscribed with the words: For Fun, Style and Excellence, which was a perfect way of summing up both his philosophy and his career. Cricket, even in the high-voltage atmosphere of modern Test matches, was never without fun while Gower was at the crease. Even those who claim he never made the fullest use of his talents would admit to an inimitable style, and you do not score 8,231 Test runs at an average of 44.25 without excelling at the game.

His first mentor at Leicester was Raymond Illingworth, a blunt Yorkshireman not much given to frivolity. Yet Illingworth recognised very early one of cricket's essential truisms. Change the man, and you change the cricketer. He had the occasional half-hearted stab, such as delivering a stern lecture over what he regarded as dress just the wrong side of acceptably casual during one away trip, whereupon Gower came down for breakfast next morning attired in full evening dress. Slightly suspicious, given the young Gower's already blossoming reputation as a *bon viveur*, Illingworth spluttered: "Bloody hell, Gower. Have you just come in?"

In a different context, the words "Gower's just come in" emptied bars in cricket grounds all around the world. Often they would be filled again soon enough, perhaps after one of those cameos in which Gower's entire career could be captured in a single over. A couple of sumptuous cover-drives for four, a languid pull to the mid-wicket boundary, two leaden-footed air shots, and finally the seemingly careless snick to gully. However, he also played innings of prolonged genius and, occasionally, just to remind his detractors, he would get his head down and graft with every bit as single-minded a purpose as the England captain who finally gave up on him, Graham Gooch. He was rarely predictable. James Whitaker recalled batting with him in a county game at Old Trafford when the West Indian, Patrick Patterson, was bowling particularly quickly and Gower three times in an over almost gave his wicket away with rash shots. Junior man or not, Whitaker felt obliged to snort that it was not a benefit match, and such was the lack of reaction he wondered whether Gower had heard him. He had. In Patterson's next over Gower struck four magical boundaries, sauntered up the wicket, and with a deadpan delivery said: "Was that a bit better, then?"

Following Gower's dismissal after his second term as England captain in 1989, the new man, Gooch, was happier without him on that winter's tour to the West Indies. But it was in Australia the following winter that Gooch, who admired Gower as a player as much as anyone, formed the terminal view of his commitment. In the 1991 Adelaide Test he watched from the non-striker's end as Gower, wafting carelessly at the last ball before lunch, fell into an Australian trap so obvious that the ball was almost delivered by registered post. This followed an aerial prank during the match against Queensland at Carrara, when Gower and John Morris nipped out during play, hired a couple of Tiger Moths from the airfield across the road, and buzzed the ground. When the management found out, Gower and Morris were fined £1,000 each, a punishment some way out of proportion to the crime, and probably owing much to pique about Gower stealing the headlines from one of the few England victories on a miserable tour. From that point, Gooch never wavered from his view that Gower was a luxury item on tour, non-conducive to team discipline, which is why he helped make sure Gower was not picked for the 1993 tour to India despite his class performances (one of them an innings of stoical self-denial to save the game at Headingley) in two of the final three Tests of the previous summer against Pakistan.

Gower was not selected against Australia the following summer, even when England were losing 4–0. And when, under the new captain Mike Atherton, he was left out of the tour to the West Indies, he decided that playing on for Hampshire was not sufficient motivation to resist offers of full-time media employment. He was comfortably the most treasured English cricketer of his generation, and possibly the most treasured ever. This puzzled even him (Gower at least recognised one or two of his more frustrating traits) but it may not have been unconnected to the Englishman's innate suspicion of perfection, plus his almost complete lack of ego.

His inherently lazy nature made him an indifferent captain, particularly at county level, where the fact that he was largely an instinctive player made it difficult for him to sympathise with and offer advice to individuals; and by his own admission he lost touch too often when away on Test duty. As a Test captain, he shone most brightly on the 1984–85 tour to India, where his bright, positive outlook rubbed off on the team in uncomfortable surroundings. Gower was tactically uninspiring, although he never wavered in his belief that Test players were good enough not to require the sergeant-majorish treatment that he latterly perceived from Gooch and the team manager, Micky Stewart.

When he started his career, he was a shy lad who liked the occasional glass of house wine. When he finished, he was an extrovert imbiber of vintage champagne. However, the reason he was loved, as well as admired, is that he finished with as few airs and graces as he had when he began, except in his batting, which was graceful to the last.

Languid grace: David Gower hits out against the Rest of the World during the MCC Bicentenary match at Lord's in 1987, watched by Allan Border (keeping wicket in place of the injured Jeff Dujon) and Desmond Haynes. Border and Gower were rival captains in the 1985 and 1989 Ashes series.

ALLAN BORDER

Mike Coward, 1995

Allan Border, who retired in May 1994 as Test cricket's highest run-scorer, committed the greater part of a long and distinguished career to re-establishing the credibility and image of Australian cricket. A self-effacing man of simple tastes and pleasures, Border served at the most tempestuous time in cricket history, and came to represent the indomitable spirit of the Australian game. As it grappled with two schisms, the first over World Series Cricket, the second over the provocative actions of the mercenaries in South Africa, it was debilitated and destabilised as never before and cried out for a figure of Bradmanesque dimensions to return it to its rightful and influential position on the world stage.

Into the breach strode earnest Allan Robert Border, a working-class boy, born at Cremorne on the north shore of Sydney Harbour, who grew up over the road from the Mosman Oval that now bears his name. At one time he was a beach bum, who was cajoled from his indolence and indifference by the noted coach and former England Test player, Barry Knight. But Border, standing just 5ft 9in, bestrode the Test match arena like a colossus for more than 15 years.

When he retired 11 weeks before his 39th birthday, after fulfilling his ambition to lead Australia in South Africa, Border was entitled to be ranked alongside Sir Donald Bradman as the greatest of Australian cricketers. Certainly no one since Sir Donald has done more to advance Australian cricket throughout the world, particularly in developing countries.

Border's batting cannot really stand comparison with Bradman but many of his achievements go far beyond the Bradmanesque – 156 Test matches, 153 of them consecutive, on 36 grounds in eight different Test-playing countries (Sir Donald played 52 Tests on ten grounds, all in Australia and England); 11,174 runs at 50.56 with 27 centuries and 63 fifties; 93 consecutive Test matches as captain; 156 catches; 273 limited-overs appearances, 178 as captain, including Australia's victory in the 1987 World Cup final. All of these accomplishments are in a league of their own and some may remain so.

Yet only in the twilight of his career did Border become even faintly interested in his statistical achievements. Essentially he was an unromantic, uncomplicated but uncompromising workman-cricketer. It is problematical whether Border, unlike Bradman, has ever understood his place in history. He reinvigorated Australian cricket and provided it with stability, direction and enthusiasm; this was the most significant of his many contributions and the one which gave him the greatest satisfaction. There is a remarkable set of figures to underscore the extent of the stability Border provided. From the time he succeeded his fragile friend Kim Hughes on December 7, 1984 until his captaincy ended on March 29, 1994, opposing countries commissioned 38 captains – 21 of them against Australia. From his first Test, at Melbourne, on December 29, 1978, he played with and against 361 different players.

To gain a true appreciation of Border, it is necessary to examine his formative years in the leadership when his team was scorned and he was disturbingly close to a breakdown. In 1985 when Australian cricket reached its nadir and a collection of leading players defected to South Africa, Border, the least political of men, was dragged into a black hole of depression. He was barely four months into his term of office – while he forgave them, he never forgot the hurt caused by those team-mates who pursued the dollar rather than the dream, and opted to play in South Africa. For a man who placed such store in team loyalty, it was a cruel lesson. When he retired, Border reflected: "I felt very let down. We were playing in Sharjah and everyone was having a beer and saying that the team was starting to get it together. There was that sort of talk. You feel such a fool when you then read in the paper that blokes you have trusted, who have told you how great the future looks, are going to South Africa."

Many of his attitudes were formed and much of his philosophy as a captain formulated at this time when Australia were not expected to win and, in the main, did not. The dire circumstances of the day compelled him to think defensively, and it was not until 1989 when he engineered a memorable 4–0 eclipse of a dispirited England that there was a measure of optimism and aggression about his leadership. But while his entitlement to the job was hardly ever questioned, the negativism of his captaincy was the area that most occupied the attention of his critics.

In mitigation, he insisted that the circumstances of his time had made it impossible for him to develop a totally positive philosophy. He evolved into an enterprising captain when he was finally in charge of able and ambitious men, as was evidenced by his thoughtful and often bold use of the leg-spinner Shane Warne. In this period, some English critics felt that Australia's approach was getting too hard; that might say more about them than about Border.

With customary candour, he often pleaded guilty to periods of moodiness and regretted that, at least in the dressing-room, his instinct was to internalise his deepest thoughts and feelings. Paradoxically, he was an expansive and articulate spokesman, and was much admired by the media for being accessible, courteous and forthright. So he had good reason to resent the "Captain Grumpy" tag foisted upon him by the tabloids. With few, if any, exceptions, his team-mates and employers indulged his contrariness; it was infrequent and irritating rather than damaging. Indeed, the fact that his actions and reactions were always so commonplace, so human, made him an endearing as well as an enduring champion. Essentially, he was an ordinary soul who accomplished extraordinary deeds. For a suburban family man, with an unselfconscious hankering for a beer around a backyard barbecue, Border became an exceptionally worldly cricketer. That he was able to expunge many of the prejudices and preconceptions amongst his team-mates about playing cricket in the Third World was another of the outstanding legacies of his captaincy.

The fact that his technique and temperament allowed him to play productively in the most extreme conditions and situations was perhaps the true gauge of his greatness. Indeed, the tougher the predicament the more resolute and more resourceful was his batting. He averaged 56.57 in 70 overseas Tests. In Australia, he averaged 45.94 in 86 Tests. And he averaged fractionally more as captain (50.94) than as non-captain (50.01) – further confirmation of his red-blooded response to challenge.

While he was never numbered among the poetic left-handers, it is erroneous to categorise him as just an accumulator of runs. In his pomp, he hooked and pulled as well as he square cut and drove in front of point. For many years he was bracketed with Javed Miandad, another eminent and indefatigable scrapper, as the foremost player of slow bowling in the world. Furthermore, Border was blessed with all-round skills. He was a sure catch anywhere, but especially at slip, and in the limited-overs game earned an impressive reputation for his ability to throw down the stumps from any angle within the circle. And while he was self-deprecating about his left-arm orthodox spin bowling, he once took 11 wickets in a Sydney Test against West Indies. But that was no balm for his disappointment at being unable to defeat West Indies in a Test series and so legitimately claim for Australia the unofficial title of world champion. At Adelaide in 1992–93 he went within two runs of attaining the goal.

His retirement from the captaincy and Test cricket was messy, an unfortunate situation caused, more than anything, by a misunderstanding between Border and the Australian Cricket Board. It should have been done with style. But he handed to Mark Taylor the most precious gift of all – a stable, committed, educated, enterprising and hard-edged elite cricket team. Australian cricket will forever be in a debt of A.B., the cricketer's cricketer, the people's cricketer and a bloody good bloke with it.

MARTIN CROWE
Eric Hill, *Five Cricketers of the Year*, 1985

At the age of 21, Martin David Crowe, who was born in Auckland, New Zealand, on September 22, 1962, achieved in his first season of county cricket what most cricketers would have considered impossible. In terms of cricket, the esteem of colleagues and public respect, he managed to fill, with poise and dignity, the enormous gap left in Somerset's ranks by the absence of Vivian Richards, who was touring with the West Indians. In any context this was a remarkable achievement. Set against the background of a broken thumb and food poisoning, suffered on the New Zealand tour of Sri Lanka, the anxiety to do well in a strange environment, homesickness and a most depressing first month, it was astonishing.

The last week in May, played out on awkward pitches, brought the nadir of his fortunes. He was dismissed for single figures in five consecutive innings. Then the character of the man, the utterly correct, "old-fashioned" batting technique, and the innate self-examination unusual in one so young, shone through into four centuries in successive Championship games, a golden June of 719 runs at an average of 143.8, and, overall, a superb season. Some 2,600 runs, 1,870 of them first-class, 44 first-class wickets, and numerous one-day triumphs which brought two match awards, plus some brilliant fielding, rounded things off splendidly.

Sport runs deep in the Crowe family, with Martin's elder brother, Jeff, a Test player, his father a first-class cricketer, and his mother 'probably our best all-round sportsman'. Martin was a rugby man at school, and now enjoys squash, tennis and golf with the rest of the family. He went through the whole cricket system, eventually becoming the youngest first-class debutant. In due course came his first experiences in England, with a "scholarship" to the Lord's groundstaff in 1981, league cricket with Bradford in 1982, and the New Zealand tour to England, combined with the World Cup, in 1983. Though he had his early heroes in Garry Sobers, Mark Burgess and Glenn Turner, he never modelled his cricket on any one individual. Giving a glimpse of the "own-man" attitude which quietly adorns a determined character, he was, he guessed, 'too busy playing my own little game'. Reminded of Glenn Chappell's early days with Somerset, he commented "It'd be nice to score half his runs."

JAVED MIANDAD
Robin Hobbs, *Five Cricketers of the Year*, 1982

It is evident after watching Javed Miandad face no more than a ball or two that he is a natural sportsman of rare talent. His relaxed but commanding attitude is immediately convincing. Extraordinarily nimble on his feet and with a superb eye, Javed in 1981 gave the Welsh cricketing public something to cheer about in what, for Glamorgan, was a moderate season. The early part of the summer being cruelly wet, it was hardly surprising that even Javed found the pitches difficult to adjust to. However, he announced himself at Leicester on June 14, with an unbeaten Sunday League hundred, and followed this with 105 on an unpredictable pitch in Glamorgan's next Championship match, against Warwickshire at Cardiff. Ten days later, against Somerset at Swansea, he scored a century in each innings. And so it went on. In the return match against Somerset, at Taunton this time, he scored 200 not out – on Royal Wedding day.

But perhaps his finest innings of the summer was against Essex at Colchester, on September 1. Set to score 325 to win, on a dusty, difficult pitch, Glamorgan lost their first four wickets for 44 runs. An early finish was visualised – until Javed took charge. When, finally, he ran out of partners, he had recorded his second double-hundred of the season, and Glamorgan had lost by only 13 runs. The Essex players were adamant that this was the best piece of batting they had ever seen. By the time the campaign ended, Javed had surpassed Gilbert Parkhouse's record of seven hundreds in a season for Glamorgan, as well as Parkhouse's 1959 aggregate of 2,071 runs, also, until then, a county record.

Javed Miandad Khan was born in Karachi on June 12, 1957, one of seven children. Cricket was the family game, his only two brothers also being destined to play top-class cricket in Pakistan. Javed made his first-class debut at the age of 16 years and five months, for Karachi Whites, and he was still only 17 when chosen for the Pakistan Prudential World Cup squad in 1975. On the recommendation of Sadiq Mohammad he was invited by Tony Greig, when the World Cup was over, to play a few matches for Sussex Second XI with a view to qualifying. Sussex were sufficiently impressed to ask him to return in 1976, when, although he appeared in only five matches, he easily headed the Sussex batting averages with 523 runs, an average of 58, and a top score of 162 against Kent at Canterbury.

At home that winter he made his Test debut, scoring 163 on his first appearance – against New Zealand at Lahore. He followed this with 206 and 85 in the third and final Test at Karachi, so becoming, at 19 years and four months, the youngest player ever to hit a Test double-hundred. Although he had a somewhat disappointing tour of the West Indies in 1977, playing in only one Test match, he was already a rising star.

In 1977, despite being at times the victim of his impetuosity, he made the number four spot his own in the Sussex side, scoring more runs than any other player and being awarded his county cap. His fielding was also a joy to watch, leaving its mark on, among others, the up-and-coming Paul Parker. By now, though, it was becoming increasingly apparent that when Kepler Wessels returned from military service in South Africa, Sussex would have a selection problem. With Imran already assured of a Sussex place, as a world-class all-rounder, Miandad and Wessels would be competing for the remaining overseas position.

In 1978 a depleted Pakistan side came to England for three Test matches. Without their Packer players, they relied heavily upon Javed and Haroon Rashid, and they were roundly defeated. The tour over, Javed rejoined Sussex, playing in eight first-class matches and again topping the county's batting averages. That winter, when he signed for World Series Cricket, he made an immediate impression in Australia, but, suffering perhaps from a surfeit of cricket, he had a depressing season for Sussex in 1979. Unable to command a regular place in the side, as had been foreshadowed two years before, he had the frustration of playing a lot of second-team cricket. Clearly he had an important decision to make regarding his future – whether or not to look for another county. In the event, with just a little persuasion, he signed with Glamorgan in 1980.

GRAHAM GOOCH

Nigel Fuller, *Five Cricketers of the Year*, 1980

It is as much a tribute to his temperament as to his undoubted skills with the bat that Graham Alan Gooch has blossomed into one of the most exciting stroke-players in the game today – a point he so ably demonstrated to a packed Lord's ground and millions of television viewers last summer when his magnificent 120 helped Essex carry off the Benson and Hedges Cup against Surrey. That was just one of several fine innings which Gooch, born at Leytonstone on July 23, 1953, unleashed to confirm his arrival as a batsman of highest class.

It is fair to say that since making his county debut in 1973, Gooch has had to endure immense pressures on his way to the top; pressure that would have got the better of players not gifted with his fierce determination to succeed. At a time when fans and media alike were demanding new blood at Test level, Gooch, following an impressive start to the season and with only a handful of first-class games behind him, was – so to speak – thrown to the lions in 1975. He was selected for his Test debut against an Australian side containing the fearsome new-ball attack of Lillee and Thomson. There was to be no fairytale baptism on the inter-national scene. Far from it. Gooch collected a dreaded pair at Edgbaston and, after one more Test, was cast aside.

That must have been a traumatic experience, but it merely hardened his resolve to make a success of a career he had set his heart on since his early days. For the next three years, he went quietly about the business of serving his apprenticeship at county level before being called up as opener for the Second Test against Pakistan at Lord's in 1978. Failure to grasp that chance would have had one doubting his ability to make the grade at the highest level. His answer was a fighting half-century to help England overcome the shock of losing their first two wickets with only 19 runs on the board. Gooch thus proved he had learnt much in the intervening years. But shortly afterwards he was under pressure to retain his place again.

A duck in the first innings of the opening Test against New Zealand at The Oval coincided with the news that Boycott was set to return to the side. With Brearley assured of his place as captain, it seemed Gooch would be the one to step aside to make room for Boycott. However, 91 not out in the second innings ensured Gooch's retention, and he responded with a half-century when opening with Boycott, the selectors having little choice but to drop Brearley down the order. Those efforts virtually clinched his selection for the 1978–79 tour of Australia, where he faced another crisis. He went into the sixth and final Test at Sydney having failed to reach fifty in the previous five and was fully aware that he could be banished to the sidelines once more if he did not produce an innings of quality. He obliged with a swashbuckling 74 to point the way to a rewarding and vastly entertaining season on the home front last year.

It was his masterpiece at Lord's against Surrey which lifted him above the ranks of the ordinary; which convinced everyone of his star status. With a mixture of frightening power and controlled fury, he not so much dictated to the bowlers as destroyed them. His 120 arrived from 140 deliveries and contained three huge sixes laced with 11 boundaries, many of them hit with lightning speed through the mid-wicket area. Those who witnessed it will treasure the innings for a long time to come, and it set the seal on a remarkable season's work in the Benson and Hedges cup. In seven innings, he totalled just under 600 runs. Apart from his gem at Lord's, he scored 133 against the Combined Universities, sharing in a competition first-wicket record of 223 with Alan Lilley, and butchered Warwickshire for 138 in the quarter-finals.

Simon Barnes, 1991

Ian Botham has, in his time, managed to make a fair amount of trouble for himself. But not even Botham managed to get himself banned from Test cricket for three years, or made himself the hate-focus of an international political campaign, or caused an entire tour to be cancelled. Graham Gooch has done all those things. How extraordinary then, how absolutely extraordinary, to consider that this is the man we must begin to think of as the most important cricketer of his generation, and the most effective captain of England since Mike Brearley.

Yes, Gooch said famously, we've got the makings of a goodish side. The point is that this was not an understatement: it was an exact assessment of the facts. Gooch's achievement has been to maximise the resources of that goodish side. It has been a triumph of nothing less than leadership, and this from a man who resigned as captain of Essex because captaincy was affecting his form. It is clear that captaincy affected his form as captain of England in the summer of 1990. To be accurate, captaincy inspired him. It took him to the enormous achievement of his innings of 333 against India at Lord's, and his breaking of Sir Donald Bradman's record for Test runs scored in an English summer.

Gooch had always been a man in search of greatness; he achieved that immodest aim last summer. He achieved greatness as a player – at the age of 37. Such preposterous scores are normally for younger men. The fitness, the reflexes, the ability to concentrate for session after session: these are things that the years take away from you. But they have not taken them from Gooch. Gooch is a fanatic for mere fitness, a passionate lover of work for its own sake, a true glutton for austerity. Furthermore, he has achieved something quite close to greatness as a leader.

Lord of Lord's: Graham Gooch on his way to 333 against India in 1990, the highest score ever made at Lord's. *Wisden* 1998 revealed that Gooch scored more runs than anyone else in history (limited-overs and first-class matches combined).

Before he was given the captaincy, England's cricket had become the material of cheap jokes: material the more discriminating joke-crackers avoided. A quip about England's defeats was simply too obvious, too hoary a joke. The joke reached its apex in 1988, "the summer of the five captains". This was perhaps the most inept display of man-management in the history of sport; a summer in which Gatting, Emburey, Cowdrey, Gooch himself and Pringle all led England in the field, four of them as official appointees. When Gooch was asked to lead England in India, the tour was promptly cancelled because of Gooch's South African connections. Disaster followed disaster. After the West Indian hammering and the Indian debacle, there came another traumatic summer. The opponents were Australia. England, captained now by Gower, were not only beaten but trampled on. For Gooch, as for Gower, the summer was a personal disaster. There was scarcely a scoreboard, it seemed, that did not carry details of Gooch lbw b Alderman, for not a lot. Gooch volunteered to stand down, to make room for fresh blood, and his offer was accepted. Perhaps that one incident summed up his summer: a personal nadir, a personal black hole. For some cricketers it would have been a disaster of career-ending proportions. Instead, Gooch used it as a springboard into greatness.

There is a case for saying that Headingley 1981 is one of the greatest disasters to have hit England's cricket. Certainly, it lunged into a pattern of self-destructiveness as the echoes of that extraordinary year died away. The England team became based around an Inner Ring, with Botham at its heart: Botham, self-justified by his prodigious feats during that unforgettable summer. To be accepted, you had to hate the press, hate practice, enjoy a few beers and what have you, and generally be one hell of a good ol' boy. Like all cliques, the England clique was defined by exclusion. Nothing could be more destructive to team spirit than a team within a team, but that was the situation in the England camp for years. It was the same at Somerset. It was the presence of an Inner Ring which created the furore in which Vivian Richards and Joel Garner were not offered new contracts, and Botham himself resigned. It needed the right man at the right time to destroy this unpleasant and destructive atmosphere in the England team. The old members of the Inner Ring were being lost to time, one by one. It needed someone to indicate that it was gone forever; that this was a new start, a new way forward. This was Gooch's moment, and he accepted it avidly.

It happened in India in the autumn of 1989. India had rejected an England team under Gooch's captaincy a year before. Now they accepted one. The Test-playing countries had at last come to an agreement about players with South African histories. Gooch was officially forgiven. The way was clear for the remaking of the England cricket team. The tour itself, a four-week trip for the Nehru Cup, a six-nation one-day tournament, was thought by all wise critics to be a complete waste of time. The widely used *mot juste* for the competition was "spurious". It was not spurious at all for Gooch. It was on a practice ground in Delhi that one became aware of strong forces at work. The weather was hot, but the pace of the practice was still hotter. It was all sweat and Gatorade: everyone was competing as to who sweated the most. Micky Stewart, the manager, was like a man come into his own, taking fielding practice with all the camp affectations of a sergeant-major. It looked as if Stewart was having his way at last, but he was not. Gooch was. The two of them plainly saw eye to eye; not something that had always been the case with Stewart and his captains. They were dubbed "the Cockney Mafia" almost within hours.

The prevailing ethic of the old Inner Ring was that if you are as massively talented as us, you don't have to work as hard as ordinary players. Gooch has always believed that the difference between ordinariness and excellence lies in hard work. And if work will make that difference, then it is folly to be idle. He does not seek mindless conformity from his players. More than most team sports, cricket requires a motley bunch of assorted shapes, sizes, temperaments, talents and social backgrounds. What Gooch has managed is to inspire his own motley bunch with the same desire to work to a common goal: what is more, to work in the belief that the goal is attainable.

That has been his miracle. The results in the West Indies in the early months of 1990 did not surprise him. It was only everybody else who was surprised by the win and the near-win under his captaincy. Gooch would, I think, have escaped from the series on level terms at worst, had it not been for the injuries to himself and to Angus Fraser. Instead, England lost 2–1. The two 1–0 wins in the following summer's three-Test series against New Zealand and India were consolidation. Suddenly, England had acquired the habit of winning Test matches. That was miracle enough to be going on with.

The central experience of Gooch's professional life was his trip to South Africa in 1982. He went to play on that "rebel" tour in the hopelessly naive belief that he would not receive any form of punishment. He was made captain of the rebel team, though not as a recognition of any leading part in the plotting and deception involved in the setting-up of this tour: it was more an expression of the dressing-room's feelings about having Geoffrey Boycott as captain. But the responsibilities of the captaincy were not restricted to cricketing decisions. Gooch did not expect that. The captaincy made Gooch the spokesman of the tour. "Gooch's men" and "Gooch's rebel tour" were phrases that tripped nicely off page and microphone. Gooch himself had to face cameras and interviews: this was, as far as the Republic was concerned, a major public relations exercise. These were muddy waters, and Gooch hid behind his role of professional sportsman. "We're just here to play cricket, we're just professional cricketers." Would that life were as simple.

Gooch and his fellow-rebels were banned from Test cricket for three years. I am sure he still feels that this was desperately unjust; I suspect that even now, he finds this "wrong" an inspiration. For whereas many of his colleagues on that South African venture were well-known players slightly over the hill, Gooch was in his prime. His adventures robbed him of three years in which he might have established himself as the greatest batsman of his generation. Instead, he played for Essex and Western Province.

Perhaps Gooch's greatest asset of all has been his ability to give equal treatment to Kipling's twin impostors, Triumph and Disaster. He remains consistent in everything in his life except shaving. His capricious changes from a clean shave, Zapata moustache, designer stubble or full beard have been the nearest he has come to a change of facial expression in 15 years. But he is not an easy person. He does not forget those who, he believes, have done wrong by him. He has no appreciation of the necessary symbiosis of professional sport and mass media. His achievement in cutting down the number of compulsory captain's press conferences during a home Test from three to one was regarded as a major coup.

The chairman of the England selectors, Ted Dexter, when in his journalistic avatar, famously described Gooch as having the charisma of a wet fish. This has been thrown back at Dexter times without number, but it is, in fact, a fair remark – from a media person. All the same, Gooch cannot have achieved his success without great gifts of communication. It just so happens that these gifts are not apparent to those outside the charmed circle of his team. Nor does his team find Gooch's gifts readily communicable to the outside world. The nearest anyone ever gets to an explanation is to say that he leads "by example". But this means little. Plenty of leaders have worked themselves silly while inspiring only contempt. Gooch simply has, at a point that must be alarmingly close to the end of his cricketing life, come into his own. He has reconstructed and re-inspired the England cricket team: and it seems that he has done a similar job on himself. Yet he remains as hostile to outsiders as ever, and the team is probably even less approachable now than it was in Botham's time. There is still an Inner Ring: the difference is that Gooch appears to have made everyone in the team a member of it.

Right from the first moment that he took charge in Delhi, Gooch made it clear that he wanted to be judged only by results. In those terms, he has established himself as a genuinely great cricketer. His achievement in remaking the England team might yet be even more significant, and in this much larger area he again bears the stamp of incipient greatness.

Christopher Martin-Jenkins, 1998

The golfer Joyce Wethered was once playing a crucial shot in a major championship when an express train suddenly thundered past. "Didn't the train put you off?" she was asked later. "What train?" she replied. The ability to forget the clutter of everything else and concentrate this completely is surprisingly rare, even among great performers in sport. But Graham Gooch had it in full measure. And this skill, more the result of mental steel than any natural gift, was the single most important reason for the fact that, by the time he started his final match for Essex on July 23, 1997, Graham Alam Gooch, born at Whipps Cross in Leytonstone exactly 44 years before, had become the most prolific player in history.

One had sensed that he must be somewhere near, when all his limited-overs runs had been added to his final tally of 44,841 in first-class games, but it took the computations of Robert Brooke to confirm for *Wisden* this stupendous fact. No single batsman, not Grace, nor Hobbs, nor Woolley, nor Boycott, nor any of his contemporaries in an age of proliferating fixtures, had made so many runs in top-class cricket as the pink-faced, heavy-limbed yeoman of Essex. He had, in fact, unnoticed overtaken Jack Hobbs's total of 61,237 runs when he reached 67 in a Benson and Hedges Cup game between Essex and Gloucestershire at Chelmsford on May 9, 1995. He finished with 65,928 at 45.81. It is hard to imagine who might overtake him.

Gooch, unfortunately, chose to release the news of his retirement through a Sunday newspaper whose chief business is scandal-mongering, but he was always acutely aware of his own worth and the need to make the most of that. In cricketing terms that made him the dedicated professional par excellence: steady, sound, sober, solid. It is still a revelation to know that he was not just the latest, perhaps the last, in a long line of that sort of English professional batsman, but, by numerical proof, the hungriest and most acquisitive of them all. He surpassed men like Sutcliffe, Hutton and Boycott from the north; Grace, Hayward, Hobbs and Mead, from the south.

It seems natural to exclude Woolley, Hendren, Hammond and Graveney of the other leading batsmen, because they were somehow different in their nature and approach: more artists than accountants. Yet Gooch himself – and this makes his achievement all the more remarkable – belongs more truly with the enter-tainers: he was a magnificent sight in full sail. This was no dabber of singles, no delicate leg-glancer or specialist in the smooth caress of a half-volley through extra cover. On the contrary, he was a bold, imposing player: a mighty driver and fierce square-cutter, who looked at the crease to be taller and bulkier than he actually was, with a bat apparently broader than the law permits.

His greatest innings was against West Indies, at Headingley in grey weather on a tricky pitch in June 1991. It took him seven and a half hours. The forces arrayed against him were fierce: Ambrose, Patterson, Walsh and Marshall. Gooch was captain and more than just the backbone of his side. Throughout England's second innings, he virtually was the side. He carried his bat for 154 out of 252 and England went on to win the Test. So they had, too, when he made his 333 and 123 in a single Test at Lord's against India in 1990. These, however, constituted easier pickings.

This does not, of course, make Graham Gooch the greatest player of his time but, even if we judge him only by the timeless yardstick of first-class cricket, ignoring the mind-wearying, sinew-stretching demands of the limited-overs game, his stature is clear. After the reduction in Championship matches in 1969, he alone scored above 2,000 runs in more than three seasons. He did so in five: 1984, 1985, 1988, 1990 and 1993; another 56 runs in his last full season, 1996, would have made it six. He made eight first-class hundreds that year and, had he not promised his dying father that he would play one more year, it would have been the right note on which to finish.

It was one of the few occasions when he allowed emotion to supersede his cricketing judgment. What made him special was his capacity for hard work and discipline. He earned every run.

DAVID BOON
Mark Ray, *Five Cricketers of the Year*, 1994

Two years ago, the pavilion at the ground in Launceston, Tasmania, was renamed 'The David Boon Stand'. Admittedly, Launceston is Boon's adoring home town but, even so, having a grandstand named after you when you are only 31 years old and in the middle of a Test career is proof that you have become a living legend. Now, two years and hundreds of runs later, Boon is rivalling Allan Border as the most respected and admired cricketer in Australia. At big matches now, banners carry the simplest of messages: 'Boonie' or, at their most verbose, 'Boon – dead-set legend'. His recently published autobiography is a best-seller and crowds have flocked to meet Boon at book-signings around the nation.

Boon had been Australia's leading batsman for some time before the 1993 Ashes tour, but it was his performances on that, his third, tour of England that elevated him to the stature of a diminutive but formidable national treasure. In ten Test innings in England in 1993, Boon made 555 runs at an average of 69.37. Importantly, he finally achieved an ambition by making his first Test century in England, an undefeated 164 at Lord's in the Second Test. This innings had followed a frustrating 93 in the First Test at Old Trafford, but Boon made up for that disappointment by following his Lord's century with another in the Third Test and another in the Fourth.

After the Ashes tour, Boon stood in fifth position on the list of all-time Test run-makers for Australia with 5,869 runs at 45.49 with 17 centuries. Against South Africa at the end of December, he reached 1,241 Test runs in a calendar year, more than any Australian has scored except Bobby Simpson, and passed Neil Harvey's aggregate of 6,149 to lie behind only Border, Greg Chappell and Sir Donald Bradman in the all-time Australian Test scoring list. If we can judge a batsman by the company he keeps in the record books, Boon's reputation is assured.

David Clarence Boon was born in Launceston on December 29, 1960. His father Clarrie was a respected sports administrator and a strong supporter of his son's career. His mother, Lesley, played hockey for Australia. Boon was educated at Launceston Grammar School, where he excelled at cricket, Australian football and swimming. His cricket career gained impetus when the Lancashire professional Jack Simmons was coaching in Launceston and predicted the lad would play for Australia. Simmons was captaining Tasmania when Boon began his first-class career as a 17-year-old. Years later Boon formally recognised his debt to Simmons by naming his son after him. Boon's achievement in becoming a fine Test player from a state which at that stage was still to enter the Sheffield Shield is strong evidence of his singular determination.

Boon's efforts on his three tours to England tell the story of his career. In 1985, he seemed anchored to the crease by indecision against the spin of John Emburey, his seven somewhat embarrassing innings producing only 124 runs at 17.71. In 1989, he made a solid 442 runs at 55.25, yet he never quite gorged himself as Mark Taylor and Steve Waugh did. In 1993, Boon was the most assured batsman in the Australian team, feasting remorselessly on wayward England bowling.

The most striking features of Boon's batting in England in 1993 were his concentration and precise shot selection. It was as if he knew that every over England's bowlers would present him with a short ball to cut for four or a half volley to clip away to the mid-wicket rope. His method was to defend patiently against any reasonable delivery, then to despatch with minimal risk the inevitable bad ball. It was a simple but ruthlessly effective strategy. Boon now knows his strengths and weaknesses as well as Border knows his. Young batsman like Slater, Hayden and Martyn talk of 'the Bible according to Boon'.

Off the field, Boon is a quiet character who does not waste words. However, he possesses a dry Australian wit and often reveals a mischievous glint in his eye. On the field, either at short leg where he is brilliant or at the batting crease, he is the rock on which Australia have built their recent good form. Border, one of his staunchest admirers, once said Boon had a heart to match that of Phar Lap, the great Australian racehorse. In Australian sport, there are few higher compliments.

GRAEME HICK
Scyld Berry, *Five Cricketers of the Year*, 1987

At any one time there are perhaps half a dozen cricketers in England who inspire people to say: "Ah, I think I'll go to that match tomorrow just to watch him play." Usually, such a compelling player is a batsman, such as David Gower or Viv Richards or Martin Crowe. In 1986, the name of Graeme Ashley Hick was added to that elite list of cricketers who actively excite followers of the game.

Nineteen years of age at the season's start, Hick was the first to make 1,000 first-class runs. A tall, broad, white-hatted wielder of a Duncan Fearnley blade, like Crowe, he went on to become one of two to score 2,000 runs, and thereby claimed another title: that of being, at 20, the youngest batsman to reach this figure in an English season. Len Hutton was 21 when he did so in 1937. It is hard to think there have been many better players at his age than Graeme Hick.

From the start he has been a prodigy. Born on May 23, 1966 in Harare, Zimbabwe, or Salisbury, Rhodesia, as the capital then was, Hick was six years and eight months old when he made his first century, with his own bat and without a box as he remembers. His 105 not out was scored against Mangula Junior School, and it contained 24 fours, the ball travelling quickly over a hard bush ground short of grass. His father, John Hick, had twice represented the district of Mashonaland as a middle-order batsman; he had already taken his son into Salisbury to watch Graeme Pollock bat in Currie Cup matches. But the schoolboy Hick, able at tennis, athletics and hockey (he came to play for the national schools team), did not give particular attention to cricket at first. He simply bowled his high, turning off-breaks for Banket Junior School in 1975 – and took 115 wickets for 347 runs, at an average of 3.02 each! As an opening batsman he had made no more than half-a-dozen hundreds by 1979, when he dropped to number three in the Prince Edward High School Under-14 team and served notice of his exceptional talent. That year he acquired the habit of making large, undefeated centuries, and averaged 185 for his school.

The following year, 1980, when living at the family home on the Trelawney tobacco-farming estate, he was found to have meningitis in its milder form. The delay was considerable, but the path already established. For the rest of his school-days Hick ascended through the various grades: from the national Junior Schools team (of which he was captain), to the Fawns, to the Senior Schools side. So rapid was the progress that at 17, while still at school, Hick was selected as a member of the Zimbabwe World Cup party of 1983 – the youngest player to have been selected for that country, or for a World Cup tournament.

In 1984 he went to Worcestershire on a Zimbabwe Cricket Union scholarship: at the season's end he was allowed a Championship debut against Surrey and had made 82 when time expired. In 1985, for Worcestershire and the touring Zimbabweans, he scored 1,265 runs at 52.70. His county, needless to say, were happy to preside over the growth of an extraordinary skill. They were especially impressed by the hungry way in which Hick approached his batting, often reaching the crease before the dismissed batsman had dragged himself from the field; by the orthodoxy and straightness of his style, tainted only by the steer through gully that has been forced upon so many by one-day cricket; by his strength, which he has developed through weight-lifting and is the strength of an amiable giant; by his pursuit of excellence, which somehow seems more attainable for a colonial than for someone bred in England; and by his method against short-pitched bowling. Hick pulls along the ground in front of square leg if he plays a shot – no top-edged hooking down to fine leg.

By the end of last season the question centred not on whether Hick was a great batsman in the making but on which country he would represent. Not Zimbabwe: reluctantly, yet understandably, Hick decided to sever the link with his native land in order to prove himself in Test cricket. New Zealand have sounded him out, offering a four-year qualification period. He was told that he could play for England only in 1991, after ten years' residence. By then many more runs will surely have flowed beneath the bridge besides New Road.

Peter Roebuck, 1999

Upon the abandonment of the match in which he scored his 100th hundred, Graeme Hick walked across a damp and emptying ground in Worcester and into the arms of his daughters. It was an ordinary thing to do, but it was noticed because it said something about a cricketer who had once seemed a fearless gladiator, but whose confidence had slowly been eroded.

Always he had seemed distant. A fellow could watch him bat a hundred times and still not feel close. Suddenly, he seemed human, warm and vulnerable, a quiet man in a noisy place. Watching him, it was hard to believe he really wanted to throw himself back into the hurly-burly. Hick was seen again, two months later, sitting alone upon the ridiculously exposed area that serves as the players' balcony in Leeds. A Test match [against South Africa] hung in the balance and much depended on his contribution. He had been recalled after scoring heavily at Worcester, an amiable place which he has made his home. The teams threw themselves at each other, and the crowd was transfixed. Here was a chance for Hick to impose himself, to use his power, to turn the match, and to secure a place in the team for Australia. It was not to be. Twice Hick fell cheaply, caught in the covers off poorly executed strokes. Throughout, he seemed stiff. Of course, he was not alone in his failures. But his failures have always been noticed, because of the expectations, and his appearance, and his extraordinary successes.

He played again at The Oval, against Sri Lanka, and hit a century. A place on the Ashes tour beckoned – until he was upstaged by a bigger hundred from John Crawley. Hedging their bets, the selectors put Hick on standby. He was duly summoned and thrown into the hotpot in Perth. After an embarrassing failure in the first innings to a stroke played with bat and body far apart, he contributed a rousing effort in a lost cause, hooking and driving without inhibition and with immense force. But power and authority are not the same. In Sydney, in the final

Test, the whole series seemed to rest on his shoulders. Perhaps it was an unfair burden. All England willed him to punch his weight. Instead, he held back: tightening, trying too hard, uncertain of his tempo. Perhaps he is too conscientious, and accordingly unable to take the brave decision or to execute it with his whole heart.

It may be his fate to be remembered as a remarkable cricketer and a monumental scorer of runs, as a player fit and reliable, yet incapable of taking the extra step; in short, a player whose finest moments came along at times of their own choosing. Considering his achievements, it might seem a harsh judgment. More leeway is given elsewhere. Sport forgives those who cannot contain themselves on the field, whose careers consist of flashes of brilliance, calling them charming and romantic and misunderstood. Sport also forgives those who must scrape around for their runs. But it will not smile upon those who do not deliver upon their promises, even if they did not make those promises themselves.

It was Hick's fate to be given an ability that did not suit his temperament. It took him on a long journey, across the world and into himself, took him further than he cared to go. His upbringing was simple and secure, and did not prepare him for the conflict. He grew up on a tobacco farm in Trelawney, not so far from Harare. His family had an English heritage and lots of Yorkshire blood, and his father played for the local cricket team, though not terribly well. Hick was confident in these surroundings with the sunshine and the emotional warmth. He hung a cricket ball from a tree and began practising in his uncreased way, building a game that had no nooks or crannies, no subtleties, a game founded upon straight lines and trust. He has always been a performer rather than a downright competitor.

Hick attended prep school and Prince Edward High School, ordered places with a sense of right and wrong. Although an uninspired student, he was obedient and respectful, as he has been throughout his career in cricket. It is hard to recall any tantrums, and he has not been greedy or vainglorious or obsessed with figures. To the contrary: he has batted at first wicket down for his club, hardly missing a match, taking catches at second slip or fielding in the deep, and showing an athleticism astonishing in such a big man. And yet something was held back. Hick has not been a leader, clapping his hands upon the field or grabbing the ball at a telling moment. Significantly, he has been reluctant to work upon his gentle off-spinners, which is not the approach taken by Viv or Sachin or Steve Waugh. Perhaps he could not imagine anyone losing his wicket to such nonsense. Or perhaps he was unwilling to put himself in places where he might be vulnerable.

The feeling arises that Hick is being criticised when he ought to be celebrated. It is hard to stop this mood creeping in. We had thought he belonged in the highest class and judged him by its standards. Perhaps we were misguided. Our expectations may have been too high. It did not help Hick that he cut such an impressive figure, and it was easy to forget that he had been a sickly stick insect in his boyhood, and that meningitis had bedevilled his teenage years. Only in young adulthood did he blossom.

Expectation did not rest easily upon him. Any hopes he had of a quiet entry into county cricket were swiftly ended. English cricket was in the doldrums. Nor did it help that Hick found himself in Worcester and not London, where he might have been pushed and cursed. And he had a long time to wait before he could play Test cricket. It would hardly be surprising if something went missing in those seven years, waiting to qualify for England. Had he played at 21 or 22, he might have risen to the heights. Most great players burst into Test cricket at an early age, before adulthood has brought its doubts. Provoked by Hick's reputation, the top bowlers of the age probed for weaknesses, waited for their man.

Conceivably, those years in county cricket lulled him, and the rest of us, into a false sense of security. Faults were not confronted and corrected. Hick may also have felt comfortable within the confines and privacies of the county game. Only the most ruthless analysts detected important faults. Most particularly, they saw a heaviness of foot and shot that made late movement an enemy. They saw, too, that Hick had a weakness against balls rising sharply at his shoulders. Torn between hooking, ducking, parrying and evading, he could appear confused, even frozen. Between them, the long wait and the problems posed by bumpers bit into Hick's confidence. At times, he has looked alarmingly baffled, bewildered by the game's betrayals and shaken by its scrutiny. He has not relished the critical world. Nor has he been able to resolve his own difficulties. Whatever his technical flaws, his limitations are mental.

Happily, there is much to be said on Hick's behalf. His cultured and forceful strokeplay has given enormous enjoyment to crowds across the world. He has hardly ever let his supporters down, or his team-mates, or the game itself. He has scored a mountain of runs, few of them given away. The regularity with which hundreds came along said much about his fitness, discipline and concentration. He has been an impressive and largely impassive professional, one of the heaviest scorers to appear in the last 20 years, and one of the best tall batsmen. His accomplishments are extraordinary. Only in Test cricket has Hick been found wanting, and even there his record is not so bad. None the less, something was missing, a spark, an ability to be himself in the most demanding situations.

It has not been Hick's fate to enjoy the fierceness of Test cricket. He was given almost all the characteristics demanded by greatness. Conviction alone was missing. It says much for him that he has remained unbowed by dismay. He has been a punishing and faithful cricketer, commanding where he is comfortable, and quiet elsewhere. Throughout, he has searched for the contentment and simplicity he knew in his early days, and he has found it in the same place, at home with his family. It might sound like a defeat but it isn't a defeat at all. Indeed, it's a sort of victory.

MOHAMMAD AZHARUDDIN
R. Mohan, *Five Cricketers of the Year*, 1991

Last summer, a new definition was given to oriental artistry as Mohammad Azharuddin, India's captain, time and again placed the ball through square leg and mid-wicket with a wristy turn of the bat at the instant of impact. Line seemed to mean little, length everything, as he feasted on England's bowling with hundreds at Lord's and Old Trafford to follow successively on one against New Zealand in Auckland. They set the crackers bursting in the cosmopolitan neighbourhood of Vithalwadi, in celebration not just of Azharuddin's success, but also of the return of the touch which five years earlier had launched his international career so spectacularly. Three hundreds against England in his first three Tests. That was early in 1985, and the 21-year-old was hailed as a prophet among the Indian pantheon of batting demi-gods. He was also beginning the struggle to cope with the expectations of a nation and his awe of his own reputation.

Mohammad Azharuddin was born on February 8, 1963, in Hyderabad, capital city of the Deccan plateau state of Andhra Pradesh. A doting grandfather was the first to spot the youngster's passion for cricket, and at the All Saints missionary school, Brother Joseph inculcated in him a love for the game. It was as a seam bowler, who could make the ball swing in a banana arc, that the young Azharuddin began playing for All Saints, but he progressed quickly to bat at No. 3, besides being the third seamer, for Hyderabad Schools in the South Zone inter-state schools tournament. In 1979–80 he turned out for South Zone Schools against the visiting English Schools side, and in 1981–82, at the age of 18, he made his first-class debut in the Ranji Trophy.

National recognition came on the heels of a double-hundred for South Zone in January 1984, in the Duleep Trophy, with a place on the Under-25 tour of Zimbabwe. He did not make the short tour of Pakistan in October that year, but only because it was thought Pakistan was no place for blooding youngsters. His breakthrough came later in the season after David Gower's team, beaten in the First Test, had come back to square the series in Delhi. In contentious circumstances Kapil Dev was dropped from the side and Azharuddin was brought in to replace Sandeep Patil for the Calcutta Test. The rest is history.

The soft-spoken, almost shy young man was also an instant hit in the limited-overs game. Critics in Australia raved about his essentially back-foot play, which they thought had gone out of fashion along with good manners on the field. His fielding, too, made him invaluable to the side, a factor which came to his aid when his form could not match the impossibly high levels he had set in his first international season.

While there were centuries to be made on the plumb pitches at home, there were none abroad until his first visit to Pakistan in 1989-90. By then, following an unhappy tour of the West Indies, where fast and short-pitched bowling had provided a searching test of his technique, his place in the side was in doubt. Indeed, it was only because Raman Lamba was forced to withdraw from the First Test because of a broken toe that he played. He saved his place in the next Test with a record-equalling five catches in Pakistan's first innings – four of them brilliant ones in the slips, where he had not always stood – but batting on a hard wicket had meant a return to the horrors of his "blind" ducking against genuine fast bowling.

Advice from colleagues to stand up and hook if bowlers were trying to corner him with bouncers was not really what an uncertain and unwilling player of the hook needed to hear. Sounder advice came from the former Pakistan batsman, Zaheer Abbas, who advocated a readjustment of his grip. By wrapping his right hand further round the handle, Azharuddin found he could stroke the ball with greater control and assurance. In the second innings of the Faisalabad Test, having been dismissed for 0 in the first innings, he made his first century away from home. In the course of it, he found his confidence and his true touch returning. Changes in selection were soon to thrust him further into the limelight, and although he had little experience of leading sides, he was made captain for the tour of New Zealand in early 1990.

Such is Azharuddin's nature, however, that he takes everything in his stride, not making a drama out of a crisis, or even a crisis out of the drama that is so often Indian cricket. He set about tackling his new responsibilities with the modesty that is a refreshing trait: the devout Muslim probably believed in just praying extra hard and leaving his young team to play to the best of their resources. Such a style was disastrous to begin with, but soon enough Azharuddin learned to assert himself as captain.

The Auckland Test, the last of the New Zealand series, brought a sensational twist to his career as a batsman, for it saw the fruition of his counter-attacking style. Suddenly, everything he did came right and a truly majestic innings of 192 unfolded. Marked by straight- and on-driving of a very high order, the innings was supreme also in that it was the highest by an Indian captain abroad. His match- and series-winning half-century at Trent Bridge in the second of last summer's Texaco one-dayers was a further indication of how completely "Azhar" had rediscovered himself.

MARK WAUGH
Colin Bateman, *Five Cricketers of the Year*, 1991

Australian cricket has two nurseries for its finest young players. One is in the verdant grounds of Adelaide's glorious Oval, where the Australian Cricket Academy prepares a balanced squad of 14 teenage prospects every year. The other is 12,000 miles away, in a country small enough to slip into Australia's back pocket, but where the opportunities for cricketers are big: England, of course, where the beer is warm, the climate cold and the Poms live.

Despite these drawbacks, Allan Border, Australia's captain, knows the value to a young cricketer's education of England cricket, with its diversity of players, pitches and pubs (for what would the game be without the bar-room analyst?). Border himself spent a few years enjoying all three with Essex, and his Australian team has benefited from the skills of such as Steve Waugh and Terry Alderman, both of them graduates of the County Championship. But while Border may have a deep affection for Essex, there was also some self-interest in the telephone call he made to Lancashire late in the summer of 1988. An investment for the future, as it were. Border was soon to leave England for training camp Down Under, prior to Australia's tour to Pakistan, and he was wondering if Mark Waugh would like to fill in at Essex for him for the rest of the season. Waugh, playing in Bolton League cricket, could hardly believe the conversation. You had to be either an established Test cricketer or a South African to get one of the plum jobs as an overseas professional at a county club. At 23, he was neither.

Waugh took the chance and did well. Well enough to be back in 1989 to watch with a mixture of anticipation and excitement as brother Steve, A.B. and his Australian mates conquered England in the Ashes series. It was becoming a formidable batting line-up to break into. Back home, however, he topped the Sheffield Shield averages with New South Wales and forced Steve out of the Australian one-day side. "One of us had to go, and brotherly love stops short when it comes to playing for your country." Last summer he returned to Chelmsford to complete his education in readiness for the call-up to Test cricket.

He scored 2,072 first-class runs at an average of 76.74 which, even in a summer of indulgence for batsmen, showed him to be a performer of the highest calibre. He is the type who can have 30 on the board without the bowlers realising he has his pads strapped on. Undemonstrative, compact and still at the crease, he works the ball rather than crashing it about. And being a high-quality cricketer, he could supplement his batting with some useful medium-pace bowling and safe, adaptable fielding. Twice he improved on his highest score, first with 204 against Gloucestershire at Ilford and then with an unbeaten 207 against Yorkshire at Middlesbrough two months later. He also turned in career-best bowling figures of five for 37 against Northamptonshire late in the season and was voted Player of the Year by Essex supporters accustomed to fine batsmen from overseas.

What gave Waugh the greatest pleasure were his innings against the best bowlers in the world. His double-hundred against Gloucestershire came off an attack including Courtney Walsh; he scored 126 against Derbyshire and Ian Bishop, 125 against Hampshire and Malcolm Marshall, a one-day century against Lancashire and Wasim Akram, and 79 not out against Surrey's Waqar Younis. "I'm confident I can handle it now," he said, explaining the satisfaction those scores had given him. "You never know as you progress in cricket how you will cope with the next step up. I realise that facing one West Indian quick at Ilford or Colchester may be different from facing four in Kingston, but the whole season has helped my confidence. I've faced those guys and survived. I feel ready for the next step when – if – it comes."

MICHAEL ATHERTON   Brian Bearshaw, *Five Cricketers of the Year*, 1991

It is quite possible that Mike Atherton would not yet have played Test cricket had Mike Gatting not taken a group of fellow-dissidents to South Africa in the winner of 1989–90. The announcement of a party which included eight players who had taken part in the 1989 series against Australia came during the Old Trafford Test. There were two Tests against Australia to go, and one of the new recruits, for the game at Trent Bridge, was Atherton, then 21 years old and having just completed his third and final year at Cambridge. His debut was the sort of which nightmares are made – out second ball to the sixth ball of the match. Atherton's reaction was to respond with, "It bothered other people more than me. I hadn't suddenly become a bad player with one duck." He was top scorer in the second innings with 47, scored 12 and 14 in the final Test, and missed out on the tour of West Indies.

There was talk of protecting him, putting him in cotton wool, and he finished up instead with the gentler pleasures of Zimbabwean bowling. He was disappointed: he did not want to be protected, and hoped he had been omitted on the simple grounds of other players being better. But Zimbabwe helped his development, which continued in England in 1990 when he played in all six Tests and scored 735 runs in 11 innings, with hundreds at Trent Bridge, against New Zealand, and Old Trafford, against India, where he joined Geoff Pullar as the only Lancastrians to score centuries for England on their home ground. This was Atherton's first season as a full-time professional after three years split between Cambridge and Lancashire, and he responded with a total of 1,924 runs in first-class cricket for an average of 71.25.

Michael Andrew Atherton was born on March 23, 1968, a Mancunian like two of Lancashire's greatest players, Archie MacLaren and Brian Statham. He learned his cricket with Woodhouses, the Lancashire and Cheshire League club where his father also played. He was at Manchester Grammar School for seven years and his batting blossomed to take him into the Lancashire Schools', English Public Schools' and English Schools' teams.

Atherton went to Cambridge in 1987 and made his first-class debut in a weak University side which sank to 20 for seven against a strong Essex team bristling with such bowling abilities as those of Neil Foster, John Lever, Hugh Page, Geoff Miller and John Childs. The team also included Graham Gooch and Keith Fletcher, who were later to play important parts in Atherton's progress. Batting at No. 3, he scored 73 not out in a total of 135 in the first innings and 33 out of 71 in the second. His first century was not far behind. In his fifth match, opening the innings, Atherton carried his bat for 109 not out in a total of 185 against Derbyshire.

His first-team debut came at Southport on July 22, 1987, and after Warwickshire had been bowled out for 116 on a soft, drying pitch, he scored 53 in 61 overs and shared in a stand of 108 with Fairbrother, helping Lancashire to a 10-wicket win in two days. He had come to stay, and he played important parts in Lancashire's run of six wins at the end of the season which almost swept them to the Championship. With 602 runs in eleven games for Lancashire to add to his 411 for Cambridge, he sneaked past 1,000 runs in his first season in first-class cricket.

For those of us witnessing him for the first time, it was not just his class which shone through; it was the temperament, his ability to adjust to any situation and play accordingly. However, 1990 was to be the true testing time: a full, demanding season with Lancashire, not just in Championship cricket but in limited-overs cricket, too. He started the Championship season with scores of 50, 191, 93 and 51, the one-day matches with 63, 44, 5, 69 not out and 76 not out, and by the end of May he had scored 856 runs in all competitions. Moreover, that did not include a century denied him in a washed-out Benson and Hedges Cup game with Hampshire. The recall to Test cricket was a near formality, although now it was as opener to leave the position of No. 3 available for Graeme Hick in 1991. Atherton showed his taste for the game at its highest level with innings of 151, 0, 54, 82 and 70 against New Zealand; 8, 72, 131, 74, 7 and 86 against India; a grand total of 735 runs and an average of 66.81. Not bad for starters.

Peter Roebuck, 2002

Throughout the 1990s Michael Atherton was the face of English cricket. Head still, eyes wary, left elbow high and feet moving neatly into position, he dedicated himself to the tasks of scoring runs, resisting bowlers and protecting his team's position. For beneath his pale, youthful and sometimes defiantly stubbled exterior could be found a wilful man blessed with skill and determination. What was wanting were the particular abilities needed by the hour; he lacked the sparkle and drive required to rouse a team from its slumbers, and if ever a team needed rousing during his years as Test cricketer and captain, it was England. But it was not his way to intone "Awake, arise, or be for ever fallen!" He was more inclined to say, in his suburban way, "Come on, lads, let's get stuck in."

In every respect Atherton remained untouched by the vicissitudes of fortune and the ravages of time. Stoicism was his most obvious quality – he played for a decade on constant medication for an inflammatory condition affecting his spine – and there was a dryness of outlook that made him as much an observer as a participant. He was tough, though, and did not flinch in the face of furious bowling or allow his spirit to wilt in adversity. Indeed he was in his element in these circumstances, as the ingredients of his Lancastrian character came together to produce a towering effort.

Just as he did not strive to appease his opponents, nor did he seek to impress the baying public, even if in time the public took him to its heart and claimed him intimately as "Athers". Not that this affected him; proud and private, he performed his duties on the field and then withdrew. Atherton enjoyed the community of the dressing-room and the fellowship of the football crowd, but otherwise he was content to be alone, reading, fishing or looking for a pair of socks in a bulging drawer. He was a tidy cricketer, and yet also expressive, for he did not depend entirely on the regimented. There was a touch of subcontinental subtlety in a manly Anglo-Saxon game, a thinness of the arm, a hint of wrist as he stroked the ball through point off back or front foot, sending it skimming to the boundary. None the less he regarded himself as a craftsman, not an entertainer, and he did not listen to the whispers of indulgence. His northern common sense outweighed the delicacies he had learnt and occasionally studied at Cambridge.

It was Mike Atherton's fate, though not his fault, to represent his country when its fortunes were at a low ebb. England had been unable to find any cricketers of Ken Barrington or Graham Gooch's calibre, players capable of dictating terms in any arena. Atherton did his utmost, especially against the Australians, whose directness stirred him: he later made friends with Ian Chappell, the most abrasive of them all. But he could not put the matter right. He worked hard, fought hard, told the unpalatable truth, and still England did not improve; so it was that his career ended as it had begun, with heavy and unavenged defeat by the Australians. Perhaps he lacked a clarity of character needed to provoke change. He was a wanderer and not a man of action.

Atherton averaged 37.69 in Test cricket and would have hoped for a little more. The top three England run-makers ahead of him – Gooch, Gower and Boycott – as well as Cowdrey, whom he passed in his farewell summer, all averaged more than 40. But, towards the end, his form fell away as his mind grew weary and his body made its complaints. It is the record of an accomplished cricketer whose contribution might be better judged from the stability he brought to the batting order during a long career that produced 7,728 runs in 115 Tests, and 16 centuries, none of them easily compiled. It was also his fate that his generation threw up some of the great bowlers of any age. There wasn't much relief. Whereas batsmen of previous generations could hope to take advantage of humdrum attacks fielded by weaker nations, Atherton was confronted by Marshall, Ambrose and Walsh, Waqar and Wasim, Donald and Pollock, McGrath and Warne. No wonder he soon lost the carefree approach sometimes seen in his early days.

In Sri Lanka in 2001, where unrelenting pace is not an option, he had particular difficulty against Chaminda Vaas as a weakness against left-arm swing bowling was revealed – precisely the failing that had tormented Geoff Boycott many years earlier. Both men remained classically side-on till the last moment and often seemed locked in this position as the ball darted back and thudded into their pads. Boycott was the consummate technician whose game didn't change much over the years. Atherton was more graceful and inclined to tinker, especially with the placement of his back foot, whose errant ways often brought unwanted trouble. Both were single-minded and watchful in the great tradition of opening batsmen.

Better than most thoughtful men, Atherton could withdraw into a cocoon of concentration, an asset as a batsman but not necessarily as a captain. He was intelligent rather than intellectual and made his decisions easily, at the crease anyhow. A purposeful man with strong opinions and principles, he did not allow his career to fritter away; instead, after last summer's Oval Test, he cut it short in the belief that his battles had been lost and won, and it is for the defiant innings he played in his country's colours that he will be remembered. His duels with Allan Donald and Glenn McGrath were cricket played at its highest pitch. These bowlers strove for his wicket because they knew it was resourcefully protected. Atherton did not give in, his wicket had to be taken from him. He had the heart for the fight regardless of conditions and obstacles.

Donald sometimes prevailed, whereupon he wore a surprised and delighted look. Sometimes the batsman had the better of him, most notably in his unbeaten 185 at Johannesburg in 1995, an innings spanning three weeks, or so it seemed, an effort of mind and body that saved a Test match. It was the innings that secured for Atherton the respect and national affection he had not sought through any artificial means.

The seeds had been sown the previous year, during another South African series, when the chairman of selectors, Raymond Illingworth, fined him for not being honest with the match referee about having dirt – an "illegal" substance – in his pocket to dry his sweaty hands. The press magnified the incident into a cause célèbre; Atherton went to ground and considered resigning the England captaincy. He didn't, and when he walked out to open the innings in the next Test, the Headingley crowd gave him a roaring reception. In similar circumstances, Fortune would have favoured lesser men with a century. Atherton was dismissed for 99.

McGrath was his nemesis. More than anyone else the Australian understood Atherton's game and knew how to pierce his defences. Atherton liked to wait till the ball was under his nose, choosing his stroke at the last, often playing with soft hands, absorbing the ball like a sponge. McGrath would relentlessly pitch on exactly the right length, moving his deliveries around unpredictably and bouncing the ball steeply so that edges would carry. Repeatedly Atherton was pushed back and, trying to adjust his stroke, often succeeded only in touching a ball others might have missed. He'd leave with a shrug and a sigh, and the Australians, respecting a fighter, were pleased to see him go. But he refused to change his game; it had been tried and tested over the years and had not let him down. He could not bring himself to chance his arm because it would be a betrayal of everything he knew and the team he represented.

Atherton was the finest English batsman of his generation, and captain in 54 Tests, a record for England. He was an even-tempered cricketer, a fierce patriot and a man prepared to fight his corner, popular with team-mates and, eventually, with distant observers. Yet he could seem aloof, even arrogant, to those who occasionally crossed his path. His retirement was well timed and he'll be able to relax now, writing books and articles, voicing his concerns, telling amusing stories and generally confirming that he is better company than he sometimes cared to show. He made an outstanding contribution to his country's cricket and his only regret must be that greatness did not bestow its largesse upon him.

A photograph of Michael Atherton batting at Johannesburg in 1995 appears on page 274.

BRIAN LARA
Tony Cozier, *Five Cricketers of the Year*, 1995

The unparalleled glut of batting records that fell to Brian Lara between April and June 1994 amazed the cricket world and gained global attention beyond the game's narrow confines. It also prompted an outpouring of national pride in his native Trinidad & Tobago where he was showered with honours and gifts. Yet, while there was understandable joy, there was no real surprise among many of his countrymen at the left-hander's achievement, simply the feeling that his inevitable date with destiny had arrived rather more suddenly than expected.

Trinidadians craved the arrival of a batting superstar they, alone of all the territories that comprise West Indies cricket, had lacked; and Lara had long since provided unmistakable signs that he would fill the void. Even the most cock-eyed optimist could not have foreseen his virtually simultaneous eclipse of both Sir Garfield Sobers's Test and Hanif Mohammad's first-class records, but those who had followed his development from the time he first played organised cricket were never in any doubt that it was within the potential of his talent and ambition. There was even talk, not entirely prompted by the euphoria of the moment, that Lara himself would surpass his own standards by the time he was through.

Such confident assessments were based on solid evidence. As a stripling of a lad at Fatima College, in Port-of-Spain, Lara had reeled off seven centuries in a single season of the national inter-school competition at the age of 15. In the annual West Indies' Under-19 championships, he created new standards, averaging over 50 in his four years. In only his second first-class match, when he was not yet 19, he held firm for more than five hours to score 92 against Trinidad & Tobago's sporting arch-rivals, Barbados, whose attack was led by Joel Garner and Malcolm Marshall.

Nor was the Trinidadian public alone in its early appraisal. Lara was made captain of the West Indies team to the Youth World Cup in Australia in 1988 and the West Indies B team to Zimbabwe the following year, ahead of older and more seasoned contenders. On his return, aged 20, he was appointed Trinidad & Tobago's youngest ever captain. If his advance to a permanent place in the West Indies Test team was inordinately delayed – he made his debut in Viv Richards' absence in Pakistan in December 1990 and did not reappear until April 1992, against South Africa, after Richards had retired – it was through no lack of claim on his part. Even after he set a new, if temporary, record for the highest aggregate in the Red Stripe Cup, with 627 runs in the five matches, he was kept on hold.

The simultaneous exits of Richards, Gordon Greenidge and Jeffrey Dujon after the 1991 tour of England finally made a place vacant and Lara immediately became the hub around which the reconstituted batting revolved. When West Indies faltered in the 1992 World Cup, he alone sparkled. Used as opener, he announced his arrival on the world stage with 333 runs in the eight matches at an average of 47.57. More than half were accumulated in boundaries as he rattled on at a striking-rate of 81.61 per 100 balls.

In common with almost all other players, Lara was not satisfied to be judged on the artificiality of the shortened game and it was his 277 in Sydney in January 1993, in his fifth Test, that confirmed what Trinidadians had long since taken for granted, that here was the newest in the long line of great West Indian batsmen. One of his predecessors, now team cricket manager, Rohan Kanhai, called it "one of the greatest innings I have ever seen". Its immediate value was that it inspired a revival of West Indian spirits that led to the conversion of a 1–0 series deficit at the time to an eventual 2–1 triumph; its long-term significance was that it established Lara as batting leader of a team still searching for a central figure in the absence of Richards.

It also reinforced Lara's self-confidence, never in short supply but always essential in the make-up of a champion sportsman. While receiving his award as Trinidad & Tobago's 1993 Sportsman of the Year, he was asked what might be his goals for 1994. "To get a few centuries, maybe a double, even a triple," he replied. He proceeded to exceed even his own expectations.

Leading Trinidad & Tobago in the Red Stripe Cup, he reclaimed his old aggregate record with 715 runs in the five matches. His 180 against Jamaica was an astonishing innings, scored out of 219 while he was at the wicket; his partners contributed 21. It was merely a preview of what was to follow. Within five months, the memory even of that extraordinary performance had been eclipsed by his 375 in the Antigua Test against England and his unique sequence of seven centuries in eight innings, the next six for Warwickshire in the English County Championship, culminating with his unbeaten 501 against Durham.

It was final confirmation for Trinidadians of what they had recognised for some time. According to Winston, one of his elder brothers, the Lara family knew he was something special even before he was ten. The second-youngest of seven sons and four daughters of Bunty and Pearl Lara, Brian Charles Lara was born on May 2, 1969 in Cantaro, a village in the verdant Santa Cruz Valley, half an hour's drive from Port-of-Spain. His father was superintendent at a government agricultural station. The boy's fascination for, and mastery of, ball games was evident almost from the time he could walk. According to Winston, he would use a broom stick and a lime or a marble as a ball and knock up against the garage door. As he got older, he would defy his brothers to get him out with a tennis ball. It was typical West Indian rural life – except that Lara was fortunate in having a family that recognised his rare talent and did everything to encourage and develop it.

When he was three, his father gave him a cut-down bat. When he was six, his father and his sister, Agnes, enrolled him at the Harvard Club coaching clinic in Port-of-Spain and would take him there and back every Sunday. Although he was good enough at soccer to gain selection to the national youth training squad – where he struck up a lasting friendship with Dwight Yorke – his father insisted his future lay with cricket and influenced him to stick to it. He was taken to major matches at the Queen's Park Oval where he saw the leading players of the day in action. Roy Fredericks, the West Indies opener, was an early favourite for he was, after all, small, left-handed and a dasher. When his father died in 1988, Lara's grief was deep and understandable. His guidance had extended beyond cricket. Dedicating his 375 to his memory, Lara said: "I had some bad influences in my time and, if my parents weren't there to straighten me out, things might have gone haywire."

Another mentor was Joey Carew, the former West Indies opening batsman. As soon as Carew saw Lara play, in Fatima College junior teams captained by his sons, he took a keen interest, gaining him membership of Queen's Park, the island's strongest club team, and carefully, but not overbearingly, monitoring his development. On leaving Fatima, Lara was academically qualified enough to consider a career in accountancy but it was only a fleeting thought. Cricket, it was obvious, would be his profession. But Lara is from the island renowned for its carnival, and he knows how to enjoy himself beyond the boundary. Like Sobers and so many other cricketers, he has become addicted to golf, which he plays right-handed and increasingly well, and is an avid fan of horse-racing. His boyish good looks and easy-going manner, not to mention his fame and fortune, render him a vulnerable bachelor.

There is another more threatening consequence of his sudden success and stardom. It places on him an awesome responsibility that not all celebrated young sportsmen can properly handle. With satellite television now spanning the globe, Lara has become cricket's first truly international megastar. Public expectations will be excessive, and the non-cricketing demands on him persistent. There are pressures that the great players of the past – even Bradman, Sobers and Viv Richards – did not have to contend with to the same extent. Temperament, as much as talent, is now likely to dictate Brian Lara's future.

A photograph of Brian Lara celebrating his world-record innings of 501 not out appears on page 1035.

SANATH JAYASURIYA David Hopps, *Five Cricketers of the Year*, 1997

Great players invariably possess an individuality that imprints itself forever on the memory: the ethereal grace of David Gower's strokeplay; the brightly scrubbed, soap-opera fantasy of Australia's leg-spinner, Shane Warne; or the brooding and intelligent menace of the West Indian fast bowler, Malcolm Marshall. Techniques might be largely unchanging, or at least evolve only slowly, but those who scale the heights do so in a distinctive manner that forever sets them apart.

Sanath Jayasuriya cannot yet be classified as a great player, which makes his influence in 1996 all the more remarkable. His World Cup exploits in an unexpected Sri Lankan triumph did not just assure him of a lasting place in the game's history, but promised – indeed, for a few heady weeks, insisted – that the course of the game would change forever. Few of The Greats have achieved that.

It is a mark of cricket's changing emphasis that Jayasuriya is celebrated not for years of consistent achievement in five-day Tests, but for a brief outpouring of intemperate strokeplay in a one-day tournament in the emotive atmosphere of the subcontinent. Traditionalists may be wary of the accolade. But all those who witnessed Jayasuriya's audacious attacking batsmanship – most particularly against India, in a group match in Delhi, and England, in the quarter-final in Faisalabad – gaped in admiration.

This was combustible strokeplay that challenged our assumptions. Steady starts. . . playing yourself in. . . wickets in hand. . . such tenets had been adapted, for sure, to the demands of one-day cricket, but never so freely abandoned. Jayasuriya's method of playing himself in seemed to consist of taking three steps down the pitch and carving the ball high over cover. He was batting as if in a baseball diamond, entirely overtaken by attacking intent. The defensive policy adopted by England's openers, Geoff Boycott and Mike Brearley, in the second World Cup final at Lord's in 1979 seemed the stuff of a different age.

It was the introduction of artificial attacking fields for the first 15 overs of a one-day international, combined with reliable batting surfaces, that provided the conditions for Jayasuriya to flourish. The term "pinch-hitter" was stolen from baseball to define an opening batsman specifically given the licence to adopt a high-risk approach in the opening overs. The very word caused some offence, but no one summoned up a more vivid description. And while other countries, notably England, viewed the new tactics suspiciously or half-heartedly, no batsman accepted their roles with more alacrity than Jayasuriya and his opening partner, Romesh Kaluwitharana.

Their joyous, uninhibited style brought starts in the first 15 overs of 90 against Zimbabwe, 117 against India (42 in the first three overs), 123 against Kenya and 121 against England. Sri Lanka were merely tapping their inclinations. As their captain, Arjuna Ranatunga, said: "They are playing their natural game. They can hit over the in-field, so we get the maximum out of them." It was Jayasuriya who was by far the classier and more successful of the two. England attempted to quell him by opening with Richard Illingworth's left-arm spin, but Illingworth was struck out of the attack within two overs as Jayasuriya breezed to 82 in 44 balls. Even after the World Cup he was not spent, recording the fastest one-day international century, from 48 balls, and then the fastest fifty, from 17, both against Pakistan at Singapore's Padang ground in April. Pakistan did gain rich recompense six months later, however, when Shahid Afridi hit Jayasuriya for 41 in two overs on his way to an even faster 37-ball hundred in Nairobi. One-day cricket recognises few barriers.

Sanath Teran Jayasuriya was born on June 30, 1969, in Matara, a fishing town which rests at the end of Sri Lanka's south-west coast railway, 100 miles from the capital, Colombo. Renowned for its local delicacy of curd and treacle, only in the last decade has it begun to make a consistent contribution to Sri Lankan cricket as the game has expanded beyond the traditional base provided by the leading Colombo colleges. His cricketing pedigree was scant: his father, Dunstan, who worked for Matara Council as a sanitary supervisor, had no active involvement in the game, and his brother, Chandana, abandoned it as a teenager to work in the council's fisheries department. St Servatius College in Matara, where Jayasuriya studied from the age of nine, also had a limited cricketing background, but the enthusiasm of the college's principal, G. L. Galappathie, and his first coach, Lionel Wagasinghe, ensured that his talents flourished.

In the late 1980s, Sri Lanka was in the grip of civil unrest. The government had invited Indian peace-keeping forces on to the island to try to suppress the terrorist activities of the LTTE, the Tamil Tigers, and that fuelled a further back-lash from nationalist groups. It was no time to be considering an international sporting career, but in such pressing circumstances the Sri Lankan cricket author-ities stalled a mass overseas migration of their top players by establishing the first-class game more firmly.

Jayasuriya, at 19, was the discovery of the first season of the new system, 1988–89. He hit successive double-centuries, in Lahore and Karachi, on a B tour of Pakistan; a Test debut followed in Hamilton on Sri Lanka's 1990–91 tour of New Zealand; and at Lord's, the following summer, he registered his first, typically enterprising, Test half-century. It was against Australia at the Adelaide Oval in 1995–96 that his maiden hundred finally followed, the ground's short square boundaries encouraging the jubi-lant square-of-the-wicket shots that have become his hallmark.

Jayasuriya's Test record remains modest, if improving. After Sri Lanka's series with Zimbabwe in September 1996, he had 830 runs in 19 Tests at an average of 34.58. Allied to that, he is a useful left-arm spinner and excellent close catcher. He has already played more than 100 one-day internationals, although only compar-atively recently has he been freed from the frustrations of the lower middle order. However unexpected his World Cup exploits were, he is no overnight sensation. Rather more, this is the story of a man who persevered in the face of consider-able hardships and, when success finally came, enthralled millions.

SACHIN TENDULKAR

Mike Selvey, *Five Cricketers of the Year*, 1997

It was one brief moment in time. The World Cup, India versus West Indies in Gwalior, and a single stroke of such exquisiteness that the old maharajah surely would have had it carved in ivory and placed on a plinth. In essence, it was no more than a leg-side flick to the boundary and, in a competition that gorged itself on hitting, might have been worth only transient acclaim. But this was a gem: a length ball from a high-class pace bowler met initially with a straight blade, and then, at the last nanosecond, turned away with a roll of the wrist and such an irresistible alliance of power, timing and placement that first of all it eluded the fingertips of a mid-wicket fielder diving to his right, and then it did the same to the boundary runner haring and plunging to his left. Skill, technique, confidence, awareness, vision: pure genius, and four more runs to Sachin Tendulkar.

The young man is probably the most famous and feted man in India, out-glitzing even the stars of Bollywood movies. With endorsements over the next five years estimated to be worth at least $US75m, he is also the highest earner in cricket. He has become public property in a country of enthusiasms that can spill over into the fanatical, but has managed to maintain a dignified, mature outlook, remaining aware of his responsibilities while protecting his privacy. When he married Anjali, a doctor and friend from his childhood, he rejected massive sums from satellite TV for live coverage, keeping the ceremony a family affair. He knows his worth, and is wealthy beyond the dreams of almost a billion Indians, but he is not a grabber. His father, a university professor, imparted a sense of perspective and a work ethic.

Tendulkar averages over 50 in Tests and is the supreme right-hander, if not quite the finest batsman, on the planet. He is a focused technician, who offers a counterpoint to Brian Lara's more eye-catching destruction, fuelled on flair and ego. He has, it seems, been around for ever. In the Third Test at Trent Bridge last summer, he scored 177, the tenth century of his Test career and his second of the series: yet remarkably, at 23, Tendulkar was younger than any member of the England team, with only Dominic Cork and Min Patel born even in the same decade. His figures have been achieved despite a lack of Test cricket, particularly at home. Seven of his centuries had been scored before his 21st birthday, a unique record. Had India not rationalised their Test match programme so much that, prior to last summer, they had played just one three-match series, heavily affected by rain, against New Zealand, in the previous 18 months, there is no telling what he might already have achieved. With time on his side and a return to a full Test programme, he could prove Sunil Gavaskar right and rewrite the records.

Sachin Ramesh Tendulkar was born in Bombay on April 24, 1973, and, since childhood, has trodden a steady, almost inevitable, path to greatness. He attended the city's Sharadashram Vidyamandir school, where the Harris Memorial Challenge Shield, a competition for Under-17s, provided the chance to bat for hours. From the age of 12, when he scored his first century for the school and came to be noticed as a special talent, he indulged himself. When 14, he compiled not out scores of 207, 329 and 346 in the space of five innings, one of them contributing to an unbroken partnership of 664 with Vinod Kambli, a record in any form of cricket.

He was 16 years and 205 days old when he made his Test debut, in November 1989, in the National Stadium in Karachi – for a young Indian, perhaps the most fiery baptism of all. The following year, at Old Trafford, he hit his first Test century – not a scintillating innings, but an exercise in technique, concentration and application beyond his tender years, which saved a game that might have been lost. Had it come 31 days earlier, he would have been the youngest century-maker in Test history. During the winter of 1991–92, he went to Australia, where they still talk in awe of the centuries he scored in Sydney and in Perth.

A few days after his 19th birthday, Tendulkar came back to England: to Yorkshire, no less, as the county's first overseas player. It would have been a massive responsibility for anyone, let alone a teenager from India, and it did not quite work, Tendulkar assumed the mantle conscientiously, and posed with cloth cap and pint of bitter, impressing colleagues and supporters alike with his under-standing of public relations. But, in the end, he failed to come to terms with the county game, scoring only one century and barely scraping past 1,000 runs in his only season. Hindsight would tell him that it was part of his education, but a mistake none the less.

In 1996 he returned to England, a teenage prodigy no longer, but a seasoned Test batsman fit to stand alongside his first hero, Gavaskar. The pair have much in common: Gavaskar was slight of build and, of necessity, a supreme judge of length. Tendulkar, too, is short. There is a lot of bottom hand, but he drives strongly, on the rise, such is his strength of wrist and the control in his hands, while he is devas-tating off his legs, pulls well and – given good bounce – can cut wide bowling to ribbons. If the delicate and unex-pected talents of Sourav Ganguly provided a distraction last season, then Tendulkar's two hundreds in three Tests

Little master: Sachin Tendulkar of India unfurls a classical cover-driven boundary against England's Alex Tudor at The Oval in 2002.

were ample demonstration of the team's premier batsman leading from the front. The first of them – at Edgbaston, where he made 122 out of 219 – was a stunning display of virtuosity in adversity.

In August, aged 23, Tendulkar succeeded Mohammad Azharuddin as captain of his country. Had he craved it and pursued it with a passion, he would surely have got the job earlier, perhaps even while a teenager. Rather, it was a position that was being held in abeyance until the time was right. His leadership has a firm base of experience to it now. His first Test in charge was against Australia. He made ten and nought but India won, just as one almost assumed they would. Some things just seem part of a wider plan.

Rohit Brijnath, 2003

Sachin Ramesh Tendulkar is now 30, he has a wife and two children, his face is wreathed in a goatee and faintly lined by time and travel, but to the world, and to India in particular, he is still a boy wonder. Thirteen years and 105 Tests have passed since he first took guard at Karachi in November 1989, but the poet's son with the almost-falsetto voice and the supremely dignified manner continues to write an elegant, belligerent and unprecedented history. When he walks to the crease – one eye occasionally turning to the sun, one hand hitching up his box –

it is cricket's equivalent of Michelangelo ascending a ladder towards the ceiling of the Sistine Chapel. He is short, 5ft 4in, and his stance is a study in stillness, his body finely balanced, his muscles relaxed. His mind has already mapped the geography of the field: as the ball is bowled, rarely does tension or indecision impede the instructions from brain to body. Only sometimes, so it seems, will he silently struggle within, caught between the responsibility he carries for his team and the force of his natural attacking instincts.

Then he plays. He is both tyrant and technician, batting with a thug's ferocity and a sculptor's finesse, though sometimes he fails to strike the necessary balance between the two. In his room, he occasionally takes one last look at his technique in front of the mirror; on the field, most days, we see that genius reflected. He will uppercut the ball gleefully for six with muscle, and next ball, in a perfect marriage of feet and bat and judgment of length, slide it softly past the bowler for four. He will generously shoulder arms and allow the ball to pass him as if it is not worthy of being struck, then explode into a flurry of shot-making that has the scoreboard ticking over like a slot machine. In full cry, his bat looks wider than the laws allow, though he hardly needs its full extent: as Greg Chappell once put it, he would do well batting with a single stump, like Bradman in the backyard. The crowd is a blur, the roar a hum, for he is too busy, as he said years ago, "reading the bowler's mind", or, better still, manufacturing shots that "compel the bowlers" to bowl where he wants them to. It is not so much that there are shots he does not have; it is merely that he has chosen not to play them.

Many things are unique to Tendulkar, and most of all the fact that the man has stayed faithful to the gifts he was given as a boy. Once, according to a possibly apocryphal story, a junior Indian team on tour was awakened by a thumping on the roof. On investigation, it was Tendulkar lost in some midnight practice. Later, too, he took little for granted. When Shane Warne toured India, Tendulkar went into the nets, scuffed the pitch on the leg side and had a spinner pitch it there; before India toured Australia, Tendulkar had the seamers deliver the ball from closer to his end, artificially manufacturing the pace and bounce he expected to face. The net has remained his temple. Asked about this once, he was gently annoyed that people felt it all came so naturally to him, thus discounting how disciplined his journey had been: his gifts, he explained, were oiled with sweat.

He will never be the greatest batsman in history: that seat is taken. But as much as Donald Bradman's Test average (99.94) outstrips Tendulkar's (57.58), the gap diminishes substantially when other factors are taken into account. Tendulkar travels more in a year than Bradman did in a decade; he has had to manage the varying conditions of 49 Test grounds, to Bradman's 10; he has already played twice as many Tests as Bradman, and over 300 one-day games, nearly all of them under the unrelenting scrutiny of television. And whereas Bradman had to cope with the expectations of a small populace, not given to idolatry, in an age of restraint, Tendulkar must play god to one billion expectant worshippers.

Steve Waugh has said, "You take Bradman away and he is next up, I reckon," though those who swear by Vivian Richards are not completely convinced. Still, his peers – Brian Lara in particular – have been pushed aside by sheer weight of consistent numbers. Tendulkar has 32 Test centuries to Lara's 18; by the end of the World Cup, he had 34 one-day centuries, with his nearest rival his captain, Sourav

Ganguly, on 22. But one statistic will please more than most. Starting when he was 20, in 1993, his Test averages for each calendar year read like this: 91.42 (8 Tests), 70 (7), 29 (3), 41.53 (8), 62.50 (12), 80.87 (5), 68 (10), 63.88 (6), 62.69 (10), 55.68 (16). The year when he averaged 29, he had only two completed innings. Otherwise, in the worst of years, his average is 41 – the usual benchmark of a very good player. This, better than anything, reflects the unwavering purity of his purpose.

He has not really known bad years, has never woken to a slump, though in the West Indies in 2002 he had successive Test scores of 0, 0, 8, 0, which – as if to prove the point – was enough to make eyebrows rise in astonishment. So true has his form been that it is easy to overlook the distinctive burdens he has carried. Wasim Akram once suggested that when Tendulkar is out, heads droop in the Indian dressing-room. Rarely has Tendulkar had the comfort of knowing that the men who follow him are as certain in rising to a challenge.

More demanding is his nation, for when Tendulkar plays, India stills, it quietens, till it is almost possible to hear a collective exhalation with every shot. In a land where governments stutter, the economy stagnates and life itself is an enduring struggle against failure, he is deliverance. For most of a billion people, unmoved by any other sport, he is escape as much as he is hope, standing like some solitary national advertisement of success. Tendulkar is not allowed to fail.

His genius has caged him, for he cannot walk any street without sparking a riot, nor sit unmolested in any restaurant. That he must indulge his passion for cars by driving through Mumbai's deserted streets in the hours before dawn points to the absurdity of his existence. It is easier written than lived. But he finds no refuge in rages or sulks; his serenity is startling for a man surrounded by an audience prostrated in hysterical worship. It points to a gift of temperament but also to his balance as a man. When a spectator invaded the field and escorted him off the ground at Lord's in 2002, he did not flinch or fuss, brandish his bat or bellow, but coolly walked on, the very picture of a warrior monk. Later, he said the fellow meant no harm.

It may well be that the sight of Glenn McGrath at the other end does not offer so much a threat as relief. If Tendulkar is India's escape, it may well be that the crease is his escape, the place where he finds his full expression. Only once, under persistent interrogation, did he admit: "People expect too much of me, a hundred every innings. They call and say, 'you scored a hundred in Kanpur, so why not in Delhi?'. They must accept my failures."

A photograph of Sachin Tendulkar with Sir Donald Bradman and Shane Warne appears on page 1163.

GRAHAM THORPE Colin Bateman, *Five Cricketers of the Year*, 1998

There are few quieter men in the England dressing-room than Graham Thorpe, and even fewer with more to shout about. The Farnham boy has the face and the demeanour of a poker player. The eyes say nothing, the straight-set mouth betrays no emotion. He does not believe in small talk. Yet the runs have piled up in front of him like columns of chips.

Ask any England follower to name the leading batsman of recent years and they will reel off Mike Atherton and Alec Stewart. Nasser Hussain might get a mention, too, and, oh yes, that little left-hander. . . Thorpe. None has contributed more consistently over the past four years than that little left-hander, who has the scoreboard ticking over before you have even noticed he has taken guard. Accumulation is the name of the game. Unspectacular and uncomplicated, Thorpe reached the end of 1997 with a Test average of 42, better than any of his contemporaries in the England side.

He ushered in the New Year of 1997 with something of a reputation as a nearly man. Since scoring a century on Test debut, he had reached 50 on 20 further occasions in 33 more Tests, but only once made it through to three figures again. Thorpe might have made a New Year's resolution to do something about it. Three centuries came in the next four Tests, two against New Zealand and one against Australia. That brought a rhetorical question from him, at one of his rare press conferences: 'I didn't notice too much of a mental barrier today, did you?' Even in an Ashes series that brought more disappointment for England, Thorpe topped the home batting with an average of 50.33, while none of his six colleagues could reach the 40s. He scored 453 runs in the six-Test series, which was bettered only by Australian opener Matthew Elliott. To round off his summer, he signed off with a career-best 222 in the vital Championship match against Glamorgan.

More than anything, though, Thorpe had faced the best team in the world and come out with his reputation enhanced. Even then, during a sticky midsummer patch while the Australians were winning three straight Tests, his place in the middle order had been called into doubt again, while other, more high-profile players escaped criticism.

Thorpe insists he will not change for the sake of the image-builders being brought in by the ECB's new regime. The only spin doctor he is interested in is one who can help him identify Shane Warne's variations. "If you're naturally enthusiastic and a showman, that's fine, but I'm not, and I think it is important not to try to be something that you are not. That way, you only fall into traps," says Thorpe. "Others may attract the publicity, but I don't need that. In sport, you can get envy and jealousy in a dressing-room, but thankfully I've never felt that. You've just got to enjoy it your own way."

Graham Paul Thorpe started in the archetypal English way. Born on August 1, 1969, into a sports-mad family, by the age of 13 he was playing with the men of Wrecclesham, a village team in the heart of Surrey. Two years later, he followed his older brothers, Ian and Alan, into the Farnham first team in the Surrey Championship, and at 16 he was invited up to The Oval.

Cricket, though, was only half of it for Thorpe, as he worked his way towards a PE diploma at Farnham Sixth Form College. By winter, he was a highly promising footballer, good enough to make the England Under-18s as a "nip-your-ankles midfielder", to use his own description. When it came to the time to make a career move, however, Thorpe had not progressed up the soccer ladder. Only Brentford had shown a passing interest, and cricket won the day.

His early development was moulded at Surrey by Micky Stewart and Geoff Arnold, two more characters interested in spit and polish rather than flash and dash. Typically, his role models were not two high-flyers but doughty opener Ray

Alikhan and left-arm spinner Keith Medlycott, a man whose own playing career nose-dived but who is now back at The Oval as coach. "It was their attitude that I admired most. I liked them as blokes," says Thorpe. "They weren't bothered about who they were playing against or who they were playing under, they were not in awe of anyone – they just got on with the job."

Apart from a broken thumb, which kept him out of the last Test of the 1993 Ashes series, and a brief spell in 1994 when he was dropped, Thorpe has been one of the few constants in the England side of the past four years. Despite problems off the field in 1997 which troubled him deeply – the death of Surrey colleague Graham Kersey in a car accident and Sunday newspaper allegations about his private life – Thorpe remained the most single-mindedly successful of English batsmen.

RAHUL DRAVID
Alan Lee, *Five Cricketers of the Year*, 2000

Think of modern Indian batsmen, and the Englishman thinks of Tendulkar. Even regular cricket followers find it hard to recognise the other members of India's top order. This may be a comment on the enduring gulfs in culture, or more simply, gaps in fixtures; but after the summer of 1999 it is an unsustainable position. India supplied two of the outstanding batsmen of the World Cup, and neither of them was Tendulkar.

Sourav Ganguly and Rahul Dravid had introduced themselves three years earlier. They made their Test debuts together at Lord's, Ganguly scoring 131 and Dravid 95 from No. 7. David Lloyd, then England coach, had been told by his observers that Ganguly would open the face of his bat outside off-stump, while Dravid's weakness was working the straight-ball to leg. This dossier was quickly consigned to the out-tray.

Three years on, and the scene changes to Taunton, its bucolic traditions given over for a day to Asian exuberance. India are playing Sri Lanka in a World Cup group match. India lose a wicket in the opening over but they will not lose another until the total has reached 324. Ganguly and Dravid's stand of 318 is, by a distance, a record for any wicket in international one-day cricket (until November, when Ganguly and Tendulkar raise it to 331). For Dravid, the day brings his second century in four days. Despite India's failure to qualify for the second round, he would complete the tournament as its leading run-scorer, and return home feted as a hero among perceived failures. To his embarrassment, Dravid fan clubs have sprung up, their membership loaded with teenage girls, and though his features may still be shamefully unfamiliar in England, they have attracted advertisers and film-makers in the land where star cricketers are national property.

Rahul Dravid was born in Indore on January 11, 1973. The son of a food scientist, he was firmly encouraged to complete his studies before branching into sport, and obtained a degree in commerce at Bangalore University. But he made his first-class debut at 18, for Karnataka, and scored 134 in his second match. He was soon identified as one of the meteors of Indian cricket. Shy and introspective, he did not seek attention, but it was to come his way naturally, through weight of runs and an impression of quiet authority that led him to captaining most of the teams he represented.

At first, his method was a painstaking one, his fierce determination to preserve his wicket matched by a desire to learn. In Toronto one year, he button-holed Ian Chappell at a party and put searching questions to him for an hour. At Lord's he learned how to succeed and how to fail, all in the same innings. Had he made five more runs, it would have been the first time in the history of Test cricket that two debutants in the same team had made centuries. "It hurt," he recalls. "But I realised it would not do me any good to keep thinking about it." He went out in the next Test and made 84.

At the start of 1999, India, a team that had spent too long confining its talents to one-day cricket, played a sudden raft of Test matches. They were beaten 1–0 in New Zealand, but the third game of that series, at Hamilton, belonged to Dravid, who made an elegant, eight-hour 190 in the first innings and followed it with 103 not out in the second. In Colombo seven weeks later, he made his fifth Test century, against Sri Lanka. By now, he had a Test average of 54 and had cemented his preferred place at No. 3.

Next, though, came the World Cup and further evidence that this pleasing player is far more capable than most of his countrymen on alien pitches, reason enough for Kent to engage Dravid as their overseas player for 2000. He was also to demonstrate that his game had moved on and that he was resourceful enough to dominate. In late November, as he waited in a Mumbai hotel for the flight to Australia and another challenging chapter in his development, Dravid reflected on his golden year. "I have improved a lot since 1996", he said earnestly, "but my game can still progress further." Taunton, he said, had been "great fun, fantastic" but the World Cup, overall, had left him with mixed emotions. "There are such expectations of us at home. We are followed very closely and people were disappointed. We had no excuses, although I thought we played well enough to reach the semi-finals."

Dravid certainly did. His total of 461 runs, 63 more than his closest challenger Steve Waugh (Ganguly was third with 379), contained not only two successive centuries but also fifties under pressure against England and Pakistan. His batting was as undemonstrative as his personality, but as eloquent, too. It spoke of a man who has the time, both in technique and age, to graduate into the very highest company, and to do it with an understated, old-fashioned grace.

A photograph of Rahul Dravid batting with V. V. S. Laxman appears on page 452.

MATTHEW HAYDEN   Greg Baum, *Five Cricketers of the Year*, 2003

Sometimes in their worthy search for the perfect alignment of talent, technique and temperament, selectors outsmart themselves by overlooking the most fundamental and blindingly obvious virtue a batsman can have: the faculty for making runs. Matthew Hayden was passed over for all manner of training institutions, squads and teams in his cricketing youth, up to and including the Australian Test team, because of a universal suspicion about flawed technique. "It always baffled me a bit, because I always, always had scores on the board," he said. "It was like I had to win the perception." When he finally established himself in the Australian team, and was asked by one of his press-box critics what had changed, he was tempted to reply: "Only your mind."

Just one man never, ever wavered in his faith: Hayden himself. By January 2003, when he was ranked the No. 1 batsman in the world, he was well placed to thumb his nose at the doubters. But he would not, because he thinks of this peak as a staging-post, not a destination. Although he has never been more content, he is as possessed now as when he was a schoolboy thumping the ball all around outback Queensland. He realised it last Australian summer when given four days off to refresh himself. He went to Stradbroke Island, a favourite haunt, with his wife, infant daughter, surfboard and fishing rod, which along with his bat and his Catholic faith constitute all that is dear to him. When he returned, he was itching for a net. "I just love the feeling of hitting the cricket ball," he said. "That's what stimulates me. That won't ever wane."

Matthew Lawrence Hayden was born on October 29, 1971, in Kingaroy, land of wide skies, beef cattle and peanuts, home also to Carl Rackemann and the former Queensland premier Joh Bjelke Petersen, who because of an infamous gerrymander ran the state for two decades and so could be said to be another who was intent on never getting out. The teenage Hayden's boon companion was his elder brother Gary, who was also his first coach. "He was always amazed at the way I just went out to hit the ball," Hayden said. "He was all about leaving it. I just wanted to bludgeon the ball everywhere." In the off-seasons, they did triathlons together.

Hayden went to school and university in Brisbane, and all the while made runs, breaking his club's scoring record in his first full season and also breaking Greenmount's record in the Bolton League as soon as he spent a winter in England. He was not picked for a youth tour of England, nor invited to the vaunted academy, but regarded that as a lucky break because he was by then on the threshold of state selection. The day before his Sheffield Shield debut against South Australia in November 1991, when another man might have been worrying about whether he belonged in this company, Hayden asked if anyone had made a double-century on debut. The next day, standing a metre outside his crease and hammering the ball back down the ground as if with a rivet gun, he made 149. "I was thinking that I wanted to be successful," he said. "That was my mindset."

At 21, Hayden toured England and made 1,000 runs without playing a Test. It was 1993 and Michael Slater was just establishing himself as Mark Taylor's opening partner. The next year, Hayden made his Test debut when Taylor was ill on the morning of the Johannesburg match. Early in the second innings, Allan Donald broke his thumb. In the next six years, he played only six Tests, all in the southern summer of 1996–97. So it was that all his first seven Tests were played against the powerful seam attacks of either South Africa or West Indies. It was hardly surprising that his performances were uneven and he could not make a permanent place for himself. He saw this period not as exile, but preparation. "The thing is, you'd have it no other way. Within myself, I knew I was gathering momentum," he said. "I knew I was good enough, but I couldn't get the opportunity." He said he felt frustration, but never despair.

He admitted to quirks in his technique, but no more than any other left-hander. "Even today, if a guy is swinging the ball into your pads, and you're trying to play straight, it's really hard to make the adjustment." Three seasons of county cricket, batting day in day out for Hampshire and Northants, helped refine his method. "The guys were bowling straight at my pads. It's the way the English bowl: at the pads and stumps and look for the LBs," he said. "Gradually, it became a strength, to the point now where, if I was to say what was my favourite shot, it would be through mid-wicket, forcing off the back foot. To get anywhere, you have to face your weaknesses."

His style still was not classical, but it worked. Tall, broad-shouldered and immensely powerful, he did not just occupy the crease, but filled it. He knew from a young age that if he remained patient and played with the full face of the bat, he had the strength to hit boundaries for days at a time. He continued to make runs in epic numbers – an opponent at this time said it was like bowling to a sightscreen – and never lost his inner conviction. "I never thought about what I could or should have been doing, but what it is that I have to do to become a better player," he said. "Even now, with one-day cricket, it doesn't stop. I want to become a better player."

Hayden regained his Test place and his vocation in New Zealand in March 2000. The next year in India, the country of reincarnation, the explosion came. In a series memorable for prodigious feats on both sides, but also for the failure of most of Australia's batting, Hayden made 549 runs in six innings. An astonishing number came from the sweep, a shot he said he always possessed, but rarely got to play on Australian pitches against Australian bowlers. "I've got a big advantage with the sweep because I've got a big stride. I can get to the length and sweep on the length," he said. "Unless it's a genuinely short ball, you can almost sweep anything."

The runs have not abated since. Hayden's tally of 1,391 in 2001 was then third only to Viv Richards and Sunil Gavaskar in a calendar year. Starting with that Indian series, Hayden made 2,560 runs in 25 Tests, with 11 centuries, including a run of eight in 13 Tests, prompting Steve Waugh to compare him with the incomparable – Donald Bradman. At the end of the 2001 Ashes tour, he and Justin Langer came together serendipitously to form an opening partnership that was instantly world-beating, yielding four double-century stands in their first seven Tests together and reducing South Africa to a quivering wreck. They set out deliberately to revolutionise the opening business; rather than simply absorb the early buffeting and dull the shine, they made up their minds to attack the puny bowlers and their piddling ball. They set out to intimidate the bowling team. "We're about really asserting ourselves. We're about making sure the opposition feel how close we are, not in a false way, but because that's the way we play cricket," Hayden said. "It starts with us."

Hayden has also emerged as a brilliant fieldsman, either in the gully or suffocatingly close to the batsman when the spinners are on. He had looked unsuited to one-day cricket – a statutory limitation on his time at the crease was anathema to him – and did not establish himself in Australia's one-day side until Mark Waugh's axing in March 2002. Yet within ten months, he was rated No. 1 in the world in both forms of the game. His temperament was such that he could thrash and dash, but also bat through the innings, as circumstances demanded.

Hayden had one other salutary experience on his way to the top. While he was fishing before dawn one morning off his beloved Stradbroke Island with an Australian team-mate, Andrew Symonds, and another friend, his boat hit a sandbar and sank. They had to swim for an hour to safety through waters where, the previous day, they had seen a school of sharks run amok among pilchards. Hayden said he had been scared. "But I controlled it. It was a good life lesson. There were three of us, and we had to support each other through it." Shaun Pollock and the new ball would never be so threatening again.

MICHAEL VAUGHAN

David Hopps, *Five Cricketers of the Year*, 2003

Michael Vaughan began 2002 keenly aware of the impatience for him to prove his worth as a Test batsman. If it emanated less from the England management than from the media, nonetheless the time was nigh for Vaughan to establish himself as a senior player and a worthy opening partner for Marcus Trescothick. Such was his response that, by the year's end, he was not just established, but had

become England's most accomplished performer since the heydays of Gooch and Gower.

The transformation was striking enough in the scorebook. In 13 Tests up to the end of 2001, he had scored 679 runs at 33.95, respectable enough without being particularly eye-catching; in 2002, in one Test more, he stacked up 1,481 runs at 61.70, with six centuries – and another in 2003, in the final Ashes Test at Sydney, for good measure. He was Test cricket's leading run-getter in 2002, an impressive feat, if not the most meaningful one in England, where the cricketing year, like the financial, traditionally begins in April. Even more impressive was the style in which he made his runs. He had always been technically sound, but a reflective, somewhat pottering, even stressful air in his formative years encouraged some to harbour suspicions that he would be overpowered by attacks of the highest class. He answered that in wonderfully emphatic style. In 2002, cricket grounds in England and Australia resounded to a new Michael Vaughan, a batsman more

Cover point: Michael Vaughan became the first person to appear on the cover of *Wisden*, after he scored 1,481 Test runs in 2002, with six centuries, plus another in the New Year Test at Sydney.

confident in his method and much more forceful in his strokeplay. Deliveries that were once sneaked into the covers now pummelled the boundary boards. Short balls, and some not very short, were pulled and hooked in a manner that must have surprised even Vaughan himself. By the end of the year, his habit of touching the peak of his helmet, like a classical batsman of old respectfully touching the peak of his cap, had become a familiar sight. Throughout, he played with a dignity that signalled him a player of true worth.

Earlier in the year, Trescothick had been the England batsman attracting the plaudits. Vaughan remained on the fringe of the team after a lengthy apprenticeship in which he had always been thereabouts but not always there. Although he had made one Test century, against Pakistan in 2001, and had contributed crucial runs to two low-scoring victories over West Indies in 2000, he had also attracted more than his share of injuries and other mishaps, culminating in being given out handled-the-ball in a Test match in India. Yet by the end of the English summer, Vaughan's four Test hundreds against Sri Lanka and India invited hopes that his opening partnership with Trescothick could be the springboard of a serious Ashes challenge. When an injury-ravaged England lost the Ashes series 4–1, Trescothick, who performed moderately, had been eclipsed; Vaughan was looking like the batsman around whom England could build for the next decade.

RICKY PONTING

Bruce Wilson, *Five Cricketers of the Year*, 2006

After that most delirious of summers, now destined to bore countless thousands of unborn grandchildren, it might seem perverse-to-absurd to include in this annual salute to excellence a batsman whose Test average dipped, who made arguably the worst decision by an Australian captain in 30 years, who was fined for what might be called excessive surliness and lost the Ashes. Yet Ricky Ponting joins this unique roll-call for any number of reasons, some of which approach the abstract; not least, for example, is the one that it takes two to tango. Without Ponting's own particular persona combating Michael Vaughan's very different one, the chemical formulae that exploded into the 2005 Ashes would not have reacted as spectacularly as they did.

Ponting's flaws and strengths were all part of the magic mix. His strengths included one of the great match-saving innings – by far the most consequential batting performance by an Australian all summer: the 156 at Old Trafford, when he stood between Australia and total Ashes meltdown. It was his 23rd Test century, made in circumstances far rougher than most of the others. Ponting's greatness as a batsman has never been in dispute, nor his place in the *Wisden* pantheon. In 2004, he was the first recipient, by acclamation rather than vote, of the almanack's newest award, the Leading Cricketer in the World. That came after a 2003 when he led Australia to victory in the World Cup, scored 11 international centuries in the calendar year and unleashed two successive double-centuries against India, the series that until last year stood as Australia's most eventful and competitive of recent times.

In 2005, there was a strong argument that, as commanding officer, he was responsible for the warship losing its teeth. The questions over his tactical captaincy, the nuts-and-bolts everyday stuff of field placings and just when to turn the screw, persisted until the last day of the Fifth Test. But Ponting's defenders went to The Oval noting that with just a couple of drops of luck Australia could have been leading the series 3–0. And the failure of so many of his team-mates to reach their normal heights was not his fault. The background noise to all this, though, was the stark fact that Ponting sent England in to bat at Edgbaston having just seen his main strike bowler, Glenn McGrath, taken to hospital. The ubiquitous "team sources" were quick to say that the decision had been made inflexibly by committee. Ponting, typically, would have none of that, and shouldered the blame.

Ricky Thomas Ponting was born on December 19, 1974 in Launceston, Tasmania's second city, in the north of that beautiful if eccentric island, son of Graeme and Lorraine. He was a sporting prodigy who at 11 scored four centuries in a Tasmania-wide Under-13 week. Promoted to the Under-16s, he promptly scored two more. His astonishing and quite natural talent has never been in doubt. At 20, he was already in the Test team. He lost his place at 21. At 22, he returned to the team to score a chanceless maiden century at Headingley – near perfection, said *Wisden*.

It was still not all smooth after that. But the bumps in his career, apart from a chastening against spin in India, were largely self-induced and off the field, until he settled down, gave up the beefsteak'n'bourbon life, and got married. He maintained, though, his love for what Australians call the dishlickers – well-bred greyhounds. His nickname remains "Punter". Marriage somehow enabled him to make runs even more regularly, and helped harden the selectors' view that he, rather than the *très méchant* Warne, was Steve Waugh's natural successor in both forms of the game. And until the Ashes series, Ponting's captaincy had kept Australia at an unfaltering position at the top of the world. But by Old Trafford last summer, a lesser man might have buckled, if from nothing else but the sheer weight of cutlery in his back. Instead, he played the defensive innings of his life to scramble the draw.

In the next Test we had the Pratt Affair, when substitute fieldsman Gary Pratt ran Ponting out and the stuff that had been rumbling away erupted in a fiery cascade of expletives. Ponting was admonished, heavily fined, and he apologised. The epilogue to this went almost unnoticed. With the Ashes just lost at The Oval, the teams were drinking together (and Ponting's personality surely played a part in that kind of fraternising) when a nervous Pratt asked if a photograph might be signed. Jokes ensued and Ponting, instead, handed the young Durham man two pairs of his initialled boots. "I think he was pleased," Ponting said. Astoundedly delighted, said an eye-witness. It was seen as a typical gesture from this understated man.

In Tasmania, just after leading a thrashing of the World XI and just before making a century in each innings against West Indies in the First Test, Ponting said that even as it all drifted away that last day in South London he was able to console himself. He was confident his position as captain was secure. "I just thought, well, they're only out on loan, the Ashes. It's less than 18 months away, and then we'll have them back."

Fast Men

BOB WILLIS   Alex Bannister, *Five Cricketers of the Year*, 1978

If Geoff Boycott's timely return made all the difference to the batting, the new-ball fire power of Bob Willis, which yielded 27 wickets, was of special significance in England's high summer of success. No England bowler of authentic speed can boast a comparable record in a home series against Australia – indeed only Jim Laker (46) and Alec Bedser (39) of different styles have done better – and, fittingly, in the final euphoric moments at Headingley when the Ashes were recaptured Willis took his 100th Test wicket.

It was singularly appropriate that team and personal triumph should go hand in hand, for few players have given such loyal and unstinting service to England as the wholehearted Willis. And he has had more than his fair share of the other side of fortune. As late as May 1975, his career was imperilled by major operations to both knees, and while in hospital he suffered a blood clot and spent several unpleasant hours. Until the middle of that season he was on crutches. In Willis' own words the operations were similar to a 50,000-mile service, but his come-back would not have been complete without his own determination and a fortu-itous meeting with Dr Arthur Jackson, an Australian disciple of the German Van Aaken's theory of the value of slow long-distance running to build stamina. Willis first met Dr Jackson during the 1974–75 tour of Australia, and formed a close friendship which has continued with phone and letter exchanges.

Pain and worry became Willis' constant companions around that period. From the first match in Australia he had knee trouble, and only drugs kept him going. He had ten injections before the inevitable breakdown, and he was flown home before the start of the last Test. Back at Edgbaston he went down again in the first Benson and Hedges Cup game, and he knew there was no alternative to surgery. After the operations there was the drudgery of daily exercises. Fast bowling is essentially a matter of rhythm and co-ordination, and the idle weeks produced a crop of niggling complaints like strained stomach muscles and bruised heels. Another restricted season meant a chance to play in only the last two Tests against West Indies, though he managed five for 42 in the second innings and eight wickets in all at Headingley.

The glamour faded when he joined the dole queue in the following winter. There had been an offer to coach in South Africa, but understandably Willis did not want to risk playing too soon on hard surfaces. The slow, cruel grind back to fitness and form had its turning point in India, traditionally anything but a bountiful hunting ground for English fast bowlers, in 1976–77. Wisely Alec Bedser and his selectors opted for a speed attack led by Willis, and with equal prudence Tony Greig, the captain, and Ken Barrington, the manager, urged Willis to abandon his somewhat circular tour to the wicket in favour of a simple and direct approach. Well-formed habits are not easy to eradicate, but it was characteristic of the man that from the moment the team arrived at Bombay Willis marked out his longest run and assiduously applied himself to his new task. He succeeded.

On pitches prepared for spinners, Robert George Dylan Willis – he added Dylan to his given names after falling under the spell of the American folk rock singer at the age of 12 – was often too much for India's batsmen. He took 20 Test wickets, including five for 27, which put England firmly on the path of victory in the second match at Calcutta. Since then Willis has had six for 53 at Bangalore, seven for 78 at Lord's, five for 88 at Trent Bridge and five for 102 at The Oval, and has put to flight any who doubted his right to be acclaimed as one of the world's foremost fast bowlers.

David Frith, 1985

Richardson had Lockwood; Larwood had Voce; Trueman had Statham; but Willis was almost alone. Just how much of an extra force for England Willis might have been, given a regular complementary strike bowler, is a question which will hang suspended in time. True, he linked with Botham for several series, and believed in his partner implicitly – until the final phase, by which time Botham had lost his thrust and Willis himself, still valiantly withstanding the hardships of ageing frame and suspect knees, sensed that the sand in his own hour-glass was nearly all in the bottom.

For one who is often outrageously convivial in a social setting, Bob Willis could be surprisingly, even shockingly, solitary when in cricket battledress. The young man flown to Australia in emergency during Illingworth's 1970–71 tour bent himself into predatory shape in the gully and held some spectacular catches; but Willis the Elder, a dozen years on, unlikely captain of England, struck a memorable and almost perpetual pose in the isolation of mid-off, thin arm across concave chest, large hand propping that promontory of a chin, blue-grey eyes seemingly glazed against what became, in 1982–83 and 1983–84, a painful scene as England's mediocre bowling was exposed by the batsmen of Australia and New Zealand. It was as well to remember, at times of exasperation at his detached air, that he merely accepted the highest honour of the England captaincy; he didn't demand it. The selectors had boxed themselves in by dropping Fletcher.

Often Willis tried to do it alone, and that was when his lone role and his uniqueness among English pace bowlers were so gallingly obvious. Inevitably in 1984, with the defeats piling up and his own condition and future in doubt, he was relieved of the captaincy. He graciously returned to the ranks and played out his last few Tests under Gower. When his bowling was hammered by the West Indians – Holding in particular – there were still those who wished to believe that it was luck on the batsmen's part, and that Willis remained a force. We were, in fact, watching the death throes of a great fast-bowling career.

Only Bob Willis's height ever encouraged any sort of belief that he would become an international fast bowler. His run-up was intimidating but slightly absurd. Even he appreciated this, especially after seeing Gooch imitate it, a fateful observation late in life which persuaded him to bring his right arm forward instead of pumping it across his rump like a frenzied jockey in the home straight. Yet irrespective of the low marks for aesthetic quality in his action, that long right arm, which came down and across at such an unlikely angle, propelled the ball at a hot pace, with steep bounce and unusually threatening movement in towards the batsman. Sometimes that batsman, as in McCosker's case at Melbourne during the Centenary Test, was pinned by it. McCosker's jaw was broken, and Willis was booed as he left the ground, in blazer and flannels, and strode up through the park towards the team's hotel. Anyone getting in his way that evening would have been squashed flat. A year later one of his bouncers hit Pakistan's night-watchman, Iqbal Qasim, a fearful blow in the mouth. Again, there was no outward show of regret, and this time his captain, Brearley, supported his tactics in bowling short.

The fast bowlers' union went into liquidation around the time that all sorts of other honourable institutions and codes were developing cracks, and Willis the tail-end batsman was as much in need of a helmet, when they came into vogue, as any opening batsman – in fact, more so. Yet he still managed to appropriate a whimsical record: most not outs in Test cricket. If he looked ungainly as he rattled in to bowl, he seemed even more of an oddity as he defied the bowling, with helmet perched on his thick mass of hair, left leg thrust down the pitch, and that curtain-rail probe with the bat – a cross-pitch slice which somehow made contact. He once hit Australian fast bowler Alan Hurst for six over cover point at Adelaide. But his finest hour with the bat was a 171-minute innings of 24 not out at The Oval in 1980, when he saw Willey to his century, shared in an extraordinary unbeaten tenth-wicket stand of 117 after England had been 92 for nine in their second innings, and held out against the sudden prospect of a West Indian victory.

Willis was awarded the MBE for services to cricket, an expression interpreted by the majority as standing for loyalty (he resisted the blandishments of World Series Cricket in 1977), patriotism (richly apparent in everything he did or said), and a displayed sense of propriety (as symbolised in his admonishment of Jackman, who had gestured to an outgoing batsman). Those tortured, pumping knees carried him in the end to 325 Test wickets, 128 of them in 35 Tests against Australia. At the time of his retirement both were records for England. That gratified the man who, as a boy, idolised Statham and dreamed, like millions before and since, of becoming one of the rare few to play cricket for his country. And yet, in the anti-climax of his withdrawal from big cricket, as illness shortened his last season and prevented him from taking an orchestrated final public bow, he privately spoke of never treading on a cricket field again. Such was his exhaustion and disenchantment.

If he was no outstanding tactical genius as captain, he could be an effective motivator. He particularly showed this quality as senior pro, chiefly in the dressing-room. But towards the end his feelings bordered on disgust at the conviction that some of England's cricketers accepted failure too readily. Nor was he able to close himself off against media comment. His finest hour was at Headingley in 1981, when his eight for 43 further stunned an Australian side already dazed by Botham's awesome 149 not out in England's follow-on innings. In the moment of supreme exhilaration Willis was less inclined to discuss the great victory with his national television interviewer than to lambast the press – not, mark you, the relevant section of it – for earlier derogatory comments. It was only much later that the full significance of his bowling feat sank in, so wound up had he been.

Over the years he resorted to hypnotherapy to relieve his inherent tension and improve his mental and physical tuning. This helps to explain the intensity of his approach: the glaring eyes, the tight lips, taut cheeks. It might even explain his oversight in the Test at Edgbaston in 1982 when he marched out, padded, helmeted and gloved, but without his bat.

He was not always quite a universal favourite at Edgbaston. Many Warwickshire supporters were resentful because he seemed to be giving more to his country than his county. But this is less of an indictment when one reflects that after John Snow's decline (he and Willis played in no more than five Test matches together) there was no English bowler for years, in the whole of the country, who came close to Willis for speed. He was the pronounced cutting edge – between bouts of reblading in the skilled hands of knee surgeons.

There was something tantalising about seeing Willis and Snow in tandem for Warwickshire when the Sussex bowler, then 38, was induced to come out of retirement in 1980 and helped his new county to win the John Player League. How different might the shape of England's Test cricket have been with those two operating with the new ball throughout the 1970s? Now both are gone, Willis with his marathon run-up and too tightly contained emotions, his bent for the zany monologue and his flat, resounding laughter. The stage is empty, and all England awaits another courageous man of speed. Preferably a pair.

JOEL GARNER — Tony Cozier and Eric Hill, *Five Cricketers of the Year, 1980*

One of the several splendid cricketers who has played his part in lifting Somerset to the pinnacle of cricket in England, and West Indies to holders of the World Cup, is Joel Garner, at 6ft 8in the tallest man to have played Test cricket. Garner and his West Indies companions in the fast bowling set, Colin Croft, Wayne Daniel, Michael Holding and Andy Roberts, all tower over six feet and they comprise the most menacing combination of fast bowlers the game of cricket was known.

What impresses most about Garner is his athleticism. Off the field he seems gangling and awkward. His legs are like stilts, and he has a slight stoop in his walk, not unnatural for one who constantly has to contort himself to get through doors and into beds designed for more conventional frames. Yet he is fast and supple as a fielder and well co-ordinated as a bowler. So far he has not been troubled by the spate of back and muscle injuries which seem to afflict so many other athletes who carry such bulk.

Joel Garner was born in December 16, 1952, bred and raised on the island of Barbados, the idyllic, 166 square miles' island in the eastern Caribbean, famous for its beaches, its rum and its cricketers. The game thrives there in magnificent climate and ideal conditions as it does nowhere else in the world. Cricket is more than just a game, it is a way of life, and the number of outstanding players born Barbadian is nothing short of a phenomenon. The most famous of all is Sir Garfield Sobers, quite simply the greatest all-round cricketer there has been.

So Garner and other young Barbadians grow up in a strong cricketing environment. Almost from the time he could walk, Garner and his mates would be hitting a ball about with an improvised bat – in the road, on the beach, anywhere with a bit of room. By the time he entered Foundation School, one of the island's leading grammar schools, at the age of 12, Garner already knew what cricket was all about. He had natural ability, and this needed only to be polished by the former Barbados Test players, employed as coaches by the government. It is a formula which has been well established over the years, churning out players as if on an unceasing assembly line.

From school, Garner went into the Barbados youth team, into a club side, into the full Barbados team and, finally, into Test cricket with West Indies. The process took ten years, but Garner was probably luckier than most. To begin with, he had as coaches Wes Hall and Charlie Griffith, who had created havoc with the world's batsmen in the 1960s. "At school we had Seymour Nurse and Everton Weekes as the main coaches, and sometimes Manny Martindale," says Garner. "We knew they were great players and we all wanted to get as far as they'd done. It was Charlie who made me change my action. I used to deliver with a round-arm, double swing which he said would not do at all. In a few months I was doing it the correct way."

His cricketing career then moved apace; it was almost as if some Fairy Godmother had waived a magic bat to clear the path for Joel Garner. First, Test duties in Australia kept Vanburn Holder and Keith Boyce away and injuries ruled out Holding and Daniel to give Garner his chance of Test selection in 1977. In his first Test series, against Pakistan, he took 25 wickets while Croft, who owed his place to the same particular piece of fate, claimed 33.

Since 1976, Garner has spent his summers in England, playing first for Littleborough in the Central Lancashire League. In his first season he took 110 wickets at under 13 apiece, and in the next two seasons, 1977 and 1978, his remarkable all-round form took the club to the top of the table. Each season his 100-plus wickets cost fewer runs, ranging from 8.54 each to 6.70, and he also topped 500 runs for the summer. His weekend League exploits attracted Somerset's attention in 1977, and Littleborough's flexible attitude brought a contract for midweek county cricket for the next two years.

His part in Somerset's double success during 1979 admits no arguments as to his potent and continuing ability to swing matches. In the four games in the Gillette Cup, which Somerset won, Garner's 43 overs brought a total of 17 wickets for 92 runs. This included the best return for a final of six for 29. In the John Player League, which Somerset also won, the West Indian played in 13 of the 16 and ended with 16 wickets for 296 in 96 overs. Curiously enough, he played in all three matches that Somerset lost, one of the quirks of the cricket game.

Garner, in fact, is not really fast. The top men generate speed through the air of between 90 and 95 miles an hour, if the scientific measurements are to be believed. Garner would be between 75 and 80. Where he is most awkward is in the sharp lift he can achieve from his immense height. The steeper the lift, the more difficult it becomes to counter – hence Garner's success. In addition, Garner also possesses the ball which complements the bouncer ideally, the yorker. Speared into the batsman's toes, it is meant to trap the batsman softened by the bouncer. England's captain, Mike Brearley, itemised another advantage of Garner's height.

"The trouble is that Garner's hand delivers over the top of the sightscreen, which makes him impossible to sight early", he said. "When you have one ball getting up chest height and another coming in at your toenails it's difficult to survive."

TERRY ALDERMAN
Brian Mossop, *Five Cricketers of the Year*, 1982

It was typical of Terence Michael Alderman that when he looked back on his remarkable bowling success in England in 1981 he attributed it to two main factors – sharing the new ball with Dennis Lillee and the state of English pitches. Certainly no blame for the failure of the Australian team in what was an unusual series could be attached to the young Perth primary school teacher. Representing his country for the first time, Alderman played in all six Tests and stamped himself not only as a seam bowler of the highest quality, with a record 42 wickets in the series, but also as a slip fielder with a sure pair of hands.

Born on June 12, 1956, Alderman, the fourth of five children, had something of a sporting start in life. His father, William, was a big-kicking Australian Rules football centre half-back, who represented Western Australia and also opened both the batting and the bowling for the Western Australian colts cricket team without ever making the first-class scene. Alderman followed naturally in his father's footsteps, playing both cricket and football during his schooldays at Aquinas College in Perth. He continued to play football as an amateur until the end of the 1978 season, when he decided that it would be foolish to continue mixing the two sports. By then he was already beginning to make his mark as a medium-paced bowler, although it would have required a crystal ball of remarkable clarity to foresee the impact he would make in England three years later.

Playing for Western Australia in colts matches in Melbourne and Adelaide in 1973–74, Alderman took six wickets against Victoria in Melbourne. That performance brought him to the notice of those who chose the state senior side and the following season, in which Dennis Lillee and Jeff Thomson made life so uncomfortable for Mike Denness's Englishmen, Alderman was picked in the Western Australian team – only to have Ian Chappell take 24 runs off his second over in a limited-over Gillette Cup match. Alderman was twelfth man for the two Sheffield Shield matches against South Australia and Victoria before making his Shield debut against New South Wales in Sydney, a match which brought him mixed fortunes. A raw 18-year-old, he took five for 63 and pulled a hamstring which led to his having to return home.

Between 1974–75 and 1980–81 Alderman was twice dropped from the state team. Looking back now he believes that it was perhaps a mistake to have been chosen for first-class cricket so early in his career. The resilience of youth, and the feeling that he had age on his side, saw him bounce back, and although he thought he had a chance of being picked for Australia's tour of India in 1979 he had to wait until the end of the 1980–81 season to win national recognition and his first tour. Not even the Australian selectors could have imagined the success that their rookie would enjoy. No one would have been more delighted with Alderman's nine-wicket Test debut at Trent Bridge than John Inverarity, the former Western Australian captain and Test batsman, who had long been championing his cause. "He was a big influence," Alderman said. "He always encouraged me and was probably the reason why I got a chance in the first place." But it was Lillee who played perhaps the most significant part in the emergence of Alderman into a Test force in England.

Always careful to bowl well within himself, Alderman had never been a pace bowler in the true sense of the word. Instead he had relied mainly on the swing generated by a seemingly lazy run-up that ends in a fairly chest-on delivery. He has never had a meanness of some of the great fast bowlers. But a spell in the Edgbaston nets just before the second Prudential Trophy match last June was a turning point. "The practice wickets were lively and Dennis told me to bowl off a long run and see what I could do. I tried to hit the seam and was unplayable in the nets. That was the first time I realised I could do more as a seam bowler than as a swing bowler. What I did after that was to try and do more off the wicket".

In the event, not only did he make the ball do more off the seam, he also bowled faster than he had in Australia. His six foot two and half inch frame, broad shouldered and tapering also came in for some lengthy spells bowling into the wind. He thrived on the challenge. "When you're bowling at the other end to Dennis, you've got to have a better chance of getting wickets."

MALCOLM MARSHALL
Alan Lee, Five Cricketers of the Year, 1983

Cricketers seldom agree on the relative merits of fast bowlers. Debates about the fastest, bounciest or most difficult to play will invariably rage unresolved through a tour or a season. But not in 1982. Then, almost without exception, the batsmen on the county circuit nominated Malcolm Denzil Marshall, born in St Michael, Barbados, on April 18, 1958, as the quickest they encountered. This accolade was remarkable enough for its unanimity, but there was more. Fast bowlers as a race are often treated with suspicion, if not outright resentment, by the men they attack day by day. But Marshall somehow earned an element of admiration, for his ability, his work-rate – if one can apply such a clichéd soccer word to him – and his cheerful Barbadian humour.

He has shown much resourcefulness since the May day in 1979 on which he made his Hampshire debut, and his sense of humour has been needed. Not long off the plane from the sand, surf and sun of his homeland, Marshall found himself running in to bowl against Glamorgan while the English climate played one of its more eccentric tricks – snow fell on the Southampton ground. Undeterred, though maybe mystified, he took nine wickets in the match, figures which he never quite lived up to during the rest of that summer. He finished with 47 wickets and less than 200 runs, missed virtually all the following season owing to the West Indians' tour, and then, in 1981, made his first significant impact on county cricket, taking 68 wickets despite missing one-third of Hampshire's matches.

The improvement accelerated dramatically in 1982. Suddenly, this man with the wispy beard, searching eyes and infectious grin was no longer just one in the pack of West Indian bowlers in the English game; he was looking like the best. He had learnt how to bowl in English conditions and he could do it for as long as he was allowed. His total of 134 wickets was 44 more than his closest challenger, Nick Cook, who also happened to be the only other leading bowler to get through more than 800 overs in the season. Marshall's total output of 822 was startling for a strike bowler; the traditional county workhorses were well behind.

This, according to those close to him, is Marshall's greatest asset, and his willingness to bowl is matched by a stamina seldom seen in the game. It was one of captain Nick Pocock's most teasing problems – just how many overs to give Marshall in the hope that he might make another break. Trevor Jesty, who led Hampshire while Pocock was absent injured, confirms: "I set out to give him spells of five or six overs, but he always wants to go on bowling, and sometimes it can be very difficult to get the ball off him."

Marshall had a great deal to live up to when he arrived with Hampshire. For the previous five years, Roberts had been taking the new ball, and with his loss of enthusiasm and subsequent departure, the county's followers quite naturally feared the worst. Who could possibly fill such boots? But Marshall came well qualified. He had just passed his 21st birthday and already he had represented West Indies, in India and Sri Lanka. What is more, he had an inbuilt affection for this new employers. As a boy in Barbados, playing cricket on the beaches and dreaming of one day bowling fast in England, his adopted counties had been Middlesex and Hampshire.

Incentive was another motivator. West Indies' quartet of pace bowlers was well established and Marshall was just one of a cluster trying hard to break in. He had time on his side, maybe, but there was a degree of impatience in him. He wanted to play Test cricket and he saw the county game as a showcase. It is said he put on a yard of pace to impress Clive Lloyd whenever the West Indies captain happened to be at the receiving end. His persistence paid off, at least to the extent that he became the regular fifth seamer in the squad.

Marshall has many of the traits of the typical West Indian. His walk is jaunty, his speech liltingly rushed, his ego large. He wears his name on a gold pendant hung round his neck, dresses sharply and remains, at 24, an eligible bachelor, delighting in soul music, reggae and a good party. But if the popular conception of the Barbadian remains dominated by mañana, then Marshall is a misfit. Tomorrow, for him, will never be good enough. He wants to be the best today and is prepared to work to achieve his aims.

A photograph of Malcolm Marshall bowling in 1991 appears on page 1218.

Mark Nicholas, 2000

From the address given at the funeral of Malcolm Marshall at the Sir Garfield Sobers Sports Complex, Barbados, on November 13, 1999. [Marshall died of cancer on November 4, 1999, aged 41.]

Many years ago my mother suggested to me, in reference to a splendid schoolteacher who had died, that in life one came across only a few truly special people. Lots of good'uns, she said, plenty of fabulous folk, but only a few who are special. Malcolm Marshall, conclusively, was one of those – one of those special people. Not so much because he was so extraordinarily good at cricket, but because of the way in which he applied the various gifts, cricket amongst them, which were given to him. Malcolm was no waster – not of time, not of talent – nor a shirker of any situation or challenge which confronted him. For as long as perhaps the last two months – maybe more, maybe less – he knew deep down, I think, that the game was up. But he was damned if he would let us know. He was such a stubborn fellow. It was as if he was more concerned about the suffering of those around him, those few intensely close friends kept by this very private man, than about the suffering he was going through himself. The qualities of thoughtfulness and caring, of courage and bravery – and didn't he often show that in his play? – were among his finest. For all the flamboyance and bravado as a sportsman, Malcolm was not one to over-dramatise off the field. He said things as they were, and he resolved that his dreadful illness would be his own problem, and as it escalated, he would not panic others with its potential end.

For everyone who lives here, on this magical island, the name of Malcolm Marshall is synonymous with the style of the place: with the game of cricket in its purest calypso form, but also in its more modern professional form; with fun and sun; with the good and simple living that is typical here; and with the honesty and generosity of spirit that characterises the people of Barbados. It is clear to a visitor his loss has stunned his nation. And yet, most fascinatingly, amazingly really, his loss has echoed all around the world, volley upon volley of shock stabbing at friends and fans wherever the game is treasured. The internet, for example is jammed with messages and memories, and telephone lines have been on heat. Among the first calls I received were from Shaun Pollock, in Natal, South Africa, who attributes so much of his success to Malcolm; from Barry Richards, the great South African batsman, now living in Australia; from Martin Crowe, who called him "the finest opponent of them all – furious, but fair, and fantastic value in the bar"; and from Ian Botham, busy on his final walk raising millions of pounds for Leukaemia Research, who for once found himself virtually unable to speak, so sad was he not to say goodbye to "the skinny wimp from the Windies", as he loved to call him.

Richards said how sorry he was not to have played with Marshall at Hampshire; he had the privilege of Gordon Greenidge and Andy Roberts but not of him. It was Captain Peter Short who brought Marshall to Hampshire, continuing the line of Barbadians who played for the county, the first of whom was another Marshall, that wonderful batsman Roy, who Malcolm used to follow in the papers.

It was funny to watch opponents greet Macko. The greats, his peers, relished the moment with hand-slapping glee and then they all tore the life out of each other on the pitch. The less good used to whisper among themselves if he was late, as he often was, incidentally, saying "no sign of Macko today? Phew!" Then when he arrived, wrapped in gold chains and fancy clothes – and boy did he dress snappy or what? – their faces would fall. Ray East and David Acfield, the Essex spinners and terrified tail-enders, used to wait by his car and offer to carry his bags to the dressing-room. "Why?" asked Malcolm, when it first happened. "Well, Mr Marshall, we thought you might consider a couple of half-volleys and, if they're nice and straight, we promise to miss them!"

Mark Nicholas, now a broadcaster and journalist, was captain of Hampshire from 1984 to 1995. Malcolm Marshall was his team-mate from 1979 to 1993.

COURTNEY WALSH

As Courtney Walsh left the field in the final Test at The Oval, Viv Richards stood up in the BBC commentary box and clapped. He didn't say a word: I daresay that there was a great lump in his throat that prevented speech. For the six others in the box, this was as eloquent a tribute to Walsh as any man could muster. Quite what the millions of listeners made of the ensuing silence, I don't know.

Understand that old cricketers can be an unsentimental, cynical lot, and that clapping in press boxes is as frowned upon as cheering a missed putt at St Andrews. But there was a tear in the Richards eye as his old colleague and friend bade farewell to his English fans after 16 years of devoted international service. Richards knew better than most what a staggering contribution Walsh had made to West Indian cricket. The captor of the most Test wickets in history, he may not have been the greatest fast bowler to emerge from the Caribbean in the modern era. Even so, it is odd that when *Wisden* conducted a poll of 100 cricketers and writers, to establish the Five Cricketers of the Century, Walsh did not receive a single vote. For there has never been a more durable pace man, or a more wholehearted one.

He did not possess the grace of Michael Holding or the swinging guile of Malcolm Marshall, but he just kept going. The gnarled Australian, Dennis Waight, his physio with West Indies for more than a decade, said in 1997: "I've got a feeling that if Courtney stops playing, he'll never get started again." Sometimes he would exasperate Waight. Between Tests, he would pop back to his home club – Melbourne in Kingston, Jamaica – and, discovering they were short, agree to turn out. There, he would at least be fortified by some of the sumptuous Caribbean dishes provided by his mother, Joan, another stalwart of the club.

So he kept playing. When he came out for his final innings of the 2000 Test series, the England players formed a guard of honour. Alec Stewart and Mike Atherton were there, long-time adversaries who had been damned sure they had seen the last of him after the Antigua Test of 1998. They were wrong. But this time they could be certain that he would torment them no more in Test cricket. After all, England were not scheduled to play against West Indies until 2004; Courtney would be 41 by then.

His one regret must be that, when his Test career was coming to a close, West Indies appeared to be in freefall. (When it began, with an innings victory in Australia in November 1984, they were invincible.) Hence the pleas for Walsh and his great friend and partner, Curtly Ambrose, to keep going beyond their natural lifespan as fast bowlers. Walsh, as ever, succumbed to those pleas and undertook yet another tour to Australia.

In the early days, Walsh was the general dogsbody of the West Indian attack. Bowling with the new ball was denied him; Holding, Marshall or Garner had earned that privilege. If there was a wind, Courtney would bowl into it. If there was a long partnership on a hot afternoon – admittedly a rare occurrence in that era – he would inevitably be tossed the ball, and he would receive it gratefully. So it took him 12 matches to acquire his first five-wicket haul in Test cricket. However, dispel the notion that facing Walsh was the soft option when playing against West Indies in the 1980s. His gangling, slightly unco-ordinated method of delivery suggested, treacherously, that the ball was coming in to the right-handed batsman. This was not always the case and led to scores of victims in the slip cordon. That distinctive, open-chested action as he glided through the crease – like many West Indian pace men raised on hard grounds, he did not bang his front foot into the turf, which may in part account for his freedom from serious injuries – made the ball hard to pick up. At least Holding had the decency to employ the perfect, classical action, which enabled an early sight of the ball.

Walsh changed his pace devilishly without any discernible change of action. As a result, he hit countless batsmen over the years, far more than Holding or Ambrose. From nowhere a lethal bouncer would appear; in his later days, he developed a brilliant slower ball that could rarely be spotted, either – especially when Graham Thorpe was at the crease. And as he grew older, he grew meaner. The inadequacies of the next generation of West Indian fast bowlers were exaggerated by the fact that Walsh and Ambrose in their final years gave the batsmen nothing to hit.

But it is his stamina and loyalty that single out Walsh, and examples abound of both qualities. In Perth in 1997, when he was leading the West Indian team, he tore a hamstring. "The doctor said he was finished," remembers Dennis Waight. "I iced him down all night and we did some static stretching the following morning. He took the field to give it a try and hobbled in off a short run. I thought he might last four or five overs; in the end he bowled 20 in a row and only stopped when the match was won. He didn't walk properly for another two weeks after that, but for Courtney the pain had all been worthwhile. That's special."

Caribbean giants: two great West Indian fast bowlers take their leave of
English cricket at The Oval in 2000. Curtly Ambrose (left) finished with 405
Test wickets, while Courtney Walsh rolled on for 519.

CURTLY AMBROSE

Mike Atherton, 2001

A cricketer's retirement, in both its timing and manner, can often tell you as much as you need to know about that player's career. In Curtly Ambrose's case, the timing, like his approach to the crease, was near perfect. He was still at the top of his game, as the 2000 series in England showed. Yet, some of his trademark pace and fire was beginning to wane, and in his final spell the ageing legs seemed to be sending him a message. Rather than risk a trip too far to Australia, which with its unremitting heat, big grounds and flat wickets is no place for old bones, he decided enough was enough and left us with memories of how great he is, rather than was.

The manner of his retirement, too, was typically Ambrose-like. He announced at the beginning of the summer, with no histrionics, that the series against England would be his last, and, with little or no fuss from the big man himself, he was true to his word. There were precious few titbits for the media to scrap over, although he did give his old pal Michael Holding one interview to ruin that oft-quoted phrase, "Curtly talks to no one". In this modern age of image and spin, with the accent on style rather than substance, he has been a refreshing change. He went, as he came and then conquered, with little to say. And yet, despite the low-key approach to retirement from Ambrose himself, rarely can a crowd or an opposition team have acknowledged a cricketer's leaving in such a fashion, an indication, if one were needed, of the high esteem in which he is held. It was one of the most touching moments I have seen on a field, when the Oval crowd rose to Ambrose and his great mate, Courtney Walsh, to applaud them off the field for an assumed last time. They left, arm-in-arm, one sensed close to tears, and halfway up the pavilion steps Ambrose symbolically removed his famous white armbands, safe in the knowledge that his legs would have to do no more pounding.

The next day, as he walked to the crease with West Indies on the brink of a famous defeat, the England team lined up and applauded him all the way to the wicket. It was a fitting mark of respect and, no doubt, a private thank you that their tormentor was finally on his way. (A few of us had remembered his wave to the Oval crowd five years before, hoping we wouldn't see him again.) In the middle of the salute he mumbled "Thanks, lads," which is about as much as I've heard him say. In cricket, even when you are losing, you can sometimes be a winner.

In statistical terms, Ambrose's career ranks amongst the very best the modern game has to offer. He took 405 Test wickets at a shade under 21, with a strike-rate of a wicket every 54 balls. Testimony to his parsimony is the 1,000th maiden in Test cricket that he notched up during last summer's series. As someone he dismissed more times than anybody else, I think I am reasonably well qualified to comment and compare him with the other fast bowlers from the last decade of the last millennium. At his best, there is no doubt he moved beyond the fine line that separates the great from the very good. Quality bowlers essentially need two of three things: pace, movement and accuracy. Ambrose had all three. He was certainly quick, especially in the mid-1990s, and the extra bounce he generated from his beanpole frame made life even more awkward for the batsman. More than anything, though, he was a mean bowler: he hated giving runs away. Twice during last summer's series it took me half an hour to get off the mark, and then it was only a nudge off the inside edge through square leg for one. But each time Ambrose was livid with himself for offering even this measly morsel.

His best spell against England was undoubtedly at Trinidad's Queen's Park Oval in 1994. On a wearing fourth-innings pitch, we needed 194 to win. But from the very first ball, which he nipped back to trap me lbw, it looked a distant target. For the final frenetic hour on the fourth evening Ambrose steamed in, reducing the England innings to tatters (40 for eight) with as good a display of hostile and aggressive fast bowling as you will see. One look at Graham Thorpe's eyes as he walked off that evening told you everything. Ambrose's performance prompted Lord Kitchener to pen a calypso about him and about that extraordinary hour, and for the remainder of the tour the whole of the West Indies could be seen dancing to its beat. Lest you think it was only the English he harassed, his spell at Perth in 1993, when on the first day he took seven wickets for one run in 32 balls on a trampoline of a pitch, was apparently even more devastating. One can only be glad not to have been 22 yards away at the time.

As West Indies became more fragile during the second half of the 1990s, they came to rely on their fast bowlers more and more. So often defeat seemed inevitable, and yet somehow Ambrose and Walsh responded to the call. They always had. Their classic comeback was probably in the inaugural post-apartheid Test against South Africa at Bridgetown, where the West Indians, outplayed for four days, roused themselves through Walsh and Ambrose to an astonishing victory on the last day in front of a deserted Kensington Oval. With South Africa, eight wickets in hand, requiring another 79 runs, Ambrose took four for 16 and Walsh four for eight.

In spite, or maybe because, of the hostility of his bowling, there was never a battle of words with Ambrose. There was no need. In the truest sense, he let his cricket do the talking. The most I ever heard him say was "Morning, skipper," and there were never any verbals during our frequent battles in the middle. Over time, however, there was a little more animation, to add spice to the contest. Before the first ball of the innings, he came to have a habit of walking down the wicket, yards from the batsman, and looking at that area of the pitch he deemed to be the "business area". He would rub his hands with anticipation, and invariably at the end of the day there would be a cluster of ball marks worrying the patch.

This discipline and professionalism typified his bowling throughout his career. With his going, and the imminent departure of Courtney Walsh, West Indies have lost the last link with their great teams of the 1980s and early 1990s. Thankfully, for batsmen, there will no longer be the sight of Ambrose stood in mid-pitch after another wicket, pumping his arms skywards.

ALLAN DONALD

Jack Bannister, *Five Cricketers of the Year*, 1992

The time was October 1986, the place Bloemfontein, the occasion a pre-season celebratory dinner, given by their supporters, for the Orange Free State team. The players, a set of enthusiastic youngsters, were headed by Corrie van Zyl, then the best young fast bowler in South Africa. But Roger Prideaux, the former England, Sussex and Northamptonshire batsman, drew my attention to someone else. "That's the bowler I would take into county cricket," he said. "He's nearly 20, and he has as much genuine potential to be fast as any bowler I've seen."

That bowler was Allan Anthony Donald, born on October 20, 1966 in Bloemfontein, where he was educated at the Technical High School and went on to be selected for the South African Schools XI in 1984, as twelfth man, and 1985. He made his debut for Orange Free State in 1985–86, against Transvaal at the Wanderers, having Jimmy Cook caught behind early on, and since then he has become one of the leading fast bowlers in world cricket.

Last summer Donald repaid Warwickshire's faith in him by bowling them to the verge of the Britannic Assurance Championship title, taking 83 wickets at 19.68 to finish behind Waqar Younis in the national first-class averages. Until the last three weeks of the season, his captain, Andy Lloyd, rigidly restricted him to spells of no more than five or six overs, even when he was taking wickets. But Donald showed great reserves of stamina and courage by bowling unchanged for 20 overs in the final home game against Northamptonshire, despite a back injury, and his six for 69 in the second innings to win that game, and another six in the first innings at Taunton, took to eight his five-wicket returns in 1991. Only Waqar Younis exceeded that figure, and twice Donald finished with ten wickets in a match.

His physical attributes are there for all to see. A magnificent natural athlete, he has a not over-long run-up, which accelerates him into a high, balanced, slightly open action. Despite this openness, he still has that priceless ability to run the ball away from the right-handed batsman, both in the air and off the pitch. He bowls a fuller length than most fast men – a deliberate change of method in 1991 – which is why some 70% of his wickets were either bowled, lbw or caught at the wicket. Occasional losses of rhythm, with their subsequent diminution of effectiveness, occurred less frequently last summer, and Donald's ability to cope with the pressure of international cricket brought him instant success in South Africa's historic week in India in November.

WAQAR YOUNIS

Peter Roebuck, *Five Cricketers of the Year*, 1992

By taking 113 wickets in 582 overs for Surrey in 1991, at a mere 14.65 apiece, and by carrying on his shoulders an otherwise moderate county attack, Waqar Younis announced himself as one of the finest contemporary bowlers and hinted that in time he may achieve the greatness which, it seems, has already been thrust upon him; with which, perhaps, he was born. In just 11 Tests for Pakistan before the last summer he had taken 55 wickets, capturing five wickets in an innings five times. Moreover, he had provoked Martin Crowe, captain of New Zealand, into saying that he had never faced pace and swing bowling of such quality. What is more, he made him attach a grille to his helmet for the first time. Not even the West Indian fast bowlers had been able to do that. And this on Pakistani pitches, under a gruelling sun.

An astonishing number of Waqar's wickets have been clean bowled or have come from leg-before decisions, for his strength lies in a deadly combination of explosive pace and late swing, with which he has regularly been able to shatter the stumps or bruise the toes of apparently well-established batsmen. Waqar's sudden dismissal of Graeme Hick at Worcester last summer with one of his specials, an in-swinging yorker, was particularly memorable for Hick, just five runs away from 150, was well and truly set fair. No modern bowler can have relied on the pitch less for help, and few have been as capable of changing the course of a game in a handful of overs. He took his wickets in 1991 despite generally slow pitches at The Oval, and despite the fact that county batsmen had been alerted to his most potent deliveries after encountering him in 1990, his first season. Surrey have long since been grateful for Ian Greig's haste in signing Waqar after a solitary net and a fulsome recommendation from Imran Khan.

Bounding in on a fast, long run, reminiscent of Malcolm Marshall in his pomp, Waqar is an immensely physical bowler. There is about him the aggression of an impassioned warrior. At delivery he jumps high, and pulling his arm through rather in the manner of Andy Roberts, he hurls himself at the batsman, often finishing his follow-through just yards from his enemy and still breathing fire. However, Waqar is by temperament more docile than his Antiguan predecessor, besides which he is young yet and unversed in the subtleties of psychological warfare. Apart from pace and swing, his greatest assets are his stamina and a flexibility of body which allows him to bowl his fastest from the first delivery of every spell, no matter what the time of day or how many overs he has already bowled.

In his early overs he concentrates on an out-swinger delivered to a full length and interspersed only occasionally with bumpers, a weapon used solely as a reminder to batsmen not to plunge too glibly forward. Because he pitches to such a full length and bowls to an unrelentingly attacking field, Waqar can in his full spell be expensive, for he invites batsmen to drive, wanting wickets not maidens. Nor is his bowling yet mechanical. Rather it is raw, though never vulgar, and he searches constantly for the extremity of what he can do. Accordingly, he is sometimes inaccurate.

If wickets do not fall in this first spell, and occasionally they do not, his captain will rest him. But if batsmen do capitulate, Waqar will want to carry on, for he is strong and willing, and inclined to the fervour of a prep school bowler who regards giving lesser fry a chance as an indication of weakness. Conservation of energy is not for him, and nor is he reluctant to bowl to great batsmen; quite the contrary in both cases. But his later spells can be just as effective; more so even, for he finds control easier with the old ball and swings it even more, much to the consternation of Occidental batsmen, who whisper about Oriental tricks. In Pakistan, it is rumoured, bowlers have been taught to interfere with the ball by roughing up one side with bottle tops and the like, a tactic which produces prodigious swing confusingly against the shine. For a time Waqar's ability to bowl searing in-swingers with a decrepit ball was thought to be due to this ruse. Umpires were on their guard in 1991 and ball checks were a regular occurrence at The Oval and elsewhere. Notwithstanding these, Waqar ran amok once more, silencing those critics and proving that he relied on such dubious tactics less, not more, than anybody else.

Beyond doubt Waqar is an outstanding bowler, probably the finest to emerge from Pakistan since Fazal Mahmood. And yet his emergence owed something to chance, for though he was born in Burewala in the Vehari area of the Punjab, breeding ground of so many courageous fighters, on November 16, 1971, he was raised in Sharjah, where his father was a contract worker. Returning to Pakistan in his adolescence, Waqar played in obscurity until, in 1988, he was noticed by Imran Khan while bowling in a televised local knockout game. As fate would have it, the Pakistan captain was convalescing in his bed in Lahore and had turned on his television set to while away a few hours. Watching this vibrant if erratic pace bowler and immediately detecting talent, Imran saw in him the means of meeting Pakistan's need for a fast bowler to support Wasim Akram. He took the 17-year-old under his wing, and played him in Sharjah and in the Nehru Cup in 1989–90 before giving him his Test debut against India. He also included him in the team for Australia, where his surging pace made an impression.

Imran refined Waqar's run and action, taught him the fundamentals of swing, and so unleashed on the cricket world a bowler of exuberance and danger. A buzz spreads around the ground as Waqar removes his sweater, and a silence descends as he begins his charges to the crease. This is a bowler of brilliance and élan, a bowler as entertaining in his way as any batsman, as enthralling as any spinner, a bowler who could become, as Imran predicted, the greatest of them all.

A photograph of Waqar Younis and Wasim Akram appears on page 547.

WASIM AKRAM
Derek Hodgson, *Five Cricketers of the Year*, 1993

Whatever the controversy surrounding their methods [the 1993 *Wisden* carried an article by Jack Bannister on alleged ball-tampering by Pakistan], there is no question that in 1992 Wasim Akram and Waqar Younis were the most successful cricketers in the world. Opening the bowling for Pakistan, they had a variety and aggression that made them as potent a pair as the game has seen.

In the Test series in England, Wasim took 21 wickets in four Tests. In the other tour matches he was even more devastating and finished with 82 first-class wickets in all at 16.21 each. He had already made his name as a batsman of sometimes astonishing power. In January 1993 he was suddenly appointed to succeed Javed Miandad as Pakistan's captain, with Waqar as his deputy. Few cricketers were so obviously destined for the game's aristocracy, but his elevation came even sooner than his admirers had expected. As captain he will be recognised more clearly and more widely as head of state than whichever general or politician holds the nominal office in Islamabad.

None of this was obvious in his boyhood. Wasim Akram was born in Lahore on June 3, 1966, to a moderately affluent middle-class family, in which his father was mostly concerned with his son's happiness rather than his success. His mother was the more ambitious for him, but her thoughts hardly embraced professional sport. They sent him to the fee-paying Cathedral School in Lahore, where all the lessons, other than Urdu, were conducted in English. In the tradition of the English public school, the Cathedral's scholars were expected to play games. Wasim, dreaming of the feats of Zaheer Abbas, Asif Iqbal and Mushtaq Mohammad, needed no urging to play cricket.

At 12 he was opening the bowling and batting for the school team. At 15 he was captain, his whole life consumed by cricket, at school, in nets at home, in the garage with his brother, and in street games played with a tennis ball. These matches were played of an evening in the lanes of old Lahore. As many as ten or more teams would compete in a tournament, each side contributing an entry fee, the eventual winners scooping the pool. It was fast, intensely competitive, as much a test of eyesight, reactions and stamina as ability. Wasim was so outstanding that local clubs took notice. When he took four wickets for Ludhiana against Lahore Gymkhana, including those of Ramiz Raja and Intikhab, he won nomination to the talent camp, a summer examination of Lahore's best 100 young players, promoted by the Pakistan board.

He was then 18 and his big in-swing and formidable hitting attracted attention. In his class were Ramiz Raja, Mohsin Kamal and Ijaz Ahmed, and he won further nomination to the Pakistan Under-19 camp in Karachi. There the sight of this tall, lively left-armer offering so much promise delighted Pakistan's former fast bowler, Khan Mohammad, who soon taught him to lift his arm in the delivery stride, adding pace. By sheer chance Javed Miandad, seeking practice, took a turn in the Under-19 net. He was so impressed by the youngster's ability to move the ball at speed, while retaining control, that he insisted Wasim be included in a squad of 14 for a three-day Patron's XI match against the New Zealanders at Rawalpindi. Wasim, again at Miandad's insistence, displaced the better-known Tahir Naqqash in the final selection and fewer first-class debuts have been more impressive: seven for 50 in the first innings, two more wickets in the second. His scalps included John Wright, Bruce Edgar and John Reid. In such circumstances a Pakistani newspaper's description of Wasim as a sensation was restrained. He then made his international début in a one-day match against New Zealand at Faisalabad and, only two months after his entry at Rawalpindi, he was chosen to tour New Zealand. According to Miandad, he did not even realise the Pakistan board would pay him. In his second Test, at Dunedin, he took ten for 128. It was early 1985 and he was 18 years old.

His reputation soon reached England and Lancashire began tracking him almost immediately. Advised by Imran Khan to seek experience of English conditions before Pakistan's 1987 tour, he spent a summer with Burnopfield in the Durham League, where he remembers a tiny, freezing flat, wet grounds, and playing on in the rain. Wasim signed an unparalleled six-year contract for Lancashire, in secret, on the first night of the 1987 tour. He burst on English cricket the following summer with a maiden first-class century in his second Championship match, against Somerset, and a performance of Sobers-like proportions against Surrey at Southport. There he took five for 15 including a hat-trick, made a half-century in the first innings and then, with Lancashire struggling, scored 98 off 78 balls. The scores were level when he was last man out, caught on the boundary.

In conversation later that summer he emphasised the point made by so many overseas professionals: "You try to play too much first-class cricket. You sacrifice quality for quantity." Wasim expressed himself much more happily in the one-day competitions where he became, probably, the most feared opponent, able to turn a one-day game, with bat or ball, in two or three overs. Championship cricket, on Old

Trafford's improving square, he found to be frustrating, culminating in an outburst in 1991 that led to an umpires' report and a £1,000 fine by the county club. For weeks there were rumours, as Wasim struggled with a recurring groin strain, that he would not return. The situation was resolved by a new contract that may have made Wasim the world's best-paid cricketer until, that is, Surrey came to settle with Waqar.

ANGUS FRASER
Mike Selvey, *Five Cricketers of the Year*, 1996

It is a sight as familiar now as once was Trueman's surge, Botham's bull-charge or Willis's manic flapping. Angus Fraser's trundle begins with a shuffle, and gathers momentum as he picks up his size thirteens and leans forward like a trawlerman breasting a brisk nor'easter. It is all rather inelegant and unathletic: a man trampling through a nettle-bed pursued by a swarm of bees. This is only the prelude, though. He hits the crease with the minimum of elevation, and his delivery stride – short by any standard, let alone a man approaching six and a half feet – scarcely spans the width of the crease. There is no resistance in his action and he bowls through his run rather than setting himself. Nor does he bend his back.

Not much for the purist so far. But now something happens. His front arm reaches out and inscribes an imaginary line to a point just outside the batsman's off stump, tugging his bowling arm after it in a replica arc so high that his knuckles could snag on the clouds and pull them down. Unencumbered by being yanked out of plane, the ball can only follow the line. The geometry of it all is simple, and the result predictable, but it is a gift given to few.

Fraser deals in parsimony and red-faced effort. He is perennially grumpy, kicks savage lumps from the turf at a conceded leg-bye, and could murder a misfielder: the opposite to the millionaire spendthrifts who buy their wickets with boundaries. Somewhere, he believes, he can always get a cheaper deal. Runs are a commodity to be hoarded, not frittered away on the undeserving. This is Scrooge in flannels. Batsmen? Bah! Humbug! There is a rationale here, though: he can dart and jag the ball around with the best of them on a sappy pitch, but when the going is tough and others do not want to know, he has another, more torturing, weapon: length and line. Throttle the lifeblood supply of runs with a garotte of accuracy and patience and you create anxiety, he will say. And where that exists so do wickets.

Angus Robert Charles Fraser was born on August 8, 1965, in Billinge, Lancashire, rugby league country, but the family came south when he was two, before his brother Alastair was born. Both went to play cricket for Stanmore and Middlesex. Alastair did not quite make the grade in county cricket. His brother is, as a succession of leaders will confirm, a captain's dream. Ever since he found his way, belatedly, into the England side at Edgbaston in 1989 and announced himself by bowling Steve Waugh at a time when the batsman was beginning to appear invincible, he has given control. Sometimes the deeds are unsung, not obvious to anyone except those in the game itself. On other occasions they manifest themselves gloriously. At Jamaica in 1990, when Gordon Greenidge and Desmond Haynes were threatening to destroy English morale terminally on the first morning of the series, it was Fraser, in only his fourth Test, who first of all held them in check and then tore them out with a spell of five for six. England won famously. Then four years on, he conjured figures of eight for 75 from the Bridgetown pitch when all around were wilting. England won again.

And yet the fates have conspired against him almost as much as his expression suggests. From his debut until the end of the 1995 season, England played a total of 65 Tests but Fraser took the field in just 29. Injury has played a large part, not least the debilitating hip ailment that manifested itself in Melbourne over Christmas of 1990, and which took two frustrating years from his cricket life. He missed 24 consecutive Tests, although when he did return for the final match of the 1993 Ashes series his match figures of eight for 131 helped bring England a consolation win at the end of a trying summer.

More mystifying, however, has been the reluctance of selectors to recognise his virtues as a thoroughbred Test match bowler, mistaking his downcast demeanour – Eeyore without the *joie de vivre* – for lack of spark. In particular, Ray Illingworth's decision not to include him in the party to Australia in 1994–95 amounted to nothing less than a dereliction of the chairman's duty. He had, said Illingworth, not bowled well in county matches. The Australians could scarcely contain their delight and pummelled England mercilessly in the first two Tests until injury to others and circumstance demanded Fraser's recall to the team. He promptly all but bowled England to victory in Sydney.

Fraser only learned of his original omission when the side was announced on the television. The captain, Mike Atherton – who, possibly through embarrassment, had not contacted Fraser prior to the announcement – confessed only to disappointment, but it carried the flavour of hospital bulletins which describe the condition of multiple fracture patients as comfortable. For his part, Fraser admits he was devastated. "I was just so disappointed at the way it was done," he says. "Playing for England means such a lot and if people treat you like that it makes it seem like it's not such a big deal after all." Even then, the lesson was not heeded. At Headingley, for the first Test of the West Indies series, Fraser was in the squad but left out on the morning of the match. Rudderless, England were pulverised. Fraser returned next match to take five for 66 in the win at Lord's.

There may not be much left now and the best has undoubtedly gone. The hip injury blunted the edge, anyone can see that. But he has still been too good, too rare a commodity, too wholeheartedly English to ignore. And for all his talent, his confidence has been dented and his pride hurt. "All along," he says, "I feel people have been doubting me. I'm proving myself all the time. Mostly I feel that I have to prove myself more than anyone else. It's a bit sad."

Glenn McGrath

Bruce Wilson, *Five Cricketers of the Year*, 1998

Friends who were there recall a day last year, deep in the Queensland bush "out the back of Longreach", on a pig-shooting weekend with the man they call "Pigeon" and the cricketing world knows as Glenn McGrath. The tall fast bowler had spotted a large boar, and he disappeared into the bush in hot pursuit. Three shots were heard, and McGrath came loping back into view, reached into the four-wheel drive, said "Out of ammo," and loped off again, all, at the same relentless, steady pace. He got the pig. It is a story many who have played against him will recognise uneasily; wild boar or batsman, Glenn McGrath tends to get what he is hunting.

He was demonstrably the best quick bowler on either side in the Ashes series of 1997 and, but for the presence of one Shane Warne, could claim to be the best bowler of all; indeed, it is a claim he might make anyway, if he were a different kind of man. To do so, though would be "big-noting" and, where McGrath comes from, there are few greater sins.

Glenn Donald McGrath was born on February 9, 1970, in Dubbo, New South Wales, first of three children of Kevin and Beverly. He carries on the great Australian bush cricketing litany, most famously represented by Sir Donald Bradman, and movingly depicted in Sir Russell Drysdale's painting of two bush kids playing against a stone wall in the sombre ochre of the Australian outback. Dubbo is a wheat and sheep farming centre a couple of hundred miles north-west of Sydney, not quite the real bush, but McGrath's father farmed in a succession of tiny settlements outside Dubbo with names smelling of gum-leaves: Eumungerie, Galgandra, Narromine. It was at the last that the young Glenn went to primary and high school, and where he started to play cricket.

McGrath recalls that there was only one turf wicket available; concrete was more usual. He was on the fringe of the game, and says that he only started to take the sport seriously when he was about 15. His captain in the local club side "thought I couldn't bowl". The captain's name is Shane Horsborough and, says McGrath, "he

Horizontal hold: an airborne Glenn McGrath catches Michael Vaughan at Adelaide in 2002. McGrath is rather better known for his metronomic fast-medium bowling, which had brought him 542 Test wickets by mid-2006.

still reckons I can't bowl". You get very little chance to become big-headed in the Australian bush. Still, someone thought he could bowl because, at 17, he was picked in the NSW Country Cup. It was then he was spotted by various good judges, above all Doug Walters. At 19, at Walters's instigation, McGrath moved to Sydney and the Sutherland club. Odd jobs and living in a caravan followed, and four seasons of weekend cricket, until, in January 1993, he was selected for New South Wales against Tasmania. He took five for 79, and was away. By November, he was playing his first Test, against New Zealand at Perth: three wickets for quite a lot.

Since then, he has become Australia's strike bowler, with Warne. At the end of 1997, McGrath had 164 wickets at the remarkable average of 23.43 from 36 Tests. It is a figure very close to the man upon whom McGrath has based his career, Dennis Lillee, whose 355 Test wickets came at 23.92. Of those Australians who have 100 or more Test wickets, the only quicks with better averages than McGrath are Lindwall, Miller and Davidson. In four series completed in 1997, McGrath took 82 wickets: 26 at 17.42 in five home Tests against West Indies; 13 at 22.23 in three against South Africa away; 36 at 19.47 against England in the Ashes series; and seven at 18.28 in one Test against New Zealand before he was injured.

He arrived in May with a huge reputation, especially after his feats against West Indies, when he had considerably better figures than Ambrose, Walsh and Bishop. Yet, after the First Test at Edgbaston and England's famous win, people were asking what all the fuss was about. McGrath's match figures of two for 149 were a fair indication of how he bowled. He failed to understand the nature of that wicket and what needed to be done on it. But he learned, as all the good ones do, very quickly. On a wicket made for line-and-length fast bowling at Lord's, McGrath had eight of 38 in England's humiliating first innings. The question "Who is this Glenn McGrath anyway?" had been roundly answered. He was integral to Australia's wins in the Third and Fifth Tests, and took seven for 76 in the first innings of a losing cause at The Oval. He was the only Australian quick to play in all six Tests. He had Mike Atherton's number, in particular, dismissing him seven times. Atherton, in fact, was McGrath's 150th Test wicket, at The Oval.

There is a thousand-dollar bet in the Australian dressing-room about whether McGrath will make a first-class fifty – ever. Yet he practises his batting with the same purpose he puts into dismissing batsmen or killing wild boars. So far his best attempt is 24. But if determination is going to count, the wise money would be on McGrath. He is a fine outfielder and, if he has a flaw, it is his apparently unstoppable habit of sledging opponents. It is odd, really, because off the field he is a quiet, modest man. He has the odd extravagance: he recently purchased 30,000 acres of wild bush in western New South Wales where he can go to be alone with his mates. Good news for them; tough on the pigs.

DARREN GOUGH　　　　　　　　Matthew Engel, *Five Cricketers of the Year*, 1999

There are two different England teams these days. This is nothing to do with the increasingly disparate Test and one-day sides, because the difference affects them both. One lot is the downbeat, fatalistic crew who have become all too familiar:

heads bowed, expecting the worst. The other is seen when Darren Gough is fit and firing. At Old Trafford against New Zealand in 1994, Gough made one of the most sensational Test debuts of modern times. He took a wicket in his first over and had figures of four for 47. Earlier, he had gone out and hit a rousing 65, with ten fours. He was 23 years old. Everyone yelled "New Botham", which was not a Yorkshire mining village but already a cliché, and later a rather sad joke.

That winter, with England having been humiliated in the Melbourne Test, they went to Sydney looking hopeless. One young man took the game by the scruff. England 309 (Gough 51, and a thrilling 51 at that). Australia 116 all out (Gough six for 49). The Test was not quite won, but its hero was suddenly the hottest property in English sport. He was young, good-looking, an authentic Yorkshireman with that air of sleeves-up defiance which the nation adores. Vast wealth as well as glory looked a certainty. But Gough had felt pain in his left foot even while the cheers were echoing. He ignored it. In a one-day international a few days later, he broke down and went home with his foot in plaster. It took four years to recapture that exuberance, in which time his career veered between wretched injuries and fated comebacks. His batting form went to pieces. And at the start of England's next Ashes tour, he became the sort of bowler everyone drops catches off, which was never Botham's fate. He was a star who twinkled rather than blazed.

And yet the omens of 1994 have been proved right. And in 1998 he delivered. At Headingley, with his home crowd roaring him on, he ripped through South Africa's second innings to settle the series: six for 42 – three of them in a dramatic opening burst. Then he was at the heart of England's epic win in Melbourne before starting 1999 with a hat-trick in the Sydney Test. In any case, Gough's contribution to the team cannot merely be computed. He is an inspirational cricketer in an uninspiring era. And his successes make the Tests he has missed even more poignant.

Darren Gough was born at Barnsley on September 18, 1970. No town in cricket has such a rich tradition of character and characters: Geoffrey Boycott, Dickie Bird, Michael Parkinson. Gough was not born straight into the tradition. His father, a pest control officer, was a sports fan rather than a performer. But young Darren quickly established himself as a breathtakingly good sportsman and, at school, was captain of football, rugby and athletics as well as cricket.

Football came first, and was the centre of Gough's early ambitions as he went through the Barnsley FC youth system and then became a government-funded trainee at Rotherham United. He was a midfielder – "stylish", he insists – modelling himself on Glenn Hoddle, and dreaming of a transfer to Tottenham. It never happened. "It was a time when football was all about quick runners, and I wasn't good enough." But then came another traineeship: this time with Yorkshire. And the club thought enough of him to give him a go in the first team right at the start of the 1989 season. The side travelled from Leeds to Lord's by train. Darren's dad took him to the station; David Bairstow, the captain, gave the lad, just 18, a big bearhug and promised Dad he would look after him. Pressure can override promises. Gough had to bowl 13 consecutive overs in the second innings. He ended up injured, and played only once more all season.

As seems to be Gough's fate, fulfilment came slower than expected. He remained a member of the first-team squad, considered too valuable to be wasted much in the Second XI, but he was not getting enough chances to be kept happy. At the start of 1993, he thought he would give it one more season before thinking about another county. Then the opportunities came, and he grabbed them: 57 first-class wickets that season, followed by an A tour to South Africa, and his Test debut. But the glory was transient. He played again in 1995 when not quite ready. For a while, he ceased to be a certain choice, and was ignored (mysteriously) through the summer of 1996. In 1997, he began to feel pains in his left leg and was forced to pull out of the West Indies tour. When he reappeared, at Edgbaston, he broke a finger.

But the selectors knew now how much they wanted him: David Graveney, the chairman, called him the pulse of the team. And when Gough came back into the South Africa series, so did England. His bowling was highly skilled by now. Though he could not match Allan Donald on the speedometer, he was consistently quicker than anyone else, and was able to offer just about every other weapon in the fast bowling armoury as well – with the possible exception of really telling bounce. Pace bowlers like Gough who are not six-footers tend to produce deliveries that skid rather than leap. Above all, though, in a team of brooders and worriers, he stood out for his bullish enthusiasm. England need Darren Gough, and not just for his wickets.

SHAUN POLLOCK
Neil Manthorp, *Five Cricketers of the Year, 2003*

Shaun Pollock has not had an outstanding year. He has had seven. Sport's Holy Grail is consistency, and Pollock found it as soon as he entered international cricket. His bowling is as straight, tight and incisive as Glenn McGrath's, and he is also an elegant, sometimes explosive batsman. And all this consistency was sustained through the daunting business of succeeding Hansie Cronje as South Africa's captain. Few players in history had as much to live up to as Shaun Maclean Pollock, born in Port Elizabeth on July 16, 1973. Father-son combinations at first-class and even Test level are not uncommon, but in most cases one or other is a fringe player. Shaun's family was already among cricket's two or three richest gene pools. His uncle Graeme was one of the greatest batsmen ever, and his father Peter was one of South Africa's finest fast bowlers. The young Shaun shouldn't have had a chance, especially with a shock of red hair making him stand out even further.

His childhood memories are understandably mixed. "It wasn't easy being a Pollock at school. I remember a lot of suspicion every time I was selected – people would say 'it's only because of his name' and then I'd have to play twice as well as everyone else just to justify my place." But selected he was, year after year through the ranks of junior school, high school, university and then his province, KwaZulu-Natal. In South Africa the annual Schools Week has always been seen as an avenue to the national side and when Shaun was chosen for that too, in 1991, people finally sat up and took serious notice.

A medium-pacer with an upright action that earned him bags of wickets on Kingsmead's green, grassy pitches, as well as an uncanny ability to find the meat of the bat immediately in the middle order, Shaun was regarded as very, very useful. The truth is, however, that while he was being taken seriously, no one spoke of him as an international prospect. The season after his debut, in 1992–93, Natal signed Malcolm Marshall as overseas professional. It was to be the making of Pollock. "He was my mentor," Pollock says with deep affection. "Everything I've learned about bowling since then has just been a refinement of something he taught me."

Perhaps Pollock's finest achievement as captain of South Africa was to secure a 2–1 series victory on their first full tour of the West Indies in 2000–01. Although Marshall died before the tour, his influence was crucial. "I was desperately keen to see his resting place in Barbados. I wanted to bowl on the wickets he bowled on, to meet the people he spent time with and to see where he grew up. Sadly I had to pay tribute to his grave rather than have dinner with him."

One of Pollock's assets is the position from which he delivers the ball – tall and upright, and so close to the stumps that he often dislodges a bail. The height exacerbates any bounce in the pitch while the gunbarrel-straight, wicket-to-wicket approach means that even the slightest seam movement can be fatal. His pace has undoubtedly dropped in recent years. But his economy-rate has become even more parsimonious and his career average remains phenomenal, at under 21.

He does tend to be referred to as a bowler, because he is so good at it, but the figures are unmistakably those of an all-rounder. By January 2003, he had a batting average of 33.45 with two Test centuries and 278 wickets at an average of 20.71. Ian Botham averaged 33 with the bat and 28 with the ball. Pollock had also worked hard to earn a coveted place in the slip cordon, a precious prize for the man more often than not bowling the most overs in the innings.

Spinners

DEREK UNDERWOOD

Doug Ibbotson, *1988*

The full significance of Derek Underwood's retirement from first-class cricket will not properly be manifest until four o'clock, or thereabouts, on the last day of a moribund Championship match at Canterbury. Tardyshire, batting as only they can when challenged to score more than four runs an over, will be entrenched at 116 for three, many of the faithful will be departing for evensong, and seasoned correspondents will have advised their sports editors that the inevitable draw warrants no more than a brief litany.

Doubtless they will be right. Whereas, in the foregoing 25 years, the remarkable Derek Leslie Underwood frequently proved them wrong. For, in his capacity and determination to take, rather than buy, wickets on an unresponsive pitch, Underwood was a rare bird among spin bowlers. Whereas, against the average slow bowler, batsmen were principally alert to the prospect of punishing loose balls, when facing Underwood they steeled themselves against the unexpected – often to discover that, when it came, neither temperament nor technique was adequate. Not the least of their problems was that Underwood was not strictly a slow bowler in the traditional sense.

And so it would come to pass, shortly after the tea interval, with the match on its sick-bed and polite adjectives thin on the ground, that Underwood would peel off his sweater, trudge out his flat-footed run-up and wheel in to bowl. Alas, to elder statesmen deck-chair deep in disconsolation, it was not an edifying sight: the approach too long, the delivery too flat. Yet, even as they hurrumphed to the heavens in the name of Alfred Percy Freeman, Underwood's unique talents were at work. The obdurate batsman pushes forward and is caught off the handle. He takes his leave, a sadder – though little wiser – man, to be replaced by another who, already impregnated with doubt, dithers, dabbles and departs. The encircling vultures resettle and Underwood toils on until, at 6.15 in the final over, the last wicket falls and Kent win by 78 runs: Underwood six for 48.

In this typical scenario lay the real mark of a master bowler; a measure of the professionalism too often overlooked when, in league with a spiteful pitch, Underwood became virtually unplayable. Canterbury, 1984, and during the Championship match against Hampshire, overnight rain crept under the covers and lay brooding on a length. Those who had played and watched cricket only in recent years had never seen Underwood, or anyone else, bowl on a sticky patch. They were in for a salutary 90 minutes. So ruthlessly did Underwood exploit the conditions that, in 11.2 overs, he claimed seven wickets for 21 runs as Hampshire collapsed to summary defeat. An easy haul? Comparatively speaking, yes. But, in the high summer and autumn of his professional career, such heaven-sent wickets had become a rare luxury. One would guess, in fact, that during a long and illustrious campaign, for each wicket plucked from a helpful pitch, Underwood quarried 50 from solid rock by the sweat of his brow and sheer tenacity of purpose.

Ironically, then, during the burgeoning maturity of his career the game's administrators, in their questionable wisdom, conspired to ensure that pitches should become as rock-like as possible; that, notwithstanding the odd, mischievous covers, they should remain dry and faithful to a new breed of batsmen who expected – nay demanded – that the ball maintain a line of such predictability that it may be cross-batted, almost with impunity, to all parts.

The declared object of the exercise was both mis-begotten and unsuccessful in that, far from providing maximum entertainment for the public (who were said to be interested only in positive results), it reduced the average Championship fixture to a two-and-a-half day bore between sides incapable of forcing a victory – followed by a limited-overs accommodation neither was prepared to lose. Under such circumstances Underwood's faculty for confounding the system was even more remarkable.

There was especial irony, therefore, when in his last season pitches were reopened to the elements. Those among us who rejoiced scanned the sullen skies and smiled in anticipation of a rich Underwood harvest. Where, after all, were the batsmen with the technique to deal with the spinning ball on a steaming pitch? In the event it transpired that the turf technicians had done their work too well. Rain it certainly did, but pitches so rigorously tailored for batsmen produced not the anticipated sticky dog but rather the Plasticine pup on to which the bowler might as well lob a ball of wool. So Underwood was back to the hard graft: 611 overs and 45 wickets at 28.77 runs apiece. No mean performance, but neither an outstanding conclusion to a career during which, in his first season, he took 100 wickets – at 18, the youngest player to do so – and repeated the feat nine times. Such are the bald statistics that all too often dominate the archives of achievement. Certainly they cannot be ignored. Underwood, D. L. – 86 Tests: First, West Indies 1966; Last, Sri Lanka 1982. Test wickets, 297; average 25.83. Best performance, against Pakistan at Lord's in 1974 – five for 20 in the first innings; eight for 51 in the second.

Most memorable, perhaps, was his match-winning seven for 50 at The Oval to square the 1968 series against Australia. Here was the young Underwood in his element. Torrential rain in the morning flooded the outfield, scores of volunteers joined the groundstaff in mopping up, and so began an agonising race against time that ended with five minutes to spare as the England spinner took his fourth wicket in 27 balls. A splendid statistic but, in perusing the Underwood curriculum vitae, it is equally pertinent to consider his analysis for the first innings of that same match – played on a pitch which yielded 494 runs for England and 324 for Australia. Underwood claimed only two wickets but, in so doing, conceded fewer than 1.7 runs for each of his 54 overs; a degree of economy, not to mention stamina, that seldom deserted him.

Facts and figures produce scope, for those so disposed, to speculate. What had he not forfeited two years of his Test career by defecting to World Series Cricket in

1977? Suppose he had not, in 1981, been banned from the international arena following an unauthorised tour of South Africa? Certainly he might have retired as the most prolific wicket-taker in Test history, which would have meant a great deal to archivists and doubtless something to Underwood himself. But if one respects individuality, honestly pursued, a generous sporting spirit and professional skill, unstintingly applied, then some may consider that many of Underwood's finest hours were spent in settings some way removed from the Ovals of Kennington or Adelaide.

He will be well remembered, albeit with somewhat grudging affection, at Bournemouth where, amid the sylvan charm of Dean Park, he invariably undid Hampshire. Likewise at Hastings where, in June 1964, he achieved a career-best bowling analysis of nine for 28 and, 20 years later, hit his maiden and only century.

Underwood's batting, like his bowling, though not a thing of beauty, was rich in intent. Essentially fundamental in style, it relied on three basic strokes; the dogged forward thrust, the square, hunch-shouldered punch to the off, and the squat, short-arm pull between square leg and mid-wicket. It was a method which served Underwood well enough over the years, not least in scoring an unbeaten 45 against Lawry's Australians at Leeds in 1968. Even so, it was stretching credibility too far to imagine that, in his 40th year and at best a paid-up member of the night-watchmen's union, Underwood could coax, from such a limited repertoire, a first-class century.

Yet he did; nudge by nudge, stab by stab, scrambling between wickets in those Chaplinesque boots. And one suspects that, not until he stumbled into the 90s, was Underwood motivated by anything other than the responsibility of doing a job for his side to the utmost of his ability. Afterwards, of course, it was different. The unconfined delight as he acknowledged the congratulatory toasts of his peers was a joy to behold and to cherish – something that cannot be expressed in a mere statistic. So it was in everything Underwood approached; he took pleasure in his craft but placed craft above all.

Is he replaceable – if indeed there is to be encouragement in a changing game for bowlers of his ilk? Unless the TCCB decrees that, in future, all pitches are to be of rolled steel, the *fourth* day of a Championship match must offer rewards for even the most modest flipper. Specialists such as Emburey, Hemmings, Marks and Gifford will undoubtedly enjoy a brisk trade. But what happens at the St Lawrence when Somerset sit on the splice? To whom do they turn at The Mote when Middlesex mount a rearguard action? No doubt the chaps in the deck-chairs will tell them.

JOHN EMBUREY   John Thicknesse, *Five Cricketers of the Year*, 1984

A bowler's first experience of taking 100 wickets in a season would normally be cause for unqualified delight. But great as was John Ernest Emburey's satisfaction in fulfilling that ambition, he would happily have traded it for the 17 extra points that would have enabled Middlesex to retain the County Championship. And with the possible exception of John Lever, whose wickets for Essex were taken at the breakneck speed of one every five and a half overs, no player in either of the top two teams contributed more than Middlesex's 6ft 2in off-spinning all-rounder.

One of their four ever-presents by dint of his England suspension, he not only took 96 wickets in the Championship and scored 772 runs, but as acting-captain in eight games, while Mike Gatting was away, he led the side to five of their 11 victories, four of them successively during the World Cup. Though he had a number of outstanding games, notably against Leicestershire at Lord's (match figures of eight for 22 in 21.2 overs and scores of 47 and 73 not out), the keynote of his season was consistency. Only once did he take more than five wickets in an innings – six for 13 against Kent at Dartford. But on 18 other occasions he took three or more, and but for a combination of wet weather and unhelpful pitches in the last four matches, when in common with his fellow-spinner, Phil Edmonds, he had to be content with seven costly wickets, he could be counted on for an analysis that would have won Middlesex an extra vital victory.

Though he relies less on variations of flight than most great off-spinners, Emburey's high arm, poise in the delivery stride, and extreme closeness to the stumps when he lets the ball go, make him in other respects a classic bowler of his type. A big spinner when conditions call for it, his wicket-to-wicket line of flight, allied to steady length and drift from leg to off, earn him many successes, either bowled off-stump or caught at slip or at the wicket, against batsmen playing for the ball to turn. His habit of hugging the stumps is a valuable asset. But from time to time he plants his front foot so far across – outside off-stump at the non-striker's end – that it lets him down by obscuring the umpire's view for an lbw decision. Let batsmen be warned, however: he was working on the fault for Western Province in South Africa last winter.

Mike Gunton, Emburey's cricket master at Peckham Manor School in South London, was the first influence on his bowling, when at the age of eleven he changed him from a medium-pacer (he once took eight for 8) into an off-spinner. But as a youngster on Middlesex's staff, his main influence was Fred Titmus. "To start with, I just learned from watching him: it wasn't his way to press opinions on young players," remembers Emburey. "But he wasn't backward when I did approach him – he hardly drew breath! The best advice he gave me was: 'Just keep it tight – eventually they'll get themselves out.' Fred used the air a lot himself – I was amazed how slowly he bowled when we played together in a benefit game a year or two ago – but it's because of that advice that I tend to bowl flatter than most off-spinners."

Emburey has mixed feelings about the venture to South Africa in 1982. "The obvious attraction was a lump sum in the bank; but I'd have thought twice about going if I'd known the ban would last three years – that stunned all of us. Assuming I would have been chosen for England's tours, and played my share of Tests at home, I have lost financially. I missed playing very much in 1982, but last year I was resigned to it. The only times I missed it then were when England were struggling and I thought I might have helped."

SHANE WARNE

Greg Baum, *Five Cricketers of the Century*, 2000

There are three elements to Shane Warne's greatness – skill, novelty and drama – and all were manifest in the one great delivery that made his name, at Old Trafford in 1993. The delivery was exceptionally skilful. It began its flight innocently so as to lull Mike Gatting, drifted to leg, pitched in the batsman's blind spot, then rounded on him fiercely and bent back off stump. It was at once pinpoint in its accuracy and prodigious in its spin, qualities that had always been thought to be irreconcilable. Later that summer, John Woodcock would write that it was doubtful if there had ever been a bowler who could aim the ball as precisely and turn it as far as Warne. This is a sentiment that has echoed down the seasons.

The delivery was something different. West Indies and their battery of pace bowlers had set the agency for 20 years; spin, particularly wrist-spin, had become nearly defunct, but suddenly here it was again in more irresistible form than ever before. Most of all, the Gatting ball was not just early in his spell, but his very first delivery – in the match, in the series, in Ashes cricket. That gave the ball a sense of theatre, and Warne a name for showmanship, that has grown at each new threshold of his startling career, and at its peak made him nearly mystical. In the modern era, only Ian Botham could compare.

The triumph of Shane Keith Warne is of the rarest kind, of both substance and style together. At his best, he has the ruthlessness of a clinician and the flourish of a performer, and his bowling is simultaneously a technical and dramatic masterpiece. It was not enough for him to take a hat-trick; it had to be in an Ashes Test on the MCG. It was not enough for him to take 300 wickets; the 300th had to be accompanied by lightning and apocalyptic thunderclaps at the climax of another consummate and match-winning performance against South Africa at the SCG.

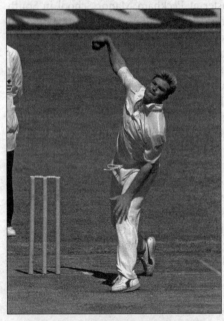

Leg-break? Googly? Top-spinner? Zooter? Shane Warne, the best leg-spinner of all time and one of *Wisden's* Five Cricketers of the Century in 2000, on the attack against South Africa at Cape Town in 1994.

Thus in 1993 a theme was established for Warne's career: extraordinary performances, extraordinary production values. He was the cricketer of and for his times. Australia's finest moments, but also their worst, their most controversial, most splendid, most dramatic, most sordid, have all revolved around Warne. From the wretchedness of the bookmakers' scandal to the glory of the World Cup triumph, from the agony of a one-wicket defeat in Pakistan in 1994–95 to the ecstasy of a come-from-behind Ashes win in 1997, he was always the central character. By cold statistics, Warne had not had such a profound influence on Australian cricket in his time as Dennis Lillee in his. Australia were already on the rise when Warne joined the team and, when they had their crowning moment, in the Caribbean in 1994–95, he was good, but not dominant. He takes fewer wickets per match than Lillee at a more profligate average. Moreover, Australia can and do win matches without him. But Warne's impact can never be understated. When he was first picked, cricket was under the tyranny of fast bowling and aching for another dimension. Soon enough, the world came to know that a man could take Test wickets by seduction as well as extortion.

And the legend grew, moment by moment, coup by coup, performance by performance. He made fools of good players, short work of fools. Australia's method was indestructibly simple: bat first, bowl last, win quickly. Always it was the stage that invigorated him as much as the challenge. For Victoria, who play in empty stadia, he averages more than 40. But for Australia, he is already by some margin the most successful spinner in Test history.

Physically, undoubtedly, his powers have declined, but not his hold on opponents. So it was that on the biggest stage of all, at the climax of the World Cup, at a moment when Australia looked impossibly behind, he came again. The only caveat on making him one of the cricketers of the 20th century is that he may yet figure in deliberations for the 21st.

A photograph of Shane Warne with Sir Donald Bradman and Sachin Tendulkar appears on page 1163.

ANIL KUMBLE
Scyld Berry, *Five Cricketers of the Year*, 1996

The summer of 1995 saw a pleasing contrast between international cricket and the domestic game. The Test series between England and West Indies was so dominated by pace bowlers, on both sides, that spinners took less than a tenth of the wickets. In first-class cricket, on the other hand, the two leading wicket-takers were Asian leg-spinners: Mushtaq Ahmed with 95 wickets, and Anil Kumble with 105.

Kumble thus became the first bowler to take 100 wickets since 1991; the first spinner to do so since 1983; and the first leg-spinner since 1971. But only nominally can Kumble be classified as a leg-spinner, for he does not specialise in temptations that end in a stumping, or a catch at long-off, and a deceived bat slammed against pad. He is a bowler of his own kind: a brisk top-spin bowler, making the ball turn a little both ways; tall at 6ft 2in and dangerously bouncy on a hard pitch; and as persistently accurate in finding his target as a mosquito. Not one of his 105 victims was stumped. Twenty were leg-before and 21 bowled, most of them making the mistake of thinking they had time to play back to this leg-spinner. All the rest were caught, seldom in the deep, largely by Richard Montgomerie at short leg, David Capel at slip, Rob Bailey at silly point and Kevin Curran at gully. Kumble paid tribute to them all, and to Bob Carter who conducted their practices, for fulfilling such a demanding task without previous experience of such bowling.

Over the first-class season he conceded 2.3 runs per over, and then the bat's edge was frequently the scorer: at times a whole session would pass without Kumble conceding a boundary in front of the wicket. He bowled more overs than anyone else as well, except Mushtaq; and as his Indian compatriots at Gloucestershire and Durham, Javagal Srinath and Manoj Prabhakar, were equally hard-working, together they did much to change the perception of Indian players, hitherto not renowned for their stamina, in county cricket. After the NatWest Trophy final at Lord's when Kumble turned on what he thought was his best one-day bowling of the season, Warwickshire's captain Dermot Reeve summarised the impression of all English cricket when he declared that Kumble was "a fabulous bowler".

There is only one bowler of the last generation to whom he could be compared. But as Anil Kumble was born on October 17, 1970, in Bangalore, he was too young to have studied Bhagwat Chandrasekhar and did not take him as a model. However, the conditions which prompted Chandrasekhar to bowl medium-paced top-spinners and googlies were those that governed Kumble's development. Club cricket in Bangalore is played on matting spread over baked mud (Kumble still occasionally turns out for his club, Young Cricketers), and the springy rather than fast surface can make a top-spinner bounce exceptionally. Kumble smiles at the recollection of wicket-keepers who were apprehensive about standing up to him. As in the case of Chandra, the batsman can sometimes hear the ball fizz after leaving Kumble's hand – although it is no easier to play for being audible as well as visible.

Kumble's father, a management consultant, had not played the game formally. Anil began by playing tennis ball cricket in the streets outside his house, a form of the game which has organised tournaments there. He moved on to bowl medium-pace until his conversion at 15, when for one reason or another, his elder brother Dinesh persuaded him to try leg-spin as a novelty, even in southern India. "There was no one to guide me or coach me or show me how to grip the ball," Kumble remembers. But with a long and energetic arm-swing, and powerful shoulders, he could soon make it bounce like a tennis ball.

He was rapidly selected for Karnataka Schools Under-15, then for Karnataka in 1989–90, when Chandra was in his last year as a state selector. On the 1990 tour of England he made his Test debut at Old Trafford, aged 19, as a bespectacled No. 10 (he has since shed the glasses for lenses, and his lowly status in the order, making hundreds for Karnataka). His first Test wicket was Allan Lamb, caught at silly point, which had long-term consequences. His 100th came in his 21st Test, on his home ground in Bangalore. In home Tests he often had turning pitches to bowl on, and large Tendulkar-fed totals to bowl at, but that is still a fine record: Shane Warne took two more Tests to reach his 100. His Indian captain, Mohammad Azharuddin, phoned Lamb to recommend Kumble when Northamptonshire wanted to replace Curtly Ambrose; and when the county contacted him at a Madras hotel, he accepted without even discussing terms.

Kumble's aim in undertaking county cricket was to develop his variety and to learn more about pitches, with a view to India's tour of England in 1996. This ambition he fulfilled. While he kept to his lower trajectory and faster speed for one-day matches, in the Championship he bowled more slowly than hitherto, and turned the ball sideways both further and more often, not just fizzing it through. He would bowl six googlies in an over against a left-hander. His county did their best to make Northampton's pitches as similar as possible to Bangalore.

He took 64 wickets at 16 runs apiece at Northampton, and 41 wickets at 27 elsewhere. If he sometimes had to come on before the seam bowlers had taken a wicket, he was always accurate, and calm, as native Kannada-speakers are reputed to be.

"I'm very satisfied with my season," he declared afterwards, and so were the county, who failed to win that elusive Championship through no fault of their overseas signing. Unmarried, teetotal and vegetarian, a graduate in mechanical engineering and speaking excellent English, Kumble would join in with his teammates at the bar, even if taking soft drinks. They would have him back any time he can get away from his public relations job for Triton Watches, his employers in Bangalore; and from the Test match game so dominated by seam.

A photograph of Anil Kumble in 1999 appears on page 447.

MUSHTAQ AHMED   Vic Marks, *Five Cricketers of the Year*, 1997

By taking 45 wickets in six Tests for Pakistan between November 1995 and August 1996, Mushtaq Ahmed confirmed his status as the final member – alongside Shane Warne and Anil Kumble – of a glittering triumvirate of wrist-spinners who adorn the modern game. Mushtaq is the most enchanting of the lot. Warne's success stems from prodigious spin and accuracy, Kumble's from prodigious bounce and accuracy; like superbly schooled sheepdogs, both pen batsmen down before picking them off with clinical ruthlessness. Mushtaq prefers to lure batsmen to their end in the traditional manner. He is the arch-deceiver, possessing every nefarious variation in the wrist-spinner's armoury. Unlike the others, he has a googly which is indecipherable to most international batsmen. His instincts are to outwit opponents rather than wear them down.

He is the most impetuous of the trio, which is often betrayed by the frenzied nature of his appealing. He cannot hide his exasperation when a batsman thrusts his front leg down the pitch in the pretence of playing a shot without being penalised by umpires, who are often equally bamboozled by his spin. "Sometimes," he says, "I tell the umpire a straight one is coming, so watch out" – a ploy that has yet to meet with conspicuous success. He has usually been the most expensive of the three in his headlong pursuit of wickets rather than maidens. Indeed, at Brisbane in November 1995, this profligacy led to his omission from the Test team.

Sometimes his variations were too pronounced and too frequent. When he was at Somerset in 1995, many opponents, following the advice of Martin Crowe, started to play him as an off-spinner because he impatiently bowled so many googlies. For a while his county colleagues nicknamed him "Tauseef" after the Pakistani off-spinner of the 1980s. In Australia he talked to Warne, more about the mental approach to wrist-spinning than the mechanics. Warne stressed the benefits of restricting batsmen and of preying on their frustration. Mushtaq took note.

Recalled for the two Tests in Hobart and Sydney, he gathered 18 wickets; there were ten more at Christchurch against New Zealand. But his maturity was confirmed in the three-Test series against England in the summer of 1996. He spun Pakistan to victory on the final afternoons at Lord's and The Oval. His innate competitiveness was now allied to patience, and this became clear to all at Lord's. Having bowled 48 overs since taking a wicket in England's first innings, he suddenly mesmerised the batsmen, conjuring figures of five for 11 from 57 balls between lunch and tea. On the last day at The Oval, he bowled 30 overs unchanged from the Vauxhall End to take six for 67, which he regards as his finest Test spell yet. He recognised that Mike Atherton was the key English batsman, and on both final days he dismissed him when bowling – Warne-style – from around the wicket. Once Atherton was gone, the rest of the English order was nonplussed as Mushtaq whirled out an assortment of unrecognisable deliveries. In the glow of victory, his grateful captain, Wasim Akram, proclaimed that Mushtaq was better than Warne.

MUTTIAH MURALITHARAN   Jim Holden, *Five Cricketers of the Year*, 1999

Maybe the whispers and rumours will never cease; maybe Muttiah Muralitharan will forever have to lure international batsmen to their doom with a murky cloud of suspicion over his twirling arm. It would be a shame, though – for cricket in general, and for the off-spin assassin who bewitched players and spectators alike at The Oval last summer when taking 16 for 220 to give Sri Lanka their first Test victory in England.

These remarkable figures were the fifth best of all time in Test cricket, yet Murali's cunning strategies, his marathon patience and his sporting instincts were overshadowed by controversy. David Lloyd, the England coach, made remarks on television that implicitly suggested a problem with his bowling action. It was another day, another victory, tainted. Murali's response to the doubters is emphatic. "I don't care what anyone says now," he protests, the insistence in his gentle voice as sharp as the spin he imparts on a cricket ball. "I know I am not a cheat. It has been medically proved that I am not chucking."

The eternal problem for Murali is that his action does look distinctly odd. First impressions are that he must be a chucker. The arm is bent, the wrist action is generous, to say the least. But that is nature, not nurture. The deformity in his right arm was there at birth. His three brothers, Sridaran, Sasidaran and Prabgaran, have exactly the same "bend". His wrist is also especially flexible, which means extra leverage on the ball. Yes, it may give him an advantage over other slow bowlers, but it is not an unfair one, according to the ICC, which commissioned many hours of analysis into Muralitharan's action and found that it conformed to Law 24 because his arm does not straighten.

Muttiah Muralitharan was born on April 17, 1972, in Kandy, Sri Lanka, the first of four sons for Sinnasami and Laxmi Muttiah, who still run the Lucky Land biscuit and confectionery firm in the city. It proved to be a lucky land for young Murali, whose first cricketing memories are of street and park games with other children. His formal sporting education came at St Anthony's College in Kandy.

"I started going to cricket practice at the age of eight," he recalls. "I was a medium-pacer, until the age of 13. But then the coach, Sunil Fernando, suggested I try off-spin and it seemed to work much better. One year I took 127 wickets in a schools competition, and the national selectors showed an interest." Until that time, Murali says, he had never considered the fact that he had a bent arm. It was just the way he was; but he soon discovered life and sport could never be simple again.

His progress through the Sri Lankan A team to the full international side was rapid, and he made his Test debut against Australia in August 1992. After one wicket in the first innings, he dismissed Tom Moody and Mark Waugh with successive deliveries in the second. Seven months later, Murali had his first bitter-sweet taste of triumph and trauma. He took five wickets in the match as Sri Lanka decisively defeated England in Colombo. However, as *Wisden* noted, there were murmurings about his action.

England's players were privately scathing, but refused to go public. Various umpires and match referees subsequently kept their suspicions out of the public domain too, until the dam burst on Boxing Day 1995, in the Melbourne Test against Australia. After 22 Tests, Murali was suddenly called for throwing seven times by umpire Darrell Hair. Ten days later, he was again repeatedly no-balled by umpire Ross Emerson in a one-day international. His world fell apart. "It affected everything, my friends and family, all those who believed in me," he says. "It was very cruel. Everyone was watching me for all the wrong reasons, thinking I was cheating. I wasn't." For a short time he considered quitting cricket and retreating to the family business, a life of selling candy to Kandy. Instead, with support from the Sri Lankan board, Murali decided to fight back.

Medical experts gave evidence about his bent arm, the bowling action was filmed from 27 different angles, and the ICC eventually sided with the Sri Lankan view that the problem was an optical illusion. The murmurings never ceased, but no umpire called him again until Emerson reappeared at Adelaide in January 1999. The general opinion was that the umpire discredited himself more than the bowler. What the whole process has done is give Murali an enviable mental toughness to complement his fiendish array of deliveries: the prodigious off-breaks, the occasional leg-break, the startling top-spinner that goes on yet bounces high at the batsman. It has made him an even more formidable cricketer.

Consistent success has flowed since, including the 1996 World Cup triumph, culminating in the waterfall of wickets at The Oval last summer. England captain Alec Stewart gave a gracious tribute afterwards, saying: "It was a very special performance, and clearly here is a bowler of great quality." Whatever the arguments, no one can deny that.

All-Rounders

IAN BOTHAM Norman Preston, *Notes by the Editor*, 1978

The potential of young talent was proclaimed by Ian Botham, the Somerset all-rounder. At the age of 21 he twice shook Australia by taking five for 74 on the first day at Nottingham and five for 21 when Australia were put out for 103 at Leeds. His success was particularly gratifying to me. He caught my eye first in a Gillette Cup tie in 1974 at Canterbury; he made only 19 runs but in a tight match showed his batting class with his upright style and when fifth-choice bowler, his persistent attack on the stumps sufficed to remove Cowdrey and Shepherd. In my notes the following year when writing on candidates for the future I said that I would particularly like to see young Botham given a chance while he was young and enthusiastic.

Eric Hill, *Five Cricketers of the Year*, 1978

Ian Terence Botham, aged 21, took five Australian wickets on his first day of Test Match cricket. By an apposite twist of chance, that day brought Brian Close's announcement of his retirement 28 years after his first England appearance at 19 years of age. Botham has tremendous respect for Close, his county captain, with whom he has much in common. He says "he kept me in order" and avers stridently, "we were always a better side with him there". They share a fierce determination to succeed, besides outstanding courage.

Within weeks of coming into the first-class game Botham, then 18, displayed all his qualities in an unforgettable performance at Taunton on June 12, 1974. The occasion was the Benson and Hedges quarter-final against Hampshire. Botham had bowled his medium paced outswingers, successfully, and had fielded – in any position – with his normal brilliance. However, shortly after arriving at the crease when Somerset at 113 for eight, needing 183, seemed doomed, Botham was hit full in the mouth by a bouncer from Roberts, then the quickest bowler in the game. Fiercely declining to leave the field, bleeding profusely, and eventually losing four teeth, he carried on, and hit two marvellous sixes while making 45 not out. He really won the match and the Gold Award in glory. Here indeed was a player to watch. In retrospect Botham thinks he should have come off the field, but still his abiding memories are of his two tail-end partners, Moseley and Clapp, who assisted him manfully.

Sport runs deeply in the family. His father, a regular in the Fleet Air Arm for 20 years spanning the war, played most sports, including cricket and soccer. His mother played cricket, too, and she remembers a match at Sherborne for the V. A. D. nursing service as captain in 1946 as one of her big days. Ian Terence Botham was born at Heswall in Cheshire in November 24, 1955 and the family moved to Yeovil before his third birthday.

His abundant talent and unquenchable enthusiasm for cricket and soccer took him into the school teams at Milford School and Buckler's Mead. A sports master, Mr Hibbert, gave him a sound start, while the Boys' Brigade at Yeovil – always keen to help young sportsmen – provided plenty of chances. It was a common sight to see Botham, about nine years old, haunting the Mudford Road Recreation Ground, kit at the ready, eager to get a game for any side that was short. He got into the various County Youth teams and, having worked his way to the MCC groundstaff at Lord's largely by his own efforts, began to attract much wider attention with some startling performances for the Somerset Second XI.

Two John Player matches in 1973 gave him his first taste of county cricket and the next year – a highly successful one for Somerset – brought his wonderful effort against Hampshire plus 441 runs and 30 wickets in first-class cricket. The development continued with 584 runs and 62 wickets in 1975, while, as his knowledge and application grew, 1976 brought his first superb century, 1,000 runs for the first time and 66 wickets. He was learning to harness his glorious straight hitting and square cutting, and beginning to vary his bowling techniques under the guidance of that doyen of medium pacers, Tom Cartwright. Bouncers of different paces, and a brisk in-swinging yorker added spice and batting danger to his out-swinger.

The 1977 season was marred only by a week's cricket idleness carrying the drinks at the Prudential matches, and a foot injury which ruined for him the end of the season and probably robbed him of a rare double. He finished with 88 wickets and 738 runs. Selection for the major winter Tour was largely taken as a formality and Botham (pronounced as in "both" by the family, although colleagues sound it as in "moth") was on his way.

John Woodcock, Notes by the Editor, 1986

Botham was never out of the news for long. Not since W. G. Grace can a cricketer, by his physical presence and remarkable exploits, have so caught the attention of the sporting world. Bradman's feats were, of course, more phenomenal, Sobers's more effortlessly versatile; but off the field they maintained a lower, more urbane profile than Botham. Bernard Darwin, in a vintage profile of W. G., wrote of his "schoolboy love for elementary and boisterous jokes. . . his desperate and undisguised keenness, his occasional pettishness and pettiness, his endless power of recovering his spirits" – all of which could apply equally to Botham.

No one can ever have sent the ball such huge distances as frequently as Botham did last summer. His 80 sixes, most of them hit with the full face of the bat, often over extra-cover, were a record for an English first-class season. He scored at something like a run a ball for Somerset, yet still averaged 100 for them, and in the six Test matches he took 31 Australian wickets and held eight catches, some of them quite breathtaking. Wherever he played he added substantially to the gate, and when the winter came he tested a recent operation on a knee by walking from John O'Groats to Land's End and raising over £600,000 for charity, an astonishing achievement. There was much else, not all of it quite so admirable. There are times when Botham needs to be saved from his unrestraint, as well perhaps as from those who would exploit him.

Graeme Wright, Notes by the Editor, 1987

Botham, it might be argued, is irresponsible; some wouldn't even bother to argue. But his lack of responsibility is more to himself that to his fellow man. He bats and bowls not with concern for averages or place but for the joy of playing and the stimulus of competition. He, too, is a "guerrilla fighter impatient of discipline. A devotee of action who thrives on challenge and crisis." Those are words used to describe Winston Churchill in the 1930s: a man at times as much loved or loathed as Botham has been in recent years.

Botham may not be everyone's ideal hero, but as Carlyle said, the hero can be poet, prophet, king, priest or whatever you will, according to the kind of world he finds himself born into. To a society that cries out for any extravagant gesture to alleviate the mediocrity, Botham by his deeds has indeed become a hero. In August, he presented the Leukaemia Research Fund with a cheque for £888,000 as a result of his great walk from John O'Groats to Land's End in 1985.

Botham's absence from the England side for all but the last Test match of the summer was due to his suspension by the TCCB from all first-class cricket from May 29 until July 31. His misdemeanour was bringing the game into disrepute by admitting to using cannabis (in a newspaper article on May 18), denying in the past that he had used cannabis, and making public pronouncements without the clearance of his county. The suspension was not severe; a week later four auxiliary nurses at a Nottingham hospital were dismissed for allegedly smoking cannabis when they were off-duty and not on hospital premises. Botham erred. In 1985 the TCCB had taken no action against him following his conviction for possession of the drug, and it was felt then that it had been lenient. Moreover, the board had agreed to support the Sports Council in its campaign against drug-taking, so it had not only to be responsible but be seen to be responsible.

John Woodcock, 1994

With the retirement last season, within a few weeks of each other, of Ian Botham and Vivian Richards, first-class cricket lost two of the greatest of all its stars. Botham and Richards were good companions. Brought together by cricket, they became firm enough friends to spend a part of their winters going round the halls, exchanging banter with much the same abandon as they showed on the field. They had no particular talent for the stage, I think; but their prowess as cricketers deserves to be remembered for as long as the game is played.

Ian Botham was strong, patently irrepressible and cheerfully insubordinate.

By the time Richards joined Somerset in 1974, Botham, although almost four years his junior, was already on the staff there. They made a flamboyant, ultimately ungovernable pair. After a while Somerset hardly knew what had hit them. Botham played the first of his 102 Test matches against Australia at Trent Bridge in July 1977, when he was 21. By the end of his fourth he had taken five wickets in an innings three times, made the first of his 14 Test hundreds and run out his captain, Geoffrey Boycott, because he thought he was scoring too slowly if the match, against New Zealand at Christchurch, were to be won (which, eventually, it was). Within two years and one month Botham had scored 1,000 runs and taken 100 wickets in Test matches – no one has ever done that in a shorter time – and was well on the way to becoming a sporting legend.

Botham's deeds against Australia in three successive Test matches in 1981 – at Headingley, Edgbaston and Old Trafford – were miraculous. Three times, with the Ashes in the balance, he snatched victory from the jaws of defeat. If his 118 in the Fifth Test at Old Trafford was even more stupendous than his 149 in the Third at Headingley that is only because it was more measured – and he still went from 28, when Australia took a new ball, to 100 in not much over half an hour with Dennis Lillee doing his best to stop him. Of its kind it was arguably the finest innings ever played. Not since Gilbert Jessop's 104 against Australia at The Oval in 1902 had such hitting been seen in a Test match. Jessop hit 17 fours off 76 balls; at Old Trafford Botham hit six sixes and 13 fours off 102 balls; at Headingley a six and 27 fours off 148 balls. To the man in the street Botham became an idol. He was as much of a sporting drawcard as Don Bradman had been, or Muhammad Ali. The bigger the occasion the better it suited him, except, to his chagrin, when it came to denying West Indies. In 38 innings Botham's highest score against them was 81, his average only 21. He took 61 West Indian wickets, however, including Richards's seven times.

Botham's 12 Tests as England's captain, from June 1980 to July 1981, were not among his happiest; but nine of them were against West Indies, and as Mike Brearley's counsellor-in-chief he had shown himself to be a good reader of the game. I suppose we should have known that it was asking too much of him to captain the side as well as doing so much else.

Only Allan Border, Greg Chappell and Richards have held more than Botham's 120 catches in Test cricket. The great majority of Botham's were taken at slip, where, contrary to accepted practice, he insisted upon standing only slightly crouched and with his hands on his thighs even when the ball was being delivered. Then there was the little matter of his 383 Test wickets. Not even Garfield Sobers had an all-round record much superior to Botham's.

Ian's bowling varied according to the state of his fitness. As a colt he was uninhibitedly aggressive and a brisk fast-medium. He came charging in off a longish run, taking wickets with a splendid out-swinger when he pitched the ball up and knocking back the bat when he dug it in. As time went by, wear and tear took their toll, though never of his enthusiasm. For his last five or six years he had to rely more on ingenuity then strength, and not least on make-believe; but even then something very often turned up, if only a catch to long leg off a long-hop. It is fashionable now, I am afraid, with short-pitched bowling so prevalent, for a bowler to station two long legs, and it was Botham who set the trend. Even when he was merely ambling up to the wicket and bowling at the gentlest of paces, he did more than anyone to help England beat Australia at Sydney in the 1992 World Cup, taking four for 31 in his ten overs and then making 53 going in first. But his batteries were pretty nearly run down by then, and once the England selectors were no longer interested in him they went flat. Despite containing the last of his 38 first-class hundreds, for Durham against Worcestershire at Stockton, his final days were more melancholy than misty-eyed.

Armed with today's heavy bats, Botham and Richards hit the ball as hard and far as it can ever have been hit. At times when they were batting together, two or three balls might be seen floating like flotsam in the River Tone, which made it all the sadder when their years with Somerset ended not in the laughter which they liked to evoke but in mounting acrimony. A parting of the ways was in Somerset's best interests.

Botham's brushes with authority, whether they concerned cricket or the law, in England or elsewhere, may have been evidence of a free spirit, but they were really no more excusable for that. Richards, for his part, had a temper to contend with, which was behind a swingeing two-year suspension, imposed in his late teens, from playing cricket in Antigua, and was another reason for his being held in fairly universal awe. It seemed to me that over the years the press generally exercised discretion in favour of both players, though I doubt very much whether they would subscribe to that view themselves.

Viv was a hard cricketer, but a chivalrous, warm-hearted and unselfish one. In the years of his maturity his love of the game and still-unwavering determination inspired Glamorgan to a season to remember. Botham was just as fiercely competitive, just as chivalrous and chauvinistic, and just as contemptuous of averages. His marathon walks undertaken to raise funds for leukaemia have been magnificent, and reflect an abundantly generous spirit. He, too, "sounded forth the trumpet that shall never call retreat". They are two of the immortals, and it is an honour to salute them as such.

A photograph of Ian Botham batting at Headingley in 1981 appears on page 230.

IMRAN KHAN

Scyld Berry, *Five Cricketers of the Year, 1983*

In the early part of last season, before he had turned into the glamorous public figure he was soon to become, Imran Khan was playing as usual for Sussex in the County Championship. During their game at Edgbaston, Imran hooked a ball from one of Warwickshire's pace bowlers down to the fine-leg fielder, who caught it but then carried it over the boundary: not out. Nothing daunted, Imran tried another hook-shot at the very next ball, and gave a simple catch to square leg. On seeing this indiscretion, a Sussex colleague commented: "He would be a great player if only he used his head."

By the end of the season Imran *had* combined thoughtfulness with a natural ability which had always been outstanding. What brought about this transformation, as Imran readily admits, was his appointment to the captaincy of his native Pakistan.

This sense of responsibility turned a fine cavalier into a great cricketer. Whether the newly transformed Imran had become the equal of Ian Botham as an all-rounder made one of the liveliest debates of the summer. On the one hand, Imran did not have the batting record in Test cricket which Botham had; on the other, Imran as a pace bowler probably had the edge over Botham as he then was. Indeed some critics, Mike Brearley amongst them, rated Imran as the best of all contemporary bowlers even at the relatively advanced age of 29.

Imran Khan Niazi was born in Lahore on November 25, 1952. His father was a Pathan landowner in the region to the north of Baluchistan. His mother was one of three sisters of the Burki tribal family: one sister gave birth to Javed Burki, who became an Oxford Blue and captain of Pakistan; the other gave birth to Majid Khan, a Cambridge Blue and captain of Pakistan. Like his cousins, Imran was born to affluent circumstances in which he could devote as much time as he wished to the development of his cricket. The school which he attended, Aitchison College in Lahore, is considered the most prestigious in Pakistan, and there he was guided by one of the country's best coaches, Abdurrabb. During his schooldays he also slipped while climbing a tree, and broke his left arm when trying to cling on to a branch. The arm was set badly in hospital and has given Imran trouble ever since – not in his bowling, but he has to practise constantly at holding his bat, otherwise his grip stiffens up.

In 1971, at the age of eighteen, he was chosen to tour England and made his Test debut there. In his one Test match, at Edgbaston, he had no success as an in-swing bowler, being far too immature at that age, as he himself knew; so much so that he returned to school after the tour, joining Worcester Royal Grammar, from where he gained admission to Keble College, Oxford. According to Imran, being university captain in 1974 was little use in giving him experience of later office, but he developed his batting at Oxford to the extent of two centuries in a match against Nottinghamshire. He also launched his reputation for being able to deliver a fearsome bouncer that would swing in at a right-handed batsman's head. Worcestershire, not surprisingly after the help they had given him, were dismayed when he decided to leave after only one full season with them.

Imran's sudden move, which brought him a three-month suspension in early 1977, took him to Brighton, where the swinging pace of life and of the Hove pitches was more to his taste. There he became a dashing No. 5 batsman, and experimented with his bowling action until he had mastered the out-swinger. He considers that his time spent with World Series Cricket was decisive in making him a complete bowler, for while Mike Procter advised him on his run-up, John Snow assisted him in turning his left shoulder more towards fine leg, to help achieve the out-swinger. Imran feels that he has been technically competent as a fast bowler only since 1979–80.

Unfortunately for Imran, Pakistan had no more than a handful of Test matches over the next two years in which he could display his full prowess. When he did have the chance to prove himself, in Australia in 1981–82, he was judged to be the player of the three-match series. During that series against Australia he overtook Fazal Mahmood's record of 139 wickets for Pakistan. Having missed their following two Tests against Sri Lanka, after joining the boycott by senior players, he took 14 wickets against them in Lahore to register his best Test performance.

His feat, therefore, against England last season, of taking 21 wickets in three Tests, was nothing extraordinary by his recent standards, which have been of the highest. He began with six wickets in England's first innings at Edgbaston, bowled with magnificent stamina in their second innings at Lord's, and took another eight wickets at Headingley. His run-up made a most exhilarating spectacle as he charged in, leaning forward from the waist, and leapt at the crease; so did the end-product of some extremely fast, in-dipping yorkers and virtually unplayable out-swingers.

This much, however, was expected of Imran Khan. The surprise was his common-sensical approach to batting now that he had the captaincy. It had been given to him as a compromise candidate in the dispute between Javed Miandad and Pakistan's senior players, but he was more tactically astute than a mere novice. He could justify not taking a new ball on the last afternoon at Lord's – a tactic which he thinks is too often a cliché – by arguing that Mudassar did not know how to use one. As to the charge of over-using Abdul Qadir in the Third Test, Imran felt it was sheer bad luck that Qadir had one of those off days to which every leg-spinner is subject. But Imran primarily places the blame for his 2–1 defeat – with much justification – on the ill-discipline of his batsmen.

Imran's own batting, meanwhile, was progressing so rapidly that his No. 7 position, and record of only one Test century, had become false labels by the time of Headingley. There he scored more runs in the match than anyone else, and he was dismissed only once, when hitting out with the last man in. The maturity with which he chose his strokes was astonishing to those who had known him only as a Sussex player.

Having won belated fame in his 30th year, Imran's private life became a regular subject of discussion in certain newspapers. As he was not married at the time, and handsome of face and build, the matter of his future wife was widely speculated upon. Imran himself, however, said that he did not intend marriage so long as he was playing full-time cricket, which could keep the females among his admirers in suspense for the next two or three years at least.

A photograph of Imran Khan batting with Sunil Gavaskar appears on page 71.

RICHARD HADLEE
Graeme Wright, *Five Cricketers of the Year*, 1982

"One of the top five fast bowlers in the world" was how his captain, Clive Rice, described Richard Hadlee as Nottinghamshire prepared for their final fixture of the 1981 Championship. Beyond the two nets, sprinklers kept the Trent Bridge grass a lush green; the blue sky overhead belied the forecasts of rain that could wash away the county's hopes. And the following day Rice invited Glamorgan to face the best fast-bowling attack at Trent Bridge since the unforgotten summers of Larwood and Voce. By lunch the Welsh county were fielding, Richard Hadlee, with four for 18 off 12 overs, had become the first, and only, bowler in 1981 to reach 100 wickets, and Nottinghamshire were on course for the victory that took the County Championship title to Trent Bridge for the first time since 1929.

Yet Richard John Hadlee, born in Christchurch, New Zealand, on July 3, 1951, might not have participated in the celebrations that followed – in the unlikely event, that is, of Nottinghamshire winning the title without his all-round contribution of 105 wickets and 745 runs. Unhappy with a disastrous 1980 season, when fitness problems limited him to seven Championship games, he was hesitant of renewing his contract in 1981. "I'm not happy playing my cricket on the sidelines," he said in his forthright way. "But the club asked me to rethink." It says much for their opinion of his ability: in his three seasons with them he had played only 23 games for his 96 wickets (from 641 overs) and 549 runs, though he missed half of his first season by joining the 1978 New Zealand touring party. Many ordinary professionals play that number of games in a season.

Richard Hadlee, however, is no ordinary performer, and he set out to prove to the English public that he was what his Test record states: a world-class fast bowler whose aggressive left-handed batting entitles him to all-rounder status. The rigours of a full Australasian summer notwithstanding – six Tests and the Benson and Hedges World Series Cup, in which New Zealand reached the finals – he embarked on a pre-season training programme with the dedication of a true professional. Its fulfilment was seen day in day out as he played in every Championship match in 1981 and missed only two of the county's 21 limited-overs matches.

Usually operating off a shorter run – 15 paces as against 23 – he bowled to telling effect: a lean, hard six-footer, with his Lillee-smooth approach to the delivery stride of a textbook high action, he was still too sharp and too uncomfortable for most batsmen, still able to "stick him on his backside or beat the bat". And he could make the ball do more; as his great rival and idol, Dennis Lillee, had shown. In 1981 he bowled 708.4 overs. No seam bowler delivered more and only five others exceeded 600. The more overs you get through, the better your chances was his philosophy, and certainly his striking-rate was evenly distributed: 31 wickets in May and June, 35 in July, and 33 in August and September. His best innings return was seven for 25 against Lancashire at Liverpool: he never once took ten wickets in a match.

Such whole-hearted effort with the ball was not Richard Hadlee's only contribution to Nottinghamshire's success. A maiden Test hundred against West Indies from 92 deliveries was testament to a hard-hitting approach, in addition to belying criticism that he was reluctant to become involved with the fastest bowling. "For Nottinghamshire," said Rice, "he was just the person to come in at number seven and belt the ball all over the place." His strokeplay took them to maximum batting points on a number of occasions, and was also used to advantage in the knockout competitions.

"The helmet makes a difference," Hadlee admitted. "No one likes being hit, but now I get into line more. Also, I've been writing a coaching manual [a reprint of his autobiography was already out of print] and I began putting the theory into practice out in the middle." The result, effective and entertaining, included a career-best 142 not out against Yorkshire, but then his theory on batting is uncomplicated. The ball should be hit as hard and as often as possible.

Fourth son of Walter Hadlee, who captained New Zealand in the post-war years and later became chairman and then president of the country's governing body, Richard Hadlee did not suffer from the expectations that accompany the sons of famous fathers. Those pressures had fallen on his elder brother Barry, a batsman like his father, and had been further absorbed by another older brother, Dayle, a fast-medium bowler who first played for New Zealand in 1969. The three brothers were in the New Zealand party for the 1975 World Cup.

Wisden's headmasterly assessment after his first tour of England, in 1973, was that "his best bowling came late in the tour, but he has considerable prospects of success ahead." Those words were not yet wet ink when he helped bowl New Zealand to a moral victory in Sydney and, a few months later in Christchurch, with returns of three for 59 and four for 75, to their first-ever victory over Australia. Still his place was not secure, and even he did not expect to play when he was included in the twelve for the Third Test against the visiting Indians in 1976. However, New Zealand excluded the spinner, Hedley Howarth, and Richard Hadlee, coming on initially as fourth seamer, finished with a match return of 11 for 58, Test record figures by a New Zealander. Later that year he led the New Zealand attack in India and Pakistan, bowling with pace and hostility in conditions that have tested the heart and stamina of more experienced fast bowlers. "Richard Hadlee has come of age," said the New Zealand captain, Glenn Turner, after the tour, and England's batsmen were to taste the fire of the new Hadlee when, with match figures of ten for 100 at Wellington in February 1978, he bowled New Zealand to their first Test victory over England. Another double-figure haul, 11 for 102, was responsible for New Zealand's dramatic win over West Indies two years later, as well as making him New Zealand's leading wicket-taker.

If a sportsman's agent in any way signifies his professional standing, then Richard Hadlee ranks among the foremost, for his affairs are handled by the prestigious Mark McCormack group. Yet when he travelled to England in 1978 to represent New Zealand in a double-wicket tournament, he had to give up his job as a sales manager in Christchurch. Time off to play for Canterbury or New Zealand in first-class cricket was all right: not so double-wicket ventures! And it was while in England that he was approached by Nottinghamshire to replace Clive Rice, sacked by the county for his involvement with World Series Cricket. Happily for all concerned, Nottinghamshire reconsidered. Rice returned, and Hadlee remained. They became firm friends, the New Zealander and the South African, both dedicated to their profession and hungry for success.

Don Mosey, 1991

The international bowling career of Richard John Hadlee KBE may, by his own assessment, be divided into three distinct periods: the first five years when he was "erratic, inconsistent and without a great idea of how to get through three days, let alone four or five"; the years 1977–80 when, according to Glenn Turner, he "came of age"; and the final decade, when he positively raced to his record number of 431 Test wickets by summoning every resource of experience and guile.

It began on February 2, 1973, at the Basin Reserve, Wellington, where he took two wickets in the match against Pakistan for 112 runs, and it ended on July 10, 1990, at Edgbaston, Birmingham, when he was handed the ball with which he had taken five wickets in a Test innings for the 36th time. From that modest start he had averaged five wickets a match over the 86 Tests in which he had played in the subsequent 17 and a half years, and he retired "very happy, relieved, proud".

That he was the most intelligent fast bowler the world has ever seen there can be little doubt or argument. He did not have the bumptious lovableness of Botham, the small boy's hero; he rarely, if ever, showed the fire and fury of Trueman in his pomp; he never besmirched his reputation with the gimmickry or histrionics of Lillee (the bowler he most admired). What Hadlee brought to fast bowling in the second half of his career was deep thought, intense academic study and immense concentration. Not only did he spend hours watching videotapes of Lillee, considering the approach, the delivery, the grip, the release; he spent even more time searching for weaknesses in the defensive armoury of the greatest batsmen of his day, in the manner of a surgeon studying X-rays before probing for the source of the problem.

Hadlee's basic delivery (if, in fact, there was one) would be the ball which moved away from the bat after pitching on to an angled seam. He called it, in southern hemisphere style, a leg-cutter – a delivery which in English terms requires a specific movement of the fingers at the moment of release – but such was his control and his ability to land the ball exactly as required that he might be said to have perfected a simplified version of the leg-cutter. He could nip one back the other way, usually from a little wider in the bowling crease to pose problems of line-judgment. Swing was not always the most potent weapon, but when atmospheric conditions were right his quicker ball moved late and away towards the slips; his slower ball, the one he called the "dangly", swung into the batsman. He used the quick bouncer sparingly, keeping it always in reserve to invest it with the additional element of surprise. There was subtlety in everything he did.

Hadlee's "placing" of those differing deliveries in the course of an over was as meticulously thoughtful as every other aspect of his campaign, for that is what a bowling spell was to him. In the manner of the great spin bowlers of earlier years, he plotted the downfall of his opponents on lines of long-term strategy, without necessarily feeling that each individual delivery deserved a wicket on its own merits. It was simply a factor in the Grand Design, a skirmish in the battle to put the batsman on the foot, front or back, where he was less assured or – the ultimate victory – to catch him in no-man's-land. There has been no greater fascination in modern cricket than watching an over from Richard Hadlee when there was some response from the pitch or some help in the atmosphere.

So great has been the impact of his bowling, for Nottinghamshire and for New Zealand, that it is possible to pay less regard to his batting than it merits. Yet on figures alone he stands among the greatest of post-war all-rounders. Only Botham, Kapil Dev and Imran Khan join him in the ranks of those who have scored more than 3,000 runs while taking more than 300 wickets in Test matches. His "double" in the County Championship of 1984 was the first to be performed in England since 1967 (by Fred Titmus), in an age when the feat seemed to be beyond modern cricketers. And consider his averages in accomplishing it: 1,179 runs at 51.26, 117 wickets costing 14.05 each. These are astonishing figures. In the 1987 NatWest Trophy final, the game seemed irretrievably lost to Nottinghamshire when it spilled over into a second day because of rain. Hadlee's 70 not out from 61 balls on the Monday resulted in a victory which was something more than improbable.

Even in a career as illustrious as his, however, there have been disappointments. "If the ultimate satisfaction for a bowler is to do the hat-trick, then the *ultimate* ultimate must be to take all ten wickets in an innings, and I never did that." The nearest Hadlee came to all ten was when he took nine for 52 in the innings victory over Australia in Brisbane in November 1985. But as he caught the tenth batsman, took six for 71 in the second innings, and in between hit 54 runs, that can scarcely amount to a deep disappointment. "No. That was, I suppose, as near-perfect a performance as one hopes to achieve, and one in which the whole team shared. Brilliant catches were held and the batting was consistent." It was a result which left Australia stunned. For the real disappointment of his Test life, one has to turn to events in his own country, most particularly a widespread failure by press and public alike to understand and accept his adoption of the short run after 1980. There was a rather naive insistence that New Zealand's principal strike bowler should *look* fast by continuing an approach from 25 yards. While sheer physical necessity demanded that he reduce this, Hadlee felt a sense of outrage that his professionalism was being questioned. The shaft which went deepest was a well-turned journalistic phrase of Don Cameron, the country's leading cricket-writer, who wrote of "New Zealand's heaviest artillery operating off a pop-gun run-up". Ten years after the words were written, Hadlee quotes them in a crescendo of indignant incredulity. It was that change which transformed him from a good Test bowler into a great one.

A photograph of Richard Hadlee bowling in 1983 appears on page 515.

KAPIL DEV
Scyld Berry, Five Cricketers of the Year, 1983

India's tour of England made a quiet start to the summer. But the Test series was lent excitement by the rivalry between Ian Botham and an Indian who, by his exuberant performances, challenged the title unofficially held by Botham of being the finest contemporary all-rounder. During the series against England, Kapil Dev again proved himself a fine fast-medium bowler, but it was his batting which secured for him the player of the series award. His scores were 41, 89, 65 and 97; and every time he went in, after the first of those innings, he seemed to be on course for the fastest Test century ever made in terms of deliveries received.

Only in recent decades have Test centuries been regularly recorded in terms of deliveries as well as minutes, and it was considered that the one by Roy Fredericks off 71 balls at Perth in 1975 was the fastest until research discovered that Jack Gregory's at Johannesburg in 1921 came from four balls fewer. Kapil Dev, in his second innings of the Lord's Test, hit 89 off 55 balls. Although he fell short of the record then, it would be surprising if he does not break it on some occasion in his career, so quick is his eye, so clean his hitting, so laughing and cavalier his manner. This amateurish, or at least old-fashioned, approach is readily comprehensible if seen against his background. Kapil Dev Nikhanj was born in Chandigarh, a model Welwyn Garden-type city in the northern foothills of India, which serves as the capital of Punjab and of Haryana, being on the border of the two states. Kapil Dev, a Punjabi, plays for Haryana. His official date of birth is given as January 6, 1959, although in that part of India the year of birth is not always registered at the time and can be altered to suit convenience. As it stands, however, Kapil Dev goes into history as the youngest man to have made 1,000 Test runs and taken 100 Test wickets.

His parents came from what is now Pakistan. They emigrated at Partition from near Rawalpindi – if they had not, Kapil Dev might have been opening the bowling for Pakistan with Imran Khan. After a while of wandering, Kapil Dev's father settled in Chandigarh to become a building and timber contractor in the new city. The family business remains prosperous: in other words Kapil Dev does not play cricket for a living but for pleasure.

Batting, however, had been no pleasure for Kapil Dev in his Test matches away from home before he arrived in England last summer. Until then his average in Tests abroad was under 13, and runs had deserted him to such an extent on India's tour of Australia and New Zealand – he made 82 runs in 11 innings, being over-careful he thinks – that some Indian critics were questioning his classification as an all-rounder. From the start, in the first Test at Lord's, he refuted them. By his own admission, India's position in their first innings at Lord's was the most awkward he faced: hounded by Bob Willis and Botham, India were 45 for five wickets. Kapil Dev had to be circumspect, but clearly the chafing shackles were going to be thrown off at the next opportunity. That came on the fourth evening, after Dilip Vengsarkar had worn down England's bowling but India were still in arrears in the follow-on. Kapil Dev then hit 89 out of the 117 runs which India added in 15 overs. Test cricket can have seldom seen such exuberance. His runs might have come off even fewer than 55 balls if Dilip Doshi had not been the last man in and Kapil Dev forced to neglect some runs in order to keep the strike. When he finished off his evening's work by taking England's first three wickets in four overs, he had enjoyed as glorious a session of play as any immortal of the game.

In the Second Test at Old Trafford, Kapil Dev reached his 50 off 33 balls, well on course again for breaking the record. India, once again, were under pressure to avert the follow-on: but after Kapil had emerged at 173 for six wickets, the remaining 53 runs required were scored in even time. Towards the end of his innings of 65 he slowed down, which does not suit him or his special talent. For Kapil Dev as a batsman has the almost unique ability to launch himself straight into fourth gear, with over-drive his variation. His cleanness of hitting and precision of timing were repeated at The Oval. Again India faced the follow-on: when Kapil Dev entered their last five wickets still had to make 147. He promptly hit, between interruptions, 97 off 92 balls in 102 minutes. When Botham offered the bait of a slower ball, the uncomplicated Kapil put it straight into the distant Vauxhall stand. During what was otherwise a promising first term of captaincy by Willis, Kapil Dev's partner-ship of 130 in 27 overs with Syed Kirmani threw England into some disorder.

Before returning to Northamptonshire after the series, Kapil Dev enjoyed a mid-season working holiday in the United States, which may again exemplify his attitude to the game. When back with his county the carefree hitting continued with two whirlwind hundreds in the Championship, one on an under-prepared pitch at Eastbourne. His 50 would arrive in even time, his century – if it came – in about two hours. Dennis Brookes said he had seen no one at Northampton with such a gift for hitting and timing since Colin Milburn.

Less to Northamptonshire's delight, the amateur attitude – playing for the pleasure of it – has manifested itself in Kapil Dev's bowling as well. Understandably, as India's one quick bowler, he has been worked to the full during an intensive Test programme. It was the opportunity to take the new ball in 25 Test matches in the space of only one year and 110 days which helped him to his world record of performing the Test double in the shortest-ever time. (Botham reached his 1,000 Test runs and 100 wickets in longer time but four fewer Tests.) The last thing he needs in India's off-season is the grind of daily bowling.

As he remains the only strike bowler on India's horizon, Kapil Dev may soon decide to devote his energies to India's cause to the exclusion of the county game. But even if he is lost to the English scene, he will not be forgotten after his all-round displays of rubbery exuberance, which were enough to evoke the memory of Learie Constantine.

Mike Selvey, 1995

Perhaps the hardest thing to appreciate about Kapil Dev finally exchanging his cricket box for the TV commentary box is the fact that he was only 35 years old when he did so. Well, give or take a bit maybe: he might be a touch more geriatric than that; it is often suggested that at the time he was born, whenever that was, it was not necessarily the custom in northern India to register the year of birth. But that misses the point: however old he was, he seemed to have been around for a lot longer, prancing in to shore up the Indian attack and joyfully retrieving an innings with uninhibited squeaky-clean hitting. An Indian team without him will never seem quite the same.

With his departure comes the end of an era that has been blessed with a quartet of all-rounders unmatched in the history of the game, beginning in the early 1970s with Richard – later Sir Richard – Hadlee and Imran Khan, progressing to the laddo Botham, and finally, with his Test debut in October 1978, to the man who became known to his countrymen as the Haryana Hurricane.

What deeds from these four! Between them, they took 1,610 Test wickets and scored 17,379 runs. With the possible exception of Hadlee, each was equipped technically to play international cricket as a specialist in either role. But what a contrast: Hadlee the Inquisitor, with a surgeon's touch and an accountant's brain; Imran, the haughty, proud Pathan; Botham, the bull elephant who lived cricket and life on the edge; and Kapil, flamboyant and cavalier, charming but deadly. Today, Wasim Akram alone is left to carry a torch for the standards set by these four.

Kapil has perhaps been regarded as the most lightweight of the group. But with 434 wickets and 5,248 runs, he is the one who proved, in the end, to be the most prolific with both ball and bat. That has much to do with the fact that he played 131 Tests compared with Hadlee's 86, Imran's 88 and Botham's 102. And, as the last to survive, he was in a position to make sure that he finished top of the heap. But he laid out his credentials as soon as he entered Test cricket. His teeth may have flashed a disarming smile but this was a formidable competitor worthy of his fierce Punjabi ancestors.

Kapil has always regarded bowling as his primary role. And on February 8,

1994 he took the wicket of the Sri Lankan, Hashan Tillekeratne, to go past Hadlee's world record haul of 431 wickets. For the latter part of his career, it had been a hard slog, chipping away bit by bit at the target, like someone climbing a rock face and gradually running out of handholds with the top of the pitch in sight. Towards the end the years caught up and he was reduced to little more than medium-pace, with away-swing going invitingly early.

But it hadn't always been so. In his prime, he was much like the young, lithe Botham, with pace enough – goaded by the irrational Indian belief that their bowlers were born only to beguile – to render footwork leaden. This was accompanied by snaking late out-swing, helped by a contortionist's action so far round that it presented his left shoulder-blade to the batsman, and a wicked break-back that struck with the speed of a cobra. Superficially, his bowling may have lacked Hadlee's relentlessly searching examination, or Imran's leaping, muscular pace, or Botham's bludgeon and will-power, but it was deceptively effective for all that.

Yet in the fullness of time, he may be remembered more for his carefree, hawk-eyed batting. He was helped by the fact that he was an all-rounder and so had the freedom to play as he did: one discipline fuelled the other. The rate at which he was capable of scoring was phenomenal. At Lord's in 1982, he brought the England bowling to its knees, hitting 13 fours and three sixes, an innings of 89 that came from just 55 balls, well on course then for what would have been the fastest Test century in history. And in his last Lord's Test, in 1990 – Gooch's match – he scored the 24 India required to save the follow-on by hitting Eddie Hemmings for four successive straight sixes while the last man, Hirwani, blinked myopically at the other end and got out next ball.

And yet perhaps his finest moment came not in a Test but in a limited-overs international against Zimbabwe, not even a Test-playing nation then, at, improbably enough, Tunbridge Wells. In 1983, it was Kapil's lot to lead India in the World Cup, and he found himself at the crease on a damp pitch, with the scoreboard reading 17 for five. He was to play what he has described as the innings of a lifetime, scoring an unbeaten 175 as India reached 266 for eight and went on to win the game. Eventually, they progressed to the final at Lord's where, against all the odds, they beat West Indies, then arguably the most potent cricket force ever to set foot on the ground. Kapil and India showed they could be taken, and an illusion was shattered: West Indies have not won the World Cup since.

A photograph of Kapil Dev batting in 1990 appears on page 438.

CHRIS CAIRNS
Richard Becht, *Five Cricketers of the Year*, 2000

Chris Cairns might be expected to nominate Lord's or The Oval as his places of the heart after a summer of cricketing content. Yet for all his glorious feats there in 1999, one of the world's less appealing venues provided a snapshot that meant just as much – Kanpur's Green Park, the dusty ground where he experienced, celebrated and then demonstratively revelled in one of the biggest moments in his cricketing life.

New Zealand were facing Sachin Tendulkar's Indians in the second of three Tests. India had the untaxing task of scoring 92 to win, an uneventful end to an unmemorable match for New Zealand. But Chris Cairns wanted to seize a moment. Sitting on 130 Test wickets, he was desperate to lift that total to 131 to go ahead of his father, folk hero Lance, on New Zealand's roll of honour. And, in the throes of defeat, came the triumph he craved, as he castled opener Sadagoppan Ramesh for five. He didn't just savour it, but made a grand statement with his next delivery. This was no rhythmical thing of cricketing beauty, rather an unco-ordinated flurry of arms, the ball unmistakeably delivered off the wrong foot – the way Bernard Lance Cairns did. As the "son of" said, it was his tribute to "the old man".

That moment meant much to the man himself, but it was his string of wondrous deeds earlier in the year that really had the cricketing world paying attention. Back home, Cairns's batting was critical against India, a half-century contributing to victory in Wellington and a restrained 126, only his second Test hundred, batting the tourists out of contention in Hamilton to secure a series win. It was also Cairns the batsman, rather than the bowler, who excited in the one day games against India, and at Christchurch he made a hundred off just 75 deliveries, New Zealand's fastest in limited-overs internationals, with seven sixes.

In such mood, he seemed destined to prosper in England, both at the World Cup, then on the tour to follow. Excel he did, boosting New Zealand's run to the World Cup semi-finals with his all-round contributions, including a blistering 60 in the famous five-wicket win over eventual champions Australia. For all that, the Test series against England was Cairns's *tour de force*. His six-wicket haul was a key ingredient in New Zealand's nine-wicket win at Lord's and, in the series decider at The Oval, he was matchless. He began with five wickets, but the jewel was his last innings of the tour. New Zealand were 39 for six and leading by just 122 when he took guard – and instantly applied the blowtorch to England's attack. When it was all over, he had 80 beside his name from only 94 deliveries, a priceless and daring innings which effectively won the series: England folded in the run-chase and lost by 83 runs. With series returns of 183 runs and at 30.50 and 19 wickets at 21.26, Cairns was unquestionably New Zealand's outstanding performer. At the start of 2000, Cairns had a claim to be considered the game's pre-eminent all-rounder. Even Hadlee struggled to stay that.

Andrew Flintoff   Tanya Aldred, *Five Cricketers of the Year*, 2004

Did you see it? That Sunday morning at The Oval when, in late-summer sunshine, a blond Apollo destroyed South Africa with a joyful 95. There always was something about Andrew Flintoff, this amiable giant who carved into the bowling, a farmhand delighting in the coconut shy. His spine-tingling whirl of the bat, exaggerated defensive shot and love of replaying his own strokes in slow-motion made him a crowd favourite and annoyingly impossible for the armchair punter to switch off. For too long, though, he had been a might-do, haunted by back trouble that threatened his bowling career, a comfortably upholstered physique, and inconsistency in the face of the hype that has surrounded every English all-rounder since Ian Botham.

But, in 2003, he became a can-do at last. First, quietly, he was England's best player at the World Cup. Then, explosively, he lit up the second half of the African summer, lifting spirits at Lord's with a bat-smashing 142 in England's grotty defeat, then setting up an improbable win with that wonderful innings at The Oval. There were other cameos in between, too. He walked off with the England Man of the Series award and averages to flaunt. Not that figures have ever done him justice: they ill-define his threat, his heart and the will of the crowd, gulping on their hasty return from the bars as he makes his jerky, proud way to the crease.

Andrew Flintoff was born on December 6, 1977 in Preston, Lancashire, where he lived until he was 21. His first game came as a six-year-old, when Dutton Forshaw Under-13s were short and he scampered around in a Manchester United tracksuit. At nine he was turning out for Lancashire Under-11s, although he did not get around to watching the first team until he was on

Folk hero: a characteristic appeal from Andrew Flintoff during the 2005 Ashes series, which he lit up with bat and ball. This time he's taken a wicket, thanks to Geraint Jones's rebound catch off Andrew Strauss's knee near the end of a tense final day at Old Trafford.

the staff: even when they came to play at Blackpool and his brother went to the cricket, he preferred to go to the amusements at the Tower.

At secondary school cricket was "for posh lads", so he played football to save face, and kept cricket for the weekends. In search of tougher competition he moved clubs to St Annes, continued playing for Lancashire age-group teams, and at 16 won a three-year county contract. The Old Trafford dressing-room, stuffed with big names, was a daunting place for a teenage beanpole. "I couldn't say anything for about three years," he recalls.

A spell behind the record counter at Woolworths was followed by an England Under-19 trip to the West Indies, where he injured his back again after bowling himself into the ground. The problem remained when, aged 20, he was picked for his Test debut against South Africa. He was greeted coolly in the dressing-room and the reception grew icier when he tried to hit Jacques Kallis over extra-cover for six in his first innings and was caught behind for 17. In the next Test he made a pair and was dropped.

What followed was a helter-skelter ride of injury, disappointment, jubilant innings – like the devastating 135 against Surrey in a NatWest Trophy quarter-final in 2000 – and humiliation, when the England management hinted publicly that Flintoff was overweight. (He followed this up with a match award against Zimbabwe, describing it as "all right for a fat lad".) At the end of a dismal 2001 season, when he had made only two Championship fifties and his love of a good time was threatening to ruin his career, he was given a rocket by his personal management team.

He asked to go to the England Academy that winter but, thanks to a Duncan Fletcher hunch, ended up in India opening the bowling, specialising in Nasser Hussain's version of leg-theory to Sachin Tendulkar. He dates his change in fortunes to that tour – even though, transfixed by Anil Kumble, he was hardly able to make a run. His maiden Test hundred came against New Zealand the following March but the summer of 2002 was botched by indecision over when he should have a hernia operation, and he missed the Ashes Tests that followed. But by the time he came back from the World Cup – he finished as the tournament's most economical bowler – he felt he knew himself and his game.

Batting is getting easier. He is learning to build an innings even when he admits he is out of touch, and is reining in his instinct to deposit every ball out of the ground. "It has probably taken quite a while longer than I and everyone else hoped," he admits. Now he wants to work on his bowling – which he admits, despite sterling performances for England as the old hand in an inexperienced pace attack, he has not given enough attention. He has his eye on developing a ball that goes out when he wants it to, and taking more Test wickets to correct a puzzlingly high average.

Flintoff is big-hearted, genial, humble, unselfish – and surprisingly shy: he still gnaws his hands in press conferences. He loves the companionship of the game, and can often be found sitting in the Old Trafford dressing-room even when banned from playing for Lancashire by England. He was 15 when John Stanworth, the former Lancashire wicket-keeper who moved on to the coaching staff, first called him Freddie. He has been stalked with cartoon expectations ever since. When he cracked it last season, it was the most heart-warming performance by an English all-rounder since. . . well, let's not go into that.

Peter Hayter, 2006

For nearly a quarter of a century, anyone who batted a bit and bowled a bit for the England team has had a label stuck round his neck. The comparison was inevitable, and somehow it always sounded like a lament. English cricket harked back to Headingley '81 even though the current team, increasingly, had no memory of it whatever. Finally, in 2005, the lament was over. Following his one-man show on the Saturday of the Edgbaston Test, Andrew Flintoff – who was three and a half in the summer of 1981 – was asked by Australian reporters what he felt about being called the next Ian Botham. "I don't see it like that," he said. "As far as I'm concerned I'm just having fun, playing cricket with my mates." Flintoff paid no heed to the past whatever. Now who does that remind you of?

Later that month, at Trent Bridge, Flintoff was able to raise his batting average above his bowling average for the first time, the statistical benchmark of the true all-rounder. Then in September came the moment when Flintoff really infiltrated

English hearts, and became the nation's Freddie. In Trafalgar Square, amid champagne, fireworks and tickertape, he was asked what he had eaten since the celebrations started the previous evening. "A cigar," he replied. "I've not been to bed," he explained to David Gower, Nelson's column and a crowd of thousands – even though he could barely tell which was which. "Behind these shades there's a thousand stories." Vintage Botham. Sporting god as one of us. No wonder the bookmakers stopped taking bets on who would win the award for BBC Sports Personality of the Year because they concluded Flintoff was a certainty for a trophy not won by a cricketer since. . . 1981.

But now that the comparison with Botham was legitimate, no one had to make it any more. Whole generations of all-rounders had been blighted by being called The Next Botham the moment they put on an England cap. That problem is over. To understand what those in between had to endure, it may be necessary to explain to the Flintoff generation exactly what Botham did. In 102 Tests, he scored 5,200 runs at an average of 33.54, taking 383 wickets (still far more than anyone else in England's Test history) at 28.40, and 120 catches, also still an England record. He also endured an up-and-down relationship with the tabloid press over his successes, his failures, his sins and his charitable saintliness that meant he constantly seemed on the brink of being worshipped or burnt at the stake. When his powers faded, he left behind a giant-sized hole: as a No. 6 batsman who could score hundreds, a bowler capable of taking five wickets in an innings regularly, a fielder able to catch flies, and a rough-and-ready table-turner straight out of the comic books.

No one who also bowled seriously was able to step into the hole at No. 6 for long, though David Capel batted there in nine Tests, and Craig White, Derek Pringle and even Ronnie Irani all had a go. But a whole series of Next Bothams were used lower down the order. The collective records of all-rounders between Botham and Flintoff who played ten Tests or more – Capel, Pringle, White, Phil DeFreitas, Chris Lewis, Dominic Cork and Alex Tudor – reads as follows: 198 matches, 5,253 runs at 18.49, 542 wickets at 34.79, and about a million comparisons with Botham, always over-optimistic when they were first chosen, and exasperated when inevitably they failed to live up to the billing.

Pringle and DeFreitas both think Flintoff has been lucky because a system was at last in place that gave him time to find himself "as a player and as a man", as Pringle put it. But Beefy is still around, of course. As a Sky commentator, he is now the one making the comparisons. He was even there on the Pakistan tour, celebrating his 50th birthday (allegedly with lashings of Pure Heaven sparkling grape juice) in the country where he famously said he should send his mother-in-law. Botham thinks there are similarities between the two of them: the low boredom threshold, for instance. "Freddie hasn't always appreciated the comparisons with me and maybe it took him a couple of years to establish his own identity as a cricketer, but he is comfortably the best all-rounder in the world now. The highest compliment I can pay him is that I enjoy watching him play. I couldn't be more pleased that he has done it by being himself and not trying to be someone else's clone."

All we have to worry about now are the future players who will have to face being described as The Next Flintoff.

The Leading Cricketer in the World, 2005 Simon Barnes, 2006

The old legend of Andrew Flintoff is The Man Who Changed: the man who belatedly came to the realisation that talent alone was not enough. So he added application and resolution to the mix and became one of the best cricketers in the world. But the new legend is better. It tells of the man who changed again, and made a still more momentous leap. He had gone from jolly good to excellent – well, many others have done that. But during the Ashes series of 2005, Flintoff then made the infinitely rarer transition – the quantum, the Beamon leap – from excellence to greatness.

How to explain the concept? Not by numbers, certainly. Great players always have great numbers: but so do many players of mere excellence. A great player is one who dominates – and wins – a great cricket competition by means of his own performances, his own nature, his own force. Flintoff and the Ashes series of 2005 will always be regarded as a perfect demonstration of cricketing greatness. He made the transition somewhere between July 24 and August 4: between the end of the First Test, and the beginning of the Second. He bowled well at Lord's. But his batting was meek and deferential, that of a man who knows he is second-best. Australia won, Flintoff made three runs in the match and was part of England's ghastly same-old-Poms collapse in the second innings.

So what happened? Like a cuckolded husband, Flintoff was the last to know. He just came out to bat on the first day of the Second Test and took over the series. He brought off the rare all-rounder's double of succeeding in both disciplines in the same match. His bowling had gone from useful-third-seamer to firecracker strike bowler. He had found pace, he had found subtlety, he had found the psychological domination he had never before possessed. His batting became filled with a massive, easy confidence. There was no swagger: just a huge relish for the confrontation, and an inner certainty about his newly acquired greatness.

This was most perfectly demonstrated in his series-turning innings of the Fourth Test, when he compiled – rather than swatted or biffed or bludgeoned – a century of murderous purpose. It was an innings that did more than score runs: it brought the beginnings of despair to the opposition. Flintoff was exceptional in the final match too, when his extraordinary last spell brought the Australians from dominance back to uncertainty. Flintoff performed well in everything he did last season, but it was his personal epic of the Ashes summer – *The Freddiad?* – that was the real expression of his greatness. Everything else was peripheral. The subtle balance between the two sides was tipped by the performances of one man.

Keepers

RODNEY MARSH   John Coomber, *Five Cricketers of the Year*, 1982

It was a source of great satisfaction to Rodney William Marsh that the catch with which he became the most successful Test wicket-keeper in history was taken off the bowling of Dennis Lillee. Few partnerships between bowler and wicket-keeper have had so profound an impact on the game. It was fitting, therefore, that in the same match, the unforgettable Third Test at Headingley in 1981, Lillee became the most prolific wicket-taker in Anglo-Australian Tests.

To the end of the 1981 series, 77 Test batsmen had begun the long walk back as the scorers entered c Marsh b Lillee beside their names. In all first-class cricket and representative one-day matches, the figure is in excess of 200, for the careers of these two remarkable competitors have gone hand in glove, as it were, since they made their debuts for Western Australia in the late 1960s. Yet Marsh, who has had few equals when standing back to fast bowling, owes his initial opportunities, at junior, club, state and Test level, to his skill with the bat.

Born in Armadale, Western Australia, on November 4, 1947, Marsh learnt his cricketing basics during innumerable "backyard tests" with his elder brother, Graham, who was later to become an outstanding professional golfer. Both represented the state at schoolboy level before pursuing careers in their chosen sport. At the age of eight Rodney was playing competitively for a team called "the mosquito fleet", an Armadale Under-16 side which seemed to attract the smallest boys in the district. "I kept wicket right from the start, but batting was my main strength," he recalled.

At 12 he was chosen for the Western Australian schoolboys' team, and captained the side the following year. He then joined the West Perth district club, travelling 18 miles into the capital city on Saturdays to play for a junior side in the morning and in senior grades in the afternoon. When he broke into the first-grade side it was as a batsman, because Gordon Becker, the state wicket-keeper, also played for the club. In order to get wicket-keeping practice Marsh joined the University club in Perth, though when he was first invited to play for Western Australia, against the touring West Indians in 1968, it was as a number five batsman. He failed to score in the first innings and made 104 in the second, against an attack containing Hall, Griffith and Sobers. Becker retired in the 1969–70 season, whereupon Marsh became the state wicket-keeper, the position he has filled ever since, apart from his two seasons with World Series Cricket.

When Marsh played his first Test in Brisbane, against Ray Illingworth's 1970–71

England team, he was not the best-credentialled wicket-keeper in Australia. But desperate to shore up the middle order, after the dreadful beating Australia had taken in South Africa in their previous series, the selectors opted for the wicket-keeper who best knew how to wield a bat. Certainly, Marsh's glovework fell some way short of being immaculate. In Brisbane he was dubbed "iron gloves" by a crowd who had grown up watching Don Tallon and Wally Grout, and in any case thought that the Queensland wicket-keeper, John Maclean, should have been playing. "I didn't know much about keeping in those days," Marsh recalled. "But I learnt a tremendous amount by watching Alan Knott." It was Knott's record of 263 Test victims which Marsh surpassed at Headingley last year, but he still rates the Kent man the finest keeper in the world.

The improvement in Marsh's technique was apparent when he came to England with Ian Chappell's team in 1972. In the next Australian season he set the first of his several batting records when he scored 118 not out against Pakistan in Adelaide, this being the first Test century by an Australian wicket-keeper. And all the time his wicket-keeping was becoming more efficient, his acrobatics more spectacular. One of the enduring memories of Australia's crushing victories over England and West Indies in the series of 1974–75 and 1975–76 is the sight of Marsh flinging his bear-like frame left and right to paw down the thunderbolts of Lillee and Thomson. He made 45 dismissals in those two series, including a world-record 26 catches in six Tests against West Indies.

Marsh's theory in standing well back to fast bowling is to get as much lateral movement as possible, allowing first slip to stand wider and thus extending the arc covered by the same number of slip fieldsmen. This worked to brilliant effect when Australia had such close catchers as the Chappell brothers, Redpath, Walters and Mallett in the mid 1970s. It was about this time that Marsh began to develop an almost psychic partnership with Lillee. He has been behind the stumps for every ball Lillee has bowled in Test matches, and for virtually every one in first-class cricket. "I've played with him so much now that most of the time I know what he is going to do before he has bowled," Marsh said. "I know from the way he runs up – the angle, the speed, where he hits the crease – where the ball is going to be. I can see the way his mind is working and I can virtually bowl his over for him, ball by ball."

ALAN KNOTT
Mike Brearley, 1986

Alan Knott was a great cricketer. In my view he was also the best wicket-keeper of his time. He had a good physique for the job – short, low-to-the-ground, agile and quick (through he himself foresees a new breed of tall keepers by analogy with tall goalkeepers, and maintains that he had to stretch so much because he was not particularly supple, especially in the hips). He had marvellous hands. Physically he kept himself extremely fit, and was an assiduous practiser. His technique was not classical; he took catches with one hand when he might have got two to the ball, and he sometimes dived when he could have reached the ball without falling. He had a sound reason for both – simply that for him these methods were more natural and more effective. His judgment about what to go for was unerring. As a first slip I always seemed to know when Alan would go for a catch in front of me, and I was never baulked by him or distracted by any tentativeness on his part. Standing up, he took the low ball without bending his knees and with his legs together. This gave him the right amount of give, against his legs. Moreover, if he missed it with his hands, the ball would not go for byes, and if the edge beat the gloves, there was no knee or elbow sticking out to obscure first slip's view, or to deflect the ball.

His constant exercising was a reflection of his perfectionism, as was the care he took to have essential equipment in perfect order. He kept and rehabilitated a favourite old bat specially for Tests; he spent the afternoon before the Melbourne Centenary Test in town getting a loose stitch from the webbing of a glove repaired, just in case he should uncharacteristically have to rely on it to make a catch. He was also prepared to be unconventional in his gear, if it helped the job in hand. He once saw the New Zealand wicket-keeper, Ken Wadsworth, struck on the inside of the knee by an awkward throw-in; his pad had swivelled round as he moved towards the ball and had left the knee unprotected. As a result, Knott took to taping his pads to his trousers rather than using the middle strap and buckle; he thereby also reduced chafing. He did not mind at all that the effect was untidy: I have never known a cricketer who was less concerned with style for its own sake. Though brilliant, he eschewed the flamboyant. He stood back to medium-pacers more than his predecessors, not at all for safety-first or to avoid error, but as the result of a cool calculation as to the overall effectiveness to the side.

He would have been, in my book, a more or less automatic selection for any team on the strength of his keeping alone. When his batting was put in the scales, all doubt fell away. For he was also a genius – a minor genius – with the bat. Here too, he was no purist for the sake of orthodoxy. Against fast bowling he realised that he had a better chance of playing a lifting delivery if he changed his grip so as to have his top hand behind the handle; this enables the batsman to hold his hands in front of his face and keep the bat straight. He evolved a kind of French cricket technique for use when he first went in against the quickest bowlers; but soon took every opportunity to attack, clipping the ball square on either side of the wicket and cutting deftly, often, intentionally, over the slips' heads. He reckons that if he were starting his career now he would learn to hook fast bowling, and cites the hours of practice Viv Richards went through, after a disastrous tour of Australia, with Andy Roberts bowling bouncers at him in Antigua.

Against fast bowlers, Knott's grip, stance and technique were totally different from those he adopted against medium-pacers and especially against spinners. He might start an innings in an orthodox vein but quickly ventured into the unusual. He played a sort of off-glide to good effect, particularly against off-spinners. His sweeping was unique; on a drying pitch at Canterbury, he once played 15 consecutive balls from Edmonds and Emburey with this shot and never missed or mis-hit one. His secret was to get low, watch the ball, and not try to hit it too hard. But many of us could follow all those instructions and still make a hash of it. I remember an innings against India at Bangalore in 1977. The pitch had deteriorated to the point where good spinners were almost unplayable. Yet the flea kept dancing down the pitch to Bedi and Prasanna and chipping them over mid-wicket or extra-cover.

The cheek and verve of this innings (he finished with 81 not out) were unmatched in my experience. Behind all his extravagances as a batsman – as with his idiosyncrasies as a keeper – there were the basic skills. His head was always steady, and he was capable of a long defensive innings as well as of impish aggression. He was completely unselfish. He was courageous too. But the courage that marked him out, for me, was of a more broad-based kind. He had the guts, the confidence and occasionally the stubbornness to stick to his method if he felt that he was right.

Personal health was one area in which these attitudes were expressed. Alan was no hypochondriac, but he was keenly interested in the state of his own body. He fell ill one evening in Delhi and in the middle of the night knocked on the physiotherapist's door, bearing a sample of what had recently been in his stomach. He wanted no sketchily based diagnosis. He was equally fussy about what went *into* his stomach. No cheese and meat at the same meal, for example. He drank little, and avoided parties. He needed eight hours of sleep, yet had to have a couple of hours clear for ablutions and exercises before breakfast (so it was not always easy to find room-partners for him on tour). After hurting his neck in two car accidents in the mid-seventies, he had his car seat remodelled. And he was so chary of draughts that he would come away from a day's play in India wearing three sweaters, an anorak with the hood up, and dark glasses. The lack of a surgical mask must have been an oversight. He was never unfit for a Test, though once, in 1976 against West Indies, he played too soon, he thought, after breaking a finger.

Tactically he was sound, though not without his biases. He had an exaggerated respect for pace, and would usually advise his captain to keep the seamers on. He sometimes overrated the players he knew best, though he was capable of hard judgments (as when he said of a colleague that he had "learned nothing during his years in the game"). Politically, he was involved in both the major cricketing rebellions of our time, Packer's in 1977 and the South African Breweries' tour of 1982. Typically, his views were well thought out, courteously expressed and tenaciously held.

The man is all-of-a-piece, and at the heart of his life lie his close family ties and religious conviction. Leaving his wife and son behind for four months at a time became an insupportable wrench; and one of the attractions of World Series Cricket for him was the welcome given to families. He was able to take a flat in Sydney with his family, and use it as his home base for the season, whereas the English establishment were less sympathetic. Their attitude often represented an unwarranted suspicion based on their inability to understand him. Some felt it outrageous that a cricketer should lay down conditions about his wife's accompanying him during an England tour. He was not, it is true, ever one of the boys; but he was a complete professional and team-man. Even his stretching exercises on the field were viewed in some quarters with a surprising hostility, as if they were for show. Nothing could have been further from the truth.

As for religion, he became a Christian in 1974. This, he has said, changed his whole attitude to life. He came to see his behaviour during the rather ill-tempered series in India in 1972–73 as reprehensible. From then on, he was on the field an unfailing example to us all. He was generous to others: Paul Downton acknowledges the many tips and kindnesses he received from Alan while on the Kent staff and since. In 1977, when we won the Ashes at Headingley, Knotty seized a bail as a souvenir for the young Ian Botham, playing in his second Test, who was off the field injured at the end of the match.

His religious beliefs also helped him to a more philosophical attitude to his own performance. He became less concerned about the *outcome* of his play, and focused more on simply trying as hard as he could in the way he felt was most likely to succeed. His view is that it is the inner attitude that counts; the results will then look after themselves. He is utterly modest, and equally without false modesty.

Alan Knott has retired from the game while still playing it at a very high standard. In 1985 he was regarded by virtually all the top players as the best keeper in England. His decision to go was based, partly, on an ankle injury which he was told could get worse if he carried on. He reaches 40 in April of this year, not long after Les Ames's 80th birthday and Godfrey Evans's 65th. He hopes to coach, to help produce, perhaps, a successor to this line of Kent and England wicket-keepers. He will be a splendid coach, wise, thoughtful, kindly and occasionally controversial. I cannot think of any cricketer, with the possible exception of Ian Botham, whose game has given me more pleasure.

JACK RUSSELL
Colin Bateman, *Five Cricketers of the Year*, 1990

At the beginning of 1989, Jack Russell had played only one Test for England and was not considered a good enough batsman to merit a place in the one-day squad to face the Australians. By the end of the year he was the only Englishman who could justifiably expect a place in anyone's World XI. In the course of a summer of England mediocrity on the field, and damaging South African recruitment off it, Russell sailed serenely through the storm, proving he could reproduce his supreme wicket-keeping performances for Gloucestershire in the intensity of Test cricket. He was one of only two ever-presents in the England side (the other was the captain, David Gower), and when he went to India for the Nehru Cup in October – now as one of the old hands in the new-look squad – Russell was outstanding.

Yet, as is often the case with the best – and Russell is, believe many experts, in the Knott-Taylor class – his work goes unnoticed until the rare fumble. The irony of Russell's year was that it was his batting, a weakness which had delayed his England selection by at least a year, that brought England's supporters to their feet during a summer when they spent most of the time sat glumly with not even a rain-cloud to provide relief. They did not have many opportunities to feel pride, but Russell the batsman produced at least a few.

Early arrivals on the first day of the Second Test at Lord's might have noticed a curious sight at the Nursery end nets. A group of MCC groundstaff boys were hurling scarlet plastic balls at an England cricketer from 15 yards. For 20 minutes, Russell did not play a shot. He simply ducked and swerved, avoiding each delivery. The Australians had decided in the First Test that the left-handed Russell was vulnerable – plain scared, if you like – to anything bowled short and fast at the body. Russell, with Alan Knott as his adviser, was determined to work it out, and subjected himself to a trial by teenagers which many of his colleagues would have found demeaning. He also decided that the best response to the verbal bouncers he was getting from the Australian close-fielders while he batted was to answer back in good, old-fashioned Anglo-Saxon. Jack, 5ft 8in and 9st 8lb with his boots on, gave the startled Aussies an earful as well as his best shots. And in the process he salvaged England's first innings with an undefeated 64. "That day I played the most important innings of my career. I crossed a mental bridge," says Russell. "They tried the short-pitched bowling and I coped, they tried all the verbals and I had a go back. You know, they didn't say another word to me out in the middle all series."

Russell gripped on to his advantage like a terrier with a bone. In the next Test, at Edgbaston, he was the second-highest scorer in England's first innings with 42, and then up at Old Trafford for the Fourth Test came his greatest moment – on a day that became known as Ash Tuesday for English cricket. England were in the throes of surrendering the Ashes amid the turmoil caused by the announcement of Mike Gatting's rebel party for South Africa, three of whom were sitting in the England dressing-room at the time. Russell had gone to the crease the previous day with the scoreboard reading 38 for five and an innings defeat looking a certainty. It seemed hopeless, but Russell played one of the gutsiest innings you are likely to see. For almost six hours he held up Australia's celebrations by scoring 128 not out, his maiden century, not only in Test cricket but in all cricket. It was an achievement matched by only one other Englishman this century, Billy Griffith against West Indies in 1948; it was a great, and almost match-saving, achievement. And yet it scarcely received the acknowledgment it deserved amid the rest of the day's news. To Jack, however, it meant the earth.

Like Knott, Russell, in his floppy white hat and taped-up pads, looks as dishevelled as a truant schoolboy behind the stumps, but he is immaculate in his preparation and work. He has the fitness of a jump jockey and the finesse of a fencer. And like most wicket-keepers – as with goalkeepers in soccer – he is cheerfully self-contained: an independent spirit in a team game. He eats nothing but steak and chips on tour – not always easy in the likes of Nagpur and Gwalior – and when he wants to relax, it is not with the headphones and lager can to which most of his colleagues turn. Rather it is an adventure out into the local surroundings, whether that be the tranquil banks of the Severn in Worcester or the teeming shanty towns of Bombay, sketchbook, pencil and camera in hand. Russell had discovered a penchant for drawing, and the hobby he took up to pass the time on rain-affected English summer afternoons has become a second profession. His work has created such an impression that he has had books published and his work exhibited in a London gallery. Jack Russell, the keeper with drawing power.

ALEC STEWART
Mike Selvey, *Five Cricketers of the Year*, 1993

It was at Lord's, midway through the morning session of the fourth one-day international last summer, that it was spotted. Alec Stewart, England captain for the day, opening batsman some days, floating middle-order batsman other days, infielder, outfielder, shake-it-all-about fielder and wicket-keeper, was standing behind the bowler's stumps, quietly buffing the ball on his flannels as, with a wave here and a flourish there, he set the field. "Omigod," said someone, "I think he's going to bowl."

He didn't, of course, but it is testament to the image that he has created that the possibility even fleetingly crossed the mind. Through sheer honest endeavour, schoolboyish "me sir, please sir" enthusiasm and a willingness to fit into any role in any circumstance, Stewart first of all made his versatility a reason to select him over others. Then, having got into the England side, he made himself indispensable. Brisk and polished, he became the very model of a modern professional. One day, perhaps, an Italian club will buy him for five million quid.

The rise of Alec James Stewart – born in Merton on April 8, 1963 – to the position of England vice-captain, acting-captain and genuine Test-class batsman has surprised many. It is not that the pedigree was absent: the fact that Micky Stewart, the recently retired England manager and former Test player and Surrey captain, is his father is unknown only to recent returnees from the planet Jupiter. That in addition his mother, Sheila, was a top netball and hockey player is less well-documented. It was a family environment conducive to the production of a young sportsman.

His cricket progress was through the ranks: Tiffin School, junior Surrey sides, Surrey second team during his final school year, and finally, when he left school at 18, actually on to the Surrey staff – Micky was manager – where he has been since 1981. Simultaneously, he began an association with Australian grade cricket, playing season after season with the Midland-Guildford club in Perth. If his batting skills were learned at The Oval, it was the Aussie school of hard knocks that instilled in him a mental toughness, a desire to give as good as he got, to mix it verbally. So when, on his first tour, and playing only his second Test, he crossed swords with Desmond Haynes at Trinidad, Haynes by no means got the better of him. And if sometimes – as in the 'ere-we-go atmosphere of the World Cup – his behaviour panders uncomfortably to the yob element in the crowd, then at least he has spark.

No one can say that success has come easily. He has always appeared to be a well-organised, busy, bat-twirling player, perky as a parrot, capable of making entertaining runs, but lacking, apparently, the commitment to register the big scores that get noticed: the first 10 years of his career had brought him just 16 first-class centuries. Had he not developed his wicket-keeping he might even now not have received the chance in international cricket.

Yet even having made the squad it was not easy to establish himself. Time after time, he played fluently and well, getting set at the crease, only to waft once too often and depart, muttering to the sky, aware that not capitalising on good form is a criminal offence in cricket, for the bad times are only just around the corner. It was, then, to his credit that he worked so hard to eliminate from his game vulnerability to the slip cordon, and became greedy for greater things. Dropped after the disastrous tour of Australia in 1990–91, he was recalled, much to his surprise, to keep wicket in the final Test against West Indies that summer. It was an opportunity he could not afford to miss; and he took it. England won memorably. Two weeks later he scored his first Test century, against Sri Lanka, and in the 17 Test innings after his return he scored 952 runs at an average of 68.00. There is an air of authority about his cricket.

Now he is also free of the shackle – real or perceived, media figment or not – of being the son of the England manager. It is a relationship that has always created debate. Nepotism, some have cried, has smoothed his progress. Nonsense, say others, if any one has been held back it has been Alec because of Micky's need to be seen to be scrupulously fair to others. Father and son, for their part, have always gone out of their way to eliminate the whole issue, with Micky insisting that, in cricketing terms, he has not had a son, and referring to Alec simply as "Stewie", while Alec has attempted to divorce himself from it by calling his father manager even at home. At times it was too much, synthetic almost.

Micky was there in Jamaica when Alec walked out to bat for the first time as an England player, and when he scored his first century. He was there when Alec, under considerable pressure to succeed, held the catches behind the wicket that helped beat the West Indies at The Oval. But never once was there a public acknowledgment of father's pride in his son. Are they really such a dispassionate family? Of course not. "He's been absolutely delighted for me," said Alec, "and he's told me so. But he was never going to show it publicly, was he? I think he always felt it could be misinterpreted, and that was the last thing he wanted. He's done nothing but treat me fairly." So now we know. Besides which it is no longer an issue. Alec Stewart has long since been his own man.

IAN HEALY
Mike Coward, *Five Cricketers of the Year*, 1994

Even though he is a wicket-keeper, Ian Healy is best described as a gloves-off crick-eter. A proud and uncompromising professional, he plays for keeps. So forceful is his personality on point-duty that he elicits strong and mixed emotions from opponents, spectators and journalists alike. Indeed, at the start of the 1993 Ashes campaign, he was regarded as much for the strength of his resolve, his unremit-ting competitiveness and an extraordinarily high threshold of physical pain as he was for his talent as a player.

However, by the end of Australia's triumphant tour he had emerged as a wicket-keeper-batsman of outstanding ability, having established a particularly memorable collaboration with the leg-spinner Shane Warne. Poised and precise, he completed 26 dismissals (21 catches and five stumpings), a record in a Test series in England, and so upheld the wicket-keeping traditions of his native Queensland which numbers Don Tallon and Wally Grout among its finest sporting sons. His batting at No. 7 was neither as technically correct nor as aesthetically pleasing but its effectiveness was undeniable and his 296 runs were gathered at 59.20 – an average beyond the reach of any of his opponents. His total included, at Old Trafford, his maiden first-class century.

No longer could it be said that Healy's words spoke louder than his actions. During a series which lifted to 53 his number of consecutive Test appearances, he elevated his performance level to the degree predicted by Greg Chappell five years before. Healy derived enormous satisfaction from his success, content that he had silenced those critics who primarily viewed him as a prickly combatant given to excessive and provocative appealing – best-known for his confrontation with

Desmond Haynes in Barbados in 1990–91 and the dubious stumping of Brian Lara in Brisbane in 1992–93.

In commensurate numbers to Healy's critics are his admirers – some in high places. Indeed, he has enjoyed support among the influential since Chappell, in his last season as a selector in 1987–88, vigorously championed his cause. At the time Healy was understudy to his friend and practice partner Peter Anderson and unsure whether to give up keeping and turn his attention to batting. Having played his entire career alongside Rod Marsh, Chappell was acutely aware of the advantages offered by a permanent, dependable wicket-keeper-batsman. In their search for the ideal successor to Marsh the selectors had called on Wayne Phillips, considered Ray Phillips, looked momentarily at Roger Woolley and briefly revived Steve Rixon's career before turning to Tim Zoehrer and then Greg Dyer. Healy's selection for the rancorous 1988–89 tour to Pakistan after just six first-class matches generally was considered to be the most surprising since the choices of wrist-spinner John Watkins in 1972–73 and off-spinner Peter Taylor in 1986–87.

Among his peers Healy is renowned for the fierceness of his loyalty and the thoroughness of his preparation. Interested in sports science and psychology since his days studying for a physical education diploma, he maintains comprehensive diaries analysing his own performance and those of his opponents. He is convinced that committing thoughts and impressions to paper makes him a calmer and more able professional. Healy had a hand in the design of the new Australian team blazer paraded before an unsuspecting public at the start of the 1993–94 season. Once employed as a salesman in his in-laws' Brisbane fashion agency, Healy welcomed the arrival of what he described as an "honour blazer". That says it all, really.

ADAM GILCHRIST   Stephen Fay, *Five Cricketers of the Year*, 2002

Adam Gilchrist had never been so nervous at the start of a Test as he was at Edgbaston last summer. This was his Ashes debut and he had always been keen to excel in England, where he had played as a young man and enjoyed himself. The nerves showed; he dropped two straightforward catches in the first session.

Gilchrist has an equable nature, but he felt he had let himself down and reparation was required. Two days later he came in to bat when Australia were 336 for five. It was a crucial moment. If England could get rid of the tail quickly, they might make a game of it. The left-handed Gilchrist transformed that hope into fantasy. He put on 160 with his Western Australian mate Damien Martyn; his own hundred came up with an unorthodox flick over the keeper's head off glove and bat.

When he was last out, having hit five sixes and 20 fours in his highest Test score of 152, Australia were 576. He had humiliated the opposition, and set a pattern that was to repeat itself through the series, except at Headingley where Gilchrist, as stand-in captain, allowed the game to slip away from Australia. That was the only dark shadow over a memorable summer. England's fans, and no doubt their cricketers, felt contradictory sensations of fear and expectation each time he strode to the crease, but he soon became the Australian the crowd most enjoyed watching.

Up and away: Australia's Adam Gilchrist, the outstanding wicket-keeper-batsman of the age, reaches his century at Edgbaston in 2001 with a characteristically unorthodox shot.

Adam Craig Gilchrist was born on November 14, 1971 in the small New South Wales town of Bellingen. His father taught in another small town, Deniliquin, before moving into schools administration at Lismore, a town, in the north of the state, that was not much larger. To the outsider, such places may not have had much to offer, but, for an aspiring cricketer, Gilchrist had a privileged upbringing. His father Stan had been a good enough leggie, when a student in Sydney, to play for New South Wales seconds and he nurtured his son's ambitions. So did his mother, who bought him a pair of wicket-keeper's gloves for Christmas before he was ten. The first time he kept with them he broke his nose, but he made the best of it. When told that Rod Marsh had also broken his nose as a boy, Gilchrist declared this proved that it was his destiny to keep wicket for Australia. (Marsh later informed him that there was no truth in the story.)

As a batsman, he was taught by his father to watch the ball, give himself time, and play naturally. "I suppose that's the way I have always thought about it. Just try to hit the ball. That's what the game's about," he says. He decided he would be a professional cricketer at the age of 17 when he had to choose between university entrance exams and a cricket scholarship to England. He chose England, and played a summer for Richmond in the Middlesex League.

His higher education was in the Australian Under-19 team that swaggered through England in 1991, with Martyn as captain and 2001 team manager Steve Bernard as coach, and at the Academy in Adelaide, where he adopted his high-on-the-handle grip. He was promising, though not a prodigy like Martyn. Moreover, he was conscious he was not a natural keeper, and when he made his debut for New South Wales, aged 21, it was as a batsman, not an all-rounder. When he failed to score many runs, Gilchrist wondered whether he should give up keeping; he decided, sensibly as it turned out, that by not keeping he would only increase the pressure on his batting.

It was clear, however, that he would have to leave his home state if he was to get on. In the mid-1990s, Australian professional cricketers could make a decent living only if they played Test cricket, and the first requirement was a secure place in a state side. In 1994–95, he found one in Perth, with his mates Martyn and Justin Langer. He succeeded a popular Test keeper in Tim Zoehrer, but he soon established a reputation as a cheerful colleague and a relentless competitor. He had to learn patience, too. Although he deputised for the injured Ian Healy in Australia's one-day side in 1996–97, and emerged a year later as a dashing opening bat, Healy still wore the gloves in the Tests. Gilchrist's inexperience let him down in the 1999 World Cup in England, where his free style was undone by seam and swing until the final, when he scored 54. But this didn't prevent the selectors from dumping Healy in November 1999. Batting at No. 7, Gilchrist scored 149 not out in only his second Test, putting on 238 with Langer to provide an improbable win against Pakistan. He became a fixture straightaway; within nine months he was Steve Waugh's vice-captain.

The significance of Gilchrist's batting is that, after the specialist batsmen have established a platform, he is capable of putting Australia's score out of reach of the opposition. He is a breaker of wills. Of course, he knows failure, having scored two runs in four consecutive innings against India in March 2001 after starting the series with a century. But at the end of the Ashes summer his average was 51.30 from 22 Tests; against England, he had just averaged 68.00. He had also taken 94 catches and made seven stumpings – more dismissals per game than Healy, the record-holder.

However, the Ashes series also revealed a flaw. To combine batting, keeping and the captaincy has stretched the talent of cricketers like Alec Stewart too far. The evidence of the Headingley Test, when Gilchrist's slack tactics on the field allowed England an easy victory, suggested that captaincy may be a step too far for him. He need not worry. Name a wicket-keeper who has played as many match-winning Test innings. Adam Gilchrist has already come a very long way.

ANDY FLOWER   Keith Meadows, *Five Cricketers of the Year*, 2002

In a country whose descent into anarchy has almost reached terminal velocity, it is hard to keep one's eye on the ball. In a perfect world, a profile of a cricketer would not carry the baggage of politics. But Zimbabwe is not like other Test-playing nations; there is not a man, woman or child there who has been unaffected by events unravelling in a land once called "a jewel in Africa". The bewildering machinations of politicians and their lackeys have permeated every fabric of society, and cricket has not been excluded.

So there was something especially piquant in Andy Flower's regeneration since being stripped of Zimbabwe's captaincy on his return from the tour of England in July 2000; a sacking that came as a "complete bolt from the blue". Lesser men might have quit. Instead, while around him his country and as often as not his team crumbled, Zimbabwe's 32-year-old left-handed wicket-keeper/batsman went about his cricketing business with his usual tight-lipped determination. Twelve months later, the Federation of International Cricketers' Associations named him International Cricketer of the Year.

Andy Flower was born on the stroke of midnight of April 28/29, 1968 in the Cape coastal hamlet of Fish Hoek, South Africa, the third-born of three brothers and a sister. Brother Grant was born some two and a half years later. Their father, a keen sports enthusiast and an accountant, traversed southern Africa in the course of his career, family in tow, and Andy was ten before the family finally settled in what was then Rhodesia. He excelled at sport throughout his schooldays, being awarded colours for hockey, tennis and cricket, and in 1986, his last year at Vainona High School in northern Harare, he toured England with the Stragglers club. They played 16 games in three weeks, and the seeds of a life in pursuit of the cricketing sun were sown.

The following year, he commenced work at the Anglo American Corporation, but after 16 months returned to England to play for Barnt Green in the Birmingham League. A spell in the Lancashire leagues came next, at Heywood, and he was already playing in the Netherlands, for Voorburg in The Hague, when Zimbabwe selected him for the 1990 ICC Trophy there. Grant, playing for Winscombe in the Somerset League, was also in the squad, and the brothers' contribution to Zimbabwe's successful tournament – they beat Holland in the final – was not inconsequential. Andy scored 311 runs at an average of 77.75, and Grant 253 at just over 63. Vital as it was to Zimbabwe's quest for Test status, this third successive ICC Trophy win also meant a place at the 1991–92 World Cup in Australasia. Against Sri Lanka at New Plymouth, Andy celebrated his senior international debut in fair style, keeping wicket and batting throughout the innings for an unbeaten 115 – only the third player to score a century on one-day debut. But while it earned him the match award, it didn't result in a Zimbabwe victory, a portent of the way things would be for the rest of the decade.

Zimbabwe's captain for two tenures, Andy Flower led them to their first Test win, a triumphant innings victory over Pakistan at Harare in February 1995. It was only their 11th Test, and saw the Flowers' stand of 269 transcend the fraternal partnership record set by Ian and Greg Chappell against New Zealand in 1973–74. Grant was not out 201, his maiden Test century, while Andy made 156, his second. Zimbabwe's inaugural Test had been against India in October 1992. From then until breaking his thumb on the last day of their Test victory over India, at Harare in June 2001 – he hit the winning boundary – Andy Flower played in every one of his country's 52 Tests and 172 one-day internationals.

He had scored 3,908 runs in the Tests at 51.42, with nine hundreds, as well as making 143 dismissals; in one-day games, he was averaging 33.54 from 5,267 runs, with two hundreds and 44 half-centuries, and had made 124 catches and 30 stumpings. His highest score, an unbeaten 232 at Nagpur in November 2000, was the best by any wicket-keeper in Tests, and the crowning achievement in a glorious run of nine post-captaincy Tests that brought 1,066 runs at 88.83. In India alone, highlighting his aptitude against spin, his scores in the two Tests were 183 not out, 70, 55 and 232 not out. A seventh consecutive Test fifty, against Bangladesh at Bulawayo, set him alongside Everton Weekes in the record books.

In his earlier years especially, commentators noted Andy Flower's obduracy. These days the talk is more about his mental stamina. "When I started taking cricket seriously," he explained, "I never actually had a high regard for whatever talent I had. Seeing the ball, hitting it, there were plenty of other cricketers who did that far better than I did. But I thought one area where I could be better than them was to be more determined, more hungry, and not give anything away." He may not be the prettiest batsman to watch, building his game around back-foot strokes square of the wicket, but he is considered by some to be the finest exponent of the reverse sweep, having added his own subtleties to that shot.

Returning after injury to play South Africa in September 2001, he did not concede a bye in an innings that lasted ten hours. He followed that up by becoming the first keeper to make hundreds in each innings of a Test, batting for almost 15 hours. His 142 and 199 not out took him to No. 1 in the PwC rankings, the first Zimbabwean and the first wicket-keeper-batsman to top the world list. Still Zimbabwe lost. No wonder Andy Flower is thought of as "The Rock" in some circles – and the patron saint of lost causes in others.

A photograph of Andy Flower batting in 1996 appears on page 612.

Captains

MIKE BREARLEY   John Woodcock, *Notes by the Editor*, 1983

After being pursued almost to the finishing line by Leicestershire, Middlesex won the 1982 Schweppes County Championship. That they did so in the year of Michael Brearley's retirement was entirely fitting. Few cricketers, if any, can have achieved so much by reading the game so astutely as Brearley, and by finding out how to get the best out of each player. With a combination of intelligence, coercion, wisdom and care he has had a profound influence on the modern game. Although a good enough batsman to have scored 45 first-class hundreds, it was less as a player than as a presence that he made his considerable impact.

John Arlott, 1983

Comfortably before lunch on Tuesday, September 14, 1982, at Worcester, Mike Brearley made the final run in Middlesex's ten-wicket win over Worcestershire. He had been applauded on to the field at the start of the match; and he was applauded off it, into the retirement he had planned and announced. He walked into the pavilion for the fourth, and last, time as captain of the county champions. There is little doubt that he was one of the best – certainly the most sustainedly successful – captain international cricket has known. A shrewd and experienced North country professional and Test selector summed it up in the words: "This man is as good a captain on the field as Illingworth; off it, he must be far and away the best we have had." He added: "If only he could get some more runs there could never be any question about him." Runs, though, are not a yardstick of captaincy, only a reinforcement of selection.

Mike Brearley's record as a Test captain is excelled only by Sir Donald Bradman who, it will be conceded, had – by comparison with his opponents – stronger sides under his command. In short, Brearley captained England in 31 Test matches, of which they won 18 and lost four; while, of nine series, seven were won, one drawn and one lost. In his 11 years as captain of Middlesex they won the County Championship three times and shared it once, against five and one shared in their previous 89 years in the competition.

His achievement that will live in the imagination of all those who lived through it – or who read of it in the future – is the taking over of the 1981 England team, one down to Australia, which had all the look of a beaten side, and transforming

774

it, almost incredibly, into the winner of the rubber by three to one. Much credit, of course, must go to Ian Botham for his amazing all-round cricket. Yet Botham had been in the losing team Brearley took over. After that Brearley stepped down from the England captaincy, as he did from that of his county a year later, on a note of triumph.

The simple explanation for his success was expressed by the Australian fast bowler, Rodney Hogg, not generally known for his perspicacity, when he said "I reckon Brearley has got a degree in people." The salient points of his make-up are intellectual quality, clarity of mind and common sense – which are by no means the same thing, nor always found in the same person – and human perception. He would not claim the finest brain cricket has known. Indeed, he has argued that Edward Craig, his contemporary at Cambridge, was superior both mentally and as a batsman. It is, though, as certain as may be that his was the most effective intellect ever closely applied to the game. His clarity of mind enabled him to pierce the woolly romanticism and anachronistic feudalism which for so long obscured the truth of cricket. His common sense was reflected in his recognition of the need for Kerry Packer to be accepted into the body of cricket; and that, if players were not better treated financially, the available talent would ebb even further away.

His understanding – both intuitive and tutored – of human beings proved a major asset in his captaincy. He was able to reach, sympathise with and – in the current term – motivate cricketers as few, if any, others have done. If that capacity proved helpful, it also led to some of his major griefs, for his depth of understanding made his failures in human relationships the more agonising. His career is absorbing to follow, if only for its many-sidedness. Invariably crick-eters who achieve so much have been single-minded about the game. Mike Brearley has never seen it as an exclusive interest so much as the finest of games, set in a world of more important matters. That has enabled him to detach himself mentally from a match in which he was deeply involved and to assess it objectively.

Yet he could not be so detached about his own performance. Throughout his career as captain of England he was deeply – often inhibitingly – concerned about his batting form in Test matches. Clear-mindedly recognising his own potential, he was idealist enough to appreciate how far he often fell short of it. Had he played under a captain as sympathetic as himself, the problem might have been solved. In the event, although he often batted freely and fluently in county cricket, when he played for England anxiety drove him constantly into over-care. This frequently cost him his wicket. In short he was, like all good batsmen, basically an instinctive player: not even he could quite impose thought on the high-speed reactions of batting against pace. Thus his best Test innings were defensive: salvage operations conducted with an eye to survival. History, surely, will say that his captaincy and fine slip-catching compensated for the deficiency.

A photograph of Mike Brearley with Greg Chappell appears on page 43.

MARK TAYLOR

Scyld Berry, 2000

When Mark Taylor came off the field for the final time in Test cricket, on January 5, 1999, he was wearing his baggy green cap, not his normal white hat, to signal that retirement was at hand. It was the end of an era not just for Australian cricket, but for the game worldwide, because he had no challenger as the finest captain of modern times.

It would be fruitless to compare "Tubby" with the leaders of other ages. Warwick Armstrong, who was tubbier still, never had to address TV viewers ten minutes after the breathless finish of a day/night international, as Taylor did with unfailing articulacy. Sir Donald Bradman did not have to calculate net run rate and work to keep the media on side: newspapers then were deferential. When Richie Benaud was captain he knew the workings of the media all right, but he did not have to speak to them about players taking money from an Indian bookmaker, as Taylor did, with the diplomacy of an elder statesman. Taylor can only be compared with other captains of the post-Packer era. And – bearing in mind that Mike Brearley led in just eight Tests in this period – among them he was unquestionably supreme. His only possible rivals, Clive Lloyd and Viv Richards had a single game-plan in the field: they did not need more with the West Indian fast bowling.

But while he had to play a more complicated game than any of these, Taylor was, like them, an autocratic captain. The wicket-keeper Ian Healy, at times Australia's vice-captain and always in a position to know what was going on, testifies that he was never consulted on any major decision. A French or Italian stranger to cricket, introduced to a ground where Australia were in the field, would surely have been able to point out who was in charge: the one who strode down the pitch between overs, carrying a helmet under his left arm, directing with his right arm here and there, and chewing gum, his very jaw the focus of Australian cricket in the field. Even in the World Cup semi-final at Mohali in 1996, when Australia were on the verge of elimination by West Indies, Taylor's jaw and eyes never wavered. The impression that he always had something left up his sleeve – if only Stuart Law's leg-breaks – was never punctured.

Being his own captain, Taylor's first act upon his appointment in 1994 was a political one. With his predecessor, Allan Border, Bobby Simpson had worked hand-in-hand, planning ahead the bowling strategies and field-placings of each session. Taylor caused Simpson to revert to being coach again, the organiser of nets and conductor of fielding practices, and determined to do all the captaincy himself – so much so that he omitted to think about his own batting and made a pair in his first Test as Australia's captain in Karachi. Soon he learnt how to compartmentalise.

He had the essential attribute of being lucky. His record of tosses – 26 wins out of 50 – was in keeping with statistical norms, but he seemed to win the ones that mattered, for instance Adelaide and Sydney in the last Ashes series. And he had two great bowlers, so he could always keep control at one end. The Australian system helped him in protecting Glenn McGrath from being overbowled; during Taylor's captaincy, McGrath played only ten Shield matches for his state, New South Wales. Shane Warne, though, needed more than the system to protect him.

On Border's last tour, to South Africa, Warne had exploded in the face of Andrew Hudson and the growing pressures of superstardom. Taylor was less of a friend to Warne than Border had been, more of a counsellor. He brought Warne under his wing, into the slips between Mark Waugh at second and Steve Waugh at gully, and relieved the pressure by explaining that as long as Australia won it didn't matter if Warne failed to take bundles of wickets.

When Taylor's form deserted him, as it did through the first half of 1997, he was still able to hang on to his catches at first slip (Mike Atherton still regrets that he did not captain England from that prime position) and therefore his position of authority. His batting could never live up to his first full series, when he scored 839 runs against England in 1989, but it recovered to the point when he scored 334 not out against Pakistan in Peshawar in 1998–99 to equal the highest score for Australia. For declaring then, he received Bradman's thanks – and some recompense from a lucrative venture of jointly signing bats. Taylor did not believe much in technique; scoring runs and taking wickets were simply the means to getting on top of the opposition and staying there.

Yet he was perhaps the least conservative captain of his era as well. In contrast to Border, his declarations were not designed to kill all hope in the opposition, and interest in the match: he set New Zealand 288 at less than five an over in Hobart in 1997, albeit when Australia were 2–0 up in a three-Test series. If his record had a weakness, it is the minor one of losing Tests after a series had been decided, the mission accomplished. Whereas he learned from his Northern District club captain Ross Turner about backing himself and his players in tight situations, his New South Wales captain Geoff Lawson showed him how to take the risk of losing in the pursuit of winning.

He also upheld the dignity of the game. If he did not abolish Australian sledging, he oversaw a reduction of the racism in it. When Dickie Bird umpired in the Tests in Australia after Salim Malik's return to the Pakistan side, he noticed that Taylor did not permit any verbals about match-fixing. In his press conferences and TV interviews, Taylor talked so well that he raised the standard of debate in Australia – and perhaps of cricket itself – in a way which was an example to all professional cricketers (except for an irritating phase when he kept referring to himself in the third person). His deeds mattered more than his words, however. His teams played such good and entertaining cricket that he strengthened its potentially vulnerable position as the No. 1 sport in Australia. Border stopped Australia losing. Taylor made them into winners, the acknowledged world champions of Test cricket.

STEVE WAUGH
Simon Barnes, 2003

Never has a cricketer had so appropriate a surname. But let us understand that aright. Steve Waugh's cricketing warfare has never been a matter of hatred, jingoism and senseless aggression, any more than a matter of chivalry, romance and the search for personal glory. No. Waugh's wars have been about the most efficient possible means of despatching the enemy. They are about a clear understanding of the opposition's strengths and weaknesses, and an equally uncluttered understanding of the strengths and weaknesses of his own side. Sometimes the results are spectacular, but that is by the way. Spectacle is a by-product of a hard head, clear vision, an analytical mind and an impersonal lust for victory.

Waugh wants to defeat you personally – but nothing personal, if you see what I mean. He has that air possessed by very few, even at the highest level of sport: that sense of vocation, that urge to beat not the opposition but the limitations of your self, your game, your world. There was something of that unearthly quality in Ayrton Senna, the Brazilian racing driver. Ellen MacArthur, the British sailor, has it too. Waugh has the gift of reducing complex matters to simple ones: he sees without prejudice how best to exploit the opposition's weakness, how best to deploy his own strengths. The approach, cold-blooded, scientific, is that of a general, rather than a character in Sir Thomas Malory.

Waugh has conducted his cricketing campaigns in a mood of dispassionate ferocity. He famously remarked that sledging was "mental disintegration"; but that is not so much the aim of Waugh's sledging as of Waugh's cricket. The batting, bowling and fielding of his teams have all had the aim of causing mental disintegration: a moment of uncertainty that leads to self-doubt that leads to defeat. Waugh always wants defeat to be personal and complete, the better to prey on the opposition mind. And in the process, he has transformed Test cricket. Over the past four years, his Australians played in a manner that was once unthinkable. A captain is usually assessed on the way he operates his bowlers and sets his field, for it is supposed to be the fielding captain who controls the tempo of a match. Waugh is, of course, spectacularly good at all that. But it is the way he manages his batting line-up that is revolutionary.

In 1990, when there had been a long-running debate about intimidatory bowling, runs suddenly flowed in county cricket through a combination of flat pitches and a different type of ball. Simon Hughes, still operating as a bowler, asked the plaintive question: "What about intimidatory batting?" Under Waugh, Australia's batting has become the most intimidating aspect of modern cricket. The Australian batsmen seek to frighten opponents every bit as much as the fast-bowling quartet of the 1980s West Indians. They all act the same way, and they're all coming to get you. Waugh's Australia bat with Waugh's dispassionate ferocity. They bat as a team, with personal glory very much a secondary matter. And above all, they bat fast. In 2001, Australia scored at 3.77 runs an over: breathtakingly fast by traditional standards. In 2002, Australia scored their Test runs at a rate of 3.99 an over. Only once in history has a team scored faster through a whole year – in 1910, Australia scored their runs at 4.47 every six balls, and there were far fewer Tests then. By comparison, England's run-rate in 2002 was 3.37 – and that was England's fastest rate in almost a century. Other nations are following the Australian lead, but they're not as good at it yet.

South Africa, once dour, now bat at a significantly faster tempo: the first thing they did in 2003 was to score 445 in a day against Pakistan. The sea-change in Michael Vaughan of England over the past year was in tempo. Speed is not an accident. It is a tactic. It can't be done without very good players, but it is not the direct result of having good players. It is the result of astute, logical, cold-blooded thought on the subject of how best to win a cricket match. We traditionally think of fast scoring as something dashing and devil-may-care: Jessop, Milburn, Botham.

It was merry and jaunty and beery, the way you batted if you were a bit of a lad. Fast scoring was not altogether serious – it came in the drive-for-show category. Waugh's Australians have put it into the putt-for-dough department. For them, fast scoring is not a bonnets-over-the-windmill slogfest: it is deadly serious. It is done first to undermine the opposing bowlers, and with them the rest of the fielding side. And then it gives Australia extra time in the quest for 20 wickets: a free session for your bowlers every innings. No wonder it took them only 11 playing days to win each of the last two Ashes series.

Most non-Australian cricket followers would admit when pressed that they can't always tell one Australian batsman from another. They all wear green helmets with the Australian coat of arms above the grille, they are all good, they are all vindictively aggressive towards anything loose, they are all hugely confident. They bat as a unit and there's always another one waiting to destroy you. A bit like the film *Zulu*. The wicket-keeper scores even faster than the top six and the tail bat seriously, always an aspect of a consistently victorious side. And just as the West Indian bowling ground the opposition down, softened them up and destroyed their confidence, so the Australian batting does the same thing.

The influence of one-day cricket is obvious, but it is not that the Australians bat in Test matches as if they were in a one-dayer. It is rather that the thought processes of one-day cricket – the need to capitalise on every error of the opposition, the presumption that you look to make runs off every ball – have been adapted to the Test context.

Hit-and-giggle? Far from it. There is no suggestion that a wicket is any less valuable to an Australian than it was before: Sydney 2003 was the first time since England's previous visit four years earlier that they had been bowled out twice in a home Test. But wickets are seen more as team than as individual possessions. Every batting tactic, including that of speed, must be adapted to the conditions. In knuckling-down conditions, Australian batsmen will knuckle down. But send them a bad ball at any time in any context and hear it thwack into the boundary board: first over of the day, last over of the day, just after a wicket, just before tea, 50 for three or 200 for nought – bam. And don't even think about a night-watchman. When Andy Bichel was moved up to No. 3 at Sydney in January 2003, night-watchman was the word that sprang to some commentators' lips, but what he was actually doing was the opposite – softening the new ball.

It is not so much a tactic as an emphasis: when in doubt, attack. Not for fun – as a thought-out ploy. As a team policy. Speed is not self-indulgence but duty. The idea is to win every session of every Test match, and mostly that is what Australia have been doing. If things go amiss, there is always the captain to come in later in the order. The only disappointment in Waugh's later career is that there have been so few occasions when he has been required to do his one-man rescue act. The tactic of speed has been enthralling, but Waugh did not do it to enthral. He did it to enslave. There was an awful lot of guff talked about "brighter cricket" in the 1960s: if that was brighter cricket, what would audiences of 40 years back have made of the Australian speed machine? Waugh doesn't employ the tactic to make cricket brighter. But – and it is an aspect of his greatness – he didn't allow his prejudice against mere entertainment to muddle his thinking. In its intention, the Australian stroke-making is as flamboyant as an atom bomb.

The definitive treatise on warfare as a science of destruction rather than a chivalric art was written by Karl von Clausewitz in Napoleonic times. It is called *On War*. If a similarly hard-nosed book were to be written on cricket, the same title could be used. With a small adjustment to the spelling.

Nasser Hussain, 2004

At the beginning of this year, the cricketing world witnessed a remarkable week in which the people of Sydney poured out their affection towards their beloved son Stephen Waugh. The members were reportedly queuing as early as four in the morning to get their favourite seats, and the streets outside the ground were gridlocked by eight, not because the enthralling series between India and Australia was coming to its conclusion, but because one man who had meant so much to Australian cricket and Australians in general was donning his dishevelled baggy green cap for the last time.

Steve Waugh was not a cricketing god or a genius, like Tendulkar or Lara, nor even technically brilliant like Rahul Dravid. Like the rest of us, he was human. But a previously unremarkable household in suburban Sydney was definitely given more than its fair share of talent when the Waugh twins, Stephen and Mark, arrived on the scene nearly 39 years ago. Their little games of backyard cricket eventually led to the pair of them playing nearly 300 Tests and scoring nearly 20,000 runs between them. Some would argue that one was given a little bit more talent than

Mind over matter: Steve Waugh, Australia's hard-as-nails captain, acknowledges his century at The Oval in 2001, accomplished despite carrying a leg injury that had kept him out of the previous match.

the other. As one member of the Barmy Army once said, as he dared to sledge the greatest sledger of them all, "Oy, Stephen, best batsman in the world? You ain't even the best batsman in your family!"

Well, for over a decade Stephen Waugh made himself into the best batsman in the world. He was given two useful cricketing skills at birth: incredible hand-eye co-ordination and the fastest pair of hands of any cricketer I have played against. The rest he has had to work for. He has proved one cricketing cliché during his career: that the higher the level you play, the more it is played in your head. And he was, mentally, the strongest player of his era.

He didn't deal with the short ball particularly well and he moved around the crease a lot as the bowler delivered, staying back and not really transferring all his weight on to the front foot when the ball was pitched up. But, hey, that is the game. Every batsman has weaknesses, and it is up to the player to overcome them and the opposition to exploit them. Waugh overcame his deficiencies because his hand-eye co-ordination meant he could keep the good ones out and put the bad ones away – and because his mental toughness helped him through every situation batting can throw up.

Many a pre-Ashes Test meeting stopped when S. Waugh's name hit the projector screen. Half the team got animated and said "Look, skip, just put in a leg gully and a short leg and we'll pepper him with the short stuff. It's only a matter of time." The other less emotional half, usually the batters and the coach, said "No, pitch it up and try to hit off stump early, because he has a tendency to get his head off-side of the ball a bit, and then there's a chance of him being bowled or lbw." The final thing always said was that, when he first came in, everyone must be on their toes as he loved to push a single and get off strike. Meeting finished. Everyone happy.

Next day, if we were doing really well and had reduced Australia to 300 for three, we would be pleased with ourselves. In comes Waugh, red handkerchief hanging out of pocket, pushes the ball (usually to someone like dopey Gough standing at mid-on) and scampers a single, smiles and stays off strike for a while. This would be followed by a few short balls (which Waugh finds uncomfortable, but never gets out to), and the bowlers begin thinking that they had better start pitching it up. They over-correct and these incredible hands start to caress the ball through the covers. Before you know it, you look up at the scoreboard and he's 30 not out, off and running. Groundhog Day! You've seen it all before, but there seems nothing you can do to stop it happening all over again.

As a player, Waugh was always at his most dangerous when confronted by a real challenge. All his great innings came in the face of adversity. Whether it was a poor wicket, or a poor calf, or a poor press hinting at the waning of his power, he felt most at at home in difficult situations. It was as if he believed in his own reputation as the "iceman" and was keen to enhance it. Nothing would give him more pleasure than reading the next day about another gutsy Steve Waugh innings.

There could not have been any more pressure on a cricketer than in January 2003 against England at the SCG. Waugh has since admitted that if he hadn't got runs in that Test it would have been his last. He was not playing particularly well in the series, and looked surprisingly nervous. He came in when Australia were 56 for three and I immediately thought: "Dangerous." Everything I tried to do that day seemed almost pointless. It was as if the script had already been written. That evening, with Waugh on 98 and the last ball of the day coming up, I ran up to Dawson, told him I had no real cunning plan but to stall things, get Waugh nervous and hope he would make a mistake. Dawson bowled a perfectly good ball and those Waugh hands just flicked it away through the covers with complete disdain.

As a captain, Waugh used the same principles that he did as a player: he made the most of what he was given. Luckily for him, he was given a remarkable collection of batsmen plus three all-time great bowlers in McGrath, Warne and Gillespie. His side played in such a way that they basically took the draw out of the equation. They would score their runs at over four an over, declare early and leave as much time as possible to bowl the opposition out twice. The days of someone like Boycott batting a day for a hundred were gone. The likes of Hayden, Ponting and

Gilchrist were scoring centuries in a session, and this attitude was infectious, spreading throughout the team with more compact players, such as Langer, becoming more expansive.

Richie Benaud believes Waugh's team has produced in the last four or five years the most exhilarating cricket in the history of the game. The three-Test series England played in Sri Lanka recently is how cricket used to be played, but it now seems ever so turgid by comparison. Whether the pace is sustainable, only time will tell. It will depend on the talent available. Three great captains have taken Australia to where they are now. Allan Border changed the culture by altering Australia's attitude. No longer were they going to be the "let's have a beer after the game" sort of men, but a much more ruthless outfit. That was the most difficult part. He was followed by the more cerebral Mark Taylor, who would quietly stand at first slip influencing the game and, more importantly, influencing some of the gems that were starting to appear in the Australian team, thanks to Border's change in culture. Taylor made sure the Australians wouldn't have to survive just on bravado, but left them with four or five all-time greats who could single-handedly turn a game of cricket. Steve Waugh combined all of this and gave them that final ingredient, belief.

Waugh's one big failure came in India, where they managed to lose a series they had for the taking. I believe that was the only time their attitude let them down. Sometimes in India you just have to sit in: slow the opposition run-rate down, keep the pressure on the likes of Tendulkar, Laxman and Dravid. Stopping them scoring gets the crowds on their backs and creates pressure. However, Australia – in search of their 17th consecutive victory had an attitude that didn't allow for "sitting in". Waugh kept attacking; enforced the follow-on and before he knew it, found his team batting last, and under pressure themselves. They lost that Test, in Calcutta, and the series. It is a blemish on his record – but it was done for all the right reasons.

I can't say I have ever got to know Steve Waugh well. He never let his guard slip for fear of letting anything penetrate his veneer of inscrutability. The nearest I came to cracking it was in a bar in Adelaide after we had failed to regain the Ashes in 1998–99, when I picked Steve's brain over his attitude to batting. Now for me there is no point in trying to talk to Lara or Tendulkar about things like that; to them it is just natural. But I have always found Waugh intriguing. How did he make himself so good? He told me that the most important aspect to him was body language. He liked to almost sprint to the crease to emphasise that he was relishing the battle ahead; he liked to give off an aura of aggression. Nothing emphasises this more than when, in Port-of-Spain nine years ago, Waugh stood face to face with one of the greatest fast bowlers of all time, Curtly Ambrose.

Now, here is a man who doesn't play the short ball particularly well, doesn't pull or hook, telling the man who has dismissed him the most in Test cricket to get back to his mark and bowl. Robert Craddock wrote in that year's *Wisden*: Waugh "stood his ground like John Wayne when Ambrose engaged him in a verbal exchange of fire from two metres; the bowler had to be tugged away by Richie Richardson. 'It's Test cricket,' the unrepentant Waugh said afterwards. 'If you want an easy game, go play netball.' " Waugh made 63 not out in that innings and went on to make 200 in the next game, when Australia won by an innings and regained the Frank Worrell Trophy.

Throughout his career, Waugh, almost on purpose, maximised the challenge – whether it be a sore calf, a last-chance-saloon innings, or a fired-up Ambrose – to bring the best out of himself. Basically, for over 20 years he has been playing mind games with himself and the opposition. The crowds did not turn up at Sydney to thank him for his statistics. They came to thank him for his character.

Nasser Hussain captained England 45 times, seven of them in Ashes Tests against Australia led by Waugh. England won one, Australia six.

NASSER HUSSAIN
Scyld Berry, *Five Cricketers of the Year*, 2003

Nasser Hussain has always been too intense to inspire mass affection. Like Nick Faldo, or Steve Redgrave, or other English sportsmen suspected of being obsessive, he has inspired respect instead. In his four years as England's captain, Hussain should have inspired gratitude too. Last winter, in the first three Ashes Tests, England were a rowing-boat overwhelmed by the mountainous waves of Australian cricket. Almost every touring side had capsized against Steve Waugh's team in Australia; but Hussain, a beleaguered skipper if ever there was, kept England afloat. If one image could sum up the tour, it came in the one-day matches before Christmas when England – 3–0 down in the Test series – had to play four one-day internationals in eight days at venues as widespread as Melbourne, Brisbane and Perth. Any other England captain might have let his exhaustion, physical or mental, show. But there was Hussain in the field, hectoring, urging, berating, then exploding in celebration at the fall of each wicket. England have not had such an ardent captain since Douglas Jardine, another cricketer whose obsessiveness was not to English taste. Spurred on by this zeal, and blessed when injuries at last struck Australia instead, England won the Fifth Test in Sydney.

It has not been zeal alone which has fuelled the England team since 1999, but a sharp intellect blended with a diplomat's skill. Hussain has helped to educate the cricket public, and media, as Mark Taylor did in Australia a few years earlier. With his honest insights into the state of English cricket (and occasional propaganda), Hussain has raised the level of debate above the platitudes which used to prevail. Using a mind that won a maths scholarship to Forest School and achieved a 2.2 in geology and chemistry at Durham University when cricket allowed, Hussain also advanced the moral argument for England not to play in Zimbabwe: it was believed to be the first time in England that team sportsmen at national level, and certainly the whole cricket team, had exercised their consciences. Above all, Hussain's legacy is that he has raised standards inside and outside the England team.

Nasser Hussain was born on March 28, 1968 in Madras (now Chennai). His father Javaid, or Joe, represented Madras in the Ranji Trophy before emigrating to England, where he married an Englishwoman, Shireen. He then returned to India to set up an electronic-components factory in Madras, where the youngest of his three sons was born. Nasser's first experiences of cricket were family visits to Chepauk, where his father was a member of the Madras Cricket Club. His elder brothers Mel and Abbas used to bat on the outfield while he chased after the ball. When Joe returned with his family to England, and took charge of the indoor cricket school in Ilford, Nasser used to bowl for hours on end at his elder brothers, and not just because he was the youngest: he found leg-spin interesting. He was keener on football at first – supporting Leeds United, as he still does, and playing for school teams – but Sunday mornings were always dedicated to cricket, and his father kept pushing him in this direction. At eight, he was bowling leg-breaks for Essex Schools Under-11s, and at 12 for their Under-15s.

Born five days apart, Hussain and Mike Atherton soon found their careers progressing in parallel as they captained, batted and bowled leg-spin for England age-group teams, while also passing enough exams to go to a leading university. In his mid-teens, however, Hussain "grew a foot in a winter" and the trajectory of his bowling was altered: "I went from bowling out Graham Gooch in the indoor school with everyone watching to hitting the roof or bowling triple-bouncers in deadly silence."

His father remembers him crying in bed at the loss of his leg-break; the son felt he was letting his father down. He was also anxious not to be left behind by his peers, boys like Atherton, Trevor Ward, Martin Bicknell and Chris Lewis. So he made himself into a batsman, moving up the order from tail-end to opening or No. 3, and becoming the first boy at Forest to score 1,000 runs in a season since 1901. Vestiges of this manufacturing process remain in his technique: he bats with little left elbow and plenty of bottom hand. In general, his runs seem to be scored as much by an exceptional effort of will as through natural talent. These characteristics have been most apparent in one-day cricket, or when Michael Vaughan at the other end has been stroking the ball around with classical orthodoxy.

He also developed a reputation. The fieriest of three brothers who had all inherited their father's short temper, he vented his frustration at being dismissed – and at being unable to bowl leg-spin? – on his equipment or anything else in sight. He came to be bracketed with Graham Thorpe and Mark Ramprakash as a brat-pack. By the time he became captain, Hussain was as unpopular as any cricketer in England. The perception, though, was worse than the reality. Self-obsessed as he may have been, driven to succeed as many migrants are, and seldom the one to depart after a run-out, he confined his tantrums to the dressing-room (including altercations with his Essex team-mates Neil Foster and Mark Ilott). He describes himself as "a fairly shy sort of bloke". According to his father, he inherited "good sense" from his mother, together with a sturdy sense of right and wrong.

The frustrations built up through his early twenties. Taken under the wing of Gooch, his Essex and England captain, who urged him to play straighter and less behind point with an open face, Hussain made his Test debut on the 1989–90 tour of the West Indies but was mostly out of the side thereafter. His Essex record was good without being outstanding. He spent the 1994–95 winter playing in South Africa, where he was prescribed a contact lens (he has since had laser treatment on his left eye). The England A-team captaincy in Pakistan the following winter was a lifeline: it took him out of himself, encouraged him to think he might be fulfilled, and proved that he was not as bad or moody as his reputation suggested. When he was recalled to the Test team at the start of the 1996 season in the problem position of No. 3, he survived a big appeal off Javagal Srinath, and went on to his maiden Test hundred. A year later, he made 207 as England for once went ahead in a modern Ashes series. Only injury has kept him out of the team since.

When Atherton resigned as England captain in 1998, Hussain had to wait while Alec Stewart had his turn. But when Stewart was sacked after the 1999 World Cup, he was matured and ready for the responsibility. His first Test in charge ended in victory as England dismantled a modest New Zealand side; his first series in failure when Hussain broke a finger in the Second Test and England fell apart. But help was on its way with Duncan Fletcher joining as coach for that winter's tour of South Africa. They had not met before but it was a fine partnership from the first. Hussain generated heat, Fletcher light. Fletcher planned and prepared the players – identifying those with the right character and refining their technique, especially when batting against spin – while Hussain led them zealously on the field. Once a new system of squad players contracted to the ECB was put in place, English cricket was set for its finest achievements – four successive Test series won – since the Ian Botham era ended in the mid-1980s.

But for Hussain himself, 2000 was also an *annus horribilis*. He did not make a first-class fifty until his final match, the Karachi Test. His place in the side was never questioned as his players and the media appreciated his captaincy, but he still couldn't make a run. Looking back, Hussain can see that he gave too little attention to his own game, that he took his own form for granted after a hugely productive tour of South Africa. It didn't matter if he didn't make runs against Zimbabwe, while against West Indies he became consumed by the prospect of England beating them in a series for the first time since 1969. By the Oval Test, completely out of form, he went out to bat in the second innings unaware that he was on a pair, and duly bagged one. Once he learned to compartmentalise, he worked out that 60% of his attention had to go on the team, 40% on his own game. And the effect on his own game may be judged by the fact that he has been England's one consistent batsman in their last five Test series. Every time, his first innings of the series has yielded at least a half-century: the captain stamping his mark.

England's series victories in 2000–01, by 1–0 in Pakistan and 2–1 in Sri Lanka, were the apogee of Hussain's captaincy – and of a generation of England cricketers, including Atherton, Stewart, Thorpe, Darren Gough and Andy Caddick. In Pakistan, England held on doggedly until the pressure told on the home team, who had never lost at Karachi before. In Sri Lanka, England overcame the stifling heat and the stifling spin of Muttiah Muralitharan. If one session marked the climax, it was when England dismissed Sri Lanka in the Third Test in Colombo in only 28.1 overs. Hussain went into the match injured and could barely walk by the end of it, but his zeal – his passion – won the day.

The hope was that England could go on to win the Ashes series of 2001. Instead, they went from apogee to nadir with a 4–1 defeat. England began a run of injuries which lasted into the following Ashes series and raised numerous questions about their medical team. Hussain himself broke a finger in the First Test against Australia at Edgbaston and missed the next two. If any good came of it, it was the plastic coating which he adopted as extra protection on his gloves. Since then, he has not missed a Test.

A mark of his captaincy has been his refusal to accept mediocrity, however often his batsmen have failed to follow his example and given their wickets away, however inaccurate his seamers have been, however little his spinners have turned the ball. Atherton in the end became resigned to his bowlers' and fielders' fallibility; Hussain has barked at every foible and thought up new ways to dismiss batsmen. His imaginative use of 8–1 fields paid off in India when the home batsmen, after their First Test win, were content to be tied down; and again at times last summer when Sri Lanka were beaten 2–0, the one win to set against three recent losses and three drawn series; but in Australia the batsmen refused to be tied down and it was widely reckoned that Hussain asked his bowlers to experiment too much. He thought his seamers had matured to the extent that he could send Australia in at Brisbane and give his bowlers best use of the pitch; he admitted his mistake long before the match ended in massive defeat. By the Third Test in Perth he was considering his position, not for the first or last time, but in the darkest hour he pushed himself as hard as ever. While England were lucky that Glenn McGrath and Shane Warne were both injured, they still had to be in good enough shape to take advantage. After the Sydney Test, Hussain received "a really nice email" from Gough, which meant a lot as an expression of esteem from his peers.

After the World Cup he retired as England's one-day captain, sensibly deciding to concentrate on Test cricket. By then his wish to be remembered as "a decent leader of men" had already been fulfilled. The only dispute is whether he has been the equal of Mike Brearley as the best England captain since World Series Cricket; or, as their fellow-captain David Gower believes, even better, in more troubled times.

A photograph of Nasser Hussain holding up the Wisden *Trophy appears on page 296.*

Characters

DEREK RANDALL   Alex Bannister, *Five Cricketers of the Year*, 1980

By any known yardstick Derek William Randall is an uncommon cricketer and an unusual character. The contrasting roles of a Chaplin, adored by the masses of India as a slapstick comedian, and a classical Olivier, heroically battling England out of defeat into an impossible victory in a Sydney heatwave, have come alike to him.

He was the perky, immortal figure scoring 174 in defiance of the fire-eating Australian fast bowlers in the Centenary Test at Melbourne, and the irrepressible fielder celebrating England's Ashes-winning victory at Headingley in 1977 with a joyous handspring. His batting technique, with its famous shuffle, can be said to be all his own, and as a fielder in the covers he is spoken of in the same breath as Colin Bland and Neil Harvey. No higher praise can be offered.

Those who admired him in the moments of high drama at Melbourne might find it hard to imagine him only weeks before playing the fool to amuse the Indian crowds. Many a police officer lost his dignity as Randall borrowed his cap and performed some outrageous imitations, or shinned up a pole in sheer exuberance. The same Randall, facing the crisis of the 1978–79 Australian series, had the disciplined determination and skill to take 411 minutes to reach a century. At that time it was the slowest century in 234 Tests between the countries. In the end he made 150 in a heat of 105°C with Bob Willis, David Gower and Ian Botham ill or injured, and by general consent it was the innings that clinched the Ashes for England. In the first innings he had been out second ball to a hook – a match to reflect the peaks and troughs of his ebullient career – and when he went in, England on that January morning in 1979, faced a deficit of 142 runs. Geoff Boycott had been out first ball.

Before he went in, he picked up his 2lb 7oz bat with its extra layer of rubber on the handle and murmured "Come on, Rags, England needs you". Over the next nine and three-quarter hours, Randall constantly upbraided himself, as is his habit, with such comments as: "Wake up, Rags, concentrate." "Get stuck in." "You idiot, Rags." "Concentrate, Rags, come on, come on." "Come on England."

The Australian bowlers were, in turn, amused and irritated, but as one said: "He's quite inconsistent. If you twice bowl the same ball to him he'll play it in two entirely different ways." Understandably they found it hard to bowl at him, particularly when he shuffled across and hid all three stumps. His movements at the crease are the despair of the purists. But Randall has his explanation: "I haven't got a long reach, and my weakness is outside the off stump. By moving across I try to get the bowler to aim at my main strengths and straight at the legs."

Australian pitches, with the ball coming on to the bat, suit Randall, and he has three gold medals – or at least his mother, Mavis, has – as Man of the Match. The first was in the Centenary match, which incidentally was his first appearance against Australia, the second at Brisbane in 1978, for his scores of 75 and 74 not out, and for the Fourth Test at Sydney. Typically, after the Brisbane Test, he talked only of the class of David Gower, and the medals were sent to his mother in appreciation of her encouragement. "She's a good'un," he says simply. A remark to typify the man.

He was born at Retford, Nottinghamshire, on February 24, 1951, and played little cricket at Sir Frederick Milner Secondary Modern School. His father, Frederick, was both an enthusiast and a noted local player. Father, younger brother Stephen, and Derek often batted and bowled in the back garden, and it was natural that Derek should join Retford, members of the Bassetlaw League. By a fortunate coincidence, Michael Hall was both captain of Retford and Nottinghamshire II, and young Randall did well for both teams. In 1970 he joined the Trent Bridge staff. There was a modest initiation in 1971 with one John Player League match, but in the following season he had 15 Championship outings, starting with an eye-catching 78, including five sixes, against Essex at Newark. Not surprisingly he set himself too hard a standard to maintain consistently, but there were frequent examples of rich promise and a refreshing desire to hit the ball hard. From the start his fielding was superb, and as time went on he became a deadly thrower, much feared by all batsmen. A prime example of his accuracy was the run out of Gordon Greenidge in the Prudential Cup final of 1979.

Randall is of comparatively slight build, standing 5ft 8½ in tall and weighing eleven and a half stone. He takes size 11 boots, and is dubbed "Arkle" after the famous racehorse. Typically, on a pre-season training run he lost his way, but arrived back first. In his never-dull career he has fallen at a few fences, but much of his appeal is that he picks himself up with a smile. He is good to be with, good to watch, and on tour is forever talking of his wife Elizabeth and family. A charismatic personality on the field, and everybody's friend off it.

A photograph of Derek Randall batting in the Centenary Test in 1977 appears on page 335.

MERV HUGHES   Bruce Wilson, *Five Cricketers of the Year*, 1994

At the end of the Ashes season, the England captain who failed to regain them, and resigned his job as a result, looked back in an interview on it all: the good, the bad, the indigestible. In the course of it, Graham Gooch spoke of "dear old Merv Hughes". What? No matter that Gooch is eight years Hughes's senior. It is not the "old" that might send the moustaches twirling; it is the "dear old". Whoever spoke of "dear old Joel Garner" at the end of a series in which he had taken 31 wickets, or "dear old Dennis Lillee"?

Perhaps it is the action. When many of us saw Hughes for the first time down at Arundel in 1989 on that blazing sunny day, there was a mixture of mirth and disbelief: the mincing little steps leading to a stuttering run, the absurd stove-pipe trousers, the pre-bowl calisthenics, the whiskers, the silent-movie bad-guy theatrics. The action is not much different today, although it might tend a little more towards out-swing and the googly variation is not used quite so often. The eyes above the hooked nose still glare with the same passion. Insults fly, though if Gooch is to be believed not especially imaginative or distressing ones, just a couple of words. Sometimes, too, a childlike smile appears, all perhaps indicating the man behind the moustache: pretty straightforward, not too gaudy.

Now Hughes has been involved in two Ashes tours, and in each he has taken key wickets at key times. Last summer, in the absence of the one man thought to separate the two sides in strike-power, Craig McDermott, Hughes showed that in fact it was he who was

Anything you can do: Australia's fast bowler and folk hero Merv Hughes loosens up – and so do many of the crowd at the Melbourne Cricket Ground in January 1989.

the difference in the seam-bowling department. If Shane Warne bowled the ball which launched a thousand paragraphs, Merv Hughes ground out the overs which gave Australia a decent front-line assault. In the course of the summer, Hughes took his 200th Test wicket and passed the Test tallies of two Australian fast bowlers, Geoff Lawson and Jeff Thomson, the second legendary and the first deeply respected. In doing this, Hughes had a strike-rate roughly the equal of Thomson's and rather better than Lawson's. Yet, until recently, it was unthinkable that he would be mentioned as being in the same class as those two. He has paid a price for his eccentricities, not least not being taken seriously.

Mervyn Gregory Hughes was born in rural Victoria on November 23, 1961, son of a schoolmaster. In Australian education, country schoolteachers are often itinerants, and Merv and his family travelled around before they settled in Werribee, south-west of Melbourne. There Hughes was preoccupied, like all good young Victorian boys, with Australian Rules football in the winter and cricket in the summer. He boasts that he is the only man to have played 96 games for Werribee First XVIII and taken 200 Test wickets. To get to Werribee from Melbourne, you must drive through Footscray, which has both a senior football team and a first-grade cricket club. It was there that Hughes naturally gravitated. At Footscray, Hughes came under the influence of two men who had short and bitter Test careers: fast bowler Ron Gaunt, who played three Tests in one-match stands between 1957 and 1961, and Ken Eastwood, a left-handed opening bat, who played just one, disastrously, in 1970. At Sheffield Shield level, though, both were outstanding and at Grade level prodigious. Furthermore, they epitomised Footscray. This is a working-class area in Melbourne's western suburbs and the Footscray footballers and cricketers are known to themselves and to the rest of the city – one which has sharp social divides – as Scraggers. If you are from outside Footscray, it is a jibe; if you are of Footscray, it is a boast. Merv Hughes was, is, always will be, a Scragger. In a way, the disappointments Gaunt and Eastwood felt have been reflected in Hughes's determination.

After Lillee and Thomson, there were always plenty of quicks off long runs around in Australia, sledging away and getting hit around the park bowling short on true wickets. Hughes ran – or minced – from the sight-screen, until wiser heads told him to cut his run. "It was simple enough," he said. "I was going to get the club fined for slow play." For the first time he learned that control was more important than sheer pace.

In the 1981–82 season Hughes made the Victorian side, and by 1985 he had been selected for Australia, playing one Test against Kapil Dev's touring Indians. He became almost, but not quite, a fixture. In 1989, Hughes came to England as the fourth seamer, behind Terry Alderman, Lawson and Carl Rackemann. An injury to Rackemann saw Hughes promoted, and he played all six Tests in a series dominated by Alderman. In the thrilling 1992–93 series against West Indies, Hughes took 20 wickets at 21.60, two more than McDermott and considerably cheaper. Yet he was still the second seamer when the party left for England, and had Bruce Reid been fit might have been the third.

The rest, as they say, is history. He took 31 wickets at 27.25, played an important innings of 38 at Edgbaston, dropped little and brilliantly helped run out Atherton at a crucial point of the Lord's Test. Recently married, he is now a sedate enough member of the side to have joined his captain in staying in the night the team went out at Leeds to celebrate the successful defence of the Ashes. Allan Border's eyes crinkle with affection when he sees "the Big Bloke" come into the bar. Hughes is one of Border's elite. He was, quite literally, exhausted by the end of the tour, but he could go back to Footscray as one proud Scragger.

DEVON MALCOLM   Paul Allott, *Five Cricketers of the Year*, 1995

Devon Malcolm is an unlikely hero. He can be erratic, he is hopelessly short-sighted, and at times he is wildly inaccurate. But he possesses an athleticism and physical strength which he combines with an ungainly, almost unco-ordinated delivery to produce bowling which at best is lightning fast and straight, and at worst searches in vain for the cut strip.

Ask any South African cricketer and they will have just one memory of the man. Fearsomely fast, searingly straight and awesomely aggressive, devastating Devon was the hero of The Oval in 1994. His nine for 57 in the second innings demolished and demoralised South Africa in a way that only outstanding fast bowling can. The analysis was the sixth-best in the history of Test cricket and it elevated Malcolm into English cricketing folklore.

Since twin tours were introduced in England in 1965, no team had ever come back to win or draw a three-match series after falling one behind. England in their selection threw caution to the wind, abandoning hope of fielding a balanced attack in favour of all-out speed. Malcolm was delivered from Chesterfield and Eastbourne and thrust into his favourite arena.

The Oval's pitch with its generous pace and bounce provided him with an ideal surface on which to perform and rejuvenate his flagging career. Malcolm felt he had been publicly humiliated when sent away from the Lord's Test match against New Zealand 24 hours before the game. Sensibly, he retained a faith in his own ability and also a respect for the England captain, Mike Atherton, who as an accomplished opening batsman realises more than most the unsettling effect of raw pace.

Devon Eugene Malcolm was born on February 22, 1963 in Kingston, Jamaica. His father, Albert, supported the family by working in England, and his mother, Brendalee, died when Devon was five, leaving him to be brought up by his grandmother in the Jamaican town of St Elizabeth. At school he enjoyed all sports, particularly sprinting, cricket and football. But it was not until he went to join his father in Sheffield in 1979, and began studying at Richmond College, that his cricketing talent was recognised. The college had a cricket team, but it was made up of old boys and staff and Devon became the first student member.

He kept taking five wickets and on his own admission kept scaring people, so much so that his prowess was highlighted in the *Sheffield Star*. In 1981 he played in the same Yorkshire schools side as Ashley Metcalfe and progressed via Sheffield Caribbean and Sheffield United to selection for the Yorkshire League XI which played the county side in April 1984. His two prized scalps that afternoon were Geoffrey Boycott and Martyn Moxon, both clean bowled.

That performance must have left Yorkshire wondering if the Kingston on Malcolm's birth certificate might be the Hull variety rather than the Jamaican. But at that stage the strict Yorkshire-born policy applied. He signed for Derbyshire later that season. He told Phil Russell, the Derbyshire coach, that he didn't want any money for playing, he would play for the love of it. His love of the game has been sorely tested since that day, his career being a constant roller-coaster of selections and non-selections for both Derbyshire and England. Derbyshire, with a large stock of seam bowlers, have had a policy of rest and rotation, believing this is in the best interests of the player, though Malcolm himself thrives on hard work.

Nevertheless, Malcolm was and always will be a raw quick bowler, who will remain indebted to Russell for encouraging him to bowl as fast as possible, and to his fellow Jamaican and team-mate at Derby, Michael Holding, who emphasised the levels of concentration that were needed to bowl fast and highlighted the one single factor that transforms Malcolm, more than any other bowler, from also-ran to danger-man: "Follow through straight."

Between qualifying to play for England, by residence, in 1987, and his triumph at The Oval, he played 28 Test matches and took 98 wickets at an average of 35. These are hardly startling figures and reflect the erratic nature of his career. But by the winter of 1989–90 his strike bowling capabilities were well recognised, and his waywardness countered and complemented by a partnership with the admirably straight Angus Fraser. The duo bowled England to an improbable victory in Jamaica, where Malcolm blew away the West Indians' key batsmen in the second innings, and to the verge of victory in Port-of-Spain where a match analysis of ten for 137 gave him his best and most aggressive performance to date.

His dislike of the generally slower and flatter pitches in England and his apparent inability to adapt to these conditions limited his appearances to the extent that by 1993 he was chosen only for the Oval Test, where he took six wickets against the hitherto rampant Australians. With a West Indies tour coming up after that, he was a natural choice to lead the attack in the winter, but the first serious injury of his career, picked up in the Jamaica Test, scuppered his chances of glory. And when he was dropped again after one Test against New Zealand in 1994, many thought that, at 31, he was finished as a Test cricketer. No one, not even Malcolm at his most resolute, could have dreamed what was to follow when he came back to face South Africa at The Oval. After a first-day argument, that he describes as healthy, with his captain over the bowling of bouncers at de Villiers and Donald (Atherton wanted them delivered, Malcolm didn't), events conspired to produce his definitive fast bowling performance. Inspired by the batting efforts of DeFreitas and Gough on Friday evening, goaded into retaliation by a blow between the eyes from a de Villiers bouncer, and kept calm by the reggae on his Walkman in the dressing-room, Devon bowled England to victory and himself into the history books.

P. S. Tradition dictates that we have to mention his batting. He was once officially described, by Conrad Hunte in his capacity as Test match referee, as "one of the worst No. 11s in the game". It is entertaining, though.

DERMOT REEVE   Alan Lee, *Five Cricketers of the Year*, 1996

Very occasionally in the game of cricket, a player emerges to defy conventional categorisation. Dermot Reeve is one such. By the accepted benchmarks of batting, bowling and fielding, he falls short of excellence, and yet the sum of the parts compels attention and admiration. The same, of course, can be said of the Warwickshire side, whose unprecedented success over the past two seasons owes so much to Reeve's inspiration.

They have been good for each other. Warwickshire, a big club with resources and ambitions, gave Reeve the broad canvas he required when they made him captain in 1993; in return, he gave them the success they craved by instilling in the players a confidence, almost a joy, in free expression. The outcome is unarguable; by winning the Championship and the NatWest Trophy in 1995, they raised the trophy count to six in Reeve's three seasons of stewardship. In the Lord's final, he was Man of the Match, and not just for his perky batting. Nobody, now, is putting it all down to coincidence.

If this past season was the best of his career, it is because he was fulfilled by the esteem of his peers. Previously, it had often been grudgingly given, and then with stinging caveats. But as 1995 progressed and it became clear even to the most star-struck that there was, after all, more to Warwickshire's rise than the presence of Brian Lara, the significance of Reeve's input received due acknowledgment and genuine respect. He had a decent enough season with bat and ball, fractionally improving his career batting average to 34 and taking 38 wickets at 17.39 to finish second, to his team-mate Allan Donald, in the first-class bowling averages. But bald statistics are not the measure of this man, whose greatest quality as a cricketer is contributing crucially when it is most urgently needed and whose gift as a captain is convincing others around him that they are capable of the same.

Donald, the South African fast bowler whose seamless takeover from Lara was critical to Reeve's strategy, sums up his captain: "Nobody should ever take Dermot for granted. He may seem to be taking the mickey and bubbling all the time but he is a very focused man and a great disciplinarian. He never lets us take our mind off the job and he has brought an arrogant, cocky attitude to the team. I wouldn't like to play against him, though, because he is such a niggling character on the field." Some say it was ever thus. Reeve's nature is to be extrovert, even confrontational, and it has not always endeared him to opponents. Many have accused him of possessing a swollen head; probably, many did so even during his schooldays.

Dermot Alexander Reeve was born in Kowloon, Hong Kong, on April 2, 1963, perhaps a day late to be truly appropriate. He was brought up in the colony by his parents, Alexander and Monica, and educated at King George V School in Kowloon. In his teens, he became something of a sporting celebrity within the local expatriate community and he represented Hong Kong in the ICC Trophy of 1982. By then, however, he was on the Lord's groundstaff and, the following season, he made his county debut for Sussex.

His five seasons at Hove were not a spectacular success, although in 1986 he did play a significant role in the winning of the NatWest Trophy, taking four for 20 in the final against Lancashire. For this, he received the first of his three Man of the Match awards in NatWest finals, an unparalleled feat. He left Sussex claiming that their conditions did not suit his swing bowling. This was only part of the truth. Reeve was intensely ambitious and wanted to play for a club that demonstrably shared his ambitions; he did not feel Sussex were proceeding in the right direction. He joined Warwickshire and played for five years under the leadership of Andy Lloyd, for whom he has an oft-repeated regard. For at least the last two of them, however, it was plain that Reeve was the captain in waiting. His accession will not have pleased everyone. Reeve is the sort of person who never will please everyone, nor seek to. But at least by then he had ticked off a number of ambitions, having played Test cricket for England and appeared in the 1992 World Cup. He fared moderately in three Tests against New Zealand, with a top score of 59 on debut, but showed himself to be an effective one-day player, especially on sluggish pitches where his stealthy swing bowling, now augmented by outrageous changes of pace, could frustrate and infuriate batsmen of all abilities.

On the second of his England tours, to India and Sri Lanka in 1992–93, his mother became the England team scorer when the official appointee, Clem Driver, fell ill. That Monica was on hand should be no surprise, for she scarcely misses a match in which her son is playing. She is Dermot's greatest fan. Those who are not presumably include Curtly Ambrose, who bowled him three beamers in swift succession during his career-best innings of 202 not out at Northampton in 1990. A certain county coach also falls into Ambrose's camp. Against himself, Reeve tells how this coach accused him, last summer, of setting out to upset his players on a regular basis. Reeve insists: "It was a misunderstanding. I don't set out to upset people, but I will be aggressive on the field. I remember at Hove going in to bat against Somerset. Ian Botham was at slip and he gave me a lot of lip, but when we walked off he clapped me on the back and said 'well played'. That's the way I play too."

It is not, however, quite as simplistic as that. Reeve is a deep thinker on the game, with a formidable memory for situations and for the weaknesses of individuals. His bowling and field changes reflect this. His analysis of each game is pressed upon his team at meetings before every session. Warwickshire have also shunned recent trends and gone back to talking cricket, as a team, when out socially or in the dressing-room. That is the strategist within Reeve. Then there is the showman, who will do the unorthodox, notably reverse-sweeping, as much for irritation as gain. And the man who will roll around in the outfield engaged in complex calisthenics for what seems an age. "I think," he says, "I am a visual cricketer." Recently, it has been unwise to take one's eyes off him, for fear of missing some new gem.

PHIL TUFNELL Andrew Nickolds, 2004

Besides being long and hot, 2003 was also the Summer of Sexing Up, and cricket dug out its rouge, false eyelashes and beauty spot in a strenuous attempt to persuade the public that the tough old mutton they'd been getting for years was in fact the freshest, most tender spring lamb. But would anybody buy it?

Judging from the media coverage, the answer was a resounding yes. England may have made an undistinguished exit from the World Cup in March, but within weeks a new hero had emerged from the swamps of the southern hemisphere. Flying the flag for the game was the winner of the ITV series *I'm a Celebrity, Get me out of Here!* Or more accurately, *Get me out of my Middlesex Contract!* Cricket's unlikely ambassador turned out to be Philip Tufnell wielding a toy bat. His survival skills in an Australian rainforest impressed several million viewers – several million more than he would have impressed at Southgate – and almost overnight the former thorn in the side of the selectors had used his easy-going nature and his willingness to put disgusting objects (in this case, witchetty grubs rather than cigarettes) in his mouth to acquire the status of lovable national hero.

This transformation caused a few raised eyebrows among Tufnell's former county and England team-mates turned media pundits, who remembered a somewhat different character and weren't afraid to say it. Mike Selvey and Angus Fraser were particularly caustic as Tufnell was wheeled out (literally, on a red sofa, at Chester-le-Street) as the acceptable face of the game. But true to fairweather form, the tabloid press rallied round their new best friend, and previously lurid front-page stories linking Tufnell with domestic violence were forgotten in the face of a bigger reconstruction job than the new Lord's outfield.

The *Daily Mail's* makeover was typical. Under the headline "The Secret of My Jungle Torment – Phil Tufnell tells of his desperate desire to meet the daughter he hasn't seen for eight years" we were introduced to a caring, sharing Tuffers who attributed the TV show victory to his experience of being a team player, a philosophy he was hoping to apply to his private life. More immediate rewards were to be found on BBC Radio 5. *Phil Tufnell's Cricket Circus* was a particularly grim example of what is normally called "zoo" rather than circus radio, where everybody jabbers at once to little effect. Almost as raucous were Tufnell's appearances on the TV sports "quiz", *They Think It's All Over*, where, significantly enough, he replaced David Gower as a team captain and the game's primetime public image.

SECTION FOUR

The World Cup

SECTION FOUR

The World Cup

The Cup Runneth Over

This may be a somewhat ludicrous question to raise in introducing a section that details the seven World Cups that took place in the period covered by this Anthology, but has the competition ever really worked? Can you, dear reader, name the winners thus far? Most of us probably know that England, feebly, have never won it, despite no fewer than half the World Cups to date being played on home territory and having a ten-year start on the rest of the world in one-day expertise. But who has won the cups – and how many matches do you truly remember?

There have been some good games – and as I trawled to decide what to include I came up with more matches than I thought I would – but the World Cup has been mortally damaged by constant changes of format and the inclusion of too many weak teams, leading to numerous mismatches. For every genuine surprise or close encounter between monster and minnow, there have been a dozen non-events, interrupting the flow of the tournament and making it unwieldy and long-drawn-out. The balance between qualifying games and knock-out phase has often been out-of-kilter: weeks are spent determining that, say, Australia are stronger then Namibia, and then the key matches are over in the blink of an eye. The ICC insists it will address these problems in future competitions.

The overriding problem may be that the cricket World Cup has to stand comparison with the soccer World Cup, which really is a global jamboree that can attract 32 national teams without the danger of too many embarrassing mismatches. In cricket – a longer, more technical, better calibrated sport – the differences in class tend to be more pronounced. Rugby union, whose own World Cup has had similar difficulties in expanding the pool, is a better point of comparison. The two sports want their cup to be a focus of global interest, a great evangelising weapon and marketing tool, but that aim simply doesn't square with putting on good, even matches.

The 1975 cup – still, in many ways, the most memorable and with a wonderful, happy, sun-drenched final – remains the most logical model: the eight strongest teams playing each other over a containable period. I don't suppose we will ever return to that – the Dubai-based ICC is committed to its evangelising mission – and, in fairness, there are plenty of cricket fans who enjoy the idea of a "carnival of cricket" that allows the minnows to swim with the piranhas (I fear I have mixed piscine metaphors). But there needs to be a balance if cricket is to be the winner and the interest (and sanity) of fans sustained. Could we say no future World Cup should last longer than four weeks? Please.   S. M.

All Hail King Viv

The second World Cup proved, like the first in 1975, a great success, and again West Indies carried off the title. Unlike four years earlier, it was not blessed throughout with blissful sunshine during the fortnight it was in progress – June 9 to June 23. Nevertheless, the three Saturdays provided fine weather and there was only one bad period – June 13, 14, 15 – when not a ball could be bowled in the match between West Indies and Sri Lanka at The Oval.

Again eight countries took part, and from a cricketer's point of view it was a shame that once more South Africa were left in the cold. To fill the two remaining places, a separate tournament was organised among Associate Members of the International Cricket Conference. From this emerged Sri Lanka, who took part in 1975, and Canada. The matches were confined to one innings of 60 overs for each side. No bowler was allowed more than 12 overs per innings, and the umpires applied strict interpretation in regard to wides and bumpers to prevent negative bowling.

Prize money amounted to £25,900. West Indies, the winners, received the Prudential Cup and £10,000; England, runners-up, £4,000; Pakistan and New Zealand, losing semi-finalists, £2,000 each; and winners of group matches £500 each. There were also Man of the Match awards: £300 to Vivian Richards (West Indies) in the final, £200 each in the semi-finals, and £100 for the nominated player in each group match. At their meeting which followed the World Cup, the International Cricket Conference agreed to make the competition a four-yearly event with the 1983 tournament again being staged in England.

SELECTED GROUP MATCHES
England v Australia
At Lord's, June 9, 1979. England won by six wickets.   1980

With all tickets sold before the match, a crowd of 25,000 saw what proved to be a comfortable victory for the home team. As usual, the meeting of England and Australia at Lord's produced its own special atmosphere of expectation and excitement. Brearley, winning the toss on a dull, grey morning, put Australia in to bat in conditions that were not easy for them. Hendrick moved the ball awkwardly and Willis, Old, Botham and Edmonds all gave the Australians a thorough test until, just before lunch, Brearley surprised many people by introducing Boycott. Yet it was Boycott who made the breakthrough immediately after interval when Hilditch touched the ball against his off stump. Next, Hendrick, racing from mid-wicket, took a great catch to remove Hughes.

When Border, after a stubborn display, edged a catch to Taylor, who previously had missed two stumpings, Australia collapsed completely. They threw away wickets with four run outs, and England needed only 160 to win. Suddenly, Australia lifted themselves again, the first two England wickets falling for five runs. Fortunately for England, Gooch was at the top of his form. He hit six magnificent boundaries in his stay of two and three-quarter hours and with Brearley, who played competently, put on 108 for the third wicket. Laughlin removed both in consecutive overs before Gower, cover driving and pulling in his best style, and Botham, full of aggression, applied the finishing touches to an absorbing day's cricket. Boycott's feat in taking two wickets posed the question: When, if ever, had the Yorkshireman taken more wickets than he made runs in the same match?

Toss: England. **Australia 159-9** (60 overs) (A. M. J. Hilditch 47, A. R. Border 34); **England 160-4** (47.1 overs) (J. M. Brearley 44, G. A. Gooch 53).

England v Pakistan

At Leeds, June 16, 1979. England won by 14 runs. 1980

This was an extraordinary match during which the bowlers held the upper hand for most of the time. That England, who set Pakistan to make only 166 to win, finally succeeded was due to a wonderful performance by Hendrick, who took four wickets in a spell of eight balls for only three runs. Finally, he held a tremendous leaping catch at mid-off from Sikander to seal England's victory.

Toss: Pakistan. **England 165-9** (60 overs) (G. A. Gooch 33; Sikander Bakht 3-32, Majid Khan 3-27); **Pakistan 151** (56 overs) (Asif Iqbal 51; M. Hendrick 4-15).

India v Sri Lanka

At Manchester, June 16, 18, 1979. Sri Lanka won by 47 runs. 1980

Sri Lanka, put in to bat, gained the only win by an Associate Member of the ICC in the competition, and it was richly deserved. The Sri Lankan batsmen enjoyed themselves on a docile pitch that was of little help to a rather harmless Indian attack. The second-wicket stand of 96 by Wettimuny and Dias off 25 overs was a joy to watch, Wettimuny excelling with stylish drives and Dias effecting many attractive wristy strokes. Mendis followed with a powerful display in which he struck Ghavri, Kapil Dev and Amarnath each for six. Pasqual, a confident left-handed schoolboy and the youngest player in the 1979 World Cup, joined in the fun with Mendis as 52 runs were added off seven overs.

Owing to a late start on Saturday, India had to wait until Monday before starting their task of 239 to win. Gavaskar and Gaekwad began with a stand of 60 and at lunch India were 117 for two, wanting 122 from the remaining 25 overs. The turning-point came when Viswanath ran himself out for 22. Afterwards, Somachandra de Silva varied his leg-breaks with such skill that he dismissed Vengsarkar, Patel and Amarnath, whereupon Opatha, who had done nothing with the new ball, returned with additional pace and swept through the tail.

Toss: India. **Sri Lanka 238-5** (60 overs) (S. R. D. Wettimuny 67, R. L. Dias 50, L. R. D. Mendis 64; M. Amarnath 3-40); **India 191** (54.1 overs) (A. D. Gaekwad 33, D. B. Vengsarkar 36; A. R. M. Opatha 3-31, D. S. de Silva 3-29).

SEMI-FINALS
England v New Zealand
At Manchester, June 20, 1979. England won by nine runs. 1980

A wonderful match played in glorious sunshine before an almost capacity crowd of 22,000 ended with New Zealand covering themselves with glory but just failing to get to Lord's for the final. Wright and Edgar began New Zealand's task of scoring 222 to win in masterly fashion, putting on 47 in 16 overs before Old had Edgar leg-before. Then Boycott, round the wicket, removed Howarth leg-before with a full toss that the batsman aimed to sweep towards square leg. Wright kept New Zealand moving the right way until he succumbed to some brilliant fielding by Randall from deep square leg. Burgess, too, was run out, but New Zealand were not finished yet. Lees lifted Hendrick over mid-on for six, and [Lance] Cairns hoisted Botham even further before Hendrick removed them both. With Willis lame, and Botham and Hendrick also limping, it was touch and go, but with 14 wanted from the last over, sent down by Botham, New Zealand went out of the World Cup with their flag flying.

Toss: New Zealand. **England 221-8** (60 overs) (J. M. Brearley 53, G. A. Gooch 71, D. W. Randall 42*); **New Zealand 212-9** (60 overs) (J. G. Wright 69, G. M. Turner 30; M. Hendrick 3-55).

Pakistan v West Indies
At The Oval, June 20, 1979. West Indies won by 43 runs. 1980

With all their leading batsmen in form, West Indies, having been invited to go in first, ran up a massive total of 293 for six. It was no day for Sarfraz, who failed with the new ball and conceded 71 runs in his 12 overs, although he did remove King towards the end of the innings. Holding struck an early blow for West Indies when Pakistan began their tremendous task with the bat. Bowling at great pace and hostile with the bouncer, he dismissed Sadiq at ten. This setback did not deter Majid and Zaheer who rose to the occasion in a wonderful partnership of 166 off 36 overs that put their side within striking distance. Croft, however, made the breakthrough by dismissing Zaheer, Majid and Miandad in 12 balls for four runs, and Richards followed by disposing of Mudassar, Asif and Imran. With Roberts proving too much for the tail, West Indies gained their deserved success. A crowd of 20,000 enjoyed the spectacle in brilliant sunshine.

Toss: Pakistan. **West Indies 293-6** (60 overs) (C. G. Greenidge 73, D. L. Haynes 65, I. V. A. Richards 42, C. H. Lloyd 37, C. L. King 34; Asif Iqbal 4-56); **Pakistan 250** (56.2 overs) (Majid Khan 81, Zaheer Abbas 93; C. E. H. Croft 3-29, I. V. A. Richards 3-52).

FINAL
England v West Indies

At Lord's, June 23, 1979. West Indies won by 92 runs.   Norman Preston, 1980

West Indies retained the Prudential Cup and the title of world champions which they first won in 1975. On another fine day the ground was completely filled by the all-ticket crowd of 25,000, and many would-be spectators were locked out. For a long time England put up a gallant fight after Brearley had won the toss and sent in the opposition to bat. The absence of Willis, injured in the semi-final, probably made the West Indies' task easier although his replacement, Edmonds, delivered his left-arm slows with much skill, and dismissed King and Murray. However, in preferring an extra batsman in Larkins, Brearley had to call on Boycott, Gooch and Larkins as his fifth bowler. Their 12 overs cost 86 runs – and brought no wickets.

Master blaster: Viv Richards, one of *Wisden's* Five Cricketers of the Century in 2000, on his seemingly effortless way to an unbeaten 138 for West Indies in the 1979 World Cup final, watched by England's Bob Taylor.

On a morning when Botham, Hendrick and Old all acquired movement, England began well enough against a side splendidly endowed with capable hitters. Moreover, England produced their highest standard of fielding and soon Randall ran out Greenidge with a deadly underarm return to the bowler's end as he dashed in from mid-wicket. Hendrick dismissed Haynes with a low-taken catch at slip off Old, and he followed this by bowling the left-handed Kallicharran round his legs, just grazing the leg stump. A superb left-handed catch by Old when Lloyd drove the ball back low meant that England had taken the first four wickets for 99 and at this stage clearly held the initiative.

Then came the partnership that turned the match. Richards, the hero of the day and rightly named Man of the Match, was already installed and he found the right ally in [Collis] King, who virtually took charge from the moment he arrived and made 86 out of 139 put on for the fifth wicket in only 77 minutes. Many of these runs came from England's three fill-in bowlers as King struck three sixes and ten fours in an amazing display. He drove, hooked and pulled with astonishing power and accuracy, so confirming the impressive form he showed when he toured England with the West Indies team of 1976, but failed to reproduce for Glamorgan the following year.

Richards, at first, was subdued by Edmonds, but he completed his hundred in the over (the 52nd) following King's dismissal, the result of a well-taken catch by Randall at deep square leg. Pressing for runs, West Indies lost their next four wickets for 48 runs. Richards remained unbeaten, having hit his 138 in just under three and a half hours. It contained three sixes and 11 fours.

England had the better batting conditions in brilliant sunshine, and Brearley and Boycott gave them a sound start by staying together for two hours ten minutes, although they never managed to take the West Indies' pace bowlers apart. Boycott occupied 17 overs to reach double figures, and when Brearley went England wanted 158 from the last 22 overs. This looked to be out of the question, and so it proved. Randall and Gooch made a brief assault, but between them Garner and Croft swept through the remainder of the innings. The 6ft 8in Garner took five wickets for four runs in 11 balls and was twice on a hat-trick as the West Indian supporters made the evening a Caribbean carnival.

England v West Indies, 1979 — World Cup Final

At Lord's, June 23, 1979. Result: West Indies won by 92 runs.

WEST INDIES

C. G. Greenidge run out	9	†D. L. Murray c Gower b Edmonds	5
D. L. Haynes c Hendrick b Old	20	A. M. E. Roberts c Brearley b Hendrick	0
I. V. A. Richards not out	138	J. Garner c Taylor b Botham	0
A. I. Kallicharran b Hendrick	4	M. A. Holding b Botham	0
*C. H. Lloyd c and b Old	13	C. E. H. Croft not out	0
C. L. King c Randall b Edmonds	86	B 1, l-b 10	11

1-22 2-36 3-55 4-99 5-238
6-252 7-258 8-260 9-272

(9 wkts, 60 overs) 286

Botham 12–2–44–2; Hendrick 12–2–50–2; Old 12–0–55–2; Boycott 6–0–38–0; Edmonds 12–2–40–2; Gooch 4–0–27–0; Larkins 2–0–21–0.

ENGLAND

*J. M. Brearley c King b Holding	64	W. Larkins b Garner	0
G. Boycott c Kallicharran b Holding	57	P. H. Edmonds not out	5
D. W. Randall b Croft	15	C. M. Old b Garner	0
G. A. Gooch b Garner	32	†R. W. Taylor c Murray b Garner	0
D. I. Gower b Garner	0	M. Hendrick b Croft	0
I. T. Botham c Richards b Croft	4	L-b 12, w 2, n-b 3	17

1-129 2-135 3-183 4-183 5-186
6-186 7-192 8-192 9-194 10-194

(51 overs) 194

Roberts 9–2–33–0; Holding 8–1–16–2; Croft 10–1–42–3; Garner 11–0–38–5; Richards 10–0–35–0;
King 3–0–13–0.

Toss won by England
MAN OF THE MATCH I. V. A. Richards

UMPIRES H. D. Bird and B. J. Meyer

805

The Shock of Shocks

The third World Cup, the last to be sponsored by the Prudential Assurance Company, began with two fine surprises, when India beat West Indies and Zimbabwe beat Australia in the opening round of matches, and ended with the greatest surprise of all, when India beat West Indies again, this time in the final at Lord's. None of the eight sides had to make do without a victory.

The competition differed from its two predecessors in that in the preliminary groups the sides played each other not once but twice. This was partly to increase revenue but also to lessen the chances of a side being eliminated through having greater misfortune with the weather than its rivals. In the event, no sooner had the sides started to arrive in England for the 1983 World Cup than the rain, which had made the month of May one of the wettest on record, cleared away.

Of the 27 matches played, only three were not begun and finished in a day. Many were played in warm sunshine, and throughout the competition, from June 9–25, interest ran high. After losing their opening match, West Indies carried all before them until failing, for the first time, to win the final. Australia had a disappointing fortnight, and with Imran Khan unfit to bowl for them, Pakistan were a shadow of the side which had trounced India and Australia in the previous winter.

New Zealand's main batting provided them with insufficient runs for a consistent challenge, while Sri Lanka, though they won their return match against New Zealand, were too short of bowling to be a serious threat. Zimbabwe, playing for the first time, having qualified as winners of the ICC Trophy in 1982, made a welcome contribution. Their side included several players with first-class experience, acquired when, as Rhodesia, their country played in the Currie Cup. Apart from beating Australia they gave West Indies a run for their money at Worcester.

India's unexpected success (they were quoted at 66–1 before the competition began) came under a young and relatively new captain (Kapil Dev) and owed much to the presence in their side of three all-rounders (Kapil Dev, Roger Binny and Mohinder Amarnath) who, at critical moments, found enough in the conditions to help form an effective attack. Who would ever have thought before a ball was bowled that the leading wicket-takers in the competition would be the Sri Lankan de Mel and Binny, with his gentle medium-pace?

SELECTED GROUP MATCHES
Australia v Zimbabwe
At Nottingham, June 9, 1983. Zimbabwe won by 13 runs.   1984

In their first appearance in the competition, the amateurs of Zimbabwe brought off a bigger surprise than any in the previous two World Cups. The Australian captain described his side as being outplayed. Having been put in, Zimbabwe made no more than a steady start, but from 94 for five their captain, Duncan Fletcher, who was once a professional with Rishton in the Lancashire League, led an acceleration, adding 70 in 15 overs with Curran and 75 in 12 overs with Butchart. Australia missed five catches, bowled moderately and, though Wood and Wessels gave their innings an adequate start, they slipped behind the required rate against Fletcher's four for 42 and some fine fielding and catching.

Toss: Australia. **Zimbabwe 239-6** (60 overs) (D. A. G. Fletcher 69*, I. P. Butchart 34*, Extras 31); **Australia 226-7** (60 overs) (G. M. Wood 31, K. C. Wessels 76, R. W. Marsh 50*; D. A. G. Fletcher 4-42).

India v West Indies
At Manchester, June 9, 10, 1983. India won by 34 runs.   1984

India began with a well-earned victory over the holders. Put in after a delayed start, they struggled in damp conditions and poor light to make 79 for three in 22 overs, but a splendid innings of 89 by Yashpal led them on to their highest score in three World Cups. Greenidge and Haynes made a confident start, scoring 49 before Haynes was run out in the 14th over. From this moment India began to take a grip on the game, and when play ended for the day West Indies were 67 for two in 22 overs. Richards was out early next day and West Indies declined so swiftly that by the 47th over they were 157 for nine. A last-wicket stand of 71 between Roberts and Garner was beginning to cause India serious concern when a smart stumping by Kirmani brought them victory. They had won only one previous Prudential Cup match, against East Africa in 1975.

Toss: West Indies. **India 262-8** (60 overs) (S. M. Patil 36, Yashpal Sharma 89); **West Indies 228** (54.1 overs) (A. M. E. Roberts 37*, J. Garner 37; R. M. H. Binny 3-48, R. J. Shastri 3-26).

England v New Zealand
At Birmingham, June 15, 1983. New Zealand won by two wickets.   1984

Such a result seemed unlikely when England, early in the day, were making a confident start, but the pitch was not entirely consistent in bounce and an experiment with Botham at No. 3 proved unsuccessful. Only Gower, with an immaculate 92 not out from 96 balls, contributed much after an opening stand of 63 between Fowler and Tavaré, and he could not stop the loss of the last three wickets for one run with 4.4 overs unused. England's score seemed adequate when Willis removed

807

Turner and Edgar with only three runs scored, and at 75 for four New Zealand were still fighting an uphill battle. But while Coney held one end, his partners, especially Hadlee, gave him support which kept New Zealand close to the required scoring-rate. With two wickets left, they needed four runs off the last over, or three if they still had a wicket intact. Off the fifth ball, with the scores level, Bracewell struck a four to settle the issue.

Toss: England. **England 234** (55.2 overs) (G. Fowler 69, D. I. Gower 92*; R. J. Hadlee 3-32, B. L. Cairns 3-44); **New Zealand 238-8** (59.5 overs) (G. P. Howarth 60, J. V. Coney 66*, R. J. Hadlee 31; R. G. D. Willis 4-42).

Australia v West Indies

At Lord's, June 18, 1983. West Indies won by seven wickets.   1984

From a start of 37 for two, Australia's innings prospered while Hughes and Hookes were adding 101, and for a time something over 300 seemed possible. In the end it needed some robust blows from Marsh for them to reach 273 for six, and it soon became clear that this was well within the reach of the West Indian batsmen on a good pitch. Haynes played on at 79, but Greenidge and Richards took the score past 200 at a pace which ensured that no undue haste would be needed thereafter.

Toss: Australia. **Australia 273-6** (60 overs) (K. J. Hughes 69, D. W. Hookes 56, G. N. Yallop 52*, R. W. Marsh 37); **West Indies 276-3** (57.5 overs) (C. G. Greenidge 90, D. L. Haynes 33, I. V. A. Richards 95*).

New Zealand v Pakistan

At Nottingham, June 20, 1983. Pakistan won by 11 runs.   1984

To qualify for the semi-final, Pakistan needed not only to beat New Zealand but to make enough runs in their 60 overs to give them a better scoring-rate throughout the tournament. They met this second requirement, achieving an overall scoring-rate of 4.01 against New Zealand's 3.94, through an unbroken fourth-wicket stand of 147 in 75 minutes between Zaheer and Imran, during which they made 47 off Hadlee's last five overs. New Zealand were soon in trouble against Sarfraz, Mudassar and Qadir and it was not until Coney led the last three wickets in a sterling attempt at making 85 off the final ten overs that Pakistan had any uneasy moments. Bracewell helped him to add 59 in five overs and 13 were needed off the last over, but Coney, attempting a second run, was run out off the first ball from Imran's throw.

Toss: Pakistan. **Pakistan 261-3** (60 overs) (Mohsin Khan 33, Zaheer Abbas 103*, Imran Khan 79*); **New Zealand 250** (59.1 overs) (G. P. Howarth 39, M. D. Crowe 43, J. V. Coney 51, J. G. Bracewell 34; Mudassar Nazar 3-43).

SEMI-FINALS
England v India
At Manchester, June 22, 1983. India won by six wickets. 1984

Though England made a brisk and promising start, this was a pitch similar to those on which India are so hard to beat at home. Binny, Azad and Amarnath had only to bowl a steady length to reduce the England batsmen, as they sought to attack, to mistimings and countless uses of the bat's edge. The fact that the faster Kapil Dev had been no great menace while Fowler and Tavaré were making 69 at four an over was an indication that the faster England bowlers would not pose the same problems to the Indian batsmen, who have plenty of experience of slow pitches of low bounce. Two run-outs – of Lamb and Gould – made a recovery of the initiative even more unlikely. For more than an hour not a four was hit, and it needed a few rough, mostly edged strokes by Dilley to lift the score above 200. India, with little need to hurry, duly found the going easier against bowling which came on to the bat more readily. Though Gavaskar and Srikkanth were out for 50, Amarnath and Yashpal added 92 with increasing belligerence, and Patil and Yashpal hurried the match to its close, at one time making 63 off nine overs.

Toss: England. **England 213** (60 overs) (G. Fowler 33, C. J. Tavaré 32; Kapil Dev 3-35); **India 217-4** (54.4 overs) (M. Amarnath 46, Yashpal Sharma 61, S. M. Patil 51*).

Pakistan v West Indies
At The Oval, June 22, 1983. West Indies won by eight wickets. 1984

Though Mohsin held one end until only three of Pakistan's 60 overs remained, their innings never promised to produce enough runs to bother West Indies. On a good, firm pitch the Pakistan batsmen, from whom Miandad was missing though influenza, struggled to such an extent that the boundary was reached only twice. Even though Mohsin and Zaheer made 54 in a third-wicket stand, the score had reached just 88 when Zaheer played on to Gomes from some way down the pitch in the last over before lunch. This was during a spell when Gomes and Richards were using up the fifth bowler's allotment economically. Greenidge and Haynes made an unspectacular start for West Indies, but Richards and Gomes finished the match with an unbroken stand of 132 and more than 11 overs to spare.

Toss: West Indies. **Pakistan 184-8** (60 overs) (Mohsin Khan 70, Zaheer Abbas 30; M. D. Marshall 3-28); **West Indies 188-2** (48.4 overs) (I. V. A. Richards 80*, H. A. Gomes 50*).

FINAL
India v West Indies

At Lord's, June 25, 1983. India won by 43 runs.   Wilfred Wooller, 1984

India defeated on merit the firm favourites, winning a low-scoring match by 43 runs. It was an absorbing game of increasing drama and finally of much emotion. The result, as surprising as, on the day, it was convincing, had much to do with the mental pressures of containment in limited-overs cricket. Amarnath was named Man of the Match by Mike Brearley for a stabilising innings of 26 against hostile fast bowling after the early loss of Gavaskar, followed by his taking three late West Indian wickets, Dujon's being especially important. Dujon and Marshall had lifted West Indies, needing 184 to win, from 76 for six to 119 for six, a recovery based on the calm application of sound batting principles and one which was threatening to achieve after all the result which everyone had expected.

Lord's, groomed like a high-born lady, bathed in sunshine and packed to capacity, was at its best when Lloyd won the toss and invited India to bat: a distinct advantage, it seemed, for his battery of fast bowlers. The Lord's wicket often inclines to extravagant morning life. Now it never lost this capacity to allow movement off the seam, sufficient to be of much significance later in the day for the medium-paced attack of Madan Lal and Sandhu, who removed the cream of the West Indian batting, and for the seemingly inoffensive Binny, who accounted for the dangerous Lloyd.

There was an explosive start to the match, Garner hurling the ball down, chest-high on the line of the off stump. Roberts, fast but flatter, had Gavaskar caught at the wicket in his third over. To score off such an attack was a problem, but Srikkanth showed how: he hooked Roberts for four, pulled him for six and square drove him to the Tavern boundary like a pistol shot. Yashpal, released from the constraints of speed, drove the slow spin of Gomes high and wide to the off, but straight to cover point. At lunch India were 100 for four. Afterwards Kapil Dev perished at deep long-on and Patil lost concentration. Madan Lal, Kirmani and Sandhu added 31 late runs, but India's total of 183 seemed many too few.

West Indies started badly. Greenidge padded up to the deceptive Sandhu and was bowled. Richards, however, swept the total swiftly and effortlessly to 50. Then, when 33, he mistimed a hook and Kapil Dev took a fine catch over his shoulder, running back towards the mid-wicket boundary. Madan Lal followed with two more quick wickets, those of Haynes and Gomes. All three fell for six runs in 19 balls. Lloyd drove Binny to mid-off and immediately after tea Bacchus was caught at the wicket. It remained for Amarnath to break the partnership between Dujon and Marshall which, just in time, he did.

India v West Indies, 1983 — World Cup Final

At Lord's, June 25, 1983. Result: India won by 43 runs.

INDIA

S. M. Gavaskar c Dujon b Roberts	2	K. B. J. Azad c Garner b Roberts	0
K. Srikkanth lbw b Marshall	38	R. M. H. Binny c Garner b Roberts	2
M. Amarnath b Holding	26	Madan Lal b Marshall	17
Yashpal Sharma c sub (A. L. Logie) b Gomes	11	†S. M. H. Kirmani b Holding	14
S. M. Patil c Gomes b Garner	27	B. S. Sandhu not out	11
*Kapil Dev c Holding b Gomes	15	B 5, l-b 5, w 9, n-b 1	20

1-2 2-59 3-90 4-92 5-110 6-111   (54.4 overs) 183
7-130 8-153 9-161 10-183

Roberts 10–3–32–3; Garner 12–4–24–1; Marshall 11–1–24–2; Holding 9.4–2–26–2; Gomes 11–1–49–2; Richards 1–0–8–0.

WEST INDIES

C. G. Greenidge b Sandhu	1	†P. J. L. Dujon c Amarnath	25
D. L. Haynes c Binny b Madan Lal	13	M. D. Marshall c Gavaskar b Amarnath	18
I. V. A. Richards c Kapil Dev b Madan Lal	33	A. M. E. Roberts lbw b Kapil Dev	4
*C. H. Lloyd c Kapil Dev b Binny	8	J. Garner not out	5
H. A. Gomes c Gavaskar b Madan Lal	5	M. A. Holding lbw b Amarnath	6
S. F. A. F. Bacchus c Kirmani b Sandhu	8	L-b 4, w 10	14

1-5 2-50 3-57 4-66 5-66 6-76   (52 overs) 140
7-119 8-124 9-126 10-140

Kapil Dev 11–4–21–1; Sandhu 9–1–32–2; Madan Lal 12–2–31–3; Binny 10–1–23–1; Amarnath 7–0–12–3; Azad 3–0–7–0.

Toss won by West Indies   UMPIRES H. D. Bird and B. J. Meyer
MAN OF THE MATCH M. Amarnath

Border Rising

WORLD CUP 1987   Scyld Berry, 1988

The fourth World Cup was more widely watched, more closely fought, and more colourful than any of its three predecessors held in England. Any doubts about it were dispelled by the opening matches when Pakistan, the favourites, were run close by Sri Lanka; when India, the holders, were beaten by Australia by one run; when England succeeded in scoring 35 off their last three overs to beat West Indies; and when the gallant amateurs of Zimbabwe lost by only three runs to New Zealand.

If the rest of the Reliance Cup, as it was officially known and seldom called, could not quite live up to such a start, the experiment of an oriental World Cup was still acknowledged to have been a great success. The semi-finals in Lahore and Bombay held the subcontinent by the ears and eyes, even if they did not produce the results desired by the tens of millions who were following the matches on radio and television. The arrangements for the final, at Eden Gardens in Calcutta, were praised to the full by the winning Australian captain, and rightly.

Any drawbacks resulted from the sheer size of the two host countries and the determination of the Indo-Pakistan joint management committee to spread the games around as many as 21 venues. It was the equivalent of staging a tournament in Europe, barring only the Soviet Union, without quite the same facility of transport and telecommunications. Fewer centres would have meant less travelling, a shorter and more compact competition – it took six weeks against less than a month for the 1983 World Cup – and increased enjoyment all round. For successive matches, the Sri Lankans were shunted from Peshawar, in the North-West Frontier Province of Pakistan, to Kanpur in central India, back to Faisalabad, then across the border again to Pune: two-day journeys every time, with hours spent in transit lounges at airports waiting for flights.

Nevertheless, in circumstances which were perhaps more arduous than they need have been, the organisers did excellently. In return, the weather was kind to them. To all intents, only one match was affected by rain, when Australia and New Zealand were reduced to 30 overs each in Indore. (Happily, the rule that a match could not be carried over to its second day was never exposed in its absurdity.) Otherwise the matches were of 50 overs per side, and on good pitches totals similar to those in the previous 60-over World Cup were raised. Viv Richards, and West Indies as a team, set up new records against Sri Lanka for World Cup innings.

If the umpiring was not of the very highest standard, its "neutrality" served to minimise grievances. Poor neutral umpiring, however, can never be a substitute for good umpiring, whether by home or neutral officials. The standard of scoring, it has to be recorded, was inadequate in many centres, done as it was by local scorers unfamiliar with visiting players, while the telegraph boards were not always kept up to date.

One especial virtue in staging the World Cup in India and Pakistan was that spin had a full part to play, whereas previous competitions in England had been dominated by repetitive seamers. Not one over of spin was risked in the 1975 final. Australia were untypical in that they usually allotted only ten overs to spin; the majority of teams fielded two spinners and benefited on the slow batting pitches that prevailed. In the qualifying rounds, seven of the nine most economical bowlers were spinners. That said, the leading wicket-takers were both fast bowlers, Craig McDermott equalling the World Cup record of 18 and Imran Khan capturing 17 in one match less.

Batsmen were not troubled by dew when batting first, as some had feared, but by the strain of batting second. Out of 27 matches, 19 were won by the side batting first. The received wisdom had been to bowl first in one-day internationals and to determine the target. Now every side wanted to bat first, then watch the opposition – fatigued by three and a half hours' fielding in the heat – make mistakes and panic as the run-rate climbed to seven and eight an over. The side batting first played the ball according to its merits; the side batting second seemed to play it according to the run-rate required.

In the context, Australia were fortunate to bat first in five of their six qualifying games, and to be able to do so again in their semi-final and final. This luck aside, they were still the team most deserving of victory: they appeared to put the most into the tournament – the sweat was dripping from the peaks of the batsmen's caps when they "warmed up" in Madras – and they gained their first success of note since 1984. England, the runners-up, arrived with a specialist in tropical diseases and a microwave oven but with only three batsmen capable of scoring at a run a ball. They won whenever their bowlers were able to make up for the deficiencies in their batting.

Co-hosts India and Pakistan, as holders and favourites, had been expected to meet in the final but never met at all, not even in a hastily conceived third-place play-off match which fell through owing to the exorbitant demands of some players. Indeed, it was perhaps as well that their paths never crossed, for there were reports of communal conflict in India after the semi-final results. Pakistan blew hot too soon, winning their first five qualifying games, largely on the basis of some overwhelming bowling from Imran Khan and Abdul Qadir, only for their luck to turn in the semi-final.

In a sense, India handicapped themselves by playing in the weaker qualifying group, much as England had in 1979. In both cases, the hosts qualified without having the weak links in their bowling exposed. India's batting was collectively the most brilliant in the tournament but not always the most effective. The demands of their crowds for spectacular hitting, and enticing awards from a sponsor for every four and six they hit, cannot have been beneficial influences; likewise, a never-settled dispute which the senior Indian players had with their board over insignia.

West Indies, in transition, missed their fast bowlers of experience. It is not inconceivable that Malcolm Marshall could have won the World Cup for them had he played. New Zealand, too, were in transition in the absence of Richard Hadlee. Sri Lanka, in the field, were utterly defensive, and confronted by mountainous totals their talented batsmen were crushed. Like the Sri Lankans, the Zimbabweans returned home without a victory, but they gained many friends by their fielding – giving themselves as professionals never quite could – and many sympathisers by their naive mistakes and run-outs. For sheer heroism, the innings of the World Cup was David Houghton's 141 against New Zealand.

The Australians had the same keen, uncynical spirit as the Zimbabweans. They worked and worked as a team; and every follower of the game had to be pleased in some measure when, at the end of the Australians' victory lap around Eden Gardens, Allan Border was raised on the shoulders of his team-mates and the gold Reliance Cup placed in his hands.

SELECTED GROUP MATCHES
India v Australia
At Madras, October 9, 1987. Australia won by one run. 1988

Kapil Dev's sportsmanship proved the deciding factor in a close-run match. One of Jones's two sixes, in his 39 from 35 balls, had been signalled as four; but between innings Kapil concurred with the Australians' insistence that the ball had cleared the boundary. That India's target was increased by two seemed insignificant when Gavaskar, Srikkanth and Sidhu sent them racing past 200 for the loss of only two wickets. McDermott's first four overs went for 31 runs, but he came back strongly to whip out the middle order. Even so, India, with four wickets in hand, needed just 15 from the last four overs; when the last over began, the requirement was six, with the last man, Maninder Singh, taking strike. He managed two twos, but along with his sangfroid went his off-stump.

Toss: India. **Australia 270-6** (50 overs) (D. C. Boon 49, G. R. Marsh 110, D. M. Jones 39); **India 269** (49.5 overs) (S. M. Gavaskar 37, K. Srikkanth 70, N. S. Sidhu 73; C. J. McDermott 4-56).

New Zealand v Zimbabwe
At Hyderabad, October 10, 1987. New Zealand won by three runs. 1988

An innings of great character, 141 from 138 balls, by Houghton, Zimbabwe's wicket-keeper-batsman, gave New Zealand a scare. Adding 117 with Butchart – a record for the eighth wicket in one-day internationals – Houghton had taken his side to within 22 of their target when he was out in the 47th over, having hit three sixes and 13 fours. Zimbabwe wanted six from the final over, but Butchart was run out off the fourth ball. New Zealand had surprisingly opened the batting with Snedden, their seam bowler, who hit 64 off 97 balls, while Martin Crowe batted elegantly as they put on 84. Everything, however, paled when set alongside Houghton's heroic attempt to lift Zimbabwe from 104 for seven to within a gasp of history.

Toss: Zimbabwe. **New Zealand 242-7** (50 overs) (M. C. Snedden 64, M. D. Crowe 72, J. J. Crowe 31); **Zimbabwe 239** (49.4 overs) (D. L. Houghton 142, I. P. Butchart 54).

India v Australia

At New Delhi, October 22, 1987. India won by 56 runs. 1988

The prospect of India finishing second in this group, and so having to play Pakistan in a semi-final in Pakistan, lessened after their convincing victory. The pitch was ideal for strokeplaying batsmen; the outfield was fast and the boundaries were not too distant. Containment, therefore, was going to be the key, and with the ball coming on to the bat, the Australians' all-seam attack proved to be vulnerable. Gavaskar and Srikkanth got India off to a flying start with 50 in ten overs. Sidhu hit his third successive fifty, and Vengsarkar and Azharuddin, batting with authority and *elan*, added 65 in ten overs. Marsh and Boon responded with 88 in 18 overs, but the introduction of the left-arm spinners, Maninder and Shastri, after 17 overs changed the complexion of the match. Turn, flight and a modicum of frustration brought about Australia's undoing. Waugh displayed technique and temperament, but while the spinners dictated the terms Australia slipped further and further behind.

Toss: Australia. **India 289-6** (50 overs) (S. M. Gavaskar 61, N. S. Sidhu 51, D. B. Vengsarkar 63, M. Azharuddin 54*; C. J. McDermott 3-61); **Australia 233** (49 overs) (G. R. Marsh 33, D. C. Boon 62, D. M. Jones 36, S. R. Waugh 42; Maninder Singh 3-34, M. Azharuddin 3-19).

England v West Indies

At Gujranwala, October 9, 1987. England won by two wickets. 1988

Lamb, with a reprise of his heroic innings against Australia in Sydney in January, and Walsh, conceding 31 runs in his last two overs, allowed England to win a match that looked beyond their grasp when they needed 91 from the last ten overs with four wickets remaining. Earlier, West Indies had themselves conjured 92 from their last ten, having been restricted by tight bowling and good fielding to 151 for four in 40 overs. Logie, Dujon and Harper (22 off Pringle's last over, the 49th) cut loose as England's control slackened. England's innings began slowly, and when Gatting and Gooch, who put on 58 in nine overs, were out to Hooper's slow-medium in the 27th over, they were in trouble. But Lamb, slow to start, found allies in Emburey and DeFreitas. The target from three overs was 35, but Walsh went for 16, Lamb scoring 15 of them. Patterson's last over realised just six, leaving 13 still required. At Sydney, Lamb had hit Reid's last over for 18; now he hit two and four from the first two balls. Then Walsh gave away four leg-side wides and followed this immediately with a no-ball, from which Lamb took a single. The hapless bowler's third attempt at his third ball, a full toss, was carved to the boundary by Foster.

Toss: England. **West Indies 243-7** (50 overs) (R. B. Richardson 53, P. J. L. Dujon 46, A. L. Logie 49; N. A. Foster 3-53); **England 246-8** (49.3 overs) (G. A. Gooch 47, A. J. Lamb 67*; C. L. Hooper 3-42).

Sri Lanka v West Indies

At Karachi, October 13, 1987. West Indies won by 191 runs.

Richards, coming in with Ratnayeke on a hat-trick, set about the Sri Lankan bowling with such savagery that his own record highest score in a one-day international (189 not out off 170 balls against England) looked certain to be eclipsed. Instead, caught when aiming for another six, he had to settle for the highest individual score in a World Cup innings: 181 from 125 balls, with six sixes and 16 fours. It was Richards's tenth hundred in one-day matches for West Indies, while Haynes's 105 was his ninth. West Indies' total was the highest in a one-day international, the previous being Pakistan's 338 for five off 60 overs in the 1983 World Cup. Then, as now, Sri Lanka's bowlers were on the receiving end. In reply, Mahanama and Kuruppu set off at a rate of 12 an over; but this spectacular flourish did not survive the third over.

Toss: Sri Lanka. **West Indies 360-4** (50 overs) (D. L. Haynes 105, I. V. A. Richards 181, A. L. Logie 31*); **Sri Lanka 169-4** (50 overs) (A. P. Gurusinha 36, A. Ranatunga 52*, L. R. D. Mendis 37*).

Pakistan v West Indies

At Lahore, October 16, 1987. Pakistan won by one wicket.

Another of the nail-biting finishes for which this World Cup was becoming renowned saw Pakistan finish their first round of group matches with an unbeaten record. Yet it could not have been closer. With their last pair at the wicket they wanted 14 from the last over, to be bowled – as in West Indies' match against England – by Walsh. He went for 112622, all but the second single scored by Qadir, whose straight-hit six raised a crowd of more than 50,000 to new heights of ecstasy. When 110 for five in the 35th over, Pakistan looked out of it. However, Imran and Yousuf added 73 in 11 overs, and with three overs remaining the target was 21 with four wickets in hand. Yousuf, who had enjoyed at least three lives, was finally caught in Walsh's penultimate over; Patterson's final over brought two wickets while only two runs were added. So came the finale. Walsh, off the very last ball, could have run out Jaffer for backing up too soon, but good sportsmanship prevailed.

Toss: West Indies. **West Indies 216** (49.3 overs) (D. L. Haynes 37, P. V. Simmons 50, I. V. A. Richards 51; Imran Khan 4-37, Saleem Jaffar 3-30); **Pakistan 217-9** (50 overs) (Ramiz Raja 42, Javed Miandad 33, Salim Yousuf 56; C. A. Walsh 4-40).

England v West Indies

At Jaipur, October 26, 1987. England won by 34 runs.

A marvellously disciplined innings by Gooch and some indisciplined bowling by West Indies, who gave away 22 runs – and extra balls – in wides, brought England the victory they needed to have a realistic chance of qualifying for the semi-finals. So profligate was West Indies' early bowling that, after 30 overs, England were 151 for two. A controlled spell by Richards, however, pegged them back to 35 from the next ten, and when Patterson returned to dismiss Lamb and Gooch, it took some inventive batting from Emburey and DeFreitas to realise 83 from the final fifth. While Richards was adding 82 in almost 18 overs with Richardson, hitting Emburey once and Hemmings twice for six, the match was swinging West Indies' way. Then Hemmings bowled him, off stump, to reward England's decision to play both spinners on a pitch sufficiently green to provide some movement off the seam for much of the day. Under pressure, West Indies cracked. They had begun the 41st over needing 65 with six wickets in hand; in eight overs they lost them for 30 runs.

Toss: West Indies. **England 269-5** (50 overs) (G. A. Gooch 92, A. J. Lamb 40, Extras 38; B. P. Patterson 3-56);
West Indies 235 (48.1 overs) (R. B. Richardson 93, I. V. A. Richards 51;
P. A. J. DeFreitas 3-28).

SEMI-FINALS
Pakistan v Australia
At Lahore, November 4, 1987. Australia won by 18 runs.   1988

Pakistan, losing semi-finalists in 1979 and 1983, again failed to reach the World Cup final. They were beaten by a superior all-round performance as Border's Australian side, scarcely rated at the start of the tournament, came of age. Until Imran returned to take three for 17 in five overs, their batsmen had contributed solidly; and at the very end, Waugh – previously the provider of heroic last overs with the ball – struck a vital 18 runs off Saleem Jaffer, beginning with a six over long-on. Jaffer had earlier conceded 39 from his first five overs (the 50th over was only his sixth) as Marsh and Boon put on 73 in 18 overs. Malik's direct hit from square leg ran out Marsh, but Boon and Jones added 82 before Pakistan broke through in the 31st and 32nd overs. Miandad, who stumped Boon, had taken the gloves when Yousuf was struck on the mouth by a deflection off Jones's pad in the 19th over. Another wicket now would have put Pakistan on top, but Border and Veletta kept the momentum going with a stand worth 60 runs.

Pakistan made a disastrous start, losing three wickets in 10.1 overs. Ramiz, sent back, was run out in the first over. Mansoor always struggled, and Malik, playing across the line, spooned the first ball of Waugh's spell to extra-cover. Miandad and Imran rebuilt the innings with 112 in 26 overs, reducing the target to 118 from 15 overs. While Miandad remained it was always possible, but his dismissal, swinging at Reid in the 44th over, left the last three wickets to muster 56 runs. Instead, McDermott, bowling fast and accurately, took all three to finish with the first five-wicket return of the tournament and dash the dreams of a nation.

Toss: Australia. **Australia 267-8** (50 overs) (G. R. Marsh 31, D. C. Boon 65, D. M. Jones 38,
M. R. J. Veletta 48, S. R. Waugh 32*, Extras 34; Imran Khan 3-36); **Pakistan 249** (49 overs)
(Javed Miandad 70, Imran Khan 58; C. J. McDermott 5-44).

India v England

At Bombay, November 5, 1987. England won by 35 runs. 1988

Kapil Dev put England in, believing that the ball would swing early in the day. In the event it did not. The pitch, slow and providing turn, was more suited to spin bowling, thought to be India's strength but countered masterfully by Gooch and Gatting. Adopting a policy of sweeping and pulling the two slow left-arm bowlers, they put on 117 in 19 overs. And when Gooch, who survived a difficult running chance to Srikkanth when 82, was fourth out, caught on the mid-wicket boundary in the 43rd over – Gatting had been dismissed in the 41st – Lamb saw that another 51 runs were added.

India, with Vengsarkar unable to play because of a stomach upset, suffered an early setback when DeFreitas knocked over Gavaskar's off stump. It was the break England wanted, and they never let India take the initiative. Srikkanth and Sidhu, both strokeplayers, did not manage a single boundary. When Azharuddin and Pandit took 27 from Hemmings' first three overs, Gooch bowled three tidy overs and Foster struck again to remove Pandit. Kapil Dev fell victim to his own impetuosity, caught on the mid-wicket boundary immediately after Gatting had stationed himself there. For Hemmings, it was the start of a 34-ball spell in which he took four for 21, his next wicket being the important one of Azharuddin. With five wickets and ten overs in hand, India were looking for five runs an over, but with Azharuddin gone, panic and recklessness set in. Shastri remained a potential threat until the last, but Lamb's marvellous running catch, to put paid to Chetan Sharma's first-ball fling, was testimony to England's all-round commitment.

Toss: India. **England 254-6** (50 overs) (G. A. Gooch 115, M. W. Gatting 56, A. J. Lamb 32*;
Maninder Singh 3-54); **India 219** (45.3 overs) (K. Srikkanth 31, M. Azharuddin 64, Kapil Dev 30;
N. A. Foster 3-47, E. E. Hemmings 4-52).

FINAL
Australia v England

At Calcutta, November 8, 1987. Australia won by seven runs. 1988

Batting first suited Australia; and when they took the field to defend a total of 253, it was in the knowledge that no side battting second had scored 254 to win in this World Cup. England, 135 for two after 31 overs, and with Australia beginning to show signs of disarray in the field, were then almost on target. But in a moment too crass to contemplate, Gatting handed back the initiative. To Border's first ball, bowled on the line of his leg stump, the England captain attempted to play a reverse sweep. Having in the semi-final swept the ball on to his leg stump, he now contrived to hit it on to his shoulder, whence it looped into Dyer's gloves. The Australians' joy was unconcealed.

England had conceded points from the start, an erratic opening spell from DeFreitas and Small helping Marsh and Boon post 52 in ten overs. Foster and the two spinners repaired the damage, with Foster's eight overs costing just 16 runs and bringing the wicket of Marsh in the 18th over. Gooch, too, was economical until coming under fire as Border and Veletta added 73 in the ten overs following Boon's dismissal. Boon's 75 was his fifth score of 50 or more in six innings. DeFreitas, brought back to bowl the last over, went for 11 to bring to 65 the runs scored from England's last six overs.

Robinson, undone by pace to no one's great surprise, was out first ball to McDermott's fourth. Gooch and Athey put on 65 in 17 overs, Athey and Gatting 69 in 13, Athey and Lamb 35 in just over eight. It was Waugh whose throw ran out Athey as he went for a third run; and with England slipping further behind the run-rate (75 from ten overs had drifted to 46 from five), he bowled Lamb in the 47th over. DeFreitas gave England renewed hope with 14 (464) in McDermott's penultimate over, but Waugh conceded just two runs, as well as having DeFreitas caught, in the 49th. That left 17 runs needed from the final over, and there was no way McDermott was going to allow that.

Australia v England, 1987 — World Cup Final

At Calcutta, November 8, 1987. Result: Australia won by seven runs.

AUSTRALIA

D. C. Boon c Downton b Hemmings 75	*A. R. Border run out 31
G. R. Marsh b Foster 24	M. R. J. Veletta not out 45
D. M. Jones c Athey b Hemmings 33	S. R. Waugh not out 5
C. J. McDermott b Gooch 14	B 1, l-b 13, w 5, n-b 7 26

1-75 2-151 3-166 4-168 5-241   (5 wkts, 50 overs) 253

S. P. O'Donnell, †G. C. Dyer, T. B. A. May and B. A. Reid did not bat.

DeFreitas 6–1–34–0; Small 6–0–33–0; Foster 10–0–38–1; Hemmings 10–1–48–2; Emburey 10–0–44–0; Gooch 8–1–42–1.

ENGLAND

G. A. Gooch lbw b O'Donnell 35	J. E. Emburey run out 10
R. T. Robinson lbw b McDermott 0	P. A. J. DeFreitas c Reid b Waugh 17
C. W. J. Athey run out 58	N. A. Foster not out 7
*M. W. Gatting c Dyer b Border 41	G. C. Small not out 3
A. J. Lamb b Waugh 45	B 1, l-b 14, w 2, n-b 4 21
†P. R. Downton c O'Donnell b Border 9	

                                                 (8 wkts, 50 overs) 246

1-1 2-66 3-135 4-170 5-188 6-218 7-220 8-235

E. E. Hemmings did not bat.

McDermott 10–1–51–1; Reid 10–0–43–0; Waugh 9–0–37–2; O'Donnell 10–1–35–1; May 4–0–27–0; Border 7–0–38–2.

Toss won by Australia	UMPIRES R. B. Gupta and Mahboob Shah
MAN OF THE MATCH D. C. Boon	

Feast for Imran's Cornered Tigers

WORLD CUP 1992

David Frith, 1993

After the manner of the Olympic Games, cricket's World Cup quadrennially grows larger and more spectacular. The event, staged in Australia (25 matches) and New Zealand (14 matches) in 1992, featured, for the first time, all eight Test-playing teams, with aspiring Zimbabwe taking the number of competing sides to an unprecedented nine. The final was the 39th match. The first two tournaments, in 1975 and 1979, featured only 15 matches, while in 1983 and 1987 there were 27.

The fifth World Cup was the first to be played in coloured clothing, with a white ball and some games under floodlights. Although it was again 50 overs a side rather than the original 60, it was generally considered to have been the fairest: each side played all the others once before the top four in the qualifying table played off in the semi-finals. Lasting 33 days from first ball to last, it could be faulted seriously only in the matter of the rules governing rain-interrupted matches. Recognising the imperfection of a straight run-rate calculation when a second innings has to be shortened after rain, and unable to schedule spare days within the time-frame of the tournament, the World Cup committee adopted a scheme whereby the reduction in the target would be commensurate with the lowest-scoring overs of the side which batted first. Against South Africa in Melbourne, England lost nine overs but their target of 237 was reduced by only 11 runs. When the teams next met, in the Sydney semi-final, another rain pause, this time at the climactic moment, led to an uproar which echoed for weeks afterwards.

Pakistan won the World Cup for the first time, beating England (twice previous finalists, never winners) by 22 runs on a memorably dramatic autumn night in Melbourne, before an Australian limited-overs record crowd of 87,182 who paid $A2m (£880,000). Almost half of them sat in the newly completed Great Southern Stand, which cost $A140m and is the largest construction ever conceived for Australian sport. It was further claimed that the global television audience exceeded one billion, in 29 countries. In Pakistan, where it was still early evening, jubilation verging on the hysterical splashed over into the streets, and upon their return the players were placed on the highest pedestals of heroism.

Imran Khan, the captain, in his 40th year and nursing a troublesome right shoulder, unsurprisingly declared this as his finest hour, a claim clearly supported by the pictures of him holding the £7,500 Waterford crystal trophy, eyes wide with exhilaration, after ICC chairman Sir Colin Cowdrey had presented it to him on the MCG dais. This accomplished all-rounder, top-scorer in the final with a measured 72, had urged his young team on through times when it seemed that qualification for the semi-finals was out of the question. They were, he said, to take on the stance and response of the cornered tiger. He dedicated the victory to the cause of a cancer hospital in Lahore for which he was fund-raising in memory of his mother. The World Cup organisers seemed content to overlook Imran's earlier remark that it was the worst-organised of all the World Cups. He and Javed Miandad (who became the highest overall run-scorer) alone have played in all five tournaments.

Excitement was high from the opening day, when New Zealand caused the first upset by beating Australia, the holders and favourites, by a comfortable margin at Auckland. Led by Martin Crowe, who made a century, New Zealand were initiating a remarkable run of victories on their slow pitches, Patel bowling off-spin at the start of the innings, followed by a bevy of harmless-looking medium-pacers challenging batsmen to come at them. Crowe's brilliant batsmanship and imaginative command in the field, augmented by the shameless six-hitting of opener Greatbatch, who earned a place only when Wright was injured, took New Zealand almost to the ultimate glory. The co-hosts won their first seven matches, and were not harmed by defeat (by Pakistan) in the eighth, for it assured them of a home semi-final. The sub-plots were multiple, for Pakistan, through this victory at Christchurch, managed to reach the semi-finals... so long as Australia (who had just lost their last chance) beat West Indies at Melbourne a few hours later. Boon's century, his second of the series, and Whitney's four wickets ensured this, putting West Indies out of the competition too.

Australia had started as favourites, but their approach was too inflexible and their form too fickle. New strategies had not so much passed them by as struck no receptive chords in captain Allan Border or coach Bob Simpson. There had been a reluctance to drop the faithful Marsh, who was taking far too much time over his runs, and Simon O'Donnell, voted top player the previous season, was not even chosen in the squad. The nation was mortified as the defeats piled up, the only victory in Australia's first four matches coming by a solitary run in the most thrilling of all the finishes: at Brisbane, when the last ball seemed successively to be a winning boundary for India, then a catch, then again a spillage into the boundary gutter, with Steve Waugh's long recovery throw perhaps too wide, but gathered by substitute wicket-keeper Boon, who made ground to beat the batsman by a few inches. Towards the end of the competition, Australians had been compelled to adopt other allegiances, with no small amount of sympathy being extended South Africa's way.

Readmitted to the international brotherhood after 21 years of political isolation, South Africa, led by Bloemfontein-born former Australian Test batsman Kepler Wessels, were an unpredictable commodity. They had won one of their three introductory limited-overs matches in India in some style three months previously. Now, overseen by coach Mike Procter, one of the world's greatest cricketers at the time of South Africa's expulsion, and spearheaded by the speedy Donald, they stepped coolly on to the stage and beat Australia by nine wickets before a clamorous crowd of almost 40,000 at Sydney, proportionate noise issuing from the throats of hundreds of South African supporters, some of them now resident in Australia. Wessels's partner at the end was Peter Kirsten, who was left out of the original tour squad but was to average 68.33 in the preliminary matches.

Setbacks against New Zealand and Sri Lanka were put behind them as South Africa won their historic encounter with West Indies in a cordially conducted match at Christchurch, following this with a rain-assisted victory over Pakistan at Brisbane, where Jonty Rhodes, already having attracted notice by his electrifying fielding, immortalised himself with an airborne demolition of the stumps to run out Inzamam-ul-Haq. Their place in the semi-finals was secured with victory over India in a shortened match at Adelaide, only for their campaign to be ended cruelly by the sudden heavy shower which fell on the SCG just before 10 p.m., transforming a requirement of 22 off 13 balls to a mocking 21 off one. The crowd's frustration and hostility focused upon the England players in lieu of the rule-makers, while the South Africans absorbed their acute disappointment with a dignified and somehow joyous lap of honour.

Beyond the bounds of cricket, it was believed that their success in the tournament had had an influence on the crucial referendum which decided whether President de Klerk's reforms were to be continued. Support for his progressive dismantling of apartheid was shown in a substantial majority of the white population's votes, some of it unquestionably swayed by live pictures from the far side of the Indian Ocean which showed the national team competing popularly and successfully after having been excommunicated for so long.

The odds after two weeks of competition were affected by the vacillating form most particularly of India and West Indies, both past winners. Reshaped after the jettisoning of several senior players, and led by an out-of-touch Richie Richardson, West Indies won their first match convincingly by making 221 without losing a wicket. This was not against the lesser Zimbabwe or Sri Lanka. It was against Pakistan, the eventual champions. Thereafter they seemed out of sorts, though Brian Lara, the flowery left-hander, finished with four half-centuries. India lost a tight opening match against England, beat Pakistan, who fell apart under the Sydney lights, but were themselves soon to fall by the wayside through poor fielding and an indecisiveness in all departments.

Sri Lanka managed two victories, scoring 313 at New Plymouth to deny Zimbabwe what had seemed a certain triumph given the weight of their own innings, centurion Andy Flower having had his effort capitalised by Andy Waller's 32-ball half-century. Sri Lanka's other success was against South Africa at Wellington, when Ranatunga steered them home by three wickets with only a ball to spare.

The most unexpected result came on the last day of the qualifying matches, when Zimbabwe, having made only 134 on a sporting pitch at Albury, overthrew England by nine runs, Eddo Brandes taking the bowling honours. England could afford to lose, as was the case in their previous match, against New Zealand, although the long run of success which began when they landed in New Zealand for their Test-match tour as the year opened was now broken and in urgent need of repair, particularly as several key players were carrying injuries. The somewhat fortuitous semi-final victory over South Africa restored their direction even if it could not dispel the accumulated weariness. In retrospect, they might have looked back upon their crushing defeat of Australia as their sweetest moment.

Graham Gooch's combination became favourites when Australia began to crack. The depth of batting and breadth of bowling alternatives made possible by so many all-rounders, together with the blend of experience and, in key positions, athleticism in the field, gave England the appearance of certain finalists and probable trophy-winners. Fatigue and Pakistan's inspired surge were to deny them on the night.

Not unexpectedly, the World Cup was given wide coverage in Australasia, though Channel Nine's television cameras were installed only at venues where the organisers felt the interest would be greatest. Matches which they did cover were comprehensively treated, although this was of little comfort to the legions of cricket enthusiasts in Britain who had no access to the BSkyB satellite television reception which was beamed almost around the clock. Apart from two-minute news segments, only half an hour of highlights of the final was shown on BBC TV. Some of the lower-shelf fixtures were staged in rural areas, Albury's reward being the historic upset when Zimbabwe beat England, contrasting with Mackay's fate after all the months of preparation, which was a washout after two balls.

The pool of umpires from the competing nations brought an added flavour of internationalism without quite ensuring the exclusion of errors, some of them quite glaring. Messrs Bucknor and Shepherd were generally regarded as the most reliable. The no-ball penalty for shoulder-high bouncers was not always consistently interpreted, but ensured that the matches were safeguarded from the excesses so often witnessed in the recent past, especially at Test level.

Perversely, as in 1987, neither host nation won through to the final. Seriously stunned in 1987 by their loss to Australia in the semi-final at Lahore, Pakistan somehow lifted themselves in the 1992 tournament after having won only one of their first five matches. Handicapped by the absence through injury of their outstanding fast bowler, Waqar Younis, they were spurred on by their rarefied captain, Imran Khan. As far as bowling strategy went they played aggressively throughout – and with the bat too, once the disciplined foundation had been laid. There was satisfaction in seeing the best two teams in the final, and, for the rare objective onlooker, a slight sadness that only one of them could triumph. For a month, the World Cup not only generated large profits but stirred many hearts and touched countless nerve-ends around the cricket world.

Selected Group Matches
New Zealand v Australia

At Auckland, February 22, 1992. New Zealand won by 37 runs.   1993

An unexpected result thrilled the home crowd and threw the Cup favourites into consternation. The Australians had reckoned on a sluggish pitch favouring New Zealand, but not on Crowe's sharp thinking: he gave the new ball to Patel, an off-spinner, and then juggled his attack so frequently that the batsmen never settled.

Yet the home team had struggled in the morning, when the pitch retained its bounce. After two wides, McDermott bowled Wright with his first legitimate ball; Reid had Latham dropped, then trapped Jones; and Healy took a low, one-handed catch. But Rutherford added 118 in 25 overs with Crowe, who ignored a knee injury to reach his century (11 fours) with one ball to spare. Next came his gambit with the ball. New Zealand's fastest bowler, Morrison, had been omitted, and the strategy soon seemed justified; while Cairns conceded 30 from four overs, at the other end Patel unnerved Boon and Marsh so much that they took only 19 from his first seven. Constant bowling changes maintained the Australians' uncertainty, and though Boon pushed doggedly on to his hundred, the asking rate crept towards double figures, Steve Waugh's attempts to hit out were cut short with 50 needed from less than five overs. When Boon was run out, the Australians disintegrated. Their last five wickets were captured for 12 runs in 17 balls.

Toss: New Zealand. **New Zealand 248-6** (50 overs) (M. D. Crowe 100*, K. R. Rutherford 57); **Australia 211** (48.1 overs) (D. C. Boon 100, S. R. Waugh 38; G. R. Larsen 3-30).

Sri Lanka v Zimbabwe
At New Plymouth, February 23, 1992. Sri Lanka won by three wickets. 1993

Away from the limelight, the cup's least-fancied teams staged a record-breaking encounter. The bare pitch and short boundaries of Pukekura Park helped them both to reach 300 for the first time in a limited-overs international, and no other team had passed that mark batting second. Their aggregate was one short of the 626 shared by Pakistan and Sri Lanka at Swansea in 1983. Of the 12 bowlers, only Traicos, the 44-year-old off-spinner, emerged with respectable figures.

Zimbabwe's opener, [Andy] Flower, scored an unbeaten 115 and earned the match award on his full international debut. He was supported first by Arnott, and then Waller in an unbroken fifth-wicket stand of 145 – a World Cup record – in 13 overs. Waller's 83 took a mere 45 balls (three sixes, nine fours), and his 32-ball 50 was also a cup record. Zimbabwe looked forward to the second win that had eluded them since 1983, but the Sri Lankans were undaunted. Mahanama and Samarasekera (50 in 33 balls) opened with 128, and though the middle order faltered, Ranatunga (61 balls) approached his task with relish, securing victory with his ninth four.

Toss: Sri Lanka. **Zimbabwe 312-4** (50 overs) (A. Flower 115*, K. J. Arnott 52, A. C. Waller 83*, Extras 30); **Sri Lanka 313-7** (49.2 overs) (R. S. Mahanama 59, M. A. R. Samarasekera 75, A. Ranatunga 88*, S. T. Jayasuriya 32; E. A. Brandes 3-70).

Australia v South Africa
At Sydney, February 26, 1992 (day/night). South Africa won by nine wickets. 1993

South Africa returned to the ground where they played their first Test in Australia, in 1910–11, and their last, in 1963–64, and won their first World Cup match with ease. Their captain, Wessels, the former Australian player, was hugged by his opposite number and former team-mate Border after hitting the winning run. But the match had a disheartening start for the returning prodigals. Donald's first ball appeared to find the edge of Marsh's bat before reaching the wicket-keeper, but umpire Aldridge thought not. The visitors' calm in disappointment was rewarded when no Australian reached 30: only Boon looked comfortable.

South Africa's medium-pacers took control, and Kuiper removed Marsh and Border with consecutive balls. The fielding, in particular that of Rhodes at cover, was universally praised. In contrast the Australians bowled and fielded untidily, and were quite unable to defend a mediocre total of 170. They were further hampered by the loss of Healy, who pulled a hamstring while batting; Boon took over behind the stumps. Victory secured, the South Africans returned to their dressing-room to receive messages of congratulation from President F. W. de Klerk and ANC leader Nelson Mandela, while cup-holders Australia digested their second defeat in their opening two games.

Toss: Australia. **Australia 170-9** (49 overs) (A. A. Donald 3-34); **South Africa 171-1** (46.5 overs) (K. C. Wessels 81*, P. N. Kirsten 49*).

England v West Indies
At Melbourne, February 27, 1992 (day/night). England won by six wickets. 1993

A convincing victory, with more than ten overs to spare, was England's eighth in succession in one-day internationals, and their fourth in a row over West Indies. England put West Indies into bat, and four top-order batsmen went for 55 runs while the white ball was moving prodigiously for the seamers. Lara, his toe still swollen, was hit on the box by Lewis's first ball and edged the second to Stewart. When Haynes, who had held firm for 20 overs, pulled to square leg, everything depended on Arthurton and Logie. The former obliged by driving and cutting to a fifty, though he offered three chances before giving Fairbrother a second catch; the same fielder had run out Logie, looking for a leg-bye when DeFreitas appealed for lbw. West Indies' 157 was their second-lowest completed total in the World Cup. In reply, Gooch opened with complete confidence while Botham scored only eight out of 50 in the first 14 overs. Hick's 54 from 55 balls dominated the later innings, until he fell to a diving return catch by Harper, whom he had just driven for six through the covers.

Toss: England. **West Indies 157** (49.2 overs) (D. L. Haynes 38, K. L. T. Arthurton 54; C. C. Lewis 3-30, P. A. J. DeFreitas 3-34); **England 160-4** (39.5 overs) (G. A. Gooch 65, G. A. Hick 54).

Australia v England
At Sydney, March 5, 1992 (day/night). England won by eight wickets. 1993

The combination of the old enemy, the bright lights and the noisily enthusiastic crowd demanded a show-stopper from Botham, and he provided it. His best bowling figures in limited-overs internationals stopped the Australian innings in its tracks, and he followed up with a confident fifty which made England's victory a formality. The match turned in the 38th over, when Botham bowled Border with the fifth ball. In his next over, Healy drove to Fairbrother at mid-wicket, Taylor was trapped lbw, and McDermott fell to DeFreitas's running catch. Botham had claimed four wickets for no runs in seven balls, and Australia were 155 for eight. They took only 16 from their last nine overs. Their only hope was to capture some early wickets, and Gooch was repeatedly beaten in McDermott's fiery opening spell. Botham's self-confidence was now complete, however, and he led the way to the hundred partnership in the 23rd over, reaching his first World Cup fifty one ball later. He hit six fours before giving Healy a low leg-side catch.

Toss: Australia. **Australia 171** (49 overs) (T. M. Moody 51; I. T. Botham 4-31); **England 173-2** (40.5 overs) (G. A. Gooch 58, I. T. Botham 53, R. A. Smith 30*).

England v South Africa

At Melbourne, March 12, 1992 (day/night).
England won by three wickets, their target having been revised to 226 from 41 overs.   1993

The first meeting of old adversaries since 1965 produced a thriller; England over-came a fine South African performance, assorted injuries, and the infamous rain rule to notch up their 12th limited-overs international without defeat. Deputising for the injured Gooch, Stewart trusted in the weather and chose to field. No wicket fell until the 36th over, when South Africa were 151. England's attack lacked Lewis, restricted by a side strain; DeFreitas bowled ten overs though he was limping so badly he left the field after each spell; Small proved too expensive to be risked; and Reeve fell, bruised his back and could not go on. His replacement, Hick, made the breakthrough, with a return catch from Hudson. Wessels batted on watchfully for 46 overs and South Africa reached 236. Stewart wasted no time: in 12 overs he was 40, and England 62 without loss. Rain transformed the target, and the match too. They were set to pass the 225 scored in South Africa's best 41 overs. Then Botham was bowled, and within seven balls Smith and Hick were caught behind. But Fairbrother added 68 in 13 overs with Stewart, 34 with Reeve and a glorious 50 in six overs with Lewis. Like Stewart, Lewis was run out by the athletic Rhodes. England then needed ten off two overs. Eight came from Meyrick Pringle's last over, but with the scores level Derek Pringle drove a full toss to short mid-wicket. DeFreitas emerged to hit the winning run with one ball to spare.

Toss: England. **South Africa 236-4** (50 overs) (K. C. Wessels 85, A. C. Hudson 79); **England 226-7** (40.5 overs) (A. J. Stewart 77, N. H. Fairbrother 75*, C. C. Lewis 33; R. P. Snell 3-42).

England v Zimbabwe

At Albury, March 18, 1992. Zimbabwe won by nine runs.   1993

In the upset of the tournament, cup favourites England were bowled out by Zimbabwe, ten runs short of a paltry target of 135. Zimbabwe earned their first points of the competition and their first win after 18 defeats since beating Australia on their World Cup debut in 1983. On that day, Houghton was dismissed for nought. Now he top-scored with 29, and the ducks were collected by Gooch and Hick, a very junior member of Zimbabwe's 1983 party. Ironically, Zimbabwe owed victory to their much-derided bowling. A bowlers' pitch was no excuse for England. Gooch departed first ball, a feather in the cap of Brandes, whose single spell plucked four prize wickets. Just as heroic were Shah and Traicos, whose 20 overs cost a mere 33 runs. At 43 for five Stewart joined Fairbrother for the biggest stand of the match, a painfully slow 52 in 24 overs. Fairbrother, still suffering from a stomach infection, batted over two hours without reaching the boundary. England narrowly ran out of wickets before overs.

Toss: England. **Zimbabwe 134** (46.1 overs) (I. T. Botham 3-23, R. K. Illingworth 3-33); **England 125** (49.1 overs) (E. A. Brandes 4-21).

Australia v West Indies

At Melbourne, March 18, 1992 (day/night). Australia won by 57 runs. 1993

Forty-five minutes into their innings, Australia's semi-final aspirations were ended by news of Pakistan's victory [over New Zealand]. But their own win eliminated the West Indians, and earned themselves a consolatory fifth place in the final table on run-rate. West Indies could blame themselves: the Australians' total was well within reach after they failed to build on an opening stand of 107 in 27 overs. Boon scored his sixth international century of the season, duplicating his 100 in the opening World Cup match in Auckland. For a mere 4.34 an over, the West Indians would have been in the last four. But only Lara met the challenge, batting 38 overs for 70. Haynes and Simmons went to consecutive balls in McDermott's fourth over, and Whitney bowled his ten straight through to remove Richardson, Arthurton, Logie and Hooper. Lara's off-drives and sweeps pushed the score on until, at 137, he called Benjamin for a run. When his colleague made no response, West Indies' last chance was shattered with Lara's stumps.

Toss: Australia. **Australia 216-6** (50 overs) (T. M. Moody 42, D. C. Boon 100; A. C. Cummins 3-38); **West Indies 159** (42.4 overs) (B. C. Lara 70; M. R. Whitney 4-34).

SEMI-FINALS
New Zealand v Pakistan

At Auckland, March 21, 1992. Pakistan won by four wickets. 1993

Pakistan reached their first World Cup final by defeating the previously invincible New Zealanders twice in four days. This win seemed unlikely when they needed 123 from 15 overs at 8.2. But the match was transformed by Inzamam-ul-Haq, whose aggressive hitting gave him 60 from 37 balls (one six, seven fours, 50 in 31) and a partnership of 87 in ten overs with Javed Miandad. When Inzamam was run out the target was 36 from five, which was passed with ease thanks to Wasim Akram, Moin Khan (20 not out in 11 balls) and Miandad, who chivvied his partners along for two hours and came in unbeaten on 57. Imran Khan ran out to welcome him as his opposite number, Crowe, limped on for New Zealand's lap of honour. He had sat out Pakistan's innings with a pulled hamstring, and Wright led in the field.

Yet Crowe's day had begun happily enough: he won the toss and re-emphasised his class with an accomplished 91 in 83 balls including three sixes. When he arrived New Zealand were tangled in Mushtaq Ahmed's leg-spin after Greatbatch's usual explosion (sixes off Wasim and Aqib Javed). Crowe accelerated smoothly, adding 107 in 113 balls with Rutherford. But when Rutherford skied the ball to Moin, the batsmen crossed and Crowe's hamstring went. He continued with Greatbatch as his runner, until this supposed aide ran him out. Still, Smith and the tail hurried on to 262. It was an imposing target, especially in mid-innings when Imran seemed bogged down. But against Inzamam's dynamism, New Zealand's successful stratagems of the past month had no power. Even their surprise weapon, Patel, whose opening eight overs of off-breaks garnered one for 28, yielded 22 when he returned for his last two.

Toss: New Zealand. **New Zealand 262-7** (50 overs) (M. D. Crowe 91, K. R. Rutherford 50); **Pakistan 264-6** (49 overs) (Ramiz Raja 44, Imran Khan 44, Javed Miandad 57*, Inzamam-ul-Haq 60).

England v South Africa
At Sydney, March 22, 1992 (day/night). England won by 19 runs.   1993

This game's closing minutes buried South Africa's World Cup hopes, and whatever credibility the rain rule had retained. By putting pressure on the team batting second, the rule supposedly created exciting finishes; on this occasion 12 minutes' heavy rain, when South Africa needed 22 from 13 balls, adjusted their target first to 22 from seven, and then to 21 from one. McMillan could only take a single off Lewis. The losers were disconsolate, the winners embarrassed, and the crowd furious. Why, they asked, were the two overs not played out under the floodlights?

The majority blamed the World Cup's organising committee, and the inflexibility which prevented a second-day resumption. (The next day was set aside only for a completely new match, to be played if the second team had not faced 25 overs.) Justice was probably done; Wessels chose to field, knowing the rules and the forecast, and his bowlers were fined for going slow and depriving England of five overs' acceleration. But it was not seen to be done, and fine performances on both sides were overshadowed by indignation.

Most of England's batsmen scored fluently, but the *tour de force* came from Hick. He survived an lbw appeal first ball, and was caught off a no-ball before scoring, but went on to 83 in 90 balls, adding 71 in 14 overs with Stewart, and 73 with Fairbrother. Reeve raced out to score 25 from 14 balls, including 17 of the 18 plundered from Donald's final over. Pursuing 5.62 an over, South Africa made 58 from their first ten. For once they did not depend on Kirsten, hampered by an

Does not compute: South Africa's impossible target – calculated by an impenetrable "rain rule" after a short weather delay – shines out from the Sydney scoreboard at the end of the 1992 World Cup semi-final against England.

injury. Hudson narrowly missed a fourth fifty, Kuiper hit three consecutive fours off Small, and Rhodes proved his worth as a batsman, reducing the target to 47 from just over five overs; McMillan and Richardson knocked off 25 from three before the rain, and the rules, made their task impossible.

Toss: South Africa. **England 252-6** (45 overs) (A. J. Stewart 33, G. A. Hick 83); **South Africa 232-6** (43 overs) (A. C. Hudson 46, A. P. Kuiper 36, J. N. Rhodes 43).

FINAL
England v Pakistan
At Melbourne, March 25, 1992 (day/night). Pakistan won by 22 runs.   1993

Imran Khan's erratically brilliant Pakistanis won their first World Cup final while Gooch and England lost their third, on the broad field of Melbourne with nearly 90,000 in attendance. Afterwards Imran said it was "the most fulfilling and satisfying cricket moment of my life". He described the victory as a triumph for his young team's talent over England's experience; he also stressed the role of his aggressive specialist bowlers rather than the "stereotyped" attack of Gooch's all-rounders. But he enjoyed an all-round triumph himself with the match's highest score and the final wicket.

Imran's role went deeper, however. He had virtually hand-picked the team, and after the disappointment of losing a key player, the pace bowler Waqar Younis, to a stress fracture before leaving Pakistan, and a disastrous start when they won only one in five matches (two of which he missed), he urged them to imitate the action of a cornered tiger before they went on to five successive wins. They reached the giant stadium in peak form, while England looked exhausted. The players who had toured New Zealand unconquered had gradually weakened in the face of constant travel and frequent injury. As Pakistan had picked up, they had been losing, first to New Zealand and then, most embarrassingly, to Zimbabwe. "It's not the end of the world," said Gooch after the match, "but it is close to it." England were worn down by the century partnership of veterans Imran and Javed Miandad, which started slowly but gathered force, and the spirit of their batsmen was broken by successive balls from Man of the Match Wasim Akram which dismissed Lamb and Lewis, one swinging in and then straightening again, the next cutting in sharply.

Remembering the baleful potential of rain, and knowing that no one had won a World Cup final chasing runs, Imran had chosen to bat. At first England prospered. In nine overs Pringle reduced Pakistan to 24 for two. Then Imran and Miandad settled down to see off the new ball. Progress was slow: Imran was nine from 16 overs when Gooch spilled a running catch. But although Pakistan were only 70 halfway through, and Miandad had summoned a runner, they accelerated to add 139 in 31 overs before Miandad attempted a reverse sweep. Soon Imran's strokeplaying proteges, Inzamam-ul-Haq (35 balls) and Wasim Akram (18 balls), took up the fight. Their 52 in six overs brought the runs from the last 20 overs to 153, though Pringle's final over cost just two and saw them both dismissed.

England's pursuit of five an over started badly when Botham was surprised to be given caught behind. The next time Moin Khan claimed a catch, Stewart escaped judgment, but not for long, and Mushtaq Ahmed's leg-spin accounted for Hick (baffled by the googly) and Gooch. With England requiring 181 from 29 overs, Lamb, preferred for his experience to Smith, whose fitness was in doubt, added 72 in 14 with Fairbrother. But Wasim returned to devastating effect. Deprived of heavyweight partners, and using a runner, Fairbrother top-edged to Moin after an hour and a half. The tail threw the bat to no avail. Imran dismissed Illingworth to complete his triumph, and pledged the proceeds of his success to the cancer hospital planned in his mother's memory.

England v Pakistan, 1992 **World Cup Final**
At Melbourne, March 25, 1992. Result: Pakistan won by 22 runs.

PAKISTAN

Aamir Sohail c Stewart b Pringle	4	Inzamam–ul–Haq b Pringle	42
Ramiz Raja lbw b Pringle	8	Wasim Akram run out	33
*Imran Khan c Illingworth b Botham	72	Salim Malik not out	0
Javed Miandad c Botham b Illingworth	58	L-b 19, w 6, n-b 7	32

1-20 2-24 3-163 4-197 5-249 6-249 (6 wkts, 50 overs) 249
Ijaz Ahmed, †Moin Khan, Mushtaq Ahmed and Aqib Javed did not bat.

Pringle 10–2–22–3; Lewis 10–2–52–0; Botham 7–0–42–1; DeFreitas 10–1–42–0; Illingworth 10–0–50–1; Reeve 3–0–22–0.

England

*G. A. Gooch c Aqib Javed b Mushtaq Ahmed	29	C. C. Lewis b Wasim Akram		0
I. T. Botham c Moin Khan b Wasim Akram..	0	D. A. Reeve c Ramiz Raja b Mushtaq Ahmed		15
†A. J. Stewart c Moin Khan b Aqib Javed	7	D. R. Pringle not out		18
G. A. Hick lbw b Mushtaq Ahmed.........	17	P. A. J. DeFreitas run out		10
N. H. Fairbrother c Moin Khan b Aqib Javed	62	R. K. Illingworth c Ramiz Raja b Imran Khan		14
A. J. Lamb b Wasim Akram..............	31	L-b 5, w 13, n-b 6		24

1-6 2-21 3-59 4-69 5-141 6-141 7-180 8-183 9-208 10-227

(49.2 overs) 227

Wasim Akram 10–0–49–3; Aqib Javed 10–2–27–2; Mushtaq Ahmed 10–1–41–3;
Ijaz Ahmed 3–0–13–0; Imran Khan 6.2–0–43–1; Aamir Sohail 10–0–49–0.

Toss won by Pakistan — Umpires B. L. Aldridge and S. A. Bucknor
Man of the Match Wasim Akram

Sensational Sri Lanka

WORLD CUP 1996   Alan Lee, 1997

There were some good, uplifting aspects to the sixth cricket World Cup, not least the style and smiles of its unsuspected winners, Sri Lanka, but overall this was not a tournament to linger fondly in the memory. Wounded by events beyond its control even before its opening, the competition proceeded to frustrate and bewilder through an interminable and largely irrelevant saga of group games in India, Pakistan and Sri Lanka before hastening frantically through its knockout games in little more than a week.

The event was poorly conceived in its format and its logistics and suffered throughout from the threat – and ultimately the reality – of crowd disorder. The abandonment of the semi-final at Eden Gardens, Calcutta, following bottle-throwing and fire-lighting on the terraces, was a shameful reflection on standards of sportsmanship in an area until recently renowned for its appreciation of all things good in the game of cricket.

Perhaps, however, we should not be too harsh on the individuals responsible for the riot in Calcutta. They were merely responding to the seductions created for them by the promoters of the Wills World Cup, an event that plainly, disastrously, put money-making above all the fundamentals of organising a global sporting competition. As the glamorising of the Indian and Pakistani cricketers reached new and absurd heights, so too did the unshakeable belief of the masses in their invincibility. Defeat, of the kind that came to India that night in Calcutta, was popularly unimaginable, with consequences for which many must share the blame.

It was all markedly at odds with the 1987 World Cup, also co-hosted by India and Pakistan and widely judged to be an organisational triumph. Players and observers alike enjoyed that competition far more than the 1996 event. Yet the paradox is that, when the accounts were complete, they showed a negligible profit. Within a decade, the profile of the game had altered substantially; so too, it transpired, had the methods and ambitions of those charged with running the tournament. Suddenly, it was deemed more important to register a company as supplier of official chewing gum – and take its money – than to pay proper attention to the welfare of the competing teams. Of course, it is possible to become too nannyish about professional sportsmen, who by and large lead a pretty pampered existence, but the wearisome travel schedules, illogical playing itineraries and inadequate practice facilities inflicted on most of the visiting teams would have caused a serious rebellion had this been a football championship.

In fact, such elementary flaws should have been dealt with at source, long before they became a millstone around the event. The reason they were not – the handing over by the International Cricket Council of all responsibility for the tournament to the World Cup committee, Pilcom – reflects poorly on all those responsible. What function does the ICC perform if it is not to be a vigilant monitor of events like this? Cricket must never permit such complacency again.

ICC must also take the blame for the format. The expansion of the field to 12, from nine in 1992, was quite right. By embracing three of the ICC's Associate Members, the non-Test countries, the World Cup was fulfilling its missionary aim (though whether the associates, wooed by financial guarantees, had too much say in the venue is another serious matter for the ICC to consider). The problem arose when the extra teams were accommodated by a complete change from the successful 1992 system, a round-robin producing four semi-finalists. Instead, the teams were divided into two groups of six, from which not four but eight sides would proceed to the knockout rounds. The effect of this, obvious in advance, was to reduce virtually a month of cricket to the status of little more than practice games: duly, almost inevitably, the three associate nations and the junior Test-playing team, Zimbabwe, were eliminated. All this could have been avoided, and a genuinely competitive group programme installed, by discarding the idea of quarter-finals and going straight to a last four. Presumably, the attraction of four big crowds, four big television games, was too great, but this was a decision taken on flawed grounds. The people were not all fooled; the group games in Pakistan, particularly, drew very small crowds.

The logistical chaos of the competition stemmed largely from the decision, laudable in theory but utterly unrealistic, to spread the tournament to virtually every corner of the vast country of India. The 17 games scheduled for the country were all staged in different cities and insufficient attention had been paid to the practicalities of moving teams (let alone television crews and media people) between games. Travel in India is problematical at best; a few specific alterations were made to airline schedules to oblige the competition organisers but nowhere near enough to surmount the problem, the size of which became clear during the first, eventful weekend. The teams were all due to gather in Calcutta for a variety of briefing meetings before the much-vaunted opening ceremony, a celebration of technology for which the organisers had outlaid considerable capital.

As it transpired, however, the weekend was dominated by the issue of two teams, Australia and West Indies, adamantly refusing to play their scheduled group games in Colombo. The bomb blast in the city, a fortnight earlier, was the clinching factor, but Australia's players were already uncomfortable about visiting Sri Lanka, with whom they had just played an acrimonious Test series. In truth, they were reluctant to participate in the cup at all, the backwash of their bribery allegations against Salim Malik having brought threats of an unpleasant nature from a number of fanatics around Pakistan. West Indies had far less reason for prudence on the Colombo issue, but the condemnatory tone of the organisers against the two defectors gave the episode an unwarranted tone, intensified by a press conference that touched heights of incoherent rancour. It was even suggested that Australia and West Indies were indulging in a vendetta against the Third World, until it was gently pointed out, by the ICC's chairman, Sir Clyde Walcott, that the Caribbean forms part of the Third World.

Positions being entrenched, the matches were forfeited, though it was a commentary on the cosiness of the format that Australia and West Indies could make such a sacrifice without seriously endangering their progress to the business end of the tournament. Sri Lanka were both winners and losers – winners because they received four points, and a comfortable passage to the last eight, without playing, but losers because their lovely island was deprived of its two biggest matches at a time when the public was most in need of rousing diversions. For them, however, the grandest of compensations awaited.

The opening ceremony was attended by more than 100,000 people, most of whom must have left wondering what on earth they had been watching. The laser show malfunctioned, the compère was embarrassing and the grand launch was a complete flop – so much so that there were subsequent calls at Calcuttan government level for the arrest of the Pilcom convenor, Jagmohan Dalmiya, on a charge of wasting public money.

At 4 a.m. the following morning, four teams gathered blearily in the lobby of Calcutta's Oberoi hotel. They were all slated for the 6 a.m. flight to Delhi (India's internal flights tend to run before dawn and after dusk), whereafter they were required to wait many hours before connecting to flights for their various first-game destinations. Had no one thought of organising a charter flight at a civilised hour? Apparently not. Given this, the choice of the unlovely city of Ahmedabad, and the teams of England and New Zealand, for the opening game of the tournament, should perhaps not seem curious. It was, however, a deflating start, and not just for England, whose obsolete one-day tactics and lack of specific preparation for the only limited-overs event that matters were exposed from the beginning. England were destined to win only two games in the competition, both against non-league opposition, and one of those, against Holland, by an unflatteringly narrow margin. Their players had come to the event tired and unfocused, which was not entirely their fault, but the need for a progressive team manager to replace Raymond Illingworth became ever clearer as their ill-fated campaign continued. England once dictated the terms in one-day cricket; unnoticed by them, other countries have caught up and left them behind, developing new and innovative ways of overcoming the essentially negative restrictions of the overs game.

The use of pinch-hitters was one such method, much discussed and granted more significance than it merited, but it was certainly the case that the successful teams no longer looked to accrue the majority of their runs in the closing overs of their innings. Instead of settling for 60 or 70 runs from the initial 15 overs, when fielding restrictions applied, teams were now looking to pass the 100 mark. On the blissful batting pitches encountered here, it was seldom impossible. Sri Lanka, through their fearless openers, Sanath Jayasuriya – later to be named the "most valued player" of the tournament – and Romesh Kaluwitharana, were the trendsetters and, as the outcome proved, nobody did it better. Jayasuriya's assault on England's bowling in the quarter-final at Faisalabad was authentic, aggressive batting without insult to the coaching manual.

There were some memorable images from the over-long group stages. Mark Taylor's sportsmanship, in refusing to claim a slip catch at a pivotal stage against

West Indies, was one; the imperious batting of Mark Waugh and Sachin Tendulkar provided more. But the majority involved the minnow nations. The best of them was the catch by Kenya's portly, bespectacled and none-too-nimble wicket-keeper, Tariq Iqbal, to dismiss Brian Lara. That it led to a Kenyan victory by 73 runs was part of the romance; here was the greatest upset the World Cup has known and, perhaps, a salutary lesson to a West Indies team that had become surly and un-attractive. Kenya played their cricket as the West Indians once loved to do, without inhibition; defeat paradoxically restored pride to West Indies. They not only rallied to reach the last eight – roused by 93 not out from their beleaguered captain, Richie Richardson, against Australia – but, there, beat the team that had hitherto looked the slickest in the event, South Africa.

The two main host nations predictably reached the quarter-finals but it was not in the preferred script that they should meet each other so soon. Bangalore had the dubious honour of staging the game and this beautiful, bustling city has never known such an event. The fact that India won it, before an intensely partisan crowd, perhaps averted the kind of disgraceful scenes witnessed four days later in Calcutta, where Sri Lanka utterly outplayed the Indians. In the other semi-final, Australia recovered from an apparently hopeless position to beat West Indies, whose collective nerve crumbled.

Thus was created a meeting, in the final, between two teams who were prevented by politics and expediency from playing each other earlier. Sri Lanka's victory was to the great approval and acclaim of much of the cricketing world. It was also a result that, to some degree, rescued this World Cup from an abiding image of bungling mediocrity. The tournament achieved one aim in increasing the profile of cricket, through television coverage on an impressive but largely uncritical scale, and undoubtedly it satisfied the organisers in the amount of money accrued. But the impression was that the cricket was secondary to the commercialism. Even in a game newly awakened to its financial opportunities, that cannot be right.

SELECTED GROUP MATCHES
India v West Indies
At Gwalior, February 21, 1996 (day/night). India won by five wickets. 1997

This match was the first real test for both teams and India won it hands down. First, they dismissed the West Indians for 173 on a decent pitch; then, inspired by Tendulkar, they knocked off the runs inside 40 overs. In fact, both innings followed the same pattern up to the halfway mark: two early wickets falling to the strike bowler, then a recovery checked by the loss of the captain, caught in the deep, with the total in the early nineties. But whereas Richardson's departure sparked the first of two West Indian collapses – curiously, both of three wickets for eight in 12 balls – India steamed on. The key moments of the match came when Lara was given caught behind fifth ball, apparently off his pad, and later when Browne dropped a skier off Tendulkar, then 22. Tendulkar advanced to 70 from 91 balls, earning his second successive match award, before he was run out in a mix-up with Kambli, who then took charge of the closing stages. Despite some tight bowling by Walsh, West Indies' task had become hopeless. A crowd of 30,000 lit torches and firecrackers, and the smoke drifted through the floodlights as they celebrated a home victory.

Toss: West Indies. **West Indies 173** (50 overs) (R. B. Richardson 47, S. Chanderpaul 38; M. Prabhakar 3-39, A. Kumble 3-35); **India 174-5** (39.4 overs) (S. R. Tendulkar 70, M. Azharuddin 32, V. G. Kambli 33*).

India v Australia
At Bombay, February 27, 1996 (day/night). Australia won by 16 runs. 1997

The first floodlit international in Bombay was also illuminated by some thrilling batting. Mark Waugh became the first man to score consecutive World Cup centuries [he had scored 130 against Kenya four days earlier], and Tendulkar treated his home crowd to an explosive 90. At first, Waugh was overshadowed by Taylor, who galloped to 59 as they opened with 103 at five an over; Australia looked capable of topping 300. But once Taylor was caught on the boundary, the spinners Raju and Kumble thwarted such ambitions. Waugh eventually went for 126 from 135 balls, having hit three sixes and eight fours, and the last seven wickets fell for 26 – four of them in the final over, which yielded only two runs. After six overs, India had lost two wickets to Fleming, while McGrath had bowled three maidens. But Tendulkar hit three fours off McGrath's fifth over, and blazed from 12 to 56 in 25 balls, with seven fours and one six. When Fleming bowled Azharuddin, Tendulkar steadied himself slightly, then raced to 90 from 84 balls, with 14 fours and a six. He was finally stumped off a wide – delivered by his rival, Mark Waugh, trying his hand at off-spin. Until then, no one could write off India, and, though Warne bowled tightly, Manjrekar and Mongia kept them in the hunt. They were always a couple of wickets adrift, however, and Fleming ended the innings by bowling Kumble, his fifth victim, with two overs to go.

Toss: Australia. **Australia 258** (50 overs) (M. E. Waugh 126, M. A. Taylor 59); **India 242** (48 overs) (S. R. Tendulkar 90, S. V. Manjrekar 62; D. W. Fleming 5-36).

Kenya v West Indies
At Pune, February 29, 1996. Kenya won by 73 runs. 1997

Kenya's victory was hailed as one of the biggest upsets in cricket history. It was the more extraordinary for being the work of their bowlers, rather than their highly rated batting. Captain Maurice Odumbe thought his team was done for when he lost the toss; once they were all out for 166, he was certain of it. But his amateur attack dismissed West Indies for 93, their lowest World Cup total and their second worst in any one-day international. Kenya had struggled to 81 for six after Walsh removed their top three. The last four, however, added 85, thanks to Hitesh Modi and the 17-year-old Thomas Odoyo, and survived into the final over, though the highest scorer was Extras, with 37. Part-time wicket-keeper Adams equalled the World Cup record of five dismissals.

West Indies' nightmare began with Richardson being bowled leg stump by Rajab Ali. Three balls later, Campbell was also bowled, by Suji. The collapse became critical when Lara was caught behind by Tariq Iqbal, whose stout figure and village-standard juggling had hitherto caused much mirth. Only Chanderpaul and Harper reached double figures and both fell to the off-spin of Maurice Odumbe, whose figures of three for 15 in ten overs exactly mirrored those of his more famous counterpart, Harper. The last wicket went the same way as the first – Cuffy was bowled by Rajab Ali, who fell into his team-mates' arms. As the Kenyans ran an exuberant victory lap, cheered on by local spectators, West Indies realised that, level on points with Kenya and Zimbabwe, they could no longer be certain of reaching the quarter-finals. The future of their captain, Richardson, looked even bleaker.

Toss: West Indies. **Kenya 166** (49.3 overs) (Extras 37; C. A. Walsh 3-46, R. A. Harper 3-15); **West Indies 93** (35.2 overs) (R. W. Ali 3-17, M. O. Odumbe 3-15).

India v Sri Lanka

At Delhi, March 2, 1996. Sri Lanka won by six wickets.   1997

A devastating assault by their openers ensured Sri Lanka first place in the group. They made 272 look a simple target, though Kumble made the middle order work hard for it. Victory by half-time seemed possible when Jayasuriya and Kaluwitharana smashed 42 in their first three overs – Prabhakar conceded 11 and 22 – and they had shot past 50 in five when Kaluwitharana, looking for his seventh four, gave Kumble a diving catch. Jayasuriya charged on, though his final statistics of 79 in 76 balls, with nine fours and two sixes, seemed sedate after his initial rampage. Having set off at twice the required rate, Sri Lanka gradually fell behind, as spin-ners Kumble and Tendulkar bowled 12 overs in harness for 48. Kumble instigated a mini-collapse as he completed the run-out of Gurusinha and then, in his next two overs, dismissed Jayasuriya and de Silva. With another slow bowler – they had opted for a four-man seam attack, while Sri Lanka augmented their spin – India might have suffocated the innings. But Ranatunga and Tillekeratne restarted the ignition in a stand of 131, winning with eight balls to spare.

India paid for their slow progress in the morning. They began batting in light mist, after play was delayed 15 minutes by dew on the outfield, and took 25 overs to score 100. After a short rain-break, the final 11 overs brought 105, thanks to Tendulkar. His run-a-ball 137, with five sixes and eight fours, was his second century of the tournament and he added 175 with Azharuddin, an all-wicket World Cup record for India. Pushpakumara's last over cost 23 – but that only prefigured the carnage to come.

Toss: Sri Lanka. **India 271-3** (50 overs) (S. R. Tendulkar 137, S. V. Manjrekar 32, M. Azharuddin 72*); **Sri Lanka 272-4** (48.4 overs) (S. T. Jayasuriya 79, A. Ranatunga 46*, H. P. Tillekeratne 70*).

Australia v West Indies
At Jaipur, March 4, 1996. West Indies won by four wickets. 1997

Four days after their humiliation by Kenya, West Indies fought back to inflict the first proper defeat of the tournament on the strongly fancied Australians. The revival was embodied by their captain, Richardson, who had 93 at the finish. He had repaired the damage to his dignity and, most importantly, salvaged the World Cup campaign. Nevertheless, he announced next day that he would retire from international cricket – saying he had made his mind up after the 1995 tour of England – and manager Wes Hall and coach Andy Roberts subsequently departed. Back in India, a lengthy meeting had focused the West Indians on their mission and they imposed themselves from the start. After Taylor chose to bat on an uneven pitch, Ambrose and Walsh bowled six maidens and conceded just eight between them in the first nine overs. But they did not convert their dominance into wickets and Australia were able to accelerate – their last 20 overs brought 135. Ponting surged to 102 in 112 balls, surviving a run-out appeal on 96.

West Indies' pursuit of 230 started badly, with Campbell edging to Healy in the second over. They were 26 for two when Richardson joined Lara, whom, it had emerged, he would have preferred not to bring to the World Cup. But the pair combined effectively to add 87 and Lara scored 60 in 70 balls, his first fifty of the tournament. Then Richardson took charge, hitting ten fours and a six, which Ponting carried over the boundary. He might have reached his century, but Adams scored successive fours for victory, and Richardson did not seem to notice as he accepted the emotional embraces of his team-mates.

Toss: Australia. **Australia 229-6** (50 overs) (M. E. Waugh 30, R. T. Ponting 102, S. R. Waugh 57); **West Indies 232-6** (48.5 overs) (B. C. Lara 60, R. B. Richardson 93*; M. E. Waugh 3-38).

Sri Lanka v Kenya
At Kandy, March 6, 1996. Sri Lanka won by 144 runs. 1997

Kenya swiftly returned to earth after their apotheosis against West Indies, while Sri Lanka were heading for the stratosphere. Determined to show that they would have scored maximum points even if Australia and West Indies had come to Colombo, they bagged a clutch of records. Most notably, their 398 for five was a world record for any one-day international, comfortably leaving behind England's 363 for seven against Pakistan in 1992 – and that total occupied 55 overs, not 50. The star batsman was de Silva, who scored his country's maiden World Cup century and went on to 145, a Sri Lankan record in all limited-overs internationals. He needed only 115 balls, hitting 14 fours and five sixes. Ranatunga, his captain, might have scored an even faster hundred; he made 75 not out in just 40 balls, with 13 fours and a six, having reached 50 in 29 balls, another World Cup record. Both de Silva and Ranatunga passed 5,000 one-day international runs – the first Sri Lankans to do so. The tone had been set right from the start, when Jayasuriya and Kaluwitharana raced to 83 in a mere 40 balls, paving the way for de Silva and Gurusinha to add 184 in 182 balls, Sri Lanka's best for any wicket in limited-overs internationals.

Kenya had opted to chase, but they could hardly have reckoned on chasing eight an over. They rose gallantly to the occasion, however; their 254 for seven was the third-highest total by a non-Test side, after Zimbabwe's 312 against Sri Lanka in the 1992 World Cup and Sri Lanka's 276 for five against Australia in 1975. Steve Tikolo was yorked four short of Kenya's first century at senior level – he hit eight fours and four sixes in 95 balls – after adding 137 for the fourth wicket with Hitesh Modi. That helped to set up a combined match total of 652 for 12, only ten behind the world record of 662 for 17 set by Sri Lanka and West Indies at Sharjah in October 1995.

Toss: Kenya. **Sri Lanka 398-5** (50 overs) (S. T. Jayasuriya 44, R. S. Kaluwitharana 33, A. P. Gurusinha 84, P. A. de Silva 145, A. Ranatunga 75*); **Kenya 254-7** (50 overs) (S. O. Tikolo 96, H. S. Modi 41).

After 30 Group stage matches, Kenya (despite their sensational win against West Indies), Zimbabwe, United Arab Emirates and Holland were eliminated and the leading eight teams proceeded to the quarter-finals.

QUARTER-FINALS
England v Sri Lanka
At Faisalabad, March 9, 1996. Sri Lanka won by five wickets.   1997

Sri Lanka continued their glorious ascent, while England sank ignominiously; they had never been knocked out before the semi-finals in the five previous World Cups. They were all but dead by the time Jayasuriya departed at 113 for one, virtually halfway to Sri Lanka's target of 236, in their 13th over. Jayasuriya had thumped 82 off 44 balls, with three sixes and 13 fours. He was most savage on the left-arm spin of Illingworth, whom he hit for four successive fours, and the seam of DeFreitas, whose second over went for 22. DeFreitas was withdrawn, having conceded 32 in 12 balls; later, he bowled some tidy off-spin, but by then there was nothing to play for. England's only real breakthrough came in the second over when Illingworth, opening the attack in an attempt to surprise the Sri Lankans, got Kaluwitharana third ball – he had hit the first two for fours. Jayasuriya's spree was finally ended when the third umpire gave him out stumped, one delivery after Reeve bowled him with a no-ball. De Silva and the rest could not keep up his momentum, but still won with nine overs in hand.

Atherton had elected to bat, hoping for 300, though even that might not have withstood the Sri Lankan assault. As it was, only DeFreitas, promoted to No. 5, managed the sustained aggression necessary. He hit 67 from 64 balls, his maiden one-day fifty for England, and looked a little unlucky to be out lbw to Jayasuriya. The run-out of Smith – also by the ubiquitous Jayasuriya, with a direct hit – was still more controversial, even after the third umpire's judgment. With the middle order crumbling, only a 62-run stand by Reeve and Gough took England past 200.

Toss: England. **England 235-8** (50 overs) (P. A. J. DeFreitas 67, D. A. Reeve 35); **Sri Lanka 236-5** (40.4 overs) (S. T. Jayasuriya 82, A. P. Gurusinha 45, P. A. de Silva 31).

India v Pakistan

At Bangalore, March 9, 1996 (day/night). India won by 39 runs.   1997

This encounter inspired high passions which boiled over back in Pakistan after India won. One fan reportedly shot his television and then himself, while captain Wasim Akram was burned in effigy. Wasim was not even playing, having ruptured his side muscles, but conspiracy theorists, fuelled by the previous year's allegations of bribery, speculated that he might have withdrawn deliberately, a charge he indignantly denied. In fact, the game looked keenly contested and turned into a thriller. India chose to bat but, though the bowlers made no gains until the 22nd over, their top batsmen never quite took control either. Tendulkar's 31 was a trifle by his standards. Sidhu, seven short of his century when Mushtaq Ahmed's flipper deceived him, steered India to an impressive-sounding 168 for two, but the scoring-rate was barely four and a half an over. It was Jadeja who played the decisive role, scoring 45 from 25 balls (four fours and two sixes), coupled with a tremendous onslaught from the tail. They smashed 51 off the last three overs. Waqar bowled two of those overs for 40 runs, after his first eight had cost just 27; when he got Jadeja he became the fourth player to take 200 wickets in one-day internationals. Meanwhile, a slow over-rate was punished by the deduction of an over from Pakistan's reply, the only such penalty in the tournament.

Even so, their openers seized the initiative. Saeed Anwar had scored 48 from 32 balls, including two sixes, when he skied to Kumble; stand-in captain Aamir Sohail was 55 from 46, with one six, when he slashed wildly at Prasad. Pakistan made 113 for two from the vital first 15 overs, putting them way ahead of India. But Prasad grabbed two more wickets and, gradually, the scoring-rate faltered. Rashid Latif, with two big sixes in a run-a-ball 26, kept Pakistan going, but his stumping sparked a collapse to Kumble. The run-out of Javed Miandad signalled the end of Pakistan's reign as one-day champions and, apparently, of a career spanning three decades. With characteristic rancour, he used the announcement of his retirement to denounce the team management for ignoring his batting and strategic expertise.

Toss: India. **India 287-8** (50 overs) (N. S. Sidhu 93, S. R. Tendulkar 31, A. D. Jadeja 45);

Pakistan 248-9 (49 overs) (Aamir Sohail 55, Saeed Anwar 48, Salim Malik 38, Javed Miandad 38;

B. K. V. Prasad 3-45, A. Kumble 3-48).

South Africa v West Indies

At Karachi, March 11, 1996. West Indies won by 19 runs.   1997

West Indies' stubborn fightback after crashing against Kenya carried them through against favourites South Africa. A century from Lara – 111 in 94 balls – set up their victory and it was completed by the spin of Jimmy Adams and Harper, who turned the game with three wickets in the first over of his second spell. At the start, though, the spinners in the news were the South Africans, Symcox and Paul Adams: uncharacteristically, South Africa played both, omitting Donald from their pace attack. But Lara, gaining confidence after a wary start, thrived on spin. Five of his 16 fours came from one over by Symcox, and a second-wicket stand with

Chanderpaul of 138 from 25 overs promised a big total. However, after Symcox returned for his belated revenge – finding Lara's top edge as he tried to sweep – the later order struggled. The final ten overs brought only 48 runs, 16 off the last one, bowled by Adams.

South Africa were also propelled by their second-wicket pair: Hudson and Cullinan, who struck three sixes, had taken the score to 118 for one at the halfway mark. It was slow left-armer Jimmy Adams, not normally a frontline bowler, who made the breakthrough, removing both of them in 15 balls and dismissing Cronje, for a hard-hitting 40, in his final over. Harper then replaced him and with his first delivery had Rhodes caught by Adams on the mid-wicket boundary. His next ball trapped McMillan lbw and, three balls later, he dived to take a left-handed return catch from Palframan. Symcox attempted to rescue South Africa's campaign with two sixes. Harper was the bowler but he had the last laugh, making Pollock his fourth victim and then catching Symcox in the very next over.

Toss: West Indies. **West Indies 264-8** (50 overs) (S. Chanderpaul 56, B. C. Lara 111); **South Africa 245** (49.3 overs) (A. C. Hudson 54, D. J. Cullinan 69, W. J. Cronje 40; R. A. Harper 4-47, J. C. Adams 3-53).

Australia v New Zealand
At Madras, March 11, 1996 (day/night). Australia won by six wickets. 1997

The Waughs relentlessly steered Australia into the semi-finals as Mark became the first batsman to score three hundreds in one World Cup. New Zealand must have been delighted with their total of 286 – it was their highest in 63 one-day games against Australia, and more than any team had chased successfully in this tournament. Their heroes were Germon, who continued to bat at No. 3, and Harris, recalled after scoring only 26 in the opening three matches. Together, they put on 168 – a fourth-wicket record for New Zealand and the World Cup – at more than six an over. Germon scored 89 from 96 balls, his maiden international fifty, and Harris his first century for New Zealand. He was finally caught, one-handed by Reiffel on the boundary, in the penultimate over, for 130 from 124 balls with four sixes and 13 fours.

With Morrison injured, Germon reverted to New Zealand's surprise tactic of the previous World Cup – giving off-spinner Patel the new ball. It had unsettled Australia in 1992, and he did have Taylor caught behind in the sixth over. But Mark Waugh was soon into his stride, with some unexpected support: Warne was promoted to No. 4 as the latest pinch-hitter, and smashed two sixes in 24 from 14 balls. It was Waugh's more familiar partner, his twin Steve, who saw him past his hundred. Mark made 110 from 112 balls with two sixes, five fours and a lot of running, before he grew tired and slightly misjudged a shot to the boundary which found Parore. However, Steve supervised the closing stages. Australia's victory, with 13 balls to spare, meant that all four semi-finalists came from Group A; their counterparts from Group B – by coincidence, the four semi-finalists of 1992 – had been wiped out.

Toss: New Zealand. **New Zealand 286-9** (50 overs) (L. K. Germon 89, C. Z. Harris 130); **Australia 289-4** (47.5 overs) (M. E. Waugh 110, R. T. Ponting 31, S. R. Waugh 59*, S. G. Law 42*).

SEMI-FINALS
India v Sri Lanka

At Calcutta, March 13, 1996 (day/night). Sri Lanka won by default after a crowd riot.   1997

Sri Lanka played brilliantly after a disastrous first over to achieve an unbeatable advantage. But the headlines were devoted to the riot which ended the match. Enraged by an Indian collapse of seven wickets for 22, some home supporters threw bottles on to the outfield and set fire to the seating. Referee Clive Lloyd took the teams off for 15 minutes, attempted a restart and then awarded Sri Lanka the game by default. Nobody questioned the result; India needed a near-impossible 132 from 15.5 overs, with only two wickets standing. But the Indian board smarted at the word default and asked for Sri Lanka to be declared winners on run-rate. The authorities – and many home fans – were intensely embarrassed by the trouble. Even as the match was abandoned, one Indian raised a banner reading "Congratulation [*sic*] Sri Lanka – we are sorry". Some took out apologetic advertisements in the Sri Lankan press. But, like the Pakistani fans four days before, others raged against their unsuccessful players and a guard was put on captain Azharuddin's house.

Azharuddin took much criticism for fielding first. He knew Sri Lanka preferred to chase, as they did to beat India in Delhi, but critics argued that he should play to his team's strengths, not his opponents' weaknesses. There were few objections, however, when Kaluwitharana and Jayasuriya, Sri Lanka's celebrated pinch-hitters, both hit straight to third man in the first four balls of the game. Gurusinha soon followed, but de Silva determinedly stuck to the strategy of scoring as heavily as possible early on: he hit 22 off Prasad's first two overs. Though he was bowled in the 15th over, de Silva had scored 66, with 14 fours, off 47 balls, and Sri Lanka already had 85. Ranatunga and Mahanama (who eventually succumbed to cramp) kept up a steady five an over.

A target of 252 was not necessarily beyond India's batting heroes, but when Tendulkar was stumped and, seven balls later, Azharuddin gave Dharmasena a return catch, the 100,000 crowd was stunned into silence. That did not last, as the collapse fuelled their fury, and no play was possible after the loss of Kapoor to de Silva's running catch in the deep. Yet the presentation ceremony went ahead as if nothing untoward had occurred, and, against the smoking backdrop, Tony Greig conducted post-match interviews so normal they were bizarre.

Toss: India. **Sri Lanka 251-8** (50 overs) (P. A. de Silva 66, R. S. Mahanama 58*, A. Ranatunga 35, H. P. Tillekeratne 32; J. Srinath 3-34); **India 120-8** (34.1 overs) (S. R. Tendulkar 65; S. T. Jayasuriya 3-12).

The day after Sri Lanka's semi-final win, in advance of the final, Sanath Jayasuriya was named Most Valued Player of the Tournament.

Australia v West Indies

At Mohali, March 14, 1996 (day/night). Australia won by five runs.　　　　1997

West Indies pulled off an extraordinary defeat, losing eight wickets in the final 50 minutes. After 41 overs, they were 165 for two, needing 43 from the last nine; Lara had gone for a run-a-ball 45, but Chanderpaul was heading for a century and Richardson for a glorious conclusion to his captaincy. Once Chanderpaul – hampered by cramp – fell, however, the innings swerved out of control. Big hitters Harper and Gibson were promoted in the order but their wickets, in quick succession, placed more pressure on the recognised batsmen, Adams and the out-of-form Arthurton, who soon followed. Australia were on top for the first time in the game and a devastating three-over spell from Warne culled three for six. But Richardson was still there to face the last over, from Fleming. When he struck the first delivery for four, West Indies required six from five balls, with two wickets left, and victory was in his grasp. The final fatal misjudgment was to set off for a single, for even if Ambrose had got home, it was Richardson who needed the strike. In fact, Ambrose was given out on a TV replay. Last man Walsh heaved at his first ball and was bowled.

Taylor had controlled the closing stages perfectly but said afterwards that West Indies had won 95% of the match. The game had seemed dead after 40 minutes, when Australia, electing to bat on one of the grassier pitches of the tournament, were 15 for four. Ambrose and Bishop had fired out both Waughs, Ponting, who scored 102 in their last meeting, and Taylor himself for a combined four runs, and a rout threatened. But Law and Bevan batted with determination and growing confidence to add 138 in 32 overs and the later order pushed the total past 200. Though Warne dismissed Browne with his first ball, West Indies seemed to have the task well in hand until panic overtook them.

Toss: Australia. **Australia 207-8** (50 overs) (S. G. Law 72, M. G. Bevan 69, I. A. Healy 31);
West Indies 202 (49.3 overs) (S. Chanderpaul 80, B. C. Lara 45, R. B. Richardson 49*;
S. K. Warne 4-36).

FINAL
Australia v Sri Lanka

At Lahore, March 17, 1996 (day/night). Sri Lanka won by seven wickets.　　Scyld Berry, 1997

Contrary to most expectations, Sri Lanka controlled their first World Cup final after the initial stages. Their batting was vastly more proficient against spin than Australia's; their catching was flawless whereas the Australians held one chance out of five; their ground-fielding was sure while the Australians frequently fumbled; and their spinners obtained enough turn on what was otherwise a batsman's pitch to stifle the Australians after their confident start. Only in pace bowling were the Sri Lankans the lesser side on the day, and their two opening bowlers did not feature again after their first 13 overs had cost 72 runs. The first day/night international in Pakistan was played in cool conditions, and there was no sun even in daytime. Storms the previous night were followed by rain just as Prime Minister Benazir Bhutto presented the Wills World Cup to Arjuna Ranatunga, one of the longest survivors among contemporary Test cricketers.

In spite of the dampness, the Australians would have batted first in any event, but Ranatunga chose to field first in the hope of some early wickets for his seamers, and because his batsmen had shown exceptional maturity of temperament in their earlier run-chases. If his plan did not work out exactly – the hitherto impressive Vaas pitching too short – his seamers did succeed in removing Australia's best player of spin, Mark Waugh, who clipped a half-volley to square leg. But the significance of his dismissal was not apparent while Taylor and Ponting took the score to 137 by the 27th over. Then Taylor was caught sweeping at de Silva, who began his various contributions with a spell of five overs for two wickets and 19 runs.

Four overs later Ponting missed his cut at an off-break, which left Australia without a settled batsman to take on the four spinners as they tightened their grip. The balance shifted, and Australia's incoming batsmen were unable to work the ball through the gaps in the infield often enough, let alone score boundaries. After 20 overs their score was 110 for one, after 40 overs 178 for five. From the 24th over to their 49th, they did not reach the boundary except for a pulled six by Law. Whereas Taylor hit eight fours and a six, his team-mates mustered just five fours between them, as Ranatunga shrewdly kept his three off-spinners and Jayasuriya going until the end.

Given the excellence of Sri Lanka's batting, the Australians had to take early wickets and catch everything. By the sixth over they did have two wickets, Jayasuriya run out by the narrowest of margins on a TV replay, and Kaluwitharana mis-pulling to square leg. That, however, was the extent of Australia's catching: Law dropped Gurusinha when 53 off a straightforward pull to deep mid-wicket, and three half-chances were not taken. Considerable dew made the ball slippery, especially for the spinners Warne and Mark Waugh, and the Australians seemed to have little left in their tank for their third high-intensity game in seven days.

Gurusinha flat-batted Warne for four to long-on and for six over long-off from consecutive balls, and provided steadily accelerating support for de Silva, who began with a model on-drive for three first ball, and whipped Fleming's straight slower ball in front of square to give Sri Lanka's innings a momentum it never lost. In mid-innings he was content to push the spinners around and hit only the bad ball hard, and he made sure of his wicket, after Gurusinha was out to a wild swing and while Ranatunga was playing himself in. Just as the required rate was climbing towards a run a ball, Mark Waugh conceded 12 runs from an over, so Sri Lanka needed just 51 off their last ten overs, which became a mere ten from five. De Silva went on to score the third hundred in a World Cup final (after Clive Lloyd and Viv Richards), and finished with 107 from 124 balls, including 13 fours, a remarkable strike-rate given his certainty of application. It was the first time in six attempts that a side batting second had won the World Cup final.

Australia v Sri Lanka, 1996   World Cup Final

At Lahore, March 17, 1996. Result: Sri Lanka won by seven wickets.

AUSTRALIA

*M. A. Taylor c Jayasuriya b de Silva	74	S. G. Law c de Silva b Jayasuriya		22
M. E. Waugh c Jayasuriya b Vaas	12	M. G. Bevan not out		36
R. T. Ponting b de Silva	45	†I. A. Healy b de Silva		2
S. R. Waugh c de Silva b Dharmasena	13	P. R. Reiffel not out		13
S. K. Warne st Kaluwitharana b Muralitharan	2	L-b 10, w 11, n-b 1		22

1-36 2-137 3-152 4-156 5-170 6-202 7-205   (7 wkts, 50 overs) 241

D. W. Fleming and G. D. McGrath did not bat.

Wickremasinghe 7–0–38–0; Vaas 6–1–30–1; Muralitharan 10–0–31–1; Dharmasena 10–0–47–1; Jayasuriya 8–0–43–1; de Silva 9–0–42–3.

SRI LANKA

S. T. Jayasuriya run out	9	P. A. de Silva not out		107
†R. S. Kaluwitharana c Bevan b Fleming	6	*A. Ranatunga not out		47
A. P. Gurusinha b Reiffel	65	B 1, l-b 4, w 5, n-b 1		11

1-12 2-23 3-148   (3 wkts, 46.2 overs) 245

H. P. Tillekeratne, R. S. Mahanama, H. D. P. K. Dharmasena,
W. P. U. J. C. Vaas, G. P. Wickremasinghe and M. Muralitharan did not bat.

McGrath 8.2–1–28–0; Fleming 6–0–43–1; Warne 10–0–58–0; Reiffel 10–0–49–1; M. E. Waugh 6–0–35–0;
S. R. Waugh 3–0–15–0; Bevan 3–0–12–0.

Toss won by Sri Lanka   UMPIRES S. A. Bucknor and D. R. Shepherd
MAN OF THE MATCH P. A. de Silva

A NIGHT TO REMEMBER   David Hopps, 1997

Colombo had known much grief in the weeks leading up to the World Cup final. The bomb on January 31 that killed about 90 people had brought terrorism back to the heart of the capital. And it undermined Sri Lanka's hopes that their co-hosting of the tournament would promote tourism and investment, as well as providing funds for an expansion of cricket facilities throughout the country.

Australia, having just been involved in a bitter series against Sri Lanka, had already voiced some reluctance to fulfil their fixtures in the country, on the grounds that some of their players had received hate mail and feared for their safety, for reasons connected with cricket rather than politics. The atrocity in Colombo justified their quick withdrawal. Even the pleas of the Sri Lankan government, whose array of security measures included an offer to fly the team in from Madras or The Maldives, failed to change their minds. West Indies soon followed Australia's example, without bothering to consult their players, leaving only two relatively minor sides, Kenya and Zimbabwe, to play fixtures which passed off without incident. That was only some compensation. In the early stages of the tournament, the mood in this most gracious and easy-going of countries was one of demoralisation and betrayal.

The night of March 17 provided handsome recompense. To be on Galle Face Green, a traditional Colombo meeting point overlooking the Indian Ocean, shortly after Sri Lanka's triumph over Australia in the final in Lahore was to witness a joyful outpouring of national pride. With most Sri Lankans preferring to watch the final in small family groups, the capital was eerily deserted for much of the day but, as night fell, the streets abruptly came alive to the blaring of car horns and the explosion of fireworks. Some people had privately expressed their reluctance to join the Galle Face parade, fearing that there could be no more crushing time for the Tamil Tigers to launch another attack than at the moment of the country's greatest sporting achievement. But many suppressed their fears as tens of thousands streamed along the sea-front in just about every form of transport known to man.

Even in its most harrowing times, Sri Lanka has rung to the sound of laughter and it was impossible to walk a few yards along Galle Face Green without another invitation to join an impromptu street party. The walk back to the hotel as the sun began to rise was made more unsteadily. Whisky and arrack (the local firewater distilled from coconut) flowed, and Bob Marley music blared from the back of cars and open-top trucks, upon which rapturous youngsters danced precariously. Among the most soulful songs was *This Land Belongs to Us*, and such lyrics cannot be sung in Sri Lanka without a sense of underlying weariness caused by years of terrorist warfare.

Cricket had always been a unifying force, offering recreation for Sinhalese, Tamil, Muslim and Christian alike. Now it had given the nation a chance to forget. The schools in Colombo had only just reopened after the Tigers' warning to the government to "build smaller coffins". Now young children wandered freely and ecstatically through the throng.

According to Sri Lankan folklore, Nadiya – the jackal – is despised as the lowest of all animals, because of its willingness to eat the crow, which is regarded as the dustbin of Sri Lanka. Australia's forfeit of their group match in Colombo had caused their high commissioner to be greeted with the call of Nadiya – "Hu, Hu, Hu" – at the prize-giving ceremony following Sri Lanka's victory against Kenya in Kandy. As televisions focused on a defeated Australian team, the jackal sounded for a final time. It was the response of a country getting even, and relishing every minute of it.

England's Debacle

 Scyld Berry, 1999

Twenty years ago – no more – England's opening batsmen walked out to bat in the World Cup final. They were the 38-year-old Geoffrey Boycott and the 37-year-old Michael Brearley, conventional batsmen both: not even at a pinch could you have called them hitters. They proceeded to prove as much: in pursuit of a target of 287 to beat West Indies, they consumed 235 balls to score 121 runs between them.

England's opening pair were not alone, however, in erring on the side of the pedestrian and conventional in that 1979 World Cup. New Zealand's batting was opened by John Wright and Bruce Edgar, India's by Sunil Gavaskar – the same Gavaskar who had batted through 60 overs in the previous World Cup for 36 runs, albeit largely out of bloody-mindedness – and the studious Anshuman Gaekwad (slow and bespectacled batsmen are always studious).

One-day international cricket in those days was for Test players letting their often-greying hair down. England's wicket-keeper in the 1979 World Cup was Bob Taylor; the only player resembling a one-day specialist was Brian McKechnie – but then New Zealand were usually short of a full hand of Test players. Nobody did anything cunning like change the batting around (England could have opened in that final with Graham Gooch and Wayne Larkins, or Ian Botham and Derek Randall). It was still an age of innocence, cricketing and commercial, and perhaps more enjoyable for being so.

Now the World Cup is a strapping young man of 24 years, who has grown and grown until he is able to look the World Cups of other sports in the eye. Every feature of cricket's World Cup has expanded enormously since those first two modest tournaments in England in the 1970s. They both consisted of 15 games played by eight teams over 15 days. In 1983, again in England, there were 27 games over 17 days. In 1987, there were still 27 matches played by eight countries, but this time they were spread over the length and breadth of India and Pakistan, regardless of the travelling hardships for the players, and the tournament took five weeks to stage.

In Australia in 1992, 39 matches were played by nine countries in the best format conceived to date, as every country played the others once. In 1996, back in the subcontinent, the number of competitors expanded to 12 as three non-Test sides were included, and Kenya produced the biggest giant-killing act of all when they defeated a disunited West Indian team. This time there will be

42 matches, the most yet, with six teams going through, and being whittled down to four via a complex system called the Super Six, to determine the semi-finalists.

Crowds have expanded too, from 158,000 to an expected 500,000 for this summer's event in England, and untold millions for the two cups staged in the subcontinent. Profits too have grown a little, from £150,000 in the original competition to millions of rupees which were again untold in the last World Cup, as the accounts were not subjected to external auditing. The International Cricket Council has decided never to repeat that mistake, and will wisely oversee this and all future World Cups.

If the entrepreneurial horizons have expanded hugely, so too have those of the cricketers themselves, and particularly of batsmen. The first three tournaments were much of a muchness, all of them 60-over events on pitches where the ball did a bit. Even as late as 1983, England were opening with Chris Tavaré – in his dogged England mode, not his sometimes free county style. You built your innings as you would in any other match, kept wickets in hand for the slog, and only clubbed and clattered in the last few overs. A rate of four runs an over after 60 overs was pretty good, except if you were whopping the likes of Canada, East Africa or Sri Lanka (yes, the 1996 winners were non-Test tiddlers in the first two cups). Only three totals above 250 were recorded in the 1979 tournament; unsurprisingly, England in the final failed to offer one of those instances.

Each of the next three cups saw a significant step forward in batting. The 1987 competition was held on the grassless pitches of India and Pakistan. The fact that the innings had to be reduced to 50 overs, to allow for shorter hours of daylight than in England in midsummer, was soon forgotten; the number of totals above 250 was now up to 16. Batsmen cut out pedantic introductions in the first ten overs. West Indies and Viv Richards went further by hitting Sri Lanka for 360 for four and 181 respectively in their Karachi qualifier.

Seam bowlers had been safe from assault in England, unless you were as aggressive as Dennis Lillee and tried to bounce out Alvin Kallicharran, even though it was a limited-overs game (Kalli hit Lillee for 35 from ten balls in a 1975 qualifier). Now, in 1987, such canny exponents as Courtney Walsh and Derek Pringle were carted, especially at the end of a long hot session: the three breaks in leisurely England had been reduced to one between innings. Line and length were no longer enough. Change of pace was in, as exemplified by Steve Waugh, who rolled his wrist and fingers and frequently got that ball up in the blockhole. But spin too had a major say for the first time in the 1987 Cup. Whereas not one over of it was bowled in the 1975 final, seven of the nine most economical bowlers in the qualifying round of 1987 were spinners.

As the 1992 tournament was staged largely in Australia, the ACB introduced floodlit cricket, coloured clothes, white balls and the fielding restriction which had been a feature of their one-day internationals at home since World Series: only two fielders allowed outside the semi-circles in the first 15 overs, so that television viewers would be glued to their seats from the start. In the previous World Cup, Geoff Marsh and David Boon of victorious Australia had been the exemplars of one-day opening, running those quick singles: their coach Bobby Simpson had calculated that 90% of internationals were won by the side which scored off the greater number of balls, never mind the boundaries. Soon that was a load of old helmet. England opened with Ian Botham, India with Kris Srikkanth, West Indies with Brian Lara, to cash in while the field was up, but none of them did so with such effect as Mark Greatbatch of New Zealand.

Nobody could legally bowl him a bouncer (the definition of what was too high and wide had been tightened up for the 1983 competition onwards), so he put his foot down the wicket and bounced the ball off the terracing of New Zealand's cricket-cum-rugby grounds. One-day batting could not be confused with the Test-match style of Boycott and Brearley any more. The vogue was to use a pinch-hitter to get that scoring-rate up and keep it up. The counter, especially in New Zealand where pitches were slow, was to take all the pace off the ball – as the Indians had done in 1983 – even to the extent of opening the bowling with Dipak Patel.

In 1995–96, Sri Lanka were playing in the one-day series in Australia when one of their regular openers, Roshan Mahanama, was injured (their other opener was called Sanath Jayasuriya). So the Sri Lankans' manager Duleep Mendis asked the coach Dav Whatmore what he thought about promoting the wicket-keeper Romesh Kaluwitharana, who had been batting down the order and getting caught in the deep. "I love it," replied Whatmore. Thus was born the Sri Lankan ploy of two pinch-hitters, except that Jayasuriya and Kaluwitharana were not in any sense mere hitters; one already had a Test century against Australia, the other would get his within a few weeks. They were able to bat with greater freedom than specialist batsmen because they were all-rounders with more than one bow-string.

With five specialist batsmen to follow – Mahanama now served as insurance against any batting collapses at No. 7 – the Sri Lankans scored freely in the 1996 cup, not only when they clattered Kenya for a record total of 398 but even when they made bad starts in the semi-final and final. Whatmore and his Australian vigour had already made Sri Lanka into the first accomplished all-round fielding side the subcontinent had produced (Asia had seen some wonderful specialists before, of course, but there was always someone less than zealous or reluctant to dive). Throw in four spinners who took the pace off the ball, and mature compo-sure from the senior players, and the World Cup was deservedly Sri Lanka's. The Australian argument that they were handicapped by dew in the day/night final in Lahore does not bear much scrutiny, as they had underperformed with the bat in broad daylight.

This growth in run-scoring may cease in 1999 as the young man reaches his mid-twenties. The three previous World Cups in England were staged in June, but this one will begin on May 14. Specialist pace bowlers will be necessary to make full use of the conditions, and specialist top-order batsmen to withstand them. Everything else should keep on growing though, like the excellence of the fielding, and the sponsorship money, and the television revenues, and the media coverage, and the worldwide interest. It will be a mature man of the world who goes to South Africa in 2003.

WORLD CUP 1999 – REVIEW

Matthew Engel, 2000

With about five playable hours of daylight remaining on the longest Sunday of the year, Darren Lehmann struck the ball towards the Lord's Grand Stand for the boundary that gave the seventh World Cup to Australia. This concluded a final so one-sided that it descended from anticlimax into bathos. A match that had started at 11.15, half an hour late, was all over by 4.35 because Pakistan, the most exciting side in the tournament, had gone to pieces when it mattered most.

The first World Cup final, at Lord's 24 years earlier almost to the day, had lasted nearly ten hours. This one was over shortly after it started. The nature of one-day cricket is such that two evenly matched teams can easily produce a lop-sided match, simply because of the breaks of the game. It was, however, true to the uniquely perverse nature of Pakistani cricket that it should happen to them on such an occasion. Thus the best Test team in the world became the world one-day champions, uniting the two forms of cricket into one undisputed title for the first time since West Indies lost their invincibility in the last Lord's final 16 years before. Hindsight made it seem like manifest destiny. It was obvious all along, wasn't it? But it was nothing of the kind.

When Australia had gone to Old Trafford three Sundays earlier for their final group match, they were in severe danger of the earliest possible exit; two Sundays after that, during the last Super Six match, Australian journalists and officials had been making calls to check on airline seat availability, which would have been firmed up had Herschelle Gibbs not celebrated too soon and literally thrown away a catch offered by Steve Waugh. In the semi-final four days later, as Damien Fleming prepared to bowl to Lance Klusener – the player of the tournament – with South Africa needing one to win, Australia were effectively goners. But that game, arguably the greatest in the history of one-day cricket, produced a final twist that no one could have foreseen or invented. Klusener and Allan Donald had a horrendous running mix-up, the match was tied, and Australia went through on net run-rate, of which, unfortunately, more later.

Australia's improbable lurch into the final was in complete contrast to their opponents' confident strut. The Pakistanis lost three successive games which did not matter, but returned to form in time to earn their place at Lord's by blowing Zimbabwe and New Zealand away by huge margins. But it has been noticed before that the way to win World Cups – and not just in cricket – is to fiddle quietly through the early matches and peak at the end. This is a lesson South Africa, who blazed their way through the early stages of all three World Cups in the 1990s without ever reaching the final, urgently need to learn. It is, however, rather diffi-cult to convert this observation into a strategy. Steve Waugh's diamond-hardness, and the bowling gifts of Glenn McGrath and Shane Warne, seem in retrospect like the determining factors of the 1999 World Cup. But it could so easily have been very, very different.

The overall quality of the Australian team meant that no one – not even an Englishman – could begrudge their right to the trophy. But Pakistan and South Africa would have been worthy winners too. The class of these three teams (one might add India's batting as well) gave the tournament enough lustre to make the whole thing seem like a triumph. Five months later, the rugby World Cup, also held in Britain, was much nearer a flop. Yet the success came against a background of travail almost as great as Australia's.

England's main objective in staging the World Cup was to reinvigorate the nation's love of the game, which had been flagging after so many years of failure by the national team. For the organisers, the worst-case scenario was that England would go out quickly. By the time they had completed no-nonsense wins over Sri Lanka, Kenya and Zimbabwe, that fear had receded to vanishing point. Some newspapers claimed that England were already through to the Super Six stage. For them to fail, Zimbabwe had to beat South Africa, which in advance seemed improbable bordering on impossible, and then England had to lose to India very badly. It all happened. Only 16 days into the tournament, with a further 21 to go, England were gone. It was an outcome wholly in keeping with many of the farcical organisational aspects of the whole competition. The hosts were reduced to just that: handing round the cucumber sandwiches at their own tea party.

The fact that the tournament maintained public interest, even in England, in spite of this disaster, represented its greatest achievement. The fact that it got into such a pickle in the first place was its biggest failure. In previous World Cups, this situation could not have arisen. The system used in Australasia in 1992, when all played all in a round robin with the top four going into the semi-finals, was widely admired and enjoyed. But this became impossible once it was decided to admit the top three non-Test countries, making 12 teams in all. In 1996, a ludicrous format was employed whereby everyone meandered around the subcontinent for three weeks simply to reduce nine serious contenders to eight. Then the competition proper, in effect, was staged as a straight knockout over a week.

For 1999, Terry Blake, the ECB marketing director, introduced a novel method. The 12 entrants were split into two groups, and the top three in each group went into the Super Six, carrying with them the points they had earned against the two teams who had also qualified from their group. They then played the qualifying teams from the other group, creating a final all-played-all league table, with the top four going into the semi-finals.

It took a while for people to cotton on. Then a perception grew that this was all rather elegant. Finally, the flaws became obvious. Notionally, ties on points were to be resolved by the result between the teams involved. Unfortunately, there were three-way ties in both qualifying groups; and New Zealand and Zimbabwe, fourth and fifth in the Super Six, had shared the one washed-out game of the entire tournament. The next determinant was net run-rate, familiar for many years from one-day cricket's triangulars and quadrangulars, but little understood, and impossible for the casual spectator to work out. This vile technicality decided the whole tournament, since the tied semi-final was resolved by the teams' positions in the Super Six, and net run-rate had put Australia ahead of South Africa. It would certainly make sense for future tournaments to use a more transparent tie-breaker: perhaps bonus points could be awarded according to the margin of victory. It might not sound ideal, but would be just as fair and much easier to follow.

The whole Super Six system had other problems, too. Zimbabwe began the second stage of the tournament top of the heap because they had beaten the teams that went through with them, but lost to two that got knocked out. It was hard to see the justice of this. The complexities turned one of the most enticing-looking games of the competition – Australia v West Indies – into a farce as both teams tried to manipulate the regulations to their advantage. Net run-rate was responsible for the failure of both England and West Indies to reach the last six. Bad luck? To an extent. But if West Indies had won more quickly against Bangladesh they would have qualified. And it is hard to see why England, with their army of officials, and who did after all make the rules as hosts, were so slow to realise the dangers.

England failures always seem like accidents waiting to happen. And, organisationally, the 1999 World Cup looked fated from the start. The ECB had turned against the idea of a sole sponsor and, as they announced long beforehand, wanted eight front-line corporate partners who would not have their name on the trophy but would commandeer all the prime advertising space. Unfortunately, they found only four, two of whom (NatWest and Vodafone) were already deeply committed as existing English cricket sponsors; another one (Pepsi) was interested only in striking a blow in the subcontinental cola wars; the fourth (Emirates Airlines) paid almost half in kind rather than cash, which represented not-always-convenient air tickets for the teams. When Outspan came on board as a subsidiary sponsor, a launch was arranged with the obligatory ephemeral celebrity, in this case a TV personality, Ms Anneka Rice, who let slip the fact that she thought cricket was as boring as fishing.

It was decided to start the tournament on May 14, desperately early in the English season. Not surprisingly, it began in drizzle, and with a quite pathetic opening ceremony. The Australian hired as tournament director, Michael Browning, specifically rejected the idea of one of those grandiloquent ceremonies that start Olympic Games, making old ladies gasp with admiration and hardened hacks groan. Instead, he went for the worst possible compromise, letting off a few cheap-looking fireworks and forcing several poor schoolgirls to stand around in the cold. The one simple, dignified, appropriate piece of ceremonial which should have been used, the 12 teams lining up in their blazers in front of the pavilion, was not. This was sad as well as stupid: there was no public moment when all the players involved were even seen to be part of the same event.

From then on, it was difficult to have any confidence at all in Mr Browning or his arrangements. Since these included a media bureaucracy notable for its dictatorial incompetence, many journalists were not going to give him the benefit of the doubt. (Local reporters with decades of experience were barred from press boxes by ignoramuses; it was rumoured, however, that a butcher from Chiswick was among those granted full accreditation.) The shortcomings were worsened by the slogan chosen. The World Cup, Browning and his staff insisted, was a Carnival of Cricket. It was a phrase that would come back to haunt them repeatedly. The trouble is that one man's carnival is another man's nightmare. It is difficult to find much accommodation between those who want to sit down and concentrate on the game, and those who want to shout, chant, cheer and sing. For English cricket, this is an intractable problem.

Given the briefness of the home team's involvement, it was the supporters of the other countries, and the Indians and Pakistanis in particular, who gave the World Cup its vibrancy. The bearded Pakistani cheerleader, Abul Jalil, was by the end of the competition more recognisable than Steve Waugh. It began to be noticed that Asians in England were the one community who had absolutely not fallen out of love with cricket. And it began to be widely accepted that the Tebbit Test – the idea, promulgated by the former Tory cabinet minister, that immigrants to Britain should switch their allegiance – was inappropriate; their loyalties were an expression of their individuality, and a perfectly legitimate one.

The 21 grounds staging the 42 fixtures were slow to recognise the importance of the Asian audience; few, for instance, made any change to their catering arrangements. When Asian teams were not involved, different cultural priorities took over. The Australia v Scotland match smashed the record for bar takings at Worcester; it was easy to get a sandwich but the queue for beer stretched about halfway to Birmingham.

There was criticism of the decision to spread the games so widely, on grounds more accustomed to catering for a few dozen spectators. All the county head-quarters staged at least one match, which meant debut one-day internationals for Hove and Northampton (both of which had opted not to take part in 1983), Canterbury and Cardiff (Tunbridge Wells and Swansea having been used last time) plus the new ground at Chester-le-Street. Three non-county grounds – Edinburgh, Dublin and Amstelveen in Holland – also joined the party. Clearly, many of these matches could have attracted bigger crowds on bigger grounds: Pakistan v Bangladesh at Northampton could have been sold at least three times over.

But English cricket has only six available stadia which can hold much more than 10,000 people. It would have been very tedious had they staged seven matches each, and would have done little for the wider cause of cricket. It is arguable that cricket would have made less money, since fewer people would have gone to their local fixtures. Nearly all the grounds coped extremely well with their big days: only Hove really seemed under-equipped, and that merely proved what the club's executive had been saying in favour of finding somewhere new. Floodlit cricket could have been tried but was unnecessary, since there were so few empty seats (except when the corporate hospitality types were finishing lunch) at any of the fixtures. In this regard, all the problems were those of success.

SELECTED GROUP MATCHES
India v South Africa

At Hove, May 15, 1999. South Africa won by four wickets. 2000

A festive atmosphere and a cracking finish were overshadowed, for the press at least, by the strange case of Cronje's earpiece. South Africa were experimenting with a one-way radio system: Cronje and Donald were wired up to coach Bob Woolmer, who sat in the dressing-room dispensing advice. The referee, Talat Ali, was not impressed and pounced at the first drinks break. The ICC later ruled out remote-control captaincy, at least for the rest of the World Cup.

India's batsmen played their own game. Though Tendulkar fell just after he had tantalised the tastebuds with a cover-drive, Ganguly, playing in his 100th one-day international but first World Cup match, hit form to add a well-crafted 130 with Dravid. They failed to capitalise fully, however, and were out in quick succession, Ganguly foolishly taking on Rhodes's arm. Donald bowled particularly well. Srinath, aggressive in turn, dismissed Kirsten and Gibbs early, but Kallis calmly powered onwards. When he was beaten by a sharp throw from Prasad – like Ganguly, just short of his hundred – South Africa needed 27 in 26 balls. Enter Klusener, who hit his first three deliveries for four. A wonderful match was marred only by a pitch invader who tried to attack Azharuddin and Dravid as they walked off.

Toss: India. **India 253-5** (50 overs) (S. C. Ganguly 97, R. Dravid 54; L. Klusener 3-66); **South Africa 254-6** (47.2 overs) (M. V. Boucher 34, J. H. Kallis 96, J. N. Rhodes 39*).

India v Zimbabwe

At Leicester, May 19, 1999. Zimbabwe won by three runs. 2000

A tumultuous crowd witnessed the closest match of the tournament so far. India needed only nine from two overs when Olonga returned to the attack. His previous three overs had cost 17, as he lost his run-up and bowled some spectacular wides and a beamer. But this time Singh was caught at cover off his second ball, Srinath yorked with his fifth, and Prasad lbw to the last. Zimbabwe had played two, won two; India played two, lost two.

Zimbabwe made slow progress with the bat, except when Andy Flower and Campbell were together, but haywire bowling donated 51 Extras, a fifth of the total. The resulting over-rate was so slow that India's reply was docked a crucial four overs. Not that Zimbabwe were misers, either: there were 90 Extras in the match. India started well enough, bringing up 44 in the seventh over before Dravid fell. Ramesh and Jadeja added 99 before Ramesh holed out to mid-on. The middle order rattled along and, when Srinath lofted two huge sixes, India seemed home and dry until Olonga's over. Mongia made five dismissals to equal the one-day international record.

Toss: India. **Zimbabwe 252-9** (50 overs) (G. W. Flower 45, A. Flower 68*, Extras 51); **India 249** (45 overs) (S. Ramesh 55, A. D. Jadeja 43, R. R. Singh 35, Extras 39; H. H. Streak 3-36, H. K. Olonga 3-22).

England v South Africa

At The Oval, May 22, 1999. South Africa won by 122 runs. 2000

England's comfortable passage thus far was put in stark perspective by the South African steamroller. The attack was reshaped, with Fraser replacing Austin. This achieved little as Kirsten and Gibbs started with a century stand at five an over. But Ealham wobbled the ball around to good effect, and three wickets tumbled for one run. Gough then took two wickets in successive balls before Klusener's inimitable clean hitting swelled the total: he clubbed an undefeated 48 in 40 balls, and took 12 off Ealham's last over.

The target was still modest but England struggled from the start. Stewart and Hussain may have been unlucky with their decisions, but there was no excuse for the middle order's performance. Donald trapped Thorpe in his first over, and removed Flintoff for a duck in his third. In between, the battle of Zimbabwe's expatriates was won by Elworthy, who had Hick caught at mid-wicket. An inspired parry and grab by Rhodes at point accounted for Croft, and England just limped into three figures. Failure to reach a respectable total damaged their net run-rate; little noticed at the time, this was to prove fatal.

Toss: England. **South Africa 225-7** (50 overs) (G. Kirsten 45, H. H. Gibbs 60, L. Klusener 48*);
England 103 (41 overs) (A. A. Donald 4-17).

India v Sri Lanka

At Taunton, May 26, 1999. India won by 157 runs. 2000

Undisciplined Sri Lankan bowling, a pitch of even bounce, short boundaries and batting which ranged from the classical to the brutal set a welter of one-day international records. Ganguly and Dravid's partnership of 318 in 45 overs was the highest in any limited-overs international. Ganguly made 183 in 158 balls, with 16 fours and seven sixes, the fourth-highest one-day international score, and the second in World Cup history behind Gary Kirsten's 188 not out against the United Arab Emirates in 1996. India's 373 for six was the second highest total in limited-overs internationals after Sri Lanka's 398 for five against Kenya in the 1996 World Cup, and thus the highest against Test opposition.

Ranatunga's decision to bowl seemed justified when Vaas cut the ball back sharply to hit Ramesh's off stump. However, Dravid, aggressively, and Ganguly, elegantly, soon gained complete dominance, with even Muralitharan unable to stem the flow of runs. Dravid established himself as the pacemaker, reaching his second successive hundred at almost a run a ball. But Ganguly made his own century, from 119 deliveries, then began to hit over the top, racing to 183 in another 39 balls. Sri Lanka restored Kaluwitharana to open the innings but, once he and Jayasuriya were out within five overs, the game was all but finished. Likewise Sri Lanka's defence of their crown.

Toss: Sri Lanka. **India 373-6** (50 overs) (S. C. Ganguly 183, R. Dravid 145; G. P. Wickremasinghe 3-65);
Sri Lanka 216 (42.3 overs) (P. A. de Silva 56, A. Ranatunga 42, R. S. Mahanama 32,
Extras 31; R. R. Singh 5-31).

South Africa v Zimbabwe

At Chelmsford, May 29, 1999. Zimbabwe won by 48 runs. 2000

The upset of the cup to date was a disaster for both England and, ultimately, South Africa, whose elimination in the semi-final could be backdated to losing this match. Zimbabwe got off to a flyer. Johnson – who had played for South Africa A before defecting back in September 1998 – and Grant Flower flailed at loose stuff from Kallis and Pollock, racing to 65 in 14 overs. It did not quite last. After hitting ten fours in his fifty, Johnson failed to manage another, and Donald grabbed three wickets; Campbell was his 200th victim in 117 one-day internationals.

No one thought 233 would be enough, but a rainstorm at lunch did funny things. Johnson's opening delivery reared up at Kirsten, and Andy Whittall took the first of three great catches. Gibbs was run out by Huckle, Boucher was caught off a Streak no-ball only to be trapped in the same over, and Kallis went fourth ball. Then Cronje was yorked by Johnson, and Rhodes snared by the inspired Streak. South Africa were in disarray and 40 for six; Zimbabwe's fielding was electric. Pollock scored a fine fifty, but when he was caught on the long-off boundary it was virtually over. Not even Klusener, who went to his fifty with a swept six, could save them. Zimbabwe were probably more stunned than South Africa; it was their first win over their neighbours at any level, and meant that they started the Super Six stage joint leaders with Pakistan.

Toss: Zimbabwe. **Zimbabwe 233-6** (50 overs) (N. C. Johnson 76, M. W. Goodwin 34; A. A. Donald 3-41); **South Africa 185** (47.2 overs) (S. M. Pollock 52, L. Klusener 52*; N. C. Johnson 3-27, H. H. Streak 3-35).

England v India
At Birmingham, May 29, 30, 1999. India won by 63 runs. 2000

England arrived at Edgbaston seemingly assured of a Super Six place, but news of Zimbabwe's surprise defeat of South Africa changed everything. Suddenly, England needed to win, and their batsmen funked the task on the second morning, after rain made this the only group match to go into the reserve day. In blazing sunshine, Stewart won his fifth toss, and again fielded first. He was happy enough with his bowlers, who restricted India well on a slowish pitch. Dravid top-scored with 53 from 82 balls.

The weather and the omens were threatening when England batted. Stewart and Hick were out to successive legal balls (separated by a wide) from Mohanty, and Hussain fell in poor light just before a spectacular downpour ended play. England needed a good start next day, but were dismayed when Javed Akhtar contentiously ruled Thorpe lbw. Fairbrother pushed and poked, but the others swished in vain. This was the first time England had failed to progress past the first stage of any World Cup. Ultimately, they paid for their abject performance against South Africa, and a lack of urgency in their three comfortable victories. For Flintoff, one of the disappointments of the tournament, the final indignity was having his bat stolen from the dressing-room.

Toss: England. **India 232-8** (50 overs) (S. C. Ganguly 40, R. Dravid 53, A. D. Jadeja 39); **England 169** (45.2 overs) (N. Hussain 33, G. P. Thorpe 36; S. C. Ganguly 3-27).

Australia v Pakistan
At Leeds, May 23, 1999. Pakistan won by ten runs. 2000

A memorable struggle tilted Pakistan's way when Shoaib Akhtar, bowling at terrifying speed in murky conditions, hurled an in-swinger into Steve Waugh's stumps. That left Australia 238 for six, chasing 276. Though the contest went to the last over, Wasim Akram then clean-bowled Martyn and McGrath to seal a ten-run win – and pass Imran Khan's record of 34 World Cup wickets. The match award went to

Inzamam-ul-Haq for his 81, the centrepiece of Pakistan's innings, although this rather overlooked the damage inflicted by his idiosyncratic running. Three times he found himself at the same end as his partner, and twice it cost a wicket. Still, Inzamam's patient stand of 118 with Abdur Razzaq paved the way for a volcanic eruption in the last ten overs, which yielded 108 runs. Moin Khan lashed an unbeaten 31 from a mere 12 balls. Australia's pursuit started confidently enough, but two wickets in three balls from Saqlain Mushtaq stalled them at 101 for four. A 113-run stand between Steve Waugh and Bevan kept the game alive, until Pakistan's quicks returned to close it out in fading light. After the finish, 21 minutes late, Waugh asked why slow over-rate penalties should apply only to teams who bowl first.

Toss: Australia. **Pakistan 275-8** (50 overs) (Abdur Razzaq 60, Inzamam-ul-Haq 81, Moin Khan 31*);

Australia 265 (49.5 overs) (M. E. Waugh 41, R. T. Ponting 47, S. R. Waugh 49, M. G. Bevan 61,

Extras 38; Wasim Akram 4-40, Saqlain Mushtaq 3-51).

Australia v West Indies
At Manchester, May 30, 1999. Australia won by six wickets. 2000

A game that in advance looked one of the most relishable of the tournament dawdled to a close amid booing, slow hand-clapping and spectators walking out. Needing only 111, Australia slowed their chase to a crawl, doing just enough to ensure they would enter the Super Six on net run-rate, while enabling West Indies to improve their own side of the equation against New Zealand. The Australians openly admitted their intention. Under tournament rules, they would retain points won against fellow-qualifiers. Against New Zealand, that meant nought; against West Indies, two. Lara angrily denied collusion; there was no need for it – the captains understood the tactics, even if spectators did not.

There had been some action for the crowd earlier in the day. McGrath got into his stride at last, collecting three wickets in 13 balls to finish with five for 14. Only Jacobs, the first man to carry his bat through a World Cup innings, got the score to 110. Beginning Australia's reply after a rain-extended break, Gilchrist batted brightly, and there was even a hint of a twist when Ambrose struck three times. But once Steve Waugh and Bevan were certain they could not lose, run-scoring became secondary to run-rate manipulation. Their final 19 runs were dragged out across 13 overs, and the victory came from a no-ball.

Toss: Australia. **West Indies 110** (46.4 overs) (R. D. Jacobs 49*; G. D. McGrath 5-14, S. K. Warne 3-11);

Australia 111-4 (40.4 overs) (C. E. L. Ambrose 3-31).

Bangladesh v Pakistan
At Northampton, May 31, 1999. Bangladesh won by 62 runs. 2000

At the last possible moment, a non-Test team felled a giant. Bangladesh had never even come close to beating a major power – while Pakistan were unbeaten in this competition. Since this was a completely dead match, accusations of Pakistani match-fixing grew louder again. Nothing diminished the Bangladeshi fans' euphoria. It was the greatest day in their cricketing history, and perhaps no event since independence had united the country with such delight. Both captains spoke of Bangladesh earning Test cricket soon; with Pakistan unaffected, the only person with reason not to enjoy the result was Gordon Greenidge, sacked as Bangladesh coach just before this game, who quietly left at lunchtime.

Put in, the Bangladeshi openers advanced confidently to 69 in 16 overs, before Saqlain Mushtaq, the only Pakistani on song, intervened. Khaled Mahmud dashed to 27 in 34 balls. But a target of 224 hardly looked a problem – until Pakistan's top order folded. Five men were out by the 13th over, three to Mahmud. Azhar Mahmood and Wasim Akram pushed towards three figures, but it was far too late. With nine wickets down, the umpires called for a TV verdict on whether Saqlain had been run out. He was, but the jubilant Bangladeshi fans were already pouring on to the field. The County Ground had never seen anything like it – at least not since the old footballing days there, when Northampton Town knocked Arsenal out of the FA Cup in 1958. The build-up was just as frenzied: Northamptonshire could have sold three times the available tickets.

Toss: Pakistan. **Bangladesh 223-9** (50 overs) (Shahriar Hossain 39, Akram Khan 42, Extras 40; Saqlain Mushtaq 5-35); **Pakistan 161** (44.3 overs) (Khaled Mahmud 3-31).

SUPER SIX STARTING TABLE

	Played	Won	Lost	No result	Points	Net run-rate
Pakistan	2	2	0	0	4	0.72
Zimbabwe	2	2	0	0	4	0.32
South Africa	2	1	1	0	2	-0.34
New Zealand	2	1	1	0	2	-0.40
India	2	0	2	0	0	0.03
Australia	2	0	2	0	0	-0.34

Super Six teams carried forward points and net run-rate already gained against fellow Super Six qualifiers, but not those gained against teams eliminated at the Group stage.

SELECTED SUPER SIX MATCHES
Australia v India
At The Oval, June 4, 1999. Australia won by 77 runs. 2000

Four exquisite overs from McGrath put this crucial game beyond India's reach. Bowling with unstinting menace and significant seam movement, he reduced India to a pitiable 17 for four. The first of McGrath's victims was Tendulkar, who followed three successive one-day hundreds against Australia with a duck, his first in 22 meetings. Jadeja, with a century – the tournament's fifth, all by Indians – and Singh rallied, putting on 141 for the fifth wicket. Despite their valiant efforts, the outcome was never in question, though the tumultuous Indian supporters appreciated one over, Warne's sixth, which yielded 21 runs.

Australia had earlier set a target of 283 – never overhauled in a 50-over international in England. A sparkling 83 from Mark Waugh was the highlight, but everyone joined in. Both teams had scraped into the Super Six without any points, so defeat for India made progress to the semi-finals highly unlikely. Two pigeons met untimely deaths during their innings. The first was shot down in mid-flight by Reiffel when he drilled the ball back from the outfield; the second, pecking the ground at short third man, was walloped by a thick edge from Jadeja's bat, leading to speculation that pigeons also had problems seeing the white ball in the evening gloom.

Toss: India. **Australia 282-6** (50 overs) (M. E. Waugh 83, A. C. Gilchrist 31, S. R. Waugh 36, Extras 35); **India 205** (48.2 overs) (A. D. Jadeja 100*, R. R. Singh 75; G. D. McGrath 3-34).

Pakistan v South Africa

At Nottingham, June 5, 1999. South Africa won by three wickets.   2000

Until South Africa met Australia, it was hard to imagine a better World Cup match than this, the meeting of the two group winners – the green giants. It had everything: subtlety, suspense, searing pace, great hitting, and a slow build-up to a pulsating finish. Pakistan chose to bat, started like snails, lost Inzamam-ul-Haq to a run-out, and left it all to Moin Khan, who took 15 off the 47th over, from Donald, flicking him nonchalantly over his shoulder for six. Of the four star fast bowlers in the match, the best was the youngest, Shoaib Akhtar, touching 95mph on the Speedster – belatedly introduced for the Super Six – and clearly alarming Cronje, who promoted himself to weather the storm and was caught at third man. At 58 for five after 20 overs, South Africa were sinking. The orthodoxy of Kallis and Pollock kept them afloat, and Klusener, once again, walked on water. But even he struggled to get a bat on Shoaib, and a target of 66 from ten overs became 41 off 27 balls. Then Shoaib made a single crucial error, slipping Klusener a bouncer which was edged for four. Scenting blood, Klusener pulled a length ball for six, and rounded off the over with four leg-byes. With only 27 now needed off 24 balls. Pakistan's last hope was to dismiss Klusener. Eventually, he did sky a chance to Saeed Anwar, who dropped it; the ball was in the air so long that the batsmen scampered the two runs needed for victory.

Toss: Pakistan. **Pakistan 220-7** (50 overs) (Abdur Razzaq 30, Moin Khan 63); **South Africa 221-7** (49 overs) (J. H. Kallis 54, S. M. Pollock 30, L. Klusener 46*, Extras 38; Azhar Mahmood 3-24).

India v Pakistan

At Manchester, June 8, 1999. India won by 47 runs.   2000

The meeting of India and Pakistan, whose armies were engaged in a stand-off over Kashmir, raised fears of a surrogate war between supporters, and security was intense. But the final statistics – three arrests, nine ejections, and one Indian flag burned during some scuffling at the close – were a very minor blemish on a thrilling day. The rival fans, flag-waving, whistle-blowing and drum-beating, created a passionate atmosphere unimaginable in English cricket. India's batsmen, though, were below their aggressive best. Tendulkar blazed briefly, passing 8,000 one-day international runs as he dominated the early stages. Dravid lost momentum, however, and Azharuddin only found top gear late on, adding 60 in nine overs with Singh.

Saeed Anwar launched his assault on a target of 228 with six fours. But Srinath was chipping away at his partners – and then Prasad took over, finishing with five for 27. His victims were Salim Malik, Anwar, Moin Khan, for an explosive 34 in 37 balls, Inzamam-ul-Haq, unusually subdued for 30 overs, and finally captain Wasim Akram, caught on the square-leg boundary. Pakistan suffered their third successive defeat, while Azharuddin had won all of the three India-Pakistan matches in World Cup history. His compatriots were euphoric, but it was their last hurrah, and later results made the victory irrelevant.

Toss: India. **India 227-6** (50 overs) (S. R. Tendulkar 45, R. Dravid 61, M. Azharuddin 59); **Pakistan 180** (45.3 overs) (Saeed Anwar 36, Inzamam-ul-Haq 41, Moin Khan 34; J. Srinath 3-37, B. K. V. Prasad 5-27).

Australia v South Africa

At Leeds, June 13, 1999. Australia won by five wickets. 2000

This was do or die for Australia. So, in a thriller, they duly did – leapfrogging over South Africa in the process, and loading the dice for the semi-final. South Africa batted first on a bouncy Headingley pitch and rattled up 271, despite the return to form of Warne, who snared his old foe Cullinan and Cronje in one over. Gibbs, with a mixture of steadiness and flair, made South Africa's only century of the tournament, and the second of his short one-day international career. Then Klusener, back to his best, masterminded a swashbuckling 47 from the final five overs.

At 48 for three in reply, Australia faced meltdown. But no one had told Steve Waugh, that iciest of icemen. He and Ponting, slogging adeptly, added 77 between overs 22 and 29. They were particularly harsh on Cronje and Boje who, in the absence of Kallis with an abdominal strain, had to muddle through ten overs, which yielded 79. Then Waugh, on 56, was unfathomably dropped by a prematurely celebrating Gibbs at mid-wicket. Waugh reportedly told him: "Hersh, you've just dropped the World Cup." Hindsight suggests he did.

Waugh raced to 120 in 110 balls, only his second century in 266 one-day internationals. Though Donald and Pollock returned with some ferocious stuff at the end, Australia's momentum carried them through; the exhausted teams headed for Edgbaston and a rematch.

Toss: South Africa. **South Africa 271-7** (50 overs) (H. H. Gibbs 101, D. J. Cullinan 50, J. N. Rhodes 39, L. Klusener 36; D. W. Fleming 3-57); **Australia 272-5** (49.4 overs) (R. T. Ponting 69, S. R. Waugh 120*).

SUPER SIX FINAL TABLE

	Played	Won	Lost	No result	Points	Net run-rate
PAKISTAN	5	3	2	0	6	0.65
AUSTRALIA	5	3	2	0	6	0.35
SOUTH AFRICA ...	5	3	2	0	6	0.17
NEW ZEALAND ...	5	2	2	1	5	-0.51
Zimbabwe	5	2	2	1	5	-0.78
India	5	1	4	0	2	-0.15

SEMI-FINALS
New Zealand v Pakistan

At Manchester, June 16, 1999. Pakistan won by nine wickets.   Harriet Monkhouse, 2000

Pakistan burst into the final after an opening stand of 194 between Saeed Anwar and Wajahatullah Wasti. They seemed quite capable of finishing the job undivided until Wasti holed out in the 41st over. Anwar pushed on to a second successive century – his 17th in one-day internationals, equalling Desmond Haynes and behind only Sachin Tendulkar. With Ijaz Ahmed smashing 28 in 21 balls, victory was delayed only by a small pitch invasion, six runs early, which stopped play for ten minutes. Then, when Anwar lofted the ball towards long-off, the crowd could be contained no longer. Twose abandoned an attempt at a running catch as the players raced to safety. Though the two runs required were never actually completed, they were awarded anyway. Ecstatic Pakistani fans let off fireworks and paraded flags, banners and a cardboard cut-out of Nelson Mandela (who had retired from the South African presidency earlier in the day). Officials, who had expected trouble for the India match eight days earlier, lost control when their guard was down. New Zealand captain Fleming called for stricter security, raising the controversial topic of fencing in spectators.

Toss: New Zealand. **New Zealand 241-7** (50 overs) (M. J. Horne 35, S. P. Fleming 41,
R. G. Twose 46, C. L. Cairns 44*, Extras 47; Shoaib Akhtar 3-55); **Pakistan 242-1** (47.3 overs)
(Saeed Anwar 113*, Wajahatullah Wasti 84).

Australia v South Africa

At Birmingham, June 17, 1999.
Match tied. Australia qualified for the Final on net run-rate.   Tim de Lisle, 2000

This was not merely the match of the tournament: it must have been the best one-day international of the 1,483 so far played. The essence of the one-day game is a close finish, and this was by far the most significant to finish in the closest way of all – with both teams all out for the same score. But it was a compressed epic all the way through, and it ended in a savage twist. The tie meant that South Africa, for the third World Cup in a row, failed to reach the final despite making

Match tied, but only one winner: all 11 Australians celebrate the run-out of the mortified Allan Donald in the 1999 World Cup semi-final at Edgbaston. The scores were level, but the Aussies knew a better run-rate would take them to the final – which they won easily.

much of the early running. The crucial fact was that Australia finished higher than them in the Super Six table, and that was determined by the obscurity of net run-rate. Many spectators were left baffled.

Klusener's brawn had powered South Africa to the brink of the final but, when he got there, his brain short-circuited. Only he could have smashed and grabbed 31 runs off 14 balls, cutting a daunting target down to a doddle: one needed off four balls, Klusener himself on strike, and a decent, experienced tailender at the other end in Donald. The bowler, Fleming, had only one thing going for him: he had bowled the final over that beat West Indies in the 1996 World Cup semi-final. Having let Klusener pummel consecutive fours to level the scores, he tightened up. Steve Waugh, knowing a tie would be enough, set a field that gave new meaning to the phrase a ring saving one. Klusener thumped the ball straight, and Donald, backing up too far, would have been run out if Lehmann had hit the stumps. The scare should have been a warning. But Klusener then repeated his straight biff and charged. Donald grounded his bat, dropped it, and finally set off, while the Australians were demonstrating the benefits of a recent visit to a bowling alley: Mark Waugh, at mid-on, flicked the ball to Fleming, who rolled it to Gilchrist, who broke the wicket, and South African hearts.

The rest of the match was studded with outstanding performances. When Australia batted, Pollock, finally finding the edge, was magnificently incisive. Donald twice took two wickets in an over. Steve Waugh and Bevan performed a repair job which showed first self-control, then controlled aggression. Kallis, carrying a stomach injury, bowled fast and tight, and held the batting together with a cool fifty. Above all, there was Shane Warne. The ball that bowled Gibbs was a miraculous replay of his most famous delivery, to Mike Gatting six years earlier. His first spell of eight overs went for only 12 runs. He pocketed three more wickets, and the match award. The game was the last as South Africa's coach for Bob Woolmer, whose blend of science and imagination had produced a 73% success rate in one-day internationals. He deserved better than to go out on a technicality.

Toss: South Africa. **Australia 213** (49.2 overs) (R. T. Ponting 37, S. R. Waugh 56, M. G. Bevan 65; S. M. Pollock 5-36, A. A. Donald 4-32); **South Africa 213** (49.4 overs) (H. H. Gibbs 30, J. H. Kallis 53, J. N. Rhodes 43, L. Klusener 31*; S. K. Warne 4-29)

FINAL
Australia v Pakistan

At Lord's, June 20, 1999. Australia won by eight wickets   Hugh Chevallier, 2000

Australia won the seventh World Cup with such single-minded ruthlessness that even an eight-wicket victory failed to do them justice. Pakistan, the most exciting team in the tournament, were totally outplayed and outwitted at the crucial moment. There were barely four and a half hours of cricket, most of it one-sided. For all but the most fervent Australian, it was not a pretty sight.

It was a sight, though, spared many Pakistanis by a controversial ticketing policy. This favoured not the fans of the competing teams but those who had ostensibly proved their loyalty to the game – and the depth of their pocket – by buying a package of tickets long before. So Lord's was awash with disinterested observers, while from outside came the klaxon, whistle and bugle of fanatical Pakistan support. About a hundred fans clambered up a building site overlooking the ground. As the police moved in, a game of cat and mouse ensued, providing an alternative spectacle for the Grand Stand opposite. Eventually, the fans, like their team, were unceremoniously bundled out of St John's Wood.

On a pitch that Steve Waugh believed was good for 260 or so, Wasim Akram chose to bat. Saeed Anwar cut the third ball of the day for four and added two more boundaries in the fourth over as Fleming struggled for consistency. For Pakistan, this was as good as it got. Next over, Wajahatullah Wasti followed a ball from McGrath that bounced and left him. Mark Waugh, at second slip, flew to his right and clung on with both hands. It set the tone for the match.

After Anwar had played on, Abdur Razzaq and Ijaz Ahmed briefly looked more at home. Razzaq benefited from Australia's one false move – McGrath dropped a comfortable catch at long-off – but minutes later was smartly caught by Steve Waugh, lunging forward at extra cover. With Pakistan faltering at 69 for three after 21 overs, Waugh brought on Warne. It was, literally, the turning point of the match.

Warne produced an astounding delivery to dismiss Ijaz, who had hung around doggedly for 22. The ball pitched on or just outside leg and hit off. It was not quite the famous Gatting ball, nor even the one that dismissed Gibbs in the semi-final, but it sent shockwaves through the lower order. Pakistan tried to get out of trouble with all guns blazing. But for every ball that ricocheted off the boards, another landed in

Australian hands. Luck was against them, too: a ball from Reiffel clipped Inzamam's pad on its way to Gilchrist. The Australians went up in appeal; umpire Shepherd's finger in judgment. An incredulous Inzamam plodded off at funereal pace. When Wasim holed out, Warne had claimed four wickets for the second game running, taking his tally to 20, a World Cup record shared with Geoff Allott of New Zealand. McGrath brought the innings to a swift end when Ponting held a superlative catch at third slip in the 39th over. The target was just 133.

Wasim later claimed he could have defended 180 but the way Gilchrist began, 300 would have been within reach. Shoaib Akhtar was desperately unlucky when his first ball was edged by Gilchrist and fell agonisingly short of long leg. Thereafter, boundaries came thick, fast and off the middle of the bat. Gilchrist's fifty took 33 balls. When he fell to the first ball of the 11th over, the broadcasters felt the end was close enough to remove the stump cameras.

In fact, it took another ten overs, in which time Mark Waugh passed 1,000 World Cup runs. Australia needed a mere 121 balls to win, and the game was over at 4.32. This, the 200th World Cup match, spanned less than 60 overs. The people who reportedly paid touts £5,000 for a pair of £100 tickets might have felt short-changed. Or maybe not: they were Australians.

Australia v Pakistan, 1999   **World Cup Final**
At Lord's, June 20, 1999. Result: Australia won by eight wickets.

PAKISTAN

Saeed Anwar b Fleming	15	Shahid Afridi lbw b Warne		13
Wajahatullah Wasti c M. E. Waugh b McGrath	1	Azhar Mahmood c and b Moody		8
Abdul Razzaq c S. R. Waugh b Moody	17	*Wasim Akram c S. R. Waugh b Warne		8
Ijaz Ahmed b Warne	22	Saqlain Mushtaq c Ponting b McGrath		0
Inzamam–ul–Haq c Gilchrist b Reiffel	15	Shoaib Akhtar not out		2
†Moin Khan c Gilchrist b Warne	6	L-b 10, w 13, n-b 2		25

1-21 2-21 3-68 4-77 5-91 6-104 7-113 8-129 9-129 10-132   (39 overs) 132

McGrath 9–3–13–2; Fleming 6–0–30–1; Reiffel 10–1–29–1; Moody 5–0–17–2; Warne 9–1–33–4.

AUSTRALIA

M. E. Waugh not out	37	D. S. Lehmann not out		13
†A. C. Gilchrist c Inzamam–ul–Haq		L-b 1, w 1, n-b 3		5
b Saqlain Mushtaq	54			
R. T. Ponting c Moin Khan b Wasim Akram	24	(2 wkts, 20.1 overs) 133		

1-75 2-112

*S. R. Waugh, M. G. Bevan, T. M. Moody, S. K. Warne,
P. R. Reiffel, D. W. Fleming and G. D. McGrath did not bat.

Wasim Akram 8–1–41–1; Shoaib Akhtar 4–0–37–0; Abdul Razzaq 2–0–13–0; Azhar Mahmood 2–0–20–0; Saqlain Mushtaq 4.1–0–21–1.

Toss won by Pakistan   UMPIRES S. A. Bucknor and D. R. Shepherd
MAN OF THE MATCH S. K. Warne

Aussies and Kenyans

WORLD CUP 2003	Tim de Lisle, *Notes by the Editor, 2003*

This World Cup was one-third party, two-thirds flop. The good things were the balance between bat and ball, the renewed power of attacking bowling, the romance of the Kenyans, and the sustained excellence, against all teams and in mixed conditions, of the Australians. They rode the loss of Warne and Jason Gillespie and found fringe players who not only filled in for absent stars but got the remaining ones out of any scrape. If Tendulkar was rightly named man of the tournament, he only just outshone Andy Bichel, who sparked fire from slow pitches, made crucial runs and even pulled off a direct-hit run-out. His desire was so great, you could see it throbbing in his veins.

The Kenyans were a big bonus. The ICC shrewdly signed up Bob Woolmer two years ago to fly around as a consultant to all four non-Test teams, and it showed in their fielding, bowling and pacing of an innings: like Brad Hogg, Australia's postman-spinner, they proved that part-timers can be highly professional. The Kenyans' story is a film waiting to happen, with its lyrical start (boys learning the game with a maize cob for a ball – corny, but true) and its heart-warming climax as a forgotten old-timer returns from his job in insurance to torment the mighty Aussies with his left-arm slows. Kenya's celebrations were irresistible: their shimmying huddle made its English equivalent look like Stonehenge.

So much for the good news. The bad things were the politics, the legal battles, the corporate bullying, the fact that there were only two good teams, and above all, the way that there were seven or eight non-events for every close contest. The decision to punish England and New Zealand for their no-shows distorted the whole tournament. The four points the ICC insisted on awarding to Zimbabwe and Kenya stayed in the system like a virus thanks to the quirky business of carrying points through to the Super Six, which should have been dumped after 1999. The Kenyans, for all their romance, were not quite the giant-killers they were made out to be: their three wins over Test opposition came against the wretched Bangladeshis, the downtrodden Zimbabweans and a Sri Lankan side with food poisoning.

Of the 14 teams, only four enhanced their standing: Australia, India, Kenya and Canada. The pool stage had just enough interesting games, and some of the mismatches were redeemed by splashes of colour from John Davison and others. But the Super Six was dire. Australia and India each went through to the semi-finals in their first match. The carrying-through of points baffled the public and wrecked any sense of suspense, and the semi-finals, once Sri Lanka's top order rolled over, fell horribly flat. The World Cup was six days of great entertainment spread over six weeks. It dragged, which is just what one-day cricket was designed not to do. It was run in the interests not of the supporters, the players and the game itself, but the sponsors, broadcasters, politicians and lawyers.

When it comes to putting on tournaments, everything the ICC touch turns to maths. The World Cup, like the Test Championship and especially the new One-Day Championship, was hard to follow: dangerous for any sport, and for cricket more than most. The intricacies of the game are part of its strange magic, but they are all the more reason for its surface to be straightforward. It should not try to shed its historic appeal to solemn 12-year-olds (of all ages) with a weakness for neat columns of numbers. But it must be attractive to other constituencies, more representative of an age in which the word anorak no longer signifies a waterproof jacket.

In some eyes, the Duckworth/Lewis system for resolving rain-affected one-day matches is a charming eccentricity. In rather more, it is a turn-off. It allows crucial matches, and the fates of captains and coaches, to hinge on pieces of paper covered in figures which not even the players always understand. Stats are one of the joys of cricket, but there is a place for them and it is not on the field. Duckworth/Lewis may be the fairest system imaginable, but it is out of tune with the game. It bewilders, where sport is supposed to bewitch. Before the next World Cup, Dave Richardson, the ICC's wicket-keeper turned gamekeeper, must find a system that is radically different and a great deal simpler.

SELECTED GROUP MATCHES
South Africa v West Indies
At Cape Town, February 9, 2003 (day/night). West Indies won by three runs.   2004

After the South African board's evangelical campaign and Olympic-standard opening ceremony the previous night (a world away from the half-hearted fiasco at Lord's four years earlier), the opening game needed to be great – and it was, thanks to a masterful performance from a great player. Unfortunately for the organisers, though, he was not South African. It was Lara: he lit up Newlands with a century that transformed a terrible West Indies start when Pollock reduced them to seven for two. Playing his first competitive innings since mysteriously falling ill in Sri Lanka five months earlier, Lara was almost out first ball when Kallis dropped a hard chance at second slip. At first he seemed to be over-cautious: it was 30 for two after 15 overs and 67 for two after 25. But then he tore into Donald and Klusener with a bat as swift as a scimitar to reach 116 off 134 balls. With Powell and Sarwan scoring even more spectacularly – Pollock's penultimate over cost 23 runs – 110 came off the last ten, and West Indies amazed themselves by reaching 278.

With one over docked because of their slow over-rate, South Africa were up against it. But Kirsten held on, Boucher hit out and then came Klusener, dragging the bitter-sweet memories of the 1999 tournament with him. His bat still as broad, his jaw still as set, he set out to improve a World Cup average of 140.50. He might have gone when Collins carried a catch over the boundary, but when his fifth six took him to his fifty, South Africa were favourites. However, with four balls remaining and eight needed, Klusener was caught by Hooper at deep mid-wicket. He and Boje failed to cross, leaving the tailenders exposed to Drakes.

Toss: West Indies. **West Indies 278-5** (50 overs) (B. C. Lara 116, S. Chanderpaul 34, C. L. Hooper 40, R. L. Powell 40*, R. R. Sarwan 32*); **South Africa 275-9** (49 overs) (G. Kirsten 69, M. V. Boucher 49, L. Klusener 57).

Australia v Pakistan

At Johannesburg, February 11, 2003. Australia won by 82 runs.   2004

This match provided a reminder, if any were needed, of why Australia began the tournament as phohibitively priced favourites. Although Pakistan had spent the winter turning capriciousness into an art, the holders looked vulnerable: Darren Lehmann was suspended for racial abuse, Michael Bevan was injured and, on the morning of the game, Shane Warne announced he would be returning home to face drugs charges. But Symonds, a player many Australians would have left out of the squad after just two fifties in 54 one-day internationals, hit a free-flowing and unbeaten 143, from 125 balls, and two other lesser-known Australians, Harvey and Hogg, provided the main support act. They shared seven wickets and each made a nuggety contribution to a valuable stand. Australia commanded at every stage, except the first hour, when Wasim Akram had Gilchrist caught off a miscued pull in his second over, then struck with consecutive balls in his sixth. Symonds entered at 86 for four and, after jogging in Ponting's slipstream, revealed the range of muscular strokes he previously reserved for county cricket. Waqar Younis's dismissal from the attack in the 49th over, for a second beamer at Symonds, encapsulated his frustration; he could not bring himself to apologise.

Toss: Pakistan. **Australia 310-8** (50 overs) (R. T. Ponting 53, A. Symonds 143*, Extras 31; Wasim Akram 3-64); **Pakistan 228** (44.3 overs) (Salim Elahi 30, Rashid Latif 33, Wasim Akram 33; I. J. Harvey 4-58, G. B. Hogg 3-54).

England v Namibia

At Port Elizabeth, February 19, 2003. England won by 55 runs.   2004

Nine thousand increasingly pro-Namibian fans watched Jan-Berrie Burger set hearts thumping nervously across England. If the technique was simple – move into line, hit as far as possible – the end result was certainly effective. Burger smashed 85 in 86 balls, and the England fielders threatened to join Nasser Hussain, laid up with a stiff neck, as they watched the ball fly over their heads. With the clouds thickening over Port Elizabeth, Namibia were ahead on Duckworth/Lewis for nearly 12 overs, though it later transpired that England were blissfully unaware of their peril: Stewart, their stand-in captain, said he had entrusted the crib sheet to Trescothick, who botched the maths and kept insisting England were ahead. A diving catch from Collingwood ended the Burger menace, but the Namibians kept fighting and when van Vuuren hit the last ball of the match for a huge six his team-mates rushed on to the field to celebrate a gutsy display. Earlier, van Vuuren, also a Namibian rugby international, had finished off the England innings, striking three times in the last over. Trescothick, Stewart and White all batted pugnaciously, but the match award could only go to one man.

Toss: Namibia. **England 272** (50 overs) (M. E. Trescothick 58, A. J. Stewart 60, P. D. Collingwood 38, C. White 35; G. Snyman 3-69, R. J. van Vuuren 5-43); **Namibia 217-9** (50 overs) (A. J. Burger 85, D. Keulder 46; R. C. Irani 3-30).

England v Pakistan

At Cape Town, February 22, 2003 (day/night). England won by 112 runs. 2004

This was England's most heartening World Cup performance for more than a decade. They had to win – defeat would have left them with only a glimmer of a chance of making the Super Six – and thanks to a precocious display of controlled swing by Anderson they did. Many thought the toss decided the game by forcing Pakistan to bat on a dewy evening. But Anderson's bowling was exceptional, and to all intents and purposes his second over settled matters: Inzamam-ul-Haq sliced an out-swinger to slip and Yousuf Youhana also went first ball, castled by an impeccable swinging yorker. Another two-wicket Anderson over – the 18th – made doubly sure: Saeed Anwar shuffled in front, Rashid Latif gloved a lifter and a star had been born. Pakistan's impotence was symbolised by Shoaib Akhtar, who bowled the first ball officially timed at 100mph (comfortably repulsed by Knight) but went for seven an over. Later, Shoaib blazed 43 off 16 balls but it was already too late to matter.

Toss: England. **England 246-8** (50 overs) (M. P. Vaughan 52, A. J. Stewart 30, P. D. Collingwood 66*); **Pakistan 134** (31 overs) (Shoaib Akhtar 43; J. M. Anderson 4-29, C. White 3-33).

Zimbabwe v Australia

At Bulawayo, February 24, 2003. Australia won by seven wickets. 2004

This should have been one of Zimbabwean cricket's greatest occasions, but politics dominated the game. The selectors tried to drop Andy Flower for "not trying" against India until he team-mates threatened to boycott the match; Olonga remained out of the side, although spectators sang his favourite song in a show of solidarity. The information secretary of the ruling Zanu-PF party bizarrely announced, "Olonga is not a Zimbabwean, he is a Zambian. Flower is also not a Zimbabwean. He is British." On the pitch, Flower somehow put the machinations to one side and top-scored with 62, before being bamboozled by Hogg's flpper. Blignaut then launched into Gillespie and Hogg, crashing eight fours and two sixes in a blistering 28-ball 54, as Zimbabwe stood up to Australia. In reply, a smash-and-grab fifty from Gilchrist, part of a rapid opening stand of 89, removed any pressure. Martyn and Lehmann cantered home and Australia made a swift exit from Bulawayo – and a game they had been urged to boycott. The English umpire Peter Willey was originally due to stand in this match, with Neil Mallender as third umpire, but both withdrew because they were unwilling to visit Zimbabwe.

Toss: Zimbabwe. **Zimbabwe 246-9** (50 overs) (A. Flower 62, G. W. Flower 37, A. M. Blignaut 54; G. B. Hogg 3-46); **Australia 248-3** (47.3 overs) (A. C. Gilchrist 61, M. L. Hayden 34, R. T. Ponting 38, D. R. Martyn 50*, D. S. Lehmann 56*).

England v India

At Durban, February 26, 2003 (day/night). India won by 82 runs. 2004

This time it was England who fell foul of the toss of a coin and a zesty young fast bowler. Beginning the match with a dicky ankle and 30 wickets in 32 one-day internationals, Nehra snatched six for 23 and wiped out England's chase with searing pace and swing – much as Anderson had done to Pakistan. It was, at the time, the third-best analysis in World Cup history – and the best away from the green fields of Headingley. It was also a kick in the guts for England, who had earlier managed to subdue India after a booming overture worth 75 from the first 11 overs. It was Flintoff who silenced the innings: Sehwag got a leading edge and Tendulkar, in effable form and hitting with silky ferocity, cut to point just after drinks. After that, the next ten overs produced 21 runs; Flintoff, straight and fast, leaked just nine in his first eight overs. However, Dravid and Yuvraj Singh broke loose, adding a run-a-ball 62, and though England filched four wickets from the last four balls, their spirits were soon flagging again. Knight underestimated Kaif's agility and was run out in the second over of the reply, Trescothick mis-hooked, and as the ball swung under the lights, Vaughan barely survived a mesmeric spell from Zaheer Khan. Nehra then made the key thrusts: in his third over, he induced a bottom-edge from Hussain, then trapped Stewart with an in-swinger; in his fourth, he had Vaughan caught behind with something equally unanswerable. The top six had made 62 between them, and only Flintoff, in his best all-round performance for England, prevented a massacre.

Toss: India. **India 250-9** (50 overs) (S. R. Tendulkar 50, D. Mongia 32, R. Dravid 62, Yuvraj Singh 42; A. R. Caddick 3-69); **England 168** (45.3 overs) (A. Flintoff 64; A. Nehra 6-23).

India v Pakistan

At Centurion, March 1, 2003. India won by six wickets. 2004

Though the players played down the first clash between India and Pakistan since June 2000, it remained the tournament's most feverishly talked-up match. Almost incredibly, the cricket lived up to the hype. Under a hot sun and in front of a crammed stadium (and a TV audience implausibly guesstimated at a billion)

Tendulkar played an astounding innings – perhaps the best of the tournament, and undoubtedly one of his best in one-day internationals. Chasing 274, on a shirtfront but against a testosterone-propelled pace attack, he hit a vivid and memorable stream of shots, none so perfect as the cut six and the two fours – one swirled into the leg side, one pushed down the ground – which concluded Shoaib Akhtar's first over. By the 12th, India had reached 100; Tendulkar, missed on 32 and struggling with cramp, went on to 98 from 75 balls. After the storm came calm, as Dravid and Yuvraj Singh eased home to maintain India's pristine World Cup record (four wins out of four) against Pakistan.

Toss: Pakistan. **Pakistan 273-7** (50 overs) (Saeed Anwar 101, Younis Khan 32);
India 276-4 (45.4 overs) (S. R. Tendulkar 98, M. Kaif 35, R. Dravid 44*, Yuvraj Singh 50*).

Australia v England

At Port Elizabeth, March 2, 2003. Australia won by two wickets. 2004

As Bichel and Bevan ran off delirious, England stood still. Hussain was on his knees, his head in his hands; Stewart stood with his back to his team-mates; both would later announce their retirement from one-day matches. How had this happened? How had Australia – chasing 205, in terrible trouble at 48 for four, and again at 135 for eight – won with two balls to spare? "Bichel" was the short answer. First, he took seven for 20 on a slow pitch and strangled England's innings; then he struck a granite-willed 34 not out from No. 10 to end their fight-back – and, as it turned out, their World Cup. With Australia needing 14 from two overs, Hussain threw the ball not to Caddick (9–2–35–4 at the time) but to Anderson (8–0–54–0). It was a hunch he later came to regret: Bichel swung the first ball for six, a four followed, and the game was gone. It was the final twist in a match full of them.

England's openers had the Barmy Army in raptures with a stand of 66 in nine overs – milking, seemingly at will, a furious McGrath. In response, Ponting brought on Bichel; half an hour later, he had four for 10, having found just enough seam movement to reward his accuracy. Flintoff and Stewart played sensibly, if slowly, adding 90 in just under 25 overs, before Bichel returned and made sure there would be no late surge. In reply, Caddick made early incisions, but it was Bichel and Bevan, with a magnificent 74, who made the headlines. Australia had won their 12th successive one-day international – a record, beating West Indies' 11 between June 1984 and February 1985. Defeat was not necessarily disastrous for England – there were tortuous mathematical calculations that suggested it might, in some circumstances, even help their chances of reaching the Super Six. In the event, it did prove their undoing. And it was yet another chapter in the 14-year saga of humiliation against their oldest cricketing enemy.

Toss: England. **England 204-8** (50 overs) (M. E. Trescothick 37, N. V. Knight 30, A. J. Stewart 46, A. Flintoff 45; A. J. Bichel 7-20); **Australia 208-8** (49.4 overs) (D. S. Lehmann 37, M. G. Bevan 74*, A. J. Bichel 34*; A. R. Caddick 4-35).

Zimbabwe v Pakistan

At Bulawayo, March 4, 2003. No result. 2004

The fate of three teams, scrapping for one place in the Super Six, hinged on the outcome here, and after persistent drizzle limited play to just 14 overs, it was Zimbabwe who emerged smiling. England would almost certainly have qualified had Pakistan won. Pakistan themselves had a faint hope, which rested on winning by a margin large enough to overhaul England's vastly superior net run-rate. But, in the event, Zimbabwe picked up two points for the no-result and pulled clear in third place. While they celebrated a spot in the second phase for the second World Cup in a row, England and Pakistan were left to rue the controversial decision not to set aside a reserve day for group matches. When Pakistan chose to bat, they needed at least 300 to give themselves a remote chance but by the second over the rain had arrived. Then, with Pakistan 73 for three, the players were driven off for the third, and final, time. The miserable Inzamam-ul-Haq was one of the batsmen to fall; he ended the competition with 19 runs in six innings. Nasser Hussain responded to England's elimination by resigning the one-day captaincy.

Toss: Pakistan. **Pakistan 73-3** (14 overs) (Saeed Anwar 40*) **v Zimbabwe.**

Australia, India and Zimbabwe led Pool A and qualified for the Super Six stage.

Bangladesh v Canada

At Durban, February 11, 2003 (day/night). Canada won by 60 runs. 2004

Nearly four years after tearing up the World Cup form-book against Pakistan at Northampton, Bangladesh were themselves humbled by a Canadian side playing their first full international since 1979 and containing players born in eight different countries. Canada's hero was Austin Codrington, a 27-year-old apprentice plumber from Jamaica with flopping dreadlocks and an open-chested action, who unplugged the Bangladeshi batting with his wobbly medium-pace. His five for 27 was the third-best by a player on one-day international debut (behind Tony Dodemaide of Australia with five for 21 against Sri Lanka in 1987–88 and S.H.U. Karnain of Sri Lanka with five for 26 against New Zealand in 1983–84). At 106 for four in the 21st over, Bangladesh were on course, only for the last six wickets to tumble for 14 in 44 balls amid a flurry of panicky strokes. The Canadians, keen as mustard, celebrated each wicket with disbelieving leaps and hugs; the Bangladeshis, who had won none of their 43 Tests and one-day internationals since Northampton, simply looked stunned.

Toss: Canada. **Canada 180** (49.1 overs) (I. S. Billcliff 42); **Bangladesh 120** (28 overs)
(A. Codrington 5-27).

South Africa v New Zealand

At Johannesburg, February 16, 2003. New Zealand won by nine wickets (D/L method). 2004

An innings of rumbustious flamboyance from Gibbs was upstaged by one of graceful power by Fleming, who hit a career-best unbeaten 134 to stun a capacity crowd into near silence. In 191 previous one-day internationals, Fleming had managed just three centuries, but now, when his team needed him most, he played the innings of his life: after defeat to Sri Lanka and with their game against Kenya likely to be forfeited, New Zealand simply had to win. They did it in style, to leave the hosts on the brink of elimination. On an ideal batting pitch, Fleming moved to a run-a-ball fifty with four consecutive fours off Kallis before surviving a simple chance to Boucher's left on 53. McMillan fell soon after, but Fleming made South Africa pay with a string of exquisite on-drives and less characteristic cuts. A 15-minute power failure was followed by two rain breaks, which brought Duckworth/Lewis into play at 182 for one in the 31st over. The recalculation meant New Zealand needed 44 in eight and a half overs for a famous win. Astle, almost anonymous, finished unbeaten on 54, but this was Fleming's match. By the time he had crashed the winning four off the ailing Donald, Fleming had faced 132 balls and hit 21 of New Zealand's 27 boundaries. He had never played better.

Toss: South Africa. **South Africa 306-6** (50 overs) (H. H. Gibbs 143, J. H. Kallis 33, L. Klusener 33*);
New Zealand 229-1 (36.5 overs) (S. P. Fleming 134*, N. J. Astle 54*).

Canada v Sri Lanka

At Paarl, February 19, 2003. Sri Lanka won by nine wickets. 2004

When Joe Harris, the Canada captain, said his side had not been able to handle the pressure, he was verging on comic understatement. Canada had been blown away for the lowest total in one-day international history: no one reached double figures; and Sri Lanka needed just 28 balls to knock off the runs. The whole match lasted less than two hours – just 23.2 overs were bowled – making it comfortably the shortest in World Cup history. Inserted on a lively track, Canada were undone by the swing of Vaas and the pace and bounce of Nissanka. The high point of Canada's innings came when Harris hit Vaas for successive fours; three balls later, he hit his own wicket after being struck in the ribs by Nissanka. A total of 36 represented a minor recovery from the depths of 12 for six, but it was still two short of the 38 Zimbabwe made, also against Sri Lanka, in Colombo in December 2001. The Sri Lankan-born Sanjayan Thuraisingam prevented a ten-wicket win by removing Jayasuriya; it was scant consolation.

Toss: Sri Lanka. **Canada 36** (18.4 overs) (W. P. U. J. C. Vaas 3-15, R. A. P. Nissanka 4-12);
Sri Lanka 37-1 (4.4 overs).

Canada v West Indies

At Centurion, February 23, 2003. West Indies won by seven wickets. 2004

If the result came as no surprise, John Davison's batting was a complete shock. In 37 first-class matches in Australia, he averaged under 11: representing the country of his birth, however, he batted like a millionaire, clobbering a sensational hundred in just 67 balls – a World Cup record – and briefly giving Canada a glimmer of hope. By the time he was out to a stunning one-handed catch at long-on by Drakes, back-pedalling furiously, Davison had made 111 from 76 balls and struck six sixes and eight fours, many of them one-bounce. There were moments of luck – he was dropped twice, and even watched open-mouthed as the ball trickled on to leg stump without dislodging a bail – but this was clean hitting par excellence. At 155 for one in the 21st over, Canada were motoring, but the departure of Chumney and, more importantly, Davison caused a terminal splutter: the last nine wickets fell for 47, five to Drakes. Taking their cue from Davison – and with an eye on net run-rate – Hinds and Lara cruised to 100 in the tenth over. For all of five minutes Hinds held the record for the fastest World Cup fifty before Lara snatched it from him and West Indies raced home with nearly 30 overs to spare.

Toss: West Indies. **Canada 202** (42.5 overs) (J. M. Davison 111; V. C. Drakes 5-44); **West Indies 206-3** (20.3 overs) (W. W. Hinds 64, B. C. Lara 73, R. R. Sarwan 42*).

Kenya v Sri Lanka

At Nairobi, February 24, 2003. Kenya won by 53 runs. 2004

A World Cup bloated by too many one-sided games needed this like a desert explorer needs a cold beer. Kenya's shock victory was memorable enough, but the style – all wide-grinning, grassy-kneed enthusiasm – was unforgettable: Kenya chased like lion cubs, backed up in gangs and jigged after every wicket. Sri Lanka, by contrast, simply moped. "The worst game of my career," admitted Jayasuriya. Violent hitting by Otieno helped Kenya to 46 for one in the seventh over, but they never really hit the balance between big shots and blocking, especially mid-innings, when Muralitharan found drift and turn. In reply to 210, Sri Lanka almost sleepwalked to defeat. Only when they lost their fifth wicket for 105 in the 28th over did they finally seem to wake to their predicament. And when de Silva went soon afterwards, it was too late to do much about it. He at least had stuck around for a while, and of the five who fell to Obuya's accurate but unthreatening leg-spin, only he could plead not guilty. Kenya's lap of honour ended up more a half-marathon.

Toss: Sri Lanka. **Kenya 210-9** (50 overs) (K. O. Otieno 60; W. P. U. J. C. Vaas 3-41, M. Muralitharan 4-28); **Sri Lanka 157** (45 overs) (P. A. de Silva 41; C. O. Obuya 5-24).

Sri Lanka v West Indies

At Cape Town, February 28, 2003 (day/night). Sri Lanka won by six runs. 2004

Like the opening match almost three weeks earlier, this was a Cape Town classic whose outcome was in doubt until the final over. West Indies looked as though they would sneak through again, but after 37 runs had flowed from the two previous overs, Muralitharan returned to concede just two from the 49th. His tight hold on the purse strings – 14 from the last six balls proved too much – took the game, and the Super Six, away from West Indies, who exited at the first opportunity, just as in 1999. Vaas won the match award for his four wickets, including Lara, caught behind for one, but the truly heroic performance came from Sarwan. Knocked out by a Fernando bouncer and stretchered off to hospital, blood pouring from the wound, he was not expected to add to his ten runs. But with West Indies in desperate trouble at 169 for seven in the 43rd over, back he came – in a maroon cap and to a whooping standard ovation. He batted from that moment with no fear, laying in to both Jayasuriya and de Silva, and being dropped by Atapattu. But this was no fairy tale. West Indies fell just short, and Hooper was too desolate to praise him. "I don't think it is too big a deal," he said. "We've seen blood before."

Toss: Sri Lanka. **Sri Lanka 228-6** (50 overs) (S. T. Jayasuriya 66, H. P. Tillekeratne 36, R. P. Arnold 34*);
West Indies 222-9 (50 overs) (C. H. Gayle 55, R. R. Sarwan 47*, S. Chanderpaul 65;
W. P. U. J. C. Vaas 4-22).

South Africa v Sri Lanka

At Durban, March 3, 2003 (day/night). Tied (D/L method). 2004

Sydney 1992, Edgbaston 1999, and now Durban 2003: South Africa have certainly acquired an unhappy knack of exiting World Cups in bizarre fashion. Late in the South African innings, with rain falling steadily, it had become a question of when – not if – Duckworth/Lewis would come into play. And so, when Boucher swung the penultimate ball of the 45th – and, as had begun to seem inevitable, final – over for six, he pumped his right fist, believing the job done. The last soggy ball of the match he pushed casually to leg, and stayed put. Crucially, though, the South Africans had misread the fine print: they had needed 229 to *tie*, when only a win would do. Sri Lanka progressed – and South Africa's world fell apart. Jayasuriya draped an arm around Pollock's shoulders as they awaited the media inquisition, compassion supplanting his own relief, however briefly.

Toss: Sri Lanka. **Sri Lanka 268-9** (50 overs) (M. S. Atapattu 124, P. A. de Silva 73; J. H. Kallis 3-41);
South Africa 229-6 (45 overs) (G. C. Smith 35, H. H. Gibbs 73, M. V. Boucher 45*).

Sri Lanka, Kenya and New Zealand led Pool B and qualified for the Super Six stage.

SUPER SIX STARTING TABLE

	Played	Won	Lost	Tied	No result	Points	Net run-rate
Australia	2	2	0	0	0	12	1.67
Kenya	2	2	0	0	0	10	1.06
India	2	1	1	0	0	8	-0.35
Sri Lanka	2	1	1	0	0	7.5	-0.06
New Zealand	2	0	2	0	0	4	-0.94
Zimbabwe	2	0	2	0	0	3.5	-0.98

Super Six teams carried forward four points each for wins against fellow Super Six qualifiers and one point each for wins (half a point for a tie or no result) against teams eliminated at the Pool stage.

SELECTED SUPER SIX MATCHES
Australia v Sri Lanka
At Centurion, March 7, 2003. Australia won by 96 runs. 2004

This was supposed to be South Africa's big day in the battle of the group winners, but history had turned a different corner and Sri Lanka were the sacrificial lambs instead. They had been the last team to beat the Australians – back in January – but by the 20th over Australia were already in the distance, 131 for one and cruising into the future; this win was enough to see them into the semi-finals. Sri Lanka had to cope with a conveyor-belt of run-a-ball partnerships – 75, 106 and 112 for the first three wickets. Gilchrist pounded 14 fours and two sixes before walking back distraught, only the third man run out for 99 in one-day internationals (after Graeme Smith of South Africa and Jayasuriya), all three involving Sri Lanka in the last five months. It wasn't even his run. But Ponting did get his hundred, moving from 52 to 101 in 30 balls. Sangakkara, who should have run him out on 35, could only watch. Lee took out Sri Lanka's talisman, Jayasuriya – chipping his thumb, then bruising his shoulder – in his first over. Sri Lanka lost four wickets in the forties, and, though de Silva did enough to wreck Lee's figures, there was no contest.

Toss: Australia. **Australia 319-5** (50 overs) (A. C. Gilchrist 99, R. T. Ponting 114, D. R. Martyn 52; C. R. D. Fernando 3-47); **Sri Lanka 223** (47.4 overs) (P. A. de Silva 92; B. Lee 3-52).

Kenya v Zimbabwe
At Bloemfontein, March 12, 2003. Kenya won by seven wickets. 2004

The Kenyan safari became ever more adventurous as they beat Zimbabwe for the first time in 15 attempts to become the least fancied side ever to reach the World Cup semi-finals. "Today is the biggest day in every Kenyan's life," enthused Tikolo. It was their third win over Test opponents in the competition – and their most convincing. On another anodyne pitch, Martin Suji's bustling, accurate medium pace accounted for three early wickets – including Campbell, summoned hastily from the commentary box because of Zimbabwe's injury list – before Obuya's leg-breaks baffled the middle order. Only Andy Flower, with a patient 63, batted with any common sense. With history beckoning, Kenya stuttered; they were 63 for three when Olonga, picked for the first time since his black-armband protest during Zimbabwe's opening game, trapped Otieno. But Odoyo and Odumbe launched a thrilling counter-attack. Odoyo was merciless off the back foot, while Odumbe repeatedly used his feet to hit inside-out over extra cover. When the two of them combined to hit six consecutive deliveries to the boundary, Zimbabwe knew their World Cup was over.

Toss: Zimbabwe. **Zimbabwe 133** (44.1 overs) (A. Flower 63; M. A. Suji 3-19, C. O. Obuya 3-32); **Kenya 135-3** (26 overs) (T. M. Odoyo 43*, M. O. Odumbe 38*).

Australia v Kenya
At Durban, March 15, 2003 (day/night). Australia won by five wickets. 2004

Another Kenyan match, another fantasy. This was the night they imagined they might beat the world's most powerful cricketing nation thanks to the exploits of a middle-aged spinner who had retired after the last World Cup but now made a Brett Lee hat-trick seem insignificant. Aasif Karim's greatest claims to fame amounted to five wickets against Bangladesh in 1997–98 and some Davis Cup tennis. After this, he could also regale his grandchildren with the tale of how, at 39, he reduced the great Australians to impotence. Karim's style on delivery suggested that he might be about to serve, not bowl. He never remotely turned a ball, but in his first two overs he had Ponting lbw, Lehmann caught at the wicket by David Obuya (deputising for the injured Otieno) and then stooped for a low return catch off Hogg. Called out of retirement barely a month before the tournament began, Karim had reduced Australia to 117 for five; Gilchrist's withering assault, that had brought 98 within 12 overs, was quite forgotten. Karim had figures of 8-6-2-3 before Symonds and Harvey took five from his last two balls to achieve victory. Ponting professed himself "bemused" that Lee's thrilling hat-trick, which had reduced Kenya to three for three, had not earned the match award.

Toss: Australia. **Kenya 174-8** (50 overs) (R. D. Shah 46, S. O. Tikolo 51, H. S. Modi 39*; B. Lee 3-14); **Australia 178-5** (31.2 overs) (A. C. Gilchrist 67, A. Symonds 33*; A. Y. Karim 3-7).

SUPER SIX FINAL TABLE

	Played	Won	Lost	Tied	No result	Points	Net run-rate
AUSTRALIA	5	5	0	0	0	24	1.85
INDIA	5	4	1	0	0	20	0.88
KENYA	5	3	2	0	0	14	0.35
SRI LANKA	5	2	3	0	0	11.5	-0.84
New Zealand	5	1	4	0	0	8	-0.89
Zimbabwe	5	0	5	0	0	3.5	-1.25

SEMI-FINALS
Australia v Sri Lanka

At Port Elizabeth, March 18, 2003. Australia won by 48 runs (D/L method).   2004

This was Gilchrist's match: not for what he did with bat or gloves but for his decision to walk, which astonished everyone unused to such Australian magnanimity. Despite being reprieved by umpire Koertzen, Gilchrist knew he had edged an attempted sweep that was caught off his pad. His departure, swiftly followed by Ponting's, gave Sri Lanka their chance to beat Australia; they blew it. Sangakkara missed a simple chance to stump Symonds, on 33, off Jayasuriya, who later removed Lehmann and Bevan with successive balls, but Symonds was not to be dismissed. He adapted well to another difficult St George's Park surface and his innings was defined by patience rather than by brute force.

Sri Lanka needed only 213, but their optimism had gone. Atapattu, their form batsman, was dropped by Hogg at cover on 14, but had his off stump ripped out by Lee's next ball, which was measured at 99.4mph. Jayasuriya hit Lee for six before being caught at square leg. Then Bichel, in his follow-through, swooped left-handed to pick up a defensive push from Sangakkara, turned, and threw down the batsman's stumps, stranding de Silva, who trudged off into retirement. The late-afternoon rain halted Sri Lanka's first decent partnership – 47 for the eighth wicket between Sangakkara and Vaas – but no one complained about Duckworth/Lewis. Australia had deservedly reached their fifth World Cup final and their third in succession.

Toss: Australia. **Australia 212-7** (50 overs) (D. S. Lehmann 36, A. Symonds 91*; W. P. U. J. C. Vaas 3-34); **Sri Lanka 123-7** (38.1 overs) (K. C. Sangakkara 39*; B. Lee 3-35).

India v Kenya

At Durban, March 20, 2003 (day/night). India won by 91 runs.   2004

The steel instilled into the Indian team and distilled by Ganguly, drop by steady drop, ensured there were no Disneyfied endings for Kenya. Captaining India for the 99th time in a one-day international, Ganguly re-emphasised his batting mastery against modest attacks to guide his team to an imposing if not unanswerable total, then sat back as his pace trio did the needful. Tendulkar seemed destined for a hundred until he pulled Tikolo to deep mid-wicket. But Ganguly matched Mark Waugh's 1996 feat of three centuries in a World Cup tournament, getting there with his fifth six, the product of a golfer's swing and that unmistakable superiority complex. Arms aloft, he drank in the acclaim. His opposite number, Tikolo, also top-scored in the Kenyan reply, before his men took a weary lap of honour, smiles intact, their place in the pantheon assured.

Toss: India. **India 270-4** (50 overs) (V. Sehwag 33, S. R. Tendulkar 83, S. C. Ganguly 111*); **Kenya 179** (46.2 overs) (S. O. Tikolo 56, Extras 39; Zaheer Khan 3-14).

FINAL
Australia v India

At Johannesburg, March 23, 2003. Australia won by 125 runs. John Stern, 2004

Ricky Ponting played a captain's innings to deliver Australia their third title. His 140, the highest individual score in a World Cup final, and his leadership through the tournament completed his ascent from underachieving Tasmanian devil to cornerstone of Australian dominance.

Just like Nasser Hussain at Brisbane a few months earlier, Ganguly raised eyebrows by putting Australia in. He was acting from fear of Australia's bowlers rather than on aggressive intent: against any other opponents, he would surely have batted first. Yet it had been 71 matches and three years since Australia last failed to defend a total of 200 or more. Gilchrist and Hayden chanced their arms, India's seamers buckled, and after nine overs Australia were 74 without loss. Ganguly turned to spin and Harbhajan Singh did send back both openers, but Australia were not reined in for long. The partnership of 234 between Ponting and Martyn was Australia's highest for any wicket in one-day internationals. So was their total. Martyn's performance was the more remarkable because he had missed the semi-final with a finger injury and was not expected to play. His batting was the perfect foil for Ponting – selfless, intelligent and perfectly tuned to the situation.

The army of Indian supporters – many from the UK – had been bemused when Ganguly asked Australia to bat. By the interval they had all but given up hope. The dream was shattered entirely when Tendulkar tried to pull McGrath's fifth ball and was caught by the bowler off a top edge. Sehwag, who was caught off a Lee no-ball on four, did his best to keep India in it with a bullish, run-a-ball 82, including ten fours and three sixes. But he was run out by a direct hit from Lehmann at deep mid-off, ending a promising stand of 88 with Dravid.

Rain had briefly threatened the unsatisfactory prospect of a replay the following day, with Australia's record-breaking performances consigned to history – so every sign of precipitation was greeted uproariously by India's fans. Knowing his side had to bowl 25 overs to ensure a result, Ponting brought on his spinners: there was a surreal period when Hogg and Lehmann were being thrashed to all parts as Indian supporters cheered and the fielders, running to their positions to speed up the over-rate, got wet. Then the umpires called a drinks break. After drinks, Bichel and McGrath returned, the lights came on, and the rain became heavy enough for the players to leave the field, with India on 103 for three. They returned 25 minutes later – no overs were deducted – and the formality of Australia's third World Cup (and 17th consecutive one-day victory) was completed under darkening skies to the sound of frequent thunderclaps.

Australia v India, 2003   World Cup Final

At Johannesburg, March 23, 2003. Result: Australia won by 125 runs.

AUSTRALIA

†A. C. Gilchrist c Sehwag b Harbhajan Singh	57	D. R. Martyn not out	88
M. L. Hayden c Dravid b Harbhajan Singh	. 37	B 2, l-b 12, w 16, n-b 7	37
*R. T. Ponting not out	140	(2 wkts, 50 overs)	359

1-105 (1) 2-125 (2)

D. S. Lehmann, A. Symonds, M. G. Bevan, G. B. Hogg, A. J. Bichel, B. Lee and
G. D. McGrath did not bat.

Zaheer Khan 7–0–67–0; Srinath 10–0–87–0; Nehra 10–0–57–0; Harbhajan Singh 8–0–49–2; Sehwag
3–0–14–0; Tendulkar 3–0–20–0; Mongia 7–0–39–0; Yuvraj Singh 2–0–12–0.

INDIA

S. R. Tendulkar c and b McGrath	4	D. Mongia c Martyn b Symonds	12
V. Sehwag run out	82	Harbhajan Singh c McGrath b Symonds . . .	7
*S. C. Ganguly c Lehmann b Lee	24	Zaheer Khan c Lehmann b McGrath	4
M. Kaif c Gilchrist b McGrath	0	J. Srinath b Lee	1
†R. Dravid b Bichel	47	A. Nehra not out	8
Yuvraj Singh c Lee b Hogg	24	B 4, l-b 4, w 9, n-b 4	21

1-4 (1) 2-58 (3) 3-59 (4) 4-147 (2) 5-187 (5) 6-208 (6) 7-209 (7) 8-223 (8)   (39.2 overs)   234
9-226 (10) 10-234 (9)

McGrath 8.2–0–52–3; Lee 7–1–31–2; Hogg 10–0–61–1; Lehmann 2–0–18–0; Bichel 10–0–57–1;
Symonds 2–0–7–2.

Toss won by India   UMPIRES S. A. Bucknor and D. R. Shepherd
MAN OF THE MATCH R. T. Ponting

SECTION FIVE

The Counties

SECTION FIVE

The Counties

Crisis, What Crisis?

The County Championship is a glorious anachronism, dating back to the 19th century, when in a geographically far less mobile age counties really mattered. You were likely to spend your entire life in the same county and moving from one to another was an event. Jane Austen's novels are full of characters going "into" Derbyshire or Hampshire – the act of crossing the county line truly meant something. In our age of flux and mutability, counties have nothing like the same resonance.

At the start of the 2006 season, *Guardian* sportswriter Barney Ronay had some fun with the notion that the County Championship was an invention of deranged minds at the ECB. "The county season has already begun," he wrote. "On Monday pictures will appear in your newspaper of a shivering county pro throwing a snowball on some frozen outfield while wearing three overcoats and a balaclava. Come September and you might catch some brief news footage of a batsman snicking the ball to the boundary while three or four people cheer loudly off camera. There goes the pennant for another year! The question is; what, if anything, happens in between?"

Then came his delightful conceit: "On the face of it, the County Championship is a massive enterprise, involving hundreds of players spending countless days in the field in front of two kebab vans and an elderly gentleman with a satchel full of old newspapers. We have no proof of any of this, of course. Scorecards are all very well, but has any independent witness ever seen one of these 'games' being 'played'? Think how much easier and cheaper it would be to cook the whole thing up over a long lunch in March."

A neat idea... and no doubt the ECB will now set up a working party to assess its possibilities. I – and you, too, if you have read this far – *love* the County Championship, but we should recognise that there are many people out there who think we are cranks, clinging to the last vestiges of Victorian England. And the county clubs have not helped themselves – with their cynical revolving-door approach to overseas imports and "Kolpak" players. The counties no longer feel like settled teams with distinct identities, but temporary agglomerations of players recruited with specific ends in mind.

And yet, and yet, I still pore over the latest county scores on Ceefax or on the internet, and follow the fortunes of my beloved Glamorgan (though I did give up in 2005, so dire and predictable were the results). I once broke my nose at Cardiff, dropping down behind the stand at the River Taff end to field a ball for Ray Illingworth (during early-morning practice!) and hitting my head on a stanchion.

So I feel I've earned my stripes in the Championship. I also go to The Oval, my nearest county ground, for Surrey games when I can, and, as members huddle in the pavilion, quite often have one entire side of the ground to myself. Bliss. Jane Austen would recognise this serenity.

Who knows if the Championship has a future? I hope so, though the dominance of international cricket is now so complete that there is little room for domestic competitions to breathe. The decline in the status of the one-day cups, reflected in the match reports in this section, is one symptom of that. The fact that once a county's best players win international recognition and are given a central contract, they in effect leave the county and become part of "Team England" is a devastating blow for the counties. Fans, especially young fans rather than elderly men with satchels full of newspapers, go to see heroes, attend county games in the hope of seeing a great player achieve something wonderful. Most county pros are capable of excellence, but many of the truly outstanding players – especially if they play for England – now make only fleeting appearances in county cricket.

I seem to recall writing an article suggesting city-based cricket as an alternative to the county system when that idea was briefly fashionable at the turn of the millennium. Even *Wisden* flirted with this notion, with editor Graeme Wright surprisingly giving it his backing in his departing notes in 2002 (see page 100). But it was never really a flyer: the counties retain a residual charm and have shown remarkable staying power. Each September, the demise of some of the weaker counties is predicted; each April they come bouncing back for more.

In this section, I have tried – through *Wisden*'s excellent annual reports from observers close to the counties – to give a sense of how each of the 18 first-class clubs has fared over the past 30 years (Durham joined the fraternity in 1992). There is not space to cover every year – and that might, in any case, become tiresome as counties get locked into, say, 14th place in the Championship for four successive seasons – so a certain amount of concertina-ing takes place. We experience the highs and lows of each county in rapid succession rather than real time.

What I hope comes across is how complex and difficult to keep on track these county clubs are. As I read through the records of past seasons, I had a strong sense of great teams coalescing, achieving their moment – or in Essex's case in the 1980s their decade – of greatness, and then dissolving. The conundrum each time is how to build another great team from the remnants of the old, how to manage change, how to blend old and new, how to deal with wonderful players now in decline. So many fine careers end in acrimony as clubs decide that it is, in that horrible phrase, time to "move on". Counties are organic entities – difficult to mould, hard to predict. But easy to love. That is why they remain in our much-changed, boundaryless world. Long may they continue. S. M.

Derbyshire

Michael Carey, 1978

At last in 1977 Derbyshire emerged from the shadows of mediocrity that had engulfed them for years. Under the inspired leadership of [Eddie] Barlow, they played cricket that was largely positive and purposeful, and their refreshing approach was reflected in a climb to seventh place in the County Championship table. Not since 1970 had the county finished as high, nor won as many three-day games. The key was Barlow's charismatic captaincy. Derbyshire did not lean heavily on his skill as a player, for though he emerged as the county's leading catcher and frequently chipped in with valuable wickets, he was often frequently out of form with the bat. Yet he welded what had been a collection of individuals into a team, starting with a winter fitness programme which produced not only stamina but discipline and self-confidence and, therefore, greater quality and consistency throughout the team. This was especially reflected in the out-cricket, which scaled new heights of athleticism and consistency.

The county's seam bowling tradition was splendidly upheld, with an injury-free Hendrick consolidating his reputation as the most effective new ball bowler in the country and also proving himself at Test level. He was well supported by the left-arm Tunnicliffe, who rarely failed to make an early breakthrough with the new ball. Miller made the most exciting progress of all. He bowled more overs than anyone and came to terms with the demands made on a young spinner by the adjustments needed for the various competitions. In contrast, Swarbrook, his left-arm spin partner, had a modest season.

Among the batsmen, Wright, a left-hander from New Zealand via Kent, looked a tremendous acquisition with a sound technique and wide range of strokes. He found the English season at first cold and damp, and towards the end tiring, but his quality was there to be seen, despite an unnerving series of run-out episodes. Taylor's wicket-keeping was, it almost goes without saying, artistry in itself and for him the reward for long seasons of selfless dedication came in his selection as first-choice keeper for the tour of Pakistan and New Zealand, along with his colleagues Hendrick and Miller.

It is worth mentioning that, with the exception of the two overseas players, the entire side usually consisted of locally produced players, while behind the scenes another one, Russell, did an invaluable job on the coaching.

Derbyshire v Middlesex

At Ilkeston, June 18, 20, 1977. Derbyshire won by an innings and 177 runs.   1978

The county champions were outplayed, virtually from first ball to last, Derbyshire obtaining their first innings win since 1968. On the first morning Hendrick, exploiting helpful conditions and well supported by Tunnicliffe, reduced Middlesex to 21 for seven before Edmonds and Selvey enabled them to reach a total which was five higher than the season's lowest at that stage. Hill's impressive 70 steered Derbyshire 121 ahead on the first day, a position which was consolidated by some brilliant, controlled aggression by Cartwright and Tunnicliffe, who added 120. At one stage Edmonds conceded 80 runs in six overs, mainly to Tunnicliffe, who reached his fifty with a straight six in an over which cost 24 runs. He batted only 85 minutes, hitting five sixes and six fours. Middlesex, going in again 315 behind, looked capable of providing much sterner resistance, but after Smith was run out off the last ball before tea, they lost their remaining nine wickets for only 49 runs.

Toss: Middlesex. **Middlesex 54** (M. Hendrick 6-19, C. J. Tunnicliffe 4-22) **and 138** (M. J. Smith 59,
C. T. Radley 32); **Derbyshire 369** (A. Hill 70, A. J. Borrington 36, H. Cartwright 77,
C. J. Tunnicliffe 82*; M. W. W. Selvey 3-71, P. H. Edmonds 3-117).

1979 – STEEP DECLINE   Michael Carey, 1980

Far from building on the fresh hope and spirit engendered by the Barlow era, Derbyshire underwent a steep decline in 1979. They were 16th in both the Championship and the John Player League. True, they did reach the semi-finals of the Benson and Hedges Cup (only to throw the match away), but a reminder that they might not have qualified for that stage but for Somerset's disqualification was firmly given when they were beaten in the Gillette Cup at Taunton. Barlow's leadership was certainly missed in a season that was all too reminiscent of the grim days of the early seventies.

For the third time in five years the captaincy was changed in mid-season when [David] Steele, who was recruited from Northamptonshire to replace Barlow, felt obliged to give it up. As a player he earned the utmost admiration for his all-round ability and dedicated approach, but he found leadership foreign to him.

[Kim] Barnett, at 19, looked the most talented batsman unearthed by Derbyshire for years. If he has learned the lessons of a demanding first county season, the cricketing world could be at his feet.

1981 – A TROPHY AT LAST   Michael Carey, 1982

By becoming the first winners of the NatWest Trophy, Derbyshire achieved their first honour since they were county champions in 1936, and only the second in their entire history. This long-awaited triumph, however, the result of some dedicated team performances under the irrepressible leadership of Barry Wood, was tempered by the departure from the county of Mike Hendrick and by further evidence of instability behind the scenes.

Few counties can have experienced so many changes in one season. At one time or another, Derbyshire's chairman, chief executive, captain and scorer all resigned. Of these moves, the most important was that of Miller, who handed over the captaincy to Wood [saying the captaincy was affecting his form] only an hour or so before the start of the Championship match against Kent on July 25. Little did anyone sense the historical significance of this at the time. Six weeks later, Wood was holding the NatWest Trophy aloft and the stigma of being one of the only two counties who had not tasted success since the war was wiped away.

Bob Taylor had a memorable 21st season, with a second benefit, the award of an MBE, a maiden century and his recall to the England side, plus selection for the tour of India. For good measure, he established a world record for catches and a Derbyshire record for dismissals.

Derbyshire v Northamptonshire NatWest Trophy Final

At Lord's, September 5, 1981.
Derbyshire won by virtue of losing fewer wickets with the scores tied. 1982

In deteriorating light, Derbyshire required seven runs from the 60th over, bowled by Griffiths, but it became apparent that six would suffice for victory if no more than eight Derbyshire wickets had fallen. Miller swatted the first delivery to mid-on for two and took a single to third man off the second. Tunnicliffe pushed the third back to the bowler but ran the next to third man for one, and with Miller getting a single to square-leg off the fifth ball, one run was needed off the final delivery. [Geoff] Cook, the Northamptonshire captain, spent two minutes placing his field, but Miller backed up well and his flying finish beat Allan Lamb's throw at the stumps.

Earlier, Cook, playing reassuringly straight, had moved with authority towards his hundred. It came during an over from Hendrick which realised 15 runs, but in the next over, the 52nd, Tunnicliffe trapped him leg-before for 111. Northamptonshire were then 204 for four. When their innings ended at three o'clock, only 31 runs had been added for the loss of five more wickets, Wood himself playing the major role in the run-outs of Willey and Yardley.

Provided that Wright and Kirsten did not fail, a target of 236 was not beyond Derbyshire. But although the New Zealand-South African partnership was both stylish and productive, neither completely dominated the tidy Northamptonshire attack, and after 45 overs Derbyshire, at 146 for one, were still behind the required rate of 3.9 runs an over. Wright improved matters when he smote Mallender into the Mound Stand for six, but trying to repeat the stroke he was lbw. So, to the last ball of the over, was Kirsten, and suddenly Northamptonshire held the upper hand. Barnett batted with distinction, but it needed the arrival of Tunnicliffe to join Miller in the 58th over to revive Derbyshire's chances. With 19 required from the last two overs and the visibility worsening, Tunnicliffe lofted Sarfraz for two, square-drove him mightily for four, and clubbed the third ball over his head first bounce into the Pavilion fence. A single and a leg-bye took the total to 229 for six and the way was paved for the final thrilling climax of an extraordinary summer [it was the summer of "Botham's Ashes"].

Toss: Derbyshire. **Northamptonshire 235-9** (60 overs) (G. Cook 111, W. Larkins 52); **Derbyshire 235-6** (60 overs) (J. G. Wright 76, P. N. Kirsten 63; N. A. Mallender 3-35).

1983 – BARNETT TO THE RESCUE   Gerald Mortimer, 1984

For the fifth time in nine years, a change of captaincy was forced upon Derbyshire during a season. Barry Wood stepped down in the first week of May. "I find it too demanding," said Wood, "to captain the team and maintain the standards I have set myself during my career as an opening batsman and a bowler." Geoff Miller stood in until the committee made the brave decision to appoint Kim Barnett, at 22 the youngest captain in the county's history.

Barnett proved an excellent choice and came through the disruption caused by Wood's withdrawal and injuries to John Hampshire, Paul Newman and Miller to lead Derbyshire to seven victories in the Championship, a total bettered only once, under Derek Morgan in 1966, in 20 seasons. While Barnett gained in stature, Wood's career disintegrated unhappily. Three consecutive Championship defeats at the beginning of June gave some substance to Wood's claim that it was an insult for him to be omitted, a remark for which he was disciplined. When later he refused to give a pledge of support to the captain and administration, it was clear that Wood would not again play for Derbyshire and his contract was terminated by mutual consent in July. It was a sad ending for a player who had represented England in 12 Tests.

1984 – BOB TAYLOR SAYS FAREWELL   Gerald Mortimer, 1985

Although there were significant individual advances, Derbyshire slipped back in 1984. There were only four Championship victories; they were bottom of the John Player League and were routed by Leicestershire in the second round of the NatWest Trophy. Their shortcomings lay in their opening attack: Michael Holding [who had played a few games for the county in 1983] was with West Indies, Steve Oldham and Colin Tunnicliffe had been released, and Derbyshire were unhealthily reliant on Ole Mortenson. Devon Malcolm bowled at a brisk pace but was hardly ready for county cricket, and Paul Taylor, a left-arm fast bowler, looked an interesting prospect in his handful of matches.

Derbyshire gained more batting points than any other team, and eight batsmen – a record for the county – shared 17 centuries. Among them was Geoff Miller's long-awaited maiden hundred, scored against Lancashire at Old Trafford in the 380th innings of his career. Kim Barnett's 1,734 runs showed him to be one of England's best young batsmen, Alan Hill completed 10,000 runs for the county,

Bill Fowler came close to 1,000 runs, and John Morris made the most spectacular improvement. Morris has a natural talent which could take him a long way in the game. The team's greatest satisfaction was gained at Trent Bridge, where Derbyshire followed on 222 runs behind and recovered to beat Nottinghamshire by 28 runs.

Victory over Hampshire in the final match also marked the end of two distinguished careers. John Hampshire spent his last three years with Derbyshire after being with Yorkshire from 1961 to 1981. Hampshire could well have played in more than his eight Tests and like the other leaver, Bob Taylor, combined a love of cricket with a respect for its traditions and courtesies. Taylor, after announcing his retirement, had a royal progress around the counties, the applause which accompanied him indicating the respect and affection in which he was held. Taylor was an artist, acknowledged as one of the greatest wicket-keepers of all time and admired for his consistency whether in front of half a dozen spectators or a full house at Lord's. He passed John Murray's world record of dismissals while in Australia in 1982–83 and Hampshire's captain, Mark Nicholas, rated it a rare privilege to be Taylor's 1,646th and final victim.

Nottinghamshire v Derbyshire

At Nottingham, August 8, 9, 10, 1984. Derbyshire won by 28 runs. 1985

Derbyshire, on the receiving end for long periods, emerged as unlikely victors after Nottinghamshire failed miserably in their bid to score 160. Nottinghamshire amassed 361 in their first innings and then comfortably enforced the follow-on as only Hampshire offered any challenge to the bowling of Hadlee and Hemmings. However, Derbyshire, 222 behind, were set an example by Barnett when they batted a second time and a sixth-wicket stand of 135 between Miller and Finney frustrated Nottinghamshire. Robinson and Randall gave Nottinghamshire a good start as they chased their target, but Moir and Miller, bowling unchanged throughout the 34 overs, ripped through the remainder of the batting. Moir finished with career-best figures of six for 60.

Toss: Nottinghamshire. **Nottinghamshire 361** (R. T. Robinson 54, D. W. Randall 57, C. E. B. Rice 64, R. J. Hadlee 56, B. N. French 42; G. Miller 4-65, D. G. Moir 4-80) **and 131** (D. W. Randall 30; G. Miller 3-69, D. G. Moir 6-60); **Derbyshire 139** (J. H. Hampshire 53*; E. E. Hemmings 4-45, R. J. Hadlee 4-30) **and 381** (K. J. Barnett 90, W. P. Fowler 30, J. H. Hampshire 33, G. Miller 86, R. J. Finney 73; R. J. Hadlee 3-47, K. E. Cooper 3-46).

1985 – A MINOR DISASTER

Gerald Mortimer, 1986

Defeat by Durham [not yet a first-class county] overshadowed what was at best a mixed season for Derbyshire. It was the first time they had been beaten by a minor county and the margin of defeat, seven wickets, was made even more embarrassing because it was at their own headquarters. Derbyshire were in the lower half of the Championship but finished strongly in the Sunday League to rise from bottom in 1984 to fourth. But players and officials felt that they should have achieved more.

The attack relied too heavily on Michael Holding, whose presence restricted the appearances of New Zealand opening batsman John Wright. When Wright was absent, Kim Barnett had an uneasy feeling that the side could crumble if he himself failed with the bat. The left-arm spinner Dallas Moir was capped in the middle of the season, but released, along with Bill Fowler and Ian Broome, at the end of it. He failed to take advantage of helpful conditions at Old Trafford and Bradford, as did Geoff Miller, who, beset by illness and worries about his benefit, had seldom been less effective with his off-spin.

1988 – NO HOLDING HOLDING

Gerald Mortimer, 1989

Derbyshire's best days came early in the season, culminating in their Benson and Hedges Cup semi-final victory over Glamorgan at Swansea. It proved to be the peak although, until then, they had played excellent cricket in three competitions. Derbyshire flopped in the Benson and Hedges final at Lord's [dismissed for 117 by Hampshire and beaten by seven wickets] and the acknowledged importance of the toss could not disguise that. Their performance in the Refuge Assurance League was poor and they slipped in the Championship from sixth in 1987 to 14th.

Michael Holding was a giant in the knockout games and established a world record for limited-overs cricket when he took eight for 21 in the NatWest Trophy elimination of Sussex at Hove. But he had a thin time in the Championship. On occasions, Devon Malcolm was startlingly fast: at others, his tendency to pitch consistently short led to severe punishment and there seemed to be no middle ground. John Morris had a respectable season but, it was felt in Derbyshire, one of underachievement. He has the talent, range of stroke and strength to be a major force in the English game.

1990 – SUNDAY SUCCESS

Gerald Mortimer, 1991

Winning the Refuge Assurance League gave Derbyshire their first success for nine years and, significantly, they avoided the mistakes which had made their victory in the 1981 NatWest Trophy final an end rather than a beginning. The team which won at Lord's under Barry Wood started to break up in a matter of days and, against a background of the smallest membership among the first-class counties, Derbyshire spent most of the 1980s in patient rebuilding.

In addition to his forthright captaincy, Kim Barnett set a Derbyshire record when he passed Denis Smith's total of 30 hundreds for the county. In his first full summer, Chris Adams was close to 1,000 runs. The Championship batting, however, relied to an unhealthy extent on Barnett, John Morris and Peter Bowler. Spectacular collapses were never far away and certain opponents, notably Essex and Hampshire, could be forgiven for wondering how Derbyshire ever won a game

The memories of 1990 will be the Sunday games, especially the successful pursuits of steep targets at Taunton, and against Kent at Chesterfield. Kuiper's savage hitting gave Derbyshire a good start and an exciting climax, while Barnett fell only one run short of his 1986 record of 700 Sunday runs.

Somerset v Derbyshire

At Taunton, May 20, 1990. Derbyshire won by seven wickets.   1991

The first-wicket partnership of 232 between Barnett and Morris was a Derbyshire record for any wicket in the Sunday League and was also the highest opening partnership for the county in one-day competitions. Barnett reached his hundred off 105 balls, while Morris's 134, a record for Derbyshire in the Sunday League, came off 116 balls. This was Morris's third of four hundreds against Somerset in the month. The previous day he had scored 122 in the Championship, and he went on to make his second of the match on the third day. On May 1 he had hit 123 in the Benson and Hedges Cup.

Toss: Derbyshire. **Somerset 258–7** (40 overs) (S. J. Cook 53; P. M. Roebuck 85, R. J. Harden 30,
N. D. Burns 30); **Derbyshire 264–3** (40 overs) (K. J. Barnett 100, J. E. Morris 134).

1991 – ARTISTRY OF AZHAR   Gerald Mortimer, 1992

Derbyshire went into the last month of the season with a chance of winning the Britannic Assurance Championship, a new experience for Kim Barnett, who equalled G. R. Jackson's record of nine years as the county's captain. Their challenge foundered against the superior all-round quality of Essex at Chelmsford, but Derbyshire's season ended with a rosy glow as they recovered to beat Yorkshire at Chesterfield. An unlikely victory enabled Derbyshire to finish third, a feat they had not achieved since 1954.

Nine Championship victories was their best tally since they won ten in 1961, and for the first time since 1971 five batsmen scored 1,000 runs. Mohammad Azharuddin, engaged in place of Ian Bishop, gave enormous pleasure and became only the second batsman to score 2,000 runs in a season for Derbyshire.

1993 – CORK POPPING   Gerald Mortimer, 1994

The exciting and emotional victory over Lancashire in the Benson and Hedges Cup final made Derbyshire's season memorable. With only three other entries on their honours board – the Championship in 1936, the NatWest Trophy in 1981 and the Refuge Assurance League in 1990 – Derbyshire do not mount the rostrum often enough to take it for granted. Barnett described the final at Lord's as the greatest day in his 11 years as captain. Lancashire, the overwhelming favourites were outfielded by Derbyshire, who do not outfield anyone that often, as well as battered by Dominic Cork's unbeaten 92.

While attaining one of their playing peaks, Derbyshire were involved in a financial crisis serious enough to threaten the club's existence. Although the players were able to distance themselves from financial worries, a problem arose in the dressing room when, in August, John Morris asked to be relieved of the vice-captaincy. At the end of the season, he tried to secure his release from a contract that had a year to run and, after initial resistance, Derbyshire succumbed and let him go [he moved to Durham]. Morris will be much missed, because his batting was often glorious.

Derbyshire v Lancashire	Benson and Hedges Cup Final
At Lord's, July 10, 1993. Derbyshire won by six runs.	1994

Toss: Lancashire. **Derbyshire 252-6** (55 overs) (T. J. G. O'Gorman 49, D. G. Cork 92*, K. M. Krikken 37*; P. A. J. DeFreitas 3-39); **Lancashire 246-7** (55 overs) (M. A. Atherton 54, N. J. Speak 42, N. H. Fairbrother 87*; A. E. Warner 3-31).

1995 – BARNETT STEPS DOWN
Gerald Mortimer, 1996

Derbyshire won their first and last Championship matches so easily as to make their performances in the intervening months the more irritating. There was high individual achievement in Kim Barnett's last season as captain, most notably from Dominic Cork, but a lack of corporate effectiveness did not give the impression of a happy summer. In retrospect, it was a mistake for Barnett to announce in the previous winter that 1995 would be his final year as captain: there was a sense of drift. He led Derbyshire for longer, 13 seasons, and in more first-class matches, 271, than anybody in the club's history. Barnett emerged heavily in credit, with two one-day trophies and the highest Championship placing, third in 1991, since the Second World War. He was central to building a new team after replacing Barry Wood a few weeks into the 1983 season. when he was not quite 23. But the final phase of his command was marked by friction. John Morris and Peter Bowler went to other counties, Chris Adams asked to be released before and after the 1995 season, and, when playing standards dipped, there were rumours that a move might suit Barnett too. There was a desire for a fresh start and, within 48 hours of the season ending, Derbyshire announced the appointment of Dean Jones as captain and overseas player.

1996 – INSPIRED BY JONES
Gerald Mortimer, 1997

Derbyshire, inspired by Dean Jones as captain and Les Stillman as coach, were runners-up in the Championship. Not since their solitary title in 1936 had they finished so high. Jones insisted that all things were possible and was ready to confront problems head on. The most extraordinary victory was at Old Trafford: Jason Gallian's painstaking 312 lasted into the sixth session, yet he finished on the losing side. A county-record eighth-wicket stand of 198 between Cork and Karl Krikken saved the follow-on and Derbyshire were able to chase a target on the final day. Krikken, noisily restless as ever, had a wonderful year as batsman and wicket-keeper.

1997 – YEAR OF CRISIS   Gerald Mortimer, 1998

As Derbyshire rounded off their season on a lovely September afternoon with a decisive victory over Yorkshire, it was almost possible to believe that all was well. The list of the disappeared at the County Ground told a different story. During an extraordinary four months, starting with defeat by Hampshire at Chesterfield, Derbyshire contrived to lose their captain, coach, cricket chairman, chairman, secretary and commercial manager. It was a horrible summer for the long-suffering membership – one which had begun with such optimism after Derbyshire were Championship runners-up in 1996.

The scale of the crisis in early June came as a complete surprise. After Hampshire won on his declaration, Dean Jones resigned as captain and overseas player, promptly returning to Australia. He issued a statement, through the club, in which he criticised the attitude of senior players. Chris Adams, too, was finally granted his release with a year remaining on his contract and became captain of Sussex. Devon Malcolm also jumped ship and signed for Northamptonshire.

2001 – THE NADIR   Gerald Mortimer, 2002

Derbyshire's inability to retain their best cricketers overtook and exposed them to a dreadful season. While more than a dozen of their former players were employed elsewhere, the county struggled along with an inadequate team that was barely competitive. Even before the final rounds of fixtures, they knew that bottom place in both second divisions was inevitable.

Demolition of the County Ground's most notable feature, the grandstand, began soon after the end of the season. Work began on new and urgently needed outdoor practice facilities, and the aim was to finance a top-quality indoor school. Trevor Bowring, the chairman, irritated by articles suggesting first-class status was in jeopardy, pointed to the development as an indication of faith in the future, while remaining fully aware of the need to improve Derbyshire's performance on the field.

Durham

Simon Hughes, 1993

Durham began their first season as a first-class county with a bang and ended it with a whimper. In between, the experience was rather like a novice's round of golf – some booming early drives and the odd good hole but plenty of double bogeys. By September, injuries to key batsmen and a lack of really incisive bowlers relegated the team to bottom place in the Championship, and there they finished. There was plenty to be proud of, though.

We are supposed to live in John Major's classless society, so he would have been pleased that for much of the season a team managed by a Cook also contained a Jones, a Smith and a Brown. Durham was a magnet for players from all corners of the country, many disillusioned with their previous counties after years trudging the same path. At first, the public school accents of some recruits jarred uneasily against the Potteries jargon and north-eastern lingo of others, but the humour and goodwill of everyone proved the catalyst. What the team lacked in pace bowling and depth, it adequately made up for with determination and charisma. It could not, however, replace Dean Jones's expertise and panache once he departed for Australia in late July.

Well as men like Larkins, Parker and Bainbridge played, they were unable to mask the overall inexperience of the team and, as injuries took their toll, the youthful Durham aspirants were cruelly exposed. Geoff Cook himself observes in his book, *The Narrow Line*: "Nothing in cricket even begins to compare with the intense psychological rupture involved in moving from a county second XI to the first XI." The gulf in standards is far wider than anything they have had to cross in the past, or will in the future; even the climb to Test cricket is less precipitous. This meant that new names like Mark Briers and Stewart Hutton were suddenly thrust into the front line and, after promising beginnings, found the sheer intensity of full-time professionalism too onerous, and the spindly body of the left-arm seamer Simon Brown eventually buckled under the strain of endless days in the field.

The remarkable thing about Durham cricket is the indomitable support. It is a common misconception that the area is typified by reclaimed slag heaps upon which people live in poky houses and eat pease pudding for tea. In fact, the county is characterised by stupendous views and a loyal, optimistic population. They soon idolised favourite members of the team, and revelled in the new identity. Importantly, the team won its first competitive game – a nail-biting Sunday encounter against Lancashire – giving it immediate credibility. There were two Championship victories to follow – one by an innings – and a mid-table position in the Sunday League. Losing to Leicestershire in the quarter-finals of the NatWest Trophy was easily the low point of the season.

The problems of setting up a new county are manifold. How would the various club wickets stand up to four-day cricket? What size might the crowds be? How many toilets would need to be installed? Many of the logistics had to be judged on a trial and error basis, and one or two home matches were lost through unfamiliarity with the pitch. Volunteers were lured to help erect marquees or drag hoardings about, and there was a touching family atmosphere about the whole venture. This effectively eliminated any barriers there might have been between players and supporters, adding to the refreshing informality of the grounds themselves. Teams and administrators mingled happily together at lunchtimes, and everywhere there were special welcomes and receptions.

The extent of regional interest in the new adventure was emphasised by eight-page pull-outs in local newspapers, grounds crawling with TV crews and a membership closed at 6,500 in early July. The county has a vast hinterland, stretching from Middlesbrough to Sunderland and from the industrial Teesside coast right across the Pennines. The players' problem was never going to be attracting spectators to the grounds but finding their own way to them. Within a complex network of wide roads various individuals became lost en route to one of the less familiar clubs like Jesmond, Hartlepool or Gateshead Fell.

Behind the scenes, Durham were quick to avoid the cumbersome infrastructure that has so stifled the advance of the county game. Instead of delegating responsibility to a catalogue of committees, Durham established a limited company controlled by a board of directors. Thankfully, the board did not meddle with team selection, which was exclusively the domain of Cook and David Graveney. Floodlit matches were organised, and leading players like Botham and Jones placed at the disposal of clubs and businesses. And when the new stadium at Chester-le-Street is completed in 1995, Durham will be endowed with the best facilities in the land.

For the participants, the County Championship had become a treadmill, as teams of weary players lurched from one venue to the next along well-worn tracks. Playing for Durham was more like an expedition, taking unfamiliar routes, touring new areas of cricketing enthusiasm. Everywhere there were fresh and not always pleasant discoveries – the biting wind off the moors at Gateshead Fell, the thieves at the Racecourse, Chester-le-Street's shirtfront wicket, the perilous scorers' crow's nest in Stockton's pavilion. At Hartlepool, the backdrop of industrial effluent and petrochemical plants contrasted drastically with the leafy ambience of the ground.

There were players' habits and methods to evaluate too. Paul Parker liked a rigorous pre-match net, while Wayne Larkins preferred to disappear into a corner of the dressing-room in a cloud of nicotine; this seemed to happen less when the match was not sponsored by Benson and Hedges. Some batsmen paced about anxiously if they were due in next, others had to be disturbed from a post-lunch snooze. The wicket-keeper Andy Fothergill had no idea how far back to stand when Botham was bowling. As a convenient departure from the norm, no unnecessary demands were made on the playing staff – they were required to report only an hour before the start rather than be forced to idle away hours completing crosswords, as most sides do. This particularly appeased Botham – not what you could call an early-morning sort of person – and, until injuries materialised, his name on the team sheet provided the ideal launching pad. Not only was his reputation still intact on the field but his mere presence lured an extra throng through the turnstiles. So, even at the end of the season when the team had not won a match for a month, home Sunday games were sold out, and there were ample crowds even on a wet Thursday in Darlington.

The first Championship win, at Cardiff, and the elimination of Middlesex from the NatWest Trophy represented the highlights of the season. Both were wholehearted team efforts and decisive victories. Glamorgan were beaten by an innings as first Larkins and Jones, then Parker, battered the bowling into submission on an unreliable wicket, which was then wickedly exploited by Brown with the new ball. Larkins's innings were regularly entertaining but always fraught with danger; Parker was less exciting but slightly more reliable. This was illustrated in the Middlesex match when, pursuing 260 against a less than fearsome attack, Larkins mis-hooked in the first over and was out for a duck – it was left to Parker and a restrained Botham to engineer victory. That such a fine performance should have been squandered by inept batting in the next round at Leicester was a travesty. On that occasion, Graveney, the captain, looked as downcast as a man can be, while Cook, though dejected, pondered the future of the team, thinking of his five-year-plan like Mao-Tse-Tung.

The long journeys to away matches and the lack of success took their toll on the players, but the extraordinary enthusiasm of the Durham faithful maintained the spirit level. To the sports fanatics of the north-east mere participation in the County Championship is a revelation, and though the end results were disappointing, they were not disheartened. At the conclusion of the last match, many came on to the field to shake each player personally by the hand. "Eet's been a canny first season," they said, "and we canner wait for the next." With the area's record of producing pedigree players, an astute management and the foundations laid in Chester-le-Street for England's first purpose-built Test match arena, there should be plenty more for them to shout about in future. Rome wasn't built in a day, either.

Simon Hughes played for Middlesex from 1980 to 1991 before signing for Durham, where he went to university.

Glamorgan v Durham

At Cardiff, May 14, 15, 16, 1992. Durham won by an innings and 104 runs.   1993

Glamorgan were completely outplayed by Durham, their successors as junior first-class county [the Welsh county had joined the club 71 years earlier], who recorded their first Championship win with a day to spare. The country's leading wicket-taker, Brown, sealed the win with his 20th victim.

Toss: Glamorgan. **Glamorgan 224** (H. Morris 46, M. P. Maynard 88; S. J. E. Brown 3-70, S. P. Hughes 3-51, P. W. Henderson 3-61) **and 193** (P. A. Cottey 112*, C. P. Metson 30; I. T. Botham 3-47, S. J. E. Brown 5-66); **Durham 521-9 dec.** (W. Larkins 143, D. M. Jones 94, P. W. G. Parker 124, I. T. Botham 40, P. W. Henderson 46, Extras 31; R. D. B. Croft 5-105).

Middlesex v Durham   **NatWest Trophy Second Round**
At Uxbridge, July 9, 1992. Durham won by six wickets.   1993

Durham's day ended in delight, but it had begun in dejection when Wood, attempting to deliver the first ball, slipped on the grass and twisted a knee so badly he was forced out of the match. After the umpires had sent for the mower, Durham's rearranged bowling line-up coped well enough. Against his former colleagues, Hughes's nip and pace earned four wickets.

Toss: Durham. **Middlesex 259-8** (60 overs) (M. W. Gatting 57, M. R. Ramprakash 46, J. D. Carr 45, K. R. Brown 44*; S. P. Hughes 4-41); **Durham 260-4** (58.3 overs) (J. D. Glendenen 57, P. W. G. Parker 69, I. T. Botham 63*, Extras 34).

1994 – A New Ground   1995

The first ground in Britain to be specifically designed with Test cricket in mind was opened in 1994 when Durham Second XI played the first of two matches at the new Riverside Ground in Chester-le-Street. Riverside is due to stage seven of Durham's ten first-class fixtures in 1995. The stadium is being built in "modules". The first is a large pavilion, including dressing-rooms, a boardroom, offices, ten hospitality suites and members' facilities. Initially, the ground will have about 7,000 seats (maybe 10,000 with temporary stands). When all five modules plus a South Stand are finished, the ground should hold 20,000

1996 – Keepers of the Wooden Spoon   Tim Wellock, 1997

Durham could scarcely have endured a more disastrous season. Other than the two victories which earned them the Costcutter Cup at Harrogate, their only win against first-class opposition was in a Sunday League match against Essex. Generally they were outplayed in one-day combat even more comprehensively than in the Championship, as their lack of all-rounders and hard-hitting batsmen was exposed. The cutlery drawer began to bulge as the third wooden spoon in five years in the Championship was joined by the first from the Sunday League.

1998 – A YOUNG MAN CALLED HARMISON
Tim Wellock, 1999

Second in the table in early June and 14th at the final curtain represented a season of unprecedented heights for Durham, who had not finished higher than 16th before. They also reached the Benson and Hedges quarter-finals for the first time and earned their first England A stripes through young pace bowlers Melvyn Betts and Steve Harmison.

They would have settled for this at the start of the season, when it was learned that Simon Brown, the spearhead of their attack, had a cruciate ligament injury. But what might have been a devastating blow was hardly felt until late in the season because of the emergence of the lanky 19-year-old Harmison and the improved form and fitness of John Wood, who took 61 Championship wickets.

Harmison, who had previously been hampered by a back injury and spent 1997 playing for Ashington Seconds as a batsman, proved deceptively quick, achieved steep bounce and bowled a deadly yorker. Early on, Harmison was second only to Betts as the country's leading wicket-taker. Betts impressed most in the Championship victory over Middlesex at Lord's, taking nine wickets in the match and hitting a six off Phil Tufnell to clinch a one-wicket win with ten balls remaining. It was quite possibly the highlight of Durham's first-class existence. David Boon [who had assumed the captaincy in 1997] was said to have leapt on to another player's back in the dressing-room. An hour later, he was telling the press: "We should not get carried away by this."

Middlesex v Durham
At Lord's, June 3, 4, 5, 6, 1998. Durham won by one wicket. 1999

Toss: Durham. **Middlesex 335** (J. L. Langer 35, O. A. Shah 47, P. N. Weekes 93*, J. P. Hewitt 53, Extras 34; M. M. Betts 4-83, S. J. Harmison 4-88) **and 216** (M. W. Gatting 66, P. N. Weekes 51*, Extras 30; M. M. Betts 5-52, S. J. Harmison 3-57); **Durham 312** (J. J. B. Lewis 68, M. A. Gough 38, D. C. Boon 68, P. D. Collingwood 66; T. F. Bloomfield 5-98, J. P. Hewitt 3-82) **and 240-9** (M. A. Gough 56, P. D. Collingwood 33; T. F. Bloomfield 3-43, P. C. R. Tufnell 3-89).

1999 – BOON'S HAPPY FINALE
Tim Wellock, 2000

An amazing season for Durham began with snow, plumbed the depths with a NatWest Trophy defeat by Holland, and ended in ecstasy as they secured a place in the first division of the 2000 Championship. It was a happy finale for Boon. "I've enjoyed every moment of my 21 years of first-class cricket, and to end it like this is the icing on the cake," said Boon, but his deadpan demeanour mirrored an inner strength which he imposed on the team.

2003 – The Riverside Rickshaw

Tim Wellock, 2004

Eleven years after becoming a first-class county, Durham achieved one of their most burning ambitions when the Riverside became the eighth English ground to stage a Test match [England v Zimbabwe on June 5, 6 and 7, 2003] and the first newcomer to the list for 101 years.

For the county side, the highlights were a double over Yorkshire, who had never previously lost to Durham in the Championship, a county-record 273 by the Australian Martin Love against Hampshire, and excitement generated for half a season by the world's fastest bowler, Shoaib Akhtar, otherwise known as the "Rawalpindi Express". After his arrival in late June, Shoaib clearly paced himself, prompting one member to call him the "Riverside Rickshaw", but his final statistics were impressive – 34 Championship wickets at 17.05. In the end, Durham finished fourth from bottom in both second divisions, which, in the Championship at least, represented a significant improvement.

2005 – Up, Up, Up North

Tim Wellock, 2006

A promotion double was the stuff of dreams for Durham after finishing bottom of the Championship the previous season. Under the inspirational leadership of their new Australian captain Michael Hussey, they were so swift out of the blocks that it was firmly on the cards by June. They lost momentum in the second half of the season, but still finished as runners-up in both divisions.

For the first time, three men passed 1,000 Championship runs – Hussey, the South African Dale Benkenstein and Paul Collingwood, whose six centuries were also a county record. Liam Plunkett became the first Durham bowler to exceed 50 Championship wickets since Simon Brown in 2000 and was named in England's squad for Pakistan. He finished up making his Test debut at Lahore at he end of November, alongside Collingwood and Steve Harmison, a county contingent that outnumbered anyone else's (Collingwood joked that they were the new Surrey). There was also Gary Pratt, who became a national folk hero for his performances as England's substitute fielder during the Ashes. This was one more source of pride in a proud year.

Leicestershire v Durham

At Leicester, April 13, 14, 15, 2005. Durham won by an innings and 216 runs. 2006

Both counties had new overseas captains, but it was Durham's Australian leader, Mike Hussey, who gave his team their biggest-ever win and their first Championship victory over Leicestershire. On his debut for his third county, he cracked 253 – Durham's second-highest score after Martin Love's 273 in 2003 – to lift his side towards 500. All eyes were on Harmison when Leicestershire batted. Making his first Championship appearance since July 2003, he needed to assure his local supporters that he could shrug off a disappointing winter and regain his reputation as England's star bowler. But he was outshone by 20-year-old Plunkett, who showed both pace and hostility. Leicestershire followed on 400 behind, and crumpled a second time after Maddy fell to the first ball of the third day. This time, Harmison did do most of the damage, inflicting pairs on Gibson and DeFreitas, who had earlier opened Leicestershire's bowling despite a combined age of 75.

Toss: Durham. **Durham 523-8 dec.** (M. E. K. Hussey 253, J. J. B. Lewis 50, G. J. Muchall 82, N. Peng 39; O. D. Gibson 3-121); **Leicestershire 123** (L. E. Plunkett 5-43) **and 184** (J. K. Maunders 50, P. A. Nixon 32; S. J. Harmison 4-30, L. E. Plunkett 3-55).

Essex

1979 – ESSEX'S FIRST TITLE   Nigel Fuller, 1980

Promise gave way to fulfilment as Essex, after 103 years of striving, at last emerged from a barren wilderness to make 1979 a year they will treasure. They did so at the double, following up their Benson and Hedges Cup triumph over Surrey by winning the County Championship. Perhaps "winning" is too simple a word to describe their Championship triumph. Their dominance was such that they finished a staggering 77 points clear of the runners-up, making sure of the title when they were still four matches short of completing their programme

The secret of their success was the shrewd tactical brain of skipper [Keith] Fletcher, allied to magnificent team work. Everyone, without exception, played a major role. On eight occasions, left-arm paceman [John] Lever finished with five or more wickets in an innings. When Essex made their historic trip to Lord's in July for the Benson and Hedges Cup final, one banner proclaimed that "Lever Walked on Water". That's certainly how it must have appeared to opponents during an outstanding June in which he claimed 53 Championship wickets. Lever's high level of performances was probably the major factor in the county's successful quest for honours. McEwan, Denness, Fletcher and Hardie topped the 1,000 mark in all matches. As one has come to accept, McEwan was again the chief contributor with 1,387 runs in first-class matches.

Essex v Surrey   **Benson and Hedges Cup Final**
At Lord's, July 21, 1979. Essex won by 35 runs.   1980

Essex carried off their first trophy since the present county club was formed 103 years earlier. They achieved it in a great match, and with the highest total ever made in a Benson and Hedges final. The main hero was Gooch, whose 120 was the first century scored in eight B&H finals. His innings was one of memorable strokes, including three mighty sixes and 11 fours.

Toss: Surrey. **Essex 290-6** (55 overs) (G. A. Gooch 120, K. S. McEwan 72, K. W. R. Fletcher 34; P. H. L. Wilson 4-56); **Surrey 255** (51.4 overs) (G. P. Howarth 74, R. D. V. Knight 52, G. R. J. Roope 39*; N. Phillip 3-42).

Essex v Leicestershire

At Chelmsford, June 9, 11, 12, 1979. Essex won by 99 runs.   1980

In a match dominated by the seam and swing of Lever, his match haul of 13 for 117 was his best performance with the ball. Denness, stylish and confident, stroked a glorious century on the opening day and received robust support from Smith, whose not out 90 took only 100 minutes. Thanks to Dudleston and Davison, the visitors looked well placed at 178 for three but then Lever made the first of his telling assaults to swing the match in Essex's favour. They finished with a lead of 71, and helped by a quick 46 from Turner and a more resolute contribution from Hardie, left Leicestershire with a target of 253 in 225 minutes. Despite another fine half-century from Davison – he hit one six and 11 fours – they never threatened to reach their objective. Lever removed Tolchard, Clift and Cook in one over and Essex gained victory in the fifth of the final 20 overs.

Toss: Essex. **Essex 303-9** (M. H. Denness 122, B. R. Hardie 30, N. Smith 90*; K. Higgs 5-72,

K. Shuttleworth 3-102) **and 181** (K. S. McEwan 39, B. R. Hardie 40, S. Turner 46; L. B. Taylor 6-61);

Leicestershire 232 (B. Dudleston 48, B. F. Davison 72; J. K. Lever 6-76) **and 153** (B. F. Davison 67;

J. K. Lever 7-41, N. Phillip 3-55).

How Essex Rose to Glory   Tony Lewis, 1980

In 1979 the Essex cricketers defied the club's long history of never winning a first-class competition by carrying off both the Benson and Hedges Cup and the Schweppes County Championship. Their friends were relieved. They had played the part of colourful, quixotic extras for so long; they had presented players of star quality along the 103 years of their first-class involvement and were cheered always by a devoted audience. Yet it looked as if they would dance forever in the shadows.

Old scorecards proved Essex's eccentricity. They could beat the best and lose to the worst. Which side was taken for 721 runs in a day by the 1948 Australians? Why, Essex of course. Which side collapsed against the rampaging Surrey in the fifties, snicked a couple of tail-end runs to escape the follow-on, then proceeded to bowl out Surrey for 119, thus leaving themselves under four hours in which to score 256 to win against the bowling of Bedser, Loader, Lock and Laker? Who would have the impertinence to do that, and win with two wickets to spare? Essex.

If you need an explanation of this Essex instability, though I doubt if it is that simple, you may blame it on the nomadic years. Their cricket was played mostly at Leyton, which was rural in the early part of the century. But when London's eastern suburbs spread, engulfing the County Ground, the Essex circus hit the road and the cricket was shared between nine grounds: Leyton, Southend, Westcliff, Romford, Brentwood, Ilford, Colchester, Clacton and Chelmsford.

On the road with the players went every piece of equipment; hundreds of yards of seven-foot screening with poles, stands, chairs and benches, score-card printing machinery, boundary boards, a heavy roller, marquees and a portable office. . . oh! and later went the famous double-decker buses: one housing the scoreboard and the other the ladies' lavatory.

You can imagine that the Essex administrators, having moved the big top to one of those venues, were keen to stay there as long as possible, and so the pattern of Essex home cricket was often set into weeks. As an opponent, it was always pleasant to find a festival spirit alive in such a week (except perhaps at Westcliff where the pitch was a bit lively), but I can understand how much it damaged the continuity of their own game. Essex, in effect, were always on tour and missed the advantage of playing most of the home matches on one ground.

The modern Essex was set into motion after the Second World War by the benign Tom Pearce. Doug Insole followed with a spell of 11 years as captain, with Trevor Bailey first the assistant-secretary and then secretary. Trevor Bailey recalls how impossible it was for him to separate his administrative and playing pursuits. "It was wonderfully impromptu stuff. I recall a game at Romford when there was a huge crowd and I had to ask the opposing captain if I could leave the field to put on my secretary's hat and attend to the late-comers. I did. I went off and helped shift some tables and found room for the people on top of the tables just in front of the sightscreen. We were always impoverished. No one got turned away."

It was Bailey, in 1965, who attended a dinner to celebrate Worcestershire's Championship. By chance he mentioned to the Warwickshire representatives that the Chelmsford ground was up for sale and that Essex were desperately seeking means of raising the asking price to buy a home of their own. It is history now that Warwickshire's Supporters' Club came up with an interest-free loan. In the year of wonderful achievement in Essex I'll bet there was a glass or two raised in the direction of Edgbaston, because there is no doubt that a settled home pitch brought stability.

Why did Essex win in this particular season, 1979? The truth is, as the old show-biz saying goes, it took them 14 years to become an overnight success. The move ahead began with the purchase of that Chelmsford ground, and then in 1967 the Essex committee turned their attention to the players. Forced to impose on their staff an act of almost savage pruning, they reduced the active strength to 13 and killed off Second XI cricket. Among those kept in regular employment were a number of youngsters still unproven. It says much for the eye which spotted them that Ray East, David Acfield, John Lever, and Stuart Turner survived to bring home the titles 12 years later. Keith Boyce, until hit by injury, played a vital part on the way to success.

There are other observations to be made. First, the fielding standards achieved by Essex have been a delight to watch. The arrival of the John Player League competition on Sundays, in which fielders became expected to throw themselves around for 40 overs, suited this new young team, I carry vivid memories of Keith Boyce racing in from the boundary, picking up and throwing the ball in one stride, leaping in the air after a throw which has not soared above or dipped below the keeper's waistline.

Secondly, it is worth noting the balance of skills which were created then and which have been maintained since. Fast bowling has been imported through Boyce and then Norbert Phillip. A high-class batsman who can gather together large innings with attractive strokes came in part with Bruce Francis of Australia, then

903

more positively with the South Africans Lee Irvine and Ken McEwan.

The spin was initially shared between Robin Hobbs, Ray East and David Acfield. In other counties the presence of a leg-spinner would stand out as a form of obsolete madness; but leg-spinning has long been Essex's personal fetish: Peter Smith, Frank Vigar, Dickie Dodds tweaked a few, Greensmith, Hobbs, of course, and Keith Fletcher. How many have noticed that Ray East is the first left-arm spinner at Essex for 20 years?

I played frequently against Essex in those days of their progress towards the unknown. They had a third quality which shone through even the worst performance: humour. They planned their one-day cricket like a war but played it like a party game. In the first three years of John Player Sunday Cricket, which began in 1969, they came third, fourth and second. The loyal Essex crowds loved it! It was a perfect stage for their fielding acrobatics: for the comic mime of Ray East, for David Acfield's treble forte asides; both playing to their most appreciative audience, John Lever.

With the utmost good sense the elders did not frown. There were noises of disciplinary caution, but those came from Brian Taylor, the captain, and he was a splendid influence on his young charges. "Pulled a muscle, Turner?" I've heard him bark in his sergeant-major's style. "Get in the shower, lad; hot water, rub soap in it. It'll be all right in the morning."

Brian Taylor was a most healthy left-over from another era of personal conduct and principles. In the field he stood Keith Fletcher next to him at slip. Fletcher had played for England and in the Essex side had proved himself a reliable advisor and clever reader of opposing batsmen. Taylor needed this advice and made him the vice-captain in 1971.

Essex had begun their move up the County Championship in 1969 when they reached a respectable sixth place. Their team was clearly designed to compete strongly in any sort of competition and, to bring the tale up to date, they had a couple of narrow misses in 1978: defeat by Somerset in the semi-final of the Gillette cup and second place in the Championship.

In 1979 everything came right. They got off to a flying start in the three-day game and would acknowledge some fortune in the fine weather they experienced in May and early June when other sides were pavilion-bound. By the close they had amassed 281 points to Worcestershire's 204 and Surrey's 192. John Lever had taken 106 wickets at an average of 17.30. Only Derek Underwood, otherwise, had made the hundred-wicket mark.

Yes, everything worked. Experience in the shape of Fletcher and Mike Denness, power from McEwan and Gooch, surprising calm and capability from Brian Hardie, and belligerent assistance along the batting order. Turner and Phillip did the all-round jobs, with Lever, East and Acfield adding the other components.

I met Keith Fletcher at Wimbledon in July. Essex were a long way ahead on points in the Schweppes Championship, but that can be an uneasy race, too. We said, almost together, that as long as Essex continued to force the pace, and get their runs quickly in the first innings, then they would always give themselves time, precious time, which so many captains undervalue. Fletcher proved that to be a good reader of batsmen is more than halfway to being an outstanding captain. Keith himself hated pressure when he batted and knew better than any how to apply it to others. What many would not suspect is that he is a bit of a gambler, too. He had confidence in his side and backed them to win in every one of his decisions.

In so many ways Essex have been the example to others. Club committees who chase their tails trying to win a major competition with a few quick overseas purchases might well contemplate the preparation which went into Essex's great year: all 12 years of it. Players from other counties who looked with scorn on their obvious enjoyment and humour failed to see how much the laughs were underlayed with serious intent.

Now the second team has been rebuilt. And if you see unknowns like Foster, Mason, Lilley, McEvoy and Pringle play, you will appreciate that it may not take Essex quite so long to come again.

1981 – RECOGNITION FOR FLETCHER
Nigel Fuller, 1982

The capture of the John Player League title, just a few days after the news that Keith Fletcher was to captain England on their winter tour of India and Sri Lanka, highlighted a very satisfying season for Essex. Having had to settle for runners-up spot on three previous occasions, Essex could view the Sunday crown as an overdue and richly deserved triumph. Fletcher's appointment was also well deserved. For some considerable time he has been acknowledged as a captain with an astute cricketing brain, and it is that quality, together with his consistency with the bat, that has been responsible for welding Essex into one of the most respected and entertaining sides in the country. For much of the season, the county were also in contention for the County Championship, though in the end they had to settle for fifth – an improvement of three places on the previous summer.

1983 – CHAMPIONS AGAIN
Nigel Fuller, 1984

In carrying off their second County Championship title within the space of five years, Essex demonstrated the ability to come from behind and conquer acute disappointment. The end of July arrived with their character to overcome adversity being questioned. They had managed to lose the Benson and Hedges Cup final against Middlesex by four runs from a position where it had seemed easier to win; they had lost by the same margin and in similar fashion to Kent in the second round of the NatWest Trophy; and they found themselves with considerable ground to make up in the title race. Yet, like worthy champions, they recovered their form and confidence to overtake Middlesex and win the Championship by 16 points.

The summer was a personal triumph for Ken McEwan, who underlined in thrilling style that he is a world-class batsman. He confirmed the point with eight championship centuries and became the first Essex player for 28 years to top 2,000 runs in a season. Yet the key to Essex's Championship success was provided by the resilient and popular Lever. To miss a third of the season and still finish with 106 wickets was a remarkable feat. Norbert Phillip, to, performed with distinction. The West Indian lost his place in mid-season, but when the absence of Lever and

Foster resulted in his recall, he responded magnificently. Foster confirmed his promise and won his first Test cap, and Pringle provided telling support to the seam attack and also produced many useful performances with the bat.

Essex v Worcestershire

At Colchester, August 24, 25, 1983. Essex won by an innings and 58 runs. 1984

McEwan once more underlined his brilliance in becoming the first Essex player to exceed 2,000 runs in a season since D. J. Insole in 1955. He also became the first batsman of the summer to reach this milestone as he plundered two sixes and 25 fours in 288 minutes. Gooch also scored a century, in just over three hours, after Worcestershire, put in, had crumbled against Lever and Phillip. The visitors showed much greater fight in their second innings, owing chiefly to Patel, whose 95 contained two sixes and 14 fours.

Toss: Essex. **Worcestershire 84** (J. K. Lever 4-43, N. Phillip 6-38) **and 271** (D. N. Patel 95, D. J. Humphries 34, J. D. Inchmore 51; J. K. Lever 3-80, N. Phillip 3-69, D. L. Acfield 3-88);

Essex 413-8 dec. (G. A. Gooch 103, K. S. McEwan 189*, S. Turner 30; D. N. Patel 3-99).

1984 – AND AGAIN! Nigel Fuller, 1985

A combination of astute leadership, youth and experience enabled Essex to crown a splendid season with the successful defence of their Championship title and the lifting of the John Player Sunday League. They thus became the first team to achieve this particular double. The Sunday competition was won with some ease. In contrast the race for the Championship proved a real cliff-hanger, being decided by a margin of 14 points from Nottinghamshire on the final day of the season.

The summer provided a golden harvest for Graham Gooch, who performed with a consistency which suggested he was at the height of his powers. Banned from Test cricket, because of his South African visit of a couple of years earlier, he averaged just over 67 and became the first player for eight years to top 2,500 first-class runs in a season. He took a hundred off the West Indian touring team when the two sides met at Chelmsford, and collected a career-best 227 against Derbyshire. Ken McEwan scored over 1,700 runs with his customary flair, and Keith Fletcher embroidered his captaincy by completing 1,000 runs for the 20th time in his career.

Essex v Warwickshire

At Ilford, June 9, 11, 12, 1984. Essex won by 35 runs. 1985

After being asked to follow on 220 runs behind, Essex pulled off a remarkable triumph with nearly ten overs to spare. It was spearheaded by Lever and Pringle, with fine support from Acfield, as the visitors crumbled to 119 after being left a target of 155. Kallicharran, having been forced to retire hurt when one for stitches to his left ear after being hit on the helmet by Foster, returned to score his sixth first-class century of the summer after Warwickshire had won the toss. A combination of conditions which helped the seam bowlers, plus an unpredictable pitch, resulted in Essex's demise in the first innings, but Gooch, Gladwin and McEwan each batted with great fluency second time around.

Toss: Essex. **Warwickshire 334** (T. A. Lloyd 72, A. I. Kallicharran 100, A. M. Ferreira 36, C. M. Old 43; J. K. Lever 5-89) **and 119** (G. W. Humpage 32; J. K. Lever 4-46, D. R. Pringle 4-13); **Essex 114** (B. R. Hardie 30; A. M. Ferreira 4-44, N. Gifford 3-6) **and 374** (G. A. Gooch 54, C. Gladwin 92, K. S. McEwan 97, P. J. Prichard 31, Extras 31; N. Gifford 4-144).

Lancashire v Essex

At Manchester, September 8, 10, 1984. Essex won by ten wickets. 1985

Essex completed an impressive double by winning in two days – a victory which enabled them to retain the Championship, though they had to wait until the following day for the outcome of Nottinghamshire's match against Somerset at Taunton. Prichard completed his maiden century, but the second morning was dominated by McEwan, whose century took 81 minutes with six sixes and 13 fours. Essex, left to score 13 in their second innings, won in the second over of the extra half-hour in poor light. Three minutes later, torrential rain flooded the ground.

Toss: Lancashire. **Lancashire 229** (G. Fowler 63, N. H. Fairbrother 77; D. R. Pringle 4-75) **and 229** (J. Abrahams 31, M. Watkinson 70, C. Maynard 49; J. K. Lever 4-81, R. E. East 3-24); **Essex 446** (G. A. Gooch 70, P. J. Prichard 100, K. W. R. Fletcher 40, K. S. McEwan 132, B. R. Hardie 41; J. Simmons 7-176) **and 14-0.**

1985 – AN UNFORGETTABLE MATCH
Nigel Fuller, 1986

The remarkable Essex success story continued in the rain-soaked summer of 1985 with two more titles to take the number in the last seven seasons to eight. In a dramatic end to the season, they not only retained the John Player Sunday League by defeating Yorkshire in the last match, but also emerged with the NatWest Trophy for the first time in a thrilling clash at Lord's when they beat Nottinghamshire by just one run. Keith Fletcher thus became the first captain to have led a county to the game's four major honours. For good measure, Essex also reached the final of the Benson and Hedges Cup, in which they were forced to admit second best against Leicestershire, and they finished fourth in the Championship.

Essex v Nottinghamshire

NatWest Trophy Final

At Lord's, September 7, 1985. Essex won by one run. 1986

A marvellous match in which Randall all but conjured up an improbable victory for Nottinghamshire, who had seen Gooch and Hardie put on 202, the highest partnership in any Lord's final, after Essex had been put in. Hardie's innings of 110 outshone Gooch's in its vigorous strokeplay, though he needed some luck early on. When Robinson, Rice and Hadlee all went trying to force the pace in Nottinghamshire's reply, Randall was joined by Martindale, appearing in his first one-day match. With 37 required and only three overs left, Essex seemed clear-cut winners. Randall, however, at last began to negotiate most of the strike, improvising to find the gaps, and Pringle bowled the last over to him with 18 needed. To defeat Pringle's leg-stump attack, Randall made room to play on the off side, taking 16 from the first five deliveries so that, remarkably, Nottinghamshire were now only one stroke away from winning. With the last ball, however, Pringle succeeded in tucking Randall up as he again tried to move inside the line, and Prichard plucked down the resulting catch at short mid-wicket.

Essex v Nottinghamshire, 1985

NatWest Trophy Final

At Lord's, September 7, 1985. Result: Essex won by one run.

ESSEX

G. A. Gooch b Pick	91	D. R. Pringle not out		29
B. R. Hardie run out	110	B 1, l-b 3		4
K. S. McEwan not out	46			
		(2 wkts, 60 overs)		280

1-202 2-203

P. J. Prichard, *K. W. R. Fletcher, A. W. Lilley, †D. E. East, S. Turner, I. L. Pont and J. K. Lever did not bat.

Hadlee 12–4–48–0; Cooper 9–3–27–0; Saxelby 12–0–73–0; Rice 7–0–38–0; Pick 8–0–36–1; Hemmings 12–1–54–0.

NOTTINGHAMSHIRE

R. T. Robinson c Hardie b Turner	80	R. J. Hadlee b Pont	22
B. C. Broad run out	64	D. J. R. Martindale not out	20
*C. E. B. Rice c Hardie b Turner	12	L-b 14, n-b 1	15
D. W. Randall c Prichard b Pringle	66	(5 wkts, 60 overs)	279

1-143 2-153 3-173 4-214 5-279

†B. N. French, E. E. Hemmings, R. A. Pick, K. Saxelby and K. E. Cooper did not bat.

Lever 12–2–53–0; Pont 12–0–54–1; Turner 12–1–43–2; Gooch 12–0–47–0; Pringle 12–1–68–1.

Toss won by Nottinghamshire
MAN OF THE MATCH B. R. Hardie

UMPIRES D. J. Constant and B. J. Meyer

1986 – CHILDS' PLAY

Nigel Fuller, 1987

In winning their third County Championship title in four years, Essex overcame problems which would have left many counties struggling in the middle reaches. England selection frequently deprived them of two or three players, and Keith Fletcher and Brian Hardie missed several matches because of injuries. In such times, however, a lack of experience was compensated for by the performances of younger players, notably John Stephenson and Donald Topley. Alan Border, signed to replace Ken McEwan who returned to South Africa in 1985, scored 1,385 runs for a first-class average of nearly 50 before setting off a month ahead of the end of the season to captain Australia in India.

Neil Foster's 105 wickets represented his most successful summer, John Lever took 70 and was recalled to Test cricket at the age of 37, and Derek Pringle again proved his qualities as an all-rounder, his seven for 46 against Yorkshire at Chelmsford and 97 against Kent at Folkestone being important match-winning contributions. But the biggest bonus for Essex was the form of John Childs, the left-arm spinner. In 1985 he took only three Championship wickets at 125 apiece. Last summer he collected 85 at an average of 15.03, four times claiming seven or more wickets in an innings. More than half his wickets were taken in the last seven weeks of the season as Essex, 54 points adrift of the leaders in the first week of August, came through to win the title by 28 points.

Somerset v Essex

At Taunton, August 27, 28, 29, 1986. Essex won by nine runs. 1987

Gooch was able to set a target of 273 in 68 overs. Richards, 94 from 94 balls with three sixes and nine fours, Marks and Botham, who left his sick-bed to hit 41 in 29 balls, made achieving it look a probability. Immediately before Botham's dismissal, 20 runs were needed in 18 overs from the last five wickets, but he disdained the opportunity to win the match in singles and was caught on the boundary, the first of five wickets to fall for ten runs as Essex won the match with a possible 53 balls remaining.

Toss: Essex. **Essex 129** (D. E. East 58*; I. T. Botham 3-77, N. S. Taylor 4-40, C. H. Dredge 3-10) **and 343-7 dec.** (G. A. Gooch 38, P. J. Prichard 38, B. R. Hardie 113*, J. K. Lever 38, D. E. East 41); **Somerset 200** (I. V. A. Richards 53, I. T. Botham 67; J. H. Childs 4-27) **and 263** (I. V. A. Richards 94, V. J. Marks 56, I. T. Botham 41; N. A. Foster 3-79).

1989 – PITCHED BATTLE

Nigel Fuller, 1990

When July dawned with Essex heading the Championship and Refuge Assurance League tables, and looking towards the Benson and Hedges Cup final, it appeared that they were destined for a season of glorious achievement. Instead, even allowing for their winning the Refuge Assurance Cup in their final match, it was to be a summer of discontent. Their Benson and Hedges hopes were dashed at Lord's when Hemmings hit John Lever for a last-ball boundary to give Nottinghamshire victory. And the pain of that defeat was matched only by the bitterness of the players when, after Yorkshire were beaten at Southchurch Park, Southend, ten days later, the TCCB stripped them of 25 Championship points because the pitch was deemed substandard. They felt they were made an example of because they were the front-runners for the title, and their belief that they had played on worse pitches outside Essex, without their opponents being penalised, compounded their anger and frustration. In the event, Essex's loss was Worcestershire's gain. The county champions went on to retain their title by just six points.

Mark Waugh, the replacement for Allan Border, emerged as Essex's leading run-maker with 1,537, including four first-class hundreds. The emergence of several young players, particularly John Stephenson and Nasser Hussain, provided much satisfaction. Derek Pringle was the county's most successful bowler with 89 wickets in the Championship. It is his misfortune to look cumbersome and sometimes uninterested, but he has an intense desire to do well and last summer he succeeded in doing that as he practised the virtues of line and length. Fittingly, the performance of the season was provided by John Lever when he took seven for 48 in Surrey's second innings at Chelmsford in what proved to be his final game for the county. The standing ovation he received after that effort, and the guard of honour afforded him by the visiting players and the umpires when he went out to bat for the last time, were a sincere tribute to his ability as a left-arm seam bowler and to his immense popularity. Lever spent 23 seasons with Essex, in which time he won 21 Test caps, captured 1,722 first-class wickets and claimed another 386, more than any other player, in the Sunday League. He was dubbed the "cricketer's cricketer" and there could be no more glowing accolade.

1991 – IN PRAISE OF DODGY KNEES
Nigel Fuller, 1992

Six victories in their last seven matches carried Essex to their fifth County Championship title in 13 years. Neil Foster was the key figure. He himself admitted to "dodgy knees", and for the last three seasons he had not been alone in wondering whether he could stand up to an arduous campaign. Yet still he managed to conquer the pain and destroy opponents with fast bowling of the highest class. His consistency left Essex members relieved that he was banned from Test cricket for his venture to South Africa early in 1990. Foster's reward was a haul of 102 first-class wickets; it was the second time he had reached three figures. Fittingly, he played a major role in the title-clinching victory over Middlesex, taking ten for 122 in the match.

Salim Malik was another outstanding success. Signed as a replacement for Mark Waugh, the Pakistani confirmed that he was one of the game's most gifted batsmen, with nearly 2,000 first-class runs for a first-class average of just over 73. Gooch scored 1,911 runs for Essex and England with his usual ease and authority, and John Stephenson, Paul Prichard and Nasser Hussain each topped 1,000 without

County champions: Essex, who had never won anything before 1979, have won 14 trophies since, more than any other county in the period covered by this Anthology. At Chelmsford for the last match of 1991, they are led out by five Test players – Graham Gooch, Derek Pringle, Neil Foster, with Nasser Hussain and John Stephenson just behind.

any difficulty. Pringle continued to confound and infuriate. Hardly a year had passed without his international career being written off, but the all-rounder announced yet another comeback with his praiseworthy contributions in the early Tests, before flu ruled him out at The Oval. Yet a mere four fifties and 47 wickets hardly did justice to his talent.

Essex v Middlesex

At Chelmsford, September 17, 18, 19, 1991. Essex won by an innings and 208 runs.   1992

The outcome was never in serious doubt after Middlesex, put in, had capitulated on a pitch that was green but never venomous. The 1990 champions surrendered for the lowest Championship score of the season in 24.3 overs, after which Gooch, at his majestic best, compiled the highest score by an Essex player against Middlesex. Essex secured the Championship shortly after lunch on the third day.

Toss: Essex. **Middlesex 51** (N. A. Foster 4-18, D. R. Pringle 3-25) **and 307** (M. A. Roseberry 99, M. W. Gatting 35, K. R. Brown 59, J. E. Emburey 37; N. A. Foster 6-104); **Essex 566-6 dec.** (G. A. Gooch 259, Salim Malik 80, N. Hussain 57, N. V. Knight 61, Extras 42).

1992 – GOOCH THE ALL-CONQUERING
Nigel Fuller, 1993

Another chapter in the Essex success story was written in 1992 when they won the Championship for the second year running and the sixth time since they broke their duck in 1979. The title was settled at Chelmsford on September 3, with two matches to spare. It had been victory against Hampshire at Bournemouth in June that had given the Essex season lift-off They had looked doomed to a resounding defeat when they followed on and then left Hampshire only 160 to win. But with the tenacity and self-belief that has characterised their play in recent years, Essex fought back to win by 79 runs.

The team were inspired throughout by Gooch and Mark Waugh, who had the highest Championship batting averages in the country. Paul Prichard had his most prolific season, Jonathan Lewis averaged over 46 and Nick Knight started to confirm his promise. Nasser Hussain did not advance his claims for a resumption of his Test career, and was disciplined and dropped for one match following a dressing-room incident at Tunbridge Wells.

1994 – INVINCIBLES NO LONGER
Nigel Fuller, 1995

Essex did not really expect to be the force they had been in recent seasons, after the retirement of Neil Foster and Derek Pringle in 1993. Bowlers of their match-winning qualities are not replaced overnight. What was surprising was the county's failure to score runs consistently and so take some pressure off an attack which lacked the penetration of old. How should one interpret a sixth-place finish in the County Championship is open to debate. Some will argue it represented a minor achievement, given the rebuilding process. Others claim that the overall strength of all the counties leaves much to be desired. Essex certainly seemed flattered to finish just one place off the prize money, but there was nothing flattering about their one-day performances. Their embarrassing ability to snatch defeat from the jaws of victory left them 17th in the Sunday League, and they bowed out of the Benson and Hedges Cup and NatWest Trophy competitions with barely a whimper.

1997 – A GOOCH-LESS WIN
Nigel Fuller, 1998

Two events dominated Essex cricket in 1997. After five years without any kind of title, and 12 without a one-day trophy, Paul Prichard lifted the NatWest Trophy at Lord's in September, a triumph which redeemed their disastrous performance there a year earlier [when Lancashire had dismissed them for 57 to win by 129 runs]. And, for the first time in the club's history, it was a competition won without Graham Gooch. After a miraculous 1996, when he was the leader run-scorer in England, Gooch found it impossible in 1997 to live up to the high standards by which he measured himself. He managed only two half-centuries before announcing in July that he was calling it a day. The only sour note, as far as the county's hierarchy was concerned, was that he chose to tell the *News of the World* first.

Instead of Gooch, Essex's rock was the mighty talent of Stuart Law, who destroyed the Warwickshire attack, including Allan Donald, in the NatWest final, with an unbeaten 80 to claim the match award. In the Championship, Law scored 1,482 runs at 57, including five centuries.

Essex v Warwickshire   NatWest Trophy Final
At Lord's, September 7, 1997. Essex won by nine wickets.   1998

Toss: Essex. **Warwickshire 170-8** (60 overs) (D. P. Ostler 34, D. R. Brown 37; A. P. Cowan 3-29); **Essex 171-1** (26.3 overs) (P. J. Prichard 57, S. G. Law 80*).

1998 – CUP NOT ENOUGH TO SAVE PRICHARD   Nigel Fuller, 1999

A traumatic summer ended with Paul Prichard resigning the captaincy, after the county had finished bottom of the Championship for only the second time. Whether he was given a gentle shove was unclear. Rumours persisted that some senior players were dissatisfied with Prichard's leadership, although the public pronouncement that he wished to concentrate on rediscovering his form and fitness was valid.

Prichard missed seven Championship matches with shin splints, but when he could play scored only 237 runs at an average of 13.16 – horrendous statistics for someone of his talent. Yet he led from the front magnificently as Essex lifted the Benson and Hedges Cup, crushing Leicestershire at Lord's in July. Prichard scored a superb 92 and was named Man of the Match. From then onwards it was all downhill, and the season ended with six successive Championship defeats – the worst sequence in Essex history. Following Prichard's abdication, [Nasser] Hussain found himself at the helm. He is widely acknowledged to possess a shrewd tactical brain, but international calls were expected to keep him away for lengthy spells.

Essex v Leicestershire   Benson and Hedges Cup Final
At Lord's, July 11, 12, 1998. Essex won by 192 runs.   Henry Blofeld, 1999

Essex's crushing victory reflected the topsy-turvy nature of county cricket. Next to bottom of the Championship, but top of the Sunday League, they outplayed Leicestershire, second in the Championship. Essex were lucky with the weather: no sooner had they completed their innings on the first day than the rain came, and Leicestershire – who had won the toss – could not bat until late on Sunday afternoon. By then, the pitch had become ideal for seam bowling. Leicestershire were dismissed inside 28 overs for 76, the lowest total in all 27 [B&H] finals, while Essex's margin of victory was the widest in terms of runs.

Toss: Leicestershire. **Essex 268-7** (50 overs) (P. J. Prichard 92, N. Hussain 88, R. C. Irani 32; A. D. Mullally 3-36); **Leicestershire 76** (27.4 overs) (M. C. Ilott 3-10, A. P. Cowan 3-24).

2001 – LAW AND DISORDER
Nigel Fuller, 2002

It might be an exaggeration to describe 2001 as the most turbulent and disastrous season in Essex's history, but the team was certainly the worst this correspondent has seen in more than 30 years reporting on the club's fortunes. It lacked a collective spirit and quality; the inevitability of its plunge into the depths left members in despair. Two Championship victories explained why Essex occupied last place in Division One. Third last in the Norwich Union League, and failure to make much progress in the Benson and Hedges Cup and Cheltenham & Gloucester Trophy, contributed further to the summer of discontent.

Off the field, the dressing-room was split asunder as Stuart Law accused teammates and management of stabbing him in the back. It was no secret that he and some of his colleagues could hardly utter a civil word to each other. And within days of meeting a delegation of angry supporters, seeking answers to the sad decline, chairman David Acfield resigned, citing pressure of business – but that was fooling no one. He was simply fed up with all the flak. A month or so later, Graham Gooch gave up a blossoming media career to take over as head coach. He succeeded Keith Fletcher, who was to adopt a scouting role.

Predictably, after his verbal blast, Law was not offered a new contract – a sad conclusion to a six-year association, during which he thrilled spectators everywhere with his majestic strokes, while scoring 8,538 first-class runs at 58.88. He was replaced by Zimbabwe's prolific wicket-keeper-batsman Andy Flower. Also shown the door was [off-spinner] Peter Such, after 12 seasons in which he took 573 first-class wickets for the county and won 11 Test caps. Paul Prichard [the former captain] also left.

2005 – DISTANT ECHO OF THE GLORY DAYS
Paul Hiscock, 2006

Thoroughbreds in the totesport League, Essex were more like carthorses in the other competitions. Their storming League season – they secured the title with three matches to go, and finished 14 points clear – came thanks to consistently disciplined performances, the sort of cricket they struggled to produce elsewhere.

In the Championship, Essex kept in touch with the second-division pacemakers for much of the season, but a combination of injury, inconsistency and a new-ball attack lacking a cutting edge ended hopes of promotion. Essex's tally of 36 bowling bonus points was the lowest in either division. The rapid development of two talented 20-year-olds, however, gave cause for satisfaction. The expansive left-hander Alastair Cook gained high praise from the former Essex and England captain Keith Fletcher, who has overseen much of his progress. In September he was named Young Cricketer of the Year, and in November joined the England squad on the tour of Pakistan [he later made a century on his Test debut against India].

Cook hit four Championship hundreds for Essex, though the innings that must really have impressed Fletcher's England namesake, Duncan, came in a non-first-class match: 214 against the Australians. In that game, Cook added 270 for the second wicket with Ravinder Bopara, Essex's second emerging talent, who made 135. Bopara also made a Championship hundred and developed into a useful seamer with the knack of breaking troublesome partnerships.

Glamorgan

1977 – END OF THE WOOLLER ERA

J. H. Morgan, 1978

The year 1977 marked the end of an era in the chequered history of Glamorgan cricket. Only four players remained of the team that won the County Championship ten years previously. Perhaps the biggest wrench was the retirement in November of Wilfred Wooller, who had served the club fearlessly and faithfully for nearly 40 years as player, captain and secretary. In many ways, he was a puzzling personality. Sometimes he gave the impression of being too aggressive. He certainly had forthright views and was never afraid to express them, but there was also a more gentle and kind-hearted side to his character.

If 1977 was the end of an era, it also opened a new and encouraging chapter. The team, under the captaincy of Alan Jones, shook off the trouble which turned the previous season into such a nightmare. Such was the transformation that Glamorgan not only obtained better results in the County Championship but also reached the final of the Gillette Cup [in which they were defeated by Middlesex].

1979 – DIRE DAYS

J. B. G. Thomas, 1980

If 1978 was never an easy summer, then 1979 was a disaster for Glamorgan with failure on and off the field. The season, which ended in disappointment and criticism, was the worst in the history of the club. No win was registered in the County Championship, and although the county had finished bottom of the table on four previous occasions it had never failed to win at least one match. Even in Glamorgan's initial year of entry in the Championship, one win was recorded.

Ten years previously, in 1969, Glamorgan won the Championship under A. R. Lewis, but the appointment of a new captain from outside Wales was not a success. Poor R. N. S. Hobbs, called out of retirement and persuaded to take over the job, tried hard enough but found the task beyond him. He did not bowl a great deal, scored very few runs, and the side slipped away. The senior players were getting older, the younger players lost form. The committee became reluctant to share their troubles and the atmosphere lacked the traditional gaiety of Glamorgan cricket. In the later stages of the season, few spectators attended matches and interest appeared to be fading fast.

1981 - MIANDAD-SHIRE

J. B. G. Thomas, 1982

For Glamorgan, 1981 will be remembered as the year of Javed Miandad [who had joined the county in 1980], a brilliant batsman in a disappointing side. Without him, Glamorgan would have been in dire straits, for as the season progressed the county became a one-man band. Javed broke records galore, with eight hundreds in Championship matches, to pass the seven by Gilbert Parkhouse in 1950, and a tally of 2,083 in all first-class matches.

Essex v Glamorgan

At Colchester, August 29, 31, September 1, 1981. Essex won by 13 runs.   1982

A memorable match ended with Essex clinching victory in the 13th of the final 20 overs. The brilliance of Miandad was responsible for setting up such a thrilling finish, for after the Welsh county had been set 325 in 323 minutes, he hit a magnificent, unbeaten 200 in five and a quarter hours. His effort ended when Lever removed his partners, shortly after taking the new ball. Miandad had earlier displayed his class in Glamorgan's first innings as, with Featherstone, he earned his side a useful lead, despite the excellent bowling of Acfield. However, Essex made light of the 87 runs' deficit, clearing it in only 48 minutes before Gooch, in just under an hour and a half, completed his third century in eight days. Hobbs bowled well against his former county, fully deserving his five wickets in their second innings.

Toss: Essex. **Essex 187** (B. R. Hardie 37, S. Turner 36; M. A. Nash 3-76, S. A. B. Daniels 3-33, R. C. Ontong 4-37) **and 411-9 dec.** (G. A. Gooch 113, B. R. Hardie 114*, A. W. Lilley 88, S. Turner 31, Extras 36; R. C. Ontong 3-102, R. N. S. Hobbs 5-85); **Glamorgan 274** (A. Jones 31, J. A. Hopkins 46, Javed Miandad 81, N. G. Featherstone 59; D. L. Acfield 6-64) **and 311** (Javed Miandad 200*, A. L. Jones 36; J. K. Lever 5-62, D. L. Acfield 3-84).

1985 - SUMMER OF SORROWS

John Billot, 1986

Assorted disappointments illuminated the fortunes – or, more appropriately, misfortunes – of Glamorgan throughout the 1985 season. Javed Miandad suffered a recurrence of a "mystery" back strain that kept him out of the team for most of August. Nevertheless, he scored more runs than any other Glamorgan batsman, and only Younis Ahmed [recruited in 1984] finished above him in the county's averages. Their exploits against the Australians virtually rewrote the record books, the most notable being Javed's 200 not out as the highest Glamorgan innings against a touring team and the highest in a first-class match at Neath. Younis scored 118 in their unbroken stand of 306, the record fourth-wicket partnership. His 177 against Middlesex was the highest innings by a Glamorgan player at Sophia Gardens and the worth of these two Pakistani batsmen was immense.

Rodney Ontong was an outstanding success in his first full season as captain, the development of Hugh Morris as a confident left-handed batsman continued, and then, late in August, came Matthew Maynard, promoted from the second team to see what a 19-year-old could do against Yorkshire at Swansea. It was a memorable day for him. He went from 84 to 102 with three successive hits for six back over he head of the bowler Carrick. There can have been few more remarkable maiden centuries in first-class cricket. He was the youngest Glamorgan century-maker on debut at 19 years and six days.

Glamorgan v Australians
At Neath, July 20, 21, 22, 1985. Drawn.   1986

After a first day of record-breaking exploits by Glamorgan, there were only 95 minutes possible on the Sunday and the final day was washed out. However, the return of first-class cricket to the Gnoll after 12 years saw a multitude of records broken with brilliant strokeplay by Javed Miandad and Younis Ahmed.

Toss: Glamorgan. **Glamorgan 409-3 dec.** (J. A. Hopkins 30, Javed Miandad 200*, Younis Ahmed 118*, Extras 32; M. J. Bennett 3-101); **Australians 105-1** (G. M. Wood 38*, D. M. Wellham 43*).

1990 – RICHARDS LEADS A REVIVAL   Edward Bevan, 1991

It was not a coincidence that the arrival of Viv Richards in Wales led to Glamorgan's most successful season for 20 years, with the club rising from bottom place in the Championship, where they had languished for two years, to eighth position. They also reached the quarter-finals of the Benson and Hedges Cup and NatWest Trophy, and the only major disappointment was in the Sunday League, in which they fell away after a promising start. Richards provided inspiration from the moment he helped his adopted county win their first Benson and Hedges tie by trapping Dermot Reeve of Warwickshire leg-before with the game's final delivery.

Richards' presence brought out the best in others, notably Maynard, who looked a far more disciplined batsman than in previous years. At Northampton in June, the pair hammered the home attack for 227 in 41 overs, which enabled Glamorgan to win with six wickets and nine overs in hand; and in the following game Richards played one of the greatest innings seen at Southampton. Glamorgan, set 364 by Hampshire, looked to be out of contention at 139 for five, but Richards, in partnership with Cowley [a former Hampshire player in his first season in Wales], initiated a remarkable recovery and Glamorgan won with two deliveries to spare.

Richards hit seven Championship hundreds, but even his outstanding deeds were overshadowed by those of Alan Butcher and Hugh Morris, both of whom exceeded 2,000 runs for the season and broke a number of Glamorgan batting records. The two left-handers proved themselves the most consistent opening pair in the country, sharing ten century partnerships, and allied to Butcher's prolific batting was his positive and thoughtful captaincy. For the second successive season he reached 1,000 runs before any other English-born player, and he fully deserved the accolade of becoming one of *Wisden*'s Five Cricketers of the Year. Morris had an outstanding season. His ten hundreds beat by two the previous Glamorgan record, set by Javed Miandad in 1981, and his aggregate of 2,276 runs surpassed by 193 another of Miandad's county records.

Steve Watkin was again Glamorgan's willing workhorse, bowling 767 overs in the first-class games, and while his wickets were more expensive than the previous year, he was again the county's leading wicket-taker. Robert Croft, in his first full season, struck 672 runs at 44.80, including an innings of 91 not out when Glamorgan failed by only two runs to reach an improbable 495 to beat Worcestershire at Abergavenny. He also emerged as an off-spinner of considerable promise. Although Steve James scored almost 1,000 runs in the short Cambridge season, he failed to maintain his form on his return to Glamorgan in July. None the less, he has the ability to succeed, and with Adrian Dale he should be available full time in 1991. Once again Colin Metson's wicket-keeping was of the highest class; yet in spite of his being rated by umpires and players as the best in the country, he was denied a tour with the England teams because of his modest batting.

Hampshire v Glamorgan

At Southampton, June 16, 18, 19, 1990. Glamorgan won by four wickets.   1991

Richards produced a masterpiece of aggression and timing to steer Glamorgan to a second successive Championship victory, successful negotiations between the captains having overcome the weather's earlier interference. Hampshire's first innings had been dominated by a magnificent 153 from Robin Smith off 155 deliveries. When the last hour was called with 112 still required, it seemed Richards might have miscalculated, but a four, six and four in Marshall's last over saw Glamorgan home with two balls to spare. Richards hit five sixes and 17 fours.

Toss: Hampshire. **Hampshire 363-8 dec.** (V. P. Terry 52, C. L. Smith 48, D. I. Gower 41, R. A. Smith 153, M. C. J. Nicholas 30; S. L. Watkin 4-84) **and 71-0 dec.** (C. L. Smith 39*); **Glamorgan 71-1 dec.** (H. Morris 38*) **and 367-6** (A. R. Butcher 51, H. Morris 44, I. V. A. Richards 164*, N. G. Cowley 58).

Glamorgan v Worcestershire

At Abergavenny, July 21, 23, 24, 1990. Drawn.   1991

A remarkable game in which a number of records were broken ended with Glamorgan failing by just two runs to score 495 for victory. On a perfect pitch and a parched outfield, 1,641 runs were scored, a record aggregate for a three-day county match and only nine runs fewer than the record established for a

Championship match by Surrey and Lancashire, over four days, earlier in the season. Hick, the first to hit a double century and century in a match since 1984, became at 24 the youngest batsman to score 50 first-class hundreds, that record having previously been held by Sir Donald Bradman, when 26. During the game, 16 sixes and 249 fours were struck on one of the smallest yet loveliest grounds on the County Championship circuit.

Toss: Glamorgan. **Worcestershire 514-4 dec.** (P. Bent 69, G. A. Hick 252*, D. B. D'Oliveira 121)

and 307-1 dec. (T. S. Curtis 111*, P. Bent 79, G. A. Hick 100*); **Glamorgan 327-5 dec.**

(A. R. Butcher 79, H. Morris 57, P. A. Cottey 100*, I. V. A. Richards 41) **and 493-6**

(A. R. Butcher 130, H. Morris 119, I. V. A. Richards 43, N. G. Cowley 63, R. D. B. Croft 91*;

P. J. Newport 3-87).

1993 – A Trophy at Last

Edward Bevan, 1994

Glamorgan staged a remarkable resurgence in 1993 when, under Hugh Morris's imaginative captaincy, they gained their first trophy since winning the County Championship 24 years before. Their AXA Equity & Law Sunday League triumph was achieved against Kent, the runners-up, in front of a capacity crowd at Canterbury, many of whom had travelled from Wales to witness a memorable and emotional occasion. They finished third in the Championship with nine wins, their highest position since 1970 by far, and also qualified for the semi-final of the NatWest Trophy. Viv Richards, in his final season, topped the club's averages and achieved his ambition of helping his adopted county win a title.

Kent v Glamorgan

AXA Equity & Law League

At Canterbury, September 19, 1993. Glamorgan won by six wickets.

1994

A crowd of 12,000 which began queuing at four in the morning watched the first season of the revamped Sunday League end in the most dramatic and romantic way imaginable. Fate had brought the two top teams together on the final day of the season; destiny ensured that Vivian Richards would round off his magnificent career by taking Glamorgan to their first trophy since 1969, after 23 seasons of often abject failure. Kent, themselves without a trophy since 1978, began the day as favourites: a wash-out would have made them champions on run-rate. But the day was fine enough for Kent to feel emboldened to bat first. With Hooper, the League's leading run-scorer, well set after reaching his ninth fifty, Kent had a chance of a good total despite a slow pitch. However, from 168 for four after 41 overs, Kent lost five wickets for 14 and only the last pair's efforts enabled them to scrape to 200. Glamorgan quickly lost James and struggled to get any runs at all against Igglesden and Ealham, before Dale and Morris eventually began to push ahead. The game was far from won when Richards sauntered to the crease in his familiar gunslinger's manner at 98 for three. He was nowhere near his best and was given an especially hard time by the pacy Anglo-Australian Spencer: he was both hit in the chest and caught off a no-ball. Richards prevailed, however, and an unbroken stand of 60 in ten overs with Cottey gave Glamorgan victory. The winning runs came from a top edge over the wicket-keeper, but by that stage the result was no longer in doubt. Richards marched off punching the air and a heavy night of Welsh celebration began.

Toss: Kent. **Kent 200-9** (50 overs) (M. V. Fleming 44, C. L. Hooper 60; S. L. Watkin 3-33);
Glamorgan 201-4 (47.4 overs) (H. Morris 67, A. Dale 31, I. V. A. Richards 46*, P. A. Cottey 33*).

1997 – WAQAR SPARKS A SURGE
Edward Bevan, 1998

When Steve James struck Graham Rose to the fine-leg boundary at 6.18 on the penultimate evening of the season, Glamorgan started to celebrate their third County Championship title, and their first for 28 years. The tenacity and self-belief which characterised their play throughout the season was present in abundance in that final game at Taunton, where they thoroughly outplayed Somerset. They began it one point ahead of Kent, needing maximum points to make sure of the title. From the moment Matthew Maynard won the toss and inserted the opposition, his team assumed complete control.

After Pakistan Test star Waqar Younis signed a two-year contract, Maynard had described the signing as "probably the best the club has ever made". But although Waqar made a huge impact, Glamorgan's success was a collective effort. The team was complemented by their coach, former Zimbabwe captain Duncan Fletcher, whose efficiency, technique and ability improved the standards of the younger players. Maynard's captaincy was another significant contribution. Not only did he inspire self-belief with his imaginative leadership, he was also prepared to gamble in pursuit of victory.

Waqar, who arrived in April with a foot injury, missed the opening game but then repaid the money invested in him by playing in the remaining 16 and heading the bowling averages with 68 wickets at 22.80. He produced two match-winning performances, against Lancashire and Sussex, taking 15 wickets for 42 in successive innings. Watkin, who for many years had to be both spearhead and workhorse, was rejuvenated by the reduced burden, while Darren Thomas improved greatly to take 50 first-class wickets in a season for the first time. The three-man pace attack was complemented by the spin of Robert Croft and Dean Cosker.

Glamorgan gained 50 batting points, more than any other county, thanks mainly to James, who had a phenomenal season. The dependable Hugh Morris was his perfect opening partner. He started the season with a career-best 233 against Warwickshire, and finished it with 165 against Somerset, his 52nd century for the county, equalling Alan Jones's record. But it proved to have been his final appearance for Glamorgan before he retired, after being appointed the ECB's technical director in succession to Micky Stewart. Fletcher, the coach, also decided against returning in 1998.

Glamorgan v Sussex

At Swansea, June 26, 27, 28, 1997. Glamorgan won by 234 runs.   1998

Glamorgan continued their extraordinary sequence of low-scoring matches and won before lunch on the third day. Since being bowled out themselves for 31 [by Middlesex at Cardiff] two weeks earlier, they had dismissed the opposition in three consecutive innings for a combined total of 172 [Lancashire had been bowled out for 51 at Liverpool, Waqar taking seven for 25]. With damp air and a damp pitch, Waqar was unplayable, and Sussex crumpled to 54 all out. James and Maynard then put on 119 for the third wicket, a remarkable effort given that no one else scored double figures. Maynard left Sussex 302 to win, and they crashed again, this time to Thomas and Croft. For the third successive Saturday afternoon, Glamorgan were able to forget the cricket and watch the Lions on TV.

Toss: Sussex. **Glamorgan 172** (S. P. James 48, A. D. Shaw 34*; R. J. Kirtley 6-60,
M. A. Robinson 3-54) **and 183-9 dec.** (S. P. James 82*, M. P. Maynard 61; M. A. Robinson 4-42);
Sussex 54 (Waqar Younis 8-17) **and 67** (S. D. Thomas 5-24, R. D. B. Croft 3-9).

Somerset v Glamorgan

At Taunton, September 18, 19, 20, 1997. Glamorgan won by ten wickets.   1998

Batting of rare brilliance from their captain, Maynard, and Morris, backed up by pointed seam bowling by Waqar Younis and Thomas, carried Glamorgan to victory and their first County Championship since 1969. They were watched by a crowd of almost 4,000, mostly Welsh. The only disappointment was that thousands more were planning to cross the Severn Bridge on the Sunday, the scheduled last day. In keeping with ancient Welsh tradition, it is possible that in years to come many will claim they really were there. Six members of the 1969 squad were definitely present: Alan and Eifion Jones, Don Shepherd, Peter Walker, Roger Davis and Kevin Lyons.

Glamorgan. **Somerset 252** (R. J. Turner 40, M. N. Lathwell 62, P. D. Bowler 63; Waqar Younis 4-41,
S. L. Watkin 3-61) **and 285** (R. J. Turner 38, M. N. Lathwell 47, G. D. Rose 67, A. R. Caddick 56*;
S. L. Watkin 3-75, S. D. Thomas 5-38); **Glamorgan 527** (H. Morris 165, M. P. Maynard 142,
R. D. B. Croft 86, A. D. Shaw 53*, Extras 35; A. R. Caddick 4-132, B. J. Trott 3-74) **and 11-0.**

1998 – SRI LANKAN SURPRISE   Edward Bevan, 1999

One of the few highlights of a disappointing and injury-ridden summer was Glamorgan's victory over the Sri Lankans at Cardiff in July. The tourists were dismissed for 54 in their first innings and never recovered. It was the only first-class defeat of their tour, Wales doing far better than England [who lost to them at The Oval]. Adrian Dale and Darren Thomas were the destroyers. Thomas, who in Watkin's absence [through injury] became Glamorgan's main bowler, ended his most successful season with 71 wickets and was rewarded with selection for the England A tour.

Toss: Sri Lankans. **Sri Lankans 54** (A. Dale 4-20, S. D. Thomas 4-10) **and 222** (M. S. Atapattu 99, H. P. Tillekeratne 36, U. D. U. Chandana 33; A. Dale 5-25); **Glamorgan 224** (M. P. Maynard 99; M. Muralitharan 5-77, U. D. U. Chandana 4-45) **and 53-5** (M. Muralitharan 5-17).

2000 – SEASIDE SPECTACULAR
Edward Bevan, 2001

At the start of his final season as captain, Matthew Maynard would have settled for an appearance at Lord's in a one-day final and Championship promotion to Division One. Not that promotion looked a possibility at the time of Glamorgan's Benson and Hedges Cup final against Gloucestershire – a joyful occasion for the club and their supporters, in spite of defeat. That was on June 10. They did not register their first Championship win for another three weeks, when Worcestershire were beaten at Swansea, the first of four successive victories that lifted Glamorgan from bottom to the head of the division. From then on, they remained in contention for a place in the top three.

The annual game at Colwyn Bay in August created new batting records, with Glamorgan declaring at 718 for three after being inserted by Sussex. Steve James broke the club's individual record with 309 not out, Glamorgan's first triple hundred, and with [Matthew] Elliott he shared a record opening partnership of 374.

Glamorgan v Sussex
At Colwyn Bay, August 22, 23, 24, 25, 2000. Glamorgan won by an innings and 60 runs.   2001

Toss: Sussex. **Glamorgan 718-3 dec.** (M. T. G. Elliott 177, S. P. James 309*, M. J. Powell 64, M. P. Maynard 67, A. Dale 48*, Extras 53); **Sussex 342** (C. J. Adams 156, U. B. A. Rashid 110; A. G. Wharf 5-68, S. L. Watkin 4-76) **and 316** (C. J. Adams 68, R. S. C. Martin-Jenkins 77, U. B. A. Rashid 54, N. J. Wilton 32*, Extras 37; A. Dale 5-46).

2002 – SUNDAY BEST
Edward Bevan, 2003

Glamorgan's disappointment at failing to gain promotion to Division One of the Championship [they had been relegated in 2001] was tempered by winning the Norwich Union League. As in 1993, when Glamorgan first won the one-day league, the title was sealed at Canterbury where, on the penultimate Sunday of the season, the hordes of travelling support once more gathered under the pavilion at the St Lawrence ground to pay tribute to their team. If the supporters were happy travellers, so were the players: they won every game away from home.

The trophy confirmed the progress Glamorgan had made in the one-day game in 2001, when they claimed the Division Two title, so it was bizarre that, for the second year in a row, they lost every single game in the Benson and Hedges Cup. They also played their part on one of the most astonishing one-day games ever seen. Set a massive 439 to beat Surrey in the fourth round of the C&G Trophy at The Oval, they failed heroically by just ten runs.

Kent v Glamorgan	Norwich Union League
At Canterbury, September 15, 2002. Glamorgan won by four runs.	2003

Glamorgan squeezed the narrow victory which confirmed them as champions. A jubilant Croft led the celebrations after Kent fell agonisingly short of the ten they needed off the last over. Nixon was run out off the first ball, and the last pair could not pinch a win.

Toss: Glamorgan. **Glamorgan 226-7** (45 overs) (M. J. Powell 74, M. P. Maynard 33, A. Dale 43, D. L. Hemp 37; J. C. Tredwell 3-28); **Kent 222-9** (45 overs) (M. A. Ealham 75, P. A. Nixon 49; A. P. Davies 3-37).

2004 – WHITE-BALL WIZARDS

Edward Bevan, 2005

Glamorgan ticked off their main pre-season objectives by returning to the first division of the Championship, after a three-year absence, and by blazing to the one-day League title with such ease that it was all over with three games left. They also reached the semi-finals of the Twenty20 Cup, where they lost out to Leicestershire – the eventual winners. For a side so good at one-day cricket, failing at the third round of the C&G Trophy was a disappointment. This is a tournament Glamorgan have never won in its 42 seasons [under varying names according to the sponsor], but news that it would be played in 2005 with the white ball the team use so well was greeted at Sophia Gardens with interested smiles.

Robert Croft had a memorable year as captain, and as an imaginative leader he made a significant and bold contribution. Matthew Elliott, who over the winter had enjoyed the most prolific season in the history of the Australian domestic competition, came close to maintaining that form, scoring 2,270 runs in all cricket and making a huge impact.

Glamorgan won four Championship games in succession in May and June, but only one match in the second half of the season, at Chelmsford. This, though, will be remembered the longest. Essex piled up 642 in the first innings – and created a world record by losing. Croft, who had become the first Glamorgan bowler to concede more than 200 in an innings, led a spirited effort by the tail: the last three wickets added 301, and Croft reached 125 from No. 9. The golden match was won with a side including ten players nurtured by the club – an ever-rarer occurrence as more and more counties employed more and more foreigners.

Essex v Glamorgan

At Chelmsford, September 2, 3, 4, 5, 2004. Glamorgan won by four wickets. 2005

Toss: Essex. **Essex 642** (A. P. Grayson 57, A. Flower 119, R. C. Irani 164, J. S. Foster 188, G. R. Napier 50; S. P. Jones 4-100, R. D. B. Croft 3-203) **and 165** (A. Flower 48, J. S. Foster 45, J. D. Middlebrook 34; M. L. Lewis 4-39, R. D. B. Croft 4-52); **Glamorgan 587** (M. A. Wallace 42, D. L. Hemp 67, M. J. Powell 31, M. P. Maynard 136, R. D. B. Croft 125, D. S. Harrison 88, Extras 43; Danish Kaneria 5-193) **and 223-6** (D. L. Hemp 83*, M. P. Maynard 32; Danish Kaneria 3-80).

2005 – WELSH LAMBS MAULED
Edward Bevan, 2006

Following promotion in 2004, Glamorgan could scarcely have made a more dismal return to the top division of the Championship. They suffered 14 defeats in 16 Championship games, an even worse record than in their very first season of county cricket in 1921. They beat only Gloucestershire, who finished just above them in the relegation zone. They retained some of their skill in the totesport League, a competition Glamorgan liked to regard as theirs, but never threatened to retain the title, and made no impact in the other one-day competitions.

The team's inexperience was continually exposed. Matthew Maynard retired after a single Championship appearance, having been plucked by Duncan Fletcher to be his right-hand man with England. And, of the two overseas players lined up, Michael Kasprowicz withdrew when picked for the Ashes tour, and a knee injury ended Matthew Elliott's season in early July. Contentiously, Glamorgan decided to replace Kasprowicz with a batsman – the then Indian captain Sourav Ganguly – but only for two months. By the time he left, Elliott had gone, and they played out the last nine weeks without any overseas help. That forced the inclusion of young players before they were ready; five made their Championship debuts.

It was possible to see this as commendable. While other counties scrambled around for short-term advantage, signing anyone who might be deemed to be qualified, the Welsh were doing their utmost for English cricket, by concentrating on bringing on their own players from the Glamorgan Academy. At The Oval the entire team was Welsh, born and bred. But some members felt the team was being neglected because the club was preoccupied with ground development. A £6m plan to transform Sophia Gardens into a Test venue was announced in August as the team went down by ten wickets against Warwickshire. More than 250 members signed a petition questioning priorities.

Gloucestershire

1977 – The Mighty All-Rounder
Graham Russell, 1978

Procter-shire took on a new meaning in 1977. For several years headline writers have found this a convenient way of linking the South African Mike Procter with Gloucestershire; a convenience based on individual performance. Now he was in charge as a captain and while his all-round ability as a player continued to come through he also, importantly, proved himself a leader of men, taking his adopted county into third place in the Championship and to their first success in the Benson & Hedges Cup.

Procter took 109 Championship wickets, backed by Brain with a hard-worked 77. In the Benson & Hedges Cup semi-final at Southampton, Procter – bowling, on his own estimation, faster than at any time in his career – took four wickets in five balls. He dismissed Greenidge and followed with a hat-trick which removed Richards, Jesty and Rice. Gloucestershire went on to win by seven runs. Procter also had a hat-trick against Essex as he went on to pass his 1,000 wickets in this country.

Zaheer, while something like 1,200 runs short of his fantastic season of 1976, still wrote himself into the record books with 205 not out and 108 not out against Sussex at Cheltenham – the third occasion that he had performed a similar feat. For a man carrying a hamstring injury, his season's total of 2,288 runs for an average of 48.68 was formidable.

Hampshire v Gloucestershire
Benson and Hedges Cup Semi-Final
At Southampton, June 22, 1977. Gloucestershire won by seven runs. 1978

Toss: Gloucestershire. **Gloucestershire 180** (54.2 overs) (Sadiq Mohammad 76, A. W. Stovold 46; T. J. Mottram 3-21, M. N. S. Taylor 3-37); **Hampshire 173** (54.3 overs) (D. R. Turner 49, N. G. Cowley 59; M. J. Procter 6-13, B. M. Brain 3-28).

Gloucestershire v Kent
Benson and Hedges Cup Final
At Lord's, July 16, 1977. Gloucestershire won by 64 runs. 1978

Toss: Gloucestershire. **Gloucestershire 237-6** (55 overs) (A. W. Stovold 71, Zaheer Abbas 70); **Kent 173** (47.3 overs) (R. A. Woolmer 64, J. N. Shepherd 55; B. M. Brain 3-9).

1981 – PROCTER RETIRES Geoffrey Wheeler, 1982

Despite the splendour of Zaheer's stroke-making, sadness was the main emotion at the end of a difficult season for Gloucestershire. For 1981 marked the end of the Procter era. Late in July it became clear that a serious knee injury would no longer allow the great South African all-rounder to continue playing for 12 months a year, and with much regret he decided to give up the captaincy and retire from the English game at the age of 34. After playing only seven first-class games during the 1981 season he ended his association with the county he had served in magnificent fashion since 1968.

Zaheer's brilliance lifted spirits, as he became only the third batsman in Gloucestershire history to make a thousand runs in a calendar month, doing so during an unforgettable June in which he scored four of his ten centuries. Chris Broad maintained his progress as an opening batsman, passing 1,000 first-class runs in his second full year.

[David] Graveney, who had the captaincy thrust upon him, responded manfully, getting the best out of a depleted side and improving his own performances at the same time. [John] Childs bowled very well throughout the last eight weeks: his return of nine for 56 against Somerset was not only the best of the season but the best for Gloucestershire since David Graveney's father, Ken, took all ten against Derbyshire in 1949.

1984 – GRAVE FOR GRAVENEY Geoffrey Wheeler, 1985

David Graveney, Gloucestershire's captain, received votes of confidence from both cricket and management committees after the county had finished bottom of the Championship for the first time since 1970. There had been calls for his removal following a disastrous end to a depressing season: five of the last six Championship games were lost, three by an innings, and the team performed as if the end of the summer could not come quickly enough. In the middle of this ruinous run Gloucestershire played Lancashire, their only serious rivals for the wooden spoon, but the win which would have taken them off the bottom of the table was not forthcoming, Lancashire's last pair safely negotiating the final 11 overs. Only Bill Athey among Gloucestershire players featured in the first 50 place in the final national batting and bowling averages.

1985 – RAPID PROGRESS Geoffrey Wheeler, 1986

Gloucestershire's rise from last to third place in the Championship was one of the features of the season. They became one of the most feared bowling sides in the competition, with David Lawrence, Courtney Walsh and Kevin Curran forming perhaps the most formidable pace attack the county has ever fielded. They claimed 213 Championship wickets between them. All the bowlers owed a debt to Jack Russell, a splendid wicket-keeper, neat and tidy even when the ball was coming through at difficult heights. Gloucestershire's cricket was refreshingly challenging, and some opponents found it hard to believe that a team could have undergone such a remarkable change between one year and the next.

Derbyshire v Gloucestershire

At Derby, June 1, 3, 4, 1985. Gloucestershire won by 226 runs. 1986

Toss: Derbyshire. **Gloucestershire 398-3 dec.** (P. W. Romaines 32, C. W. J. Athey 170, P. Bainbridge 151*)
and **291-4 dec.** (A. W. Stovold 112, C. W. J. Athey 58, B. F. Davison 47, P. Bainbridge 36*;
K. J. Barnett 3-84); **Derbyshire 381-5 dec.** (B. J. M. Maher 46, K. J. Barnett 83, B. Roberts 100*,
R. J. Finney 82) and **82** (D. V. Lawrence 5-38, C. A. Walsh 5-44).

1988 – DROPPING THE CAPTAIN
Geoffrey Wheeler, 1989

Near the end of a somewhat disappointing yet far from disastrous season, Gloucestershire shot themselves in the foot when the cricket committee voted to dismiss David Graveney as captain and replace him with Bill Athey. Unfortunately, the decision was made public as Graveney was engaged in taking 14 wickets against Worcestershire in a Championship match at Bristol. The timing of the announcement and the insensitive way it was handled upset not only Graveney, one of the most popular cricketers in the county game, but also the players and many members. It caused at least one potential sponsor to break off negotiations. The selection of Jack Russell and David Lawrence for the Test match against Sri Lanka made them the first Gloucestershire-born players to play for England while on the county staff since 1966.

1989 – THE CAPTAIN DROPS HIMSELF
Geoffrey Wheeler, 1990

The controversial change in the captaincy failed to bring about an improvement in Gloucestershire's fortunes and the season ended with the county cricket committee back to square one when Bill Athey, their choice to succeed David Graveney, resigned after a 12-month tenure "for the benefit of the club". Hopes that Athey would mould the side into a force in the Championship were not realised. He was not even able to lead by personal example, for his batting form was wretched by his own standards. He made one century and failed to reach 1,000 runs for the first time since joining Gloucestershire in 1984.

1990 – TROUBLES COME NOT AS SINGLE SPIES Geoffrey Wheeler, 1991

Gloucestershire finished the season in such good style, winning four of their last nine Championship matches, that in normal circumstances it would have been possible to look forward to 1991 with a degree of optimism. Unhappily, however, the season again ended on a note of discord, following the decision to dispense with the services of Kevin Curran, one of the best all-rounders in the county game. The first official announcement, after some weeks of rumour, said that Curran was leaving by "mutual consent". But a day or two later, Dickie Rossiter, the club chairman, revealed that the decision had been taken because Curran was perceived to be a disruptive influence. Eddie Barlow, coming to the end of his first season of a three-year contract as chief coach, said: "It was a difficult decision, but one we felt had to be made in the interests of the club."

Curran certainly presented impressive playing credentials to potential employers in the two remaining games of the season, with scores of 144 not out, 78 and 101 not out, as well as capturing nine wickets. In the same two games David Graveney, who had said earlier in the season that he would be ending his long association with the county, took 15 wickets. Then, at the end of September, Phil Bainbridge announced his retirement to concentrate on his business interests. These three departures, allied to the near certainty that Courtney Walsh would be touring with the West Indians in 1991, left a daunting task of rebuilding facing Barlow and the captain, Tony Wright, who had joined forces at the start of the summer. [The task was, indeed, daunting: Gloucestershire performed moderately in 1991, and Barlow left as coach without completing the third year of his contract.]

1994 – THE WONDER OF WALSH David Foot, 1995

Gloucestershire, who had been desperate to retain the services of Courtney Walsh, logically and astutely gave him the captaincy. Nothing could have been more felicitous. He grew marvellously into the job, full of enthusiasm, surprising energy – ignore that seemingly languid persona – and with a gentle touch of discipline when it was needed. His players listened to his words, and visibly doted on his deeds.

Although 1994 was hardly a memorable summer for the county, the wise influence of Walsh – allied for the most part to sound tactical judgment – was always apparent. Unlike a number of fellow West Indian Test players, he seldom looked weary and often bowled quite magnificently. He won and nearly won matches for Gloucestershire on his own, taking 89 wickets at an average of 17.24, second only to Curtly Ambrose. But for an injury caused by a car accident, and a brief return to the West Indies to discuss his role and responsibilities as Test captain, he would surely have taken 100 wickets.

Gloucestershire v Somerset

At Bristol, April 28, 29, 30, May 1, 1994. Gloucestershire won by 83 runs.   1995

Gloucestershire followed their win over Somerset at the back-end of 1993 with another unexpected triumph, which was almost wholly due to the bowling of their captain Walsh. His figures of 11 for 143 reflected his enthusiasm for leadership as well as considerable skill – and stamina after an onerous winter in the Caribbean. He achieved pace and lift on a slowish wicket. A back spasm prevented Caddick bowling after the first day. Somerset were forced to recruit a club cricketer from the crowd to act as 12th man; he was forgiven when an over-eager return went for four overthrows.

Toss: Gloucestershire. **Gloucestershire 203** (S. G. Hinks 42, T. H. C. Hancock 33, R. C. Russell 34;
A. R. Caddick 4-40, Mushtaq Ahmed 4-88) **and 284** (S. G. Hinks 68, T. H. C. Hancock 55,
R. C. Russell 66*; Mushtaq Ahmed 4-104); **Somerset 229** (A. N. Hayhurst 49, N. A. Folland 79*,
Extras 30; C. A. Walsh 5-71, A. M. Smith 3-68) **and 175** (G. D. Rose 31, V. P. Clarke 38,
N. A. Mallender 43*; C. A. Walsh 6-72).

1998 – IMPROVING FORTUNES   Graham Russell, 1999

For the second year running, Gloucestershire shaped up as if they might win their first Championship since it took official form in 1890. No county won more games than their 11 but, as so often, they lost their chance in the final weeks. Still, fourth place was three up on 1997.

Gloucestershire debated long whether to go for a top overseas batsman or turn again to the pace and knowledge of Courtney Walsh. They took the right decision: Walsh, arguably the most durable overseas player any county has had in modern times, had a magnificent year. He finished with 106 wickets, the highest return for any county since the Championship was reduced to 17 matches a side in 1993. With the back-up of Mike Smith and a fast-improving Jon Lewis, who bowled himself to his county cap, Gloucestershire took 65 bowling points; no county managed more. For Walsh it was a last hurrah. Negotiations over a new contract broke down acrimoniously in midwinter, and it was clear that the long love affair was over.

Gloucestershire's new coach, John Bracewell, arrived from New Zealand on a two-year contract. Team spirit soared quickly and captain Mark Alleyne, cheery and unflappable, moulded a team largely unfancied outside their own shire into a winning combination.

Behind the stumps, Jack Russell passed another milestone – he has now held more catches for Gloucestershire than anyone else. The season saw the end of fast bowler David Lawrence's attempt to revive his career after his terrible knee injury in New Zealand six years earlier, while former captain Tony Wright announced his retirement and moved into coaching.

Gloucestershire v Surrey

At Cheltenham, July 22, 23, 24, 1998. Gloucestershire won by two wickets. **1999**

Toss: Surrey. **Surrey 297** (J. D. Ratcliffe 38, A. J. Hollioake 112, J. A. Knott 35, Extras 36; C. A. Walsh 3-57,
A. M. Smith 6-66) **and 135** (A. J. Hollioake 30; C. A. Walsh 6-47); **Gloucestershire 167**
(T. H. C. Hancock 37, D. R. Hewson 52, Extras 32; M. P. Bicknell 5-34, Saqlain Mushtaq 4-84)
and 266-8 (R. J. Cunliffe 53, M. G. N. Windows 60, M. C. J. Ball 48*, Extras 46; M. P. Bicknell 3-81,
Saqlain Mushtaq 3-94).

1999 – THE CUPS THAT CHEER

Graham Russell, 2000

Two cups and relegation after finishing bottom of the County Championship made for a strange switchback season. Gloucestershire entered it with some trepidation, twice reached exultant heights at Lord's and then collapsed through exhaustion, mental and physical. An open-bus tour of Bristol and drinks with the Lord Mayor were deserved tributes to Mark Alleyne's side, who brought home silverware for the first time in 22 years. Alleyne's majestic century helped him to lift the Benson and Hedges Super Cup, and his shrewd captaincy led to triumph in the NatWest Trophy.

Gloucestershire v Yorkshire   Benson and Hedges Super Cup

At Lord's, August 1, 1999. Gloucestershire won by 124 runs. **2000**

Toss: Gloucestershire. **Gloucestershire 291-9** (50 overs) (T. H. C. Hancock 35, R. J. Cunliffe 61,
M. W. Alleyne 112; P. M. Hutchison 3-30, C. White 4-51); **Yorkshire 167** (40 overs) (C. White 38;
J. Lewis 3-32, M. C. J. Ball 3-39).

Gloucestershire v Somerset   NatWest Trophy Final

At Lord's, August 29, 1999. Gloucestershire won by 50 runs. **2000**

Toss: Somerset. **Gloucestershire 230-8** (50 overs) (K. J. Barnett 49, T. H. C. Hancock 74,
R. C. Russell 31*; P. W. Jarvis 5-55); **Somerset 180** (45.1 overs) (K. A. Parsons 42, R. J. Turner 51;
I. J. Harvey 3-23, A. M. Smith 3-25, M. W. Alleyne 3-37).

2000 – TROPHY TREBLE

Graham Russell, 2001

A "Trophy" was once a beer that Gloucestershire sold in the club bars, not something they put in the committee-room cabinet. But times have changed at Nevil Road. Two cups in 1999 seemed a feast, but they were simply the *hors d'oeuvre* for 2000 when, in their best summer ever, the county made a unique clean sweep of the three limited-overs competitions, and missed Championship promotion by two points.

Getting to the two Lord's finals was not without scares. They scrambled through the Benson and Hedges qualifying stage after losing the opening tie to Glamorgan, their eventual opponents at Lord's. Eleven days after retaining that title, they looked to have lost their hold on the NatWest Trophy when Worcestershire beat them by three wickets. But a journalist spotted an ineligible player [Kabir Ali, ruled out on arcane technical grounds] in their neighbours' ranks, the ECB decreed a replay, and Gloucestershire lived again, winning by five runs.

A troika of coach John Bracewell, captain Mark Alleyne and veteran Jack Russell moulded the side so that it was always more than the sum of its parts. For the coach, the vital thing was that his team stepped out of the shadow of Courtney Walsh. Bracewell was rewarded with an extended contract and the title of director of cricket, while Alleyne's leadership qualities were again recognised by the England A selectors. Kim Barnett, who turned 40 mid-season, set aside both his years and tendonitis in a knee as he harnessed his experience in the hunt for trophies.

Glamorgan v Gloucestershire

Benson and Hedges Cup Final

At Lord's, June 10, 2000. Gloucestershire won by seven wickets.

2001

Toss: Glamorgan. **Glamorgan 225** (49.3 overs) (M. J. Powell 48, M. P. Maynard 104; I. J. Harvey 5-34); **Gloucestershire 226-3** (46.5 overs) (T. H. C. Hancock 60, K. J. Barnett 39, M. G. N. Windows 53*, M. W. Alleyne 40*).

Gloucestershire v Warwickshire

NatWest Trophy Final

At Lord's, August 26, 27, 2000.
Gloucestershire won by 22 runs (D/L method).

Matthew Hancock, 2001

Rain washed out the scheduled day, truncated the reserve one, and brought Duckworth/Lewis into play for the first time in a Lord's final. It may have made history – doubly so with Gloucestershire winning their fourth successive final – but it was an unsatisfactory and anticlimactic way for the curtain to fall on the NatWest Trophy after 20 years.

Toss: Gloucestershire. **Warwickshire 205-7** (50 overs) (A. F. Giles 60, Extras 34; A. M. Smith 3-18); **Gloucestershire 122-3** (29.4 overs) (K. J. Barnett 45, I. J. Harvey 47).

2003 – VICTORY FOR DAD'S ARMY

Graham Russell, 2004

Some perceived a thickening in the players' waistlines, and the evidence of their birth-dates was incontrovertible. Everyone seemed to agree Gloucestershire were cricket's Dad's Army. The sobriquet amused the dressing-room as they celebrated victory over Worcestershire in the C&G Trophy final. It was their sixth one-day trophy in five years. Given that they also won promotion to Division One of the Championship, finished runners-up in the National League and reached the semi-finals of the Twenty20, they could afford to laugh. They bore all the hallmarks of a mature side knowing exactly what was required of them.

Mark Alleyne, captain for the past seven years, had to cope with personal loss of form in 2003 and eventually moved at least partially upstairs to the job of head coach. The change was precipitated by the departure of John Bracewell, director of cricket and the architect of Gloucestershire's rise to one-day glory, who left to coach New Zealand. He left behind a remarkable record.

Gloucestershire v Worcestershire
C&G Trophy Final

At Lord's, August 30, 2003. Gloucestershire won by seven wickets.
2004

Toss: Gloucestershire. **Worcestershire 149** (46.3 overs) (V. S. Solanki 40); **Gloucestershire 150-3** (20.3 overs) (W. P. C. Weston 46, I. J. Harvey 61).

2004 – GRIM START, GLORIOUS FINISH
Graham Russell, 2005

Gloomy head-shaking turned into smiles as, defying all predictions, Gloucestershire stayed up in the Championship's first division, retained the C&G Trophy, and saw Craig Spearman hit the county's highest score.

Foreboding was understandable after the loss of several significant figures from 2003. John Bracewell, who had seen Gloucestershire to six one-day titles, had left to coach his native New Zealand; of two key overseas players, South Africa's Jonty Rhodes had retired, while Australian Ian Harvey took his considerable one-day skills to Yorkshire. Club captain Mark Alleyne became head coach and Chris Taylor unexpectedly became captain of the first-class side. Jack Russell, that cult figure among wicket-keepers, played three games, agreed an extension to his contract, and was then forced to retire by a chronic back problem.

It was a daunting inheritance for Taylor, whose first match in charge was a seven wicket defeat by Kent. By the end of May, Gloucestershire were in the relegation zones of both first divisions. Even when they turned things round with three Championship wins out of four in June carrying them into second place, the critical view was that they were punching above their weight and they did end up having to fend off relegation. They redeemed a disastrous start to the totesport League – five defeats out of six – by winning five in a row to finish fifth. And an eight-wicket thrashing of Worcestershire in the C&G Trophy final confirmed their status as knockout kings.

Gloucestershire's Championship turnaround was epitomised when Spearman batted himself into history with a county record 341 against Middlesex at Gloucester. He was only the club's third triple-centurion, after W. G. Grace and Wally Hammond. A couple of months later, Spearman took 237 off champions-elect Warwickshire.

Gloucestershire v Middlesex

At Gloucester, June 9, 10, 11, 12, 2004. Gloucestershire won by ten wickets. 2005

At 2.36 on the sunny third afternoon, Craig Spearman pushed through mid-wicket to reach the highest score in Gloucestershire's 135-year first-class history. It was two and a half years after he was lured back to cricket from a planned career in the City and 498 minutes after his epic innings began. Along the way he eclipsed two towering giants: the previous record-holder was W. G. Grace (318 not out against Yorkshire at Cheltenham in 1876); four balls earlier Spearman had passed Hobbs's record for the biggest first-class innings against Middlesex (316 not out for Surrey at Lord's in 1926). "You are talking about the father of cricket as he is known the world over," said Spearman, who admitted targeting Grace's record, "so it is quite something." Even umpire Kitchen shared his pleasure. "Get rid of the old man," he said. "He used to pick the bails up and put them back on the stumps."

Toss: Middlesex. **Middlesex 383** (S. G. Koenig 45, O. A. Shah 34, P. N. Weekes 50,
J. W. M. Dalrymple 49, L. Klusener 63, Extras 45; Shabbir Ahmed 4-96) **and 358** (O. A. Shah 72,
E. C. Joyce 71, P. N. Weekes 53, L. Klusener 68*, Extras 40; J. Lewis 3-36, I. D. Fisher 4-110);
Gloucestershire 695-9 dec. (W. P. C. Weston 85, C. M. Spearman 341, C. G. Taylor 100,
A. P. R. Gidman 51, S. J. Adshead 35*, Extras 51; C. T. Peploe 4-199) **and 47-0.**

Gloucestershire v Worcestershire   C&G Trophy Final

At Lord's, August 28, 2004. Gloucestershire won by eight wickets.   Paul Weaver, 2005

The reprise of the previous year's final was less hopelessly one-sided, but Gloucestershire's victory margin was even wider, and the result not in serious doubt for most of the day. The fact that the teams were the same as in 2003 detracted from the sense of occasion, as did around 7,000 empty seats, and the game maintained the recent anticlimactic pattern of Lord's finals. Those twilight thrillers that made the Gillette Cup and NatWest Trophy finals famous seemed the stuff of nostalgic memory.

Solanki and Leatherdale rescued Worcestershire from the ruins of eight for three, and a late flurry would have given them a competitive total, but they collapsed again. Six wickets fell for 32 runs, with Averis completing a hat-trick, only the second in a domestic cup final, after Ken Higgs for Leicestershire in the 1974 Benson and Hedges. This was one split across two overs, which muted its impact. On a true pitch a total of 236 was unlikely to be enough, and Spearman and Weston put on 141 for Gloucestershire's first wicket to settle the destiny of the trophy. One-day cricket is supposed to be more capricious than the longer game, but when Gloucestershire are involved, matches are often about as balanced as Laurel and Hardy on a see-saw.

Toss: Gloucestershire. **Worcestershire 236-9** (50 overs) (V. S. Solanki 115, D. A. Leatherdale 66;
J. Lewis 3-32, J. M. M. Averis 4-23); **Gloucestershire 237-2** (43.5 overs) (W. P. C. Weston 110*,
C. M. Spearman 70).

2005 – CHEAP AND CHEERLESS

Graham Russell, 2006

Gloucestershire denied that their 2005 policy was "Save the pounds and let the points look after themselves", but there were times during what turned out to be a disastrous campaign when that seemed to be very much the case. With their repurchased Bristol headquarters to run, and doubts over the future scale of their academy, thrift was in the decision-makers' minds. It led to international cricket's bargain basement for the overseas spots, and the signing of two Sri Lankan leg-spinners – Upul Chandana to start with, then Malinga Bandara as his mid-term replacement.

Craig Spearman had domestic troubles and twice took time off, but his form had gone. Phil Weston picked up a rib injury. The malaise was deep, and Gloucestershire made a rapid exit from the C&G Trophy – a competition regarded as their personal fiefdom in recent years. It was clear that the burning intensity in the field that John Bracewell had instilled as coach had gone too.

The low point of a dire Championship campaign came at Trent Bridge, with defeat inside two days, which followed shortly after a 322-run home massacre by Glamorgan, the only side to finish below them in the Division One. There was just one win, and even that was tinged with controversy when Steve Kirby, the fast bowler recruited from Yorkshire, was found guilty of scuffing the ball on the tarmac of a Cardiff car park. An inquiry tapped him on the wrist with a velvet glove, giving him a suspended ban and ordering him to pay £125 costs. There was just one win. The season ended with Mark Alleyne announcing his retirement as a player after 19 years. Earlier in the summer, Chris Taylor had reluctantly departed the captaincy, grumbling that he had been let down by the club's management structure and given little support.

Hampshire

1978 – Farewell to the Legends

Brian Hayward, 1979

The 1978 season set Hampshire a most searching test of character. Barry Richards and Andy Roberts walked out from the county, but the players left behind overcame their traumas, hardened their resolve, and came through with great credit to win the John Player League for the second time in four years

The Sunday success brought deep satisfaction to Richard Gilliat, the captain, his players, and their supporters. There were still five matches to go when Richards and Roberts departed and, without them, many felt the task would be beyond Hampshire. The disenchantment shown by Richards and Roberts did not come as a real surprise. Richards had been out of form since 1977, but before then his contribution had been considerable and this should be remembered; Roberts, however, although invaluable in the one-day game, had only one good season: his first.

Whereas the form and departure of Richards and Roberts bred ill-feeling, the form and behaviour of another Test cricketer, Gordon Greenidge, was exemplary. He remains totally loyal to the county which discovered him as a lad playing in Berkshire. He topped the county's batting averages in both the first-class game and the John Player League, and without question he is now one of the world's great batsmen.

1982 – Marshall Lays Down Law

Brian Hayward, 1983

Hampshire's commitment to positive cricket saw them finish third in the Championship and thus enjoy their best season since 1975. The improvement of 1981 had been meaningful and was further continued with a brand of exciting cricket which produced a series of thrilling finishes and a climb of four places up the table. Without doubt players and supporters would have settled for third place at the start of the season and the team's performance certainly pleased Nick Pocock, an enterprising captain. Yet he was left with a lingering disappointment that Hampshire had not won the Championship.

Hampshire's good performances owed much to the individual achievements of Malcolm Marshall and Trevor Jesty. Marshall, a genuinely fast bowler with a fine, rhythmic action, was the only bowler in the country to take 100 wickets, and his total of 134 wickets broke the record for a 22-match Championship season. He took five or more wickets in an innings 12 times, and his century against Lancashire furnished evidence of his emergence as an all-rounder.

Marshall's hostile and penetrating bowling was undoubtedly the biggest single factor in Hampshire's high finish, but this in no way detracts from the splendid batting of Jesty, who must be considered unlucky not to have been called up for Test duty. He scored centuries against Pakistan and India, and his total of eight hundreds was the most in a season by a Hampshire batsman since Phil Mead collected ten in 1933.

Hampshire v Somerset

At Bournemouth, July 31, August 2, 1982. Hampshire won by ten runs. 1983

Hampshire gained a remarkable win in two days after seemingly facing certain defeat when Somerset needed only 83 for victory. The "Big Birds" ruled the first day: Somerset's Joel Garner and the Red Arrows. A nearby display by the RAF team appeared to upset Hampshire's concentration, but Garner disturbed them even more, at one stage taking six wickets for nine runs in 8.1 overs. Somerset's task of scoring 83 seemed a mere formality, but at 38 for two Jesty came on to take four for eight and, with Marshall bowling throughout, Hampshire took the final wicket off the last ball of the extra ten overs.

Toss: Somerset. **Hampshire 119** (J. Garner 6-23) **and 157** (T. E. Jesty 50; J. Garner 5-57, C. H. Dredge 3-40); **Somerset 194** (J. Garner 40*; M. D. Marshall 3-47, K. S. D. Emery 3-53, T. E. Jesty 4-31) **and 72** (M. D. Marshall 5-37, T. E. Jesty 4-8).

1985 – DROPPING THE TITLE

Brian Hayward, 1986

The 1985 season brought a resurgence to Hampshire cricket [1984 had been disappointing in the absence of their great West Indian duo on Test duty]. They were runners-up in the Championship, third in the Sunday League, and reached the semi-finals of the NatWest Trophy and the quarter-finals of the Benson and Hedges Cup. Much of the credit must go to Mark Nicholas, who was in his first full season as captain. He had taken over in August 1984, when Nick Pocock announced his retirement, and all was not smooth. Trevor Jesty, feeling he should have been offered the job, left to join Surrey; but Nicholas proved Hampshire right in their decision. He led the team with a refreshing keenness and a quickly found maturity.

Hampshire possessed perhaps the most formidable batting line-up in the county game. They were never bowled out twice in a first-class match. This considerable potential was given consistency by Chris Smith, who was the third highest run-getter in the country and the first Hampshire batsman to score 2,000 first-class runs in a season since Barry Richards in 1968. Smith's younger brother, Robin, who qualified as English at the start of the season, confirmed his talent by scoring over 1,500 runs and could well become an international cricketer of some repute.

The return of Malcolm Marshall was vital to Hampshire's bowling. He overcame a succession of slow pitches to take 95 wickets, a performance which his captain described as remarkable. There were notable contributions, too, from the ever willing Tremlett, who was the first bowler in the country to reach the 50 mark, and from Rajesh Maru, the slow left-arm spinner.

But for the weather Hampshire could well have amassed an almost unassailable lead in the Championship by mid-June. However, the weather could not be held totally to blame, for their own lapses in the field cost Hampshire dearly. Middlesex should have been beaten at Bournemouth, where the eventual champions, having been set 265 in 63 overs, stared defeat in the face at 82 for eight, before being helped in saving the match by at least two dropped catches. And in their penultimate Championship fixture of the season, they let slip a total of nine chances in Northamptonshire's two innings.

Hampshire v Northamptonshire

At Southampton, September 11, 12, 13, 1985. Northamptonshire won by one wicket. 1986

This was a vital game in Hampshire's bid for the Championship, and although it went to the last ball, their failure to win could be attributed to poor catching. With Greenidge in fine form, Hampshire were able to gain maximum batting points before making early inroads into the Northamptonshire batting. Marshall took three wickets in five balls to reduce Northamptonshire to 30 for four, and half the side were out for 61. But Hampshire put down five catches, and Cook, Capel and Harper changed the complexion of the game. Hampshire's second-innings declaration set a target of 241 in 55 overs and in a tense finish Harper hit the last ball, bowled by Maru, for six. His unbeaten 27 was made off only 15 balls and contained four sixes. Earlier, Lamb's 60 had kept Northamptonshire in the hunt, although at nine and at 38 he survived chances.

Toss: Northamptonshire. **Hampshire 300-8 dec.** (C. G. Greenidge 143, M. C. J. Nicholas 33;
B. J. Griffiths 4-64) **and 244-4 dec.** (C. G. Greenidge 68, R. A. Smith 55*, M. D. Marshall 66*);
Northamptonshire 304 (G. Cook 73, D. J. Capel 81, R. A. Harper 76; M. D. Marshall 4-75,
T. M. Tremlett 4-53) **and 241-9** (G. Cook 36, W. Larkins 48, A. J. Lamb 60; R. J. Maru 5-114).

1986 – Sunday Consolation

Brian Hayward, 1987

Hampshire's winning of the John Player League for the third time was a deserved success in a season which was tinged with the disappointment of the team's failure to play to full potential in the other major competitions. Having finished second in the Championship the previous season, the county had entertained high expectations of challenging for the season's premier title, but these were not always matched by performance and they finished sixth.

Hampshire were splendidly served by Gordon Greenidge and Malcolm Marshall. Greenidge, whose aggregate of runs in the first-class game, 2,035, was the highest by a Hampshire player since B. A. Richards's 2,395 in 1968, topped the national batting averages, and Marshall, taking 100 wickets for the second time, led the bowling to give the county a first-time double.

1988 – It's a Knockout
Victor Isaacs, 1989

In Hampshire, 1988 will be remembered as the year when they at last rid themselves of the tag of being the only county not to have appeared in a Lord's final. Moreover, it was the year in which they won their first knockout trophy, for on their first visit to Lord's they beat Derbyshire by seven wickets to lift the Benson and Hedges Cup. Their South African opening bowler, Steve Jefferies, had set up the victory with a return of five for 13, the best figures in a Lord's final. A month later, Hampshire could have made it two finals in the same season but went down by 29 runs in the NatWest Trophy semi-finals to Worcestershire, the county they had beaten in the quarter-finals of the Benson and Hedges Cup.

However, Hampshire's successful season in the two knockout competitions contrasted with their performances in the Championship, in which they finished 15th, their lowest placing since 1984 when, as last season, they were without Gordon Greenidge and Malcolm Marshall.

Derbyshire v Hampshire   **Benson and Hedges Cup Final**
At Lord's, July 9, 1988. Hampshire won by seven wickets.   1989

Toss: Hampshire. **Derbyshire** 117 (46.3 overs) (J. E. Morris 42; S. T. Jefferies 5-13); **Hampshire** 118-3 (31.5 overs) (M. C. J. Nicholas 35*, R. A. Smith 38).

1991 – Triumph in the Face of Adversity
Mike Neasom, 1992

Winning the NatWest Trophy at Lord's made the summer of 1991 one of fond memories for Hampshire supporters. The build-up to Lord's was hardly propitious. Chris Smith, the centrepiece of their batting, had retired [mid-season] to become marketing manager of the Western Australian Cricket Association, and a quirk of the fixture list took Hampshire to The Oval to face their fellow finalists, Surrey, immediately before the encounter at Lord's. The Championship match lasted until noon on the third of the four days: Waqar Younis destroyed their batting – and kept their captain, Mark Nicholas, out of the final by breaking the little finger of his left hand. [Hampshire were captained at Lord's by David Gower, who had joined the county from Leicestershire in 1990.] But while Surrey inevitably went to Lord's as favourites, once again the odds were mocked. Hampshire restricted their opponents to 240, and the scourge of Waqar Younis was denied, though in the end it was perilously close. Two balls remained when Jon Ayling hit the winning boundary, after Tony Middleton's solid foundation had filled the gap left by Chris Smith, and Robin Smith had provided much-needed acceleration.

Hampshire v Surrey	**NatWest Trophy Final**

At Lord's, September 7, 1991. Hampshire won by four wickets. 1992

Toss: Hampshire. **Surrey 240-5** (60 overs) (A. J. Stewart 61, G. P. Thorpe 93, D. M. Ward 43; C. A. Connor 3-39); **Hampshire 243-6** (59.4 overs) (V. P. Terry 32, T. C. Middleton 78, R. A. Smith 78).

1992 – A TROPHY... THEN A COLLAPSE   Mike Neasom, 1993

Hampshire won the Benson and Hedges Cup and finished third in the Sunday League, a record that would have provided enough of a glow to keep the members of most counties warm all winter. Most Hampshire members felt a chill instead. Unfortunately, the Cup final came in mid-July when Hampshire were lying second in the Championship. It was the two months after that which will linger in the memory: Hampshire failed to win another Championship match and collapsed to 15th in the final table.

Even the triumph at Lord's itself – convincing and well-executed though it was – was something of an anticlimax. The weather forced the match into a second day and by the time Mark Nicholas received the trophy the ground was half-empty. By then, it was already possible to discern the signs of a collapse in the form of what Nicholas regarded as the strongest and best-balanced squad he had led in his eight years as captain.

Robin Smith's appearances were inevitably restricted by Test matches, but when he did play he had his least successful season in county cricket. David Gower's early-season form ensured that he won back his England place; after that he seemed to lose his appetite for humdrum occasions and he failed to score a fifty in his last 12 Championship innings. The unluckiest player was Paul Terry, who looked in his best form since he was picked for England in 1984 but suffered a dislocated thumb against Surrey and then had his season prematurely terminated by an attack of sciatica.

Hampshire's attack was also inconsistent. Marshall bowled as enthusiastically as ever but, at 34, his figures became a little more mundane: only 49 Championship wickets from 529 overs at 27.51. The most encouraging progress was made by Shaun Udal, who won the opening match against Sussex by taking eight for 50 and passed a hundred wickets in all competitions; he was especially effective in one-day cricket.

In September, Hampshire announced that Bobby Parks, the most successful wicket-keeper in the county's history, had no further part in their plans. He had already lost his first-team place in 1990. However, a knee injury to his successor Adrian Aymes in June enabled him to return to the team for five games when he took the opportunity, which he feared he would miss, to beat Neil McCorkell's Hampshire record of 688 dismissals. Parks finished with exactly 700. Another, even longer-lasting era came to an end in August after the Middlesex match, when Hampshire left Dean Park, Bournemouth for economic reasons. First-class cricket has now ceased on one of the best-loved grounds on the circuit and one deeply embedded in the soul of Hampshire cricket.

Hampshire v Kent   **Benson and Hedges Cup Final**
At Lord's, July 11, 12, 1992. Hampshire won by 41 runs.   1993

Toss: Kent. **Hampshire 253-5** (55 overs) (V. P. Terry 41, R. A. Smith 90); **Kent 212** (52.3 overs)
(M. R. Benson 59, M. V. Fleming 32; M. D. Marshall 3-33, S. D. Udal 3-67).

1994 – END OF THE MARSHALL ERA   Mike Neasom, 1995

It was never going to be an easy season for Hampshire – and for much of it, that seemed like an understatement. The retirement of David Gower, even the Gower who had generally underachieved in his four years with the county, and the departure of the legendary Malcolm Marshall made it inevitable that it would be a summer of retrenchment. In fact, it was rather worse than that: Gower's departure left an upper-order gap which was hard to fill and the man brought in to succeed Marshall, Winston Benjamin, did not come off.

1996 – JAMES' SOLO ROLE   Mike Neasom, 1997

Transition can be painful, and Hampshire were in the midst of transition. Under a new captain, John Stephenson [the long-serving Mark Nicholas had stepped down the previous season], and a new coach, their former star bowler Malcolm Marshall, they slipped one place down the Championship table, winning just three games to finish 14th. They climbed three places from the foot of the Sunday League, while neither knockout competition held much satisfaction. Yet the summer was lifted out of the mundane by an individual performance by Kevan James, who entered cricket's record books with a unique match double.

His previous claim to fame had been his six for 22 to dismiss the 1985 Australians for 76. This time it was the Indians who got the James treatment. On a sunny afternoon in June, they had eased to an impressive 207 for one. Seven minutes later, it was 207 for five. In four deliveries, left-arm seamer James removed Rathore, Tendulkar, Dravid and Manjrekar – the first four in four in Hampshire's history. Next day, James completed a century, and a place in cricket's hall of fame was his.

Hampshire v Indians

At Southampton, June 29, 30, July 1, 1996. Drawn.   1997

Toss: Hampshire. **Indians 362-5 dec.** (A. D. Jadeja 91, V. Rathore 95, S. C. Ganguly 100*,
A. Kumble 59*; K. D. James 5-74); **Hampshire 458-9** (J. S. Laney 100, K. D. James 103,
M. Keech 36, M. J. Thursfield 37*, S. M. Milburn 54*, Extras 57; S. A. Ankola 4-120).

1999 – EARLY WARNE-ING   Pat Symes, 2000

Hampshire's season grabbed the headlines in the last week of what had been a
largely unspectacular summer. While the team were ensuring a place in the first
division of the County Championship for 2000, with a two-run win at Derby so
controversial it sparked an unsuccessful complaint from Warwickshire about collusion, an announcement was made which stopped the entire cricket world in its
tracks. Hampshire had signed Shane Warne.

The club said it was the largest contract ever awarded over a single season by
a county: estimates of £150,000 for one summer's work were not denied. Soon
afterwards, there was confirmation of another big-money signing in Alan Mullally,
Leicestershire's Test bowler (there were also rumours about Andrew Flintoff, ended
when he came to terms with Lancashire), while the club began the task of building
a side worthy of the new stadium taking shape on the northern outskirts of
Southampton. Hampshire were to vacate the County Ground, their home for more
than a century, at the end of 2000, when Nigel Gray's square – much-loved (especially by batsmen) – would disappear under housing.

2000 – THE REVOLUTION STARTS HERE   Pat Symes, 2001

Hampshire have not had many seasons, if any, quite as revolutionary or extraordinary as the one they experienced in 2000. From the moment Shane Warne
touched down in the dawn of a wet April morning – to unprecedented publicity
as the club's overseas player – through to the emotion-charged last days at
Northlands Road in the gloom of a September evening, this was a summer never
to be forgotten.

On the field, little went right, in spite of Warne's presence and the international-
calibre bowling of Alan Mullally. Off the field, it was a case of bidding farewell to
the comfort of three familiar old grounds as Hampshire prepared to move to the
new £17m stadium taking shape, somewhat slowly, on farmland at West End on the
eastern outskirts of Southampton.

Warne enjoyed his county season, taking 109 wickets in all cricket, and said
he would like to return in 2002. He responded to the sympathetic handling of the
captain, Robin Smith, with a willingness to bowl beyond the call of duty. The
other Hampshire players, once they overcame being star-struck, responded positively to him, and the fielding was better than for some years.

Warne and Mullally accounted for half the club's Championship wickets, and with only Yorkshire matching Hampshire's achievement of maximum bowling bonus points in every match, the bowling was not the problem. The batting was. There was no doubting the talent available to new coach Jimmy Cook, but the application left much to be desired. Some of their performances were abject, devoid of confidence and resolution, and the trail of supine collapses left the bowlers little scope to force a winning position.

2001 – MILLIONAIRE TO THE RESCUE

Pat Symes, 2002

Hampshire moved into their spacious new headquarters at the Rose Bowl to high expectations, but only after an acrimonious and difficult winter during which the club's survival came under threat more than once. The projected cost of the stadium rose beyond the budgeted £17m to nearer £25m, and the prospect of bankruptcy was staved off only by the timely intervention of Rod Bransgrove, a multi-millionaire entrepreneur. Bransgrove was elected chairman without opposition in March, after he had volunteered vital financial support, and his control was completed at an EGM two months later, when members voted to turn the club into a private limited company. Bransgrove himself underwrote the first £4m of a share issue.

It was against this turbulent background that first-class cricket was staged for the first time in the still uncompleted stadium, in front of woodland and fields and surrounded by a collection of Portakabins and temporary marquees. After nine months of uncompromising rain, groundsman Nigel Gray had performed miracles in fashioning a cricket square from mud, puddles and high grass. His new pitches were a source of concern at times, with some lateral movement, swing and uneven bounce; four Championship matches failed to go beyond three days. Life could be hard for opening batsmen, but Hampshire were never docked points, and official criticism was levelled not at the pitches but those who batted on them. In December, the ECB announced that the Rose Bowl would stage one-day international cricket from 2004. Hampshire made new-home advantage count by winning five games and losing none at the Rose Bowl, where visiting teams often struggled to cope with alien conditions.

Hampshire v Worcestershire

At Southampton, May 9, 10, 11, 2001. Hampshire won by 124 runs.   2002

Hampshire celebrated the inaugural first-class match at their new headquarters with a confidence-boosting victory. Despite a three-day finish, the umpires praised the quality of Nigel Gray's pitch, blaming instead poor batting technique for the 20 wickets that fell on the last day. On the first day, Mascarenhas rescued Hampshire from 79 for six, hitting 18 fours in the second hundred of his county career. Hick responded in kind, making the Rose Bowl the 44th ground on which he had reached three figures. in the process, he overtook

Allan Lamb's first-class aggregate of 32,502 to become the highest African-born run-scorer.

Toss: Hampshire. **Hampshire 309** (J. P. Stephenson 51, A. D. Mascarenhas 104, A. C. Morris 32, Extras 43; A. Sheriyar 4-85, S. R. Lampitt 3-45) **and 159** (D. A. Kenway 30, A. N. Aymes 37*; A. Sheriyar 4-30); **Worcestershire 236** (G. A. Hick 120, D. A. Leatherdale 34, Extras 31; A. C. Morris 4-39) **and 108** (A. Singh 33, A. J. Bichel 30; A. C. Morris 4-27, S. D. Udal 4-32).

2004 – WARNE THE TALISMAN   Pat Symes, 2005

This was Hampshire's best year in terms of results since they left the old county ground in 2000. While one man does not make a team, Shane Warne came close. Chairman Rod Bransgrove fought with determination to persuade Warne to return as captain, talisman and master tactician, and Warne lit up Hampshire cricket as no man since Malcolm Marshall in his prime.

After his year's suspension, the great leg-spinner approached the task of raising the club's playing profile with a gusto and depth of involvement which inspired consistent underperformers by exuberant example, and his reward was much-improved results in all competitions. While his 51 wickets in 12 Championship matches may not have been exceptional, his fierce desire to win every game and his sharp tactical acumen were major factors in Hampshire's success. His mere presence was often enough.

The highlight of an efficient campaign, in which coach Paul Terry was an astute and thoughtful foil for the captain, was a remarkable victory at Taunton where Somerset, chasing 351, were 300 for three until Warne got among them. The low point was a crushing home defeat by Essex, the 384-run margin Hampshire's biggest-ever in terms of runs.

2005 – GLITZVILLE-ON-SOLENT   Pat Symes, 2006

Hampshire had their most successful summer in at least 20 years, finishing second in the Championship and winning the C&G Trophy. They also continued their metamorphosis from Happy Hampshire into domestic cricket's most fashionable, glamorous county. They regularly supplied players to international squads and the Rose Bowl's distinctive architecture became a familiar sight on television. Hampshire may have moved just five miles from Northlands Road, but in other respects they have come a long way in a short time.

As September began, it looked as if Hampshire would win the Championship for the first time since 1973. Then a controversial deal between David Fulton, the Kent captain, and Nottinghamshire's Stephen Fleming took the matter out of Hampshire's hands after Kent lost. Warne reacted fiercely, accusing Fulton of bringing the game into disrepute. The ECB was unmoved. It was especially frustrating for Hampshire, who twice beat Nottinghamshire inside three playing days.

Hampshire v Warwickshire

At Lord's, September 3, 2005. Hampshire won by 18 runs.

C&G Trophy Final

Paul Weaver

County cricket's big day out enjoyed a revival after the poor crowds and worse matches of previous years. Perhaps it was the Ashes effect. Or it might have been because Hampshire had not been to a Lord's final since 2000. Either way, both counties enjoyed good support, and the frisson of anticipation among the near-full house evoked memories of epic end-of-season finals from the tournament's golden years. The game did not match some of the grand old Gillette climaxes, but provided a good spectacle on a delightful summer's day. The day belonged to the overseas allsorts that make Hampshire resemble a latterday version of the International Cavaliers: only three of their players – Crawley, Tremlett and Udal – were born and raised in England. It was one of their ready-baked imports, Ervine, who played the match-winning innings, while another, Watson, produced a telling all-round display. Knight made 118 for Warwickshire but had no support as Hampshire's brace of all-rounders, Watson and Bichel, swept through the side. In the end, they won with some comfort. It made for a sad end to Knight's time as captain, John Inverarity's as coach and Dennis Amiss's as chief executive. For Hampshire, though, it seemed to be the first triumph of an era of resurgence.

Toss: Warwickshire. **Hampshire 290** (50 overs) (N. Pothas 68, S. M. Ervine 104; N. M. Carter 5-66, I. J. L. Trott 3-35); **Warwickshire 272** (49.2 overs) (N. M. Carter 32, N. V. Knight 118, I. R. Bell 54; A. J. Bichel 3-57, S. R. Watson 3-34).

Kent

Dudley Moore, 1978

Kent had to wait until the very last day of the season to know that they had won something – a shared County Championship with Middlesex – and so yet again they had overcome successfully all the problems that face them annually. Certainly it was compensation for their defeat in the Benson and Hedges final, their exit at the first hurdle in the Gillette Cup and a less prominent summer than usual in the John Player League.

With Luckhurst and [Colin] Cowdrey retired and Denness having moved to Essex, there was a heavy responsibility on the new captain Asif. He took it all in his stride and his personal form never suffered. He scored runs consistently, and as always entertainingly, in all competitions and his younger players developed well as the season progressed. They all received their chances because Kent were continually hit by Test calls. Knott and Underwood were always certainties for the series against Australia, and Woolmer's early form – three centuries for the county in five innings – booked his place in the England side.

In a season in which all-round team work counted for so much, it was still very justifiable to pick out one man who did so much – and that was the West Indian all-rounder [John] Shepherd. He got useful runs at the right time – he virtually batted Middlesex on his own in the Gillette Cup, hitting a magnificent century – but his seam bowling will be remembered most in 1977. How he bowled – so well and for such long spells throughout the summer. In one match he sent down 77 overs and in eight other games he bowled more than 40 overs in a match. On six occasions he took five wickets in an innings and surely would have crowned such a fine season by taking 100 wickets had it not been for a dreadful rain-soaked spell in August.

Kent v Essex
At Folkestone, July 20, 21, 22, 1977. Kent won by one wicket.   1978

Kent had to make 184 to win in two and three-quarter hours on a wicket which helped the bowlers all day. Ealham hit 50 in an hour with two sixes and four fours, and Kent seemed assured of victory, needing 16 off the last five overs with six wickets in hand. Yet five wickets fell, four of them for three runs, and Kent scrambled home in the last over.

Toss: Essex. **Essex 322-4** (M. H. Denness 59, M. K. Fosh 66, K. S. McEwan 92, K. W. R. Fletcher 42, G. A. Gooch 32*; J. N. Shepherd 3-117) **and 150** (K. R. Pont 40; J. N. Shepherd 4-44, D. L. Underwood 4-22); **Kent 289** (G. S. Clinton 57, Asif Iqbal 90; J. K. Lever 3-57, D. L. Acfield 3-38) **and 184-9** (R. A. Woolmer 48, Asif Iqbal 30, A. G. E. Ealham 54; R. E. East 5-75).

1978 – OUTRIGHT CHAMPIONS
Dudley Moore, 1979

Kent had a truly wonderful season. They won the County Championship outright and compensated for the 1977 disappointment of losing in the final of the Benson and Hedges Cup by lifting the trophy for the third time in six years. It was a dream first season as captain for [Alan] Ealham, who had been appointed to the task only a fortnight before the campaign started against a background of controversy surrounding the future of the four Packer players – Asif, the previous captain, Underwood, Woolmer and Knott. In the event, all but Knott played, and two days before the Benson and Hedges Cup final the county announced that their Packer players would, after all, be retained at the end of the season, instead of being released as had been the intention.

For the first time in many years, Kent were not handicapped by continual Test calls on their key players, either by England or countries touring here. The situation was exploited to the full. Underwood, with pitches regularly to his liking, took more than 100 wickets for the county for the first time since 1967. Woolmer scored more than 1,000 runs, while [Chris] Tavaré, in his first full season with the county, quickly established himself in the number three position and became the county's leading run-getter.

[Paul] Downton, also in his first full season, sustained his high promise behind the stumps, but for the next two seasons he will probably be spending the first half of the season continuing his law studies at university. However, as Kent and Knott, who mutually agreed that the former England wicket-keeper would not play in 1978, have amicably agreed that he should reappear at least in the first half of the season, the problem of Downton's absence appears to be solved.

Surrey v Kent
At The Oval, June 28, 29, 30, 1978. Kent won by an innings and 102 runs. 1979

Surrey fell foul of the best wet-wicket bowler in the world, Underwood, who returned the first nine-wicket haul of the season, for 32 runs, and took 13 for 49 in the two innings as Surrey were shot out for 95 in 50.5 overs and 75 in 39.2. Surrey lost 18 wickets for 140 runs in four hours 20 minutes on the final day after the second had been almost washed out by rain.

Toss: Kent. **Kent 272-8** (R. A. Woolmer 30, C. J. Tavaré 64, A. G. E. Ealham 58, G. W. Johnson 45; R. D. V. Knight 3-45); **Surrey 95** (D. L. Underwood 4-17, G. W. Johnson 4-22) **and 75** (D. L. Underwood 9-32).

Derbyshire v Kent   **Benson and Hedges Cup Final**
At Lord's, July 22, 1978. Kent won by six wickets.   1979

It proved a one-sided contest after Barlow had won the toss and decided to bat. Derbyshire struggled for runs before a full house of 24,000 and made only 60 from the first 30 overs.

Toss: Derbyshire. **Derbyshire 147** (54.4 overs) (P. N. Kirsten 41, G. Miller 38; J. N. Shepherd 4-25);
Kent 151-4 (41.4 overs) (R. A. Woolmer 79; P. E. Russell 3-28).

1980 – A TEAM IN DECLINE
Dudley Moore, 1981

For an unseemly length of time after the end of the 1980 season, the record book was being investigated to reveal how long it had been since Kent had endured such an unsuccessful summer. It was found to be 1956, this being the last time they had finished 16th in the Championship; but not since 1897 had they won only two Championship matches.

They slumped also to a worst-ever 11th position in the John Player League table, fell at the first hurdle in the Gillette Cup, and failed to qualify for the knockout stages of the Benson and Hedges Cup. It was a poor way to start the 1980s for a side which had dominated all spheres of cricket throughout the previous decade. It had been decided, before the end of May, to embark on a policy of giving young players the best possible chance to develop. A period of transformation, inevitable in sport, was to begin, with senior players left out of the side from time to time. That was the plan, and it was Asif Iqbal who was sidelined most. Thus the best side was not always selected and a certain amount of confusion and frustration resulted. Some two months after the season ended, [Alan] Ealham's frustrations were climaxed by the decision to relieve him of the captaincy and reinstate Asif.

1986 – KNOTT'S FAREWELL
Dudley Moore, 1987

It was a testing summer for the new captain, Christopher Cowdrey. The county again suffered from a lack of consistency [finishing ninth in the Championship and equal tenth in the John Player League], and by the beginning of August the wind of change was blowing. It was announced that Graham Johnson, in his 21st season with the county, would not be offered a new contract for 1986. By the end of the month, Johnson's contract had been cancelled forthwith, disciplinary action taken on account of his refusal to play against the Australians at Canterbury. The decision inevitably had an unsettling effect in the dressing-room, and this was to spill over well into the close season.

Alan Knott still kept wicket so consistently and well that he was close to an England recall. Towards the end of the summer, however, his ankle injury manifested itself again, and it was a sad day when, on the penultimate afternoon of the season, he announced his retirement. The club acknowledged his "outstanding services to the county and to English cricket", adding that "his ability and professionalism have ranked him among the truly great players in the history of the game." [The following season, Derek Underwood retired, too. "It was," wrote Dudley Moore, "the end of an era", and the final echo of the "glory days" of the 1970s.]

1988 – A SURPRISE SECOND IN TITLE RACE

Dudley Moore, 1989

For Kent it had all the trappings of a Championship-winning season – almost bottom of the table after three successive defeats; a team meeting at which there was plenty of straight talking. Such facets had been present in 1970, albeit at the halfway stage of the summer, and the title was won. In 1988 it was lost, by the agonising margin of one point, after the field had been led since the middle of June. Disappointment? Of course. But there was pride, too, at finishing second and confounding the critics who had written off the side early in the season.

The excitement mounted from late May, when at Canterbury Kent squeezed home with a three-wicket win over Yorkshire and began a winning sequence of six Championship matches in succession, the best since 1920. The last of these was at Edgbaston, where in the Warwickshire first innings Kent gained only three bonus bowling points instead of four because they could take only eight wickets. Warwickshire had two batsmen injured. It was a point that rankled all season, but the authorities were insistent that the rule stated that the fourth bonus point was awarded only when a side took the ninth wicket.

Chris Penn emerged as the county's leading strike bowler, with 80 Championship wickets. Richard Ellison returned after missing the 1987 season [through injury] and took 71 first-class wickets, a tremendous performance. Alan Igglesden [another injury-prone bowler] took the bowling honours in the second half of the summer, with 37 wickets in six matches, leaving Kent wondering what might have been achieved had he been fit all summer.

The batting was led, appropriately in his benefit year, by Chris Tavaré. Starting slowly, he scored four centuries, was twice dismissed in the 90s, and played with assurance and confidence. Roy Pienaar, the South African batsman signed in an emergency the previous summer because he also bowled medium-fast, batted superbly and also took wickets at important stages.

1994 – HOPES PINNED ON HOOPER

Andrew Gidley, 1995

Kent supporters, perennially waiting for something to turn up, voiced even more optimism than usual at the start of the season. By the end of June, however, Kent were winless and perilously close to the bottom of the Championship. When they did start winning, they could hardly stop. Starting in Maidstone Week, at the beginning of July, they won six of their last ten Championship fixtures and began a surge in the Sunday League that brought them nine consecutive victories and their second consecutive near-miss for the title. They eventually finished third.

Throughout the season Carl Hooper's role was immense with both bat and ball, and he was without doubt Kent's player of the year. He scored 1,579 first-class runs at 54.44 – apart from him, only Neil Taylor and Trevor Ward reached 1,000 – and on Sundays he was consistently brilliant. He scored 773 at 51.53 with six fifties and two hundreds, becoming the top scorer in the league for the second season running.

But it was the performance of Min Patel that offered most encouragement. With Richard Davis leaving for Warwickshire, he found hmself the principal left-arm spinner and responded magnificently. He was the leading wicket-taker in England, with 90 at 22.86, two years after a knee injury nearly ended his career.

1995 – TOP... AND BOTTOM
Andrew Gidley, 1996

Kent's recent history has been full of near-misses. They have finished as beaten finalists or runners-up nine times in the 17 seasons since their days of regular trophy-collecting came to an end in 1978. When they lost their fifth successive Lord's final, to Lancashire in the Benson and Hedges Cup in July, the sequence looked set to continue indefinitely. September 17, 1995, was the day they finally came good, becoming Sunday League champions and bringing home a piece of silverware at last. It may be a turning point.

The last match, against Warwickshire, was lost, and Kent won the title because Worcestershire's match was rained off. And the Sunday League went together with bottom place in the Championship, a bizarre double previously completed by Yorkshire in 1983. Kent, who last came bottom in 1895, failed to win a single Championship match after June 5.

As a result, some Kent members were not inclined to join in the general celebrations, and one wrote to all the papers in the county trying to drum up support for an extraordinary meeting. The necessary numbers appeared not to be forthcoming and the committee rejected the idea of calling such a meeting itself. However, the club chairman, David Kemp, insisted: "There is absolutely no complacency about our performances in the Championship. How could there be?"

Aravinda de Silva was a huge success as the county's one-season overseas replacement for Carl Hooper, and in the Benson and Hedges final at Lord's he played arguably the best innings of the whole summer [112 off 95 balls in an unsuccessful attempt to make 275 to win against Lancashire]. De Silva scored 1,781 first-class runs at 59.36, with seven centuries, and was Kent's Player of the Year. No other batsman passed 1,000.

1997 – THE ART OF COMING SECOND
Andrew Gidley, 1998

Nobody remembers who comes second in sport – victors celebrate while the vanquished slip away. In 1997, Kent turned coming second into an art form, finishing runners-up three times. A poor performance in the Benson and Hedges Cup final in July saw them lose to Surrey. But they put that behind them to mount concerted challenges for the Championship and the Sunday League. On September 9, with 12 days of the season to go they led in both.

They faltered at Headingley. First, they drew their penultimate Championship game, allowing Glamorgan to take a one-point lead. Then, they lost their final League game by seven wickets to Yorkshire, and their biggest one-day foes, Warwickshire, pipped them to the Sunday title. he following weekend, a five-wicket victory over Surrey was not enough to claim the Championship, as Glamorgan achieved a ten-wicket success against Somerset on the same evening.

It was difficult to know whether such a season should be celebrated or mourned? And questions were directed at coach John Wright and captain Steve Marsh: why had the county yet again been bridesmaids? Both pledged that the side would learn from the experience.

2001 – FULTON IN FULL FLOW

Andrew Gidley, 2002

Kent, so often the "nearly men" of county cricket, enjoyed a successful season in 2001, culminating in winning the Norwich Union League, the county's first trophy for six years. Finishing third in the County Championship was another notable achievement for a team offered as rank outsiders, at the start of the summer, to win any major honours. They made less progress in the knock-outs, but are now one of only three counties, Leicestershire and Yorkshire being the others, who have never experienced second-division cricket in either Championship or League.

The form of David Fulton was a revelation. He scored eight hundreds in the Championship, including a career-best 208 not out as he scored two in one match, against Somerset at Canterbury. He finished the summer as the leading English run-scorer. Robert Key and Ed Smith also passed 1,000 runs for the season, while Matthew Walker finished just 15 short. All told, Kent batsmen registered 23 first-class hundreds, the most popular being Mark Ealham's career-best 153 not out against Northamptonshire – his first century at Canterbury since 1997. The loss of overseas player Daryll Cullinan through a knee injury was overcome by recruiting Andrew Symonds, the county's import in 1999, who was already in England with the Australian one-day squad. He averaged 46.91 in the Championship, scored useful runs in the League and held some stunning catches.

Warwickshire v Kent   **Norwich Union League**
At Birmingham, September 16, 2001. Kent won by nine runs (D/L method).   2002

Kent held their nerve to capture the title for the fifth time. The architect of their win was Birmingham-born Symonds, who took five for 18 and also ran out Hemp off his own bowling, after Warwickshire had needed 60 from the last ten overs with seven wickets in hand. The decline began when Brown was stumped in

Symonds' first over. Rain reduced the match to 40 overs a side, and Warwickshire's revised target was 218.

Toss: Warwickshire. **Kent 216-6** (40 overs) (J. B. Hockley 90, R. W. T. Key 50; D. R. Brown 3-30);
Warwickshire 208-9 (40 overs) (M. A. Wagh 58, I. R. Bell 48, N. M. K. Smith 38; A. Symonds 5-18).

2004 – UNHAPPY SHIP CAUGHT IN A SQUALL   Mark Pennell, 2005

This was an odd season for Kent, runners-up in the Championship but relegated for the first time in the one-day league. While an inexperienced side were proud of seven Championship wins (two more than the winners, Warwickshire), 2004 will be remembered more as a bleak summer of unrest.

By the last game, the club were consulting solicitors to quell a members' revolt. Persistent stories of dressing-room infighting through the season were followed by the news that the stylish and consistent Ed Smith was leaving for Middlesex and, much more surprisingly, that Alex Loudon, promising as an off-spinner, batsman and potential captain, was going to Warwickshire. Both cited a lack of faith in Kent's coaching and management structure, prompting members to demand action. It was a sad end to a season of great promise. And when the St Lawrence Ground lime tree was blown down in the New Year, some might have sensed a hint of symbolism.

The crisis emerged in early June, when a resounding win over Lancashire lifted Kent to second, with four wins from six starts, and they should have been in good heart at Worcester four days later. A bruised hand forced Fulton to drop out, delegating the captaincy to Smith. But as Worcestershire piled up 453, it became obvious that Smith was getting no support from Symonds or, to a lesser extent, Key. By mid-afternoon, the atmosphere had degenerated so much that Fulton attempted to take charge as twelfth man. The umpires told him he was flouting Law 2.3 (a substitute shall not act as captain) and he went off again. Smith's authority had been fatally undermined.

The aloof and intellectual Smith and the abrasive Symonds were never natural soulmates, but their mutual dislike soon got out of hand. A fortnight later, Symonds raised the stakes. As acting captain for the Twenty20 campaign [with Robert Key away on Test duty], he dropped Smith, who had scored fifties in his last two one-day games. Former England captain Mike Denness resigned as chairman of cricket, hoping to "send a message to the lads that I thought their behaviour was despicable". Graham Johnson, another Kent stalwart of the 1970s, took over, and disciplined Key and Symonds. To their credit, Fulton, Smith and a much-changed side rose above the squabbles to get through their last six Championship games unbeaten, regaining the runners-up spot.

Lancashire

1977 – Desperate Days
John Kay, 1978

Lancashire endured their worst-ever season in 1977, winning only two Championship games. Only two batsmen, [Frank] Hayes and [Barry] Wood, made 1,000 runs, although [the captain] David Lloyd was only four runs short; only two bowlers, [Peter] Lee and [Jack] Simmons, managed to capture more than 50 wickets. It must be said that the absence of Clive Lloyd for most of the summer was a shattering blow to the morale of the side, and the West Indies captain had a doleful time in his benefit season. He batted only three times in first-class matches and scored only 164 runs because of recurring knee trouble which ended with him having cartilages removed from each knee. [Farokh] Engineer was also much missed. In the end, David Lloyd decided to resign as captain, and Hayes was appointed to lead the side in 1978.

1984 – Jekyll and Hyde
Brian Bearshaw, 1985

A Jekyll and Hyde performance saw Lancashire recapture the glorious days of the 1970s in the one-day competitions, yet have their worst season ever in the Championship. They won the Benson and Hedges Cup for the first time, came fourth in the John Player Sunday League, and were knocked out of the NatWest Trophy in the quarter-finals by the eventual winners. Yet they were in the bottom two of the Britannic Assurance Championship all summer, and although they just managed to avoid finishing last for the first time, they won only one game. For the ninth successive year they were in the bottom six, finishing in 16th place [out of 17] for the fourth time. It was the first season in 110 years that they had won only one game.

Lancashire started the season without Clive Lloyd, who was leading the West Indians, and David Lloyd, who had retired in 1983. Within a few weeks they also lost Frank Hayes, who announced his retirement, on medical advice, after playing in only one match. Graeme Fowler played in all England's matches, which meant his being available for Tests and one-day internationals for 36 days against his 30 days of Championship cricket. In addition, Paul Allott forced his way back into the England team: coupled with a late injury, this limited his Championship appearances to only two of the last 11 games. Eight of Lancashire's nine

953

Championship defeats came in those last 11 matches. Lancashire were a different team in limited-overs games when their fielding, eager and athletic, provided a reminder of their great days a decade earlier. They had to overcome heavy odds to win the Benson and Hedges Cup from Warwickshire in the Lord's final, having been drawn away against Essex in the quarter-final and against Nottinghamshire in the semi-final.

Lancashire v Warwickshire	Benson and Hedges Cup Final
At Lord's, July 21, 1984. Lancashire won by six wickets.	1985

Toss: Lancashire. **Warwickshire 139** (50.4 overs) (A. I. Kallicharran 70; P. J. W. Allott 3-15, S. T. Jefferies 3-28); **Lancashire 140-4** (42.4 overs) (D. P. Hughes 35*, N. H. Fairbrother 36*).

1987 – JUST JEKYLL
Brian Bearshaw, 1988

Lancashire had a marvellous season, one that will be remembered for many years despite their not winning anything. For the first time in 12 years, they did not finish in the bottom six of the Championship, rising from 15th place in 1986 to the giddy heights of second, only four points behind the winners [Nottinghamshire] and their best position since 1960. Their transformation was remarkable, especially after much of the close season had been a shambles. Their first-team coach, Peter Lever, manager Jack Bond, and the captain, Clive Lloyd, had all been relieved of their positions. Lloyd later decided to retire, and at the beginning of February Cedric Rhodes, chairman since 1969, was forced to resign by intense pressure from an action group who were intending to call a special meeting of members. This might well have overthrown the committee.

Lancashire, therefore, approached the season with a new captain, David Hughes, a new coach/manager Alan Ormrod, and a new chairman in Bob Bennett. All three can take a huge amount of credit for a season which restored interest, pride and enthusiasm in a great club which had been in decline for too long. Lancashire kept Nottinghamshire waiting until the penultimate day of the season before they could claim the Championship, and were left to rue two matches at Old Trafford in June when Yorkshire's last pair held out for 17.5 overs to secure a draw, and when they lost to Derbyshire by three runs after needing five to win with three wickets standing.

Ian Folley and Mike Watkinson came of age in the summer, and they and the West Indian fast bowler Patrick Patterson were capped in the closing stages of the season. Graeme Fowler also had his best season in ten years with Lancashire, his total of 1,800 runs in first-class matches being the highest by any batsman for the county in 22 years. Only Worcestershire's Graeme Hick scored more, yet Fowler was not chosen for any England team or for a winter tour. Gehan Mendis, Neil Fairbrother and Michael Atherton, who was in his debut season, also scored more than 1,000 runs in the season.

Lancashire v Derbyshire

At Manchester, June 27, 29, 30, 1987. Derbyshire won by three runs. 1988

Lancashire had 73 overs in which to score 276 to win. After a faltering start they were rallied by a fifth-wicket stand of 154 in 37 overs by Fairbrother and Watkinson, and looked to be on course for victory when Barnett came on with his leg-breaks and dismissed them both. Lancashire went into the last over wanting four with two wickets standing, but Allott's spirited innings ended when he was stumped off Barnett's third ball. Patterson, failing to beat Barnett's throw, was run out off the next.

Toss: Derbyshire. **Derbyshire 226** (K. J. Barnett 39, J. E. Morris 64; J. Simmons 3-43, I. Folley 5-67)
and 101-4 dec. (K. J. Barnett 36, J. G. Wright 39*; M. Watkinson 3-22); **Lancashire 52-2 dec.**
(S. J. O'Shaughnessy 30*) **and 272** (N. H. Fairbrother 82, M. Watkinson 91, P. J. W. Allott 32;
O. H. Mortensen 3-65, K. J. Barnett 4-43).

Essex v Lancashire

At Chelmsford, September 12, 14, 15, 1987. Lancashire won by 89 runs. 1988

Lancashire won with 7.1 overs to spare to make certain of finishing runners-up to Nottinghamshire in the Championship. Their sixth successive victory, it was never really in doubt from the moment that their spinners, Folley and Simmons, captured four wickets in six overs immediately after tea on the third day. If they were to go ahead of Nottinghamshire, Lancashire had to take maximum points from this match, but losing the toss meant batting first on a pitch of inconsistent bounce in conditions favouring the Essex seam bowlers. [John] Abrahams stayed almost four hours for his 64, but their fate was settled when the last five wickets fell in ten overs.

Toss: Essex. **Lancashire 220** (J. Abrahams 64, W. K. Hegg 31; I. L. Pont 5-73) **and 220-5 dec.**
(G. Fowler 76, M. A. Atherton 60; G. A. Gooch 3-32); **Essex 201-5 dec.** (A. W. Lilley 88, I. L. Pont 39)
and 150 (I. Folley 3-43, M. Watkinson 3-33).

1989 – COMING UP ROSES
Brian Bearshaw, 1990

Lancashire's best season for 18 years saw the Sunday League return to the club which won the 40-overs competition in its first two years. However, the Championship, which they have not won outright since 1934, eluded them again. They had a good season, staying among the front-runners all summer, and three wins in the last four matches enabled them to finish among the prize money in fourth place. The most satisfying part of the season probably came in the penultimate match, at Scarborough, when Lancashire completed a Championship double over Yorkshire for the first time since 1960 and for only the second time in 96 years. Moreover, the victories were overwhelming – by 184 runs at Scarborough to follow the 181-run win at Old Trafford only three weeks earlier.

Yorkshire v Lancashire

At Scarborough, September 8, 9, 10, 11, 1989. Lancashire won by 184 runs. 1990

Toss: Lancashire. **Lancashire 347** (G. Fowler 58, N. H. Fairbrother 161; J. D. Batty 3-75, P. Carrick 4-69)
and 369-8 dec. (G. D. Mendis 66, G. Fowler 123, M. A. Atherton 39, N. H. Fairbrother 67, T. E. Jesty 35;
P. W. Jarvis 3-103, J. D. Batty 5-118); **Yorkshire 237** (M. D. Moxon 54, C. S. Pickles 62,
A. Sidebottom 40; J. D. Fitton 5-53) **and 295** (M. D. Moxon 41, A. A. Metcalfe 30, P. E. Robinson 117,
A. Sidebottom 40*; P. J. W. Allott 3-59, M. Watkinson 3-36).

1990 – DOUBLE TRIUMPH
Brian Bearshaw, 1991

Lancashire became the first county to win both Lord's finals, finished runners-up in the Refuge Assurance League, and were sixth in the Championship. They were virtually invincible in all forms of the limited-overs game, losing only four out of 28 matches. The formidable line-up of batting was enough to carry them to victory on most days, and high among the list of Sunday wins was the seven-wicket victory, with 11 balls to spare, when set to score 268 in 39 overs at The Oval. But the most crushing win of the season was their 241-run victory over Gloucestershire in the quarter-finals of the NatWest Trophy. Lancashire's 372 for five was the highest in any limited-overs game between first-class counties. Another record was denied Lancashire when the weather forced their Benson and Hedges Cup tie against Hampshire to be expunged after they had scored 352 for six, following a third-wicket partnership of 244 between Neil Fairbrother and Mike Atherton.

By winning the two one-day finals, Lancashire took to four their total of trophies won in the four years of David Hughes's captaincy. His batting and bowling contributions continued to be modest in 1990, but his fielding was as alert as ever and his enthusiasm for the game and for Lancashire cricket never flagged. Not surprisingly, he was asked to captain the county again in 1991 in his 25th season.

Fairbrother, who captained the team whenever Hughes was absent, was appointed vice-captain for the first time, a clear pointer to the day when Hughes decides to retire. He had his best-ever season for Lancashire with 1,681 runs and an average of 80.04. His 366 against Surrey at The Oval was the third-highest innings in England after fellow Lancastrian A. C. MacLaren's 424 [in 1895] and G. A. Hick's 405 not out. Atherton, too, had an outstanding summer, playing in all six Tests – in which he scored two centuries – and falling just short of 2,000 runs in his first full season since completing his studies at Cambridge. He is unquestionably Lancashire's best batting find since Cyril Washbrook was discovered nearly 60 years ago.

Surrey v Lancashire
At The Oval, May 3, 4, 5, 7, 1990. Drawn. 1991

This record-breaking match will long be remembered and chronicled for its quite phenomenal feats of scoring on a pitch exemplifying the tougher standards laid down by the Test and County Cricket Board. [Ian] Greig, the Surrey captain, drove an extremely hard tactical bargain by amassing 707 for nine declared in the hope that his bowlers could take 20 wickets for an innings victory. However, it presented Lancashire with a *fait accompli*. Needing 558 to avoid the follow-on, and realising that victory was for them out of the question, they settled down to revel in the sumptuous batting conditions. The home bowling was savaged for a colossal 863, the highest Championship total of the century and second only to Yorkshire's 887 against Warwickshire at Birmingham in 1896. Fairbrother thrashed 366 to pass by two runs the previous best score at The Oval – 364 by Sir Leonard Hutton in the 1938 Test match against Australia. The aggregate for the match was 1,650 runs, a new mark in Championship cricket and the second-highest for a match in England.

Surrey v Lancashire, 1990
At The Oval, May 3, 4, 5, 7, 1990. Result: Drawn.

SURREY	*First innings*			*Second innings*
R. I. Alikhan st Hegg b Fitton	55			
G. S. Clinton c Patterson b DeFreitas	8	–	c Watkinson b Atherton	15
A. J. Stewart c Fowler b Patterson	70	–	(1) not out	54
M. A. Lynch c and b Watkinson	95	–	(3) not out	6
G. P. Thorpe c Atherton b Fitton	27			
†D. M. Ward c Hughes b Fitton	36			
*I. A. Greig c Jesty b Hughes	291			
K. T. Medlycott c Fairbrother b Patterson	33			
M. P. Bicknell c Hegg b Hughes	42			
N. M. Kendrick not out	18			
B 6, l-b 16, n-b 10	32		B 2, l-b 1, n-b 2	5
(9 wkts dec.)	707 1-57		(1 wkt)	80

A. J. Murphy did not bat.

1-10 2-118 3-187 4-261 5-275 6-316 7-401 8-606 9-707

First innings – Patterson 27–4–108–2; DeFreitas 26–4–99–1; Watkinson 23–2–113–1; Fitton 45–6–185–3; Atherton 22–5–75–0; Hughes 22.1–0–105–2.
Second innings – DeFreitas 4–0–10–0; Fitton 16–4–42–0; Atherton 13–5–25–1.

LANCASHIRE	*First innings*			
G. D. Mendis run out	102	P. A. J. DeFreitas b Murphy	31
G. Fowler run out	20	*D. P. Hughes not out	8
M. A. Atherton c Greig b Kendrick	191	J. D. Fitton c Stewart b Murphy	3
N. H. Fairbrother c Kendrick b Greig	366	B. P. Patterson c Greig b Medlycott	0
T. E. Jesty retired hurt	18	B 8, l-b 15, w 1, n-b 9	33
M. Watkinson b Greig	46		
†W. K. Hegg c Ward b Bicknell	45		863

1-45 2-184 3-548 4-745 5-774 6-844 7-848 8-862 9-863   T. E. Jesty retired hurt at 665.

Murphy 44–6–160–2; Bicknell 43–2–175–1; Kendrick 56–10–192–1; Medlycott 50.5–4–177–1; Lynch 5–2–17–0; Greig 19–3–73–2; Thorpe 7–1–46–0.

Toss won by Surrey   UMPIRES B. Dudleston and A. A. Jones

Lancashire v Worcestershire   **Benson and Hedges Cup Final**

At Lord's, July 14, 1990. Lancashire won by 69 runs.   1991

Toss: Worcestershire. **Lancashire 241-8** (55 overs) (M. A. Atherton 40, M. Watkinson 50, W. K. Hegg 31*);
Worcestershire 172 (54 overs) (I. T. Botham 38; Wasim Akram 3-30).

Lancashire v Gloucestershire   **NatWest Trophy Quarter-Final**

At Manchester, August 1, 1990. Lancashire won by 241 runs.   1991

Lancashire followed the highest total in any limited-overs game between first-class counties with the highest victory margin. It was Watkinson's 29th birthday and he celebrated with the biggest innings and the best bowling return in the match.

Toss: Gloucestershire. **Lancashire 372-5** (60 overs) (G. Fowler 52, G. D. Mendis 88, N. H. Fairbrother 86,
M. Watkinson 90); **Gloucestershire 131** (30 overs) (G. D. Hodgson 52; Wasim Akram 3-29,

M. Watkinson 3-14).

Lancashire v Northamptonshire   **NatWest Trophy Final**

At Lord's, September 1, 1990. Lancashire won by seven wickets.   1991

Phillip DeFreitas determined the course of the final in an opening spell of 8–4–19–5, exposing technical weaknesses in Northamptonshire's top-order batting.

Toss: Lancashire. **Northamptonshire 171** (60 overs) (D. J. Capel 36, C. E. L. Ambrose 48;
P. A. J. DeFreitas 5-26); **Lancashire 173-3** (45.4 overs) (M. A. Atherton 38*, N. H. Fairbrother 81).

1992 – THE MISERY RETURNS   Brian Bearshaw, 1993

Lancashire had a miserable year. They finished 12th in the Championship and joint 11th in the Sunday League, were knocked out of the NatWest Trophy in the second round, and the Benson and Hedges Cup in the quarter-final. It all culminated in the manager, Alan Ormrod, being sacked and former England players Paul Allott and Graeme Fowler being released by the committee at a meeting held on August 10, five weeks before the end of the season. Yet this was Ormrod's first poor season since taking over as manager in 1987. Neil Fairbrother, in his first season as official captain [he had taken over from David Hughes halfway through the previous season], was severely restricted by injury and played in only 12 first-class matches. In October, Hughes, who had been Ormrod's assistant, was appointed manager and David Lloyd, captain from 1973 to 1977, became coach.

1993 – MANCUNIAN GLOOM
Brian Bearshaw, 1994

Another miserable season for Lancashire, in which they lost seven of the last ten Championship matches, ended with the departure of David Hughes, the manager, and the resignation of the captain, Neil Fairbrother. After winning four of their first seven games to hold third place in the table, Lancashire failed to win again and slipped to joint 13th, their lowest position since 1986. The batting was inconsistent, although there were regularly ten players in the side who had scored first-class centuries; the bowling lacked balance and was too often denied by the opposition's middle order. Only Hampshire had fewer bowling points.

A change of leadership was essential and, in appointing Mike Watkinson, Lancashire might just prove to have made an inspired choice similar to that of Hughes in 1987. Hughes [as manager] suffered the fate of his predecessor Alan Ormrod the previous year. Both carried the can, in the manner of a football manager, for the failure of the team in a club with vociferous and impatient supporters. David Lloyd survived and was given a more prominent role for 1994, but without the title of manager.

1995 – WASIM THE WIZARD
Brian Bearshaw, 1996

When Lancashire won the Benson and Hedges Cup on July 15, many observers felt sure there would be other trophies to follow. They were lying fourth in he Championship and in the Sunday League, and were due to meet Yorkshire in the quarter-final of the NatWest Trophy. Disappointingly, that was as far as they got, losing to Yorkshire in the NatWest and remaining fourth in both the other two competitions, after sitting on the shirt-tails of the leaders all summer. Their unquestioned ability was shown in their victories over the other four teams in the top five in the Championship – Warwickshire, Middlesex, Northamptonshire and Essex.

Wasim Akram was in inspirational form throughout the season until he had to return home for Pakistan's Test series against Sri Lanka. In 14 games he took 81 wickets, far and away his best performance for Lancashire and the highest number of wickets for the county since Peter Lee took 112 in 1975.

Kent v Lancashire   **Benson and Hedges Cup Final**
At Lord's, July 15, 1995. Lancashire won by 35 runs.   Steven Lynch, 1996

Lancashire took the first of the season's domestic trophies, but Kent's overseas player, Aravinda de Silva, claimed the Gold Award and the headlines with a dazzling century. His memorable 112, made from 95 balls, was only the third century in a Benson and Hedges final (following Graham Gooch's 120 in 1979 and Viv Richards's 132 not out in 1981), and the first not to bring about victory.

Toss: Kent. **Lancashire 274-7** (55 overs) (M. A. Atherton 93, J. E. R. Gallian 36, J. P. Crawley 83);
Kent 239 (52.1 overs) (P. A. de Silva 112; M. Watkinson 3-42, G. Yates 3-42).

1996 – ONE-DAY WONDERS

Brian Bearshaw, 1997

A poll of Lancashire supporters on their impressions of the season would produce a mixed bag. For those who go for the one-day game and its quick cricket, this was a great year, with Lancashire striking the golden double of winning two Lord's finals for the second time. For the out-and-out traditionalist, the abject performance in the County Championship made this a wreck of a summer. In between, there are the loyalists who despair of winning the Championship but draw grudging comfort from the one-day successes. But there are four trophies on offer, and to win two of them – even the two easiest – twice in seven years is something of a triumph. Even the dyed-in-the-wools would have to admit 1996 was a thrilling, entertaining season.

The quarter-finals and semi-finals of both [cup] tournaments were staged at Old Trafford in front of huge crowds. Both semis were against Yorkshire and both were thrillers, particularly the game in the Benson and Hedges Cup, which Lancashire took by one wicket when Peter Martin drove the last ball for two to win. Martin gave Lancashire another one-wicket win, over Northamptonshire, in the second round of the NatWest Trophy, while the quarter-final, against Derbyshire, went to the last ball before Lancashire won by two runs. In contrast to the closeness of the earlier rounds, Lancashire won both finals quite easily.

Lancashire's form in the Championship was desperately disappointing after their challenge for the title and final position of fourth in 1995. Fifteenth place was their worst finish for ten years. Jason Gallian [who left to join Nottinghamshire a year later after falling out with the club] and Graham Lloyd looked like being the only batsmen to score 1,000 runs until Neil Fairbrother swept past with a double century in his final innings. Gallian scored 312 against Derbyshire, the highest-ever innings at Old Trafford, but finished on the losing side. Lloyd made a career-best 241 at Chelmsford, which included the fastest hundred of the season in 70 balls.

Lancashire v Derbyshire

At Manchester, July 18, 19, 20, 22, 1996. Derbyshire won by two wickets. 1997

Jason Gallian finished on the losing side after scoring 312, the highest innings ever played at Old Trafford in its 139 years. Only Percy Perrin of Essex, 92 years earlier, had ever scored a triple-century for a losing side in England – also against Derbyshire. Gallian's innings, the longest in Championship history, occupied 11 hours ten minutes and 583 balls; he hit 33 fours and four sixes. He beat Bobby Simpson's 311 for Australia in the Old Trafford Test of 1964 and his score was the fourth-highest for Lancashire

Toss: Lancashire. **Lancashire 587-9 dec.** (J. E. R. Gallian 312, J. P. Crawley 54, S. P. Titchard 96, M. Watkinson 46, G. Chapple 32) **and 174-3 dec.** (J. P. Crawley 97*, G. D. Lloyd 46);
Derbyshire 473-8 dec. (C. J. Adams 119, C. M. Wells 35, K. M. Krikken 104, D. G. Cork 83*, Extras 46; G. Chapple 4-83) **and 289-8** (K. J. Barnett 92, D. M. Jones 107, D. G. Cork 34*; G. Chapple 3-55, G. Keedy 3-91).

Lancashire v Yorkshire — Benson and Hedges Cup Semi-Final

At Manchester, June 11, 12, 1996. Lancashire won by one wicket. 1997

The contest went to the last ball and will stand as not only one of the great modern Roses matches but as a contender for any list of best-ever limited-overs matches.

Toss: Lancashire. **Yorkshire 250-5** (50 overs) (M. G. Bevan 95*, R. J. Blakey 80*); **Lancashire 251-9** (50 overs) (N. J. Speak 34, N. H. Fairbrother 59, W. K. Hegg 81).

Lancashire v Northamptonshire — Benson and Hedges Final

At Lord's, July 13, 1996. Lancashire won by 31 runs. Matthew Engel, 1997

A match in which half the men taking part were Test players was decided by perhaps the least charismatic man on the field. Ian Austin, who looks, in Mike Selvey's words, like "a stoker on a merchant steamer", broke through the Northamptonshire batting at both the start and finish to settle the final in Lancashire's favour. The result was what everyone expected, given the teams' records. It was Northamptonshire's tenth Lord's final and their seventh defeat. It was Lancashire's ninth win in 14. The victory also continued their extraordinary recent record in this competition excluding one washout, they have won 15 consecutive matches.

Toss: Lancashire. **Lancashire 245-9** (50 overs) (M. A. Atherton 48, J. P. Crawley 34, N. H. Fairbrother 63); **Northamptonshire 214** (48.3 overs) (R. J. Bailey 46, R. R. Montgomerie 42, K. M. Curran 35; I. D. Austin 4-21).

Essex v Lancashire — NatWest Trophy Final

At Lord's, September 7, 1996. Lancashire won by 129 runs. Paul Weaver, 1997

Essex, needing a modest 187, thought the game was won, a notion not immediately dispelled when Grayson, Hussain and Prichard fell cheaply to Martin. Gooch was still there. But he was a hapless bystander as Irani, Robinson and Rollins – whose off stump was knocked back by a ball pitching on leg – succumbed to [Glen] Chapple. Then, at 33, Gooch was seventh out for a tortuous ten scored in 20 overs and Essex knew their day was in ruins. They were bowled out in 27.2 overs. Nos. 9 and 10, Williams and Cowan, were joint top scorers. Chapple's figures of six for 18 replaced Joel Garner's six for 29, for Somerset in 1979, as the best in a September final. The Sunday newspaperman who had started his mid-afternoon first-edition report by writing: "Ronnie Irani was the only happy Lancastrian at Lord's yesterday," turned pale, lit a cigarette and rewrote frantically.

Toss: Essex. **Lancashire 186** (60 overs) (J. P. Crawley 66; R. C. Irani 3-25, A. P. Grayson 3-24); **Essex 57** (27.2 overs) (P. J. Martin 3-17, G. Chapple 6-18).

1998 – TEAM OF THE SEASON?

Colin Evans, 1999

Again, frustratingly, there were no Championship celebrations. But Lancashire could lay claim to the unofficial title of Team of the Year, having carried off the NatWest Trophy and the Sunday League, and come close to the most desired component of the treble. Old Trafford was definitely the place to be, on a glorious Sunday morning in September, when captain Wasim Akram waved goodbye to the crowd gathered under the dressing-room balcony. Although Lancashire's Championship bid had just ended in anticlimax – Leicestershire's triumph at The Oval the previous day left them trailing – there were emotional scenes as the fans paid tribute to their team and to Wasim, in his first and only season as captain. Leaving the club after ten years, he had to fight to clear himself of the match-fixing allegations engulfing cricket in Pakistan, but at least he had a rousing send-off.

John Crawley enjoyed the most prolific season of his career, with 1,681 Championship runs, a wonderful comeback century for England against Sri Lanka, and 849 runs in one-day matches, which had much to do with Lancashire's double triumph. He hit eight first-class centuries, three in successive innings, and finally 239 in the game against Hampshire just before he was proclaimed Lancashire's new captain.

The tall, lean Crawley was the outstanding figure, but many others hit high notes and five played for England: Andy Flintoff joined Mike Atherton and Crawley in playing Tests, while Peter Martin was picked for one-day internationals, as was Ian Austin, called up at short notice. The seam attack of Wasim, Martin, Austin and Glen Chapple was a potent force, notching up 176 wickets between them. Spin had little chance in 1998, but 19-year-old leg-spinner Chris Schofield captured eight wickets in his second game and off-spinner Gary Yates totted up 18 in his four appearances. [Warren] Hegg's improved batting – 628 runs at 36.94 – won him a place in the Ashes squad and Test caps at Melbourne and Sydney.

Derbyshire v Lancashire

NatWest Trophy Final

At Lord's, September 5, 6, 1998. Lancashire won by nine wickets.

Mike Selvey, 1999

Lancashire won what was arguably the most one-sided final in the history of a competition that specialises in them. Rain prevented any play before 4.30, but even so the game was concluded, in front of a sparse crowd, by Sunday lunch. Lancashire lost just one wicket in attaining their target of 109. Only 67 overs were bowled in the match. The winners had batted second in 12 of the past 13 finals, and the damage – to Derbyshire's morale if nothing else – had been done when Wasim Akram won the toss. Early autumn darkness and the time the pitch had spent under cover always made it likely that seam would hold sway over bat from the start, even though Derbyshire's terrible collapse eventually gave them the advantage of bowling in morning conditions. The surprise was that Lancashire, with all their experience of such occasions, allowed Derbyshire a dream start. The new-ball bowling of Wasim Akram and Peter Martin was uncontrollably tense and wild, and the openers had 70 on the board after 18 overs. [Michael] Slater, who had flown to Brisbane the previous week and returned specifically for the final, had just taken ten off two balls from Chapple – a six driven over extra cover and a four pulled through mid-wicket – and expectation had been turned upside down.

For Derbyshire, that was as good as it got. Their nemesis, in the rotund, metronomic form of [Ian] Austin was already operating at the Pavilion End. He and Martin, visibly more relaxed in his second spell, were moving the ball wickedly. Austin had Slater lbw for 34, to precipitate an astounding collapse that saw four wickets fall for one run and, ten runs later, another three for none: 70 for nought became 81 for seven. In a six-over spell, Martin took four for seven. But Austin hardly bowled a bad ball and his figures of three for 14 from ten overs were distorted by four overthrows. Derbyshire's total of 108 was the lowest by a team batting first in the final.

Toss: Lancashire. **Derbyshire 108** (36.4 overs) (M. J. Slater 34; P. J. Martin 4-19, I. D. Austin 3-14); **Lancashire 109-1** (30.2 overs) (J. P. Crawley 53*, N. H. Fairbrother 38*).

1999 – THE MAGIC OF MURALI

Colin Evans, 2000

Lancashire's 1999 season will always be associated with Muttiah Muralitharan. His dazzling performances were the spark that lit a winning streak which eventually earned them runners-up honours in the Championship for the second year in succession, and the inaugural National League title to follow one the previous year in the final Sunday League.

Muralitharan finished with 66 wickets from the six Championship games in which he bowled. He became an instant hero: a world-class match-winner on the pitch, a smiling chatterbox in the dressing-room, a co-operative and courteous ambassador for the club. He even put on Bavarian lederhosen for a publicity stunt when Lancashire agreed a sponsorship deal with a lager company.

Take away Muralitharan and what do you have left? Quite a lot, actually. The comeback of Atherton, marked by his career-best 268 not out against Glamorgan at Blackpool, was a major bonus. Hegg, angry at the way England had discarded him, responded with another impressive season, with the gloves and the bat, and in a fairly lean year for the seamers, Martin bowled consistently well for 50 wickets. Graham Lloyd finished in brilliant form, passing 1,000 first-class runs in his final innings, which brought his third century.

2001 – NONE-TOO-FOND FAREWELLS

Colin Evans, 2002

Lancashire will want to forget 2001. Relegation became a real possibility in the Championship and they plunged to near-oblivion in two of the one-day competitions. If not, statistically, the worst season in the club's modern history, it was probably the most depressing, with poor performances on the field aggravated by a quarrelsome tone off it.

By early August, the recriminations were flying thick and fast, with a quickly widening rift between the Bob Simpson-John Crawley [coach and captain] axis and an influential section of the Old Trafford establishment. Almost inevitably, Simpson left after two years as coach. Crawley lost the captaincy to Hegg; by the end of the year he was threatening to sue the club if they would not release him from the remaining three years of his contract. Ian Austin retired with a verbal blast in Simpson's direction and Joe Scuderi, a controversial signing two years earlier, was sacked. The cricket secretary, Dave Edmundsen, was also a casualty, while Mike Atherton packed in the game without a farewell appearance or a flicker of regret. Lancashire, looking to the future, handed ex-captain Mike Watkinson a three-year contract as cricket manager, and he began with the club at its lowest ebb for many years.

Leicestershire

A season of almost unprecedented injuries ended on a note of triumph for Leicestershire when they won the John Player League for the second time in four years. Also, their position of fifth in the County Championship, only one place lower than the previous year, represented no small measure of success considering that eight players, at one time or another, suffered fractured bones.

The batting was full of ups and downs, and it was left to those two stalwarts, Illingworth and Higgs, to provide the real highlight of the season by setting a county batting record for the last wicket of 228 which played a major part in saving the game against Northamptonshire at the end of August. [Ken] Higgs, once more, proved a wonderful asset to the side, bowling as accurately as ever with the new ball. His hat-trick, the third of his career, helped Leicestershire to defeat Hampshire by six wickets in July. It was the second hat-trick for the county of the season, [Ken] Shuttleworth, in his first year after leaving Lancashire, achieving the other when Surrey were beaten at The Oval in May.

Leicestershire v Northamptonshire

At Leicester, August 27, 29, 30, 1977. Drawn. 1978

A last-wicket stand of 228 by Illingworth and Higgs, easily the best for Leicestershire and only seven short of the Championship record, highlighted the match. Illingworth put Northamptonshire in and must have been satisfied with the outcome, but disappointed by Leicestershire's reply – at one stage they were 45 for nine. He and Higgs remedied the situation. Both were dropped, but late in their innings, and they took full advantage of a pitch made easier by drying sun. Illingworth hit his only century of the season, but Higgs failed to score his first-ever county hundred, being run out when two short. Cook made sure Leicestershire would be denied victory with an accomplished century in the Northamptonshire second innings.

Toss: Leicestershire. **Northamptonshire 172** (Mushtaq Mohammad 44, B. S. Bedi 38; K. Higgs 5-51) **and 278** (G. Cook 126, W. Larkins 38, Sarfraz Nawaz 35; J. Birkenshaw 4-55, J. C. Balderstone 3-66); **Leicestershire 273** (R. Illingworth 119*, K. Higgs 98; Sarfraz Nawaz 4-27, B. J. Griffiths 3-30) **and 3-0.**

1982 – COOK FINDS RIGHT RECIPE

Martin Johnson, 1983

Despite the absence of any tangible evidence in the way of trophies, Leicestershire enjoyed their most satisfactory season since 1975, when they won both the Championship and the Benson and Hedges Cup under Ray Illingworth's leadership. Their run of eight victories in 12 matches at one point pulled them to within two points of the eventual county champions, Middlesex, with two matches left; but they then produced perhaps their worst performance of the season, at Trent Bridge, and conceded the title.

Leicestershire's charge began, after a good May but a thoroughly unhappy June, with a six-wicket victory over Middlesex, the runaway leaders, at Uxbridge in the first week of July. That win owed much to some fine spin bowling by Nick Cook, who went into the game with only 20 Championship wickets under his belt yet was to take his tally for the county to 87 by the end of the season, persuading many that the England selectors would have been well advised to take him to Australia.

There were hints, too, that Brian Davison, Rhodesian-born but recently qualified as "English" by registration, might make the tour. He proved a sparkling exception to the rule that players do not prosper in their benefit seasons, totalling 1,800 runs, only 18 short of his best-ever aggregate in 1976. His aggressive batting played a major part in Leicestershire's success.

Davison had sound support from three other batsmen who passed 1,000 runs for Leicestershire in the season, including David Gower, who achieved it in his last innings. Gower scored his runs in only 21 visits to the crease, his appearances being restricted by the heavy demands of Test cricket. Nigel Briers confirmed the promise he had shown the previous season, and Chris Balderstone had his best-ever season with the bat, scoring nearly 1,500 runs. Les Taylor, Andy Roberts and Gordon Parsons all took 50 wickets or more, and Jonathan Agnew impressed with his pace and new-found control until injury ruled him out midway through Leicestershire's strong surge.

Middlesex v Leicestershire

At Uxbridge, July 7, 8, 9, 1982. Leicestershire won by six wickets.   1983

Toss: Middlesex. **Leicestershire 399** (J. C. Balderstone 148, B. F. Davison 100, R. W. Tolchard 80*; W. N. Slack 3-17) **and 75-4** (J. E. Emburey 3-26); **Middlesex 160** (P. R. Downton 40, K. P. Tomlins 51; L. B. Taylor 3-42, N. G. B. Cook 6-32) **and 313** (W. N. Slack 57, K. P. Tomlins 44, P. R. Downton 65, J. E. Emburey 61; A. M. E. Roberts 4-53).

1985 – CUP FAILS TO SATISFY

Martin Johnson, 1986

Leicestershire's pleasure at winning the Benson and Hedges Cup, their first major trophy since the John Player League title in 1977, was tempered by their lowest Championship placing since 1964 and a spate of late-season departures by discontented players [Gordon Parsons and Nick Cook and Mike Garnham retired but offered to turn out "in emergencies".] Leicestershire looked to have unearthed a very useful replacement [for Parsons] in the 19-year-old Phillip DeFreitas, Dominican-born but English-qualified, who was signed from the Lord's ground-staff. He impressed many observers with his high, whippy action and ability to extract bounce and movement from the pitch.

[Peter] Willey [recruited from Northamptonshire 1984] topped the averages and played a succession of crucial innings in the Benson and Hedges Cup. He also bowled with great economy in the one-day games, besides taking 35 first-class wickets. For the second year running, he won the Leicestershire Player of the Year award.

Essex v Leicestershire	Benson and Hedges Cup Final
At Lord's, July 30, 1985. Leicestershire won by five wickets.	1986

Gower put Essex in on an overcast morning and a slow pitch still damp from preparation, and Willey's wily off-spin and Taylor's accurate medium-pace made runs hard to come by, especially in the morning. Needing to score at just under four runs an over to win, Leicestershire lost their openers for 33, Butcher to a brilliant catch at mid-wicket by Prichard. Gower went to another fine catch, this time by Lilley at cover point. When Whitaker and Briers fell cheaply, Leicestershire still had 81 to make in 15 overs, which was no easy matter. Willey, however, was finding gaps on the leg side by now, and Garnham made him a confidently dashing partner. They won the match for Leicestershire with three overs to spare, making Denis Compton's choice of Willey for the Gold Award a mere formality.

Toss: Leicestershire. **Essex 213-8** (55 overs) (G. A. Gooch 57, P. J. Prichard 32; L. B. Taylor 3-26);

Leicestershire 215-5 (52 overs) (D. I. Gower 43, P. Willey 86*, M. A. Garnham 34*).

1986 – THE GOWER DILEMMA
Martin Johnson, 1987

Injuries and a lack of balance in the bowling produced a somewhat disappointing season for Leicestershire; one which culminated in the removal of David Gower as captain less than three months after his being replaced as England's captain. Gower had just announced that he was to miss the county's last three matches because of "mental and physical exhaustion" when Mike Turner, the secretary-manager, recommended to the committee that he be given a "rest" from the position to which he was appointed at the end of the 1983 season. Gower's absences because of his England commitments had become increasingly detrimental, Turner felt, and there was evidence that he found it difficult to motivate himself adequately on his return to county cricket. In addition, Gower had a benefit in 1987, which could have proved a further distraction to his captaincy. Gower described the decision as "disappointing but understandable".

1987 – THE GREAT SALT SCANDAL

James Hunt, 1988

There can hardly have been a time when the county experienced so much media attention and speculation [as in 1987]. Unhappily, much of it had little to do with playing performances, which a times were considerable, but with personal and personnel problems. Rumours frequently overshadowed the side's actual achievements, and this marred what would otherwise have been recognised as a highly successful season.

By finishing in the top three in the Championship, they achieved something only four previous Leicestershire teams had managed, and by reaching the semifinal of the NatWest Trophy they equalled the club's best progress in 60-overs competition. Both these achievements were peppered with some fine individual performances, the most notable of which were the bowling of Jonathan Agnew and the batting of Nigel Briers. Agnew, bowling off a shorter run and with a wicked slower ball added to his armoury, became the first Leicestershire player since J. Birkenshaw in 1968 to take 100 first-class wickets in a season. Briers, after a poor start in the middle order, moved up to open the innings and scored 806 runs in the final month and a half, totalling 1,257 first-class runs in all.

Leicestershire began the season with an optimism born of having their strongest and largest squad for many years. However, keeping such a talented gathering happy and playing was bound to be a problem, and so it proved. Before the season was a month old, all-rounder Paddy Clift, in his last term at the club, threatened to resign after being omitted from a limited-overs match. After talks with the management, the threat was never carried out, and Clift went on to enjoy one of his best years at Leicestershire. Ian Butcher, also dissatisfied at failing to command a regular first-team place, asked the committee not to renew his contract and he later joined Gloucestershire.

But it was the county's England all-rounder, Phillip DeFreitas, who posed the greatest problem. There were rumours of a dressing-room rift and conflict with the new captain, Peter Willey. However, the rumours would have remained no more than that but for a notorious incident in which DeFreitas poured a pot of salt over Agnew's lunch on the final day of the Championship match against Sussex late in June. Agnew responded by throwing DeFreitas's kit over the dressing-room balcony, and the all-rounder left the ground for two hours before returning and, in dramatic fashion, helping Leicestershire to their first Championship victory. For DeFreitas, the troubles did not end there. He lost his England place and was then dropped from the county's first team for disciplinary reasons. It was a sorry state of affairs, and in the end it proved too much for Willey. During the close season, he resigned the captaincy.

Leicestershire v Sussex

At Leicester, June 20, 22, 23, 1987. Leicestershire won by four wickets.

1988

Toss: Sussex. **Sussex 251** (R. I. Alikhan 45, I. J. Gould 43, G. S. le Roux 72*, P. Moores 31; P. B. Clift 6-64) **and 64-4 dec.; Leicestershire 32-0 dec. and 288-6** (R. A. Cobb 46, N. E. Briers 54, J. J. Whitaker 55, T. J. Boon 61).

1994 – CALM AFTER THE STORM
Jon Culley, 1995

Leicestershire's achievement in finishing second in the Championship, their highest final placing since 1982, confounded almost every pre-season forecast. Like the champions, Warwickshire, they were a team whose collective efforts amounted to more than the sum of its parts. No individual was deemed good enough to play Test cricket, although the wicket-keeper, Paul Nixon, was chosen for the England A tour. A paucity of players of the highest calibre, however, was balanced by a clutch of those on the better side of average.

Even though they exceeded all outside expectations, the team ended up disappointed not to win the Championship. In mid-August, they cut Warwickshire's lead to nine points with a game in hand. But they lost their next three matches, starting with a two-day capitulation against Sussex. None the less, considering that the county had finished in the top three only five times in 89 previous attempts, they could hardly grumble. Even in the Sunday League, they escaped the bottom five for the first time since 1983, though they achieved little in either of the knock-outs.

It was possible to link advances on the field with a change of climate off it. The unhappy end of the Mike Turner era did at least conclude a period of bitter infighting, which inevitably affected morale. There was a widespread feeling that the former chief executive, who resigned in 1993, had not had a proper acknowledgment [from the club] for his achievements. Ironically, Turner was made an MBE in June for his services to cricket.

Jack Birkenshaw strengthened his position as cricket manager and signed a contract lasting until 1998. After he dispensed with Winston Benjamin and signed Phil Simmons as overseas player, Birkenshaw's ruthless streak reappeared in June when he excluded four senior men – Tim Boon, James Whitaker, David Millns and the captain, Nigel Briers – from the Sunday side in favour of "some eager youngsters who want to throw themselves about and chase everything".

Leicestershire v Northamptonshire
At Leicester, April 28, 29, 30, 1994. Leicestershire won by ten wickets. 1995

International attention was focused on Edgbaston where the new Test record-holder Lara was beginning his Warwickshire career. But, while Lara was forced to spend the opening day in the field, his fellow-Trinidadian Simmons stole the headlines with a sensational innings to mark his arrival as Leicestershire's overseas player. He became the first player to score a double-century on Championship debut and passed not only his own highest score, 202 for Trinidad, but the 80-year-old Leicestershire record, Sam Coe's 252 not out, also against Northamptonshire.

Toss: Leicestershire. **Leicestershire 482** (P. V. Simmons 261, J. J. Whitaker 55, P. A. Nixon 106; J. P. Taylor 3-82, A. R. Roberts 3-147) **and 9-0; Northamptonshire 224** (A. J. Lamb 70, A. L. Penberthy 41; A. D. Mullally 3-57, G. J. Parsons 3-30, A. R. K. Pierson 3-57) **and 266** (A. Fordham 102; D. J. Millns 3-40).

1996 – YEAR OF THE FOX (1)

Martin Johnson, 1997

Homespun, unfashionable, unglamorous, prosaic. . . all these descriptions were applied to Leicestershire in 1996, and when the County Championship went to Grace Road, it was greeted with the kind of embarrassed silence associated with a rag-and-bone man's horse winning the Derby. In fact, if they ever built a ring road next to Leicestershire's ground, they would probably have to call it the Charisma By-Pass.

Not that there were ever many traffic jams when Leicestershire were playing. They won the Championship by using only 13 players all season, and were roared on towards the coveted pennant by much the same number of spectators. Not the least of Leicestershire's achievements was in clinching the title against Middlesex at home in their final game, when they faced the unfamiliar pressure of performing in front of an audience which almost qualified as a crowd.

It was a long way removed from Leicestershire's only previous Championship, in 1975, even though there were parallels involved, such as having a Yorkshireman as captain and losing only once, to Surrey at The Oval. However, if James Whitaker became known for orchestrating the mid-pitch "huddle", the only time Raymond Illingworth was ever likely to call for a huddle was when a bit of loose change dropped out of his trouser pocket. Under Illingworth, the 1975 side was as close to glamorous as Leicestershire have ever got. Apart from Illy, they had players of the stature of Ken Higgs, Graham McKenzie, Brian Davison, Roger Tolchard, and the embryonic David Gower. There were times in those days when getting around the ground was harder work than elbowing your way through Marks and Spencer on Christmas Eve, whereas the average 1996 spectator required a loud-hailer to converse with his neighbour. This had more than a little to do with the side being all but ignored by the local evening newspaper, for whom sport appeared to begin and end at Filbert Street. A booking for Leicester City's No. 5 would be greeted with the largest headline available, while a double-century for Vince Wells could just about be located with the aid of a magnifying glass.

There was a different atmosphere in 1975, when no home match was complete without a local character nicknamed The Foghorn, who would announce his impending presence from the front door of his house a couple of hundred yards away. "I'm on me way" he'd bellow, at about five past eleven, and would regularly circumnavigate the ground clutching (or to be more accurate, spilling) a pint of mild, yelling: "Get Birky on!" He knew full well, of course, that Jack Birkenshaw, the present manager, would be bowling only if Illy had first ascertained that the pitch was in no danger of taking spin.

Those were the days when Leicestershire not only had crowds, but sponsored marquees on the outfield. Illy protested on a daily basis that "t'bloody tents" were compromising the long boundaries he demanded for a team that had no less than five decent spin bowlers, and, on one memorable occasion when a down-the-order slogger had launched him into a plate of salmon mousse, Illy stalked up to the committee balcony and launched into a five-minute,

Double huddle: as Leicestershire's players adopt a familiar team-bonding pose during their match against Middlesex in 1996, the umpires decide to follow suit.

finger-wagging tirade. They were also the days, long gone now, one imagines, when players used to combine two professional sports. Graham Cross was Leicester City's centre-half as well as a county player, and when Leicestershire won the Championship in their final match at Chesterfield, Chris Balderstone interrupted an innings of 51 not out at close of play, dashed up the M1 to play soccer for Doncaster Rovers, and returned to complete his century the following morning.

After Illingworth left in 1978, Leicestershire had their moments, but made more headlines for the number of players heading for the exit gate than for their exploits on the field. Nick Cook, Phillip DeFreitas, Chris Lewis, Peter Such and, finally, David Gower, all left for various reasons, and Leicestershire slipped back into their previous existence as a team with no stars. The structure known as The Meet, a sort of cross between an aircraft hangar and a farmer's barn, symbolised a kind of cobwebbed decrepitude, where a handful of elderly punters peered through opaque windows, swapping stories about the good old days.

It was this general perception of a run-down club that masked a succession of highly respectable seasons in the early nineties, and presumably persuaded some bookmakers to quote them at 40-1 for the 1996 Championship. Even when they began the season well, and remained at or near the top of the table as it went on, the general belief was that they would eventually slide away into mid-table anonymity.

Their failure to do so had a lot to do with the newly elected captain. Admirable cricketer though Nigel Briers, Whitaker's predecessor, had been, he was a more natu-rally cautious leader than the gung-ho Whitaker, who, as a youngster in his first season, had greeted the first three deliveries that Ian Botham had ever sent down to him with thundering off-drives for four. Leicestershire are known as the Fox County, and if Briers and Whitaker had both belonged to the Quorn Hunt, Whitaker would have been out front with the bugle, while Briers would have been more practically engaged at the back, collecting fertiliser for the roses.

Whitaker had taken inspiration from the idiosyncratic methods employed to such good effect by Dermot Reeve at Warwickshire, and also concluded (partly as a slightly nervous newcomer to captaincy) that team spirit would best be fostered by democracy rather than dictatorship. This led to the famous huddle, as Leicestershire plotted their tactics for the next man in. Quite how and when the huddle first started, even Whitaker is not sure, though he thought it might have been against Yorkshire. "They were top of the table at the time, but we posted a massive first-innings total and then started running through them. Everyone was on such a high that suddenly we all had our arms around one another, and would start talking about how to bowl at the next man in."

There were times, Whitaker admits, when the conversation ran along more traditional lines, such as: "Where shall we go for dinner tonight?" or "Have you seen that girl in front of the pavilion?" But mostly, he said, it was about tactics. "It was never planned, it just happened. I like to think it reflected the way we all played for one another, and how everyone was made to feel that their input was important."

Whitaker also backed his admiration for Vince Wells – an apparently workaday cricketer transferred from Kent as someone who could bowl a bit, bat a bit, and keep wicket a bit – by promoting him to open the batting. Wells then proceeded to make two double-centuries and a 197 in the space of six weeks. David Millns and Allan Mullally formed a formidable new-ball partnership. Meanwhile, Gordon Parsons, whose one-time belief that he was at least 40mph quicker than Jeff Thomson was rarely shaken, even when he had to wait for the ball to be thrown back by a pedestrian from the adjacent Milligan Road, had developed into a cagey, and highly effective, medium-pacer. However, the individual who most of all turned Leicestershire from an averagely decent side into a title-winning one was, according to Whitaker, the West Indian Phil Simmons. He made runs, took a lot of wickets with his deceptive pace, and had flypaper hands in the slips, but it was his infec-tious enthusiasm and tactical input that made him so valuable.

Birkenshaw reckoned that the 1996 side would have been more than decent opposition for the one he played for in 1975; as someone who watched them both, I would take minor issue with that. However, I would not quibble with his contention that the 1996 model was out in front in terms of team spirit.

As for Whitaker, he missed the boat as a Test player after winning his one and only cap in Australia on Mike Gatting's 1986–87 Ashes tour. But he now regards himself as a cricketer fulfilled. "If I had to point to one single factor for our success," he said, "it would be enthusiasm. At the start of the season we sat down and asked ourselves why we were all playing professional cricket, and the answer was obvious. To enjoy it. Once you've focused in on that, the game doesn't seem half so difficult."

Yorkshire v Leicestershire

At Bradford, June 20, 21, 22, 24, 1996. Leicestershire won by an innings and 151 runs. 1997

Toss: Leicestershire. **Leicestershire 681-7 dec.** (V. J. Wells 200, P. V. Simmons 69, J. J. Whitaker 218,
P. A. Nixon 77*, Extras 45); **Yorkshire 342** (D. Byas 42, M. G. Bevan 82, D. Gough 50,
C. E. W. Silverwood 44, R. D. Stemp 51*; G. J. Parsons 4-83, M. T. Brimson 3-57) **and 188**
(M. P. Vaughan 54, M. G. Bevan 65*, A. McGrath 32; D. J. Millns 4-67, G. J. Parsons 3-40).

Leicestershire v Middlesex

At Leicester, September 19, 20, 21, 22, 1996. Leicestershire won by an innings and 74 runs. 1997

Leicestershire clinched the second Championship title in their history over a pot of tea and ham sandwiches on the penultimate day of the season. The tea interval had just started when supporters tuning into radios heard that Surrey had forfeited their first innings against Worcestershire, and thus could not get the maximum points they needed to take the title. Within minutes, 3,000 jubilant fans had gathered under the players' balcony. Ultimately, Leicestershire did not need Surrey's capitulation: they crushed Middlesex for their tenth victory of the season and their fourth in succession – three of them by an innings.

Toss: Middlesex. **Middlesex 190** (M. R. Ramprakash 71, Extras 32; A. D. Mullally 4-53) **and 248**
(P. E. Wellings 42, M. R. Ramprakash 78, Extras 40; D. J. Millns 4-48, A. D. Mullally 3-40);
Leicestershire 512 (D. L. Maddy 30, J. J. Whitaker 89, A. Habib 49, P. V. Simmons 142*, D. J. Millns 40,
A. D. Mullally 75, Extras 57; R. A. Fay 4-140).

1998 – YEAR OF THE FOX (2)
Chris Goddard, 1999

After Leicestershire's second County Championship in three years, a journalist friend said: "Done well your boys, haven't they? Leicestershire, though. . . Not *really* that good, are they?" I enquired how many times he had watched them. "Well, er, none actually," he said sheepishly.

This attitude is not unusual. Leicestershire are never mentioned in the same breath as counties that play on a Test ground. Because the team is short of "stars" and Grace Road does not boast a tree on the outfield, or a cathedral on its doorstep, while fans still eat in the run-down Meet and the crowds are among the lowest on the circuit, Leicestershire are deemed unfashionable. Even the Saatchi brothers would struggle to improve their image.

But in 1998 Leicestershire proved their win in 1996 was no fluke. They are a good team – not great, because the Championship is not a great competition. But their record now shows they can play a bit. They became only the fourth side since the war to win the title unbeaten, having lost just one game in each of the previous two seasons. Their last home Championship defeat was by Lancashire in August 1995.

The title was the second in three years under the captaincy of James Whitaker. This time, Whitaker did not face a single ball in the competition, because of a knee injury that required two operations. He did, however, play every ball his team faced, bowl every ball they bowled and catch every catch. Once back on his feet, Whitaker did not miss a match and often paced the boundary, smoking nervily. At the Benson and Hedges final at Lord's [in which Leicestershire lost heavily to Essex], he was ejected from the field as he tried to encourage his players.

Whitaker had resisted interfering with the running of the side by acting-captain Chris Lewis. But he dropped both Lewis and fast bowler David Millns when they arrived late for practice [at Worksop in August]. Simmons then took over as acting-captain and led Leicestershire to a title that had earlier seemed a long shot. They won eight of their last nine games. Two of those wins were particularly significant. Against Northamptonshire in July, they successfully chased an unbelievable 204 in 20 overs, thanks to Wells and Lewis, in what became his last match as captain; Wells scored 58 and Lewis 71, both off 33 balls. Then, in early September, they beat Warwickshire just after tea on the last day, under threat of rain which never arrived. With Surrey losing to Yorkshire, Leicestershire went top for the first time, with two matches to go.

But the most satisfying victory was the one over Surrey in the final game, which clinched the title. There was a touch of irony here. In 1996, Leicestershire's only defeat had been inflicted by Surrey. This time. Leicestershire beat them by an innings and 211 runs. Appropriately, the win was set up by a double-hundred from [Ben] Smith and a century from [Aftab] Habib, their best batsmen of the season, and some devastating fast bowling by Millns and Mullally, who reduced Surrey to eight for four. Surrey captain Adam Hollioake, whose team had led the table for most of then season, graciously said Leicestershire were the best Championship side he had faced.

Leicestershire v Northamptonshire

At Leicester, July 14, 15, 16, 17, 1998. Leicestershire won by four wickets. 1999

After Northamptonshire's tail had held out until after tea on the final day, and with the crowd drifting away, Leicestershire embarked on one of the most remarkable run chases in Championship history. That they attempted to make 204 in 20 overs, even on a good pitch, was daring; that they won by four wickets with five balls to spare was outrageous. Northamptonshire coach John Emburey said he had "never seen anything like it in all my years". "You could try that a thousand times and only pull it off once", said Leicestershire's acting-captain Chris Lewis.

Toss: Northamptonshire. **Northamptonshire 322** (M. B. Loye 76, G. P. Swann 92, J. P. Taylor 41, Extras 37; A. D. Mullally 5-62) **and 365** (D. Ripley 32, G. P. Swann 111, J. P. Taylor 56, Extras 62; A. D. Mullally 4-48, M. T. Brimson 3-88); **Leicestershire 484** (B. F. Smith 153, A. Habib 198, Extras 48; F. A. Rose 5-123) **and 204-6** (V. J. Wells 58, C. C. Lewis 71*; F. A. Rose 3-93).

Surrey v Leicestershire

At The Oval, September 17, 18, 19, 1998. Leicestershire won by an innings and 211 runs.   1999

Smith and Habib transformed Leicestershire's innings with a stand of 252, an all-wicket county record against Surrey. Smith batted eight minutes short of nine hours for a maiden double-hundred. A third century, from Nixon, allowed Simmons to declare. Four overs later, Surrey had lost their top three for ducks.

Toss: Leicestershire. **Leicestershire 585-6 dec.** (B. F. Smith 204, A. Habib 114, P. A. Nixon 101*, C. C. Lewis 54*, Extras 42; B. C. Hollioake 3-106); **Surrey 146** (A. J. Stewart 33, A. J. Hollioake 40, B. C. Hollioake 46*) **and 228** (N. Shahid 34, A. J. Hollioake 54*, M. P. Bicknell 31; M. T. Brimson 3-62, P. V. Simmons 3-50).

2002 - A MESSY DIVORCE   Neville Foulger, 2003

Leicestershire's modest summer on the field was followed by a shambolic winter off it. Though the trophy cabinet remained bare, they could be forgiven for feeling satisfied at staying up in both leagues after starting the season as undisputed favourites to go down. But their performances veered between the admirable and the abject, and not everyone agreed that congratulations were in order. A letter in the local paper summed up the feelings of a section of the membership: "There are celebrations at Grace Road at retaining Division One status," it said, "but it is a celebration of mediocrity. Leicestershire looked what they were, an ageing team. What is needed is a shake-up." By January, there had been one. Having already lost four key players – James Ormond, Ben Smith, Aftab Habib and Jon Dakin – at the end of the 2001 season, they now lost more, in ugly circumstances.

Perhaps the most contentious departure was that of wicket-keeper Neil Burns. Although approaching 37, he had enjoyed another excellent season: his 63 dismissals were the most in Division One, and he scored 720 runs at nearly 33. Even so, he was not offered a new contract. He found the explanation offered by the club unsatisfactory and resolved to take his case to an industrial tribunal.

Controversy surrounded the captaincy, too. Vince Wells, who had led the side for three years, was dogged by niggling injuries and endured a difficult summer. He occasionally recaptured the form of the Championship-winning days of the late 1990s – he hit a magnificent 150 against Hampshire and took eight wickets against Yorkshire – but was no longer the same all-round force. At the end of the summer, the club sacked him as captain; Wells said he had been given an oral offer of the job, and he turned down a one-year playing contract in disgust, preferring to move to Durham. The captaincy was duly offered to Iain Sutcliffe, who was expected to be a vital part of Leicestershire's future. But Sutcliffe was so disillusioned by the treatment of Wells that he abandoned the county that had groomed him for eight years and joined Lancashire. Phillip DeFreitas, the senior pro, was asked to plug the gap in 2003.

2004 – TWENTY20 VISION

Paul Jones, 2005

Late on the hot evening of August 7, after a dramatic and draining day, Jeremy Snape hit a boundary through mid-wicket to win the hippest trophy in English cricket for Leicestershire, just 11 months after they had limped to the end of a miserable 2003 season. The Twenty20 Cup, the county's first one-day trophy for 19 years, was a deserved reward for a club that put its heart and soul into making the competition a success on and off the pitch.

Compared with the usual scattering at Grace Road, the support for Twenty20 was phenomenal. The ground was jam-packed with 5,806 spectators for the zonal match against Nottinghamshire, and the two other home games were well attended. The crowds were rewarded with sound, disciplined cricket, and the odd dash of batting brilliance from Brad Hodge and Darren Maddy.

Still almost everyone expected the little club to come unstuck at Edgbaston on finals day. But Maddy, the competition's heaviest scorer in 2004 with 356 runs, played another masterful innings in the semi-final. Hodge then took centre-stage in the final against Surrey. Under intense pressure he hit a glorious unbeaten 77 from 53 deliveries and, to the delight of many neutrals, Leicestershire chased down a taxing target of 169. It ended Surrey's unbeaten record in Twenty20.

Leicestershire v Surrey   **Twenty20 Cup Final**

At Birmingham, August 7, 2004 (day/night). Leicestershire won by seven wickets.   2005

Toss: Surrey. **Surrey 168-6** (20 overs) (A. D. Brown 64); **Leicestershire 169-3** (19.1 overs) (B. J. Hodge 77*, J. N. Snape 34*).

Middlesex

Terry Cooper, 1978

Middlesex confirmed that they are currently the strongest county by again finishing at the top of the table [joint first with Kent] and comfortably winning the Gillette Cup. These successes followed the two cup finals in 1975 and the Championship in 1976.

[Wayne] Daniel provided most of the menace, becoming a full member of the Thomson-Holding generation of lightning-fast bowlers who can bounce the ball chest-high from any length. Many batsmen rated him the quickest bowler they had faced. [Mike] Selvey's consistent improvement as a tireless, hostile swing-and-cut bowler is illustrated by his recent returns – 64 wickets at 28 in 1975, 61 at 21 in 1976 and now 72 at 19.

[Mike] Brearley played in half the Championship games, but contributed big scores between Tests, and six of the nine wins came in his 11 appearances. His career between June 1976 and September 1977 is certainly unparalleled. In that time he won his England place, led his country to their emphatic Ashes victory and masterminded Middlesex's triumphs. Brearley may well have been influential in Gatting's selection for [England's] winter tour. In his first full season the confident Gatting looked a commanding player, but he flew to Pakistan without a first-class century. His urge to maintain an accelerating rate throughout an innings accounted for him being dismissed 11 times between 40 and 82. Mixing with Test players should teach him how to graft on for the hundred.

Glamorgan v Middlesex   **Gillette Cup Final**

At Lord's, September 3, 1977. Middlesex won by five wickets.   1978

The tall left-handed Llewellyn gave the best batting display of a rather dreary day's cricket. His first three strokes were four, six, four off Gatting. Later he hoisted a ball from Emburey over mid-on which dropped into the guttering beside the broadcasting box near the top tier of the pavilion – a colossal carry. As Middlesex managed to restrict Glamorgan to a total of 177 from their 60 overs, they did not face a tall task, but they lost Brearley to the second ball of their innings, whereupon Radley took charge, though he was fortunate to be missed when two at second slip by King off Nash and had other escapes as Glamorgan paid dearly for poor fielding.

Toss: Middlesex. **Glamorgan 177-9** (60 overs) (J. A. Hopkins 47, M. J. Llewellyn 62; N. G. Featherstone 3-17); **Middlesex 178-5** (55.4 overs) (C. T. Radley 85*).

1980 – A WINNING IMPORT
Terry Cooper, 1981

Observers who believed that Middlesex's 14th place in 1979 was a freakishly false one were vindicated when Brearley's team clinched the Schweppes County Championship on September 2, four years to the day after their 1976 triumph. Having resisted Surrey's persistent challenge, they denied them again four days later by beating them in the Gillette Cup final, and next day Middlesex finished third in the John Player League. Having also reached the semi-finals of the Benson and Hedges Cup, they could look back on the most successful year by any county in the nine seasons that have offered four trophies. The previous best record was their own in 1977.

Brearley referred to Vintcent van der Bijl as "the biggest single factor behind our success". He was initially recruited as a replacement for Daniel, who was expected to be chosen for the West Indian team in England. When West Indies decided to do without Daniel, Middlesex were left with one of the most dangerous attacks in their history.

John Emburey and Phil Edmonds did not play a full county season, but van der Bijl surpassed even the high expectations aroused by his South African record. He brought the ball down from around nine feet, more swiftly than many opponents imagined, moved it, made it lift, and bowled unerringly straight. A measure of his stump-riveting line was that 49 of his 85 Championship victims were bowled or lbw, and he had 17 more caught behind.

In contrast to van der Bijl's brief stay, both Simon Hughes and Paul Downton promised years more service. Brearley called Hughes "the best fast-bowling prospect in England". After being dropped for a number of matches, Roland Butcher shrugged off the disappointment in astonishing fashion. He made a match-winning 153 against Hampshire at Lord's, and went on to produce similar strokes against Yorkshire and Essex. These outstanding innings won him a place in England's Prudential Trophy side. Emburey, as artistic in the longer game as he is restrictive in the shorter, became England's premier spinner. His highlight came when he destroyed Nottinghamshire with 12 wickets in a day.

Middlesex v Surrey　　　　　　　　　　　　　　　**Gillette Cup Final**
At Lord's, September 6, 1980. Middlesex won by seven wickets.　　　　　1981

Toss: Middlesex. **Surrey 201** (60 overs) (D. M. Smith 50, G. R. J. Roope 35, Intikhab Alam 34; S. P. Hughes 3-60); **Middlesex 202-3** (53.5 overs) (J. M. Brearley 96*, R. O. Butcher 50*).

1982 – END OF THE BREARLEY ERA — Terry Cooper, 1983

The Middlesex players were determined that their retirement gift to Mike Brearley should be a trophy – all four if possible. They embarked on their prize-gathering so skilfully, remaining unbeaten until the middle of June, that the four-timer began to look something less than an impossibility. But this inspired start could not be maintained. Lancashire, in the Benson and Hedges Cup quarter-final, and Surrey, in the NatWest Trophy semi-final, ended hopes of a farewell Lord's appearance for Brearley. A run of three consecutive John Player League defeats also transformed a six-point lead into a six-point deficit, although four wins in the last five games kept Middlesex in second place [behind Sussex], their highest in the League's 14 seasons.

There remained the Championship. With Leicestershire closing fast, Middlesex managed an important victory over Surrey. They then lost at Hove before moving to the verge of the title in the last home match by beating Hampshire at Uxbridge and clinching it at Worcester on September 11. The captain made the winning hit of that final game, ending another fruitful season with the bat.

So Brearley departed after a dozen years of captaincy, festooned with honours at Test and county level. The Middlesex successes were crammed into his final eight seasons, the necessary spade-work having been undertaken in the previous four years. In 1971 he inherited a side disunited and unsuccessful, with, at times, an aversion to attacking cricket that was the despair of their dwindling supporters. Brearley restored purposeful cricket to Lord's, while winning four Championships (one shared) and two Gillette Cups. As the best county side of a generation they were also a credit to their coach, Don Bennett.

Worcestershire v Middlesex

At Worcester, September 11, 13, 14, 1982. Middlesex won by ten wickets. 1983

Brearley fittingly hit the winning runs in his final game for Middlesex, who coasted home by ten wickets with two sessions to spare. Humphries and Patel had provided the only resistance as Middlesex dismissed the home side for 168 in their first innings to clinch the four points they needed to be sure of the Championship title.

Toss: Worcestershire. **Worcestershire 168** (D. N. Patel 44, D. J. Humphries 56; N. G. Cowans 3-50, J. E. Emburey 3-18) **and 263** (M. S. Scott 37, P. A. Neale 50, M. J. Weston 64; S. P. Hughes 3-59, M. W. Gatting 4-43); **Middlesex 382** (J. M. Brearley 31, M. W. Gatting 61, R. O. Butcher 94, P. H. Edmonds 92; R. M. Ellcock 3-80, M. J. Weston 3-42) **and 50-0** (W. N. Slack 32*).

1983 – A SEAMLESS TRANSITION — John Thicknesse, 1984

If another season of high achievement ended in anticlimax through their being overtaken in the home straight of the Championship, Middlesex still had reason to look back on 1983 with satisfaction. Mike Gatting [the new captain] and John

Emburey, who deputised during the World Cup and the last two Tests, led the side so soundly that the retirement of Mike Brearley was absorbed with a minimum of difficulty. To finish second in the Championship, win the Benson and Hedges Cup, and be deprived of a second final only by a masterly 96 not out for Somerset by Ian Botham in the NatWest Trophy semi-final, reflects a high level of consistency in view of the fact that they were constantly weakened by representative calls and injuries [Butcher suffered a fractured cheekbone in July which ended his season.] Only in the John Player League, where they dropped six places, did they fail to leave their mark.

Essex v Middlesex	Benson and Hedges Cup Final
At Lord's, July 23, 1983. Middlesex won by four runs.	1984

In a thrilling finish, Middlesex saved themselves from what for most of the day had seemed like impending defeat. Middlesex, having lost the toss, were put in. With the ball moving around a good deal they had to work hard for their runs, and were greatly indebted to Radley, whose adhesive qualities were never better demonstrated. Batting was easier by the time Essex began their reply, soon after four o'clock [the game had been delayed for 50 minutes by rain], and Gooch and Hardie raced to 79 with only 11 overs bowled. Cowans' first over cost 16 runs. In the 12th over Gooch was caught at the wicket, but by tea, taken as late as 6.20, Essex had reached 113 for one. Even after McEwan had gone to a diving catch in the covers and Fletcher to a bat and pad catch at silly-point, Essex, at 135 for three, looked to have plenty in hand. But they now lost their last seven wickets for 57 runs. When Pringle and Turner took the score to 185 for five, with four overs left, it seemed that Essex would win after all. But with the light fading and the tension rising, Middlesex, astutely led by Gatting, took Pringle's wicket in the 52nd over, Turner's in the 53rd, those of both Easts in the 54th and Foster's off the first ball of the 55th. The match ended at 8.50.

Toss: Essex. **Middlesex 196-8** (55 overs) (C. T. Radley 89*; N. A. Foster 3-26); **Essex 192** (54.1 overs)

(G. A. Gooch 46, B. R. Hardie 49, K. S. McEwan 34; N. G. Cowans 4-39).

1984 – AT HOME AT LORD'S

Terry Cooper, 1985

As a gratifying consolation for failing to justify pre-season Championship favouritism [they came third after a poor start], Mike Gatting was again able to brandish a trophy after a one-day final. Success in the NatWest Trophy emulated the 1983 Benson and Hedges Cup final victory in terms of a Middlesex recovery preceding a cliff-hanging, twilight finish.

Gatting was again phenomenal [during the season]. Among English batsmen he ranks with Gooch and Boycott as the most reliable run-scorer. For the fourth consecutive season he was the most highly placed Test-qualified Englishman in the national averages. His other noteworthy achievements included the fastest century of the season [in 79 minutes against Kent at Lord's] and becoming only the eighth player – the first since Eric Russell in 1964 – to make 2,000 runs in a summer for Middlesex.

Kent v Middlesex   **NatWest Trophy Final**
At Lord's, September 1, 1984. Middlesex won by four wickets.   1985

Middlesex won off the last ball of the match, a delivery of full length from Ellison which Emburey turned to the square-leg boundary for four. It was then almost 7.45 p.m. and the lights of the scoreboards and neighbouring buildings shone brightly through the gloom. Had Middlesex not scored off the last ball, Kent would have won [because, with wickets equal, they had a higher score after 30 overs].

Toss: Kent. **Kent 232-6** (60 overs) (M. R. Benson 37, N. R. Taylor 49, C. S. Cowdrey 58); **Middlesex 236-6** (60 overs) (M. W. Gatting 37, C. T. Radley 67, P. R. Downton 40; K. B. S. Jarvis 3-47).

1985 – THE UNSTOPPABLES   Terry Cooper, 1986

For the fifth time in ten seasons Middlesex won the County Championship, probably the most satisfying of their successes since the first title of this modern era back in 1976. Before the start of the 1985 season it was considered that the Championship might be beyond a county squad certain to be weakened by Test calls. Mike Gatting and Phil Edmonds had spent the winter establishing themselves in the England side and John Emburey was again available for Tests [after being banned because of the "rebel" tour to South Africa]. Paul Downton and Norman Cowans were also almost sure to be required. In these notes last year, I presumed to wonder – "Are the reserves adequate?" The answer came that they were.

Gatting again scored substantially, though his major innings were for England. The huge quantities of runs that he produced for Middlesex from 1981 to 1984 were not there. In contrast to 1984, however, the batting coped effectively without Gatting's constant big scores. Those principally responsible for this were Barlow, Slack and Radley. The openers' reliable form was a bonus, for Barlow had struggled to complete his benefit season the previous year because of a hip injury and had become pessimistic about his playing future. Happily, a faith healer restored him and he employed his regained physical freedom to join with Slack in a string of substantial starts. Down the order Radley, Downton and Emburey enjoyed more profitable seasons with the bat, Radley enhancing his already high reputation for excavating runs from the deepest pit.

Daniel and Neil Williams provided the extra wickets that were needed with the spinners so often absent. Daniel, fully earning his benefit, was as dedicated as ever. He shortened his run, but there was no noticeable reduction in speed or hostility.

Warwickshire v Middlesex

At Edgbaston, September 14, 16, 17, 1985. Middlesex won by an innings and 74 runs.   1986

Middlesex clinched the Championship title with an emphatic win in a match which they dominated from the start. After bowling out Warwickshire with a mixture of seam and spin in just 63 overs, they reinforced their early advantage by taking a lead of 258 through forceful contributions from Slack, Brown, Gatting and Emburey. The result was a fitting one for both sides, Middlesex deservedly taking the title and Warwickshire slumping to 15th place from ninth in 1984.

Toss: Warwickshire. **Warwickshire 187** (T. A. Lloyd 32, R. I. H. B. Dyer 52, A. M. Ferreira 34;
W. W. Daniel 3-51, N. F. Williams 3-43, J. E. Emburey 4-47) **and 184** (D. L. Amiss 39;
J. E. Emburey 4-64, P. H. Edmonds 4-63); **Middlesex 445** (W. N. Slack 74, K. R. Brown 67,
M. W. Gatting 76, P. R. Downton 40, J. E. Emburey 68, N. F. Williams 46; A. M. Ferreira 3-94,
N. Gifford 5-128).

1986 – "SUPPORTERS QUICKLY FORGET"   Terry Cooper, 1987

There was universal surprise and local disappointment at Middlesex's non-existent defence of their Championship pennant. It had been expected that they would again overcome the loss of key players to England duties, but neither the full-strength side nor the second-string team performed to the level achieved in 1985. The mid-summer weeks near, or at, the foot of the table brought grumblings from impatient supporters.

The reality was that, having been denied a winning start with Mike Gatting, John Emburey and Phil Edmonds, Middlesex had little prospect of winning without them. "Supporters quickly forget", ruminated Middlesex's coach, Don Bennett, referring to criticism even after the Benson and Hedges Cup had been won. Gatting said: "Our Benson displays included some of the best cricket in my Middlesex career."

Kent v Middlesex   Benson and Hedges Cup Final

At Lord's, July 12, 1986. Middlesex won by two runs.   1987

A dramatic finish, in murky light and heavy rain, was adequate compensation for a match which, though tightly fought, had been a somewhat dull affair until late in the day. Kent needed 31 runs from the last three overs, but the dismissal of Cowdrey in the first of them was the turning-point. Edmonds came back to bowl the penultimate over, dismissed Ellison and gave away just five runs, leaving 14 to be scored off the 55th over. Hughes, despite Marsh's six, kept his head and his line.

Toss: Kent. **Middlesex 199-7** (55 overs) (A. J. T. Miller 37, C. T. Radley 54; R. M. Ellison 3-27);
Kent 197-8 (55 overs) (G. R. Cowdrey 58; P. H. Edmonds 3-58).

1988 – TWO NEW STARS ARE BORN
Terry Cooper, 1989

Middlesex returned to the winners' enclosure, after a rare year on the outside, when they beat Worcestershire in the NatWest Trophy final. It was the fifth time in his six years as captain that Mike Gatting had accepted a prize and it provided a gratifying end to an encouraging season. Middlesex were seventh in the Championship, quarter-finalists in the Benson and Hedges Cup, and fourth in the Refuge Assurance League

The position in the Championship reflected a considerable improvement from 16th in 1987, and there were hints that Middlesex might challenge for the title sooner than was expected during two previous mediocre seasons. In the NatWest final, two of the young players responsible for the renewed optimism, Mark Ramprakash and Angus Fraser, demonstrated their talents to a wide audience. In 1987 most areas of the team had given cause for concern; last season, Fraser and Ramprakash helped ease anxieties about the pace bowling and the batting.

Middlesex v Worcestershire
NatWest Trophy Final
At Lord's, September 3, 1988. Middlesex won by three wickets.
1989

Winning the toss gave Middlesex a decisive advantage on a pitch containing suffi-cient moisture to help the seam bowlers throughout the day. Ramprakash, two days away from his 19th birthday, took them to within three runs of victory, batting throughout in his cap with confidence, style and rare charm. Emburey stayed with him till the 53rd over, by which time Ramprakash had reached 50 from 118 balls.

Toss: Middlesex. **Worcestershire 161-9** (60 overs) (P. A. Neale 64, M. J. Weston 31; A. R. C. Fraser 3-36, S. P. Hughes 4-30); **Middlesex 162-7** (55.3 overs) (M. R. Ramprakash 56, J. E. Emburey 35; G. R. Dilley 5-29).

1990 – HAYNES THE HERO
Terry Cooper, 1991

Two unconnected decisions taken in 1989 were decisive factors in Middlesex winning the 1990 Championship. Firstly, Mike Gatting and John Emburey committed themselves to a tour of South Africa, which carried a suspension from Test cricket and meant they would be available for their county throughout the season. Second, the TCCB, having finally begun to penalise counties for poor pitches, also legislated for a reduced seam on the ball. This ensured that only attacking bowlers would earn regular reward, and proved advantageous to Middlesex, whose attack was not made up of trundling medium-pacers. Middlesex also benefited from their policy over two decades of invariably choosing two spin-ners. Where once Edmonds and Titmus, and then Edmonds and Emburey had held sway, now another left- and right-arm alliance, Tufnell and Emburey emerged as a match-winner.

The top five in the batting remained constant. In a particularly rare occurrence in the County Championship, Desmond Haynes, Mike Roseberry, Gatting, Mark Ramprakash and Keith Brown played in all 22 games. Roseberry could hardly fail to profit from opening with Haynes, and they launched the innings with such commanding strokeplay that the opposition was forced into premature defence. Middlesex expected much of Haynes when he joined them in 1989, and he fulfilled their expectations in both Championship and limited-overs cricket.

1992 – SUNDAY BEST
Terry Cooper, 1993

Mike Gatting's tenth season as captain gave him yet another chance to flourish a trophy before Middlesex supporters. But unexpectedly this one was for winning the Sunday League, the competition which had eluded the club for 23 years. The 40-overs title completed a Grand Slam for Gatting, who has led the team to two Championships, two NatWest Trophies and two Benson and Hedges Cups. Only Keith Fletcher of Essex has previously captained a team to all four competitions. When Gatting succeeded the honours-laden Brearley, he naturally wanted to maintain his predecessor's achievements, which comprised three Championships (and one shared) and two Gillette Cups in the period 1976–82. Gatting will not regard the books as quite balanced until another Championship is achieved.

1993 – SPINNING TO ANOTHER TITLE
Norman de Mesquita, 1994

If ever confirmation was needed of the cricketing adage that bowlers win matches, Middlesex's 1993 Championship success provided it. They won the title without a single batsman scoring 1,000 Championship runs. John Emburey, in particular, had a year to remember. He took 68 wickets at 18.39 apiece and scored 638 runs at an average of 49.07 in his unique style. In Emburey and Philip Tufnell, Middlesex had the best pair of spinners in the county game.

The Championship represented the eighth title during Gatting's 11-year tenure of office, but the appointment of John Carr as vice-captain indicated that Gatting expected his captaincy to end sooner rather than later. Carr acquitted himself well when suddenly forced to lead the side – after Gatting had put his arm through a dressing-room door during a one-day game with the Australians – and he responded particularly well with the bat.

It was very much a team effort, though one drawback was the limited number of opportunities to introduce new, young blood to the side. Eleven players made 13 or more Championship appearances and the average age of those players at the end of the season was 31. Life may have begun at 40 for John Emburey, but if the Middlesex success story is to have future chapters, that average must surely be drastically reduced.

Middlesex v Hampshire
At Lord's, July 22, 23, 24, 1993. Middlesex won by nine wickets.   1994

A month away from his 41st birthday, Emburey recorded his best figures in 20 years of cricket to transform what had been an even contest. Beginning the second innings only 30 behind, Hampshire were routed for 88, with Emburey, getting bounce and turn from the Pavilion End, taking eight for 40; Tufnell helped by securing the vital wickets of Gower and Terry.

Toss: Hampshire. **Hampshire 280** (R. S. M. Morris 54, D. I. Gower 91, M. J. Thursfield 36*;
J. E. Emburey 4-75) **and 88** (J. E. Emburey 8-40); **Middlesex 310** (M. W. Gatting 84, K. R. Brown 45,
N. F. Williams 44; M. J. Thursfield 4-78) **and 59-1** (D. L. Haynes 41*).

1994 – JOHNSON'S MATCH   Norman de Mesquita, 1995

Fourth place in the Championship would be seen by some counties as representing a successful season. For Middlesex, winners of eight trophies in the previous 11 years of Mike Gatting's captaincy it was a disappointment. There were several reasons for underperforming, principally a series of injuries that prevented the county from fielding its strongest attack. Chas Taylor had two knee operations during the year and did not make a single Championship appearance. Richard Johnson, having taken all ten wickets in the second innings at Derby, then played only one more first-class match before he, too, needed surgery on his knee. Neil Williams did not play between the middle of June and the end of August, while Philip Tufnell did not appear in the Championship until the end of June because of personal troubles.

Derbyshire v Middlesex
At Derby, June 30, July 1, 2, 1994. Middlesex won by an innings and 96 runs.   1995

Nineteen-year-old seamer Richard Johnson became the first bowler to take all ten wickets in the Championship for 30 years, since Ian Thomson, for Sussex against Warwickshire at Worthing in 1964. In Derbyshire's second innings, Johnson captured seven for 17 in his first nine overs, rested after 12 and completed the task after tea when Taylor was caught at third slip. The opening batsman Haynes bowled the last two overs from the other end, in an attempt to ensure that Johnson took the final wicket, and had a fright when Malcolm almost played on.

Although Johnson was helped by reckless batting, it was an outstanding feat by a young man in his first full season. Only one player younger than Johnson had taken ten in a first-class innings: 18-year-old Imran Adil of Bahawalpur in 1989-90. Johnson's previous best was four for 64 against Durham a week earlier – though he had attracted attention by dismissing Lara in both the Benson and Hedges Cup and the Championship. "It hasn't quite sunk in," he said afterwards. "The ball did a little bit off the seam, but it didn't really swing."

Derbyshire v Middlesex, 1994

At Derby, June 30, July 1, 2, 1994. Result: Middlesex won by an innings and 96 runs.

DERBYSHIRE	*First innings*		*Second innings*	
*K. J. Barnett c Brown b Johnson	148	–	c Emburey b Johnson	4
M. J. Vandrau b Feltham	31	–	b Johnson	0
C. J. Adams c Gatting b Shine	17	–	(4) c Carr b Johnson	8
T. J. G. O'Gorman c Gatting b Emburey	39	–	(3) c Emburey b Johnson	18
D. G. Cork run out	0	–	c Feltham b Johnson	4
†A. S. Rollins not out	53	–	c and b Johnson	2
C. M. Wells c Shine b Feltham	8	–	b Johnson	32
A. E. Warner c Haynes b Emburey	0	–	c Brown b Johnson	2
S. J. Base c Carr b Feltham	7	–	lbw b Johnson	20
M. Taylor b Feltham	1	–	c Ramprakash b Johnson	5
D. E. Malcolm c Roseberry b Feltham	4	–	not out	1
L-b 17, w 1, n-b 18	36		B 2, l-b 4, w 1, n-b 2	9

1-96 2-124 3-219 4-220 5-285 6-313 7-313   344   1-4 2-9 3-30 4-34 5-35 6-36 7-43 8-93   105
8-326 9-334 10-344   9-104 10-105

First innings – Johnson 20–5–65–1; Shine 17–0–93–1; Feltham 29.5–8–69–5; Emburey 30–14–43–2; Tufnell 30–9–57–0.
Second innings – Johnson 18.5–6–45–10; Feltham 12–4–37–0; Shine 6–2–15–0; Tufnell 2–1–2–0; Haynes 2–2–0–0.

MIDDLESEX   *First innings*

D. L. Haynes c Rollins b Malcolm	46		J. E. Emburey b Wells	0
M. A. Roseberry lbw b Base	18		K. J. Shine b Cork	0
*M. W. Gatting run out	147		P. C. R. Tufnell b Wells	5
M. R. Ramprakash c sub b Malcolm	131		B 11, l-b 16, n-b 54	81
J. D. Carr not out	108		1-43 2-128 3-330 4-433 5-452 6-495 7-519	545
†K. R. Brown lbw b Base	2		8-519 9-520 10-545	
M. A. Feltham b Wells	4			
R. L. Johnson lbw b Wells	3			

Malcolm 25–4–102–2; Warner 19–4–53–0; Base 20–2–88–2; Cork 22–4–108–1; Wells 22–5–52–4; Vandrau 18–2–58–0; Taylor 10–1–57–0.

Toss won by Derbyshire   UMPIRES R. Palmer and P. Willey

1995 – EMBUREY'S FAREWELL…   Norman de Mesquita, 1996

Middlesex came desperately close to winning their eighth Championship in 20 years in 1995 and they made Warwickshire wait until the very last round to be sure of retaining their title. They travelled to Taunton for the last game 15 points adrift, but rain in Somerset and Kent's feeble performance against Warwickshire kept them in second place – their fifth finish in the top four in seven years. The Somerset match was John Emburey's last for the county he joined in 1973. He began a new career in coaching by taking England A to Pakistan, and it was soon confirmed that he would become Northamptonshire's chief coach in 1996. In 23 seasons, he had taken 1,250 first-class wickets at 24.06 for Middlesex. He was still their most successful bowler in 1995, with 74 wickets. His departure seemed likely to turn the following season into a watershed year.

1997 – ... AND GATTING'S TOO
Norman de Mesquita, 1998

It was a watershed year which saw a change of captain and the end of Don Bennett's 29 years as coach. Mike Gatting, captain since 1983, already intended to step down in favour of Mark Ramprakash. But at the end of May, with new responsibilities as an England selector, he decided to do it immediately. In contrast with bloody coups at other counties, the handover could not have been smoother [but see below!].

1998 – NIGHTMARE FOR BUCHANAN
Norman de Mesquita, 1999

Middlesex had a dreadful season, culminating in five consecutive defeats and their worst-ever Championship placing – 17th. Even veteran Middlesex watchers, who remember the barren period before the Brearley era, could not recall so many embarrassing displays. An August Saturday at Hove, when Middlesex were bowled out twice in less than two sessions, was the nadir.

After such a year, it was tempting to find a scapegoat. First-team coach John Buchanan, recruited from Queensland to bring a fresh approach, was the popular choice. The fact that he was not asked to return was seen by some as an indictment. Mike Gatting, who retired as a player in September, was appointed director of coaching, with the task of trying to restore the Middlesex glory years.

2000 – MELTDOWN
Norman de Mesquita, 2001

The harsh realities of modern county cricket finally caught up with Middlesex after difficulties on and off the field in 2000. It was a sorry enough time when the end of August brought the unexpected departure of two icons, Mike Gatting and Ian Gould. But the loss of Mark Ramprakash in the New Year, to join traditional rivals Surrey, cut much deeper. He was a recent captain [he had resigned the previous year after another disappointing season under his leadership], had just enjoyed a benefit year and, in its hour of need, was turning his back on the club to pursue his ambition for England honours. This, he claimed, required first-division cricket – something he had not experienced with Middlesex in either the Championship or the League. Gatting and Gould, as director of coaching and club coach respectively, had paid the price for the county winning nothing since the 1993 Championship, and for never looking as if they would end that barren run over the past three seasons. Both first played for Middlesex in 1975 and were so strongly identified with the county that it was hard to imagine neither having a role there any more.

Northamptonshire

1980 – PRIME LAMB   Fred Speakman, 1981

The highlight of Northamptonshire's season was their victory at Lord's where they won the Benson and Hedges Cup for the first time, thus continuing their successful Cup run of recent years. In 1976 they gained their first-ever major trophy when they won the Gillette Cup, and in 1979 they were again finalists, losing to Somerset.

Claiming one of the four major trophies was a fitting climax to the long career of their captain, Jim Watts, who retired in August after three spells with the county, the first of them beginning in 1957. Having trained as a teacher, he returned for the last time in 1978 to stabilise the club after the upheaval caused by the departure of four leading players in 1977, among them the previous captain Mushtaq Mohammad [Bishan Bedi was another]. The captaincy has been passed to opening batsman Geoff Cook.

Wayne Larkins, Allan Lamb [recruited as the county's overseas player in 1978] and Richard Williams enjoyed splendid seasons. Lamb [scored] 1,797 runs in first-class matches at an average of 66.55, and the delight his batting gave contributed to his inclusion as one of the Almanack's Five Cricketers of the Year. He won the Gold Award in the Benson and Hedges Cup final. Larkins was in fine, aggressive county form with 1,682 first-class runs and an average of over 50, hitting four hundreds. He and Williams shared a second-wicket stand of 322 against Leicestershire in August, a record for the county.

With the ball, the fast-medium combination of Jim Griffiths, Sarfraz and Tim Lamb was an effective attacking force. Sarfraz, though hindered at times by injuries, bowled economically and was a commanding figure in the Benson and Hedges Cup matches at Lord's, both in the semi-final [in which he took five for 21 to secure victory by 11 runs over Middlesex] and the final.

Essex v Northamptonshire   **Benson and Hedges Cup Final**

At Lord's, July 19, 21, 1980. Northamptonshire won by six runs.   1981

Toss: Northamptonshire. **Northamptonshire 209** (54.5 overs) (A. J. Lamb 72, S. Turner 3-33, K. R. Pont 4-60); **Essex 203-8** (55 overs) (G. A. Gooch 60, K. S. McEwan 38, N. Philip 32*; Sarfraz Nawaz (3-23).

1981 – UNSUITABLE TIE
Fred Speakman, 1982

Northamptonshire reached the NatWest Trophy final, losing the game when the scores were tied because Derbyshire had more wickets in hand. In their progress to the final, they beat strong opposition in Somerset, Leicestershire and Lancashire. Otherwise it was an unhappy season for Geoff Cook and his team. They finished 15th in the Championship, bottom in the John Player League, and did not qualify for the knockout stages of the Benson and Hedges Cup, which they won the previous season.

The best batting came from the South African Allan Lamb, who will be eligible for England in 1982. He was in tremendous form, becoming the first Northamptonshire batsman to total 2,000 runs in a season for 26 years and only the fourth in all. In bowling the summer brought a best-ever return of 70 wickets for [Jim] Griffiths and the discovery of [Neil] Mallender, a young Yorkshire-born bowler.

At one stage the Indian Test bowler, Kapil Dev, was signed for midweek matches, but he played only three times and was then more successful with bat than the ball. Tim Lamb was the hero of the exciting NatWest semi-final against Lancashire with his bowling, fielding and finally his batting as he controlled a memorable, match-winning last-wicket stand.

1986 – IN SEARCH OF AN ATTACK
Andrew Radd, 1987

That a season which featured many outstanding individual performances – mostly with the bat – should produce so little improvement in the team's final placings was a source of disappointment. In the three-day game, the problem was a familiar one: that of bowling sides out in the absence of a consistently effective pace spearhead. David Capel, who matured considerably as an all-rounder, showed promise as a strike bowler, but Neil Mallender failed to find his rhythm for much of the season and his potential remained unfulfilled.

Much was expected of the spinners, Nick Cook and Roger Harper. They finished as the county's leading wicket-takers in first-class matches, sending down nearly 1,700 overs between them. [Harper took 62 wickets; Cook 61.] However, they rarely looked sufficiently threatening when operating in tandem in Championship matches, and this greatly reduced Northamptonshire's chances of success. The dismissal of Essex for only 44 at Colchester rewrote some records, but in the context of the season it was more a curiosity than an accurate gauge of bowling strength.

Despite Lamb's brilliance, the player of the year was Robert Bailey. He enjoyed a memorable summer, tainted only by the absence of a Test call to play against India or New Zealand, or of a place in the touring party for Australia. Hitting the ball with obvious power but little apparent effort, the 22-year-old Bailey registered two double-hundreds in four weeks and narrowly missed reaching 2,000 runs in only his third full season.

Essex v Northamptonshire

At Colchester, August 16, 18, 19, 1986. Northamptonshire won by 102 runs.   1987

On a pitch which crumbled rapidly, Essex [who were in the process of winning their third Championship in four seasons], needing 147 to win in a minimum of 56 overs, were dismissed for the lowest score of the season in 85 minutes, or 20.1 overs. Nick Cook and [Neil] Mallender were the destroyers, with only Gooch managing to reach double figures. Northamptonshire claimed the last eight Essex wickets for 13 runs.

Toss: Northamptonshire. **Northamptonshire 302** (A. J. Lamb 81, R. J. Bailey 63, D. J. Capel 40;
N. A. Foster 5-83) **and 181** (W. Larkins 34, R. A. Harper 39; J. H. Childs 8-61); **Essex 337**
(G. A. Gooch 87, P. J. Prichard 72, B. R. Hardie 66; N. A. Mallender 5-110, N. G. B. Cook 4-76)
and 44 (N. A. Mallender 4-22, N. G. B. Cook 5-14).

1987 – TREBLE DISAPPOINTMENT   Andrew Radd, 1988

When the Northamptonshire side arrived at Lord's on the second Saturday in July for the Benson and Hedges Cup final against Yorkshire, a historic hat-trick of titles looked within the realms of possibility. Yet by the time the same players began the return journey to Northampton after losing to Nottinghamshire in the NatWest Trophy final eight weeks later, the dream had been shattered. Richard Hadlee's heroic innings on that momentous Monday afternoon ensured that Northamptonshire shared Middlesex's unhappy experience of 1975, reaching both major one-day finals, only to lose them both. And seventh place in the Championship, although an improvement of two places on 1986, was a disappointing outcome after being among the pace-setters for a good part of the season.

The signing of the West Indian fast bowler, Winston Davis, proved a successful move, and Northamptonshire's belief in him was rewarded with 70 Championship wickets, the county's best individual return for ten years. Despite Davis's tendency to overstep – 211 no-balls in 19 three-day matches – his penetrative, hostile bowling brought a new edge to the seam attack.

1988 – LILLEE'S BRIEF BURST   Andrew Radd, 1989

After the near-misses of the previous year, Northamptonshire's failure to challenge for any of the major trophies in 1988 was especially disappointing. Nothing better served to illustrate the unfulfilled hopes of the season than the striking contrast between the high-profile arrival in May of Dennis Lillee, thrusting the club into the national spotlight, and the small, low-key press conference to witness Geoff Cook's resignation in September.

The decision of Cook, a leader respected throughout the county game, to stand down after eight years in charge was hardly a surprise following a season in which little had gone right for him, or his team. Cook admitted that the side had been found wanting in commitment and application; hence his desire for someone with "fresh ideas and fresh motivation" to replace him.

Lillee earned much admiration for his determination to fight back from an injury which threatened to end his career within three weeks of his taking six for 68 in the second innings of his Championship debut against Gloucestershire. He was an admirable ambassador for the club, liberal with his advice to colleagues and opponents alike.

1992 – SUCCESS AT LAST
Andrew Radd, 1993

Two victories over Leicestershire in September ensured that 1992 would be remembered as a season of outstanding achievement for Northamptonshire. The first, at Lord's, earned Allan Lamb's side the NatWest Trophy, and brought to an end the club's frustrating and sometimes fractious 12-year wait for a major title. Then, in beating their old rivals at Grace Road ten days later, Northamptonshire secured third place in the County Championship, their highest finish since 1976.

Lamb himself was, in every sense, the central figure throughout the summer. He comfortably topped Northamptonshire's first-class averages with 1,406 runs at 66.95, including six centuries, while in his fourth year as captain he displayed a greater tactical awareness, particularly in the NatWest Trophy run, and was duly re-appointed for 1993. His allegations of ball-tampering against the Pakistani tourists, which led to him being fined and suspended for two matches by the county, threatened to distract his Northamptonshire colleagues at a critical point of the season, although director of cricket Mike Procter said that the effect of the whole affair on dressing-room morale had been, if anything, a positive one.

The bulk of the first-class runs came from Lamb, Alan Fordham and vice-captain Rob Bailey, with Fordham once more unfortunate to miss out on an England tour overseas. His opening partnership with Nigel Felton was again a key element in the overall strategy, both in one-day cricket and the Championship.

Curtly Ambrose was at his best in the NatWest Trophy, taking eight wickets for 82 runs in 50.5 overs spread over the county's five games – a scoring-rate against him of just 1.6 runs per over. He was troubled for much of the season by a knee injury that required surgery after the NatWest final. This was also the year which saw Richard Williams's retirement. Williams's cleverly flighted bowling and pugnacious batting were part of the Northamptonshire scene for nearly 20 years, and his well-crafted skills will be missed in the county and beyond.

Leicestershire v Northamptonshire
At Lord's, September 5, 1992. Northamptonshire won by eight wickets.

NatWest Trophy Final
Matthew Engel, 1993

The county used to being criticised for fouling up promising situations won this match with such uncompromising efficiency that it could be remembered as the most boring of all the Lord's finals, if anyone outside Northamptonshire bothers to remember it. If so, that was entirely to the winners' credit. They did just about everything right on the day and Leicestershire, who played far above themselves simply to get this far, were in the end simply overmatched. What chance they might have had was probably wrecked the previous night when the all-rounder Wells collapsed in the team hotel and was taken to hospital. Leicestershire again approached [Jonathan] Agnew, the improbable hero of the semi-final [who had come out of retirement in response to an injury crisis and bowled a tight spell], and obtained an emergency registration for another former player, Peter Willey, who was working alongside Agnew in the BBC commentary box. In the end, they opted to play their fast bowler Millns, but he was barely even quarter-fit.

The score of 208 for seven was nowhere near enough to withstand the assault it received from Fordham and Bailey, who put on 144. Fordham hit 13 fours in his 91 and struck the ball as sweetly as was possible on a slow surface. Ray Illingworth rightly made him Man of the Match. The inevitability of the result made the closing stages very routine. From the start the atmosphere had been lifeless: for the first time in many years the final was not a sell-out. Most people put this down to the presence of two of the smaller counties. More relevant were the weeks of bad weather before the event, the high prices (£35 for a half-decent view) at a time of recession, and a certain loss of novelty value: for Northamptonshire this was their eighth Lord's final in 17 years. Those who did pay were able to watch skydivers in the lunch interval; they might have been more entertained had they been privy to events behind the scenes, especially when Lamb, the Northamptonshire captain, received a writ for libel from his former team-mate Sarfraz Nawaz because of allegations about ball-tampering. When he went out to bat, Lamb was accompanied through the Long Room by two county officials to prevent anyone choosing that moment to hand over another writ.

Toss: Northamptonshire. **Leicestershire 208-7** (60 overs) (J. J. Whitaker 84, P. E. Robinson 62; K. M. Curran 3-41); **Northamptonshire 211-2** (49.4 overs) (A. Fordham 91, R. J. Bailey 72*).

1994 – AMBROSE THE ACE
Andrew Radd, 1995

Rarely in Northamptonshire's history have the performances and the personality of one cricketer dominated a season to the extent that Curtly Ambrose's did in 1994. His non-appearance at the start of the season, when chief executive Steve Coverdale was left baffled and embarrassed at the airport, left the club in turmoil and contributed significantly to a depressing start. But he did appear four days later and by the time he returned to Antigua, one match early because of a shoulder problem, he had largely redeemed himself in the eyes of team-mates and supporters with a succession of superb bowling performances, enabling the side to finish the Championship campaign with a flourish.

Ambrose's haul of 77 first-class wickets – at 14.45, comfortably on top of the national averages – was the best for the county since 1976, when Sarfraz Nawaz took 82. He collected 47 of them in seven games between mid-July and early September which brought six wins.

Hampshire v Northamptonshire

At Southampton, July 28, 29, 30, August 1, 1994. Northamptonshire won by 24 runs.   1995

Four men dominated the match: the two captains with the bat and two West Indian pace bowlers. But Ambrose settled the issue. Bowling in short bursts because of a side strain, he returned seven for 44, improving on his best analysis for Northamptonshire for the second time in nine days. As in the previous game, against Derbyshire, he finished with ten in the match.

Toss: Northamptonshire. **Northamptonshire 164** (A. L. Penberthy 56*; C. A. Connor 7-47) **and 358**
(A. J. Lamb 131, M. B. Loye 48, A. R. Roberts 30, N. G. B. Cook 43*; C. A. Connor 3-79, S. D. Udal 5-119);
Hampshire 229 (G. W. White 38, M. C. J. Nicholas 53, K. D. James 49*; C. E. L. Ambrose 3-44,
J. G. Hughes 5-69) **and 269** (M. C. J. Nicholas 107, A. N. Aymes 31; C. E. L. Ambrose 7-44).

1995 – LAMB'S LAST HURRAH   Andrew Radd, 1996

Northamptonshire failed to lift a trophy in 1995, but if that suggests business as usual at Wantage Road, nothing could be further from the truth. Victory over Leicestershire on June 26 – their sixth successive Championship win, equalling the county's best-ever sequence – left Allan Lamb's side 43 points clear at the top of the table. A month later, they defeated Warwickshire by seven runs in an unforgettable contest at Edgbaston. Even Northamptonshire's traditionally sceptical supporters began to believe that a first Championship title, the club's Holy Grail, was within reach.

It was not to be, however. Despite winning 12 matches, more than any champion county since 1989, they had to settle for third place. Defeat in the NatWest Trophy final – another triumph for Warwickshire – denied them a consolation prize. No one could deny, though, the team's contribution to the season as a whole. Conventional cricketing wisdom was undermined time and time again as a burgeoning sense of self-belief helped to secure a string of triumphs that ranged from the unlikely to the almost impossible. Northamptonshire were dismissed for the two lowest totals of the summer – 46 against Essex at Luton and 59 against Surrey at Northampton – but went on to win both matches. They also built up the season's biggest score, 781 for seven declared, to set up an innings victory after Nottinghamshire had made 527.

The results reflected clearly Lamb's style of captaincy: a blend of confidence, arrogance, enterprise and sheer will-power. Conscious that this was his last year in charge, he never gave up hope of some silverware until it became a mathematical impossibility. To Lamb, too, went the credit for the decision to bring the Indian leg-spinner Anil Kumble to Northampton. It was an inspired move. He captured 105 first-class wickets, becoming the first bowler to reach three figures since Neil Foster and Waqar Younis in 1991, and the first to achieve the feat for the county since another Indian, Bishan Bedi, in 1973

Warwickshire v Northamptonshire

At Birmingham, July 27, 28, 29, 31, 1995. Northamptonshire won by seven runs. 1996

This nerve-shredding encounter was described by both captains as the best Championship game they had ever played in. It was probably one of the best of all time. Northamptonshire won at 2.45 on the final day. Had they lost, Warwickshire would have been near-certain champions already; victory reduced the gap between them to two points. A match of dramatic twists was exemplified in the final innings. Chasing 275, Warwickshire slumped to 53 for six against Kumble, recovered to 201 for six, thanks to Reeve and Smith, lost their ninth wicket with 47 required and still fell only eight short. "It was like a little bit of a war out there," said Lamb, "but that's the way county cricket should be played."

Toss: Northamptonshire. **Northamptonshire 152** (D. J. Capel 50; A. A. Donald 4-41, T. A. Munton 4-47) **and 346** (A. Fordham 101, K. M. Curran 30, R. J. Warren 70, Extras 41; A. A. Donald 6-95); **Warwickshire 224** (R. G. Twose 140; A. Kumble 3-69, D. J. Capel 7-44) **and 267** (D. A. Reeve 74, N. M. K. Smith 75; A. Kumble 7-82).

2002 – FROM BAD TO WORSE
Andrew Radd, 2003

If double relegation in 2001 indicated that Northamptonshire did not possess the strength in depth to compete with the best counties, their results in 2002 hinted at even starker shortcomings. A return to both top divisions had naturally been the target, but promotion in the Championship was ruled out as a serious possibility in July, while the chances of a top three finish in the Norwich Union League evaporated with the loss of the last six matches.

It was depressing enough to finish seventh in Division Two of the Championship, three off the bottom of the league, and suffer early exits from both the B&H and C&G. But other issues gave substance to the perception that Northamptonshire were an increasingly accident-prone club. One of their longest-serving players, Russell Warren, was dropped in June following a domestic imbroglio, apparently involving a team-mate's fiancée, of which the management had been aware for some months. Then, a fortnight later, Mal Loye, Warren's near-contemporary, announced his intention to leave after 13 years on the staff. The breakdown in his working relationship with the director of cricket, Bob Carter, was at the heart of Loye's decision. He later agreed a four-year deal with Lancashire; Warren left for Nottinghamshire.

Of Carter's six close-season signings, only one – the fast bowler Carl Greenidge, from Surrey – made much of an impact in the first team. These factors combined to convince the committee that a change of direction was required, and Carter was sacked in September with a year of his contract remaining. In December the former South African captain Kepler Wessels was hired as Carter's replacement.

Nottinghamshire

1977 – RICE WITH EVERYTHING
Harry Richards, 1978

After showing signs of a revival over the previous two seasons, Nottinghamshire had a disastrous summer and finished firmly at the bottom of the County Championship with only one victory – and that at the end of the season in a match of declarations against Worcestershire. All the promise held out for their budding young talent crumbled, and only the efforts of their brilliant South African all-rounder [Clive] Rice gave any hope.

Rice enjoyed his best season in English cricket and provided a brilliant inspiration to the team, which unfortunately proved incapable of backing him up. He finished top of the batting and bowling averages not only in first-class games but in one-day competitions as well. Without Rice, Nottinghamshire cricket would have been a shambles and it was good news for the county when he signified his intention to renew his contract.

1979 – HADLEE'S ARRIVAL
Harry Richards, 1980

Before a ball had been bowled in 1978, the Nottinghamshire season was plunged into controversy and disarray. This was because Clive Rice, newly appointed captain in the winter months, announced on his return from his native South Africa that he had agreed to play for Kerry Packer's WSC. It led to his instant dismissal by the club committee. Backed by World Series Cricket, Rice sought redress in the High Court, but before the case came up for hearing Nottinghamshire had second thoughts and reinstated Rice as a player but not as captain.

Before this happened, however, the club gained an unexpected bonus. No sooner had they given Rice his marching orders than they signed the New Zealand fast bowler, Richard Hadlee, as a replacement. It gave Nottinghamshire an opening attack as penetrative as that possessed by any county in the Championship, and the results were immediate. In his first five Championship games, Hadlee collected 34 wickets, including match figures of seven for 90, 11 for 141 and eight for 55, in the three consecutive victories over Derbyshire, Yorkshire and Warwickshire. Hadlee, too, proved most capable with the bat and his hard-hitting maiden century against Derbyshire revealed him as a genuine all-rounder.

1981 – GREEN TOPS
John Lawson, 1982

Not since the days of Harold Larwood and Bill Voce had Trent Bridge hosted such celebratory scenes as those that greeted Nottinghamshire's final victory of the season over Glamorgan. The win – the ninth in their last 11 games of the summer – gave them the County Championship for the first time for 52 years.

It was a title-winning effort that, as in the Nottinghamshire days of old, owed much to the devil and destruction of a formidable new-ball attack. Richard Hadlee and Clive Rice exploited to the full Trent Bridge wickets that were always well-grassed; they capitalised, too, on Rice's good fortune in winning all but the first toss of the season in home fixtures. Rice's all-round play led to his being labelled as the most complete player in world cricket, Botham included. He scored 1,462 runs at an average of 56.23, and his positive and vibrant leadership created winning situations where none seemingly existed.

The performances of off-spinner Eddie Hemmings also deserve special mention. His 90 first-class wickets included several productive spells at Trent Bridge that defied the criticism which Nottinghamshire attracted for preparing wickets to suit the needs of their pace attack. On many an occasion it was Hemmings who eventually spun Nottinghamshire to victory at home – as when producing career-best match figures of 13 for 129 against Derbyshire at Trent Bridge.

Nottinghamshire's batting failed to measure up to their bowling. Unlike in previous years of failure, however, they mustered some useful scores under pressure. Once more, too, much depended on Rice, who scored six hundreds. The only other player to complete 1,000 runs was Derek Randall, attempting to reconstruct an England future amid Nottinghamshire's success. At his best he remained a composed and uninhibited stroke-player, but he still had those moments of indecision and recklessness that were such a frustration to his admirers.

Nottinghamshire v Glamorgan

At Nottingham, September 12, 14, 1981. Nottinghamshire won by ten wickets. 1982

Nottinghamshire clinched the County Championship when they destroyed Glamorgan inside two days. They underlined their intentions to leave nothing to chance by bowling out Glamorgan for 60 on the first morning, with Hadlee reaching 100 wickets for the season in his four for 18.

Toss: Nottinghamshire. **Glamorgan 60** (R. J. Hadlee 4-18, K. E. Cooper 4-25) **and 149** (Javed Miandad 75; R. J. Hadlee 4-38, E. E. Hemmings 4-51); **Nottinghamshire 180** (M. A. Nash 4-48, R. C. Ontong 3-47) **and 30-0**.

1984 – ANYTHING BUT A BORE

John Lawson, 1985

Few people remember who comes second: that was the tragedy of Nottinghamshire's 1984 season, which must go down as one of the most successful in the club's history. Ironically, their performances and results were better than in 1981, when Clive Rice's side ended a 52-year drought by winning the County Championship. In 1984, after one of the most fascinating, fluctuating and frenetic finishes to a season, Nottinghamshire had to settle for second place behind Essex in the Championship.

They entered the final day of the season against Somerset at Taunton knowing that if they won that match they would pip Essex, who had just overtaken them by accounting for Lancashire in two days. Somerset's declaration was challenging, leaving Nottinghamshire chasing 297 against the clock. With Clive Rice playing a captain's innings, they kept in touch with their target for most of the way, but 27 were needed off the last two overs and 14 off the last. Mike Bore, who has rarely had pretensions to being anything other than a No. 11 batsman, was the unlikely figure Nottinghamshire looked to in this gripping climax to the season, and he looked capable of achieving the unexpected when he reduced the target to four from three balls. Having blocked the first, he gambled all on hitting the penultimate delivery for six, but was caught on the long-off boundary.

Somerset v Nottinghamshire

At Taunton, September 8, 10, 11, 1984. Somerset won by three runs.   1985

Toss: Somerset. **Somerset 274** (P. M. Roebuck 44, M. D. Crowe 57, J. W. Lloyds 94; R. J. Hadlee 4-59, K. E. Cooper 4-57) **and 244-5 dec.** (P. M. Roebuck 78, M. D. Crowe 45, J. W. Lloyds 63*; E. E. Hemmings 4-123); **Nottinghamshire 222-7 dec.** (B. C. Broad 88*, D. W. Randall 64) **and 293** (B. C. Broad 45, C. E. B. Rice 98; V. J. Marks 6-111, S. C. Booth 4-138).

1987 – SUPERCHARGED SWANSONG

John Lawson, 1988

A scriptwriter could not have devised anything better for the swansong of Clive Rice and Richard Hadlee, the South African and New Zealander who had done so much to transform Nottinghamshire into one of the most successful county sides. At one time, with the Championship, NatWest Trophy and Refuge Assurance League in their sights, it looked as if they would capture a remarkable treble. Then, for an agonising fortnight at the end of August, all the old doubts and uncertainties returned. However, determination had always been as significant a quality of Rice and Hadlee as their natural talent, and they were determined to capture honours as proof of the best season in the club's history. So it was. First came the NatWest Trophy, then the Championship, and they were denied the treble by Worcestershire's winning the Sunday League, having to settle for the runners-up prize money.

Northamptonshire v Nottinghamshire NatWest Trophy Final

At Lord's, September 5, 7, 1987. Nottinghamshire won by three wickets. 1988

When play resumed at 1.30 on Monday afternoon, overnight rain having prevented a false start, Northamptonshire were heavily backed to win. In 21 overs on Saturday evening, they had reduced Nottinghamshire to 57 for four, with Rice 20 not out, Birch nine not out, and only Hadlee of the recognised batsmen to come. Only Hadlee! When Birch was bowled in the 29th over and the New Zealand all-rounder walked bare-headed to the middle, neither his determination nor his self-belief could be denied. He and Rice added 62 in 12 overs. Northamptonshire were jubilant when Rice was caught at mid-on, but it was from then on that they lost their grip on the game.

Their cricket had been superb: 15 overs had passed before the day's first boundary. But the 44th over, Williams's last, realised 15 runs and Hadlee might have been caught any one of three times – once when Lamb lost the ball as it was crossing the mid-wicket boundary for six. When Davis was brought back to complete his spell, French set about him with full-blooded drives and confident flicks, and as the pressure mounted, Northamptonshire's fielders fumbled and conceded overthrows. A target of 51 off five overs was brought down to eight off the last, to be bowled by Capel, who was nursing a back strain. Off the first ball he ran out French when his off-drive was deflected off Hadlee's boot towards the bowler; but now Hadlee had the strike. Capel's next ball he drove high and straight for six, and then he pulled the third to the Tavern boundary. It was a magnificent finale to a calculated innings: 70 runs off 61 balls with two sixes and four fours. He and French had added 75 in eight overs to dash the cup of victory from Northamptonshire's lips.

Toss: Nottinghamshire. **Northamptonshire 228-3** (50 overs) (W. Larkins 87, A. J. Lamb 41, R. J. Bailey 39*);
Nottinghamshire 231-7 (49.3 overs) (C. E. B. Rice 63, R. J. Hadlee 70*, B. N. French 35).

1989 – ROBINSON TO THE RESCUE John Lawson, 1990

In 1989 Nottinghamshire took the opportunity to prove to the prophets of gloom that the club could manage without Richard Hadlee and Clive Rice – and successfully at that. Beating Essex in the final of the Benson and Hedges Cup at Lord's in midsummer, and contesting the final of the Refuge Assurance Cup, after finishing fourth in the Sunday League, was the strongest evidence that Nottinghamshire, under the leadership of Tim Robinson and the astute off-the-field management of Ken Taylor, remained a team to be respected.

Robinson, after a traumatic first year as captain when he was faced with dressing-room unrest, emerged positively from the experience as a captain with the ability to lead by example. In the Benson and Hedges final, he [produced] a marvellous innings of 86 to set Nottinghamshire on course for victory and also earn himself the Gold Award. Fittingly, he was their leading run-maker in both the first-class game and one-day games and boasted the highest average from their first-class matches.

Robinson's greatest allies were Derek Randall and Chris Broad, both of whom scored more than 1,400 first-class runs for the county. Franklyn Stephenson, with his outstanding double of 1988 still fresh in the memory, was again the leading strike bowler, finishing with 92 wickets at 18.77 each. His seam partner, Kevin Cooper, did not have quite the same level of penetration as the previous summer, when he took 101 wickets.

Essex v Nottinghamshire   **Benson and Hedges Cup Final**

At Lord's, July 15, 1989. Nottinghamshire won by three wickets.   1990

A match which was often dull began amusingly when Stephenson bowled Hardie with his renowned slower ball in the third over and ended excitingly with Nottinghamshire requiring nine runs from the last over and four from the final delivery. Had the scores finished level, Essex would have won as they were ahead after 30 overs. The last over was bowled by Lever, whose first eight overs had cost just 15 runs for two wickets. Gooch was an age setting the field for Lever's last ball, to Hemmings, and ended up with all but one man on the on side. Hemmings made room, drove, and the ball raced to the backward-point boundary with Hardie in vain pursuit.

Toss: Essex. **Essex 243-7** (55 overs) (G. A. Gooch 48, A. W. Lilley 95*, M. E. Waugh 41, Extras 32);
Nottinghamshire 244-7 (55 overs) (R. T. Robinson 86, P. Johnson 54, D. W. Randall 49).

1991 – ALL-ROUND SUCCESS   Nick Lucy, 1992

Nottinghamshire swept aside the seeds of doubt in 1991 and demonstrated a fierce determination to remain at the forefront of English cricket. They captured their first Sunday League title and finished a creditable fourth in the Britannic Assurance Championship. The county crowned a heartening year by signing two of the world's most exciting young all-rounders, Chris Lewis of England and the New Zealander, Chris Cairns. Such a vivid upturn in fortunes dispersed the memory of the gloom that descended on Trent Bridge in late 1990, when seven of the last 11 Championship games ended in defeat.

1996 – SLUMP (EXCEPT ON SUNDAYS)   Nick Lucy, 1997

Nottinghamshire's near miss in the Sunday League title race could not paper over ever-widening cracks during 1996, especially in the catastrophic second half of the Championship campaign. The fact that Surrey pipped them for the Sunday prize only on superior run-rate seemed pretty hollow when surrounded by so much gloom and despondency. As well as making the earliest possible exits from the two knockout competitions – they lost by a humiliating 205 runs to Yorkshire in the first round of the NatWest Trophy – Nottinghamshire suffered eight defeats in their last ten Championship matches, after their sole win in June. That left them languishing one place off the bottom of the table, their worst finish for 19 years.

Some discontented members tried to instigate an extraordinary general meeting. Their concern was justified, since the slump followed a similar capitulation in 1995, which featured heavy losses in each of the last six Championship games. Nottinghamshire officials, however, remained defiant, insisting that too much upheaval at the top in he early 1990s [when two managers, first John Birch and then Mike Hendrick had been abruptly sacked after short periods in the job] had contributed to the decline in fortunes and that only a period of continuity, with Alan Ormrod consolidating as cricket manager following his promotion from senior coach in late 1995, would lead to happier times.

1998 – RICE'S RETURN
Nick Lucy, 1999

Nottinghamshire's greatest desire is to recapture the glory days of Clive Rice's captaincy. After a season which yet again fell well below expectations and plunged into a steep decline, Alan Ormrod lost his job as cricket manager. Everyone agreed that there was only one man for the job, the inspirational leader who had lifted Nottinghamshire out of the doldrums two decades ago. Initially, Rice offered little encouragement. He said it was two years too early, given his circumstances at home in South Africa. Nottinghamshire were determined, however, to get their man. When they dangled a financial carrot that was too good to resist, he reorganised his other commitments and accepted.

2001 – A GIANT CALLED PIETERSEN
Paul Fearn, 2002

Hopes and ambitions kindled by an encouraging start were never realised as Nottinghamshire ultimately underperformed again in 2001. Many had installed Clive Rice's new-look team as promotion favourites in the Championship after seeing their impressive early-season form, particularly in the Benson and Hedges Cup. But a first semi-final appearance in 11 seasons in the major cup competitions would be the highlight of their summer. They managed only three Championship wins, one more than the previous year, but their ranking remained unchanged at seventh in Division Two, and they fared little better in the League.

The most impressive cricket came from [Kevin] Pietersen, who scored 1,275 Championship runs at a remarkable 82 per 100 balls. At times, the giant 21-year-old from KwaZulu-Natal was impossible to bowl to, and he impressed not only with the sheer power of his hitting but also with the way he played with a ramrod straight bat. It may be 2005 before he meets the residency requirements to play for England [in fact, he was able to make his international debut in November 2004] but, if he can maintain his first season's form, the name of Pietersen should be pencilled in for future Test squads.

2002 – A Dual Farewell
Paul Fearn, 2003

Two managers, promotion in the Championship, relegation in the Norwich Union League: Nottinghamshire's season was certainly eventful. Members paid tribute to the much-admired and popular Paul Johnson, who joined the coaching staff after 22 years' sterling service and dashing strokeplay. He was a natural entertainer, whose arrival at the crease generated an air of expectancy; his diminutive figure will be sadly missed on the circuit. By his exceptional standards, Johnson went out with a whimper, but he did reach the rare double of 20,000 first-class and 10,000 one-day runs.

It was a fitting farewell for him that Nottinghamshire won promotion in the Championship on the strength of an unstinting run of high-class cricket in the second half of the season. The late surge was prompted by the departure of Clive Rice, a Trent Bridge legend, from the manager's post in June. The committee took this toughest of decisions after ignominious exits from both knockout competitions and a miserable run in the Norwich Union League. On the field, Rice was the club's most successful captain and arguably its greatest leader-by-example, but he could not exert the same influence from the pavilion. His straight talking and single-minded approach ruffled feathers, and his all-too-frequent practice sessions seemed to lack a clear objective. Few connected with Nottinghamshire cricket dared believe Rice was the reason for the underperformance, but results did point that way.

He was replaced by Mike Newell, who had been in charge of all cricket outside the first team. Where Rice had been autocratic, Newell chose group discussion and democracy. His impact was almost immediate: after defeat in the Championship at Northampton, Nottinghamshire reeled off an unbeaten run of nine games, including six victories. It lifted them from eighth to the brink of the Division Two title, which they would have won had they beaten Essex at Chelmsford on the final day.

2004 – An Entrance and an Exit
Paul Fearn, 2005

At the AGM in February 2004, Nottinghamshire's director of cricket, Mike Newell, announced his target for the season: promotion in both league competitions [they had been relegated from Division One of the Championship in 2003]. Not many believed it possible. The county's form of 2003 had been miserable, and plenty of supporters dismissed Newell's talk as morale-boosting bluster. But by September his predictions had proved astute rather than over-ambitious.

A key part of Newell's strategy was to bring in what he called "winning characters": the all-rounder Mark Ealham from Kent, the batsman Anurag Singh from

Worcestershire and the left-arm Ryan Sidebottom from Yorkshire. It worked: Nottinghamshire did win far more matches, and each newcomer contributed. But so did the existing staff, who had struggled through 2003.

Eight batsmen averaged more than 40 but the find of the season for Nottinghamshire, perhaps even the best find in county cricket, was the inexperienced Australian David Hussey, who rattled up 1,208 Championship runs – including six centuries – and finished third in the national first-class averages. [Chris] Read was peerless as a wicket-keeper, and a revelation with the bat. After some brutal treatment over the winter of 2003–04 from the England selectors, who doubted his run-scoring powers, he reacted by hitting two hundreds and averaging 50.

The long-running Kevin Pietersen saga ended with him moving to Hampshire. Pietersen had been in dispute with Nottinghamshire since 2003, a feud which erupted when Gallian threw his kit off the Trent Bridge balcony, and continued into 2004, with Pietersen at one point threatening legal action for unfair dismissal, despite never actually being sacked. By the start of the season the rift seemed to have been bridged, and Pietersen indicated he might stay. But in October he finally turned his back on Trent Bridge.

2005 – FLEMING ADDS FIZZ Simon Cleaves, 2006

Nottinghamshire got the best of both worlds when they persuaded Jason Gallian to step down as captain and make way for arguably the best leader in the world game. Stephen Fleming's contribution to Nottinghamshire's first Championship triumph in 18 years was immense, but since he was away the whole of August touring Zimbabwe with New Zealand, it might have been very different.

Gallian was understandably put out when, after leading Nottinghamshire to a double promotion in 2004, he was deprived of the chance to test his leadership skills in the top flight. However, he accepted the decision with dignity, concentrated on his batting – he scored 1,220 first-class runs at 53.04 in his benefit year – and willingly stepped up when Fleming was away, earning three wins and two draws in that crucial phase of the season.

Fleming weighed in with the bat, averaging 60, and his captaincy was astute, thoughtful and always aggressive. The best example came in September, when Fleming stood firm and left Kent no choice but to attempt to chase 420 in 70 overs to keep themselves in the title race. Andrew Harris claimed his third five-wicket haul of a productive summer, and the title celebrations began a week before the expected showdown with runners-up Hampshire.

That game infuriated Hampshire captain Shane Warne, who seemed to have forgotten the similar scenario that set up a thrilling final day at Trent Bridge in June. With Nottinghamshire in first place and Hampshire second at the time, Fleming gamely agreed to reciprocal declarations. And he faced up to the criticism afterwards, when six wickets fell for 11 runs and Warne's side won by just 14. Without that victory, Hampshire would never have been in the running at the end.

Kent v Nottinghamshire

At Canterbury, September 14, 15, 16, 17, 2005. Nottinghamshire won by 214 runs.

Toss: Nottinghamshire. **Nottinghamshire 486-8 dec.** (D. J. Bicknell 64, J. E. R. Gallian 199,
C. M. W. Read 75, M. A. Ealham 72) **and 170-3 dec.** (J. E. R. Gallian 74*, C. M. W. Read 63);
Kent 237-5 dec. (D. P. Fulton 35, R. W. T. Key 43, N. J. Dexter 79*, N. J. O'Brien 56*; G. P. Swann 3-66)
and 205 (M. van Jaarsveld 64, M. M. Patel 37; A. J. Harris 6-76).

Somerset

1977 – RICHARDS'S RICHES

Eric Hill, 1978

Somerset's hopes of winning something were once again frustrated, but there were memorable points about a season which, although maintaining high public interest, was curiously unfulfilled. The first-ever victory over the Australians gave the season a splendid send-off [since it was May, the writer may have meant start-off]. The astounding batting of Richards, throughout, the elevation of Botham to Test match status, and the selection of him and Rose for the winter Tour were individual distinctions which made Somerset an attractive, interesting side which nevertheless failed somehow to live up to expectations.

Somerset v Australians

At Bath, May 18, 19, 20, 1977. Somerset won by seven wickets. 1978

Somerset won by seven wickets off the first ball of the final 20 overs. A splendid match played in superb weather brought Somerset their first win over the Australians in 22 fixtures played since 1893. After Garner took a wicket with his fifth ball for Somerset, [Greg] Chappell, reaching 99 before lunch and hitting three sixes and 12 fours in a brilliant display, dominated a third-wicket stand of 120. Then Garner and Burgess caused a collapse as the last eight wickets fell for 55 runs. Thomson bowled 15 no-balls in seven overs as Denning led a fine opening stand of 81. Botham hit three sixes and six fours and Slocombe, missed when three, hit one six and ten fours. All the while Rose batted patiently and steadily, hitting 15 fours while escaping difficult chances at 63 and 96. After the loss of two early wickets with his side still 90 behind, Hookes batted superbly, making 108 with four sixes and 15 fours. Somerset needed 182 to win in three and three-quarter hours. Richards hit 11 fours while racing to 53 and then Botham struck boldly to finish this memorable match with an hour to spare.

Toss: Somerset. **Australians 232** (G. S. Chappell 113, G. J. Cosier 44; J. Garner 4-66, G. I. Burgess 5-25) **and 289** (C. S. Serjeant 50, D. W. Hookes 108, G. S. Chappell 39; I. T. Botham 4-98); **Somerset 340-5 dec.** (B. C. Rose 110*, P. W. Denning 39, I. T. Botham 59, P. A. Slocombe 55*, Extras 36) **and 182-3** (P. W. Denning 34, I. V. A. Richards 53, I. T. Botham 39*).

1979 – HONOURS AT LAST

Eric Hill, 1980

In a year memorable for many reasons, the abiding memories will be of victories in the Gillette Cup and the John Player League on the last two days of a season which brought Somerset their first major successes since their foundation in 1875. In Rose's second year as captain [Brian Close had retired in 1977], and following the ignominy of expulsion from the Benson and Hedges Cup for the well-intentioned but ill-advised declaration at Worcester, the team really found itself.

The availability of the giant Garner for the whole season was a critical factor, and this, together with the increasing maturity of Botham as all-rounder and Rose as captain, was vital. Marks continued his excellent progress as off-spinner and batsman in his first full year. Garner's record of 17 Gillette Cup wickets for 92 runs and Richards', with 266 runs in the same four games, culminating in a superbly disciplined century at Lord's, cannot be overvalued.

Worcestershire v Somerset   **Benson and Hedges Cup**

At Worcester, May 23, 24, 1979. Worcestershire beat Somerset by ten wickets.   1980

The Somerset captain, Rose, sacrificed all known cricketing principles by deliberately losing the game. His declaration after one over from Holder, who bowled a no-ball to concede the only run, enabled Somerset to maintain their superior striking-rate in the group. Rose won the battle of mathematics but lost all the goodwill which Somerset had gained by playing attractive cricket in the preceding years. Worcestershire refunded admission money to 100 paying spectators after Turner had scored two singles to complete their victory in a match which lasted 16 deliveries and only 20 minutes, including the ten minutes between the innings. Worcestershire chairman, Mr Geoffrey Lampard, commented: "It is a great pity when the supreme game of cricket is brought down to this level." The TCCB met at Lord's on June 1 and Somerset, for bringing the game into disrepute, were disqualified from the Benson and Hedges Cup by 17 votes to one (Derbyshire).

Toss: Somerset. **Somerset 1-0 dec.; Worcestershire 2-0** (1.4 overs).

Northamptonshire v Somerset   **Gillette Cup Final**

At Lord's, September 8, 1979. Somerset won by 45 runs   1980

While Somerset's triumph was a team effort, two of their West Indies players achieved outstanding performances. Richards scored 117 and when Northamptonshire faced the enormous task of getting 270 [four and a half an over was then seen as a phenomenal rate of scoring], Garner took six wickets for 29. Richards, whom Cyril Washbrook named as Man of the Match, batted superbly from the seventh to the last over; he did not offer a chance. Most of his 11 boundaries came from powerful leg hits and straight drives during an innings which lasted three hours and nine minutes.

Toss: Northamptonshire. **Somerset 269-8** (60 overs) (B. C. Rose 41, I. V. A. Richards 117);
Northamptonshire 224 (56.3 overs) (G. Cook 44, A. J. Lamb 78; J. Garner 6-29).

1981 – THE RICHARDS AND GARNER SHOW (AGAIN) Eric Hill, 1982

Somerset's story of success continued resoundingly in 1981 with victory for the first time in the Benson and Hedges Cup, second place in the John Player League, and a convincing third in the County Championship. The immense performances of Joel Garner and Vivian Richards could hardly be overvalued. Garner, with a total of 132 wickets in all matches, despite missing five Championship games, took 63 of his 88 first-class wickets in the seven victories in which he participated. He missed the two Championship defeats, and in them, significantly, Richards failed. In his inimitable style, more often than not starting against a virtually new ball, Richards made nearly 2,500 runs overall, with nine centuries. The pair's performance in the Benson and Hedges final was matchless.

Somerset v Surrey Benson and Hedges Cup Final

At Lord's, July 25, 1981. Somerset won by seven wickets. 1982

On the day, Somerset were much the better side, restricting Surrey to 194 for eight, a total they passed with 10.3 overs to spare. As he makes a habit of doing, Vivian Richards carried off the main honours, including the Gold Award, with a brilliant innings of 132 not out. When Somerset lost Denning and Rose in the first three overs of their innings, Richards was obliged to play himself in with some care. Having done so, he finished by treating the bowling much as he pleased.

Toss: Somerset. **Surrey 194-8** (55 overs) (R. D. V. Knight 92; J. Garner 5-14); **Somerset 197-3** (44.3 overs) (I. V. A. Richards 132*, I. T. Botham 37*).

1982 – CUP IS HALF FULL Eric Hill, 1983

It is a measure of current Somerset expectations that a season containing the first-ever successful defence of the Benson and Hedges Cup and sixth position in the Championship was regarded as something of a disappointment. Being made favourite for all four competitions hardly assisted a realistic appraisal: especially, as it happened, in view of many injuries. Most of the team were affected at some time, but, most critically, Joel Garner missed much of the year with knee and shoulder ailments. Vivian Richards, troubled by a nagging finger injury, testimonial year duties and understandable cricket-weariness after nine crowded years, had some unusually thin periods. He made more first-class runs than anyone else in the team, but his one-day batting was well below his best. Garner and Richards, at peak form, make the difference between a good side and a winning one.

Nottinghamshire v Somerset   **Benson and Hedges Cup Final**

At Lord's, July 24, 1982. Somerset won by nine wickets.   1983

Toss: Somerset. **Nottinghamshire 130** (50.1 overs) (J. Garner 3-13); **Somerset 132-1** (33.1 overs) (P. M. Roebuck 53*, I. V. A. Richards 51*).

1983 – ROEBUCK'S RISE   Eric Hill, 1984

Despite many difficulties, both expected and unforeseen, Somerset enjoyed another in their heartening sequence of successful seasons. They won the NatWest Trophy without the advantage of a single home tie, and again finished second in the John Player League. Those successes outweighed the disappointments of early removal from the Benson and Hedges Cup and one of the poorest County Championship records of recent years. The World Cup took away four players (Botham, Marks, Garner and Richards) for an important period, while long-term injuries to Brian Rose, Hallam Moseley and Hugh Wilson severely disrupted team plans.

Two of the most improved players were Peter Roebuck and Nigel Popplewell. Roebuck's thoughtful captaincy of weakened sides drew well-deserved praise, and his batting was rewarding. Popplewell's improved all-round application, coupled with some dazzling catches, found its high point in the five NatWest Trophy matches. He was closely concerned in the great recovery in the semi-final against Middlesex [when Somerset reached 222 from an apparently hopeless 52 for five to win with the scores tied], led unerringly by Botham.

Middlesex v Somerset   **NatWest Trophy Semi-Final**

At Lord's, August 17, 1983. Somerset won by virtue of losing fewer wickets with the scores level.   1984

Toss: Somerset. **Middlesex 222-9** (60 overs) (W. N. Slack 57, M. W. Gatting 49, K. P. Tomlins 58; J. Garner 3-23, N. F. M. Popplewell 3-34); **Somerset 222-8** (60 overs) (I. T. Botham 96*, N. F. M. Popplewell 46; N. G. Cowans 3-48).

Kent v Somerset   **NatWest Trophy Final**

At Lord's, September 3, 1983. Somerset won by 24 runs.   1984

Toss: Kent. **Somerset 193-9** (50 overs) (I. V. A. Richards 51, N. F. M. Popplewell 35; G. R. Dilley 4-29); **Kent 169** (47.1 overs) (C. J. Tavaré 39; V. J. Marks 3-30).

1985 – Heroic Failures

Eric Hill, 1986

Expected by many to be a challenging force, Somerset suffered one of their worst seasons since the 1970s resurgence, despite the return of Vivian Richards and Joel Garner [who had been with the touring West Indies side during the 1984 season] and the astonishing batting exploits of the captain, Ian Botham, and Richards. One of the outcomes of a somewhat bizarre season came in early October. Citing his many interests outside Somerset cricket as the reason, Botham resigned the captaincy, Peter Roebuck being appointed, and accepted a one-year contract instead of the two years he was offered.

While achieving the highest number of batting points in the Championship, Somerset were bottom of the table for the first time since 1969, with only one victory. Besides some superb one-day batting, Botham made the first three of his five centuries from 76, 76 and 50 balls respectively, creating a new record of sixes in a first-class season, and averaged 100 in the Championship. His friend Richards, with nine centuries, including a memorable 322, averaged 76. Together they scored 3,047 Championship runs.

In this context the season's final results were remarkably disappointing, but the reasons are fairly clear. Principally, a savage spate of injuries upset team plans' also, the bowlers, with the exception of the vice-captain, Vic Marks, could not match expectations.

Somerset v Warwickshire

At Taunton, June 1, 3, 4, 1985. Drawn.   1986

Everything was dwarfed by a magnificent 322 out of 479 by Richards, who came in when Bail had retired after a blow on the helmet and Felton was out next ball. His first 100 came from 105 balls, his second from 76, and his third in 63. He hit eight sixes and 42 fours.

Toss: Somerset. **Somerset 566-5 dec.** (N. F. M. Popplewell 55, I. V. A. Richards 322, R. L. Ollis 55, V. J. Marks 65) **and 226-5 dec.** (T. Gard 47, N. A. Felton 45, V. J. Marks 66*);
Warwickshire 442-9 dec. (T. A. Lloyd 61, R. I. H. B. Dyer 33, A. I. Kallicharran 36, D. L. Amiss 81, P. A. Smith 93, A. M. Ferreira 101*; M. S. Turner 4-74) **and 181-2** (R. I. H. B. Dyer 63*, A. I. Kallicharran 89).

1986 – Season of Strife

Eric Hill, 1987

After a start of some promise under the new captain, Peter Roebuck, Somerset again failed to live up to expectations and, worst of all, the season ended with the club in the grip of internal strife. The crux of this was the decision of the committee, in late August, not to renew the contracts of Vivian Richards and Joel Garner, who had played such a large part in the successful years from 1978 to 1983. The cricketing reasons for this bold move were sound, but they quickly became swamped by the sentimental response of a large number of members. Ian Botham, who had come back from nine weeks' suspension by the TCCB [for drug taking] with some thunderous performances, even by his standards, threatened to leave the county if the two West Indian Test players were not reinstated.

In due course, a special general meeting was requisitioned, calling for the resignation of the committee – and by inference the re-engagement of Richards and Garner. However, at Shepton Mallet on November 8, a motion of no confidence in the committee was defeated by 1,828 votes to 798, and a motion for the committee to stand down was defeated by 1,863 to 743.

1987 – PICKING UP THE PIECES
Eric Hill, 1988

Following the bitterness of the winter, the remodelled Somerset side of 1987 had an encouraging season. To lose three of the world's best players [Botham carried out his threat and decamped to Worcestershire], and yet to improve the playing record was a major achievement – a tribute to all involved with the club and notably to the captain, Peter Roebuck.

Showing a wider range of strokes, Roebuck started superbly in all competitions, suffered a hand injury which put him out for seven weeks, but returned with another flow of runs. Martin Crowe was first in the country to 1,000 Championship runs and to 2,000 in all competitions; yet the importance of his return [he had played for Somerset, in Richards' absence, in 1984] cannot be measured only by his output of classically made runs. When Crowe was required by New Zealand for their suddenly arranged – but soon to be abandoned – tour of Sri Lanka, Somerset hastily signed the young Australian all-rounder, Stephen Waugh, as cover. He played in only four Championship matches, but two superb match-saving centuries indicated his class, and his bowling was also of fine quality.

1991 – COOK'S GRAND GOODBYE
Eric Hill, 1992

Too few wins, too many farewells, and the officially acknowledged prospect of a heavy financial loss made 1991 another season for Somerset to forget. There were, none the less, some remarkable individual performances, almost inevitably dominated by the South African opener, Jimmy Cook, who was in his third and final season for the county. Recording only two Championship victories, Somerset finished bottom of the table. They registered the highest but one number of batting points, and the lowest but one number of bowling points. However, it may be appropriate to remind the county's supporters that the last time they were 17th [Durham were yet to join], Viv Richards, Joel Garner and Ian Botham played in a total of 45 Championship matches.

The 6ft 5in Andrew Caddick's 96 wickets, at an average of 12.84, suggested an interesting prospect. The batting, centred around Cook, the captain Chris Tavaré [who had joined from Kent in 1989], Richard Harden and Peter Roebuck, rarely faltered. Regrettably, Roebuck announced his retirement in August. The year was clouded by the death of the president, Colin Atkinson, by the premature retirement of Roebuck, and by Cook's return to South Africa. Each, in his own way, made contributions of great importance to the county. Cook's remarkable three seasons demand expansion. He was 35 years old when he arrived in 1989. In all his matches for Somerset, he compiled 10,639 runs at an average of 62.21, including 7,604 in first-class games at 72.41, with 28 hundreds. He will be fondly remembered by friend and foe, and many were glad on the November day in 1991 when he stepped on to the field at Calcutta to represent South Africa in recognised international competition for the first time.

1998 – CADDICK'S LONE HAND

David Foot, 1999

Andy Caddick of Somerset and Gloucestershire's Courtney Walsh, just up the M5, were by some distance the best fast bowlers in the 1998 County Championship. Caddick narrowly pipped Walsh to 100 first-class wickets (though he finished with 105 to Walsh's 106) and was the first to achieve the target for Somerset since Tom Cartwright in 1971. He produced some marvellous marathon bowling stints and repeatedly had the opposition in trouble, so that it is surprising his county won only six Championship matches and finished ninth – just missing qualification for the Super Cup. The batsmen were the primary culprits.

Marcus Trescothick got nearest 1,000 first-class runs, with 847, at least showing some improvement on his inexplicable recession since 1994. But there was a painful paucity of backbone in the higher order. The captain, Peter Bowler, took a worrying time to get going and dropped himself for some of the one-day games in June. Mark Lathwell did not play until mid-May and too occasionally demonstrated his exquisitely instinctive batsmanship. Adrian Pierson found little in the summer's strips for his off-breaks, but did graft for his maiden century.

Pondering on the experiences of Somerset's slow bowlers brings us with some sadness to Pakistani leg-spinner Mushtaq Ahmed, who turned up at Taunton in 1993 to create an immediate frisson. Here was a magician and an incorrigible entertainer, a cheerful personality who never wanted to let go of the ball. In 1998, Mushtaq played just six Championship games, took 14 wickets, and looked almost jaded. He was no longer beating the bat, no longer visibly chuckling, as he used to when he varied his deliveries at will. The troublesome knee was a burden. He had worries at home over his wife's confinement and was given compassionate leave. He was hardly seen in Taunton, and it was increasingly evident that his career with Somerset was over. Jamie Cox of Tasmania was signed as both overseas player and captain for 1999.

2001 – BEST-EVER SEASON

David Foot, 2002

By general agreement, certainly in every parish across the Mendips and the Quantocks, Somerset's season was the best in their variegated history. Perhaps there were more flash, pulsating days when players of mighty individual talent such as Botham, Richards and Garner were around; when, in 1979 for example, the county picked up two trophies. But 2001 was better, a more balanced triumph from lesser souls. Somerset finished runners-up in the Championship, higher than ever before – at one point, poised on the shoulders of Yorkshire, they actually looked capable of winning the pennant – and, amid much West Country elation, they vanquished Leicestershire in the Cheltenham & Gloucester Trophy final at Lord's.

Keith Parsons, an authentic Somerset lad from Taunton, unable to command a regular place in the Championship side, enjoyed a marvellous match. He figured in a significant stand with Rob Turner, rounded off the innings with two stunning sixes, took important wickets and deservedly won the match award. It could be said he was an unlikely match-winner; yet that symbolised one of the county's virtues during a heady season.

Astute recruitment was another factor in Somerset's successes. Ian Blackwell, boyish of features and comfortable of build, arrived from Derbyshire in 2000, primarily as a slow bowler. But a year later he hit four Championship centuries with well-judged, timely, beefy strokes to suggest he is a genuine all-rounder. After him came the Middlesex pair, Richard Johnson and Keith Dutch. They had moved west in 2001 at the persuasive behest of Kevin Shine, the accomplished coach who, probably to his surprise, had found himself succeeding Dermot Reeve.

Leicestershire v Somerset	C&G Trophy Final
At Lord's, September 1, 2001. Somerset won by 41 runs.	2002

Toss: Somerset. **Somerset 271-5** (50 overs) (P. D. Bowler 42, J. Cox 44, K. A. Parsons 60*, R. J. Turner 37*, Extras 34; Shahid Afridi 3-47); **Leicestershire 230** (45.4 overs) (T. R. Ward 54, D. L. Maddy 49; P. S. Jones 3-40).

2002 – AND ONE OF THE WORST	David Foot, 2003

Explanations do not come easily for Somerset's embarrassing decline. By the end of the season they had been relegated in both the Championship and the Norwich Union League. Their chief executive, Peter Anderson, was sufficiently mystified by the team's miserable form to send a letter of apology to each member. "Too many of our performances," he wrote, "seemed to lack enthusiasm, urgency and the requisite application expected of professional players." He said some members might feel puzzled or even resentful that such a successful team in 2001 should underperform so badly. In uncompromising tones, he added that every coach and player within the club was being interviewed. The message was simple: "You got us down; now you get us up." The players were left smarting by this very public rebuke.

Surrey

1978 – Knight-Mare
Harold Abel, 1979

Surrey experienced probably the worst season in their history in 1978. They plunged to new depths at 16th in the Championship, and at times even the spirit looked unwilling. Roger Knight, the new captain, found himself submerged in a wave of mediocrity. Certainly that was the case in the last match when Surrey threw in the towel to their perennial enemies from across the water, Middlesex. A blood match turned anaemic as Brearley put Surrey in and saw his side win in two days. To rub salt in the wound, Selvey took the occasion to reach 100 wickets in a season for the first time. *Wisden* ten years earlier had said of him in the preface to the Surrey section: "Selvey, a lively medium-quick bowler, seemed to be a cricketer worth encouraging." Recent history is filled with instances of Surrey players who left and succeeded elsewhere.

1979 – Stewart (Senior) Leads Revival
Harold Abel, 1980

Surrey cheerfully turned their world upside down in 1979. They jumped from second from bottom in 1978 to third from top in the Championship and were in at the death of the Benson and Hedges Cup, losing to Essex in the final. Not yet, perhaps, anywhere approaching the dizzy heights of the 1950s, but a least they took a step in the right direction.

There was a renewed feeling of hope at The Oval, and it was no coincidence that the change of spirit came about with the return as manager of Micky Stewart and the arrival of Sylvester Clarke to join Roger Knight, who had suffered a season of frustration after taking over the leadership 12 months earlier. In their separate ways, the trio contributed much to make the team begin to believe in themselves.

1982 – A Cup at Last
Harold Abel, 1983

Surrey finished the 1982 season with something in their hands at last. After three abortive visits in three years to Lord's, for the 1979 and 1981 finals of the Benson and Hedges Cup and the 1980 Gillette Cup final, they walked away with the NatWest Trophy. Rounding off the season so successfully created justifiable optimism at a time of gradual change. Monte Lynch, David Smith and Jack Richards are firmly established; Dave Thomas, Andy Needham, Graham Monkhouse and Kevin Mackintosh are following along the right lines – and they are all in their early or middle twenties. Graham Roope, after the best part of 20 years of excellent service, had had to make way for the younger school and was looking for another county.

Sylvester Clarke and Robin Jackman proved as good an opening pair of bowlers as any in the country, taking 85 and 73 wickets respectively in three-day cricket and 25 and 22 in one-day games. Jackman, in his late thirties, was spared the Sunday frolics but did better than anybody in the knockout tournaments. His six for 22 against Hampshire in the NatWest Trophy was an outstanding performance. This was followed by selection for his first home Test appearance and subsequently a place in the side for Australia.

Surrey v Warwickshire	NatWest Trophy Final

At Lord's, September 4, 1982. Surrey won by nine wickets. 1983

Warwickshire were outclassed and after 29 overs they were 74 for eight. Thomas, left arm over the wicket and distinctly fast, removed Smith, Amiss and Humpage for one run, and two superb slip catches by Howarth saw to it that by noon the result, barring a remarkable turnabout, was disappointingly inevitable.

Toss: Surrey. **Warwickshire 158** (57.2 overs) (Asif Din 45, G. C. Small 33; D. J. Thomas 3-26); **Surrey 159-1** (33.4 overs) (A. R. Butcher 86*, G. P. Howarth 31).

1983 – ALL OUT FOR 14! Harold Abel, 1984

Surrey suffered more than most from a wet May. They were unable to bowl a ball in two of their first three Championship games and did not bat or bowl in four of their first five Sunday League matches. They were then hit by a "hurricane" at Chelmsford when Essex bundled them out for 14, the lowest total in Surrey's history, and only two runs more than the lowest in the annals of the first-class game. Such a happening could have knocked them sideways. Instead, Surrey answered back immediately by beating Worcestershire for their first Championship win, and although the final reading in the premier competition was not all that pleasant, it could have been worse. Seven victories brought eighth place in the table, which represented a very reasonable recovery.

Essex v Surrey	

At Chelmsford, May 28, 30, 31, 1983. Drawn. 1984

On the second afternoon Surrey were skittled out for the lowest score in their history, their first innings lasting a mere 14.3 overs. Phillip and Foster, making the ball swing in the humid atmosphere, were their tormentors and only a boundary from Clarke, the sole one of the innings, spared them the humiliation of recording the lowest-ever first-class score. Five wickets fell with the total on eight. The next day a fine century from Knight, well supported by Clinton, enabled Surrey to win back some self-respect. After a barren opening day because of rain, Fletcher showed that there was nothing wrong with the pitch with a century full of grace and elegance after Knight had gambled on putting the home side into bat.

Essex v Surrey, 1983

At Chelmsford, May 28, 30, 31, 1983. Result: Drawn.

ESSEX — First innings

G. A. Gooch b Thomas	1
B. R. Hardie b Clarke	16
*K. W. R. Fletcher c Lynch b Monkhouse	110
K. S. McEwan c Lynch b Knight	45
K. R. Pont b Pocock	12
N. Phillip b Pocock	8
S. Turner c and b Knight	20
R. E. East c Lynch b Clarke	19
†D. E. East c Butcher b Pocock	17
N. A. Foster not out	19
D. L. Acfield run out	0
B 4, l-b 10, n-b 6	20
	287

1-1 2-27 3-113 4-156 5-179 6-222 7-238 8-252 9-276 10-287

Clarke 20–3–58–2; Thomas 20–2–78–1; Monkhouse 13–2–49–1; Knight 17–6–33–2; Pocock 19.5–6–49–3.

SURREY

	First innings	Second innings
A. R. Butcher c D. E. East b Phillip	2	– c Gooch b Foster . . . 5
G. S. Clinton c D. E. East b Foster	6	– not out . . . 61
A. Needham b Foster	0	– lbw b Phillip . . . 4
*R. D. V. Knight lbw b Phillip	0	– not out . . . 101
M. A. Lynch lbw b Phillip	0	
†C. J. Richards c Turner b Phillip	0	
D. J. Thomas lbw b Foster	0	
I. R. Payne b Phillip	0	
G. Monkhouse lbw b Phillip	2	
S. T. Clarke b Foster	4	
P. I. Pocock not out	0	
B 1, l-b 8, w 2, n-b 3		14
	14	(2 wkts) 185

1-2 2-5 3-6 4-8 5-8 6-8 7-8 8-8 9-14 10-14   1-11 2-18

First innings – Phillip 7.3–4–4–6; Foster 7–3–10–4.
Second innings – Phillip 13–2–39–1; Foster 13–2–33–1; Turner 7–3–16–0; Gooch 22–6–45–0; Acfield 17–7–23–0; R. E. East 1–0–5–0; Pont 5–1–10–0.

Toss won by Surrey   UMPIRES W. E. Alley and J. W. Holder

Surrey's first innings total of 14 is the fifth lowest first-class innings in history (there have been two totals of 12 and two of 13) and the lowest since 1907.

1989 – HOPE AFTER A DISMAL DECADE
David Field, 1990

A solitary trophy in the 1980s and a volume of unfulfilled ambitions throughout the decade did not leave Surrey entertaining pessimistic thoughts about the past, present or future. Instead, they were preparing to reap the harvest from a flourishing youth system sown more than ten years earlier by their former manager Micky Stewart, and now handsomely providing 80% of Surrey's current pool of players. While the club was naturally disappointed with results in 1989 which had produced a worse record than the previous season, the future, moulded around Graham Thorpe and the Bicknell brothers, was all that mattered when the last ball was struck in the Oval gloom on September 16. A feeling of optimism was backed by a growing opinion within the game that Surrey had the potential and the capacity to emerge as one of the teams of the 1990s.

1990 – THE WONDER OF WAQAR
David Field, 1991

In a year when batsmen reigned supreme, Surrey spent much of the summer of 1990 admiring their unexpected and rare gift from the Orient, a teenage Pakistani fast bowler, Waqar Younis. Club coach Geoff Arnold polished the magic lamp provided by the great all-rounder Imran Khan, the genie Waqar appeared, and, granting three wishes in one, he provided a treasure chest of 95 wickets in all cricket. The Surrey committee prudently recognised the benefits of such a special talent and granted him a five-year contract.

The compactly built Younis, of the two-way swing and devastating yorker, was Surrey's most effective Championship bowler, with 57 wickets at just under 24 apiece. In the Refuge Assurance League, he was top of the national averages and the leading wicket-taker with 31 at 12.77. [His figures in 1991 were even more impressive: 151 wickets in all competitions, with two-thirds of his victims bowled or lbw. In the Championship he took 113 wickets at 14.36, with 13 returns of five wickets or more.]

Indeed, Surrey's season was highlighted by Waqar and Ward, a cricketing double-act with an entrepreneurial ring which produced its most profitable business in the middle. David Ward, hitherto regarded as a useful county professional, became one of ten players in the country to pass 2,000 runs in a prosperous summer for strokemakers. In his previous five years at The Oval, he had made only three hundreds, but now he rubbed shoulders with such international "heavyweights" as Gooch, Cook, Hick and Haynes. Of his seven hundreds, two were doubles, including a career-best 263 against Kent at Canterbury, and he became the first Surrey player since J. H. Edrich in 1962, and the 13th in all, to score 2,000 for the county alone. Greats such as Hayward, Hobbs, Sandham and May had achieved the same feat, but in the days when more matches were played.

1996 – A Triumph Overshadowed
David Llewellyn, 1997

For the first time since 1982, there was a glint of silver in The Oval trophy cupboard, after Surrey won their first Sunday League title. But, as 1997 began, cricketing success was put into perspective by the death – after a car crash in Australia – of wicket-keeper Graham Kersey, the most popular player on the staff. The news left everyone at Surrey stunned.

Back in mid-August, the mood at The Oval had been more buoyant than for many years: the county had been on course to complete a treble by collecting the Championship and NatWest Trophy as well. But the disappointment of their semi-final capitulation to Essex, despite Alec Stewart's unbeaten hundred, was a foretaste of future failure. The Championship slipped from their grasp, first with a draw in the rain at Trent Bridge, then with a dusty share of the spoils at Cardiff, where Surrey's need for a top-class spinner was starkly revealed. The rain-soaked final match against Worcestershire was reduced to a money-chase; second place was the best they could hope for and, despite a brave effort, they ended up third. At last Surrey had rid themselves of the monkey that had clung to their backs for the last 14 years, in which they won nothing but criticism for unfulfilled potential. They ended the season with the belief that the Sunday League should be the first of many trophies for this talented team, but Kersey's death will make 1997 much harder.

The contribution of Australian bite to Surrey's summer cannot be under-estimated. The shrewdest signing was that of former Test fast bowler David Gilbert in the role of manager-cum-coach. He began by ordering the demolition of the wall between the capped and non-capped players' dressing-rooms. Having taken that first, dramatic step towards uniting his squad, Gilbert saw the players respond swiftly to his canny man-management skills. Another key figure was Australian all-rounder Brendon Julian, who overcame an alarming propensity to bowl no-balls and wides and completed an impressive double by passing 500 runs and 50 wickets. Meanwhile, Australian-born Adam Hollioake began the season at Taunton with a century in each innings – the 12th Surrey batsman to achieve the feat – and, while Stewart was on England duty, led Surrey to four of their eight Championship victories and five Sunday League wins. He was rewarded by being named captain of England A's winter tour – to Australia.

1997 – Starry Underachievers
David Llewellyn, 1998

In 1997, Surrey took the season's first trophy when they crushed Kent by eight wickets in the Benson and Hedges Cup final, but such was the pre-season level of expectation that their year went down as only a heavily qualified success. Many counties would have been delighted with joint eighth place in the Championship and fifth in the Sunday League, but not a side which could boast ten interna-tionals. When they were eliminated from the NatWest Trophy in the second round, bowled out for 154 by a modest Nottinghamshire attack, accusations of complacency were quickly levelled.

Among the bowlers, only Saqlain Mushtaq excelled. He finished fifth in the first-class averages – higher than any other spinner – with 32 wickets at 19.28, and would have taken more if his season had not been interrupted by one-day appearances for Pakistan.

1999 – THE WAIT IS OVER

David Llewellyn, 2000

Surrey left the 20th century as they entered it – as champions. One hundred years after winning the 1899 Championship, Surrey did it again. But the more significant date in everyone's minds was 1971, Surrey's last Championship. It took 28 years for the sequence of failure to be broken, but, when success finally happened, it arrived in spectacular fashion. They finished unbeaten, only the 15th time a county has gone through a Championship season without losing. Even the legendary Surrey sides of the 1950s, who lifted the title seven years running, never managed this.

Three Surrey bowlers figured in the national top 10, five in the top 30. Saqlain, after returning from the World Cup, took 58 wickets in seven matches at a staggering 11.37; Salisbury, one of three ever-presents, did his bit, as 60 wickets bore witness; and so did Martin Bicknell, who finished with 71, the eighth time he had reached 50 first-class wickets in an injury-plagued 14-year career.

Surrey v Nottinghamshire

At The Oval, September 1, 2, 1999. Surrey won by ten wickets.   2000

Surrey won the 1999 Championship in convincing style when they beat Nottinghamshire by ten wickets inside two days. It was their eighth consecutive win, a sequence they had not surpassed since 1957. The club had endured 27 seasons without a Championship: the last had been won on September 13, 1971, when Adam Hollioake was eight days old. As in 1998, they led the 1999 table for most of the summer, but this time they held their nerve, playing hard, uncompromising cricket until the finish. And what a finish it was. Set 150 for victory, and the crown, with just 19 scheduled overs left on the second day, they gave it everything. In a display of savage strokeplay, [Mark] Butcher and [Ian] Ward cracked on to 110 without loss before they claimed the extra half-hour and hit 43 off the next 22 balls. It was glorious, heady stuff from the openers, who eclipsed a meticulous and gutsy performance from Afzaal, top scorer in both Nottinghamshire's innings. Saqlain Mushtaq and Salisbury split 14 wickets between them. In their first innings, Surrey themselves found runs a struggle, and missed a batting point by one. But in the end there was no denying them; it was, at last, their season.

Toss: Nottinghamshire. **Nottinghamshire** 115 (U. Afzaal 47; M. W. Patterson 3-25, Saqlain Mushtaq 3-15, I. D. K. Salisbury 3-29) **and 233** (U. Afzaal 104, P. Johnson 41; Saqlain Mushtaq 4-100, I. D. K. Salisbury 4-66); **Surrey 199** (A. D. Brown 34, A. J. Stewart 49, Extras 41; V. C. Drakes 4-53, M. N. Bowen 3-30) **and 153-0** (M. A. Butcher 81*, I. J. Ward 55*).

2000 – CHAMPIONS AGAIN

David Llewellyn, 2001

While there will always be someone proclaiming that Surrey's Championship-winning side of 2000 had to beat only eight other counties – that it was half a Championship – the teams in Division One were the best, and had to be played twice. In that this represented a truer test, it could be argued that there was more merit in lifting this second successive Championship – Surrey's 17th title since 1890 – than there was in winning it the previous year. Surrey were unbeaten then; in 2000, there were defeats by Durham and Derbyshire before Adam Hollioake's men asserted themselves with seven consecutive wins. Even so, the trophy was not theirs until the final game.

[Martin] Bicknell scored 500 runs for the first time, giving him credence as an all-rounder, and while his 60 wickets at 17.53 were apparently not enough to catch the eye of the England selectors, they went a long way to securing the Championship for Surrey. He had a memorable game against Leicestershire on his home ground, Woodbridge Road, Guildford, claiming the best match return by an England bowler – 16 for 119 – since Jim Laker's 19 for 90 against Australia in 1956. In recent years, his flawless seam bowling has been singularly neglected by his country. Instead, the selectors returned their attention to Ian Salisbury's leg-spin for England's winter tours to Pakistan and Sri Lanka, attracted by his 52 Championship wickets at 18.92. As a foil to Saqlain Mushtaq's masterful off-spin and bewitching variations, which brought 66 wickets at 15.39, Salisbury enjoyed an impressive domestic season, but was found wanting in Pakistan, doing neither himself nor his county figures justice in the three Tests. He was not taken to Sri Lanka.

Surrey v Leicestershire

At Guildford, July 19, 20, 21, 2000. Surrey won by ten wickets. 2001

Bicknell turned the game on its head with the best match return in England since 1956. But the bare figures, 16 for 119, scarcely capture the drama of his superb seam and swing bowling on a near-perfect pitch. With hundreds from Smith and Ward – both demonstrating what could be achieved with discipline and concentration – matched by seven first-innings wickets for Bicknell and six for Ormond, Leicestershire held a slim advantage when they batted again in the last hour of the second day. By the close, the game was as good as settled. Bicknell had captured five for 24 in seven overs, the first two, Maddy and Sutcliffe, with deliveries that would have bowled the best. Next morning, Wells and DeFreitas threw the bat at everything until, in the fourth over, Bicknell began a spell of four for four in 16 balls that brought him Championship-best figures of nine for 47 and made him the first to 50 first-class wickets in the season. Ward followed the third hundred of his career with an unbeaten 61 as Surrey wrapped up victory by mid-afternoon.

Toss: Leicestershire. **Leicestershire 318** (I. J. Sutcliffe 37, B. F. Smith 102, D. Williamson 47, Extras 53; M. P. Bicknell 7-72) **and 87** (M. P. Bicknell 9-47); **Surrey 288** (I. J. Ward 107, N. Shahid 47, A. D. Brown 34, Extras 41; J. Ormond 6-87, A. Kumble 3-68) **and 119-0** (M. A. Butcher 47*, I. J. Ward 61*).

2002 – A TRAGEDY AND A TITLE
David Llewellyn, 2003

The death of Ben Hollioake cast a dark cloud over the start of the season, yet the effect of the tragedy was to draw the club closer together, and the collective sense of purpose and spirit played a big part in Surrey's success – a third Championship title in four years [their defence in 2001 had been feeble], and promotion in the Norwich Union League. Almost as exciting was the rapid rise of two stars of the future: Rikki Clarke and Scott Newman both scored maiden hundreds, and Clarke looked useful with the ball too.

The early part of the season took place without the captain, Adam Hollioake, who remained with his family in Australia until June, by which time his wife Sherryn had given birth to their daughter, Bennaya. When he did return, he played with unfettered ease and confirmed his reputation as one of the most astute, innovative and flexible captains in the modern game. His philosophy was to entertain, and several sensational innings rekindled memories of the way he had burst on the scene in the early 1990s. His unbeaten 117 in the C&G at Hove was not unlike his brother Ben at his best: brutal but beautiful. "Adam played," wrote one observer, "like a man possessed."

The frequent absences of Saqlain Mushtaq on international duty were a blessing in disguise because his replacements, both fellow Pakistanis, proved astute signings. Azhar Mahmood claimed 20 wickets in three Championship matches, including a stunning eight-wicket haul to beat Lancashire. And near the end of the season, Mushtaq Ahmed's leg-spin was crucial in the victory at Leicester. Not even an injury to Martin Bicknell – out for eight weeks from late June after stumbling in his delivery stride against Sussex and breaking his right wrist – could stop an exhilarating team from lifting the title. They headed the table after every round save one.

2003 – SHORT BUT NOT ENTIRELY SWEET
David Llewellyn, 2004

Winning is an exhausting business. Surrey made that plain, losing the last three Championship matches very wearily, as they staggered to the finish. In the wake of winning the inaugural Twenty20 Cup, and plodding on to win the National League, they lost their way in the one competition they really wanted – the County Championship – and finished third. Surrey's ultimately unsuccessful defence of their title became the focus of their whole season.

On his own admission, Adam Hollioake found it hard to motivate himself, let alone the team. It was hardly a surprise that, having announced he would retire after 2004, his benefit season, Hollioake relinquished the captaincy. At least he would be around to support his successor, Jon Batty, for the next year. However,

Keith Medlycott, the cricket manager, resigned in November, saying he had taken Surrey as far as he could. There were undercurrents suggesting senior players felt Batty, like Stewart before him, would find captaining, keeping wicket and opening too onerous. The task of repairing these cracks, as Medlycott's successor, now falls to the Australian Steve Rixon.

The most prominent absentee in 2004 will be Stewart, who announced his retirement in September. He had wanted one more year, but Surrey had been granted planning permission to develop the Vauxhall End, at a cost of £22m, and claimed there was no spare cash – or sentiment. Stewart was therefore denied a chance to add to the 14,440 Championship runs he had scored since 1981. He was, however, appointed the club's director of new business.

2004 – A BATTY SUMMER

David Llewellyn, 2005

The discontent of the previous winter, when Surrey's senior players had objected to departing coach Keith Medlycott appointing wicket-keeper/batsman Jon Batty as captain, turned into an inglorious early summer of ignominy and underachievement. Surrey won only one of their first 11 Championship matches, and crashed out of the C&G Trophy with a shock defeat by Ireland. Not until it was too late did they function as a competitive unit, reaching their second successive Twenty20 Cup final and making a fight of it for the Championship runners-up spot. Batty can take some of the credit for this belated revival. But the damage had been done much earlier, leaving the new coach, Steve Rixon, with a Herculean headache.

Batty's situation was unenviable: leading a side which doubted he was the man for the job in the footsteps of Adam Hollioake, one of the county's more brilliant captains. The old hands' worst fears were quickly realised – Batty's three-dimensional role as captain, opener and keeper did prove too much. He eventually dropped to No. 5, although that was often above Alistair Brown and Hollioake, whose career averages were about ten runs higher than his. Batty did manage three hundreds and three more half-centuries, but by August the runs were drying up. It was mystifying that Rixon had not insisted on picking his own man when he first arrived. Still, he got his chance after Batty was sacked, and Mark Butcher looked a sound choice.

The batting centred around the relentless run machine that is Mark Ramprakash. Surrey's first three Championship victories were all ensured by his bat, and he completed 1,000 runs for the 14th time in his career. Brown turned a thin summer around and reached four figures, as did Scott Newman, whose consistency was reassuring in his first full season.

2005 – VAUXHALL FARCE

David Llewellyn, 2006

There were times, on the way to relegation in the Championship, when it was more Whitehall than Vauxhall, or more Rix than Rixon, at The Oval. At other times in a monumentally disappointing season, farce gave way to darker forces. The main example was when Surrey were found guilty of ball-tampering, against Nottinghamshire early in May. To Surrey's shame, an internal investigation headed by Micky Stewart was unable to identify the culprit(s). It was not their first offence: in the early 1990s they received a suspended fine. This time they were docked eight points, which ultimately cost them their place in the first division. In the last season of three-down, they finished third-bottom, just one point behind Middlesex.

Mark Butcher, the captain, missed three-quarters of the campaign with a wrist injury, and returned too late to prevent the drop. Graham Thorpe had a quiet final year, struggling with injury and motivation: he was eventually left out of the side altogether. But the chief cause of Surrey's on-field failures was the lack of capable replacements when a succession of bowlers fell by the wayside and reduced the attack to one of the most ineffectual in the Championship. Mohammad Akram did not have the anticipated impact at his fourth county, while the resurrection of Saqlain Mushtaq, repaired knees and all, was misguided. His beard and burgeoning midriff gave him gravitas, but the mystique had gone from his off-spin.

Rixon felt that there were too many long-term contracts, so he had no ultimate threat against any perceived slackers. Not surprisingly, he decided not to push for an extension to his own contract (which sources suggest might well not have been forthcoming anyway), and returned to Australia. He was replaced by a home-grown coach, Mark Butcher's father Alan. Things were patently wrong at The Oval in 2005, and the family Butcher has a lot to do to put it right.

Sussex

1977 – Mr Packer Comes to Hove
Jack Arlidge, 1978

Not for many a year had a season opened with such justifiably high hopes of success. Players, committee and followers of the club felt that Sussex would win one of the competitions, and the captain Tony Greig spoke confidently of the splendid spirit right throughout the camp. There was the right approach, and a very good side, he emphasised. The way Sussex opened the campaign strengthened and confirmed these hopes and predictions. They won the first two Benson and Hedges matches, the first three John Player League fixtures and the first County Championship game. Although Kent then dared to end this run of success, Sussex promptly won three matches in a row to show just how determined they were to make this a memorable season. And then came the Packer affair.

The Australian TV tycoon visited the Hove County Ground and conferred with Greig in the captain's room at the top of the pavilion. Greig followed by holding the most extraordinary press conference ever likely to be staged on the ground and the Sussex boat was well and truly rocked. Just what an adverse effect the whole business had on the club we do not know, but with Greig obviously Packer's right-hand man over here, and Snow and Imran Khan also signed up, Sussex were closely involved. There was uncertainty in the air, and the earlier spirit of hope and confidence disappeared. Several poor results, including a dismal Gillette Cup display against Derbyshire, matched the wretched weather. There was precious little sunshine during the summer, and the sparkle vanished from Sussex.

1978 – Greig's Sudden Goodbye
Jack Arlidge, 1979

At one time the 1978 season seriously threatened to prove one of the unhappiest and last successful in the history of Sussex. Snow had gone; Greig left in mid-season; numerous injuries weakened the playing strength and generally an air of pessimism prevailed at Hove. But there was an upsurge of spirit and determination later in the summer, culminating in the winning of the Gillette Cup against a formidable Somerset side. A position midway in the John Player League, ninth place in the Championship table after looking likely "wooden spoonists", and the encouraging emergence of several fine young players saw the season end with Sussex looking ahead with justifiable confidence.

It was on July 11 when Sussex announced that they had "acceded to a request from Tony Greig to be released forthwith from the remainder of his contract, which would have expired in September 1978". The controversial career, which had started back in 1966, was over. It was not until late September, however, that the secret of Greig being an epileptic, which a few of us had known from an early match with the Second XI, was revealed. His association with Packer proved a great blow to the club and the game, but we can still admire the spirit and will-power which enabled him to become so fine a player despite such a handicap.

It was obviously a traumatic season for the new captain, but wicket-keeper Long, so different from Greig in temperament, persevered in cool and admirable fashion, steadily rebuilding the old team spirit and reaping a thrilling reward when he was hoisted on to the shoulders of his team-mates, with the Gillette Cup raised aloft, on the balcony a Lord's.

It was the blend of youth with ripe experience that finally lifted Sussex out of the doldrums. Imran Khan revealed his world class in some matches, and his batting, often at times of crisis, was a model of skill and assurance. He hit three centuries and topped the half-century mark six times, and there were some thrilling partnerships with his Pakistan team-mate Miandad. The batting of Phillipson was a revelation. A medium-pace bowler who failed to make great progress in that sphere, he improved considerably as a middle-order batsman. He played many creditable innings, including one in the Gillette Cup final, and passed 50 five times, aggregating more than 1,000 runs in all matches.

The way the young players performed did much to raise Sussex spirits. The average age of their first four batsmen – Barclay, Mendis, Miandad and Parker – was only 21. Barclay and Mendis proved a dependable opening pair, and Miandad and Parker possessed the ability and confidence to consolidate or hurry the score along. Mendis was particularly impressive against fast bowling and played some gritty innings against speed merchants. He fractured a thumb shortly before the Gillette Cup final, and it was broken again in the third over of his innings at Lord's, but he battled on with Barclay to give his side a great start.

Somerset v Sussex   **Gillette Cup Final**

At Lord's, September 2, 1978. Sussex won by five wickets.   1979

Toss: Sussex. **Somerset 207-7** (60 overs) (B. C. Rose 30, I. V. A. Richards 44, I. T. Botham 80); **Sussex 211-5** (53.1 overs) (J. R. T. Barclay 44, G. D. Mendis 44, P. W. G. Parker 62*, C. P. Phillipson 32).

1981 – PIPPED TO THE TITLE   Jack Arlidge, 1982

The season ended in a thrilling battle for the County Championship, with Nottinghamshire finally clinching the title by only two points from Sussex, who were in the process of beating Yorkshire at Hove when they learned, on the penultimate day of the season, that their rivals had made certain of the prize.

The 1981 Sussex side must have been one of the best balanced they have ever fielded, batting right down the order, possessing a really hostile pace attack, and generally excelling in the field. Once again Sussex owed much to the all-round qualities of their overseas players, Imran Khan and Garth le Roux, who provided a fearsome attack when the wicket gave them any sort of encouragement. Ian Greig had a fine season, emerging as an all-rounder of immense promise. Paul Parker and Gehan Mendis were the leading run-getters, and Ian Gould an efficient and exuberant wicket-keeper.

1982 – Sunday Success
Jack Arlidge, 1983

At the start of the season there was justifiable confidence that Sussex were strong enough, with the right balance of youth and experience, to win one of the four competitions. As the County Championship had always eluded them, and following their spirited bid to foil Nottinghamshire the previous season, it was hoped that this would be the 1982 prize. After an encouraging start, hopes soared, but later in the season inconsistency proved to be a fatal handicap, while Imran Khan's great all-round ability was badly missed when he took over the captaincy of Pakistan. Time after time the early batsmen failed, and only in the John Player League did Sussex produce really reliable form. In this competition they lost only one match, picking up 58 points, a record for the League, and finishing 12 points ahead of runners-up Middlesex.

1983 – Hopes Go Out the Window
Jack Arlidge, 1984

The season opened disastrously for Sussex with a home Championship defeat by Nottinghamshire, heavy reverses against Somerset in both the Benson and Hedges Cup and the John Player Sunday League, other matches washed out and a wait until mid-May before victory came. The unfortunate opening set the general pattern for a season ranking with he worst in post-war years, a crop of injuries following and several players failing completely to produce anything like their best form. Ian Greig was first on the casualty list when he fell from his flat window, trying to gain entrance there after snapping his key in the lock. This was in early June, during a match with Kent at Hove; with Imran Khan unable to bowl until the end of the season because of a stubborn stress fracture of the left shin, and Garth le Roux out of action from the start of August with a chronic groin condition, the pace battery was seriously depleted.

1986 – Covering the Cracks
Jack Arlidge, 1987

Sussex finished the season with a flourish, beating Lancashire decisively and handsomely at Lord's to win the NatWest Trophy and record their fourth victory in seven appearances in the final of the 60-over competition. All very exciting, this grand finale none the less tended to cover over the cracks of a disappointing performance in the Championship, the county slumping from seventh in 1985 to a place dangerously near the bottom of the table.

Lancashire v Sussex	NatWest Trophy Final
At Lord's, September 6, 1986. Sussex won by seven wickets.	1987

No team batting second had previously scored 243 to win either of the two domestic one-day finals at Lord's, and yet so commonplace was Lancashire's bowling that Sussex never looked like falling short, achieving their target with ten balls to spare. Reeve, their medium-pace bowler, made their victory possible, taking four wickets for 12 runs in 25 balls after Fowler and Mendis had put on 50 in 13 overs to question Gould's decision to insert Lancashire. The most important wicket was that of Lloyd, who was given a standing ovation, in which the Sussex players all joined, as he made his way to the wicket in what seemed likely to be his last appearance in Lord's final. With the first ball of this over, his third, Reeve had trapped Mendis; with his fifth he dismissed Lloyd for nought.

Toss: Sussex. **Lancashire 242-8** (60 overs) (N. H. Fairbrother 63, A. N. Hayhurst 49, Extras 30; D. A. Reeve 4-20); **Sussex 243-3** (58.2 overs) (A. M. Green 62, P. W. G. Parker 85, Imran Khan 50*).

1987 – ROCK BOTTOM
Jack Arlidge, 1988

With only seven matches won in all the major competitions, this was a most disappointing season for Sussex. They were last in the Championship, last but one in the Sunday League, and were soon out of the Benson and Hedges Cup and the NatWest Trophy. Only one match was won in the Championship, at Worcester at the beginning of May.

The summer ended on a definite down, with Sussex winning only one of their final 26 matches and Ian Gould, who had led them to victory at Lord's 12 months earlier, resigning after only one full season in charge. It had been a demanding season for a small staff, weakened by the loss of Imran Khan – with the Pakistani touring team – and by injuries to several key players. The absence of a full-time coach to replace Stewart Storey, who was dismissed during the close season, was also felt. It was among the reasons Gould gave for his resignation. He also felt that the pressure of captaincy and the handicap of a stubborn knee injury were preventing him from producing his best form.

Colin Wells was considered by many shrewd judges to be unfortunate to miss selection for one of the winter tours. He scored more than 1,000 first-class runs for the fifth time in eight full seasons and took 52 wickets, a better record than some of the all-rounders chosen.

Over and out: as the game became more centralised on counties' headquarters, several charming outposts disappeared from the fixture list. This match, in 1989, was Sussex's last at the old Central Ground in Hastings, where they had played since 1865. The ground is now a supermarket.

1994 – THE DROUGHT GOES ON
Jack Arlidge, 1995

Sussex went into 1994 believing that a first Championship title was within their grasp at last. Expectations were high following the signing of fast bowler Paul Jarvis as "the last piece in the jigsaw" but, once again, the club could only reflect on disappointment after an eighth year passed by without a trophy. It was ironic that, after his leanest season for years, captain Alan Wells was upgraded to lead England A's tour of India. Sussex, who had come to rely heavily on Wells's consistency, were found wanting as no one took over the mantle. Bill Athey, top-scorer with 1,600 first-class runs in 1993, scraped into four figures in the final match, against Yorkshire. Martin Speight was just short [of 1,000 runs] and led the county's first-class averages with a modest 34.17.

1996 – A FIRST-CLASS ROW
Andy Arlidge, 1997

A year which started with renewed optimism under new coach Desmond Haynes ended with a team threatened by disintegration. In October, Alan Wells returned from a benefit tour in the Caribbean to learn that the captaincy had been given to his deputy, wicket-keeper Peter Moores. Wells had been a model of consistency over his 16 years with a the club, passing 1,000 runs ten times. But his five seasons as captain attracted increasing criticism. At times he lacked imagination, and he was said to be unwilling to listen to experienced colleagues. Wells felt he had been less pig-headed in 1996, but the committee, concerned by the lack of success on the field and tensions in the dressing-room, opted for change.

It did not prevent a general rush to the exit. In November, the long-running rumour that leg-spinner Ian Salisbury was planning to leave for Surrey was confirmed, though Sussex were so keen to keep him that they offered him a five-year contract with the promise of a benefit. A day later, all-rounder Danny Law signed for Essex. Sussex had already released pace bowler Ed Giddins, after the TCCB banned him for 18 months for failing a random drugs test. Wells himself signed for Kent. It appeared that Sussex might have trouble fielding a team at all in 1997, never mind a team with ambitions, which is what some of the departing players coveted. [They did field a team in 1997, though one that finished bottom of both the Championship and Sunday League. The season was dominated by the replacement of the committee by a new body headed by former captain Robin Marlar, as chairman, and Sussex stalwart Tony Pigott as chief executive and director of cricket.]

2001 – ADAMS LEADS RECOVERY

Andy Arlidge, 2002

The wheel turned full circle for Sussex in 2001. Twelve months after a two-day defeat by Gloucestershire condemned them to the Championship wooden spoon, they beat the same opponents in three days to secure the Division Two title. Fittingly, Murray Goodwin, one of the stars of the summer at Hove, hit the runs that completed a 10-wicket win.

No one enjoyed the success more than Chris Adams. A year earlier, his future as captain was under scrutiny when Sussex capitulated in the closing weeks, having gone into August as second division leaders. They were similarly placed in 2001, but this time there was no loss of form or focus. Goodwin, who had retired from Test cricket after Zimbabwe's tour of England in 2000, was an inspired choice as overseas player, scoring 2,465 runs in all cricket, including eight centuries, a phenomenal performance by someone reluctantly agreeing to open in the absence of a specialist. Adams passed 1,000 runs for the second time in his four seasons with Sussex.

James Kirtley's match-winning performance against Gloucestershire, ten for 93 and an unbeaten half-century, helped guarantee the title and closed an outstanding personal season, capped by selection for England's one-day series in Zimbabwe. Doubts over his bowling action resurfaced there, but Kirtley, who had been cleared by the ECB in 2000, was confident he would be allowed to continue his international career. The country's leading first-class wicket-taker with 75, he claimed 102 in all cricket, the second time he had reached 100 wickets in a season.

2003 – THE HISTORY-MAKERS
Andy Arlidge and Bruce Talbot, 2004

Sussex had to wait 164 years for their first Championship title but, when the moment of history arrived, it was perfect. They made certain of their triumph during a crushing victory in the last game of the season, at their Hove headquarters. Some of those present spoke of the dreamlike atmosphere. But for Sussex supporters, for years the butt of jokes about their love of dozing in deckchairs regardless of events in the middle, it was glorious reality. When Murray Goodwin pulled Leicestershire's Phil DeFreitas for four to earn the bonus point that clinched the title, play halted for several minutes. A lap of honour by the squad, accompanied over the loudspeakers by "Sussex by the Sea", gave a packed house a memory to treasure.

Sussex were hardly tipped as Championship contenders, but in 2003 it all came right. A youngish side with tremendous belief, who had been playing together for three or four years, performed above themselves to win 10 Championship matches. After seven weeks in second place, behind defending champions Surrey, they inched ahead in late August.

The key ingredient was the signing of Mushtaq Ahmed, the Pakistani leg-spinner, who took 103 Championship wickets and won games that Sussex would have drawn without him. Mushtaq collected ten or more in a match five times, all of them leading to victory. He was the first bowler for five years to take 100 first-class wickets in the English season. "The most important signings we made were two world-class overseas players," said Adams. "They should have been playing international cricket, and we were lucky that they didn't."

The other overseas player was Goodwin, the former Zimbabwean Test batsman. His championship aggregate was 1,496, his average just under 60, and he crowned Sussex's day of title glory in spectacular fashion, hitting 335 not out against Leicestershire, beating Duleepsinhji's 73-year-old county record.

Sussex v Leicestershire
At Hove, September 17, 18, 19, 2003. Sussex won by an innings and 55 runs. 2004

Toss: Leicestershire. **Leicestershire 179** (D. L. Maddy 55, B. J. Hodge 36; R. S. C. Martin-Jenkins 3-20, Mushtaq Ahmed 4-71) **and 380** (D. D. Masters 119, J. L. Sadler 145, Extras 38; J. D. Lewry 8-106); **Sussex 614-4 dec.** (M. W. Goodwin 335*, P. A. Cottey 56, C. J. Adams 102, T. R. Ambrose 82).

Warwickshire

1980 – WILLIS TAKES CHARGE
Geoff Beane, 1981

Having undergone a wretched season in 1979, Warwickshire staged a partial recovery by winning the John Player League in 1980. But in the Championship early hopes were not realised and the team only finished 14th; an improvement of just one place. They made no real mark in the Benson and Hedges Cup and the Gillette Cup. The season began with a new look, Willis replacing Whitehouse as captain, and David Brown, the county's former England pace bowler, taking over as team manager. Warwickshire were seldom short of runs. Dennis Amiss totalled 1,626 in the Championship, David Smith had an excellent season, Andy Lloyd came to the fore and Geoff Humpage again made his presence felt. John Whitehouse, relieved of the burden of captaincy, returned in the second half of the season to show the form which had once made him an England prospect, finishing second in the first-class averages with 725 runs at 65.90. His match-saving 197 not out in the draw with Glamorgan was especially memorable.

1981 – DESPERATE DAYS
Geoff Beane, 1982

Warwickshire had a dismal season. For the first time since 1919 the county finished in last place in the Championship and there were poor performances in the one-day knockout competitions. Their problems can be tracked down to their deficiencies in bowling. Because of Test calls Willis played in only seven matches and it was of limited comfort to suffering supporters to know that he was putting on match-winning performances against Australia.

In the absence of Willis, the burden of captaincy fell on Amiss and it was to his credit that he continued to make runs consistently. He scored 1,722, with six centuries, and at Derby in June topped three figures twice in the match for the second time in his career. Humpage, who played for England in the Prudential series as a wicket-keeper/batsman, also hit six centuries and averaged 50.02 off 1,701 first-class runs. When he hit his second century of the match at Gloucester he became only the second post-war wicket-keeper to perform this feat in Championship cricket.

1987 – AMISS BOWS OUT
Jack Bannister, 1988

Warwickshire's most shapeless season of the 1980s produced just five wins against first-class opposition from 44 attempts. It ended with a members' petition calling for a special general meeting to debate a vote of no confidence in the chairman and the committee, following the resignation of Bob Willis as chairman of cricket [Willis's playing career had ended in 1984].

Given the atmosphere of administrative disunity, it was not surprising that the club finished 15th in the Championship and bottom of the Refuge Assurance League, having also failed to qualify for the knockout stages of the Benson and Hedges Cup. In the NatWest Trophy, they went out in the quarter-finals after beating Minor Counties teams in the first two rounds. Warwickshire's wooden spoon in the Sunday League was their fourth since 1979 and the third since they won the title in 1980.

Amiss scored two hundreds in his 1,300 – the 23rd time he reached 1,000 runs in 28 seasons of county cricket. His final position of 11th in the all-time list of run-makers is a true indication of an approach to batting that has never been short of dedication and skill. He broke every Warwickshire batting record and more than an era ended with his retirement.

1989 – SUCCESS AFTER A DIRE DECADE
Jack Bannister, 1990

A startling transformation of Warwickshire's fortunes was triggered by three wins in five days at the end of July and the beginning of August. The victories came in three competitions after only five wins in four competitions from the previous 29 games; a record that left them in 16th place in both the Championship and the Refuge Assurance League. The about-turn, bringing them 11 wins from their next 17 games, lifted them to a respectable eighth in the Championship and led to their first victory in a Lord's final for 21 years. Winning the NatWest Trophy from holders Middlesex was due reward for Andy Lloyd and a side which became a tightly welded unit, compared with the unco-ordinated team which had stumbled through the first three and a half months of the season.

Whence the metamorphosis? Essentially, the top-order batsmen performed more consistently and solidly, with the result that the penetrative fast bowling of Allan Donald, Gladstone Small and Tim Munton was no longer wasted. Lloyd, Moles and Humpage all passed their thousand runs for the season. Alvin Kallicharran had a poor summer, though he finished strongly with his 86th and 87th first-class hundreds in the club's purple month of August.

Donald's 86 wickets at 16.25 put him at the top of the national averages; as well as bowling out good batsmen, the South African had the priceless quality of ripping out tailenders. Munton's steady progress as a third seamer won him a [county] cap, and his high proportion of maidens (178 from 613.4 overs) was evidence of an unusual economy for such a penetrative bowler.

Middlesex v Warwickshire

NatWest Trophy Final

At Lord's, September 2, 1989. Warwickshire won by four wickets.

1990

An exciting and, in its way, story-book finish was the high point of a match in which tight bowling, tigerish fielding and a slow pitch had combined to limit strokeplay. Haynes, who hit eight fours, needed 98 balls for his pre-lunch 50, and Middlesex required the experience of Downton and Emburey to see them past 200. But if 210 did not seem a large total, their bowlers defended it with miserly control. Attempts to raise the tempo cost Lloyd, Smith and Humpage their wickets, and even in the crucial partnership between Reeve and the elegant Asif Din, the run-rate fluctuated as they mixed caution with aggression. They added 69 in 15 overs before Reeve, backing up too far, was run out by Haynes's smart return to Emburey, the bowler. This brought to the wicket the inexperienced Neil Smith, with 20 wanted from 18 balls; and when Hughes began the final over, Warwickshire still required ten runs. A single to Asif Din gave Smith the strike; nothing he had done so far, not even his maiden first-class hundred the day before, indicated what he would do now. A full swing of the bat sent the ball soaring over long-off for the only six of the match. Hughes, trying to contain him, conceded a leg-side wide two deliveries later, whereupon Smith, son of the former England captain, straight-drove the next ball for the winning runs.

Toss: Middlesex. **Middlesex 210-5** (60 overs) (D. L. Haynes 50, P. R. Downton 43*);

Warwickshire 211-6 (59.4 overs) (T. A. Lloyd 34, G. W. Humpage 36, D. A. Reeve 42, Asif Din 34*).

1991 – DEADLY DONALD

Jack Bannister, 1992

Warwickshire ended one of their most successful Championship campaigns as runners-up for the third time. Nevertheless Andy Lloyd and his players were disappointed that, after leading the table from May 28 to August 26, and winning as many games as champions Essex, they were still 13 points adrift. It says much for the spirit of the side, and Lloyd's leadership, that they pushed Essex's stronger all-round squad to the last match, though in Allan Donald, Tim Munton, Gladstone Small and Dermot Reeve, they did possess the strongest fast-bowling attack in English cricket.

The season was a personal triumph for Donald and Lloyd, after both had featured in the storm which bedevilled the club during the winter. Some members had been highly critical of Lloyd, and of the committee's decision to retain Donald as their overseas player at the expense of the Australian batsman, Tom Moody. The South African responded with the best fast bowling of his career in the first part of the season. Of the regular county bowlers, only he and Surrey's Waqar Younis secured their wickets at under 20 apiece, and his 83 wickets at a strike-rate of one every 37.77 balls suggested that he would have been an automatic selection for any Test country, even West Indies.

1993 – REEVE THE REDEEMER
Jack Bannister, 1994

Warwickshire's magnificent last-ball win against Sussex in the NatWest Trophy final redeemed an otherwise poor season in which they fell from sixth to 16th place in the Championship, from eighth to tenth in the Sunday League, and failed to survive their first Benson and Hedges match. The winning hit at Lord's by Roger Twose, off the only ball he faced, accomplished a unique double: both knockout finals were won by sides which, on the day, did not have an overseas cricketer.

The match was a triumph for the new club captain, Dermot Reeve, who could easily have won his third Man of the Match award in as many finals. The win epitomised his rare combination of all-round talent and innovative approach – qualities which inspired his ordinary-looking side to overcome injuries to key bowlers, as well as the loss of Allan Donald, on tour with South Africa, after the quarter-final. Typical of the team's resilience in the face of the highest total ever scored in a final were the performances of Asif Din and Paul Smith, two experienced players who were still not sure of their place in the side. Both scored over 500 runs in one-day cricket, with Asif Din's season resurrected in the last six weeks by the NatWest campaign.

Sussex v Warwickshire   **NatWest Trophy Final**

At Lord's, September 4, 1993. Warwickshire won by five wickets.   Paul Weaver, 1994

The 53rd one-day final at Lord's was widely regarded as the greatest ever played. Off the last ball, Warwickshire overhauled the Sussex total of 321 for six, the highest score in a Cup final. The result has to be judged in the context of poor Sussex fielding and some unimaginative captaincy by Wells, but the magnificence of the victory and the thrilling nature of the cricket was beyond dispute.

David Smith, who averages over 50 in the competition after a career spanning 20 years and three counties, returned from injury to score 124, full of powerful drives. Sussex scored 83 from the final ten overs, with Smith run out off the final ball – which hours later attained far more significance than anyone imagined at the time.

Warwickshire's task looked hopeless, the more so when they lost both openers with the score on 18. Paul Smith, all long hair and long handle, then added 75 in 16 overs with Ostler and, when Ostler clipped Salisbury to mid-wicket, Asif Din entered to play the innings of his life. It was only after tea that Sussex first realised the awful possibility of defeat. Smith, with flowing off-drives, and Asif Din, with wristy improvisations, added 71 in 15 overs. Sussex, bowlers and fielders, were haemorrhaging runs. Smith was fourth out at 164 in the 36th over, and Asif Din and Reeve were required to score at more than a run a ball. They kept going, but, with 20 needed from two twilit overs, Sussex still held a slender advantage. They strengthened their position in the 59th when Giddins conceded just five runs and had Asif Din caught at deep cover. He had scored 104 from 106 balls and added 142 in 23 overs with his captain Reeve. Fifteen were needed from the last over: Reeve, without Ian Botham's outrageous talent but with much of his competitive sense, scored 13 from the first five deliveries. Twose, facing

THE COUNTIES

his first and last ball, sliced it through the close off-side field for two to give Warwickshire their victory; stumps were pulled at both ends before the completion of the second run, and Warwickshire should have been awarded the match through losing fewer wickets. However, it was a day for romance rather than technicalities.

Toss: Warwickshire. **Sussex 321-6** (60 overs) (D. M. Smith 124, M. P. Speight 50, A. P. Wells 33, N. J. Lenham 58, Extras 45); **Warwickshire 322-5** (60 overs) (P. A. Smith 60, Asif Din 104, D. A. Reeve 81*, Extras 35).

1994 – THE GREATEST SEASON
Jack Bannister, 1995

Warwickshire recorded the most remarkable season by any side in the history of English county cricket. Uniquely, they won three trophies and, arguably, were only denied the fourth by the toss of a coin. They won their fourth County Championship, their second Sunday League title and their first ever Benson and Hedges Cup. For the ninth successive time, and the 18th in the last 21 years, the NatWest Trophy went to the side batting second in the final; otherwise Warwickshire might have defeated Worcestershire to complete a clean sweep.

Warwickshire's unforgettable season came from meticulous planning and a stroke of luck in being able to sign Brian Lara when Manoj Prabhakar withdrew because of injury. The publicity surrounding Lara's 375 against England in Antigua started a bandwagon which rolled into Edgbaston 11 days later when he scored 147 against Glamorgan, the first of what were to be six Championship hundreds in seven innings, culminating in his world record 501 not out, and nine in all. By June 6, he had scored 1,176 runs in those seven innings.

Crucial for a good, but not outstanding, county attack was Lara's scoring-rate: his 2,066 Championship runs came off 2,262 deliveries; that is five and a half runs per six balls faced. The extra time he created contributed materially to several of the wins, and his presence widened the horizons of his team-mates. The influence of Bob Woolmer, director of coaching, was incalculable. His fourth season at Edgbaston brought to fruition a rare ability to communicate technical advice and it was no surprise when he was given a similar appointment with the South African Test team just after that triumphant end of the season.

Warwickshire v Durham
At Birmingham, June 2, 3, 4, 6, 1994. Drawn.
1995

The astonishing record-strewn Monday, including Lara's 501 not out – the highest score in the history of first-class cricket – that concluded this game was possible only because the third day was lost to rain. Having narrowly missed joining Bradman, Fry and Procter in scoring six successive first-class hundreds, Lara became the first man to score seven in eight innings. When he ran off, the first man ever to have scored 500 runs in an innings, with one ball of the day to spare, Lara had set a string of

1034

other records. His 501 took six minutes under eight hours, in which he faced only 427 balls and hit 308 in boundaries – 62 fours and ten sixes. He shared two partnerships over 300, with Penney scoring 44 out of 314, and Piper scoring a career-best 116 not out from 322 – the highest stand for Warwickshire's fifth wicket. The circumstances that allowed his assault on the record derived from Durham's own total, 556 for eight declared, injuries to two of their bowlers, Graveney and Saxelby, and a playing surface which was reported to Lord's by the umpires as too heavily in favour of batting. Bainbridge would not risk setting Warwickshire a target, and once Durham decided, after the loss of the third day, to play only for bonus points, Lara was given an open cheque to bat. But Lara was unaware of the playing conditions by which the game had to end half an hour early, because there could be no result. Only when Piper informed him, four balls into the last over, that he had two balls left, did he blaze the four to pass Hanif Mohammad's 499 at Karachi in 1958–59. His first reaction afterwards was, "I am not yet a complete player."

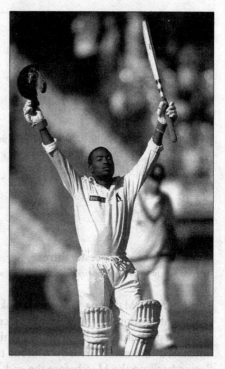

Where no man has gone before: Brian Lara celebrates his amazing 501 not out for Warwickshire against Durham in 1994, which came just six weeks after he had broken the Test record with 375 against England in Antigua.

Warwickshire v Durham, 1994

At Birmingham, June 2, 3, 4, 6, 1994. Result: Drawn.

DURHAM

W. Larkins c Penney b Munton	13	A. C. Cummins lbw b Twose	62
M. Saxelby b Small	19	D. A. Graveney not out	65
J. E. Morris c Lara b P. A. Smith	204	B 2, l-b 17, w 3, n-b 6	28
S. Hutton b Davis	61		
*P. Bainbridge c Reeve b N. M. K. Smith	67	1-35 2-39 3-225 4-365 5-393 (8 wkts dec.)	556
J. I. Longley lbw b N. M. K. Smith	24	6-420 7-422 8-556	
†C. W. Scott lbw b Small	13		

D. M. Cox and S. J. E. Brown did not bat.

Small 22–8–80–2; Munton 28–4–103–1; Reeve 5–2–12–0; P. A. Smith 15–5–51–1; Davis 36–12–105–1; N. M. K. Smith 32–6–97–2; Twose 9.5–1–42–1; Lara 11–1–47–0.

WARWICKSHIRE

D. P. Ostler c Scott b Cummins	8	T. L. Penney c Hutton b Bainbridge	44
R. G. Twose c Cox b Brown	51	P. A. Smith lbw b Cummins	12
B. C. Lara not out	501	†K. J. Piper not out	116
		B 28, l-b 22, w 2, n-b 26	78

1-8 2-123 3-437 4-488   (4 wkts dec.) 810

*D. A. Reeve, N. M. K. Smith, R. P. Davis, G. C. Small and T. A. Munton did not bat.

Cummins 28–1–158–2; Brown 27–1–164–1; Bainbridge 33–4–169–1; Graveney 7–1–34–0; Cox 30–5–163–0; Larkins 5–0–39–0; Morris 5.5–1–33–0.

Toss won by Durham	UMPIRES T. E. Jesty and P. B. Wight

Warwickshire v Worcestershire   Benson and Hedges Cup Final

At Lord's, July 9, 1994. Warwickshire won by six wickets.   Derek Hodgson, 1995

The Al Fresco Marching Jazz Band, making its debut at Lord's, provided perhaps the brightest moments of a mundane cup final. Despite a capacity 29,000 crowd and a blissful summer's day, Worcestershire failed to enjoy it. They were outgunned, outclassed and sunk virtually without trace, and many of their supporters were fleeing back up the M40 before the end. All records of this contest could be swept away from New Road in the next Severn Flood. Small and Munton were a high-class double act, commanding the first 17 overs. It was English fast-medium bowling on an English morning and enabled Warwickshire to put a stranglehold on the game in which their opponents barely wriggled.

Toss: Warwickshire. **Worcestershire 170-9** (55 overs) (T. M. Moody 47; P. A. Smith 3-34); **Warwickshire 172-4** (44.2 overs) (D. P. Ostler 55, R. G. Twose 37, P. A. Smith 42*).

1995 – RECORD-BREAKERS   Jack Bannister, 1996

Warwickshire almost repeated their unique treble of 1994, winning the County Championship and the NatWest Trophy and finishing second to Kent in the Sunday League – beaten only on run-rate. If anything, Warwickshire's perform-ances in the Championship were even more remarkable than before. Their 14 wins in 17 matches constituted the highest percentage of wins in Championship history, shading the 23 out of 28 by Surrey in 1955. The good summer helped. But the margins of their victories and the fact they were equally divided home and away were testimony to the county's all-round strengths.

In 1994 Brian Lara had provided a rare batting impetus. This time, Allan Donald produced the best and most consistent fast bowling seen in county cricket for years. His strike-rate was over six wickets in each Championship match and he headed the national bowling averages with 89 at 16.07. The captain, Dermot Reeve, and his deputy, Tim Munton, joined him in the top five.

After Lara, there was always a question of whether Warwickshire could score enough runs. But the arrival of Nick Knight, whose form earned him a Test place, from Essex, together with outstanding performances from Trevor Penney and Roger Twose, who both passed 1,000 runs at an average over 45, ensured they were never short. Dominic Ostler scored a maiden double-century against Surrey and got over a disappointing period mid-season to score 909 at 43.28. Neil Smith's all-round form earned recognition when he was added to the preliminary squad for the World Cup, along with Reeve.

The NatWest victory meant Warwickshire had won five trophies in two seasons and six in 24 months. The smooth replacement of Bob Woolmer as director of coaching with Phil Neale, who moved from Northamptonshire, and the way that Reeve adjusted his tactics to maximise Donald's performances suggested that this was not a glorious fluke.

Northamptonshire v Warwickshire — NatWest Trophy Final

At Lord's, September 2, 3, 1995. Warwickshire won by four wickets. Matthew Engel, 1996

Allan Lamb spat in the face of cricketing history when he chose to bat; history exacted the customary penalty. For the tenth year running, the NatWest final went to the team batting second and for the second year out of three that team was Warwickshire. Lamb's decision was quite logical and legitimate: rain delayed the start until 3 p.m. on the Saturday thus, in effect, reversing the normal sequence – the team batting second could expect to have to contend with any morning juice in the wicket. However, except that it added further to the superstitions surrounding this extraordinary sequence, the toss itself made no difference. Warwickshire won a tight, low-scoring context primarily because, as in the 1987 final, Northamptonshire wilted when the heat was on. Even so, Northamptonshire would probably have won if umpire Bird had shared the majority opinion that Reeve was out lbw to Kumble in the 52nd over. Reeve survived and Warwickshire began an unstoppable surge towards victory.

Toss: Northamptonshire. **Northamptonshire 200** (59.5 overs) (R. J. Bailey 44, K. M. Curran 30, R. J. Warren 41; A. A. Donald 3-33); **Warwickshire 203-6** (58.5 overs) (D. P. Ostler 45, R. G. Twose 68, D. A. Reeve 37*).

1997 – SUNDAY CONSOLATION

Jack Bannister, 1998

Warwickshire's strength in depth paid dividends in 1997. They won the Sunday League – their seventh trophy in five years – and reached the NatWest Trophy final [in which they were easily beaten by Essex]. They also came joint fourth in the County Championship and lost the Benson and Hedges Cup quarter-final, despite topping 300 at Canterbury. Yet they ran into injury problems that other clubs would have found insuperable even before the opening game. Club captain Tim Munton broke down during pre-season training in the Cape, and missed the entire campaign. Opening batsmen Nick Knight and Andy Moles and pace bowler Allan Donald missed 15 Championship matches between them. It says much for the various captains – Knight, Moles and Neil Smith – that the side challenged so strongly for three trophies.

1998 – LARA'S UNHAPPY RETURN
Jack Bannister, 1999

Rarely in recent years have Warwickshire ended a season wanting to forget it; they did in 1998. Second place in the Sunday League was the only redeeming feature of a campaign sullied by a public fine and reprimand for captain Brian Lara. A substantial minority of the membership had expressed reservations about Lara's appointment, despite his record-breaking feats for the club in 1994. But the committee believed the responsibility of captaincy would prevent the time-keeping lapses which marred that stay. In May, however, after a trip home to Trinidad, Lara caught a later plane than arranged, without the club's permission. He arrived too late for a Sunday game at Taunton, where the team crumbled for 96; Lara was fined £2,000.

For the choice to work, Lara needed another outstanding season. Nobody expected a repeat of 1994, when he scored 2,066 in 25 innings, with nine hundreds, including the world record 501 not out. But both Lara and the club hoped for more than they got – 1,033, precisely half his previous aggregate, in one more innings. Poor home pitches showed up his technical deficiencies; he did not score a hundred in 39 first-class innings between June 1997 and August 1998. Then, a double-hundred at Lord's started a run of three centuries in as many matches. But Lara's lack of form until the final quarter of the season was at the heart of a general batting slump.

Lara and coach Phil Neale never forged a relationship to match the Reeve–Woolmer axis that won the treble in 1994. The team lost the knack of squeezing victory from difficult situations, and finished eighth in the Championship; they were beaten eight times, having lost only 11 matches in the previous four seasons.

1999 – THE GLORY DAYS END
Jack Bannister, 2000

Warwickshire, on some reckonings the team of the 1990s – with two Championships, two Sunday League titles and three knockout trophies – ended the decade condemned to the second division of both Championship and National League. The season's final 48 hours sealed their fate, amid much controversy. The club unsuccessfully accused Derbyshire and Hampshire of collusion in their Championship match, when both got exactly what they needed to squeeze ahead of Warwickshire. Warwickshire tied on points with Derbyshire, but were relegated because they had one less win. The next day, a wet Sunday, Hampshire arrived at Edgbaston for the last National League game. Warwickshire were heading for victory when the umpires took them off, five balls short of the minimum needed for a result. They went down to the second division on net run-rate.

It was Warwickshire's worst season for years. They also made an early exit from the NatWest Trophy, and lost to Yorkshire in the semi-final of the spurious Super Cup. In mid-June, it was announced that director of coaching Phil Neale would be replaced in 2000 by Bob Woolmer, who had held the post before leaving to coach in South Africa.

2002 – WOOLMER DEPARTS
Paul Bolton, 2003

Warwickshire enjoyed their best summer since 1995, winning the last Benson and Hedges Cup and finishing as runners-up in their first season in Division One of the Championship – all of it against a background of unsettling political intrigue. Victory over Essex at Lord's allowed Bob Woolmer to end his second spell as director of coaching as he had his first – with a trophy, the county's first in five years – and to leave with some dignity. But there was nothing dignified about the machinations that led to his departure. Within two weeks of the B&H triumph, Woolmer announced that he would not be seeking a renewal of his contract. This was ostensibly because he wanted to spend more time at home in Cape Town, but it soon became apparent that he had jumped before he was pushed. John Inverarity, the former Australian all-rounder, was appointed as his replacement before the end of the season. Woolmer's parting shot told a tale. "I have found the last three years very educational," he said, "but I can't pretend that they have been the most enjoyable three years of my career."

Essex v Warwickshire   **Benson and Hedges Cup Final**

At Lord's, June 22, 2002. Warwickshire won by five wickets.   2003

Toss: Warwickshire. **Essex 181-8** (50 overs) (A. Flower 30, A. P. Grayson 38*);
Warwickshire 182-5 (36.2 overs) (I. R. Bell 65*, J. O. Troughton 37, S. M. Pollock 34).

2004 – A BATHETIC TRIUMPH
Paul Bolton, 2005

The manner in which Warwickshire clinched their sixth County Championship summed up their summer. The title was secured not in the grand manner, with victory on the pitch, but on a day off. They monitored events at Hove, where Middlesex ended Sussex's mathematical hopes of overhauling the leaders, via television and computer scores. The players staged champagne celebrations at a deserted

Edgbaston for the sponsors' benefit. And a day later, they were relegated in the totesport League.

Warwickshire spent most of the season talking down their Championship prospects, as if they never quite believed they were good enough. They may have completed only five wins, a record low for any Championship side, but they could not be faulted for playing the system. New captain Nick Knight was quick to appreciate that the points were weighted so that not losing was almost as important as winning. He was justifiably proud that Warwickshire were the first county since Surrey in 1999 to survive a season unbeaten.

They insured themselves against defeat through big first-innings totals – a sequence of ten consecutive 400-plus scores was a Championship record – which put the opposition on the defensive. Knight combined captaincy and his benefit without any obvious deterioration in form, passing 1,000 runs, including a maiden triple-century [against Middlesex at Lord's], for the fifth time. Ian Bell finally converted promise into consistency with six centuries and almost 1,500 Championship runs, which earned him a Test cap. Michael Powell regained confidence after relinquishing the captaincy; he was one of nine men who made centuries. No one typified Warwickshire's fighting spirit and refusal to admit defeat more than Brown, who enjoyed another outstanding all-round season. He contributed 911 Championship runs, mostly scored according to his side's needs, and 38 wickets.

Worcestershire

1979 – YOUNIS SPARKS REVIVAL
Michael Beddow, 1980

By finishing second in the County Championship – an improvement of 13 places compared with 1978 – and third in the John Player League, Worcestershire exceeded all expectations and encouraged their members to approach a new decade in optimistic mood. Younis Ahmed, having arrived from Surrey in circumstances which caused him to make a forlorn attempt for compensation from his previous employers, made a strong case to be recognised as the batsman of the season. He scored seven centuries in all cricket – including three-figure innings against Surrey on two occasions – and challenged Turner's long-held status as the county's most prolific scorer.

1985 – HICK'S FIRST HUNDRED
Chris Moore, 1986

If there were an award for talent-spotting it would surely have gone to Worcestershire in 1985. The signing of Neal Radford was one of the more inspired transactions of recent times, the former Lancashire paceman becoming the only bowler in the country to finish the season with more than 100 first-class wickets. No one had achieved that feat at New Road since Norman Gifford in 1970. Equally successful in his debut season was the 21-year-old wicket-keeper Steven Rhodes, whose 57 dismissals and 538 runs were rewarded with selection for the England B tour during the winter of 1985–86.

Then there was Graeme Hick, the prolific young Zimbabwean who looks set to follow in Glenn Turner's footsteps and become Worcestershire's leading overseas batsman. He started the summer with seven centuries outside the first-class game before joining up with the Zimbabweans. For them he scored 230 in the opening game against Oxford University, one of the highest maiden first-class centuries ever made, and followed this with 192 against Glamorgan. On returning to Worcestershire he hit his first Championship century, an innings of 174 not out against Somerset, to which he added 128 against Northamptonshire.

1987 – BOTHAM THE INSPIRATION

Chris Moore, 1988

A new era dawned at New Road in 1987 as Worcestershire, inspired almost inevitably by Ian Botham, captured their first trophy for 13 years by becoming the first winners of the Refuge Assurance League. Much of their improvement on the previous season in the Sunday competition, when they finished 16th, could be credited to the England all-rounder. In 11 Sunday innings, he scored 578 runs, as well as taking 19 economical wickets. Owing to injuries and Test calls, he appeared in only 11 Championship matches and made just one first-class century. That, almost predictably, came against his former county on his first return to Taunton.

Yet, over the season, not even Botham could match the supreme talents of Graeme Hick, who was only 30 runs short of scoring 3,000 in all matches for the county. But for the weather, he would surely have exceeded 2,000 runs in first-class cricket for the second year running. Eight hundreds, the last three in consecutive matches, took his tally to 16 in 89 Championship innings for Worcestershire.

Graham Dilley's first season [having joined from Kent] was restricted by Test calls and continued problems with a side injury. He appeared in only six Championship matches, but his 21 wickets, at 18.42 apiece, included a Championship-best six for 43 against Leicestershire the day he and Ian Botham were awarded their county caps.

1988 – HICK'S WONDER SEASON

Chris Moore, 1989

It was the season Worcestershire had planned for. And but for the toss of a coin, it might have been possible to argue that, in 1988, theirs was the most successful side of modern times. Instead, exposed to batting first on an autumnal morning at Lord's, they lost the NatWest Trophy to Middlesex by three wickets and with it the chance of an unprecedented treble. The previous Sunday, they had retained their Refuge Assurance League title, having claimed 38 of the possible 40 points from their last ten games; a fortnight later, despite an attempt to sabotage the pitch at New Road, they were the County Champions.

Few counties have been as indebted to one player as Worcestershire were to Hick. In their final Championship match, against Glamorgan, they required 24 points to be certain of pipping Kent. It was Hick's 197 on the second day that secured maximum batting points and left the bowlers with almost two days in which to win the match. Yet Worcestershire were by no means a one-man team.

Neal Radford and Graham Dilley started the year as England tourists; Tim Curtis and Phil Newport graduated to the Test team during the season; and Steven Rhodes's contribution was recognised with selection for the ill-fated winter tour of India. Phil Neale's contribution, in his benefit season, was a significant one, both as a respected captain and with the bat. His 1,036 first-class runs contained four hundreds, including a career-best 167 against Sussex. Richard Illingworth, the left-arm spinner, enjoyed his best season to date, twice taking ten wickets in a match. Ian Botham appeared in just four Championship matches, four Refuge Assurance matches and three Benson and Hedges matches before announcing on May 20 that, because of a back condition, he required an operation to fuse two vertebrae. And yet, such was the depth of talent assembled at New Road, he was probably missed more by England than by Worcestershire.

Radford's 71 wickets increased his tally in the Championship to 356 in 81 matches since his "free transfer" from Lancashire, while Newport went from strength to strength. His 85 Championship wickets included five or more in an innings seven times, with a career-best eight for 52 in the win over Middlesex. Curtis passed 1,000 runs for the fifth successive season.

And so to Hick. He scored 3,586 runs for the county in all cricket; his first-class aggregate of 2,713 runs beat G. A. Gooch's previous record of 2,559, the highest aggregate since the Championship was reduced in 1969; and his ten hundreds equalled G. M. Turner's record for Worcestershire in 1970. His monumental 405 not out at Taunton was the second-highest innings in the history of the county Championship [later relegated to third by Brian Lara's 501 for Warwickshire] and erased from the record books Turner's 311 not out against Warwickshire in 1982, the previous highest score by a Worcestershire batsman. When the West Indians took the field at Worcester on May 28, Hick needed a further 153 runs to become the first player since Turner in 1973 to reach 1,000 runs by the end of May. He got them, from 253 balls, and went on to make 172. One man might not make a team, but no one at New Road was prepared to suggest what Worcestershire would have achieved in 1988 without Graeme Hick.

Somerset v Worcestershire

At Taunton, May 5, 6, 7, 9, 1988. Worcestershire won by an innings and 214 runs.   1989

All else in the match was overshadowed by the immense achievement of the Worcestershire batsman, Hick, who 17 days before his 22nd birthday became one of only seven batsmen to score 400 in an innings. W. H. Ponsford performed the feat twice. Hick went in at 78 for one, and having steered his side from the dangers of 132 for five – Rose had taken three for nine in 27 balls – he dominated play until tea on the second day. The weather was fine when he batted and, on a pitch encouraging movement off the seam, he survived very sharp chances when 67, 101 and 141. Yet there were only two other scores over 50 in the match. The first, by Rhodes, occupied 274 balls as a new Worcestershire record was set for the sixth wicket (265); the county's eighth-wicket record was also broken as Hick and Illingworth added 177 before the declaration. On the third and fourth days, under heavy cloud, Newport and Radford steadily overcame considerable defiance by the Somerset batsmen in adverse conditions. The match finished 90 minutes into the final day.

Somerset v Worcestershire, 1988

At Taunton, May 5, 6, 7, 9, 1988. Result: Worcestershire won by an innings and 214 runs.

WORCESTERSHIRE — *First innings*

T. S. Curtis b Rose	27		†S. J. Rhodes c Felton b Dredge	56
G. J. Lord c Mallender b Dredge	49		P. J. Newport b Marks	27
G. A. Hick not out	405		R. K. Illingworth not out	31
D. B. D'Oliveira c Roebuck b Rose	0		B 6, l-b 16, n-b 4	26
*P. A. Neale c Marks b Mallender	0			
I. T. Botham b Rose	7		1-78 2-112 3-112 4-119 5-132 (7 wkts dec.)	628
			6-397 7-451	

N. V. Radford and G. R. Dilley did not bat.

Jones 32–4–97–0; Mallender 32–9–86–1; Marks 50–6–141–1; Rose 31–8–101–3; Dredge 34.5–8–133–2; Roebuck 10–0–48–0.

SOMERSET — *First innings* — *Second innings*

N. A. Felton c Radford b Hick	24	– c Rhodes b Newport	36
*P. M. Roebuck lbw b Radford	0	– lbw b Radford	17
J. J. E. Hardy c Rhodes b Radford	39	– b Newport	0
M. D. Crowe c Rhodes b Newport	28	– c Lord b Radford	53
R. J. Harden lbw b Hick	2	– lbw b Newport	3
V. J. Marks c Botham b Newport	42	– c Hick b Newport	7
†N. D. Burns c Botham b Radford	32	– c Illingworth b Hick	11
G. D. Rose c Curtis b Newport	12	– c Rhodes b Newport	30
N. A. Mallender c Rhodes b Newport	3	– lbw b Radford	1
C. H. Dredge b Radford	16	– c Curtis b Newport	17
A. N. Jones not out	8	– not out	3
L-b 6, n-b 10	16	B 2, l-b 1, n-b 11	14
1-1 2-70 3-70 4-75 5-147 6-152	222	1-49 2-59 3-62 4-74 5-90 6-111	192
7-166 8-173 9-203 10-222		7-154 8-167 9-185 10-192	

First innings – Dilley 12–0–40–0; Radford 23.5–1–77–4; Newport 17–4–59–4; Hick 8–3–18–2; Illingworth 1–0–4–0; Botham 9–3–18–0.
Second innings – Dilley 14–2–40–0; Botham 6–2–25–0; Radford 17–6–39–3; Newport 15.3–3–50–6; Illingworth 11–4–20–0; Hick 11–4–15–1.

Toss won by Worcestershire — UMPIRES R. Julian and R. Palmer

Worcestershire v Glamorgan

At Worcester, September 14, 15, 16, 1988. Worcestershire won by an innings and 76 runs. 1989

Not even a vandal's attempt at sabotage could prevent Worcestershire from taking the maximum points needed to clinch their first Championship title for 14 years. Play on the third day was delayed for an hour while a mixture of petroleum jelly and engine oil, spread over the pitch during the night, was cleared with the help of industrial heaters. Then, after Worcestershire had extended their lead to 179, Glamorgan were promptly dismissed for 103 in 36 overs, leaving Worcestershire victors with more than a day to spare. Newport's five wickets came in a spell of 26 balls in which he conceded just two runs, and took his tally for the season to 93. But once again it was Hick, with a majestic 197, including 29 fours, who made it all possible.

Toss: Glamorgan. **Glamorgan 244** (A. R. Butcher 35, M. P. Maynard 69, J. G. Thomas 40; N. V. Radford 4-84, R. K. Illingworth 3-31) **and 103** (G. C. Holmes 33; P. J. Newport 5-23); **Worcestershire 423** (G. J. Lord 42, G. A. Hick 197, S. J. Rhodes 46, P. J. Newport 30, Extras 34; J. G. Thomas 3-130, J. Derrick 3-91).

1989 – CHAMPIONS BY DEFAULT

Chris Moore, 1990

Worcestershire, it has to be said, would not have retained the County Championship in 1989 but for the TCCB's decision to deprive Essex of 25 points for providing a substandard pitch at Southend in July. To be seen to have won the Championship "fair and square", and not by default, Worcestershire needed to beat Glamorgan in their final match. Instead, rain washed out the last three days at Pontypridd to leave them just six points ahead of Essex.

Yet beyond Essex's borders there would have been few who could deny Worcestershire their right to the crown. Against a succession of injuries to key players and Test calls that would have crippled other counties, Phil Neale's side recovered from a mediocre start to win 12 Championship matches, two more than the previous year. They failed by six points to win the Refuge Assurance League for the third successive year, having to settle for runners-up spot. They also had a remarkable first-ever win over the touring Australians, whose first-innings total of 103 was their lowest against the county. Worcestershire went on to win inside two days by three wickets, with Phil Newport returning match figures of 11 for 127.

Worcestershire v Australians
At Worcester, May 13, 14, 1989. Worcestershire won by three wickets. 1990

Toss: Australians. **Australians 103** (N. V. Radford 3-32, P. J. Newport 6-43) **and 205** (A. R. Border 48, S. R. Waugh 63; N. V. Radford 4-58, P. J. Newport 5-84); **Worcestershire 146** (T. S. Curtis 46, I. T. Botham 39; T. M. Alderman 4-33, G. F. Lawson 3-50) **and 163-7** (G. A. Hick 43, I. T. Botham 42; T. M. Alderman 4-61).

1991 – TWO CUPS (ALBEIT LITTLE ONES)

Chris Moore, 1992

Worcestershire were the only county to win two trophies in 1991; yet there was no denying that they could have done better. Victory by 65 runs over Lancashire in the Benson and Hedges Cup finally ended the hoodoo surrounding six defeats in a Lord's final, and the county triumphed again, by seven runs, against the same opponents to win the Refuge Assurance Cup at Old Trafford. But rain hampered them in the early summer, wiping out nearly a quarter of scheduled play in their first six Championship matches, and their eventual sixth place in the table, with only six wins, was a disappointment.

The Refuge Assurance Cup final was Ian Botham's farewell appearance for Worcestershire, and it was no coincidence that his five years at New Road were the most successful in the county's history, with two Championships and two Refuge Assurance League titles before 1991. Ironically, Botham left for Durham after re-establishing himself as England's all-rounder in his best season for Worcestershire. As the West Indians arrived, he nudged the selectors with a Championship century against Lancashire, and he celebrated his call-up for the Texaco Trophy series with his first hundred against a West Indian team, reaching 100 in 83 balls and going on to 161, his highest score for the county. Later in the year he returned career-best Championship figures of seven for 54 against Warwickshire, and he also won the Gold Award after taking three for 11 against Essex in their Benson and Hedges Cup semi-final. Botham's early release inevitably dismayed some members, as did the announcement in August that the captain, Phil Neale, had been asked to stand down in favour of Tim Curtis in 1992. Neale had led Worcestershire for ten seasons and openly wanted to continue.

The player with greatest cause for satisfaction was Tom Moody, who started where he had left off the previous year at Warwickshire. In all cricket, Moody scored 3,274 runs and hit 12 hundreds: six in the Championship, four in the Refuge Assurance League and two in the Benson and Hedges Cup. He hit a career-best 210 against Warwickshire, and by the time he left to join an Australian XI in Zimbabwe, thus missing three Championship games, he had scored 1,887 first-class runs at an average of 62.90. In the Sunday League he became the first player to score four hundreds in a season, and beat Jimmy Cook's record aggregate of 1990 with 917 runs at 70.53.

What might Worcestershire have achieved had Graeme Hick carried on his own rich vein of form? After struggling to adjust to the pace and bounce of Australian wickets as he wintered in Queensland, Hick gave his long-awaited international career an early boost with his unbeaten 86 against West Indies in the Lord's one-day international. But his first four Tests yielded just 75 runs in seven innings, and this inevitably undermined his form for Worcestershire, for whom he scored only 986 first-class runs at a modest average, by his standards, of 37.92.

Lancashire v Worcestershire **Benson and Hedges Cup Final**
At Lord's, July 13, 14, 1991. Worcestershire won by 65 runs. 1992

Hughes, who had captained Lancashire to victory in both Lord's finals in 1990, omitted himself a year later in order to strengthen their batting. However, Fairbrother's inexperience told against him, not least in his decision to bowl his steady openers, DeFreitas and Allott, until the 14th over, by which time Hick had settled to play a match-winning innings. Well though Wasim Akram bowled to him in his opening spell, it was too late by then.

Toss: Lancashire. **Worcestershire 236-8** (55 overs) (G. A. Hick 88; Wasim Akram 3-58);
Lancashire 171 (47.2 overs) (G. Fowler 54; N. V. Radford 3-48).

1994 – MOODY MAGNIFICENT

John Curtis, 1995

In many respects, Worcestershire's season went as expected. They prospered in the limited-overs game and struggled in the four-day game. One trophy, another Lord's final and second place in the Sunday League, up from 16th in 1993, exceeded their wildest hopes in one-day cricket. But in the Championship, their crash from runners-up to 15th was worse than anyone feared.

Their choice of overseas player had a significant influence. The previous season, they had signed young West Indian pace bowler Ken Benjamin, who shone all too briefly before succumbing to injuries. His departure left an ageing attack short of a new-ball cutting edge. Though Worcestershire had several opponents on the ropes, they could rarely deliver the killer punch and recorded only four Championship victories. But the return, after a year's absence of aggressive Australian all-rounder Tom Moody was the catalyst for a very successful one-day season, culminating in the county's first ever NatWest Trophy, after 32 years of the 60-overs competition.

That eight-wicket win at Lord's halted Warwickshire's hopes of achieving a grand slam of all four domestic titles. But Worcestershire themselves were not so far off treble glory of the kind which fell to their neighbours up the M5. They were beaten by Dermot Reeve's side in the Benson and Hedges Cup final when, just as in the NatWest Trophy final eight weeks later, the toss of the coin proved decisive. Worcestershire also ran Warwickshire very close on Sundays.

Graeme Hick's old confidence in his technique returned as he finally came of age as a Test batsman. He scored 1,101 first-class runs for Worcestershire at 57.94 and became the youngest player, at 28 years and 19 days, to register 50 Championship centuries. The sight of Hick and Moody in tandem at full throttle was a fearsome prospect for bowlers, as Warwickshire found to their cost in the NatWest Trophy final: they shared an unbroken stand of 198 during the surge to victory.

Warwickshire v Worcestershire

NatWest Trophy Final

At Lord's, September 3, 4, 1994. Worcestershire won by eight wickets.

Paul Weaver, 1995

Warwickshire's wonderful adventure, in which they went so close to winning all four domestic titles, ended here, two days after they had secured the Championship. Instead, in what became a one-sided final through luck, keen bowling and magnificent batting, Worcestershire completed a quadruple of their own; victory meant they had won all four trophies in seven years.

Hick and Moody shared a magnificent stand of 198 off just 212 balls – the second-highest for any wicket in 32 finals. Moody, who won the Man of the Match award, hit one six, off Paul Smith, over the Grand Stand roof. Earlier, he had bowled 12 overs off the reel for only 17 runs.

Toss: Worcestershire. **Warwickshire 223-9** (60 overs) (B. C. Lara 81; P. J. Newport 4-38); **Worcestershire 227-2** (49.1 overs) (G. A. Hick 93*, T. M. Moody 88*).

2001 – A Fresh Start

John Curtis, 2002

Worcestershire, after too many years of minimal success, took the first steps towards rebuilding under their new director of cricket, former captain Tom Moody. Brought back to New Road after the resignation of Bill Athey, and given a free hand in all cricketing matters, he set out the guidelines for a five-year plan [though he actually left in 2005 to become Sri Lanka's coach] aimed at restoring Worcestershire as a force to be reckoned with. Crucial to Moody's thinking was a revamped cricket academy, due to be launched in early 2002, after he had pinpointed the paucity of homegrown talent breaking into the senior side in the past decade. Admittedly, the break-up of the side that won six trophies in the late 1980s and early 1990s had been a tardy process; the county had rested on its laurels for too long instead of capitalising on the golden years of Ian Botham and Graham Dilley. But only Graeme Hick and Steve Rhodes from that era were likely to play a full part in 2002.

2004 – Exit One Captain

John Curtis, 2005

County captains come and go in all kinds of mysterious ways. But what happened at Worcester in mid-August was particularly baffling. Ben Smith gave up the job, without notice or logical explanation, in the middle of a match against Northamptonshire. His deputy, 40-year-old Steve Rhodes, had to take charge for the rest of the game and the season, before he retired after 20 years as Worcestershire's first-choice keeper. It was a confusing episode in a confused season which ended with the county – tipped by some as outsiders for the title – relegated in the Championship but promoted in the totesport League, and searching for two new overseas players as well as a new captain and vice captain.

Australia's Andy Bichel was released after three seasons at New Road, with South African all-rounder Andrew Hall allowed to go to Kent. Promising batsman Kadeer Ali sought fresh pastures at Gloucestershire and, though chief executive Mark Newton squashed rumours that Smith, Gareth Batty and Stephen Peters were looking to move, it appeared the dressing-room was not completely harmonious.

Yorkshire

1977 – War Breaks Out
John Callaghan, 1978

The disappointment of a sad summer for Yorkshire spilled over into an angry autumn as the selector Don Brennan waged a public campaign to replace Boycott as captain with Cope. Another member of the committee, Mel Ryan, also threatened to resign as a selector unless dramatic changes were made in the running of the team, adding to the air of crisis which hung over a sequence of unsatisfactory results.

The matter came to a head at a committee meeting at Headingley on November 9 when it was decided to reappoint Boycott as captain and engage Ray Illingworth, the Leicestershire and former England captain, as team manager from April 1, 1979. After Boycott's triumphant return to Test cricket in 1977 public opinion swung behind him, especially in Yorkshire. This may have influenced the committee, who [later] tried to remove some of the more onerous responsibilities from the captain. Illingworth, who left his native Yorkshire in 1968 over a contract disagreement, said he expected to have a happy relationship with Boycott. Following Boycott's unanimous reappointment, Brennan, who was not at the meeting, announced his resignation from the committee.

1978 – Boycott v Hampshire
John Callaghan, 1979

Manoeuvring behind the scenes involved a rearguard action by the anti-Boycott lobby, who seized on a welcome run of good results under [John] Hampshire and devalued it by using it as a weapon in the captaincy argument. Thus, by the middle of June, the county was sadly split by the suggestion that the team did better under Hampshire, whose batting also prospered as he deputised for the injured Boycott.

The climax came at the end of September when Boycott was dismissed as captain after eight years in command. He was replaced by Hampshire. It had been a shattering week for Boycott. He had been passed over as vice-captain of the England team to visit Australia, the honour being given to Bob Willis, and only four days before the Yorkshire decision his mother, with whom he lived, died after a long and painful illness.

1980 – HAMPSHIRE FAILS TOO

John Callaghan, 1981

Another disappointing season for Yorkshire was followed by the resignation of their captain, John Hampshire, who will be replaced in 1981 by Chris Old. Richard Lumb has been appointed vice-captain to cover for Old's possible absence on Test duty. A measure of the confusion which has clouded the county's prospects during several years of political intrigue can be gained from the fact that Lumb made it clear he did not want to become captain. With two former captains, Boycott and Hampshire, remaining in the dressing-room, the likelihood of complications is obvious. Old thus comes into an uneasy inheritance.

1981 – UNBELIEVABLY, IT GETS WORSE

John Callaghan, 1982

Yorkshire spent another winter locked in bitter internal conflict after further failures on the field created circumstances in which a campaign to have Ray Illingworth sacked as team manager developed. The central issue became the suspension of England batsman Geoff Boycott, who had publicly criticised Illingworth. But there were many other issues floating beneath the surface. These were officially acknowledged when the committee instituted an "in-depth investigation" into all aspects of the club's affairs.

Boycott and John Hampshire, who asked for his release at the end of the season and joined Derbyshire, were left out of the Sunday League side as a matter of policy, and after a dismal spell the younger members of the side rallied impressively to indicate what might have been with greater application in June and July. Martyn Moxon, with a century on his first-class debut, emerged as a batsman of the highest promise. Kevin Sharp emphasised the extent of his recovery from illness, and Jim Love played some innings of power and authority.

1982 – ILLY MAKES A COMEBACK

John Callaghan, 1983

The erratic nature of Yorkshire cricket was reflected in the fortunes of their former England seam bowler, Chris Old, who began the summer as club captain only to find himself surplus to requirements in September. The decline in his fortunes resulted from an unhappy start to the programme, particularly in the one-day competitions, with only one victory in nine games – and that against the Minor Counties. In one of the most controversial moves of even Yorkshire's trouble-strewn recent history, Old was replaced [as captain] by the manager, Ray Illingworth, who resumed his playing career at Ilford 15 days after his 50th birthday. Not even Illingworth's experience and tactical skill, however, could compensate for the lack of consistency and, in some cases, application as the side continued to perform some way below expectations.

1983 – A Trophy and a Wooden Spoon
John Callaghan, 1984

Yorkshire's satisfaction at winning the John Player Sunday League, their first major trophy for 14 years, was more than counterbalanced by the embarrassment of finishing at the foot of the County Championship table and by the row which followed the sacking at the end of the season of Geoff Boycott. The county's leading batsman was sacrificed to a youth policy which was the committee's answer to their drop from tenth place in the major competition, and the position was further complicated when Bill Athey refused a new contract and left to join Gloucestershire. The pro-Boycott campaigners forced Yorkshire to reconsider their decision, made by 18 committee votes to seven, but despite threats of action by members of the county club, a second committee meeting brought a comparable vote, thus setting the stage for what seemed likely to be a long and bitter winter. [Boycott survived, Illingworth was sacked as manager, David Bairstow became captain, and Yorkshire carried on struggling.]

1986 – Boycott Finally Leaves the Crease
John Callaghan, 1987

After a disappointing season, Yorkshire ended their association with Geoff Boycott, and in November David Bairstow was replaced as captain by Phil Carrick. The cricket committee voted 4–1 against offering Boycott another year's contract, and when this recommendation was put before the general committee, an amendment aimed at extending his career failed by 12–9. Boycott, whose final record with Yorkshire in the Championship was 29,485 runs at an average of 58.27, again headed the county's averages, despite missing nine Championship matches with a broken bone in his left wrist. County officials paid due tribute to the 45-year-old opener, while stressing that the committee wanted to give younger talent the chance to develop, particularly as several outstanding prospects had gone to other counties in the past.

1987 – A Cup for Carrick
John Callaghan, 1988

Yorkshire, who began 1987 under a cloud of doubt, put most – if not all – of it behind them and exceeded the expectations of even their most optimistic follower. The highlight of the season was the triumph in the Benson and Hedges Cup, in which they defeated Northamptonshire in an absorbing final from which both sides emerged with credit. It was a success which put Yorkshire in the company of Essex, Kent and Lancashire as the only counties to capture all four major honours. In addition, they recorded seven victories in the Championship, the most since 1978. But there was a worrying decline in the second half of the summer as they faded – after heading the table for a long time – to finish eighth, only two places better than 1986.

Following the decision not to renew Geoffrey Boycott's contract, the most important move was the appointment of Phil Carrick as captain in place of David Bairstow. Bairstow quickly settled into the role of senior professional, which suited his temperament. And, without the ultimate responsibility in the field, he refound much of his best form behind the stumps until injury, with which he wrestled bravely over a lengthy period, reduced his effectiveness.

Paul Jarvis had easily the best striking-rate for Yorkshire in the Championship with a wicket every 47.7 balls, and his 75 wickets underlined both his potential and his importance to the county's attack. Among the batsmen, Richard Blakey made remarkable progress. The 20-year-old Young England opener, who effectively stepped into Boycott's shoes, even though he batted at No. 3, became the youngest since Len Hutton to make 1,000 runs in a season for Yorkshire and the youngest ever to complete a double-century.

Northamptonshire v Yorkshire   **Benson and Hedges Cup Final**

At Lord's, July 11, 1987.

Yorkshire won, having taken the greater number of wickets with the scores tied.   1988

Requiring an average of 4.45 runs per over, Yorkshire had paced their reply almost to perfection, and when the scores were level with one ball remaining Love coolly blocked it. Yorkshire were 240 for six when Davis began the last over, and if Bailey's shy from mid-on had run out Sidebottom off the fifth ball, one run would still have been needed. Instead, Love, having hit five boundaries, was not required to score from the 93rd delivery he faced.

Toss: Yorkshire. **Northamptonshire 244-7** (55 overs) (D. J. Capel 97, R. G. Williams 44;

P. W. Jarvis 4-43); **Yorkshire 244-6** (55 overs) (M. D. Moxon 45, A. A. Metcalfe 47, J. D. Love 75*;

R. G. Williams 3-32).

1989 – BACK TO THE TRENCHES   John Callaghan, 1990

The general level of Yorkshire's performance throughout the season was so poor that, before the end of the programme, the dressing-room sent up a distress signal in the shape of a letter from the captain, Phil Carrick, urging the committee to seek outside help. Inevitably this attempt to break with a cherished traditions [of fielding only Yorkshire-born players] provoked an angry response from many members and began another round of debates and arguments – the regular winter activity in troubled times. Ultimately, the widespread concern prompted a "crisis" meeting of the full committee which involved some heated exchanges, notably between members of the cricket committee and Geoff Boycott, who led the criticism of the way the county was being run. The players added to the controversy by making it clear, in a meeting with leading officials, that they took no particular pride in representing Yorkshire and would just as soon offer their talents elsewhere if the money was right. Operating under the shadow of this unpalatable fact, the cricket committee spent seven weeks putting together a blueprint for the future. In the end, though, they came up with very little. Steve Oldham was appointed cricket manager, and Doug Padgett became club coach.

1990 – A FUDGE
John Callaghan, 1991

Yorkshire cricket was a mass of contradictions at the end of yet another worrying season. On the one hand, leading officials took public comfort from an overall statistical improvement reflected in the county's rise from 16th to 10th in the Championship and 11th to sixth in the Refuge Assurance League, arguing that important strides had been made in the right direction. In contrast, however, other members of the committee were so concerned at the poor quality of the cricket that they echoed the dressing-room plea from the previous year for outside assistance. And the loss of around 1,000 members caused the overseas-player issue to be debated once more. The outcome was that in November, by 18–1, the committee voted to relax the county's "Yorkshire born" policy and make eligible those cricketers who, although not born in Yorkshire, had grown up there.

1991 – THE END OF THE TRADITION
John Callaghan, 1992

Yorkshire were in such disarray by the end of June that the general committee, under the decisive leadership of their new president and chairman, Sir Lawrence Byford, broke with the tradition of relying exclusively on players from within the county. The majority view was that defeat by Warwickshire in the first round of the NatWest Trophy had effectively ended their season – they were bottom of the Championship table and could only hope for Sunday League success; the outcome was that on July 10 the committee agreed to employ an overseas player. And with remarkable speed and efficiency, the county announced on July 19 the signing of the Australian fast bowler, Craig McDermottt, for 1992.

It proved to be a fairly painless process, with members generally accepting that Yorkshire cricket was in a desperate state. Spelling out the harsh financial facts, Sir Lawrence indicated that the club were facing a £100,000 loss on the year and that membership had declined by 3,000 since their last trophy in 1987. The threat of bankruptcy clouded the future, with little prospect of any improvement until things took a turn for the better on the field. In addition, the players and the cricket manager, Steve Oldham, were very much in favour of recruiting outside help.

1992 – A SUB CALLED TENDULKAR
John Callaghan, 1993

Yorkshire's decision to break with cherished tradition and sign an overseas player brought some commercial success, checking the worrying decline in membership.

However, the county endured a disastrous season in the field, emphasising that there are no easy or short-term answers to long-standing problems. They slipped from 14th to 16th in the Championship and from seventh to 15th in the Sunday League, suffering seven successive defeats in the process. They lost interest in the Benson and Hedges Cup at the qualifying stage, while Northamptonshire humiliated them in the second round of the NatWest Trophy.

Australian fast bowler Craig McDermott, the original choice as Yorkshire's first officially recognised "outsider", broke down during the winter and required an operation for groin trouble, so, with little room for manoeuvre, the club turned their attentions at the last minute to Sachin Tendulkar. The 19-year-old Indian's appearance on the scene a least silenced those who, from a distance, accused Yorkshire of being racist, and he proved extremely popular with the public and his fellow players. Tendulkar collected his runs with a good deal of style, scoring quickly in limited-overs competitions and being prepared to apply himself diligently in the Championship, but he lacked the experience to dominate. Tendulkar topped 50 in eight of his 25 Championship innings, yet he managed only one century, which won the match against Durham.

Martyn Moxon shouldered a heavy responsibility as the captain and leading batsman, particularly as an opener. Despite a lean spell in August, he remained the most reliable run-maker. Overall, however, Yorkshire batted without much conviction. There were a number of spectacular collapses and, even when the side compiled a substantial total, the runs came too slowly.

1996 – BYAS TAKES CHARGE
John Callaghan, 1997

In one sense, Yorkshire enjoyed their best season since 1972, when the county game was expanded to take in a fourth major competition, for they challenged strongly on all fronts. They failed, however, to win on any of them, and seemed to have the makings of a good side while remaining no more than a useful one. The fact that under their new captain, David Byas, they enjoyed some bursts of excellent form understandably encouraged high hopes among the members. In the final analysis, however, the improvement on 1995 was marginal.

Byas was able to retain an unchanged side for most of the season. The only real setback was the departure of vice-captain Michael Bevan in mid-August, called up by Australia for a one-day tournament. Darren Gough proved the most effective bowler, with 67 first-class wickets adding up to his best total yet. The emergence of Chris Silverwood as a quick bowler of obvious ability was a godsend.

1998 – PROGRESS AT LAST
David Warner, 1999

A rousing start and a storming finish made this Yorkshire's most successful first-class season in years. And there was promise of even better to come from a young and enthusiastic squad, with a battery of talented fast bowlers. A ten-wicket win at Hove in the last match gave Yorkshire their fifth consecutive Championship victory, a sequence they had not equalled since 1967, and third place in the table was their highest since coming second in 1975.

Left-arm swing bowler Paul Hutchison led the way with 57 Championship wickets, one ahead of Gavin Hamilton, whose all-round form was a revelation. Doubt about whether Hamilton was good enough evaporated as, in three successive matches, he improved on his career-best analysis; it finally settled at seven for 50 as he claimed 11 wickets against Surrey. His batting also progressed beyond recognition; he scored five centuries. While Hamilton impressed with his sheer determination, Matthew Hoggard secured a regular place with bowling which became ever faster, more accurate and more hostile. Tall, with a sturdy frame and a smooth, well-controlled run-up, he bagged 31 wickets in the last six matches.

If Hoggard was the bowling find of the season, then 21-year-old Matthew Wood was the batting discovery. He began with one first-class match behind him, but went on to join Michael Vaughan as the only Yorkshire batsman to complete 1,000 runs.

2001 – THE WAIT IS OVER David Warner, 2002

At 13 minutes past midday on August 24, with two matches still to play, Yorkshire became County Champions and ended 33 years of anguish. Fittingly, Brian Close and Vic Wilson, two of Yorkshire's previous Championship-winning captains, were on the pavilion balcony at Scarborough when David Byas crowned his own leadership by holding the catch that brought victory over Glamorgan by an innings and 112 runs. It was Yorkshire's ninth win of the season, out of 14 matches, and made them uncatchable.

Darren Lehmann's brilliance was the single biggest factor [in Yorkshire winning the Championship], his five hundreds and five half-centuries helping him to 1,416 Championship runs and an average of 83.29. His batting throughout the summer was a delight to watch, never more so than when he was compiling his 252 against Lancashire at Headingley, the highest innings in a Roses match, and he remained as well balanced, irreverent and audacious as ever. No one who saw his 191 off 103 balls against Nottinghamshire at Scarborough, in the League, is likely to forget it.

Another factor was the sensational arrival of Steve Kirby, formerly with Leicestershire Seconds, who was signed during the Kent match at Headingley so he could replace Matthew Hoggard, requisitioned by England after taking four first-innings wickets. The red-headed pace bowler, giving every indication of nerves as he fielded on the boundary, was quickly transformed from lamb to lion once introduced to the action. Genuinely hostile bowling, backed up by glares and stares at astonished batsmen, earned him figures of seven for 50, the joint second best by a Yorkshire bowler on Championship debut. Kirby went on to become Yorkshire's leading wicket-taker, with 47 dismissals at 20.85 runs apiece.

Yorkshire v Lancashire

At Leeds, July 27, 28, 29, 30, 2001. Yorkshire won by seven wickets. 2002

Yorkshire's first Championship win over Lancashire in six years preserved their 14-point lead at the top of the table with a game in hand. It was achieved through a phenomenal innings by Lehmann, whose 252 was the highest in Roses history, beating Maurice Leyland's 211 not out in 1930 and Graham Lloyd's 225 in the 1997 non-Championship "friendly". In 365 minutes, facing 288 balls, he never offered a chance, and at times toyed with the bowling, periods of relative calm being followed by salvos of audacious shots fired off to all parts of the ground.

Toss: Lancashire. **Lancashire 373** (J. P. Crawley 73, J. C. Scuderi 56, W. K. Hegg 76, C. P. Schofield 55, G. Chapple 33; D. Gough 4-65, S. P. Kirby 3-103) **and 314** (J. P. Crawley 113, C. P. Schofield 34, P. J. Martin 51*, J. Wood 35, Extras 32; C. White 4-57); **Yorkshire 531** (M. J. Wood 86, D. S. Lehmann 252, D. Gough 96; G. Chapple 5-83) **and 158-3** (M. J. Wood 51, D. S. Lehmann 48; G. Keedy 3-67).

Yorkshire v Glamorgan

At Scarborough, August 21, 22, 23, 24, 2001. Yorkshire won by an innings and 112 runs. 2002

At 12.13 on the final day, Byas took the catch that returned the Championship title to Yorkshire after 33 years. He also contributed one of three centuries to his side's impregnable total, but – not for the first time in the season – he had refused to be hurried into his declaration by gloomy weather forecasts, preferring to go by his farmer's instincts. Even so, he cut it fine, for heavy rain was setting in as the jubilant winners left the field. When Glamorgan were six down on the third evening, it was decided to fling open the gates on the final morning, although the 5,000 crowd had to watch a spectacular counter-attack by Jones before acclaiming the new champions. Tearing into Lehmann's bowling, he lashed 46 off 14 balls, hitting six sixes and two fours before slicing to backward point where Byas, having dashed from slip, held the catch that sent the champagne corks popping.

Toss: Glamorgan. **Glamorgan 223** (J. P. Maher 36, A. Dale 59, M. A. Wallace 31; R. J. Sidebottom 3-34, R. K. J. Dawson 6-82) **and 245** (K. Newell 30, A. Dale 45*, S. P. Jones 46, Extras 34; S. P. Kirby 4-40, D. S. Lehmann 3-56); **Yorkshire 580-9 dec.** (C. White 183, M. J. Wood 124, M. P. Vaughan 45, D. Byas 104, R. J. Blakey 54, Extras 30; D. A. Cosker 4-168).

2002 – FLUCTUATING FORTUNES

David Warner, 2003

In sharp contrast with normal practice, Yorkshire's latest revolution broke out during the season rather than waiting for the winter months. Their fortunes fluctuated wildly both on and off the field. After the long-awaited Championship triumph in 2001 came humble pie: anchored to the bottom of the table from early June, Yorkshire raised their game a little but could not avoid relegation. Some compensation came in the form of a Lord's cup win in the C&G Trophy – just like the 2001 Championship, it came after a 33-year gap – but it was the spectacular failure to defend their Championship crown that lingered in the memory. The coach, Wayne Clark from Western Australia, refused to offer excuses and acknowledged that dreadful form early on had left them with much to do. He did, however, concede that the players had not been able to concentrate 100% on their game because of problems elsewhere. It was a valid point. But in January 2003, it was announced that Clark, who had turned down the position of bowling coach after failing to agree a revised contract, was leaving the club by mutual consent a year early. His replacements were expected to be Kevin Sharp, as batting coach, and Arnie Sidebottom for the bowling, as Yorkshire turned back to their own.

Dark clouds had gathered over Headingley at the annual meeting the previous March when the treasurer, Peter Townend, apologised to members for "our abysmal failure to conduct business successfully last year". He also admitted that the wiping out of profits in the marketing department had highlighted several serious deficiencies in the way the club shop was run. Soon afterwards, the fraud squad were called in to investigate a black hole of up to £100,000. No evidence was found of criminal wrongdoing, but there were mounting fears that Yorkshire were heading for bankruptcy. On August 12, it was announced that the chairman, Keith Moss, had agreed to stand down and that a new, four-strong management team had, at the bank's insistence and with the committee's approval, taken over the running of the club's affairs. Later in August, an extraordinary general meeting voted in a rule change which allowed the club's borrowing ceiling to rise to £10m in order to meet the spiralling costs of Headingley's redevelopment.

Somerset v Yorkshire

At Lord's, August 31, 2002. Yorkshire won by six wickets.

C&G Trophy Final

Tim de Lisle, 2003

A close encounter between two teams having a nightmare in the Championship was decided by the one man on the field who had not spent months worrying about relegation. When he strode out to bat in a mini-crisis, Matthew Elliott had been a Yorkshire player for only two and a half weeks and had not even followed this year's C&G, let alone played in it. After a watchful start, he rediscovered the booming strokeplay that had rung out in the Lord's Test of 1997. He reminded a capacity crowd why the Australian selectors had once preferred him to Matthew Hayden, and played out a trailer for the Ashes by singling out Caddick for rough treatment. Caddick went wicketless for the third time in four Lord's finals, and the only sign of a cutting edge came in a spell of big-hearted swing from his new-ball partner, Johnson. Somerset, fielding the XI that had won the cup the year before, were comfortably beaten, and Yorkshire lifted their first Lord's trophy in 15 years.

Toss: Somerset. **Somerset 256-8** (50 overs) (P. D. Bowler 67, J. Cox 34, K. A. Parsons 41; M. J. Hoggard 5-65); **Yorkshire 260-4** (48 overs) (M. T. G. Elliott 128*, M. P. Vaughan 31, A. McGrath 46*; R. L. Johnson 3-51).

SECTION SIX

The Bigger Picture

SECTION SIX

The Bigger Picture

Cricket Round the World

Will cricket ever be a truly global game? *Wisden*, judging by its current views, doubts it. Soccer's dominance is safe. It seems unlikely that cricket will ever sweep Brazil or Germany. But some cricket seems to be played more or less everywhere in the world – even in Antarctica, as we discover below. When he became editor, Matthew Engel instituted a "Cricket Round the World" section to cover these curious outcrops of the game. This section samples some of those intriguing items – reports from such unlikely cricketing hotbeds as Russia, Japan, Uganda and the Falkland Islands. It also includes items from more established cricketing countries such as Holland, Kenya and the US, and a delightful essay on cricket in the Pacific. Taken together, they make a persuasive case for cricket being almost a global game. Who knows, perhaps one day soccer will be pushed aside.   S. M.

CRICKET IN THE PACIFIC   Scyld Berry, 1981

The two epicentres of cricket in the Pacific – or so it seemed to me during the travels I was fortunately able to make after England's last two tours to Australia – lie in Fiji and Papua New Guinea; the island of Lakeba in the former and the villages along the south coast of the latter. These two countries are the only two in the region that are currently Associate Members of the International Cricket Conference, and between them they could perhaps turn out a team with a potential of good minor county standard. However, cricket is played, in some form or other, in most countries of the South Pacific, and it struck me as an interesting question why the game is so widespread and relatively popular.

The primary sport in the Pacific is usually rugby union or rugby league, because of Australia's influence, or football. But there is a fairly compelling reason why cricket comes first in Lakeba (pronounced "Lakemba"), a small island 200 miles to the east of Suva, the capital, on Fiji's main island. The prime minister, a native of Lakeba, banned all forms of rugby there; he banned it because its close physical contact led to outbreaks of tribal warfare. So the islanders, 2,400 of them, all built like rugby players – though the more slender women might only make fly-halves – have long devoted their leisure energies to cricket.

Lakeba has eight villages, and each village has an "A" and a "B" team. Wednesdays are given over as devotedly to cricket as Sundays are to religion; the majority practise Methodism, the rest Catholicism, while everyone practises cricket as the original missionaries brought both bats, and bibles. The island's collective fervour has its focus on the Dewar Shield, which is challenged for annually by one of the various district associations – Suva, Lautoka, etc. It is the most splendid cup I have seen: huge and silver on a platform of wood. To the great pride of Lakebans, the cup has taken up almost permanent residence in the prime minister's house, which stands on the fine leg boundary of the island's main ground.

Of all Lakeba's and Fiji's players, the star is Peni Dakai, thick-set, square-jawed, and in his eyes is the killer instinct that great batsmen have. He is a nephew of Bula, who was acknowledged in his day as the finest of Fijian batsmen, the maker of hundreds against provincial sides in New Zealand. Dakai also lives next to the main ground, which is of the village-green type, roughly grassed, with only the canvas-spread concrete wicket left untouched during the week. Dakai lives at mid-wicket, in a three-roomed house on stilts, and can beat a regular thud every match day on his corrugated roof.

The new ball swings violently in Lakeba, either because of the humidity or the wind off the ocean a hundred yards away. Dakai also opens the bowling and swings it both ways. But it is his batting which is celebrated: not only his mid-wicket pull but his lofted straight drive over the prime minister's house and a variety of cuts. I did not see him bat during my visit (he had hurt his leg on coral while snorkelling after fish), but in 1979 I saw him hit a straight six in England that went off his bat like a tracer bullet. I can believe Peter Roebuck of Somerset, who has coached in Lakeba, when he says positively that Dakai can hit the ball as far and as hard as either Viv Richards or Ian Botham.

His lifestyle would partly explain it. Lakeba is only starting to be integrated into the cash economy, and most of Dakai's time, as a villager, is taken up in subsistence farming. He goes fishing, too, for a couple of days at a time with his spear, and grows copra, his only cash-crop which brings him an income of a few hundred dollars a year. He also cuts down pine trees as part of one of those community projects which characterise the Polynesian and Melanesian lifestyle. Such work must have given him good eyesight and immense strength of limb. For his sixes he needs but a short backlift, which is also a help against the late, oceanic swing.

If Dakai is the champion of Fiji – and his failure to prove himself as such during the "mini" World Cup in England in 1979 was an immense disappointment to him; in mitigation, he was rather a fish out of water as he cannot speak English – then Papua New Guinea's champion is Kila Alewa. He comes from that other epicentre; the villages, centred on Hula on the south coast of the island, that jut into the muddy waters of the Coral Sea. Even today Hula is four hours' drive from the capital, Port Moresby, through thick coastal savannah along a winding track. It is easy to understand why the first missionaries arrived by sea in the second half of the 19th century.

Today the clergy maintains as strong a hold on the game in Papuan villages as ever it did in the rural England of Cardus's imagination. The pastor of Hula – here again most missionaries were low church, Unitarians now – is not only captain of the village team, he also leads his flock by opening the batting and bowling, a monopoly which no one is going to challenge as long as he keeps all the kit in his house. It is the same pattern as in Lakeba: one day a week set aside for religion, another for cricket, and another couple for community projects in lieu of rates and taxes. The simplicity is appealing, the lifestyle ideal for exercising a cricketer.

However, because there is no employment other than as a villager or pastor, most young men of the area, having learned their cricket, migrate to Port Moresby and the few other towns. But they come together again for the few international matches that Papua New Guinea has played and form the bulk of the side: players like Kila Alewa, a fast-medium bowler with an action like Imran Khan's, hostile when he wants to be, Vavine Pala, his left-arm opening partner, and Brian Amini, the first native-born to captain a representative side – when they beat Fiji in 1977 by eight wickets.

Although organised cricket is a minority interest elsewhere in the Pacific, five other countries were able to send teams to the South Pacific Games held in Suva in late 1979: Tuvalu (formerly the Ellice Islands), New Caledonia, the weakest team for having to play the game in a French culture inimical to it, the Solomon Islands, where Australian expatriates have nurtured the game, New Hebrides and Tonga.

Papua New Guinea won the limited-overs tournament by beating the New Hebridean outsiders by nine wickets in the final. In the following months New Hebrides were otherwise engaged in becoming the independent state of Vanuatu, but several factors promise a future for cricket in the islands, apart from the fact that the secessionist Jimmy Stevens has a beard like W.G's. Their new president, Walter Lini, is said to encourage the game, and the two secondary schools on the main island both teach it. In consequence there are some good native batsmen, while bowling is mostly in the hands of expatriates. In New Hebrides, as elsewhere, those coming late and uncoached to the game are prone to throw.

Tonga was the surprise of the competition. For a start, few were aware that cricket is played in Tonga. But it is, if in a fairly unconventional form: the umpiring a highly subjective process, the bowling more a matter of throwing. If the canons have not been inculcated, then it is partly because there were very few British officials in Tonga in colonial days, and those who were posted there were not interested in cricket coaching. More recently, Tonga has been the victim of that lack of interest which the ICC has shown all too widely. To promote cricket in Tonga it has done nothing. The first team to visit there was from the University of California, only a few years ago. Indeed, apart from New Zealand's interest in Fiji, and some generous help given by New South Wales to Papua New Guinea, the Pacific story is one of total neglect by the game's established authorities.

Given this, it is remarkable that cricket has made the headway it has in the Pacific. Compared with the state of the game in former British colonies in East and West Africa, cricket is much more popular amongst Polynesians and Melanesians than amongst Africans. The reason why appears to lie with those missionaries. They came principally from the London Missionary Society, and apart from a few castaways and beachcombers they were the first white men to settle in the South Pacific; courageous men, too, for the cooking pots took a toll of them. According to their reports, they found cannibalism and inter-tribal warfare to be endemic. Frequent, indiscriminate massacring of entire villages made refinements like birth control superfluous. How were these missionaries to stop the natives butchering each other? By teaching them cricket, they decided; it was as simple as that. To quote chapter and verse of the missionaries' strategy: "We transformed their spears into wickets, their shields into cricket bats." This was written by Charles Abel, the Missionary Society's leading evangeliser in Papua New Guinea.

Facts fall in with this theory. Fiji's prime minister bans rugby in Lakeba because it led to tribal violence – and even tiny Lakeba has 32 tribes. The clergy of Hula and its surroundings propagate the gospel and cricket, leading the community in both. Cricket, in short, was introduced into the Pacific as a surrogate for war, and it is still capable of serving that purpose today.

Non-conventional cricket in the Pacific confirms this. There is a mass form of the game – where whole villages of a hundred or more play one another, with one ball per over, thrown not bowled, and made of wood made familiar by a recent film on cricket in the Trobriand Islands of Papua New Guinea. It is played by men and women alike, from Kiribati (the former Gilbert Islands) to Pitcairn Island, and even in non-British colonies like Samoa. This form of the game is even more manifestly a surrogate for war. Where in the past a village would take up its spears and go raiding its neighbour, now the inhabitants go armed with bats for a festival of eating, dancing and "krikiti". Cultural imperialism it may have been on the part of those missionaries, but they certainly did a good job in imposing the peace. So the next question is: has cricket everywhere been a substitute for war?

NEPAL – A TV SET FOR THE SUPERSTAR
Jai Kumar Shah, 1993

In Nepal cricket is second only to soccer in popularity. A festival of daily matches in Kathmandu in early 1992 was watched by crowds of up to 4,000, with 8,000 watching the final. In 1989 at least 15,000 people in Biratnagar, south of Everest in the Eastern Region, watched two teams from India, Patna and Benares, in the final of an invitation tournament. More than 25 teams are now competing in Kathmandu alone and eight of them competed for the Rameshwore Memorial Shield in April. This was won by Kathmaridu Khel Mandal. Their player Sri Nivas Rana was named as Man of the Series and he was awarded a television set, courtesy of Khetri Sausages. The tenth national tournament for the JAI Trophy took place in Birgunj with teams from nine zones; Koshi Zone were the winners. All matches are played on matting.

BOOM IN THE US
Gerald Howat, 1993

As American cricket approaches the centenary of its greatest moment, it is enjoying a boom in popularity, caused by the large number of immigrants from the cricket-playing countries. In October 1893 the Philadelphians beat the

Australian Test team by an innings. In 1993 Philadelphia's clubs – with their grand clubhouses – are enjoying a revival, although the major centres of the sport are now in New York and New England.

Once again teams of Test stars came to New York to play heavily sponsored, well-attended exhibition matches at Randall's Island. India beat West Indies while the Pakistanis, under Imran Khan, lost by four runs to a Rest of the World team containing Malcolm Marshall, Richie Richardson and Sachin Tendulkar. But the strength of the game lies in the leagues across the country. New York's oldest league, the Metropolitan, which flourished in the 1890s, was won by Westbury, ahead of the New York West Indians. Somerset A won the American League, with the help of 537 runs from Hubert Blackman, while the Brooklyn Championship went to Carricou and Cambridge. Emite Evertz, with a century against New England and six wickets for six against Mahasabha, contributed most to Norwalk's success in the Connecticut League. Hillside's two formidable batsmen, Amanath Ramcharitar, with three centuries, and Khamal Singh, ensured them the Eastern American President's Trophy. Eclipse won the New Jersey League in which Ram Budhu of Mirror took ten wickets for four, including a hat-trick, against General Electric. New York Eagles, for whom Amjad Khan scored over 600 runs, won the Commonwealth League. Representatives of all these leagues played in the Eastern Zone competition, which the Metropolitan League won, beating the Commonwealth League by 56 runs in the final.

The season in Philadelphia included a completely rain-ruined visit from Bermuda while cricket in Southern California was beset by both floods and the Los Angeles riots. The interrupted League was eventually won by Corinthians. Stanford University won the North California League. Southern California beat the North to retain the Raisinland Trophy and also won the inaugural match at Under-21 level.

HUNGARY'S KIT CRISIS   1994

In May [1993], the *Hungarian Times* reported the formation of the Magyar Cricket Club, which intended to play three other teams of expatriates, with kit provided by the British Embassy, on a matting wicket at Obudai Island. Two months later, however, it was reported that the kit had been stolen.

BEATING BASEBALL   Peter Foster, 1994

A third team, the Good Men Cricket Club, has now been founded in the Philippines to join the Manila Nomads (founded 1912) and the Manila Anzacs (founded 1980). All three teams are made up largely of expatriates and most matches are against clubs from elsewhere in East Asia; The Philippines, as a former US colony, plays baseball. However, there are some signs of local interest and a game between GMCC and Nomads was recently televised. All matches are at the Nomads ground, which doubles up as a rugby pitch during the rainy season. The wicket is matting. Scores tend to be high as the boundaries are rather short and the outfield is fast as the grass is kept to a minimum by the goats that graze on it during lunch and tea breaks. However, the matting itself is worn and the bounce somewhat irregular. For that reason, there is normally a rule that batsmen cannot be out first ball.

RUSSIA'S MCC
1994

In July [1993], an English touring team, the Explorers, played what was reported to be the first formal match in Moscow since the Bolshevik Revolution. Their opponents were the MCC: the newly formed Moscow Cricket Club. Owing to a misunderstanding, the pitch was originally laid out for a croquet match. Broomhandles had to be used in place of stumps: the man bringing some of the kit was stopped at Heathrow because he had forgotten to get a visa.

DO CRY FOR ME, ARGENTINA
1995

The annual North v South match, played over three days and the highlight of the Argentine calendar for over a century, fizzled out into a draw.

BRUNEI'S SOLITARY CRICKETER
Derek Thursby, 1995

Cricket is almost totally an expatriate game in Brunei; it is a matter of some regret that only one Bruneian plays cricket on a regular basis. The season roughly follows the northern hemisphere summer. In 1994, six teams competed: Manggis and Cavaliers were joint league champions, and Cavaliers won the knockout cup. The annual fixture against Sabah was played in Kota Kinabalu in September – Sabah won by eight wickets.

BOWLING CHINAMEN
1995

The first games in Shanghai since 1948 were reported to have been played over the weekend of November 12 and 13 between the Craigengower Cricket Club of Hong Kong and a Shanghai team, captained by Richard Graham. The teams played on a matting wicket on a football pitch borrowed from the Shanghai Sports Institute.

THE MYTH OF THE TRIAL BALL   Peter Knight, 1995

Fiji's results in the ICC Trophy in Kenya were disappointing, especially after the relative success in the Netherlands in 1990. Two leading players were unavailable – one of them, Neil Maxwell, gained a place in the New South Wales team. There has also been a lack of good competition since 1990; Fiji is so isolated it is very expensive to travel anywhere. The annual Crompton Cup competition, played over Easter, was won in its 43rd year by the New South Wales Police team, which beat Suva in a close-fought final. Suva won the Colonial Mutual Inter-District competition, beating Moce, an island team, in the final.

This year marked the retirement of Philip Snow as Fiji's ICC representative after 30 years' service and consecutive attendance. He has done a wonderful job for Fiji and will be sadly missed, but has been ably replaced by his son-in-law Peter Wain. Umpiring continues to be a problem, but we have managed to eradicate the misconception that the first ball of an innings is "a trial ball" and our coaching programme has led to a better understanding of the laws. Our plans for 1995–96 are to continue with our development programme, with emphasis on coaching schools and grassroots, and to send the national and Under-21 teams to New Zealand or Australia. To do this, we have to rely on Fiji's share of the World Cup proceeds. Without this, the future of cricket in Fiji would not be very bright.

THOMMO IN JAPAN   Trevor Bayley, 1995

Though expatriates still account for the bulk of cricket played in Japan, the game is now being played all over the country and locals are gaining in numbers and enthusiasm. We are seeing at least one new university team a year and all but two of the positions in the Japan Cricket Association are now held by Japanese. Japan's only cricket magazine, *The Straight Bat*, sponsored a competition of two-day matches, with five teams entered. The winning team, Tokyo Bay CC, was founded only two years ago by one of the new pioneers of Japanese cricket, Mr Fumito Miyakawa.

Having previously experienced only 35-over cricket, it took some time for the locals to become accustomed to the longer game, but Mr Miyakawa, who had been to New Zealand to study cricket, led his team to a well-deserved victory over Senshu University. *The Straight Bat* also sponsored the second annual Challenge Cup for beginners, with 65 players vying for honours. The cup was won by Ms Miki Koyama for her dedication, enthusiasm and all-round cricket skills. The Yokohama Country and Athletic Club's fourth annual six-a-side competition had to be held over two days to accommodate all those who wanted to play, and even then some missed out; victory went for the second year running to the Edogawa Falcons. The season ended with a bang when Jeff Thomson came to Tokyo and conducted three days of coaching on behalf of the JCA.

MAIL SHIP STOPPED PLAY

Fraser M. Simm, 1995

The cricket season on St Helena (population 5,500) runs from January to July. Eight teams play one-day matches of two innings a side on a matting pitch at Francis Plain, where in 1886 a fielder is alleged to have died chasing a ball over the cliff; a repetition is still theoretically possible. After many years of ascendancy by Jamestown B, Western B won the 1994 championship ahead of Levelwood A, who won the knockout. Jamestown B, however, provided two individual highlights: left-arm spinner Eric George, the chairman of the Cricket Association who is in his 60s, took eight for 39 before announcing his retirement at the end of the season; his son Gavin averaged 71 with the bat. Play traditionally continues in the rain, but two matches had to be postponed in 1994 because the Royal Mail ship, the only link with the outside world, was in port for its bi-monthly visit.

VIETNAM'S FIRST CENTURY

1995

The Sri Lankan Nalliah Sellathurai was reported to have become the first batsman to score a century in the Vietnamese capital, Hanoi, scoring 106 for an Indian subcontinent team against an Australian-English side on a matting pitch.

DUTCH DODGY DEALING

David Hardy, 1996

Dutch cricket had an intermediate year between the national team's historic qualification for the World Cup at the ICC Trophy in 1994 and participation in the World Cup itself in 1996. But 1995 was also an historic year in its own right: Holland became the first team from outside the British Isles to compete in an English domestic competition, when they played Northamptonshire in the NatWest Trophy.

Holland lost, but they scored 267 for nine and had one of the strongest counties worried, even though they were without all three of their players with experience of county cricket: Paul-Jan Bakker, now playing again in the Netherlands, was injured, and Roland Lefebvre and Andre van Troost were ineligible because they were still contracted to counties. For the record, the Dutch team on the day contained more foreigners – five – than ever before, including South African newcomer Billy Stelling.

What followed was an anticlimax, as only one game out of nine was won, against Scotland, but Young Australia – who won by just one run in Haarlem on July 14 – were nearly added to the long list of impressive scalps. Earlier, the team had returned to Kenya for a triangular tournament with the other two qualifiers for the 1996 World Cup: Kenya and the United Arab Emirates. This time Holland came out on top, winning two games out of three against Kenya, and one out of two against the UAE. There was also a tour to India, which produced three wins out of six and invaluable experience in local conditions.

Following a match-fixing scandal in 1994, the domestic season was again blemished, this time by violence on the field. There was actual fighting between a player from Bloemendaal and one from Shaheen, and even between two from the same side, Sparta. On another occasion an elderly umpire was kicked, and the police had to be called to calm down a player from the Gandhi club. Unfortunately, cricket in the Netherlands is no longer immune from developments that are commonplace in other sports.

The shameful events of 1994, when HCC tried to achieve promotion by arranging a 702-run win over their own second team, led to the creation of a Reserve Premier League, in which the Second XIs were separated from the rest. This league was promptly won by HCC Second XI, bowled out for one in the infamous 1994 match, who registered 17 wins out of 17. In the Hoofdklasse, it was close all season before Excelsior won the Championship for the second time in their 75-year history. HCC were promoted ahead of Gandhi, their rivals in 1994 when Gandhi won a match by 797 runs before officials took action against everyone involved.

BEWARE THE CLIFF   Canon Nicholas Turner, 1996

Plans are afoot to return cricket to one of the world's most distinctive grounds. The barren, volcanic rock of Ascension Island in the South Atlantic is believed to be the only place where "wedding stopped play" – to be resumed 40 minutes later as the last of the congregation left for the reception. The little Church of St Mary the Virgin is inside the boundary and, when it was restored in 1993, with a new slate roof, cricket moved to a new and larger ground at the island's RAF camp, where floodlit play is possible. However, the move has not been popular with the crowds (all things are relative – the total population is only 1,200) and Dr Sukhtanker, the resident surgeon and cricketing supremo, intends to take the game back to its traditional venue.

Cricket on Ascension, uninhabited until the Royal Navy landed in 1815, took off when West Indian workers arrived in the mid-1960s to build a relay station. They started league cricket, which has been kept going by South Africans working for the cable company, and the RAF, who returned during the Falklands War. They have provided teaching input for the workers from St Helena who are employed here. Saint Helenians have a natural aptitude for the game, and have developed good technique, with two exceptions: the concrete strip offers little chance of spin, and the short boundaries – combined with American influence – have encouraged some towards the high baseball slog. The cricket field by the church, which used to be the army parade ground, is actually rolled volcanic ash, with not a blade of grass in sight, and the outfield is very fast.

The ball used is a composite – a leather ball would be torn to shreds – and we need several per game there, to replace those which get stuck on the church roof or among the stores waiting to be loaded on the next ship. A dusty trade wind always blows across the pitch, but it is what people seem to prefer and it is indeed a fine setting, if you can find some shade: the four sides comprising the small white church, a smooth, dark red, volcanic cone, the ageing, arcaded barracks, and the dark blue ocean with its waves crashing in towards the anchorage below.

REVOLUTION IN HONG KONG
Russell Mawhinney, 1996

Cricket in Hong Kong is going through a period of change: 1997, when Hong Kong reverts from British to Chinese sovereignty, looms as a threat to the future of the game. Already some grounds are being lost to cricket as the British forces continue their withdrawal and municipal councils reclaim facilities for sports which have greater Chinese representation. The Hong Kong Cricket Association has realised that if the game is to survive, it must cease to be an expatriate domain and be taken to the local Chinese. If they are to be attracted to the sport, bearing in mind Hong Kong's unique challenges, especially lack of space and time, this must mean shorter, faster versions of the game. The association is making strenuous efforts to expand the base of players and is having some success against a backdrop of resistance from certain sections of the expatriate community, intent on protecting their own patch.

The Hong Kong Sixes, held at Kowloon in October, was again a success and there was much delight when Eddie Tse, the first Chinese player to take part, dismissed Mohammad Azharuddin with his second ball in international cricket. At the 1995 AGM of the Hong Kong Cricket Club Rodney Miles was elected president at 6.45 p.m. Immediately after the AGM an EGM was held which approved a change in the structure, making the president a titular head and giving responsibility to the chairman. At 7.30 Miles became chairman. He thus ceased to be president after 45 minutes. This may be a record.

ITALY MAKES THE GRADE
Simone Gambino, 1996

On July 13 [1995] the Associazione Italiana Cricket achieved its cherished goal of becoming an Associate Member – the 22nd – of ICC, thus gaining the right to take part in the 1997 ICC Trophy in Malaysia. The success on the field of the national side, coached by Doug Ferguson and captained by Andrea Pezzi, explained the reasons behind the elevation. Italy, at that time still an Affiliate Member, scored an historic win over Argentina at the Hurlingham Club in Buenos Aires. They also, not without a slice of luck, enjoyed the best of Israel's visit to Rome in September, easily winning the one-day game and saving the "Test", despite entering the last hour at 54 for eight, having been 103 behind on first innings.

KENYA'S PROGRESS
Jasmer Singh, 1998

Kenyan cricket perhaps recorded its best year, and in July 1997 took another step up the game's ladder. Along with Bangladesh, Kenya were granted a special one-day international status by the ICC, enabling them to arrange both internationals and first-class matches. They marked their promotion by organising a three-nation tournament in October with both Bangladesh and Zimbabwe, the newest of the Test-playing countries. It was not as financially successful as the four-nation tournament a year earlier and it showed that Zimbabwe were a class above their two rivals, their experience and professionalism shining through. However, it also enabled the Kenyans to consider themselves once again the best of the non-Test countries.

Kenya's promotion came after a successful run in the ICC Trophy in Kuala Lumpur. They won all their matches leading up to the final, barring one no-result, but then lost a rain-affected match to Bangladesh on the last ball. They had the consolation of providing the Man of the Match in the final, Steve Tikolo, and the Man of the Tournament, Maurice Odumbe, who made 493 runs in all. In Nairobi six months later, in more familiar conditions, they looked clearly superior and easily beat the Bangladeshis twice. In the opening game, at the Gymkhana ground, the Kenyan openers Kennedy Otieno and Deepak Chudasama got the tournament off to a remarkable start and broke the hearts of the Bangladeshi bowlers with a first-wicket stand of 225, beating the 11-year-old one-day international record of 212 set by David Boon and Geoff Marsh of Australia. Six days after that, Thomas Odoyo and Tony Suji beat the seventh-wicket record, with a stand of 119 against Zimbabwe. This did not save the Kenyans from defeat, however.

Just before the tournament, New Zealand stopped in Nairobi, on their way to Zimbabwe, and played a three-day match and two one-day matches, which did not have international status. The three-day match was drawn and New Zealand won the one-dayers. These games have made Kenya aware that they still have some way to go before they can compete with the very best. But there have been enough successes and individual achievements to enable the game to maintain its momentum, as the efforts continue to develop it at grassroots level and spread it across the country.

TAKE ME TO CUBA
John Duncan, 1998

There is a trophy cabinet in the Havana Golf Club that hasn't been opened for 39 years. When the deposed ruler Batista left the island in the hands of Fidel Castro and Che Guevara on New Year's Eve 1958, someone took the keys to Miami. But if you look long enough through the dust and the rust you can see that there, among the baseball and golf trophies, is unmistakably a silver cup with a man wielding a cricket bat on top.

Cricket was brought to Cuba by black sugar workers and slaves from the English-speaking Caribbean. And, until the 1960s when private sports clubs were abolished, the game was widely played in the sugar regions of the east. "We had a proper team and ground in my town, Manati," said Donald Pancho Muir. "It's a car workshop now. The local Cubans never really took to the game, but the club kept going because of the immigrant interest. We had a great time. There were teams in five other places that we used to play. There was always a party after the match."

In 1955 and 1960, Club Manati were invited to play in Montego Bay, Jamaica. "We lost more than we won," said Pancho, "but we had genuinely good players like Hilary 'Drinki' Pendas, and Rafael Bood. I think there is still a team in Baragua, and I heard of something going on in Cayo Mambi. But it is sad the game isn't played here much any more. We could have been good."

In the past 12 months, however, the game has shown signs of a comeback. A British journalist, Ian Katz, working on a story at the Guantanamo airbase, was approached by the Anglo-West Indian Cultural Association to explain the rules of cricket to their youth section, with a view to starting a team. When he got back to England he sent them a bat and a ball. Months later, another British journalist brought them pads and gloves and another bat. And the British Embassy sent one of their men in Havana, Ed Hobart, who plays for the expats and diplomats' team in the capital, to give them a training session.

"It was a chastening experience," said Hobart. "They were so eager to learn they copied everything you showed them exactly. There was one lad who after ten minutes' practice on a stone courtyard was playing classic cover drives and square cuts as if he had been coached from five years old." The Guantanamo team had their first game against another eastern team, Ciego de Avila, late in 1997. "We can't predict when games will be," said Robertson Claxton, the club president. "It depends when the opposition can get the petrol."

There are 11 million people living in Cuba, an island that dwarfs every other in the Caribbean. They play baseball to a high enough standard to suggest that the art of throwing a ball and using a bat to hit it comes very naturally. And the idea of a game that can take five days would not frighten a population accustomed to queuing four hours to travel on the back of a lorry to the next town. If the Cubans can find a Spanish translation of the laws, the West Indies and the world had better watch out.

FRANCE WIN BY A HEAD
Simon Hewitt and Brian Fell, 1998

France retained the European Nations Cup at Zuoz, Switzerland, in astonishing circumstances. They beat Germany by one run in a pulsating 50-over final. The unwitting hero was France's last man, David Bordes, who was hit on the forehead, and staggered through for a single at the end of the French innings before collapsing with a fractured skull. With two balls left, Germany, chasing 267, were 260 for nine: a top-edge fumbled by third man plopped over the rope for six. The Germans completed the two runs they needed for victory while the last ball was still skying to mid-on, where Valentin Brumant eventually caught it. So the Bordes head-bye proved a match-winner. He had to spend the next two weeks in hospital, and was ill for some time but, happily, was able to resume playing indoor cricket before Christmas. Bordes normally bats with a helmet but did not bother this time because he had only the one ball to face. In a group game against Switzerland, Germany scored 467 for one in their 50 overs including an unbroken stand of 349 between Shamaz Khan, a Pakistani-born naturalised German, and Abdul Bhatti. Shamaz scored 200 not out and Bhatti 179 not out.

SURVIVING AMIN
1998

Uganda is unique in African cricket: it is the only country where the game is played mainly by the African community. When the country was enduring its national nightmare of tyranny and civil war in the 1970s and early 1980s, and nearly all Asians and Europeans left the country, a small group of enthusiasts kept the game alive in near-impossible circumstances. Under the Amin regime, cricket was regarded as elitist and the team was often denied permission to play abroad. Once, the square used by the national team was churned up by being used for the start and finish of a motor rally – at the insistence of the sports minister. Now, with the country reviving, Ugandan cricket is reviving too. In 1997 Uganda won the annual quadrangular tournament against the other countries affiliated to the ICC as East and Central Africa (Malawi, Tanzania and Zambia) for only the second time in three decades. In 1998 Uganda hope to break away from this group and achieve associate membership of the ICC in their own right. Playing standards are not a match for neighbouring Kenya, but the Ugandans' tour of England in 1995, when they won ten games out of 12 against strong club sides, suggests that the team could be a force in future ICC trophies.

BENAUD AMONG THE BOARS
Simon Hewitt, 1998

Richie Benaud, who has French ancestry and a home near Nice, delighted Gallic cricket in October by agreeing to become honorary patron of France Cricket, the new ruling body of the game in France, and offering to advise on coaching and development. The Benaud *oui-oui* came soon after a two-day, 700-mile, inspection by the ICC chief executive David Richards and Jorgen Holmen, chairman of the associate members, in connection with French hopes for promotion from affiliate to associate status in 1998.

Five new grounds were built in 1997. Three of these were at St-Aulaye (Dordogne), and Wimereux and Arras in the north. The most notable was at the Domaine des Ormes in Brittany, on a site that includes a golf course, a hotel and the national cricket office. The unluckiest was Robin Marlar's ground (complete with turf wicket) at Mollans-sur-Ouveze, Provence, which was wrecked by wild boar, who dug their snouts into the turf and almost ploughed it up. "Hampshire Hogs on tour, I expect," said Marlar. The ground has had to be temporarily abandoned.

DRAMA AT THE OVAL

Richard Heller, 1999

The annual match in the Falkland Islands between the Governor's XI and the Forces resulted in a thrilling one-run win for the Governor's XI, reducing the Forces' lead in the series to 4–3. The contest is played on the world's southern-most cricket field, Mount Pleasant Oval, for a handsome trophy, mounted on rock, representing a penguin's beak emerging from an egg. The Oval can hold the entire population of the Falklands: 4,000. The matting wicket traditionally favours bowlers, but only when they have the wind behind them. Those bowling into the wind regularly struggle to reach the opposite end.

SCHOOL OF HARD KNOCKS

Guy Parker, 2000

Cricket in Bahrain has been described as the hardest – perhaps even the worst – in the world. It is a reputation the cricket authorities on this desert island find easy to live down to. The standard of play is not the issue. Indeed, Bahrain won a four-nation six-a-side tournament involving Sri Lanka, India and Bangladesh at the Isa Town football stadium in November. Luminaries such as Vinod Kambli, Robin Singh, Sanjay Manjrekar, Roshan Mahanama, Kumara Dharmasena and the entire Bangladesh World Cup squad were swept off the park by Bahrain's robust wham-bam cricket. Instead, the reputation has more to do with local conditions. The cricketers who brave the appalling outfields (made up of stony, bumpy desert), the cracked concrete strips which are inadequately covered with tatty coir mats and patched with canvas, and the derisory umpiring are forced to develop hard-edged tactics to win the 25-over matches. Winning is paramount. Some sides would rather walk off the field than lose.

Field placing is simple: eight or nine men are often placed on the boundary, with the emphasis on making the batsmen work for their runs in the heat. Sixes (the favourite shot) are greeted with car horns from the partisan spectators. Totals of 200-plus are chased with contrasting emotions of elation and despair which reach a violent crescendo. The top teams import professionals from the subcontinent. Failure can mean prompt repatriation – tough when you get only one chance a week. The Bahrain Cricket Association league is, of course, only the tip of the sand-dune. There are junior, amateur, hotel, and gentlemen's leagues, all playing in even worse conditions. The old low-tide league seems to have succumbed to global warming but, with the dearth of pitches, it is likely to resurface in some form.

One hero did rise above the rest in 1999. Ajay Kumar, playing in two separate league matches every Friday, notched almost 3,000 runs in the year, including 11 centuries. One took him 25 balls, and, in a rare 50-over match, he scored 293. Friendly cricket lives on at Awali CC, where regular Thursday "Taverners" games are enjoyed by players of all levels. This is where visiting ships' XIs cut their desert cricket teeth (or knees). In the last couple of years, though, cucumber sandwiches have been replaced by *shawarmas*.

WHEN ICELAND BEAT ENGLAND   2001

The most northerly and most remarkable of cricketing nations arrived on the scene in 2000, not, in the normal fashion, through the efforts of exiles, but owing to the extraordinary vision of a handful of Icelanders. The story of Icelandic cricket began at the University of Iceland a few years ago when some students caught a glimpse of the game on Sky News. "Everyone was dressed in white," said one of them, Ragnar Kristinsson, "with pressed trousers, and we wanted to do the same." But none of the TV channels available in Iceland showed more than snatches of this mysterious game. However, in 1999 Kristinsson was on holiday in Cyprus during the great World Cup semi-final between Australia and South Africa, and was entranced again. The following Sunday he and a friend were in London, and decided they had to be near Lord's for the final. Outside, they met some Pakistanis, leaving in disgust as their team hurtled to defeat, who readily handed over their tickets. Kristinsson was now firmly hooked.

He wrote to the European Cricket Council, who sent a starter set of equipment, and a couple of teams emerged: Kylfan (Icelandic for "the bat") in Reykjavik and Ungmennafelagid Glaumur in Stykkisholmer (believed to be the world's most northerly club, as well as the most unpronounceable). The teams mostly comprised native Icelanders, with coaching from some better-informed expats. Iceland's entry into international cricket came in September 2000 when Manchester barrister and aspirant Liberal Democrat politician Jonathan Rule decided this was the perfect venue for his stag night. He assembled a group of friends in a beautiful valley outside Reykjavik to take on the locals. With the help of the emigrés, the Icelanders scored 107 on a bumpy football pitch. The visitors (said to be swaying slightly at the crease after the previous evening's entertainment) lurched to 94 in fading light, watched by rather more journalists and cameras than their cricket usually justifies. The headline "Iceland beats England at cricket" appeared in the following morning's paper.

REVIVAL IN NIGERIA   Patrick Opara, 2002

The West African Cricket Conference's decision in 2001 to support the Nigerian Cricket Association's bid for individual ICC membership was tangible proof of cricket's regeneration here after two decades of decline. And the NCA received another boost when the Nigerian government agreed to hand back the Tafawa Balewa cricket ground, which had been held by the Ministry of Defence for 27 years. These decisions were deserved reward for the country's former cricketers who had vowed to salvage the game from the brink of extinction. In January, ICC development officer Hossain Ayob conducted coaching and umpiring courses, and Nigeria subsequently contributed ten players to the West African Under-19 squad that contested the ICC Associates' Youth Africa Championship in Uganda. In a group game, West Africa beat eventual winners Namibia. Nigeria also sent teams to the second African Championship, in Kenya, and to a quadrangular tournament in Freetown, where they played hosts Sierra Leone, Gambia and Ghana. The Howzat Foundation, a non-profit organisation for the development and promotion of cricket, attracted more than 200 aspiring cricketers between the age of five and 22 to a holiday coaching clinic in August, offering further grounds for confidence in the game's future. The Lagos League, which has been running for more than 40 years, saw Foundation CC head off nine other clubs.

How Many Jumpers?

John Rich, 2003

The packed slip cordon at the annual Casey Base cricket match has little to do with swing, seam or – with temperatures hovering around freezing – conserving body heat. It's more a question of knowing that a missed catch will condemn the guilty fielder to a trek down treacherous icy slopes to fetch the ball from a small meltwater lake. The fixture is traditionally played each Casey Day (February 12), the anniversary of the founding of the Australian Antarctic Research Station, some 3,880km due south of Perth and 2,580km from the South Pole. Teams comprise Australian scientists and visitors of varying nationalities. The pitch is a cement helipad, ensuring generous bounce. Naturally, local rules apply: should the tennis ball – this isn't the place to break the triple-glazed windows – ricochet off the Red Shed, the two-storey living quarters, it's four; over the roof is six; hitting the station leader at the barbecue brings instant dismissal, which still somehow proves an irresistible target. Post-match analysis is often fuelled by ample quantities of Antarctica's own home brew, known as Penguin's Piss.

Bats, Not Guns

Khalil Khan and Andrew Bank, 2004

The boom in Afghan cricket, which began when the first refugees returned from their camps in Pakistan after the fall of the Taliban government, continued in 2003. There are now more than 2,500 players and leagues spread across 16 of the country's 21 provinces. Nearly all the players are Afghan with almost no expat participation except from the British forces team. The British Embassy, with support from several counties and sponsors, handed over a large quantity of kit, and the ECB donated six Kwik Cricket sets which are now used on a regular basis in schools in Kabul.

A new limited-over contest, the Olympia Lube Oil tournament, was held in May. It featured the first use of coloured clothing and white balls in Afghanistan: Khost beat 13 other teams to win a hard-fought competition. And in June, Afghanistan were made Associate Members of the Asia Cricket Council. The senior Afghan squad made several visits to Pakistan during the year, with mixed but encouraging results. Afghan government support for the development of cricket continues at all levels. Problems remain: for instance, Khost, near the Pakistan border, is a keen cricketing province but is still troubled by fighting between Al-Qaeda and coalition forces.

However, cricket is helping provide hope in Afghanistan. Allah Dad Noori, the founder of the Afghanistan Cricket Federation, was playing one day in Kabul when a young man walked by carrying an AK47. He watched for a while before being invited to join in. Afterwards, he asked if he could play next time. When he returned he was without the rifle. "Where's your AK47?" asked Noori. "Oh, I don't need that," the youth replied, " playing cricket!" The aim of the ACF is to get all the men of Afghanistan to choose cricket instead of guns.

Beyond the First-Class Game

There is a rich world beyond the first-class game – of cricket in schools, clubs, villages and the Lancashire leagues. This chapter offers a glimpse of each of those sub-cultures: Alan Lee's journey through modern, hyper-efficient village cricket; Andrew Longmore's examination of the way public schools were coming to terms with limited-overs cricket; a more leisurely "time" match between Eton and Harrow at Lord's; three pieces on the leagues; and John Woodcock's homage to I Zingari. I reprint their results from 1977, too, on a whim – and because their fixtures encapsulate the way this upper-crust "social" cricket was for a century.   S. M.

VILLAGE CRICKET SPLITS IN TWO

Alan Lee, 2005

As a boy, my life revolved around the village cricket club. Indeed, the power of the attachment lasted well into adulthood and might never have slackened but for the intrusion of a job that diverted me to far pavilions. There was, about that club on the common in rural Hertfordshire, a spirit of community and camaraderie that I have never replicated in any subsequent environment. It enveloped people's lives, dictated their diaries, and provided their social, as well as sporting, outlet. It fostered relationships, even marriages – fractured some, too. Matches were the focus, the headline items, but the idea that members did not meet from one weekend to the next was laughable. The club was the hub of life: our village, our soap opera.

It follows, nostalgia being the force it is, that when I set out last summer to discover the health of village cricket in the 21st century, I longed for every club to be as I remembered mine. And of course they weren't. How could they be? The beauty of the village game lies, as it has always done, in its infinite variety of settings and communities and characters.

There were trends apparent, though, some of them alarming to those of us with no desire to see everything quintessentially English expire. Despite its quaint image, village cricket reflects the world we live in. Sport in Britain is more competitive, more outwardly aggressive and less sociable than it was 30 years ago, and nowhere is immune. The incompetent overweight who once held his place because he was reliable, popular and happy to serve behind the bar every week is no longer necessarily tolerated. Characters are being lost, along with stalwart servants, putting the very future of many clubs in jeopardy. Most villages now play in leagues, with the rigours of travel and player transience that this brings. The ambitious clubs continue to thrive, though with a sterner philosophy than was practised in my youth, but those that, by choice or circumstance, remain faithful to tradition are dropping in number and profile. Even more than before, their survival is dependent on the selfless work of one or two individuals.

My boyhood memories of early May are of Sundays that started clear blue – though seldom stayed that way – and of walking through the woods to be at the club by breakfast time. The pitch might need rolling, the pavilion sweeping, the scorebook brought up to date. The same few people were always there early. Although it scarcely occurred to me at the time, they did virtually all the work. On a comparable May Sunday last year, I arrived at Godshill, a setting to match its name. This is a ground carved out of the New Forest. And shifting the ponies off the outfield, then sweeping up what ponies do, is just one of the jobs that Alan Cousins does routinely and uncomplainingly before each game. Cousins is captain, groundsman, team and fixture secretary. He would doubtless run the bar if Godshill possessed such a luxury, but the rudimentary shack of a pavilion has no showers, electricity or phone line, and no evident hope of attaining them. Cricket survives because enough clubs still love visiting the place, and because Cousins works so hard to accommodate them. It is the more heroic for what is happening nearby: Fordingbridge, the nearest town, has seen its cricket club fold through lack of interest, and many Forest village teams have gone the same way.

Godshill is in Hampshire, but neighbouring Dorset is no better off. Of the 492 clubs who entered the 2004 National Village Cup (sponsored by npower and administered by *The Wisden Cricketer*), not one gave an address in Dorset. This does not mean that there is no village cricket played in the county, but it is indicative of the shrinkage. Perhaps, though, it also says something about apprehension, about a sense of reluctance to expose oneself to embarrassment? For the fact is that village cricket is no longer a comfortably uniform game. The span of standards, and of ambitions, is greater than at any time since the first shepherd boys whacked balls with their crooks.

The winners of the npower Cup in 2004 were Sully Centurions from Glamorgan, whose ground sits on the Barry peninsula, looking across the Bristol Channel. They were worthy winners. In all probability, this was the best team ever to play in the 33 years of the competition. But Sully, though physically and geographically a village, had outgrown the generally accepted criteria of village cricket. Having made swift and remarkable progress under the inspired leadership of a single, committed family – the Sylvesters – they not only played in the top league in Wales last year but won it, and the cup for good measure.

Several of the side had played for Wales. Four had played at Lord's before. Though they insist, heatedly, that none of their players is paid, some are certainly found accommodation and jobs. Sully are not alone in this – the best clubs around the country, towns and villages, now attract players this way – but, for them, the village cup was not so much a romantic adventure as a ruthless mission, duly accomplished. In the course of it, and in their eyes by doing nothing more heinous than playing competitively, Sully caused an uncomfortable stir, leaving a succession of opponents and some vocal observers disillusioned not only with the tournament but the direction in which village cricket was being taken.

There are those within English cricket's administration who may consider this to be an admirable sign of progress and wish for nothing more than the continued culling of the weakest clubs. Social cricket, in these eyes, is anathema, and it does not exist elsewhere in the world. The idea of village cricket in Australia would be derided. There, club players meet up to practise and to play, uncompromisingly hard in both cases. Lingering in a pavilion bar, chewing the fat with the opposition over a few pints, is simply not part of the psyche. Nor is the building of community spirit through a cricket club environment. The strong get on, the weak can go hang.

That, increasingly, is the norm here. Village cricket is splitting in two: the old and the new. But the old-style clubs cannot be allowed to vanish. Any further diminution of their numbers and influence will be detrimental to the game, for it will close another door of entry to the majority of teenagers, for whom schools cricket is already off the curriculum. One of the joys of my tour of Britain in search of the village game was seeing how many clubs now have highly developed colts sections, benefiting not only their own future but that of cricket in general.

Shireshead & Forton from Lancashire (mainly famous for an M6 service station) was a shining example. There, a professor of environmental biology named Terry Mansfield organises 70 boys at practice every weekend. Shireshead field three teams and it is their policy to have at least six under-16s in the third XI. The future seems assured. A grittier atmosphere awaited me at Hopkinstown in south Wales. This was a colliery village, devastated by the closure of the local pit in the late 1970s, and it is no exaggeration to say that village spirit was saved by the cricket club. Its pavilion, extended three times, is now a social centre, an arm around the shoulders of local youths who might otherwise run out of control. Here, they run teams from under-11 upwards, all keenly subscribed. Hopkinstown is no rural idyll – indeed, it is as far away from the picture postcard stereotype of the village game as can be imagined. Yet it is the finest example I found of village cricket as community therapy.

If the village cup is a barometer of health for the game it represents, it is worrying that the entry has dropped from a peak of more than 800. The 2004 final, in which the more bucolic Exhall & Wixford (the dual names may themselves be signs of the times) from Warwickshire fought valiantly against Sully and the odds, was of startlingly high standard. This, the organisers acknowledge, was a mixed blessing. Measures have now been taken to redress the balance and any clubs playing in ECB premier leagues, including Sully, have been excluded from the 2005 competition. The hope is that this will take the cup back to the places where it truly belongs – places like Godshill, and the indefatigable Alan Cousins. He reminded me of similar men at my own club in Hertfordshire. The majority of village cricketers will always wish only to turn up with the pitch marked out, the sightscreens in place and the bar (where such a thing exists) fully stocked. Most clubs are still sustained by the efforts of a handful of people. Some things in village cricket are utterly unchanged. It's still the stage for local heroes.

Alan Lee spent the summer of 2004 visiting village cricket grounds for The Times, *as a break from his job as the paper's racing correspondent. He was its cricket correspondent from 1988 to 1999, and has written more than 30 books on the game.*

JUDGE HITS CRICKET BAN FOR SIX

A village cricket club on April 6, 1977 won the support of the Appeal Court in London to carry on playing – and hitting boundaries. By a 2–1 majority the court lifted a legal ban on the hitting of sixes into a neighbouring garden. Lord Denning, Master of the Rolls, said that if Mr John Miller, whose house adjoined Lintz Cricket Club, Burnopfield, Durham, did not like it, he should sell his house and move elsewhere.

"For over 70 years the game of cricket has been played on this ground to the great benefit of the community as a whole, and to the injury of none," said the judge. The court allowed an appeal by the cricket club from a decision of Mr Justice Reeve, in December 1976. On an application by Mr Miller and his wife, Brenda, the judge had banned cricket matches until adequate steps were taken to prevent balls being hit on to their property.

Lord Denning said Mr Miller had bought the house four years ago in midsummer when the cricket season was at its height. He might have guessed that there was a risk that a hit for six might possibly land on his property. If he found he did not like it he ought, when cricket was played, to sit on the other side of the house or in the front garden – or go out. Or take advantage of the offers the club had made of fitting unbreakable glass. "Or, if he does not like that, he ought to sell his house and move elsewhere," the judge said. "I expect there are many who would gladly buy it in order to be near the cricket field and open space. At any rate, he ought not to be allowed to stop cricket from being played on this ground."

MINOR COUNTIES V AUSTRALIANS
At Sunderland, August 4, 5, 1977. Minor Counties won by six wickets.

On a windy day Bailey won the toss and put in the Australians on a sporting pitch from which the ball came through at varying heights. After a sound start the Australian batsmen became rather reckless, but Walters gave a fine display on a well-grassed surface. Two splendid innings by Nurton and Gill took the Minor Counties to 133 for four at the end of the first day and with 75 minutes lost at the beginning of the second, Bailey declared 37 behind. Davis and Hookes hit in brilliant fashion, but Walters required seven stitches in his chin when hit by a rising ball. O'Keeffe took over the captaincy and set the Minor Counties to make 207 in two and three-quarter hours. Thanks to a superb 92 by Gill, who hit 17 fours in just under two and a quarter hours, the Minor Counties were always up with the clock. Riddell, the Durham left-hander, struck Bright for six, and 19 runs were required from the last five overs. In the end a stolen leg-bye brought Minor Counties success with one over to spare in a sporting contest which, confined to two days, did not rank as a first-class fixture.

THE VAGRANT GYPSY LIFE – 150 YEARS OF I ZINGARI   John Woodcock, 1995

The widespread increase in competitive club and village cricket in the late 1960s and through the 1970s presented many long-established and well-run private clubs with an awkward problem. I am thinking, for example, of the constituent county clubs with euphonious names, such as the Devon Dumplings and the Hampshire Hogs, as well as the more nomadic Free Foresters, Incogniti, Cryptics, Buccaneers and Arabs, and the oldest and perhaps most illustrious of them all, I Zingari. Even MCC, with their 300 out-matches a year, began to find it more difficult to put a strong side into the field.

In 1960 there was very little league cricket south of the Midlands. Now, the great majority of town and village clubs throughout the country are in a league of some kind or other, and need to find, in so far as it is possible, a settled side. There is also the national club knockout, the national village championship, and countless other relatively new competitions. The wandering clubs suddenly found it more difficult to fulfil their commitments to the extent to which they were accustomed, or to recruit suitably competent and socially suitable members. The sort of players they had always relied upon became less regularly available. Fixture lists had to be cut back; in some cases, dissolution threatened. None has ridden the crisis – for that, to many, is what it was – more surely than IZ, founded 150 years ago and still with a language and a status of its own.

On July 4, 1845, its founders, J. L. Baldwin, Frederic and Spencer Ponsonby (to become the Earl of Bessborough and Sir Spencer Ponsonby-Fane respectively) and R. P. Long, dined together at the Blenheim Hotel in Bond Street, following a match that day against Harrow School. There and then they formed a club, for the purpose of fostering amateur cricket, christened it and framed the rules. Next day they informed William Boland, a barrister with an extensive practice and a formidable presence, that he was perpetual president and 20 of their friends that they were now members of I Zingari (the gypsies).

The rules were half-serious and half-comic ("The Entrance fee be nothing and the Annual Subscription do not exceed the Entrance") and many of them survive today, including the ordinance to keep your promise, keep your temper and keep your wicket up. The affirmation of amateurism was important, mainly because most sides in those days employed professionals, or "given men", to bolster them, whereas the Zingaros preferred to do without one. Colours of black, red and gold ("out of darkness, through fire, into light") were chosen, and attracted such attention that in the late 1860s MCC appropriated them, except that they kept to the red and gold and left out the black. (For the next 100 years or so the MCC egg and bacon tie and cravat were rarely worn – it was considered bourgeois to be seen in them. Today, however, on the first morning of a Test match at Lord's, the pavilion is a blaze of red and gold.)

Excellence was of the essence to IZ. Patronised by royalty, acknowledged in high society and careful whom they chose to play for them, they were very soon able to turn out a side strong enough to hold its own against any professional XI, besides reading like a table of precedence. By 1877, IZ were beating Yorkshire at the Scarborough Festival, and in 1882 and 1884 they had a fixture against the touring Australians. Their last first-class match was against a Gentlemen of England XI at Lord's in 1904. At the time, a fully representative Gentlemen's side would have consisted mostly of IZ. But the days of quite such high glory were numbered. With their activities being suspended during the two wars, when many of the country house grounds on which they played came under the plough, the club had to rely upon its renown – one could justifiably say its mystique – and the devotion of its senior members to hold its place.

Since 1867, *Wisden* has made a point of publishing the results of all I Zingari matches, a service provided for no other private club. In 1884, in its heyday, IZ played 52 days' cricket (one three-day, 19 two-day and 11 one-day matches). In 1994 they played 24 one-day matches and one of two days. Because Boland was made perpetual president in 1845, the club's senior living officer is called not the president but the governor, who is currently the former Middlesex and England captain, George Mann. To Sir William Becher, though, IZ owes its greatest modern debt. In 1839, six years before the dinner in Bond Street, one of Becher's forbears gave his name to the brook at which so many hopes have been dashed in the Grand National at Aintree. Billy Becher himself, secretary from 1953 to 1993, has given much of his own life to keeping the Zingaric spirit alive, and ensuring that in 1995, its 150th year, IZ remains the most urbane of clubs.

John Woodcock was cricket correspondent of The Times *from 1954 to 1987 and editor of* Wisden *from 1981 to 1986.*

I Zingari Results 1977

Matches 27: Won 9, Lost 5, Drawn 9, Abandoned 4.   1978

Date	Opponent	Result
May 14	Honourable Artillery Company	Won by 67 runs
May 21	Royal Engineers	Won by four wickets
May 28	Eton Ramblers	Won by 44 runs
May 28	Charterhouse	Drawn
May 29	Royal Military Academy	Drawn
June 2	Harrow School	Lost by 92 runs
June 11	Hurlingham Club	Abandoned
June 12	Lord Porchester's XI	Abandoned
June 14	Winchester College	Lost by 18 runs
June 18	Guards Cricket Club	Won by eight wickets
June 19	Staff College	Won by seven wickets
June 25	Green Jackets Club	Drawn
June 26	Lavinia, Duchess of Norfolk's XI	Drawn
July 2	Eton College 1st XI	Drawn
July 2	Eton College 2nd XI (XXII)	Drawn
July 3	I Zingari (Australia)	Won by seven wickets
July 9	Royal Artillery	Won by six wickets

Date ctd.	Opponent ctd.	Result ctd.
July 14	Lloyds C.C.	Drawn
July 16	Bradfield Waifs	Lost by one wicket
July 16	Gentlemen of Leicestershire	Won by seven wickets
July 17	Capt. R. H. Hawkins' XI	Drawn
July 24	Royal Armoured Corps	Drawn
August 6	J. H. Pawle's XI	Abandoned
August 6, 7	South Wales Hunts XI	Lost by nine runs
August 27	Hampshire Hogs	Abandoned
August 28	Yellow Hammers	Lost by four wickets
September 11	Rickling Green C.C.	Won by 104 runs

UNREST IN THE LANCASHIRE LEAGUES

John Kay, 1980

For almost the first time since both the Lancashire and Central Lancashire Leagues were established in 1892 there are signs of unrest. The Central Lancashire League, in which Oldham won the championship and the Wood Cup to complete a tremendous double, have a "steering committee" considering ways and means of reviving interest. In the Lancashire League, where Burnley retained the championship and Enfield won the Worsley Cup, officials were surprised and dismayed to find several clubs calling and attending a specially convened meeting to discuss the future. It was entirely an unconstitutional gathering and it brought forth no real suggestions, but it was a clear indication that some clubs have thoughts about change. Be that as it may, the support for cricket in the Lancashire League remained consistent, despite the often treacherous weather. And although gates in the Central Lancashire League remained unpredictable, there is an obvious feeling that new faces, both among clubs and playing personnel, might produce more public interest and support.

At the same time, one clear factor emerges. Given good weather, league cricket still has its adherents, and it is still being presented at charges that have not kept up with either inflation or the cost of living. With the price of everything – and most noticeably cricket balls – rapidly rising, slight increases in admission charges and club membership fees are not enough. It is a sign of the times when a professional makes it known in mid-season that he is available for the following year at a salary of £2,000 or more. The game has come a long way since such memorable figures as Sydney Barnes, Learie Constantine and Frankie Worrell, to mention just a few, played for much less.

Burnley's success in the Lancashire League was heartening for the very fact that it produced an amateur bowler who broke all Turf Moor records for an unpaid player, and for some consistent returns from Pakistan professional, Mudassar Nazar, whose contribution of 841 runs and 43 wickets did much to provide the foundation for a second championship success. Trevor Jones was the amateur bowler who made the season memorable by collecting 72 wickets at 11.87 runs each. A left-arm spinner, now turned 30, with a vast experience of league cricket behind him, the deadly Jones gave the lie to the frequently expressed opinion that league cricket, with its limited-overs format, has no use for the spin bowler. As Jones proved with his steady command of length, line and spin, there is no substitute for skill, and a slow bowler will be just as successful as any other kind provided he can supply the basic essentials.

Jones has picked up 141 wickets in two years at Turf Moor and it is good to hear him still paying tribute to the experience he gains from playing with and against good professionals. He played for Lowerhouse for six years and says he owes a lot to the advice given to him by the former England batsman, Colin Milburn. Milburn had one somewhat dismal season in Lancashire League cricket in 1976 but still managed to pass on some useful tips for up and coming players. Jones also pays tribute to the team spirit in the Burnley ranks and considers it no mere coincidence that he had, in Roland Harrison, a captain who not only hit 618 runs but led the side with considerable skill and flair.

Only one batsman in the Lancashire League reached the 1,000-runs mark, and no bowler came within the 100-wickets target. The Todmorden professional, Aftab Baloch, reached 1,000 runs in his last innings of the season. By far the most successful bowler was Mike Malone, Haslingden's recruit from Australia who signed for Lancashire and has already made a tremendous impression at Old Trafford. Malone captured 88 wickets at a little over 12 runs each and did much to steer his side to runners-up position in the Lancashire League. Malone also hit 546 runs to earn the title as the summer's leading all-rounder, although the Indian Test player, Madan Lal, was always among the runs and wickets with a return of 683 runs and 64 wickets for Enfield.

The Central Lancashire League season was dominated by the all-round prowess of Oldham's Australian professional, John Buchanan, who hit 666 runs for an average of 31.71 and collected 101 wickets at a cost of 11.50 runs each to provide the basic foundation for a side that completed the league and cup double in impressive manner. Derek Parker, of Ashton, was also among the wickets, and his haul of 103 at 10.24 runs, plus a batting return of 435 runs, earned him an appointment with Nelson in the Lancashire League for the coming season. He leaves the Central Lancashire League with the distinction of being one of the most consistent bowlers in the history of a league that has seen many great performers.

Heywood went to Australia and stretched themselves financially to sign Geoff Lawson from New South Wales. He obliged with 93 wickets and 487 runs to emerge as a cricketer of much potential. He was offered but could not accept, because of university commitments in Sydney, a contract by Lancashire, for whom he played on occasions at both first- and second-class level. Littleborough unearthed yet another impressive young West Indian fast bowler in Francis Stephenson, who captured 95 wickets at a cost of 13.94 runs, but he was allowed to leave Hare Hill for an engagement at Royton this summer following the slump of a side never far away from the top of the table in recent years to a bottom-half position.

Royton, incidentally, could claim to be the unluckiest team of the season inasmuch as they were pressing Oldham hard for the championship when their professional, the controversial Colin Croft from the West Indies, walked out on them with several matches still to play. As a result, he earned himself a ban on all future CLL engagements. Leading run-scorer in the League was Rohan Kanhai, whose return of 826 runs for an average of 45.88 took Crompton to the Wood

Cup final and a middle-of-the-table league position. Kanhai's class was obvious every time he went to the wicket, but there were also some good returns from unpaid batsmen with Leon Taylor (Middleton) and Stuart Wales (Milnrow) both topping the 600 mark.

Yet it was a man of much league experience and a record of long service, both as a professional and amateur in various leagues, who really hit the headlines. Bob Bartels, who came to England from Sri Lanka when it was known as Ceylon, captured 72 wickets at 11.59 runs each on behalf of Castleton Moor. He attributed his success to the old-fashioned belief that length and direction are still of paramount importance in cricket at all levels.

HOOPER IN A LEAGUE OF HIS OWN
Chris Aspin, 1987

From time to time there arrives in one of the Northern leagues a virtually unknown professional who proves to be a cricketing genius. Last season, Werneth in the Central Lancashire League enjoyed the exhilaration of just such a discovery – Carl Hooper, a 20-year-old from Guyana who will one day play for West Indies and, in all forms of cricket, score a lot of runs. Hooper missed the last two games of the season, but he still beat the record aggregate of 1,694 runs accumulated 35 years earlier by Sir Frank Worrell when he was professional for Radcliffe. At the start of his final weekend, Hooper needed 282 for the record. Against Royton he made 127 not out; the following day at Norden he struck an unbeaten 175, which gave him a total of 1,715 runs and an average of 77.95. In all, he hit eight hundreds, including an unbeaten 187 at Heywood where, on the large ground, he hit nine sixes and 19 fours as his side scored a record 311 for three. Werneth's gate receipts quadrupled and the club quickly re-engaged their young star for 1987.

LANCASHIRE LEAGUE CELEBRATES ITS CENTENARY
Chris Aspin, 1992

When east Lancashire was full of cotton mills, you could sometimes see 78 tall black chimneys from the old wooden scorebox in the top corner of Church cricket ground. I counted them once, during the local holiday week. On other days, sharp-eyed spectators could discern about a dozen through the sooty haze, and it would surprise me if as many as that now rise above Accrington, Great Harwood and the distant brickfields of Clayton-le-Moors. The smoking mills, familiar for so long to spectators at Lancashire League matches, have gone. The Pennine air is refreshingly clean this centenary year, though it will probably be too sharp at times for the overseas professionals who have followed in the steps of Learie Constantine, Ray Lindwall, Everton Weekes, Clive Lloyd, Dennis Lillee, Viv Richards and a host of other immortals in order to play in what is widely regarded as the world's foremost league.

There have been many times when I have wondered why cricket ever took root in these parts. Snow has more than once prevented play, and the sight and feel of cold Lancashire rain falling from a pewter sky is almost enough to put people off the game for ever. But on a sunny afternoon, with noble hills providing the backcloth to a keenly contested game involving two world-class professionals, there are few better cricketing occasions. Though Lancashire League clubs are often criticised for paying large fees for Test stars, few are likely to abandon a tradition which began with men like McDonald, Headley and Constantine during the inter-war years, and which now provides amateurs with a rare chance to pit their skills against the world's best. Long before the League was formed in 1892, clubs regularly engaged English professionals with first-class and Test experience. And for important matches they occasionally included three or four paid men, causing resentment among opponents who could afford only one or two. The control of professionalism was one of the stated aims of the Lancashire League. Two pros were allowed in the early years, but since 1900 the number has been one.

Many of the older clubs can trace their roots to the enthusiasm for cricket which was fired at public schools attended by the sons of mill owners and professional men. The Blackburn club, East Lancashire, is unusual in having been started by officers of the town's volunteer corps, and its stars, included A. N. (Monkey) Hornby, the Lancashire and England player, who was a member of one of the county's oldest cotton families. Most of these players were batsmen. Professionals were engaged to coach and to bowl, with working men occasionally helping out in the nets. Some of the enthusiasts became good enough to be included in the teams, and by the time the League was formed, artisans were well represented both on the field and in the committee rooms.

Mills worked till noon on Saturdays well into this century; and to enable spectators to see a full match, wickets were pitched at two o'clock. Today, the starting time is 1.45, but since limited-overs cricket came in 20 years ago, there has been no fixed finishing time. As many games are now played on Sundays as on Saturdays. Sponsorship has become increasingly important, though bar takings and the renting of rooms provide most of the income.

If I could choose one match from the thousands which have been played during the past 100 years, it would be that between Rawtenstall and Nelson in 1931. It brought into conflict the great Sydney Barnes, aged 59, but still a bowler without equal, and the young Learie Constantine, the cricketing phenomenon, who was the greatest single attraction any league has known. "Connie", as everyone called him, often said that the 96 he scored in front of a vast crowd that afternoon was the best innings he ever played. The duel with Barnes, who took seven for 68, was cricket at the very highest level and was remembered vividly long after the result of the match was forgotten. Nelson won by 72 runs. Constantine was professional for Nelson from 1929 to 1937; and in those nine seasons he gained seven championship medals. Against Accrington in 1934 he took all ten wickets for ten runs.

Looking over the club records, one sees that bowlers had their best years in the early decades of the competition. One would certainly have liked to watch Sam Moss, the Manchester shoemaker, who burst into league cricket in the 1890s. In his first game as professional for Haslingden in 1896, he took five wickets in eight balls – all bowled – and for Bacup four years later he finished with 143 wickets at 8.2. Publicans throughout the district put up glass cases to display the stumps he broke, and those who saw Moss were in no doubt that they had never come across anyone faster. Nowadays batsmen have the upper hand, and the recent policy of rearranging games hit by the weather has helped them to score more runs than ever before. The Australian, Peter Sleep, professional for Rishton, and the Rawtenstall amateur, Peter Wood, both achieved Lancashire League aggregate records last season.

Over the years, the Lancashire League has provided Lancashire and England with many fine players. Eddie Paynter, who worked in the brick-fields at Clayton-le-Moors and who played for Enfield at both the start and the end-of his career, was one of the best known. After his performances for England during the Australian tour of 1932–33, the League presented him with a pair of silver candlesticks. Accrington have the distinction of nurturing David Lloyd and Graeme Fowler, two other left-handers who have played for their country, and many League players have gone to other counties. In 1939, five Bacup-born players were in the first-class game.

ETON V HARROW

At Lord's, June 24, 1992. Drawn. 1993

The oldest surviving fixture in the Lord's calendar was threatened with extinction, because its traditional Saturday was unavailable. A compromise shifted it to Wednesday, coincidentally the 80th birthday of Etonian and broadcaster Brian Johnston, who made Lord's the venue of his celebrations. His old school put Harrow in and within nine overs had reduced them to 13 for three; Douglas's pace dismissed Harrap and Danby in successive overs. Foster and Renshaw batted cautiously, reaching 81 by lunch. But in the afternoon their partnership gathered momentum, swelling to 196 over nearly four hours, despite the tidy spin of Wemyss and Lightfoot. The chief honours went to Foster, who scored the first hundred since T. M. H. James's unbeaten 112, also for Harrow, in 1978. He hit 13 fours in 239 balls. A few minutes later Hill declared, setting a target of 210 in what became 44 overs. It was a tall order for an inexperienced Eton side, none of whom had appeared at Lord's before. Evidently Harrow were wary of a third consecutive defeat, and they briefly scented victory when Hawkins claimed five wickets, for the second year running. But too little time was left, and Walsh steered Eton to the close with three wickets in hand.

NEXT – SCHOOLBOYS IN PYJAMAS?

Andrew Longmore, 1996

It was only a matter of time before the last barricades of proper cricket came tumbling down. In the West Country in the summer of 1995, seven public schools formed their own 55-overs league, marking a significant move away from the traditional game in the schools. The league produced some bright, positive cricket too, with masters reporting a greater sense of involvement within teams and increased enthusiasm for the game. "There was a real buzz about the place when we had an overs game," Ray Codd, head of games at King's College in Taunton, said. This was bad news for those who believe that overs cricket will poison tender minds just as surely as it has ruined professional techniques.

Five months earlier, in late spring, Codd had sat in the Long Room at Lord's, underneath the portrait of W. G. Grace and alongside 140 other cricket masters and school representatives listening to a lament delivered by Dr Tim Woods of Trent College at a forum organised by MCC. Dr Woods warned that cricket was losing credibility in the schools because the timed game produced too many dull draws. Cricket was therefore regarded as boring by many teenagers, who were turning to sports offering more instant excitement. The game, he added, had to become brighter and sharper to capture the more demanding imaginations of the young.

Dr Woods advocated matches of 110 overs, split 60–50 in favour of the side batting first, as a way of eliminating stalemate and stimulating competition. The idea triggered a lively discussion about the pros and cons of limited-overs cricket for schools. On the one hand: bad batting habits, defensive bowling and unambitious field placing – the formulaic cricket which had ruined many of the leagues in Yorkshire and Lancashire. On the other hand: improved standards of fielding, better running between the wickets and more aggressive batting. The arguments on both sides were largely adapted from the county game. The real message of the evening, though, was more fundamental.

The assembled cricket masters – consciences clicking, excuses whirring – stood accused of the professional vice of elevating the result above the game, of deliberately playing not to lose. Some, privately, defended their negative attitudes on the grounds that, like football managers, they would be dismissed if their teams lost too often; success at sport is one of the best ways for schools to attract publicity in a competitive market. Others scoured their souls and found no guilt. "Me? Negative? Ah yes, but we were 20 for four and the wicket was poor and, goodness, did we bat that long? Well, we were playing Harrow and the previous year they'd batted on after tea. . ." Feuds are surprisingly commonplace in schools cricket.

David Walsh, of Tonbridge School, who chaired the meeting, said that it did not matter whether the game was limited-overs or timed, attitude was all-important. "Challenge your cricketers," he said. "Give them a sense of enjoyment and adventure." He saw no harm in having a balance of fixtures, some limited-overs, some timed, which would satisfy the twin – and often conflicting – aims of attracting the young to cricket, boys and girls, while developing the best of them into potential Test cricketers.

One game, in particular, brought out the best of overs cricket. At 98 for five at lunch after 34 overs against Sherborne, Clifton had no option but to force the pace in the afternoon; they made 212 and won the match by 60 runs. "Based on previous experience, I could have envisaged a dull draw," wrote Mike Nurton, the Sherborne cricket master. "The match was an endorsement of limited-overs cricket at school level."

Overs cricket, though, has a habit of starting brightly only to stagnate as tactics become more sophisticated. Cricket masters and coaches must know where to draw the line, or Eton will soon be strolling out to play Harrow at Lord's dressed in light blue pyjamas and sponsored by a brewery.

Women's Cricket

The women's game normally sneaks into *Wisden* on about page 986. Even when England's women win the Ashes, as in 2005, it is seen as an adjunct to the men's triumph. But they were on the victory bus – and gradually the women's game is gaining greater acceptance. They are winning over the doubters. This chapter explores some of those doubts, charts the battles women cricketers have had to face, and records key moments – notably MCC's long-delayed acceptance of women members. There is still a long way to go – press coverage of women's cricket is at best grudging – but the women's game has sponsorship money, some TV coverage and flash new kit. All to play for.   S. M.

ENGLAND'S CAPTAINCY CRISIS   Netta Rheinberg, 1979

The Women's Cricket Association underwent some rough handling during the end of the 1977 season and in the first few months of 1978 as a result of the England captaincy crisis. In the consequent glaring and unwelcome searchlight of the press, its administrators, uncomfortable and unhappy, chose to weather the storm in comparative silence. This lack of defence inevitably resulted in the widespread view that the association either lacked solid ground for their action, or that the ability was lacking with which to state their case. Early in 1978 a further blow was suffered when England lost the World Cup to Australia in India, and this particular phase of the association's misfortunes caused the resignation of the patron, Jack Hayward, through whose great generosity the first World Cup had been made possible.

With regard to the second World Cup tournament in India, England had in past years always been the pioneer of overseas tours, but on this occasion both Australia and New Zealand had sampled Indian women's cricket (together with Indian generosity and hospitality) and there were great expectations in England of this first tour to India by the WCA. In the months before the World Cup, information from that country was scarce, so that progress with preparations became difficult. Six teams had indicated their willingness to take part, but owing to political and financial difficulties, both Holland and West Indies withdrew, leaving only Australia, New Zealand, England, and India.

By the time these teams arrived, there had been a change of management in India and political innuendos had crept into the organisation, which unfortunately left much to be desired. Furthermore, too little cricket had been arranged for the visitors. Nevertheless, this was a pioneering venture by India, the youngest member of the International Women's Cricket Council, and much was learned from the experience, not only by the hostess country but also by their visitors.

The eighth meeting of the International Women's Cricket Council was held at Hyderabad on January 11, 1978, attended by delegates from Australia, England, India, New Zealand, and South Africa. The chairman, in her report, referred to Kerry Packer and remarked that in these days of equality of the sexes, one wondered how long it would be before there is a female counterpart.

This report is strangely coy about the sacking of Rachael Flint, by far the best player of her generation but never a favourite of the authorities, which prompted the "captaincy crisis" that Netta Rheinberg seems barely able to bring herself to mention. This, in extreme form, was not untypical of the Wisden *of the period – when the sport was deemed to have some god-like quality that should not be besmirched by controversy, self-interest, or money. Admirably batty in its way – though it sometimes made for rather obscure reporting.*

WOMEN IN CRICKET
Teresa McLean, 1992

"What is human life but a game of cricket?" asked the 3rd Duke of Dorset, fervent cricket fan and supporter of the Hambledon club, in a letter to "a circle of Ladies, his intimate Friends" in 1777. "And if so, why should not the ladies play it as well as we?" Unreliable though he was in most of his dealings with the female sex, the 3rd Duke was unfailingly generous towards women's cricket. He liked his women sporty and rangy, in the outdoor mode, and his support for women's cricket was only one of his many efforts to help women play the game, however, much opposition they met.

At this early stage in the life of cricket there was little concerted opposition to women taking part in the game. The standard attitude was one of ignorance with a vague predisposition to believe that cricket was, as W. G. Grace still considered it more than a century later, "not a game for women, and although the fair sex occasionally join in a picnic game, they are not constitutionally adapted for the sport!"

Even so, 18th- and early 19th-century women's matches were popular as freakish amusements and attracted large crowds, Married Women v Maidens being one of the favourites. On October 5, 1811, a *Times* reporter described a serious women's match at Newington, between a Hampshire XI and a Surrey XI, which lasted three days and was played for 500 guineas a side. It was won by Hampshire, by 15 notches (runs), and led to another match being fixed immediately, as there had been "some very excellent play, and much skill". Nevertheless, it was the burlesque element which appealed most to the public, and "a great concourse of people attended to witness this singular contention", which they would not have done had it not been so exotically singular.

Most women lacked the patronage, interest or incentive to play the game as the Newington ladies played it. Most kept busy in the tavern, preparing refreshments for the men on the field of play. Most preferred, or at least accepted, this state of affairs. However, female support sometimes extended beyond washing clothes and making tea. Women cricket writers have been a small and intermittent but talented minority since Mary Russell Mitford first published her article "The Cricket Match" in *The Lady's Magazine* in 1823, then again, with great success, in her book *Our Village* in 1824. Just over a century later Majorie Pollard completed her career in an era of enthusiasm for cricket and for all women's sports by writing a regular cricket column for the *Morning Post* and *London Evening News*. There are one or two female correspondents today, enjoying being presented with press packs of ties and men's T-shirts.

Before cricket writing had become as inflated an operation as it is now, the only way women who did not want to be tea ladies could participate actively in men's cricket was as teachers. John Willes of Kent, famous as the pioneer of round-arm bowling, is often said to, have picked up the idea of this new "march-of-intellect system", radical and widely mistrusted all through his lifetime, from his sister. She is supposed to have started bowling round-arm when her voluminous skirt got in the way of her under-arm action. There is, however, no clear evidence for this and Christina Willes, John Willes's daughter, knew nothing of it; though she took a lively interest in the game, as her cricketing aunt had before her. Martha Grace was an amazon among cricket enthusiasts, watching, coaching, and commenting on her five sons' performances on the field of play. Three of them, E.M., G.F., and W.G., played for England in the first Test in England against Australia, at The Oval in 1880. The late 19th century was a high point of female efforts to improve men's cricket and a starting point of serious women's cricket, played as a sport rather than being an amusing spectacle.

The White Heather Club, founded in 1887 and surviving until 1959, was the first women's cricket club, its members mostly Yorkshire ladies, with enough money to pay their own expenses. Even after the Women's Cricket Association was founded in 1926, and women's cricket had enjoyed a flourishing decade in the 1930s, the game was still expensive for those taking part. It was no longer weird enough to attract big, curious crowds, nor well enough established to count as a major sport and so attract sponsors. It has, however, always had some distinguished male supporters, such as the 3rd Duke of Dorset, C. B. Fry, Frank Chester in the 1920s, and Jack Hayward, the outstanding patron of women's cricket in the 1970s. But a minor sport, with few women knowing anything about it, still less how to play it, is not a recipe for prosperity.

Cricket is fighting to keep going in boys' schools; it is almost non-existent in girls' schools. The WCA is, in the words of Cathy Mowat, its current chairman, "either staying static or holding its own, depending on how you look at it". The 1970's were high-profile years, with England's women under the captaincy of Rachael Heyhoe-Flint and the patronage of Jack Hayward. Since then things have been quieter. Women's cricket clubs have to inspire and teach their own juniors, although the National Cricket Association provides qualified coaches, and the Lord's Taverners provide some funds. And in the last 30 years or so, women's cricket has been given more institutional help. Women playing for

Oxford and Cambridge – sometimes with more will than skill – are given only half-Blues, but Cyril Coote, the incomparable groundsman at Fenner's, gladly let women play there when I asked him, on behalf of Cambridge, in 1978. Similarly, women in the last 30 years have been allowed the use of the nets at Lord's and a growing share in the MCC coaching awards. Above all, England's women have been allowed the use of Lord's for Test matches since 1976, when Rachael Heyhoe-Flint first persuaded MCC to let women tread the hallowed turf.

Cricket is doing particularly well in Europe, where England retained the European Culp at Haarlem, in the Netherlands, in July 1991, against spirited opposition from Denmark, Ireland and the host country. However, England is the only country where first-class women's games are umpired by women, without payment. Women also umpire a few men's games in the Lancashire League, and in local and village matches, as I know from nerve-racking personal experience.

Women's cricket is extremely popular in India, where it was taught, maybe even introduced, at Kottanam in 1913 by an Australian teacher, Ann Kelleve, who made it compulsory in the school she set up. Mrs Gandhi was a strong devotee of women's cricket and it is widely played. When Young England toured there in 1980–81, crowds of 20,000 to 25,000 attended the major matches in some centres. In Australia it has always had more of a pioneering spirit. The sex war is a hard-fought inheritance in antipodean cricket, and it was a great achievement when Peggy Antonio, the great lady spin bowler from Victoria, was christened "Girl Grimmett" by the Australian press after taking six English wickets for 49 in the Third Test at Melbourne in 1934–35. She inspired Neville Cardus to ask: "Suppose one day the greatest slow left-handed bowler in England is discovered to be a woman, will any male selection committee at Lord's send her an invitation?" The 3rd Duke of Dorset would laugh in his grave if a woman played for England, flour-ishing against the odds. "Mind not, my dear ladies, the impertinent interrogato-ries of silly coxcombs, or the dreadful apprehensions of semi-men. . . Go on, and attach yourselves to the athletic."

ENGLAND WIN 1993 WORLD CUP
Carol Salmon, 1994

England finally broke Australia's stranglehold on women's cricket when they beat New Zealand in the final at Lord's by 67 runs. After England's win in the inau-gural competition, at home in 1973, they had lost the next three finals to Australia. This time the Australians lost two crucial preliminary matches and went out; not only was it refreshing to see someone other than an Australian lift the World Cup, it was a fine achievement by New Zealand to deny their trans-Tasman rivals a final place for the first time.

Around 4,500 people attended the final, beyond all expectations, thanks to excellent media coverage. With England's men 3–0 down against Australia, English newspapers, television and radio eagerly portrayed the women's team as the country's cricketing salvation. But only an eleventh-hour contribution of £90,000 from the Foundation for Sports and the Arts had enabled the tournament to go ahead in the first place, though later it received substantial support from the Sports Council and MCC.

New Zealand had a magnificent qualifying run, winning all their seven games and conceding just 1.61 runs an over. Their 25-run victory over England at Beckenham featured the best fielding – there were five run-outs – and bowling of the tournament, when they prevented England performing the seemingly routine task of scoring 128 in 60 overs. England were no match for New Zealand that day; nor, surprisingly, were the Australians in their final qualifying match. Having lost to England, Australia needed to win to have a chance of reaching the final. Instead they lost by ten wickets, bowled out for 77. Going for their shots, New Zealand reached their target in only 18.2 overs.

The Australians' fall from grace was spectacular; coach Peter Bakker acknowledged that their late arrival in England, reducing the opportunity for warm-up matches, was a major factor. But too many players did not perform up to past standards and there was a feeling that they had enjoyed too much success and lost their appetite. Denise Annetts, who came with a formidable reputation, played only one significant innings and their highest scorer was Belinda Clark, with 199 runs at 33.16, while their chief wicket-taker was leg-spinner Sharyn Bow, with 11 at 12.36.

The leading run-scorer of the competition was England's 34-year-old opener Janette Brittin, with 410 runs at 51.25. During the final at Lord's she became the first player to pass 1,000 World Cup runs; she earlier overtook Rachael Heyhoe-Flint's record of 2,457 runs in all internationals for England, reaching 2,789. She hit only 16 boundaries in her eight innings but her approach throughout was mature and thoughtful. She scored two hundreds, one against Denmark, who conceded 286 and lost their first-ever World Cup match by 239 runs; the second came in a much closer game with India, which England won by three runs in the final over.

Carole Hodges, who also scored two centuries, was second in the run aggregates, with 334 runs at 47.71. Her match-winning 105 not out in 141 balls against Australia at Guildford was probably her finest for England. The other heroine of the victory over Australia – which was seized on by the press, as it came on the day England lost the Ashes and Gooch resigned – was Gill Smith, who destroyed their batting with five for 30. The all-rounder Jo Chamberlain played below her best in the early matches, but hit peak form by the final, where she won the match award for a spectacular 38, followed by a wicket, a run-out and a catch. Captain Karen Smithies was England's player of the tournament. Her 77 overs of seam cost just 1.54 runs each and she took 15 wickets at 7.93. Her contribution to women's cricket was recognised with an OBE in the New Year's honours. Clare Taylor, who conceded just 1.81 an over, and Smith had 14 wickets each, and off-spinner Hodges, who often opened the bowling, had a hat-trick against Denmark. Wicket-keeper Jane Smit justified her surprise selection ahead of Lisa Nye with quiet efficiency, making 12 dismissals, nine caught and three stumped.

JOINING THE ECB

Carol Salmon, 1998

The 1997 season was probably the last for the Women's Cricket Association in its present form. Negotiations were advancing inexorably towards amalgamation with the England and Wales Cricket Board, which was already involved on the marketing front and expected to take full control in 1998. The benefits of operating under the ECB umbrella were demonstrated when Vodafone's sponsorship of the England men's team was extended to the women, a tremendous boost, which permitted a full week's preparation for their series with South Africa. At grassroots level, the biggest change will be that all local organisations must be aligned with men's county clubs, whether first-class or minor.

THE YEAR THE CITADEL FELL

Peter Hayter, 1999

What was a woman to think? Or a chap? The messages being thrown at women in cricket during 1998 were so confused and confusing that they made the head spin. In the early months of the year came three items of news that suggested that all the old attitudes were alive and well and living at Lord's.

In March, an industrial tribunal upheld a claim for sex discrimination by Theresa Harrild, a receptionist formerly employed by the England and Wales Cricket Board, who said she had been pressured and paid by the Board to have an abortion after becoming pregnant by a colleague. Harrild's evidence, regarding the attitude of certain high-ranking Board officials towards women in their offices and in cricket at large, was damning. The ECB got into even more trouble when it denied her allegations after the hearing, having declined to contest them. This came only weeks after a case in which Geoffrey Boycott, one of the game's most public figures, was convicted by a French court of assaulting a girlfriend in a Riviera hotel room.

To the public, the conclusion that there was no smoke without fire was all but irresistible. Why would the man, or woman, in the street think otherwise? To them, all the available evidence, outside as well as inside the courtrooms, pointed to the same conclusion: the majority of men in cricket regarded women as simply fodder for jokes about maidens, tickles to fine legs and bouncers – or worse.

It was made all the more relevant because of events in the Marylebone Cricket Club barely a fortnight before the Harrild case. A blocking minority of the all-male MCC membership had voted against the proposal of their committee – pushed by the president, Colin Ingleby-Mackenzie – to admit persons of the opposite gender. They thus reaffirmed the club's 211-year-old position: not in here, madam.

By the end of the year, so much had changed that those of a cynical disposition might have been tempted to believe Rachael Heyhoe-Flint had been busy putting something in the gin-and-tonics at NW8. Ingleby-Mackenzie, having refused to take no for an answer, urged the members to think and vote again and, on September 28, they did, momentously. Just how influential in their final decision was the president's warning that no women meant no lottery money, who can tell? In the meantime, the Women's Cricket Association had voted to become an integral part of the ECB, thus establishing a single governing body for all cricket in the country. Women in MCC, and the ECB, as equals? Whatever next?

In the short term, some answers please, for those who play. Shirley Taylor, the manager of the England women's cricket team that was defeated 5–0 in their one-day international series with Australia but battled to draw the three-Test series 0–0, believes that although some progress has been made, the road to real recognition will be long and arduous. "I do think we are being taken more seriously," she says, "but there is a lot of work to be done. You will still find the armchair critics with nothing better to do than have a go. Everyone who has taken the trouble to come and watch us play has been impressed, not only with our enthusiasm and commitment, but also with the level of skill we reach."

My own experience of the women's game was, until 1998, limited to one match at Lord's in 1987, a one-day game between England and Australia ruined by rain and by grim clichés about naked ladies in the pavilion. But when I went to watch the 1998 Ashes Test at Worcester, I was enormously impressed by the quality of play. Clearly, the bowling is not as fast as in the men's game, but the batting, in particular, was of a high standard. Indeed, the thought occurred and then grew that, given the opportunity, almost all of the Australian bats, and many of the English, had the technical skill not only to survive in men's county cricket, but to prosper. Predictably, when I put that proposition to a current England Test cricketer (male), his reaction was: "Oh, yes. And how would they deal with the quick stuff?" It would be interesting to find out.

ECB figures suggest that interest, at least, is on the increase. They state that 3,600 women are playing, as are 475,000 school girls, three-quarters of them at primary school. There are more than 150 women's clubs, and women's sections in nearly 100 other clubs – 27 clubs or sections have been formed in the past two years.

All well and good. But the disparity between England's cricketers and their Australian counterparts is best illustrated by some other statistics. There are 80 women's cricket clubs in Melbourne alone, and Australia, with a third of the population, has almost seven times as many women playing: 23,000. At the start of the 1998–99 season, the cover of the big-selling *Australian Women's Weekly* proclaimed that a full list of Australian domestic and international cricket fixtures (male) was included. Admittedly, the magazine is owned by Kerry Packer, who has a vested interest. But it is hard to believe cricket would be used as a selling point in any English equivalent.

For the lot of the English woman cricketer to be significantly improved, it will not be enough for a few token members to be admitted to MCC. Nor is it enough for the board – and their Test sponsors Vodafone who, for no obvious publicity benefit, pushed money the way of the women in 1998 – to repeat the dose and leave it at that. At the moment, it seems that women in cricket are themselves unsure how to pitch their campaign for recognition. To some, Vodafone's publicity gimmick to drum up media interest in the women's Ashes might have been considered retrograde in tone: journalists were sent a bunch of red roses with a card reading Eleven English roses playing cricket – watch this space. And even Rachael Heyhoe-Flint's comments in celebrating women's admission to MCC sounded peculiar: "Perhaps now," she suggested, "you will be able to buy MCC nighties and fluffy slippers as well as pyjamas." If there is an inferiority complex at work here, it will only be shattered by strong women with confidence and belief in their place in the sport – separate, but entitled to equal respect and opportunity. That's why, the extraordinary nature of its events notwithstanding, 1998 must be only the beginning.

Matthew Engel's Editor's Note on MCC and women is on page 95.

BAT BURNING
Carol Salmon, 1999

England and Australia's women created their own Ashes by burning a miniature bat, autographed by both teams, before their Test series. The trophy was shared, as the three Tests were drawn, but there was no doubt as to the superior team: Australia won all five one-day internationals, and held a clear advantage in the Tests. They were bowled out only once in 16 fixtures in England and Ireland – by England A, for 596. Their top five batsmen all averaged over 50 in the Tests; Joanne Broadbent scored a double-hundred at Guildford, and there were also centuries for Melanie Jones, Kim Rolton, who scored 327 runs for twice out, and captain Belinda Clark.

England's response was to occupy the crease for as long as possible. Janette Brittin's courage and concentration – she was the leading run-scorer on either side, batting more than 24 hours for an aggregate of 450 – undoubtedly saved them from defeat. Brittin announced her retirement from international cricket after the Third Test, finishing her career as the leading run-scorer in women's Tests, with 1,935 at 49.61 in her 27 matches since 1979.

Off the field, the England squad was more secure than ever, thanks to sponsorship from Vodafone, while coverage on Sky television continued to raise their profile. But they need to play with more style: England's scoring-rate of 2.27 an over in the Tests – compared with Australia's 3.34 – was not pretty to watch. Some of the Australian officials said that Test cricket would die in their country if they adopted England's approach. New Zealand have already lost interest in the four-day game, and plan to concentrate on one-day cricket; financial constrictions were likely to force Australia to schedule future series with just one Test and a plethora of limited-overs games.

BOOMING OR BORING?
Sarah Potter, 2005

In March 2004, at the National Stadium in Karachi, Pakistan opener Kiran Baluch bagged a coveted record. Her 242, compiled in 584 minutes, against West Indies became the highest individual score in women's Test cricket, eclipsing 214 by India's Mithali Raj at Taunton in 2002. In the same game Pakistan captain Shaiza Khan collected 13 wickets, another Test record, including a hat-trick. And West Indies saved the match by scoring 440 after following on. Women's cricket across the globe must be in rude health.

Well, perhaps. The bald truth is that there are yawning gaps in standards. Pakistan had not even qualified for the World Cup in South Africa in March and April 2005. West Indies did but, like Sri Lanka and Ireland, were not expected to lift the trophy unless something jaw-droppingly improbable happened, such as the five major teams (Australia, New Zealand, England, India and South Africa) not turning up. Baluch, of course, could only play against what was before her. At least her innings had the chance to happen. Women's Test cricket is an endangered species. Only three Test matches have been played worldwide since the end of the 2003 season. India met New Zealand in November 2003; Baluch's Test followed in March; and England played New Zealand in August. All three ended in stalemate. That New Zealand featured in two of them is odd, as they had avoided Test cricket since their tour of England in 1996.

Why so few? Partly cost, partly preference and partly, too, because it seems to be the modern perception that, if it isn't over in a day, nobody will be interested. I've heard that nasty little bouncer delivered from the lips of international coaches who ought to know better. Also, it has to be admitted, too many Tests end in draws. Boring, whisper the few who turn up to watch. The women have four, not five days, to nail a result, but lack of time is not the sole culprit. Simply put, not every team sets out to win.

So should women's Test cricket be killed off? Absolutely not. If international sides give up on 70 years of history, something more valuable than tradition will be lost. It's called credibility. Won't play it, or can't play it? The question may as well merge into one damning sneer. The way forward, both for standards and acceptance, is to play more Tests. The International Women's Cricket Council is due to merge with the International Cricket Council in April 2005, during the women's World Cup, which the ICC has funded. It may seem like a small step for the men's governing body; it represents a thrilling shimmy for womankind.

If the similar marriage in 1998 between the old Women's Cricket Association and the England and Wales Cricket Board is anything to go by, the distaff side can tighten their thigh-pads for an exciting innings. Since then, the England team have been transformed beyond recognition (through their play, rather than the new sponsored trousers and wrap-around shades); grassroots women's cricket is healthier than at any time in its history (in 2003, the ECB announced that more than two million girls were playing cricket); a record number of clubs are affiliated (ECB figures showed a 33% increase in 2003) and – the key to it all – the growth is sustainable.

The necessary high-level merger throws up some tricky politics. Australia, New Zealand and Ireland are, like England, already fully affiliated to their men's governing bodies; South Africa and West Indies are in the throes of the process. India, Pakistan and Sri Lanka are not, but the ICC has stipulated that they must be. It is a particular problem for Pakistan. Two rival women's associations are in bitter dispute about who controls the game: how they can even open talks with the Pakistan Cricket Board is unclear.

The ICC has promised a period of transition in which these nations will, in theory, still be able to play Test cricket – if they want to. If they do not, another raft of countries will eventually emerge to take their places, courtesy of the ICC's power and money. In April and May 2004, for example, tournaments for emerging African nations were held in Uganda and Namibia, funded by the ICC. Such tournaments could never have happened on the IWCC's shoestring resources, and women stand to benefit from many more such development plans.

The broken records in Karachi may at first glance seem like the extra top-spin you put on the truth, but, all things considered, there is much to be cheerful about whenever the mind wanders during the tedious parts of the Test matches.

ENGLAND WIN THE ASHES
Sarah Potter, 2006

England's women had waited even longer than the men to beat Australia in a Test series. Mary Duggan had led them to their last series win at The Oval in July 1963, when the country was more interested in the Profumo Affair. Of the 22 Tests since then, they had won just one, at Adelaide in December 1984 – Australia's last Test defeat by any side. But in 2005, England held out to save the First Test at Hove and then overturned the odds to beat Australia at Worcester.

Their triumph was celebrated alongside the men's: Clare Connor and her side were presented with the Ashes – the first time England had ever held the trophy, which was created only during the 1998 series – during the men's final Test, and given a lap of honour round The Oval. A few days later, they rode in their own open-top bus right behind Michael Vaughan's men, cheered on by the crowds filling every vantage point en route to the rally in Trafalgar Square. In the New Year's honours, Connor, like Vaughan, was awarded the OBE.

There was drama aplenty in the two Tests. Holly Colvin became England's youngest-ever Test player, a month short of her 16th birthday, and took two wickets with successive balls at Hove, where Arran Brindle saved the team with a last-day hundred. And at Worcester, 20-year-old Katherine Brunt scored a maiden fifty and took nine wickets to humble Australia. At the start of the summer, Brunt said her role model was Darren Gough, whose older brother, Adrian, has captained her in Barnsley's Second XI. By the end of August, clutching her Player of the Series award, her allegiance was torn: "I want to be a baby Freddie Flintoff now," she said.

The one-day matches were equally thrilling, and the sides went into the fifth and final game at Taunton all square, but here England failed to complete their first limited-overs series win over Australia since Rachael Heyhoe-Flint's success in 1976. The tourists had gone 2–0 up after Shelley Nitschke's left-arm spin snared seven for 24 at Kidderminster. But England pulled off their first one-day win over Australia since the 1993 World Cup at Stratford, with a brass band playing across the Avon and an enthusiastic crowd ringing the tree-lined ground. Australia needed seven runs from the final over to win both that match and the series, but Brunt had Cathryn Fitzpatrick stumped, ran out Julie Hayes first ball, and denied Australia the boundary they required off the final delivery. Then Claire Taylor's wonderful 116 levelled the series at Taunton. But in the final match half-centuries from Lisa Keightley – her fifth in as many games – Karen Rolton and Lisa Sthalekar helped

Australia to a four-run win, and they also won a Twenty20 international the following day. This match, like the last 50-over game, was televised live by Sky; the left-handed Rolton scored a scintillating, unbeaten 96 from just 53 balls, which helped earn her the award for Player of the Tour.

A raft of retirements followed. Australian captain Belinda Clark, arguably the greatest batting star the women's game has ever seen and the only player of either gender to score a double-hundred in a one-day international, finished with a bafflingly meagre tour – only 105 runs from ten innings against England. She departed to become head of Cricket Australia's Centre of Excellence in Brisbane. Keightley gave up her playing career for a coaching post in New South Wales. And on England's side, all-rounder Clare Taylor (not to be confused with the younger Claire), called it a day. She had played 105 one-day internationals since her debut in 1988.

Umpires

Recent *Wisden* editors have had difficulties with umpiring. John Woodcock was resolutely opposed to "neutral" or – the preferred term – third-country umpires; Graeme Wright and Matthew Engel vociferously pro. Rightly so – their introduction has immeasurably improved the spirit in which the game is played. Equally contentious is the gizmos-for-umpires issue: should Simon Taufel arbitrate on appeals for caught behind, or should Snicko? Wright, in his concluding Notes, called for more gizmos; Engel has made "keep it human" his mantra. Battle is joined and, as with the phased introduction of neutral umpires, we can probably expect a decade's-worth of wrangling.

A matter on which there is no debate is that one umpire became a national hero in the 1980s and '90s – Dickie Bird, whose innocence and glowing love for the game made him a household name, even in households where cricket was not necessarily a prominent pastime. His autobiography sold in bucketloads – sufficient for him to buy a flashy, sporty Jaguar which he was reputed to drive at a maximum of 60mph on motorways; his Lord's farewell was as emotional an occasion as John Arlott's; he remained, in retirement, a much-loved presence; he proved cricket's continuing capacity to throw up magnificent one-offs. Tony Lewis's piece, reprinted below, marking his retirement is a delightful and measured homage to this curious, diffident man who found love in cricket's warm embrace.   S. M.

WHO WOULD BE AN UMPIRE?   John Woodcock, *Notes by the Editor*, 1981

One way and another it was a difficult year for umpires. With such large amounts of prize-money at stake, and a levelling-out of standards in Test and other first-class cricket, the game is becoming ever more fiercely competitive and the umpire's job correspondingly more demanding. Not only that. Every decision a Test umpire makes is subjected to a slow-motion television replay. In the Jubilee Test Match which England played in Bombay on their way home from Australia in February (50 years had passed since the Board of Control for Cricket in India was officially constituted), an umpire was constrained to change a decision. Having shown his surprise at being given out to an appeal for a catch at the wicket, Taylor, the England wicket-keeper, was reprieved upon the request of the Indian captain. That this, however well intentioned, was a misguided gesture became more clear in England's second innings when the same umpire, having given Boycott out, leg before wicket, changed his own mind when the batsman stood his ground. An umpire without confidence is worse than no umpire at all.

I am opposed to the idea of neutral umpires for Test matches. By the very nature of their job all umpires are fallible, whoever they may be, and on the rare occasions that I have wondered about the integrity of an umpire it has usually been because one side or the other has been harassing him. Remember, too, that if ever neutral umpires are introduced into Test cricket, England will never again have the benefit of playing under those who by common consent are the best of all umpires – the two dozen or so who stand day in and day out in the English county game. By the John Langridges of the world, that is. After 52 years as player and umpire in first-class cricket, Langridge has gone into honourable retirement.

NEED FOR "NEUTRAL" UMPIRES
Graeme Wright, *Notes by the Editor*, 1987

The answer to the problem of short-pitched bowling appears simple: a strict application of the law. On a number of occasions last summer I saw bowlers threaten the batsman's person with no appearance of caution from the umpires. Umpires are not appointed simply to count the number of balls in an over any more than policemen are there to direct traffic. Their job is to uphold all the laws: by no means a simple task and one full of responsibility. It requires, also, the full backing of the authorities, which applies both in this country and overseas.

That is why I would prefer independent umpires for Test matches, by which I do not mean "neutral" umpires; rather, umpires who are not appointed by the home country's board of control. I would advocate an international panel of leading umpires, appointed by and responsible to the ICC, which in turn would have to show a more positive attitude. It would cost money, but Test matches are cricket's money-spinner. They are also the world's window on the sport. Such a panel will stand later this year for World Cup matches. I feel that an international team of umpires, paid in accordance with their responsibilities, would feel less the servants of the national authorities who appoint them at present and, as a body, would have the confidence to enforce the laws.

NEUTRAL UMPIRES IN ACTION
R. Mohan, 1991

Two cricketers made a quiet and yet very effective contribution to the tenth series between India and Pakistan. They were not players. John Hampshire and John Holder, both from England, were the third country umpires invited to officiate in the four Test matches, and their presence changed the nature of cricket contests between these two Asian neighbours. The frisson was missing. Events on the field were far less contentious, with both teams accepting the umpires, and their rulings, in good faith. The occasional mistakes, some glaring, did not lead to flare-ups, with the result that the atmosphere was refreshingly free of suspicion. Teams had been touring Pakistan for years without any firm belief that they could, or even would be allowed to, win a Test. In this series, the relations between the two sides were cordial and the cricket, if not spectacular, was highly competitive.

OF UMPS AND REFS
Matthew Engel, Notes by the Editor, 1993

> Chaos umpire sits,
> And by decision more embroils the fray.
> *Paradise Lost, Book II*

It was clear to anyone watching the England–Pakistan series that the relationship between the Pakistanis and English umpires had, as they say in the divorce courts, "irretrievably broken down". As in a marriage, not all the blame can be heaped one way. Pakistani cricketers are indeed paranoid, but that does not mean people are not out to get them. However hard umpires try to be fair, years of niggling from one country's team must start to affect their subconscious judgment.

The world umpiring system is now a shambles. ICC has willed a solution, an international panel of umpires, but has refused to will the means, i.e. how to pay for it. Instead, with great solemnity, they have created the completely irrelevant system of referees. It is very nice that so many affable and deserving former Test players not at the time employed in television are able to take part in this makework scheme. But they can serve only one purpose; indeed their terms of reference, shorn of ICC jargon, boil down to only one purpose: to reinforce the authority of the umpires.

Competent Test match umpires do not need anyone to reinforce their authority; they already possess enough. However, because the game has refused to rid itself of the 19th-century delusion that a system of home-country officials can function effectively, Test match umpires round the world have been (all too frequently) incompetent or (just occasionally) corrupt. Even men supremely good at giving out and not out have not been in a strong enough position to run against the prevailing local culture, such as the West Indian notion that endless intimidation of batsmen is an acceptable form of play.

There are practical problems in setting up the panel. The longer people persist in believing there is a sensible alternative the harder it will get. The situation is not helped by the umpires themselves. English umpires have argued that such a panel would diminish their career prospects, when in fact it would enhance them immeasurably. Overseas associations are just as obstructive in a different way, by doing far too little to encourage former first-class players to join them. Everyone should now be aware that the empirical skills, instincts and sheer nous acquired playing first-class cricket are a far better preparation for top-level umpiring than years spent passing exams. Yet still some umpires' unions prefer recruits who can recite the law on seam-picking word-perfectly instead of someone who knows how it is done.

Into the current vacuum have come various nonsenses; first, the turn-and-turn-about three-umpire matches tried in Zimbabwe and South Africa; and then, South Africa's unique contribution, the TV umpire. This involves an official sitting in the stand to adjudicate on run-outs and, if they still exist, stumpings, by watching the replay if requested by the umpire in the middle. As a stunt, it gave the Durban Test a little publicity, not that it helped the attendance much. It also sowed the first harmless-looking seed of something that could grow to be thoroughly pernicious.

If cricket has contributed to society as a whole, it is the notion that the umpire's decision is final and that cricketers do not argue with it. Anything else is not cricket. The idea is totally foreign to, for instance, baseball. Wise professional cricketers have always known that the good decisions and the bad ones balance out over time. Wise selectors, who presumably exist somewhere, do not ruin a player's career for one bit of bad luck. And above all, cricket teaches us that, in the end, whether you are in or out does not matter much. What matters is the ability to accept the decision. As a rule of thumb, cricketers should have that firmly understood by the age of 11.

This only works at a professional level if umpiring is recognised as fair-minded, competent and authoritative. That, however, is considered too expensive, though it is hardly more expensive to fly umpires around the world than to fly the referees round and have a man paid to sit and watch television on the off-chance. Only the tiniest percentage of cricket matches would ever be able to have TV umpiring. Yet the doubt and dissent will spread to every English village, every corner of the Bombay maidan and the Port-of-Spain savannah. If Steve Bucknor is called idiotic, as he was in Johannesburg, for giving someone not out without calling for a replay, how can old Fred from Middle Snoring make such a decision. Proponents had said TV umpiring worked in American Football. News travels slowly to South Africa. The National Football League had just decided to scrap it all and go back to basics.

THE CULT OF BIRD
Derbyshire v Gloucestershire
At Ilkeston, June 1, 2, 1978. Gloucestershire won by an innings and 35 runs.   1978

Without Miller and Hendrick, who were on Prudential Trophy duty though not actually playing, and Barlow, who was injured, Derbyshire were bowled out in three hours by Brain, well supported by Procter and Shackleton. The pitch, which had a bounce varying from ankle to knee height, left much to be desired. Wisely, Gloucestershire took no risks and built a lead of 178 on the second day, which also produced two unusual incidents. In the first, Shepherd was, it transpired, caught behind off Tunnicliffe but no fielder appealed. Later, Stevenson, in his delivery stride, caught umpire Bird a painful blow in the face causing a hold-up for a few moments. On the resumption, Bird awarded the bowler an lbw decision from his next ball!

The Man who Stole the Show

Tony Lewis, 1997

Harold Dennis Bird, known to the cricket world as Dickie, retired from Test match umpiring in 1996, aged 63. He had completed 23 years at the top and his 66 Tests were a record; he stood in three World Cup finals and 68 one-day internationals. His career coincided with the advent of television coverage of cricket by satellite to many parts of the world; consequently his fame was global. Frank Chester, who umpired in England between 1924 and 1955, was once described as "the most famous of all umpires". There is no doubt that this accolade now belongs to Dickie Bird.

Personal celebrity, however, was never thought to sit easily alongside excellence in a professional cricket umpire, and so Bird's retirement provoked debate. Was he television-made? Was he better known for his eccentric, theatrical behaviour than for his wise judgments? Administrators of the British game used to throw their hands to their faces, hoping to mask the sight of Dickie running to the boundary behind the bowler's arm to deliver loud Yorkshire strictures to someone disturbing the batsman's concentration. Hands on hips, he would address a hospitality box three floors above, informing them that their open glass door was reflecting sunshine into a player's eyes. Everything he said was in the manner of the lugubrious northern over-the-garden-wall comedian. "Shut that door. Shut it. Where d'yer think you are?"

Sometimes he himself seemed to be the interruption. When he prepared to umpire in Sharjah, in the Gulf, for the first time, he was advised not to subject his eyes to the dazzle of the sun which bounced up off the shiny pitch. Instead he was told to look away from the playing surface between balls, and to divert his eyes to the grassy surrounds. So after the first ball from his end, he set off on a crouching, circular walk, like someone searching for a lost contact lens within a 15-yard radius of the stumps, and kept that up all day. Afterwards, he thanked his adviser: "Me eyes were great, they were. Great they were, me eyes." The conclusion was that he was not performing theatricals but that it was "just Dickie".

In Frank Chester's day, umpires were seen but rarely heard. They had been brought up as players on ground staffs in counties captained by amateurs but heavily influenced by the senior professional. There was hierarchy and discipline, and so the control they exerted as umpires was by the odd word to the captain or senior pro – and perhaps only a whisper: "Have a word

"The man who stole the show": an emotional Dickie Bird during his 66th and last Test as an umpire, at Lord's in 1996.

with your fast bowler. He's pushing his luck with that appealing."

Chester virtually created the modern profession of umpiring by his serious approach to the smallest detail. After him, Syd Buller was outstanding: massively unobtrusive, entirely dependable. His decisions were quick and clean. Players were happy with his judgments; even if they had not been, no one would have dared leave the field with a shaking head. Charlie Elliott, another protector of the spirit of cricket, was often Buller's companion in Tests, and also operated without fuss or palaver. And so it must have been a fascinating umpires' room at Headingley in England's Third Test against New Zealand in 1973 when Elliott, of the old school, welcomed Dickie Bird to Test cricket.

"I have never seen anyone so nervous in my life," Elliott recalled. "I thought he would never make it to the middle let alone give good decisions. Then I saw something which was a clue to his future reputation. He gave Ray Illingworth out lbw. The bowler was the New Zealand seamer Bruce Taylor and he was bowling round the wicket. I thought from square leg – 'How can that be out? A seamer bowling right-arm round the wicket?' But I saw it later on television and I liked what I saw. Dickie was absolutely correct: the ball had moved back into Illingworth from the line of off stump. It was a top-class instant decision."

There are not many secret corners to Dickie Bird's life; he has written autobiographies and has been the subject of many written and broadcast profiles. Son of a Barnsley miner, still cared for by his sister; nervous, dithery off the field, highly strung. A former Leicestershire teammate of his, Ray Julian, remembers how Bird needed help to strap on his pads and put his sausage-fingered gloves on the right hands before walking out to bat. "And not a lot has changed when we share an umpires' dressing-room now." Julian, like Charlie Elliot, talks of a different Dickie once he is crouched behind the stumps.

There is no doubt that his failure to become an established county cricketer heightened his appreciation of being an umpire. But it was the cricket he did play – from 1956 to 1959 with Yorkshire, from 1960 to 1964 with Leicestershire – that helped him become such an outstanding umpire. So has it been with most first-class umpires in England. Bird carried over from his playing days a strong sympathy for the legion of cricketers who plied their daily trade. He cared for professional standards.

Everyone agrees that he has been a very good umpire for a long time. It is the other little choices he has always found so difficult. But there is a special relationship between Bird and other umpires. His colleagues have been willing to take over when Bird's nerves are twanging at the thought of making tricky decisions about bad light or resuming play after rain. Where Dickie has been unique is in his rapport with players, and with the crowds watching at the ground or on television. The message emanating from Bird's whole being is his complete understanding of the spirit of the game, and his ability to preserve sporting play. Charlie Elliot agrees that international umpiring is more difficult these days. These is far more shouting, far more concerted appealing; as fielders, protected by helmets and padding, have moved in closer to the bat, the appeals for catches off bat and pad are now acted out in order to deceive the umpire. This is cheating.

If there was similar trouble in the old days, Buller or Elliot or Harry Baldwin would simply address the captain and tell him to control his players; the captain, after all, is responsible for preserving the spirit of the game. Bird, however, was able to chide individuals who specialised in sledging opponents and cursing umpires. He had their respect. Merv Hughes, Dennis Lillee and Javed Miandad, who were all verbally bellicose, accepted that he could laugh with them and yet caution them. They knew Dickie Bird put cricket above his own life.

As he leaves the Test match scene, the job has become more and more burden-some. Decisions made by humans in white coats are checked endlessly against technology on television and they are sometimes proved wrong. The use of a third umpire to pass judgment may bring about correct decisions but it undermines the authority of the umpire in the middle and erodes his confidence.

We are left looking back at the Dickie Bird phenomenon. His huge appeal was based on his personal vulnerability. He was a magnet for minor disasters. But the watching world was affectionate; old ladies wanted to mother him. Here was a real character, fun to observe in days when the cricketers themselves had become anonymous under helmets and behind visors. In a busy main street in Colombo he once got out of a car on the wrong side and found himself in the middle of hooting Ambassador cars, fast bicycles, slow ox-carts, and listing Leyland buses, all bearing down on him. Suddenly everyone stopped. They began pointing and shouting: "Mr Dickie Bird". He played to the crowd and gave them his funny hunched run to safety, repeating louder than any of them, "Mr Dickie Bird. Mr Dickie Bird".

His final exit at Lord's, 1996, was incredible. He was given a Hollywood-style reception which has never been afforded to any player, let alone an umpire. Don Bradman and Viv Richards were applauded to the crease when they played their last innings in England, and The Don was given three cheers. Umpire Bird walked out of the Long Room and the whole of Lord's stood and applauded. Even more, the players of the England and India sides were out on the grass to form a corridor of appreciation. Frank Chester would not have recognised the scene nor, I guess, would he and his contemporaries have approved the elevation of an umpire so far above the real craftsmen who bat, bowl and field.

But if you wanted the essence of Dickie Bird encapsulated in a few minutes, you could have seen it that day. One moment he was dabbing at his tears with a handkerchief; then at the fifth ball of the match he gave a rock-solid decision for lbw against Mike Atherton, the England captain. It is probably true that Dickie was a natural character who became a conscious character. But he never allowed anything to stand in the way of the fair conduct of the game. This is why he retained the trust of the players and stayed at the top so long.

THROWING MUD
Matthew Engel, *Notes by the Editor*, 1999

Two more of our new Cricketers of the Year began 1999 mired in controversy. The Australian umpire Ross Emerson called Muttiah Muralitharan for throwing in a one-day international against England at Adelaide; the vigorous and uncricketlike response of his captain, Arjuna Ranatunga, caused widespread criticism. The main blame must attach to Emerson, who ignored both the ICC and common sense by no-balling Muralitharan from apparent premeditation, rather than because one ball was delivered in a different way from any of the others. This was the behaviour of a man with his own agenda. The quality of Australian cricketers may be unsurpassed at present, but their umpires could use a little humility concerning their own limitations. Australia cannot even reliably provide competent TV umpires – not an especially arduous duty – for Test matches.

The issue of throwing recurs in cricket history like outbreaks of flu. In 1898 and 1899 these Notes were simply headed "A Note By the Editor", and it was solely on this subject. Yet the real problem in modern cricket is not the persistent thrower, who has mostly been eradicated, but the occasional deceitful chucker who throws the odd faster ball or bouncer. Such people are never called.

Muralitharan is a special case. Assuming his assertion – that he cannot unbend his arm – is correct, and it has not been disproved, then under Law 24 his action is legal. In my view, the law is badly drafted, and there is a case for changing the wording. A bowler whose arm is bent has an extra advantage because he can clearly get extra snap from his wrist. But a man's entire career is at stake here. It is not a matter that can sensibly be dealt with by an umpire/show-off at a one-day international.

KITCHEN'S BAD DAY
Jack Bailey, 1999

Although you still get the impression that first-class umpires generally enjoy their work – being part of the game and its bonhomie – there is little doubt that the demands imposed by the all-seeing eye of the television camera have knocked off a sizable amount of gilt from the gingerbread. Witness Mervyn Kitchen's unguarded words to Simon Hughes of the *Daily Telegraph*, when he wondered aloud whether he was up to the job after a poorish day during the England v South Africa Test at Trent Bridge. The erosion of the umpire's confidence during this match was so complete that nothing was done about the intimidatory bowling levelled by Donald at Atherton when he had been given not out caught off his glove. The Donald/Atherton duel was of riveting intensity and millions thrilled to it. But the laws were temporarily suspended while it went on.

The final match against South Africa raised criticism of the ICC's method of appointing umpires. Javed Akhtar was drafted in for this crucial game with only one Test outside Pakistan behind him, and recent experience of just one rain-affected Second XI match at Uxbridge. A number of seemingly arbitrary decisions, the majority to the South Africans' disadvantage, caused one critic to liken the whole thing to a game of Russian roulette. Since then, Akhtar has umpired in the Pakistan v Australia series and earned much praise.

Akhtar had in fact stood in 16 Tests before Headingley. In any case, the ICC say they have to give relatively inexperienced Test umpires every chance to do themselves justice. They strive to give them two warm-up games before a Test and at least two Tests in a series. Neither happened in the summer of 1998; weather and scheduling problems were blamed.

The method of selecting umpires has evolved since the early days when the

ICC strove to do something about constant complaints of home bias. The system of one home umpire and one visiting umpire has been established since 1994. (No home umpires were being used at all in the Asian Test Championship early in 1999.) But the 20-man international panel – two from each Test-playing country with an extra two from England – now includes an elite band, headed by David Shepherd, Steve Bucknor and Venkat, who are constantly on the go. They are supplemented by those of lesser experience; the aim is to pair the tyro with a senior umpire. The logistical problems are such that the system will never be perfect. But ten out of ten for effort.

YES, GIVE THEM THE GIZMOS
Graeme Wright, *Notes by the Editor*, 2002

It is so obvious that it bears repeating: umpires are only human and, being human, can always make mistakes. This is not to say that umpiring should be hit or miss; simply that, when they do err, umpires deserve better than histrionics from the players and opprobrium from the media. Similarly, the players deserve the best umpires. They have not always had them. Back in 1987, *Wisden*'s Notes advocated an independent panel of leading umpires, appointed by and responsible to the ICC, which in turn would have to show a more positive attitude in supporting them. Fifteen years later we are about to get it. In the interim, we have had that constant companion of cricket administration, compromise, along with the usual diet of fudge.

Having one ICC umpire in a Test match was a start, but it neither tackled the problem of erratic standards nor eradicated the cause of so much player dissent – the suspicion that, deep down, the home umpire was biased. Referees were a recognition of the problem without solving it. They focused on player behaviour in order to sustain the shibboleth that the umpire is always right. Television has thrown that into confusion, and an elite panel will not solve the problem unless cricketers – and this applies at every level – accept that the umpire is integral to the game, not as an authority figure but an arbiter.

So it was worrying when the chairman of the first-class umpires' association, Allan Jones, complained that their representations to the ECB over increasing incidents of dissent were falling on deaf ears. New regulations were introduced last season to stop intimidatory appealing, but umpires feel these were toothless. When they reported players to the board, there was no indication what penalty, if any, had been imposed. "Youngsters see these things taking place on the field and, when nothing is done, they think it's appropriate behaviour," Jones said. It would help if the board dealt out the penalties, but they leave this to the county that employs the offender. It's the procedure, apparently – and very convenient it is, too.

Meanwhile the debate rumbles on over television's role as an umpiring aid. Is there any reason why the talking should not be replaced by trials? For cricket and television to have a meaningful relationship, cricket has to keep up with television. Already there are virtually two games: one watched by those at the ground, the other dissected by millions getting all the gizmos. The technological wizardry does not provide all the answers, but used intelligently it could help umpires avoid errors. Maybe there can never be certitude that a ball would have gone on to hit the stumps, but the umpire could receive advice on where the ball pitched and where the pad was when it was struck. Similarly with catches: it does not matter if there is doubt. The laws cater for that; if in doubt, not out. Television's opponents argue that it will slow the game, but there is already a hiatus after every delivery during which the umpire could phone a friend, let alone receive a word in his ear from a colleague in the techno-trailer, with immediate access to different camera angles and replays. No-balls could be scrutinised this way, and a larger penalty – four runs or even six – would concentrate bowlers' minds wonderfully.

No, Keep Cricket Human
Matthew Engel, *Notes by the Editor*, 2005

Both the ICC and MCC have acquired a taste lately for high-flown talk about "The Spirit of Cricket", and MCC now has an annual Cowdrey Lecture devoted to the subject. Last year it was given by Clive Lloyd, who used the occasion to call for much greater use of technology in all manner of umpiring decisions. "It is time to use technology to the fullest extent," he said. "There is a lot at stake in international cricket these days: what matters is that we get it right."

Well, up to a point. What matters is the spirit of cricket, which insists that – whether it is a playground or a Test ground – what's important is that the umpire's decision should be a fair one, and that the players should accept it. Personally, I would rather spend eight hours a day undergoing root-canal surgery than function as an international umpire, but it is gratifying that there are men willing to do the job and who are not rushing to have their lives made simpler the Lloyd way.

"I would like to have my skills tested. You know, the players' skills get tested in the match. Why not the officials?" said Simon Taufel, the ICC umpire of the year. "Players make mistakes, umpires make mistakes," said his colleague Billy Bowden. "Let's just get on and move on." Quite so. This does not preclude the sensible use of technology: there seems to be a case for further experiments with third umpires monitoring the front-foot law. But cricket is a game between humans, which should be controlled by humans.

It is possible that the argument may be ended for ever if the new trend towards self-regulation takes hold. The Australians have begun walking when they believe they are out. Maybe we soon won't need umpires at all. But I shall suspend judgment until we reach the final Test this summer with the Ashes series poised 2–2, the Test in the balance, when an out-of-form Aussie batsman, battling to maintain his place in the side, gets the thinnest of nicks while still in single figures. If he walks then, I will walk too: home from The Oval in my underpants.

Pundits

This is perhaps a curious, uneasy section – in that it must look both back and forward. Back to the great writers and broadcasters who flourished after the war – Arlott, Swanton, Johnston. And forward to the internet age. I grew up with John Arlott and – call me a reactionary – but these days find it difficult to listen to long stretches of *TMS*, unless the cricket is utterly riveting and can more or less speak for itself. How, 30 years ago, we listeners used to long for rain breaks to take us away from some tedious Test between England and New Zealand and into an intimate, rambling, utterly beguiling conversation between Arlott and Fred Trueman.

But enough nostalgia. Mike Brearley's fond farewell to Arlott, reprinted below, is superb – honest, beautifully written, all-seeing. Had he so chosen, Brearley, as well as being a nonpareil captain, could have been our greatest cricket writer. Swanton's death is mourned by his friend and colleague John Woodcock – a lovely piece written by a natural stylist. Tim de Lisle, ace media-watcher, discusses the merits of cricketers who become correspondents, roots out the man who has seen most live Tests, and traces the rise and rise of the internet. Marcus Berkmann assesses media reactions to England's dismal showing in 1999; Quentin Letts does the same for the tumultuous summer of 2005. Perhaps we should take a midpoint between meltdown and magnificence, and say that is where English cricket currently resides.

S. M.

JOHN ARLOTT – A LOVER OF CRICKET AND LIFE   Mike Brearley, 1992

It is not an empty cliché to say of John Arlott [who had died in December 1991] that he was the voice of cricket. In his early days at the BBC, the house style was pukka, formal and, whenever possible, scripted. John brought the eye and tongue of a poet; the accent and timbre of a Hampshire grave-digger's son; and the courage to describe a whole scene, to give a rich game its setting. He knew cricket more in the way of the lover than of the critic, and as such tended to romanticise the performers.

His own disappointed aspirations as player (he appeared for Hampshire Club and Ground in 1937 as an opening batsman) never soured into envy or rancour. He saw professional cricketers, with few exceptions, as honest and likeable craftsmen in a worthy tradition. He regarded the invitation from the Cricketers' Association to be its first president, a post he held from 1968 to his death, as a great honour. In his later years as a member of the Radio 3 Test match team – by which time the individuality and informality, which his own example among others had encouraged, had often descended to triviality and egocentricity – John gave the commentary a needed ballast of objectivity and seriousness.

John Arlott was born in Basingstoke in 1914. He was an only child in a happy family. Hating his sadistic headmaster, he left school at 16 after failing the School Certificate "spectacularly". He worked in local government; then as a clerk in a mental hospital, calculating the amounts of each item of food needed daily by the wards. In 1934 he joined the Southampton police force. He enjoyed his 11 years on the beat, but his interests were wider. He must have been an unusual policeman, composing poetry on quiet duties and writing programmes freelance for the BBC. This led in 1945 to his first job with the BBC, as a staff producer.

Soon the opportunity came to broadcast cricket. He toyed with the idea of modifying his country accent but, thankfully for him and the rest of us, was dissuaded. He started, too, his prolific cricket-writing career, which continued beyond his retirement in 1980 from radio and TV until his death. In 1949, when he stopped off in Sicily on his way home from the MCC tour of South Africa, he was introduced to the local wines. Thus began yet another passion and career, on the fruit of the vine, and on the food, particularly cheeses, to be eaten with it. He always regretted that cricket is not played in the Latin countries.

John Arlott managed to combine qualities that do not often come together. He was both passionate and moderate in his opinions. He was a lover of tradition – policeman, cricketer, historian, collector – and a rebel against many authorities: he was outspoken in his antagonism to the regime in South Africa, and had little time for sports administrators, dismissing Lord's as feudal. Among all else, he found the time and energy to stand as the Liberal candidate in two parliamentary elections in the 1950s. He regarded his part in bringing Basil D'Oliveira to England in 1960, to play in the Central Lancashire League, as one of the best things he did in his life. As a diplomat and negotiator, he sometimes found that the need for restraint was tested by his sentiment and conviction, but he nevertheless steered the Cricketers' Association towards a constructive role in both the major divisive issues of the past 20 years – South Africa and Packer.

In his personal life, John suffered two untimely losses. On New Year's Eve of 1965 his eldest son, Jimmy, was killed at 21 in a motorbike accident. Then in March 1976 came the death at 42 of his much-loved second wife, Valerie. His son's death changed John's vision; at a deep level he felt thereafter that there could not be any underlying meaning in life. The second loss increased his tendency to lugubriosity. The pleasures of life, of friendship, family, cricket, wine, food, poetry, were real enough, but even the best moments were tinged with an awareness of their inevitable ending. So a claret or an innings became "desperately" good, and those protruding eyes would fill with tears.

He became less healthy. Too much tobacco, wine and food left him with chronic bronchitis. He would emerge panting from his cellar at lunchtime, clutching armfuls of dusty bottles. He became overweight and less handsome. His move to Alderney in 1981 was in part motivated by the need for clean air, though living on a small island also satisfied some longing for solitude, for the rhythm of the sea and no doubt for much else.

Over the past two to three years, John suffered badly from the deterioration in his health, and needed constant care. This he received with steadfast love and patience from his third wife, Pat. Others, too, were tolerant and affectionate, moved by the hints of the person he had been and by the shell that he had almost become. Now he often demanded company and feared being alone. He was also afraid of dying, but the end came peacefully, in his sleep in the early morning on Saturday, December 14, 1991. Pat and his much-loved sons, Tim and Robert, were with him in the house and had spent the previous evening at his bedside.

Until the last painful phase, despite the grief and the ill health, and despite the increasing tendency to monologue, John remained immensely generous and lovable. He was a marvellous raconteur, ranging brilliantly over past and present while from time to time shaking his head and hand as if to say: "But what does it all matter?" And he did feel that cricket mattered not a jot in comparison, say, with the death of one person in the violence of Ulster. He acknowledged that cricket and wine and aquatints are in the last resort marginal, so, recognising this, he would in mid-flow subtly (with, as I say, this characteristic little demurring, self-dismissive, pushing-away gesture with his hand and fingers) undermine the importance of his story before embarking on another.

As to generosity, I think of it as a wide-ranging attitude of thought and of deed. His hospitality was rich. He liked strong foods, patés, smoked eel, meat, matured cheese; he was not bothered about delicacies much – sweets, salads, chocolates. I suppose you could call it a man's taste – with perhaps an apple pie permitted as a robust dessert. He was generous in thought, too, though he could be savage about those he found to be beyond the pale of decency and kindness.

He was generous with his time. In the company of friends, John never made one aware of his other commitments and anxieties; he wanted to talk over a meal and long beyond. I once sat down to Sunday lunch with John, his family and some friends at two o'clock, and we did not get up from the table until ten at night.

On leaving South Africa in 1949, John left blank the section marked "race" on a form provided by the immigration authorities. When an Afrikaner official insisted that the space had to be filled, John spat out: "I am a member of the human race."

Much of this article first appeared in the Sunday Times. *Wisden's obituary of Arlott, together with a photograph of him commentating at Lord's with Keith Miller, appears on page 1158.*

BRIAN JOHNSTON'S MEMORIAL SERVICE 1995

More than 2,000 people gathered in Westminster Abbey on May 16, 1994, to celebrate the life of the commentator Brian Johnston, who had died on January 5. Sir

Colin Cowdrey spoke of the cry "Good luck, Cowders" that sent him out to bat in his first Test and quoted the broadcaster Wynford Vaughan Thomas on Johnston: "That gallant Guards officer who could talk the turret off one of his own tanks." He was followed by the prime minister, John Major, who spoke of Johnston's essential Englishness and his ability to make everyone feel better for meeting him. He quoted the citation for Johnston's Military Cross: "His dynamic personality, his determination and cheerfulness under fire proved an inspiration to all those around him." Among the other speakers was a blind listener, Melvin Collins: "He was a friend to those who never knew him. Eyes to those who cannot see. Warmth to those who were alone and depressed".

Wisden's *obituary of Brian Johnston appears on page* 1204.

CRICKETERS AS CORRESPONDENTS
Tim de Lisle, 1995

At the end of 1994, Australia's Channel Nine, the company which leads the way in cricket coverage, unveiled a new presenter: Shane Warne, the hottest property in Australian cricket. From the Second Test against England onwards, Warne was entrusted with fronting the eve-of-Test preview on the evening news, and took time off from the nets to interview his team-mates. The questions he lobbed up were jokey and anodyne (you would never have known he was a spinner). Viewers who tuned in to hear about the pitch, the weather or the line-ups were disappointed. The only thing to be learnt from Warne's first report was that Tim May had joined the fashion for goatee beards.

Cricketers have been going into the media for longer than the word "media" has been common currency. And stars of Warne's wattage have long had ghost-written columns in popular newspapers. But this may have been the first case of a player acting as a reporter while still standing centre-stage. For Channel Nine, the loss in information was evidently offset by the reflected celebrity. It was the way things seemed to be going. It ain't what is said, it's the person that's saying it.

During the English season, the trend blew up into a storm about who is better qualified to cover cricket, the ex-player or the lifelong journalist. The touchpaper was lit by Michael Henderson, a cricket writer on *The Times* [he later became cricket correspondent of the *Daily Telegraph*]. Henderson was invited on *The Back Page*, a programme on BBC Radio 5 Live devoted to sports journalism. Asked what he thought of players-turned-writers, Henderson said some were good, and named names – Peter Roebuck, Mike Selvey, Mark Nicholas. Then he said some were bad, and named names. "Simon Hughes can't write. . . He was a very poor player and he's an *execrable* writer." The stress on "execrable" was more than mere italics are capable of conveying. But there was more. "Vic Marks hasn't got a clue. He's palpably out of his depth and it's an embarrassment." Henderson then described Marks as "a lovely chap", to add compliment to injury.

There are not many new things under the sun, but one cricket writer savaging two others on national radio is probably among them. The victims reacted in different ways. Hughes let down one of the tyres of Henderson's car. Marks kept his own counsel, but was stoutly defended by his sports editor [on *The Observer*], Alan Hubbard. In his weekly column, Hubbard accused Henderson of bitterness, paranoia, bleating, pomposity, bitchery, prejudice, mean spirits, palpable ridiculousness, and sour grapes: he had been an *Observer* contributor, but a previous sports editor had felt that "he wrote pretentious twaddle and did not merit a place in *The Observer* first XI".

Fleet Street tradition holds that dog does not eat dog. But that presupposes that all journalists are members of the same species. Henderson's attack was intemperate, arrogant and ill-directed; but it raised a legitimate issue. Former players, for years confined to column and sidebar, are now landing plum jobs. But only on the broadsheets – with one exception, which proves the rule. David Gower joined the tabloid *Sunday Express* straight from Hampshire in 1993, dislodging the respected old-school reporter Pat Gibson. Gower found the job harder than either batting or television commentary, and in 1995 switched to writing a column, on the *Sunday Telegraph*.

His experience points to the paradox of big-name reporting. The bigger the name, the keener editors will be to get him on board. But the bigger the name, the less opportunity he will have had to learn his new craft. All those winters that Gower was on tour all over the place with England, Roebuck spent in Australia, writing columns for the *Sydney Morning Herald*. Gower knows more about Test cricket; Roebuck knows more about journalism.

Sports writing is harder than it looks. The specialist correspondent regularly takes on what would be four jobs in, say, politics: news, comment, features and colour. (In politics, only one of these, comment, would normally be entrusted to a former practitioner, and then only if he or she wrote conspicuously well.) In Australia, the story of the year was the allegation of bribery made by three current Test players, including Channel Nine's man, against the then Pakistan captain. It was broken by Phil Wilkins of the *Sydney Morning Herald*, another respected member of the old school. Journalistically, it had less in common with a match report than it did with Watergate. Would it have been published, let alone reported thoroughly, if the call from cricket's Deep Throat had been made to an ex-player?

NEVILLE OLIVER DECLARES
Simon Briggs, 1999

One familiar Aussie voice was missing from the 1998–99 Ashes series. Neville Oliver, head of sport on both ABC Radio and Television, was also *Test Match Special's* overseas player in the last three Ashes series in England. But in March, he suddenly announced his resignation, cleared his desk within three days and, at 53, was out of a job. "It had been mulling over in my mind for a year or 18 months," he says. "There comes a time when you have to look at a wider expanse of life than just tootling around doing cricket. By that stage I was also in a senior management position at the ABC. I won't say I despised a lot of the people around me, but I certainly didn't agree with them, and I'm a fairly forthright person. That made my decision easier, put it that way."

Oliver stood as a Labor candidate for the Tasmanian state parliament in August, but narrowly missed election. Instead, he is spending most days at his local golf club in Hobart, where he is the honorary secretary: "It fills in my time, but I'm looking for something more meaningful than that, I can assure you." Oliver says he will miss seeing his friends around the world, but when it was suggested that he might feel a pang of regret at missing the World Cup, he laughed. "Anyone who has listened to me for long will know my very deep loathing of one-day cricket and all that it stands for. To miss any kind of one-day tournament strikes me as more of a reward than a fine."

RADIO WAVES
Matthew Engel, Notes by the Editor, 2000

Over the past year, English cricket followers have had to get used to being separated from the BBC, which lost the rights to televise home Tests until 2002 [and well beyond, as it transpired] and, for one winter at any rate, the radio rights as well. Their increasingly half-hearted TV coverage was not much missed, and Channel 4 brought a welcome sense of adventure to proceedings, though overall, I thought, the newcomers were a touch over-praised. Aside from the iconic figure of Richie Benaud, they were short on commentators with real authority and bite.

Talk Radio, aka Talk Sport, who covered the series in South Africa, solved that last problem by hiring Geoff Boycott. They offered far more commitment than has been possible for years on the BBC, with no breaks for shipping forecasts and the like (the BBC were hampered because so many of their spare wavelengths were lost to outfits like Talk Radio). And I didn't even mind the adverts. Unfortunately, Talk fell down on the basics. You couldn't trust their commentators to read out the score or fill you in on developments. Often, one felt like an eavesdropper, trying to piece together the scraps of information they occasionally let slip. Some thought the coverage improved as the series went on, but by then the bond of trust had snapped as far as I was concerned.

Talk insisted that their commentators had to be ex-cricketers. This is now the norm; anyone who wants to commentate on the game probably has to play for England first (though maybe only a few times). This has had two disadvantages. Firstly, we have lost the lovely balance between professional broadcaster and professional cricketer – the one subtly deferring to the other – that made a combination like John Arlott or Brian Johnston with Freddie Brown or Trevor Bailey so right. Secondly, the essential journalistic skills of covering the cricket have been lost. Talk was fine on technicalities but failed to convey the mood – and, very often, the facts.

HAWKS V DOVES
Marcus Berkmann, 2000

England's early elimination from the World Cup elicited a predictable response. "Let's get things fully in perspective," wrote John Etheridge in *The Sun*. "This was only the most catastrophic day ever for English cricket." Photos of eight English batsmen were accompanied by the headline "Guilty of wrecking English cricket".

The Sri Lankan captain Arjuna Ranatunga, in his characteristically shameless *Guardian* column, asked: "What is so wrong with English cricket? The answer is simple: everything." Mike Selvey in the same paper: "This is the land, remember, where the most important cricket event ever staged here has been greeted with general indifference. . . The English get the team they deserve."

Farewell, then, Alec Stewart; welcome Nasser Hussain. "Before he does anything else, he can improve the team's conduct," wrote Michael Henderson, the new cricket correspondent of the *Daily Telegraph*, "and he can make a useful start by speaking properly. Somebody who went to a good university has no excuse for speaking in that ghastly estuary sludge." As Francis Wheen remarked in *The Guardian*, "England may be a second-rate cricketing nation but we are still world champions at the ancient game of missing the point." Henderson, though, had barely started. With an energy that dismayed much of the cricketing establishment, he maintained a tone of apoplectic rage that reached its zenith when Graeme Hick was recalled for the Third Test at Old Trafford. "This is the most feeble, witless, craven of all possible selections. It is buttock-clenchingly grim." This was strong stuff for a readership accustomed to the patrician restraint of Christopher Martin-Jenkins, now at *The Times*.

As England's performances declined yet further ("A great British game is being gradually eroded" – Vic Marks in *The Observer*), only CMJ continued to believe that things weren't quite as bad as they seemed. "At Old Trafford, as at Lord's, England won what turned out to be a toss that would better have been lost. On both occasions they had much more difficult conditions in which to bat on the first day than New Zealand did on the second." Gradually, two factions began to form: CMJ's doves (trust the men in charge, they're doing their best) and Henderson's hawks (sack the lot of them, then run them through with red-hot pokers).

Even E. W. Swanton was drawn into the argument. "Strong criticism within limits has been deserved this summer, and to both selectors and players," he wrote in the *Telegraph* in August. "Some of it, however, from respectable quarters has been so unbalanced and immoderate as to destroy faith in the writers' judgment." In among his usual columns about the strength of Eton's batting, this amounted to a stern warning, and it was noticeable that Henderson mollified his tone for his early despatches from South Africa. Anger, though, seemed a perfectly reasonable response to England's performances. Beyond it lay only indifference.

CRICKET ON THE WEB Tim de Lisle, 2000

In the Hobart Test on November 21, 1999, Australia set off in pursuit of a fourth-innings target that only a romantic, or an Australian, would consider, feasible: 369, against Pakistan on one of their good days. They were 126 for five when Justin Langer was joined by Adam Gilchrist. The two of them added 238 and ensured a famous victory. It was probably the best run-chasing partnership of modern times – and certainly the best by two internet diarists.

Neither of these amiable Western Australia players was established in the Test side, but each was already a fixture on the worldwide web. Langer had been sending email postcards to the Australian Cricket Board website, www.BaggyGreen.com, for three years; Gilchrist had had a column on www.thePavilion.com.au, run by the Fairfax group of newspapers, since before his Test debut. Both brought to cyberspace the bright-and-breezy air of Perth.

If Gilchrist was the more exciting player, Langer was the more accomplished columnist, with an eye for detail and a line in trenchant opinion which reflected well on the ACB censor. Soon after the Hobart thriller, reporters covering England's tour of South Africa were astonished to hear the England bowling coach, Bob Cottam, claim that Chris Silverwood had bowled faster in the nets than Allan Donald had in taking 11 wickets at Johannesburg. They might have been less taken aback if they had spent more time online: Langer had informed his readers four months earlier that Silverwood was the fastest bowler he had faced in the English season.

By the time these words are published, those correspondents may well be up and surfing. In 1999, according to a survey conducted in mid-December, by the pollsters ICM, the proportion of British adults with access to the internet rose from 29% to 37. By the end of 2000, the 37% was projected to swell to 48%, or 21 million adults. The web was pronounced the fastest-growing medium in history, far ahead of radio or television. If some still smelt a certain amount of hype, no one could doubt that we were talking about a revolution.

And, for once, cricket lovers were among those storming the winter palace. In 1996, readers of *Wisden Cricket Monthly* were asked in a poll if they were on the web: 21% said yes even then. At the end of 1999, the website CricInfo had 108,000 subscribers to its free daily email newsletter, CricInfo365, run in partnership with the company behind Football365 and Music365. If that doesn't sound a huge number, bear in mind that the football newsletter had 37,000 subscribers and the rock-music one 5,000. CricInfo as a whole claimed an average of five million users a month in 1999, giving it twice the reach of the leading football site, Soccernet (2.3 million users in April 1999). During the World Cup, CricInfo claimed an audience of 14 million.

Earlier in its six-year life, CricInfo had been the be-all and end-all, except that on the web, the be-all is never the end-all. The last business field to come along with such low barriers to entry was probably busking. All it takes to start a website is a computer, a telephone, some software, a domain name and an idea. Doing a good one is harder, but not even one-tenth as hard as, say, launching a magazine or an almanack.

The web could have been invented with cricket in mind. The game is both concentrated and far-flung: it is played professionally in only five areas of the world, but they are all in different time zones. As addictive as the web itself, cricket is followed with especial passion in the world's second-biggest country – India, with a population of around a billion. It is played in several countries that feature on lists of the world's most wired nations: Australia, New Zealand, India, Pakistan and Britain. Cricket is all about national teams rather than local clubs, often takes place during working hours, and has a public which is used to following the action from afar, at a high level of both literacy and numeracy.

THE GREAT SAGE

For the whole of the second half of the 20th century E. W. (Jim) Swanton was, as it were, the conscience of cricket; and because he lived to a great age, and retained his wits and enthusiasm right to the end, he became an ever-rarer, ever-more precious source of reference and enlightenment.

Affecting everything he did was a strong and forceful personality, and a love of cricket that withstood, sometimes painfully but always objectively, the constant and countless changes that come with evolution. With the passing years came benevolence, and a standing in the game, worldwide, that very few, if any, have enjoyed who have not themselves, at some time or other, been famous players. I suppose the only other sporting journalist to have commanded such attention and had so influential a following was Bernard Darwin, who wrote about golf, mostly for *The Times*, for 46 years, ending, in 1953.

It would be as wrong to give the impression that Jim was an absolute paragon as it was for one of his obituarists to say that he was a man of little humour. I am one of many who were introduced into the world of sports journalism as his amanuensis, a job which was underwritten by the *Daily Telegraph* when he was their cricket correspondent, and entailed being typist, chauffeur, chronicler, batman and butt. Among others whom he helped to bring forward were Christopher Martin-Jenkins (now a household name), Brian Moore (of TV footballing fame) and, briefly, the erudite Scyld Berry (who found secretarial work not to be his strongest suit). The chances are, too, that only by breaking the male line and filling the post herself did Daphne Surfleet become Mrs Richie Benaud back in the 1960s.

We all came to know what drove Jim to become the towering figure he was: attention to detail; discretion; the strength of his convictions (not least spiritually); a potentially daunting presence (not least physically); an eye for the main chance (not least socially); goodwill towards cricketers in the making; not the longest of fuses; great kindness and generosity; a wonderful memory; unwavering loyalty, both to the game and his friends; a proper knowledge of the technique of cricket; a prolific output; and a thinly disguised preference for getting his own way.

Those who opposed Swanton, perhaps through jealousy or perceived exclusion, were inclined to see him either as a reactionary or as being too high and mighty. In fact, though honouring the past, he was always looking to the future. He abhorred Kerry Packer – not personally (they never met) but for the vulgarity and militancy with which, in the late 1970s, he hijacked the game. On the other hand, he loved with a passion to see cricket hard, skilfully and sportingly played and, if it was at Lord's or during the Canterbury Week or in Barbados, so much the better. So far as the highness and the mightiness goes, that may not entirely be a myth – but neither did it affect in any way what he wrote.

Many people meeting Jim for the first time were surprised to discover what fun and what riveting company he was. Never was that more evident than at the Cricket Writers' Club Golden Jubilee Dinner in the Long Room at Lord's in 1996: a majestic speech, brimming with cadence, wit and wisdom; brought him a standing ovation from by no means the least cynical of audiences. He was 89 at the time.

His writing, like his broadcasting, had clarity and resonance, and was never forced. His reports were informative, his commentaries judicial. "Have you read what Swanton said today?" was a question posed by a majority of cricketers from the time he joined the *Daily Telegraph* [immediately after the Second World War] until he wrote his last piece for them, a full page of recollections, shortly before he died. The game will miss him badly, his sense of perspective perhaps most of all.

Wisden's *obituary of E. W. Swanton appears on page 1247.*

BEING THERE
Tim de Lisle, 2003

If you want to know who has played the most Tests, the answer is easily found here. In 2003 Steve Waugh passed Allan Border at the top. But what if you were wondering who has seen the most Tests? We decided to work it out. Given the inflation in the international game, it was probably someone involved in a professional capacity over the past 30 years. We decided not to count watching on television, nor any Tests but official ones between male teams. During the winter, while professional cricket-watchers were scattered around the world, we fired off emails to a few likely suspects. Some didn't fancy the idea; others were too busy – watching cricket. But enough were intrigued for answers to trickle in.

Tony Cozier, voice of the Caribbean since time immemorial, came in at 266 Tests. Patrick Eagar, doyen of cricket photography, worked out the figure from his computer reference system ("what a dweeb"): he had watched, more closely than most, 265 Tests. Bill Frindall, *Test Match Special's* Bearded Wonder since 1966, could be relied upon to keep his own score: 252 ("I have also watched an entire Women's Test in Adelaide"). D. J. Rutnagur, who specialises in India, knew he had started in 1951–52, but could only guess at his tally – "over 300". Graham Morris, the photographer, thought he was in the 300s too: "Sorry to be so vague, only I have never been a bedpost notcher. This is like being asked to do one's expenses for the last 20 years – without the obvious advantages."

The first definite 300 came from Qamar Ahmed, the Pakistan expert: he had just reached his triple-century, with a wave of the pen, at Cape Town. Christopher Martin-Jenkins did some sums ("1972–2002: all Tests in England") and came up with 302. It was the highest exact figure so far, but if even CMJ wasn't much above 300, who would be?

The same three names kept coming up: Richie Benaud, a fine player who has been commentating ever since, in England and Australia, in one never-ending summer; E. W. (Jim) Swanton, whose cricket-writing career ran from the 1930s to his death, aged 92, in 2000; and John Woodcock, today's elder statesman of cricket writing, who was the *Times* correspondent from 1954–87 and still pops up there, radiating genial authority.

I rang Woodcock at home in Longparish. How many Tests had he been to? "About 400 for the *Times*, so it would be over 400 now. There was a time I think when I had watched half the Test matches ever played, or very nearly. It came and went very quickly, can't remember when." His most recent Test had been at Lord's last summer, against India. The first had also been against India – 66 years earlier, in 1936. "I went up from my prep school."

What about Swanton, his old friend? "Oh, Jim's way behind. We discussed it once and he was on about 270. He never went to Pakistan, and I think he only saw two Tests in India – on Tony Lewis's tour [1972–73], when England won on Christmas Day. He did it in style of course: he was met by the Maharajah of Baroda's driver."

Who might be ahead? "Richie. I'd have thought he would be way ahead." Richie Benaud, naturally, was in the commentary box, in Melbourne, for the Australia-England one-day finals. We sent a message via Ian Healy. For a couple of weeks, there was silence: Richie's signature tune. One morning, an email landed: "From: Richie Benaud." It was like getting a postcard from the Pope. "Sorry to be so long coming back to you, but it has all been slightly hectic out here." He had a figure, but needed to check it when he was back home in Sydney. "Cheers, Richie." Next morning, another email. "I hope the following might fit in with what you want, and I hope I've got the figures right"

He had totted them all up, scrupulously: 63 Tests as a player, three as twelfth man, one on tour that he didn't play in (Lord's, 1961), one at the MCG in 1964, when he had broken a finger and covered it for the Sydney Sun, "68 in my playing time, 11 covered in the West Indies, 8 in South Africa, 5 in New Zealand, 223 in England, 171 in Australia, 0 in India, 0 in Pakistan, 0 in Sri Lanka, 0 in Zimbabwe, 0 in Bangladesh." He listed all the ducks as if he planned on breaking them.

In Australia and England together, he had seen 394 Tests, out of 733: more than half. His grand total was 486, a phenomenal figure. There had been 1,636 Tests in history, and Richie had been there for nearly a third of them, weighing his silences, composing his understatements, keeping his cool, distilling all that experience. Within a year, he should reach 500.

It made you wonder how he had sprung so swiftly from the top of one tree to the top of the next. Anticipating this, he had added an informal CV. "Did a three-week BBC television course devised for me by Tom Sloan at the end of the 1956 tour of England, then joined the team in Rome to fly to Pakistan and India for four Tests. On return to Australia, started as a journalist on Police Rounds and Sports at the Sydney Sun.

"Covered the five 1960 Tests E v SA for BBC Radio whilst still an Australian player. Captained the side to England in 1961, and BBC TV asked me back to cover E v WI 1963. Retired from cricket after the 1963–64 series A v SA. Didn't cover E v P and I in 1971. Didn't cover Tests during World Series Cricket [which he helped set up]. I watched Tests at the SCG 1946–47 to 1951–52, but haven't counted them as I was playing club cricket on the Saturdays and then was in the NSW team on tour. I thought Johnny Woodcock would have considerably more than the figure he has given you." A nice touch, deflecting the spotlight.

One last question. When was his first glimpse of Test cricket? "1946–47, Sydney, Second [Ashes] Test. Great disappointment, Lindwall had chicken-pox, but Ian Johnson and Colin McCool were there, taking nine of the ten wickets. Australia were 159 for four when Bradman, injured and ill, came out at No. 6 and put on 400 with Barnes. McCool took another five wickets to reinforce the thought that leg-spinners were great. I had just turned 16. Over 40,000 spectators the first three days." Australia won by an innings, but Benaud's recollection skips that to focus on the fans. He always was on our side.

All Hail! The Wazzock with the Skunk! Quentin Letts, 2006

For a quarter of a century, Britain's news editors yawned at the mention of cricket. At Fleet Street morning conferences, where tales of death and valour and love and betrayal are weighed coldly in the scales of news-stand saleability, cricket was dismissed as mere "back-of-the-book" fare. It was for the sports pages, the sports pages alone. Between late July and early September 2005 Fleet Street did what it does well, and changed its mind. Cricket started to nibble, chew and, finally, gnaw its way into the national consciousness.

In mid-August a senior executive at one of Britain's best-selling dailies wrinkled his nostrils at the thought of an editorial-page article on the Ashes. "Nah!" came the verdict. "Cricket's too poncey for us, and they'll only go and lose the bloody thing anyway." Two weeks later the same executive was to be heard screaming recriminations at junior commissioning editors, demanding to know: "Why aren't we doing more on cricket and why haven't we signed up Rachael Flintoff for a skincare spread, you poxy plonkers?" Not even the Aussies sledge like our beloved newspaper chiefs.

By the time of Kevin Pietersen's century in the Fifth Ashes Test ("That wazzock with the skunk hairdo – let's splash with him!"), cricket was a "front-of-the-book" story for the dailies, a "top-of-bulletin" story for television and radio, and was giving millions of new followers (and newsdesk juniors) the screaming abdabs. The closeness of the Ashes series did not just make for exciting cricket and tight-knotted abdomens. It was good for TV ratings and newspaper circulations. The Fourth Estate was duly thankful and gave cricket a wonderful show in print and on air. The build-'em-up/knock-'em-down press even forgave Andrew Flintoff for being so gloriously blotto the day after the Ashes were regained. "Off his Fred!" cried both The Sun and the Daily Mirror, cheerfully concluding that Flintoff had earned the right to drink London dry.

What a different world we inhabited on the last Monday of July. England's flattening of roadkill Bangladesh had attracted little more coverage than a lower-division football match. The one-dayers went widely ignored, batting way down the news bulletins. Cricket won less coverage than the unsuccessful Lions tour of New Zealand and the farcical US Grand Prix.

A modest tumescence before the Lord's Test soon disappeared when the match was won comfortably by Australia. The few marketing types and editorial executives who had encouraged their organisations to "buy into cricket big-time" were left feeling silly. Before the end of the Lord's Test, England's players were being pulled to pieces by the know-alls of Punditshire.

Tabloids and broadsheets, as one, showed their contempt or lack of interest. Channel 4's Today at the Test highlights were often broadcast at 1 a.m. and therefore broke the Trade Descriptions Act. It should have been called Yesterday at the Test, or Cricket for Insomniacs, or And Now Some of that Sport We've Just Lost to

Sky. And from every direction came the egregious sound of balding, broad-hipped ex-Test cricketers telling the young 'uns they didn't have a clue how to play the game. Part whine, part trumpet-blast; what a niggardly noise it is. "We'll never beat Australia carrying dead wood, and Ashley Giles and Geraint Jones are dead wood," asserted Derek Pringle from E. W. Swanton's old pulpit in the *Daily Telegraph*. Geoffrey Boycott, one of the regular vowel-murderers on Channel 4's Ashes team, was the sparse essence of Yorkshire charity: Boycs would come on for the start of his shift, drop that lower right lip, and deplore the batsman's lack of technique – only for said batter immediately to thwack the ball for four. "That's more like it," Boycs would then say, as though taking the credit for the shot. Bob Willis, over on Sky, was little cheerier. "Overexposure to Willis can bring you to question why you liked cricket in the first place," the *Independent* would later murmur.

When Derbyshire's coach, Dave Houghton, suggested that, by using Giles, England were playing with ten men, the England spinner replied aggressively in his column in *The Guardian*. The manner of his response, touchy though it seemed at the time, was evidence of a spirit of counter-attack in the England dressing-room. Australia should have taken note. "Can't bat, can't bowl, can't field," snorted Giles. "Famously, they said that about the last England side to win the Ashes. Now they are saying it about me. I suppose I should take it as an omen. I don't expect media cheerleaders. I just think I have a right to some fair criticism."

On my study wall is a cartoon from the 1920s. A man in a trilby cheekily approaches a white-flannelled player during the tea interval with the words: "I say, old man, that was a splendid article of yours in last Sunday's *Hoot*. Who wrote it?" Eighty years on, not much has changed, except there are more *Hoots*, and more fake bylines. The Ashes series saw an unprecedented number of newspaper columns "by" senior players, nearly always bashed out by jobbing sports-desk hacks, often for no extra money.

Regular scribblings which appeared under the names of Matthew Hoggard, Matthew Hayden and Glenn McGrath certainly carried a flavour of editorial top-spin. Just as players will exhort their bowlers from mid-off, so sports editors are likely to bawl at their scribes, suggesting macho, aggressive lines of attack. This can make for fiery journalism, but it does not do the reputation of the players much good. In the *Mail on Sunday*, McGrath (billed immodestly as "the world's top fast bowler"), or someone purporting to be McGrath, wrote that "Shane Warne will be unplayable when we have our turn to bowl on this Old Trafford pitch for a second time." Alas! Warne did not take a wicket in England's second innings. McGrath also predicted after Lord's that Australia would win the series 5–0. "The world's top fast bowler" had made himself the world's ripest banana.

TV and radio were just as obsessed with having the players' voices at any cost. One of the fallacies of modern sports broadcasting is that players have something fascinating to say immediately after a contest. All we heard during the summer of 2005 were the latest clichés – "we've got our noses in front" and "we got over the line" (i.e. "we won") – from Michael Vaughan and a few sporting inconsequences from Ricky Ponting. If producers want post-match reaction, how about interviewing a few spectators, or the umpires, or the groundsman? When Pietersen climbed the pavilion steps after his Oval century he was clapped on the back by a delighted policewoman. An enterprising TV producer might have sent a camera off to interview the policewoman, and seek her views on KP.

And there was a sense of it all getting worse. Summer 2005 was Richie Benaud's last in England as a television commentator. Benaud's skills at the microphone were discussed during numerous tributes, colleagues such as Mark Nicholas praising his economy, professionalism and lack of bias. A typical Benaud touch came after Ian Bell had dropped a catch. By the end of that over Channel 4 had assembled a package which showed how today's fielders invariably react after they have fluffed a sitter. They clap their hands and shout at their team-mates to try harder. Bell had done just the same thing. Benaud wondered gently if perhaps Bell's team-mates might be justified in telling him that he, not they, was the one who should try harder.

Despite all Benaud's excellence, no one emulated the old boy. Television's new generation of cricket commentators have not made themselves irreplaceable. Verbal diarrhoea is endemic and the tone too little varied. There is none of the gruff poetry of an Arlott or the snuffling calm of a Laker. If a wicket fell when Benaud was away from the mike there was the danger of a guttural eruption of "Goodnight Charlie!" from Tony Greig, a man who speaks as though newly arisen from the dentist's chair, or a sequence of hyperbole from little Master Sunbeam, Mark Nicholas.

BBC Radio Four's *Test Match Special* stuck to its game, as dogged as Jason Gillespie lumbering in with an old ball. Before the final Test there was a kerfuffle because the programme's fruitiest voice, that of Henry Blofeld, was scheduled to miss the game. His absence was caused by the rota and by Blofeld's desire to fulfil some freelance speaking engagements, neither of which might have arisen had the bean-counters at Radio Four not been so stingy at the start of the season and given *TMS* a bigger budget.

A "Bring Back Blowers" campaign started on the internet and was soon picked up by newspapers. Blofeld is not universally loved. Yes, the dear old thing sometimes works too hard at his eccentricity, but the merest lift of his larynx on the breeze is a signifier of summer. Cricket commentary should not be the preserve only of former professional cricketers. There must be a place for wry and warm observers of the human condition, and that is where the flawed, bus-spotting, seagull-watching, posh-burbling Blofeld scores. There was, sadly, no "Bring Back Nicholas" campaign. Channel 4, which happily uses the absurd but watchable John McCririck for racing, seemed to be paralysed by a desire to be classless and go-ahead in its cricket coverage. The reporting was never quite amiable or eccentric enough.

It is hard to select highlights of the newspapers' coverage of the Ashes, so good was the standard. For the *Daily Telegraph* the resourceful Simon Hughes (whose Analyst slot on Channel 4 was consistently informative) took Pietersen off for a net and tried bowling to the big hitter. In *The Observer*, Vic Marks showed that, although county cricket is disappointingly under-reported, today's papers do not lack the artistry of Neville Cardus. Reporting from Trent Bridge, Marks described a flashing stroke by Adam Gilchrist off Flintoff. "Four runs surely. Four more runs in another frenetic session. Hang on. A blur of white is coming into view. It is Andrew Strauss, England's auxiliary second slip, diving to his left. He's read the manual – 'two hands whenever possible' – so both are outstretched. But mid-dive he recognises he can't reach that way. So, still horizontal, he sticks out his left hand, his stronger one, and, glory be, there the ball resides." This continued for another 100 words or more, catching the athleticism, the drama, the see-saw of fortunes and players' emotions. It was in the same game that Gary Pratt, the little-known player from Durham, came on as a sub for England and famously ran out Ponting. "The Pratt Intervention", Marks named it, "which is not a Robert Ludlum novel".

Newspapers loved this series. They loved the tension, the success, and they loved the cricketers' wives – in particular willowy Mrs Flintoff and her baby. One could sense picture editors yelping that cricket had found its own, far prettier Victoria Beckham. Simon Jones found himself the object of a broadsheet's fashion spread, and Warne and Pietersen started to appear in celebrity columns. Londoner's Diary in the *Evening Standard* snapped the two leaving a Knightsbridge disco early one morning. We were back to the days of Compton and Miller (minus the young Princess Margaret). What fun, what unreservedly good news it all was. Was. And will be? Would the thousands turned away from the gates of Old Trafford Test ever have made the effort to get there had they not been able to see the previous day's dramas on free-to-air television?

By the end of the Ashes, cricket was gaining bigger ratings than *Big Brother* and was being watched by half the terrestrial audience. Unprecedented numbers of young women and children became interested, the ratings for Channel 4's coverage rising by about half a million with each Test. Radio Five Live, that temple of soccer worship, was pumping out programmes direct from The Oval and almost every hack columnist in the land seemed to be asking, "Is cricket the new football?" (To which the answer, please, is "good grief, we hope not!".)

But the game has been changed. And so has England. At the start of the season cricket was not thought to be mainstream. Its players did not misbehave, did not drive Ferraris, were not courted by New Labour, and did not count. Just a few weeks later, Vaughan and his men had helped to glue the country together.

The Great Unsung

When I was about 14, for the one and only time in my life, I helped to operate a proper scoreboard. My memory of the occasion is dim, but the ground was at Rodney Parade, Newport, where Glamorgan used to play and where Wally Hammond once made a triple-century against them. I was attending a charity game involving some decent Newport players and maybe the odd Glamorgan "star", and was roped into helping with the scoreboard. It was a complete nightmare, the score was rarely correct, and since then I have always had great respect for those who keep scoreboards up to date. That experience also gave the lie to that absurd phrase, "out without troubling the scorers". It was immediately apparent to me that a player who makes nought causes infinite trouble to the scorers – the wickets change, the batsman's score changes, the last man's score changes... the board has to be transformed. Far better the man who makes a serene hundred. He is the one who does not trouble the scorers.

I am a very bad batsman, as my team-mates in the several geriatric teams for which I still turn out (play would be an overstatement) will attest. But I am a worse scorer. Do not give me the book under any circumstances, or the game will be reduced to farce. How anyone manages simultaneously to fill in batsmen's scores, bowlers' analysis, extras, the running total, and the rest of the actuarial detail I have never understood. It is the arithmetical equivalent of rubbing your head while patting your stomach. I recall scoring in one game and having to make all sorts of compromises to square the various totals at the end. I could not guarantee to be within 20 of the "real" score. So I stand in awe of good scorers and dedicate this section, which hails cricket's unsung heroes, to all the Frindalls who keep the game ticking over.   S. M.

AN ALTERNATIVE FIVE
David Hopps, 1995

Every year *Wisden* chooses Five Cricketers of the Year and often the selection includes one of the game's lesser stars, who has worked away in county cricket for many years without the glamour of international recognition. They usually get called stalwarts and salt of the earth. But, as well as all the cricketers, there is a far bigger band of stalwarts who keep the professional circuit alive without getting any recognition, sometimes without getting any money. There are the umpires, scorers and groundsmen, of course. But there are hundreds of others, as well, in all kinds of jobs. This year, as well as the Five Cricketers, we have chosen five other people. Without them, in different ways, first-class cricket would be impossible. But they are only a sample, chosen almost at random. They stand for dozens of others. There are people like Vince Miller, who has been printing the scorecards under the Grand Stand at Lord's since 1958, Lilian Byrne, who has answered the MCC telephones since 1972, Peter Lees, long-time presiding genius of the Lord's press bar, Graham Jones, the steward, and Eddie Rickard, the dressing-room attendant, both at Swansea from just after the war into the 1990s. There are many more. We could only pick five.

The first of them is undoubtedly the best-known. Amongst professional cricketers she is a legendary figure. Last year, **Nancy Doyle** was made an honorary MBE and received her honour inside the Long Room at Lord's, which was a far more appropriate setting than Buckingham Palace. Her domain, however, is upstairs, where she is manageress of both the players' and committee dining rooms. Nancy Doyle has never read a cookery book, claiming she could never follow a written recipe. She never uses scales, much preferring guesswork, and has changed little from the basic method taught to her by the nuns at her convent school in Mullingar. That means a typical menu, as on one day of the Lord's Test against New Zealand last summer, might read: roast chicken with chips and two veg, followed by jam roly-poly with a choice of custard, cream or ice cream. The players love it.

Nancy first worked at Lord's as a casual waitress in 1961, transferring to the players' dining room the following year. In all those years, she says, she has never had a complaint, not even the time when she dropped hot apple pie and custard over Wilf Slack's lap during a Middlesex Championship match. Wilf quietly assured her it was no problem, accepted another helping and, after changing his trousers, went back out to complete a double-century. During Tests, Nancy prepares about a hundred meals for players, committee and office staff and about 60 at every county match. She unfalteringly protects the Lord's dress code: no jeans, tracksuits or shorts in the players' dining room, no jackets to be removed in the committee dining room. During Tests against India, Pakistan or Sri Lanka, her daughter Jeanette, a nurse, takes leave to help her; Nancy cannot cook curries.

She professes scant knowledge of cricket, although Sir Colin Cowdrey first taught her that "it wasn't rounders", which has left her with a soft spot for Kent ever since. Her loyalty to her players is unshakeable. She claims never to have been asked for a hangover cure. Nancy plans to serve out the 1995 season, then "see what happens". Everyone hopes retirement is a good while away yet, but when it comes woe betide anyone who makes a fuss of her by baking her a cake.

Bert Barden was also contemplating retirement as the season drew to a close last September. At 83, he was one of the county game's most senior servants and beginning to suspect that age was catching up with him. In the hectic build-up to a big limited-overs occasion, there are few more taxing jobs than that of manning the Chelmsford members' car park. Bert, as Essex's chief car parking steward, has been responsible for keeping order when tempers are becoming frayed. There have been times when merely not being run over in the rush for parking places has been some kind of achievement. If 33 years as a bus driver for Eastern National left him with a poor opinion of driving standards, he is equally unimpressed at the parking skills of the great cricketing public.

"They all know they have to park properly," he said, "but some of them have to reverse three or four times to get into a space, even if it's at the end of a row. When I was on the buses, I used to complain about women drivers, just like everybody else, but I've come to learn that the women park much more neatly than the men do. Perhaps it's because they know I'm keeping a keen eye on them."

Since the death of his wife, Kathleen, more than ten years ago, the camaraderie of the county circuit has been a blessing. He admits openly to long, lonely winters, which he is able to escape each spring with the first smell of freshly-mown grass. "I get very depressed in the winter, he said, but Essex have been good to me. There are one or two nasty pieces of work about, and we have to watch out for the West Ham mob on Sundays down at Ilford, but 99% of people are well behaved and friendly. It's good company; in fact, it's been good company since I watched my first Essex match more than 70 years ago."

His active involvement with Essex began in the early 1980s. Bert was in the garden shed, doing some carpentry and listening to the football on the radio; Kathleen was in the greenhouse, tuned instead to the local BBC station, where an appeal for stewards went out. "I went down for an interview," he said. "They didn't ask me much. It seemed that if you could walk and breathe, you were up to the job." In his quieter moments, Bert Barden has had the fortune to see some excellent cricket in the past 13 seasons. He has also had the chance to utter, more than once, that immortal line: "You can't come in here without a pass."

Consider the history of Trent Bridge, and the Dalling family should, by rights, immediately spring to mind. The name figures prominently in the county's history, with four men boasting more than a century's service to Nottinghamshire. **Harry Dalling** served as ground superintendent at Trent Bridge (responsible for everything outside the boundary rope) for 42 years until 1991. No one ever believed that retirement would end his connection with the club and last season, aged 73, he was still performing a variety of supporting roles, most recognisably as one of the voices on the Trent Bridge public address.

Harry Dalling was born in Nottingham and has never had any inclination to leave it. Today, he still lives only six minutes' walk from the ground. His father, Frank Dalling, was ground superintendent for 22 years; Harry's younger brother, also Frank, was head groundsman for 26 years until the mid-1970s; and now Frank's son, know as Frank junior, is assistant to the present groundsman, Ron Allsopp.

Harry has never married. "I've often been asked why," he said, "but I don't know a woman who would have tolerated the hours that I've spent at the ground. My first love has always been cricket and I don't feel that I've missed anything. I've had so many happy memories." Those memories include the Championship win in 1929 when, as a child, he glimpsed Harold Larwood and Bill Voce, and the day he dismissed Jim Laker for 49 in a benefit match. "I thought I fired one in just short of a length. He called it a long hop, but I was proud of it all the same," he said.

"The family have been privileged to serve Nottinghamshire over the years," he said. "Trent Bridge is an exquisite sight and has a very special atmosphere, even when it's empty. When it's full, the place sends a shiver down your spine. And what's pleasing is that it has retained its character throughout all the changes."

More than a decade has passed since computerised scoreboards began to change the face of English county grounds. For detailed information, the advantages of the best of them are undeniable, but if they remain for a century and more, they will never achieve the same solid and restful qualities of their manual predecessors. Wooden scoreboards, in all their alternative forms, help to form the character of the ground they grace.

Steve Howes therefore gains prominence, not just for himself, but for the building he represents. For the past 13 years, he has been particularly responsible for the smooth running of the scoreboard at The Oval, the most efficient in the country. Only in cricket, and perhaps only in England, could a scoreboard encourage such affection. But cricket is a statistical game, its conclusion revealed over a considerable period of time. When major records are broken – Lancashire's 863 against Surrey in 1990, the highest Championship total this century; or Devon Malcolm's nine wickets for 57 runs against South Africa last year – The Oval scoreboard unfailingly poses for another round of photographs.

For most of the 1980s, Steve worked the box alongside his brother, Andrew, and they drew pride from their reputation for speed and accuracy. The advent of a second, electronic scoreboard on the ground a few years ago provided another incentive to maintain the highest standards. Recognition can easily depart and Steve admits that he used to feel a flutter of nerves before the start of a Test. One year a number on the hundreds fell horizontal and no one could see it, he said. I watched the Test highlights that evening and nearly had a heart attack.

The Oval box is now more than 40 years old and struggling to disguise its age. Figures have been known to drop from the windows without warning – thankfully, there have been no recorded incidents of spectators being injured by Last Man's score – and are temporarily repaired with a hastily applied nail or screw. The box is spartan: a couple of chairs, a stool (Steve's preference), and a portable radio, tuned whenever possible to *Test Match Special*. There is not even a kettle in the box; they tried it once, but remembering to bring along a pint of fresh milk proved too challenging.

Steve took time out in 1990 to gain a degree in leisure management at Thames Valley University. But he returned in 1994, and the retirement in the autumn of Harry Brind caused him to move up a rung to No. 4 on the groundstaff. The only drawback with his promotion is that it might end his scoreboard duties, traditionally the novice's role. Approaching his mid-thirties, Steve wonders about a proper job. But The Oval exerts a powerful pull: the renewal of old acquaintances, the charting of a player's career from its infancy, the discovery of the same old boys in the same old seats year upon year. "And you have to be mad on cricket to watch as much as I do," he said.

In his two passionate loves, cricket and classical music, **Keith Partridge** has something in common with Sir Neville Cardus. When he is not at Hove or Horsham watching his beloved Sussex, Keith listens to Mozart and Brahms. There, the similarities must end. Cardus never tramped around a county ground all day selling lottery tickets. But he would have recognised that it is the untiring and unheralded contribution of cricket lovers like Keith that guards the future of the game.

Keith is handicapped and partially sighted, but he has consistently risen above such misfortune to be one of Sussex's staunchest and most committed supporters. He is a familiar sight during Sussex home matches, and sells lottery tickets throughout the county, from Chichester to Crawley to Rye. The only payment he receives is his train fare and the cost of his lunch. He was a young man when he moved, with his parents, to Brighton from London in the early 1960s, just before Sussex won their first trophy, the inaugural Gillette Cup, in 1963.

"It was a great time to be a Sussex member," he recalled. "Ted Dexter and Jim Parks were batting, John Snow played for England for the first time in 1965 and then we had Tony Greig." But Keith was not satisfied with taking an inactive pleasure in the county's success. In 1968, he began to attend the Sussex Cricket Society's monthly winter meetings and then started to raise money for the club. He has barely stopped for breath since. He now raises about £5,000 a year for Sussex: Christmas draw tickets, the Derby draw and the year-round lottery tickets. It may be small beer compared to the modern might of the TCCB handout, but it is community involvement at its finest.

GROUNDSMEN
David Hopps, 1996

Rarely has the desire for central control been as apparent as in the Test and County Cricket Board's instructions in the past couple of years for the preparation of first-class pitches. At times it has been possible to imagine that the appearance of a single wormcast on a county square would bring an immediate edict on how it should be countered.

It can be argued that the attitude of some counties invited such unyielding guidelines. There is little point in having a four-day Championship designed to foster the long-term development of players if counties, with an eye to short-term gain, continue to produce three-day pitches. But groundsmen are a notoriously individualistic breed, resistant to the imposition of bureaucracy. Preparing pitches is more of an art than a science, and an inexplicable art at that. It is no surprise therefore that two of England's leading Test groundsmen, Ron Allsopp at Trent Bridge and Keith Boyce at Headingley, retired at the end of last season with an air of dissatisfaction.

Boyce laboured to combat the ground's unpredictability for 17 years, and his resignation to concentrate on the Rugby League side of the Headingley operation arose out of painful emotions. He was very upset that Yorkshire took him to task for his preparation of a Benson and Hedges Cup quarter-final strip against Worcestershire on the day of his wife's funeral.

"In my bleakest period in the mid-1980s, when they wouldn't let me dig up the square, Margaret was out there with me all hours of the night," he said. "I had to accept criticism as part of my life. Until I was allowed to re-lay the square in 1988, we had to keep moisture in to stop it cracking. Too little moisture, as in 1981, and the pitch would crack; too much, like for Pakistan in 1987, and it would seam too much on the first morning. Then we didn't re-lay deep enough, and we used over-light soils. I think we've begun to get it right."

It is Boyce's dissatisfaction with modern TCCB restrictions which will strike a chord with his fellow groundsmen. "Umpires should be the only people to judge a pitch," he said, "and their only criterion should be whether it has provided an even contest between bat and ball. Each groundsman has his specific problems and a way of dealing with them. We shouldn't be regimented. We shouldn't be fretting over moisture content, amount of grass or colour. Last season we were asked to fill in a detailed report before a ball was even bowled. It didn't half vex me."

Allsopp, who will be retained by Nottinghamshire as a consultant, retired without regret. He produced his first Test pitch in 1973 and after unveiling his final strip condemned the TCCB's marking system as "a complete shambles". "They expect them to seam a little to begin with, flatten out into good batting tracks for two days and then turn, as if by magic, on the third afternoon. It's not always as simple as that," he said.

Allsopp remained loyal to the memory of Clive Rice, the South African, who led the club in the 1980s to its first successes of the modern era. When Allsopp once resisted Rice demands for a green top, he got the response: "What's the matter – have you gone bloody religious?" "The biggest compliment anyone ever paid me was to say that to play Notts was to face Rice, Hadlee and Allsopp," Ron concluded. "I was proud of that. Always will be."

Scorers
Graeme Wright, *Preface*, 1988

If cricket's history is not to be rewritten, those who compile it have a duty to ensure that it is written accurately initially – or corrected quickly. I am, therefore, grateful to the county scorers and statisticians who have checked *Wisden*'s first-class scorecards throughout the 1987 season. That there were times when two scorers offered differing views merely highlights the difficulty of striving for accuracy.

It would help if the game's authorities saw the office of scorer as one of greater importance. Pakistan came to England last year without a scorer; as I understand, no country took its own scorer to the World Cup; and when England tour, the scorer has to pay his own travel and accommodation expenses. The number of versions of scores emanating from the World Cup, with sometimes little way of knowing which was right or wrong, is testament to the need for an official scorer with any touring team.

Extras

This section is, in the nicest possible sense, a ragbag – items that didn't seem to fit into the logical, ordered (sic) structure that underpinned the book, but pieces I was still keen to include. Quirky items from Notes by the Editor, David Frith on cricketana, and at the end of the chapter, some of the best entries from the chronicle of offbeat cricketing stories that Matthew Engel, characteristically, introduced when he became editor in 1993. All utterly barmy (except the occasionally tragic ones) and utterly unmissable.   S. M.

VOTE FOR CRICKET   1984

No fewer than seven fixtures were casualties of the general election campaign in June and its immediate aftermath. In fact bat was not put to ball until the new charity fixture on June 26 against Old England, when, in an enjoyable day's cricket, more than 450 runs were scored. Basil D'Oliveira's 72 was top score for Old England; for Lords and Commons Michael Rawlinson, son of a former attorney general, made 96. Matches cancelled owing to the general election were those against St Paul's School, ACAS, Diplomatic Service, the Mandarins, Conservative Agents and BBC.

IN FANTASYLAND   Matthew Engel, *Notes by the Editor*, 1995

Maybe, in the end, 1994 will be remembered as the year when Fantasy Cricket took a grip of the land. Four of Britain's national newspapers ran competitions in which readers were invited to compile their own XIs made up of any of the players in the County Championship; the runs and wickets they got in the Championship then counted in the competition.

The best-organised of these was in the *Daily Telegraph*, which attracted 132,537 entrants, who all had to pay 75p each. The sole prize was a trip to Australia, costing, say, a thousand pounds or two. It is not necessary to be Einstein to work out that this constitutes a rather less favourable form of gambling than a bent fruit machine or the three-card trick.

But it was an awfully good game, infinitely better than the footballing equivalent, because cricket's individual and statistical nature is perfect for the purpose. It began to take over cricket conversation: "Poor old Bloggins of Loamshire has just fallen downstairs and broken every bone in his body." "Damn, he's in my fantasy team." The editor of *Wisden* came 36,952nd. As I was saying, no one has a monopoly of cricketing wisdom.

HATS OFF
Matthew Engel, *Notes by the Editor*, 1994

If cricketers want to be better-paid, they could work harder at justifying it. When actors take their bow at the end of a performance, they do not turn round and face the wings. It is hard to imagine anything more insulting to the paying public than a batsman who scores fifty or a hundred and waves his bat only at his team-mates.

Since many modern cricketers are so anonymous, it might also be in their interests – as well as good manners – to take their helmets off as they do so. It should certainly be accepted etiquette that players remove their helmets before leaving the field, especially after a long innings, so spectators can see them as they applaud them in.

In return, spectators could start to behave better too. But cricket has some difficulty addressing the problems caused by drunks: Yorkshire's announcement that they would eject anyone who caused trouble by chanting was printed on a letterhead bearing the Tetley Bitter logo. And I suppose there may be someone, somewhere, who goes along with the notion that the ground is actually called Bass Headingley.

The popularity of the dreary old Mexican Wave remains baffling, especially as its arrival seems to bear no relation to the state of the game. Why it should have started on the Sunday afternoon at Old Trafford when Warne and Mike Gatting were staging one of the most magnificent duels in modern Test cricket is completely bewildering.

SPOOFS AND SPIES
Matthew Engel, *Notes by the Editor*, 1994

There have, thank heaven, been some more pleasingly surreal moments in the past year. There was the story about Botham getting into trouble for not going into pubs enough – he was supposed to be doing promotion work for a brewery. Gooch, the man who did more than anyone to push Gower towards retirement, called for his return to the Test team the day before the Israelis and Palestinians signed their peace treaty. The *Yorkshire Post* ran an April Fool spoof about the formation of an alternative county club, to be led by Geoff Boycott. It fooled me: I have heard many more far-fetched stories in Yorkshire that have turned out to be true.

And then there was the genuine revelation that the late spy Kim Philby kept the 1972 edition of *Wisden* in his Moscow flat. Did the old traitor particularly enjoy reading about the Empire shuddering as India won a Test in England for the first time? Or did he get nostalgic and regretful pleasure from reading the details of England's recapture of the Ashes?

Perhaps he would dwell, on those dull Moscow evenings, on the obituary of W. H. Copson, the Derbyshire and England fast bowler, who would never have come to cricket but for the General Strike; with the colliery closed, he took part in a game on the local recreation ground. I digress, but then old *Wisdens* get you that way, wherever you are in the world.

ILLY BANS GOD   1995

Cricket and Christianity had an improbable collision at the Trent Bridge Test in June when it was reported that Ray Illingworth, the chairman of the England selectors, had sacked the Oxford Blue, Rev. Andrew Wingfield Digby, as the team's chaplain, saying that if England players needed a shoulder to cry on, they should not be in the team. This brought forth the memorable headline: "Illy Bans God."

The story was only slightly spoiled later when it became clearer that Wingfield Digby did not hold a formal chaplaincy from which he could be sacked. He had been invited by Illingworth's predecessor, Ted Dexter, to act informally as the team's spiritual adviser. The TCCB later apologised and Illingworth said the vicar would still be welcome in the dressing-room. On the eve of the Oval Test, Wingfield Digby switched sides to take the Bible class which is a regular feature of touring life for several of the South African players. Six of them attended; they were not rewarded with worldly success in the game that followed.

In the winter, Wingfield Digby joined the England A team in India and, as director of the organisation Christians in Sport, took part in a tour to Zimbabwe, captained by the Northamptonshire batsman Alan Fordham. Christians in Sport had previously run tours to India, and plan to repeat the Zimbabwe visit in 1995–96.

Six of the 18 first-class counties did have official chaplains at the end of 1994, not counting Worcestershire, whose secretary Mike Vockins is an ordained minister. "People are recognising that having professionals on all different levels is a good thing to do in sport," said Wingfield Digby. "Having people to look after the staff spiritually, if and when required, is part of running a good professional set-up."

THE CEEFAX SUMMER   Matthew Engel, *Notes by the Editor*, 1996

For some of us, 1995 was the Ceefax summer. The Press Association/TCCB scores computer, after an appalling start in 1993, began to provide an efficient service, enabling Championship scores to be updated every few balls instead of every half-hour. The upshot was that watching a game on teletext could be almost as exciting as being there: Northamptonshire's marvellous matches against Warwickshire and Nottinghamshire were just as draining on the screen as they must have been for the players. (Note to the BBC: this summer, can you just mention how many overs are left, please?)

THE MISSING CENTURION
Matthew Engel, Notes by the Editor, 1996

I probably ought to say something in these Notes about Laws 24 and 42, and Brian Lara's battles against the problems of mega-stardom, mixed in with some perceptive thoughts on Sky TV, the internet and Darren Gough's left foot. Some other time, maybe. It is gratifying (though occasionally alarming) to know how many *Wisden* readers rummage conscientiously even through the mustiest corner of the Almanack. Several have noted that Cota Ramaswami of Madras is apparently due to celebrate his 100th birthday this year, a feat not yet achieved by any Test cricketer. His date of birth is recorded as June 18, 1896, and there is no record of his death.

Ramaswami toured England in 1936, played two Tests on the tour though he was already over 40, and indeed scored rather well: 40, 60, 29 and 41 not out. And his centenary falls just two days before the start of this year's Lord's Test against India. Unfortunately, the odds seem to be against him being around to enjoy it. In 1985, aged 89, Ramaswami left his home, wearing shorts, T-shirt and slippers, and has never been seen since. He had already tried to commit suicide several times. But no body has ever been found, and some people believe he must still be alive. In *Wisden*, though, he will now have to be presumed dead.

BOOM IN TEST GROUNDS
1996

In the first century of Test cricket, between 1877 and 1977, 48 different cricket grounds round the world staged Test matches. But in the past couple of decades the number has exploded. There was an average of a new ground every year in the 1980s; in the 1990s the rate has been two a year. The number of grounds now stands at 76. The growth is partially explained by the arrival of two new Test-playing countries, Sri Lanka and Zimbabwe – especially Sri Lanka, with its confusing proliferation of stadiums in and around Colombo. But since 1977 there have been seven new grounds built in both India and Pakistan, partly because new stadiums have been built, partly because the authorities have moved games into the hinterland to counter falling enthusiasm for the five-day game in the more sophisticated centres. Forty of the 76 are in the subcontinent and, like most of them, the Arbab Niaz Stadium in Peshawar, which recently joined the list, is a featureless concrete bowl. There is said to be a distant view of the Khyber Pass on the rare occasions the smog lifts.

GOODBYE TO OUT-GROUNDS

Matthew Engel, *Notes by the Editor*, 1997

One of the minor sadnesses of modern county cricket is the way in which the game is being withdrawn from so many of the out-grounds, and moving closer towards the point when nearly all the matches will be played at the 18 county headquarters. In 1996, most drastically, Yorkshire abolished their traditional fixtures in three of Britain's largest cities – Sheffield, Bradford and Middlesbrough – and one of its liveliest festival grounds, Harrogate. Simultaneously, Somerset made the long-expected decision to abandon the Weston-super-Mare festival. Further retrenchment is expected elsewhere in the years ahead.

Any argument against these changes is usually dismissed as soppy sentimentalism by county officials who like to present themselves as shrewd managers making sensible economic decisions in keeping with cricket's modern needs. The reverse is the case. Of all branches of the game, county cricket is the one that has most dismally failed to market itself – hence its appalling public image.

The festival games have long been the one great exception, the time when county cricket comes alive, and draws in a wider public. In Yorkshire's case, it would have been one thing to get rid of their outposts in the context of a move to a spanking new stadium, which everyone would want to experience. They hope to move to Wakefield by 2000. This may or may not happen; it will be terrific for English cricket if it does. But for the next few seasons they will be playing almost all their cricket at Headingley, which they have effectively condemned. Unless the team is very successful indeed, at least three very downbeat years are in prospect; it is impossible to see how this can work to the advantage of either Yorkshire or cricket – except in the narrow terms of saving small amounts of cash. I hope Lord MacLaurin tells them Tesco did not succeed by closing down shops without opening new ones.

CRICKETANA

David Frith, 1997

If 1996 was an unremarkable year for English cricket, this was not the case in memorabilia trading. It was the year of the Big Names. Record prices were paid for books, bats and letters, all with highly important associations, while the staple fare of *Wisdens*, autographs, postcards and photographs continued to swell in value. The most desirable *Wisdens* ever offered inspired frenzied bidding at Bearne's, Exeter in July. They once belonged to W. G. Grace, who had signed many of them. The run, from the 1864 first edition to 1915, the year of WG's death, went to a collector from Maidenhead who paid £94,100 (all prices include premium) and excitedly proclaimed, unchallengeably, that WG and *Wisden* were cricket's ultimate combination. Over 100 lots were contested by eager collectors and dealers, the spectacular realisations justifying the auctioneers' decision to abstain from publishing estimates.

CRICKET IN THE CLASSROOM

Peter Mason, 1997

A ruler and a serviceable Biro may have been essential prerequisites for school exams of the past; now you must take along a decent piece of willow and a pair of whites. Studying cricket at A-level may once have seemed a fanciful schoolkid's dream, but now it is reality. The first cricket A-level courses began in September 1996, with the first examinations due in 1998. They are not devoted entirely to cricket, and go under the general heading of physical education, but they do offer a new-look syllabus which allows 15% of all marks to be devoted to practical performance in the summer game. There will be no questions about the origin of the Ashes or the size of The Oval boundary, and no last-minute cramming on Test averages, but cricket is at last on the academic map.

DUCK SOUP

Matthew Engel, *Notes by the Editor*, 1998

It is of course desirable that a cricket match should produce the fairest possible result. But that cannot be the only consideration. This volume faithfully reports that Glamorgan, batting second in a rain-affected Sunday League match against Warwickshire, scored 81 for three against 147 for seven, and thus won by 17 runs.

As editor of *Wisden*, I would like to be able to explain why this is so. Trouble is, I haven't got the foggiest idea. It is, of course, all tied up with the Duckworth/Lewis system that is used on these occasions and tormented the lives of players, umpires, scorers, journalists and spectators alike in 1997. It is said to be fairer than any other system yet devised.

Unfortunately, virtually everyone except the inventors have to take that on trust, because if we understand the principles which govern the system, we get lost when it comes to its implementation. If the average, reasonably well-informed spectator cannot understand what is happening at an event, then it is not a credible entertainment.

A GRACELESS ANNIVERSARY

Matthew Engel, *Notes by the Editor*, 1998

This *Wisden* includes an article [see section F8] to mark the 150th anniversary of the birth of W. G. Grace, which falls on July 18 this year. The author, Geoffrey Moorhouse, has his own view of the great 19th-century champion. My own line would be more charitable. But even Moorhouse wants to raise a glass to the greatest of sporting Victorians. Cricket, it seems, does not. WG's 50th birthday in 1898 was marked by a special celebration Gents v Players match at Lord's with the man himself playing. A similar match was arranged for his centenary in 1948 (without his presence). By happy chance, July 18, 1998 is a Saturday with no Test or cup final, when Middlesex are away and, indeed, a special MCC v Rest of the World fixture at Lord's has been scheduled.

Nothing to do with WG though. It is a memorial match for Diana, Princess of Wales. Her tragic death last year affected millions of people (though only one county was sufficiently affected to postpone a home fixture the day it happened). But her connection with cricket was somewhat remote, it has to be said, and, of all the many worthy causes which deserve support, her Memorial Fund is perhaps not the one in most urgent need of cricket's patronage. I am sorry that MCC has, uncharacteristically, opted for the obsession of the moment, rather than a rare chance both to honour English cricket's most lustrous star and to choose its own charitable priorities.

A RECORD FOR EVERY BATSMAN 1998

Players in the one-day internationals [between New Zealand and England] were asked to select a piece of music to be played as they went out to bat:

New Zealand

Nathan Astle *Unbelievable* – EMF
Chris Cairns *Back in Black* – AC/DC
Heath Davis *Wild Thing* – The Troggs
Simon Doull *No Second Prize* – Jimmy Barnes
Stephen Fleming *Omen Theme* (Carmina Burana)
Lee Germon *That's the Way (I Like It)* – KC and the Sunshine Band
Chris Harris *Relax* – Frankie Goes to Hollywood
Matt Horne *New Sensation* – INXS
Gavin Larsen *Movin' On Up* – M People
Danny Morrison *Start Me Up* – Rolling Stones
Adam Parore *Danger Zone* – Kenny Loggins
Dipak Patel *U R the Best Thing* – D:Ream
Blair Pocock *Alive and Kicking* – Simple Minds
Craig Spearman *Whatta Man* – Salt 'N' Pepa
Justin Vaughan *Hit Me With Your Best Shot* – Pat Benatar
Bryan Young *Start Me Up* – Rolling Stones

England

Mike Atherton *Some Might Say* – Oasis
Nick Knight *Some Might Say* – Oasis
Nasser Hussain *Zombie* – The Cranberries
Graham Thorpe *Swamp Thing* – The Grid
Alec Stewart *Summer of '69* – Bryan Adams
John Crawley *Wonderwall* – Oasis
Dominic Cork *Return of the Mack* – Mark Morrison
Robert Croft *Delilah* – Tom Jones
Darren Gough *Walking on Sunshine* – Katrina and the Waves

Ronnie Irani *Two Tribes* – Frankie Goes To Hollywood
Andrew Caddick *I Feel Good* – James Brown
Chris Silverwood *Supersonic* – Oasis
Alan Mullally *Even Better than the Real Thing* – U2
Craig White *Son of a Gun* – Jx
Jack Russell *How Much is that Doggie in the Window?* – Lita Roza
Phil Tufnell *Cigarettes & Alcohol* – Oasis

BARBADOS – OH NOT AGAIN
Matthew Engel, *Notes by the Editor*, 1999

Neville Cardus first went to Australia to report the 1936–37 tour. He was not far
off 50. When the ambition of a lifetime is fulfilled, he wrote later, when a boy's
dream comes true, something has gone from one's life. These days, as our Schools
section makes clear, teams of teenagers regularly fly off to matches in the furthest
corners of the globe. There are Under-19 Tests, an Under-15 World Cup even. This
may help explain why professional cricketers who come up through the system
get so blasé about the opportunities for travel that are part of their job, and turn
into bored and boring tourists. "Where are we going on our tour?" one public
schoolboy was overheard asking another last year. "Barbados" he was told. "Oh,
no!" came the reply. "Not again!"

BEHIND THE GLASS
Matthew Engel, *Notes by the Editor*, 2000

The 1901 *Wisden* Notes included a whinge by Sydney Pardon about press facilities
at Lord's – although even then, conditions had moved on since the time of one
of Pardon's predecessors, W. H. Knight, who had to report games from a shrubbery. Now we have a media centre, built at vast expense in pole position behind
the bowler's arm. It has won a major architectural award, though not everyone
shares the enthusiasm. The building has been compared to an alien spaceship, a
barcode reader, Wallace's teeth (from Wallace and Gromit), Tony Blair's smile, Mrs
Blair's smile, a digital alarm clock and a pickled gherkin. Those of us allowed
inside don't have to worry about how it looks, however. We ought to be eternally
grateful to MCC, and promise never to write horrid things about them ever again.

There is a problem, though. None of the windows (except in the Test Match
Special box) opens at all. We watch from behind plate glass as though in a cataleptic
fit: able to see what goes on but wholly removed from it. If Lord's is full, we have
nowhere else to go. It confirms my view of architects: they win awards for grand
conceptions, not concern with the comfort of a building's users. The new media
centres at Taunton, Nottingham and Leicester are enclosed in the same wretched
way. It is said that health and safety officers are worried that, if a window opens,
one of us might throw himself out. (The *Evening News* did once hurl the *Sunday
Times* typewriter off the balcony at Leyton, but that's as near as we've got.) I
became a cricket writer partly because I wanted to spend my summer days in the

fresh air, rather than cooped up in an office. These new arrangements are deeply depressing. End of this whinge. Could someone direct me to the shrubbery, please?

THE OLD MOANERS AND THE VEGAN   Matthew Engel, *Notes by the Editor*, 2004

The world's cricketers, we are constantly told, have never been fitter. They spend hours in the gym. They receive constant attention from all manner of specialists. Yet they keep falling down. In 13 Test matches in 2003, England had to field 11 different new-ball pairings. As soon as a fast bowler emerged, he collapsed in a heap. Even Australia were not immune and their attack was unusually hard-hit.

The older generation of cricketers have long had an explanation for this. The likes of Sir Alec Bedser and Fred Trueman have moaned for years about the issue, with lots of eye-rolling and "Idunnos" and "inmydays". They have now received improbable support from another all-time great with a very different outlook on life. Since retiring from cricket, Greg Chappell, who once dickered with conservative politics, has embraced veganism (he prefers the term "pure vegetarianism") and become an animal rights activist. His approach to cricketing fitness is based on reading the works of nutritionists, educational experts and fitness gurus, but they have led him right back to the world of Alec and Fred. "Gymnasiums should be banned," he said in an unguarded moment.

On further questioning, he rowed back, but only a bit. "A lot of what cricketers are doing in the gymnasium is creating problems, not solving them," Chappell said. "Many of the leg machines are incorrectly set up and put pressure on the lower back. For a batsman, too much weight work can have quite drastic effects on movement patterns. Nobody's done any real research on what's right for cricketers. And I believe a lot of what we do is setting players up to be injured. We're going blindly down modern paths and ignoring what's served us so well in the past. The best way for young people to prepare for cricket is by playing cricket." As you read the papers, you note that yet another quick bowler has done yet another part of his anatomy, and you begin to think Chappell may be on to something.

A TIME TO MOURN   Matthew Engel, *Notes by the Editor*, 2004

On the final day of the Sydney Test this year, Steve Waugh's last day in Test cricket, the Australian players took the field wearing black armbands. There was no obvious reason for this. However, enquiring pressmen were informed it was to mark the death of Brett Lee's grandmother. The crowd were just left puzzled. And it was notable that, on his big day, Waugh chose not to join in.

Now the Lee family has all our sympathy in their loss, and I would never belittle it. But players these days seem to wear black armbands more often than not, and it is time the authorities stamped out this dressing-room indulgence. There were 27,000 people at the SCG that day, all of whom either have lost or will expect to lose their grandmothers. There is a difference between private grief and public grief. Black armbands represent an important tradition: a shared emotion between player and spectator. They should be reserved for the deaths of famous cricketers or major public figures and for national or global tragedies. Otherwise, if a future Flower and Olonga try to draw the world's attention to their nation's plight, people will just assume it concerns one of their team-mates' elderly relatives.

GROUND RULES   Matthew Engel, *Notes by the Editor*, 2004

Unfortunately, cricketing authorities are more concerned about stopping what shouldn't be stopped. When England won the *Wisden* Trophy by beating West Indies at The Oval in 2000, the crowd were welcomed on to the pitch to share a perfect moment of national cricketing joy. A full house cheered, and kids celebrated by playing on the outfield – not football, but cricket. There was not a hint of a problem. Three years later, on the same ground, when England squared the series against South Africa with a tremendous win, the crowd were sent a different message by phalanxes of cold-eyed stewards.

I was in the Peter May stand at the time, as were a large proportion of a substantial crowd. The rostrum was erected with its back to us, and the symbolism was very clear: "This is for telly, not for you. You can go home now." And most people did, deflated, disgruntled and rather insulted. Thus ends a beautiful English end-of-summer tradition. Of course, it is right to be stern about the players' security. Of course, we cannot go back to the old days of stump-grabbing mayhem. But there is no good reason why, say, ten minutes after play in the final Test of summer, when the players are safely corralled and stewards have had time to cordon off the square, the crowd cannot be allowed on to the outfield. This is an over-zealous ruling by Tim Lamb, the ECB chief executive, and I beseech him to think again. It alienates the people cricket should cherish most.

INITIAL REACTION   Matthew Engel, *Notes by the Editor*, 2004

It is possible that not every *Wisden* reader will make it through to page 1,415, the Sri Lankan domestic scores. This seems a pity, because you might be missing the following: At FTZ Sports Complex, Katunayake, February 14, 15. Kurunegala Youth won by an innings and four runs. Toss: Kurunegala Youth. Antonians 100 (A. R. R. A. P. W. R. R. K. B. Amunugama 4–39) and 121 (A. R. R. A. P. W. R. R. K. B. Amunugama 4–34, A. W. Ekanayake 4–18); Kurunegala Youth 225 (K. G. S. Sirisoma 5–40).

The successful bowler in this game, as we all know, is Amunugama Rajapakse Rajakaruna Abeykoon Panditha Wasalamudiyanse Ralahamilage Ranjith Krishantha Bandara Amunugama – Ranjith to his friends, apparently. With ten initials, he has now established a commanding lead over his nearest rival, A. K. T. D. G. L. A. S.

de Silva (I won't spell it out, if you don't mind: I'm getting tired) and the leading international player W. P. U. J. C. Vaas. This is an area where England used to fancy it could hold its own with any other cricketing country, but such stars of yesteryear as J. W. H. T. Douglas, M. E. J. C. Norman and R. I. H. B. Dyer have long been eclipsed by these ex-colonial upstarts. Only the Essex newcomer A. G. A. M. McCoubrey carries on the tradition – and he's Irish.

Amunugama is not a newcomer. As far back as 1990–91 *Wisden* reported him taking match figures of 12 for 91 for Tamil Union against Sebastianites. But in those days he was plain old R. K. B. Amunugama, which just makes me wonder. Is this an elaborate joke, along the lines of Llanfairpwllgwyngyllgogerychwyrndrobwllllantysiliogogogoch? *Wisden*'s policy is that players may suppress embarrassing middle names if they wish without fear of being outed by researchers bearing birth certificates, and the reverse should also apply (after all, Bob Willis added the middle name Dylan). But our patience is not infinite. You can call yourself what you like, but not if we have to omit the Laws of Cricket again just to make room.

HORSE PLAY
Matthew Engel, *Notes by the Editor*, 1994

Regular readers of our Chronicle feature know that over the past ten years *Wisden* has developed a considerable fascination with exotic reasons for stopping play: boy falling out of tree, rogue hang glider, galloping elk – we've had the lot. On my very first weekend back in England last summer, I went down to the New Forest for a family party. On the Saturday there was a game – Brockenhurst v Ellingham – being played on a lovely cricket ground on a heavenly afternoon. I settled down to enjoy it but the over after I arrived, a herd of New Forest ponies suddenly galloped out of the woods and on to the outfield around deep extra cover. Wild Horses Stopped Play. I watched a lot of baseball in the US, and loved that too, but somehow only cricket produces stuff like this.

TEMPUS FUGIT
Matthew Engel, *Notes by the Editor*, 2005

In the Wanderers media centre, in the midst of the splendidly eventful January Test match between South Africa and England, I was passed one day by a familiar figure, bustling out of the TV commentary box, far too cross about something to say "Good morning". I did hear him say (to himself, I think) the words "Extraordinary behaviour!" in a voice reminiscent of Lady Bracknell or Bertie Wooster's Aunt Agatha. Perhaps someone had put a mouse under his chair or uttered a profanity like "Darn!" or "Drat!" On November 24 this year, Ian Botham, the greatest tearaway ever to win the Ashes for England, will be 50. All England will be hoping the Ashes come back home before he gets there. In the meantime, go easy, Beefy. And welcome to middle age.

OH, WHAT'S THE POINT? Matthew Engel, *Notes by the Editor*, 2006

If there is one thought that I've tried to bang home most from this pulpit, it's this: a complex game needs simple structures. That's one reason why the Ashes were so appealing: you didn't need to be an expert or a statistician to work out who needed to do what. Yet administrators remain addicted to trying to achieve too many objectives at once. Thus, with all the bonus points and fractional over-rate penalties, the ECB has made the County Championship fairly incomprehensible. But that's nothing. Take a look, if you can face it, at our Cricket in South Africa section: "Bonus points awarded for the first 85 overs of each team's innings. One bonus batting point was awarded for the first 100 runs and 0.02 of a point for every subsequent run... Gauteng 20.18 pts, Northerns 4.94."

It got worse. Consider Sri Lanka: "... 0.1 pt for each wicket taken and 0.005 pt for each run scored up to 400... Galle 11.925 pts, Ragama 3.795." The attendance for one Sri Lankan provincial match in early 2005 was reported as zero; I'm surprised they got that many. Under the circumstances, congratulations to Zimbabwe Cricket, who were unable to tell us, despite repeated requests, what points system, if any, was in operation for their domestic tournament. I was rather relieved, frankly.

BRIEFLY NOTED

Soon after Matthew Engel assumed the editorship, he introduced a chronicle of "remarkable and eccentric cricket happenings outside first-class cricket". It was a rich seam. Here is a selection:

• An elderly woman pushing her bicycle past the ground at Burghill, Herefordshire, was taken to hospital after being hit by a six in a game against Hay-on-Wye. "It was certainly very unlucky," said the Burghill club chairman Len Sparrow, "especially as the lad who hit it normally can't play leg-side."

• Andrew Flintoff, 15, a pupil at Ribbleton Hall High School, Preston, hit 234 not out in only 20 overs with 20 sixes and 20 fours, for St Anne's against Fulwood and Broughton.

• Dave Cutting, 26, was bitten by an adder as he went out to bat at Hastings, Sussex.

• More than 60 people offered to give a home to a stray mongrel who ran on to the pitch at Trent Bridge as Merv Hughes was about to deliver the first ball of the Third Test. Graham and Sally Bosnall from Derby, who adopted him, followed the example of the staff at the RSPCA shelter and called him Merv.

- Ian Harris, of the Veryan club near Truro, who continued playing after losing a leg in a farm accident in 1987, was told by the Cornwall Umpires' Association that he could not bat with a runner under Law 2.5, which only covers injuries received during the match. MCC said their interpretation was over-zealous and the umpires relented.

- Despite many protests, the name of the Bat and Ball pub at Broadhalfpenny Down, traditional resort of the Hambledon players, was changed by the landlord to Natterjacks.

- Sharon Scott of Kington, Herefordshire, was taken to hospital for observation after being hit on the head by a six struck by her husband, Clive, while she was wheeling their baby round the boundary. "She probably cost me a century," Clive said. "I went into my shell for a while after that."

- The former England captain Brian Close, playing for Norma Major's XI against the EMP Bunburys, was caught one-handed in the gully by the former Rolling Stone Bill Wyman, who had a cigarette in his other hand.

- A London insurance broker paid £6,000 at a benefit auction for a short-sleeved shirt said to have been worn by Brian Lara during his innings of 375. Tipped off by a friend, he later watched the video and discovered that Lara wore a long-sleeved shirt throughout.

- Blair Sellers, playing for South Melbourne in the Dowling Shield Under-16 competition, hit a lofted drive that was stopped by the back of a seagull's head, turning a certain four into two. He was not unduly upset by this until he was bowled for 98. The seagull recovered.

- Prince Charles was bowled first ball by 10-year-old Wajid Khan at a Kwik Cricket demonstration at The Oval.

- Local councillors in Ripon, Yorkshire, rejected an attempt to name the new bypass Sir Leonard Hutton Way. It will be called the Ripon By-Pass.

- A cage has had to be erected on the square of the Earl of Bessborough's ground, Stansted Park in Hampshire, to protect a green-winged orchid, one of only 13 specimens known to have grown in England in 1996.

- A fielder who chased a ball hit out of the ground down a steep hill brought it back by bus. Paul Crabb, playing for Ilfracombe Rugby Club in Devon against Woolacombe, caught up with the ball a quarter of a mile from the ground at Hele. When he saw the bus coming, he decided to hop on it. The driver was sporting enough to overlook the fact that he did not have the 46p for his fare.

- November 14 was officially declared David Boon day by the premier of Tasmania, Tony Rundle.

- Philip Halden, a British businessman kidnapped in Colombia and held in the jungle by guerrillas for eight months, taught his captors cricket after carving a bat with a machete. But he said his kidnappers and his fellow hostages preferred playing soccer and, when the bat broke, he was not encouraged to carve another one.

- Geoffrey Boycott's TV commentaries have made him a cult figure in India. One group of schoolboys were given six of the best by their headmaster for constantly imitating Boycott and describing everything as "roobbish".

- The Prince of Wales declared himself "absolutely knackered" after facing three balls from a schoolboy at the Sinhalese Sports Club on a royal visit to Colombo.

- Jennifer Christian drove on to the field in the middle of a match in Dorset, slid to a halt, flung her car keys at the man fielding in the gully and ran off, leaving their two children strapped in the car. Her husband Eric drove off after her and took no further part in the game, between the Dorchester Third XI and the Parley Montys from Wimborne. He refused to comment, but team-mates believed he had promised to look after the children that afternoon.

- The village team from Stoke Canon, Devon, has disbanded after other teams refused to play them because of the quality of their teas. The club had failed to replace their regular tea-maker, Vi Dolling, after she retired in 1993. Younger wives and girlfriends were less keen, and the men were forced to make the teas themselves. "Some of the players made really terrible sandwiches," said the captain Tim Keehner. "Our teas became notorious."

- Dave Kachargis, 40, collapsed and died of a heart attack moments after making his highest ever score. Kachargis, captain of Old Parkonians in Essex, weighed 19 stone and was known as "Honey Monster". His wife Suzanne said: "It was the perfect way for him to go."

- Gregson CC and the Pressbox's XI of Lancaster claimed to have played the last match of the old millennium in the UK after continuing under floodlights until 4.55 p.m. on December 31, 1999. Soup was served at teatime.

- Paul McIntosh, a cricket-mad 11-year-old from Northampton, named his new pet rabbit "Hansie" after the South African captain, Hansie Cronje, three days before Cronje's downfall for his role in the match-fixing scandal. "We couldn't believe it," said Paul's mother, Elaine. "Our nine-year-old, Lauren, has been telling everybody that our rabbit has been arrested."

- MCC has been selling an "official Lord's ball" stamped "made in England", which turned out to be almost entirely made in Pakistan.

- The Graces, Britain's first openly homosexual team, have applied to join the Surrey Cricket Board. The side includes former Yorkshire League and minor county players. "People think we're just a load of old queens who think we look good in white, but actually we can and do play well," said captain Ian Crossland. "Sport is one of the last bastions of male homophobia." One of WG's great-granddaughters, Rosemary Douglas, complained: "They are cashing in on the Grace name and it is unsuitable for this team to do so."

- A horse chestnut that Geoff Boycott practised against as a schoolboy has been shortlisted for the title "Greatest Tree in Yorkshire".

- Tom Gueterbock approached the Wisden.com website to help publicise the sale of his £495,000 home in Battersea, south London, which he thought might particularly appeal to Indian cricket fans. The address was 10 Dulka Road.

- Charlie Watts, the Rolling Stones drummer, nominated John Arlott's commentary of Jim Laker taking 19 wickets against Australia at Old Trafford in 1956 as one of his *Desert Island Discs*.

- Carlisle Cricket Club held a minute's silence in memory of their former player and groundsman, Leonard Brunton, and then rang his home to ask if flowers should be sent. Mr Brunton answered the phone; there had been a misunderstanding.

- Minor Counties umpire Steve Kuhlmann, in Torquay to take charge of the game between Devon and Berkshire, was kicked out of his hotel after asking for fresh fruit instead of a cooked breakfast.

- Players from the Nerrena club in Victoria were served green-speckled cupcakes for tea by rivals Inverloch. They later claimed the cakes were laced with marijuana. "I thought, gee, this is pretty good, they usually feed us crap," said Nerrena player Tim Clark. He ate five, other players also tucked in and then their game went to pieces. One player took nearly 20 minutes to put on his pads, while two others broke out in hysterical laughter and fled the pitch for drinks of water. Nerrena lost by 50 runs and were relegated.

SECTION SEVEN

Farewells

INCLUDING:

Close of Play

T he obituaries are one of the enduring joys of *Wisden* – cogent summings-up of the great, the good, and the occasionally marginal and eccentric figures who have left their mark on cricket. Before Matthew Engel became editor in 1993, they could be a little hit and miss, with truly major figures promoted to the front of the book and left in the hands of one writer, who might or might not provide an adequate summation of the career. Since Engel assumed control they have simply glittered – beautifully written and paced, charming, sometimes funny, and always deeply humane, an attempt to see the whole person. Before, they were often – in Old *Wisden* style – recitations of facts and numbers; by my average shalt thou know me. Now, they divine the man (or woman – women are not ignored) behind the statistics, and trace the life – often difficult – after cricket, that all-consuming world which, once one's playing days are over, can leave a vacuum.

There are some fine leave-takings here – Compton, Cowdrey, Hutton, Godfrey Evans. I have had to compress *Wisden's* farewell to Don Bradman, but hope I have retained some of its epic quality. A good dozen of the entries are of players who were in their prime in this period and died tragically – in the case of Ben Hollioake unbearably – young. Chris Balderstone, Sylvester Clarke, Malcolm Marshall, Keith Boyce, Phil Carrick, Roy Fredericks, David Hookes, and more, too many more. How soon the sun sets. Yet those men whose pomp we remember rub shoulders with figures from a distant era – Frank Woolley, Percy Fender, Bill Ponsford, legendary players who one forgets lived into this modern era. This period also marks the deaths of many of those who communicated the game to the public – Arlott, of course, Johnston, the monolith that was E. W. Swanton, the brilliant but brittle Alan Gibson, the forever smiling Peter West.

Wisden's treatment of public figures who had some involvement in cricket is always a source of delight. Great writer, sometime cricketer, lifelong fan Samuel Beckett, for example, who "had two first-class games for Dublin University against Northamptonshire in 1925 and 1926, scoring 35 runs in his four innings and conceding 64 runs without taking a wicket." So much more important than *Waiting for Godot*. In the 1990 *Wisden*, wherein Beckett is memorialised, it amused me that a groundsman called William Bowles was given an obituary three times the length of the great writer. Terence Rattigan, "the famous play-writer", is also included here. "He was an elegant stroke player, but unsound" seems a definitive summing up of the career. And who else but *Wisden* would, in its obituary of an Archbishop of Canterbury, choose as its most salient fact that he "was a useful schoolboy cricketer at Merchant Taylors, Crosby, where he was opening bat and captain".

But perhaps my favourite obituary is of the Worcestershire and England leg-spinner Roly Jenkins, whose skill, commitment and love of the game are, in death, brought beautifully to life. That, in many ways, is the test of a great obituary: we do not weep at the loss but celebrate the life; not dwell in the past but catch a glimpse of a perpetual present. "He will forever be associated with long afternoons at Worcester, running up to bowl his leg-breaks in his cap (though he batted without one) with a seaman's gait (though his furthest posting during the war was fire-watching at the top of Worcester Cathedral) and punctuating the game with a very mellow sort of humour." If only the conclusion to this obituary were true of them all: "He never lost his love of cricket, or cricket talk. 'We're given memories so we can have roses in December,' he once said."   S. M.

ANTHONY AINLEY   2005

AINLEY, ANTHONY, who died on May 3, 2004, aged 71, was an actor and a keen club cricketer for The Stage and London Theatres CC. "He was an eccentric and very effective opening bat who appeared in full body padding, sunblock, helmet and swimming goggles," according to his fellow-actor Christopher Douglas, "and he had a penchant for charging down the track and smashing the ball back over the bowler's head." Ainley followed his father Henry on to the stage, but found his greatest success on television as The Master, the arch-enemy of Doctor Who, in the 1980s. At one club game at the time, Ainley's fame preceded him, and the *Sutton & Cheam Herald* ran a headline above its match report proclaiming that "Inter-Galactic Terror" had been visited upon Surrey. A complex character, he usually took his cricket teas alone in his car – possibly because, according to one report, he "despised cheeses of all kinds".

GUBBY ALLEN   1990

ALLEN, SIR GEORGE OSWALD BROWNING (GUBBY), CBE, TD, who died on November 29, 1989, aged 87, had a stronger influence on the welfare and development of cricket than anyone since Lord Harris over a period of more than 50 years. For his services to the game he was made CBE in 1974 and knighted in 1986.

Sir George ("Gubby", as he was universally known) was born in Sydney on July 31, 1902. His father, believing firmly in the value of an English education, brought the family to England when he was six. A mere 27 years later he was elected to the committee of MCC. By impressing his seniors with his strong views and a general interest in the game, he had quickly been recognised as good committee material, and by 1933 he was treading the corridors of power, familiarising himself with the inner workings of Lord's.

After service in the Second World War, early on in an anti-aircraft battery and later as an intelligence officer, rising to the rank of lieutenant-colonel, Allen returned to Lord's fully aware that cricket needed revitalising and determined to bring this about. With the help of other like-minded spirits he was soon disturbing the peace. In 1949 Allen launched his campaign for action by proposing the election of famous retired professionals to honorary life-membership of MCC, an imaginative and popular move. In the same year he successfully nominated H. S. Altham for the key post of Treasurer against strong opposition, a measure of his growing influence, and he became the driving force behind the formation of the MCC Youth Cricket Association and its related coaching scheme.

This brought to an end Allen's first period of administrative activity. By now he was ready to assume the chairmanship of the Test Selection Committee, a post he held for seven momentous years from 1955 to 1961. Most of the selectors' deliberations in this period had a successful outcome. Some of their choices were inspired, notably Washbrook, Sheppard and Compton in the last three Tests in 1956 against Australia. The loss of the Ashes in 1958–59 and the failure to regain them in 1961 were major disappointments, but winning home series at the expense of West Indies, India, South Africa and New Zealand was ample compensation. Allen laid down one principle for selection: class before averages. Everything was now falling into place for him.

He was President of MCC in 1963–64, and in 1964 he became Treasurer, holding this influential post for 12 years. As Treasurer he had much to do with the setting up of the Cricket Council and with its subordinate executive bodies, the Test and County Cricket Board and the National Cricket Association. During all this time he was England's representative on ICC. His period of office at Lord's was full of incident. At one time or another he had to give his attention to the over-rate, the lbw law (he always regretted not having opposed the 1935 change more vigorously), the size of the ball, improvements to Lord's, the Packer affair, the problem of bouncers, the front-foot no-ball law and, not least, the throwing crisis of 1958–61, for which he enlisted the help of Sir Donald Bradman.

Allen's deep knowledge and unique ability to advise on any aspect of cricket was based on his playing experience at the highest level, although he could never find the time to make either 1,000 runs or take 100 wickets in a season. At Eton the groundwork was laid for future success. His housemaster, C. M. Wells, a notable all-round sportsman, was in charge of cricket and an important influence in his development, and there was George Hirst to give encouragement in moments of stress. In school matches Winchester rather than Harrow felt the full fury of his onslaughts.

By 1921, his third year in the XI, he was a genuinely quick bowler who could make useful runs, and he was chosen to play for Middlesex in two matches before going up to Cambridge. In 1922 he had a match analysis of nine for 78 in the innings defeat of Oxford at Lord's, taking expert advantage of a helpful pitch, and his total for the Cambridge season was 49 wickets at 15 each. The following year he took a further 45 wickets at 18.88 each for the University, but at Lord's he suffered a recurrence of a muscle strain in his side and bowled only 15 overs without a wicket.

After going down after his second year, Allen remained a true amateur and played first-class cricket only when his work in the City permitted. He took trouble to keep himself fit by playing squash regularly and playing good-quality club cricket at weekends. That he was able to step up a gear and invariably make his mark was a tribute to his natural ability and dedication. He had a superb action with a rhythmical run-up and full follow-through, and it needed only a little fine-tuning to be running smoothly. In 1924, at Trent Bridge, his six for 31 in 13 overs wrecked Nottinghamshire's second-innings and helped Middlesex win a memorable match by 27 runs after being forced to follow on 209 runs behind.

In 1925 he made the first of his 11 first-class centuries: Allen (130) and Haig (98) put on 193 for the ninth wicket for the Gentlemen at The Oval. Selection for the Test Trial followed in 1926, but the sudden emergence of Larwood was to delay his first taste of Test cricket. In June 1929 he achieved his most spectacular analysis, ten for 40 at Lord's against the reigning champions, Lancashire, having been brought on as first change because he did not take the field until almost midday. He had been working earlier in the day. All but one of his ten wickets were taken after lunch, and his achievement remains unique in a county match at Lord's.

In 1930 his chance finally came against Australia at Lord's, but it proved to be a torrid baptism with Australia amassing more than 700 on the plumbest of pitches. He conceded 115 runs, failed to take a wicket and did not play again in the series. He did, however, score 57 in the second-innings and help his captain, Chapman, add 125 for the sixth wicket, and the following year, going in at No. 9, he made 122 against New Zealand at Lord's, putting on 246 with Ames (137) for the eighth wicket.

Five for 14 in New Zealand's first innings at The Oval in the Second Test emphasised his potential as a Test player. Even so, Allen's selection for the 1932–33 tour of Australia was widely criticised, yet by normal, orthodox methods he played a leading part in regaining the Ashes, claiming 21 wickets at 28.23 apiece and more than once making useful runs. His refusal to have any truck with Bodyline and his general conduct made him the prime candidate for the captaincy on MCC's next visit.

The 1936 series against India saw him captain England to a 2–0 victory in the three Tests, his personal contribution being 20 wickets for an average of 16.50, and thus the greatest prize in cricket was his: the captaincy of MCC in Australia. England lost the series 2–3 after leading 2–0 against all the odds. Bad luck with the weather and Bradman's wonderful batting tipped the scales against Allen, and yet the tour was a triumphant success. By his efforts on and off the field, the proper relationship between the old antagonists was restored and goodwill abounded once again. At Brisbane in the First Test, and before his exertions had drained his reserves of energy, he took eight wickets for 107 and made 103 runs. Allen could have been available for the 1938 series, but Hammond, newly turned amateur, found favour with Sir Pelham Warner, the chairman of selectors.

After the war, at the age of 45, he undertook to lead MCC in the West Indies in 1947–48. Though he was never fully fit and the opposition, with Worrell, Weekes and Walcott in their ranks, were too strong, he again proved to be the ideal touring captain. Nothing was too much trouble for him in seeing to the needs of his men. At home he confined himself to a few games for Middlesex and an annual return to Fenner's for the Free Foresters, when as often as not he made a century, a reminder of how many runs he would have made had he not largely concentrated on high pace. His highest score of 180 was made for them against the University in 1948.

In all he played in 265 matches, making 9,232 runs for an average of 28.67, capturing 788 wickets at 22.23, and taking 131 catches; he was a splendid close fielder. He took ten wickets in a match on nine occasions. His Test record was 750 runs at 24.19 and 81 wickets for 29.37. With his death cricket lost one of its most devoted and dedicated servants. Active almost to the end, he returned to his home from hospital to die only a pitch's length from the Pavilion at Lord's and the stand next door now named after him.

BILL ALLEY   2005

ALLEY, WILLIAM EDWARD, died on November 26, 2004, aged 85. Bill Alley became a Somerset legend, although he was born in Australia and did not make his county debut until 1957, when he was 38. In 1961 he was the last man ever to score 3,000 first-class runs in a season. He later became a Test umpire, and one of the game's most durable characters.

Alley arrived in Sydney in the 1940s, working as a labourer, nightclub bouncer, blacksmith's assistant and oyster fisherman. He was also making a name as a New South Wales batsman, and as a boxer: he was unbeaten in 28 fights as a welter-weight. But boxing – and almost cricket too – came to an end after a gruesome accident in the Adelaide nets in 1946. His team-mate Jock Livingston hooked a ball that went through the net and poleaxed Alley in the adjacent one. He needed 60 stitches in his jaw and was in a coma for two days. He pulled through, but the accident set back his hopes of touring England in 1948. A year earlier, Bradman had hinted that Alley was likely to win a spot on Australia's first post-war tour, to New Zealand early in 1946 – but Ron Hamence went instead. Alley had even acquired a dozen new white shirts for the trip.

After his first wife died in childbirth (their son, Ken, also died young in an army accident), Alley decided to take up an offer to play in the Lancashire leagues, and enjoyed ten prolific seasons with Colne and Blackpool. Apart from a tour of India with a strong Commonwealth XI in 1949–50, when he plundered two unbeaten double centuries, it appeared that Alley's first-class days were over: some counties made offers, but the sums involved were hardly more for six-days-a-week cricket than for Saturdays only in the leagues. Finally, though, he decided to give county cricket a go – with Somerset, he later wrote, "because of the sheer magic of the name".

Alley was no stylist, a left-hander who favoured the leg side and the horizontal bat; but every now and then he would play a beautiful cover-drive. The man himself summed up his own philosophy succinctly: "If the ball is there to be hit, for Christ's sake hit it." And in 1961 he hit it everywhere. "The crease was his God-given territory," wrote David Foot. "He occupied it with the mannerisms of a lusty, lovable black-sheep squire." In 1960, Alley had made only 807 runs at 23. But now, aged 42, he was relentless. His 3,019 runs at 56.96 included 11 centuries, among them his career-best 221 not out against Warwickshire at Nuneaton. His Somerset team-mate Roy Virgin preferred his 156 at Northampton: "Malcolm Scott, the left-arm spinner, was bowling, and Bill was almost placing his field for him. He'd say 'No, you want that bloke at mid-wicket a bit squarer', and then he'd smash the ball over the chap's head anyway." He even made 134 and 95 against the touring Australians.

The following year Alley persuaded his captain to use his right-arm seamers rather more, and he finished with 112 wickets (at only 20.74 apiece) to go with 1,915 runs. He was record-conscious enough to rue the missing 85 runs that cost him an even rarer double. His bowling fell away a little in later seasons, though team-mates remember how nimbly he would run in. And he continued to field brilliantly in the gully ("Bill just plucked legitimate cut-shots out of the air," said Virgin) and collect his annual 1,000 runs every year bar one until 1968.

Bill kept talking too. Once he waved a handkerchief at Fred Trueman, and said it would do as a thigh-pad against him. His forthright manner offended some of his team-mates, and this appears to have cost him the chance of the county captaincy in 1965 after he had deputised the previous year. He played on and would have been there after his 50th birthday, except that Somerset offered him terms for one-day games only. He angrily turned them down and stomped off to join the umpires' list. Fearless in that role too, he stood in ten Tests and nine one-day internationals between 1974 and 1981. But he was too trigger-happy for some batsmen and he had several seasons off the international list, which he put down to aggrieved captains' reports; he finally retired in 1984.

Alley retreated to a smallholding in Somerset with Betty, his second wife, and was happy raising chickens and shooting rabbits. Ill-health marred his later years, although knee replacements gave him temporary relief: spotted striding up the pavilion stairs at Lord's in his mid-seventies, he announced that his brand-new knees were tempting him to make a comeback. To umpiring? "Stuff that, mate – I'm talking about playing!" His funeral service was held in St James's Church, next to the ground in Taunton. Merv Kitchen, another Somerset player-turned umpire, observed that the setting was appropriate, as Alley had hit so many balls into the graveyard.

LALA AMARNATH   2001

AMARNATH, NANIK BHARDWAJ, died on August 5, 2000, aged 88. "Lala" Amarnath scored India's first Test century and went on to become Indian cricket's patriarchal figure: as selector, manager, coach and broadcaster, as well as in a literal sense – his three sons became first-class cricketers and two played in Tests. Amarnath, a Punjabi, was also the first to kick against the stifling domination of Indian cricket by the local princes and their imperial backers. It severely damaged his career. Amarnath's figures in his 24 Tests are nothing special, but they do no justice to either his spasmodic brilliance or his enduring influence.

From a poor background in Lahore, when it was still part of India, he rose to prominence by scoring 109 ("a brilliant display" – *Wisden*) for Southern Punjab against MCC in 1933–34, and a few weeks later became a star with a century on his Test debut, India's first Test at home, at the genteel old Gymkhana ground in Bombay. With India facing an innings defeat, he took on the England attack and played, so he said later, "as if possessed by a mysterious power". He hit 83 in 78 minutes, hooking Nichols and Clark with confidence and going down the pitch to hit Hedley Verity. Slowing just a fraction, he reached his century in 117 minutes. According to Mihir Bose: "Amarnath was engulfed with spectators, garlanded and congratulated while the band played *God Save the King*... As the day's play ended, women tore off their jewellery to present it to him, Maharajahs made gifts of money, and India hailed a hero." England's eventual easy win was almost forgotten in the hysteria.

Though he did little in the remaining two Tests of that series, Amarnath was by far the best player – with bat and ball – in the early stages of the unhappy Indian tour of 1936, captained by the Maharaj Kumar of Vizianagram ("Vizzy"). Furthermore, Amarnath knew he was the best player and, having waited, padded up, during an unusually big partnership in the match against Minor Counties at Lord's, he was infuriated to be told that other batsmen would be promoted ahead of him. He swore at the captain and tour treasurer, and was sensationally sent home. The team's subsequent failures, a commission of inquiry, and history as written by people with a more egalitarian world-view than Vizzy have all combined to exonerate him. But it meant a 12-year gap between his third Test and his fourth. He remained a force in Indian cricket, however, scoring 241 for Hindus v The Rest in 1938–39. But when he visited England with the 1946 team, by then rehabilitated, his bowling was more potent than his batting, most dramatically in the first post-war Test, at Lord's, when he reduced England's first innings to 70 for four by dismissing Hutton, Washbrook, Compton and Hammond. "After a shuffling run of only three paces, he bowled off the wrong foot," said *Wisden* with slightly shocked admiration, "but he kept an almost impeccable length, moved his in-swingers probably more than any bowler in England, and mixed these with a cut leg-break of some venom."

The following year he was appointed India's captain for their first tour of Australia when Vijay Merchant withdrew. But with Bradman at his most merciless, India were understandably overwhelmed. Amarnath did little himself in the five Tests, averaging 14 with the bat, and taking 13 wickets, although he was magnificent against state sides. His 228 against Victoria contained, Neil Harvey said, the best cover-driving he ever saw. He remained captain against West Indies in 1948–49 and in Bombay narrowly failed to lead India to their first Test victory. Then cricket politics again turned against him. There were arguments about money and second-class treatment (the visitors were treated royally; Indian players were dumped in second-class hotels). Amarnath fell foul of the powerful board secretary, Anthony De Mello, who was furious with the man he had dragged "out of the gutter and made captain of India" and had him suspended for "continuous misbehaviour and breach of discipline".

Amarnath sought refuge in the Lancashire League. But he was buoyed by support from Bradman, who called him "a splendid ambassador", and by De Mello's subsequent fall from power. He was restored, though reduced to the ranks, in 1951–52 and took part when India at last won a Test, against England in Madras; passed over for the humiliating 1952 tour of England; and then given back the captaincy against Pakistan in 1952–53, apparently at the insistence of – of all people – Vizzy.

Although India won their first series, Amarnath's contributions as a player were minor, and yet more internal machinations meant he left the job in anger. However, the wheel keeps spinning in Indian cricket and Amarnath's reputation grew with the years. He became chairman of selectors, most famously insisting on the inclusion of off-spinner Jasu Patel at Kanpur in 1959–60, which led to an historic win over Australia. Lala also supervised the development of his sons: Surinder, too, made a century on debut; Mohinder ("Jimmy") played 69 Tests. He was a well-informed and humorous commentator, and in old age he acquired widespread affection as the nation's leading source of cricket anecdotes. But he never lost his habit of speaking his mind. "He was an impetuous man," said his contemporary, Mushtaq Ali, "quick to love and quick to fight." The Indian prime minister, A. B. Vajpayee, called him an icon.

LES AMES 1991

AMES, LESLIE ETHELBERT GEORGE, CBE, who died suddenly at his home in Canterbury on February 26, 1990, aged 84, was without a doubt the greatest wicket-keeper-batsman the game has so far produced; and yet, at the time he was playing, it used to be said there were better wicket-keepers than Ames, and that he was in the England team because of his batting. If this was so, would Jardine, for example, have preferred him to Duckworth in Australia in 1932–33? Surely not.

When fully fit, Ames was England's first-choice wicket-keeper from 1931 to 1939, when he virtually gave up the job. For Kent, he was an integral part of their Championship side from 1927 to the first match of 1951, when a sharp recurrence of back trouble, which had dogged him for so long, brought his career to an end while he was actually at the crease. By this time he had amassed 37,248 runs, average 43.51, made 102 hundreds, including nine double-hundreds, and passed 1,000 runs in a season 17 times, going on to 3,000 once and 2,000 on five occasions. He had had a direct interest in 1,121 dismissals, of which more than 1,000 were effected when he was keeping wicket. His total of 418 stumpings is easily a record.

Ames represented England in 47 Tests, making 2,434 runs, including eight hundreds, and 97 dismissals (74 catches and 23 stumpings). He toured Australia with MCC in 1928–29 as reserve wicket-keeper to Duckworth, and would have played in the final Test at Melbourne, purely as a batsman, but for breaking a finger keeping to Larwood. Instead, he made his debut against South Africa at The Oval in 1929 and toured the Caribbean under F. S. G. Calthorpe in the following winter. In the second of the representative matches (since granted full Test status) he helped Hendren in a match-winning stand of 237 for the fourth wicket in England's second innings, his 105 being the first century by an England wicket-keeper. In the fourth and final match, at Kingston, he hit his highest Test score of 149. Against New Zealand in 1931, Ames (137) and G. O. B. Allen (122) put on 246 together for the eighth wicket at Lord's, which has remained a record in Test matches for that wicket. The runs, which rescued England from a paltry 190 for seven, were made in under three hours, while at Christchurch in 1932–33 he and

Hammond "flogged the bowling all over the ground" to the tune of 242 in 144 minutes for the fourth wicket.

More restraint was expected of him at Lord's in 1934 against Australia on the first afternoon, when he and Leyland came together and added 129 in what was to prove a crucial partnership. Failure then, and England instead of Australia would have been caught on the sticky wicket so brilliantly exploited by Verity. Ames used to say that he was more proud of this innings of 120 than of all his others; *Wisden* simply described it as "inspiring". In 1935, against South Africa at The Oval, he made 123 before lunch on the final day, a tremendous effort and still the most runs in the morning session of a Test match. In 1938 at Lord's, Hammond (240) and Ames (83) added 186 for England's sixth wicket against Australia, and that winter in South Africa, on his last major tour, Ames again helped his captain in a major partnership. At Cape Town, in the Second Test, the pair put on 197 in 145 minutes for the fourth wicket, both scoring hundreds. Ames finished the series with an average of 67.80 and a career average in Tests of 40.56.

Ames was a correct player with a fluent classical style; a magnificent driver, especially when moving out to the pitch. When set, he employed the lofted drive over the inner ring of fielders with rare judgment and skill, and he could turn good-length balls into half-volleys on lightning feet. Woe betide any bowler who started dropping short: he would be hammered to the cover boundary, or despatched to leg with powerful hooks or pulls.

On the Bodyline tour he took the thunderbolts of Larwood and Voce with quiet efficiency. His style was unobtrusive; there were no flamboyant gestures. He saw the ball so early that he was invariably in the right position without having to throw himself about. His glovework was neat and economical, his stumpings almost apologetic.

During the Second World War, Ames rose to the rank of Squadron-Leader in the RAF and played a little one-day cricket, even taking a hat-trick against Epsom CC with his slow spinners. In the five post-war seasons before his retirement, playing now as a batsman, he enjoyed an Indian summer, adding nearly 10,000 runs to his already formidable aggregate. In 1947, and again in 1948, he made seven hundreds, his total of 2,137 runs in the Championship in 1947 being reminiscent of 1933.

In 1950 he reached his 100th hundred in brilliant style to win the match against Middlesex during the Canterbury Week, becoming only the twelfth player to achieve this milestone. His batting had lacked none of its old virility and panache, but that winter, captaining the Commonwealth team in India, he was often worried by the back trouble which was soon to end his playing days.

From 1960–74 he was secretary/manager of Kent, a post he filled with conspicuous success, commanding the respect of the players by his sense of discipline and absolute fairness. From years of failure Kent improved steadily until they won the Championship in 1970. In retirement he remained fit and active, spending many pleasurable days on the golf course, where his natural sense of timing stood him in good stead. If ever there was a true Man of Kent it was he. The attendance of a thousand people at his memorial service in Canterbury Cathedral was a worthy tribute to him.

BILL ANDREWS

ANDREWS, WILLIAM HARRY RUSSELL (BILL), who died on January 9, 1989, aged 80, welcomed strangers with the cheery greeting, "Shake the hand that bowled Bradman", after he performed the feat at Taunton in 1938. Andrews was always honest enough to record that this happened only after the Australian captain had helped himself to 202 against Somerset. He was in the true tradition of county all-rounders – a tall, right-handed fast-medium bowler, who kept a good length and moved the ball sharply, and a dangerous late-order bat. But in the extra tradition of the slightly rebellious or eccentric characters in which Somerset cricket has specialised, Andrews led a chequered career, almost proud of the fact that he had been sacked four times by the county: twice as player and twice as coach. In his autobiography, *The Hand That Bowled Bradman*, published in 1973, he declared generously that he bore the county no grudge. He recorded a first-class career running from 1930 to 1947 before returning to Somerset as coach, as well as playing with Devon.

JOHN ARLOTT

Signing off: John Arlott commentating on his final Test match, at Lord's in 1980, accompanied by Keith Miller.

ARLOTT, LESLIE THOMAS JOHN, OBE, died at his home on Alderney on December 14, 1991, at the age of 77. Few men who have concentrated the interests of a lifetime on cricket have commanded as wide and thorough a knowledge of the game as John Arlott. When he was doing a commentary, or composing a portrait of a Tate or a Trueman, or writing a match report for *The Guardian*, he was at or near the centre of affairs. But he was equally an expert on interests connected with the game: its vast literature, extensive history and collection of artefacts were all within his purview. To fuel his activities he had great energy, the ability to work at speed, and the charm to elicit information from whatever source he was investigating. Add in the fact that he was a poet of some stature and that he enjoyed the laughter and company of friends, whom he loved to entertain in the most civilised way, and you have a man of deep humanity.

Of all Arlott's talents, it is his unique gift for commentary which will bring him lasting fame. And nothing became him more than the manner in which he quietly slipped away from the scene at the end of his final commentary at Lord's while the crowd stood and, along with the players of England and Australia, applauded.

Mike Brearley's tribute to John Arlott appears on page 1111.

GROUP CAPTAIN SIR DOUGLAS BADER 1983

BADER, GROUP CAPTAIN SIR DOUGLAS, CBE, DSO, DFC, the famous airman, who died on September 5, 1982, aged 72, was captain of St Edward's School, Oxford, in 1928. A good attacking bat and a useful fast-medium bowler, he later played for the RAF and in 1931 made 65, the top score, for them against the Army, a fixture which in those days had first-class status. He gained greater distinction at rugger, and at the time of the accident the following winter which cost him his legs he was in the running for an England cap.

DAVID BAIRSTOW 1998

BAIRSTOW, DAVID LESLIE, was found hanged at his home on January 5, 1998. He was 46. Reports said he had been suffering from depression: his wife was ill, he had financial troubles, he faced a drink-driving charge and was in pain from his own injuries. The news stunned cricket, especially as Bairstow had always seemed the most indomitable and least introspective of men, and led to much comment on the problems faced by retired sportsmen.

CHRIS BALDERSTONE 2001

BALDERSTONE, JOHN CHRISTOPHER, died suddenly at his home on March 6, 2000, aged 59; he had been suffering from cancer. Chris Balderstone – "Baldy" – was a formidably fit man who became a Test cricketer and an international umpire after a successful career in football. In the 1960s, he was a stylish inside-forward for Huddersfield Town and Carlisle United who played occasionally as an all-rounder for Yorkshire in the close season. However, when he passed 30, he was brought to Leicestershire by Ray Illingworth, and became primarily a cricketer. It quickly paid dividends: his cool-headed 41 not out won Leicestershire the inaugural Benson and Hedges final, and Balderstone the Gold Award.

However, his most famous day came a year later, and it was also Leicestershire's. On September 15, 1975, he was playing cricket at Chesterfield but had also committed himself to turn out for Doncaster Rovers against Brentford. This was the day Leicestershire won their first-ever Championship, which they secured with bowling bonus points. Towards the close, Balderstone was still batting and the Doncaster manager, Stan Anderson, was pacing the Belle Vue ground with increasing agitation. With the Championship decided, Balderstone could easily have given his wicket away and headed off to football, but it was not in his nature. He stayed till stumps were drawn, had to change in the car, played his usual solid game of football, then came back to complete his century next morning.

EDDIE BARLOW   2006

BARLOW, EDGAR JOHN, died on December 30, 2005, aged 65. Though not the most gifted or elegant of his outstanding, and largely lost, South African generation, Eddie Barlow was the most combative. Barlow came into Test cricket as a 21-year-old in December 1961, and was able to play 30 times before South Africa's exclusion in 1970. In Tests, he nearly always opened, but he was also an effective out-swing bowler, brilliant slip and dynamic personality who invested each game with such energy that one felt he could bat, bowl, field and organise the teas simultaneously. "He rolled up his sleeves high above his elbows, flexed his muscles and bounced on to the field like a prize fighter," wrote Rodney Hartman.

KEN BARRINGTON   Appreciation by Robin Marlar, 1982

There should be no need for reticence in anyone paying tribute to Ken Barrington. He died [aged 50] of a heart attack in his hotel room at the Holiday Inn in Barbados on March 14, 1981, the Saturday night of the Barbados Test, while serving as assistant-manager on the England tour of the West Indies. As a player, as a friend, as a businessman and latterly as a leader of England's cricketers in the field, he was a man who always did what he could and, when the chips were on the table for all to see, one who could be relied upon to give of his best, his uttermost. The world and especially the cricketing world cannot ask for more. That is why Ken Barrington, master of the malaprop, the man who slept not like a log but "like a lark", commanded such affection all over the world.

To my mind, the story of Ken's death is as heroic as so many of his innings. It came as a great shock in the spring of 1969 to learn that the chest pains which had led him to withdraw from a double-wicket competition in Melbourne had in fact been a heart attack. After due reflection, taking into account not only his family but the fact that, at 38, batting in Test matches, always Ken's particular forte, was not going to get easier, Ken Barrington retired. Immediately the cares of carrying England's rickety batting through the uncertain and far from satisfying 1960s slipped off his shoulders, like some leaden cloak. As he took to the village greens of charity cricket and to the golf courses where his game was good enough to be successfully competitive – and therefore a source of pleasure to a man who hated to be beaten – Ken Barrington's step seemed lighter and his stature in cricket enhanced. His admirers, both far and near, began to realise just how much private effort had gone into coping with "chuckers" and bouncers, as well as the vagaries of form and the whims of selectors.

None the less, a heart attack is a warning, a red light that never joins with amber and turns to green. Although he had managed tours to India, Pakistan and New Zealand, and indeed had had the well-deserved honour of leading the England party at the Melbourne Centenary Test, nothing in his managerial career had tested him quite like this final West Indian ordeal. As a player he had not only plundered bowlers on the great Indian subcontinent but, the son of a soldier who might well in other times have done tours in India of a different nature, he established such a good-humoured relationship there that win or lose, come triumph or disaster, the pressures of touring were easily absorbed. In Australia, where the results mattered more, his role was that of coach, so that the burdens were shared first with Doug Insole and then with Alec Bedser.

He was playing that same familiar part in the West Indies. Ironically, he had not been one of the early selections, but as an old player scarred in earlier wars against Hall and Griffith, he knew better than most the perils that a new manager, Alan Smith, and an inexperienced captain, Ian Botham, were flying into as they took on the world champions with their fast bowling quartet in the increasingly stormy Caribbean. In Guyana the heavy and persistent rain meant that the practice sessions which were his charge were suspended. They had been difficult in smaller islands like Antigua and St Vincent in the early weeks of the tour.

And then he had to take the team, badly defeated in the First Test and now with their morale increasingly affected by the start of the Jackman affair, as well as their collective lack of practice and form, to the one-day beating at Berbice, while Alan Smith began to play one of his best innings with the politicians. The events of those few days deeply disturbed Barrington. He was also worried about [his wife] Ann's imminent arrival if the tour was to be cancelled.

But once the party arrived safely in Barbados he seemed to relax. My own last, long and treasured conversation with him was in the happy atmosphere of a Cunarder's bridge, a party in the harbour which he himself had organised. Whatever he felt, he was full of hope for the more distant future, his absolute faith in the ability of Botham and Gatting made more significant by the summer of '81. He knew there were gaps in the England side, but he was old enough in the ways of cricket to know that they are not easily filled.

It was a little thing, at least in the context of that global conversation, that piled all the pressure back on to this caring man. At fielding practice it was Barrington who hit the ball that split Gooch's hand. Gooch was due to bat that day, and in fact played better than anyone – as he told me, without too much discomfort. However, Ken took it badly, as he was bound to do, but it was the way in which he said to Bernard Thomas, "I didn't mean to hurt him", that in retrospect gave the party's medical superintendent the first indication that events were getting out of proportion, upsetting the nervous balance. It was that night, with the Barringtons ready for bed, that the attack struck Ken down. Ann Barrington summoned Bernard Thomas, who was next door, and he knew at once that the attack had been instantaneously fatal. Next morning, when the team stood in Ken's memory, there were many tears.

SAMUEL BECKETT

1990

BECKETT, SAMUEL BARCLAY, who died in Paris on December 22, 1989, aged 83, had two first-class games for Dublin University against Northamptonshire in 1925 and 1926, scoring 35 runs in his four innings and conceding 64 runs without taking a wicket. A left-hand opening batsman, possessing what he himself called a gritty defence, and a useful left-arm medium-pace bowler, he had enjoyed a distinguished all-round sporting as well as academic record at Portora Royal School, near Enniskillen, and maintained his interest in games while at Trinity College, Dublin. Indeed, Beckett, whose novels and plays established him as one of the important literary figures of the twentieth century, bringing him the Nobel Prize for literature in 1969, never lost his affection for and interest in cricket.

KEITH BOYCE

1997

BOYCE, KEITH DAVID, who died on October 11, 1996, his 53rd birthday, played in 21 Test matches for West Indies in the early 1970s but was better-known for being one of the most exciting and successful imports into county cricket. He spent 12 years with Essex from 1966 to 1977, and it was appropriate – and maybe no coincidence – that these were years when Essex won nothing but had an enormous amount of fun.

He was an uncomplicated, aggressive fast bowler, sometimes slowed down by no-ball problems, and an equally aggressive if not always disciplined batsman, whose *tours de force* were all the more memorable for their irregularity. He was an obvious power in one-day cricket and was the first player to reach the 1,000 runs/100 wickets double in the Sunday League. But he occasionally translated his methods into Championship cricket: he scored a hundred in 58 minutes against Leicestershire in their Championship year of 1975, with no contrivance involved whatever. He then took 12 for 73 in the match. Perhaps only Essex of the 1970s could have failed to win such a contest.

SIR DONALD BRADMAN

2002

BRADMAN, SIR DONALD GEORGE, AC, the most effective batsman in cricket's history, died in Adelaide on February 25, 2001, at the age of 92, having been ill with pneumonia. He was born on August 27, 1908, with Australia, as a nation state, but seven years old; 25 years later, he had become and would remain its most illustrious citizen. A legion of obituarists recorded and analysed his skills, and such was his impact on the game and on society that some of their analogues – Winston Churchill, Jack Kennedy, Shakespeare, Diana, Princess of Wales, the Pope – did not appear unduly extravagant.

Donald Bradman was the youngest of the five children of George and Emily

One room, three greats: Don Bradman, one of *Wisden*'s Five Cricketers of the Century in 2000, at his home in Adelaide with Shane Warne (another of the Five) and Sachin Tendulkar, a batsman whose style The Don felt similar to his own.

Bradman. His father, a farmer and carpenter, was the son of Charles Bradman, who emigrated from East Anglia in 1852. Born at Cootamundra in the south-east corner of New South Wales, the young Don lived for three years on a farm at nearby Yeo, whereupon the family moved to Bowral, some 80 miles from Sydney and now the home of the Bradman Museum and Trust. These were humble beginnings. It was here that the legendary practice with golf ball and single stump was undertaken, employing the brick stand of the family water tank.

In 1920–21, the 12-year-old Bradman scored 115 not out for Bowral High School against Mittagong School, his first century, and when, a season later, one of the Bowral club first team failed to turn up, Bradman, their scorer, played instead and made 37 not out. It was his first game with adults. After a convincingly successful flirtation with tennis, he settled down determinedly to cricket and, in 1925–26, scored a triumphant 234 for Bowral against Wingello, for whom Bill O'Reilly was bowling. He joined the St George club in Sydney for the 1926–27 season and made 110 on debut against Petersham in the more sophisticated realms of city club cricket. He had adjusted seamlessly from dirt pitch to coir matting to turf, and, in December 1927, he made his first-class debut at Adelaide for New South Wales against South Australia. Not long past his 19th birthday, Bradman made 118.

Such marked achievement quickly led to Test selection a year later, but, as Australia were trounced by England at Brisbane by 675 runs on a sticky wicket alien to his youthful experience, he made only 18 and one, and was dropped for the first and last time in his international career. Returning for the Third Test at

Melbourne, he scored 79 and 112 amid tumultuous scenes as the crowd recognised the emergence of a genius and a likely upturn in Australian cricketing fortunes. They were not disappointed: Bradman hit another century at the MCG in the Fifth Test. Between these hundreds, he completed a marathon 340 not out against Victoria at Sydney; the following year, again at the SCG, he established a world first-class individual record of 452 not out in New South Wales's second innings against Queensland. Almost three-quarters of a century later, it remained the highest innings by an Australian and in Australia.

His introduction into the international arena was crowned by an astonishing first tour of England in 1930, when he assembled what remains the record sum for a series: 974 runs, with an average of 139.14, in the five Tests. This included 334 at Leeds, his highest Test score and then the highest such score ever, an innings watched by the young Len Hutton, who observed how carefully Bradman found the spaces between the fielders. But it was the 254 in his first Test at Lord's that Bradman considered his perfect innings, in that every shot, including the one when he was out, was exact in its technical assessment and operation. That fabled summer he made 2,960 runs, with a thousand before the end of May, and ten centuries. At the more material level, there was also a gift of £1,000, worth something like 40 times as much today, from the soap magnate, Arthur Whitelaw, which indicated that, although he was an amateur, his cricket was the serious key to Don Bradman's livelihood.

The West Indians were his next victims when they toured Australia in 1930–31, with 447 more Test runs flowing from his quicksilver blade. Then came the notorious Bodyline series against England. He missed the First Test of 1932–33 through illness, and Bill Bowes bowled him first ball in the Second, but he responded well with 103 not out in the second innings, his only hundred, as it transpired, of that controversial rubber. Douglas Jardine, the autocratic English captain, employed, as has been well rehearsed, intimidating leg-theory bowling, with Harold Larwood, along with Bill Bowes and Bill Voce, delivering short-pitched balls at high speed to a packed on-side field. There is little doubt that this ruthless campaign arose from an English despair over the ascendancy of Bradman. His riposte was to shift leg-wards and rap the ball through an almost deserted off side. England won the battle but lost the war, for Jardine's tactics were condemned as unsporting and perilous. Although Bradman's average was pared to 56.57 for the series, and this was considered a measure of containment, it is worth noting that the next best Test career average to Bradman's 99.94 (from a minimum 20 innings) is the 60.97 of South Africa's Graeme Pollock. Len Hutton's Test average is 56.67.

The rancour of the Bodyline series lingered, but there was a substantive element of reconciliation on the 1934 tour of England, when Australia regained the Ashes. After a comparatively tentative beginning to the tour, Bradman scored 304 in the Headingley Test, followed by 244 at The Oval, where he shared a record second-wicket stand of 451 with Bill Ponsford. Such heavy scoring sent his average for the series soaring to 94.75 from 758 runs, and he made 2,020 runs in that English summer. However, his health, which had for a year or so been troublesome, became critical when he fell victim to acute appendicitis. The cricketing world held its breath, but he recovered, although it was a year before he played first-class cricket again.

In pursuit of his business concerns, he moved to Adelaide and commenced playing for South Australia in 1935–36. The following season, when MCC toured under Gubby Allen, he was appointed captain of Australia. After an uneasy baptism, with two lost Tests, he rallied in characteristic fashion and saved the Ashes with spirited knocks of 270 at Melbourne (putting on 346 for the sixth wicket with Jack Fingleton after reversing Australia's batting order to counter a rain-affected pitch), 212 at Adelaide and 169, again at Melbourne. He averaged 90 from 810 runs in the series, and huge crowds cheered him on in noisy admiration.

Visiting England in 1938, he began excellently with a thousand runs by the end of May in an amazing seven innings, and overall he scored 2,429 on the tour, with 13 hundreds. In the Tests, he hit centuries at Nottingham, Lord's and Leeds and enjoyed an average of 108.50, although his exploits were overshadowed by Hutton's monumental endeavour in the final Test when he accumulated 364 to eclipse Bradman's Ashes record. Undaunted, Bradman launched into his own domestic season, 1938–39, with a stream of six consecutive centuries to equal C. B. Fry's record from 1901, and he ended it with a phenomenal average of 153.16 from seven innings in seven games. Soon, war came to rob him, as others, of manifold opportunities to add to his laurels. Statisticians may only muse over what his record might have been.

There were question marks over both the fitness and availability of the now 37-year-old Bradman for post-war cricket. He had an uncomfortable start to the 1946–47 MCC tour. In the First Test at Brisbane, he had laboured over 28 runs when, on the English submission, he was caught at second slip by Jack Ikin, the premier close-in fielder of his day and a chevalier among sportsmen. To Wally Hammond's chagrin, both Bradman and, more crucially, the umpire believed it was a bump ball; Bradman eschewed his ring-rustiness and flourished in what Neville Cardus termed a "Lazarus" innings of 187. In the next match, at Sydney, chiefly in a massive partnership of 405 with Sid Barnes, he scored 234, and went on to total 680 runs at an average of 97.14 for the series, a calamitous one for England.

The touring Indian party of 1947–48 was treated to even greater exercises in dominance, with Bradman notching 715 runs for an average of 178.75. It was also against these visitors, for an Australian XI at Sydney, that he completed his 100th century, all done and dusted in 295 innings. He was the first non-English batsman to reach this target, as well as the quickest to the mark before or since.

As well as nonpareil batsman, he was also now recognised as an astute and unbending captain. In 1948, he led the famed "Invincibles", a team still acknowledged by many commentators as the finest international combine ever fielded, on their unbeaten tour of England. Bradman himself made 2,428 runs at an average of 89.92, while in the Tests he scored 508 runs (72.57), including the 173 not out at Headingley that enabled the Australians to speed to a winning total of 404 for three on the final day. He celebrated his 40th birthday with 150 against the Gentlemen in his *adieu* to Lord's. But a fortnight earlier, in the final Test at The Oval, Eric Hollies had bowled him second ball for "the most famous duck in history" when, to cite perhaps the best-known cricket statistic, he required only four runs to preserve an overall Test average of 100.

Apart from three more first-class games in the 1948–49 season, including a valedictory century, that was, from the straightforward cricketing angle, that. An adequate compendium of his figures is difficult to draft. The awe and the majesty of this exceptional sportsman did lie more in his serial acquisition of runs than in the manner of his doing. Other cricketers might be prettier or more regal in demeanour (although it would be unfair to hint that he was unattractive to watch, such was the balance and command of his technique), but none could realistically expect to keep the scoreboards rattling so peremptorily.

Bradman totalled 28,067 first-class runs in 234 matches and 338 innings at an average of 95.14 including 117 centuries, 37 of them double centuries. In 62 Sheffield Shield games, he averaged 110.19 from 8,926 runs, with 36 hundreds. Of his 29 Test hundreds, there were 12 doubles including triples at Leeds in 1930 and 1934. Within those parameters may be traced a thousand intricacies of mathematical astonishment, but in the end they all subscribe to the one fundamental truth: that a man who is able to score a century every 2.88 innings and a double century every 9.13 innings has perfected a skill beyond normal imagining.

A photograph of Sir Donald Bradman with Harold Larwood and Dennis Lillee appears on page 1209.

Sir Eric Bullus

2002

BULLUS, SIR ERIC EDWARD, died on September 8, 2001, aged 94. As MP for Wembley North for almost a quarter of a century, he was the doyen of the Lords and Commons cricket team and in 1959 published a history of its activities. Although himself a virulently right-wing Tory, it is said he mourned the electoral defeat of Labour members with cricketing prowess.

Harry Calder

1996

CALDER, HARRY LAWTON, who died in Cape Town on September 15, 1995, aged 94, was both the youngest ever and the oldest surviving *Wisden* Cricketer of the Year. Calder was chosen as one of the "School Bowlers of the Year" in 1918 when there was no regular selection because of the war. He was in the Cranleigh XI for five years as a bowler of varied medium-paced spinners. But he played little cricket after leaving school, when he went to South Africa, and did not know he had ever been a Cricketer of the Year until he was tracked down in 1994.

Phil Carrick

2001

CARRICK, PHILLIP, who died of leukaemia on January 11, 2000, aged 47, was captain of Yorkshire from 1987 to 1989. The highlight of his 24-year career with the club came when he led them to the Benson and Hedges Cup in 1987, perhaps Yorkshire's proudest day since they last won the County Championship 19 years earlier. Carrick played on until 1993, and was desperately keen to become the fifth player to reach 10,000 runs and 1,000 wickets for Yorkshire: he failed by just six runs. A Surrey player even dropped a catch to help him in the final match, but play had to be abandoned. He went on to captain Pudsey Congs in the Bradford League and was still playing in August 1999 when he became ill. By this time, he had reached the first-class umpires' reserve list as a prelude to possible full-time umpiring, the perfect job for such an enthusiast. Carrick's premature death came only two years after that of his predecessor as Yorkshire captain, David Bairstow.

SYLVESTER CLARKE   2000

CLARKE, SYLVESTER THEOPHILUS, died suddenly on December 4, 1999, aged 44. He died the day after Sir Conrad Hunte and a month after Malcolm Marshall, completing a terrible treble for Barbadian cricket. Yet it was estimated that Clarke's funeral was the best-attended of the three. "You see," said one Bajan, "he was one of us." Clarke played in only 11 Test matches, and six of those were when West Indies were weakened by the absence of their World Series players. But he was an exceptional fast bowler, and in ten years with Surrey rapidly acquired a reputation as perhaps the most feared of them all.

PADDY CLIFT   1997

CLIFT, PATRICK BERNARD, died of bone marrow cancer on September 2, 1996, aged 43. Paddy Clift played Currie Cup cricket for Rhodesia before being recommended to Leicestershire by his compatriot, Brian Davison. He spent a year qualifying before making an astonishing impact in Leicestershire's match against MCC as champion county in April 1976. Against a team containing nine past or future England players, he took eight for 17 – five bowled and three lbw. Clift said he just bowled straight. In the next five sessions, only three wickets fell. He played for the county until 1987 without ever doing anything quite as spectacular, though his cricket was often dramatic. He took two hat-tricks, and one of his two centuries, made in 50 minutes at Hove in 1983, was the fastest ever made for Leicestershire.

CLAUDE COLLEY   2006

COLLEY, CLAUDE ARNOLD, who died on June 2, 2005, aged 98, had an extraordinary career in Australian club cricket, making his debut in the fearsome Brisbane A grade aged 55. Having been a successful leg-spinner in the lower grades, he was promoted to the first team by Sandgate-Redcliffe three times in 1961–62. He took 89 wickets at 10.76 eight seasons after that, and finally retired, at 84, after a mild heart attack in the dressing-room.

DENIS COMPTON 1998

COMPTON, DENIS CHARLES SCOTT, CBE, who died on April 23, 1997, aged 78, was not just a great cricketer but a character who transcended the game and became what would now be called a national icon. In the years after the war, when the British were still finding the joys of victory elusive, the exuberance of Compton's batting and personality became a symbol of national renewal. Almost single-handed (though his pal Bill Edrich helped), he ensured that cricket returned to its pre-war place in the nation's affections. Only Ian Botham has ever come remotely close to matching this achievement.

Compton was a remarkable batsman: loose-limbed with broad shoulders and powerful forearms. He could play all the strokes, though he rarely straight-drove. What made him special was his audacity: he would take risks, standing outside the crease even to quickish bowlers, challenging them to bowl anything other than the length he wanted. He took 622 wickets, mostly with his chinamen, and any other player might have turned this skill into a career; Compton regarded them as a bit of a party trick. His running between the wickets was never good, but it seemed to get worse after he retired and became the source of a thousand after-dinner jokes. In reality, it was never a disastrous weakness.

Denis Compton was born in Hendon, on May 23, 1918, and described his childhood as both "poorish" and "happy". His father was a self-employed decorator who became a lorry driver when his business floundered. He was also a keen cricketer, as was Leslie, Denis's elder brother. They played against the lamp-posts in Alexandra Road and at Bell Lane Elementary School, and Compton's talent was obvious at once. At 12, he was playing for his father's team, and North London Schools against South London Schools at Lord's. He made 88. Two years later, watched by Sir Pelham Warner, he made 114 at Lord's for the Elementary Schools against C. F. Tufnell's XI and led his team to a crushing victory. He joined the Lord's staff in 1933, and three years later got a game for the county, as an 18-year-old against Sussex in the Whitsun match. Compton batted at No. 11: he scored 14 in an important last-wicket stand with Gubby Allen that gave Middlesex first-innings points; the umpire Bill Bestwick supposedly said later that he only gave Compton lbw because he was desperate for a pee.

Next match he was No. 8 and facing Larwood with confidence. Then he was No. 7, scoring 87 against Northamptonshire. In one game, the captain Walter Robins came down the pitch after he had driven a fast bowler for two consecutive fours. "You know what to look out for now, don't you?" "No, skipper." "Well, he'll bounce one at you." "If he does, I shall hook him." And he did – into the Mound Stand. Before June was out he scored a hundred, in an hour and three-quarters, at Northampton. By the time the season was over and he had passed a thousand runs, Warner, then chairman of the Test selectors, called him "the best young batsman who has come out since Walter Hammond was a boy".

But Compton had no time to relax. In September he made his Football League debut for Arsenal on the left wing against Derby County, scored the opening goal in a 2–2 draw, and was called "the success of the afternoon" by the *Daily Express*. Soon he was being marked out as a future England footballer as well as cricketer, despite criticism, which Compton always accepted, that he was inclined to prefer pretty ball-play to anything else.

In cricket, the golden youth's progress turned out to be stoppable only by the Germans. In 1937 he scored 1,980 runs and was picked by England against New Zealand at The Oval. He scored 65 and was run out, flukily, while backing up. That year, as Pasty Hendren retired, Bill Edrich qualified for Middlesex. Len Hutton also made his Test debut. Thus started both the great partnership and the great rivalry that were to dominate post-war cricket. The contrast between the serious-minded Hutton and the insouciant Compton would be the great divide in English cricket for years, and small boys of all ages invariably inclined to one or the other.

There is no telling what this generation of batsmen might have achieved had they not been so rudely interrupted [by the war]. Possibly, in the absence of equally compelling bowlers, they might have got bored. They never had the chance to find out. Soon Compton was a special constable and then a member of the Royal Artillery, posted first to East Grinstead which still allowed the chance of weekend football. In 1944 he was sent to India as a sergeant-major supposedly in charge of getting men fit to defeat Japan; his lenient approach to this task enhanced his popularity with the men, and the Allies still won the war. He was able to fit in 17 first-class matches in India as well. His performances included a century for East Zone against the Australian Services, which was interrupted by rioters for several minutes when he was in the nineties. The line "Mr Compton, you very good player but the game must stop" became one of the catchphrases of his friendship with Keith Miller, which ended only with Compton's death. Compton also appeared, in the casual manner of that era, in the extraordinary Ranji Trophy final of 1944–45, then the highest-scoring match ever, between Holkar and Bombay.

Compton struggled at first in 1946, and his first 12 months of post-war cricket are sometimes thought of as a failure. He was still the leading scorer with 2,403 runs in 1946, and made a hundred in each innings at the Adelaide Test the following February. Because Compton had been touring, he missed that icy, fuel-rationed winter which for many people in Britain was tougher than anything produced by the war. Thus the stage was set for the greatest cricket season any individual has ever had.

Compton did not really hit form until the season was a month old, and did not emerge into his full glory until the sun came out, and the series against South Africa began. He scored 753 of his 3,816 runs that summer in the Tests. But somehow, in the mind's eye of a generation, he was always batting at Lord's in a county match: hair tousled, the ball racing past cover point or backward of square. An exile in Australia complained: "I hardly expected him to score 18 hundreds in a season. I thought him too good a player for that sort of thing." He was assured that Compton had just played his natural game and the centuries – like his aggregate,

Four aces: Denis Compton (left) makes a point to his old mate Bill Edrich at Lord's in 1982, watched by two more all-time greats, Len Hutton and Keith Miller. All four feature in this section.

a record for any season – had been almost incidental. Even more incidentally, Compton and Edrich took Middlesex to the Championship. The only cloud in that perfect summer came in the very last county match at Lord's: Compton had to retire to the pavilion because of knee trouble. He came out to make a second-innings century, another against the South Africans, and a further 246 – the knee strapped – for Middlesex against The Rest at The Oval.

But from then on the words Compton and knee were to go together almost as easily as Compton and Edrich. Apparently, it was first damaged in a collision with Charlton goalkeeper Sid Hobbins in 1938, but it now became increasingly troublesome to him, and a constant source of worry for the public too. There were still many great innings – two big Test hundreds in 1948 against Bradman's invincible Australians, an astounding 300 in three hours against an admittedly weak North-Eastern Transvaal team a few months later – but they came less certainly. As a cricketer his zenith had been so high that the only possible way was down.

He was, however, now much more than a cricketer. On the 1948–49 tour of South Africa, he approached the journalist Reg Hayter with a suitcase full of unopened letters. Hayter started to go through them and found one from the *News of the World* offering £2,000 a year for a weekly column. Then he found another, written a few months later, withdrawing the offer because there had been no reply. Hayter introduced Compton to Bagenal Harvey, who became the first sportsman's agent, and did the famous deal in which Compton slicked down his hair and became forever identified with Brylcreem.

He left county cricket as triumphantly as he entered it, hitting 143 in three hours in his final match as a professional for Middlesex in 1957. Thereafter he made occasional appearances as an amateur, scored his 123rd first-class hundred for the Cavaliers on a sociable trip to Jamaica in January 1964, and finally bowed out with a fifty for MCC against Lancashire later that year.

By then, he had become a thoroughly successful ex-cricketer, commentating for the BBC, writing pieces for the *Sunday Express* that were usually absurdly optimistic about the talents of iffy young cricketers, and using his natural readiness to have a drink and a chat with anyone to win accounts (successfully) for advertising agencies, first Royds then McCanns. He remained a bit of a roisterer into old age and maintained the friendships of his playing days until death. Edrich and Miller were at the top of this list; but it extended to all the South Africans he had found such chivalrous opponents and generous hosts. This led him to take the pro-white South Africa side in the disputes that followed his retirement and to be used on occasion – such as the 1983 debate over sending an MCC team to South Africa – by those with dubious motives.

He never lost the slightly chaotic ingenuousness that was responsible for the suitcase of letters: he was always unpunctual and would arrive, as Michael Parkinson put it, in a cloud of dust even when he was walking with a stick. His home life was successful only serially, but his third and last wife provided two daughters to add to his earlier families, which helped keep him young. He was always young at heart, even towards the end when the pain from his hip merged with the pain from his knee. He died in hospital at Windsor on St George's Day, following complications from his third hip operation. His memorial service at Westminster Abbey created more applications for tickets than any in 30 years.

COLIN COWDREY   2001

COWDREY of TONBRIDGE, Baron, died on December 4, 2000, aged 67, after suffering a stroke earlier in the year. Michael Colin Cowdrey was successively known to the world as Michael Cowdrey – when *Wisden* reported on him as a 13-year-old schoolboy prodigy – Colin Cowdrey, Sir Colin and finally Lord Cowdrey, when he became the first English cricketer to be given a peerage. In an era of outstanding English batsmen, he was the most durable, with a Test career spanning more than two decades.

On his journey from teenage phenomenon to sporting statesman, he was at the heart of the game for half a century: Cowdrey was the first man to play 100 Tests, captained England 27 times and scored almost 43,000 first-class runs – 7,624 of them in Tests. In later years, he played a major role behind the scenes in marrying the traditions of international cricket with modern demands. Yet it was still possible, and only mildly unkind, for one of his contemporaries, Fred Trueman, to describe Cowdrey on his death as "a terrific talent who never fulfilled his potential". Amid the triumphs there was often a vague sense of unease: of unexpected failures, opportunities not taken. Despite everything, Cowdrey never achieved the greatest accolade English cricket can offer: he toured Australia six times, which equalled a record held by Johnny Briggs, but never once was he selected as captain; every time a more forceful figure shoved him out of the way when it mattered.

His entire early career, and most of the rest of it, was the stuff of male fantasy. His father, Ernest, a tea planter in India, was a first-class cricketer too, scoring 48 for the Europeans against MCC at Madras. Colin's parents met at a cricket club and, when he was born on Christmas Eve 1932, he was – famously – given the initials MCC, just in case anyone doubted his destiny. On the plantation Colin would play with an Indian boy eight years his senior, with occasional supervision from his father who initiated a rule, to encourage correct technique, that all leg-side shots would be given out. Colin was sent to a sporty prep school, Homefield, and apparently reached a century in his first proper match, only to give his wicket away and then discover that he had only 93.

A modern thinker might be more conscious of the traumas rather than the triumphs. An only child – and not an insensitive one either – in the stern English schools of the 1940s, Colin did not see his parents for seven years owing to the twin tyrannies of distance and war. If, as countless spectators and writers later theorised, he had psychological flaws as a cricketer, who could be surprised? But skill at games is a great consolation to a boy, and Cowdrey was a natural: at golf, rackets and squash, as well as cricket. Within weeks of arriving at Tonbridge, he was in the First XI, though more for his leg-spin than his batting, and in the annual match against Clifton, then still played at Lord's, he scored 75 and 44, and took eight for 117. At 13, he was thought to be the youngest player ever at Lord's.

His leg-spin did not develop: Cowdrey later theorised that he could not grip a larger, adult, ball so well with his small hands, and that he lacked the necessary "bottle". But his batting began to flower gloriously: it was said that Maurice Tate, the last of his coaches at Tonbridge, would forget to signal while umpiring because he was so engrossed in Colin's strokeplay. At Oxford, his batting was impressive rather than earth-shattering. But he scored a century in the 1953 University Match, which prompted E. W. Swanton, in the *Daily Telegraph*, to compare him to Walter Hammond, the same thought that had struck Hutton two years earlier.

Cowdrey did not, between Tests, impose himself on county cricket: as with Hobbs, a hundred was enough, and he also found slow, constricting seamers rather tiresome (he would later name Barry Wood, the Lancashire dobber, as the bowler he hated facing most). He was arguably more impressive when the England ship sank in Australia in 1958–59 than against weak New Zealand the previous summer, and his century at Sydney saved England from a 5–0 whitewash.

No one ever doubted Colin Cowdrey's cricketing ability. Fred Titmus has talked with awe about how, in dead county games, he would let John Murray behind the stumps nominate in advance the shot he would play: "Amazing talent, done without showing off." But there was always that enigmatic quality. Trevor Bailey said that he was too nice to demolish an attack truly, and that he worried too much.

His character also caused some debate. Every cricket fan knew that Cowdrey walked when he thought he was out, and every prep school master thought this made him a hero. Professionals muttered darkly that he behaved differently on soft days in county cricket than at moments of crisis, banking on his reputation with umpires to get him through. "He was not generally liked by cricketers," said Ray Illingworth. This had to be balanced against the thousands of people – high and low – who were charmed by his kindness and thoughtfulness. The unanimous judgment, though, was that he was indecisive, a captain incapable of inspiring his players and a ditherer.

His later life shed unexpected light on all these speculations. In 1978, he left his wife and went to live with Lady Herries, a daughter of the Duke of Norfolk, causing temporary rifts with his children. They later married and she became famous in her own right as a racehorse trainer. In 1986, after some years pottering inconsequentially doing PR for Barclays, Cowdrey became president of MCC for the bicentenary year. He turned this Buggins' turn sinecure into an improbable platform for dynamic change. He forced out the long-serving secretary, Jack Bailey, to end an institutionalised feud with the Test and County Cricket Board, and meanwhile made the first moves to sever the umbilical cord between MCC and the ICC, remaining as ICC chairman after giving up the presidency. It was possible to have differing views of Cowdrey's actions – pro-Bailey members voted down the committee report and accounts – but dithery they were not.

Through his last years, he would often travel hundreds of miles to make beautifully crafted speeches to cricketing gatherings, expecting no money at all. "He loved to be loved," said a friend, and perhaps a man, however great, needs reassurance forever when he spends seven years of childhood apart from his parents. He was loved. And the memory of him in later years – portly, a fraction stooped, his fey voice ever solicitous about all-comers – will remain, almost as indelibly as the memory of him in his pomp: fairly portly even then, caressing the best bowlers' finest efforts past cover as though it were the simplest trick in the world.

ROBERT CRISP   1995

CRISP, ROBERT JAMES, DSO, MC, who died in Essex on March 3, 1994, aged 82, was one of the most extraordinary men ever to play Test cricket. His cricket, which is only a fraction of the story, was explosive enough: he is the only bowler to have taken four wickets in four balls twice. Born in Calcutta, he was educated in Rhodesia and, after taking nine for 64 for Western Province against Natal in 1933–34, which included his second set of four in four, was chosen for the South Africans' 1935 tour of England. He took 107 wickets on the tour at a brisk fast-medium, including five for 99 in the Old Trafford Test. Crisp played four further Tests against Australia in 1935–36 and appeared eight times for Worcestershire in 1938 without ever achieving a huge amount.

But it is astonishing that he ever found a moment for such a time-consuming game as cricket. He was essentially an adventurer – he had just climbed Kilimanjaro when he got news that he was wanted for the 1935 tour – with something of an attention span problem. Like other such characters, his defining moment came in the Second World War when he was an outstanding but turbulent tank commander, fighting his own personal war against better-armoured Germans in Greece and North Africa. He had six tanks blasted from under him in a month but carried on fighting and was awarded the DSO "for outstanding ability and great gallantry". However, he annoyed authority so much that General Montgomery intervened personally and prevented him being given a Bar a year later; his second honour was downgraded to an MC. Crisp was mentioned in despatches four times before being invalided out in Normandy. The King asked if his bowling would be affected. "No, sire," he is alleged to have replied. "I was hit in the head."

Crisp never did play again and found that the tedium of peacetime presented him with a problem far harder than anything offered by the Germans. He was briefly a journalist for a succession of newspapers, and went back to South Africa where he founded the now firmly established paper for blacks, *Drum*. But he wanted a magazine about tribal matters rather than something appealing to urban blacks and rapidly fell out with his proprietor. He returned to England, tried mink farming and, for an unusually long time by Crisp standards, worked as a leader writer on the *East Anglian Daily Times*. While there he wrote two accounts of his war exploits, *Brazen Chariots* (1957) and *The Gods Were Neutral* (1960). Then he suddenly left and lived in a Greek hut for a year. Told he had incurable cancer, he spent a year walking round Crete, selling accounts to the *Sunday Express*. He died with a copy of the *Sporting Life* on his lap, reportedly having just lost a £20 bet, a risk-taker to the last. Crisp's 276 career wickets came at an average of only 19.88, but statistics are absurd for such a man.

RICHARD DAVIS 2004

DAVIS, RICHARD PETER, who died on December 29, 2003, aged 37, had been suffering from a brain tumour since 2001, the season he became the first cricketer to play for five first-class counties. At 22, Dickie Davis, born in Margate, succeeded Derek Underwood as Kent's left-arm spinner, daunting enough even without the end of uncovered wickets, which made his task near-impossible. In 1992, he was the leading slow bowler in the country, taking 74 wickets and finishing sixth in the national averages. But that was the only year his average dipped below 30 and a year later the younger Min Patel was challenging for a place, so Davis, turning down a one-year contract, signed for Warwickshire. He appeared in most of their Championship matches in the county's miraculous 1994 season and played an important role by solving what had been the team's great weakness. But he quickly came under challenge from another young pretender, Ashley Giles, and moved on to Gloucestershire.

Retirement from first-class cricket in 1997 (to become cricket development officer for Greater London) opened an even more peripatetic chapter. Likeable and sympathetic, he showed increasing promise as a coach, working with the England women's team, St Edmund's School, Canterbury and, as player-coach, Berkshire. Davis also played a few one-day games for Sussex in 1998 and in August 2001 relegation-rattled Leicestershire obtained a special registration so he could strengthen their meagre spin bowling on a Northampton dirt track; he repaid their confidence with a first-innings half-century and six for 73, his 17th five-for. Two weeks later he had a seizure and the tumour was diagnosed. He was buried in his Kent blazer.

MARTIN DONNELLY 2000

DONNELLY, MARTIN PATERSON, who died on October 22, 1999, aged 82, left an indelible impression on cricket despite the brevity of his career. As a New Zealander at Oxford, he entranced cricket-followers in the immediate post-war years in a manner surpassed only by Compton. He proved that reality matched appearance with a magnificent double century against England in the Lord's Test of 1949. C. B. Fry said he was as good a left-hander as any he had seen, including Clem Hill and Frank Woolley. Then Donnelly retired and became a businessman in Sydney.

For New Zealanders, his career was even more tantalising, since he played only 13 of his 131 first-class games in the country. None the less, he did enough in his seven Tests to raise the country's cricketing profile and, establish himself among the country's best-remembered sporting heroes. When he was elevated to the New Zealand Sports Hall of Fame in 1990, the citation read: "They said he had everything as a Test batsman: style and grace; confidence and determination; success and modesty." The words "they said" encapsulate the sense of loss that surrounded Donnelly, despite his long life. His cricket was a victim of the war, the lowly cricketing status of his country at the time, and the game's financial circumstances.

ALEC DOUGLAS-HOME 1996

HOME OF THE HIRSEL, The Baron, KT, PC, who died at his home on October 9, 1995, aged 92, was the only British prime minister to have played first-class cricket. As Lord Dunglass, he was a useful member of the Eton XI. In the rain-affected Eton-Harrow match of 1922 he scored 66, despite being hindered by a saturated outfield, and then took four for 37 with his medium-paced out-swingers. He played ten first-class matches for six different teams: Middlesex, Oxford University, H. D. G. Leveson Gower's XI, MCC (with whom he toured South America under Pelham Warner), Free Foresters and Harlequins. His two games for Middlesex were in 1924 and 1925, both against Oxford University while he was actually an Oxford undergraduate; he did not represent the university until the following year. His cricket was gradually overtaken by politics, and he entered the Commons in 1931.

From 1977 to 1989 Lord Home was governor of I Zingari. The general opinion is that, even if he had devoted himself to the game, he would not have been a regular county player, but then no one expected him to rise so high in politics either. H. S. Altham, in his review of public schools cricket in the 1923 *Wisden*, said Lord Dunglass was a better batsman on wet pitches – "he had the courage of his convictions and could hook and pull the turning ball effectively". Much the same could be said for his politics: he was always at his best on a sticky wicket.

TED DRAKE 1996

DRAKE, EDWARD JOSEPH, died on May 29, 1995, aged 82. Ted Drake was an apprentice at the Southampton Gasworks before he made his debut for Hampshire in 1931 and shared a vital stand of 86 with Phil Mead against Glamorgan. He made 45 but never reached this score again in the 15 further matches he played over the next six years, first as an amateur and then as a professional. However, he found greater glory in the winters, when Hampshire would have paid him ten shillings a week, as one of the great centre-forwards of his era, first with Southampton and then with Arsenal, where he was transferred in 1934 for £5,000. He only won five England caps, but scored 42 goals in the 1934–35 season, an Arsenal record, and went on to manage Chelsea to the 1955 League Championship. He married the girl he met at the gasworks dance, not a detail associated with modern football stars of his magnitude.

SIR ROBERT DUNDAS 1983

DUNDAS, SIR ROBERT WHYTE MELVILLE, BT, died on October 10, 1981, within three weeks of his 100th birthday. He was captain of an unbeaten Glenalmond Eleven in 1899. At the age of 90 he caught, at cover-point, while playing for Comrie, an opponent 70 years his junior.

BASIL EASTERBROOK 1996

EASTERBROOK, BASIL VIVIAN, who died on December 15, 1995, aged 75, was cricket and football writer for Kemsley (later Thomson Regional) Newspapers from 1950 to 1983 and thus covered all the major domestic matches for many of Britain's largest regional papers. He was a regular writer for *Wisden* and contributed an article every year from 1971 to 1980. Easterbrook was a much-loved member of the press corps with a puckish humour. He claimed that while covering a match from the old Lord's press box, he leaned out of the window to throw away his pencil shavings and the Nottinghamshire batsmen walked in, thinking it was the signal to declare. Once he phoned his office to dictate his copy, announced his name to the telephonist – "Basil V. Easterbrook" – to be greeted by the response "What league is that in?"

BILL EDRICH 1987

EDRICH, WILLIAM JOHN (BILL), DFC, who died at Chesham as the result of an accident on April 23, 1986, aged 70, was a cricketer who would have been the answer to prayer in the troubled England sides of today and especially in the West Indies in 1986. Endlessly cheerful, always optimistic and physically courageous, he was a splendid hitter of short-pitched fast bowling and took the blows he received as a part of the game. When he made 16 in an hour and three-quarters on a hideous wicket at Brisbane in the first innings of the first Test in 1946–47, an innings which *Wisden*'s correspondent described as "one of the most skilful batting displays I have ever seen", it was reckoned that he was hit ten times by Lindwall, Miller and Toshack.

So far from being demoralised by this experience, he scored in the series 462 runs with an average of 46.20, and that for a side which lost three Tests, two of them by an innings, and drew the other two. Moreover, his cricket did not end with his batting. Though he stood only 5ft 6in tall, and had a low, slinging action, he could off a run of 11 strides bowl genuinely fast for a few overs. In first-class cricket he scored 36,965 runs, with an average of 42.39 and made 86 centuries, nine of them double-centuries: he took 479 wickets at 33.31 and held 526 catches. His highest score was 267 not out for Middlesex against Northamptonshire at Northampton in 1947. For Middlesex his figures were 25,738 runs with an average of 43.40 and 328 wickets at 30.41, and in Tests he made 2,440 runs with an average of 40, including six hundreds: he also took 41 wickets at 41.29 and held 39 catches.

A photograph of Bill Edrich with Len Hutton, Keith Miller and Denis Compton appears on page 1170.

GODFREY EVANS   2000

EVANS, THOMAS GODFREY, CBE, died on May 3, 1999, aged 78. Godfrey Evans was arguably the best wicket-keeper the game has ever seen. Debates about wicket-keepers cannot be stilled by statistics in the way that a challenge to Don Bradman might be. What is beyond question is that Evans was the game's most charismatic keeper: the man who made the game's least obtrusive specialism a spectator sport in itself. His energy and enthusiasm brought the best out of other fielders, whatever the state of the game. But he added to that a technical excellence that has probably never been surpassed.

Evans was born in North London, but moved to Kent when he was a baby and was brought up by his grandfather after the death of his mother. At Kent College, he was an all-round sportsman, and played in the school team mainly as a batsman: the games master thought wicket-keeper was a good place to hide one of the team's less mobile fielders. He made his Kent debut in July 1939 as a batsman, but kept wicket in three of his next four games before the war came. His reputation only flourished when the former England captain, A. E. R. Gilligan, saw him in a Services match in 1942 and ensured that he received invitations for the major wartime matches.

By the end of the first post-war summer, Evans had displaced Paul Gibb as England's wicket-keeper, after an excellent performance for the Players at Lord's when he did not concede a bye. He let through one on his Test debut at The Oval, which irritated him years later: "a silly little blighter" from Jim Langridge, outside off stump. That kind of perfectionism ensured that there was no serious challenge to his pre-eminence for the next 13 years.

Evans was not ashamed to tumble, perhaps making the comparatively easy look difficult. But he also executed stumpings with lightning speed, making the difficult look absurdly easy. He was one of the most theatrical of cricketers but, as with all the great performers, the apparent ease masked a self-discipline that the audience never suspected. His greatest secret was the meticulously observed lunchtime siesta ritual, which enabled him to keep fresh and focused. This gave him the ability to conduct the team like an orchestra, and he could flog life from the tired limbs of his team-mates at the end of the hottest day. He had a remarkable physique: strong, sturdy, squat and astonishingly resilient, plus a keen eye, remarkable concentration and sharp reflexes. Evans might have taken up boxing for a career: he flattened several opponents before the Kent authorities intervened and told him to choose between the sports. He chose.

At home, he missed only five Tests in 12 seasons between 1947 and 1958, and in all played 91. After the 1946–47 tour, Bill O'Reilly wrote that wicket-keeping was the only department where England matched Australia. In 1950–51, according to Trevor Bailey, Evans did not miss a chance, and took one at Melbourne that still amazed Bailey years later, when he caught Neil Harvey standing up to Bedser "one-handed, horizontal, and airborne down the leg side off a genuine leg-glance". But Evans's value to his side and his popular appeal also hinged on his batting. At Adelaide in 1946–47, he famously batted for 97 minutes without scoring, to help Denis Compton to his second century of the match, and avoid likely defeat. More often, his batting was as flashy as his wicket-keeping: highlights included a century in the Old Trafford Test of 1950 and another against India at Lord's two years later, when he scored 98 before lunch.

He remained on his pedestal until 1959 when he was felt to have lapsed against India, and lost his place to Roy Swetman. The need for "team building" was cited. He promptly retired. There is evidence that he did so too early. In 1967, just short of his 47th birthday, he made a comeback during Canterbury Week while Alan Knott was playing for England and there was no available deputy. Huge crowds saw him keep, according to Wisden, "superbly". The England bowler Mike Selvey, now The Guardian cricket correspondent, played with him nine years later in a fun seven-a-side at The Oval. "My experience was an education. Late out-swing just whispered into his gloves. I slipped in a full-length in-swinger on leg stump – the most difficult to take – and there he was, down the leg side as if by telepathy, flicking the bails away as the batsmen changed feet." Selvey said he had never seen a better display of wicket-keeping.

Keeping alone could not account for his popularity. He made his highest score, 144, at Taunton in 1952. Afterwards, it was announced that there would be a collection for Somerset's beneficiary, Harold Gimblett. Evans at once volunteered to go round with the box, which he did with his cheery smile and banter, making the takings far larger than they would have been. He was always generous himself for good causes. He was equally famous for his night-time roistering, some of which would – in a sterner age – have got him into terrible trouble with the tabloids.

His standard shipboard party piece, as Carmen Miranda leading the team in a fancy-dress conga, has never quite been forgotten.

Many who knew him well believe that behind the extrovert lay a rather sadder figure: he never quite settled into steady post-cricket employment. "For all that Godfrey was a cricketing Falstaff," said his biographer Christopher Sandford, "there was a touch of Hamlet too. He thought and fretted about life more than he let on." But any sadness was well hidden, in later years, behind exuberant mutton-chop whiskers. He became best-known as resident expert for the bookmakers Ladbrokes, reassessing the odds at each twist and turn of a Test match, usually getting it right, but, at Headingley in 1981 when he offered England at 500-1, famously getting it wrong. He remained – even for cricket-lovers too young to have seen him – a symbol of some of the happiest times for English Test cricket, on the field and off it. His CBE, he blithely proclaimed, stood for Crumpet Before Evensong.

GAVIN EWART 1996

EWART, GAVIN BUCHANAN, who died on October 23, 1995, aged 79, was a well-known poet and a lifelong cricket enthusiast. He produced many poems on cricket, penning A Pindaric Ode on the 1981 Headingley Test as well as shorter lyrics of wry nostalgia and a squib on the radio commentary team.

His most substantial piece, The Sadness of Cricket, was a poignant elegy for the players of the Golden Age:

> We'd one at Wellington, that A. E. Relf,
> who'd bowled for England – long since on the shelf –
> in 1937 stalled and shot himself.
> Remembered bowling in the nets,
> a little irritable (I thought – but one forgets),
> doling out stumps to junior games, like doubtful debts,
> from the pavilion's mean back door.

FAZAL MAHMOOD 2006

FAZAL MAHMOOD, who died on May 30, 2005, aged 78, was Pakistan's first great bowler, inspiring his country to several famous victories in the 1950s. "He was the torch-bearer," said his modern counterpart Shoaib Akhtar. Tall and handsome, with a Comptonesque mop of hair that led him to feature in advertisements as Pakistan's own Brylcreem Boy, Fazal's ability to cut and seam the ball at a fair pace led him to be compared – in style and stamina – to England's Alec Bedser. He was especially difficult to handle on the artificial pitches widely used in Pakistan in the 1950s: Neil Harvey, the great Australian batsman of the time, said that Fazal "could make the ball talk" on matting.

When Pakistan beat India by an innings on the mat at Lucknow in October 1952 – only their second official Test – Fazal took 12 wickets, seven for 42 in the second innings. Then, on the inaugural tour of England in 1954, he again took 12 wickets as Pakistan pulled off a stunning series-levelling win at The Oval. England were 109 for two, chasing only 168, but lost their last eight wickets for 34. He took 13 for 114 at Karachi when Pakistan won their maiden Test against Australia, "varying his swing with a mixture of leg-cutters and breakbacks" according to *Wisden.*

Overwork dulled his edge after that: he bowled 250 overs in the first three Tests of the 1957–58 series in West Indies. Fazal still managed eight wickets in the final Test, which Pakistan won. And the following season he became the first Pakistani to reach 100 Test wickets, in only his 22nd match, and added 12 more as they won the next game, against West Indies at Dacca. By then he was Pakistan's captain, and led them in ten Tests in all. He retired after the 1962 England tour with a first-class bowling average of under 19. Hanif Mohammad, Pakistan's first star with the bat, recalled: "He was a great human being, always willing to help anyone who sought his advice. All our wins since we started playing Test cricket were indebted to him."

He had a long career in the police force, running the sports department where he groomed several top-class hockey players, and was still working, as director of a textile firm, when he had a heart attack in his office.

PERCY FENDER 1986

FENDER, PERCY GEORGE HERBERT, who died at Exeter on June 15, 1985, aged 92, was the last survivor of those who had played county cricket regularly before the Great War: more important, he was one of the most colourful figures in the cricket world for many years after it and was widely regarded as the shrewdest county captain of his generation.

In a career of 26 years he scored 19,034 runs with an average of 26.66, took 1,894 wickets at 25.05, made 21 hundreds and caught 599 catches. Six times he did the double. But he was not a cricketer who could be judged on figures. *Wisden* has never been a slave to statistics and, when in 1915 he appeared as one of the Five Cricketers of the Year, it was after a season in which both his bowling and batting averages had been approximately 23 and he had not scored 1,000 runs nor taken 100 wickets. Yet the honour was fully deserved. Surrey had won the Championship and Tom Hayward had said that Fender was the making of their XI. In a crucial match, for instance, against Kent, the reigning champions, at Lord's in August (The Oval was occupied by the military), going in on a pitch made for Blythe, who took nine for 97, with a scoreboard reading 147 for four, he made 48 in 20 minutes, thus securing Surrey a lead of 94: he also took in the match five for 43 and thus played a big part in his side's victory.

Throughout his career Fender's policy was to hit fiercely, regardless of the state of the pitch, even of the quality of the bowling. He was a tremendous driver and also delighted in the pull, and he cut or slashed ferociously outside the off stump:

he once slashed the ball over cover out of The Oval. It was difficult to set a field for him. His century in 35 minutes against Northamptonshire in 1920 remains a record; though it was equalled in farcical circumstances in 1983. His highest score, 185 against Hampshire in 1922, took 130 minutes and against Kent later that season he made 137 in an hour and a half, 52 of them off 14 consecutive balls. It was not to be expected that one batting on these principles would be as consistent as a more sedate player, but in the very strong Surrey batting sides of those days another solid bat would have been neither here nor there: Fender the hitter was invaluable.

His attitude to bowling was the same. His object was to get the batsman out, and the tactics fostered by the modern one-day game would never have suited him. He had at his command a great variety of pace, spin and swing and all were fully employed. Inevitably his length sometimes suffered. Yet it was unwise to assume that because a batsman was out to a full toss it was a lucky wicket: almost as likely as not it was bowled for that very purpose. Probably he was least expensive when he concentrated on leg-breaks and googlies.

IAN FOLLEY   1994

FOLLEY, IAN, the former Lancashire left-arm spin bowler, died in hospital on August 30, 1993, aged 30. He had been struck under the eye trying to hook a short ball while captaining Whitehaven in a North Lancashire League match against Workington. He jogged off the field and it was assumed he would only need a few stitches but, while under anaesthetic, apparently suffered a heart attack. Folley played for Lancashire from 1982 until 1990 and was regarded as a promising medium-pace bowler before the manager Jack Bond encouraged him to switch to spin. At first the change worked magnificently, and he took 68 Championship wickets in 1987, including seven for 15 against Warwickshire at Southport. He took 57 wickets in 1988 but then began to suffer "the yips" and found bowling almost impossible. In 1991 Folley moved to Derbyshire, but played in only four matches. In 140 first-class games he took 287 wickets. At the time of his death he was managing a night club.

JOHN FOWLES   2006

FOWLES, JOHN ROBERT, who died on November 5, 2005, aged 79, was a novelist whose work included *The Magus* and *The French Lieutenant's Woman*. Cricket remained a lifelong interest from the time Fowles learnt the game from the Essex captain, Denys Wilcox, at Alleyn Court prep school in Westcliff-on-Sea. He and Trevor Bailey used to cycle there together. As a fast bowler, Fowles took plenty of wickets for Bedford School, which he captained in 1944, and had a trial for Essex. His off-cutter remained a source of pride – though demonstrations of how he achieved this were lost on American film directors.

While watching England nervily bat to victory over West Indies at Lord's in

2000, he was joined in his living-room in Lyme Regis by a stranger asking the score. When Fowles told him, his visitor sat down and watched with him until Dominic Cork had hit the winning runs. Only when he subsequently asked how much Fowles charged for bed and breakfast, did both men realise that the stranger had walked uninvited into the wrong house.

ROY FREDERICKS

FREDERICKS, ROY CLIFTON, who died of cancer on September 5, 2000, aged 57, was one of the handful of batsmen who distinguished themselves by counter-attacking the great pace bowlers of the 1970s. He is remembered best for his blazing performance at Perth in 1975, when he raced to one of the most astonishing of all Test centuries. This series was eventually won 5–1 by Australia, with Lillee and Thomson at full pelt. But in the Second Test, on an incredibly fast WACA pitch, Fredericks took them on in amazing fashion. The harder they banged the ball in, the harder he cut and hooked. Into the second morning, he opened what might have been a diffident reply to Australia's 329: at lunch West Indies were 130 for one off 14 eight-ball overs; the 200 came up in the 22nd. Fredericks went on to reach a hundred from 71 balls and, though he grew tired, turned it into a match-winning 169. This was merely a distillation of his entire career. "There has," as Mike Selvey wrote, "probably never been a better or more willing exponent of the hook." His most famous single shot was a failure, however: right at the start of the first World Cup final, he hooked a ball from Lillee over long leg – only to tread on his wicket in the process.

A small (about 5ft 6in) left-hander from Berbice, Fredericks made his debut for what was then British Guiana in 1963–64, and for nine years and 59 Tests – from 1968–69 until the World Series schism of 1977 – he provided half the answer to the conundrum of who should open for West Indies. This had been intractable even when Conrad Hunte was playing, and remained a source of constant change and argument until Gordon Greenidge emerged to join Fredericks in the mid-1970s. He preferred to tilt his cap back, rock on to his left foot and smash the ball hard. Though he scored eight Test hundreds in his 109 innings, this was a low ratio for a player who averaged above 40 – he preferred the blistering 50.

Fredericks averaged 63.83 for Guyana. In his three years with Glamorgan (1971–73), he was less consistent but spasmodically magnificent and extremely popular – not least with his opening partner Alan Jones, even though Jones described his calling as "terrible" and suffered from his musical tastes when they roomed together. On an amazing day at Swansea, they put on 330 against Northamptonshire, at the time a record for any Glamorgan wicket; they still lost.

Fredericks announced his retirement in 1978, while playing World Series, but five years later, aged 40, he made a comeback for Guyana, batted twice, and scored 103 against Trinidad & Tobago and 217 against Jamaica. It was an astonishing way to finish. By then, he was already a junior minister in Forbes Burnham's left-wing

Guyanese government, responsible for youth and sport, and known as Comrade; earlier in his playing days he had generally endeared himself by calling everyone "old chap". He remained attached to the government, but later concentrated on coaching. By then, openers around the world were batting in anonymous helmets. Fredericks was one of the last players who not only relished facing the best bowlers but looked as though he did.

SIR JOHN PAUL GETTY 2004

GETTY, SIR JOHN PAUL, KBE, who died on April 17, 2003, aged 70, described himself in *Who's Who* as simply a "philanthropist". Paul Getty inherited a fortune from the family oil business but, unlike his tycoon father, had little interest in adding to it. Instead, he settled in Britain and gave away huge chunks of his money to a vast array of beneficiaries, most of them institutions representing what he saw as the country's threatened heritage, including cathedrals, art galleries, the British Film Institute's archive and the Conservative Party. Cricket was close to the top of the list.

Born at sea off Italy and originally called Eugene Paul, he came to the game by an unbelievably circuitous route after an unhappy American childhood, a tumultuous youth and reclusive middle years. For nine years he worked for the Italian subsidiary of Getty Oil before being seduced by the distractions of the 1960s, divorcing his first wife, Gail, and marrying a Dutch beauty, Talitha, who died of a heroin overdose in Italy in 1971. He moved to London and lived as a recluse in Chelsea, subject to depression and his own drug dependence, a period that included the terrible kidnap of his eldest son, Paul. During this period Mick Jagger, a friend since the 1960s, visited him, insisted on switching the TV over to the cricket and explained what was going on. Getty got the bug.

Gubby Allen, *eminence grise* of MCC and at one time a fellow patient at the London Clinic, described by Getty as being "like a father", encouraged him into the cricketing community. Men like Brian Johnston and Denis Compton became friends, and he took delight in the game's history, traditions and etiquette, which were at one with the concept of Englishness that he embraced. So he sprinkled cricket with some of the stardust that his wealth made possible. He gave an estimated £1.6m to build the Mound Stand at Lord's, but this was the tip of an iceberg of donations: to every county, to countless clubs, to individuals fallen on hard times and to organisations like the Arundel Cricket Foundation, which received £750,000 from him to help disadvantaged youngsters play cricket.

Even his pleasures were inclusive ones. At Wormsley, his estate nestling in the Chilterns, he created his own private cricketing Eden project: a square like a billiard table with a thatched pavilion. Getty built his field of dreams, and they really did come: the Queen Mother and the prime minister, John Major, attended Wormsley's inaugural match in 1992; touring teams made it a regular stopover; and cricketers ranging from the great to the gormless delighted in playing there or simply sharing the idyll. There was a touch of Scott Fitzgerald's West Egg about the place, but that was not inappropriate for a ground where the most coveted sidetrip was to the library to see the host's rare first editions. The Getty box at Lord's also became a London salon where celebrities, cricketing and otherwise, rubbed shoulders.

His ownership of *Wisden*, sealed in 1993, brought together the two great passions: cricket and books. In 1994 Getty sealed his own personal happiness by marrying Victoria, who had nursed him through the bad years, and four years later tied the knot with the country he had come to love, becoming a British citizen, which allowed him to use the knighthood that had been bestowed on him for his charitable services 12 years earlier. His presidency of Surrey, in 1996, was another honour he cherished. Those who knew him valued him as a generous spirit, a quality that has nothing to do with money. And cricket repaid him a little by giving him a sense of his own self-worth as a man, not just as a benefactor.

ALAN GIBSON
1998

GIBSON, NORMAN ALAN STANLEY, died on April 10, 1997, aged 73. Alan Gibson was one of the most remarkable men ever to broadcast or write about cricket. He was president of the Oxford Union and gained a first in history. Perhaps no one has brought more literacy or classical knowledge to the reporting of any game. Men with his background expect to become cabinet ministers at least, and Gibson often seemed conscious of this; a sense of failure may explain the demons that regularly afflicted him.

He came from an unmoneyed background – his father was a Baptist preacher – and joined BBC West Region in 1948 in search of security. It became clear that he was a natural broadcaster, with a honeyed voice, a wonderful sense of cadence, a turn of phrase and an eye for the telling detail. In 1962 he was finally promoted to *Test Match Special*. When Gibson commentated on the same match as John Arlott, listeners were given a stream of description, wit, and both general and cricketing erudition that remains unsurpassed.

Unfortunately, Gibson had the same weakness as Arlott without the same capacity to conceal it. Finally, the incidents of drunkenness on air became too reckless, and he was dropped – without ever being told why. He did, however, have a second flowering as his county match reports in *The Times* attained cult status. He described his experience at or going to the cricket with occasional, tangential references to the actual game. There was generally some disastrous experience to report from Didcot station, where he usually had to change trains. There was the mysterious GRIP (The Glorious Red-headed Imperturbable Pamela), the barmaid in the Hammond Bar at Bristol. And he baffled Peter Lees, who ran the press bar at Lord's, by rechristening him Bardolph. The overall result was usually uproarious. He was, however, capable of ignoring some peripheral event like a century or a hat-trick; and as the years went by, humourless sub-editors lost patience.

Despite his taste for drink – perhaps a reaction against his Nonconformist background – Gibson was not a clubbable man. He rarely went into press boxes, and would sit alone, fending off bores, writing his copy in fountain pen while nursing a gigantic whisky, cleverly diluted so that it looked like a half of lager.

Eventually, after his second marriage had broken down, he drifted into a nursing home, and in the last years the shadows took over. Much of his life – Didcot might have been a metaphor – was a source of torment as well as humour. He had a spell in a psychiatric hospital, which he wrote about in his autobiography *A Mingled Yarn*. His history, *The Cricket Captains of England*, was a wonderful read. He was a Liberal candidate in the 1959 election and remained a Baptist lay preacher.

Gibson spoke at Sir Neville Cardus's memorial service in 1975 and read from William Blake:

> Joy and woe are woven fine
> A clothing for the soul divine.
> Under every grief and pine
> Runs a thread of silken twine.

It perhaps summed up Alan Gibson's own life better than Sir Neville's.

EDWARD GILBERT   1979

GILBERT, EDWARD, who was the best-remembered aboriginal cricketer to play first-class cricket in Australia, had been long absent from the scene of his some-times sensational fast bowling feats of the 1930s and in ill health for many years before his death in the Wolston Park Hospital near Brisbane on January 9, 1978, aged 69. Nevertheless, this notably quiet but well-spoken product of Queensland's Cherbourg Aboriginal Settlement has remained a legend down the years.

After successfully graduating through the Queensland Colts XI in 1930, Eddie Gilbert quickly reached the headlines in the 1931 Sheffield Shield match against New South Wales in Brisbane by his first-over dismissals of Wendell Bill and Bradman without scoring. Both were caught by wicket-keeper Len Waterman within seven deliveries, but not before one ball rising from a green-top had flicked off Sir Donald's cap and another knocked the bat from his hands. Sir Donald has since recalled that the six deliveries he faced on this occasion were the fastest expe-rienced during his career.

Lightly built and only a little over 5ft 7in in height, Gilbert possessed excep-tionally long arms and could bowl at great pace off a run sometimes no longer than four paces. It was this, allied with a somewhat whippy forearm action, which led to suggestions that his right arm bent on occasions during a pronounced arc action which finished with his hand almost touching the ground and his head at knee level. Strong advocacy for Gilbert's Test selection was nullified by the suspect action, a view several times shared and acted on by umpires. Nevertheless, the same officials completely accepted his delivery on most other occasions.

Several films were taken without conclusive decision and controversy continued throughout Gilbert's career which was undoubtedly affected by the publicity. He faded out of the game in 1936 after showing fine form while taking six wickets in his final match – against Victoria at the Brisbane Cricket Ground in 1936. In 19

Shield matches he took 73 wickets at an average of 29.75, while a further 14 wickets were gained in Queensland matches against touring MCC, West Indies and South African sides.

ROY GILCHRIST 2002

GILCHRIST, ROY, died at Portmore, St Catherine, in his native Jamaica on July 18, 2001, aged 67. The image of a bowler of genuinely high pace stricken with Parkinson's disease is a dolorous one, but such was Roy Gilchrist's fate. Following his brief but dramatic Test career, he had lived in England for many years, marrying and, not always in peaceful accord, rearing seven children before returning to the West Indies in 1985. He was accorded a ready welcome, but he was troubled by his health and by persistent hard times. His childhood on a sugar plantation had been impoverished and rough, and, in Michael Manley's sympathetic analysis, he was "burdened by those tensions which so often run like scars across the landscape of the personalities of people who come from poverty".

Certainly he was awkward to manage, insufferably so at times, and his Test career came to a precipitate termination in 1959 when his hard-pressed captain, Gerry Alexander, with the support of the senior players, dispatched "Gilly" home from India before the Pakistan leg of West Indies' tour of the subcontinent. Constant friction with Alexander off the field, coupled with over-aggressive bowling on it, including the unacceptable use of the beamer, was the cause.

Banished from the international scene, he found professional slots in England, where he had toured in 1957 with mixed fortune. He played in the Lancashire leagues for a variety of clubs, including Middleton (for whom he took a total of 280 wickets in 1958 and 1959), going on to take 100 wickets every year until 1979. However, tales of atrocity, some perhaps arising from the proverbial tendency to give a dog a bad name, continued to emerge about his violently over-reactive attitude to batsmen and his unsparing use of the bouncer. Even charity matches were not free from his ferocious assaults: on one such occasion, at Werneth, that resolute Australian Cec Pepper luridly but successfully remonstrated with Gilchrist in terms not suitable to print.

Gilchrist's venomous bowling was the expression of a fiery, hostile personality. Of medium height, but long-armed and strong, he spearheaded, along with the young Wes Hall, the late 20th-century West Indian phalanx of unremittingly fast bowlers. Not since the heady days of Learie Constantine and Manny Martindale had they enjoyed so forceful an attack. Although Gilchrist's 21 wickets had cost almost 31 each when Pakistan toured the Caribbean in 1958, he was demonic in India, taking 26 in his four Tests at 16.11. In his best Test figures of six for 55, at Calcutta, five were bowled. All told, his 57 Test wickets in 13 outings averaged 26.68, while in 42 first-class matches his haul was 167 at 26, including one astonishing return of six for 16 at Nagpur when the West Indians bowled out a Combined Universities XI for 49. Roy Gilchrist played only five times for Jamaica, between 1956–57 and 1961–62, and he also had six games for Indian sides in 1962–63, when a number of West Indians were recruited to harden Indian batsmen to pace bowling.

HAROLD GIMBLETT

GIMBLETT, HAROLD, who died at his home at Verwood, Dorset, on March 30, 1978 aged 63, was the most exciting English batsman of his day. Years ago, C. B. Fry wrote of MacLaren, "like all the great batsmen, he always attacked the bowling!" If that view was once shared by the selectors, they had abandoned it by Gimblett's time. They preferred soundness and consistency. Gimblett played in three Tests only, two against India in 1936, the first of which at Lord's he finished with a dazzling 67 not out, culminating in five consecutive boundaries, and one against the West Indies in 1939. Those who saw the inexpressibly feeble English batting against Ramadhin and Valentine at Lord's in 1950 shown up for what it was by the bold tail-end hitting of Wardle, longed for an hour of Gimblett, and indeed he was picked for the next Test, but was unfortunately ill and unable to play.

The start of his career was so sensational that any novelist attributing it to his hero would have discredited the book. Given a month's trial on the Somerset staff in 1935 after a number of brilliant performances in local matches, he was told before the period had expired that there was no future for him in county cricket and was sent home. Next day there was a last-minute vacancy against Essex at Frome and he was recalled to fill it, mainly as a young man who could chase the ball in the field and perhaps bowl a few overs of mild medium pace. In fact, coming in to face Nichols, the England fast bowler, then at his best, with six wickets down for 107, he reached his 50 in 28 minutes and his 100 in 63, finally making 123 out of 175 in 80 minutes with three sixes and 17 fours. The innings won him the Lawrence Trophy for the fastest 100 of the season. In the next match, against Middlesex at Lord's, though lame and batting with a runner, he made 53 against Jim Smith, Robins, Peebles and Sims, three of them England bowlers.

It was hardly to be expected that he could keep this up and his record at the end of the season was modest, but his second summer dispelled any notion that his early successes had been a fluke, as he scored 1,608 runs with an average of 32.81. People sometimes talk as if after this he was a disappointment. In fact his one setback, apart from being overlooked by the selectors, was when in 1938, probably listening to the advice of grave critics, he attempted more cautious methods and his average dropped to 27. But can one call disappointing a man who between 1936 and his retirement in 1953 never failed to get his 1,000 runs, who in his career scored over 23,000, more than any other Somerset player, and 50 centuries, the highest 310 against Sussex at Eastbourne in 1948, and whose average for his career was over 36? Moreover after his first season he habitually went in first and yet he hit 265 sixes, surely a record.

Naturally, as time went on, his judgment improved with experience, he grew sounder and in particular became the master of the hook instead of its slave, though he never abandoned it, as did Hammond and Peter May. To the end, he might have said, as Frank Woolley used to, "When I am batting, I am the attack."

ALF GOVER

GOVER, ALFRED RICHARD, MBE, the Mr Chips of cricket teachers, died in south London on October 7, 2001, at the age of 93. With his death, the mantle of being England's oldest living Test player passed to Norman Mitchell-Innes, born in 1914, while G. L. (Lindsay) Weir of New Zealand, born like Gover in 1908, became the oldest Test cricketer worldwide. During the 1939–45 war, Alf Gover served as a company sergeant major with the Army Physical Training Corps, before rising to the rank of major in the Pioneer Corps. As well as cricketer and coach, he was a journalist, although whether he would wish to be remembered as the technical adviser to the leaden-footed 1953 film, *The Final Test*, is a moot point. He was president of the Lord's Taverners in 1974 and of Surrey in 1980, and manager of two Commonwealth cricket tours to the subcontinent in the 1960s.

After a spell on the Essex ground staff, 19-year-old Alf moved to The Oval in 1927, making his debut for Surrey at Horsham against Sussex in 1928. These were the summers of "Bosser" Martin's impeccably groomed Oval wickets and of Surrey batting graced by Jack Hobbs, Andrew Sandham and others; bowling resources, not surprisingly in the circumstances, were scarce. Born on the same leap year day (February 29) as Frederic in *The Pirates of Penzance*, he was, like that ambivalent buccaneer, "a Slave to Duty", forced to act both as shock and stock bowler, galloping up his inordinately lengthy and somewhat ungainly run and hurling his thunderbolts hour after hour and over after over. Yet when he was opening the bowling in harness with Eddie Watts, his brother-in-law, Surrey were a formidable proposition for any county line-up in the second half of the 1930s.

Of Gover's 362 first-class matches, 336 were for Surrey in a career lasting until 1947. By the time he had put in 27 overs for an All England XI against Glamorgan in 1948, he had bowled a prodigious 77,269 deliveries and taken 1,555 wickets (1,437 for Surrey) at an average of 23.63. He took 100 wickets eight times, going on to 200 in 1936 and 201 in 1937 – the first fast bowler to reach 200 since Surrey's Tom Richardson in 1897. At Worcester in 1935, he had taken four in four balls to complete his best analysis of eight for 34, having conceded 22 runs before getting a wicket. He scored only 2,312 runs, never made a fifty and held 171 catches. Catches, however, were regularly dropped off his own luckless bowling, so that he seemed doomed, like an Ovalite Flying Dutchman, to bowl eternally, the hand of foe and butter-fingered friend alike against him.

He played only four Tests: all were at home, against India in 1936 and 1946, and two against New Zealand in 1937. He was not too successful, managing no more than eight wickets for 359 runs, but he found some consolation in being the joint leading wicket-taker with Lord Tennyson's team in India in 1937–38. It was on this trip that, stricken with dysentery in an up-country match, he continued his long run-up beyond both wickets, over the boundary and into the safety of the pavilion lavatory.

For many years, Alf Gover was the proprietor of a legendary indoor cricket school in Wandsworth, south London, whither came for tuition not only the lowly but the mighty, including Tom Graveney, Ken Barrington, Viv Richards, Frank Tyson, Sunil Gavaskar, Andy Roberts and Brian Lara. It had been financed in 1928 by his future father-in-law, Bill Brooke, with Andy Sandham and Bert Strudwick as the active partners. Gover married Marjorie Brooke in 1932, and one of their sons, John, later ran the cricket retail side of the school. Alf's real interest began in 1938, and by 1954 he had obtained sole control of the premises, with its four low-slung nets. He was shrewd in his choice of fellow-tutors, employing coaches like Arthur Wellard, and he continued to bowl there until he was over 80. He finally retired in 1989, still kindly, smartly attired and upstanding. His coaching ensured that his fame was less dimmed in middle and older age than that of his peers, some of whom, without such a focus, faded from memory. At the last, none the less, it is as part of the Surrey scene of the 1930s that he will and should be remembered.

BENNY GREEN
1999

GREEN, BERNARD, died on June 22, 1998, aged 70. Benny Green was a jazz musician, broadcaster, writer and wit who had the rare ability to make unexpected connections between his various enthusiasms, and delighted millions of people in the process. Among those enthusiasms were cricket – he grew up watching Compton at Lord's – and, most specifically, *Wisden*, which he regarded as a work of glorious social history. He reviewed the Almanack one year in *The Spectator*, and suggested there ought to be an anthology. There was only one candidate for the job. In 1979, he began work, reading the entire canon cover-to-cover before slimming down the first 119 editions into four (chunky) volumes, brought alive by Green's eye for telling and quirky detail. This turned into a cottage industry: spin-offs included *The Wisden Book of Obituaries* (1986), *The Wisden Papers* (1989) and *The Concise Wisden* (1990), originally published two years earlier especially for Marks & Spencer, a very Greenish connection itself. His various introductions are mini-classics. He also published a number of other cricket books, including a notably eclectic non-*Wisden* anthology, *The Cricket Addict's Archive* (later retitled *Benny Green's Cricket Archive*). He talked about everything with an auto-didact's zest, and in an unchanging Cockney accent. "The effect," wrote Dave Gelly in *The Observer*, "was as though a particularly grumpy taxi-driver had started quoting Dr Johnson while sorting out your change."

CLARRIE GRIMMETT
Appreciation by Bill O'Reilly, 1981

Born in Dunedin in the South Island of New Zealand on Christmas Day 1891, Clarence Victor Grimmett [who died in Adelaide on May 2, 1980, aged 89] must have been the best Christmas present Australia ever received from that country. Going to Australia in 1914, on a short working holiday which lasted for 66 years, he joined the Sydney club, which had its headquarters at Rushcutters Bay. Three years in Sydney District cricket were sufficient to warn him that Arthur Mailey, another great spinner, had literally been given the green light towards the New

1189

South Wales team and all fields beyond. This, and marriage to a Victorian girl, took Grimmett to Melbourne, where he played with the South Melbourne club. During his six years in Melbourne he was given only three invitations to play for Victoria, the third of which was against South Australia when, providentially, he collected eight wickets.

It was after his visit to Sydney with the Victorians, for the first Shield match after the Great War, that I managed to see him for the first time. In Sydney, in the match against New South Wales, Ted McDonald had performed outstandingly for Victoria and was consequently the cynosure of all eyes when the Victorian team, on its way home to Melbourne, played an up-country match in the mountain city of Goulburn. Not quite all eyes, however. The attention of one pair, belonging to a 13-year-old boy named O'Reilly, was riveted on a wiry little leg-spinner whose name on the local scoreboard was "Grummett". To me, from that day onward, "Grummett" he remained, and my own endearing name for him throughout our later long association was "Grum".

We played together for the first time in an Australian team at Adelaide against Herbie Cameron's South Africans in 1931, and for the last time in the Durban Test of 1936 when Vic Richardson's Australian side became the first ever to go through a tour undefeated, a feat paralleled by Bradman's 1948 team in England. On that 1935–36 South African tour, "Grum" set an Australian record for a Test series with 44 wickets, yet he came home to be dropped for ever from the Australian side. He was shoved aside like a worn-out boot for each of the five Tests against Gubby Allen's English team in Australia in 1936–37 and he failed to gain a place in the 1938 team to England, led by Bradman.

It was illogical to assume that age was the reason for his discard. He was 47, it is true, when the touring side was chosen, yet two years later, at the age of 49, he established an Australian record of 73 wickets for a domestic first-class season. Which raises, rather pointedly, the question of "why the hell was he dropped?" By now Don Bradman was Grimmett's captain for South Australia, and also Australia's captain. As such he was an Australian selector, and Bradman, it seemed, had become inordinately impressed with the spin ability of Frank Ward, a former club-mate of his in Sydney. It was Ward who was chosen for the first three Tests against Allen's side in 1936–37 and who caught the boat for England in 1938. Bradman, it seemed, had lost faith in the best spin bowler the world has seen. "Grum"'s departure was a punishing blow to me and to my plans of attack. His diagnostic type of probing spin buttressed my own methods to such a degree that my reaction to his dismissal was one of infinite loss and loneliness.

Unlike Arthur Mailey, the first of the Australian spin trilogy of the inter-wars era, Grimmett never insisted on spin as his chief means of destruction. To him it was no more than an important adjunct to unerring length and tantalising direction. Grimmett seldom beat a batsman by spin alone. Mailey often did. I cannot remember Grimmett bowling a long-hop, whereas Mailey averaged one an over. So much, in fact, did inaccuracy become a feature of Mailey's success that he himself came to believe that it was an essential ingredient. Such wantonness was anathema to Grimmett, who believed that a bowler should bowl as well as he possibly could every time he turned his arm over. And Grimmett was perhaps the best and most consistently active cricket thinker I ever met.

He loved to tell his listeners that it was he who taught Stan McCabe how to use his left hand correctly on the bat handle – and I never heard Stan deny it. The "flipper" was originated by "Grum" and he used it to good effect in his record-breaking last season before the Second World War. He passed it on to men like Bruce Dooland and Cecil Pepper. He seldom bowled the "wrong'un", because he preferred not to toss the ball high. On hard, true pitches he would bowl faster than his usual pace, taunting good batsmen to get to him on the half-volley. He was a genius on direction, and his talent for preying on a batsman's weakness was unequalled. He never let a batsman off the hook; once you were under his spell you were there to stay.

Grimmett joined South Australia from Victoria in 1923, just in time to bowl his way into the final Test in Sydney against Arthur Gilligan's 1924–25 England team. In his baptismal effort he took 11 wickets. In 79 Sheffield Shield games he tallied 513 wickets, an Australian record that will probably last for ever. The most successful Shield spinner in modern times, Richie Benaud, totalled 266 wickets in 73 matches, a relatively insignificant performance. Of Grimmett's 106 Test wickets against England, nearly 70 were collected on English pitches in a land where savants say leg-spinners are ineffective. One wonders what colossal figures he would have amassed had he played all his first-class cricket in England. Had he done so, you can be sure there would not be half the present insistence on pacier finger-cutting.

It was lucky for me that I preferred to bowl downwind, an unusual trait in a spinner's character. It allowed our partnership to develop and prosper. No captain ever had to worry which bowling end was whose. We competed strongly with each other and kept a critical eye on one another's performances. In Johannesburg in 1936, all-rounder "Chud" Langton hit me clean over the top of the square-leg grandstand of the old Wanderers ground. Cackling gleefully, "Grum" left no doubt in my mind that it was the biggest hit he had ever seen. Silently I was inclined to agree. In Clarrie's next over, "Chud" clouted him straight over the sightscreen and so far into the railway marshalling yards that the ball was never returned. From that delivery, until hostilities ceased for the afternoon, I never managed to get within earshot of my bowling mate.

Social life meant little to "Grum". Not until late in his career did he discover that it was not a bad idea to relax between matches. In England in 1934 I bought him a beer in the Star Hotel in Worcester to celebrate his first ten wickets of the tour. It took him so long to sink it that I decided to wait for his return gesture till some other time on the tour. Later he told me, with obvious regret, that on previous tours he had been keeping the wrong company and had never really enjoyed a touring trip. That I thought was sad, but not half as sad as I felt when, at the very zenith of his glorious career, he was tipped out of business altogether. With "Grum" at the other end, prepared to pick me up and dust me down, I feared no batsman. Our association must have been one of cricket's greatest success stories of the 20th century.

Bill O'Reilly played with Clarrie Grimmett in 15 Tests for Australia. O'Reilly's obituary is on page 1227.

SUBHASH GUPTE

GUPTE, SUBHASH PANDHARINATH, died in Port-of-Spain on May 31, 2002, aged 72. He had suffered from diabetes and was unable to get about without a wheelchair or walking frame. Sir Everton Weekes had recently said Gupte was "easily the best leg-spin bowler of all time", and certainly between 1953 and 1956 he was peerless. In 15 successive Tests for India he beguiled his way to 82 wickets at 23.57, averaging a wicket every 70 balls. At a comparable stage in his career, Shane Warne's strike-rate was 75.

In contrast to his burly younger brother Baloo, who also bowled leggies and won three caps in the 1960s, Subhash Gupte was small and slight. But he had a high arm action and the wrist-spinner's predilection for experimenting with flight and rotation. Unlike some, he possessed the control and patience to afford his variations. Unhappily, his close catchers struggled to pick his repertoire almost as much as the batsmen, so chances often went begging. He would have taken all ten wickets, instead of nine for 102, against West Indies on jute matting at Kanpur in 1958–59 had the wicket-keeper Naren Tamhane not dropped Lance Gibbs. It was the first time an Indian bowler had taken nine wickets in a Test innings – and still India lost by a large margin. There was one ten-wicket return in his career bag, however: for the Bombay CA President's XI against a visiting Pakistan Services and Bahawalpur side in December 1954, at a cost of 78 runs. While most of his domestic cricket was for his native Bombay, he also played for Bengal and Rajasthan.

Gupte was considered the best of his kind when India went to England in 1959, but the strain of carrying India's attack was beginning to tell. Gerry Alexander's West Indians had recently made him pay 42.13 apiece for his 22 wickets; India's next highest wicket-taker claimed only five and Gupte's workload of 312 overs was almost three times that of anyone else. Though he remained India's leading wicket-taker, he did not always come up to expectation on the hard pitches of that sun-baked English summer. And the Indians' slothful fielding didn't help; he was patently dispirited by the poor standard.

Gupte missed that winter's Tests against Benaud's Australians because he was coaching in the West Indies. When Pakistan visited India in 1960–61, his brother replaced him halfway through the series. But the old familiar flight and fizz were much in evidence when he was recalled for the Kanpur Test against Ted Dexter's MCC side in December 1961. He took the first five wickets and, for the first time, India made England follow on. But the comeback did not last long. During the next Test his room-mate, Kripal Singh, phoned the hotel receptionist to ask her for a date. She complained to the hotel management who, claiming they did not know who made the call, suspended both players. Even worse, the Indian board president, himself an acquaintance of the lady, told the selectors not to pick Gupte for the forthcoming tour of the West Indies.

Bitter and disillusioned, Gupte quit India for good at 33 and emigrated to Trinidad, where he worked in the sugar refinery and as a sports officer within the industry. Two Beaumont Cup finals for South Trinidad and one appearance for Trinidad in 1963–64 closed his first-class career after 115 games with 530 wickets at 23.71. In 36 Tests, he took 149 wickets at 29.55 – only Benaud and Grimmett among leg-spinners had taken more – with five in an innings 12 times and ten in a match once.

ASHLEY HARVEY-WALKER   1998

HARVEY-WALKER, ASHLEY JOHN, was shot dead in a bar in Johannesburg on April 28, 1997, aged 52. A gunman apparently walked in, shouted his name and fired when he responded. It was a bizarre end for an engaging cricketer associated with the good humour of the Derbyshire dressing room in the 1970s. Harvey-Walker made an immediate impact when he became the first Derbyshire player to score a century on debut. This came on the less than fierce occasion of a match against Oxford University at Burton-on-Trent in 1971 when he was already 26. Though he played 81 matches over eight seasons, he was rarely sure of his place, and his successes were spasmodic. He was a fine striker of the ball and once hit Pat Pocock on to the top deck of the Oval pavilion; the fast bowlers, however, usually found him out.

John Arlott once christened him "Ashley Hearty-Whacker", though the Derby press box usually preferred "Ashley Harvey-Wider", a reference to his occasional off-breaks. These, however, came good spectacularly at Ilkeston in 1978. Derbyshire went into the match without a recognised spinner and found themselves on a disintegrating pitch; Eddie Barlow gave Harvey-Walker the new ball, and he took seven for 35 as Surrey collapsed for 77 – though Derbyshire still lost. Harvey-Walker will be best remembered for the incident in the famous match at Buxton in 1975, when Derbyshire were caught on a snow-affected pitch with the ball bouncing dangerously. He handed something wrapped in a hanky to umpire Dickie Bird: his false teeth. As the ball looped to short leg when he was seven, Harvey-Walker is supposed to have let out a gummy cry of "Catch it!"

After retirement, he played in the Bradford League then emigrated to South Africa. He worked as assistant groundsman at The Wanderers and only a month before his death helped prepare the pitch for the Test against Australia. He also had an interest in an inner-city bar, a business prone to produce murderous disputes.

LINDSAY HASSETT   1994

HASSETT, ARTHUR LINDSAY, MBE, died on June 16, 1993, aged 79. Lindsay Hassett followed Bradman both as captain of Australia and as the embodiment of the national tradition of pocket-sized batting geniuses. He was of course nowhere near Bradman's class as a batsman, but the two men differed most in their approach to life: Hassett was far more light-hearted and puckish. In 1953 he surrendered the Ashes to England but his team won many friends.

In 1948 he became Bradman's vice-captain and his 137 played an important role in the victory at Nottingham that set the tone for the series. It was said he was chosen as Bradman's successor by only one vote. It may have been remembered that, among other pranks, he had once tied a goat to Bradman's bed. But he was highly successful against South Africa, West Indies and England and his batting remained absolutely staunch. He was 40 at the end of the 1953 tour of England but had scored centuries at Trent Bridge and Lord's. When he finally lost the Ashes, he made a gracious and humorous speech, having been introduced as "The Happy Warrior".

It was his fourth defeat in 24 Tests as captain, against 14 wins and six draws. In retirement, he ran a sports goods business and commentated until 1981 when, he said, he could stand modern players' behaviour no more. In 216 matches he hit 16,890 runs at 58.24, an average bettered (amongst players with 10,000 runs or more) only by Bradman, Merchant, Ponsford and Woodfull. He scored 59 centuries in his 290 completed innings, 27 of them overseas. His Test record was 3,073 runs in 43 matches, at 46.56.

He was a quick, smart fielder. Cardus described his century at Lord's in 1953 as "four and a half hours of cricket so fashioned that the watchmaker's eye was required to detect a loose screw or loose end here or there". He once remarked in a press box during a boring passage: "I'm glad I wasn't up here when I was down there."

VIJAY HAZARE   2005

HAZARE, VIJAY SAMUEL, died on December 18, 2004, aged 89. Vijay Hazare was one of the few Indian batsmen of his time who could translate prolific domestic form into success at Test level, and who could perform equally well on turf and on matting pitches. Despite coming late to international cricket because of the war – he was 31 when he made a subdued debut in England in 1946 – Hazare went on to play 30 Tests and score seven centuries and, above all, skipper India to their first Test victory, over England at Madras in 1951–52.

Hazare was one of eight children of a Maharashtra schoolteacher and, unusually in India, was not merely Christian but Protestant. He was picked for the first unofficial Test at Lahore against the very strong touring team brought over by Lord Tennyson in 1937–38, mainly for his medium-paced bowling, but was only allowed two overs, and batted No. 9. He soon, however, became a protege of the Maharaja of Dewas, who took him on his personal staff and brought Clarrie Grimmett over as well, hoping he might make Hazare into a leg-spinner. Grimmett soon decided that would not work; but what he did teach Hazare, according to the historian Mihir Bose, was patience and judgment as a batsman.

He succeeded in that. In January 1940, Hazare became the first Indian (excluding Duleepsinhji, who was playing as an Englishman) to hit a triple century: 316 not out for Maharashtra against Baroda at Poona. He made 619 runs in five Ranji Trophy innings that season, and Indians proclaimed that the great Vijay Merchant had a rival. It was the age of the two Vs. Unlike the silky, stylish Merchant, Hazare was a functional batsman with few flourishes, and his habit of tucking the bat between his pads in the stance worried the purists. But he liked to hook and cut, and in an age of formidably high scores in Indian domestic cricket vied with

Merchant on the topmost peaks. They exchanged the batting record in the Bombay Pentangular tournament – then as important as the Ranji Trophy – four times in the early 1940s, including three times in a week late in 1943. Hazare was helped by a move to Baroda, where princely patronage enabled him to devote himself to cricket. This paid off when he put together an extraordinary sequence from March 1943 to February 1944 of 264, 81, 97, 248, 59, 309, 101, 223 and 87.

That 309, in the Bombay Pentangular final, was an extraordinary innings, made out of a total of only 387 as the Rest followed on against the Hindus. He shared (if that is the word) a stand of 300 with his brother Vivek, who scored just 21. The Hindus still won by an innings. Three years later, playing for Baroda in the Ranji final against Holkar, Hazare made 288, and put on 577 for the fourth wicket with Gul Mahomed, the highest partnership in all first-class cricket.

When Test cricket returned to England in 1946, Hazare made his debut in front of a packed Lord's; his first real flourish as a Test batsman came at Adelaide in 1947–48 when he scored two centuries in the match. These also came in an understandably losing cause: Bradman had made 201, and Hazare's second-innings 145 was more than half the total. But this made him a member of what was then a very exclusive club, and the feat enhanced both his own reputation and India's. A century at Bombay against West Indies a year later left India six runs short of their maiden Test victory.

It was nearly three years before they had a chance to try again, and by now Hazare was captain against what was not much more than England's third team. He made big but slow centuries in the first two Tests, at Delhi and Bombay, and India's win finally came – at the 25th attempt in all – in the Fifth, at Madras. But this was the prelude to their disastrous 1952 tour when the full England team blew them away, and Hazare's reputation as a leader never recovered. "With all due respects to Hazare, a thorough gentleman and a great cricketer," said *Wisden*, "he was far from the ideal captain. His shy, retiring disposition did not lend itself to forceful authority." Indeed, according to Bose, he was a ditherer, taking 15 minutes to decide whether to bat or field before he scored his century against England at Bombay, and then being ordered back on to the field by the chairman of selectors, C. K. Nayudu, after hooking a bouncer from the fiery Fred Ridgway on to his pith helmet and trying to retire hurt.

Merchant later observed: "Hazare was always a disciplined soldier, never a commander. Captaincy affected his otherwise unflagging concentration and he was never the same batsman again. It was a tragedy of Indian cricket." But he made another Test century, at Bombay against Pakistan, and regained the captaincy for the 1952–53 tour of the West Indies, when the team performed respectably, though his batting indeed went to pieces. He still averaged more than 47 in Tests overall and 58 in first-class cricket, and was also an underrated bowler, whose 20 Test wickets included Bradman twice in 1947–48. But he will be remembered above all for his batting. "He had an impregnable defence and a wide array of strokes," said the Indian cricket eminence Raj Singh. "The manner in which he held the bat, hands spread slightly apart, made him different. He had great hands, and could move them up or down the handle, like a flute player."

GEORGE HEADLEY

HEADLEY, GEORGE ALPHONSO, MBE, who died in Jamaica on November 30, 1983, aged 74, was the first of the great black batsmen to emerge from the West Indies. Between the wars, when West Indies' batting was often vulnerable and impulsive, Headley's scoring feats led to his being dubbed "the black Bradman". His devoted admirers responded by calling Bradman "the white Headley": a pardonable exaggeration.

In 22 Tests, when the innings could stand or fall on his performance, Headley scored 2,190 runs, including ten centuries – eight against England – with an average of 60.83. He was the first to score a century in each innings of a Test at Lord's, in 1939, and it was a measure of his ability that from 1929 to 1939 he did not have a single bad Test series. By the start of the Second World War he had totalled 9,532 runs in first-class cricket with an average of 72.21. Afterwards, though not the power that he had been, he extended his aggregate to 9,921 runs, with 33 centuries and an average of 69.86.

Headley was of medium build, compact, balanced and light on his feet. Like most great batsmen he was a superb back-foot player and seldom made a hurried shot. Sir Leonard Hutton, who saw him at his best in 1939, declares he has never seen a batsman play the ball later. It was hard to set a field for him, such was his genius for collecting runs with his precise placement of the ball. In League cricket in England Headley also excelled. At every level of the game, in fact, he scored an avalanche of runs with a style and brilliance few of any age have matched. His contribution to the strength and power of modern West Indies teams cannot be exaggerated.

MOLLY HIDE

HIDE, MARY EDITH, died in hospital on September 10, 1995, aged 81. Molly Hide was a farmer's daughter from Surrey (though she was born in Shanghai) who became one of the great pioneers of women's cricket in England. She played in the first ever women's Test in Brisbane in December 1934 and was England captain for 17 years. Tall and lithe, she could drive the ball beautifully, but her batting had a strength as well as a style that astonished sceptical male spectators, many of whom in her era thought women's cricket was like a dog on its hind legs.

BEN HOLLIOAKE

HOLLIOAKE, BENJAMIN CAINE, died in Perth, Western Australia, on March 23, 2002, when his Porsche 924 left a freeway exit road, made slippery by light rain, and crashed into a brick wall. He had been driving home from the customary family dinner that preceded his and his brother Adam's return to Surrey for the

English season, having spent much of the winter with England's one-day squad in Zimbabwe, India and New Zealand. Ben was just 24 years and 132 days old: no England Test cricketer had died so young.

The England captain, Nasser Hussain, flew from the Test series in New Zealand for his funeral, which was attended also by Surrey colleagues and Australian players, testimony to his immense popularity. "Ben was the most naturally gifted cricketer that I have ever played alongside," said Alec Stewart, who captained him for Surrey and England. Everyone recalled his easy-going approach to life and the friendships he fostered with his gentle nature and whimsical sense of humour; Adam, in his funeral address, described him as "a beautiful work of art, a classic sculpture". And in the game's collective memory, the picture of Ben Hollioake remained fixed on a spring afternoon in 1997 when, making his England debut at 19, this tall, loose-limbed all-rounder set Lord's alight with 63 in 48 balls against Australia to take the Man of the Match award.

Would he have gone on to greater things? A record of 2,794 runs at 25.87 and 126 wickets at 33.45 from 75 first-class games, alongside 2,481 runs (24.98) and 142 wickets (28.22) in 136 one-day games, is no true indicator. His 309 runs and eight wickets in 20 one-day internationals, his obvious métier, give few clues. Simply seeing him play was the real measure: he gave genuine pleasure to all who watched, whether from the dressing room or the stand. Perhaps the 2003 World Cup – he was there or thereabouts in England's thinking – would have brought out the best in him. He loved the big stage. But while the sense of unrealised potential added extra poignancy to his death, his life, as a character in Tom Stoppard's play *Shipwreck* says of another young death, "was what it was. Nature doesn't disdain what lives only for a day. It pours the whole of itself into each moment. Life's bounty is in its flow; later is too late." Still, 24 was much too soon, even for someone who insouciantly declared himself too cool to grow old.

DAVID HOOKES

HOOKES, DAVID WILLIAM, died on January 19, 2004, aged 48, after becoming involved in an argument with a bouncer outside a Melbourne pub, where, as coach of the Victorian state team, he had been celebrating a victory with his players. Hookes was allegedly hit in the face and smashed his head on the road. News of his death stunned Australia and the cricketing world, partly because of its brutal suddenness and partly because of his larger-than-life personality. He had an impact on the game as cricketer, coach and character that transcended his patchy career record, and more than 10,000 mourners attended his funeral at Adelaide Oval which was televised across Australia. At Hookes's funeral, his bat was placed against the stumps, with his cap and gloves alongside; it was a trademark gesture of his when he was batting at an interval, a sign that he would be back. In these circumstances, it was almost unbearably poignant.

SIR CONRAD HUNTE 2000

HUNTE, SIR CONRAD CLEOPHAS, died of a heart attack after playing tennis in Sydney on December 3, 1999, aged 67. Conrad Hunte was one of the greatest West Indian batsmen of a great generation; he also played a major role in the reconstruction of South African cricket, and was a figure of moral authority in the wider world. As a batsman, Hunte could match anyone stroke-for-stroke, especially on the leg side, if he wanted. But he subdued his attacking nature in Test cricket to let his team-mates play their shots, a decision which was vital in making the West Indian side of the early 1960s one of the most complete of all time. It was an early signal of the determined thoughtfulness that was to stamp his whole life.

JIM HUTCHINSON 2001

HUTCHINSON, JAMES METCALF, died on November 2, 2000, 22 days short of his 104th birthday and 80 years and 62 days after his county debut. A Derbyshire miner, Jim Hutchinson doubled up as a stalwart member of the county team in the 1920s. He was a gifted, if not always disciplined, batsman best known for his athleticism in the field; the Derbyshire history names him as the club's finest cover. He made five hundreds, including 143 against Leicestershire at Chesterfield in 1924. None of them, however, was as famous as his last: in 1996 he became only the eighth first-class cricketer known to have reached his 100th birthday, and in 1999 overtook R. W. de Smidt of Western Province to become the longest-lived of all. Hutchinson ascribed his longevity to pork chops and onion rings.

SIR LEONARD HUTTON 1991

HUTTON, SIR LEONARD, who died in hospital at Kingston-upon-Thames on September 6, 1990, aged 74, was one of the greatest batsmen the game has produced in all its long history. In the Hall of Fame he sits at the high table with the elite, and if English cricket alone is taken into consideration he was one of the two most accomplished professional batsmen to have played for his country, the other being Sir Jack Hobbs with Walter Hammond and Denis Compton coming next *haud longo intervallo*.

He was born at Fulneck near Pudsey into a family in which there was a healthy respect for the old virtues of discipline and self-denial. It was also a keen cricketing family, and the boy seems to have nursed ambitions deep in his heart to become a great player. He devoured anything he could lay his hands on about the art of batting, and by the time he had come to the notice of George Hirst he was already a complete player. Indeed, Hirst proclaimed that there was nothing to teach him; Sutcliffe, more extravagant in his praise, predicted that he would play for England.

In 1941 Hutton injured his left arm so badly in a gymnasium during commando training that three bone grafts were needed to repair the damage done by the compound fracture. He was in hospital for eight months before he was finally discharged, his left arm weakened and some two inches shorter than the other. However, he set about restoring the strength to the withered arm, and by 1943 he was making plenty of runs in the Bradford League. His top hand was once more in control, as he always insisted it must be, and when in the summer of 1945 he played in the Victory matches against the Australian Services, and one or two other first-class games, all were agreed that his technique was in good working order and promised well for the future.

In the post-war seasons he made runs in full measure, exceeding the 2,000 mark comfortably from 1947 to 1953 and never allowing the strain of Test cricket to interfere with his commitment to Yorkshire. In the summer of 1949 he excelled himself. Two years earlier Compton and Edrich had held the stage, and Hutton had merely had a good season. Now it was to be the turn of the Yorkshireman. His total of 3,429 runs, including 12 hundreds, was the fourth-highest aggregate in the all-time list. Furthermore he passed 1,000 runs in two separate months, breaking the record for a single month with 1,294 in June.

A batsman's worth must always by judged by his performances in Test matches. Hutton was chosen to represent his country for the first time in 1937 against New Zealand. He had a rough start to Lord's, making 0 and 1, but he was quickly into his stride with 100 at Old Trafford. A year later he was destined to make history and capture the public's imagination with his 364 at the Oval. Hammond wanted 1,000 on the board to be certain of victory and Hutton, suiting his game perfectly to the needs of the occasion, obliged by staying at the crease for 13 hours 17 minutes until 770 had been scored. The following winter in South Africa, without scoring heavily in the Tests, he delighted spectators wherever he played by the sheer quality of his batting. Back at home he was in irresistible form against the West Indians with 196 at Lord's, the last 96 coming in 95 minutes, and he rang down the curtain on Test cricket for six years with 165 not out at The Oval.

MCC's tour of Australia in 1946–47 was reluctantly undertaken, for the prospect of a humiliation as complete as that of 1920–21 was abhorrent to them. But Hutton, although often not in the best of health, had a splendid tour, scoring 1,267 runs and averaging 70. In the Second Test, at Sydney, he savaged the Australian fast bowlers in an innings too scintillating to last, making 37 out of 49 before he unluckily hit his wicket, and he finished on a high note with an unbeaten 122 in the final Test at Sydney before being laid low with tonsillitis between the close of first day's play and the resumption three days later.

When West Indies comprehensively defeated England in 1950, Hutton alone seemed able to fathom the wiles of Ramadhin and Valentine, and his undefeated 202 at The Oval, when he carried his bat, was a magnificent fighting innings. Now he was nearing the final phase of his career, and he seemed to be playing better than ever. With Compton immobilised, Washbrook past his best and Edrich no longer the player he was, Hutton had to carry England's batting. He responded by averaging 88.83 in the 1950–51 Test series in Australia, 50 more per innings than the next Englishman; he again carried his bat, for 156 at Adelaide, and at Melbourne he had the satisfaction of making the winning hit in England's first post-war victory over Australia. But at The Oval in 1951, against South Africa, he had the misfortune to become the first player given out "obstructing the field" in Test cricket.

In 1952, against India, Hutton became England's first professional captain, although he had never captained his county. He at once showed his mastery of the job and kept his side splendidly on their toes. His handling of the young Trueman was exemplary, keeping him sharp and full of energy by restricting him to short bursts. Three of the four Tests were won, rain depriving England of victory at The Oval. In 1953, when the Ashes were regained in a low-scoring but nevertheless absorbing series, his leadership throughout was firm and confident, and with no one else averaging 40 he, with 55, was much the best batsman on either side.

He had to decline the offer of the captaincy for all five Tests against South Africa in 1955, owing to ill health, and early in 1956 he announced his retirement. He had captained England 23 times, winning 11 Tests, drawing eight and losing only four. Recognition of his achievements was swift. The previous year MCC had made him an honorary member while he was still playing, and in June he received a knighthood for his great services to the game.

In 513 first-class matches, Sir Leonard Hutton compiled 40,140 runs for an average of 55.51. He reached 100 centuries in 619 innings, the lowest ratio by an Englishman, and of his eventual total of 129 hundreds, 11 exceeded 200. Twelve times in England and five times on tour overseas he passed 1,000 runs in a season. A useful leg-spinner in his early days, he claimed 173 wickets, average 29.51, and made 400 catches, generally in positions near the wicket. In 79 Test matches he scored 6,971 runs for the impressive average of 56.67, hitting 19 hundreds and twice carrying his bat; he alone had passed 400 runs in a series eight times. He was a selector in 1975 and 1976 and had accepted the presidency of Yorkshire not many months before he died.

John Woodcock, 1991

Between the end of the First World War in 1918 and the start of the Second in 1939, English cricket produced three great batsmen – Walter Hammond, Leonard Hutton and Denis Compton. Each one was endowed with a wonderful talent, Hammond's enabling him to play with a rare splendour, Compton's with an irresistible *joie de vivre* and Hutton's with a style that was all-embracing. Although Herbert Sutcliffe had a comparable record, compiled between the wars, he was not in the same way a product of the 1920s or 1930s, having been on the point of breaking through in 1914.

Len Hutton died on September 6, 1990, at the age of 74. He had slipped into Lord's only five days earlier, to watch the final of the NatWest Trophy from Paul Getty's box in the Mound Stand. He had been there, too, for the Test match against India in July, and seen Graham Gooch get to within 31 runs of his own most famous record, the 364 with which he tormented Australia at The Oval in 1938.

Hutton retained until the end the unassuming manner which marked his apprenticeship. Sir Jack Hobbs had been the same; as disarmingly unboastful after being knighted as before. There was also about Sir Len an apparent frailty at the crease, a characteristic which caused his son, Richard, who also played for Yorkshire and England, frequent anxiety until he was old and wise enough to recognise the artistry it disguised.

For the benefit of those who never saw Hutton bat, I have been trying to think of someone playing today who puts one in mind of him, and I am not sure that I can. This is surprising, for he was essentially orthodox and resolutely conventional. Except that he gives more of an impression of hitting the ball, and less of stroking it, than Hutton did, Stephen Waugh, the gifted Australian of similar build, probably comes as near to it as anyone. Mohammad Azharuddin is another who possesses that intuition which gives the great natural players such a start to life. There was something quite uncanny about the way, for example, in which Hutton coped with the mysteries of Sonny Ramadhin's spin while carrying his bat against West Indies at The Oval in 1950, just as there was in his handling of Jack Iverson's when doing the same against Australia at Adelaide only six months later. He was, hereabouts, at the meridian of his powers. So, besides Ramadhin and Iverson, were Keith Miller and Ray Lindwall. In fair weather and foul, at home and overseas, if Len failed the chances were that England would.

Whether his character was influenced by being born at Fulneck, the village near Pudsey where there was an isolated Moravian community ("Protestants of rare missionary zeal") is a matter for conjecture. To some extent it probably was, their significance being quite considerable. But cricket, too, was a family religion. Those who didn't take to it would have been put back if that had been possible, and being chosen for Yorkshire when still a month short of his 18th birthday – his first match was against Cambridge University at Fenner's in May 1934 – made Hutton the youngest player to appear for the county since George Hirst in 1889.

He came into a side that had won the Championship for the previous three years – Yorkshire had not been out of the first four since 1911 – and, although they finished a disappointing fifth in 1934, to play regularly for them in those days gave a young man a distinct advantage. In Hutton's case, the transition from callow youth, cap steeply tilted, to one of the world's most accomplished batsmen was achieved in an extraordinarily short time. Within four years, Hutton had become a household name. Nothing was more remarkable about his *tour de force* at The Oval than that he was only just 22 at the time.

For a decade Len Hutton was the model for English batsmen. As a first movement he slid his right foot back and across towards the middle stump, from where, basically, he did what came naturally. He had a lovely stance, as still as it was relaxed. He would play right back but seldom right forward, preferring to let the ball come to him and playing it very late. Between bat and pad there was sometimes, dare I say it, a gap – the forward "prop" had yet to come into fashion – and through it he was liable to be bowled by an off-break. Early in the season, undergraduates at Oxford and Cambridge were known to get him out this way.

There were occasions, too, when, because of his [shortened] arm, he played his cover drive not leaning into the ball so much as reaching for it. But his timing and balance were such that it was still pleasing to the eye. He had all the strokes if he wanted them, though only when no risk was involved did he loft the ball. In his 19 Test hundreds he hit only two sixes, and one of those was to what was then the shortest straight boundary in Test cricket – Jamaica's Sabina Park. It was a drive off Garry Sobers, bowling orthodox left-arm spin.

Hutton never greatly cared for leaving his crease to the spinners, of whom there were vastly more then than there are now. Had he done so, the chances are that the generation which followed him, led by Peter May, Colin Cowdrey and Tom Graveney, would themselves have ventured forth rather more. Like all instinctively good judges of a run, he never looked to be in any hurry between the wickets. Studying under Sutcliffe in his early days for Yorkshire would have shown him the need for conviction in calling and let him into the secrets of the short single.

A broken nose gave Len a misleadingly rugged appearance. But to go with it he had a winning smile and blue eyes which regularly twinkled with his own brand of sometimes cryptic humour. He was full of paradoxes: self-contained yet vulnerable, reserved yet quizzical, shrewd yet enigmatic, gentle yet tenacious. He wanted to be judged as a person as much as in his role as a cricketer, and it may truthfully be said that, like Hobbs before him, he attracted widespread and genuine affection.

I see him on board ship in 1950 and again in 1954, bound for Australia and wrapped in contemplation. I see him working the ball around, seldom plundering the bowling, rather picking up runs as he went – a late cut here, a placed single there, and then, sometimes after a long wait, the cover drive that was his special glory. The modern game would have given us, inevitably, a different player: he would have had no chance to surpass himself, as he sometimes so memorably did, on drying pitches, and it is as dreadful to think of him in a helmet as it is to think of Compton, Hammond or W. G. in one.

I see him near the end of his tether, as a lot of us were, before the Ashes were safely in England's keeping in Australia in 1954–55. And I shall remember him at the Lord's Test match against India last year, going quietly and a little wearily off into the twilight, content, I fancy, that his record score for England was still intact, though certain to have been just as affable had it not been. He was not one to shower compliments around, but by then he knew when they were due and duly paid them. A cricketing legend, he won as many hearts with his beguiling, albeit watchful, charm as with the mastery of his batting.

A photograph of Len Hutton with Bill Edrich, Keith Miller and Denis Compton appears on page 1170; another of him with Geoffrey Boycott and Herbert Sutcliffe appears on page 1246.

C. L. R. JAMES 1990

JAMES, CYRIL LIONEL ROBERT, died on May 31, 1989, at the age of 88 in his tiny Brixton home in South London which, in his final years, had become a place of pilgrimage for admirers of both his cricket and his political writings. Born just outside Port-of-Spain, Trinidad, C. L. R. James was a scholarship boy who became deeply involved in politics with a strong Marxist flavour at a time when West Indian nationalism began to burgeon and black cricketers of the Caribbean looked for more acknowledgment of their place in society and in the sport.

James was a close friend of the great all-rounder, Learie Constantine, who invited him to Lancashire in 1932 when he was playing league cricket with Nelson. Neville Cardus helped make it possible for James to contribute to the *Manchester Guardian*, and his writing flourished; in addition to his own books on black radicalism, he helped Constantine to produce *Cricket and I*.

James returned to the United States, where he increasingly wrote and lectured, with great clarity of language and deep conviction, on social and political reform. It was perhaps inevitable he should be expelled in 1953 when America was gripped by Senator McCarthy's obsession with un-American activities, but this meant his efforts were channelled into West Indies politics, especially the move towards a Caribbean federation. However, in 1963 he leapt from his considerable status in the world of radical politics to fame as a writer on cricket with *Beyond a Boundary*, widely regarded by many as the greatest book on the game yet written. Its argument that cricket was a delight, but must always be set in context against more significant matters, and written in near classic language, made it one of the few books on cricket qualified to rank as literature.

ROLY JENKINS
1996

JENKINS, ROLAND OLIVER, died on July 21, 1995, aged 76. Roly Jenkins was one of the most popular, and skilful, county cricketers of the years just after the war. He will forever be associated with long afternoons at Worcester, running up to bowl his leg-breaks in his cap (though he batted without one) with a seaman's gait (though his furthest posting during the war was fire-watching at the top of Worcester Cathedral) and punctuating the game with a very mellow sort of humour. However, he was a fundamentally serious cricketer, indeed almost obsessive. He played nine Tests, but in the end his career may have been damaged by his constant search for perfection – as well as his propensity to make remarks that were not always appreciated by starchy authority.

Jenkins was the youngest of a family of ten, and was spotted playing in a knockabout on Worcester racecourse. He made his debut in 1938, was capped in 1939 and, when cricket resumed, established himself as a gutsy middle-order batsman as well as a fierce spinner of the ball. He finished the 1948 season with 1,356 runs and 88 wickets and was just finalising plans for his wedding when he received a telegram asking him to replace Eric Hollies in the touring party for South Africa. The wedding was postponed and he had a hugely successful tour, dismissing Eric Rowan with his third ball in Test cricket, and topping the England bowling averages for the series. However, Jenkins did not play against New Zealand the following summer, though he took 183 wickets (including two hat-tricks in one match, against Surrey) and scored 1,183 runs: he may have made an ill-advised remark to someone important. Once, while batting with his captain, Bob Wyatt, who was alleged to be rather disdainful about calling, he said: "Say something, even if it's only goodbye." "I'll see you at lunch, Jenkins," came the stern reply.

Jenkins is said to have changed his grip after he came back from South Africa and switched to something more normal for a seamer; previously, he had been ripping both his fingers and the ball. But even after this change he still turned the ball prodigiously, possibly as much as Shane Warne, though at a slower pace. His googly was comparatively easy to pick: asked how many of the 183 victims in 1949 came through googlies, he replied: "About 14 – and they were all jazzhats." But he continued taking large quantities of wickets, was recalled by England in both 1950 and 1952, when he did the double again, and remained a force in county cricket until he retired in 1958. Still he worried constantly about his bowling. He was sometimes spotted in the nets at 7 a.m. and once remarked to Eric Hollies after he bowled Warwickshire out: "But I can't hear it fizzing." "I shouldn't worry about it, Roly," said Hollies. "Six of our blokes did." Tony Lewis said he was bowled out in Worcester by a ball that pitched in Hereford.

Jenkins played on in the Birmingham League as the pro for West Bromwich Dartmouth until his mid-fifties. By then, he was a revered figure and one umpire insisted on letting him deliver a ten-ball over for the sheer pleasure of watching him bowl. He ran his own sweet shop next to Worcester bus station, before they moved the bus station and trade declined. Then he took a job as foreman in a canning factory. A manager once asked him why he was wearing two coats. "I'm doing two men's jobs," he told them, twinklingly, but pointedly all the same. For some years, he umpired village matches for Ombersley – and coached as he did so. He never lost his love of cricket, or cricket talk. "We're given memories so we can have roses in December," he once said.

BRIAN JOHNSTON   1994

JOHNSTON, BRIAN ALEXANDER, CBE, MC, who died on January 5, 1994, aged 81, was among the best-known and best-loved of all cricket broadcasters. Along with John Arlott, who died in 1991, he was the central figure of BBC's *Test Match Special* and responsible for its unique style. Brian Johnston's major contribution to the game was to maintain that it was wholly fun, like life itself; cricketers were never incompetent, they were always unlucky ("He's just dropped three catches, poor chap").

This could only be a partial view of cricket and his broadcasting thus never had the richness or depth of Arlott's. But he was a tremendous all-round professional – among the greatest ad-lib outside broadcasters – who upheld his standards and his enthusiasm until his heart attack a month before he died. Even then, he was on his way to do another edition of his one-man touring show, *An Evening with Johnners*. He was mourned by many millions.

His cricket commentaries began when Test cricket resumed on television in 1946 and he remained on TV until he was abruptly sacked – without a word of thanks – in 1970, when executives decided they wanted ex-players instead. At once, he switched to radio and, aged 58, began his stint of almost a quarter of a century on Test Match Special, during which he reached the height of his fame.

His double entendres ("Neil Harvey, standing at leg slip with his legs wide apart, waiting for a tickle") became legendary enough to attract their own

Apocrypha: there is no record of him or anyone else ever saying live "the bowler's Holding, the batsman's Willey". After Arlott retired in 1980, some people felt that the frivolity had taken over the programme too much; indeed all Johnston's professionalism may not be remembered as much as the minute and a half of bizarre radio history created in 1991, when he broke down laughing after Jonathan Agnew had described a dismissal by noting that Botham didn't quite get his leg over.

Only very, very rarely did the humour drain away: he made an extraordinarily vehement speech against the boycott of South Africa at a special meeting of MCC in 1983. However, he will be remembered by friends, acquaintances and listeners alike for his sunny disposition. Even people who only heard him felt for certain he had a twinkle in his eye. It takes a superb performer to convey that on radio.

HENRY JORDAN   1982

JORDAN, LT-COL. HENRY GUY BOWEN, died in hospital at Tonbridge on October 5, 1981. A member of the Marlborough XI from 1914–16, he played as a batsman for Derbyshire against Essex in 1926, but was unfortunate enough to make a pair.

DANNY KELLEHER   1996

KELLEHER, DANIEL JOHN MICHAEL, was found dead at his home on December 12, 1995, aged 29. It was reported that a note was by the body. Danny Kelleher was a popular and extrovert medium-pacer who played 34 matches for Kent between 1987 and 1991 without firmly establishing himself. He was later engaged on a match basis for Surrey, but failed to reach the first team.

GRAHAM KERSEY   1997

KERSEY, GRAHAM JAMES, died in hospital in Western Australia on January 1, 1997, after being injured in a car crash on Christmas Eve. Kersey was a wicket-keeper who played occasionally for Kent in 1991 and 1992 before moving to Surrey the following year. He quickly established himself at The Oval as the first-choice keeper, except on the big one-day occasions when the captain, Alec Stewart, did the job. Kersey was not an especially stylish keeper – apart from anything else, his cap regularly fell off – but he rarely dropped catches, and was a battling batsman who could irritate opposing bowlers with effective use of the sweep. Above all, he was a dedicated team man whose cheerful attitude and combative approach were an important part of Surrey's revival in 1996. Stewart described him as "the most popular member of the staff – a true player's player." The Surrey vice-captain Adam Hollioake said: "You could rely on him totally. You could get the best wicket-keeper in the world, but he couldn't possibly fill the gap."

JIM LAKER   1987

LAKER, JAMES CHARLES (JIM), who died at Putney on April 23, 1986, aged 64, will always be remembered for his bowling in the Test match at Old Trafford in 1956, when he took 19 Australian wickets for 90, nine for 37 in the first innings and ten for 53 in the second. No other bowler has taken more than 17 wickets in a first-class match, let alone in a Test match. The feat is unique and, rash though it may seem to say, may well remain so. Ten wickets in an innings, more than any other achievement in cricket, must contain a large element of luck: however well a man bowls, the odds must always be that his partner will pick up a wicket. In this case these odds were heavier than usual because Lock at the other end was, on such a wicket, as great a spinner as Laker and bowled superbly. What turned the scale was that Laker was bowling off-breaks whereas Lock relied on the left-armer's natural leg-break, and the Australians at that period were wholly inexperienced in playing off-breaks, especially on a wicket which, heavily marled and almost devoid of grass, might have been designed for an off-spinner.

The Australians had had a foretaste earlier in the season of what might happen when, for Surrey at The Oval, Laker had taken ten for 88 in the first innings, the only instance of a bowler performing the feat twice in one season. Altogether that summer he played seven times against the Australians and took 63 wickets for ten runs each.

In 1957 Laker played in four Tests against West Indies, missing one through illness, and again in 1958 in four of the five against New Zealand. In 1956–57 he was one of the MCC side in South Africa, where he met with fair success, and at last in 1958–59 was picked for a tour of Australia, where he topped the bowling averages both in the Tests and in all first-class matches. But he was by now feeling the strain and opted out of the New Zealand part of the tour which followed.

In England in 1959 he was not the bowler he had been: his 78 wickets cost 24.61 runs each and he was much handicapped by an arthritic finger. At the end of the season he retired from the Surrey side, having taken for them, over 13 years, 1,395 wickets at 17.37 in 309 matches: 11 times he had more than 100 wickets in a season. However, in 1962 he was persuaded by his friend, Trevor Bailey, to turn out for Essex, and for three years he appeared for them in 30 matches as an amateur. He was still capable of discomfiting the best players.

In the immensely strong Surrey sides which won the Championship season after season, Laker and Lock proved themselves one of the greatest combinations on a turning wicket in cricket history. He may well have thought that, when he took eight for two for England against the Rest at Bradford in 1950, his place in the England side was secure, but in the next six years he went on only one tour abroad to the West Indies.

In 1960 he had published a book, *Over to Me*, which gave so much offence to the authorities at Lord's and The Oval that they withdrew his honorary membership of MCC and Surrey, although these were restored some years later, and at the time of his death he was chairman of Surrey's cricket committee. Meanwhile, he had found himself a new career as a television cricket commentator: he had, of course, a deep knowledge of his subject, he was admirably clear and, though outspoken, never unfair.

RAMAN LAMBA 1999

LAMBA, RAMAN, the former Indian Test player, died in a Dhaka hospital on February 23, 1998, aged 38. Three days earlier he had been hit on the temple while fielding, without a helmet, at short leg in front of a substantial crowd at a big club match at the Bangabandhu Stadium. Lamba walked off the field and the injury appeared not to be serious, but he suffered an internal haemorrhage and his condition worsened dramatically. A neurosurgeon was flown in from Delhi but it was already too late. The news caused widespread grief in both India and Bangladesh. Lamba was a popular cricketer in India, but in Bangladesh he was a legend.

He first went there to play club cricket in 1991, and was a key figure in the revival of interest in the game there. "I am the Don of Dhaka," he would joke to his Indian friends. The tragedy happened in Dhaka's traditional local derby between Mohammedans and Abahani, when Maharab Hossain, the Mohammedans' opener, played a full-blooded pull shot. Lamba had only moved in from the outfield that delivery and it was reported that he had already signalled for a helmet. Lamba was known to be fearless, though, as well as an exceptionally committed and enthusiastic player. The commitment sometimes went too far: he was banned for ten months after provoking Rashid Patel, who charged after him brandishing a stump in the 1990–91 Duleep Trophy final.

Critics also pointed to his technical shortcomings, but he always hoped for a recall to the Indian team after his four indifferent Tests in the late 1980s: "Runs I am going to make," he would say, "then we shall see." And he did make runs. His career average was over 50: in 1996–97, his 19th season, he scored 1,034 runs in just 14 innings for Delhi in the Ranji Trophy. He was one of only two Indians (with Vijay Hazare) to score two triple-centuries: 320 for North Zone in the 1987–88 Duleep Trophy final, and 312 for Delhi against Himachal Pradesh in 1994–95. He had been chosen to tour England in 1986, but failed to make the Test team.

He did, however, establish a lasting rapport with Ulster: he played club cricket there for 12 years, appeared four times for Ireland, and married an Irish girl. They had two children. "I admired his guts," said his former teammate Maninder Singh. "He never believed he could be defeated." Only two cricketers are known to have died as a result of on-field injuries in a first-class fixture. Both were hit while batting: George Summers of Nottinghamshire on the head at Lord's in 1870; and Abdul Aziz, the Karachi wicket-keeper, over the heart in the 1958–59 Quaid-e-Azam final. The last first-class cricketer to die after being hit in any match was Ian Folley of Lancashire, playing for Whitehaven in 1993.

JOHN LANGRIDGE 2000

LANGRIDGE, JOHN GEORGE, MBE, who died on June 27, 1999, aged 89, was one of the best English cricketers of the 20th century never to play a Test match. He turned out for Sussex from 1928–55, and came into contention at the worst possible moment, earning selection for the 1939–40 tour of India which was cancelled by war.

Langridge was an opening batsman with an unclassical, open stance that made him strongest on the leg side. "His batting was as idiosyncratic as it was stoical," said *The Times*. "He was not only one of the game's great accumulators, he was one of the great fidgeters, adjusting every part of his equipment before each ball, a ritual which could never be omitted. He was only ever seen without his Sussex cap when he took it off in acknowledgment of applause, a doffing which revealed a head bereft of hair above his small, round and rosy face."

Langridge removed it on reaching a hundred 76 times, a figure unmatched by any other non-Test cricketer. Eight of these were double hundreds. He remains 40th in the all-time run-scoring list; Alan Jones of Glamorgan is the only non-Test player above him. Langridge also took 784 catches, mainly in the slips, where his huge, disproportionate hands missed hardly anything; 69 of them came in his last season, 1955, when he was well into his forties.

However, the figures understate his real standing in cricket. The Langridges – John, his elder brother James and James's son Richard – are one of the great locally rooted families who have characterised Sussex cricket. John was born in Chailey, lived in Brighton for 50 years and died in Eastbourne. After his playing career, he became a first-class umpire for 25 seasons; his concentration, his affability, and his quiet but old-fashioned insistence on standards made him universally respected. In this incarnation, he finally did make it on to the Test field; seven times. As he aged, his complexion grew more apple-red and he seemed, alongside Sam Cook, to represent everything that was best about county cricket. It was not an illusion.

HAROLD LARWOOD
1996

LARWOOD, HAROLD, MBE, who died in hospital in Sydney on July 22, 1995, aged 90, was one of the great fast bowlers of all time. This will forever be over-shadowed by his role in the cricketing controversy of the century, the Bodyline affair. It is a dispute that retains its extraordinary potency even though nearly all the participants are now dead. It came close to rupturing cricket; indeed, it might have ruptured relations between Britain and Australia. But it was in the nature of cricket that Larwood should eventually settle happily in Australia, the country whose batsmen he once haunted.

Harold Larwood was a miner's son from Nuncargate outside Nottingham. He left school at 13; at 14 he was working with the pit ponies at Annesley Colliery near Nottingham and would doubtless have become a miner himself had he not already been showing promise at cricket; at 18 he had a trial at Trent Bridge. This was the classic instance of a county whistling down the nearest coal mine when they wanted a fast bowler.

In 1924, at 19, Larwood was starring in the Second XI and making his Nottinghamshire debut; in 1925 he was a first-team regular; in 1926 he was in the England team at Lord's and, more significantly, the one that regained the Ashes

Bodyline revisited: Don Bradman and Harold Larwood, the main protagonists in the infamous 1932–33 Ashes series, tell Dennis Lillee what all the fuss was about, during the 1977 Centenary Test at Melbourne.

at The Oval. In that match he took six wickets, all front-line batsmen, and consistently troubled everyone with pace and lift from short of a length. The word was already going round that "Lol" Larwood was the quickest bowler seen in years. In 1927 he came top of the national averages. By 1928 he was in harness with the left-armer Bill Voce and together they would become the world's most feared pair of opening bowlers.

Larwood began the 1928–29 series in Australia with a match-winning six for 32 on the old Exhibition Ground in Brisbane (in addition to scoring 70). The only batsman in the top seven that he did not get out in that match was the debutant D. G. Bradman and, though England comfortably retained the Ashes, Bradman asserted his authority as the series progressed. By the time he came to England in 1930, he was almost unassailable.

Larwood played only three of the Tests that summer, and took just four wickets. Australia regained the Ashes. The combination of shirt-front wickets and the greatest batsman of all time was enough to break the spirit of any bowler. Larwood's urge to find something, anything, that would enable him to defeat Bradman, was crucial in rendering him a willing instrument in the crisis that was to come.

Bodyline, or leg-theory bowling, with bowlers aiming at the body with a ring of predatory leg-side fielders, was not unknown at this stage; Arthur Carr, the Nottinghamshire captain, would sometimes unleash Larwood in that manner in county matches. Several batsmen were carried off unconscious after being hit by

Larwood even when he was bowling normally. Carr used Bodyline as a tactic. Douglas Jardine, who led England in Australia in 1932–33, elevated it into a strategy. But Larwood was not just his dupe. "The game had become so biased in favour of the batsmen, there was no pressure on them at all," he said in 1983. "If we got four wickets down in a day, we'd done a good day's work. If we got five we had an extra drink. Our way was the only way to quieten Bradman. I knew that if we eased up, we'd have to pay for it."

The controversy reached boiling point in the Adelaide Test when Larwood hit Bill Woodfull over the heart and Bert Oldfield over the temple. "Larwood again the unlucky bowler", as the newsreel commentator famously said. It was the feeling that Larwood, far from being unlucky, had achieved his side's objectives by inflicting injury that incensed the Australians. However, when he made 98 as a night-watchman in the final Test in Sydney he was, according to *Wisden*, "loudly cheered". Larwood damaged his foot while bowling in that match, though Jardine made him stay on the field until Bradman was out.

The foot injury meant he could bowl only ten overs in the 1933 season, and by the time the Australians came to England in 1934 the full implications of Bodyline had sunk in. A combination of poor communications, inadequate newspaper coverage and imperial arrogance, especially at Lord's, had prevented English cricket understanding immediately what had been going on in Australia. But once opinion had changed, Larwood is understood to have been given a letter of apology and told to sign. He refused and never played another Test match, alienating MCC once and for all by giving frank opinions on the subject to the *Sunday Express*. At the time he paid the penalty rather than Jardine, who captained MCC again in India in 1933–34. History has reversed the judgment, and Jardine is usually painted as the villain. Larwood's loyalty to his skipper remained unshaken until he died. He continued to play county cricket to devastating effect and topped the national averages for the fifth time in 1936, two years before he finally retired. Bodyline had almost disappeared after Jardine's tour and was formally outlawed two years later. Larwood, though, was good enough, even if he was slowing down, to achieve success without it.

He was only about 5ft 8in, less than 11 stone, and his training regime seemed to consist largely of beer and cigarettes. But he was stocky, and his technique was magnificent: "He ran in to bowl with a splendid stride," wrote Neville Cardus, "a gallop, and at the moment of delivery his action was absolutely classical, left side showing down the wicket, before the arm swung over with a thrillingly vehement rhythm." Later generations, observing only a few newsreel clips, have wondered whether Larwood threw; contemporary critics echoed the Cardus line – and in any case his Australian victims might just have raised the subject if there was any doubt at all. His bouncer was truly terrifying to unprotected batsmen, but it was employed only sparingly for most of his career. Of his 1,427 first-class wickets, more than half – 743 – were bowled. Larwood's average was 17.51, which was outstanding in a batsman's era; in his 21 Tests he took 78 at 28.35. His batting average was close to 20, and he scored three centuries.

After retirement, he went into eclipse and was living in Blackpool with his wife and five daughters, running a sweet shop, when he decided to emigrate to Australia. In 1949, he sailed on the Orontes, the ship which had taken him there, more famously, 17 years earlier. Encouraged by a former opponent, Jack Fingleton, and helped by a former Australian prime minister, Ben Chifley, Larwood settled in an obscure Sydney suburb, got a job on the Pepsi-Cola production line, and worked his way up – "not because I was a cricketer but because I could do the job" – to managing the lorry fleet.

It was possible to hear the noise of the Sydney Cricket Ground from his bungalow when the wind was right, and it became a place of pilgrimage for visiting Englishmen with a sense of history; Darren Gough delighted the old man by calling there during the 1994–95 Ashes series. By then Larwood was blind, and long before that visitors were baffled by the idea that this shy, stooped, kindly man could ever have terrorised cricket. There was never a hint of animosity in Australia, and Larwood had no regrets either, although he repented of his old view that Bradman was frightened of him. "I realise now he was working out ways of combating me." John Major signalled the British Establishment's forgiveness by awarding him the MBE in 1993. Larwood was most proud of the ashtray given him by Jardine: "To Harold for the Ashes – 1932–33 – From a grateful Skipper."

See also an appreciation of R. E. S. Wyatt and Harold Larwood on page 1258.

RAY LINDWALL   1997

LINDWALL, RAYMOND RUSSELL, MBE, died on June 23, 1996, aged 74. Ray Lindwall was undeniably one of the great fast bowlers, arguably the greatest of all the Australian practitioners, and perhaps the man who established fast bowling's role in the modern game. In the 1930s the game had been dominated by batsmen, with the brief, unacceptable, interlude of Bodyline. Lindwall began a new era in which bat and ball were more evenly matched, when the bouncer (or "bumper" as it was then called) was an accepted weapon, provided it was not overused. He bowled the bumper sparingly but brilliantly, and the mere possibility of it made batsmen uneasy. He thus paved the way for all the other great fast bowlers of the post-war era, from Trueman to Ambrose. But in fact more than two-fifths of Lindwall's 228 Test victims were bowled.

Ray was a Sydney boy and watched Larwood during the Bodyline series. He played with other kids on patches of green and in the streets, choosing – it is said – the street down which the great leg-spinner Bill O'Reilly walked home in the hope of catching his eye. He was also a promising batsman, scoring a double century and a century in different junior matches on the same day. At the St George club, he came under the wing of O'Reilly, who used the novel technique of photography to help the lad correct his faults. But Lindwall was a smart learner and dedicated to practice; during the war, when he was in the South Pacific and suffered horribly from tropical diseases, he marked out his run-up between the palm trees and got his bowling into a beautiful groove.

Halfway through the home 1946–47 series against England, he and Keith Miller emerged as the undisputed leaders of Australia's attack; on top of that Lindwall actually beat Miller to a Test century, scoring 100 at the MCG in the New Year

Test of 1947, batting at No. 9. At Sydney two months later, Lindwall took seven for 63 and, after getting seven for 38 against India in 1948, came to England in 1948 an established star.

On that tour, he rose to even greater fame as the leader of the attack in Australia's 4–0 triumph. And though Bradman used him carefully, his very presence dictated the terms. Lindwall was injured during the First Test, but in three of the subsequent four he was devastating, reaching his peak at the Oval when he took six for 20 as England were bowled out for 52. He had a clever slower ball and, though his arm was too low to satisfy the sternest purists, he was close to being the complete fast bowler. The low arm meant his bowling had a skidding effect, which made the bouncers all the more fearsome. Sir Pelham Warner once exclaimed "Poetry!" and Lindwall, watching himself on film, discovered that all the effort and pain failed to transmit itself to anyone else. "I don't look tired," he murmured with surprise.

Lindwall never quite reached such a peak after 1948, but he played Test cricket for more than another decade. Jack Fingleton said Lindwall never liked bowling much, and always preferred batting, but he was opening Australia's attack as late as January 1960, when he was 38, and played the last of his 61 Tests a few weeks later. Lindwall simply would not go away. Inevitably, his shock effect had declined by then but, like his eventual heir Dennis Lillee, he compensated by his canniness, mastery of technique – he began to use the in-swinger far more – and utter determination. He captained Australia once and, for several seasons, Queensland, having moved from New South Wales, before finishing with 228 Test wickets at 23.03 and 794 first-class wickets at 21.35.

He was a phenomenal all-round sportsman: had he not played cricket, Lindwall could easily have been a rugby league international, and he ran 100 yards in 10.6 seconds. But when he retired he ran a flower shop with his wife in the centre of Brisbane. If anyone in Australia ever imagined floristry was unmanly, his presence in the shop provided an answer, though he concentrated on the figures, and his assistant claimed he could not tell a rose from a dandelion.

While still playing for New South Wales, he once saw the young Alan Davidson bowl a bouncer at an opposing No. 8. "You've just insulted all fast bowlers," Lindwall told him. "You've admitted No. 8 can bat better than you can bowl. Get into the nets and learn how to bowl." And he took him there, and taught him.

***

TONY LOCK 1996

LOCK, GRAHAM ANTHONY RICHARD, died on March 29, 1995, aged 65, in Perth, Western Australia where, in the 1960s, he enjoyed a career as rewarding as that pursued throughout the previous decade for Surrey and England. Tony Lock was an aggressive, attacking left-arm spinner, who complemented ideally the subtleties of Jim Laker's off-spin when Surrey were winning the County Championship every year from 1952 to 1958 and England regained, then retained, the Ashes; their names were twinned in cricket lore in a way usually associated with opening batsmen and fast bowlers. The final phase of his playing days saw him as a more orthodox slow bowler, relying on guile and flight as much as spin, and as a driving captain of Western Australia and Leicestershire.

Recommended to Surrey by H. D. G. Leveson Gower, Lock made his Championship debut in 1946, a week after his 17th birthday, against Kent at The Oval, and marked it with a hot catch at backward short leg off Alf Gover: the first of 830 in his career. In 1948, while doing National Service, he took six for 43 at Pontypridd when the Combined Services beat Glamorgan, that summer's champions. Back at The Oval in 1949 he ousted the recently capped South Australian, John McMahon, as the left-arm spinner.

Next year, when Surrey shared the Championship with Lancashire, his contribution was 72 wickets at 22.38 and his reward – belatedly in his opinion – was his county cap. In 1951 he took 100 wickets for the first time. But the 1952 *Wisden* said he would struggle to gain higher honours "unless he imparts more spin to his leg-break". After two winters working at an indoor school in Croydon, he emerged with a lower trajectory that produced vicious spin at around medium-pace. Now the ball spat from leg stump to hit the top of the off, or spun devilishly and jumped shoulder high. Gone were his original high-arm action and the classical spin bowler's loop, victims, it was said, of a low beam in those Croydon nets that had forced him to drop his arm.

His new method was far more effective but produced mutterings about its legitimacy. In 1952 he was called up for the Old Trafford Test against India, and took four for 36 in the second innings. But a week later, when Surrey played the tourists at The Oval, he was no-balled three times in two overs for throwing his quicker ball. Raising the beam at the Croydon nets helped restore something of Lock's original action, but he was again called for throwing in the West Indies in 1954 and for a time he refrained from bowling his faster ball. It was this delivery which drew the legendary lament from Doug Insole, the Essex captain, to the square-leg umpire when he was bowled by Lock in fading light: "How was I out then – run out?"

Although picked for the First Test against Australia in 1953, he wore his spinning finger raw the day after selection and played in only the last two Tests. At Headingley, his resolute batting served England better than his bowling, but at The Oval his return of 21–9–45–5 on the third afternoon, along with Laker's four for 75, was instrumental in Australia's dismissal for 162. Next day, England regained the Ashes for the first time since 1932–33, and in the spring *Wisden* named him as one of the Five Cricketers of the Year.

It was a different story at Old Trafford in 1956, when Laker took 19 Australian wickets while Lock had to be content with the left-over, and economical match figures of one for 106 from 69 overs. He had enjoyed his own ten-wicket return three weeks earlier. After taking six for 29 in Kent's first innings at Blackheath, he demolished their second innings with figures of 29.1–18–54–10. In 1957 he had a match return of 11 for 48 from 37.4 overs in the Oval Test against West Indies, and in the wet summer of 1958 he was utterly ruthless against the weak New Zealanders, taking 34 wickets at just 7.47 apiece.

On overseas tours, he was not quite the same threat, except on the soft pitches of New Zealand in 1959. There he took 13 Test wickets at less than nine apiece, but also saw himself on film, and was genuinely shocked by the imperfection of his action. "Had I known I was throwing I wouldn't have bowled that way," he said later. So he remodelled his action once more, but he still took his 100 wickets every year until 1962, his penultimate year at The Oval. He was no longer such a fearsome proposition in England but emerged as a better bowler overseas.

He was the leading wicket-taker on MCC's tour of India and Pakistan in 1961–62 and, when he was omitted from the side for Australia in 1962–63, he went instead to play for Western Australia, where he took 32 wickets in the Sheffield Shield and immediately became a fixture. In 1966–67, he was the first post-war bowler to take 50 or more Shield wickets in a season. He assumed the captaincy in 1967–68 and led Western Australia to only their second Shield. Meanwhile, he had been recruited by Leicestershire for mid-week games in 1965, and captained them in the next two seasons with such infectious enthusiasm that they rose from 14th in 1965 to second in 1967, then their highest position in the Championship. He was, Trevor Bailey wrote, "the ideal person to walk out to the crease when the match seemed lost".

Lock continued as a coach in Perth and from 1987 to 1991 was a cricket professional at Mill Hill School in north London. His final years were overshadowed by two allegations of sexual abuse involving young girls, the second only months before his death from cancer. Cleared of both charges, he was nevertheless forced to sell some of his cricket memorabilia to meet his legal costs, and while the second court case was pending his wife died of a heart attack. He said bitterly just before he died that he would be remembered only for the charges and not for his cricket, but he will be proved wrong.

"There never has been a more aggressive spin bowler," wrote David Frith in *The Slow Men*, and the aggression came out in his captaincy, his famous full-throated appealing ("When Lock appeals at The Oval," as the old joke said, "someone's out at Lord's.") and his marvellous catching. "The spectacular ones, the sudden full-length dives, were the easy ones," recalled his Surrey teammate Micky Stewart. His best were when he took the rockets, close in, without anyone noticing. Only W. G. Grace and Frank Woolley have taken more catches. Lock is also ninth in the list of all-time wicket takers with 2,844 at 19.23; 174 of those came in his 49 Tests, at 25.58. He was a volatile, vulnerable man but he was an astonishingly durable cricketer and the memory of that will endure too.

BRIAN LUCKHURST   2006

LUCKHURST, BRIAN WILLIAM, died of cancer on March 1, 2005, when he was in office as president of Kent, the culmination of a 50-year rise he recorded in his autobiography, *Boot Boy to President*. He was 66. Luckhurst was devoted to Kent, and seemed set for a contented playing career opening the batting for them, but was plucked from county cricket, aged 31, to face the top-class Rest of the World attack in the hastily arranged quasi-Tests of 1970.

"Lucky" had already been with Kent 15 years, having been signed from school as a slow left-arm bowler. His bowling disappeared but – although his team-mate Derek Underwood says Luckhurst started with only two shots, the square cut and the work to fine leg – his batting developed, and he was called up from the second team during an injury crisis to face Somerset at Gravesend in 1962. After helping save the game with 71 not out, he soon found himself as regular opener. A year later he was capped, and started to earn his reputation as one of the most tenacious batsmen on the circuit. Even so, few judges were convinced he was top-drawer until he proved it.

Luckhurst began his England career alongside another newcomer, Alan Jones of Glamorgan, who never did get the chance to play in a real Test. But unlike Jones, he compensated for a first-innings failure with a fighting half-century at the second attempt. And in the second match, he defended stoutly and scored an unbeaten 113 to lead England to their only victory of the series. Luckhurst kept his place all summer and for the real Tests in Australia that winter, when England adopted a three-opener policy, mainly using Luckhurst to open with Geoff Boycott, and John Edrich coming in at No. 3. Routing the doubters who thought he might be undone by the bounce on hard wickets, Luckhurst became, according to *Wisden*, "an outstanding success". He looked set for a century on debut until Alan Knott ran him out for 74. He made up for it next game by scoring 131, the first-ever Test century at the WACA, and followed with a heroic 109 at Melbourne when his little finger was broken. Coming in at tea, he refused to let the physio, Bernard Thomas, take his glove off. "You'll never get it back on again."

Underwood insisted that Luckhurst was the best batsman in England between 1969 and 1971, and added that, throughout his career, "he was the gutsiest cricketer I ever came across". The Melbourne innings did as much as anything to win the Ashes, blunting the game and thwarting Australia's hopes of squaring the series. He continued his form in England that summer, with hundreds against Pakistan and India. But he lost his place in 1972, and hardly played until Boycott dropped out of the 1974–75 tour, and Luckhurst was sent out to Australia to face Dennis Lillee and Jeff Thomson. He was not Lucky this time: now rising 36, his courage was no longer enough. His Test career ended amid the general carnage, and his misery was compounded when Barry Wood was flown out as a late replacement and given preference when soft runs were on offer in New Zealand. He asked to go home, but was turned down.

Luckhurst played for Kent until 1976, but he was not even halfway through his association with the county. He was cricket manager from 1981 to 1986 (though some thought he was not a good enough communicator to be much of a coach), and made a startling comeback, aged 46, against the 1985 Australians. Several men were injured and as ever Luckhurst was the man for a crisis: he held the Aussies up for an hour, batting No. 10. Affable, equable, unassuming, he imagined no higher honour than the presidency of Kent, which he reached in 2004. Weeks later, he was diagnosed with cancer, and he died before he could have the honour of planting the new lime tree inside the Canterbury boundary.

VINOO MANKAD 1979

MANKAD, MULVANTRAI, affectionately known to cricketers throughout his life by his schoolboy nickname of "Vinoo", died in Bombay on August 21, 1978, aged 61. He was the greatest all-rounder that India has yet produced [this was written before the emergence of Kapil Dev in the 1980s]. In Tests he scored 2,109 runs with an average of 31.47 and took 162 wickets at 32.31. He made five centuries and twice took eight wickets in an innings. Against New Zealand at Madras in 1956 he scored 231, and with P. Roy put on 413 for the first wicket. His average for that series was 105.

When India at Madras in 1952 gained their first victory over England, his bowling was almost wholly responsible. On a wicket which gave him little assistance he took eight for 55 and four for 53. But his most famous feat was against England at Lord's in 1952 when, going in first, he scored 72 and 184. In the second innings he went straight to the wicket after bowling 31 overs that day. In the whole match he bowled 97 overs and took five for 231. England won by eight wickets, but Mankad's performance must surely rank as the greatest ever in a Test by a member of the losing side. Indeed in assessing his record one must remember that of the 44 Tests between 1946 and 1959 in which he played India won five only.

As a batsman, he had great powers of concentration and a strong defence. His record stand with Roy lasted over eight hours and they were not separated till after lunch on the second day. At the same time, if a ball wanted hitting, he hit it. Many will remember how at Lord's in 1952 the match had barely been in progress half an hour when he hit Jenkins high over the screen at the Nursery End. He had a fine cover-drive and hit well to leg. Like many players of great natural ability he did not in attack worry overmuch about the straightness of his bat.

As a bowler, he was a slow left-hander of the old-fashioned orthodox type, varying his natural leg-break with a faster one which came with his arm and got him lots of wickets. As a boy he had experimented with the chinaman but was fortunately persuaded by that shrewd coach, Bert Wensley, to abandon it. For some years he was undoubtedly the best bowler of his type in the world.

MALCOLM MARSHALL 2000

MARSHALL, MALCOLM DENZIL, who died of cancer on November 4, 1999, aged 41, was one of the greatest fast bowlers of all time. Even in the formidable line-up of West Indians whose speed and ferocity dominated world cricket for the last quarter of the 20th century, Marshall stood out: he allied sheer pace to consistent excellence for longer than anyone else; he was relentlessly professional and determined; and he was also the best batsman of the group, coming nearer than any recent West Indian to being an all-rounder of the quality of Garry Sobers. Though batsmen feared him, he was exceptionally popular among his peers: his death was mourned throughout the cricket world, but his fellow professionals, who knew him best, were most deeply affected.

Marshall was born in St Michael, Barbados. As with Sobers, his triumphs grew out of childhood tragedy: his father was killed in a road accident when he was a baby, and he learned the game from his grandfather as well as at the beach and the playground. He began as a batsman, then discovered his ability to strike back. After playing just one first-class match for Barbados as a 19-year-old, he was taken to India amid the confusion of the World Series schism in the weakened team captained by Alvin Kallicharran. He made his Test debut, aged 20, in December 1978 at Bangalore. Marshall made no immediate impact at that level but showed enough to be taken on by Hampshire as successor to Andy Roberts.

Although not physically imposing – he was 5ft 11in – he had a natural balance and athleticism. Furthermore, he applied himself to his craft. In 1982, he was devastating, taking 134 wickets for Hampshire – a figure no one else touched in county cricket in the last 32 years of the century – and building a reputation as the bowler best avoided by anyone with a sense of self-preservation. Careful observers noted that he also bowled more Championship overs than anyone else. His first really dominant Test performance came at Port-of-Spain the following March, when he took five for 37 against India. When West Indies played Pakistan in the 1983 World Cup semi-final at The Oval, he worked up top speed even in a one-day game, and it was obvious – though he was still first-change – that the global fast-bowling crown now rested on his head.

And there it stayed. Batsmen agreed that Marshall was hardest of all to face because of the way he used his ordinary height to produce telling rather than exceptional bounce. He was, they said, a skiddy bowler. His out-swinger was magnificently controlled. And when he dropped short of a length – he was never shy of doing that – especially from round the wicket, he produced deliveries that were as physically intimidating as anything the game has seen.

In 1983 he was the prime avenger for the World Cup final defeat by India, taking 33 wickets in a six-Test series which West Indies won 3–0. Less than four months later, he overpowered Australia's batsmen, taking five for 42 when they were 97 all out at Bridgetown, and five for 51 at Kingston. But it was at Headingley in July 1984 that he produced his most astonishing performance: on the first day, he broke his left thumb in the field and was assumed to be out of the game. When the ninth West Indian first-innings wicket fell, the England players were about to stroll off. Suddenly, Marshall marched down the dressing room steps and batted one-handed long enough for Larry Gomes to score a century. Then, with his lower arm encased in pink plaster, Marshall took seven for 53: bowling first at his normal pace, then swinging the ball in the heavy northern air, throughout showing an indomitable ability to play through pain that in itself helped force England into submission. He recovered from the injury to blast England out with a fusillade of bouncers at The Oval: his seventh five-for in ten Tests, a sequence he took to 11 in 14 a few months later when he took command of the series in Australia.

At this point, Marshall was in his unbeatable prime. He set the tone for the 1986 series against England by breaking Mike Gatting's nose in a one-day international, just as he had done when he hit Andy Lloyd (who never recovered as a top-level cricketer) at the start of the 1984 series. And he led an assault on the New Zealand batsmen at Kingston in 1985 that may well have been the most intimidatory of

the lot. No umpire in the world – and certainly none in the West Indies – had the courage to limit properly the number of bouncers. But venom was only part of his armoury. Marshall acquired ringcraft at an early stage: he developed the in-swinger and the leg-cutter. And he became capable of playing vital Test innings as well, at No. 8 or even higher (he made 92 against India in 1983, and scored seven first-class centuries) without ever quite losing his fast bowler's relish in batting as a hobby. Marshall's average of 20.94 is unsurpassed by any bowler who has taken 200 Test wickets.

After play, he was affable among his fellow-pros and polite to all-comers. He was contemptuous of his West Indian contemporaries who went to South Africa to bolster apartheid in 1982–83 but, when the politics changed in the 1990s, he went to play and coach in Natal, where he became as revered as in Southampton or Bridgetown. Across the continents, to a generation of cricketers unused to the death of their friends, the loss of Marshall came as a savage blow.

The greatest of all West Indian fast bowlers? Malcolm Marshall fizzes one down at Edgbaston in 1991. Marshall, who took 376 Test wickets at 20.94, died of cancer in 1999, aged only 41.

PETER MAY   1995

MAY, PETER BARKER HOWARD, CBE, died at his home in Hampshire on December 27, 1994, four days short of his 65th birthday. In the 1950s P. B. H. May – the initials were part of the style of the man – came to represent the *beau ideal* of English batsmanship and sportsmanship. He was tall and hand-some with a batting style that was close to classical, and he was the hero of a generation of schoolboys. To his contemporaries at Charterhouse he was a heroic figure much earlier: from a very young age it was clear that he was going to play for England and he glided towards greatness in an effortless-looking manner.

Peter May was born at Reading on December 31, 1929. He was an instinctive cricketer, though there was no background of the game in his family. When he was 13, the headmaster of Charterhouse barred him from the First XI for his own good. By 1947, his last year at school, he was clearly the best schoolboy batsman in the country, scoring an unbeaten 183 against Eton and 148 and 146 in the representative matches at Lord's. He then had to do two years' national service, but his duties were being heavily interspersed with cricket and in 1949 he played enough to come third in the national averages behind Hardstaff and Hutton. By 1951 he had made enough runs in every type of cricket – including a century for the Gentlemen – to be picked for the Fourth Test against South Africa at Headingley. He scored 138, an innings that seemed like a revelation.

May became a crucial member of two of the most successful teams English cricket has ever seen: Surrey, who won the Championship every year between 1952 and 1958, and an England team that never lost a series in the same period. May adapted his method and his mental approach to Test cricket and moved from being a promising batsman to a great one. In Australia in 1954–55, May was Hutton's vice-captain, and the following year, when Hutton became ill, inherited the leadership. He captained England in 41 Tests, and was an unchallenged figure of authority. England won 20 of those Tests and lost only ten.

May's stature as a batsman increased each year, even on the indifferent pitches of 1956. In the First Test at Edgbaston against West Indies in 1957, he scored 285 not out, sharing a stand of 411, England's highest ever, with Colin Cowdrey, saving the match and blunting Sonny Ramadhin's mastery of English batsmen once and for all. England went on to win the series 3–0. In 1958, in the wettest, most bowler-friendly summer of the century, he averaged almost 64, 17 more than any other batsman. In both these years, he followed on where Stuart Surridge had left off in 1956 and captained Surrey to the Championship.

That was May's apogee. England went to Australia in 1958–59 as hot favourites, but were met by bowlers widely suspected of throwing, and slumped to a 4–0 defeat. May was greatly upset by newspaper criticism of the presence on tour of his fiancée, Virginia Gilligan, especially when one report said they had been secretly married. They actually married that April, and from then on his enthusiasm for the game seemed to wane.

He missed much of the 1959 season with an abscess, which also forced him home from the West Indies tour that winter. It was 1961 before he returned to cricket and, when he was bowled round his legs by Richie Benaud at Old Trafford, his dismissal sealed the fate of the Ashes. Three weeks later he played his last Test and in 1962 effectively retired from first-class cricket, though there was always the hope, in other minds, that he might return, and *Wisden* delayed its retirement tribute until 1971.

May became an insurance broker and underwriter at Lloyd's and concentrated on his growing family: four girls, all of them sharing their mother's love of horses, which their father, though no horseman, happily took on. For many years his cricketing involvement was low-profile, though he served as a Test selector from 1965–68, and was president of MCC in 1980–81. However, in 1982 he agreed to return to the limelight by becoming chairman of selectors with a specific brief to get a grip on the players' behaviour. He never gained a rapport with a new generation of cricketers and did not seem to have much disposition to choose between them. Had he stuck to the original plan and retired after the 1985 Ashes series, his reputation would have been largely undamaged, but he stayed on until 1988, working through four captains in the last summer alone. By the end, players were being picked and dropped with bewildering rapidity.

Peter May will be remembered best as a batsman, upright in everything he did, especially the on-drive which, famously, he perfected as a schoolboy. In 66 Tests he scored 4,537 runs at 46.77; in first-class cricket he scored 27,592 runs at 51.00 with 282 catches. He scored 85 centuries, his early retirement preventing him becoming the first amateur since W. G. Grace to score 100 hundreds. His gifts were sublime, indeed mysterious, and he bore them with honour, modesty and distinction. The fear that we will never see his like again meant his early death was felt all the more keenly.

ALAN McGILVRAY   1997

McGILVRAY, ALAN DAVID, AM, MBE, who died on July 16, 1996, aged 86, was the voice of Australian cricket. He first commentated on an Ashes series in 1938, sitting in Sydney and interpreting cables from England accompanied by sound effects such as a pencil on the tabletop to simulate bat on ball. He retired at The Oval in 1985, after 225 Tests, including more than a hundred between Australia and England. His popularity was such that in the midst of the schism between Kerry Packer and official cricket, the ABC advertised traditional cricket with a jingle – The Game Is Not the Same Without McGilvray.

Alan McGilvray was a fine left-hand batsman and sturdy right-arm medium-pacer himself, playing 18 games for New South Wales. In 13 of those games he was captain, starting in only his third match in February 1934. He took over again when Bert Oldfield was with Australia in South Africa in 1935–36, and continued when Stan McCabe was playing against England the following year. However, when New South Wales dropped him, he changed direction and became the exemplar of the Australian style of radio commentary: precise, factual and statistically oriented with only faint traces of humour.

In England, amid the sometimes irreverent hilarity of the BBC commentary box, he could sound a rather po-faced, disapproving, guest and he often saved his best anecdotes for the evenings. The nearest thing he had to a catchphrase was a firm: "That's by the by, as Lillee [or whoever] comes in to bowl. . ." His greatest professional disaster was when he flew home early from the Tied Test at Brisbane in 1960–61, believing Australia were certain to lose. It was an aberration. His professional standards were exceptionally high. He expected the same of the game he loved, and was often appalled by sloppy dress or bad behaviour.

But he still had Australian tastes. There is a story that during a one-day international in 1983, a brewery donated two dozen cans of beer to the ABC commentary team, who agreed to save them until after the match. No one remembered to tell McGilvray, though. He drank 23 of the cans – and never slurred a word.

MILBURN, COLIN (OLLIE), who died on February 28, 1990, aged 48, after collapsing at Newton Aycliffe, Co. Durham, enjoyed all too brief a career in first-class cricket. On May 23, 1969, he was involved in a car accident and lost the use altogether of his left and master eye. His other eye was slightly damaged as he was thrown forward into the windscreen. This cruel blow was a tragedy not only for the player himself but for the whole world of cricket. For he was a devastating attacking player, with a wide range of orthodox strokes to supplement his cutting and pulling. He was nearing his peak when his injury removed him from the scene he had illuminated during a period of depressing mediocrity.

Milburn was a heavyweight. One winter, after a rigorous course of dieting, he turned the scales at 16 stones; he normally hovered around the 18-stone mark. He was the largest man to play first-class cricket in England since Warwick Armstrong in 1921, but like many large men he was light on his feet, and he never had any difficulty in positioning himself for the shot he wanted to play.

Born at Burnopfield, a mining village near Durham, he inherited his large frame and cricketing ability from his father, who was a big hitter in local cricket. By 1953, 11-year-old Colin was playing in the Burnopfield second team, and two years later he was batting and bowling for the senior side and representing Durham Schoolboys. By 1959, impatient to measure himself against stronger opposition, he moved to Chester-le-Street, where he was a sensation: a string of spectacular performances earned him selection for Durham county against the touring Indians, and he seized on the occasion to make an impressive hundred. Warwickshire and Northamptonshire were soon competing for his services, but Ken Turner, the secretary at Northampton, with an eye for talent, was the one to snap him up.

The season of 1960 was spent qualifying and learning his craft. He gained a regular place in the senior side in 1961, and his maiden hundred came at Northampton against Cambridge University. His 129 contained two sixes and 19 fours, and with Mike Norman he put on 227 in 170 minutes for the first wicket. Such was his weight of stroke that almost 70% of his runs had come in boundaries, a proportion typical of his larger innings. His other century was made on an awkward pitch at Buxton: coming in with the scoreboard reading 23 for four, he hit 18 fours in his 102 and with Norman (58) put on 152 for the fifth wicket. The other nine batsmen scraped 13 runs between them.

In 1966 Milburn took the step up into Test cricket and quickly showed that he had both the temperament and technique to succeed at the highest level. Against the formidable West Indies side, he hit 94 in England's second innings at Old Trafford in the First Test, and with a memorable 126 not out at Lord's he saved the game by his brilliant attacking strokes. He had come off on the most famous of stages, but to his acute disappointment he was dropped for the final Test at The Oval on the grounds that he was too much of an encumbrance in the field.

His answer to the selectors' caution was to put the Essex bowlers to the sword with a superb double century at Clacton. His 203, which was the lion's share of a county record opening stand of 293 with Roger Prideaux, was an object lesson in how to set up a victory by attacking cricket. Milburn, already first to 1,000 runs that year, finished second in the national averages with an aggregate of 1,861 at 48.97. He was one of *Wisden*'s Five Cricketers of the Year in the 1967 edition.

That winter came a new departure: he was engaged to play for Western Australia in the 1966–67 Sheffield Shield competition. The enterprise proved an enormous success both on and off the field. Milburn's jovial manner and love of his fellow human beings made him immensely popular in the dressing room and beyond the boundary. The Australians acclaimed him. He made 571 runs in the Shield for an average of 40.79, and spectators who saw it have not forgotten his hundred in only 77 minutes at Adelaide. The following winter he went to the West Indies with Cowdrey's side, but in 1968–69, omitted from the team to Ceylon and Pakistan, he was able to play once again in Australia.

This time he made a royal progress through the states, and at Brisbane he played the most extraordinary innings seen there in Shield matches. On the first day he made 243, and before he was out in the first over after tea, having scored 181 between lunch and tea, he had hit four sixes and 38 fours. He was fifth in the Australian averages that season with 940 runs at 62.66, and when England were in trouble on their riot-torn tour of Pakistan, Milburn was summoned to help out. The players formed a guard of honour as he descended from the plane. Coming into the side for the Third Test at Karachi, he gave England a marvellous start with 139, his hundred arriving off 163 balls. But it was to be his last Test innings. On the third day the match was abandoned because of the civil disturbance, and the team flew home to England. Two months later, in Northamptonshire's first match of the season, he made his final hundred, 158 against Leicestershire, just a day or two before his injury.

There were those who liked to say that he was a mere slogger. Nothing could have been further from the truth. He was fundamentally an orthodox player with a sound defence. He could drive well, but his shots square on either side of the wicket were his special hallmark. He could cut and pull with brutal power and would literally batter an attack into submission. He was only 28 when he lost his eye and there is no knowing what heights he might have reached. He and Botham, who was, appropriately, a pall-bearer at his funeral, might even have joined forces for England.

The cold statistics show that Milburn made 13,262 runs in first-class cricket for an average of 33.07, a figure which would have been substantially higher if he had not attempted a comeback in 1973–74. They give little idea of the pleasure and excitement he gave to thousands. The records also show that he took 99 wickets at 32.03 and made 224 catches, mostly close up on the leg side; that he passed 1,000 runs in six English seasons; that for Northamptonshire he made 100 before lunch on four occasions; and that he holds the county's record with 43 catches in 1964. In his nine Tests he made 654 runs for an average of 46.71.

KEITH MILLER   2005

MILLER, KEITH ROSS, MBE, AM, died on October 11, 2004, aged 84. He was, Neville Cardus wrote, "Australia in excelsis". Free-spirited, generous, sometimes bloody-minded, altogether bonzer, Miller was the most colourful cricketer of his post-war generation, driving sixes beyond imagination, bowling fearsomely fast and catching with a predatory instinct, playing to and for the crowd. Off the field, his zest for life and natural charm attracted friendship from every quarter, be it country house or street-corner bar. He was, moreover, Hollywood handsome, over six feet tall, broad-shouldered, with dark brown hair worn longer than the times approved. Little wonder women wanted to be with him and men wanted to be him.

Associated mainly with New South Wales and captaining them to three successive Sheffield Shield titles, Miller was in fact Melbourne-born and raised. He was named after Australian aviators Keith and Ross Smith who at the time were making the first flight from England to Australia. His hard-hitting batting for South Melbourne led to selection for Victoria Second XI while he was still attending Melbourne High, where Bill Woodfull, the former Australian captain, taught maths. Two months after turning 18, in 1937–38, he made an impressive if restrained first-class debut, scoring 181 (with only five fours) against Tasmania at the MCG. But his Shield debut was held back another two years until 1939–40. He made a century when South Australia came to Melbourne, but war soon took priority over cricket, and in 1942 Miller enlisted in the RAAF, qualifying as a pilot.

When Lindsay Hassett's Australian Services team set sail for India in 1945, *Wisden* was rating Pilot Officer Miller "the liveliest opening bowler seen in England during the summer". There were eulogies, too, for his upright, full-flowing batting that had *The Times* correspondent musing whether Lord's was big enough for his mighty hitting. Unimpressed with Lord's on first sight – a crummy little ground, he thought – he subsequently blessed it with his best. His three hundreds there in 1945 included a magnificent 185 to set up the Dominions' victory over England. The first of his seven sixes carried to the top tier of seats between the Pavilion turrets; an on-drive crashed into the roof of the broadcasting box above the England dressing room.

The first of Miller's 55 Tests – the 1946 annihilation of New Zealand at Wellington – was not recognised as such until March 1948. By then he had returned Test-best figures of seven for 60 at Brisbane against England, made a maiden Test hundred at Adelaide, and forged the hostile pairing with Ray Lindwall that spearheaded Bradman's Invincibles through England in 1948. At least Lindwall was orthodox. All a batsman had to think about was searing pace, late swerve, skiddy bouncer, the phalanx of fielders behind the bat and a new ball every 55 overs. Miller was unpredictable. A pitch-perfect ball, snaking off the seam, might easily be followed by a leg-break or googly or a round-arm off-cutter. His run-up comprised nine easy paces – ostensibly. As likely as not he would come off a few yards and let loose a snorting bouncer that sucked the crowd breathless – or, when he bounced Len Hutton five times in eight balls at Trent Bridge, encouraged a protracted chorus of booing. Miller's response was a toss of his thick mane and, next day in atrocious light, bumping Denis Compton, supposedly a mate, back on his stumps to end a rearguard innings of 184.

But his seven Trent Bridge wickets had a price. Miller's pace, the product of immense torque, put a terrible strain on a back damaged when he crash-landed late in the war. (Bored with hanging about the airfield, he had taken his mechanic up for a "flip" and an engine caught fire. "Nearly stumps drawn that time, gents," he said as they walked away from the wreckage.) He did not bowl at Lord's or in the first innings at Old Trafford. When Bradman threw him the ball, Miller tossed it back, kindling rumours of a rift between them and embellishing the rebellious Miller image. He took only six more wickets in the series, and failed to top his 74 at Lord's.

Who cared? His style counted more, contrapuntal to Bradman's relentless advance into immortality. "He'll learn," Bradman muttered to Trevor Bailey at Southend after Miller, coming in at 364 for two, disdained the plunder and gave his wicket away first ball. Bradman was wrong. War, and with it the death of friends, had taught Miller there was more to life than easy runs. But Bradman, godfather of Australian cricket, was unforgiving. Miller was omitted from the 1949–50 side to South Africa. And for all his success as New South Wales captain, he was never appointed to lead his country in Tests. The stories of Miller telling his players to "scatter", instead of setting a field, masked New South Wales's pre-match planning and his intuitive leadership.

In 1956, Jim Laker and spin-friendly pitches made Miller's final tour a nightmare, reducing his classical batting to mockery as hair, pad and bat flopped forward in futile defensive lunges. Yet there were consolations. At Lord's, ignoring his 36 years, he bowled Australia to victory with peerless fast-medium bowling and his only 10-wicket return in Tests. Showman to the last, he acknowledged the Lord's ovation by picking the umpire's pocket and tossing the bails into the crowd. A fortnight later, while captaining the tourists against Hampshire, he was invited to nearby Broadlands by Lord Mountbatten, whose guests included Princess Margaret. Miller had met the princess in 1948 when the Australians visited Balmoral; now he found himself being asked to sit beside her during the after-dinner film. "The bluest eyes I have ever seen," Miller noted, but rumours of an affair gained no currency from him. "No gentleman ever discusses any relationship with a lady," he chastised the curious.

He continued to visit England every summer, working initially as a journalist for the *Daily Express*, maintaining friendships and pursuing his love of classical music. A cousin had introduced him to Beethoven early on – returning from a wartime mission he reputedly diverted over Bonn to see Beethoven's birthplace – and music, as much as cricket, was integral to his friendship with Sir Neville Cardus. Hallé maestro Sir John Barbirolli wrote the foreword to one of Miller's books. But passing years and ill-health took their toll, and he was in a wheelchair when the statue of him at the MCG was unveiled in February 2004. It didn't matter. The legend and the memories were intact; the mourners who packed Melbourne's cathedral for his state funeral testified to that.

Richie Benaud, 2005

Keith Miller's statistics – a Test bowling average just under 23, a batting average just below 37 – are maybe those of a very good cricketer, but not a great one. Those who look at them, examine them closely and then give something of a wave of the hand, miss the point in the way some people now dismiss Victor Trumper.

Trumper's batting average is ordinary compared to those who spent vastly more time at the crease, but much less time enthralling, entertaining, bemusing and imprinting themselves on the minds of cricket followers.

It was the same with Miller. In 1946 *Wisden* named him as the fastest bowler seen in England the previous summer. The war had just ended and the Victory Tests were played, and Miller was outstanding for the Australian Services' team with his prodigious hitting and innovative pace bowling. He became an overnight star in England, as he was to be in Australia after he returned and resumed playing Sheffield Shield. He became Australia's greatest all-round cricketer. To that you can add that he was also a much-loved character in both countries. Miller was a one-off. I saw no one else in the time he played in Australian cricket who managed to be a great cricketer and a star at the same time. And that was without television, which began in Australia in 1956, the year he retired.

Everyone has heroes. Bradman was my first because, as a small boy, I listened on the giant-sized radio in Jugiong as he captained Australia and turned around a 0–2 deficit to a 3–2 victory in the 1936–37 Ashes series. Then Grimmett, because I saw him take six for 118 at the SCG in the first Sheffield Shield match I ever watched. After them it was Miller who, when playing for the Services against New South Wales, hit 105 off an attack which included Bill O'Reilly. Miller remained the hero even when I played in the same NSW and Australian side with him.

I was able to watch him at close quarters for the last six years of his career, and there were four things about him: skill, unpredictability, kindness and charisma. His skill, even when standing languidly at slip, was the reason young people do have heroes. As a batsman he made full use of his height and reach for the drive off both front and back foot. No one hit the ball harder. That didn't preclude him from the most delicate late cutting.

That mixture of grace and power was also the essence of his often devastating bowling. Miller's action was close to flawless, consisting of a wonderful delivery stride from a short run-up, his left arm high while looking over his left shoulder. He always had his bowling hand going in a full sweep past his front knee. He was genuinely fast, but also unorthodox in his thinking, always trying to stay two steps ahead of the batsmen. He had studied the art of swing by watching George Pope of Derbyshire and England, and there was no one who learned it better than Miller. With either bat or ball in hand, his thoughts were always attacking, a role model for any youngster watching either from the dressing room or the Sydney Hill.

His approach to some matters, however, was less orthodox. In 1955–56, we twice played South Australia, the first time at the SCG and the second at the Adelaide Oval. In the Sydney match, Miller won the toss and then, bored with proceedings late in the day, closed our innings at 215 for eight. The South Australian openers successfully appealed against the light and "Nugget" was livid as he left the field. Also in our team was Peter Philpott. Like Miller, he lived in Manly, and Miller gave him a lift to the ground each morning. A few hours after that declaration, Miller's wife Peg gave birth to a son, Bob. After a few celebratory drinks it was no wonder he was running late for the ground the next morning, and only remembered Philpott, standing on the Manly street corner, as he was speeding over the Harbour Bridge. Miller did a quick Jack Brabham V-turn, which was possible on the Bridge 50 years ago, and arrived at the SCG as I was very slowly, and rather reluctantly, leading the team on to the field in his absence. Somehow, he and Philpott made it in time, whereupon Miller, from the Paddington End, proceeded to take seven for 12 to bowl out South Australia for 27.

Twenty-five days later, in Adelaide, South Australia won the toss and batted. It was an action replay of Sydney with Miller bowling so superbly that they were five down for 31, with left-hander Tim Colley, making his debut, yet to face a ball. Three wickets and 30 times past the outside edge were enough for Keith, and he decided the crowd should have a bit more batting entertainment. He had a casual look around the field and waved to Norman O'Neill, who was also making his Sheffield Shield debut. "Come and have a bowl, Normie, Colley hasn't faced a ball in Shield cricket." "I've never bowled one, Nug."

"Should be a good contest!"

It was an interesting debut for both of them. Colley made 57 but only played three games in his career, O'Neill didn't take a wicket and made a duck, then became one of Australia's finest batsmen. Miller was an outstanding captain, the finest never to have captained Australia in an era where speech-making and public relations sometimes rated above all else with the aptly named Australian Board of Control. But his kindness was overwhelming. It covered everyone from those in prominent places to the guy who worked at the fishmonger's stall down the road from where he lived in London. Others away from sport were recipients: people he knew in both England and Australia who might have been down on their luck, or simply having a bad trot. It extended as well to young cricketers trying to make a way in the sporting world, and it was my personal good fortune to have as mentors Miller and his two great friends, Arthur Morris and Ray Lindwall. For me, it was priceless luck that those three were there when I started in cricket.

He was sentimental too. Eight years ago I asked Nugget about the Victory Tests played when the war had just finished. The matches were fun, but sad as well because of those who weren't able to be there. He told me about one of the players, Graham Williams, the tall, broad-shouldered, bustling pace bowler, who was in the side having just been repatriated from a German prison camp after being shot down during the Libyan campaign.

Williams had been four years in the camp and had spent most of that time teaching Braille to fellow prisoners, also to Germans blinded by the war. Williams, as he walked slowly out to bat on the Lord's ground, looked around at the 30,000 spectators, most of whom had read his harrowing story in the newspapers and heard it on the wireless over the past few days. He was still tall but there was nothing broad-shouldered about Williams that day. He was gaunt. Miller said he would never forget that instant when Williams came out to bat. Thirty thousand rose to their feet and clapped softly from the moment he appeared until the moment he reached the centre of the ground. The only sound to be heard was that soft, unbroken applause. "It was the most touching thing I have ever seen or heard, almost orchestral in its sound and feeling. Whenever I think of it, tears still come to my eyes."

A photograph of Keith Miller commentating at Lord's with John Arlott appears on page 1158; another, with Bill Edrich, Len Hutton and Denis Compton, appears on page 1170.

BILL O'REILLY

O'REILLY, WILLIAM JOSEPH, OBE, who died in a Sydney hospital on October 6, 1992, aged 86, was probably the greatest spin bowler the game has ever produced. Bill "Tiger" O'Reilly was unquestionably one of cricket's great figures: as a player, as a character and later as a writer on the game. His cricket was proof that spin bowling was not necessarily a gentle art. He was 6ft 2in tall, gripped the ball in his enormous right hand and released it at a pace that could be almost fast-medium. It would then bounce ferociously on the hard pitches of his time and, on occasion, knock wicket-keepers off their feet. He bowled leg-breaks and, especially, top-spinners and googlies, backed up by an intimidating manner. Jack Fingleton said he was "a flurry of limbs, fire and steel-edged temper". It has been suggested that his action and the general commotion before delivery were born of a deep sense of frustration at not being able to bowl fast enough to knock the batsman down. Off the field, his gruffness was mitigated by his intelligence, erudition, wit and twinkling eyes.

He played 27 Test matches and took 144 wickets – 102 of them Englishmen and the vital wicket of Walter Hammond ten times – averaging 22.59. But his figures have to be judged by the fact that all but one of his Tests came in the 1930s, when other bowlers were dominated by batsmen to an unprecedented extent. No one ever dominated O'Reilly. Even when England made 903 at The Oval in 1938, he bowled 85 overs and finished with figures of three for 178. And before that, he had secured the Ashes by taking five for 66 and five for 56 at Headingley.

O'Reilly was born in White Cliffs in the New South Wales bush into a large Irish family on December 20, 1905. His father was a small-town schoolmaster and young Bill was above average at several sports, including tennis, athletics and rugby. Cricket was harder to arrange. According to Jack Fingleton in *Cricket Crisis*, the four O'Reilly brothers played with a gum-wood bat and a piece of banksia root chiselled down to make a ball. Since the others were older, Bill inevitably bowled more than he batted. The brothers also cuffed him a lot, possibly because he was starting to show them up.

In 1917 the family moved to Wingello. When he played his first match for Wingello Juniors, the team walked to the opposition's ground seven miles away in Tallong, with their dogs chasing rabbits along the way. In 1919, he went to the high school in the larger town of Goulburn, where he concentrated on his athletics as much as his cricket. And when he went to the teachers' college at Sydney University in his late teens he was more interested in such events as the hop, step and jump, in which he held the state record. According to Fingleton's account he would probably have been lost to cricket had he not been asked to make up the numbers in a Sydney junior match and, with a method that at first made everyone giggle, whipped out the opposition.

In the summer of 1925–26, the young O'Reilly, by now an undergraduate at the teachers' college in Sydney University, met the man whose destiny was to be linked with his for ever. O'Reilly's own account of this remains a classic. He was passing through Bowral Station on his way home to Wingello for his summer holiday when he heard his name being called down the platform. He put his head out of the carriage window and was told to get out at once: Wingello were playing at Bowral and needed him.

"How was I to know that I was about to cross swords with the greatest cricketer that ever set foot on a cricket field? He didn't have it all his own way, let me tell you. Well, not for the first couple of overs, anyway." By the close of play, 17-year-old Don Bradman was 234 not out. The match resumed a week later, according to the local custom. "The sun shone, the birds sang sweetly and the flowers bloomed as never before. I bowled him first ball with a leg-break which came from the leg stump to hit the off bail. Suddenly cricket was the best game in the whole wide world."

In 1926–27 O'Reilly was chosen for the New South Wales state practice squad on the strength of one match for North Sydney. A year later he made his first-class debut against the New Zealanders. But teachers in New South Wales work for the state rather than an individual school and the newly qualified O'Reilly was despatched to three different bush towns. This may have cost him the chance of a Test against England in 1928–29 and, very probably, a tour in 1930. He was transferred back to Sydney in time for the 1931–32 season and after four more matches made his debut for Australia. He performed quietly in a match in which Bradman scored 299 not out and Grimmett took 14 wickets, but he had arrived.

In the 1932–33 Bodyline series he took 27 wickets, without anyone noticing much, given what else was happening. In the series in England in 1934 he took 28 wickets, including seven in an innings twice. At Trent Bridge he won the match with seven for 54, achieved by what *Wisden* called "clever variation in flight and pace combined with spin off the worn turf". He took 109 wickets on the tour, including nine for 38 against Somerset. He went back to Australia and suddenly announced his retirement. He had married in 1933, had a daughter and was anxious about his teaching career. However, Sydney Grammar School offered him a job that enabled him to play on. He toured South Africa in 1935–36 and took 27 wickets again, 25 in the great series against England in 1936–37, and 22 back in England in 1938, despite the unforgiving wickets ("dosed up to the eyeballs", said O'Reilly) of Trent Bridge and The Oval.

He played only one more Test, the one-off game against New Zealand at Wellington in March 1946 when he was already 40. The opposition barely beat his age: they were bowled out for 42 and 54, and O'Reilly took five for 14 and three for 19. It was the 11th time he had taken five in an innings in Tests.

O'Reilly then began writing on cricket for the *Sydney Morning Herald* with a muscular, very Australian prose style flavoured with wit and imagery ("You can smell the gum-leaves off him", he wrote of one country boy just starting with Queensland). Until he finally retired in 1988, he was as revered in Australian press boxes as he had been on the field. His opinions often came more from the heart than the head, especially if it was a question of attacking the selectors for playing safe and ignoring a young player, most especially a young leg-spinner. But he was consistent, loved quality and hated one-day cricket ("hit-and-giggle") which he generally refused to watch. He was hot-blooded and humorous which perhaps explains why his relationship with the cooler Bradman is believed to have been based on intense mutual respect rather than the profoundest form of Australian mateship. While Sir Donald walked the corridors of cricketing power, O'Reilly was the rumbustious backbencher.

KERRY PACKER · 2006

PACKER, KERRY FRANCIS BULLMORE, AC, who died on December 26, 2005, aged 68, was the media tycoon whose intervention in cricket created the finances, shape and tone of the modern game. In 1977, Packer bought up more than three dozen of the world's best players after Australian administrators refused to countenance the idea of his Channel Nine network televising the game. Within two years, after the game's bloodiest civil war, he emerged triumphant. Before his victory, the game's authorities, and most of cricket's loyal followers, regarded Packer as the devil incarnate. When he died, there were black armbands and a minute's silence at the Melbourne Test, and the tributes – from the Australian prime minister and the president of the ICC downwards – verged on the unctuous.

There were good reasons for this: Channel Nine, now under the aegis of Packer's son James, remained an exceptionally potent force in both cricket and Australian society. And after nearly 30 years, the bitterness engendered by Packer had long dissipated, and there was almost universal acceptance that the changes he wrought were, if not wholly beneficial, then at the very least inevitable. Affection, however, was generally confined to his associates and the players, whose lives he transformed.

Packer was the younger son of the rumbustious, right-wing, Sydney newspaper owner, Sir Frank Packer. He was a sickly, unhappy, dyslexic and – on the face of it – stupid child; his father called him Boofhead. Kerry's most obvious childhood achievement was to overcome polio and become school heavyweight boxing champion. When he joined the family business, he was regarded as a joke: "a gangling dill", as one journalist put it. Everyone, including Sir Frank, assumed the elder son, Clyde, would succeed. But Clyde fell out with his father, emigrated to California and, in 1974, Kerry inherited.

He was big, ugly ("the man in the stocking mask"), crude and unintellectual. But everyone soon learned that he was sharp as a tack. He was not interested in the day-to-day influence that comes from owning newspapers, and – even before his father's death – had engineered the sale of the Sydney *Daily Telegraph* to Rupert Murdoch, who shared Sir Frank's taste for shaping public policy. Kerry still had Australia's biggest collection of magazines, and above all the market-leading Channel Nine stations in Sydney and Melbourne. His interest in power was at once narrower and broader; he judged politicians mainly on their attitude to him, and saw television as the medium of the future.

Colour TV was only just about to hit Australia; there was pressure to produce home-grown programmes to leaven the network's Hollywood pap. What better than sport? Packer had already shown his commitment by sponsoring, revamping and televising the Australian Open golf championship, which had been close to collapse; he did it by putting cameras on every hole, previously considered unthinkable. Unlike his commercial rivals, he saw Australian cricket as ripe for the same kind of makeover. But cricket was not collapsing, and its officials were perfectly happy with its comfy if not lucrative long-standing partnership with the government-owned ABC channel, which offered national reach, showed domestic matches as well, and made no waves. In 1976, they had an agreed but, as yet, unsigned deal for the next three years. Board officials airily offered Channel Nine the possibility of some kind of shared arrangement in three years' time. Packer wanted an exclusive deal, he wanted it now, and he was willing to offer $A500,000 a year, seven times the ABC figure. He was rebuffed. The exact wording of what he said next is in dispute; their import is not. According to Packer, he told the gentlemanly pair, Ray Steele and Bob Parish: "There's a little bit of the whore in all of us. Gentlemen, name your price." According to Steele, he said: "We're all harlots. Name your price." But they wouldn't.

Packer took a while to react, and did so only after a chance conversation with his associate John Cornell, who suggested Packer should sign up the world's best players for his own competition. This proved astonishingly easy. The administrators – and the game's regular followers – may have been happy with the status quo: indeed, perhaps the best-ever cricket match, the Centenary Test, was about to take place, in March 1977, at the MCG. But the players, eking out their uncertain careers on little more than a working man's wage, emphatically were not happy. Packer flattered them by approaching them as the world's best, cowed them by swearing them to secrecy and bowled them over by offering $A25,000 for 12 weeks' work. There were hardly any refusals.

The true story of the Centenary Test was the unseen one: the collusion involving nearly all the Australian team signing secretly for Packer. After the great game, Packer's lieutenant Austin Robertson moved under the noses of officials, handing brown envelopes ("Here are your theatre tickets") round the victorious Aussies in their dressing-room. Then the England captain Tony Greig was approached, and the brown envelopes spread round the cricketing world.

The news broke in May like a thunderclap, and would dominate the newspapers for the next two years. The reaction was strongest in Britain, where it was coloured by sentimentality, indignation, anti-colonial arrogance and a not unjustified feeling that the team had been betrayed by the South African-born Greig. But the original Australian miscalculation was now compounded. The various governing bodies misjudged both Packer's strengths and his weakness. They misread his intentions – he was not interested in running cricket – and above all his readiness to give up everything else, if only he could have had the exclusive rights he craved. They also underestimated his implacability. If it was to be war, he would fight it with far more resources and resourcefulness than his opponents.

They also misunderstood the solidity of his position. Packer players were now barred from Test cricket and, in England, from domestic cricket, although they had broken no contracts. The ban was, however, an attempt to get them to break their contract with Packer, which left the authorities disastrously exposed legally. When Packer and some players sued in the High Court in London, even those who loathed him thought he made a more impressive witness than the Lord's officials ranged against him. "Is it right that you went into the Supertest business to make money?" asked Michael Kempster QC, cross-examining. "Of course," said Packer suavely. "I have never said anything else." The bans were struck out.

The cricket itself was not at first a success. The rebels were banned from Australia's main grounds and the first season of World Series Cricket flopped miserably, with small audiences in the grounds, and on the box. From inside the Packer empire came reports that money was haemorrhaging to the point of jeopardising the business, and that the boss was privately ranting and raging. The one tiny glimmer of success came at VFL Park, Melbourne. Packer had seen floodlit Australian Rules football there, and he could see no reason why cricket shouldn't be floodlit too. The first attempt (played in whites) drew a reasonably encouraging 7,000.

Yet the venture was saved, arguably more than anything, by that last resort of a beleaguered media tycoon: a political fix. Neville Wran ("Nifty Nev"), the premier of New South Wales, decided a good turn for Packer was in his interests. He forced out the Establishment-minded trustees of the Sydney Cricket Ground and brought in replacements willing to let in both Packer and floodlights. Capturing the temple was the key to victory. The first day/night match there was packed (except in the members' enclosure) to overflowing, and Packer's success was assured, a triumph sealed as the weakened official Australian team collapsed in the 1978–79 Ashes in front of dwindling crowds. Meantime, Packer promoted his own Australians as "the real thing" with the slogan "C'mon, Aussie, c'mon." Traditional cricket had never seduced the masses so effectively.

In May 1979, the Australian Cricket Board capitulated and gave Packer an infinitely better deal than he would have accepted a year earlier. As in all the great victories, there had been a substantial element of fluke; Packer did not dream up one-day internationals – the first was in 1971 – and floodlit cricket was a chance by-product of the schism. The pattern of Australian cricket was now set, though, and has remained essentially unchanged to this day when the formula seems tired: relentless one-day cricket, mostly under lights, brought to the nation by Channel Nine with a mixture of innovative technical wizardry and shameless, sometimes nauseating, hype.

Packer personally held an effective veto over Australian cricket for more than a quarter of a century until his death, with a brief interregnum between 1987, when he sold his TV interests to his less smart rival Alan Bond for $A1 billion, and 1990, when he bought them back for a song after Bond over-reached himself. But Packer displayed little interest in the world he conquered. His admirers have relayed accounts of him joining in slip practice in the early days, and talking knowledgably and lovingly about the game. He certainly had a red-blooded Australian's interest in the national sport. Sceptics say he enjoyed the company of cricketers because he found them unthreatening. But he was never seen on the grounds he tacitly controlled. He was livid in the mid-1980s when the South Africans copied his tactics, and bought up many top Australian players, which threatened his investment; but there was no public sign of enthusiasm for the game itself.

His business deals grew shrewder and shrewder and soon he could buy almost everything and everyone in Australia. But personal popularity he could never buy. His reputation among the sniggering classes never wholly recovered from unconvincing allegations that he was a major figure (codenamed "Goanna") in organised crime. He was, in many ways, a monster: a mix of Citizen Kane and Henry VIII, and he tyrannised his employees with his mood swings. But he could inspire unbelievable loyalty in some of them, like his helicopter pilot Nick Ross, who in 2000 donated a kidney so Packer could have a transplant.

Ten years earlier, Packer lay clinically dead for eight minutes after having a heart attack playing polo. The fact that he came back, authoritatively announcing that there was "fucking nothing" on the other side, only added to his aura. But illness took its toll. He became more like Howard Hughes than Henry VIII. He was a restless, seemingly lonely and often sickly figure, watching TV endlessly, and so rich that he could only get kicks by gambling on a scale that made him the highest of high rollers. He reputedly won $US24m in Las Vegas in 1995; one night at the Ritz in London, he dropped £2m, ate a boiled egg and raw onion, then won £3m. Australian casinos could not face such opposition, so he turned to owning them instead; under the next generation, these look like becoming the new centre-piece of the Packer empire.

It is intriguing to speculate what might have happened had 1970s administrators been less boof-headed and given Packer what he wanted in the first place. Somehow, somewhere, the game would have changed, possibly in a way that better preserved its most endearing qualities. His motives were positively not altruistic. As the former ACB secretary Graham Halbish pointed out, Packer did far better out of cricket than cricket did out of him: he got hours of high-rating TV incredibly cheap. And his stations have not always been loyal to the game itself, refusing to show the 2005 Ashes because they stretched across Australia's evening prime-time. But the consequences of his involvement were immediately beneficial for the long-downtrodden professional cricketer. England players' fees (£210 per Test in 1976) rapidly quintupled because the split galvanised the official game enough to bring about Test match sponsorship. Professional cricketers across the globe might wish to pay Kerry Packer homage; but if cricket ever erects a statue, there will be plenty of passers-by who will have an irresistible urge to spit on it.

A photograph of Kerry Packer with Tony Greig appears on page 22.

IAN PEEBLES   1981

PEEBLES, IAN ALEXANDER ROSS, who died on February 28, 1980, aged 72, was for a short time one of the most formidable bowlers in the world and one of the few who could make Bradman look fallible. A tall man with a beautifully easy run-up and a high action, which gave him a particularly awkward flight, he bowled leg-breaks and googlies, and in an age of fine leg-spinners he was, for a while, the equal of any. The start of his career was unusual. Coming south from Scotland in the hope of getting a chance in the cricket world, he was engaged as Secretary at the Aubrey Faulkner School of Cricket and so impressed Faulkner himself (to whose coaching he always acknowledged a great debt) and also Sir Pelham Warner that, when difficulty was found in raising a good enough Gentlemen's side against the Players at The Oval in 1927, he was given a place. On this occasion he bowled Sandham, but that was his only wicket; nor was he more successful later in the season at the Folkestone and Scarborough Festivals.

However that winter he was sent with the MCC side to South Africa: ostensibly he went as secretary to the captain, but he bowled well enough to secure a place in the first four Tests and, without doing anything spectacular, made it clear that his possibilities had not been overestimated. In 1928 he played a few matches for Middlesex, but it was in 1929 that he really came to the fore, taking 120 wickets at just under 20 runs each and being one of three amateurs to take 100 wickets for the county that season – a unique performance.

In 1930 he was up at Oxford, for whom he took 70 wickets, 13 of them against Cambridge; then, after taking six wickets (including Hobbs, Sutcliffe and Leyland) for 105 for the Gentlemen v the Players, he was picked for the Fourth Test at Old Trafford. Here, as soon as Peebles came on, Woodfull, who was well set, became acutely uncomfortable, on one occasion leaving a ball which just went over his middle stump; Bradman, coming in, was all but bowled first ball by Peebles, who then had him dropped in the slips and finally caught at slip for 14. The first three balls Kippax received from Peebles produced three confident but unsuccessful appeals for lbw. For such bowling three for 150 was a wholly inadequate reward. In the final Test at The Oval six for 204 may not look much, but in an Australian total of 695 it was better than anyone else.

That winter Peebles went again with MCC to South Africa and both there and against New Zealand in the following summer he was one of the most effective bowlers. Already, though, the amount of bowling he had had to do in matches, followed by countless hours in the nets in winter, was affecting him: his leg-break was losing its venom, he was becoming increasingly dependent upon his googly, and his great days were passing, though he was picked for the last Test in 1934, an invitation which he had to refuse owing to injury.

When, after several seasons of intermittent appearances, he returned to regular county cricket in 1939 to captain Middlesex, Peebles was really no more than a change bowler, and though he played occasionally until 1948, the loss of an eye in a war-time air-raid had, to all intents and purposes, ended his serious cricket career.

After his playing days were over he entered the wine trade and also became a notable cricket writer and journalist. When writing of players he had played with or seen, he was in the top class; to a deep knowledge of the game he added rare charm and humour. For any student of cricket history over the last 60 years, his many books are compulsory and delightful reading.

BILL PONSFORD
1992

PONSFORD, WILLIAM HAROLD, died at Kyneton, Victoria, on April 6, 1991, at 90. He was Australia's oldest living Test cricketer and the sole survivor of H. L. Collins's 1926 team in England. He made 162 in his second first-class game, for Victoria against Tasmania at Launceston in February 1922, but did not play for the state again until selected against the same opposition a year later in Melbourne. Then, in what was only his fourth innings, he created a sensation by hitting 429 in 477 minutes: it was the world's highest first-class score until he bettered it five years later. Furthermore, Victoria's 1,059 was the first four-figure total in any first-class match, and Ponsford, who was captaining his side, stayed until he made the 1,000th run himself, having gone in at 200 for three.

He was soon to prove that his 429 was something more than money for old rope against moderate bowling, as some would have it. The previous record holder MacLaren had protested peevishly at the status of the match. Four centuries for Victoria in 1923–24, including 248 out of 456 with Edgar Mayne for the first wicket against Queensland sounded a warning note of what was in store for bowlers. The next season he played in all five Tests against England and scored 110 and 128 in the first two, an unprecedented achievement. His tour of England in 1926 was less successful, but early in December a veritable torrent of runs began to flow from his bat. Never before had anyone strung together such a series of colossal scores as Ponsford did in 1926–27 and 1927–28. In 1926–27, his innings were 214 and 54, 151, 352, 108 and 84, 12 and 116, 131 and seven, producing an aggregate of 1,229 runs at 122.90; in 1927–28 he scored 133, 437, 202 and 38, 336, six and two, and 63 – an aggregate of 1,217 at 152.12. His 336 against South Australia in January 1928 was his 11th first-class hundred in consecutive matches in Australia.

Only phenomenal powers of concentration, a high degree of physical fitness and an insatiable appetite for runs could have sustained him through so many hours at the crease. Over Christmas in 1926, Ponsford was in especially devastating form. On the second day of Victoria's match against New South Wales at Melbourne, he dominated an opening partnership of 375 with Woodfull, and his 352, of which 334 were made in a day, contained 36 fours. It was the foundation of Victoria's 1,107, still the record first-class total. But in reviewing 1927–28 the gods must have deemed Ponsford guilty of hubris, after he had had the temerity to amass 1,013 runs in only four innings. Nemesis was soon to follow: his new world-record score of 437, made in 621 minutes against Queensland at Melbourne, was eclipsed two years later by the young Bradman's 452 not out.

The difference between Ponsford's career and Test averages is 17 runs. In his first and last series, those of 1924–25 and 1934 against England, he made nearly half of his total of Test runs for an average of 64.81 whereas in his other six series he made his runs at under 40. This calls for an explanation. Although a member of the supporting cast in England in 1930, Ponsford played two fine innings – 81 at Lord's and 110 at The Oval; and in 1930–31, he took heavy toll of the West Indies attack, just pipping Bradman in the averages. But in his other three series against England, the rhythm and progress of his Test career was disrupted by illness, injury and Bodyline.

Ponsford is the only player to have exceeded 400 twice. He and Hammond, apart from Bradman who made six, are the only players to have hit four triple hundreds, and his 281 not out against MCC at Lord's in 1934 is the highest score by an Australian on the ground. He shared in five partnerships of 375 or more; with Woodfull, whose career record so closely matched his own, he put together 23 three-figure partnerships, 18 of them for the first wicket and 12 over 150. In 162 first-class matches, he scored 13,819 runs at 65.18, an average only Bradman and Merchant have bettered among batsmen with more than 10,000 runs, and he hit 47 hundreds. In the Sheffield Shield his runs totalled 5,413 at 83.27, and in 29 Tests he made 2,122 runs for an average of 48.22. A superb outfielder in any position, he had 71 catches to his credit – although, when examined for war service, he was found to be red-green colour-blind.

"Ponny" was a man of few words outside the dressing room: shy, modest and shunning publicity at all costs. When he was "postered" in Sydney in 1928 after his extraordinary four-innings sequence, it must have given him nightmares; the flow of runs suddenly stopped. Few, however, have been more eloquent with the bat than the great Victorian.

NORMAN PRESTON

1981

Born March 18, 1903. Died March 6, 1980. Editor of Wisden *1951–80. The following tribute was paid by Denis Compton at Norman Preston's memorial service.*

Throughout my cricketing career I regarded Norman Preston as one of my best friends. His jovial face, lively sense of humour and infectious laugh endeared him to all cricketers. How true it was when he was affectionately described by John Woodcock in *The Times* as the Mr Pickwick of cricket.

Norman Preston was not one to present different faces to different people. Rather, he could be described as a definite man: definite in appearances, definite in his opinions, and definite in his likes and dislikes. He was also a man of great humanity and pride, in the best sense of that word.

That pride showed itself in his pleasure at being honoured by the award of the MBE in the Queen's Jubilee Honours List in 1977 – an award he regarded as belonging as much to his beloved Almanack as to himself. Pride, too, in his profession, which he showed on receiving his MBE from the Queen when, on being asked what he did, replied: "I am a sporting reporter, Your Majesty." Sporting reporter he certainly was, with a career spanning 47 years which began when he joined the old Pardon's Cricket Reporting Agency in 1933 and took in three overseas tours as Reuters' correspondent.

The 28 editions of *Wisden Cricketers' Almanack* published under his editorship are also testimony to the truth of that statement. They cover a period which saw more changes and innovations than any other in the history of the game. Norman saw to it that *Wisden* faithfully recorded events as they occurred and never forebore to comment forthrightly whenever he thought such comment was called for. Norman Preston is rightly assured of a place in cricket history, not because of prowess on the field of play, nor indeed because of the power of his pen, but because for 28 years he ensured that every detail of cricket was duly compiled, collated and published without fear or favour.

Appreciation by Harold Abel, 1981

To have lived 35 years knowing Norman Preston, first as my employer, then as a close colleague, and finally, I like to think, as a trusted friend, means that his passing leaves a deep chasm. Here was a man who within half an hour could chastise you, console you and take you for a drink. To be able to forgive is one of life's great virtues – and Norman could do that. To bear a grudge was not for him. He was an extrovert, ever ready to enter a conversation, invited or uninvited. Nobody needed to be lonely in his presence, and no one was for long.

Norman's voice was heard more than once from the choir stalls of St Paul's Cathedral. He sang better than he played sport, though in his 76 years he entered wholeheartedly into many pastimes. Towards the end of his days he bore a strong facial resemblance to his father, Hubert, known, likewise with affection, as "Deafy". Both spent most of their working days in Fleet Street as partners in the Cricket Reporting Agency, from whence, until it was merged in 1965 with the Press Association, came the majority of *Wisden*'s editors. Hubert was in the editorial chair from 1944 until 1951, and Norman from 1952 (when *Wisden* cost twelve shillings and sixpence) until his death. The book was never far from the minds of either of them.

SIR TERENCE RATTIGAN 1978

RATTIGAN, SIR TERENCE MERVYN, CBE, the famous play-writer, who died in Bermuda on November 30, 1977, aged 66, was, like his father and his uncle, in the Harrow XI. He won his place in 1929 as an opening bat, but next year, though he played in the XI, was not in the side at Lord's. He was an elegant stroke player, but unsound.

ALAN ROSS 2002

ROSS, ALAN, CBE, cricket writer and litterateur, died suddenly of a heart attack on February 14, 2001, aged 78. He was born in Calcutta, whence he was dispatched to private schools in Falmouth and East Grinstead, and on to Haileybury, where his medium-paced bowling served the XI well. His time at Oxford was fleeting, but he did play in the hastily arranged one-day game with Cambridge in 1941; some 7,000 turned up at Lord's, and £120 in gate money was donated to the Red Cross. Then it was off to the Royal Navy and convoy duties in the Arctic. His cricket writing stemmed chiefly from his spell as cricket correspondent of *The Observer* from 1950–71, and was in direct line of descent from R. C. Robertson-Glasgow. His account of the 1954–55 antipodean tour, *Australia 55*, and his 1983 biography, *Ranji: Prince of Cricketers*, are perhaps the best of his cricket books, along with the tasty pickings of *The Cricketer's Companion*, the anthology of prose and verse he first edited in 1960. From 1961, he took on the lifelong, spirited if rarely trouble-free editorship of the influential *London Magazine*.

Much as Ross enjoyed the bohemian and metropolitan life, Sussex, and in particular the Hove ground, also played host to his spirit. With Bert Wensley, the Sussex professional, having been rich in anecdote as his coach at Haileybury, his poetry and prose were both redolent of that county's pre-war flavours, as in these lines from *Cricket at Brighton*:

Today Langridge pushes the ball for unfussed
Singles; ladies clap from check rugs, talk to retired colonels;
On tomato-red verandas the scoring rate is discussed.

Romanticist and averse to the trite arithmetic of the game, Alan Ross might well
have chosen St Valentine's Day as an apt moment for his widely mourned demise.

LORD RUNCIE

2001

RUNCIE of CUDDESDON, The Rt Rev. Baron, MC, PC, who died on July 11,
2000, aged 78, was Archbishop of Canterbury from 1980–91. Robert Runcie was a
useful schoolboy cricketer at Merchant Taylors, Crosby, where he was opening bat
and captain. He also played for his Oxford college, Brasenose, and remained a lifelong lover of the game. After retiring from Canterbury, he became one of the best
of all cricketing speakers, crafting witty, erudite and self-deprecating speeches with
loving care. He spoke beautifully at the 1997 *Wisden* dinner and then, though he
was already very ill, delivered a masterful eulogy at E. W. Swanton's funeral in
February 2000. His father-in-law, J. C. W. Turner, played for Worcestershire.

WILLIE RUSHTON

1997

RUSHTON, WILLIAM GEORGE, who died on December 11, 1996, aged 59, was a
well-known TV and radio humorist and a passionate follower of cricket. He regularly
drew cartoons for *The Cricketer* – including the January 1997 cover illustration –
and his novels included *W. G. Grace's Last Case*, a fantasy in which W. G. and
Dr Watson foil a plot to take over the world by Martians.

ANDREW SANDHAM

1983

SANDHAM, ANDREW, who died in hospital on April 20, 1982, aged 91, might,
had things turned out differently, have been for years a regular and successful Test
match batsman. It was his misfortune that, slow to develop, owing partly to the
great pressure for places as batsmen in the Surrey side, partly to the Great War,
he was over 30 when he first came into serious consideration, and by then his
rival as Hobbs's partner was Sutcliffe. By the time Hobbs retired from international cricket Sandham was too old to be his replacement. And so he will be
remembered as a wonderful servant of Surrey and as Hobbs's partner for the
county for 15 years.

He had formed his style in his early days by watching Tom Hayward, much
of whose skill on the leg side he had inherited, and he perfected it by association
with Hobbs. Like many small men he was quick on his feet and a fine and fearless

hooker: this, with his mastery of the cut, in which he always made full use of such height as he had, made him a particularly good player of fast bowling. Of his other strokes perhaps the best was a square drive. He was also a magnificent outfield with a fast and low return, whose value was even greater in the days when the whole area of The Oval was used more often than it is now.

MARK SAXELBY   2001

SAXELBY, MARK, died on October 12, 2000, aged 31, having apparently committed suicide by drinking weedkiller. It emerged that he had been suffering from chronic clinical depression almost throughout his cricketing career, and the baffled comments of team-mates about his inability to match achievement to promise could be seen in a new and poignant light. In dressing-rooms, he was thought to be likeable but withdrawn, and his cricketing ups and downs were often attributed to his back problems.

A tall, gifted left-handed batsman, he followed his older brother, Kevin, on to the Nottinghamshire staff, with limited success, then suddenly blossomed after moving to Durham in 1994. On his Championship debut for them, he scored a brilliant 181 against Derbyshire at Chesterfield and followed with 63 and 131 at Stockton-on-Tees on his home debut. Though his form inevitably dwindled, he still scored more than 1,000 Championship runs that season, and things only started to go seriously wrong after the arrival of Mike Roseberry the following year. This forced Saxelby to drop down the order, which he disliked, and he was released.

He began playing league cricket for Heanor Town, to such effect that in 2000 Derbyshire hurriedly registered him for their home Championship match against Lancashire. Kevin Saxelby said his brother disliked Sunday cricket because there were often large crowds; he also felt uncomfortable if someone praised his batting. "It came as a terrible, terrible shock," he said, "but we knew he'd been through torment."

SHAKOOR RANA   2002

SHAKOOR RANA, who found his few minutes of fame in an unedifying spat with Mike Gatting in the 1987 Faisalabad Test, died of a heart attack in Lahore on April 9, 2001, aged 65. As much as three-quarters of his press obituaries were consumed by the squabble after he halted play because, Shakoor Rana alleged, Gatting had moved a fielder without the batsman's knowledge. Umpire and England captain had a toe-to-toe, finger-jabbing confrontation, there were reciprocal charges of cheating and swearing, and the third day's play was lost, helping Pakistan escape with a draw. The match did not resume until an apology was forthcoming from the English camp.

A right-hand batsman and medium-fast bowler in his playing days, Shakoor Rana made his first-class debut for Punjab in the 1957–58 season, and between then and 1972–73 he also played for Lahore, Khairpur and Pakistan Railways, with whom he held a post as a sports officer. In 11 first-class games, he scored 226 runs, took a dozen wickets and held 11 catches. Three of his brothers, Shafqat, Azmat and Sultan, also played first-class cricket (the first two at Test level), and two of his sons, Mansoor and Maqsood, played one-day cricket for Pakistan.

Burly of frame and jocose by nature, he stood in 18 Tests and 22 one-day internationals from 1974–75 to 1996–97, and was reckoned to be upright and bold in his decision-making. It seems he could be self-important, too. In the 1984 Test at Karachi, he quarrelled with the New Zealand captain, Jeremy Coney, when he ignored an appeal for a catch at the wicket against Javed Miandad, and the outraged New Zealander threatened to lead his team from the arena. But former Sussex captain John Barclay remembered a much friendlier character from the 1981 summer, when Shakoor Rana was umpiring in England. Barclay had been told by an Indian taxi-driver to ask "Where's Allah?" (rather than the customary "Howzat?") when appealing; the response would be a finger pointing to the sky. Shakoor Rana was having none of it. "Not that silly trick again," he said *sotto voce* as Barclay walked back to his mark.

A photograph of Shakoor Rana arguing with Mike Gatting appears on page 156.

ROY SHEFFIELD
1998

SHEFFIELD, JAMES ROY, died in New Zealand on November 16, 1997, aged 90. Roy Sheffield was probably the only Essex wicket-keeper ever to be arrested on suspicion of being a Bolivian spy. He was a small, agile man who kept wicket in 177 games for Essex between 1929 and 1936. Though he was an efficient keeper, Sheffield's batting shone only intermittently – he scored 85 not out on his debut against Warwickshire, and made a century at Hove in his last season, but did little in between.

Sheffield was more notable for his off-season adventures. In 1932–33, while England's most famous cricketers were involved in the Bodyline series, he was working as a cowboy in South America and trying to canoe down the River Paraguay. There was a war going on between Paraguay and Bolivia, and the Paraguayans arrested Sheffield and locked him up until a British businessman intervened. He later wrote a novel based on the incident, entitled *Bolivian Spy*. A year later he spent two months walking through the Drakensberg Mountains and Basutoland. Essex did not retain him after 1936 and he left for New Zealand, meeting his future wife on the boat, and never returned to England. He played three games for Wellington in 1938–39, but later concentrated on his canoeing. He competed in the 50-mile Waikato River Marathon when he was well into his eighties; the Essex secretary Peter Edwards visited him in 1992 and described him as astonishingly fit. He died a few days after his daughter, a BBC producer who had been visiting him, was knocked off her bike and killed.

DAVID SHEPPARD

Baron SHEPPARD of LIVERPOOL (Rt Rev. David Stuart Sheppard) died on March 5, 2005, the day before his 76th birthday. Rev. David Sheppard, as he was known for most of his playing career, was one of the most remarkable men ever to play cricket to a high level. His involvement was intermittent but always eventful. He captained England in two Tests in 1954. Had he devoted himself to cricket, Sheppard would have captained more often, and could easily have scored a hundred hundreds. Instead he devoted himself to the Church, where he rose to become a long-serving, distinctive and, by most reckonings, outstanding Bishop of Liverpool. Politics cost him his chance of becoming an archbishop.

Unlike his exact contemporary, Peter May, Sheppard was no schoolboy prodigy. At prep school, he was a slow left-armer and tailender, and he was 17 before he broke into the team at his public school, Sherborne. But, under the tutelage of Micky Walford and Len Creese, he blossomed as a batsman as he grew from a shrimp into a strong young man, good enough to get three games for Sussex just after he left school, and 204, 147 and 130 in 11 days for them as a 20-year-old late in 1949. The next year, when Sheppard and May arrived at Cambridge together after National Service, it was Sheppard who was first to sparkle, gaining national attention in 1950 when he shared an opening stand of 343 with John Dewes, and went on to a chance-less 227, against the mighty 1950 West Indians. That helped catapult Sheppard into the Test team at The Oval and both men on to the tour of Australia.

He scored heavily for Cambridge and Sussex in 1951, though now May was ahead of him in the selectors' minds, and Sheppard did not return to the Test team until 1952, when he took a century off the weak Indian team at The Oval without looking in touch. By now, after hearing an American Presbyterian preach in Cambridge, he had turned to an intense form of evangelical Christianity, and the two poles of his life were starting to pull him in contrary directions. He agreed, after some hesitation, to captain Sussex in 1953, leading them from 13th to a near-miss second. "We always said he was the best captain we ever had," said Alan Oakman. "He led by example and he supported everyone. He was the first captain we'd ever had who applauded your good bits of fielding. He didn't swear at us either."

Now he did put the church first, and studied for the priesthood at Ridley Hall, Cambridge. But his success at Sussex had given him a national reputation as a potential captain and, in 1954, when Len Hutton was ill, England asked Sheppard to take charge at Trent Bridge and Old Trafford against the infant Pakistan team. The Archbishop of Canterbury, Geoffrey Fisher, encouraged him to defer his ordination to obey this call: "Here is a piece of what I should regard as direct service to the wider interests of the Kingdom of God. . . And as I understand it there really is a crying need for someone to bring back into the higher ranks of English cricket a sort of moral decisiveness which has been slipping."

Now, with the 1954–55 Ashes tour looming, came one of those great captaincy controversies that so often convulse English cricket. To the discomfort of both men, the arguments raged between the claims of the gritty northern pro and the genteel southern amateur. It was resolved in Hutton's favour because he returned to cricket, and form, in the nick of time, which enabled him to beat the old-fashioned class prejudice that might have defeated him.

Sheppard returned to his studies, was ordained in 1955 and became curate of St Mary's in Islington. But still he could not wholly resist the call of cricket, and the selectors could not resist him. Despite minimal match practice, he was recalled for the 1956 Old Trafford Ashes Test made immortal by Jim Laker's 19 wickets. It is largely forgotten that England's position was set up by centuries from Peter Richardson and Sheppard – chanceless and showing no signs of rust. He did, however, ask May, now the captain, if he could move from short leg: "My reactions aren't what they used to be."

He made another 62 at The Oval and 68 against West Indies the next year. But that really did seem like his last hurrah. Gradually, the church took over. Sheppard could have been a comfy country vicar, and still become a bishop. But he opted for the sharp end, being appointed warden of the Mayflower Family Settlement in the East End, working, alongside his wife Grace, with the poor and the new migrants who were starting to pour in. Still, cricket pulled him back. And in 1962 he went on sabbatical, returned to the England team for the last two Tests, scored two half-centuries, and sailed to Australia.

If he was being self-deprecating about his reactions in 1956, they really had become dulled now. Throughout a freezing winter, English cricket followers would habitually wake in icy bedrooms to burst pipes and news that the Rev. had dropped yet another catch ("abiding in the field" was the joke). In Melbourne, he got a first-innings duck, dropped two catches, was dropped on a pair in the second innings – then went on to stroke a match-winning century. On Sundays, he would preach in the local cathedrals. "He drew bigger crowds than we did," noted Tom Graveney. After the tour, he returned to the East End and never played seriously again.

In 1969, Sheppard became Suffragan Bishop of Woolwich, and in 1975 Bishop of Liverpool, where for 22 years he became almost synonymous with the city and its troubles. He became an articulate spokesman for the poor, credited with anticipating the inner-city riots of the 1980s and turning into a more forceful opponent of the Thatcher government's policies than the official opposition. No one could have embraced the gritty north more completely. He was vice-chairman of the committee that produced a much-discussed report on urban poverty, *Faith in the City*, in 1985, and had to defend it at a lunch with Mrs Thatcher, who kept interrupting him. Sheppard said his mouth went dry, just as it had done when he faced Lindwall and Miller.

When Archbishop Runcie retired six years later, Sheppard had no chance, even though normal Anglican politics dictated that the evangelical wing should provide Runcie's successor, and Sheppard was an outstanding figure. His views had also created a distance between him and Establishment cricket figures such as May; he was an implacable opponent of sporting links with South Africa long before it became fashionable, refusing to play against them as early as 1960. He never wavered. He retired in 1997 and became a life peer, alongside Colin Cowdrey, but was soon diagnosed with cancer, and his last years were difficult, although cricket was a great solace.

As a very young man, his evangelising could irritate his team-mates. He tempered his enthusiasm and became a popular dressing-room figure. "On a very hot day in Dubbo," recalled A. C. Smith, a team-mate on Sheppard's last tour, "we all went into the bar. Most Australian beer glasses are rather small, and there was just one English-style pint mug. Who won the race for it? DSS." His sermons sometimes had a little too much God and too little humour in them for the taste of fellow-cricketers, but when he spoke at the 1995 *Wisden* dinner, he made a speech of outstanding grace and charm. His memorial service took place at a packed Liverpool Cathedral, with a bat placed on a table alongside his ordination Bible.

WILF SLACK 1990

SLACK, WILFRED NORRIS, the Middlesex and England left-handed opener, collapsed and died while batting in Banjul, capital of The Gambia, on January 15, 1989, at the age of 34. He had suffered four blackouts on the field or in the nets in the two previous years, but exhaustive tests had failed to identify the cause. Born in St Vincent, Slack came to England at the age of 11 and learned his cricket at High Wycombe. He played for various local teams and in 1976, when 21, he was Buckinghamshire's leading run-scorer with 748 in his debut season. The Middlesex coach, Don Bennett, marked him as first-class county material, and he was signed by them the next year.

However, he did not establish himself until 1981, partly because he was asked to bat down the order. Promoted to open against Kent at Lord's when Brearley was recalled to lead England at Headingley, Slack hammered a maiden century in an unbroken second-innings, first-wicket stand of 367. His unbeaten 181 contained three sixes and 20 fours, and with Graham Barlow (174 not out) he bettered the county record of 312 by W. E. Russell and M. J. Harris. He followed with a career-best 248, again not out, in the second innings of the next match, against Worcestershire, and went on to finish the season with a settled place, his county cap and 1,303 Championship runs at 48.25.

Quiet, even reserved, Slack prospered with the aid of a good understanding with Barlow, and in the seasons that followed he was often Middlesex's leading scorer. In 1985 his aggregate of 1,900 runs at 54.28 was bettered only by three others in the country, and that winter he went to Sri Lanka with the England B side, scoring heavily and consistently. Late in the tour he was called to the West Indies after Mike Gatting had his nose broken in the first one-day international of England's Caribbean tour.

The dauntingly abrupt change in conditions and quality of opposition saw Slack make just two and nought (run out) in his Test debut at Port-of-Spain. Dropped from the next two Tests, he made a brave 52 in an opening stand of 127 with Gooch in the Fifth, but an astonishing century by Richards – the fastest in Test history in terms of balls faced: 56 – rushed England to defeat by 240 runs and to a 5–0 defeat in the series. That experience, the loss of his partner when Barlow retired, and domestic problems affected Slack's form, and in his only other Test, at Headingley against the 1986 Indians, he again looked a good county player out of his depth.

However, he battled on to record his 1,000 runs with a late-season revival, and rather surprisingly won a place in the England team for Australia in 1986–87. He ran into some good early bowling and did not play in any Tests or internationals. He gave Middlesex good service in 1988, hitting centuries in both innings against Glamorgan at Lord's and completing 1,000 runs in a season for the eighth time.

In addition to his three Tests, Slack played twice in one-day internationals, and while he never made the climb from domestic cricket, he tried hard, kept cool and was regarded with warm affection, especially by Middlesex crowds. He held nearly 200 catches – many in the demanding bat-pad position – and was always eager to bowl medium pace, especially in limited-overs matches. He was particularly popular among fellow-cricketers, who spoke feelingly of their respect and sorrow when he died. He was mourned, too, in New Zealand, where he coached in five English winters. Slack was buried in his prized England blazer, bat at his side, and as the funeral cortege drove past Lord's, the Grace Gates bore a sign reading "Farewell Wilf". In 237 first-class games he scored 13,950 runs at 38.96, with 25 centuries, and took 21 wickets at 32.76.

NEIL SMITH 2004

SMITH, NEIL, died of cancer on March 3, 2003, aged 53. Smith served a four-year apprenticeship as Yorkshire's Second XI wicket-keeper and seemed the natural successor to the long-serving Jimmy Binks in 1970, but, after a shaky start, was usurped in mid-season by 18-year-old David Bairstow, who took his A levels at 7 a.m. so he could play. Bairstow established himself, and Smith moved to Essex to succeed Brian Taylor in 1973 and spent the next eight years as a stalwart of that famously perky dressing-room. Technically, many thought him a better gloveman than Bairstow, but he was on the large side, and irritated Graham Gooch by eating a lot and getting larger. This helped his often beefy batting, which had minimal backlift but considerable power: Essex occasionally used him as a pinch-hitter long before the term was ever used. In 1981, he lost form and was again ousted in mid-season, this time by David East. Smith captained the second team for a season and then went back north to go into business.

BETTY SNOWBALL 1990

SNOWBALL, ELIZABETH ALEXANDRA (BETTY), who died December 13, 1988, aged 82, was an all-round sportswoman who played squash and lacrosse at international level as well as cricket. But it was as one of the major figures of women's cricket for two decades from 1930 that she is best remembered, being a fine opening bat and generally accepted as the outstanding wicket-keeper of her generation. She had something of Australia's Bert Oldfield in her style; always immaculate in turnout, and neat and tidy in technique, although enthusiasm added a flourish to efficiency.

Born in Burnley, she was coached after leaving school by Learie Constantine, from whom she gained what she termed "aggressive inspiration". She played ten times for England, and toured Australia twice, recording a Test average of 40.86 and effecting 21 dismissals. Just over 5ft tall, Betty Snowball was an effective foil to the powerful all-rounder Myrtle Maclagen, both as fellow-opener and taking her spin bowling. Her outstanding innings was 189 in 222 minutes against New Zealand in 1935, which remained a Test record for half a century. She retired to Colwall, the Worcestershire village often called "the cradle of women's cricket", and the venue of an annual women's cricket week.

BRIAN STATHAM   2001

STATHAM, JOHN BRIAN, CBE, died from leukaemia on June 10, 2000, aged 69. Brian Statham was one of the best of all English fast bowlers, and beyond question the best-liked. A gentle man who had to be persuaded to bowl a bouncer, he was a mainstay of the England team in its vintage period between 1951 and 1963: he took 252 wickets in 70 Tests. His name will be forever coupled with that of Freddie Trueman, though they actually played together in only half his Tests. Statham's name always came second because he was the foil to Trueman's sabre – and the more reticent man.

In cricketing folklore he is remembered primarily for his accuracy: "If they miss, I hit," he would say. This diminishes his astonishing skill. He was indeed accurate; so are many fast-medium bowlers. Statham kept his line and length at a very high pace indeed, comparable with all but the very fastest of Test match bowlers. A batsman hit by Statham – even on the foot, which was more likely than the head – knew all about it. In Statham's case the area around off stump was more a corridor of certainty than uncertainty, but if the ball hit the seam it jagged back in very sharply. The results were always formidable, and occasionally devastating. Year after year he was Lancashire's leading bowler, despite lacking anyone to give him the support he himself provided so unstintingly for England. Until the emergence of Ken Higgs in 1958, he sometimes had to do all the work himself. At Coventry in 1957, he bowled Lancashire to an innings win with match figures of 15 for 89. Though he dipped in and out of the England team, through injuries and the whims of selection, his form remained remarkably constant, whether or not it was reflected in the statistics. A half-volley remained a major event.

His methods remain a matter of some debate. His action was certainly too chest-on to be accepted as classical. He swung the ball only rarely, and perhaps never by design. Part of the secret seems to have been that Statham was not merely supple but double-jointed. "He could put his right arm round his face and touch his right ear and do the same with his left arm and his left ear at the same time," said an admiring Geoff Pullar. He was certainly an impressive athlete: a beautiful outfielder and an occasionally effective left-handed tailender.

His bowling quality was never in dispute. Nor was his character: he had an enchantingly easy-going temperament. "I only saw him lose his rag twice," said

Pullar, his Lancashire and England team-mate. "Both times he was certain they had gloved a catch. One was Easton McMorris in the West Indies – he hit him on the chest and made him spit blood. The other was 'Pom-Pom' Fellows-Smith, and he knocked his cap off." Even the accuracy seems to have been a reflection of his temperament: "I'm not going to run in 30 yards and watch a batsman shoulder arms," Statham once said. "It's a waste of energy."

Despite his huge popularity, his life after cricket was a difficult one. He was employed by Guinness to go round pubs and clubs – more celebrity PR than selling. But after the company was taken over, a stern new management tried to force timetables and paperwork on him, and Statham's life was made intolerable. He became ill and in 1989 his financial plight was such that his friend Trueman organised some benefit dinners for him. More than 1,000 turned up at the Grosvenor House in London. He was a cricketer who engendered admiration and affection from both those who saw him from a distance, and those who knew him best. "I knew him for 50 years and we never had a wrong word," said Trueman.

HERBERT SUTCLIFFE
J. M. Kilburn, 1979

Herbert Sutcliffe was one of the great cricketers and he brought to cricket as to all his undertakings an assurance and capacity for concentration that positively commanded success. His technical talent matched his character and his achievements were therefore on the highest plane. In a career extending from 1919 to 1939 Herbert Sutcliffe scored more than 50,000 runs and averaged 52. He never knew a season of failure, except by the standard of his own astonishing peaks, and at the zenith of his career he scored 16,255 runs in five years as a measure of mastery in all conditions and over the world's best bowling of the time.

The First World War delayed his entry into county cricket until he was 24 years old when, after demobilisation from a commission in the Green Howards, he was given a place in the Yorkshire side. His quality was never in doubt and by the end of the 1919 season he had scored five centuries in an aggregate of 1,839 runs. He had also established a first-wicket partnership with Percy Holmes. For 14 years these two batsmen opened the innings for Yorkshire, representing a partnership of unparalleled success in which they put up the hundred on 74 occasions. Equally happy was Sutcliffe's Test match association with J. B. Hobbs, for this became the most accomplished of all opening partnerships. Sutcliffe's good fortune, however, was only in the presentation of opportunity. Seizure of it was his own merit and with one partner or another he constructed 145 first-wicket century stands.

His artistry and efficiency in difficult conditions became legendary in his lifetime, with his centuries against Australia at The Oval in 1926 and at Melbourne in 1929 as historic examples. Matches against Lancashire stirred him to nine centuries. His defensive patience and skill became a byword, yet at need his hitting was brilliant in the extreme. Against Northamptonshire at Kettering he met spin on the sticky wicket with an innings of 113 which included ten sixes. At Scarborough against the fast bowling of Farnes and Nichols, Sutcliffe took his personal score from 100 to 194 in 40 minutes. His 100th first-class century was the 132 he hit in less than two hours at Bradford when Yorkshire were hurrying to defeat Gloucestershire.

Courage and concentration were his basic attributes. No prospect daunted him, no difficulty dismayed him, no crisis upset him. He was an artist of the dead bat and an uncompromising hooker of fast bowling. He sought solution to his batting problems by taking them as they came, one at a time. He never allowed the present to be influenced by the alarms of the past or fears for the future. In the means and manner of his performances he raised enormous prestige for himself throughout the cricketing world. He was admired and respected wherever he played and by his refusal to depreciate his own value he raised the status of his profession.

He took the supplementary rewards of his distinction with polished grace and unfailing consideration for colleagues. Herbert Sutcliffe the individual always made it clear that he was Herbert Sutcliffe inseparable from Yorkshire and England. He was as punctilious in acknowledgment of obligations as he was single-minded towards the immediate task in hand.

After the retirement of A.W. Lupton in 1927, Sutcliffe was offered the Yorkshire captaincy as a professional player. Although he was on tour in South Africa when the invitation came he appreciated the possibility of divided opinions and with characteristic diplomacy declined the appointment, giving an assurance of his willingness to play under any captain.

Three Headingley greats: Geoff Boycott, Herbert Sutcliffe (in wheelchair) and Len Hutton celebrate Boycott's 100th first-class hundred, which came in style during the 1977 Ashes Test at their home ground.

During his playing days he founded and developed a sports outfitting business. After his retirement from the field he took a managerial appointment in the paper trade. He showed himself as successful in commerce as in cricket and for the same reasons of application and reliability. His repayment to the game which had given him so much was service on the Yorkshire committee, as an England selector, and as sponsor for many good causes in cricket. Though he was born in Summerbridge, Sutcliffe was a Pudsey native in cricket association. There, as a schoolboy, he began league cricket and from there he advanced to the county, but neither Pudsey nor any other nursery could have claimed Herbert Sutcliffe as a typical product. He was a Yorkshireman in his loyalty and training, but he was cosmopolitan in approach and outlook. His manner fitted Lord's expressively as it fitted Leeds.

Immaculate, alert, brisk of movement, serene in repose, he carried his character with a clear label wherever he appeared. His off-drive wore a silk hat and his hook was a ready response to the aggressive intent of any bumper. His defensive play was the reduction of risk to the minimum and his self-confidence was unshakable. In his first-class career he scored 149 centuries. He shared with Holmes a partnership of 555 for Yorkshire, and with Hobbs a partnership of 283 for England against Australia. Second in the nominal batting order, Herbert Sutcliffe was second to none in stead-fastness on all occasions. He was esteemed for accomplishment, he was acclaimed for his unfailing resolution. His name will always stay in the headlines.

This tribute by J. M. Kilburn first appeared in the Yorkshire Post.

E. W. SWANTON   2001

SWANTON, ERNEST WILLIAM, CBE, who died on January 22, 2000, aged 92, was the most influential and most durable cricket writer of the 20th century. In the columns of the *Daily Telegraph*, he was always E. W. Swanton; to his friends and enemies alike, he was "Jim". There were plenty of enemies and he was called many other names besides over the years, but he was never ignored. In the 30 years after World War II, as the *Telegraph* cricket correspondent, he carried an authority both in print and in person that perhaps no writer can have surpassed in any sport. And the glory never faded. In a quarter-century of nominal retirement, he continued to write columns that were read with eagerness and some trepidation in the game's committee-rooms.

In an unusual moment of self-deprecation, Swanton cheerfully referred to himself as a dinosaur. In fact, he was the reverse: he hated many of the changes in cricket, but he adapted to them, and retained the ability to comment on them confidently, relevantly and pertinently without ever losing sight of cricket's eternal values – hence his enduring importance. Swanton's literary style was basic – "halfway between the Ten Commandments and Enid Blyton", as J. J. Warr famously put it. But that suited the *Telegraph*, which disapproved of Cardusian fancy. Just before he died, Swanton recited his writing method: "First, briefly, the basic facts – what happened. Next, a critical view – why it happened." Finally, came the chronological detail, which grew in length once newsprint came off the ration. The significant part was the critical view, which was always delivered magisterially, if not pontifically. Part of its power came from Swanton's own sonorous voice and air of grandeur. But he could not have carried off the act if he had not had a profound – and ultimately matchless – knowledge of cricket and cricketers.

Though he was imbued with the values of cricket's establishment, he was often a voice for change. He welcomed overseas players in the County Championship, and one-day cricket. ("This 'instant cricket' is very far from being a gimmick," he wrote after the first Gillette Cup final in 1963, "and there is a place in it for all the arts of cricket.") Swanton was appalled when Gloucestershire sacked Tom Graveney as their captain in 1960 in favour of the Old Etonian, Tom Pugh, and was an early convert to the idea of boycotting South Africa over apartheid. He had become uneasy on the 1956–57 tour, and his strong connection with the West Indies – he led two private tours there and had a holiday home on Barbados – helped propel him into the progressive camp. He abhorred sledging, coloured clothing and the four-day Championship.

It was his personal style that brought him the most detractors, and he did not always treat social inferiors graciously. The historian Rowland Bowen rechristened him Pomponius Ego. Ray Illingworth remarked that he was too snobbish to travel in the same car as his chauffeur. Swanton reported only rarely from the more down-market county grounds: he is believed to have visited Leicester and Northampton only once each, and these occasions had to be treated like state visits, with elaborate preparations so that both he and his amanuensis would not have to endure routine privations. He expected a gin and tonic on cue. Once, when told the bar had run out of ice, he responded irritably, "Didn't you tell them who it was for?" This is a well-sourced story. The *Telegraph* sub-editors were not allowed to change a solitary comma of his copy, and they waited gleefully for his mistakes. These were, however, infrequent. His excesses were softened by both his belated marriage, in 1958 – to Ann Carbutt, a widow and an accomplished pianist and golfer – and the passing years. He was a much nicer man in old age. As Lord Runcie said at his funeral: "The solemnity, prickliness and, yes, arrogance that were part of the serious perfectionist gave way to the gentle self-mockery and kindly wisdom which never seemed to fail us."

PETER TINNISWOOD 2004

TINNISWOOD, PETER, who died of cancer on January 9, 2003, aged 66, was a prolific and original comic writer with an eye for the minutiae of English life. His genre was initially abrasive northern surrealism, but in the 1980s he turned his attention to cricket and through one character, a crusty cricket obsessive known as the Brigadier, created *Tales from a Long Room*, a fantasy on "our summer game" riddled with puns, verbal abuse and whimsical name-play. It began as a radio monologue with Robin Bailey, who had played Uncle Mort in Tinniswood's television masterpiece *I Didn't Know You Cared*, as the Brigadier, recalling the MCC tour of the Belgian Congo in 1914: "There were at least two outbreaks of cannibalism among spectators... which I am convinced were responsible for the loss of our most promising young leg-spinner, M. M. Rudman-Stott. He was sent out to field at deep third man in the match against an Arab Slavers' Country XI, and all we found of him after the tea interval was the peak of his Harlequins cap and half an indelible pencil."

In time, Tinniswood transported listeners to the Snug hamlet of Witney Scrotum, introducing them to Granny Roebuck who ran the cake shop, Mr Bruce Woodcock of *The Times*, E. W. "Gloria" Swanton, Winston Place, the former

Lancashire batsman and one of Tinniswood's real-life heroes, and the recurrent Mr H. D. "Dickie" Bird. There was also romance. "Into my view she glided; a tall, slim sylphlike figure in purest white. My heart missed a beat. The sap rose in my loins. Dear God, she was the spitting image of Herbert Sutcliffe. Call it the impetuosity of youth if you will, but remember I had been out of the country for many years, serving my King and country in some of the remotest and most primitive outposts of his Empire. I had not seen a first-class cricketer for seven years."

The monologues spawned several books, a stage play with Willie Rushton as the Brigadier, recalling army times in the Far East and the massive earth works at Botham's Gut, a column in *The Cricketer*, even a shortlived television version. Though seriously ill, and able to communicate only through an electronic voicebox, Tinniswood continued to write prodigiously and was *Wisden*'s book reviewer in 2000.

ALF VALENTINE

VALENTINE, ALFRED LOUIS, died in Orlando, Florida, on May 11, 2004, shortly after his 74th birthday. He had suffered a stroke while recovering from a back operation, and spent his last days in a wheelchair. A toothy Jamaican, Alf Valentine had a meteoric rise to fame, being selected for West Indies' 1950 tour of England aged just 20, after only two first-class matches, and then, along with the Trinidadian off-spinner Sonny Ramadhin, spinning West Indies to three successive and sensational victories. This was the first hint of the new world order that would dominate the game for much of the next half-century. It also spawned perhaps cricket's most famous song: Lord Beginner's calypso about "Those two little pals o' mine, Ramadhin and Valentine".

Valentine was a brisk left-armer who gave the ball a prodigious tweak and sometimes made it fizz audibly. On that tour, he bowled nearly 1,200 overs and took 123 wickets, but he started steadily rather than spectacularly, and might not have played in the First Test at Old Trafford had it not been preceded by a match there against Lancashire, in which he took 13 wickets for 67. Understandably retained for the Test, he grabbed five wickets before lunch on the first day and, uniquely, claimed the first eight to fall on his debut. He finished with eight for 104, took three more in the second innings, and 33 in all in a four-match series.

West Indies lost at Old Trafford but then took command. At Lord's, he bowled 71 overs in the second innings, then 92 in the second innings at Trent Bridge, a Test record later beaten by Ramadhin. Doug Insole played in that game, and had his Test debut rather ruined by the two spinners as he made 21 and nought: "Valentine wasn't a graceful-type bowler, he'd chunter up to the wicket and rip it." Clyde Walcott was keeping wicket: "Val in 1950 was extremely accurate, and he concentrated on pure spin with no gimmicks. The result was that he turned the ball more in helpful conditions than any left-arm bowler I have ever seen," he said. "Those who thought that batsmen got out to Valentine merely in reaction to playing Ramadhin at the other end underrated Val badly."

Halfway through the tour a team-mate asked him the score, but he couldn't read the board. He was despatched for some National Health specs, which he wore from then on, secured by sticking-plaster when he bowled. They did little for his batting – he ended up with more first-class wickets (475) than runs (470). The big rip Valentine gave the ball took its toll on his fingers, which he bathed in surgical spirit and later, following a tip from Richie Benaud, a mixture of calamine lotion and boracic acid powder. England 1950 remained the pinnacle of his career: although he took 24 Test wickets in Australia in 1951–52, the harder pitches allowed the batsmen to combat the spin twins more effectively.

Valentine had little subtlety beyond the fizzing spin, and rarely bothered top batsmen again, although he was still a fine containing bowler. At Georgetown in February 1954 he became the first West Indian to reach 100 Test wickets, in only three years and eight months, on his way to a final tally of 139. But a youngster called Garfield Sobers made his debut in the last match of that England series, and although his left-arm spin was altogether gentler than Valentine's, the other aspects of his game were infinitely superior.

Valentine carried on, touring England in 1957, when a broken nose and loss of confidence hampered him, and played in the tied Test at Brisbane in 1960, where his sensible piece of backing-up in the final over saved what would have been the winning overthrows. He faded out of Test cricket, still only 31, after the final match of West Indies' clean sweep over India in 1962, although he toured England one last time without making the Test team in 1963.

After a few years in the Birmingham League, he returned home, and moved to Florida in 1978 with his second wife Jacquelyn (his first wife Gwendolyn, who bore him four daughters, had died). A chance visit to a Sydney care home during that 1960–61 tour had made him want to devote his life to helping underprivileged children, and the Valentines became foster parents to a succession of what are known in Florida as "adjudicated children" – those in need of special care and counselling while their parents are in prison or rehabilitation. Sometimes they would have as many as 12 at a time, and Valentine lost count of the total number who passed through their care.

CYRIL WASHBROOK   2000

WASHBROOK, CYRIL, CBE, who died on April 27, 1999, aged 84, was an always staunch and sometimes brilliant opening batsman for Lancashire and England. He flourished either side of the Second World War, and his name will forever be paired in history with that of Len Hutton, with whom he opened for England 51 times. Their average partnership was 60, which from this distance seems like unparalleled riches, although they played in often perilous times for England. In the popular imagination, he is remembered for two other things. One was his comeback in 1956 when, as a selector, he made a dramatic return to the Test team, aged 41. The other was the jaunty angle of his cap, which hinted at a carefree nature. In fact, he was a diffident man, and he masked this by acquiring a rather forbidding exterior as he gained authority.

His cricket, however, gave pleasure right from the start. In his second match for Lancashire, as an 18-year-old in 1933, Washbrook made 152, and Neville Cardus wrote in the *Manchester Guardian*: "He looks like a cricketer, has a cricketer's face and wears his flannels like a cricketer." He went on to become the very embodiment of a Lancashire cricketer, and remained deeply associated with the county until his sad and lingering final illness.

In Australia in 1946–47, he and Hutton had three successive century stands, and Washbrook emerged as one of the recognisable cricketers of a heroic cricketing age. "The chin, always square and thrust out a little," wrote Cardus, "the square shoulders, the pouting chest, the cock of cricket cap, his easy loose movement, his wonderful swoop at cover and the deadly velocity of his throw in. The tensing of his shoulders as he prepared to face the bowling, the preliminary champing of his feet – every sign of determined awareness, every sign of combined attack and defence, his mind ready to signal swiftly either to infantry, cavalry, or for cover behind the sand bags." He was, from the start, strongest on the leg side and was one of the great hookers and pullers; he also had a ferocious square cut. No fast bowler ever changed his demeanour. "He was like concrete," said Wilfred Wooller.

Washbrook was in his pomp in the late 1940s. He scored six Test centuries of varying moods, but roughly equal quality. The first came against Australia at Melbourne in 1946–47, where a huge crowd saw him battle six hours for 112. He got another at Headingley in 1948, where he hit what *Wisden* called an "almost faultless" 143 in the Ashes match where England reached 423 for two but still lost. Five months later, in South Africa, Hutton and Washbrook put on 359 in 290 minutes on the first day of Test cricket at Ellis Park. Washbrook made a chanceless 195, his highest Test score. He hit an unbeaten 103, mostly with a runner, against New Zealand at Leeds in 1949 and scored two more centuries, both in defeat, in the 1950 series against West Indies. He was apparently reluctant to tour Australia in 1950–51, and it showed; he was also troubled by the "mystery spinner", Jack Iverson. From then on, he faded out of the Test team (apparently against Hutton's wishes when he was captain). In 1954 he became Lancashire's first professional captain and in 1956 a Test selector.

The historic moment came that July, after England had lost to Australia at Lord's. More than five years after his last Test appearance, his colleagues on the selection panel requested him to leave the room. On his return, they asked if he would play at Headingley. He was 41, and the decision was greeted first with astonishment and then with delight. Washbrook made 98, sharing a stand of 187 with May after England had been reduced to 17 for three. England won the game, and Washbrook stayed in the team to play less heroic roles as Jim Laker worked his magic at Manchester and gave England the best of a draw at The Oval.

He remained Lancashire captain until retiring in 1959; a strong team never managed to challenge Surrey's domination, but they usually played cricket that reflected Washbrook's iron discipline – and self-discipline. In 1964, Washbrook became the club's cricket manager and he was an England selector again in 1971 and 1972. This time he was not asked to make a comeback – though even when he was near 50, he scored 85 for MCC in a centenary match against Lancashire. Washbrook remained close to Old Trafford until illness overtook him; the feeling was mutual – his benefit, of £14,000 in 1948, remained a record for more than two decades before inflation rendered comparisons meaningless. John Major, in his first year as prime minister, awarded him a very belated CBE in 1991. Washbrook was the last survivor of the Lancashire team that won the Championship outright in 1934 but, though he lived another 65 years, did not see a repetition.

DONALD WEEKES 2004

WEEKES, DONALD RUDOLPH, died on November 29, 2003, aged 63. This Bajan blaster was never a first-class cricketer but a yarn-spinner of international calibre who was the subject of a lengthy profile in *The Cricketer* in 1975, headlined "The best batsman never to have played Test cricket?" Among various implausibilities, the description of his century "for Barbados against Trinidad" as "one of the most brilliant" seen on the Bridgetown ground omits the detail that it was for Barbados B.

Tony Cozier, who worked with Weekes on the *Daily News* sports desk in Bridgetown in the mid-1960s, remembers him holding listeners spellbound with "descriptions of fantastic innings in far-flung places, a first-hand assessment of Muhammad Ali's cross (he claimed he had sparred with Ali in Tokyo) and analysis of the young Viv Richards. I see a lot of Don Weekes in that boy." Certainly, they were similar in build, method and power.

But Weekes's cavalier batting was given fullest expression outside the Caribbean. Living in California, he captained the United States against Canada in 1969 and 1970, and in 1972 hit their first hundred in the series since 1898. *Wisden* also records him making double-hundreds for American clubs touring British Columbia and England in 1970. But neither *Wisden*, nor any other source, authenticates his claims to have scored 700 not out in an innings in India, totalled 2,879 runs for Blackpool in his first English season, or played Othello in Moscow.

ARTHUR WELLARD 1982

WELLARD, ARTHUR WILLIAM, died peacefully in his sleep on December 31, 1980, aged 77. In a career extending from 1927 to 1950 he scored 12,575 runs with an average of 19.73 and took 1,614 wickets at 24.35 – figures which suggest a valuable county all-rounder. In fact he was more than that. Though he was a good enough opening bowler to be selected in that role for a Test against Australia, and once took nine for 117 in an unofficial Test in India, it is as a batsman that he will be chiefly remembered. In the course of his career he hit some 500 sixes, thus accounting for a quarter of the runs he made. But he was no mere slogger: he had a sound defence and was, for one of his type, remarkably consistent. His record was not boosted by large innings. He made only two hundreds, his highest score being 112 against Lancashire at Old Trafford in 1936. A tall, strong man, he bowled fast-medium with a vicious break-back, and a large number of his victims were clean-bowled. For variety in a second spell, or when the pitch was taking spin, he could bowl just as efficiently slow off-breaks round the wicket. He was a fine field anywhere close in. Above all, whatever he was doing he was an indefatigable trier.

Born at Southfleet, near Gravesend, he originally played for Bexley and as early as 1921 took six for 21 against Kent Club and Ground. When the sides next met in 1926, he took five for 36. But despite this, and although he headed the Bexley batting and bowling averages for three years, Kent were not interested and tradition has it that, when he asked whether there was any chance of a trial for them, he was told he had much better be a policeman. It was Arthur Haywood, late of the Kent staff and then professional at Taunton School, who suggested that he should approach Somerset and he started to qualify for them in 1927. That year and the next he showed promising form against the touring side, and in his first full season, 1929, he took 131 wickets at 21.38.

In 1933 he did the double, a feat he repeated in 1935 and 1937. A good example of what he could do was the Hampshire match at Portsmouth in 1933. Coming in when six wickets were down for 38, he made 77 out of 94, took seven for 43, made 60 in the second innings and then took three more wickets for 66. In 1936 he hit Armstrong of Derbyshire, a slow left-armer, for five sixes off consecutive balls. He had already taken nine wickets in the match and his 86 in 62 minutes brought his side a one-wicket victory. In 1938 he again hit five consecutive sixes, this time off Frank Woolley, being dropped just in front of the screen off the sixth ball. On this occasion his scores were 57 and 37 and he took 13 for 115. These feats, at that time unparalleled, were both performed on the small ground at Wells.

In 1937 he played in the Test at Old Trafford against New Zealand without any particular success and in 1938 was in the side against Australia at Lord's. On this occasion he certainly bowled well and in the second innings made 38 vital runs, including a pulled drive for six off McCabe on to the Grand Stand balcony. When he joined Compton at 142 for seven, an Australian victory was possible: when he was out at 216 for eight, the match was safe. This was his last Test, but he was due to go to India in the winter of 1939–40 had war not intervened. He had already been a member of Lord Tennyson's unofficial side there in 1937–38 and had had a successful tour. After the War he continued for another four seasons to be a valuable member of the Somerset side, finally dropping out in 1950.

E. M. WELLINGS   1993

WELLINGS, EVELYN MAITLAND, died in hospital at Basingstoke on September 10, 1992, aged 83, his ashes by his own request being cast into the Channel. E. M. ("Lyn") Wellings was cricket correspondent of the now-defunct *London Evening News* from 1938 to 1973 and was one of the most idiosyncratic of all writers on the game.

He was a very good games player at school and university, and was successful both as a batsman and as a bowler of off-breaks and off-cutters. For Cheltenham against Haileybury at Lord's in 1927, he took seven for 113, bowling unchanged, and then carried his bat through his school's first innings for 44 not out, though Cheltenham still lost. At Oxford he won a golf Blue (he later reached the last 32 of the English Championship). He failed to make much impression as a cricketer in his first year at Oxford but won Blues in 1929 and 1931, taking five for 118 in the first innings of the Varsity match in 1929 and five for 25 in the second innings in 1931. He did not play in 1930 because of loss of form, according to the official history, though it was widely believed, in a year when Oxford was riven by faction-alism, that he could not get on with the captain, P. G. T. Kingsley. This sort of falling-out was to be more of a pointer to his future than his successes on the field.

He played four matches for Surrey in 1931 and 36 first-class matches in all, making a century for H. D. G. Leveson Gower's XI against Cambridge in 1933 and finishing with 836 runs at 20.39 and 108 wickets at 30.14. More significantly, he took a job with the *Daily Mirror* and then moved to the *Evening News* and, as Ian Wooldridge put it, "dipped his pen in vitriol". Wellings reported more than 200 Tests with a trenchancy that has never been matched. He attacked inefficiency on or off the field in indignant terms. He hated one-day cricket, overseas players in county teams, South Africa's isolation, faulty technique and, in later years, every-thing to do with the Test and County Cricket Board. He was right more often than many people cared to admit but the tone of his argument was so forceful that it usually upset more people than it won over. From 1945 to 1972 he also wrote on public schools cricket for *Wisden*, which he did with a magisterial sweep that no one else can ever have brought to the subject.

He retired to Spain but returned to live in Hampshire and to write unmel-lowed articles for *Wisden Cricket Monthly* until shortly before his death. Personally, he was cantankerous and his temper became legendary amongst his colleagues. Once the telephonist who was supposed to send over his reports for successive editions of that day's *Evening News* failed to appear at The Oval. Wellings wrote his reports as usual but let them pile up on the desk and then posted them. A lesser journalist would have been fired instantly. A greater one would have behaved differently.

PETER WEST
2004

WEST, PETER ANTHONY, who died on September 2, 2003, aged 83, was the beaming and unflustered front man for BBC's televised cricket coverage for nearly 20 years until his retirement in 1986. The smile was genuine: Peter West was a charming and courteous man with a boyish enthusiasm for sport that never left him. But he had an acute sense of the need to marry sport and commerce, and his most lasting contribution may well be as a pioneer of sporting sponsorship.

WILFRED WOOLLER
1998

WOOLLER, WILFRED, who died on March 10, 1997, aged 84, was one of the greatest all-round sportsmen Wales ever produced. More than that, he was one of the nation's richest – and certainly most combative – characters. He was captain of Glamorgan for 14 years, secretary for 30 and club president for the six years before he died. He had 18 rugby caps for Wales, played soccer for Cardiff and was later fearsome at bowls. Even when he was in his seventies, it was always likely that Wilf's latest exploit would be the talk of the principality. He was brave and bull-headed, on and off the field. There will never be another.

FRANK WOOLLEY
Norman Preston, 1979

FRANK EDWARD WOOLLEY, who died on October 18, 1978, aged 91, was beyond doubt one of the finest and most elegant left-handed all-rounders of all time. In a first-class career extending from 1906 to 1938 he hit 58,969 runs – a total exceeded only by Sir Jack Hobbs – including 145 centuries, to average 40.75; he took 2,068 wickets for 19.85 runs each, and he held 1,015 catches, mainly at slip, a record which remains unsurpassed.

Even more impressive than the number of runs Woolley amassed was the manner in which he made them. Standing well over six feet, he was a joy to watch. He played an eminently straight bat, employed his long reach to full advantage, and used his feet in a manner nowadays rarely seen. His timing of the ball approached perfection and he generally dealt surely with all types of bowling. Master of all the strokes, he was at his best driving, cutting, and turning the ball off his legs. He was described by Sydney Pardon as the cleanest driver since F. G. J. Ford, but he often started badly and there was something wanting in his defence. As a bowler he made good use of his height and bowled with a graceful easy swing.

As a small boy he was always to be found on the Tonbridge Cricket Ground, and his natural ability as batsman and bowler attracted so much attention that, in 1903, he was engaged to take part in the morning practice and play in a match or two in the afternoon if required. In the following year he became a regular member of the Tonbridge Ground staff, which in those days was the official Kent nursery. When given his first chance in the Kent XI in 1906, he was almost unknown to the public, and his all-round form in his third match, against Surrey at The Oval, came as nothing less than a revelation. To begin with, he took three Surrey wickets, clean bowling Hayward, Hayes, and Goatly. He then made 72, and when Surrey batted again he took five wickets for 80 runs. Finally he scored 23 not out, helping to win a wonderful game for Kent by one wicket. The match established his reputation.

R. L. Arrowsmith, 1979

Frank Woolley was a slow left-arm bowler with a beautiful action who took over 2,000 wickets and was at one time perhaps the best of his type in the world. He caught during his career far more catches than anyone else, except wicket-keepers, yet it is as a batsman that he is primarily remembered. Few now alive have seen a player who approached him in ease and grace, and his average rate of scoring has been exceeded only by Jessop and equalled by Trumper. His philosophy was to dominate the bowler. "When I am batting," he said, "I am the attack." I was lucky enough to see him innumerable times. Obviously I often saw him out for small scores, but I never saw him in difficulties. If a ball beat him, the next would probably go for four or six.

This was made possible not only by his wonderful eye and sense of timing but by his range of strokes. All types of bowler came alike to him personally, but, if he saw his partner in trouble, he would make it his business to settle the bowler responsible. At Tunbridge Wells in 1924, he came in at 29 for two to join George Wood, who was in grievous difficulties with Tate, then at his best. As he passed Wood, he said: "Push a single, Mr Wood, and leave me to deal with Chubby." The single was duly obtained and Tate's next two balls were driven for four. Great trier though he was, Tate, always demonstrative, flung the ball down, exclaiming, "I can't bowl to this chap." Wood, a useful though not great bat, went on to make 49, Woolley made 87, and together they put on 103 out of a total of 190. Though Kent won by 200 runs, it is not fanciful to suggest that those two early fours had a considerable effect on the course of the match.

At Folkestone in 1928, an England XI required 286 to beat West Indies. There was a bit of feeling in the air, and the three fast bowlers, Francis, Constantine, and Griffith, set out to intimidate the batsmen. Lee and Hammond were quickly out and Wyatt, though struggling with typical determination, was acutely uncomfortable. Woolley, as if unconscious of any trouble, set about the bowlers from the start and hit them to every corner of that large ground. Never have I seen fast bowling so massacred. He scored 151 in three hours. Wyatt compiled a gallant 75, and against all the odds the England side won by four wickets. Years later Constantine said it was the worst hammering he ever received.

The feelings of an opposing captain on such occasions were succinctly expressed by Woodfull: "He made the game look so untidy. It appeared as if the wrong bowlers were on and the fieldsmen all in the wrong places." One can see why Woolley could be a far greater menace to the opposition than players with higher averages, and why 40 years after his retirement he is mentioned in print more than any other batsman of his time except Bradman. And if some statistically minded reader says, "But wouldn't he have been a greater player had he exercised a bit more caution?" I am sure that all who saw him, and, even more, all who played with him, would answer firmly, "No".

CHRISTOPHER WORDSWORTH   1999

WORDSWORTH, CHRISTOPHER WILLIAM VAUGHAN, who died on October 15, 1998, aged 83, epitomised the breed of eccentrics who used to report county cricket for the posher Sunday papers. In his younger days he was an adventurer who tried to eke out a living in Wales by his skill as a fly-fisherman; later he eked out an even more precarious living reviewing books for *The Guardian* and *The Observer*. On Saturdays, he would write erudite and literate reports on rugby or cricket, dictated in a booming voice, and was a familiar, shambling figure on the country circuit, liked by his colleagues, except by those who remembered him as The Man Who Broke The Only Phone At Horsham.

JEFFREY WORNHAM   2006

WORNHAM, JEFFREY RICHARD TRISTAN, was killed tackling a fire on February 2, 2005, aged 28. Jeff Wornham and a fellow fireman were trying to rescue a woman trapped by a blaze in a tower block in Stevenage, Hertfordshire. All three died. Cricket was Wornham's enduring love. As a boy, he spent much of the summer dressed in whites on the off chance that he might find a game he could join. A teacher, faced with a moderate academic record, explained Wornham's school year: spring term to prepare for cricket, summer term to play it and autumn term to relive the matches. He also played for Reed CC, helping them to the Hertfordshire Colts Championship in 1990, and rejoining the club after college. He made useful runs with his correct, left-handed batting and kept wicket after a snowboarding accident hampered his bowling. "Soul Limbo" – the signature tune for the BBC's cricket coverage – was played at his funeral, and his ashes scattered over the Lord's outfield. On the evening of the fire, he was knocking in his new bat, bought earlier that day.

DOUG WRIGHT   1999

WRIGHT, DOUGLAS VIVIAN PARSON, died on November 13, 1998, aged 84, after several years of ill-health. Doug Wright was the finest English leg-spinner, perhaps the most dangerous of all English bowlers, in the years just before and after the [Second World] War. A Kentishman, from Sidcup, he made his debut for the county in 1932 aged 17, but did not become a regular for another four years until "Tich" Freeman's final season. By 1938, he was in the Test team against Australia, and at Leeds came close to bowling them to a remarkable victory, dismissing Bradman, McCabe and Hassett as Australia sought a mere 105 for victory. For most of his 34 Tests, he was bowling in difficult circumstances with little support. Often he was the spin attack, as in Australia in 1946–47 when he and Bedser bowled almost 500 eight-ball overs between them. Against South Africa at Lord's in 1947, he took ten for 175, but there were many more days of abject frustration.

He took seven hat-tricks, more than anyone else in history, and 100 wickets in a season ten times. In 1954, Doug Wright became Kent's first professional captain, though his natural diffidence did not obviously lend itself to leadership and, as so often in his career, he had a weak team around him: Kent slid nearer the bottom each season. At the end of each day, he would take his shoes and socks off and apologise to his poor old feet. "Sorry, boys," he would say, "but you're going to be needed again tomorrow."

Cowdrey remembers him being asked about the best over he ever bowled. "Bowling to the Don at Lord's," he said. "Every ball came out of my hand the way I wanted and pitched where I wanted. I beat him twice. It went for 16."

BOB WYATT

David Frith, 1996

An appreciation of R. E. S. Wyatt and Harold Larwood.

The generations slip gently away. All the Edwardian Golden Age cricketers are gone. And in 1995, within 93 days, the last two truly eminent English survivors of the 1920s and 1930s died. R. E. S. Wyatt and Harold Larwood were not the last living pre-war Test cricketers, but they were clearly the most outstanding of the oldest soldiers, and symbolic of the two English divisions, the two castes: amateur and professional, Gentleman and Player.

All about them was contrast: their backgrounds, their speech, their education, their financial standing. Yet united they stood as two of the toughest and most resilient cricketers ever to have represented England: Larwood (H.), the Nottinghamshire express bowler, and Mr. R. E. S. Wyatt, the very serious Warwickshire and later Worcestershire captain, who was vice-captain during England's notorious 1932–33 Bodyline tour of Australia.

The former miner finished that explosive venture with a broken foot, which might have been coupled with a broken heart had he been made of lesser stuff, for he was expected to shoulder all the blame when those who ran English cricket finally came to comprehend the malodorous nature of D. R. Jardine's strategy.

Larwood was accessible in his Sydney home, where he spent more than half his life after emigrating in 1950 with his wife Lois and their five daughters. In short-sleeved shirt, braces and slippers, liberated from the drudgery of a sweet shop in Blackpool, he would tell visitors of his pride in his achievements as a cricketer, of his respect for his vilified skipper, of his undying love for his home-land and his gratitude to Australia, where he had once been hated and abused during that acrimonious 1932–33 tour, when his bumpers crashed into Australian flesh. He never lost that sense of wonder at the warmth of welcome extended to him by his former adversaries, though in truth Australia was proud to accommodate a sporting icon of such dimension and vintage. England had been the losers, not just in their refusal to open the way for Larwood's return to the Test side later in the 1930s.

In a faintly anachronistic panama hat, and latterly in need of sturdy walking-sticks, Mr Wyatt was also accessible whenever he left his remote home in Cornwall to watch cricket or attend functions in the metropolis. In spite of his physical discomfort he journeyed till the end with his wife Mollie – South Africa in 1989, Lord's summer after summer, at ease in Paul Getty's box in the new Mound Stand. From that vantage-point, the action out in the middle gradually became a blur, though the memory – of olden days if not of last week – never failed. Didn't Percy Chapman make a century here against Australia in 1930 when Bob Wyatt was not playing? Yes – missed before he'd scored a run!

The nonagenarian with the basset-hound eyes and slightly glottal voice, in common with the old fast bowler who now lived on the other side of the world, was firm in his opinions. Mr Wyatt loved theory. He would talk at length and with passionate conviction on the iniquities of the lbw law (among other things, he believed it discouraged backplay). Larwood, for his part, was good on whether a batsman stood up to fast bowling or revealed a shortfall in courage. At his most animated he could still be scathing in the matter of Australian heart in that particular Test series with which, alas, he will always be linked. Always, though, he referred to his old captain as Mr Jardine (or the Skipper) and to the MCC vice-captain as Mr Wyatt. Decades in Australia's egalitarian environment came too late for him to throw off the code of etiquette into which he had been born in 1904.

That they held each other in deep respect is beyond question. Visualise cricket's 1995 Legion of the Departed as they shuffled up the steps of the Greatest Pavilion: "After you, Lol. Naw, after you, Mr. Wyatt". If there was any final imbalance, it was that prime minister John Major, he who wished to create a classless society, gave Harold Larwood an MBE by way of long-overdue atonement. Bob Wyatt was never thus recognised. It was as illogical and unjust as Larwood's ostracism by Lord's following Bodyline.

See also Harold Larwood obituary on page 1208.

Chronology

Compiled by Steven Lynch

1977

March: Centenary Test between Australia and England is played at Melbourne, to celebrate 100 years of competition: despite Derek Randall's fighting 174, Australia win by 45 runs, exactly duplicating the result of the first match in 1877. **May:** Details emerge of Kerry Packer's breakaway World Series Cricket, featuring 50 of the world's top players: set up after the Australian board refuses Packer's offer for broadcast rights of home Tests. **July:** John Edrich of Surrey scores his 100th first-class century. **August:** Geoff Boycott, who had returned to international cricket after a three-year self-imposed exile with a century in the third Ashes Test, scores another in the fourth at Leeds – his 100th hundred in first-class cricket. England go on to win the Ashes series 3–0, against an Australian side mostly composed of Packer signees. **November:** World Series Cricket starts, on non-recognised grounds in front of indifferent crowds, while a makeshift Australian side struggles in the Test series against India, eventually winning it 3–2.

County Championship: 1st Middlesex and Kent (shared title).
Gillette Cup: Middlesex beat Glamorgan.
Benson and Hedges Cup: Gloucestershire beat Kent.
John Player League: 1st Leicestershire, 2nd Essex.

1978

January: Australia win the women's World Cup in India. **February:** New Zealand beat England in a Test for the first time, after 48 years and 48 matches of trying: at Wellington, Richard Hadlee (six for 26) bowls England out for 64 as they chase 137. England win the Second Test to square the series. **June:** Ian Botham scores 108 and takes eight for 34 in Lord's Test against Pakistan. England win that series 2–0, and all three of the Tests that follow against New Zealand. English Tests are sponsored for the first time, by Cornhill Insurance. **September:** India tour Pakistan for the first series between the two neighbours since 1961–62: they had fought two wars in the interim. Pakistan win two of the three Tests. **December:** One-sided Ashes series starts in Australia: England, captained by Mike Brearley, win 5–1 against a second-string side lacking all the Packer players.

County Championship: 1st Kent, 2nd Essex.
Gillette Cup: Sussex beat Somerset.
Benson and Hedges Cup: Kent beat Derbyshire.
John Player League: 1st Hampshire, 2nd Somerset.

1979

APRIL: The Australian Cricket Board grants TV rights for home Tests to Kerry Packer's Channel Nine, and he disbands World Series Cricket. The players gradually return to the Establishment game. **JUNE:** The second World Cup takes place in England: West Indies retain the title they won at the inaugural event in 1975, beating England by 92 runs in the final. **DECEMBER:** As part of the Packer "peace", England undertake another tour of Australia, losing all three Tests – but not the Ashes, which the TCCB declined to put at stake – to a full-strength Australian side. The first annual Australian three-way one-day series, this time involving the hosts, England and West Indies, gets under way.

County Championship: 1st Essex, 2nd Worcestershire.
Gillette Cup: Somerset beat Northamptonshire.
Benson and Hedges Cup: Essex beat Surrey.
John Player League: 1st Somerset, 2nd Kent.

1980

FEBRUARY: Ian Botham dominates the Golden Jubilee Test against India at Bombay, scoring 114 and taking 13 wickets as England win with a day to spare. **MARCH:** *Wisden* editor Norman Preston dies, shortly before publication of the 1980 Almanack, his 30th: John Woodcock takes over for 1981. **JUNE:** West Indies win First Test at Nottingham: the other four games in the series are drawn. **AUGUST:** Centenary Test played at Lord's to mark 100 years of Test cricket in England: rain spoils the game, which was enlivened by the batting of Australia's Kim Hughes but marred by a clash between angry MCC members and the umpires after a lengthy stoppage. Legendary radio commentator John Arlott makes his last broadcast from a Test. **SEPTEMBER:** English cricket's longest-running major sponsorship deal comes to an end with the last Gillette Cup final at Lord's, won by Middlesex: the NatWest Bank took over the competition, which Gillette had sponsored from the start in 1963 but reluctantly gave up after market research suggested more people associated their name with cricket than razor blades.

County Championship: 1st Middlesex, 2nd Surrey.
Gillette Cup: Middlesex beat Surrey.
Benson and Hedges Cup: Northamptonshire beat Essex.
John Player League: 1st Warwickshire, 2nd Somerset.

1981

FEBRUARY: With New Zealand needing six to win a one-day international at Melbourne, Australia's captain Greg Chappell instructs his brother Trevor to roll the last ball along the ground to ensure victory: he is widely criticised, and the regulations are soon changed to avoid a repeat. Later in the month New Zealand beat West Indies by one wicket at Dunedin, and go on to win a bad-tempered series 1–0. It was New Zealand's first series victory at home, and West Indies' last defeat in any Test series until 1994–95. MARCH: England's assistant manager, Ken Barrington, dies of a heart attack on the eve of the Barbados Test against West Indies: England lose the match, and the series 2–0. The Georgetown Test was cancelled after the Guyanese government objected to the "South African connections" of England's Robin Jackman. JULY: England beat Australia at Leeds after following on, only the second such instance in Test history: inspired by Ian Botham, recently deposed as captain, and Bob Willis, the side now led by Mike Brearley confounds the bookmakers, who offered odds of 500/1 against England during the match. Two weeks later England win again at Birmingham, and go on to take an enthralling series 3–1. DECEMBER: Geoff Boycott becomes the leading Test run-scorer, passing Garry Sobers's tally of 8,032 during the series in India: shortly afterwards Boycott left the tour, and never played for England again, finishing with 8,114 runs.

County Championship: 1st Nottinghamshire, 2nd Sussex.
NatWest Trophy: Derbyshire beat Northamptonshire.
Benson and Hedges Cup: Somerset beat Surrey.
John Player League: 1st Essex, 2nd Somerset.

1982

FEBRUARY: Sri Lanka play their inaugural Test match, losing to England by seven wickets in Colombo; their side included the teenager Arjuna Ranatunga, who also featured in Sri Lanka's 100th Test, against Pakistan in June. Australia retain the women's World Cup, beating England in the final at Christchurch. MARCH: "Rebel" England tour of South Africa starts, captained by Graham Gooch and including Geoff Boycott and several of the team which had recently been playing in India and Sri Lanka: all the players are banned from Test cricket for three years. MAY: Glenn Turner scores his 100th first-class hundred, extending it to an innings of 311 not out. JULY: Ian Botham hits 208 at The Oval as England clinch series against India. AUGUST: Pakistan win a Test at Lord's for the first time: but England win the Third Test, and a close-fought series, despite missing several players banned for touring South Africa. DECEMBER: Zaheer Abbas scores his 100th first-class century, for Pakistan against India at Lahore. England, captained by Bob Willis, win nail-biting Melbourne Test by three runs – but Australia regain the Ashes by taking the series 2–1.

County Championship: 1st Middlesex, 2nd Leicestershire.
NatWest Trophy: Surrey beat Warwickshire.
Benson and Hedges Cup: Somerset beat Nottinghamshire.
John Player League: 1st Sussex, 2nd Middlesex.

1983

MARCH: Australia's Sheffield Shield domestic competition introduces a final, between the top two teams in the table: New South Wales beat Western Australia at Perth to win the Shield for the 37th time. **JUNE:** India upset West Indies by 43 runs to win the third World Cup, successfully defending a modest target of 183 in the final at Lord's. **AUGUST:** New Zealand win the Leeds Test, their first win in England after 17 defeats and 11 draws – but England go on to win the series 3–1. **SEPTEMBER:** Yorkshire, who had just finished 17th and last in the Championship for the first time, announce the sacking of Geoff Boycott, then almost 43, as part of a youth policy: his supporters rally round and eventually force the committee to resign. Boycott played on until 1986, finishing with 151 first-class centuries and an average of 56.83. **NOVEMBER:** Sunil Gavaskar passes Boycott's record of 8,114 Test runs, during the third match of India's home series against West Indies (who won 3–0): in the sixth match Gavaskar made his 30th Test century, passing Don Bradman's record of 29.

County Championship: 1st Essex, 2nd Middlesex.
NatWest Trophy: Somerset beat Kent.
Benson and Hedges Cup: Middlesex beat Essex.
John Player League: 1st Yorkshire, 2nd Somerset.

1984

JANUARY: Dennis Lillee and Rod Marsh retire from Test cricket, with record tallies of 355 wickets and 355 dismissals respectively. **FEBRUARY:** New Zealand bowl England out for 82 and 93 in Christchurch Test, and go on to their first series victory over England, who had to counter newspaper allegations that some of the players had smoked pot during the tour. **MARCH:** Pakistan also beat England 1–0 in Test series. **APRIL:** Sharjah becomes the first ground outside a Test-playing country to host official one-day internationals: it eventually stages a record 198 (and four Pakistan "home" Tests) before being supplanted by Abu Dhabi. **AUGUST:** West Indies, captained by Clive Lloyd, complete a 5–0 "blackwash" of England, the first by any away team in Test history.

County Championship: 1st Essex, 2nd Nottinghamshire.
NatWest Trophy: Middlesex beat Kent.
Benson and Hedges Cup: Lancashire beat Warwickshire.
John Player Special League: 1st Essex, 2nd Nottinghamshire.

1985

JANUARY: England, captained by David Gower, come from behind to win Test series in India 2–1. **AUGUST:** Bolstered by the return of some of the players previously banned for touring South Africa, England win a high-scoring Ashes series 3–1. **SEPTEMBER:** Sri Lanka record their first Test win, at the 14th attempt, over India in Colombo. **NOVEMBER:** Australia's turn to lose players to a "rebel" tour of South Africa: a team captained by Kim Hughes incurs three-year bans after signing up. **DECEMBER:** Richard Hadlee takes 33 wickets in three Tests – including 15 at Brisbane – as New Zealand win a series against Australia for the first time.

County Championship: 1st Middlesex, 2nd Hampshire.
NatWest Trophy: Essex beat Nottinghamshire.
Benson and Hedges Cup: Leicestershire beat Essex.
John Player Special League: 1st Essex, 2nd Sussex.

1986

APRIL: John Woodcock steps down as editor of *Wisden*: Graeme Wright takes over for 1987 Almanack. With Viv Richards making a 56-ball hundred in the final Test, West Indies complete their second successive 5–0 "blackwash" of England, this time at home. **JULY:** Dennis Amiss of Warwickshire scores his 100th first-class hundred, aged 43. **AUGUST:** Ian Botham returns from a three-month ban after admitting to drug use, and takes a wicket with his first ball, to equal Dennis Lillee's Test record of 355 wickets: he soon passes it. **SEPTEMBER:** India and Australia contest cricket's second tied Test, at Madras: Australia's coach, Bob Simpson, played in the first tie against West Indies in 1960–61. **DECEMBER:** England clinch the Ashes series at Melbourne: they eventually take the series 2–1, and also win two one-day competitions in what becomes known as captain Mike Gatting's "Grand Slam" tour.

County Championship: 1st Essex, 2nd Gloucestershire.
NatWest Trophy: Sussex beat Lancashire.
Benson and Hedges Cup: Middlesex beat Kent.
John Player Special League: 1st Hampshire, 2nd Essex.

1987

MARCH: Sunil Gavaskar becomes the first player to score 10,000 runs in Tests, against Pakistan during his final series: he finishes with 10,122. **JULY:** Victory in the Leeds Test gives Pakistan, led by Imran Khan, their first series win in England. **AUGUST:** Star-studded match against the Rest of the World played at Lord's to mark the Bicentenary of MCC. **NOVEMBER:** The World Cup is staged outside

England for the first time: Australia beat England by seven runs in the final at Calcutta. DECEMBER: A day's play is lost in the Faisalabad Test after a face-to-face argument between the England captain, Mike Gatting, and the Pakistani umpire Shakoor Rana: Pakistan eventually win a rancorous series 1–0.

County Championship: 1st Nottinghamshire, 2nd Lancashire.
NatWest Trophy: Nottinghamshire beat Northamptonshire.
Benson and Hedges Cup: Yorkshire beat Northamptonshire.
Refuge Assurance League: 1st Worcestershire, 2nd Nottinghamshire.

1988

FEBRUARY: England and Australian draw special Test played in Sydney to mark Australia's Bicentenary: Chris Broad, later a stern match referee, smashes down his stumps after being bowled for 139. MARCH: New Zealand and England draw uninspiring three-match Test series 0–0. MAY: Graeme Hick completes 1,000 first-class runs in English season before the end of May. AUGUST: West Indies win Test series against England 4–0. SEPTEMBER: Franklyn Stephenson, a Barbadian playing for Nottinghamshire, becomes the last player to date to do the double of 1,000 runs and 100 wickets in a season in England, completing it in style with two centuries and taking 11 wickets in the final match. OCTOBER: England tour of India called off due to the "South African connections" of some of the players, notably the selected captain, Graham Gooch, and vice-captain John Emburey. NOVEMBER: Viv Richards scores his 100th first-class century, during West Indies' tour of Australia. DECEMBER: Australia beat England to win the Women's World Cup – the first for almost seven years – in the final at Melbourne.

County Championship: 1st Worcestershire, 2nd Kent.
NatWest Trophy: Middlesex beat Worcestershire.
Benson and Hedges Cup: Hampshire beat Derbyshire.
Refuge Assurance League: 1st Worcestershire, 2nd Gloucestershire.
Refuge Assurance Cup: Lancashire beat Worcestershire.

1989

JANUARY: West Indies win Test series in Australia 3–1. JULY: The South African Jimmy Cook, in the middle of a prolific stint with Somerset, carries his bat for centuries in both innings against Nottinghamshire. AUGUST: Australia, captained by Allan Border, regain the Ashes – and don't surrender them again until 2005. Mark Taylor scores 839 runs in the series, an aggregate only ever exceeded by Don Bradman and Wally Hammond: in the Fifth Test at Nottingham he and Geoff Marsh bat through the first day's play, finishing it at 301–0, an unpromising start for England debutants Mike Atherton and Devon Malcolm. NOVEMBER: Sachin Tendulkar makes his Test debut for India in Pakistan, aged 16 years 205 days. Gubby

Allen, former England captain and long-time administrator, dies aged 87. **DECEMBER:** Javed Miandad scores 145 in his 100th Test for Pakistan, against India at Lahore.

> *County Championship:* 1st Worcestershire, 2nd Essex.
> *NatWest Trophy:* Warwickshire beat Middlesex.
> *Benson and Hedges Cup:* Nottinghamshire beat Essex.
> *Refuge Assurance League:* 1st Lancashire, 2nd Worcestershire.
> *Refuge Assurance Cup:* Essex beat Nottinghamshire.

1990

JANUARY: A "rebel" England side, captained by Mike Gatting, incurs five-year bans after undertaking a disapproved tour of South Africa: the tour ends prematurely as political change sweeps the country. **FEBRUARY:** Richard Hadlee becomes the first bowler to take 400 Test wickets, against India at Christchurch, his home ground. **MARCH:** England beat West Indies in a Test for the first time since 1973–74, narrowly fail to go two up. . . but lose the series 2–1. **APRIL:** Gordon Greenidge scores 149 in his 100th Test for West Indies, against England in Antigua. **JULY:** Hadlee, who was knighted between the First and Second Tests, finishes his career with 431 wickets as England take series against New Zealand 1–0. In the First Test against India, at Lord's, Graham Gooch establishes a host of records by scoring 333 and 123: England go on to win the series 1–0. Gooch scores 1,058 runs in six Tests during the summer, another record. **SEPTEMBER:** Len Hutton, the first professional to captain England in the modern era, leading them to Ashes success in 1953 and 1954–55, dies, aged 74.

> *County Championship:* 1st Middlesex, 2nd Essex.
> *NatWest Trophy:* Lancashire beat Northamptonshire.
> *Benson and Hedges Cup:* Lancashire beat Worcestershire.
> *Refuge Assurance League:* 1st Derbyshire, 2nd Lancashire.
> *Refuge Assurance Cup:* Middlesex beat Derbyshire.

1991

FEBRUARY: Australia complete 3–0 victory in Ashes series. **MAY:** Gordon Greenidge plays his 108th and last Test, ending an association with Desmond Haynes that yielded 6,482 runs together in partnership (still a Test record in 2006). **JULY:** ICC meeting agrees to restrict the amount of fast, short-pitched bowling. **AUGUST:** England beat West Indies at The Oval to square the Test series 2–2. **NOVEMBER:** South Africa return to official international cricket after more than 21 years, playing three one-day internationals in India under the captaincy of 42-year-old Clive Rice. **DECEMBER:** Broadcaster and writer John Arlott dies, aged 77.

CHRONOLOGY

County Championship: 1st Essex, 2nd Warwickshire.
NatWest Trophy: Hampshire beat Surrey.
Benson and Hedges Cup: Worcestershire beat Lancashire.
Refuge Assurance League: 1st Nottinghamshire, 2nd Lancashire.
Refuge Assurance Cup: Worcestershire beat Lancashire.

1992

FEBRUARY: England win 2–0 in New Zealand: Ian Botham, who missed the start of the tour because he was starring in a pantomime, joins in time to play his 100th Test match. **MARCH:** Pakistan win the fifth World Cup, beating England by 22 runs in the final at Melbourne. **APRIL:** South Africa, who had just participated in their first World Cup, return to Test cricket with a close-run defeat against West Indies at Bridgetown. Durham become the 18th first-class county in the Championship – the first new team since Glamorgan in 1921. Graeme Wright steps down as editor of *Wisden*, to be replaced for 1993 by Matthew Engel. **JUNE:** Botham plays the last of his 102 Tests, finishing with 383 wickets (still an England record in 2006), 5,200 runs and innumerable headlines. **AUGUST:** Pakistan win Test series in England 2–1, amid claims of ball-tampering made against their fast bowlers. **OCTOBER:** Zimbabwe play their inaugural Test match: captain Dave Houghton scores a century in a draw against India at Harare.

County Championship: 1st Essex, 2nd Kent.
NatWest Trophy: Northamptonshire beat Leicestershire.
Benson and Hedges Cup: Hampshire beat Kent.
Sunday League: 1st Middlesex, 2nd Essex.

1993

JANUARY: West Indies beat Australia at Adelaide by one run, the closest definite result in Test history, and go on to win the series 2–1. Graham Gooch scores his 100th first-class century, early on England's tour of India. **FEBRUARY:** England lose all three Tests on tour in India: in March they lose a Test to Sri Lanka for the first time. **JUNE:** Shane Warne's first ball in an Ashes Test, at Manchester, turns prodigiously and bowls Mike Gatting: it is later dubbed "The Ball of the Century". **JULY:** Graham Thorpe marks the first of his 100 Tests with 114 not out against Australia. New ICC offices, independent of MCC, are set up at Lord's. **AUGUST:** Australia win the Ashes series 4–1. England, captained by Karen Smithies, win the Women's World Cup, beating New Zealand by 67 runs in the final at Lord's. **SEPTEMBER:** Middlesex win the County Championship, the first composed entirely of four-day matches.

County Championship: 1st Middlesex, 2nd Worcestershire.
NatWest Trophy: Warwickshire beat Sussex.
Benson and Hedges Cup: Derbyshire beat Lancashire.
AXA Equity & Law League: 1st Glamorgan, 2nd Kent.

1994

JANUARY: South Africa beat Australia by six runs at Sydney, and draw series 1–1. **FEBRUARY:** Kapil Dev passes Richard Hadlee's record total of 431 Test wickets, and later retires with 434. **APRIL:** After being bowled out for 46 in the Third Test, England win the next one at Bridgetown – West Indies' first defeat there since 1934–35 – but lose the series 3–1. Brian Lara breaks the Test record with 375 in the final Test at St John's: the previous record-holder, Garry Sobers, is one of the first to congratulate him. **MAY:** Five weeks after his Test record, Lara beats the first-class mark with 501 not out for Warwickshire against Durham at Birmingham. Allan Border announces his retirement, after 11,174 Test runs (a record passed by Lara in 2005). **JULY:** South Africa, playing their first Test at Lord's for 29 years, win it by 356 runs: Michael Atherton, England's captain, is caught by TV applying dust to the ball, and fined. **SEPTEMBER:** Warwickshire, captained by Dermot Reeve and with Lara in rare form, complete an unprecedented county season, winning three of the four major competitions and losing in the final of the fourth. Pakistan beat Australia by one wicket in Test at Karachi.

County Championship: 1st Warwickshire, 2nd Leicestershire.
NatWest Trophy: Worcestershire beat Warwickshire.
Benson and Hedges Cup: Warwickshire beat Worcestershire.
AXA Equity & Law League: 1st Warwickshire, 2nd Worcestershire.

1995

FEBRUARY: Australia win final Test at Perth to take Ashes series 3–1: Graham Gooch (8,900 runs) and Mike Gatting (4,409) announce their international retirements afterwards. Henry Olonga is called for throwing during his Test debut for Zimbabwe. Shane Warne and Tim May allege that Salim Malik of Pakistan tried to bribe them to perform badly during recent tour. **MARCH:** Chairman of selectors Ray Illingworth becomes England "supremo" after Keith Fletcher is sacked as coach. Queensland win Australia's Sheffield Shield for the first time, at the 63rd attempt. **MAY:** Australia win 2–1 in the Caribbean, West Indies' first Test series defeat anywhere since 1979–80. **JULY:** Harold Larwood, the chief exponent of Bodyline bowling, dies aged 90. **AUGUST:** England beat West Indies in final Test at The Oval to draw series 2–2. **OCTOBER:** Lee Germon captains New Zealand on his Test debut. **DECEMBER:** Michael Atherton's 643-minute rearguard helps England draw at Johannesburg, but South Africa win the final Test to take series 1–0.

County Championship: 1st Warwickshire, 2nd Middlesex.
NatWest Trophy: Warwickshire beat Northamptonshire.
Benson and Hedges Cup: Lancashire beat Kent.
AXA Equity & Law League: 1st Kent, 2nd Warwickshire.

1996

FEBRUARY: Kenya bowl West Indies out for 93 to win their World Cup match at Pune. **MARCH:** Sri Lanka upset Australia by seven wickets in the final of the sixth World Cup, inspired by Aravinda de Silva's unbeaten 107. **APRIL:** Wicket-keeper Wayne James makes a record 13 dismissals in a domestic match in Zimbabwe – and also scores 99 and 99 not out. **JUNE:** Dickie Bird umpires his 66th and last Test, at Lord's: Sourav Ganguly makes 131 on debut for India (and Rahul Dravid 95) in a draw, but England go on to win series 1–0. **AUGUST:** Pakistan, captained by Wasim Akram, who takes his 300th wicket during the series, beat England 2–0. **OCTOBER:** Shahid Afridi smashes a century in 37 balls in his first one-day innings for Pakistan, against Sri Lanka in Nairobi. Pakistan's Hasan Raza, allegedly only 14, makes his Test debut for Pakistan against Zimbabwe. **DECEMBER:** Zimbabwe's first Test against England at home, at Bulawayo, ends with the scores level. The second Test – and with it the series – is also drawn.

County Championship: 1st Leicestershire, 2nd Derbyshire.
NatWest Trophy: Lancashire beat Essex.
Benson and Hedges Cup: Lancashire beat Northamptonshire.
AXA Equity & Law League: 1st Surrey, 2nd Nottinghamshire.

1997

JANUARY: Eddo Brandes takes a hat-trick as Zimbabwe win all three one-day internationals against England. **FEBRUARY:** England win 2–0 in New Zealand, their first overseas Test-series victory for five years. **MARCH:** David Graveney named chairman of England's selectors. **APRIL:** England legend Denis Compton dies aged 78. **MAY:** Saeed Anwar scores 194 in a one-day international for Pakistan against India at Chennai (still a record in 2006). **JULY:** Edgbaston stages first floodlit one-day National League match. **AUGUST:** Australia win Ashes series 3–2, despite losing first and last Tests. Sri Lanka score 952 for six declared against India in Colombo, the highest Test total: Sanath Jayasuriya and Roshan Mahanama share a partnership of 576. **NOVEMBER:** Floodlights used during play in Australia–New Zealand Test at Perth. **DECEMBER:** England, captained by Adam Hollioake, win four-nation one-day tournament in Sharjah. Australia win the Women's World Cup, beating New Zealand in the final at Calcutta.

County Championship: 1st Glamorgan, 2nd Kent.
NatWest Trophy: Essex beat Warwickshire.
Benson and Hedges Cup: Surrey beat Kent.
AXA Life League: 1st Warwickshire, 2nd Kent.

1998

JANUARY: The First Test between West Indies and England at Kingston is abandoned after 56 minutes when the pitch is deemed unsafe. MARCH: England lose 3–1 in West Indies, and lose their captain too: Michael Atherton resigns. Makhaya Ntini becomes South Africa's first black Test player. MAY: Graeme Hick scores his 99th and 100th first-class hundreds in the same match, for Worcestershire against Sussex. AUGUST: England, now captained by Alec Stewart, come from behind to win series against South Africa 2–1. Muttiah Muralitharan takes 16 wickets as Sri Lanka beat England in one-off Test at The Oval. SEPTEMBER: Cricket played in Commonwealth Games in Kuala Lumpur: South Africa beat Australia in the final. MCC vote to admit women members. OCTOBER: Ian Healy breaks Rod Marsh's record of 355 Test dismissals by a wicket-keeper: he retires later with 395. Australia win their first series in Pakistan for 39 years: Mark Taylor, their captain, scores 334 not out in the Second Test. NOVEMBER: South Africa beat West Indies in a Test for the first time; Zimbabwe beat Pakistan, their first series victory. DECEMBER: Counties agree to two-division Championship from 2000. Shane Warne and Mark Waugh admit to accepting money from a bookmaker for "information" in 1994.

County Championship: 1st Leicestershire, 2nd Lancashire.
NatWest Trophy: Lancashire beat Derbyshire.
Benson and Hedges Cup: Essex beat Leicestershire.
AXA League: 1st Lancashire, 2nd Warwickshire.

1999

JANUARY: Australia win Ashes series 3–1: Mark Taylor retires afterwards. Muttiah Muralitharan called for throwing in one-day international against England at Adelaide: Sri Lanka team walks off in protest. FEBRUARY: Anil Kumble becomes the second man (after Jim Laker) to take all ten wickets in a Test innings, against Pakistan at Delhi. MARCH: Wasim Akram takes second hat-trick in successive Tests, as Pakistan win Asian Test Championship. APRIL: Australia share exciting series in West Indies 2–2. MAY: Channel 4 cover live Tests in England for the first time, after BBC lose the contract. The seventh World Cup starts in England: the hosts crash out at the group stages, and Alec Stewart loses the captaincy. JUNE: Australia win the World Cup, demolishing Pakistan in the final by eight wickets: the tournament's best match is the semi-final, when Australia tie with South Africa but progress thanks to their superior run-rate in the earlier matches. AUGUST: England, now captained by Nasser Hussain, lose home series to New Zealand for the first time, and go bottom of the *Wisden* World Championship, the unofficial ranking table which was adopted shortly afterwards by the ICC. SEPTEMBER: Lancashire retain the National League, which this year is split into two divisions for the first time: Sussex win the Second Division. Sri Lanka win a Test – and later a series – against Australia for the first time. OCTOBER: John

Buchanan appointed Australia's coach, **NOVEMBER:** Malcolm Marshall dies of cancer, aged 41.

County Championship: 1st Surrey, 2nd Lancashire.
NatWest Trophy: Gloucestershire beat Somerset.
Benson and Hedges Super Cup: Gloucestershire beat Yorkshire.
CGU National League: 1st Lancashire, 2nd Worcestershire (Div. 2 winners: Sussex).

2000

JANUARY: England win Fifth Test at Centurion after both sides forfeit an innings: South Africa still take series 2–1. Writer and broadcaster E. W. Swanton dies, aged 92. **MARCH:** England announce first batch of 12 players to be given central contracts. Zimbabwe, chasing only 99 to win their inaugural Test in West Indies, are bowled out for 63 at Port-of-Spain. **APRIL:** Millennium edition of *Wisden* names the Five Players of the Century: Don Bradman (who received a vote from each of the 100 experts consulted), Jack Hobbs, Viv Richards, Garry Sobers and Shane Warne. Delhi police charge Hansie Cronje and others with match-fixing: after initially denying the charge, Cronje later admits it, is replaced as South African captain, and subsequently banned for life. **MAY:** Salim Malik and Ata-ur-Rehman banned for life after Pakistani investigation into match-fixing allegations. **AUGUST:** England beat West Indies inside two days in the Leeds Test: they go on to win the series 3–1, and lift the *Wisden* Trophy for the first time since 1969. Alec Stewart scores 105 in his 100th Test, against West Indies at Manchester: it is Michael Atherton's 100th Test too (he makes 1 and 28). First indoor one-day internationals played, between Australia and South Africa at Melbourne's Docklands Stadium. **SEPTEMBER:** Surrey win the first two-division County Championship. **NOVEMBER:** Bangladesh's first official Test, against India at Dhaka: they score 400 in the first innings, Aminul Islam making 145, but collapse in the second and lose. **DECEMBER:** Former England captain and ICC chairman Colin Cowdrey dies, aged 67. England beat Pakistan at Karachi – their first Test defeat there – to take the Test series 1–0. Mohammad Azharuddin and Ajay Sharma banned for life after Indian investigation into match-fixing. Playing at home, New Zealand beat Australia to win the Women's World Cup final for the first time.

County Championship: 1st Surrey, 2nd Lancashire
(Div. 2 winners: Northamptonshire).
NatWest Trophy: Gloucestershire beat Warwickshire.
Benson and Hedges Cup: Gloucestershire beat Glamorgan.
Norwich Union National League: 1st Gloucestershire, 2nd Yorkshire
(Div. 2 winners: Surrey).

2001

JANUARY: Australia complete 5–0 whitewash of West Indies. FEBRUARY: Sir Donald Bradman dies, aged 92. MARCH: India beat Australia at Kolkata after following on, only the third such instance in Test history (Australia were on the receiving end each time), and go on to take exciting series 2–1: Australia had won their previous 16 Tests, another record. England also come from one-down in Sri Lanka to win series 2–1. Courtney Walsh becomes the first bowler to take 500 Test wickets: he retires shortly afterwards with 519. Sachin Tendulkar passes 10,000 runs in one-day internationals. APRIL: Graeme Wright returns as *Wisden* editor while Matthew Engel is working in the USA. MAY: Hampshire play their first match at their new Rose Bowl ground: the first day is washed out. AUGUST: Australia win the Ashes series 4–1. SEPTEMBER: Yorkshire clinch their first County Championship title since 1968. Mohammad Ashraful, 17, becomes the youngest player to score a Test century, on his debut for Bangladesh against Sri Lanka. NOVEMBER: Test between South Africa and India is stripped of official status after a dispute about the referee, Mike Denness, who fined six Indians for various offences in the previous match. DECEMBER: India beat England 1–0 in three-match series.

County Championship: 1st Yorkshire, 2nd Somerset (Div. 2 winners: Sussex).
Cheltenham & Gloucester Trophy: Somerset beat Leicestershire.
Benson and Hedges Cup: Surrey beat Gloucestershire.
Norwich Union League: 1st Kent, 2nd Leicestershire (Div. 2 winners: Glamorgan).

2002

JANUARY: Sharjah hosts its first Test, after West Indies decline to tour Pakistan for security reasons. MARCH: ICC announces its first panel of full-time international umpires. MAY: Inzamam-ul-Haq scores 329 for Pakistan v New Zealand at Lahore: shortly afterwards the tour is abandoned following a bomb-blast near the tourists' hotel. JUNE: Hansie Cronje is killed in a plane crash in South Africa. England beat Sri Lanka 2–0. Warwickshire win the 31st and last Benson and Hedges Cup. SEPTEMBER: England draw 1–1 with India. Yorkshire are relegated to Division Two of the County Championship, finishing bottom of the table the year after winning the title. DECEMBER: Australia retain the Ashes, winning the first three Tests inside 11 days of actual play: they eventually take the series 4–1.

County Championship: 1st Surrey, 2nd Warwickshire (Div. 2 winners: Essex).
Cheltenham & Gloucester Trophy: Yorkshire beat Somerset.
Benson and Hedges Cup: Warwickshire beat Essex.
Norwich Union League: 1st Glamorgan, 2nd Worcestershire
(Div. 2 winners: Gloucestershire).

2003

FEBRUARY: Shane Warne banned for a year after positive drug test – he claimed he was given a slimming pill by his mother. During the World Cup, Andy Flower and Henry Olonga wear black armbands protesting at the "death of democracy" in Zimbabwe: neither has played for the country since the tournament finished. In the eighth World Cup itself, Canada beat Bangladesh – but are then skittled for a record-low 36 by Sri Lanka. England refuse to play in Zimbabwe, which ends up costing them a place in the later stages. **MARCH:** Australia retain the World Cup, despite Warne's absence, hammering India by 125 runs in the final at Johannesburg: captain Ricky Ponting makes 140 not out. **APRIL:** Tim de Lisle edits *Wisden* for one year, before the return of Matthew Engel: the Almanack features a photograph (of Michael Vaughan) on the cover for the first time. **MAY:** West Indies score a record 418 to beat Australia in Antigua Test – but still lose the series 3–1. **JUNE:** England win both Tests against Zimbabwe inside three days. New 20-over competition – the Twenty20 Cup – introduced in England and catches the public imagination. **JULY:** Nasser Hussain resigns as England captain after first Test against South Africa (in which Graeme Smith makes 277) and is replaced by Michael Vaughan. **AUGUST:** England win final Test to draw series against South Africa 2–2. **OCTOBER:** Matthew Hayden breaks the Test record with 380 for Australia against Zimbabwe at Perth. **DECEMBER:** Sri Lanka beat England 1–0 after innings victory in Colombo. Australia score 556 in Adelaide Test – but lose it to India.

> *County Championship:* 1st Sussex, 2nd Lancashire (Div. 2 winners: Worcestershire).
> *Cheltenham & Gloucester Trophy:* Gloucestershire beat Worcestershire.
> *National League:* 1st Surrey, 2nd Gloucestershire (Div. 2 winners: Lancashire).
> *Twenty20 Cup:* Surrey beat Warwickshire.

2004

JANUARY: Steve Waugh retires, after a record 168 Test matches: the series against India is drawn 1–1. **MARCH:** Virender Sehwag hits 309, India's first triple-century, against Pakistan at Multan. Steve Harmison takes seven for 12 as England bowl West Indies out for 47 at Kingston, in a four-match series England go on to win 3–0. **APRIL:** Start of long-running bitter dispute between Zimbabwe's board and players, who are reportedly concerned at the board's "racist" policies: Zimbabwe eventually withdraw temporarily from Test cricket, and several of the "rebels" have not played since. Brian Lara regains the Test record by scoring 400 not out for West Indies against England in Antigua. **MAY:** Muttiah Muralitharan passes Courtney Walsh's record tally of 519 Test wickets. Nasser Hussain announces his retirement after hitting a century and the winning runs in the Lord's Test against New Zealand. **AUGUST:** England finish the summer with a 100% record in Tests, winning all four against West Indies and three against New Zealand. **SEPTEMBER:** West Indies beat England in Champions Trophy final at The Oval which ends in near-darkness. OCTOBER: Shane Warne passes Muralitharan's tally (533) to become Test cricket's leading wicket-taker. DECEMBER: Galle Test ground devastated by the tsunami disaster that cost thousands of lives in Sri Lanka.

County Championship: 1st Warwickshire, 2nd Kent
(Div. 2 winners: Nottinghamshire).
Cheltenham & Gloucester Trophy: Gloucestershire beat Worcestershire.
totesport League: 1st Glamorgan, 2nd Lancashire (Div. 2 winners: Middlesex).
Twenty20 Cup: Leicestershire beat Surrey.

2005

JANUARY: England win close-fought series in South Africa 2–1. Bangladesh win their first Test, at the 35th attempt, against Zimbabwe at Chittagong. FEBRUARY: Australia beat New Zealand in the inaugural Twenty20 international. MARCH: Inzamam-ul-Haq scores 184 in his 100th Test for Pakistan, against India at Bangalore. Steve Bucknor becomes the first umpire to stand in 100 Tests. APRIL: Australia win the Women's World Cup for the fifth time, beating India in the final at Centurion. MAY: England brush Bangladesh aside 2–0, winning both Tests by an innings: England take 40 wickets and lose only six themselves. JUNE: Bangladesh beat Australia in one-day international at Cardiff. AUGUST: England level Ashes series with nail-biting two-run win at Birmingham. Shane Warne becomes the first bowler to take 600 Test wickets. ICC offices move to Dubai, after 96 years at Lord's. SEPTEMBER: England regain the Ashes for the first time since 1989, winning an action-packed series 2–1 to great national acclaim, including a victory parade that ended in Trafalgar Square. England's women regain their Ashes too, beating Australia 1–0. OCTOBER: Australia beat a World XI in three one-day internationals and a Test match, controversially all given official status by the ICC. NOVEMBER: Brian Lara becomes Test cricket's leading run-scorer, passing Allan Border's aggregate of 11,174. DECEMBER: Sachin Tendulkar makes his 35th Test century, beating Sunil Gavaskar's record. Pakistan beat England 2–0, ending their run of six successive series victories. Kerry Packer dies, aged 68.

County Championship: 1st Nottinghamshire, 2nd Hampshire
(Div. 2 winners: Lancashire).
Cheltenham & Gloucester Trophy: Hampshire beat Warwickshire.
totesport League: 1st Essex, 2nd Middlesex (Div. 2 winners: Sussex).
Twenty20 Cup: Somerset beat Lancashire.

WISDEN CRICKETERS OF THE YEAR 1978–2006

1978 I. T. Botham, M. Hendrick, A. Jones, K. S. McEwan, R. G. D. Willis.
1979 D. I. Gower, J. K. Lever, C. M. Old, C. T. Radley, J. N. Shepherd.
1980 J. Garner, S. M. Gavaskar, G. A. Gooch, D. W. Randall, B. C. Rose.
1981 K. J. Hughes, R. D. Jackman, A. J. Lamb, C. E. B. Rice, V. A. P. van der Bijl.
1982 T. M. Alderman, A. R. Border, R. J. Hadlee, Javed Miandad, R. W. Marsh.
1983 Imran Khan, T. E. Jesty, A. I. Kallicharran, Kapil Dev, M. D. Marshall.
1984 M. Amarnath, J. V. Coney, J. E. Emburey, M. W. Gatting, C. L. Smith.
1985 M. D. Crowe, H. A. Gomes, G. W. Humpage, J. Simmons, S. Wettimuny.
1986 P. Bainbridge, R. M. Ellison, C. J. McDermott, N. V. Radford, R. T. Robinson.
1987 J. H. Childs, G. A. Hick, D. B. Vengsarkar, C. A. Walsh, J. J. Whitaker.
1988 J. P. Agnew, N. A. Foster, D. P. Hughes, P. M. Roebuck, Salim Malik.
1989 K. J. Barnett, P. J. L. Dujon, P. A. Neale, F. D. Stephenson, S. R. Waugh.
1990 S. J. Cook, D. M. Jones, R. C. Russell, R. A. Smith, M. A. Taylor.
1991 M. A. Atherton, M. Azharuddin, A. R. Butcher, D. L. Haynes, M. E. Waugh.
1992 C. E. L. Ambrose, P. A. J. DeFreitas, A. A. Donald, R. B. Richardson, Waqar Younis.
1993 N. E. Briers, M. D. Moxon, I. D. K. Salisbury, A. J. Stewart, Wasim Akram.
1994 D. C. Boon, I. A. Healy, M. G. Hughes, S. K. Warne, S. L. Watkin.
1995 B. C. Lara, D. E. Malcolm, T. A. Munton, S. J. Rhodes, K. C. Wessels.
1996 D. G. Cork, P. A. de Silva, A. R. C. Fraser, A. Kumble, D. A. Reeve.
1997 S. T. Jayasuriya, Mushtaq Ahmed, Saeed Anwar, P. V. Simmons, S. R. Tendulkar.
1998 M. T. G. Elliott, S. G. Law, G. D. McGrath, M. P. Maynard, G. P. Thorpe.
1999 I. D. Austin, D. Gough, M. Muralitharan, A. Ranatunga, J. N. Rhodes.
2000 C. L. Cairns, R. Dravid, L. Klusener, T. M. Moody, Saqlain Mushtaq.
2001 M. W. Alleyne, M. P. Bicknell, A. R. Caddick, J. L. Langer, D. S. Lehmann.
2002 A. Flower, A. C. Gilchrist, J. N. Gillespie, V. V. S. Laxman, D. R. Martyn.
2003 M. L. Hayden, A. J. Hollioake, N. Hussain, S. M. Pollock, M. P. Vaughan.
2004 C. J. Adams, A. Flintoff, I. J. Harvey, G. Kirsten, G. C. Smith.
2005 A. F. Giles, S. J. Harmison, R. W. T. Key, A. J. Strauss, M. E. Trescothick.
2006 M. J. Hoggard, S. P. Jones, B. Lee, K. P. Pietersen, R. T. Ponting.

Note: Awards are based on influence on the previous English season. However, from 2000 to 2003 the award was made on the basis of all cricket round the world.

THE LEADING CRICKETER IN THE WORLD

This was instituted in *Wisden 2004*. Players can be chosen more than once for this award, which is made on the basis of all cricket round the world in the previous calendar year.

2004 R. T. Ponting.   2005 S. K. Warne.   2006 A. Flintoff.

CRICKETERS OF THE 20TH CENTURY

Selected by a panel of 100 leading cricket experts and announced in *Wisden 2000*.

D. G. Bradman, J. B. Hobbs, I. V. A. Richards, G. S. Sobers, S. K. Warne.

Statistical Highlights 1977–2005

Compiled by Philip Bailey

From the start of the Centenary Test, Melbourne, March 12, 1977 until January 1, 2006
[WR] all-time record at January 1, 2006   [WR =] joint all-time record at January 1, 2006

FIRST-CLASS MATCHES

Highest Individual Scores

501[*WR]	B. C. Lara	Warwickshire v Durham at Birmingham	1994
405[*]	G. A. Hick	Worcestershire v Somerset at Taunton	1988
400[*]	B. C. Lara	West Indies v England (4th Test) at St John's	2003–04
394	Naved Latif	Sargodha v Gujranwala at Gujranwala	2000–01
380	M. L. Hayden	Australia v Zimbabwe (1st Test) at Perth	2003–04
377	S. V. Manjrekar	Bombay v Hyderabad at Bombay	1990–91
375	B. C. Lara	West Indies v England (5th Test) at St John's	1993–94
366	N. H. Fairbrother	Lancashire v Surrey at The Oval	1990
366	M. V. Sridhar	Hyderabad v Andhra at Secunderabad	1993–94
355[*]	G. R. Marsh	Western Australia v South Australia at Perth	1989–90
353	V. V. S. Laxman	Hyderabad v Karnataka at Bangalore	1999–2000

Five Hundreds in Succession

B. C. Lara   1993–94 and 1994   M. E. K. Hussey   2003

Ten Fifties in Succession

R. S. Kaluwitharana   1994–95

Fastest Hundreds (*balls faced*)

34	D. W. Hookes	South Australia v Victoria at Adelaide	1982–83

Most Runs in a Day

390[WR]	B. C. Lara	Warwickshire v Durham at Birmingham	1994
322	I. V. A. Richards	Somerset v Warwickshire at Taunton	1985
317	K. R. Rutherford	New Zealanders v D. B. Close's XI at Scarborough	1986
311	G. M. Turner	Worcestershire v Warwickshire at Worcester	1982
311	N. H. Fairbrother	Lancashire v Surrey at The Oval	1990

Six Sixes in a Six-ball Over

36[WR =]	R. J. Shastri off Tilak Raj	Bombay v Baroda at Bombay	1984–85

Most Sixes in an Innings

16[WR]	A. Symonds (254[*])	Gloucestershire v Glamorgan at Abergavenny	1995
14	Shakti Singh (128)	Himachal Pradesh v Haryana at Dharmasala	1990–91

Longest Innings (*minutes batted*)

1,015[WR]	R. Nayyar (271)	Himachal Pradesh v Jammu and Kashmir at Chamba	1999–2000
878	G. Kirsten (275)	South Africa v England (3rd Test) at Durban	1999–2000

Highest Partnerships

576 for 2nd wicket	S. T. Jayasuriya and R. S. Mahanama, Sri Lanka v India (1st Test) at Colombo 1997–98
475 for 2nd wicket	Zahir Alam and L. S. Rajput, Assam v Tripura at Guwahati 1991–92
470 for 4th wicket	A. I. Kallicharran and G. W. Humpage, Warwickshire v Lancashire at Southport 1982
467 for 3rd wicket	A. H. Jones and M. D. Crowe, New Zealand v Sri Lanka (1st Test) at Wellington 1990–91

Highest Partnerships (*continued*)

464	for 1st wicket	R. Sehgal and R. Lamba, Delhi v Himachal Pradesh at Delhi	1994–95
464*	for 5th wicket	M. E. Waugh and S. R. Waugh, New South Wales v Western Australia at Perth	1990–91
462*	for 4th wicket	D. W. Hookes and W. B. Phillips, South Australia v Tasmania at Adelaide	1986–87
460	for 7th wicket	Bhupinder Singh and P. Dharmani, Punjab v Delhi at Delhi	1994–95
459	for 1st wicket	W. Jaffer and S. K. Kulkarni, Mumbai v Saurashtra at Rajkot	1996–97
451*	for 1st wicket	S. Desai and R. M. H. Binny, Karnataka v Kerala at Chickmagalur	1977–78
451	for 3rd wicket	Mudassar Nazar and Javed Miandad, Pakistan v India (4th Test) at Hyderabad	1982–83

Highest partnership for other wickets

372*	for 6th wicket	K. P. Pietersen and J. E. Morris, Nottinghamshire v Derbyshire at Derby	2001
313	for 8th wicket	Wasim Akram and Saqlain Mushtaq, Pakistan v Zimbabwe (1st Test) at Sheikhupura	1996–97
268	for 9th wicket	J. B. Commins and N. Boje, South Africa A v Mashonaland at Harare	1994–95
239	for 10th wicket	Aqeel Arshad and Ali Raza, Lahore Whites v Hyderabad at Lahore	2004–05

All Ten Wickets in an Innings

10–28	Naeem Akhtar	Rawalpindi B v Peshawar at Peshawar	1995–96
10–41	G. P. Wickremasinghe	Sinhalese SC v Kalutara PCC at Colombo	1991–92
10–45	R. L. Johnson	Middlesex v Derbyshire at Derby	1994
10–46	D. S. Mohanty	East Zone v South Zone at Agartala	2000–01
10–59	S. T. Jefferies	Western Province v Orange Free State at Cape Town	1987–88
10–74	A. Kumble	India v Pakistan (2nd Test) at Delhi	1998–99
10–78	P. Sunderam	Rajasthan v Vidarbha at Jodhpur	1985–86
10–92	Imran Adil	Bahawalpur v Faisalabad at Faisalabad	1989–90
10–175	E. E. Hemmings	International XI v West Indies XI at Kingston	1982–83

Sixteen Wickets in a Match

17–137	J. M. Davison	Canada v United States of America at Fort Lauderdale	2004
16–99	A. Kumble	Karnataka v Kerala at Thalassery	1994–95
16–119	M. P. Bicknell	Surrey v Leicestershire at Guildford	2000
16–130	A. R. Tait	Northern Districts v Auckland at Hamilton	1996–97
16–136	N. D. Hirwani	India v West Indies (4th Test) at Madras	1987–88
16–154	P. Sunderam	Rajasthan v Vidarbha at Jodhpur	1985–86
16–167	R. Dhanraj	Trinidad and Tobago v Leeward Islands at Charlestown	1995–96
16–220	M. Muralitharan	Sri Lanka v England (Only Test) at The Oval	1998

Four Wickets in Four Balls

S. S. Saini	Delhi v Himachal Pradesh at Delhi	1988–89
D. Dias	Western Province Suburbs v Central Province at Colombo	1990–91
Ali Gauhar	Karachi Blues v United Bank at Peshawar	1994–95
K. D. James	Hampshire v Indians at Southampton	1996
G. P. Butcher	Surrey v Derbyshire at The Oval	2000
Fazl-e-Akbar	PIA v Habib Bank at Lahore	2001–02

Five Wickets in Six Balls

Yasir Arafat	Rawalpindi v Faisalabad at Rawalpindi	2004–05

Most Balls Bowled in an Innings

588	98–24–203–5	Arshad Ayub	Hyderabad v Madhya Pradesh at Secunderabad	1991–92
582	97–15–259–5	D. Sharma	Haryana v Punjab at Faridabad	1987–88
564	94–26–180–1	A. R. Bhat	Karnataka v Delhi at Delhi	1981–82
563	93.5–30–191–6	R. K. Chauhan	Madhya Pradesh v Mumbai at Indore	1996–97
552	92–18–210–6	R. K. Chauhan	Madhya Pradesh v Railways at Gwalior	1991–92
527	87.5–18–204–3	Maninder Singh	Delhi v Karnataka at Delhi	1981–82
518	64.6–18–96–4	Zafar Mehdi	Sind A v Habib Bank at Karachi	1977–78
516	86–49–94–4	P. M. Such	Essex v Leicestershire at Colchester	1997

Most Balls Bowled in a Match

702	117.0–46–161–11	Mohammad Nazir	Pakistan Railways v Lahore City at Lahore	1985–86
684	114.0–46–176–5	Mohammad Nazir	Pakistan Railways v United Bank at Lahore	1982–83
683	113.5–41–220–16	M. Muralitharan	Sri Lanka v England (Only Test) at The Oval	1998
680	85.0–22–174–12	Iqbal Qasim	National Bank v Muslim Commercial Bank at Karachi	1977–78
660	110.0–26–265–6	Arshad Ayub	Hyderabad v Madhya Pradesh at Secunderabad	1991–92

Most Wicket-Keeping Dismissals in an Innings

9 (8ct, 1st)^{WR} =	Tahir Rasheed	Habib Bank v PACO at Gujranwala	1992–93
9 (7ct, 2st)^{WR} =	W. R. James	Matabeleland v Mashonaland Country Districts at Bulawayo	1995–96

Most Wicket-Keeping Dismissals in a Match

13 (11ct, 2st)^{WR}	W. R. James	Matabeleland v Mashonaland Country Districts at Bulawayo	1995–96

Most Catches in an Innings in the Field

6	Gulfraz Khan	Pakistan Railways v Muslim Commercial Bank at Sialkot	1981–82
6	Masood Anwar	Rawalpindi v Lahore Division at Rawalpindi	1983–84
6	J. D. Carr	Middlesex v Warwickshire at Birmingham	1995
6	C. M. Wickremasinghe	Sebastianites v Police at Colombo	1995–96
6	G. P. Thorpe	Surrey v Kent at The Oval	1998

Most Catches in a Match in the Field

8	Masood Anwar	Rawalpindi v Lahore Division at Rawalpindi	1983–84
8	M. C. J. Ball	Gloucestershire v Yorkshire at Cheltenham	1994
8	J. D. Carr	Middlesex v Warwickshire at Birmingham	1995
8	G. A. Hick	Worcestershire v Essex at Chelmsford	2005

No Byes Conceded in Total of 700 or More

R. C. Russell^{WR}	Gloucestershire v Northamptonshire (746–9 dec.) at Bristol	2002
S. Reuben Paul	Tamil Nadu v Karnataka (716) at Bhadravati	1995–96
T. Taibu	Zimbabwe v Sri Lanka (713–3 dec.) (2nd Test) at Bulawayo	2004

Highest Innings Totals

952–6 dec.	Sri Lanka v India (1st Test) at Colombo	1997–98
944–6 dec.	Hyderabad v Andhra at Secunderabad	1993–94
912–6 dec.	Tamil Nadu v Goa at Panaji	1988–89
868	North Zone v West Zone at Bhilai	1987–88
863	Lancashire v Surrey at The Oval	1990
855–6 dec.	Bombay v Hyderabad at Mumbai	1990–91
810–4 dec.	Warwickshire v Durham at Birmingham	1994
802–8 dec.	Karachi Blues v Lahore City at Peshawar	1994–95

Lowest Innings Totals

14	Surrey v Essex at Chelmsford	1983
19	Matabeleland v Mashonaland at Harare	2000–01
20	National Bank v Pakistan Customs at Karachi	1998–99
23	Jammu and Kashmir v Haryana at Rai	1977–78
24	Oxford University v Leicestershire at Oxford	1985
27	Habib Bank v PIA at Lahore	2001–02
28	Goa v Kerala at Thalassery	1998–99
29	Andhra v Tamil Nadu at Coimbatore	1978–79
29	South Australia v New South Wales at Sydney	2004–05
30	Andhra v Punjab at Mohali	2003–04
30	Bangladesh A v Pakistan Customs at Karachi	2003–04

STATISTICAL HIGHLIGHTS 1977–2005

Highest Fourth-Innings Totals

513–9	Central Province v Southern Province at Kandy (set 512)	2003–04
	(*the highest-ever fourth-innings total to win a match*)	
506–6	South Australia v Queensland at Adelaide (set 506)	1991–92
503–4	South Zone v England A at Gurgaon (set 501)	2003–04
500–7	South African Universities v Western Province at Stellenbosch (set 499)	1978–79

Highest Match Aggregates

1,945 for 18	Canterbury (496 and 476–2 dec.) v Wellington (498–2 dec. and 475–4)	
	at Christchurch	1994–95
1,869 for 32	Bombay (390 and 719) v Delhi (389 and 371–4) at Delhi	1990–91
1,835 for 20	Bombay (855–6 dec. and 446–4 dec.) v Hyderabad (498 and 36–0) at Mumbai	1990–91
1,815 for 28	Surrey (608–6 dec. and 324–5 dec.) v Somerset (554 and 329–7) at Taunton	2002
1,808 for 20	Sussex (591 and 312–3 dec.) v Essex (493–4 dec. and 412–3) at Hove	1993

Win Without Losing a Wicket

Kerala (141 and 124) v Karnataka (451–0 dec.) at Chickmagalur		1977–78

Large Margin of Victory

By Runs Margin

609 runs: Muslim Commercial Bank (575 and 282–0 dec.) beat WAPDA (98 and 150)		
at Hyderabad		1977–78
585 runs: Sargodha (336 and 416) beat Lahore Municipal Corporation (77 and 90)		
at Faisalabad		1978–79
573 runs: Sinhalese (395–7 dec. and 350–2 dec.) beat Sebastianites (63 and 109) at Colombo		1990–91
556 runs: Nondescripts (397–8 dec. and 313–6 dec.) beat Matara (65 and 89) at Colombo		1998–99

By an Innings

Inns and 472 runs: Assam (684–7 dec.) beat Tripura (129 and 83) at Guwahati		1991–92
Inns and 430 runs: Habib Bank (731–8 dec.) beat Sargodha (80 and 221) at Faisalabad		1977–78
Inns and 425 runs: Allied Bank (600–8 dec.) beat Dadu (102 and 73) at Karachi		2002–03

Tied Matches

England XI (296–6 dec. and 104) v Central Districts (198 and 202) at New Plymouth	1977–78
New Zealanders (301–9 dec. and 174–3 dec.) v Victoria (230–5 dec. and 245) at Melbourne	1982–83
Muslim Commercial Bank (229 and 238) v Pakistan Railways (149 and 318) at Sialkot	1983–84
Kent (92 and 243) v Sussex (143 and 192) at Hastings	1984
Kent (250–6 dec. and 204–5 dec.) v Northamptonshire (124 and 330) at Northampton	1984
Eastern Province B (189 and 278) v Boland (211 and 256) at Grahamstown	1985–86
Natal B (367 and 204–5 dec.) v Eastern Province B (279 and 292) at Pietermaritzburg	1985–86
Australia (574–7 dec. and 170–5 dec.) v India (397 and 347) (1st Test) at Madras	1986–87
Derbyshire (340 and 226–5 dec.) v Gloucestershire (288 and 278) at Bristol	1987
Peshawar (263–9 dec. and 249) v Bahawalpur (325–8 and 187) at Bahawalpur	1988–89
Wellington (398 and 250–4 dec.) v Canterbury (381 and 267) at Wellington	1988–89
Kent (381 and 408–7 dec.) v Sussex (353 and 436) at Hove	1991
Worcestershire (203 and 325–8 dec.) v Nottinghamshire (233 and 295) at Nottingham	1993
West Indies A (370 and 266–7 dec.) v Somerset (183 and 453) at Taunton	2002
Warwickshire (446–7 dec. and 0–0) v Essex (66–0 dec. and 380) at Birmingham	2003
Worcestershire (262 and 247) v Zimbabweans (334 and 175) at Worcester	2003

Most Extras in an Innings

	b	l-b	w	n-b		
99	9	10	16	64	Lahore City (502–8 dec.) v Gujranwala at Gujranwala	1997–98
98	17	17	16	48	Northamptonshire (579) v Essex at Northampton	1999

TEST MATCHES

From the start of the Centenary Test, Melbourne, March 12, 1977 until January 1, 2006
WR all-time record at January 1, 2006   WR = joint all-time record at January 1, 2006

Highest Individual Scores

400*WR	B. C. Lara	West Indies v England at St John's	2003–04
380	M. L. Hayden	Australia v Zimbabwe at Perth	2003–04
375	B. C. Lara	West Indies v England at St John's	1993–94
340	S. T. Jayasuriya	Sri Lanka v India at Colombo	1997–98
334*	M. A. Taylor	Australia v Pakistan at Peshawar	1998–99
333	G. A. Gooch	England v India at Lord's	1990
329	Inzamam-ul-Haq	Pakistan v New Zealand at Lahore	2002
317	C. H. Gayle	West Indies v South Africa at St John's	2004–05
309	V. Sehwag	India v Pakistan at Multan	2003–04

Note: when they were scored, Hayden's 380 and Lara's 375 were all-time records.

Three or More Hundreds in Succession

4	R. Dravid	India	2002 and 2002–03
3	S. M. Gavaskar	India	1978–79
3	Mudassar Nazar	Pakistan	1982–83
3	Zaheer Abbas	Pakistan	1982–83
3	D. L. Haynes	West Indies	1989–90 and 1990–91
3	G. A. Gooch	England	1990
3	A. H. Jones	New Zealand	1990–91
3	V. G. Kambli	India	1992–93 and 1993
3	P. A. de Silva	Sri Lanka	1996–97
3	A. C. Gilchrist	Australia	2004–05

Hundred Runs Before Lunch

76* to 176	G. S. Chappell	Australia v New Zealand at Christchurch	1981–82
112* to 215*	M. A. Taylor	Australia v Pakistan at Peshawar	1998–99
103*	Inzamam-ul-Haq	Pakistan v Zimbabwe at Harare	2002–03
77* to 191	B. C. Lara	West Indies v Zimbabwe at Bulawayo	2003–04
57* to 162*	I. R. Bell	England v Bangladesh at Chester-le-Street	2005

Fastest Hundreds (balls faced)

56WR	I. V. A. Richards	West Indies v England at St John's	1985–86
69	S. Chanderpaul	West Indies v Australia at Georgetown	2002–03
74	Kapil Dev	India v Sri Lanka at Kanpur	1986–87
74	M. Azharuddin	India v South Africa at Calcutta	1996–97

Fastest Double-Hundreds (balls faced)

153WR	N. J. Astle	New Zealand v England at Christchurch	2001–02
211	H. H. Gibbs	South Africa v Pakistan at Cape Town	2002–03
212	A. C. Gilchrist	Australia v South Africa at Johannesburg	2001–02
220	I. T. Botham	England v India at The Oval	1982

Most Runs in an Over

28WR	B. C. Lara off R. J. Peterson	West Indies v South Africa at Johannesburg	2003–04
26	C. D. McMillan off Younis Khan	New Zealand v Pakistan at Hamilton	2000–01

Out Handled the Ball

A. M. J. Hilditch	Australia v Pakistan at Perth	1978–79
Mohsin Khan	Pakistan v Australia at Karachi	1982–83
D. L. Haynes	West Indies v India at Bombay	1983–84
G. A. Gooch	England v Australia at Manchester	1993
S. R. Waugh	Australia v India at Chennai	2000–01
M. P. Vaughan	England v India at Bangalore	2001–02

Highest Partnerships

576 for 2nd wicket[WR]	S. T. Jayasuriya and R. S. Mahanama, Sri Lanka v India at Colombo	1997–98
467 for 3rd wicket	A. H. Jones and M. D. Crowe, New Zealand v Sri Lanka at Wellington	1990–91
451 for 3rd wicket	Mudassar Nazar and Javed Miandad, Pakistan v India at Hyderabad	1982–83
438 for 2nd wicket	M. S. Atapattu and K. C. Sangakkara, Sri Lanka v Zimbabwe at Bulawayo	2003–04
429* for 3rd wicket	J. A. Rudolph and H. H. Dippenaar, South Africa v Bangladesh at Chittagong	2003

Highest partnership for other wickets

368 for 1st wicket	G. C. Smith and H. H. Gibbs, South Africa v Pakistan at Cape Town	2002–03
353 for 4th wicket	S. R. Tendulkar and V. V. S. Laxman, India v Australia at Sydney	2003–04
385 for 5th wicket	S. R. Waugh and G. S. Blewett, Australia v South Africa at Johannesburg	1996–97
317 for 6th wicket	D. R. Martyn and A. C. Gilchrist, Australia v South Africa at Johannesburg	2001–02
248 for 7th wicket	Yousuf Youhana and Saqlain Mushtaq, Pakistan v New Zealand at Christchurch	2000–01
313 for 8th wicket	Wasim Akram and Saqlain Mushtaq, Pakistan v Zimbabwe at Sheikhupura	1996–97
195 for 9th wicket	M. V. Boucher and P. L. Symcox, South Africa v Zimbabwe at Johannesburg	1997–98
151 for 10th wicket	Azhar Mahmood and Mushtaq Ahmed, Pakistan v South Africa at Rawalpindi	1997–98

Nine Wickets in an Innings

10–74	A. Kumble	India v Pakistan at Delhi	1998–99
9–51	M. Muralitharan	Sri Lanka v Zimbabwe at Kandy	2001–02
9–52	R. J. Hadlee	New Zealand v Australia at Brisbane	1985–86
9–56	Abdul Qadir	Pakistan v England at Lahore	1987–88
9–57	D. E. Malcolm	England v South Africa at The Oval	1994
9–65	M. Muralitharan	Sri Lanka v England at The Oval	1998
9–83	Kapil Dev	India v West Indies at Ahmedabad	1983–84
9–86	Sarfraz Nawaz	Pakistan v Australia at Melbourne	1978–79

Fifteen Wickets in a Match

16–136	N. D. Hirwani	India v West Indies at Chennai	1987–88
16–220	M. Muralitharan	Sri Lanka v England at The Oval	1998
15–123	R. J. Hadlee	New Zealand v Australia at Brisbane	1985–86
15–217	Harbhajan Singh	India v Australia at Chennai	2000–01

Wicket with First Ball in Test Cricket

R. K. Illingworth	England v West Indies at Nottingham	1991
N. M. Kulkarni	India v Sri Lanka at Colombo	1997–98
M. K. G. C. P. Lakshitha	Sri Lanka v Bangladesh at Colombo	2002

Hat-Trick

M. G. Hughes	Australia v West Indies at Perth	1988–89
C. A. Walsh	West Indies v Australia at Brisbane	1988–89
D. W. Fleming	Australia v Pakistan at Rawalpindi	1994–95
S. K. Warne	Australia v England at Melbourne	1994–95
D. G. Cork	England v West Indies at Manchester	1995
D. Gough	England v Australia at Sydney	1998–99

Hat-Trick (*continued*)

Wasim Akram	Pakistan v Sri Lanka at Lahore	1998–99
Wasim Akram	Pakistan v Sri Lanka at Dhaka	1998–99
D. N. T. Zoysa	Sri Lanka v Zimbabwe at Harare	1999–2000
Abdul Razzaq	Pakistan v Sri Lanka at Galle	2000
Harbhajan Singh	India v Australia at Kolkata	2000–01
G. D. McGrath	Australia v West Indies at Perth	2000–01
Mohammad Sami	Pakistan v Sri Lanka at Lahore	2001–02
J. J. C. Lawson	West Indies v Australia at Bridgetown	2002–03
Alok Kapali	Bangladesh v Pakistan at Peshawar	2003
A. M. Blignaut	Zimbabwe v Bangladesh at Harare	2003–04
M. J. Hoggard	England v West Indies at Bridgetown	2003–04
J. E. C. Franklin	New Zealand v Bangladesh at Dhaka	2004–05

Four Wickets in Five Balls

C. M. Old	England v Pakistan at Birmingham	1978
Wasim Akram	Pakistan v West Indies at Lahore	1998–99

Match Double (*100 runs and ten wickets*)

I. T. Botham	114; 6–58; 7–48	England v India at Bombay	1979–80
Imran Khan	117; 6–98; 5–82	Pakistan v India at Faisalabad	1982–83

Most Wicket-Keeping Dismissals in an Innings

7 (7ct)[WR] =	Wasim Bari	Pakistan v New Zealand at Auckland	1978–79
7 (7ct)[WR] =	R. W. Taylor	England v India at Bombay	1979–80
7 (7ct)[WR] =	I. D. S. Smith	New Zealand v Sri Lanka at Hamilton	1990–91
7 (7ct)[WR] =	R. D. Jacobs	West Indies v Australia at Melbourne	2000–01

Most Wicket-Keeping Dismissals in a Match

11 (11ct)[WR] =	R. C. Russell	England v South Africa at Johannesburg	1995–96
10 (10ct)	R. W. Taylor	England v India at Bombay	1979–80
10 (10ct)	A. C. Gilchrist	Australia v New Zealand at Hamilton	1999–2000

Most Catches in an Innings in the Field

5	M. Azharuddin	India v Pakistan at Karachi	1989–90
5	K. Srikkanth	India v Australia at Perth	1991–92
5	S. P. Fleming	New Zealand v Zimbabwe at Harare	1997–98

Most Catches in a Match in the Field

7	H. P. Tillekeratne	Sri Lanka v New Zealand at Colombo	1992–93
7	S. P. Fleming	New Zealand v Zimbabwe at Harare	1997–98
7	M. L. Hayden	Australia v Sri Lanka at Galle	2003–04

Highest Innings Totals

952–6 dec.[WR]	Sri Lanka v India at Colombo	1997–98
751–5 dec.	West Indies v England at St John's	2003–04
747	West Indies v South Africa at St John's	2004–05
735–6 dec.	Australia v Zimbabwe at Perth	2003–04
713–3 dec.	Sri Lanka v Zimbabwe at Bulawayo	2003–04
708	Pakistan v England at The Oval	1987
705–7 dec.	India v Australia at Sydney	2003–04

Lowest Innings Totals

46	England v West Indies at Port-of-Spain	1993–94
47	West Indies v England at Kingston	2003–04
51	West Indies v Australia at Port-of-Spain	1998–99
53†	Pakistan v Australia at Sharjah	2002–03
53	West Indies v Pakistan at Faisalabad	1986–87
54	West Indies v England at Lord's	2000
54	Zimbabwe v South Africa at Cape Town	2004–05
59	Zimbabwe v New Zealand at Harare	2005–06
59	Pakistan v Australia at Sharjah	2002–03

† *one batsman absent*

Highest Match Aggregates

1,747 for 25	India (705–7 dec. and 211–2 dec.) v Australia (474 and 357–6) at Sydney	2003–04
1,702 for 28	Pakistan (588 and 490–8 dec.) v India (603 and 21–0) at Faisalabad	2005–06
1,648 for 28	South Africa (532 and 335–3 dec.) v West Indies (427 and 354–5) at Cape Town	2003–04
1,614 for 30	England (519 and 320–4 dec.) v India (432 and 343–6) at Manchester	1990
1,603 for 28	England (653–4 dec. and 272–4 dec.) v India (454 and 224) at Lord's	1990

Large Margin of Victory

By Runs Margin

491 runs:	Australia (381 and 361–5 dec.) beat Pakistan (179 and 72) at Perth	2004–05
408 runs:	West Indies (328 and 448) beat Australia (203 and 165) at Adelaide	1979–80
384 runs:	Australia (492 and 296–5 dec.) beat England (325 and 79) at Brisbane	2002–03
379 runs:	Australia (435 and 283–2 dec.) beat West Indies (210 and 129) at Brisbane	2005–06

By an Innings

Inns and 360 runs:	Australia (652–7 dec.) beat South Africa (159 and 133) at Johannesburg	2001–02
Inns and 324 runs:	Pakistan (643) beat New Zealand (73 and 246) at Lahore	2002
Inns and 322 runs:	West Indies (660–5 dec.) beat New Zealand (216 and 122) at Wellington	1994–95
Inns and 310 runs:	West Indies (536) beat Bangladesh (139 and 87) at Dhaka	2002–03

Win after Following-On

England (174 and 356) beat Australia (401–9 dec. and 111) at Leeds by 18 runs		1981
India (171 and 657–7 dec.) beat Australia (445 and 212) at Kolkata by 171 runs		2000–01

ONE-DAY INTERNATIONALS

All-time records are not listed for one-day internationals.

Highest Individual Scores

194	Saeed Anwar	Pakistan v India at Chennai	1996–97
189*	I. V. A. Richards	West Indies v England at Manchester	1984
189	S. T. Jayasuriya	Sri Lanka v India at Sharjah	2000–01
188*	G. Kirsten	South Africa v United Arab Emirates at Rawalpindi	1995–96
186*	S. R. Tendulkar	India v New Zealand at Hyderabad	1999–2000
183*	M. S. Dhoni	India v Sri Lanka at Jaipur	2005–06
183	S. C. Ganguly	India v Sri Lanka at Taunton	1999
181	I. V. A. Richards	West Indies v Sri Lanka at Karachi	1987–88
175*	Kapil Dev	India v Zimbabwe at Tunbridge Wells	1983

Highest Partnerships

331 for 2nd wicket	S. R. Tendulkar and R. Dravid, India v New Zealand at Hyderabad	1999–2000
318 for 2nd wicket	S. C. Ganguly and R. Dravid, India v Sri Lanka at Taunton	1999
275 for 4th wicket	M. Azharuddin and A. Jadeja, India v Zimbabwe at Cuttack	1997–98
263 for 2nd wicket	Aamir Sohail and Inzamam-ul-Haq, Pakistan v New Zealand at Sharjah	1993–94

Seven Wickets in an Innings

8–19	W. P. U. J. C. Vaas	Sri Lanka v Zimbabwe at Colombo	2001–02
7–15	G. D. McGrath	Australia v Namibia at Potchefstroom	2002–03
7–20	A. J. Bichel	Australia v England at Port Elizabeth	2002–03
7–30	M. Muralitharan	Sri Lanka v India at Sharjah	2000–01
7–36	Waqar Younis	Pakistan v England at Leeds	2001
7–37	Aqib Javed	Pakistan v India at Sharjah	1991–92
7–51	W. W. Davis	West Indies v Australia at Leeds	1983

Hat-Tricks

Jalal-ud-Din	Pakistan v Australia at Hyderabad	1982–83
B. A. Reid	Australia v New Zealand at Sydney	1985–86
C. Sharma	India v New Zealand at Nagpur	1987–88
Wasim Akram	Pakistan v West Indies at Sharjah	1989–90
Wasim Akram	Pakistan v Australia at Sharjah	1989–90
Kapil Dev	India v Sri Lanka at Calcutta	1990–91
Aqib Javed	Pakistan v India at Sharjah	1991–92
D. K. Morrison	New Zealand v India at Napier	1993–94
Waqar Younis	Pakistan v New Zealand at East London	1994–95
E. A. Brandes	Zimbabwe v England at Harare	1996–97
Saqlain Mushtaq	Pakistan v Zimbabwe at Peshawar	1996–97
A. M. Stuart	Australia v Pakistan at Melbourne	1996–97
Saqlain Mushtaq	Pakistan v Zimbabwe at The Oval	1999
Mohammad Sami	Pakistan v West Indies at Sharjah	2001–02
W. P. U. J. C. Vaas	Sri Lanka v Zimbabwe at Colombo	2001–02
W. P. U. J. C. Vaas	Sri Lanka v Bangladesh at Pietermaritzburg	2002–03
B. Lee	Australia v Kenya at Durban	2002–03
J. M. Anderson	England v Pakistan at The Oval	2003
S. J. Harmison	England v India at Nottingham	2004
C. K. Langeveldt	South Africa v West Indies at Bridgetown	2004–05

Most Wicket-Keeping Dismissals in an Innings

6 (6ct)	A. C. Gilchrist	Australia v South Africa at Cape Town	1999–2000
6 (6ct)	A. J. Stewart	England v Zimbabwe at Manchester	2000
6 (5ct, 1st)	R. D. Jacobs	West Indies v Sri Lanka at Colombo	2001–02
6 (5ct, 1st)	A. C. Gilchrist	Australia v England at Sydney	2002–03
6 (6ct)	A. C. Gilchrist	Australia v Namibia at Potchefstroom	2002–03
6 (6ct)	A. C. Gilchrist	Australia v Sri Lanka at Colombo	2003–04

Most Catches in an Innings in the Field

5	J. N. Rhodes South Africa v West Indies at Bombay	1993–94

Highest Team Totals

398–5 (50 overs)	Sri Lanka v Kenya at Kandy	1995–96
397–5 (44 overs)	New Zealand v Zimbabwe at Bulawayo	2005–06
391–4 (50 overs)	England v Bangladesh at Nottingham	2005
376–2 (50 overs)	India v New Zealand at Hyderabad	1999–2000

Lowest Team Totals

35 (18 overs)	Zimbabwe v Sri Lanka at Harare	2003–04
36 (18.4 overs)	Canada v Sri Lanka at Paarl	2002–03
38 (15.4 overs)	Zimbabwe v Sri Lanka at Colombo	2001–02
43 (19.5 overs)	Pakistan v West Indies at Cape Town	1992–93
45 (40.3 overs)	Canada v England at Manchester	1979
45 (14 overs)	Namibia v Australia at Potchefstroom	2002–03

Highest Match Aggregates

693 for 15	India 349–7 (50 overs) v Pakistan 344–8 (50 overs) at Karachi	2003–04
664 for 19	Sri Lanka 349–9 (50 overs) v Pakistan 315 (49.4 overs) at Singapore	1995–96
663 for 15	Australia 331–7 (50 overs) v New Zealand 332–8 (49 overs) at Christchurch	2005–06
662 for 17	West Indies 333–7 (50 overs) v Sri Lanka 329 (49.3 overs) at Sharjah	1995–96
660 for 19	Pakistan 371–9 (50 overs) v Sri Lanka 289 (49.5 overs) at Nairobi	1996–97

Largest Margins of Victory

256 runs	Australia 301–6 (50 overs) v Namibia 45 (14 overs) at Potchefstroom	2002–03
245 runs	Sri Lanka 299–5 (50 overs) v India 54 (26.3 overs) at Sharjah	2000–01
233 runs	Pakistan 320–3 (50 overs) v Bangladesh 87 (34.2 overs) at Dhaka	1999–2000
232 runs	Australia 323–2 (50 overs) v Sri Lanka 91 (35.5 overs) at Adelaide	1984–85

Index by Edition of *Wisden*

"Top. . . and Bottom" – Kent in 1995 950

Warwickshire v Northamptonshire 1995 995

"Wasim the Wizard" – Playing for Lancashire in 1995 959

International cricket

Australia v England 1994–95 267

"The Bribes Crisis" – Salim Malik alleged to have offered bribes 168–70

England v West Indies 1995 271–2

New Zealand v Sri Lanka 1995 585–6

Pakistan v Australia 1994 550–1

South Africa v New Zealand 1994–95 520–1

South Africa v Pakistan 1995 491–2

"The View from Pakistan" – Salim Malik alleged to have offered bribes 171

West Indies v Australia 1995 361–5

Zimbabwe v Pakistan 1995 608–9

Other articles and extracts

"Beware the Cliff" 1069–70

"Boom in Test Grounds" 1135

"Dutch Dodgy Dealing" 1068–9

"Italy Makes the Grade" 1070

"Next – Schoolboys in Pyjamas?" 1088–9

"Revolution in Hong Kong" 1070

1997

Notes by the editor

"Alas, Poor Raymond" – Illingworth as manager and chairman of selectors 278

"The English Disease" – Consistent failure of England team 277–8

"Goodbye to Out-Grounds" 1136

"Handle with Care" – County matches 85–6

"Tomorrow the World?" – Future of international cricket 86–7

People/players

Alan McGilvray – Obituary 1220

Graham Kersey – Obituary 1205

Keith Boyce – Obituary 1162

Mushtaq Ahmed – A Cricketer of the Year 739–40

Paddy Clift – Obituary 1167

Ray Lindwall – Obituary 1211–12

Sachin Tendulkar – A Cricketer of the Year 695–7

Sanath Jayasuriya – A Cricketer of the Year 693–5

Willie Rushton – Obituary 1237

County cricket

"Byas Takes Charge" – Yorkshire in 1996 1054

Essex v Lancashire 1996 961

"A First-Class Row" – Sussex in 1996 1027–8

"Inspired by Jones" – Derbyshire in 1996 892–3

"James' Solo Role" – playing for Hampshire in 1996 941

"Keepers of the Wooden Spoon" – Durham in 1996 897

Lancashire v Derbyshire 1996 960

Lancashire v Northamptonshire 1996 961

Leicestershire v Middlesex 1996 973

"One-Day Wonders" – Lancashire in 1996 960

"Slump (Except on Sundays)" – Nottinghamshire in 1996 1000–1

"A Triumph Overshadowed" – Surrey in 1996 1017

"Year of the Fox" – Leicestershire in 1996 970–2

International cricket

Australia v New Zealand – 1996 World Cup 841

Australia v Pakistan 1995 552–3

Australia v Sri Lanka 1995–96 588–91

Australia v Sri Lanka – 1996 World Cup 843–5

Australia v West Indies – 1996 World Cup 838, 843

England v Pakistan 1996 553–7

England v Sri Lanka – 1996 World Cup 839

India v Australia – 1996 World Cup 836

India v Pakistan – 1996 World Cup 840

India v Sri Lanka – 1996 World Cup 837, 842

India v West Indies – 1996 World Cup 835–6

Kenya v West Indies – 1996 World Cup 836–7

"A night to remember" – 1996 World Cup 845–6

Pakistan v Sri Lanka 1995 586–8

South Africa v England 1995–96 273–5

South Africa v West Indies – 1996 World Cup 840–1

Sri Lanka v Kenya – 1996 World Cup 838–9

"A Wind Blows from the East" – Cricket in India 88–91

"The Wisden World Championship" 81–2

"World Cup Hangover – The 1995–96 Season" 553

World Cup 1996 832–46

Zimbabwe v South Africa 1995 609–10

Other articles and extracts

"All Change at the Top" – West Indies leadership changes completely 402–3

"Cricket in the Classroom" – Cricket A-levels 1137

"Cricketana" – Memorabilia trading 1136

"English Cricket – A Manifesto" 278–9

"The Man who Stole the Show" 1105–7

1998

Notes by the editor

"Cricket's Place in Cool Britannia" 279–80

"Duck Soup" – Duckworth/Lewis scoring system 1137

"A Graceless Anniversary" 1137–8

"If You're Broke, Fix It" – Allegations of match-fixing 171–2

"Mr Dalmiya Goes to Lord's" 92

"A Tightrope Walk" – TV rights to Test cricket 128–9

People/players

Alan Gibson – Obituary 1184–5

Ashley Harvey-Walker – Obituary 1193

"Cricket's No. 1 Run Machine" – Graham Gooch 678–9

David Bairstow – Obituary 1159

Denis Compton – Obituary 1168–71

Derek Underwood 732–4

Glenn McGrath – A Cricketer of the Year 726–8

Graham Thorpe – A Cricketer of the Year 699–701

Index of Key Players and Topics